THE CLASSICAL TRADITION

HARVARD
UNIVERSITY
PRESS
REFERENCE
LIBRARY

THE CLASSICAL TRADITION

ANTHONY GRAFTON

GLENN W. MOST

SALVATORE SETTIS

Editors

The Belknap Press of Harvard University Press
Cambridge, Massachusetts, and London, England

2010

Printed in the United States of America

Library of Congress Cataloging-in-Publication Data
The classical tradition / Anthony Grafton, Glenn W. Most, Salvatore Settis, editors.
p. cm.
Includes bibliographical references and index.
ISBN 978-0-674-03572-0 (alk. paper)
1. Civilization, Classical—Handbooks, manuals, etc.
I. Grafton, Anthony. II. Most, Glenn W. III. Settis, Salvatore.
DE60.C55 2010
938—dc22 2010019667

CONTENTS

Preface

vii

List of Articles

xiii

THE CLASSICAL TRADITION

1

Contributors

1003

Index

1011

PREFACE

THIS BOOK aims to provide a reliable and wide-ranging guide to the reception of classical Graeco-Roman antiquity in all its dimensions in later cultures. Understandings and misunderstandings of ancient Greek and Roman literature, philosophy, art, architecture, history, politics, religion, science, and public and private life have shaped the cultures of medieval and modern Europe and of the nations that derived from them—and they have helped to shape other cultural traditions as well, Jewish, Islamic, and Slavic, to name only these. Every domain of post-classical life and thought has been profoundly influenced by ancient models. True, these models have not always been interpreted in ways that a sober modern scholarship would consider correct. On the contrary: it has often been creative misunderstandings that have preserved the ancient heritage and made it useful for later needs. All too often a pedantically restrictive determination of the truth of the matter concerning some nebulous ancient mystery has emptied it not only of its mistakes and distortions, but also of every trace of its once fascinating aura. The history of the reception of classical antiquity, as of any work of the human spirit, must balance, delicately and not unproblematically, between an unwavering commitment to uncovering as far as possible the truth of both ancient and modern cultural formations on the one hand and an undogmatic appreciation of the endless resourcefulness and inventiveness of human error on the other.

One cannot understand the history of the post-classical world without constant reference to the classical cultures by which it has never ceased to define itself—in assent and dissent, in defiance and imitation, in veneration and in willed but futile forgetfulness. At one extreme, modern cultures have sought to identify themselves as fully as possible with these ancient ones; at the other, they have defined themselves precisely by their sense of radical extraneous-ness and alienation from antiquity. At both extremes and in all intermediate cases, modern Europe and the Americas have unfailingly found in ancient Greece and Rome an "other" ideally well suited for understanding, criticizing, and redefining themselves. For that very reason, no account of the history of the reception of antiquity could possibly aim at comprehensiveness. Even those rare episodes when the ancient heritage has apparently been ignored would in fact form part of the full story of the reception of that heritage, so that an exhaustive exposition of the ways in which the world has defined itself with regard to Graeco-Roman antiquity would be nothing less than a comprehensive history of the world.

That is why we have conceived our work not as a Lexicon or Dictionary or Encyclopedia, but rather as a Guide. It has strategically chosen a large but limited number of paradigmatic topics and cannot claim for itself any kind of totality. Instead, it hopes to point to the variety of ways in which the post-classical tradition has drawn sustenance and inspiration from (revering, but also misunderstanding and opposing) classical antiquity. This volume seeks to make accessible to an audience of experts and educated non-experts alike, in an intelligible and interesting form, both what has always been known and what has recently been learned about the continuing influence of ancient Greek and Roman culture in the post-classical world. It conceives the classical tradition broadly—to include not only the texts, but also the images and objects, the ideas and institutions, the monuments and cultural artifacts, the rituals and practices that have so profoundly influenced the Western traditions and some non-Western ones. But it does not do so universally—it does not aim to provide a global dictionary of all cultures in all times, but only to focus upon empirically identifiable cases of appropriation and transformation of the classical heritage. As a guide, it does not pretend to exhaustiveness—not only practical considerations of feasibility, but also the many gaps in the scholarship on the field suggest the advisability of aiming at a more modest goal. Rather, it hopes to provide, for the general reader, a first place to turn in order to satisfy doubts and curiosity and to suggest further reading and, for the scholar, a work of reference indicating the current state of research in a number of disciplines as well as productive avenues of further work. For both kinds of readers, our Guide hopes to be both authoritative and accessible, learned and entertaining, reliable and surprising. If we may permit ourselves to compare small things with great ones (this formulation is itself a central topos of the classical tradition), we would hope to serve, in our own small way, as guides for the interested and perplexed, as the Sibyl did for Virgil's Aeneas, and as Virgil then did for Dante, bringing to renewed life the only apparently dead and restoring a voice to those who had given us ours but had temporarily lost their own.

Never, perhaps, has such guidance been as urgently needed as now. For in all contemporary industrial societies, intensive study of the ancient languages is in decline in the educational institutions that have traditionally formed both social and intellectual elites. As a result, the easy familiarity with the classical tradition that used to be the identifying mark of those who had benefited from a civilized, and civilizing, education has become increasingly rare. And yet the disappearance of this widespread erudition has not made the questions whose answers it had facilitated vanish with it. On the contrary, many people in modern societies remain curious about the countless traces of antiquity still visible in their world and about the ancient sources of various modern phenomena, but they do not know where to turn to satisfy their curiosity. Some of the facts and adages, images and examples that were once the object of a tacit knowledge will, we hope, be at least partially elucidated by our Guide. Perhaps, it might even help to contribute, in its own small way, to reestablishing the unity of classical culture which is being lost in the modern world—or at least to slowing down somewhat its rapid disappearance. Perhaps, too, looking back to the ways in which individuals and cultures, Western and non-Western, have studied and used the classics over the centuries may suggest new angles from which modern scholarship can view antiquity itself.

For the decline in classical education of the traditional kind has not been accompanied by a decline in classical scholarship. On the contrary, research into both the ancient world and the classical tradition has burgeoned at an unprecedented rate in recent decades. New approaches have transformed our understanding of realms as distant from one another as literary criticism and art history on the one hand, and medicine and mathematics on the other. Our understanding of critical aspects of ancient art and architecture, and material and social life, has also been radically changed by archaeological discoveries. And specialized research into the classical tradition has taught us a vast amount about everything from the transmission of individual texts to the afterlife of ancient forms of urban life and trade. New information and new kinds of questions are profoundly changing the scholarly picture of both the details and the general outline of the nature and structure of the classical tradition. But the notorious difficulty of communication among scholarly specialties and between the scholars and the general public makes it difficult to coordinate and measure progress across different fields and all but impossible to make such progress available to the ordinary educated readers who need and want it. This purpose, too, is one we hope our Guide will serve.

Thus, our volume is addressed in the first instance to various kinds of fellow members of our own European and North American cultures—but certainly not to them alone. Ideally, this Guide would have been entitled not *The Classical Tradition* but rather *A Classical Tradition*, for one of the things we have all learned from our recent history is that Europe is only one part of a complex and interlocking world. Europe's cultural heritage can be understood fully only when it is replaced within the larger context of other cultures with which it has always been in dialogue. The Graeco-Roman classical tradition is only one of the limited number of classical traditions that define the history of world culture, and its important affinities and divergences with such other classical traditions as the Islamic, Judaic, Chinese, and Indian ones mean that it cannot be fully understood without systematic reference to them. Ultimately, we have had in mind as potential readers for this volume not only the direct beneficiaries of the Graeco-Roman classical tradition but also interested members of other cultures. Our hope is that scholars who understand those other, non-European cultures better than we do will be stimulated by work like ours to explore, together with us and with those who we hope will follow us, the similarities and differences between all these traditions, so that we will someday be in a position to understand better what it is that makes a classical tradition classic. To what extent are ideas of the classical throughout our world the fruit of interaction between various cultures, to what extent are they indigenous products? What if anything differentiates the classical tradition in the West from the histories of other canons? Toward the remote but not unimaginable goal of a truly comparative history of all classical traditions, our volume is intended as an invitation and as a preliminary contribution.

This book has been long in the conceiving and even longer in the making, and along the way it has, and we have, accumulated debts of all kinds. Our first, and deepest, debt of gratitude goes to four editors without whom it could never have seen the light of day: Harry Haskell, then of Yale University Press, who first conceived of the possibility of this highly improbable project and who managed to convince one of the editors, and then helped to convince the other two, that it could indeed be done; Peg Fulton, then of Harvard University Press, who rescued this project when all reasonable hope for it had been lost and succeeded in guiding it through enormous difficulties toward a happy conclusion; and Jennifer Snodgrass and Mary Ann Lane of Harvard University Press, who brought it, with almost infinite patience, gentle obstinacy, canny flexibility, and extraordinary skill to the final form in which, dear reader, you hold it now in your hands. Without all four of these godparents, this volume would never have been born: we, and you, owe them our sincere thanks. We also thank the Delmas Foundation for an initial planning grant and the Warburg Institute and the Scuola Normale Superiore for their hospitality at early organizational sessions. Beyond this, we thank the advisory editors who believed in this project from the beginning and gladly put to its service their time, energy, and individual and collective wisdom; and the hundreds of authors who, often with good humor, allowed us to push them and prod them, to blackmail and cajole them, and then, when they had delivered their extraordinary articles, to carp and cavil at them. And finally we thank our friends, relatives, and institutions. They have always had to put up with a lot from us, but never more than this time. If, dear reader, you find some surprise and pleasure in perusing the volume open before you, then you have many others besides us to thank for it.

ANTHONY GRAFTON, *Princeton University*

GLENN W. MOST, *Scuola Normale Superiore di Pisa, University of Chicago*

SALVATORE SETTIS, *Scuola Normale Superiore di Pisa*

May 2010

LIST OF ARTICLES

Academy
Achilles
Actaeon
Adam, Robert
Adonis
Aeneas
Aeschylus
Aesthetics
Affecti
Ajax
Al-Fārābī
Alberti, Leon Battista
Alcestis
Alchemy
Alcuin
Alexander the Great
Alexandria
Alexandrianism
Allegory
Amazons
Amphitryon
Anacharsis
Anacreon and Anacreontics
Ancients and Moderns
Annius of Viterbo
Anthology and Florilegium
Anthropology
Antigone
Antiquarianism
Aphrodite
Apollo
Apollo Belvedere
Apuleius
Arachne
Arcadia
Archimedes
Architecture
Argonauts
Ariadne
Aristocracy
Aristophanes
Aristotle and Aristotelianism
Armenian Hellenism
Art History and Criticism
Asterisk
Astérix
Astrology
Astronomy
Atheism
Athens
Atlantis
Atlas
Atoms and Atomism
Atrium
Atticism
Augustine
Augustus
Automata
Averroës
Avicenna
Baalbek
Bacchanalia and Saturnalia
Baghdad Aristotelians
Barbarians
Barberini Faun
Basilisk
Baths
Bellori, Giovan Pietro
Belvedere Torso
Bentley, Richard
Bessarion of Nicaea
Biography
Boccaccio, Giovanni
Böckh, August
Boethius
Book, Manuscript: Development and Transmission
Book, Manuscript: Production
Book, Printed
Botany
Bronze
Brutus
Budé, Guillaume
Burckhardt, Jacob
Byzantium
Caesar, as Political Title
Caesar, Julius
Caesars, Twelve
Calendars, Chronicles, Chronology
Cameos and Gems
Carpe diem
Cartography
Caryatid
Casaubon, Isaac
Cassandra
Castor and Pollux
Catacombs
Catharsis
Cato the Younger
Catullus
Cavafy, C. P.
Censorship

Centaur
Cento
Chaos
Chartres
Chaucer, Geoffrey
Chrēsis
Christine de Pizan
Cicero and Ciceronianism
Cinema
Circe
Cities, Praise of
City Planning
Classical
Cleopatra
Coins and Medals
Collecting
Colony
Color
Colosseum
Comedy and the Comic
Comic Books
Commentary
Concord, Philosophical
Consolation
Constantine
Constantinople
Constitution, Mixed
Corneille, Pierre
Cosmology
Cupid
Cyclops
Cynicism
Dacier, Anne
Danaë
Dante Alighieri
Daphnis
David, Jacques-Louis
Delphin Classics
Demeter and Persephone
Demiurge
Democracy
Demon
Demosthenes
Despotism, Oriental
Deus ex Machina
Devil
Dialectic
Dialogue
Dictatorship
Dido
Diels, Hermann
Dilettanti, Society of
Diogenes Laertius
Dionysus
Diophantus
Dioscorides
Diotima
Divination
Domus Aurea
Donation of Constantine
Donatus
Doxography
Dramatic Unities
Dream Interpretation
Dulce et decorum est pro patria mori
East and West
Ecphrasis
Education
Egypt
Electra
Elegy
Elgin Marbles
Emblem
Empedocles
Empire
Endymion
Epic
Epictetus
Epicurus and Epicureanism
Epigram
Epigraphy
Erasmus, Desiderius
Estienne, Henri II (Henricus Stephanus)
Ethics
Ethnography
Etruscans
Etymology
Euclid
Euripides
Europe
Eustathius
Fascism
Fashion
Fathers, Church
Faun
Ficino, Marsilio
Fin de Siècle Art
Forgery
Forma Urbis Romae
Fortune
Forum
Founding Fathers, American
Fragments
Fraternities and Sororities
Freud, Sigmund
Galatea
Galen
Galileo Galilei
Gandhara
Ganymede
Gellius, Aulus
Genius
Genre
Geography
Gesture and Dance
Giants
Gibbon, Edward
Glass
Goethe, Johann Wolfgang von
Grammar
Grand Tour
Greek, Ancient
Greek, Modern
Greek, Modern Uses of Ancient
Greek Anthology
Greek Revival
Grotto
Guidebooks to Ancient Rome
Gymnasium
Gynecology
Hadrian's Villa
Hagia Sophia
Hannibal
Harmony of the Spheres
Heidegger, Martin
Helen of Troy

Hellenes
Hellenistic Age
Heraclitus
Herculaneum
Hercules
Herm
Hermaphroditus
Hermes Trismegistus and Hermeticism
Hero
Hero and Leander
Herodotus
Hesiod
Heyne, Christian Gottlob
Hieroglyphs
Hippocrates
Hippocratic Oath
Historicism
Historiography
History Painting
Homer
Homosexuality
Horace
Households and Householding
Humanism
Humors
Hunayn ibn-Ishāq
Hydra
Hypnerotomachia Poliphili
Iconoclasm
Imitation and Mimesis
Immortality of the Soul
India
Inscriptions, Greek and Latin
Interpretatio Christiana
Iphigenia
Iranian Hellenism
Irony
Isagoge
Isidore of Seville
Islam
Janus
Jesuits
Judaism
Julian
Juvenal
Knossos
Korais, Adamantios
Labyrinth
Lachmann, Karl
Laocoön
Latin and the Professions
Latin Language
Law, Roman
Leda
Lessing, Gotthold Ephraim
Letters and Epistolography
Liberal Arts
Liberty
Libraries
Ligorio, Pirro
Livy
Locus Amoenus
Lodging
Loeb Classical Library
Logic
Lucan
Lucian
Lucretius
Lyceum
Lyric Poetry
Macaulay, Thomas Babington
Machiavelli, Niccolò
Macrobius
Maecenas
Maenads
Magic
Magna Graecia
Maison Carrée
Mars
Marsyas
Martial
Martianus Capella
Marxism
Masada
Matriarchy
Mausoleum
Maxims
Medea
Medicine
Melancholy
Melanchthon, Philipp
Menander
Mercuriale, Girolamo
Metaphrasis
Metaphysics
Meteorology
Michelangelo
Midas
Milton, John
Mime and Pantomime
Mirabilia Urbis
Mithras
Mnemonics
Modernism in Art
Mommsen, Theodor
Monsters
Montaigne, Michel de
Mosaic
Moschopoulos, Manuel
Muses
Museum
Music
Musical Instruments
Mycenae
Mystery Religions
Mythology
Names
Narcissus
Natural History
Neo-Latin
Neoclassicism
Neoplatonism
Neptune
Nero
Nicetas Codex
Niebuhr, Barthold Georg
Nietzsche, Friedrich
Notitia Dignitatum
Novel
Nudity
Numbers, Numerals, Notation
Numismatics
Obelisk
Ode
Odysseus
Oedipus
Olympia

Olympic Games
Olympus
Opera
Optics
Oracles
Ornament
Orpheus
Ovid
Paestum
Paganism
Palace
Palimpsest
Palladio, Andrea
Palmyra
Pan
Pandora
Panegyric
Pantheon
Paper Museum
Papyrology
Parasite
Parmenides
Parnassus
Parody and Burlesque
Parthenon
Pasquino
Pastoral
Pausanias
Pederasty
Pegasus
Penelope
Pergamon
Persia
Petrarch
Petronius
Phaedra
Phaethon
Pharmacology
Philhellenism
Philo
Philosophy
Photius
Physiognomy
Physiologus
Picasso, Pablo
Pico della Mirandola, Giovanni
Pindar
Piranesi, Giovanni Battista
Plague
Planudes, Maximus
Plaster Casts
Plato and Platonism
Plautus
Pléiade
Pliny the Elder
Pliny the Younger
Plutarch
Poetics
Political Theory
Poliziano, Angelo
Pompeii
Pope, Alexander
Popular Culture
Pornography
Porphyry
Portico
Portraits, Reception of Ancient
Praeneste
Presocratics
Professionalization of Classics
Progress and Decline
Prometheus
Pronunciation of Greek and Latin
Propertius
Prosody
Psellus, Michael
Ptolemy
Purple
Pygmalion
Pyramid
Pyramus and Thisbe
Pythagoras and Pythagoreanism
Rabelais, François
Racine, Jean Baptiste
Raphael
Ravenna
Renaissance
Replicas
Republicanism
Revolution, French
Rhetoric
Rhōmaioi
Roads, Roman
Roman Monuments, Reuse of
Romance, Medieval
Romanticism
Rome
Ronsard, Pierre de
Roswitha
Rubens
Ruins
Sacrifice in the Arts
Sallust
Sappho
Sarcophagi
Satire
Scaliger, Joseph Justus
Scaliger, Julius Caesar
Schinkel, Karl Friedrich
Schlegel, Friedrich
Sculpture
Seneca the Elder
Seneca the Younger
Seven Sages of Rome
Seven Wonders of the World
Sewers
Sexuality
Shakespeare
Sibyls
Sicily
Sirens
Sisyphus
Skepticism
Slavery
Soane, John
Socrates
Sophocles
Sparta
Spartacus
Speculum Romanae Magnificentiae
Split
Spolia
Sports
Squaring the Circle
Stadium
Statius
Stoicism
Suda

Suetonius
Suicide
Symposium
Syriac Hellenism
Tacitus and Tacitism
Tantalus
Television
Temperament
Temple
Terence
Teubner
Theater Architecture
Thermopylae
Thomas Magister
Thucydides
Thyestes
Toga
Topos
Tourism and Travel
Tragedy and the Tragic
Translatio Imperii
Translation
Triclinius, Demetrius
Triumphal Arch
Triumphal Bridge
Troilus
Tzetzes, John
Ut pictura poesis
Valla, Lorenzo
Vegetarianism
Venice
Venus de Milo
Veterinary Medicine
Vico, Giambattista
Virgil
Vitruvius and the Classical Orders
Volcanoes
War, Just
Warburg, Aby
Warfare
Water Supply
Widow of Ephesus
Wilamowitz-Moellendorff, Ulrich von
Winckelmann, Johann Joachim
Wolf, Friedrich August
Wonders
Writing
Xanthippe
Xenophon
Zeno's Paradoxes
Zoology

THE CLASSICAL TRADITION

Academy

The word *academy* owes its origin to Greek antiquity. It served first as the name of the place where Plato taught his students, on the outskirts of Athens near a grove sacred to a Greek hero known as Academus. The term soon came to signify both an actual place where teaching and learning occurred and a school of thought, one that changed with the times.

After Plato's death in 347 BCE, leadership of the school changed hands, and the Academy took on various philosophical orientations in succeeding epochs. It was in Cicero's day and beyond that the term *academy* began to indicate two things in a philosophical sense: a variety of skepticism (something one could infer from the Socratic practice of bringing interlocutors into doubt), and a relation to the Platonic heritage (which took on certain definitive contours only in late antiquity). The Academy itself also served as a model for future gatherings of learned people. The late 4th century CE saw a revival of the specifically Platonic Academy, after the Neoplatonism of Plotinus grew in popularity in the Mediterranean world.

Though the emperor Justinian closed the Platonic Academy in 529, the word's association with Platonism remained intact in the Middle Ages, just as the skeptical connotation also formed part and parcel of the notion of the academy. This conflation of Platonism and skepticism can be seen in Isidore of Seville (ca. 560–636 CE), whose *Etymologies* became a standard text in the Middle Ages. He wrote: "The Academics are so called because of Plato's villa, the Academy of the Athenians, where Plato himself taught. They believed that all things were uncertain. However, just as it must be admitted that many things are uncertain and hidden (things that God meant to exceed human understanding), nevertheless there are many things that can be grasped by the senses and understood by reason" (*Etymologies* 8.6.11). From then on, *academy* served as a stand-in for skepticism and Platonism, even as it signified, in the Byzantine world and the West, the original model for an informally organized group dedicated to learning.

The 15th century in Italy saw a number of intellectuals use the term to refer to gatherings of intellectuals. Poggio Bracciolini (1380–1459) referred at different times to his own villa, to the intellectual environment of the papal court, and to the intellectual circle surrounding Coluccio Salutati (1331–1406) as an academy (Chambers 1995, 2). An observer of an attempted Council of Union between the Greek and Roman Catholic churches in 1438, Lapo da Castiglionchio the Younger, marveled at the visiting Greek intellectuals. "When I am present at one of their talks," he wrote, "I seem to dwell in that ancient Academy or Lyceum" (*De curiae commodis* 5.4). The presence of the Greeks induced a feeling of Greek antiquity in him, as if he were present at one of the two great classical places of learning, Plato's Academy and Aristotle's Lyceum.

The word had other meanings in 15th-century Latin, running the gamut from a place where intellectuals gathered to an elementary school to a set of books (Hankins 2003, 2:224). The Platonist Marsilio Ficino (1433–1499), for example, defined his academy in a loose way: the Platonic Academy of Florence was an ideal rather than an actual place, a location of the mind where the multileveled truths contained in Plato and Platonic wisdom could be accessed in flexible ways.

Rome in the 15th century had at least two academies. One, a loose configuration of members formed around the Byzantine émigré Cardinal Bessarion (ca. 1403–1472), was dedicated to the rediscovery of Greek wisdom. The academy in this case represented gatherings in Bessarion's household, and the members eagerly used Bessarion's substantial library of Greek texts. Another, the Roman

Academy of the flamboyant Pomponio Leto (1428–1498), was more controversial. Its members were at one point imprisoned by Pope Paul II, accused of paganism, sodomy, and conspiracy. The late 15th century saw the beginnings of clerical fears about orthodoxy, as people began to realize the potential of the printing press to disseminate possibly heretical ideas, and the fact that Leto's academicians studied "dangerous" texts could have been a cause for concern. One of their objects of study, for example, was the great Epicurean poem of Lucretius, *On the Nature of Things,* in which the immortality of the individual human soul is denied.

The multifaceted 15th-century use of *academy,* together with the rather informal gatherings of intellectuals such as those in Rome and Florence, provided the background for the 16th- and 17th-century flourishing of academies, first in Italy and then throughout Europe. The philosophical connotation of the word, with its overtones of skepticism or Platonism, remained in force; as specialized philosophical terms, those meanings continue even today. But in the development of the early modern European academies, it was Humanists of the Italian 15th century who revived its meaning as a loose gathering of intellectuals. This small verbal act can be seen as signifying a larger import of the Humanist movement, one intimately tied to the later burgeoning of academies. One thread that linked many Renaissance Humanists was their rhetorical tendency to dissociate themselves from institutionalized learning. After the 15th century the term *academy* often reflected the desire of intellectuals to have a separate space—sometimes only ideologically separate—not affiliated with existing institutions, in which to carry out their work.

The 16th century saw these sometimes vague yearnings become reality. Two academies in Florence are good examples. The first, called the Orti Oricellari, or Rucellai Gardens, was a learned discussion group sponsored by the Rucellai family of Florence. It later captured the imagination of the 19th-century author George Eliot in her novel *Romola.* It was there that Niccolò Machiavelli presented, as he was writing it, his groundbreaking *Discourses on Livy.* One can assume that, just as Machiavelli's *The Prince* was shaped by his epistolary friendship with Francesco Vettori, so his *Discourses* was developed in the rich context of social interaction and intellectual community represented by the Rucellai Gardens. It is further indicative of the community's importance that Machiavelli set his *Art of War,* a dialogue, in the Rucellai Gardens. It was a key site in the development of the Italian madrigal as well, and the associates who gathered there also had an abiding interest in another topic of great concern: the development of the Tuscan vernacular (Cummings 2004, 35–36).

Rucellai Gardens was referred to most often informally, as the Gardens. In contrast, the Sacred Academy of the Medici, also in Florence, defined itself as an academy, kept membership lists, and engaged in formally organized projects. A certain project included among its proponents one "Michelangelo *schultore*" (Michelangelo the sculptor), as a key document demonstrates (Cummings 80). The academicians wanted to have Dante's remains moved from Ravenna to Florence, and their petition was directed to Pope Leo X (himself a Medici and sympathetic to the group). The petition reveals that, in addition to Michelangelo, the Sacred Academy's members included a number of prominent Florentines. Their aim in this case went unfulfilled, but their effort shows some of the directions in which early modern academies were to travel.

One of these directions related to language. The 16th and 17th centuries saw the increased growth of sovereign states, and an important aspect of this growth was the attempt to define suitable national languages. Throughout Europe there arose increasingly refined, rule-bound, and classicizing conceptions of vernaculars. Certain early modern academies took the lead. The Accademia della Crusca (Academy of the "Bran") took as its primary mission the definition, regulation, and protection of the Italian language. Its members published a dictionary, the *Vocabolario degli accademici della crusca,* in 1621, basing it on three classic works from the 14th century: Dante's *Divine Comedy,* Boccaccio's *Decameron,* and Petrarch's *Canzoniere.* This seeming archaism was criticized, and the dictionary underwent revisions. The project's aims signaled a desire to plumb the origins of common language.

The French followed this language-based lead. Founded in 1635 during the reign of King Louis XII by Cardinal Richelieu, the Académie Françoise (now known as the Académie Française, the French Academy) also took as its mission the establishment of fixed rules for the national language. It too published a dictionary; the academicians published the first version in 1694. Like the Italian *Vocabolario* of the Accademia della Crusca, it has been continuously revised and republished. Both academies still exist today as repositories of learning and monitors of their national language.

Language was one concern of the academies, science was another. "Natural philosophy" (natural science) separated itself gradually from philosophy as a whole in the early modern period. Many practitioners of this new science found institutional structures unable to accommodate the new methods they employed to carry out their scientific agendas. They often did not fit in at universities and were compelled to seek patronage from other sources.

Elite patrons played a lead role in fostering the new science. Federico Cesi (1586–1630) founded the Accademia dei Lincei, the Academy of the Lynxes, in 1603 (Freedberg 2002). The lynx was emblematic because it was presumed to have extraordinary powers of sight, exactly what it was hoped the new science would provide. Attracted by the power of the printing press to provide representations of natural phenomena, the Linceans were drawn first to botanical studies. This scientific area remained a central concern, culminating in the 1651 publication of the academy's *Tesoro messicano* (*Mexican Treasury*), which communicated the flora and fauna of the New World to a broad audience. In 1611 Galileo Galilei (1564–1642) became a Lincean. Galileo's membership meant that the new heliocentric view of the known and observable universe put forth by Nicolaus Copernicus (1473–1543) had support. It was with the backing of the academy that Galileo published both his groundbreaking treatise on sunspots and his *Saggiatore*. The Accademia dei Lincei went into a period of dormancy after the death of Cesi in 1630. Revived in the 19th century, it continues today, housed in the Palazzo Corsini in Rome.

The Accademia dei Lincei served as inspiration for a young German doctor, Johann Lorenz Bausch (1605–1665), from the free imperial city of Schweinfurt. After spending some youthful years traveling in Italy, he returned to Schweinfurt, where he and three friends founded the Academia Naturae Curiosorum (Academy for those Curious about Nature) in 1652. Eventually this group increased in number (it had 73 members by 1677), developed its own statutes, and gained recognition from the Habsburg Holy Roman Emperor Leopold I (r. 1658–1705). Known thenceforth informally as the Leopoldina, the academy began publishing a journal (the *Ephemeriden*), soon included Goethe as a member, and became the longest continuously running academy for research in the natural sciences. It still exists today, headquartered in Halle.

A propensity to inquire into the "new philosophy" also drove the members of the Royal Society in Britain. The chemist Robert Boyle (1627–1691) mentioned in various letters an "Invisible" or a "Philosophical" college whose members began meeting as early as 1645. Another member, the mathematician John Wallis (1616–1703), wrote that, around that time, the English civil wars were causing interruption to "academical studies . . . in both our universities [Oxford and Cambridge]." He was "acquainted with divers worthy persons, inquisitive of natural philosophy, and other parts of human learning . . . We did . . . meet weekly in London on a certain day and hour" (Lyons 1944).

After the Restoration of the monarchy in 1660, the members of the Royal Society sought the backing of Charles II, and in 1662 and 1663 they received charters establishing royal support for the society. In 1672 Isaac Newton (1643–1727) was elected to membership after he donated a telescope to the society. Newton's first scientific publication, concerning light and color, appeared that year in the Royal Society's journal, *Philosophical Transactions.* Still published today, *Philosophical Transactions* is the world's oldest continuously published scholarly journal. Much of Newton's work was conducted in the Royal Society's give-and-take environment, leading to the 1687 publication of his *Mathematical Principles of Natural Philosophy,* or the *Principia,* as it is now known.

The two charters that the Royal Society received included the king as a member, a fact that represents an important aspect of almost all early modern learned societies: their aristocratic or indeed royal leaning. From the vague inclinations of the 15th-century Humanists to the late early modern period, academies possessed strong links to society's socioeconomic elites. Not until 1847, for example, did the Royal Society officially decide that election was to be determined by scientific merit alone (as opposed to a combination of merit and social standing). Its learned and wealthy amateurs were counted on not only to understand the purposes of the learned society but also to support those purposes financially.

As natural philosophy separated itself from philosophy as a whole, professionalization in the sciences became the norm. This development was accompanied by more state patronage of the many academies founded in the early modern era. The academies went on to become key elements of modern intellectual life.

BIBL.: David Chambers, "The Earlier Academies in Italy," in *Italian Academies of the Sixteenth Century,* ed. David Chambers and François Quiviger (London 1995) 1–14. Anthony M. Cummings, *The Maecenas and the Madrigalist: Patrons, Patronage, and the Origins of the Italian Madrigal* (Philadelphia 2004). John Dillon, *The Heirs of Plato: A Study of the Old Academy,* 347–274 BC (Oxford 2003). David Freedberg, *The Eye of the Lynx* (Chicago 2002). James Hankins, *Humanism and Platonism in the Italian Renaissance,* 2 vols. (Rome 2003). Isidore of Seville, *Etymologiarum sive originum libri XX,* ed. Wallace M. Lindsay (Oxford 1957). Lapo da Castiglionchio the Younger, *De curiae commodis,* in *Renaissance Humanism and the Papal Curia: Lapo Da Castiglionchio the Younger's De curiae commodis,* ed. and trans. Christopher S. Celenza (Ann Arbor 1999). Henry G. Lyons, *The Royal Society, 1660–1940* (Cambridge 1944). C.C.

Achilles

Achilles (Greek *Achilleus*) occurs as a common masculine name in Greek documents as far back as the late Bronze Age. At that time a man so named may have become one of the main figures of the story of Troy, the outlines of which we know mainly from post-Homeric epics of the Epic Cycle (7th–6th cents. BCE; only late summaries survive). The first author to flesh out the character was clearly Homer, who made Achilles the central figure of his *Iliad* (5.1: "Rage, Goddess—sing the rage of Peleus' son Achilles," Fagles trans.). The Epic Cycle provides (fictitious) details of Achilles' biography (including the love affairs so popular with later commentators, e.g., those with Deidameia, daughter of Lykomedes; with Penthesilea, queen of the Amazons; and with Polyxena, daughter of Priam). Homer, by contrast, concentrates on portraying Achilles' character, in what W. Kullmann has called a "psychologization of the saga's events." In Homer's treatment Achilles becomes the embodiment of the ancient ideal of nobility—"to be always best in battle and pre-eminent beyond all others" (*Iliad* 11.784, Lattimore trans.)—and the symbol of a genuine hero, who prefers an early death with glory to a long but dull life (*Iliad* 9.410–416).

The reception of Achilles in this sense began in the visual arts by the early 7th century (Kossatz-Deissmann 1981). The literary reception first became available to us in early Greek lyric poetry in the work of Sappho and Alkaios (ca. 600 BCE), who praised Achilles as an exemplary young war hero (Sappho fr. 105a, 218V; Alkaios fr. 42V). It continues in the same vein with Pindar (*Nemean Odes* 3.43–63; *Olympian Odes* 2.79–83) and Bacchylides (13), reaching its first culmination in Attic tragedy: Aeschylus devotes an entire tetralogy to Achilles (*Achilleis;* only fragments survive); it dramatizes the second half of the *Iliad,* in particular Achilles' grief over the death of Patroclus (a homosexual component being emphasized for what may be the first time), Achilles' revenge on Hector, and the return of Hector's corpse to Priam (later imitated by the Roman tragic poet Accius, 2nd cent. BCE). During the 5th century BCE at least eight tragedians produced plays on Achilles; one is Sophocles' satyr play *The Loves of Achilles* (of which, unfortunately, only the title and a few fragments are known). In all these versions the fundamental attitude is the same admiration set forth in the ancient epic. It is reflected in the cultic veneration of Achilles as a hero or god in the entire Greek world, from lower Italy across the Greek mainland to Asia Minor and the region of the Black Sea, as well as in the tradition that he spent the afterlife in the Elysian Islands (e.g., Pindar, Olympian Odes 2.79). Later, this admiration had an effect on events in world politics; for example, the royal dynasty of Epirus, to which Alexander the Great belonged, claimed descent from Achilles.

Toward the end of the 5th century BCE a new strand began to emerge, which deviated from that of admiration; this minor thread mocks, defames, and trivializes Homer's heroic "idea of Achilles" or makes a concerted attempt to discredit it. This tendency—probably a result of the disillusionment arising from the general decay of values during the Peloponnesian War—first became palpable in Euripides, who on several occasions adopted a defensive, ironic, or bitter tone when referring to the idea of Achilles (*Hekabe, Elektra, Iphigenia in Aulis*). The process of disparaging him continued in Roman literature, particularly in the Augustan period. The rulers of Rome claimed descent from the Trojans; although they and their sympathizers praised Achilles' *summa virtus* through gritted teeth (Horace, *Satires* 1.7.14f.; cf. *Ars poetica* 120–122), ultimately they could see in the "best of the Achaeans" (*Iliad* 1.244; 2.761f.; 17.164f.) only negative traits. In Virgil's *Aeneid* he appears as a savage (*saevus*), merciless (*immitis*) butcher of men (2.29; 1.30; 3.87), whereas in Horace he is the incarnation of inhuman brutality (*Odes* 4.6.17–20). A second strand of disparagement runs from Catullus (poem 64) via Propertius (2.8.29–30), Ovid (*Ars amatoria* 1.681–704), and Statius; the last-named transforms Achilles the heroic warrior into a ladies' man (*Achilleis* fr.). This strand continues with the late Latin translations of trivialized Greek versions of Homer by writers such as Dictys and Dares (probably 2nd cent. CE) and runs all the way to the Middle Ages, in Benoît de Sainte-Maure's *Roman de Troie* (ca. 1160) and its Latin translation, *Historia destructionis Troiae* by Guido delle Colonne (1287). There Achilles the Greek, a menacing barbarian, is contrasted with the cultivated Trojans, the supposed ancestors of the medieval European nobility, and his most interesting feature is his supposed erotomania, evinced in his obsessions with Briseïs, Penthesilea, and Polyxena, as well as his alleged homosexual relationship with Patroclus. Since Benoît's and Guido's versions were translated or retold countless times in the most prevalent vernacular languages, as late as the 17th-century Europeans saw Achilles primarily through Benoît's eyes.

Even after the original *Iliad* appeared in print (1488), this view remained influential through retellings in verse and prose, handbooks of mythology, lexicons, and novels. The best-known example is Shakespeare's play *Troilus and Cressida* (ca. 1602), a mordant and sometimes cynical antiheroic comedy, which derives from Benoît and Guido by way of Boccaccio's epic *Filostrato* (1335), Chaucer's verse narrative *Troilus and Criseyde* (ca. 1360), the *Troye Book,* an abridged treatment of the same material by Chaucer's pupil J. Lydgate (ca. 1420), and the *Recuyell of the Historyes of Troye* (a translation of a French prose version) by the first English printer, William Caxton (1475). Shakespeare did not know Homer's original *Iliad,* and clearly he was also unfamiliar with George Chapman's first experimental translation of seven books of the *Iliad,* which appeared in 1598; the world of Greek heroic poetry of the 8th century BCE remained closed to him. It was replaced by the world of medieval knighthood and minnesang (lyric songwriting), although Shakespeare did not seek to glorify it. Rather, he unmasks its hollowness and depravity (including veiled references to contemporary political events). Both Greeks and Trojans act equally immorally in the service of their highest values, war and lasciviousness; the most frequently mentioned value category is lechery. Achilles has only a minor role in this drama of love and betrayal between Priam's son Troilus and Cressida, daughter of a Trojan priest (originally named Cryseïs in Homer); he serves here as a prime example of an egomaniac, a man of great physical superiority who is inwardly corroded by pride and conceit. His humiliation by Agamemnon serves only as a justification of his idle and dissolute life with his lover Patroclus ("Achilles' brach": 2.1.112) so long as the woman he loves passionately from afar—Polyxena—remains inaccessible. Achilles is introduced by Cressida's go-between uncle Pandarus as "a drayman, a porter, a very camel" (1.2.240); the other Greek leaders (Odysseus, Ajax, Agamemnon, Nestor) regard him as "lion-sick—sick of proud heart" (2.3.85), a man who is throwing away what good reputation he still possesses by continuing to boycott the battle (Agamemnon: "Much attribute he hath, and much the reason/Why we ascribe it to him; yet all his virtues,/Not virtuously on his own part beheld,/Do in our eyes begin to lose their gloss": 2.3.115–118). After Hector has killed Patroclus, Achilles seeks vengeance but, as he faces his enemy in single combat, his rage subsides; he retreats with a cowardly excuse: "Be happy that my arms are out of use:/My rest and negligence befriends thee now,/But thou anon shalt hear of me again" (5.6.17–19). In keeping with this behavior he lets his myrmidons kill the defenseless Hector shortly afterward and then proclaims himself the victor: "On, Myrmidons, and cry you all amain/'Achilles hath the mighty Hector slain'" (5.9.13–14). No later writer would ever surpass Shakespeare's brutal moral annihilation of Homer's idea of Achilles.

Continuing ignorance of the original *Iliad* up to the 19th century caused the image of Achilles to remain distorted in comparison with the original, with few exceptions. A further essential contribution was the controversy over the merit of Homer's poetry that blossomed after the Renaissance and reached a peak around 1700 in the battle of the ancients and moderns throughout Europe. In the hard-fought conflict between supporters and critics of Homer, the figure of Achilles played an important role, because his behavior and character proved particularly unappealing to complex modern sensibilities (see Finsler 1912).

No agreement was ever reached. Treatment of the figure in the arts thus tended to remain superficial: of the 50 or so paintings of Achilles produced in Europe between 1500 and 1850 (by artists including van Dyck, Rubens, Poussin, Tischbein, and Tiepolo), half are devoted to the subject of "Achilles with the daughters of Lykomedes," and the majority of the approximately 20 operas and operettas composed on this theme between 1650 and 1900 deal with his love affairs (including Handel's *Deidamia* of 1739, still performed today). The roughly 25 epic and dramatic versions of the material do not look much different. It is true that the groundbreaking translations of the *Iliad* (1783) and *Odyssey* (1781) into German by Johann Heinrich Voss and the study by Friedrich August Wolf of the epics' historical background (*Prolegomena ad Homerum,* 1795) led to a much better informed assessment, and thus occasionally a far more positive one, particularly in German classicism:

> Goethe: "the best of the Greeks, the worthy favorite of the gods" (*Achilleïs,* 1797–1799, line 274)
> Hölderlin, "At the fig tree my Achilles died" (*Mnemosyne,* 1803)
> Kleist, "Achilles, son of the gods" (*Penthesilea,* 1807).

Nevertheless, the approach remained selective and simple; Achilles was portrayed as a lover rather than as a complex and tragic figure within the larger heroic context of his time. In Goethe's *Achilleïs,* a fragment, the title character would die of love for Polyxena, according to the surviving outline. In Kleist's *Penthesilea* it is the hero's passion for the Amazon queen that prompts him to abandon his heroic role and succumb to her; in the end it is this passion that, like a maenad, rips him apart and devours him.

Not until the 20th century is the Achilles of the *Iliad* (and not of *Iliad* reception history) rediscovered—at least occasionally, although not to anywhere near the same extent as the figure of Odysseus, who is much more congenial to the modern temperament. In the aftermath of both world wars and the Holocaust, however, modern treatments have tended to place a one-sided emphasis on Achilles' uncompromising nature and obsession with revenge (as had been the case at the end of the 5th century BCE), portraying it as moral turpitude, an almost sadistic indolence. Thus, in his play *Cement* (*Zement,* 1972) the German playwright Heiner Müller presents Achilles' revenge on the dead Hector as the ultimate in cold and mercenary brutality, with visual and acoustic suggestions of a lust for blood ("the skin in shreds—the flesh torn apart—the bones splintered"). It represents a strand of reception history that completely bypasses the essence of Homer's idea of Achilles and has reached its pinnacle to date with Christa Wolf's *Kassandra* (1983), in which Achilles is reduced to "the swine." A notable departure from the usual black-and-white depictions of the character is offered by Derek Walcott in his epic poem of the Caribbean, *Omeros* (1990). There he transforms Achilles into a fisherman named Achille who is competing with a taxi driver, Hector, for a fickle woman named Helen. Achille and Helen are united in the end, just like the Achilles and Helen of antiquity on the Elysian Islands. The most recent attempt to return to something like the sophistication and subtlety of Homer's characterization of Achilles, at least in places, is Wolfgang Petersen's film *Troy.* Though such an assessment of a blockbuster costume epic may appear paradoxical at first glance, deeper analysis reveals an approach that is not altogether trivial and even a bit subversive.

BIBL.: Georg Finsler, *Homer in der Neuzeit von Dante bis Goethe* (Leipzig 1912). Herbert Hunger, *Lexikon der griechischen und römischen Mythologie, mit Hinweisen auf das Fortwirken antker Stoffe und Motive in der bildenden Kunst, Literatur und Musik des Abendlandes bis zur Gegenwart,* 8th rev. ed. (Vienna 1988). Catherine C. King, *Achilles: Paradigms of the War Hero from Homer to the Middle Ages* (Berkeley 1987). Anneliese Kossatz-Deissmann, "Achilleus," in *Lexicon Iconographicum Mythologiae Classicae* (Zurich 1981). Joachim Latacz, *Achilleus: Wandlungen eines europäischen Heldenbildes,* 2nd ed. (Stuttgart 1997) and "From Homer's Troy to Petersen's Troy," in *Troy: From Homer's Iliad to Hollywood Epic,* ed. Martin M. Winkler (Oxford 2007) 27–42. R. P. Martin, *The Language of Heroes: Speech and Performance in the Iliad* (Ithaca 1989). Bernd Seidensticker, "Die literarische Rezeption Homers in der Neuzeit," in *Homer: Der Mythos von Troia in Dichtung und Kunst,* ed. J. Latacz et al. (Munich 2008).

J.LA.

Translated by Deborah Lucas Schneider

Actaeon

Greek Aktaion, Etruscan Ataiun, Latin Actaeon, mythic hero and hunter. Among the many Greek myths that explore the paradoxically intimate relationship between hunters and their prey, the story of Aktaion draws the most explicit parallel between the two; when the goddess

Artemis suddenly transformed the young man into a stag, his own hunting dogs turned on him and devoured him. In the earliest known versions of the myth, Artemis punished Aktaion for boasting that he was a better hunter than she: this version can be seen on the vase by the Pan Painter and the metope from Temple E at Selinunte, both ca. 470–460 BCE, and also appears in Euripides' *Bacchae;* it is also presumably the story implied in Etruscan vase paintings showing a stag-headed Ataiun set upon by his dogs. A sexier Hellenistic retelling of the myth (by Callimachus) claimed that Aktaion incurred the wrath of the goddess when he spied her bathing with her nymphs. This version of the tale, with its dramatic tensions between male and female, human and animal, predictably caught the fancy of poets and artists alike and became the definitive version of the myth for the Romans, most memorably, and wittily, in Ovid's *Metamorphoses* (3.138–252).

Ovid was made palatable for medieval European readers in "moralized" versions that turned his ancient myths of transformation into Christian allegories; in this *Ovide moralisé* tradition, Actaeon stood for Christ. His fate as a heroic victim, wounded, killed, and eventually granted heroic status, prefigured Jesus' Passion and Resurrection. Furthermore, chivalric tradition considered stags royal animals; as the most regal of victims, they prefigured Christ's kingship as well as his suffering and death. Thus, two medieval chivalric saints, Hubert and Eustace, were each converted to an actively Christian life after seeing visions of the Cross shining between the antlers of a magnificent stag. Stags also appear as Christ figures in 16th-century frescoes for the Benedictine convents of San Benedetto Po and San Paolo in Parma, both in northern Italy.

Christian allegory also remodeled Actaeon's nemesis, Artemis/Diana. No longer a nature goddess with a vindictive streak, she became, as a divinity sworn to virginity, an image of divine purity, all the more so when naked at her bath. Actaeon's pursuit of her, inadvertent in ancient myth, became a deliberate hunt in chivalric romances like Giovanni Boccaccio's *Ninfale fiesolano* (ca. 1345) and Jacopo Sannazzaro's *Arcadia* (first published 1504).

Not much later the Augustinian prelate (and future cardinal) Giles of Viterbo, a friend of Sannazaro's, retold the Christianized myth of Actaeon with a deliberately Neoplatonic slant in an influential theological commentary, the *Sentences according to the Mind of Plato* (written 1506–1512, it survives only in manuscript form). He also composed a more secular verse rendition, "The Most Beautiful Hunt of Love" (*La caccia bellissima dell'amore*), in which Diana becomes an image of the human soul, and Actaeon an aspiring philosopher who searches the physical world for traces of divinity; in spying the goddess, the soul is transported to a higher level of awareness and dies to its old ways. In 1585 the Italian philosopher Giordano Bruno further developed this philosophical version of Actaeon in his dialogue *On the Heroic Frenzies.*

Thereafter Actaeon appeared in art and literature mostly as a hero of classical myth rather than an allegorical figure, and as an excuse, most especially, to portray Diana and her nymphs at their bath (Correggio, Titian, Domenichino), or to explore the boundaries between human and animal in a human being who is becoming a four-hoofed, horned creature. The transformation from man to beast, for example, animates the Art Deco sculptor Paul Manship's small bronze *Actaeon* (now in the American School of Classical Studies, Athens). Ancient Romans and their modern Italian descendants have never been unaware of another image that stag-horned Actaeon suggests: the horns that mark out a cuckold, a *cornuto.* Modern Romans joke about the men who are married near the Pantheon in the church of Sant' Eustachio (Saint Eustace), with its horned stag on the summit of the facade; these poor bridegrooms are supposedly destined to "wear the horns," not as heroic hunters but as inadequate husbands.

BIBL.: H. Casanova-Robin, *Diane et Actéon: Éclats et reflets d'un mythe à la Renaissance et à l'âge baroque* (Paris 2003). W. Cziesla, *Aktaion Polyprágmon: Variationen eines antiken Themas in der europäischen Renaissance* (Frankfurt 1989). L. R. Lacy, "The Myth of Aktaion: Literary and Iconographic Studies" (PhD diss., Bryn Mawr 1984). I.D.R.

Adam, Robert

Scottish architect and designer, 1728–1792. One of the most prolific and versatile designers in European Neoclassicism, Adam was the creative force, in collaboration with his three brothers, in promoting a stylistic revolution in architecture and the decorative arts, based on a wide range of classical sources. Ultimately the impact of their consciously devised, consumer-led style extended from North America to the Russia of Catherine the Great.

After training with his father, William Adam, the leading Scottish architect in the first half of the 18th century, Robert made a well-documented Grand Tour, mainly in Italy (1754–1757). His extremely varied studies covered not only the classical antiquities of Rome and Herculaneum but also the decorative language of Renaissance designers such as Raphael, Peruzzi, and Giulio Romano, as well as contemporary architects such as Salvi and Vanvitelli. These experiences were catalyzed and reinforced by the teachings of his contemporary Piranesi, whose unique approach to the creative range offered by the classical tradition countered the exclusive attitude of the early Greek Revival. Piranesi advocated a flexible system of modern design, based on an eclectic use of classical material that embraced not only Etruscan culture and late imperial Rome but, eventually, ancient Greece as well as Egypt. During his return journey to Britain in 1757, Robert surveyed the remains of Diocletian's marine palace (ca. 305 CE) overlooking the Adriatic at Spalato (Split) in Dalmatia, which was to feature in a handsome illustrated folio volume, partly promotional as well as offering new sources and concepts for design, dedicated to George III in 1764.

While James, his younger brother, made a less productive Grand Tour (1760–1763), Robert established their practice in London, aided by their father's financial acumen. The brothers swiftly developed a fashionable reputation, applying Robert's idiosyncratic style in a highly efficient atelier and exploiting the new processes and synthetic materials of the early Industrial Revolution. Robert's ornamental vocabulary of classical motifs would be applied to an unprecedented range of media from facades to interior decorative schemes in plasterwork and stucco (with a novel concern for the effect of color as found in antiquity) and incorporating furniture, metalwork, textiles, and ceramics. In the decorative arts the furniture of Chippendale, the earthenware of Wedgwood, and the metalwork of Matthew Boulton all reflected this classical idiom. Notable among a group of major country houses representing Adam's new style is Kedleston Hall, Derbyshire (1760–1777), where the south front marks a radical break with established neo-Palladian design, introducing the Piranesian conception of a combined triumphal arch and domed rotunda, approached by a dynamic curved staircase. The remodeling of Syon House, Middlesex (1760–1767), was inspired by the complex scenic qualities of Roman thermal planning (that is, relating to the Roman public baths) as well as by the sumptuous decoration and color of Roman imperial interiors.

In the 1770s the Adam firm carried out a series of skillfully designed town houses in London, also inspired by antique spatial forms and characterized by an increasing refinement and delicacy of ornament. The monumental influence of Diocletian's palace was expressed in the highly influential Adelphi housing scheme overlooking the Thames (1768–1772, largely demolished in 1937), built by William Adam as contractor; it became the world's first comprehensive block of luxury apartments. Meanwhile, in reaction to rival designers such as William Chambers and James Wyatt, Robert Adam devised a series of particularly controversial interior schemes, notably demonstrated by the Red Drawing Room at Northumberland House (ca. 1773–1775), with its simulated porphyry and richly gilded metal decoration, as well as a series of Etruscan rooms. The latter displayed an exceptionally diverse combination of influences from classical antiquity, including painted vases (as published by Sir William Hamilton, they were believed at the time to be Etruscan), the Domus Aurea (ca. 65 CE, via Raphael's interpretation), and the wall paintings of Herculaneum. The most ambitious example was the Etruscan Dressing Room at Osterley Park (ca. 1775). Here for the first time in Europe was a highly conscious contemporary style, based on antiquity and applied throughout an interior in all its decorative aspects from walls, ceiling, and floor to window fittings and furniture.

Toward the end of a productive career, apart from undertaking major public buildings and parts of the New Town in Edinburgh, Robert designed a remarkable sequence of neo-medieval castles in Scotland (exemplified by Culzean, 1777–1790), which are distinguished by a play of abstract geometrical forms and thought to have been partly inspired by the Roman military architecture of Hadrian's Wall. Ultimately, the theoretical justification of the Adam style was effectively expressed and disseminated through the text and illustrations of *Works in Architecture of Robert and James Adam* (3 folio vols., 1773, 1779, 1822); its influence spread rapidly, notably to the Federal style in North America.

BIBL.: John Fleming, *Robert Adam and His Circle in Edinburgh and Rome* (London 1962). Eileen Harris, *The Genius of Robert Adam: His Interiors* (New Haven 2001). J.W.-E.

Adonis

The beautiful son of Myrrha and her father (Theias, king of Smyrna). Loved by Venus, the goddess who conquers all, he is human: a shepherd and hunter with a boy's down on his cheeks in Theocritus (Idyll 15), but a man in Ovid's *Metamorphoses* (10.523). The story usually focuses on the goddess's grief at her mortal beloved's death, incurred while hunting a boar sent by the vengeful Artemis. Bion's lament for Adonis (Idyll 1) aestheticizes the wound made by the boar's tusk in the young man's white thigh. The plot inversion—a goddess falling in love with a mortal—also became an important part of the myth.

In Jean de Meun's *Romance of the Rose* (1280), when Adonis dies, the narrator draws the moral that men should heed the women they love (15.659–778). In most renditions, however, Venus tends to blame fate rather than her beloved. In Ronsard's "Adonis" (1563), she does lament, "Alas! If only you'd believed me"; but even so, she blames herself: "In need my counsel failed you." At Adonis' death, she follows another shepherd, proving how shallow female affection is, converting the mutability of the mortal to the mutability of the feminine.

Shakespeare's narrative poem *Venus and Adonis* (1593) makes love's inversion of hierarchy comic. Venus, an older, more experienced woman, "like a bold-faced suitor" plucks unhappy Adonis from his horse and stands with "Over one arm the lusty courser's rein/Under her other . . . the tender boy" (31–32). When she learns he means to hunt the boar, she falls on her back, dragging him into a parody of intercourse. The beauty of his wound makes her think the boar tried to kiss Adonis, "nuzzling in his flank" (1,115); given tusks, and the chance, she might have killed him too. In Spenser's *Faerie Queene* (1590) Adonis' story fills the tapestries on the walls of the Castle Joyous (3.1.34–38); the Garden of Adonis (3.6.29–50) anticipates the Garden of Pleasure in Giambattista Marino's epic *Adone* (1623)—a work that outsold Shakespeare's First Folio. Marino's treatment is explicit about the pleasures of love and has Adonis hit the boar with Cupid's arrow; his hip is crushed by a loving tusk.

Venus's desperate love influenced many Elizabethan depictions of courtship, of any beloved, male or female. Shakespeare's homoerotic descriptions of the beauty of

Adonis, and of Venus's masculine pursuit of the boy, eventually led to a novel by Rachilde (Marguerite Valette-Eymery), *Monsieur Vénus* (1884), in which a woman named Raoule pursues a feminine man who works in a flower shop; inevitably he is killed in a duel.

Ecphrasis (elaboration of one artistic medium by another; for example, a poem's portrayal of a sculpture) is an enduring part of the tradition. Ovid's Venus in hunting attire became a popular subject in fine art. In paintings by Phillips Gale, Jacob Matham, Jacopo Amigoni, Ferdinand Bol, Titian, Annibale Carracci, and Abraham Janssens, she gazes up at her Adonis, adoring him. Paintings of Adonis' death restore the divine hierarchy, with Venus standing over his body. Anthony van Dyck, however, painting George Villiers and his wife, Katherine, as Venus and Adonis ca. 1620, shows the nobleman gazing down at his love, who is naked from the waist up. Another recurrent motif is Adonis' dogs, which can express his own itch to be off hunting the boar, or Venus's grief; in a marble sculpture by Canova one even lifts his nose to the couple's backsides.

Opera loved the story, and still does (see Hans Henze's work of 1996). Calderón's *La púrpura de la rosa* (1660) was one of the first wholly sung Spanish dramas. With new music by Tomás de Torrejón, it was performed in Lima, Peru, in 1701, 34 years before opera came to Britain's colonies in North America. A *loa,* or choral praise poem based on the story, and possibly on Calderón's libretto, was written in Mexico by Sor Juana Inés de la Cruz ca. 1681.

BIBL.: W. Atallah, *Adonis dans la littérature et l'art grecs* (Paris 1966). E.M.H.

Aeneas

Son of the Trojan Anchises and the goddess Aphrodite; the strongest Trojan hero after Hector. With his father and his son Ascanius, Aeneas fled Troy and after long wandering reached Italy, where he founded the city of Lavinium and became the forebear of the Romans. He is immortalized in Virgil's *Aeneid* as a virtuous and pious national hero. Three main factors have influenced Aeneas' place in the classical tradition.

First, as the saga of Rome's origins, the *Aeneid* had ideological significance and was very widely read, which secured Aeneas' place in literature from the Augustan age onward. Even after Rome lost political dominance in late antiquity, the *Aeneid* remained a canonical text both for learning Latin and as a source for Roman history; it became a central reference text for literary history, as the figure of Aeneas was invoked directly and indirectly or transported to a different setting (see, e.g., the reception of Virgil and Aeneas in the "Inferno" of Dante's *Divine Comedy* or the parallels to the *Aeneid* in the narrative and imagery of Milton's *Paradise Lost*). Second, the popularity of the Aeneas figure rests on its use by the Julian clan in Rome to support its claim to political power; from the time of Julius Caesar and Augustus the family traced its lineage directly to Aeneas and made him a symbol of a *pius imperator.* In the Middle Ages and early modern period this tradition was taken up by aristocratic and royal families such as the Habsburgs, who could thus follow their genealogy through Aeneas all the way back to Troy. Third, the ambivalent characterization and symbolism of the figure, especially in connection with the Dido episode, provides room for later interpretation, as Aeneas appears on the one hand as a model hero and on the other as a faithless lover responsible for the suicide of the queen of Carthage. Both points of view exist side by side in the tradition, wherein the following emphases are displayed.

The image conveyed by Virgil of Aeneas as a blameless and noble hero dominated reception history in antiquity; in his commentary on Virgil, which dates from the time of the Roman Empire, Fulgentius depicts Aeneas as a model of virtuous conduct. This thread is continued by Cristoforo Landino in his somewhat Neoplatonic interpretations of the *Aeneid,* the *Disputationes camaldulenses* (1480, books 3–4), where he has Aeneas trace a journey of the soul from vice to wisdom. The most influential literary work in this tradition is the *13th Book of the Aeneid,* written by Maffeo Vegeo in 1428, which was first set as an addendum to Virgil's text and came to be included in numerous editions of Virgil, with its own commentary and illustrations by Sebastian Brant added in 1502. This continuation of the *Aeneid* tells of Aeneas' marriage to Lavinia and his peaceful rule in Latium and concludes with his apotheosis, transforming the image of the brutal Aeneas—who at the end of Virgil's 12th book mercilessly kills his opponent, Turnus—into an image of a prince of peace. In addition, the *13th Book,* with its motifs of the marriage and apotheosis, increases the possibilities for allegorical Christian exegesis of his life's journey. Such an interpretation of Aeneas as a symbol of the moral life finds artistic expression in the allegories of the *Sala dell' Eneide* in the Palazzo Spada in Rome (1550), although the most extensive reworking of the material in a Christian sense is probably found in the *Galleria di Enea* and the *Sala di Enea e Didone* in the Roman palace of the Doria Pamphili (1653–1656), where an emphasis on the role of Providence shows Aeneas as a prefiguration of the papacy. This fits with the integration of the figure of Aeneas into the *Fire in the Borgo* in the rooms of Raphael (1514–1517) in the Vatican, which were created in honor of Pope Leo X. The depiction links the literary theme of Aeneas' flight from the burning city of Troy with the action of Pope Leo IV, allegedly historical, when he is said to have put out a fire in Rome in 847 by speaking a blessing. The two are shown as acting both in the service of Rome (by either founding or rescuing the city) and in the service of piety (by saving people in danger), so that the pope is portrayed as an *alter Aeneas.* An opening for this modern religious parallel is offered by the iconography of the hero, who is shown with his father and son; the three figures become an allegory of tradition (the father), the present (Aeneas), and the future (the son). A further link is offered by the rescue of the *penates* (household gods) during the flight from Troy. Raphael only hints at this aspect by depicting Ascanius carrying them in a coffer, but later artists give this motif a particularly prominent place, as Bernini did in his sculpture *Aeneas and Anchises* (Galleria Borghese, ca. 1618).

In addition to Aeneas' piety, his heroism is emphasized when this theme is taken up in historiographic works such as the *Histoire ancienne jusqu'à César* (*Ancient History up to Caesar;* early 13th cent.) and when he is portrayed as a courtly knight in the transformation of the *Aeneid* into a courtly "mini-roman" entitled *Roman d'Énéas* by an anonymous author (ca. 1160). This work in turn influenced Heinrich von Veldeke's *Eneide* (1170–1190).

Also in the 13th century we find the first evidence of a negative view of the Aeneas figure as an antihero; the criticism arises in connection with his flight from Troy, but particularly because of his treatment of Dido. The starting points for the first criticism are the chronicles of Dares and Diktys, which date from the period of imperial Rome and are critical of Troy. Highly esteemed in the Middle Ages, they could be read to imply that Aeneas had betrayed Troy, and the story was continued in works such as Guido delle Colonne's *Historia destructionis Troiae* (1287), which was translated numerous times (including an English version by John Lydgate, *Troy Book,* 1412–1420).

The second point of criticism, Aeneas' betrayal of Dido, arose from the seventh of Ovid's *Epistulae heroidum* (*Letters of Heroines*), which takes Dido's perspective and shows her in despair, vainly pleading with her faithless lover to change his mind. The influence of this tradition appears as early as 1160, in the anonymous *Roman d'Énéas,* where Aeneas is characterized as faithless, and also in the *Roman de la rose* (13th cent.), where he is shown as not keeping his word. This critical tradition extends from the *Ovidius moralizatus* (ca. 1340) and Boccaccio's *Amorosa visione* (1342–1343) and *De claris mulieribus* (1356–1364), through Chaucer (*House of Fame,* 1381, and *The Legend of Good Women,* 1385–1386), C. de Pizan (*Epistre au dieu d'amours* [*Epistle to the God of Love,* 1399], and J. Lydgate (*Fall of Princes,* 1430), all the way to Christopher Marlowe's posthumously published play *The Tragedy of Dido, Queen of Carthage* (1594).

A contrary tendency began to develop during the Renaissance, above all in dramatizations of the Dido episode. Beginning with A. Pazzi de' Medici's *Dido in Cartagine* (1524), playwrights showed Aeneas as less and less culpable and emphasized that Dido's love for him is either a mistake (G. B. Giraldi Cinczio, *Didone,* 1541) or excessive and uncontrolled (W. Gager, *Dido,* 1583). In Petrus Ligneus' Dido play (1559) she is pursued by one of the Furies as the personification of evil. Against this background Dido is sketched more and more negatively, up to the complete devaluation of her character as a schemer in J. E. Schlegel's play *Dido* (1739) and two 19th-century adaptations of it by E. H. Gehe (*Dido,* 1821) and W. Jensen (*Dido,* 1870). By contrast, Latin plays for use in schools (P. Ligneus, 1559; H. Knaust, *Dido,* 1566) often make Aeneas' behavior appear more pious by including a warning that he must be obedient to the gods, and the hero's behavior appears justified, as in Shakespeare's *Troilus and Cressida* (1602) or Hector Berlioz's *Les Troyens* (1886). A middle position between the two extremes of Aeneas as hero and antihero is occupied by Henry Purcell's frequently performed opera *Dido and Aeneas* (1699), in which he emphasizes the tragedy of both figures without depicting either as morally superior.

Artistic works that do not center on the Dido episode clearly portray Aeneas as a hero. Although artists make use of aspects of the Dido episode (N. Poussin, *Aeneas and Dido,* 1630s; G. B. Tiepolo, *Aeneas Presenting Amor with the Features of Ascanius to Dido,* 1757; P.-N. Guérin, *Dido and Aeneas,* 1815), almost all the episodes described in the *Aeneid* appear as themes of paintings that show Aeneas as a hero from various perspectives and in different phases of his life.

Motifs that gained popularity during the Renaissance other than the flight from Troy and the Dido episode include the first encounters in Italy (D. Dossi, *Aeneas and Achates,* 1520) and the scene of combat with which the *Aeneid* ends (J. Amigoni, *The Combat of Aeneas with Turnus,* 1721–1722). Since Monteverdi's *Le nozze d'Enea con Lavinia* (1641), opera composers have concentrated on the hero's experiences in Latium, such as J. W. Franck in *Aeneae, des trojanischen Fürsten Ankunft in Italien* (*Aeneas; or, The Arrival of the Trojan Prince in Italy,* 1680), and A. M. G. Sacchini in *Enea e Lavinia* (1779).

Comparatively little attention was paid to Aeneas during the Enlightenment and Romantic periods, and creative adaptations, such as Victor A. C. Le Plat's travesty of the *Aeneid: Virgile en France ou la nouvelle Eneid,* which transfers the ancient plot to the events of the French Revolution, remain the exception. This could be due to the characterization of Aeneas—begun in the *Aeneid* and largely dominant up to the Renaissance—as a hero tied to established traditions who must follow a chain of events that has been teleologically determined. Furthermore, the type of hero Aeneas represents, a man who successfully achieves what the gods have destined for him, appears outmoded in the modern period. Thus, in his *ABC of Reading* Ezra Pound relates an anecdote from W. B. Yeats about a sailor who is learning Latin. When asked about Virgil's hero, the man cannot recognize Aeneas as such a figure, identifying him as a priest instead—probably influenced by the Christian understanding of the Virgilian attributes *pius* and *pater.* In Turgenev's *Torrents of Spring* (1871) Aeneas is invoked as a contrast to the hero, Sanin, who fails to reach his political and ethical goals and is defeated by society.

A new notion of the Aeneas material develops when an author stresses the constant shifting between past and future that the figure of Aeneas represents and interweaves prospective and retrospective points of view in the narrative, as Hermann Broch does for the modern reader-hero in search of an identity in *Der Tod des Vergil* (*The Death of Virgil,* 1945).

BIBL.: G. Binder, ed., *Dido und Aeneas: Vergils Dido-Drama und Aspekte seiner Rezeption* (Trier 2000). A. Geyer, *Die Genese narrativer Buchillustration: Der Miniaturzyklus zur Aeneis im Vergilius Vaticanus* (Frankfurt 1989). C. Kallendorf, "The *Aeneid* Transformed: Illustrations as Interpretation from the Renaissance to the Present," in *Poets and Critics Read Vergil*, ed. S. Spence (New Haven 2001) 121–148. W. Taegert, *Vergil 2000 Jahre: Rezeption in Literatur, Musik und Kunst* (Bamberg 1982). *Virgilio nell'arte e nella cultura Europea* (Rome 1981).
M.BA.

Translated by Deborah Lucas Schneider

Aeschylus

Athenian tragedian, ca. 525–456 BCE. Aeschylus is the earliest of the surviving tragic poets. Indeed, if it is true, as Aristotle asserts in the *Poetics,* that he added a second actor to a dramatic form that had previously employed only chorus and a single actor, he can be considered the "inventor" of tragedy as we understand it. Successful in his lifetime, both at the festivals of Dionysus at Athens and beyond (his last plays were written for Sicily, where he died), Aeschylus became an instant classic. Sophocles and Euripides each responded to the *Choephoroe* (the second drama of the *Oresteia*) with a very different *Electra.* And the ancient *Life of Aeschylus* reports a decree of the Athenian popular assembly, passed shortly after Aeschylus' death, that "granted a chorus" (i.e., gave the requisite means for a festival production) to anyone who wished to revive his plays.

Among the indirect evidence of such revivals is the disappointment expressed by the comic hero of Aristophanes' *Acharnians* (425 BCE) that he has recently been subjected to tragedies by the feeble Theognis when he was expecting Aeschylus (lines 9–11). Aristophanes' *Frogs* (405 BCE) stages a contest in which Aeschylus defeats Euripides, further testifying to the older poet's continuing prestige. In the earlier decades of the 4th century BCE, Plato still cites Aeschylus more frequently and more favorably than his rivals, but by the time of the *Poetics,* Aristotle gives pride of place to Sophocles and Euripides, a sign of changing tastes. And to judge from citations and papyrus fragments, Greek speakers in later antiquity clearly preferred Euripides. The revival of tragedy by Roman poets of the 2nd and 1st centuries BCE was also relatively little indebted to Aeschylus (only four titles clearly indicate Aeschylean originals), although he was obviously still known and read. In addition to some adaptations of Aeschylean lines in surviving fragments of Roman tragedy, we have Cicero's translation of lines from the lost *Prometheus Unbound* (*Tusculan Disputations* 2.10.23). The tragedies of Seneca (probably written in the 60s CE) are also indebted chiefly to Sophocles and Euripides.

In Byzantine times the seven plays we still possess continued to be copied and studied, but in the West Aeschylus went into hibernation (along with other Greek authors) for nearly a millennium and a half, only to reawaken in the Italian Renaissance, with the arrival of manuscripts from the Greek-speaking world and the dissemination of early printed texts. The Aldine edition was the first (Venice 1518), although its sources offered a defective *Agamemnon;* Victorius provided the complete text (Geneva 1557). Meanwhile, Sanravius had published a Latin version (Basel 1555), but unlike the more approachable Euripides, whose translation into European vernaculars began in the 1500s, Aeschylus did not appear in French, German, or English until the late 18th century. The first complete translation into English, by Robert Potter, was published in 1777.

From that time forward, interest in Aeschylus blossomed. The character of his language and thought ("quelque chose d'énorme, de barbare et de sauvage"—"something huge, barbarous, wild"—as Diderot put it in an essay on dramatic poetry, 1758), formerly a stumbling block, became a virtue for the new Romantic sensibility, aided perhaps by the fact that the Age of Revolution saw the Aeschylean Prometheus as the archetypal hero of defiance. In this regard, the "continuations" of *Prometheus Bound* by Herder (*Der entfesselte Prometheus,* 1802; choruses set to music by Liszt, 1850–1855) and Shelley (*Prometheus Unbound,* 1820) are of particular importance. And Shelley offered his "lyric drama" *Hellas* (1821), whose subject was the Greek struggle for freedom from Ottoman dominion, as "a sort of imitation of the *Persae* of Aeschylus." In the end, however, the *Oresteia* was more profoundly, if less obviously, influential. One need only think of figures such as Schiller (e.g., the *Wallenstein* trilogy, 1800) and Wagner (especially *Der Ring des Nibelungen,* 1853–1874, with its aspiration to be a *Gesamtkunstwerk* of cosmic scope, its use of the *Leitmotiv,* and much more). For Hugo, Aeschylus was "Shakespeare l'ancien." Swinburne considered the *Oresteia* "the greatest spiritual poem in the world"; Marx reread it every year, and Engels made it a central text in his study of the origins of the family and the state. Aeschylus has come into his own not only as a dramatist and poet, but as a thinker.

Translations and adaptations have multiplied throughout the last two centuries, and this trend shows no signs of abating. Two well-known examples from the 1930s give some sense of the variety of purposes adaptation can serve. O'Neill's heavily Freudian trilogy *Mourning Becomes Electra* resets the *Oresteia* as a drama of inherited guilt in an unrelievedly bleak post–Civil War New England; Eliot's *The Family Reunion* offers an explicitly Christian drama of expiation and redemption based on *Eumenides* and presented in the guise of a drawing-room melodrama. Composers, too, were drawn to Aeschylus, notably Taneyev (an ambitious *Oresteya* first performed in St. Petersburg in 1895), Fauré (*Prométhée,* a *tragédie lyrique* with spoken dialogue originally written for outdoor performance, 1900), Milhaud (settings, 1913–1922, of Claudel's translation of the *Oresteia,* 1892–1916, initially performed separately, and first presented as a three-act opera in 1949), Krenek (*Das Leben des Orest,* 1928–1929), Xenakis (incidental music for the *Suppliants,*

1964, and the *Oresteia,* 1966), and Orff (*Prometheus,* 1966).

Continued interest in Aeschylus has been assured by a number of important and influential stagings over the last thirty years, including versions of the *Oresteia* directed at Epidauros by Karolos Koun (1980), in Berlin by Peter Stein (1980), in London by Peter Hall (1981), and in Paris and elsewhere by Ariane Mnouchkine (*Les atrides,* including the Oresteia and Euripides' *Iphigenia in Aulis,* 1990–1991). Tony Harrison, Hall's translator, went on to write and direct a challenging film version of the *Prometheus* (1998), the most recent in a series of politically engaged adaptations that include Richard Schechner's *Prometheus Project* (New York 1985) and Tom Paulin's *Seize the Fire* (commissioned by the Open University for a film directed by Tony Coe, 1989). Peter Sellars staged a similarly radical *Persians* at the Salzburg Festival in the wake of the First Gulf War (1993). Whatever one's opinion of these and other contemporary productions, they demonstrate Aeschylus' ability to speak powerfully to audiences now about their own concerns.

BIBL.: P. Burian, "Aeschylus," in *Encyclopedia of Literary Translation,* ed. O. Classe (London 2000). P. E. Easterling, ed., *The Cambridge Companion to Greek Tragedy* (Cambridge 1997) 228–323. J. A. Gruys, *The Early Printed Editions of Aeschylus* (Nieuwkoop 1981). E. Hall, F. Macintosh, and A. Wrigley, eds., *Dionysus since 69* (Oxford 2004). M. J. Lossau, *Aischylos* (Hildesheim, 1998) 151–163. M. Mund-Dopchie, *La survie d'Eschyle à la Renaissance* (Louvain 1984). P.BU.

Aesthetics

Greek *aisthēsis* fused such modern ideas as sensation, perception, and intuition. It was the ongoing apprehension of particular things, as opposed to *noēsis,* which was reflective and analytical, general and rational. Alexander Baumgarten cited this distinction when he christened a new philosophical field with the publication of his *Aesthetica* in 1750. Modern aesthetics was thus associated from the beginning with prerational and intuitive judgment, and it retained its essential relation to the particular. Modern aesthetics is concerned with taste, with judgments of beauty and quality, but the term also quickly assumed much broader dimensions, becoming in effect the collective imagination, worldview, style, or sense of form of cultures, peoples, and historical periods. It thus became possible to speak, as we still do, of 17th-century aesthetics or Egyptian aesthetics, referring to prerational, formative principles that might explain both the cogency of cultures and differences among them. Aesthetics, in short, was a major means by which the modern equivalency of cultural expressions was achieved.

The history of aesthetics itself must be acknowledged, even so briefly, because the Western classical tradition, seen as a culture among cultures, became identified with rule, reason, and proportion, with principles rather than with their actual realizations. To be sure, rule, reason, and proportion have been major themes and issues in Western classicism, but sole emphasis on them has cut the classical tradition off from those specific, circumstantial values that were vital to it. Classical aesthetics, in short, sought the accommodation of *noēsis* and *aisthēsis.*

In earlier Greek writers, *kallos* (beauty) and *kalos* (beautiful) were used for things that please on sight: physical beauty, for example, but also virtuous actions, or, rarely, works of art. Socrates and Plato made beauty a central philosophical issue, giving it a powerful and persistent *vertical* dimension as something like the earthly visibility of the good and true in themselves. The given world is the material shadow of higher, true, and eternal ideas. *Idea* usually meant "look" or "appearance," and the philosophical metaphor is carried through, in that, although reflective thought is described as a kind of vision, its objects are invisible. This paradox is solved, and physical and mental vision linked, by beauty, which, Plato wrote (*Phaedrus* 250D), is "brilliant . . . shining most clearly through [sight], the clearest of our senses." Moreover, beauty of all kinds begets love and desire. Earthly beauty—especially that of adolescent boys—must be sublimated if its experience is to lead the soul homeward, to the source from which visible beauty emanates, and in which it participates. When Plato argued (*Philebus* 51B–52B) that forms made with lathes, compasses, and rulers were beautiful in themselves, he meant that they provide a unique pleasure relative to no lack on our part, and that their simplicity and purity testify to the final unity of the good and the true—more generally, the ideal—with the beautiful. These arguments were to have a long life.

The object of desire might vary considerably, but the conviction that all beauty enabled transcendence provided the basis not only for the love of wisdom, but also for major strands of Western culture as seemingly unrelated as allegory—truth set out in a fair and fitting garment of fiction, in the formula of late medieval poets—and romantic love. Plato's theory of beauty, expanded by late classical Neoplatonists like Plotinus, merged easily with early Christian theology (principally Augustine). Plato's own writings had a slender but important tradition in the Middle Ages—principally a Latin translation of the first half of the *Timaeus*—that was most influential from the 12th century onward. After his works were recovered and translated by Marsilio Ficino, Renaissance Neoplatonism could take form around compatible ideas of both theology and the great poetry of Dante and Petrarch.

Plato's beauty is ultimately One, and in general unity and purity were fundamental themes of classical aesthetics. In the discussion just cited from the *Philebus,* Plato writes that we enjoy the beauty of unity and purity—even in the "less divine" sense of smell—because unity and purity are soullike. In the late *Timaeus* these soullike forms assume macrocosmic proportions: "He [the Demiurge, the divine craftsman] made it smooth and even and equal on all sides from the center, a whole and perfect body compounded of perfect bodies. And in the midst thereof he set Soul, which he stretched throughout the whole of it." The universe is made up of circles contained in a living sphere, and the human being is alone among animals in being able to turn its eyes to the heavens; the human soul is housed in a round skull, fitted to the heavens' perfect and healing motions. This grand concentric stereometry, not only the cosmos itself but the "Platonic solids," the constituents of the four elements, would fuel the imaginations and early modern cosmological speculations of Luca Pacioli, Leonardo da Vinci, and Johannes Kepler.

Relations among Plato's spheres and orbits were held to be harmonic, and, more specifically, Pythagorean. *Harmony* itself is a metaphor adapted from the art of joining, and the story is told in several versions that the legendary philosopher Pythagoras noticed a relation between harmonies—sounds, or relations of sounds, that please the ear—and ratios of whole simple numbers. By an extraordinary leap of imagination, it was proposed that similar numbers governed relations in the world at large. With adjustments and modifications (see Aristotle, *On the Heavens,* or Macrobius, *Commentary on the Dream of Scipio*), Plato's universe persisted to early modern times, and because the laws of Pythagorean harmony were essential to both, music and astronomy were sister arts in the Quadrivium of the liberal arts from the early Middle Ages through the Renaissance. The ideal of simplicity of circle, sphere, and square, all based on ratios of 1:1, persisted, giving universal sanction to these forms in art. Vitruvius (*On Architecture* 3.1.1–2) wrote that *symmetria* and proportion can be achieved only by scrupulously observing the members of a "well-shaped human body," which Nature has composed according to particular ratios, established by the consonance of human height and span with the perfect forms of the square and circle. Leonardo da Vinci illustrated Vitruvius' words in his famous drawing *Vitruvian Man* (1487), which shows a male form posed within a circle, within a square; the drawing has become an emblem of the Western classical tradition. Leonardo's older contemporary Leon Battista Alberti (*On the Art of Building* 9.5) wrote that the same ratios please ear, eye, and mind, and that (7.4) Nature also "delights primarily in the circle. Need I mention the earth, the stars, the animals, their nests, and so on, all of which she has made circular?" Such ideas laid the principles for neoclassical architecture from Brunelleschi (and Alberti himself) to Palladio and Jefferson. On the macrocosmic level, even Galileo refused to believe that the movements of the heavens would not be resolved in terms of circular forms.

A teleological definition of beauty clearly emerged in the writing of Aristotle, according to which a thing is most beautiful when it is best suited to its purpose or end (Plato, *Republic* 601D, *Greater Hippias* 295A; Aristotle, *Parts of Animals* 645a, *Rhetoric* 1361b11). It was possible in these terms to extend the idea of unity and give new definition to relation as *organic* or *functional.* As organic, this definition entailed the idea of *life* and complemented the Platonic idea of participation in the beautiful as such with the idea of beauty as fully realized participation in life. The teleological definition of beauty could be applied to works of art and architecture, and Aristotle (*Poetics* 1451a, *Rhetoric* 1409a–b) compared the plot of a tragedy to an animal, and the development of the art of tragedy to the life cycle of an animal. The physician Galen (*On the Usefulness of the Parts of the Body,* 2nd cent. CE) hymned the human body in teleological terms. In the 16th century classicizing artist-anatomists such as Vincenzo Danti (and perhaps Michelangelo) defined beautiful forms as "pure intentional forms of Nature."

The idea of beautiful form as evident *telos* or final cause merged fairly smoothly with the Platonic *idea* in a long tradition. Plotinus (*Enneads* 1.6) rejected the common belief that beauty was defined by proportion (*symmetria*) and pleasing color (Aristotle, *Topics* 116b; Cicero, *Tusculan Disputations* 4.31; Augustine, *City of God* 22.19). He objected that proportion is tainted by association with measurable, divisible matter; and if proportion was essential, then single colors or tones cannot be beautiful, and parts could not be beautiful in themselves. This, he argued, would lead to the absurd conclusion that the beautiful was made up of the un-beautiful. Instead, the beauty of forms is evident at once, on sight; it is experienced as a unity, which is a manifestation of *higher* indivisible and soullike form. By the same token, the imagined form of a work of human art is higher than its realization in matter, at the same time that this higher form is evident when the work is beautiful.

Plato and Plotinus could explain the intrinsic beauty of forms in terms of the affinity of the human soul to things possessing a unity similar to its own. Aristotle literally added another dimension by extending the idea of proportion to the apprehension of the world itself, that is, to *aisthēsis.* Things are pleasing when they are proportional to the bodily instruments of the soul, the organs of sense. In his *De anima* (*On the Soul*), the foundation of the Western science of psychology, Aristotle characterized the organs of sense as embodying "means": excessive light and dark, or heat and cold, will foil or damage sense, whereas our natural pleasure in moderation constitutes a positive judgment.

Both Plato and Aristotle argued that most immediate judgments are not made by the five external senses, which, Socrates jokes (Plato, *Theaetetus* 184), cannot simply be supposed to be like soldiers in the Trojan Horse. Rather, they are linked by a single common principle, *psychē,* which judges good and bad, beautiful and ugly. Aristotle called this principle *koinē aisthēsis,* the common sense, which is also a "mean" (*On the Soul* 431a15–20). Furthermore, the common sense "sees" that we see (and more broadly, that we sense) and thus is a principle of consciousness of one's own sensation. Human beings are unique among animals in their capacity to reflect on their own perceptions (and so might be said to be aesthetic as well as rational by nature). The common sense correlates and judges what is apprehended by more than one sense; such things are the "common sensibles," such as movement or rest, size, number, and unity. Judgments about common sensibles are adequate for most activities, but they may also be clarified by reason in ways that lower sensations may not be. In late antiquity and the Middle Ages, the common sense became the core of the system called "internal senses" (because, like external senses, they treat particular things). The list of these faculties included imagination and memory, but also "estimation," capable of intuitions regarding individual things in themselves. Internal sense was given its fullest definition, and expressly developed as aesthetic in a proto-modern sense, in the *Optics* (2.3–4, 200–232) of Ibn al-Haytham, called Alhazen by his Latin translators. Alhazen's *Optics* was well known by the late Middle Ages. "Internal senses" were advanced to account for post-sensationary perception well into the modern period; they figured prominently in the investigations of Leonardo da Vinci, Giovanni Pico della Mirandola, and Descartes and provided a precedent for later kinds of possible immediate intuitions about particulars—the 18th-century "moral sense," for example, or the "sense of beauty."

If the common sense is a mean, then perhaps Aristotle's argument that nothing is beautiful that is too small or too large (*Nicomachean Ethics* 1123.5–6) describes a condition for beauty in relation to perception, although the distinction might also be that between refined and popular taste, for the latter of which sheer size was most impressive. We need only consider the Seven Wonders of the Ancient World. The contrast could thus be political. Alberti (*On the Art of Building* 6.3) would condemn huge buildings such as pyramids in favor of Greek buildings, in which "the artist's skill attracted more praise than the wealth of the king."

Plato (*Statesman* 284E) wrote that the mean is essential in the practice of all arts, both arts of numerical measure—architecture, for example—and arts that measure "in relation to the moderate, the fitting [*to prepon*], the opportune, the needful, and all the other standards that are situated in the mean between the extremes." If Aristotle might be said to have lodged the Delphic inscription "Nothing in excess" in *aisthēsis* itself, and extended such judgment to his definition of practical reason and virtue (*Nicomachean Ethics* 1106b27), Plato's words also point to the appropriateness of, and to the corresponding ability to judge the appropriateness of, actions to circumstances and occasion.

Cicero translated *to prepon* as *decorum,* which was one of the deepest principles of classical aesthetics. Just as a beautiful body attracts and delights the eyes, Cicero wrote, by its apt composition and mutual consent of parts, so decorum in the conduct of life shines forth to attract the approval of all (*On Duties* 1.93). In Greek, *to prepon* meant something like "right-appearing" and so was closely related to the beautiful itself (Plato, *Greater Hippias* 294A). Aristotle (*Rhetoric* 3.6.7) turned the idea toward rhetorical style, which should be in proportion (*analogia*) to subject matter; we may solemnly address Madam Fig in a comedy, he says, but not in a funeral oration. *Decorum* also made a direct connection between art and social order. According to Vitruvius (*On Architecture* 1.2.5, 1.2.9, 6.5.2–3), *decorum* presupposes usage and tradition; social and architectural practice meant that the kind and degree of decoration of buildings had to be visibly appropriate to the nature of the deity enshrined, or to the status of patron or institution.

The aesthetics and ethics of *decorum* were by far most fully developed in the large instructional, theoretical, and critical literature of rhetoric, the art of persuasion. Degree of ornament and the closely related display of art and ingenuity were always central issues. For most audiences a plain (unornamented) or a middle (unobtrusively ornamented) style was deemed appropriate, but for an audience of connoisseurs, those who appreciated the art of rhetoric itself, all possible artifice and ingenuity might be displayed. Someone who dismissed Myron's *Discobolus* (*Discus Thrower*) as "twisted and elaborate," criticizing it because it was neither stiff nor upright, would simply reveal an ignorance of the sculptor's art, in which "novelty and difficulty" are prized by those who know. Departures from "straight," ordinary diction also give a certain "grace and delight" (Quintilian, *Education of the Orator* 2.13.10–11). However differently it has been interpreted, Horace made his famous comparison of poetry to painting—*ut pictura poesis,* "As is painting, so is poetry" (*Art of Poetry* 361)—to the point that both must be treated in ways appropriate to their audiences.

As may be gathered from the discussion so far, the importance of the sense of sight in ancient discussions of art can hardly be exaggerated. Sight, however, is not one thing, and important critical differences emerged regarding notions of real and metaphorical "vision." Sheer delight in visible surface is evident in the variety and resolution of the best Greek sculptures, as it must also have been in the coloring originally applied to them (now lost). For Platonists, however, beauty should address both the eye and the mind's eye, and although the guardians of Plato's imagined republic were to be trained in the discrimination of beautiful things, and were to be surrounded by them (*Republic* 400E), he dismissed the "lovers of spectacle and novelty" who seek out beautiful tones, colors, and shapes, and all art fashioned from them. Because they cannot approach the beautiful in itself (476B), such aesthetes (as we might call them) live in a dream.

Similar issues arose around the idea of what might be called the eye of the imagination (including memory). Plutarch (*On the Fame of the Athenians* 347A) tells us that the early poet Simonides called painting mute poetry, and poetry spoken painting, explaining his words to mean that the writer, "by a vivid representation of emotions and characters, makes his narration like a painting." The common ground for the two arts is the inner vision of imagination, and as many after Aristotle (*Rhetoric* 1401b) would repeat, the goal of the art of rhetoric—which arose as painting, sculpture, and theater were reaching their classical formulations—was to persuade by placing the matter before the eyes of the listener; hence the continual visual metaphors of writers on rhetoric—colors, figures, and tropes. Plato objected that just as the beautiful might lead us into dreams of sensuality, so sophistic rhetoric might persuade us of the false.

As for painting itself, Plato's contemporary Apollodorus of Athens, called the Shadow Painter, is said to have been the first to model forms in virtual space (that is, to depict them as if in relation to a source of light). Plato himself was perhaps the first to use the word *mimēsis* for the imitation of appearances (as opposed to mimicry of one kind or another). The simple power and fascination of the illusion of "convexity and concavity" achieved by modeling, which Plato strenuously rejected (*Republic* 602 C–D), is conveyed in the story of the painter Zeuxis, who depicted grapes so lifelike that birds flew up to them (Pliny, *Natural History* 35.36.65–66). Fooling birds is one thing, but fooling the sense of sight we share with birds is another, and wasting time on "playthings," exploiting the weakness of the rational soul, was once again not suitable for the guardians of Plato's republic.

Aristotle took a characteristically more modulated view, stating that we are drawn to *mimēsis* because we ourselves are imitative. If paintings that imitate appearances are, like dreams, false by nature, we still take pleasure in the recognition of things well imitated, even unpleasant things like corpses (*Poetics* 1448b, *Rhetoric* 1371b). In images of living human beings, imitation of appearances raised the question of the inwardness also made apparent, that is, of the actions, passions, and character of the soul. Socrates (Xenophon, *Memorabilia* 3.10) convinced the painter Parrhasius and a sculptor that movements of the body cannot be imitated without also revealing the soul. Plato (*Republic* 401D) and Aristotle (*Politics* 1340a) agreed that music imitates and influences the life of the soul most effectively and powerfully, and that music should be carefully controlled if education is to shape right states of mind. We are told (Pliny, *Natural History* 35.36.98) that Aristides (a contemporary of Aristotle and Apelles) first painted character and emotion; in the education of the young, Aristotle wrote, the works of Polygnotus and other "ethical" painters are to be preferred. Alberti (*On Painting* 41) would assume that soul—emotion and character—are evident in the movements of the body, and Leonardo da Vinci called such imitation the purpose of painting.

Greek illusionistic painting grew up in close association with theater and with the beginnings of geometric optics. The first *skēnographia* (architectural scene painting) was attributed to Agatharchus of Samos (mid-5th cent. BCE) (Vitruvius, *On Architecture* 1.2.2, 7.pref.11) The receding diagonals converging on a single point (what is today called perspective) in such painting also implied a *point of view* and specifically raised the question of the relation between quantities and their appearances, which were now defined by the visual angle under which they are seen.

Symmetry did not assume its modern meaning—reflection in a plane relative to an axis of rotation—until after the Renaissance. In earlier writers *symmetria* meant proportion, but more simply it meant correctness in terms of a single measure. It soon passed beyond the technical, however, as the sculptor's goal passed from accuracy to beauty and the representation of movement. *Symmetria* thus provides an excellent example of the expansion of vision and the deepening of point of view in the ancient practice and theory of art. Diodorus Siculus (*Historical Library* 1.98.5–9) tells the story of two early Greek sculptors who learned the measures of their Egyptian colleagues, which were so exact that each sculptor working separately made half of the same statue, which was then perfectly joined. The Greeks themselves, however, Diodorus observed, usually determined the *symmetria* of their statues "according to the appearances (*phantasias*) which are presented to the eyes"; that is, they adjusted their measures to the circumstances in which they appeared.

Phantasia is an excellent example of the transformation of external to internal vision. Aristotle noted (*On the Soul* 429a) the ancestry of *phantasia* in *phaos*, "light," and the word most simply meant an appearance in light. It soon, however, came to denote the capacity to make the past, or the absent, present to the mind, in the mind's own light.

According to Pliny the Elder (*Natural History* 34.19.55), the *Canon* (*Rule*) of Polyclitus was the most famous system of sculptural proportion, an indispensable model for later sculptors. Polyclitus' *Doryphorus* (*Spear Bearer*) exemplifies this canon. Greek archaic figures, like their Egyptian predecessors, were bilaterally symmetrical on a central vertical axis, apparently alive in being upright and posed, one leg advanced. The more complex, apparently lifelike figure of the *Doryphorus* was achieved by breaking the vertical symmetry of the body, then recomposing the parts in a resolution of weights (the modern term is Italian, *contrapposto*, or "counterpoise"); this standing, hipshot posture became one of the signatures of classical figural art. Three subjectivities emerge; first (as Socrates urged), the apparently living presence of the subject; second, the appearance of that life as being *like* the life of the observer; and third—because the new resolution of movement must depart from any simple modularity—the animating skill and *phantasia* of the sculptor. Still, Pliny continues (34.19.65), the sculptor Lysippus also studied *symmetria* but abandoned the older, "square" proportions of Polyclitus for a slenderer canon, saying that, whereas earlier sculptors had made men as they were, he made them as they appeared to be. That is, Lysippus adjusted proportions to achieve the appearance, or effect, of *symmetria*. As Giorgio Vasari would write of sculpture in his *Lives of the Artists* (1550), if the numbers are right but the eye is offended, the eye will not cease to be offended.

These examples suggest that if *symmetria* creates beauty, then the *appearance* of beauty might be equivalent to *symmetria*, whether or not it was achieved by actual measure. Position highlights this problem, which Plato (*Sophist* 235E–236D) was by far the earliest writer to consider. If sculptors (and painters) adjust the proportions of figures to the height at which they are seen, what is the status of their apparent *symmetria*? Plato decided that it is a *phantasma* (236C), comparing it to the falsehoods of sophistry, making a distinction between "phantastical" imitation and a truer imitation of images whose measures can be directly compared to their subject. Plato made a backward-looking choice, and what he characterized as "phantastical," the immeasurable supplement to the measurable, was a new region into which ancient art would continue to develop.

To understand an important dimension of the development of *phantasia,* we must turn to the fundamental distinction between *ars* and *ingenium,* art and natural talent. In the premodern and early modern West, *ars* referred to a discipline with teachable practices and principles; the more general and abstract these principles, the more "liberal" (and not manual) the art. *Ingenium* was seen as varying greatly from person to person; only some are able to put the art, once learned, into practice at a high level, or actually to contribute to it. By the same token, of course, the art must be mastered as the basis for extraordinary practice.

Vitruvius (*On Architecture* 6.2.1) states that although nothing is more important to the architect than *symmetria,* additions and subtractions must be made once the design of a building has been calculated. Things appear different in one or another circumstance, and great judgment is necessary to make these adjustments. The successful result is *eurhythmia,* which might be approximately translated as "good form," which creates beauty (*venustas,* 1.2.3), one of the three attributes of architecture, following *firmitas* (strength) and *utilitas* (1.3.2). Only by "acuteness of individual talents, not merely by rule," may a *venustas* not unlike true *symmetria* be realized (6.3.1). Sight, Vitruvius says (3.3.13), follows *venustates,* and if sight is not accommodated by adding measure, or by taking it away, the building will appear *vastus et invenustus,* uncouth and graceless. By contrast, the presence of *eurhythmia* will be apparent beyond doubt to all viewers.

Vitruvius attached the greatest importance to *venustas.* The Latin noun *venus, veneris,* meant "charm," "beauty," or qualities exciting love, and *venustas* meant "charm," "grace," or "beauty." The personification of this feminine noun was Venus, the goddess of love. Venus might be a beautiful or pleasing woman, but she could also be "Mother of Aeneas and his race, pleasure of men and gods, nurturing Venus," the generative force of Nature invoked by Lucretius to give eternal charm to his poetry (*On the Nature of Things* 1.1). Marsilio Ficino, commenting on Plato's *Symposium* (180D), distinguished between Natural Venus and Celestial Venus: the first is comparable to the Venus of Lucretius, a terrestrial principle of reproduction; the second is higher, sublimated love, the goal of the Platonic "desire for beauty," drawing the soul upward, now given feminine form.

Vitruvius associated slender proportions with refinement and grace, which he characterized as feminine. Briefly recounting the history of the columnar orders of architecture (*On Architecture* 4.1.6–8), he described the oldest, the Doric, as "virile in appearance, bare and unadorned," and the Ionic as "womanly." The Doric column—six column diameters high—had the *firmitas* and *venustas* of the male body; the Ionic—eight column diameters high—was taller and more slender, with fluting like a matron's robes, and a capital with volutes like curling hair. As judgment advanced, Vitruvius wrote, a measure was added to the height of each.

Socrates (Xenophon, *Memorabilia* 3.10.2) was assured by the painter Parrhasius that because perfect beauty is seldom found, he selected the most beautiful parts of several models, then made the whole appear beautiful. Zeuxis, in order to paint a Helen for a temple of Minerva, examined the (unclothed) young women of Croton and combined in his design the most beautiful parts of the five most beautiful (Pliny, *Natural History* 35.36.64; Cicero, *On Invention* 2.1.1). This tirelessly repeated anecdote made the point that beauty is scattered, and that the principle of selection and unification is the imagination of the artist. Raphael called this principle (with some irony) his *idea;* it was shaped by the study of nature and by the imitation of the best art of the past. The story thus had important implications for the training of artists (see Alberti, *On Painting* 55–56).

Scale, like *eurhythmia,* is apparent, a variant adjustment of proportions, and so again falls under the category of Plato's "phantastical imitation." A new scale is evident in the "gravity" and "majesty" of the pedimental sculpture of the Athenian Parthenon, and Strabo (*Geography* 8.3.30) reports that the sculptor Phidias said he learned from the epic poet Homer how best to represent the majesty of Zeus at Olympia. The painter Zeuxis amplified the members of bodies to make them appear fuller and more august; he too was said to have followed Homer, "who even in women prefers most powerful (*validissima*) forms" (Quintilian, *Education of the Orator* 12.10.5–9). Parrhasius said that in his dreams he had often seen himself painting a Hercules (Pliny, *Natural History* 35.36.71–72). In reply to the question "Did Phidias and Praxiteles go up to heaven to copy the forms of the gods?" Apollonius of Tyana is claimed to have replied, "No, *phantasia* wrought those, an artificer much wiser than imitation. For imitation will represent that which can be seen with the eyes, but *phantasia* will represent that which cannot" (Philostratus, *Life of Apollonius* 6.19).

The interactions of poetry, painting, and sculpture raise the older question of divine inspiration, the *mania* or *furor* long associated with the poet (Plato, *Ion* 533D, *Phaedrus* 245A). The sculptor Scopas was said to have been thus possessed while carving a bacchante (Callistratus, *Descriptions* 2). *Furor* was associated with execution and performance, but also inevitably with imagination. Renaissance Neoplatonists were fascinated with *furor,* and it was in these circles that it became fused with the *melancholia* of Greek medicine, preparing the way for the later notion of *genius* (in the modern sense) and for the appropriation of the biblical metaphor of creation for human making.

It was proverbial from antiquity onward that poets and painters are permitted to "lie," that is, that they have license to create images or portrayals of things that do not exist, such as harpies and hippogriphs, combinations arising from "the free play of fantasy" but pointing to a more general delight in *metamorphōsis*. The most famous and influential repetition of the idea of transformative "poetic license" is found in the opening lines of Horace's *Art of Poetry*. A painter has painted a feathered equine mermaid, which Horace dismisses as ridiculous. When it is objected that "painters and poets alike have the right to dare," his reply is that even so, the limits of the natural should not be transgressed. Horace's position, which seems "classical" to modern eyes, was clearly an alternative to another position, also condemned by Vitruvius. Grotesques (as they came to be called in the Renaissance, when such paintings were found in grottoes) abound in ancient art, especially in Roman art, and in fact have persisted in one form or another from antiquity to the present. Michelangelo, whose Florentine architecture was termed *alla grottesca*, is quoted as having cited Horace in support of fantastic, "poetic" invention.

Pliny the Elder (*Natural History* 35.36.79–80) tells us that Apelles (4th cent. BCE) stood out even in an age of great painters because his works possessed "what the Greeks call *charis*," which Pliny translates not as *gratia* (grace) but as *venustas*. Pliny also linked this quality with the avoidance of the appearance of laboriousness, the flaw Apelles found in the work of his rival Protogenes, who did not know when to stand back from the panel, and therefore made his art too visible. This raises the important question of the "art of concealing art."

Without the benefit of either the treatises or the great paintings of antiquity, Alberti wrote his *On Painting*, finished in 1435, much under the influence of the rhetoric of Cicero and Quintilian. His "new art" was based on a more practical version of the perspective demonstrated by Filippo Brunelleschi, in its turn a reconstruction of the scene painting described by Vitruvius. Within this framework of clarity, the "composition" of Alberti's Humanist "history" was modeled on rhetorical *compositio*, pleasing artificial order, and the contribution of the orator's art and *ingenium:* "An elegant harmony (*concinnitas*) and grace, which they call beauty (*pulchritudo*)," he writes, "arises in bodies from the composition of surfaces." The painter should study the "surfaces of the most beautiful bodies *composed* by Nature" (*On Painting* 35). Nature is an artist, and in her most beautiful things there is *concinnitas*, which we have the capacity—the sense (*On the Art of Building* 9.7)—to apprehend through diligent study. A certain mean or restraint in artfulness is also enforced by Nature, which may be violated by the excessive display of art, and the vice of the "stubborn and bizarre" Protogenes is to be avoided.

Writers from Aristotle onward warned orators that in most circumstances ornate diction (an overt display of art) must be used sparingly, because—as is still the case—it makes the hearer suspicious and thus works against the goal of persuasion. The trick is to speak vividly, sweetly, and forcefully without evident artifice. One of the most striking translations of an aesthetic ideal into an ideal of social—including artistic—performance is the central virtue of *sprezzatura* in Baldassare Castiglione's *Book of the Courtier* (1528). When he defined *sprezzatura*, the difficult done with ease, avoiding affectation, Castiglione again cited the bad example of Protogenes. The idea of apparently natural artifice still underlies Immanuel Kant's notion of "fine art" (*Critique of Judgment* 45), which "must be clothed with the aspect of nature, with an absence of labored effect (without academic form betraying itself)."

If, as E. H. Gombrich has argued, the classical tradition offers certain choices, and critical debate within the tradition has been shaped by these alternatives—Attic versus Asian, classic versus baroque, naturalism versus mannerism—it is important to recognize that all of these choices are part of the classical tradition itself. In general, the Latin rhetorical writers were more restrained in their attitudes toward ornament and evident art than their later Greek counterparts. "Longinus," for example, while continuing the appeal to imaginative vision, wrote that "as lesser lights vanish in the surrounding radiance of the sun, so an all-embracing atmosphere of grandeur obscures rhetorical devices" (*On the Sublime* 17.2). That is, art should be concealed by dazzling brilliance, and assent achieved by sheer, overwhelming display of art and imagination, which at once transports its audience and remains appropriate to great themes. Michelangelo's Sistine Chapel ceiling is the great example of such brilliance in Renaissance art.

Plato's suspicion of appearance and fantasy, although perhaps the most familiar strand of ancient aesthetics, was never the only alternative and was in important respects polemical. His older contemporary the sophist Gorgias of Leontini is quoted—in the midst of Plutarch's remarks about the excesses of Athenian theater productions (*On the Fame of the Athenians* 348C)—as saying that "he who deceives is more honest than he who does not deceive, and he who is deceived is wiser than he who is not deceived." That is, the deceiver is more honest because he has done what he promised to do—deceive by art—and the one deceived is wiser in appreciating the art of deception itself. There are circumstances, and a realm of art and appearance, in which the skills of illusion, and the acceptance of illusion, are to be valued in themselves.

As we have seen, *charis* and *gratia*—charm, grace, favor—are words used by ancient writers, and *grazia* continued to be used in the Renaissance. In the Christian context of the Renaissance, however, grace also assumed an expanded vertical dimension, compatible with Platonic beauty but also different from it. In his brief *Book on*

Beauty and Grace, Benedetto Varchi, writing in the mid-16th century, summarized the long Neoplatonic tradition from Plotinus to Giovanni Pico della Mirandola. The true form of the human body, he says, is the soul, in the unity of which true beauty is found. Beauty of soul is higher, spiritual beauty, which Varchi, however, identifies with grace. The example discussed is from Catullus (86), whose Quintia is well proportioned and fair, but without *venustas.* For Pico della Mirandola and Varchi she is without *grazia.* Lodovico Dolce compared the qualities of Raphael's painting to the *venusta*—the *charis*—of Apelles, and, citing Petrarch, he called it the *non so che*—the *je ne sais quoi*—so pleasing in painters and poets, the grace beyond the reach of art.

The aged Michelangelo was named honorary head of the Florentine Accademia del Disegno, founded in 1563. (The name "Academy" is of course a reference to the famous school of Plato.) His grand style, "difficult" in meaning and "terrible" in conception and execution, was already under attack, however, in favor of the more restrained and teachable art of Raphael. Counter-Reformation writers emphatically rejected the too-evident art of Michelangelo, and by the mid-17h century G. P. Bellori was stating a kind of Platonic orthodoxy when he wrote of the classical orders, and of the normative works of antiquity in general, that "they became laws of a marvelous Idea and ultimate beauty that, being only one in each species, cannot be altered without being destroyed." J. J. Winckelmann extolled the "noble simplicity and quiet grandeur" of Greek art. Jacques-Louis David made a stern, moralizing classicism emblematic of the French Revolution, a prototype for later state classicisms.

Once set, the themes and alternatives of the Western classical tradition held remarkably firm. The disappearance of the ancient "harmony of the spheres" in the early modern period, however, meant the negation of the millennial concentricity of microcosm and macrocosm, removing the universal sanction of the preference for unity and proportion. This fruitful crisis served to relocate the basis of classical values in the structures of perception itself, or in the conditions of human embodiment (empathy). It was at this point that all art, including Western classical art, became "aesthetic."

Sublimity first referred to the lofty style of ancient rhetoric, but it assumed entirely new meanings in the post-Newtonian 18th century. The remains of classical antiquity, while continuing to stimulate reconstructive, idealizing imagination, came to fascinate as ruins, subject to the vast processes of nature and the Earth's long history, processes dwarfing human effort, even the most timeless. As this new sublimity flowed into Romanticism, Western artists turned increasingly to pre-classical styles, archaic Greek art and pre-Raphaelite painting, the "primitive," "artless" art of their own tradition.

In the 19th century Winckelmann's Greek art became a dream of reason; for Hegel the balance of the classical was exemplary, but also in the past; for Schopenhauer classical beauty represented human reflection on its own Idea, brief respite from the ultimate and endless striving of the Will; and for Nietzsche this became *The Birth of Tragedy from the Spirit of Music,* a contest between what he called Apollonian and Dionysian principles, restraining order and reason in tense, intermittent union with disorder and dark, irrational energy. Nietzsche's vision of the classical has been deeply influential, aligning art, and the sources of creativity in general, with the unconscious, broadly paralleling the opposition between the academies and the self-consciously modernist avant-garde.

Western artistic modernism was in large part a repudiation of the classical tradition, which, after the 16th century, had become closely associated with national academies of art and with state patronage. Optical naturalism was dismissed as the basis of painting, and the figure became a secondary theme of sculpture. Allegory was rejected, and ornament was another major casualty. Ancient themes and principles were not so easily set aside, however, and it is not clear that the old standards of unity—geometric and arithmetic, organic and anthropomorphic—did not continue to animate much of the expressly modernist painting and sculpture of the 20th century. As the best examples of modernist architecture took their place in the broader history of architecture, they might also be seen to have approached—however unintentionally—more traditional standards of proportion, scale, and accommodation to sense and circumstances. Taken as a whole, modern Western culture has produced a dizzying array of new forms, and Postmodern architects, reacting in their turn against the essentialist severity of Modernism, have incorporated these forms (and variants of the traditional orders) as ornament. In classical aesthetics, ornament states the nature of a building and addresses public spaces. Modern materials and technology have also lent themselves to buildings and spaces of unprecedented scale. In the context of such technological sublimity, of spaces shaped by the structural potentials of steel and glass, by high-speed transportation, commerce, and exchange of information, the most important responsibility of classical aesthetics may be the resolute insistence on human scale and activity as the primary criteria for selection among so many choices.

BIBL.: Leonard Barkan, *Unearthing the Past: Archaeology and Aesthetics in the Making of Renaissance Culture* (New Haven 1999). Michael Baxandall, *Giotto and the Orators: Humanist Observers of Painting in Italy and the Discovery of Pictorial Composition, 1350–1450* (Oxford 1971). E. H. Gombrich, *Studies in the Art of the Renaissance,* vol. 1, *Norm and Form* (London 1966), vol. 2, *Symbolic Images* (London 1978). John Onians, *Bearers of Meaning: The Classical Orders in Antiquity, the Middle Ages, and the Renaissance* (Princeton 1988). Erwin Panofsky, *Idea: A Concept in Art Theory* (Columbia, S.C., 1968) and *Renaissance and Renascences in Western Art* (New York 1972). Nicholas Penny and Francis Haskell, *Taste and the Antique: The Lure of Classical Sculpture, 1500–1900* (New Haven 1981). Joseph Rykwert, *The Dancing Column:*

On Order in Architecture (Cambridge, Mass., 1996). Robert A. M. Stern (with Raymond W. Gastil), *Modern Classicism* (New York 1988). David Summers, *The Judgment of Sense: Renaissance Naturalism and the Rise of Aesthetics* (Cambridge 1987). D.S.

Affecti

The *Affecti* (Affections) are categories of human passions aroused and sustained in listeners through rhetorical and especially musical means.

Classical mythology is replete with stories of music's powers both to arouse and to soothe human passions, the legend of Orpheus being among the most famous. Plato (*Republic* 3; *Laws*) explained that it was the choice of modes (*tonoi*) and, to a lesser extent, of rhythms and musical instruments that determined the *ethos* of music. The Phrygian mode, for example, was said to move the hearer to anger, whereas the Dorian mode induced gravity and temperance. Consequently for Plato, music, much like rhetoric (to which it was often compared) needed to be carefully regulated because of its volatile and potentially disruptive powers. In his *Politics* (8) Aristotle suggested a cathartic function for music, by which it was capable through *mimēsis* of both arousing and purging specific passions.

Questions of musical *ethos* did not generally seem to interest Roman writers, who mostly subordinated music as a species of rhetoric (Cicero, *De Oratore;* Quintilian, *Institutio Oratoria* 7). Nonetheless, the capacity of music to stir (*flectere*) the emotions remained an undisputed axiom among Roman and, later, medieval writers, for whom the topos became a key element of the ubiquitous *Encomium musicae* (Praise of Music).

It was only in the first Humanistic writings of the 15th century that a more substantive doctrine of musical affection was again addressed. Spurred by the numerous translations and publications of ancient texts related to music and rhetoric, a number of musical Humanists speculated broadly concerning the affective powers of music and the possibilities of recapturing such powers in the music of their own day. One of the most obvious means to do this, it was thought, was to align each of the church modes (which were frequently misunderstood as representing the Greek *tonoi*) to a specific musical affect (Gaffurio, 1492; Glarean, 1547). Ficino in his *De vita libri tres* (*Three Books on Life,* 1489) argued that it was through the influence of individual planets that the modes achieved their respective affective powers. Later music theorists such as Zarlino (*Istituzioni harmoniche,* 1557) gave compositional advice by recommending the use of specific musical intervals and rhythms when setting texts to convey the *affetti.* Still, there was little agreement as to the number and kinds of affections, let alone the musical means for arousing them.

If Renaissance Humanists were largely responsible for reviving the theory of musical affection from their reading of ancient sources, it was Italian composers in the 17th century who were most responsible for putting the theory into practice. Inspired by the animated discussions of members of Count Bardi's Florentine *camerata* and supported by the philological studies of Francesco Patrizi and Girolamo Mei, composers such as Jacopo Peri and Claudio Monteverdi attempted to replicate the purported affective marvels of Greek music through their own experiments with dramatic monody, the precursor to modern opera. (Not surprisingly, it was the story of Orpheus that both composers chose to set first.)

In these earliest monodies, composers employed music-rhetorical mimesis in their continuously sung recitatives (*recitar cantando*) to express the emotional nuances of the text: large melodic leaps for expressions of joy and surprise; falling and chromatic motion for sadness or resignation; and so forth. By midcentury a number of German music theorists had begun to rationalize and codify this compositional practice within a system of prescriptive "figures" (based loosely on models of rhetorical pedagogy) by which given affects might be expressed, including works by Athanasius Kircher (1650), Christoph Bernhard (ca. 1660), and Johann Heinichen (1722). (Their efforts received intellectual support from Descartes, who in 1649 offered a highly influential mechanistic theory of the passions which attempted to show how physical stimuli such as music could affect the bodily humors or "animal spirits.") The Baroque *Affektenlehre* reached its climax (and one might say its ossification) in Johann Mattheson's *Der vollkommene Capellmeister* (1739), in which virtually every parameter of music—modal, harmonic, rhythmic, and melodic—was broken down into subgroups of individual "figures" that could be applied didactically by a composer to achieve a desired expressive end.

Over the second half of the 18th century, musicians gradually abandoned the systematic *Affektenlehre.* The received theory of classical mimesis by which music was subordinated to textual imitation became subject to widespread criticism in the wake of a growing appreciation of nontexted instrumental music. The development of a transcendental aesthetics in the writings of Kant and his followers likewise called into question the naive sensualism upon which traditional affect theory had been based. In the early 20th century, however, a few aestheticians (notably Hermann Kretzschmar and Hans Mersmann) attempted to reanimate less mechanistic models of musical affection in order to account for music's expressive capacities, and more recently a number of music psychologists (including Leonard Meyer and Eugene Narmour) have proposed Gestalt-like models of musical cognition by which varying affective qualities of music might be empirically measured.

BIBL.: Dietrich Bartel, *Musica Poetica: Musical-Rhetorical Figures in German Baroque Music* (Lincoln 1997). George Kennedy, *Classical Rhetoric and Its Christian and Secular Traditions from Ancient to Modern Times,* 2nd ed. (Chapel Hill 1999). Leonard Meyer, *Emotion and Meaning in Music* (Chicago 1956). Claude V. Palisca, *Humanism in Italian Renaissance Musical Thought* (New Haven 1985). T.CH.

Ajax

Son of Telamon, the ruler of Salamis, Ajax was the strongest Greek fighting at Troy, after Achilles. After the latter died and Ajax lost the struggle over Achilles' armor, he tried to kill the leaders of the Greek army, but he went mad, slaughtered a herd of sheep, and finally committed suicide out of shame. The most important versions of this story have come to us in Sophocles' tragedy *Ajax* and its Latin reception in Ovid's *Metamorphoses* (12.624–13.398); there are also numerous creative adaptations of the figure and his tragic life in almost all ancient genres (e.g., in the characterization of Turnus in Virgil's *Aeneid*) up to the recreation of Ajax as an epic hero in *Posthomerica* (5.128–412) by Quintus Smyrnaeus in the 3rd century CE.

The struggle between Ajax and Odysseus for Achilles' armor and the injustice of the resulting decision always dominate in the post-Homeric reception history. Ajax appears as the ideal of an archaic hero, either because Odysseus' rhetoric is exposed as deceptive (Pindar) or because stress is laid on Ajax's own honest and virtuous nature. Dramatic potential is provided by the inner conflict of a man who goes mad after suffering dishonor, but also by the theme of a conflict of interest that leads to individuals' isolation in society.

Visual representations of Ajax's deeds are plentiful; his heroic battles with different Trojans dominate the ancient iconography, whereas from the classical period onward the most frequent scenes depict the struggle for Achilles' weapons and Ajax's ensuing madness and suicide.

After antiquity two strands regarding Ajax can be identified. At first the material taken from Sophocles dominates the adaptations for the stage. Though the original work was not presented publicly as part of the Cambridge Greek Plays until 1882, creative adaptations of it appeared on European stages from the early 17th century on. They include versions by Juan de la Cueva (*Tragedia de Ayax Telamón,* 1582) and Pieter Hooft (*Achilles en Polyxena,* 1614), as well as James Shirley (*Contention of Ajax and Ulysses for the Armor of Achilles,* 1645–1658), which was probably intended for use in schools. The story was used as the basis for operas by Pietro d'Averara (*L'Aiace,* 1694–1697) and Bertin de la Doué (*Ajax,* 1712), followed by Jean-George Noverre's ballet *La mort d'Ajax* (1758). Ajax was also introduced in other dramatic contexts, such as the aria in Mozart's *Idomeneo* in which Electra underscores her threat to kill herself by citing the example of Ajax. Only rarely did a dramatist focus on the story of Ajax's love for his slave Tecmessa, as August C. Borheck did in his adaptation of 1789. Ugo Foscolo's tragedy *Ajace* (1811) offers the first instance of a revision with decidedly political overtones, as Napoleon was preparing to invade Russia; Ajax appears there as a hero motivated by virtue, patriotism, and hatred of tyranny, in contrast to Odysseus and Agamemnon, representing Napoleon. Further dramas with contemporary political and social references followed: H. J. Rehfisch's tragedy *Die goldenen Waffen* (*The Golden Armor,* 1913) and Heiner Müller's *Germania 3: Gespenster am Toten Mann* (*Germania 3: Ghosts at The Dead Man,* 1995), in which Ajax is reborn in the figure of a Communist functionary named Ebertfranz. Similarly, Robert Auletta and Peter Sellars adapted Sophocles' play in the United States in 1986, presenting it as a political drama against the background of the conflict with Libya, in which Ajax falls victim to the intrigues of CIA agents (Odysseus) and high-ranking Pentagon generals and politicians (Agamemnon).

The second strand involves satirical use of the material, which can be traced to Ovid's *Metamorphoses.* At the beginning stands John Harington's *New Discourse of a Stale Subject, Called the Metamorphosis of Ajax* (1596), in which he gives his invention of a flush toilet the name Ajax; the author uses Ajax's "heroic" deed, the slaughter of a herd of sheep, as a symbol in his polemic against English society. Cervantes also makes reference to Ajax's madness when he has Don Quixote mistake a herd of sheep for two armies in battle (*Don Quixote* 1.18). It is possible that Cervantes was influenced not only by direct knowledge of ancient literature but also by Alciato's well-known *Emblematum liber* (*Book of Emblems,* 1531); in the 1546 edition of this work, emblem 176, *Insani gladius* ("The Madman's Sword"), shows Ajax killing pigs. Satire is also the object—although not related to Ajax's madness—in Jacques Offenbach's use of the material in his operetta *La Belle Hélène* (1864), which offers an exposé of modern society with figures and costumes from antiquity. "The great Ajax" appears at a festival of Adonis with his young namesake (the son of Oileus in Homer) and kills time by playing dice.

Although Shakespeare's *Troilus and Cressida* (1602) is not often performed, it has played a significant role in Ajax's history. Ajax is only a minor character in the play, based on Chaucer's *Troilus and Criseyde* (1375); his tragic life and suicide thus receive no mention at all. Nevertheless, Shakespeare makes use of the conflict with Odysseus by depicting him as the pawn in Odysseus' intrigues. Shakespeare also exploits the comic potential in the characterization of Ajax as "dull" and "brainless" (1.3.382), particularly in dialogue with Thersites. As the victor in the combat with Hector, however, Ajax regains some of his Homeric heroic status.

Johanna Niemann's novel *Ajax* (1905) represents a unique instance of creative interpretation; Niemann gives her heroine, an author of books for young people, the nickname Ajax to stress the character's isolation from society.

In the visual arts Ajax is frequently depicted as a minor character in connection with the Trojan War (e.g., a fresco by Giulio Romano in the Sala di Troia of the Ducal Palace in Mantua, 1535–1539). Otherwise he appears occasionally in scenes showing the battle over the armor (Leonaert Bramer, *The Quarrel between Ajax and Odysseus,* ca. 1625) or his madness and suicide (Giovanni Battista Castello's *Ajax Runs on His Sword,* 1579, and a series of works by Johann Heinrich Füssli). A rare exception to the classical treatment of the material is found in the fresco by Romano in the Ducal Palace in Mantua, which shows Ajax being struck dead by Athena with a thunderbolt (not a sword) as punishment for his hubris toward her.

The name further occurs—stripped of all connection to antiquity but retaining a connotation of exceptional strength—as the name of a Dutch football club, Ajax Amsterdam, and a popular brand of household cleanser.

BIBL.: Jon Hesk, *Sophocles: Ajax* (London 2003). Erika Simon, *Aias von Salamis als mythische Persönlichkeit* (Stuttgart 2003). M.BA.

Translated by Deborah Lucas Schneider

Al-Fārābī

Very little that is reliable is known about the life of al-Fārābī (Abū-Nasr al-Fārābī, d. 950–951), an Aristotelian philosopher of Baghdad called the Second Teacher (after Aristotle) by posterity. His origins are said to be either in Fārāb on the Syr Darya (Jaxartes) in modern Kazakhstan, and probably coming from a Turkish background, or in Faryāb in modern Afghanistan, and of likely Persian background. There is not enough evidence to decide the matter. Whatever his background, it is clear that he was either born in Baghdad or went there very early, where he studied logic with a certain Christian cleric, Yūhannā ibn-Haylān, who died in that city sometime between 908 and 932. Baghdad was the center of the Graeco-Arabic translation movement, during the course of which (ca. 770–1000) almost the entire Greek philosophical and scientific corpus that had survived in the Eastern Mediterranean until the 8th century was translated on demand into Arabic. Al-Fārābī's works reflect intimate knowledge of this corpus, a knowledge that could have been acquired in the late 9th century only in Baghdad.

He spent almost his entire life in the ʿAbbāsid capital, where he composed some of his works for known personalities there. Nothing is known about the means by which he earned his living. He stayed in Baghdad until September 942, at which time he left Iraq and traveled to Damascus. In Syria he also lived and worked for some time in Aleppo, at the court of the local Hamdanid ruler, Sayf al-Dawla, though there is no information about how long and in what capacity. At some point he also visited Egypt, but shortly before his death he returned to Syria, where he died in Damascus in December 950 or January 951.

His philosophy is directly affiliated with the Greek Neoplatonist school of Ammonius in Alexandria, in the form in which it survived as a philosophical curriculum among Syriac-speaking Christian clerics and intellectuals in the centers of Eastern Christianity in the Near East. The school of Ammonius, though Neoplatonist in its metaphysics through its acceptance of Plotinian emanationism at its pinnacle, was essentially Aristotelian in its basic orientation, structure, and content. By al-Fārābī's own account, the Nestorian Christian Yūhannā ibn-Haylān, his immediate teacher, and Mattā ibn-Yūnus (d. 940), his older contemporary and colleague in Baghdad, were direct descendants in this tradition. To Mattā apparently belongs the credit for reviving Aristotelian studies in Baghdad and establishing both a curriculum of school texts and a method for their study, as a response, it would seem, to the eclecticism of al-Kindī (d. ca. 870), who had resuscitated philosophy in Baghdad in the first third of the 9th century.

Al-Fārābī sought to present philosophy as a coherent system, promulgate emanationist Aristotelianism as the one true philosophical doctrine, and rationalize its practice and show its validity for contemporary ʿAbbāsid society. With this purpose in mind, he taught philosophy and wrote about it in a number of ways. At an elementary level and apparently for a wide audience, he popularized certain existing translations of Greek texts through adaptation and paraphrase. He also wrote extensive commentaries on the works of Aristotle. Most important, he created a philosophical system of his own, on the basis of principles and orientations that he had inherited from the late antique tradition and by using as his material the entire array of Greek philosophical thought that was available to him in translation. A précis of that system is offered in two of his major works, *The Principles of the Opinions of the People of the Excellent City* and *Governance of the City* (with the alternative title *Principles of Beings*), in which he describes the entire universe as an interrelated whole, deriving ultimately from the supreme principle, and presents in great detail all its component parts in descending order: the One; the eternal supralunar world, consisting of the spheres with their souls and intellects; Earth, with its minerals, plants, animals, and humans; the mental and physical constitution of humans; and a classification of the various state formations.

He treated philosophy as it was understood and classified in late antiquity. Logic is considered the instrument with which to study philosophy, which is in turn divided into theoretical and practical parts. The theoretical part consists of physics, mathematics (the *quadrivium*), and metaphysics, while the practical part includes ethics, household management (economics), and politics. His work on the subject of classification, *The Enumeration of the Sciences,* enjoyed wide circulation both in Arabic and in a medieval Latin translation. Though he wrote on all the parts of philosophy, including a few essays on medicine and geometry, his main contributions lie in logic, music, metaphysics, and the theory of the perfect and imperfect states, based on an analysis of the intellectual development and metaphysical knowledge of the ruler.

He was the most prominent member of the Baghdad Aristotelian school, which flourished in the 10th and 11th centuries and revived an Aristotelian tradition going back to Alexander of Aphrodisias (2nd century CE). He was the first philosopher to internationalize Greek philosophy, by creating in a language other than Greek a complex and sophisticated philosophical system that influenced subsequent philosophy as much in the Arabic East as in the Latin West. In the East, he established philosophy as a discipline of utmost intellectual rigor, based on Aristotelian logic, which could on the one hand explain and account for all human activity in all its aspects, including the religious, and on the other provide ultimate happiness (the Aristotelian *eudaimonia*) to individuals able to pursue its methods. His philosophical views and insight were further systematized in the works of Avicenna, which through their sheer penetration into the very heart of Islamic intellectual life gained for philosophy a central position in it. In the West, al-Fārābī's philosophy formed the basis of the thought of Andalusian philosophers and eventually of Averroës and, in this way, exerted formative influence on the renewal of philosophical activities in Latin after the 12th century. In a very real sense he stands at the beginning of the post-classical philosophical tradition, East and West.

BIBL.: Patricia Crone, "Al-Fārābī's Imperfect Constitutions," *Mélanges de l'Université Saint-Joseph* 57 (2004) 191–228. "Fārābī," *Encyclopaedia Iranica* 9:208–229. J. Lameer, *Al-Fārābī and Aristotelian Syllogistics: Greek Theory and Islamic Practice* (Leiden 1994). D. C. Reisman, "Al-Fārābī and the Philosophical Curriculum," in *The Cambridge Companion to Arabic Philosophy,* ed. Peter Adamson and Richard C. Taylor (Cambridge 2005) 52–71. R. Walzer, *Al-Farabi on the Perfect State* (Oxford 1985). F. W. Zimmermann, *Al-Farabi's Commentary and Short Treatise on Aristotle's De Interpretatione* (London 1981).

D.G.

Alberti, Leon Battista

A Humanist architect, artist, and writer on many subjects (1404–1472); no intellectual of the 15th century showed more enthusiasm for modernity. As a young man he praised the dome that Brunelleschi had raised over the Florentine cathedral as a feat of technology "unknown and unthought of among the ancients." As an old man, he walked the Vatican gardens with his old friend Leonardo Dati, enthusiastically discussing the new art of printing. He wrote innovative books in Italian as well as in Latin. Yet no one did more to show that ancient forms could take on new life when applied to modern topics and problems.

Born in Genoa, the illegitimate son of an exiled member of a great Florentine family, Alberti learned the crafts of Humanism at the school of Gasparino Barzizza and may have studied law at Bologna. In the 1420s he became an abbreviator at the papal curia, and in the 1430s, when the ban on his family was lifted and the curia of Eugenius IV moved north to Florence, he returned to his family's native city. The new Florentine art of Brunelleschi, Ghiberti, Masaccio, and della Robbia astonished and delighted him. A skilled Latinist, Alberti had already tried his hand at a number of genres, including a saint's life and a treatise on the state of letters, when he went to Florence. But his Florentine years saw him create radically new kinds of classicism.

Struck by the transformation of painting and sculpture in Florence, he wrote a treatise, *On Painting* (*Della pittura,* 1435), which defined the painter's task in a new way. Using one-point perspective (analyzed at length), with rigorous treatment of the geometry and optics required, the painter was to create an illusion of three-dimensional space on a two-dimensional surface, and to dispose figures in a dramatic but decorous way that would affect viewers emotionally, just as a superb classical speech would affect listeners. A master of ancient rhetoric, Alberti modeled his treatise on the *Institutio oratoria* of Quintilian. The painter—in his prophetic view—should be less a craftsman than a good man skilled in painting, the practitioner of a learned art. His work should be purely classical, every figure balanced, symmetrical, anatomically correct but more than humanly beautiful. Alberti produced two versions of this: a first one in Italian, dedicated to Brunelleschi and evidently aimed at painters; then a second in Latin, probably meant for scholars like himself and informed patrons. In the same years, he wrote a series of four connected Ciceronian dialogues in Italian, *On the Family* (*Della famiglia,* 1435–1444). Here he drew on ancient moral philosophy to explain how one should go about preserving a great clan like his own in the shark-filled waters of Florentine economic and political life—a dazzling demonstration, in a very different sphere, of the contemporary uses of the classics.

He would never cease to experiment with the techniques of Humanism. His writings during the 1440s included Lucianic dialogues, the *Intercenales,* and a strange satire, also Lucianic, on the papacy and the curia, the *Momus;* a late treatise, *On Statuary,* in which he pursued his interest in the proportions of the ideal human body; and a grammar of Italian, in which he applied the Humanist grammarian's technique of direct observation, for the first time, to a vernacular language.

In the 1440s Alberti's interest in the visual arts began to dominate his career. In Ferrara he advised the young ruler Leonello d'Este on artistic questions. A bronze plaque he created with his own self-portrait in profile, classically dressed and set off by a winged eye and his motto, *Quid tum?* (What then?), may well have helped to create the fashionable new genre of classicizing portrait medals that became a Ferrarese specialty. In Urbino he advised Federico da Montefeltre on his great palace complex. In Rome, often working with Flavio Biondo, he became a skilled antiquary. Alberti devised new ways to survey and map the ancient city. He even tried, in 1446, to raise one of the sunken Roman ships from the bottom of Lake Nemi in the Alban hills.

Above all, Alberti studied ancient ways of building and city planning. In the field, he surveyed the Pantheon from porch to roof and examined Rome's ancient bridges, arches, and *insulae* (apartment buildings) with minute care. In his study—and in the new Vatican Library of Nicholas V—he gathered information from a vast range of texts, Greek as well as Latin. Everything that he learned, he used, both in three dimensions and in writing. As an architect, he worked with Matteo de' Pasti and other builders who could translate his proposals into stone and brick. His major architectural works, which variously occupied him from the later 1440s until virtually the end of his life, included the classical, symmetrical outer shell of the Malatesta Temple in Rimini; the Rucellai Palace in Florence, with its facade, intricately alluding to the Colosseum; the decorated facade of Santa Maria Novella in Florence, the tiny Holy Sepulchre inside the Florentine church of San Pancrazio; and two major churches in Mantua. He pioneered in the use of the ancient temple porch as a prominent element in church design, experimented with inscriptions, and planned to top off the Malatesta temple with an immense dome—an unrealized project, but one that other architects would bring into being elsewhere.

Alberti also assembled his findings on the built world of the Greeks and Romans in a massive, systematic study, *Ten Books on the Art of Building* (*De re aedificatoria*). Here he set out both to emulate, and to replace, Vitruvius, whose work he denounced, unfairly but effectively, as both unintelligible and corrupt. Alberti's book, completed in the 1450s, was the first of his major works to be printed. It helped to shape the tastes of patrons and architects working in what they saw as classical styles down to the 18th century and after.

Bitter, ironic, perpetually critical of his predecessors and contemporaries, Alberti showed that ancient literary genres could be reconfigured to deal with radically modern topics, and that ancient forms could be reused to create new, classicizing environments for private life and public worship. His work made clear that Humanist scholarship could be productively applied to technical fields like mathematics and architecture—and thus opened up realms that others would explore for two centuries after his death.

BIBL.: Michael Baxandall, *Giotto and the Orators* (Oxford 1971). Francesco Paolo Fiore, with Arnold Nesselrath, *La Roma di Leon Battista Alberti: Umanisti, architetti e artisti alla scoperta dell'antico nella città del Quattrocento* (Milan 2005). Anthony Grafton, *Leon Battista Alberti* (New York 2000). Joseph Rykwert and Anne Engel, eds., *Leon Battista Alberti* (Milan 1994). Rocco Sinisgalli, *Il nuovo "De pictura" di Leon Battista Alberti: The New "De Pictura" of Leon Battista Alberti* (Rome 2006). Christine Smith, *Architecture in the Culture of Early Humanism: Ethics, Aesthetics, and Eloquence, 1400–1470* (Oxford 1992). A.G.

Alcestis

Euripides' tragedy *Alcestis,* which is fourth in a tetralogy of 438 BCE, possesses all the qualities for attaining the highest success in the modern theater. Attic tragedy was encumbered by an ideology mistrustful of sex, and *Alcestis* was unique in staging a beneficent thaumaturgy of love: of all the *philoi* of her husband Admetus, only the protagonist is willing to sacrifice her own life to prolong his, thus fulfilling the terms of a legendary privilege granted him by Apollo. Furthermore, the tragedy has a happy ending, as Alcestis is brought back to life by Heracles, who, touched by the hospitality Admetus has offered him even in his period of mourning, struggles victoriously with Thanatos, the god of death.

The play's numerous adaptors in the 17th and 18th centuries, however, were faced with resolving a difficulty that did not exist for Euripides and his many-sided, kaleidoscopic conception of humanity: the contradiction between the idealization of the couple's relationship, which the tragedy prolongs after death through Admetus' promise of fidelity to Alcestis (as *charis* for the benefit he has received), and Admetus' liability to moral censure for having requested such a sacrifice, for which he is reproved by his father, Pheres. The modern solution is to make Admetus unaware of his wife's decision, so that, for example, in Quinault's *Alceste,* set to music by Lulli (1674), he learns of it only after her death. This is a costly solution, as it necessitates eliminating the grand scene of the spouses' parting from one another. In Gluck's *Alceste,* with a libretto by Calzabigi (1767), the parting scene is kept, but Alcestis' clear and painful decision is contrasted with the desperate refusal of Admetus, who even accuses his wife of having broken the conjugal pact with her sacrifice. In the much-revised French version of Gluck's opera (1776), whose libretto is by the knight Le Blanc du Roullet and whose musical text is also quite innovative, Admetus fights with Alcestis to the very end, on the banks of the Acheron, about his right to die. It is his desperation, in addition to Alcestis' heroic virtue, that persuades the divinity to restore her to life—as in the version recorded in Plato's *Symposium*—thus eliminating both the character of Heracles and the triumph of physical force he embodies. The same happens in Herder's *Admetus Haus* (1801), whereas Pier Jacopo Martello's *Alceste* (1709), the *Alceste* of Wieland (1773), and Vittorio Alfieri's *Alceste seconda,* while preserving the same perspective, retain the roles of Heracles and Pheres.

In particular, Wieland's ennobling of Admetus gave rise to a bitter controversy with the young Goethe, who, accusing it of being an antihistorical fake, claimed that the Greek love of life was the central idea of Euripides' tragedy (but not altogether pertinently: Euripides' Admetus considers the life left to him "worse than death").

It is in an altogether different culture, and with an altogether different perspective, that Robert Browning took up the *Alcestis* in his *Balaustion's Adventure* (1871). It sets a quite faithful translation, recited *per voce sola,* into a commentary that energetically accuses Admetus of meanness, and it interprets his path toward happiness as the progress of penitence and conversion. Browning adds a modern variant on the myth at the end, where Alcestis' sacrifice can be accepted because it is the only way for Admetus as sovereign to effect an ethical and social palingenesis. (Benito Pérez-Galdós's interpretation is similar in his *Alcestis,* 1914.)

One of the more significant experimental adaptations of the 20th century was Alberto Savinio's *Alcesti di Samuele* (1949). It updates the myth, setting it in Nazi Germany, portraying the savior Heracles as President Roosevelt, and placing the emphasis on the second term of the love-death duality: instead of returning to life, Savinio's Alcestis entices her husband to death, understood, on the model of Wagner's *Tristan,* as the proper and sole site of love. Marguerite Yourcenar (*Le mystère d'Alceste,* 1942) has provided a feminist version of the myth: Admetus is portrayed as a tired and frustrated intellectual who disregards the concrete aspects of people in order to study the totality of the world; Hercules restores his wife to him, giving her the mission of protecting his weakness. A little later, T. S. Eliot's *The Cocktail Party* (1949) recast the plot of Euripides' play in terms of psychoanalysis and a desire for religious salvation, beginning as a drawing-room comedy but gradually achieving ever-widening circles of tragic significance. G.P.

Translated by Patrick Baker

Alchemy

The origins and development of alchemy form a complex topic whose details cannot be ascertained without some measure of conjecture. The term comes from the Arabic *al-kīmiyā',* which in turn probably derives from the Greek *chymeia* or *chēmeia,* having as its root sense "the art of fusing metals" and bearing the extended sense of transmuting them. There are competing etymologies, however, such as an eponymous one from a supposed *Chymēs,* and another that refers to the black earth of the Egyptian homeland (Egyptian *chemi*). According to A. J. Festugière, Greek alchemy can be divided into three stages: a protoalchemical stage, represented for example by the jewelry-making and textile-dyeing recipes found in the late antique papyri Leidensis X and Graecus Holmiensis (now respectively in Leiden and Stockholm); a more philosophical stage represented by the use of sympathies and antipathies to explain such recipes, as in the *Physika kai mystika* of pseudo-Democritus (ca. 1st cent. CE); and a religious stage, in which alchemical recipes became intertwined with Gnostic and Hermetic motifs in an effort to transform matter and to redeem it from its fallen state. The last stage found its main representative in Zosimos of Panopolis (ca. 4th cent. CE), an obscure figure whose works had a major influence on later alchemists.

Greek alchemy was appropriated by Arabic authors in the early centuries of Islam, and the discipline was in a burgeoning state by the 9th century. Three authors in particular stand out: the author who styled himself Balīnās and wrote an early *Book of the Secret of Creation;* the semi-fabulous Jābir ibn Hayyān (supposedly 8th cent., but most of the 3,000-odd works attributed to him were composed much later); and Muhammad ibn Zakariyyā al-Rāzī (9th–10th cents.). Balīnās is famous for introducing the hugely influential sulfur-mercury theory, according to which the known metals are all compounds of sulfur and mercury that vary in their purity, fixity, color, and relative quantity. The works of Jābir (in Latin, Geber) are known for their attempt to quantify alchemy by arithmological methods; Rāzī, a famous medical figure in his own right, systematized alchemy and denuded it of the complicated, riddling language employed by its Greek-speaking framers.

The alchemy inherited by the Latin West of the 12th and 13th centuries was a vastly more comprehensible discipline than it had been when in the hands of pseudo-Democritus, Zosimos, and their peers. Scholastic authors continued in the rationalistic vein of Rāzī, whose genuine and pseudonymous works provided models for Roger Bacon and Albertus Magnus in the 13th century. At the same time, Bacon saw alchemy as a means of reforming medicine, both in terms of the grand ambition to extend human life to a millennium or more and in terms of more mundane purifications of medicines carried out by distillation and other laboratory processes. Bacon's contemporary Albertus Magnus had little interest in the medical applications of alchemy, but his remarkable *Liber mineralium* (also known as *De mineralibus*) used the aurific art as the basis for an experimental approach to mineralogy and metallurgy. The *Liber mineralium* had a significant effect, in turn, on the bible of the medieval alchemists, the *Summa perfectionis* ascribed to Geber but actually written by a pseudonymous Latin author around the end of the 13th century, probably the little-known Franciscan Paul of Taranto. Although Geber's work contained a massively influential corpuscular theory of matter that the author employed to explain both geological and laboratory processes, the 14th century also saw a huge explosion in the realm of medical alchemy, probably related to the emergence of the Black Death in midcentury. The Franciscan author John of Rupescissa (14th cent.) composed the enormously popular *Book Considering the Fifth Essence [Quintessence] of All Things* (*Liber de consideratione quintae essentiae omnium rerum*), extant in more than 200 manuscript copies today, which was still a formidable force in early modern medicine. His work would in turn heavily inform the authors who wrote under the name of the Catalan philosopher Ramon Lull. The huge Lullian corpus, comprising more than 100 separate works, would serve as a major conduit for spreading John of Rupescissa's medical reform.

Although the 16th century is usually credited with the emergence of iatrochemistry, or chemical medicine, it is quite clear that the movement begun by John of Rupescissa had spread throughout Europe by the time that Theophrastus von Hohenheim, or Paracelsus (1493–1541), had appeared on the scene. Paracelsus' *Archidoxis,* an influential work devoted to the rectification of materia medica and the separation of the four elements, employs techniques manifestly borrowed from the tradition of John of Rupescissa, though perhaps partly appropriated indirectly through the pseudo-Lullian corpus. Nonetheless, Paracelsus displayed originality in his view of the cosmos as a whole and its individual members as all being composed of three principles—mercury, sulfur, and salt. The principles of mercury and sulfur were obviously borrowed from the alchemical tradition inaugurated by Balīnās, but the third principle, salt, was added by Paracelsus himself, partly to supply a trinitarian component to alchemical theory. His material theory was not merely a rewriting of Aristotle's four elements in terms of three, because he introduced the important idea that his three principles existed as the ingredients of bodies and could be separated from them by "chymical" analysis. The Thomistic and Scotist interpretations of Aristotelian mixture long dominant in the universities maintained, to the contrary, that the ingredients of a mixture (including the four elements) could not be recaptured in number, because they had been effectively destroyed by the process of *mixis.* Paracelsus' emphasis on what he called *spagyria* or *Scheidung,* that is, analysis, was fundamental to the formation and identity of "chymistry" as the analytical discipline par excellence.

In the 17th century this direction received a new emphasis in the works of Andreas Libavius, Jean Beguin, and especially Jan Baptista van Helmont, who were all instrumental in reformulating Paracelsian *spagyria* so that it included synthesis as well as analysis. Indeed, in the work of Van Helmont, *spagyria* came to acquire a quantitative aspect, and the conservation of weight displayed during the analysis and resynthesis of substances led Van Helmont to formulate in clear terms what is now called the principle of mass balance. The Helmontian reformulation of chymistry would still resonate at the end of the 18th century, when Antoine Laurent Lavoisier employed his related balance-sheet method to derive the first list of chemical elements in the modern sense.

Despite the great changes that alchemy underwent between the Roman imperial period and the 17th century, a number of theories, practices, and general themes still prevalent in early modern alchemy can be traced back to the Greek origin of the discipline. Remnants of the artisanal recipes and techniques such as those we see in the Leiden and Stockholm papyri, for example, found their way into the countless "books of secrets" and works on natural magic copied and printed in the 16th and 17th centuries. Processes for surface enrichment and coloration (bronzing) of metals were transmitted from ancient origins, along with processes for making artificial precious stones and pearls, as well as textile dyes. These were augmented with newer recipes for the manufacture and purification of "salts" inherited from the Arabic tradition, such as sal ammoniac, borax, niter, and salt of tartar. Gunpowder, unknown to the West until the 13th century, was also associated with alchemy by Roger Bacon, an unsurprising connection given the need for purifying potassium nitrate found as a mineral efflorescence. An additional industrial impetus grounded itself on the technology of distillation. The earliest recognizable stills appear in the works of Zosimos, where they are linked to the separation of *pneuma* from gross terrestrial matter. By the 9th century distillation technology had become industrialized to the degree that it formed the basis for manufacturing commercial perfumes, such as rosewater. The earliest clear recipes for distillation of alcohol, however, had to wait for the Latin Middle Ages: extraction of *aqua ardens* ("burning water") from wine is first described in 12th-century texts stemming from the School of Salerno. Ethanol's usefulness as a solvent for extracting mineral and botanical essences allowed the originally alchemical technology of distillation to reenter the pharmaceutical branch of the discipline in the works of John of Rupescissa, pseudo-Lull, and Paracelsus. In the course of the 16th century a huge trade in alcoholic "strong waters" sprang up in the West, still largely medicinal in character. Another industrial offshoot of alchemy may be seen in the transformation of old recipes for "sharp" and "pontic" waters, often involving corrosive salts and weak acids, into recipes for the mineral acids proper—hydrochloric, nitric, and sulfuric acids and the mixture of the former two usually known as *aqua regia.* Clear recipes for these remarkable substances first appear in the early 14th century; pseudo-Geber's *Summa perfectionis,* composed about a generation earlier, is still ignorant of them. In the course of the 15th and 16th centuries the mineral acids would receive wide dispersion in mining and metallurgical literature, and their use led to major technological breakthroughs in the early modern assaying and refining of metals.

The fruits of Greek alchemy may also be seen in the theoretical realm. The concept of a "philosophers' stone" that could transmute vast quantities of base metal into silver or gold is already found in the later treatises of the Greek alchemical corpus. Similarly, the term *xērion* appears in Greek alchemy as a term for a transmuting powder: this word would later become *al-iksīr* in Arabic and thus *elixir* in Latin. Similarly, the notion that the philosophers' stone is produced by a series of "regimens" leading from a black "first matter" to a white material and then to a red or purple one is founded on the Greek alchemists' quest for *melanōsis, leukōsis, xanthōsis,* and *iōsis.* The technical processes leading to these color changes are not clearly described in the Greek alchemical corpus, but they may have involved successive depositions of oxides, sulfides, and other thin layers on the surfaces of metals. By the early modern period, however, these induced color changes had fused together to become an organic process of development often conceived of as occurring over many months in a single sealed flask subjected to slow heating. As a final debt to Greek alchemy, one must add that the striking figurative language of the art, especially prominent from the 15th through the 17th centuries, was already present in the work of Zosimos. He depicted metals as miniature humans within flasks and developed elaborate enigmata employing fiery swords, dragons, temples, and sacrificing priests—all topoi that would receive considerable development in the early modern period, when they became the stock in trade of the riddling language for which alchemy is famous today.

BIBL.: Georges C. Anawati, "Avicenne et l'alchimie," in *Oriente e occidente nel medioevo* (Rome 1971) 285–341. Marcelin Berthelot and O. Houdas, *La chimie au moyen-âge,* 3 vols. (Paris 1893). Marcelin Berthelot and C.-E. Ruelle, *Collection des anciens alchimistes grecs,* 3 vols. (Paris 1887–1888). Denis I. Duveen, *Bibliotheca alchemica et chemica* (London 1949).

André Jean Festugière, *La révélation d'Hermès Trismégiste,* 4 vols. (Paris 1949–1954). Robert Halleux, *Les textes alchimiques* (Turnhout 1979) and *Les alchimistes grecs: papyrus de Leide, papyrus de Stockholm, fragments de recettes* (Paris 1981) vol. 1. Arthur John Hopkins, *Alchemy: Child of Greek Philosophy* (New York 1934). Paul Kraus, *Jābir ibn Hayyān: Contribution à l'histoire des idées scientifiques dans l'Islam,* 2 vols. (Cairo 1942–1943). Claudia Kren, *Alchemy in Europe: A Guide to Research* (New York 1990). E. O. von Lippmann, *Entstehung und Ausbreitung der Alchemie,* 3 vols. (Berlin 1919–1954). Bruce Moran, *Distilling Knowledge: Alchemy, Chemistry, and the Scientific Revolution* (Cambridge, Mass., 2005). Robert Multhauf, *The Origins of Chemistry* (London 1966). William R. Newman, *Promethean Ambitions: Alchemy and the Quest to Perfect Nature* (Chicago 2004) and *Atoms and Alchemy: Chymistry and the Experimental Origins of the Scientific Revolution* (Chicago 2006). William R. Newman and Lawrence M. Principe, *Alchemy Tried in the Fire: Starkey, Boyle, and the Fate of Helmontian Chymistry* (Chicago 2002) and *George Starkey: Alchemical Laboratory Notebooks and Correspondence* (Chicago 2004). Lynn Thorndike, *A History of Magic and Experimental Science,* 8 vols. (New York 1923–1958). W.NE.

Alcuin

Carolingian writer, ca. 735–804. Alcuin was an Anglo-Saxon who was educated at York and later taught there. In 781 he met Charlemagne and became part of his circle. The Frankish king appointed him abbot of Tours Abbey in 796, which became a center for the production of biblical and classical manuscripts.

In his concern with classical antiquity, Alcuin was in line with the Church Fathers, Saint Augustine in particular, who all advocated the "proper use" (*usus iustus*) of the antique heritage, and thus reinforced the idea of interpreting heathen values in Christian terms. In his major work, *Disputatio de vera philosophia* (PL 101.849–854), as well as in other writings (e.g., epistle 280), Alcuin established a strong link between classical culture and Christian thought: "You can only acquire more or less perfect knowledge (*perfecta scientia*) by hoisting yourself with the support of seven pillars or steps" (PL 101.853). By the seven steps Alcuin meant the seven liberal arts, which formed the basis on which to carry out true research into the Divine word as imparted in the Bible—that is to say, research both linear and hierarchical, from the bottom (study of classical texts) to the top (comprehension of the Holy Scriptures). Alcuin's occasional criticism of Virgil (epistle 309) can be easily explained. The context matters: after all, as he says, Saint Paul made use of the "gold of wisdom he found in the faeces of poets" as a mainstay of true religious belief (epistles 203, 207).

Alcuin wrote several dialogues about the trivial disciplines (grammar, rhetoric, and dialectics). (It is unknown whether he wrote, or planned to write, on all the liberal arts.) Dialogue is a traditional Anglo-Saxon literary form, though it is noteworthy that Alcuin's *Grammatica* represents a turning away from insular grammar to classical grammar. Especially important are Alcuin's writings on logic; indeed, his great contribution was to make *logica vetus* even theologically fruitful for the Middle Ages.

His dialogues about rhetoric and dialectics, which are held between himself and Charlemagne, already hint at the humanistic link between the intellectual elite as purveyors of the antique heritage and political power. When Alcuin described for Charlemagne, just before the latter's coronation in Rome, his tasks with the words "Spare the lowly and keep the high and mighty down" (*parcere subiectis et debellare superbos,* epistle 178), he naturally had recourse to Virgil by way of Saint Augustine. Charlemagne himself, in various decrees he issued up to 800 CE (*Epistola de litteris colendis; Admonitio generalis*), declared that the knowledge of Latin ought to be improved to make divine worship more worthy of God. This was quite consonant with Alcuin's thinking, though it is not easy to tell how far he had a hand in the formulation of those decrees. The return to correct Classical Latin, which Alcuin did his utmost to foster (but did not always practice, e.g., in his hagiographic works), had far-reaching consequences in Western Europe, for it led to a heightened awareness of the long-standing difference between spoken and written language.

In Alcuin the writer we see a pairing of the theory and practice of "proper use" with a sound knowledge of classical literature. He proved to be a genuine connoisseur of Virgil. He also quoted Statius and Lucan but only seldom Ovid and Horace, despite being nicknamed Flaccus on account of his close relationship with Charlemagne. But some of his pupils bore Virgilian names, such as Damoetas and Menalcas, and some other courtiers were called Homer or Naso. In this way classical antiquity came back to life in virtually physical ways.

BIBL.: Wolfgang Edelstein, *Eruditio und sapientia: Weltbild und Erziehung in der Karolingerzeit* (Freiburg 1965). Louis Holtz, "Alcuin et la Renaissance des arts liberaux," in *Karl der Große und sein Nachwirken,* ed. Paul Butzer, Max Kerner, and Walter O. Oberschelp (Turnhout 1997) 45–60. Hans-Joachin Werner, "*Meliores viae sophiae:* Alkuins Bestimmung der Philosophie in der Schrift 'Disputatio de vera philosophia,'" in *Was ist Philosophie im Mittelalter?* ed. Jan A. Aertsen and Andreas Speer (Berlin 1998) 452–459. Gernot Wieland, "Alcuin's Ambiguous Attitude towards the Classics," *Journal of Medieval Latin* 2 (1992) 84–95. M.C.F.

Alexander the Great

Few if any personalities of the ancient world, fictional or historical, have so captured the imagination of subsequent centuries as has Alexander the Great. Oliver Stone's controversial epic film *Alexander* (2004) may have bombed with the American critics and failed at domestic box offices, but it went on to recoup around the world even more than the staggering $155 million it had cost to produce. Alexander's continuing political significance as a source for national identity and pride is demonstrated by the remarkable tensions between Greece and its northern neighbor, a country that would like to call itself the Republic of Macedonia (but at Greek insistence was admitted to the United Nations only under the provisional name Former Yugoslav Republic of Macedonia) and that puts Alexander's name and monumental statues on its airport, motorways, and city squares. Indeed, even in geographical terms Alexander's fame exceeds that of most other classical figures, for it has extended far beyond Europe and Asia Minor, throughout Central Asia, and all the way to the Far East. Alexander's exploits had an enormous diffusion in a plethora of cultural, religious, and linguistic traditions from the Mediterranean to China, and there is no clear distinction between history and myth. In the East the great Persian poet Firdausi's *Book of Kings* (*Shanahmeh,* 10th cent.) played a central role in the diffusion of the legend of Alexander (Iskandar); it also contributed to the "Islamicization" of his figure. As early as the 7th century the Byzantine historian Theophylactus Simocattes had depicted Alexander's expedition as continuing all the way to China. In late antiquity and after, biblical history and prophecy intertwined with the classical stories about Alexander to produce strange hybrid legends. Many thousands who never read a word of Greek history knew Alexander as the heroic figure who had saved Christianity from unclean northern peoples, led by Gog and Magog, whom he had penned up beyond the Caucasus by constructing the Gates of Alexander, a huge protective wall stretching between two mountains. And millenary fantasies that Alexander would someday return flourished, at least until fairly recently, in some parts of Afghanistan and India—fantasies to which Rudyard Kipling gave memorable expression in his short story "The Man Who Would Be King" (1888), adapted by John Huston in 1975 for a celebrated film.

Not only did the telling of Alexander's history begin in his own lifetime, but so did his legend and the construction of his myth. The young king made sure to have with him a train of poets, historians, and secretaries with the task of recording the events of his enterprise as they happened. These first, direct witnesses, however, have been almost completely lost, and they are known to us only by way of fragments and later versions composed centuries after the events. The accounts of direct witnesses and contemporaries—treatises about the expedition, letters and documents, some more and some less authentic, such as the controversial *Testament of Alexander*—and the school exercises based on those materials gave rise to two grand lines of historiography that ran parallel to each other for centuries: "the historiography of love for Alexander and that of hatred for him" (Mazzarino 1965–1966, 2:24–27). The very same details derived from the dry, diary-like annotations of the *Ephemerides* (the daily journals kept by the chief secretary, Eumenes of Cardia) were dramatized to construct the cult of Alexander and to create his legendary biography.

True and false documents thus intertwined with oral traditions, anecdotes about Alexander's incredible physical and moral qualities, and the fabulous accounts of those who had returned from the marvels of the East. In turn, all these materials—authentic, forged, or frankly spurious—converged in the Alexandrian schools, where a central place was occupied by rhetorical exercises based on Alexander's speeches to his soldiers and generals and on the epistolary correspondence between Alexander and his mother, Olympias, his teacher Aristotle, his generals, and enemy kings (Darius and then Porus, king of India).

Alexander, who became king of tiny Macedonia at 21 years of age, in no time found himself king of the world. After having arrived at the far end of the Indus and at the Indian Ocean, he began a difficult march home. In 323 BCE, when he died in Babylonia, he was barely 33 years old. The empire he constructed in such a short time had only a fleeting existence. Immediately after his death, his successors, the Diadochi, divided his immense territory into the various Hellenistic kingdoms. But Alexander's enterprise, although so fragile and short-lived, threw the geopolitics of the Middle East and Central Asia into confusion. More important, it triggered a process of cultural contamination that imparted a quality of Greekness to peoples and civilizations quite far afield, who for centuries felt the imprint on their art and culture left by Alexander's lightning rule. One thinks, for example, of the Indo-Hellenic art of Gandhara, which flourished beginning in the 3rd century BCE; of the iconography of the Buddha himself, which arose in the 3rd century BCE and was decisively influenced by Hellenic statuary models; but also of the introduction into Indian culture of subjects taken from Greek mythology and of the entrance into its literature, for example, of the genre of drama based on the model of Menander's comedy.

These cultural consequences, although secondary with respect to the plane of politico-military conquest, were a coherent result of the visionary objectives that, even if they could not possibly have been planned in detail, all the sources indicate Alexander pursued. His deeds were performed in a time and on a mental horizon that transcended the historical plane, that exceeded literary narration itself, and that in its scope included even a mythopoetic dimension (Goukowsky 1978).

According to various sources, Alexander decided to entrust the task of representing his likeness to the best artists of the time, whom he wanted to have in his entourage. To the painter Apelles, the sculptor Lysippus, and the engraver Pirgoteles we owe the construction of iconographic models suited to the most diverse media—from coins to gems, from paintings to statuary—that went on to be mass-produced and diffused throughout the empire.

Coins in particular became an important vehicle for the widespread diffusion of Alexander's likeness. A standard numismatic type was established at the beginning of the age of the Diadochi, one side portraying the profile of the sovereign's head, the other an exploit of his or a divine counterpart. This typology ended up prevailing in the Hellenistic era and in the imperial age of Rome, and it was then taken up in the 15th century, first by Pisanello in Renaissance medals.

But it was the stranger and more exceptional bodily traits recorded in biographies and especially in fabulous historiography and hagiography that became popular in the tradition: the incredible scent that emanated from Alexander's skin and mouth and permeated his clothing (Plutarch, *Alexander* 4.2–4); his very short stature, which made him resemble a child; his hair like a lion's mane; his teeth, sharp as a snake's fangs; his different-colored eyes, the right dark and the left light (*Alexander Romance* 1.13).

Alexander's moral qualities were also marked by excesses (positively and negatively), by lack of restraint, by exceptionality. The sources mention his extravagant material and emotional generosity toward his friends, his lack of interest in material goods, his courage to the point of exposing himself to mortal danger, his extraordinary personal charisma, his loyalty, and his magnanimity toward his enemies. All these traits entered into the construction of a heroic and chivalric personage, making him first a paladin ahead of his time, a protagonist of medieval romances, and then one of the *viri illustres* of antiquity, a source from which to draw excellent paradigms of moral virtue.

But the same sources that extolled Alexander's exceptional virtues often emphasized his negative excesses as well: unbounded ambition; cruelty against Greek Thebes and its citizens; the elimination of generals and close collaborators suspected of conspiring against him; intolerance of criticism, even from his friends and comrades in arms; outbursts of rash anger—the anger that brought him, for example, to murder Cleitus, the intimate friend who had saved his life on the battlefield. If one strand of historiography (Plutarch, for example) presents Alexander as sober and temperate in the pleasures of the flesh and table, some sources insist on his weakness for wine, which was supposedly a determining factor in his murder of Cleitus, as well as in the unfortunate burning of the royal palace of Persepolis, which happened at the drunken climax of a Dionysian debauch. The sources also refer to his awe of prodigies and prophecies, which is said to have become an obsession in the last period of his life, a superstitious phobia that tormented his last months with anxiety (Plutarch, *Alexander* 75.1–3).

Stories about Alexander are animated not only by his exceptional traits, but also by the various other characters who contributed to the construction of the legend.

In describing the relations between Alexander and his father, Philip II, the sources oscillate between Philip's feelings of affection and pride as well as suspicion and wariness toward his son, and Alexander's respect and emulation but also rancor toward Philip. In a popular legendary tradition more attention was paid to those voices that insinuated that Philip was not his real father, and credence was given to a tale, apparently of Egyptian origin, according to which Alexander was the natural son of Nectanebus II—the last pharaoh of Egypt (who bore the title Son of Amon-Ra) and a fugitive in Macedonia after the Persian occupation of his country—and was therefore the "son of Zeus-Ammon."

Alexander's mother, Olympias, a descendent of Achilles through Neoptolemus, had been initiated into the mysteries of Samothrace, and all the sources mention her strange relationship with snakes. In late antique and then medieval iconography, the scene of Alexander's birth (following the scene of the Christian Nativity) has Philip off to one side, in the melancholic pose of the putative father, as was already typical for Saint Joseph. Renaissance culture, however, dredged up Plutarch's anecdote about Philip being blinded by a divine thunderbolt while spying on his wife's intimate relations with snakes and the snakelike Zeus-Ammon.

Another important figure in the history and legend of Alexander is the philosopher Aristotle, summoned by Philip II to the court in Pella to educate his son. The relationship between the philosopher and the young prince was close and lively. One of the stories that was especially popular in literature and iconography regards a copy of the *Iliad,* which Aristotle gave as a gift to his young pupil upon his departure for Asia, and which Alexander always carried with him and considered his most precious treasure (Plutarch, *Alexander* 26). The sources record an ever-widening rift in the relations between king and philosopher. For his part, Aristotle disapproved of the enlargement of Alexander's objectives and horizons and the hybridization of Greek and barbarian customs that he pursued. Alexander, on the other hand, became increasingly critical of and detached from the philosopher, "who had nevertheless taught him to live" (Plutarch, *Alexander* 8). According to a rumor recorded in various sources, Aristotle was involved in the death of Alexander, who was supposedly killed in Babylonia by a poison prepared by his own teacher. Oriental versions of romanticized biographies provide the source for a medieval anecdote in which the youthful Alexander amusedly rebukes his elderly teacher, whom he has surprised on all fours during an erotic game with the courtesan Phyllis. The story was popular in European literature and art between the 13th and 16th centuries, from Henri d'Andeli's short French poem *Le lai d'Aristote* to Hans Baldung Grien's moralizing engravings.

All the sources mention Alexander's dear friend Hephaestion, the "other Alexander." Upon Hephaestion's death in Ecbatana, which preceded his own by a few short months, Alexander organized funeral games—just as Achilles had for Patroclus—which were as memorable as those of the epic tale.

Alexander's horse Bucephalus occupies an important place among the characters featuring in stories about him. The wild beast (in legends it became anthropophagous) was miraculously tamed by the adolescent Alexander. It accompanied its master throughout the entire course of his exploits to the borders of India, where it died in battle and was honored with a city dedicated in its name (Bucephala, on the banks of the Hydaspes River).

Alexander's posthumous fortune, the transmission of his history and his myth, is the product, in the world of literature, of histories, anecdotes, and romances and, in the world of the visual arts, of the formal revolution introduced by Hellenistic art and diffused across an extremely vast area. But Alexander's importance in Hellenistic and Roman times is measured less by the historical and military consequences of his exploits than by the secondary consequences produced by this symbolic and political model of an unprecedented figure of power.

In a historical interpretation proposed in the 19th century, Gustav Droysen—the first modern historian to grasp the political and cultural significance of Alexander's undertaking and to create the very definition of "Hellenism"—indicated the influence that the paradigm established by Alexander had on Roman history. But the illuminating studies of the Italian historian Santo Mazzarino have also made an important contribution to the historiographical recovery of the role and figure of Alexander. He clearly demonstrates that, down to Julius Caesar, Alexander provided a model of individual heroism; Augustus, however, found in Alexander's cosmocracy the political outline for his own *renovatio imperii:* his transformation, also constitutionally, of the *res publica* into a principate. The phenomenon of *imitatio Alexandri* formed the backdrop of the entire history of the Roman Empire. It was a constant that was magnified at intervals (e.g., under the Severan dynasty) but that always influenced political and military strategy, expansionistic decisions, and the cosmocratic symbolism of the Roman emperors. It is no accident that the 2nd century CE (one of the periods in which the paradigm of Alexander had the greatest political importance) produced the majority of the histories of Alexander that have come down to us: Plutarch's *Alexander,* Arrian's *Anabasis Alexandri* and *Indica,* and the redaction of the *Alexander Romance.*

At the very beginning of Rome's imperial age, however, Alexander's exploits and figure also became the object of serious attacks, on the level of historiographical reconstruction and beyond. Livy and Seneca formed part of the historiographical tradition of antipathy for Alexander; they were the chief sources denigrating his personal life and reducing the political importance of his exploits. Livy, with the evident intention of celebrating the new Roman model of the *Pax Augusta,* diminished the myth of Alexander's cosmocracy. He suggested that Alexander's glorious and invincible image would surely have been much dimmed if his early death had not prevented Macedonia from continuing with its western campaign, and thus if Alexander had encountered the Romans: the Hellenic *arete* that had made sport of Eastern armies "of eunuchs and women" would have yielded in the face of Roman *virtus* (Livy 9.17–19). Livy's attack is ideological and propagandistic, supporting a Roman model of cosmocracy and undermining the Hellenistic one. Seneca, on the other hand, launched a more direct and personal attack. In his eyes, Alexander was a victim of the intemperance of excesses and passions and thus incapable of mastering his extraordinary fortune. Plainly worried about the facile (and, as it turned out, effective and dangerous) analogy of Aristotle : Alexander :: Seneca : Nero, Seneca stigmatized the tyrant's savagery and cruelty, his ruinous drunkenness, his inability to set a limit to his projects and horizons, and his insatiable rage to destroy other people's possessions. Especially in works preceding Nero's rise to power, Seneca insisted on the hazards of the king's intemperate character, on his failure to adhere to the lesson of his teacher, and on the excesses that brought him sorrows and ultimately led to his premature death. In the 14th century, after a positive image of Alexander as the first emperor and a quasi-Christian paladin ahead of his time had been dominant for centuries, Francesco Petrarch reintroduced this morally negative interpretation. For him, Alexander was the Macedonian "conqueror of the Persians, himself conquered by Persian vices" (*Persarum victor Persarum vitiis victus*); reproved in vain by Aristotle, he ultimately died in Babylonia "utterly effeminate and as if transformed into some kind of monster" (*funditus enervatus et ceu in monstrum aliquod transformatus*), never having had the opportunity to encounter the Romans, that is, an army of men and not of Eastern "women" (*De viris illustribus, Alexander,* 51). In the new spirit of Humanism, Petrarch proclaimed that his interpretation was based not on fables but on "ancient" sources, on the authority of the testimonies of Seneca and of Livy, *historicorum princeps* (*De viris illustribus, Alexander,* 49).

Another negative interpretation important for the late ancient and then the proto-humanistic tradition is the one deriving from Paulus Orosius. In his *Historiae adversus paganos,* finished in 417, he refocused the historiographical vein opposed to Alexander through a Christian lens, taking his inspiration from the few mentions made of the Macedonian in Scripture. One such passage is the recapitulation of Alexander's exploits contained in the prologue to the first book of Maccabees, which culminates thus: "The earth fell silent before him [Alexander], and his heart became proud and arrogant" (1:1–10). But Orosius based his interpretation especially on the prophetic vision of Daniel in which "a male goat appeared from the west . . . and ran at [the ram] with savage force . . . The goat had a horn between its eyes . . . but at the height of [the goat's] power, the great horn was broken, and in its place there came up four prominent horns . . . The male goat is the king of Greece, and the great horn between its eyes is the first king. As for the horn that was broken, in place of which four others arose, four kingdoms shall arise from his nation , but not with his power" (Daniel 8:3–26). The Christian historian used the figure of Alexander to attack the paradigm of pagan cosmocracy, which performed its deeds and made its conquests only to satisfy its own blind ambition and vanity, taking no part in the design of providence. Alexander was a scourge who brought death and destruction throughout the whole world, a fierce beast "insatiable of human blood" (*humani sanguinis inexsaturabilis*) (*Historiae adversus paganos* 3.18.10). This wholehearted condemnation had precedents in Saint Jerome and Fulgentius, and it projected a demonic and satanic image of Alexander, the would-be "son of God." This image was destined for centuries to leave significant marks on patristic texts, on orations and sermons. It even reached the German mystics and Dante, who, following in the footsteps of Livy and Orosius, maintained that only Alexander's early death saved him from a doubtlessly disastrous encounter with the *coathleta Romanus* (*De monarchia* 2.8.8), the one people that could have competed with him in his plan for world domination.

Alexander's cult, however, continued to the end of late antiquity. The masses continued to believe religiously in the prophylactic and apotropaic power of gold and silver medals bearing his image (*Historia Augusta, Tyranni Triginta* 14.4.6), and at the end of the 4th century John Chrysostom warned the Christians of Antioch to stop wearing amulets with Alexander's image around their necks and ankles (Homily 26 on the Second Epistle of Paul to the Corinthians). The last temple dedicated to Alexander was closed by Justinian in the 6th century and replaced by a temple dedicated to the Madonna. But the superstition and magical practices related to Alexander's cult persisted for centuries: in an 11th-century letter to a doctor in Constantinople, the Byzantine theologian and philosopher John Italus mentions that talismans with images of Alexander were thought capable of making bearers "immune to the plague."

For the centuries between late antiquity and Humanism, just about the only vehicle transmitting Alexander's myth was the *Alexander Romance*. The Greek text, which had first been translated into Latin by Julius Valerius in the 3rd century CE, existed in various redactions. These can be traced to no common archetype, but an inextricable ramification of versions, translations, and redactions spread the *Romance* far and wide and made it extraordinarily popular in literature and iconography. In the 10th century the archpriest Leo brought a new translation of the text back to the West from Byzantium, the *Historia de preliis,* and it served as the basis for all medieval versions in Western languages. At the same time the *Romance* was translated into various other languages: Syriac, Armenian, Coptic, and Arabic. It has been noted that "of all the textual traditions growing out of Graeco-Roman antiquity (excepting the New Testament), the *Alexander Romance* has had the most important diffusion in space and time" (Baumgartner 1998). In particular, the story of Alexander's flight to heaven, charged with precise symbolic meaning, enjoyed its own success, and it is perhaps the one image from stories about Alexander that for centuries was known even to those who could not read (Frugoni 1973). Images of Alexander's journey are found on gems, in miniatures, on religious hangings (such as the border of a French reliquary cushion of the 8th century, on which the phrase *Alexander Rex* alternates with the phrase *Agnus Dei*), on capitals of Romanesque churches, and in floor mosaics. Alexander's flight is used as a prefiguration of the relationship between the earthly king and God, and as a symbolic narrative key for history as shaped and ordered by Divine Providence.

But the allegory of the journey also took on a strong political and ideological significance. The Byzantine emperors recognized in Alexander the model of cosmocracy from which the Roman *principes* and they themselves, as legitimate successors of the Rhomaioi, derived their own pattern of rule. In Byzantium and in the Byzantine area of influence, Alexander and his celestial journey were evoked as an archetype of the cosmocratic power of the emperor, who ruled over the Earth by divine mandate and in imitation of the one Pantokrator.

The image of Alexander in flight was also used, and precisely as a symbol of Byzantine imperial authority, by the Normans in their 12th-century fight against Byzantium for control over the Adriatic. In Norman Puglia—in Trani, Taranto, and Otranto—the flight with griffons appears as a negative allegory, along with other examples of arrogance that are punished in biblical history, such as the sin of Adam and Eve and the Tower of Babel.

Alexander's flight reappeared in Venice, once again with a positive meaning directly imported from Byzantium. After the Fourth Crusade of 1204 and the despoiling, material and symbolic, of Constantinople on the part of the Crusaders led by the doge Enrico Dandolo, the image was reintroduced in the renovated Basilica of St. Mark. The triumph of Alexander's sovereignty symbolized the authority of the empire of Rome, then of Byzantium, and finally of Venice.

Here we have confirmation of the vitality and ideological usefulness of the figure of Alexander in the 13th century: Byzantines and Venetians on the one hand, and Normans on the other, were still waging a battle around images of the flight, which had earlier been interpreted as a positive allegory, but which had also been understood by late ancient Christian sources as an example of arrogance.

Leo's 10th-century *Historia de preliis* was the source of countless reworkings, versions, and translations of the *Romance*. The first, in chronological order, is the French *Roman d'Alexandre,* from the early 12th century, the work of an otherwise unknown cleric by the name of Albéric de Pisançon. It is perhaps the first case in which the subject for an epic poem was taken not from the hagiography of a saint or knight but from a story dating back to classical antiquity. The poem's pagan subject was saved from the risk of *vanitas* by its invocation of the *auctoritas* of antiquity (Baumgartner 1998, 11).

Albéric's text is the likely source for the first German version of the *Romance,* the *Alexanderlied* of the priest Lamprecht, dated to the mid-12th century, and then for Gautier de Châtillon's popular work in verse, *Alexandreis.* These first medieval versions featured, in moralized form, Alexander's extraordinary infancy (comparable to the infancies of Christ, Arthur, and Roland), the chivalric tone of his enterprise, and the protection, unbeknown to the hero, of Divine Providence over his conquests. In short, they depict Alexander in the form of a knight, wearing the clothes of a paladin, a prototype of the wise monarch, courageous and valiant, driven to the ends of the Earth to give proof of his exceptional chivalric virtues, but also to enact a plan willed by Divine Providence. (The Christianization of the legend, however, was already present in Greek redactions in Alexandrian territory of the first centuries CE.) Thus, the vernacular versions of the *Romance* in French, in German, and in Spanish passed into the epic cycles of the *Chansons des gestes* together with the various versions of *The Romance of Troy, The Romance of Thebes,* and *The Romance of Aeneas:* pagan heroes entered our libraries, providing the ancient model for the new ethics of chivalry.

Advancing in step with the literary diffusion of the *Romance* was the spread of iconography related to the more striking episodes of the legend. For the most part it was transmitted through the precious miniatures that accompanied the text of the *Romance*'s medieval versions, both Eastern and Western. In these illustrations Alexander appears dressed in contemporary medieval clothes, and the elements of the compositions are often indistinguishable from those of other chivalric cycles.

This iconographical history of the episodes of the *Romance* in the West had a very precise chronological duration. It began with the first miniatures in vernacular manuscripts, which did not appear in the West until the end of the 13th century. It ended with tapestries showing the *Tales of Alexander,* whose formal motifs and medieval themes remained popular among clients and in the textile production of artisanal masters until the end of the 15th century, or even to the first decades of the 16th. The most noteworthy example of this genre is provided by the two grand tapestries with episodes from the *Romance* that were recently transferred from the Doria-Pamphili Gallery in Rome to the Palazzo del Principe in Genoa. Almost certainly commissioned from the Flemish shops in Tournay by Charles the Bold in the last quarter of the 15th century, the tapestries depict all the most important episodes of the *Romance* as recounted in one of the innumerable versions based on the medieval *Roman d'Alexandre* (to be precise, the one composed in 1440 by Jean Wauquelin, one of the leading intellectuals at the Burgundian court). They show a Charles of Burgundy who is clearly so eager to identify himself with Alexander that he lends him his own bodily features. These tapestries are an extraordinary example of the persistence, well into the Renaissance, of chivalric themes and international gothic stylistic elements, according to a taste that was still entirely courtly, clearly lagging behind the artistic and cultural revolutions of the time.

But in the 14th century, with the Humanist rediscovery of the texts of the great classical authors—including Seneca and Livy—an issue had arisen that was destined to have important consequences in the tradition of tales about Alexander. As has been seen, Petrarch had proudly proclaimed in the proem to his *De viris illustribus,* "My object is not to fashion fables but to retell history" (*Neque michi fabulam fingere sed historam rinarrare propositum est*). This is the humanist premise that would bring about the reintroduction of Plutarch, Curtius Rufus, and Arrian (published by the first decade of the 16th cent.)—texts considered authentic and ancient—to the detriment of the various versions of the *Romance,* which in the preceding centuries had enjoyed extraordinary popularity and which, precisely on that account, are all considered, en bloc, medieval fables. In the sixth book of his treatise *De politia litteraria,* the Humanist Angelo Decembrio (brother of Pier Candido Decembrio, who in 1438 had translated Plutarch's biographies, which were printed in the 1470s) attacked anecdotes and fantastic episodes handed down by tradition, such as "the fables of Trajan, Pope Gregory, and Alexander" that constitute the subjects of opulent northern tapestries. Decembrio ended up lamenting that in the libraries of courts and intellectuals, medieval fables are often shelved next to the authentically ancient Greek and Latin originals, thus causing confusion.

These judgments and prejudices resulted in an emphatically critical revaluation of the entire romance tradition of tales about Alexander, and therefore in censorship of their sources. Thus, a copyist of the *Historia de preliis* prefaced his transcription with the declaration that the text was "based on apocryphal tales." Another copyist interrupted his transcription, writing, *Nolui plura scribere quondam nimium fabulosa narrat in sequentibus* ("I did not want to write more because the rest is too fabulous"). Finally, in 1538, the Humanist Melanchthon noted with regard to Alexander's fantastic exploits, *Nemo sine risu legisset* ("No one would have read this without laughing").

The spell of Alexander's myth was broken, and little by little that myth lost its power. In iconography, too, Alexander was stripped of the medieval clothing in which he had appeared in reliefs and tapestries. This was the case, for example, in a famous "sanguine" by Raphael (in the Albertina Museum, Vienna), whose theme is Alexander's marriage to the Bactrian princess Roxana, according to a description by Lucian.

In mature Renaissance painting and until the end of the 18th century, the Macedonian king was dressed in "ancient" clothing. And he was no longer portrayed as a legendary character, but as a military leader at the head of his armies in grandiose battles, or in other scenes, taken for the most part from Plutarch (but also from Pliny, Curtius Rufus, and Arrian), which become topoi of royal magnanimity.

Until the end of the 18th century the cultural imagery of the age reserved for Alexander a place of moralized exemplarity, and it reduced him to the iconographic subject of various edifying episodes and curious anecdotes.

But the figure of Alexander had not yet lost its vitality. Before surfacing in the 19th century as the subject of Droysen's historiographical rediscovery, before providing inspiration and atmosphere to the aesthetically pretentious exoticism of late 19th-century painting, before returning in the 20th century to provide material for literature and film, novels and fables, the image of Alexander made one final triumphal appearance, restored, as he had been in Roman and then Byzantine times, as an archetype and model of an imperial ideology of power.

Napoleon Bonaparte imitated Alexander's visionary designs to the point of retracing his footsteps in the sands of Egypt. When sculpting his own image as world ruler, he took as his model a fresco (a copy of a painting by Apelles) found shortly before under the ashes of Pompeii, in which Alexander is depicted in the pose and with the attributes of Zeus's sovereignty. Thus, in 1806 the new emperor chose to have his portrait painted by Ingres in the exact pose of the ancient Alexander-Zeus.

BIBL.: *Alexander the Great: East-West Cultural Contacts from Greece to Japan* (exhibition catalogue) (Tokyo 2003). C. Alfano, ed., *Alessandro Magno: Storia e mito* (Rome 1995). E. Baumgartner, "La fortuna di Alessandro nei testi francesi medievali del secolo XII e l'esotismo del Roman d'Alexandre," in *Le Roman d'Alexandre: Riproduzione del ms. Venezia, Biblioteca Museo Correr 1493*, ed. R. Benedetti (Tricesimo 1998). L. Braccesi, *L'ultimo Alessandro* (Padua 1986). G. Cary, *The Medieval Alexander* (Cambridge 1956). C. Daniotti, "Il mito di Alessandro dall'ellenismo al Rinascimento," in *L'originale assente: Introduzione allo studio della tradizione classica,* ed. M. Centanni (Milan 2005). C. Frugoni, *Historia Alexandri elevati per griphos ad aerem: Origine, iconografia e fortuna di un tema* (Rome 1973). P. Goukowsky, *Essai sur les origines du mythe d'Alexandre,* 2 vols. (Nancy 1978–1981). R. Lane Fox, *Alexander the Great* (London 1973). S. Mazzarino, *Il pensiero storico classico,* 2 vols. (Bari 1965–1966). R. Merkelbach, *Die Quellen des griechischen Alexanderroman* (Munich 1954). L. Pearson, *The Lost Histories of Alexander the Great* (New York 1960). Richard Stoneman, *Alexander the Great: A Life in Legend* (New Haven 2008). M.C.

Translated by Patrick Baker

Alexandria

Founded by Alexander the Great on the Nile delta in 331 BCE, Alexandria became one of the finest cities of the classical world, the site of the celebrated lighthouse and famed for its library and museum. Its reputation as a center of religion, learning, and commerce inspired the imagination of succeeding millennia in both East and West.

With its double harbor and grid plan, the city was enthusiastically described by several ancient writers. The Mouseion, a center of arts and sciences, was visited by such famous scholars as Euclid and Archimedes. Pliny the Elder mentioned the obelisks and the gigantic lighthouse known as the Pharos. The two giant obelisks that marked the entrance to the Caesareum, the temple complex founded by Cleopatra, now stand prominently in Western cities: one was reerected on the Embankment in London in 1887, the other in Central Park in New York City two years later.

The Pharos, one of the Seven Wonders of the Ancient World, was probably completed in 297 BCE. Square at the base, octagonal in the center, and circular at the top, it was lit by a great fire that was reflected far out to sea by a system of mirrors. The lofty white silhouette was to inspire bell towers and minarets in both East and West for centuries to come. After Alexandria fell under Muslim rule in 641–642 CE, the population of Alexandria declined, and the monuments of the ancient city fell into disrepair. The Pharos suffered from two partial collapses and was several times remodeled; it was eventually destroyed when the Mamluk Sultan Qa'it Bay erected a fort on the site in 1480. Immediately after its demolition, the bell tower of the Cathedral of Venice, San Pietro di Castello, was reclad in white stone in three tiers (square, octagonal, and circular) by the architect Mauro Codussi, as if to claim for Venice the legacy of Alexandria as a great center of religion, learning, and commerce. Today, the underwater ruins of the Pharos in the harbor of Alexandria are still the subject of intense archaeological exploration.

In the early centuries of the first millennium Alexandria was the site of conflict between pagans and Christians, and several ancient temples were converted to Christian worship. Eusebius attributes the origins of Christianity to Saint Mark, who was martyred in Alexandria; his relics remained there until stolen by Venetian merchants in 828–829. The *translatio* of the Evangelist's body to Venice gave the Adriatic port the confidence to evoke aspects of Alexandria in its townscape, for example, in the construction of bulbous superstructures over the domes of St. Mark's Church to recall the profile of funerary structures in Islamic Egypt. Other celebrated Christian martyrs associated with Alexandria include Saint Catherine and Saint Athanasius.

Alexandria's reputation as a center of learning rests on the fame of the ancient library, which is believed to have housed around 700,000 titles on papyrus scrolls by the 1st century BCE. It was supposedly ignited accidentally when Caesar set fire to the Egyptian fleet in the nearby harbor in 48 BCE; other books were reputedly destroyed by fire in the time of Aurelian (ca. 272 CE). Arab historians claim that many more books were burned to fuel the furnaces of the city's 400 public baths under Muslim rule. The Bibliotheca Alexandrina has now been refounded on the seafront, just to the east of the Eastern Harbor. The new building, designed by the Norwegian architectural practice Snøhetta on a circular plan with an inclined roof, was opened in 2002. Its global identity is highlighted by the inscriptions in many different alphabets on its outside walls.

The literary legacy of Alexandria is an international one. The most popular source for the city's foundation myth in medieval Europe was the *Life of Alexander* by pseudo-Callisthenes, also known as the *Alexander Romance;* lives of Alexander also feature in medieval Arab literature, often preserved in richly illuminated manuscripts. The alexandrine, a poetic form based on 12 syllables per line, dominated heroic French verse of the Middle Ages. Shakespeare gave renewed literary life to the story of Anthony and Cleopatra, and the tragic heroine Cleopatra has remained a potent figure in the Western imagination in literature, drama, and cinema.

By the time of Napoleon's expedition to Egypt in 1799 the city had shrunk to just 6,000 inhabitants, but it revived as a cosmopolitan cultural and commercial center under Mohammed Ali in the 19th century, and the Greek community remained strong until Colonel Nasser's revolution in 1952. The work of the Greek poet Constantine P. Cavafy (1863–1933) revived the use of demotic Greek as a literary language. Many of his poems reflect on the ancient historical figures evoked by the townscape. By the time Lawrence Durrell arrived in Alexandria in 1941, Cavafy was dead, but the Greek poet's memory was still a potent inspiration. Durrell's four-part novel, *The Alexandria Quartet,* gives a vivid picture of the combination of seediness and nostalgia that characterized Alexandria in the mid-20th century.

BIBL.: Narratives of the founding of the city are provided by Plutarch (*Life of Alexander* 26.1–5), Diodorus of Sicily (17.51, 52), and Strabo (17.1, 6). For descriptions of the city see Strabo (*Geography* 17.1, 6–12), Achilles Tatius (5.1), Ammianus Marcellianus (22.16.7–22), and Pliny (*Natural History* 36.11, 14, and 18). The multivolume Napoleonic *Description de l'Egypte* (1821–1830) includes a detailed description of Alexandria and its antiquities.

C. P. Cavafy, *Before Time Could Change Them: The Complete Poems of Constantine P. Cavafy,* trans. T. C. Theoharis (New York 2001). Jean-Yves Empéreur, *Alexandria Rediscovered* (London 1998). E. M. Forster, *Alexandria: A History and Guide* (1922), new ed. with introduction by Lawrence Durrell (London 1982). P. M. Fraser, *Ptolemaic Alexandria,* 3 vols. (Oxford 1972). John Marlowe, *The Golden Age of Alexandria* (London 1971). Gareth L. Steen, ed., *Alexandria: The Site and History* (New York 1993). Hermann Thiersch, *Pharos: Antike, Islam und Occident: Ein Beitrag zur Architekturgeschichte* (Leipzig 1909). D.H.

Alexandrianism

A style, manner, or movement associated with the culture, literature, and art of ancient Alexandria. Founded by Alexander the Great in 331 BCE, on the Mediterranean coast of Egypt, Alexandria quickly became one of the largest cities of antiquity. It was the leading cultural center of the Hellenistic Greek world, famous for its Great Library and the Museum, an institution sacred to the Muses that housed a research community of scholars supported by the Ptolemaic rulers of Egypt.

Alexandrian culture is regarded as that of a post-classical age, the product of Greeks living in a non-Greek land in a city containing a rich ethnic mix and characterized by an antiquarian and scholarly interest in the literature and arts of the Greek cities of the classical age. Callimachus (3rd century BCE), the greatest of the Alexandrian writers, is typical of the scholar-poets who wrote highly allusive and learned poetry, explicitly intended for a small and discerning audience, although modern scholarship has arguably exaggerated the degree to which Alexandrian literature was written in an ivory tower, detached from the civic and social performance occasions of earlier Greek literature. Alexandria was also the center for important developments in Jewish thought and, in the CE centuries, in pagan philosophy and Christian theology, and the term *Alexandrian(ism)* has specialized applications in those areas.

In a more general way the label has been applied, with a greater or lesser awareness of the actualities of historical Alexandria, to the culture and literature of later periods with one or more of the following connotations: belated, post-classical, learned and allusive, imitative, art for art's sake, artificial, esoteric, obscurantist, decadent. Many uses of the term predate (or are oblivious to) classical scholars' recent positive revaluation of the quality and interest of Alexandrian literature. In modern times the city of Alexandria itself, once again a flourishing commercial and cultural center, became the setting for a different kind of Alexandrian revival, albeit not without connections to the first set of meanings.

The term *Alexandrian* (often used interchangeably with *Callimachean* or *neoteric*) is applied by modern literary historians to the group of Latin poets of the 50s and 40s BCE, including Catullus, Calvus, and Cinna, who practiced a learned and highly crafted poetry, self-conscious of its debt to Callimachus and other Hellenistic poets, such as Theocritus, Apollonius of Rhodes, and Euphorion, aimed polemically at an audience of the cultural elite, and turning from the more public areas of Roman culture and politics to an interest in private emotions and leisured pursuits. In the late 19th century the Roman historian Theodor Mommsen dismissed Roman Alexandrianism (in which he included poetry of the Augustan age) as "a thoroughly degenerate, artificially fostered, imperial literature." More recent students of Latin poetry celebrate the intricate and sophisticated allusiveness of these texts. Like all period labels, Roman Alexandrianism runs the risk of being overschematic: in a Roman culture that had been Hellenized from the start, the influence of Alexandrian literature and scholarship was present long before the later 1st century BCE. Furthermore, the "Alexandrian" learning, refinement, and self-consciousness of Catullus and his friends was continued by the poets of the triumviral and Augustan periods, not only the more politically committed writers like Virgil and Horace but also the love elegists and Ovid, the last and in many ways the most Alexandrian of all Latin poets.

The term was also used by various early commentators on Modernism, who perceived an analogy between the Hellenistic and the modern worlds. For Friedrich Nietzsche in *The Birth of Tragedy* (1872) "Alexandrian man," who turns away from the Dionysiac truths to the pursuit of science and scholarship, dominates the culture of the modern world, reinventing art through scholarly imitation (section 18). In *The Decline of the West* (1918–1923)

Oswald Spengler, in a Nietzschean vein, speaks of "the [present, i.e., 20th] century of scientific-critical Alexandrianism," which will be followed by decline into a second religiousness.

More narrowly the label has been applied to movements in modern literature regarded as analogous to those of the Alexandrian poets themselves or their Roman followers. In France the term was used of 19th- and early 20th-century adherents of "art for art's sake" and related movements, such as Banville, Mallarmé, and Valéry. A character in Oscar Wilde's "The Critic as Artist" (1891) says that "there is really not a single form that art now uses that does not come to us from the critical spirit of Alexandria," where the Greek spirit became most self-conscious; Wilde is acutely aware that Alexandria, not Athens, supplied Rome, and hence later European civilization, with her models. In a more negative spirit the anonymous author of the essay "An Alexandrian Age" in *Macmillan's Magazine* for November 1886 opined that "the literary tendencies of the age . . . are distinctly Alexandrian. Literature has become an industry, more or less polite; mannerism and affectation have . . . taken entire possession of it."

The term has been applied notably to the founders of Modernism in Anglo-American poetry, above all to T. S. Eliot and Ezra Pound, both products of the American "colonies" rather than old Europe, writing in the wake of a war seen as having put an end to an old order of things, and sharing with poets like Callimachus a combination of poetry and scholarship, a reverence for the past combined with iconoclasm, a defamiliarizing juxtaposition of the lyrical and the realist, and a complex and ironic self-awareness. Recent proponents of the analogy, often professional classicists, have used it positively. An early reviewer of *The Waste Land,* F. L. Lucas, found the poem "disconnected and ill-knit, loaded with echo and allusion, fantastic and crude, obscure and obscurantist—such is the typical style of Alexandrianism." Rather later, in 1942, Randall Jarrell observed that the modern poet's "erudition and allusiveness (compare the Alexandrian poet Lycophron) consciously restrict his audience to a small, highly specialized group; the poet is a specialist like everyone else"; and the classicist J. K. Newman describes *The Waste Land* as "that great masterpiece of purely Alexandrian art (even down to the pseudo-serious notes appended)."

The term has also gained some currency in the criticism of modern art through its use by the influential art critic Clement Greenberg, who in "Avant-garde and Kitsch" (1939) saw the avant-garde as a reaction against "a motionless Alexandrianism, an academicism in which all the really important issues are left untouched because they involve controversy, and in which creative activity dwindles to virtuosity in the small details of form, all larger questions being decided by the precedent of the old masters." But Greenberg is also aware that in the turn from the everyday world of representation to an obsession with its own medium and with "the imitation of imitating," the avant-garde "contains within itself some of the very Alexandrianism it seeks to overcome"—so pointing up the slipperiness of the term. More recently *Alexandrianism* has been used as a derogatory term for ironic, self-reflexive, quotational, and trivializing tendencies in modern or postmodern art.

Reduced to the size of a small village by the time of Napoleon's arrival in 1798, Alexandria was rebuilt by Mohammed Ali (viceroy 1805–1848) and in the later 19th century grew to be a flourishing commercial and cultural center. From 1882 until 1936 it was under British occupation and administration. The cosmopolitan golden age that lasted from the 1860s to the 1950s produced a number of writers who used the city and its history as the setting and subject for their works. Most important is the Greek poet Constantine Cavafy (1863–1933), of international importance in the history of Modernism, who was born and died in Alexandria, but was educated largely in England. His poetry often takes as its subject the history of Hellenistic Greece, Alexandria (down to the Arabic conquest of 642), and Byzantium. Cavafy's is a self-consciously alternative Hellenism: in "The Poetry of C. P. Cavafy" E. M. Forster comments that "Alexandria, his birthplace, came into being just when Public School Greece decayed . . . his literary ancestor—if he has one—is Callimachus." Cavafy combines learning with poetry, practicing small-scale neo-Alexandrian forms such as the epigram, and with a focus on the remembered intensity of private passions and sensations. In his celebration of homosexual love Cavafy exploits a perception, going back to Roman antiquity, of Alexandria as a city of sensual indulgence: one of his best-known poems, "The God Abandons Antony," is based on an anecdote in Plutarch's *Life of Antony* that is also dramatized in Shakespeare's *Antony and Cleopatra,* the play that created an image of Alexandria for centuries of English-speaking culture.

Cavafy became an icon of the Alexandrian for a series of English writers who spent time in his native city. E. M. Forster, stationed there for three years during the First World War, knew Cavafy personally and introduced his poetry to T. S. Eliot, T. E. Lawrence, and others. His *Alexandria: A History and a Guide* appeared in 1922; the 2nd edition, in 1938, was dedicated posthumously to Cavafy. Forster took especial care over the section entitled "The Spiritual City," in which he examined the ways in which Jews, Greeks, and Christians in Alexandria constructed philosophical and theological answers to the question "How can the human be linked to the divine?" For Forster Alexandria is as much the city of the author of the *Wisdom of Solomon,* of Plotinus, Origen, and Hypatia, as it is of Callimachus and Cleopatra. (An earlier English novelist, Charles Kingsley, had also focused, in *Hypatia,* published in 1853, on late-antique Alexandria as a turning point in the history of spirituality.) Elsewhere ("The Lost Guide") Forster comments on another aspect of the modern city that links it to its ancient past: "that city symbolises for me a mixture, a bastardy . . . I . . . feel Cavafy its representative. It has been a mixture, a bastardy, for nearly 2000 years." Forster also published a collection of essays on Alexandrian subjects, *Pharos and Pharillon* (1923).

Forster's Alexandrian writings in turn fed the works of Lawrence Durrell, who fled to Alexandria from Nazi-occupied Greece in 1941. A strong interest in the mystical tradition of Alexandrian Gnosticism informs his *Alexandria Quartet,* in which the character Balthazar is a thinly veiled Cavafy. Unlike Cavafy and Forster, Durrell takes the whole history of Alexandria as his canvas, from Pharaonic Egypt down to the period after the Muslim conquest. The line of English Alexandrian writers has continued with Robert Liddell and D. J. Enright.

The physical Alexandria has for centuries been the lost city: travelers before the 19th century found few substantial remains of what had been one of the greatest ancient cities, and much of the archaeological record is now buried under the modern city. The Great Library itself was probably lost early on, burnt accidentally, according to some sources, in 48 BCE during the war between Julius Caesar and Ptolemy XIII. Just recently the ancient city has started to reemerge through a stunning series of discoveries, in the harbor, of Ptolemaic palaces and other structures, by underwater archaeology teams led by Jean-Yves Empereur and Franck Goddio. The Library has also risen again through the construction of a new Bibliotheca Alexandrina (1995–2002).

BIBL.: P. M. Fraser, *Ptolemaic Alexandria* (Oxford 1972). F. Goddio and A. Bernand, *Sunken Egypt: Alexandria* (London 2004). M. Haag, *Alexandria: City of Memory* (New Haven 2004). A. Hirst and M. Silk, eds., *Alexandria, Real and Imagined* (Aldershot 2004) 337–352. J. K. Newman, *Augustus and the New Poetry* (Brussels 1967), with appendix "Alexandrianism in Modern English Poetry." J. L. Pinchin, *Alexandria Still: Forster, Durrell, and Cavafy* (Princeton 1977). On the new Library of Alexandria see www.bibalex.org/English/index.aspx.

P.R.H.

Allegory

Literary allegory and allegorism. The activity of the poet (broadly defined) who incorporates into a text secondary meanings, things hinted at (in Greek, *hyponoiai,* and later *allēgoriai*), and the activity of the interpreter who discovers, articulates, and comments on those secondary meanings are categories of literary activity that are distinct but deeply implicated one in the other. Although this whole issue is fraught with problems on the level of vocabulary, we may take *allegory* to refer primarily to the former—the activity of the author (whether poet, rhetor, or mythoplast)—and *allegorism* to that of the allegorical interpreter. Even so, we will find ourselves calling both Prudentius and Origen allegorists and saying that both allegorized, although the former practiced only the first activity and the latter only the second. The ambiguity reflects the process by which the interpreter usurps the poet's role in the creation of meaning; and yet without a poet who allegorizes, an interpreter who discovers allegories has no credibility. Indeed, allegorical interpreters are seldom more than a step ahead of those eager to brand them as frauds, intellectually dishonest readers, imposing their own notions on texts innocent of those notions.

Given the interdependence of the two activities, we might expect the issue of priority to be fraught with difficulties as well as a chicken-and-egg problem. Common sense dictates that there can be no allegorical interpreter before there is an allegorizing author to interpret, but 20th-century theory, starting as early as the work of Walter Benjamin, pointed to an allegorism inherent in all texts and emphasized the complexity of the act of interpretation—a focus and an orientation that tend to break down the commonsense distinction. Certainly there exist "literary" genres that belong to preliterate tradition—notably the beast fable (Greek *ainos,* compare *ainigma* and *ainittesthai*)—in which the narrative itself, cultivating a paradoxical (if conventionally structured) mode of representation, calls attention to its own incompleteness, its own need for interpretation. The *Panchatantra* and the Fables of Aesop, both clearly literary adaptations of traditional, oral material, reach us with interpretations securely attached—explicit articulations of the ethical allegories contained in each fabulous narrative.

Thus, allegory and allegorical interpretation are already difficult to separate clearly in their preliterate manifestations. Indeed, it is this fundamental allusiveness—playful or serious, and present in a wide range of verbal performance—that both provides the foundation for the claims of allegorical readers and renders difficult if not impossible the task of testing such claims. This is the point Plato's Socrates makes in the *Protagoras* (347E) when he dismisses the interpretation of poetry as an activity subject to no *elenchos* (testing, refutation) and therefore unlikely to be useful in the pursuit of truth.

There is little indication in ancient literary theory of a systematic attempt to distinguish between plausible and implausible claims about the meaning of texts, until a surprisingly late date, and when we first encounter such distinctions it is in an agonistic context. The Stoics are the usual targets, and although we are led to believe that their odd claims about the veiled cosmological notions to be found in the early poets go right back to Zeno and the beginnings of the Stoa in the 4th century BCE, the indignant voices that denounce those claims are those of Cicero, Plutarch, and Galen centuries later. This delayed response is significant, and it is a reminder that however tantalizing the archaic and classical antecedents of allegorical interpretation may be, they are just that: interpretive acts situated in a continuum of claims in a growing literature of interpretation, but not yet differentiated from interpretations of other sorts by any clear or trenchant criteria. Thus, allegorism properly speaking—understood as the systematic claim that some texts characteristically represent what they represent in a veiled, oblique manner, seldom if ever saying what they mean, but rather "saying something else" (the common etymology of *allēgoria*)—was a product of the early Roman Empire and became a clearly defined activity only in the context of the culture wars between the polytheist tradition and the monotheists (the "peoples of the book")—that is, from the 1st century CE to the 6th.

Before those centuries, we nevertheless have some striking accounts of interpretive claims, some of these unquestionably allegorical. These claims usually address the text of Homer, which (given its preeminent role in pedagogy) attracted the lion's share of preserved polytheist Greek interpretive activity. Of these early protoallegorists, a 5th-century BCE follower of Anaxagoras known as Metrodorus of Lampsacus is the most notorious. His most credibly documented claim was that by *Agamemnōn* Homer designated the *aithēr,* the bright, dry element in the upper atmosphere (Hesychius, at *Agamemnōn*), but a longer list of equivalences was attached to this one by Philodemus (*On Poems* 2), without specifying the interpreter. The 2nd-century Christian apologist Tatian (whose veracity and accuracy are in doubt, given the agonistic context) is significantly the earliest author to speak of "allegory" in Metrodorus—indeed, no polytheist author seems ever to have called Metrodorus an allegorist. Even Philodemus' shotgun blast at interpreters who made "insane" claims (*mainontai*)—apparently including Metrodorus—has to be understood as invective rather than as a serious assessment of interpretive claims. The Epicurean and the Christian would have agreed about little else, but each for his own reasons found in the physical allegory associated with Metrodorus a handy target for ridicule.

It was in the context of those same culture wars that someone—perhaps Porphyry, the student of Plotinus who wrote influentially against the Christians in the 3rd century—formulated a sketch of the early history of allegorical interpretation. The B scholiast (medieval annotator) on the battle of the gods in *Iliad* 20 offers first a physical allegory (in which the battling gods stand for fire, water, the moon, air, etc.), then an ethical one (Athena versus Ares = judgment versus folly) and concludes: "This mode of response [to accusations of impiety in Homer] is very old and goes back to Theagenes of Rhegium, the first to write about Homer, and takes the language itself (*lexis*) as its point of departure" (*Scholia Graeca in Homeri Iliadem* (Dindorf) 4:231, on *Iliad* 20.67). The term *allegory* does not appear here, but clearly the "mode of response" (*tropos apologias*) in question is precisely that. This "mode" is here defined in contrast to others based on custom (*apo ēthous*)—that is, on traditional representations of the gods (in the mysteries, etc.). Allegory, then, is inherent in the poetic language (*lexis*) itself—significantly, it is *not* conceptualized as the intrusion of notions from outside the text—and according to the scholiast the decipherment of such oblique systems of representation was as old as the first defenders of Homer against his first detractors (Xenophanes of Colophon and such) in the 6th century BCE.

This is a belated formulation, a history of literary interpretive practice dependent on categories ("modes") defined centuries later, but Plato would have us believe that a little more than a century after Theagenes wrote, the explication of "hinted secondary meanings" (*hyponoiai*) constituted a significant element in the contemporary discussion of Homer, and specifically in pedagogic discourse (*Republic* 2.378D; cf. *Ion* 530C and passim). Late in the 20th century a papyrus of the 4th century BCE containing part of a commentary, sometimes allegorical, on an Orphic text was found at Derveni, near Thessaloniki (Laks and Most 1997). The "Derveni commentator" has been plausibly placed in the late 5th century BCE, and although his identity, along with his purpose and goals, remains obscure and in dispute, he does at the very least provide tangible support for the general picture we find in Plato of the role of the interpretation of poetry—allegorical and otherwise—in the intellectual discourse of the age of Socrates.

Allegory in literature, religion, and myth. The allegorism whose early history has occupied discussion up to this point is an essentially literary phenomenon, and one that can be understood within the categories of rhetoric, the dominant literary discourse of the Graeco-Roman tradition. So viewed, allegory is one of a group of tropes and figures that include irony and sarcasm. These have in common the fundamental principle that the speaker says one thing in order to communicate another. Dramatic context or extratextual features may impinge on that communication. For instance, if I look out the window at a blizzard and say "What a beautiful day!" that sarcastic communication is likely to be complete and satisfactory if addressed to a listener who is present and aware of all the relevant phenomena. All these tropes do, however, entail risks, most of all the risk of obscurity (*asapheia*), which may very well result if the connection between what is said ("What a beautiful day!") and what is meant ("What an awful day!") is broken.

Another way to view this is to say that allegory and related tropes incorporate a complex structure of meaning. Texts characterized by these procedures are not limited to the relatively straightforward and generally nonproblematic sense or meaning (*dianoia*) of most literary texts (according to Aristotle and others). Rather, such texts incorporate secondary meanings (*hyponoiai*, "undermeanings" or "things hinted at" but not explicitly or clearly stated). Beyond the risk of obscurity, where for whatever reason the listener or reader fails to grasp the secondary meaning, there lurks as well the risk of "frigidity" (*psykhrotēs*), against which rhetors warn their pupils, a known effect of—among other things—excessive recourse to the trope of allegory.

From an early date, it becomes very difficult to draw a clear line of demarcation between, on the one hand, this literary trope of allegory along with its risky but conceptually straightforward interpretation and, on the other, a different mode of oblique signification specific to religion. The connection is made explicit in the discussion of allegory in "Demetrius," *On Style* (*De elocutione,* 1st cent.

CE?), where the discussion is firmly focused on modes of diction, and the relationship of allegory to religion is invoked to communicate the qualities of the trope: "Anything expressed indirectly (*pan to hyponooumenon*) is all the more imposing and disturbing (*phoberoteron*), and different listeners imagine different things . . . This is why the mysteries are expressed in allegories, to inspire awe and dread such as are created by darkness and night, since allegory in fact resembles darkness and night" (101).

Myth, in this sense the mediator between literature and religion, lies somewhere in between. Traditional stories, widely viewed as authorless, escape the rhetorical model of signification outlined above, and several alternative models were applied in the service of making them yield their significance. The later Platonists invoked "mythoplasts" (myth-shapers) of privileged insight and understanding, standing at the remote source of the tradition. Like the traditions of the explanation of problems in Homer, the allegorical decipherment of myth was an ongoing and cumulative process, but the evidence in this instance is even more scattered. We have a single substantial interpretive compendium or manual (*Epidromē*) of Greek myth, from the 1st century CE, addressed to a young student (*paidion, teknon*) and attached to the name of Annaeus Cornutus, perhaps best known as the teacher of the satirist Persius (Ramelli 2003). It is rich in material known to have interested many Stoics (etymologies and "physical" allegories) and represents the most substantial evidence we have for a serious concern with such matters on the part of a Stoic philosopher, though it remains unclear how such allegories could play a role in any sort of credible intellectual project. Cornutus's purpose here seems to be to alert his young charge—it has been suggested, naturally, that this might have been Persius himself—to the allegorical resonances of the traditional stories, particularly as encountered in literature. The relative importance of Homeric and Hesiodic material supports this thesis, but the compendium remains focused on explication of myths, not texts, citing a range of authors in support of various claims, while treating the poems cited as evidence rather than texts to be explained.

Into the same hermeneutic limbo with myth fall a few other categories of texts of obscure or "supernatural" authorship, most notably oracles. That this was a category fraught with problems and anxieties is shown by the skepticism associated with oracles and oracular signs, found in the earliest evidence (e.g., Hector at *Iliad* 12.237–250) and widespread in Aristophanes. Herodotus' familiar tales of hermeneutic hubris reflect another aspect of this ambivalence concerning authorless or "divinely authored" texts: it seems that we are rarely able to make use of such privileged information, and when it is before us we are condemned to misinterpret it, leaping to conclusions dictated by our own limited perspective and our lack of knowledge both of self and of the world.

Philosophical concern with such matters in the archaic Greek world begins early. Thanks to Plutarch, who cites the evidence (and who was himself obsessed with signification), we know that Heraclitus, in the 6th century BCE, had already observed that "the god of the oracle at Delphi neither tells nor conceals, but rather delivers signs" (*sēmainei*, fr. 93 Diels-Kranz; Plutarch, *De Pythiae oraculis* 404D).

An episode in the early history of the hermeneutics of myth deserves our attention at this point. The traditional stories created a short circuit in the rigorously intentionalist model of interpretation embraced by the rhetorical tradition because they were authorless. But in Plato we encounter for the first time myth that is self-consciously fabricated and calls attention to that fact. The "mixed" thinkers in Aristotle's history of inquiry (*Metaphysics* A, 1091a–b), including Pherecydes (6th cent.), seem to have exploited fabricated or revisionist myth for philosophical ends. Aristotle represents them doing something of the sort, putting *some* things "mythically," but not everything. The 5th-century Sophists also anticipated Plato's practice. But Plato exploited the elusive and playfully imaginative semiotic structures of myth as a complement to the other rhetorical registers of the dialogues. He not only invented new myths, he dramatized the fabrication of parodic philosophical myth (in Aristophanes' speech in the *Symposium*). In some instances, notably the Creation myth of the *Timaeus,* there is good reason to believe that for pedagogic reasons he wrote the opposite of what he thought to be true. The result is that the uninformed reader who misses the point and reads the myth as a straightforward presentation of what the author takes to be the truth is in danger of serious error (and of thinking, for instance, that Plato thought the universe to have had a beginning in time). Those didactic myths incorporated into Plato's dialogues were a magnet for the hermeneutic imaginations of his successors. Their influence on the larger history of the interpretation of myths and texts in Platonism has been enormous.

The polytheists. The texts that give us our first substantial evidence concerning literary interpretation in the Greek tradition date to the 1st and 2nd centuries CE—a period of extraordinary literary accomplishments in Greek and in Latin. Homer, the core of the educational canon, attracted a growing literature of commentary built on a foundation of Homeric "questions" or "problems," typically representing classroom solutions to specific issues of interpretation and ranging from the level of vocabulary and morphology to plot and significance. The first collection of such "Homeric questions" was attributed to Aristotle, and a few interpretations are attributed to this collection in the scholia. The collection made late in the 3rd century CE by the Neoplatonist Porphyry (now usually referred to as his *Homeric Questions*) has fared better, but like its predecessor, along with many other interpretive texts or collections both named and nameless, it is known primarily from excerpts in the scholia.

As we might expect, these marginal notes that preserve many centuries of the reception of Homer and address questions ranging from the philological to the theological represent a considerable range of interpretive techniques.

Allegory—explanations based on the claim that in a given passage Homer says one thing but means, or hints at, something else—has a circumscribed but important role in this interpretive material.

The corpus of the Homeric scholia is too vast and too varied to provide a clear indication of how the *Iliad* and *Odyssey* were read in any particular context. But a related text, the *Essay on the Life and Poetry of Homer* attributed to Plutarch, can help to put the role of allegory in ancient Homeric interpretation in perspective, relative to other modes of explication (Keaney and Lamberton 1996). This introduction to the epics, probably the work of a grammarian (*grammaticus*) of the 2nd century CE, presents a considerable array of interpretive material, much of which shows up as well in the scholia. The author repeatedly tells the reader that Homer "hints at" (*ainittetai*) ideas that are not made explicit, and, though much less often, that Homer "allegorizes" or speaks "allegorically" (*allēgorikos*). In the discussion of Homer's tropes and figures, he defines allegory as the trope that "represents one thing by another" (ch. 70). If we ask when and where, according to "Plutarch," Homer allegorizes, we find that the field is surprisingly narrow, and virtually limited to theology. Allegory is invoked to explain passages found theologically unacceptable, recalling the critiques of Xenophanes and Plato: Hera's (erotic and incidentally incestuous) deception of Zeus (ch. 96, where she = *aēr,* the damp gaseous element; he = *aithēr,* the bright, hot one; their union produces the universe) and the theomachy of *Iliad* 20, where "Plutarch" supplies a list of decipherments (Hera versus Artemis = mist versus moon, etc.) which has significant overlap with the one in the possibly Porphyrian scholion cited above (Dindorf 4:231). In the erotic epyllion on Ares and Aphrodite in the *Odyssey,* the story (*mythos*) itself "hints at" the Empedoclean cosmology of love and strife (ch. 101). There are some other "hintings," some, like the transformation of Odysseus' crew, pointing to edifying lessons of reward and punishment (ch. 26, bestial reincarnations for foolish men). The pattern that emerges is clear: allegory as such is to be invoked in Homeric explication specifically to resolve theological issues—points at which Homer had long needed some sort of defense—and secondarily to articulate moral lessons implicit in the text. These traditional solutions to traditional problems had been embedded in the pedagogical tradition for centuries when "Plutarch" wrote his introduction to the poems. Aside from those passages where Homer's anthropomorphic gods irrevocably violated behavioral boundaries dear to Homer's readers and had to be neutralized into allegorical representations of something other than gods, Homer, it seems, was seldom speaking allegorically. In fact, for this grammarian, Homer's principal value lay in his eloquence, and for "Plutarch" the *Iliad* and *Odyssey* were first and foremost a propaedeutic (preparatory requirement) to the study of rhetoric, not theology.

Another collection of Homeric interpretive material that may be roughly contemporary with that of "Plutarch" offers a striking contrast to his reticence with regard to allegory. This collection of "Homeric Problems, relating to Homer's allegorizing about the gods" (as it is designated in the best manuscript), assembled by Heraclitus (1st cent. CE, perhaps a namesake of the early philosopher), is a focused compilation of interpretive material, largely (but by no means exclusively) devoted to defending specific passages of the poems against the charge of impiety (Buffière 1962). Heraclitus' language is florid and encrusted with ornament and recherché vocabulary, and his eulogy of Homer risks "frigidity." But Heraclitus makes broader and more interesting claims for allegory itself and for Homer's use of it than any other author before Proclus in the 5th century. "Allegory" here encompasses a wide range of obscure or allusive language. It is applied to poems of Alcaeus and Anacreon that a modern reader would hardly call allegorical (though the illustrations do contain metaphors), and to the language of philosophy in the extreme cases of Heraclitus of Ephesus (the early philosopher) and Empedocles. Athena's visit to Ithaca to advise Telemachus at the beginning of the *Odyssey* is allegorical: a colorful way of saying that the ideas in question simply came into Telemachus' head. Even here, however, it remains clear that the core of the "allegorical" Homer is the poet who uses the names of the gods and the actions he attributes to them to designate truths about the physical universe.

The 3rd-century Neoplatonist Porphyry, whose *Homeric Questions,* mentioned above, seems to have been largely limited to philological matters, shows himself a Homeric commentator of a very different sort in his essay *The Cave of the Nymphs in the Odyssey* (Westerink 1969). Porphyry was exceptional among the Platonists for his literary studies and has this in common with the other great ancient Platonist to concern himself with allegory, Proclus, two centuries later. The essay is devoted in large part to a recital of lore about nymphs, shrines, and cave sanctuaries, especially Mithraic ones, providing keys to decipher each element of the Homeric passage, which itself eventually proves to be a metaphor for the world and the key to the larger significance of the entire epic poem. This is something quite different from the piecemeal allegorical interpretations produced thus far. Porphyry situates the allegory of the cave in the center of an allegorical *Odyssey:*

> Homer says that all outward possessions must be deposited in this cave and that one must be stripped naked and take on the persona of a beggar and, having withered the body away and cast aside all that is superfluous, and turned away from the senses, take counsel with Athena, sitting with her beneath the olive, to learn how he might cut away all the destructive passions of his soul. No, I do not think Numenius and his friends were off the track in thinking that, for Homer, Odysseus in the *Odyssey* was the symbol of man passing through the successive stages of *genesis* and so being restored to his place among

those beyond all wavecrash and "ignorant of the sea":

until you reach men who do not know the sea
and put no salt on their food.
(*Odyssey* 11.122–123)

Whether this interpretation was first fully developed by Porphyry, or by the obscure Numenius a century earlier, it represents a new departure. The essay is unique, but it represents a tradition of the reading of Homer among the later Platonists that is next documented among the Athenian scholarchs in the 5th century.

Porphyry's interest in symbolism, mythic, religious, and literary, was far-reaching. He also produced *On Statues,* of which a generous series of fragments survives (preserved, significantly, by Eusebius in his *Preparatio evangelica*).This collection of interpretations is to the "reading" of statues of the gods what Cornutus's compendium, two centuries earlier, was to the "reading" of myth generally. Porphyry and Cornutus provide the most important surviving evidence for the cumulative allegorization of the Greek myths that seems to have begun in the Stoa, to be nurtured by Platonists in the later Roman Empire, down to the last days of polytheism.

Proclus (d, 485) was one of the last leaders of the Platonic school in Athens. The extensive collection of Homer interpretation in his commentary on Plato's *Republic* is explicitly intended for the use of a closed group. In the world beyond the Platonists' school, the poems were daily taught by Christians who knew well how to discredit and dismiss Homer's theology while appropriating the poems as cultural capital. Our last glimpse of the Neoplatonists' understanding of the *Iliad* and *Odyssey* we owe to Proclus's determination to save Homer from Socrates' condemnation in the early books of the *Republic.* What is most remarkable about Proclus's accomplishment is that he developed an infrastructure to explain just how and why Homer's text was allegorical—a hierarchical semiotics of poetry, built on the foundation of late Platonic metaphysics and establishing the text alongside the human microcosm as yet another manifestation of the universal triad of soul, mind, and the One. Proclus also, quite incidentally, offers a reading of the Troy tale that incorporates Porphyry's allegory of the *Odyssey* and turns the two epics into a single story of emananation and return: "The myths want to indicate, I believe, through Helen, the whole of that beauty that has to do with the sphere in which things come to be and pass away and that is the product of the Demiurge. It is over this beauty that eternal war rages among souls, until the more intellectual are victorious over the less rational forms of life and return hence to the place from which they came" (*In Platonis Rempublicam commentarii* 1.175.15–21). This, or some variant of it, was the story Homer had to tell, according to what may have been his last polytheist readers.

Commentary on the *Aeneid* mimicked Homeric criticism, and Servius's 4th-century commentary on Virgil's epic makes frequent appeal to allegorical interpretations of isolated passages, without invoking any grand allegorical scheme in the manner of Porphyry and Proclus on Homer. Nevertheless, in Macrobius' *Saturnalia* (1.24.13), where a young and rather unobtrusive Servius is portrayed, the *Aeneid* is already a "sacred poem" of "arcane meanings"—in other words, a Roman epic to equal Homer's and with a similar complexity of signification. Perhaps a century later, a certain Fulgentius (probably a North African bishop who died in 533) had taken allegorical commentary on the *Aeneid* that next step: the shipwreck in book 1 is a metaphor for birth, and the poem and its encrypted philosophical message turn out to have, so to speak, a life of their own (Rosa 1997). This commentary, in the form of a dialogue between the author and Virgil, was one of the seminal texts for the development of the visionary and allegorical Virgil who emerged in the Middle Ages. As Virgil tells Fulgentius at the start: "In all of my works, I have inserted ideas about the order of the natural world" (*physici ordinis argumenta induximus,* 90–91, Rosa).

The monotheists. The historical relationship between the traditions of polytheist allegorical readings of myth and Christian allegorical exegesis remains obscure. Christians like Origen and Eusebius were intensely concerned with the polytheist material, and they preserve much of it for us. This interest was in part fueled by its usefulness in discrediting the polytheist cults, but that was not their only motive.

Christian interpretations of Scripture as such lie beyond our concerns here, as does Philo's elaborate allegorical reading of the Pentateuch, for all its influence on subsequent Christian hermeneutics. Nevertheless, Philo's enterprise of cultural appropriation (claiming Greek wisdom and culture for the Jews on the basis that it is all contained in and derived from the writings of Moses) was informed in part by the literature of commentary we have been exploring. In his dialogue *On Providence,* Philo embraces the principle that Homer and Hesiod were allegorizing poets and offers some of the specific interpretive commonplaces we have encountered repeatedly—Hera = air, Hermes = reason, etc. (*De providentia* 2.40–41).

The roots of Christian allegorical reading no doubt tap the polytheist tradition of allegorism, but the canonical texts of the New Testament contain their own foundation and antecedents for the practice. The parables and the notion, repeatedly invoked, of a privileged interpretation unavailable to the outsider are at least as important for Origen's practice as his knowledge of "Stoicizing" allegory. It is clear, however, that in the early centuries of Christianity, Christian intellectuals followed in the footsteps of Philo in appropriating elements of Greek thought by claiming to find them in their own Scripture (which of course included the already appropriated Jewish Scripture).

In his rebuttal to the anti-Christian writer Celsus, Origen reveals that Celsus's categorical refusal to admit the validity of allegorical readings of Scripture is an important element in their differences. To Origen such a refusal is simply ungenerous, given Celsus's apparent commitment to the allegorical reading of at least some traditional myth, Homeric and otherwise. What they are arguing over, then, is rights to allegorical reading, rights to the hermeneutic enterprise that had long played a role in the preservation of Greek tradition by mediating between archaic poetry and new audiences with new values, who found elements of that poetry ethically and theologically offensive. As Origen tells the story, Celsus of course does appear ungenerous and unreasonable, but we have only Origen's side of the debate, along with his own sketchy and self-interested account of Celsus's original arguments. Celsus may well have seen clearly that Christian scriptural allegory, on the Philonian model, was a weapon of appropriation.

Whatever the reason, it is during the first centuries CE that the polytheists seem rather suddenly to embrace the allegorical interpretation of cultural material on a scale far beyond anything documented earlier. It is impossible, for instance, to imagine a book like that of the Hellenistic allegorist Heraclitus in an earlier cultural context, and Cornutus's manual, though it taps an old and cumulative tradition, is nevertheless something quite new. There is good reason to suspect that the Christian strategy of allegory as appropriation was one stimulus behind the polytheists' burst of allegorizing of their own cultural heritage.

The fate of allegorism. As we have seen, by the 6th century, when Christianity had effectively completed the absorption of the classical tradition, Christians like Fulgentius had become the bearers of the allegorical tradition of interpretation of polytheist material.

We might ask at this point why Christian education and culture embraced the classical tradition at all, irrevocably encumbered as it was with those superseded gods whose cults the early Christians had confronted and destroyed. The answer seems to be that the Hellenized culture of the Roman Empire had a momentum (or an inertia) that was too powerful for even Christianity to displace. There were no other models of eloquence with which to replace the educational canon, and once the cults were effectively suppressed, and polytheism no longer a threat on an institutional level, the way was clear for precisely what Julian the Apostate had tried to prevent: the absorption of the great books of Hellenism into a Christian *paideia.* In fact, we seem to have in the example of Fulgentius (if we can accept the identification mentioned above) a historical illustration of the process. For that other North African bishop, Augustine, a century earlier, the polytheism of the *Aeneid* was still a threat, the poem itself pernicious in its message and dangerous. Certainly it was nothing a Christian should read. By the time of Fulgentius, those concerns seem to have evaporated. The polytheism of classical literature could not be removed, but it could be ignored or explained away. It was ultimately to be aestheticized, transformed from threatening alien religion into harmless art, but that was a process not completed before the Renaissance.

The claim has been made that the tradition of allegorism, born in classical antiquity and enthusiastically appropriated by the Christians at a very early date, had an important role in this transition. Allegory, in the hands of rhetors and grammarians, had clearly had a role in earlier transitions and accommodations between archaic texts and "modern" values. It is important to keep in mind, however, that these Christians as "people of the book" had a sophisticated arsenal of techniques for dealing with texts. The Greeks had no scripture before they embraced the Old Testament along with the New. The authority of the *Iliad* and *Odyssey* was a cultural, not a religious authority (though some developments in later Platonism, clearly influenced by the confrontation with Christianity, confer on Homer that sort of authority). The Christians themselves were heir to a tradition that privileged certain texts to an extraordinary degree, and they made claims concerning those texts that were utterly foreign to anything in the Graeco-Roman culture they appropriated. Along with that privileging of texts came a high level of sophistication in the use of those texts. There are few documents that go to the heart of the issue, but a text contemporary with Julian, Basil's *Ad adulescentes,* offers a glimpse of that sophistication. In Basil's discussion of the use of polytheist texts in Christian education there is very little that could be called allegorical. His more impressive tools lie in manipulation of the expectations of the young as they read polytheist texts. If you select the texts and tell the readers what sort of message to look for, they will find it. The alien religious framework shrinks to the margin. There is not even a need to explain it away. Other tools of appropriation included *centones* (pastiches of Homer's language, used to retell biblical stories) and perhaps most important of all, the constant citation of Homeric lines and phrases to ornament and illustrate Christian tracts.

This is also the context of the rise of the uniquely Christian genre of allegorical epic. Prudentius' *Psychomachia* (ca. 405) takes the "personification allegory" that was a part of epic right from the *Iliad*—where its role is small but memorable, as when, for instance, Strife visits the Greek camp (*Iliad* 11.1–14)—and makes it the vehicle for an entire epic narrative. In Prudentius' epic, the Christian virtues, led by Faith, defeat the vices and construct a heavenly city in the mind. Personification allegory as such has little beyond the name in common with the notions of allegory that concern us here, but it did open up one possibility for a Christian epic to replace Homer and Virgil. Prudentius' imitators were many in the Middle Ages and Renaissance.

In the East, the 12th-century commentaries of Eustathius on the *Iliad* and *Odyssey* constitute the great medieval compendium and summation of Homeric scholarship. They were written, as the author indicates, at the request of his students. Eustathius recognizes a role for allegory in explaining some of the mythic material but warns against excessive recourse to such explanations. Even the *Homeric Allegories* of his contemporary John Tzetzes are not what their title might suggest but, rather, a metrical paraphrase of the two epics for the edification of the teenaged German bride of Emperor Manuel I. The paraphrase incorporates many allegories, but its goal is not to allegorize the entire poem, and certainly not to Christianize it. This is something that the Byzantines never sought to do, always recognizing the Homeric poems as a cultural property simultaneously their own and alien (Browning 1992).

In the Latin West the *Iliad* is intermittently visible in the form of the *Ilias latina,* an epitome in 1,070 verses that probably dates from the early 1st century CE. This was included in the elementary curricula of the cathedral schools of the high Middle Ages. Otherwise, the poems of Homer faded from memory—or rather, back into memory and into the oral tradition, whence they reemerged in such remote retellings as the *Roman de Troie.* The classical authors most famously allegorized in the Latin Middle Ages were Ovid and Virgil, though in both instances the evidence for this development is relatively late.

A 12th-century commentary on *Aeneid* 1–6, dependent on Fulgentius and more broadly on the Platonist texts that elaborated the allegorized Troy tale, finds in Virgil's poem a narrative not unlike the one Porphyry found in the *Odyssey:* the journey of a soul through a human body (Jones and Jones 1977). The appropriation of Virgil, however, like that of Homer where Homer was still read, was accomplished more through *centones* and through citation in illustration of specifically Christian values than through claims about the allegorical meaning of the poems. By the early 4th century Virgil had been cited as a proclaimer of Christianity before the fact, his Fourth Eclogue assimilated to prophecy of the birth of Christ. The story of the evolution, both on the level of popular legend and in learned literature, of this 4th-century Virgil into Dante's guide in his own cosmic allegory a millennium thereafter has been told by Domenico Comparetti in one of the monuments of literary history, *Virgilio nel medioevo* (1872, English translation 1895). Properly allegorical claims have a role in that story, but a relatively modest one alongside the appropriation of Virgil the *magus* (along with the Sybil) to the select company of pagans who foretold the coming of Christ.

Ovid (though he as well was clothed in legend) is another story. The 14th-century allegorizing translation of the *Metamorphoses* known as the *Ovide moralisé* taps a range of traditions of allegorizing polytheist divinities and myth that includes Macrobius, Fulgentius, the Vatican mythographers, and Isidore of Seville, as well as a medieval tradition of allegorizing commentary on Ovid that had existed at least since the 12th century (Engels 1945). This translation or adaptation, embellished with voluminous interpretive commentary, became in turn the true Ovid for the poets of the late Middle Ages and Renaissance and, for a vernacular reading public, the source for the whole range of classical myth, in a heavily mediated and assimilated form.

The Renaissance was the golden age of allegory, when commentary aimed at deciphering the "mysteries" of ancient religion, myth, and literature proliferated and generated a reaction that largely signals the end of our story. Allegories—those of the *Ovide moralisé* as well as a host of others, etymological, euhemeristic, physical, moral and typological—were everywhere. The fascination with cracking the code, with recovering the truths behind the screen of fiction (a favorite metaphor ever since Proclus) was enduring, but in the 16th century this enthusiasm was dampened by a growing chorus of skeptics. The most famous is Rabelais, who in the preface to *Gargantua* (1534) mocked the entire tradition, from Cornutus and "Plutarch" to Eustathius and the *Ovide moralisé.* The Christianization of antiquity was a favorite target, and an easy one. Rabelais's dismissal of the discovery in Homer of the "sacrements de l'évangile" is echoed in Joseph Scaliger's criticism of his own teacher Jean Dorat for "seeking the whole Bible in Homer" (Grafton 1992). But along with the Christianizing side of the process, allegory itself was falling into disrepute.

The story of the gradual stripping away of the ancient interpretive material from the early modern printed editions of Homer provides a graphic illustration of the decline of allegorical interpretation. Much as the 18th and 19th centuries pared Neoplatonic commentary away from the text of Plato, so Homer emerged from behind the introductions of "Plutarch" and others, unmediated. The process ran parallel to the Reformation and was in a sense related. Martin Luther himself was one of the declared enemies of allegory, whose invention he ascribed to "stupid, lazy monks" (Brisson 2004, 148).

Allegorism has never entirely recovered from the scorn heaped on it by Rabelais and Luther, though allegory as a literary genre is protean and constantly recurring in new forms. Twentieth-century literary theory, by problematizing all hermeneutic activity and the very possibility of reading, prepared the way for a more sympathetic reassessment of the allegorists. That, combined with increased attention to the reception of ancient authors and to the history of that reception, has gone far to restore allegoresis and the allegorists to their legitimate place in European intellectual history.

BIBL.: R. G. Boys-Stones, *Metaphor, Allegory, and the Classical Tradition* (Oxford 2003). Luc Brisson, *How Philosophers Saved Myths: Allegorical Interpretation and Classical Mythology* (Chicago 2004; German, Darmstadt 1996). Félix Buffière, *Allégories d'Homère* (Paris 1962) and *Les mythes d'Homère et la pensée grecque* (Paris 1956). Domenico Comparetti, *Virgilio nel medio evo* (2d ed. Florence 1895; English, London 1908). David Dawson, *Allegorical Readers and Cultural Revision in Ancient Alexandria* (Berkeley 1992). J. Engels, *Études sur l'Ovide moralisé* (Groningen 1945). J. W. Jones and E. F. Jones, eds., *The Commentary on the First Six Books of the Aeneid Attributed to Bernardus Silvestris* (Lincoln, Neb., 1977). J. J. Keaney and Robert Lamberton, eds., *"Plutarch": Essay on the Life and Poetry of Homer* (Atlanta 1996). André Laks and Glenn W. Most, eds., *Studies on the Derveni Papyrus* (Oxford 1997). R. Lamberton, *Homer the Theologian: Neoplatonist Allegorical Reading and the Growth of the Epic Tradition* (Berkeley 1986). R. Lamberton and J. J. Keaney, eds., *Homer's Ancient Readers* (Princeton 1992). Jean Pépin, *Mythe et allégorie: Les origines grecques et les contestations judéo-chrétiennes* (Paris 1976). Pophyry, *The Cave of the Nymphs in the Odyssey* [ed. and trans. L. Westerink] (Buffalo 1969). Ilaria Ramelli, ed. and trans., *Anneo Cornuto: Compendio di teologia greca* (Milan 2003). F. Rosa, ed., *Fulgenzio: Commento all'Eneide* (Milan 1997). Donald Russell and David Konstan, eds. and trans., *Heraclitus: Homeric Problems* (Atlanta 2005). Gordon Teskey, *Allegory and Violence* (Ithaca 1996). Jon Whitman, *Allegory: The Dynamics of an Ancient and Medieval Technique* (Cambridge, Mass., 1987). Jon Whitman, ed., *Interpretation and Allegory: Antiquity to the Modern Period* (Leiden 2000). R.L.

Amazons

A race of warrior women. In ancient sources their homeland is variously situated at the edge of the known world; its capital, Themiscyra, is set on the River Thermodon or on the Tanais or at the Caspian Gates. Amazon society consisted of women and girls. Men were valued only as sperm donors, so conception was achieved at occasional meetings with men of another race, and baby boys were either killed or mutilated. Folk etymology connected the name Amazon to *maza* (breast), and it was therefore thought to mean "breastless." Amazons were believed to cauterize the right breast to ensure that it did not impede javelin-throwing or (in later traditions) the drawstring of the bow. In epic the function of Amazons is to fight men; this combat, which is known as Amazonomachy, always ends in victory for males.

Named Amazons include the queens Penthesilea and Hippolyta. Penthesilea was the daughter of Mars and the Amazon queen Otrere. She accidentally killed Hippolyta, her sister in arms, in the battle that ensued after the marriage of Theseus to Antiope. After the death of Hector, Penthesilea led an army of Amazons to assist the Trojans and was killed in battle by Achilles. In an alternative tradition, the Amazon that Theseus married was Hippolyta, not Antiope. In Shakespeare's *Midsummer Night's Dream* Theseus and Hippolita (princess of the Amazons, so spelled) are portrayed as betrothed.

In art Amazons are normally portrayed in Scythian dress (a cap and trousers). They are commonly represented from the mid-6th century onward on friezes and metopes (e.g., at the Temple of Apollo at Bassae, the heroum at Gyölbashi, and the Mausoleum at Halicarnassus); in sculptures by Phidias, Polyclitus, Cresilas, and Phradmon for the Temple of Diana at Ephesus; on painted pottery (notably a kylix, now in Munich, depicting the death of Penthesilea: the *Lexicon iconographicum mythologiae classicae* (1981–) records 819 depictions of Amazons. Penthesilea's death at the hands of Achilles was also portrayed in Renaissance art (e.g., by Rubens, Giulio Romano, and Jordaens). Renaissance writers attributed to the Amazons the invention of the battle-ax, and the term persists in English usage as a pejorative epithet for a formidable woman. The conquistador Francisco de Orellana, who in 1542 sailed downstream the length of what is now the Amazon River (Brazil), named it thus in acknowledgment of the female warriors whom he claimed to have encountered on his journey. Countries of warrior women based on the Amazons feature in Renaissance literature (e.g., in Ariosto's *Orlando furioso*).

In Arthur Ransome's *Swallows and Amazons* (1930) the Amazons are Nancy Blackett and her younger sister, Peggy, two girls so called because their dinghy is called *Amazon*. Beginning in 1941 the Amazon legend was adapted in the American comic book series *Wonder Woman,* the work of William Moulton Marston: the heroine is Princess Diana of the Amazons, daughter of Hippolyta and niece of Antiope. In the late 1970s the character migrated to the television screen both as an acted part (by Lynda Carter) and as a cartoon character in *Super Friends* and *Justice League*. Amazons also featured frequently in the television series *Xena: Warrior Princess* (1995–2001); Xena's companion Gabrielle was an Amazon. Isolated instances include a Tarzan film (*Tarzan and the Amazons,* 1945) and a Buck Rogers episode (*Planet of the Amazon Women*, 1979).

In chess the queen has sometimes been known as the Amazon. In 1992 an abstract strategy game based on chess, called El juego de las Amazonas (invented in 1988 by Walter Zamkauskas), was published in an Argentinian puzzle magazine, *El acertijo;* an English version by Michael Keller subsequently appeared in the chess magazine *NOST-Algia;* as Game of the Amazons it is now widely played on the Internet. In the game, which is played on a chessboard, each player is allocated four Amazons, who capture territory by shooting arrows.

The term Amazon is now commonly used to denote armed women. Female soldiers in the Israeli Defense Force are known as the Amazon Brigade, and in Libya President Qaddafi's corps of female bodyguards is known as the Amazonian Guard.

BIBL.: F. G. Bergmann, *Les Amazones dans l'histoire et dans la fable* (n.p. 1853). Josine H. Blok, *The Early Amazons: Modern and Ancient Perspectives on a Persistent Myth* (Leiden 1995). D. von Bothmer, *Amazons in Greek Art* (Oxford 1957). A. Klugmann, *Die Amazonen in der attischen Literatur und Kunst* (Stuttgart 1875). H. L. Krause, *Die Amazonensage* (Berlin 1893). P. Lacour, *Les Amazones* (Paris 1901). A. D. Mordtmann, *Die Amazonen* (Hanover 1862). J. A. Salmonson, *The Encyclopedia of Amazons* (New York 1991). W. Stricker, *Die Amazonen in Sage und Geschichte* (Berlin 1868). W. B. Tyrrell, *Amazons: A Study in Athenian Mythmaking* (Baltimore 1984). G.C.

Amphitryon

Human foster father of Hercules. Zeus took Amphitryon's form in order to deceive his wife, Alcmene; Hercules was the offspring of that union. Post-classical authors and artists focus on that phase of Amphitryon's story, barely attending to his earlier adventures as a young man.

Since Plautus' tragicomedy *Amphitruo* (ca. 200 BCE), Amphitryon's situation has given rise to comic dramatic renderings that exploit motifs of disguise, trickery, mistaken identity, cuckoldry, broad sexual humor, and marital sexual jealousy. The most influential of these after Plautus was Molière's verse *Amphitryon* (1668), widely performed, imitated, and studied throughout Europe. Molière's play ridiculed the gods' voraciousness and venality but also explored the problems confronting Amphitryon and his servant Sosia, who fight to establish their identities against the gods' impersonations; Amphitryon is saddled with the ambiguity of marital trust and the rearing of a son who will always remind him of Zeus' intimacy with his wife. (It is Molière's play that gives us the now proverbial sense of an Amphitryon as a fine host, with the famous line "Le véritable Amphitryon est l'Amphitryon où l'on dîne"—"The real Amphitryon is the one who gives you dinner"). John Dryden's English *Amphitryon, or The Two Sosias* (1690) followed Molière's play, lyricizing and expanding it with music by Henry Purcell. Expansive musicalizations of the Amphitryon story have continued ever since, including (in the 18th cent.) adaptations with musical interludes, ballets, songs, dances, and new theatrical versions in the media of opera and (in the 19th cent.) operetta and vaudeville. Cole Porter wrote a musical, *Out of This World* (1950), inspired by Amphitryon, from which we now remember the song "From This Moment On," and 1986 saw the Broadway production of Barry Harman and Grant Sturiale's *Olympus on My Mind,* in which Amphitryon nobly defends his wife's purity of heart in order not to accuse her of adultery, thus inspiring a rare compassion in Jupiter.

The events in the Amphitryon story continually provoke examinations of the relations between power, sexuality, and knowledge. It is likely that the story lies behind Geoffrey of Monmouth's influential account in *History of the Kings of Britain* (mid-12th cent.) of the conception of King Arthur: Uther Pendragon begot Arthur upon Igraine when, with Merlin's assistance, he took the form of her husband Gorlois. Heinrich von Kleist's German play *Amphitryon* (1807), which began as a blank-verse translation of Molière's work, adopts the broad comic motifs and continues the tradition of expanding Molière's tight play, but it darkens and embitters the comic tone: Amphitryon's troubles with Jupiter and Alkmene give rise to social critique of the ways that possessors of power control what counts as truth, and to philosophical discourse about doubt and certainty as he is driven to self-alienation (perhaps an oblique ironic reflection on the Christian account of the Annunciation). Kleist's Alkmene in particular gestures toward the tragic in the contradictory circumstances in which she finds herself; the play's final scene, in which she is required to identify the true Amphitryon in the presence of all the other characters, and in which she discovers her fate of bearing a son to two fathers, focuses what the play represents as a deep and painful ambiguity. Jean Giraudoux's French play *Amphitryon 38* (1929) represents deception and inability to avow the truth as pervasive: his Amphitryon is passive, easy to dupe, without the fiery temper of earlier portrayals. Reinhold Schünzel's greatest film, his 1935 *Amphitryon,* sends up and parodies certain Nazi figures; the exiled Georg Kaiser wrote his play *Twice Amphitryon* (*Zweimal Amphitryon,* 1944) as an antiwar polemic.

In late 20th-century popular culture Amphitryon represents the virtues of monogamy and family life. In the television series *Hercules: The Legendary Journeys* Amphitryon is a ruggedly handsome, middle-aged spouse to Hercules' mother, trying to create stability for his mortal family while their immortal relations, chiefly the vindictive Hera, create recurrent suffering. In the Walt Disney animation *Hercules* (1997)—also a musical, making much of the Gospel-music idiom—Amphitryon is a stolid, happy peasant, and emphatically not a cuckold, for the human couple has adopted Hercules after his fall from Olympus. These versions interestingly allow opportunities to imagine new accounts of ongoing and middle-aged married life, thus providing a temporal extension of Amphitryon's story.

BIBL.: Charles Passage and James Mantinband, *Amphitryon: The Legend and Three Plays. Plautus, Molière, Kleist* (Chapel Hill 1974).

T.KR.

Anacharsis

Scythian wise man of dubious historical authenticity. There are evanescent figures who, beginning early in their literary existence, manage to inscribe their identity in two particular cultural meanings that are diametrically opposed to one another. Their many connoisseurs—that is, the readers of the texts to whom their existence is tied—therefore find themselves presented with the dilemma of choosing between two antithetical "truths," or with the necessity of attempting to synthesize two opposites. Anacharsis is an example of this mechanism of reception. In fact, we could say that antiquity has passed down to us the image of two Anacharses. On the one hand, there is the "ill-starred Westernizer" (L. Canfora), who, as Herodotus recounts, traveled Greece far and wide to learn its customs and, when he returned to Scythia and tried to introduce the worship of the mother of the gods, was killed. On the other hand, we have the "internal outsider" (R. P. Martin), to whose Scythian roots—an expression of the most extreme form of otherness—Greek cultural imagery accorded the function of its own critical self-portrait. This second face, probably as archaic as the first, surfaced—but only to be confuted to the advantage of the other—as early as Herodotus and was destined to be imposed firmly on all the more important witnesses to whom Anacharsis' survival was entrusted: in particular the Hellenistic collection of ten fictional letters addressed by the Scythian wise man to various recipients.

It was precisely his critical stance toward the most deeply rooted customs of Greek society that, along with his barbarian origin, "naturally" destined him to become a kind of archetypal noble savage, as well as a guru for all seasons: one of the Seven Wise Men, the ancestor of the sophists, the Cynic philosopher, the Christian ascetic, and, at the beginning of modernity, the wise man of good old antiquity ready to dispense highly ethical maxims for every occasion. It was, in fact, the apothegms passed down under his name both in the Greek and in the Latin tradition that guaranteed his (admittedly sporadic) presence in the works of medieval and Renaissance moralists. "Laws are like spider webs: they catch the small animals, but let the big ones go": this maxim, which was supposedly Anacharsis' reply to Solon's legislative activity, struck John of Salisbury with such force that he used it three times in the course of his works. "What is good and at the same time bad in man? His tongue": it was thus, by making use of the Scythian guru, that Erasmus admonished the religious.

Giovanni Pico della Mirandola thought he had instead found a literary model in Anacharsis: one of his letters of 1485 took ostentatious inspiration from the first of the *Anacharsidis epistulae,* known to Pico from a manuscript source (the *editio princeps* dates to 1499). And it is precisely as the archetype of a literary genre (the philosophical letter) that Anacharsis made his entrance in the 18th century. This is the period that deserves credit for having fully resuscitated the figure of Anacharsis, turning him into the prosopopoeia of its more typical cultural attributes: naturalistic rationalism, the libertarian and revolutionary spirit, cosmopolitan universalism. It is in fact the *Anacharsidis epistulae* that Montesquieu's famous *Lettres Persanes* (1721) took as a direct model. His Rica and Usbek were "new" Anacharses, that is, the expression of Nature's criticism of the errors of culture.

Under the entry "Scythians" in the *Encyclopédie* (1765)—where that people's infamous inclination to the "crime atroce et momentané" was celebrated as the opposite of European society's "corruption policée et permanente"—Anacharsis' assimilation to the myth of the noble savage was formalized. What is more, following Tertullian's earlier forced interpretation, the Scythian wise man was made the exemplum of the superiority of the contemplative to the active life. A new Anacharsis, a descendant of the ancient one, then became the protagonist of J. J. Barthélemy's powerful *Voyage du jeune Anacharsis en Grèce* (1788), in which the modern alter ego of the ancient wise man was imagined as spending 26 years in 4th-century Greece to admire its greatness and at the same time to reveal its weak points (above all, religious superstition). But the new Anacharsis also took a critical stance toward Scythia (which at the end of his voyage was chosen as his final residence) and its people. In other words, the two contrary images of the ancient Anacharsis seem to be fused here, for the first time, in terms of an "impartial" cultural relativism.

Ultimately Anacharsis descended in cultural status, becoming the nearly exclusive property of philologists and scholars or transformed into the object of "secondhand" reception—as in the case of Barthélemy's wildly popular *Voyage* (followed, for example, in 1801 by P. J. B. Chaussard's *Supplément aux voyages d'Anacharsis et d'Antenor*). Before this happened, however, his literary history had yet another chapter, in the form of an experiment in true and proper living theater. In 1790 the Prussian baron J. B. Cloots—a fervent supporter of the revolutionary ideals of which, according to Barthélemy, the anti-tyrannical Anacharsis represented a dedicated forerunner—appeared before the legislative assembly at the head of a delegation of foreigners, using the name Anacharsis Cloots. Thus, without any conscious intention, the reconciliation of the two original faces of the Scythian wise man underwent another important and novel transformation: to the most radical cosmopolitanism.

BIBL.: J. F. Kindstrand, *Anacharsis: The Legend and the Apophthegmata* (Uppsala 1981). Julia Kristeva, *Strangers to Ourselves,* trans. L. Roudiez (New York 1991). R. P. Martin, "The Scythian Accent: Anacharsis and the Cynics," in *The Cynic Movement in Antiquity and Its Legacy,* ed. R. Bracht Branham and M. O. Goulet-Cazé (Berkeley 1996) 136–155. M.T.

Translated by Patrick Baker

Anacreon and Anacreontics

Early Greek lyric poet (ca. 570–ca. 485 BCE), of whose work a few dozen fragments survive. Some 60 Greek lyrics, composed over a period of perhaps six centuries, give voice to the purportedly Anacreontic view of life.

In antiquity Anacreon was influential as the spokesman for a mature and gently melancholy philosophy of sensual longing and alcoholic festivity; a metrical line (⏑⏑–⏑–⏑––) was called the Anacreontic after him. This meter, in simplified form, serves a number of purposes in Byzantine literature, including a fair amount of religious poetry ("Father, Son, and Holy Ghost" can be phrased in Greek as a perfect anacreontic line); it is also the principal meter of the Anacreontics (Anacreon himself is a character in the first of them). The manuscript in which the collection survives (Paris. suppl. gr. 384, 10th cent., the same that preserves the Palatine version of the Greek Anthology) attributes them to the original Anacreon. That attribution was accepted by Henri Estienne, who published the *editio princeps* in 1554 and, with a glance at the difficulties of reading Pindar, recommended them to those who were *philomousos,* fond of poetry, but not *philoponos,* fond of work. The volume established "Anacreontic" as a popular category for lyric poetry in several European vernaculars over the next two centuries.

Individual poems from the collection were translated into almost every major European language (including Greek, Polish, and Russian), sometimes by poets of considerable note, including Ronsard, Herrick, and Goethe.

Complete translations were done by Remy Belleau (into French) and Thomas Stanley and Thomas Moore (into English). Numerous other poems label themselves Anacreontic or concern themselves with Anacreon's own fortunes; in a generalized way, the category served for expressions of a code of carpe diem perceptibly less urgent or grave than that of Horace, let alone Catullus:

> Yes, ere the airy dance I join
> Of flitting shadows, light and vain,
> I'll wisely drown, in floods of wine,
> Each busy care, and idle pain.
> (Christopher Smart, "Beneath This Fragrant Myrtle Shade," 1756)

Leporello's catalogue of his master's erotic conquests in Mozart's *Don Giovanni* expands on a particular Anacreontic conceit (Anacreontea 14). Alternatively, in something of a return to Byzantine precedent, some poets—such as Wilhelm Alardus and Caspar Barth in 17th-century Germany—rewrite Anacreontic poems to more edifying ends as *Anacreon christianus.* In the early 19th century the setting for a popular song, "To Anacreon in Heaven" ("And long may the sons of Anacreon entwine/The myrtle of Venus and Bacchus's vine"), became the melody for the U.S. national anthem.

The popularity of such poetry reached its peak in the late 18th century, but its themes blend readily into those of Romantic literature. Goethe's famous epitaph, from the 1780s, makes the affinities clear:

> Where the rose is in flower, where vines interlace with the laurel,
> Where the turtle-dove calls, where the small cricket delights,
> What a grave is this, which all the gods have embellished,
> Graced and planted with life? It is Anacreon's rest.
> Springtime, summer, and autumn blessed the fortunate poet:
> And from winter the mound kept him secure in the end.
> (trans. Christopher Middleton)

The epitaph itself stands in a tradition, and derives from one in the Greek Anthology (7.30); Robin Skelton's translation of it (1971) is incisively modern:

> This is Anacreon's grave. Here lie
> the shreds of his exuberant lust,
> but hints of perfume linger by
> his gravestone still, as if he must
> have chosen for his last retreat
> a place perpetually on heat.

BIBL.: John O'Brien, *Anacreon Redivivus* (Ann Arbor 1995). Patricia A. Rosenmeyer, *The Poetics of Imitation: Anacreon and the Anacreontic Tradition* (Cambridge 1992). G.B.

Ancients and Moderns

The war between ancients and moderns—or, more precisely, between modern people who argued for the unchallengeable superiority of classical texts and modern people who insisted that knowledge of the world and human nature had grown and improved since ancient Greece and Rome—dates from the humanistic revival of learning, if not from earlier times. But a famous skirmish abruptly broke out at the Académie Française in 1687, when Charles Perrault read a poem in celebration of the century in which he lived.

> The Ancients I behold with unbent knee,
> For they, though great, were men as well as we,
> And it is just as right for us to praise
> The Age of Louis as Augustus' days.

One member of the audience, Nicolas Boileau-Despréaux, rose to his feet in outrage. Boileau had long championed the ancients, especially in *The Art of Poetry* (1674), a poem that set out to draw enduring critical principles from the works of great classical authors. Now Perrault had dared to suggest that even Homer might sometimes be coarse and long-winded. This demanded a rejoinder. The ensuing "Quarrel of the Ancients and the Moderns" engaged not only Boileau and Perrault, who elaborated his ideas in *A Parallel of the Ancients and Moderns in Regard to the Arts and Sciences* (4 vols., 1688–1692), but many of the leading literary figures in France. Jean de La Fontaine, in a poetic "Epistle to Huet" (1687), paid tribute to his ancient masters, though insisting, "my imitation is not slavery"; and Jean Racine, whose tragedies had used Homer and Euripides as models to shape himself into a classic, commented wryly in verse that Perrault had managed to make Cicero, Plato, Virgil, and Homer all sound like Perrault. On the modern side, in *A Digression on the Ancients and the Moderns* (1688), Bernard le Bovier de Fontenelle proclaimed that "Nothing so limits progress, nothing narrows the mind so much as excessive admiration of the ancients."

Eventually Boileau and Perrault declared a truce. But in the meantime the quarrel had spread to England. Offended by Fontenelle's gibes at ancient pastorals, as well as by Thomas Burnet's enthusiasm over recent advances in knowledge, Sir William Temple sprang to the defense. *An Essay upon the Ancient and Modern Learning* (1690) contends that the ancients surpassed the moderns not only in poetry and oratory but even in the sciences (though much of that learning, sadly, had been lost): "The oldest books we have are still in their kind the best." As evidence Temple offers "the two most ancient that I know of in prose," Aesop's fables and Phalaris's epistles, which "have more race, more spirit, more force of wit and genius, than any others I have ever seen, either ancient or modern." The examples were not well chosen. The great classical scholar Richard Bentley, in "A Dissertation upon the Epistles of Phalaris," appended to the second edition of William Wotton's *Reflections upon Ancient and Modern Learning* (1697), conclusively proved that the epistles ascribed to the Sicilian tyrant Phalaris (6th century BCE) were actually crude forgeries written more than 700 years later; and the antiquity of Aesop's fables was dubious too. Temple had many friends who honored his distinguished diplomatic career as well as his elegant prose; they ridiculed Bentley's pedantry and arrogance. And Jonathan Swift, who served as Temple's secretary, recast the quarrel as farce. *The Battle of the Books* (written in 1697) describes a mock-epic clash between ancient and modern books in the royal library; after Bentley steals the armor of two sleeping ancient heroes, Phalaris and Aesop, he and Wotton are skewered by Charles Boyle, an ally of Temple in the ancient armies. Thus modern learning was trounced by the counterattack of wit—at least for a moment.

Despite the comic excess of the war, however, its issues were both serious and lasting. A veneration for Greek and Roman authors formed the basis of Renaissance education; they were the giants, and moderns walked in their shadows. Most Europeans believed that nature and human beings had declined since the golden age of the ancients. "Authority" resided in canonical authors; learning depended on gathering their wisdom, not on striving for a phantom originality. Yet when Humanists rediscovered major works of antiquity in 15th-century Italy, the manuscripts they found were often corrupt and incomplete. To repair classical texts, editors such as Lorenzo Valla sought to understand not only their words but also the history and spirit that informed them. Hence, some modern scholars began to think of the ancients as men like themselves—who might need to be corrected. As early as Leonardo Bruni's *Dialogues* (1406–1408), a few Renaissance writers believed that they too might contribute to literature and knowledge. Dante, Petrarch, and Boccaccio had shown that masterpieces could be written in the vernacular; perhaps the best way to honor the ancients was to emulate, not merely to imitate, what they had achieved. Gradually, during the 16th and 17th centuries, the view of history as a steady degeneration from classical times was supplemented or challenged by cyclic views, in which learning might rise and fall and rise again, or by ideas of progress, in which learning might rise to heights far above the past.

The supremacy of the ancients was challenged most of all by unprecedented discoveries in science (or "natural philosophy"). When Galileo turned his telescope to the heavens in 1609, the new invention revealed wonders unknown before: mountains and valleys on the moon, a Milky Way dispersed into a multitude of stars, four "planets" circling Jupiter, and, later, spots on the sun. The perfect, unchanging cosmos envisioned by Aristotle and Ptolemy had been shattered forever. Ancient authority would have to yield to a more reliable source of truth, the book of nature. "Is it possible for you to doubt," Galileo asked, "that if Aristotle should see the new discoveries in the sky he would change his opinions and correct his books and embrace the most sensible doctrines, casting away from himself those people so weak-minded as to be induced to go on abjectly maintaining everything he had ever said?" Galileo did not defeat the doubters; the ancient forces proved to be strong. But in the long run modern scientists were stronger. In England, Sir Francis Bacon's *Great Instauration* (1620), inspired by the voyages that had opened new worlds, proposed an exploration of nature that would replace ancient hearsay with rigorous experiments and fresh observations. In a famous paradox—*antiquitas saeculi juventus mundi* ("ancient times are the youth of the world")—Bacon pointed out that the true old age of the world was his own era, which over generations had accumulated stores of new experience and knowledge. The Royal Society of London, founded in 1660, put Bacon's experimental method into practice. A still more drastic modern program to depose the ancients was formulated by René Descartes, whose *Discourse on the Method of Rightly Conducting the Reason and Seeking Truth in the Sciences* (1637) set out rules for finding "the principles or first causes of everything that is or that can be in the world" without "deriving them from any source excepting from certain germs of truth which exist naturally in our souls." The ancients, Descartes insisted, had been ignorant of the geometry and pure mathematics he had discovered, which were capable of explaining all natural phenomena. Hence, the full exposition of his system, *Principles of Philosophy* (1644), was intended to replace Aristotle as a standard text in the schools; and though that did not happen, ancient authority in the sciences had been fatally wounded. The next generation ended the war. When Newton revolutionized the laws of nature, the giants on whose shoulders he stood were not the ancients but his fellow moderns.

In literature, however, the war went on. The prestige of the Classical age remained so dominant that even in such arts as painting and music, of which very few ancient examples survived, modern achievements were often held to be pale simulacra of a lost glory. Above all, that glorious past lived on in Greek and Latin poems. Critics idolized Homer as the father and spirit of poetry, and Virgil was taught to students as simply "The Poet." Some writers avoided comparison with classical models by writing in modern forms such as tragicomedy or devising lyrics with intricate rhyme schemes. But others tried to compete with their models. For Ben Jonson, the ancients best served "as Guides, not Commanders"; and in the poem he supplied to the First Folio of Shakespeare (1623), Jonson boasted that the comedies of his fellow playwright surpassed "all, that insolent *Greece*, or haughty *Rome*/Sent forth, or since did from their ashes come." A few audacious poets even challenged the ancients in epic poetry, the genre in which they had most excelled. In *The Lusiads* (1572), the Portuguese national epic, Luís Vaz de Camões claims preeminence because the exploits he celebrates (Vasco da Gama's seafaring adventures) are true, not myths, and because he exalts a whole people, not merely one hero. And in *Paradise Lost* (1667) John Milton converts the ancient gods and the glories of poetry into adumbrations of the eternal truth known to Christians alone. Yet ancient partisans did not surrender. The Quarrel of the Ancients and the Moderns resumed in the early 18th century, when Anne Dacier's French translation and defense of the *Iliad* (1711) ran afoul of a version by Antoine Houdar de La Motte that modernized and "corrected" Homer's text. Dacier's reply, *On the Causes of the Corruption of Taste* (1714), argued that moderns were blind to true and pure classical art; later she also denounced the English translation by Alexander Pope, who falsely posed as an ancient. Homer could never be improved, and moderns could only surrender to his perfections or try to comprehend them.

Nor did the ancients and moderns come to terms in the war over education. Most people conceded supremacy to the ancients in eloquence: Demosthenes' and Cicero's oratory and Quintilian's rhetoric were still unmatched. But these were not merely technical achievements; they depended on understanding what human beings desire and what they should be. To make oneself into an ancient implied being absorbed and inspired by timeless wisdom. Thus, for Temple, whether Phalaris's epistles were authentic mattered far less than what they could teach about the mind of a tyrant. Moderns like Bentley might know much more about classical texts, but Temple's statesmanship *embodied* ancient learning. The purpose of humanistic education in Greek and Latin was to mold a certain kind of person, devoted to good works and civic virtue. Moderns, according to Swift, were spiders, spinning frail threads of speculation wholly from themselves; ancients were bees, searching the finest blossoms to bring home honey and wax, "thus furnishing Mankind with the two Noblest of Things, which are *Sweetness* and *Light.*" Or so it was in theory. But many moderns contended that, in practice, rote lessons in dead languages could only stifle thought; advances in learning were needed to keep up with changing and heterogeneous times. Meanwhile, a classical education put students between two worlds: the ancient world they studied in texts and the modern world in which they lived and in which they sometimes felt like strangers. In this respect the war between ancients and moderns went on for centuries, and still goes on, in the divided minds of schoolchildren and scholars.

BIBL.: Thomas M. Greene, *The Light in Troy: Imitation and Discovery in Renaissance Poetry* (New Haven 1982). Richard Foster Jones, *Ancients and Moderns: A Study of the Rise of the Scientific Movement in Seventeenth-century England,* 2nd. ed. (Berkeley 1961). Joseph M. Levine, *The Battle of the Books: History and Literature in the Augustan Age* (Ithaca 1991).

L.LI.

Annius of Viterbo

Annius, ca. 1432–1502, born Giovanni Nanni, was the most infamous Renaissance forger of ancient texts. A Dominican, Annius served at Viterbo, Genoa, and Rome. Having gained renown in the 1480s for commentaries on Christian subjects, by 1493 he was seeking the patronage of the newly elected Pope Alexander VI. Organizing fraudulent excavations near the papal summer residence at Viterbo, Annius produced statues and inscriptions purporting to document the presence at Viterbo of important primordial figures from Roman, Egyptian, and biblical mythology. Two of his forged inscriptions survive in the civic museum at Viterbo.

Annius's early "discoveries" showed familiarity with the Etruscan alphabet and vocabulary gleaned from Etruscan funerary objects. He identified Etruscan language with Hebrew, and claimed to translate it, revealing the centrality of Viterbo to the earliest world history.

Between 1493 and 1498 Annius perfected his revision of universal history by forging 11 ancient chronicles. His voluminous commentaries synchronized his forged evidence with the chronologies given by genuine ancient authorities such as Pliny the Elder, Livy, and Diodorus Siculus. Annius's *Commentaria super opera diversorum auctorum de antiquitatibus loquentium* (*Commentaries on the Works of Various Authors Who Spoke of Antiquity,* 1498) rewrote ancient history, marshaling evidence that Rome had usurped the place of Viterbo as capital of the world.

Annius's forgeries bore the names of prestigious ancient authors whose works had perished except for fragments or admiring mention by other ancient writers. Pseudo-Berosus of Chaldea quoted documents in the library of Babylon proving that Noah, a giant, had founded Viterbo barely a century after the Flood, as the capital of his world empire. Noah later left colonies elsewhere in Europe and the Middle East, but he remained in Viterbo among his favorite descendants, the Etruscans. As *pontifex maximus,* Noah prefigured the Roman priesthood, the papacy, and important Christian rituals: his surname, Janus, revealed his discovery of wine (*Iain*). Annius's other pseudo-authors were Manetho of Egypt, Metasthenes (not Megasthenes) of Persia, Philo of Judea, Archilochus, Xenophon, and Myrsilus Lesbius of Greece, and the Romans Cato the Elder, Quintus Fabius Pictor, Caius Sempronius Tuditanus, and Antoninus Pius. Even without Annius's meticulous commentaries, these texts implied that ancient Rome forsook the pious theology of Noah's Etruscans for the philosophical quibbling of Greece, thereby erasing the true history of the world and replacing it with a pagan lie of Greek superiority.

Annius's knowledge of Greek and Hebrew was very limited; he forged his texts in Latin, claiming to have received them from two intermediaries, an Armenian monk named George who visited him in Genoa, and one William of Mantua, who collected texts around 1315. Since the fictitious originals were lost and the intermediaries dead or absent, Annius's readers had to rely on his good faith.

Respected scholars incessantly denounced Annius's collection as a forgery, yet it had been reprinted 20 times by 1612. Moreover, dozens of patriotic writers from France, Spain, Germany, England, and other countries cited Annius's texts and commentaries out of context, easily supplanting his imperialistic Etruscans with invincible Gauls, Celts, Britons, Teutons, and others. Serious scholars, intent on recovering and interpreting genuine lost texts of antiquity, had to debunk Annius's legacy repeatedly until nearly 1800.

BIBL.: R. E. Asher, *National Myths in Renaissance France: Francus, Samothes, and the Druids* (Edinburgh 1993). Anthony Grafton, *Forgers and Critics: Creativity and Duplicity in Western Scholarship* (Princeton 1990). Walter Stephens, *Giants in Those Days: Folklore, Ancient History, and Nationalism* (Lincoln 1989) and "When Pope Noah Ruled the Etruscans: Annius of Viterbo and His Forged *Antiquities*," *Studia Humanitatis: Essays in Honor of Salvatore Camporeale, MLN Italian Issue* 119, no. 1 Supplement (2004) S201–S223. W.ST.

Anthology and Florilegium

A collection of secular or religious citations in verse or prose excerpted from literary or theological writings and arranged under broad or specific subject headings. Although the terms are interchangeable (and only two of the dozens that have been used), *anthology* is applied more often to secular collections, *florilegium* to theological ones.

The poetic anthologies include excerpts from classical poetry, epigrams, and moralizing verses, whereas the prosaic ones contain maxims, *apophthegmata,* and aphorisms or sayings of Epicurus. The primary purpose of these anthologies was didactic; aesthetic aims were secondary. The earliest reference to an existing anthology is found in Plato's *Leges* (811A), but the first artistically and thematically arranged anthology of epigrams is the *Garland* of Meleager from Gadara (1st cent. BCE). The *Garland* formed the basis for later poetic anthologies that were finally incorporated in the Greek Anthology. Extensive parts of the Greek Anthology survive today in the Palatine Anthology, a collection that takes its name from its unique codex, which was separated into two manuscripts now known as *Palatinus Heidelberg* 23 (preserving books 1–13 of the Greek Anthology) and Parisinus suppl. gr. 384 (books 14–15). Book 16 of the modern editions contains an additional 388 epigrams of the Greek Anthology collected by a scholar of the 14th century, Maximus Planudes, and transmitted by the autographed codex Venetus Marcianus gr. 481 of 1301 CE. This great Greek Anthology was the result of putting together smaller compilations by Byzantine scholars and poets such as Agathias, Diogenianus, Palladas, Strato, Constantine Cephalas, and others. Its books include epigrams on a number of disparate (and sometimes incompatible) topics such as Christian epigrams (book 1); epigrams that describe the statues in the baths of Zeuxippus in Constantinople (book 2); the sexually explicit pederastic poetry of Strato (books 11 and 12); and the epigram verses of Gregory of Nazianzus (book 8).

In the early 5th century John Stobaeus put together another anthology of excerpts from prose and poetry in order to educate his son Septimius. Stobaeus' very lengthy anthology contains fragments from Hermetic and Neoplatonic texts, Plutarch, and verses from Aeschylus and Euripides, but no Christian author was excerpted in it. Finally, Photius in his 9th-century *Bibliotheca* summarized another anthology by the 4th-century philosopher Sopater of Apamea that included, among others, excerpts from Apollodorus, Athenaeus, Diogenes Laertius, Herodotus, a history of music by Rhuphus, and others.

The purely religious florilegia (such as the collection of "Golden Words" ascribed to Pythagoras, or the oracle collections) were originally composed both in Greek and Latin by pagans. They became very common, however, with the spread of Christianity. The Apostle Paul, Clemens of Alexandria, Origen, Gregory of Nazianzus, and other, later authors had no scruples in using maxims from pagan anthologies to illustrate a point. Clemens of Alexandria in his *Stromata* indiscriminately mixed citations from Plato or Pythagoras with Bible verses and juxtaposed Hesiod to David's Psalms. The earliest, and exclusively Christian, florilegium is found in Cyprian's *Testimonia ad Quirinum* (Corpus Scriptorum Ecclesiasticorum Latinorum 3.1). In the first two books the citations come from the Old Testament, whereas the New Testament has also been used in the third. The primitive antecedents of this florilegium are the early Christian collections of *testimonia,* which are passages from the Old Testament that supported the Christian claim against Jews and pagans that in Christ all scriptural prophesies and promises were fulfilled. After these, the first nonbiblical Christian florilegium is the *Philocalia,* a collection of quotations from works of Origen compiled by Gregory of Nazianzus and Basil of Caesarea. All these florilegia, and especially the testamental ones, responded to a new necessity Christians were facing: to substantiate their claims on the basis of a superior ideological or dogmatic authority, which is the Scripture. This trait continued with the dogmatic florilegia that emerged from the 5th century onward within the frame of Christological confrontations. Patristic authority was invoked and the appeal of both heretics and mainstream Christians to these authorities found its expression in the incorporation of florilegia in the *acta* of the Ecumenical Church Councils. Conciliar (dogmatic) florilegia are the tip of the iceberg compared to what circulated among the apologists of Orthodoxy and heretics after the 5th century.

The *Doctrina patrum de incarnatione Verbi* is a typical example of an Orthodox florilegium that was compiled in various stages, but its edited version must reflect a date of editorial additions carried out around the first quarter of the 8th century. In its 45 chapters the *Doctrina* includes quotations from Greek (Cyril of Alexandria, Gregory of Nyssa) and (to a lesser extent) Latin Fathers, such as Pope Leo I and Ambrose of Milan, on topics such as the position of Christ within the Holy Trinity, the two natures of Christ, and so on. Few of the quotations found in chapter 45 (on the veneration of holy images) are also included in the Acts of the Seventh Ecumenical Council. In the same period John of Damascus compiled a number of florilegia, of which the most extensive and well known was the *Sacra parallela,* in three books. The first was dedicated to the Divinity, the second to humanity, and the third to virtues and vices. Numerous florilegia composed later on—such as the *Florilegium rupefucaldianum*—contain parts from or versions of the *Sacra parallela.*

After the 11th century anti- and pro-Latin florilegia (on the procession of the Holy Spirit, Purgatory, unleavened bread, etc.) were created, alongside a proliferation of "sacro-profane" florilegia that are based on the *Sacra parallela* and the anthology of Stobaeus or recensions of an anthology of citations from Democritus, Isocrates, and Epictetus. Typical examples of this kind of florilegia are Pseudo-Maximus' *Loci communes* and the *Gnomologium* of John Georgides, preserved by at least two 11th-century manuscripts.

The significance of florilegia and anthologies for later and modern audiences and scholarship cannot be understated: by their nature florilegia and anthologies tend to preserve for posterity what is essential in terms of content from lengthy, tedious, and otherwise lost secular and religious writings. Without the Greek Anthology our knowledge of Greek poetry would have been much more limited; the anthology of Planudes exercised enormous influence in Renaissance Europe. The formation of Christian dogma and its crystallization through Church councils owes much to florilegia. European morality was also informed by the medieval moral florilegia. During the Renaissance and at later times Humanist educators such as Leonardo Bruni and Battista Guarino (14th–15th cents.) encouraged florilegia based on classical works and advised their students to construct their own florilegia of noteworthy rhetorical expressions. Even today one can still see the modern descendants of florilegia and anthologies in the collections of sayings by Oscar Wilde and Lord Byron, or in books that bear titles such as *Romanticism: An Anthology* and *The Norton Anthology of Poetry,* not to mention the anthologies of various Great Books in the curriculum of Ivy League and other universities in the United States.

BIBL.: Alexander Alexakis, *Codex Parisinus Graecus 1115 and Its Archetype* (Washington, D.C., 1996) 1–42. Alan Cameron, *The Greek Anthology: From Meleager to Planoudes* (Oxford 1993). Sir Henry Chadwick, "Florilegium," *RAC* 7 (1969) 1131–1160. Marcel Richard, "Florilèges spirituels," in *Dictionnaire de spiritualité, ascétique et mystique* 5 (1962) 435–512.

A.A.

Anthropology

The term *anthropology* itself has a history. It does not occur in antiquity (the adjective *anthropologos,* used once by Aristotle, *Nicomachean Ethics* 1125a5, means "gossipy"), and is first attested ca. 1600 to denote theories about human nature. Its specific modern association with evolutionism and with the study of "primitive" societies, on the assumption that it would throw light on the evolutionary process, developed in the late 19th century and led in the following century to the practice of intensive ethnographic fieldwork in small-scale societies. Some use was made of data from ancient history by evolutionists in the 19th century (most notoriously by J. G. Bachofen in his theory of primitive matriarchy), but the functionalist ethnographers of the 20th century reacted strongly against historical speculation.

It would therefore be misleading to maintain that modern anthropology (whether evolutionist or functionalist) derives from a classical tradition. If, on the other hand, we consider the older use of the term (to which some postmodern anthropologists are now returning) and ask about the long-term influence of ancient Greek ideas about the nature of man, the inquiry becomes more fruitful.

I begin with a Kantian question: How is anthropology possible? What is the starting point for a theory about the specific situation and qualities of human beings? The Greeks started by distinguishing humans from animals and from gods.

Our evidence for the development of their ideas in contexts other than the specialized arguments of philosophers is scrappy, but the difference between humans and other sentient living beings probably was conceived partly in terms of social institutions (the central role of justice in human societies) and partly in terms of afterlife (there were no animal *psychai* in Hades or the Islands of the Blessed). Ideas about gods, who were normally unobservable, were vaguer and less consistent: in addition to being immortal, they were not subject to constraints of time and space; although represented in human form, they could change shape; they could influence events in the world of humans; the same gods were worshiped under different names in other parts of the world.

The elements in this conglomerate of ideas that particularly stimulated speculation were the fate of the human psyche after death and the attitude of the gods to justice and morality. Even in nonphilosophical circles the two questions tended to be linked, through ideas about reward and punishment after death and techniques of improving one's chances of salvation, and through a tendency to treat myths in which gods behaved immorally as poetic fantasy. The Homeric *Hymn to Aphrodite* enjoys the paradox of the goddess of love succumbing to her own powers.

Philosophers went much further, rejecting anthropomorphic conceptions of god and constructing the difference between men and animals on the possession of reason, a capacity shared by man with the philosophers' god. This led Plato, in the *Republic,* to explore the analogy between the parts of the soul, now divided into *nous, thumos,* and *epithumiai* (reason, will, appetites), and the functional divisions of the citizens of a well-ordered city. The implication was that the contemplative life of reason was superior to the life of action; thus, subsequent discussions of the good life tended to concentrate on cultivation of the self to ensure rational control of emotions and appetites.

Whereas philosophers thought in terms of the individual's success (or failure) in controlling emotions, tragic poets were implicitly developing a much more dialogic understanding, in which emotions escalate as tragic characters interact with each other, taking ever more extreme positions, in what Gregory Bateson would later term *schismogenesis*. Plato was opposed to the representation of undesirable behavior in poetry and onstage, but Aristotle suggested that the vicarious experience of emotion could have a cathartic effect, the experience of extremes in fiction promoting moderation in real life. This hint of the dangers of repression would later be developed by Freud.

Plato also developed in the *Phaedrus* and *Timaeus* a theory of the afterlife that combined reward and punishment with reincarnation; like the Pythagoreans, he seems to envisage reincarnation of human souls in animals (a view that led some groups to vegetarianism; see Obeyesekere 2002).

The question of intercultural variation in human types was handled, from the 5th century on, partly by assertion of the superiority of Greek law over barbarian monarchy, and partly by theories of the influence of climate on ethnic characteristics (both physical and moral), which recur in the work of Jean Bodin, Montesquieu, and H. T. Buckle. Climatic variation was seen in terms of the elemental oppositions hot/cold and dry/wet; these were also manipulated in medical theory to account for individual variations both in health and in character (which led eventually to elaboration of the theory of the four humors). Both doctors and philosophers also reflected on the influence of habitual occupations on physique and character (to the advantage of the leisure classes).

Most Greek cities thought that they had passed from a period of monarchy into constitutional government; if the question of premonarchic social forms was raised, conceptions were based either on the family or on the (animal) herd controlled by its strongest male (Cole 1967). The idea that primitive societies were vegetarian was influenced by conceptions of a golden "age of Kronos," in which no effort was required.

Observations of animal behavior and anatomy were oriented toward questions about humans, even though doctors relied largely on butchery and dissection of animals for their understanding of human anatomy. Researchers were interested in the capacities of the animal soul (desire, emotion, perception, memory, imagination) and were influenced by folk analogies between human and animal character (Lloyd 1983), which covered qualities associated with *thymos* (anger, courage) as well as more vicious traits. Nubile girls, like foals, had to be tamed (male adolescence, though lasting much longer, was not considered so problematic); Hesiod and Semonides make systematic comparisons between types of women and animals, praising only the bee.

Anthropology, as defined here, changed in the course of the *longue durée* of antiquity and, of course, later. The changes that most affected it were perhaps:

1. The development in the Classical and especially Hellenistic periods of a distinctive urban culture
2. Changes (from the Hellenistic period through late antiquity) in conceptions of divinity and man's relation to it, especially the crystallization of sects around monotheistic attachment to a personal god, and the repeopling of the gap between god and man with intermediate beings, *daemones* and holy men of various types
3. The rise of new conceptions of rationality and of nature in the Enlightenment, and reconstruction of the Greek legacy to fit them
4. Darwinian evolutionism
5. Freudian psychology
6. Late modern reassessments of the relation between man and nature, and between religion and public life.

Urbanization reinforced the view that reason was man's defining characteristic, encouraged concentration on collaborative qualities such as generosity and friendship, and, since danger was now seen as abnormal and undesirable, favored generalization of the philosophers' model of the good life as free from emotion. Cities had less scope in the Hellenistic period for political action, and sociability was increasingly focused on sectlike groups, whether these were philosophical schools or cult associations. Relations between city and countryside became more tense: city dwellers were afraid of brigands and pirates and had difficulty ensuring adequate food supplies. There was an increased sense of the unpredictability of fortune, which perhaps encouraged the growth of mystery cults promising security in the afterlife. The discourse of sects presented each as having a privileged truth, even though (as the term *hairesis,* choice, indicated) they did not force exclusive loyalty on their members.

Jews, however, had always insisted that theirs was the only god, and Christians followed them, as later did Muslims. Gods recovered a susceptibility to emotion that they had lost in philosophical (if not popular) paganism: they could be jealous, angry, loving, and feel grief or pity. This made the question of evil problematic; the animal side of man's nature no longer seemed a sufficient explanation. There was a convergence between philosophical and religious sects: first, the leaders of these sects were increasingly seen mainly as teachers, whereas teachers of philosophy were expected to have the charisma of the holy man (Shaw 1995); second, at least some religious sects imposed on their followers a comprehensive way of life like that required of philosophers; third, this way of life, in philosophical sects and Christianity, was connected to the possibility of mystical union with God both in this life and hereafter. These orientations directed anthropological speculation to the relation between body and soul, and the special qualities of soul that linked it to God (the figure of the holy man posed peculiar problems to Christian thinkers reflecting on the dual nature of Christ, and to Muslims concerned with the privileged insight of the Prophet). It should be stressed that this was a period when men and ideas moved widely, across the boundaries of both sects and states (Fowden 1993).

The Enlightenment consolidated a process of internalization and privatization of religion that had begun in the Reformation, and this drove a wedge between the problems of the good society and the good life. Theology, increasingly a specialization of priests, was separated from the study of nature (even if nature had been designed by God). Society, like nature, exhibited lawlike regularities, and scientific study would enable man to control both; social control would be achieved through the design of self-regulating institutions (both Marx and Herbert Spencer expected the state to wither away). Association in "civil society" would promote the Greek urban virtues of benevolence and friendship; even relations between men and women would be reshaped by the "polite" standards of this civic public sphere. The Greeks were reconstructed as having anticipated Enlightenment political thought, philosophy, and science.

The decisive shift from an ancient to a modern conception of anthropology was Darwin's argument (1871) for the evolution of humans from apes. From that point humans were distinguished from animals by their brain structure and their capacity to pass on cultural innovations through language. The human mind became social rather than divine, its contents (even, for Durkheim, its faculties) shaped by social experience. In the context of disciplinary proliferation in the 19th-century university (and museums) the new anthropology had to define itself in relation to archaeology (responsible for the study of early hominids, now very remote in time), sociology, psychology, and linguistics. It came to be associated principally with the observation of "primitive" societies and traditional village communities relatively little affected by modernity, both being nostalgically seen as culturally and socially integrated and stable.

Psychology continued to work on the Greek problem of the relation between animal and human faculties and emotions, and on questions about mental illness and the conditions for stable selfhood. A strikingly Platonic theory of personality development emerged in Freud's model of the three-part psyche (id, ego, and superego); he was also Platonic in recognizing the role of desire in intellectual pursuits (a point further developed by Lacan). On the other hand, his views on the dangers of repression seem distinctly un-Greek (though he was not responsible for introducing the term *catharsis* into modern psychology).

Lévi-Strauss's attempt to move from the study of kinship and myth to generalizations about the structure of the human mind has not convinced many modern anthropologists, but it was important for showing (through analyses of myth and totemism) that speculative and original thought occurs in societies at all levels of technical and social development.

Reflexivity—the habit of critically examining one's own practices and assumptions—is increasingly emerging as a characteristic postmodern preoccupation and a core element of anthropology as a discipline (sometimes traced back to Herodotus). Reflecting in the early 21st century on the trajectory of Greek anthropological ideas, I note that new questions are emerging about man's relation both to animals and to gods, in the form of anxieties about man's exploitation of nature (see Coetzee 1999) and rejection of the modern treatment of religious affiliation as solely a private matter.

BIBL.: M. Arkoun, *Rethinking Islam* (1989, repr. Boulder 1994). J. M. Coetzee, *Elizabeth Costello* (London 1999). T. Cole, *Democritus and the Sources of Greek Anthropology* (Ann Arbor 1967). M. J. C. Crabbe, ed., *From Soul to Self* (London 1999). C. Darwin, *The Descent of Man* (London 1871). M. Ficino, *Three Books on Life,* ed. C. V. Kaske and J. R. Clark (Tempe 1998). G. Fowden, *Empire to Commonwealth* (Princeton 1993). J. Heath, *The Talking Greeks: Speech, Animals, and the Other in Homer, Aeschylus, and Plato* (Cambridge 2005). G. E. R. Lloyd, *Science, Folklore, and Ideology* (Cambridge 1983). G. Obeyesekere, *Imagining Karma* (Berkeley 2002). M. M. Sassi, *The Science of Man in Ancient Greece* (1988), trans. Paul Tucker (Chicago 2001). G. Shaw, *Theurgy and the Soul* (University Park, Pa., 1995). R. Sorabji, *Animal Minds and Human Morals* (London 1993). R. Thomas, *Herodotus in Context: Ethnography, Science, and the Art of Persuasion* (Cambridge 2000).

S.HU.

Antigone

Daughter of Oedipus, mythical king of Thebes, and his wife, Jocasta. She has been known to post-Renaissance writers, theater audiences, and visual artists primarily from three tragedies: Euripides' *Phoenician Women* (most popular from the Hellenistic to the Byzantine era), Sophocles' *Oedipus at Colonus,* and Sophocles' *Antigone.* (Euripides' *Antigone,* though influential in antiquity, has not survived.) During the Middle Ages and early Renaissance it was Statius' *Thebaid* and the (incomplete) *Phoenician Women* by Seneca the Younger that were best known; these two 1st-century CE sources are the basis for Boccaccio's rendition of Antigone in his *On Famous Women* (*De mulieribus claris,* ca. 1375), chapters 23 and 27. Since the 18th century, however, Sophocles' treatments have come to eclipse all others.

The most distinctive features of Antigone's character and actions are these: (1) intense loyalty to her father and to her brother Polynices (sometimes contrasted with the more pragmatic attitude of her sister, Ismene); (2) burial of her brother in defiance of Creon's edict forbidding this; and (3) betrothal to Creon's son, Haemon, which provokes his intervention on her behalf but (in most versions) does not save her—or him—from death. Of course, her portrayal as a character varies greatly. Sometimes she is fierce, prickly, and unreasonable, quarreling with her sister, disregarding her fiancé, and insulting the king; but many authors and interpreters (and modern directors of

Sophocles' play) emphasize instead her warmth of feeling (both toward her brother and toward Haemon) in contrast with Creon's cold authoritarianism, her piety and otherworldliness in contrast with his emphasis on the state and its laws, and her idealism as a young woman resisting male domination and oppression.

She appears in such dramas as *La Thébaïde* (of J. de Rotrou in 1638 and of J. Racine in 1664), but it was J.-J. Barthélemy's description of a performance of Sophocles' play in Revolutionary Paris (1788) that marked the beginning of an outpouring of poems, letters, and essays (Shelley, De Quincey, Goethe, and many others; see Steiner 1984, 4–12). Since then the Sophoclean version has dominated Western consciousness. In the 19th century, scores of poets, playwrights, and painters presented her as the embodiment of virginal purity, sisterly love, and self-sacrifice. F. Hölderlin's almost modernistic translation of Sophocles' play (1804), though unpopular when it first appeared, became increasingly influential as the 20th century dawned. More widely popular for 19th-century audiences was the opera by F. Mendelssohn (1841, libretto by J. C. Donner). Essayists such as Matthew Arnold (1849), George Eliot ("The *Antigone* and Its Moral," 1856; also *Middlemarch,* 1872), and S. Kierkegaard (*Either/Or,* 1843, and elsewhere) continued to extend discussion of the political, religious, and moral themes.

Most significant of all have been G. W. F. Hegel's lectures on aesthetics, ethics, and religion (1795–1805; accessible in Paolucci and Paolucci 1962; see also Steiner 1984, 19–42), which often refer to Sophocles' *Antigone* as the most perfect and representative tragedy ever written. Hegel sees Antigone as embodying in one person the claims of family, the feminine, natural law, and traditional religion, in dialectical opposition to Creon's male principle of arbitrary/civilized political law and order. On this reading, Antigone and Creon are equally right and equally limited in their positions, and the tragedy comprises their mutual destruction in the course of bringing about (in a form that Hegel never quite makes clear) a synthesis of higher "ethical substance." This "theory" of tragedy has loomed large in the subsequent history of both dramatic criticism and political theory.

In the 20th century (with Hölderlin or Hegel—or both —as well as Sophocles, often providing a key point of focus or departure), translations, adaptations, restagings, and critical theories have continued. M. Heidegger is among those who see Sophocles' "ode to humankind" ("Many are the wonders/monstrous things . . . ," *Antigone* 332–364) as expressing the inscrutability and dangers of the human capacity for good or evil. But most performers, critics, political scientists, and philosophers have tended instead to take Antigone as an unequivocally righteous figure of individual resistance to an evil totalitarian regime, or as a martyr to the cause of family, or religion, or women's rights: so, for example, Brecht's East German adaptation (1947), the operas by A. Honegger (1927) and C. Orff (1949), and innumerable restagings of Sophocles' play in the West, including the movie versions by G. Tsavellas (1961, in Modern Greek) and Don Taylor (1989). The play is often selected—or banned—as an effective vehicle for more or less overt criticism of a repressive government (e.g., in Greece during the junta of the 1970s; and A. Fugard's brilliant two-man play, *The Island,* set in Apartheid South Africa, 1973). Jean Anouilh's *Antigone,* first produced in Nazi-occupied France in 1944 and often restaged (even televised) since, was thus unconventional (but acceptable to the regime) in presenting a mindlessly idealistic Antigone who, despite the efforts of a pragmatic, long-suffering (and generally more sympathetic) Creon, sacrifices herself for no good reason. Likewise Satoh Makoto's Japanese *Ismene* (*Isumene,* 1966) presents Antigone's younger sister as the focal, tragic figure, while Antigone herself postures uselessly in the name of the paternal authority of "traditional" Japan.

J. Lacan's influential Seminar VII, "The Ethics of Psychoanalysis" (delivered in 1960 but not much noticed outside France until the 1990s), combined Hegelian ethics with post-Freudian psychoanalysis, arguing that Antigone's "desire for the impossible" (Sophocles, *Antigone* 90–92), along with the many references in Sophocles' play to the family's incestuous "madness/disaster" (*atē*), conjure up a notion of human (especially female) insufficiency and ill-repressed desire that Lacan locates ultimately with Jocasta. Several feminist post-Lacanians and philosophers have responded with critiques (e.g., J. Kristeva, L. Irigaray, P. Phelan, J. P. Butler). In the 21st century the debate regarding Antigone's true nature and her ethical status continues unabated, on the page and on the stage.

BIBL.: A. Paolucci and H. Paolucci, eds., *Hegel on Tragedy* (New York 1962). George Steiner, *Antigones* (Oxford 1984).

M.GF.

Antiquarianism

The term applied to a variety of ways of interpreting the past and studying classical antiquities. It describes a wide range of overlapping historical practices pioneered in antiquity. At its narrowest, antiquarianism can refer to the collecting and study of the material remains of the classical world; it is also used for the historical examination of institutions and customs; and most broadly it denotes a variety of approaches to the past outside the purview of narrative history in the Thucydidean mode. It often has derogatory connotations, targeted at the practices of scholars (usually known as antiquaries) with unfocused historical interests who collect evidence for a given phenomenon indiscriminately without evaluating its relevance to a particular question. As a result, antiquarianism won little scholarly attention in any of its guises until the later 20th century. Since then, researchers have shown that the work of antiquaries played a vital role in the emergence of modern historical scholarship, by expanding the range of evidence and subjects available to the historian and by illustrating the importance of careful source criticism. They have also shown that, far from being unworldly, antiquarianism was often an explicitly political undertaking. Furthermore, the questions raised and the techniques used by premodern antiquarians prefigure the practices of many modern fields and disciplines, most obviously archaeology and ancient history but also art history, anthropology, and sociology.

Scholars in antiquity discussed historical sources and questions about their past in a variety of genres. They made up an erudite tradition of antiquarianism often independent of narrative history writing, although both Thucydides (especially in his "archaeology," 1.2–19) and, more important, Herodotus showed on occasion how the study of material culture or institutions could be placed in a historical narrative. The most famous and influential classical antiquary was Marcus Terentius Varro, who in 47 BCE published his *Antiquities of Things Human and Divine* (*Antiquitates rerum humanarum et divinarum*), which provided a model for the systematic discussion of the origins of Roman civilization (Varro's humans were Romans). The first and longer part of this work was divided into sections for peoples, places, times, and things. The second part, presenting an anthropocentric view of religion, placed first the author's material on priesthoods and holy sites, and only then turned to the deities. Cicero in his *Later Academics* (*Academica posteriora* 9) wrote that Varro enabled the Romans to understand "who and where we were," a particularly potent, and politically relevant, achievement in the chaos of the triumviral period. Varro's work informed poetic treatments of the Roman past, including Ovid's *Fasti,* provided much raw material for the elder Pliny's encyclopedic *Natural History* and Aulus Gellius' miscellany *Attic Nights,* and later influenced the works of the 6th-century Byzantine John Lydus, who wrote on Roman history. Very little, however, of Varro's book survived into the Middle Ages: our knowledge of its contents and structure comes from authors including Censorinus and, most significantly, Saint Augustine, who described the work and used information from it to attack Roman paganism. As a result his influence within the classical tradition lies in his creation of an institutional history, rather than in specific treatments of particular offices or customs.

After Lydus, antiquarianism flourished again in Byzantium during the Palaeologan period. A number of 10th-century treatises connected with the emperor Constantine VII Porphyrogenitus examine the historical foundations of various imperial traditions, among them *De ceremoniis* and *De administrando imperio,* the latter combining historical information on the nature of imperial rule with didactic ideas about how that ruling should be done. There are isolated Western medieval examples of antiquarian musings on the classical past, including the 12th-century *Mirabilia urbis Romae,* a historical reflection on Rome inspired by the city's ancient remains. Around 1346 Cola di Rienzo appealed to the tangible example of the engraved *lex de imperio Vespasiani* (which he understood as the Roman Senate's assertion of its authority over the emperor Vespasian) when trying to lead a rebellion against papal power in Rome.

It is only with the flowering of Humanism in the 15th century, however, that we can really identify a vigorous antiquarian tradition dealing fundamentally with the Roman world. This tradition emerged in step with Humanist philological investigations: treatises on Roman ruins and institutions could explain arcane references in classical authors and the texts of Roman law, and coins and inscriptions offered examples of Latin grammar and orthography uncorrupted by medieval scribes, as well as of the public offices mentioned in other classical texts. The most famous 15th-century antiquary was Flavio Biondo, whose *Rome Restored* (*Roma instaurata,* 1446), a topographical history of the city of Rome, far surpassed the *Mirabilia* in precision and detail, and whose *Rome Triumphant* (*Roma triumphans,* 1459) included surveys of various ancient Roman institutions. Although he devoted much time to the identification of ruins, Biondo was little interested in other *realia* (physical remains); in this respect he seems to have been like Varro. Various contemporaries, however, most notably Cyriac of Ancona, began to make extensive compilations of records of inscriptions, and the second half of the 15th century saw the first extensive Renaissance collections of antiquities, including coins, gems, and statues as well as inscribed monuments. From that point onward, collections were intended to inform, to inspire, and in some cases to provide employment for antiquaries.

In the 16th century Humanists continued to expand the range of topics they investigated from the Roman world and the information with which they did so. Johannes Rosinus' *Romanae antiquitates* (1583) is an impressive summa of 16th-century antiquarian writing, divided into 10 books that include treatises on juridical, military, and religious institutions. Like Biondo, Rosinus did not reveal much interest in material remains, but his contemporaries did. Particularly in the years following 1550, Humanists engaged in a process of description, illustration, and classification of the classical objects that they and their predecessors had discovered. Their work resulted in a stream of books about coins, the most analytical of which arranged their material chronologically for coin issues struck under Roman emperors, by family of the moneyer for issues made during the Republic, and by originating city for Greek examples. In the field of epigraphy, Jan Gruter edited and in 1603 published a vast compilation of inscriptions from across the former Roman Empire, building on his contemporaries' and predecessors' collections. Gruter's representations of inscriptions, along with his classificatory systems, provided the model for future collections.

Various Renaissance artists interested in representing classical antiquity used and expanded the work of antiquaries. Andrea Mantegna is the most important example: he worked alongside epigraphers. In his *Introduction of the Cult of Cybele at Rome* (ca. 1506), inspired by details in coins and bas-reliefs, he imitated a classical frieze to show an event in Roman religious history; most spectacularly, he used Biondo's *Roma triumphans* as the major source for his visualization, in a series of canvases, of a classical victory parade, the *Triumphs of Caesar* (ca. 1486).

Mid-16th-century antiquaries responded to the visual interests of their artist colleagues and began to examine bas-reliefs and other objects for what they could reveal about topics only briefly treated in classical textual sources, such as dining, dress, and slaves: Pirro Ligorio, for example, who had trained as a painter, adopted the appearance of Roman reliefs for his reconstructions of classical ceremonies. The difficulty and expense of integrating text and image in print, combined in some quarters with philologists' distrust of the qualifications of artists to interpret antiquity, limited the influence of Ligorio's example. The collaboration of Peter Paul Rubens with his brother Philip is a striking exception; Peter Paul illustrated Philip's work on Roman costume and used what he learned with his brother in later paintings. Some other 17th-century antiquaries, such as those associated with Cassiano dal Pozzo, also built on Ligorio's work, and Bernard de Montfaucon's *Antiquity Explained* (*Antiquité expliquée,* 1717–1721) is an impressive summation of that tradition.

The work of the 15th- and 16th-century antiquaries (like Ligorio) who dealt with material remains was characterized by a commitment to description and empirical examination of material sources; the work of their philologically inclined counterparts, from Varro to Rosinus, revealed how a culture could be described historically. In the 17th century various scholars built on these two strands of effort to apply the methods and questions of antiquaries to the medieval past. The intellectual journey of William Camden in England provided an influential model. He began by examining traces of the Roman past in Britain but then applied the same scrutiny to later physical remains. In his *Britannia,* a historical and geographical survey of the British Isles first published in 1586, the Roman material is dwarfed by evidence from the medieval period. Along with his colleagues in the Society of Antiquaries (who as a group rarely considered classical questions), Camden also examined the origins of various English institutions, including law and language.

As Camden and his successors, such as Ole Worm in Denmark, uncovered new vistas for historical research, 17th- and 18th-century classical antiquaries continued to gather information and write about the Roman, and increasingly the Greek, worlds. Prominent scholars like Scipione Maffei in Italy and Ludwig August von Schlözer in Germany argued for the importance of antiquarian methods and materials in historical training, the latter with some success. But even as some historians recognized the importance of the antiquarian tradition, others opposed its erudition (even as they built on it) to the new philosophical history of the Enlightenment. A range of writers from Johann Winckelmann (who exploited previous antiquaries' commitment to empirical examination and connoisseurship) to Edmund Gibbon (who put their commitment to source analysis to the service of his narrative history) seemed to some to render the antiquarian tradition obsolete.

To consider antiquarianism dead by the beginning of the 19th century, however, is mistaken. For example, the two most important projects of Theodor Mommsen developed precedents set by the antiquaries of the early modern period: he planned the monumental *Corpus inscriptionum latinarum* (begun in 1861) to replace the epigraphical collections of Gruter and others, and his *Roman Constitutional Law* (*Römisches Staatsrecht,* 1871–1888) stands within a tradition of historical examinations of the Roman constitution, even if Mommsen's analysis surpasses his predecessors'. In landmark cultural histories, Mommsen's contemporary Jacob Burckhardt asked questions about ceremonies and customs similar to those that antiquaries had previously asked concerning Rome. It is through scholars such as Burckhardt and Mommsen, via followers such as Max Weber, that we can see traces of antiquarianism in the disciplines of anthropology and sociology.

Arnaldo Momigliano was responsible for the 20th-century move to rehabilitate and reevaluate antiquarianism. In 1950 he published his authoritative and enormously influential article "Ancient History and the Antiquarian," in which he drew attention to the importance of antiquarianism as a phenomenon, viewing it primarily in terms of its contribution to historical method. Building on Momigliano's example and working under the influence of the cultural turn in scholarship, late 20th-century historians began to look at antiquarianism anew. Their work, expanding Momigliano's focus, makes clear how central a role antiquarianism has played in Western civilization's understanding of the past.

BIBL.: P. Miller, ed., *Momigliano and Antiquarianism: Foundations of the Modern Cultural Sciences* (Toronto 2007). A. Momigliano, "Ancient History and the Antiquarian," *Journal of the Warburg and Courtauld Institutes* 13 (1950) 285–315, and *The Classical Foundations of Modern Historiography* (Berkeley 1990) esp. 54–79. E. Rawson, *Intellectual Life in the Late Roman Republic* (London 1985) esp. 236–246. A. Schnapp, *The Discovery of the Past* (London 1996). W.S.

Aphrodite

Roman Venus, also Cypris, Cytherea, and a dozen other epithets or cult titles. As the embodiment of sex, love, and ideal feminine—and above all, naked—beauty, she is the most common symbol of love and desire from antiquity. Citations of Venus simply as a metonym for "sex" in the major European literatures would run into the tens, if not hundreds, of thousands. Artistic representations fill every museum and concert hall.

If these prepotent meanings were not enough, Aphrodite was allegorized at least since Empedocles. She was split in two by Plato in the *Symposium:* a common Aphrodite (earthly, reproductive) and the Uranian (heavenly, nonreproductive, and hence pederastic). Fulgentius (2.1), Boccaccio (*Genealogy of the Gods* 3.22–23), Landino (*Disputationes camaldulenses,* 61), and Ficino (*Commentary* 2.7, passim) elaborated, turning the latter into the study of "Humanitas," among other meanings.

Her presence in classical literature was so all-pervasive that *Quellenforschung* is mercifully impossible in most cases. Venus and Adonis took on a separate erotic, narrative, and allegorical life. Venus reentered literature more as a person than a metaphor, notably in the legend of Tannhäuser: Tannhäuserlied (ca. 1200–1270); opera by Wagner (1845); movie about the opera, *Meeting Venus* (1991); and Swinburne, "Laus Veneris" (1861).

Numerous statues—Belvedere (based on the Cnidian), Doidalses, Esquiline, Genetrix, Capitoline, Medici—have survived from antiquity, providing a basic language. The *Venus di Milo* was discovered in 1820 and promptly became one of the most famous images of antiquity.

Literature and art intersect in two of the most famous and influential images, Botticelli's *Birth of Venus* (1484–1485, Uffizi) and Giorgione's *Sleeping Venus* (ca. 1510, Gemäldegalerie, Dresden). Giorgione created a new pose from the pudica ("modest") type and drew on Claudian ("Epithalamium of Palladius and Celerina") to paint a talisman for married love culminating in a male heir. The attribute of Cupid was painted over in 1843, but Titian's variant *Venus of Urbino* (1538, Uffizi) had already dispensed with any overt marker of antiquity. Mark Twain labeled it "the foulest, the vilest, the obscenest picture the world possesses" (*A Tramp Abroad,* 1880, chap. 50). The path was now open for female nudes unsupported by mythology, such as Goya's *Maja Desnuda* (ca. 1799–1800, Prado) and, most scandalously, Manet's *Olympia* (1863, Musée d'Orsay).

Allegorization dominated in Bronzino's still mysterious *Venus and Cupid* (ca. 1510–1520, National Gallery, London), Titian's *Sacred and Profane Love* (ca. 1514, Borghese Gallery), and Tiepolo's *Allegory with Venus and Time* (1754–1757, National Gallery, London). The toilet of Venus allowed play with light, nudity, reflection, allusion, representation, and domestic luxury, as in Titian's *Venus and Mirror* (ca. 1555, National Gallery, Washington) and Velázquez's "Rokeby Venus" (1647–1651, National Gallery, London).

Venus's mythology is exceptionally rich, providing countless opportunities for narrative, still more for allegory and display of naked bodies. The contrast of male and female spheres of activity and styles of beauty has always been popular: Botticelli, *Venus and Mars* (1483, National Gallery, London); Veronese, *Mars and Venus United by Love* (ca. 1570, Metropolitan); Poussin, *Venus and Mars* (1629, Museum of Fine Arts, Boston); Lagrenée, *Mars and Venus, an Allegory of Peace* (1770, Getty, Malibu).

Other popular incidents include the Judgment of Paris, contrasting three types of feminine beauty: Lucas Cranach the Elder (several versions), Rubens (ca. 1639, Prado), Claude Lorrain (1645–1646, National Gallery of Art, Washington), Watteau (ca. 1718, Louvre). Venus as mother of Aeneas has a textual and artistic life of its own.

The goddess is still powerful in popular culture: the movies *One Touch of Venus,* with Ava Gardner (1948), and *Mighty Aphrodite,* by Woody Allen (1995); the song "Venus," recorded by Frankie Avalon (1959); the self-help book *Men Are from Mars, Women Are from Venus,* by John Grey (1992).

BIBL.: Kenneth Clark, *The Nude: A Study in Ideal Form* (New York 1956). Jane Davidson Reid, ed., "Aphrodite," in *The Oxford Guide to Classical Mythology in the Arts, 1300–1990s* (New York 1993) 1:112–162.

H.PA.

Apollo

One of the chief gods of Greek mythology; Olympian god of prophecy, of the arts and sciences, of medicine, of shepherds and animal husbandry, and since the 5th century BCE also the sun god.

Although only a few sources deal with him in detail (among them a 7th-cent. BCE hymn attributed to Homer and another hymn of the 3rd cent. BCE by the Alexandrian poet Callimachus), Apollo is one of the most beloved gods of the pagan pantheon in the post-antique tradition. He is particularly prized as the god of the Muses and the arts. In the opening poem to Martianus Capella's *De nuptiis Philologiae et Mercurii* (before 439), Apollo advises Mercury to marry Philologia, who receives the Seven Liberal Arts as a gift from the gods. In a subtle allusion to Apollo's love for the nymph Daphne, who in her flight from the god was transformed into a laurel tree, Petrarch consistently plays in his *Canzoniere* (1370) with the notion of himself as a poet laureate and thus compares himself to Apollo, to whom the laurel is sacred. Cervantes, on the other hand, parodies the cult of laurel-crowned poets in his epic poem *Viage del Parnaso* (1614). There the indignant Cervantes makes a complaint against Apollo and denies him a place on Parnassus.

In the Middle Ages, when pagan gods were generally discountenanced, Apollo, for instance, is nevertheless seen as an allegory for Wisdom. In the *Ovide moralisé* (1316–1328)—a bowdlerized adaptation of the Roman poet's *Metamorphoses* for a Christian audience—the python defeated by Apollo is compared to the devil, and his slaying is equated with Christ's victory over Evil. Similar allegorizing occurs time and again; for example, in Milton's *Paradise Lost* (1667), Python is identified with the serpent in Paradise. And it is within this tradition that Rodin interpreted the myth when he portrayed *Apollon vainqueur du serpent Python* (1894–1896) on the base of a monument honoring the Argentine president Domingo Sarmiento. There Apollo, the "god of light," symbolizes the Enlightenment's victory over ignorance. Numerous works of art depict him as a deity of light. For example, Rubens's oil sketch *Apollo im Sonnenwagen* (1621–1625) and Redon's symbolic portrayal in *Le char d'Apollon* (various versions 1905–1910) show him driving the chariot of the sun. This motif was used quite frequently for ceiling paintings, like those of François Boucher in the Palais de Fontainebleau (1753). In Louis XIV's France Apollo embodied a political program: the Sun King granted the sun god the chief place in the park of Versailles, thereby underscoring his own status as an absolute monarch. Apollo's love affairs provided material for numerous operas, such as Martin Opitz's *Dafne* (1640, music by Hans Schütz), Jean-Baptiste Lully's *Apollon et Daphne* (1698), and Mozart's *Apollo et Hyacinthus seu Hyacinthi metamorphosis* (1767).

From the end of the 15th century the god's significance was heavily influenced by the striking impression made by the discovery of the Apollo Belvedere (ca. 350 BCE, named after its display location in a wing of the Vatican). An engraving by Raimondi (ca. 1530) made the sculpture famous all over Europe. The Apollo's pose was widely copied as a model of stylistic perfection and was thereby also transferred to other contexts: in his marble group *Apollo and Daphne* (1625), Bernini shows the god grasping in vain with his outstretched arm for Daphne; and the stance of Dürer's Adam varies only slightly from Apollo's in an engraving portraying the fall of man (*Adam und Eva,* 1504). The importance of the Apollo Belvedere also manifests itself in poetry (e.g., Giambattista Marino's *Apollo in Belvedere,* 1619) and culminates in J. J. Winckelmann's essay *Geschichte der Kunst des Altertums* (1764), which sees sculpture as the epitome of beauty and harmony: "Of all the works of antiquity, the statue of Apollo is the highest ideal of art, . . . for in it there is nothing mortal, nothing presupposing human wretchedness . . . I forget everything else when I behold this miraculous work of art." This elevation of the god to an aesthetic ideal reveals a tendency toward philosophical abstraction, a tendency that was strengthened in Romanticism, and which in Friedrich Creuzer's *Symbolik und Mythologie der alten Völker* (1810–1812) is expanded to a primordial antithesis between the religion of Apollo and that of Dionysus. From then on the two gods were regularly elevated to representatives of contrary principles. Thus, for Ruskin they become the polar opposites of a metaphysical ethics: Apollo was "the spirit of light, moral and physical," and Dionysus was "the spirit of pure human life" (*The Ethics of the Dust,* 1865). This antithesis finds its most influential formulation in Nietzsche's polarity of the Apollonian (which he compares to the dream state) and the Dionysian (which corresponds to intoxication), the interaction between which he identifies as the generative force of drama in his *Geburt der Tragödie* (1872).

"Apollo" as the aesthetic paradigm of Winckelmann and of classical antiquity ends up being largely displaced by Dionysus and the Dionysian. Even when Apollo inhabits the thematic center, as in Hauptmann's dramatic fragment *Helios* (1899) or in Rilke's poem *Archäischer Torso Apollos* (1908), he is still characterized in terms of his opposite. One of the most convincing attempts in the realm of art to create a foil to the anarchic Dionysian is Stravinsky's ballet *Apollon musagète,* choreographed by George Balanchine (1928).

Under the auspices of National Socialism there was a program to revaluate Apollo, this time based on the fragments of the pediment of the Temple of Zeus at Olympia, which was excavated between 1878 and 1881. Like Raimondi's engraving and the Apollo Belvedere, Walter Hege's photographs made the archaic sculptures of the west pediment famous. During the 1936 Olympic Games, magazine covers and posters with images of Apollo were meant to substantiate the ancient relationship, asserted by the racial politics of the day, between Germany and Greece. Largely discredited since then as a model of purity, Apollo underwent a surprising rehabilitation at the hands of the sociologist Richard Sennett in *The Conscience of the Eye* (1990). As "a god of calm but not of permanence, a deity carrying within it its own seeds of change," Apollo provides the mythical example for a nondogmatic humanism in the culture of modernity.

BIBL.: Fritz Graf, *Apollo* (New York 2009). Antje Heissmeyer, *Apoll und der Apollonkult seit der Renaissance* (Tübingen 1967). Karl Kérenyi, *Apollon: Studien über antike Religion und Humanität* (Leipzig 1937). William F. Lynch, *Christ and Apollo: The Dimensions of the Literary Imagination* (Wilmington, Del., 2004). John Solomon, ed., *Apollo: Origins and Influences* (Tucson 1994). T.G.

Translated by Patrick Baker

Apollo Belvedere

According to historians of ancient sculpture, the Apollo Belvedere is a marble copy made during the Hadrianic period from a Hellenistic bronze original, but such a description fails to do justice to the centuries of fascination that this statue has exerted on lovers of the classical tradition. Its ancient provenance is unknown, nor are we certain when and where it was found in the Renaissance. By the end of the 15th century it was in the private garden of Giuliano della Rovere, who would become Pope Julius II in 1503, and in the course of his pontificate it was transferred to the Vatican. It was displayed there in a niche within the Cortile Belvedere, where, with the exception of the period from 1798 to 1815, when it was seized by Napoleon and displayed in Paris, it has remained ever since.

Although the figure has always been identified as Apollo, there has been no agreement as to the narrative moment that is being depicted—whether, for instance, the god is in the process of shooting an arrow and, if so, under what circumstances. It may be that this uncertainty contributes to the work's appeal, suggesting to viewers that it is the representation not of a specific mythological episode but of the Apollonian divinity itself, possibly in the midst of a *theophany,* the sudden appearance of a god among mortals. This effect is perhaps heightened by the statue's complex *contrapposto,* which seems to put the figure both frontally and in profile. The statue was widely sketched, copied, and translated into other media during the Renaissance, by artists including Michelangelo, Bandinelli, Dürer, and Goltzius.

It was not until the 18th century that the *Apollo* became one of the world's most famous art objects. For Winckelmann, it represented the perfection of the Greek ideal. But while he ascribed to the work a "noble simplicity and quiet grandeur" that became the watchwords of Neoclassicism, he also experienced stormier emotions in its presence: "Before this miracle of art I forget the entire universe . . . From admiration I pass to ecstasy; I feel my breast dilate and expand as if at the height of prophetic frenzy." With Winckelmann's passionate imprimatur and given the associations of the god himself, the statue became an icon of the Enlightenment, adulatory responses coming from Goethe, Schiller, and Byron ("in his eye/And nostril beautiful disdain, and might,/And majesty flash their full lightnings by,/Developing in that one glance the Deity," *Childe Harold* 4.161). In a striking portrait from 1752 Sir Joshua Reynolds staged the elegantly dressed Commodore Augustus Keppel in the posture of the Apollo, and a widely circulated lithograph of Goethe done by Kaulbach in 1769 depicts him in a similar pose—but on ice skates.

With the advent of Romanticism, the tide of opinion turned against the statue. Hazlitt declared the work to possess "a faultless tameness, a negative perfection," and he dismissed it as "positively bad. A theatrical coxcomb." Ruskin found it disappointingly mortal, rather than divine. Walter Pater was the first in a long line of modern commentators who see the glorification of the Apollo Belvedere as having to do with the statue's homoerotic appeal, which he traces back to Winckelmann himself. In a decidedly different vein was the adoption of the statue's head as part of the official emblem for the Apollo XVII spacecraft. Eugene Cernan, who headed the mission, offered an analysis of the visual quotation: "Apollo gazes to the right toward the galaxy to imply further exploration" —though in fact the mission (December 1972) turned out to be the last moon landing to date.

BIBL.: Phyllis Bober and Ruth Rubinstein, *Renaissance Artists and Antique Sculpture* (London 1986). Francis Haskell and Nicholas Penny, *Taste and the Antique: The Lure of Classical Sculpture, 1500–1900* (New Haven 1981). Alex Potts, *Flesh and the Ideal: Winckelmann and the Origins of Art History* (New Haven 1994).

L.B.

Apuleius

Roman literary author, philosopher, and rhetorician, ca. 125–ca. 170. Apuleius was a lucky man. He cultivated the arts of all nine Muses, married a rich widow, defended himself brilliantly against a charge of practicing magic, and—by his own account—achieved fame and fortune as a Sophist and Platonic philosopher. His works enjoyed similar good fortune, most coming through the Middle Ages unscathed. The philosophical works—*De deo Socratis* (*On the God of Socrates*), *De Platone* (*On Plato*), and *De mundo* (*On the Universe*)—were preserved in northern Europe; the *Apology, Metamorphoses* (*The Golden Ass*), and *Florida* survived in a separate tradition, slumbering through the centuries in a single manuscript in the library of Monte Cassino. The two traditions came together in Italy in the 14th century: the earliest manuscript to contain both the literary and the philosophical works was owned and annotated (ca. 1340–1345) by Petrarch. A few years earlier (by 1339) Giovanni Boccaccio was reading and annotating a manuscript of *The Golden Ass* (though he did not discover it, as is often claimed). He went on to transcribe both *De deo Socratis* (ca. 1339–1340) and the literary works (ca. 1350).

The works from both traditions probably owe their survival to Augustine, who in *The City of God* (books 8–9) both praised and criticized Apuleius' Platonism, thus ensuring the inclusion of the author's philosophical writings in the canon of Latin Platonic works transmitted through the Middle Ages. His influence on the survival of Apuleius' literary works is more indirect. The oldest surviving manuscript containing them was copied at Monte Cassino in the 11th century, when the monks engaged in a campaign of recopying their ancient manuscripts—especially those that were mutilated or damaged, and most especially those associated with Augustine. Augustine also transmitted the title of Apuleius' novel as *The Golden Ass* (the oldest manuscripts call it *Metamorphoses*), and he assumed that the work was either real or fictitious autobiography (*City of God* 18.18). Both that title and his assumption were taken over by 14th-century pre-Humanists and passed unquestioned into later interpretations.

In the 15th century the Florentine Platonists eagerly studied the Latin Platonic writers, including Apuleius. Fifteen manuscripts of Apuleius' philosophical works (including some owned by Marsilio Ficino and the Medici) still remain in Florentine libraries. The importance of these works declined as the writings of Plato himself became available, but Apuleius remained a symbol of Platonism. In 1469 he became only the second classical author to be printed in Italy, when his complete works were published as a salvo in the Platonist controversy—to announce and promote the publication of Cardinal Bessarion's *Defense of Plato* a few months later.

Apuleius' mannered language in the literary works (and particularly in *The Golden Ass*) brought him into another Renaissance controversy, over Latin style. The battle between the Ciceronians and the Apuleians raged well into the 16th century (when the Ciceronians prevailed).

Apuleius' most famous and durable legacy is *The Golden Ass*. Interpreters have generally concentrated on its two principal stories: the narrative of young Lucius, transformed into an ass by incompetent use of magic and redeemed by eating a rose garland; and, embedded within that, an account of Psyche's romance with Cupid. The ass story is very similar to the *Onos* (*Ass*) of pseudo-Lucian; the plots of both are derived from the lost Greek *Metamorphoses* ascribed to a certain Lucius of Patrae. The Psyche story seems to be Apuleius' invention.

Both stories lend themselves to allegory. The names in Psyche's tale suggest a union of the Soul with Love. Among Christian allegorists, Fulgentius (6th cent.) treated Psyche as a type of Adam, driven from Paradise by the sins of curiosity and lust, whereas Boccaccio, writing in a different age, saw her marriage as a union of the immortal soul with God. In an influential (but now contested) Jungian allegory, Erich Neumann (1956) treated the story as reflecting "the psychic development of the feminine." Lucius' story was often seen as autobiographical because of its first-person narrative style, so much so that from the 14th century until late in the 20th, Apuleius was regularly given the *praenomen* Lucius. The allegory adduced by Filippo Beroaldo (1500) was typical and influential: Lucius' transformation results from his bestial behavior and desires, and the redeeming roses represent either knowledge or wisdom. Modern interpreters have noticed parallels between the stories of Lucius and Psyche (both curious, both punished, both redeemed by divine favor), but much else is disputed. Questions include the genuineness of Lucius' conversion to Isis and the reliability of the narrator (Winkler), and whether Psyche's story bears a Platonic interpretation (Kenney).

In 1999 *The Golden Ass* was presented as an opera, with music by Randolph Peters and a libretto by Robertson Davies. Beginning in the Renaissance, Boccaccio (d. 1375), Matteo Maria Boiardo (d. 1494), and others had imitated the adultery tales of book 9. Most imitators, however, have turned to the Psyche story. Niccolò da Correggio (1491) used it in a poem with Cupid as the narrator; Thomas Heywood made it into a Neoplatonic masque, *Love's Mistress* (1634), for the court of Charles I; La Fontaine (1699) turned it into a romance in prose and verse. In the 19th century Walter Pater translated it in a chapter of his *Marius the Epicurean* (1885), and William Morris incorporated it in his *Earthly Paradise* (1870). Twentieth-century versions include Eudora Welty's fairy tale *The Robber Bridegroom* (1942), H.D.'s "Psyche: 'Love drove her to Hell,' " and C. S. Lewis's novel *Till We Have Faces* (1956), narrated by one of Psyche's sisters.

Cupid and Psyche appear in Constantinian art on a painted ceiling in Trier. The story was painted on Medici wedding chests (ca. 1470) and in fresco cycles by Raphael and his pupils at Villa Farnesina (ca. 1518) and by Giulio Romano at Palazzo Te in Mantua (1527–1528). Other famous Psyche cycles include those by the Master of the Die (mid-16th cent.), Edward Burne-Jones (1870s–1890s), and Max Klinger (1880). There are important paintings of individual episodes by Anthony van Dyck (1638), Angelica Kauffmann (1800), and Jacques-Louis David (1817).

BIBL.: Sonia Cavicchioli, *The Tale of Cupid and Psyche: An Illustrated History* (New York 2002). John D'Amico, "The Progress of Renaissance Latin Prose: The Case of Apuleianism," *Renaissance Quarterly* 37 (1984) 351–392. Julia Haig Gaisser, *The Fortunes of Apuleius and the Golden Ass: A Study in Transmission and Reception* (Princeton 2008). Elizabeth Hazelton Haight, *Apuleius and His Influence* (New York 1927). E. J. Kenney, "Psyche and Her Mysterious Husband," in *Antonine Literature,* ed. D. A. Russell (Oxford 1990) 175–198. Hugh J. Mason, "Greek and Latin Versions of the Ass Story," *Aufstieg und Niedergang der römischen Welt* 2.34.2 (1994) 1665–1707. Erich Neumann, *Amor and Psyche: The Psychic Development of the Feminine,* trans. Ralph Manheim (New York 1956). John J. Winkler, *Auctor and Actor: A Narratological Reading of the Golden Ass* (Berkeley 1985). J.H.G.

Arachne

Daughter of a dyer in purple from Colophon, Arachne (from the Greek *arachnē,* "spider") was a famous weaver who presumed to challenge the goddess Athena to a competition in the art of weaving. Both wove a tapestry, but Athena, jealous of her rival's great workmanship and angry at her portrayal of the gods' amorous escapades and human weaknesses, destroyed Arachne's work and transformed her into a spider.

The only exhaustive ancient account of this myth is found in Ovid's *Metamorphoses* (6.5–145), where the story can be interpreted metapoetically as a commentary on Ovid's own literary-agonal reworking of the traditional myth. Visual representations, for their part, are absent in antiquity. The relationship between image and text is reversed in the story's reception: since the Renaissance the tale of Arachne has been a beloved subject in art, but a creative reception in literature has failed to materialize. A possible explanation for this literary reticence is the myth's uniformity. The lack of competing versions might have aided in the canonization of Ovid's text and hindered any reshaping of the story. At the same time the broad diffusion of the *Metamorphoses,* which can be considered the most important source of inspiration for early modern artists and writers, promoted especially the artistic representation of this myth. For its content presents a particular artistic challenge: not only are the jealousies of the gods and the portrayal of man's hubris a beloved subject in Renaissance art, but Ovid's ecphrasis of the two works of art woven by Arachne and Athena invites the viewer to visualize the tapestries and even to transform them into paintings. Thus, the competition between the two women turns into a struggle between Ovid and his artistic interpreters, extending to three aspects of the myth: the warning given to Arachne by the goddess Athena in the disguise of an old woman, which is illustrated in numerous text editions of the *Metamorphoses* from the 16th and 17th centuries; the competition itself, which is depicted, for example, in Tintoretto's *Minerva and Arachne* (1579) and in the *Stanza dei Lanefici* in the Palazzo Farnese in Caprarola; and Athena's punishment of Arachne. The destruction of Arachne's loom is portrayed in the *Stanza* and by Rubens (*Pallas und Arachne,* 1636–1637). The best-known version of Arachne's metamorphosis into a spider is Gustave Doré's woodcut illustration of Dante's *Purgatorio* 12.16–24, which instills in observers a mixed sense of eroticism and horror.

Especially interesting is Velázquez's adaptation of the myth (*Las Hilanderas,* or *The Tapestry Weavers,* ca. 1657). Velázquez invites the viewer to read the myth across multiple image layers, like acts of a play. The foreground contains a portrayal of contemporary weavers, while the background depicts Athena standing punitively before Arachne's completed tapestry. By portraying the tapestry as a copy of Titian's *Rape of Europa,* Velázquez connects in his painting the reflection on the ancient myth's contemporary significance with a rivalry between old and young generations of artists over the creation of art.

Literary adaptations of the myth gained strength in the 20th century, as in Hanns H. Ewers's novella *Die Spinne,* in which its negative characteristics are embodied in a femme fatale. Another example is Christoph Ransmayr's *Die letzte Welt,* in which Arachne is a deaf-mute weaver who incorporates Ovid's tale into her tapestry. In poetry, on the other hand, Arachne's name lives on nobly as a pure synonym for "spider," as in George Meredith's *A Garden Idyl* (1909) and Robin Hyde's *Arachne* (1939). In the realm of psychoanalysis (Karl Abraham), the myth has been interpreted as an oedipal conflict between mother and daughter. In the popular imagination Arachne has an ambiguous persona whose positive function is as a giver of direction or aid to man. This could have a basis in the ancient myth, since there she plays the role of enlightener, giving mankind a more "correct" view of the gods. Thus, the many digital networks, Web sites, and e-journals that take their names from Arachne, such as Arachne@ Rutgers, also function as aids.

BIBL.: S. Ballestra-Puech, *Métamorphoses d'Arachné: L'artiste en araignée dans la littérature occidentale* (Geneva 2006). M. L. Welles, *Arachne's Tapestry: The Transformation of Myth in Seventeenth-century Spain* (San Antonio 1986). M.BA.

Translated by Patrick Baker

Arcadia

The idealized setting of Western pastoral literature, Arcadia is the name of both a real and a fictional place. The real Arcadia is a mountainous and rather barren district in the central Peloponnesus. The fictional Arcadia is a verdant and fertile land inhabited by shepherds, nymphs, satyrs, and demigods under the tutelary rule of the goat god Pan. In Western imagination the real Arcadia is the fictional one.

Centuries of pastoral poetry inspired by classical models turned Arcadia into a place of primeval plenitude and happiness resembling a secular version of the Garden of Eden. Shepherds' main occupation is tending their flocks and singing love songs, often in friendly competitions, while resting in the shadow of a tree. Love is the only cause of suffering. And whenever love is destined to remain unfulfilled, song is the only remedy. The poetic and musical talent of the inhabitants of Arcadia is one of the distinctive traits of their existential condition (Polybius, *Historiae* 4.20–21; Virgil, *Eclogues* 4.58–59, 10.32). Nature provides for all human needs, spontaneously and abundantly.

The two central classical sources for bucolic poetry, Theocritus's *Idylls* and Virgil's *Eclogues,* actually offer a somewhat less idealized vision of pastoral life. References to an Arcadian setting are present in only four of Virgil's eclogues (4, 7, 8, and 10); rural leisure, no matter how nostalgically escapist it may appear to us today, is hardly devoid of labor. The Eden-like image of Arcadia is, rather, the result of a cyclic reelaboration of a cluster of related ideas in which the pastoral poetic tradition merged with various currents of naturalism and primitivism connected with the classical myth of the Golden Age (Ovid, *Metamorphoses* 1.102–131; Virgil, *Eclogues* 4). In this easily malleable form, the dream of a superior existence in perfect harmony with nature was often evoked in support of both pessimistic and optimistic views on the destiny of humankind. Thus, Arcadia could be construed as the site of a nostalgic retreat in a past forever lost, or just as easily as the emblem of a utopian faith in the return of a new Golden Age.

From a literary standpoint, the most important postclassical work is Jacopo Sannazaro's *Arcadia* (1504). Although closer to Virgil's melancholic spirit than to late Renaissance hedonism, Sannazaro's humanistic rediscovery of classical Arcadia influenced generations of poets, from Torquato Tasso to Philip Sidney and Lope de Vega. In the late 16th and early 17th centuries, Arcadia became the setting of uncountable pastoral poems and plays that explored the paradox of love or the propagandistic celebration of rulers responsible for the return of an era of political and social concord. But the Arcadian imaginary also resurfaced in contemporary descriptions of the New World such as in Captain Arthur Barlowe's account of his journey to the "countrey now called Virginia" (1584). Recast in differently accepted or refuted guises, an Arcadian subtext celebrating nature's spontaneous lushness and agrarian values exerted a long-lasting influence on the construction of American identity. In Italy the foundation of the literary academy of Arcadia in 1690 gave new impulse to a neoclassical ideal rooted in the expressive and elegant simplicity of the pastoral code. In more recent times, the literary uses of the Arcadian theme have multiplied and diversified in works whose setting is not necessarily or strictly pastoral. Arcadia has become synonymous with a world of the imagination that has been variously recreated, in contrast with the real world, as a world of lost innocence, ancient values, sweet nostalgia, spiritual rebirth, contemplative withdrawal, or artistic communality.

It is difficult to trace the many ramifications of the Arcadian ideal outside the domain of a literature consciously imitating or reworking classical models. Arcadia provided Western imagination with the coordinates of an alternative world. As such, it served as one of the main ideological catalysts for utopian thought, despite the fact that its existence was traditionally located in a primeval and lost past. But at the same time, it differed from other forms of utopian criticism of society in at least three respects. Arcadia did not offer the blueprint for a perfect and orderly city-state, but rather a model of living outside the boundaries of urban civilization. Accordingly, its community of shepherds thrived on the opposition between the country and the city, or the court, or any social structure regarded as unnecessarily complex, constrictive, and unnatural. The image of a labor-free society associated with the myth of Arcadia was not predicated on man's technological dominion over nature, but on the idea of a harmonious and mutually respectful bond between man and nature. And finally, Arcadia-inspired utopias promoted not so much a change of contemporary society as a retreat from contemporary society.

Because of this emphasis on the human relationship

with nature, ideas and images of Arcadian origin have repeatedly influenced worldviews advocating a return to nature, where the concept of "nature" may variously stand for what is perceived as genuine, authentic, traditional, or familiar. The theme of a simpler but more fulfilling "rural" life, for example, continued to resonate, albeit in different forms, in Western aristocracy's interest in country villas and gardens artificially reproducing the luxuriant fertility of a secular Earthly Paradise, as well as in environmentalist movements celebrating nature as a benevolent and nurturing mother. In the visual arts, the Arcadian symbolism fostered a distinctive representation of nature emphasizing order, abundance, tranquility, and erotic bliss. The mental and intellectual coordinates of this influential construction of the landscape can best be appreciated when compared with the Romantic view of nature as a violent, terrifying, uncontrollable, and potentially dangerous force.

BIBL.: Robert C. Cafritz, Lawrence Gowing, and David Rosand, *Places of Delight: The Pastoral Landscape* (Washington, D.C., 1988). Terry Gifford, *Pastoral* (London 1999). Bryan Loughrey, *The Pastoral Mode* (London 1984). Leo Marx, *The Machine in the Garden* (Oxford 1981). Bruno Snell, "The Discovery of a Spiritual Landscape," in *The Discovery of the Mind: The Greek Origins of European Thought* (Cambridge, Mass., 1959). G.G.

Archimedes

Even in antiquity Archimedes of Syracuse was a symbol of intelligence and discernment beyond all human proportion, comparable in modern times to Newton and Einstein. Accordingly, several different images of Archimedes can be discerned, behind which the actual historical figure lies somewhere concealed. All we know for certain is that Archimedes died in 212 BCE as an old man during the Roman capture of Syracuse. The report that he was 75 at the time of his death comes from the Byzantine historiographer Tzetzes, who lived about 1,400 years after Archimedes.

During the reign of Hiero II, Archimedes was probably a technical adviser in the king's inner circle. According to ancient sources, he was active in that capacity in the shipbuilding, farming, defensive fortification, and artillery works of Syracuse.

Like Newton and Einstein, Archimedes used mathematics to describe his investigations of nature and its laws. Also like Newton, but unlike Einstein, Archimedes made major contributions to the mathematics of his time; his extant writings are exclusively mathematical. His accomplishments as a mathematician, however, would not have sufficed in antiquity to secure him the status of a superhuman genius. For that his deeds as a military engineer were responsible. As the man in charge of the defense of Syracuse, Archimedes succeeded in resisting the capture of the city for two years against a besieging Roman force under the command of Marcellus, one of the most capable Roman generals. It is no longer possible to determine the extent to which the technical accomplishments ascribed to Archimedes are truly the work of the historical figure (e.g., a mechanical apparatus for launching a manned and fully loaded ship, and the development of the Archimedes' screw, which was used for irrigation in farming). One reason for this difficulty is a tendency, already discernable in antiquity, to assume that a mathematical innovation found in his writings must have been based on a corresponding practical activity, such as shipbuilding for the treatise *On Floating Bodies*. It has also been claimed that the practical activities in which he is known or even merely believed to have engaged were accompanied by related theoretical writings. This is the case, for example, with the planetariums built by Archimedes, with which the motion of the heavenly bodies then known to be in the solar system could be duplicated. Their description by Cicero, who saw two of them with his own eyes and considered them Archimedes' grandest accomplishments, testify to their existence, but there is no trace of the writings that, according to Carpus of Antioch, accompanied them. Archimedes' supposed employment of a mirror as a secret weapon for setting fire to Roman ships at great distance has been shown to be a legend that sprang up about 300 years after his death. In the same vein, Apuleius (2nd cent. CE) describes the contents of a large work on optics by Archimedes, but the supposed author's near-contemporary Diocles, an expert on the subject, does not know it.

Even the authenticity of the writings contained in the Heiberg edition of Archimedes is problematic for several reasons. All editions of Archimedes are based on Byzantine collections of his works, beginning in the 6th century with the commentaries of Eutocius of Ascalon and the compilation of Isidore of Miletus, and ending with the 10th-century manuscript collections of codices A, B, and C. In the more than 1,000 years separating Archimedes from the writing of these codices, works such as the *Measurement of the Circle*, the original version of which was more comprehensive than the one known today, were altered with respect to language, didactics, and content. Archimedes wrote his works in the Doric dialect used in the Syracuse of his day, whereas in most parts of the Greek Mediterranean Koine was spoken. Most of Archimedes' works were later translated into Koine. Yet when certain of the mathematical texts were incorporated into collections of his writings in Byzantium, only versions in the original Doric dialect were available. It remains an open question, then, to what extent all the texts included in these collections are actually by Archimedes.

An analysis of his work suggests that Archimedes did not know Euclid's *Elements*. It could therefore be concluded that Euclid lived not before Archimedes, as is usually thought, but after him.

The influence of the writings and deeds attributed, correctly or incorrectly, to Archimedes was manifold. As early as Anthemius of Tralles, faith in Archimedes' technical achievements was encouraging others to search for solutions to technical problems otherwise considered insoluble.

In his *Arenarius,* a work on a numerical system for representing very large numbers, Archimedes gave the most detailed description of the heliocentric worldview of Aristarchus. Copernicus, the first modern proponent of heliocentrism, learned of Aristarchus' system from Archimedes or Plutarch.

Although Archimedes' writings are of a purely technical and mathematical nature, and no statements of his on the four great schools of Greek philosophy have been preserved, it is clear that he was no Aristotelian. This much emerges from the contempt he expressed for the Aristotelian dogma about the incomparability of curved and straight lines in his *Quadrature of the Parabola* and from his concept of nature in *On Floating Bodies.* Accordingly, Archimedes appeared to leading representatives of the Scientific Revolution such as Galileo and Kepler to be an ideal model for overcoming the Aristotelian worldview once and for all. Until Newton, who completed the development begun by Copernicus, the geometry employed by Archimedes remained the standard form of description in natural philosophy. Archimedes' importance for the development of mathematics and natural philosophy in the 16th and 17th centuries was made possible by the availability of his works, from the middle of the 16th century, in printed form. The slow diffusion of a few of his writings, such as *Measurement of the Circle* and *On the Sphere and Cylinder,* as well as late medieval Arabic texts inspired by Archimedes, did not lead to advancements in mathematics in the West before that time. Not even William of Moerbeke's 1269 Latin translation of those writings of Archimedes contained in codices A and B had any effect. Archimedes remained a source of inspiration from the Sicilian abbot Maurolyco in the 16th century to the days of Leibniz and Newton, and he was a symbol of mathematical precision until the 19th century.

Leibniz points to Archimedes' writings on determining area and volume and to *On Spirals* as the only works from antiquity that, because of the concrete problems they tackle, carried within themselves the seed of a new kind of mathematics: infinitesimal calculus. In reality, Leibniz's infinitesimal calculus went well beyond Archimedes' method for determining area and volume, just as the new algebra of Viète and Descartes far exceeded that of Apollonius.

But Leibniz, like Western mathematicians before and after him, did not know Archimedes' *Method of Mechanical Theorems,* which was missing in codices A and B. Not until 1906 did Johan Ludvig Heiberg, the Danish philologist and historian of mathematics, find this writing in a palimpsest in a monastery near Constantinople. The manuscript, which he called codex C, had been copied with a collection of Archimedes' texts in the 10th century and then overwritten in the 13th century with a liturgical text. Since its auction in 1998, codex C, and with it the *Method of Mechanical Theorems,* can once again be studied. A conjecture has recently been spread by the news media that knowledge of the *Method of Mechanical Theorems* in the Renaissance or early modern period sped up the development of natural science and mathematics by centuries, but this is pure speculation. It underestimates the capabilities of 16th- and 17th-century mathematicians, which allowed them to develop equivalents to Archimedes' procedure for determining the properties of surfaces and solids. And it ignores that Archimedes' method, which was based on a precise weighing of objects, relies on special knowledge of the location of centers of gravity, and that it at any rate exhibits none of the fundamental features of infinitesimal calculus. Neither Leibniz's notion that differentiation and integration are inverse operations, nor the algorithmic form that these operations have, has any basis in Archimedes' method. As for the extent to which Archimedes' prescription (in the *Method of Mechanical Theorems*) for dealing with infinitesimal magnitudes by comparing two infinite quantities can be seen as a precursor to Cantor's theorem, that will be up to future research to decide.

BIBL.: Marshall Clagett, *Archimedes in the Middle Ages,* vol. 1 (Madison 1964), vols. 2–5 (Philadelphia 1976–1980). E. J. Dijksterhuis, *Archimedes* (1956; Princeton 1987); supplement, Wilbur R. Knorr, "Archimedes after Dijksterhuis: A Guide to Recent Studies," 419–451. T. L. Heath, *The Works of Archimedes,* 2nd ed. (Cambridge 1912). Ivo Schneider, *Archimedes* (Darmstadt 1979).

I.S.

Translated by Patrick Baker

Architecture

Classical architecture in its broadest sense refers to any buildings inspired by the architecture of ancient Greece and Rome from the 6th century BCE to the present. The reference may be explicit by using the architectural vocabulary of the columnar orders, found in the Parthenon and Pantheon; implicit in the use of particular proportions, such as the Golden Section; or even merely alluded to in the use of materials and symmetrical composition. Architecture is the most public art, and the art most intimately connected with power and wealth. Architects can usually realize their designs only by the intervention of rich and powerful patrons. Classicism has an obvious appeal to ruling elites or those aspiring to power and legitimacy, as a way of expressing authority, and is commonly invoked by individuals, groups, or governments wanting to restore order and inspire confidence after a period of insecurity or unrest, such as civil war or revolution. To a large extent the appeal is inherent in the regularity of the architectural forms and compositions, but it also depends on the accretion of associations evoked by classical architecture from Periclean Athens, the Roman Republic through the Roman Empire, the early Christian period, the Italian Renaissance, Baroque absolutism, Enlightenment Neoclassicism, and more recent applications. The wide range of associations and the different dialects of the classical architectural language have allowed popes and monarchs, democrats and demagogues, all to feel comfortable using it to express their authority. These various classicisms are discussed below in generally chronological order.

The fundamental element of classical architecture is the

upright column. The Roman architect Vitruvius (fl. late 1st century BCE), on whom we depend for almost all we know of ancient architectural theory, tells us that the fluted or striated cylindrical column shafts tapering slightly toward the top are derived from tree trunks; but he also says that the two principal column types are related to humans, which explains their proportions and ornaments. The stockier Doric (height between six or seven times the diameter of the shaft) has no base; its capital is thought to derive from the helmet of a Dorian soldier. This column type developed in mainland Greece and southern Italy beginning in the 7th century BCE. The more slender Ionic (height between eight and nine diameters), its capital styled as downward-curling volutes (said to represent a woman's hair), originated in the Greek cities of Asia Minor. The entablatures (horizontal beams resting on the columns) of each type also differed, their ornaments again said by Vitruvius to derive from wooden structural effects such as purlins and rafters. The columns were used to create porticoes around the rectangular cellas of temples with a roof extending lengthwise, ending in low-pitched gables (pediments). Both Doric and Ionic column styles reached their classic forms in the Parthenon, the Propylaeum, and the Erechtheum, during rebuilding of the Athenian Acropolis under Pericles' leadership in the late 5th century BCE. It is likely that there was a deliberate attempt by the participating architects to establish canonical versions, just as the sculptor Polyclitus, their contemporary, set out to establish in his *Spear Bearer,* also known as the *Canon* or *Rule,* the perfectly proportioned male form. At this same time a third capital type appeared, the Corinthian, said by Vitruvius to have been inspired by an acanthus plant growing through a basket on the tomb of a girl; this inspired a column style (base, shaft, and capital) slightly more slender than the Ionic. It did not originally have its own entablature but was usually combined with the Ionic. During the Hellenistic period, the Corinthian style became established as the third canonical Greek column type.

The Romans adopted all three types. The Doric gradually became assimilated with the native Tuscan column type, thus acquiring a base. But the borrowings were by no means slavish, and the Greek styles were adapted to Roman taste. Although trabeated (column and crossbeam) colonnades remained the norm for temple exteriors, arches were admitted inside, as in the apse of the cella of the Temple of Mars Ultor in the Forum of Augustus (inaugurated 2 BCE). Even more important were the exterior walls of public buildings, such as the Theater of Marcellus (inaugurated 13 or 11 BCE), consisting of superimposed rows of arches articulated by a network of engaged nonstructural columns and entablatures. This *Theatermotif* was extremely versatile and proved immensely attractive to later architects from the Renaissance onward. The same combination of elements appears in the honorific or "triumphal" arches, one of the most enduring Roman additions to the canon. The Romans also invented a new capital type (1st century CE) that combined the Corinthian and Ionic styles, which is found on a few highly prestigious buildings, such as the Arch of Titus (81 CE). Its present name, Composite, bestowed by Serlio, dates from the Renaissance (see below). The vast expansion of the Roman Empire, especially into North Africa, encouraged the trend toward use of hard, colored marbles for column shafts and also for decorating walls and floors, both interior and exterior. Most such buildings were destroyed or fell into ruin during the succeeding centuries, but the Pantheon (erected by Hadrian, 118–125 CE), which owes its survival to early conversion into a church (in 609), gives us an accurate impression of how richly polychromatic much of Roman architecture was. It is even more important for its perfectly hemispherical dome (150 Roman feet, or 44.4 meters, in diameter), resting on a rotunda. This structure was made possible by the Roman development of concrete vaulting, which allowed the opening up of interiors in a way that the Greeks never achieved. The great public baths (*thermae*) of the imperial era, such as those of Caracalla (central block built 211–216 CE) and of Diocletian (dedicated ca. 305–306), contain sequences of vaulted halls and pavilions that remain awe-inspiring even today. The entrance portico of the Pantheon, a pedimented, trabeated temple front, displays the Roman genius for extending the traditional canon by tempering radical innovation with archaic elements that convey prestige and authority.

Although much the same architectural vocabulary was in use until the end of the Western Roman Empire in 476, not all periods in antiquity were as "classical" as others. Several revivals can be identified over the centuries. The most important occurred during the reign of Augustus (31 BCE–14 CE); having defeated all his rivals and gained sole power, he looked back to Pericles (ca. 495–429) as inspiration for his architectural program. He even imported Athenian craftsmen to carve copies of the Erechtheum caryatids for the porticoes of his forum. Vitruvius' treatise, *De architectura,* dedicated to Augustus, is part of this call to order, appealing to classical Greek and Hellenistic practice and theory and condemning in several places the licentiousness of contemporary architecture. He probably had in mind such innovations as an entablature in Arelate (present-day Arles, in Provence), which combines a Doric and an Ionic frieze. Many of Vitruvius' prescriptions were old-fashioned even at the time of his writing. For instance, he treats Ionic as the normative column type and barely touches on Corinthian—at just the point that the latter was becoming by far the most-used order in Roman architecture.

Architecture again shows adventurous developments in the decorative split pediments of Trajan's Market (Mercatus Traiani, 107–110) and in the arcuated lintels on the Library of Celsus at Ephesus (117–120), which has been characterized as "baroque" (see below). Yet in between are "classical" revivals, most notably those under the emperors Hadrian (117–138) and Constantine (306–337). The latter's triumphal arch erected in Rome (dedicated in 315) is notably conservative in comparison, for example, to the virtually contemporary Arch of Galerius (298–299) in Thessalonica, commissioned by Constantine's near contemporary and counterpart, the caesar of the eastern half of the Roman Empire (r. 293–311), which abandoned the use of engaged columns. Constantine's Arch is instead modeled on earlier arches like that of Septimius Severus (awarded in 203). The reuse of columns, parts of entablatures, and sculptures from earlier structures may have been partly caused by shortage of resources, but the technique also seems to have been used to confer an age value on the arch as a way of endowing it with authority. It is notable that these *spolia* (spoils) elements all come from structures of "good" emperors such as Hadrian and Antoninus Pius (138–161), that is, predecessors worthy of imitation in classical terms. Constantine also built the churches of Saint John Lateran and Saint Peter in Rome according to a uniquely Roman form, the basilica—a long nave flanked by colonnades and arcades and ending in an apse, originally designed to house magistracies and business, but which became archetypal for churches in western Europe. Constantine is fundamental to the survival of classicism in architecture because, as the first Christian emperor, he was the role model for all subsequent rulers and so effectively sanctified its use.

The ten centuries of the Middle Ages were formerly thought to be the nadir of classical architecture, but the dominant architectural style of the first 600 years is now called Romanesque, that is, "Roman-like." By the late 7th century in Anglo-Saxon Northumbria (site of Hadrian's Wall, former frontier of the Roman Empire), crude churches with squared stones (sometimes *spolia* from Roman structures) were being erected; a few, such as St. Paul's at Jarrow, displayed small, round-arched windows. We know from the Venerable Bede, who lived there at the time, from a request of the Pictish king in neighboring eastern Scotland for the help of masons from Northumbria, that these churches were considered "in the manner of the Romans." At the other end of the spectrum, the church built to replace the original Basilica of San Clemente in Rome, destroyed by the Normans in 1084, was such a successful imitation of early Christian style that it was mistaken for the original church until the latter's remains were discovered in the 19th century. The second Basilica of San Clemente was built during the 12th-century Renaissance, the last and greatest of the "medieval renaissances," which differed from most of its predecessors in not being initiated by a monarch. Paradoxically, the Gothic style, often considered the antithesis of classical architecture, also arose in the 12th century. Yet its earliest manifestations, simple, round columns (as opposed to the complex clustered piers often characteristic of late Romanesque architecture) with corinthianizing capitals, as found in Abbot Suger's new choir for the Abbey of St. Denis near Paris (begun ca. 1040), can be related to the original classical impulse, since the columns of its choir represent humans, namely the apostles and the prophets. Later Gothic styles moved toward greater complexity, and it was this that was challenged by the Italian Renaissance.

To the east, Islamic architecture had for centuries been influenced by the classical monuments it encountered on first conquering the Mediterranean world from Syria to Spain in the 7th century. At the most basic level, classical buildings became convenient quarries for stone to be reused for new constructions. But the first great monuments of Islamic architecture, the Great Mosque in Damascus (completed 715) and the Dome of the Rock in Jerusalem (completed 691), built by Byzantine craftsmen for the Umayyads, took over forms from the Roman and early Christian basilica and domed, centrally planned tomb. There was also a curious revival of Roman forms and masonry building techniques during the 12th century in Syria and Anatolia, exemplified by such monuments as the Great Mosque in Diyarbakir. Finally, following the conquest of Constantinople in 1453, the late antique domed and vaulted Hagia Sophia became the model for the imperial mosques of Sinan and countless lesser monuments throughout the Ottoman Empire.

In architectural terms the founder of the Renaissance is acknowledged to be Florentine Filippo Brunelleschi, whose Foundling Hospital began construction in 1419, its front arcade supported on classically proportioned Corinthian columns, with pedimented windows above. In his two churches, San Lorenzo (begun 1421) and San Spirito (begun 1436), he used the same basic plan of a Latin cross (three short arms and one longer), exploring the use of the module derived from the diameter of the round arch of a single bay to determine all the proportions. It is now realized, however, that Brunelleschi's sources were Tuscan Romanesque buildings, such as the Florentine Baptistery and the Church of San Miniato in Florence, rather than genuinely antique models. His motivation can be characterized as "nationalist," a rejection of the Gothic style favored by Florence's then principal enemy, Milan, where the cathedral was being erected under the direction of French and German Gothic masons.

Nevertheless, Brunelleschi paved the way for Leon Battista Alberti, who designed the first full-blown classical revival buildings and outlined his architectural principles and design method in his treatise *On Building* (*De re aedificatoria,* written ca. 1443–1452). It was explicitly meant to surpass Vitruvius' *De architectura,* which had been brought to the attention of Italian Humanists by Poggio Bracciolini around 1414. Alberti advised architects to sketch the parts of ancient buildings they admired—just as Humanists copied from ancient sources particular turns of phrase worthy of imitation—and to combine these elements to compose new buildings in the antique style but fitting the different needs of contemporary society. A good example is his facade of the Gothic church of Santa Maria Novella in Florence (ca. 1456–1470), where he wove together elements from three Roman monuments—the Pantheon, the Arch of Septimius Severus, and the Basilica Aemilia—in the lower zone, which supports a temple-like upper part with four pilasters under a pediment, flanked by scrolls (to hide the roofs of the side aisles). This became the classic Renaissance and Baroque solution for the facades of basilical churches.

Alberti found Vitruvius' reliance on Greek examples of temples described in Greek technical terms particularly baffling in the context of the Roman remains in Italy. Instead, he recommended the use of circles, polygons, and squares for the plans of sacred buildings, which should then have vaulted roofs or domes. This stipulation probably largely depends on his observation of Roman remains, of which the best preserved, and hence most impressive, tended to be structures with vaults, often thermal buildings. However, the influence of Hadrian's Pantheon, the most impressive example of the type, led Alberti and his contemporaries to interpret other circular domed buildings, such as the thermal pavilions around the Phlegrean Fields near Naples and late antique mausolea, like Santa Costanza outside Rome, all as having been temples. Another immensely influential building was the barrel-vaulted ruin of the Basilica Nova (built 306–313 CE) in Rome, through its misidentification as Vespasian's Temple of Peace, which Pliny the Elder had cited as one of the three most beautiful buildings in Rome (one of the others was Agrippa's Pantheon, the predecessor of Hadrian's, which was probably a normal rectangular temple).

By 1511, when Fra Giocondo published the first illustrated edition of Vitruvius, demonstrating that ancient temples were predominantly rectangular with columns outside, it was too late to influence Renaissance architects, who found the possibilities afforded by central plans, vaults, and domes much more exciting. Donato Bramante is reputed to have said that his concept for the new St. Peter's (begun 1506) was to put the Pantheon on top of the Basilica Nova. Hence this happy misreading of antique remains vastly enriched the canon of classical architecture.

One problematic feature of early Renaissance architecture was that its appearance was much plainer than the late Gothic style. It was a language, like Latin, learned and appreciated by scholars but whose attractions were not always apparent to others. Particularly puzzling was the dictum, according to Vitruvius, that the plainest of the column types, Doric, was the most prestigious, because it represented a strong and capable man, a sentiment that conflicts with the more usual perceptions that status is indicated by greater variety and complexity, and that strength is a necessity only for those whose work is of low status. The Florentine architect Antonio Filarete tried to square the circle in his treatise (ca. 1465) by labeling as "Doric" his most ornamented and slender column type, which had a Composite capital. But as architects explored more Roman remains and became more familiar with Vitruvius (the first printed edition appeared in 1486), genuine Doric was better recognized. The first correct use of Doric columns was by Bramante in his circular Tempietto in Rome (begun 1502), as appropriate for the shrine of a male martyr and saint, in this case Saint Peter. The Tempietto, which became an instant classic, marks the beginning of the High Renaissance. Andrea Palladio included it as the only modern building in the fourth book of his *Four Books on Architecture* (*Quattro libri dell'architettura*, 1570), which is devoted to temples. But despite Doric's theoretical prestige, Bramante abandoned it in his rebuilding of St. Peter's, employing instead the showier Corinthian. He also frequently juxtaposed several column types, as he did in the cloister of Santa Maria della Pace (begun 1500) in Rome and in several works in the Vatican, including the Cortile del Belvedere (begun 1504) and the Cortile del San Damaso (ca. 1509–1518), exploring hierarchical relationships between the types and adding arcades and rustication (roughly carved masonry blocks) to extend the lower end of the scale, as at Palazzo Caprini (begun ca. 1510), which was later owned by Raphael.

Raphael was the first to call the column types "orders," in a famous letter to Leo X (dating from between 1515 and 1519). He also extended the palette further by introducing colored marble into architecture, as in the Chigi Chapel (begun ca. 1513) at Santa Maria del Popolo in Rome. This revival of ancient practice had been anticipated in early Renaissance architecture in Venice, competing with the rival attractions of late Gothic buildings such as the multicolored Ca' d'Oro.

It was in Venice that the final systematization of classical architecture was accomplished, with the publication of an immensely influential treatise by Sebastiano Serlio and the erection of three buildings in or near St. Mark's Square by Jacopo Sansovino, both men having fled to Venice after the Sack of Rome in 1527.

Serlio was the first to illustrate the Five Orders, as they had come to be called, in an engraving published in 1528 and reprinted in what became the fourth book of his treatise (the title varies; the completed work ran to seven books), first published in 1537. The plate shows each column type with its own pedestal and entablature, beginning with the Tuscan, crude and squat, and moving through Doric, Ionic, and Corinthian to the most slender and ornate, the Composite. In the treatise this plate is accompanied by another showing masonry rustication ranging from rough, undressed blocks to clean, diamond-cut stones. Serlio's text expounds how the orders and masonry type and materials can be used to communicate the function or the status of a building. Thus, Sansovino's Zecca (1536–1547, the mint of the Venetian Republic), a public but industrial building, had rusticated arcades below and a rusticated Doric colonnade above (the third story was added after 1558). Both the Zecca and the nearby Biblioteca Marciana (1537–1564) are built of monochrome Istrian limestone, but the superior status of the library is signified by its greater height, smooth ashlar masonry, and refined Doric *Theatermotif* arcade below and Ionic arcade above. On the other side of the library stands the Loggetta, diminutive in comparison but displaying its higher status (it served as a rendezvous for the aristocracy) by the use of Composite capitals and polished colored marble and bronze. Variegated Corinthian columns on the facade of the medieval Basilica San Marco, across the square, complete the series.

By 1540, when he published the third book of his treatise (they were not published in order), on the antiquities of Rome, Serlio was insisting on the necessity of observing the rules of classical architecture, denouncing those who ignored the authority of Vitruvius as "heretics," even if precedent could be found in physical remains. His attack is directed at the Mannerists, like Giulio Romano in the Palazzo del Te at Mantua (ca. 1525–1535) or Michelangelo in the Laurentian Library in Florence (begun 1525); the latter, apparently bored with repeating the correct classical formulae established by Bramante, deliberately subverted the conventions, introducing, for example, crude rustication into an otherwise refined pedimented aedicule, or apparently supporting a column on a bracket and pilasters tapering toward the bottom. The influence of Mannerism, however, depends on spectators who are educated enough in the classical language of architecture to recognize that the rules are being broken.

Serlio's attitude was reinforced by later codifiers such as Palladio and Giacomo Barozzi da Vignola, whose manual, published in 1562, is significantly titled *Regola delle cinque ordini dell'architettura* (*Rule* [*or Canon*] *of the Five Orders of Architecture*). Together they succeeded in fashioning an architectural language that both acknowledged the original classical values of restraint, thus satisfying scholars and connoisseurs, and conformed to more general conventions for expression of status enough to appeal to popular and uneducated taste. Their books also acted as pattern books, which allowed patrons and builders across Europe and the New World for the next five centuries to achieve passably correct classical architecture. Yet it should be pointed out that for the first hundred years of this new architectural movement, northern European taste tended to apply *all'antica* ornament thickly and with little apparent regard for classical restraint or rules, in a style often called Northern Mannerism. The Palladian purity of works such as the Queen's House at Greenwich (begun 1616), by the English architect Inigo Jones, is exceptionally precocious.

The hard line on architectural rules was in tune with the clampdown by the Catholic Church on license in all aspects of life and culture as a response to the Reformation. Not until the 17th century, when it became clear that the tide of Protestantism had somewhat receded, did Rome relax restrictions enough to permit the development of Baroque architecture by masters such as Gian Lorenzo Bernini and Francesco Borromini, who were so thoroughly fluent in the language of classicism that they felt able to bend the rules with impunity to achieve whatever architectural effect they desired, abandoning the simple geometries favored by the Renaissance in the process. Bernini chose Tuscan columns to support an Ionic entablature in the colonnades enclosing his elliptical St. Peter's Square (1656–1667). Borromini went much further. His San Carlo alle Quattro Fontane (begun 1638) has an oval central dome, but the complexities of the ground plan are incomprehensible to the casual observer—suggesting a profoundly anticlassical ethos. Similarly, the column types in the cloister are impossible to pigeonhole within the canonical orders. Borromini's insouciance toward rules was a direct precursor of the 18th-century Rococo style, best seen in the stucco and gilt confections of the southern German pilgrimage churches such as Wies (1745–1754, by Dominikus Zimmermann) and Vierzehnheiligen (1743–1772, by Johann Balthasar Neumann), where all certainties are dissolved, providing a glimpse of the heaven of the God who can break His own laws. The aesthetic is instantly accessible and lingers today in the decoration of fairground attractions and casinos, which pander to a similar need for escapism from the rules of everyday life.

Bernini's attempt to export Italian Baroque during his visit to France in 1665 met with resistance. The insecure Louis XIV needed to assert the authority of his absolute monarchy, and the Italian's designs for the east front of the Louvre were rejected as too weak and capricious. The commission went instead to Claude Perrault, whose design (a screen of coupled columns supporting a central pediment and set on an ashlar basement) restrained the Baroque spirit within a classical cage. This hybrid style, Baroque Classicism, endured in France well into the following century in public architecture.

Neither full-blown Baroque nor Baroque Classicism was popular in Britain or the Netherlands, where they were too much tainted by their associations with Catholicism and absolutism, although Christopher Wren's St. Paul's Cathedral in London (begun ca. 1675), and John Vanbrugh's Blenheim Palace (1705–ca. 1722) offer a taste of what might have been. A revival of interest in Palladio, arising in the Netherlands in the late 17th century, spread to Britain after William of Orange and his wife, Mary Stuart, were offered the crowns of England and Scotland in 1688–1689. Part of the attraction was associational, in that Palladio's patrons were from the maritime Republic of Venice, whose constitution was admired by both the Dutch and the British as a model of the balance of powers. Similar associations led to the popularity of Palladianism among the founders of the United States, as exemplified in Thomas Jefferson's residence Monticello (built 1768–1782, remodeled 1796–1808).

By the mid-18th century, however, the more radical revival known as Neoclassicism was beginning to sweep through Europe, stimulated by the travels of hordes of patrons and architects not only to the long-known Roman remains in Italy, on the Grand Tour, but also to the newly discovered sites of Pompeii and Herculaneum. The Roman revival, pioneered in Britain by Robert Adam, revolutionized interiors especially; Syon House (1762–1769), for example, near London, had sequences of varied room plans derived from Roman imperial bath and palace complexes and startling "Pompeian" and "Etruscan" decorative schemes for walls, ceilings, and furnishings. In exterior treatments, as demonstrated by his triumphal arch on the south front of Kedleston Hall (1759–1765) in Derbyshire, Adam reintroduced motifs from Roman architecture rather in the manner that Alberti prescribes.

Neoclassicism in France, bound up with wider questions of philosophical rationalism, considered Gothic structural principles as well as Roman and Greek. Marc-Antoine Laugier's *Essai sur l'architecture* (1753) examined the origins of essential elements of architecture such as columns, roof beams, and doorposts. The second edition (1755) included the famous engraving of the primitive hut that exemplifies architecture deriving its authority from nature. The use of engaged columns or pilasters was condemned as mere decoration and hence rejected, as can be seen in Jacques-Germain Soufflot's Church of Ste.-Geneviève in Paris (1764–1789), where the columns are all freestanding and structurally necessary. The main front is a simple pedimented portico, like a Roman temple, although for the dome Soufflot looked to the Renaissance Tempietto of Bramante. The church was secularized during the French Revolution and renamed the Panthéon, becoming a mausoleum to great French citizens. This in part led to the modern misconception that neoclassicism is a style appropriate for revolutionaries, which has made it popular during the 20th century. In fact, the two greatest French Neoclassical architects, Claude-Nicolas Ledoux and Étienne-Louis Boullée, both worked chiefly in royal service, respectively in France and Prussia. Most of Ledoux's inventive tollgates around Paris were demolished during the Revolution as hated symbols of the Ancien Régime.

The Roman Revival was soon joined by the Greek. Ancient Greek architecture became increasingly known, as Grand Tourists found their way to the Doric temples of Paestum, south of Naples, and then on to Sicily. Few had yet made the journey to mainland Greece and Asia Minor, but the first publications of measured drawings, such as Julien Leroy's *Ruines des plus beaux monuments de la Grèce* in 1758 and James Stuart and Nicholas Revett's *Antiquities of Athens* (beginning in 1761), made an enormous impression, not always benign. Adam despised the pedantry of some of the Hellenophiles, seen at its extreme in the St. Pancras Parish Church (1819–1822) in London, by Thomas Inwood and his son, Henry, where quotations from large elements of buildings, such as the caryatid porch from the Erechtheum and the Tower of the Winds, are juxtaposed with little subtlety. Nevertheless, the Greek Revival did inspire masterpieces such as Thomas Hamilton's Royal High School (1825–1829) in Edinburgh, and Leo von Klenze's Walhalla (1831–1842) near Regensburg, both examples of Romantic Classicism, where function is subordinate to effect. The eminent 19th-century German architect Karl Friedrich Schinkel produced some of his best work in the Greek idiom, such as the Neue Wache (1816–1818) and Altes Museum (1823–1830), both in Berlin, and these in turn inspired perhaps the greatest 19th-century Scottish architect, Alexander "Greek" Thomson, whose St. Vincent Street Church in Glasgow (1857–1859) is startlingly original.

The explosion in knowledge of ancient Greek and Roman architecture that originated in the mid-18th century made possible the Neoclassical hegemony in architecture. It equally led to the collapse of classical authority, however, for the sheer wealth of examples made it clear that there was not a monolithic classical architecture but several alternatives—archaic, "classic," or Hellenistic Greek, Republican or imperial Roman, and so forth, from which the patron or architect could choose or occasionally mix. Such choice was anathema to the classical concept of intrinsic objective beauty. Thenceforward, the appeal had to be to the associations of the style; this led to the pluralism and eclecticism of the 19th century, during which several varieties of classicism vied for popularity with other styles, such as Gothic and Romanesque, and could even be combined in a single building.

The associations of Greek architecture made it particularly popular with educational institutions and with museums such as William Burn's Edinburgh Academy (1823–1824) and Robert Smirke's British Museum in London (1823–1847). The richness of Roman architecture was at first favored for banks, such as John Soane's work for the Bank of England (1788–1833). Later, financial institutions tended to prefer the Italian Renaissance palazzo, partly because of the associations (the Florentine Medici had been the preeminent banking family of Europe), but it no doubt helped that the palazzo was also a more flexible and cheaper building type to imitate than temples or baths. Similarly, residences adopted the Renaissance villa style, which afforded more comfort and did not demand absolute symmetry or the expense of columnar porticoes. Baroque came back into favor in the later 19th century, particularly in imperial European capitals such as Paris (Jean-Louis-Charles Garnier's Opéra, 1862–1875), London (William Young's War Office, 1898–1906), and Berlin (Julius Raschdorff's Lutheran Cathedral, 1894–1905). Thomas Ustick Walter's dome (ca. 1860) added to the Capitol in Washington, D.C., however, can be categorized as Baroque Classicist, that style thereafter being associated as much with democracy as with monarchy.

With the eclipse of the Gothic Revival in the late 19th century and the failure of its offshoots, Arts and Crafts and Art Nouveau, to have much influence on public architecture, academic classicism influenced by the École des Beaux-Arts in Paris enjoyed a renaissance, especially in America, where it dominated the Chicago Columbian World Exposition of 1893; it maintained its hold until the Second World War, led by such accomplished practitioners as McKim, Mead and White (Pennsylvania Station, New York, 1910; demolished 1964–1965); Daniel Burnham (Union Station, Washington, D.C., 1908); and Cass Gilbert (Supreme Court, Washington, D.C., 1935).

More idiosyncratic was the Viceroy's Palace (1914–1929) the central edifice in New Delhi, then the capital of British Imperial India. (It is now the Rashtrapati Bhavan, or Presidential Palace, home of India's head of state.) The masterpiece of Sir Edwin Lutyens, it succeeds in enculturating classicism by supporting the stupa-like central dome and Mughal-inspired side pavilions on colonnades bearing capitals derived from Hindu temples.

Reaction against the political establishments of countries involved in the First World War (1914–1918) such as Britain, France, and Germany saw a retreat from full-blown classicism to a stripped version pioneered especially in Scandinavian states to represent their prevailing social democratic aspirations. The plan of Erik Gunnar Asplund's Stockholm Public Library (1918–1927), its circular reading room at the center of a square, recalls the British Museum and Schinkel's Altes Museum; the cylindrical drum that lights the reading room looks back to the Roman Mausoleum of Hadrian and to Ledoux's Barrière de la Villette. Yet it appears accessible to the ordinary citizen, being built largely of warm brick and cement and approached on a ramp rather than steps. Doric was the order favored for this stripped classicism because its simplicity and Athenian associations appeared to embody democratic and egalitarian values. These qualities also made it a strong contender to be the official style for the Soviet Union immediately after the Russian Revolution of 1917. It lost out at first, however, to the Constructivist architects who were part of the European avant-garde known as the Modern Movement, which included Le Corbusier in France and the Bauhaus group in Germany, led by Walter Gropius and Ludwig Mies van der Rohe, which believed the form of buildings should be dictated solely by their functions.

By the early 1930s the tide of Modernism seemed to be ebbing. In the Soviet Union, Stalin rejected the avant-garde as unintelligible to the masses, and full classicism returned as the architectural counterpart of Socialist Realism in painting and sculpture. Hitler favored a stripped Doricism, as he perceived the ancient Dorian Greeks to be cognate with the primitive Germans. He employed the young architect Albert Speer to realize his dreams, notably in the Zeppelinfeld in Nuremberg, with its square Doric columns massed like soldiers on parade. Hitler's plan for rebuilding Berlin entailed a new central axis with an enormous triumphal arch at one end and a national assembly building at the other, the dome of which would be large enough to incorporate the whole of St. Peter's in Rome. Not surprisingly, Mussolini also favored stripped classicism for the Fascist monuments around Rome, best seen at the new suburb of E.U.R., intended to be the site of a world exhibition for 1940.

After 1945 the taint of totalitarianism discredited most overt displays of classicism, except where such regimes survived, as in North Korea, where the triumphal arch (1982) and the monumental buildings surrounding Kim Il Sung Square in Pyongyang show its continuing appeal for demagogues. Elsewhere the International Style (as the Modern Movement was renamed for American consumption) succeeded in becoming the mode for reconstructing the postwar world. Despite the claims of Modernists to be rejecting the past and reinventing architecture, many of their buildings appear to incorporate hidden classical values that could be termed crypto-classical. Le Corbusier's *Five Points of a New Architecture* (1925), on architectural design, was meant to replace the long-standing convention of the Five Orders, yet Colin Rowe (1976) has demonstrated how Le Corbusier's early villas owed a great debt to Palladio's. Similarly, his postwar Assembly Building of Chandigarh, the new capital of the Indian state of Punjab, depends on Schinkel's Altes Museum. Le Corbusier's proportional system, *Le Modulor,* used for his Unités d'Habitation (postwar multistory housing blocks constructed in several European locations), owes as much to Vitruvius as to what he declared to be his inspiration—ocean liners.

Even Mies van der Rohe's German Pavilion for the 1929 Barcelona Exhibition, which could not be more asymmetrical in plan and whose chrome cruciform-section columns seem designed to appear unclassical, negates its novelty by using Roman travertine and polished onyx (which cannot help evoking classical associations), reinforced by the presence of a bronze statue of a female nude. After the rise of the Nazis and the closure of the Bauhaus, Mies moved to America. In his inaugural address as director of architecture at the Armour (later Illinois) Institute of Technology (IIT) in 1938, he appealed to tradition and ended by quoting Saint Augustine: "Beauty is the radiance of truth"—an amazing intellectual turnaround within a decade. His master plan for the IIT campus reflects this conversion; the plan's format resembles a Hellenistic agora or Roman forum, the principal buildings being sited symmetrically and having the proportions of temples, albeit constructed from steel, glass, and brick.

Modernism's dominance was short-lived. By the 1950s Italian architects such as Ernesto Rogers and Paolo Portoghesi were reintroducing historical references in an attempt to make their buildings communicate more. The American Robert Venturi, while on a fellowship in Rome, was inspired by their work, and by Mannerist and Baroque monuments, to do likewise; his *Complexity and Contradiction in Architecture* (1966) set out a theoretical manifesto for what became known as Postmodernism. Venturi is interested purely in the associational values rather than the intrinsic character of classicism. This is well exemplified in his facade for the Sainsbury Wing of the National Gallery in London (1991), where the strongest classical references are clustered closest to the original building on the east and gradually fade in frequency and detail toward the west.

Much more profound is James Stirling's comparable extension of the Staatsgalerie in Stuttgart (1978–1984). Although there is no superficial attempt to imitate the classical style of the original, the mostly travertine cladding evokes the appropriate association, and the building is infused with references to the canon of Western architecture from Egyptian antiquity to Frank Lloyd Wright's Johnson Wax Headquarters in Racine, Wisconsin. The plan of the Staatsgalerie, with its circular courtyard, pays homage not only to Raphael's Villa Madama but also to Schinkel's Altes Museum; its double spiral staircase recalls Bramante's elegant stairway to the Belvedere Courtyard.

Postmodernism has also permitted the return of more conventional classicism. At one end of the spectrum is the neorationalism of Aldo Rossi, whose simple, unadorned geometrical projects derive from vernacular archetypes such as Italian farm buildings as well as Neoclassical models. At the other end is the full-blown, dogmatic classicism of Quinlan Terry, who argues that the orders were given by God to Moses for building the Tabernacle. Though much of his work has been houses for wealthy clients, at Richmond Riverside in London (1984–1987) Terry proved that the classical language of architecture could be applied successfully in a modern speculative development of offices, shops, and dwellings.

Between the two extremes, many nondoctrinaire architects have demonstrated that the classical style can still produce humane, functional buildings, not only for traditional types such as Thomas Beeby's Harold Washington Library Center in Chicago (1988–1991), but also for new projects such as the Seville Airport (1989–1991) by Rafael Moneo, and mixed developments like Demetri Porphyrios' Brindleyplace in Birmingham, England (1996–1998).

Whether the prevailing stylistic pluralism in contemporary architecture will continue is unclear, but it seems unlikely that the classical tradition in architecture will die out. Its flexible framework of rules ensures its attraction to those seeking to structure the built environment with order and reason, and its still-expanding canon in so many different contexts means that the associational values are immensely attractive to all sorts of institutions and individuals. One or another variety of classical architecture can appeal to reactionaries and revolutionaries and all shades of opinion between.

BIBL.: Georges Gromort, *The Elements of Classical Architecture* (New York 2001). Robin Middleton and David Watkin, *Neoclassical and Nineteenth-century Architecture,* 2 vols. (London 1980). John Onians, *Bearers of Meaning* (Princeton 1988) and *Classical Art and the Cultures of Greece and Rome* (New Haven 1999). Andreas Papadakis, *Classical Modern Architecture* (Paris 1997). Colin Rowe, *The Mathematics of the Ideal Villa* (Cambridge 1976). Robert A. M. Stern, *Modern Classicism* (London 1988). John Summerson, *The Classical Language of Architecture,* rev. ed. (London 1980).

I.C.

Ares. *See* Mars.

Argonauts

The Greeks who sailed with Jason on the *Argo,* bound for Colchis to secure the Golden Fleece. The myth of the Argonauts is widely represented in the art of classical antiquity. In 1382 a short-lived and unrecognized military order of the Argonauts of Saint Nicholas emerged in Naples. The voyage of the Argonauts adumbrated the modern naval mission, so there have been four ships called *Argonaut* in the Royal Navy (the first in 1782, the last decommissioned in 1993), and another three called *Argonaute* in the French navy (the first in 1794, the last decommissioned in 1910). Simon Lake's submarine of 1894 may have been named after the genus Argonauta (a kind of octopus) because of its propulsion system; its later namesakes, which include two American World War II submarines and the two French submarines called *Argonaute,* recall both the name of Lake's prototype and the sense of a naval voyage. The Argonauts are also seen as early exemplars of the team, and the term has been used in that sense for events such as the Yalta Conference of 1945 (which was known originally as the Argonaut Conference) and for the Canadian football team. The story has been reworked by modern writers such as Robert Graves (*Hercules, My Shipmate,* 1945) and John Gardner (*Jason and Medeia,* 1975), and there have been two films called *Jason and the Argonauts* (1963 and 2000). A hugely popular American television series called *Hercules: The Legendary Journeys,* in which many of the characters are Argonauts, ran from 1995 to 1999.

BIBL.: Janet Bacon, *The Voyage of the Argonauts* (London 1925). B. K. Braswell, *A Commentary on the Fourth Pythian Ode of Pindar* (New York 1988). Karl Meuli, *Odyssee und Argonautika* (Säckingen am Rhein 1921). Francis Vian, ed., *Argonautiques/Apollonios de Rhodes,* 3 vols. (Paris 1974–1981).

G.C.

Ariadne

Mythological figure, princess of Crete, daughter of Minos and Pasiphaë. Ariadne betrayed her family by helping Theseus conquer the Minotaur (her half brother) and escape the Labyrinth. She fled with Theseus to the island of Naxos, where he abandoned her, but (according to most versions of the myth) she was ultimately rescued by the timely arrival of the god Dionysus (Bacchus). The tale is given its fullest exposition in Catullus' Poem 64, where it appears as interruptive ecphrasis in the central portion of the poem on the marriage of Peleus and Thetis. The varied images of Ariadne were likely transmitted to modern times through Ovid (*Ars Amatoria* 1.524–564; *Fasti* 3.459–516; *Heroides* 10; *Metamorphoses* 8.169–182) and particularly the authors who borrowed heavily from him (such as Chaucer), as well as through translations with commentaries such as *Ovide moralisé* (14th cent.) or Giovanni Andrea dell'Anguillara's widely disseminated 16th-century editions of the *Metamorphoses.*

The ubiquity of the Ariadne myth in medieval, early modern, and modern visual arts, poetry, opera, and theater may be a result of its suitability as a cautionary tale (warning both maidens and heroes about the dangers of love, betrayal, and female vengeance), an allegory of marriage (through Ariadne's union with Bacchus), and a celebration of unabashed Bacchanalian pleasure and sensuality. Artists and their patrons in the Renaissance and Baroque eras seem to have been particularly drawn to the boisterous, chaotic, and highly sensual scenes depicting the arrival of Bacchus. Tintoretto's *Venus Officiating at the Marriage of Bacchus and Ariadne* (1576), one of four allegories now housed in the Sala Anticollegio in the Ducal Palace in Venice, recalls not only the city's annual marriage to the sea, but the gift of Venetian liberty from the divine gods. Ovid's vivid description in *Ars Amatoria* of the marvelous cacophony and chaos of Bacchus's arrival in his cart, accompanied by panthers, satyrs, and nymphs, certainly inspired works such as Annibale Carracci's *Triumph of Bacchus and Ariadne* (ca. 1602), the commanding ceiling fresco in the gallery of the Palazzo Farnese, Titian's *Bacchus and Ariadne* (ca. 1520), Peter Paul Rubens's fleshy and parodic *Bacchus and Ariadne* (1638), and Giovanni Battista Tiepolo's elegant but earthy depiction of the same scene (ca. 1745). The expressive, introspective power of the abandoned Ariadne also captured artists' imagination, as is apparent in Claude Lorrain's *Bacchus and Ariadne* (1656), which depicts the lone maiden contemplating a stormy sea, or in Angelica Kauffmann's desolate *Ariadne Abandoned by Theseus* (1774). Artists were also fascinated by the stillness of the sleeping Ariadne, as is apparent in such works as *Ariadne* (1913) by the Surrealist painter Giorgio de Chirico, which was no doubt inspired by the statue of the sleeping nymph in the Vatican Museums (ca. 250 CE), identified as Ariadne in the late 18th century.

As the quintessential lamenting woman, who (like Virgil's Dido) bemoans her fate and curses her lost lover, Ariadne—along with her unique rhetorical style—was used as the model for abandoned women in Italian epic poems (Ariosto's *Orlando furioso* and Tasso's *Gerusalemme liberata*). It was on female rhetoric in opera and theatrical music, however, that she exerted her most profound influence. "Lasciatemi morire," the only surviving excerpt from Claudio Monteverdi and Ottavio Rinuccini's *Arianna* (first performed as part of the 1608 Gonzaga wedding celebrations) used the newly expressive musical style of the early 17th century to capture Ariadne's disordered psyche. This not only created a burgeoning market for female laments in the 17th-century repertoire but also launched the operatic convention of the lamenting woman and established the myth as a standard operatic subject.

Perhaps the most innovative and ironic treatment of the tale is Hugo von Hofmannstahl's libretto for Richard Strauss's opera *Ariadne auf Naxos* (1912). This opera within an opera juxtaposes a serious presentation of Ariadne's abandonment with a commedia dell'arte improvisation; comic and serious characters interact, creating startling stylistic frictions that drive the high-minded Composer (a member of the dramatis personae) to despair. The opera ends with a glorious apotheosis as Ariadne, awaiting death, is safely escorted to heaven by Bacchus.

In 1995 Alexander Goehr wrote a modern setting of Rinuccini's 1608 libretto for Monteverdi's lost opera. Scholars still cling to the hope that Monteverdi's score, abandoned by fate, like its eponymous heroine, will eventually be returned to us.

BIBL.: Karen Forsyth, *Ariadne auf Naxos by Hugo von Hofmannstahl and Richard Strauss: Its Genesis and Meaning* (Oxford 1982). Charles Martindale, ed., *Ovid Renewed: Ovidian Influences on Literature and Art from the Middle Ages to the Twentieth Century* (Cambridge 1988). David Rosand, *Myths of Venice: The Figuration of a State* (Baltimore 2001). Ellen Rosand, *Opera in Seventeenth-century Venice: The Creation of a Genre* (Berkeley 1991). T. B. L. Webster, "The Myth of Ariadne from Homer to Catullus," *Greece and Rome* 13 (1966) 22–31.

W.H.

Aristocracy

An aristocracy, in the sense of an elite dominating the social order, was a general phenomenon in premodern society after the rise of complex civilizations in the Neolithic age. An aristocracy existed in Greece and Rome. Europe also was dominated by the aristocracy, politically and culturally, but also economically, at least until World War I. Older generations of historians tended to believe that the Renaissance and the rise of the modern state in Europe marked the beginning of the decline of the aristocracy and the rise of the bourgeoisie. In the past decades, however, historians have found that this view, propagated most influentially in the work of Tocqueville and Marx, is by and large wrong. There was indeed a crisis of the aristocracy, beginning in the Renaissance and reaching its climax in the late 16th and early 17th centuries, but it was successfully overcome and ushered in a period of renewed aristocratic predominance, which lasted into the 20th century.

During this period the aristocracy, everywhere in Europe, was deeply influenced by classical ideas and ideals; they shaped its views of life, society, and politics. This can be seen first of all in its education. The medieval aristocracy had held learning in contempt. What a gentleman needed was practical training that prepared him for warfare, for honorable service to his lord, and for elegant courting. Bookish learning was considered servile and not proper for men of the world. In the 16th century this attitude changed drastically, as it became clear that, because of its ignorance, the aristocracy was about to lose its role as the governing elite. It was obvious that the traditional education of the nobleman needed modification and augmentation, and that the anti-intellectual ethos of the aristocracy had to be cast off. Accordingly, more and more nobles sent their sons to school and to the universities. Most noble scions went to what in France was called a *collège* and in Britain a public school, the most famous of which were, respectively, the collège Louis-le-Grand and Eton. These became models for many others, and all had more or less the same curriculum, which was overwhelmingly classical in orientation. Most of the students' time went into studying the ancient Latin and, to a much smaller degree, Greek authors. When they had finished their formal education, they were steeped in the ancient writers and in little else. Even those who went on with their studies in order to get a higher degree, such as a rule in law, did not leave the ancients behind, since Roman and canonical law were at the heart of legal studies.

The European aristocracy's classical orientation was visible in many ways. Its libraries were frequently stocked with works from the ancient poets, orators, historians, and philosophers. Noblemen adorned their houses with pilasters and porticoes, filled their rooms with urns and busts, and placed temples, statues, and satyrs in their gardens. Their minds were imbued with classical images and models, which deeply affected both their behavior and their lifestyles. In short, as even a brief glance will reveal, aristocratic culture, from the late Renaissance to World War I and beyond, was permeated by the ancients.

It is hardly surprising then that aristocratic political and moral discourse also owed much to the ancients. One can even speak of it as a classicist tradition in moral and political thought, one that was very influential for centuries. Yet it has hardly been investigated and charted until now. This is not surprising: historians of ideas have concentrated on the thinkers who seemed to them to represent the new thought of the new ruling class of the bourgeoisie.

Aristocratic political analysis consistently employed a variant of the classical scheme of political regimes, such as that of Polybius, who distinguished among six different kinds of regime, three good and three corrupt, and who argued that a mixed regime of the three good regimes—monarchy, aristocracy, and democracy—was the best possible. Hence the aristocracy's permanent vindication of such a mixed regime. In every such regime, it was argued, the aristocracy should be the preponderant element, as it had been in the Roman Republic, where it had been represented by the Senate. The aristocracy stands as an indispensable tempering force between the monarchical and the democratic element. Without its influence, a monarch would degenerate into a tyrant, and democracy into mob rule. Thus, the aristocracy is the prop that keeps the ship of state afloat: the doings of the most prominent men determine the fate of the whole res publica. These doings can be either virtuous or vicious. Therefore, as long as the aristocracy is virtuous, the state will flourish and be great. As soon as it comes under the sway of vice, it will flounder and decay. What virtue and what vice? The virtues and the vices that could be found in the ancient authors, particularly in the Romans. No author was more widely read than Cicero, whose *De officiis* was standard fare in the noble scions' schools and regarded as the handbook par excellence of noble morals. It is in this book that one finds the most influential and elaborate exposition of the four cardinal virtues—prudence, justice, courage, and decorum, or temperance—that are at the center of aristocratic moral thought.

BIBL.: J. Dewald, *The European Nobility* (Cambridge 1996). A. A. M. Kinneging, *Aristocracy, Antiquity, and History* (New Brunswick 1997). D. Lieven, *The Aristocracy in Europe, 1815–1914* (London 1992). H. M. Scott, ed., *The European Nobilities in the Seventeenth and Eighteenth Centuries*, 2 vols. (London 1995).

A.K.

Aristophanes

Greek comic dramatist (d. ca. 386 BCE). His 11 surviving plays are the only extant examples of Athenian Old Comedy. The genre was becoming obsolete in his own lifetime, and there seem to have been few performances of his plays in antiquity after his death. By the end of the 4th century BCE Old Comedy had been definitively replaced by Menandrian New Comedy. The dramatic legacy of New Comedy, through Plautus and Terence to the European Renaissance, is immense, whereas Aristophanes' comic mode—a dramatic free form with an almost improvisational feel, great poetic and linguistic inventiveness, highly topical satire (public figures being named and personated on stage), and obscenity beyond almost any subsequent standard of acceptability—never again became a major theatrical tradition. Plutarch, comparing Aristophanes and Menander in the late 1st century CE, views the former with educated distaste. Yet his judgment is also testimony to the durability of Aristophanes' plays as reading texts. They received intensive scholarly study at Alexandria and Pergamum, acquired a body of commentary second only to that on Homer, and were regarded by many as touchstones of Attic Greek. Interest in Aristophanes gained new life in Byzantium; he figures frequently in the great Byzantine lexicon, the Suda, and three of his plays (*The Clouds, The Frogs,* and *Wealth*—the last by far the most popular) became regular school texts. Byzantine manuscripts secured his survival into the age of printing; the *editio princeps* of nine plays from the Aldine press (1498) used the text of the 14th-century Byzantine editor Demetrius Triclinius. The remaining plays (*Lysistrata* and *Thesmophoriazusae,* their descent more perilous than that of the others) were printed in 1516; a complete edition appeared in 1535, and a complete set of Latin translations in 1538.

A collection of Italian translations was published in 1545, but otherwise vernacular versions were slow to arrive, and for centuries Aristophanes remained difficult of access in the West. The problem was in part slow progress in Aristophanic scholarship. His Greek is loaded with words unattested elsewhere, his topicality requires strenuous decoding, and the received text is full of acute and chronic problems; the scholia attached to that text have also proved a mixed blessing, as full of disinformation and misdirection as enlightenment. Serious work on the text began in the 16th century—its challenges attracted talent on the order of Pier Vettori, Willem Canter, and Joseph Scaliger—but progress has remained slow and still cannot be said to have reached its goal. Readers have encountered other disincentives. Those drawn to classical Greek culture in the first place have often been appalled by the mocking, possibly lethal portrait of Socrates in *The Clouds.* The Byzantine critic John Tzetzes was unhappy with it, and it was a particular scandal in philhellenic Germany, where it either was grounds for dismissing the author altogether (Moses Mendelssohn thought him a hack hired by Socrates' enemies) or needed to be theorized into harmlessness (F. A. Wolf proposed that Aristophanes was satirizing an early phase of Socrates' career, before he came into his real calling). In *Aristophanes' Apology* (1875) Robert Browning allows the playwright a lengthy, drunken self-justification before confronting him with a stern arraignment by Browning's heroine Balaustion, primarily because of his mockery of Euripides. More generally, Aristophanes' vaudevillian messiness and sexual and scatological joking fit uneasily with some notions of what great literature—especially classical literature—is supposed to provide. Even for those without such compunctions, the unguarded laughter needed to enjoy the original has a hard time surviving the work needed to understand it—"sally after sally," in Stephen Leacock's annoyed description, "each sally explained in a note calling it a sally." Appreciation of Aristophanes continually threatens to be a highly restricted affair.

Against these odds Old Comedy has nevertheless since the 16th century made its mark in Western literature. It is uncertain whether Rabelais read Aristophanes, but he might as well have; Joachim DuBellay happily hailed him as "he who has made Aristophanes be born again" (*Défense et illustration de la langue française,* 1549). Repeated attempts have been made to effect that rebirth onstage. There is a long tradition of academic performances, some quite ambitious; John Dee, later to be astrologer to Elizabeth I, secured his reputation as a magus with a spectacular staging of *Peace* at Cambridge in 1546 (the flying dung beetle made an especially strong impression). Niccolò Machiavelli, author of some skillful updatings of New Comedy to 16th-century Italy, composed ca. 1505 an adaptation of *The Clouds* called *Le Maschere* (*The Masks*); the decision of his literary executor not to preserve it because of the scabrousness of its attacks on powerful contemporaries suggests that Machiavelli understood the genre and took it seriously. There is less seriousness (and little obscenity) in Pierre le Loyer's *Le Néphélococugie* (1579), a recasting of *The Birds* as the story of two cuckolds who leave Toulouse to live among the cuckoos. Ben Jonson studied Aristophanes carefully, and in *The Devil Is an Ass* (1616) has a character quote *Wealth* in the original ("He curses/In Greek, I think," says another character). Jonson's disciple Thomas Randolph composed a modestly topical Londonization of *Wealth* called *Hey for Honesty, Down with Knavery* (ca. 1626, published with some updating of the satire in 1651). Jean Racine's single, unrepeated venture into comedy, *Les plaideurs* (1668), reworks *The Wasps*. There is a notable string of such reworkings in German, beginning with Hans Sachs's *Pluto* (1551, the satire against wealth taking an anti-Semitic turn), and continuing through the 19th century; Robert Misch's widely played 1901 version of *Lysistrata* has the Goethean title *Das Ewig-weibliche* (*The Eternal Feminine*). The politics and the theatrical experimentalism of the 20th century on occasion made Aristophanes a natural inspiration. A version of *Peace* aggressively updated to the Vietnam War (with a text by Tim Reynolds and minstrel-show music by Al Carmines) played in New York in 1969. Vasily Aksyonov's *Aristophaniana s lyagushkami* (*Aristophaniana with Frogs,* performed in Moscow in 1968) expands the conceit of *The Frogs* to include a new regime in Athens: the dictatorship of Alcibiades and a chorus of hacks. That chorus is eventually displaced by the traditional frogs, but only in Hades, where the true poets—Pushkin, Shakespeare, and Aristophanes himself, as well as Aeschylus and Euripides—are at the end eternally confined.

BIBL.: Edith Hall and Amanda Wrigley, eds., *Aristophanes in Performance, 421 BC–AD 2007* (London 2007). Louis E. Lord, *Aristophanes: His Plays and His Influence* (Boston 1925).

G.B.

Aristotle and Aristotelianism

The influence of Aristotle (384–322 BCE) on Western intellectual life is immense, so much so that once one begins to track it, no field of inquiry can be identified that it would be safe to overlook. Aristotle laid the foundations for not one but two sciences, logic and biology, an achievement unmatched by any thinker before or since; on both, he conferred a meticulously thought-out methodology and then implemented it, providing enough raw material along the way for thinkers to digest over two millennia. The reach of Aristotle's influence on every branch of intellectual enterprise is equally as long. If one were *ex hypothesi* to imagine surgically removing the Aristotelian strand from the history of Western philosophy, or science, or theology, it is difficult even to imagine what the end result would look like. An Aristotelian analysis of this predicament would be that the thought experiment has been conducted strictly *per impossibile.* The development of Western ethical and political theory is likewise inextricably intertwined in its engagement with Aristotelian notions of virtue, sociability, and worldly and otherworldly happiness. And Western rhetoric and letters owe a great deal to the philosopher from Stagira.

As a consequence, much of our basic theoretical vocabulary is Aristotelian in provenance. Energy, actuality, and potency; necessity, possibility, and contingency; matter and form, substrate and substance, genus, species, and differentia; essence and accident; subject and predicate; catharsis and weakness of will: all of these and a score more (*ex hypothesi* and *per impossibile,* indeed!) were first introduced as technical terms by Aristotle and continue to exert an influence. Whether wittingly or unwittingly, the way in which a person today dissects reality will almost certainly carry Aristotelian overtones. Aristotle would have thought that this is because his choice of terminology replicates with reasonable accuracy both the intuitions captured in everyday language and the nature of the reality underlying it. Those with more individualistic predilections will see instead evidence of an exceptionally forceful mind.

Once all this is acknowledged, Jonathan Barnes's onetime estimate that "an account of Aristotle's intellectual afterlife would be little less than a history of European thought" (1982, 86) begins to look positively subdued. For Aristotle has never belonged to Europe alone. The life of the Arabic Aristotle in particular is long and storied, with riches yet to be mined. The part that Aristotle played in the development of Islamic high culture was every bit as central as his role in medieval Europe—perhaps more so, given that philosophy of a recognizably Aristotelian stamp continues to be taught in present-day Iran. (There are teachers in present-day Qum who claim to be able to trace an unbroken lineage of philosophical teaching through Baghdad and Alexandria all the way back to Aristotle's Athens.) Indicative of the depth of this felt connection is that the renowned Iraqi poet Saadi Youssef in a recent poem ("A Roman Colony," 2004) can evoke the image of Aristotle's disciples visiting the great school at Kinnesrin (now in northern Syria), taking manuscripts to Mesopotamia, "on the borders of the Arabian desert." War-ravaged locals protest that they, too, were "Greeks, and peasants": but they had no idea that in the West a new sun was rising, a mighty conquering power also trained by Aristotle: Alexander the Great. Aristotle thus emerges as a man of science and a teacher of princes, a figure simultaneously uniting and dividing Europe and *dār al-Islam,* the world of Islam—the two dominant cultures of the Mediterranean and the Levant. But for this to happen, a long road had first to be traversed.

Aristotle founded his school in Athens, the Lycaeum, in 335 BCE. From its beginnings the Peripatos, as the school alternately became known (for its covered colonnade), was conceived of both as a teaching and a research institution. Sometimes the original research conducted by Aristotle's students took them well beyond what their master had taught. Theophrastus (372–287) expanded Aristotle's biological program into the field of botany and provided pioneering treatments of the hypothetical syllogism, demonstrating that not even the jewels in Aristotle's scientific crown were considered out of bounds for improvement. He also deployed Aristotle's own analysis of final causes in a critique of his master's teleological cosmology, effectively charging Aristotle with not being Aristotelian enough. Peripatetic naturalism was carried further by Strato, the school's second successor. In the first century BCE, with Aristotle's fortunes at an all-time low, Xenarchus "the Peripatetic" is known not for defending Aristotle at all, but for criticizing his famous theory of *aether,* the stuff of the heavenly spheres or the "fifth element"—this last term being of Hellenistic provenance. This willingness on the Peripatetics' part to deviate from their master's teaching gained them notoriety in antiquity. It contrasts pointedly with the later caricature of Aristotelians as a generally subservient group and may have contributed to the school's demise in the Hellenistic era. With the stiffening competition between the philosophical schools, the Peripatetics' relative lack of ideological commitment and clear-cut doctrine worked against them.

Perhaps Aristotle would have smiled on such independent-mindedness. The ancient biographers recount a tale where he ruthlessly pressed Plato, much to the distaste of the loyal students Speusippus and Xenocrates. Aristotle's supposed rejoinder, "Plato is a friend, but truth is a truer friend," was cited by critics ranging from al-Ghazālī in the 11th century to Gianfrancesco Pico della Mirandola in the 16th to indicate that the best way to honor Aristotle was to remain critical toward him. (The titles alone are telling: Ghazālī wrote *The Incoherence of the Philosophers,* Gianfrancesco *The Vanity of the Gentiles' Teachings.*) In some ancient and medieval accounts Aristotle's relentless drive for truth even drives him to suicide. Unable to decipher the mystery of the shifting tides at Euripus (for which see *Nicomachean Ethics* 1167b6–7), the philosopher despondently throws himself into the sea. In the 19th century Nietzsche, who personally preferred Plato's poetic genius, would consider Aristotle's very commitment to truth his supreme folly; in the 20th, the same facet would again endear Aristotle to scientists and philosophers of a more analytic persuasion.

Aristotle was thus known to the ancients as a scientist and logician first and foremost, just as he is today. Famous examples of his seemingly insatiable intellectual appetite are the catalogues (sadly lost to us) of Greek constitutions and Olympic heroes. Pliny the Elder in his *Natural History* (8.44) even reports that Alexander the Great shipped animals from the ends of the Earth for Aristotle's inspection: the story is fabulous, but it reveals an ongoing fascination both with Aristotle's encyclopedic tastes and with his tutelage of Alexander. The royal connection inspired countless legends and instigated a genre of medieval "counsels for kings" literature, chiefly in the form of spurious correspondence.

Continuing the variegated research program of Aristotle's school, Hellenistic Alexandria produced the grammarians Apollonius Dyscolus and Herodianus, the geographer Dicaearchus, and the astronomer Aristarchus, among others. Even Galen's scientific approach to medicine is best understood against a Peripatetic backdrop, though Galen himself preferred to think that Aristotle was merely following Hippocrates in his empiricism. All this is indicative of the extent to which the Peripatetic school's commitment to specialized, methodologically autonomous research had become a commonplace in the Hellenistic era, enough that Aristotle could easily become lost along the way. Cicero in his *Topics* reports that most philosophers in his age were ignorant of Aristotle, and probably at this stage the Peripatetic school itself was no longer in existence. In the competitive and catty intellectual climate of early imperial Rome, Aristotle was painted as a dandy and a connoisseur, fond of jewelry and fine clothes. This picture reflected the Peripatetics' general reputation as moneyed and indulgent in worldly matters. Still, the emperors Octavianus (Augustus) and Nero had Peripatetic teachers, and enough respect for Aristotle remained that the emperor Marcus Aurelius (r. 161–180), upon instituting imperial subsidies for the teaching of philosophy, included Peripatetic learning among the schools to be supported.

Alexander of Aphrodisias' ascension to this newly founded Peripatetic chair represents a seminal moment in the revival of Aristotle's fortunes. Andronicus of Rhodes' collection of Aristotle's scholarly works had steadily gained in popularity over two centuries (they form the foundation of our Aristotelian corpus even today). Alexander now purported to reveal their hidden unity as a complete and coherent world system. When subsequent generations praised Aristotle for his panoptic view of reality, it was Alexander's Aristotle whom they had in their sights. And with Alexander, the notion that a Peripatetic's primary vocation lay in Aristotelian apologetics set in. Of course, originality and brilliance could be cloaked under such activity; this too we find in Alexander. Alexander's sober and sharp observational skills and his analytic propensities set a high standard for all future Aristotelian commentary.

Curiously, this first Aristotelian renaissance came to fruition under the banner of Platonism. Plotinus (205–270), in explicating his highly sophisticated, systematized brand of Platonism, made extensive use of Aristotelian concepts (in his school not only Aristotle but also Alexander was studied); his student Porphyry (234–305) then undertook to show that this was no chance appropriation but rather that Aristotle's worldview was essentially in harmony with that of Plato. The move reflects a growing desire on the part of late ancient thinkers to view, and present, the Greek (and Egyptian, and Babylonian) intellectual heritage as being essentially of a piece, as well as their wish to see even the more mundane disciplines contribute to a sweeping cosmic vision with some distinctly transcendent goals—paradoxically, the best bulwark against a world-denouncing Gnosticism that was antithetical to its own basic metaphysical optimism. Thus, even as Platonism rose to dominance among the late imperial schools, so too were Aristotelian studies (primarily logic and natural philosophy) advanced as a preliminary to the higher mysteries of Plato and the Chaldean oracles. In this recovery of all ancient learning, Aristotle's extensive descriptions of earlier Greek thinkers were an invaluable study and research tool.

How far the harmony between Plato and Aristotle extended was a matter of dispute. Most scholars recognized at least some degree of difference between the two thinkers' approaches: Simplicius in a 6th-century commentary to Aristotle's *Categories* (6.27–30) puts the matter wonderfully concisely, stating that Aristotle "always refuses to deviate from nature; he considers even things which are above nature according to their relation to nature. By contrast, the divine Plato, according to Pythagorean usage, examines even natural things insofar as they participate in the things above." This is the image captured later in Raphael's *School of Athens* (1511). Standing next to Plato, Aristotle motions down toward the ground, while his teacher points up toward the sky.

Such differences notwithstanding, the late ancients were convinced that Plato and Aristotle chose complementary rather than opposing lines of investigation and that their worldviews were fundamentally compatible. Aristotle was regarded as a reliable guide to sensible reality, to logic and language, and stories abound of the high regard in which Plato held Aristotle. A later tradition related by al-ʾĀmirī (d. 992) has Plato nicknaming his student simply The Intellect, which simultaneously flatters Aristotle and points out his limitations. For the Neoplatonists there were realities, truths, and delights beyond the intellectual ones: Aristotle might have been "daemonic" ("spiritual," in Āmirī's terms), but only Plato was "divine."

Even as the schools of Athens and Alexandria produced their masterworks of Aristotelian commentary, the scene began to shift outside the bounds of the Greek-speaking world. In the early 6th century the Syriac clergyman Sergius and the Latin senator Boethius, working at opposite ends of a divided empire, both announced their intention of translating all of Aristotle. Initially these would prove false starts, each project reaching only as far as the first few logical works; still, the impetus was there, and this curiously curtailed version of Aristotle proved ultimately significant: the Aristotle encountered by the early Islamic empire and the Latin monks was a master of skilled disputation rather than scientific demonstration. Here there was space for open-ended exploration once again, for a spell, even as a more comprehensive body of work lay tantalizingly just beyond the horizon.

Farther to the east, the Sasanian empire (Persia) also expressed an interest in Aristotelian teaching. Though ultimately short-lived, documents issuing from the court of Chosroes I (d. 578) project this curiosity as going back several centuries. It formed part of an effort to reclaim what the Sasanids maintained were parts of a universal Zoroastrian wisdom, originally codified in the Avesta but scattered in the four winds by the plunderer Alexander the Great. Here the myth of Alexander and Aristotle receives a fresh twist, the latter now being portrayed as preserving an ancient wisdom that the former was keen on destroying. Centuries later, when the philosopher al-Suhrawardī (1154–1191) resuscitated the idea of a Persian Illuminationism, the notion of Aristotle as an essentially Eastern thinker resurfaced. Aristotle appeared to Suhrawardī in a dream and commended Sufism, not Arabic Peripateticism, as the real wisdom (*Opera* 1.70); he pointed to pure self-awareness as a necessary first step in its acquisition.

That Suhrawardī could put such words in Aristotle's mouth reflects the extent to which in the Arabic tradition Aristotle had become an all-purpose sage. The Aristotle of Arabic folklore, like his later Latin counterpart, is a protean figure, a grammarian, a magus, an alchemist, and more. (According to the 12th-century Englishman Alexander Nequam, to pick an example, Aristotle had decreed that his more subtle writings be buried with him, and cast a spell around his tomb so that none would get to them.) Authentic and spurious details mix freely in the lives, florilegia, and gnomological treatises that promise to relate all those crucial details that Aristotle's scholarly works failed to provide. Thus in the medieval treatise *On the Apple* (*De pomo*) Aristotle on his deathbed gets to argue for the immortality of the soul, a most un-Aristotelian position. In a thematically related Jewish legend, Alexander upon conquering Jerusalem comes across Solomon's writings and promptly sends them off to Athens, whereupon Aristotle becomes a proselyte to the Hebrew religion and denounces his previous this-worldly beliefs.

So was the Arabic Aristotle a theist? Yes and no. In the 10th-century *Letters of the Brethren of Purity* (4.179) we find a saying attributed to Muhammad proclaiming that had Aristotle but lived to witness the Prophet's teaching, he would have converted to Islam—but this of course presupposes that he in fact had not. As a Greek, Aristotle early on came to symbolize all manner of secular, foreign learning. (The picture proved enduring: in Enlightenment Germany, for instance, Aristotle again was held up as an example of dangerously secular thought, his views equated with those of Spinoza.)

Then again, the Arabs had learned from the Alexandrians that Aristotle recognized some divine Creator, if not Muhammad's. This fanciful notion had originally been advanced by Ammonius Hermiae in order to bolster Aristotle's standing among the Platonists; in the medieval tradition, it could be used to measure the real distance between the positions of Aristotle and Abraham. Thus we hear of an 8th-century refutation of "Aristotelian theology" by one Hishām ibn al-Hakam. Ghazālī speaks for the emerging consensus when he says that Aristotle is to be counted among the theists (*al-ilāhiyyūn*); that he had provided refutations of all his predecessors, Plato and Socrates included, and he had systematized all previous Greek learning to an unprecedented degree; but that he "was still unable to purge himself entirely of the remnants of their vicious unbelief and innovation." In forming this picture the pseudonymous 9th-century *Theology of Aristotle* (in actuality a paraphrase of Plotinus' *Enneads*) and *Treatise on the Highest Good* (selected theses of Proclus, later known as the *Book of Causes*) were of the highest importance. Without these works, Aristotle does not appear to say much about matters divine: in their light, he appears quite the Platonizing monotheist, another "Moses to the Attics," missing only the light of divine revelation. Even as late as Mulla Sadrā (1571–1640) and the Italian Renaissance one finds appeals to Aristotle's *Theology*, made seemingly in earnest.

These two depictions, Aristotle the theist, Aristotle the scientist, combine in the famous dream of al-Mā'mūn (786–833), in which Aristotle urged the caliph to profess divine unity and to establish in Baghdad a House of Wisdom (*bayt al-hikma*) dedicated to the transmission of Greek learning. The Graeco-Arabic translation movement proved to be of the utmost importance to the nascent Islamic civilization and ultimately to Europe. At its heart stood a series of translations and then retranslations of Aristotle, often made through the mediation of Syriac (Nestorian) teachers. The wide range of commentary works, paraphrasing treatises, and refutations both translated and independently produced testifies to the pride of place that Aristotle occupied in Arabic learning. The same can be said of the more popular summaries that present Aristotelian philosophy as the first stop for logic (for this see *Sophistical Refutations* 183b16–184b8) and the last word for all the other sciences, newly organized and holistically oriented. (Now Plato is made to serve Aristotle!) According to this picture, all that remained for later thinkers to do was to elaborate and amplify, essentially as Alexander of Aphrodisias had done.

That the Aristotelian corpus was nonetheless given a comprehensive reworking for an Arabic-speaking audience by the brilliant Ibn Sīnā (in Latin, Avicenna, 980–1037) speaks volumes about the latter's intellectual confidence and independent-mindedness. Though broadly Peripatetic in outlook and structure, the resulting synthesis can more properly be termed Avicennian than Aristotelian. Subsequent Muslim thinkers began to build on Avicenna, not Aristotle, and so here our story shifts to the Latin world—not, however, before taking into account the contributions of the Andalusian commentator Ibn Rushd (in Latin, Averroës, 1126–1198). It was primarily through Averroës' exhaustive commentary works that the achievements of the Arabic Aristotelians and their Greek predecessors came to be appreciated by medieval Christian and Jewish thinkers. According to Averroës' doting *Proemium to the Physics*, Aristotle either invented or completed the three arts of "logic, natural philosophy, and metaphysics." That nobody since had been able to add to them, or to subtract a word, signified a divine provenance, making of Aristotle "an exemplar given by nature to demonstrate the utmost perfection humanity can reach" (*Commentary on the Soul* 3, comm. 14). Averroës' reverence did much to establish Aristotelian teaching as the apex of rational inquiry for the Latin world. To the 14th-century Averroist John of Jandun (*Questions on Metaphysics*, fol. 84), for instance, subsequent generations were to Aristotle as apes are to a human being—a curious analogy to be drawing in a pre-Darwinian age.

Flowing back into the Latin West, the Arabic (Avicennian as well as Averroist) Aristotle did not encounter a vacuum, of course. Though 12th-century Latin scholars had known Aristotle chiefly as a logician, their close study of these few texts (aided by Boethius' commentary) made of them Aristotelians in a deeper sense willy-nilly, as the *Categories* had already evoked numerous metaphysical issues and *On Interpretation* had touched, for instance, on questions of necessity and contingency. The comprehensive nature of Aristotle's pursuits was already known to John of Salisbury (1120–1180), who saw fit to affix to him above all others the appellation The Philosopher (*Policraticus* 7.6), which soon became a common convention. Thanks to reports from Cicero and Ambrose, the early Middle Ages also knew of Aristotle's belief in the eternity of the world; and his name had become associated with a certain psychological determinism early on. The Arabic philosophers' heavily systematized and theistically interpreted (yet theistically suspect) Aristotle was thus readily recognized by the Europeans. Translations from the Arabic and also from the original Greek proliferated through the late 12th century, and a host of commentary activity followed soon after.

This encounter brought to the surface old, familiar

questions concerning Aristotle's presumed piety. Initially the signs looked promising: the anonymous *Theology* and *Book of Causes,* mentioned above, had provided Aristotle's cosmos with a Neoplatonic superstructure; the similarly spurious *On the World* connected it with Stoic notions of providence and divine rule; the plainly bizarre *Secret of Secrets* gave credence to the notion that Aristotle would have stressed the importance of revelation and prophecy. All this amounted to a picture whereby, for instance, Roger Bacon (1214–1294) could present Aristotle as divinely inspired after his own fashion, as being intuitively acquainted with the notion of the Trinity, and as having commended prayers and sacrifices to it. But Bacon's (and thereafter, e.g., Thomas Bradwardine's) defenses of Aristotle betray the fact that serious doubts were accumulating as to whether such pious portrayals held water. An anonymous 14th-century Franciscan friar could resolve a disputed question on *Whether Aristotle Is Saved* resoundingly in the negative, easy in the knowledge that this was a common opinion. Even Dante, who famously eulogized Aristotle as the "master of those who know," could not bring himself to lift the philosopher above the gloomy recesses of Limbo (*Inferno* 4).

In light of these misgivings it is understandable that the teachings of the potentially explosive natural sciences would be prohibited in Paris in 1210, and again in 1215 and 1220. The bans appear not to have been especially effective, as by 1255 the study of all Aristotle's works was part of the arts curriculum (*Chartularium Universitatis Parisiensis* 1.n. 246). With Paris and Oxford leading the way, this trend ushered in an era of unprecedented Aristotelian dominance throughout the European school system. First the study, then the analytic probing, of all aspects of Aristotle's philosophy came to be considered the backbone of a secular higher education: countless disputations, commentaries, and sets of questions were produced by all the leading Scholastics, sometimes as an end in itself (witness the case of John Buridan, all his life an arts master) but more often as a stepping-stone toward a career in divinity. The question then became whether the Scholastics' broad acceptance of Peripatetic philosophical principles might affect the Church's understanding of Scripture, especially the interpretation of some of its more controversial theses. To some, like the aforementioned Latin Averroists, Aristotle's teachings seemed to have become simply equated with the voice of unfettered natural reason. The famous Parisian condemnations of 1270 and 1277 were clearly directed against such radical Aristotelians, although, as before, the net effect of these crackdowns seems to have been merely a further explosion in the teaching and minute analysis of Aristotle.

What the condemnations did in the end was to liberate Aristotle's Scholastic commentators from the need to treat the philosopher's works as a complete, hermetically sealed package, to be either taken or discarded *in toto.* Rather, the broad backdrop of Aristotelian teaching could then be viewed as a loose set of common principles out of which any one piece could be picked up for detailed examination and scrutiny, improvement, and (in extreme cases) repudiation. Probably the most profound seismic shifts occurred in the field of modal theory (Aristotle's theory of impossibility, possibility, and necessity, the backbone of his more advanced logical investigations and crucial to multiple aspects of Peripatetic metaphysics and physics), but equally significant developments in subjects as diverse as dynamics and moral psychology began to lay the foundations for what much later came to be identified as the modern European worldview. It can plausibly be argued that the post-1277 European philosophical climate more effectively than any period before or since captured the spirit of Aristotle's original Peripatetic school, with its freewheeling mixture of accepted Aristotelian principles and bold intellectual developments. This departure could even be couched in Aristotelian terms: Pierre d'Ailly (1350–1420) pointed out that Aristotle's works contain more dialectic than demonstration and hence, according to Aristotle's own stipulations, more opinion than scientific knowledge.

With the 14th-century translation of Aristotle's works, complete with illustrations, into the French vernacular the Peripatetic conquest of Europe was largely complete. Such dominance inevitably bred resentment: in the late Middle Ages popular encomia of Aristotle the sage were balanced out by tales that portrayed Aristotle the man in distinctly unflattering terms, notably emphasizing his overbearing arrogance. One popular tale has Aristotle fall from grace in particularly humiliating fashion. Hopelessly in love with a courtesan, or else with one of Alexander's female acquaintances, or yet again with his own concubine Herpyllis (who was in point of fact touchingly remembered in Aristotle's genuine and extant will, for which see Diogenes Laertius, *Lives* 5.11–16), Aristotle submits to the woman's riding on his back as one would mount a horse. The tale neatly illustrates the vulnerability to bouts of worldly desire that could afflict the kind of rarefied intellectualism that Aristotle had so forcibly come to represent—a vulnerability that Aristotle would readily have appreciated but that his public image at the time scarcely permitted. Even echoes of the one-intellect controversy found their way into the public consciousness, as Aristotle's supposed fatalism regarding the afterlife acted as a justification for licentiousness in one much-publicized late 13th-century trial. This would prompt questions about Aristotle's suitability for a general education and a Christian Europe.

It was with the advent of the Italian Renaissance that such criticisms of Aristotle really increased in volume. The reasons initially had to do with a rise in fortunes of Platonism, spearheaded by the Byzantine Hellenophile Gemistos Plethon (1360–1452). There had been precedents: even during high Scholasticism, an Augustinian like Henry of Ghent (d. 1293) could declare Platonism more suited to Christian doctrine than Aristotle, and Francis Meyronnes (d. 1328) could at once term Aristotle the best physicist (*optimus physicus*) and worst metaphysician (*pessimus metaphysicus*). But the Renaissance Platonists' resurrection of these old charges, coupled with their added jeers that the Schoolmen preferred Aristotle only because of their limited exposure to the ancient texts, unfortunately had the ring of truth to them. The lines of combat were drawn quickly and (initially at least) fairly clearly: on the one side were the admirers of the full range of ancient culture and learning who resented the prominence given to one thinker (Aristotle) and his garbled legacy (Scholasticism); on the other were the Schoolmen, who under a guise of subservience to Peripatetic teaching were used to having a rather large degree of intellectual latitude, certainly more than the Humanists, with their at times antiquarian interests, seemed ready to give them.

Aristotle's style, too, came under attack from the Humanists. Where Cicero had once praised Aristotle's popular dialogues (now lost to us, save for some fragments) for their fluency, the Humanists, who of course revered Cicero, had in front of them only the crabbed and elliptic scholarly writings. Reviving an ancient simile—Atticus by way of Eusebius—they likened Aristotle to a cuttlefish, which will release an effusion of black ink rather than be captured. This information about cephalopod habits they of course derived from Aristotle (*De partibus animalium* 678b37–679a8).

What to make of these failings in content and presentation? Some were satisfied merely to point out Scholastic infidelities in interpreting the text. Others adopted Ammonius' old explanation, insinuating that deliberate obfuscation was an appropriate tactic in warding off unsubtle minds. Yet others, like Leonardo Bruni (1370–1444) and Ermolao Barbaro (1454–1493), followed Petrarch in blaming stodgy and faulty word-by-word translations, insisting on the need for newer, more eloquent ones. These sometimes lost the technical nature of Aristotle's prose, however, and so the new translations often found their principal audience outside the universities. In the latter, more traditional study methods continued to predominate. Picking up on the controversy depicted in Raphael's *School of Athens,* Jacopo Zabarella (1533–1589) could still put Aristotle forward as a thinker perfectly poised between the sensible and the intelligible, empiricism and rationalism, and both Agostino Nifo and Philipp Melanchthon could find great strength in Aristotle's careful distinction between the disciplines and the approaches appropriate to each. One did not argue for theological precepts in philosophy, after all, and to expect preciseness in ethics or eloquence in the teaching of geometry was to misunderstand the nature of these arts (*Nicomachean Ethics* 1094b12–27, *Rhetoric* 1404a1–12).

The give-and-take had a generally salutary effect, resulting in a new breed of Scholastics who had had to hone their philological skills (and perhaps even learn some Greek!). The Humanists' understanding of the philosophical subtleties of Aristotle also appreciably deepened, resulting in some measure of collaboration or at least healthy cross-pollination. In the universities ancient Greek commentaries were reintroduced to supplement, correct, and (where necessary) oppose Scholastic authorities. The commentators' complex Neoplatonism added heat to the old debate concerning Aristotle's relationship to both Plato and Scripture: every possible permutation was canvassed in a quest to rank not only the three but their interpreters, *graeci, arabes,* and *latini* alike. As regards the former, both *comparatio* and *concordia* became established literary forms in this period. Typical was Pletho's accusation that Aristotle was more interested in the life of shellfish than in the fate of the immortal soul: all in all, a fair charge, though Aristotle would find able defenders, such as the Greeks Gennadios Scholarios (later patriarch of Constantinople) and George of Trebizond (1395–1484).

As far as the latter relationship is concerned, 16th-century Italian Aristotelians—Agostino Nifo, Nicoletto Vernia, and Pietro Pomponazzi, to name but a few—were zealous in their efforts to show the essential compatibility of Aristotle and Scripture: it is here that the late ancient, Arabic, and Latin traditions truly converge. Aristotelians came in all hues in this period, not only Thomist and Scotist but (for example) Themistian and Simplician as well. Averroists might become anti-Averroists at the drop of a hat, and vice versa, provided only that a satisfactory reconciliation between Aristotle and Saint Paul could be found. In the process the authorship of some works was called into question—*Theology, On the World, On the Virtues, On Indivisible Lines*—though some went unquestioned for surprisingly long, and the doubts sometimes extended to authentic works, like the *Nicomachean Ethics.* Erasmus could praise Aristotle but heap scorn upon the Schoolmen who deified him; the net effect of the Humanists' efforts was once again to relegate Aristotle to the headmastership of a particular school, albeit the one that still commanded by far the most institutional support. In fact, through the rise in the number of universities and printing presses, Aristotelian commentaries proliferated as never before. Whole fields of inquiry—zoology, rhetoric, poetics—opened up for renewed attention and commentary activity, and paraphrases like those of Jacques Lefèvre allowed for a condensed assimilation of Aristotle, where previously years of study and dedication had been required. Aristotelian rhetoric and poetics came into their own, the latter in quite spectacular fashion, having previously languished under the banner of logic but now emerging for the first time since Hellenistic Greece in the wider context of ancient literary and oratory theory.

The Reformation further added to the upswing in Aristotelian studies. To Luther, trained by Ockhamists but wary of a fully rationalist theology, Aristotle represented everything that was wrong with Catholicism; yet through Melanchthon's ameliorations, Evangelicals returned to a broadly Aristotelian teaching, omitting only the offensive *Metaphysics.* The Counter-Reformation sought refuge in Thomism: thus, for example, Jesuit missionaries in the *Ratio studiorum* (1585) were enjoined to promulgate Aristotelian philosophy, and especially the syllogistic, in its entirety—a practice that led to early first translations of Aristotle into Chinese. The Coimbra commentators produced many fine works in the old mold, and Aristotelian natural philosophy for a time enjoyed a late blooming both in the Roman Catholic south and through the Protestant north. (To take but one example, at the school of Padua discussions about scientific method contributed to the tradition that would eventually produce Galileo.)

It was not to last. Though Aristotelian curricula in European universities survived well into the 17th century, what emerged out of the tumult of the 15th and 16th centuries was a sullen refusal by those who would style themselves reformers to submit to anything like Aristotle's past predominance ever again. The protest rings loud and clear in Francis Bacon's *New Organon* (1620), from the title onward (see especially 1.63). Where Aristotle had let his own perceptions be contaminated by a flawed methodology, and his followers let themselves be fooled by claims to authority and promises of absolute deduction, the dawning new age of science would be free of such misguided notions, preferring instead independent study and patient induction. Such was the newly found rhetoric of independence, and soon it was everywhere. The philosophers, as ever, were the first on the scene. Descartes maintained a tactful silence, whereas the ever-diplomatic Hobbes expressed outright contempt: "I beleeve that scarce anything can be more absurdly said in naturall Philosophy, than that which is called *Aristotle's Metaphysiques;* nor more repugnant to Governement than much of that hee hath said in his *Politiques;* nor more ignorantly, than a great part of his *Ethiques*" (*Leviathan* ch. 46).

The Schoolmen's blind allegiance to Aristotle had made of philosophy an "Aristotelity": it was the task of modernity to cut through vacuous talk of "entities," "essences," and "substantial forms." This desire to frame a newfound freedom of thought in terms of a break from the Schoolmen and their dreaded "dictator," as Bacon names him, is distinctive of much modern philosophy. At times it appears disingenuous: just as the Schoolmen had cloaked even their most daring innovations in appeals to Aristotle, so the moderns would sometimes blithely pass on traditional teachings as new inventions. (While Locke berates the futility of syllogisms, for instance, it is still the 14 valid Aristotelian moods that he utilizes.) Leibniz is an exception, confessing that his system owes a larger debt to Aristotle's *Physics* than to any modern philosophy: and even if in the end he favors Plato over the "empiricist" Aristotle (compare Kant, *Critique of Pure Reason,* A854/B882), the entelechy of his forceful substances stands out as Aristotelian, all the more so because of most modern theorists' and practicing scientists' comprehensive rejection of Aristotelian final causes.

Kant's lectures on logic are illustrative of attitudes in this supremely shallow period of Aristotelian appreciation. According to Kant, Aristotle had no students of note, only slavish followers: and though he was a brilliant man, in the end Aristotle's dogmatism and his emphasis on demonstration harmed more than helped the cause of philosophy. Scholars in the 21st century will scarcely recognize this caricature, but it is notable how pervasive it was for a while. Even as gentlemen of character and distinction continued to be educated in accordance with the principles spelled out in Aristotle's *Ethics,* and even as the *Poetics* and the *Art of Rhetoric* continued to influence their respective fields to an extraordinary degree, the perceived theoretical value of Aristotle for some time was close to nil. Even Aristotle's logic gradually came to be supplanted during the 19th century, a feat previously considered unthinkable.

Still, at least Kant grudgingly acknowledges that "Aristotle is a serious work" (*Akademie-Ausgabe* 8.393), and it was this seriousness that eventually attracted German philosophers to Aristotle again. Hegel famously remarked that for the earnest philosopher no worthier pursuit existed than to lecture on Aristotle (*Werke* 19.148), and his *Encyclopaedia of the Philosophical Sciences* (1817) closes with an unadorned Greek quote from Aristotle's *Metaphysics* book 12 (Lambda). Furthermore, although Hegel's idealism is a far cry from Aristotle's naturalism, his fusing of inner teleology with life and reason does operate within a genuinely Aristotelian continuum. Unapologetic adoration came from Franz Brentano, who in *Aristotle and His Worldview* (1911) presents himself as brother to Eudemus and Theophrastus, successor to Jacob and the Apostle John—late-born, perhaps, but, he hopes, best-loved. In pursuing a genuinely philosophical psychology, Aristotle thus comes to act as godfather to phenomenology as well.

Yet the 19th-century rehabilitation of Aristotle owes more to German philologists than to the philosophers. What the world gained through the classicists' efforts was not only a set of greatly improved editions but also a renewed appreciation of, and attention to, Aristotle's cultural context in 4th-century Athens. Bekker, Bonitz, Brandis, Trendelenburg, and Zeller all figure into this philological revolution: when Brentano revived Ammonius' presentation of Aristotle as a Creationist, for instance, Zeller rose up in opposition, pointing out that the whole question did not make sense in Aristotle's own intellectual milieu. The controversy was soon joined by the Thomists, reinvigorated by Pope Leo XIII's endorsement of Aquinas (*Aeterni Patris,* 1879, a move that made the Roman Catholic Church a major center for 20th-century Aristotelian studies) and put to rest only with the arrival of Ross's edition of the *Metaphysics* in 1924. The philologists came to reconsider even the possibility that Aristotle's thought might have evolved over the years. On the model of critical biblical scholarship, after all, they had been trained to detect disunity and fault lines, where previously sympathetic scholars tended to seek preestablished harmony.

At the same time, Aristotle's naturalistic inclinations began to be appreciated anew. Darwin in his correspondence calls Aristotle "a wonderful man" (to William Ogle, 1882) and "one of the greatest observers, if not the greatest, who ever lived" (to Crawley, 1879). Though his reliance on final causes continued to be depreciated, Aristotle could at least be championed as an empiricist and analytically minded thinker in opposition to the speculative idealism of Plato. With the rise of logical empiricism in philosophy, the Anglo-American Aristotle acquired a remarkably modern character in contradistinction to the German one (the latter also continued to thrive in the wake of Heidegger and Gadamer). The developmental picture coincides with the empiricist one in Werner Jaeger's *Aristoteles: Grundlegung einer Geschichte seiner Entwicklung* (1923), which was to set the tone for much of the 20th century. In Jaeger's view, Aristotle evolved from a Platonic youth to a mature scientist. Scholars have since come to question almost every aspect of Jaeger's developmental thesis, but few have managed to escape its pull altogether.

In the best 20th-century scholarship Aristotle comes alive as a thinker wrestling with the full weight of the Greek philosophical tradition. The engagement it envisions is affirmative rather than destructive in character: though scholars have learned not to take Aristotle's accounts of early Greek philosophy quite at face value, they still provide our closest, and often philosophically most acute, guide to Presocratic thought and the early life of Plato's Academy. Owing to Aristotle's methodological commitment to finding things to appreciate in the observations of his predecessors (the many, as well as the best), he will also find some in Plato. Contemporary scholars thus concede that the late ancients may have had a point. If Plato's aim had been to unveil the stable and abiding structural features of reality, then Aristotle can be said to have extended this project in the direction of the natural world. The difference would then lie not in the ideals that the two pursued, but in the direction in which their satisfaction was sought. Aristotle believed that the patterns of change in the natural world themselves are susceptible to rational analysis and that this world itself provides the means of its own explanation. No wonder that scientific realists and functionalists of various designations have found in Aristotle an important forerunner.

That most enduring of romantic images, Aristotle tutoring the future conqueror Alexander, likewise has survived into the current age. More evocative than any cinematic portrayal (of which there are several) is an editorial cartoon by the title of *Aristotle Teaches Alexander,* in which the Stagirite solemnly cites B. B. King's *The Glory of Love:* "You've got to give a little/take a little/let your poor heart/break a little." The lesson is not only poignant but to the point, for it is indeed distinctive of Aristotle's brand of ethics not only to enjoin moderation but also to acknowledge the vagaries of fortune and our need to throw ourselves into the pursuit of happiness nonetheless. This seeming openness and malleability of Aristotelian ethics has recommended it to a wide array of otherwise disparate contemporary thinkers, ranging from Martha Nussbaum to Alasdair Macintyre. Likewise, metaphysical inquiry in the sense of a general ontology is still, perhaps more than ever, fixated on Aristotelian questions regarding the nature of being qua being, and this precisely because of Aristotle's aporetic and quizzical (some would say quixotic) manner in pursuing these most subtle matters of "first philosophy." By contrast, it is the firm rules of Aristotelian dramatic theory that have secured a place for Aristotle's *Poetics* in Hollywood; it seems as though our assimilation of Aristotelian teaching is not yet complete, nor is it only of a single character.

BIBL.: Jonathan Barnes, *Aristotle: A Very Short Introduction* (Oxford 1982). Enrico Berti, *Aristotele nel Novecento* (Rome 1992). Ingemar Düring, *Aristotle in the Ancient Biographical Tradition* (Gothenburg 1957). Dimitri Gutas, *Avicenna and the Aristotelian Tradition* (Leiden 1988). Eckhard Kessler, Charles H. Lohr, and Walter Sparn, eds., *Aristotelismus und Renaissance* (Wiesbaden 1988). Jill Kraye, W. F. Ryan, and C. B. Schmitt, eds., *Pseudo-Aristotle in the Middle Ages: The Theology and Other Texts* (London 1986). Norman Kretzmann, Anthony Kenny, and Jan Pinborg, eds., *The Cambridge History of Later Medieval Philosophy* (Cambridge 1982). Paul Moraux, *Der Aristotelismus bei den Griechen,* 3 vols. (Berlin 1973–2001). Riccardo Pozzo, ed., *The Impact of Aristotelianism on Modern Philosophy* (Washington, D.C., 2004). Richard Sorabji, ed., *Aristotle Transformed: The Ancient Commentators and Their Influence* (London 1990). Jürgen Wiesner, ed., *Aristoteles. Werk und Wirkung,* vol. 2, *Kommentierung, Überlieferung, Nachleben* (Berlin 1987).

T.KU.

Armenian Hellenism

"I do not hesitate to call Greece the mother or nurse of the sciences," wrote Moses Khorenats'i (*History of Armenia* 1.2). The Armenians as a distinct people within the greater Iranian empire are attested from the 6th century BCE onward. Following the conquests of Alexander the Great, Armenia emerged as a kingdom in contact with the Greek culture of the eastern Mediterranean, ruled by monarchs of Parthian origin. By the 1st century BCE Greek was well enough known—at least in courtly circles—for King Tigranes' son Artavazdes to gain renown as an author of tragedies and histories, some of which, according to Plutarch, were extant in his day. Greek styles of architecture, mosaic decoration, and coinage were adopted. Nonetheless, even the embrace of Christianity in the early 4th century brought no dramatic break with social organization or traditional ways of life rooted in Iranian culture. The use of an individual script for Armenian and the development of an indigenous literature in the 5th century, however, gradually brought about a more definite orientation toward the Greek-speaking world, though the influence of Christian Syria remained strong.

Before the invention of the script by Mashtots, an ascetic missionary active within and beyond the borders of Armenia, Armenians wrote in Greek, Aramaic, or Syriac. Young Armenians attended the famous schools of Antioch (as pupils of Libanius, for example), Athens, Beirut, or Alexandria; some made careers abroad, such as Prohaeresius in Athens. The lasting influence of Hellenism in Armenia was thus not the result of direct contact with ancient Greece—though Armenians formed part of Xerxes' army in his attack on Greece in 480 BCE—but rather with Greek culture as expounded in the schools of late antiquity and as interpreted in Christian guise. In the 5th century CE a great deal of Greek Christian literature was translated into Armenian, notably the writings of famous patristic writers such as Basil of Caesarea, Gregory of Nazianzus, and John Chrysostom. The playwrights, philosophers, poets, and historians of ancient Greece were known only indirectly, through secondary works of compilation and exposition that circulated as textbooks in the schools of the eastern Mediterranean, and some of that heritage percolated into Armenia. Aphthonius' and Theon's *Progymnasmata* (probably 1st cent. CE) served for rhetoric; Dionysius Thrax's *Grammar* (2nd cent. BCE) was adapted for the Armenian language and sparked a long series of ever more complex original commentaries; Alexandrian commentaries on Aristotle introduced the basics of philosophy, the writer David being adopted as a native Armenian; and the works of Philo exercised considerable influence. Ptolemy, through the intermediary of Pappus, influenced the only serious Armenian *Geography* (ca. 300 CE), and knowledge of the natural world was influenced by Basil of Caesarea's *Hexaemeron* (ca. 378), a cornucopia of ancient lore.

History too was studied, mostly through Christian writers. Thus, the *Ecclesiastical Histories* of Eusebius (ca. 324) and Socrates Scholasticus (ca. 439) in translation provided a broad background for the presentation of Armenian church history. The comprehensive *Chronicle* of Eusebius (1st ed. ca. 310) gave a backdrop for ancient legendary heroes and the exploits of early kings, while the brief *Chronicle* of Hippolytus (early 3rd cent.) set a pattern for later Armenian works of a similar cast. Josephus was admired for his narrative of Armenian participation in international affairs, and the Alexander Romance added less reliable details. But the later Byzantine historians were neglected; Procopius, for example, despite his knowledge of Armenia, was not translated. In the writing of original history and biography, however, Armenians incorporated Hellenistic models into a Christian outlook. Their greatest writers are thus indebted to the Bible, hagiography, homiletics, and theological works of both Greek and Syriac composition as much as to pagan Greek authors.

The significant number of Armenian translations of important texts, some now lost in the original, such as the *Chronicle* of Eusebius, prompted scholarly research in the 19th century. In recent years more attention has been paid to how these translations influenced the development of an original Armenian outlook on the world. Mention must therefore be made of Moses Khorenats'i, the most learned and enthusiastic pro-Greek Armenian historian, who set his country firmly in the ancient past and despised Persian culture; the anonymous author of the *Buzandaran* and Elishe, in contrast, who emphasized the Iranian milieu in which the Armenian church developed; and a host of other scholars and historians who integrated Hellenistic and Christian traditions into an ancient indigenous culture, creating an original matrix for their people.

BIBL.: Richard H. Hovannisian, ed., *The Armenian People*, vol 1, *From Antiquity to the Fourteenth Century* (New York 1997). Jean-Pierre Mahé, "Quadrivium et cursus d'études au VIIe siècle en Arménie et dans le monde byzantin d'après le *K'nikkon* d'Anania Sirakac'i," *Travaux et Mémoires* 10 (1987) 159–206. Abraham Terian, "The Hellenizing School," in *East of Byzantium: Syria and Armenia in the Formative Period,* ed. Nina G. Garsoïan, Thomas F. Mathews, and Robert W. Thomson (Washington, D.C., 1982) 175–186. Robert W. Thomson, *A Bibliography of Classical Armenian Literature to 1500 AD* (Turnhout 1995) esp. 29–88 and 233–287, and *Moses Khorenats'i: History of the Armenians* (Cambridge, Mass., 1978).

R.W.T.

Art History and Criticism

Art history, as a historical narrative, as the categorization or classification of the products of the figurative arts and their producers, presupposes the modern notion of "art," a cultural creation that came about in the 18th century, and that has its heart in artistry as a value and in the delimitation of "art" to creations of the highest quality. Such a notion is more restricted than those covered by the Greek *technē* or by the Latin *ars,* which were commonly used to refer to every kind of know-how or "ability to do" something specific (the cobbler and the physician thus had a *technē,* as did the architect and the painter, the orator and the breeder of horses); classical civilizations, although certainly not shying away from judgments about quality and value, never raised the barriers familiar to us between what deserves to be called art and what does not. The Western tradition of art history is only one part of the literature of art, a much larger sphere that includes treatises on technique, paints, and iconography, such as Theophilus' *Schedula diversarum artium* in the West, and Dionysius of Furna's *Hermeneia* in the East; writings on artistic topography, such as the *Mirabilia urbis Romae* or the *Patria* of Constantinople; the descriptive tradition in poetry and in prose, where each instance of *ekphrasis,* as was the case in classical literatures, can be (rarely) autonomous, or inscribed within a wider textual context; and still other possibilities.

The production of images, including those that could be understood as works of art and often had mixed functions (e.g., magical, religious, aesthetic, political), is an attribute of all known human cultures, all the way back to prehistory. Very few civilizations, however, have developed any kind of art history, in the sense of a specific literary genre or subgenre or a sphere of discourse that arranges in a sequential (historical) narrative the lives of artists, their works, the context in which they operated, and the changeable judgment of their value. The well-established character of art history as an academic discipline in cultures rooted in Europe obscures this basic fact; but it is useful to remember that art has always been done, art history much more rarely. (A parallel can be seen in the Chinese tradition beginning with the Tang era, 618–907.) Therefore the question about the origins of art history, about how it has been understood in the Western tradition, both in the past and in modern times, takes on greater importance. Schlosser's deeply influential *Kunstliteratur* (*Literature on Art,* 1924) identifies its infancy in Lorenzo Ghiberti's three *Commentarii* (ca. 1450), the second of which contains, among other things, biographies of artists. These are, significantly, arranged chronologically and thus follow or imply the unfolding of an evolutionary arc, whose beginning in Graeco-Roman antiquity, taken from Pliny the Elder's *Naturalis historia,* is described in the first *Commentario,* which offers a kind of epitome of Pliny's art historical information. By the Middle Ages Pliny's observations on the arts had been occasionally cited, especially after the Venerable Bede renewed his popularity, and there are nearly 200 extant manuscripts of his work. In particular, Petrarch (who possessed the ms. Paris lat. 6802) used Pliny in two chapters of his *De remediis utriusque fortunae* (ca. 1356–1357), one *"De tabulis pictis"* (ch. 40), the other *"De statuis"* (ch. 41), where he comes to feel admiration for ancient art, although this is corrected by the Augustinian reproof of *vana curiositas.*

The first translator of Pliny into the vernacular, Cristoforo Landino (1476), included brief observations on artists (especially Florentines) in his commentaries on Horace and Dante. A direct or indirect knowledge of Pliny's (but also of Vitruvius') categories and expository style was the necessary prerequisite for every other Italian writing of the 15th and 16th centuries, such as, for example, Antonio Billi's *Libro* (before 1520), which also centered on Florence, and the Magliabechian Anonymous (before 1542). For its part, Ghiberti's *Commentarii,* which although remaining in manuscript form was nevertheless available to various readers—among whom Vasari stands out—increased awareness of Pliny's text and its authority. In the 15th and 16th centuries, historical sketches, compendia of information, and lists of artists and works abounded, always with a strong local emphasis. Let it suffice to recall the presence and tastes of the Neapolitan court reflected in Bartolomeo Facio's *De viris illustribus* (ca. 1456), the poem in terza rima written from the perspective of Urbino by Raphael's father, Giovanni Santi (in particular the *Disputa della pittura,* ca. 1490), Raffaello Maffei's lists of Romans (1506), and, for Venice, the unfinished composition of Marcantonio Michiel (who also sought information from the rest of Italy, requesting, for example, the aid of his correspondent in Naples, Pietro Summonte, 1524). A separate place is occupied by Leon Battista Alberti's original theoretical proposals and linguistic usages. In his *De re aedificatoria* (ca. 1452), he vies with Vitruvius and does not shrink from giving a brief historical digression (book 6). And although he does not offer a historical profile of art in his *De pictura* (ca. 1435) and *De statua* (ca. 1440), he does presuppose the skeleton of one along the lines of Pliny.

These and other pioneering efforts set the stage for Giorgio Vasari's foundational work, the *Vite.* Focusing on Florence and following a tradition that also belonged to historians of the city such as Filippo Villani (ca. 1380), the first and especially the second edition reveal a plan of previously unheard-of proportions. This work is linked to a crowd of forerunners—in addition to those cited above, we can add, for example, Giovan Battista Gelli in Florence and Paolo Giovio in Como—and its immediate and uninterrupted success shows just how much it responded to the expectations of a cultivated public, one that was spurred by the competition among artists and patrons, and especially among collectors, to construct for itself some idea of connoisseurship. This also provides the explanation for why writings on artistic topography, beginning with Francesco Albertini's *Memoriale di molte statue e pitture* of Florence (1510), although following the model of the medieval *Mirabilia urbis,* were tinged with historical observations and recorded attributions to this or that artist. The biographical structure that Vasari chose does not negate a holistic vision (which, on the contrary, runs throughout and hinges on the neat certainty that with Michelangelo art had reached an insurmountable apex); rather, this is articulated by means of individual treatments replete with details and dates, paradigmatic anecdotes, filiations according to schools and workshops, lists of works—the same elements that make up Pliny the Elder's compendium of ancient art history. The Italian model of art history, with its developmental and biographical approach (cultivated in a bumper crop of *vite* like those by Baglione, Passeri, and Baldinucci), gave rise to similar writings in the rest of Europe, such as Karel van Mander's *Schilderboek* (1604), André Félibien's *Entretiens sur les vies et les ouvrages des plus excellens peintres* (1668–1688), Joachim von Sandrart's *Teutsche Akademie* (1674), and Antonio Palomino's *El Parnaso español pintoresco laureado* (1724). A monographic narrative, which absorbed the individual biographies into the broad frame of a unitary artistic development, was achieved only in Germany, with J. J. Winckelmann's *Geschichte der Kunst des Alterthums* (1764). The historical and theoretical structure of this work is truly astounding, but perhaps even more so is the fact that while limited to ancient art history (the Egyptians, Greeks, Romans, Etruscans), and thus making use of classical sources beginning with Pliny, it actually signaled the birth of a new kind of art history: focused on but not restricted to the ancient world, informed by antiquarian erudition but inspired by ethical and pedagogical aims that struck a chord throughout all of Europe. Having at his disposal only the "statues of Rome" and not those of a still nearly unknown Greece, Winckelmann divined ancient art history from an ingenious assortment of classical texts. Their authority was such, and the richness and fascination of Winckelmann's work were such, that his narrative was destined to endure for a long time, even after the marbles of Athens, Aegina, Pergamon, and Samos came to light, and after originals (even if fragmentary) took the place of copies (even if intact). Indeed, new discoveries, from the pediments of Olympia to the Riace bronzes, were used and are still being used to provide confirmation or disproval of the paradigm constructed between the 1st and 3rd centuries and transmitted by the pen of Pliny and other authors (Pausanias, for example). Even the technique of description (*ek-*

phrasis), exemplified especially by Philostratus but also by a host of ad hoc epigrams, "petits musées en vers" (which in the Greek Anthology occupy books 2 and 3 and recur among the votive epigrams of book 6 and the epideictic ones of book 9), reveals in Winckelmann's text not only its evocative capabilities, but also those for hermeneutics and for stylistic analysis.

The enormous panorama that Luigi Lanzi organized by school in his *Storia pittorica della Italia* (1792–1796) is unthinkable without a new cross between Vasari and Winckelmann. Here began evolutionary lines that run all the way to the present, including developments and conflicts of approach and method that it would go beyond our present purpose to describe. We ought nevertheless to recall the shift in the writing of art history, which appears complete at the end of the 18th century, from artists (e.g, Ghiberti, Vasari, Baglione, van Mander, Sandrart, Palomino) to antiquarians and scholars (e.g., Félibien), who sometimes had curatorial responsibilities at major courts (such as Filippo Baldinucci in Florence and especially Winckelmann in Rome). Meanwhile, the once-solid tie between artistic practice and antiquarian research (of which Mantegna and Raphael, Rubens and Poussin were and remain the foremost representatives) was being unraveled; and ultimately antiquarian research, on the one hand, and the historiography of art, on the other, moved from the artist's workshop to the scholar's desk, still informed by the categories and formulas inherited from (and filtered through) Greek and Latin literature. Art history's process of professionalization (with two principal variants: connoisseurs working in museums and in the market, and teachers employed in universities) is exemplified perfectly by the Italo-German Johann Dominicus Fiorillo. Trained as a painter in Rome and Bologna, he taught drawing at the art academy of Göttingen, and, after publishing his five-volume *Geschichte der zeichnenden Künste* (1798–1808), which he based on Lanzi, he held the first chair of art history in all Europe at the university in the same city (1813). Winckelmann's history of Greek art, with its Graeco-Roman ideas and modes of thinking, thus gave birth to a new stage in art history, which the academic culture of the 18th and 19th centuries would enrich without obscuring its original imprint.

This long and desultory process involved the progressive development and stabilization of an art historical discourse that, allowing for a thousand variations in time, place, and distinctive authorial style, is characterized by the recurrence of five principal attributes: (1) the idea of the historical development, or progress, of art, which sometimes is accompanied by the corollary of art's fatal decline; (2) the subdivision of artists into regional schools; (3) the distinguishing and identification of individual artistic personalities, accompanied especially by the related practices of constructing biographies, establishing the lineage of workshops, and making attributions; (4) the judgment of art (or of quality), and related terminologies; and (5) the description (*ekphrasis*) of works of art, out of which only very recently has the study of iconography been developed. All these ideas and practices are rooted in Greek and Latin texts, especially Pliny: the dawning of the historiography of art in Greece and Rome thus acted as a foundation for the entire European tradition. In this sense, for example, many terms borrowed from rhetoric became central elements of art historical terminology; what is more, the very idea of a historical narrative of art, beginning at least with Ghiberti, was taken from Pliny. That Pliny had as sources (and listed most of them as such) a mass of Greek writings on the arts and their history was forcibly stressed as early as Franciscus Junius's *De pictura veterum* (1637), where his list of ancient writers on art has the explicit function of exalting the nobility of painting. (This certainly appealed to his friend Rubens, who received one of the first exemplars of the book as a gift.) Even now art history bears the deep imprint of its origins in Hellenistic-Roman culture, although this is rarely noticed because of the division in the discipline between antiquity and later periods. It will therefore be worthwhile to identify certain characteristic traits in the trajectory of this earliest form of art history, which arose in Greece; otherwise, later developments would be less comprehensible.

Serving as prerequisites for the birth of art history in Greece were the oldest writings of the architects, which were listed by Vitruvius (7.praef.1–9). These texts—for example, those of Theodorus on the Heraion of Samos, of Chersiphron and Metagenes on the Artemision of Ephesos (both before 550 BCE), of Iktinos on the Parthenon, of Philon of Eleusis on the arsenals of the Piraeus—were not historical in character but rather justificatory and descriptive (of the techniques and contrivances of building sites). Only in the mid-5th century BCE was the sphere of technical writing extended to painting (with Agatharchus of Samos's description of the scenery he painted for Aeschylus, ca. 460 BCE) and to sculpture (with Polyclitus' famous *Canon,* small fragments of which survive). Both efforts had theoretical implications that provoked comment from non-artists, for example (according to Vitruvius) Anaxagoras and Democritus. In addition to the description and justification of one's own work, a new element gradually came into play, that of prescription: treatises like the one Apelles dedicated to his student Perseus bear witness to the fact that oral teaching, part and parcel of the practice of the workshop, could now be carried over into the written dimension; even more so does the fact that Apelles' master, Pamphilus of Amphipolis, had written treatises prescribing to his students the study of geometry and mathematics. The entrance of discourse on art into literary space, which implied a potential audience that included non-artists, involved the adoption of specific expository conventions and technical vocabulary, both of which were derived from the *technē* that dominated the cultural horizon: rhetoric. The historico-developmental dimension, perhaps already present in those treatises that held up a particular artistic practice as exemplary (such as the proper proportions of the human body in Polyclitus' *Canon*), came into the foreground in works on renowned painters (or sculptors); this perhaps was already the case in one of Pamphilus' writings, and it certainly was in the two treatises *On Painters* and *On Bronze Sculpture* by Duris of Samos, himself not an artist but a student of Theophrastus and a political leader (ca. 340–280 BCE). Here the decisive step was taken: a true and proper literature of art history, produced outside the workshop, came on the scene and was offered to a more general public. (Polyclitus' text would be cited by Plutarch, Galen, Lucian.) From this point forward works of professional artists had a place on this new horizon, works dedicated to one lone *technē* (the most common titles were *On Painting* and *On Famous Painters, On Sculpture* and *On Renowned Sculptors*) and, needless to say, never to a general history of art in the modern sense. Such were the works of the sculptor Xenocrates of Athens (first half of the 3rd cent. BCE), of the school of Lysippus and Pliny's most important source, and those of his contemporary Antigonus of Carystus, a sculptor as well but also a philosopher and biographer of artists and philosophers. It is on these texts and others like them (all lost) that the later profiles and compendia drew. The most substantial of these are books 34–36 of Pliny's *Natural History*, though quicker syntheses are found, for example, in Cicero and Quintilian.

By the 3rd century BCE, then, the principal elements of the Greek historiography of art were established: the codification of the vocabulary for judging art, the words having been taken from the language of rhetoric (*symmetria, rhythmos, akribeia; prepon* or *convenientia*, translated into English as "suitableness"; *charis* or *gratia*, which by way of a comparison between Apelles and Correggio would live on in Winckelmann's *Grazie;* the pair *ethos* and *pathos*, and so on); the comparison of the development of the various arts; precision in the chronological indications for connecting artistic productions to events (therefore a local calendar was often not used, time being reckoned instead according to the Olympiads); the "artistic biography" that for every artist identified masters, relevant cities and schools, characteristics of his style, and a list of works organized with reference to his period of flourishing (*akmē* or *floruit*). The epideictic and prescriptive use of "exemplary" anecdotes enjoyed special prominence, in part through its rebirth and perpetuation in *Künstlernovellen* from Boccaccio onward, and then in biographies of a Vasarian stamp. A few of the more popular ones in the Renaissance and afterward: Zeuxis' grape, mistaken for a real one by birds; the competition between Apelles and Protogenes over who could draw the finer line; Apelles silencing the cobbler: *ne supra crepidam!* (no further than the sandal!). No less noteworthy was the frequent contrast of drawing to painting, which calls to mind that between Venice (for painting) and Florence-Rome (for drawing). This opposition is firmly rooted in an ancient tradition, depicted first by Quintilian (*Institutio oratoria* 12.10.4), where Zeuxis is the champion of painting and Parrhasius that of drawing: the split between Titian and Raphael thus had an ancient precedent. The definition of special talents in drawing, including contour lines and foreshortening, was an aspect of this contrast, as Pliny recounts in detail (citing Xenocrates and Antigonus) with regard to Parrhasius, who knew that "the extreme outline, to be properly executed, requires to be nicely rounded, and so to terminate as to prove the existence of something more behind it, and thereby disclose that which it also serves to hide" (*Natural History* 30.68, trans. J. Bostock and H. T. Riley).

Two related aspects of ancient art historiography enjoyed the highest prominence in the modern period, recurring in all sorts of texts in the Humanist tradition in Italy and then in the rest of Europe, from Dante and Boccaccio to Filarete: faith in the progress of art (which appears in complete form in the surpassing of Cimabue by Giotto described in *Purgatorio* 11.94–96) and periodization into three grand ages, which can be seen quite clearly in Antonio Manetti's *Vita di Brunelleschi* (ca. 1480). In this popular scheme, the highest achievements of the ancients (the Greeks and Romans, sometimes also the Etruscans) give way to a barbarous and dark *media aetas* in which "oltremontani" (northerners) corrupt the arts in Italy (and concurrently, according to Ghiberti, the Greek, that is Byzantine, style is diffused in Italy), until a new style arises that looks to renew the ancient one; and its founder can be Nicola Pisano, Giotto, or Brunelleschi. The idea of linear progress was thus mixed with a parabolic conception of art's development, and the periodization of art history (among other things) in Europe came to be constructed around its relationship to classical antiquity.

In particular, the idea of a "biological" development of art had a great deal of influence. Modeled on the course of human life, it necessarily had to have "a beginning, a period of growth, a transformation, a decline, and an end" (thus Winckelmann regarding Greek art). This scheme contains in itself the idea not only of progress, but also of symmetry and, equally important for the historiography of art, of decline. Winckelmann adapted to the artistic taste of his own time an evolutionary model that he found already mature in Vasari and destined to be repeated often (but already present in Ghiberti). His contribution was to make it more systematic and thus more effective, having also learned on the authority of Joseph Scaliger's *Thesaurus temporum* (1606) that it was legitimated not only by Pliny but also by other ancient sources. These consonances among Ghiberti, Vasari, Scaliger, Winckelmann, and many others can easily be explained: all were readers of Pliny, and Pliny, like other writers (among them Vitruvius), organizes his information on art history according to a biologico-parabolic scheme, which also happened to be used for rhetoric and poetry in numerous ancient sources (e.g., Cicero and Quintilian).

The rise of this interpretive-expository scheme, which enjoyed great success at least from Ghiberti onward, is explained by Pliny's Greek sources, especially Xenocrates and Antigonus. They placed themselves and their age on the descending part of the parabola, thus taking a retrospective view. This worship of the past, the idea that the apogee of Greek civilization now lay behind them, along with the resulting devaluation of the present, belongs to the cultural horizon of the Hellenistic cities, to the mourning for the classical form of the *polis* after the coming of the Hellenistic monarchies and then of Rome. But it established itself firmly in the Greek historiography of art, and through Pliny it became an essential component of writing on art history from the 15th century onward. The work of Aristotle gave rise to specialized histories of various *technai* (painting and sculpture, but also rhetoric, geometry, philosophy, and medicine), which often adopted the evolutionary principle of which Aristotle himself furnishes an example in his description of the development of tragedy (*Poetics* 1449a): born as improvisation, it grew slowly as the poets developed its capabilities; it thus underwent many changes and finally reached its finished form, at which point its development stopped. His pupil Dicaearchus of Messina adds a final element to this still-nascent conception in his *Life of Greece,* which starting with its very title compares the history of a civilization to the life of an individual. But it was only in the 15th and 16th centuries that the full scope of the biologico-parabolic model theorized by the ancients could be fully reached, with the addition of a new component: after decline or death, rebirth.

It is solely against the background of the biological paradigm adopted from the ancient historiography of art that the idea of Renaissance was able to be born. Indeed, beginning in the 15th century it was based on a terse passage in Pliny's *Natural History* (34.52), according to which in the 121st Olympiad (296–293 BCE) art *cessavit,* and then *revixit* in the 141st Olympiad (156–153 BCE). Pliny, as is clear from the context, was not talking about art in general but about bronze casting. But Lorenzo Ghiberti, translating Pliny's *revixit* as "rinacque" ("was reborn"), contributed to the legitimation of a cyclical periodization, in which classical civilizations, having once passed away, could be roused to new life, or rebirth (*rinascita*). Poliziano's epigram for Giotto, later cited by Vasari in his *Vita,* also contains a citation from Pliny: *Ille ego sum, per quem pictura extincta revixit* ("I am the one who brought painting back from the dead"). The *Proem* of the *Vite* runs along the same lines. There Vasari speaks of the "perfection and ruin and restoration, or better, rebirth" of the arts, and he insists on the parallel between their arc and that of human life. The idea that the decline characteristic of the Middle Ages (already called such) was followed by a "new life of the arts" is clearly expressed in Voltaire's *Siècle de Louis XIV* (1751), but it gained new force after Winckelmann provided a coherent picture of the development of the arts in the ancient world (1764). The 18th-century insistence on decline, exemplified on a large scale by Gibbon's masterpiece (*Decline and Fall of the Roman Empire,* 1776–1788), led to Séroux d'Agincourt's periodization in his *Histoire de l'art par les monumens* (1811–1823), which treated the *décadence* of the 4th century and the *renouvellement* of the 15th. This was a necessary precursor to Michelet's (1840) and Burckhardt's (1860) diffuse genealogy of "Renaisssance."

Here, too, it is possible to see how the Hellenistic historiography of art, even though every one of its texts is lost, has exercised great power in the modern period by way of the citations and compendia of later authors. They have contributed to the formation of the very idea, and the undertaking, of writing a history of the artists and of the arts, but also the categorization of the terminology for describing and judging art, as well as the general lines of a periodization into grand epochs, which found its justification and its popularity in the death and the rebirth of classical art.

In this framework, from the Renaissance onward historical writing on art, which the ancients were accustomed to divide by *technai,* gave way to a synoptic vision of art history as a unitary process. Nevertheless, even this decisive step sought support in the authority of the ancients. Vasari's theory of the arts of design (painting, sculpture, and architecture) presupposes the conceptualization, which Benedetto Varchi (1547) attributes to Aristotle and to a "learned commentator" of his, of a mental form (for Vasari, "design") in the mind of the creator, the originator of every finished art object. Finally, though the artists' rise in social status and their autonomy found eloquent support in the glory (reflected in the sources) of the ancient Greek masters, the diffusion of figurative culture found encouragement not only in the ancient practices of collecting and of discourse on art, but also in even more explicit texts. One such is a passage of Aristotle (*Politics* 8.3.1337b251ff., esp. 1338a18), which for the education of the citizen lists, alongside knowledge of grammar and music and a program of physical exercise, the study of drawing (*graphike*), as "useful for better judging the works of craftsmen." The reborn literature on art history, which took its own legitimation from the ancients, was directed toward the same end.

BIBL.: A. Blunt, *Artistic Theory in Italy, 1450–1660* (Oxford 1940). G. Boehm and H. Pfotenhauer, eds., *Beschreibungskunst-Kunstbeschreibung: Ekphrasis von der Antike bis zur Gegenwart* (Munich 1995). K. Borinski, *Die Antike in Poetik und Kunsttheorie,* 2 vols. (Leipzig 1914–1924). R. Krautheimer, "The Beginnings of Art-Historical Writing in Italy" (1929), in Krautheimer, *Studies in Early Christian, Medieval, and Renaissance Art* (New York 1969) 257–273. P. O. Kristeller, "The Modern System of the Arts: A Study in the History of Aesthetics" (1951–1952), in Kristeller, *Renaissance Thought and the Arts,* 2nd ed. (Princeton 1990) 163–227. U. Kultermann, *The History of Art History* (New York 1993). P. Ganz, M. Gosebruch, N. Meier, and M. Warnke, eds., *Kunst und Kunsttheorie, 1400–1900* (Wiesbaden 1991). M. J. Marek, "Die Rezeption der antiken Kunstliteratur und ihre Voraussetzungen," in Marek, *Ekphrasis und Herrscherallegorie* (Worms 1985) 1 ff. É. Pommmier, ed., *Histoire de l'histoire de l'art,* 2 vols. (Paris 1995–1997). R. Prange, *Geburt der Kunstgeschichte: Philosophische Ästhetik und empirische Wissenschaft* (Cologne 2004). É. Prioux, *Petits musées en vers: Epigramme et discours sur les collections antiques* (Paris 2008). J. von Schlosser, *La letteratura artistica: Manuale delle fonti della storia dell'arte moderna* (1924), ed. O. Kurz (Florence 1974). S. Settis, "La trattatistica delle arti figurative," in *Lo spazio letterario della Grecia antica,* ed. G. Cambiano, L. Canfora, and D. Lanza (Rome 1993) 1.2:469–498. J. Tanner, *The Invention of Art History in Ancient Greece* (Cambridge 2006). S.S.

Translated by Patrick Baker

Asterisk

From the Greek *asteriskos,* "small star"; a polyvalent critical sign in manuscripts or printed texts. Aristophanes of Byzantium and his pupil Aristarchus of Samothrace, the fathers of textual criticism in Ptolemaic Alexandria (3rd–2nd cents. BCE), provided their editions of Homer with a certain number of marginal signs. From the corpora of Homeric scholia and from evidence scattered in the papyri, we learn that the asterisk marked repeated lines in the *Iliad* and *Odyssey.* Diogenes Laertius (ca. 2nd cent. CE) attests (3.66) that asterisks were also used by the editors of Plato's text to mark passages that expounded similar doctrines.

A few centuries later Origen introduced asterisks into the philological study of the Old Testament, to indicate words or *pericopae* (selected passages) that had not been translated in the Septuagint version but whose existence could be inferred by comparison with other Greek translations in the synoptical edition called Hexapla. The passages between asterisks thus appeared twice on the same page, once in Theodotion's version, and once in the Septuagint, where Origen had restored them. The deep meaning of Origen's philological procedure was summarized by Jerome (epist. 106.7): *Origenes signum posuit asterisci, id est, stellam, quae quod prius absconditum videbatur, inluminet, et in medium proferat.* Similar etymological interpretations of the asterisk are given in Epiphanius, *De mensuris et ponderibus* (*On Weights and Measures*) 299; Isidore, *Etymologiae* 1.21.2.

The use of asterisks in the Bible is very important not only because the practice made its way through the Middle Ages (Wyclif in the mid-14th century still speaks of "asterischos" in the prologue to his English version of Chronicles 2), but chiefly because it explains why asterisks soon became the sign of omission par excellence. Starting with the early 16th century, from Marcus Musurus to Justus Lipsius and beyond, it became common for editors of printed texts to use asterisks to indicate textual corruptions or insanable lacunae. This usage, quite popular in critical editions of ancient texts well into the early 20th century, was often parodied by authors pretending to reproduce the defects of their manuscripts, such as Jonathan Swift's *Tale of a Tub* and *Battle of the Books* (both 1704) and Laurence Sterne's *Tristram Shandy* (1760). A special case is Cyrano de Bergerac's joke in Rostand's homonymous drama (1897): descending from Roxane's balcony, Cyrano pretends he is falling down from heaven, adding, "I mean to write the whole thing in a book;/The small gold stars, that, wrapped up in my cloak,/I carried safe away at no small risks,/Will serve for asterisks in the printed page!"

Even today asterisks often "cover for" something. They cover random characters working as "jollies" in computer strings; they cover passwords when we write them on a keyboard; they cover names in top-secret files or in historical novels. Jane Osman's *An Essay in Asterisks* (2004) is a collection of poems devoted to unsaid or inexpressible things.

Yet, perhaps on account of its innate vagueness, through the centuries the sign served other purposes as well. An asterisk placed in the margin to mark the end of an ode by a lyric poet, especially if the following one is in a different meter, a notation seen as early as Aristophanes of Byzantium (Heph. ench. p. 74.5–14 Consbr.), lasts to our day in books of poetry and prose. The asterisk as a sign to connect footnotes, scholia, or integrations to the main body of a text appears in Medieval Greek and Latin manuscripts, from which the usage was passed down in printing to modern times. The sign was introduced in the early 19th century into Indo-European studies to indicate unattested or reconstructed words; more recently it has been used in generative grammar to mark agrammatical words or phrases.

It would be impossible to list all the other countless applications of this sign (multiplication in mathematics, symbol for "born" in typography, multifunction key on telephone keypads, etc.). These attest to the asterisk's potential for infinite evocativeness, which was acutely grasped by Emily Dickinson in 1885: "What are stars but asterisks/to point a human life?"

BIBL.: E. J. Kenney, *The Classical Text* (Berkeley 1974) 155. M. B. Parkes, *Pause and Effect: An Introduction to the History of Punctuation in the West* (Aldershot 1992) 57. F.M.P.

Astérix

A French cartoon character drawn by Albert Uderzo and scripted by René Goscinny. Astérix made his first appearance in the magazine *Pilote* in 1959, and two years later featured in a book, *Astérix le Gaulois.* As of 2007 there have been 32 more books (Uderzo being responsible for the writing after Goscinny's death in 1977), eight animated and three live-action films (with Gérard Depardieu), and numerous other manifestations, including a Disney-like Parc Astérix near Paris and a line of potato chips. The series has also been one of France's main exports in popular culture; the books have been translated into more than 100 languages (including Latin, classical Greek, and Esperanto) and local dialects (Occitan, Mirandese, and Low German, among others), and proved successful in many foreign markets (though less so in the United States and Japan). An official Web site (www.asterix.tm.fr) comes in five languages; detailed research into the series is available through several fan sites. Book-length scholarly analyses have also appeared—most recently Nicolas Rouvière's *Astérix ou les lumières de la civilisation* (2006).

The guiding conceit of the series is that in 50 BCE one village in Gaul has held out against Julius Caesar after the surrender of Vercingetorix in 52. The short, feisty Astérix (who bears some visual resemblance to the American Popeye) and his large, slower-witted companion Obélix—

their names derive from the asterisk (*) and the obelus (†), as if two footnotes to history—sustain this defiant independence in adventures at home and abroad. Roman imperial hegemony is both resisted and twitted. In *Les lauriers de César* (1972), for instance, a need to improve the local cuisine sends Astérix and Obélix to Rome to steal the bay leaves (laurels) that make up Caesar's victory crown; they do so, replacing them with fennel. The switch is not detected in Rome, although Caesar in his triumphal chariot wonders why he keeps thinking of *poisson grillé* (grilled fish). Throughout the series Obélix repeatedly observes, *Ils sont fous ces romains!*—"These Romans are crazy!" or, in Italian, *Sono pazzi questi romani!* (this last phrase abbreviates as SPQR, the time-honored official Latin acronym for the Senate and People of Rome). The ancient conflict shimmers with contemporary relevance, and sometimes the satire is quite direct. In *Obélix et compagnie* (1976) Caius Saugrenus, a recent graduate of the Nouvelle École d'Affranchis de César, subjects the village to an ultimately catastrophic plan of economic modernization; he is unmistakably Jacques Chirac, then Premier of France. The joke even improves slightly in the German edition, where his name becomes Technokratus.

The linguistic and historical playfulness is pervasive. The rule that Gallic names end in *-ix* relies comically on memories of Caesar's *Commentarii* on his campaigns in Gaul (58–52 BCE), as do many of the place names: for example, the four forward Roman posts in Astérix's Gaul are Petibonum, Laudanum, Aquarium, and Babaorum. Characters occasionally speak Latin; at his first appearance in *Astérix le Gaulois* Caesar greets the news of the continued rebellion with an annoyed "*Quid?*" ("What?"). There is a fair amount of proleptic ethnic joking, much of it having to do with food and drink. In *Astérix chez les Bretons* (1966) the tribe across the English Channel takes a break every day at the same hour—even during battle—for a cup of hot water with a bit of milk in it. Astérix introduces them to the herbs they did not know they were waiting for. In *Astérix en Corse* (1973) Corsicans are enmeshed in complicated multigenerational vendettas and make a bad-smelling cheese that is also an explosive. The usual underlying message is genially chauvinist. In *Astérix et Cléopâtre* (1965) Astérix tells the famous queen of Egypt to call on his countrymen if she ever needs anything—such as a passage between the Mediterranean and the Red Sea: the proper readership would need no reminding that it was a French engineer who built the Suez Canal in the 19th century.

BIBL.: N. Rouvière, *Astérix ou les lumières de la civilisation* (Paris 2006). G.B.

Astrology

The study of the heavenly bodies' various influences on the earth. Drawing on fundamental Babylonian contributions, Graeco-Roman culture refined and developed a particular instrument for schematically representing the heavens in relation to a particular time and place on earth (an astrological figure or horoscope) and a systematic doctrine for interpreting the influences of each particular configuration on people and events. The basic elements of classical astrology are the two luminaries (the Sun and Moon) and the five planets (Mercury, Venus, Mars, Jupiter, and Saturn), the twelve signs of the zodiac, and the small set of significant angular relationships among the planets, the planetary aspects. Over the centuries a complex tradition of doctrine and technique developed to enrich astrological practice.

When a person is described as saturnine, jovial, or mercurial, as having a sunny disposition or as being a lunatic, or when arts are described as martial and diseases venereal, these are all linguistic vestiges of a time when astrology was a primary mode of understanding the worlds of nature, politics, and individuals. Of course, astrology continues to exist, in however truncated a form. Although the ubiquitous daily newspaper horoscope is its most well-known representative, there are people today who take astrology very seriously indeed and practice it primarily as a tool for psychological self-understanding.

Astrology employed what were called great conjunctions, originally developed in Sasanid Persia. Saturn (with its 29.5-year orbit) and Jupiter (with its 12) join and rejoin roughly every 20 years in strikingly triangular patterns called great, greater, and greatest conjunctions, which occur every 20, 240, and 960 years; the greatest conjunctions are thought to inaugurate new world orders. Although still considered harbingers of change to astrologers today, great conjunctions no longer refer to Jupiter and Saturn, but to the new "outer planets," Uranus, Neptune, and Pluto, discovered in 1781, 1846, and 1930, respectively, evidence that astrological elements and doctrine have transformed over the years.

But these changes should not blind us to astrology's profound continuity. Developed in antiquity by Babylonians, Greeks, Romans, and Hellenized Egyptians, the astrology articulated in its fullest classical form by Ptolemy in his 2nd-century CE *Tetrabiblos* is easily recognized as much the same discipline, art, or science as that found in astrology textbooks today. With its strikingly consistent structures, astrology has been studied and practiced in—and deeply influenced—many different cultures, East and West, over the last two millennia, and within profoundly different sociopolitical, religious, and scientific contexts.

Classical astrology was created in the Hellenistic Mediterranean, most probably in Egypt around 100 BCE. Its doctrines were framed within the context of contemporary syncretic religious traditions, Aristotelian and Stoic physics, and Babylonian and Greek astronomy.

In Mesopotamia scribes were for centuries deeply involved in the activity of recording, analyzing, and interpreting astral and meteorological phenomena. Their prognostications originally concerned only the fate of rulers or of an entire nation, but in the 6th and 5th centuries BCE a basic form of personal horoscopy developed. Extant Babylonian birth horoscopes (28 in number) span the period

410–69 BCE, the first being three full centuries before our earliest Graeco-Roman examples. These proto-horoscopes provide a list of planetary positions at an individual's time of birth, sometimes with additional data and, in a few cases, basic prognostications.

The most conspicuous element of Babylonian celestial science later incorporated into Greek astrology was the zodiac, which appears in our sources during the 5th century BCE. The zodiac was divided into 12 units of 30 degrees, each as a convenient reference system for mathematical astronomy. These zodiacal units were named after neighboring constellations that had been defined long before.

Babylonian astronomy also exerted a strong influence in the Hellenistic world. The method of calculating the rising times of zodiacal signs proposed by Hypsicles of Alexandria (before 150 BCE), for example, is completely Babylonian in origin. Alexander Jones's recent analysis of Greek papyri from Oxyrhynchus in Egypt provides compelling evidence for the knowledge and popularity of Babylonian planetary theory among hellenized astrologers in Egypt in the early centuries CE.

Babylonian horoscopy reached the Greek world during the last three centuries BCE, but it was not until the Roman period that astrology developed into a full-fledged doctrine with a philosophical rationale rooted in the Greek tradition. From its beginnings in the late 2nd or early 1st century BCE, the science of astrology gradually acquired an astounding level of technical complexity and an elaborate interpretive system. Toward the very end of the Roman Republic (1st cent. BCE) and especially with Augustus (63 BCE–14 CE), astrology attained its mature sociopolitical role in Roman public life. Indeed, the earliest complete astrological text we possess from antiquity is Manilius's Latin epic poem the *Astronomica* (ca. 25 CE).

Astrologers played a conspicuous and notorious role in the public life of late republican and especially imperial Rome. The most powerful individuals came to employ their own personal diviners, turning increasingly to astrologers, including Cicero's friend Nigidius Figulus, for detailed prognostications. In the early empire, Thrasyllus and Balbillus, astrologers to Tiberius and Nero respectively, attained great prominence. Augustus Caesar published on coins his powerful ruling sign, Capricorn, to further legitimate his claims to absolute power. Firmicus Maternus (fl. 330–354 CE) is one of the most influential Roman astrological authors.

Among the important astrological authors who wrote in Greek are Dorotheus of Sidon (1st cent. CE) and Vettius Valens of Antioch (2nd cent.). The former's most important work is the *Pentateuch* (four books on genethlialogy, one on catarchic astrology), whose original is also lost, but which is almost completely preserved in Arabic, though in versions substantially affected by Pahlavi additions.

The most influential text from antiquity is Ptolemy's *Tetrabiblos* (ca. 150 CE). With this book, Ptolemy completed the first phase of astrology's history by systematizing and criticizing earlier contributions, thus placing the subject on a firmer foundation and causing earlier treatments to fall into oblivion. Another text long attributed to Ptolemy was the *Centiloquium,* an influential collection of aphorisms with significant medical application. That it was translated three times into Arabic attests to its great popularity in the Near East and Iran before Islam. The work's pseudonymity was not fully established until the late 19th century by the philologist Franz Boll.

At the beginning of the learned tradition of scientific astrology, Ptolemy in the *Tetrabiblos* formulated the canonical distinction between astronomy and astrology, even though he referred to both by the same term, *astronomia,* which may be neutrally translated as "the science of the stars." Astronomy, aspiring to be an exact science, studies and predicts the *motions* of the sun, moon, and planets using mathematical methods. Astrology, which requires the knowledge gained from astronomy and can never be an exact science, is concerned with the *influences* of the heavenly bodies on the Earth and its inhabitants. Although astrology is a conjectural (stochastic) science, Ptolemy argued strenuously for its utility, comparing it with another useful conjectural body of knowledge, medicine (*Tetrabiblos* 1.2–3). Indeed, medicine and astrology were closely related for the next 1,500 years; there was a particular discipline (*iatromathematics*) devoted to medical astrology.

Ptolemy described two astrological practices in detail: genethlialogy, the science of nativities, which seeks to interpret the celestial configuration at an individual's time of birth or conception, and general or universal astrology, which is concerned with the celestial influences on countries and cities, the causes of major natural and political events, and atmospheric phenomena such as the weather. A third practice, catarchic astrology (elections), which aims to provide the most astrologically propitious time to perform certain actions, developed simultaneously with genethlialogy. Not explicitly dealt with in Ptolemy's *Tetrabiblos,* however, this type of astrology was treated more fully in Dorotheus' *Pentateuch*.

Ptolemy taught that the major celestial bodies, the zodiacal signs, and additional significant points of the ecliptic (including the ascendant and midheaven) form varied and ever-changing combinations that affect the sublunar world.

The basic astrological tool is the horoscope, a schematic diagram representing the ecliptic at the time of the nativity (or other event) in relation to a particular place on earth. The zodiac sign (or degree) rising on the eastern horizon is called the horoscopus, or ascendant. Its inclusion in Greek horoscopes distinguishes them from their Babylonian predecessors; our earliest integral extant example (with a diagram) is a papyrus from 15 or 22 CE. The vast majority of Greek horoscopes preserved in papyri or literary sources, however, lack diagrams, which do not appear regularly until the Byzantine period. The four cardinal points (the cardines) are marked at the left, bottom, right, and top of this diagram, representing the ascendant, lower midheaven, descendant, and upper midheaven, respectively. Each quadrant has three subdivisions, making a total of twelve astrological places (or houses), each representing different features of a person's life—for example, children, friends, and death. (These terrestrial houses should not be confused with the celestial houses, a term often used for the signs of the zodiac.)

Once the structure of the horoscope has been oriented for time and place, the longitudes for each planet (and sometimes the lunar nodes) are then inscribed at the appropriate places on the zodiac, along with other significant ecliptic points, including the lot of fortune and the prorogator, which is used primarily to predict the length of life. The completed horoscope is then interpreted according to a complex series of rules and protocols.

The astrolabe was (and still is) iconic of astronomical and astrological practices. Developed originally in late antique Alexandria, astrolabes had numerous astrological uses, discussed in many treatises, beginning with those of Severus Sebokht (Syriac, 7th cent.) and al-Khwārizmī (ca. 830), and continuing well into the 17th century. An astrolabe allowed the astrologer to determine instantly the ascendant and midheaven and easily work out the further house divisions. In addition, Eastern Islamic astrolabes often had astrological tables engraved on them.

Hellenistic astrology reached India from Graeco-Roman Egypt during the 2nd century CE, where it took root in fertile soil and still plays a vital role today. On the basis of catarchic astrology, the Indians developed the fourth major type of astrological practice, called interrogations, wherein an astrologer answers a wide range of questions using horoscopes. Interrogations often concerned love and money, as well as the sex of expected children. Medical interrogations were an increasingly significant subset.

Between the 3rd and 5th centuries CE, Greek genethlialogical, universal, and catarchic astrology and Indian interrogational astrology were transmitted from India to Sasanian Iran, where Greek astrological and astronomical lore had also arrived directly.

The early decades of the Abbasid dynasty (beginning in 750), with its new capital, Baghdad, offered many exciting opportunities at court for astrologers, most of whom were Iranian. Not surprisingly, Sasanian historical astrology, with its Zoroastrian imperial ideology, found a receptive audience at the Abbasid court, where it was used effectively by the caliphs to further their political agenda. Theophilus of Edessa was court astrologer for the third Abbasid caliph, al-Māhdī (r. 775–785). His putative associate in Baghdad, Stephanus the Philosopher, later went to Constantinople, where he revived the study of astrology and other mathematical disciplines. A number of mathematicians, astronomers, and astrologers active in the 9th and 10th centuries originated from Harran (Roman Carrhae, in northwestern Mesopotamia), home to a surviving sect of pagan astral worshipers and a center of Hellenistic astronomical and astrological learning.

The astrologer par excellence of the Middle Ages was Abū Maʿshar (787–886), known as Albumasar in the Latin world, a prolific and eclectic author who lived in Baghdad. His major contribution was to situate astrology more solidly in the framework of Aristotelian natural philosophy. Also extremely famous was his contemporary al-Kindī, "the philosopher of the Arabs," a true polymath who wrote on a vast range of topics, from metaphysics to magic, including astrology and astrometeorology. His work *De radiis stellarum,* preserved only in its early 13th-century Latin translation, was fundamentally important for providing the natural philosophical foundations of astrological practice in the medieval West.

Many fundamental astrological and astronomical texts —as well as those by Aristotle and the physicians—were translated from Arabic and Greek into Latin, primarily in Italy and Spain, ca. 1130–1250. The major institutional foundation for perpetuating this learning, the medieval universities, was then created in the 13th century. As taught in the best European universities from the 13th into the 17th centuries, astrology was configured as natural knowledge within three distinct scientific disciplines: mathematics, natural philosophy, and medicine. An excellent source for understanding these structures is the 1405 statutes for the University of Bologna, where the multiyear course of study in arts and medicine is spelled out in detail. In addition to mandating the curriculum, the statutes required the professor of astrology at Bologna to make an annual public prognostication, to participate in formal public disputations, and to provide astrological services—free, and in a timely manner—for the scholars of the university. Indeed, if they did not make their annual prognostication, they would not receive their salary.

Astrology served to integrate the highly developed mathematical sciences of antiquity—mathematical astronomy and geography, and geometrical optics (*perspectiva*)—with natural philosophy. Taking a lead from al-Kindī's *De radiis stellarum,* Robert Grosseteste, Albertus Magnus, and Roger Bacon in the 13th century integrated these mathematical disciplines with Aristotelian natural philosophy by developing a geometrical-optical model of planetary influences within the broader cosmological framework provided by mathematical astronomy and geography. This mathematical natural philosophy provided fundamental patterns of interpretation and analysis.

Aristotelian heliocentric structures were fitted into a fundamentally Ptolemaic cosmographic framework composed of mathematical astronomy calibrated with mathematical geography. This framework allows the planetary movements to be uniquely located for any time at any place by means of the horizon. Once the planets can be mapped in this way, and related to each place on earth, their influences may then be analyzed using a geometrical-optical model of planetary influences. The angular relationship of the planets to each other—the planetary aspects—and their collective relationship to each place on earth may then be fully articulated.

But astrology was not only concerned with conceptual

structures and abstract patterns of knowledge; it was also profoundly involved with action and power in the world. We now return to the four main types of astrological praxis—nativities, revolutions, elections, interrogations—and explore some ways astrology interacted with individuals and society in early modern Europe.

Nativities have had many uses throughout their long history. In the 16th century Girolamo Cardano used his own nativity to explore the mysteries of his peculiar autobiography, published for all to see. The first duke of Tuscany, Cosimo I de' Medici (1519–1574), on the other hand, followed Augustus's imperial example in the 16th century by liberally sprinkling Capricornian motifs throughout his iconographic programs. Kepler and Galileo used their patrons' nativities as prefatory motifs in the dedicatory letters to their respectively epoch-making *Astronomia nova* (1609) and *Sidereus nuncius* (1610).

Nativities could also be used—illegally—to predict the death of powerful individuals. The head of an astrologico-political research institute in Rome in the 1620s, Orazio Morandi (d. 1630), publicly predicted Urban VIII's death at a tense political moment, which landed him in prison and inspired some ineffective anti-astrological legislation. A professor of astrology at the University of Padua in the mid-17th century, Andrea Argoli (1570–1657), collected and published the nativities of many powerful people who had died along with a horoscope for the onset (decumbiture) of their last illness, thus providing an empirical sourcebook of potentially valuable political information.

Revolution horoscopes (a type of universal astrology), on the other hand, provided the basis for annual prognostications both before and after the dawn of printing. With printing, however, annual almanacs burst on the stage of European culture as one of the most successful print genres, and one whose message many people in and out of power tried to control. For example, Galeazzo Maria Sforza, duke of Milan (r. 1467–1477), threatened to cut into pieces a professor of astrology at the University of Bologna for a perceived negative prognostication. In England the Stationer's Company had a monopoly from the Crown to print almanacs during the 16th and 17th centuries. During periods of social instability, however, such controls evaporated, and uncensored almanacs were able to dramatically affect public opinion, as William Lilly's *Merlinus Anglicus* did so effectively for the Parliamentarian side during the English civil war.

Elections were used to time the baton of command's transfer in 15th-century Florence and the setting of St. Peter's cornerstone in 16th-century Rome. Perhaps surprisingly, even modern political leaders—most famously Ronald Reagan and François Mitterrand—still consult astrologers for propitious political timing.

Manuscript records of astrological interrogations can be a rich source for both social and medical history. The notorious Simon Forman (1552–1611) kept meticulous records during his many years of medical practice in Elizabethan and Jacobean London. These records include hundreds of interrogations on medical and other topics. Many other rich manuscript resources, including the vast collection acquired by Elias Ashmole (1617–1692), Charles II's astrological adviser, await detailed analyses.

Influential not only in intellectual and political circles, astrology also played a significant cultural role throughout its history. Indeed, astrology permeated Western European culture thoroughly, ramifying broadly and deeply through many domains, literary, visual, monumental, and otherwise. During the Middle Ages astrology informed visual representations in seats of civic power, such as the Sala della Ragione in Padua. Among astrology's most glorious visual expressions during the Renaissance are the fresco cycle at the Palazzo Schifanoia in Ferrara, the astrological iconography of which Aby Warburg so brilliantly deciphered, and the magnificent representation of Agostino Chigi's nativity on the ceiling of the Villa Farnesina in Rome.

Several 15th-century poets, including Lorenzo Bonincontri and Giovanni Gioviano Pontano, composed epic poems on astrological themes inspired by the discovery of Manilius's *Astronomica.* The challenges of this text also attracted the editorial attentions of three extraordinary classical scholars, Joseph Justus Scaliger (1540–1609), Richard Bentley (1662–1742), and A. E. Housman (1859–1936). Writers of history, including Matteo Villani (d. 1363) and Paolo Giovio (1483–1552), adapted astrological structures to explain the patterns of history. Even in philosophy, scholars of the caliber of Marsilio Ficino (1433–1499) wove astrological motifs into their varied writings.

Throughout its long history, astrology also inspired its share of critics, even when it was a dominant form of knowledge. These include Cicero toward the end of the Roman Republic, Sextus Empiricus around 200 CE, and Saint Augustine in the 4th century, who famously challenged astrologers with the case of twins born to the same mother in the same place at nearly the same time, but who nonetheless led completely different lives. There is substantial anti-astrological literature in Arabic, mostly from theologians and philosophers: there are critiques of astrology by Ali ibn Isa (mid-9th cent.), al-Fārābī (d. 950), Avicenna (d. 1037), Averroës (d. 1198), Maimonides (d. 1204), and Ibn Taymiyya (d. 1328). The most articulate defense of astrology was by Abū Maʿshar in his *Great Introduction.* Several late philosophers and theologians, such as Fakhr al-Din al-Razi, Qotb al-Din al-Shirazi, and al-Suhrawardī, were sympathetic to astrology. Most religious scholars, however, especially in Sunni Islam, condemned astrology or discouraged its study.

Astrology's relation to the Western religion is also complex. The Catholic Church was concerned mainly about deterministic astrological practices that threatened to undermine an individual's free will (*liberum arbitrium*). Indeed, Galileo's first brush with the Inquisition in 1604 stemmed from this charge, which was dropped when he was found to be practicing an astrology with appropriate latitude for free will. In a defense of astrology, the widely read *Speculum astronomiae* (ca. 1260) confronted this difficulty head-on. The anonymous author (later taken to be Albertus Magnus) argued that astrology not only did *not* undermine free will but, rather, supported it by providing more information on which to base one's decisions.

Moreover, Roger Bacon and Pierre d'Ailly (among others) taught that astrology could be used positively in the Church's service. Indeed, d'Ailly presented ideas in 1414 to help resolve the Great Schism (1378–1414) by interpreting that situation in terms of the great conjunctions central to historical astrology, proving to his satisfaction that the end would not arrive until 1789. Still, many in the Church opposed referring the origins of the different religions to the doctrine of great conjunctions, since they thought it would thereby limit God's own free will. Likewise, for some churchmen another problematic astrological practice was the repeated attempt to construct and interpret Christ's horoscope.

Within Protestant circles, Calvin and Luther both rejected astrology. Philipp Melanchthon (1497–1560), on the other hand, Luther's ally and the architect of curricular reform within the Lutheran universities, advocated the study of astrology in mathematics, natural philosophy, and medical courses as the best way to understand God's providence. This conflict between Luther and Melanchthon was never resolved.

Some of astrology's more famous critics in the late Middle Ages and the Renaissance were Nicole Oresme and Henry of Hesse in the 14th century, and Giovanni and Gianfrancesco Pico della Mirandola in the late 15th and early 16th. Giovanni Pico's extensive *Disputations against Divinatory Astrology* (1496) is perhaps astrology's most famous critique, however overrated its actual influence. Using a broad range of arguments, Pico aimed to obliterate astrology for primarily religious motivations, including the liberation of religion from its subordination to historical astrology. Fuel for later attacks were the notorious prediction of a great flood in 1524, which never materialized, and the deafening silence concerning the peasants' revolt of 1525, which did.

In the long wake of Pico's *Disputations,* many figures, some of the highest intellectual caliber, responded directly to his legitimate criticisms (in their view) and rejected the spurious. In Italy, Placido Titi (1603–1668), professor of astrology at the University of Pavia, was among the most significant. He set out to reform the nature of the astrological houses. His student Girolamo Vitali published the deeply astrological *Lexicon mathematicum astronomicum geometricum* in Paris in 1668. In England, John Goad (1616–1689) studied in detail the effects of the heavens on the weather for thirty years in his *Astrometeorologica* (1686).

As for astrology and the Scientific Revolution, it has long been thought that the one-two punch of Giovanni Pico's attack on astrology and Copernicus's reorientation of the heavens brought astrology to its knees. The inadequacy of this account becomes obvious once we realize that both Galileo Galilei (1564–1642) and Johannes Kepler (1571–1630), the two main warriors for the Copernican cause, were both practicing astrologers decades after Copernicus's *On the Revolutions of the Heavenly Spheres* was published (1543).

Influenced by Pico's critique, Kepler wanted to reform, not reject, astrology by placing it on a more solid astronomical and natural philosophical foundation, as did Tycho Brahe (1546–1601). Although a practicing astrologer during most of his career, Galileo seems to have been concerned with reforming only natural philosophy, not astrology. Francis Bacon, on the other hand, sought to reform astrology and make its practice more sound, primarily in the two domains of his greatest concern, nature and politics. We can see this clearly in a section of his late *De augmentis scientiarum* (1623), which is devoted to astrological reform.

With Isaac Newton (1642–1723), although a committed alchemist for most of his career, we find no evidence whatsoever of his interest in astrological theory or practice. On the contrary, he seems to have wanted to remove astrology entirely from the realms of legitimate natural and political knowledge.

Although astrology remained in the mathematics, natural philosophy, and medical curricula of the universities of Padua and Bologna until well into the 17th century, we can see a major transitional moment in its removal from the teaching of mathematics in the writings of Christoph Clavius (1537–1612), the primary textbook writer for the vast Jesuit educational network. We can see astrology's rejection most clearly in the works of the Cartesian Jacques Rohault and in Newton. Astrology seems to have lasted longest within the medical curriculum, but the precise contours of its removal have yet to be studied. Political astrology's high-water mark came with the English civil wars and the Interregnum (1643–1660), when William Lilly was the most dramatic and successful of a vast and colorful cast of characters.

With the articulation, reception, and institutional establishment of Newton's natural philosophical reforms, astrology was effectively delegitimized as a form of natural knowledge, which could thus no longer support its claims to political knowledge. An important event in this transformation was Newton's naturalization of comets from an expression of God's direct action in the world, and especially of his wrath, to yet another regular feature of the natural world containing no particular political relevance. Likewise, often subjected to ridicule, almanacs and their annual prognostications became increasingly marginalized in the 18th century, as astrology began its precipitous fall from the highest cultural echelons to the grubbier regions of popular culture on its way to the much more questionable company of the occult and other pseudo-sciences.

Reconfigured as occult or hidden knowledge in the 19th century by the likes of Francis Barrett (*The Magus,* 1801), Eliphas Levi (1810–1875), and Aleister Crowley (1875–1947), astrology joined the other unsavory denizens of the mystical underground, magic, alchemy, and the cabala, with which it is still most often configured today. Lately, however, and at various times in the last century, astrology has had significant recrudescences and periods of broader acceptance. Fears of such resurgences, with their deleterious effects on the weaker-minded, inspired Wayne Shumaker in an influential study (*The Occult Sciences in the Renaissance,* 1972) to explicitly refute contemporary astrology, which he saw all around him at the University of California at Berkeley. Such concerns also prompted 186 scientists to sign a declaration condemning astrology in a 1975 issue of the *Humanist.*

Although astrology in the 20th and early 21st centuries seems to be moving from the occult underworld into the somewhat more respectable neighborhood of Jungian psychology and New Age philosophy, it also occasionally still finds its way into the highest echelons of political power. Astrology thus continues to thrive in contemporary Europe, America, and the East, despite the profound changes in its scientific, religious, and sociopolitical environments, thereby evincing its extraordinary adaptive flexibility, vitality, and longevity. Who knows what its future will bring?

BIBL.: Tamsyn Barton, *Power and Knowledge: Astrology, Physiognomics, and Medicine under the Roman Empire* (Ann Arbor 1994). Bernard S. Capp, *English Almanacs, 1500–1800: Astrology and the Popular Press* (Ithaca 1979). Anthony Grafton, *Cardano's Cosmos: The Worlds and Works of a Renaissance Astrologer* (Cambridge, Mass., 1999). Otto Neugebauer and H. B. van Hoesen, *Greek Horoscopes* (Philadelphia 1959). David Pingree, *From Astral Omens to Astrology: From Babylon to Binaker* (Rome 1997). Francesca Rochberg, *Heavenly Writing: Divination, Horoscopy, and Astronomy in Mesopotamian Culture* (Cambridge 2004). H. Darrel Rutkin, *Reframing the Scientific Revolution: Astrology, Natural Philosophy and the History of Science, ca. 1250–1750* (Dordrecht forthcoming). Aby Warburg, *The Renewal of Pagan Antiquity: Contributions to the Cultural History of the European Renaissance,* trans. David Britt (Los Angeles 1999). David Juste, "History of Western Astrology—Bibliography" (updated 14 February 2008), www2.sas.ac.uk/warburg/institute/astro_bibliointro.htm.

D.RU. & F.CH.

Astronomy

Astronomy's classical heritage consisted of a number of parts. First of all, there was a cosmology that had been built up over five centuries, from the 4th century BCE to the time of Ptolemy (2nd century CE). The key works were Aristotle's *On the Heavens* and Ptolemy's *Planetary Hypotheses.* And then there was the lore of popular astronomy, embodied in poetic works such as Hesiod's *Works and Days* and Aratus's *Phenomena,* in encyclopedic works such as Pliny's *Natural History,* and in textbooks of liberal learning such as Martianus Capella's *Marriage of Philology and Mercury.* A third branch of astronomical learning, mathematical planetary theory, was cultivated by relatively few. Applied astronomy, which constitutes a fourth branch of the subject, included not only *parapegmata* (star calendars) and treatises devoted to specialized subjects, such as the making of sundials, but also a complex material culture consisting of celestial globes, armillary spheres, and instruments designed for observation or for avoiding tedious calculation, such as the astrolabe.

In ancient views, the spherical Earth is located at the center of a spherical cosmos. Each planet is carried along by a spherical shell in which it is embedded. These shells are nested one inside the other, forming a sort of cosmic onion. In earlier times, there had been a debate about the order of the planets, but the standard order was well in place by the 1st century BCE.

Theon of Smyrna (early 2nd century CE) showed how the deferent circles and epicycles of mathematical astronomy are incorporated into the three-dimensional cosmology. The definitive treatment of this issue was Ptolemy's *Planetary Hypotheses,* which not only discussed the physical arrangement of the cosmic spheres, but also worked out the distances of all the celestial bodies from the Earth.

The same cosmos could embody different cultural values. Plato's version of the nested spheres is discussed in book 10 of his *Republic.* Three centuries later, Cicero wrote his own *Republic,* inspired by Plato's but dedicated to an examination of the Roman Republic. Cicero's text, like Plato's, ends with a cosmic vision, the dream of Scipio. Cicero's *Republic* dropped out of circulation and was rediscovered in the 19th century. The "Dream of Scipio," however, circulated separately and attracted a commentary by Macrobius in the 4th century. Macrobius's *Commentary on the Dream of Scipio* enjoyed a great popularity in the Middle Ages. Macrobius also served as one of Dante's sources for the cosmic journey in the *Divine Comedy,* where the concentric levels of hell are an inverted image of the nested celestial spheres.

Transmission of the ancient cosmos across cultural boundaries required surprisingly little adjustment. Macrobius described the outermost sphere as *empyrean,* from the Greek word for "fiery." But by the time of Dante, the Empyrean heaven was regarded as the habitation of God and of the elect. The cosmic onion of the ancient pagans was simply inserted into the Empyrean without any modification of its internal parts. But there was a debate about how the movements of the spheres are regulated. For the ancients, the forms of the motions were prescribed geometrically, but appeal was made to transcendental agents to explain the fact and regularity of the motions themselves; Christian commentators sometimes proposed that the orbs are turned by angels.

The constellations of the ancient sphere represent a mixed tradition. The 12 zodiacal constellations were of Babylonian origin and were adopted by the Greeks, with a few modifications, by the 5th century BCE. But the rest of the now-familiar northern constellations are probably of Greek origin. The oldest known complete description of the celestial sphere was the *Phenomena* of Eudoxus. This has not survived, but it inspired Aratus of Soli to produce a poetic *Phenomena* (ca. 280 BCE), which was extraordinarily popular. The work inspired artistic representations of the sky and was translated into Latin at least four times. Only a few constellations were added later, such as Equuleus and Coma Berenices. Aratus's influence is evident in the *Catasterisms* attributed to Eratosthenes (ca. 230 BCE), who, in turn, was a source for Hyginus's *De astronomia* (perhaps 2nd cent. CE). Among technical astronomers, the ultimate authority was the star catalogue in Ptolemy's *Almagest,* which gave coordinates for more than 1,000 stars. Ptolemy probably based his catalogue on an earlier work of Hipparchus, which has not survived. But, as Ptolemy tells us himself, he altered the figures and descriptions of some of Hipparchus's constellations. Between them, Aratus and Ptolemy did the most to stabilize the names and forms of the constellations.

The Greek constellations were adopted as a matter of course in the Islamic Middle Ages. One of the most important works of Islamic uranography is the *Kitab suwar al-kawakib al-thabita* (*Book on the Constellations of the Fixed Stars*) of al-Sufi (ʿAbd al-Rahman Ibn ʿUmar al-Razi al-Sufi, ca. 974 CE). Al-Sufi gave a catalogue of coordinates, which was simply Ptolemy's star catalogue updated for precession. But he added a paragraph of discussion to each constellation, in which he included old Arabic star names that predated Arabic contact with Greek science. Finally, for each constellation he gave two paintings, one showing the constellation as viewed from inside the celestial sphere (as we see it on the sky) and one showing it as viewed from outside (as we see it on a celestial globe). In an important development, al-Sufi numbered the individual stars in each of his constellation drawings and keyed them to the list of stars in the catalogue.

Though most of the constellation names come from classical antiquity, the same is not true of star names. The ancient Greeks had names for few individual stars—generally just the exceptionally bright ones, such as Sirius, Arcturus, Antares, and Canopus, or those that were important as weather indicators or signs of the seasons, such as the Pleiades and Vindemiatrix (which the Greeks called Protrugeter). Most of the other stars were indicated in Ptolemy's star catalogue in terms of their positions in the constellations (e.g., "the star on the end of the tail" of Leo). Arabic astronomers then tended to make literal translations of these descriptions, and when their works were translated into Latin these names were often compacted or corrupted. For example, the same star was called in Arabic *dhanab al-asad,* "the tail of the lion," from which we get the modern European name Denebola. But some modern star names descend from Arabic names that have no counterpart in the classical tradition. For example, our Vega is a corruption of [*al-nasr*] *al-waqi*ʿ, "the swooping [vulture]." In 1603 Johann Bayer, in his celestial atlas, *Uranometria,* introduced the modern custom of labeling the stars in each constellation with Greek letters. A particular star is indicated by its Greek Bayer letter and the Latin constellation name in the genitive case. Thus Rigel = β Orionis. (The recent trend is to use a three-letter abbreviation of the constellation name: β Ori.)

The classical tradition proved remarkably resistant to change. In 1627 Julius Schiller published his *Coelum stellatum Christianum,* in which the classical constellations were renamed in an attempt to Christianize the sphere. For example, the 12 zodiacal constellations became the 12 apostles. Blatantly political imagery was sometimes introduced in an attempt to flatter royal patrons. For example, Johannes Hevelius (1611–1687) introduced a constellation called Scutum Sobiescianum (Shield of Sobieski), after Jan Sobieski, the king of Poland. But neither religion nor politics has succeeded in breaking the hold of the ancient Greeks and Romans on the night sky.

The strength of the classical tradition is also evident in the nomenclature for planets and their satellites. In 1609, using the newly invented telescope, Galileo discovered four satellites moving around Jupiter. He thought to cash in by naming them for his prospective patron, Cosimo de'Medici. Galileo wrote to inquire whether the duke would prefer to have them named *Cosmian* stars, after himself, or, since they were four in number, *Medicean* stars, after the duke and his three brothers. The duke opted for the latter, and this is the name that appeared on the title page of Galileo's *Siderius nuncius.* The astronomical community of the 17th century refused to go along, and these bodies acquired classical names, Ganymede, Io, Europa, and Callisto. Collectively, they are informally called the Galilean satellites.

A similar instance occurred in 1781, when William Herschel discovered an object that he first took to be a comet, but which was soon shown to be a new planet. Taking advice from the English scientific community, he proposed to name it *Georgium sidus,* "the Georgian star," so that it would always be remembered that this planet had been discovered during the reign of George III. There was a classical precedent, *Julium sidus,* the Julian star mentioned by Horace and Virgil. Not surprisingly, continental astronomers refused to go along with Herschel's proposal. Cybele and Neptune were both proposed as names—the latter would be resurrected the next time a planet was discovered. In 1783 Johann Elert Bode proposed the name Uranus; Bode wrote to Herschel that it would be better to go back to mythology.

In 2003 Michael Brown, Chad Trujillo, and David Rabinowitz photographed a dim object that their analysis soon revealed to be a small and very distant planetlike object with a satellite. These they named Xena and Gabrielle, after the pseudoclassical characters in a popular television series, *Xena: Warrior Princess.* The International Astronomical Union, which has authority over the naming of celestial objects, took a dim view of this proposal and assigned to Xena the temporary name 2003 UB313. Finally, in September 2006, accepting an official proposal by the discoverers themselves, the IAU assigned the name Eris to the new minor planet and Dysnomia to the companion. Eris ("strife") is personified in the *Theogony* of

Hesiod, who also makes Dysnomia ("lawlessness") one of her offspring. Michael Brown, in his Web site, points out that the name Eris still makes a nod to *Xena,* since the Roman version of this goddess's name, Discordia, was that of a minor character who appeared from time to time on the television show.

Ptolemy's key devices for explaining the motions of the Sun, Moon, and planets are deferent circles and epicycles. To take the simplest case first, the Sun travels on a perfect circle at a constant speed. It is a fact, however, that the four seasons are not all of the same length, so it is necessary to place the Sun's circle slightly off-center from the Earth. Though the general idea may have been proposed by Apollonius of Perga (ca. 220 BCE), the first derivation of the amount and direction of the eccentricity (or off-centeredness) was that of Hipparchus, about 150 BCE. Ptolemy in his *Almagest* adopted the same theory. Indeed, this theory of the motion of the Sun prevailed until Kepler's time. Copernicus put the Sun at rest in the middle of things, but he let the Earth travel at a constant speed on an off-center circle. An off-center solar circle was often figured on the backs of European astrolabes.

Ptolemy's introduction of nonuniform motion into the theory of the planets represented a severe violation of Aristotelian physical principles, for which he was to be criticized in the Middle Ages. The planets really do move nonuniformly, however, and Ptolemy's manner of handling this fact turned out to be very accurate. In a later work, the *Handy Tables,* Ptolemy extended his work; the tables were designed for convenience and quick, routine calculation—by a working astrologer, for example.

The *Almagest* and the *Handy Tables* represent the high road of Greek planetary theory and come from its final, most mature stage. During the period between Hipparchus and Ptolemy, Greek astronomers experimented with a variety of theories. In particular, they learned and creatively adapted arithmetical methods borrowed from the Babylonians. The dates and locations in the zodiac of important events in the planet's cycle (for example, the beginning of Mars's retrogradation) are calculated directly, without any need to visualize a physical model. Papyri from Egypt show Greek writers using Babylonian arithmetical theories with complete facility in the 2nd century CE, right alongside the methods based on Ptolemy's *Almagest* and *Handy Tables.* But in the writings by later Greek astronomers and philosophers, such as Theon of Alexandria (4th cent. CE) and Proclus (5th cent.), the numerical methods were never mentioned: the earliest histories of Greek astronomy were written by thinkers of the high road, who emphasized geometry and philosophical principles.

Babylonian astronomy entered India from Persia in the late 5th century BCE, following the Achaemenid dynasty's conquest of northwestern India. Examples of Babylonian influence include the equal-sign zodiac and arithmetical rules for calculating the length of daylight. A greater wave of transmission occurred during the Seleucid period (roughly the last three centuries BCE). Babylonian arithmetical methods were again transmitted, but this time often in modified forms showing Greek influence. The history of this transmission is complex. Greek geometrical theories from the time between Hipparchus and Ptolemy also made their way into India. This was the period in which Greek astronomers were still struggling to find a satisfactory way of handling the planets. One attempt, based on a double epicycle, was modified in India in highly original ways. This material is of the greatest complexity and heterogeneity and is often difficult to sort out. Nevertheless, it provides information about the status of Greek astronomy during a vital period concerning which the classical texts have little to tell us.

In the 8th century Arabic Muslim astronomers came into contact with this complicated astronomical material. Models and procedures that had passed from the Babylonians and Greeks through Persia and into India now came back to the West. A good example is provided by the *zij* of Muhammad ibn Musa al-Khwarizmi (early 9th cent.). (The original Arabic version no longer exists, but the text is preserved in a 12th-century Latin translation by Adelard of Bath). Al-Khwārizmī's work helped establish an important genre, that of the *zij.* A *zij* is a handbook of astronomical tables, including tables for working out positions of the Sun, Moon, and planets, often accompanied by auxiliary material, such as trigonometric tables and chronological lists, as well as the all-important directions for using them. The ancient prototype of such a work is Ptolemy's *Handy Tables.*

In the 8th and 9th centuries Ptolemy's *Almagest* was translated, first into Syriac and then at least four times into Arabic. With the pure, geometrical form of Greek planetary theory now available, Arabic astronomers worked to master it and then to improve on it. The important *zij* of al-Battānī (Abu ʿAbd Allah Muhammad ibn Jabir ibn Sinan al-Raqqi al-Harrani al-Sabi, ca. 910) shows full mastery of Ptolemaic planetary theory. Scholars now know of about 200 Arabic *zij*es, spanning the period from the 9th to the 15th century. Some are based on the Indian methods, but the great majority are in the tradition of the *Almagest* and the *Handy Tables.* The *zij* most influential in the development of European astronomy was the *Toledan Tables,* compiled in Spain by a group of Muslim and Jewish astronomers, put into final form by Ibn al-Zarqallu around 1080, and translated into Latin soon after. It contains new tables for the mean motions, but most of the rest of the material was borrowed from the *zij*es of al-Khwārizmī and al-Battānī.

As one of the "foreign sciences" borrowed from the Greeks, astronomy had an ambiguous position in Islam. It could be attacked by the pious as unnecessary, or even as dangerous to faith and culture. Mathematics and theoretical astronomy, however, were never as vulnerable to such attacks as were astrology and Greek philosophy of nature. Through a process of Islamization, astronomy was comfortably integrated into the culture. Moreover, astronomy soon began to render technical services to the faith, in three specific ways: calculation or measurement of daily prayer times based on shadow lengths, tables for the first visibility of the crescent Moon (which governed the beginnings of months), and techniques for determining the direction of Mecca at an arbitrary location on the surface of the Earth. Large numbers of specialized treatises on these problems are preserved in manuscript.

With the revival of astronomy and the passage of time, new discoveries came to be made, notably those that depended on the detection of slow changes in the heavens. In the early 9th century the Baghdad astronomers observed that the obliquity of the ecliptic had decreased from the value given in Ptolemy's *Almagest.* The obliquity of the ecliptic is the angle between the celestial equator and the tropic of Cancer. It corresponds to the northward displacement of the Sun between the equinox and the summer solstice. It is one of the easiest parameters to measure in all astronomy, and it can be determined simply by means of noon altitudes of the Sun taken at key times of the year. Between Ptolemy's day and our own, the obliquity of the ecliptic has decreased by about a quarter of a degree.

In some cases Arabic astronomers had to grapple with the effects of uncertainty in measurements left by their Greek predecessors. For example, Ptolemy had put the rate of precession at one degree in 100 years, but by the 9th century it was easy to see that Ptolemy's rate was too slow. (Precession is the slow apparent eastward rotation of the sphere of stars about the pole of the ecliptic. Today it is regarded as due to a toplike motion of the axis of the Earth.) In the 9th century Thabit ibn Qurra devised an ingenious scheme to account for both the decrease in the obliquity of the ecliptic and the variable rate of precession. (The attribution to Thabit has been questioned.) It is ironic that Thabit's theory explained both a real phenomenon (the decrease in the obliquity of the ecliptic) and an illusory one (the supposedly variable rate of precession). For in fact the precession rate is steady, to the precision of ancient and medieval astronomy, and Thabit had been misled by faith in Ptolemy's measurements. Thabit's theory had little influence in the East, where, for example, al-Battānī adopted a uniform precession of one degree in 66 years. But it was more influential in Moorish Spain, where it appeared in the *Toledan Tables,* from which it passed into European astronomy. In Thabit's theory, the sphere of fixed stars does not precess steadily forward, as Ptolemy claimed, but rather rocks back and forth over an interval of plus or minus 8 degrees, called trepidation.

It soon became apparent, however, that the stars would not be restricted to the 8-degree excursions prescribed by Thabit. Thus, in the 14th-century *Alfonsine Tables* (the dominant European planetary tables for the last centuries of the Middle Ages), the trepidation invented by Thabit was combined with the steady precession described by Ptolemy. The theory of trepidation continued to disfigure European astronomy until Tycho Brahe showed that the precession rate really had been uniform since the time of Ptolemy. This misguided theory is extremely interesting for the light it throws on the efforts of the medieval astronomers to properly evaluate, and to become independent of, the ancient astronomical heritage.

A tradition of criticism of Ptolemy's planetary theory eventually emerged. Minor disagreements between Ptolemy's tables and the actual motions of the planets did not play a significant role in this criticism. Rather, most of it centered on Ptolemy's violation of the Aristotelian principle of the uniformity of the celestial motions. Such was the case in *Doubts about Ptolemy* (ca. 1000), by Ibn al-Haytham (Al-Hasan ibn al-Hasan ibn al-Haytham, known as Alhazen in Latin Europe). Ibn al-Haytham was not, however, a complete skeptic about the ancient system of the world, since he also wrote *On the Configuration of the World,* an elementary survey of Ptolemaic astronomy.

Ibn al-Haytham's doubts about the technical details of Ptolemaic planetary theory inspired some creative mathematical modeling by 13th-century astronomers associated with the observatory of Maragha (in northwest Iran). Nasir al-Din al-Tusi (Abu Jaʿfar Muhammad ibn Muhammad ibn al-Hasan Nasir al-Din al-Tusi, 1201–1274 CE) described a construction whereby two circular motions can give rise to the oscillation of a point back and forth along on a straight line. Ptolemy's theories of Mercury and of the Moon involved oscillatory movements for which the standard mechanisms seemed philosophically questionable. Tusi was able to apply his two-circle mechanism (called a Tusi couple by modern scholars) to produce essentially the same phenomena in what seemed a physically more plausible way. These constructions were described in his *Memoir (Tadhkira) on the Science of Astronomy.* In the next century Ibn al-Shatir of Damascus (1304–1375) built on the works of the Maragha school in his *Final Inquiry concerning the Rectification of Planetary Theory,* which was also characterized by the elimination of nonuniform motions in favor of minor epicycles. Ibn al-Shatir was also the author of two *zijes*. An early one that has not survived was based on standard Ptolemaic theory. But a later one, still extant in manuscript, was based on his own non-Ptolemaic models. These efforts did not succeed in transforming common practice, however, since the overwhelming majority of late medieval planetary tables are Ptolemaic in their underlying theory.

But in the 16th century Nicholas Copernicus, in his *Commentariolus* and *On the Revolutions of the Heavenly Spheres,* employed models identical to those of Ibn al-Shatir and the Maragha school. How he came by them we do not know, but there are too many of them for independent discovery to have been. These technical "improvements" on Ptolemy do not bear in any way on the heliocentric hypothesis. But they remind us that Copernicus was heir to a tradition of critical engagement with Ptolemy.

In the Latin West of the early Middle Ages, neither Ptolemy nor Aristotle was available. The teaching of astronomy depended on several low-level texts of Roman antiquity, including the astronomical portions of Pliny's

Natural History. Three other works provided somewhat more detail: Macrobius's *Commentary on the Dream of Scipio,* Calcidius's (4th cent. CE) work on Plato's *Timaeus,* and Martianus Capella's *Marriage of Philology and Mercury* (5th cent. CE). Calcidius made a translation of the first half of Plato's *Timaeus,* which he equipped with a commentary that included remarks on epicycles and deferents. In the Middle Ages this was sometimes a source of confusion, since the *Timaeus* belonged to the earliest (and prescientific) stages of Greek cosmology. In Martianus' work, Mercury is wedded to Philology in two introductory allegorical books. These are followed by seven further books, in which each of the seven liberal arts, personified, speaks about her specialty, thus providing a compendium of universal learning that was widely admired. All these works played a role in the study and teaching of astronomy in the 9th-century Carolingian renaissance.

The desire to recover ancient Greek astronomy was a stimulus to the translation movement of the 12th century. Many people made translations, but one of the most prolific and influential was Gerard of Cremona. Gerard translated, from Arabic versions, not only Ptolemy's *Almagest,* but also Aristotle's *On the Heavens,* Euclid's *Elements,* and about two dozen other works of astronomy and geometry. In a single generation, most of the key works of ancient astronomy became available.

With the establishment of the universities, beginning around 1200, astronomy received a crucial stimulus through its place in the Quadrivium, the upper-level tier of the liberal arts curriculum. The mathematical arts of the Quadrivium (arithmetic, geometry, music theory, and astronomy) went all the way back to Plato's *Republic,* where they were prescribed for the education of the guardians of Plato's ideal state. The level of astronomical instruction in the arts curriculum was rather low. Students might be taken through an introduction to the theory of the celestial sphere, such as the *Sphere* of Sacrobosco (John of Holywood, early 13th cent.). Sacrobosco's text paralleled the ancient primers of astronomy by treating day and night, the annual motion of the Sun, and the circles of the celestial sphere. But it reflected the concerns of its own time by taking up the question of whether the eclipse of the Sun that, according to the Gospels, followed the crucifixion of Jesus should be considered miraculous, since it came during the Jewish Passover—around the time of a full (rather than a new) Moon. Sacrobosco might be followed by an introduction to the planets, perhaps with the aid of the anonymous 13th-century *Theorica planetarum,* which was sometimes wrongly attributed to Gerard of Cremona, and which introduced the notions of deferent circles and epicycles. This level of instruction would not prepare a student to read Ptolemy with understanding or to do original work in astronomy. But it did guarantee a certain level of astronomical activity in the late medieval world, since every university town had to have a mathematician capable of teaching the subject.

By the 15th century the inadequacies of the standard teaching texts were keenly felt. In the 1450s Georg Peurbach (1423–1461) wrote *Theoricae novae planetarum,* so titled not because it contained any new theories, but because it was intended as a teaching text to replace the earlier *Theorica planetarum.* Peurbach's text was printed posthumously in 1472 as the first book off the press of his student Regiomontanus (Johann Müller, 1436–1476), who established at Nuremberg the first publishing house devoted to scientific works. Peurbach's text very clearly explained the basics of Ptolemy's planetary theory, as well as the Ptolemaic version of solid-sphere cosmology, for which Peurbach drew on Ibn al-Haytham's *On the Configuration of the World,* or some source dependent on it. Peurbach's text became extraordinarily popular, and no fewer than 56 editions, including translations and commentaries, were printed between 1472 and 1653. It was not until Regiomontanus's own *Epitome of the Almagest* (begun by Peurbach, completed by Regiomontanus in the 1460s, but not published until 1496), however, that western Europe produced an astronomer able to confront Ptolemy as an equal. Regiomontanus did not hesitate to criticize Ptolemy. For example, he pointed out that the twofold variation in the distance of the Moon implied by Ptolemy's lunar theory far exceeded the actual variation in distance revealed by the Moon's variation in apparent size. Although this fact had earlier been pointed out in Arabic astronomy, this was its first mention in a text produced in the Latin West.

The tools of astronomy in the Middle Ages and the Renaissance were largely (though not exclusively) those that had been developed by the close of antiquity. These included the astrolabe, which became the very symbol of astronomical learning in the Middle Ages. It was once thought that the astrolabe was an invention of medieval Islam, since the earliest datable examples all come from eastern Islam, but it was in fact an invention of Greek antiquity. A manual describing the construction and use of the astrolabe may have been written by Theon of Alexandria. This does not survive, but a list of its contents does, along with two later treatises that were obviously dependent on it, one in Greek by John Philoponus (ca. 625) and one in Syriac by Severus Sebokht (ca. 650). In the Islamic Middle Ages the astrolabe was developed into an instrument of great beauty and flexibility. New kinds of scales and curves were added to the instrument, facilitating the calculation of prayer times, and whole new varieties of astrolabes (e.g., the universal astrolabe, good for any latitude) were invented. Treatises on the astrolabe were written in Arabic, and then in Latin. By the 12th century the astrolabe had arrived in Paris, where it must have made quite an impression, for Abelard and Héloïse named their only son Astrolabe. The oldest moderately sophisticated scientific work in the English language is a *Treatise on the Astrolabe,* written by Geoffrey Chaucer and addressed to his 10-year-old son, Lewis.

A second noteworthy instrument is the equatorium. A planetary equatorium functions as a specialized analogue computer, which permits the user to rapidly determine the position of a planet in the zodiac for any desired date. Such instruments could be made of wood or, more often, of paper or parchment. It is possible that the ancient Greeks made planetary equatoria, for Ptolemy remarks, in his introduction to the *Handy Tables,* that it is possible to calculate the positions of the planets by drawing scale diagrams. It is but a short step further to make the diagrams reusable by adding moving parts. The oldest extant works on planetary equatoria are 13th-century Castilian translations of two 11th-century Arabic works from Spain, one by Ibn al-Samh of Granada and the other by al-Zarqallu, who is best known for his canons (or directions) to the famous *Toledan Tables.*

Equatoria entered medieval Latin astronomy right along with Ptolemaic planetary theory itself. The first comprehensive introduction to Ptolemy written in the Latin West was the *Theorica planetarum* by Campanus of Novara (13th cent.) (not to be confused with the anonymous *Theorica planetarum* mentioned above). Campanus's text contains directions for making and using an equatorium, and the best of the extant manuscripts contain actual equatoria with movable paper circles called volvelles. The earliest work on the subject in English is an anonymous 14th-century treatise, *The Equatorie of the Planetis.* Derek J. Price (1955) argues, on the basis of handwriting and other evidence, that it was composed and written by Geoffrey Chaucer. The first printed equatoria were designed and published by Johann Schöner (1477–1547).

The works of Nicholas Copernicus (1473–1543) and Johannes Kepler (1571–1630) represent the culmination of the ancient astronomical tradition. Copernicus announced the motion of the Earth in *On the Revolutions of the Heavenly Spheres* (1543). But his preliminary sketch of the theory, the *Commentariolus,* had earlier circulated in manuscript in the astronomical community of central Europe. And in 1540 Copernicus's disciple Georg Joachim Rheticus (1514–1574) had offered the first printed glimpse of the theory in his *Narratio prima.* Rheticus was fully aware of the importance of Copernicus's ideas, for he said that Copernicus was worthy of comparison to Ptolemy, as he was preparing the reform of all of astronomy.

Although Copernicus made some observations of the planets, new observations played no role in the discovery of the motion of the Earth. The essential clues lay there in the *Almagest* for all to see. For example, in Ptolemy's theory, the three outer planets (Mars, Jupiter, and Saturn) remain in lockstep with one another and with the Sun as they move around their epicycles. In ancient astronomy, there was no natural explanation of this rather amazing coincidence. But, in book 9 of the *Almagest,* Ptolemy points out that it can be used to reduce the number of calculations if one wants to work up the positions of all the planets for a given date: if you have worked out the position of Mars on its epicycle, there is no need to calculate the positions of Jupiter and Saturn on their epicycles, for they must be just the same. It was Copernicus's insight to realize that when there are several motions that stay in step with the motion of the Sun, they might all, in fact, be manifestations of the Earth's motion around the Sun. Thus, in the case of the outer planets, the large epicycles of Ptolemy do not exist. Rather, as we move around the Sun in our own circular orbit, we see these bodies *apparently* moving in lockstep with one another in circular motions that we *interpret* as motions on epicycles. Their motions on their epicycles are really our projection of our own motion onto them.

Similar considerations apply to the inner planets, Mercury and Venus. They are always close companions of the Sun; that is, they complete their motions around their deferent circles in exactly one year. But their motions on their epicycles are free. Historically, it was much easier for people to see the heliocentric possibility in the case of the inner planets. Even in antiquity, Theon of Smyrna had proposed that Venus and Mercury might circle the Sun, while the Sun and the other planets circle the Earth. Copernicus's boldness lay in a systematic treatment of all the planets, so that every motion that had a period of one year was eliminated and recognized as a manifestation of the Earth's motion.

As a consequence, Copernicus was able to deduce the actual distances of the planets from the Sun, taking the Sun-Earth distance as the unit of measure. In Ptolemy, astronomical observations can be used in the case of each planet to determine the ratio of the epicycle's radius to that of the deferent. But the systems for the individual planets are astronomically separate: there is no way to tell how big the deferent of Jupiter is compared to the deferent of Mars. Copernicus criticized this aspect of Ptolemy's theory in the introduction to *On the Revolutions.* He realized that the epicycles of the superior planets and the deferents of the inferior planets (in Ptolemy's system) should all be the same size—for they were all merely reflections of the Earth's own circle (in Copernicus's system). In Copernicus's theory, the systems of the individual planets form a coherent whole, united by a common scale of measure. This is an aspect of his theory on which Copernicus placed great importance.

In the technical details of his planetary theory, however, Copernicus was much more conservative. Indeed, he regarded himself as a purer Aristotelian than Ptolemy. Rejecting nonuniformity of motion, Copernicus replaced Ptolemy's equant point with a minor epicycle. This results in a theory that is nearly equivalent to Ptolemy's, with no real increase in accuracy. In fact, the minor epicycle is a step backward, for the planets really do move uniformly and the equant point is actually more accurate than the minor epicycle. The revolutionary part of Copernicus's work—the heliocentric hypothesis—is presented in book 1, which constitutes about 5 percent of the text of *On the Revolutions.* The other 95 percent is a sort of revision of the *Almagest,* in which Copernicus is in constant conversation with his ancient predecessor. Kepler later remarked that Copernicus would have done better if he had emulated nature rather than Ptolemy.

In *New Astronomy* (1609) Johannes Kepler, working with observations made by Tycho Brahe, showed that the path of Mars around the Sun is not an off-center circle, but an ellipse, with one focus at the Sun. Moreover, the speed of the planet varies in such a way that a line drawn from the Sun to Mars sweeps out equal areas in equal times. Kepler had begun as a convinced Copernican who believed that the Sun is at rest. But, unlike Copernicus, he was prepared to admit that the planets really do speed up and slow down. Thus, he abandoned Copernicus's minor epicycle and returned to Ptolemy for technical details. It was better to adopt an equant point, which acknowledged the variation in speed, rather than hide it behind the guise of uniform motion. In his first versions of the theory of Mars, Kepler treated the planet as moving in an off-center circle according to the law of the equant. It was only with the greatest reluctance, and after repeated failures, that he abandoned the circle for the ellipse and the equant for the area law. In our solar system the elliptical orbits of the planets depart from circularity by only a small amount, which explains why the circles had worked well enough for 200 years. Moreover, it turns out that Kepler's area law makes only a small correction to Ptolemy's equant law. Indeed, the empty focus of the Keplerian ellipse is almost equivalent to an equant point. Copernicus and Kepler can be considered the last and the most accomplished astronomers of the Ptolemaic tradition, the last for whom the *Almagest* was still a vital part of the research literature.

In the early 18th century it was still—just barely—possible to make discoveries by comparing modern observations with ancient Greek ones. In the *Philosophical Transactions* of the Royal Society for 1718, Edmond Halley announced that two stars, Arcturus and Sirius, had slightly shifted their positions with respect to their neighbors. Halley reached his conclusion by comparing the modern positions of these stars with data in Ptolemy's *Almagest.* This was the first detection of what is called the proper motion of a star. For two other stars (Aldebaran and Betelgeuse) Halley made a similar claim but was mistaken, having been led astray by errors in the ancient star positions. By the end of the 18th century proper motions had been detected for a substantial number of stars, simply by comparing positions measured early and late in that century. Thus, with the rapid advances in the precision of astrometry, the ancient data ceased to be of value.

In 1780 the young Jean-Baptiste-Joseph Delambre was attending astronomy lectures given by Lalande at the Collège de France. One day Lalande happened to mention a passage in the *Phenomena* of Aratus. Delambre attracted the astronomer's attention by reciting the whole passage from memory and summarizing the opinions of various scholars and commentators. Delambre soon became Lalande's assistant and then his scientific collaborator. Delambre had a distinguished career as an astronomer, devising new tables for Jupiter, Saturn, Uranus, and the satellites of Jupiter, as well as new techniques of calculation. In the 1790s, under the revolutionary government, he and Pierre Méchain surveyed the arc of the meridian between Dunkerque and Barcelona that was used to define the meter (one ten-millionth of the distance between the pole and the equator). Later in life, Delambre made full use of his early training in classical languages by taking up the history of astronomy. Between 1817 and 1821 he published a five-volume history, including the two-volume *Histoire de l'astronomie ancienne.* A sixth volume, on the history of astronomy in the 18th century, was published posthumously. Although other astronomers, including Jean-Sylvain Bailly, had written histories of their field, Delambre's account was at a far higher level. He had read all the principal works in Greek and Latin and did not hesitate to make detailed calculations to analyze some aspect of an ancient astronomer's work. He did not attempt a historical synthesis, but rather discussed all the important works of ancient astronomy known to him, treating each ancient author almost as a living contemporary whose work might be subjected to a searching review and evaluation. Astronomy had entered a new phase in its relationship to the classical tradition.

In our own day, historians are far more likely to find ancient astronomical data of use than are astronomers. Indeed, historians of astronomy use the errors in ancient astronomical data to try to figure out something about the ancient astronomers themselves—about the instruments and techniques they used, as well as their reliability as witnesses and reporters. In the 21st century practically the only category of ancient observation that continues to be of astronomical use is the solar eclipse. Ancient eclipse data are most useful in analyzing the secular deceleration of the Moon in its orbit and of the Earth on its axis. The length of the day is slowly increasing as the Earth slows down on its axis—the result being that the Earth, considered as a clock, has lost about two and a half hours (in comparison to a theoretical, uniformly running clock) since the days of the ancient Greeks. The places at which eclipses of the Sun were seen in ancient times cannot be accounted for without taking this fact into account.

BIBL.: E. J. Aiton, "Peurbach's *Theoricae novae planetarum:* A Translation with Commentary," *Osiris,* 2nd ser., 3 (1987) 5–44. Francis S. Benjamin Jr. and G. J. Toomer, *Campanus of Novara and Medieval Planetary Theory* (Madison 1971). Geoffrey Chaucer, *A Treatise on the Astrolabe,* ed. Sigmund Eisner (Norman 2002). Alison Cornish, *Reading Dante's Stars* (New Haven 2000). James Evans, *The History and Practice of Ancient Astronomy* (New York 1998). Edward Grant, *Planets, Stars, and Orbs: The Medieval Cosmos, 1200–1687* (Cambridge 1994). Michael Hoskin, ed., *The Cambridge Illustrated History of Astronomy* (Cambridge 1997). David A. King, *In Synchrony with the Heavens: Studies in Astronomical Timekeeping and Instrumentation in Medieval Islamic Civilization,* 2 vols. (Leiden 2004). Y. Tzvi Langermann, *Ibn al-Haytham's "On the Configuration of the World"* (New York 1990). Michel-Pierre Lerner, *Le monde des sphères,* 2 vols. (Paris 1996). Steven C. McCluskey, *Astronomies and Cultures in Early Medieval Europe* (Cambridge 1998). John North, *Chaucer's Universe* (New York 1988) and *The Norton History of*

Astronomy and Cosmology (New York 1994). Marijane Osborn, *Time and the Astrolabe in the* Canterbury Tales (Norman 2002). Olaf Pedersen, trans., "The Theory of the Planets," in *A Sourcebook in Medieval Science,* ed. Edward Grant (Cambridge, Mass., 1974). David Pingree, "The Recovery of Early Greek Astronomy from India," *Journal for the History of Astronomy* 7 (1976) 109–123, and The *Yavanajataka of Sphujidhvaja* (Cambridge 1978). F. J. Ragep, *Nasir al-Din al-Tusi's Memoir on Astronomy* (New York 1993). George Saliba, *A History of Arabic Astronomy: Planetary Theories during the Golden Age of Islam* (New York 1994). Peter Whitfield, *The Mapping of the Heavens* (San Francisco 1995). J.EV.

Atheism

The relationship between atheism and the classical tradition is somewhat perplexing. Early modern atheism frequently refers to ancient models, yet then (as now) barely anything was known about the teachings of those ancient thinkers who were regarded at the time as atheists, such as Diagoras of Melos and Theodorus of Cyrene. It is not even clear whether one can really speak of atheism in the strict sense, that is, the denial of the existence of God or gods, in Graeco-Roman antiquity.

A good example of an early modern text that looks backward is a treatise now considered to be the first real atheist tract: *Theophrastus redivivus* (*Theophrastus Revived*), from the 1650s. The unknown author of this clandestine manuscript, which survives in only a few copies, alludes in the title to a lost work by Theophrastus of Eresus (4th cent. BCE), *Peri theōn* (*On the Gods*), in which (it was assumed) the existence of the gods was refuted from a naturalist point of view. Whether this was actually the case is by no means certain.

Genuine influences based on substantial arguments therefore need to be separated from mere attributions, legends, and denunciations. Without doubt, the most prominent example is Epicurus. A victim of denunciation as an atheist on the part of the Stoics, he had long been considered an arch-atheist until his reputation was eventually restored in the modern era. Cosma Raimondi made the first attempt in the 15th century, but not until 1647 did Pierre Gassendi achieve some degree of success on this front. Locating authentic atheistic influences from antiquity is, however, a difficult and complex undertaking. Sometimes, lines such as *Stulte, verebor ipse cum faciam deos* ("I would be a fool to fear the gods, since it is I who create them")—originally assigned to the character Nero in the pseudo-Senecan tragedy *Octavia* (449)—or the passage in Seneca's *Trojan Women* (*Troades* 390–402) on the mortality of the soul, developed a life of their own and had an influence on the atheism of modern times.

The origins of the notion that religion was created out of political considerations can be seen in the theories of the Sophist Critias (5th cent. BCE)—if he was the author of the drama *Sisyphus.* This idea went through numerous stages and transformations up to the notorious treatise *De tribus impostoribus* (*The Three Impostors,* ca. 1700) and beyond. In the course of this process, however, the focus shifted from a shrewd make-believe divine authority, which guarantees the legitimacy of the law, to the far more negative accusation of plain fraud.

The first signs of a history of divine worship are found in Prodicus (5th cent. BCE), according to whom the elements of nature were originally revered as gods and later supplemented by cultural innovators who had been raised to divine status. Such hypotheses could equally provide material for an atheistic interpretation and, in fact, became effective through Euphemus, Lucretius, and others from antiquity down to Nicolas Fréret's elaborate reconstruction of the history of religion in his clandestine *Lettre de Thrasybule à Leucippe* (ca. 1725) and to numerous later genealogies. The Epicurean argument that a belief in gods originated in human fear (of thunder and lightning, for example) plays a major role in Lucretius' *De rerum natura* (1st cent. BCE) and can still be found in a 19th-century thinker like Ludwig Feuerbach. Although in the early modern period Epicurean philosophy was used (by Giambattista Vico, e.g.) to explain only the *superstitio* of heathens, its reach extended further and further to *religio* in general and thus also to Christianity.

The catalogues of atheists that already existed in antiquity (in Clitomachus, Cicero, or pseudo-Aetius) were expanded during the early modern period into entire "histories of atheism," as found in the works of Gottlieb Spizel, Jenkin Thomas Philipps, Jacob Friedrich Reimmann, and others. Nevertheless, the 17th and 18th centuries produced extremes of both kinds. Pierre Bayle, for instance, believed that antiquity as a whole should be called atheistic, yet he thought that this should not prevent us from reading ancient authors and taking them seriously. Other thinkers, seeking to identify *Spinozismus ante Spinozam* (Spinozism before Spinoza), attempted to extract, with the precision of a scalpel, individual ancient intellectual tendencies from the broader tradition, on the grounds that they were especially dangerous—for example, the Presocratic materialists or the Stoa, as well as Neoplatonism, which was thought to feed into pantheism. At the opposite end of the spectrum were those such as the Jesuit Michel Morgues, who denied that atheists had ever existed (because all human beings are endowed with the knowledge of God), and liberal-critical historians who, following Gabriel Naudé, wanted to restore the reputation of thinkers who "had unjustly been accused of atheism." In this vein Johann Jacob Zimmermann from Zurich wrote his immense but never published *Apologia virorum illustrium falso atheismi suspectatorum* (*Defense of Illustrious Men Falsely Suspected of Atheism* (1730s, now in the Zentralbibliothek Zürich, MS F. 200).

During the Enlightenment two different types of atheism developed: one that was skeptical-agnostic in form, another that was materialist. Pyrrhonist skepticism influenced the former, as, for instance, when the author of the clandestine *Symbolum sapientiae* (ca. 1700), stating that the question of God's existence cannot be resolved, put the burden of proof on the faithful, or when David Hume developed his arguments against the physico-theological proofs for the existence of God. Materialist atheism surfaced in a systematic way in Denis Diderot and Baron d'Holbach. In the sense of the latter's act of unmasking, Nicolas Boulanger, in his *Antiquity Unveiled* (*L'antiquité dévoilé,* 1766) "exposes" antiquity; but this is an antiquity that is less atheistic than superstitious, in the grip of a fear generated by the trauma of the Flood, which caused various cults of deities to mushroom.

Many writers of the 18th and 19th centuries viewed themselves as decidedly "modern" and considered atheism to be a distinctly modern phenomenon, as it was the worldview that seemed most appropriate to the new science of Newton and the new philosophies of Descartes and Spinoza. For that reason, references to the ancients became scarce. Nietzsche, too, viewed atheism as the final outcome of a 2,000-year-old European development.

BIBL.: Michael Hunter and David Wootton, eds., *Atheism from the Reformation to the Enlightenment* (Oxford 1992). P. O. Kristeller, "The Myth of Atheism and the French Tradition of Free Thought," *Journal of the History of Ideas* 6 (1968) 233–243. Pierre Lurbe and Sylvie Taussig, eds., *La question de l'athéisme au dix-septième siècle* (Turnhout 2004). W. Schröder, *Ursprunge des Atheismus: Untersuchungen zur Metaphysik- und Religionskritik des 17. und 18. Jahrhunderts* (Stuttgart 1998). M.MU.

Athens

Various cities and regions of the ancient world became symbols of self-actualization in the collective consciousness of modern Western civilization, serving to anchor current identity in a distant past. In the process they were accorded foundational status, each with different values; they were often characterized metaphorically as "roots" and "foundations"; and they were deemed to constitute a cultural patrimony. In this sense Athens competes for prominence with Egypt, Jerusalem, and especially Rome.

Unlike Egypt, Athens could not impress posterity with the duration of its cultural framework, much less with the beliefs and rites of its religion. In contrast to Jerusalem, Athens could not function as a foundational cipher for the Christian culture of the West. And great respect for ancient Greek science aside, it was Rome that stood for distinction in technology and civilization. The same applied to Athens' form of government, ruling practices, and law. In modern times Athenian democracy has rarely been seen in an unqualifiedly positive light.

Instead, Athens has achieved a unique status in what is generally called culture, not in the anthropological sense of cultures, but as a singular term of value, in the sense of high or low culture. It is a particular appreciation for beauty, artistry, and education that has been ascribed to the Greeks and especially to the Athenians throughout the tradition. This idea of a people of artists, poets, and philosophers is paired with the ideal picture of a community of free and self-aware individuals who consciously accept the polarity of their lives and seek to bring it into a harmonious equilibrium. The term *classical,* which embodies this ideal, has become the stamp of Athens. That all these attributes are of a notional character, indeed that they evoke a distorted view of Athenian society, has not lessened their influence in the slightest.

These attributes are not based on a consistent appraisal of Athens' nature throughout its entire history, but merely on its classical period, the 5th and 4th centuries BCE. The stress, moreover, is on the 5th century. That was when, in the wake of the Persian Wars of 490–480 BCE, Athens played the leading role in the resulting naval alliance and fashioned its democratic structures. As a consequence of these developments, the city effectively gained a hegemonic position within Greece.

Athens' role as an icon of the classical per se begins not in the Middle Ages or modernity but in antiquity, directly upon the city's reaching its economic and political zenith. In a speech in honor of the first Athenians killed in the Peloponnesian War (430 BCE), the statesman and general Pericles drew his countrymen's attention to the balanced life and appreciation of beauty for which they would become known, saying, "We are lovers of the noble and the beautiful and yet remain simple, we are lovers of the mind without becoming effeminate." As individuals the Athenians were gifted with a "many-sided gracefulness" that raised them above other Greeks, which led to the culminating assertion that "the city is the teacher of all Hellas" (Thucydides 1.40–41). These phrases, written down 30 years later, were addressed to Thucydides' contemporaries but seem equally intended as a legacy to posterity.

With Athens' defeat at the end of the Peloponnesian War (404 BCE), the city lost its supremacy once and for all. It is true that the following century endowed Athens with renewed prosperity and an abundance of elegant architecture, but it shared these distinctions with other Greek cities. Only in the realm of philosophy (Plato, Aristotle) and rhetoric (Isocrates, Aeschines, Demosthenes) did Athens remain the center of culture, which is what has encouraged posterity to think of it as "classical" in that century as well.

The tradition of honoring the classical age of the city began in Athens itself as early as the 4th century BCE, at which time Athens became its own memorial and museum. An example can be seen in the fate of the famed mythological and political dramas of the likes of Aeschylus, Sophocles, and Euripides. At the time of their conception (5th cent. BCE) they were all intended for a single production, they treated important societal issues of the day, and they were all staged in the open without any special architectural frame. A century later the situation was altogether different. Athens received a magnificent stone theater on the southern slope of the Acropolis. When performed there, the plays lost their contemporary meaning, serving instead as vehicles for nostalgically recalling the city's former greatness. They ended up being appreciated as exemplars of classical drama and from then on were regularly staged as canonical literary texts. In an act of cultural politics, the statesman Lycurgus convinced the popular assembly in 330 BCE to have bronze statues of the old poets erected in the Theater of Dionysus. Even the gymnasia that were instituted all over Greece in the 4th and 3rd centuries BCE turned into sites for the diffusion and transmission of classical Athenian education.

In the Hellenistic period Athens lay far from the magnificent capitals like Alexandria and Antioch. That it did not decline into an insignificant provincial city was due entirely to its dazzling past. The ever-vibrant cultural life of the philosophical and rhetorical schools and of the theater, as well as widely known festivals like the Panathenaia and the Eleusinian Mysteries, maintained Athens' appeal. Hellenistic kings, especially the Attalid dynasty of Pergamum, donated buildings and sculptural monuments in the city and partially based their architecture elsewhere on the Parthenon and the Propylaea, buildings on the Acropolis that had over time attained the status of models to be imitated.

In the period of the Roman empire Athens attained a double appeal as the site of classical art and literature. The city was despoiled, but at the same time its patrimony was spread far and wide and passed down over centuries. Various ancient works of art were carried off to Rome, and others were copied in large numbers and imitated in other, now specifically Roman, contexts: not only sculptures such as the famed caryatids of the Erechtheion, which were put to new use in the Forum of Augustus in Rome (3 BCE) and in Hadrian's Villa in Tivoli, but also innovative forms of architecture and ornamentation. Roman intellectuals like Cicero visited Plato's Academy in Athens as tourists. In the 2nd century BCE Pausanias put together a proper handbook of ancient Greek cultural monuments that served as a traveler's guide. Even Roman emperors—especially Hadrian—made cultural pilgrimages to Athens. They displayed their reverence for the city by restoring buildings such as temples and libraries and had themselves admitted to the Eleusinian Mysteries on the occasion of their visits. In 230–240 CE statues of important generals and statesmen of the 5th century BCE were still being set up in an Athenian gymnasium. Meanwhile, the teachers at this educational institution modeled their demeanors and their hairstyles on those of classical Athenian intellectuals and had corresponding portrait busts made of themselves.

But museums gather dust, and so did Athens. The scientific teachings, philosophical ideals, and aesthetic values associated with the name of Athens—and not least the proud physicality and display of nudity in life and art that was perceived as classical—had run their course. It was not the rapid destruction of the city in the 3rd century at the hands of invading Germanic tribes, but simple indifference that brought about the disruption of this long tradition.

With the transfer of imperial power from Rome to Constantinople and the subsequent banning of pagan cults and the violent closing of sanctuaries under the emperor Theodosius (379–395), Athens lost any and all significance. In any case, Christian memory latched on to other places, such as Jerusalem, Bethlehem, Ephesus, Philippi, Corinth, and naturally Rome, which became attractions for swarms of pilgrims. Conversely, the tenets of Athens' classical education became suspect to certain Christian dogmatists. There is a hymn to Mary, probably written in the 6th century and still recited today in the Greek Orthodox liturgy, whose verses embody the suspicion generally harbored toward Athens throughout the Middle Ages:

> Hail Mary, you who show that the philosophers are unwise!
> Hail, you who teach that the orators are speechless and thoughtless!
> Hail, you who rent the webs of the Athenians!
> Hail, you who unmasked the deceit of the idols!

Even in Hartmann Schedel's *Weltchronik* (1493), Athens is labeled both as "lover of the liberal arts and of wisdom" and as "nurturer and worshiper of pagan devilry."

Works of art that remained in the city until the end of pagan antiquity were carried off to Constantinople between the 4th and 6th centuries, where they later fell victim to plundering and fires. The Byzantine emperors had almost no interest in Athens, which for them was merely one of hundreds of bishoprics. When the cleric Michael Choniates (Akominatos), an expert in classical literature, was appointed bishop of Athens in the 12th century, he found upon his arrival in the city not gleaming marble buildings but ruined walls and hovel-like houses lining dingy alleys. He transferred his official residence to the Parthenon, which had been converted into a church, and found there a "library" stocked with very few books. His inaugural address, delivered in Byzantine literary style and composed of ancient Greek phrases, was incomprehensible to the inhabitants. The art and ideas of Athens had been sent abroad. In this period they were diffused throughout Byzantium and the Arab world, but Athens itself played no role in the process.

Except for a few scant pieces of news, the very concept of the city's physical presence was lost in the West. Athens was the "city of Minerva," the goddess of artistry. It became an abstract repository for classical philosophy and literature. Even after the Fourth Crusade (1204), when Athens came under Burgundian, then Catalonian, and finally Florentine rule and travel there became easier for Western Europeans, it remained relevant at most as a place of strategic military value, far from the cultural eye. The short visit of the Italian scholar Cyriac of Ancona, who in 1436 copied numerous ancient inscriptions there and also made a cursory sketch of the Parthenon, was a solitary exception.

It is true that the widely diversified reception of antiquity in the Renaissance included an abundance of ancient Greek texts, many of which were written in Athens. Athenian art also played a part, but not consciously as such. Instead, it was understood as ancient in a general sense, and at any rate it was received by way of Rome. Raphael's fresco *The School of Athens* (1509–1511), in the Vatican Palace, gathers together great Athenian minds, but the architectural setting is derived from Roman baths and the Basilica of Maxentius in Rome, not from Athenian buildings.

A renewed interest in the architectural remains of Athens began, ironically, at a time when Greece lay behind an iron curtain for Westerners. With the establishment of Ottoman rule in 1458, local authorities suspected travelers to Greece of espionage, and they were accordingly hindered. French expeditions ultimately started things off: in 1645 Jesuits and Capuchins came to the city, bought the area around a late classical choragic monument (the Lysicrates monument), and drew and measured the structure. In 1675 the doctor Jacob Spon of Lyon, together with George Wheler of England and other traveling companions, visited Athens and obtained permission to view the Acropolis. Spon and Wheler's reports about the extensiveness of the preserved ruins caused a stir and were translated into several languages. The French diplomat Marquis de Nointel had viewed the Acropolis a year earlier and had engaged the artist Jacques Carrey to make detailed drawings of the sculptures at the Parthenon. This visual document constitutes a deciding moment in the history of the Acropolis: Carrey's 1674 drawings are both the first and the last reliable depictions of the Parthenon before several phases of destruction, which began in the same period.

In 1687 the Venetian general and future doge Francesco Morisini occupied Athens. The Turkish garrison entrenched itself on the Acropolis, which then came under fire. The besieged soldiers used the Parthenon, which had been converted into a mosque, as a powder magazine. The store took a direct hit and burst into flames, and the Parthenon—the icon of Greek architecture and sculpture par excellence for the following centuries—was blown up. Initial joy at the quick victory swiftly gave way to consternation in learned circles across Europe. And ultimately the tide of war turned: the Venetians were forced to retreat, and Athens fell again under Turkish rule, where it remained until the wars of independence.

Interest in ancient Athens and especially the Acropolis having been awakened—and hindered—it became caught up in a yearning for civic freedom that captured all of Western Europe. In the process ancient Athens, the cradle of democracy, was promoted to the historical symbol of this modern utopia. The idealization of Greek antiquity was commingled with an enthusiastic transfiguration of the modern Greeks, who increasingly were seen as descendants of the ancient freedom fighters from Eastern rule. In this new reverence for Greece, Athens' classical monuments became an emblem for the fight against a purportedly despotic Orient, but they were equally an emblem for liberation from repression at home. The past became a vision for the future.

The oldest tradition of this kind of understanding of antiquity is found in England. By the 17th century the castle of a Duke of Buckingham or an Earl of Arundel contained important collections of antiquities. England had long had a parliamentary system of government, and its educated gentry had quite early come to cultivate a civic philosophy. Independence from the papacy and its specifically Roman tradition had also encouraged the English to cast their glance on the ancient Greeks. The views of philhellenic English noblemen were in reality not all that disparate from those of the ancient Athenians, and the peers of the realm were aware of this fact. In their youth they undertook extensive journeys to the south: the Grand Tour led not only to the well-established holiday destination Italy, but also to Greece and the Near East. The Society of Dilettanti—a kind of dining club composed of scholars, adventurers, seasoned travelers, and enthusiasts for antiquity—was responsible for the first concerted effort to investigate the ancient monuments of Athens and have them drawn. The success and influence of this mission were stunning. The architects James Stuart and Nicholas Revett provided a work that exceeded all expectations with their opulent, three-volume publication *The Antiquities of Athens* (London 1787, 1794, 1830), which featured romantic views and, more important, precise and detailed floor plans and elevations.

The measurement and meticulous drawing of the remains led to a boom in "Greek" architecture in Europe and soon thereafter also in America. The graceful Ionic forms of the Erechtheion seemed to 19th-century architects especially suited for the facades of private homes and the interior design of public buildings. For weightier structures like cenotaphs, courthouses, banks, and train stations they preferred the Doric order, which could be seen in the exterior architecture of the Propylaea and the Parthenon.

Famous examples of copies of the Propylaea (on the Acropolis) are the Brandenburg Gate in Berlin (1788–1791), the gate complex on Königsplatz in Munich (1848–1862), and the cast-iron Moscow Triumphal Gate in St. Petersburg (1834–1838). Architecture modeled on the Erechtheion (also on the Acropolis) includes St. Pancras Parish Church in London (1819–1822), Canada House on Trafalgar Square (1822–1824), and, in the United States, the State Capitol in Nashville, Tennessee (1845–1859). Numerous villas in the southern United States cite the columnar decoration and the famed caryatids of the Porch of the Maidens. Prominent copies of the Parthenon are the Second Bank of the United States in Philadelphia (1818–1824) and the Walhalla, constructed in 1830–1842 near Regensburg in Germany.

Ancient Greek sculpture also held the same fascination. When Lord Elgin removed the sculptures of the Parthenon from the Athenian Acropolis and took them to England in 1809, they swiftly achieved world fame. The pedimental sculptures, despite their fragmentation, became *the* premier art attraction. Classical Greek sculpture was understood as the expression of a free way of living—freer than the situations in most European countries then permitted. This view of the past had a utopian character and was connected with a yearning for the future. The

Parthenon sculptures emblematized for early 19th-century European viewers the natural free movement of the body; freedom from the confining norms of courtly dress, from the wasp waist and the corset, from the rigid collar and the calculated gait; but also freedom of thought and political action. Nudity presented itself in the Parthenon sculptures as if it were perfectly natural. Even the clothing that, as if wet, partially sticks to the bodies does not dampen but rather enhances the sense of forcefully flowing movement. Casually lounging or vigorously in action, the gods self-confidently put their own physicality on display. Should all people be allowed to behave in this way at least once, freed from the constraints imposed by tradition and the state? In Germany these were the dreams of Johann Gottfried Herder and Wolfgang von Goethe.

Classical Greek sculpture, and as a consequence architecture, too, came to be equated with naturalness in two senses: as the perfection of nature and as a metaphor for freedom. Fragments of the Greek art of sculpture had become available from that period in Athens' history designated as the cradle of democracy and of Western freedom, where it had appeared as a foil for purported Eastern despotism.

That the scholars of the day saw these works of art in this way and judged them accordingly is no accident. Decades earlier Johann Joachim Winckelmann had made this bold comparison—between classical Greek art and naturalness, and between nature and freedom—and had therewith sent out a signal that was enthusiastically received all across Europe. From Winckelmann's time onward, the meaning of the word *classical*—although it still referred to all of Greek and Roman antiquity—was focused on the Greek, and especially the Athenian, art of the 5th and 4th centuries.

The classicist focus on Athens' monuments lost its utopian character over the course of the 19th century. The ideas of naturalness and freedom were eclipsed by the view that the rigorous perfection of form was the expression of control and order. Above all the Doric order of the Parthenon, but also the lighter and more elegant Ionic order of the Erechtheion, came increasingly to symbolize what Sigmund Freud aptly called the superego: discipline and self-discipline as an expression of human civilization. The Greek *habitus* came to be seen as a state-serving mechanism. As a result, since the middle of the 19th century the artistic avant-garde has seldom made recourse to Athens' classical buildings and sculptures, turning instead to other styles as mediums of expression.

Athens, however, with its monuments and sculptures, has remained the preeminent icon of the classical. After a turning point in the 1970s, it becomes a cipher for the noble and the sublime in postmodern art and media, admitting of citation in manifold contexts and capable of conveying all kinds of messages and aims. Meanwhile, in the United States especially a tendency can be recognized toward a rather conservative, stern neoclassicism based on elements of Athenian architecture.

But what happened to the place of origin of this long tradition of influence? Thanks solely to its ancient heritage, in 1834 Athens—then a paltry village—was chosen as the new capital of the Greek state. On the model of central European metropolises, the new capital of Greece was provided with classicizing buildings designed by German architects citing the architecture of the Acropolis (the university, 1839–1842; the Academy, 1859–1879; the National Library, 1885–1891): no less than a reimportation of Athenian forms to Athens.

As for the Acropolis, at the (provisional) end of its history of influence not only was it archaeologically investigated and preserved, but its physical condition was simultaneously adapted to the classicizing ideals, desires, and yearnings described above. The varied accretions of its millennial history, still present in 1830, have been washed away to the extent permitted by the scientific thoroughness of German and Greek archaeologists, in what now amounts to their more than 175 years of work: prehistoric remains and Roman, Byzantine, Frankish, and Turkish additions have been methodically shaved away, so that now the skeleton of the four classical buildings stands, as desired, alone atop naked rock, framed by the sky: "ideal" art atop "pure" nature.

BIBL.: E. Bastéa, *The Creation of Modern Athens: Planning the Myth* (Cambridge 2000). F. Gregorovius, *Geschichte der Stadt Athen im Mittelalter* (Stuttgart 1889). C. Habicht, *Athens from Alexander to Antony* (Cambridge, Mass., 1997). M. McKenzie, *Turkish Athens: The Forgotten Centuries, 1456–1832* (Reading, U.K., 1992). L.S.

Translated by Patrick Baker

Atlantis

Legendary submerged island-continent. Plato introduced the Atlantis legend in two of his dialogues, composed in the mid-4th century BCE. In the *Timaeus* (20C–27B), he described an enormous island, larger than the whole area between the Maghreb and Asia Minor, which about 9,000 years earlier had been situated in the Atlantic Ocean, somewhere to the west of the Pillars of Hercules (now the Strait of Gibraltar). This island, known as Atlantis, disappeared beneath the sea, destroyed by violent earthquakes and a great flood. In the *Critias* (108E–109A, 113B–121C), Plato described the exact configuration of Atlantis and the customs and political constitution of its inhabitants, semimortal children of the sea god Poseidon, whose descendants lost their divine nature after becoming intoxicated by avarice.

Controversy has surrounded the Atlantis legend almost from its birth: thus, although Aristotle (Plato's most famous pupil) seems to have rejected his teacher's account as fictional, Crantor (Plato's first commentator, ca. 300 BCE) reportedly accepted the whole story at face value. Indeed, for most of its history Plato's account of Atlantis has generally been interpreted either as a politically motivated account of an ideal but nonexistent realm—a utopia—or as the literal description of a real place. According to the first interpretation (the "mythical" reading), the original story of Atlantis functioned simply as a literary device that enabled Plato to contrast an unjust and vast imperial opponent with the wise and virtuous Athens. A mythological understanding of the Atlantis story is supported partly by the fact that Plato himself located the lost island in a remote space and distant time and partly because, as a philosopher, he tended to favor the persuasive power of myth over empirical argumentation. On the other hand, according to the second interpretation (the "geophysical" reading), Plato's description of Atlantis has been taken to signify the existence of a real place, the location of which could, in principle, be pinpointed after sufficient exploration.

During the Renaissance, when European voyagers were encountering territories beyond the limits of their known world, the geophysical interpretation of Atlantis led several thinkers, such as Giambattista Ramusio (*Navigationi et viaggi,* 1556), Girolamo Fracastoro (*Syphilis, sive morbus Gallicus,* 1530), and Hieronimo Garimberto (*Problemi naturali e morali,* 1549), to claim that the newly discovered landmass on the western side of the Atlantic Ocean was in fact the lost continent described by Plato. Thus, when Francisco Lopez de Gomara (*Historia general de las Indias,* 1552) asserted Spain's dominion over this region, he referred to it as Atlantis. Other scholars, however, wishing to adhere precisely to Plato's account of Atlantis as a submerged island, advanced more subtle theories of its former whereabouts. Both Agustin de Zarate (*Historia del descubrimento y conquista de la provincia del Perú,* 1555) and Pedro Sarmiento de Gamboa (*Historia general llamada Indica,* 1572), for example, speculated that it had once served as a passage of land linking America and Europe—allowing Peru to be populated—before disappearing beneath the waves. This idea was also embraced by Justus Lipsius (*De constantia,* 1584), Tommaso Campanella (*Epilogo magno,* 1595), and later the Jesuit Athanasius Kircher (*Mundus subterraneus,* 1664), who suggested that the inhabitants of the Canary Islands might be descended from the survivors of Atlantis. Other commentators of the time regarded Atlantis as the ancestral home of the native peoples who came to inhabit the Americas, though some contemporaries—most notably Montaigne (*Essais,* 2nd ed., 1588) —rejected this view.

Although Plato's story of a lost continent could be invoked to explain the origin of the Americas in a way that corroborated the biblical account of a single human line of descent from Noah, it also had the effect of propagating a historical and geographical narrative that was not to be found in Scripture. Not surprisingly, such an ambiguous amalgamation of sacred and profane history came to be treated with suspicion by men such as Benito Arias Montano (*Phaleg,* 1572) and José de Acosta (*Historia natural y moral de las Indias,* 1590), who both feared the danger of diminishing the uniqueness and universality of the Bible. Later, in the 18th century, other Christian scholars, such as Jacques-Julien Bonnaud (*Hérodote historien du peuple hébreu sans le savoir,* 1786), claimed that when Plato referred to Atlantis he was in reality describing, though imperfectly, the biblical Holy Land.

Political and even chauvinistic concerns have also been at work, especially since the Enlightenment, in the writings of those who have sought to revive the Atlantis story. The Swedish polymath Olof Rudbeck the Elder (*Atlantica,* 1679–1702) claimed to possess archaeological and etymological evidence that Atlantis had once been situated in Scandinavia, the ancient birthplace, he believed, of all language, mythology, and culture, and that his hometown of Uppsala had been at its center. By contrast, the Italian Gian Rinaldo Carli (*Lettere americane,* 1770–1781) maintained that Italy had once been part of the vast continent of Atlantis; as for the Germans, Albert Hermann (*Unsere Ahnen und Atlantis,* 1934) pointed to an old manuscript as indubitable evidence that it was a Germanic-Atlantic Empire that had disappeared under the ocean in the second millennium BCE. Geophysical interpretations of Plato's account gained much ground in the 19th century when putative archaeological evidence was discovered for other legendary sites, such as Homeric Troy and biblical Babylon. A typical work in this vein from the period is Ignatius Donnelly's *Atlantis: The Antediluvian World* (1882), a speculative and occult-inspired investigation into a lost continent in the middle of the Atlantic.

Despite their differences, the mythical and geophysical approaches to the Atlantis story have often coalesced. After the Renaissance, the geographical proposition that Plato's lost island could be physically identified with the newly discovered America led to imaginary speculations about the nature of utopian states such as those advanced in Francis Bacon's *The New Atlantis* (1626). By contrast, the theory that Atlantis was a real place within the Mediterranean basin (perhaps Santorini, Crete, or Troy) has been based on the assumption that Plato projected into the Atlantic, under the guise of a fictional tale, the memory of a past civilization. Beyond the Mediterranean, other locations for this former island have been proposed, including the seas around the Bermudas, the Azores, the British Isles, and islands such as Madagascar, Sri Lanka, and Iceland. More recently, Atlantis has been alleged to have been located using satellite photography and submarine radar in places as diverse as Ireland, the south of Andalusia, and even 1,500 meters below the sea between Cyprus and Syria.

The Atlantis myth has endured in literature and music. It was adopted, for example, by Jules Verne (*Vingt mille lieues sous les mers,* 1869) and transformed into operas not only by Viktor Ullmann and Peter Kien (*Der Kaiser von Atlantis,* 1944) but also by Henri Tomasi (*L'Atlantide,* 1954). The story has recently been the inspiration for a feature-length Walt Disney animation, *Atlantis: The Lost Empire* (2001), in which the main character, Milo Thatch, is portrayed as the organizer of an adventurous archaeological expedition that sets out in search of the ruins of the lost civilization of Atlantis and discovers that its inhabitants still exist.

BIBL.: Christopher Gill, ed., *Plato, the Atlantis Story: Timaeus 17–27, Critias* (Bristol 1980). Giuliano Gliozzi, *Adamo e il Nuovo Mondo* (Florence 1977). Edwin S. Ramage, ed., *At-*

lantis: Fact or Fiction? (Bloomington 1978). Pierre Vidal-Naquet, *L'Atlantide: Petite histoire d'un mythe platonicien* (Paris 2005). A.S.

Atlas

A Titan, in myth a participant in the unsuccessful revolt against the Olympian gods; as punishment he was condemned to support the heavens (the celestial globe) for eternity. To carry out his sentence, he settled near the Hesperides at the borders of the Earth, on the westernmost horizon where day and night meet. His name means He Who Bears, or Who Endures. He figures in Hercules' quest to fetch the Golden Apples from the Garden of the Hesperides; Atlas obtains the apples while Hercules temporarily assumes his burden; once the deed is done, Hercules must trick the reluctant Atlas into resuming his eternal task of supporting the vault of the heavens.

Ovid relates that Perseus too asked Atlas the way to the Garden of the Hesperides, or perhaps simply for hospitality. Fearing a prophecy foretelling the theft of the Golden Apples, Atlas was hostile and disrespectfully refused. In anger Perseus showed the Titan the severed head of the Gorgon Medusa, which literally petrified him. Atlas's conversion to stone is said by Ovid and Virgil to be the origin of the Atlas Mountains in northwestern Africa, though this conflicts with the tradition that has him assisting Hercules a couple of mythical generations later.

From earliest times Atlas has proved a pliable repository for different meanings and associations. Homer stressed Atlas's wisdom; Diodorus, Vitruvius, Virgil, Pliny, and Diogenes Laertius claimed him as the first astrologer. Plato believed that Atlas was the first king of Atlantis, and other classical writers found him a worthy sovereign for other mysterious kingdoms as well. Numerous authors emphasized his wisdom and considered him a sage. A later tradition claimed that he founded the science of astronomy, discovered the secrets of the stars or laws governing the celestial bodies, fashioned the first celestial sphere, and fathered several constellations, including the Pleiades (his name is now given to a triple-star cluster in their vicinity).

Servius's medieval commentary on Virgil popularized the motif of Hercules' assuming Atlas's burden as a metaphor for the transfer of knowledge from Atlas to Hercules. Atlas was said to have instructed Hercules in the science of astronomy or mystery of the heavens, such that the weight of the celestial globe, seen as a symbol of divine wisdom, represented great learning, the weight of wisdom. This attitude differed from Greek interpretations, which had characterized the incident between Atlas and Hercules as a duel of wits or a study in contrasts. In the 16th century the two main themes, Atlas as world-bearer and as cosmically wise, would merge in allegory representing the transmission of knowledge of astronomy to Hercules. By acquiring from Atlas the celestial sphere, representing divine wisdom, Hercules became a philosopher. That is how the 17th-century biographer Bellori interpreted Annibale Carracci's fresco in the Camerino (1596) of the Palazzo Farnese.

Among post-classical efforts at reconciling pagan and Christian learning and culture, Bersuire's *Ovide moralisé* (1340) related Atlas to the Christian God: *Dieu le Père est le grant tout puissant Athlas, qui soutient tout le firmament.* This theme was picked up by Boccaccio and Salutati and expressed succinctly by Ronsard (*Dieu c'est le très fort Atlas*). And just as God was compared to Atlas in terms of strength and support, sustenance and foundation, so Christ was associated with Atlas's patient suffering. In early prints of the Passion, Christ is sometimes depicted carrying a globe on one shoulder, the Cross resting on the other.

Atlas's punishment possesses an inherently functional aspect of support that was easily transferred to ideas on architecture, specifically the column. In antiquity the world itself was sometimes conceived as a building, and occasionally Atlas supports the sky, which is symbolized by a beam or architrave. The idea of Atlas's acting literally as a column or architectural support on a colossal scale appropriate to his Titan status appears on the Temple of Zeus at Agrigento, Sicily (ca. 480 BCE). Atlantids or atlantes, male figures modeled on Atlas, for use as architectural supports (like caryatids, their female counterparts), have featured in architecture and objects of decorative art continuously from antiquity to the present. Michelangelo's unfinished *Atlas' Slave* and the atlantids supporting the balcony at the Hôtel de Ville, Toulon (by Pierre Puget) are spectacularly imaginative examples. Expanding on the ancient use of bronze atlantids as furniture legs, Renaissance artists such as Riccio fashioned bronze statuettes of Atlas as Humanist inkstands and paperweights. Male architectural support figures eventually became dissociated from their mythological origins, but Atlas himself remained a favorite iconographical theme.

In fact, Atlas and his story appealed to Renaissance scientists and artists from a variety of perspectives. Francesco di Giorgio Martini's 15th-century drawing of Atlas in the role of astrologer shows him standing on the disc of the Earth while supporting the disc of the heavens. The signs of the zodiac above correspond to the planetary influences inscribed on the disc below. Functioning as intermediary between the two spheres, Atlas accounts for the influence of the stars on earthly existence. This tradition culminates in the frontispiece of Nostradamus's *Prophecies* (1568), which uses an image of Atlas to testify to the author's expert understanding of the mysterious workings of the stars. Atlas was also associated with scientific and technical advances in the observation of the skies and is represented with compass and the armillary sphere, attributes of astronomy. He bears the heavens in the form of an armillary sphere on a tapestry commissioned by the Portuguese king John III (now in the Palacio Real, Madrid) and in the frontispiece to *The Cosmographical Glasse* by William Cunningham (1559), where the crown signifies his status as "prince of astrologers."

Contrary to the ancient view of Atlas as an eternally

condemned rebel, in the Renaissance and early modern periods he became a model for authority, the paragon for bearers of power. Erasmus, writing in the early 1500s, summarized this attitude in his *Adages*. For the emperor Charles V (r. 1516–1556), Atlas was a metaphor for the burdens of state, and he used Atlas imagery to symbolize the transfer of power to his son Philip II on commemorative medals (Poggini) and in triumphal entries into Milan (1548) and Antwerp (1549), when those municipalities were transferred to the prince. Exhausted by his burden like Atlas, Charles V needed rest and so abdicated to Philip II, the new Hercules. The theme had appeared in the writings of Juan Luis Vives (1529) and became a constant in the iconography of imperial succession. Atlas's globe was also interpreted by rulers and popes to imply universal rule or dominion. The bronze Atlas figure on Amsterdam's Town Hall (1655) represents authority in a general way. French political figures of the 17th century had a more sophisticated, peculiar reading of the relationship between Atlas and Hercules. Ruzé, Marquis d'Effiat and Superintendent of Finances and Commander of the French army, had a medal cast that portrayed himself in the guise of Atlas assisting Hercules, the French king, to carry the burdens of state, symbolized by the globe (1629). Claude Lefebvre's portrait of the French finance minister Colbert (1666), with a figurine of Atlas in the background, implies similar identifications and ideas of support of the Crown. Jonathan Swift ridiculed this pompous artistic convention in his satirical poem directed at the Earl of Oxford (1712).

Atlas's characteristic long hair and beard referred in antiquity to the eternal duration of his punishment or to his status as a wise man. Medieval and Renaissance cultures tended to appreciate Atlas's wisdom, whereas the early modern period favored his association with time. He was connected with the measurement of long spans of time, and the celestial globe he holds aloft displays signs of the zodiac. He featured as a common decorative motif on luxury clocks of the Ancien Régime. If he instead supports a terrestrial globe, the instrument is termed a geographical clock.

The 16th-century cartographer Gerard Mercator entitled his collection of maps *Atlas* (1578) and featured the Titan as his frontispiece. It is thanks to this work that the Titan's name has become, ever since, the standard term for a book or collection of charts or maps. Atlas's relation to images of the world in its entirety and the tradition of his divine wisdom have subsequently been transferred to images or works illustrating universal or exhaustive knowledge of specialized topics, such as an anatomical atlas.

In the early modern period Atlas became an allegory for the science of geography and began to serve as his own atlantid figure supporting terrestrial or celestial globes, such as the one made for Louis XVI (1778); the figurine in Colbert's portrait (1666), mentioned above, also appears to be in that mode. During the Ancien Régime he also expanded his range of associations to include economic and financial concerns. In the 1770s Great Britain issued in its colonies in North America a 50-dollar bill bearing an image of Atlas. The French more humorously used a diminutive figure, buckling under its globe, as an allegory of the common man overburdened by taxation (e.g., on a *brisé* fan, 1788–1789, now in the Museum of Fine Arts, Boston).

In present-day usage the name Atlas is associated with any person or thing that supports a great burden or considerable weight. The first vertebra of the neck, supporting the skull, is called Atlas. His enduring association with space and the heavens has strengthened with advances in technology. According to ancient authorities, he was the father of several constellations, such as the Pleiades, and became one himself. In the 20th century his name was given to lunar craters and, in 1980, also to the 15th moon of Saturn, newly discovered by the Voyager spacecraft. During the Cold War the Atlas missile was used by the United States to launch space vehicles.

He remains an enduring, widely recognized figure in the popular culture as well. In 1922 the enterprising bodybuilder Angelo Siciliano legally took the name Charles Atlas and soon made his self-improvement exercise business into a household word, connoting physical power and strength, still recognized today. In a 1927 cartoon the New York press crowned J. P. Morgan the Atlas of Finance. Ironically, the barons of commerce and industry paid greatest tribute to Atlas during the Depression. The colossal cast bronze statue of a youthful Atlas erected in 1937 at Rockefeller Center in New York City proudly displays the exaggerated musculature common to sculpture of the era. The image was an Art Deco beacon of stability, strength, promise, and eternal hope at a time when the national economy and psyche were heavily burdened.

BIBL.: "Atlas," *Lexicon iconographicum mythologiae classicae* 3.1:2–16. Malcolm Bull, *The Mirror of the Gods* (Oxford 2005) 116–119. D. P. Snoep, "Van Atlas tot Last: Aspecten van de betekenis van het Atlasmotief," *Simiolus: Netherlands Quarterly for the History of Art* 2, no. 1 (1967) 6–22. M.PE.

Atoms and Atomism

Greek scientific concept and philosophical system. Because we think today of Greek atomism as a precursor to our modern scientific worldview, it may come as a surprise to discover its roots in the puzzles of Eleatic metaphysics. Parmenides of Elea (early 5th cent. BCE) argued that coming-to-be and ceasing-to-be were self-contradictory and therefore unreal. He went on to dismiss all forms of change as illusory; only the changeless One is truly real. The first atomists, Leucippus (5th cent. BCE) and Democritus (ca. 460–ca, 370 BCE), replied that the only intelligible form of change is local motion or change of place: the apparent qualitative changes, coming-to-be and ceasing-to-be, that we observe around us must ultimately be reducible to the local motions and combinations of unchanging units or atoms. These atoms are characterized only by size, shape, and motion or rest; they do not have such properties as color, taste, smell, or heat and cold. The observed properties of compound bodies result from the complex arrangements and internecine motions of their constituent atoms.

The Greek word *atomos* means "not cuttable," so an atom is by definition indivisible. The notion of splitting the atom would have been dismissed by the ancient atomists as a conceptual confusion, showing only that we had incorrectly described something as atomic that was in fact not so. But something can be indivisible for very different reasons. We know that Democritus thought of his atoms as physically indivisible because of their lack of inner void (there is nowhere they can be divided); whether he also believed in conceptual or mathematical minima is unclear from the surviving fragments and continues to divide the commentators. In the case of Epicurus (ca. 341–270 BCE), the textual evidence is much clearer. His atoms are physically indivisible and consist of serried ranks of minimal parts, which are mathematical indivisibles, occupying the smallest parts of an essentially granular space.

Much of what we know of Democritean atomism comes down to us from the critical discussion in Aristotle's works, notably his *Physics* and *On Coming-to-Be and Passing Away.* In the former Aristotle argues for an account of the continuum that rejects indivisible magnitudes; in the latter he argues against Democritus's account of coming-to-be and ceasing-to-be as the mere aggregation and segregation of atoms. For Aristotle an organic body like a cat or an oak tree has a substantial form that is irreducible to the mere arrangement of atoms and that demands both a hylomorphic account (explaining it as a combination of the matter, *hylē,* from which it is made and the form, *morphos,* which that matter takes) and a teleological one (explaining its design, purpose, and directive principle or end, *telos*). Instead of thinking in terms of mere rearrangement of already actual atoms, we should think of the coming-to-be of a cat in terms of a form seeking to impose actuality on the potentiality of some mere formless (and hence not independently intelligible) matter.

Epicurus responded to Aristotle's critique of Democritean atomism, producing a new version of atomism that included a detailed naturalistic cosmology and ethics. The Epicureans admitted the existence of the gods but held that they played no role in the formation or governance of worlds, which simply come to be and cease to be—like all complex bodies—as a result of the chance combinations of atoms. The human soul too is a complex subtle body that can exist only in its proper environment, namely the human body. Thus, when the body dies, the soul too dissolves back into its constituent atoms. This worldview was most eloquently expressed in the Latin poem *On the Nature of the Universe* by Lucretius (ca. 95–ca. 52 BCE).

During the so-called Dark Ages, learning declined in the Latin West, and many of the works of antiquity were lost forever. In the Moslem world, a version of atomism survived among the Mutakallimun, a school of Islamic theology, but that variant was theistic and occasionalist in its metaphysics, far removed from the naturalism of Democritus and Epicurus. These Islamic scholars emphasized the radical dependence of all things on God's absolute power and concluded with a picture of the world as consisting of a sequence of instantaneous freeze-frames, each in principle independent of every other. The influence of this Islamic occasionalism can be seen in the work of Nicholas of Autrecourt (1300 CE). In the Latin West, philosophy began to revive in the 12th century, based first on Plato and Augustine and later on Aristotle. As Aristotle came to set the scholastic curriculum, his discussions of the continuum, of matter and form, and of coming-to-be and ceasing-to-be, were widely discussed, and the rival Democritean theory became generally known by way of Aristotle's criticisms. What was lacking, however, was any systematic presentation of atomism as a worked-out philosophy of nature.

The Middle Ages also saw the development of a variety of other particulate or corpuscular theories of matter, quite distinct in their origins and their claims from Greek atomism. A particulate theory of matter could be derived from Plato's *Timaeus,* or even—surprisingly—from Aristotle's *Physics.* In *Physics* 1.4 Aristotle sketches an argument against Anaxagoras that seems to presuppose the existence of natural minima of flesh and blood and bone. This theory of natural minima could easily be extended to the four elements: fire, air, water, and earth. The theory was developed by a number of Aristotelian commentators and gave rise to an important tradition independent of atomism in the strict sense. On this account, the minima of the four elements still possess the properties of heat and cold, moisture and dryness, and still interact with one another to produce compounds with new forms: so this remains a qualitative matter-theory with a picture of chemical interaction quite distinct from the mere mechanical aggregation posited by Democritus. The natural minima tradition was to provide a congenial theoretical framework for the emerging science of chemistry, in figures such as Daniel Sennert (1572–1637).

In the 15th century, the work of Humanist scholars helped provide more direct access to the remaining sources for ancient atomism. Diogenes Laertius' *Lives of the Most Eminent Philosophers* (ca. 3rd cent. CE) was translated into Latin in 1433. Although anecdotal in tone and largely unreliable in content, it did provide a great deal of information about Epicurus and his school. The most important breakthrough, though, was the discovery in 1417 by the Italian humanist Poggio Bracciolini of a manuscript of Lucretius. When *On the Nature of the Universe* was eventually published in 1473, it became clear to the scholarly world that Epicureanism was a systematic philosophy incorporating metaphysics, cosmology, and ethics that could provide a serious rival to the dominant Aristotelian and Platonist schools.

The obvious problem, of course, was that the Epicurean philosophy flatly contradicted Christian teaching on such key issues as Creation, Providence, and immortality. Any philosopher who wanted to defend an atomist natural philosophy would have to come to terms with the objection that this amounted to teaching atheism. Atomism had to be stripped of this association before it could become respectable. Francis Bacon began the process in his *Novum organum* (1620), in which he praised Democritus and denied that atomism led to atheism. The crucial role, however, was played by Pierre Gassendi (1592–1655), who in a series of important writings sought to "baptize" Epicurus. He argued at length that Epicurus's ethics were not as bad as they had been portrayed and that his matter-theory could be divorced from his views about the gods. If God created a large but finite number of atoms, set them initially in motion, and gave them their initial motive force (*pondus*), the Christian doctrines of Creation and Providence could be reconciled with Epicurean matter-theory. Immortality was rather more difficult: Gassendi had to argue that the Epicurean account of the soul captures only its "lower" aspects and that an immaterial soul was needed in addition to the vapor or breath of the Epicureans.

Once Gassendi had taken the crucial step, others could more easily follow. His works were popularized in France by François Bernier (1625–1688) and in England by Walter Charleton (1620–1707), whose *Physiologia Epicuro-Gassendo-Charletoniana* (1654) influenced scientists of the caliber of Robert Boyle (1627–1691) and Isaac Newton (1642–1727), who found themselves able to proclaim their acceptance of versions of atomism without any fear of theological censure, and even to incorporate atomism into their revised accounts of Creation and Providence. Boyle's "corpuscular philosophy" was intended to occupy a neutral ground between the rival systems of Gassendi and Descartes, so he did not commit himself on the question of whether his smallest corpuscles were strictly indivisible or merely "scarce ever divided" in the course of nature; but many of Boyle's opinions on key issues were closer to those of Gassendi than of Descartes. As for Newton, we know that he studied Charleton closely and even considered introducing a number of "classical scholia," based on his own reading of Lucretius, into the text of the *Principia* (1687). Perhaps the most famous statement of all is in Query 31 of his *Opticks:* "All these things being consider'd, it seems probable to me, that God in the Beginning form'd Matter in solid, massy, hard, impenetrable, moveable Particles, of such Sizes and Figures, and in such Proportion to Space, as most conduced to the End for which he form'd them." From being a suspect body of natural philosophy, atomism had become a widely accepted (and theologically innocuous) background assumption for much of natural science.

After Newton and Boyle, it is much harder to discern direct links and lines of influence from ancient atomism to modern science. It is possible to see a clear continuity of themes and concepts from Democritus to Newton, but arguably not from Democritus to Rutherford. Physics has emerged as a distinct discipline with its own norms and traditions, owing little to the great tradition of natural philosophy. Two developments from the post-Newtonian age do, however, demand at least a mention. In the *Theory of Natural Philosophy* (1758) of the Croatian Jesuit Roger Boscovich (1711–1787), the atoms of Newton are shrunk down to mere mathematical points, loci for concentric spheres of alternating attractive and repulsive forces. This revised version of atomism supplied workable solutions to pressing problems about atomic contacts and collisions and helped provide the philosophical foundations for the development of field theories in the 19th century. And in *A New System of Chemical Philosophy* (1808), by the English Quaker John Dalton (1766–1844), a system of chemical atomism was introduced that linked the Democritean tradition with the chemistry of Antoine-Laurent Lavoisier (1743–1794) by postulating atoms of the various chemical elements, thus integrating atomism with chemistry in a manner more reminiscent of Sennert than of Boyle and Newton.

BIBL.: Cyril Bailey, *The Greek Atomists and Epicurus* (New York 1964). David Furley, *Two Studies in the Greek Atomists* (Princeton 1967) and *The Greek Cosmologists* (Cambridge 1987). Robert Kargon, *Atomism from Hariot to Newton* (Oxford 1966). Christoph Lüthy, John E. Murdoch, and William R. Newman, eds., *Late Medieval and Early Modern Corpuscular Matter Theories* (Leiden 2001). William R. Newman, *Atoms and Alchemy: Chymistry and the Experimental Origins of the Scientific Revolution* (Chicago 2006). Margaret Osler, ed., *Atoms, Pneuma and Tranquility: Epicurean and Stoic Themes in European Thought* (Cambridge 1991). Andrew Pyle, *Atomism and Its Critics: Democritus to Newton* (Bristol 1995). A.PY.

Atrium

Its name improbably derived by Varro (1st cent. BCE) from the Etruscan people of Atria, the atrium appeared as a feature of houses by the 6th century BCE, at Marzabotto and Rome, but its classic examples are from Pompeii, where the form dominated domestic architecture by the early 1st century BCE. Typically rectangular and close to the front entrance, the atrium is easily confused with its central feature, the *cava aedium,* of which Vitruvius distinguishes five types, characterized by an opening in the roof (*compluvium*), which provided light for inner rooms and through which rainwater fell into a basin (*impluvium*) bordered by columns. Atria remained a standard feature of upper-class house design into the imperial period, although few surviving examples show the room's ideal proportions prescribed by Vitruvius (3:5, 2:3, or 1:$\sqrt{2}$). They symbolized status and patriarchal structure, being well-furnished and housing wax images of male ancestors (Pliny, *Natural History* 35.6–7), and were used for family ceremonies or for receiving clients. Vitruvius considered atria of grand style unnecessary for "those of modest income," but men of rank with social obligations to their fellow citizens required "lofty entrance courts in regal style and very spacious atria and peristyles" (*De architectura* 6.5.1). By the 2nd century CE the term meant little more than "vestibule" (Gellius, *Attic Nights* 16.5.3), although atrium houses are found up to the 6th century CE.

Georg Dehio (1850–1932) developed a theory that the Christian basilica evolved from the Roman atrium house:

the atrium corresponded to the nave; the *lararium* and *tablinum* to the altar and apse; the flanking *alae* to the transept. This theory now has few supporters. The Christian building at Dura-Europos shows a different kind of transformation of private house into church (White 1990). The front courts of early churches in Italy, France, and Germany from the 4th through the 9th centuries, which preserved not only the name *atrium* but also the atrium's status and range of social functions, seem to have derived their term not from domestic atria but from public halls of that name, such as the Atrium Regium in the Roman Forum, a prototype for basilicas where foreign dignitaries were received, and the Atrium Libertatis, a "large and capacious" space (as Servius described it) housing public records.

By the later Middle Ages the term referred to private loggias or halls located off public spaces, such as the Broletto Nuovo in Milan (1233), called *atrium* on its 14th-century inscription. But the domestic use of the term was properly revived only in the Renaissance, when Humanists and architects, unaware of the Pompeian examples, used ancient texts and nondomestic archaeological material to reconstruct many different atrium types that influenced contemporary house design but never reproduced the authentic ancient form. Flavio Biondo (1392–1463), influenced by church atria, interpreted the Roman atrium as a transitional space between street and house; Pirro Ligorio (ca. 1510–1583) depicted it as a peristyle courtyard behind the vestibule. Leon Battista Alberti (1404–1472), following Vitruvius, recognized the atrium as an internal space, the "bosom" (*sinus*) or "forum" of the house, which he identified with the *cava aedium,* an image reflected in Giuliano da Sangallo's Palazzo Scala in Florence (ca. 1476) and the palace he designed for the king of Naples (1488). Raphael's Villa Madama (1518–ca. 1525) had an atrium "in the Greek manner," a narrow, vaulted passageway, following Fabio Calvo's belief that *aula* was the Greek word for *atrium.* For Daniele Barbaro (1514–1570) and Andrea Palladio (1508–1580), the atrium combined the three-aisled form with the light well of the *cava aedium.* Palladio's evocation of the tetrastyle atrium replaced the three-aisled form as inspiration for 16th-century villas and palaces, and the belief that monasteries were built over ancient houses encouraged Palladio's design for the Carità in Venice as a Vitruvian *domus.* The atrium was thus reformulated as a grand internal courtyard, as in the Palazzo Farnese at Rome by Antonio Sangallo the Elder (begun in 1515) and the Palazzo Reale at Genoa by Pier Francesco Cantone and Michele Moncino (1643), or a domestic sculpture court, as in the Atrium of the Four Winds at the Villa Visconti Borromeo, at Lainate (ca. 1620). Vanbrugh's front halls at Blenheim Palace (1705–1724) and Seaton Delaval (1718–1728) combined both concepts, with classicizing statuary around an inner entrance hall.

The church atrium experienced a brief revival in post-Tridentine Rome in buildings such as San Gregorio Magno al Celio (1629–1633), as the Church, encouraged by Carlo Borromeo's *Instructions for Ecclesiastical Construction and Furnishings* (*Instructiones fabricae et supellectilis ecclesiasticae,* 1577) sought to recover its early roots. The idea of a walled, open-air atrium, discernible in the Great Mosque at Córdoba (which had been converted to a church in 1236), was favored in the New World, where such areas were used to house large crowds of converts, as illustrated in the *Rhetorica* (1579) of Fray Diego de Valadés.

Since the 19th century the atrium has undergone a further revival. Atria became a popular design feature in domestic architecture in the 1950s. In the United States, beginning in the 1960s, John Portman developed the atrium-type hotel, characterized by a large central atrium surrounded by multiple stories of guest rooms (Saxon 1986). In London the Coutts building (1979) introduced a style of bank design that became widespread. The IBM World Headquarters Atrium in New York (1983) and the restored Queen Elizabeth II Great Court of the British Museum (2000) have given the classical atrium renewed prominence.

BIBL.: Eugene Dwyer, "The Pompeian Atrium House in Theory and in Practice," in *Roman Art in the Private Sphere,* ed. Elaine K. Gazda (Ann Arbor 1991) 25–48. Linda Pellecchia, "Architects Read Vitruvius: Renaissance Interpretations of the Atrium of the Ancient House," *Journal of the Society of Architectural Historians* 51 (1992) 377–416. R. Saxon, *Atrium Buildings: Development and Design,* 2nd ed. (London 1986). L. Michael White, *Building God's House in the Roman World* (Baltimore 1990) 12–17. E.T.

Atticism

Attikismos, at first denoting in a political sense "siding with Athens" (Thucydides), later in a linguistic and literary sense (Cicero, Dionysius of Halicarnassus, Plutarch) came to mean the use of an Attic style and idiom, that is, the style and idiom of the Athenian writers of the 5th–4th centuries BCE. Atticism dominated the literature of the Roman imperial era and was transmitted into late antiquity and beyond by rhetoricians, from Aelius Aristides in the 2nd century and onward, with the help of Atticistic lexica, up to the *Selection of Attic Names and Words* compiled by the Byzantine scholar Thomas Magister in the 14th century. Thus, mimesis as emulating the ancient authors has always been a consistent factor of learned Byzantine literature. In the Latin West, the apologist Clement of Alexandria (2nd–3rd cents.) was the first learned Christian writer widely enough acquainted with pagan Greek literature to adopt Atticizing language. He was followed by the Church Fathers of the 4th and 5th centuries, such as Gregory of Nazianzus.

Particularly when characterizing Atticism during the Byzantine period, we must pose two questions. First, can any developments be discerned in the Atticism? And, second, how consequential was the separation of such works from those written in a more colloquial or vernacular style? An at least provisional answer to the first question is that Atticist vocabulary clearly shows development, especially in creating new composita (compounds) in the traditional manner. This tendency toward "modern Atticism" or "inner Byzantine mimesis" can clearly be traced in the 11th through 13th centuries in a series of works showing lexical and stylistic imitation, beginning with the polyhistor Michael Psellos, continuing with Theophylactus of Ohrid, including among others Eustathius, archbishop of Thessalonica, and culminating with Nicetas Choniates. Especially noteworthy is Nicephoros Basilaces, an advocate of personal style who boasted that he "wrote like Basilaces." The second question can be approached in a variety of ways. As to the conventional distinction between Atticizing authors and writers in other styles and in vernacular language, it is worth noting that Eustathius was not only an outstanding Byzantine scholar and an excellent writer, but also—and this was quite unusual for an Atticist—deliberately showed interest in the vernacular Greek of his time. Theodore Lascaris, a philosopher on the throne (as emperor of Nicaea, early 13th cent.), went a step further by sometimes using vernacular words in his letters as a stylistic device.

Aside from these, it is also worth noting that authors (especially historians) who were strongly committed to the old literary heritage and the use of an archaizing style began to transpose names of contemporary peoples into ancient ones (for example, writing "Persians" for "Turks" or "Scythians" for "Russians"). But these same authors also introduced current Latin or Italian terms (e.g., *cardinal, bailo, podesta*) into their work. A peculiar example of these divergent tendencies appears in the work of George Pachymeres (ca. 1300), who in his history of Byzantium used Attic names for the months (in quite an arbitrary order) instead of the Latin ones. He was followed in this 150 years later by Theodore Gaza, a Greek emigrant teacher and translator in Italy. Besides his introduction to Greek grammar, a standard reference work for Humanists, he composed a work on the Attic months (*De mensibus*), although likewise not completely according to the order of the ancient calendar.

Toward the end of the 10th century Symeon Metaphrastes reworked many early saints' lives by purifying and rhetorically embellishing the language. A similar example is the case of Theodore Phialites, who in the first half of the 14th century rewrote the *Dioptra* of Philip Monotropus, Atticizing both syntax and vocabulary. This is all the more interesting because in late Byzantine literature we also find just the opposite tendency, of simplifying highbrow style and works (Anna Comnena, Nicetas Choniates, Nicephorus Blemmydes).

BIBL.: G. Horrocks, *Greek: A History of the Language and Its Speakers* (London 1997). H. Hunger, *Die hochsprachliche profane Literatur der Byzantiner,* 2 vols. (Munich 1978). *The Oxford Dictionary of Byzantium* (New York 1991) 229–230. E. Trapp, "The Role of Vocabulary in Byzantine Rhetoric as a Stylistic Device," in *Rhetoric in Byzantium,* ed. E. Jeffreys (London 2003) 137–149. G. Ueding, ed., *Historisches Wörterbuch der Rhetorik* (Tübingen 1992) 1:1163–1176. E.TR.

Augustine

Augustine of Hippo, bishop and saint, notable Latin writer (354–430 CE). The son of a provincial squire, he almost lived up to his father's dreams for him, then abandoned those dreams for reasons of faith. Though survived by no children, he became a father in the eyes of many; his reputation long surpassed his time. Intellectually he was trained in the old ways, then taught himself the new ones, of Christianity, and lived amphibiously between those worlds. He both accepted and rejected the Graeco-Roman tradition and was a creative influence in shaping it into a classical past.

As a young man he was schooled in the Latin and Greek classics (the latter without much lasting effect) and mastered the arts and skills such an education sought to impart in his time. His reading in Latin literature was fairly broad and mainly shallow, but Virgil and Cicero absorbed his full attention, and he profited from the experience. Cicero's philosophical works in particular exercised a powerful influence on him, as on some of his Latin contemporaries, inasmuch as the Greek philosophical tradition was mainly opaque to them by reason of their limited linguistic skills. It can be argued that Augustine is the best reader that Cicero the philosopher ever had. Until his 33rd year, the cultural stage of Latin antiquity was the only milieu Augustine really knew, and he knew how to play his own minor part on that stage as orator, teacher, and writer.

Inordinately successful for a provincial academic, Augustine had become by that age professor of rhetoric at the imperial court in Milan and harbored hopes, obvious to all, of advancing appropriately to a governorship or beyond. (His older contemporary Ausonius had in fact advanced to the praetorian prefecture, and a flotilla of lesser public intellectuals had sailed in his wake to offices of preferment.) But then Augustine abandoned his hopes and his past in favor of Christian baptism and retirement to his father's estates. There he showed every sign of a permanent rustication that would have brought him mild literary renown at best. If he was idiosyncratic, it showed in his choice of literary pastimes and texts and in his avoidance of the usual hearty prerogatives of wealthy country life. We know today, what most of his contemporaries would not have seen, that he had already changed his textual allegiances for the most part and now found his intellectual nourishment in the texts from Hellenistic Judaism that formed the pretexts for the Christian movement, which was receiving decisive government support at just the moment of Augustine's retirement.

In 391, the year in which traditional (non-Christian) religious observances were banned by the emperor, Augustine abandoned his past to accept an entirely new social identity as a priest (and five years later, as a bishop) in the Christian community in Hippo Regius on the coast of North Africa. There he served almost 40 years, picking fights, writing books, and saving souls. The fights had long afterlives and helped define important doctrinal preoccupations of Western Christianity—even when later generations have not always espoused the Augustinian position—and the saving of souls had its own afterlife in books that shaped spiritual reading and understanding for many centuries to come, into the present day. And the books more than anything were the making of his reputation. Through them, he defined a position that has remained essential to understanding the place of the classical in medieval and modern times.

We would not pay much attention to Augustine if it were not for the books he wrote. Even during his lifetime, he used his authorship to create a persona that became widely known in the world of socially and intellectually advanced Latin Christianity. Jerome, a rival with whom he avoided open conflict, became only in later years a grudging ally against Pelagianism, but Paulinus of Nola, the well-connected patron of wealthy Italian Christianity, promoted Augustine's works as long as it seemed useful, and Augustine benefited. Even after Augustine's death, there arrived a letter of invitation to the ecumenical council to be held at Ephesus in 431, which would invent and condemn Nestorianism from the sketchy and quite orthodox materials provided by Nestorius, the impolitic patriarch of Constantinople.

But Augustine the Christian was never the antithesis of Augustine the rhetorician. Not for him a forsaking of the past, or self-absorbed nightmares of being found out for his classical heritage (like the dream Jerome claims to have had): with Augustine, the past stayed on.

His version of Christianity inherited Graeco-Roman antiquity and, by its own admission, surpassed it. The books of the past could be matter-of-factly pillaged for useful information, and their stories reshaped (by Augustine in the subtle, even operatic *City of God;* by Orosius, the boneheaded disciple he never managed to disown, in a *History against the Pagans*, tinny melodrama by comparison) into a history for the present moment. If the classical is always somehow not the thing one possesses *now,* then Augustine made that past quite explicitly classical. He admired many things about it, despised others, but convinced himself that he could tell a persuasive story of the continuities that connected that past to the present, even when marked by certain important discontinuities.

The classical that he knew is much the same as the classical that we know today. He knew archaic Latin literature only slightly (other than Terence, a schoolroom text), and the first century BCE was for him the classic age. Greek literature, insofar as he knew it, consisted of authors of golden authority, universally recognized, barely more than Homer and Plato. The cultural riches of Hellenistic antiquity he knew barely enough to hold in suspicion, except for the fragments embedded in the Christian Scriptures. His ignorance of ancient history, in particular, is impressive. But he knew his past just well enough to be sure that he knew all that he needed to know.

The first books of his *City of God* embody his creation of that version of the classical within a Christian context. A deliberate rejoinder to Cicero's *De re publica* and Plato's *Republic,* the book has a range of classical reference and quotation that Augustine was sure would have impressed his teachers and all their forebears. It is a virtuoso performance in the old style, a proof that the failed imperial courtier now stuck in a provincial town could still play the part of a gentleman, even while he sought to disown the culture that had created those gentlemen. The later books of the work diverge back toward the more pedestrian ecclesiastical style that Augustine had been forming in the 20 years of churching that preceded it, but they preserved the ideological ambition of taming, domesticating, and explaining away the miracles of Roman grandeur into a world-historical narrative that was more ambitious and comprehensive in every way.

When Augustine was done with the Graeco-Roman past, it was classical in the respect in which he regarded it, and classical in the way that he had reduced it to be a piece of the past, not the whole. Even the most ambitious restorers of classical learning and education in later centuries would still have to admit that the past was over, and that there were other human pasts that needed to be attended to in order to have a full understanding of the cultures that claimed classical ancestry.

BIBL.: P. P. Courcelle, *Les Confessions de saint Augustin dans la tradition littéraire: Antécédents et posterité* (Paris 1963). H. I. Marrou, *Saint Augustin et la fin de la culture antique* (Paris 1937) and *St. Augustine and His Influence through the Ages* (New York 1957). G. B. Matthews, ed., *The Augustinian Tradition* (Berkeley 1999).

J.O.

Augustus

Born Gaius Octavius 63 BCE, upon adoption by his uncle Julius Caesar he was named Julius Caesar Octavianus (Octavian); died 14 CE. Augustus rose to become sole ruler of Rome and its empire through ruthlessness, firm control of the military, and exercise of patronage. Few contemporary writers dared mention the brutality of his climb to power or the subsequent constitutional tinkering that signaled the end of the Roman Republic. Such was Augustus' concern for his legacy that he himself documented—highly selectively—his achievements. His *Res gestae divi Augusti* (*Deeds of the Divine Augustus*) emphasized Augustus' munificence and empire building. Though wielding supreme power, Augustus himself never employed the title *Imperator* (Emperor). Virgil, Horace, and Livy were among the members of a literary stable who helped hone the carefully crafted Augustan image of *princeps* (first citizen) and *pater patriae* (father of his country). It was Virgil who lauded Augustus for his restoration of a Golden Age of Latin letters. Literary texts and public monuments alike celebrated the Augustan virtues: peace, clemency, and a united empire.

It was not until the second century that a reassessment of Augustus' career and achievements became politically possible. This was undertaken most notably by Tacitus. His bitter indictment of Augustus as a cruel and corrupt usurper of republican liberty voiced the frustrations of a Roman senatorial class excluded from power under the principate. This view, together with Tacitus' claim that

Augustan secrecy and censorship had made historical truth impossible, resonated loudly with later students of the classical world.

By contrast, Greek writers, acutely aware of the benefits a stable empire conferred on the Hellenic world, stressed instead the administrative system Augustus had created and his institutional legacy. Christian authors from Origen to Paulus Orosius merged a benign image of Augustus as peacemaker with the providential view of an emperor sent by God to allow the unfettered spread of the Gospel. Orosius read much into the fact that Octavian received the title *Augustus* (revered) from the Roman people on January 6—the feast day of the Epiphany. In later Byzantine legend and in the medieval *Mirabilia urbis Romae* (*Marvels of Rome*), Augustus was reported to have himself seen a vision of a virgin standing in the sky holding the infant Jesus. This Christianized view of Augustus no doubt encouraged Holy Roman Emperors from Charlemagne onward to style themselves *Imperator Augustus*.

During the early modern period a pitched battle raged over the merits and shortcomings of Augustus. Political leaders of all stripes dared to compare themselves—or were compared by others—with the first Roman emperor. When ruling Rome during the Avignon papacy of the mid-14th century, Cola di Rienzo proclaimed himself tribune of the people on Augustus' example; rebuilding Rome nearly a century and a half later, Pope Sixtus IV modeled himself rather differently on Augustus the patron of Vitruvius. Charles V as Holy Roman Emperor not only conducted imperial business as *Imperator Augustus*, but dressed the part as well, frequently appearing at state ceremonies in a fine suit of neoclassical armor. James I, Charles II, and George I in England and Louis XIV in France invited comparison with Augustus through both their styles of government and patronage of the arts. A strong monarchy, it was argued, brought about peace, prosperity, and the advancement of the arts and sciences. Echoing Virgil, some called the literary flowering of early 18th-century Britain an "Augustan Age."

The Renaissance rediscovery of Tacitus allowed for alternative visions of Augustus. Republican writers from Leonardo Bruni to Machiavelli saw in the example of Augustus persuasive arguments against the concentration of power in the hands of a single individual. Sole rule was portrayed as the first act in a drama of public corruption and moral decline that concluded in tyranny; the result was loss of political liberty and the suppression of free thought. Enlightenment opponents of absolutism argued with ever greater command of historical detail that his brutal rise to power not only failed to justify the accomplishments of Augustus, but that his suppression of liberty sowed the seeds of Roman decline that followed. Edward Gibbon, in his *Decline and Fall of the Roman Empire*, charged that Augustus maintained power only by deceiving the people with the illusion of civil liberty and the military with the illusion of civil government.

Others charted a middle road. The discovery of the *Res gestae* in the 16th century allowed for a seemingly empirical assessment of the Augustan achievement. When combined with the newly unearthed texts of Cassius Dio and other Greek historians of empire that were packed with administrative detail, Renaissance thinkers such as Justus Lipsius, while never quite excusing Augustus' political style (Lipsius was too much a student of Tacitus for this), nonetheless found comfort in the institutions of state that he had created.

In the 19th and 20th centuries classical scholars working in the glow of German and Italian unification and British imperialism were once again willing to excuse Augustus' excesses in light of the perceived brilliance of his political and administrative achievements. Politics and scholarship collided most forcefully under Mussolini, who held a yearlong celebration leading up to the bimillenary celebration of Augustus' birth on September 23, 1938. Preparations involved major archaeological excavations of imperial Rome and the restoration of Augustan monuments. But if Augustus furnished a mirror for fascist ambitions, so did contemporary politics from the Russian revolution to the rise of fascism illuminate the Augustan state. In his *Roman Revolution* of 1939, Ronald Syme—like Lipsius and Gibbon, a deep admirer of Tacitus—exposed the Augustan achievement as one based on ruthlessness and the manipulation of constitutional traditions.

BIBL.: John M. Carter, "Augustus Down the Centuries," *History Today* 33 (March 1983) 24–30. Howard Erskine-Hill, *The Augustan Idea in English Literature* (London 1983). Emilio Gabba, "The Historians and Augustus," in *Caesar Augustus: Seven Aspects*, ed. Fergus Millar and Erich Segal (1984, corrected ed. Oxford 1990) 61–88. Paul Nelles, "The Measure of Rome: André Schott, Justus Lipsius and the Early Reception of the *Res gestae divi Augusti*," in *History of Scholarship*, ed. C. R. Ligota and J.-L. Quantin (Oxford 2006) 113–134. Ronald T. Ridley, *The Emperor's Retrospect: Augustus' Res gestae in Epigraphy, Historiography and Commentary* (Louvain 2003). Howard D. Weinbrot, *Augustus Caesar in Augustan England* (Princeton 1978).

P.N.

Automata

Automata, or self-moving machines, have played an important role in literature and the sciences since ancient times. They were known and manufactured in antiquity, featured prominently throughout the Middle Ages in both Romance literature and court festivals, and revived with particular vigor in the Renaissance, paving the way for Descartes's reflections on the nature of self-movers and the sophisticated machines of the 18th century and beyond.

References to automata abound in ancient literature. The remarkable self-moving tripods of Vulcan, reputedly the founding father of automaton making, are described at length in the *Iliad*, and several accounts survive of the "bronze birds" of Boethius, Archytas' "wooden dove," the sphere of Archimedes, and several self-movers constructed by Daedalus. Aristotle refers to automata in the *Metaphysics* as wondrous devices that provoke curiosity (and hence philosophy) in men, and in the *Politics* as part of a discussion about slavery. The fullest account of ancient automata to have come down to us, however, is to be found in the works of the 1st-century engineer Hero of Alexandria, particularly in his *Pneumatics* and *Automaton-Construction,* the latter of which describes an automaton theater in considerable detail. Though fragments of Hero's works were published by Giorgio Valla in 1501, it was the efforts of the mathematical Humanist Federico Commandino and his pupil Bernardino Baldi that led to the editing and translation into Latin and the vernacular of the *Pneumatics* (first Latin ed. 1575) and *Automaton-Construction* (first Italian ed. 1589). Both texts had a wide-ranging influence on the reception of automata, each providing a strong classical precedent for the study of such devices.

The classical heritage of self-moving machines was of particular importance because at around the time these works were published the status of automata was at a low ebb. The Middle Ages never entirely lost sight of automata (which often featured as part of the *entremet* at banquets), but by the 16th century their standing had been tarnished by a strong association with sorcery. This stemmed principally from the story of Thomas Aquinas's destruction of Albertus Magnus's "oracular head," supposedly manufactured through the harnessing of astral influences or, far worse, black magic. In his narration of the event in *Trattato dell'arte de la pittura* (1584), the Italian art theorist Giovanni Paolo Lomazzo claimed that Aquinas obliterated the head because "he thought it the devil."

The pejorative status of self-movers, however, was vigorously contested by late 16th- and early 17th-century apologists for automata who claimed that the art of automaton making was a noble one and that their study was worthy of liberal status. The reception of self-moving machines in the Renaissance was determined by a wide range of factors, such as the local availability of texts on automata (and indeed automata themselves), technical or mathematical education, and religious confession. But the first hurdle that automata's apologists had to overcome was convincing their audience that self-movers were real rather than fictional. Increasingly their arguments partook of a rhetoric of witness. For example, Lomazzo describes an automaton in the form of a lion made by Leonardo da Vinci for Francis I of France, the sight of which made the king and his courtiers believe that "Architas Tarentinus his wooden dove flew; that the brasen Diomedes, mentioned by Cassiodorus, did sound a trumpet; that a serpent of the same material was heard to hiss; that certain birds sang; and that Albertus his brasen head spoke to St Thomas Aquinas." Thus, it was only after the experience of seeing an actual automaton in action that the wondrous feats related in ancient literature could be thought to be possible rather than fictional.

Once the plausibility of ancient self-movers had thus been established, automata's apologists were presented with an excellent opportunity to situate self-movers within an august, classical tradition. The fullest example of this is Bernardino Baldi's lengthy *Discorso sopra le machine se movente* prefaced to his Italian translation of Hero's *Automaton-Construction* (1589). After having provided automata with an appropriately classical vocabulary, he placed modern automata manufactured by contemporary craftsmen at the end of a long line of distinguished automaton makers going back to antiquity, noting that since he could find no mention of automata in sacred history, they must have been invented by someone in ancient times. By linking ancient and modern automaton makers in a continuous tradition, Baldi was able to promote contemporary artisans, defending the craftsman's skill against accusations that such labor was vulgarly mechanical.

The devices supported by automata's Renaissance apologists fall broadly into two categories: large-scale, hydraulically or pneumatically powered automata designed as set pieces for the princely garden or grotto, and small-scale, clockwork automata fashioned from precious metals. The first variety was principally produced by Italian engineers and their pupils, and may be associated with the machines described by Hero and Ctesibius. The second, derived from medieval traditions of the automaton-clock and ornaments for the dinner table, was made by the master clockmakers of German-speaking Central Europe.

Perhaps the most important defense for these machines was that they were, in Lomazzo's words, "merely mathematical." Increasingly, learned opinion on automata tended toward the acceptance of self-movers as harmless, natural magic. For instance, in the widely read *Disquisitiones magicae libri sex* (1599), the Jesuit Martín del Rio identified automata as legitimate "mathematical magic," whereas Baldi associated them with the mixed mathematical science of mechanics. Indeed, following Aristotle, Baldi claimed that such devices were perfect pedagogic tools, and that by making men "wonder that things are as they are," automata could be used to teach the mechanical principles necessary for a host of useful arts.

Debates about automata did not, however, end in the utilitarian rhetoric of the 16th century. In the 17th century Descartes's application of the automaton model first to animals and then to humans prompted protracted arguments over the nature of motion, cognition, and the soul. In fact, the increasing sophistication of self-moving machines, particularly after the advent of the computer, has ensured that the automaton remains a subject of fascination, particularly in relation to questions pertaining to artificial life.

BIBL.: S. A. Bedini, "The Role of Automata in the History of Technology," *Technology and Culture* 5 (1964) 24–42. A. Chapuis and E. Droz, *Automata: A Historical and Technological Study,* trans. A. Reid (Neuchâtel 1958). O. Mayr, *Authority, Liberty, & Automatic Machinery in Early Modern Europe* (Baltimore 1986). O. Mayr and K. Maurice, eds., *The Clockwork Universe: German Clocks and Automata, 1550–1650* (Washington, D.C., 1980).

A.M.

Averroës

Abū ʿl-Walīd ibn Rushd, Andalusian philosopher (1126–1198). One of the most influential Muslim philosophers in the Latin West, where he was widely known as Averroës, he became renowned for his commentaries on Aristotle's works and for his own contributions as an original thinker.

Born into a family of juridical and religious authorities in Cordoba, he was educated in Islamic law, theology, philosophy, and medicine. Around 1157 he wrote his earliest compendia of Aristotelian philosophy. The philosopher Ibn Tufayl introduced him in the late 1160s to the court of the Almohad Caliph Abu Ya'qub Yusuf, where he became a philosopher and physician. As a high-ranking judge, he played a leading role in political society. During the last years of his life he fell out of favor with Abu Ya'qub's successor, Abu Yusuf al-Mansur, for reasons that are not entirely clear. His engagement with the classical tradition seems to have played a role, but a power struggle among the jurists may have been more decisive. His philosophical works were burned, and he was banished from court but readmitted shortly before his death.

He was the author of more than 100 works on theology, jurisprudence, philosophy, astronomy, and medicine, many of which have not been preserved in the Arabic original, though some survive in Hebrew and Latin translations. His lasting influence lies in his role as commentator on Aristotle's works; these were commissioned by the caliph, probably for propaganda purposes, as the Almohads defended an interpretation of the Islamic religion that gave great weight to a rational understanding of its basic truths. Along similar lines, Averroës' only commentary on a work by Plato (on the *Republic,* which he knew in Galen's epitome), emphasizes the obligation of the ruler to educate his people. In his *Fasl al-maqal* (*Decisive Treatise*) he explained that revelation required the use of the rational syllogism and that ancient philosophers should be relied on for this purpose, except in cases where they were clearly mistaken. His short and middle-length commentaries on Aristotle abbreviated and reformulated the original works and were probably aimed at a wider audience, whereas in the later long commentaries the complete Aristotelian text is divided into individual sections accompanied by detailed interpretations. The quotations in these long commentaries sometimes provide the unique testimony to the Arabic translations of such works as the *Metaphysics* and give important evidence for the way the Aristotelian corpus was presented in the Arabic-speaking world. Not knowing Greek himself, he used different Arabic translations and manuscripts, and he turned to the Arabic versions of the Greek commentators on Aristotle (Alexander of Aphrodisias, Nicholas of Damascus, and Themistius, via the last of whom he gained access to Theophrastus) to enhance his understanding of the original wording, which was frequently unintelligible in the Arabic translations of Aristotle. His method was literal and thus not unlike the verbatim exegesis of the Qur'an propagated by the Almohads. His purist attitude is obvious in his interpretation of Aristotle, where he blamed earlier Greek authors for having distorted the philosopher's terminology, causing Arab authorities such as Avicenna and Avempace to misunderstand his ideas. He criticized Avicenna for introducing new ideas that he could not find in Aristotle's works; and for similar reasons he turned against the addition of Neoplatonic elements (such as Plotinian emanationism) to later Aristotelianism. With his anti-Avicennian stance, Averroës belonged to a group of like-minded Andalusian philosophers of the same period (such as Avempace and Maimonides) who were influenced by al-Fārābī. Among the ancient medical authorities, he was familiar with Galen and Dioscurides.

Whereas other exponents of Arabic philosophy, above all al-Ghazālī and Avicenna, had a considerable effect in the Muslim world, Averroës' influence remained marginal. This was perhaps because he was a member of a small elite, because of the nature of the patronage he enjoyed, because Almohad Spain was too fragile and isolated, or because his specific approach to Aristotelian philosophy did not sufficiently lend itself to fusions with Islamic religious thought. In the East the influence of Avicenna was overwhelming. The only one of Averroës' numerous disciples to devote a work to the classical tradition was Ibn Tumlus, author of a logical compendium. Averroës' works were also known by the 13th-century theologian Ibn Taymiyya and the 14th-century historian Ibn Khaldūn, and in the 15th century at the court of the Ottoman Sultan Mehmed II; Safavid scholars in Persia also copied some of his texts.

In the medieval West, a number of his works were translated into Latin during the 13th century, especially by Michael Scot in Spain and at the court of Frederick II. Subsequently, Averroës became one of the most important authorities for Aristotelian philosophy in the West; his reputation and honorary title, The Commentator, persisted throughout the Renaissance. Among his original works, *Tahāfut al-Tahāfut,* a refutation of a critique of Avicenna in al-Ghazālī's *Incoherence of the Philosophers*, was translated into Latin, but other key texts remained unknown. His influential medical treatise *Kulliyāt fī ʿl-tibb* (*Generalities,* known in Latin as *Colliget*) followed the Galenic paradigm, so that Averroës also gained significance as an interpreter of Galen. Many of the same works were translated into Hebrew, enabling him to attain a comparable importance among Jewish thinkers.

In the West he became the founding figure of a set of ideas referred to as Averroism. Some of these represented a radical Aristotelianism, directly concerning the classical tradition (the eternity of the world, based on Aristotle's *Physics*), whereas others referred to views that Averroës had allegedly produced himself, such as the "double truth": the idea that philosophy and religion have separate truths. This, however, was clearly a misrepresentation of his position. The University of Padua was one of the main centers of support for Averroism, as was the University of Paris, where in 1277 his works became one of the targets of a condemnation issued by the bishop of Paris. His authority was also challenged by Thomas Aquinas, who referred to him as the *depravator* ("distorter").

In modern scholarship Averroës still enjoys a reputation as the last defender of the philosophical tradition in Islam (Renan 1852). His key role in the rise of Aristotelian studies in the West is widely acknowledged, but so too is the significance of his philosophical thought within his own environment. In the Muslim world, in particular in North Africa, he is celebrated as the champion of rationalism by present-day philosophers seeking a revival of his thought in order to promote intellectual reform (von Kügelgen 1994).

BIBL.: Jamāl al-Dīn al-ʿAlawi, *al-Matn al-Rushdī, Madkhal li-qirāʾa jadīdah* (Casablanca 1986). Gerhard Endress and Jan A. Aertsen, eds., *Averroës and the Aristotelian Tradition: Sources, Constitution and Reception of the Philosophy of Ibn Rushd (1126–1198)* (Leiden 1999). Arthur Hyman, "Averroës as Commentator on Aristotle's Theory of the Intellect," in *Studies in Aristotle,* ed. Domonic J. O'Meara (Washington, D.C., 1981) 161–191. Barry S. Kogan, "Eternity and Origination: Averroes' Discourse on the Manner of the World's Existence," in *Islamic Theology and Philosophy: Studies in Honor of George F. Hourani,* ed. Michael E. Marmura (Albany 1984) 203–235. Josep Puig, "El proyecto vital de Averroës: Explicar e interpretar a Aristóteles," *al-Qantara* 32 (2002) 11–52. Ernest Renan, *Averroès et l'averroisme: Essai historique* (Paris 1852). Dominique Urvoy, *Ibn Rushd (Averroës)* (London 1991). Anke von Kügelgen, *Averroës und die arabische Moderne: Ansätze zu einer Neubegründung des Rationalismus im Islam* (Leiden 1994). A.AK.

Avicenna

Avicenna is the Latinized name of Abū-ʿAl al-Husayn ibn-ʿAbdallāh Ibn-Sīnā (b. before 980–d. 1037), the greatest and most influential philosopher in the Islamic world.

Avicenna lived during the period of the uncontested supremacy of medieval Islamic civilization. He came of age at the end of the 10th century, a time when the philosophical and scientific movement in Islam, and the Graeco-Arabic translation movement it fostered and sustained, had been in progress for more than two centuries. The vast majority of Greek philosophical and scientific texts had already been translated into Arabic upon demand from scientists and scholars, and in all intellectual fields new advances had been made in works originally composed in Arabic that surpassed the achievements of their Greek prototypes.

The outlook in which philosophical and scientific research was seen as a cultural good was developed in Baghdad, along with the beginnings of the Graeco-Arabic translation movement, in the second half of the 8th century, during the first decades of the rule of the new Arab dynasty of the Abbasids. With the decentralization of political power that followed the gradual erosion of caliphal authority by the middle of the 10th century, there arose in the vast Islamic empire, from the Iberian Peninsula to central Asia, local dynasties that took over regional governance while acknowledging the caliph in Baghdad as the ultimate overlord. With the decentralization of power there also came decentralization of culture, and the several capitals of the local dynasties began to imitate and rival Baghdad for intellectual and cultural supremacy, adopting the same tastes and fashions as those in the Abbasid capital.

Avicenna grew up in Bukhara, the capital of the Muslim Persian dynasty of the Samanids (819–1005) in central Asia. His precise date of birth is not known, though it is certain that it was quite a few years before 980, the year given in some sources. His father was governor of nearby Kharmaythan, and Avicenna grew up in the company of the Samanid administrative elite. His education began early, as was customary, and continued throughout his teens. He studied the traditional subjects—the Qur'an, Arabic literature, and arithmetic—and had a particular propensity for legal studies (Islamic canon law) as well as medicine (Galenic). In his famous autobiography, which is our sole source for this information, he reports that he had started practicing both law and medicine by the time he was sixteen.

In the autobiography Avicenna also says that, at the same time, he was studying all the branches of philosophy at increasingly advanced levels. The course of study or philosophical curriculum he says he followed was patterned on the classification of the philosophical sciences in the Aristotelian tradition of Alexandria in late antiquity and of the Baghdad Aristotelians under the early Abbasids: logic came first, with the Organon, as the instrument for the study of philosophy, followed by theoretical philosophy, which consisted of physics (Aristotle's physical and zoological treatises), mathematics (the Quadrivium: arithmetic, geometry, astronomy, music), and metaphysics. His studies were crowned by advanced research in the royal library of the Samanids, which he describes as follows in the autobiography:

> [The ruler of the Samanids] gave me permission and I was admitted to a building with many rooms; in each room there were chests of books piled one on top of the other. In one of the rooms were books on the Arabic language and poetry, in another jurisprudence, and so on in each room with a separate science. I looked through the catalogue of books by the ancients and requested those which I needed. I saw books whose very names are unknown to many and which I had never seen before nor have I seen since. I read those books, mastered their teachings, and realized how far each author had advanced in his science. So by the time I reached my eighteenth year I had completed my study in all these philosophical sciences. At that time my retention of knowledge was better, but today my grasp of it is more mature; otherwise the knowledge is the same, nothing new having come to me since. (Gutas 1988, 29)

Avicenna's description of the Samanid library and its contents is a significant witness for the spread and dominance of the Greek philosophical and scientific culture that was created in Baghdad in its first two centuries of existence (the city was founded in 762). As for his statement concerning his extraordinary performance in his studies, it is no conceited boast but is intended as a concrete illustration of his epistemological theory, which is centered on the ability of some individuals with a powerful intellect to acquire knowledge of the intelligibles—that is, theoretical knowledge—all by themselves, without the help of a teacher.

After a youth spent in tranquility, Avicenna was forced to abandon his native land as a result of the political troubles that led to the fall of the Samanid dynasty around the turn of the first millennium. He moved west and spent the rest of his life in the courts of local rulers in the Iranian world, predominantly in Hamadan and Isfahan. Though his services to these rulers were both political and medical, he spent most of his free time on philosophy, composing works on demand from disciples and patrons alike, holding philosophical sessions, and responding to philosophical questions presented to him by other scholars or former disciples. He died in 1037 in Hamadan and was buried there.

The work he left behind is immense and has yet to be properly inventoried. His contributions lie predominantly in philosophy, but in medicine he produced the monumental *Canon of Medicine,* which for many centuries remained the standard textbook of medicine both in Arabic in the East and in its Latin translation in the West. In philosophy he wrote more than a hundred works, ranging from brief essays to multivolume summae, in a wide variety of styles, including analytical studies, expository works, commentaries, abridgments, allegories, responsa, didactic poems, and works in a format he introduced to Arabic philosophical literature, the allusive and suggestive genre of "pointers and reminders" that he employed in the homonymous work *al-Ishārāt wa-t-tanbīhāt.* His magnum opus is the book he called *The Cure* (of the soul, that is; in Arabic, *ash-Shifā'*, most of which was translated into medieval Latin as *Sufficientia*), a summa of philosophy that includes, in 22 large volumes (Cairo edition, 1952–1983), all the parts of philosophy as classified in the Alexandrian tradition in late antiquity.

Avicenna treated practical philosophy very briefly in *The Cure* as an appendix to his section on metaphysics. He had little interest in these subjects, and other than some short essays on ethics and politics that are extant, he wrote a major work on ethics only in his youth, and it is now apparently lost.

The philosophical work of Avicenna is characterized by the attempt to create a philosophical system that would integrate, in a consistent whole based on Aristotelian logic, all the parts of philosophy as classified above. In practice this meant erecting a system that harmonized, rationalized, and completed all the discrete traditions of Aristotelian philosophy both among those traditions and with the Plotinian, Proclean, and other Neoplatonic accretions that accumulated over the ages. As a result, his works display a highly systematic and deeply rational structure and an all-encompassing comprehensiveness: whereas philosophers between Plotinus and Avicenna, writing in both Greek and Arabic, preferred the commentary as a form of expression, Avicenna eventually developed the *summa philosophiae* as his favorite genre. From this point of view he can be seen as the last philosopher of antiquity and the first Scholastic. In addition, he sought to express his new synthesis of philosophy in a way that would also respond to philosophical concerns of his age and society, which explains his experimentation with the wide variety of compositional styles listed earlier. He aimed at reaching audiences with different backgrounds and preparations in order to communicate the contents of his philosophy more effectively.

Avicenna's influence was monumental. Within Islam, he shaped the development of not only philosophy but also all subsequent intellectual life. His logic, a revised and expanded form of the Aristotelian Organon, achieved the status of the single scientific method of conducting research, and it penetrated—and dominated—modes of argumentation in Islamic jurisprudence and theology. It became the basis for further elaboration of numerous details, and it was cast and recast in various handbooks intended for pedagogic use. These handbooks by later systematizers were read in the traditional schools of the Ottoman Empire until the beginning of the 20th century, and they are still being read in religious schools throughout the Islamic world and especially in Iran. His physics, thoroughly Aristotelian, was the only physical doctrine to pose a serious challenge to the occasionalism of the Ash'arite theologians for the allegiance of intellectuals throughout the Islamic premodern period. His theory of the soul, going well beyond Aristotle's *De anima* and its late antique commentators, introduced novel theories on the function of the intellect, the internal senses, and the self-awareness that stand at the beginning of modern psychology. And his metaphysics, a systematic reorganization of the Aristotelian work by that name with significant developments in all major areas—causality, and the theories of essence, substance, and existence—which anticipate the modern approach to the subject, quickly became the major metaphysical doctrine of the Islamic world, penetrating Islamic theology and conditioning all later developments.

Avicenna's influence was no less substantial in the Latin West. Although relatively few of his works were translated into Latin, his ideas—often anonymously—shaped much in the way of terms and contents of discussion in both Scholastic philosophy and theology. In an interesting ironic twist of history, some of his ideas, which were attacked by Averroës for being un-Aristotelian, were used by the Latin Schoolmen to argue against Averroës himself during the height of the anti-Averroist controversy in Western Europe. His influence in European medicine was even more long-lived. His *Canon* was at the center of controversy in the Renaissance, with its new approaches to medicine, and new translations or revisions of its old approaches were still being made in the 17th century.

With regard to the classical tradition, Avicenna's influence is paradoxical. On the one hand he is without doubt the one thinker who is most responsible for integrating and, even more significantly, naturalizing classical Greek philosophical and medical thought into Islamic intellectual life. To put it differently, he made premodern Islamic intellectual life the natural extension of the classical tradition. By the same token, however, the very success of his efforts was also responsible for the gradual attenuation of interest in the original works of the Greek authors: after Avicenna, intellectuals by and large no longer read Aristotle and Galen; they read Avicenna instead. Even during the philosophical revival of the Safavid period in Iran (16th and 17th centuries), when scholarly interest in the translated philosophical literature was clearly evident—to this revival we owe the survival of many a philosophical manuscript that otherwise might not have been recopied—the Greek classics that were read were studied in the context of Avicenna's philosophy and his formulation of the problems. Nevertheless, the popularity of his thought and the long shadow of his influence, East and West, lent classical ideas, in whatever guise, a longevity they would not have otherwise enjoyed.

Avicenna, however, has hardly been credited for this accomplishment in either the East or the West. In the Islamic world, about a century and a half after his death there began to develop a tradition that presented his teachings as having esoteric and exoteric aspects, the esoteric part claiming to represent his true, and mystical, philosophy. Although he never ceased to be regarded as the unchallenged representative of Arabic Peripateticism, this aspect tended to fade into the background (or, among more conservative scholars, it tended to be indulged), as the allegedly mystical side was seen to represent his true teachings. In support of this thesis a number of pseudepigraphic works began to be attributed to him, and with the passage of time the "mystical" persona of Avicenna became dominant in popular perception. Especially in Iran, where in later centuries (and also because of his Persian origins) he was elevated to a most revered status, he was considered—and is considered to this day—the master of mystical illumination and esoteric gnosis, *irfān,* the origins of which allegedly go back to a pre-Islamic Persian spirituality. In this way, the classical heritage that Avicenna systematized, rationalized, and integrated into Islamic intellectual life is not recognized, and the vast majority of Muslim scholars to this day remain unaware of this accomplishment. As an example one need mention only the contemporary Moroccan philosopher Mohammed al-Jābirī, who, in his effort to introduce traditional rationalist thinking into modern Islamic discourse, presents Averroës as the true champion of rationalism and pits him against an allegedly obscurantist Avicenna, the source and origin of the plight of modern Islamic intellectual life.

Western scholarship has been hardly less guilty in this regard. In the 19th century, European scholars took their cue from the traditional Muslim view of Avicenna as mystic, and, aided by the European predisposition of their time to view "orientals" as mystical and irrational, concentrated on an investigation of the "esoteric" aspects of his philosophy. Most influential in this regard have been, in the 20th century, the studies by the French orientalist Henri Corbin. With the current resurgence of Islamic apologetic and anti-Western discourse, there are some in Western academia who, following Corbin's lead, present the mystical side of Avicenna as part of the age-old "oriental spirituality" that is far ahead of the West in its apperception of eternal truths. Avicenna has thus become a cult figure.

This state of affairs has delayed the serious study of Avicenna the philosopher and the translation and presentation of his works for an audience that is interested in philosophy. In the past two decades a younger generation of scholars has begun to look critically at his works in the context of the classical tradition and to reclaim for him the position of eminence that is his due in the history of philosophy in general and of Aristotelianism in particular.

BIBL. "Avicenna," *Encyclopaedia Iranica,* ed. Ehsan Yarshater (London 1982–) 3:66–110. A. Bertolacci, *The Reception of Aristotle's Metaphysics in Avicenna's Kitāb al-Šifā': A Milestone of Western Metaphysical Thought* (Leiden 2006). D. Gutas, *Avicenna and the Aristotelian Tradition* (Leiden 1988) and "The Heritage of Avicenna: The Golden Age of Arabic Philosophy, 1000–ca. 1350," in *The Heritage of Avicenna,* ed. J. Janssens and D. De Smet (Louvain 2002) 81–97. D. N. Hasse, *Avicenna's De anima in the Latin West* (London 2000). J. Janssens, *An Annotated Bibliography on Ibn Sīnā (1970–1989)* (Louvain 1991) and *First Supplement (1990–1994)* (Louvain-la-Neuve 1999). D. Reisman, *The Making of the Avicennan Tradition* (Leiden 2002). N. Siraisi, *Avicenna in Renaissance Italy* (Princeton 1987). T. Street, "Arabic Logic," in *Handbook of the History of Logic,* vol. 1, ed. D. M. Gabbay and J. Woods (Amsterdam 2004) 523–596, and "An Outline of Avicenna's Syllogistic," *Archiv für Geschichte der Philosophie* 84 (2002) 129–160. R. Wisnovsky, *Avicenna's Metaphysics in Context* (Ithaca 2003).

D.G.

B

Baalbek

The sheer size and splendor of the temple complex at Baalbek (Lebanon) have captured the imagination of every generation. The site has been referred to as "one of the very great monuments in the history of European architecture" (Wheeler 1962). Known in more recent times as a stronghold of the militant Shiite Hezbollah movement, it once centered on worship of a deity called in Latin *Iuppiter Optimus Maximus Heliopolitanus,* Jupiter Most High and Greatest of Heliopolis (the City of the Sun), Heliopolis being the Greek name under which Baalbek was known in the Roman period.

The temple complex may have been the exception to the rule that Near Eastern sanctuaries in Roman times were constructed through accumulated individual dedications by local benefactors. Its magnitude, most notably expressed in a row of six columns that remain standing in the main temple area (among the tallest extant from Antiquity) and in the gigantic monoliths used in the podium, has long raised questions about which authorities could have conceived such a project. The epigraphic evidence is scant, and the suggestion by the 6th-century chronicler John Malalas of Antioch—that the main temple was built by the 2nd-century Roman emperor Antoninus Pius—is otherwise unsupported. Suggested answers by modern scholars range from the Ituraean dynasts of Chalkis ad Libanum (in whose territory Baalbek was situated in the 1st century BCE) and other tribal leaders to an earlier Roman emperor. More fanciful legends that sprang up around the ruins include ancient stories about the involvement of the mythical figure Nimrod, and the modern "theory" by the Russian/Israeli author Zecharia Sitchin that Baalbek was used for landing and parking by the divine space travelers who visited Earth from another universe.

Monoliths unearthed in a nearby quarry show that the podium was meant to have been even larger. For unknown reasons, the famous "stone of the pregnant woman," as it is still popularly referred to, and another, more recently discovered monolith never made it to the temple. But because three others did, the site was known for centuries as the Trilithon, "site of the three stones." By the time that the first European travelers arrived (such as the Spanish rabbi Benjamin of Tudela in 1170), the Arab fortress into which the temple complex had been turned initially obscured its Roman past as a major sanctuary. Even in the late 16th century, when the Polish prince Radzivil visited Baalbek on his way to Jerusalem, it was as the legendary palace of King Solomon, described in 1 Kings 7:2–7, that the site was recognized, and it would be a long time thereafter before it was properly identified. An illustrated folio by Robert Wood, published in 1757, made Baalbek's splendor known to a larger public in the West, and so did paintings by David Roberts, who visited the site in 1839. The first proper archaeological explorations of Baalbek took place under the auspices of the German emperor Wilhelm II, whose visit to the ruins in 1898 inspired him to order the excavations that are now forever linked to the name of Otto Puchstein, accounts of which were published by Theodor Wiegand after the former's premature death.

BIBL.: Margarete van Ess and Thomas Weber, eds., *Baalbek: Im Bann römischer Monumentalarchitektur* (Mainz 1999). Friedrich Ragette, *Baalbek* (London 1980). E. M. Ruprechtsberger, *Vom Steinbruch zum Jupitertempel von Heliopolis/ Baalbek (Libanon)* (Linz 1999). Mortimer Wheeler, "Size and Baalbek," *Antiquity* 36 (1962) 6–9. Theodor Wiegand, ed., *Baalbek: Ergebnisse der Ausgrabungen und Untersuchungen in den Jahren 1898 bis 1905,* 3 vols. (Berlin 1921–1925). Robert Wood, *The Ruins of Balbec, Otherwise Heliopolis in Coelosyria* (London 1757).

T.K.

Bacchanalia and Saturnalia

The festival known as the Bacchanalia took place in Attica and Rome in honor of the god of wine, Dionysus or Bacchus. Originally confined to women, the festival involved drinking, dancing, masks, and a procession in which an ithyphallic image of the god was pushed along on a ship on wheels. The festival was prohibited in Rome in 186 BCE as a threat to public order. After centuries without evidence, we find references to festivals like the Bacchanalia in the Middle Ages; it is difficult to determine whether this was a case of continuity in social practices or of learned observers viewing rural customs through classical spectacles. The 13th-century *Chronicle of Lanercost,* for instance, refers to village girls dancing in honor of "Father Bacchus."

Some folklorists have claimed that Carnival derives from the Bacchanalia and even that it takes its name from the wheeled ship (*currus navalis*) containing the god's image; ships of this kind were drawn through the streets during Carnival in 15th-century Florence, for instance, and in Nuremberg. In any case, some early modern observers noted the classical parallels. Pieter Brueghel's painting of the battle between Carnival and Lent (1559) represents Carnival as a Bacchus-like figure astride a barrel. A Lutheran pastor from Bavaria, Thomas Kirchmeier, and the archbishop of Milan, Carlo Borromeo, were among those who described and condemned Carnival as a modern version of the Bacchanalia. What had once been viewed as *orgia,* "rituals," were now seen as "orgies." So wrote the Anglican clergyman Conyers Middleton in his *Letter from Rome* (1729). Whether or not he was aware of these early modern predecessors, Richard Dawkins, an English professor of Greek who observed the Carnival in rural Thrace at the beginning of the 20th century—noting especially the wooden phallus, the mock wedding, and the mock flaying—believed that he was witnessing a survival of the worship of Dionysus.

The European Carnival also resembles the classical Saturnalia and may owe something to that tradition too. The Saturnalia was the name of a Roman festival, celebrated on 17 December and marked by various rituals of inversion, notably the liberty given to slaves, who were waited on by their masters. Turning the world upside down in this way may have been a celebration of the renewal of the cosmos or a way of ensuring this regeneration. A mock king presided over the proceedings, which consisted mainly of eating, drinking, and playing a variety of games. This festival continued into early Christian times, providing the setting for the dialogues by Macrobius known as the *Saturnalia* (5th cent. CE). As in the case of the Bacchanalia, after centuries from which virtually nothing is known about festive practices, we find late medieval and early modern festivals of a broadly similar kind. The twelve days of Christmas, like the Saturnalia, were marked by massive eating, drinking, and game playing and also by rituals of inversion, with a Lord of Misrule or mock king presiding. When the "king" drank, for instance, everyone had to drink. Within these twelve days, 28 December, the day on which the Church commemorated the Massacre of the Innocents (Herod's slaughter of infants in the days after Jesus' birth), was celebrated in parts of medieval Europe, notably in France, with a particular ritual of inversion known as the Feast of Fools. A "bishop" or "abbot" of the fools would preside, the clergy would wear masks or women's clothes or put their vestments on back to front, and a mock Mass would be enacted in which the congregation might be cursed instead of blessed. Dancing in church formed part of the festivities from December into January.

In the 16th century Catholic and Protestant reformers, some of whom had had a good education in Greek and Roman literature, competed to suppress the Feast of Fools and also to reform or even to abolish Carnival. They did this not only on moral grounds but precisely because they saw it as a "pagan" (in other words, classical) survival, just as they saw May Day as a relic of the ancient feast of Flora. What had once been viewed as regenerative was now seen, by the clergy at least, as diabolical. A similar view of continuity, though without the condemnation, was held by the Cambridge anthropologist Sir James Frazer (who had indeed read Kirchmeier and other reformers). He noted that "traces" of the Saturnalia "long survived" in Britain, "in the practices of May Day and Whitsuntide, if not of Christmas." As for the Italian Carnival, he remarked, with some exaggeration, "We may well ask whether the resemblance does not amount to identity."

The efforts of the early modern reformers were partially successful. In some parts of Catholic and Protestant Europe, Carnival virtually disappeared, only to be revived in the 19th century (it is surely no accident that the continuities noted by Dawkins were to be found in the world of Eastern Christendom). Whether they go back to this revival or are much older, a few vestiges of these classical traditions are still to be found today. When adults or children wear paper crowns or British officers wait on their men on Christmas Day, they are, without knowing it, reenacting the Saturnalia.

BIBL.: Sandra Billington, *Mock Kings in Medieval Society and in Renaissance Drama* (Oxford 1991). R. M. Dawkins, "The Modern Carnival in Thrace and the Cult of Dionysus," *Journal of Hellenic Studies* 26 (1906) 191–206. James Frazer, *The Golden Bough,* 12 vols. (London 1911–1936). Jacques Heers, *Fêtes de fous et carnivals* (Paris 1983).
U.P.B.

Baghdad Aristotelians

Generations of Arabic-writing philosophers in Baghdad during the 10th and 11th centuries who propagated the preeminence of Aristotle in philosophical matters and adopted a scholarly approach to the study of his works and the Greek commentatorial tradition.

Al-Kindī (d. 873) and his successors won for philosophy a secure place in the intellectual environment of Baghdad, but by the time of their last representative, al-

Āmirī (d. 992), they had slowly lost their distinctiveness as philosophers through a gradual decline into Islamic apologetics. The cause of philosophy was then taken up by a new generation of thinkers, who essentially reintroduced it to Baghdad. This second line of Arabic philosophers is that of the Aristotelians of Baghdad, founded by the Nestorian scholar and translator Mattā Ibn-Yūnus (d. 940). His Aristotelianism can be traced directly to the Alexandrian commentators of late antiquity and reaches beyond them to Alexander of Aphrodisias and Themistius.

The philosophical curriculum adopted by the Baghdad Aristotelians followed the classification of the sciences current in Alexandria in late antiquity, a classification that had developed from that of Aristotle's works. Aristotle's Organon, including the *Rhetoric* and *Poetics,* and prefaced by Porphyry's introduction (*Eisagōgē*), constituted the canonical nine books of logic, the instrument of philosophy. Philosophy proper was then divided into theoretical and practical; theoretical philosophy was further subdivided into physics, mathematics, and metaphysics, and practical into ethics, economics (household management), and politics. This entire curriculum, including all the extant works of Aristotle, was translated into Arabic, in some instances by these philosophers themselves. The corpus of Aristotle's writings (with the sole exception of the *Politics,* which was apparently made available only in excerpts), together with the complete range of commentaries from Alexander of Aphrodisias onward, were established as the Arabic curriculum of school textbooks in logic, physics, metaphysics, and ethics by Mattā Ibn-Yūnus, who also provided the guidelines of a method for their study.

His colleague al-Fārābī (d. 950), al-Fārābī's student Yahyā Ibn-ʿAdī (d. 974), and the wide circle of disciples of the latter, prominent among whom were Abū-Sulaymān al-Sijistānī (d. ca. 985), Īsā ibn-Zura (d. 1008), al-Hasan Ibn-Suwār (d. ca. 1030), ʿAlī Ibn-al-Samh (d. 1027), and Abū-l-Faraj Ibn-at-Tayyib (d. 1043), engaged in rigorous textual analysis and philosophical interpretation of Aristotle's works and composed commentaries and independent monographs on all branches of philosophy.

The significance of the Baghdad Aristotelians lies not only in their cultivation and dissemination of a rigorous Aristotelianism but also, and perhaps more important, in their development of a scholarly and philological approach to the study of the translated texts in the Aristotelian tradition. In their efforts to understand precisely the meaning of these texts, they frequently prepared new translations of the key texts themselves, compared and collated earlier Syriac and Arabic translations, and annotated lavishly the school textbooks of their tradition. To their diligence we owe the survival of the most important (and, for some treatises, the only extant) manuscript of the Arabic Aristotelian Organon (MS Paris, Bibliothèque Nationale 2356) and the *Physics* (MS Leiden, Warner 583). They established Aristotelianism as the dominant philosophical current in Baghdad and, by extension, throughout the Islamic world. Their teachings traveled to Islamic Spain, where they formed the foundation of the development of Arabic philosophy, and in particular of the philosophy of Averroës (d. 1198). In the East, Avicenna (d. 1037) benefited from their texts, but he criticized them severely for their pedantry and lack of philosophical insight. His philosophy, which quickly dominated intellectual life in the Islamic world, put an end to the independent existence of their line by the end of the 11th century.

BIBL.: G. Endress, "Mattā b. Yūnus," in *Encyclopaedia of Islam* 6:844–846, and *The Works of Yahyā Ibn ʿAdī: An Analytical Inventory* (Wiesbaden 1977). C. Haddad, *Īsā Ibn Zura, philosophe arabe et apologiste chrétien* (Beirut 1971). Joel Kraemer, *Humanism in the Renaissance of Islam: The Cultural Revival during the Buyid Age* (Leiden 1986) 104–165, and *Philosophy in the Renaissance of Islam: Abū Sulaymān al-Sijistānī and His Circle* (Leiden 1986). E. Platti, *Yahyā Ibn ʿAdī: Théologien chrétien et philosophe arabe* (Leuven 1983). R. Walzer, *Greek into Arabic* (Oxford 1962).

D.G.

Barbarians

J. M. Coetzee's novel *Waiting for the Barbarians* (1980) is narrated from the perspective of an aging provincial governor who, while serving on an imperiled frontier more and more openly defies the state that has stationed him there. His gradual change of heart results in, and partly stems from, a physical relationship with one of the barbarians, a young woman to whom he loyally attends in an inversion of the usual master-servant relationship. Sexual, cultural, and political identities intersect in complex ways, so that the novel constantly addresses the relation of civilization and barbarism, exploring its ethical dimensions. Coetzee's spare style frustrates any desire to pinpoint a historical setting: some readers have understandably seen the novel as a thinly veiled parable for the apartheid South African society in which Coetzee was writing. But there is another intertext, elusive as it is suggestive: namely, the later Roman empire in the West. Behind Coetzee's milieu of state functionaries, soldiers, and barbarians stands a lengthy historiographic tradition that embraces Ammianus Marcellinus and Gibbon.

The very title, borrowed from the poem of the same name by Constantine Cavafy (1897–1908), points to Rome. Written at Alexandria amid the decline of the Ottoman empire, Cavafy's poem dramatizes the end of the Roman empire, which, in its death throes, has preened itself so as to be proud in surrender. But, in the end, the news of the barbarians' non-arrival only removes the pretext for final grandeur: "So now what will become of us, without barbarians./Those men were one sort of resolution" (tr. T. C. Theoharis, 93) The end of the Roman empire has thus been, by turns, both a historical event and a timeless symbol.

In their different ways, Coetzee and Cavafy are heirs to a long tradition of classical barbarians; equally pertinent examples can be found in historiography, such as J. G. A. Pocock's multivolume *Barbarism and Religion* (1999–), itself a reading of Gibbon and the Enlightenment. If ideas of the barbarian have metamorphosed between Homer and Coetzee, that is because of the ever-present, ever-changing need for self-definition by people using them. The flexibility of the concept cannot be overstated. By one definition, barbarians were simply foreigners known by the generic Greek or Latin term; by another they are marked by savagery that puts them at or beyond the edges of human culture. Any survey of the idea must identify a continuum from negative to neutral and even to the positive senses found when barbarians are presented as implicit criticism of civilization.

Homer's designation of the Carians as *barbarophōnoi* (*Iliad* 2.867) is the earliest attested Greek use of the term for "foreigners" who are literally "foreign-speakers"; tellingly, Homer uses a compound form of the word, pointing to the centrality of language to the ancient concept. Indeed, language was one criterion by which Greeks of the archaic period came to distinguish themselves from their Greek neighbors (Hall 1997, ch. 6). No such term is used of the Trojans. It is ironic that the term *barbaros,* used by Greeks of non-Greeks, itself seems to be a loanword from Anatolian languages. It appears that until the early 5th century BCE the term was, if not exactly neutral, then at least lacking the full measure of its later pejorative connotations. The Ethiopians in Homer are a clear case of good barbarians, for they are pious and beloved of the gods; but their image is vague and caricatured. It is no coincidence, further, that they are located on the outskirts of the known world (*oikoumenē*).

At the time of the Persian Wars, Greek views about foreigners became more charged, a change that must be seen alongside the evolution of the historiographic and dramatic genres. The Achaemenid empire provided subject matter not only for Aeschylus' *Persians* (472 BCE) and Herodotus' *Histories* (ca. 430 BCE) but also for Simonides' newly discovered fragment on the battle of Salamis. Such texts show that they "were one sort of resolution": it is in relation to them that classical Athenians developed a new sense of themselves as a polis. By the early 5th century BCE there were also more foreigners in Athens, following Solon's reforms relieving the conditions that had oppressed its poorest citizens. Many of the foreigners were slaves. A further factor was Athenian control over the Delian League: their leaders' drive for a united Greek front against the enemy (i.e., the Persians) was an attempt to strengthen their status among the city-states. Increased Athenian self-confidence after the war perhaps accounts for Aristotle's famous dictum that barbarians are "slaves by nature" (*Politics* 1, esp. 1252b8, quoting Euripides' *Iphigenia at Aulis* 1400). In Aristotle's time slaves were mainly the product of warfare.

In practice, of course, there was more to the Persians than the emerging ethnic stereotype allowed. Their empire united many people over a large area, and their courts were places where people, goods, and ideas came together to an unprecedented degree. Greeks are known to have been present in the Achaemenid empire, not merely as mercenaries but also in other capacities, such as the doctor Ctesias around 400 BCE. But a stereotype has hung heavily over ideas of ancient (and more recent) Iran, particularly when the Ottoman Empire was seen through the enduring frame of the Achaemenid. It is only since the 1980s, particularly with the Achaemenid History Workshop, that integrated attempts have been made to understand this period of Persian history in its own terms, rather than falling prey to Greek prejudices. In fact, inscriptions and reliefs (notably the treasury at Persepolis) show that the Persians themselves had a vivid sense of the distinctiveness of their subject peoples. Around the early 5th century the Athenians had a marked interest in imitating Persian styles in their art and everyday objects, a kind of *Perserie* that has been posited by analogy with the *Turquerie* of 17th- and 18th-century France (Miller 1997). At this time a word for "going Persian" entered the Greek vocabulary, namely *mēdizein,* which usually carries a negative connotation. Montesquieu, in his *Persian Letters* (1721), was one writer whose deployment of the old themes of Eastern luxury allowed critique of his own French society.

Herodotus' *Histories* brought to life not only the Persians but such a wide palette of foreigners that Plutarch, in his treatise *On the Malice of Herodotus,* would denounce him as a "barbarian lover" (*philobarbaros*). The Egyptians, though of minor importance to the main narrative, are the subject of his entire second book. The fascination exercised by Egypt and its people would mark it out for exceptional status, revealed by Western fascination for things Egyptian that never completely died but received a massive injection of interest around Napoleon's short-lived campaign. The *Chronique d'Égypte* (1809–1828), with its 23 volumes, is the largest of several scholarly and artistic enterprises arising directly from the expedition. The contrast between past grandeur and present dereliction found here is characteristic of the representation of Middle Eastern people in general (as Edward Said claimed in *Orientalism*), but is true also of Mediterranean locales in Greece and Italy. Over the long term, much of this interest has been antiquarian in nature, the emphasis being on collecting objects large and small, as well as imitating Egyptian styles in the broadest range of contexts. But in its Herodotean beginnings Egyptomania is strongly linked to place and inhabitants.

Pastoral nomads, most notably the Scythians of Herodotus' fourth book, are something else again. These Scythians emerge as a paradox: militarily powerful, they nonetheless lack the accoutrements of human culture, such as agriculture and houses, and certainly monuments (Hartog 1988). This type of barbarian is crucial to later conceptions of barbarians as the antithesis of culture, or even enemies thereof. Nearly 1,000 years later, Ammianus would reveal the force of tradition with regard to pastoral nomads. For Herodotus, the theory of environmental determinism was one means of making sense of these strange people, with reference to their indigenous climate. From this point of view his ethnology bears comparison with that of the roughly contemporary Hippocratic treatise, *Airs, Waters, Places*. The Scythians form a strong contrast with the Egyptians, in that their image is related not to commodities and collecting but to certain rugged qualities. One Scythian, the 6th-century BCE sage Anacharsis, receives an admiring description from Herodotus (4.76–77), in which he is marked out as a figure of primitive wisdom. This idea is later developed by the Cynics. Following extensive travels he was executed for trying to introduce the cult of Magna Mater among the Scythians. According to various versions Anacharsis was a friend of Solon, the son of a Greek mother, and one of the Seven Sages (Diogenes Laertius 1.101–105). His legendary status caused letters and sayings to be circulated under his name, in which the simple life of the Scythians is praised (Cicero, *Tusculan Disputations* 5.90). His life thus brings both the wisdom and the savagery of the Scythians to the fore, paving the way for the Enlightenment idea of the noble savage. The allure of barbarian wisdom is evidenced in Abbé Barthélemy's fictive account of his descendant in *Voyage du jeune Anacharsis en Grèce* (1788). Again, travel is a dramatization of intercultural exchange, undertaken in this case by a non-Greek.

Alexander's expedition, though brief in duration, brought an unprecedented degree of encounter between non-Greeks and Greeks by its sheer volume of human relocation. Interest in foreigners received strong support: Alexander took a number of scholars with him, and the early Ptolemies at Alexandria were active patrons of scholarship and the arts. For all its richness, however, Hellenistic ethnography reveals precious little attempt by Greeks to learn non-Greek languages, an indication of the ongoing cultural cachet of the Greek language (Momigliano 1971). Instead, the learning of Greek was a crucial step in upward mobility within the Hellenistic world, as a number of papyri suggest. It was in this period that the Jews entered Greek consciousness, becoming certainly one of the most distinctive and resilient *ethnē* of the Mediterranean in this period. The term *barbaros* does not, however, seem to be used of Jews in antiquity.

The earliest use of the term *barbarus* is by Romans of themselves: thus Plautus (e.g., *Curculio* 150; *Miles gloriosus* 211). This is a reminder of the degree to which Latin literature took its lead from Greek, and particularly the proximity of early Roman comedy to the Greek New Comedy of Menander and others. This self-stigmatization gives way, with the growth of Roman power in the Mediterranean in the 3rd and 2nd centuries BCE, to the use of the term for non-Romans—though not for Greeks, even though some Romans of the middle and late Republic, such as the elder Cato, resented the growing influence of Greeks at Rome. Cicero, in keeping with the rhetorical trope of hyperbole, uses the language of barbarism to describe the enemy within: both Antonius and Verres receive the appellation (*Philippics* 3.15; *Verrine Orations* 2.4.112).

Hellenistic ethnography would live on into the Roman empire in works such as Strabo's *Geography* and Pliny's *Natural History* (books 3–6). With them come highly systematized and even institutionalized views of barbarians. Such scholarly projects should be seen in contrast to other responses to foreigners at a time when the cosmopolitan city of Rome may have been home to as many as a million inhabitants from far afield. Juvenal's *Satires* (especially no. 3) and Martial's *Epigrams* give some sense of the ill feeling their presence sometimes engendered in the crowded city, particularly among the poorer inhabitants. The high degree of connectivity visible at various points in ancient history thus render the question of barbarians no less relevant at home in the large cities than on the peripheries. Juvenal's xenophobic tone is matched by Samuel Johnson's comment that his own 18th-century metropolis "suck[ed] in the dregs of each corrupted state" ("London").

In the late empire, the decline of Roman arms meant commensurately more power for the barbarians who had moved westward over a long period, across eastern and central Europe. The widespread use of the term, even by historians today, at once reflects the importance of foreign people in changing Rome's political landscape and belies the variety of ethnic groups that were appearing on the horizon. Many of these were Germanic peoples, but there were others too, such as the Huns, from farther east. The Roman military disaster against the Goths at Adrianople in 378 was sorely felt by contemporaries, some of whom resorted to the sharp language of barbarism. Like the sack of Rome by Alaric's forces in 410, it also stimulated a degree of soul-searching: Jerome (in the preface to his *Commentary on Ezekiel*), Augustine (*City of God*, especially books 1–3), and Orosius (*History against the Pagans*) all saw the barbarians as catalysts of change, but they responded with varying degrees of horror or resignation. After the death of Constantine, in both East and West a large number of military commands went to non-Romans and particularly to Germans. Such 4th- and 5th-century careers were sometimes shrouded in controversy. Thus, the general Stilicho, son of a Vandal, rose to the office of commander or *magister militum* in 392–393 under Theodosius I and then acted as regent for the youthful Honorius, only to be executed later. An irony of negative views of barbarians is that, in practice, many of them sought to acquire or emulate features of Roman culture, as Cavafy's poem suggests. Examples are the adoption of Christianity (often in its heretical Arian form, however) and of Roman law, and even the influence of the Latin language in the evolution of proto-Romance, precursor to the Romance languages. In such ways some barbarians would prove to be more Roman than the Romans.

The Huns had a special place amid the changes of late antiquity and have been vividly remembered as barbarians par excellence. It was their speedy appearance that caused the Goths to cross the Danube at Adrianople, with disastrous effect for the Romans, including the death of the emperor Valens. Ammianus offers a full-blown ethnographic excursus (31.2), in part as an explanation of events. As he and others recount, their appearance was distinctively frightening, and their habits marked them out as maximally far from Roman *civilitas*. Their subsequent leader, Attila (d. 453), has long been a source of lurid fascination. But one example is Franz Liszt's symphonic poem *Hunnenschlacht* ("Battle of the Huns," 1857), inspired by Wilhelm von Kaulbach's mural depicting the battle of the Catalaunian fields. Both Kaulbach and Liszt present Attila's defeat by Theoderic as a victory of Christianity over paganism. The film *Sign of the Pagan* (1955) demonstrates its appeal to 20th-century popular culture and again shows religion as a marker of barbarism. The image of the Huns has increasingly been challenged by historical and archaeological work of the 20th century, including the ethnoarchaeological fieldwork of Otto Mänchen-Helfen.

Admiration for barbarians reaches a new level with Salvian of Marseilles in the 5th century: in *De gubernatione Dei* the barbarians' high moral character is contrasted with Roman laxity and decadence (esp. 7.7). They are in fact tools by which God instructs Christians of his providential scheme. By means of explicit comparison, barbarians are sources of Roman self-criticism; implicitly, they had already had that role in the early empire, as for example when Tacitus in his treatise *Germania* presents the Germans as bastions of the *libertas* that the Romans had lost. Tacitus' positive view of the Germans, though conceived in relation to Rome, would be enthusiastically adopted in the guise of German Romantic nationalism: the victorious chieftain of the Cherusci people, Arminius or Hermann, would become central to the new ideology. If barbarians were good for Greeks and Romans to think with, then they would provide Europe's emerging nation-states with an ancient, primordial framework in which to create their own pasts.

BIBL.: P. J. Geary, *The Myth of Nations: The Medieval Origins of Europe* (Princeton 2002). J. M. Hall, *Ethnic Identity in Greek Antiquity* (Cambridge 1997). F. Hartog, *The Mirror of Herodotus: The Representation of the Other in the Writing of History* (Berkeley 1988). M. C. Miller, *Athens and Persia in the Fifth Century: A Study in Cultural Receptivity* (Cambridge 1997). A. Momigliano, *Alien Wisdom: The Limits of Hellenization* (Cambridge 1971). P. Vasunia, *The Gift of the Nile: Hellenizing Egypt from Aeschylus to Alexander* (Berkeley 2001).

G.PR.

Barberini Faun

Statue depicting a sleeping satyr, seated on a boulder, his right arm raised above his head and his legs splayed; a wolf's hide hangs from his left shoulder to the base (now at the Glyptothek, Munich). The sculpture, a creation of the 3rd century BCE, has also been deemed a copy or a reworking from Roman times. It was found ca. 1627 in Rome, at Castel San Angelo—at the Mausoleum of Hadrian—and was given by Urban VIII to his nephew Cardinal Francesco, who was setting up an antiquarium at the new family palazzo. The Faun remained in that room until 1640. Cassiano dal Pozzo compared it to the masterpieces in the Vatican's Belvedere Court (the Laocoön, the Apollo, etc.) and to the Farnese Hercules; Tezi, in his *Aedes Barberinianae* (1642), described it as the most beautiful sculpture of the collection. A 1644 letter from Poussin to Chantelou, who had commissioned a copy of it (now lost), reveals a great appreciation for the work, whose style is compared to that of the most beautiful Greek statues. Tezi's text and the engraving that illustrates it show that at that time the Faun was placed on his back, in a nearly horizontal position. Only in 1679, after a fresh restoration, did the figure assume the seated position, at which time it was given a base decorated with a vine and a flute (Montagu 1989). The supine position chosen by the restorer in 1628 was connected to an iconography of drunkenness, attested both for Noah and for satyrs starting in the 15th century, and it moreover recalls the Satyr attributed to Montorsoli and once owned by the Barberini (ca. 1532; now in St. Louis). A torso of a sleeping Endymion (now in St. Petersburg), which at that time was exhibited alongside the Faun, influenced the restoration as well.

The statue gained renown in the 18th century. In 1704 it was presented as one of the most important ancient sculptures in Maffei's *Raccolta di statue*—an ennobling interpretation, and this was accepted in Montfaucon's *Antiquité expliquée* (1722). Between 1726 and 1730 Bouchardon sculpted a copy in marble, now in the Louvre, that initially graced the Parc Monceau, a decorative use envisioned also for the Château de Menars and realized in 1861 at Peterhof, the Russian imperial residence. In the first half of the 18th century opinions of its value were not unanimous. Winckelmann considered it far from the perfection of the Belvedere statues, though he appreciated the finesse of its workmanship and its realistic rendering of sleep. This is the sense in which Henry Fuseli cites it in the figure of Bottom in his *Titania's Awakening* (1795). But in 1786 Giovanni Volpato and Raffaello Morghen included it in their *Principi del disegno,* a collection of engravings of ancient statues chosen as excellent models and a work based on Winckelmann's own aesthetics; Volpato also marketed a reproduction of the statue in bisque. Restored in marble by Pacetti in 1799, it was then sold to Ludwig of Bavaria, and, after a long lawsuit, it reached Munich in 1821. In the 20th and 21st centuries it has been taken up in figurative works that reflect on the relationship between the arts (J. S. Sargent; L. Renner), but it has also become an icon of drunkenness, of sleep, and of eros, in artistic production as well as in mass communication.

BIBL.: F. Haskell and N. Penny, *Taste and the Antique* (New Haven 1981) 28, 202–205. J. Montagu, *Roman Baroque Sculpture: The Industry of Art* (New Haven 1989). B. Sismondo Ridgway, *Hellenistic Sculpture* (Madison 1990) 1:314–321. H. Tetius, *Aedes Barberinae ad Quirinalem descriptae,* ed. L. Faedo and T. Frangenberg (Pisa 2005) 36, 46, 484–487. L.F.

Translated by Patrick Baker

Basilisk

Derived from the Greek *basilískos* ("small king," Latin *regulus*), the name for a small poisonous snake originally native to Libya. According to ancient sources (esp. Pliny 8.33, 29.19), this animal's distinctive features included its half-erect, regal manner of locomotion, its deadly venomous breath, and a petrifying gaze. This last quality, which elevates the basilisk to an animal counterpart of the Medusa, especially excited later imaginations, which made an enormous monster out of the small snake, mythologized it, and, following Isidore of Seville's definition of it as "king of snakes" (*rex serpentium*), believed it could be found throughout Europe. In the few ancient sources that treat it, however, the basilisk is a strictly local phenomenon. Moreover, it is either described concretely as a poisonous desert snake (for example in Lucan, *Pharsalia* 9.724–726; 825–833) or, as in Heliodorus' *Aithiopika* (3.8), used metaphorically for malevolent interpersonal behavior. The unraveling of this tradition resulted in large part from uncertainty regarding the basilisk's birth; according to ancient sources, it could hatch from the egg of a snake or a bird. For the basilisk to be accepted in northern Europe, however, it had to be procreated by means unrelated to Africa and the animals native to it. The idea that the basilisk hatches from a rooster's, or cock's, egg was first contrived by Alexander Neckam in his *De naturis rerum* (1180); it thereafter became standard and gave rise to the alternative name "cockatrice." This does not seem to be an arbitrary explanation, but rather probably stems from ancient accounts that the cock's crow is a proven counteragent to the basilisk (Aelian 3.31). In addition, the term *basilisk* was then applied to the rooster because of the visual similarity between the rooster's comb and a king's crown.

Poison and antidote, basilisk and rooster, from then on become inseparable. Into the 17th century popular belief envisioned the basilisk as a chimera composed of a rooster, snake, and dragon, hatched from a yolkless chicken egg that had been incubated by a snake or toad. It dwelled in caves, well shafts, and cellars, posing a threat to humans, and could grow to eight meters in length. It could be combated most effectively with the aid of a mirror, which would reflect the monster's deadly gaze and petrify it—numerous local legends report such Perseus-like deeds of heroism, which seem to have their source in a medieval account of an episode in the life of Alexander (*Gesta Romanorum,* chap. 139). The two counteragents known from antiquity, however—the odor of a weasel and the cock's crow—retreat more and more from view. Like the Gorgon's head, the basilisk's carcass had apotropaic properties, and illnesses could be cured with its blood.

The basilisk's allegorical meaning is closely linked to biblical exegesis and Christian animal symbolism. The basilisk appears seven times in the Vulgate, always in the context of apocalypse and sin. It is associated with injustice, lying, envy, and lust, and even with the devil and the Antichrist, for which it is often seen as an allegory. Accordingly, there are many depictions in sacred church spaces (baptismal fonts, apsidal friezes) showing the basilisk in conflict with Christ the Savior. A connection between allegorical Christian interpretation and popular tales came to the fore in etiological legends and town histories in which the heroic vanquishing of a threatening monster in the form of the basilisk (a Perseus motif) is related to the symbolic exorcism of the devil. A conquered basilisk can have a positive connotation in this context: for example, as the bearer of the coat of arms of Basel, it not only has apotropaic functions but also keeps the viewer mindful of a great deed of the local populace. Literary adaptations and mentions of the basilisk are numerous. The most popular is found in J. K. Rowling's *Harry Potter and the Chamber of Secrets,* in which the protagonist succeeds in killing the basilisk only with the aid of the phoenix Fawkes. A much less dangerous but, on the other hand, actually existing species of basilisk is found in the iguana family. The common basilisk (*Basiliscus basiliscus*), for example, takes its name from its striking similarity to snakelike depictions of basilisks from antiquity, as well as to the dragonlike ones, often crowned, which appeared beginning in the early modern period.

BIBL.: Laurence A. Breiner, "The Basilisk," in *Mythical and Fabulous Creatures: A Source Book and Research Guide,* ed. Malcolm South (New York 1987). Marianne Sammer, *Der Basilisk: Zur Natur- und Bedeutungsgeschichte eines Fabeltieres im Abendland* (Munich 1998). M.BA.

Translated by Patrick Baker

Baths

Although they existed in classical Greece, public baths are associated particularly with Roman civilization. Bathing in public was an essential part of all Roman daily life, for relaxation, social interaction, health, and hygiene. Nevertheless, few coherent accounts of either process or setting exist in the ancient literature, apart from the description of a bathhouse by Vitruvius (5.10), from the late 1st century BCE. Roman medical writers and encyclopedists, such as Pliny the Elder, discussed the use of baths as preventative and curative health measures. Public baths were a ubiquitous physical presence in urban landscapes, and the buildings are easily recognizable, even from ruins today, by their pools and heating systems. Structures ranged from the vast and complex *thermae* of Rome. built by the emperors, to the simple domestic-scale buildings which sufficed in forts or in urban neighborhoods. The practice and the associated technology all but disappeared in the West after the 6th century but continued in the East throughout the Byzantine period, directly influencing Arabic culture and surviving today in Islamic hammams.

In the West the habit of bathing persisted longest in palaces and among the clergy, but it was no longer meant to be a pleasure or a focus of social life. Christian mores were not, however, opposed to cleanliness in principle, and the maintenance of health was an acceptable rationale for the use of baths and thermal spas. Thus, the ancient writings on the medical uses of bathing were widely copied throughout the Middle Ages and continued to inform medical treatises even down to the early 19th century.

Interest in how the baths worked and their wider role in ancient society developed in the Renaissance and was based largely on Vitruvius' account and anecdotal evidence from the ancient sources. Exceptionally, the imposing remains of the imperial *thermae* of Rome were repeatedly studied and drawn by leading artists and architects of the Renaissance, particularly Palladio, for quite other reasons. Their interest was in the buildings as exemplars of the architectural practices of the ancients and as inspiration for their own designs. This interest in the public architecture of the baths continued through the 19th century, as can be seen in winning entries for the Grand Prix de Rome sponsored by the École des Beaux-Arts, and it culminated in the design of New York City's Pennsylvania Station (1910), heavily influenced by the Baths of Caracalla, and other Neoclassical railway termini.

Generally, however, the lack of fit between the available ancient written sources and the physical remains posed a stumbling block—until the excavation in 1824 of the Forum Baths of Pompeii, which appeared to match Vitruvius' prescriptions exactly. This led to a new, more archaeological, interest in the many small baths that had appeared in excavations throughout the Roman world but had been largely ignored except by local antiquarians. The wealth of detail these studies provided, combined with the opportunity for portraying the naked body, gave rise to many late Victorian depictions of ancient baths by artists like Lawrence Alma-Tadema and Edward Poynter. The renewed interest in ancient bathing also coincided with sanitary reforms of the mid-19th century, when public bathhouses were built in many industrial cities of Western Europe as a form of social control for the urban poor. Such attitudes to contemporary public baths in turn informed the scholarly literature on ancient practices; Roman emperors and aristocrats who funded baths were seen as acting from the same concerns for the health and welfare of their subjects as their modern counterparts. Since bathing was not generally considered part of the "high" culture of antiquity, many such anachronistic assumptions went unquestioned well into the 1900s.

BIBL.: Janet DeLaine, "Historiography: Origins, Evolution and Convergence," in *Bains curatifs et bains hygiéniques en Italie: De l'antiquité au moyen âge,* ed. Marie Guérin-Beauvois and Jean-Marie Martin (Rome 2007). F. K. Yegül, *Baths and Bathing in Classical Antiquity* (New York 1992). J.D.

Bellori, Giovan Pietro

Antiquarian and art historian, 1613–1696. A Roman by birth, he was reared in a circle of *érudits* such as Francesco Angeloni and Giovan Battista Agucchi, who had continued into the mid- and late 17th century the cult of antiquity and art begun by Annibale Carracci (1560–1609). Bellori entered the studio of Domenichino around 1629 but did not continue on to become a painter, devoting his life instead to art criticism and literature. In 1670 he accepted the position of Commissioner of Roman Antiquities. Joining forces with the engraver Pietro Santi Bartoli and the printer de' Rossi, he developed a project to catalogue, and thus to safeguard, the immense archaeological patrimony of Rome. This team produced a series of illustrated books devoted to ancient topography, to the great imperial monuments (the Columns of Trajan and Antoninus Pius, the triumphal arches), to painting, and to the customs of the ancients. A number of numismatic publications constituted a first attempt at a corpus of imperial coins and medals. Thanks to his extensive connections on the international scene, Bellori realized that European public opinion could be influenced to perceive the monuments of Rome, from the smallest to the largest, from a coin to the Colosseum, as forming a seamless garment, one that was shamefully rent by expropriations and sales and stood in need of protection. He stressed the importance of Latin as the international language, and of engraving as the medium by which the monuments became common intellectual property, taking the place of privatization and clandestine movement. Into the pages of the *Giornale de' letterati,* one of the first learned journals of Europe, he introduced both archaeology (including accounts of ongoing excavations) and contemporary art as matters fit for the attention of a learned public without borders.

Bellori's important lecture on the ideal in art (*L'Idea del pittore, dello scultore e dell'architetto scelta dalle bellezze naturali superiore alla natura,* 1664) sealed his enduring reputation, into the present, as the lamp-tender of 17th-century classicism and as a rigid theorist of ideal beauty. The essay is in fact a theoretical and historical analysis of the creative process in art. Bellori offers an Aristotelian correction to the Platonic theory of Ideas, downplaying the transcendent and metaphysical side of artistic creation and instead emphasizing the artist's relation to experience. The Carracci reform of painting had turned attention to nature, and now that reform was given theoretical form. The point of Bellori's lecture was to clarify the intellectual dimension of art for the artists themselves—not to flatten it out as a paradigm valid for eternity, but to exalt the specificity of the figurative enterprise.

This is borne out in his most important and influentual work, *Vite de' pittori, scultori et architetti moderni* (Rome 1672). Through it he became the Vasari of his century, though in a more focused way, avoiding short lives and concentrating on only 12 artists. His biographies, with their careful structure and ideology, and their famous ecphrases, showed the international learned community that the history of images and of artists was an inescapable part of European culture. Thus Bellori's writings marked a step toward the liberation of the figurative arts from the old Platonic prejudice. They brought to the attention of the République des Lettres a group of artists whose concern was not simply to take over the values of a nobler art (such as poetry) but rather to reflect and cherish the values of their own art and history.

BIBL.: Evelina Borea and Carlo Gasparri, eds., *L'Idea del bello: Viaggio per Roma nel Seicento con Giovan Pietro Bellori* (Rome 2000). Elizabeth Cropper, "'La più bella antichità che sappiate desiderare': History and Style in Giovan Pietro Bellori's Lives," in *Kunst und Kunsttheorie 1400–1900* (Wiesbaden 1991) 145–173. Tomaso Montanari, "Introduction," in G. P. Bellori, *The Lives of the Modern Painters, Sculptors and Architects: A New Translation and Critical Edition,* trans. A. Sedgwick Wohl, notes by H. Wohl (New York 2005) 1–43. Erwin Panofksy, *Idea: A Concept in Art Theory* (German ed. 1924, English trans. New York 1968). Giovanni Previtali, "Introduzione," in G. P. Bellori, *Le vite de' pittori, scultori e architetti moderni,* ed. E. Borea (Turin 1976) ix–lx. T.M.

Translated by Joseph Connors

Belvedere Torso

Portion of a Hellenistic sculpture (now in the Vatican Museum); its discovery was a major influence on Renaissance art. Giorgio Vasari declared in 1550 that along with several other famous Vatican antiquities, the Torso was responsible for the transition from a crude and arid style of art in the 15th century to the kinds of perfect design and grace that were characteristic of the High Renaissance. Though it was often considered in the company of other famous masterpieces from the classical period, including the Laocoön and the Apollo Belvedere (it remains near them today), the Torso was viewed as distinctive, first of all, because it was signed. The inscription "Apollonius, son of Nestor, from Athens has made it," located on the drapery at the front of the pedestal, made the *Torso* virtually unique among the classical antiquities known and revered in the Renaissance. Not that this attribution was able to shed much light on the work. Because Pliny's *Natural History* (1st cent. CE), avidly read during the Renaissance for its information regarding the history of ancient art, makes no mention of such a sculptor, the Torso's early modern admirers were left to assume that lost works by truly famous ancient artists, like the sculptors Phidias and Praxiteles, were even greater in some unimaginable way. The Torso was also to be distinguished from its celebrated companions because it was radically fragmentary and—what is even more remarkable—because no effort ever seems to have been made to restore it. All these circumstances, combined with persistent doubts about assigning the statue a definite identity (at first generally supposed to be Hercules; later scholarship has suggested Philoctetes or Marsyas), eventually led to recognition of the Torso as an icon of artistry itself. In particular, it seems to have been canonized by its association with Michelangelo. According to a story attributed to Bernini, Michelangelo was discovered enraptured and on his knees in front of the Torso, declaring that it was the work of a sculptor who knew more than Nature. Such an encounter is probably legendary, but the oeuvre of Michelangelo himself, from the *Ignudi* on the Sistine Ceiling to the *Victory* to Christ and Saint Bartholomew in the *Last Judgment,* makes it clear that the Torso exerted a major influence on him. Countless other artists and aesthetes have celebrated this work. It was drawn by Goltzius and Rubens; numerous statuettes in various degrees of completeness were made in imitation of it; and in a 1524 portrait of the Licinio family, a little replica of the statue (partly restored) is placed in the hands of the eldest son, presumably to indicate that this was a family of artists. Among the many paeans to ancient art by Winckelmann, the eminent 18th-century scholar of classical culture, perhaps none is more eloquent than his account of the Torso: "I have the sensation as though the statue's back, bent over by lofty acts of contemplation, manages to create for me the image of a head which is busied with happy recollection of its extraordinary deeds. And just as this head, so full of majesty and wisdom, rises before my eyes, so the other missing limbs start to form themselves in my thoughts. Out of the present condition of the work a new creation assembles itself, producing, as it were, a sudden complete restoration." Equally passionate was the response of Sir Joshua Reynolds: "What artist ever looked at the Torso without feeling a warmth of enthusiasm, as from the highest efforts of poetry? From whence does this proceed? What is there in this fragment that produces this effect, but the perfection of the science of abstract form?" This fascination endured into the 19th century, with J. Q. A. Ward's sculptural portrait of a freed slave (*Freedman,* New York, Metropolitan Museum) and appears in the present day in works of the sculptor Aaron Quinn Brophy, who has said, "At the age of 19, I vividly remember seeing the *Belvedere Torso* in the Vatican Museum. It is a fragment of an ancient figure that I find more compelling than any complete figure I have ever seen."

BIBL.: L. Barkan, *Unearthing the Past: Archaeology and Aesthetics in the Making of Renaissance Culture* (New Haven 1999). C. Schwinn, *Die Bedeutung des Torso vom Belvedere für Theorie und Praxis der bildenden Kunst vom 16. Jahrhundert bis Winckelmann* (Bern 1973). R. Wünsche, *Il torso del Belvedere* (Vatican City 1998). L.B.

Bentley, Richard

English classical scholar, 1662–1742. Probably the most celebrated classicist of his day and certainly one of the most polemical, Bentley has enjoyed a complicated but lively reputation to the present day. His constant experimentation with new approaches and materials for publication, along with his manifest desire to attract attention as a public intellectual, made him particularly remarkable in the period around 1700. Few contemporary classicists aimed for a well-defined personal style; no one, especially, would have expected a scholar of such prominence to emerge from England. Strictly speaking, Bentley invented no new method or technique, yet he left distinctive marks on the study of literary history, the technical field of poetic meter, and the practice of textual criticism.

In professional terms, Bentley spent his entire life in the more exclusive reaches of the English Church and universities, making additional forays into the court and the book trade. Failing to win a college fellowship following his baccalaureate in 1680 at St John's, Cambridge, and still too young to take clerical orders, he was hired in 1683 by the influential London churchman Edward Stillingfleet, nominally as tutor to Stillingfleet's younger son. Actually, Bentley also had some responsibility for Stillingfleet's enormous library; more broadly, he observed at close range and may have assisted in Stillingfleet's politically charged publishing campaigns. London further exposed Bentley to active scholars such as Thomas Gale, Edward Sherburne, and Paul Colomiès, whose interests included the classics; he worked in the important manuscript library of Isaac Vossius (today in Leiden) and succumbed to the cult of Joseph Scaliger, whose printed letters he read with pen in hand.

Yet Bentley's scholarly projects lacked direction until his year in Oxford, where he accompanied Stillingfleet's son in 1689. Manuscripts, Greek, patristics, historical chronology, and textual criticism were important studies there: Bentley's first signed publication, the *Epistola ad Millium* (1691), was commissioned as an appendix to the first printing of Joannes Malalas' 6th-century world chronicle from a Bodleian manuscript. The *Epistola* revealed Bentley's lifelong taste for controversy, for minute erudition, and for breathtaking connections between disparate subjects. Picking out Malalas' very occasional references to the history of poetry, Bentley quarreled with him and with celebrated early modern scholars over the titles of lost tragedies, the attribution of fragments, the eras of poets, and the prosody of the anapestic line. The *Epistola* established Bentley in England and northern Europe as a brilliant and decisive scholar—and as one still in search of a publication project that could give a more constructive form to his mastery of Greek literary history.

In 1690 Bentley was named domestic chaplain to Stillingfleet, who was then a bishop. Returning to London, Bentley spent the 1690s establishing himself as a writer in English and, gradually, as an organizer of the capital's intellectual life. As he delivered the prestigious sermon series known as the Boyle Lectures, won the post of Royal Librarian, and orchestrated a new series of classical editions for the Cambridge University Press, his own scholarly publications neither accelerated nor showed the mark of personal initiative, even if they began to take a more intelligible form than the deeply miscellaneous *Epistola ad Millium.* His collection of Callimachus' fragments (1697) was produced on request, as was the *Dissertation on the Epistles of Phalaris* (1697, 2nd ed. 1699), regarded then and now as one of Bentley's outstanding works. By the 1690s few people, and no scholars, really believed that Phalaris, a 6th-century Sicilian tyrant, was the author of the wildly histrionic, stylistically suave epistles that circulated under his name. But a multiplayer pamphlet war, of the endlessly ramifying kind that regularly swept Church, university, and political circles, now demanded a contribution from Bentley, to whom it appeared the right course rigorously to disprove the Phalaris letters' authenticity. Eschewing stylistic argument, he focused on historically suspect *realia* in the letters, from toponyms to the names of drinking vessels to the lifespan of Pythagoras, one of Phalaris' alleged correspondents. In the 1690s it would have been more usual to publish on such topics in Latin; the *Dissertation* thus marked an important experiment in English classical publishing as well as a powerful new way for Bentley's erudition to reach his compatriots. Perhaps for the same reason, the elegant and concise first *Dissertation* provoked a hail of hectoring pamphlets in reply; Bentley's decision to issue a grossly expanded second edition, in 1699, shows the difficulty and novelty he faced in presenting philological argument to a vernacular public.

Bentley became Master of Trinity College, Cambridge, in 1700, where he enjoyed more than a decade of relative peace and prosperity. Most visibly at the time, he organized and aided younger scholars who produced intensively worked editions for his Cambridge University Press: the most famous of these protégés, Ludolf Küster, edited the Suda (Cambridge 1705) and Aristophanes (Amsterdam 1710). Bentley himself began editing Horace in 1702, marking a sharp change of scholarly direction. He published for the first time not a multifarious treatise but a focused study of a single text. He studied an entire corpus of attractive poems, turning away from fragment collection. And he made his interventions not on a little-known Greek source, but on a Latin school poet beloved by the genteel. Still more remarkably, Bentley presented strong intellectual reasons of his own for undertaking the Horace project. Discussing his editorial method at copious and combative length, he loudly reanimated older Humanist debates that pitted emendation by conjecture against emendation from manuscript. In declaring himself conjecture's most loyal defender and most brilliant exponent, Bentley cemented a central part of his reputation for contemporaries and for readers ever since—a reputation that tends to eclipse the many individual readings he favored that have remained well regarded, a great number of which he actually derived from manuscripts. When the Horace edition appeared, after many printing difficulties, in the first weeks of 1712, it produced the outrage Bentley had evidently hoped for. Alternately satirized and praised in the English-language press, it called forth questioning responses from scholars abroad, and it inspired a rash of less expert conjecturers to publish highly experimental Latin editions in ensuing decades.

Meanwhile, Bentley's bitter conflict with the fellows of Trinity was beginning, and his research team disappeared through dispersion and deaths. He also quarreled in print with the scholar and journalist Jean LeClerc over the fragments of Menander. Chiefly, however, Bentley sought to remake himself in the 1710s as a learned theologian, reprinting his Boyle Lectures at the Cambridge University Press, joining a pamphlet war in defense of the textual authority of the New Testament, capturing the rich Regius Chair of Divinity in Cambridge, and in 1716 beginning his own New Testament edition. Yet if this project was motivated by a desire to provide a definitive account of the text's early history—a lively issue that focused, at the time, on the possibility that Christian factions had inserted or removed passages around the time of the Council of Nicaea—in practice Bentley found nothing new in the manuscripts concerning the most controversial passages. No hint of a general theory or argument emerges from his working papers. With two assistants, he collated a large number of manuscripts in England, France, and Italy. But Bentley ultimately decided either that it was pointless to publish without more manuscript readings, or that it was pointless for him personally to publish without making some intervention in contemporary debate over the textual bases for Christianity, or perhaps both.

His return to classical study was provoked by the Terence edition of Francis Hare (1724), who claimed that his new theory of Terence's meter came directly from Bentley's mouth. Clearly Hare had heard something very like what Bentley eventually wrote, but his exposition was neither clear nor coherent. In Bentley's own edition of Terence (1726), he introduced the terms *rhythmus, accentus, ictus,* and *arsis* as the structural principles of Terence's verse—developments that were meant to supersede earlier, inconclusive debates over the permissible feet of the Old Comedy, and that exercised powerful inspiration for theorists of prosody in the 19th century and beyond. For Bentley this new focus on meter not only exploited and systematically applied what had been a lifelong topic of interest; in terms of textual criticism, meter also provided him with a clear methodological platform that went beyond the infamous categories of manuscripts and conjectures. His reprinting of Gabriele Faerno's 16th-century emendations alongside his own signaled that Bentley now wished to present himself not necessarily as the most interventionist or even the most original textual critic in history, but as the one with the deepest understanding of poetic form.

Bentley's *Paradise Lost* (1732), one of the strangest textual editions ever produced, was the shocking culmination of his desire to bring philology to a broad literary public, as well as his fascination with systematic approaches to textual criticism. In the preceding decades others had made it fashionable to edit 16th- and 17th-century English poetry with textual apparatus, editorial notes, and frequent invocations of Bentley's name as the example of what an editor should or should not do. Now, in explaining why Milton's 60-year-old epic required his wholesale revision, Bentley displayed logical consistency, if little else: the blind poet had dictated *Paradise Lost* to clumsy amanuenses, sent his poem to inaccurate printers, and, above all, entrusted its proofreading to a perfidious friend who had inserted countless spurious passages. With the possible exception of Bentley, no one believed this in 1732 any more than today. Yet the edition was valuable for forcing a question too often overlooked by contemporaries: was it right to take it for granted that English poetry should be edited in just the same way as classical poetry? Strictly speaking, what would "the same way" be?

Bentley's Manilius (1739), published by his nephew after Bentley was incapacitated by a stroke, was an abandoned project of Bentley's youth, and although it made only moderate advance with the text compared to Joseph Scaliger's editions, it reveals the provenance of Bentley's alarming theory concerning *Paradise Lost.* Accepting Scaliger's argument that Manilius' astrological poem had been substantially interpolated, Bentley not only identified new passages to be excised but attempted generalizations about the interpolator's historical milieu, literary taste, and habitual failures of understanding. Still, despite respectful words from subsequent editors, Bentley's Manilius never exerted the influence of his Horace or Terence. A. E. Housman's effulgent praise—deeply formative for Bentley's reputation in the 20th century—seems largely to have rested on his admiration for Bentley's detailed account of the interpolator, as perhaps also for Bentley's magisterial, not to say bullying, editorial voice.

Bentley died, then, with an immediate legacy of disappointing publications, discontinued directions, and failure to establish a durable school—not to mention a reputation for obstreperous rudeness in print and in person. In 1742, indeed, his personal image probably stood at its lowest in England and abroad, in contrast with his celebrity in the 19th and 20th centuries. Bentley's publications still reward attention. Yet it may be precisely as a celebrity classicist that he influenced the field even more broadly: Bentley graphically showed his successors, in Humboldt's Germany and beyond, that erudite professors could also become influential, controversial, and compelling, on a national and international stage. In England, more specifically, Bentley must be counted among the *Ur*-dons. His style of written argument—opprobriously brilliant, endlessly insistent, and scathing to his enemies—continues to receive regular *hommage,* whether deliberate or inadvertent, in print and in academic conversation. For his great 19th-century biographers, J. H. Monk and R. C. Jebb, it was nonetheless Bentley's scholarship that mattered above all, and it is Bentley's scholarship that has led many to depict him as the founder of a continuous and distinctive English tradition.

BIBL.: R. C. Jebb, *Bentley* (London 1882). J. H. Monk, *The Life of Richard Bentley, D.D.*, 2nd ed., 2 vols. (London 1833). Christopher Wordsworth, ed., *The Correspondence of Richard Bentley, D.D.*, 2 vols. (London 1842). K.H.

Bessarion of Nicaea

Byzantine Humanist, philosopher, and cardinal, 1400–1472. Bessarion is a key figure in the mediation and cultural transfer between Byzantium and Italy, and between the Orthodox and Catholic Churches, in the 15th century.

His education and life as a scholar evolved entirely within the framework of the Orthodox Church and, later, the Catholic Church. In 1416 or 1417 he began his studies in Constantinople under John Chortasmenos and George Chrysokokkes, forging lifelong friendships with his fellow students Francesco Filelfo, Giovanni Aurispa, and George Scholarius. He later studied in Mistra under Georgios Gemistos Pletho. In 1423 he became a monk and changed his birth name, Basil, to Bessarion, after one of the Egyptian desert church fathers, and eventually he was ordained to the priesthood (1430), appointed abbot of a monastery in Constantinople (1436), and elevated to metropolitan of Nicaea (1437). In 1438 he was part of the imperial delegation to negotiate a union between the Catholic and Orthodox Churches at the Council of Ferrara–Florence and soon changed allegiance to the Catholic Church, where he held prominent positions. He was created cardinal (1439) and twice considered a candidate for the papacy (1455, 1471). He was appointed abbot of the Basilian monastery in Grottaferrata (1462) and—10 years after the fall of the city to Muslim rule—Catholic patriarch of Constantinople (1463). The last two decades of his life were shaped by the Ottoman conquest of Byzantium and threat to Western Europe, which Bessarion aimed to combat both as a scholar, by intensifying his efforts to support the copying of Greek manuscripts, and as a diplomat and papal envoy, by traveling to Germany, France, and England to build an anti-Turkish alliance.

Bessarion's lasting influence on Humanist scholarship lies in his contribution to the revival of Platonic studies. In 1469 he published *In calumniatorem Platonis* (*Against the Slanderer of Plato*) in response to George of Trebizond's *Comparationes Aristotelis et Platonis* (*Comparisons of Aristotle and Plato*), the first attack on Plato in Latin. In his treatise, originally written in Greek but published in Latin translation, Bessarion maintains that Plato can be reconciled with Aristotle and with Christianity; he highlights especially the importance of Neoplatonic thought in Christian theology. At the same time, he rejects those concepts in Plato that are incompatible with Christian teaching, such as the preexistence of souls and the multiplicity of gods. Following Pletho, he endorses Plato's views on politics and the formation of society, advocating the ideal of the philosopher-king.

Bessarion also paved the way for Platonic studies in the Renaissance through his activities as a manuscript collector. The 1524 inventory of his library records 80 codices of Plato and "Platonici" (Platonists), many of which constitute the most important, or indeed the only, textual witnesses of Middle and Late Platonic authors. He also owned manuscripts of Aristotle and his commentators and translated the *Metaphysics* into Latin. Bessarion donated his manuscript collection to the library of San Marco in Venice in 1468. By this time it had grown to 746 codices, including 482 in Greek, constituting one of the largest collections in Italy at the time (the library of Pope Nicolas V, his contemporary, consisted of 824 manuscripts). Begun as Bessarion's private reference library of liturgical and theological texts, augmented by his interest in ancient Greek history and science, especially astronomy (he was a patron of the German founder of modern astronomy, Johannes Regiomontanus, who dedicated a treatise to him and made an astrolabe for him that still survives), the collection was further enlarged by his acquisition, in 1459, of the library of Giovanni Aurispa, which contained Cassius Dio, Athenaeus, Hesiod, manuscripts now known as Homerus Venetus A and Homerus Venetus B, the Anthologia Planudea, Eustathius' autograph *Commentary on the Odyssey*, Photius, and Demosthenes. About 40 manuscripts in his collection were copied (at least in part) by Bessarion himself, and an additional 70 have his annotations. Many of his manuscripts were used for the production of first editions of classical Greek texts in the printing house of Aldus Manutius, the Aldine Press.

In modern scholarship he has been treated as a figurehead of the Council of Ferrara–Florence (by W. von Goethe, the grandson of the German poet), as a hero of Catholicism (Mohler), as a Byzantine Humanist (Monfasani, Vast, Wilson), as an important figure in the revival of Platonic studies in the Renaissance (Hankins), and as a manuscript collector (Labowski, Mioni).

BIBL.: G. Fiaccadori, ed., *Bessarione e l'umanesimo: Catalogo della mostra* (Naples 1994). W. von Goethe, *Studien und Forschungen über das Leben und die Zeit des Cardinals Bessarion 1395–1472, Abhandlungen, Regesten und Collectaneen,* vol. 1, *Die Zeit des Concils von Florenz,* part 1 (Jena 1871). J. Hankins, *Plato in the Italian Renaissance,* vol. 1 (Leiden 1990) 163–263. L. Labowski, *Bessarion's Library and the Biblioteca Marciana: Six Early Inventories* (Rome 1979). E. Mioni, "Vita del Cardinale Bessarione," *Miscellanea Marciana* 6 (1991) 13–197. *Miscellanea Marciana di studi Bessarionei* (Padua 1976). L. Mohler, *Kardinal Bessarion als Theologe, Humanist und Staatsmann,* 3 vols. (Paderborn 1923–1942, repr. Paderborn 1967). J. Monfasani, *Byzantine Scholars in Renaissance Italy: Cardinal Bessarion and Other Émigrés: Selected Essays* (Aldershot 1995). H. Vast, *Le cardinal Bessarion (1430–1472): Étude sur la chrétienté et la Renaissance vers le milieu du XVe siècle* (Paris 1878). N. G. Wilson, *From Byzantium to Italy: Greek Studies in the Italian Renaissance* (Baltimore 1992) 57–67.

C.R.

Biography

Genre of writing inherited from classical antiquity and devoted to the literary representation of lives either individually or collectively, though the term *biography* is a term of modern origin. It was not a monopoly of the classical tradition: Chinese literature has a strong biographical tradition, as does Islam, though the latter was arguably influenced more directly by late antique practices. In Greek culture biography was seen from as early as the 5th century BCE as quite separate from historiography—Plutarch would reflect long-standing wisdom in declaring his intention to write not history but "lives." The first Greek biographers include two contemporaries of Herodotus, Skylax of Caryanda and Xanthus of Lydia, but little has remained of such early writings apart from fragments by the poet Ion of Chios (5th century BCE). The rhetorician Isocrates wrote the first extant biographical work, *Evagoras,* which he called an encomium. Isocrates' contemporary Xenophon, who wrote widely of lives, utilized a variety of genres, for instance in the *Cyropaedia,* the *Memorabilia,* and the *Agesilaus,* an encomium of the great Spartan king composed shortly after its subject's death in 360 BCE (Cox 1983, 8–12). In all these fiction was liberally intermixed with fact, the real person with an ideal. There was, however, neither a dominant model nor a poetics.

The full maturation of ancient biography did not occur before the Roman late republican and imperial periods. The purposes of Graeco-Roman biography were varied, ranging from instructive praise of a subject's virtues, to panegyric, to providing insurance against the jaws of oblivion by immortalizing the *fama,* good or ill, of notable individuals.

In summarizing Greek and Roman biography, the German scholar F. Leo once postulated the existence of two quite separate streams of ancient biography, a chronological Plutarchan (or "peripatetic") variety, mainly suited to the lives of generals and statesmen, and a nonchronological Suetonian (or "Alexandrian") type, invented by grammarians to cover literary and philosophical figures, but extended by Suetonius to include his Caesars (Momigliano 1993, 19). This rather rigid classification has not been universally accepted, nor have its origins (both varieties in fact have earlier precursors); even if true, the differences between the streams may have less to do with specific ancient originators than with a wider tension between chronologically organized history and topically organized antiquarianism. There is no doubt, however, that by the late imperial period a rich and multistranded heritage of biographical writing was reasonably well known.

Early Christian culture was a syncretistic mélange of Jewish, Graeco-Roman, and Near Eastern traditions, and biography was no exception to this pattern: the author of the *Acts of the Apostles,* for instance, was clearly influenced both by earlier oral traditions, via the Gospels, and by Hellenistic or Roman biographies. Most of the subgenres of biography inherited from antiquity were adaptable, in one way or another, to Christian evangelical purposes. Earlier lives of wise and moral men such as Socrates and Pythagoras proved readily adaptable, pagan philosopher being easily transmuted into Christian holy man (a process exemplified in a work like Philostratus' early 3rd-cent. *Life of Apollonius*). Moreover, compendia of lives like Diogenes Laertius's 3rd-century *Lives of the Philosophers* provided a useful template for similar Christian collections. And in the political realm, ruler-focused imperial biography was well suited to the depiction of latter-day princes and lay notables. Within a century or so, Christian life-writers would be faced with a tension between what Augustine called *res* and *verba*—roughly speaking, the conflict between the actual deeds of a subject, not all of which might be worthy of emulation, and their rhetorical presentation, which if strictly verisimilar might not adequately perform its didactic function.

The pattern of the godly life was established during the early 4th century in two paradigmatic works, Athanasius' *Life of Saint Anthony,* which depicted its subject's upbringing to include rejection of formal learning and Christlike survival of diabolic temptation; as was true of most subsequent examples, the stress lay on the reflection of divine intervention through the deeds of the saint. A decade or so earlier, the Church historian Eusebius of Caesarea had set the tone for secular biography in his *Life of Constantine,* in which he combined panegyric, polemic, theology, and history in a manner that later historians often found deplorable. Eusebius saw *vita* as vessel for *apologia;* the life of a spiritual figure, Origen, which he included in book 6 of the *Ecclesiastical History,* would literally be based on an earlier *Apology,* a work that summarized Origen's life before providing a defense of his theology (Cox 1983, 137). The practice of collecting lives together in the manner of Plutarch received early Christian treatment in such 4th-century works as Eunapius' *Lives of the Philosophers and Sophists* and the anonymous *History of the Egyptian Monks.*

Leaving aside autobiographical forms such as Augustine's *Confessions,* the principal tasks of patristic-age biographers were the commemoration and sanctification of the holy. Though it was a new genre, hagiography, or "sacred biography," as it has sometimes been called, cannot be viewed separately from the classical forms on which it built, and in any case medieval culture from the 5th to the 15th centuries remained in direct possession of ancient biographical writers, including Suetonius and Plutarch. A corresponding medieval line of Christian secular biography, descended from Eusebius, began with Einhard's *Life of Charlemagne;* the "lives of kings and emperors" genre would eventually include such notable specimens as Asser's *Life of Alfred* and Joinville's *Life of Saint Louis,* both works as effusive about their respective subjects' Christian piety and learning as about their military prowess. Sacred biography proper was inherently more socially inclusive than royal biography, since sanctity did not limit itself to the noble. Beyond the purely hagiographic, there were lives of celebrated clergy and even pious members of the laity, many of which were as concerned with their subjects' earthly deeds as with their godliness. The accounts of the holy in many medieval chronicles (e.g., Bede's *Ecclesiastical History of the English People,* early 8th cent.) were supplemented by occasional outstanding examples of "freestanding" biographies, such as Bede's own *Life of Saint Cuthbert* and Eadmer's 12th-century *Life of Anselm.* Popes, too, were suitable subjects for biography, at first in a Carolingian format known as the *gesta* (a kind of papal counterpart to the *res gestae*—literally "things done" of emperors), later by *gesta*'s successors. These included certain chronicles organized by lives rather than by years (e.g., William of Malmesbury's *Deeds of the Kings of England* and *Deeds of the Bishops of England*) and specialized genres such as the *Vitenliteratur,* lives of spiritual leaders written by nuns in medieval German convents.

The most influential and characteristic of all medieval biographical genres in the Middle Ages, hagiography, would not survive unscathed the sharp criticism of Renaissance Humanists such as Erasmus, many of whom doubted the veracity of much that was contained in some of the more popular collections of saints' lives, such as Jacobus de Voragine's famous compilation, *The Golden Legend.* But endure it did, bifurcating after the Reformation into Protestant and Catholic forms. On the one hand, Protestant martyrologists such as Jean Crespin, Adrian Cornelis van Haemstede, and John Foxe, while repudiating the miraculous aspects of medieval saints' lives, nonetheless adapted their stress on the preternaturally divine into praise of virtue and steadfastness in the face of persecution (borrowing especially from Eusebius and Lactantius); using the full power of the printing press to good effect, they illustrated the deaths of Protestant martyrs through woodcuts and engravings accessible even to the illiterate. Others used such ancient vehicles as the funeral oration (for which precedent exists as far back as the *Iliad*), publicly declaimed and subsequently printed, as a rhetorical opportunity to eulogize the learning and piety of reformed leaders such as Luther and Melanchthon; this was a significant genre given that the Reformers did not often write "straight" lives of their leading figures, preferring such commemorative media as collected letters or sayings. On the other hand, the Counter-Reformation response, employing rather than rejecting Humanist philology, and affected by 16th-century skepticism and its Cartesian response, set about restoring faith in the veracity of saints' lives by renewed emphasis on *res* instead of *verba.* This critical approach to sacred biography was epitomized in the work of the Bollandists and Maurists, beginning in the mid-17th century. It is important to distinguish such works of scholarship from much earlier Renaissance biographies of spiritual figures; these were a kind of cross between hagiography and secular biography, concerned as they were with their subjects' this-worldly deeds rather than their sanctity. Often written as collective biography, this tradition embraces at least two famous *Lives of the Popes,* the first in the 15th century by Bartolomeo Platina, born Sacchi—a work whose criticism of certain pontiffs provided grist for the mill of Protestant polemic in later decades—and the second a century later by Onofrio Panvinio.

But the Renaissance reinvigoration of some classical models, and the Humanist fusing of the medieval inheritance with the newly discovered texts of other ancient authors, provided fresh opportunities for writing the lives of eminent secular individuals from the recent or remote past. The common goal of much early modem life-writing, as it had been in medieval times, was exemplarity—that is, providing a model life from the past for the sake of illustrating encapsulated human characteristics within the concrete vessel of a specific individual, whose historicity (in the sense of a detailed connection to external events specific to time and place) was necessary but of less importance than the timeless value of the virtues he, or she, embodied. That which was being exemplified could of course vary considerably: the type of Renaissance despot or soldier-of-fortune evaluated by a Machiavelli was not suitable for the writer interested in promulgating more conventional notions of Christian virtue.

Regardless of its purpose or subject, classical biographical forms were crucial in the writing of early modern lives, during a period long cited for its discovery of the "individual." The great 19th-century proponent of the latter view, Jacob Burckhardt, once famously opined that Renaissance biography retained its distance from history, and that the new contribution of Humanism was the depiction of lives because they were interesting, not because they fit the rigidities of chronological narrative (rigidities notably rejected in Burckhardt's own history writing) (Bietenholz 1966, 52); but he allowed that they could in sequence illustrate historical progress, as in the case of Vasari's account of the improvement of art from Cimabue to Michelangelo. (In any case, the tendency of early modern methodologies of history, the *artes historicae,* to treat biography as a subdivision of history belies the firmness of this distinction.) More recently, Cochrane (1981, 393–395) has distinguished two major late antique sources for Humanist biography, the first being the Church Father Saint Jerome (who in turn had borrowed from Suetonius in constructing his foundational *De viris illustribus*) and the second Diogenes Laertius. Looking back at Renaissance life-writing from the vantage point of the present, however, it is possible to see that the classical inheritance did not stay intact in either stream but was split at the end of the Middle Ages into a much greater variety of subgenres, further modified by the confessional motivations of the Reformation, and thus transmitted to the late 17th and 18th centuries, when many of these offshoots would come to a dead end.

In the early modern era, from roughly 1400 to 1700, one can distinguish the following subgenres (once again excluding the autobiographical), each of which owed something to classical form: the Plutarchan exemplary life, designed to immortalize the character, more than the deeds, of either individuals or groups of individuals; the Suetonian courtly tradition (earlier deployed in Einhard's *Charlemagne*), a format in which the deeds of the individual were recited and then his character summarized separately; a hybrid of this and the "secret history" genre of Procopius, wherein the private lives of famous figures, especially rulers, were exposed in critical and often salacious detail; the Humanist *vita,* or life, of a celebrated literary individual, often written in the vernacular rather than in Latin (e.g., Boccaccio's *Life of Dante* and Machiavelli's *Life of Castruccio Castracani*); a collected version of this subgenre wherein several lives were contained, a tradition that commenced with Petrarch's *Concerning Fa-*

mous Men and continued with 15th- and 16th-century compendia such as Enea Silvio Piccolomini's *Of the Celebrated Men of His Own Time* and Paolo Giovio's *Lives.* This last is the stream that would lead through Izaak Walton's 17th-century lives of John Donne and George Herbert to an Enlightenment successor, Samuel Johnson's *Lives of the Poets.*

There were also other variants of the collected lives approach applied to particular crafts (a "low" subject not really provided for in ancient poetics), most famously in Giorgio Vasari's vernacular *Lives of the Artists,* and in lives of notable merchants, clerics, and civic figures. The set of short biographies written by the bookseller Vespasiano da Bisticci in the later 15th century, organized according to profession, again owes something to the Diogenes Laertius model. One must be cautious in postulating these literary forms as discrete and self-contained, since there are plentiful examples of overlap and cross-fertilization: a much-lauded case, William Roper's *Life of Sir Thomas More,* is part hagiography of a secular saint and part account of a moral man living and dying in the cutthroat world of early Tudor *realpolitik.*

By the late 16th century some of the educational fervor and moral confidence of Humanist biography had been blunted in the wake of a century of religious war and mounting skepticism (itself the revival of another classical tradition) toward knowledge of the past. One consequence was the adaptation of classical biography into dramatic and especially tragic versions, which tended to bring out the flaws in their heroes rather more directly than prose lives. The most famous synthesis of the biographical with the tragic is Shakespeare's use of Plutarch, as translated by Jacques Amyot and retranslated by Thomas North, as the source of his Roman plays. There was also an increased tendency to blur the boundary between biography and history in accounts of the "life and times" of a great person, most often a ruler. This sort of hybrid (and its autobiographical counterparts, the memoir and "history of his own time") would prove highly durable in northern Europe, for instance in the "politic histories" of late Tudor and early Stuart England. Francis Bacon's *History of the Life and Reign of King Henry the Seventh* (1622) is not the most learned of its species, but it is among the best at treating its subject tragically, as a good king weakened by serious flaws of avarice and distrust, and thus both model and cautionary tale for Bacon's intended reader, the future English King Charles I.

A second consequence was the flourishing of sectarian spiritual biography, especially in England and colonial America, arguably another Protestant adaptation of the hagiographic, shorn of its miraculous aspects; the doppelgänger of this form was provided by the genre of criminal lives, accounts of notorious brigands, rogues, and pickpockets that poured forth from the popular press in the later 17th and 18th centuries. Finally, a third, and quite different outcome, a harnessing of philology and skepticism to life-writing, was the development of the sort of erudite biographical treatment to be found in Pierre Gassendi's *Life of Peiresc.* This would be given a more radically doubtful hue in Pierre Bayle's late 17th-century *Historical and Critical Dictionary,* in which the deeds of individuals were systematically debunked.

The old Plutarchan tradition, broadly conceived, remained powerful during the 18th century. It thrived in the flourishing genre of "biographical lexicography" (dictionaries in which individuals could be looked up in some order, most often alphabetical), and in prominent collections such as Samuel Johnson's *Lives of the Poets,* though not, ironically, in the very different life of Johnson himself by James Boswell. This latter work has been called the "great dividing point in the history of biography" (Whittemore 1988, 125). It veered in the direction of the intimate detail, the casual anecdote, and inclusive comprehension of the "trifling," quotidian, or even vulgar, balanced by a lingering sense that true verisimilitude—and literary art—demands that some things simply be left out. This tension between inclusiveness and selectivity has become a hallmark of modem biography (though Boswell's magpie quality owes something to the *Brief Lives* of John Aubrey a century earlier). Although this problem superficially resembles the old early medieval quandary of *res* versus *verba,* the issue is no longer principally the risk of perverting the reader with a flawed example, but rather balancing the historically accurate with the rhetorically persuasive and aesthetically pleasing.

In creating his *Life of Johnson,* Boswell anticipated biographies of the Romantic era by authors such as Thomas Carlyle. These in turn built on Enlightenment "sentiment," an aesthetic of melancholy, and a sense of interiority. In the wake of Goethe and Rousseau, literary biographers highlighted the character as a psychologically complex and emotive entity, rather than an amalgam of virtues and vices. They emphasized private life, feeling, and reflection as much as outward public actions—certainly a departure from the classical heritage as it had developed all the way up to the late 18th century, which had focused resolutely on the public. Both Carlyle and his American contemporary Ralph Waldo Emerson developed an intense devotion to biography as the ideal genre for capturing a past filled with political and poetic heroes, such as Carlyle's *Schiller.* Carlyle's *Heroes and Hero-Worship* virtually collapsed the history-biography distinction in its famous articulation of what has become known as the "Great Man Theory." Emerson, a childhood admirer of Plutarch, went a step further in declaring flatly that "There is properly no history, only biography."

The 19th century, the first age of true mass-market literacy, was witness to an enormous increase in the popularity of biography, including a relatively new phenomenon, the published compilation of lives of women by female authors such as England's Agnes Strickland and the American Elizabeth Fries Ellet. The appeal of biography among a general readership has continued unabated to the present day in defiance of trends within academic historiography. Biography is notoriously a safer bet for publishing houses than its learned cousin, and the interwar period in Europe and America was notable for a sharp slippage of readership away from history and toward biography, from which the former has only partly recovered. Indeed, although history proper has flirted with the social sciences and the study of groups, numbers, and trends for three-quarters of a century, it too has recently turned back to the life, as synecdoche for a period, in the form of the "microhistory."

André Maurois (1929, 46) commented perceptively that biography shares with tragedy a sense of magnificent inevitability that the novel generally lacks. This may account for the equal success of accounts of lives that ended badly and those that ended well. For all its many transmutations, the classical roots of the genre still lie visible below the surface and can be found, acknowledged or not, in so homespun a life-writer as the mid-19th-century journalistic biographer James Parton (1822–1891), a self-confessed admirer of Homer (Whittemore 1989, 133). It can be observed in a satirical form (first promulgated in Lucian of Samosata's critique of philosophical asceticism) in Lytton Strachey's subversive *Eminent Victorians* and the brief lives in his later *Portraits in Miniature,* a work descended from Plutarch via John Aubrey and Samuel Johnson (Nadel 1984, 64). Finally, the biographical compilation, first rendered by Suetonius and Plutarch, is alive and well in scholarly collections such as Leslie Stephen and Sidney Lee's *Dictionary of National Biography,* its early 21st-century successor, and its numerous counterparts around the world.

BIBL.: Judith H. Anderson, *Biographical Truth: The Representation of Historical Persons in Tudor-Stuart Writing* (New Haven 1984). Peter G. Bietenholz, *History and Biography in the Work of Erasmus of Rotterdam* (Geneva 1966). Eric Cochrane, *Historians and Historiography in the Italian Renaissance* (Chicago 1981). Patricia Cox, *Biography in Late Antiquity: A Quest for the Holy Man* (Berkeley 1983). Tomas Hägg and Philip Rousseau, eds., *Greek Biography and Panegyric in Late Antiquity* (Berkeley 2000). Thomas J. Heffernan, *Sacred Biography: Saints and Their Biographers in the Middle Ages* (New York 1988). André Maurois, *Aspects of Biography,* trans. S. C. Roberts (New York 1929). Thomas Mayer and D. R. Woolf, eds., *The Rhetorics of Life-writing in Early Modern Europe: Forms of Biography from Cassandra Fedele to Louis XIV* (Ann Arbor 1995). Arnaldo Momigliano, *The Development of Greek Biography,* expanded ed. (Cambridge, Mass., 1993). Ira Bruce Nadel, *Biography: Fiction, Fact, and Form* (New York 1984). Reed Whittemore, *Pure Lives: the Early Biographers* (Baltimore 1988) and *Whole Lives: Shapers of Modern Biography* (Baltimore 1989).

D.R.W.

Boccaccio, Giovanni

Italian Humanist and writer of poetry and short stories (1313–1375); best remembered for his *Decameron,* a collection of short fictions composed in Italian. He also wrote, in Latin, encyclopedic books of history, biography, geography, and mythography that earned him fame throughout Europe in the 15th and 16th centuries.

After early schooling in Florence he studied canon law at the University of Naples, where he came into contact with intellectuals at the royal court of Robert of Anjou. From the outset his writings there were bilingual. Latin works include his *Elegy of Costanza,* from the ancient epitaph of Homonoea and Atimetus; an Ovidian "Mythological Allegory"; and epistles that display the influence of the medieval *ars dictaminis* (the rhetorical art of prose composition, specifically of letter writing). Italian works include *Diana's Hunt; Filostrato,* the source of Chaucer's *Troilus and Criseyde* and, via Chaucer, of Shakespeare's *Troilus and Cressida; Filocolo,* following in the footsteps of Virgil, Lucan, Statius, Ovid, and Dante; and *Teseida delle nozze d'Emilia* (*Thesiad on the Nuptials of Emilia*), the first epic in Italian, later adapted in Chaucer's "Knight's Tale." Back in Florence by the 1340s, he served the city with his oratorical skills, completed a translation into Italian of the third and fourth decades of Livy, and composed a string of imaginative vernacular fictions: *Ameto* and *Ninfale fiesolano,* the first Tuscan pastorals; *Elegia di Madonna Fiammetta,* a psychological romance inspired by Ovid's *Heroides* and Senecan tragedy; *Amorosa visione,* an amusingly Dantesque allegory with debts to Macrobius, Boethius, and Thomas Aquinas; and his masterpiece, the *Decameron.*

In the friendship he enjoyed from 1350 onward with Petrarch (whose biography he had penned long before), Boccaccio defines a transitional era between the Middle Ages and the Renaissance. In a written self-portrait (*Buccolicum carmen,* Florence, Biblioteca Medicea-Laurenziana, MS Plut. 34.49) he depicts himself as cleric *in cathedra* explicating his eclogues. In his Petrarchan period he abandoned Gothic conceits (numerical composition, the poetic mistress Fiammetta) and moved in a proto-Humanistic direction by composing ambitious encyclopedias, among them the geographical gazetteer *De montibus, silvis, fontibus, lacubus, fluminibus, stagnis seu paludibus et de diversis nominibus maris* (*On Mountains, Woods, Springs, Lakes, Rivers, Lagoons or Swamps, and on the Different Names of the Sea*). Cicero's oration *Pro Archia,* recently recovered by Petrarch, together with Donatus' life of Virgil, in its transmitted and augmented state, lies behind his short work in praise of Dante, *Trattatello in laude di Dante.* Such direct access to previously undiscovered classical works culminated in his pioneering study of Homer, whose works he read in the Latin translation of Leonzio Pilato. In *Genealogies of the Pagan Gods* (*Genealogiae deorum gentilium* 15.6–7) he proudly took credit for restoring Greek to Tuscany. His impoverished last years were spent in his ancestral village, Certaldo, revising the *Decameron* and two widely circulated biographical compilations: *The Fall of Illustrious Men* (*De casibus virorum illustrium*), a parade of Lady Fortune's victims in a universal moralizing framework provided by Orosius; and *Famous Women* (*De mulieribus claris*), the first collection of biographies of women in Western literature.

Highly eclectic, as is often true of autodidacts, Boccaccio possessed phenomenal creative energies that impelled him to revive an ancient heritage in innovatively forged modern composite forms. He asserted his membership in the time-honored sodality of poets and passionately defended their mission in his monumental and influential *Genealogies of the Pagan Gods* (14–15), euhemerist mythology decorously veiled by Christian allegory. Poetry for Boccaccio was the highest form of human expression, a vehicle for moral truth that hides its lesson beneath a fanciful narrative, much as the pith of a tree lies covered inside its bark. True to the medieval allegorical mode, this aesthetic also resonates with Horace's ideal of art that is both "sweet and useful."

BIBL.: Giovanni Boccaccio, *Famous Women*, ed. and trans. Virginia Brown (Cambridge, Mass., 2001), and *Tutte le opere*, ed. Vittore Branca, 10 vols. (Milan 1964–1998), with facing Latin and Italian texts. Attilio Hortis, *Studj sulle opere latine del Boccaccio* (Trieste 1879). Victoria Kirkham, "Giovanni Boccaccio, Latin Works," in *Routledge Encyclopedia of Italian Literary Studies*, ed. Gaetana Marrone and Paolo Puppa (New York 2007). V.K.

Böckh, August

A German classical scholar and antiquarian (1785–1831), he played a prominent role in German classical studies for more than 50 years. After finishing school in Karlsruhe, he went to Halle, where he first studied theology but then transferred to philology under the influence of Friedrich August Wolf. At Halle Schleiermacher also made a deep and lasting impression on him. Accordingly, Böckh's first publication was on the subject of Plato, a topic to which he returned repeatedly in later years. In 1809 he received a professorship at Heidelberg, which he left to accept a position at the newly founded University of Berlin in 1811. He played a decisive role in its organization and administration, and he served five times as rector. As a professor of rhetoric he defended academic freedom in numerous speeches. From 1814 onward Böckh was also a member of the Prussian Academy of Sciences, where he worked actively to ensure that it functioned not merely as a society for the learned but also as a sponsor of major scholarly projects.

In more than 120 semesters of uninterrupted teaching and in his publications Böckh staunchly advocated a restrained and unemotional approach to antiquity, in which the study of classical literature was to be combined with an overall view of social "realities" based on empirical foundations. His work *The Public Economy of Athens* (1817) was conceived as a preliminary study for just such an overview of Greek culture, but that larger project was never carried out.

The Public Economy offers a comprehensive survey of the Athenian economy in the classical period. Böckh broke new ground chiefly by making use of all the inscriptions available at the time. At his urging the Prussian Academy in Berlin began a collection of Greek inscriptions, which he subsidized for decades. Thus began the scholarly study of Greek epigraphy. He believed, however, that printed texts and copies would be sufficient, not yet recognizing the necessity of direct examination of the objects themselves. (Given the fact that Greece was still under Turkish rule, scholars would have faced practical difficulties in traveling there.) Nevertheless, his later insistence on maintaining his approach considerably delayed the start of the Roman inscription project proposed by Mommsen.

Böckh was compelled to defend this stance against criticism from the philologist Gottfried Hermann in Leipzig, who began a long-lived controversy that drew in students and colleagues from both camps. Böckh's defense of classical studies on a broad, cross-disciplinary basis—as opposed to Hermann's narrower philology emphasizing grammar and textual criticism—involved a definite modification of classical studies that Wolf had advocated. His approach had some continuity with Wolf's, since it was necessary to draw on all genres in which classical civilization had been transmitted. Böckh, however, dropped the Neohumanist superstructure, which was intended to establish the absolute supremacy of Greek (and Roman) culture, arguing that studies of Hebrew, Indic, Chinese, and other Oriental philology possessed the same fundamental importance. Only the fact that the roots of all European culture lay in Graeco-Roman antiquity justified giving them priority. He investigated the links between ancient Oriental and Graeco-Roman cultures in his *Metrological Studies* (1838), on ancient weights, coins, and measures.

Böckh's lecture series the Encyclopedia of Philology, which he delivered 26 times, was posthumously edited and published as the *Enzyklopädie und Methodologie der philologischen Wissenschaften* (*Encyclopedia and Methodology of Philological Studies*). In it he developed a general hermeneutics for the humanities (based in part on the work of Schleiermacher), which was in principle not bound to the subject of classical studies that he used to elucidate it. The influence of Böckh's hermeneutics can be observed in Droysen's *Historik* (*The Principles of History*).

BIBL.: Benedetto Bravo, *L'Enciclopedia di August Böckh*, *ASNP* 3rd series, 16 (1986) 171–204. Christine Hackel, *Dei Bedeutung August Böckhs für den Geschichtstheoretiker Johann Gustav Droysen* (Würzburg 2006). Axel Horstmann, *Antike Theoria und moderne Wissenschaft: August Böckhs Konzeption der Philologie* (Frankfurt 1992). Wilfried Nippel, "Philologenstreit und Schulpolitik: Zur Kontroverse wischen Gottfried Hermann und August Böckh," in *Geschichtsdiskurs*, vol. 3: *Die Epoche der Historisierung*, ed. Wolfgang Küttler, Jörn Rosen, and Ernst Schulin (Frankfurt 1997) 244–253.

W.N.

Translated by Deborah Lucas Schneider

Boethius

Roman philosopher and scholar, ca. 476–ca. 524 CE. Standing at the crossroads of ancient and medieval times, between pagan philosophy and Christian faith, between Greek learning and Western Latinity, Boethius shaped medieval thinking and writing in a number of important ways. His *Consolation of Philosophy* was almost uninterruptedly translated and commented on from the 8th century onward, and it inspired internationally renowned poets such as Dante and Chaucer. It was, moreover, the text that Sir Thomas More, among many others, took as his guide to life. Boethius' translations of and commentaries on the Aristotelian corpus of logical texts provided the Scholastics with the basic tools of reasoning and argumentation. And in his theological treatises he showed the Scholastics how to use these tools of reason in explaining Christian dogmas such as the Trinity.

Boethius' education and cultural background prepared him for this role as mediator of ancient learning. He was educated in the best of Roman aristocratic households, where study of the Roman classics and Neoplatonic philosophy went hand in hand with a reading of Christian authors. Boethius saw himself primarily as a scholar, but given his aristocratic background, it was natural for him to take up offices under the Ostrogothic king Theoderic, who ruled over Italy. Boethius was consul in 510 and later, probably, prefect of Rome. In 522 he rose to prominence by becoming Master of Offices at Theoderic's court in Ravenna. Soon thereafter, however, he was accused, surely unjustly, of leading a conspiracy against the king and condemned to death. In prison he wrote his masterpiece, finding consolation in the lessons of Lady Philosophy.

Boethius' plan to translate and comment on the works of Aristotle and Plato was entirely in line with the program of his Neoplatonic masters, including Plotinus, Porphyry, and Proclus. It was especially from the writings of Porphyry (d. ca. 305) that he learned how to reconcile the philosophies of Plato and Aristotle by interpreting Aristotelian logic and the doctrine of the 10 categories as pertaining to the sensible world, and Plato's metaphysics as concerned with the realm of intelligible being. From his study of these Neoplatonic texts Boethius inherited and passed on a number of philosophical problems, such as the status of universals, future contingency, and the relationship among words, thoughts, and things. Though his attempts to resolve these problems were not always successful, they inspired later thinkers to come up with their own theories. His commentaries on, for instance, Porphyry's *Isagoge,* Aristotle's *Categories* and *De interpretatione,* and Cicero's *Topics* formed the backbone of the curriculum in the schools of early medieval Europe and later in the arts faculties of the universities. The structure of this curriculum, too, owed much to Boethius, who had coined the term Quadrivium, that is, the Fourfold Path, by which he meant the four mathematical disciplines: astronomy, geometry, arithmetic, and music. As the cosmos was believed to be structured in a mathematical way, the quadrivial arts were the sine qua non for a deeper knowledge of the cosmos and the place of human existence in it. Here, as well, Boethius was a crucial transmitter of ancient learning. His textbooks on music and arithmetic were widely read and commented on. In the 12th century the Platonic notion of the mathematical structure of the cosmos would lead to a rationalist exploration of nature by thinkers such as Adelard of Bath, William of Conches, and Thierry of Chartres.

The belief that study of the liberal arts leads to a higher understanding of the cosmos is also the central theme of the *Consolation of Philosophy.* Lady Philosophy appears to Boethius in his prison, showing him that true happiness resides not in the transitory world we live in but beyond it, in the eternal abode of God. By discursive reasoning Boethius is led to understand that behind this apparently disordered and unjust world there is a fundamental stability imposed by the Creator. The philosophical problems from Boethius' earlier studies recur here: the nature of true happiness, necessity and chance, the eternity of God, and divine providence versus human freedom.

The influence of the *Consolation* on medieval thought and literature was immense. It was translated into all the major vernacular languages and therefore reached a massive readership, virtually unparalleled in the Middle Ages. Among its translators were King Alfred, Notker III of St. Gall, Chaucer, Jean de Meun, and Queen Elizabeth I. These translations, often accompanied by Latin commentaries (sometimes translated into the vernacular as well), became a source of knowledge of mythological lore (the fable of Orpheus, Ulysses and his comrades, the labors of Hercules), of Roman history and literature, and various other kinds of information, dutifully expounded by glossators. The literary genre of the work—a dialogue in *prosimetrum,* prose alternating with verse, which Boethius may have derived from Martianus Capella's *The Marriage of Philology and Mercury* (late 5th cent.)—was often imitated in later centuries: for instance, in Adelard of Bath's *De eodem et diverso* (*On the Same and the Different*), Bernardus Silvestris' *Cosmographia* (*Cosmography*), and Alan of Lille's *De planctu Naturae* (*The Complaint of Nature*), all in the 12th century alone. More generally, the *Consolation* is an important source for the medieval penchant for personification and visionary poetry. This can also be seen in the works of Chaucer, who exploited various Boethian motifs and ideas such as necessity, chance, destiny, and cosmic love, most notably in the *Knight's Tale* and *Troilus and Criseyde.* For the poet Dante, the *Consolation* was the book that won him over to the love of philosophy. Dante's conception of the force of love owes much to Boethius' hymn on the "love by which heaven is ruled" (2, metrum 8). As a token of gratitude, he placed Boethius in Paradise, alongside Augustine and Thomas Aquinas.

In the Renaissance Boethius continued to be read and praised, even though some Humanists found his Latin faulty. Erasmus could not believe that the jejune prose sections and the well-crafted poems of the *Consolation* were written by one and the same author. Lorenzo Valla accused Boethius of having disfigured Latin by encouraging the development of abstruse metaphysics and technical dialectic. Other Humanists were uneasy about the rejection of the Muses by Lady Philosophy at the bedside of the sick Boethius (1, prose 1). He was defended, however, by important Humanists such as Albertino Mussato, Petrarch, Boccaccio, and Coluccio Salutati, who solved the problem by distinguishing between two kinds of Muses: the "theatrical tarts," who represented low, obscene poetry, and those who had Lady Philosophy's approval ("*my* Muses"), that is, those of serious poetry conveying philosophical or scientific truths.

The search for philosophical truths underlying the text of the *Consolation* became all the more pressing: the work contains no allusions to Christian faith or to Christ himself, while it advocates heterodox Platonic teachings such as the preexistence of the soul. In the 19th century this pursuit culminated in a thoroughly "pagan" reading of the *Consolation* and a denial of the authenticity of the theological treatises traditionally attributed to Boethius. With the discovery of a fragment from a lost work by Cassiodorus, a near contemporary, in which Boethius is referred to as the author of "a book on the Holy Trinity and some chapters of dogmatic theology and the book against Nestorius," that interpretation had to be rejected. Modern scholars continue to debate the precise character of Boethius' Christian faith and its relationship to Neoplatonic philosophy. What is beyond doubt is Boethius' importance for the continuity of classical learning in the Middle Ages.

BIBL.: Henry Chadwick, *Boethius: The Consolations of Music, Logic, Theology, and Philosophy* (Oxford 1981). A. Galonnier, ed., *Boèce, ou la chaîne des savoirs* (Louvain-la-Neuve 2003). Margaret Gibson, ed., *Boethius: His Life, Thought and Influence* (Oxford 1981). Maarten Hoenen and Lodi Nauta, eds., *Boethius in the Middle Ages: Latin and Vernacular Traditions of the "Consolatio Philosophiae"* (Leiden 1997). John Marenbon, *Boethius* (Oxford 2003). Lodi Nauta, "*Magis sit Platonicus quam Aristotelicus:* Interpretations of Boethius' Platonism in the *Consolatio Philosophiae* from the Twelfth to the Seventeenth Century," in *The Platonic Tradition in the Middle Ages*, ed. Stephen Gersh and Maarten Hoenen (Berlin 2002) 165–204. L.N.

Book, Manuscript: Development and Transmission

One of the most relevant consequences of the change from roll to codex for the transmission of classical texts was that many corpuses underwent a process of selection. This was true in several ways. First, texts were selected in order to fit the average size of a codex. This happened with the New Testament for what might be called ideological reasons: all the Apocrypha were simply no longer copied into the same book as the canonical texts that still appear in present-day Bibles; for pagan texts the same occurred for practical reasons. The codex format might thus be a clue to the peculiar order of Demosthenes' extant speeches or of Terence's plays, and for the survival of 5 books by Polybius, 10 by Dionysius of Halicarnassus, and 15 by Diodorus Siculus, or of only 7 plays by Aeschylus and Sophocles but 21 by Plautus. For all this, one must bear in mind that many authors whose editions are now lost or mutilated survived into the 7th century (Sappho, Callimachus) or even the 12th (Hipponax, Pindar). More generally, a codex was often planned to embrace all the doctrines relevant to a single branch of life: an emblematic instance is the selection and standardization of the Roman law corpus within volumes designed for the instruction of the ruling elite; down to our own day "codes" of laws owe their name to this phenomenon.

Second, commentaries, which in ancient times circulated on separate rolls from the texts they were explaining, in the new book format could easily be accommodated in the page margins. This practice probably had its roots in some late antique experiments, as a few papyri seem to attest, but the standard form was reached in the medieval manuscripts with scholia. The process of excerpting and abridging annotations of different origin into one and the same margin made consultation much easier and quicker but also entailed a large amount of cutting, adapting, and rewording, which had important bearings on the textual facies of the scholiastic corpuses that have survived to the present—and thus on present-day images of ancient scholarship.

Third, not all texts preserved in rolls were transcribed into codices. This danger is probably what the rhetor Themistius referred to when in 357 he praised the emperor Constans II for having engaged professional scribes to copy the works of ancient authors threatened by time and oblivion. This act was the first instance of an institutional interest in the preservation and transmission of written pagan culture, an interest that was to enjoy a long life in the Greek schools of the Mediterranean, well into the 6th century (from Athens to Gaza, from Antioch to Berytos), and that was not to fade alongside the secular history of the Byzantine empire.

In the Greek East the imperial elite (civil servants, magistrates, bureaucrats, and even military officers) was represented by educated men whose instruction often embraced some degree of contact with books and with classical texts. According to later historians, the emperor Theodosius II (the famous lawgiver and husband of the poetess Eudocia in the early 5th century) was an excellent calligrapher and attended to the copying of books (sometimes in golden ink) instead of watching horse races in the Hippodrome: "thus," he said, "I can hold my life in my hands." Imperial and (small) private libraries never ceased to exist, and modes of literacy and alphabetism, even in urban centers of the provinces, were manifold. We learn from hagiographies that even during the Dark Ages most Eastern saints could read. Monasticism, though initially hostile, slowly changed its attitude toward books: in the early 7th century the edifying narration of John Moschus has a chapter on the Alexandrian scholar Cosmas, who is praised for keeping in his house just "books, stools, a bed, and a table." The ecclesiastical elite (bishops, patriarchs, and other high officials) was often directly involved in book production and collection; evidence of religious censorship is rare and uncertain. A form of mild secular

Hellenism (favored by soft Christianizations of classical authors, such as Epictetus and Heliodorus), though practiced only by few more or less distinguished intellectuals, was not seen as a real danger to Christianity, from the age of the patriarch Photius and bishop Arethas in the 9th and early 10th centuries down to the archbishop Eustathius in the 12th and Planudes, a monk, in the 13th and early 14th centuries.

The situation developed rather differently in the West. From the 4th century down to the Gothic wars the copying of classical texts and preservation of the ancient tradition was the affair of single (and nostalgic) aristocratic families or individuals, not of the state. Members of these same families were responsible both for the production of some luxury codices and for philological activity on Latin texts: from subscriptions added by editors or scribes to works that they copied we learn that a text of the Vergilius Mediceus was corrected throughout by a consul named Asterius, and that a text of Macrobius' *Commentary on the Dream of Scipio* (as related in Cicero's *De re publica*) was edited in the late 5th century by Symmachus, the great-grandson of the Symmachus named in Macrobius' *Saturnalia.* This declining Latin elite could of course read Greek as well: the Vienna Dioscorides was commissioned in 512 by Anicia Juliana, the daughter of a former emperor of the Western empire; but by then, like other Roman aristocrats, she had found refuge in Constantinople.

Later the old senatorial families collapsed, the book trade sank abruptly, and the West entered the Dark Ages: the transmission of Latin classics was left to the fluctuations of fate, as schools collapsed, the new ruling elites became basically ignorant of the liberal arts, and the only institutions that cared about the preservation of written culture were monasteries. In this new context reading and writing were practiced almost exclusively by the same people, namely monks, who obviously concentrated on religious texts and ruminated on written words rather than reading them, *lugentes non legentes,* "mourning, not reading," according to Saint Jerome (d. 420). Books became a distant object of veneration: on the vault of the Neonian Baptistry in Ravenna (mid-5th cent.) a Gospel book is depicted standing on the altar; the copy of Pseudo-Dionysius the Areopagite sent by the Byzantine emperor Michael II to the French king Louis the Pious in 827 (now in the Bibliothèque Nationale, Parisinus Graecus 437) was said to have performed miracles and healings in the Abbey of St. Denis; in art, saints and evangelists tended more and more to be shown carrying closed books rather than open ones. Furthermore, the only collections of books were now housed in monasteries (with the exception of some capitular, that is, chapter, libraries in cathedrals, as in Verona). The cultural primacy of monastic scriptoria arose from the convention that knowledge should not pass the walls of the monasteries themselves: this atmosphere of conservation without divulgation, of monastic libraries "unfathomable as the truth they host, deceitful as the lies they hide" is brilliantly described by Umberto Eco in his best-selling novel *The Name of the Rose* (1980).

Collateral effects of this situation were a decreasing interest in Latin secular literature; even such a remarkable experiment as Cassiodorus' library at Vivarium (mid-6th cent.) embraced very few pagan authors, aside from purely grammatical or technical ones, and a complete standstill in the copying of Latin classical texts occurred from the mid-6th century through the 8th. Early Benedictine monasticism was rather suspicious of books, and the new medieval Christian culture accepted pagan writings only as technical tools for disciplines such as grammar, rhetoric, law, and medicine. The sinking degree of literacy—"Make your tongue a codex," Gregory the Great (pope, 590–604) instructed his Christian preachers, for the benefit of the illiterate masses—and the gradual differentiation of national languages from Latin forced scribes to enhance the "grammar of legibility," that is, to introduce special devices (accurate word division, punctuation, and diacritical signs) to make the reading and writing of Latin easier. But the lack of a general cultural paradigm was also mirrored by the development of the "national hands," semiuncial-derived scripts that became peculiar to one or another region of the former Roman empire: Visigothic script in Spain and Merovingian script in France were seldom used for manuscripts of classical authors, and the same is true of the earlier stage of Beneventan script in southern Italy.

The Insular scripts in Britain and in Ireland were among the neatest of these national hands: they were not frequently used for classical texts, but from the 7th through 9th centuries the British Isles produced some of the most interesting personalities of European culture, such as Aldelmus, Bede, and later Alcuin himself (d. 804), whose poem in praise of York is an eloquent witness to the presence of good libraries on English soil. Yet the seminal role of Irish monks and British scholars was the spreading of written culture in new monastic centers of continental Europe, especially in France, Germany, and northern Italy: this was an indispensable preparation to the Carolingian renaissance.

The general economic crisis in the Dark Ages impaired both the supply of parchment and the production of new books. Down to the 15th century, manuscripts were never a cheap object in either East or West, which explains why medieval private and monastic libraries appear generally rather limited to modern eyes. Resorting to an expedient already widespread in antiquity, monks often decided to reuse a written manuscript by wiping out its text. Each sheet was bathed in milk for a few hours and then dried with a sponge and some flour; this process led to the creation of a palimpsest book (the Greek word, meaning "rubbed over," is not exact, as no scraping or erasure was practiced). In this way classical texts were often superseded by Christian ones (famous cases of succumbing texts are Cicero's *De re publica,* Sallust's *Histories,* the Ambrosian Plautus, the Archimedes once at Istanbul, and a recently discovered fragment of Menander in a Syriac manuscript), but there was no ideological bias in this phenomenon. The texts chosen for deletion were generally the little read, the no longer fashionable (including collections of outdated documents), and the readily available; in fact, many Gospels and sacred texts underwent the same treatment, although a canon of the Quinisext Council (692) explicitly forbade this.

But where, and how, were books copied and produced? Most big monasteries had one large room, generally with more than one window, so that light might flood in during the day. Specialist monks sat in this scriptorium early in the morning and spent several hours in the silent task of copying (the practice of dictation is attested for antiquity but was exceptional in the Middle Ages). They worked under the direction of another monk, who was in charge of providing the writing materials and the exemplars to be copied, as well as of revising and correcting the scribes' work. An average scribe could copy roughly three folia per day (up to ten in extreme circumstances). An edict by Charlemagne in 784 discouraged the overexploitation of monks as scribes.

A similar system was operating in the Greek East, although monasteries housing a scriptorium were less numerous. The rule of the Constantinopolitan monastery of Studios (founded by Theodore, himself a calligrapher, in the late 8th century, perhaps as an iconophile reaction to the supremacy of iconoclastic patriarchs and intellectuals of that era), prescribed severe punishment for the careless scribe who damaged the exemplar or the copy he was writing or made gross mistakes in copying. The protocalligrapher (supervisor) was also to be sanctioned if he did not coordinate the teamwork properly. Neither in Studios nor in other important monasteries such as those of Patmos and of the Holy Mountain (Athos), however, were classical authors normally copied.

Our major source for the study of the life and activity of scribes is the subscriptions (also called colophons) that they added at the end of manuscripts that they copied. Just as the colophons in late antique Latin codices (described above) help modern scholars detect the influence of aristocratic families on book production, during the Middle Ages, at least down to the 13th century, they reveal that most scribes were monks, and more so in the West than in the Greek East, where we also find, albeit exceptionally, lawyers, doctors, and schoolmasters who copied manuscripts, and even monastic scriptoria that sometimes carried out copies for laymen. Monks are generally reluctant to divulge their names and status or mention the date and place of their activity: when they do, especially in the Greek world, they add a conspicuous amount of self-humbling epithets and exhort the reader to pray for their soul and salvation. Reconstructing scribes' personalities and, beyond that, tracing the provenance of manuscripts (with the help of other clues such as scripts, ruling methods, and the like) is so hard a task that it comprises its own branches of modern scholarly discipline, palaeography and codicology. But ordinary readers can often grasp copyists' measured complaints about the hardships of their life, their physical toil ("three fingers are at work, but the whole body is aching"), and simply the tedium of the texts they are copying.

Among the most important scriptoria of the Latin West, the great Irish foundations on the Continent—Bobbio in northern Italy, Corbie and Luxeuil in France, and St. Gall in Switzerland—stand out. It was precisely in these monasteries that in the wake of experiments in other French and Italian centers (among these Fleury, Lyon, and Nonàntola) a new, clear, and elegant handwriting originated during the late 8th century, Caroline minuscule. Not a mere script but the bearer of a new cultural and political paradigm, Caroline or Carolingian minuscule is tightly connected to Europe's cultural renaissance under Charlemagne's empire, and in fact this script enjoyed a rapid international success in France, Germany, and later northern Italy. Several important manuscripts of classical authors copied in scriptoria at major houses such as Corbie, Lorsch, and Fulda were written in Caroline (the more traditional rustic capitals, uncials, and half-uncials being confined to titles and headings). A curious case in this respect is the Carolingian Aratea manuscript (9th cent., now in Leiden), a lavishly illustrated copy of an astronomical work by Aratus (3rd cent. BCE).

Prepared by the activity of Insular scholars such as Alcuin, who taught at the cathedral school in York and was later summoned by Charlemagne to reorganize the Palatine school attached to his court at Aix-la-Chapelle (Aachen), the Carolingian renaissance still conceived of classical instruction as propaedeutic (preparatory) training for more advanced study in Christian doctrine. Yet the new transcription of many classical authors prompted by Alcuin's innovative educational program proved vital to ensuring their survival into the Middle Ages. A first if quantitatively modest philological effort was also performed by scholars such as Sedulius Scotus, Hrabanus Maurus, Heiric of Auxerre, and (above all) Lupus of Ferrières (d. 862). Lupus's motto, "Knowledge must be pursued for its own sake," had ramifications both in his zeal for the library of his monastery and in his work of emending manuscripts of Cicero, Livy, Macrobius, and other classical and late antique authors.

For different reasons, the 9th century was an important age in the history of Greek books as well. Here the great change was represented by the transliteration of texts from uncial handwriting (all capitals, more and more confined to titles and special headings) into the new Greek minuscule script that prevailed during the 9th century. The date and place of origin of Greek minuscule are still debated: some have argued for Studios, but its spread, as recent finds on Sinai seem to certify, certainly dates back at least to the 8th century. The advantages of the minuscule over the obsolete ogival script it superseded can be summarized in three features: greater speed of transcription, greater clarity (especially by virtue of the consistent use of accents and breathings, though systematic word division would not be completed until the late 10th century), and space saving. If one takes into account the overall uniformity of Greek minuscule down to the present day (something inconceivable, for example, in the fragmented Latin world), this was probably the crucial formative stage in the tradition of Greek literature: the texts that were not copied into the new script were doomed to oblivion.

The 9th century witnessed in the East the beginning of a humanistic trend that later gave life to the Macedonian renaissance (from the name of the ruling Byzantine dynasty). We know of Cometas, who taught in the imperial school in the mid-9th century and worked at the emendation and punctuation of newly transliterated manuscripts of Homer. Sometime around 850 the future patriarch Photius wrote a work conventionally known by the titles *Bibliotheca* (*Library*) or *Myriobiblos* (*Thousand Books*), in which he gathered summaries of no fewer than 279 works of classical and Christian authors. It has been surmised that this work actually grew out of a reading circle conducted by Photius in Constantinople; be that as it may, the very plausibility of such an institution in Byzantium marks a clear-cut difference from the cultural climate in the Latin West during the same period. Among the achievements of the Macedonian renaissance one can mention a remarkable series of philosophical manuscripts (from Plato down to Aristotle's commentators) produced in a scriptorium in Constantinople in the second half of the 9th century. And at the beginning of the 10th century, Arethas the archbishop of Caesarea had many manuscripts of ancient prose writers copied for him (Plato, Aristotle, Euclid, Lucian, and others): some of these codices survive today, including the Clarkianus Plato in the Bodleian Library at Oxford, bearing marginal notes in the hand of Arethas himself.

Yet in both East and West these 9th-century renaissances were short-lived and ended in less exciting decades, more oriented to the production of lexicons, compilations, florilegia, anthologies, and the like. These works had the advantage of being more functional to easy consultation and of physically aggregating the gist of several or many books into one volume (at the expense of the originals). Many miscellaneous codices, embracing different texts of different authors in an incoherent way, were also produced in this period. But in the 10th century some of the most important extant manuscripts of the ancient Greek poets were copied (Homer, Aristophanes, Aeschylus, Sophocles, and others). Michael Psellus in the 11th century was a great connoisseur of ancient literature and philosophy, and a very prolific writer himself. In the West, Ratherius of Verona read rare texts like Plautus and Catullus and commissioned a beautiful exemplar of Livy. The abbey of Montecassino flourished in the 11th century (especially under the abbot Desiderius), producing important codices of Varro, Tacitus, Juvenal, Apuleius, and other classical authors, written in the new Beneventan script.

A new renaissance of written culture in the Latin West came about in the course of the 12th century, culminating in a general renewal of Western cultural institutions. In the frame of a sweeping social evolution, books began to be produced and sold in cities: most significantly the rise of universities implied a progressive secularization of culture, despite fierce opposition from authorities of the monastic world such as Bernard of Clairvaux. Monasteries gradually lost their dominant position as the depositories of knowledge, partly to the advantage of capitular (chapter) schools in the cathedrals. Mentalities changed too: when some monks showed the French king Louis IX (d. 1270) a luxurious, wonderfully preserved old codex, he replied that in his view books should be less sumptuous and more read.

This process was fostered not only by learned individuals among the clergy, such as John of Salisbury or Wibald of Corvey (both living in the 12th century). Especially from the 13th century onward books in general were no longer conceived as objects of veneration or of private rumination but rather as a public good that should be produced in bulk; paper, much cheaper and more convenient than parchment, played a crucial role in this respect. Expectations arose regarding design: the two-column arrangement became dominant, and Bolognese law books with their massive marginal glosses, miracles of functional *mise en page,* influenced the layout of the first incunables. And prices were expected to be economical: guilds of book artisans and booksellers were created, and important markets arose in Paris, London, Venice, Florence, Bologna, Lübeck, and other cities. Books were stored more conveniently (the mendicant orders and their libraries amassed the largest collections down to the Humanistic age) and made accessible to a wider public of young people.

A perfect example of this evolution was the pecia system, used in Italian, French, and German universities: once a textbook (exemplar) had been examined and approved by a special committee, the authorized copy was handed over to stationers, who in their turn, according to the demand from students, rented single quires to different scribes, so that more copies of the same book could be produced simultaneously and then sold. These books were often of poor quality, written on bad paper and without any illustration or decoration; when they were bound, misplacement of quires occurred fairly frequently.

But this process concerned primarily the great works of law and scholastic philosophy, the most important textbooks (on which hosts of commentaries were produced) being Abelard's *Dialectica,* Gratian's *Decretale,* and Peter Lombard's *Sententiae.* The transmission of Latin secular literature was greatly enhanced by the proliferation of cultural centers and by the growing number of scholars who could produce their own copies, yet it did not make a leap forward in terms of quality—much less, as some works circulated in very corrupt copies (in the mid-13th century Roger Bacon complained about the sheer ignorance of Parisian scribes). In most cases the basis of textual transmission was still the selections and editions of the Carolingian age. And we lack precise information about the structure of late medieval urban book markets: even Europe's largest bookshop, that of Vespasiano da Bisticci in mid-15h-century Florence, remains largely unknown.

In material terms this age of great expansion in the book trade needed a new material and a new handwriting. In the West the production of paper was enhanced from the beginning by the use of watermarks, whereby each sheet was impressed during manufacture with the symbol of the mill that produced it, a design which could (and can today) be discerned by backlighting the page—a tremendous aid in dating manuscripts. The advance in handwriting was the advent of Gothic script, characterized by very few curves and a sharp contrast between thick and thin strokes, partly due to a new method of cutting the nib of the pen. This script, which had evolved from Caroline minuscule in the second half of the 11th century, triumphed across Europe in the following three centuries, though with slight regional and functional variations—among the latter, *bastarda* was used for documents, scholars' drafts, university books, and vernacular literature.

The new two-column page layout and the need for clearer and more frequent subdivisions of each work—the main purpose was *statim invenire,* "to find immediately" a given passage—along with the larger average format of books also influenced the characteristics of book illumination. Initial letters were more lavishly historiated (sometimes with gold, foliage, and floral decorations) than in the Romanesque period, grotesques became less frequent, and narrative illustration was often confined to smaller scenes; in secular works pictures were conceived less in terms of decoration and more in terms of visual commentary, or gloss, to the illustrated texts. Illuminators became very specialized (and very well-paid) artists, whose interaction with scribes and commissioners of manuscripts took various paths; yet only rarely did illustration concern secular Latin literature.

The 12th century brought fresh air in the Greek East as well. Under the Comnenian dynasty many books were copied, and such important philologists as John Tzetzes and Eustathius of Thessalonica devoted their efforts and their huge knowledge of doctrine to the transmission and interpretation of ancient pagan authors. (An imperishable example is Eustathius' bulky commentary on Homer; his autograph manuscripts are preserved in Florence, Paris, and Venice.) The work of these scholars relied primarily on the books preserved in the imperial library in Constantinople or available through the book trade in that capital; the circulation of books in other regions of the Byzantine empire did not increase, owing to the difficult political and military situation.

When Byzantium fell to the Crusaders in 1204, not only were many books lost or destroyed but the whole system of education and cultural transmission favored by the state collapsed. Despite the generous efforts of the emperors of the Nicaean empire (a new school and library were created in Nicaea in the mid-13th century) it was not until the recovery of the capital in 1261 that a proper institutional interest in books and culture resumed.

The role of one particular province must be highlighted in this context: southern Italy, which toward the end of the 11th century the Byzantines definitively lost to the Normans, enjoyed a rich production of Greek books from the 10th through the 14th centuries. Though this production of course evolved over time, some consistent material features distinguish these codices from Constantinopolitan ones of the same period, from the lower quality of their parchment (and frequent use of palimpsests) to their special decorations, including brighter colors and frequent animal or human figures. Whereas most of these south Italian manuscripts contained works of theology or liturgy, from the 12th century onward, and especially under the reign of Frederick II, the transcription of many ancient classical texts was undertaken in the province of Otranto (where Greek communities subsist down to the present day). Both learned laymen and ecclesiastics such as Nicholas (Nectarius), abbot of the important monastery of Casole in Otranto (whose rule was modeled on the rule of Studios, mentioned above), ensured the survival of ancient technical texts, mainly of grammatical, lexicographical, and medical content but also of remarkable editions of philosophers and poets (including the *Odyssey* richest with scholia, Hesiod, Lycophron, and Aristotle). These Greek texts derived either from contemporary Constantinopolitan prototypes or, more rarely, from an indigenous Italian branch of transmission. Contamination with Latin and Western book production is obviously to be expected in the Terra d'Otranto, but precisely the defense there of Greek culture in a more philistine age can be read as an ethnic reaction to the ongoing assimilation of Latin culture, which by then was almost complete in Sicily and Calabria.

In the heart of the Byzantine empire, the late 13th and early 14th centuries were the era of the so-called Palaeologan renaissance, a period of renewed interest in ancient authors and of wider book circulation (more than 50 percent of the scribes were now laymen; Thessalonica, Trebizond, and later Mistra become first-rank cultural centers). A relatively large number of philologists—first and foremost Maximus Planudes and Demetrius Triclinius—produced new editions and commentaries of important, chiefly poetical pagan texts, from Pindar to the tragedians, from Plutarch to the Greek Anthology. This activity met either private scholarly purposes (small, cursive, and exact Palaeologan hands can be detected in the marginal annotations of many classical manuscripts) or the needs of school teaching: for instance, the *syllogē* compiled by Manuel Moschopoulos at the turn of the century gathered into one book an anthology of basic Greek poetry from Homer to Lycophron that became an established canon in Byzantine education. In this age a few women worked as illuminators (for example Irene, the daughter of Theodore Hagiopetrites) and scribes (the noblewoman Theodora Palaeologina), something unheard of in the West. Constantinople and Thessalonica were the main centers of book production and trade during this last acme of Byzantine culture before the fall of Constantinople to Ottoman forces in 1453.

A radical change in the attitude of the Western world toward manuscripts of ancient secular literature arrived with Italian Humanism. Despite some forerunners in northern Italy (especially Padua), the man whose influence was decisive in this respect was Petrarch (1304–1374): his stay at Avignon, to which the papal court had repaired for political reasons, put him in touch with the glorious tradition of French monastic libraries. His indefatigable activity in the recovery, study, and transcription of manuscripts led to such brilliant results as the physical gathering into one codex (now at the British Library in London, Harley 2493) of three decades of Livy previously scattered in different books, the patient collection of many of Cicero's letters, orations, and philosophical works, the textual restoration of Propertius and Pomponius Mela, and the production of an impressive annotated Virgil containing the best of ancient doctrine along with Petrarch's own notes.

Petrarch was followed to a certain extent by Boccaccio, who paid special attention to less obvious authors such as Tacitus, Martial, and Apuleius; in the latter decades of his life Petrarch tried to tackle Greek works as well, with the aid of a Greek-speaking Calabrian monk. Petrarch can be considered the model and forerunner of early 15th-century Florentine Humanists such as Coluccio Salutati and most notably Poggio Bracciolini, whose merits in the discovery of pagan Latin literature (Cicero, Lucretius, Statius, Petronius, and many others) were greater than those of all his predecessors.

The history of Latin writing reflects this cultural revolution: Petrarch had grown weary of the Gothic script, even in its more rounded Italian form (*rotunda*), which evoked the old Caroline minuscule as a model of elegance and clarity. He thus invented a new style of handwriting, semi-Gothic, itself partly imbued with Caroline features. A further attempt in this direction was made by Coluccio Salutati, but the true "archaeological" recovery and adoption of the Caroline script for the writing of books was achieved in early 15th-century Florence by Poggio Bracciolini, with the help of the Humanist and book trader Niccolò Niccoli. The return to ancient models was completed around the middle of the century, when (thanks to the researches of antiquarians such as Felice Feliciano) the Roman epigraphic capital was adopted for majuscule letters. Poggio's *littera antiqua,* despite being designed for the needs of a cultural elite, was adopted by scholars all over Europe: in England Duke Humphrey (d. 1446) had manuscripts copied for him by Italian Humanists, and Italian scribes were also engaged by the Hungarian king Matthias Corvinus. The *antiqua* then made its way into print, and its success explains why the style is still used today in printed books, including the present one.

The 15th century in Italy was a golden age for the history of manuscript books of ancient authors. Many old manuscripts were discovered, many new manuscripts were copied, and some beautiful manuscripts were produced thanks to innovative illuminators. Examples range from the Ferrarese chorals and the splendid Bible of Borso d'Este to secular works such as Livy, Virgil, Seneca, and Martianus Capella. In northern Europe in the same era the International Gothic style of illumination was producing such masterpieces as the Books of Hours of the duc de Berry and of Étienne Chevalier (both now at the Musée Condé in Chantilly). This enthusiasm soon affected Greek studies too, as the firm idea of a Graeco-Latin Humanism prompted scholars to acquire Greek books from the Byzantine empire, either by direct acquisitions during personal travels or through the mediation of Greek scholars fleeing their embattled fatherland. Cardinal Bessarion's donation of Greek books to what was to become the Marcian Library in Venice (1468) was a landmark in this field, but large collections of Greek manuscripts were also amassed in Florence (thanks to Humanistic trends among the Medici), Rome (thanks to the efforts of various popes), and later in Paris (especially by impulse of Francis I).

The renewed prestige enjoyed by older manuscripts explains both the Humanists' special care for the physical aspect of newly produced codices (good parchment, elegant illumination, etc.) and, from a different approach, some important discoveries in the newly opened realm of philology, such as Politian's notion of the *eliminatio codicum descriptorum,* a guiding rule, in collating manuscript readings, that examplars must be presumed superior to their copies. Indeed, Humanists sometimes went so far as to forge nonexistent manuscript sources of their own works: examples range from Leon Battista Alberti's comedy *Philodoxeus* (1424), allegedly written by a certain Lepidus, to Annius of Viterbo's fake translation of Berossus' and Manetho's historical works (1498); in Germany, John Trithemius similarly forged a manuscript of the Frankish historian Hunibald. At the same time, Humanists perceived books as a common good and agreed to lend manuscripts to any scholar wishing to consult them: this is epitomized by the addition *et amicorum* that often follows the owner's name on bookplates and other ownership notations of the period.

The star of manuscripts continued to shine even within the Gutenberg galaxy: the effect of print on the history of books was gradual. All first editions of ancient works of course depended on manuscripts, and indeed many incunables resemble old codices in striking ways. The older medium enjoyed wide popularity both among Humanists and among princes and collectors particularly sensitive to the external charms of books: Duke Federico da Montefeltro did not admit any printed book into his library at Urbino; the bookseller Vespasiano da Bisticci continued to deal exclusively in manuscripts until his death in 1498; the erudite German John Trithemius wrote an entire book (*De laude scriptorum,* 1492) against printing and in praise of manuscripts.

Obviously not all texts were printed immediately; yet the Humanistic quest for classical antiquity prompted scholars and editors (especially in Italy and in Central Europe) to concentrate their efforts precisely on the works of Latin (and, to a certain extent, Greek) authors, which in most cases appeared in print before their vernacular counterparts. A collateral effect of the new medium was that some manuscripts became lost after publication: this was the fate of glorious codices such as the Vetus Cluniacensis Cicero and the Veronensis Catullus, for whose readings we now rely solely on printed editions or Humanistic collations.

In the special case of Greek texts the development of satisfying typographic characters was particularly slow: manuscripts continued to be copied in the West until the mid-16th century, and in the East the powerful tradition of monastic scriptoria (as on Mount Athos) lasted well into the 19th. Aldus Manutius' beautiful editions of the Greek classics, a turning point in the history of typography, were deeply connected with their manuscript antecedents both for the design of letters and layout of pages, and in many cases also for their bindings, which were decorated with the geometric patterns typical of Byzantine books.

But in the long run the far-reaching psychological and cultural implications of print changed irreversibly readers' approach to the written word. Manuscripts became more and more an object of archaeology or antiquarianism, and European Humanists started studying them in order to improve their editions of classical authors. Among the scholars who took an interest in the shapes of letters and the fate of ancient books were Joseph Justus Scaliger and Willem Canter in the second half of the 16th century, though of course scattered remarks occur in the writings of many philologists, from Turnèbe to Bentley.

It was not until the turn of the 18th century, however, that two major works inaugurated the age of scientific study: Jean Mabillon's *De re diplomatica* (1681; supplement, 1704) and Bernard de Montfaucon's *Palaeographia Graeca* (1708). The new discipline of palaeography focused on the dating of codices and on the history of libraries and collections; the first catalogues of manuscripts (Montfaucon, Zanetti, Bandini) were produced in France and Italy during the 18th century. Studies of manuscripts with reference to their philological value in constituting the text of ancient authors dominated the 19th century, but an interest in manuscript books as documents of peculiar historical moments and milieux emerged only with the pioneering work of Ludwig Traube and others at the end of that century. Codicology became autonomous from palaeography in relatively recent times, and the organic study of manuscripts as the functional products of social, economic, and cultural factors has been practiced only since the 1960s.

Yet throughout modern times manuscripts have changed our perception of the past: Villoison's discovery of Venetus A of the *Iliad* in 1788 revolutionized perceptions of ancient scholarship and literary criticism; Angelo Mai's deciphering of Cicero's *De re publica* in 1819 (from a palimpsest) greatly enhanced our knowledge of Roman history and political theory; the Sinaiticus codex of the Bible was the object of an international intrigue in the late 19th century; two Leiden manuscripts of Lucretius were the starting point for Karl Lachmann's reshaping of textual criticism; in the second half of the 20th century, the discovery of the lexicon of Photius in a Macedonian monastery supplied many new fragments of the ancient poets. Another chapter in this recent history concerns the achievements of papyrology, a discipline that developed mainly thanks to the Egyptian excavations of the late 19th century: we owe to recently recovered fragments of ancient rolls the knowledge of substantial portions of Greek literature, ranging from archaic lyric down to Hellenistic poetry and late antique epic, from Orphic literature down to Athenian historiography and Epicurean philosophy—not to mention the wealth of documentary evidence covering and illuminating the history of Ptolemaic and Graeco-Roman Egypt.

Even in the present day, while waiting for the continuous and unpredictable surprises coming from papyrological finds, the world hopes that new techniques of palimpsest analysis will enable the recovery of some of Archimedes' mathematical doctrines as well as some lost scenes of Menandrean comedy, from manuscripts currently preserved in Baltimore and in Rome.

BIBL.: M. L. Agati, *Il libro manoscritto* (Rome 2003). L. Avrin, *Scribes, Scripts and Books* (Chicago 1991). L. E. Boyle, *Medieval Latin Palaeography: A Bibliographical Introduction* (Toronto 1984). M. Buonocore, ed., *Vedere i classici: L'illustrazione libraria dei testi antichi dall'età romana al tardo medioevo* (Rome 1996). *Byzantine Books and Bookmen: A Dumbarton Oaks Colloquium* (Washington, D.C., 1975). G. Cavallo, ed., *Libri, editori e pubblico nel mondo antico* (Rome 1975), *Libri e lettori nel Medioevo* (Rome 1977), and *Libri e lettori nel mondo bizantino* (Rome 1982). C. A. Chavannes-Mazel and M. M. Smith, eds., *Medieval Manuscripts of the Latin Classics: Production and Use* (Los Altos Hills, Calif., 1996). J. Glenisson, ed., *Le livre au Moyen Âge* (Paris 1988). A. Grafton and M. Williams, *Christianity and the Transformation of the Book* (Cambridge, Mass., 2006). M. Maniaci, *Archeologia del manoscritto* (Rome 2002). E. Pöhlmann, *Einführung in die Überlieferungsgeschichte und in die Textkritik der antiken Lietratur,* vol. 2 (Darmstadt 2003). L. D. Reynolds and N. G. Wilson, *Scribes and Scholars,* 3rd ed. (Oxford 1991). K. Weitzmann, *Illustrations in Roll and Codex* (1947, repr. Princeton 1970).

F.M.P.

Book, Manuscript: Production

The oldest extant manuscript books, which can be assigned to the late 4th century BCE, are rolls of papyrus, the vegetable writing material obtained from the plant of the same name. These rolls have sufficiently well-defined characteristics to suggest that this form had already been in use for some time. The introduction of papyrus to Greece from Egypt in an earlier period had enabled the manufacture of manuscripts of this kind for several hundred years before the 4th century, a conclusion supported by considerable evidence: literary sources, inscriptions arranged as *volumina,* rolls painted on Attic vases. But before papyrus became a standard writing material used in producing rolls in Greece, literary texts were apparently inscribed on hard surfaces, on which they were usually scratched and laid out in some fashion: strips of leather, schist plates, thin sheets of lead, wax tablets. These last continued to be used long beyond the archaic period. For the 4th century BCE we have testimony from Diogenes Laertius (3.37) that the text of Plato's *Laws* existed on wax tablets, and that these were transcribed by Philip of Opus, most likely onto rolls of papyrus.

When we speak of manuscripts in roll form in the Greek and Roman period, we are usually referring to papyrus rolls, since rolls of parchment—the other writing material used in the ancient and medieval periods, which was obtained from animal skins—are rarely attested. But how was a papyrus roll made, written, and read? Leaves, called *kollemata* in Greek, made of thin strips of papyrus—obtained from the stalk of the plant, layered at right angles (first horizontally and then vertically), then pressed to make them stick together and dried in the sun—were joined lengthwise to form *volumina,* or rolls, of a standard length (about 3.40 m) that were then sold for various writing purposes. By cutting or joining commercial rolls, one appropriate for literary content was created. The typology of this kind of roll from the 4th century BCE until its definitive eclipse in the 4th century CE, when it was replaced by manuscripts in codex form, has been the subject of various studies based both on surviving materials and on literary and iconographical sources. It was a roll unfurled horizontally; its length varied depending on the size of the text it was supposed to contain, and on the types of writing and columnar arrangement (*mise en colonne*) it employed; writing was normally done on the side of the roll with the horizontal papyrus fibers and was organized into a series of regularly spaced columns; the height of the roll and the width of the columns varied according to time period, place of production, type of text, and quality and use of the book. Latin book rolls seem to have had wider columns than their coeval Greek counterparts. However the text was arranged, a roll normally contained either one lone book of a specific work (e.g., a book of Thucydides or of Livy) or one autonomous work (a tragedy of Sophocles or a comedy of Aristophanes). In the case of short texts, such as books of Homer or Demosthenes' *symbouleutikoi* speeches, a roll could contain more than one textual unit; on the other hand, very long books could be divided into two rolls. Not infrequently, rolls that ceased to serve their purpose—not only those containing books, but also documents—were reused by writing a text on the other side, that is, on the side with the vertical fibers. Certain ancient literary works—Euripides' *Hypsipyle* and Aristotle's *Constitution of the Athenians,* for example—have been preserved only on reused rolls. Words were written continuously without spaces between them (*scriptio continua*), and sentences were barely distinguished by empty spaces or punctuation signs; the sense of the text emerged from being read aloud, which was much more prevalent in the ancient world than silent reading. Once written, the book was rolled up—sometimes around wooden rods, called *umbilici*—and was ready for reading. To read the text, the reader held the roll in the right hand and unrolled progressively with the left, which then rolled up and held the part already read; after reading, the book remained rolled up on the left, so it was necessary to roll it back to the beginning to read the work again.

Beginning in the late 1st century CE, the roll began to be replaced by a new form of manuscript, the codex. Of Roman origin, the codex was modeled on tablets joined as polyptychs, which are attested in literary works of the period by Cato the Censor (3rd–2nd cent. BCE). When the tablets were replaced by leaves of parchment (as they were in the Western Roman world) or papyrus (as was often the case in the Graeco-oriental world, especially in Egypt), the codex was born. At the end of the 1st century CE Martial's compositions circulated in this form (Martial 1.2.1–4); and Martial himself makes reference to parchment manuscripts of Homer, Virgil, Cicero, Livy, and Ovid in codex form (Martial 14.184, 186, 188, 190, 192). The manuscript of Virgil bore a portrait of the author on its title page. The codex's success was assured by the various opportunities it afforded: saving writing material, since the codex was written on both sides of the page, unlike the roll, usually written on only one side; greater practicality of handling and use, since it could be held and read with only one hand or placed on a stand; expanded capacity, since the codex could hold a much greater amount of text than the roll and thus could contain more books of a single work (e.g., all eight books of Thucydides, or a decade of Livy) or many works of a single author (for example, a good number of plays by Sophocles, Aristophanes, or Plautus); the pages of the codex were numbered, which facilitated reading and consultation and made it possible to find given passages easily or to return to them later. Between the late 1st and the 4th centuries the manuscript codex spread throughout the Graeco-Roman world. This happened more quickly for biblical texts and the new Christian literature, more gradually for profane literature, but at the end of the 4th century the codex had definitively taken the place of the roll.

Accompanying this development was another change in the technology of the book: parchment's progressive replacement of papyrus as a writing material. (It is not correct, however, to posit a necessary relationship between roll and papyrus on the one hand, and codex and parchment on the other.) Parchment was much stronger than papyrus. It was obtained from the skins of animals, especially sheep and cattle, but the sources also mention deer, gazelle, antelopes, and even snakes, although no examples are extant. In a curious medieval epigram human skin is said to be of lesser value than that of animals; after the death of a human being its skin decays together with its flesh and bones, whereas animal skin can be turned into writing material. A specific tanning procedure was followed to produce parchment: the skin was soaked in water and lime, then stretched on a frame, scraped on both the hair and the flesh side, left to dry, and finally smoothed with pumice stone. This was the most widespread procedure in the Middle Ages, but there were other methods of preparation: in the East, for example, the parchment was sometimes smeared with egg white to lighten it. Parchment was believed to have been invented in Pergamon as a response to the embargo on Egyptian papyrus, imposed by the Ptolemies to keep the library in the Attalid city from growing and competing with theirs in Alexandria. Parchment, since it was obtained from animal skins, could be made everywhere, unlike papyrus, which was produced only in Egypt. Thus the use of parchment ended up spreading together with the codex, first in Rome and in the West, and later in the Greek world. After the 4th century papyrus codices are attested frequently only in Egypt, whereas elsewhere they are quite rare.

Sometimes papyrus or parchment was reused by erasing or washing away the text and writing a new one; such manuscripts are called palimpsests. Their use was quite common in the Middle Ages particularly and in certain places, especially the peripheral territories of Byzantium (Syria, Palestine, and the Greek Terra d'Otranto) and of the Latin West (Ireland, but also Continental monastic institutions founded by the Irish, such as Bobbio). Fragments of certain works that would otherwise be lost, such as John Malalas's *Chronography* or Cicero's *De re publica,* have been recovered from palimpsests.

It was also in the Middle Ages that a new writing material, paper, eventually gained a place alongside parchment. Made by soaking rags, paper was invented in China in the 1st century CE and was familiar in the Arab world in the 8th. It was then introduced first to Byzantium, by way of Syria, Palestine, and Egypt, and later to the West, by way of Spain. A distinction should be made between paper without watermarks and Italian paper, which had them. A watermark is an alphabetic or, more often, figural motif inserted into the weft of the frame in which sheets of paper are made. Since it is pressed into them permanently, a watermark makes it possible to identify the papermaker and, with a good deal of certainty, the date of manufacture. Eastern paper never had watermarks. In Greek manuscripts paper appeared as early as the 8th to 9th century; in Latin ones it was widespread beginning in the 13th century.

Writing on both papyrus and parchment was done with a calamus, a short section of a reed sharpened and dipped in ink. An anonymous epigram in the Greek Anthology (9.162) describes it thus:

> I was a useless plant, a reed,
> I bore neither figs, nor apples, nor grapes.
> But someone sharpened my lips and made there a thin cut,
> turning me into an adept of the Muses.
> Since then when I drink a black potion, as if possessed
> I say every word with this mute mouth.

The calamus was used as a writing instrument for the whole of the Byzantine era in the East; in the West it was gradually replaced beginning in the 4th century by the quill.

How was a manuscript codex put together and organized? It was normally made up of a group of fascicules bound together, themselves made up of folded sheets of parchment or, in more ancient times, of papyrus or, in the Middle Ages and the Renaissance, of paper; only early on could one find papyrus codices made up of only one large fascicule. The folded sheets—called bifolia—were placed one inside another in varying numbers to form fascicules, mostly of four bifolia (quaternion); but there were also fascicules of two (duernion), three (ternion), five (quinternion), six (sextern), and rarely a greater number of bifolia. In the case of parchment, the animal skin could also be folded and then cut to form gatherings of a given number of bifolia directly. The older kind of papyrus codex was constructed so that pages with horizontal fibers faced those with vertical fibers, but later they were made so that pages with fibers in the same direction faced one another. In the parchment codex, regardless of how the fascicule was made, facing pages—except in rare cases—were of the same side of the skin, flesh side to flesh side, hair side to hair side (known as Gregory's law, from Caspar René Gregory, the scholar who first noted this correspondence). In eastern Greek codices the fascicule normally began with the flesh side of the parchment, whereas in the Latin world this practice is found above all in the most ancient manuscripts and in the Renaissance; in the Middle Ages fascicules generally began with the hair side, a practice that can sometimes be found also in Greek codices produced in southern Italy. The correct order of the fascicules was indicated by a number placed either at the beginning or at the end of each one, or even both; but it was also possible to use *reclamantes* (catchwords), writing at the end of one fascicule the beginning of the text (first word or several words) contained in the next.

Before copying, it was necessary to rule, that is, to trace a series of lines on, the pages to guide the writing. The rules also served to limit the space designated for the text or to divide the space itself between text and commentary. Parchment was usually ruled by making an imprint with the dry point of a rod or metallic instrument that sometimes left its mark on many pages at once; but lines could also be traced with lead or ink, and this was the normal practice on paper. The course of the lines was guided by a series of regularly spaced, small pricks made on the page —almost always on the margins—with a kind of small wheel with teeth, but also, in certain contexts, with a special *tabula ad rigandum.* The different systems by which ruling was carried out (sheet by sheet or a certain number of sheets at once), as well as the types of rulings (the layout resulting from the traced lines) were quite numerous. They have been classified and are normally indicated by means of a sequence of numbers and letters that indicate the number, arrangement, and length of the lines, which allows the page format to be reconstructed.

The next step was to transcribe the text, after which the

fascicules were gathered and bound together according to techniques that varied by time and place. Bindings were generally made of wooden boards covered with leather and furnished with brass studs and clasps. There were also precious bindings (of ivory, silver, and ivory with gems), but they were not used as much for manuscript books of the classics as for luxury codices of sacred works.

BIBL.: Bernhard Bischoff, *Paläographie des römischen Altertums und des abendländischen Mittelalters* (Berlin 1986). Alain Blanchard, ed., *Les débuts du codex* (Turnhout 1989). Jacques Bompaire and Jean Irigoin, eds., *La paléographie grecque et byzantine* (Paris 1977). Guglielmo Cavallo, *Dalla parte del libro: Storie di trasmissione dei classici* (Urbino 2002). Paul Géhin, ed., *Lire le manuscrit médiéval: Observer et décrire* (Paris 2005). William A. Johnson, *Bookrolls and Scribes in Oxyrhyncus* (Toronto 2004). Marilena Maniaci and Paola Munafò, eds., *Ancient and Medieval Book Materials and Techniques*, 2 vols. (Vatican City 1993). Armando Petrucci, ed., *Libri, scrittura e pubblico nel Rinascimento. Guida storica e critica* (Rome 1979). L. D. Reynolds and N. G. Wilson, *Scribes and Scholars*, 3rd ed. (Oxford 1991). Eric G. Turner, *The Typology of the Early Codex* (Philadelphia 1977). G.CA.

Translated by Patrick Baker

Book, Printed

The printing of the classics began in a definite year, 1465. The Gutenberg Bible had been finished 10 years before, and other Bibles followed, along with a wide range of theological, patristic, lexicographical, prophetic, and astronomical texts and works of liturgy and ecclesiastical administration. But if we exclude the medieval schoolbook "Donatus," with which children took their first steps in Latin, and which was much printed in the earliest phase, nothing strictly classical appeared in print until the almost simultaneous publication of Ciceronian works in Germany and Italy. There is no certainty as to the absolute priority. The Mainz edition of Cicero's *De officiis* and *Paradoxa stoicorum* is dated 1465, without day or month, but a copy was presented by the publisher, Johann Fust, in July of that year, and a second edition was called for as early as 4 February 1466. The edition of *De oratore* assigned to the German printers Conrad Sweynheym and Arnold Pannartz at the Benedictine monastery of Subiaco, 50 miles east of Rome, bears no date. One copy, however, often wrongly reported as lost or destroyed, was thickly annotated by the Parma Humanist Antonio Tridentone, work that he concluded on 30 September 1465. The book had therefore (allowing time for Tridentone's "correction and emendation," as he put it) been in print for some time, perhaps some months, before the end of September. There is even a chance, from the evidence of its type and technique, that another, undated edition of *De officiis* (alone), printed at Cologne by Ulrich Zel, may date from the same year.

This outbreak of Cicero was presumably not the result of a sudden vogue but the outcome of the steady percolation of Humanist influence, north of the Alps as well as in the homeland of Humanism. In retrospect, the choice of author was inevitable. Cicero was the quintessential Latin prose author, as Virgil was in verse, and the variety of his writings catered to many different interests. There were 30 editions of Ciceronian works in print by 1470, before most Roman authors had received even one, and by the end of the century, more than 330. The early German editions of Cicero were isolated experiments to test the market; they later reappeared in another guise (as they also did in the Low Countries), as small books with ample room for annotation, texts used for reading in schools and in the early stages of the arts course at universities. In Italy, by contrast, the volumes were typically large and imposing, for the scholar's desk and lecturer's lectern, and after about 1480 these were often equipped with one or more commentaries, arranged around the larger type of the text.

The dominance of Cicero and, in poetry, of Virgil, with nearly 200 editions in the 15th century, did not preclude the printing of a wider range of texts than we might now expect in a classical corpus. In the earliest days it was difficult to print an edition of a classical author that was not an *editio princeps*. The most notable pioneers in this field, after they moved to Rome in 1467, were again Sweynheym and Pannartz, to whom are due the first editions of several Ciceronian works, Caesar, Livy, and the Elder Pliny, Virgil, Ovid, and Lucan. But they also printed Apuleius, Aulus Gellius, Suetonius, Silius Italicus, Justin's *Epitome*, and Donatus on Terence (as well as Terence himself) and, in translations from the Greek, Strabo and Polybius. All this was alongside extensive printing of the Church Fathers, for the Quattrocento saw itself as the fortunate, if sometimes conflicted, inheritor of a glorious patristic tradition as well as a pagan classical one, and insofar as the first purchasers of the products of the early Roman presses are identifiable, they were very largely churchmen and religious foundations. Sweynheym and Pannartz's in-house editor, Giannandrea Bussi (himself a bishop and papal secretary), remarked in the preface to Pliny that printing itself was one of the very few advances that the modern age had made on antiquity. The others were sugar and gunpowder.

The pronounced classical and patristic accent of Sweynheym and Pannartz's editorial program found ready rivals at Rome, and soon enough at Venice, when printing started there in 1469. The sheer amount of classics now in print (by the end of the century, at least 100,000 copies of Cicero, doubtless several times the number of manuscripts of the author then in existence) resulted in a crisis of overproduction observable at both Venice and Rome in the years 1472–1473. At this time, too, many smaller printing centers in Italy ceased to support presses, and thereafter safer courses were followed. The famous Venetian printer Nicolas Jenson, for example, made a marked retreat from the production of classical texts, standard or marginal, turning instead to law, liturgy, and theology. Retrenchment and consolidation were the order of the day, though the classics never ceased to be printed in Italy. Venice in particular soon outstripped Rome as the center of classical printing, with an alert eye on the rich German markets beyond the Alps. Something similar happened in the other countries of mainland Europe, where an early concentration on classical and Humanistic texts in France (Paris) and Spain (Barcelona and Valencia) and the roman types associated with them gave way to a more varied output and increasing reversion to gothic types as time went on. The Low Countries tended to follow Germany in printing educational texts for local consumption, more so toward the end of the century, and in importing more scholarly works from abroad. England never printed classical texts in the original language in the incunable period, except for Terence's plays and a solitary speech of Cicero; English scholars who wanted printed books necessarily relied on imports, for which there is abundant evidence. All in all, classical printing accounts for no more than 5 percent of extant production to the end of the 15th century, and the much greater rate of attrition of vernacular and liturgical texts suggests that that figure is itself inflated.

A minute but highly prestigious corner of the trade was in the making of Greek books, the exclusive preserve of Florence and Northern Italy in the early period—there was no Greek printing in Ottoman Greece itself for centuries. The very first greek type is found in Fust and Schoeffer's *De officiis* and *Paradoxa* (Mainz, 1465), but the letters were so ill-formed and randomly set that only a reader who already knew what they were could make out the scattered Greek. A much more satisfactory rendering appeared in the extensive Greek quotations of the Sweynheym and Pannartz Lactantius, the first dated book printed in Italy (Subiaco, 29 October 1465). This simplified "quotation greek"—usually accentless—continued to be used by various printers in Latin books, but very little printing of whole works in Greek took place until the 1490s, and most of that was aimed at students wishing to acquire the language. In the meantime scholars and amateurs could turn to the many Latin translations, medieval and contemporary, of Greek works that the Humanists found useful and instructive, primarily Plato, Aristotle, and the historians. The first major work to appear in the Greek language was the Florentine Homer of 1488, *Iliad* and *Odyssey* together, edited by the local professor of Greek, the Athenian Demetrius Chalcondylas. Florence continued to produce a modest series of literary classics over the next decade, but Greek printing took firm and enduring root only with the establishment of the Aldine press at Venice.

Aldus Manutius (1451–1515) was at bottom a teacher possessed of a burning desire to communicate what he held to be the best lessons that the ancient world had to offer, its Greek writings. The Aldine firm was first set up to issue all of (obtainable) Aristotle in the original language, a massive undertaking that was published in five large folio volumes over the years 1495–1498 in a cursive type specially designed for them. These were squarely aimed at a market that hardly as yet existed, the serious scholar of Greek with a deep pocket, and the very large numbers of the Aldine Aristotle still extant are perhaps testimony to the quixotic nature of the enterprise. But Aldus, in other respects a shrewd businessman, cross-subsidized his erudite publishing (including on the Latin side Poliziano's *Opera,* 1498) with more salable items, as well as much private presswork.

Apart from his program of bringing the ancient Hellenic sources directly to the reader, Aldus's second great contribution was the series of italic octavo classics issued from the beginning of the 16th century. By that time there was considerable segmentation of the market, different readerships that could be targeted more closely. The typical incunable classical text was being submerged under the weight of commentary, prefaces, indexes, and other paratexts—some of these massive variorum editions could incorporate four or five commentaries on a single text. Aldus swept it all away, producing small, plain texts with the briefest of forewords in the elegant new type we call italic: to Erasmus they seemed "the neatest types in the world." This was in itself an important development in printing a canonical text, one that gave pagan classics the appearance of biblical authority and power.

These books were evidently not for scholars, or not for scholars on duty; their intended audience was, rather, politicians, prelates, diplomats, and the cultivated courts of Northern Italy, persons like Isabella d'Este, the learned marchioness of Mantua, or Jean Grolier, the French treasurer of Milan. The series that began with Virgil in 1501 expanded its range to include besides Latin classics the Greek tragedians (Sophocles, 1502, never before printed; Euripides, 1503, the first collected edition) and the "modern classics," the Italian Trecento poets. So we find Machiavelli in rustic garb in his famous 1513 letter to Vettori: "Leaving the grove, I go to a spring, and thence to my aviary. I have a book in my pocket, either Dante or Petrarch, or one of the minor poets such as Tibullus, Ovid, and the like." These pocket books will have been octavo Aldines or imitations. When Machiavelli returned to his study, he settled down with serious folios of Livy and other ancient worthies. Not that Aldus shied away from continued scholarly publication in these years, for there are plenty of folio editions of obscure Greek authors, as well as some very central ones—the *editiones principes* in Greek of Thucydides and Herodotus, for example, in 1502, Plutarch's *Moralia* in 1509, the long-heralded Plato in 1513—and he certainly had no prejudice against commentators in general, provided they were respectably ancient. But it was the octavo classics, the *libri portatiles*, designed to be held in the hand, that set a style and formed a taste for small-scale fine printing that led to many contemporary imitations, sometimes outright piracies, and down the years to the Elzeviers and Baskerville.

By 1475 the bulk of the Latin classics had been put into print. By the time of the death of Aldus 40 years later, practically all classical Latin and most of classical Greek literature had reached print. Of the Greek writers now considered major, or part of the "canon," only Aeschylus

—not an author likely to appeal to Quattrocento tastes—remained in manuscript, and he was printed by the successors of Aldus in 1518. The Aldine house also put out the collected works of the most voluminous ancient author, Galen, in 1525, though he had been partially printed in Greek and (much more) in Latin before 1501. The year 1515 saw the publication at Rome of a work only recently rediscovered, the first six books of the *Annales* of Tacitus (again, not an author much to the taste of the 15th century). Apart from that, and apart, of course, from texts hidden in papyri and palimpsests, the only significant additions to the classical corpus were the Roman history of Velleius Paterculus (Basel: Froben, 1521), the last five extant books of Livy, 41–45, in the edition by Simon Grynaeus (Basel: Froben, 1531), and some letters of Cicero's *Epistulae ad Brutum,* included in Cratander's Cicero, *Opera* (Basel 1528), the last finds of the great age of rediscovery.

The place of publication of these works marks an important and in the long run decisive shift in the locus of classical printing away from Italy and to the north. From amateurish beginnings of like-minded scholars, grouped in self-styled sodalities or academies, and with powerful impetus from newly established chairs of rhetoric or "humanity" at seats of higher education in France, Switzerland, and the German Reich, transalpine Europe began to develop its own brand of classical scholarship, very soon to a highly professional level. Many of these Humanists had been schooled in Italy or taught by Italian professors abroad; but a growing self-confidence soon enabled them to match or surpass contemporary Italian achievement in many areas of classical learning. By the 1520s the presses of Basel had become the leading center for the dissemination of Greek literature and scholarship, building on the earlier classical and patristic work of Johannes Amerbach and Johann Froben, the latter being Erasmus's printer of choice. Professors of the caliber of Grynaeus, Oecolampadius, and Oporinus were active participants in the work of the press, as everything from publishing directors to proofreaders, just as Beatus Rhenanus, Badius Ascensius, and Erasmus had been before them. Erasmus's stint at the Aldine press in 1508–1509, when he was working on the much-improved second edition of his *Adagia,* is a token of the way the north absorbed Italian lessons and ideals.

The *Adagia,* a large collection of classical proverbs and maxims with extensive commentary, rapidly became indispensable as a window on the ancient world. It can also stand as an exemplar of the sort of self-standing contribution to classical learning and literature, derived by a process of detachment from continuous commentary and through a great many *Emendationes, Annotationes,* and *Miscellanea* (notably Poliziano's acute philological inquiries) until scholars came to devote monographs to particular aspects of the ancient world. Thus, at Paris we find Guillaume Budé producing works on Roman coins and measures in *De asse* (1514) or on the Greek language in his *Commentarii linguae Graecae* (1529). Such monographs were the product of the age of printed books: their viability depended entirely on the trade and distribution that the printers had opened up. Budé also took the leading part in persuading François I to found a new institute for teaching the ancient languages (and other subjects), the Collège Royal (1530), which rapidly gave Paris primacy in classical, especially Greek, studies. One outcome was a vast increase in production of short texts in the original language for the use of studious youth. These books were often bare Greek texts intended for *viva voce* commentary—sometimes of very out-of-the-way authors—or commented Latin ones, of Cicero above all. Gathered together in *Sammelbände,* these unpretentious (and now very scarce) booklets have much to tell of the teaching of the *lecteurs royaux.*

The printers of these books were men who, if not always learned themselves, disposed of learned press-correctors and learned advisers—the very professors for whom they were printing on commission. But for a large-scale enterprise that could match the glamour and prestige of the Aldine printing dynasty in Italy, Paris (and in the latter half of the century Geneva too) could show the members of the Estienne (or Étienne) family. One of them, the younger Henri Estienne (Henricus Stephanus) stands out as not just the leading scholarly printer of his day but absolutely the leading scholar. His uncle François and father, Robert, had been the first to employ, from 1543 onward, the *grecs du Roi,* a famous cursive greek font newly designed by Claude Garamond, whose family of roman fonts became equally standard in editions of the classics. Robert had produced a three-volume folio dictionary of the Latin language, long unreplaced; his son's most notable achievement was a Greek–Latin lexicon that to this day has not quite been replaced: the five folio volumes of the *Thesaurus Graecae linguae* (Geneva 1572). This was on top of a remarkable run of Greek texts, many of them first editions, of which he is reckoned to have printed some 4,000 pages a year at the peak of production. His 1578 edition supplies the standard system of reference to Plato's text in use today (often referred to as Stephanus numbers). But both these editions proved unremunerative and brought him to financial ruin.

The move (for confessional reasons) of one branch of the Estiennes to Geneva is emblematic of the way that scholarship and, hand in hand with it, scholarly printing spread, flourished, and decayed. A biological model of rise and decline is no doubt oversimplified, but it does correspond to something real in the fluctuations of both classical scholarship and printing history. Venice continued to publish works of genuine value, not least in the person of Aldus's son, the classical scholar Paulus Manutius, but the cutting edge now lay elsewhere. Basel's preeminence in Greek printing was a thing of the past by the last quarter of the 16th century. The leading Italian classicist of that century, Pier Vettori, had many of his editions, especially of the Greek dramatists, printed in Paris, but by the time of Henri Estienne's death in 1598 the center of classical learning had moved northward again, to the Low Countries, where Justus Lipsius and his successor Joseph Scaliger (a Frenchman) gave luster to the new university of Leiden.

Christophe Plantin, another Frenchman, set up a long-running press in Antwerp, and one of his former apprentices founded the book business of the Elzeviers at Leiden, later at Amsterdam as well, which came to dominate publishing in the northern Netherlands throughout the 17th century. The Plantin firm and the Elzeviers by no means devoted themselves exclusively to classical publications, but there were many Greek and Latin editions among their total output. Both houses were known for the high quality of their typography, presswork, and editing. The Golden Compasses device of Plantin (and his son-in-law and successor, Jan Moretus) was in some measure a guarantee of a solid, scholarly product when affixed to such works as the celebrated editions of Tacitus and Seneca issued by Lipsius in 1585 and 1605. Plantin actively sought support for the unremunerative editions of marginal Greek authors like Stobaeus, both through internal cross-subsidy from his profitable printing of liturgies and from outside sources. Another son-in-law of Plantin, Franciscus Raphelengius, himself a considerable orientalist, acted as the publisher of Scaliger's forbiddingly technical monographs in his early years at Leiden. Like the work of the Golden Compasses, the Elzevier classical texts, many of them finely printed duodecimos (typically some 12 cm × 6 cm), early attracted the attentions of collectors and bibliophiles: to the inviting smallness of the editions was added scholarship sometimes of the highest order—16 editions of Virgil's *Opera* in the 17th century, for example, edited by such luminaries as Daniel and Nicolaus Heinsius. An "Elzevier" came to have the same sort of cachet that attached then, and still does, to an "Aldine." The Plantin-Moretus and Elzevier firms had the further advantage of being run by a succession of hard-headed businessmen, which kept both at the top of their trade for a century or more.

Schoolbooks were always needed. A remarkable late 17th-century enterprise in this sphere was the publication of the Delphin classics (1674–1691), a uniform series of 68 Latin authors published in Paris with state subvention and designed in the first place *in usum serenissimi Delphini*, "for the use of the Dauphin," that is, the eldest son of Louis XIV. Edited by Pierre-Daniel Huet and others (including the learned Anne Lefèbvre, Mme Dacier), they provided a text, a Latin paraphrase, extensive notes, and, very usefully, a word index. The popularity of the series led to several reprints over the next two centuries, and it even traveled as a brand name to England, where the printer A. J. Valpy issued 141 solid octavo volumes, with newly adopted texts, between 1819 and 1830.

If the Delphin classics at first represented a clear pedagogical advance, their presentation increasingly suffered from the weight of commentary that accumulated around and eventually suffocated the few lines of text on each page. This was all very much in the style of the endless Netherlandish and English quarto editions *cum notis variorum*, that is, with notes of various scholars. Yet the fact that the variorum editions were well and often printed, sometimes splendidly bound for school prizes, suggests that they were valued by many readers who liked erudition. Several reactions to this development were possible: a return to the modest, chaste classical text that put forth a single scholar's views of its emendation and interpretation, in the manner of Richard Porson's terse editions of the Greek tragedians (1795–1801), free of the Pelion on Ossa of a couple of centuries of commentary; or one could ditch comment altogether and aim instead for an unblemished purity of text, well-printed, free of all misprints, such as we find in the Virgils of Baskerville (Birmingham 1757) or Didot (Paris 1798), or the heavy and individual greek and roman types of the Parma master printer Giambattista Bodoni, all of whom sought to recover certain "classical" values in printing that they felt had been lost to sight in recent centuries. These were books for gentlemen, ideally aristocrats, not scholars as such. Somehow the image of an English parson settled down with a plain text of Horace seems to capture the flavor of the classical book of the 18th century.

One 19th-century development that persists even now was the outcome of the dissolution of a pan-European sense of the Republic of Letters and the rise of nationalism, in scholarship as elsewhere. With increasing professionalization of the classics, especially with the institution of German *Altertumswissenschaft* (ancient studies, especially classical), the days of the variorum edition were definitively over. There was a perceived need for rigorous, concise, reasonably cheap, and above all *reliable* editions of the Greek and Roman authors, not just for educational purposes but for serious scholarly work. The need was initially met by the Bibliotheca Scriptorum Graecorum et Romanorum Teubneriana, whose first volume was issued by the Leipzig publishing house of B. G. Teubner in 1849. As such, it is the longest-running of the several national series that aim to cover (and replicate, and duplicate) the ancient authors; but it is no longer a showcase of German-speaking scholarship, and many Anglophone and Romance-language editors have been engaged in the last century. Its distinctive typefaces (the greek "dull and lumpish," according to Victor Scholderer) and format give a Teubner text instant recognizability and authority. The same can be said of the Oxford Classical Texts series, and the French Collection Budé, both, like the Teubner, equipped with an *apparatus criticus* of manuscript variant readings. This minimum is very largely dispensed with in the series of texts perhaps most familiar to present-day students of the classics, the squat, comforting volumes of the Loeb Classical Library, with their much-consulted right-hand pages that bear English renditions of the texts. With the widespread use of Scholderer's own New Hellenic font, most commonly seen (though usually unacknowledged) in the Cambridge Greek and Latin Classics series, Greek at last has a typeface fit to stand beside the roman fonts that have remained essentially unchanged since the days of Jenson and Garamond.

BIBL.: Martin Davies, *Aldus Manutius, Printer and Publisher of Renaissance Venice* (1995, repr. Tempe, Ariz., 1999). Howard Jones, *Printing the Classical Text* ('t Goy-Houten 2004). E. J. Kenney, *The Classical Text: Aspects of Editing in the Age of the Printed Book* (Berkeley 1974). Otto Mazal, *Die Überlieferung der antiken Literatur im Buchdruck des 15. Jahrhunderts,* 4 vols. (Stuttgart 2003). Christopher Stray, ed., *Classical Books: Scholarship and Publishing in Britain since 1800* (London 2007). M.D.

Botany

The classical influence on botany seems evident in the use of Latin for scientific names. But this survival is misleading. Botany (*res botanica*) in the modern sense is a coinage of the Renaissance, when the scientific discipline was invented. Modern botanical Latin marks a decisive break with the classical tradition.

The Greek word *botanikos* appears first in a medical context. Plutarch and Dioscorides used it to refer to the study of herbs and herbal remedies. Plant materials were the primary source of materia medica in classical antiquity and the Middle Ages, and most plants were studied for their medicinal uses. Dioscorides' *De medica materia* (1st cent. CE) is the most important ancient source of medical botany, but Nicander, Galen, Celsus, and Pliny the Elder also left writings on simple or compound medicines made from plants. A common source for many of these authors was Cratevas (2nd–1st cents. BCE), whose works have been lost. These authors codified a rich oral tradition connected with the *rhizotomoi* (root-cutters) who supplied classical pharmacists with raw materials. In medieval Europe, Dioscorides circulated in an epitomized Latin translation, but by Carolingian times ancient descriptions of plants had been largely superseded by recipe lists that gave mere names, without descriptions, for the plants that composed them.

Agriculture was another context in which ancient sources discussed crop, forage, and decorative plants. As with medical botany, most of this knowledge was local, informal, oral, and practical. Theophrastus of Eresos drew on agricultural lore in his *Inquiry into Plants* (4th cent. BCE; a later Latin rendition is known as *Historia plantarum*); treatises on agricultural and household administration, in particular the works of Roman agrarian writers (*scriptores rei rusticae*) Cato, Varro, Columella, and later Palladius, codified such knowledge; Palladius in particular was widely copied and read in the medieval Latin West.

The study of plants was pursued as part of natural philosophy by Aristotle and Theophrastus, but they had few successors. Aristotle's *De plantis* has been lost, though a pseudepigraphic work by that title survives. Theophrastus' two works on plants (his *Inquiry,* mentioned above, and *Causes of Plants*) were unknown in the Latin Middle Ages but had a great influence on Renaissance botany. His *Inquiry* or *Historia plantarum* discussed the parts of plants, classified them in four major kinds, and outlined their differences and uses; the *Causes of Plants* examined them within the framework set forth by Aristotle in his biological works, though Theophrastus was more skeptical of teleological explanations than his master. Theophrastus interrogated farmers and root-cutters to learn about plants, but it is unclear whether he expected his philosophical study to bear any practical fruit. Aside from the pseudo-Aristotelian *De plantis* and occasional references in Stoic and Epicurean treatises, Aristotle and Theophrastus had no successors in the philosophical study of plants until Albertus Magnus, who in the 13th century composed a treatise, *De vegetabilibus,* as a commentary on pseudo-Aristotle's *De plantis,* with an appendix of plant descriptions.

Elements of the Greek traditions were gathered in the encyclopedic *Natural History* (*Naturalis historia*) of the elder Pliny (1st cent. CE), but without any systematic framework. The *Natural History* was excerpted and copied throughout the Middle Ages in the West, providing one of the chief conduits of classical knowledge about plants for medieval writers. It was an important source for Vincent of Beauvais and other medieval encyclopedists, who in turn furnished Albertus Magnus with his descriptive list of plants. The encyclopedists, however, did not identify the study of plants as a distinct discipline. Even Giorgio Valla's Humanist encyclopedia of 1501 discussed plants under three separate headings corresponding to the ancient literary traditions: natural philosophy, medicine, and household management (including agriculture).

Botany emerged in the Renaissance specifically through an engagement with these classical texts, especially Dioscorides and Theophrastus, and attempts to collate their information with the actual flora of 15th- and 16th-century Europe. The immediate context was the teaching of materia medica. The Renaissance return to Greek medical texts was accompanied by a learned suspicion of medieval pharmacological and Arabic medical learning. This new, medically oriented study of classical knowledge of plants quickly gained a distinctive character and became a relatively autonomous discipline with a distinct corps of practitioners.

The Humanist recovery and translation of Greek literature played an important role in this process, as did incunabular editions and critiques of Latin authors. Ermolao Barbaro claimed to have corrected more than 5,000 errors in the received text of Pliny (1492), relying mostly on Dioscorides and other Greek authors. He also produced posthumously published annotations on Dioscorides. Further translations of Dioscorides by Jean Ruel (1516) and others were joined by substantial commentaries, including those by Valerius Cordus (1549), Andrés Laguna (1555), and most notably Pier Andrea Mattioli

(1544), in whose successive editions Dioscorides' original text was often the mere pretext for extensive new descriptions.

Renaissance botanists from the 1490s onward were initially concerned with identifying the plants described by the ancients. In his collection of illustrations from living plants (*Herbarum vivae eicones,* 1530–1532), Otto Brunfels placed ancient descriptions next to modern woodcuts. The growing realization that the ancients' descriptions, chiefly based on flora of the Mediterranean lands, did not always correspond to transalpine flora in northern Europe led to Leonhart Fuchs's hypercritical attempt to reconcile them (1542) but also to attempts by Valerius Cordus (posthumous, 1561) and Hieronymus Bock (1539) to write new descriptions of plants, while still proposing tentative identifications with plants mentioned by ancient writers. Carolus Clusius continued this regionalizing practice in a work on flora of the Iberian Peninsula (1576) but, in a harbinger of later developments, abandoned the attempt to find ancient synonyms in his volume on Austrian flora (1583). The ancients had described fewer than 1,000 plants; by 1623 Gaspard Bauhin could enumerate 6,000.

Nonetheless, classical influences could still be found in the styling of botanical descriptions, which were mostly modeled on Dioscorides, though some botanists, like Andrea Cesalpino (1583), adopted a Theophrastean approach of causal explanation. By the 17th century these influences were waning. As classification became a pressing problem, the limits of classical taxonomies became clear. And as botany became a clearly defined scientific discipline that generated its own problems and methods, classical texts ceased to be points of reference for botanists.

In this regard Linnaeus's reformulation of the technical vocabulary of botany in the 18th century marked a distinct break with the classical past. Botanists in the Renaissance had been concerned with recovering the classical vocabulary for describing plants. Early Renaissance botanical works, like Fuchs's herbal, contained glossaries of such terms, and later Renaissance writers added terms that would not have seemed unusual to Cicero or Pliny. But Linnaeus added wholly new terms, redefined others, and gave them newly precise meanings. For him and his successors, botanical Latin was a technical tool whose value was its precision and its separation from ordinary language.

BIBL.: Arno Borst, *Das Buch der Naturgeschichte: Plinius und seine Leser im Zeitalter des Pergaments* (Heidelberg 1994). Edward Lee Greene, *Landmarks of Botanical History,* ed. Frank N. Egerton (Stanford 1983). Ernst H. F. Meyer, *Geschichte der Botanik* (Königsberg 1854–1857). Charles G. Nauert, Jr., "Humanists, Scientists, and Pliny," *American Historical Review* 84 (1979) 72–85. Brian W. Ogilvie, *The Science of Describing: Natural History in Renaissance Europe* (Chicago 2006). Karen M. Reeds, *Botany in Medieval and Renaissance Universities* (New York 1991). John M. Riddle, *Dioscorides on Pharmacy and Medicine* (Austin, 1985). Jerry Stannard, *Herbs and Herbalism in the Middle Ages and the Renaissance,* ed. Katherine E. Stannard and Richard Kay (Brookfield, Vt., 1999). William T. Stearn, *Botanical Latin: History, Grammar, Syntax, Terminology and Vocabulary,* 3rd ed. (Newton Abbot 1983).

B.O.

Bronze

An alloy of copper and tin; like all metals, it was understood, from the Middle Ages to the Scientific Revolution, through Aristotle's *Meteorologica.* Early readers, who typically studied this text alongside Hippocrates's *On Airs, Waters, and Places* and Plato's *Timaeus,* would have concluded that the ingredients in bronze were forms of water, exhaled beneath the earth, and that bronze itself contained a *pneuma* or spirit that verged on life. Postclassical writings on bronze ranged from Albertus Magnus's alchemical speculations on the metal's occult properties, to Vanoccio Biringuccio's and Benvenuto Cellini's descriptions of the craftsman's techniques used to transform it, to Georg Bauer's scholarly Latin treatment of mining and metallurgy; but what these writers shared was a collective if sometimes indirect foundation in ancient Greek ideas. The common culture is reflected in the early small bronze objects made for Humanists to keep on the desks and shelves of their studies, which included not just figurines of ancient deities but also casts of frogs, crabs, and other creatures of the mud: the material from which these were made, like the animals themselves, would have seemed to be the product of spontaneous subterranean generation, and the casting process, which involved the infusion of glowing liquid metal into a matrix of earth, would only have reinforced the parallel.

Bronze has traditionally been used for everything from andirons to liturgical instruments, from coins and bells to harnesses, but the idea of the substance was inexorably shaped by the awareness that it had been one of the premier materials of ancient Greek and Roman sculpture. By the late Middle Ages, surviving examples of such works were among the rarest and most prestigious of antiquities, and thus all the more likely to be studied and copied. As early as 1400, Filippo Brunelleschi's *Sacrifice of Isaac* was quoting the *Spinario,* then to be seen outside the Lateran Palace in Rome. Equestrian monuments from Donatello's and Verrocchio's 15th-century depictions of warlords to Girardon's and Coyzevox's late 17th-century royal portraits were all ultimately inspired by the *Marcus Aurelius* on the Capitoline Hill in Rome. And when, in the 19th century, Antoine-Louis Barye's small bronze bulls, rams, boars, and stags helped create a sensation for animal sculpture, he was using ancient prototypes, including small Roman and Etruscan bronzes then in the Caylus collection.

Still, the earliest modern artists and viewers to reflect on the classical legacy must have realized that they were seeing only a fraction of what the ancients had done with bronze; anyone who wanted to learn more would have had to turn to texts, especially Pliny's *Natural History.* Pliny surveyed bronze sculpture in a chapter on metals that also discusses their sources, value, and medicinal uses, encouraging readers to reflect further on the substance from which bronze sculptures were made. Still more significant, though, was the attention he gave to famous works and common formats, most of which linked the massively expensive and laborious process of bronze casting to civic enterprises and state power. Pliny's remark that the Greeks dedicated bronzes not just to gods but also to mortal heroes anchored a tradition that extended from early bronze statues of saints to the ubiquitous 19th-century monuments to local and national heroes in city squares. His comment that the doors to ancient temples were bronze allowed the inference that the bronze doors of the cathedrals of Hildesheim and Pisa, and even the doors of modern museums and government buildings, took up ideas first encountered in the ancient world. His statement, finally, that Spurius Carvilius made a devotional bronze statue using the breastplates, greaves, and helmets of the defeated Samnites introduced a topos that was reemployed in works ranging from Giambologna's *Equestrian Monument to Henry IV* (16th cent.), cast from artillery that came from Livorno, to Vivant Denon's 1810 bronze imitation of Trajan's Column for the Place Vendôme in Paris, cast from cannons captured in Ulm and Vienna, to Klenze's 1833 Obelisk in Karolinenplatz in Munich, cast from the guns of sunken Turkish battleships.

For much of its post-classical history, the international circulation of bronze distinguished it from other common sculptors' materials. The most abundant copper mines were in Central Europe and the major tin mines in England, so the very existence of the metal, when not derived from the destruction of previously cast bronzes, depended on trade and on shared knowledge. The fact that bronze was also essential for weapons guaranteed that the expertise its manipulation required would be widely diffused, and many of the formats associated with bronzes from the 15th century onward—the medal, the plaquette, the small statue—were designed for travel. This may help explain why bronze artworks, far more frequently than those made in local materials like wood or marble, involved classical subject matter, a kind of lingua franca in regions divided by language, politics, and, increasingly, religion. Nearly all the major early modern bronze workshops (those of the Vischer and Jamnitzer families in Nuremberg, of Leone and Pompeo Leoni in Milan, of Guglielmo della Porta in Rome, or of Willem Daniëlsz. van Tetrode in Delft and Cologne, to name a few) produced portable pieces with ancient themes, intended for exchange.

In antiquity it was not uncommon for artists to make marble copies of bronzes, and many ancient bronze statues are now known only through these replicas. Yet the fact that bronzes were cast in molds that could themselves be taken directly from the original works ensured that in later periods the opposite relation would hold, and that bronze would itself become the prestige material for reproductions. Initially, only the rare patron who could both afford bronze and win uninhibited access to the antiquities themselves could hope to obtain bronze copies of them; when King Francis I of France had Primaticcio make molds from famous statues in Rome and then cast them at Fontainebleau, he was undertaking something particularly novel and ambitious. By the 19th century, though, new technologies, including Achille Collas's pantograph, allowed the reproduction of statues to be mechanized and the cost of bronzes to be significantly lowered. Together with his collaborator Ferdinand Barbedienne, Collas commercialized the entire process, and other entrepreneurs began assembling stocks of molds from which bronzes could be produced in series and offered for sale through catalogues and retail dealers. Today any wealthy person can purchase bronze copies of antiquities from venerable operations like the Chiurazzi Foundry in Naples and the Marinelli Foundry in Florence.

In the 20th century a primary attraction that bronze might once have seemed to offer—its capacity to be shaped in nearly any way its designers could imagine—was overshadowed by still more flexible artificial materials. The popularity and accessibility of bronzes, meanwhile, has demystified their making, changing the ways that those who have remained in the trade have fashioned their own identities. In the Middle Ages casters of bells and cannons had been among the first European craftsmen to sign their works, associating objects with named individuals as the Greeks and Romans had done. Later artists and their viewers made more pointed comparisons between the labors of the early modern bronze caster and the artists, real and mythical, of antiquity: Vincenzo Danti and Adriaen de Vries, for example, both compared themselves explicitly to Vulcan. Now, by contrast, the working of bronze is perceived above all as a historical craft, the only mysteries of which are the trade secrets that the families who practice it protect.

BIBL.: Glenn Benge, *Antoine-Louis Barye, Sculptor of Romantic Realism* (University Park, Pa., 1984). Michael Cole, *Cellini and the Principles of Sculpture* (Cambridge 2002) and "The Medici *Mercury* and the Breath of Bronze," in *Large Bronzes in the Renaissance,* ed. Peta Motture (New Haven 2003) 128–153. Martina Droth and Penelope Curtis, eds., *Bronze: The Power of Life and Death* (Leeds 2005). Sybille Ebert-Schifferer, ed., *Natur und Antike in der Renaissance,* exh. cat., Liebieghaus Museum Alter Plastik (Frankfurt am Main 1985). Dietrich Erben, "Die Reiterdenkmäler der Medici in Florenz und ihre politische Bedeutung," *Mitteilungen des Kunsthistorischen Instituts in Florenz* 40 (1996) 287–360. Norberto Gramaccini, "Zur Ikonologie der Bronze im Mittelalter," *Stadel Jahrbuch* 2 (1987): 147–170. Edgar Lein, *Ars aeraria: Die Kunst des Bronzegiessens und die Bedeutung von Bronze in der florentinischen Renaissance* (Mainz 2004). Thomas Raff, *Die Sprache der Materialien: Anleitung zu einer Ikonologie der Werkstoffe* (Munich 1994). Monika Wagner, *Das Material der Kunst: Eine andere Geschichte der Moderne*

(Munich 2001). Whitney Walton, *France at the Crystal Palace: Bourgeois Taste and Artisan Manufacture in the Nineteenth Century* (Berkeley 1992). M.CO.

Brutus

Marcus Junius Brutus (ca. 85–42 BCE), Roman politician; best known as the assassin of Julius Caesar in 44 BCE and as opponent of Antony and Octavian at Philippi in 42. He was heir to a long historical tradition and inspired a more impressive one. He claimed paternal descent from Lucius Junius Brutus, who half a millennium earlier had overthrown the tyrannical king of Rome and become one of the first consuls of the Roman Republic. Lucius's head appeared on the coins that Marcus Brutus issued as a moneyer, the reverses featuring either the head of the goddess Libertas or that of Marcus's maternal ancestor C. Servilius Ahala, revered for killing an aspiring tyrant. Marcus Brutus himself was adopted by a relative of his mother, Servilia, but a more profound influence was that of her half-brother, Marcus Porcius Cato.

Though his father had been killed in civil strife by Pompey, whose dictatorial ambitions he attacked as a young man, Brutus joined Pompey's side in 49 BCE against Caesar, who had been his mother's lover. After Pompey's defeat at Pharsalus, however, Brutus did not join him to serve under Cato in Africa. He accepted a pardon from Caesar, now dictator, and also accepted high office. But after Cato's suicide in 46, he wrote a eulogy of him; the next year he married Cato's daughter Porcia. When Caesar, victorious in the civil wars, accepted the title of Perpetual Dictator and proposed leaving Rome on campaign instead of restoring the Republic, Brutus was persuaded by Cassius to join an assassination plot. Afterward his dry oratory failed to win over the public and, with Cassius, he was forced to leave Rome. At the Battle of Philippi, though initially victorious, he was defeated by Antony and Octavian and, like Cassius, committed suicide.

Unlike his uncle Cato, a Stoic, Brutus adhered to the Academy and followed Antiochus of Ascalon. His consistent hostility to tyranny was compatible with, but not dictated by, his philosophy; and he eventually convinced himself that, despite Plato's *Phaedo,* suicide was not inconsistent with his creed. This is what his biographer Plutarch reports, and the contradictory story from a later historian, that he died disillusioned with virtue, is to be rejected. He wrote works on virtue, on endurance, and on duty: they gave the impression of intense sincerity and were still being read 150 years later. Brutus's reputation for virtue was besmirched only by his harshness in extorting money from Rome's subjects.

Response to his part in the killing of Caesar has always been mixed. Among his contemporaries some, like Cicero, commended his public spirit; others, like Cicero's friend Matius, condemned his breach of friendship. In early imperial times the assassination of Caesar was condemned mostly as an act of ingratitude or political myopia, but the purity of Brutus's motives was acknowledged. The young radical poet Lucan, however, made Caesar the villain of his epic poem *Pharsalia* (mid-1st cent. CE) and viewed Brutus's motives and action with approval. The emperor Marcus Aurelius (2nd cent.) in his writings included Brutus among those who inspired the ideal of a monarchy that cherished the liberty of the subject.

To the imperialist Dante, more than a millennium later, Brutus was guilty of the ultimate treachery (betraying his emperor) and thus worthy of the lowest place in the Inferno—a verdict that many of Dante's contemporaries deplored or tried to explain away. Brutus was always more controversial than the two historical characters with whom he is commonly associated: Cato, whom Dante made a judge in Purgatory; and the founding republican ancestor, Lucius Junius Brutus.

Though in times of political unrest Roman republicanism became a potent memory, even among republicans Brutus was problematic. The persecution of Protestants in 16th-century France produced a defense of tyrannicide, *Vindiciae contra tyrannos* (1571), published under the pseudonym Stephanus Junius Brutus; by inserting himself into that austere family line, however, the author shows less enthusiasm for Marcus than for Lucius. The British political crises of the mid-17th century likewise evoked Roman analogies. The royalist Thomas Hobbes deplored the radicalizing effect produced by reading classical texts, but the Bible was a more popular source of precedents, and there was little unqualified praise for Brutus. Even Milton, who defended the execution of Charles I, had reservations about the assassination of Caesar. An exception was the aristocratic republican Algernon Sidney, executed for his alleged part in a plot to murder Charles II: he identified himself with Caesar's assassin and was soon referred to as the British Brutus.

Paradoxically, there was more enthusiasm for Brutus in England after the age of revolution. In the less scripturally minded 18th century, Roman republicanism became something of a fashionable taste—Jonathan Swift granted his Gulliver a vision of Brutus in the afterlife, grouped with four other classical figures (and Sir Thomas More) as a hero of liberty and public spirit. But republican rhetoric took on greater resonance in the New World. The American colonists fighting for independence found Brutus an inspiring figure: "Caesar had his Brutus," declared Patrick Henry, with obvious implications. In France revolutionary leaders expressed admiration for Brutus (though only his ancestor Lucius rated a bust in the Convention Hall). But the French Revolution ended in the imperial rule of Napoleon (a fervent admirer of Caesar), and the general European drive toward empire in the 19th century, combined with more scholarly study of the ancient records, led to a drop in Brutus's reputation. Historians such as Wilhelm Drumann and Charles Merivale castigated him for both ingratitude and adherence to an outworn tradition in the face of inevitable change.

In 1918 Lenin suggested replacing figures from the old tsarist regime with statues of Brutus and 30 other revolutionary heroes, but none actually went up, and later Soviet ideology dismissed the killing of Caesar as a reactionary gesture carried out for an aristocratic clique. The political ideas of Brutus and his friends were too distant from the egalitarianism of modern radical thought.

The death of Caesar has always been the crucial issue for Brutus's reputation. By the violence of the action and the closeness of his relationship with its victim, he seems to embody the conflict of personal versus public duty in its sharpest form. If we retrace the same history through writers less centrally concerned with the political issues, we see the moral problem expressed in terms of personal complexity. The most famous literary treatment in any language is Shakespeare's *Julius Caesar* (1599), evoking varied critical responses since at least the 18th century. Is Brutus here supposed to be right or wrong? The case he makes for resistance to tyranny made the play a favorite among South African opponents of apartheid; but when asked to identify his favorite passage from Shakespeare, Nelson Mandela chose a brave speech by Caesar, not Brutus. Writers often found themselves divided in their sympathy—for example, the playwrights John Sheffield, Duke of Buckingham (late 17th century), and Antonio Conti (early to mid-18th), each wrote two versions of Brutus's story, one more and one less favorable to him. Other dramatists, including Voltaire and Alfieri in the 18th century and Enrico Corradini in the 20th, were attracted by the ancient rumor (recorded by Plutarch) that Brutus was Caesar's son and adopted it in their plotlines, to heighten his personal dilemma to the maximum.

As he appears in literary representations of the mid- and later 20th century and into the present, Brutus has tended to be more of a troubled soul than a public symbol. The confidently self-righteous figure who emerges from contemporary sources even finds a place in the history of psychoanalysis: Sigmund Freud's perception of a painful emotional conflict in the Brutus–Caesar relationship surfaced in one of his own most complicated dreams, as recorded in *The Interpretation of Dreams* (1900).

BIBL.: M. L. Clarke, *The Noblest Roman* (London 1981). F. Gundolf, *The Mantle of Caesar,* trans. I. W. Hartmann (London 1964, German 1924). John Ripley, *Julius Caesar on Stage in England and America, 1599–1973* (Cambridge 1980).

J.B.G & M.GR.

Budé, Guillaume

Pioneering scholar and a central inspiration for the growth of classical studies in the kingdom of France, 1468–1540. His contemporaries and successors recognized him as one of the greatest humanists of his generation, particularly because of his study of Greek.

As a young man Budé studied civil law, but he was not inspired by legal practice and underwent a self-described conversion to Humanism and the study of classical texts in 1491. His new passion by no means disqualified him from royal service: he served Charles VIII and Louis XII, then briefly retired, only to return with renewed patriotic enthusiasm to advise Francis I. He strove to inculcate in the young king the same devotion to classical studies that he himself enjoyed, and urged him to establish an institution that would teach young Frenchmen Latin, Greek, and Hebrew. He tried in vain to bring Erasmus to Paris to head the putative college, but his promptings eventually bore fruit when Francis established royal lecturers, the forerunners of the Collège de France, who began teaching in 1530. Budé himself served as Royal Librarian, a post created especially for him. He became a model for French classical scholars of his time and subsequent generations, both because of his devotion and because he showed how to apply Humanistic learning to a successful secular career.

Although he has been best known for his institutional achievements, Budé was also a scholar of individual brilliance. Influenced by Lorenzo Valla (ca. 1407–1457), he combined an acute historical sensitivity with philological genius. He brought his gifts to bear on the text of the *Digest,* the central text of Roman law, in his *Annotationes in Pandectas* (*Notes on the Pandects,* 1508). By situating the institutions that the *Digest* described firmly in the milieu of the Roman Empire, he was to found the juridical tradition of *mos gallicus* (Gallic custom), which aimed to place civil legal texts in their historical context. He went on to produce *De asse* (*On the As* [a Roman coin], 1515), ostensibly an investigation of ancient weights and coinage but in practice a meandering encyclopedic treatment of various facets of the classical world; the work took references in texts to measurements as its starting point. Most influentially, he published *Commentarii linguae Graecae* (*Commentaries on the Greek Language,* 1529), his guide to Greek usage, which he compiled with an autodidact's passion for the language that he rated more highly than Latin, and which set the standard for all subsequent works of Greek lexicography.

Budé wrote with one eye firmly on the history of the French state, the development of the French language, and contemporary political events. He provided his readers with equivalents of ancient numerical terms and demonstrated how Roman juridical institutions shaped medieval French counterparts. In his *Commentarii* he tried to demonstrate that Greek, rather than Latin, was the source for some French words. More controversially, he took the opportunity to use classical antiquity as a means of criticizing the world around him, making reference, for example, to the corrupting effect of money on the Church. It was no surprise that he later wrote *De transitu Hellenismi ad Christianismum* (*On the Progression from Hellenism to Christianity,* 1535), defending humanism and dissociating himself from Protestant reformers. Budé's unusually pointed classical scholarship, a reaction in particular to intellectual and political developments in Italy, was to prove greatly influential on the French late 16th- and early 17th-century *politiques* such as François Hotman and Jacques-Auguste de Thou, who supported monarchical authority and proclaimed the independence and importance of the French kingdom.

BIBL.: Gilbert Gadoffre, *La révolution culturelle dans la*

France des humanistes: Guillaume Budé et François 1er (Geneva 1997). Marie-Madeleine de la Garanderie, "Budé (Guillaume)," in *Centuriae latinae,* ed. Colette Nativel (Geneva 1997) 221–231. Anthony Grafton, "Is the History of Reading a Marginal Enterprise? Guillaume Budé and His Books," *Papers of the Bibliographical Society of America* 91 (1997) 139–157. Luigi-Alberto Sanchi, *Les* Commentaires de la Langue Grecque *de Guillaume Budé: L'oeuvre, ses sources, sa préparation* (Geneva 2006). W.S.

Burckhardt, Jacob

Swiss art and cultural historian (1818–1897). Along with Bachofen and Nietzsche, Burckhardt is one of the most important representatives of an anti-classicizing vision of antiquity in German-speaking areas, and he is among the first to apply the methods of cultural history to the study of antiquity in the 19th century.

Burckhardt owed his intellectual formation to the social, political, and cultural milieu of the Swiss city-state of Basel, where he was born. He initially wanted to become a minister, like his father, but his experience with historical and critical biblical scholarship caused him to abandon his study of theology. He turned instead to history and art history, which he studied in Bonn and Berlin under Welcker, Kugler, Ranke, Böckh, and Droysen. In his student years he had liberal political leanings. After his return to Switzerland he took a conservative turn as the politics editor for the *Basler Zeitung* (1844–1845), which made him the representative of an "aristocratic liberalism" (Kahan 1992). Burckhardt taught history and art history from 1854 to 1858 at the ETH (Eidgenössische Technische Hochschule) in Zurich and from 1858 to 1893 at the University of Basel. He died in Basel in 1897.

Burckhardt's historical judgment is characterized by skepticism, irony, and laconism. In contrast to the historiography of his time, including both historicism and the Hegelian philosophy of history, he insisted on respecting the ambivalences and antinomies of historical development. He focused his attention on historical crises and the processes of transformation to which they gave rise. His judgments were informed by the critical stance he took to the modernizing trends of the 19th century: the movements for political and social emancipation brought about by the French Revolution; the rise of modern mass society; the decrease in importance of small, independent states with respect to the mighty nation-states; and the subordination of culture to the needs of the state and the economy in the wake of industrialization.

Burckhardt's criticism of modernity also molded his view of antiquity, and it brought him into conflict, as it did Nietzsche, with the classicism of Goethe and Winckelmann as well as with neohumanism in the tradition of Humboldt.

Burckhardt's importance as a historian lies in his development of a method of cultural history as an alternative to the strict narration of political events. He replaced the chronologically structured, linear historical narrative with a panoramic tableau of significant elements, out of which emerged the general picture of an epoch. Alongside the two other historical "forces," state and religion, Burckhardt theorized in his *Reflections on History* that "culture" (or "civilization") operated as the historically productive and symptomatic element: "its action on the two constants (state and religion) is one of perpetual modification and disintegration"; "it is the critic of both, the clock which tells the hour at which their form and substance no longer coincide" (93).

Burckhardt's study of antiquity was corner- and capstone to his work as a historian. His first book, *The Age of Constantine the Great* (1853), deals with the "end" of antiquity and its transformation in the transition to the Middle Ages. Late antiquity, whose formation Burckhardt puts in the 2nd and 3rd centuries CE, is depicted as a period of crisis but also of continuity for the European cultural tradition. The sum of Burckhardt's thought on the aims and methods of cultural history is found, after his exemplary *Civilization of the Renaissance in Italy* (1860), in his lectures on Greek cultural history (originally held in 1872, published between 1898 and 1902).

Besides its influential description of the *polis*—Burckhardt introduced the term into modern scholarship as a designation for the specific political and sociocultural organizing principle of Greek civilization—*The Greeks and Greek Civilization* brought together a plethora of new perspectives, judgments, and insights: for example, the emphasis on the fundamental importance of rhetoric for understanding ancient culture; a fair assessment of the Sophists; the identification of Roman philhellenism and of Rome's importance for the continued influence of Greek culture; the theory of *agon* as a dynamic element in Greek cultural development; insight into the correlation between cultural development and slavery; and the investigation of popular religion (dream interpretation, belief in spirits) and the relationship of the Greeks to the irrational.

Burckhardt's and Nietzsche's emphasis on the "dark sides" of ancient culture are in many respects complementary as critiques of historicism and philhellenism. Their views have been supplemented and carried forward by Erwin Rohde, Hermann Usener, and Aby Warburg, among others.

BIBL.: S. Bauer, *Polisbild und Demokratieverständnis in Jacob Burckhardts "Griechischer Kulturgeschichte"* (Basel 2001). J. Burckhardt, *The Age of Constantine the Great,* trans. Moses Hadas (New York 1949); *The Civilization of the Renaissance in Italy,* trans. C. G. C. Middlemore (New York 1958); *The Greeks and Greek Civilization,* trans. Sheila Stern, ed. Oswyn Murray (London 1998); *Reflections on History,* trans. Marie D. Hottinger (1943, repr. Indianapolis 1979); *Werke,* 27 vols. (Munich 2000–). L. Burckhardt and H.-J. Gehrke, *Jacob Burckhardt und die Griechen* (Basel 2006). A. Casaba and L. Gossman, eds., *Begegnungen mit Jacob Burckhardt/Encounters with Jacob Burckhardt* (Basel 2004). L. Gossman, *Basel in the Age of Burckhardt: A Study in Unseasonal Ideas* (Chicago 2000). W. Kaegi, *Jacob Burckhardt: Eine Biographie,* 7 vols. (Basel

1947–1982). A. Kahan, *Aristocratic Liberalism: The Social and Political Thought of Jacob Burckhardt, John Stuart Mill, and Alexis de Tocqueville* (New York 1992). B.V.R.

Translated by Patrick Baker

Burlesque. *See* Parody and Burlesque.

Byzantium

Successor state to the Roman Empire in the eastern Mediterranean. As with Rome, the name Byzantium (Greek Byzantion) originated with a founding city. Unlike Rome, the city of Byzantium was rechristened at a crucial point in its history, and only the state with its spreading dominions retained the name of its origin.

Byzantium received, adapted, and suppressed the many strands of knowledge that came to it from classical antiquity, at first with little sense of separation from the ancient world. The end of the Byzantine Empire is clear—the Ottoman conquest, the fall of Constantinople in 1453, and shortly thereafter the subjugation of the few remaining lands of the empire. Its beginning, however, might be fixed at several moments. For the eastern Mediterranean area the reign of Constantine the Great was a watershed period, because of the Edict of Toleration (Milan, 313 CE), which made Christianity one of the official religions of the Roman Empire; another important juncture was the founding of the new eastern capital at the city of Byzantium, renamed Constantinople after the emperor's death in 337. The center of subsequent Byzantine culture, this second Rome supplanted ancient Rome. Significant transformations also occurred later. In the late 4th century the Roman Empire was divided into eastern and western halves, and Christianity was proclaimed the sole official religion of this dual empire. The emperor Justinian (r. 527–565) won back significant western territories, establishing a pan-Mediterranean empire for the last time, but he also closed the philosophical schools in Athens (529). During the reign of Heraclius (610–641) and continuing through the 7th century, Muslim conquests closed the southern coasts of the Mediterranean away from the classical world; the economy and material culture of the empire deteriorated, and the great cities of antiquity declined so far that some never recovered. This was truly a Dark Age, but to set the beginning of Byzantine history in the later 7th century is to ignore crucial earlier changes in the classical tradition: hence the utility of the traditional date of origin in the reign of Constantine.

Formerly, discussions of Byzantium and the classical tradition focused on what survived the end of antiquity, but recent scholarship has considered instead what later centuries did with ancient culture. In some cases the assimilation was initially unproblematic. For example, in the new city of Constantinople, a statue of the emperor as Apollo—Helios with a radiant crown—was placed atop a tall column of porphyry in the newly constructed Forum of Constantine; when the statue fell, in the early 12th century, it was replaced with a cross. In other cases Christian appropriation resulted in destruction, as when a bishop in 5th-century Gaza campaigned against a nude statue of Aphrodite, venerated by local women. Throughout the late antique empire, cult statues were destroyed and temples were abandoned or occasionally converted into churches (as was the Parthenon in Athens).

In contrast, a large bronze statue of Hercules, formerly in the Hippodrome in early Constantinople, passed easily into the Middle Ages. This pensive rendition of the hero, seated on a basket covered with a lion skin, had a long history. It was created by Lysippus in the 4th century BCE for the southern Italian city of Tarentum. After the Romans conquered Tarentum, they installed the bronze at the Capitol in Rome; its base is still preserved in the Capitoline Museum. Taken next to Byzantium sometime between the city's refounding (324) and dedication (330) as Constantinople, the statue was set up in the Basilica, a large public building with a considerable library and the principal intellectual and cultural center of the city. Sometime before the later 5th century, Lysippus' bronze Hercules was transferred to the Hippodrome, where it joined other antiquities, including a tripod from Delphi, and remained there until the Fourth Crusade and the Latin (Western) sack of the city in 1204.

The criteria that governed the acceptance or destruction of ancient sculpture are not detailed in Byzantine sources but probably bore some relation to that which governed the acceptability of ancient literature. An often-cited text in this regard is the essay that Saint Basil, a bishop of Caesarea in the 4th century, addressed to his nephews about how to benefit from pagan literature. His advice was simple and pragmatic: take what is useful and abandon the rest. His advisees should be like Odysseus, who fled from the songs of the Sirens, or (referring to another common simile) like the bee that chooses the best flower and takes only its nectar. They should disregard poets, who find happiness in a full table or speak of the gods in the plural.

Basil recommended cultivating authors, especially Plato and the philosophers, who wrote about virtue. One example, taken from Xenophon (*Memorabilia* 2), concerns Hercules when he was about the age of Basil's nephews. The young hero, on a journey, had paused to decide which of two roads to take, when two women approached. Vice, beautiful and voluptuous, promised pleasure and happiness. Withered and poorly dressed, Virtue offered only hard work but also the reward of becoming a god. By choosing to follow the latter, Hercules constituted a worthy example for Christian youth to emulate and for the citizens of Constantinople to see prominently displayed in the Hippodrome. (This motif would be copied in later Byzantine art.)

Basil's essay remained an important justification for the Christian study of ancient literature throughout the Byzantine period and later proved useful to Renaissance Humanists, but more was at stake here than personal development. Even in the pre-Constantinian period, Christianity had cautiously embraced the dominant Greek intellectual heritage. Pagans and Christians shared a common education and hence larger patterns of thought. The Greek *paideia* (conventions of education) can be observed in the New Testament and the early Christian apologists, so that by the time of the 4th-century Cappadocian Fathers—Gregory of Nazianzus, Gregory of Nyssa, and the aforementioned Basil—an education in grammar, rhetoric, literature, and the sciences was the norm for the upper classes.

A proper classical education was essential to gain entry into the governing class in the early Byzantine state, as the Theodosian Code (438 CE) made clear: "No person shall obtain a post of the first rank unless it shall be proved that he excels in long practice of liberal studies, and that he is so polished in literary matters that words flow from his pen faultlessly" (14.1.1). What was to be cultivated was an Attic Greek based on the aesthetics of the Second Sophistic (1st–3rd cents. CE). Attempts to substitute classicizing versions of Christian texts for the classics did not succeed, and higher education in Byzantium remained mainly secular, unlike that in the Latin West, where monasteries became the main continuators of the classical tradition. By the 6th century in the East, classical culture and Christianity had become a nearly harmonious blend. For example, John Lydus, a civil servant in the reign of Justinian, was both an antiquarian and a Christian; it is said that in a single day he "might read Plato, be healed at a saint's shrine, deliver a panegyric in Latin, praise or criticize the emperor, and sing the Trisagion hymn—without any sense of contradiction" (Maas 1992). The Latin would soon drop away, but the basic combination of a classical education, Christian faith, and government service characterized the Byzantine elite until the end of the empire.

This is not to say that the classical tradition emerged from late antiquity unaltered. The border between magic and religion was redrawn by the Church Fathers. Astrology and astronomy continued to be studied, but cautiously and not without criticism from the Church. Other sciences fared better. The pharmacological treatise by the ancient physician Dioscorides, *De materia medica* (1st cent. CE) survives in 10 illustrated manuscripts that include the famed copy now in Vienna, a gift to the daughter of the empress Galla Placidia in the early 6th century. In the 10th century the Byzantine emperor sent an illustrated Dioscorides to the caliph of Cordoba. Knowledge passed in the other direction as well, for ancient science in Byzantium at times was influenced by Arab refinements on ancient sources taken from and returned to Byzantium.

In late antiquity, canons of literature changed. Theater, for example, slowly disappeared. The Church's disapproval is apparent in Saint Basil's essay, when he writes that his young readers should leave the loves, adulteries, and sexual acts of the gods to the stage. Even though theater was banned by the end of the 7th century, ancient Greek drama, if not the Hellenistic corpus, continued to be read as literature for centuries afterward, and the dramatic dialogue survived in ecclesiastical hymns and poetry.

The pattern is the same for other bodies of knowledge: that which was absorbed into the imperial, Christian tradition of Byzantium survived. For philosophy, the 5th-century Church historian Socrates suggested one process that was at work. Because the Bible alone did not provide adequate logical tools to refute the pagans, he advocated studying classical reasoning in order to use it against pagan opponents. The emperor Justinian took another approach. He sponsored persecutions of those who would not convert to Christianity, prohibited pagans from teaching anywhere in the empire, and in 529 closed the philosophical schools of Athens; as a result, uncompromising philosophers sought sanctuary in the Sassanian capital of Ctesiphon. But Greek philosophy compatible with Christianity continued to be read and taught down to Plethon and Bessarion in the 15th century and thus into the Italian Renaissance.

Although Byzantine historians aspired to write in the language of Herodotus, they did not share the same interests or worldview. Writing more as apologists than historians, they maintained a close personal interest in their subject matter. The Byzantine chronicle tradition that began in the 6th century with John Malalas understood the past in terms fundamentally different from those in ancient writings on history. These chronicles merged biblical and ancient history, emphasized Egyptian and Assyrian history over details relating to ancient Greek city-states, demythologized the ancient gods, and made Rome the precursor to Constantinople. Nevertheless, the Byzantines regarded themselves as Romans (*Rōmanoi*), and their emperor was formally considered to be the *basileus* of the Romans until 1453. The name applied to a territory as well as a people and government. When the Seljuk Turks conquered Anatolia in the late 11th and 12th centuries, they became the Seljuks of Rum.

The later 6th and 7th centuries witnessed the demise of many aspects of classical life and culture, and a Dark Age began that lingered into the 9th century. The Christian authorities successfully inveighed against gladiator contests and animal fights as well as the theater. Public baths, long the mainstay of classical culture, declined when the bishops criticized them as sites of immorality, and standards of personal hygiene changed. In the cities public spaces were subdivided and privatized, and urban life shifted to neighborhoods and local churches. The outbreak of plague in the mid-6th century and the loss of significant territories in the 7th century contributed to a demographic and economic decline. The smaller, more modest medieval cities could no longer support the same level of cultural activity as before, and the written word itself became more expensive after the loss of Egypt blocked access to inexpensive papyrus.

As the empire shrank to Anatolia and parts of Greece and the Balkans, Greek became the dominant language. But Slavic incursions deep into the Balkan Peninsula, beginning in the 6th century, interrupted cultural and ethnic continuity. Classical learning and education retrenched, and Church unity fractured over the legitimacy of religious images. After the Iconoclastic controversy ended in the mid-9th century, the Church took active control of practices relating to images. The preferred artistic media became two-dimensional mosaics, frescoes, and icon paintings. Sculpture would never again be as important as it had been in antiquity. The 7th and 8th centuries were Byzantium's Middle Ages, in the sense that an uninterrupted classical tradition was broken and, when eventually revived, took different forms.

That process began during Iconoclasm, an ecclesiastical and cultural civil war. Its vigorous debates drove partisans to discover old manuscripts, find or invent better arguments, and compose new texts. Aristotelian reasoning reappeared during the first half of the 9th century in Iconophile writing. A new script came into use, a cursive minuscule. With it scribes formed letters with fewer strokes and joined them together more quickly with ligatures. Because writing in minuscule entailed punctuation, word division, and the addition of accents to letters, the change from ancient uncial to medieval minuscule led to the editing and interpretation of texts.

Individual copyists and book collectors from this era of revival in literary culture can be traced even today. In 895 Arethas, later the archbishop of Caesarea, paid the scribe John to copy a manuscript of Plato and himself added marginal notations. The same scribe prepared for Arethas a copy of Aelias Aristides, a Second Sophistic author popular in Byzantium. Arethas also composed scholia on Porphyry and Aristotle; his manuscripts of Lucian and the Organon of Aristotle are the earliest surviving versions of those texts. Putting his classical learning to use, Arethas revised an earlier commentary on the Apocalypse (the Book of Revelation) by inserting passages from Homer and Aristotle, thus making it more compatible with the style of his own era.

The 10th century saw new copies of some of the oldest and often the best versions of classical orators (e.g., Isocrates, Demosthenes), dramatists (Aeschylus, Aristophanes), historians (Herodotus, Xenophon, Polybius, Plutarch) and scientists (Archimedes, Aristotle, Theophrastus). Also from the same period is the only surviving manuscript of the poetic collection known as the Palatine Anthology, as well as the oldest complete manuscript of the *Iliad,* the Venetus A (now MS gr. 454 in the Bibliotheca Marciana in Venice), dated to the first half of the century by the style of its decorative initials and its script. Some scribes specialized in producing classical texts; the same copyist, for example, prepared important manuscripts of Strabo and Dio Cassius. The vocation of the scribe, however, does not necessarily correlate with the genre copied. One of the best scribes of the day was the monk Ephraem, who copied New Testament manuscripts as well as Aristotle's Organon.

Arethas may have been a pupil of the patriarch Photius, who has been called "the most important figure in the history of classical studies in Byzantium" (Wilson 1996) and the best representative of Byzantine civilization (Lemerle 1986). Patriarch twice in the second half of the 9th century, Photius was a major figure in the revival of learning. In his early career he taught Aristotelian logic. His fascinating series of reading notes, titled the *Bibliotheca,* though not a great work of Byzantine literature, is a major source for the survival of the classical tradition in Byzantium. Omitting commonly read texts, Photius commented on lesser-known works: 386 in all, 110 of which are now lost; others are preserved only in other languages. Slightly more than half of the works included were classical or secular. Photius discussed writing styles, generally valuing Attic Greek. In his reading of ancient historians he attended, like others before him, to the history not of the Greek city-states but of the Persians, an understandable preoccupation of the Byzantines given the powerful kingdoms to their empire's east and south.

What Lemerle (1986) has termed the encyclopedism of the *Bibliotheca* characterizes the 9th and 10th centuries more generally. The Suda presented alphabetically ordered entries on words, sayings, people, and places, based mainly on ancient sources. The Basilika codified Roman law, and other texts summarized earlier learning about agriculture and military tactics. The emperor Constantine VII Porphyrogenitus (r. 945–959) took a personal interest in this type of scholarship and sponsored or collaborated on treatises about imperial administration and protocol (*De administrando imperio, De ceremoniis*).

A similar antiquarian regard for synthesis and compilation can be seen in the art of the period. An illustrated Psalter (now MS gr. 139 at the Bibliothèque Nationale in Paris) portrays the authors of the Psalms and Canticles in company with classical personifications that draw attention to author or text. In one of these miniature scenes, David, as Orpheus, strums his lyre, accompanied by his muse, Melodia, who silently affirms the power of the unheard melodies. She catches the eye of the beholder and points to animals soothed by the words and music. Another vignette shows David as king, flanked by personifications of Wisdom and Prophecy, the attributes of a just ruler. David presents a book open to Psalm 71, one of two psalms that he addressed to his son and successor, Solomon. The unique appearance of this psalm at the beginning of the manuscript suggests an association with the family of Constantine VII. The prologue of *De administrando imperio* employs language similar to this psalm and begins: "Constantine in Christ the eternal Emperor of the Romans, to his son, Romanus . . ." On the pages of this probable gift from father to son, the biblical and classical provide the verbal and visual codes of power.

The same mixture appears in other contexts as well. Panels on the front and back of a small ivory box (10th cent., now in the Church of St. Thomas in Xanten, Germany) depict a commanding, enthroned Joshua, warriors, and two scenes of Hercules (first struggling with the Nemean Lion, then seated, head in hand, on a lion's skin). The latter composition is thought to refer to the Lysippan bronze Hercules at the Hippodrome in Constantinople. Joshua and Hercules here serve as examples of manly virtue, a long-standing motivation for classical or biblical citations. Joshua, the Israelite general who led his people into the Promised Land, was of particular interest in the middle years of the 10th century, when Byzantine forces were battling the Arabs in Syria. The Joshua Roll now in the Vatican illustrates the Israelite conquests in a continuous narrative that recalls the reliefs on spiral columns in Rome and Constantinople. Like Joshua, Hercules served in panegyric as a metaphor for contemporary imperial prowess.

Other classicizing objects from the 10th century are difficult to decode. The Veroli Casket, an ivory box now in the Victoria and Albert Museum in London, is covered with classical motifs, all unlabeled. These may have denoted Antiquity generally or provided erudite puzzles for learned Byzantine intellectuals. One modern interpretation has connected the imagery with the 5th-century CE poet Nonnus. Other luxury objects of the period have even less programmatic coherence. The head of a Gorgon guards the lid of a gold inkwell now in Padua, made for the calligrapher Leo. Around its sides are a nude figure with a lyre, a reclining river god, and perhaps Ares. The figures are separated by columns of intertwined snakes that recall the bronze Delphic tripod that still stands in the Hippodrome, its serpent heads lost (except for one preserved in the nearby Archaeological Museum). The classicizing figures painted on a glass bowl (10th cent., now in Venice) are similarly obscure and not identified. The classical pastiches on these objects do not so much narrate ancient myths as evoke that past by discrete, unconnected quotation, much like the anthologies and dictionaries that characterize this period of encyclopedism.

Building on the preceding period of retrieval and revival, scholars of the 11th and 12th centuries analyzed, extended, and reworked the classical tradition. The major intellect of the 11th century was Michael Psellus. This protean personality lacks a comprehensive modern study, and it will not be an easy one to prepare. A recent bibliography credits him with 1,176 works, many unedited. Best known as the author of a political history of Byzantium, the *Chronographia,* Psellus served in high government office during a period of military decline and was an imperial tutor and professor. He briefly became a monk but lacked monastic humility and took great pride in his scholarly attainments, boasting that Celts, Arabs, Persians, and Ethiopians came to study with him. In the *Chronographia* (book 6), he credits his initial position to his eloquent, learned speech, which made him known to the imperial bodyguards. They in turn recommended him to the emperor Constantine Monomachus, who at their first meeting was almost overcome by the sound of the young man's voice.

Psellus describes his study of philosophy as starting with Plato and Aristotle and concluding with Plotinus, Porphyry, and Iamblichus. Next he moved to mathematics, music, astronomy, and "more advanced studies." About literature he is less specific. Later he taught everything—philosophy, logic, literature, theology, medicine, geometry, mathematics, optics, astronomy—and with a certain flair, performing experiments during lectures. At the end of his encomium for his mother, he again details his wide reading and employs the same image of the bee and the flowers that Saint Basil had used.

Though he was a highly learned man, Psellus' values were not those of today. In one treatise he compares Euripides and the 7th-century Byzantine poet George of Pisidia, at times to the latter's advantage. Elsewhere he discusses the writing styles of the Church Fathers, comparing John Chrysostom's sermons to ancient oratory and valuing especially Gregory of Nazianzus and Proclus. He praises and follows the ancients up to or just beyond the limits set by Church authorities but in the end affirms orthodox doctrines and avoids censure, unlike his pupil John Italus, an overly enthusiastic admirer of Plato for this period.

In the 12th century Eustathius, bishop of Thessalonica, is the scholar of greatest interest for students of the classical tradition. He wrote about Pindar and other poets but is best known for a lengthy commentary on Homer, an autograph copy of which was identified and owned by Cardinal Bessarion in the 15th century. The treatise is the record of lectures that Eustathius gave at the Patriarchal School, located at the Church of Hagia Sophia in Constantinople. Other intellectuals in the period (Theodore Prodromus, John Tzetzes, Constantine Manasses), though accomplished and likewise possessed of a good classical education, devoted themselves to flattering aristocrats or composing original works of literature, though Tzetzes did offer allegorical interpretations of Homer and wrote several long poems about the *Iliad* and the *Odyssey.*

Among the many factors that separated the eastern and western Middle Ages was knowledge of Homer. Only Byzantium knew the *Iliad* and the *Odyssey* directly; the former was fundamental to general education, as the manuscript evidence suggests. In his *Chronographia* (book 6) Psellus provides a telling and often-cited anecdote about the common knowledge of his day. He says that Constantine Monomachus broke with tradition by installing his mistress Sclerena at court. A courtier seeing Sclerena for the first time pronounced, *sotto voce,* two words in Greek, *Ou nemesis!*— "It would be no disgrace!" The reference was to a passage in the *Iliad* (3.156–157), in which the old men of Troy catch sight of Helen and declare it would be no disgrace were Trojans and Achaeans to suffer because of such a woman. Afterward, Sclerena asked for the person who had spoken these words, repeating them exactly, but without understanding the reference. For Psellus the incident showed that she was intelligent but not well educated and hence did not belong in such an exalted company. For modern commentators it is evidence of the courtiers' deep knowledge of Homer, regardless of whether the incident happened as described or Psellus invented it for readers well versed in the *Iliad.*

Medieval Byzantium combined the classical and the

Christian in novel ways, as can be seen from an intriguing, archaizing text, the *Christos Paschon* (*Christ Suffering*), a Christian tragedy that dramatizes the life of Christ from the Passion to the Resurrection and gives roles to Mary, John the Evangelist, Jesus, and a chorus. About a third of its 2,600 lines are taken from Attic tragedy, mainly Euripides. Who might have composed the *Christos Paschon* remains an unresolved question, and attributions have ranged from Gregory of Nazianzus in the 4th century to court intellectuals in the 12th. Byzantine art may be of help in this regard. The description of Mary crying at the entombment of her dead son and embracing his body (lines 1273–1274) recalls a Lamentation scene popular in Byzantine art from the 11th century. The focus on Holy Week and the general emotional treatment of the Passion are features of the later 11th and 12th centuries, when new images and liturgies were created for elite monasteries in the capital.

By the end of the 12th century, although Constantinople had long since ceased to be a classical city, it nonetheless had an unbroken connection with antiquity. The Venetian-led Fourth Crusade in 1204 sacked the city, installed a Latin emperor in Constantinople for nearly six decades, disrupted intellectual communities, and left the city in ruins. Writing not long after the conquest, the historian Nicetas Choniates described in detail the Lysippan Hercules that the Latins had overturned in the Hippodrome; he used phrases from the *Odyssey* (11.539, 18.27) to lament how the city once so grand, striding far and wide, and handsome in stature had become squalid and dirty like an old servant woman. The decline continued. Shortly before the Latin conquest, great fires had swept across the city; then came looting and destruction during the sack, followed by protracted neglect during the period of Western rule. The Latins could not afford to maintain buildings or institutions, because they did not control the hinterland necessary to sustain a great city.

After 1204 scholars went into exile, and cultural production declined until the Byzantines repossessed Constantinople in 1261. The city they entered required several generations to refurbish. The Latins had left in ruins the Great Palace that had been the home of emperors since Constantine the Great. It was replaced by the palace at Blachernai near the city wall. Late Byzantine Constantinople shrank to two principal areas, one at Blachernai and the other surrounding the cathedral of Hagia Sophia at the end of the peninsula. Just as the urban fabric of the city needed to be rebuilt, so did the productive networks of students, teachers, and libraries that had existed before 1204 and would make Constantinople again the center of Greek culture.

The reign of Michael VIII (1259–1282), who began the Palaeologan dynasty, was fraught with ecclesiastical controversy over his advocacy of union with the Latin Church. The long reign of Andronicus II (1282–1328) witnessed internal unity and significant external threats from renegade Catalan mercenaries, who caused significant damage to central Byzantine lands, and from the rise of the Ottoman Turks, who would overwhelm Byzantium in the next century. Despite or because of this turmoil the reign of Andronicus was the high point of late Byzantine history and a period when arts and letters flourished for the last time.

The career of the monk Maximus Planudes (ca. 1260–ca. 1330) anchors the beginning of the period. He taught the sons of the aristocracy and wrote extensively. He lived in different Constantinopolitan monasteries, including the Chora, near the Blachernai Palace. While hunting for manuscripts at the Chora monastery ca. 1295, he discovered a copy of Ptolemy's *Geography,* a text that had been little read for centuries. Some scholars have suggested that, because it did not contain the essential maps, he commissioned a set that impressed Andronicus II, who had a copy made for himself. In the same period Planudes traveled to Venice on diplomatic business. Then or before, he learned Latin and translated Augustine and Boethius (*Consolation of Philosophy*), as well as Ovid's *Metamorphoses,* predictably neutralizing its erotic passages.

Planudes produced commentary on the difficult mathematics of Diophantus and prepared a new edition of Plutarch, but he is best known for his work on the Greek Anthology. He rearranged the contents of the 10th-century Palatine Anthology, deleted poems with sexual references, and added 388 more poems, which modern editions relegate to an appendix. He was one of few since the 10th century to have read Pausanias, and he made a compilation of writings by John Lydus (6th cent.) and other scholars. His many letters discuss the preparation and writing of manuscripts and detail the networks of fellow scholars, who supported each other's work by lending, borrowing, and for the most part returning manuscripts. Planudes was an active teacher. His pupil Manuel Moschopoulos was one of several early Palaeologan scholars interested in ancient poetry and drama. He had access to several manuscripts of Sophocles and Euripides and commented on both.

Poetry was an interest as well of Thomas Magister, active during the first half of the 14th century in Thessalonica, the second city of the empire. He assembled earlier commentaries on the dramatists but, like Moschopoulos, understood little of ancient meter. The Byzantine expert on metrics was Demetrius Triclinius, who also resided in Thessalonica and may have been a pupil of Thomas Magister; but he was also associated with Planudes in Constantinople. Considered as remarkable in his day as Casaubon was in the 16th century (Dawe 1973–1978) and the "first genuine [textual] critic produced by the middle ages" (Wilson 1996), Triclinius revised the Planudean Anthology, corrected Ptolemy's *Geography,* wrote about lunar theory, and made emendations to the only early manuscript of the fables of Babrius.

His real contribution, however, was to the study of ancient drama. Triclinius produced editions of Aeschylus, Sophocles, Euripides, and Aristophanes. He prepared not only the standard plays but rarer ones as well, including the second series of Euripides' plays, known to but a few earlier scholars. Working from a deeper knowledge of meter than any of his contemporaries, he emended freely but was overly confident in his abilities. He consulted multiple manuscripts for his editions and cited passages from old books. Because Triclinius was able to make qualitative distinctions among his sources, one recent editor of Sophocles has argued that his readings "should be systematically reported in any apparatus" (Dawe 1973–1978)—high praise for a 14th-century scholar. The survival of most of Aeschylus' *Agamemnon* is due to Triclinius, who discovered a manuscript containing both that play and the *Eumenides,* neither of which was known to scholars of the period. That manuscript has since disappeared, and the *Agamemnon* is known only from Triclinius' emended text—hence the necessity for philologists to understand Triclinius' working methods, and the careful studies made of his scholarship.

Contemporary with Planudes and Triclinius was Theodore Metochites, the most politically powerful of all Byzantine intellectuals. His life demonstrates that the intent if not the legal force of the Theodosian Code remained in effect, for he excelled in the "long practice of liberal studies" and achieved posts of the "first rank." The son of a disgraced, exiled official in the reign of Michael VIII, he began his rise through the government in 1290, when Andronicus II heard his oration on the city of Nicaea and took him into his service. Thereafter he held progressively more important positions until he became prime minister and the second most powerful person in the empire. Closely allied with the emperor, he fell with him in 1328 and was exiled.

Metochites defined his oeuvre as consisting of oratory, poetry, and philosophy and boasted that it treated all branches of wisdom and culture. He arrived in Constantinople in the last decade or so of Planudes' life and benefited from his scholarship. He supported the Chora monastery and, after Planudes' death, restored it. Planudes had lived at the Chora, and it was there that he had prepared his edition of Plutarch, who became a favorite of Metochites. Later, when he took up the study of astronomy, Metochites worked from a manuscript that Planudes had left in the monastery's library.

Metochites' *Semeioseis gnomikai,* a text not easily classified, reveals his attitude toward the classical tradition and issues of his own time. After a full day of governmental business, as a pupil of his described, Metochites pondered the classics, and the *Semeioseis* suggests that they were a refuge for him, not merely the necessary erudition for a Byzantine mandarin. The prologue compares the pitiful present to the glories of antiquity and laments that nothing new can be said. Metochites nevertheless continues for more than 100 chapters, musing about diverse topics in a manner that anticipates Montaigne's *Essais.* Plato and Aristotle appear often, and Metochites took a particular interest in Aristotle's works on science and logic. In one chapter he concludes that mathematical studies lack conflict, because their abstractions are eternal and beyond the vagaries of this world, surely the reaction of someone who had experienced more than his share of the latter. Like other Byzantines, Metochites attends to the style of classical authors, discussing the simple language of philosophers and finding in Plato a great talent for rhetoric, even though he wrote dialogues.

Metochites' prose can be verbose and obscure and does not find favor with many. His masterpiece is not what he wrote but what he created at the monastery of the Chora, especially its first-rate library, a sure refuge that he could only imagine from exile. The mosaics and frescoes that he commissioned for the narthexes and side chapel at the Chora are the finest works of late Byzantine art but have little relation to the classical tradition. There the Bible and the Church alone rule. The 10th century's creative fusion of the biblical and the classical was in the past, although late Byzantine artists did copy the Paris Psalter and the Joshua Roll.

Knowledge and appreciation of the classics continued in Byzantium until the end. From ca. 1400 onward the history of Byzantium and the classical tradition intersect with the rise of Humanism in Italy. Initially, the key figure is Manuel Chrysoloras, a learned Byzantine intellectual and diplomat who specialized in negotiations with the West. Contacts in Italy led to an offer to teach Greek grammar and literature in Florence, a well-paid position that he assumed from 1397 to 1400. There he ably taught the prominent Humanists of the day, creating a simplified grammar for the purpose. Translated into Latin by one of his students, this work became the best-selling textbook for the study of Greek. Also to aid his teaching, Chrysoloras took manuscripts to Florence; one survives, a large, luxury codex of the *Geography* of Ptolemy that soon passed to the library of Federigo da Montefeltro (now Vat. Urb. gr. 82). The *Geography* was translated into Latin in the early 15th century. Copied and later printed on folio-size pages, it became an essential part of aristocratic libraries; Columbus was able to consult a copy before his voyage to America.

For further education in Greek, Italian Humanists traveled to Constantinople to seek tutors and manuscripts. As the demand for Greek texts rose in Italy, enterprising Humanists also traveled east in search of old books. Among the most successful collectors was Giovanni Aurispa, who made two expeditions in the first quarter of the 15th century. The second yielded 238 pagan texts, an immense quantity that would have cost far more than a simple teacher could have afforded. He must have had financial backing from Italy. Nevertheless, he did not always succeed. He tried to purchase the 6th-century copy of Dioscorides' *De materia medica* (now in Vienna, mentioned above) from a Constantinopolitan monastery, but the monks would not part with it. The manuscript instead passed in the 16th century to the Jewish physician of Süleyman the Magnificent and finally to the Holy Roman Emperor.

The greatest individual collector of Greek manuscripts in the later 15th century was Cardinal Bessarion, a man of great learning and considerable influence in Renaissance Italy. Born in Trebizond and educated in Constantinople and Mistra, he had a career first in the Greek and then the Latin Church. After Constantinople fell in 1453, he despaired for the fate of ancient culture and spared no expense to assemble a collection of Greek literature, which he donated to the Republic of Venice in 1468. Among his many important manuscripts was the aforementioned Venetus A of Homer. His fine Byzantine education served him well in Humanistic debates about Plato and Aristotle. After the fall of the empire, Bessarion supported refugee scholars, who found roles within Renaissance culture, copying manuscripts and teaching Greek.

The canon of Greek literature that the Humanists initially came to know was Byzantine rather than classical, but as direct knowledge of the empire waned, Humanistic studies advanced, and Greek began to be printed, judgments changed. In 1557 the German scholar Hieronymus Wolf published the history of Nicetas Choniates. In his preface he distinguished antiquity from the 12th century by using the name Byzantium, the Latin form of Byzantion, to denote the ancient Greek colony that later became Constantinople. Only slightly more logical than the label America on a map of the New World, this ancient Greek city name came to be accepted for the medieval empire. With none of the *Rōmanoi* left to protest, Byzantium thus separated from antiquity and entered the realm of scholarship, where it continues to be remade according to the needs and desires of scholarship, nationalism, and the classical tradition.

BIBL.: S. Bassett, *The Urban Image of Late Antique Constantinople* (New York 2004). R. Browning, "Homer in Byzantium," *Viator* 6 (1975) 15–33. H. Buchthal, "The Exaltation of David," *Journal of the Warburg and Courtauld Institutes* 37 (1974) 330–333. G. Clarke, ed., *Reading the Past in Late Antiquity* (New York 1990). R. D. Dawe, *Studies on the Text of Sophocles,* 3 vols. (Leiden 1973–1978). K. Hult, *Theodore Metochites, On Ancient Authors and Philosophy* (Stockholm 2002). H. Hunger, "On the Imitation of Antiquity in Byzantine Literature," *Dumbarton Oaks Papers* 23–24 (1969–1970) 15–38. K. Ierodiakonou, ed., *Byzantine Philosophy and Its Ancient Sources* (New York 2002). P. Lemerle, *Byzantine Humanism: The First Phase, Notes and Remarks on Education and Culture in Byzantium from Its Origins to the 10th Century* (Canberra 1986). Michael Maas, *John Lydus and the Roman Past: Antiquarianism and Politics in the Age of Justinian* (New York 1992). C. Mango, "Antique Statuary and the Byzantine Beholder," *Dumbarton Oaks Papers* 17 (1963) 53–75. P. Moore, *Iter Psellianum: A Detailed Listing of Manuscript Sources for All Works Attributed to Michael Psellos* (Toronto 2005). M. Mullett and R. Scott, eds., *Byzantium and the Classical Tradition* (Birmingham, U.K., 1981). R. S. Nelson, "The Italian Appreciation and Appropriation of Illuminated Byzantine Manuscripts, ca. 1260–1450," *Dumbarton Oaks Papers* 49 (1995) 209–235. O. L. Smith, *Studies in the Scholia on Aeschylus,* vol. 1, *The Recensions of Demetrius Triclinius* (Leiden 1975). N. G. Wilson, *Scholars of Byzantium,* 2nd ed. (Cambridge, Mass., 1996).

R.NE.

C

Caesar, as Political Title

Gaius Julius Caesar, *dictator perpetuus,* passed on his cognomen, Caesar, to his adopted son, Gaius Octavianus, the emperor Augustus. Thereafter, *imperator* was used as a praenomen, accompanied by the cognomen Caesar of the *gens Iulia.* After this family line died out it was taken up by the succeeding emperors and became the distinctive title of imperial power. From Hadrian onward, the emperor-designate was called Caesar. With the tetrarchy of Diocletian (293 CE), the title Caesar indicated the junior rulers and that of Augustus the two senior emperors. If in antiquity Caesar was consistently used by the emperors, it was, however, neither distinctive of nor exclusive to their office, nor was it preponderant; nevertheless, without referring any longer to Julius Caesar, it became synonymous with emperor and identified the state and temporal power. And in Persia the proper name of certain important kings, like that of Chosroes (ancient Persian Kisra, 531–576) of the Sassanid dynasty, ran a somewhat parallel course to that of Caesar, eventually taking on—even if not so categorically—the general sense of epithet of the sovereign.

With the fall of Rome (476 CE), Virgil's earlier prophecy of an *imperium sine fine* (Aeneid 1.279) was fulfilled in the transcendence of its spatial limitations.

In the West, thanks to a *translatio imperii* by way of the Church in February 962, Otto I the Great had himself crowned emperor of the Romans and king of Italy by Pope John XII. Ever since Caesar's campaigns the Germans had known his name, which retains the ancient form with the diphthong, *kaiser,* although in imperial Rome it was pronounced kesar (in old high German kaisar). Kaiser was used by the German emperors of the Holy Roman Empire in various dynasties until its abolition by Napoleon in 1806. It was then reestablished after the Congress of Vienna, and German sovereigns would be called kaiser from 1871, the year of the proclamation of the German Empire (*Deutsches Kaiserreich*), until the abdication of Wilhelm II in 1918.

In the East, thanks to the *translatio imperii,* the privileges and functions of the empire were transferred from the old capital to Constantinople, New Rome. Starting in 629 with Heraclius I, the Byzantine emperor was called *basileus* (king of kings), but the title caesar remained characteristic of the Roman emperor in the East, the dominant political figure in eastern Europe and central Asia. From Byzantium the title caesar spread to the neighboring peoples in its cultural orbit, who kept their sights set on Constantinople. For the immense prestige it afforded, these rulers adopted it after an invasion of Constantinople, or by self-proclamation, or even with the consent of Byzantium itself. The first to do so was Tervel, khan of Bulgaria 695–715, who helped Justinian II reconquer Constantinople after his ousting in 695; in return, the emperor promised him his daughter, certain territories, and the title of caesar. In their efforts to secure their own borders, the Byzantine emperors often made recourse to the granting of titles and marriages to Byzantine princesses. Caesars sprang up, and a corresponding devaluation of the title's meaning ensued. Therefore, starting with Alexios I Komnenos (1048–1118), the Byzantine emperors used different titles supposedly superior to caesar (*sebastocrator, despotes,* and so on).

In the Slavic world the Bulgars, Serbs, and Russians proclaimed themselves caesars, using the denomination czar, which arrived with the Goths, who ruled the area inhabited by the Slavs between 200 and 375 CE. The word probably derived from the Gothic *kaisr* (Russian *car',* Bulgarian, Ukranian, and Polish *car,* Serbian and Croatian *căr*). It is probable that the word derived from the Greek and came through Byzantium. In both cases this transformation has been legitimized by the second palatization.

The two Bulgarian empires of the 10th and then the 12th and 13th centuries, like the Serbian one of the 12th century, aspired to the conquest of Byzantium. After Tervel, the first Slavic caesar was Simeon I of Bulgaria (893–927), who yearned to conquer the territories subject to Byzantium and have himself proclaimed czar of the Greeks; the Bulgars unsuccessfully encamped many times beneath the walls of Constantinople, which the Slavs called Czargrad (city of the czar). Kalojan (1197–1207), the creator of the second Bulgarian empire, fared better. After his attack on New Rome, the emperor Alexios III had to officially recognize the independence of the revived state. Kalojan had also appealed to Rome, requesting the rank of czar, but the pope granted him only that of *kral'*, or king, a title inferior to emperor. Nevertheless, czar would be used by all the successive Bulgarian rulers until 1397, when the Ottomans definitively conquered their territories. In 1908, its sovereignty completely recovered, Bulgaria once again used the title of czar, which lasted until the abolition of the monarchy in 1946.

Serbian developments were analogous, where the two czars, Stefan IV Dušan and his son, Stefan V Dušan, created an empire that was then destroyed by the Turks in 1371. Though these are the only Serbian czars, preceding rulers were also depicted with the same attributes and the same crown as Byzantine ones: before the title an image had already been created of the Serbian ruler equal to that of the *basileus* of Czargrad.

The expansion of Byzantine terminology and caesar's prestige also reached Georgia, where, for example, George II (1072–1089) had his imperial title of caesar put on the verso of his coins, modeled on Byzantine ones. The only Slavs who did not have official pretensions to the rank of czar were the grand princes of Kievan Rus', for whom caesar remained an honorary title bestowed on particularly wise or powerful princes, such as Saint Vladimir (Christianizer of Russia, crowned *basileus* and czar by Basil II and Constantine II in 988). The situation changed toward the middle of the 13th century, when the Rus' fell under the dominion of the Tartars: the khan, head of the Golden Horde, was called czar. The transfer of this title from the Byzantine emperor to the head of the khanate also occurred on account of the capture of Byzantium by the Crusaders in 1204, considered by the Russians to be the death of the *czarstvo* (empire). From then on both the khan and the Byzantine emperor were considered czars, whereas the Russian grand princes lost this appellation, which at the time was considered to belong only to an independent governor.

The czar or khan was regarded a superior and in the right if he charged the grand prince with wanting to usurp his power. Nevertheless, starting at the end of the 14th century the Russians fought the Tartars for their independence: the caesarian dignity of grand prince Ivan Vasilevič began to be emphasized, while that of the Tartar Achmat was diminished, "evil and rejected by God, for he had proclaimed himself Czar." The line of Genghis Khan did not descend from the Caesars, whereas the rulers of Kievan Rus', according to Russian writings of the 16th century, were considered descendants of Prus, the legendary brother of Augustus; they were made emperors by Constantine, who had given the regalia to Vladimir Monomakh. Ivan the Terrible officially adorned himself with the title of czar in 1547, the first time the title was used in the Russian state. Nevertheless, as the Jesuit Antonio Possevino writes, many Catholics did not recognize him since "such titles would have no worth without the authorization of the Supreme Pontiff, who would never permit such an injury to be done to Caesar, the emperor of the Romans."

Only an emperor legitimized by the pope was an actual emperor. This is why Pius II was willing to recognize the caesarian rank of Mehmed II, who conquered Constantinople in 1453, only on the condition that he convert to Catholicism.

The concept of the *translatio imperii ad Mahumetem,* expressed by Pius II in a letter that was actually never sent to Mehmed, is a repetition of the idea of Augustan peace that the pope had cited to exalt the unlimited sovereignty of Frederick III, emperor of the Holy Roman Empire, but this time for the sultan.

According to many people, including George of Trebizond, the Florentine agent in Constantinople, "no one doubted that he [Mehmed II] was by right the emperor of the Romans. Indeed, the emperor is the one who possesses just title to the imperial seat." The sultan would be recognized as czar by the Bulgars, Ottoman subjects. "I intend to surpass by far Caesar and Alexander and Xerxes," declared Mehmed II, who gave himself the title Caesar of the Romans, *Kayser-i-Rûm,* which was then passed down to numerous Ottoman rulers until 1900. Some sultans affixed the inscription Kaiser to their effigies.

In Russia, starting with the intensification of relations with the West, for diplomatic reasons and so as not to translate the title of czar as rex, the title changed. In 1721 Peter the Great became *imperator,* and the heir to the throne was *czarevic:* by referring in this way to the ancient Roman custom, the Russian desire to appear an heir to the first and second Rome was emphasized. Thanks to the foundation of a new city, St. Petersburg, the Russians paid homage to their caesar, but also to the apostle Peter, and they considered themselves the guardians of the values of the empire and of Christianity.

If in the East Caesar legitimized the historical continuity of autocracy, in the West the deeper the discovery and reappraisal of republican Rome went, the more the reputation of Julius Caesar declined as the one responsible for the destruction of the republic. Beginning in the 13th century the glory of the commander and tyrant Caesar was famously contrasted with the figure of Cato, the symbol of virtue, and that of Brutus, especially in republican Florence. They become paladins of freedom, contrasted with the yoke of absolutism. In 1599 William Shakespeare, following Plutarch, demythologized Caesar in his *Julius Caesar.* His killer, Brutus, exclaims:

And let us bathe our hands in Caesar's blood
Up to the elbows, and besmear our swords;
. . . And waving our red weapons o'er our heads,
Let's all cry, "Peace, freedom, and liberty!"
(*Julius Caesar* 3.1).

These themes enjoyed great success. The Shakespearean *Caesar* was translated and freely adapted by Voltaire, and it was later revisited in an anti-Hitlerian key by Orson Welles in 1937. The myth of Caesar the glorious commander, like the analogy Caesar : tyranny :: Brutus : freedom, is still a topos today.

Now, in the names of all the gods at once
Upon what meat doth this our Caesar feed
That he is grown so great? . . .
What should be in that "Caesar"? (*Julius Caesar* 1.2).

BIBL.: L. D'Ascia, *Il Corano e la tiara: L'epistola a Maometto di Enea Silvio Piccolomini* (Bologna 2001). J. V. A. Fine Jr., *The Late Medieval Balkans: A Critical Survey from the Late Twelfth Century to the Ottoman Conquest* (Ann Arbor 1987). G. Gentili, ed., *Giulio Cesare: L'uomo le imprese il mito* (Milan 2008). A. Stender Petersen, *Slavisch-Germanisch Lehwortkunde* (Hildesheim 1974). *Roma-Costantinopoli-Mosca,* papers from the conference Da Roma alla terza Roma, 1981 (Naples 1983). P. Schramm, *Kaiser, Rom und Renovatio* (Leipzig 1929). W. Vodoff, "Remarques sur le valeur du terme 'tsar' appliqué aux princes russes avant le milieu du XV siècle," in *Oxford Slavonic Series* (Oxford 1978) 11:8–14. M. Wyke, *Caesar: A Life in Western Culture* (Chicago 2008). S. Yerasimos, *Constantinople: De Byzance à Istanbul* (Paris 2001).

F.R.

Translated by Patrick Baker

Caesar, Julius

Born on 12 July 100 BCE, killed on 15 March 44, Caesar dominated the political scene in Rome and the entire Roman world for 16 years, from 60 BCE (first triumvirate, with Pompey and Crassus) until his assassination. But as early as the year of Cicero's consulship and Catiline's conspiracy (63 BCE), Caesar played an extremely important role in Roman political life. His career unfolded between the two conspiracies, that of Catiline (to which Caesar was no stranger) and that of the "Caesaricides" (who labeled themselves liberators). His assassination marked an epoch. It also gave birth to the legend that Romulus, the first *rex,* had also been murdered in the Senate in the same way (Dionysius of Halicarnassus, *Roman Antiquities* 2.56.4). Despite the claim of tyrannicide, Caesar's conduct did not fit the topos of the tyrant at all. Not only was he no friend of censorship, but he also accepted the challenge of public debates that were much more political than historical in nature (*Anticato*). He was a great writer, unlike all those who held supreme power after him (with the possible exception of Julian the Apostate, four centuries later).

Although Caesar's name became the universal denominative of power (czar, Kaiser), the fate of his myth fluctuated greatly. His heir and adopted son, Octavian, took power by exploiting his special role as son. He gathered armies in the name of avenging the death of his father; in the *Res gestae divi Augusti* he states that he took up arms only to punish his father's murderers. But he never says that he wanted to restore the confused dictatorial regime that Caesar had established.

Indeed, it was Octavian—Augustus—who ensured that the political model represented by Caesar was eventually forgotten. In the politically most important book of the *Aeneid,* book 6, Caesar is barely glimpsed at verse 789, whereas the whole long political-imperial prophecy that Anchises recites for Aeneas in Hades regards Augustus (790–805); its tone is so servile as to justify Naphta's indignant anti-Virgilian invective in Thomas Mann's *Magic Mountain.* Ovid puts the apotheosis of Caesar at the end of the *Metamorphoses* (15.745–759), but he hastens to herald the apotheosis of Augustus, too (15.852–870)—and with a rather infelicitous phrase at that (15.868–70), considering that "becoming a god" and "dying" were becoming synonyms precisely in relation to the practice of the sovereign's apotheosis upon his departure from this world. On his deathbed Vespasian said ironically, "I think I am becoming a god" (*Puto deus fio*) (Suetonius, *Life of Vespasian* 23.4). At any rate, that Ovid was not politically savvy can be seen in his later personal misfortunes.

In the *Bellum civile* of Lucan (the nephew of Seneca the Younger), Caesar is a sinister and entirely negative figure. It is significant that Lucan demonstrated his extremely harsh attitude toward Caesar at the most "tyrannical" moment in the long rule of the Julio-Claudians, that is, in the worst period of Nero's reign. In Lucan's poem Caesar is the prototype for the aberrant, tyrannical arrival of the principate. What is more, making Caesar wholly responsible for what happened later also meant unmasking the republican restoration staged by Augustus (and proclaimed with the steady support of the *Res gestae,* copies of which were distributed to the four corners of the empire).

Lucan's portrayal of Caesar also hit at the myth of *clementia Caesaris.* Surveying the battlefield of Pharsalus (48 BCE), then covered with thousands of bodies, Caesar supposedly said, according to Plutarch, "They wanted this, they forced me to this" (*Life of Caesar* 46). According to Lucan, however, Caesar actually prohibited the burial of the defeated (*Bellum civile* 7.786–803). Nor can the scene be forgotten, described in detail by Lucan, in which Caesar feigns sorrow but secretly rejoices at the sight of Pompey's severed head (9.1037–1043)—an episode that also influenced Petrarch's conception of Caesar (*Canzoniere* 102).

At this point, it goes without saying that the monarchic

tradition, from Charles V to Louis XIV—both of whom struggled with the text of the *Commentaries*—had a stable point of reference in the name and the myth of Caesar, and that conversely the much weaker but nevertheless uninterrupted republican tradition was never able to "get this Brutus out of its head" (*cavarsi di testa questo Bruto*), as Pietro Paolo Boscoli famously said at his execution in Florence in 1513 for having taken part in a conspiracy against the Medici.

With the French Revolution Marcus Brutus became the hero par excellence. His act became a universal symbol of the fight against tyrants, and various of the 48 Paris sections were named after him. Caesar was in the dust. The chapter on the Roman Republic in the *Tableau historique,* written, perhaps under the Robespierre government, by "citizen Bulard," a fierce militant of the section Brutus, concludes with a call to repeat, whenever necessary, the assassination of Caesar: "O vous, jeunes républicains français, braves et vertueux sans-culottes, que des imposteurs voudroient tromper, que les intrigans voudroient corrompre, profitez de cette leçon de l'histoire . . . et s'il paroissoit quelque ambitieux, qui voulût imiter César, soiez tous autant de Brutus et Cassius" (Bulard, *Brutus, ou Tableau historique,* 1794); not knowing which month of year 2 in which the work was written, we could surmise that the dreaded "tyrant" is Robespierre himself.

On the other hand, it is well known that after the Revolution the Caesarian politico-institutional model was reclaimed by Napoleon Bonaparte. Even in his march toward increasing personal power (first consul, consul for life, emperor), he followed the lead of that model. But Caesar, after the consulship and the dictatorship, stopped at the further step of perpetual dictatorship; Napoleon drew the logical conclusion and thus took the leap toward a sui generis form of monarchic power, empire.

The solution adopted by Caesar at the end of his political career was incomplete, provisional, almost a refusal to choose. By proclaiming himself emperor, Napoleon followed the path of development taken by the Roman constitution after Caesar—empire; but he, too, rigorously avoided the word *monarchy.* He went beyond Caesar, and yet he cultivated, in defeat, the myth of Caesar. To this end he dictated a literary work, the *Précis des guerres de Jules César* (1835), which is a kind of "rendering of accounts" between the emperor and his Roman prototype, not only militarily but also historiographically and politically. Indeed, Napoleon did not limit himself, as the title might suggest, to reconsidering the grand military campaigns of his great model, mixing praise with critical observations; he also discusses Caesar's politics, the regime he established. And he pays particular attention to the character that Caesarism came to assume, as a kind of "third way" between oligarchy and popular rule. Napoleon was in full agreement with one aspect in particular of the choices Caesar made: his attempt to reconstitute, to reach an accord with, the nobility that had opposed him. Indeed, he went even further in this regard, formulating a maxim that seems to anticipate Michels's "iron law of oligarchy": "In peoples and in revolutions aristocracy always exists: eliminate it in the nobility, and you will see it reappear in the rich and powerful houses of the Third Estate; eliminate it here, too, and it subsists in the aristocracy of laborers" (*Précis* 16.1). These lines contain, among other things, a clear enough reference to those pages of the *Commentaries* of the civil war that describe how Antony, Caesar's *magister equitum,* very harshly repressed the movements in favor of the cancellation of debts that had exploded in Italy when the defeat of Pompey seemed nigh.

It should therefore come as no surprise that Alphonse de Beauchamp (1767–1832), who began as a Jacobin and ended his career by writing the *Mémoires* that Fouché circulated under his own name, diffused in 1823, after Napoleon's death (5 May 1821), a *Vie de Jules César* that he intended as a history à clef whose subject was also Napoleon.

The fact that Napoleon sought to give life to a form of charismatic military power, one of whose sources of inspiration had been Caesar, helped clarify that the Caesarian regime had not been a monarchy *sic et simpliciter.* Napoleon studied that far-off experience, he extracted its fundamental and peculiar traits, and he constructed a model—Bonapartism—such that his contemporaries well understood how different it was from the "salutaires et protectrices des monarchies modernes," to use the words of Alphonse de Beauchamp.

Nevertheless, for the ruling classes of late republican Rome (who thought they had ended the game with the tyrannicide of the Ides of March), the Caesarian experiment could be seen only in the constitutional terms of monarchy, which in Rome was utterly illegal. What is more, it bore marks of usurpation, and thus of tyranny. If *regnum,* and especially aspiring to it, was a crime in Rome, an attempt on the constitution, then tyranny was the notion closest to it in the tradition of Greek political thought. King-usurper and tyrant ended up coinciding and were, from the point of view of the Roman ruling classes, present both in the figure of Caesar and in the type of power he established in the perpetual dictatorship. In this regard, it is not out of place to add that the tyrant, before becoming the antithesis of *politeia* and thus of democracy, had also been the mediator (sympathetic to the people) in the irresolvable conflicts of 6th-century BCE Greece.

Just how tilted toward monarchy—and thus untenable—Caesar's experiment appeared is clearly visible in the way Octavian distanced himself from it. And although it necessitated enduring a protracted conflict with Antony (who was enamored of the Hellenistic model), Octavian achieved a political tour de force when he succeeded in winning the support and allegiance of the legions and of the Caesarian *pars,* and yet at the same time in establishing a form of rule capable of being presented as a "restoration of the Republic."

Moreover, in simplifying things and excising from Caesar's experiment its distinguishing Bonapartist feature of the "third way," Eduard Meyer, in one of his most renowned works (*Caesars Monarchie und das Prinzipat des Pompeius,* 1918), classified Caesar's regime as monarchy, and Pompey's mode of being *in re publica* as a principate, thus anticipating the kind of government devised by Augustus.

Meyer wrote his book in 1917. Meanwhile in Russia, revolutionized by the war and by various shocks, Lenin was busy asserting his personal rule, a "left-wing Bonapartism" of which Meyer declared himself an admirer in his essay "Das neue Russland" (1925). And a few years later in Italy, with the inability of the revolutionaries to "do as in Russia" and of the bourgeois state to "crush the revolution," a "right-wing Bonapartism" asserted itself: Mussolini's dictatorship.

Reflecting in prison on the defeat suffered by the "revolution" in Italy and, in a barely veiled way, on the dictatorial forms that Bolshevism had assumed in the U.S.S.R., Antonio Gramsci arrived at the distinction between *progressive* Caesarism (Caesar and Napoleon I) and *regressive* Caesarism (Napoleon III and Bismarck). This distinction is perhaps questionable, but one must not lose sight of the premise that immediately precedes it and that is common to both its terms. In Gramsci's felicitous definition, "Caesarism always represents the arbitral solution, entrusted to a grand personality, of a situation characterized by an equilibrium of forces whose outlook is catastrophic." And: "Caesarism represents a situation in which there is a catastrophic equilibrium of contending forces, such that the continuation of their struggle can end only in mutual destruction." "The point," Gramsci continues, "is to see whether in the dialectic of revolution/restoration it is the element of revolution or of restoration that prevails, since it is certain that in the movement of history there can be no turning back ever, *and there are no restorations 'in toto'*" (*Prison Notebooks,* written 1929–1935).

Caesar is the character around whom these patterns revolve. The enthusiasm with which Marx speaks about Caesar in a well-known letter to Engels, written in the months when Marx was certainly reading (as can be drawn from other letters) Mommsen's *Römische Geschichte* (vol. 3, 1889), may seem strange. This is the letter of 27 February 1861, better known for its oft-cited judgment of Appian, the Greek-Egyptian historian from Alexandria, and Spartacus—"a great general, but no Garibaldi!" (*grosser General, kein Garibaldi!*). In the letter Marx goes on to demonstrate quite emphatically his appreciation for Caesar's military daring, the proof of his unquestionable superiority over his adversaries: "Pompey was a real shithead [*Scheisskerl*] who rose under false pretenses as Sulla's 'young man,' . . . a disgrace as soon as he had to go head-to-head with Caesar. Caesar committed the grossest military errors on purpose, like some crazy man, in order to confuse the philistine opposing him. An ordinary Roman general, let us say Crassus, would have destroyed him six times during the battle in Epirus" (*Marx-Engels Correspondence, 1861–1866*).

This letter emanates a sympathetic, pro-Caesarian exaltation that goes beyond even Napoleon's admiring tone. In this domain at least, Napoleon did not hesitate at times to denounce Caesar's tactical errors, especially in the civil war. And capital among these is exactly his hazardous conduct in Epirus. Napoleon writes, "At Durazzo Caesar used extremely reckless maneuvers, and for these he was punished" (*Précis* 11.4).

Mommsen's enthusiasm for Caesar is well known. I mention it only in passing and emphasize that it coexisted with his liberal *forma mentis* (especially in the period in which he wrote the *Römische Geschichte*). It is possible that Marx was influenced by his reading of Mommsen's *History,* but there was surely something else going on in his enthusiastic appraisal of Caesar's stature and unscrupulousness: he had no hang-ups about dictatorship.

Attempts to write the history of Rome from a Marxist point of view have also had to take account of Caesar, and not rarely is he given the historical role of having ushered in a new age by putting an end to the untenable contradictions of the oligarchic city-state, which was no longer capable of ruling such a large empire. The fullest and most balanced attempt at this kind of synthesis is that proposed by Francesco De Martino in the third volume of his *Storia della costituzione romana.* De Martino, however, is also convinced that Caesar was opposed by "a political class, the senatorial nobility, which had become incapable of assuring the proper government of the State and whose only object was not to renounce any of its privileges" (1973, 194).

BIBL.: F. E. Adcock, *Caesar as Man of Letters* (Cambridge 1956). T. R. S. Broughton, *The Magistrates of the Roman Republic,* vol. 2 (Cleveland 1952), and vol. 3, *Supplement* (Atlanta 1986) 105–108. L. Canfora, *Julius Caesar: The Life and Times of the People's Dictator,* trans. M. Hill and K. Windle (Berkeley 2007). I. Cervelli, *Rivoluzione e cesarismo nell'Ottocento* (Turin 2003). F. De Martino, *Storia della costituzione romana,* vol. 3 (Naples 1973). W. Drumann, *Geschichte Roms in seinem Übergange von der republikanischen zur monarchischen Verfassung oder Pompeius, Caesar, Cicero und ihre Zeitgenossen,* ed. P. Groebe (Leipzig 1906) 3:125–684, 696–827. E. S. Gruen, *The Last Generation of the Roman Republic* (Berkeley 1974). C. Meier, *Caesar,* trans. D. McLintock (New York 1995). Napoléon III, *Histoire de Jules César,* 3 vols. (Paris 1865–1866). R. Syme, *Roman Papers,* ed. E. Badian and A. R. Birley, 7 vols. (Oxford 1979–1991), and *The Roman Revolution* (Oxford 1939). T. P. Wiseman, *New Men in the Roman Senate, 139* B.C.–A.D. *14* (Oxford 1971). L.C.

Translated by Patrick Baker

Caesars, Twelve

The Twelve Caesars was a decorative theme of wide appeal in post-classical Europe, thanks especially to the sheer number of imperial images surviving from antiquity (in the form of busts, cameos, and coins), the political power these images evoked, and continued interest in Suetonius's biographies. The Caesars became popular subjects in *all'antica* painting and sculpture, and the desire to collect them in sets made their imagery particularly suitable for serial reproduction in prints, plaquettes, and other media. From the 14th century to the 16th, interest in the Twelve Caesars spread the use of antiquarian methods, as myriad textual and visual sources were compiled and compared to rediscover "authentic" portraits of the emperors. By the later 16th century displays of the Twelve Caesars seemed to symbolize the encyclopedic knowledge of collectors; the ruling dynasties of Europe exhibited portrait cycles in grandiose settings as emblems of imperial might.

In the medieval era portraits of the Caesars were greatly prized by the popes, the Byzantine emperors, and the Carolingians, who claimed Roman *imperium* as the source of their own authority. Antique cameos with portraits of the emperors were kept in princely and ecclesiastical collections or incorporated into treasuries. A particularly splendid example is the Cross of Lothar in Aachen (ca. 1000). Antiquarian research into imperial portraits is first seen in northern Italy during the 14th century, when ancient coins—conveniently equipped with both the names and effigies of the emperors—provided the models for portraits used to illustrate Suetonius's text (e.g., Fermo, Biblioteca Comunale Ms. 81, ca. 1350). New attitudes toward antique *Uomini illustri* emerged in the writings of Petrarch and his followers, who promoted their exemplary value; it soon became a Humanist trope that portraits of the ancients put good and bad examples before the eyes of learned men, inspiring them to imitate their virtues and avoid their vices. Such moral overtones bolstered interest in portraits of ancient worthies among scholars and justified their appropriation by aristocrats. The lavish illuminations of the Kane Suetonius *Twelve Caesars* at Princeton University, made in 1433 for Duke Filippo Maria Visconti of Milan, acknowledge Humanist ideals while reveling in the imperial splendor of Italian court life.

In the medium of sculpture, artists in 15th-century Florence invented a new type of rectangular relief featuring Caesars, empresses, and other *illustri* in elegant profiles, of which Desiderio da Settignano's *Julius Caesar* in the Louvre (ca. 1460) is the most famous example. Alfonso I of Naples and Ercole I d'Este in Ferrara ordered these in sets of twelve: they seem to have excluded the "bad" or lesser-known emperors (such as Caligula or Otho) and incorporated "good" Caesars who did not appear in Suetonius's twelve biographies (such as Trajan and Hadrian), but nevertheless held to the canonical number twelve, acknowledging the authority of Suetonius's text and drawing parallels with traditional Christian motifs, like the Twelve Apostles or the Twelve Months. Sculpted images of the ancient emperors appealed to elite Italian patrons as an art form that intermingled antique and modern with great subtlety, in the manner of the *all'antica* portrait busts and medals also invented in the Quattrocento. By the later 15th century the imagery of the Caesars gained in popularity, appealing to patrons as diverse as city governments, men of letters, and *condottieri.* Andrea Mantegna painted them on the ceiling of the Camera degli Sposi and, after the Sforza promoted the cult of the ancient Caesars in Milan, Lombard sculptors adopted them as a decorative leitmotif (at the Certosa di Pavia, the tomb of Bartolommeo Colleoni, and the Loggia of Brescia), always in the form of medallion busts.

By the late 15th century the Italian fascination for the Caesars had spread to other parts of Europe. In France, England, and the Holy Roman Empire, galleries of imperial portraits created a sense of unbroken continuity between ancient emperors and modern-day kings: when Maximilian I planned the monumental display of ancestral sculpture for his own tomb at the Innsbruck Hofkirche, he hoped to include more than 30 bronze busts of ancient Caesars. Not only rulers, but also noblemen, scholars, and merchants across Europe avidly collected antique and modern portraits of the Caesars. Major sculptors such as Guglielmo della Porta supplied sets of the Twelve Caesars for the high end of the market, and other artists specialized in inexpensive prints: in 1520 Marcantonio Raimondi issued the first printed series of the Twelve Caesars, depicting them in a rather modest medallion format, whereas later portrait books by Antonio Tempesta (Rome 1596) and Stradanus (Antwerp 1600) reflect new trends by showing them dressed in full armor and on horseback.

In the 16th century the preferences of aristocratic patrons shifted toward large canvas paintings, sculpted busts, and full-length statues of the Twelve Caesars, displayed as a complete Suetonian set. Among the most influential of this type was the half-length set painted by Titian for Duke Federico Gonzaga to decorate a Gabinetto dei Cesari in the Palazzo Ducale in Mantua (1537–1538). Though the canvases have since been destroyed, they were widely known through copies and prints. Eventually, cycles of Twelve Caesars became unabashed expressions of imperial power in the princely residences of Europe, as new types of exhibition spaces—especially art galleries and large gardens—allowed for their display in imposing settings. Commissions for sets of these could inspire competition among artists, as when Frederik Hendrik (1584–1647), Prince of Orange, ordered a set of bust-length portraits from Rubens and eleven different Netherlandish painters. King Philip II of Spain (r. 1556–1598) owned a copy of Titian's cycle and at least six sculpted series, combining antique works, images commissioned from living artists, and others received as diplomatic gifts. These decorated Philip's vast palaces and gardens, such as the Jardín de los Emperadores at the Alcazar, always with reference to Habsburg claims on Roman *imperium.* Spain also heralded the expansion of its empire to the New World by exporting cycles of the Twelve Caesars to the colonies.

The theme of the Twelve Caesars inspired new inventions in the decorative arts, as is seen in the Aldrobrandini Tazze (ca. 1560–1570), silver-gilt cups decorated with small statuettes of the Twelve Caesars and narrative reliefs illustrating their deeds. For the Kunstkammer collections artists produced small statuettes of the emperors, often in precious stones and metals. The fashion for encyclopedic collections gave the Twelve Caesars particular resonance for antiquarians, who displayed full sets as a reflection of their complete, well-ordered knowledge of the past. Around the same time that King Charles I of England bought Titian's *Twelve Caesars* from the Gonzaga collection, the bibliophile Sir Robert Cotton (1571–1631) arranged the contents of his extraordinary library in cases crowned by busts of the Twelve Caesars, together with Cleopatra and Faustina. Today Cotton's manuscripts number among the greatest treasures of the British Library, where they still are catalogued according to emperor pressmarks.

BIBL.: Francesco Caglioti, "Fifteenth-century Reliefs of Ancient Emperors and Empresses in Florence: Production and Collecting," in *Collecting Sculpture in Early Modern Europe,* ed. N. Penny and E. D. Schmidt (Washington, D.C., 2008) 67–109. Claudio Franzoni, "*Remembranze d'infinite cose:* Le collezioni rinascimentali di antichità," in *Memoria dell'antico nell'arte italiana,* ed. S. Settis (Turin 1984) 298–360. Gerald Heres, "Kaiserserien in den Kunstkammern des Barock": *Römisches Porträt (Conference Acts), Gesellschafts- und Sprachwissenschaftliche Reihe* 31, no. 2/3 (1982) 209–210. Heinz Ladendorf, *Antikenstudium und Antikenkopie* (Berlin 1953). Milan Pelc, *Illustrium Imagines: Das Porträtbuch der Renaissance* (Leiden 2002). Annegrit Schmitt, "Zur Wiederbelebung der Antike im Trecento: Petrarcas Rom-Idee in ihrer Wirkung auf die Paduaner Malerei: Die methodische Einbeziehung des römischen Münzbildnisses in die Ikonographie 'Berühmter Männer,'" *Mitteilungen des Kunsthistorischen Institutes in Florenz* 18 (1974) 167–218. Reinhard Stupperich, "Die zwölf Caesaren Suetons: Zur Verwendung von Kaiserportät-Galerien in der Neuzeit," in *Lebendige Antike. Rezeptionen der Antike in Politik, Kunst und Wissenschaft der Neuzeit,* ed. R. Stupperich (Mannheim 1995) 39–58. Max Wegner, "Bildnisreihen der Zwölf Caesaren Suetons," in *Migratio et commutatio: Studien zur alten Geschichte und deren Nachleben,* ed. H.-J. Drexhage and J. Sünskes (St. Katharinen 1989) 280–285.

K.W.C.

Calendars, Chronicles, Chronology

Petrarch's favorite books—the manuscripts that he cherished most, and in the margins of which he inscribed his intimate thoughts—included Virgil's *Aeneid* and Livy's history of Rome. But they also included a work that few philosophers or general readers look at now: the *Chronicle,* a history of the world from the time of Abraham to the 4th century CE, compiled by the Greek Christian writer Eusebius and translated and adapted in Latin by Jerome. In this richly informative text, parallel columns list the rulers of Assyria and Israel, Athens and Rome, and interspersed is information about the invention of poetry and the trireme, athletic contests and the fall of cities. It offered Petrarch both information that he needed and scholarly puzzles that he enjoyed trying to solve (how Aeneas could have met Dido, for example, given the century and more that separated them in what he took as the historical record). No wonder, then, that he filled the margins of his copy of the *Chronicle* with parallel notations and queries.

In this instance Petrarch's tastes were not unusual. Today chronology, the subdiscipline of classical philology that reconstructs the calendars used in the ancient world and establishes the dates of events, seems a subject so dry, so lacking in human interest, that it demands the adjective "mere." Over the millennia, however, ancient chronicles and calendars have fascinated and engaged erudite, innovative, and combative scholars, from Eratosthenes and Varro in the ancient world, to Eusebius and Bede, Isaac Newton and Giambattista Vico, to Eduard Schwartz and Felix Jacoby. Through much of the history of the classical tradition, books on chronology preserved a vast amount of information found nowhere else, and cutting-edge scholars studied the field. Many of the erudite 14th-century clerics and jurists who shared Petrarch's interest in ancient texts and Roman ruins also shared his partiality for the work of Eusebius and Jerome.

In antiquity, chronicles and calendars both began as public projects. Cities and temples maintained lists of rulers, magistrates, priests, and winners of athletic contests. Priests and magistrates—sometimes the same individuals—laid out the months and set the dates for the festivals of the gods. By the 5th century, Greek astronomers understood the 19-year lunisolar cycle discovered in Mesopotamia. They could have laid out the Athenian year, which was nominally lunar, so that each month actually began at the new moon. In practice, however, civil calendars followed more arbitrary rules, as we know from the complaint of the gods, in Aristophanes' *Clouds,* that the Athenians failed to feed them in a timely way. The calendar systems used in different cities across the Greek world varied widely. Boeotians, Spartans, and Athenians, for example, dated differently events in which they all had been involved. Nonetheless, 5th-century antiquarians did their best to work out exactly when such events had taken place, in the terms of the calendar systems they knew best, and even to fix precise calendrical dates for such events from the distant past as the fall of Troy.

From the late 4th century BCE, Greek historians collated lists of rulers and accounts of events. Timaeus, Eratosthenes, and others drew up synchronistic tables. They distinguished people and events of what Eratosthenes called the "mythical time" before the Trojan War, in which chronology was necessarily uncertain, from those of later periods, for which they thought it possible to establish firm dates, and they linked the histories of cities across the Mediterranean to one another. The depth and rigor of their work remain in dispute; though they drew at times on official records like the Athenian archon lists, they also put forward arbitrary conjectures. Still, their results circulated in many forms, from the chronicle inscribed on stone in Paros in 264–263 BCE, still known as the Marmor Parium, to the popular verse chronicle that the Athenian Apollodorus composed a few decades later.

In the Roman world the great crisis of the 1st century BCE was accompanied by projects, some individual and some orchestrated by Caesar and Augustus, to set order in both the calendar year and the historic past. Throughout the Mediterranean, chronology mattered. The *Astronomicon* of Manilius and the *De die natali* of Censorinus—a strange text, written in 238 CE, that combined antiquarian scholarship with natural philosophy—preserve fragmentary records of the great antiquary Varro's efforts to date the founding of Rome. Astronomers used an artificial calendar, based on the Egyptian year of 365 days, which they could run backward and forward, seamlessly, for hundreds of years before and after their own time. Varro consulted an astrologer, Lucius Tarrutius of Firmum, who inferred from Romulus's character traits the appropriate celestial charts for his conception and birth. He provided Egyptian dates for both, as well as for the solar eclipse that had supposedly accompanied the conception. Varro's enterprise seems quixotic now, but it did not to Cicero, who praised him for bringing the Romans, who had been wandering like visitors in their own city, home at last, and teaching them the chronology of their own history, as well as the development of their institutions and rituals (*Academica posteriora* 3.9). Roman scholars' new visions of the past and the calendar, as Caesar and Augustus had reordered both, were carved on stone for public display in the time of Augustus and after. The structure of time mattered, especially in an age of crisis.

In the 3rd and 4th centuries CE, as the Roman Empire passed through a new series of crises and transformations, both pagans and Christians began to weave new syntheses of information about time. Some had polemical motives. Christian scholars, tying their tradition to its Jewish predecessor, used chronology to argue that their Scriptures were older than the oldest Greek and Latin texts. Some hoped to provide a cultural background for the new, undereducated rulers of both state and church. And some—like the patron and scribe who produced the so-called Calendar of 354—simply set out to preserve and codify local traditions. All these goals seem to have been at work in the years around 300 CE, when Eusebius, the learned bishop of Caesarea in Palestine, assembled his *Chronicle* and, a century later, when Jerome translated and adapted it in Latin. In its original form, which was widely read and adapted in eastern Christendom, this massive work contained the records of the many nations whose histories he investigated and also a long, complex table in whose parallel columns he synchronized Jewish and Near Eastern history with the histories of Greece and Rome. Eusebius knew that he could not solve all the contradictions in his records: his Egyptian and Chaldaean king lists, derived from Manetho and Berossus, respectively, stretched too far back to be accommodated to the biblical account of past time. Though he suggested that the years mentioned in some of these records had actually been lunar months, he admitted that he could not draw up a single coherent table that stretched from the Creation to his own day, and he started his second book after the Flood. Jerome avoided these problems in his version of the work by omitting the first book, and his updated adaptation became the model of chronological writing in the medieval West.

Eusebius's work was exemplary in another way. Its parallel columns vividly dramatized the providential order of history. States rose and fell, rose and fell, until they fell away and Rome became the universal empire—just in time to unify the world to hear the message of Christianity. It took special resources, and the scribes whom Eusebius had trained at Caesarea, to create this demanding, visually complex book. Jerome's version of it was endlessly copied and updated, studied and imitated. Other chronologies from this period as well—such as the Calendar of 354, with its elegant images of the toils of the months—were similarly labor-intensive—and, like the *Chronicle,* were copied and studied by Carolingian rulers. From late antiquity onward, in other words, complex, elegant, neatly executed design became a standard feature of chronological writing—one that set it apart from narrative histories and made its lessons especially accessible and its contents especially easy to commit to memory.

As late as the 6th century, scholars like the Byzantine official John Lydus could still read some of the original works of ancient chronological scholarship. But few of these works survived intact. The Christian world chronicles, however, became the models for one of the standard genres of medieval historical writing. These late-antique texts and the later works that adapted and imitated them—such as the Greek chronicle of George Syncellus (ca. 800)—preserved, in the Christian world, some of the results of Hellenistic and Roman scholarship about the past—including the vital fact that debates had raged, long before, about the exact dates of such epochal events as the fall of Troy and the founding of Rome. No encyclopedia was complete without its chronicle of events from Creation to the present.

Debates of a different kind, mostly about the proper date for celebrating Easter, spurred Christians to learn as much as they could about the motions of the sun and the moon, and to study the ancient calendars of the Jews, the Romans, and the Greeks. The desire to convert those they saw as pagans induced erudite ecclesiastics to learn about the calendars of contemporary peoples, from the Gothic north to the Islamic Mediterranean. Christian writers who dealt in depth with calendrical questions—Dionysius Exiguus in the 5th century, Bede in the 8th—knew a surprising amount about ancient calendars, as well as about the chronology of ancient kingdoms. Through the Middle Ages, texts on the computus—the ecclesiastical calendar—preserved rich and complex information about antiquity (though this literature also spread the legend that Julius Caesar had devised not the calendar he actually created for civil use in Rome, but the Julian ecclesiastical calendar as a whole). Even humble works of reference, such as bilingual glossaries and dictionaries, made clear that the ancient world had known many ways of dividing the year into months. Like chronology, the study of calendars always represented something more elaborate and demanding than a simple list of known facts.

Astronomers had their own distinctively precise ways of dealing with time. Varro was by no means the only scholar who attempted to use his data and techniques to bring a new level of precision to the study of the past. The Alexandrian chronologers Annianus and Panodorus tried, a century after Eusebius, to reconfigure his work, using the very detailed canon of Babylonian, Persian, Macedonian, and Roman rulers that circulated with Ptolemy's *Handy Tables,* and fragments of their work survived, along with fragments of Eusebius, in later Byzantine texts. In the 13th century Roger Bacon called on his contemporaries to use Ptolemy's precise intervals of years and days to fix absolute dates for the Incarnation and other axial events of Christian history.

In the 14th and 15th centuries, both Byzantine and Western scholars began to explore these ruinous realms in a newly active way. George Gemistus Pletho devised a modern version of an ancient Greek ritual calendar as part of his apparent plan to revive ancient paganism. Theodore Gaza, more modestly, did his best to reconstruct the calendar of ancient Athens—and helped inspire generations of scholars who wrote in Greek, as many did, to date their letters to one another not in June, for example, but in Hekatombaion. Cyriac of Ancona drew up a short treatise on the Roman calendar, in Greek, and encouraged what would become a massive effort to compare all ancient calendars. On 7 November 1468, so Marsilio Ficino claimed, he and other members of a Platonic academy held a banquet in honor of Plato's birthday. He had found the date in question, 7 Thargelion, in Diogenes Laertius and Plutarch, both of whom derived it from Apollodorus (Jacoby, *Fragments of the Greek Historians* 244, fr. 37). Unfortunately, when Ficino looked up Thargelion in a glossary, he consulted one whose author had set Hekatombaion, the first month of the Attic year, next to the Roman January, rather than next to June or July. This source placed the 11th month of the Attic year in the late fall rather than, as it should have, in the late spring. Ficino, accordingly, mistimed his party—making a mistake replicated by dozens of Humanists who worked out Attic dates for modern events in the same way.

In the 15th and 16th centuries, far more material was accessible on Roman chronology than on Greek. Pomponio Leto and his followers scrutinized and published epigraphic evidence on the Roman calendar. The rising demand for calendar reform—which came to a first climax during the preparations for the Lateran Council of 1513—called into being a rich literature on the structure and history of ancient calendars. Erudite polyglots such as Paul of Middelburg, Sebastian Münster, and Erasmus Oswald Schreckenfuchs collected information on the ancient calendars in a newly systematic way and tried to work out ways to convert early Greek and Roman dates to the astronomers' Egyptian calendar.

Jerome's version of Eusebius survived, in the manuscript book trade of the Humanists and in the world of print that gradually supplanted it, as both a popular source and a model for new chronicles. Printers revived and replicated all the visual devices that traditional chronologers had deployed to represent the course of time. But new questions also arose. Valla and other students of Roman history, especially Johannes Cuspinianus and Heinrich Glarean, compared the chronology of Jerome with those attested by the surviving books of Livy and the Greek historian Dionysius of Halicarnassus. Soon they realized that in this realm, too, the ancients' testimony was rarely uniform and sometimes contradictory. By the 1540s, when the fragments of the *fasti consulares,* official chronicles, were discovered in the Roman Forum, Pirro Ligorio and Michelangelo fought for the right to set them up, restored, in the Palazzo dei Conservatori on the Capitoline. Unfortunately, Michelangelo, who understood their original arrangement less well than his rival, won the contest. Learned antiquaries such as Carlo Sigonio and Onofrio Panvinio filled the gaps in the *fasti* with conjectural supplements, printed them, and surrounded the texts with massive commentaries. They debated whether such lists represented official records that deserved absolute credence or reflected the theories of individual scholars, such as Verrius Flaccus—even as some of them sold credulous clients genealogies that traced their ancestry back to the Roman republic. Chronology became both fashionable and contentious.

Gradually scholars recognized that no surviving chronicle, not even the *fasti,* could claim absolute authority. Petrus Apianus and Gerardus Mercator, Paulus Crusius and Joseph Scaliger, imitated Varro and collated the written record with the evidence of datable eclipses. By the end of the 16th century, most scholars agreed that only astronomical evidence could fix absolute dates for past events. Some radicals, such as the wonderfully named Jean du Temps, went further. He argued that most of the early recorded history of Rome deserved no credence since it must have been created retrospectively, long after the city fell to the Gauls, who would have destroyed all early records. Others, like François Baudouin, argued that oral tradition—notably the banquet songs mentioned by Cicero—might have preserved some salient details. Scaliger and many successors offered rival reconstructions of the ancient calendars, many of them equipped with tables that supposedly enabled the modern reader to convert an Attic or early Roman date into an Egyptian or Julian date. But conflict continued.

In 1606, when Joseph Scaliger published the fragments of the first book of Eusebius's *Chronicle,* he caused a scandal by printing the dynasty lists of Manetho and Berossus and insisting that they were neither forgeries nor fantasies, even though they seemed to begin before the creation of the world. Endless debates ensued, impossible to resolve without doing violence to some of the sources. Gradually scholars realized that ancient calendars could not be reconstructed with absolute precision, nor could all the key dates of ancient history be fixed to a seamless timeline. It also became clearer and clearer that it was not possible to reconcile all the ancient data with those of the Bible. The Jesuit Denis Petau, who summed up the discoveries of the Renaissance chronologers in his *De doctrina temporum* of 1627, stole Scaliger's discoveries, arranged them with far greater clarity—and made clear, as Scaliger had not, the limitations that chronological scholarship must accept.

Through the 17th and 18th centuries, new materials continued to be discovered and edited. John Selden, for example, published the earliest Greek chronicle to survive, the *Marmor Parium,* in 1628, and he equipped it with a detailed commentary. Though chronology had always had a strong visual component, Selden's publication—and the presence in Oxford of the Arundel Marbles, the collection to which the Marmor Parium inscription belonged—did much to convince scholars of the central importance of inscriptions to the field. Chronology still appealed to thinkers of great sophistication and learning: Kepler, Leibniz, Riccioli, Bianchini. New theories still took shape. Newton reframed the entire history of the world on the basis of an astronomical reading of the myth of Chiron the Centaur (and a reconstruction of his celestial sphere), causing an international scandal. Across Europe, Vico insisted that only a sophisticated understanding of the language, the prejudices, and the fears of the ancients could enable one to follow the evolution of the human race, and he found at first little interest. Yet Vico's theory implied, as he admitted, that all chronological tables were fundamentally flawed, since they embodied not facts but the ambitions and prejudices of the pagan peoples, who had known little about their own early history—an argument far more radical in substance than Newton's. Massive new treatises that offered comprehensive accounts of past time continued to roll from the presses. Debate moved slowly and often covered what was already in part old ground. When B. G. Niebuhr set out to undermine the traditional chronology of Rome, he repeated critical arguments made long before—though he used them to advance a vision of the course of early Roman history that was quite distinct from those of his predecessors.

Slowly, the limits of what the surviving sources could reveal about the outlines of ancient history were more and more firmly drawn; so too the limits of what could be understood of ancient ways of organizing the year. In a world in which scholars such as Henry Fynes Clinton and August Böckh were still familiar with ancient astronomy, and astronomers like Christian Ludwig Ideler and Friedrich Karl Ginzel could still draw on the classical learning of their schoolboy years, lively technical debates persisted on certain issues—for example, the identification of particular eclipses mentioned by historical sources. The discovery of papyri, many of them dated, at Oxyrhynchus and elsewhere gave the working calendars of ancient Egypt—Egyptian, Roman, and Alexandrian—a new interest as far more primary data became available. By the middle years of the 20th century, however, chronological scholarship in its traditional form had become the recondite preoccupation of a few particularly erudite philologists and historians, such as E. J. Bickerman and K. J. Dover.

In the past three decades scholarly interest in these fields has revived, but its emphasis has undergone a vital shift. Many classical scholars now study ancient understandings of the calendar, and even more are at work editing and interpreting the surviving chronicles and reconstructing their lost sources. But few hope to establish when Troy fell or on what dates the plays of Sophocles were first performed. They want to understand what their ancient predecessors believed about the past and the present—and to find out how those beliefs did so much to shape ancient art and literature.

BIBL.: E. J. Bickerman, *Chronology of the Ancient World,* 2nd ed. (Ithaca, N.Y., 1980). Roberto Bizzocchi, *Genealogie incredibili* (Bologna 1995). H. J. Erasmus, *The Origins of Rome in Historiography from Petrarch to Perizonius* (Assen 1962). Denis Feeney, *Caesar's Calendar* (Berkeley 2008). Anthony Grafton, *Joseph Scaliger: A Study in the History of Classical Scholarship,* vol. 2, *Historical Chronology* (Oxford 1993). Anthony Grafton and Megan Williams, *Christianity and the Transformation of the Book* (Cambridge, Mass., 2006). Frank Manuel, *Isaac Newton, Historian* (Cambridge, Mass., 1963). William McCuaig, *Carlo Sigonio* (Princeton 1989). Paolo Rossi, *The Dark Abyss of Time,* trans. Lydia Cochrane (Chicago 1984). Anna Schreurs, *Antikenbild und Kunstanschauungen des neapolitanischen Malers, Architekten und Antiquars Pirro Ligorio (1513–1583)* (Cologne 2000). Gerrit Walther, *Niebuhrs Forschung* (Stuttgart 1993). A.G.

Cameos and Gems

A gem is a precious or semiprecious stone, bearing an engraved design or inscription either in relief (cameo) or in a carved surface (intaglio).

The best gems are usually made of corundum, quartz, or jade. Cheaper media are feldspars, obsidian, amber, coral, and shells. Diamond gems, engraved from the 16th century onward, are very rare. Imitations in glass or faience have been made since antiquity.

Lenticular, cylindrical, and scarab-shaped intaglios have been found in collars, rings, and dresses from prehistoric societies and were used in many ancient civilizations. Held to be endowed with magic powers because of their optical and thermic properties, they were worn as talismans, applied as healing medicaments, and offered as votive gifts (a custom still alive in the Middle Ages). Their incised cavities also made them suitable as signets.

Inscriptions on gems may bear the name of the owner or magic formulas indicating the particular stone's use.

Animals, gods, warriors, and fighting and mythological scenes were the most common subjects. These figures shifted from propitiatory to allegorical functions, often being employed to convey personal devices. It is also interesting to note that the first coinage marks are thought to originate from authenticating seals. As a matter of fact, from the 7th century BCE onward Greek and Roman gems shared some representational aspects with contemporary coinage.

Cameos, which exploit differently colored layers in opaque stone, made their appearance around the 6th century BCE.

Gem engravers in 5th-century BCE Greece, having increased their technical ability, reached a higher social position, as testified by their signatures. The apogee of the art was attained during the Hellenistic age with Pyrgoteles (4th cent. BCE), a fact still recognized by Pliny in his *Natural History* (book 37) in the 1st century CE.

During the Middle Ages antique gems were preserved in ecclesiastical and royal treasuries or set into saints' shrines. (The most important cameos and vases surviving from antiquity are thus not to be found in archaeological excavations.) These relics from antiquity bore venerable images and imperial portraits invested with aulic (high political and juridical) connotations, which often led to their adoption as attributes of sacred and secular powers. Nevertheless, gem engraving had become very rare in the West, although it survived better in the East under the Byzantines and Sassanians. Jewelers' demands for precious stones, still significant, were better answered by reusing antique gems in new settings. Inscriptions engraved in the collets that secured a gem to its mounting often turned a pagan subject into a Christian one, adapted a signet into an appliqué, or converted a generic image into a portrait or a device of the owner.

Some 15th-century Italian dynasties (the Medici, the Barbo, the Grimani) gave a new impulse to gem collecting, reviving these venerable status symbols with new Humanistic connotations. Sulphur impressions and brass casts answered an increasing request for pendants and bookbindings *all'antica*, in the ancient style. The fashion for antique forms encouraged artists to copy ancient originals in miniatures, supellectiles (vases, luxury items, etc.), furniture, and monumental sculptures. Engravers such as Valerio Belli (1468–1546) and Giovanni Bernardi (1496–1553) and the 16th-century Milanese school brought the emulation of antique gems and cameos to incomparable heights of technical and stylistic quality.

The first effort to produce a printed work illustrating a glyptic (engraved gem) collection, launched by Battista Franco and Enea Vico in the mid-16th century, coincided with the earliest attempts to interpret the stones' iconography. Especially after the publication of Leonardo Agostini's *Figured Ancient Gems* (*Le gemme antiche figurate,* Rome 1657), studies in glyptography, closely related to numismatics, attracted a wealth of antiquarian and ethnological debate for at least two centuries, involving such personalities as Paolo Alessandro Maffei, Antonfrancesco Gori, Pierre Jean Mariette, and Johann Joachim Winckelmann. At the end of the 19th century art historians turned special attention to gems believed to reproduce lost masterpieces of antique sculpture and painting. More recently cameos and intaglios have obtained an important place in the chapter of artistic reuse and in the scholarship of the classical tradition.

BIBL.: E. Babelon, *La gravure en pierres fines* (Paris 1929). J. Boardman, *Greek Gems and Finger Rings: Early Bronze Age to Late Classical* (London 1970). C. M. Brown, ed., *Engraved Gems: Survivals and Revivals* (Washington, D.C., 1997). N. Dacos, A. Giuliano, and U. Pannuti, *Il tesoro di Lorenzo il Magnifico: Le gemme* (Florence 1973). E. Kris, *Meister und Meisterwerke der Steinschneidekunst in der Italienischen Renaissance* (Vienna 1929).

W.C.

Carpe diem

"Seize the day!" (a phrase from Horace, *Odes* 1.11.8). Horace's words are an injunction to abandon attempts to predict the future in order to savor the present; the addressee is a woman, and sexual pleasure is implicitly part of what is at stake. Later adaptations of the phrase figure in appeals to a resisting addressee (usually a woman) to accept an erotic invitation (usually the speaker's own). Horace's phrase mingles with phrases from more overtly erotic poems: Ovid's *carpite florem* ("Pluck the flower," *Ars amatoria* 3.79) makes explicit the metaphor suggested by Horace's *carpe* ("pluck"), and the pseudo-Virgilian *De rosis nascentibus* concludes with a figuration for the surrender of virginity: *collige, virgo, rosas* ("Gather roses, maiden"). The most influential poem on the topic is Catullus 5, which without any phrase analogous to Horace's serves as the most forceful development of this argument: awareness of human mortality ("the night is endless, unbroken, and must be slept out") induces a fierce sense of the urgency of sexual love ("Give me a thousand kisses, then a hundred").

The topic was widespread during the Renaissance, when it involved an obvious if rarely overt sense of resistance to Christian faith in the afterlife. *De rosis nascentibus* has a particularly clear descent: "Let us gather the fair rose of the garden" (Angelo Poliziano, *Canzoni a ballo,* before 1487); "Here we will in time gather both roses and flowers" (Gaspara Stampa, *Rime* 158, 1554), a woman writing to a male beloved; "Starting today, gather the roses of life" (Ronsard, *Sonnets pour Hélène* 2.24, 1578); "Gather ye rose-buds while ye may" (Herrick, "To the Virgins, to make much of Time," 1648). Horace's phrase is detectable in more generalized injunctions—"Therefore take the present time" (Shakespeare, *As You Like It* 5.3.30, 1599)—and in English can acquire a felicitous double meaning: "Young folks, take time while you may" (Philip Sidney, *Astrophil and Stella,* Fourth Song, ca. 1582), that is, Hurry up and slow down. Individual instances show a range of tone and decorousness; Herrick's poem is an avuncular recommendation of marriage for all young women. In some cases, the mortality that makes present pleasure urgent is not death but the lapse of female attractiveness or the inherent brevity of erotic interest itself:

> Beauty like a shadow flies,
> And our youth before us dies.
> Or, would youth and beauty stay,
> Love hath wings, and will away.
> (Edmund Waller, "To Phyllis," 1640)

On the other hand, Andrew Marvell's "To His Coy Mistress" (first published in 1681) juxtaposes a lurid vision of death as a rival lover—"worms shall try/Thy long preserved virginity"—with a ferocity in the lovemaking being urged—"tear our pleasures with rough strife/Thorough the iron gates of life"—for a memorable equivalent to Catullus.

Saul Bellow has used *Seize the Day* as the mordant title for a novella (1956) about a middle-aged man confronting the wreckage of his life. Bobby Seale put the phrase to political use in *Seize the Time* (1970), his account, written from prison, of Huey Newton and the Black Panthers. The Latin tag gained recent currency through the film *Dead Poets Society* (1989), in which a charismatic teacher cites it as the lesson of all poetry, though mainly with reference to 19th- and 20th-century examples; a Web site centered on the movie continues to propagate the message. An epigram appropriated by the American poet Jonathan Williams in a poem of his own (*In England's Green &c,* 1962) summarizes the topic with a deeper sense of literary history: "Sappho died the other day . . . /all ass is grass, so let's make hay." G.B.

Cartography

In 1569 the Jesuit José de Acosta sailed across the Atlantic to serve in his order's mission in the New World. As he crossed the equator, he found that he was cold. The experience surprised and amused him. As a well-educated modern traveler, Acosta knew both how to trace his own progress on a map of the world and what to expect, in terms of climate, from each region he entered. In Europe his professors had taught him, following Aristotle, that the equator bisected a larger torrid zone, an area that the sun's heat made uninhabitable. Acosta could not help laughing, he told readers of his *Natural and Moral History of the Indies* (1590), to think of the teachers solemnly spreading ancient misinformation to their eager pupils.

Yet though Acosta made clear that modern experience trumped ancient authority in this case, he also acknowledged that the ancients had disagreed about the habitability of the torrid zone. Ptolemy, the greatest ancient geographer and cartographer and a formidable Aristotelian in his own right, thought it might be possible to live near the equator. The experience of sailing to the New World, in short, did not rid Acosta of his respect for all ancient authorities in the realm of geography and cartography. Rather, it taught him that he could use empirical evidence to distinguish between authorities that made valid claims and those that did not. Acosta's response to the ancient cartographical tradition was typical of the larger experience of Europeans in the Renaissance. For they found themselves the first learned men in almost 1,000 years to confront the complex and varied traditions of ancient cartography, and as they attacked this rich body of theories and data, technical instructions and complex images, they found in it not only inherited mistakes, but also some of the tools with which they corrected these and some of the inspiration to do so.

The history of cartography in antiquity was complex, and its legacy reflected that. Formal cartography began in the Near Eastern monarchies of Babylon and Egypt, but the earliest maps known to Westerners until recently were those sketched by Anaximander (6th cent. BCE) and other early Greek thinkers, most of whom took the inhabited world as circular and represented it as surrounded by ocean. Later, more detailed maps called these early schemata into question. Herodotus (5th cent. BCE) made fun of the traditional image of a round *oikumenē,* though instead of offering a full replacement he modestly confessed his inability to offer detailed maps of the north and west parts of the inhabited world. By the 5th and 4th centuries BCE, maps and globes—the latter representing both the heavens and the Earth—had become commonplace enough in Greece that Athenians studied them en masse as they discussed the wisdom of dispatching the Sicilian expedition.

Formal cartography really took shape, however, in the time of Alexander (d. 323 BCE) and his successors. Qualitative images of the Earth's surface—such as Aristotle's influential scheme of frigid, temperate, and torrid zones—still circulated. But Alexander's expeditions acquainted Greeks with a vast range of lands previously unknown to them. As streams of information flowed into the new Alexandrian library, scholars and natural philosophers—above all Eratosthenes (d. ca. 195 BCE)—searched for rigorous ways to measure the actual distances that separated major cities. Eratosthenes was very likely the first to set out a map with a full system of coordinates and to locate places on it precisely. The astronomer Hipparchus and the geographer Marinus of Tyre, who worked in Rhodes and elsewhere in the late 1st and early 2nd centuries CE, improved maps in vital ways. Marinus devised a form of projection and assigned two coordinates, a longitude and latitude, to every place he attempted to locate on a cartographic grid. He also collected a vast amount of information and used it to draw up his maps. But much is still unknown. The only formal map that survives from this period is a partial map of Iberia in the *Geography* of Artemidorus of Ephesus, preserved on a papyrus roll that has become the object of intense study since 2006, when it went on exhibit in Turin. Distinguished specialists disagree sharply about its status. Map and text alike have been denounced as a product of the 19th-century forger

Constantine Simonides. Though most specialists hold that the work is authentic, the relation of the map to the text remains entirely unclear, as does the identity of the landscape of rivers, towers, and buildings that it represents (which was originally identified, wrongly, with Iberia). The duration and complexity of this debate both suggest how obscure substantial segments of the history of cartography remain.

Ptolemy, who made datable observations in Alexandria in the middle of the 2nd century CE, produced a massive compendium, the *Geography*. It defined the discipline, offered a critique of the methods of his predecessors, described and explained a number of different map projections, and listed 8,000 places with their longitudes and latitudes, as well as qualitative information about their climates, resources, and inhabitants. Most of this material came, by his own testimony, from Marinus. Ptolemy regularly criticized his predecessor. In particular, he insisted that Marinus had made the inhabited landmass of the world longer than it really was; Ptolemy held that the whole *oikumenē* was only 180 degrees in longitude. But his instructions for the 26 regional maps meant to accompany the *Geography* adapted Marinus's cylindrical projection.

At the core, Ptolemy's approach to geography was quantitative and cartographical. He worked extensively on astronomy, instruments for measurement, and methods of projection, and much of what he wrote bore on technical problems in geography and cartography. In the *Geography*, accordingly, Ptolemy analyzed the possible forms of cartography in detail. He made clear that maps could be drawn either on globes or on flat surfaces. The latter, moreover, could be drawn in accordance with various geometrical schemes—each of which had disadvantages as well as advantages. His work offered admirably clear instructions on how to put these principles into cartographic practice.

Specialists disagree as to whether Ptolemy's original work contained a set of maps that represented the world as a whole and of individual lands from Europe to Taprobane, as Renaissance manuscripts and editions of it do. The Byzantine scholars who put the *Geography* back into circulation found copies equipped with maps that they regarded as ancient. A note transmitted in certain manuscripts tells us that an Alexandrian engineer named Agathodaimon drew up one or more maps, but this could have happened in the age of Ptolemy or centuries later. No ancient Ptolemaic map survives. But scholia in some copies offer practical directions for the form and content of particular maps, and some late antique and early medieval writers refer to the work in very suggestive terms. In the sixth century, Cassiodorus praised Ptolemy for "representing all places so vividly that it seems as if he inhabited every region at once" (*Institutiones* 1.25). It seems highly likely that the original *Geography* was illustrated and certain that with Ptolemy's work, ancient cartography reached its technical peak.

In many other complex disciplines—including astronomy and music, Ptolemy's other central fields of interest—core texts dictated the later history of the field. The *Geography*, however, was a large, densely technical work and had no clear place in formal education. Accordingly, though Ptolemy's work was copied and occasionally annotated and other cartographical projects continued to be undertaken, his model seems to have inspired relatively little imitation. In the Roman world, interest in cartography had burgeoned as the city's empire grew, and military experience created a rich body of information about roads and territories. Well before Marinus or Ptolemy, Marcus Vipsanius Agrippa planned to use this material to "make a spectacle of the world for the city of Rome" in a portico near his house on the Quirinal. Left incomplete at his death, this massive project was finished by Augustus. Under the emperors, new forms of cartography took shape: severely practical ones, for the most part, either in the form of collected route maps, as used by the army and the administration, or in that of instructions and model maps for surveyors. Ptolemy drew on this material, but it nourished other forms of mapping as well. Under Severus, early in the 3rd cent., a great plan of the entire city of Rome, 13 by 18 meters in size and carved on 160 separate pieces of marble, was set up in the Temple of Peace. The Christian writer Eusebius drew on Roman practical maps and itineraries when he wrote his book about the geography of Palestine, which was accompanied by a map of some sort, now lost.

In the philosophical and literary tradition, as time passed, cartography became more a matter of schemata than of technical methods and empirical evidence. In the late antique heyday of encyclopedism, maps of the world, which laid out lands and oceans with only approximate regard to sizes and distances, illustrated the views of Macrobius (who saw the inhabited world as a body of land in the Northern Hemisphere, surrounded by water and separated by it from the Antipodes in the southern hemisphere). Probably in the same period, Christian scholars devised the very influential T-O schema, a formalized representation of the three known continents, Europe, Asia, and Africa, described in the *Etymologies* (14.4) of Isidore of Seville (7th cent.). He and other Christian cosmographers introduced Paradise and Jerusalem—the situation of the former varying widely, as the cartographer's imagination dictated—into these world maps, which found their way, as illustrations, into the works of Macrobius, Sallust, and other pagan writers.

For centuries few other maps seem to have been drawn in Byzantium or the Latin West—and most of those were not made according to the ancient models. No one could have sorted out the mysteries of the discipline's development, even to the extent that readers of Aristotle could follow, through the distorting lens of his polemical accounts, the development of mathematics or metaphysics. Even the scholarly 10th-century emperor Constantine Porphyrogenitos, whose overview of the administration of the Byzantine empire took account of its larger ancient size as well as its reduced format that time, does not seem to have tried to revive formal cartographic methods, though they could have helped to impose visual order and clarity on the masses of political and ethnographic information that he collected in textual form.

Muslim writers, by contrast, regularly mentioned and cited the *Geography.* Tradition holds that Ptolemy's work reached the Islamic world under caliph al-Mā'mūn, early in the 9th cent. CE, and was translated a few decades later by al-Kindī or Thābit ibn Qurra. Many Islamic scholars read the book as a whole, and experts on the exact sciences, like the astronomer al-Battānī and the ethnographer and historian al-Bīrūnī, used his work both to draw up maps and to compose lists of places with latitudes and longitudes. Although Ptolemy's detailed, analytical discussion of his different methods of projection was not translated, Islamic cartographers drew heavily on his work, using his methods even when they applied them in a different way or disagreed with his conclusions—as several of them did when they argued that his maps made the Mediterranean far too long from east to west. His work served as one model for the Balkhi school of cartographers in the 10th and 11th centuries and was still used by al-Idrisi, an Arab geographer who belonged to the court of Roger II of Sicily in the 12th century. His depictions of the course of the Nile and much else remained standard in Islamic cartography for centuries.

In the medieval West, libraries preserved the practical cartography of the Romans. As late as the 13th century, a monk in Colmar copied, on a parchment scroll, a schematic map of the Roman Empire now known, from a Renaissance owner, as the *Tabula Peutingeriana.* He probably followed a late antique original, based on official itineraries, which derived in turn from Augustan prototypes such as Agrippa's map in Rome, as he drew up his striking, elongated image of the Roman world. But the new forms of practical mapmaking that took shape in the Middle Ages—such as the portolan charts developed by Mediterranean navigators, which used a schematic cartography to show sailors how to find their way from one port to the next—did so without using ancient sources and methods. The often contradictory schemata of Macrobius and Orosius, Aristotle and Isidore, continued to circulate. They appeared again and again in manuscript illuminations and then, as script slowly yielded to print, in woodcuts. But even the splendid *mappae mundi,* or great world maps, drawn up in the 12th and 13th centuries, with their detailed and vivid illustrations of marvels and monstrous races, did not substantively reflect Ptolemy's effort to minimize the necessary distortions of cartography by treating it as a rigorous, quantitative field.

The *Geography* came back to life in Palaeologan Byzantium—a world in which scholars regularly combined an intense devotion to ancient literature and rhetoric with a serious interest in highly technical subjects, while emperors engaged in wars and negotiations with outside powers of every kind, from Latin Christendom to the Ottomans and Mongols. A number of Greek manuscripts of the texts date to around 1300. They probably owed their creation to Maximus Planudes (ca. 1255–1305), who recorded his discovery "through many toils of the *Geography,* which had disappeared for many years." Planudes did more than recover the text. He examined and collated multiple manuscripts, in particular one that he described as both very old and very splendid. It seems likely that his reconstruction of the maps in what he called Ptolemy's "Great work of wonder" derived from this, presumably late antique, original.

By the early 15th century numerous copies of the Greek text of the *Geography* were in circulation, some of them large, physically splendid, and equipped with a full set of maps. Among those who studied the work with special zeal were Manuel Chrysoloras, the scholar whose pioneering lectures, held in Florence 1397–1400, introduced several influential scholars to the study of Greek, and George Gemisthos Pletho, the Platonic prophet of Mistra, whose studies helped inspire Bessarion and Ficino with their passion for the Platonic tradition. Cyriac of Ancona, the greatest of the early Italian antiquaries, spent the winter of 1447–1448 in Mistra, where he learned from Pletho to compare Strabo's prose account of the *oikumenē* with Ptolemy's text and maps. More important, Chrysoloras himself saw the interest of Ptolemy's book and began to translate it into Latin. The Tuscan scholar Jacopo d'Angelo, a papal secretary who became one of Chrysoloras' first pupils, produced a complete Latin version by 1410. Later —so the Florentine bookseller Vespasiano da Bisticci tells us—maps were added, transforming the book into a colorful Latin atlas. Patrick Dalché is very likely correct when he suggests that the Florentine bibliophile Niccolò Niccoli—book collector, antiquarian, calligrapher, student of ancient sites, and connoisseur of ancient art—played a major role in this process.

The Latin *Geography* became a bestseller. Connoisseurs of beautiful books, like Cosimo de' Medici and Poggio Bracciolini, enjoyed inspecting particularly handsome copies of the work—such as those produced, with attractive schematic maps of Rome and other cities in addition to the standard Ptolemaic maps, in the atelier of Pietro del Massaio after 1460. The vogue for Ptolemy's atlas even attracted satire. Leon Battista Alberti argued, in a mock encomium of the fly, that Ptolemy had modeled the maps in the *Geography* on the beautiful, multicolored wings of the fly. He was right to suggest that many readers could appreciate the beauty of the maps better than their technical qualities. In the early decades of the 15th century, Humanists often treated Ptolemy's maps as an authority not to be questioned, a source of indisputably accurate information—though Alberti himself drew on Ptolemy in a more consequential way when he constructed his own method for mapping Rome using a polar coordinate system. His *Descriptio urbis Romae* applied Ptolemy's methods on a microscopic scale—and, like the *Geography,* showed as much concern for teaching techniques as for recording data. But one should not exaggerate the impact of Ptolemy's work on Alberti and his contemporaries. No clear evidence supports the theory, put forward by some

Adam, Robert (1)

When the Adam brothers designed the block of unified **Neoclassical** terrace houses known as the Adelphi Buildings, overlooking the river Thames, their sources of inspiration were antique spatial forms and the ornamental vocabulary of classical motifs. Particularly remarkable is the influence of Diocletian's **Palace** in Dalmatia, which Robert Adam had the opportunity to visit and survey extensively on his return trip from Italy to Britain in 1757.

Adonis (2)

The story of **Aphrodite** and Adonis usually focuses on the goddess's grief at her mortal beloved's death while hunting a boar sent by the vengeful Artemis. Titian's reworking of the myth stresses the role of the youth as author of his own ruin when he leaves the safe embrace of Aphrodite to run toward the quirks of Fate, in the risky adventure of the hunt. **Cupid**, still asleep and unaware of Adonis' parting, remains powerless and cannot prevent the tragic choice.

1 Robert and James Adam, Adelphi Buildings, London, 18th century.

2 Titian, *Venus and Adonis*, 1553.

3 Gian Lorenzo Bernini, *Aeneas and Anchises*, 1618–1619.

Aeneas (3)

The story of Aeneas' flight from burning Troy, as told by **Virgil** and often represented in Roman art, inspired Gian Lorenzo Bernini to design an extremely complex composition, with the hero supporting his elderly father, Anchises, on his shoulder and followed by his child Ascanius, who carries the rescued household gods. This marble group demonstrates extraordinary technical virtuosity in the way that it carefully differentiates the velvety softness of the child's complexion, the powerful musculature of Aeneas, and the wrinkled skin of the eldest fugitive.

Ajax (4)

One of the favorite themes in the story of Ajax has always been his heroic deeds in the war with Troy, where he proved himself the strongest Greek fighter after **Achilles**. Red-figure vase paintings inspired the style of this lithographic print that depicts the well-known episode in which Ajax valiantly mounted resistance against the Trojans, who were attacking the Greek fleet. His enormous size made him a target for many enemy lances and arrows while he defended the ships until the timely arrival of additional Greek troops.

4 John Flaxman, *Ajax defends Greek ships against the Trojans*, 20th century.

5 Leon Battista Alberti, Basilica of S. Andrea, Mantua, Italy.

Alberti (5)

Leon Battista Alberti's knowledge encompassed a broad range of subjects; above all, he studied the ancient ways of building and city planning, gathering information from both the extant ruins of Rome and a wide array of Greek and Latin texts. His Basilica of S. Andrea in Mantua is a significant example of Alberti's architectural principles, with its facade based on the elaboration of the **triumphal arch** motif (following a scheme that has been linked to the Arch of Titus) and its internal barrel vault likely modeled on the Basilica of Maxentius in Rome.

6 Frederic Leighton, *Hercules Wrestling with Death for the Body of Alcestis,* ca. 1869–1871.

Alcestis (6)

Among all the Greek myths, that of Alcestis was unique in staging a beneficent thaumaturgy of love: not only is the heroine willing to sacrifice her own life to prolong that of her husband, Admetus, but a happy ending is assured by the intervention of **Hercules**, whose victory over Thanatos, the god of death, brings Alcestis back to life. All the protagonists are depicted in Lord Leighton's painting, in which the composition is organized around Alcestis on her deathbed. Her dignified expression is in marked contrast with the desperate grief of her husband and her maidens, as well as with the fight raging between her savior and Thanatos.

7 Anonymous, *The Arch of Einhard,* 17th century.

Alcuin (7)

One of the most prominent intellectuals in Charlemagne's circle, Alcuin advocated the proper use of the classical heritage through an interpretation of heathen values in Christian terms. A comparable philosophy was visualized on a monument, unfortunately lost, of which only later anonymous drawings exist: the silver base of an altar cross given to the monastery of St. Servatius in Maastricht by Einhard, another scholar belonging to Charlemagne's court. The base imitated the form and architecture of a Roman **triumphal arch** and is decorated with personifications drawn from the ancient repertoire to embody Christian concepts.

8 Pantaleone, *Alexander the Great on a Chariot Supported by Griffins,* 1163–1165.

9 Giulio Romano, *Zeus Approaches Olympias in the Form of a Snake,* ca. 1526–1535.

10 Jean Auguste Dominique Ingres, *Napoleon on His Imperial Throne,* 1806.

Alexander the Great (8–10)

The story and image of Alexander enjoyed widespread popularity throughout the Middle Ages and modernity. The legend of his ascent to heaven, handed down by a long tradition, came to embody a precise set of political and ideological meanings. Under **Byzantine** rule, Alexander's celestial journey was invoked as an archetype of the cosmocratic power of the emperor. In Western Europe, however, this story was constantly freighted with a negative moral judgment and interpreted as an insolent attempt to emulate the power of God. Images of Alexander's flight were remarkably widespread in Norman southern Italy; the best known and oldest preserved example is Pantaleone's mosaic in the floor of the cathedral in Otranto. In territories controlled by the Normans, who were involved in a struggle with the Greeks, depictions of Alexander carried to the sky by griffins became a symbol of the arrogance of Byzantine imperial authority. Another famous legend relates to Alexander's birth. Giulio Romano's painting shows the entire episode, with Jupiter-Ammon, in the shape of a snake, seducing the queen, Olympias, while Alexander's putative father, Philip, is blinded by a divine thunderbolt. Since antiquity, Alexander has remained an ideal prototype for kings and emperors who often shaped their images after his. For example, Ingres's portrait of Napoleon as a world ruler was influenced by a fresco that had recently been found under the ashes of **Pompeii,** in which Alexander is depicted in the pose and with the attributes of Jupiter's sovereignty.

11 Johann Bernhard Fischer von Erlach, *Lighthouse at Alexandria,* 1721.

12 Peter Paul Rubens, *The Battle of the Amazons,* ca. 1615.

13 Eugene Guillaume, *Anacreon,* 1851.

Alexandria (11)

Founded by **Alexander the Great** on the Nile delta, Alexandria owed its millennial reputation as a center of learning to its famous library and *Mouseion.* Its lighthouse, called Pharos after the name of the tiny island where it stood, was equally interesting to posterity. The lighthouse has been deemed one of the **Seven Wonders of the World** since its construction at the end of the 3rd century BCE.

Amazons (12)

In ancient myth, Amazons were a race of warrior women whose homeland was variously situated at the edge of the known world. A tale such as the one about the battle by the river Thermodon between the Amazons and Theseus' Athenians allowed the young **Rubens** to show the full impetuosity of his talent. In *The Battle of the Amazons,* Rubens staged a whirlwind composition in which men, women, and horses charge into a tumultuous frontal attack.

Anacreon (13)

Only a few dozen fragments of the work of the Greek lyric poet Anacreon survive, and his fame is tightly connected to his drinking songs and hymns. Anacreon's purportedly hedonistic view of life is the central feature of Eugene Guillaume's marble portrait of the poet, who appears confident in his relaxed posture and concentrated on the cup full of wine that he raises above his head.

14 Giorgione, *Sleeping Venus,* ca. 1509–1510.

15 Antonio Canova, *Perseus,* ca. 1800.

16 Giulio Romano, *Wedding Banquet of Psyche and Cupid.*

Aphrodite (14)

Giorgione's *Sleeping Venus* interprets the classical symbol of love, desire, and ideal feminine beauty with revolutionary novelty. While the viewer is allured into a close inspection of her exposed nudity, the goddess remains absent in her sleep, inaccessible in her lack of any conscious expression. Her raised arm, which allows a full view of her breasts, and the placement of her left hand on her groin underline the erotic implications of the scene, portraying not only Venus' beauty but also her sensual nature.

Apollo (15)

The role of Apollo in classical imagery became even more prominent beginning at the end of the 15th century, owing to the major impact made by the discovery of the **Apollo Belvedere.** The influence of this statue was enormous, particularly during the 18th century when **Neoclassicists** considered it a model of stylistic perfection and the very embodiment of classical aesthetic ideals. The Perseus carved by Antonio Canova holds up the severed head of Medusa in a pose recalling the attitude of the Apollo Belvedere so vividly that its first version was acquired by Pope Pius VII as a replacement for the Apollo itself, which Napoleon had removed from the Vatican.

Apuleius (16)

In **Renaissance** painting, the story of Psyche's romance with **Cupid** enjoyed more popularity than any other tale by Apuleius. For a banquet hall in Palazzo Te, in Mantua, Giulio Romano chose to represent this myth in its full length. From the uncommon relationship between the two lovers, the narration goes on to the discovery of Cupid and to Psyche's repentance, culminating in the magnificent scene of their wedding banquet.

17 Diego Rodriguez Velazquez, *The Spinners,* ca. 1657.

Arachne (17)

According to the narrative of **Ovid's** *Metamorphoses,* Arachne was a famous weaver who presumed to challenge Athena to a competition that eventually led to a tragic outcome when the enraged goddess turned the conceited human into a spider. This tale inspired one of Velazquez's most interesting paintings, *The Spinners,* which suggests a many-layered interpretation and plays skillfully on the ancient myth's contemporary significance regarding the nature of art and the multifold rivalry between creation and imitation, divine and human, master and pupil.

18 *Atlas Holding up the World,* Hellenistic sculpture, 2nd century.

Atlas (18, 19)

In Greek mythology, the Titan Atlas was sentenced to support the heavens for eternity as a punishment for having participated in the unsuccessful revolt against the Olympian gods. The most famous ancient representation of this legend is a 2nd century CE Roman copy of a Hellenistic sculpture of Atlas kneeling under the weight of the celestial globe on his shoulders, known as the Farnese Atlas. Modern reception of the myth often replaced the ideas of effort, exertion, and hopeless damnation found in the original story with those of strength and stability, as suggested by the Farnese statue. Such is the message of the Art Deco **bronze** Atlas in front of Rockefeller Center in midtown Manhattan who enthusiastically holds up the celestial globe with his powerful muscles.

19 Lee Lawrie, *Atlas,* 1937.

20 Giovanni Bellini and Titian, *The Feast of the Gods,* ca. 1514/1529.

21 "Roman citizens" enjoy an end of term party at Goldsmiths College, London, 1948.

22 *Barberini Faun,* ca. 220 BCE.

Bacchanalia and Saturnalia (20, 21)

The Bacchanalia festival in honor of **Dionysus,** the god of wine, was originally confined to women and involved drinking, dancing, masks, and a procession in which an ithyphallic image of the god was pushed along on a ship on wheels. **Ovid's** *Fasti,* a poem about ancient Roman rites and their origins, provided the inspiration for Giovanni Bellini and Titian's painting. In this canvas, gods, nymphs, and other creatures of Dionysus' circle enjoy the delights of a feast in the countryside. Literary accounts and images of Bacchanalia inspired endless revivals, with more or less accurate re-creations of ancient costumes and historical settings. So-called toga parties became part of popular culture during the 20th century, as shown by this picture of a group of "Roman citizens" enjoying the end of term party at Goldsmiths College in London in 1948.

Barberini Faun (22)

A Roman copy after a Hellenistic original dated around 220 BCE, this statue depicts a sleeping satyr, seated on a boulder, with his right arm raised above his head and his legs splayed. Its impudent pose, uncouth expression, and ostentatious nudity have turned the Barberini Faun into an icon of drunkenness and erotic abandon in both artistic production and mass communication.

23 *The Basilisk of Magdeburg*, 1549.

24 Princeton University Library MS Garrett 158 (Marcanova), fol. 7v: Rome. Baths of Diocletian, ca. 1470.

Basilisk (23)

Ancient legends on a snake with this name excited later imaginations to the point that the basilisk was turned into a gigantic, poisonous being with the combined shapes of a reptile and a rooster. During the Middle Ages, it was commonly believed that basilisks could be found throughout Europe. A dramatic sighting was reported in 1548 in the German town of Magdeburg, where the beast was alleged to have killed several men.

Baths (24, 25)

To the Romans, bathing in public was an essential part of everyday life, for relaxation and social interaction as much as for the obvious purpose of hygiene. Ancient writings on the medical use of bathing continued to be widely copied during the Middle Ages. At the same time, the monumental remains of imperial public baths in Rome fascinated those who saw them. The baths also became a source of high-quality architectural ***spolia*** for new buildings such as this capital, originally from the Baths of Caracalla, that was reused in the construction of the cathedral in Pisa, which was initiated in 1064.

25 A capital of the cathedral in Pisa that was taken from the Baths of Caracalla

26 Benvenuto Cellini, *Perseus with the Head of Medusa,* 1545–1554.

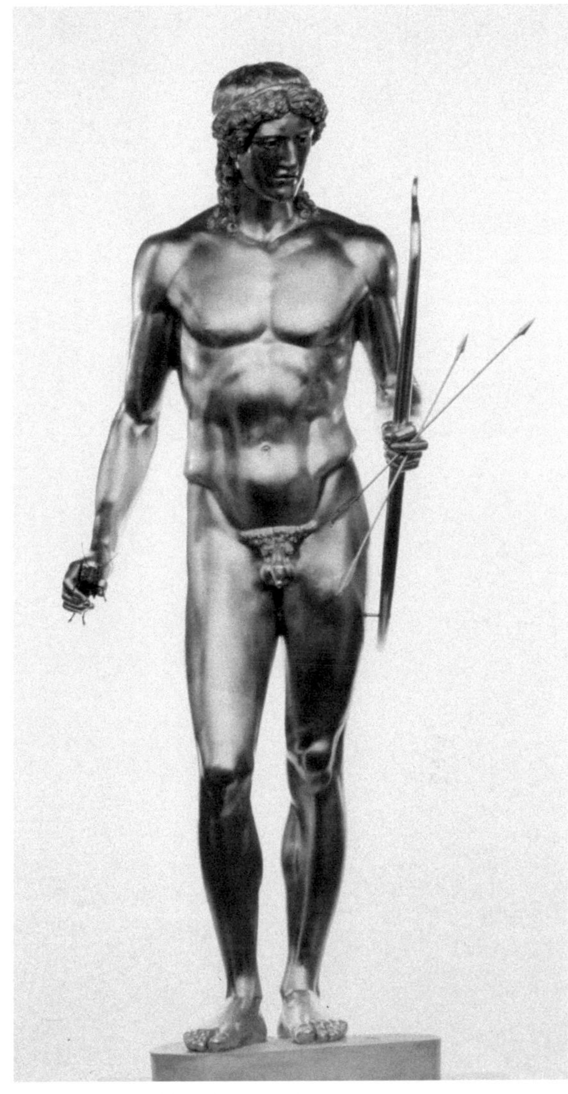

27 The *Apollo of Kassel,* bronze-colored cast of a Roman copy after a 5th century BCE original.

Bronze (26, 27)

Phidias is one of the most celebrated classical artists mentioned by Greek and Roman sources. Bronze-colored casts have often been employed to re-create the effect of his statues, which we know only through later **replicas** like the *Apollo of Kassel.* Benvenuto Cellini's *Perseus with the Head of Medusa* is one of the most striking examples of the growing interest in ancient bronze statuary and its technique during the **Renaissance.** In his accounts, Cellini describes the atmosphere of tension and uncertainty that accompanied his virtuoso attempt at casting the bronze Perseus using a single large mold.

28 The *Capitoline Brutus,* 4th–3rd century BCE.

29 Caryatids at St. Pancras Parish Church, London, 1819–1822.

Brutus (28)

Marcus Junius Brutus, the most famous of **Caesar's** assassins, belonged to a family which claimed as an ancestor Lucius Junius Brutus, the mythical founder of the Roman Republic. In the 1st century CE, Marcus Brutus issued inscribed silver coins that bore the image of Lucius Brutus on one side. The features of a bronze portrait bust known from the 16th century resembled those on the coins, thus suggesting a fictional identification with the Father of the Republic. This statue therefore became known as "Brutus Capitolinus," and its stern expression was thought to symbolize the virtues of ancient Rome. Soon after the outbreak of the **French Revolution,** Jacques-Louis David took inspiration from the Capitoline bust for the image of the Roman leader in his *The Lictors Bring to Brutus the Bodies of His Sons.* According to legend, Brutus had to order the death of his sons in order to avert their attempt to overthrow the new republican government and restore the monarchy. Obviously, the story was a **republican** symbol, and **David's** painting thus had powerful meaning at that time in France.

Caryatid (29)

In the early 19th century, Lord **Elgin** had one of the sculptures from the southern porch of the Erechteion in **Athens** removed and transported to London where it became accessible to a wider audience. The effect of this sculpture on public taste in art was nearly immediate, and only a few years later a row of caryatids, restrained in an accurate Greek form, made its appearance on the porch of St. Pancras Parish Church in London, designed by William and Henry Inwood (1819–1822).

Castor and Pollux (30)

According to the *Mirabilia Urbis Romae,* two colossal statues of horse tamers were already extant on the Quirinal by the mid-12th century and were counted among the major sights in Rome at that time. In 1589, Domenico Fontana incorporated these antique statues into Pope Sixtus V's remodeling of the Piazza del Quirinale in Rome. The youths were interpreted as the Dioscuri, mythical twins and a symbol of heroic concord. The high esteem accorded to these sculptures was closely connected with their fictional attribution to two famous Greek masters, Phidias and Praxiteles, as indicated by two inscriptions carved on the bases.

30 Obelisk with the Dioscuri.

31 Sandro Botticelli, *Pallas and the Centaur,* ca. 1480–1489.

32 Visitation with the Prophet Daniel, North Portal, Chartres Cathedral, ca. 1220.

Centaur (31)

The animal component of these mythical creatures, which feature a human head and torso above the body of a horse, has fascinated artists and writers from antiquity to the present day. In his painting *Pallas and the Centaur,* Botticelli stages an **allegory** of virtue, victorious over sensuality through the use of reason, depicting a wicked centaur who has trespassed on forbidden territory and is being brought under control by the armed Pallas.

Chartres (32)

The cathedral school at Chartres played a crucial role in the transmission of classical culture, in particular for the **Platonic** tradition. It rose to great prominence in the first half of the 12th century, when, under Bernard of Chartres, it became one of the foremost educational centers in Europe. Classical styles and subjects provided important sources of inspiration for the rich sculptural program that embellishes the cathedral of Chartres. In the voussoirs of the Royal Portal, **Aristotle, Cicero, Euclid, Pythagoras, Boethius, Ptolemy,** and **Donatus** (or Priscian) are represented as the founding authorities over which stand the Seven **Liberal Arts** (dialectics, **rhetoric,** geometry, arithmetic, **astronomy, grammar,** and **music**).

33 Elizabeth Taylor in her role as Cleopatra, 1963.

34 Sebiastiano del Piombo, *Polyphemus,* 1511.

Cleopatra (33)

Cleopatra VII Philopator, daughter of Ptolemy XII, became joint ruler of **Egypt** with her brother Ptolemy XIII in 51 BCE. Her alliances with **Julius Caesar** and Mark Antony, her defeat by Octavian at Actium, and her subsequent **suicide** not only became cornerstones of the founding myth of the Roman Empire but also rendered the queen a millennial symbol of irresistible charm, seduction, and the flaunting of conventions. Since the 1960s, the face of Cleopatra has been visualized as that of Elizabeth Taylor, who played the title role in the 1963 film directed by Joseph L. Mankiewicz.

Cyclops (34)

For his Villa Farnesina in Rome, Agostino Chigi commissioned the artists Sebastiano del Piombo and **Raphael** to create two frescoes depicting the Roman myth of **Galatea** (see **62**), a beautiful Nereid, and Polyphemus, the Cyclops she rejected. The image of Polyphemus, painted by Sebastiano, is the very antithesis of ideal beauty and stands in striking contrast to his graceful beloved as portrayed by Raphael on the adjacent panel.

35 Correggio, *Danaë,* 1531–1532.

36 Correggio, *Leda and the Swan,* 1531–1532.

37 Correggio, *The Abduction of Ganymede,* 1531–1532.

38 Correggio, *Jupiter and Io,* 1531–1532.

Danaë, Ganymede, Leda (35–38)

Ovid's tales about the metamorphic Loves of Jupiter became the source of inspiration for a famous set of canvases painted by Antonio Allegri (better known as Correggio) in 1531–1532, under the patronage of Frederick II Gonzaga of Mantua. Seduction and sensuality are notable themes of all four paintings, which depict, in turn, Danaë receiving the golden shower, **Leda** and the swan, the abduction of **Ganymede,** and the passionate embrace between and Io and the cloud. The erotic overtone emerges vividly in the image of Leda's love with the divine swan, as well as in the scene of Io. In the latter, attention is conspicuously drawn to the woman's sensual body and her erotic rapture as she is seized by an immaterial lover.

39 Louis Hersent, *Daphnis and Chloe*, 1817.

Daphnis (39)

Daphnis is the mythological model shepherd of Graeco-Roman pastoral poetry and the protagonist of Longus' pastoral romance in which he happily loves a neighboring shepherdess named Chloe, despite his poverty and the various misadventures that threaten their union. This canvas by Louis Hersent retains all the lightness, merriness, and erotic allusiveness of the ancient sentimental novel.

40 Jacques-Louis David, *The Oath of the Horatii,* ca. 1784.

David, Jacques-Louis (40)

On his return from Rome, David inaugurated a series of historical paintings based on classical subjects that electrified his contemporaries. Among the most famous is *The Oath of the Horatii,* in which an episode from Rome's ancient history becomes, on the eve of the **French Revolution,** the source of inspiration for a vivid depiction of political concepts. The unanimous determination of all three sons, swearing their oath in compliance with their father, is a powerful embodiment of the **republican** ideal of the general will.

41 Sarcophagus depicting the Rape of Persephone, Roman, 2nd century CE.

42 Rembrandt, *The Rape of Persephone,* 1632.

Demeter and Persephone (41, 42)

The heart of their myth is the violent seizing of Persephone by Hades, lord of the underworld, who made her his queen. Demeter, goddess of harvest and fertility, fought desperately to rescue her daughter. The struggle was eventually resolved when Persephone was restored to life on earth for part of each year, but during the rest of the year she rules in her new realm. This eschatological **allegory** was particularly celebrated in Roman funerary art, as illustrated by several **sarcophagi** depicting the story. Modern imagery privileged the highly emotional content of the abduction, which emerges with striking evidence in a painting by Rembrandt.

43 William Blake, *The Ancient of Days*, 1794.

Demiurge (43)

Demiurge is a term for a deity or divine artisan responsible for the creation of the physical universe, a character which figures prominently in **Plato's** mythical account of the world's creation in the *Timaeus*. The revival of the ancient Gnostic notion of an evil Demiurge has had a remarkable role in Romantic and modern literature. For example, William Blake's prophetic books, beginning with *The Book of Urizen* (1794), call on man's revolutionary spirit to rise up and dethrone Urizen, the old and evil Demiurge, symbol of the tyrannical power of alienated reason.

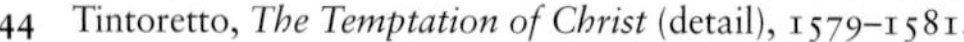

44 Tintoretto, *The Temptation of Christ* (detail), 1579–1581.

45 Jan Saenredam, *Marriage for Wealth Officiated by the Devil,* 1595.

Devil (44, 45)

In the painting by Tintoretto, Christ in the desert is tempted by gluttony and lust, proffered by a young and handsome devil who is unsuccessfully disguised with wings and the appearance of an angel. More often though, modern interpretations of the Devil draw from the classical imagery of **Dionysus'** hybrid followers: **Pan, fauns,** and satyrs. Based on a grotesque conflation of their features, the Devil came to develop a highly recognizable set of characteristics such as goat-like ears and horns, cloven hooves, a goat's tail, and a hairy lower body.

Dialogue (46)

As a literary genre, dialogue had its origins in the conversations of **Socrates,** whose pupils **Plato** and **Xenophon** wrote works in which philosophical topics are debated in a fictional historical setting. Among Plato's dialogues, the one that is best known in popular culture is probably the *Symposium* and, within it, the scenes centered around the obviously attractive character of Alcibiades. In this 19th century painting by Anselm Feuerbach, conversation ceases at the entrance of the late arrival Alcibiades, and the tragedian Agathon welcomes him into his house. Alcibiades is portrayed according to the classical model for the drunken **Dionysus.**

Dilettanti, Society of (47)

The Dilettanti Society was founded as a London dining club by a group of noblemen and gentlemen who had been on the **Grand Tour** and wished to encourage the study of ancient art at home. The expeditions, collections, and publications of these 18th century connoisseurs laid the groundwork for the **Neoclassical** revival and for the scholarly study of Graeco-Roman antiquity. Sir Joshua Reynolds, who painted a portrait of some of the society's members during a meeting, was himself a Dilettante.

46 Anselm Feuerbach, *Plato's Symposium,* 1869.

47 *Meeting of the Society of Dilettanti,* engraving after Sir Joshua Reynolds, dated 1777–1778.

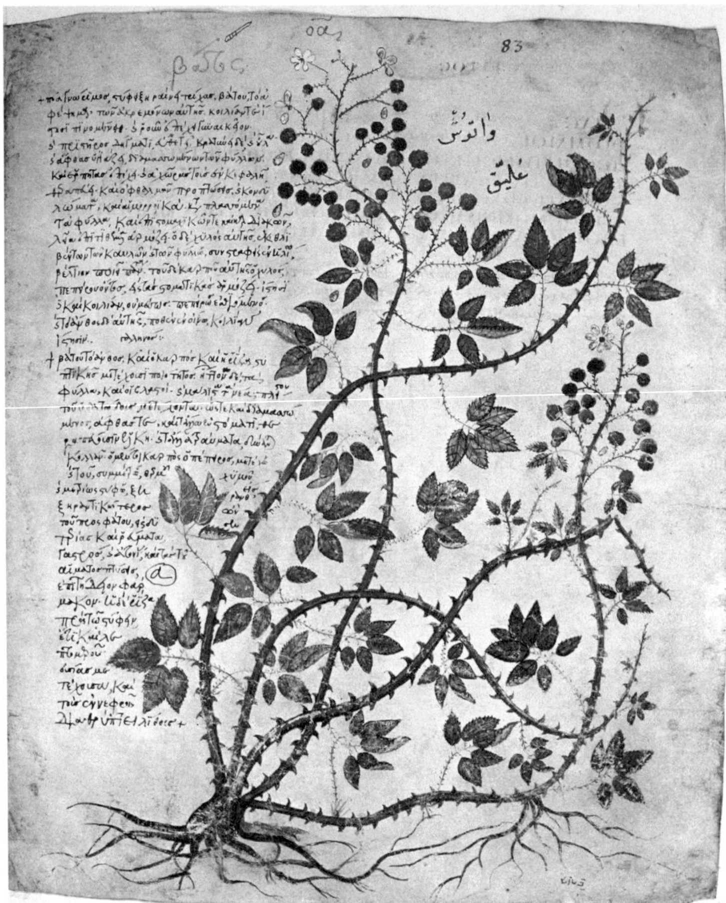

48 Dioscorides, *De materia medica,* manuscript at the Austrian National Library, Vienna, fol. 83r, ca. 512.

Dioscorides (48)

Dioscorides' five books, *De materia medica,* compiled around the 1st century CE, aimed at providing a comprehensive account of the use of plants, animals, and minerals for medicinal purposes. Unlike other classical texts, Dioscorides' treatise never went out of circulation, and it remained one of the most influential herbal books throughout the Middle Ages and Renaissance, until the early 17th century. Moreover, Dioscorides' essay on medicaments is one of the very few instances in which book illustrations from antiquity were preserved and remained available through the following centuries, as shown by the oldest and most famous of its manuscripts, now at the Austrian National Library in Vienna.

Domus Aurea (49)

The word *grotesque* originally referred to an extravagant style of ancient Roman decorative art, which was rediscovered and then enthusiastically copied in Rome during the 15th century. The **"grottoes"** where artists could see these decorations were in fact rooms and corridors of the Domus Aurea, the unfinished **palace** complex started by **Nero** after the great fire in 64 CE. They had become overgrown and buried for many centuries until they were broken into again, mostly from above. The rich repertoire of images, fantastic figures, and ornaments displayed in these paintings enjoyed extraordinary popularity for a very long time and was constantly reinvented from the 16th century onward.

Donation of Constantine (50)

During the 4th century CE the emperor Constantine and his family enriched the Church with vast gifts of property. These later became the basis for still larger claims by the popes to political power and temporal jurisdiction over Christianity. The legendary donation, represented on a Romanesque fresco in the basilica of the Quattro Santi Coronati in Rome, was recorded in a set of (fictional) documents later incorporated into the basic corpus for canon law, Gratian's *Concordance of Discordant Canons.* In 1440, **Lorenzo Valla** proved that the text was a forgery in his *Treatise on the Donation of Constantine.* Valla's work did not circulate widely at first, however, and many continued to defend the legend.

49 Bernardino Pinturicchio, Ceiling with *grotesques* (detail of the Delphic Sibyl), 1508–1510.

50 Donation of Constantine, Romanesque fresco, ca. 1246.

ILLUSTRATION CREDITS [1–50]

1. Vanni/Art Resource, NY.

2. Museo del Prado, Madrid, Spain. Erich Lessing/Art Resource, NY.

3. Galleria Borghese, Rome, Italy. Scala/Art Resource, NY.

4. Private Collection/Ancient Art and Architecture Collection Ltd./ The Bridgeman Art Library.

5. Scala/Art Resource, NY.

6. The Ella Gallup Sumner and Mary Catlin Sumner Collection Fund. 1982.46. Wadsworth Atheneum Museum of Art, Hartford, CT/ Art Resource, NY.

7. Bibliothèque Nationale, Paris, France, MS 10440. Foto Marburg/ Art Resource, NY.

8. Mosaic floor of the Cathedral of Otranto, Italy. Erich Lessing/Art Resource, NY.

9. Detail of the Hall of Amor and Psyche. Palazzo del Te, Mantua, Italy. Erich Lessing/Art Resource, NY.

10. Musée de l'Armée, Paris, France/Dist. Réunion des Musées Nationaux/Art Resource, NY.

11. Private Collection/ The Stapleton Collection/ The Bridgeman Art Library.

12. Alte Pinakothek, Munich, Germany. Scala/Art Resource, NY.

13. Musée d'Orsay, Paris, France/Giraudon/ The Bridgeman Art Library.

14. Staatliche Kunstsammlungen, Dresden, Germany. Erich Lessing, Art Resource, NY.

15. Museo Pio Clementino, Vatican Museums. Scala/Art Resource, NY.

16. Palazzo del Te, Mantua, Italy. Scala/Art Resource, NY.

17. Museo del Prado, Madrid, Spain. Scala/Art Resource, NY.

18. Museo Archeologico Nazionale, Naples, Italy. Alinari/Art Resource, NY.

19. Rockefeller Center, NY. Vanni/Art Resource, NY.

20. Widener Collection. Image courtesy of the Board of Trustees, National Gallery of Art, Washington, DC.

21. Getty Images.

22. Staatliche Antikensammlung, Munich, Germany. Vanni/Art Resource, NY.

23. Erasmus Alberus, *Von Basilisken zu Magdeburg* (Hamburg, 1549).

24. Robert Garrett Collection of Medieval and Renaissance Manuscripts No. 158. Manuscripts Division. Department of Rare Books and Special Collections. Princeton University Library.

25. Archivio Franco Cosimo Panini Editore.

26. Loggia dei Lanzi, Florence, Italy. Vanni/Art Resource, NY.

27. Museumslandschaft Hessen Kassel, Kassel, Germany. Bildarchiv Preussischer Kulturbesitz/Art Resource, NY.

28. Musei Capitolini, Rome, Italy. Erich Lessing/Art Resource, NY.

29. © Michael Nicholson/Corbis.

30. Piazza del Quirinale, Rome, Italy. Alinari/Art Resource, NY.

31. Uffizi Gallery, Florence, Italy. Alinari/Art Resource, NY.

32. Foto Marburg/Art Resource, NY.

33. Getty Images.

34. Villa Farnesina, Rome, Italy. Scala/Art Resource, NY.

35. Galleria Borghese, Rome, Italy. Scala/Art Resource, NY.

36. Staatliche Museen, Berlin, Germany. Bildarchiv Preussischer Kulturbesitz/Art Resource, NY.

37. Kunsthistorisches Museum, Vienna, Austria. Erich Lessing/Art Resource, NY.

38. Kunsthistorisches Museum, Vienna, Austria. Erich Lessing/Art Resource, NY.

39. Louvre, Paris, France. Réunion des Musées Nationaux/Art Resource, NY.

40. Louvre, Paris, France. Réunion des Musées Nationaux/Art Resource, NY.

41. Uffizi Gallery, Florence, Italy/ Giraudon/ The Bridgeman Art Library.

42. Staatliche Museen, Berlin, Germany. Bildarchiv Preussischer Kulturbesitz/Art Resource, NY.

43. Frontispiece, plate 1, from *Europe, a prophecy.* The Pierpont Morgan Library/Art Resource, NY.

44. Scuola Grande di S. Rocco, Venice, Italy. Scala/Art Resource, NY.

45. Harvard Art Museum, Fogg Art Museum, Gift of Robert M. Light, M24395. Photo: Imaging Department © President and Fellows of Harvard College.

46. Staatliche Kunsthalle, Karlsruhe, Germany. Bildarchiv Preussischer Kulturbesitz/Art Resource, NY.

47. Private Collection/The Stapleton Collection/The Bridgeman Art Library.

48. Austrian National Library, Vienna. © ÖNB, Picture Archive, Cod. med. gr. 1, fol. 83r.

49. S. Maria del Popolo, Rome, Italy. Scala/Art Resource, NY.

50. Quattro Santi Coronati, Rome, Italy. Scala/Art Resource, NY.

historians and art historians, that Alberti and others drew their new systems of perspective from Ptolemy's work.

Still, once Ptolemy's atlas became accessible, it attracted the interest of new intellectual circles—especially after clerics and scholars of many different varieties met at the Council of Constance (1414–1418)—and in some of them it met with more varied and critical responses. Ptolemy's maps attracted attention in late Scholastic universities and monasteries whose inmates took a serious interest in mathematics and cosmology. In France, for example, Pierre d'Ailly and Guillaume Philastre, both learned clerics, studied the *Geography* critically. They noted that Ptolemy's maps conflicted with the views of other ancient authorities, and they collated them with information drawn from medieval and contemporary texts. Scholars in the Holy Roman Empire did their best to solve the technical riddles posed by Ptolemy's methods of map projection. Gradually the Italian Humanists followed suit. Intrepid travelers and antiquaries like Flavio Biondo admired Ptolemy for the daring with which he had depicted and described the whole world, but they felt free to correct the information he provided as they would that of any other source.

In the second half of the 15th century annotated copies, adaptations, world maps, and textbooks began to show central features of Ptolemaic geography, suitably adapted to the ends of Christian world history. By the time these maps became popular, the picture of the Earth's surface that Ptolemy had presented had become seriously out of date. Though Herodotus knew, from Phoenician reports, that the African peninsula was surrounded on three sides by water, Ptolemy still represented it as connected to a vast, nonexistent southern landmass, and he showed the Indian Ocean as closed, not open, to the south. Portuguese navigators of the 15th century proved that Herodotus was right: ships could circumnavigate Africa. Editors of Latin editions of Ptolemy in the late 15th and 16th centuries strove to find sensible compromises between preserving his tightly coherent structure and inserting up-to-date additions and corrections. For example, they added sections of "modern maps" to the ancient ones in the *Geography.* Ancient and modern images and data swirled and combined, sometimes in strange forms.

The Venetian cartographer Fra Mauro drew information from Ptolemy as well as from earlier schematic maps when he created the last great *mappa mundi* in the middle of the 15th century. Hartmann Schedel included in his *Nuremberg Chronicle* (1493) a handsome version of Ptolemy's world map, which he integrated with the Old Testament. Schedel correlated each of the three sons of Noah (Shem, Ham, and Japheth) with one of the three Ptolemaic continents, Asia, Africa, and Europe. He thus suggested that ancient science agreed with the biblical history of the races of mankind—though the supposed connection between Ham and Africa actually took firm shape, like the European and Atlantic slave trade, in this period. This reconfigured Ptolemaic model would give intellectual support to the enslavement of black Africans for centuries. Martin Waldseemüller, whose world map of 1507 included both the continent and the term America, still used a revised Ptolemaic projection and portrayed Asia, Europe, and Africa much as Ptolemy had. But by 1500 some cartographers did not hesitate to correct Ptolemy even as they drew on his work. Some printed versions of Ptolemy's world map included legends pointing out that the Indian Ocean was open to the south, not closed, as Ptolemy's image indicated. Waldseemüller made the same point, even more dramatically, by representing the Cape of Good Hope as overlapping the ornamental border of his map, and showing the Indian Ocean as open to the south. After 1475, when the first printed editions of the Latin text appeared at Bologna, and 1477, when it was printed with the maps at Bologna, multiple reprints made it widely accessible. Even in textbooks, where Ptolemaic maps coexisted with much simpler schemes from Aristotle and Macrobius, they were not always passed on uncritically.

One reason that Ptolemy attracted critical attention was that Angeli's translation often departed from the literal sense: even the title was transformed in his hands from *Geography* to *Cosmography,* a formulation that emphasized the connection between the heavens and the surface of the Earth, thereby ignoring Ptolemy's own special interest in cartography. Joannes Regiomontanus, who mastered astronomy in Vienna and Greek in Italy, argued that Angeli's version did particular injustice to the maps: "The maps of the specific provinces do not preserve the appearance intended by Ptolemy, but have undergone frivolous transformations." Regiomontanus settled in Nuremberg, where he hoped to bring out corrected editions of the classics of Greek science. In the case of the *Geography,* he planned to reconstruct the instruments Ptolemy had used and the exact details of the maps he had drawn with them, as part of a larger effort to reconstruct ancient geography and cartography. Though he died too soon to carry out this plan, other German Humanists printed up-to-date, technically rigorous versions of the work at Strasbourg in 1513 and 1525.

The accretion of new information and the growing criticism of existing versions of Ptolemy left the status of the *Geography* oddly undefined, its powerful, coherent model still in command of the visual field even as its obsolescence became notorious. Even the Portuguese used a Ptolemaic framework when they reported their discoveries about the coast of Africa to the Vatican. A generation later Leonardo da Vinci still took the *Geography* as the model for the anatomical atlas of the human body that he hoped to create. And in one quarter at least, the evidence that Ptolemy preserved about ancient cartography had an explosive effect. Columbus—a dedicated reader—studied the 1490 Rome edition of Ptolemy and Pierre d'Ailly's *Imago mundi,* which used more recent Islamic and Western writings to comment on the *Geography.* Many points from Ptolemy reappear in Columbus's journals and other writings: for example, the notion that there were two "Indies," one beyond the Ganges and one to the far east, in

China, which helped inspire Columbus's nomenclature for the New World. But it was a set of otherwise lost Greek texts and maps quoted by Ptolemy that proved crucial. Ptolemy justified his world map by arguing that Marinus, the predecessor from whom he had learned the most, had employed far too large a value for the length, from east to west, of the inherited surface of the Earth. Reinterpreted through a complex scrim of Islamic and medieval texts, Marinus's view suggested that one might reach Asia relatively quickly by sailing westward across the Atlantic. Columbus seized on and quoted Marinus's dangerous idea. No other fragments of a lost classical text, in all probability, have played so large a role in world history.

Though the *Geography* dominated the formal discussion of cartography, humanists rediscovered other ancient traditions as well. Italian antiquaries brought the *agrimensores* to light. These richly illustrated texts on surveying helped inspire Angelo Colocci and others to undertake vast projects in measurement. They even hoped to use ancient metal images of the standard Roman *pes* (foot), which they eagerly collected, as a standard for taking the dimensions of the entire universe, city by city and building by building. The *Tabula Peutingeriana,* which was owned by the poet and scholar Conrad Celtis and published, in 1598, by the Augsburg scholar Markus Welser, revealed that not all useful ancient maps had employed the sorts of projections used by Ptolemy. In some ways, though, these other forms of cartography were chiefly of antiquarian interest. The Roman antiquary Pirro Ligorio undertook his spectacular *Antiquae urbis imago*—a brilliant, vivid effort to recreate ancient Rome, seen from above, circus by circus and temple by temple—without knowledge of the fragments of the *Forma urbis Romae,* which were not collected or published, even in part, until 1582.

Antiquaries, who boasted expert knowledge of the history of communities' names, of roads and buildings, and took travel as one of their central modes of information gathering, were ideally equipped to use the historical information that maps preserved. Many of them were also skilled cartographers, more than able to collate variant versions of maps and work out how the ancient doctrines and practices that underpinned them had developed. In 1570 Gerardus Mercator, now remembered as a cartographer but equally famous in his own day as a historical scholar, produced an atlas that relegated all of Ptolemy's maps to a "historical" section. Mercator distinguished sharply between these venerable but no longer definitive maps and his own innovative charts of the continents as they were in the late 16th century. The status of Ptolemaic cartography was now clear: it belonged to the beloved past, every bit as much as the Roman military route maps and schematic plans of the five or seven zones. As Lazius and Mercator, Camden and Cluverius began to map the provinces of the Roman Empire and trace the route that Hannibal had traveled with his elephants, a new form of scholarship took shape—one that deployed textual and archaeological evidence and applied the changing methods of earth science to both, and that relegated Ptolemy firmly to the past. Everyone could now see, as Regiomontanus and Mercator had long before, that Ptolemaic cartography offered the key not to describing the face of the Earth as it was in modern times, but to understanding ancient views about how the world was divided into different continents and climatic zones.

In the 17th and 18th centuries, a modern cartography emerged, independent of ancient sources and methods. In the same period, Francis Bacon and other polemicists bent on asserting the importance of innovation, played down—and sometimes denied—that Columbus's discovery had rested on classical foundations. From their standpoint, which many historians adopted, ancient cartography, with its errors, its limited vision of the inhabited world, and its unearned authority, had been a mere obstacle to the exploration of the world. In more recent times, by contrast, historians of art and culture have seized upon the *Geography* in the belief that its reappearance explained much of the intellectual innovation that took place in early 15th century Florence. Each of these positions rested on exaggerated and polemical theses.

Only in recent decades have historians of cartography fully accepted that, in Dalché's words, "Ptolemy could represent either a rigid corpus of knowledge or an opening toward innovation," as determined by the form in which his maps were transmitted and the circumstances in which they were studied, and come to appreciate the richness of the ancient images of the world's surface, fantastic and scientific, that confronted Alberti and Biondo, Regiomontanus and Columbus, as they tried to sort out the tradition that Ptolemy's work crowned. And only in the last few decades have scholars collaborated to recreate the history of cartography and retrace the history of Ptolemy's text and maps, and to produce a genuinely critical edition of both. Even now, however, the process of historicization begun by Regiomontanus and Mercator remains incomplete. Many dark places remain in our mental maps of ancient cartography and its fate.

BIBL.: Howard Burns, "Pirro Ligorio's Reconstruction of Ancient Rome: The *Anteiquae Vrbis Imago* of 1561," in *Pirro Ligorio: Artist and Antiquarian,* ed. Robert Gaston (Florence 1988) 19–92. Patrick Dalché, *La Géographie de Ptolémée in Occident (IVe–XVIe siècle)* (Turnhout 2009). J. B. Hartley and David Woodward, eds., *The History of Cartography,* 3 vols. in 6 parts to date (Chicago: University of Chicago Press, 1987–). Florian Mittenhuber, *Text und Kartentradition in der Geographie des Klaudios Ptolemaios* (Bern 2009). Ingrid Rowland, *The Culture of the High Renaissance: Ancients and Moderns in Sixteenth-century Rome* (Cambridge 1998). Alessandro Scafi, *Mapping Paradise: A History of Heaven on Earth* (Chicago 2006). R. J. A. Talbert and R. W. Unger, eds., *Cartography in Antiquity and the Midele Ages: Fresh Perspectives, New Methods* (Leiden 2008). Nicolás Wey Gómez, *The Tropics of Empire: Why Columbus Sailed South to the Indies* (Cambridge, Mass., 2008).

A.G.

Caryatid

Greek term indicating a column or pilaster with its shaft carved in the form of a draped female. The term literally means "maiden of Caryae," an ancient town in Laconia, and the origin of its use in architecture is unclear. It is first recorded in the 1st century BCE in Vitruvius' *De architectura* (1.1.5); according to his fictional account, the sculpted supports known by this name were invented during the Persian Wars, in the 5th century BCE, and allegedly represented the punishment of the women of Caryae, condemned to slavery after betraying Athens and conspiring with the enemy. The best-known examples are in the southern porch of the Erechtheion on the Acropolis in Athens (421–407 BCE), but the form has been traced to the 6th century BCE. The Erechtheion caryatids enjoyed great fame in the Roman world, and copies were set up in public and private buildings, including the Forum of Augustus in Rome and Hadrian's Villa in Tivoli.

Caryatids had a rich but checkered history in post-antiquity. Anthropomorphic supports seem never to have gone out of use, yet it is not possible to establish a direct relation between the relatively rare medieval figures with this function and ancient examples. Only at the turn of the 12th to the 13th century did columns and pilasters in the shape of men become more frequent in religious buildings, where they usually represented prophets, saints, evangelists, or allegories of virtues.

The classicizing revival of caryatids is directly tied to the rediscovery of Vitruvius by Renaissance scholars. Until at least the 1480s, in fact, there were only rather unreliable Vitruvius manuscripts, where Greek words were distorted or omitted. As a consequence the ancient meaning of anthropomorphic supports was ignored, and they were only cursorily dealt with in 15th-century treatises on architecture. Fra Giocondo's (1511) and Cesare Cesariano's (1521) editions of Vitruvius contain the first attempts to illustrate the caryatids as described by the Latin author: prisoners supporting the load of a trabeation (horizontal weight or lintel) on their heads. These reconstructions, though totally unrelated to ancient figurative models, played a decisive role in establishing the caryatid as a main decorative element in Renaissance art and architecture. Roman copies of the Erechtheion maidens, on the other hand, were well known during the 16th century and served as models for shaping new types of classicizing caryatids. Since then, the practice of integrating caryatids into monuments, building facades, and interiors has remained commonplace in the decorative vocabulary of sculpture and architecture.

A new phase in the modern history of caryatids began in the early 19th century, when Lord Elgin had one of the Erechtheion sculptures removed and taken to London. The Greek prototype thus became available to a greater public, whose keen interest had already been raised a few decades previously by the widely circulated *Antiquities of Athens* (1787) by James Stuart and Nicholas Revett. The presentation of caryatids restrained in accurate Greek forms on the porch of Saint Pancras Church in London (1819–1822), designed by William and Henry Inwood, can be read as an immediate expression of the new taste that was rapidly taking hold. Other eminent architects of the era—among them John Soane, Karl Friedrich Schinkel, and Leo von Klenze—made extensive use of caryatids fashioned according to classical models. The success of these design elements was such that draped figures supporting an acanthus capital became a familiar cliché in decorative arts, often sustaining chimneypieces or serving as candlesticks and table supports.

No less revealing of wider-ranging cultural attitudes is the afterlife of this classical motif during the late 19th and 20th centuries. While losing its preeminence in architecture and decorative arts, the caryatid has grown into a favorite subject for sculptors and painters. The classical reference is immediately apparent, for example, in a large set of drawings by Amedeo Modigliani aimed at exploring the contortions of the female form under an overwhelming weight. Auguste Rodin's crouching nude caryatid, crushed by a massive stone, is a vivid and thoughtful allegory of the human condition. Abstract forms are preferred in the caryatids sculpted by Constantin Brancusi and, later on, by Fritz Koenig, which reduce the theme to its basic components and to the core idea of statics: a vertical element supporting a horizontal one.

BIBL.: Magdalena Bushart, Sylvaine Hänsel, and Michael Scholz, "Karyatiden an Berliner Bauten des 19. Jahrhunderts," in *Berlin und die Antike*, ed. W. Aronhövel and C. Schreiber (Berlin 1979) 531–555. Giulio Carotti, "Le cariatidi nel Medio Evo" and "Le cariatidi nel Rinascimento e nei tempi moderni," *Arte Italiana decorativa e industriale* 12 (1903) 58–60, 65–67, 74–76, 79–83. George Hersey, *The Lost Meaning of Classical Architecture: Speculations on Ornament from Vitruvius to Venturi* (Cambridge, Mass., 1988). Klaus Parlasca, "Motive antiker Stützfiguren an Kaminen des Frühklassizismus," *Zeitschrift für Kunstgeschichte* 37 (1974) 269–283. Evamaria Schmidt, *Geschichte der Karyatide. Funktion und Bedeutung der menschlichen Träger- und Stützfigur in der Baukunst* (Würzburg 1982).

A.AN.

Casaubon, Isaac

Hellenist and scholar, 1559–1614. Casaubon was born in Geneva to French Protestants who had sought asylum there. Initially a professor of Greek at the Geneva Academy (1582–1599) he later became professor of literature at Montpellier (1597–1599). In 1600 he was summoned to Paris by Henry IV to mange the Royal Library. Upon the death of King Henry, in 1610, Casaubon was called by James I to England, where he died four years later.

A superb Hellenist as well as a scholar of Arabic and Hebrew, Casaubon edited approximately 10 ancient texts. Although he produced few first editions (the *Strategemata* of Polyaenus in 1589, five unpublished chapters of Theophrastus *Characters* in 1599), his philological talents are fully apparent in the quality of his commentaries; he drew on his profound knowledge of every aspect of ancient tradition, from zoology to military art and theology, to clarify or correct textual issues. Although powerfully drawn to Scripture and the work of the Church Fathers, as a Protestant he could not openly devote himself to their study while under the protection of Henry IV. Once in England, however, he was able to apply his patristic culture to works of religious controversy. In particular, the *Exercitationes contra Baronium,* a work refuting the *Annales ecclesiastici* of Cardinal Cesare Baronio, was meant to be a Protestant history of the early Church.

Casaubon was first and foremost a reader, and a major part of his work on ancient texts remains buried in his manuscripts. His annotated books and the 60 volumes of *adversaria,* preserved at Oxford, reveal the way in which he read ancient texts: pen in hand, he corrected the text as he went, by conjecture or following manuscripts, constantly comparing with other sources. He also took notes and copied extracts on separate pages. Some notebooks were dedicated to words or to little-known or problematic aspects of civilization, and these were carefully indexed; subsequently, over several years, he added notes based on his reading and complementary research. It is thus possible to see how, step by step, a master philologist applied his vast knowledge. For example, in writings thought to be very early and attributed to Hermes Trismegistus, he detected a later text and thereby refuted the very widely accepted idea that truth had been revealed to the Greeks in a veiled fashion before Christianity (*prisca theologia*).

BIBL.: Anthony T. Grafton, "Protestant versus Prophet: Isaac Casaubon on Hermes Trismegistus," *Journal of the Warburg and Courtauld Institute* 46 (1983) 78–93; Hélène Parenty, *Isaac Casaubon helléniste, des* studia humanitatis *à la philologie* (Geneva 2009). Mark Pattison, *Isaac Casaubon, 1559–1614* (London 1875). H.P.

Translated by Jeannine Routier Pucci and Elizabeth Trapnell Rawlings

Cassandra

Cassandra is one of the best-known figures of Greek mythology. The seer who predicted calamity and her unheeded warning cries are anchored deep in general consciousness and linguistic usage. Nevertheless, today she suffers a fate common to several mythological figures (such as Sisyphus): her rich fictive biography, full of variations and constantly new motifs and facets, has been largely reduced to the "vestige" (Karlheinz Stierle) of a metonymic allegory, which in addition to having positive connotations can also take on the negative tincture of "pessimist, fatalist, killjoy."

The most beautiful of Priam's daughters was desired by Apollo and received from him the power of prophecy. She rejected him, however, and he turned his gift into a curse: from then on no one would believe what she foretold. Thus, her warnings—before the birth of Paris and again before his voyage to Sparta, upon his return with Helen, and at the reception of the wooden horse—had no effect. After Troy's capture she took refuge in the temple of Athena, but she was hauled away from the goddess's statue by Ajax and (according to later sources) raped. Ultimately Agamemnon took the beautiful seer home as a war trophy and a lover, where she was then killed along with him by Clytemnestra (and Aegisthus).

In the Homeric epics Cassandra plays only an insignificant bit part. Otherwise, her reception has been especially influenced by Aeschylus' *Agamemnon* and Euripides' *Trojan Women,* as well as Virgil's *Aeneid* and Seneca's *Agamemnon.* The only ancient work featuring Cassandra as title heroine, the Hellenistic writer Lycophron's *Alexandra* (= Cassandra), has had no influence.

Although the stories surrounding Troy were widely diffused in the Middle Ages, Cassandra played only a rather limited role in the numerous romances, epics, and tales. This is due to the facts that the grand depictions of her in Greek were not known at the time, and that the two most important late antique sources for her reception, the historical prose paraphrases of Dictys and Dares, marginalize her. It is also a result of Cassandra's having played a small role or none at all in the Latin texts that were central to the early phase of antiquity's literary reception. In Virgil's account of the fall of Troy she is overshadowed by Laocoön. Ovid uses her as an example a few times in his love elegies, but he mentions her only twice in his *Metamorphoses,* as a victim of Ajax, without even giving her name. Moreover, as prophet of calamity, Cassandra—unlike the Sibyls—does not lend herself well to the medieval Christianization of pagan mythology. An exception is her treatment by Herbort von Fritzlar, who makes her a prophet of salvation and has her foretell the birth of Christ.

Since the Renaissance, tragic depictions of Cassandra from Seneca (in the 16th and 17th cents.), Euripides (esp. since the 18th cent.), and Aeschylus (esp. since the 19th cent.) have been influential. Up to the turn of the 19th century Cassandra appears in many, although hardly important, literary guises. And when she plays a part in a great work—as in Shakespeare's *Troilus and Cressida*—it is merely a bit one. The dramatic works of these centuries featuring Troy and Cassandra, as well as the sundry influential poems of Platen, Schiller, and Meredith, are today as forgotten as the corresponding operas and the few sculptures, paintings, and drawings of the seer who had been a popular subject of art in antiquity.

Only in the 20th century did Cassandra gain emphatically and persistently in importance. The reasons for this are obvious. The rediscovery of the dark sides of antiquity, and especially the great wars and crises of the century endowed the unheeded prophet of impending calamity with new timeliness. The adaptations of Euripides' *Trojan Women* before and after the two world wars (Werfel, Braun, Sartre, Jens), and the grand productions of Aeschylus' *Oresteia* from Max Reinhardt to Karolos Koun, Peter Hall, Peter Stein, and Ariane Mnouchkine put Cassandra back on center stage. Pacifism, historical pessimism, skepticism about progress, and feminism found an ideal medium for their fears and concerns, warnings and appeals in the ancient harbinger of disaster whom no one believed. All these themes are impressively joined in Christa Wolf's story *Cassandra.* The wide success of this book, along with Marion Zimmer Bradley's feminist novel about Troy, *Firebrand,* provides the clearest evidence of the seer's modern boom. It can also be seen in many sectors of the art world as well as in the political, journalistic, and social discourse of the age, and it informs Woody Allen's *Deconstructing Harry* (1997). It remains to be seen, however, whether in the long run this development will result in the mythological figure's once again becoming more than a mere metonymic cipher for the foreteller of disaster.

BIBL.: T. Epple, *Der Aufstieg der Untergangsseherin Kassandra* (Würzburg 1993). S. Jentgens, *Kassandra: Spielarten einer literarischen Figur* (Hildesheim 1995). "Kassandra," in *Lexicon Iconigraphicum Mythologiae Classicae,* ed. H. C. Ackermann and J. R. Gisler (Zurich 1981–1999). K. Ledergerber, *Kassandra: Das Bild der Prophetin in der antiken und insbesondere in der ältern abendländischen Dichtung* (Buochs 1941). D. Neblung, *Die Gestalt der Kassandra in der Literatur der Antike* (Stuttgart 1997). J. D. Reid, ed., *The Oxford Guide to Classical Mythology in the Arts, 1300–1990s,* 2 vols. (New York 1993).

B.S.

Translated by Patrick Baker

Castor and Pollux

In Greek, Castor and Polydeuces; collectively known as the Dioscuri (from *dios kouroi,* "sons of Zeus") or, in Latin, the *Castores.* Twin brothers, they were also brothers to Helen and Clytemnestra, all four born from two eggs produced by Leda, wife of Tyndareus, king of Sparta, after an encounter with Zeus in the form of a swan. The Dioscuri were characterized by a profound duality. Pollux, a boxer, was traditionally regarded as the son of Zeus, and therefore immortal; Castor, a horseman, was thought to be sired by Tyndareus (hence the brothers' alternative name, the Tyndaridae). This ambiguous status is explored by Pindar in his 10th Nemean Ode, which tells of Castor's death in a fight with Idas and Lynceus, nephews of the Messenian king Leucippus, and Pollux's grief-stricken request to share his own immortality with his brother. In respect for their fraternal bond, Zeus granted that they might live "half the time beneath the earth and half in the golden homes of heaven" (87–88).

The redemptive power of this story of brotherly love and the potential conflict it raises between duty and desire formed an inspirational theme in 18th-century Europe, as explored in Jean-Philippe Rameau's opera *Castor et Pollux* (1737, revised 1754) and Johann Evangelist Holzer's facade fresco of *Brotherly Love Shown through the Fable of Castor and Pollux* in Augsburg (1737). In a later era, as children in Vólos, the artist Giorgio de Chirico and his brother, the writer and composer Alberto Savinio, explored their rich relationship to the Greek past through an identification with the Dioscuri. More recently, the complexities of brotherhood and shared identity have been tackled through the characters Castor and Pollux Troy in John Woo's film *Face/Off* (1997).

The dual nature of the Dioscuri as twins exists in tension with their ambiguous status as individuals. They are commonly represented as handsome youths, or by a symbolic pairing of stars (as befits their association with the constellation Gemini). In Sparta, where their cult originated, they were closely linked to the practice of double kingship, and in Attica they were worshiped as the Anakes, divine twin horsemen. As prominent heroes of the generation before the Trojan War, the Dioscuri distinguished themselves in both the voyage of the Argonauts (Apollonius Rhodius, *Argonautica* 2.1–153) and the hunt for the Calydonian boar. A popular myth (and the most commonly cited cause for Castor's death and apotheosis) saw the brothers abducting Phoebe and Hilaeira, the daughters of Leucippus, and so gaining twin brides. The double abduction scene provided erotic inspiration for artists from the Athenian Meidias Painter (ca. 420–400 BCE) to Rubens (*Rape of the Daughters of Leucippus,* 1617). The power of the Dioscuri to exceed the limits of mortality made their iconography appropriate both for funerary contexts and for deified rulers, especially for princely brothers in Hellenistic Greece and imperial Rome.

The Dioscuri were commonly invoked as epiphanic gods. As "saviors" (*sōtēres*), they appear to storm-tossed sailors as the constellation Gemini (the Twins) or the electrical phenomenon known as Saint Elmo's fire and are celebrated for their vigilance at sea in songs from the 33rd Homeric Hymn and Theocritus' 22nd Idyll to Franz Schubert's 1816 setting of Johann Baptist Mayrhofer's *Lied eines Schiffers an die Dioskuren* (*Song of a Sailor to the Dioscuri*). Their salvific appearance in warfare was commemorated by the Romans, after the Battle of Lake Regillus (496 BCE), with the foundation of the Temple of Castor in the Forum Romanum.

In 1589 Domenico Fontana incorporated colossal antique statues of the Dioscuri into Pope Sixtus V's remodeling of Rome's Piazza del Quirinale. These subsequently provided a model of ideal masculinity for several Neoclassical monuments, including Richard Westmacott's 1822 bronze *Achilles,* commissioned in honor of the Duke of Wellington, which had the dubious honor of being the first male nude statue publicly displayed in London.

BIBL.: Richard Hunter, *Theocritus and the Archaeology of Greek Poetry* (Cambridge 1996) 46–76. Leila Nista, ed., *Castores: L'immagine dei Dioscuri a Roma* (Rome 1994). W. W. K. Pritchett, *The Greek State at War* (Berkeley 1974) 3:11–46. E. M. Steinby, ed., *Lacus Iuturnae I* (Rome 1989). V.P.

Catacombs

Underground passages and rooms once used for the burial of the dead, catacombs are found throughout the Mediterranean world. The most famous catacombs are outside

Rome, but other significant ones are located in southern Italy, northern Africa, and Syria.

When funerary custom in the Roman world shifted from cremation to inhumation about the 2nd century CE and increased extramural burial space was needed, miles of underground cemeteries gradually developed. The early Christians called their burial places *coemeteria,* places of repose. The first use of "catacomb" is a reference of 354 CE to a *coemeterium ad catacumbas,* identified as the cemetery of St. Sebastian on the Via Appia Antica, about two miles outside Rome's Aurelian Wall. *Kata kymbas* in Greek means something like "near the hollows," generally taken to be the pozzolana quarries nearby. From this one site, associated with Christian worship of the saints Peter and Paul since the mid-3rd century, the term catacomb came to refer, at least since the 9th century, to all underground cemeteries.

Catacombs continued to be used for individual burials even after Constantine's official recognition of Christianity in 313. Never places of habitation or refuge, they were used for funeral feasts on anniversaries of the dead, as well as places of "repose" for martyrs and confessors. They were not limited to Christians, but the increasing numbers of converts meant an ever-rising percentage of Christian burials. The majority of the dated funerary inscriptions from Rome are from this period (4th and 5th cents.), which coincided with concentrated efforts by bishops and emperors to foster the cult of the martyrs. Monumental modifications were made to tombs of the martyred in the catacombs. Of special note is the work of Pope Damasus (366–384) at Rome; he revamped monuments and added grand metrical commemorative inscriptions, incised on large marble slabs in splendid capital letters. His efforts supported the increasingly popular phenomenon of burials *ad sanctos* (near the bodies of the martyrs).

The use of catacombs for burials declined by the late 5th century; the last securely dated inscription found in situ is from 535 CE at the catacomb of St. Sebastian (Osborne, 280 n. 11). This change in funerary practice, however, did not mean the end of the importance of the catacombs. Pilgrims and tourists continued to come to see them and venerate them as cult sites through the 8th century. From the early 6th century we find altars used for Eucharistic purposes placed in the catacombs. And aboveground *basilicae ad sanctos,* such as those built in the late 6th and early 7th centuries at St. Agnes and St. Lorenzo, confirm the devotional nature of these sites.

By the mid-8th century a process had begun of removing the relics of the early saints and martyrs from their suburban burial sites and "translating" them into the city. Knowledge of the catacombs was kept alive by guidebooks that recounted the marvels to be seen in and around Rome, notably the *Mirabilia,* a ca. 12th-century guide that listed these cemeteries, some of which presumably could still be visited. Probably only in the late Middle Ages, with the removal of the papacy from Rome in the 14th century, was the very existence of the catacombs largely forgotten.

Thus, the rediscovery of a catacomb on Via Anapo on 31 May 1578 understandably created a sensation. This interest in the ancient roots of the Roman Church was fueled, in part, by the Counter-Reformation. Among those inspired to visit the catacombs was A. Bosio (1575–1629), deemed the "Christopher Columbus of Roman Catacombs" by the archaeologist G. B. De Rossi (1822–1894), himself often viewed as the father of Christian archaeology. Bosio made detailed drawings, documenting some 30 new catacombs in 40 years of work; these were posthumously published in his *Roma sotteranea* (1632). His careful, systematic annotations were ahead of his time. By the mid-17th century, and continuing for the next two centuries, the catacombs were studied for mere antiquarian interest. Much iconographic material and grave goods were removed, and a pontifical decree of 1668 made such removal legal.

Only in the mid-1800s did the systematic recording of information about the catacombs resume, principally as a result of De Rossi's work. Today the catacombs of Rome are under the control of the Vatican, which maintains them and fosters their scientific study.

BIBL.: L. Duchesne, ed., *Liber Pontificalis* (Paris 1955) esp. 151, 207, 227, 305–306. V. F. Nicolai, F. Bisconti, and D. Mazzoleni, *The Christian Catacombs of Rome: History, Decoration, Inscriptions,* trans. C. C. Stella and L. Touchette (Regensburg 1999). I. Oryshkevich, "The History of the Roman Catacombs from the Age of Constantine to the Renaissance" (PhD diss., Columbia University 2003). J. Osborne, "The Roman Catacombs in the Middle Ages," *Papers of the British School in Rome* 53 (1985) 278–328. J. Stevenson, *The Catacombs: Re-discovered Monuments of Early Christianity* (London 1978).

M.R.S.

Catharsis

A Greek term for "cleansing" or "purgation," it covers a wide spectrum of meanings, from ritual baths and medical and psychological treatments for constipation to moral cleansing from guilt or the clarification of intellectual concepts. In the sixth book of his *Poetics* Aristotle applies the term to tragedy. The goal of tragedy is "through pity and fear" to effect "the proper purgation of these emotions." This formulation is new in the context of Greek poetics. Aristotle makes use of the fundamental opposition between clean or pure and unclean or impure to defend tragedy against its critics (Plato) as a cleansing process.

The problem of defining catharsis lies in Aristotle's isolated use of the term: he gave no explanation whatsoever of tragic catharsis. The central position he gave to it and his evocative brief description have contributed significantly to the term's fascination, which has lasted into the modern era. After rediscovery of the *Poetics* during the Renaissance (it was first published in 1498), 16th- and 17th-century commentators (such as Francesco Robortello, Antonio Sebastiano Minturno, Lodovico Castelvetro, Giovanni Antonio Viperano, Daniel Heinsius, and Alexander Donatus) developed the following three main interpretations. The tragic emotions (fear and pity) give rise to catharsis, which is transferred to other passions. Or catharsis refers to the tragic emotions themselves, which are preserved in a cleansed (or cultivated) form. Finally, catharsis can be interpreted as elimination of the emotions aroused by tragedy and liberation from them.

In French classicism (Pierre Corneille, Charles de Marguetel de Saint-Denis de Saint-Évremond, Jean Racine, Bernard le Bovier de Fontenelle) theoretical interest was concentrated on the aspect of acquiring a stoic attitude. Tragedy allows spectators to practice freedom from passion as a form of Christian stoic impassivity. As art grew more bourgeois in the 18th century, the accent shifted from fear to pity. Possibilities for increased sensitivity were sought in place of stoic attitudes. Gotthold Lessing sums up this tendency in a passage that locates the emotion of pity at the center of his reflections on poetics: "The person who feels the greatest pity is the best person, most inclined to all social virtues, to all forms of generosity. Thus whoever makes us feel pity makes us better and more virtuous, and the tragedy that does the one also does the other" (letter to Friedrich Nicolai, 13 November 1756).

As art became more autonomous and a poetics that stressed the effect on audiences was increasingly discarded, catharsis began to lose its central position in the discourse on tragedy. Goethe and Hegel attempted to rescue it as "equilibrium" (Goethe) and "reconciliation" (Hegel). Finally in 1857 Jakob Bernays emphatically rejected the moral interpretation, observing that Aristotle had used a medical model as the basis for poetic catharsis and that in the course of tragic drama pity and fear were first aroused and then eliminated like noxious bodily secretions. This analogy has explosive connotations; at the height of German idealism, philhellenism, and emphasis on the humanistic tradition in secondary education, Bernays created a dubious association between the effects of classical Greek tragedies and emetic medicines. A profound philological argument ensued. At the same time, however, the discussion of catharsis was expanded to include new contexts. Josef Breuer and Sigmund Freud applied Bernays's interpretation of poetic catharsis as abreaction to modern psychology: the "cathartic cure" became a precursor to psychoanalysis. Friedrich Nietzsche gave the contemporary discussion a new turn by separating the concept of catharsis from the discussion of tragedy, saying that "Aristotle's great error" was "to see two *depressive* affects, fear and pity, as the affects of tragedy, and furthermore that the hypothesis on the purging of affects was "simply not true" (posthumous fragments, 1888–1889). Anthropologists such as William Robertson Smith, Jane Ellen Harrison, and James G. Frazer investigated early forms of catharsis in other cultures. In the course of the 20th century the term became even broader and entered a wide variety of fields, including art history (Warburg school), communications studies and reception aesthetics (Jauss), political discourse, and the debate on whether violence in the new media—film, television, and the Internet—increases or diminishes aggression.

BIBL.: Leon Golden, *Aristotle on Tragic and Comic Mimesis* (Atlanta 1992). Stephen Halliwell, *Aristotle's "Poetics"* (London 1986) 168–201. Donald W. Lucas, ed., *Aristotle: "Poetics"* (Oxford 1968) 273–290. Matthias Luserke, ed., *Die Aristotelische Katharsis: Dokumente ihrer Deutung im 19. und 20. Jahrhundert* (Hildesheim 1991). Thomas J. Scheff, *Catharsis in Healing, Ritual, and Drama* (Berkeley 1979). M.V.

Translated by Deborah Lucas Schneider

Cato the Younger

Marcus Porcius Cato (95–46 BCE), known as Cato the Younger and Cato Uticensis (Cato of Utica), was the great-grandson of Cato the Elder (234–149 BCE). He earned renown for his dedication to the Republic, unwavering morality, and strict Stoicism. He sided with Cicero against the conspiracy of Catiline and worked in the Senate to ensure that the death penalty was given to the conspirators. His various state-sponsored duties gained him a reputation for scrupulous honesty.

Cato opposed Caesar's triumvirate with Pompey and Crassus, eventually transferring his support to Pompey when the latter broke with Caesar. Cato continued to oppose Caesar's policies and later his eastern military campaign. After the Battle of Pharsalus (48 BCE), in which Caesar defeated Pompey, Cato's opposition to Caesar's ambitions became even more unyielding. At Utica (in what is now Tunisia), following Caesar's victory over Metellus Scipio at the Battle of Thapsus, Cato found himself unable to imagine living in a world in which Caesar would rule and committed suicide. It was said that the last book he read was Plato's *Phaedo,* in which Socrates willingly goes to his own death rather than act contrary to virtue.

Ancient interpretations of Cato's actions set the tone for the way he was understood in the millennia to come. Cicero maintained admiration for his colleague in the defense of old republican institutions, yet a comment in his letters to Atticus (well before the events that led to Cato's suicide), leads one to believe that Cato could be seen as a representative of a somewhat naive ultraconservatism: "He speaks in the Senate as though he were living in Plato's *Republic* instead of Romulus's cesspool" (*Letters to Atticus* 2.1.8). Sallust (86–34 BCE) wrote that in his time two outstanding men had appeared, Caesar and Cato, as outstanding in virtue as they were different in character. They shared intelligence and eloquence, but "Caesar grew eminent by generosity and munificence; Cato by the integrity of his life" (*Conspiracy of Catiline* 54). Caesar sought glory through his spectacular deeds, Cato gained glory because he tried to remain austere, to stay away from spectacle.

Lucan (39–65 CE), toward the beginning of his unfinished account of the Roman civil war, the *Pharsalia,* expresses uncertainty about the merits of each side in the war. Who could be certain who had taken up arms rightly, Pompey or Caesar? "It is unlawful," Lucan writes, "even to know." However that may be, "the winning cause pleased the gods, the vanquished, Cato" (1.126–128). Is

Cato a patron of a lost cause, and thus a foolish, stubborn conservative? Or, faced with the indeterminacy of human life, that is, with the fact that we can never really know what pleases the gods and so are compelled instead to seek good moral exemplars, is Cato, instead, a symbol of virtue?

Plutarch (46–127 CE) presents one of the fullest accounts of Cato's life in his laudatory *Life of Cato the Younger.* Plutarch tells us that when Caesar heard of Cato's death, he remarked, "Cato, I begrudge you your death, because you begrudged me the sparing of your life." Even if the statement is apocryphal, the sentiment it reveals is important. Thereafter Cato would be seen as a martyr both for devotion to philosophy and wisdom and for republican principles in the face of tyranny. The historian Cassius Dio (165–229 CE) wrote in his *Roman History* that "Cato, who had proved himself at once the most democratic and the strongest-minded of all the men of his time, acquired great glory even from his very death" (43.11).

Saint Augustine (354–430 CE), in one of the most widely read books in the Middle Ages, the *City of God,* poses a difficult question: What was it that allowed the one true God to favor the Romans as he did, permitting them to acquire such power and prestige, even as they worshipped countless false gods, honoring those gods with sacrifices that ultimately (if unwittingly) went not to gods but to demons? Relying heavily on Sallust's account, Augustine answers this question by suggesting that it was the moral qualities of certain Romans, such as Caesar and Cato (4.12). Yet, of the two, Cato received higher praise, Augustine judges, because he sought virtue not for glory but for its own sake.

One of the most lasting and well-known medieval depictions of Cato comes in Dante's *Divine Comedy.* Dante has ascended out of Hell along with Virgil, his guide; they enter Purgatory and Dante is overwhelmed by the sky, wondering at four marvelous stars. Dante does not say this explicitly, but the reader realizes that these stars must represent prudence, justice, fortitude, and temperance, that is, the four cardinal virtues, the best to which a human being can aspire (*Purgatorio* 1.23–24). Immediately thereafter Dante sees "an old man, alone, who in his aspect was worthy of such reverence that no son could owe his father more" (*Purgatorio* 1.31–33). The man has a long beard streaked with white, and his hair too is white, and "the rays of those four holy stars so adorned his face with light that the sun seemed to be right in front of him" (*Purgatorio* 1.37–39). Cato, in short, is for Dante the guardian of the realm of Purgatory, a noble position for a pagan, especially since Cato died by his own hand. Dante's Cato is quite old, even though ancient sources suggest Cato was 48 years old at his death.

Was Dante simply a poor reader of ancient sources, or did he represent Cato as an old man to symbolize the greatest human wisdom that comes through human experience, through having lived a complete life? This question became a point of controversy for early 15th-century Humanists in Florence. One of these, the wealthy dilettante Niccolò Niccoli, is represented by Leonardo Bruni in that Humanist's *Dialogues to Pier Paolo Vergerio* as criticizing Dante for "lacking Latinity" and for not understanding from the ancient sources that Cato was in fact not an old man when he died. Bruni's work is structured in two books and set dramatically on two different days. The second day sees Niccoli reverse sides and argue that Dante was only using poetic license. One can tell nothing from a dialogue such as this about the fixed opinions of the historical characters represented as interlocutors, but one sees that Cato's symbolic value became a matter for discussion.

Thereafter, Cato could be used in a number of ways, all connected to classical interpretive trajectories. "Cato" could be used as a kind of shorthand for the impossibility of a truly Stoic life, that is, a life that remained unemotional and seemingly unmoved by the normal human passion for glory. Michel de Montaigne (1533–1592) wrote, in this vein, that he must at some level accept his own nature. To be excessively dissatisfied with his natural temperament or to try unduly to change himself would be like "being dissatisfied that I am not an angel or Cato. My actions are regular, and conformable with what I am, and to my condition. I can do no better" (*Essais* 13.14).

This same tendency is reflected when certain writers use Cato almost as a topos of a lost, golden, heroic age. Giambattista Vico (1688–1744) praised the nature of ancient aristocratic commonwealths as heroic. He writes in his landmark work, the *New Science,* however, that "such heroism is impossible today." The Roman republican period saw only one hero: Cato, "whose reputation reflected his aristocratic spirit. The death of Pompey left Cato to head the party of the nobility; and when he could not bear to see it humiliated by Caesar, he killed himself" (trans. D. Marsh, 304–305)

Montesquieu (1689–1755), in his 1734 *Considerations on the Causes of the Greatness of the Romans and Their Decline,* wrote that if Cato had not committed suicide, "he would have given a completely different turn to events." Montesquieu believed there was a salient difference between Cato and his contemporary Cicero: "With Cicero, virtue was the accessory; with Cato glory." Jean-Jacques Rousseau (1712–1778) also saw Cato as a signal figure. In his 1755 *Discourse on Political Economy* Rousseau compared Socrates and Cato. Socrates, the perfect philosopher, is faithful to himself, whereas Cato considers the interests of his fellow citizens: "Socrates instructed a few individuals . . . but Cato defended his country."

A more revolutionary Cato appears in an Anglophone guise in *Cato: A Tragedy,* written by Joseph Addison (1672–1729), cofounder of the *Spectator.* This play, quite successful in its day, presented Cato as the proponent of liberty versus tyranny, of enlightened republicanism versus monarchy, basing its dramatic action on Cato's final days in Utica. It was an inspiration to many, including George Washington, who had it performed for his troops as they were encamped in Valley Forge in 1777–1778.

The army that would later triumph at Yorktown against Cornwallis must have appreciated Addison's entertainment, even as Cato continued to resonate in other cultural contexts. In revolutionary France the "Death of Cato" became an artistic theme, sculpted and painted a number of times. The sculpture of that subject completed in 1832 by Jean-Baptiste Roman and François Rude stands today in the Louvre. Inspired by Cato, the French statesman Alphonse de Lamartine in 1848 quoted the famous line of Lucan, that "the winning cause pleased the gods, the vanquished, Cato," as he argued, against his own interests, that the French Republic's president should be chosen not by the Assembly but by the whole nation of France.

Cato, like many classical, emblematic figures, took on various guises in the course of Western history. His name will always be associated, however, with Stoicism, self-sacrifice, firm (sometimes stubborn) devotion to an unpopular cause, and republican politics.

BIBL.: R. Sklenar, "Nihilistic Cosmology and Catonian Ethics in Lucan's *Bellum Civile,*" *American Journal of Philology* 120 (1999) 281–296. G. Vico, *New Science,* trans. D. Marsh (New York 1999).

C.C.

Catullus

Catullus (ca. 82–ca. 52 BCE) was Rome's first great lyric poet. His small corpus (around 2,300 lines) includes 113 poems ranging in length from a couplet to 400 verses, of diverse content and in every register: from passionate love to obscene (and sometimes very funny) abuse, from austere and moving emotional restraint to recherché Greek Alexandrianism. Most important for his later fortunes, however, is the Catullan persona, which is so vivid, sympathetic, and realistic that it persuades readers both to believe in its sincerity and to identify with it, painting their vision of Catullus as self-portraits.

Catullus was admired and imitated by the Augustan poets. Horace borrowed motifs from Catullus' two poems in the sapphic strophe (poems 11 and 51) in one of his most famous odes (1.22, *Integer vitae scelerisque purus*). Virgil's Dido has much in common with the abandoned Ariadne of poem 64 and utters a similar lament. The Roman elegists (Tibullus, Propertius, and Ovid) based their theme of love-struck poet and faithless mistress on Catullus and his Lesbia. But Catullus' most influential reader was the Silver Age epigrammatist Martial, who created the picture of Catullus that would survive the Middle Ages and form the basis of the Renaissance Catullus. Martial promoted Catullus as a racy epigrammatist, and the image perhaps contributed to Catullus' eclipse after the 2nd century. Martial, after all, was the racy epigrammatist par excellence, and he was easier and more fun to read than his by then old-fashioned and difficult model.

No one knows how or where Catullus' poetry survived the Middle Ages. One of his poems (62) appears in a 9th-century French anthology. He is ambiguously mentioned in the 10th century by Bishop Rather of Verona, who may have been reading his poetry. A single corrupt manuscript of his poetry finally emerged in the Renaissance around 1300, probably from France. But no one can be sure: only corrupt copies of it survive. More copies were made in the 15th century, and the first edition was printed in Venice in 1472, in a large quarto edition that also contained Tibullus, Propertius, and Statius' *Silvae.*

Humanist scholars studied and corrected Catullus from the outset of his rediscovery, but poets contributed equally to his reception. The genre of Renaissance Catullan poetry was invented by Giovanni Gioviano Pontano (1429–1503). Pontano accepted the portrait of Catullus he found in Martial, read Catullus' poetry through Martial's imitations (but with Renaissance eyes), and wrote Latin verse using Catullus' themes and meters. He created a new Catullus—a Renaissance sensualist. He did so imitating a mere handful of Catullus' poems: the sparrow poems, the kiss poems to Lesbia, and poem 16, in which Catullus argues that light poetry must be titillating and also distinguishes the poet from his poetry: "It is right for the true poet to be chaste/himself, but his verses need not be so" (16.5–6). Pontano set the terms for Renaissance imitation of Catullus: explicit eroticism, focus on kisses and sparrows, and use of poem 16 as a manifesto. (More than a century later Ronsard would use 16.5–6 as the epigraph announcing the Catullan program of his *Folastries,* in 1553.) Pontano's Catullan poetry inspired hosts of talented (and not so talented) Latin poets. Among the best are Pontano's younger contemporaries Marullo and Sannazaro and the Dutch poet Janus Secundus (1511–1536). Secundus is probably the most famous Neo-Latin lyric poet. His sensuous and complex *Basia* (*Kisses,* 1541), a cycle of 19 poems in various meters, influenced European lyric poetry in several languages.

The most notorious Renaissance interpretation of Catullus was the obscene reading of the sparrow in poems 2 and 3. The interpretation was derived from Martial, taken up by Pontano, and made famous by Poliziano (*Miscellanea* 1.6):

> That sparrow of Catullus in my opinion allegorically conceals a certain more obscene meaning . . . Martial persuades me to believe this in that epigram [Martial 11.6] of which these are the last verses:
>
> Give me kisses, but Catullan style
> And if they be as many as he said,
> I will give you the sparrow of Catullus. [14–16]
>
> For he would be too inept as a poet (which it is wrong to believe) if he said he would give the sparrow of Catullus, and not the other thing I suspect, to the boy after the kisses. What this is, for the modesty of my pen, I leave to each reader to conjecture from the native salaciousness of the sparrow.

Poliziano's interpretation was hotly contested (it is still debated today), and many contemporary readers also rejected the excuse for obscene poetry in Catullus 16.5–6. The controversies were played out in essays and commentaries, but especially in both Latin and vernacular poetry.

In England poets began to notice Catullus only in the late 16th century. They focused on the poems on kisses and sparrows (but not exclusively); but the times made them less enthusiastic about obscenity than their continental counterparts. The earliest translation (1614) was written by Sir Walter Raleigh while he was imprisoned in the Tower of London. Those verses (Catullus 5.4–6) were probably taken from his commonplace book:

> The Sunne may set and rise:
> But we contrariwise
> Sleepe after our short light
> One everlasting night.

Individual poems were translated by Thomas Campion (who set them to music), and by Ben Jonson and Richard Lovelace, but the first collection of translations appeared in *The Adventures of Catullus* (1707). This work, translated from the French *Les amours de Catulle* (1680), was a novel based on Catullus' poetry that included translations by various authors. (Several later authors have also presented Catullus' "story" in prose and verse, including Benita Kane Jaro in *The Key,* 1988.) The first complete translation was that of John Nott (1795).

Later poets, like their Renaissance counterparts, created a Catullus like themselves. In *The Adventures of Catullus* he was a 17th-century French courtier in English translation; in George Lamb's translation (1821), a man of aristocratic manners living in an uncongenial age; in Theodore Martin (1861), an embodiment of Victorian "manliness." Richard Burton's picture (1894) of "the toga'd citizen, rough, haughty, and careless of any approbation not his own" is (apart from the toga) very like what is known of Burton himself. The drawing of Catullus that Aubrey Beardsley made to accompany his translation of poem 101 (1896) actually incorporates his own image (Beardsley's beaky profile is outlined by the folds of Catullus' garment, with his eye sketched in Catullus' navel). Yeats's famous portrayal ("The Scholars," 1915) depicts himself and his friends, rebelling against bourgeois scholarship and morality. Their identification with Catullus, however, sometimes made it difficult for poets and scholars to treat his obscenity, and almost always prevented them from dealing honestly with his homosexual romance with Juventius (only Burton did so).

In the 20th century Catullus inspired many translators and imitators, including Ezra Pound, Dorothy Parker, Stevie Smith, Louis Zukofsky, Basil Bunting, and Anne Carson. Readers still tended to see a Catullus in their own image. Especially after the 1960s scholars and translators emphasized and explicated his obscenity and homoerotic themes, often pushing the Lesbia poems into the background. Scholarship in the 20th century moved from preoccupation with the short lyrics to New Criticism and a focus on Catullus' Alexandrianism, and onward to studies of masculinity, self-positioning, and reception.

BIBL.: Gordon Braden, "*Vivamus mea Lesbia* in the English Renaissance," *English Literary Renaissance* 9 (1979) 199–224. James Butrica, "History and Transmission of the Text," in *Blackwell's Companion to Catullus,* ed. Marilyn Skinner (Oxford 2007) 13–34. Julia Haig Gaisser, *Catullus and His Renaissance Readers* (Oxford 1993) and *Catullus in English* (Harmondsworth 2001). James A. S. McPeek, *Catullus in Strange and Distant Britain* (Cambridge, Mass., 1939). T. P. Wiseman, *Catullus and His World: A Reappraisal* (Cambridge 1985).

J.H.G.

Cavafy, C. P.

Konstantinos Petrou Kavafis (1863–1933), known to most of his readers as C. P. Cavafy (in either case the stress in the last name falls on the second syllable), of Alexandria in Egypt and the most widely recognized Greek poet since Theocritus. With Angelos Sikelianos (1884–1951), Cavafy is perhaps the most original of the modern Greek poets who have sought inspiration in antiquity; and (with James Joyce) he remains among the most enduringly iconic of Modernists, as well as the one whose recourse to Homer has proved most memorable. He is now essential reading for anyone concerned with the classical tradition, and indeed many readers with a classical education have been inspired to learn Modern Greek for the sole purpose of reading his work. All this rests on the basis of a corpus of 154 collected poems, none longer than three pages, most much shorter, and published in book form only posthumously (1935).

The equipment Cavafy brought to the task of engaging with the classical tradition could be described in much the same terms that the renowned historian Gibbon had once applied to his own qualifications: "a stock of erudition that might have puzzled a doctor, and a degree of ignorance of which a schoolboy would have been ashamed." But Cavafy's education, partly at private schools in England, exposed him early on to Victorian appropriations of the classical heritage that he found engaging but, as a Greek and as a poet, fruitfully open to challenge. Four aspects of his work may be singled out as representing his greatest contributions to the classical tradition.

First, and unavoidably, along with other subtle responses to Homer, there is "Ithaca" (1911), now familiar to thousands worldwide (though often in the unpromising setting of a commencement address or a funeral). Historically, the poem represents a radically new reading, Epicurean in character, of the Odyssean *nostos* (journey toward home). Its underlying message is a rebuttal of Tennyson's "Ulysses" (1842), as Cavafy himself implicitly acknowledged in an unpublished essay contemporaneous with a proto-version of his poem (1894). The last lines of "Ithaca" have become virtually a commonplace: "Wise as you have become, with such experience,/by now you will have come to understand what Ithacas mean."

A second notable aspect of Cavafy's involvement with the classics was his Alexandrian origin. He was born in Alexandria and died there, and to Greeks he is known simply as "the Alexandrian." But that attractively cosmopolitan society of the modern era appears in his work only obliquely: rather, an Alexandria of the past is refracted through an aesthetic of brevity and restraint that recurs to the epigrammatists of the Greek Anthology. The increasingly open homoerotic strain in Cavafy's work, however, owes little to the risqué Musa Puerilis of that tradition (though it is also free of the rather wan "Greek love" found in Pater and Wilde). A much more developed textual relationship is found in his reworking of the sepulchral epigrams. An indirect response to the Great War (1914–1918), these are far more original than Edgar Lee Masters's epitaphs in *Spoon River Anthology* (1915), likewise based on J. W. Mackail's rather post–Pre-Raphaelite *Select Epigrams from the Greek Anthology* (1890, later editions). Cavafy indeed rehabilitated the idea of Alexandrianism, freeing it from being a critical tendency or mere custodianship of the classics and making it a live force in poetry.

A third link in Cavafy's connection with the classics was his sustained concern with late antiquity (a field largely fallow in earlier poetry) and in particular with the vexed and ambiguous transition from paganism to Christianity. Following Browning, but pursuing the chase with the instincts and insights of his own Greek Orthodox heritage, Cavafy presents us with the elation and the contradictions, the resolutions and the backslidings, of pagan, Jew, and Christian over several centuries, encapsulating the matter of weighty monographs and ponderous historical novels in miniatures as beguiling as the then newly excavated Fayyum portraits. (He would be an important poet for his poems on Julian the Apostate alone.) In his involvement with that pivotal era in ancient history he of course sets out to undermine any simple idea of the classical—and, for good measure, the subtler nostalgia of Arnold.

Cavafy's fourth and perhaps most far-reaching contribution to classical traditions is his technique of reading history as a palimpsest. In this spirit—he saw the role of historical poet as a high vocation—he reads the classical through the strata of later experience. "Darius" (1920), for example, is not about Marathon, as one might expect from a Greek poet, but about Phernazes, a fictional poet of Persian origin who is writing a Greek epic, *Darius,* for Mithridates VI Eupator in 74 BCE, when the Roman forces invade Pontus. Similarly, "Demaratus" (1921) does not rehearse Herodotus' story of the famous turncoat but rather centers on an imagined rhetorical exercise on that subject proposed by the Neoplatonist Porphyry to a young sophist in the late 3rd century AD. For Cavafy, history's major actors are best seen through minor ones, history's classical peaks best described from post-diluvian foothills. (For Czeslaw Milosz, this made Cavafy a great poet of empire.) In the same vein, Cavafy opens up his idiom to subtle shifts of register, as lexical items or larger gobbets of antique Greek jostle with colloquialisms, and history reveals itself as a palimpsest. The most exquisite example of Cavafy's laying bare of documentary sources (here, as often, invented), the poem "In the Month of Hathor" (1917), exemplifies—even in a translation that fails to capture some of the wordplay—his enterprise of interrogating the tradition. The square brackets in the passage below have a progenitor in Browning's "A Death in the Desert" (1864); the ellipses have a parallel in Pound's "Papyrus" (1915); the fissure in the stone evokes the character of that venerable Alexandrian genre, the pattern poem—but the ramifications are at once more painful and wholly original:

> With difficulty I read   on the ancient stone
> "LO[R]D JESUS CHRIST." A "SOUL" I can make out.
> "IN THE MON[TH] OF HATHOR" "LEUCIU[S]
>   FELL ASLEEP."
> In the mention of his age   "LI[VED] YEARS"
> The Kappa Zeta shows   it was young he fell asleep.
> There among the worn characters I see   "HI[M] . . .
>   AN ALEXANDRIAN."
> Then there are three lines   extremely mutilated;
> but I can make out some words—   like "OUR T[E]
>   ARS," "PAIN,"
> then once more "TEARS"   and "TO [U]S HIS [F]
>   RIENDS SORROW."
> It seems to me that over Leucius   love went very deep.
> In the month of Hathor   Leucius fell asleep.

BIBL.: C. P. Cavafy, *The Poems of C. P. Cavafy,* trans. John Mavrogordato (London 1951); *Collected Poems*, trans. Edmund Keeley and Philip Sherrard, ed. G. P. Savidis, rev. ed. (Princeton 1992); *Collected Poems,* trans. and ed. Daniel Mendelsohn (New York 2009); and *Unfinished Poems,* trans. and ed. Daniel Mendelsohn (New York 2009). David Ricks, *The Shade of Homer: A Study in Modern Greek Poetry* (Cambridge 1989) and "Cavafy's Alexandrianism," in *Alexandria, Real and Imagined,* ed. Anthony Hirst and Michael Silk (Aldershot 2004) 337–352.

D.RI.

Censorship

Although the word *censor,* from which we derive the concept of censorship, originated in Rome, the idea of censorship in the strict modern sense—the official vetting of literary or other forms of expression, especially before dissemination—does not really obtain in antiquity, perhaps in part because of the limited literacy and the informal means of publication that existed in ancient cultures.

Nonetheless it is likely that something resembling what we call censorship has been in operation since there have been public means of expression, literary and otherwise, and governments to disapprove of them. Socrates, for instance, was condemned to death in 399 BCE on grounds of corrupting the youth of Athens and because his teachings were viewed as impious, even though he had produced no written texts. Because notions of impiety and corruption of youth have been central to arguments for censorship of artistic works in modern times, the trial of Socrates may be considered one of several early instances of governmental censorship at work. The writings of the Presocratic philosopher Anaxagoras had previously led to a charge of impiety under a decree specially drafted for his case (ca. 437 BCE); found guilty, he spent the remainder of his life in exile.

Imperial Rome instituted a form of what we call censorship under the aegis of the *lex maiestatis,* under which crimes against the majesty of the Roman people were prosecuted. Julius Caesar and, following him, Augustus took this notion of majesty personally and added to the law the category of defamatory works (*famosi libelli*). According to Tacitus, it was Augustus who applied this concretely for the first time, sending Cassius Severus into exile in 12 CE for having attacked illustrious men and women in his works. Tiberius, annoyed by poetry critical of his behavior, decided formally to apply the *lex maiestatis* to *dicta* (words) as well as to *facta* (acts); in 25 CE the historian Cremutius Cordus was prosecuted for having depicted Brutus and Cassius as "the last Romans." Still, this application of the *lex maiestatis* never gained acceptance among the citizens of Rome, and each successive emperor renounced it before eventually reinstating it. The Senate, presided over by the emperor, judged these cases and decided on the sentence, which ranged from deportation with confiscation of property to execution. Under Domitian, in the case of the historian Hermogenes of Tarsus (a different man from the later rhetorician with the same name) the sentence went so far as not only to demand execution of the writer but also to have his scribes crucified, to make sure the ideas contained in his *History* would not be repeated elsewhere. The literary works themselves were publicly burned. Pythagorean works had already been burned by order of the Senate as early as 181 BCE.

Perhaps the most famous case of what might be termed censorship in imperial Rome is the banishment of Ovid. Augustus, under the first part of whose reign writers such as Virgil, Horace, and Propertius had enjoyed favor, in 8 CE sent Ovid to spend the rest of his life in exile in Boeotia, along the Black Sea, under circumstances that have never been fully elucidated. His crime, at least in part, was the licentious tone of his *Ars amatoria,* all copies of which were removed from public libraries. The episode remains shrouded in mystery; he may also have been somehow implicated in an adultery scandal involving the emperor's granddaughter Julia, herself banished in the same year.

In the Middle Ages the art and literature of antiquity, even as it was being saved from oblivion, fell under severe suspicion because of its pagan origins. There were occasional strange efforts at recuperation, such as the early 14th-century *Ovide Moralisé,* a French work that recast Ovid's *Metamorphoses* as Christian allegory. The attempt to reconcile classical writings with Christian doctrine has its roots in a tradition going back at least to Eusebius, a 4th-century bishop of Caesarea, and aiming to demonstrate that the writings of Plato and Virgil in particular anticipate the coming of Christ; Dante's *Divine Comedy* also participates in this trend. Some of the same unease persisted into the Renaissance, particularly in regard to sexual matters. The first translators of Plato repeatedly expurgated the text; when Marsilio Ficino produced the first complete translation at the end of the 15th century, he provided as well confidently allegorical interpretations of the scandalous (mostly homoerotic) passages.

In the 18th century, with the discovery of Herculaneum and Pompeii, the art of antiquity began to cause a new round of trouble. By midcentury, with excavations ongoing, rumors had begun to fly about lascivious frescoes unearthed, as well as, among similar objects, a small marble statue of a satyr, or the god Pan, in sexual congress with an apparently consenting goat. *Lupanaria* (brothels) were uncovered from time to time as work on the excavations progressed, but it is also true that the great number of fertility symbols in the shape of phallic objects found in a variety of contexts led scholars to overestimate the number of places specifically devoted to sexual activity. Such discoveries were kept hidden in the Museo Borbonico, later to become the National Museum of Naples, which first produced a systematic catalogue of them in 1866 under the rubric "pornographic collection." They were not available for viewing by the general public, but their existence was well known; it fueled the idea, put forth most famously in Gibbon's *Decline and Fall of the Roman Empire* (1776–1788), that the empire had been felled by rampant moral depravity and corruption.

The excavations at Pompeii and environs, which stimulated enormous interest in archaeological discovery, also coincided with the great age of prudery beginning in the late 18th century and continuing well into the 20th. As a result, generations of scholars were faced with the problem of what to do about the large proportion of sexually explicit artifacts found there. In 1732 John Horsley's *Britannia Romana* imposed a vine leaf over a phallus featured in an ex-voto engraving; 1757 saw the first of a series of illustrated volumes on the finds at Herculaneum that provided a separate volume for sexually explicit material. From the late 18th century onward, increasing numbers of guidebooks, catalogues, and descriptive accounts dealt with this quandary by using various degrees of euphemism and censorious circumlocution in their attempts to juggle classical erudition with modern sensitivity. In 1780 Pierre Sylvain Maréchal produced a nine-volume catalogue of Pompeian discoveries, excluding the satyr-and-goat statue but including some priapic artifacts, with the observation that "the simplicity of our ancestors found nothing indecent in objects which today make modesty blush," adding Rousseauistically that "one blushes, perhaps, only to the degree to which one has strayed from nature."

In 1786 Richard Payne Knight, a well-known English

collector and antiquarian and later a major benefactor of the British Museum, published his *Discourse on the Worship of Priapus,* a highly erudite work on the survival in Christian times of the ancient use of phallic votives made of wax in Isernia, a small town near Naples. Despite its scholarly nature, this work, which its author tried unsuccessfully to withdraw from circulation, was reprinted many times and continued to arouse censure for decades to come. In 1808 it was termed "one of the most unbecoming and indecent treatises which ever disgraced the pen of a man who would be considered a scholar and a philosopher," and a British Museum curator wrote about it several decades later: "of this work it is impossible to speak in terms of reprobation sufficiently strong: it is a work too gross almost to mention; and it is quite impossible to quote the indignant but too descriptive language of the critics in their severe but just remarks upon this disgusting production." Thus, in the mid-19th century a specialist in the field heaped opprobrium even on the critics who described, in the course of decrying, the work of a scholar attempting to account for the survival of ancient phallic votive use. In 1865 Knight's *Discourse on the Worship of Priapus* was reprinted by a publisher of pornographic works. The collection Knight left to the British Museum on his death in 1824 was set aside, as was the practice at the time for "indecent" artistic and literary material—the latter being reserved in the Private Case of the British Museum Library (now British Library), which had its counterpart in the Enfer of the French Bibliothèque Nationale.

Modern censorship of ancient artifacts has not been confined to the plastic arts; the literature of antiquity has also been censored in modern times. Throughout the 19th century and well into the 20th, Greek and Roman literature formed the cornerstone of upper-class education for boys in Europe and Anglophone countries, but the texts used were carefully chosen, vetted for sexual content, and expurgated accordingly. Homosexuality (for which there exists neither a term nor a category in Greek; the word itself is a Greek-Latin hybrid coined in the second half of the 19th century) was one of the major problems. In E. M. Forster's *Maurice* (1914; first published 1971), for instance, an Oxford tutor is depicted instructing his students translating Plato to "omit the reference to the unspeakable vice of the Greeks." This was far from being the sole source of difficulty, though, and the early 20th century saw a number of fine editions of Greek and Latin literary works in translation, most notably Aristophanes' *Lysistrata* and the *Satyricon* of Petronius, refused admission into the United States by the Post Office under pressure from the Society for the Suppression of Vice.

A French proverb states that *Femme qui parle Latin ne fit jamais une bonne fin* (A woman who knows Latin will come to no good end). The idea that the knowledge of Latin was to be restricted to boys of the dominant classes and withheld from women and the working classes coincided, over the course of the 19th century, with rising literacy rates among those groups and, as a result, increased anxiety about the consequences of educating those whose education was felt to be dangerous to the status quo. Debates about the perils of educating women and the working classes often centered on the question of who should be allowed to learn Latin. It was felt that the knowledge of that language encouraged the sons of the working classes as well as women in general to be discontented with their lot: the former would aspire to the clergy, it was feared, and the latter would no longer be happy with their domestic role. A number of 19th-century writers insisted that the learning of Latin was appropriate among women only for nuns, old maids, and widows; clearly there existed a necessary if unexplained negative link between Latin and female sexuality. In the early 20th century such debates began to subside along with the decline of teaching of classical languages.

Until then, though, the knowledge of Latin, and even more so of Greek, was viewed as the mark of an educated man of the upper classes. In his ca. 1696 dictionary Pierre Bayle observed that "those who understand Latin are better fortified than other men against the malign influence of dirty objects." In prerevolutionary France the idea of censorship had itself been referred to using a delicate Latin periphrasis, expurgated works being termed *ad usum Delphini* (for the use of the dauphin). Latin and Greek were for centuries the languages of privilege, as witness the fact that diarists had for centuries confided their most intimate secrets in those languages so as to keep them opaque to the prying eyes of both spouses and servants. The most famous example of this form of private encoding is the diary of Samuel Pepys (1633–1703) with its macaronic notations on his erotic life using shorthand in Latin, French, and Spanish. Other practitioners include two prominent classicists who kept significant parts of their journals in Greek: Martin Crusius (1526–1607) for recording his dreams, Karl-Benedikt Hase (Charles Benoît Hase, 1780–1864) for describing his adventures with prostitutes and dildos in the back streets of Paris.

Latin in particular for centuries served as the official language of whatever could not be expressed in the vernacular, including what we now term pornography. (The word derives from an ambiguous Greek term meaning "prostitute-writing" but is hardly to be found in Greek, gaining currency only in the late 18th century in reference to writing about the social conditions of prostitutes; it was not used in its current meaning before the mid-19th century.) Around 1660 *The Ladies' Academy,* which quickly became a bestseller of European pornographic literature, was written and published directly in Latin by a Grenoble lawyer, Nicolas Chorier, but posed as a memoir written in Spanish by a Spanish noblewoman and translated into Latin by a philosopher. A huge international success, it enjoyed many editions in various languages and as late as 1881 was reprinted in a four-volume edition mixing French with a simplified form of Latin easily recognizable to a French-speaking public with little or no knowledge of that language.

By the 18th century it had become the usual practice to publish works deemed potentially dangerous entirely in Latin, or at least with particularly offensive passages set in that language. A salient example is offered by the anti-masturbation treatises that gained great currency over the course of the 18th century and into the 19th. The anonymous *Onania* was first published in England in the 1720s in Latin, as was the Swiss physician Samuel-Auguste Tissot's extremely influential work *L'Onanisme ou dissertation physique sur les maladies produites par la masturbation* (1760), first published two years earlier in Latin under the title *Tentamen de morbis ex manstupratione.* In his preface to the French-language version Tissot remarks on how much more difficult it is to speak of such matters in the vernacular; accordingly, in many editions of the French text some particularly embarrassing case studies are described in Latin (in other editions these passages are omitted entirely).

A century later, Ambroise Tardieu, an eminent physician and later dean of the medical school of Paris, published a work entitled *Étude médico-légale sur les attentats aux moeurs* (1857), on what would later be called sex crimes; he felt compelled to note that he had chosen to write in French because it was important to deal frankly with absolutely everything, adding: "I have not even felt it necessary, except in one instance, to have recourse to the veil of Latin." Of the one case described in that language he writes: "I would hesitate before these horrible details were it not possible to hide them under Latin circumlocution." Decades later, the German sexologist Richard von Krafft-Ebing cited this same passage, preserving the Latin "for obvious reasons."

In addition to medical works (which continued into the 20th century to use Latin to deal with such topics as venereal disease), theological treatises, especially dealing with practical advice to priests, resorted to Latin when dealing with touchy subjects such as sins *contra naturam.* Historians too had recourse to Latin at times: Gibbon's *Decline and Fall of the Roman Empire,* for instance, avoids the use of the vernacular when describing the Empress Theodora's wilder moments, and the author boasted that his English was entirely chaste, all licentious passages left to the obscurity of a learned language. As late as the mid-20th century, writers and scholars were still inclined, when in doubt, to take refuge in Latin. A 1953 German translation of the *1001 Nights* gives nine problematic lines in Latin rather than German, and several volumes in the Loeb Classical Library—Catullus, Martial, and the *Greek Anthology* among others—long declined to translate certain passages into English, using Latin or in some cases Italian in the parallel texts to its classical editions. This tendency has not in fact disappeared: English translations of Freud's works, among others, still learnedly resort to Latin terms when referring to certain sexual matters.

The practice of resorting to Latin and sometimes Greek as a form of implicit internal censorship, to obscure the meaning of passages or whole texts, making them accessible only to those with a certain level of classical education, is almost never explained in the works in question; the reasons for it have always gone without saying. Those who understand, it is understood, understand; those who do not, do not (or else, of course, they get themselves a good dictionary). As a result, Latin, designated in principle the language of science and theology, became for a very long time in practice the standard vehicle of obscenity. Under "Latin" in Gustave Flaubert's *Dictionary of Received Ideas* (1880), the entry reads: "Beware of quotations in Latin: they always hide something unseemly." Generations of classicists may well have been spurred on to the study of Latin and Greek because of this; as Anthony Burgess notes about such use of foreign and classical languages, "Thus are we led to learning." The filmmaker Derek Jarman had fun with this phenomenon in his soft-core pornographic film *Sebastiane* (1976), which recounts the life of Saint Sebastian, Christian martyr and gay icon, with dialogue entirely in Latin.

As noted above, it is somewhat inappropriate to apply the term *censorship* in the modern sense to the ancient world; similarly, it would be inexact to say that all subsequent arguments around the issue of literary and artistic censorship can be directly traced to Plato and Aristotle. Those writers never actually deal with the subject of censorship as we know it. Nonetheless, the conceptual framework underpinning all the various arguments that have been put forth over the centuries comes back to ideas first advanced by Plato and Aristotle.

Plato goes so far as to banish poets entirely from his *Republic,* because of his well-known suspicion of artistic representation of all sorts. He also suggests expurgating Homer for immature audiences. (According to Suetonius, Caligula later toyed with the idea of suppressing Homer altogether, but this was never actually put into practice.) For Plato the morality of storytelling is always suspect both because of the problem of mimesis—always an imitation of something that is itself no more than an imitation—and because of the moral problem posed by the tendency of people to imitate what they see. Narrative is thus by its nature unreliable: good examples might alone be admissible, but good examples are not known to make interesting narrative. The poets are therefore out.

This viewpoint has, with variations, provided the major argument for censorship of narrative forms ever since, from Saint Augustine to Catharine MacKinnon. Once one has posited that people tend to imitate what they see and often lack the discernment to determine whether what they see is good or bad, one ends up following the Platonic line and assuming that representations of bad behavior inspire actual bad behavior and should therefore perhaps be suppressed for the good of the greater society.

Plato, in any case, pronounced on the subject of what should and should not be allowed in an ideal society. Aristotle, on the other hand, is not interested in this sort of moral category in either his *Poetics* or his *Politics.* Nonetheless, and despite having been Plato's student, he developed his famous theory of *catharsis,* according to which tragedy, by inspiring pity and terror in its audience, purges negative emotions and allows the spectators to achieve spiritual equilibrium. Aristotle was not trying to establish an ethics of what should and should not be shown in the theater; instead, he was describing, using contemporary medical terms (purging of bad humors), the effects of tragedy on the audience so as to provide guidelines for the potential writer of tragedy. Despite his lack of interest in the ethical dimension of these matters, his followers established on the basis of Aristotle's pronouncements on tragedy, and especially his theory of catharsis, arguments against censorship that have obtained ever since. Notable proponents of Aristotelian arguments for freedom of representation include Saint Thomas Aquinas and John Milton in his *Areopagitica* (1644).

Most of these arguments have, historically, focused on the question of the morality of theater. From the 17th through the 19th centuries in particular, polemics raged around the question of the morality of theatrical representation, because, as in Athens during the time of Plato and Aristotle, during that time theater was the most readily accessible form in which the greatest number of people, regardless of class and education, were exposed to narrative art. For the same reason such conflicts tended to concentrate on theater and novels in the 19th century; novels and the cinema in the 20th century; and various media such as video games and the Internet today. It is to be noted that the major arguments advanced never stray far from the essential lines initially established by Plato and Aristotle in the 4th century BCE.

BIBL.: Catherine Johns, *Sex or Symbol? Erotic Images of Greece and Rome* (London 1999). Walter Kendrick, *The Secret Museum: Pornography in Modern Culture* (New York 1987). Françoise Waquet, *Latin, or the Empire of a Sign: From the Sixteenth to the Twentieth Century* (London 2001). E.L.

Centaur

A mythical creature composed of a human head and torso above the body and legs of a horse. Although these fantastical animals are half human and half horse, it is the animal, equine component that has fascinated artists and writers from antiquity to the present.

Centaurs are ubiquitous in Greek art and myth. Although half human, they lived at the margin of civilization in the forests and caves of Mount Pelion in Thessaly. Described by Homer as wild beasts, these aggressively masculine creatures were rude, savage, and brutal and inclined to excessive drinking, unbridled sexual appetites, and outbursts of unthinking violence. They appear in myth as uncouth, lawless, strapping lecherous drunks. Ovid's description of the Battle of the Lapiths and Centaurs (*Metamorphoses* 12.210–535) epitomizes the centaurs' character and behavior and their significance. Invited to a wedding banquet, they become intoxicated, rape the bride and female guests, and attack their Lapith hosts. The offending centaurs are massacred or exiled.

Centaurs feature in numerous narratives involving Hercules. The most popular, again from Ovid, concerns Hercules, his wife Deianeira, and the centaur Nessus, who aims to rape Deianeira as he carries her across a river (*Metamorphoses* 9.101–133; see also Sophocles' *Trachiniae*). With a single poisoned arrow Hercules dispatches Nessus in midstream. Generic images of Hercules vanquishing a centaur with cruel violence (and without the presence of Deianeira) probably refer to the vicious rout he wreaked among the centaurs on Mount Pholoë, which led to the injury and death of Chiron.

The centaur's physical form symbolizes the ambivalent nature of human existence and has been interpreted as a metaphor for the struggle between civilization and barbarism, reason and chaos. Yet two centaurs, Chiron and Pholus, were hospitable, gentle, and wise, noble paragons of aristocratic virtue. These two exceptions highlight the dual nature of the centaurs that arises from the beast in humans and the humanity in beasts. Chiron's complex character blurs the boundary, so cleanly marked on his body, between human and equine. Homer calls the immortal Chiron the "justest of the centaurs" (*Iliad* 2.832), and Pindar celebrates him as a "lover of humanity" (Pythian Ode 3.5). He was the mentor of several gods and heroes, including Peleus, Achilles, Jason, Actaeon, Meleager, and Asclepius. Accidentally poisoned by Hercules' arrow, Chiron exchanged his immortality for Prometheus' mortality, thus ensuring his eminence as a father figure. After death Chiron was placed by Zeus in the night sky, as the constellation Sagittarius (the Archer).

Centaurs flourished throughout the medieval period. They overran their original ancient confines to settle in the imaginations of artists of the Indian subcontinent, through Hellenistic influence, and then in the expanding Islamic world, while in Europe their appearance and significance changed in a new Christian interpretative context. The centaur was commonly represented in European, Ottoman, and Persian illuminated manuscripts as a galloping archer, deriving ultimately from ancient Near Eastern models. The archer centaur was identified visually with the constellation Sagittarius, which appears in this form in Islamic astrological illuminated manuscripts earlier than in Europe. In medieval Europe, Sagittarius inhabited manuscript illuminations, stained glass windows, and decorative frescoes. Archer centaurs also figured as decorative motifs for manuscript marginalia in Christian and Jewish texts and for wall decoration, as in the mosaic at the Palazzo of the Normans, Palermo, which probably refers to an Islamic decorative vocabulary. Centaurs less comfortably served as Romanesque portal sculpture.

The archer centaur's inclusion in medieval bestiaries served Christian purposes. According to the moral interpretations offered by bestiaries, the centaur's double nature symbolized the sin of hypocrisy. As vehicles for Christian teaching, centaurs embodied the idea of the human condition, suspended between good and evil, or represented the individual's internal struggle between spiritual and animal nature. Inevitably, negative traits triumphed in medieval commentaries, and the centaur's bestial qualities eventually came to symbolize lust and adultery.

In the *Divine Comedy* Dante places the centaurs in the Inferno, with murderers and thieves, but also in Purgatory, among the gluttons. Other medieval writers simply labeled centaurs as pagans and heretics. Through Dante these Christianized centaurs passed directly to innumerable artists, among them Botticelli and William Blake, who over the centuries taxed their imaginations endeavoring to illustrate the *Divine Comedy.* In a fresco of the Inferno for the basilica of Santa Maria Novella in Florence, Andrea Orcagna surrounded heretics and the violent with menacing centaurs.

Jacobus de Voragine's *Golden Legend* (ca. 1260), a popular collection of saints' lives, portrayed a centaur as the beneficent and knowledgeable guide of Saint Anthony Abbott on his search for Saint Paul the Hermit. Because Anthony Abbott is a minor saint, however, this refreshing image was rarely represented, although Giovanni Bellini's *Sacred Allegory* (ca. 1490–1500) guarantees the durability of this positive vision of the centaur in Christian narrative.

Centaurs underwent further changes in form and meaning during the Renaissance. Neoplatonism and the imagery it inspired, like Botticelli's *Pallas and the Centaur* and Pollaiuolo's *Hercules and Deianira* (both later 15th cent.), gave renewed prominence to the centaur as symbol of sensuality and barbarism in contrast to reason and civilization. The centaur embodied Ficino's concept of the dual, conflicting nature of humanity that could be transcended only by divine wisdom. For Mantegna, the lowly centaur constituted one of the irascible Vices that Minerva had to chase from the Garden of Virtue.

The emphasis on the heroic male nude in Renaissance art returned the centaur to its ancient heroic stature. Michelangelo's *Battle of the Lapiths and the Centaurs* (ca. 1492) celebrates the virility and muscular harmony of the centaurs engaged in combat, without explicit moralizing overtones. Although courageous, possessed of otherworldly might, and always willing to brawl, the rude, often intoxicated centaur invariably succumbs to civilized heroes like the Lapiths or Hercules. In imitation of ancient practice, aggressive masculinity is likewise showcased on the battle scenes and fights found on ceremonial helmets, shields, and saddles of the period made for such figures as Henri II (in the Metropolitan Museum of Art, New York) and Alessandro Farnese (Vienna).

On the Parthenon (5th cent. BCE), defeat of the centaurs by Greek soldiers symbolized the victory of Greece over Persia. Similarly, representations of Hercules' destruction of the centaur Nessus assumed an intimidating political valence in the sculptural rendition that Giambologna executed in 1599 for the Medici in the Loggia dei Lanzi. Here conflict and struggle have been eliminated in favor of absolute, punishing domination, an obvious reference to firm Medici rule. Giambologna also executed bronze statuettes of a centaur raping a woman and of a centaur fighting a lion that highlight the centaur's natural impulses of unrestrained lust and animal savagery (both are now in the Museum of Fine Arts, Boston). Their virtuoso craftsmanship, bronze material, and small scale, however, indicate that the objects were intended to function as conversation pieces in refined settings, implying that Renaissance man had mastered these human flaws.

From idiosyncratic perspectives, the painters Filippo Lippi and Piero di Cosimo endowed the centaur with a sympathetic humanity unknown in antiquity. Lippi's *Wounded Centaur* (ca. 1500) gently conveys the suffering of the typically savage creature as he contemplates his impending demise. Centaurs appear in a pair of paintings by Piero that represent the growth of civilization. Although he shows centaurs engaged in their expert activity of hunting, he suggests that they actually contribute, however primitively, to the formation of civilization. The tender, human element of the centaur emerges in Piero's *Battle of the Lapiths and the Centaurs* (1490s), where despite the melee raging in the background, a female centaur embraces and kisses her dying centaur lover. The expression of centaur affection and compassion gained currency as representations of female centaurs and centaur families fascinated artists, like Dürer, who worked from Lucian's ecphrastic description (2nd cent. CE) of a centaur family and from a salacious account of the female centaur form by Philostratus.

Centaur-related themes and imagery figure on furniture of this period, such as elaborately decorated marriage chests. Panels on these cassoni feature centaurs that turn wedding banquets into battlefields, attempt to rape brides, embark on hunting and military adventures, and even participate in wedding processions (in an example by Bartolomeo di Giovanni, now in the Louvre). This was seen as appropriate visual entertainment and moral instruction for young brides, as narrative representations of centaur myths were considered guides for right action.

Centaurs most often appear in Renaissance art in tapestry and fresco cycles depicting the Labors of Hercules and, in illuminated manuscripts and fresco and architectural decoration, in cycles illustrating the zodiac, seasons, or months. Boccaccio was partly responsible for the proliferation of images of Hercules confronting centaurs, for he incorrectly believed that Hercules had joined the Lapiths in battle. For the Renaissance, Hercules was the ubiquitous nemesis of centaurs. Also, intensifying a trend from antiquity, centaurs permeated Renaissance visual culture as ornamental motifs divorced from narrative myths.

Chiron is depicted in art as a tutor, and his education of Achilles remains the preferred subject. In the Renaissance he represented the ideal of Humanist education, an enormous tribute. He was renowned for his moral and practical wisdom, especially in music, medicine, hunting, and warfare. For Francis I and his painter Rosso Fiorentino, at the Palace of Fontainebleau, Chiron's aristocratic curriculum epitomized ideal princely education. Renaissance elites took to heart Euripides' remark that the learned centaur instructed Achilles in proper behavior so that "he might not learn vile men's ways" (*Iphigenia in Aulis* 709). Yet the more politically shrewd minds of Erasmus (*Ad-*

ages), Machiavelli (*The Prince*), and, under their influence, Alciato (*Emblems*), perceived Chiron as an evil adviser, stressing instead his sensuality and treachery. Erasmus thought Chiron's curriculum fostered tyrants; Machiavelli interpreted the myth to advocate the use of brute force by princes.

Stripped of the personality and emotional complexity they had acquired in the 14th century, centaurs continued to thrive in the early modern period as unambiguous embodiments of strength and virility and lust and barbarity while providing artists such as Rubens and Jordaens with opportunities for magnificent banquet scenes and dramatic battle panoramas.

With typical Baroque humor, centaurs furnished opportunities for witty, lavish aristocratic play on a small and large scale, in private and public spaces, and their bestial nature was paradoxically animated by advances in technology. Rudolf II owned a silver gilt automaton clock in the form of an archer centaur carrying Diana with two dogs (now in Vienna), which was used for sophisticated drinking games: the person to whom the centaur's arrow pointed was to offer a toast before imbibing his drink, emulating the centaur's insatiable appetite for wine. At the Teatro dell'Acqua in the Villa Aldobrandini near Rome, the centaur "makes a terrible roaring with a horn" (John Evelyn). Although centaurs retained their fearsome, threatening qualities, they were also employed to elicit reactions of surprise and amusement.

Guido Reni used centaurs to explore the psychological implications and power dynamics of sexuality, whereas Antonio Canova reduced the Battle of the Lapiths and the Centaurs to a statement of victorious resolve and uncontested potency of European male culture. A new genre of lyrical love scenes emerged in the 18th century from excavations at Herculaneum and in the art of Giandomenico Tiepolo, who pictured centaurs cavorting with satyrs, nymphs, and fauns. Although present in the preceding periods, scenes of the education of Achilles by Chiron won new prominence and acquired erotic overtones. Few artists of the Romantic period ignored the centaur as the most eloquent evocation of the world of myth, but the creature was especially dear to Moreau and Redon. Picasso was likewise attracted to the centaur as representative of sexuality and the mythic universe. Freud employed the centaur as a metaphor for the marriage of the id and the ego, much as others since antiquity had used the centaur as a metaphor for the binaries of nature/civilization and barbarism/reason. As a vehicle for metaphor, the centaur's popularity is unsurpassed by any other composite creature or humanized animal from Greek myth. Throughout the 20th century, centaurs permeated science fiction and popular culture, including Disney's full-length animation *Fantasia* (1940). Centaurs appear in works by Thornton Wilder and John Updike as well as in a remarkable number of modernist texts by T. S. Eliot, W. B. Yeats, H.D., and D. H. Lawrence. Centaurs have been reinvented in multifarious, unanticipated forms in the explosion of Internet sites. In modern Italian, *centauro* is the standard vernacular term for a motorcyclist.

BIBL.: Ernst Gombrich, "Botticelli's Mythologies: A Study in the Neo-Platonic Symbolism of His Circle," *Journal of the Warburg and Courtauld Institutes* 8 (1945) 7–60. Heather Ingman, "Machiavelli and the Interpretation of the Chiron Myth in France," *Journal of the Warburg and Courtauld Institutes* 45 (1982) 217–225. J. Michael Padgett, ed., *The Centaur's Smile: The Human Animal in Early Greek Art* (New Haven 2003).

M.PE.

Cento

The cento, whose name is derived from Greek *kentron*, "needle," and which is often called a "patchwork," is most easily described as poetry consisting of short units taken verbatim from earlier poets. The genre was probably invented in the 2nd or 3rd century CE and flourished in late antiquity, with some presence through the Middle Ages, a revival during the Renaissance, and occasional use in the modern period. The most famous centos are those of late antiquity, composed from the texts of Homer and Virgil. In Latin these include the *Cento Nuptialis* of Ausonius, written to commemorate the wedding of the Emperor Gratian in 374, and the *Cento* of Proba, of debated date, a retelling of Christian salvation history in epic form. In Greek the outstanding examples are the Homeric centos of the Empress Eudocia, written in the early 5th century CE and, like the *Cento* of Proba, a casting of biblical narrative into classicizing form. Other ancient examples are found in the Latin Anthology and in the Palatine Anthology.

The generic purpose of the cento and its compositional rules are debated. The clearest programmatic statement of centonist practice from antiquity is Ausonius' preface to the *Cento Nuptialis*. He suggests that the cento is to be laughed at rather than praised, and the parodic aspects of his work, with its notoriously graphic depiction (in epic Virgilian language) of a bride's deflowering, may be intended humorously. Other centos, however, such as the 3rd-century *Medea* of Hosidius Geta, have clearly serious intent. Ausonius also lists what are often taken for rules of cento composition: "two half-lines are joined in a single line or one-and-a-half lines are joined to a half-line. It is clumsy to put together two full lines, and utter nonsense to put down three in a row." Yet despite Ausonius' opprobrium, it is common for centonists to join full lines, and to achieve striking poetic effects, for instance in the use of enjambment, by doing so.

Ausonius' characterization of the cento as *solae memoriae negotium,* "strictly a matter of memory," nonetheless clarifies the form's place in the history of classical literature. The genre requires writer and reader to remember displaced fragments of poetry and their original contexts; this reveals the influence of traditional educational practice, in which short units from canonical poets were painstakingly analyzed in the teaching of literacy. Such dissection promoted the use of literary intertexts in learned discourse: the cento is the logical extension of this use. Yet cento composition also raises larger issues of cultural memory. The genre showcases the manipulation of prior texts, suggesting that such texts served as compacts between readers who understood them as common sources of authoritative language. At the same time, this active manipulation suggests cultural fragility. Ancient criticisms of the cento focus on fidelity to authorial intent: Jerome accused centonists of misrepresenting their source texts; a similar criticism had been made before him by Irenaeus of Lyon. Such criticisms reflect ambivalence over the instability of cultural remembrance as represented by the cento.

The floruit of the cento in the post-classical period, and the ambivalence surrounding it, thus reveals the genre's status as a cultural commentary, both indicating and negotiating the authority of particular canonical texts within a specific cultural milieu. As literary retrospection and introspection, the cento fundamentally defines for its readers the literary tradition in which they stand.

BIBL.: J. Octave Delepierre, *Tableau de la littérature du centon*, 2 vols. (London 1875). Filippo Ermini, *Il centone di Proba e la poesia centonaria latina* (Rome 1909). Scott McGill, *Virgil Recomposed: The Mythological and Secular Centos in Antiquity* (New York 2005). M. D. Usher, *Homeric Stitchings: The Homeric Centos of the Empress Eudocia* (Lanham, Md., 1998). C.CH.

Chaos

The notion of chaos was introduced into Western cosmology around 700 BCE by Hesiod. Telling the story of the origin of the world in his poem *Theogony*, he explained that "first of all, Chaos came to be" (116). The term *chaos* did not signify confusion or disorder; rather, deriving from a verb meaning "to gape, or yawn," its basic meaning was "a chasm." Hesiod seems to have conceived of the beginning of the world as the opening of a vast, gaping expanse between earth and sky; this may have influenced Plato's creation myth in the *Timaeus* (ca. 360 BCE), especially his account of *chōra* (the space or place that is the receptacle of becoming), a subject of much recent reflection by Julia Kristeva and Jacques Derrida.

The idea of chaos had an enormous influence on Western thought. Interpretations of the term, however, varied considerably. Hesiod's conception of chaos was soon replaced by the notion that the world, before it was made into an orderly cosmos, was chaos, in other words, confusion and disorder. Expressing a view held by many ancient authors, Ovid described it as an "indistinct and disorderly mass," *rudis indigestaque moles* (*Metamorphoses* 1.7), "a jumbled mass of things without order," *rerum confusa sine ordine moles* (*Art of Love* 2.467). This belief became widespread in later centuries. It is still current today.

Christian cosmology inherited the notion of chaos from pagan antiquity but adroitly set it aside. Although God had created the world from nothing (*ex nihilo*), there was also the biblical account: "In the beginning God created the heaven and the earth. And the earth was without form, and void [Hebrew *tohu va-bohu*]" (Genesis 1.1–2). In a semantic move of enormous importance, Christian theologians identified *tohu va-bohu*—translated in the Vulgate as "void and empty," *inanis et vacua*—with chaos. This meant that chaos was no longer considered to be the beginning of the world but instead a consequence of the world's creation. Yet chaos continued to trouble Christian thinkers. Why was God's creation not perfect from the very beginning? Was chaos perhaps inseparable from creation even for almighty God? This, however, would be a contradiction in terms. How, then, could the problem of chaos in God's creation be resolved? The early Greek Church Father Origen looked to the "wisdom that was always with the Father": since everything was made in wisdom, everything always existed within wisdom, in a state of prefiguration and preformation, before it was eventually created. Consequently there was no chaos in God's creation of the world (*On First Principles* 1.4.4–5). In the 13th century Thomas Aquinas, drawing on Saint Augustine, attempted to dispose of the problem of chaos definitively by distinguishing between the time at which the world was formed and the logical order according to which it was formed. The confusion called chaos by the ancients, he maintained, preceded the world's formation, not in time, but merely in logical terms (*Summa of Theology* 1.q.66, art.1).

New perceptions of chaos arose in the Renaissance. One of the most original was evoked by Cardinal Nicholas of Cusa. Writing in 1440, he referred to a "dark chaos of pure possibility" that descends on the soul that has turned away from truth and toward uncertainty and confusion, thereby failing to attain God. Separated forever from the immutability and certainty of eternal life, the soul is thrown into the "chaos of confusion," in which it will die an agonizing death without extinction or termination (*On Learned Ignorance* 3.10.241). In the 16th century the Friulian miller Menocchio was tried by the Inquisition for his heretical belief that the world had congealed from a churning chaos composed of the four elements, like a ball of cheese in milk, and that, just as cheese produces worms by spontaneous generation, so too the world had produced angels.

In the opening of book 1 of Maurice Scève's cosmological poem *Microcosme* (1562), God makes a "great chaos" that opens out into the visible light to show that it is the first manifestation of his creative power. In Edmund Spenser's *Faerie Queene* (1596), all things belonging to the world draw their existence from a chaos within the world:

> For in the wide wombe of the world there lyes,
> In hateful darknesse and in deepe horrore,
> An huge eternall Chaos, which supplyes
> The substaunces of natures fruitful progenyes. (3.6.36)

John Milton, in his great biblical epic *Paradise Lost* (1667), straining language almost to its limits, described chaos as

> . . . the hoary Deep—a dark
> Illimitable ocean, without bound,

Without dimension; where length, breadth, and height,
And time, and place, are lost; where eldest Night
And Chaos, ancestors of Nature, hold
Eternal anarchy. (2.892–896)

This chaos, an infinite Beyond, surrounds heaven and hell, earth and paradise, and yet it exists within the world: the "womb of Nature" and "perhaps her grave" (2.911).

Like Milton, the German mystic Jakob Böehme attempted to find appropriate imagery to express the sheer majesty of chaos. In his spiritual cosmology, as presented in chapter 33 of *The Great Mystery* (1623), chaos is the preeminent source of all reality, the hidden world (*verborgene Welt*) from which the realm of the outer nature of this world (*Reich der aeussern Natur dieser Welt*) emerges. Chaos is the root of nature (*Wurzel der Natur*) that produces only the good. Though hidden, it opens itself to our vision through the rainbow, whose colors reflect the four elements or qualities of being as they exist in the depths. Boehme explains, in *The Key* (1624), that chaos has existed from eternity as the origin of the spiritual world, of light and darkness, of heaven and hell (22–23).

Friedrich Schelling, in his *Philosophy of Mythology* (1842), acknowledged the leap in perception achieved by Hesiod, whose notion of chaos in the *Theogony* represented, Schelling believed, the first steps by which philosophy began to disentangle itself from mythology. In the late 19th and 20th centuries chaos became a central category for understanding the world. Nietzsche valued it as a Dionysian source of creativity. Hedwig Conrad-Martius formulated a theory of space, from the perspective of philosophy, that focused on "primordial" or "boundless space" (*Ur-Raum* or *apeirischer Raum*), resembling Hesiod's chaos, and Ilya Prigogine, an authority on chaos theory in the sciences, proclaimed the "end of certainty." Chaos, which has been with us from the very beginning of Western thought, still influences our thinking about reality. At the end of the 20th century, chaos theory, a branch of mathematics and physics developed to describe why certain nonlinear dynamic systems appear to behave randomly, inspired popular novels like Michael Crichton's *Jurassic Park* (1990), films like *The Butterfly Effect* (2004), and even certain forms of literary and cultural criticism, whose authors claimed to find in chaos theory a scientific counterpart or grounding for postmodernism.

BIBL.: Hedwig Conrad-Martius, *Der Raum* (Munich 1958). Olof Gigon, *Der Ursprung der griechischen Philosophie: Von Hesiod bis Parmenides* (Basel 1945). Carlo Ginzburg, *The Cheese and the Worms: The Cosmos of a Sixteenth-century Miller* (Baltimore 1980). Alexander Gosztonyi, *Der Raum*, 2 vols. (Freiburg 1976). Thomas Kratzert, *Die Entdeckung des Raums. Vom hesiodischen "chaos" zur platonischen "chōra"* (Amsterdam 1998). Donald H. Mills, *The Hero and the Sea: Patterns of Chaos in Ancient Myth* (Wauconda, Ill., 2002). "Mythological Structures of Chaos," *Diogenes* 42, no. 165 (1994). Ilya Prigogine, *The End of Certainty: Time, Chaos, and the New Laws of Nature* (New York 1997). Tilo Schabert et al., *Strukturen des Chaos* (Munich 1994). Florian Schenk, *Mechanics: From Newton's Laws to Deterministic Chaos* (Berlin 2005). Hans Schwabl, "Weltschopfung," in *Realencyclopädie der classischen Altertumswissenschaft*, Suppl. IX (1962).

T.S.

Chartres

The cathedral school at Chartres has played a crucial role in the transmission of classical culture, in particular of Platonist tradition. First becoming a significant educational center under Fulbert (ca. 950–1029), Chartres acquired particular fame under Bernard of Chartres (d. ca. 1126) and a cluster of brilliant disciples in the first half of the 12th century. Although Richard Southern provoked considerable controversy by questioning its importance, a consensus is emerging that while Chartres was never as important an educational center as Paris, its school did provide a stimulus for a remarkable series of scholars in the first half of the 12th century.

Bernard of Chartres, active as a teacher there ca. 1110–1120 and its chancellor 1124–1126, was praised by John of Salisbury (ca. 1115–1180) as "the most copious fount of letters in Gaul in modern times." John invoked Bernard as exemplary in the way that he identified grammatical, dialectical, and rhetorical elements in any text, in addition to drawing out what ethical and religious instruction it could offer (*Metalogicon* 1.24). John, who probably learned about Bernard only through his own teachers in grammar, namely William of Conches (d. ca. 1154) and Richard "the Bishop," reports that Bernard was profoundly Platonist in his ideas, holding that "native forms" mediated between pure ideas on the one hand and more specific forms existing in the world of matter (*Metalogicon* 4.35) on the other. The same ideas are expounded in a widely diffused set of glosses on the *Timaeus* that Paul Dutton has convincingly argued to be the work of Bernard of Chartres.

Less is known about the career of Thierry of Chartres, whom both Otto of Freising and Peter Abelard allude to as Bernard's brother, other than that he was archdeacon of Dreux in the 1130s, became chancellor of Chartres in 1142, and was still active in 1149. John of Salisbury does not mention any kinship between Bernard and Thierry, whom he describes as "a most studious investigator into the arts" and as less than fully clear in his teaching on rhetoric (*Metalogicon* 1.5, 2.10). In his *Tractatus in Hexameron* Thierry goes further than Bernard in relating Plato's *Timaeus* to the Genesis creation, postulating that the world soul is identical to the Holy Spirit, a position that Abelard criticized in his *Dialectica* (before 1117) and with more nuance in his *Theologia "Summi boni"* (1120). Thierry subsequently commented several times on the *De Trinitate* of Boethius. His great familiarity with sometimes rare texts from both classical and scientific traditions is evident in his *Heptateuchon*.

William of Conches was another distinguished disciple of Bernard of Chartres. In his early glosses (from around 1120) on the *Consolatio Philosophiae* of Boethius, William shared the same ideas as Thierry about the identity of the world soul and the Holy Spirit, but he moved away from this in his later glosses on Macrobius and Plato. Allusions to Chartres in his commentary on Priscian's *Institutiones grammaticae* make it likely that this is where he taught, although it is not certain where John of Salisbury actually pursued his studies under William. Gilbert of Poitiers (d. 1154) extended Bernard's interest in native forms into an elaborate metaphysical system in his commentary on the *Opuscula sacra* of Boethius. Gilbert, chancellor at Chartres 1126–1142 (when he relinquished the position to Thierry, on becoming bishop of Poitiers), seems to have been teaching in Paris by the late 1130s. Though Paris was a center for Aristotelian learning, Chartres preserved a reputation as a seat of Platonist and scientific study, not least through its rich and valuable library. Unfortunately, the destruction in 1944 of many manuscripts from Chartres has made its full contribution to preserving the transmission of classical culture difficult to assess.

BIBL.: Bernard of Chartres, *Glosae in Platonem*, ed. Paul E. Dutton (Toronto 1991). A. Clerval, *Les écoles de Chartres au Moyen Âge* (Paris 1895). Peter Dronke, "New Approaches to the School of Chartres," *Annuario de Estudios Medievales* 6 (1969) 117–140. Robert Giacone, "Masters, Books and Library at Chartres According to the Cartularies of Notre-Dame and Saint-Père," *Vivarium* 12 (1974) 30–51. Nikolaus Häring, "Chartres and Paris Revisited," in *Essays in Honour of Anton Charles Pegis*, ed. R. O'Donnell (Toronto 1974) 268–329. E. Jeaneau, *"Lectio philosophorum": Recherches sur l'école de Chartres* (Amsterdam 1973). R. W. Southern, *Medieval Humanism and Other Studies* (Oxford 1970) and "The Schools of Paris and the School of Chartres," in *Renaissance and Renewal in the Twelfth Century*, ed. R. L. Benson and G. Constable (Cambridge, Mass., 1982) 113–137. C.J.M.

Chaucer, Geoffrey

English poet, ca. 1340–1400. Born into a London mercantile family, he began his association with the English ruling classes as a page in the household of the Countess of Ulster, afterward achieving the rank of esquire under Edward III. In his later life he became an important member of the royal household of Richard II, serving as a diplomat and civil servant until the end of his life.

In his envoi to *Troilus and Criseyde* Chaucer's narrator urges his poem to "kis the steppes where as thow seest pace/Virgile, Ovide, Omer, Lucan, and Stace" (5.1791–1792). Such display of devotion to these classical poets might suggest to modern readers that Chaucer turned directly to their works as models. Yet he usually relied on Italian and French redactions of classical poetry as sources for his own art. This is not to say that he failed to see how classical narratives could inspire and contribute to the ambitious projects of medieval poets; rather, he turned to his immediate literary predecessors for his classical material partly because he was interested in exploring how they packaged it for Christian readers, namely, through glossing, amplification, abbreviation, censorship, and allegorization. In other words, his focus is often on the medieval reception of classical literature, as he imitates, parodies, and sometimes overtly mocks the strategies of Dante, Boccaccio, the French court poets, and others who brought classical material to their contemporary readers. His own approach to classical material, then, is always accompanied by acknowledgment of its mediated presence in medieval culture.

Nonetheless, his debt to classical literature is immense. In his earliest works he demonstrates familiarity with Ovid's *Metamorphoses* and *Heroides,* Virgil's *Aeneid,* and the rhetorical and philosophical works of Cicero. For example, in his *Book of the Duchess* (1369–1372) the narrator reads Ovid's story about Ceyx and Alcyone, discovering that the character of Morpheus, who resurrects the dead Alcyone, can serve as a counterpoint to his own attempt to "resurrect," poetically speaking, the dead spouse of John of Gaunt, Chaucer's patron for the work. In *The Parlement of Fowles* (1380?), he again meditates on his poetic task by portraying his narrator in the act of reading Macrobius' commentary on Cicero's *Somnium Scipionis* while searching for material to use in his own poem about love. In the opening lines of *The House of Fame* (1379–1380) his dreaming narrator tersely (to the point of comedy) rehearses events from the *Aeneid,* viewing them at one point, inappropriately, from Dido's sentimental, Ovidian perspective. Such comic treatment of his classical sources displays Chaucer's skepticism about the stability and coherence of the classical tradition as it was received by medieval culture. Later in the same poem the record of events from ancient history is shown to be garbled during its transmission, and truth becomes entangled with fiction. Standing in as an image of the inevitability of such corruption is Lady Fame herself (based on Ovid's Fama), a monstrous dispenser of lies and promulgator of unjust reputations whose judgments about which narratives will remain alive in the literary tradition, and what their authors' reputations will be, make a mockery of any culture's belief in the truth value of narratives that have been passed down through time. Chaucer's *Legend of Good Women* (late 1380s) makes a similar point: when asked by an ignorant but powerful Christian patron to write an anthology of short exemplary narratives about classical women true in love, the poem's narrator comically ends up forcing his classical sources into unsuitable hagiographical forms and also radically pruning and censoring them to fulfill the requirements of his reader. Such is the fate, suggests Chaucer, of classical narrative in its new medieval context; not only did a major change in religion make classical literature difficult to justify as reading matter for Christians, but a number of social factors surrounding the production of literature (such as the system of patronage and the ruling canons of taste among consumers of classical stories) also made tenuous the survival of classical literature in any true form in the medieval period.

Two of Chaucer's later poems, *Troilus and Criseyde* (1382–1386) and *The Knight's Tale* from his *Canterbury Tales* (1380–1400), are attempts to imagine life in the Trojan and Theban past. Both are modeled on works by

Boccaccio (*Il Filostrato* and *Teseida* respectively, both ca. 1340), but Chaucer also occasionally directly consulted texts by Virgil, Statius, and Boethius. Many of the themes and social mores visible in these poems exhibit medievalizing strategies (such as the inclusion of chivalric ideals and the focus on courtly love); further, intrusive remarks by the poems' narrators raise arguments about the superiority of Christianity to pagan belief. Nonetheless, in these poems Chaucer wanted to convey a sense of the dignity of classical epic and the moving plights of its characters. Both works are profoundly searching experiments in the representation of the classical world, and both constitute sophisticated acts of historical consciousness.

Other works by Chaucer also pay homage to the ancients. His "Complaint of Mars," "Complaint of Venus," and *Anelida and Arcite* are rhetorical exercises in pagan voicing. *The Manciple's Tale* tells the story of Phoebus and his raven from Ovid's *Metamorphoses* (with a new application to medieval courts), and *The Physician's Tale* rehearses a story originally found in Livy's historical works (though Chaucer may have relied on French and Italian retellings of it). *The Merchant's Tale* ends with a comic marital squabble between Pluto and Proserpina; Dorigen, in *The Franklin's Tale,* alludes to a large number of classical heroines who were faced with the choice of saving their honor or committing suicide; and *The Monk's Tale* rehearses, in severely abbreviated form, a number of tragic stories from the classical canon, each designed to illustrate the teller's rather simple-minded thesis that the goddess Fortuna is unpredictable.

Chaucer's admiration of classical poetry, and the lessons he learned from it about irony, tragedy, history, fate, and love, made him a major conduit, and fashioner, of the classical tradition in England. Yet his engagement with it was always accompanied by a profound awareness of how medieval authors, himself included, betrayed it in the course of presenting it to contemporary audiences.

BIBL.: Christopher Baswell, *Virgil in Medieval England: Figuring the Aeneid from the Twelfth Century to Chaucer* (Cambridge 1995). John M. Fyler, *Chaucer and Ovid* (New Haven 1979). Lisa J. Kiser, *Telling Classical Tales: Chaucer and the Legend of Good Women* (Ithaca 1983). A. J. Minnis, *Chaucer and Pagan Antiquity* (Woodbridge, Suffolk, 1982). Winthrop Wetherbee, *Chaucer and the Poets: An Essay on Troilus and Criseyde* (Ithaca 1984).

L.J.K.

Chrēsis

From the Greek for use, (proper) utilization. With the concept of proper utilization (*usus iustus*), or simply with words for "to use" (often modified by adverbs regarding intention), the Church Fathers designated their method of dealing with ancient culture. They thereby employed a teaching that had a long history in pre-Christian thought. The insight that the worth of a thing depends on the way it is used is rooted in everyday experience, but it gains special strength in scientific discussion (for physicians) and in philosophical thought beginning in the time of the Sophists (Plato and Aristotle, and in the Stoa). The concept of proper utilization requires that behavior be dictated by guiding values, and that a choice necessarily be made between true and false, right and wrong.

In this way, *chrēsis* took on a meaning that made it a suitable tool for the Church Fathers. As early as Tertullian, Clement of Alexandria, and Origen (2nd–3rd cents.), the concept of proper utilization took on terminological coherence. The method it designated was bolstered by the New Testament, and it was developed through the allegorical exegesis of the Old Testament as well as through analogies with nature. The Christian sees himself placed in a world that is the work of God and in that respect good, but also a world of idolatry and moral perversion: the components of God's divine order have been thrown into confusion and are therefore abused. The result is that appropriate utilization becomes a general duty of everyday Christian behavior. *Chrēsis* of pagan knowledge is one aspect of this comprehensive duty, a practical example of which was provided by the apostle Paul's speech on the Areopagus. The method requires first of all the ability to make proper distinctions. For although the seeds of truth existed in pre-Christian thought, they were always mixed there with falsehood and evil. Justin Martyr (ca. 150) attempted to explain the state of affairs using the Stoic teaching of *logos spermatikos*. The elements of the True, the Good, and the Beautiful had to be sifted out and "restored" to God, who is their true possessor. Just as the Israelites, following God's command during the Exodus from Egypt, took with them Egyptian vases and vestments of silver and gold with which to furnish the Holy of Holies, thus the Christian must turn the goods incorrectly used by the pagans to the worship of God. This exegesis is first found in Irenaeus, then in Origen, Gregory of Nyssa, Augustine, and others. *Chrēsis* is understood, however, not only as a useful tool but also as a creative, unifying power. An example from nature is provided by bees: they collect useful material from alien flowers, making out of it new structures (honeycombs) and a new substance (honey). Related to *chrēsis* but not identical with it is *synkatabasis* (*condescensio*), the assimilation to certain habits of thought and life for pedagogical or missionary purposes. The greatest model for both is God, who descended to earth to give human expression to his Word, and who uses everything well, even evil.

Using the exegesis of the treasures of the Egyptians as his basis, Cassiodorus (6th cent.) successfully defended the reading of profane authors for the training of monks, as Hrabanus Maurus (780–856) later did for the education of clerics. Christian Humanists (Petrarch, Erasmus, and others) fought with the same weapons, although their goal was quite different from that of the Church Fathers. *Chrēsis* remains a vital principle within the Catholic Church, intrinsically connected to the theory and execution of its mission. It continues therefore to be adhered to even in more recent church documents—including those of the Second Vatican Council.

BIBL.: Christian Gnilka, ΧΡΗΣΙΣ/*Chrēsis: Die Methode der Kirchenväter im Umgang mit der antiken Kultur,* vol. 1, *Der Begriff des "rechten Gebrauchs"* (Basel 1984), and vol. 2,

Kultur und Conversion (Basel 1993). Paul Hacker, *Theological Foundations of Evangelization* (St. Augustin 1980). C.GN.

Translated by Patrick Baker

Christine de Pizan

French author (1364–1430). Though born in Venice, she was raised in Paris, where her father, Tommaso da Pizzano, served as astrologer to Charles V. During his reign (1364–1380), Charles V promoted the translation of Latin texts into French and commissioned manuscripts for an extensive royal library that laid the foundation for the vernacular humanism of late medieval Paris and helped shape Christine's career as a writer.

In her autobiographical text, *Avision-Christine* (1405), she recounts her childhood interest in intellectual pursuits. Although her gender excluded access to formal education, she did receive some informal instruction, presumably from her father, over the objections of her mother, who thought it more suitable that she learn to spin rather than acquire literacy in Latin. Whatever Christine's educational opportunities were, they ended with her marriage at age 15 to Etienne du Castel, a royal secretary, and she devoted herself to the tasks of running a household until she was widowed at the age of 25. With dependent children and a mother to support, she turned to composing poetry and prose treatises, many on topics drawn from the classical tradition. As a woman writing in French, Christine offers a unique perspective on the reception of classical texts in the medieval vernacular.

Describing her entry into the profession of letters, she speaks of the remnants of Latin she retained from her education. Though Christine could read Latin, she knew most classical texts in their French versions, versions that often included commentary as part of the translation. She read Nicole Oresme's translations of Aristotle's *Ethics* and *Rhetoric;* she knew Ovid's *Metamorphoses* in the anonymous *Ovide moralisé,* Ovid's *Ars amatoria* in the anonymous *Art d'amours,* and the story of Troy—including the narrative of the *Aeneid*—in the second redaction of the prose compilation of universal history, *Histoire ancienne jusqu'à César.* She frequently appealed to the authority of such texts to address the political and social issues of her day. Her *Epistre Othea* (1399) develops a reading of classical mythology as a tutorial in chivalric values; since Christine was involved in the production of illustrated manuscripts of the *Othea,* this text offers a visual interpretation of the classical tradition and marks the origin of the iconography of the "children of the planets." Her *Mutacion de Fortune* (1403) offers a narrative of universal history in verse, and her *Livre de la cité des dames* (1405), a prose treatise in defense of women, includes an extensive survey of women from classical myth and history, so that *Cité des dames* can be read as a feminist critique of the classical tradition. In the *Livre du corps de policie* (1406–1407), she drew on Oresme's translations of Aristotle in a prose treatise on political theory. She also composed a large number of texts on courtly as well as devotional themes, but her contributions to the *translatio studii* that is vernacular humanism—and her awareness of the gendered structures of literary history—constitute a significant aspect of her literary legacy.

BIBL.: Marilynn Desmond and Pamela Sheingorn, *Myth, Montage, and Visuality in Late Medieval Manuscript Culture: Christine de Pizan's "Epistre Othea"* (Ann Arbor 2003). Thelma Fenster, "'Perdre son latin': Christine de Pizan and Vernacular Humanism," in *Christine de Pizan and the Categories of Difference,* ed. Marilynn Desmond (Minneapolis 1998). Sandra L. Hindman, *Christine de Pizan's Epistre Othéa: Painting and Politics at the Court of Charles VI* (Toronto 1986). Charity Cannon Willard, *Christine de Pizan: Her Life and Works* (New York 1984). M.DE.

Cicero and Ciceronianism

Theodor Mommsen's *History of Rome* (1854–1856) excited readers for many reasons. Mommsen mobilized the new philological, historical, and legal scholarship of his time to produce an innovative history, not just of the city of Rome but of Italy as a whole. Like Darwin and Marx, whose great syntheses appeared not long after his, Mommsen was a master stylist. Like them, he provided readers in an age of rapid social, political, and social change with what seemed a comprehensive, rigorous, and challenging synthesis of materials and approaches that no one before him had brought together. Yet Mommsen brought Roman history back to dramatic life less by analysis than by crafting brilliant, vivid portraits of Roman statesmen and writers. He used deliberately anachronistic language to emphasize that these men had been just as human, just as weak or strong, fallible or brilliant as his own contemporaries. And he made Cicero his antihero. Mommsen transformed Cicero from an exemplar of antique republican virtue into the very model of a modern poseur, a politician without principles and a writer without originality. His speeches were bombastic and manipulative. His philosophical works were a patchwork of borrowings from the Greeks, crude mosaics hastily assembled. Even his letters were only the weak-minded outpourings of a pathetic political exile, like the German or Russian exiles of Mommsen's own time, condemned to poverty and isolation in Paris or London, "stale and empty as was ever the soul of a feuilletonist newspaper columnist banished from his familiar circles."

Mommsen damaged Cicero's reputation, and, for a time at least, many scholars accepted his view that Cicero had been a sleazy politician whose ambitious-looking treatises were chiefly valuable as sources for the lost texts he had pillaged, and whose career as orator and politician exemplified not the civic and republican values he had claimed to defend but the self-seeking, personal politics that had destroyed the Roman Republic. In the course of the 20th century, however, Cicero recovered. The scholarly rediscovery of the rhetorical tradition after the Second World War restored his reputation as a literary theorist and clarified his achievement as an orator. Renewed interest in republican values and in the schools of Greek philosophy that flourished in the Hellenistic period gave

Cicero's thought a new historical interest—and made clear why generations of medieval, Renaissance, and Enlightenment thinkers had taken him so seriously. Areas of activity that earlier scholarship had largely ignored, such as the antiquarian passion for information about Roman traditions and rituals that Cicero shared with Varro and others, also came back to light. Cicero, in short, is back. Soon, no doubt, a new generation will set out to shove him back down the slopes of Parnassus, but for the present, what matters is that the scholarly struggle over Cicero that took place during the past century and a half, though dramatic, was only one chapter in the long and fascinating history of his afterlife. From the early imperial period onward, Cicero's contentious life and vast literary production provoked admiration and criticism in nearly equal proportions: Seneca, who would enjoy great authority in the Middle Ages and the Renaissance, viewed him critically, but Quintilian—whose treatise on rhetoric would have an enormous influence when the full text was recovered in the 15th century—admired him unreservedly and took him as an absolute model. The sine-curve pattern of Cicero's reception was set early, and it lasted for more than 1,500 years—though the period of his greatest glory was, perhaps, the Renaissance, when he became not only a historical figure and a writer but also the object of the literary cult known as Ciceronianism.

The Christian and pagan thinkers of the 4th and 5th centuries shared a passionate interest in Cicero, but they expressed it, and used his work, in a wide variety of ways. Lactantius admired Cicero unreservedly, taking him as the model for his own decision to spend the latter part of his life in contemplation and praising him for his elegant proof of the existence of divine providence. Ambrose, the patrician bishop of Milan, adapted Cicero to Christian ends. He took Cicero's treatise *De officiis* as the model for his own treatise *De officiis ministrorum* (*On the Duties of the Clergy*). But he changed Cicero's message fundamentally, insisting that the pursuit of wisdom ranked higher than any form of activity—though he found a Ciceronian way to make the point, noting the importance of *otium,* leisure, for true mental activity. Augustine, who deeply admired Ambrose, noted that almost all students of rhetoric admired Cicero's language, "but not his heart." Yet he praised Cicero's protreptic work *Hortensius,* now lost, and credited it with inspiring him to love wisdom and study philosophy (*Confessions* 3.4).

It was Augustine's contemporary and correspondent Jerome, however, who most clearly revealed the paradoxes of the Christian response to Cicero. Splendidly educated in pagan literature, he went to Syria with a friend, planning to study monastic life. But he found himself unable to give up reading his classical texts, and fasted in advance in order to expiate a future encounter with Cicero's writings. During Lent, Jerome later recalled, racked with fever, he found himself caught up in the spirit and brought before God's judgment seat, where he fell prostrate, blinded by the light. Asked about his condition, he said, "I replied that I was a Christian. 'You lie,' answered He that sat upon the throne. 'You are a Ciceronian, not a Christian: for where your treasure is, there will your heart be.' " Eventually, Jerome found an application for his classical education in translating and explicating the Scriptures. Yet he never made clear, to others or to himself, exactly how he or any other Christian could reconcile a passion for secular learning and eloquence with a commitment to the true religion. The problem would torment many later scholars in the Christian tradition.

Even as late antique Christians worried about whether they could legitimately read and admire Cicero, a pagan thinker took a decisive step toward showing that they could and should. Macrobius excerpted from Cicero's *De re publica* his account of Scipio's dream, to which he appended a lengthy commentary. By focusing on this text, which offered something like a survey of the cosmos, he gave the impression that Cicero's primary concern had been less with what happened on earth than with the perfect heavens that surrounded it. Macrobius also emphasized the passage in which Cicero remarked that the chief God who ruled the universe approved of human assemblies and societies as much as anything that took place *on earth*—and took it as a statement that the pursuit of eternal truths was a higher-level activity, for Cicero, than participating in the political and civic sphere. Though Macrobius emphasized the civic and military career of Cicero's hero, Scipio, he also sketched Cicero as a sage whose message was compatible with Christian thought—a view only enhanced by Ambrose's assertion that Cicero had described marriage as incompatible with the life of a philosopher.

In the early Middle Ages, accordingly, many Christian thinkers found it easier than Jerome had to praise Cicero and recommend the study of his works. His speeches, his rhetorical treatises, and his philosophical works had a vast, inchoate distribution, often in mutilated or incomplete form. And with the rise of more formal centers of learning, he rapidly regained a central position in the Latin corpus. Collections of his speeches circulated widely: the Catilinarian Orations were read at the Carolingian court, and the speeches against Verres were annotated by the great 9th-century critic and scholar Lupus of Ferrières. Many of his philosophical works were also read in centers of learning from Montecassino to northern France, where Einhard, the biographer of Charlemagne, read the *Tusculan Disputations.* The letters circulated as well, though often in incomplete corpora: Lupus not only studied them but also modeled his own correspondence at least partly on Cicero's. Later, as schools took shape, two works in particular, one of them spurious—the *De inventione,* and the *Rhetorica ad Herennium* wrongly ascribed to him—became the central textbooks for rhetoric. Reproduced hundreds of times, they also became the objects of numerous commentaries, often partly derivative. The history of Latin schooling in the Middle Ages and Renaissance is, to a large extent, the history of these texts and the tricks that teachers made them perform.

By the 13th century, as stable collections of Cicero's most important writings took shape in major centers, the sheer scope and richness of his work became clear. The encyclopedist Vincent of Beauvais, for example, drew directly from a wide range of texts as he assembled Cicero's arguments in favor of both the active and the contemplative life. And though Vincent had little sense of Cicero's own career or of his fundamental commitment to the active, civic life, scholars in the Italian cities, who knew republican regimes firsthand, realized by the 13th century that the author of *De officiis* espoused a civic, activist morality that fundamentally contradicted the ascetic teachings of medieval Christianity. The conflict between Ciceronianism and Christianity had come back to life, in a new form, and was resolved in different ways; some maintained that Cicero's testimony proved the independent value of the civic life, whereas other authorities—above all Thomas Aquinas—insisted that the Christian contemplative life excelled all others.

Petrarch, who felt this conflict in his bones, dramatized it as brilliantly as Jerome had. At the same time, he helped give Cicero an intellectual dominance that would last for centuries, a position comparable only to that of Aristotle in the medieval university curriculum. A passionate reader and collector of Cicero's works, Petrarch found in him all the wealth of resources—and all the problems and paradoxes—that previous Christian readers had uncovered. Convinced that true philosophy must not only reveal the truth to its readers but also make them desire to do good, he saw Cicero's eloquent dialogues as a model more useful and powerful than the systematic treatises of Aristotle and his scholastic followers. Acutely conscious of the historical difference between paganism and Christianity, Petrarch continually found himself frustrated by Cicero's habit of writing sometimes in monotheistic terms, sometimes in polytheistic—a constant reminder that his favorite ancient writer had not known the true God.

In 1345 Petrarch discovered a manuscript of Cicero's letters to Atticus in the Chapter Library at Verona. Horrified by the discovery that his beloved Cicero had abandoned politics only when Caesar's ascendancy forced him to do so, and disgusted by the maneuvers that these texts revealed, he denounced Cicero for pursuing false glory when he should, as a true philosopher, have devoted himself to leisure and contemplation (*Epistolae familiares* 24.3). Throughout Petrarch's life, he insisted that Cicero's chief glory consisted in the literary works that he had written in the lonely, intense solitude of his last years. And yet Petrarch modeled his own literary production in part on Cicero's. Like the Roman, whose *Epistolae ad familiares* provided the title, as well as the model, for his own *Epistolae familiares* (*Familiar Letters*), he made his letters, which he carefully rewrote and edited, into a kind of autobiography and a partial history of his own life and time. Even as Petrarch rebuked Cicero for being too Ciceronian, in other words, he helped establish Cicero as a uniquely powerful stylistic model and intellectual resource. His followers—the younger writers, such as Boccaccio and Coluccio Salutati, who made Petrarch's ways of reading and imitating ancient books into the intellectual program of the larger movement known as Humanism—shared his sense that Cicero was indispensable.

For the next two centuries and more, Cicero remained a best seller, in manuscript and then in print. Of the 400 surviving manuscripts of *De senectute,* for example, 350 were written in the 15th century—clear witness to Cicero's role as the hero and founder of a new brand of moral philosophy. Once printing was introduced, Cicero's works found new channels of diffusion and new audiences. The first classical text to be printed was *De officiis,* which appeared in Mainz in 1465. And through the first century of print and beyond, Cicero retained his preeminence.

At the same time, however, Cicero also became the object of a sharp controversy—one that began in the realm of style but expanded to involve the full range of religious issues that had worried Petrarch. In the later 15th century, Humanists like Angelo Poliziano and Filippo Beroaldo began to widen the range of Latinity: they commented on and sometimes imitated Quintilian, Statius, Apuleius, and others. But the same enhanced consciousness of Latin style that drove these men to eclecticism inspired others with the conviction that moderns should pursue a purer style based on a single model. When Paolo Cortesi protested that Poliziano, who refused to follow a single model, wrote unclassical Latin, Poliziano was unmoved: "'You do not write like Cicero,' someone says. So what? I am not Cicero. Yet I do manage to express myself, I think." Poliziano insisted that each writer should frame his own style—and suited his action to the word by using the Latin verb *exprimo,* for the first time, in its modern sense. Cortesi, in contrast, insisted that "nothing in these times could be said with elegance and variety except by those who set out a model for themselves to imitate." The debate continued, sometimes bitterly, in Florence and elsewhere, and was renewed a generation later in more complex terms. In 1513 Gianfrancesco Pico della Mirandola wrote a set-piece letter to Pietro Bembo, insisting that true eloquence came not from the imitation of a single model but from creative emulation, directed by an Idea of style or beauty. Bembo, a peerless Ciceronian, demurred, insisting that Pico's Idea was too vague to guide artistic practice, which had to begin from imitation of a single model.

At this point the question was more than theoretical. Thanks to the patronage of humanistically inclined popes like Julius II, Leo X, and Clement VII, and the cardinals, ambassadors, and bankers who emulated them, the papal Curia and the city of Rome became a center of classicism in the arts. In Leo's eyes, as Martin McLaughlin has shown, Bembo and his allies such as Jacopo Sadoleto won the debate over Ciceronianism. Accordingly, Leo appointed them papal secretaries, whereas the "Apuleian" G. B. Pio had to leave Rome, and these discriminating scholars set the seal of Ciceronianism not only on the Latin writings they published in their own names but also on the language of the Church. Curial Humanists began to refer to God as "Jupiter Optimus Maximus," to call churches "temples," and to introduce classical forms into the Catholic liturgy.

Erasmus—the greatest Latinist of the day and a creative eclectic in the style of Poliziano—saw these practices as intrinsically absurd. Worse still, they seemed to lend credence to Martin Luther's denunciation of the established Church as corrupt and pagan. In a brilliant polemical dialogue of 1528, the *Ciceronianus,* Erasmus etched an acid portrait of the Roman Ciceronians. He depicted them as neurotic aesthetes, unable to write unless they locked themselves in darkened rooms and terrified to set any Latin word on paper if it was not attested, in the necessary form, in one of Cicero's works. More seriously, he argued that no Christian could or should base his style exclusively on that of a single pagan. Christians, after all, lived not in antiquity but in their own historically distinct world—a world that boasted churches rather than temples; a world illumined by the sacrifice of Jesus and the subsequent development of the Christian religion. Only a Latin that took account of history—that used the language of the Christianity its writers and speakers believed in—could serve the moral and philosophical needs that Christian Humanists since Petrarch had sought to meet with classical culture. In fact, of course, Erasmus exaggerated. He caricatured his opponents, who did not engage in the extreme forms of Ciceronian pedantry that he brilliantly mocked. In some sense, too, as more than one of his critics pointed out, the logical consequence of his argument was not that moderns should bring their Latin up to date, but that they should use their vernaculars. Yet his polemic reveals how central was the role Cicero continued to play, not only in the realm of style but also at the deeper level at which Christian thinkers tried to justify their passion for Greek and Latin thought and art.

Over time, a moderate Ciceronianism, generally classical but not extremist, became the norm, in Protestant *Gymnasien* in North Germany, Jesuit schools from Paris to Prague, and English grammar schools alike. Despite the late 16th-century vogue for Tacitus, Cicero retained his central position as a school author and a model for good writing of many kinds. He also served new purposes. From the 15th century on, as natural philosophers debated the value and status of astrology, his own *On Divination* served as a source and model, especially for those who rejected such pursuits. In the 16th-century heyday of skepticism, his *Academica,* which offered information to be found nowhere else, attracted intensive philosophical analysis.

In the late 17th and 18th centuries, finally, Cicero regained something of the central cultural status he had enjoyed in the Florence of Salutati and Leonardo Bruni. His works continued to be committed to memory in schools, and his pious, generally optimistic vision of the cosmos endeared him to the Cambridge Platonists. But it was above all the civic Cicero who now came back to life. In the British political system of the mid-18th century, he served as a model of civic engagement and effective oratory. The Bostonians who agitated against British rule imagined themselves as so many Catos and Ciceros, and their enemies as so many Catilines. These Roman visions rose so vividly before them that when Dr. Joseph Warren stood to speak in the Old South Church about the Boston Massacre, he wore a "Ciceronian Toga." John Adams was fascinated throughout his life by the "Sweetness and Grandeur" of the sound of Cicero's Latin, especially as exhibited in the Catilinarian Orations.

The French radicals of the 1780s and 1790s drew even sharper lessons from the Latin texts they had read in school. As the radical journalist Camille Desmoulins recalled,

> The republicans were for the most part young men who, nourished by reading Cicero in the colleges, conceived a passion for freedom there. We were brought up in the schools of Rome and Athens, and in the pride of the Republic, only to live in the abjection of the monarchy and under the reign of a Claudius and a Vitellius. It was foolish to imagine that we would be inspired by the fathers of the fatherland of the Capitol, without feeling horror at the maneaters of Versailles, and that we would admire the past without condemning the present.

Robespierre, like Adams, had a passion for Cicero, from whom he learned the art of denouncing his own opponents as enemies of the people and the Republic.

In the wake of the republican movements of the 18th century and their less powerful replay in 1848, Mommsen and others devalued Cicero and his role in the history of the Roman Republic. Yet even the Roman orator's sharpest critics did not try to remove him from the classroom. For generations, those who mastered *Latin for Americans* would then make forced marches through the Catilinarian and Verrine Orations, often with little or no sense of the political issues at stake. Even in America Cicero has retained, if not the status of a great philosopher, at least the reputation of the greatest of orators. When George W. Bush's handlers wished to prepare the press and the public for what they believed would be Senator John Kerry's victories in the 2004 presidential debates, they explained that Kerry was another Cicero—a name that still suggested, as no other could, the mastery of persuasive language and political argument that Cicero's words, over the centuries, have both taught and exemplified.

BIBL.: Hans Baron, "The Memory of Cicero's Roman Civic Spirit in the Medieval Centuries and in the Florentine Renaissance," in *In Search of Florentine Civic Humanism,* 2 vols. (Princeton 1988) 2:94–133. Marc Fumaroli, ed., *Histoire de la rhétorique dans l'Europe moderne, 1450–1900* (Paris 1999). Howard Jones, *Master Tully: Cicero in Tudor England* (Nieuwkoop 1998). Martin McLaughlin, *Literary Imitation in the Italian Renaissance: The Theory and Practice of Literary Imitation in Italy from Dante to Bembo* (Oxford 1995). Ingrid Rowland, *The Culture of the High Renaissance: Ancients and Moderns in Sixteenth-Century Rome* (Cambridge 1998). T. Zielinski, *Cicero im Wandel der Jahrhunderte,* 3rd ed. (Berlin 1912).

A.G.

Cinema

Images of classical antiquity occupied the motion picture camera almost from its invention. The roster of early silent experiments and short features includes a large number of classical subjects; the first *Last Days of Pompeii* dates from 1900. The genre comes into decisive focus with Giovanni Pastrone's *Cabiria* (1914), a sprawling story of the Punic Wars—nearly three hours long—centered on the adventures of the endangered young woman who gives the film its title. A large budget was well spent: on the use of four cameras (one of them innovatively mobile), location work in Sicily and North Africa, imposing sets (notably the Temple of Moloch in Carthage), and spectacular effects (an eruption of Etna, Archimedes' defense of Syracuse), as well as some florid intertitles by Gabriele D'Annunzio. The film's galvanizing effect on early American cinema is on view in D. W. Griffith's *Intolerance* (1916). From this point on the movie industry claimed a version of the ancient world as a prime site for some of its most ambitious efforts (they came to be called epics). The classical world on view is more exotic than ancient; outsized and strange and recklessly opulent, it serves as something of a mirror for the industry itself. By the end of the 20th century much of what most people knew about antiquity came to them by this route.

America and Italy have dominated the production of films set in the classical world. Mussolini saw to the building of Cinecittà, still the best studio setting for classical Roman exteriors; he also, as propaganda for his Ethiopian campaign, provided the purse for a grandiose reenactment of the battle of Zama in *Scipio l'Africano* (1937). In general, though, Italian classical films have had modest budgets; the stunning profitability of Pietro Francisci's *Le fatiche di Ercole,* marketed internationally as *Hercules* (1957), opened the way for a broad stream of classical strongman films, made with polyglot casts for dubbing into several languages. The genre descends from the popularity of Maciste, the heroine's muscular guardian in *Cabiria;* his later incarnations are sometimes mythological, like Hercules, sometimes characters in an episode from Roman history. In the latter case they are often gladiators; gladiatorial combat is a common occasion for spectacle in these films, and the influence of that combat on Roman politics is a frequent plot point. The ability of some directors to compensate for meager financing with cinematic ingenuity is part of the lore of the business; Mario Bava's effects for *Ercole al centro della terra* (*Hercules in the Haunted World,* 1961) are especially famous.

Hollywood films in this line are fewer and progressively more expensive, often at the leading edge of the industry's technical development. The climax of the 1935 *Last Days of Pompeii* was engineered by Willis O'Brien, who had directed the effects for *King Kong* two years earlier; the 15-minute chariot race that Yakima Canutt staged for William Wyler's *Ben-Hur* (1959; in competition with a famous precedent in the silent version of 1925) remains one of the most complicated and intense action sequences ever filmed. Henry Koster's *The Robe* (1953) was the first film in Cinemascope. Wyler's *Ben-Hur* in its initial release was shown in a large-format 65mm print; it was shown twice a day with reserved seating, and several other films of the type followed suit over the next few years. Studios became eager to claim historical authenticity, and the films testify to sometimes considerable efforts at research, though the results are always in service to cinematic effect. In the most spectacular scene in Joseph Mankiewicz's *Cleopatra* (1963), the title character enters the Forum at Rome through a costly replica of a triumphal arch that was not to exist for another three and a half centuries. The legendary expensiveness of that film was an event in cinema history; it almost bankrupted its studio, and its disappointing box office and that of Anthony Mann's *The Fall of the Roman Empire* (1964) and George Stevens's *The Greatest Story Ever Told* (1965) effectively terminated the genre in its high-end form for several decades. In the early 21st century it has been reborn, aided by the ability of computer-generated imagery to reduce the expense and risk associated with massive sets and large battle scenes. Ridley Scott's *Gladiator* (2000) was a great success—like *Ben-Hur,* it won the Academy Award for Best Picture. Some successors on the same scale—Wolfgang Petersen's *Troy* (2004) and Oliver Stone's *Alexander* (2005)—did not fare as well, but Zack Snyder's *300* (2007), a violent presentation of the battle of Thermopylae stylized to resemble, very closely, the graphic novel on which it is based, set box-office records. There has also since the late 1990s been a run of internationally produced films for television with classical settings; some of these have been given theatrical release in certain markets.

Manckiewicz's script for *Cleopatra* draws on Plutarch and Shakespeare, but in general these movies seldom rely on older sources. A number are based on popular novels (*The Robe, Quo Vadis, Ben-Hur*). The preeminent influence, however, is Hollywood's own history of conventions and expectations, which constitute a powerful filter; publicity material for Robert Wise's *Helen of Troy* (1955) refers to the *Iliad* as "one of the greatest love stories ever written." The Homeric poem is more of a presence in *Troy*—the scene between Achilles and Priam is kept—but romance still dominates: Helen flees with a still-living Paris at the end, and Achilles' death is linked to his love for Briseis ("You gave me peace in a lifetime of war," he tells her). The most serious strain in the genre shows when the setting is, as is usually the case, imperial Rome; American filmmakers regularly present Roman civilization as a moral and political failure, for its luxury and greed or for its cruelty and hollowness. Up through the 1950s the dramatic contrast is normally with Christianity, to which the principal characters eventually give their allegiance. With *Spartacus* (1960; directed by Stanley Kubrick, though many key decisions were made by the star, Kirk Douglas) the frame of reference becomes largely secular, though martyrdom remains a key theme. *Spartacus* ends with the crucifixion of its title character as the Roman Republic ends in a fascist coup d'état, and in *Gladiator* the hero's redemptive death opens the way for the restoration of the Republic at the end of the 2nd century CE. By widely observed though not entirely rigorous convention, the more powerful Romans in these films speak with English accents, and initially the contemporary empire being evoked is the British one, fading in reality but with a strong hold on the imagination. By *Gladiator,* the implied template is America's own worldly dominance.

Hollywood has also had its own line of mythological films, usually playful and often comic. *Jason and the Argonauts* (1963) and *Clash of the Titans* (1981; the story, more or less, of Perseus) contain some distinguished effects by O'Brien's protégé, Ray Harryhausen. The Walt Disney studio produced a witty animated *Hercules* (1997). A minor tradition transports figures from classical mythology into the modern world, often in musicals: Terpsichore in *Down to Earth* (1947) and *Xanadu* (1980), Venus in *One Touch of Venus* (1948; from a Broadway play with music by Kurt Weill). The best example of the genre is Danish: Torben Anton Svendsen's *Mød mig på Cassiopeia* (*Meet Me on Cassiopeia,* 1951), in which Polyhymnia falls in love with a modern composer and helps make his operetta a hit. Arnold Schwarzenegger debuts as a movie actor in *Hercules in New York* (1970), with the name and the voice that would later be famous incongruously disguised. Time warps in the opposite direction in *The Three Stooges Meet Hercules* (1962). Serious reenactment of a classical myth in modern dress has not been a significant Hollywood genre, but filmmakers elsewhere have been attracted to the possibility: Jean Cocteau's *Orphée* (1949), Marcel Camus's *Orfeu Negro* (1959; in Portuguese, set in Brazil), Jules Dassin's *Phaedra* (1962) and *A Dream of Passion* (1978; centering on a modern Greek theatrical production of *Medea*).

A few cinematic recreations of the ancient world have been mounted outside the studio mainstream, and they do things that would not be attempted there. Bob Guccione, the publisher of *Penthouse* magazine, financed *Caligula* (1979), directed by Tinto Brass from a script by Gore Vidal (reportedly with serious intervention from Guccione himself). The most extreme cinematic representation of imperial Rome as a site of sadism and erotic license, it combines some distinguished acting talent with sexual scenes of pornographic explicitness (though with less male homosexuality than would have seemed called for). Two notable films are acted in the ancient languages themselves. Derek Jarman's *Sebastiane* (1976; the title is a vocative) dramatizes the story of Saint Sebastian's death in the 3rd century CE, less as a religious martyrdom than as a parable of male homoerotic suffering and violence. Latin, spoken in a deliberately harsh classical pronunciation, contributes to the effect through its long-standing associations with discipline and punishment. In Mel Gibson's *The Passion of the Christ* (2004) the Judaeans speak Aramaic and the Romans Latin, in this case in Church pronunciation; the focus is on the torturing of the male body, at length and with a graphic intensity exceeding that of Jarman's film, though the intent is orthodoxly Christian (indeed, polemically so).

Spoken Latin has on occasion been used to striking local effect. In Gibson's directorial debut, *The Man without a Face* (1993), the title character's final instruction to the boy whom he has led through a neo-Socratic education is spoken in Latin and not translated for the modern audience. At a key moment in Paolo and Vittorio Taviani's *Padre Padrone* (1977), the efforts of a 20th-century Sardinian peasant to master modern Italian merge with the learning of Latin, and lines from the *Aeneid* (recited over a military radio, with Italian subtitles) manifest an uncanny transparency to his own situation. A sword-to-the-throat Latin lesson from a centurion enraged at a Palestinian graffiti writer's bad grammar is a high point of *Monty Python's Life of Brian* (1979).

The diffusion of classical material into moviemaking at large is in some regards very broad and general, but it can also be very specific and unpredictable. The imperial theme plays an important role in science fiction; George Lucas's first *Star Wars* trilogy (1977–1983) dramatizes the end of antiquity and the beginning of the Middle Ages as an evil empire is brought down and the rule of the galaxy handed over to a religiously devout order of knights. The conceit of Stanley Donen's musical *Seven Brides for Seven Brothers* (1954) turns on the male lead's discovery of the story of the Sabine women in Plutarch. The character sets out the idea it gives him (with credit) in a song about the "sobbin' women" of history and his own time; the abducted brides-to-be later read aloud from the *Life of Romulus* in their communal bedroom. The premise that an American frontier wife's inherited library would consist of the Bible and Plutarch is not a fantastic one.

A relatively small number of films can be considered cinematic treatments of specific works of classical literature. Homer's *Odyssey* is by far the most popular in this regard. Among the lost films of Georges Méliès was a three-minute *L'Île de Calypso,* subtitled *Ulysse et le géant Polyphème* (1905). Italy produced silent and sound films of the entire poem (*L'Odissea,* 1911; *Ulisse,* 1955, with Kirk Douglas in the title role), as well as a television version (1968; the Cyclops segment directed by Mario Bava); there has been an English-language television version, directed by Andrei Konchalovsky (1997). The film-within-a-film being shot in Jean-Luc Godard's *Le Mépris* (*Contempt,* 1963) is an *Odyssey* directed by Fritz Lang (playing himself). The poem is invoked by the title of Kubrick's *2001: A Space Odyssey* (1968), and that of Theo Angelopoulos's *To vlemma tou Odyssea* (*Ulysses' Gaze,* 1995), where the mantle of Odysseus falls on a Greek film director journeying through Balkan history of the 20th century (climaxing at the siege of Sarajevo). Joel and Ethan Coen's *O Brother, Where Art Thou?* (2000) opens with the first lines of the *Odyssey* and brings Homer on-screen as a character. The film's hero, Ulysses Everett McGill, is a fugitive from a Depression-era chain gang making his way across the American South, outwitting adversaries and trying to win back his divorced wife, Penny; at the close, he is still trying.

Other classical epics do not have much in the way of a cinematic history. Most films about the Trojan War are only spottily related to the *Iliad; L'ira di Achille* (*The Fury of Achilles,* 1962) and *Troy* stand out for retaining the

Homeric focus on Achilles. *La leggenda di Enea* (1962; released in English as *Last Glory of Troy* and *The Avenger*) treats the second part of the *Aeneid* with reasonable fidelity to the plot; despite the popularity of the Dido story in other venues, the rest of Virgil's epic has been filmed only for television (Franco Rossi's *Eneide,* 1971). *Jason and the Argonauts* bears little relation to the ancient account by Apollonius of Rhodes. *Hoshi no Orpheus,* a Japanese animated film by Takashi Yanase (1979; released in the West as *Winds of Change*), consists of five stories from the *Metamorphoses* (linked by a modern cartoon character) and gives Ovid screen credit. Lucan, Statius, and Nonnus have yet to interest filmmakers.

Xenophon's *Anabasis* becomes the story of a New York street gang's dangerous trek from the Bronx back to Coney Island in Walter Hill's *The Warriors* (1979); the classical subtext is made more explicit in a director's cut released on DVD (2005). The most distinguished film based on a classical narrative is Federico Fellini's *Satyricon* (1968), in which elements from Petronius' work interact with the director's distinctive cinematic style. The film mimics the state of the ancient text by opening in medias res and ending with interrupted narration and a freeze-frame that becomes a fragmented wall painting. Petronius' comedy and satire are tilted toward the phantasmagoric, often grotesque, sometimes lyrical, with if anything a heightening of the original's polymorphous sexuality (Fellini adds an episode about a sacred hermaphrodite). The strangeness of it all suggests not historical distance but continuity with Fellini's depictions of contemporary Italy. His next theatrical release, *Roma* (1972), a quasi-documentary fantasia about the modern city, is effectively a sequel. Fellini's example informs Julie Taymor's *Titus* (1999), a film of Shakespeare's *Titus Andronicus,* for which a nightmare version of late imperial Rome is created by shooting both at Cinecittà and in the streets outside.

Otherwise, the most impressive cinematic adaptations of classical literature come from drama. *A Funny Thing Happened on the Way to the Forum,* Burt Shevelove and Larry Gelbart's conflation of a half-dozen or so plots from Plautus with the kind of contemporary shtick represented by the title, had a successful run on Broadway and was made into an antic film by the director of the early Beatles movies, Richard Lester (1966). Among its pleasures is an ancient street scene (under the opening credits) more convincingly real than the better-financed equivalents in more serious films. There have been several responses to the challenge of giving cinematic form to Greek tragedy. George Tzavellas's *Antigone* (1961; in modern Greek) opts for undistracting period decor and a modest opening up of the action around the main palace set; only at the end, as Creon wanders alone into the landscape, does it attempt the note of archaic starkness that characterizes other efforts in the genre. Tyrone Guthrie's *Oedipus Rex* (1957; using W. B. Yeats's English translation) is the austere record of a Canadian stage production attempting the re-creation, in a modern, intimate setting, of Greek theatrical resources: the set unadorned, the actors masked, the acting stylized and at times ritualistic. Michael Cacoyannis has filmed a trio of plays by Euripides in a distinctive style: *Electra, The Trojan Women,* and *Iphigenia* (1962, 1972, 1977; the second with a particularly distinguished anglophone cast, the first and third in modern Greek). The texts are severely pared (though not beyond recognition), with much weight given to silent close-ups (especially of Irene Pappas, who is in all three films). The bleakness of the action is reinforced by location filming in harsh southern landscapes; the effect is that of core human experiences excavated in some primal form. Lars von Trier uses Nordic locations to the same end in his harrowing *Medea* for Danish television (1987)—completing a project originally planned by Carl-Theodor Dreyer.

Two filmed tragedies in Italian by Pier Paolo Pasolini share something of the same aesthetic but have a conceptual boldness that sets them apart. The inhabitants of their archaic landscapes have few of the trappings of classical Greeks as usually imagined; the world is generally that of tribal primitivism, with a fair amount of screen time devoted to religious ritual (including human sacrifice and dismemberment). In *Medea* (1970; with Maria Callas in her one movie role) the primitive world is Colchis, and Greece is the leading edge of Western civilization; as the action plays out, Medea's revenge on Jason is also the revenge of the archaic world on a modernity that is losing its sense of the sacred. In *Edipo Re* (1967) the encounter is internalized by presenting the otherwise chronological action (Sophocles' play constituting *secondo tempo*) with anachronistic framing: the title character is born in rural Italy of the early 20th century, matures in the ancient world, and at the end is a blind flute player on the streets of a modern city. Antiquity is the subconscious of the present day; the tragedy of modern man is routed through primordial conflict.

BIBL.: Sandra P. Joshel, Margaret Malamud, and Donald T. McGuire, eds., *Imperial Projections: Ancient Rome in Modern Popular Culture* (Baltimore 2001). Jon Solomon, *The Ancient World in the Cinema,* 2nd ed. (New Haven 2001). Martin M. Winkler, ed., *Classical Myth and Culture in the Cinema* (New York 2001). Maria Wyke, *Projecting the Past: Ancient Rome, Cinema, and History* (New York 1997). G.B.

Circe

Greek goddess, daughter of Helius (the sun god) and Perse (the daughter of Oceanus); resided on the mythical island of Aeaea, later identified with the promontory of Circeii in Latium (now San Felice Circeo, south of Rome). In *Odyssey* 10 she invites the companions of Odysseus to a feast on the island, which is populated with wild beasts who fawn on visitors (in *Aeneid* 7 the beasts are said to be earlier visitors whom she has transformed). After feeding the crew, Circe transforms them into pigs. One crewman (Eurylochus) escapes and warns those (including

Odysseus) who have remained on the ships. Odysseus mounts a rescue attempt after procuring, on the advice of Hermes, an herb (moly) that will protect him. When Circe's attempt to transform Odysseus fails, she becomes his lover and agrees to reverse the transformation of his men. Odysseus and his crew remain on the island for a year, and before they leave Circe suggests possible routes by which they might return home. In later literature Telegonus is said to be the son of Odysseus and Circe; in Hesiod they are given three sons. Moralists such as Horace (*Epistles* 1.2.23–26) treated the story as a fable about how the pursuit of women and luxury could turn men into beasts.

The transformation of Odysseus's companions is a common motif in Greek art, especially in vase paintings. The most famous image of Circe in the Renaissance, Dosso Dossi's painting (1531, now in the Galleria Borghese, Rome) may in fact be an image of the nymph Melissa rather than of Circe. Annibale Carracci painted *Ulysses and Circe* (1597–1604) on a ceiling in the Palazzo Borghese. From Victorian art the best-known images today are those of John William Waterhouse, whose interest in the figure of the enchantress led him to portray her repeatedly, most famously in *Circe Offering the Cup to Ulysses* (1892), *Circe invidiosa* (1892, now in the Art Gallery of South Australia), and *Circe* (1911–1915). She was also portrayed by Edward Burne-Jones in *The Wine of Circe* (1869). In sculpture the best-known rendition is that of the Australian Sir Bertram Mackennal, who exhibited the plaster version of his *Circe* (1892) in Paris and London.

Renaissance literature contains many figures modeled on Circe, such as Spenser's Acrasia, Tasso's Armida, and Trissino's Acratia. In the 19th century Nathaniel Hawthorne included the story in *Tanglewood Tales* (1853). Modern treatments include the Circe episode (episode 15) in James Joyce's *Ulysses,* in which the goddess is presented as the brothel madam Bella Cohen. In Carol Ann Duffy's collection *The World's Wife,* the poem entitled "Circe" records the cooking of the body parts of the sailors that Circe has changed into pigs. In 1949 John Myers Myers published *Silverlock,* a novel in which Circe changes the protagonist into a pig in recognition of his gluttony and lechery. In popular culture, Circe is a prominent enemy of Wonder Woman in the DC Comics series, in which she first appeared in 1949; elsewhere in DC Comics publications she encounters Superman (who surmises that she may be from Krypton) and Batman (as a member of Lex Luthor's Injustice Gang).

In chess, circe is a variant game in which captured pieces are reborn on their starting squares; the game is seldom played but figures instead in chess problems in many variants (e.g., anticirce, assassin circe, chameleon circe). In cosmology, 34 Circe is the name of an asteroid discovered in 1855.

BIBL.: B. Kuhn, *Mythos und Metapher: Metamorphosen des Kirke-Mythos in der Literatur der italienischen Renaissance* (Munich 2003). S. Tochtermann, *Der allegorisch gedeutete Kirke-Mythos: Studien zur Entwicklungs- und Rezeptionsgeschichte* (Frankfurt 1992). J. Yarnell, *Transformations of Circe: The History of an Enchantress* (Urbana 1994). G.C.

Cities, Praise of

The practice of composing formal speeches in praise of cities has a rich history spanning at least two millennia. Some constant themes of these speeches include the relationship of individual to group and of past to present, and the depiction of the experience of the city as place and of the sources and effects of political power in the city's history. The nature and relative importance of these themes and their interaction with one another varies greatly, however.

The first glimpses of the rhetorical praise of cities in Greek literature are to be found in the funeral speeches (*epitaphioi logoi*) of the classical city-state. The most famous example is the speech in praise of the war dead pronounced by Pericles in Thucydides' *History* (2.35–46), where praise of the unnamed soldiers is subsumed into an account of the moral and political virtues of the city of Athens, for which they gave their lives.

In the Hellenistic and Roman periods the balance between individual and city was transformed. Speeches in praise of an individual often contained praise of his city of origin, and the praise of cities itself became a developed genre of epideictic oratory as described in the first portion of the 3rd-century CE treatise *On Epideictic,* attributed to Menander Rhetor. Menander's recommendations apply elements familiar from the praise of countries (such as geographical location and climate) and from the praise of individuals (such as origins and achievements). Various traditions are put to use: the discussions of the site and climate of the city draw on geographical and medical lore; political and philosophical traditions are evident in the discussion of the government of the city; and accounts of the city's origins draw on local history. This last category reveals the importance of the classical past in creating a sense of identity for the citizens of the post-classical world. Praise of cities is frequently modeled on the praise of individuals (as advised by Quintilian 3.7.26). This conception of the city as an organic unity is used most strikingly in the speeches of lament (*monōidiai*) for cities destroyed by natural disasters or by war.

The single most famous and influential speech in praise of a city is the *Panathēnaikos* by the orator Aelius Aristides (2nd cent. CE), who interweaves the mythological and historical past of Athens with praise of its location and its continuing cultural importance. Standard speeches of praise for other cities pay a great deal of attention to the physical appearance and monuments. Such laudatory descriptions of buildings often serve as a means of paying tribute to their patron, as in the case of the first book of Procopius' *Buildings* (6th cent. CE), in which praise of the beauties of Constantinople reflects ultimately on the emperor Justinian. In this way praise of cities may contribute to praise of an individual patron.

The importance of monuments in speeches of this type provoked a reaction from some philosophers who chose to emphasize the virtue of the citizens over and above the appearance of the city. In Philostratus' *Life of Apollonius of Tyana* (3rd cent. CE) the sage tells the inhabitants of Smyrna that their citizens, not their monuments, represent the true value of the city (4.3). Dio Chrysostom (1st–2nd cents. CE) plays on the same contrast in his speech to the Alexandrians (*Orations* 32), in which his initial praise of the city is purposely undercut by his criticisms of the citizens' behavior.

In Roman literature the city itself could be a subject of *psogos,* or blame, particularly when contrasted with the ideal of the simple pastoral life (an exercise mentioned by Quintilian 2.4.24). In Juvenal's Third Satire the speaker lambastes the noise, confusion, and cultural mix in the city of Rome, which have led to his sense of alienation. (Ovid's *Tristia,* by contrast, expresses nostalgia for the life and entertainment of Rome.) The conception of the countryside as a place of original Roman simplicity and purity, however, is frequently undercut by the very fact that it is evoked in terms that owe much to Greek rhetorical and poetic traditions.

Criticism of the city took on a new significance in the Christian ascetic tradition, in which the city came to represent evil and debauchery. But the paradoxical claim in Athanasius' *Life of Antony* (mid-4th cent. CE) that "the desert became a city" because of the large number of Christian ascetics who sought refuge there reveals the tenacity of the idea of the city as a model for human life.

In Byzantium church buildings took over from cities as the focus of speeches of praise, though these sometimes evoked the church's situation within a city, as in the *ecphraseis* of the Church of the Holy Apostles by Constantine the Rhodian and Nikolaus Mesarites. In the last centuries of the Byzantine empire there was a revival in the practice of composing speeches of praise and lament for cities such as Constantinople, Nicaea, Thessalonica, and Trebizond, reflecting both a classical revival and the importance of these cities in the shrinking empire. Of particular cultural and political interest is the comparison of Rome and Constantinople written by the Greek scholar Manuel Chrysoloras in 1411 at a time when the beleaguered Byzantine empire was looking for help from the West. The classical tradition of praise for cities was not influential in the medieval West, but Chrysoloras' introduction of the Greek rhetorical tradition to Italy inspired Leonardo Bruni in 1404 to compose his *Laudatio Florentinae urbis.* The choice of Aristides' *Panathēnaikos* as a model reinforced Bruni's emphasis on the benefits of the Florentine Republic, presented as the heir to democratic Athens. The classical tradition of praise for a city also allowed Bruni to emphasize the importance of monuments as the physical embodiment of civic qualities. This innovative adoption of a classical form proved influential and was also applied to the praise of rulers of city-states. But Bruni's use of the panegyric mode of writing was also criticized by Lorenzo Valla and Pier Candido Decembrio, who saw the amplification, typical of rhetorical praise, as a form of untruth.

Formal praise of cities is rare in modern literature. However, 19th- and 20th-century writers (such as Baudelaire and Walter Benjamin) praise the city as a place of freedom, variety, and self-actualization; compare too the film *Berlin: Symphony of a Great City* (1927) and Kander and Ebb's *New York, New York* (1977). Here the individual's random path of discovery contrasts with the fixed monumental routes that articulate many Roman and Byzantine city descriptions. The opposite current is also strong in various media, as in the representations of the city as a place of corruption and alienation to be found in Hogarth's and Dickens's depictions of London and in the horror of the crowd expressed in Engels's *Condition of the Working Class* (1845).

BIBL.: W. Benjamin, "On Some Motifs in Baudelaire," in *Illuminations* (London 1970) 157–202. L. Bruni, *Laudatio Florentinae urbis,* ed. S. U. Baldassarri (Florence 2000). C. J. Classen, *Die Stadt im Spiegel der Descriptiones und Laudes urbium in der antiken und mittelalterlichen Literatur bis zum Ende des zwölften Jahrhunderts* (Hildesheim 1980). C. Edwards, *Writing Rome: Textual Approaches to the City* (Cambridge 1996). C. Foss, *Nicaea: A Byzantine Capital and Its Praises* (Brookline 1996). N. Loraux, *The Invention of Athens: The Funeral Oration in the Classical City* (Cambridge 1986). L. Pernot, *La rhétorique de l'éloge dans le monde gréco-romain* (Paris 1993). D. A. Russell and N. G. Wilson, *Menander Rhetor* (Oxford 1981). C. Smith, *Architecture in the Culture of Early Humanism: Ethics, Aesthetics and Eloquence* (New York 1992).

R.W.

City Planning

The cities of the Roman Empire established the urban base of a significant part of medieval and early modern Europe. But with only a few exceptions the sprawling fabric of the ancient city has remained hard to know. Excavations beginning in the 18th century have given us the plans of abandoned sites like Pompeii and Ostia, but ancient Rome itself has never fully emerged from beneath the living city. For most continuously inhabited sites, scattered finds and the ambiguous testimony of the ancient texts have had to suffice. Nonetheless, as the most eloquent surviving witness to the greatness of the Empire, the ancient city has fascinated all succeeding generations.

At the rebirth of urban culture in the late Middle Ages, it was an idealized and abstract city to which builders had access. Authors imagined contemporary cities as simulacra of ancient ones. For its 14th-century chronicler Giovanni Villani, Florence was *la piccola Roma,* the Little Rome. Although he knew that the ancient city lay just below the modern one, he had a limited idea of its plan. He could identify the site of the Forum on the basis of contemporary toponyms, but imagination provided most of the physical details (*Cronache* 1.38). Medieval city planners were on firmer ground when they culled the ancient authors for ritual. Frederick II traced the perimeter of Victoria, a siege camp outside the city of Parma, with a plow and oxen in imitation of the rite described by Varro, Plutarch, and others. The Corpus Agrimensorum, a collection of texts on field survey first assembled in the 4th century CE, was known and copied throughout the Middle Ages. Illustrations accompanied at least some of the manuscripts and together with the text spell out the same principles of spatial organization based on straight lines and right angles that were used in the new towns founded across the Continent and in Great Britain from the 9th through the 14th centuries. Beyond the orthogonality of their street grids, however, the plans of these towns bear few resemblances to the colonies of the Romans. The absence of a relationship is dramatically illustrated by the early 9th-century plan for the town of Winchester in England, refounded by Alfred the Great on the site of the Roman Venta Belgarum. The plan makes use of the old defensive perimeter, but it is redrawn to maximize rental frontage on the market street that runs down the center of the town and to mark out great tracts of land for assignment to the king's feudatories. The function of cities had changed dramatically enough by the 9th century to make the physical structure of the Roman model obsolete.

The systematic study of antiquity begun in the Renaissance brought the skills of both scholars and designers to bear on the investigation of the city. Antiquarians studied the topography of ancient Rome in the texts of the classical authors, in coins, in inscriptions, and in the ruins themselves. Architects measured the buildings and reconstructed them in drawings. Leo X (r. 1513–1521) initiated a project that would have integrated these disciplines and produced a graphic record of the ancient city. The artist Raphael was put in charge of the work and received advice from members of the pope's circle, including the historian Andrea Fulvio and the Humanist polymath Fabio Calvo. He proposed to record the monuments in drawings according to a system that became the modern triad of architectural representation: plan, section, and elevation. He used a primitive theodolite, adapted from the medieval astrolabe in the middle of the preceding century by Leon Battista Alberti (d. 1472), to measure the plans of irregularly formed buildings and may even have begun a plan of ancient Rome. Nothing of this survives, but a distant reflection of the project may appear in the earliest surveyed map of the city. Prepared by the military architect Leonardo Bufalini in 1551, the map records the ruins of the ancient monuments—often in fanciful reconstruction—within the plan of the modern city. The architect Pirro Ligorio, a serious antiquarian, reconstructed the ancient city in 1561 in an image made pictorial by the addition of representations of the monuments derived from ancient coins.

None of these representations attempted to map the streets of ancient Rome or to reconstruct the details of the spatial relations among its monumental complexes. Though by 1562 fragments were known of the Forma Urbis Romae (205–208 CE), a marble map of the city that documented the presence of streets as structuring elements, the first attempt to reconstruct a part of ancient Rome in plan, Piranesi's *Ichnographia Campi Martii* of 1762, presented an urban fabric organized exclusively as a series of building complexes based around central courtyards or plazas. The elaborate symmetries of these compositions, which Piranesi described as inventions based on contemporary design principles, even forced the relocation—on the basis of an elaborate historical argument—of a street (the Via Flaminia/Via del Corso) that was demonstrably ancient.

Only one ancient text, Polybius' account of a Roman military camp, dealt comprehensively with the plan for a complex, urbanized environment. The orthogonal format of the camp made its plan easy to reconstruct, and the values of hierarchy and order embedded within its military structure fell on sympathetic ears. Albrecht Dürer's detailed scheme for the city around the residence of a prince in the *Etliche Unterricht* of 1527 has Polybius' meticulous description of the quartering of troops to thank for the license it takes to order every detail of inhabitation, from the palaces of the nobility to the foundries of the armorers. The Sienese mathematician and military architect Pietro Cattaneo published a graphic reconstruction of Polybius' scheme in his *Architettura* of 1554, but when he proposed a camp "in the modern manner" he organized it very differently. For Polybius enough formal order had been achieved by putting the *praetorium* at the head of the main street. Cattaneo's camp, driven by the need to separate the armies of the nations that contributed to the imperial forces of his era, set the commander's accommodations in a square at the symmetrical center of the encampment and defined each of the surrounding quarters as a self-contained unit with an open space at its center. In his treatise *On Castramentation,* Sebastiano Serlio (d. 1554) brought a Renaissance sensibility to the ancient camp itself. He introduced a 50-foot-wide space between the *praetorium* and the tents of the tribunes because "as an architect [one] must always look to grandeur and decorum."

Of all the parts of the ancient city, it was the Forum that held the greatest fascination for Renaissance designers. The starting point was Vitruvius' text (5.1); Alberti quotes another passage (8.6) almost verbatim. A regular form and a unified facade of porticoes were the distinguishing features of a kind of square that the post-antique world could have known only at San Marco in Venice, whose 12th–13th-century remodeling seems to have been directly inspired by the surviving ancient fora in Constantinople. As in almost every other detail of his text, Alberti modifies the ancient author's formula. He proposes alternative proportions—sides 2:1 rather than 3:2—and introduces a formula for the height of the porticoes that is based on the width of the square. In a great leap of creative archaeology he reimagines the triumphal arch as the gateway into the forum, an interpretation that established a Renaissance type in projects like Ludovico Sforza's rebuilding of the market square at Vigevano (1494) and the clock tower astride the Merceria at its entry to the Piazza San Marco (1496). In 1556 Andrea Palladio and Daniele Barbaro read Vitruvius in contemporary terms when they aligned the forum and the adjacent basilica along a single axis. Authority for so symmetrical an arrangement may come from the fora of Augustus and Nerva, whose plans Palladio published in his *Quattro Libri* of 1570. A synthesis of Vitruvius and the imperial fora had already been made by Bramante in his plan (by 1509) for the Apostolic Palace at Loreto, which served as the atrium and forum for the adjacent shrine of the miraculously translated site of the birth of the Virgin. Serlio, again, gives the most literal statement of the modern forum type. In his version of the legionary camp, the forum had become a palace. It had a seven-foot-thick external wall and a ground level, reached by an external stair that passed below a triumphal arch five feet above the street.

Vitruvius' descriptions of the forum of a port city (1.7, 5.12) had a special appeal to the Renaissance urban imagination. He located it at the edge of the city, fronting on the harbor and immediately visible to the visitors whose good opinion was so avidly courted in the early modern period. A temple to Venus ornamented this forum, and the arms of the harbor's breakwater preceded it. Warehouses, boat sheds, and porticoes lined both areas. Renaissance architects, beginning with Francesco di Giorgio, reconstructed this scheme, and in the 16th century antiquarians and architects (Baldassare Peruzzi, Pirro Ligorio) integrated it with ancient evidence from the harbor at Portus, next to Ostia. The type made its way into urban design in a scheme for a secondary harbor at the port of Ancona offered to Sixtus V (1585–1590) by the artillery officer Giacomo della Porta. Even closer to the type is Bernini's final project for St. Peter's Square (1656).

Projects derived from the classical texts always seemed like intrusions into the living fabric of the city. Planners were never able to adapt city forms of the ancient world with the ease and productivity that architects experienced in their adaptations of ancient buildings. Even in Athens, whose 19th-century architecture was the most antiquarian of all European Neoclassicism, planning for the capital of the newly independent Greek state (begun in 1832) followed 18th-century models exclusively. The elements of the ancient city most easy to integrate into the postclassical urban fabric were the memorial structures. The triumphal arch and honorific column first appeared as temporary ornaments when cities decorated streets to structure processions for the reception of distinguished visitors. Permanent versions appeared in the early 16th century. The facade of the papal mint at the first fork of the ceremonial route on the Rome side of the Tiber was built as a triumphal arch during the papacy of Leo X (1513–1521); the same motif was reinterpreted with gun embrasures for the Porta Santo Spirito in the Vatican Borgo (1542–1545). Later in the century antiquities themselves were reinstalled on the contemporary street plan. Sixtus V reerected the Egyptian obelisks that had anchored the *spina* of the imperial circuses as markers on the new system of avenues that opened the eastern side of the city to development. In the next century (1658–1659) Alexander VII remodeled the space around the Column of Marcus Aurelius as the site for the residence of his nephews and an ornament to the city along the principal route of entry from the north.

In the age of scientific archaeology, excavations that established ground levels well below the modern streets were defined as ornaments of the urban fabric. The idea of an archaeological park around the Roman Forum was first proposed in 1871. One of the projects of the city's planning commission included the idea of a suspension bridge over the site to facilitate circulation through the city but also to allow the Roman levels to be viewed by the public.

The monuments of antiquity (whether authentic or artificial) have always been displayed as trophies. They can mark continuity (the 12th-cent. Baptistry of Florence imagined to be an ancient temple of Mars) or change (Sixtus V's obelisks and their celebration of the triumph of Christianity). In the modern era the message of the monuments has often been overtly political. Napoleon contemplated the relocation of the Column of Trajan to his own capital but settled for a modern simulacrum celebrating the military campaign that culminated in the victory at Austerlitz (designed 1808). That column was erected on the site made available in the Place Vendôme by the destruction of an equestrian statue of Louis XIV. Only a few decades later (1833) the Restoration monarch Louis-Philippe raised the Luxor obelisk, acquired from the Egyptian government of Muhammad Ali, as the centerpiece of the transformed Place de la Concorde (formerly the Place de la Révolution and the site of the execution of Louis XVI).

When, in the course of the 19th century, urban planning became an autonomous discipline, it was hygiene and traffic that drove design, not history. Camillo Sitte's *Die Städtebau nach seinen künstlerischen Grundsätzen* (Vienna 1889) flew in the face of his professional colleagues and distilled aesthetic principles for modern design from traditional cities. His models, however, were mostly medieval and early modern. The ancient city offered, at best, abstract concepts. With Aristotle he asserted that the city should be designed "to make its people at once secure and happy." Formal lessons were few. One is about the enclosure of urban space by construction at the edges (colonnades), the second prescribes an open area at the center of the square. Temples and the monuments to heroes respected the free center. But the forum and the agora, he acknowledged, could not provide direct models: "So much has changed since then."

The ambitious urban programs of Fascist Italy reflect the same reality. Despite the tirelessly repeated rhetoric equating the modern regime with the ancient empire, Italian urban environments of the 1930s and early 1940s reflect very little of the design ideas being uncovered in the excavations in Rome and Ostia. Aside from a general symmetry and monumentality, the plans of the new towns in the Pontine marshes (Littoria in 1932, Sabaudia in 1933, among others) and the African colonies (1936–1943), and the areas of expansion in Rome itself (the E42 [now EUR], begun in 1937) reflect the expertise of traffic planners more than that of archaeologists. Rather than the closed fora of imperial Rome, the urban environments of the Fascist towns have an openness more like that of Frank Lloyd Wright's Broadacre City, and scenographic qualities whose origins are indeed Roman but 17th-century. In the center of Rome, ancient monuments (the Colosseum, the Tomb of Augustus) were stripped of their post-classical additions and established as the centers of new public spaces and grand boulevards. The medieval and Renaissance neighborhoods that covered the imperial fora were torn down and a new avenue, the Via del Impero (1932), laid out across the newly excavated archaeological site. The road completed the sequence of avenues that crossed the city from the Vatican in the west to the train station at Termini in the east, but unlike the remainder of the route it was kept free of office and apartment buildings. Only one architectural project was proposed for the site: a building that would have united all the organs of the Fascist Party in the capital, the Palazzo del Littorio (for which a competition was held in 1934).

BIBL.: A. Sutcliffe, *The History of Urban and Regional Planning: An Annotated Bibliography* (London 1981). D.F.

Classical

The use of the term *classical* is not exclusive to "classical antiquity." Rather, it is in European languages applied to numerous spheres (for example "classical music") that have only the most tenuous connection (if any) to Graeco-Roman antiquity, and even to completely unrelated cultures (there are Chinese "classics," "classical" periods in pre-Columbian art, and so on). Nevertheless, there is a privileged connection between *classical* and the realm of Graeco-Roman culture that admits of three converging explanations: (1) the exemplary value that Graeco-Roman civilization long enjoyed in the education of elites; (2) the fact that the word *classicus* is Latin; and (3) the fact that the retrospective cult of antiquity that characterizes "classical" education derives from Graeco-Roman antiquity itself. *Classicus,* an adjective derived from *classis,* is a component of political, economic, and military terminology (it designates first and foremost the classes of Rome's Servian order); but *classis* can also be a "class of pupils" (thus Juvenal and Quintilian), and *classicus* a student (Ennodius).

There is only one ancient author at the root of the evolution of the term *classicus* into classical: Aulus Gellius, a writer of marked archaizing tendencies, especially regarding language and grammar. He makes reference to the rare and obsolete meaning of *classicus* as "a taxpayer in the highest bracket" (*Noctes Atticae* 6.13); and elsewhere he relates that Fronto was *classicus scriptor, non proletarius* (a first-rate writer, not one from the masses) (*Noctes Atticae* 19.8.15), who was also *adsiduus* (another census designation, "wealthy taxpayer") and *antiquior;* being anterior to the present was thus a requisite of "classicism." This metaphorical usage, based on technical language perhaps exclusive to Fronto and Gellius, does not correspond to the lists of *enkrithentes* (approved) authors given by the Greek grammarians but nonetheless presupposes them; it is, moreover, consistent with the understanding of Cicero, who in a comparison to Democritus describes certain philosophers (such as Cleanthes and Chrysippus) as *quintae classis* (*Academica posteriora* 2.73).

The term disappeared in late Latin and in the Middle Ages, first reappearing in Filippo Beroaldo's *Commentarii quaestionum Tusculanarum* (1496) and then in his commentary on Apuleius (1500). There Beroaldo makes explicit reference to Gellius's text and draws a contrast between *classici*—writers like Livy and Quintilian—and a *proletarius* like Fulgentius. Guillaume Budé, a correspondent of Erasmus, used Gellius in his *Annotationes* on the Pandects (1508), and reference was made to Greek and Latin literature by Matthias Schürer (1509), Beatus Rhenanus (1512), Melanchthon (1519), and Alonso III Fonseca (1528). Thomas Sebillet transferred the term to the realm of French literature in his *Art poétique* (1548), in which "les bons et classiques poètes françois" were Jean de Meun (13th cent.) and Alain Chartier (15th cent.), whereupon it entered into general use, especially after the foundation of the *Académie française* (1635). It was also adopted, with reference to literature, in English and in other European languages.

Much slower and more desultory was its diffusion with regard to the figurative arts. (Winckelmann, who contributed more than anyone else to the definition of classical art, makes occasional and nonsystematic use of the term *klassisch,* but only in his letters and only with regard to literary works.) Goethe's dictum ("I call classic that which is healthy, romantic that which is sick," 1829) added a new, essential ingredient; meanwhile, F. A. Wolf's *Darstellung der Alterthums-Wissenschaft* (1807) consecrated a definition of classical antiquity as Graeco-Roman, to distinguish it from other antiquities, such as the Egyptian or the Hebraic.

Wladislaw Tatarkiewicz (1958) has distinguished four meanings of *classical* in current use: (1) to denote value: first-class, perfect, to be used as a model (as opposed to imperfect, mediocre); (2) to denote a chronological period, as a synonym for Graeco-Roman antiquity (or even just the apogee of Greek civilization: in this sense, notes Tatarkiewicz, it would be permissible even to say that, of the three canonical tragic poets, Aeschylus is not yet, and Euripides is no longer, classical); (3) to denote a historical style, with reference to moderns who have imitated ancient models; (4) to denote an aesthetic category, with reference to authors and works that possess harmony, measure, and equilibrium. This range of meanings is also the source of closely connected terms, such as *classicism* and *neoclassical,* which are often used to refer to movements or cultural phases in which particular weight is given to Graeco-Roman models.

In the language of advertising, *classic* has recently been applied to products that have been surpassed by new versions of the same thing but are still desired by certain customers (for example MacIntosh Classic, Coca-Cola Classic). The attempt to find equivalents for the concept of classical in other great cultural traditions belongs especially to the 20th century. In China recourse has consciously been made to two traditional concepts in order to translate classical. These are *gudian* and *jingdian* (Zhu Guangqian, 1935, which is based on Sainte-Beuve), where *gu* means "ancient," *dian* "canon," and *jing* "plot, story." The character for *dian* is written as two hands supporting a surface for writing, thus referring to books; *jing* designates sacred texts as well ("Bible" is translated as *Shengjing,* "sacred Scripture"). The Chinese *classical* places emphasis on tradition's anonymous force, not on the presence of the author; it is normative and analogical, not analytical and classificatory. Other intercultural comparisons in the future will be able to clarify better the nature and history of this product of the European tradition, *classical.*

BIBL.: H. O. Burger, *Begriffsbestimmung der Klassik und des Klassischen* (Darmstadt 1972). M. Citroni, "The Concept of the Classical and the Canons of Modern Authors in Roman Literature," in *Classical Pasts: The Classical Traditions of Greece and Rome,* ed. J. A. Porter (Princeton 2006) 205–234, and "Gellio 19, 8, 15 e la storia di classicus," *Materiali e discussioni per l'analisi dei testi classici* 58 (2007) 181–205. S. E. R. Curtius, *Europäische Literatur und Lateinisches Mittelalter* (Bern 1948). T. S. Eliot, *What Is a Classic?* (London 1945). F. Kermode, *Classic: Literary Images of Permanence and Change* (Cambridge 1983). S. Rizzo, "Il latino nell'umanesimo," in *Letteratura italiana,* ed. A. Asor Rosa, (Turin 1986) 5:379–408. P. L. Schmidt, "Classici und Klassiker als Begriff und Vorstellung," in *Beatus Rhenanus (1485–1547),* ed. J. Hirstein (Turnhout 2000) 49–60. Settis, *The Future of the "Classical"* (Cambridge 2006). W. Tatarkiewicz, "Les quatre significations du mot 'classique,'" in *Revue internationale de philosophie* 12, no. 43 (1958) 5–22. R. Wellek, "The Term and Concept of Classicism in Literary History" (1966), in *Discriminations: Further Concepts of Criticism* (New Haven 1970). Zhu Guangqian, *Shenme shi classics* (1935), in *Zhu Guangqian quan ji* (Hefei 1993) 8:91–392.

S.S.

Translated by Patrick Baker

Classical Orders. *See* Vitruvius and the Classical Orders.

Cleopatra

Cleopatra VII Philopator (69–30 BCE), daughter of Ptolemy XII, became joint ruler of Egypt with her brother Ptolemy XIII in 51 BCE. Her alliances with Julius Caesar and Mark Antony, her defeat by Octavian at Actium, and her subsequent suicide became a cornerstone of the founding myth of the Roman Empire. In book 8 of Virgil's *Aeneid* Cleopatra appears on Aeneas's shield as the "shameless Egyptian consort" of Antony, the analogue of Dido, the queen of Carthage; but in book 4 Aeneas avoids the fate of Antony by adhering to his Roman duty and abandoning Dido. Accounts by Plutarch and Lucan proved to be the most influential in post-classical representations of Cleopatra. Plutarch's *Life of Antony* emphasizes her bewitching attractiveness, which seduced and unmanned Antony; this account, translated in the 16th century by Jacques Amyot and Sir Thomas North, greatly influenced Shakespeare. In book 10 of Lucan's *Civil War* (*Pharsalia*), to which can be traced the 17th-century accounts by Thomas May, Pierre Corneille, and Katherine Philips, as well as Handel's opera *Giulio Cesare in Egitto,* the ambitious and extravagant Cleopatra is contrasted to the chaste and sober Roman wives Cornelia and Marcia.

Medieval representations of Cleopatra are almost entirely negative: in canto 5 of Dante's *Inferno* (1308–1321), "lustful" Cleopatra appears in the catalogue of lovers between Dido and Helen. Boccaccio in his *Famous Women* (*De claris mulieribus,* 1359) excoriates "wicked" Cleopatra for transgressive excess. In addition to the well-known account of Cleopatra's suicide, Boccaccio gives another, less common version of her death, in which Antony forced her to drink the poison she intended for him. Yet in *The Legend of Good Women* (1386–1388), which Chaucer supposedly wrote as penance for having defamed women through his account of the inconstancy of Criseyde, Cleopatra is included as one of the martyrs on Cupid's calendar and is praised for her constancy to "her knyght," Antony.

Representations that emphasize the political aspects of Cleopatra's queenship featured in both French and English drama during the Renaissance: Etienne Jodelle's *Cléopâtre captive* (1552) was followed by Robert Garnier's *Marc Antoine* (1578), translated by Mary Sidney as *The Tragedie of Antonie* (1595). Samuel Daniel wrote *The Tragedie of Cleopatra* (1594) as a companion to his patron Sidney's *Antonie,* casting his work in the tradition of *de casibus* tragedy (on exemplary fallen rulers). He accordingly focused on the political conflict between Octavian and Cleopatra, representing her suicide as a political act that opposed Caesar's conquest.

Shakespeare's *Antony and Cleopatra* (1609) includes the most memorable and most influential post-classical representation of Cleopatra. His heroic portrayal of Cleopatra bespeaks a nostalgia for Elizabeth (by contrast to the colorless Octavian, who represents James I). Shakespeare's Cleopatra is at once a comedic lover and a stately if paradoxical figure, whose "infinite variety" Enobarbus famously celebrates.

Women writers in the English Renaissance considered Cleopatra to be a negative *exemplum:* Aemilia Lanyer in *Salve Deus Rex Judaeorum* (1611) criticizes Cleopatra as a mistress who did not pay heed to her political responsibilities; she also racializes Cleopatra as "the Blacke Egyptian," as does Elizabeth Cary in her *Tragedie of Mariam* (1613), in which the title character calls her a "brown Egyptian." By contrast, Thomas May's *Tragedie of Cleopatra* (1654), at times echoing Shakespeare, represents Cleopatra as heroic and capable, especially in Caesar's extended tribute to her as queen. Book 2 of May's *A Continuation of the Subiect of Lucans Historicall Poem* (1657) depicts Caesar as having become "enflamed" by his love for Cleopatra; by contrast, Cleopatra desires "Soveraigntie" above all else.

In France, Corneille in the *Examen* to his *Mort de Pompée* (1644) specifically stated that he intended to depart from the negative portrayal of Cleopatra; Katherine Philips's translation, *Pompey* (1663), produced in both Dublin and London, was well received by the Restoration court. Margaret Cavendish's defense of Cleopatra in *The World's Olio* (1655) anticipates Dryden's *All for Love* (1677) in challenging her reputation as a "whore" and praising her constancy to Antony. Dryden's version of Cleopatra, which domesticates her as a wife, became more influential than Shakespeare's during the 18th century, for example in Restoration portraits of fashionable wives as Cleopatras. Yet Handel's opera *Giulio Cesare in Egitto* (1724) follows Corneille and Philips in contrasting Cleopatra with Cornelia the exemplary wife; he emphasizes the paradoxical nature of Cleopatra in the famous aria "Piangerò," in which she alternates between hauntingly lamenting her defeat and captivity by her brother Ptolemy and energetically vowing to torment him after her death.

Cleopatra has also been the subject of memorable renderings by visual artists, beginning in the Italian Renaissance. In Michelangelo's drawing of her head with a serpent, on which Vasari based a later painting, the snaky locks associate Cleopatra with Medusa. Lavinia Fontana's *Cleopatra* (1585) significantly deviates from the seductive yet sinister allure of Michelangelo's and Vasari's renderings to represent Cleopatra as an "exotic" but meditative or serene ruler in rich headdress and clothing. A snake coils upward from an urn, rather than resting on her body, unlike later representations by Guido Reni (1630) and Guercino (1621, 1648) that exploited the eroticism involved in depicting a woman applying an asp to her exposed breast. Artemisia Gentileschi's two paintings of Cleopatra's suicide (1621–1622, 1630s) resemble those of her male contemporaries in depicting an unclothed Cleopatra. Giambattista Tiepolo diverged from this tradition to focus on the magnificence of Cleopatra as queen, capturing the moment of her meeting with Antony (1746–1747) as well as depicting her entertaining Antony (1743–1744). Notable 19th-century examples include Delacroix's *Cleopatra and the Peasant* (1838) and Gérôme's *Cleopatra and Caesar* (1866).

In the 20th century Cleopatra was revived on the stage by George Bernard Shaw's *Caesar and Cleopatra* (1901), which became the basis of the 1945 film directed by Gabriel Pascal and starring Vivien Leigh and Claude Rains. In this and other adaptations Cleopatra became a central figure in the history of cinema in the 20th century: six films featuring Cleopatra were made between 1912 and 1999. Among these, the best known are the 1917 version with Theda Bara; the 1934 production, directed by Cecil B. DeMille, with Claudette Colbert; and, most iconic, the 1963 *Cleopatra* directed by Joseph L. Mankiewicz, with Elizabeth Taylor and Richard Burton.

The continuing fascination with Cleopatra can be gauged in the many books that appeared in the 1990s on Cleopatra as a historical figure as well as on the history of her representations. A major exhibition launched by the British Museum in 2001 addressed both aspects of the question.

BIBL.: Michael Chauveau, *Cleopatra: Beyond the Myth*, trans. David Lorton (Ithaca 1998). Michael Grant, *Cleopatra* (New York 1972). Mary Hamer, *Signs of Cleopatra* (London 1993). Lucy Hughes-Hallett, *Cleopatra: Histories, Dreams, and Distortions* (London 1990). Susan Walker and Peter Higgs, *Cleopatra of Egypt: From History to Myth* (Princeton 2001).

M.SU.

Coins and Medals

A form of money fabricated according to a specific standard weight and material. Produced in large quantities, coins bear features (format, inscriptions, special marks, obverse and reverse designs) that identify the issuing authority, which guarantees its nominal value. Medals, on the other hand, are small portraits in relief inscribed on metallic disks and, though similar to coins, were invented as historic records and devised for social communication. Unlike coins, they are not meant as units of economic value or as a means of exchange.

The first Western coins, stamped in an alloy of gold and silver known as electrum, appeared in western Asia Minor sometime before ca. 560 BCE. Although not Greek in origin, coinage had a quick diffusion throughout the Hellenized Mediterranean, where Greek silver money spread widely. The conquests of Alexander the Great extended the use and the scale of coinage throughout much of central Asia, and the coinage of Alexander's successors introduced the portrait as a standard device. Under Greek influence the Romans adopted a cast bronze coinage as well as a struck silver and copper one (3rd cent. BCE), but the former was abandoned after the Second Punic War. The Roman Empire imposed a standardized coinage produced in Rome and in regional mints. Its formal and technical tradition had a long influence, but its first metallic system underwent profound economic transformations and was repeatedly reformed in the 3rd and the 4th centuries. Radical changes occurred in four subsequent eras: the period of the Barbarian invasions, early medieval feudalism (8th–12th cent.), the Communal Age (13th–15th cent.), and the Renaissance, which introduced mechanical minting presses. The issue of banknotes and the notion of fiduciary circulation in the 18th century marked the passage to the contemporary monetary system.

Since antiquity coins have been collected as objects of

art, reused as jewels or decorations, and buried in building foundations to date a monument or to commemorate its patron. According to the first Humanists, ancient coins visualized the features and the character of illustrious men from the past. Being the most praised form of celebrative portrait, since the 14th century ancient coins have also provided artists and epigraphers with models for historical illustrations, moral examples, or mere ornaments. Published in 1517, the *Illustrium imagines* by Andrea Fulvio was the first printed collection to reproduce ancient coins of illustrious men with these purposes, initiating a very lively genre. Fulvio's work, however, mixed true portraits with fanciful restitutions, the authenticity of which was attested by little more than their adherence to a coinlike format.

Modern imitations of ancient coins and original medals of Graeco-Roman characters seem to have appeared in Venice as early as the last decade of the 14th century. Jean, duc de Berry (by 1402), and Francesco II da Carrara (first half of the 15th cent.?) were portrayed, respectively, in embossed and cast medals.

Nevertheless, it was only in 1438–1439 that the passage through Italy of a Palaeologan emperor, John VIII, led the painter Pisanello to cast a large medal that became a model for a new genre. The reverses of modern medals, very often signed and inscribed with a motto, represented historical scenes, landscapes of political significance, or personal devices. Their issue was closely connected with contemporary courtly, military, and civic life. Medals of this type were soon disseminated in the main Humanistic centers as gifts, badges, or jewels. In the same period, by engraving steel dies, the Milanese Caradosso Foppa succeeded in adapting the minting technique to smaller medals.

The hybrid allegorical imagery of the reverses soon evolved into more specific visual codes (emblems, devices, exemplary stories, coinlike representations). Rulers of the 16th century in particular adapted the abstract language and range of institutional occasions transmitted by the Roman coinage for civic pageantry and their own self-celebration. Variety and flexibility soon extended the medal to new social classes, not only rulers, Humanists, and artists, but even bankers, merchants, and institutions. A survey of the different functions of medals—illustrative, celebrative, loyalist, promotional, honorific, and decorative—is still needed.

It is noteworthy that in the inventories of early modern art collections the Latin word *medalia* (medal, or a coin that is no longer in circulation) and its translations were often extended to refer to any kind of circular portrait in hard media (cameos, pastiglias, miniatures, embossed leathers, and wall reliefs).

In 1517 Guillaume Budé published a treatise in metrology, illustrating how the value of ancient coins was based on a system of ponderal fractions. At the same time, Sebastiano Erizzo argued that the artistic quality and iconic complexity of the best Roman types could not have been intended for currency circulation. His *Discorso sopra le medaglie antiche* (*Discourse on the Ancient Medals*, 1559) gave a first, tentative interpretation of the imagery stamped in the reverses. Starting with Guillaume du Choul and Pirro Ligorio, attempts were also made to solve topographical and architectural problems by means of the monuments represented on coins. As contemporary material sources, coins were used as evidence to supplement and correct accounts of historical events by ancient authors.

In the second half of the 16th century, counterfeiters, art dealers, and collectors developed a specific connoisseurship focused on numismatic materials and styles. Criticizing the previous iconographic literature, Antonio Agustín, Fulvio Orsini, and others initiated a more philological study of coins. Systematic studies of coinage also emerged at this time; the foundations of the science of numismatics was laid by authors such as Hubert Goltzius, the father of numismatics.

The 17th and 18th centuries saw the commodity of antique coins and medals reach any erudite historian or monarch. The first scientific catalogues of collections appeared, and antiquarians across Europe, such as Giovan Pietro Bellori and Johann Friedrich Gronovius, focused on coins to solve problems of chronology, iconography, and computation. Between 1792 and 1798 Joseph-Hilaire Eckhel's *Doctrina numorum veterum* (*Doctrine of Ancient Coins*) provided an influential synthesis of the discipline, and the 19th-century numismatic societies extended the systematic description of types to every ancient coinage, as well as medieval and modern ones. Theodor Mommsen and François Lenormant showed the importance of numismatics in studying ancient economic and juridical systems, and thus may be considered the ancestors of many 20th-century investigations into monetary theory and circulation.

Recently a linguistic interest in coins and medals has arisen in the history of ancient art, and the numismatists' early approach to material sources and to autoptic methods has inflected antiquarian history.

BIBL.: R. A. G. Carson, *Coins: Ancient, Mediaeval, and Modern* (London 1971). M. H. Crawford, C. R. Ligota, and J. B. Trapp, eds., *Medals and Coins from Budé to Mommsen* (London 1990). F. Haskell, *History and Its Images: Art and the Interpretation of the Past* (New Haven 1993) 13–25. G. F. Hill and J. G. Pollard, *Medals of the Renaissance* (London 1978). C. J. Howgego, *Ancient History from Coins* (New York 1995). M. Jones, *The Art of the Medal* (London 1979).

W.C.

Collecting

By the time Augustine (354–430 CE) wrote in his *Confessions* of the "worldly things" that take possession of men's souls (10.34), the proliferation of collections in the Roman world—from the emperor Hadrian's villa at Tivoli to the imaginary gallery described by Philostratus in the late 2nd or early 3rd century CE—made the city at the center of this empire into a vast and dynamic museum whose objects were rearranged by a succession of emperors and patricians in order to make their understanding of the magnificence of Rome visible. Early Christian emperors, including Constantine I (272–337 CE), expressed a growing ambivalence toward the pagan statuary that embellished the empire. Rather than cultivating this past, as previous emperors had done, they began to repudiate aspects of it. Statuary became a form of idolatry. The Tuscan poet Petrarch (1304–1374) would wander through Rome 1,000 years later, famously lamenting the events that had transformed such magnificence into a broken city (*Epistolae familiares* 6.2.15).

Despite Petrarch's view that his age had utterly neglected its Roman inheritance, there are ways in which medieval collecting practices continued important elements of the ancient traditions of collecting. Medieval cathedrals and princely treasuries also housed natural curiosities, gems, objects fabricated from precious materials, and trophies of conquest. If their relics primarily evoked a world of Christian saints rather than Greek gods and heroes, they shared the desire to collect and sanctify human remains. The marvelous objects of the Treasury of San Marco in Venice and the Abbey of Saint Denis near Paris may not have been quite as openly displayed to visitors as those in the great temples of the Forum Romanum, but they were no less important as state and church collections.

While retaining the general idea of a collection, the medieval treasury did not proclaim itself to be a specific revival of Graeco-Roman collecting practices. Despite important moments in the Middle Ages in which rulers such as Charlemagne invoked the specter of the Roman Empire as a model to be revived, there was very little impetus to rediscover the ancient world in its specificity. It was this lack of self-conscious affiliation and recognition of incomplete knowledge that Petrarch lamented. In the 14th and 15th centuries the rise of a new kind of antiquarian sensibility created several generations of patrons, scholars, and artists fascinated with the material and literary remains of the ancient world. Renaissance Humanists such as Niccolò Niccoli (1364–1457) and Poggio Bracciolini (1380–1459) reveled in the possibilities of reconstituting antiquity through things. They collected Greek and Latin manuscripts from monasteries and cathedral libraries and unearthed ancient statuary, sarcophagi, inscriptions, coins, and engraved gemstones; they embedded fragments of ancient buildings in the walls of their palaces to claim a lineage with the Romans. Pausanias in hand, they traveled to Greece, Egypt, southern Italy, and Asia Minor to rediscover the Hellenistic world, just as Petrarch and many others had made the pilgrimage to Rome to see what remained of the world described by such writers as Cicero, Virgil, and Quintilian, whose works they were rediscovering. The merchant and diplomat Cyriac of Ancona (1391–1452) regularly returned from his overseas travels with artifacts, drawings, and notes that greatly increased knowledge of Greek learning and antiquities in the mid-15th century.

Collecting took on a decidedly historical function in this era, as it became a reflection of the Renaissance's evolving relationship with antiquity. The activities of especially well-known collectors such as Cosimo de' Medici (1389–1464) in Florence, who readily displayed his precious manuscripts, coins, and gems to visitors as a form of cultural capital, helped create a thriving market in antiquities by the late 15th century. While Roman patricians gathered inscriptions to invent illustrious family genealogies, the cardinals and Humanists who flocked to Rome fueled their passion for the antique through the creation of courtyards and gardens filled with ancient statuary. With Sixtus IV's restitution of some of Rome's ancient monuments to the Capitoline in 1471 and Julius II's creation of the Belvedere Courtyard in the first decade of the 16th century, the papacy also began to present itself as a guardian and restorer of antiquity in Rome. A series of spectacular discoveries—most notably the 1506 unearthing of a group statue identified as the *Laocoön* described by Pliny—helped cement the image of ancient Rome as a seemingly endless resource for Renaissance collectors in search of new things.

When the Bolognese scholar Ulisse Aldrovandi (1522–1605) composed his *Delle statue antiche, che per tutta Roma, in diversi luoghi, e casa si veggono* (1556) after an extensive visit to Rome in 1549, he catalogued almost 100 collections in the Eternal City, overwhelmingly in the palaces of Roman patricians and cardinals. This influential guidebook, the first to document the extensive growth of antiquarian collecting, explicitly demonstrated how Pliny's image of Rome as a city-museum had been revivified by the early 16th century. A similar impulse also informed new kinds of editorial projects that collected every written trace of those ancient authors whose legacy was especially important to Renaissance Humanists. Carlo Sigonio (ca. 1524–1584) published his *Fragmenta Ciceronis variis in locis dispersa Caroli Sigonii diligentia collecta et scholiis illustrate* (Venice 1559) with the goal of publishing every remaining fragment of Cicero's lost writings. The Greece and Rome that emerged in the cabinets of antiquities found their complement in the paper museums of these ancient civilizations.

In the course of the 16th century the idea of collecting antiquities became a passion for collectors who lived far away from Rome. Indeed, distance from the source made the reconstitution of antiquity all the more gratifying for collectors whose fondest desire was to immerse themselves in the past. Collectors such as the cardinal and Humanist Pietro Bembo (1470–1547) in Padua, the Marchioness of Mantua, Isabella d'Este (1474–1539), and the Patriarch of Aquileia, Giovanni Grimani (1501–1593), created significant collections of antiquities to rival the Roman and Medicean collections. By the early 17th century some of the greatest collections could be found in northern Europe, as wealthy German princes and diligent scholars, such as the Aix antiquarian Nicolas-Claude Fabri de Peiresc (1580–1637) and the English ambassador Thomas Howard, Earl of Arundel (1585–1646), used their connections, influence, and firsthand experience of

Italy to increase their store of antiquities or, in the case of the Delft collector Abraham Gorlaeus (1549–1609), his collection of gems and coins. Though collectors were increasingly fascinated with more modern artifacts, no early modern cabinet of curiosities could be complete without some talisman of the Graeco-Roman past. In the hands of collectors such as the German Jesuit Athanasius Kircher (1602–1680), the idea of antiquity expanded to include a taste for Egyptian and pseudo-Egyptian artifacts (already anticipated in the famous inscribed tablet in Bembo's collection later known as the *Tabula Bembina*).

As collecting antiquities became a widespread pursuit, some collectors began to consider the public value of antiquities. Inspired by his uncle Domenico's donation of several statues to the Republic of Venice in 1523, Grimani bequeathed the majority of his ancient statues to the Venetian Senate in 1587 on the condition that they be publicly displayed in an appropriate location. The *Statuario pubblico* opened in the antisala of the Biblioteca Marciana in 1597, the first public antiquities collection in any early modern city. Despite the often-repeated claim that the Capitoline Museum in Rome was the first public museum, Sixtus IV's donation in 1471 was not given with the explicit intent to create a public collection in Rome, nor can we describe the sculpture garden in the Vatican Belvedere Courtyard (1503) as a fully public collection, though it was certainly seen and drawn by visitors. It was not until Clement XIV opened the Capitoline Museum in 1734, following his spectacular acquisition of Cardinal Alessandro Albani's (1692–1779) first collection in 1733, that Rome had its first public museum of antiquities. This museum, a product of papal ambitions to proclaim Rome the cultural capital of Europe in response to the ever-increasing numbers of Grand Tourists who came to Italy to see and buy it all, inaugurated a new era of displaying antiquities, which culminated in the creation of the Museo Pio-Clementino, the papal collection of antiquities created by Clement XIV in 1771 and completed under Pius VI.

This same period saw the emergence of well-publicized excavations of such famous sites as Hadrian's Villa, and the recently rediscovered remains of Herculaneum (1738) and Pompeii (1748), which soon filled the king of Naples' museum in Portici. The romance of archaeology inspired antiquarian-adventurers such as the members of the London-based Society of Dilettanti (f. 1732) to fund increasingly far-flung collecting expeditions to Turkey and Greece, while professional *ciceroni* (antiquarian tour guides) and art dealers such as Francesco Ficoroni (1664–1745) lined their pockets providing Grand Tourists with mementos of their voyage into the past. By 1755 the papal antiquary Johann Joachim Winckelmann (1717–1768) had begun to produce an influential series of publications that explained the origins and purpose of art through a close examination of antiquities, especially Greek statues such as the Apollo Belvedere and Laocoön, which embodied his idea of aesthetic perfection. Such a climate deeply influenced the habits of Sir William Hamilton (1730–1803), British envoy to Naples 1764–1800, who developed a special fondness for painted vases and acquired many, some of which the British Museum purchased in 1772. The marble collection of the great British antiquary Charles Townley (1737–1805), as well as Lord Elgin's famous despoiling of the Parthenon between 1801 and 1812 to create his collection known as the Elgin marbles, eventually joined Hamilton's vases as the nucleus of the Graeco-Roman collection in the British Museum.

By the 19th century collecting antiquities was a highly political endeavor, as major western European nations and the papacy all competed to lay claim to the idea that their states continued the legacy of ancient Greece and Rome. Napoleon's conquest of much of Italy in 1796 forced many Italian states, including the papacy, to cede their best antiquities to the newly formed Musée de Louvre (f. 1793). The desire to compete with Napoleon led the British Parliament to invest hefty sums in the acquisition of the best private collections to ensure that the British Museum would compare favorably with its French counterpart. It similarly inspired King Ludwig of Bavaria's Glyptothek (f. 1830) and Staatliche Antikensammlungen (f. 1848) in Munich, two great antiquarian collections designed to make Munich the new Athens. The formation of the Prussian royal family's Altes Museum in Berlin (f. 1830), whose Pantheon-inspired rotunda would initially house the Pergamon altar after its sensational arrival in Berlin in 1880, also suggests the way in which antiquarian collecting had become a measure of the power and privilege of the modern state.

BIBL.: Alexandra Baunia, *The Nature of Classical Collecting: Collectors and Collections, 100* BCE–*100* CE (Aldershot 2004). Horst Bredekamp, *The Lure of Antiquity and the Cult of the Machine: The Kunstkammer and the Evolution of Nature, Art, and Technology* (Princeton 1995). Giovanna Ceserani and Andrea Milanese, eds., *Antiquarianism, Museums and Cultural Heritage: Collecting and Its Contexts in Eighteenth-century Naples,* special issue of the *Journal of the History of Collections* 19, no. 2 (2007). Raymond Chevallier, *L'artiste, le collectionneur et le faussaire: Pour une sociologie de l'art romain* (Paris 1991) esp. 132–177. Kathleen Wren Christian, *Empire without End: Antiquities Collections in Renaissance Rome, 1350–1527* (New Haven forthcoming). Paula Findlen, "Possessing the Past: The Material World of the Italian Renaissance," *American Historical Review* 103 (1998) 83–114. Lionel Gossman, "Imperial Icon: The Pergamon Altar in Wilhelminian Germany," *Journal of Modern History* 78 (2006) 551–587. Ian Jenkins and Kim Sloan, *Vases and Volcanoes: Sir William Hamilton and His Collection* (London 1996). Suzanne Marchand, *Down from Olympus: Archaeology and Philhellenism in Germany, 1750–1970* (Princeton 1996). Adrienne Mayor, *The First Fossil Hunters: Paleontology in Greek and Roman Times* (Princeton 2000). Arnaldo Momigliano, "Ancient History and the Antiquarian," *Journal of the Warburg and Courtauld Institutes* 13 (1950) 285–315. Glenn Most, ed., *Collecting Fragments = Fragmente sammeln* (Göttingen 1997) esp. 1–33. Krzysztof Pomian, *Collectors and Curiosities: Paris and Venice, 1500–1800,* trans. Elizabeth Wiles-Portier (London 1990).

Alain Schnapp, *The Discovery of the Past* (New York 1997). Jonathan Scott, *The Pleasures of Antiquity: British Collectors of Greece and Rome* (New Haven 2003). A. W. van Buren, "Pinacothecae with Especial Reference to Pompeii," *Memoirs of the American Academy in Rome* 15 (1938) 70–81. Roberto Weiss, *The Renaissance Discovery of Classical Antiquity* (Oxford 1969).

P.E.F.

Colony

The modern European language of colonization derives from Roman models. The word *colony* derives from Latin *colere,* "to cultivate or farm." A *colonus* was originally a tenant farmer, and although not all colonists were farmers, the association with agriculture and land remained closely tied both to what kind of society a colony was and, crucially, to arguments for the legitimacy of its existence. Roman colonies (*colonia*) were essentially settlements of Roman citizens in either vacant or, more often, occupied territory. In some cases and in some periods the colonists retained their Roman citizenship, and in some cases not. The practice of moving and resettling populations has, however, been common to all peoples everywhere. It had been practiced by the Achaemenids and was the basis of Alexander's empire in Asia. The Greek colony, *apoikia,* differed from the Roman *colonia,* however, in being a distinct *polis* established beyond the territorial limits of the mother country, or *mētropolis.* (This distinguished it from *klērouchiai,* settlements on confiscated territories of former allies, whose settlers remained citizens of their respective metropolises.) The commonly perceived distinction between Greek and Roman colonization, however, was between one kind of settlement, the *apoikia*, which was independent of the metropolis while still retaining close ties with it, and another, the *colonia*, which remained a part of the mother country.

The earliest post-classical European settlements overseas were the Crusader states of the Levant between 1098 and 1291; the Venetian empire in the Mediterranean, which at its greatest extent included Corfu, Crete, Cyprus Euboea, several of the Aegean islands, and for while outposts in mainland Greece; and merchant communities within the Ottoman Empire. There are other cases, such as the German settlements to the east of the Elbe in the 12th century. Although these, in particular the Crusader states, were described as "colonies" in the 19th century, in particular by the French in search of a legitimizing genealogy for their conquest of North Africa, they were never regarded so, or described as such, by contemporaries. The Crusader states were fully independent feudal kingdoms whose subjects came from many different parts of Europe and Asia, and the Venetian settlements in the Mediterranean were, as were such Portuguese "factories" in Africa and Asia, little more than fortified trading stations. The history of modern colonization really begins with the "discovery" and settlement the Americas after 1492.

The Spanish, first in the Canary Islands and later in the Americas, created settler societies that were intended, as far as was possible, to replicate those of Castile and to transform the indigenous inhabitants, as far as was possible, into Europeans. In this respect their objectives closely resembled Roman *coloniae.* Our king, wrote the Spanish Humanist Sebastiano Fox Morcillo in 1536, speaking of the Spanish residents in the Netherlands, "will likewise send colonies of his citizens to the provinces in order that they . . . not only act as a garrison to the kingdom but also keep the others [i.e., the native inhabitants] always faithful. This was exactly what our countrymen did in the New World when we sent numerous colonies from Spain; and what the Romans did in Egypt, Gaul, Hispania and many other provinces." Yet until the 18th century, when the administration of the empire, and the languages in which it was described, changed radically to emulate French and British practices, Spanish America (and the Philippines), although formally integrated into the Crown of Castile in 1523, were looked on as distinct kingdoms; even Charles V listed then separately among his titles. By the 17th century America was even being described by some as if it constituted a separate empire. It was also the case that, as numerous unsympathetic observers remarked, the Spanish had not gone to America, as had both the French and the English, to cultivate the land. They had gone to occupy and to benefit from the labor of others. In a memorandum of 1797 on the possible future of the French islands in the Caribbean, Napoleon's foreign minister, Charles-Maurice de Talleyrand, scathingly observed that for this reason the Spanish could never be said to have had true colonies since they had merely invaded "the first lands they encountered. They wished not to cultivate, but to devastate."

The French, who followed swiftly in the wake of the Spanish, created in America what were in effect dependent feudal territories ruled, in the case of New France (Canada), by local Parisian administrative law, the Coutume de Paris. French India, by contrast, was essentially, as were the Portuguese and the British settlements in India until the 18th century, "factories" rather than true colonies. Similarly, the possessions in America and in Asia held by the Dutch East and West Indian Companies were administered as if they were parts of the republic, and Dutch settlers never ceased to think of themselves as anything other than Dutch citizens residing temporarily overseas.

The English settlements in America, by contrast, were rather different. Although their legal association with the metropolis was complex and changing, they were widely referred to as colonies, and as frequently conceived as agricultural settlements in what, rightly or wrongly, were held to be "unoccupied" lands. For this reason, the term *colony* rapidly became synonymous with *plantation.*

It was generally recognized that all forms of colonization had the threefold purpose that the ancient colonies were believed to have had: they provided valuable, and generally unused, agricultural land; they were a means of asserting political control over occupied regions; and they offered places in which to relocate what the English geographer Richard Hakluyt called the "superfluous peoples" of the metropolis. From the outset all the European powers seem to have regarded their overseas settlements as either simple depositories for the waste products of the metropolitan society or, more farsightedly (and more humanely), as places where the disadvantaged could find lives for themselves that they were denied in Europe. Colonization, Hakluyt thought, was the human equivalent of the swarming of bees. The absence of extensive overseas colonies in which to dump potentially disruptive populations during the Wars of Religion was believed to be one of the sources of the persistent unrest in France. "It is an established fact," wrote the French Humanist Henri de la Popelinière in 1582, "that if the Spaniard had not sent to the Indies discovered by Columbus all the rogues in the realm . . . those would have stirred up the country"—as their counterparts had done in France for nearly half a century.

The relationship between the settler populations and the indigenous populations, and between the settlers and the metropolis, became (and remained, until colonization effectively disappeared in the 1960s) a source of acute anxiety. All the European colonizing powers, to varying degrees, claimed that although their colonists might be primarily agriculturalists, one of the justifications for their presence in lands over which they could make no unassailable, or even very compelling, claims to sovereignty was religious and political. For the Spanish, whose initial claim to legitimacy rested on a papal donation, this was evidently crucial. (In 1493 Pope Alexander VI had granted the Catholic monarchs of Spain, Ferdinand and Isabella, the right to occupy a region vaguely defined as "such islands and lands . . . as you have discovered or are about to discover," with the express, and sole, purpose of converting their inhabitants to Christianity.) But even the English, with no obvious evangelizing program and certainly no papal sanction, were prepared to argue that (as Hakluyt nicely put it) the objectives of the Virginia colony were "to plant Christian religion, to traffic, to conquer"—in that order. The charter for what was to become the French West India Company stated that its purpose was to "discover in those lands and countries . . . some habitation capable of sustaining colonies, for the purpose of attempting, with divine assistance, to bring the peoples who inhabit them to the knowledge of the true God, to civilize them." Furs, the main staple of the company, came second. Both the French and the English, and to some degree the Dutch, also represented themselves for the most part as those who, unlike the Spanish, had settled on territories acquired through either charter or treaty and who had always been concerned with peaceful commerce and agriculture. "I like a *Plantation*," wrote Francis Bacon, "in a pure soil; that is. where People are not displanted to the end, to Plant others. For else it is rather an Extirpation, than a Plantation."

Such conquests as had occurred had been secondary and defensive. The Utopians, explained Thomas More, in this respect stout English yeomen, founded colonies in true Greek fashion, when the "population should happen to swell above the fixed quotas." They would then "join with themselves the natives [of some adjacent island], if they are willing to dwell with them," and, if not, make war on them, for "they consider it a most just cause for war when a people which does not use its soil but keeps it idle and waste nevertheless forbids the use and possession of it by others who by the rule of nature ought to be maintained by it." This, wrote Verron de Forbonnais, the author of the long and complex article "Colonie" in the *Encyclopédie,* had been "the sole reason for the establishment of modern colonies."

No matter what truth these claims might offer—and that was far from obvious—they heavily influenced the subsequent relationships between the colonist and the metropolis. The French had, since the beginning, asserted that the colonists were transplanted French citizens. "The people of Saint Domingue," the settlers (*colons*) informed the National Assembly in 1792, "form part of the French people constituted by the sovereignty of the French empire." And what had always applied to the settlers themselves also applied, in varying degrees, to the indigenous populations of the colonies. In 1664 the founding charter of the French West India Company went so far as to decree that all American Indians who had converted to Christianity should "be registered and counted as denizens and French natives, and as such entitled for all rights of succession, goods, laws and other dispositions." This sense of the French empire as a single territory was to last until the end of the French overseas empire in the mid-20th century. The peoples of Algeria, French Indochina, and the French colonies in the Caribbean and Africa were all, at different times, and to differing degrees, considered to be French. Even today all that remains of the French overseas empire—the Départements and Territoires d'Outre-mer—are not colonies but departments of metropolitan France.

The English situation was legally at least not so very different. The claim that "New England lies with England" may have been a social myth, but it corresponded to a legal reality. The English colonies in America were, like the later "crown colonies" in Africa and Asia, an inseparable part of the royal demesne. In practice, however, the colonists exercised virtual autonomy in their own internal affairs. "The colonies," wrote John Campbell disapprovingly in 1755, "have in reality . . . acted as if they thought themselves so many independent states, under their respective charters, rather than as provinces of the same empire." By the early 18th century, as tension between the colonists and the Crown mounted, many began to look to the distinction between Roman and Greek colonization as a means of explaining, if not resolving, the growing dispute over the proper relationship between colony and metropolis.

The Spanish and the French may have set out to emulate the Romans, but Britain's empire, argued the English pamphleteer Andrew Fletcher in 1704, more closely resembled the leagues of the Greek city-states—a model that was later applied by James Madison and James Wilson to their proposals for a federal structure for the United States. In the terms dictated by this image, the English colonies had been private ventures, unlike both the French and the Spanish settlements, which had been very largely engineered by the state. It could be argued, therefore, that like the Greek colonies before them, the British settlements in the New World had been constituted from the beginning as semi-independent political, and possibly even cultural, communities. The implication of this was that the colonies would remain attached to the aptly named mother country only so long as they needed her. Colonies in both the ancient and the modern worlds, observed the *philosophe* Anne-Robert-Jacques Turgot, who was at the time (1776) comptroller general of France, were "like fruit." They clung to the tree only until they were mature. After that they should be allowed to drop. That same year, Adam Smith urged the British Crown to abandon what he called the "doomed attempt to hold the British colonies by force." Such a gesture would, he was confident, "certainly persuade turbulent and factious subjects, to become our most faithful, affectionate and generous allies; and the same sort of parental affection on the one side, and filial respect on the other, might revive between Great Britain and her colonies, which used to subsist between those of ancient Greece and the mother city from which they descended."

In the aftermath of the American and French revolutions the entirety of European overseas imperial projects, conceived along broadly Roman lines, seemed to be at a much-deserved end. The French Crown, complained Talleyrand, had always thought of its imperial ventures in Roman rather than Greek terms. This had been its fatal error. For whereas the colonies established by the Greeks, which had been precisely autonomous states of the kind that the British now had in India, had flourished, the Roman ones had in the end "achieved almost nothing." Postrevolutionary France would, he concluded, be well-advised to abandon its remaining colonies in the Caribbean and create new ones after (what he supposed to be) the English model in Bengal.

In fact, however, the English presence in India was not in any ancient sense colonial at all. The great expansion of the European powers after the end of the Napoleonic Wars took a very different direction. Gone now was any attempt to create a cohesive Roman-style empire. The new empires that grew up during the 19th century involved a wide variety of novel, often improvised political forms. "I know of no example of it either in ancient or modern history," wrote Benjamin Disraeli in 1878 of the British Empire, for whose image he was largely responsible. "No Caesar or Charlemagne ever presided over a dominion so peculiar." And, crucially, very few of the colonies, dominions, protectorates, or mandates that the 19th-century empires comprised involved extensive overseas settlement. The major colonizers, the French and the British, always preferred if possible to rule their subordinate territories by what came to be known as "indirect rule," or the *politique des races,* in which government was left to compliant local elites. British India remained until the end a place visited rather than settled. "The English," observed the French essayist and art historian Élie Faure in 1931, "seem to be camping. One only ever sees them from behind a wall of steel"—a reference to the railways. In South Africa, which was one of the most densely settled regions of that continent, whites accounted for only 21 percent of the population in 1936. In Southern Rhodesia the figure was less than 5 percent. Even in Algeria, which had been meant to be, in Alexis de Tocqueville's words, "an extension of France itself on the far side of the Mediterranean," the *colons* in 1931 made up less than 13 percent. Although the term *colony* continued to be applied to a number of different settlements, and *colonialism* and *postcolonialism* continue to be used to describe the forms of exploitation pursed by many European states in Africa and in some parts of Asia, very few of the territories that made up the great 19th-century European overseas empires were ever colonies in any sense the ancients would have recognized.

BIBL.: Brett Bowden, *The Empire of Civilization: The Evolution of an Imperial Idea* (Chicago 2009). Anthony Padgett, *Peoples and Empires: Europeans and the Rest of the World, from Antiquity to the Present* (London 2002). A.P.

Color

Antiquity's legacy in color was to both theory and practice, but the relationship between the two was an uneasy one, particularly in the Renaissance, as evidenced by the respectful nods made by virtually every writer in the direction of the Aristotelian science of color, and then the quick abandonment of the discussion in favor of technical concerns. As Leon Battista Alberti said: "For what help is it to the painter to know how colour is made from the mixture of rare and dense, or hot and dry or cold and wet? . . . It is enough for the painter to know what the colours are, and how they should be used in painting" (1991, 45). The constant references to classical sources in theoretic writing is an indication of the authority of antiquity, but the more interesting instances of influence are indirect rather than direct citations. There was no possibility for artists to imitate Greek painting because all they had were descriptions and no examples. Until the discoveries of the Golden House of Nero (Domus Aurea) and, later, Pompeii and Herculaneum, examples of Roman painting were fragmentary and faded. And it was not recognized until 19th-century archaeological discoveries that Greek and Roman sculpture was polychromed. The use of colored marble in ancient architecture, on the other hand, was apparent from surviving examples in Rome, notably the Pantheon. Its marble revetment was imitated by Raphael in Agostino Chigi's chapel in Santa Maria del Popolo, and such decoration became increasingly popular in the later 16th century, beginning in the chapels in the new St. Peter's and Sixtus V's chapel in Santa Maria Maggiore. Aristotle's seven-color system was canonical in theory but useless in practice. Pliny's description of Apelles' four-color palette, which he said was used by certain other renowned Greek painters, made constant reappearances in theoretical discussions from the Renaissance on, but the interpretation changed according to the practice of the time. The palette was described as comprising black, white, red, and yellow, but the absence of blue—a color indispensable to Renaissance sacred paintings for the draperies of Christ and the Virgin Mary—made its adoption impossible.

Cennino Cennini (*Il Libro dell'Arte,* ca. 1390) had little interest in theory, but he felt he had to make some gesture toward it, so he began his discussion with the Aristotelian distinction between three natural and four artificial colors, then quickly jumped to a technical description of the pigments and how to prepare them. Leon Battista Alberti was the first theorist of the Renaissance to make use of antique sources. In his *De pictura* (1435) Alberti identified his own choice of four colors as the *genera* of color, from which all other colors could be created, and he equated them with the elements: red is the color of fire, blue of the air, green of the water, and gray and ash of the earth (1991, 45). The last, *cenereum* or *bigio,* has been interpreted by some scholars to mean a kind of yellow, perhaps an unsaturated earthy color, because without yellow it is difficult to imagine how other colors could be mixed. Alberti adapted his theory to practice, modifying the abstract philosophical discussion of his ancient sources.

Of greater service and influence was Alberti's use of the rhetorical model from Cicero and Quintilian. His treatise follows generally the outline of a good oration as described by Cicero, omitting only the refutation of other positions. Alberti began a tradition that remained at the other end of the Renaissance: Lomazzo modeled his theoretical works on Cicero. Cicero (*De oratore* 3.57.216–217) made an analogy between the colors of art and the facial expressions, vocal tone, and gestures the orator uses to arouse emotion in his hearer. Following Cicero, Alberti advised the painter to use color to affect the emotions of the viewer, though he did not make his reference to Cicero explicit. More interesting is the influence of Pliny, who, although he is never cited by Alberti, is the source of some 29 references in *De pictura.* The keynote of Alberti's treatise derives from Pliny's concern with simplicity and a noble seriousness. Just as Pliny wished to use Greek practice to chasten the proliferation of gaudy and expensive materials in his day, so Alberti counseled artists to use moderation and restraint in all aspects of painting, including color. Specifically, he advised them to abjure gold and to paint the effect of gold, ostensibly because it would be more naturalistic, but also as part of his agenda of restraint. His recommendation that black as well as white be used in modeling (instead of Cennini's white only) would have the effect of muting the palette, creating more sober paintings. Alberti may have had in mind Pliny's celebrated account of Apelles' dark varnish (*Naturalis historia* 35, 97), *atramentum,* which Pliny claimed had the effect of toning down the "florid colors." The moral overtones of Pliny's austerity are present in Alberti when he recommends the substitution of artistic skill for sumptuous color. Renunciation of gaudy color's cheap appeal to the senses suggests greater dignity and moral superiority. As Michael Baxandall has documented, increasingly in the later Quattrocento skill replaced expensive materials as the most valued commodity in contracts between painters and patrons. The restraint Alberti counseled did in fact have an influence on practice, though as a rule painters found their own ways of creating the effect he called for. Modeling down with black was widely introduced in central Italy, but a dark underpainting like that employed by Leonardo da Vinci in his unfinished *Adoration of the Magi* (Florence, Uffizi) could produce a similarly muted color. Gold did disappear for a while in the second half of the 15th century, and mixed or layered coloring replaced the pure and brilliant tones of the Cennini system.

Beginning around 1480, the most important discovery of ancient Roman painting before Pompeii introduced an alternative model to Alberti's sobriety. Excursions into the grottoes of the Esquiline Hill provided visitors the opportunity to see magnificently well-preserved vaults of the 1st century CE. Nero's extravagant Domus Aurea had been such an embarrassment to later emperors that Trajan had it filled with rubble, which by the late 15th century had settled sufficiently in places for holes to open and permit entrance. Although the explorers mistook these caves for the Baths of Titus, they understood that they were viewing what had previously been available only in faded fragments at the Colosseum and at Hadrian's Villa at Tivoli. The motifs copied from these grottoes, dubbed *grotteschi,* became the fashion for decorating the borders and frames in chapels and palaces. Pinturicchio, who left his name inscribed on a wall of the grottoes, displayed the new art in the Borgia Apartment of the Vatican and the Piccolomini Library in Siena. Perugino (Collegio del Cambio, Perugia), Filippino Lippi (Caraffa Chapel, Santa Maria sopra Minerva, Rome; Strozzi Chapel, Santa Maria Novella, Florence), and Signorelli (Brizio Chapel, Orvieto) were among the first painters to accommodate their patrons with this newest expression of the continuity of antiquity with their own time. The opulence and radiant color found in the antique paintings brought back into favor gold, ornament, and brilliant color, at least for peripheral areas and in vaults. A watercolor by Francisco da Hollanda of the Volta dorata (1538) gives us a sense of the source of Renaissance creations such as the Sala dei Pontifici in the Vatican Palace. The sudden and unexpected appearance of gold in the frescoes of the Sistine Chapel (1481–1483) may be a reflection of a new aesthetic of sumptuousness resulting from the experience of the Domus Aurea. A more restrained version was offered by Giovanni da Udine under Raphael's direction in the Vatican Loggia of Cardinal Bibbiena (1516) and the Loggia of Leo X (1518), where the background is white and the colors quite subdued.

Albertian restraint was replaced in the second quarter

of the 16th century in central Italy with a delight in fantasy and ornament that included color. There is very little direct commentary on color by the Counter-Reformation critics of midcentury, but the *all'antica grotteschi* became a symbol for pagan frippery that was condemned in sacred images on the basis of Horatian decorum. The Counter-Reformation call for didactic painting that remained true to Scripture discouraged for a time color inventions in religious art such as those produced with *cangiantismo* (hue shift in a modeling sequence) and *grotteschi*. Lomazzo, for example, discouraged the use of *cangianti* for the draperies of the Virgin, arguing from a Horatian standpoint that it was inappropriate. *Grotteschi* of the kind invented by Raphael and his workshop were acceptable to Counter-Reformation critics like Gilio and Armenini because they appeared to them to contain "nothing repugnant to nature," that is, nothing fantastical. Under Sixtus V (1585–1590) *all'antica* ornaments were revived, somewhat chastened, and treated as evidence of the continuity of the classical tradition. The Sistine wing of the Vatican Library and the vaults of the Lateran Palace were covered with *grotteschi* in the style of Raphael's loggias. Decorum had become the prime criterion for judging acceptability.

Although all these theorists made constant reference to classical sources, the conflict between abstract Aristotelian theory and practice is apparent. Leonardo attempted to reconcile empirical observation, painting practice, and Aristotelian science. He adapted Aristotle in constructing his color scale, but he made scant use of other classical sources, except to cite the usual clichés about deceptive illusionism from Pliny. Lomazzo undertook a full-fledged theory of color toward the end of the 16th century, in which he revisited the model of rhetoric and made the same kind of uncomfortable accommodation between the Aristotelian seven-color system and practice as Alberti. He returned to Aristotle in his definition of color and its species (*Trattato* 3.3), constructing a color scale on a theoretical, not experiential, basis. In selecting his examples of color symbolism he drew them almost entirely from antique literary sources (chaps. 12–18). The trappings of the classical tradition provide the frame for his practical discussion of pigments and their proper use. In Venice it was commonplace to compare Titian to Apelles, who was the exemplar of ancient painters, although a four-color palette was never attributed to Titian, and the classical tradition again was given only lip service by Pino, Dolce, and Aretino. These fanciful uses of Aristotle and other ancient authors would be abandoned in the 17th century, when Rubens's and Aguilonius' system of primary and secondary colors would prevail, thus finally spelling an end to the appropriations of ancient color systems (Gage 1993).

Another example of an indirect but fundamental influence on the thinking of the Renaissance is the development of multiple modes of color. Poussin in his famous letter to Chantelou (1647) described a system of modes of painting by analogy with the Greek modes of music, again making use of the concept of decorum. This was the first time such a system had been fully articulated, but it is a way of thinking that had been operating in the Renaissance. Although it is nowhere expressed in theoretical terms, it appears from practice that the categories of rhetoric distinguished by Cicero gave the model for multiple options that had not been conceived in the early Renaissance. Alberti does not discuss genres of painting, but by the second decade of the 16th century the painter in Rome had available to him a choice of color styles, which he could match to his commission, in the same way Poussin described matching the mode to subject. Just as the orator would choose a style for a funeral different from that he would use to address the Senate, so a painter could select the chiaroscuro mode of coloring for a dramatic narrative, or the gentler and more harmonious *unione* mode for a devotional work. This situation came about because of the increased mobility of artists, so that painters from different workshop traditions came to Rome and worked side by side. In the first years of the new century, Michelangelo had come from Florence, Raphael from Umbria, Sebastiano del Piombo from Venice, and a few years later Leonardo da Vinci, who had been working in Milan, arrived. Each of them had developed distinctive styles, particularly of coloring, which then were on display as alternatives to any who cared to observe. When artists began coming to Rome, either to seek work or just to study the antiquities and the wonders of art being commissioned by the pope and his court, such as the Sistine Chapel and the Stanze by Raphael, they could choose among the modes of color on display or match the mode to the commission. By the 1520s Polidoro da Caravaggio was practicing a kind of monochrome painting, akin to a manner described with approval by Pliny, simulating relief sculpture on exteriors. These facades would become another of the wonders that painters would seek out to study. In fact, by the time of Armenini (ca. 1533–1609), young painters were exhorted to complete their education by drawing from these four sources: the antique, Michelangelo, Raphael, and Polidoro. Eclecticism of this sort was something new, and its roots can be found in rhetorical theory, which generated a new sensitivity to matching style to conditions and function, in the same way that Poussin described (Hall 1992).

An interesting attempt to link color harmony to music theory was made when Comanini described how the Milanese painter Arcimboldo had undertaken to create the Pythagorean musical harmonies in paint by matching the proportions of black and white to the mathematical proportions of tones that create the octave, the fifth, the twelfth, and the fifteenth discovered by Pythagoras.

> What I say of the colours white and black is true of all the other colours as well, because just as Arcimboldo progressed bit by bit shadowing white and reducing it to sharpness, so he has done with yellow and with all the other colours, employing white for the lowest part found in the singing, and green and

> also blue for the middle ranges, and purple and brown for the highest parts—since in these colours one follows and darkens the others. White is shaded by yellow, and yellow by green, and green by blue, and blue by purple, and purple by brown as the bass is followed by the tenor, and the tenor by the alto, and the alto by the soprano. (Comanini 2001)

Italian theory was disseminated across Europe and in the centuries succeeding the Renaissance was expanded everywhere by authors drawing on antique sources, but color did not fare particularly well in this art theory. Franciscus Junius, a Dutch physician and scholar, gathered together every surviving text to create *The Painting of the Ancients* (1638), with the intention of influencing contemporary painting. He reinforced Pliny's endorsement of simplicity with quotations from Aulus Gellius and Vitruvius condemning the lavish use of costly materials (2.6). Bellori continued and extended the Plinian prejudice against beautiful color, which he characterized as the taste of the vulgar, as opposed to beautiful form, the nobler preference (*Ideal in Art,* 1664). Johann Winckelmann, although he was obsessed with the beauty of Greek art, did not consider color because, he said, "The essence of beauty consists not in color but in shape, and on this point all enlightened minds will at once agree" (*History of Ancient Art among the Greeks,* 1764). In the area of practice, on the other hand, the excavations of Pompeii and Herculaneum, beginning in 1748, provided a vast new cache of wall paintings from which painters could draw inspiration, as the Domus Aurea had done for the Renaissance. "Pompeian red" entered the vocabulary and was used in decoration all over Europe.

In modern times the most significant legacy of the classical writers has been centered on Pliny's description of Apelles' dark varnish. Pliny described this *atramentum* as "a dark coating so thinly spread that, by reflecting, it enhanced the brilliance of the colour while, at the same time, it afforded protection from dust and dirt and was not itself visible except at close quarters. One main purpose was to prevent the brilliance of the colours from offending the eye, since it gave the impression as if the beholder were seeing them through a window of talc, so that he gave from a distance an imperceptible touch of severity to excessively rich colours" (Gombrich 1962). In the 1950s and 1960s, when controversy raged over the postwar cleaning of Old Master paintings by the National Gallery in London, some claimed that the conservators were stripping away original varnishes and glazes. Those who favored subdued coloring sought support in Pliny and the fame of his text in the Renaissance, stating that such tinted varnishes would surely have been imitated by painters for whom Pliny and Apelles represented the ultimate authority. This is an issue that has proved impossible to resolve because in all likelihood any such tinted varnish would have been removed in the harsh cleanings that took place before modern technology made it possible to analyze the layers of paint microscopically and chemically. The arguments surfaced again with the cleaning of Michelangelo's Sistine vault in the 1980s, but they were harder to support in the case of fresco, where no corroboration from a classical source such as Pliny could be adduced.

BIBL.: Leon Battista Alberti, *On Painting,* trans. Cecil Grayson (Baltimore 1991). Gregorio Comanini, *The Figino; or, On the Purpose of Painting,* trans. A. Doyle-Anderson and G. Maiorino (Toronto 2001). Nicole Dacos, *La découverte de la Domus Aurea et la formation des grotesques à la Renaissance* (London 1969). John Gage, *Colour and Culture* (London 1993). Jonas Gavel, *Colour: A Study of Its Position in the Art Theory of the Quattro- & Cinquecento* (Stockholm 1979). Ernst Gombrich, "Dark Varnishes: Variations on a Theme from Pliny," *Burlington Magazine* 104 (February 1962) 50–51. Marcia B. Hall, *Color and Meaning: Practice and Theory in Renaissance Painting* (New York 1992). Rensselaer W. Lee, "*Ut Pictura Poesis:* The Humanist Theory of Painting," *Art Bulletin* 22 (1940) 197–269.

M.B.H.

Colosseum

The largest and best-preserved amphitheater of imperial Rome, begun by Vespasian and dedicated in 80 CE by his son Titus.

From the moment of its inauguration, the Colosseum became the symbol of Roman architectural achievement. Over the centuries its stubborn resistance to wear and tear has made it the icon of the Eternal City. Pomponio Leto acknowledged the authoritative status of the Colosseum in a lecture published in 1510, in which he echoed Suetonius by describing it as being in the middle of the city, *in media Urbe amphitheatrum,* even though the Colosseum then stood on the fringes of the papal capital. Nevertheless, as Pomponio recognized, despite the uncertainties of time and fortune, the Colosseum continues to represent the symbolic heart of Rome.

Originally called the Flavian Amphitheater, the Colosseum acquired its now universally familiar name in the Middle Ages, perhaps as an invented term inspired by an adjacent colossal statue built by Nero. Gladiatorial combat there ended in the 5th century, and the amphitheater began to decay as scavengers extracted the metal clamps pinning its stones together. As early as the 8th century, a catastrophic earthquake destroyed more than half of the external arcades, creating a gigantic pile of rubble called the Coscia Colisei. In the 12th century the Colosseum served as a fortress for the Frangipani, a Roman baronial family, who built their *palatium* at the eastern end of the arena, but eventually the monument was restored to the public domain. From the early 15th century onward two-thirds of the amphitheater was subject to the jurisdiction of the civic government; the remaining third belonged to a religious confraternity, the Compagnia del Salvatore.

The Colosseum always provided a convenient quarry for new construction in Rome, and during the Renaissance building boom the scale of excavations increased exponentially. In 1452 alone, under Pope Nicholas V, more than 2,500 cartloads were hauled from the site. Landmark structures such as the Palazzo Venezia and the Palazzo della Cancelleria exploited the Colosseum for its building stone while also emulating the design of its superimposed arcades. But the presence of the civic government as official custodian of the ruins limited demolition at the Colosseum. Civic officials protected the surviving arcades, delegating the Coscia Colisei to the Salvatore confraternity, which sold off rubble to support their charitable works. Stone was removed from the Colosseum as late as 1796, just before the construction of the monumental buttresses. The remarkable survival of the arcades testifies not only to their rugged construction but to the vigilance of the Roman civic guardians who preserved them intact.

Religion played a more prominent role at the Colosseum after 1490, when the Gonfalone confraternity began to stage their annual Passion plays in the arena. Successive popes proposed consecrating the Colosseum—with the notable exception of Sixtus V, who proposed either rehabilitating it as a textile mill or leveling it—and in 1749 Benedict XIV dedicated the monument as a public church, erecting a crucifix and tabernacles marking the Stations of the Cross in the arena. Modern excavations have effaced much of this religious atmosphere, but the Colosseum still provides the setting for the reenactment of the Via Crucis on Good Friday.

Contemporary sports stadiums often claim to be the modern equivalents of the Colosseum (Americanized as *coliseum*), but the design of such mega-structures continues to move away from the ancient model. The primary external feature of the Colosseum was its masonry shell, whereas domed roofs, or cantilevered boxes, now dominate stadium design. But the Colosseum's amphitheater remains a popular setting for films. For *Gladiator* (2000), a cast of 2,000 filled a full-scale model of the lowest tier, encompassing nearly a third of the original circumference; the upper tiers, and the remaining 33,000 spectators, were recreated using digital technology.

BIBL.: Stefano Antonetti and Rossella Rea, "Inquadramento cronologico delle tracce del riuso," in *Rota colisei, la valle del Colosseo attraverso i secoli,* ed. Rossella Rea (Milan 2002) 283–327. Michela Di Macco, *Il Colosseo: Funzione simbolica, storica, urbana* (Rome 1971). Keith Hopkins and Mary Beard, *The Colosseum* (London 2005). Nerida Newbigin, "The Decorum of the Passion: The Plays of the Confraternity of the Gonfalone in the Roman Colosseum, 1490–1539," in *Confraternities and the Visual Arts in Renaissance Italy,* ed. Barbara Wisch and Diane Cole Ahl (New York 2000) 173–202. D.KA.

Comedy and the Comic

The word *comedy* derives probably from the Greek *kōmos,* "revel," or "a company of men singing," or its likely source *kōmē,* "village," + *aoidos,* "singer." From ancient times communities gathered together for comedy, singing, and dancing, sometimes in costume according to routines. These activities produced *to geloīon,* "laughter." Throughout the ages communal processions, parties, parades, folk gatherings, local celebrations, musical revues, satirical skits, and holiday festivals have all been various descendants of the original revels and, therefore, various expressions of the comic.

One popular type of quasi-literary comedy, mime, from *mimēsis,* "imitation," deserves notice at the outset. Surviving evidence suggests that mimes appeared early in the 6th century BCE and presented farcical scenes from daily life or mythological travesty. Mimes could consist of skits, songs, dialogues, dances, animal imitations, acrobatics, and juggling by costumed performers, including women. Pantomime (the art of silent mime) appears to have derived from interpretive dances and developed as an ancient, especially Roman, variation. Mimes combined with other native art forms, such as the Atellan farce (originally in Oscan), which featured stock characters in masks: Maccus, the stupid clown; Bucco, the glutton or braggart; Pappus, the foolish old man; and Dossennus, the clever hunchback. Mimes appeared regularly at the Roman Floralia (perhaps as early as the 3rd cent. BCE) and became a popular entertainment at banquets and other gatherings.

Descendants of mime in the Middle Ages had become itinerant entertainers, working as vagrant actors, traveling minstrels, and song-and-dance performers. In France they were *jongleurs,* in England *gleemen,* in Denmark *scalds,* in Germany *scops,* or singers of tales. Elements of Graeco-Roman mime made their way into the Turkish Karagoz theater, popular until the 17th century, and into the Italian *commedia dell'arte,* an improvisatory style that flourished from the 15th through 18th centuries and featured stock characters in masks and farcical action, including dances, beatings, acrobatics, and *lazzi,* or comic routines. From 1570 the Théâtres de la Foire (fairground theaters) in Paris presented Italianate farces, dumb shows, marionette plays, rope dancing, tumblers, and trained animals. The English pantomime developed from the popular, largely silent, harlequinade afterpieces of 18th-century plays. It appeared as the dumb show, entr'acte entertainment, and satirical sketch.

In France the arts of mime and pantomime reached their highest forms of development. In the 19th century Gaspard Deburau transformed the masked, lazy, and mischievous Pedrolino of the *commedia dell'arte* into a new figure, Pierrot, white-faced, expressive, capable of poetic emotion. His innovations continued in the creations of the Cercle des Funambules. In the 20th century Jacques Copeau and his student Etienne Decroux started a school of corporeal mime, a pure style of bodily expressivity that abandoned conventional gestures as well as accompanying music and setting. His innovations flowered in the work of later modern masters such as Marcel Marceau and Jacques Lecoq. Throughout its history, practitioners of mime have featured great clowns whose laughter and tears capture something of the comic (and tragic) in human life. Modern mime clowns include the stars of vaudeville, Emmett Kelly ("Weary Willie" of Barnum and Bailey Circus), the clowns of the Moscow Circus, and the film stars Charlie Chaplin, Buster Keaton, and Harpo Marx. Today mime companies flourish throughout Europe and the United States.

On the origins of more formal, literary comedy, Aristotle provides an early witness. Though misattributing the work to Homer (it is now thought to be by Pigres of Halicarnassus), he praises *Margites* as the archetypal comedy: "Just as Homer was a supreme poet in the serious style, since he alone made his representations not only good but also dramatic, so, too, he was the first to mark out the main lines of comedy, because he made his drama not out of personal satire but out of the laughable as such. His *Margites* indeed provides an analogy: as are the *Iliad* and *Odyssey* to our tragedies, so is the *Margites* to our comedies" (*Poetics* 1448b–1449a). Now lost, *Margites* appears to have been a poem featuring a dense and foolish hero, "knowing many things, but knowing them all badly." The name derived from *margos,* "gluttonous, wanton," and the poem featured both epic hexameter and iambic trimeter, the latter a meter regarded as suitable for treating the base and ridiculous. This, the earliest comedy that we know of, was thus a mock-epic: it evoked laughter by presenting elevated treatment of a foolish or trivial subject.

As such, *Margites* resembled in spirit at least the pseudo-Homeric parody of the *Iliad, Batrachomyomachia* (*The Battle of the Frogs and the Mice*). This poem features the epic vaunts of its mouse hero, Crumb-snatcher, son of Bread-nibbler, and the best of the frogs, Puff-jaw, son of Mud-man. Zeus and Athene intervene, and the battle ends with a final assault by mailed warriors with curving claws, crooked beasts who walk sideways on eight legs—that is, crabs.

The mock-epic has a long and distinguished history, appearing in elevated descriptions of the cock and hen (Chanticleer and Pertelote) in Chaucer's 14th-century *Nun's Priest's Tale.* Rabelais transformed the epic catalogue, quest, and other conventions in his riotous *Gargantua and Pantagruel* (1532–1552). There the Picrocholine episode constitutes a mock-epic rehearsal of a local dispute and widens into consideration of other issues—war, the treatment of prisoners, and regulation of the social order. In the final poem of Ben Jonson's *Epigrams* (ca. 1612), "On the Famous Voyage," two Londoners take a grand journey by boat through the sewage-clogged Fleet Ditch in quest of a Holborn brothel. Alessandro Tassoni records the struggle of two Italian towns over a stolen water bucket in *Secchia Rapita* (1614). Lope de Vega's *Gatomaquia* (1634) sings of two tomcats, Marramaquiz and Micifuz, who battle for the fair female cat Zapaquil. In *Dulot vaincu* Jean François Sarrazin (1614–1654) mocks a minor French poet who composed sonnets by selecting end rhymes (*bouts-rimés*) and then filling in the lines.

The neoclassical age produced many mock-epics. Nicolas Boileau's *Le lutrin* (*The Lectern,* 1667), for example, begins as a quarrel between clerics about the placement of a lectern in a chapel and ends in a bookstore with ancients and moderns hurling their favorite books at each other. In England neoclassical writers such as John Dryden, Jonathan Swift, and Alexander Pope brought this kind of comedy to its highest point of development. In Dryden's *MacFlecknoe* (1684) the poetaster Richard Flecknoe passes his kingdom over to Thomas Shadwell:

> At his right hand our young Ascanius sat,
> Rome's other hope, and pillar of the state.
> His brows thick fogs, instead of glories, grace,
> And lambent dullness played around his face.
> As Hannibal did to the altars come,
> Sworn by his sire a mortal foe to Rome;
> So Shadwell swore, nor should his vow be vain,
> That he till death true dullness would maintain. (108–115)

Dryden substitutes thick fog for Virgil's divine flame of destiny, and the kingdom of dullness for the *imperium sine fine* of Roman empire. Swift, like Boileau, wrote a mock-epic account of the war between the ancients and moderns. *The Battle of the Books* (1704), a prose satire, starts with a tour de force, an extended quarrel in the King's library between a bee (representing the ancients) and a spider (representing the moderns). Aesop speaks, explaining that the bee ranges over the world and produces honey and wax while the spider, filled with dirt and excrement, spins from itself only cobwebs. The battle then rages:

> Homer appeared at the head of the cavalry, mounted on a furious horse, with difficulty managed by the rider himself, but which no other mortal durst approach. He rode among the enemy's ranks, and bore down all before him. Say, goddess, whom he slew first and whom he slew last. First Gondibert advanced against him, clad in heavy armor, and mounted on a staid, sober gelding, not so famed for his speed as his docility in kneeling whenever his rider would mount or alight. He had made a vow to Pallas that he would never leave the field till he had spoiled Homer of his armor. Madman, who had never once seen the wearer, nor understood his strength! Him Homer overthrew, horse and man to the ground, there to be trampled and choked in the dirt.

Extolling Homer, Swift mocks here William Davenant, author of a dull chivalric epic, *Gondibert* (1651), and by extension all moderns, for witless pretension.

Alexander Pope wrote two mock-epics that remain triumphs of English literature. *The Rape of the Lock* (1712–1717) treats in epic style an actual incident: Robert, Lord Petre, cut off a lock of Arabella Fermor's hair, which started a quarrel between their families. Seeking to heal the rift by evoking laughter at the incident, Pope calls upon the muses and describes the arming of the heroine, Belinda (Arabella), at her toilette, "Each silver vase in mystic order laid" (1.122):

Now awful beauty puts on all its arms;
The fair each moment rises in her charms,
Repairs her smiles, awakens every grace,
And calls forth all the wonders of her face. (1.139–142)

Airy sylphs take the place of the Olympian gods but cannot prevent the rape; Belinda is horrified:

Then flashed the living lightning from her eyes,
And screams of horror rend th'affrighted skies.
Not louder shrieks to pitying heaven are cast,
When husbands or when lap-dogs breathe their last. (3.155–158)

Pope personalizes and moralizes the epic journey to the underworld, which here takes the reader to the Cave of Spleen, home of female affectation and foul humors. The poem ends with an apotheosis of the lock, now a blazing star in heaven.

Pope's *Dunciad* (1728–1743) starts out as an attack on the Shakespeare scholar Lewis Theobald, crowned ceremoniously king of dunces. Pope several times expanded this work, shifting the focus to Colley Cibber, actor, dramatist, theater manager, and poet laureate, Pope's new King of Dullness. In the final version epic games featured in book 2 include contests in urination, flattery, and noisemaking. Cibber descends to the underworld, where he meets his poetic father, Elkanah Settle, who gives him a vision of the past and future glories of Dullness. The ending of the poem, the triumph of Dullness, suggests the loss of Britain's intellectual and artistic heritage and the general decay of culture under Hanoverian rule.

Religion blushing veils her sacred fires,
And unawares, morality expires.
Nor public flame, nor private, dares to shine;
Nor human Spark is left, nor glimpse divine!
Lo! thy dread empire, Chaos! is restored;
Light dies before thy uncreating word;
Thy hand, great Anarch! lets the curtain fall;
And universal darkness buries all. (4.649–656)

From the *Margites* onward the mock-epic has proved a rich vein for satirists and humorists. In the preface to his *Joseph Andrews* (1742), Henry Fielding alludes to Aristotle's comments on *Margites* as warrant and precedent for his "comic romance" or "comic epic poem in prose . . . differing from comedy as the serious epic from tragedy":

its action being more extended and comprehensive; containing a much larger circle of incidents, and introducing a greater variety of characters. It differs from the serious romance in its fable and action, in this: that as in the one these are grave and solemn, so in the other they are light and ridiculous; it differs in its characters, by introducing persons of inferior rank, and consequently of inferior manners, whereas the grave romance sets the highest before us; lastly in its sentiments and diction; by preserving the ludicrous instead of the sublime.

The result is a rollicking yet sentimental exaltation of male virtue, especially chastity, and a series of adventures that end in the providential discovery of lost identity. But the novel maintains only an oblique relationship with its epic forebears, particularly the *Odyssey.*

The lines of filiation are only slightly clearer in another mock-epic adaptation, *The Hasty Pudding* (1796), by Joel Barlow, one of the "Hartford wits" (named for the town in Connecticut).

Despise it not, ye bards to terror steeled,
Who hurl your thunders round the epic field;
Nor ye who strain your midnight throats to sing
Joys that the vineyard and the stillhouse bring;
Or on some distant fair your notes employ,
And speak of raptures that you ne'er enjoy.
I sing the sweets I know, the charms I feel,
My morning incense, and my evening meal,
The sweets of Hasty Pudding. (1.9–16)

This celebration of cornmeal mush won Barlow more fame than his lugubrious *Columbiad* (1809), an epic praise of Columbus and America.

Lord Byron works yet another change on the mock-epic in his celebrated *Don Juan* (1819), where he mixes colloquialism with the high style and epic conventions to portray and to lampoon his hero, the fabled lover and seducer of women, Don Juan.

Most epic poets plunge 'in medias res'
(Horace makes this the heroic turnpike road),
And then your hero tells, whene'er you please,
What went before—by way of episode,
While seated after dinner at his ease,
Beside his mistress in some soft abode,
Palace, or garden, paradise, or cavern,
Which serves the happy couple for a tavern.
That is the usual method, but not mine—
My way is to begin with the beginning. (1.41–56)

Byron's mock-epic contends with earlier epics, even as it imitates them; the result is a digressive, conversational, fantastic, episodic, romantic, and satirical romance.

One genre related to the mock-epic that has flowered through the centuries is the mock-encomium, the praise of unworthy subjects; this genre extols cowardly figures such as Thersites (from the opening of the *Iliad*), vicious actions such as lying, or trivial things—the gout, pots, pebbles, even Nothing itself. The earliest examples appear in the works of Greek rhetoricians, notably Isocrates' ironic praise of Helen. Influential Latin examples include the pseudo-Virgilian *Culex* (*Mosquito,* or *Gnat*), the pseudo-Ovidian *Nux* (*Nut*), and, from the 2nd century CE, Marcus Cornelius Fronto's *Praise of Smoke and Dust,*

Lucian's *Praise of a Fly,* and pseudo-Lucian's *Trapopodagra* (a tragedy on the gout). In the 4th century Claudian wrote several mock-encomia, and Synesius of Cyrene produced *Praise of Baldness,* which became a favorite in the Renaissance and thereafter. Erasmus wrote the masterpiece of the genre, *Moriae Encomium* (*Praise of Folly,* 1509), a wide-ranging satire on the manners and morals of early modern Europe. Rabelais distributed various mock-encomia throughout *Gargantua and Pantagruel* (1532–1552), including celebrations of debt and debtors (3.3–4), the codpiece (3.8), and the stomach (4.57). Examples multiply in the works of the Marotic poets (named for Clément Marot, 1496–1544), those of the Pléiade (especially Du Bellay), and the work of Bruscambille (the comedian Deslauriers, d. 1634), a farceur who influenced Molière. The reaction against Petrarchanism resulted in a related subgenre, the parodic mock-blazons of poets such as Francesco Berni, Anton Doni, Agnolo Firenzuola, and William Shakespeare (Sonnet 130).

Anthologies of mock-encomia appeared in the 17th century, for example, *Delle rime piacevoli* (Venice 1603), and, importantly, Caspar Dornavius' *Amphitheatrum sapientiae socraticae joco-seriae* (*Amphitheater of Lighter Socratic Wisdom,* Hanover 1619), which presented more than 500 Latin examples from leading Humanists. Here Daniel Heinsius praised the louse; Philipp, the ant; Janus Dousa, shade; Justus Lipsius, the elephant. Mock-encomia also took the form of paradoxes, or defenses of outrageous propositions, in the works of Charles Estienne, Philibert de Vienne, and the young John Donne, whose juvenile *Paradoxes* (1633) argue "That nature is our worst guide," "That the gifts of the body are better than those of the mind," and so on. Cavalier poets such as Sir John Suckling and Richard Lovelace dabbled in the paradoxical argument while William Cornwallis similarly praised Richard III, the French pox, Nothing, and debt in *Essays of Certain Paradoxes* (1616). The works of John Taylor, the Water Poet, variously laud bawds, whores, thieves, jail, and hempseed, culminating perhaps in *Ale Ale-Vated into the Ale-Titude* (1651). John Dunton collected many of these works in *The Athenian Sport; Or, Two Thousand Paradoxes Merrily Argued* (1707).

In the 18th century some imitated the Earl of Rochester's witty and deeply cynical poem, "Upon Nothing" (1691):

> The great man's gratitude to his best friend,
> Kings' promises, whores' vows, tow'rds thee they bend,
> Flow swiftly into thee, and in thee ever end.

Henry Fielding wrote an "Essay on Nothing" (1743), and Laurence Sterne also composed a meditation on the subject (1760). In *Tristram Shandy* (1759–1767) Sterne included panegyrics on the battering ram, whiskers, a proposed praise of buttonholes, and a sustained exaltation of noses. Joseph Addison praised nonsense in his political writings (1710). Anonymous essayists sang the virtues of the dumpling (1726), ugliness (1751), and living in a garret (1751), as Dr. Johnson did more seriously in *The Rambler* (also 1751). The mock-encomium came to its greatest fruition in 18th-century England, often blending with other satirical forms. Henry Knight Miller detects its shaping presence in the works of Swift, Pope, Wycherley, Gay, Smart, Gray, Cowper, and Sheridan. The Romantic essayist Charles Lamb (1775–1834) provided late examples in several essays, including "Praise of Chimney-Sweepers" and "The Ass."

Whereas the mock-epic and mock-encomium present low subjects in high style, travesty (from *trans* + *vestire,* "to cross-dress") presents high subjects in low style: not the mock-epic per se, but rather the epic mocked. Matro of Pitane (4th century BCE) and after him Hellenistic writers ridiculed Homeric subjects and style. Paul Scarron first used the word *travesty* in this specific literary sense in his French *Virgile travesti* (1648–1653). Scarron's version of the nightmarish book 2 of Virgil's *Aeneid* features the servants and chambermaids simply leaving the burning city by other routes; the harpy's prophecy of a terrible hunger that will cause the Trojan exiles to eat their tables comes true in spades as they devour their plates and napkins, too. In England Charles Cotton followed suit with *Scarronides* (1664, 1665), English-verse travesties of *Aeneid* 1 and 4, deflating the immortal opening lines as "I sing the man (read it who list,/A Trojan, true, as ever pist)." Dido's love is reduced to a sexual itch for Aeneas, "For which she did so scald and burn,/That none but he could serve her turn." The first work written wholly in the Ukrainian language is also a travesty of the *Aeneid,* Ivan Kotlyarevsky's *Eneida* (1798), wherein Aeneas and the wandering Trojans become dispossessed Cossacks. Much enjoyed, this work has inspired adaptation in the form of plays, musicals, and even animated cartoons. The long tradition of epic travesty includes Stephanus' *Homerou kai Hesiodou Agon* (*The Duel of Homer and Hesiod,* 1573) and Thomas Bridges's irreverent translation of the *Iliad* (1889).

Mock-epic, mock-encomium, and travesty may all be considered forms of burlesque, which treats any subject in an incongruously comic manner. Classical mythology and classical tragedy were popular subjects of burlesque, early and late. Elements of burlesque appear to have been regular features of satyr plays (6th–5th cents. BCE), which followed tragic trilogies and featured legendary heroes along with a self-centered, lecherous chorus of 11 satyrs led by Silenus. Few survive, fragments of Sophocles' *Ichneutae* and most of Euripides' *Cyclops.* In the latter, the cowardly chorus cannot help Odysseus plunge the stake into Polyphemus' eye because, they complain, they have suddenly sprained their ankles. Aristophanes sends up tragic style and subject regularly in his plays. *The Frogs,* for example, features a hilarious and abusive contest between Aeschylus and Euripides.

Sophocles' *Oedipus Rex,* the archetypal tragedy for Aristotle and many others since, has proved through the ages to be an irresistible target for burlesque. One of the most-performed German plays, Heinrich von Kleist's *Der zerbrochne Krug* (*The Broken Jug,* 1805–1806), parodies *Oedipus* as Adam presides over his own trial for the attempted rape of Eve. There have been many modern burlesques. The American musical satirist Tom Lehrer wrote a theme song for his imagined *Oedipus Rex: The Movie* (1959):

There once lived a man named Oedipus Rex.
You may have heard about his odd complex.
His name appears in Freud's index
'Cause he loved his mother.

The Egyptian writer Ali Salem's *Comedy of Oedipus: You Killed the Beast!* (1970) adapts the myth to satirize Gamal Abdel Nasser's role in Arab–Israeli politics. The play features many comic characters, including Cassandra as a meddlesome emcee. As part of his film *New York Stories* (1989), Woody Allen presented *Oedipus Wrecks,* the story of Sheldon, a middle-aged, neurotic lawyer, and his overbearing Jewish mother. P. D. Q. Bach (Peter Schickele) reimagined the tragedy as *Oedipus Tex* (1990), a dramatic oratorio set in the Wild West. Anne Fliotson and Bob Johnson produced *Oedipus! A New Musical Comedy* (1999) with the tune "Something just ain't right in Thebeville, West Virginia"; at the end Eddie and Jo decide to sell their story to the tabloids. No account of tragic burlesque can omit mention of A. E. Housman's hilarious send-up, *Fragment of a Greek Tragedy* (1901):

Why should I mention Io? Why indeed?
I have no notion why.
. . .
Eriphyle (within). O, I am smitten with a hatchet's jaw;
And that in deed and not in word alone.
Chorus. I thought I heard a sound within the house
Unlike the voice of one that jumps for joy.
Eri. He splits my skull, not in a friendly way.

Burlesque as a genre has roots in antiquity and branches in many later ages and literatures. Post-classical examples relevant to the classical tradition include Bottom and company's production of *Pyramus and Thisbe* in *A Midsummer Night's Dream* (1595–1596). Here Shakespeare mocks Ovid, Arthur Golding's translation (1567) of the *Metamorphoses,* and Elizabethan neoclassical tragedy. Bottom the weaver, playing Pyramus, finds Thisbe's bloodied garment:

Eyes, do you see?
How can it be?
O dainty duck! O dear!
Thy mantle good,
What, stained with blood?
Approach, ye Furies fell!
O Fates, come, come,
Cut thread and thrum;
Quail, crush, conclude, and quell! (5.1.275–283)

Charles Cotton aimed barbs at another classical author, Lucian, in his *Burlesque upon Burlesque, or The Scoffer Scoft* (1675).

As succeeding post-classical generations redefined the heroic, their burlesques shifted focus and target. Romance notions of chivalry come under attack in Luigi Pulci's epic *Morgante* (1482) as well as in Miguel de Cervantes' great novel *Don Quixote* (1615). Imitating *Don Quixote*'s motif of the maladapted knight-errant, Samuel Butler produced the mock-epic *Hudibras* (1668–1672) in tetrameter couplets, satirizing Puritan hypocrisy and the culture of his age. As an Augustan conservative, Butler also ridiculed the suspect innovations of "romantic" epics by Ariosto, Spenser, and Davenant. John Dryden's neoclassical tragedy and his conception of the heroic inspired various burlesques, notably George Villiers's *The Rehearsal* (1671) and Henry Fielding's *Tom Thumb* (1730), which parodies other tragedies as well. Fielding published the work with a learned preface that analyzes it according to Aristotle's observations on tragic action, character, diction, and the like. Thumb, a six-inch warrior, is beloved by the normal-sized Queen Dollalolla and her daughter, Huncamunca, and eventually kills his rival Noodle, only to be swallowed up alive by a "cow, of larger than usual size." Like some Senecan *umbra,* the Ghost of Tom Thumb returns at the end and precipitates eight murders in about as many lines, and a suicide. Classical themes and figures also appear sporadically in Victorian burlesques, particularly in the works of H. J. Byron, J. R. Planché, and W. S. Gilbert.

Beyond providing sanative burlesque to ancient tragedy, the satyr play, featuring horse figures carrying musical instruments or dancing, illustrates comedy's fascination with the human animal, or humans as animals. Aesop told fables about anthropomorphic animals and insects, which received new life in the French expansions by Jean de la Fontaine (1621–1695) and the Russian adaptations by Ivan Andreyevich Krylov (1769–1844). Aristophanes delighted audiences with choruses of frogs, wasps, and birds. Avian progeny include the swans of Wagner's *Lohengrin* (1850) and the Swan Queen Odette in the classic ballet *Swan Lake* (1875–1877), as well as the parrotlike courtship of Papagena and Papageno in Mozart's earlier *Magic Flute* (*Die Zauberflöte,* 1791). The *argumentum ad bestiam* (dialogue of beasts) has proven especially rich for satire. In *Volpone* (1605) Ben Jonson exhibits human predators—Voltore the vulture, Corbaccio the crow, and Corvino the little raven—circling around the supposedly dying Volpone, or Fox, and his servant Mosca, the gadfly. In *Gulliver's Travels* (1726) Jonathan Swift depicts humanity as trapped between the degenerate bestiality of the Yahoos and the cold reason of the Houyhnhnms, a superrational race of horses that represents the most complete inversion of the satyr archetype. George Orwell's *Animal Farm* (1945) satirizes the Russian Revolution by presenting the rebels as pigs in a farmyard who become corrupted by power and establish a tyranny, under their leader, Napoleon (Stalin): "All animals are equal but some animals are more equal than others." The possibilities of theriomorphosis have enabled darker explorations of human nature. Franz Kafka starts his polyvalent fable about modernity, *The Metamorphosis* (1915), with the famously shocking opening: Gregor Samsa awakes to find himself transformed into a giant insect. Vladimir Mayakovsky mocked the Soviet regime in his futuristic parable *The Bedbug* (1929). And Eugène Ionesco exposed the cowardliness of the crowd in *Le Rhinocéros* (1959), where everyone except the hero, Berenger, is content to turn into a galloping rhino. T. S. Eliot, of course, traversed safer, more pleasant ground in *Old Possum's Book of Practical Cats* (1939), magically transformed by Andrew Lloyd Webber into the long-running musical comedy *Cats* (1981).

In addition to subsisting as a mockery of epic, tragedy, or serious subjects, comedy also appeared in ancient times as a dramatic genre, which, according to Aristotle, presented "an imitation of characters of a lower type—not, however, in the full sense of the word bad, the ludicrous being merely a subdivision of the ugly. It [comedy] consists in some defect or ugliness which is not painful or destructive. To take an obvious example, the comic mask is ugly and distorted, but does not imply pain" (*Poetics* 1449a). No Greek comic mask has survived, but representations of them—broad of forehead, with eyeholes and open mouths to allow for speech—exist in terra-cottas, reliefs, mosaics, wall paintings, and statues. Comedy for the ancients, then, meant laughter at, not laughter with, ugly and base characters. Aristotle's treatise on comedy—the subject of Umberto Eco's *Name of the Rose* (*Il nome della rosa*, 1980)—is lost, but a fragmentary 10th-century manuscript, the *Tractatus Coislinianus*, represents a creditable expansion of his discussion. The *Tractatus* analyzes comedy in terms of plot, character, thought, diction, melody, and spectacle, the components of tragedy given in Aristotle's *Poetics*. As characters for comedy it names the *alazōn* (impostor), the *eirōn* (self-deprecator), and the *bōmolochos* (buffoon), along with (perhaps a later addition) the *agroikos* (boor).

These kinds of characters appear prominently in ancient comedy, Old and New. *Alazōn* in Greek has a range of meanings (impostor, pretender, charlatan, braggart), but Aristotle particularly defines the *alazōn* as a boaster who pretends to creditable qualities that he does not possess (*Nicomachean Ethics* 1127a). Aristophanes presents a specialized kind of *alazōn*, the braggart soldier, in the figure of Lamachus in *The Acharnians*, whose descendants have since swaggered across many stages in many forms, especially in the influential soldiers of Roman New Comedy—Plautus' Pyrgopolynices (*Miles gloriosus*) and Terence's Thraso (*Eunuchus*), both would-be lovers as well as would-be warriors. In later centuries the braggart soldier appeared often as a rambunctious Spaniard on the Italian stages of the *commedia erudita* and as Capitano Spavento della Vall'Inferno (Captain Fright of Hell's Valley) in the improvisations of the Italian *commedia dell'arte*. In France de Turnèbe's Capitaine Rodomont retreats ignominiously but brings down the house in *Les Contents* (1584). Pierre Larivey changed his soldier into a duelist in *Les Jaloux* (1597). In Spain the character took various forms in the *comedias de capa y espada* (cloak-and-sword plays) of the Spanish Golden Age. In England Nicholas Udall staged *Ralph Roister Doister* (1552), where the eponymous hero unsuccessfully besieges his beloved, Dame Custance. John Lyly's mythological *Endymion* (1588) presents Sir Thopas, whose hypothetical enemies include sheep and wrens and who has two paramours, the crones Dipsas and Bagoa. George Peele has Huanebango bluster martially and amorously in *The Old Wives' Tale* (1595). The original version of Ben Jonson's *Every Man in His Humour* (1598) featured Bobadilla, who affected great skill in the new science of fencing only to be cudgeled by the choleric Giuliano. Jonson presents Bobadilla's *alazoneia* as a humor, a ruling folly of self-love that receives comic exposure. Shakespeare's *alazōns* include the blustering Armado of *Love's Labor's Lost* (1594), Parolles in *All's Well That Ends Well* (1603), and the great Falstaff of *Henry IV*, Parts 1 and 2 (1597, 1598).

Shakespeare's Falstaff is the most complex adaptation of the type in the classical tradition—*miles gloriosus*, parasite, Lord of Misrule, medieval figure of Vice, and, grandly, himself. He possesses a quick-witted inventiveness that raises bluster to a theatrical art. Eating, drinking, and making merry, he revels in extempore performance and in making excuses for himself: "Thou knowest in the state of innocency Adam fell; and what should poor Jack Falstaff do in the days of villainy? Thou seest I have more flesh than another man, and therefore more frailty" (*1 H IV* 3.3.165–169). He robs some travelers at Gad's Hill, relinquishes the spoil to friends in disguise, then makes up fantastic lies about his courage against the "men in buckram" during the exploit. He misuses the king's press to draft wealthy men in order to collect bribes for exemptions; he feigns death to avoid fighting. And yet he pointedly challenges the entire ethos of honor in the *Henry IV* plays:

> Can honor set to a leg? No. Or an arm? No. Or take away the grief of a wound? No. Honor hath no skill in surgery, then? No. What is honor? A word. What is in that word "honor"? What is that "honor"? Air. A trim reckoning! Who hath it? He that died o' Wednesday. Doth he feel it? No. Doth he hear it? No. 'Tis insensible, then? Yea, to the dead. But will it not live with the living? No. Why? Detraction will not suffer it. Therefore I'll none of it. Honor is a mere scutcheon. And so ends my catechism. (5.1.131–140)

Falstaff's catechism rejects the value of military valor and many centuries of cultural investment in war heroes. Traditional laughter at the cowardly soldier turns here to reconsideration of war and its costs. Looking at a fallen soldier, Falstaff comments, "I like not such grinning honor as Sir Walter hath. Give me life" (5.3.58–59). Shakespeare gave Falstaff additional life later as the soldier-turned-lover in *The Merry Wives of Windsor* (1597–1600). Here Falstaff woos two good wives and, for his pains, suffers the fate of the comic scapegoat—ritualistic ridicule and expulsion from the community.

The *alazōn*'s opposite number is the *eirōn,* or self-deprecator, who pretends to be less, not more, than he is (*Nichomachean Ethics* 1127a). Appearing sporadically in Old Comedy (e.g., as Aristophanes' Xanthias in *The Frogs*), the *eirōn* took distinctive and popular shape in the tricky slave of New Comedy, Greek (Menander) and Roman (Plautus and Terence). Dissimulating his powers and perceptions, this *callidus servus* relies on wit and a quick tongue to dupe various authorities. At times he exults in his own *ingenium* in private, as Chrysalus does in Plautus' *Bacchides* (925 ff.), comparing his deeds to those of the Greeks at Troy. Often he assists his youthful master in a love intrigue. Descendants include Shakespeare's Tranio (*The Taming of the Shrew,* 1594), a direct borrowing from Plautus' *Mostellaria,* and his wise fools, Feste (*Twelfth Night,* 1602), Touchstone (*As You Like It,* 1599), and the Fool in *King Lear* (1603–1606). Putting on an antic madness, Hamlet enacts the original role of the *eirōn* who pretends to be less than he is. Like the classical *servus,* Hamlet intrigues, improvises, frets, and urges himself on in soliloquy. Cervantes worked another variation in Don Quixote's earthy, commonsensical sidekick, Sancho Panza. Calderón's Fabio is a tricky servant who works against, not for, his master in *El secreto a voces* (1650). William Wycherley's Fidelia, disguised as a pageboy and secretly in love with her master, nonetheless helps him to the bed of the lustful, hypocritical, and married Olivia in *The Plain Dealer* (1676). Molière gallicized the clever slave into a figure of outrageous wit and fun in *Les Fourberies de Scapin* (1667). Beaumarchais took this character type to new heights in the person of Figaro in *Le Barbier de Séville* (1773) and *Le mariage de Figaro* (1778). In the first of these plays, Figaro's impertinent question pertains to many centuries of New Comedic tradition: "On the basis of the virtues commonly required in a servant, does Your Excellency know many masters who would pass muster as valets?" Napoleon called *Le Mariage de Figaro* "the revolution in action."

Modern variations of the *eirōn* include both Huck and Jim in Mark Twain's masterpiece, *Adventures of Huckleberry Finn* (1884). There the ignorant boy outwits the educated townspeople, and the runaway slave shows more decency and humanity than his captors. Self-deprecation took a new turn in the careers of homespun American humorists such as Artemus Ward (Charles Farrar Browne, 1834–1867): "It ain't so much the things we don't know that get us in trouble. It's the things we know that ain't so"; and Will Rogers (1879–1935): "There's no trick to being a humorist when you have the whole government working for you." The *eirōn* appears surprisingly in Beckett's *Waiting for Godot* (1953) as the slave Lucky speaks a dithyrambic monologue that mocks the cherished beliefs of his society. In the novels of P. G. Wodehouse (1881–1975), we find the *eirōn* in a starched collar as the imperturbable Jeeves. And the ancient *eirōn* animates various roles of comedian Eddie Murphy in a number of films, *48 Hours* (1982) and its sequel (1990), *Trading Places* (1983), and *The Distinguished Gentleman* (1992). Disadvantaged by race or social status, Murphy's characters trick, impersonate, improvise, fast-talk, and laugh their way into and out of trouble with all the cheek and wit of any New Comedic *servus.*

As defined by Aristotle and the *Tractatus Coislinianus,* the comic plot often culminates in a *pistis,* "proof," that leads to *anagnōrisis,* "recognition." In New Comedy the recognition often involves the discovery of true identity: the slave girl, perhaps, is actually the long-lost daughter of a citizen and therefore is eligible for marriage. Identical twins discover that each has been getting mistaken for the other. This second premise drives Plautus' *Menaechmi,* wherein the resident brother's dream of a holiday from work turns into a nightmare, while the visiting twin enjoys misdirected gifts and pleasures. Shakespeare more than doubles the fun in *The Comedy of Errors* (1594) with two sets of identical twins. He expands the female roles and emphasizes the wonder of reunion here and in his next adaptation, *Twelfth Night* (1602), where one of the twins is a girl in disguise.

> *Sebastian:* Were you a woman, as the rest goes even,
> I should my tears let fall upon your cheek
> And say, "Thrice welcome, drownèd Viola!"
> *Viola (disguised):* My father had a mole upon his brow.
> *Sebastian:* And so had mine. (5.1.241–245)

Usually in a comic plot, a proof produces *anagnōrisis,* brother finds brother (or here, sister), families get started or reunited, losses are restored, and sorrows end.

Variations on the formulas, of course, have multiplied over the centuries, beginning with the practitioners of New Comedy themselves. Plautus' *Casina* has a boy disguised as a girl and plays the *anagnōrisis* for bawdy slapstick as the would-be lover gets a comeuppance. Adapting that play, early modern Italians such as Machiavelli, Dolce, and Lanci follow suit, expanding the raucous tone and genital jokes. Aretino's *Il marescalco* (1533) features a duped suitor who, as a closet homosexual, is delighted with the trick. Ben Jonson adapts this recognition in *Epicoene* (1609), where the gender surprise culminates a scene of legal satire and comic confusion. Cross-dressing has remained a staple for comedy and supplied various recognition scenes in drama and in comic films such as *Some Like It Hot* (1959), *La Cage aux Folles* (1978), and *Tootsie* (1982). Discovering that his beloved is actually a man in *Some Like It Hot,* the millionaire Osgood (Joe E. Brown) remains undeterred: "Well, nobody's perfect."

Victorians and moderns parodied and inverted the conventional *pistis* and *anagnōrisis.* John Maddison Morton rewired the classical recognition scene in *Box and Cox: A Romance of Real Life* (1847):

Box: Cox! *(About to embrace, Box stops, seizes Cox's hand, and looks eagerly in his face.)* You'll excuse the apparent insanity of the remark, but the more I gaze on your features, the more I'm convinced that you're my long lost brother.
Cox: The very observation I was going to make to you!
Box: Ah, tell me, in mercy tell me, have you such a thing as a strawberry mark on your left arm?
Cox: No!
Box: Then it is he! (They rush into each other's arms.)

Oscar Wilde's sparkling *The Importance of Being Earnest* (1895) has the dotty Miss Prism climactically produce the handbag left in Victoria Station, Brighton Line, which confirms the identity of the lost child. Jack Worthing discovers that his real name is indeed Ernest and that he does have a brother, as he has been pretending all along: "It is a terrible thing for a man to find out suddenly that all his life he has been speaking nothing but the truth." George Bernard Shaw inverts multiple classical formulas in *Major Barbara* (1905), wherein Cusins confesses that he is, after all, an illegitimate foundling. His parents' marriage is invalid (except in Australia), he reveals, because his mother is his father's deceased wife's sister. As a foundling Cusins can then inherit Undershaft's business, fortune, and gospel of money and gunpowder. Eugène Ionesco staged perhaps the ultimate parodic inversion, *La cantatrice chauve* (*The Bald Soprano,* 1949), which inaugurated the Theatre of the Absurd. Here, apparently meeting by chance, Mr. and Mrs. Martin discover that each of them comes from the same town, lives at the same address, occupies the same bedroom, and has the same daughter. Their polite and banal conversation, punctuated with exclamations—"*C'est curieux!*" and "*Quelle coincidence!*"—leads to the revelation that they are none other than husband and wife.

Eros has always driven comic plots and comic characters, as is evident from the phalluses prominently displayed in the early mimes (especially the *phylakes* of southern Italy) and in Greek Old Comedy, notably Aristophanes' *Lysistrata,* where women too have their desires. *Eros* drives the young and the old in New Comedy as well, firing domestic conflicts and complications. Comedy tends to present the frustration of desire as well as its fulfillment, either in illicit (fornication and rape) or licit (marriage) forms. The bed trick, wherein one partner is disguised during sex, represents a popular combination of the two forms. Machiavelli tried a different kind of combination of the licit and illicit in his brilliantly cynical version of New Comedy, *La Mandragola* (1520): there the virtuous young wife, seduced by an elaborate deception, credits the success of the ruse to Divine Providence and resolves to keep her new lover permanently.

Often in comedy of the classical tradition, however, "the catastrophe is a nuptial," as Armado says in *Love's Labour's Lost* (4.1.76–77), using the technical term for the "overturning" that leads to resolution. Though connubial bliss is deferred for the characters in this play, many other plays—*A Midsummer Night's Dream* and *As You Like It,* for example—end in the celebration of multiple marriages, Hymen herself even appearing in the latter. Beatrice and Benedick of *Much Ado about Nothing* (1600) finally conclude their witty combat at the altar, as do their descendants, Millamant and Mirabel in Congreve's *The Way of the World* (1700), but not before these two negotiate a legal contract so that Millamant may "dwindle into a wife" and Mirabel not be "beyond measure enlarged into a husband." Such precautions do not, of course, ensure felicity, as many couples in comedy live unhappily ever after. August Strindberg staged marital misery as darkly comedic in his *Dance of Death* (1901), which features ferocious spousal warfare; his Edgar and Alice anticipate the vitriolic George and Martha of Edward Albee's *Who's Afraid of Virginia Woolf?* (1962).

Harry Levin observes: "When the object is matrimony, the plot is a courtship, and the tone is blithe. When the *donnée* is matrimony, the plot is an adultery, and the tone is cynical" (1987, 103–104). Infidelity and witless cuckolds get laughs in medieval tales, in the Italian *commedia erudita,* and in Restoration comedy. William Wycherley's Horner is liberal with his "china" and other men's wives in *The Country Wife* (1675); Sir John Vanbrugh's *The Relapse* (1696) presents Loveless's transformation from husband back to rake. The Austrian playwright Arthur Schnitzler multiplied love affairs cynically and scandalously in *Reigen* (*Roundelay,* 1901), which consists of 10 pre- and post-coital dialogues. One interlocutor always appears in a subsequent scene with a new partner. Infidelity real or pretended is a staple of Screwball Comedy, including Alfred Hitchcock's only venture in the genre, *Mr. and Mrs. Smith* (1941), which features a battling couple who discover that they are not legally married. In a recent film of the same name (2005), starring Brad Pitt and Angelina Jolie, the infidelity is occupational and the comic *anagnōrisis* occurs when husband and wife discover that they are both professional assassins and have been hired to kill each other ("I missed you"—"I missed you, too"). After an explosively literal scene of homewrecking, they renew their vows and join forces against their employers.

BIBL.: Daniel C. Boughner, *The Braggart in Renaissance Comedy* (Minneapolis 1954). K. J. Dover, *Aristophanic Comedy* (London 1972). George E. Duckworth, *The Nature of Roman Comedy* (Princeton 1952). Northrop Frye, *Anatomy of Criticism: Four Essays* (Princeton 1957). Marvin T. Herrick, *Italian Comedy in the Renaissance* (Urbana 1960). K. M. Lea, *Italian Popular Comedy,* 2 vols. (1934; repr. New York 1962). Harry Levin, *Playboys and Killjoys: An Essay on the Theory and Practice of Comedy* (New York 1987). Annette Lust, *From the Greek Mimes to Marcel Marceau and Beyond* (Lanham, Md., 2000). David Marsh, *Lucian and the Latins* (Ann Arbor 1998). Henry Knight Miller, "The Paradoxical Encomium with Special Reference to Its Vogue in England, 1600–1800," *Mod-*

ern Philology 53 (1956) 145–178. Robert S. Miola, *Shakespeare and Classical Comedy* (Oxford 1994). Annette Tomarken, *The Smile of Truth* (Princeton 1990). R.MI.

Comic Books

The parallels between gods and superheroes make the history of comics a long improvisation on classical legend, but some books explicitly use classical themes or figures.

Classic Comics (1941–1947), created by Albert Lewis Kanter, adapted literary works for young readers, but almost none were classical. The first title in the renamed Classics Illustrated series was Edward Bulwer-Lytton's Victorian take on Roman imperial excess, *The Last Days of Pompeii* (issue 35). Later came Homer's *Iliad* (77) and *Odyssey* (81), followed by *Caesar's Conquests* (130). An adaptation of Virgil's *Aeneid* was published in Britain, but not in the United States.

The most exuberant use of classical material is the French comic *Astérix,* first published in the magazine *Pilote* (1959), then in volumes beginning in 1961 with *Astérix the Gaul.* Thriving on elaborate multilingual puns and welcomed in language classrooms, the series tells of a tiny, mustachioed Gaulish rebel traveling a world that combines elements of the classical with satire on the modern. Much use is made of Latin tags and allusions to Caesar's *Gallic Wars,* though Tacitus sneaks in when the Roman legions complain about their retirement plan (*Astérix and Caesar's Gift,* 1).

The British novelist Neil Gaiman's *Sandman* (Vertigo 1988–1996) mixes classical stories with those of other historical periods. *Sandman*'s 75 issues spiral around Sandman, Oneiros, and Morpheus, the "shaper of forms." In *Calliope* (issue 17), a present-day novelist (in 1927) captures Calliope, the ancient Muse of epic poetry, with moly (a mythical herb) and fuels his creative inspiration by imprisoning and raping her; eventually (in 1986) he sells her to a younger novelist. She calls on the Camenae, and on Melete, Mneme, and Aiode, who invoke Oneiros, the father of her son Orpheus. Threatened by Dream, the offending novelist pleads: "I *need* her. If I didn't have her I wouldn't be able to write. I wouldn't have ideas." Justly tortured by an avalanche of ideas, including "a man who inherits a library card to the library in Alexandria," he finds that all ideas cease with her freedom. The modern writer has stolen and brutalized what the epic poet Homer prayed to—or perhaps Homer once did the same. Orpheus tells the bard's tragedy, amplified by that of Dream, who kills his son, and in the multi-issue collection *The Kindly Ones* (1996) is punished for it by three Hecatae, set on him by Hippolyta Hall, known as Fury on the 1980s DC Comics team Infinity Inc.

Classical figures pervade American comics. Shazam, the wizard's name that when uttered turns young reporter Billy Batson into Captain Marvel, is an acronym for Solomon's wisdom, Hercules' strength, Atlas' stamina, Zeus's power, Achilles' courage, and Mercury's speed. These powers, along with Prometheus, Vulcan, Ajak, Aegis, Gaia, Ganymede, Hyperion, Icarus, Roma, Polaris, Triton, Venus, Antaeus, Andromeda, Arion, Orpheus, Artemiz, and Hero and Leander (a gay couple), fight for good; Calypso, Ares, Cybelle, Nox, Phalanx, Thanos, Proteus, Selene, Agamemno, Nemesis, Naiad, Nero, Elektra, and Lacuna (who creates gaps in time) fight for evil. (Characters whose names sound Greek or Latin are more frequently evil than good.)

DC Comics' *Wonder Woman* (1941–present) reflects the classical world almost obsessively. Princess Diana belongs to an Amazon tribe protected by Aphrodite, part of whose girdle made their Lasso of Truth. Enamored by Eros imitating an American intelligence officer, Diana enters World War II, confronting Ares, Herakles, and the sorceress Circe; at the end of the 1960s Diana resigns her powers, then regains them (at Gloria Steinem's urging) after undergoing twelve trials. One Amazon queen, Antiope, falls in love with the series' Theseus character. The great strength of *Wonder Woman,* and of comic books' use of classical themes in general, is how their creators revel in classical material, while adapting it first for World War II, then Vietnam, and recently for a world of computers and conflict ruled not by Zeus but by Athena and Ares.

BIBL.: Brian Walker, *The Comics: Before 1945* (New York 2004) and *The Comics: Since 1945* (New York 2002). E.M.H.

Commentary

Commentary is nearly as ancient as writing. The Phoenician writer Sanchuniathon, whose works were given currency in Greek by Philo of Byblos (2nd cent. CE), thought that Taaut (whom the Egyptians called Thouth, the Alexandrians Thoth, and the Greeks Hermes) invented both letters and "the writing of commentaries" (Eusebius, *Preparation for the Gospel* 1.9.24). We cannot confirm or rebut this conjecture, but we do know that the oldest preserved commentary on a Greek text appears in one of the oldest written documents in Greek, the Derveni papyrus. The unidentified author of this document, composed in the 5th century BCE and copied in the 4th century, explicates an Orphic text as commentators have explicated other works for millennia after him: by atomizing it. He divides it into short quotations and then comments on them, citing parallels. His work uses most of the techniques of explication that later became standard in the Hellenistic world in commentaries on Homer and other canonical authors, and that also appear in many other premodern traditions, from China and India to Persia.

Today some of the same techniques are still in regular use, though readers often encounter them on computer screens rather than in books. A beginning student of Latin or Greek can call up a text from a database and use online resources to parse, translate, and explain the syntactical function of every word, just as readers 500 or 1,000 years ago learned to do, though they relied on Greek *epimerismoi,* or parsings, of classical texts or on the immense, line-by-line commentary on Virgil's *Aeneid* by

Tiberius Donatus (early 5th cent.). The vast range of commentaries produced in the ancient world offered vital resources and models for post-classical readers of Greek and Latin texts, as they still do for scholars. The labyrinthine processes by which they were preserved, reworked, and emulated were as long, complex, and rich in historical interest as any other chapter in the history of the classical tradition.

Ancient commentaries took many forms and addressed a wide variety of subjects. Originally the commentator was a parasite. He nested in and tried to dictate the uses of an existing text that claimed authority in some field. Day by day and school by school, teachers explicated the classics that schoolboys needed first to master and then to emulate. They buried the texts in glosses that explained grammar, syntax, usage, and prosody, identified mythical and historical characters, places, and events, and warned the young not to imitate the liberties that the mighty dead had taken with the normal rules of grammar and taste. Literary and philological specialists explicated and corrected canonical classics like the works of Homer. Teachers of rhetoric explained the ancient customs and identified the ancient people mentioned by orators like Demosthenes and Cicero. Philosophers elucidated the works of Plato and Aristotle. The character and quality of these enterprises varied radically. But the industry of their makers established commentary as the standard medium for elementary and advanced instruction in a vast range of subjects, and the materials that they collected were used and reused in fascinating, complex ways by the learned poets of Alexandria and Rome.

But commentators, like sheep in trees, could be dangerously ambitious. Many wanted to do more than preserve and protect their authors. Pergamene commentators explained Homer's apparent breaches of taste and decorum as clues to a higher meaning. From the 3rd century CE onward, philosophers used the form of running commentary on their canonical texts to carry out a novel fusion of Platonic and Aristotelian methods.

Students of the natural world regularly used the genre of commentary to revise, as well as to explicate, the knowledge offered by texts. In the 2nd century BCE Hipparchus drew up a commentary on the astronomical work of Aratus in which he sharply criticized his predecessor and insisted on the superiority of his own data. Galen, in the 2nd century CE, wrote extensive commentaries on Hippocrates in which he presented the older writer as the model of a medical man; but he also updated Hippocrates' work in the light of later schools of medical thought and his own experience in practice and dissection. Didymus, working at Alexandria in the 1st century BCE, addressed (and misinformed) an audience of his fellow specialists as he explicated the speeches of Demosthenes. Lawyers spun endless webs of commentary around the rules and applications of the Roman law, a process that the emperor Justinian vainly tried to bring to a stop by creating a mammoth anthology of older works, the Corpus Iuris Romani, and forbidding further interpretation. In Hellenistic Greece and in the Greek and Roman culture of the imperial age, commentary was a recognized literary genre that sought to demonstrate the commentator's, as well as the author's, profundity, originality, and erudition. For two millennia to come, commentaries would do more than explicate existing forms of knowledge. In fact, they became and remained a genre whose authors produced new knowledge, and one of the most prominent ones at that.

Many ancient commentaries had at least a few formal properties in common. In an age of rolls, they were normally written out not on the margins of the texts they explicated but on separate rolls of their own. Many of them began with some form of introduction, in which the commentator addressed general questions about the work in question: its author, its genuineness, its purpose. In other respects, however, they varied radically. Some, like the philological commentaries of the Alexandrian scholars Aristarchus and Zenodotus, dealt with a narrow band of selected problems and were clearly presented as the intellectual property of one author. Others, like the Virgilian commentaries of Aelius Donatus (4th cent. CE), ranged widely in content and claimed to offer their readers not one single interpretation but rather a range of possibilities. The intelligent reader, said Donatus, must test these and accept or reject them as a skilled money changer tests currency (see Jerome *Contra Rufinum* 1.16)—a definition of commentary that found favor with later authors, from Donatus' pupil, the Christian scholar Jerome, to the 16th-century Jewish philologist and exegete Azariah de' Rossi.

Some commentaries, like those of the 1st-century Roman grammarian Asconius Pedianus on the speeches of Cicero, were brief, pointed, and impersonal in tone. Others, like those of Galen, made room for long digressions on everything from the nature of commentary itself to the author's life and experiences. Some made every effort to defend the text they explicated, as some Homeric commentators did, by using allegory to explain away apparent offenses against taste and reason. Others challenged and even refuted the arguments they presented, as the 6th-century scholars Simplicius and Philoponus did in their commentaries on Aristotle's *Physics*. The commentary could be a textual lichen, a moldlike growth that could flourish only in the crevices of a grander, more lasting text. But it could also become a freestanding work that proclaimed its author's originality. Some commentators, like Galen, proudly proclaimed their authorship: others complained that students had put notes on their lectures into circulation and forced them to publish what they had meant only for limited circulation. The possible variants of this protean form were endless.

Not all those who studied and emulated these commentators applied their methods to pagan texts. Greek-speaking Jews and Christians learned the fundamentals of grammar and the higher arts of interpretation from the classical commentaries that they too mastered in school, and soon new bodies of commentary grew up around the Old and New Testaments. The 3rd-century Christian scholar Origen, for example, composed elaborate critical commentaries on Old and New Testament books. He followed the Jewish writer Philo (1st cent. CE), who had Hellenized the existing Jewish tradition of biblical exegesis, and the Neoplatonists of his own day when he insisted that the Bible had a higher sense which only allegorical exegesis, rather than the literalism he ascribed to the Jews, could unlock. But he also emulated the philologists of Alexandria when he collected variant versions of the biblical texts and laid out four Greek versions of the Old Testament, as well as the Hebrew and a Greek transliteration of the Hebrew, in parallel columns in his Hexapla. Jerome continued Origen's enterprise in the Latin world; Augustine agreed, and he made clear to Christian readers in his authoritative books that the Christian scholar needed to apply the methods of ancient scholarship to Christian sacred texts. Thus, the practices of the ancient commentators survived, partly because they served entirely new purposes.

As ancient culture and society were transformed in the 4th through 6th centuries, the conditions of scholarship and teaching underwent radical changes of their own. In the Greek world the vast bodies of commentary that had accumulated around Homer, Hesiod, Demosthenes, and the tragedians were gradually abridged into far shorter compilations, most of them anonymous, and entered as scholia, or marginal notes, in codices like the famous Venetian MS A of Homer. Though many details of this process are known, its larger history remains obscure. It was probably connected with the transition from the roll to the codex, or modern form of book, in which commentaries could be entered more conveniently in the margins of the text they dealt with, and perhaps also with the gradual change from majuscule to minuscule script that took place in the 8th and 9th centuries. At all events, the appearance of the scholia marked a slow but radical transformation of the enterprise of exegesis. In Byzantium, the new center of the Greek world, students continued to use these shorter commentaries to master the ancient Greek which they still tried to write. New commentaries were chiefly devoted to the Bible and the works of the Fathers. Philosophical and scientific commentary continued into the 6th and 7th centuries, but it too seems to have ceased in the Greek world after the emperor Justinian closed the philosophical schools of Athens in 529 CE.

These older genres were actively continued, however, in the new world of Islam, as scholars in Baghdad and elsewhere, most notably the Nestorian Hunain ibn Ishaq, translated and explicated ancient texts, for the most part Greek philosophical, medical, and scientific works. Galen's own commentaries on Hippocrates and the later commentaries of Porphyry, Alexander of Aphrodisias, and Simplicius on philosophical and scientific texts proved essential to Muslim scholars, some of whom found these systematic, step-by-step commentaries more cogent and useful than the texts they explicated and thus decided that they must master the full body of commentaries before they could surpass the ancients. Abū l-Faraj Abdallāh (Ibn at-Tayyib), for example, explained in his commentary on Aristotle's *Categories* that according to Hippocrates, "the arts develop in the following way: an original creator transmits what he has devised to a follower, and this follower tests it critically and improves it to the best of his ability, and matters continue in this way until the art reaches completion." In accord with this schema he noted: "I have followed the trail of my predecessors and done my best to understand their works well. In addition, I have discovered a number of ideas in connection with their unclear remarks and explanations, and these go beyond what they said. Therefore, I would like to add my own few remarks to their numerous ones and set down all of this material in a single commentary. This will spare the user the great effort involved in having to consult the older commentaries." Though he offered the reader a variorum, he also professed that "since I love the truth and prefer to use the method of the ancients, we must begin as they did. All commentators have concerned themselves, before studying the *Categories* of Aristotle, with the ten chief categories."

Commentary in the Islamic world took many forms, especially when scholars set out, as many did, to explicate the Koran, with its rich content and relevance to so many topics. Commentaries on technical and mathematical works, however, were faithful, to a considerable extent, to the systematic, technical model forged in the late antique schools, and they preserved and discussed a vast amount of classical scientific and philosophical matter.

In the Latin world, commentary changed phase and style when the Roman Empire fell. The 4th and 5th centuries saw the production of immense and exemplary commentaries on Virgil by Servius and by Tiberius Donatus. Calcidius' translation of and commentary on Plato's *Timaeus* became a primary source for Western understanding of the Platonic (or Neoplatonic) universe. On the whole, though, the Christian scholars who created the Western tradition of monastic learning made relatively modest efforts to carry on these enterprises. They drew up commentaries on the Bible, but when they turned to ancient learning they found encyclopedic guides to all the disciplines more useful than line-by-line investigations of individual ancient books. Macrobius' *Commentary on the Dream of Scipio* (mid-5th cent.), with its overview of the universe and the forms of human learning, won widespread popularity because it did not resemble most other commentaries but instead offered a coherent and appealing vision of the cosmos.

In the middle and later centuries of the first millennium, scholia wreathed the margins of some classical Latin texts, such as Ovid's notoriously obscure *Ibis* and the *Satires* of Juvenal. Readers were guided through Virgil by the 4th-century commentary of Servius, and through Horace by that of pseudo-Acro. One enterprise of this transitional period would prove transformative in the long term. Boethius, in his commentaries on the logical works of Aristotle and Porphyry, drew heavily on Porphyry's own exegesis. He introduced into the Latin world a basic conceptual apparatus, a formal terminology for logic and semantics, and a model for technical commentary that focused on argument rather than style. For the moment, however, his work had only a modest effect. The great Carolingian scholars who practiced a sophisticated, critical study of the Latin classics, such as Lupus of Ferrières, wrote few new formal commentaries on literary or historical texts. Fewer still were compiled in the 9th and 10th centuries, when Europe's borders came under attack from many directions and the production and study of all classical texts declined.

Gradually, commentary of a different form, Latin commentary on the Scriptures, began to take shape. Theological controversies over the nature of the Eucharist and other technical problems forced clerics to explicate the biblical text. And though every great question continued to spark controversy, consensus grew about the form that commentary on the Bible should take and the technical functions that it should perform. A standard set of glosses and explanations took shape, between the lines and in the margins of the Bible: this came to be known, and vested with authority, as the Glossa Ordinaria. When scholars began to read ancient medical texts at Salerno and the Corpus Iuris Romani at Bologna, and when they collected and began to interpret the Church's own canon law, they configured these authoritative ancient texts as their clerical predecessors had treated the Bible and equipped them with standard glosses of their own. Elaborate specialized commentaries showed how to apply each of these texts to the contemporary world, often using creative anachronism to make them fit changed circumstances.

As population and trade revived and education spread in the 11th and 12th centuries, monasteries and cathedral schools began to foster the study of the classics as well. Once again Western scholars began to read ancient texts with ancient commentaries. Calcidius' 4th-century Latin rendition of Plato's *Timaeus,* with his Latin commentary, became particularly popular in the Holy Roman Empire and in France. Over time the two texts began to be studied separately and for different purposes, and new glosses were drawn up to explicate both the ancient author and his translator and commentator. Calcidius had used diagrams to explicate Plato's vision of the universe and the musical harmony that ruled it, and these received elaborate visual commentaries of their own.

In the long run, Boethius proved the most influential of models. The new approach to theology, law, and medicine emphasized the application of formal dialectic to authoritative texts. It soon reshaped the study of the ancients as well. Texts that could play a role in an education that culminated in the study of formal philosophy and theology, such as the late antique Aristotelian commentaries and their Islamic continuators, now found their way into Latin and the curriculum. A rich body of commentaries grew up around such core texts of the new scholastic curriculum as the medical *Canon* of Avicenna and Peter Lombard's *Sentences.* Commentaries on the Greek and Roman writers began to diverge from the ancient models, though in doing so they normally adopted ideas and methods from other sectors of the ancient world. For example, commentators began to emulate Boethius and offer lucid, rigorous accounts of the authors they planned to explicate. What came to be called the *accessus ad auctores* fell into two forms: either the commentator inquired into the authorship, authenticity, and matter of his text, as ancient writers of prolegomena had done, or he analyzed the work at the outset in the Aristotelian terms of the four causes. Commentaries on the ancients developed, in part, into inquiries into argument and meaning that looked not at all like their ancient predecessors, at least at the start.

Yet ancient models of commentary also began to enjoy a revival. In the 14th and 15th centuries Humanists across Europe began both to study the ancient commentators with a new interest in historical and philological details and to compile new commentaries of their own on ancient authors. Members of the mendicant orders in France and Britain ransacked Servius, Macrobius, and other late antique authors for the materials which they could arrange into their own erudite commentaries on Livy, Ovid, and other ancient writers. Petrarch, the most influential of the early Italian Humanists, used as his working copy of Virgil a magnificent, large-format manuscript (now in the Biblioteca Ambrosiana in Milan) in which the comments of Servius surrounded the text, which was written in much larger letters. In the margins he entered his own commentary: not mere notes, but complex responses to both the poet and his commentator, carefully written and designed to be preserved. As Petrarch read other classics, he emulated Servius to the fullest extent of his abilities, filling the margins of texts as radically different as Propertius, Livy, and the *Chronicle* of Eusebius and Jerome with rich comments of his own. Later scholars (most famously, Lorenzo Valla) studied many of these partial commentaries intensively.

As Humanistic schools took shape across Italy and teachers offered formal instruction on a wider and wider range of texts, commentary in the late antique style became popular once more. In schools and university arts courses, teachers presenting texts that had been the backbone of the medieval curriculum often recycled the work of their medieval predecessors. Commentaries on the *Rhetorica ad Herennium* and Cicero's *De inventione* show a continuity of content that sometimes seems out of keeping with the Humanists' claims that they were offering revelations, to those willing to pay the price of entrance, about the wisdom and piety of the ancients—and certainly reveals how exciting it seemed, in a newly sophisticated urban world, to revive the secular system of education that had presumably produced Cicero and Virgil themselves. Much duplication and triplication took place: not just the normal recycling of glosses from lexica into commentaries and then back into a new generation of lexica, but the formal, and almost literal, repetition of lectures and glosses, sometimes for generations. As late as the 16th century, when Erasmus drew up his innovative, philologically precise commentary on the New Testament, his work included a striking number of observations drawn from the Glossa Ordinaria.

For all the mind-numbing repetition of facts and anecdotes, experimentation flourished. By the middle of the 15th century some scholars were addressing commentaries to texts deliberately chosen because they had previously lain outside the standard curriculum, or even for their difficulty. Lorenzo Valla commented brilliantly on Quintilian's rhetoric, drawing on his own independent reading in history, dialectic, and rhetoric rather than on the predigested tags of earlier scholiasts. Domizio Calderini attacked Ovid's difficult, demanding *Ibis* as well as his more accessible, if allusive, *Epistolae Heroidum.* Poliziano lectured on Suetonius, Quintilian, and the *Silvae* of Statius and sharply defended these nonstandard choices: texts different from the most famous canonical ones, he explained, were not necessarily less worthy.

Eventually a more focused and technical form of commentary began to emerge. When the ambitious, learned, and polemical Calderini and Poliziano lectured on Roman poets, they concentrated on identifying the Greek sources from which Virgil, Ovid, and Statius had drawn and adapted so much. When the philosopher and philologist Ermolao Barbaro commented on the greatest of ancient encyclopedias, Pliny's *Natural History,* he concentrated on questions of textual criticism as well as the text's relation to Greek sources. Filippo Beroaldo the Elder deliberately produced a hybrid commentary and monograph on Virgil. He chose only passages on which he disagreed with Servius and made them the object of sharp, erudite discussions that cumulatively challenged the authority of the most influential ancient commentator.

Commentary could even provide, as Galen had shown, an unlikely but effective forum for that almost Californian self-revelation that is so central a theme in Renaissance literature. Professors at the 15th-century University of Rome filled their courses not only with grammatical and philological observations but also with anecdotes of witches they had seen burnt, healing springs they had discovered in the Roman Forum, and complaints (modeled on those of their ancient predecessors) that students were putting notes on their lectures into circulation and forcing them into print against their will. By the end of the 15th century formal innovation had produced some masterpieces, difficult to tie to any ancient model, such as Niccolò Perotti's *Cornucopiae,* a commentary of some 1,000 folio pages on one book of Martial, which concerned itself almost exclusively with lexical matters. In the same period a number of ancient Latin writers whose students had no body of antique commentary or medieval glosses to draw on (notably Catullus, Propertius, and even Apuleius) were equipped with individual commentaries or, in some cases, complex, contentious bodies of exegesis.

Not many of the Greek texts translated in the course of the 15th century came with commentaries that could readily be adapted into Latin use. Leonardo Bruni worked out a Humanistic version of Aristotelian commentary, concentrating on historical and moral issues, to accompany his own new version of the pseudo-Aristotelian *Oeconomica.* Lorenzo Valla attached translations from the scholia to Thucydides to his own Latin translation, adding only a few new remarks of his own, as when he noted that the ancient revolution in Corcyra, and the consequent degradation of political language throughout Greece, recalled revealing parallels in his own time (Vat. lat. 1801, 66v).

But in the second half of the 15th century commentators began to tackle Greek writers who almost demanded more explication and who in some cases came already encased in ancient exegesis. Marsilio Ficino drew on Proclus and other late antique Neoplatonists as he elaborated his discursive Latin commentaries on the *Timaeus* and other Platonic texts, learned works that became so popular and authoritative that, for a century and more, most readers in the Latin West encountered Plato through the veils that Ficino wove. Regiomontanus, similarly, drew on Proclus as he finished an epitome, or running paraphrase, of Ptolemy's *Almagest* that had been a major work in progress by his teacher Georg Peurbach (d. 1461). This work, first published in 1496, reached a far wider public than Regiomontanus' formal commentary on the text, which spent more time thrashing the Latin version by George of Trebizond than explaining planetary theory. The *Epitome Almagesti* gave Copernicus and all other astronomers of the late 15th and early 16th centuries a rigorous, accessible version of Ptolemaic planetary theory.

The middle and later decades of the 15th century thus became an age of commentary. Manuscripts and printed editions of the classics, especially the Latin classics, took on a set form, modeled on the manuscript biblical and legal commentaries of the later Middle Ages. At the center of each page, a few lines of the text in question appear, set in a large font. In manuscripts or printed editions meant for schools, the lines are separated by blank spaces, in which the student could enter a prose paraphrase dictated by the teacher. Around the text wound one or more formal commentaries, closely written or printed in tiny letters. Editions of Virgil, by the end of the 15th century, came with seven of these, a format that proved so attractive, in an age of glossators, that Jewish scholars and Christian printers replicated it when they created the canonical form of the Rabbinic Bible. In all these texts the margins of the page invited the student or reader to enter a teacher's remarks or his own personal responses.

Commentary, in fact, became so fashionable that it provoked criticism and debate. Battista Guarino, son of the great teacher Guarino of Verona, noted that critics had appeared "who deny that, given the vast supply of books that the marvelous and speedy method of printing has made available in a few years, scholars have any need of this sort of precise, detailed commentary, since by working at it they could have done a better job of mastering these questions on their own. . . . Moreover, they say, this kind of reading actually harms the mind, since it loses the taste for carrying out inquiry on its own, devises no hypotheses, and creates nothing worthy of a free intellect." The appearance of dissenting views like these was only natural, given the uniform appearance and sometimes turgid content of the commentaries that had filled the Muses' gardens like so much learned kudzu. They may also have been inspired by one especially and diabolically suggestive commentary: the massive one in which the Dominican Annius of Viterbo wrapped a vast range of supposedly ancient historical texts, almost all of them his own forgeries, in 1498. This pullulating mass of glosses fitted its exegesis so transparently to the texts that Beatus Rhenanus condemned the work with one devastating quotation from Erasmus: "One of them milks the he-goat, the other holds out the sieve."

Battista himself disagreed with the critique he described, and he offered a panoramic account of Italy's great commentators in support of his view that commentaries were valuable, even necessary, for the ordinary reader of the classics. Others, like Beroaldo, Calderini, and Poliziano, disagreed more or less forcefully. These men began to write short, miscellaneous series of observations on textual cruces and interpretative problems about which they had something new to say, a specialist form of classical scholarship modeled on the work of Gellius, and one that made it easier for an author to stand out from the herd. Often given such titles as *Miscellanea* or *Variae lectiones,* these works represented a transition from full-text exegesis to a more monographic form of scholarship with its own classical models.

But the commentary was far too useful to abandon, and in the 16th century both Italian and northern scholars imaginatively extended its forms. Erasmus made a specialty of one particular kind of commentary: a massively learned, even encyclopedic essay that expanded on a single line or phrase. He tried both to explicate ancient texts and to show their direct relevance to modern political and moral questions. Guillaume Budé applied the Humanist method of erudite commentary (and a great deal of material drawn, often without acknowledgment, from earlier Humanist commentators) in his learned, digressive commentary on the 6th-century Digest, which appeared in 1508 and marked the beginning of radical change in legal scholarship. Many other practitioners of the so-called *mos gallicus* would emulate Budé, drawing up commentaries on the Corpus Iuris Romani designed not only to draw out the current relevance of each law or juridical statement but also to set it back into its original historical context. Valla and Erasmus, for their part, used the methods of classical commentary to explicate the New Testament, thus initiating a process of transformation which would last through the next two centuries, even as the Reformation definitively split the Catholic Church. Both Protestant and Catholic scholars did their best, in the centuries to come, to explicate the historical sense of the Old and New Testaments, using philological and historical evidence to fix the meaning of every disputed word and line—only to discover, in the end, that history and philology could define the scope of interpretative problems but could not solve them.

Pierio Valeriano, meanwhile, turned his own *Corrections and Variations in the Text of Virgil* (1521) into something like a formal critical apparatus: not a text, but materials for creating one, in the form of a line-by-line record of the readings of the great Roman manuscripts of Virgil, which he studied systematically in the Vatican Library and elsewhere. Valeriano's precedent did not find consistent emulation, but he did help to inspire such systematic and businesslike textual critics as Beatus Rhenanus (editor of Tacitus and Velleius Paterculus), Piero Vettori (editor of Cicero), and Gabriele Faerno (editor of Terence) to concentrate on textual matters in their commentaries. When the young Joseph Scaliger, in the 1560s and 1570s, produced a series of commentaries on Varro, Ausonius, Festus, Catullus, Propertius, Tibullus, and Manilius, he generally followed Valeriano's model, concentrating on textual questions rather than the wider range of literary ones canvassed, for example, in Denis Lambin's immense and influential commentaries on Horace and Plautus. Yet Scaliger also added elements from the work of legal Humanists to the mix, making his notes on Ausonius a fascinating study of the late antique Roman Empire and the ways of education and literary life cultivated there.

The forms of commentary traditionally practiced in universities continued to flourish alongside the philological exegesis of the Humanists. Throughout the 16th century medical men wrote massive commentaries on the *Canon* of Avicenna, and the Jesuits of Coimbra produced the most searching and meticulous of all commentaries on the works of Aristotle. Like the Humanists, however, these commentators often knew a wide range of classical texts in Greek and Latin, and their methods often amounted to a synthesis of Scholastic and Humanist methods that brought ancient forms of exegesis together in radically new ways. In medical commentary, for example, the formalized questions and disputations of the medieval university made way for more essayistic forms of exegesis. No one plied this genre more energetically, or found more readers, than the medical man and polymath Girolamo Cardano, who drew on both Scholastic and Humanistic traditions as he developed Galen's self-reflexive and digressive model of scientific commentary into a rich and flexible medium—one with which he sought to prove that Hippocrates offered a better model than Galen for medical theory and practice.

Of the many experiments in commentary that the 16th and early 17th centuries witnessed, two proved especially influential. A long series of commentaries on Aristotle's *Poetics,* beginning with those of Francesco Robortello and Pier Vettori, encased that short, endlessly fertile text in a vast mass of exegetical amber. Every word was examined, corrected, translated, compared with the evidence about Greek tragedy, fused with related or apparently related passages from Horace, and argued over, again and again. Clunky and immense, these commentaries, which basically applied the discursive model of late antique philosophical commentary to literary ends, still made the *Poetics* live—just as academies began to revive and stage Greek tragedies and modern plays modeled on them. The 16th-century commentators succeeded in drawing attention, more systematically than any of their predecessors, to the need to lay a philosophical foundation for the practices of writing and criticism in the classical tradition. The lesson was not lost on Racine, who loved and annotated these editions, or on the other creators of 17th-century classicism.

If the commentaries on Aristotle filled one stately shelf, those on the ancient historians, especially Tacitus, proliferated into whole libraries. In the 1520s and 1530s, acute observers of contemporary politics felt the need for a new kind of commentary on ancient historians, one that would draw the practical lessons that ancient statesmanship and military practice had to offer without worrying about philological questions or confining itself to the straitjacket of line-by-line exegesis. Machiavelli's *Discourses on Livy* (1513–1517, the first of his works to be published, and the only one to appear in his lifetime) offered a new model: topical discussions of political, social, religious, and military matters, in the form of substantial essays that orbited around narratives from Livy, rather than normal glosses. Tacitus and Polybius (especially the former) materialized on cue as the preferred objects of this sort of commentary. By the end of the 16th century scholars and political specialists all over Europe had realized that, as Francesco Guicciardini pointed out, Tacitus had much to teach both absolute rulers and their rebellious subjects. Elaborate discourses like Machiavelli's and pungent series of aphorisms drawn from Tacitus' work and laid out in deliberately meaningful groups circulated everywhere. Commentary on Tacitus became the core of an up-to-date training in politics. It could even become subversive, as Isaac Dorislaus found when he drew what he saw as the republican implications of Tacitus in his history lectures at Cambridge in the 1620s, only to be silenced and deprived of his office by the authorities. But Tacitean commentary remained the common currency of political discourse until new kinds of treatise replaced it in the 17th century.

Through the 16th and 17th centuries commentary played a major role in philosophy as well as in philology. Both naturalists and philologists strove to explicate Pliny's *Natural History.* Humanists and Scholastics alike produced massive exegeses of Aristotle and Plato, and mathematicians continued to equip the works of Euclid and Archimedes with ever more up-to-date commentaries. Johannes Kepler, William Harvey, and Giambattista Riccioli all combined substantial scientific arguments with the exegesis of ancient texts.

Even in the 16th century some scholars worried about the vast glossematic hedges that now lined (and obscured) the highways and byways of ancient literature. The influential Parisian educational reformer Petrus Ramus argued that commentators needed to follow a single textual thread if they and their readers were to arrive at the mystery in the heart of each text. Ignore all questions of style and format, he suggested, and treat all texts, poems as well as speeches, plays as well as histories, as arguments, as working examples of dialectic. Close attention to the writer's argument, accompanied, whenever possible, by formal diagrams, could make commentary rigorous in a way that the endless proliferation of information and argument in traditional commentaries could not. Many a Ramist in Paris and Cambridge enlightened his students and lightened his labors by explaining Horace's *dulce et decorum est pro patria mori* as a formal refutation of the argument that it might be preferable to flee the battlefield and seek safety rather than stand fast and die in glory. Yet Ramus's views, like their author, remained controversial, especially after his brutal death at the hands of Catholic rioters on Saint Bartholomew's Day in 1572 made him a Protestant martyr.

Above all, commentary grew—and grew. Printers in Holland specialized in what the book trade came to call variorum editions, in which multiple commentaries, or selected bits from multiple commentaries, accompanied the reader through a text, thus dispensing with the need to buy a library before attempting to read Cornelius Nepos or Sallust. Later in the 17th century, Pierre-Daniel Huet created a series of editions, comprising the Greek poet Callimachus and 62 Latin writers down to the 6th century CE, for the dauphin of France, for whose capacities the bulky variorum editions were at once too demanding and too informative. Each of these Delphin editions, as they were called, came equipped with a Latin prose paraphrase of the text as well as a running commentary, often partly derivative. A bibliophilic and pedagogical success, the Delphin collection was reprinted as late as the early 19th century. Yet even Huet's ingenuity was not sufficient to save the commentary as a modern literary form.

By the middle decades of the 17th century the commentary had finally begun to lose its roles in the presentation of contemporary ideas. Scientists and philosophers, as their work departed slowly but definitively from ancient models, held that textbooks and treatises written from a coherent, modern standpoint could present a subject more effectively than a commentary on any ancient text. Many propagandists of the New Philosophy, most notably Bacon, Galileo, and Descartes, insisted that knowledge of nature was the most important of all studies and that textual study could never yield new or effective knowledge in the sphere of nature. Political thinkers of the era still referred constantly to the ancients: Hobbes drew much of his understanding of human nature in and outside society from Thucydides, whose histories he translated brilliantly into English. But Hobbes, like Grotius before him and Locke after him, cast his work in the new form of the treatise on politics, a genre that insisted on its coherence, originality, and independence from existing models. On the whole, the most sophisticated classical scholars (Richard Bentley, for example) concurred. The ancient texts belonged to an older world, one that could be studied for aesthetic or ethical purposes but could never again be brought back to life. Commentary, in this context, was necessarily a second-order discipline. It served, at best, to correct and explicate—to stand and wait, rather than to make statements of its own.

Many of Bentley's contemporaries were even more scathing. Alexander Pope reissued his great satire the *Dunciad* as a self-embellished *Dunciad Variorum* (1735), a vast denunciation of scholars in general and commentators in particular, which took the parodic form of a poem equipped with massive, point-missing notes. For Bentley, so Pope held, choosing to live in the margins of a great text meant not finding a privileged place from which to understand one's own world, but rather retreating from it into dry-as-dust obsessions and sterile pedantry. Satirists have continued to find this theme attractive, notably Vladimir Nabokov, whose *Pale Fire* (1962) includes the deadliest parody of a commentary since Pope, and David Lodge, one of whose characters dreams of creating a literary commentary on the novels of Jane Austen so rich with every possible interpretation that it will silence all other critics.

For all its polemics against excess and trivial glosses, the Enlightenment was no more able than the age of the New Philosophy had been to do away with the commentary entirely. Indeed, the genre moved, once again, into new realms. As scholars began to apply the techniques of classical philology, suitably modified, to the national classics of the modern European nations, commentaries on modern national literatures flourished like grass in a rainy spring. Shakespeare became the object, first of many quarrelsome individual scholars, and then of a variorum commentary all his own. Goethe's *Faust* and Montaigne's *Essays* almost disappeared under the weight of erudition brought to bear on them, line by line, in editions and commentaries. French secondary schools adopted as their central exercise a formalized *explication de texte.* Students learned to use set passages from canonical classics, ancient and modern, as the objects of both literary evaluation and encyclopedic exegesis, neatly conveyed in essay form.

If classical scholarship lost prestige and support in much of 18th-century Europe, ancient and medieval commentaries reoccupied a position of special prominence in what remained of the field. Scholars in Holland and Germany, in particular, honed and polished the tools with which they dissected scholia. They made themselves expert at separating medieval commentaries into their earlier and later components. They mined older scholia for new fragments and used their evidence to reconstruct the assumptions and methods of ancient scholars. In 1788, when D'Ansse de Villoison published the first edition of the Venice A and B scholia on the *Iliad,* Christian Gottlob Heyne, Friedrich August Wolf, and others as well leapt on the new material. Wolf used it as the principal basis for the radical arguments he advanced in his 1795 *Prolegomena,* about the nature of the Homeric text. The apparent unity of the text, Wolf insisted, in fact resulted not from the inspiration of a single author but from the critical talents and efforts of generations of Alexandrian scholars. Wolf took as his model for the analysis of the Homeric scholia the work that biblical scholars had done on the Jewish textual commentary to the Old Testament, the Masorah, and later biblical scholars emulated what they saw as his iconoclastic, fiercely historical approach to a canonical text. Scholia and their analysis continued to be at the center of the Homeric question for decades after Wolf wrote, though they served scholars only as sources, not as models.

Classical texts of all sorts continued to be taught and edited, and the edition with commentary continued both to serve as the mainstay of school and university instruction and to attract scholars toward crafting new models for the study of texts. Some of the greatest classical scholars of the 20th century, figures as diverse as A. E. Housman and Eduard Fraenkel, devoted the best of their lives and work to massive commentaries on difficult texts. Others, like Robin Nisbet and Margaret Hubbard, have continued to set new standards for what a formal commentary can do. All of this activity, however, like the vast majority of critical writing not cast in the form of commentary, takes place within the world of higher education and professional scholarship. Not only has the commentary on secular texts, ancient or modern, ceased to function as a scientific genre, it has also ceased to play any role in the intellectual lives of ordinary educated men and women once they leave school or university. "Commentary," in current American English, often refers not to a written text at all, but to oral reporting on or reaction to a public ceremony or athletic contest: a fancy way of saying "comment."

Within the world of humanistic scholarship, however, the commentary has begun to occupy a distinctively new position, especially since World War II. The historicist scholars of the 19th century (even Wolf and his pupils) generally regarded ancient commentaries and scholia less as works to be studied in their own right than as sources from which the critical scholar might retrieve new fragments of lost authors or new historical information. Byzantine and Western medieval commentaries were ransacked for the information they might provide about lost ancient predecessors or sources. Few scholars made much effort to think themselves into the mind of an ancient or medieval commentator, or to use such works as evidence for larger historical questions.

Since the 1930s this branch of scholarship has changed radically. Philologists have provided new editions of the Homeric scholia, Servius, Eustathius, and other major bodies of commentary. Historians have begun to use these texts, moreover, as something more than quarries. Henri-Irenée Marrou, Louis Holtz, Nigel Wilson, Robert Kaster, and others have drawn from ancient commentaries and scholia the evidence for their histories of ancient education and its social and political setting. Medievalists have devoted close scrutiny to the fates of Calcidius and other ancients in medieval schools and the rise of the *accessus ad auctores,* and now treat them, in the manner of their classical colleagues, as evidence for cultural and intellectual history. Byzantinists and Arabists have also found new ways to appreciate the meanings and uses of commentary in premodern societies. Students of Renaissance and later intellectual history have also begun to treat the commentaries produced in their periods as substantial intellectual achievements and to study them in detail. Much remains undone: notably a systematic, comparative, and collaborative study of all premodern commentary traditions. But in the world of scholarship, at least, the genre of commentary, with its millennial history and multiple functions, no longer demands the adjective *mere.*

BIBL.: Ottavio Besomi and Carlo Caruso, eds., *Il commento ai testi* (Basel 1992). August Buck and Otto Herding, eds., *Der Kommentar in der Renaissance* (Boppard 1975). Jean Céard, "Les transformations du genre du commentaire," in *L'automne de la Renaissance, 1580–1630,* ed. Jean Lafond and André Stegmann (Paris 1982) 101–115. Martine Furno, *Le Cornu Copiae de Niccolo Perotti: Culture et méthode d'un humaniste qui aimait les mots* (Geneva 1995). Wilhelm Geerlings and Christian Schulze, eds., *Der Kommentar in Antike und Mittelalter,* 2 vols. (Leiden 2002–2004). Roy Gibson and Christina Shuttleworth Kraus, eds., *The Classical Commentary: Histories, Practices, Theory* (Leiden 2002). Marie-Odile Goulet-Cazé, ed., *Le commentaire entre tradition et innovation* (Paris 2000). Ralph Häfner and Markus Völkel, eds., *Der Kommentar in der frühen Neuzeit* (Tübingen 2006). John Henderson, *Scripture, Canon, and Commentary: A Comparison of Confucian and Western Exegesis* (Princeton 1991). Craig Kallendorf, *Virgil and the Myth of Venice: Books and Readers in the Italian Renaissance* (Oxford 1999). Robert Kaster, *Guardians of Language: The Grammarian and Society in Late Antiquity* (Berkeley 1988). Jaap Mansfeld, *Prolegomena* (Leiden 1994). Glenn W. Most, ed., *Commentaries—Kommentare,* Aporemata 4 (Göttingen 1999). Per-Gunnar Ottosson, *Scholastic Medicine and Philosophy: A Study of Commentaries on Galen's Tegni* (Naples 1982). Marianne Pade, ed., *On Renaissance Commentaries* (Hildesheim 2005). Deborah Parker, *Commentary and Ideology: Dante in the Renaissance* (Durham, N.C., 1993). Stefano Perfetti, *Aristotle's Zoology and Its Renaissance Commentators (1521–1601)* (Leuven 2000). Franz Rosenthal, *Das Fortleben der Antike im Islam* (Zurich 1965), and *The Classical Heritage in Islam,* trans. Emile and Jenny Marmorstein (London 1975; repr. 1992). Bruno Sandkühler, *Die frühen Dantekommentare und ihr Verhältnis zur mittelalterlichen Kommentartradition* (Munich 1967). Catherine Volpilhac-Auger et al., eds., *Le collection Ad usum Delphini,* 2 vols. (Grenoble 2000–2005).

A.G.

Concord, Philosophical

The concept that there is a fundamental agreement between all or, at any rate, the most important philosophical beliefs and systems has roots in classical antiquity. It was developed during the Middle Ages by Western and Arabic thinkers and came to have a profound influence on Renaissance and early modern thinkers and the ways in which they interpreted earlier philosophical texts.

The tradition has its beginnings in the question of the relationship between the philosophical doctrines of Plato and his most famous student, Aristotle, which was perceived as closer than is commonly accepted today, perhaps on the basis of lost works by Aristotle, especially his dialogues. The earliest claim of the overall agreement between Plato and Aristotle may be that of the Middle Platonist Antiochus of Ascalon (130/120–68 BCE), whose student Cicero repeatedly states that the Academics and Peripatetics "differed in words while agreeing in fact" (*Academica* 1.17; *De finibus* 4.5).

Following Antiochus, Platonic–Aristotelian concordism became more prevalent, though it did not win universal approval. The 2nd-century CE *Didaskalikos* (*Handbook of Platonism*), sometimes attributed to Albinus, argued for the fundamental agreement of Plato's theory of transcendent Forms with Aristotle's concept of immanent forms within physical bodies. This work was translated into Latin by the Italian Renaissance Platonist Marsilio Ficino in the 15th century and appeared in several printed editions, contributing to the resurgence of interest in concordism in early modern Europe.

With the development of Neoplatonism the question of Aristotle's relation to Plato became a major issue. Could Aristotle's philosophical and scientific writings, far preferable in an instructional context to Plato's dialogues, be properly used as texts within a Platonic setting? Plotinus (3rd cent. CE), the leading figure in early Neoplatonism, was ambiguous on this point. His student Porphyry, however, was one of the major proponents of Platonic–Aristotelian concordism in the classical world; his treatise *That the Doctrine of Plato and Aristotle Is One* influenced many thinkers, perhaps surviving among Arab scholars as late as the time of Al-Fārābī (ca. 870–950). Spurious works of a Platonic character that circulated under Aristotle's name in the Arab world and were transferred to the West in Latin translation—such as the *Theology of Aristotle* and the *Book of Causes,* based on Plotinus and Proclus (5th cent.) respectively—also helped to make concordism seem plausible.

Among classical Latin authors who adopted a concordist position, the most influential was Boethius. In his longer commentary on Aristotle's *De interpretatione* (*Patrologia Latina,* 64:43c–d), he announced that he wished "to reduce the opinions of Aristotle and Plato to a single concord and demonstrate that they, unlike most, do not disagree about everything, but rather agree to a great extent on the majority of subjects which comprise philosophy." The six centuries following the death of Boethius, whose concordist project never got beyond its early stages, saw little direct study of Plato and Aristotle in the Latin West. In the 12th century a brief reference by John of Salisbury indicates that Bernard of Chartres and his students "labored hard to compose Aristotle and Plato, but I think they came too late and labored in vain to reconcile dead men who disagreed as long as they lived" (*Metalogicon,* 2.17.875d). Henry Bate of Malines, a late 13th- and early 14th-century thinker devoted to reconciliation, wrote in his *Mirror of Divines and Certain Naturals* that the verbal differences between Plato and Aristotle could be reconciled, frequently quoting in support of this view the writings of Greek commentators such as Themistius (4th cent. CE) and Simplicius (6th cent.) that were available in Latin. Bate's treatise was an important source for the concordist movement in the Renaissance, as we know that Giovanni Pico della Mirandola possessed a copy.

During the 15th and 16th centuries philosophical concord became a major theme in the Latin world. A crucial source for this was the Byzantine scholar George Gemistos Pletho, who composed in Florence in the spring of 1439 the treatise *On How Aristotle Differs from Plato,* which sought to reintroduce Platonic views into a realm then dominated by Aristotelian doctrine. This gave rise to a polemical debate, involving such prominent figures as George of Trebizond and Cardinal Bessarion, and proved a key source for the leading Platonic scholar of the Italian Renaissance, Marsilio Ficino, whose translations and studies of Plato's works were enormously influential. In a letter of 1489 Ficino praised Pico's demonstration three years earlier, in his *Nine Hundred Conclusions,* that "Plato and Aristotle are in wondrous agreement (*concordes*) on the soul," adding, "You as well as I have long sought the concord of philosophers (*concordia philosophorum*) on this issue." Ficino was less pleased when Pico —known as "the Prince of Concord" (*Princeps concordiae*) both for his interest in concordism and because his family were the rulers of the principality of Concordia as well as of Mirandola—produced a treatise in 1491 entitled *On Being and the One,* part of a planned but never completed program to demonstrate the philosophical concord of Plato and Aristotle. In this work Pico expressed a view that ran contrary to the entire Neoplatonic tradition, dear to Ficino's heart, by maintaining that the two philosophers agreed even in the contentious area of metaphysics. In Raphael's famous fresco *The School of Athens* (1510), painted for Pope Julius II in the Vatican Stanza della Segnatura, Plato, holding a copy of his *Timaeus,* and Aristotle, with a copy of his *Ethics,* occupy center stage, presiding over a philosophical congress of Greek thinkers. The painting may reflect a concordist vision of the two great philosophers of antiquity, handing down complementary and ultimately reconcilable doctrines. The genre of comparing the philosophies of Plato and Aristotle continued into the 16th century, though the aim was often to pinpoint dissimilarities as well as to highlight similarities.

Another strain of concordism that gained ground during the Renaissance, in the writings of Bessarion, Ficino, and Pico, stressed the broad agreement between pagan philosophy, especially Platonism and Neoplatonism, and Christianity. In his treatise *On the Perennial Philosophy* (1540), Agostino Steuco, an Augustinian biblical scholar, bishop, and prefect of the Vatican Library, drew on an impressively wide range of works, from the Old Testament to the suppositious writings of "ancient theologians" such as Hermes Trismegistus, to prove that Jews, Chaldaeans, Egyptians, and other early peoples had transmitted to the Greeks a body of doctrines that, beneath a diversity of forms, contained the same truths, including the creation of the world and the immortality of the soul. Though Steuco was attacked by defenders of Counter-Reformation orthodoxy, especially Jesuits, for blurring the distinction between Christian dogmas and pagan doctrines, his ideas were repeated, usually without acknowledgment, by 16th- and 17th-century authors who shared his vision. The most notable proponent of this tradition was Leibniz (1646–1716), whose philosophy of harmony, built on eclectic foundations and broadly ecumenical in spirit, attempts to provide a sophisticated metaphysical underpinning for the notion of philosophical concord.

BIBL.: Anthony Cutler, "The *Disputà* [*sic*] Plate in the J. Paul Getty Museum and Its Cinquecento Context," *J. Paul Getty Museum Journal* 18 (1990) 5–32. Glenn W. Most, "Reading Raphael: 'The School of Athens' and Its Pre-Text," *Critical Inquiry* 23 (1996) 145–182, and "Athens as the School of Greece," in *Classical Pasts: The Classical Traditions of Greece and Rome,* ed. James I. Porter (Princeton 2002) 377–388. F. Purnell, Jr., "The Theme of Philosophic Concord and the Sources of Ficino's Platonism," in *Marsilio Ficino e il ritorno di Platone: Studi e documenti,* ed. Gian Carlo Garfagnini (Florence 1986) 2:397–415. Ingrid Rowland, *The Culture of the High Renaissance: Ancients and Moderns in Sixteenth-century Rome* (New York 1998). Charles B. Schmitt, "Perennial Philosophy from Steuco to Leibniz," *Journal of the History of Ideas* 27 (1966) 505–532. F.PU.

Consolation

In prose and verse the classical world spawned a rich tradition of consolatory genres: the *epistola consolatoria,* the longer *oratio consolatoria* or *consolatio,* the funeral oration, the consolatory dialogue, elegiac poetry, and the remedy book or consolation manual. Although bereavement was the dominant focus (e.g., in Crantor's lost *On Grief,* Cicero's lost *Consolation,* and Seneca's *To Marcia, On Consolation,* and *To Polybius*), this tradition also encompassed a wider array of travails, including the fear of death, illness, imprisonment (Boethius' *Consolation of Philosophy*), exile (Ovid's *Sorrows*), and general misfortune (the pseudo-Senecan *On the Remedies of Misfortunes*). As Cicero reveals in the discussion of *aegritudo* (sickness, sorrow) in his *Tusculan Disputations* (itself a type of consolation manual), the Stoic, Peripatetic, Cyrenaic, and Epicurean schools posed distinct therapeutic approaches to remedying distress, and he eclectically drew on all of them in his attempt to console himself for the death of his daughter, Tullia, in his *Consolation* (*Tusc.* 3.31.75–76).

Although some writers in the patristic period readily adapted the genres of the consolatory letter (Chrysostom, Jerome) and the funeral oration (Ambrose) to a Christian context, Christian theology also added a skeptical perspective on secular sorrow—as is evident in Paul's distinction (2 Cor. 7:10) between a worthy "sorrow according to God" (contrition) and a dangerous "worldly sorrow," and in Augustine's guilt over his grief at his mother's death (*Confessions* 9). Indeed, the principal therapeutic concern of the medieval Church would be sin, as the confessor's treatment of contritional sorrow dominated pastoral care.

With the revival of rhetoric in the medieval *ars dictaminis* and in Renaissance Italian Humanism, consolation reclaimed a prominent cultural place. The dictaminal writer Boncompagno da Signa included 35 sections on administering solace in his *Ancient Rhetoric* (1215). In the following century Petrarch in his letter collections (emulating those of Cicero and Seneca) fully restored the *epistola consolatoria,* drawing on classical topoi and exempla and incorporating Christian themes as well. In some cases, such letters could articulate timely social views, as in the Florentine chancellor Coluccio Salutati's defense of the active lay life in a series of consolatory letters in 1393 to an acquaintance who contemplated religious retreat following the loss of six children and six grandchildren in a recent plague. Renaissance Humanists also revived the *consolatio,* most notably in Francesco Filelfo's 80-page *Consolatory Oration to Jacopo Antonio Marcello on the Death of His Son Valerio* (1461). Filelfo devoted almost one-third of his treatise to a largely philosophical exposition of the theme of the immortality of the soul, a treatment he prided himself on in his own bid for secular immortality and fame. Humanists also widely cultivated the funeral oration, which not only praised the dead but also often offered consolation; the coalescence of these genres was confirmed by a parody by Leon Battista Alberti (d. 1472), who wrote a funeral oration for the death of his dog. The vitality and range of Renaissance consolatory genres is exemplified by an anthology of writings compiled in Florence following the death of Cosimo de' Medici in 1464: this miscellany, the *Cosmian Collections,* included six consolatory letters and a reply to one of them, a funeral oration, an elegiac verse, a *consolatio* (on the death of Cosimo's mother), and a consolatory dialogue (on the death of his son).

Perhaps the most creative revival of the classical consolation in the Renaissance comes in the exploration of the subjective psychological realm. In his *Secret Conflict of His Cares* (ca. 1347–1353), Petrarch—in part inspired by Boethius' *Consolation of Philosophy*—presents a dialogue between himself and Saint Augustine, in which Augustine not merely cautions him to meditate on death and to cultivate a spiritual contempt of the world but also offers him worldly consolation for the sin of *accidia,* conceived here not as the traditional spiritual torpor or sloth but as a classical *aegritudo* caused by worldly frustration (over career) and characterized by an indulgent "sweet grief." Renaissance Humanists also developed the genres of the self-consolatory letter or dialogue on bereavement, culminating in Giannozzo Manetti's *Consolatory Dialogue on the Bitter Death of His Cherished Son* (1438), in which Manetti forcefully counters harsh Stoic (and Christian) proscriptions on grieving with Peripatetic (and Christian) arguments on the legitimacy and naturalness of sorrow. (In the 1460s such a repudiation of Stoic *apatheia* and all stern rationalism was even ghostwritten for a mourner: the grieving Venetian nobleman to whom Filelfo had addressed his *Consolatory Oration* arranged for a Humanist surrogate to respond to his 14 consolers with a lengthy treatise defending the prerogatives of unrestrained parental grief.) In the following century Thomas More explored the self-consolatory motif in the context of his imprisonment in his Boethian, but pointedly Christian, *Dialoge of Comfort Agaynst Trybulacion* (1534).

Renaissance Humanists also restored, and amplified, the genre of the remedy book or consolation manual. Taking the brief pseudo-Senecan *On the Remedies of Misfortunes* as his model, Petrarch composed a massive *On the Remedies of Both Kinds of Fortune* (1366), adding to the "Senecan" consolations of bad fortune cautions concerning the good. The second book of his treatise, in which Reason ministers to 132 misfortunes of Fear and Grief, constitutes a major consolation manual. In one chapter, "On Misery and Sadness" (93), Petrarch counters the medieval *contemptus mundi* with the remedy of happiness owing to the "dignity of the human condition," which would flower into a prominent Renaissance theme in the following century. Also much in the tradition of Cicero's *Tusculan Disputations,* this treatise reveals Petrarch's interest in applying the "medicine of words" to the "illnesses of minds," and in this adumbrates the modernizing shift from the spiritual cure of sin to the psychological cure of sickness. Nearly two centuries later, the Milanese physician Girolamo Cardano, citing the precedent of Petrarch's *On Remedies* (and hoping to supply the Ciceronian *Consolation* lost to the world) wrote his own *On Consolation* (1542), which encompassed not only bereavement and the fear of death but also illness, poverty, exile, imprisonment, and other hardships. (In fact, the Renaissance fascination with emulating and replacing Cicero's treatise culminated in a forgery and publication of the lost *Consolation* in Venice in 1583.) The early modern encyclopedia of sorrow, Robert Burton's *Anatomy of Melancholy* (1621), which included a lengthy "Consolatory Digression, containing the Remedies of all manner of Discontents" that drew on Petrarch's *On Remedies* and Cardano's *On Consolation,* is both testament to the legacy of the classical consolation and harbinger of the modern era's embrace of worldly sorrow.

In the realm of verse, the revival of elegy in the Renaissance and beyond provided a venue for probing the reaches of loss in tones now plaintive, now defiant, now consolatory. In forms such as the epitaph (Ben Jonson's "On My First Sonne" of 1616), the sonnet (Donne's Holy Sonnet 17, on the death of his wife in 1617), the pastoral

(Milton's "Lycidas" of 1637 and Shelley's "Adonais" of 1821), and the extended lament (Tennyson's *In Memoriam* of 1850), elegiac poets contended with the conventions of emotional restraint, confessed to worldly attachments unworthy of logic or religious belief, challenged traditional consolations, questioned the possibility of expressing grief with words, proclaimed the necessity of doing so against criticisms of weakness and literary ambition, praised the dead, and offered solace.

In the 20th century the consolatory realm admitted a new practitioner when the professional clinician began to fully objectify sadness and grief as psychological conditions or illnesses (as signaled by Freud's *Mourning and Melancholia* of 1917). That century's tragedies also prompted the emergence of new genres of collective sorrow, remembrance, and consolation, both in works witnessing the Holocaust, such as Elie Wiesel's *Night* (1958), and in those posing existential responses to those horrors, such as Viktor Frankl's *Man's Search for Meaning* (1946). The modern world has also shown an increasing interest in the public memorialization of grief and the dead in monuments and museums. The sometimes contested views concerning such monuments reveal the degree to which, at least in one way, consolation vitally remains part of the public, collective, and political realm, even as classical consolation's rhetorical and literary legacy (except for the funeral eulogy) has largely receded.

BIBL.: M. L. King, *The Death of the Child Valerio Marcello* (Chicago 1994). P. O. Kristeller, "Francesco Bandini and His Consolatory Dialogue upon the Death of Simone Gondi," in his *Studies in Renaissance Thought and Letters* (Rome 1984) 411–435. G. W. McClure, *Sorrow and Consolation in Italian Humanism* (Princeton 1991). J. M. McManamon, *Funeral Oratory and the Cultural Ideals of Italian Humanism* (Chapel Hill 1989). G. W. Pigman, *Grief and the English Renaissance Elegy* (Cambridge 1985).

G.M.

Constantine

Roman emperor, 306–337 CE. His life can be briefly summarized here. He was born to Constantius, soon to be emperor, and Helena, probably a concubine; upon his father's death in 306, he was proclaimed emperor. In 312 he converted from paganism to Christianity after having seen a cross in both a waking vision and a dream. Defeating his rival emperors, Maxentius and Licinius, he gained control of the entire empire in 324. The following year he summoned and participated in the first ecumenical council at Nicaea, which excommunicated Arius for his subordinationist views and formulated the Nicene Creed. Around the same time he initiated construction of a new capital at Byzantium, which he renamed Constantinople. In 326 he ordered the execution of his wife Fausta and his son Crispus, possibly for adultery. In the late 320s his mother toured the Holy Land to find the site of Jesus' nativity, and Constantine ordered the construction of a church over what was believed to be the location of Christ's passion and burial, the Holy Sepulcher. At the beginning of a military expedition against Persia, he took ill and died after having been baptized by the Arianizing bishop Eusebius of Nicomedia.

Constantine became a pivotal figure in the historiographical tradition beginning shortly after his death. Eusebius of Caesarea composed a panegyrical biography, *The Life of Constantine,* which elevated him to the level of a prophet or saint. A counterreaction started with his pagan nephew, the emperor Julian (r. 361–363), whose critique was magnified by the late 4th-century pagan historian Eunapius and his early 6th-century epitomizer Zosimus. They criticized, inter alia, Constantine's confiscation of treasuries from pagan shrines and his family murders, in repentance for which, they argued, Constantine chose to convert. Late antique Christian writers joined the debate by attempting to counter these pagan detractions (esp. Sozomen), to supplement them with charges of Constantine's tendency toward Arianism (esp. Jerome), or, in the case of Arianizing historians, to claim the emperor as an ally (esp. Philostorgius).

Legends also appeared quickly, the first relating to Constantine's refashioning of the Holy Land. Although by the 350s Christians believed that the True Cross on which Christ was thought to have been crucified had been discovered, in 395 Ambrose of Milan first reported that Constantine's mother, Helena, was responsible for its excavation (*De obitu Theodosii* 43–47), and only a few years later Rufinus of Aquileia (*Historia eremitica* 10.7–8) offers a full narrative of the *inventio crucis*. These late 4th-century accounts spawned a series of more elaborate legends in Latin, Greek, and Syriac involving the revelation of the cross's whereabouts by a Jew named Judas, who converted and as bishop of Jerusalem took the name Cyriacus.

In the mid-5th-century West another legend invented a new narrative for Constantine's problematic conversion and baptism: Constantine, a pagan emperor engaged in ruthless persecutions, had been afflicted with leprosy and was advised by the pagan priests of Rome to bathe in the blood of infants; disgusted, he refused and was visited by a dream in which Saints Peter and Paul encouraged him to summon Pope Sylvester, by whom he was baptized and converted into a champion of the Church. By the late 8th century the Sylvester story spawned a further elaboration in the form of a document, supposedly given to Sylvester by Constantine upon his departure for Constantinople, which granted the pope supremacy over the entire Church and ceded to him control of all western territories. This document, the Donation of Constantine, was regarded as a mainstay of papal authority in both East and West until it was definitively proven to be a forgery in the 15th century by Lorenzo Valla, Nicholas of Cusa, and Reginald Pecock, with obvious repercussions for Reformation arguments against papal supremacy.

The figure of Constantine also generated a rich legendary tradition in the East, where it had a much a greater influence because of the continuation of his empire from his capital. Beginning in 574 the emperor Tiberius II adopted the imperial name Constantine, thereby initiating an onomastic tradition that was continued in the Heraclian and Macedonian dynasties. The 9th to 11th centuries saw the proliferation of a variety of interrelated romances featuring elaborate stories of Constantine's illegitimate birth, his conversion and baptism, his foundation of Constantinople under the guidance of the clever eunuch Euphratas, and his chivalrous exploits among the Persians (Lieu and Montserrat 1998). Because of the availability of Eusebius' biography, however, these legends always followed the basic outlines of Constantine's life.

Enlightenment interpretations tended to downplay the veracity of Constantine's vision, the genuineness of his conversion, and his significance to world history. Voltaire (1767) excoriated Constantine as an opportunistic fraud whose fame outpaced that of his more virtuous nephew Julian only because he professed Christianity. Gibbon's (1776) Constantine exploited the advantages of a monotheistic religion for political ends but became sincere in his Christian belief in the wake of his successes. Burckhardt (1853) portrays a realist Constantine who only feigned religious conviction in order to claw his way to supremacy. By the early 20th century many openly denied the authenticity of Eusebius' *Life* and the reality of Constantine's conversion altogether. A papyrus discovery laid to rest suspicions about Eusebius' veracity, and the bulk of more recent scholarship has abandoned skepticism about Constantine's spiritual conviction while laying more emphasis on the complexity of his religious worldview.

BIBL.: G. Bonamente and F. Fusco, eds., *Costantino il Grande: Dall'antichità all'umanesimo,* 2 vols. (Macerata 1992). Constantine I, *Constantine and Christendom: The Oration to the Saints, The Greek and Latin Accounts of the Discovery of the True Cross, the Edict of Constantine to Pope Sylvester,* trans. M. Edwards (Liverpool 2003). S. Lieu and D. Montserrat, eds., *Constantine: History, Historiograpy, and Legend* (London 1998). P. Magdalino, ed., *New Constantines: The Rhythm of Imperial Renewal in Byzantium, 4th–13th Centuries* (Aldershot 1994).

N.L.

Constantinople

Capital of the Roman and Byzantine Empire, 330–1453 CE, Constantinople was important to the classical tradition in several ways: as the last great urban creation of antiquity, which survived as the greatest Christian city of the Middle Ages; as the main, and for long the sole, center of education in the Greek classics during the Middle Ages, where nearly all the ancient Greek texts read today were preserved; and as the home of early classicizing tendencies in ideology, art, and literature.

Among the new Roman imperial capitals established in late antiquity, the city of Constantine, begun in 324 and inaugurated in 330, was novel mainly in the scale and the permanence of its foundation. The emperor Constantine the Great, developing a previous Roman extension to the ancient Greek polis of Byzantion, laid out a vast new monumental complex along and around the main access routes. It was a showcase of traditional urban planning that looked for inspiration to Rome itself and, more immediately, to eastern cities such as nearby Nicomedia. Unlike the layout of Constantine's building program at Jerusalem, that of his eponymous city was not shaped by his adoption of Christianity: it included two or at the most three churches, but it also included temples to pagan deities at central locations, in addition to those long situated on the ancient acropolis. Its dominant features were the secular structures that commemorated the founder and echoed the civic topography of Rome: the circus or hippodrome for chariot racing and the adjacent palace and public bath, the circular forum with a senate house and a colossal column in porphyry marble bearing a bronze statue that represented Constantine, the capitol at the convergence of the access roads from the main land gates, and, near the northernmost gate, Constantine's own mausoleum at the center of a porticoed recreational complex. The founder's commitment to traditional Graeco-Roman civic ethics and aesthetics was further evident in the numerous porticoes that lined its streets and squares, and the concentrations of public statuary, including some famous masterpieces, gathered from older centers of the Greek world. The choice and deployment of these statues suggests that the intention was not so much to expose pagan "idols" to ridicule, as claimed by Constantine's Christian apologist Eusebius of Caesarea, but to appropriate the mythological identities and origins of other cities for Constantinople, conceived as the fulfillment of their past.

The continued expansion of Constantinople in the century after Constantine's death, in 337, gave greater emphasis to its Christian identity, with the construction of new urban churches, the importation of holy relics in preference to statues, the emergence of suburban monasteries, the religious organization of social welfare, and the closure of temples. The greatest building projects were still secular, however, enlarging, on the one hand, the city's infrastructure of harbors, granaries, aqueducts, cisterns, and fortifications and, on the other hand, its monumental armature of colonnaded streets and squares, triumphal arches, commemorative columns, assembly halls, public and private palaces, and opulent thermal baths, all of which enhanced the increasingly strident claim that Constantinople was a New (and better) Rome. It was not until the late 5th century that the New Rome began to merit consideration as a New Jerusalem. From this point, however, the city progressively lost its classical character, as churches and pious foundations proliferated, monks and monasteries entered the urban scene, the erection of new secular monuments declined and eventually ceased, and old structures fell victim to frequent fires, earthquakes, and quarrying of their building materials. Both the contraction of the urban population between 542 and 747 and its revival over the following centuries played their part in the transformation of the late antique fabric.

Yet in Constantinople, as in Rome, the remains of this fabric continued to excite admiration as late as the 15th century, even after many of the city's antiquities, including its still substantial collections of bronze statuary, had been destroyed or pillaged in the conquest by the Fourth Crusade and the resulting Latin occupation (1204–1261). Until 1204 Constantinopolitans lived in what was the best-preserved urban environment from the ancient world, thanks to two factors: its successful resistance to foreign invasion, and its continuity as the seat of imperial government. This continuity further ensured the survival of some aspects of ancient civic ritual in the ceremonies of the imperial court, and especially in the chariot races and other public festivities organized on major feast days and special occasions in the hippodrome.

Continuity of government also ensured continuity of secular literacy and therefore the survival of ancient Greek *paideia* at a level sufficient to permit a more ambitious revival from the end of the 8th century. Constantinople had not been one of the great intellectual hubs of late antiquity; indeed, under Justinian (527–565), it had been at the center of intellectual repression. The decline, disruption, or destruction of provincial cities, along with the extinction of Greek as the language of literary and philosophical discourse in Latin Europe and the Arabic Near East, however, eventually left Constantinople as the only place where the Greek classics were read, copied, and taught. Schools attached to churches provided the basic curriculum of grammar, rhetoric, and philosophy, which had been standard since Hellenistic times. The more learned teachers provided advanced tuition, both at school and in their homes. Some individuals (for example, Photius, Arethas, Michael Psellus, Anna Comnena, Eustathius of Thessalonica, and Theodore Metochites) acquired a prodigious knowledge of Greek literature. It was in large part from Constantinople that translations of Greek works began to reach Western Europe in the 12th century, and that Byzantine scholars in the 15th century brought to Italy all the texts that would form the basis of Greek studies in the Renaissance and later.

While perpetuating and preserving the classical heritage in these ways, however, the culture of Constantinople also experienced a progressive sense of detachment from its classical roots. This expressed itself at one extreme in ignorant suspicion of ancient authors and works of art and, at the other, in a tendency to idealization and stylistic imitation of the classics, broadly defined. An early example of this classicism was the museum of pagan statues that the imperial chamberlain Lausus, a patron of Christian holy men and ascetic writings, assembled in his house around 420. The development of classicism in later centuries is perhaps best exemplified by the successive compilations of epigrams collected from public monuments all over the Greek world, including Constantinople, that make up the Greek Anthology.

Literary perceptions of Constantinople from its foundation to the Ottoman conquest reflect the transformation of the classical heritage from living tradition to alienation and finally rediscovery. In the 6th century Hesychius of Miletus could still write about the city's origins, and Procopius and Paul the Silentiary could describe Justinian's additions to the built environment, in the language and genres that Greek authors had always used to celebrate their native or adopted polis, with little sense of division, in the civic environment, between the Christian present and the pagan past. The 8th-century anonymous *Parastaseis* (Brief Historical Notes), however, tells a different story with much less classical literary elegance: the city's ancient sculptured monuments are exotic "spectacles" (*theamata*) and "wonders" (*thaumata*), whose hidden meaning and menace have to be decoded by "philosophers" and whose identities are largely invented by the anonymous author or authors of these brief notes. Invention is taken still further in 9th- and 10th-century texts, the *Narration of the Building of Hagia Sophia* and the *Patria,* which spin legendary origins even for the Christian monuments of Constantinople. Not until the early 13th century, with Niketas Choniates' lament on the statues destroyed by the Latin conquerors of Constantinople in 1204, did Byzantine authors begin to show an appreciation of these objects as works of ancient art. Thereafter, the increasing dilapidation of the city's ancient buildings, which accompanied the empire's political decline, led some late Byzantine intellectuals to view their capital with a more critical sense of historical antiquity: it was in this spirit that Theodore Metochites wrote his long oration in praise of Constantinople, the *Byzantios* (ca. 1315), and that Manuel Chrysoloras wrote his *Comparison of the Old and New Rome* (1411). The ideology of empire, however, prevented medieval Byzantines from being fully antiquarian about the Constantinople of Constantine and Justinian, a civic past in which they invested their present and future political identity. It was left for Western travelers of the Renaissance to rediscover Constantinople as an *ancient* city.

Before the 15th century, there is little to distinguish the accounts of westerners from those of other foreign visitors, apart from the sharpness and the criticism of their comments. Like the Arabs, they were fascinated by the intricate splendors of the court; like the Russian pilgrims, they were interested in churches and relics; and like all visitors as well as the Byzantines themselves, the source of all "tourist" information, they regarded the city's ancient sculptures as exotic wonders. The urbane Latinists Liudprand of Cremona and Odo of Deuil were in this respect no more classical in their observations than the Arab prisoner Harun ibn Yahya, the Spanish rabbi Benjamin of Tudela, the Russian archbishop Anthony of Novgorod, and the vernacular French chronicler of the Fourth Crusade, Robert of Clari. The change came with the Humanists Cristoforo Buondelmonti and Cyriac of Ancona in the decades before the Ottoman conquest of 1453. They visited Constantinople, among other places, not to admire churches and palaces but to record ancient monuments and inscriptions. They thus anticipated the work of Pierre Gilles (Gyllius), the polymath scholar who came with the

French mission to the court of Süleyman the Magnificent in 1544 and gathered material for the two books, *On the Thracian Bosphoros* and *On the Topography and Antiquities of Constantinople,* that were published after his death. Though primarily interested in the ancient city, Gilles did use Byzantine sources and recorded the topography and remains of the medieval period. His work was an invaluable resource for the future development of Byzantine studies, as well as an indispensable handbook for all later European travelers to Constantinople.

By Gilles's time, the remains of Byzantine Constantinople were fast disappearing in the development of the new Ottoman capital, but this development did owe something to the Roman and Byzantine legacy. The conqueror of 1453, Sultan Mehmed II, was a cultivated man who had both Byzantine scholars and Renaissance Humanists working for him, and he enjoyed hearing about the exploits of Alexander, Hannibal, and Julius Caesar. In refounding Constantine's city as an Islamic imperial capital, he was conscious and proud of the precedent he was following. The city's name officially became Istanbul in 1930.

BIBL.: S. Bassett, *The Urban Image of Late Antique Constantinople* (Cambridge 2004). A. Bauer, *Stadt, Platz und Denkmal in der Spätantike: Untersuchungen zur Ausstattung des öffentlichen Raums in den spätantiken Städten Rom, Konstantinopel und Ephesos* (Mainz 1996). Averil Cameron and J. Herrin, eds. and trans., *Constantinople in the Early Eighth Century: The Parastaseis syntomoi chronikai* (Leiden 1984). Niketas Choniates, *Historia,* ed. J.-L. van Dieten, 2 vols. (Berlin 1975), and *O City of Byzantium: Annals of Niketas Choniates,* trans. H. Magoulias (Detroit 1984). G. Dagron, *Constantinople imaginaire: Études sur le recueil des Patria* (Paris 1984). P. Gilles, *On the Antiquities of Constantinople,* trans. J. Ball, ed. R. G. Musto (New York 1988). R. Macrides, ed., *Travel in the Byzantine World* (Aldershot 2002). P. Magdalino, *Constantinople médiévale: Études sur l'évolution des structures urbaines* (Paris 1996). C. Mango, *The Art of the Byzantine Empire, 312–1453* (Englewood Cliffs, N.J., 1972; repr. Toronto 1986) and *Le développement urbain de Constantinople, IVe–VIIe siècles,* 3rd ed. (Paris 2004). C. Mango, ed., *The Oxford History of Byzantium* (Oxford 2002). G. Necipoğlu, *Architecture, Ceremonial, and Power: The Topkapi Palace in the Fifteenth and Sixteenth Centuries* (Cambridge, Mass., 1991). Paul le Silentiaire, *Description de Sainte-Sophie de Constantinople,* trans. Marie-Christine Fayant and Pierre Chuvin (Drôme 1997). Th. Preger, *Scriptores originum Constantinopolitanarum* (1901–1907; repr. Leipzig 1975). Procopius, *Works,* ed. and trans. H. Dewing, vol. 7, Loeb Classical Library (Cambridge, Mass., 1940). P.MG.

Constitution, Mixed

A modern term with no counterpart in antiquity, *mixed constitution* denotes a political order in which elements from the basic types of constitution (monarchy, aristocracy, democracy) are combined to produce a new form of government. The concept rests on the development of a typology of constitutions that began in the 5th century BCE. It was claimed that a mixed form promoted stability, since it guaranteed that various social interests would be kept in a state of equilibrium. The goal was to regulate the composition of a politically active citizenry so that the tensions between the broad mass of citizens and a social elite would be neutralized; historians believed that a mixed constitution had existed in Sparta, since the plurality of institutions—dual kingship, gerousia, ephorate, and the popular assembly—guaranteed both social equilibrium and mutual oversight by officials. Polybios (6.11–18) further developed this model, which he understood as a system of political organs exercising control over one another, and applied it to the Roman constitution, with its consuls, Senate, tribunes of the people, and popular assembly. Cicero followed him in part.

For reception history it is particularly important, first, that ephors and tribunes were presented as "democratic" elements in the context of a mixed constitution, although otherwise "democracy" referred to the immediate participation of the people in political affairs; second, that though the ephorate was regarded as an institution kept in check by the monarchy in Sparta (Plato, *Leges* 629A), this very situation also contributed to its continuing existence (Aristotle, *Politica* 1313a23–33; Plutarch, *Lykurgos* 7.2); and, third, that the institution of tribunes of the people made it possible to tame the popular will (Cicero, *De legibus* 3.19–26).

The notion of the mixed constitution reemerged in political theory after the reception of Aristotle's ideas began in the 13th century, even though at first it was thought to have no direct connection to the current times. In the context of city-states it was taken up chiefly in Florence and Venice. The debate on the constitution of Florence after 1494 included a discussion of the extent to which the granting of political rights to a broader group of citizens had to be balanced by other political organs, according to the Venetian model. The idea that Venice, with its institutions of Doge, Senate, and Major Council, represented a mixed constitution on the pattern of Sparta and, like the ancient city-state, owed its stability to a division of powers was then turned into one element of the myth of Venice as a model republic by Contarini.

The theory of the mixed constitution and the ephors played a particular role in discussions of the relationship between the crowns and estates in a number of European countries from the 14th to the 17th centuries, as well as in the conciliar movement, which sought to limit the power of the pope. By comparing the role of representatives of the different estates with that of ephors, political thinkers could argue that including them in government lay in the interest of monarchs themselves. Reformers such as Butzer, Calvin, Luther, and Melanchthon accepted variations of the idea that the political organs of the estates possessed the right to resist a tyrannical ruler. Scottish and English Monarchomachs used this as a basis for their protest against Catholic rulers in the mid-16th century, and after the St. Bartholomew's Day Massacre French Huguenots used it to justify their resistance. By assigning the right of resistance to "ephors," they avoided legitimizing the killing of tyrants by private individuals.

These ideas enjoyed a particular vogue in the English constitutional debates of the 17th century. The conflicts between the Stuarts and their parliaments initially took the form of legal disputes, but this changed abruptly after 1641, when the issue became one of sovereignty. The response of Charles I to the Nineteen Propositions of Parliament (June 1642) took on a fundamental significance: the king declared that the English constitution was a "mixture of absolute monarchy, aristocracy, and democracy which by the experience and wisdom of your ancestors had been moulded as to give this kingdom . . . the conveniences of all three, without the inconveniences of any one, as long as the balance hangs even between the three estates." For that reason he could not accede to Parliament's demands, as he was unwilling to destroy the "ancient, equall, happy, well-poised, and never enough commended constitution of the government of this Kingdom" and ultimately to promote the subjugation of Parliament by the unbridled power of the people. This line of argument, which harks back to Polybios' model of equilibrium, emphasizes the internal logic of a system that depended on compromise for its continued existence. The House of Lords was declared the necessary factor to provide a balance between the king and commons, and its legitimacy was thus based not on the titular rights of the aristocracy but rather on its function as an upper house of the legislature. This proclamation was a sharp but double-edged sword in the war of propaganda. Charles I could present himself as a constitutional monarch, but he had placed himself on the same level as the two houses of Parliament. The king's answer was immediately taken up by pamphleteers for both the parliamentary and the royalist causes. As the civil war proceeded, the comparison with the ephors grew more radical, since the mixed constitution appealed to by the king became a hindrance to the parliamentary cause. Hence, when Charles I was brought to trial, the precedent of Sparta was cited, where the ephors could bring an action against a king, a right that had led to the execution of King Agis IV in 241 BCE. By 1658 the failure of the constitutional experiments during Cromwell's Protectorate appeared to make a restoration of the monarchy inevitable. It was clear even to committed republicans that adhering to unrestricted rule by Parliament was not possible. Various authors, including James Harrington, broached the idea of creating equivalents to ephors and tribunes through a bicameral system, in order to keep a check on Parliament.

Indeed, the Restoration of the monarchy and House of Lords in England in 1660 was a return to the traditional constitutional order. The image of the mixed constitution that had become established by then lent itself to the situation; it fit with the sovereignty of the king-in-Parliament and the associated insulation from the direct popular will. This theory remained generally accepted well into the 19th century; debate occurred only with regard to the question of whether the Crown's patronage of offices and parliamentary constituencies enhanced or detracted from the balanced interplay of the constitutional organs of government.

During the American Revolution it was John Adams especially who took up this conception, observing, however, that it needed to be better implemented than had been the case in antiquity and in England. Adams connected this with the idea of a "natural aristocracy" that would have to be represented in the Senate. But in the course of the Constitutional Convention the idea of a mixed constitution was divested of its social implications and converted into the principle of checks and balances between institutions whose authority was derived solely from the constituent power of the people (and which would at the same time link individual states with the federal government). This amounted to retention of the fundamental idea that mutual oversight of government organs served the freedom of the people, but at the same time an abandonment of the notion that these institutions stood for different constitutions, each with its own independent legitimation.

A mixed constitution could remain a topic of discussion as long as the goal was solving the problem of a constitution by combining the monarchical principle with representation of the estates, as was the case in early German liberalism. Once the kind of democratic constitutionalism established by the American and French revolutions was accepted, the type of constitution inherited from antiquity necessarily became obsolete. The idea of the mixed constitution is occasionally invoked today to stress that in a constitutional government the democratic-majority principle is subject to legal restrictions. This recognizes the continuity of the principle of limitation of power, but at the same time it obscures the epochal break with the past that the rise of democratic constitutionalism represents.

BIBL.: James M. Blythe, *Ideal Government and the Mixed Constitution in the Middle Ages* (Princeton 1992). Eco O. G. Haitsma Mulier, *The Myth of Venice and Dutch Republican Thought in the Seventeenth Century* (Assen 1980). Wilfried Nippel, "Ancient and Modern Republicanism: 'Mixed Constitution' and 'Ephors,'" in *The Invention of the Modern Republic,* ed. Biancamaria Fontana (New York 1994) 6–26, and *Mischverfassungstheorie und Verfassungsrealität in Antike und früher Neuzeit* (Stuttgart 1980). John G. A. Pocock, *The Machiavellian Moment* (Princeton 1975). Alois Riklin, *Machtteilung: Geschichte der Mischverfassung* (Darmstadt 1975).

W.N.

Translated by Deborah Lucas Schneider

Corneille, Pierre

French dramatic author, 1606–1684. Corneille, the dominant French playwright of the middle of the 17th century, is an excellent example of the effect of Jesuit Humanist education in France. A Norman, educated in Rouen for a legal career, he left an impressive body of plays in all major genres as well as the French 17th century's liveliest and most intelligent text on dramatic writing, *Three Discourses on the Dramatic Poem* (1660). He presented himself as a brilliant maverick, and yet his tragedies subsequently provided the models for what is now often called French classical tragedy, preparing the way for Jean Racine, a younger rival who eclipsed Corneille in the 1660s.

Corneille first specialized in romantic comedies, but he made a breakthrough with his hugely popular 1637 tragicomedy, *Le Cid* (later revised and republished as a tragedy). During the "quarrel of *Le Cid*" the French Academy criticized the play as implausible and morally indecent. Corneille retrospectively provided a theoretical justification for this work and for his subsequent variations on its theme when he issued his *Three Discourses* in 1660. This major neo-Aristotelian treatise on poetics argued that all great tragic stories must be implausible and must have their foundation in a conflict between love and ethical codes. Seizing on a passage in chapter 14 of Aristotle's *Poetics,* Corneille found there authorization for historically real but improbable events that provide models of this conflict. Corneille argued that the playwright's task is to take an implausible story and then provide psychological and contextual details that make the story believable to an audience. His preference for true but implausible stories led him to use historical subjects rather than mythological ones for almost all his major plays: classical sources such as Livy, Tacitus, Seneca, Lucan, Plutarch, Dio Cassius, and Appian of Alexandria, as well as post-classical historians such as Paul the Deacon and Baronius. The subjects of Corneille's tragedies and heroic comedies, a historic panorama, cover more than 1,000 years of Roman and Byzantine history, ranging from the combat of Horatius against the Alban champions under Tullus Hostilius (7th cen. BCE) to the Lombard king Perctarit (7th century CE). His heroes and heroines include the emperors Augustus Caesar, Otho, Titus, and Heraclius, and the empress Pulcheria, as well as Attila the Hun. Corneille and many of his contemporaries saw the sweep of Roman history without sharp distinction between classical Rome and Byzantium.

A second major innovation of Corneille's poetics is the promotion of romantic love to a status equal to family ties. This approach, which is the core of *Le Cid,* led to tragedies in which a man and a woman are attracted to each other in large part by their heroic adherence to duty, and yet that very duty puts them in opposition. Corneille saw himself as differing from Aristotle in preferring plots in which the principals are perfectly aware of identities, as opposed to the recognition-based plots favored by Aristotle.

Corneille wrote a small number of tragedies on mythological subjects, including *Medea, Andromeda, The Conquest of the Golden Fleece, Oedipus,* and—in a collaboration with Molière and Quinalt—*Psyche.* These, however, have not been widely performed or read.

BIBL.: B. Ariosto Croce, *Shakespeare e Corneille* (Paris 1920). G. Forestier, *Essai de génétique théâtrale: Corneille à l'oeuvre* (Paris 1996). A. Gasté, *La querelle du Cid* (Paris 1898). G. Lanson, *Corneille* (Paris 1898). H. Merlin-Kajman, *Public et littérature en France au XVIIe siècle* (Paris 1994). Voltaire, *Commentaires sur Corneille* (Geneva 1764).

J.D.L.

Cosmology

The image of the universe created in ancient Greece, adopted practically without modification by Latin authors, remained dominant in the West until the 17th century. With greater or lesser friction it was incorporated into the cultures of the societies of the book (Christianity, Judaism, and Islam). It was only as a result of the Scientific Revolution, which began in the West with the publication of Copernicus's work in 1543, that this older system was replaced by the modern image of the universe enshrined in Newton's *Principia mathematica philosophiae naturalis* (1687). The traditional representation of the universe, prevalent for two millennia, thus constitutes a paradigmatic expression of the classical tradition and of its fortunes through the ages. This is even more evident when one considers that the representation of the universe was intimately related not only to the content of natural science, but to every aspect of culture: from religion and theology to anthropology and history, medicine, literature, and art. Even the demolition of the traditional conception of the cosmos and its replacement by the modern, scientific image of the universe in the 16th and 17th centuries was made possible largely by philosophical and scientific concepts originating in the Stoic cosmology and Epicurean atomism of Graeco-Roman antiquity. Through these Stoic and Epicurean concepts, the classical tradition—albeit in diminished form—remained operative even after the 17th-century battle of the ancients and moderns decreed the superiority of the latter.

The traditional image of the universe is expressed in the very notion of the cosmos as an ordered and permanent structure endowed with an immanent rationality, a hierarchy of being and of value, and in which natural processes are teleologically determined. All those features originated in the philosophy of Plato and Aristotle, whose cosmology in turn represented the culmination of a tradition of natural philosophy that began with the Presocratics and drew on Near Eastern thought. The cosmology of Plato and Aristotle (with which Stoic cosmology coincides in its basic features) endowed the West with a notion of the cosmos whose plastic representation is enormously more complex than the mythical representation of the ancient Egyptians (in which Shu, the air god, separates Geb, the Earth, from Nut, the starry sky). The cosmos that the Platonic, Aristotelian, and Stoic tradition bequeathed to the West presents some distinct features: it is a finite, spherical, and unique world, closely linked to the divine (or, for Stoics, immanent) intelligence, and divided into an eternal dualist hierarchy of supralunar/celestial and sublunar/elemental levels. It is centered on an immovable

Earth, around which the planets and the stars trace the perfectly circular and regular orbits that express their divinity and that mathematical astronomers from Eudoxus (4th cent. BCE) to Ptolemy (2nd cent. CE) tried to reproduce. Eternal and uncreated (in Aristotle) or engendered (according to Plato's *Timaeus,* but *ab aeterno* according to the Platonic tradition), the universe is a stable and permanent structure by virtue of its governing laws. This general convergence does not, however, rule out the existence of differences, occasionally of some importance. Thus, the Stoics affirmed the existence of an infinite void beyond the finite and unique cosmos, periodically consumed by fire (*ekpyrosis*). Epicureans revived atomism and the conception of an infinite void or space with innumerable worlds participating in an incessant process of generation and corruption, free from any sort of divine providence or goal.

Excepting the Latin translation and commentary on Plato's *Timaeus* by Calcidius (4th cent.), the cosmology of the high medieval Latin West was constructed in the absence of both Plato's and Aristotle's works. Until the 12th century, the reigning image of the world was derived instead from indirect sources of a Platonic and Stoic character. Macrobius's commentary (5th cent.) on Cicero's *Somnium Scipionis,* Martianus Capella's encyclopedic *De nuptiis Philologiae et Mercurii* (6th cent.), and Pliny's *Historia naturalis* (1st cent.) were the fundamental authors and works. Together with the information available in the writings of the Church Fathers, these authors and works established the representation of the universe—Platonic in its essence, with some Stoic contamination—that the authors of the European West adopted as their own. This representation of the universe found magnificent expression in Boethius' *De consolatione philosophiae* (6th cent.)—particularly in the extremely influential verse 3.9: *O qui perpetua mundum ratione gubernas* (O you who in perpetual order govern the universe)—as well as a far-reaching metaphysical articulation in Johannes Scotus Eriugena's *De divisione naturae* (9th cent.). It culminated in the Platonism of the school of Chartres (12th cent.), with authors such as William of Conches, Thierry of Chartres, and Bernard Silvestris.

In the Islamic world, meanwhile, the Aristotelian formulation of ancient cosmology—more or less contaminated by Neoplatonism, and complemented by the (more or less contradictory) astronomy of Ptolemy—constituted the nucleus of philosophical activity until the end of the Middle Ages. Here the fundamental reference works were Aristotle's *De caelo* (together with his other writings on natural philosophy and the 12th book of his *Metaphysics,* which contributed, as a theological complement, the doctrine of the Divine Intelligence and the doctrine of the celestial spheres and their motive intelligences) and Ptolemy's *Almagest* and *Hypotheses on the Planets.* Ptolemy's *Tetrabiblos* also served as a fundamental authority within the field of astrology, a discipline intimately linked to Aristotelian cosmology and which, through various channels, had permeated the Islamic world. On the basis of the Aristotelian conception of the sublunar world's inferiority and dependence on its celestial counterpart, astrology experienced an enormous efflorescence in Islamic culture, with particular application to the fields of anthropology and medicine (in conjunction with the correspondence of macrocosmos/microcosmos), as well as in that of history (the succession of empires and religions) with the theory of the "great planetary conjunctions." This theory was developed by Albumasar (9th cent.) in *De magnis coniunctionibus,* a work that was to enjoy great success in the West beginning in the 12th century. In the context of astrology, the motif of the celestial images (both the 48 constellations into which, beginning with Ptolemy, the 1,022 stars constituting the cosmos were organized, and the seven planets) offers a splendid example of the endurance of the classical tradition, and of its gradual diffusion across cultures of different languages and religions. Its presence was as important for astronomy, medicine, and art as it was for religion and spirituality. It was, in effect, the foundation of the religion practiced by the Harranian Sabeans. This motif is also present in the important 13th-century manual of magic known as the *Picatrix,* which was assembled from eastern materials in Arabic Spain and subsequently enjoyed great success in Christian Europe during the late Middle Ages and Renaissance.

The transmission of Aristotelian-Ptolemaic cosmology (in both its original sources and the form to which it had evolved in the Muslim world) to the Latin West began in the 12th century, through Sicily and Spain. Even though the Platonic cosmos shared fundamental features with those of Aristotle and Ptolemy, the arrival of this new system revolutionized the intellectual panorama and brought about a thorough change of authorities and reference works. It also enabled the assimilation of a theoretical corpus far richer than the Platonic one: namely, Aristotle's encyclopedia and the works of its Islamic commentators.

The assimilation of this Graeco-Arabic cosmology, which coincided with the consolidation and expansion of the universities, continued throughout the 13th century. It was a difficult process, and it sparked significant doctrinal conflicts along the way. These culminated in the famous condemnation of 1277, in which the bishop Etienne Tempier prohibited 219 propositions in circulation at the University of Paris, particularly among members of the arts faculty—that is, the philosophers. The assimilation in the Latin West of Arabized Greek cosmology raised numerous problems stemming from its conflict with Christian dogma. Above all else was the clash of certain cosmological theses with Christian notions of divine liberty and omnipotence: namely, the eternity of the world, necessitarianism in the universe's divine production, the undeniable finitude and (most important) uniqueness of the world, and the Earth's centrality and immobility. The condemnation of 1277 affirmed the primacy of divine liberty and omnipotence over and against the necessitarianism central to Graeco-Arabic cosmology, establishing that the uniqueness of the world, the centrality and immobility of the Earth—in general, the structure of the Aristotelian universe—were not absolutely necessary, but rather were the result of divine free choice among a variety of initial possibilities. Beyond this ontological devaluation, however, the universe's basic structure and functioning remained recognizably Aristotelian and traditional. The most patent demonstration of this continuity is Dante's *Divine Comedy* (14th cent.); the poet's itinerary through the three kingdoms of the afterlife (Inferno, Purgatory, and Paradise) is mapped onto the Christianized cosmos of Aristotle and Ptolemy.

The cultural revolution of the Renaissance initially had little effect on the field of cosmology. Humanists of the 16th century contemplated the same classical cosmos inherited from Aristotle and Ptolemy (and adapted to suit Christianity) as their forefather Petrarch had known in the 14th century. The Humanists' recovery of the corpus of ancient philosophical currents did little to alter the situation. Though they introduced some significant modifications, Renaissance Platonism (especially in the works of Marsilio Ficino) and the so-called ancient theology (especially Hermeticism) did not affect the fundamental components of classical cosmology. Thus the celestial ether came to be seen less as a fifth element distinct from the four sublunar elements than as purified air, at the same time as the celestial bodies were conceived as pure fire. Likewise, the increased familiarity with the ancient Stoic sources (Cicero, Seneca's *Naturales quaestiones*) in the 16th century allowed for proposals for specific modifications within the structure of the geocentric cosmos, which undermined the credibility of the Aristotelian cosmos and were incorporated into the new cosmology. In his preface, *De usu optices,* to the 1557 Latin translation of Euclid's *Optica,* the Frenchman Jean Pena rejected the existence of solid celestial spheres, affirming instead the existence of a fluid sky of air extending to the stars. Pena also bestowed celestial rank on some comets. The recovery of Epicureanism, begun in the 15th century as a result of the discovery of Lucretius's *De rerum natura* and the Latin translation of Diogenes Laertius's *Lives of the Philosophers,* initially had little significance in cosmological circles. Epicureanism's incompatibility with the Aristotelian-Ptolemaic, Platonic, and Stoic cosmos was so great that it could be marshaled effectively only after an entirely new image of the world had begun to circulate.

This new image was Copernicus's heliocentrism, first presented in the 1543 edition of *De revolutionibus orbium coelestium.* Copernicus, however, did not offer his proposal to the reader as a novelty. Rather, he described it as an attempt to correct an error within the existing cosmological tradition, to restore the truth already known to the ancient Greeks. Copernicus knew that the cosmological principles of his astronomy (the centrality and immobility of the Sun and the daily and annual movement of the Earth) had been postulated by Aristarchus of Samos (3rd cent. BCE). Moreover, Copernicus identified these principles with the cosmology of the Pythagorean Philolaus of Croton (5th cent. BCE) and with other Pythagorean and Platonic authors' notion that the Earth undergoes a daily rotational motion. Thus, to its early partisans (Thomas Digges, Giordano Bruno, Johannes Kepler) the new Copernican cosmology represented the restoration of the ancient cosmology of the Pythagoreans. Kepler even asserted that Aristotle's critique of Pythagorean cosmology was based on an erroneous interpretation, an error caused by his failure to grasp its true meaning (as Copernicus defined it). As late as the second half of the 17th century Newton still affirmed that his theory of the planetary system merely recapitulated the cosmological wisdom of the ancients, buried within mythological fables like Pan's flute or Apollo's lyre.

The rapid transformation of the Copernican cosmos—originally finite, unique, and organized into an internal hierarchy, like the Aristotelian universe—propagated a cosmological revolution that established a radically different image of the universe within Europe. At the same time, however, this new representation remained rooted in the classical tradition, insofar as it integrated Platonic, Stoic, and even Epicurean components. On the authority of Seneca's *Naturales quaestiones,* comets were redefined as celestial bodies and said to trace closed orbits around the sun. The immobilization of the sphere of fixed stars permitted Giordano Bruno, as Lucretius's heir, to open the universe to the infinite and conceive of the stars as other suns, each one orbited by its own planets and comets (the plurality of worlds). Galileo's application of the telescope to astronomical observation beginning in 1609 inaugurated a new era in cosmology that seemed to confirm these theories by means of scientific experiments. The 17th century also witnessed the incorporation of atomist ontology in the new cosmology: the vacuum and atoms definitively arrived as components of the universe, at the same time as the mechanicist representation of physical processes called into question the traditional teleological vision of nature. Yet the old geocentric cosmology was not the only competitor with which Copernicanism had to contend. In the 1580s various authors (including Tycho Brahe) postulated that the true "system of the world" is geoheliocentric—in other words, that both the Sun and the Moon orbit a central and unmoving Earth, while the remaining five planets orbit the Sun. The adoption of this Tychonic system by the powerful Society of Jesus in the wake of the Church's 1616 condemnation of the idea of terrestrial motion guaranteed its wide acceptance in the 17th century.

Yet by then a variety of developments had already begun to destroy the classical notion of the cosmos and to contribute the outlines of a new conceptualization of the universe. These included Kepler's celestial dynamics, with its three laws of planetary motion; Galileo's conception of a universal, mathematical science of motion; the various speculations about the infinity of space and time; the atomist ontology restored by Gassendi and Pascal's experimental demonstration of the vacuum; and the principle of inertia. All these came together in the vast Newtonian synthesis, crowned by the law of universal attraction.

Newton's *Principia mathematica philosophiae naturalis* brought the Scientific Revolution to a close and established the cosmology that would remain dominant in the West until the end of the 19th century. It spread across Europe throughout the 18th century. The French translation of the *Principia* was a decisive factor in the incorporation of Newtonian mechanics and cosmology into the ideology of the European Enlightenment. So, too, was the support of Voltaire, author of *Les éléments de la philosophie de Newton* (1738) and the supremely brilliant *Lettres philosophiques* (1734), in which the Newtonian universe replaced Descartes's cosmological "novel" (*roman*).

Before this moment, the evolution of modern cosmology had been guided by a fundamentally synchronous perspective—that is, its objective had always been knowledge of the current structure of the universe, without regard to its genesis. The sole exception was Descartes's attempt in *Principes de la philosophie* (1644) and *Le monde* (published posthumously in 1664) to narrate the generation of the contemporary universe as a function of the action of the laws of motion on primordial matter—that is, as a mechanical process. According to Descartes, God must have created matter and its laws, but not the existing order of the world. Yet Newton strongly rejected Descartes's theories, arguing that "this most elegant system of the sun, planets, and comets could not have arisen without the design and dominion of an intelligent and powerful being" (*Principia,* 2nd ed., 1713, General Scholium, trans. I. B. Cohen and A. Whitman). In this way, Newton's cosmology retained teleology and providentialism, both of which were abundantly developed in the "natural theology" that flourished in the 18th century (particularly in England, where its intent was apologist).

By the end of the 18th century scholars also had begun to direct their attention to the genesis and history of the solar system, the galaxy, and, thus, of the universe. Immanuel Kant's *Allgemeine Naturgeschichte und Theorie des Himmels* (1755) and Pierre Simon Laplace's *Exposition du système du monde* (1796, with various subsequent editions) constituted the first great milestones in that direction. Both attempted to derive the current system of the universe from the action of the Newtonian laws of mechanics, without divine intervention. In this conflict, we can recognize a new expression of the ancient Greek dispute between the mechanicist physicists (atomists, Anaxagoras) and those philosophers who, beginning with Socrates, had inserted intelligence and final causes (the "argument from design") into their cosmological explanations. This tension—and, by extension, the fading presence of the classical tradition—may, in fact, have survived to the present. Nevertheless, since the 19th century the classical tradition has ceased to be the direct and necessary source of inspiration for the most accomplished European intellectuals working in this field. By this time, the battle of the ancients and moderns had been decided definitively in favor of the latter, whose intellectual emancipation was practically complete. This process of emancipation coincided with another development absent from the classical tradition: the divorce of natural science from philosophy.

BIBL.: Rémi Brague, *The Wisdom of the World: The Human Experience of the Universe in Western Thought,* trans. T. Lavender Fagan (Chicago 2003). Noriss S. Hetherington, ed., *Encyclopedia of Cosmology: Historical, Philosophical, and Scientific Foundations of Modern Cosmology* (New York 1993). Michael Hoskin, ed., *The Cambridge Illustrated History of Astronomy* (Cambridge 1997). Alexandre Koyré, *From the Closed World to the Infinite Universe* (Baltimore 1957). Thomas S. Kuhn, *The Copernican Revolution: Planetary Astronomy in the Development of Western Thought* (Cambridge, Mass., 1957). Michel-Pierre Lerner, *Le monde des sphères,* 2 vols. (2nd ed., Paris 2008). Fritz Saxl, *La fede negli astri: Dall'antichità al Rinascimento* (Turin 1985). M.A.G.

Translated by Adam G. Beaver

Cupid

Personification of amorous desire and fertility, from the Latin *cupido,* also called Amor or Eros (Greek). In Hesiod's *Theogony* Cupid is conceived of as an elemental force of the cosmos, but since the classical period, as the son of Aphrodite and Ares, he has symbolized sexual love. An exception is his philosophical invocation as an intellectual striving for knowledge of the Ideas, as in Plato's *Symposium* and other texts. This work is also the basis for the symbolic dichotomy between a heavenly Cupid, seeking divine contemplation, and an earthly one, beholden to sexuality. From the classical period onward, Cupid is depicted as a winged youth. Only in the Hellenistic period did he receive the bow and arrow and boyishly round figure that would remain his characteristic attributes in his post-antique reception. These can be seen frequently in Pompeian wall paintings and on gems.

Cupid appeared in ancient literary texts mostly as a minor character or as a mechanism for advancing the plot, as when he is sent by his mother to kindle the love affair between Dido and Aeneas in Virgil's *Aeneid.* Except for Apuleius' tale *Cupid and Psyche* (2nd cent. CE), in which Cupid is struck by his own weapons and thus becomes the protagonist of a love story, he lacks his own mythology or any wider cultic worship independent of Aphrodite (the only known cult site is in Thespiae). Both aspects enhance Cupid's power as an allegorical symbol and offer welcome gaps for creative reception. Besides purely ornamental depictions, then, there are two main types of reception that, usually based on Apuleius and ancient mythographers, fill out Cupid's *vitae:* allegorical and mythological narrative. The two are not mutually exclusive, but rather collaborate in achieving the enduring triumph of the boy with bow and arrow from antiquity to modernity. Virgil's *omnia vincit amor* (*Eclogues* 10.69) provides a fitting motto to their manifold success. All the while Cupid—and the sentiment he embodies—remained ambivalent: ancient lyric poetry speaks of Cupid as *glukupikros* ("sweet-bitter"); he shifts between carnal (*amor carnalis*) and spiritual (*amor spiritualis*) love depending on the significance given to his symbolic power; he often seems inconsistent and rather undiscriminating.

In medieval and early-modern reception, Cupid was frequently found in manuscripts as an ornamental embellishment as well as an illustration of the passion of love. His iconography was initially based entirely on the ancient tradition, but the childlike Cupid came increasingly to be accompanied by the youthful god of love. The reason seems to lie in the division of his reception into pagan-mythographical and Christian-metaphysical branches, which, in connection with Neoplatonic interpretations (e.g., Ficino, *De amore,* 1469), uses Cupid as a symbol for pure, sensual love and assimilates his iconography to that of angels. This tendency had already found literary expression in Heinrich von Veldeke's *Eneasroman* (ca. 1187), which distinguishes between the names of Cupid, who stands for carnal love, and Amor, who embodies metaphysical desire, as well as in minnesang and troubadour verse. Other influential works were Dante's *Vita nuova* and the popular *Roman de la rose* (13th cent.), contemporary illustrations of which depict Cupid as an angelic youth in courtly dress.

In this form the figure of Cupid is thus firmly integrated into the Christian tradition, but his pagan, childlike aspect can at the same time be used as a negative symbol for *Amor carnalis.* Intimately related to this development was the emergence of blindness as one of Cupid's attributes in texts and illustrations. Beginning in the 13th century with Thomasin von Zerclaere's didactic poem *Der Wälsche Gast,* and continuing in French and Latin versions of the *Ovidius moralizatus* and Boccaccio's *Genealogia Deorum gentilium* (1350–1367), this new tradition contrasted *Amor spiritualis* with arbitrariness and unpredictability, whose negative symbol was the inspiration for Baptista Fulgosus' *Anteros* (1496). With his blindfold, Cupid became associated with other negative symbols of Christian iconography, such as Night and Fortune.

In the transition to the Renaissance, the angelic Cupid figure receded especially in Italy and yielded to the youthful, naked version, whose rather negative symbolic significance is transformed into an ambivalent one, capable of embodying all aspects of amorous desire. One of the earliest returns to the ancient Hellenistic type is Piero della Francesca's *Blind Cupid* in Arezzo. The image of Cupid became iconographically unified, and as a result his concrete significance in various contexts and with different attributes can be more clearly interpreted. Thus, the same figure can have negative connotations when blindfolded, but without a blindfold or in the process of removing it (Lucas Cranach the Elder, *Amor nimmt sich die Augenbinde ab,* ca. 1530, and illustrations of Plato's *Symposium*) can be understood as a personification, or the inchoate comprehension, of divine love. New attributes also emerged that suggest definite connotations, such as talons on his feet, iconography otherwise known from depictions of the devil (such as the fresco depicting the allegory of chastity in the Basilica of San Francesco in Assisi, ca. 1320).

From the Renaissance onward Cupid was omnipresent in art and embodied a multitude of meanings. We find him sleeping as a symbol for absent love (Michelangelo, *Sleeping Cupid,* 1496, now lost), crying in disappointment (Rembrandt, *Danaë,* 1636), fighting or playing with Anteros (Alciato, *Emblemata,* 1534), as a symbol of heavenly and earthly love (Titian, *Sacred and Profane Love,* 1512). Frequent subjects of painting, which had earlier provided popular material for Hellenistic verse, were Aphrodite's punishment or disarming of Cupid (Correggio, *Venus Disarming Cupid,* 1524; François Boucher, *Venus Disarming Cupid,* 1749) and his education (Titian, Correggio, Giulio Romano, and others). Anacreon's poetry is the source for the motif of the god being stung by a bee, as drawn by Dürer (*Venus and Cupid, the Honey-Thief,* 1514). Cupid often served to lead the viewer's eye and arouse amorous desire (Botticelli, *Primavera*) or functioned as the escort of Venus/Aphrodite—whether personified or figuratively cited on the goddess's belt (Francesco del Cossa, *Allegory of April,* Palazzo della Schifanoia).

Beginning in the 15th century Cupid merged iconographically, but without concrete significance, with the putto figure initiated by Donatello and became an ornamental genre figure for gracing garlands and friezes. Cupid is also found in this form on numerous *memento mori* paintings (e.g., Pieter Moninckx's *Amor Sleeping on a Skull,* mid-17th cent.), although he can also symbolize death by holding an inverted torch, as on the tomb of Antonio Canova (1819). New finds from antiquity occasionally give rise to new impulses. For example, the 1759 discovery in the Villa of Ariadne in Stabiae of a Roman mural showing a woman selling Cupids quickly made its way into contemporary art (Joseph-Marie Vien, 1763).

Cupid's literary reception has unfolded on different levels since the Renaissance. Strongest by far is his presence in numerous poetic descriptions of his character. Fired by the reception of ancient love poetry (Sappho, Anacreon, Ovid, Catullus), they use his figure to play through all the facets of amorous desire and its adventures, and they can be found in all national languages, from Petrarch's *Il trionfo dell'Amore* (1340–1344), to Ronsard's *Le petit enfant Amour* (1553), to the Amor-inspired poetry of *Genieästhetik.* In broader narrative contexts, Cupid appears as a main character mostly in creative adaptations of Apuleius' much-read tale of *Amor and Psyche,* such as in Galeotto del Carretto's *Le nozze di Psiche e di Cupidine* (1520), Hercole Udine's epic *Avvenimenti amorosi di Psiche* (ca. 1598), and numerous plays on the subject, such as Calderón's *Ni Amor se libra da Amor* (ca. 1640). He takes on smaller roles in love novels, which—following ancient and Byzantine tradition—use his help to bring couples together (e.g., Boccaccio, *Filocolo,* ca. 1338). Cupid also has a secure place in (neo-Latin) epithalamia, where he fulfills the same function.

Cupid appears onstage in Jacobean masques (e.g., Ben Jonson, *The Hue and Cry after Cupid,* 1608, *Love Restored,* 1612; James Shirley, *Cupid and Death,* 1653). His proverbial blindness is a central theme in Shakespeare's *A Midsummer Night's Dream.* Opera discovered him as a subject in the 17th century (e.g., Filiberto Laurenzi and Andrea Mattioli, *L'esiglio d'Amore,* 1651; B. Ferrari, *Le ali d'Amore,* 1660; Maurizio Cazzati, *Le gare d'Amore e di Marte,* 1662; Pietro Cesti, *Le disgrazie d'Amore,* 1667; Cherubini, *Anacreon,* 1803). The tradition of madrigals and chansons about Cupid began early (Francesco Landini, *Questa fanciulla, Amor,* 1397). Ballet became the most popular form of his musical reception in the 19th and 20th centuries; examples include Auguste Vestris, *Mars et l'Amour* (1815), Lev Ivanov, *Cupid's Pranks* (1890), Mary Skeaping, *Cupido* (1956), and Erick Hawkins, *The Birth of Eros from the World Egg* (1987), which returns to the Orphic origins of Eros's birth by way of modern dance. The popular reception of Cupid at the beginning of the 21st century is completely detached from such origins: today he is found for the most part on Valentine's Day cards and gifts as a banal symbol of love.

BIBL.: G. Niccoli, *Cupid, Satyr, and the Golden Age: Pastoral Dramatic Scenes of the Late Renaissance* (New York 1989). E. Panofsky, "Der blinde Amor," in *Studien zur Ikonologie. Humanistische Themen in der Kunst der Renaissance* (Cologne 1980) 153–202. R. Stuveras, *Le putto dans l'art romain* (Brussels 1969).
M.BA.

Translated by Patrick Baker

Cyclops

The mythical one-eyed giant, blinded by Odysseus during his travels returning from Troy. One of a clan of Cyclopes inhabiting a distant island (later identified as Sicily). Subsequently a pastoral shepherd, lover of Galatea.

For the story of the most famous Cyclops, the inhospitable and man-eating Polyphemus, see Homer, *Odyssey* 9.105–566: after inebriating and blinding Polyphemus, Odysseus and his crew escape from the giant's cave strapped to the underbellies of his livestock. But the Cyclops recurs in countless different folktales the world over, and classical traditions themselves were also varied (for the Cyclopes as craftsmen see Hesiod, *Theogony* 139–146, 501–506).

The Homeric version of the blinding of the Cyclops can be seen to have lain behind most ancient visual representations. It also inspired the invention of earlier episodes in the character's life. For ancient and modern authors alike, the myth has proved particularly useful as a means of literary self-positioning, that is, of negotiating relations with former poetic traditions. Euripides' satyr play *Cyclops,* for example, wholly burlesques the Homeric episode; Theocritus' 11th Idyll alludes to the Homeric story but sympathetically reveals the Cyclops in his youth, a naive shepherd desperately in love with Galatea; Virgil has one of Odysseus's comrades, Achaemenides, haplessly abandoned on Sicily, recount the story to Aeneas after the event (*Aeneid* 3.568–683); Ovid mocks the Virgilian "post-Homeric" stance by having the now aged Achaemenides recount the episode to a different member of Odysseus's crew (*Metamorphoses* 14.154–222). Such literary stratification of the story forms the backdrop for the most famous modern retelling of the myth, in the second book (episode 12) of James Joyce's *Ulysses* (see Scott 1995, 62–75): in the showdown between Leopold Bloom and the glassy-eyed regulars of Barney Kiernan's pub, Joyce alludes to the full gamut of previous renditions of the episode in order to ponder his own situation within a Western tradition of epic poetry.

A plethora of subsequent traditions has also centered on the figure. The 12th-century allegorist Bernardus Silvestris, following Fulgentius (5th–6th cents.), interpreted the blinding of Polyphemus as a parable for the extinction of myopic vanity by fiery intellect. After the discovery of the Americas, other writers compared the traits of the Cyclopes with those demonstrated by the inhabitants of the New World, sometimes deemed to share—as George Sandys put it in 1632—their "folly of barbarous strength, feebled with vices." Artists of the 17th and 18th centuries, foremost among them Poussin, Lorrain, and Turner, treated the land of the Cyclopes in a more idealizing fashion, associating it with an age of natural abundance and fulfilled love (compare with Góngora's Spanish poem *Polifemo,* written ca. 1614). The Cyclops has also appeared in less obvious guises: as the epitome of human arrogance and impiety he is evoked in the character of Satan (in the works of Tasso, Spencer, Milton, and Cowley, among others); and as a cannibalistic monster he is recalled in the figure of Hairy Carl, Spenser's allegory of Lust (*Faerie Queene* 4.7.5).

Most influential of all, however, has been the Theocritean tradition of the bucolic Cyclops, as developed in Ovid's *Metamorphoses* 13.838–897. Ovid's Polyphemus, rejected by Galatea in favor of Acis, is the subject of numerous paintings (among them, by Carracci, Fuseli, and Moreau), poems (for example, Castellejo's *Canto de Polifemo* and Ronsard's *Le Cyclope amoureux*), and music (most famously, Handel's masque *Acis and Galatea*). Reworkings of the episode are also included in Petrarch's *Triumphus Cupidinis* and Ariosto's *Orlando furioso.*

The end of the 20th century saw numerous new Cyclopes, from the Orwellian Great Shepherd of Derek Walcott's *Odyssey: A Stage Version* (1993) to the one-eyed Ku Klux Klan leader Big Dan of *O Brother, Where Art Thou?* (2000), directed by Joel and Ethan Coen. More puzzling is the Cyclops of contemporary popular culture: numerous science fiction comics and movies (for example, *X-Men, Krull, Futurama*) can boast a Cyclops all their own. Whatever the relationship of these Cyclopes to their classical prototypes, they nevertheless testify to the figure's continuing grip on the Western imagination.

BIBL.: E. W. Leach, "Polyphemus in a Landscape: Traditions of Pastoral Courtship," in *The Pastoral Landscape,* ed. J. D. Hunt, Studies in the History of Art 36 (Washington, D.C., 1992) 63–87. M. E. Lehrer, *Classical Myth and the Polifemo of Góngora* (Potomac, Md., 1989). H. M. Richmond, "Polyphemus in England: A Study in Comparative Literature," *Comparative Literature* 12 (1960) 229–242. S. C. Scott, "Man, Mind, and Monster: Polyphemus from Homer through Joyce," *Classical and Modern Literature* 16 (1995) 19–75. M.S.

Cynicism

Literally "Philosophy of the Dogs"; personified by the legendary Diogenes of Sinope (4th cent. BCE). Surprisingly, given its ambiguous status in the ancient world—socially marginal yet symbolically central—the afterlife of Cynicism (from *kuōn,* "dog") is the liveliest and most varied of any of the ancient philosophical sects, extending from philosophy (e.g., Diderot, Nietzsche, and Foucault) to politics (e.g., anarchism), literature (e.g., Menippean satire, the aphorism), and the visual arts (from Raphael, Velázquez, Poussin, and Rubens to Daumier and political cartoons) to journalism and pop culture. The famous story of Diogenes' taking a lantern in broad daylight to search in vain for an honest man—actually a "human being" (*anthrōpos*) in the ancient version—while apocryphal, is one of the best known, and most widely appropriated, of all anecdotes from classical antiquity.

The protean and still proliferating legacy of Cynicism reflects its wayward nature as a philosophical movement: it was atypical in all respects. Nietzsche called the Cynics "the humorists of antiquity," because their teachings are preserved not in dialogues and treatises but in seriocomic anecdotes and aphorisms culled from the lost Cynic classics of the 4th century BCE and attributed to the founders of Cynicism: Antisthenes, Diogenes, Crates, and Menippus. Rejecting the prevailing conceptions of the good life, both conventional and philosophical, they promoted a radical alternative exemplified by the eccentric exile, Diogenes, whose quixotic determination to live out his heterodox philosophy of "life according to nature" in full public view—eating, urinating, masturbating, sleeping, teaching, and begging on the streets of Athens and Corinth—made him both an intellectual scandal and a touchstone of philosophic authenticity rivaled only by Socrates. Indeed, Plato called him "a Socrates gone mad."

Though Cynicism was never institutionalized as a school like the Stoa or the Academy, it was the closest the ancient world ever came to a popular philosophical movement open to all. The Cynics considered gender and class irrelevant to the practice of philosophy, and poverty as positively edifying; in the same vein, the traditional conception of patriotism, of being a loyal citizen of the fatherland (*patria*), was rejected in favor of "cosmopolitanism," of being a citizen of the cosmos, perhaps Diogenes' most far-reaching invention.

The fascination exerted by the iconic figure of Diogenes, freely dispensing his topsy-turvy wisdom while living in his doghouse (more accurately, a *pithos,* a large wine cask), is the most obvious reason for the longevity of Cynicism as a cultural phenomenon. But the salient ideas of his philosophy have had a trajectory and velocity of their own. Three are fundamental: first, the founding metaphysical claim that nature, not culture (the gods and laws of society), is the sole authority on how to live. As adapted first by the Stoics and later by Romantics like Rousseau and, in our own time, by ecologists, animal rights activists, and many environmental interests, the significance of this idea can hardly be exaggerated. Second, the practical, ethical corollary of this claim: a mental and physical regimen (*askēsis*) designed to free the human animal from the misguided and superfluous demands of society by making the individual as adaptable and self-sufficient as any other creature. This idea has appealed to ascetics and social rebels, beginning with the Christians. The third idea is entailed by the first two: the need for active resistance to the social control of cognition, through defiant acts of truth-telling (*parrhēsia*) addressed to those in power (e.g., Alexander) and the innovation of a seriocomic literature designed to deface the idols of the tribe, these being myth and religion, law and custom, and, not least, philosophy itself. The Cynics made laughter and fearless speech the hallmark of the true philosopher.

It is important to remember that "ancient Cynicism" actually refers to a process of transmission and reception that begins (for us) with Greek authors of the Roman imperial era such as Plutarch (ca. 50–120 CE), Lucian (ca. 120–180), and Diogenes Laertius (fl. early 3rd cent.). When we first meet the Cynic Diogenes in the pages of our most important extant source, book 6 of Diogenes Laertius' *Lives and Opinions of Famous Philosophers,* his image and its meaning have already been shaped by oral and written traditions for more than 500 years. Thus, unlike Platonism, for example, Cynicism cannot be separated from the history of its reception. And that reception itself was rarely free of ambivalence, even in antiquity. Lucian, for example, took a dim, even cynical, view of the practicing Cynics of his own day (e.g., *On the Death of Peregrinus, The Runaways*) even while reviving and ventriloquizing the legendary Cynics of old in his Menippean works—such as *Menippus, Icaromenippus,* and *Dialogues of the Dead.* Some associations of the modern concept of cynicism (which does in fact derive from ancient Cynicism)—irreverence, superiority, shamelessness—were always there and could be seized on by critics. Beginning at least with Augustine (*City of God* 14.20.23) there was among some Christians a deep suspicion of Cynic shamelessness, an indispensable canine virtue; but that did not stop Dante from placing Diogenes among the greatest philosophers in the first circle of the Inferno, the Limbo reserved for virtuous pagans, or Boccaccio in his *Fall of Great Men* (*De casibus virorum illustrium,* 1355–1360) from citing Diogenes cheek by jowl with John the Baptist.

Although the Cynic philosopher was evidently known in the Middle Ages from a variety of Arabic and Latin sources (e.g., Cicero, Valerius Maximus, Seneca, Macrobius), the modern history of his reception begins with the recovery of book 6 of Diogenes Laertius in Ambrogio Traversari's Latin translation (1433) and the first printing of the Greek text (Basel 1533). In the early 16th century the publication of Cynic-inspired literary texts such as the Latin translations of Lucian by Erasmus and Thomas

More and François Rabelais's *Histories of Gargantua and Pantagruel* (1530s) ignited an unprecedented vogue for Menippean satire throughout Renaissance Europe. Ironically, the enormous popularity of Lucian's Menippean works, which inspired original satires as well as imitations and translations in the vernacular languages, would make his reception the primary literary mode for the survival of Cynicism in Europe. Also important were anthologies of apothegms, a popular Renaissance genre (a prominent example is Erasmus's *Adages*); these routinely gave more entries to Diogenes than to any other philosopher. Antisthenes, Crates, and even Demonax were also well represented. It was in this cultural context that Velázquez chose to paint a full-length portrait of Menippus (now in the Prado, Madrid).

More systematic scrutiny of the Cynics began with Pierre Bayle, famous for his *Historical and Critical Dictionary* (1697); his work cast doubt on the historical credibility of the anecdotal tradition (e.g., of Alexander the Great having met Diogenes). But the Cynics did not lose the prestige they had enjoyed in the Renaissance until Hegel (1770–1831), the founder of the history of philosophy in the modern sense, dismissed the importance of biography in favor of the rational content of a philosopher's work—thus reducing the history of philosophy to the history of ideas. Yet it is precisely because Cynic thought has been conveyed primarily in literary form—anecdotes and aphorisms—that the most illuminating stages of its reception are not scholarly treatments in histories of philosophy but the topical and literary responses of philosophers who were artists. This aspect of the reception reached its apogee in Diderot, who not only wrote the article on the Cynics for the *Encyclopédie* (1751–1772) but also produced the literary masterpiece of the Cynic tradition, *Rameau's Nephew* (1761?), a work so radically original that he refrained from publishing it. Among modern thinkers only Nietzsche grasped the modern significance of Cynicism as profoundly: he boasts ironically in his late autobiographical work, *Ecce Homo* (1888), that his own books attained here and there "the highest thing that can be attained on earth—Cynicism."

It would be a mistake, however, to suggest that modern reception of Cynicism ended with Nietzche. In the 20th century the mythical Diogenes searching in vain for an honest man lived on in political journalism and cartoons, and Cynic mockery of the idols of the tribe lives on in many forms, from the novel to sketch comedy. At a more reflective level, four moments stand out: the heterodox argument of Mikhail Bakhtin (1895–1975) that ancient Menippean satire is crucial to the genealogy of the modern novel; the attempt to understand modern cynicism by contrasting it systematically with its ancient prototype, which produced a philosophical best seller in Germany, Peter Sloterdijk's *Critique of Cynical Reason* (*Kritik der zynischen Vernunft,* 1983; trans. 1987), but was more philosophically successful in H. Niehues-Pröbsting's *Diogenes' Cynicism and the Concept of Cynicism* (*Der Kynismus des Diogenes und der Begriff des Zynismus,* 1979); the late work of Michel Foucault on the theory and practice of *parrhēsia* in antiquity; and, in classical studies, the recent work of M.-O. Goulet-Cazé, which has reinvigorated the study of Cynicism as an ethically original and philosophically demanding practice (*askēsis)* or way of life.

BIBL.: R. Bracht Branham, *Unruly Eloquence: Lucian and the Comedy of Traditions* (Cambridge, Mass., 1989). R. Bracht Branham and M.-O. Goulet-Cazé, eds., *The Cynics: The Cynic Movement in Antiquity and Its Legacy* (Berkeley 1996). D. R. Dudley, *A History of Cynicism from Diogenes to the 6th Century* A.D. (London 1937). M. Foucault, *Fearless Speech* (Los Angeles 2001). P. Marshall, *Demanding the Impossible: A History of Anarchism* (London 1992). H. Niehues-Pröbsting, *Der Kynismus des Diogenes and der Begriff des Zynismus,* 2nd ed. (Frankfurt 1988; 1st publ. 1979). J. C. Relihan, *Ancient Menippean Satire* (Baltimore 1992). S. Schmitt, *Diogenes: Studien zu seiner Ikonographie in der niederländischen Emblematik und Malerei des 16. and 17. Jahrhunderts* (Hildesheim 1993). P. Sloterdijk, *Kritik der zynischen Vernunft* (1983), trans. M. Eldred as *Critique of Cynical Reason* (Minneapolis 1987).

B.BR.

D

Dacier, Anne

In an era disdainful of learned women, Anne Dacier (1647–1720) emerged as a highly respected scholar whose role in the Homeric controversy was significant. Both as an editor and, more important, as a translator, she did more to popularize the classics than to advance philology and history; by emphasizing skill and accuracy in translation over aesthetics, she broke with the tradition of the *belles infidèles.*

Anne Dacier was the daughter of the great Protestant scholar Tanneguy Le Fèvre, and she benefited from his instruction. Following her father's death in 1672, she continued the work of that indefatigable philologist, chiefly by producing an edition of Callimachus (1675); the volume, which enjoyed some success (Graevius's edition in 1697 included certain passages), clearly owed more to the research of the father than to that of his inexperienced daughter. She was penniless, but she had the support of Pierre-Daniel Huet, assistant tutor of the dauphin, son of Louis XIV. Between 1674 and 1683 Huet assigned her the task of preparing several short, simple volumes on the minor historians for the collection *Ad usum Delphini:* Florus, Dictys of Crete, and Dares the Phrygian (regarded at the time as historians), as well as Aurelius Victor and Eutropius. In 1681 she chose a new path, trying her hand at translating Anacreon and Sappho, the latter a brief work that allowed her to defend the poet against charges of immorality (which Pierre Bayle would ridicule). She thereafter made a name for herself as a translator of Greek and Latin and pursued, alongside her husband, André, a brilliant career, made easier when they denounced Protestantism in 1685.

She soon moved on to more important works that were the core of classical culture, with translations of Plautus (*Amphytryon, Rudens, Epidicus,* 1683) and the complete works of Terence (1688). These established her reputation as a translator, or popularizer, and with an essay on the evolution of antique comedy she brought the Latin plays to a large public, particularly to women. Her interest in Plautus, at a time when Molière was drawing inspiration from this author, is also remarkable in an era that considered Terence clearly superior. She also translated Aristophanes (*The Clouds* and *Plutus*) in 1684: although in these, as in other translations, she sometimes settled for approximations, the work showed unquestionable audacity since Greek humor was considered almost intolerably crude.

It was a translation of Homer that gained her the most fame, beginning with a prose *Iliad* in 1711, followed by the *Odyssey* in 1716; her work was often considered scattered, inelegant, and lacking forcefulness—but after her no one in France dared to translate Homer for half a century. It was she who returned the poet to preeminence, unleashing the "second Homeric controversy," which continued the quarrel of the ancients and moderns (involving Houdar de La Motte). That quarrel prompted a response from Anne Dacier, *Des causes de la corruption du goût* (1714) and then a *Défense d'Homère* (1715). Whereas Pope's translation (1715–1720) claimed to restore Homer's brutality, Anne Dacier saw in the Greek poet only harmony and regularity (*Réflexions sur la préface de Pope,* 1719), and in what her contemporaries found shocking she discovered the traces of a golden age; she thus appeared as the official champion of the ancients, defending Homer against all criticism, sometimes even at the expense of common sense.

BIBL.: Eugène Haag and Émile Haag, *La France protestante,* 10 vols. (1846–1859; rept. Geneva 1966). Noémi Hepp, *Homère en France au XVIIe siècle* (Paris 1968). F. Létoublon and Catherine Volpilhac-Auger, eds., *Homère en France après la querelle, 1715–1900* (Paris 1999). G. S. Santangelo, *Madame*

Dacier, una filologa nelle "crisi" (1672–1720) (Rome 1984). Catherine Volpilhac-Auger, ed., *La collection "Ad usum Delphini": L'antiquité au miroir du Grand Siècle* (Grenoble 2000).

C.V.-A.

Translated by Jeannine Routier Pucci and Elizabeth Trapnell Rawlings

Danaë

Daughter of Acrisius, king of Argos; lover of Zeus, who appeared before her as a rain of gold. She had been imprisoned because her father had learned of a prediction that he would meet his death at the hands of his grandson. After she nevertheless bore Zeus a son (Perseus), Acrisius made another futile attempt to prevent the oracle from being realized: he put his daughter and his infant grandson into a boat and set it afloat in the open sea.

In antiquity two scenes from the myth of Danaë were often expressed in poetry and painting. The first, of Danaë in a boat, was popular in Greece: the heroine's pitiful fate was movingly uttered by Simonides of Ceos (in a dirge known as the *Lamentation of Danaë*) and portrayed by Artemon the painter (Pliny, *Natural History* 35.139). The second, of Danaë with Zeus as the rain of gold, was popular in Rome (Martial 14.175). It was this second scene that remained popular in the post-classical West.

Roman poets associated the myth of Danaë with the image of a venal woman whose love can be bought for money. In misogynistic tirades these poets often pointed to Danaë's reception of Jupiter transformed into a rain of gold as a demonstration of the omnipotent influence of gold as a monetary value (Horace, *Odes* 3.16.9–11), an interpretation that ignored the noble quality of the metal and its association with royalty. In one of his comedies Terence employs the myth's image as a wall painting in a courtesan's house, placed there to suggest to the protagonist that he satisfy his lust by aping Jupiter and bribing the girl with gold (*The Eunuch,* 584–590). Terence's allusion to a picture of Danaë was later used by Saint Augustine to demonstrate the immorality of ancient theology (*City of God* 2.7).

Like most classical myths, the story of Danaë was interpreted in various, often contradictory ways, and like other myths recounting the adventures of the Olympian gods on earth, it too became Christianized during the 14th century. A woodcut from the printed edition (1490) of Franciscus de Retz's *Defense of the Inviolate Virginity of Mary* (*Defensorium inviolatae virginitatis Mariae,* written ca. 1388) shows a clothed, upright Danaë in a tower with rays from a Jupiter-sun directed toward her. The rhymed inscription below the woodcut raises the issue that if Danaë had conceived a child by Jupiter disguised as a rain of gold, it was possible for the Virgin to have given birth when impregnated by the Holy Spirit. This rhyme is followed, paradoxically, by a reference to Terence's play.

Attitudes toward the myth of Danaë were decidedly ambivalent, particularly as expressed in depictions of her as a royal daughter encountering the ruler of the ancient gods. Several artists, including Correggio and Titian, mitigated the pessimistic interpretation of the myth as primarily illustrative of money's power in the seduction of a desired woman; they instead rendered a nude, recumbent Danaë accompanied either by Cupid or her own maidservant: the presence of the former attests to the divine force of love, whereas the latter is shown collecting money, the former drops of gold now solidified into coins. This presentation renders Danaë as an innocent virgin welcoming Jupiter, visibly conveying a mortal being's longing toward a union with the divine.

Some uncertainty still remains as to whether depictions of Danaë that were created for rulers or their courtiers were representations of royal mistresses in this mythological guise, as a socially codified avenue possibly approved for employing this particular subject in art.

BIBL.: A. Wirth, *Danae in christlichen Legenden* (Vienna 1892).

L.FR.

Dance. *See* Gesture and Dance.

Dante Alighieri

Florentine poet (1265–1321). His extensive debts to and complex engagement with the classical world are emblematically captured in Virgil's unexpected role in the *Divine Comedy* (*Divina commedia,* 1306/1307–1321) as guide through the first two realms, Hell and Purgatory, of the Christian afterlife. His choice of the Roman poet highlights the strength of the bonds that Dante believed united pagan antiquity and the Christian era, the two epochs forming complementary parts of a single providential plan for humanity's salvation. Thus, in fashioning the moral structure of Hell, he fused Christian ideas about sin with the moral thought of Aristotle and Cicero, which reached him filtered through a Christianizing exegesis. Equally, his political and social views were fundamentally shaped by Roman notions of empire and justice (his principal sources were Virgil, Lucan, Augustine, and Orosius), which he adapted to conform to the Church's spiritual and ethical doctrines.

His admiration for classical culture and society was profound, and nowhere did he express this more effectively than in his description of Limbo in *Inferno* 4, which he presents as a quasi-Virgilian Elysian Fields peopled by the heroes and major intellectuals of the Greek and Roman world. At the same time, however, he never fails to stress that the achievements of the ancients were ultimately flawed. Though monuments to the power of human reason, they were imperfect, as their creators remained untouched by divine grace. Despite helping and instructing the Christian wayfarer, Virgil must eventually return to Limbo, while his ward, the Dante within the poem, ascends to Paradise. The relationship between the character Dante and his guide thus stands as a microcosm of the poet's sense of the connections between Christianity and paganism, whereby the latter is never judged on its own terms but always and reductively in terms of the former. More specifically, the relationship between the two poets serves to reveal Dante's opinion of their relative standing as writers.

Notwithstanding the vital influence that classical culture exerted on Dante throughout his career, how he acquired his knowledge of it remains a matter of some conjecture and dispute. Since the 1990s the extent of his firsthand familiarity with the works of even quite major classical authors whom he cites and mentions by name has increasingly and persuasively been called into question. Dante almost certainly learned Latin sometime in the late 1270s or early 1280s, during his time as a grammar-school student in Florence, when he also first came into contact with Latin literature. (As had long been common, Greek was not taught, and Dante never became even minimally proficient in the language.) As recent studies have shown, the number of Latin authors and texts circulating at the time in Florentine schools and, more generally, in Italy was restricted. Furthermore, despite unfounded claims to the contrary, it is almost certain that Dante neither attended university nor was given access in the 1290s to the relatively well-stocked libraries of the religious orders in Florence, though he did attend the orders' public lectures, which introduced him to Christian Aristotelianism and Neoplatonism. As a result, the works he wrote before his exile in 1302 (*La vita nuova,* 1292–1294, and the majority of his lyric verse) normally reveal a narrow and conventional appreciation of classical culture. It was only after Dante had left his native city and had started to move around the Italian Peninsula that he seems to have read more widely and independently. This is especially apparent in *Convivio* (1303–1306/1307), a major development in the form of the classically based poetic commentary, in which he engaged seriously, for instance, with the epic poetry of Statius, Virgil, Ovid, and Lucan (4.25–28), as well as with Aristotle, the source of much of his scientific information, and with Plato, who lies at the basis of his semiotic thought—both of whom he read in Latin translations.

Yet his direct knowledge of classical writing remained patchy; and the texts that he did read were always mediated by the extensive commentary tradition that had accumulated around them. His acquaintance with Plato was limited to the *Timaeus,* the only one of the dialogues available in the Middle Ages; of Aristotle he knew only the *Nicomachean Ethics, Physics, Metaphysics, Meteorologica, De caelo, De anima,* and probably the *Politics.* The situation was similar when it came to the poets; for example, as regards Horace, he was familiar only with the *Ars poetica;* Ovid to him was the "Ovid of the *Metamorphoses*" (*De vulgari eloquentia* 2.6.7). With the exception of Cicero and Seneca, he was largely ignorant of Latin pagan prose, though he was rather better versed in Christian prose writers of late antiquity, such as Augustine and Boethius. The bulk of his knowledge of the classical world came from medieval sources, and many of the passages that he cited were taken from contemporary works of compilation or were popular authoritative quotations (*auctoritates*). In this he was no different from the majority of his lettered contemporaries.

Revealingly, it was also only after he had been exiled that he began to compose texts in Latin. First, *De vulgari eloquentia* (1304–1306), which, though ostensibly written under the aegis of Horace (2.4.4), in fact is quite unlike any classical work on language and poetics; and then, a decade or so later, *Monarchia* (1317–1318), which, relying heavily on borrowings from classical authors bolstered by the Bible, proves the divinely ordained character of the Roman Empire. Although Dante appreciated the order, sophistication, and rigor of Latin as a language, his primary aim throughout his life was to reveal the efficacy of the vernacular as a language of culture, and specifically of poetry. Indeed, with the *Divine Comedy,* and directly challenging established opinion, his goal was to show that at least his vernacular, as the language of modern Christian culture, was actually more effective as a literary medium than Latin. To achieve this he needed to demonstrate that as a poet he was superior to the great canonical authors of antiquity who for centuries had served as the highest models of literary endeavor. Quite early in the *Commedia,* in the fourth canto, he presents himself as welcomed in Limbo by the foremost classical poets, Homer, Virgil, Horace, Ovid, and Lucan, "so that I became the sixth amidst such wisdom" (*Inferno* 4.102). In granting himself this exalted status—a status that no post-classical writer had previously achieved—he usurped the position among the classical *auctores* conventionally occupied by Terence, the recognized authority on comedy, but whose plays, interestingly, like those of the other Roman dramatists, he had not read. His new, contemporary, Christian, and vernacular "comedy" (*Inferno* 16.128, 21.2)—the epithet "Divine" was added in 1555—was about to replace a hallowed tradition.

Dante was intent not only on challenging Terence, however, but also on challenging classical literature as a whole. Thus, while he openly acknowledged his debts to Latin literature, beginning with Virgil, he emphasized the fact that classical literature could only partially serve a poet like himself, whom God had chosen to inspire a moral revival in a society that had lost "the straight way" (*Inferno* 1.3). Although in the *Commedia* he borrowed extensively from classical writing—from single words to complete episodes—he circumscribed his appreciation of that tradition by invariably highlighting its artistic and ideological flaws—flaws that essentially stemmed from its being the product of a culture unenlightened by the divine. In writing his own epic, therefore, he declined to follow the model canonized by Latin poetry, creating an innovative text whose rhyme scheme, carefully partitioned structure, and linguistic and generic range were all unprecedented.

Dante's bold experimentation was unparalleled in Western letters; and it is significant that many of his 14th-century Italian readers openly recognized his mastery over even Homer and Virgil. There is little doubt that medieval vernacular culture desperately needed a Dante to grant it the confidence to distinguish itself from the classical tradition. Yet it is impossible to imagine Dante without his pagan "guides." Thus, Horace offered him the model of the poet who was also a critic; Virgil, whose three major works Dante had read, showed him that it was possible for a poet to write successfully in different genres; Orpheus confirmed that poets could act as the moral leaders of their societies; and the arrogant single-mindedness of Ulysses, whom, like Orpheus, Dante considered a figure of history, revealed to him the errors that, as a serious thinker, he needed to avoid. In *Inferno* 26, however, the Greek hero, known to Dante through Latin and medieval reworkings of the Homeric myth, is not simply a negative exemplar. He embodies the allure, pathos, dangers, and lasting relevance of classical humanism. Although Dante was zealous in asserting his own and his culture's independence and value, he was acutely aware that the past continued to inform the present—a belief that he made concrete when he chose Virgil to accompany him as his teacher on his great journey of salvation.

BIBL.: Z. G. Baranski, "Dante Alighieri: Experimentation and (Self-)Exegesis," in *The Cambridge History of Literary Criticism,* vol. 2, *The Middle Ages,* ed. Alastair Minnis and Ian Johnson (Cambridge 2005) 561–582. Teodolinda Barolini, *Dante's Poets* (Princeton 1984). C. T. Davis, *Dante and the Idea of Rome* (Oxford 1957). Edward Moore, *Studies in Dante, First Series: Scripture and Classical Authors in Dante* (Oxford 1896).

Z.B.

Daphnis

Daphnis is the mythological model shepherd of Graeco-Roman pastoral poetry, universally admired and praised by other inhabitants of the pastoral world. His origins predate the advent of the pastoral genre: the choral poet Stesichorus (Davies 1991, fr. 279) narrated his story in the early 6th century BCE. Daphnis swears fidelity to an amorous nymph, pledging loss of his eyesight as the penalty for violating his oath; but a princess later uses wine to cause him to break his vow, and the tradition of "bucolic songs" develops to lament his ill fortune. The first idyll of Theocritus (3rd cent. BCE) preserves just such a lament, which portrays Daphnis wasting away on a riverbank, visited and mourned by animals, men, and gods alike. Theocritus leaves the exact reason for Daphnis' suffering unspecified, as if the earlier tradition would explain it. Allusions to absent nymphs, an eager maiden, and a fateful vow are all compatible with the Stesichorean account, but Theocritus' twist on the tradition is to present Daphnis as an embittered rebel against love generally. Melodramatic variants are attested in other Hellenistic sources. Daphnis figures prominently in only one of Virgil's eclogues, but there all nature mourns his death (5.20–44); his subsequent apotheosis engenders a rustic cult (5.56–80), in a probable allegory for the catasterism (elevation to the stars) of Julius Caesar. Daphnis appears in the *Eclogues* never as a tangible figure in the flesh but rather as a distant, quasi-legendary quintessence of pastoral life.

Longus' pastoral romance *Daphnis and Chloe,* probably datable to the 3rd century CE, transfers the setting from Sicily to the island of Lesbos, and this Daphnis happily loves a neighboring shepherdess named Chloe, despite his poverty and various misadventures that threaten their union. He has little in common with the Daphnis of earlier Greek tradition save his universal appeal to all who know him. This highly sentimental novel deploys the pastoral world as a metaphor for childhood innocence and depicts the couple's growth into sexual maturity.

Although Edmund Spenser's *Daphnaida* (1591) was a pastoral lament in the tradition of Theocritus and Virgil, it was Longus' novel of adolescent self-discovery (translated into French by Jacques Amyot in 1559, and thence into English by Angel Day in 1587) that framed Daphnis' image for later tradition. The theme of childhood innocence appealed to Rousseau, who commenced a libretto on Daphnis and Chloe (1779), but the project of an operatic rendition had to await the attention of Offenbach (1860). The most successful musical treatment was Maurice Ravel's ballet (first performed in 1912 by Diaghilev's Ballets Russes), with its powerful sound painting of adolescent sexual awakening and a choreographic scenario based closely on Longus. The love story also inspired visual artists, particularly in France, including figures no less significant than Corot (1845), Gérôme (1852), Rodin (1886), and Chagall (1956).

Literary treatments have tended toward irony, as in Andrew Marvell's poem "Daphnis and Chloe" (ca. 1650): far from innocent, his Chloe is a cruel mistress who withholds her favors but vainly offers them at the last minute to coax Daphnis into staying, while Daphnis combines the proud defiance of Theocritus' shepherd with the cynicism of a cavalier roué. Earlier, John Fletcher's drama *The Faithful Shepherdess* (ca. 1609) had presented Chloe as a not very faithful nymphet and Daphnis as a repressed, straitlaced youth not much to her liking. John Gay set to music a frivolous ballad (1720) in which each blames the other's rejection. The saccharine character of Longus' narrative did not appeal to all.

BIBL.: Malcolm Davies, *Poetarum Melicorum Graecorum Fragmenta* (Oxford 1991). D. M. Halperin, "The Forebears of Daphnis," *Transactions of the American Philological Association* 113 (1983) 183–200. Gunter Wojaczek, *Daphnis: Untersuchungen zur griechischen Bukolik* (Meisenheim 1969).

T.HU.

David, Jacques-Louis

French painter and politician, 1748–1825. Born into a prosperous Parisian bourgeois family, David received a classical education at the Collège de Beauvais and the Collège des Quatre Nations, elite preparatory schools where many future leaders of the French Revolution also studied. The curriculum was heavily weighted toward ancient poetry and history, above all Homer, Virgil, Ovid,

Livy, and Suetonius. He entered the Royal Academy in 1766 as a student of Joseph-Marie Vien, and he submitted *Combat between Minerva and Mars* to the Prix de Rome competition in 1770. David was no prodigy; he won the coveted prize that funded four years' residence at the French Academy in Rome on the fourth attempt, with *Antiochus and Stratonice.* In 1775 he accompanied Vien, the new director of the French Academy, to Rome, where he remained for five years, making hundreds of drawings after ancient sculptures and classicizing works of the Renaissance and Baroque eras.

In 1780 David returned to Paris and for the next decade executed a series of historical paintings based on classical subjects that electrified his contemporaries, including *Andromache Mourning Hector* (1783), *Oath of the Horatii* (painted in Rome during a second sojourn there, 1784–1785), *Death of Socrates* (1787), *Paris and Helen* (1787–1788), and *Lictors Bringing to Brutus the Bodies of His Sons* (1789). David's bold tenebrism and corporeal expressiveness were a complete rejection of the academic late rococo and established neoclassicism as the dominant mode in French art for the next generation.

At the outbreak of the revolution in 1789, the liberal David initiated the epic *Oath of the Tennis Court* to celebrate the defiance of royal authority. The radicalization of events, however, prevented him from completing it, and by 1792 the painter was deeply involved in radical politics. Elected to the national legislature, in 1793–1794 he became an associate of the Jacobin dictator Maximilien Robespierre and served on the Committee of General Security, which supervised the network of police spies and conducted trials for counterrevolutionary activities. When the Jacobins fell in 1794, David was imprisoned and narrowly escaped execution. During the more moderate Directory government, from 1795 to 1799, he turned to the politically less controversial genre of portraiture. His major achievement during this period, however, was the colossal *Intervention of the Sabine Women* (1799), a metaphorical plea for national reconciliation.

Corruption and war brought down the Directory in 1799 and established Napoleon Bonaparte as the dictator of France under the classical title First Consul. David was initially enthusiastic about the regime and became First Painter of the Empire in 1804. His major works for Napoleon were propaganda machines with antique allusions, since Bonaparte based his rule on classical precedents. In *Napoleon Crossing the Alps* (1800–1801), the general is shown on a rearing horse with his name newly carved on a stone that also bears the names of past conquerors—Hannibal and Charlemagne. David was less enthusiastic about the empire than he had been about the consulate, and his imperial commissions are bombastic and less progressive than his previous work.

After the Bourbons reclaimed the throne following the demise of the empire in 1815, David went into exile in Brussels, where he spent the last ten years of his life painting portraits and erotic mythologies such as *Cupid and Psyche* (1816) and *Mars Disarmed by Venus and the Three Graces* (1824). Absence from Paris and the rise of the Romantic painters Théodore Géricault and Eugène Delacroix lessened his influence, but David's profound effect on the early modern French school cannot be overestimated.

BIBL.: A. Brookner, *Jacques-Louis David* (London 1980). E. J. Delécluze, *Louis David, son école et son temps* (Paris 1855). D. Johnson, *Jacques-Louis David: Art in Metamorphosis* (Princeton 1993). C.S.M.J.

Decline. *See* Progress and Decline.

Delphin Classics

The first state-sponsored edition of Latin classical texts, the collection *Ad usum Delphini* was undertaken at the request of Louis XIV between 1674 and 1691. From its inception early in the 1670s, under the guidance of the Duke of Montausier, governor of the dauphin, son of Louis XIV, and Pierre-Daniel Huet, assistant tutor of the dauphin (Jacques Bossuet, the primary tutor, took no part in it), this collection was meant to complete a gentleman's education: the texts with notes and *interpretatio* are instruments of culture rather than erudition. There are no Greek texts in a corpus that probably aimed at integrating all authors of any importance from the 2nd century BCE to the 6th century CE. The absence of agronomists and of Pomponius Mela, Solinus, Martianus Capella, Boethius, and others who, along with Seneca, were never edited, is due to the shortcomings of the Delphin authors. Antiquity, as it is seen through these 68 volumes, is huge; but what started as a very ambitious project did not quite succeed, as it lacked competent contributors, time, money, and a specific scientific purpose. The project was actually rather anachronistic; it marked the end of a period when classical culture was the only culture possible for a gentleman.

The Delphin editions follow a fixed model: the frontispiece depicts a dolphin ready to save Arion, under the motto *Trahitur dulcedine cantus* (He is attracted by the sweetness of her song); then follows the title page, which indicates that the book is done *Jussu Regis* (under the king's order), *In* (or *Ad*) *usum serenissimi Delphini,* and a paratext in Latin (a preface, a letter, or the like), all of which gives unity to the collection. Then there is the text, in two or three orders: the text itself with numbered lines, the *interpretatio* or full rewriting in Latin prose of verse texts, or partial rewriting of difficult prose texts (only some easy authors such as Eutropius or Dares had no *interpretatio*), and the *annotatio.* Everything is in Latin. At the end is an index that attempts to gather and reproduce all the conjugated forms and declensions of all the words of the text. (Ovid's index occupies all of the fourth volume; other indexes are more succinct.)

There is no real philological work done on the texts, and the Delphin authors, particularly those who were dilettantes or inexperienced, like Anne and André Dacier, relied on previous editions. One exception was Pliny the Elder, remarkably edited by Father Hardouin. The *interpretatio* not only facilitated the reading, but also improved the competence of the reader and offered new expressions and new constructions; the purpose of *interpretatio* was mostly pedagogical, just as *annotatio* opened the doors to classical culture and instructed the reader, even morally. Initially the intention was to gather all the indexes together to produce a general index of Latinity, but in any case the disparity among indexes would have made that impossible.

Completing the collection were several dictionaries published by Pierre Danet between 1673 and 1698, and these, like the collection itself during the 18th and 19th centuries, were reissued several times. The collection was expanded in 1730 by one "Ausonius," but by that time the collection had become obsolete.

The expression "Delphin collection" continues in the French language as a term for watered-down or censored works. Yet this was never intended: although all the words referring to sexuality were replaced by asterisks, they were collected at the end of each volume. Not only was this collection a failure, but it was doomed to be misunderstood.

BIBL.: Martine Furno, ed., *La collection "Ad usum Delphini": Catalogue raisonné* (Grenoble 2005). Catherine Volpilhac-Auger, ed., *La collection "Ad usum Delphini": L'antiquité au miroir du Grand Siècle* (Grenoble 2000). C.V.-A.

Translated by Jeannine Routier Pucci and Elizabeth Trapnell Rawlings

Demeter and Persephone

Greek gods, mother and daughter; Roman Ceres and Proserpina. The central myth tells of the violent seizing of Persephone (or Kore, "the maiden") by Hades (or Plouton, "the rich one," Roman Dis), lord of the underworld, who made her his queen. Demeter then caused the earth to become barren. Through Zeus's intervention, Persephone was restored to her mother for part of the year; Demeter relented, returning fertility to the earth and establishing her cult.

In the agrarian world of the Greek city-states the worship of Demeter and Persephone was very widespread; its best-known sanctuary was at Eleusis, near Athens. There, as elsewhere, secret rites (termed mysteries) offered mortals the hope of prosperity and a blessed existence after death. The myth of the Two Goddesses contained strong agricultural and eschatological metaphors, and because it offers explanations of several opposing concepts (e.g., summer/winter, fertility/barrenness, love/hatred, life/death), the story has retained its interest and power. The major ancient texts are the Homeric *Hymn to Demeter* (7th century BCE, known in the modern era from 1777), where the myth is a rich source of religious ritual, and the highly literary Roman accounts of Ovid (*Metamorphoses* 5.341–571, *Fasti* 4.393–620) and Claudian (the unfinished *De raptu Proserpinae,* ca. 400 CE), both of whom situate the capture of Persephone in a flowery Sicilian meadow near Enna. Late antique Christian writers such as Fulgentius, Firmicus Maternus, and Isidore of Seville provide much information about the cult, which they wished to discredit; interpretations reducing the gods to allegorical concepts or euhemeristic human prototypes were later influential. There is no iconographic continuity with the many images of the Two Goddesses in ancient art; 11th-century manuscript illustrations of the encyclopedia of Hrabanus Maurus curiously depict Proserpina as a draped figure, standing on wheels to indicate movement and contrasting with depictions of the other gods represented in *nuditas criminalis* (codex 132, Montecassino).

In the 14th century the Ovidian story of the rape of Proserpina was recast in French as an allegory in *Ovide moralisé* (ca. 1290–1320), later latinized in Pierre Bersuire's *Ovidius moralizatus* (1343). Also influential was Christine de Pizan's *Épitre d'Othéa* (late 14th century). In such allegorical narratives Proserpina might be viewed as fallen human nature and Hades as Satan, whereas Ceres was identified with abundance or the Church. Proserpina's redemption and return to Demeter, as told in the ancient story, were of less interest than her role as queen of the underworld (Boccaccio, Chaucer, Gower). As in Dante (*Purgatorio* 10.49–51), Proserpina can have the conflicting aspects of a grim-faced spouse of death and an innocent personification of spring. The demonic dimension of the story is emphasized in the anonymous *Enlèvement de Proserpine* (1430), and it survives both in Dürer's etching of Persephone seized by a wild, naked Hades mounted on a fiery unicorn (1516) and in an eerie early painting of the rape by Rembrandt in Berlin, following Claudian. The allegorical reading of the myth is still perceptible in Spenser, but in famous lines of *Paradise Lost* (4.268–272) Milton sees "that fair field of Enna" as analogous to Eden, and Proserpina to Eve; the myth is accepted on its own terms, exemplifying a lesser truth.

The Roman accounts of Proserpina's descent were emancipated from imposed allegory in the 16th century. Tasso lovingly described the natural setting (*Loda una vaghissima montagnetta*), drawing on Claudian for details. The vivid narrative of the *Metamorphoses* was a more common source, as seen in paintings by Rubens (now in the Prado Museum, Madrid) and Veronese (now in the Gardner Museum, Boston), and in the sculptures of Bernini (Galleria Borghese, Rome) and Girardon (Versailles). Claudio Monteverdi's lost opera *Proserpina rapita* (1630, one aria survives) was preceded by his brother Giulio Cesare's *Rapimento di Proserpina* (1611, also lost); later operas based on Ovid's account include a *Proserpine* by Lully (1680) and also by Saint-Saëns (1887).

In contrast to the details of her daughter's narrative, Demeter/Ceres can be depicted as a timeless, idealized figure adorned with the attributes of agricultural fertility, as we see in paintings by Peruzzi (Villa Farnesina, Rome), Tintoretto (National Gallery, Washington, D.C.), and Pietro da Cortona (Castel Fusano, near Rome). Similar in idea is Hiram Powers's much-copied neoclassical bust of Proserpina crowned with wheat sheaves (1844, Philadelphia Museum of Art). The poet Shelley's "Song of Proserpine," written for Mary Shelley's play *Proserpine* (1820), evokes the fertility and innocence that precede (but also follow) the fall.

The myth's potential for evoking a wide range of human experience has been exploited in modern poetry since the 18th century, new material from antiquity finally being provided by the chance discovery in Moscow of the single surviving manuscript of the Homeric *Hymn to Demeter* (first published 1780; English and Latin translations 1782; German 1826). Goethe's monodrama *Proserpina* (1776, commissioned by C. W. Gluck, who regrettably composed no score) consists of the young goddess's bitter, passionate lament over her imprisonment with a hated spouse in a loveless Hades. The myth could also be reworked from a male standpoint: George Meredith gives Persephone and Hades a "shadow-born" daughter, Skiogeneia, who in turn has a youthful admirer, Callistes, in "The Day of the Daughter of Hades" (1883). For Swinburne ("Hymn to Proserpine," 1886) the myth was a convenient vehicle for lamenting the loss of pagan values and a celebration of death. In Tennyson's quiet, late poem "Demeter and Persephone" (1880), the mother muses over her daughter's tragic fate and foresees the coming of Christianity. The Homeric *Hymn to Demeter* is the source for both Robert Bridges's *Demeter: A Mask* (1904), which probes the moral dimensions of myth and cult, and André Gide's play *Persephone* (1912), which with much freedom stresses the cyclic aspect of the story. Gide's text was revised in 1932 when Stravinsky provided a strong musical score in neoclassical style. Other major 20th-century poets attracted to the myth include Osip Mandelstam (*Tristia,* 1916), W. B. Yeats ("Colonus' Praise," 1928), Ezra Pound (*Pisan Cantos,* 1948), and Donald Davie, evoking Ovid as the source ("The Fountain of Cyanë," 1981).

Like Goethe, recent poets have found analogues for women's experience in the story of Persephone; examples include Robert Lowell in the long narrative "The Mills of the Kavanaughs" (1951), Margaret Atwood in *Two Persephones* (1962), and, most eloquently, Louise Glück in the related lyrics of *Averno* (2006). William Carlos Williams had earlier used the myth as a metaphor of escape from winter entrapment ("Kore in Hell," 1920). Persephone's return can be evoked as a biological metaphor, as in Thom Gunn's "The Goddess" (1968).

One of the governing metaphors of the myth of the Two Goddesses—the relationship of mother and daughter—led C. G. Jung in the 1940s to his theory of archetypal forms of human experience; in this he was inspired and aided by Carl Kerenyi, who wrote extensively on the Eleusinian cult. The myth has also attracted the Italian prose writers Cesare Pavese (*Dialoghi con Leuco,* 1947) and Roberto Calasso (*Le nozze di Cadmo e Armonia,* 1988).

BIBL.: Herbert Anton, *Der Raub der Proserpina: Literarische Traditionen eines erotischen Sinnbildes und mythischen Symbols* (Heidelberg 1967). Nikolaus Himmelmann, *Antike Götter im Mittelalter,* Trierer Winckelmannsprogramme, vol. 7 (Mainz am Rhein 1985). Jane Davidson Reid, *The Oxford Guide to Classical Mythology in the Arts* (New York 1993). M.BL.

Demiurge

Demiourgos in Greek means a craftsman or technician, originally someone who did not earn his living from the soil, though in Homer the term is also applied to soothsayers and heralds. A mysterious figure called the Demiurge, however, figures prominently in Plato's mythical account of the world's creation in the *Timaeus* 28Aff., where he is also called the "father and begetter," and most frequently "the god" (with the definite article) to differentiate him from younger gods to whom he delegates the task of fashioning mortal bodies. His work is that of an intellect, for he is faced with assembling, and imposing order and beauty on, a preexistent stuff that is in constant unregulated motion and is to some degree unmalleable or intractable, though not evil as such. Plato, or rather Timaeus, the dialogue's eponymous speaker, refers to this stuff as "the mother of becoming," "place," "nurse," "necessity," and "receptacle." The Demiurge emerges therefore not as an omnipotent god but as a craftsman who does the best he can, because he is good, to make a good world, which, being from "the best of causes," is the best possible effect. Though it is "the fairest of creations," that is, a "living visible creature . . . comprehending within itself all other living creatures," it remains imperfect because its stuff contains an irreducible element of waywardness. To create the cosmos at all, the Demiurge must have looked up to a model "which is eternal" and "contains in itself all intelligible beings," that is, the Platonic Forms or Ideas. Although Plato certainly does not identify the Demiurge with this intelligible model, Augustine and a succession of medieval interpreters, most notably those associated with the 12th-century School of Chartres, were drawn, understandably, to identifying the Forms with the Ideas in God's mind and the Demiurge with the Creator of Genesis. As a consequence, the *Timaeus*—essentially the only dialogue whose actual text, at least up to 53C, was known to the Latin West via Calcidius' Latin commentary and lemmata—became for Christians throughout the Middle Ages the ancillary cosmological treatise to Genesis.

Proclus' *In Timaeum* 2 gives us a detailed history of the succession of ancient interpretations of the Demiurge, with their increasing elaboration, beginning with Numenius, who called the world itself a third god and distinguished between the "father" and the "creator," a distinction with a decisive role to play. Plotinus, the founder of Neoplatonism, identified the Demiurge with the second hypostasis in his metaphysical system, that is, with Mind; the Demiurge thus became double, one part of him being in the intelligible realm, the other being the fabricating and ruling principle of the universe. Plotinus identified these dual roles with Cronos and Zeus (Zeus as a "royal intellect"); and a long-running debate ensued as to which references in Plato's works referred to this higher intellectual Zeus. Sundry post-Plotinians introduced a triplicated demiurge, and Iamblichus held the Demiurge to be the third monad in a seventh, purely intellectual triad between the created world and what he saw as three triads of intelligible-intellectual gods and three triads of intelligible gods.

Finally, from Syrianus and Proclus emerged the most complicated ancient interpretation of all. As the god who stands at the lowest limit of the intellectual gods, the Demiurge possesses the intelligibles even as he extends his creative power to fashion the world of souls and of ensouled matter: he is a demiurgic monad and a demiurgic triad (mythologically a Cronos and his three sons, Zeus, Poseidon, and Hades). Because he produces intellect from himself but creates soul, he is superior to, and cannot be identified with, the World Soul (though some had espoused this interpretation). As creator, Proclus argued, he is the cause of encosmic beings; but as creator-and-father he is the cause of hypercosmic and encosmic beings; as father-and-creator, of intellectual, hypercosmic, and encosmic beings; and as purely father, of intelligible, intellectual, hypercosmic, and encosmic beings. He is the Zeus of various Orphic verses and of Plato's *Cratylus* 396B, *Gorgias* 523B–524A, *Laws* 4.716A, *Philebus* 30D, and *Statesman* 272B, 273B. Proclus also explored the notions of an old and a new demiurgy and of Pluto as the third demiurge. Of these proliferations, the most arresting is the arcane notion of the (or a) sublunar Demiurge, variously identified in the Proclian tradition with this Pluto or, alternatively, with Poseidon or even Hephaestus.

The great Renaissance Neoplatonist scholar and philosopher Marsilio Ficino (1433–1499), who was steeped in the history of Neoplatonic interpretation, revived many of these Proclian ideas. Most notably, his study of the *Sophist* prompted him to postulate a Proclian sublunar craftsman who is simultaneously a daemonic "many-headed" sophist, a magus, an enchanter, a fashioner of images and reflections, a shape-changer of himself and of others, a poet in a way of being and of not-being, a royal Pluto. And yet as a master of distinction-making, this Demiurge is "a purifier of souls" who presides over the magic of love and generation and who uses a fantastic counter-art to mock, but also strangely, as his art too is "most eminent," to supplement, the divine icastic or truly imitative art of the sublime translunar Demiurge.

From this intriguing nexus of associations it is an obvious short though hazardous step to the notion of a bumbling or even an evil demiurge. Plato himself seems to have anticipated this possibility by way of his circumlocutionary *if*-clauses in the *Timaeus* at 29A: "If the world is beautiful and if its maker is good, he obviously looked to an eternal pattern; but if they are what it is even blasphemous to utter, then he looked to a pattern that has come to be." A demiurge (or demiurges) who gazes at such a temporal pattern must either be doing something impious (the reference to blasphemy suggests this) or at least working as a subordinate and incompetent craftsman far removed from the supervision of the good Demiurge.

In post-Renaissance times the revival of the ancient Gnostic notion, once attacked by Plotinus, of an evil or incompetent demiurge (whether he is named such and whether he is to be identified in some way with Satan) has had a remarkable role to play in Romantic and modern literature—though the central concerns of modern theodicy go back, of course, to the very origins of dualism in various cosmological and eschatological myths, as do current quasi-demiurgic arguments based on the theory of intelligent design. William Blake's prophetic books, for example, beginning with *The Book of Urizen* (1794), call on man's revolutionary spirit to rise up and dethrone Urizen as an old and evil demiurge, associated with Locke and Newton, of a mechanistic and exploitative order; and to turn instead to Los, the creative power within, in order to build the new Jerusalem. A number of subsequent assaults, by Nietzsche and others, on the conventional notion of a good Creator or creation have indeed made the antithetical notion of an evil (or Darwinian!) demiurge an increasingly familiar one; and it has become integral, by way of opposition, to a number of revolutionary, cultic, and antinomian ideologies and to the narratives they generate.

Meanwhile, the good Demiurge has been relegated to Platonic exegesis, though some might argue for its having had an influence on the emergence of 17th-century Deism.

BIBL.: Michael J. B. Allen, *Icastes: Marsilio Ficino's Interpretation of Plato's Sophist* (Berkeley 1991) chaps. 3, 5. F. M. Cornford, *Plato's Cosmology* (London 1937). W. K. C. Guthrie, *A History of Greek Philosophy*, vol. 5, *The Later Plato and the Academy* (Cambridge 1978) 253–280. Anthony D. Nuttall, *The Alternative Trinity: Gnostic Heresy in Marlowe, Milton, and Blake* (Oxford 1998). Jan Opsomer, "Demiurges in Early Imperial Platonism," in *Gott und die Götter bei Plutarch*, ed. Rainer Hirsch-Luipold (New York 2005). Proclus, *In Platonis Timaeum commentaria*, ed. Ernst Diehl, 3 vols. (Leipzig 1903–1906).

M.A.

Democracy

Since the middle of the 20th century democracy has been considered the only legitimate form of government; virtually every country claims to be a democracy, whatever its actual governing practices may be. Well into the 19th century democracy was largely identified with the historical example of Athens in the period between Kleisthenes' reforms (508–507 BCE) and the imposition of an oligarchic constitution by the Macedonians (322 BCE). As the concept of *dēmokratia* evolved over the course of the 5th century BCE, it came to reflect Athens' unique political order, in which the popular assembly and courts made up of citizens played a central role. Every citizen could participate in political affairs, and exercising this right was made possible by compensation for such service and selection by lot. In later times this model was rejected to a large extent, even though Athens' cultural achievements remained greatly admired. This came about, first, because no ideology was developed to legitimate it (or at least no extended text on the subject has survived) and, second, because Plato and Aristotle painted a critical picture of democracy on the whole in their works on political theory. Thus, the image was created of a "rule of the poor," in which demagogues' influence rendered the popular assembly incapable of devising rational policies. Furthermore, the assembly was unwilling to accept any legal limitations on the principle of majority rule, while at the same time the popular courts followed a policy of plundering "the rich." As a result democracy appeared to be a form of collective tyranny.

This understanding dominated the reception of Aristotle's work from the 13th century onward. Quite apart from the fact that democracy was not realizable in most commonwealths, since they were governed by monarchs, it was not even considered desirable. In the context of city-states one finds reference to the Aristotelian conception of "citizens," but its limited application to only a portion of the population was taken virtually for granted (e.g., Marsilius of Padua). Well into the 18th century democracy was consistently condemned, with few possible exceptions (Spinoza and Pufendorf). At the most, mixed constitutions with a "democratic element" found acceptance: this consisted of bodies representing the various estates; it definitely did not mean self-rule by citizens. Though the Levellers' movement during the English civil war was democratic in tendency, it was based on an understanding of equality in primitive Christianity, the covenant theology of the Old Testament, and the invocation of time-honored English liberties and inviolable rights granted by God. The Levellers did not invoke the concept of democracy transmitted from antiquity.

In Scottish and French political theory of the 18th century—linked because each group read the works of the other—the idea was repeatedly raised that the self-government practiced in ancient city-states and contemporary republics in Switzerland and the Netherlands depended on their small size, which made it possible for all citizens to attend a single assembly. (This notion is ultimately derived from Aristotle.) John Millar observed that almost all the republics of antiquity owed their inner freedom to the limited extent of their territory (1779, 5.3). And the author of the article on democracy in the *Encyclopédie* could not name a single example from his own time (1754), with the exception of San Marino, where "500 peasants rule over a miserable rock, a possession for which no one envies them." David Hume turned this idea on its head so to speak in his *Idea of a Perfect Government* (1752), where he noted that the constitution in a small state must of necessity be unstable, since here the danger of a tyranny of the majority could arise. In a state that covers a large area, on the other hand, citizens could participate only through representatives with delegated powers. Representation in nations of the size of France or Great Britain also made possible a new and better form of democracy, in which the instability of democracies in small nations could be avoided because the geographical dimensions of the country would prevent the establishment of a single majority party. It was further argued that in ancient times citizens' orientation toward war and the use of slave labor instead of peaceful commerce and trade prevented the development of a "commercial society" that guaranteed progress for all over the long term. Certainly there were opposing voices, theorists who used the idea of citizenship in antiquity to criticize the individualism and striving for material goods dominant in their own era. Rousseau adhered to the ideal of the *citoyen*, but he was aware that it had become obsolete in a society composed of bourgeois (*Lettres écrites de la montagne* 1764, 9). Only a nation of gods would be able to govern itself democratically (*Social Contract*, 1762, 3.4).

In the revolutions of the 18th century many diverse doctrines from antiquity were cited, but in practice the Athenian model was dismissed. The American Founding Fathers attributed to direct democracy, on the pattern of Athens, a tendency to tyranny of the majority, which would disregard individual liberties and private property. John Adams (certainly the member of that group with the best grasp of ancient constitutional history) went so far as to characterize the brutal rule of the "Thirty Tyrants" in Athens in 404–403 BCE not as the antithesis of Athenian democracy but as the unavoidable result of a system based on government by assembly (*Defence of the Constitutions of Government of the United States of America*, 1787, 3.6). In the opinion of Alexander Hamilton, the assumption that a pure democracy represented the best form of government was refuted by the experience of history. In ancient democracies, he observed, popular assemblies were made up of mobs easily manipulated by presumptive tyrants ("Speech in the New York Ratifying Convention," 1788). James Madison wrote: "In all numerous assemblies, of whatever character composed, passion never fails to wrest the scepter of reason. Had every Athenian citizen been a Socrates, every Athenian assembly would still have been a mob" (*Federalist* no. 55). Because the democracies of the past had collapsed as a result of the confusion and injustice prevailing in the popular assemblies, it was important to create a constitution for the Union that offered "a republican remedy for the diseases most incident to republican government" (*Federalist* no. 10).

As the debate over a federal constitution progressed, ever greater emphasis was placed on the gap between the forms of political organization existing in ancient times and the political order to be established in the United States of America. Even though the Fathers of the Constitution enjoyed comparing themselves with the great lawgivers of antiquity like Solon and Lycurgus, they understood themselves as architects of an entirely new world order. At the ratifying convention in Pennsylvania, James Wilson declared in November 1787 that for the first time in the 6,000 years of world history a system of government was being established on the basis of general consensus, in an orderly process after impartial debate. By deriving the political system from the constitutive power of the people (through the creation of constitutional conventions), Americans were truly practicing popular sovereignty, whereas the ancient lawgivers had possessed dictatorial authority.

Alexander Hamilton and James Madison declared that —despite Montesquieu's claim, which the anti-federalists cited—it could be demonstrated for the first time that, thanks to the principle of representation, a republic could be established in an extensive territory and acquire a kind of stability unattainable by the pure democracies of the Athenian stamp. For the Fathers of the American Constitution the election of representatives was not merely a practical means to compensate for the impossibility of all citizens gathering in a single place. Had this technical problem been the sole issue, they could have followed the practice of Athenian democracy and chosen a decision-making body by lot. Rather, they believed that transferring the power of decision to suitable elected representatives offered far greater chances for policies that would serve the general good than if the popular will were to be expressed without any filter.

The new political order, in which the institutions created by the constitutive power of the people were embedded in a system of checks and balances, was generally referred to as a republic, less often as a democracy. (The word *democracy* does not occur in the U.S. Constitution.) Once doubts about the fundamental distinction between antiquity and the new form of government had ceased to exist, over the passage of time the idea of democracy could be reconciled with the principle of representation, especially in the era of Jacksonian democracy. The new usage was then reflected especially in Alexis de Tocqueville's famous description of the United States in *Democracy in America* (1835–1840), in which he equated the American political and social order with democracy. There the nation appears as a model for a representative democracy—including both its chances for success and its potential hazards—that no longer has anything in common with the ancient form.

In competition with the ideals of the creators of the American constitution, the leaders of the French Revolution also regarded themselves as founders of an entirely new order in world history. Robespierre declared that the people of France seemed to be 2,000 years ahead of the rest of mankind; they could be considered a separate species (speech at the National Convention, 7 May 1794). References to antiquity generally served a specific agenda; they evoked certain associations for polemical effect but did not reflect a deeper examination of ancient models. The term *republic* acquired great significance when contrasted with *monarchy,* and figures from antiquity, familiar from Plutarch's biographies of famous Romans, became paradigms for a republic, which had to consist of virtuous citizens. The terms *democracy* and *democrat,* which until that time had been used mostly in a pejorative sense, were used by Jacobins as a positive self-description, but above all they served as antonyms for *aristocracy* and *aristocrat.*

In principle the Jacobins' aim was the establishment of a representative constitution, but they used section meetings in Paris to exert pressure on deputies to the Convention. The lower-class sansculottes expressed more radical demands for direct democracy, including public debates in primary assemblies, imperative mandates and recall of deputies at any time, and public casting of votes; these were hardly inspired by classical models, even though they do not differ greatly from Athenian practices. They were fed rather by a vulgar form of Rousseauism that took seriously the idea that the will of the people could not be delegated. Robespierre was an adherent of direct democracy, but he used his charisma to obscure the tensions between the supporters of differing conceptions of popular rule. He did not regard citizen assemblies as a fundamental alternative to the representative system. He claimed that the French were the first people to have established a "true democracy"—by this reckoning Athens and the United States did not count—but made it clear that democracy could not be a government "in which the people constantly assemble and regulate all public matters themselves . . . Democracy is a government in which a sovereign people acts in accordance with laws that are its own work, doing everything that it can do well itself, and letting its deputies do what it cannot do itself" (speech at the National Convention, 5 February 1794).

As a result of the experience of the Jacobin Reign of Terror, the idea of democracy fell into discredit in Europe for a long time. The (dubious) claim that the Jacobins had espoused a "cult of antiquity" led Benjamin Constant to formulate a distinction in 1819 between a "liberty of the ancients," which signified political participation without any guarantee of individual civil rights, and a "liberty of the moderns," which primarily guaranteed individuals protection from the state. (Constant's ideas were more differentiated, however, than is often recognized.)

A new appreciation for the idea of democracy resulted from Tocqueville's depiction of the United States. As John Stuart Mill noted, the concept had been detached from its ancient image as "pure democracy," limited to states covering a small area, and could now be applied to "modified democracy" in the form of representative systems. The American constitution appeared to many European liberals—although not all—as a realization of democracy under modern conditions. Most of the constitutional movements of the first half of the 19th century wanted to combine the democratic and monarchical principles (in varying forms), but in the revolutions of 1848 demands for a "democratic republic" grew louder. The early communists developed the idea of a "true democracy" that would be attainable only in the future, after passing through the intermediate stage of "bourgeois democracy." At that point the term *democracy* no longer meant demands for political participation alone, but also for social equality. Looking back at the year 1848, Guizot and Tocqueville lamented the fact that the term was now claimed by all political camps and had thus lost all distinctive force. And though they observed a general acceptance of the democratic principle, whatever might be understood by that in detail, it is well known that this phenomenon quickly disappeared throughout Europe. From the mid-19th century onward the idea found expression in the "Caesarism" or "Bonapartism" of Napoleon III that democracy could be realized only if there was a consensus on rule by one particular man.

The general discourse on democracy continued largely without reference to Athens but affected contemporary scholars' view of antiquity. Over the course of the 19th century numerous accounts were written in which Athenian democracy was interpreted in the light of the authors' own experiences with revolution. The Athenian courts in particular were presented as a sort of revolutionary tribunal, where the *demos* unleashed terror and redistributed income. The works of Fustel de Coulanges and Jacob Burckhardt are particularly prominent examples of a widespread tendency. The response came mainly from England. According to John Stuart Mill, George Grote's *History of Greece* represented a "triumphant vindication of the Athenian Democracy"; at the same time it supplied historical legitimacy for calls to reform the English parliamentary system. Grote and Mill did not advocate a return to the Athenian model, but they did see in it a standard by which even the English system had to be measured with regard to citizens' participation and liberty. When German classicists such as Eduard Meyer, Ulrich von Wilamowitz-Moellendorff, or Karl Julius Beloch welcomed Grote's portrait of Athens as a necessary correction of accepted clichés, even though they stood far to the right of him politically, this is an indication that a clear-eyed, positivistic view of Athenian democracy prevailed. The difference between ancient and contemporary circumstances appeared so great that positive or negative judgments of Athenian democracy could no longer automatically be taken as comments on the contemporary political situation.

The general political discourse of the late 19th and early 20th centuries was also carried on by and large without mention of Athens (apart from scattered instances of political rhetoric). This is as true for debates on the relationship between "direct" and "indirect" democracy, with their allusions to the popular referendums in Switzerland or Napoleonic plebiscites, as for the abandonment of traditional ideas of democracy and acceptance of the inevitable dominance of a "political class" (Gaetano Mosca, Robert Michels, et al.), and finally it applies as well to the alleged symbiosis between a leader and his followers in Italian fascism and German national socialism.

In the period following World War II antiquity occasionally came under suspicion of having provided a model for "totalitarian democracy," although the accusation was more often directed at Sparta rather than Athens. The general triumph of the idea of democracy—at least on paper—corresponded to a mostly positive assessment of Athenian democracy among historians; nevertheless, the academic reconstruction of a distant past in ever greater detail was not usually regarded as a forum of discussion on the appropriate political order in the scholars' own era.

Since the 19th century "democracy" has been used to denote both a society that existed at the beginnings of European history and at the same time a goal still to be realized: an ideal form of government and society. In this overlapping of historical, descriptive, and normative aspects comparisons with Athens can be used to serve contrary arguments. One group (in broad terms) rejects the notion that democracy can mean only a free choice between political elites, pointing out that the degree of political participation achieved in Athens has not been equaled in modern times. Hence, this group calls for the ideal of the ancient citizen as a point of orientation and wants to see the principle of representation complemented or even replaced by forms of direct democracy (citing even the workers' council or soviet movements of the 19th and 20th centuries as well as the referendum model practiced in Switzerland, some states in the United States, and elsewhere). Recently forms of "electronic democracy" have also been proposed that would make a return to citizen participation on an Athenian scale. The other group (just as broadly), however, noting that in Athens slaves and women had no political rights, concludes that by the standards of the 19th and 20th centuries Athens was not a real democracy at all. (Usually a third group excluded from participation is mentioned, namely foreigners residing in Athens, overlooking the fact that such rights are also linked to citizenship in the modern era.) There are many indications that despite the fundamental difference from antiquity, comparisons with Athens will continue to be made as long as societies keep striving to realize democracy under modern conditions and their successes and failures are discussed.

BIBL.: Moses I. Finley, *Democracy Ancient and Modern* (London 1973). Lucian Guerci, *Libertà degli antichi e libertà dei moderni: Sparta, Atene e i "philosophes" nella Francia del '700* (Naples 1979). Mogens Herman Hansen, *The Tradition of Ancient Greek Democracy and Its Importance for Modern Democracy* (Copenhagen 2005). Bernard Manin, *The Principles of Representative Government* (Cambridge 1997). John Millar, *The Origin of the Distinction of Ranks* (London 1779). Wilfried Nippel, *Antike oder moderne Freiheit? Die Begründung der Demokratie in der Antike und in der Neuzeit* (Frankfurt 2008). Paul A. Rahe, *Republics, Ancient and Modern: Classical Republicanism and the American Revolution* (Chapel Hill 1992). Peter J. Rhodes, *Ancient Democracy and Modern Ideology* (London 2003). Jennifer Tolbert Roberts, *Athens on Trial: The Antidemocratic Tradition in Western Thought* (Princeton 1994). Pierre Vidal-Naquet, *La démocratie grecque vue d'ailleurs: Essais d'historiographie ancienne et moderne* (Paris 1990).

W.N.

Translated by Deborah Lucas Schneider

Demon

In philosophical (mainly Platonist and Neoplatonist) thinking of the Hellenistic and Roman periods, demons (*daimones,* singular *daimōn*) were intermediate beings, sharing immortality, or at worst extreme longevity, with the gods, and susceptibility to emotion with humans. Cosmologically, by inhabiting the space between earth and the moon, they ensured that no zone of the cosmos was devoid of living creatures. Theologically, they accounted for traditional religious beliefs and cults, including the identities of the Olympian and other lesser deities, and were responsible for maintaining contact between humanity and higher power (via oracles, dreams, portents, and prayer). In the individual's life quest, they acted as guardian spirits, and (in some versions) constituted the higher community which the virtuous could hope to join at death. Part of this picture is developed already in Plato's *Symposium* (202E–203E), but its systematization came later, with the pseudo-Platonic *Epinomis* (984b–d) and the Middle Platonist Xenocrates. The starting point in Plato, however, guaranteed that the personal *daimōn* of Socrates was always a central instance and talking point (perhaps most influentially in the 2nd-century Latin of Apuleius' *On the God of Socrates*).

For classical authors *daimones* were positive beings, subservient to a benevolent supreme divinity. The only partial exception were the gloomy or even malevolent *daimones* hypothesized by Xenocrates to account for the more sinister forms of traditional religious observance. Christian writers, however, from the 2nd century onward, exploited the classical doctrine equally vigorously in both positive and negative directions. The combination of Jewish ideas with the religious functions of classical *daimones* (especially in Xenocrates' version) allowed for the construction of a damning picture of pagan religion as a malevolent fraud practiced on humanity by rebel angels; and the classical perception of the emotionalism and appetites of *daimones* helped flesh out thinking about the character and modus operandi of the Devil's subordinates more generally. But, equally, a purified version of *daimōn* theory fed into the construction of late antique and medieval angelology. A key text in this latter connection was the *Celestial Hierarchy* of pseudo-Dionysius the Areopagite, a 6th-century Christian transposition of Neoplatonic demonology that defined the nine canonical orders of angels. Translated into Latin and enriched with a commentary by Eriugena in the 9th century, this work made a major contribution to the teaching on angels of Albert the Great, Bonaventure, Duns Scotus, and Thomas Aquinas, even as at the same time they were taking other aspects of the classical nexus into their theorizing about demons.

The ambivalent heritage of classical demonology was thus made available to later thinkers for a range of different purposes. Marsilio Ficino expounded the Platonic material (in his essays on Plato's *Theages* and *Symposium*) and explored the relevance of *daimones* to higher, "theurgic" magic, aimed at the purification of the intellect (*On Arranging One's Life According to the Heavens,* 1489). Cornelius Agrippa (*Occult Philosophy,* 1533) and Paracelsus (*On Nymphs, etc.,* 1515) adapted different strands of the tradition in accounts of nature and the orders of living beings; Agrippa took the high Neoplatonic line, whereas Paracelsus preferred the elemental spirits of *Epinomis,* which blended better with popular beliefs. Others used classical theory to help map the hierarchy of evil spirits, especially as involved in witchcraft and black magic, as Jean Bodin did in his *On the Demonology of the Sorcerers* (1580)—though King James I's *Daemonologie* (1597) shows much less dependence on classical, as opposed to biblical, authorities. At the same time, classical demons continued to be used, as by the early Christians, in explanations of the origins and typology of pagan religion (e.g., Gerardus Joannes Vossius, *Pagan Theology,* 1641). From all these sources, shards of classical demonology have remained in circulation in 19th- to 21st-century esoteric and neo-pagan writing.

Throughout, special attention has continued to be paid to the question of the demon of Socrates, which has been reinterpreted at regular intervals in a startling variety of ways: as a true guardian angel (e.g., Giannozzo Manetti, *Life of Socrates* 28); as Socrates' own half-understood moral consciousness (Hegel); or (Nietzsche, with a characteristically reductive inflection) as an infection of the inner ear. The case of Socrates has also stimulated some notable attempts to represent a *daimōn* in visual form: for example, Nicolai Abildgaard's depiction of a contemplative Socrates accompanied by not one but two contending *daimonia* (1784, drawing on Manetti); or Simeon Solomon's provocatively witty sketch of the *daimonion* as a naked ephebe (youth) leaning elegantly on his older protector's shoulder (ca. 1865).

BIBL.: J. Daniélou, *Gospel Message and Hellenistic Culture* (London 1973). J. Dillon, *The Middle Platonists* (London 1977). D. P. Walker, *Spiritual and Demonic Magic* (London 1958).

M.B.T.

Demosthenes

Greek orator and politician (384–322 BCE); the most famous orator from ancient Athens. Most of his speeches (some 60 survive) were written for others to present in the law courts; he built his reputation in both rhetoric and politics on his opposition to the emerging power of Macedon. Philip II gained control of Athens in 338, after the battle of Chaeronea; during the remainder of his reign and in early years under Alexander, Demosthenes kept a low political profile. But in 330, against an attack by his political opponent Aeschines, he defended his entire career in the oration *On the Crown,* generally regarded as his masterpiece. In 324 he was briefly exiled during the Harpalus scandal; in 322 he fled political reprisals in Athens and committed suicide on the island of Calauria (Poros).

In his rhetoric as in his politics his style was confrontational and uncompromising. He developed his ideas in sharply antithetical terms, representing the war between Athens and Macedon as a personal contest between Philip and himself, in which he was the wise, incorruptible adviser of a free, democratic state fighting to preserve liberty for all Greeks against a perfidious and depraved military autocrat. He contrasted Athens' glorious past and present inactivity with Philip's insignificant origin and boundless ambition. At home he branded all who opposed him as traitors, corrupted by Philip's bribes. The evidence suggests that his delivery was dramatic, almost violent. His vocabulary was rich, strongly metaphorical, and often vituperative.

Even during his lifetime opponents promulgated negative accounts, charging him with (among other things) undermining peace negotiations with Philip and advocating confrontational policies that led to the defeat at Chaeronea. His later involvement in political scandal tarnished his image as an incorruptible adviser. After his death the Peripatetics, who had no fondness for democracy and were close to Macedon, attacked his reputation, especially as an orator; Demetrius of Phaleron developed many elements in the traditional (probably fictional) picture that eventually appeared in Plutarch's *Life of Demosthenes,* of a man without natural oratorical ability who acquired his skill through hard work and practice—the austere, bookish Demosthenes we see in the well-known statue by Polyeuktos (ca. 280 BCE), which survives in a Roman copy (Carlsberg Glypothek, Denmark). As the rhetorical schools gained influence throughout the Hellenistic period, the notion that he had achieved greatness only by study became instead a strong point in his favor; by the 1st century BCE, though few still cared about his politics, he was recognized as the greatest of the canon of 10 Attic orators. The particular quality that critics in that era saw in his unique style was *deinotēs* (denoting both the terrible and the clever, often translated as "intensity").

It was as the greatest of the Greek orators that he was introduced to the Italian Humanists, like Leonardo Bruni, when the Greek texts of his works were brought back to the West by Byzantine scholars at the end of the 14th century. The first printed edition of his speeches, by Aldus Manutius in 1504, proclaimed that "no one disputes that Demosthenes holds the highest position in oratory amongst the Greeks and Homer in poetry." Their counterparts in Latin were Cicero and Virgil. This quartet was still the mainstay of classical instruction at Oxford almost five centuries later. Throughout that long period, except for a backlash against the authority of ancient authors that occurred during the 17th century, Demosthenes was touted as the Greek whose style had to be mastered by anyone who wished to excel at rhetoric. Paradoxically, in the fashion set by the Reformation educationalists Erasmus and Sturm, his texts were also commonly used as a medium for teaching the Greek language. Over the centuries great men from Bruni to Brougham, and great women like Elizabeth I, have sharpened their knowledge of Greek by translating Demosthenes, but few have attempted to imitate his passionate rhetoric. Cicero's more balanced, fulsome style has found greater favor. With the decline of interest in classical rhetoric that began in the 20th century, Demosthenes' expertise in oratory has ceased to be valued.

His political legacy is more checkered. After the eclipse of Athens by Macedon, the ancient world had little sympathy for Demosthenes or the cause of democracy. Even in the 15th and 16th centuries, when his rhetoric was so admired, only two instances can be found where his themes were exploited for contemporary use (by Cardinal Bessarion in 1470 against the Turks, and by Reuchlin in 1495 against Charles VIII), but in both cases the message was a rather general summons to resist an invader. The first use of a specific Demosthenic theme was in Elizabethan England, where John Cheke, Thomas Wylson, and others adopted his persona of wise counselor to the *dēmos* as a model for their role as advisers to the queen. Not until the 18th century was his great issue revived, when the rise of Frederick the Great of Prussia led to a positive reevaluation of Philip of Macedon, with a concomitant devaluation of Demosthenes. The resultant battle between democracy and autocracy continued, largely between English and German scholars (although the French statesman Clemenceau saw himself as a sort of Demosthenes incarnate), right up until World War II. Not all German scholars were for Philip; Schaefer produced his unsurpassed *Demosthenes und seine Zeit* in 1885. On the other hand, the most bitter conflict over the soul of Demosthenes was between two English historians, William Mitford and George Grote. Grote was victorious, and late-Victorian and Edwardian England persuaded itself that it was a second Athens, and in that spirit fought the two world wars. Since then, despite the popularity of democracy, writing on Demosthenes, its champion, has been strangely hostile and largely biased in favor of Philip.

BIBL.: Craig Cooper, "Philosophers, Politics, Academics," in Worthington 2000, 224–245. Phillip Harding, "Demosthenes in the Underworld," in Worthington 2000, 246–271. Ulrich Schindel, *Demosthenes im 18. Jahrhundert,* Zetemata 31 (Munich 1963). F. Turner, *The Greek Heritage in Victorian Britain* (New Haven 1981). I. Worthington, ed., *Demosthenes: Statesman and Orator* (London 2000). P.H.

Despotism, Oriental

Throughout its long history, the concept of oriental despotism has, with few exceptions, carried pejorative connotations derived from the Eurocentric perspective of its users. Since the end of the 18th century, despotism has been conflated with tyranny, a term from which it had previously been distinguished. But for two millennia tyranny and despotism were the principal types of regime used to classify governments in which a single person was said to exercise total domination over subjects, the political equivalent of slavery.

Although the classical Greek concept of oriental despotism had first appeared during the wars of the 5th century BCE with the Persian Empire, it was most thoroughly developed in the next century by Aristotle, who found in it similarities to and differences from tyranny. Although both despotism and tyranny treated the ruled as slaves, tyranny, in Aristotle's view, was the usurpation of power from Greek freemen accustomed to ruling themselves. Despotism was the normal form of rule for Asian barbarians, who, because they were slaves by nature, submitted willingly to an absolute ruler. Such oriental empires were described as both extensive in area and long-lived. Stable because resting on tacit consent, they were said to be governed by law and principles of hereditary succession.

Thus, Aristotle's concept of oriental despotism derived from three polar oppositions: between Hellenes and barbarians, between freemen masters and natural slaves, and between Europeans and Asians. Oriental despotism became the first concept used by Europeans in an adversary anthropology that grouped together indiscriminately all Asian governments, whatever their histories, locations, and relationships, past, present, or nonexistent. This pejorative category of unfree peoples, said to be naturally inferior to Europeans, was used to legitimate conquest and rule by those allegedly superior.

Beginning with the 15th century, the claim to domination based on the assumption of European superiority found new applications, sometimes combined with the alleged right to convert heathens to Christianity. Aristotelianism, revived once again, was applied by Sepúlveda to the debate among Spanish conquerors about the justice of enslaving Native Americans. In their increasingly extensive travels, Europeans often classified societies in terms of Aristotle's invidious polarities.

Early modern European theorists often justified sovereignty, slavery, and colonial conquest by reconceptualizing theories of despotism, as did Bodin, Grotius, Pufendorf, Hobbes, and Locke. Bodin made new uses of Roman legal arguments justifying slavery, conquest, and seizure of property as a matter of right by victors in a just war. Grotius and Pufendorf certified as legitimate those modes of enslavement consented to by either servile or conquered peoples. Hobbes defined despotical dominion as power consented to by the conquered, and he argued that conquerors providing peace and security ought to be obeyed. Locke distinguished political from despotical power, defined as that of a lord over those who have been stripped of all rights because they forfeited them by waging unjust war. And classical republicans such as Algernon Sidney followed Machiavelli in asserting that free European republics produced citizen-soldiers with greater virtù than the armies of Asian despotisms. Free states, such republicans concluded, should rule lesser peoples to whom liberty was unknown.

In the 17th and 18th centuries French aristocratic and Huguenot critics of Louis XIV took the momentous step of extending the concept of oriental despotism to a European state. While reinforcing earlier uses of the term as an invidious category for all Near- and Far-Eastern regimes, the new strategy further entailed condemning certain characteristics of European absolutisms as identical with practices long attributed to oriental despotism. Montesquieu's *Persian Letters* (*Lettres persanes,* 1721) epitomized this mode of tacit attack on the absolutism, bureaucracy, aggressive foreign policy, and religious persecution of Louis XIV and his successors. Despotism was depicted, not just as a structure of state power and offices, but as a triangular system of fear, jealousy, and mutual suspicion. Thus employed, the concept of despotism became a potent weapon of opposition groups alleging that the monarchy had become this type of Asian government, alien to ancient French constitutional tradition.

Throughout the 18th century the prominence of despotism as a regime type, and its continuing association with the East, was in no small part due to Montesquieu. In *The Spirit of Laws* (*De l'esprit des lois,* 1748) he made despotism into one of the three basic types of government and relegated tyranny to a lesser place, relevant only to republics, a type of regime that he thought had become archaic in modern commercialized Europe. At the center of Montesquieu's typology of regimes was his stipulated definition of monarchy as constitutional, sharing power with intermediate groups, based on the separation of powers, and guaranteeing liberty to its subjects. Despotism he defined as a dreaded Asian dystopia, the polar opposite of modern European limited monarchy. Like the other two regimes, it was defined in terms of its nature (or structure) and its principle (or operative passion). He held the structure of a despotism to consist of the despot, ruling through his viziers or ministers, who exercise virtually absolute power over subjects. The ruled are equal in that they and all property belong to the despot. As for the principle of despotism, this requires that subjects be so dominated by fear that they obey completely and passively. As contrasted to free societies, the characteristics peculiar to despotism are its suppression of conflict in the name of order, its refusal to recognize the legal status of intermediate groups and classes, and its insistence on immediate and unquestioned passive obedience to the sovereign's commands. Whereas disagreements and even conflict are essential to free societies, they are fatal to despotisms.

In the second half of the 18th century Montesquieu's reclassification of governments made "despotism" into the most important category of vitiated, that is, illegitimate, one-person rule. In book 19 he reinforced the connection of despotism with the Orient by contrasting the positive model of England with what he presented as its antithesis, the Chinese empire, often viewed in his time as an ideal form of government. The concept of despotism continued to be prominent in political discourse both before and during the French Revolution.

As government and society were reconstructed between 1789 and 1815, some theorists such as Constant and Tocqueville argued that despotism and tyranny, whether European or oriental, were outmoded regime types. As such, they were applicable only to the ancien régime, but not to modern commercial or egalitarian societies.

Both Hegel and Marx found uses for the concept of oriental despotism, depicted in their respective philosophies of history as diverging from the patterns of Western civilization. Although despotism continued to carry negative connotations, these authors redescribed it as stagnant, as opposed to Western progressive development. Hegel depicted the movement of history as traveling from East to West. Despotism was the first stage of history, the final goal of which was European, that is, Prussian monarchy. The unchanging Orient knows that only one, the despot, is free, but the progressive West knows that all are free.

Marx also treated oriental societies as identical and unchanging, qualities he attributed to their mode of production and consequent political organization. The first human mode of production was the "Asian," in which there was no private property in land. Rather, a despotic centralized power executed such indispensable public works as irrigation. Asian society was based on self-sufficient villages, which preserved the unchanging oriental mode of production. The Orient could be brought into the destructive but progressive conflicts of the capitalist economy only by European colonial expansion, which was both destructive and regenerating.

Using another political economy and philosophy of history, British utilitarians such as James and John Stuart Mill worked out still different versions of the relationship between Western political liberty and oriental despotism. Mill argued that backward Asian societies such as India could be civilized and enabled to progress only by Western governments' exercising despotism to change the stagnant institutions and customs of those it had conquered and now ruled as colonies.

Today both despotism and tyranny have been reduced to vague synonyms connoting arbitrary, coercive, and exploitative rule incompatible with political liberty, constitutional government, the rule of law, and individual rights. To the extent that the term *oriental despotism* evokes any response, it is because of the notion of orientalism as rephrased by Edward Said in his book by that name (1978). But in his usage the political and economic dimensions of that term are subordinated to the sweeping cultural claims made by Said, who scarcely mentions the history of oriental despotism as a political concept.

BIBL.: P. Anderson, *Lineages of the Absolute State* (London 1974). S. Avineri, *Karl Marx on Colonialism and Modernization* (New York 1969). R. Koebner, "Despot and Despotism," *Journal of the Warburg and Courtauld Institutes* 14 (1951) 275–302. J. Pitts, *A Turn to Empire* (Princeton 2005). M. Richter, "Despotism," *Dictionary of the History of Ideas,* ed. P. P. Wiener (New York 1973), vol. 2, and "Aristotle and the Classical Greek Concept of Despotism," *History of European Ideas* 12 (1990) 175–187.

M.R.

Deus ex Machina

The phrase *deus ex machina* (Latin, "god from machine") is used colloquially to describe the sudden intercession of a person or event that resolves seemingly irresolvable problems. In its purest form, it refers to the theatrical device used in Greek tragedy—particularly those by Euripides—in which a deity or divine being miraculously appeared at the last minute, usually suspended from a crane or machine, and used his or her ostensibly supernatural powers to bring a resolution to the plot. The device has been criticized since ancient times. Aristotle (*Poetics* 1454b) and Horace (*Art of Poetry* 192) decried its implausibility as a symptom of authorial failure; modern commentators have criticized its negation of tragic effect and its artificiality. Nevertheless, the deus ex machina was a powerful spectacular and authoritative force in Greek tragedy, reconfiguring the relationship between gods and men, conferring punishment, preventing disasters, foretelling the future or interpreting the past, and even—as in the case of Euripides' *Medea*—allowing an unexpected escape.

Critics are by no means in agreement over the theatrical legacy of the deus ex machina. Some consider comedy to be the natural inheritor of the device, seeing its vestiges in recognition scenes, timely rescues, and the other surprise endings that have become clichés of comic plotting in a variety of genres. Arguably, it was most exploited in musical theater and opera, both as plot device and as spectacular effect, particularly in the 17th and 18th centuries. Technological innovations in Renaissance stagecraft made possible the staging of airborne deities that could invoke wonder in the context of Neoplatonic ideals, with the concomitant demonstration of earthly power. The descent of Harmony from the clouds, for example, in the first of the Florentine *intermedi* (1589) during the marriage celebrations for Ferdinand de' Medici and Christine of Lorraine, is only one of numerous early modern spectacles—English masques, French court ballets, and the like—in which the dazzling appearance of an immortal god in the upper reaches of the theater enhanced the temporal power of the real and very earthbound ruler.

The deus ex machina found its natural home in opera, where sung drama already challenged notions of verisimilitude, and happy endings were favored well into the 19th century. Many ancient sources adapted by librettists either used the device or were easily adapted to do so. Operatic settings of the Orpheus tale, for example, usually avert the tragic death of the singer and emphasize his power to triumph over death. Though Alessandro Striggio's original version of the libretto concluded with the hero's dismemberment, the version set and published by Monteverdi in 1607 features Apollo *ex machina,* who escorts his son to the heavens. The differing operatic treatments of Euripides' *Alcestis* and *Iphigenia in Tauris* reveal much about the ways in which the deus ex machina could be used to praise royalty (Louis XIV in Lully's *Alceste,* 1674), to create ambiguity (Handel's *Admeto,* 1727), or, as in the settings crafted by Gluck and his librettist Calzabigi in the 1770s, to suit French neoclassic notions of tragedy in an operatic context.

Changing political fortunes likewise altered the way in which the deus ex machina was used. In Metastasian librettos of the mid-18th century, such as *Il clemenzo di Tito,* the benevolent monarch assumes the role of the god whose magnanimity saves the day, whereas the fashion for so-called rescue operas in the 19th century—most notably Beethoven's *Fidelio* (1805)—invoked the mechanism to vanquish tyranny. The unexpected rescue of the villainous MacHeath in John Gay's *Beggar's Opera* (1728) and, later, Bertolt Brecht's *Three-Penny Opera* (1928) uses the innate artificiality of the convention to criticize not only the genre of opera and its audiences but also the class distinctions implicit in the device itself.

BIBL.: Julie Cummings, "Gluck's Iphigenia Operas: Sources and Strategies," in *Opera and the Enlightenment,* ed. Thomas Bauman and Marita McClymonds (Cambridge 1995) 217–240. Francis M. Dunn, *Tragedy's End: Closure and Innovation in Euripidean Drama* (Oxford 1996). Wendy Heller, "The Image of the Beloved: Handel's *Admeto* and the Statue of Alcestis," *Journal of the American Musicological Society* 58 (2005) 559–638. Andreas Spira, *Untersuchungen zum Deus ex machina bei Sophokles und Euripides* (Kallmünz 1960).

W.H.

Devil

Many cultures have devils, but the Devil with a capital *D* is best defined as the polar opposite of Jesus: he is initially a Christian creation. Because the first certain images of the Devil emerged in the 800s, centuries after classical Greece and Rome had disappeared, it might be imagined that classical culture had little influence on the Devil's appearance. But that would be a mistaken view.

We would not expect to find the Devil in classical art or texts, and we do not. Some representations of Pan, however, through ignorance and distorted interpretations by the early Fathers, and conflations with satyrs, were used by medieval artists, and these did affect the appearance of the Devil. This bewildered the poet Shelley: "It is inexplicable why men assigned [the Devil his horns and hoofs] as circumstances of terror and deformity. The sylvans and fauns with their leader, the great Pan, were the most poetical personages." But the Church Fathers evidently had felt quite differently from Shelley. And what Shelley found inexplicable is not so hard to explain.

When Isaiah (13:19–21) described ruined Babylon as a place where "hairy ones" danced, Saint Jerome, reading late in the 4th century, interpreted this as a reference to satyrs. This view survives in the King James Bible: in addition to the passage in Isaiah, "hairy one" or "goat" is also typically translated as "devil" in Leviticus 17:7 and 2 Chronicles 11:15. Even today Peter Pan is still with us, a developed fragment of pastoral Pan playing his flute. In ancient myth and literature young Pan and old Silenus were satyrs: ready to fight, gifted musically, sometimes wise, and often randy. Half man and half goat with a large phallus, Pan had pointed, goatlike ears and usually a dense beard, and he was in appearance sometimes not very different from his satyrs and fauns. In many depictions from satyr plays, actors portraying the satyrs wear what look like the animal-skin "skirts" that modern convention assigns to cavemen. Much later these same skirts were often worn by the Devil and his cohorts. Like Pan, satyrs and fauns had goatlike ears, sometimes a goat's tail, cloven hoofs, a pair of horns, and a hairy body (but in many instances, unlike Pan, they had human bodies). These distinctions were of no interest to theologians.

Five typical characteristics of the Devil derive from the classical Pan: the horns, hoofs, ears, tail, and hairy lower body. For people remote in time or circumstance from classical culture, satyrs seemed bestial, lustful, and unclassifiable in the Christian scheme of the world (for would God have created such creatures?). Pan was a servant of the Devil in disguise. The conventional notion that Pan is the main source for the Devil, however, does not fit the facts. This is particularly true of many sculptures of the Devil in Romanesque churches and cathedrals in France (Conques and Autun are important examples). And classical influence cannot be found in most Last Judgment tympans of Romanesque and Gothic cathedrals.

Another classical influence was the shaggy, flamelike hair that is a defining element of the Devil. This feature came partly from the Egyptian household god Bes but mainly from portraits on Greek and Roman coins. Today the Devil sports a pitchfork, but that came from Poseidon's trident. We first find the shaggy hair, trident, and "caveman" skirts in many illustrations in the influential 9th-century Utrecht Psalter (Psalm 38 is one example). A fascinating detail is that the Devil holds a trident at his first appearance owing to classical influence, but almost never again until the Renaissance. Between those two points in time, the Devil usually is shown holding a grapnel (a medieval instrument of torture) to punish the damned.

Perhaps the single most important connection between the Devil and classical culture is reflected in the Devil as nude or, more precisely, as naked. Because Christian ecclesiastics considered pagan gods as "devils" and those gods in classical sculpture were often nude, devils were depicted likewise. Christian art avoided nudity so strongly that the first naked Christ-child does not appear until 1325. From the 12th and 13th centuries there are nude classical figures (such as Hercules), but very few. For hundreds of years, the only naked figures were those being baptized, Jonah swimming in the ocean, Adam and Eve, and the Devil. The crucial difference is that Adam and Eve were created naked; the Devil, originally a beautiful archangel, became naked.

More precisely, the Devil was often not totally naked but wore the animal-skin skirt derived from paintings of satyr plays, though sometimes (e.g., the Soriguerola altarpiece) the skirt was derived from the Egyptian *shenti.* Literary texts may tell tales of the Devil's formidable sexual powers; but if an artist were to show the Devil totally naked, he would then have to decide how to portray the genitalia, and this was not a pleasant prospect. As a result, the Devil's genitalia were never shown in sculpture and rarely in painting.

BIBL.: François Garnier, *Le langage de l'image au Moyen Âge* (Paris 1982). Erwin R. Goodenough, *Jewish Symbols in the Greco-Roman Period,* 10 vols. (New York 1953–1964). Chanoine Denis Grivot, *Images d'anges et démons* (Paris 1981). L. F. Kaufmann, *The Noble Savage: Satyrs and Satyr Families in Renaissance Art* (Ann Arbor 1984). *Library of Christian Classics,* 10 vols. (London 1953–1957). Luther Link, *The Devil: A*

Mask without a Face (London 1995). Jeffrey Burton Russell, *The Devil; Satan; Lucifer,* 3 vols. (Ithaca, N.Y., 1977–1984). Gertrud Schiller, *Ikonographie der Christlichen Kunst,* 4 vols. (Gütersloh 1966). L.L.

Dialectic

Dialectic has a range of meanings within classical philosophy, primarily: the method of philosophy; the technique of debate; arguing with premises that are plausible or widely agreed rather than certain; and logic itself. Within the classical tradition dialectic is best understood today as the art of arguing in a convincing manner. It may be thought of as distinct from logic, the science of reasoning with certainty, or as including logic (for the most plausible arguments of all are those that are certain). In the Middle Ages dialectic and logic were synonyms. In the 19th and 20th centuries the term has generally been used to refer to the logical method of Hegel and, following him, of Marxism. This usage is connected to the classical Greek idea of dialectic but separate from the mainly Latin ancient, medieval, and Renaissance tradition.

Aristotle, who defined formally correct reasoning in his *Analytics,* thought that dialectic was useful in everyday conversations, in arguing on subjects (such as politics or questions of practical behavior) on which certainty was not attainable, and for debating the merits of generally held opinions in order to establish the principles from which reliable scientific reasoning could proceed. Whereas certain reasoning was guaranteed by the forms of the syllogism, plausible reasoning depended on the topics.

Classical thinkers provided three versions of the topics. Aristotle's *Topica,* which was recovered shortly before 1150, provides a list of 337 rules for arguing with an opponent, usually suggesting that if the opponent argues in a certain way it may be possible to oppose the argument by considering a particular aspect of what has been said. Cicero's *Topica,* which was available throughout the Middle Ages, gives a list of headings (such as definition, genus, species, part and whole, cause, effect, consequence, contrary, difference, authority) that a speaker can mentally run through to devise plausible arguments. So, for example, if one wished to formulate arguments about poetry, one might start from its definition, its genus, its cause, or its effect. At first students would run through this list systematically and in order; later they would internalize the list and develop an instinct for which topics might generate strong arguments about a particular subject. Boethius' *De differentiis topicis,* which was the principal medieval authority on the topics, gives a list of headings like Cicero's but integrates them into the science of argument by adding a rule that justifies the argumentative link implied (e.g., on the topic of genus, "what is present to the genus, is present to the species"; on the topic from the greater, "if what appears more likely to belong does not belong, nor will what seems less likely to belong").

Boethius' topics were widely taught in medieval universities because of their usefulness in training pupils for disputation, which was the main academic exercise required of students in their obtaining their degrees until at least the 18th century. Medieval commentators, whose works are admirably surveyed by Green-Pedersen (1984), were understandably concerned with the truth status of Boethius' maxims (e.g., of the two quoted above, the first must always be true if the formal reasoning of the Aristotelian syllogism is to be regarded as reliable, whereas the second has scarcely any independent truth value), the nature of the headings, and the kind of statement being made by the maxims. In general, medieval commentators attempted to read Aristotle's *Topica* through the lens of Boethius.

Lorenzo Valla, whose *Repastinatio dialecticae et philosophiae* (1439) attacked both Aristotle and Boethius, argued that the practical problems facing people could rarely or never be resolved through the formal reasoning of the syllogism. He urged people to study the practical use of arguing in classical Latin, concentrating on the implications of the combinations of particular words and on the relations of inference set out in the topics. For him the topics (for which he extracted the version in Quintilian's *Institutio oratoria* 5.10, itself an expansion of Cicero's *Topica*) generated the arguments that the writer could then choose to express in a number of forms (including hypothetical syllogism, dilemma, and sorites, as well as the syllogism and the enthymeme).

Rudolph Agricola believed that dialectical invention encompassed the whole process of planning a composition. He placed the topics at the center of his *On Dialectical Invention* (1479), explaining that they label a series of relations between the things in the world and providing training in their use. He wrote a new version of the topics that explained the nature of the relation involved in each topic, described ways of exploring that relation, and considered examples of arguments based on each topic. He showed that narratives and expositions could be organized to instruct audiences, and he set out a method of reading a text dialectically, uncovering the chains of argument implicit in a text, which influenced a school of Humanist commentators, including Latomus, Melanchthon, and Ramus. This approach facilitated an absorption of dialectical techniques within 16th- and 17th-century rhetoric textbooks. In the second book of his influential *De copia* (1514), Erasmus used dialectical techniques to transform preexisting material in order to generate *copia* of things.

The continuing importance of dialectical training for disputation ensured that early modern political and religious arguments exploited the probabilistic arguments of the topics. Dialectic encouraged writers to explore the implications of statements and to formulate reservations and counterstatements. Many of the comments in Montaigne's *Essais* (1580) are dialectical reactions to an opinion already expressed either by an author he has read or by Montaigne himself. Montaigne's method of additive composition and his penchant for qualifying and even rejecting positions he has just stated exploit the possibilities of the topics of invention, particularly those connected with contraries and distinctions. Descartes and Bacon used dialectical arguments to clear the ground and establish the propositions from which deductive argument could proceed, thus using dialectic in one of the ways envisaged by Aristotle. Dialectic was a dynamic feature of the classical tradition, providing techniques that enabled inherited ideas to be elaborated, applied, questioned, and turned in new directions.

According to Hegel, who explicitly compared his new dialectic with Plato's style of argument, especially in the *Parmenides,* "The dialectical moment is the self-sublation of these finite determinations on their own part, and their passing into their opposites" (*Encyclopaedia Logic,* paragraph 81). Dialectic is the process by which some phenomenon turns of its own accord into its opposite. Engels enshrined this idea in his laws of dialectical materialism. Although Marx and Engels rejected Hegel's idealism, they preferred his philosophy to the mechanicism of Feuerbach's empirical philosophy because it allowed for conflict and change. In their view change is the result of conflicts inscribed in the nature of a thing that are resolved and repeated when this nature is transformed and the thing reaches a new stage of development. So a Marxist analysis would find that the internal contradictions of capital produce a change in the nature of society (e.g., from a national economy to globalized capitalism) that will resolve and repeat those contradictions. For Hegel and Marx the key characteristic of dialectic is its capacity to explicate change.

BIBL.: N. Green-Pedersen, *The Tradition of the Topics in the Middle Ages* (Munich 1984). G. W. F. Hegel, *Encyclopaedia Logic,* trans. T. F. Geraets et al. (Indianapolis 1991). P. Mack, *Renaissance Argument: Valla and Agricola in the Traditions of Rhetoric and Dialectic* (Leiden 1993). E. G. Rose, *Hegel contra Sociology* (London 1981). Eleonore Stump, *Boethius's De Topicis Differentiis* (Ithaca, N.Y., 1978). P.M.

Dialogue

The Greek noun *dialogos,* "discussion," derives from the verb *dialegesthai,* "to discuss," although a mistaken etymology, associating it with *duo,* defined the term as a conversation between two people. As a literary genre, the dialogue had its origins in the conversations of Socrates, whose pupils Aeschines, Antisthenes, Plato, and Xenophon wrote works in which philosophical topics are debated in a historical if fictionalized setting. Based on the Socratic question-and-answer method, this "dialectical" form of the genre was practiced by subsequent members of the Academy. By contrast, the Peripatetic school followed their founder, Aristotle, in composing dialogues in which a private discussion provides the dramatic forum for communicating ideas to a wider public; but most of their works have not survived. After a period of decline the Greek dialogue was revived by Plutarch (ca. 50–120 CE), whose "symposiac" dialogues, modeled after Plato's famed work, depict a banquet as the scene of learned disquisitions. An innovative approach to the genre was taken by the sophist and satirist Lucian (ca. 120–180 CE), who saw the comic potential of dialogue using mythological interlocutors as a vehicle for social comment.

In Rome the greatest practitioner of dialogue was Cicero, who chose Platonic themes for his *On the Republic* and *On Laws* but imitated Aristotle in the formal organization of his works, in which single books are introduced by authorial prefaces, and lengthy exposition replaces dialectical exchanges. Trained as a rhetorician, Cicero conceived of debate as "presenting arguments on both sides of a question" (*in utramque partem disserere*); and as a philosopher in the Academic tradition, he generally preferred to leave the conclusion of such debates unresolved within his dialogues, allowing readers to judge for themselves. After Cicero, the dialogue was used sporadically in Latin works such as Tacitus' *On Orators* and Macrobius' *Saturnalia.* With the rise of Christianity, apologists for the new faith at first employed the dialogue as a useful means of persuasion—Minucius Felix's *Octavius* (3rd cent.) is a notable example—but the rhetorical freedom characteristic of dialogue inevitably led to its condemnation by Church authorities. Sometime before his conversion in 386, Augustine used the dialogue form in his *Against the Academicians,* a work that undermines the skeptical approach to debate that had been employed by Cicero and others. The last great dialogue of antiquity, Boethius' *Consolation of Philosophy* (ca. 524) presents the author in conversation with Philosophy herself and alternates exchanges of dialogue with passages of poetry.

During the Middle Ages, Latin dialogue was generally conceived as a catechism in which a master instructs his pupil. A new start was made in the 1340s by Petrarch, whose *Secret* depicts the author in conversation with Augustine. In 1402 the Ciceronian model was revived by Leonardo Bruni's *Dialogues to Pier Paolo Vergerio,* which relate a contemporary debate about the merits of Dante and Petrarch. Other Italian Humanists soon followed suit and made Cicero the principal model for the Latin dialogue of the Quattrocento. In the 1430s the use of Italian was championed by Leon Battista Alberti, whose *Books on the Family* follow the Ciceronian model. In his Latin works Alberti also revived the satirical style of Lucian, whose works had been among the first Greek texts to be translated in Italy after 1400.

The renewed popularity of Cicero's dialogues is not surprising. The Roman orator's philosophical skepticism attracted thinkers who shared Petrarch's disdain for abstract disputation, and his portrayal of learned Romans engaged in moral discussions confirmed both the Humanists' ideal of eloquent and cultured discourse and their predilection for social and ethical questions. By the 16th century the use of the vernacular challenged the supremacy of the Latin dialogue, and works like Baldassare Castiglione's influential *Book of the Courtier* (1528) spawned numerous imitators in France and England. In Italy the discussion of literary theory and philosophy was central to dialogues by men of letters such as Sperone Speroni

(1500–1588), Torquato Tasso (1544–1595), and Giordano Bruno (1548–1600). But after the Council of Trent, Augustinian strictures again prevailed, and the dialogue in Catholic countries often reverted to instructive catechism. The ambiguities of the two-sided exposition in Galileo's *Dialogue on the Heavenly Systems* (1636) could not protect the scientist's Copernicanism from the condemnation of the Roman Inquisition.

The Enlightenment brought a renewed appreciation of classical dialogue both as learned conversation and as imaginative satire. (The same era witnessed the rise of the epistolary novel, a genre that illustrates the ancient definition of a letter as "half a dialogue.") The civilized model of Ciceronian discussion was imitated in England by Addison, Shaftesbury, and Berkeley, and in France by Descartes, Montesquieu, and Diderot—to name but a few illustrious practitioners of the genre.

Lucian, in turn, served as a model for *Dialogues of the Dead* by Fontenelle (1683) and Fénelon (1712) and for Voltaire's multicultural dialogues, including his *Dialogue between Lucian, Erasmus, and Rabelais* (1765). Between 1770 and 1793 the German writer Christoph Martin Wieland (1733–1813) published original Lucianic works such as *Dialogues of Diogenes* and *Dialogues of the Gods,* as well as a complete translation of Lucian.

After the French Revolution, the dialogue waned as Western thinkers employed more systematic and scientific modes of discourse. But the tradition never completely died out. In Italy the Lucianic tradition flourished somewhat later: witness several of the *Short Moral Works* (1824) by the scholar and poet Giacomo Leopardi (1798–1837), the complete translation by Luigi Settembrini (1813–1876), and the *Dialogues with Leucothea* (1947) of Cesare Pavese (1908–1950), which recast figures from Greek mythology as Existentialist thinkers. And the 20th century saw sporadic revivals of Platonic dialogue in works like the *Dialogues in Limbo* (1925) by the philosopher George Santayana (1863–1952) and *Acastos: Two Platonic Dialogues* (1986) by the novelist Iris Murdoch (1919–1999).

BIBL.: Virginia Cox, *The Renaissance Dialogue* (Cambridge 1992). Simon Goldhill, ed., *The End of Dialogue in Antiquity* (Cambridge 2008). David Marsh, *The Quattrocento Dialogue* (Cambridge, Mass., 1980). Michael Prince, *Philosophical Dialogue in the British Enlightenment* (New York 1996). D.M.

Dictatorship

The term has survived from antiquity, though its meaning has changed substantially. It is now used to describe a state-level system that defies the rule of law, abolishes any separation of powers, and represents the opposite of democracy. The original distinction, between an emergency government installed with defined competences and a régime without legal restraints, seems to have been forgotten. Accordingly, *dictator, tyrant,* and *despot* are now used interchangeably and express at best degrees of moral condemnation.

Until the 18th century, dictatorship was understood as applying to a peculiar institution of the Roman Republic. Roman dictatorship was considered to have been an ingenious solution to the problem that an emergency might occur that demanded extraordinary means be used for the preservation of the commonwealth, but which required in the end a return to the constitutional system that had previously prevailed. The method of appointment, which separated the roles of initiator (the Senate), nominator (a consul), and nominee (the candidate for the office of dictator), was intended to guarantee the nominee's lack of personal ambition. Once chosen, the dictator was bound by a strict time limit of at best six months; and the record of the early and middle Republic shows that indeed the task, once assumed, was not used as a means to seize permanent power for the dictator or his faction. It further appears that this institution had become obsolete by the 2nd century BCE; in the 1st century BCE first Sulla in 82–81 and then Caesar in 48–44 broke with law and tradition and usurped the title of dictator, keeping the office beyond the conventional terms—Caesar ultimately being named Dictator in Perpetuity—and thus inaugurating a development that finally led to the replacement of the Republic by a new kind of monarchy.

Machiavelli in his *Discorsi* (book 1, ch. 34) expresses interest in the original notion of dictatorship as an institution for coping with serious conflicts within the citizenry. (He passes over dictatorship as an instrument of unifying military command during a war.) Such a purpose avoids the deadly alternatives either to be helpless against enemies of the constitution or to resort to unconstitutional means of coping with the crisis. Machiavelli rejected the opinion that dictatorship, as demonstrated by the cases of Sulla and Caesar, would inevitably lead to tyranny: a man like Caesar would in any case have seized power, whatever title he used to camouflage his intentions. Writing about 250 years after Machiavelli, Rousseau in his *Contrat social* (book 4, ch. 6) argued that it had been a mistake for the Roman Senate and consuls to have allowed the traditional institution of dictatorship to fall into disuse. It would have been a provision to stop Sulla and Caesar before it was too late.

Other discussion has referred to the problem of sovereignty and dictatorship. Writers of various stances have argued that the delegation of power to a dictator did not diminish the role of the sovereign. Thomas Hobbes (*De cive,* ch. 17, section 16) and Algernon Sidney (*Discourses concerning Government,* ch. 2, section 13) assumed that the office of dictatorship could be abrogated. They made this point with respect to the curious decision of 217 BCE whereby the *magister equitum* (head of the knightly class) was elevated by the Senate to the status of equality with the dictator. Livy (22.25.10) makes the proposing tribune say that he could have alternatively demanded the abrogation of the dictator's *imperium,* his mandate to absolute rule. Other theorists considered preserving the essence of Roman dictatorship in an ideal commonwealth but pleaded for institutional reorganization. Thus, Harrington, Spinoza, and Hume preferred a collective body that could be entrusted with this function.

All in all, early modern theorists concentrated on dictatorship in the early and middle Roman Republic and evaluated it as a model for an emergency government that could temporarily suspend certain elements of the constitution but under no circumstances alter it for future times.

The American Founding Fathers, however, did not want to follow the Roman example of a limited dictatorship. Against (narrowly defeated) motions in the Virginia House of Delegates to install a dictator (in December 1776 and in June 1781) Jefferson argued that a true republican system did not need such provisions (*Notes on the State of Virginia,* query 13). The Constitution of the United States makes no explicit provisions for temporary suspension of rules in times of emergency.

In the course of the French Revolution the concept of dictatorship became subject to a new understanding. The Jacobins (with the exception of Marat) did not refer to it, as that would have destroyed the image of collective leadership. Their opponents, however, evoked dictatorship to denounce the Jacobin regime. By decrying Robespierre as a dictator, they evoked the example of Caesar. The distinction between dictatorship and tyranny became blurred.

In the revolutionary upheavals of 1848 the concept of dictatorship came to be dissociated from any aspect of constitutional government and began to be used with respect to the collective dominance of a social class. In a speech delivered to the Spanish Parliament in January 1849, Donoso Cortés advocated a "dictatorship of the sword," to be led by the legitimate monarchs, as the only possibility for avoiding the masses' "dictatorship of the dagger." His ideas were echoed by counterrevolutionary authors all over Europe.

At the other end of the political spectrum, Karl Marx projected a "dictatorship of the proletariat" that would crush the "dictatorship of the bourgeoisie." This dictatorship of the proletariat would be a transitional stage, though for an indefinite time, until the social conditions for real democracy could be achieved. Marx and Engels later declared the Paris Commune of 1871 to be the first realization of the dictatorship of the proletariat. Lenin had no doubt that it was an illusion to rely on self-organization of the masses; one needed the strong leadership of professional revolutionaries. In his view dictatorship of the proletariat is "democracy on behalf of the poor," necessarily connected with restricting the liberties of the "suppressors, exploiters, capitalists" (*A Contribution to the History of the Question of the Dictatorship,* 1920).

An alleged fusion of dictatorship and democracy was also implied in the coinage Caesarism or Bonapartism. It was developed in the era of Napoleon III (r. 1852–1870) to describe one-man rule founded on usurpation but later legitimized by popular ratification of the constitution. The term spread across Europe. Some used it in an affirmative sense, stressing the democratic aspect, others polemically underlined the autocratic features.

Since the 19th century the term *dictatorship* has been used in a great variety of ways, in most cases without reference to the Roman model. The idea of a constitutional dictatorship was debated until the 1950s or so; the understanding of dictatorship only in a polemical sense was a more recent development.

BIBL.: Peter Baehr and Melvin Richter, eds., *Dictatorship in History and Theory: Bonapartism, Caesarism, and Totalitarism* (Cambridge 2004). Ernst Nolte, "Diktatur," in *Geschichtliche Grundbegriffe* (1972) 1:900–924. Carl Schmitt, *Die Diktatur. Von den Anfängen des modernen Souveränitätsgedankens bis zum proletarischen Klassenkampf* (1921; repr. Berlin 1994).

W.N.

Dido

Dido, Queen of Carthage, also called Elissa, was daughter of the King of Tyre. After her husband was killed, Dido fled the city with a group of followers to the coast of Africa, where she founded and ruled Carthage. According to legend as recounted by Timaeus of Taormina (d. ca. 269 BCE), she committed suicide when pressured into marriage by an African king (Iarbas) in order to preserve her vow of chastity to her deceased husband. Virgil (d. 19 BCE) alters this history in the *Aeneid,* making Dido's Carthage contemporaneous with the fall of Troy. When Aeneas lands at Carthage, Dido, through the intervention of the goddesses Venus and Juno, succumbs to his charms. Aeneas loves Dido in return; but reminded of his duty to found Rome, he leaves Carthage, and Dido, after raining curses on his head and his lineage, kills herself. Although Virgil characterizes Dido as an impediment to Aeneas' mission, his compassionate portrayal of her in book 4 left many readers sympathizing more with her abandonment than with the hardships faced by Aeneas. Augustine (4th–5th cent. CE) wept for her fate (*Confessions* 1.13). As early as in the *Heroides,* however, Ovid (d. 17 CE) presented Virgil's Dido apart from Aeneas' epic history, giving voice to a loving and aggrieved queen wronged by a callous ingrate. Thus, classical legend and literature presented three distinct Didos to the modern world: the historical, chaste Dido, Virgil's captivating Dido, and Ovid's abandoned Dido. Each claims a separate representational afterlife.

The historical Dido survived less as a figure for artistic elaboration than as an emblem of chastity. Macrobius (*Saturnalia,* 400 CE) supports her virtue against Virgil's ahistorical portrayal, and this theme continues in the 14th-century catalogues of exemplary women by Petrarch (*Trionfo della Castità*) and Boccaccio (*De claris mulieribus*). Andrea Mantegna (ca. 1450) depicts the historical queen holding the ashes of her husband in an urn. The chaste Dido took particular hold in England and acquired special significance in the late 16th century, symbolically representing the chastity of Elizabeth I. Dido vigorously defends herself against Virgil in George Tuberville's "Of Dido and the Truth of Her Death," in his *Epitaphs, Epigrams, Songs and Sonnets* (1567).

This emblematic Dido was superseded in the Baroque

era largely by theatrical and operatic portrayals of the epic Dido, emphasizing the perils of female rule. Christopher Marlowe's *Dido, Queen of Carthage* (1594) plays dangerously with this image during the end of Elizabeth's reign. In 17th-century Italy opera found female usurpation a congenial theme, sometimes domesticating the queen by having her marry King Iarbas after Aeneas leaves, as happens in Francesco Cavalli's *Didone* (1641, libretto by Giovanni Francesco Busenello), where she prevents Iarbas' suicide. Thomas Bridges gave this story line a comic turn in *Dido, a Comic Opera* (London 1771), where Dido fails to hang herself on her own garters and agrees to marry Iarbas, the burlesque tone perhaps influenced by Charles Cotton's ribald parody of *Aeneid* book 4, published in 1665 and reprinted well into the 18th century.

The full, epic breadth of Virgil's *Aeneid* appears in the painting *View of Carthage with Dido and Aeneas* (1676), by Claude Lorrain, whose influence can be strongly felt nearly 150 years later in the monumental series by J. M. W. Turner based on the Dido and Aeneas story (ca. 1850). The love of epic also resonates in Hector Berlioz's five-act opera *Les Troyens* (1858), in which the first two acts portray the fall of Troy and the death of the unheeded prophetess Cassandra. This foreshadowing of Dido's fate and the fall of Carthage gives unusual poignancy to the celebrated depiction in act 4 of Dido and Aeneas' mutual love.

Without either the trappings of epic or the mantle of chastity, abandoned Dido is a lonely figure. Peter Paul Rubens (1640) and Sir Joshua Reynolds (1779) distinctively render her final isolation in oil, both paintings entitled *The Death of Dido*. Her voice can be heard in the beautiful but little-known motet "Dulces exuviae," attributed to Josquin des Prez (d. 1521) and based directly on Virgil's text of Dido's lament (*Aeneid* 4.651–654). As depicted more famously in Henry Purcell's opera *Dido and Aeneas* (1685–1689, libretto by Nahum Tate), Dido struggles primarily with her own emotion, her alter ego perhaps personified by the evil Sorceress. Aeneas serves as little more than a symbol of everyman. Dido's final aria, with an obsessively repeating bass and slowly rising melodic line—which reaches its climax on the poignant cry "Remember me!"—epitomizes the anguish of her death.

BIBL.: Michael Burden, ed., *A Woman Scorn'd: Responses to the Dido Myth* (London 1998). René Martin, ed., *Énée et Didon: Naissance, fonctionnement et survie d'un mythe* (Paris 1990).

E.H.

Diels, Hermann

Hermann Diels (1848–1922) was a classical scholar in the tradition of the German *Altertumswissenschaft*. His immense philological labors laid the foundations for modern research on the history of early Greek philosophy.

Diels was born in Wiesbaden, the son of a railway official. His interest in classical philology was awakened early under the guidance of a maternal uncle. He pursued his university studies mainly in Bonn, where he was a fellow student of Ulrich von Wilamowitz, Georg Kaibel, and Carl Robert. His revered mentor was Hermann Usener, a leading proponent of the method of *Quellenforschung*, which used source criticism to reconstruct earlier and more original writings that had not survived. The same method was practiced by the librarian at Bonn, Jakob Bernays, but in his memoirs Diels claims that Bernays obstructed his progress. Through Usener's researches on Theophrastus, Diels was first put on the track of the corpus of doxographical writings, which provides important information about early Greek philosophy. This became the subject of his dissertation (1870), prepared under Usener's supervision. Another important influence was Eduard Zeller, the great historian of Greek philosophy. Though not a philologist, Zeller saw the value of Diels's researches and supported him both in his studies and in the pursuit of an academic career.

Diels's first research project culminated in his monumental *Doxographi Graeci* (1879). He was able to disentangle the complex strands of the doxographical tradition by analyzing the works of numerous later authors and tracing their information back via the shadowy figure of Aëtius to Theophrastus and the Peripatetic school. Although much of his research had been prefigured in scholarship going back to the 16th century, his presentation immediately superseded all previous studies. Recent research has confirmed much of Diels's findings. A weakness is that he underestimated the role of Aristotle, whose invention of the dialectical method in the *Topics* set in motion the doxographical method developed by Theophrastus and the later tradition.

In 1877 Diels moved to Berlin, where he soon gained a university position. In 1881 through Zeller's recommendation he was placed in charge of the huge project of the Prussian Academy to edit the writings of the Aristotelian commentators of late antiquity (*Commentaria in Aristotelem Graeca*), of which 25 volumes would be published from 1882 through 1909. Diels contributed the two volumes on the *Physics* commentary of Simplicius and proofread all the others, which amounted to 15,000 pages in all. These writings too contain much valuable information on the earlier period of Greek philosophy. The English translations currently being published in the Ancient Commentators on Aristotle project directed by Richard Sorabji are based on this edition.

But Diels's best-known contribution to classical scholarship was his edition of the fragments of the Presocratic philosophers, *Die Fragmente der Vorsokratiker*. The first edition was published in 1903 as a textbook for his teaching, but subsequent editions were considerably expanded. For each philosopher the material available was divided into two main sections. The first section presented the A-fragments, which contain the biographical and doxographical evidence. In the second he published the citations of the actual words of each author as B-fragments, marking off their extent through the use of different kinds of type and including a full textual apparatus and a German translation for each one. He did not aim at exhaustive completeness, but all the important evidence is there, and it is remarkable how little material of any importance can be added to his collection (excluding later finds). The project was continued after his death by his pupil Walther Kranz. The sixth edition (1951–1952) has become standard and continues to provide an indispensable textual basis for the study of the early Greek philosophers.

Diels's interests were wider than just source criticism and the history of philosophy. He also published a number of studies on ancient technology and lexicography. His papyrological editions, though valuable, are marred by excessive speculation. An interest in ancient medicine led to his involvement in the *Corpus Medicorum Graecorum,* the project to publish the corpus of Greek medical writings, which remains unfinished.

From 1886 until his retirement in 1920 Diels held the chair of classical philology at the University of Berlin. Unlike his colleague and friend Wilamowitz, he was not an inspiring teacher and writer. His main achievement lay in the organization and execution of fundamental textual research. His lasting legacy is the foundation that he laid for the study of Greek philosophy. Modern research will honor Diels not by accepting that foundation uncritically, but by examining it with care and modifying it where necessary.

BIBL.: W. Burkert, ed., *Hermann Diels: Kleine Schriften zur Geschichte der antiken Philosophie* (Darmstadt 1969) (with a complete list of Diels's writings). W. M. Calder III and J. Mansfeld, eds., *Hermann Diels (1848–1922) et la science de l'antiquité,* Entretiens sur l'antiquité classique 45 (Vandœuvres 1999). J. Mansfeld and D. T. Runia, *Aëtiana: The Method and Intellectual Context of a Doxographer* (Leiden 1996). W. Schütrumpf, "Hermann Diels, 1848–1922," in *Classical Scholarship: A Biographical Encyclopedia,* ed. W. W. Briggs and W. M. Calder III (New York 1990) 52–60.

D.T.R.

Dilettanti, Society of

This was a group of 18th-century British connoisseurs whose expeditions, collections, and publications laid the groundwork for the Neoclassical revival and for the scholarly study of Graeco-Roman antiquity.

In 1736 a group of young male patricians, all of them alumni of the Grand Tour, began to meet regularly at a London tavern and to set about "encouraging, *at home,* a taste for those objects which had contributed to their entertainment *abroad.*" The name they chose for themselves introduced the word *dilettante* into English and celebrated the lively curiosity of the amateur. As they devised suitable rituals and regalia, the Dilettanti turned for inspiration to such groups as the Hell Fire Clubs, the Freemasons, and the Accademia dell'Arcadia, whose Bosco Parrasio on the slopes of the Janiculum in Rome created private spaces for pastoral play. The Society's choice of mottoes signaled the founders' priorities: "Viva la Virtù" (with its call for collecting), "Grecian Taste and Roman Spirit" (with its antic celebration of antiquity), and "Seria Ludo" ("Serious Matters in a Playful Vein," with its echoes of Virgil's *Eclogues* and Horace's *Satires*).

During their first two decades, the Dilettanti devoted most of their energies to the worship of Bacchus and Eros. As Horace Walpole waspishly observed, "The nominal qualification [for membership] is having been in Italy, and the real one, being drunk." Sobriety began to mix with inebriety during the 1750s, when the Dilettanti subsidized the scheme formed by the painter James Stuart and the architect Nicholas Revett to publish "a new and accurate Description of the Antiquities, etc., in the Province of Attica." Thanks to the Society's support, Stuart and Revett were able to spend three years in Athens, measuring, drawing, and excavating. They distilled their findings into a monumental folio, *The Antiquities of Athens* (1762), which upheld the highest standards of clarity, accuracy, and exactitude. In both text and image the authors were inspired by the passionate precision of Antoine Desgodetz's *Édifices antiques de Rome* (1682) and Robert Wood's *The Ruins of Palmyra* (1753), which continued to exemplify the dictum of Wood, "The principal merit of works of this kind is truth."

Encouraged by the success of *The Antiquities of Athens,* the Dilettanti sent Revett, along with the epigrapher Richard Chandler and the artist William Pars, on an ambitious expedition to Asia Minor. The Society exhorted them to "procure the exactest plans and measures possible of the buildings you shall find, making accurate drawings of the bas-reliefs and ornaments, and taking such views as you shall judge proper." This charge was magnificently fulfilled by *Ionian Antiquities* (1769) and its sequel (1786).

Galvanized by two of its most influential members, Sir William Hamilton and Richard Payne Knight, the Society made an equally ambitious but much more subversive contribution to classical studies by publishing *A Discourse on the Worship of Priapus* (1786), which drew on recent discoveries in southern Italy. This work straddles the divide, as Arnaldo Momigliano has defined it, between "a book of history and a book of antiquities": on the one hand, it aims for "factual truth"; on the other, it keeps in mind that "history is a re-interpretation of the past which leads to conclusions about the present." The Dilettanti returned to the proto-archaeological folio with *Specimens of Antient Sculpture* (1809), whose attributions have not stood the test of time but whose illustrations remain unrivaled. Although the Society continued to send expeditions to the Levant and to publish imposing architectural and archaeological reports, it lost its status as classical arbiter par excellence when it dismissed Lord Elgin's marbles as Hadrianic imitations. Nevertheless, the achievements of the Dilettanti from 1760 to 1810 mark what the 19th-century historian Friedrich Kruse called "a new period in the rediscovery of Greece."

The Society's projects and publications exemplify the Enlightenment ideal of the gentleman amateur, which is linked in turn to a culture of wide-ranging curiosity. Such works as *Priapus* and *Specimens* are hybrid texts, coterie productions that also reach out to a wider intellectual community. As their role in the Elgin controversy makes clear, the Dilettanti both prepared for and conflicted with the culture that replaced them, that of the soberly specialized professional.

BIBL.: Michael Clarke and Nicholas Penny, eds., *The Arrogant Connoisseur: Richard Payne Knight* (Manchester 1982). Lionel Cust and Sidney Colvin, *History of the Society of Dilettanti* (London 1914). Arnaldo Momigliano, "Ancient History and the Antiquarian," *Journal of the Warburg and Courtauld Institutes* 13 (1950) 285–315. Bruce Redford, *Dilettanti: The Antic and the Antique in Eighteenth-century England* (Los Angeles 2008).

B.R.

Diogenes Laertius

Greek writer, 3rd century CE. Because of an irony of fate, no biographical details survive about the foremost biographer of Greek philosophers. Diogenes Laertius is a mere label attached to the ten books of the *Lives and Doctrines of the Philosophers,* our best indirect source of knowledge for classical philosophy. The *Lives* comprises both a biographical and a doxographical account, basically focused on Greek thinkers from the 6th to the 3rd centuries BCE (from Thales to Epicurus), although references to schools and individuals extend to at least the 2nd century CE, and the topics covered include the barbarian origins of philosophy, an issue that some Renaissance thinkers would place high on their intellectual agenda.

The importance of the *Lives* as a source cannot be overestimated, though its very richness gave rise to a scholarly debate when 19th-century philologists called into question Diogenes' strategies of collecting and assembling information. The shift from thinking of the *Lives* as a gallery of opinions to approaching it as an organic whole required a concept of authorship that Diogenes seemed unable to live up to. In addition to criticizing Diogenes' lack of philosophical talent, Hegel categorized the *Lives* as a mere compilation, though an important one. It was Hermann Usener, however, in his *Epicurea* (1887), who sanctioned the image of Diogenes as a "complete ass" (*asinus germanus*) in the course of a long debate over his sources (single or multiple, direct or indirect), whose results some scholars have not hesitated to call a fiasco. Partly redeemed by subsequent readings committed to emphasizing a Hellenistic background and claims of literary consistency, the *Lives* has still not received adequate philological attention, both critical editions by H. S. Long (1964) and M. Marcovich (1999) having attracted considerable criticism.

Yet long before German philologists started dissecting the *Lives,* the canonization of Diogenes Laertius had already taken place. Evidence for this is provided by Victor Hugo (*Les Misérables* 4.9.3), whose character M. Mabeuf sadly resolves on 4 June 1832 to sell the last volume surviving in his bookcase for 100 francs. This was an edition of Diogenes' *Lives,* supposedly printed at Lyon in 1644, including some variant readings as well as all the passages in Doric dialect preserved only in a 12th-century manuscript in the National Library of Naples. This "famous manuscript" (Burbonicus Graecus III B 29) is actually one of the oldest and best among nearly 40 surviving. It was probably the exemplar used by Henricus Aristippus for his Latin translation, made in southern Italy in the late 1150s, now unfortunately lost. That version was employed by Geremia da Montagnone in his *Compendium moralium notabilium* (1285) and by an anonymous Italian author whose *Liber de vita et moribus philosophorum,* written ca. 1317–1320 and falsely attributed to the Englishman Walter Burley, gained wide popularity.

The Latin version produced by Ambrogio Traversari in Florence between 1424 and 1433 is far more richly documented. It began to circulate immediately in several manuscript copies, as is shown by Leon Battista Alberti's early borrowings in book 2 of his *Libri della famiglia,* which was certainly finished by 1433–1434. Also noteworthy is Alberti's use of Diogenes' *Life of Thales* as a model for his autobiography (whose traditional dating to 1438 has recently been challenged). The Latin Diogenes might, however, have had an even earlier indirect effect on the Humanist Leonardo Bruni, whose laudatory *Life of Aristotle* (1429) preempted the unsympathetic portrait of Aristotle that Traversari's translation would soon make available. In fact, among the Italian Humanists the Latin version of the *Lives* met a fate marked in equal measure by strong criticism and widespread circulation. The latter is exemplified by the presence of Traversari's translation in the library of the Byzantine émigré Cardinal Bessarion, the outstanding Hellenist of the 15th century, whose magnificent collection of Greek philosophical manuscripts, including Diogenes' *Lives,* hardly needed to be supplemented by a Latin version.

As for Diogenes' text, it could not help being affected by skilled philologists and sloppy editors. An instructive example involves Machiavelli's *Life of Castruccio Castracani* (1520). Putting into Castruccio's mouth some thirty sayings that Diogenes had ascribed to the Socratic philosopher Aristippus, Machiavelli implicitly paid tribute to the first printed editions of the Latin Diogenes (Rome ca. 1472, Venice 1475), but he also paid the price of their misunderstandings. In Diogenes' *Life of Aristippus,* just as fishermen "allow the sea to drench them in order to catch a gudgeon," so Aristippus endures Dionysius of Syracuse's spitting on him "in order to take a blenny," that is, to gain Dionysius' favor. In Machiavelli's adaptation, however, a clever flatterer endures Castruccio's spitting on him "in order to catch a whale": *balena* was Machiavelli's vernacular reading of *balenus,* a Latin word invented by the editors of the Latin *Lives* who did not understand Traversari's *blenus,* a calque of the original Greek *blennos.*

Diogenes' *Lives* was repeatedly issued in Latin and Italian in the late 15th and the early 16th centuries. It was only in 1533 that Hieronymus Froben and Nicolaus Episcopius printed the Greek text at Basel; in 1570 Henri Estienne (Stephanus) published a bilingual Greek and Latin edition in Geneva. Traversari's text remained at the center of scholarship on Diogenes, as can be seen in *Notes to Diogenes Laertius* (1583) by Isaac Casaubon, and the *Annotations* (1594) by Tommaso Aldobrandini (d. 1572), who also provided a new Latin translation. In 1692 Traversari's Latin version (the so-called *versio Ambrosiana*) was reissued in Amsterdam in a bilingual edition revised by Marcus Meibom, including annotations by Isaac and Méric Casaubon, Aldobrandini, and Gilles Ménage—an edition studied by Giacomo Leopardi, among others.

The progressive philological improvements in the editions of the *Lives* were followed by diffusion of their contents, first of all those concerning otherwise little-known doctrines. Indeed, Diogenes' doxographical accounts offer long excerpts from primary texts not transmitted elsewhere, such as Epicurus' *Principal Doctrines* and letters to Herodotus, Pythocles, and Menoeceus. Epicurus eventually had his day in the 17th century: his monument was Pierre Gassendi's *Observations on the Tenth Book of Diogenes Laertius* (1649), which includes facing Greek and Latin texts of Diogenes' *Life of Epicurus,* followed by Gassendi's extensive and philosophically engaged commentary. Yet there is good evidence of an earlier dissemination of Epicureanism: a case in point is an anonymous censure of the 1570s that reproached Girolamo Cardano for drawing attention to Diogenes Laertius as a source of otherwise prohibited authors such as Epicurus.

Although condemned to perpetual exploitation by scholars and thinkers, the *Lives* proved itself to consist of something more than raw materials serving higher purposes. The section of *Apophthegms* (1531) that Erasmus devoted to Diogenes of Sinope drew heavily on Diogenes Laertius' account of the Cynic school, an account that was also instrumental in shaping the Cynicism that colored the French Enlightenment. Furthermore, Erasmus acknowledged Diogenes' curiosity, as did Montaigne, indirectly, when lamenting that "we do not have a dozen Laertiuses." Two centuries elapsed, however, before Jakob Brucker redirected this very curiosity toward a critical historiography of philosophy based on eclectic grounds. In fact, beginning with G. J. Vossius' *Sects of Philosophers* (*De philosophorum sectis liber,* 1657), through Thomas Stanley's *History of Philosophy* (1655–1662) in Gottfried Olearius' Latin translation (1711), and notably in Brucker's *Critical History of Philosophy* (*Historia critica philosophiae,* 1742–1744), Diogenes' *Lives* ended up embodying the eclectic roots of the history of ideas. Modern scholarship took up Diogenes' pattern of philosophical successions (which relates thinkers to each other in a descending line of master and pupil) as a basic framework for his accounts (which discuss each philosopher's biography, writings, doctrines, documents, followers, and so on) and used it to lay the foundations of an unprejudiced treatment of philosophical opinions—a treatment whose virtues of "modesty, justice, caution and courage" (Olearius), from the 18th century onward, became the central features not of a specifically eclectic philosophy, but of the historiography of philosophy in general.

BIBL.: Tiziando Dorandi, *Laertiana: Capitoli sulla tradizione manoscritta e sulla storia del testo delle "Vite dei filosofi" di Diogene Laerzio* (New York 2009). Wolfgang Haase, ed., *Aufstieg und Niedergang der Römischen Welt* (Berlin 1992), vols. II.36.5 and II.36.6. G.M.C.

Dionysus

Greek god of vegetation, wine, ecstasy, and the theater, son of Zeus and Semele. As the god of wine and the theater, Dionysus was one of the major culture bearers who freed the life of ancient man from its daily toil. And he led it across its own boundaries into religious ecstasy, opened it to the divine or the animalistic, and thereby shook its cultural foundations. The ancient sources (Greek and Latin texts, archaeological evidence) for his myth are numerous, but two particularly have given decisive form to his reception: Euripides' tragedy *Bacchae* (performed after 406 BCE), whose influence overshadows that of all other depictions to date, and Plato, whose interpretation of religious inspiration in the language of the Dionysian and Orphic mysteries (*Phaedrus* 244 ff.) had a great influence on both Neoplatonic and Renaissance thought.

Christian culture was hostile to the pagan gods and fought their worship. Joining the polemic of other Church Fathers, Augustine singled out "Liber" (a Latin name for Dionysus, like "Bacchus") as responsible for the divinely ordered fall of Rome, since the festival of the Bacchanalia, celebrated in his honor, had unleashed the immorality of the people to the utmost degree. Despite the ban on cult practice, pagan deities survived in niches of the literary tradition and made partial headway into Christian writings. Thus, the play *Christos paschon,* written by an anonymous Byzantine author of the 11th or 12th century, was a compilation of several ancient works, including Euripides' *Bacchae.* In it the suffering of Dionysus is replaced by the suffering of Christ.

In the Renaissance Dionysus' myth fell under Orphic-Neoplatonic influence and seemed at times to presage Friedrich Nietzsche's Apollonian-Dionysian dualism. In his *De hominis dignitate* (1496), Giovanni Pico della Mirandola compares the highest knowledge of nature and God with the initiation into the Bacchic mysteries: at one moment the philosopher descends a ladder to the deep, where with the force of the Titans he rips apart "unity" in the form of Osiris (who after Herodotus 2.48 was considered equivalent with Dionysus and whose death at the hands of the Titans is described in the passage); the next moment he ascends to the heights, where with the strength of Phoebus Apollo he reassembles the multitude of Osiris's rent limbs into a unity. A burlesque side of Dionysus came to the fore in Angelo Poliziano's *Fabula di Orpheo* (1480). As in Euripides' *Bacchae,* the protagonist is dismembered by the god's female adherents, but here the drama ends as a rollicking satyr plays with a chorus of drunken Bacchantae.

In Baroque poetry Dionysus appears as a god of abundance, joy, idyll, and festivities—for example in Martin

Opitz's *Lobgesang Bacchi* (*In Praise of Bacchus,* 1622). Above all, however, this is also his guise in the rich emblematics of the time, as well as in numerous paintings, such as Jacopo Tintoretto's *Bacchus and Ariadne* (1577) and Peter Paul Rubens's *Bacchus* (ca. 1636), which regularly accented his unruly vitality, his youthfulness, and his beauty. In this context Bacchus and his retinue, the satyrs, were intermingled again and again with Golden Age myths and Arcadian pastoral bliss. The god's dark side barely played a role and was first emphasized from time to time in the Enlightenment. Thus, Christoph Martin Wieland waged a barely disguised polemic in his *Geschichte des Agathon* (1766) against the ruling power of the "government of lascivious princes," whose lives were "an everlasting Bacchanal" (9.1). Soon thereafter these excessive parties were overwhelmed by the Bacchic antipode of riotous pleasure, namely the excessive violence of the French Revolution. Heinrich Campe, an eyewitness to the events, reported from Paris in 1789 that he wanted to "shout out with delight" and "rush to meet the approaching spring of the general well-being of nations" with "a Thyrsus [an attribute of Dionysus] in hand." Saint Just spoke of the "revolution en bacchante." And Heinrich Heine greeted the beginning of the February Revolution of 1848 with the Bacchantae's shout of joy, in which he replaced Dionysus with the names of two revolutionaries from 1789: "Evoe Danton! Evoe Robespierre!"

The idea of revolution, which drives the conflict between Dionysus and Pentheus in Euripides' *Bacchae,* remained a focal point of interest in the course of the events in France, and in Romanticism it took on utopian features. Friedrich Hölderlin, who translated portions of Euripides' tragedy, reflected intensely on the god. His considerations found their most forceful expression in his elegy *Brod und Wein* (*Bread and Wine,* 1807), whose title was initially supposed to be *Der Weingott* (*The Wine God*). Dionysus is apostrophized there as "the coming God," the harbinger of a new epoch whose advent is expected after the night in which the current age of man is found. Friedrich Schelling's introduction to *Philosophie der Offenbarung* (*Philosophy of Revelation,* 1841/1842) interprets him the same way, as does, finally, the work that became decisive for the later reception of his myth: Friedrich Nietzsche's *Geburt der Tragödie aus dem Geiste der Musik* (*Birth of Tragedy from the Spirit of Music,* 1872). Following Richard Wagner, Nietzsche developed the concept of the artwork of the future, in which—according to his interpretation—the Dionysian and the Apollonian, inebriation and moderation, would be united as they once were in Greek tragedy. Thanks to the cult of Nietzsche in National Socialism, the revolutionary aspect of Dionysus also had a place there, although Alfred Rosenberg, the editor of the *Völkischer Beobachter* (*People's Observer*), saw him (as a god coming from Asia) as a "symbol of miscegenation" that did not fit into the ideology of the "pure Aryan race" (*Der Mythus des 20. Jahrhunderts,* 1930). In another perspective, Dionysus provided the source for an aesthetic of inebriation that found expression in works of Charles Baudelaire (*Le Thyrse,* 1863), Walter Pater (*Denys l'Auxerrois,* 1887), and Thomas Mann (*Death in Venice,* 1912). In the 20th century anthropology and psychoanalysis caused the dark side of his myth, namely its aspects of foreignness and ecstasy, to be emphasized. Examples can be found in Hans Werner Henze's opera *Die Bassariden,* whose libretto was written by W. H. Auden and Chester Kallman (*The Bassarids,* 1966), in Richard Schechner's *Dionysus in 69* (1968), and in Botho Strauss's *Kalldeway Farce* (1981).

BIBL.: Achim Aurnhammer and Thomas Pittrof, eds., "*Mehr Dionysos als Apoll": Antiklassizistische Antikerezeption um 1900* (Frankfurt 2002). Burghard Dedner, "Die Ankunft des Dionysos," in *Die andere Welt: Studien zum Exotismus,* ed. Thomas Koebner and Gerhart Pickerodt (Frankfurt 1987) 200–239. John Burt Foster, *Heirs to Dionysus: A Nietzschean Current in Literary Modernism* (Princeton 1981). Manfred Frank, *Der kommende Gott: Vorlesungen über die neue Mythologie* (Frankfurt 1982). R. D. Stock, *The Flutes of Dionysus: Daemonic Enthrallment in Literature* (Lincoln 1989). T.G.

Translated by Patrick Baker

Diophantus

Greek mathematician (fl. ca. 250 CE), working in Alexandria, author of a large algebraic treatise, the *Arithmetica.* A small fragment of a treatise on polygonal numbers is also attributed to him. Because he is not mentioned in sources earlier than the 4th century, he is thought to have lived in the 3rd, and the Dionysius he addresses in the introduction to the *Arithmetica* may have been Saint Dionysius. An epigram from the *Anthologia Graeca* (14.126), which retraces some of his life (marriage at 33, birth of son at 38, death of son four years before his own, at 84), seems contrived.

Ten of the 13 books (*biblia*) of the *Arithmetica* have come down to us. Books 1–6 arrived in Europe in the 15th century; in 1968 four more books were found in an Arabic translation. As these latter are in fact the original books 4–7, the last three Greek books (4–6) should follow them, presumably corresponding to books 8–10. Books 12 and 13 must be considered lost. The Arabic version (covering originally books 1–7) is notably more prolix than the Greek text we know, for it preserves a late Greek commentary, giving details of the computations and verifying that the solutions found fulfill the equations. Most probably this commentary is by Hypatia, the daughter of Theon of Alexandria.

After an introduction giving general instructions, Diophantus proceeds with problems (some 250 in the extant part). Book 1 contains elementary (school) problems that are, however, solved in the new, algebraic way. Books 2 and 3 teach Diophantus' fundamental methods, which are extended to further problems in books 4–7, the purpose of which is, he says, "experience and skill" (rather than new knowledge). This explains why the lacuna in the middle of the six Greek books escaped notice. The problems in the last three Greek books are of a notably higher level.

The historical importance of the *Arithmetica* is twofold. First, it is the only surviving testimony of a higher algebra in antiquity and the first occurrence of an algebraic symbolism (with signs to denote the unknown, its powers, and a few operations, all of which are explained in the introduction and clearly originate in scribal abbreviations). Second, the six extant Greek books gave the impetus, principally through the observations of the French mathematician Pierre de Fermat (1601–1665), to modern number theory. One of Fermat's assertions in particular (namely his remark, on Diophantus' problem 2.8, that the equality $x^n + y^n = z^n$ with n any integer larger than 2 is impossible with rational numbers) was to occupy mathematicians for more than three centuries before being proved in 1993–1995.

The reason for such observations is that, mathematically, the *Arithmetica* raises more questions than it answers. Most of the problems are indeterminate, thus with more unknowns than equations and, as such, may or may not be soluble. But apart from the guidelines in the introduction, only a few generally applicable methods are explained, and it is only through Diophantus' skillful assumptions that a proposed problem is made determinate and reduced to a simple case, or to some problem or method seen before. Difficult in itself, the *Arithmetica* remained largely inaccessible, and departing from Diophantus' assumptions was beyond the capabilities of most mathematicians until modern times. This explains the fascination still exerted by his name, which is associated with numerous fields in modern-day mathematics.

BIBL.: Thomas Heath, *Diophantus of Alexandria* (1910; repr. New York 1964). Jacques Sesiano, *Books IV to VII of Diophantus' Arithmetica in the Arabic Translation Attributed to Qusta ibn Luqa* (Berlin 1982). Paul Tannery, *Diophanti Alexandrini opera omnia,* 2 vols. (1893–1895; repr. Stuttgart 1974).

J.SS.

Dioscorides

Dioscorides' *De materia medica,* compiled around the 1st century CE, was divided into five books, according to medicinal affinities. Though some plants were discussed together under natural groupings, others of the same family were scattered across chapters. Dioscorides' aim was to provide a comprehensive account of the use of plants, animals, and minerals for medicinal use.

Latin translations of the *De materia medica* were available in the Middle Ages, as were alphabetical redactions with additional material from Arabic sources. The study and use of Dioscoridean material were mostly carried out indirectly through various pharmacological manuals, however, such as the *Liber medicinae ex herbis feminis,* Matthaeus Platearius' *Circa instans,* and Matthaeus Sylvaticus' *Opus pandectarum medicinae.* Except for Petrus Padubanensis' commentary on the alphabetical redaction (ca. 1300), there appears to be no medieval commentary on *De materia medica. De materia medica* did not form part of the *Articella,* nor is there direct evidence that it was used as a principal text for examination by the medical faculty of universities, perhaps because it did not contain the Galenic theory of degrees of simples.

The Latin text (alphabetical redaction) of *De materia medica,* with Petrus Padubanensis' commentary, was the first to be printed, in Colle in 1478. Hermolaus Barbarus completed a translation by 1481, which was not printed until 1516. The Greek text was first printed in 1499, and a revised version in 1518. Further editions followed throughout the 16th century (by Janus Cornarius, Basel, 1529; by Jacobus Goupylus, Paris, 1549; by Janus Antonius Saracenus, Frankfurt, 1598). Latin translations from the Greek were made by Barbarus (1516), Johannes Ruellius (1516), Marcellus Virgilius (1518), Cornarius (1557), and Saracenus (1598).

It is the 16th century that can truly be called the century of the revival of Dioscorides. *De materia medica* was read and studied not just for antiquarian and philological interest, but primarily because it was believed to improve medical knowledge and practice. Commentaries of the 16th century show efforts to identify Dioscorides' plants in contemporary Europe, to establish whether the exotica flooding in from all parts of the world were new, and to make available through vernacular translations these findings to medical practitioners (for instance, Andrés Laguna's Castilian translation and commentary, 1555). Dioscorides became a medical authority whose work should be taught in medical faculties, for instance at the universities of Padua, Wittenberg, Montpellier, and Bologna. Universities set up botanical gardens for medical instruction; a lecturer was assigned to point out herbs, and prefects of these gardens, such as Luca Ghini (Pisa), Aloysius Anguillara (Padua), and Melchior Guilandinus (Padua), also composed commentaries on *De materia medica.* The foremost commentator on Dioscorides was Pier Andrea Mattioli (1501–1577). In 1544 Mattioli first wrote on *De materia medica;* the text (based on Ruellius' edition) was followed by a crisp discussion of practical matters rather than lengthy exposition on philological niceties. The Latin edition, first printed in 1554, followed a similar format. The major addition here was the illustrations, perhaps inspired by the illustrated herbals of Otto Brunfels and Leonhart Fuchs. Together with various indexes—of properties of drugs, of afflicted parts of the body, and of types of diseases—Mattioli's commentary (always illustrated after 1554) was designed to be used by practicing physicians and apothecaries. In successive editions, Mattioli's annotations grew, rebutting criticisms by others, rebuking other commentators for their mistakes, and thanking some for their help. More than 30 imprints of Mattioli's commentary appeared in the 16th century, and there were vernacular translations into Italian, French, Czech, and German.

Toward the end of the 16th century a growing realization that Dioscorides described only a fraction of the world's plants, together with an interest in applying Theophrastus' morphological taxonomy, shifted the focus of the study of plants. Interest in Dioscorides' *De materia medica* on its own declined in the 17th century, except for the republication of the works by Mattioli and Lacuna.

BIBL.: Paula Findlen, "The Formation of a Scientific Community: Natural History in Sixteenth-century Italy," in *Natural Philosophy and the Disciplines in Early Modern Europe,* ed. Anthony Grafton and Nancy Siriasi (Cambridge, Mass., 2000) 369–400. Karen M. Reeds, *Botany in Medieval and Renaissance Universities* (New York 1991). John M. Riddle, "Dioscorides," *Catalogus translationum et commentariorum* 4 (1980) 1–143.

S.K.

Diotima

Greek priestess, ca. 400 BCE. The figure of Diotima first appeared in Plato's dialogue the *Symposium.* She is the only woman who participates actively in a Platonic dialogue. Her appearance resolves the difficulty that Socrates, who claims to know nothing, here preaches a positive doctrine; Socrates' teachings on love come from her mouth. The core of her doctrine is presented in the famous ascent of the lover, which can be understood as a process of intellectual development and became a significant element in the reception of Plato's philosophy. The love of a beautiful person leads, through several intermediate steps, to the love and view of the idea of the beautiful itself. Whether Diotima is a historical figure or fictional character remains uncertain. In the *Symposium* she is depicted as a priestess whose offering of a sacrifice preserved Athens from a plague for 10 years (201D).

During late antiquity and the Middle Ages references to Diotima were sparse. In Proclus' commentary on Plato's *Republic* she numbers among the Pythagorean women who achieved renown through their learning and virtue (8.248.25–30). The reception of the *Symposium* during the Renaissance led to a revival of the figure of Diotima; Ficino, for example, praises her as a divinely inspired sibyl in *De amore* (1469), his commentary on the *Symposium.* From then on Diotima came to stand for a female participant in philosophical discussions, but one whose doctrines may in some circumstances depart considerably from those expressed in Plato's text, as in Francesco Patrizi's 16th-century dialogue *Amorosa filosofia.* There Tarquinia Molza appears in the role of a female teacher, a "nuova Diotima" who imparts her knowledge on the subject of love. Since this knowledge has a physiological orientation, however, it can be described as virtually anti-Platonic in character.

Toward the end of the 18th century, as authors of the late classical and early Romantic period in Germany absorbed Plato's ideas, interest in the figure of Diotima was reawakened. She served both Platonists and anti-Platonists to illustrate contemporary emancipated women who expressed their own independent philosophical ideas. Friedrich Schlegel, motivated by a desire to show that women of high social status with philosophical training had existed in antiquity, devoted a historical study to her entitled *Über die Diotima* (1795). There he argued that Diotima was neither a courtesan nor a slave but rather a priestess whose teachings derived from the philosophical tradition of Pythagoras. In his epistolary novel *Aristipp* the author Christoph Martin Wieland takes a critical view of Plato's Diotima. The work contains a description of a banquet characterized as an "anti-symposium," and Wieland, calling Diotima a "mystagogue of love," introduces a female figure who criticizes Diotima's teachings and wants to hear speeches denouncing Eros. Over time the name Diotima became a kind of code word when real persons are superimposed on fictional characters, as when Frans Hemsterhuis addresses the learned Princess Amalie Gallitzin by this name and depicts her as Diotima in his dialogue *Simon* (1787). The figure of Diotima had a special significance for Friedrich Hölderlin, and he dedicated a number of poems to her. In his unfinished novel *Hyperion oder der Heremit in Griechenland* (*Hyperion; or, The Hermit in Greece,* 1797–1799), Diotima becomes the central female character, inspired by and modeled on Susette Gontard.

Interest in the figure of Diotima during the 19th and 20th centuries was slight. Robert Musil introduced a character by that name in his novel *Der Mann ohne Eigenschaften* (*The Man without Qualities,* 1930–1942) in order to depict other characters—Romantics and enemies of learning—in an ironic light. Diotima herself is referred to as a "docent of love" (1.22). No irony is intended in the title of the composer Luigi Nono's *Fragment—Stille, An Diotima* (Fragment—Silence, to Diotima, 1980), a string quartet inspired by Hölderlin.

BIBL.: Ulrich Gaier, "Diotima, eine synkretistische Gestalt," in *Hölderlin: Christentum und Antike,* ed. Valérie Lawitschka (Tübingen 1991) 141–172. David M. Halperin, "Why Is Diotima a Woman? Platonic *Eros* and the Figuration of Gender," in *Before Sexuality,* ed. D. M. Halperin et al. (Princeton 1990) 257–308. Stefan Matuschek, ed., *Wo das philosophische Gespräch ganz in Dichtung übergeht: Platons Symposion und seine Wirkung in der Renaissance, Romantik und Moderne* (Heidelberg 2002). Friedrich Schlegel, "Über die Diotima," in *Kritische Friedrich Schlegel Ausgabe,* vol. 1, ed. Ernst Behler et al. (Paderborn 1979) 70–115. Kurt Sier, *Die Rede der Diotima: Untersuchungen zum platonischen Symposion* (Stuttgart 1997).

S.E.

Translated by Deborah Lucas Schneider

Divination

The attempt to interpret what the gods have in store for the future, or to reveal what lies hidden in the present, using either natural signs offered to the interpreter from the outside world or artificial signs that the interpreter devises, for instance by casting lots (*sortes,* a term more widely applied to various techniques). Such concerns figured prominently in antiquity, and some of the ancient techniques of divination and many of the ancient arguments for or against it laid the ground for later discussions. Cicero defined divination as "the experience in advance (*praesensio*) and knowledge of future things" (*De divinatione* 1.1). For the Romans, he said, *furor* (being "out of one's mind") and dreams were the main means of predicting the future. Using the term "magic," Pliny (*Natural History* 30.5) refers to making predictions with water, with balls, by the aid of the air, of the stars, of lamps, basins, hatchets, and numerous other appliances. Writing ca. 600 CE, Isidore of Seville (*Etymologies* 8.9.12–14) relates, from Varro's account (1st cent. BCE), a division according to the four elements, earth, water, air, and fire, which gave rise to geomancy, hydromancy, aeromancy, and pyromancy, but of these he describes only hydromancy: "the evocation of the shadows of demons by looking at the surface of water, or seeing images or their illusions, or to hear something from them, or, by using blood, to summon the inhabitants of the nether world." Of diviners he says that "they pretend that they are full of divinity, and by a certain fraudulent cunning they guess future events for men." He distinguishes two modes of divination: through *furor* and by *ars* (skill, art). These definitions were taken up and developed in the Middle Ages and the Renaissance (e.g., by Thomas Aquinas, *Summa theologiae* 2a.2ae.q95,a3) and can still be discerned in the *Malleus maleficarum* (1486), the Inquisitors' handbook on magic, in which are described (bk. 1, q. 16) three kinds of divination, from which all branches of magic derive: "The first of these occurs through the manifest invocation of demons (divided into sorcery, oneiromancy, necromancy, oracles, geomancy, hydromancy, aeromancy, pyromancy, and the cult of soothsaying), the second through the silent consideration alone of the disposition or movement of some object, such as the stars, the days, the breezes, and so on (horoscopy, haruspicy, augury, observation of omens, cheiromancy, and spatulamancy), the third is through the consideration of some human act for finding out something hidden, and is called by the name of 'lots' (e.g., the consideration of pricks and straws, and molten figures in lead)."

Saint Augustine's description of hydromancy (*City of God* 1.7.35) shows that it served as a term for lecanomancy, by which the diviner saw portents in the shapes produced by oil poured onto water in a cup or bowl. In the *Romance of Alexander* (3rd cent. CE), for example, the magician Nectanebus sees an entire fleet of ships in his bowl. Related to lecanomancy was catoptromancy, or divination by mirrors or other luminous objects, which had a literary tradition in Byzantine, Jewish, and Arabic cultures but for which there is also evidence of practice in the West, for example in the story that John of Salisbury (*Policraticus* 2.28) tells of his experience, as a young boy, when he was obliged by his priest to look into fingernails moistened with sacred oil or chrism, or into the smooth, polished surface of a basin sprinkled with oil, and descry images in them. Other shiny objects for seeing, such as crystal balls, swords, and ivory knife handles, are also frequently mentioned in medieval sources, both in order to condemn their use and in anecdotes referring to their use.

Two ancient forms of divination remained widespread and licit, namely bibliomancy and "books of fortune." Bibliomancy was the random opening of a book to reveal a significant message. The Greeks used Homer, the Romans, Virgil (*sortes Virgilianae*); but Christians would naturally use the Bible (*sortes biblicae* or *revolutio foliorum*). Augustine's course of life was changed when he received the instruction to do this: *Tolle, lege,* "Take, read" (*Confessions* 8.12.29). In 12th-century England the *revolutio foliorum* became an official part of the ceremony for consecration of a bishop.

Books of fortune derive written predictions through a set of procedures from a randomly acquired datum (usually a number generated from turning a wheel or randomly sketching dots in a line). This classical genre (as we see in the Greek *sortes Astrampsychi* from 3rd-century Egypt) received Christian endorsement from the casting of lots by the Apostles to find a replacement for Judas (Acts 1:29) and is extant in several early medieval texts called variously *sortes Sangallenses, sortes apostolorum, sortes sanctorum,* and *experimentarius* (the last attributed to Bernardus Silvestris, mid-12th cent.). The random element (the *sors* or lot) was thought to be divinely controlled, and some books of this nature begin with a prayer asking that the practitioner's *sortes* be placed "in God's hands" (*in manibus tuis sortes meae,* Montero and Alonso 2004, 70).

Nature too could provide clues as to what to expect in the future. From antiquity, a continuous tradition can be traced for divining the weather from celestial phenomena and various terrestrial occurrences. The predictions of Aratus (*Phaenomena*), Virgil (*Georgics* 1), and Theophrastus (*On Signs*) were included in Pliny's *Natural History* (18) and Ptolemy's *Tetrabiblos* (2.13). These signs, such as a red sky at night indicating rain within three days, and ants carrying their eggs out of their nests in anticipation of inundation, were repeated in Arabic texts dependent on the *Tetrabiblos,* and also in the Latin West (a translation of *On Signs* was made by Bartholomew of Messina in the mid-13th century under the title *De astronomia navali* or *De signis aquarum*); but they also became mingled with (or percolated to the level of) folklore. Unexpected happenings in the environment could also be significant. The so-called Table of Solomon (*tabula pronostica Salomonis*) gives predictions according to events occurring under each sign of the zodiac: the house creaking, ears ringing, a crow cawing, a cock crowing, a dog howling, a wild animal appearing, and so on. John of Salisbury (*Policraticus* 1.13) pours scorn on such observations: hares, he says, are better met with on the dinner table than on the road.

Astrology was regarded as the preeminent of the divinatory arts. It is the first one mentioned in Cicero's *De divinatione,* and Pliny asks the rhetorical question "Who is not ready to believe that knowledge [of the future] may with the greatest certainty be obtained by observing the face of the heavens?" (*Natural History* 30.2). But whereas astrology as a whole indicates the dispositions of individuals to certain fates and of nations to certain destinies, some branches of astrology are more clearly divinatory in nature than others. One of these is "interrogations," in which the client, suitably prepared, asks the astrologer a question concerning something hidden from immediate knowledge, or the outcome of an enterprise, and the answer is given according to the condition of the heavens at the time of the question. Interrogations of this kind appear in the West in writings as early as the 1st century CE (in Dorotheus of Sidon, *Carmen astrologicum* 5.17.1–2) and developed into their own genre in the Islamic world (with the influx of Indian astrology) and traveled thence into medieval Western astrology. According to the 13th-century *Speculum astronomiae* (chaps. 9 and 14), a guide to the astrological texts then available in France, the validity of the interrogation depends on intense concentration at the moment of questioning on the part of the interrogator (*intentio radicalis* and *sollicitudo*) and the agreement of the interrogator's horoscope with the horoscope of that moment. An example of a reverse form of this interrogational astrology is a curious letter purported to have been written by "Argafalau" for Alexander the Great and dating back at least to Hellenistic times, in which the astrologer is able to guess what the client is going to ask about (as well as what he holds in his hand) from the planetary hour of his approach.

Likewise directly traceable to classical precedents are techniques involving the conversion of the letters of the client's name into numbers: The Spheres of Life and Death (attributed to Pythagoras and Apuleius), in which the resultant numbers can be looked for within a circle divided into the quadrants Great Life, Small Life, Great Death, and Small Death; and The Victorious and the Vanquished, in which the resultant numbers "fight" each other to determine the victor. A similar method determines who will overcome an illness or get the better of his wife. One version of The Victorious and the Vanquished was included in the *Secret of Secrets,* a manual of statesmanship said to be addressed by Aristotle to his royal pupil, Alexander. Although the text cannot be traced farther back than its Arabic version, it does fall within a Hellenistic genre of letters purportedly exchanged between the philosopher and Alexander.

Another section of the *Secret of Secrets* is devoted to physiognomy, by which the ruler can divine the character of a prospective servant or client. A lively classical tradition for this too can be discerned, starting with the Greek texts of Philemon and pseudo-Aristotle, which found a fertile field in Arabic and bore fruit again in medieval Latin writings. In respect to the physiognomy of one particular part of the body, the palm, Aristotle himself alludes to the significance of its major lines (*History of Animals* 493b32), but one may surmise that an oral tradition of cheiromancy preceded the writing down of the first texts in Latin, which date from the mid-12th century. A peculiar concentration on the lines of the forehead (metoposcopy) developed in the Renaissance.

Although several kinds of divination continued unabated from the classical period into the Middle Ages and beyond, through learned and popular channels, others had only antiquarian interest. Still others lent their names and terms to new forms of divination introduced in the Middle Ages. For example, in the mid-12th century Hugo of Santalla purported to be rediscovering in Arabic texts the Varronian technique of divination by each of the elements, when he identified as "geomancy" the Arabic practice of divination by sand (*ʿilm al-raml*), whereby three-tiered geomantic figures are construed from random lines of dots sketched on sand, parchment, or paper. He promised in the preface to his translation of an Arabic text on this form of divination to tackle hydromancy next, "having put aside aeromancy and pyromancy" (Haskins 1927, 78–79). Other texts on divination in Arabic, Greek, Hebrew, and Latin that emerged in the Middle Ages were ascribed to classical authorities such as Pythagoras, Socrates, Plato, Apuleius, Ptolemy, and especially Hermes. Divinatory works attributed to Hermes that clearly have no classical precedents include *Lectura geomantiae, Liber de spatula* (involving the scapulae of sheep), and *Tractatus de iudicio urinae.* Antiquarian interest in ancient forms of divination reached its fullest expression in the *Commentary on the Chief Forms of Divination* (*Commentarius de praecipuis divinationum generibus,* 1553), which included ample interpretations of Greek texts by the German Reformer Kaspar Peucer. The subtitle expresses the general tone of the 500-page volume: *The book in which, by prophecies handed down by divine authority and by deductions from natural science, diabolic wiles and impostures are seen clearly for what they are, along with observations arising from and conjoint with superstition. The sources and cases of predictions from nature are shown, while diabolic and superstitious predictions are confuted and condemned.*

The renewed interest in divination at the beginning of the early modern period was not merely antiquarian: it was also part of the Humanistic effort to recover the classical sources of ancient learning. As Aby Warburg pointed out in an influential essay, "Pagan-Antique Prophecy in Words and Images in the Age of Luther" ([1920] 1999), behind the forays into the field of divination made by such diverse personalities as Martin Luther, Johann Lichtenberger, and Albrecht Dürer lay a mentality in which anxiety about the future was accompanied by the hope of finding intellectual consolation in predictive knowledge. Because of widely diffused fears of impending floods, eschatological expectations, and the sense of being surrounded by a large-scale demonic conspiracy, the interpretation of heavenly signs, monstrous births, and natural omens could easily take on political and religious resonances. In such a context both theoretical and practical motives acted as a catalyst for divinatory investigations, as is apparent in the case of Girolamo Cardano, who was interested in a broad range of divinatory subjects, from the loftiest (divine prophecy) to the most trivial (gambling).

In *De rerum praenotione* (written in 1502 and published in 1506), Francesco Pico della Mirandola theorized about the beneficial uses of divination and recognized the importance of establishing criteria for discriminating between licit and illicit knowledge of the future. He distinguished four kinds of precognition (*praenotio*): prophecy, superstition, natural precognition, and vain curiosity ([1506] 1557–1573, 2:378). Within the limits imposed by traditional concerns of an ethical and religious nature, Pico allowed a certain latitude to divination because of the numerous practical needs in everyday life and the unavoidably inferential character of human knowledge (2:395). Finally, at the highest level, he conferred an absolute degree of cognitive and moral reliability to divine prophecies in their power to establish laws and religions (2:404). At the beginning of the 17th century, in his *Trattato della divinatione naturale* (1614), Paolo Antonio Foscarini maintained that the validity of divination rested on the interplay of three reliable causes: nature, understood as the principle of necessity; man's intellect, as the keeper of freedom in the created world; and, above these, God as the prescient and provident cause of everything ([1614] 1615, 105–106).

In the early modern period the canonical distinction between natural and artificial divination gained new meaning and momentum with the progressive establishment of forms of empirical and experimental knowledge. Conjecture, the basis of artificial and inductive divination, gained epistemological respectability. In the various classifications of divinatory disciplines, human learning continued to be presented as ambiguously suspended between nature's faultless but insentient activity and God's absolutely transparent knowledge. Natural divination and the direct revelation of the future through prophecy remained the standards of divinatory knowledge. In *De sapientia* (1544), Cardano distinguished four kinds of wisdom (divine, natural, human, and demonic) and conceded divinatory trustworthiness only to the disciplines that relied on nature's and God's perfection (men and demons deal with appearances) ([1544] 1663, 1:500b).

Because of their emphasis on the temporal dimension (especially the future and the past), the divinatory disciplines, astrology in particular, contained the seeds of full-fledged philosophies of history, centered on theories of cosmic causality and views of divine providence. Rudolph Goclenius the Elder wrote his *Urania divinatrix* (1614) with the express purpose of providing a survey of various forms of divinatory knowledge to be used as proof of God's providential rule of the world. The possible use of astrology as an intellectual tool to probe the course of human history had already been pointed out by Thomas Aquinas. Drawing on a tradition of astrological history that had its roots in the classical period and had been articulated in the conjunctions of Saturn and Jupiter by Persian and Arabic astrologers, he argued that through their knowledge of these conjunctions, sages and philosophers were able to understand and anticipate the major turning points in human history; this was so because, statistically speaking, only a few men are in control of their affects and use their reason, whereas for the great majority of humankind the senses and appetites are influenced by the stars (*Summa Theologiae,* 2a.2ae.q95,a5). On the other hand, the disruption of Europe's religious unity and the escalation of the confrontation between the Catholic Church and Protestant Reformers brought back into favor the Augustinian model of philosophy of history, centered on the idea of a cosmic conspiracy led by demonic forces and based on the assumption that all kinds of divination were forms of idolatry and vain observances. The boundaries between magic, paganism, and heresy, which had never been clearly defined, had to be redrawn each time new issues of theological legitimacy arose. As a consequence, the tension between divinatory rituals and the pastoral and soteriological aspects of the official religions increased. If during the Middle Ages there had been a certain level of acculturation and assimilation between magic and religion, in the early modern period insistence on the absolute transcendence of divine nature and the unidirectional movement of God's redeeming action (exclusively from God to man) led to an increasingly wider chasm between the sphere of nature and that of God, and to the progressive futility of inquiries into the nature and value of divination.

In his unfinished treatise *The New Atlantis* (1627) Francis Bacon concludes his account of the various activities that take place on the utopian island of Bensalem, under the supervision of Salomon's House, with an acknowledgment of the usefulness of natural divination. All sorts of diviners were kept ready there for "the prevention and remedy" of such natural phenomena as "diseases, plagues, swarms of hurtful creatures, scarcity, tempests, earthquakes, great inundations, comets, [and] temperature of the year." But it was not only in the ideal setting of Bensalem that Bacon found a place for divination. In his all-encompassing survey *On the Proficience and Advancement of Learning* (*De dignitate et augmentis scientiarum,* 1623), divination can be found in several provinces of the system: astrology is under the rubric of *scientia naturae;* physiognomy and oneiromancy are in the section *doctrina de indicationibus;* natural divination represents one of the numerous ramifications of the doctrine of the faculties of the soul; the importance of *prudentia* is stressed in the discussion concerning *philosophia civilis.* Given his idiosyncratic role in the formation of the modern idea of science, Bacon cannot be used as a paradigm to test the persistence of divinatory practices in the development of early modern natural philosophy. But the fact remains that conjecture and prediction maintained a key role in the empirical and inductive traditions of experimental science.

During the 18th and 19th centuries the history of divination came to coincide with accounts of superstitious and irrational beliefs provided by Enlightenment and positivist savants interested in paving the way to the full affirmation of reason. This critical and demystifying tradition is still recognizable in Theodor Adorno's essay "The Stars Come Down to Earth" (1953). For all his subtle criticisms of Enlightenment reason and its self-destructive tendencies, Adorno interpreted the persistent popularity of astrological forecasts in contemporary society as a form of institutionalized superstition produced by authoritarian and totalitarian patterns of behavior still in place in postwar democratic regimes. Augustine had long since explained (*De doctrina Christiana* 2.24), however, that the success of the symbolic universe enacted by divinatory practitioners did not depend on the fulfillment of their predictions or on the real effect of the divinatory ritual on someone's life, but on the sense of safety and affective force caused by ritual performances. In the same essay, Adorno failed to acknowledge that the law of supply and demand had always accompanied the development of divinatory practices and that the existence of a divinatory market did not necessarily imply the fulfillment of the destructive dialectic inherent in capitalistic rationality. And as Johannes Kepler had already recognized more than three centuries before, casting horoscopes can be a way of rounding out one's own income ([1604] 1937–, 1:211).

BIBL.: M.-T. d'Alverny, "Récréations monastiques: Les couteaux à manche d'ivoire," in *Recueil de travaux offert à M. Clovis Brunel,* Mémoires et documents publiés par la Société de l'École des Chartes 12 (Paris 1955) 10–32. A. Bouché-Leclercq, *Histoire de la divination dans l'antiquité,* 4 vols. (Paris 1879–1882). C. Burnett, *Magic and Divination in the Middle Ages* (Aldershot 1996). C. Burnett and W. F. Ryan, eds., *Magic and the Classical Tradition* (London 2006). Girolamo Cardano, *De sapientia* [1544], in *Opera omnia* (Lyon 1663) 1:493–580, online at http://filolinux.dipafilo.unimi.it/cardano/testi/opera.html. A. Delatte, *La catoptromancie grecque et ses dérivés* (Liège 1931). Paolo Antonio Foscarini, *Trattato della divinatione naturale* [1614] (Basel 1615), online at http://fermi.imss.fi.it/rd/bdv?/bdviewer/bid=387147. G. Giglioni, "Man's Mortality, Conjectural Knowledge, and the Redefinition of the Divinatory Practice in Cardano's Philosophy," in *Cardano e la tradizione dei saperi,* ed. M. Baldi and G. Canziani (Milan 2003) 43–65. A. Grafton, *Cardano's Cosmos: The Worlds and Works of a Renaissance Astrologer* (Cambridge, Mass., 1999). C. H. Haskins, *Studies in the History of Mediaeval Science,* 2nd ed. (Cambridge, Mass., 1927). G. Henderson, "*Sortes Biblicae* in Twelfth-century England: The List of Episcopal Prognostics in Cambridge, Trinity College MS R.7.5," in *England in the Twelfth Century: Proceedings of the 1988 Harlaxon Symposium,* ed. D. Williams (Woodbridge, U.K., 1990) 113–135. *Hermetis Trismegisti astrologica et divinatoria,* ed. G. Boss et al. (Turnhout 2001). Johannes Kepler, *De stella nova in pede Serpentarii* [1604], in *Gesammelte Werke* (Munich 1937–) 1:313–356. E. Montero Cartelle and A. Alonso Guardo, ed. and trans., *Los "Libros de suertes" medievales: Las sortes sanctorum y los Prenostica Socratis Basilei* (Madrid 2004). O. Niccoli, *Prophecy and People in Renaissance Italy,* trans. L. G. Cochrane (Princeton 1990). Francesco Pico, *De praenotione* [1506], in *Opera omnia* (Basel 1557–1573). R. W. Scribner, "The Reformation, Popular Magic, and the 'Disenchantment of the World,'" *Journal of Interdisciplinary History* 23 (1993) 474–494. Theophrastus of Eresus, *On Weather Signs,* ed. D. Sider and C. W. Brunschön (Leiden 2007). L. Thorndike, *History of Magic and Experimental Science* (New York 1923–1958). J. R. Veenstra, *Magic and Divination at the Courts of Burgundy and France: Text and Context of Laurens Pignon's "Contre les devineurs" (1411)* (Leiden 1998). A. Warburg, "Pagan-Antique Prophecy in Words and Images in the Age of Luther" (1920) in *The Renewal of Pagan Antiquity,* trans. D. Britt (Los Angeles 1999) 597–697.

C.BR. & G.GI.

Domus Aurea

The Domus Aurea (Golden House), Nero's palace in Rome, constructed 64–68 CE, was the perfect embodiment of Nero's narcissistic ego, the pinnacle of artistic creativity. In addition to a conventional Hellenistic palace on the Palatine Hill, it also included a vast park and a rural luxury villa, notorious because Nero had seized much of the city for their creation after the great fire of 64 CE (Suetonius, *Nero* 31; Tacitus, *Annals* 15). The park included an artificial lake, created by diverting an aqueduct through a fountain, covering one whole side of the Caelian Hill. The park re-created picturesque countryside, with villages, fields, forests, and even wildlife. The villa was sited above the park, terraced into the Esquiline Hill, surveying the view. The whole palace was notoriously grand and novel, even though other patrician villas were even more spectacular. Nero trumped them all in convenience: his Golden House was just a brief stroll from the Forum.

Nero's architects, Severus and Celer, created a truly visionary design. Their genius lay in the brilliant use of Roman concrete, a strong, flexible medium suitable for large, vaulted interiors. Previously concrete had been used primarily for utilitarian structures, but Severus and Celer exploited it with panache. The best example is the Octagon Suite, an octagonal rotunda with rooms radiating from its sides, including the first known groin vaults in Roman concrete. Hidden skylights and a surrounding corridor make the dome appear very light. Waterworks and the vista of the park emphasized the dramatic main axis. The decoration was spectacular, including colored stone revetment and pavements, painted relief stucco ceilings, and colorful glass mosaics on the dome. The brilliant interplay of spaces, lighting, and decoration was revolutionary. More important, the contrast between Nero's vaulted architecture and Greek architectural orders was patent. The Domus Aurea demonstrated that splendid new design concepts could be executed in Roman concrete. Thereafter, simply reusing Greek architectural orders would appear passé, even dull.

The Domus Aurea changed the Roman conception of architecture. In its wake the greatest Roman architecture was of vaulted concrete, emphasizing grand ulterior spaces. In Rome itself the Pantheon is the most famous example, but Domitian's palace, the great public baths, and the Basilica of Maxentius are just a few of the other examples. Great vaulted interiors then became Rome's architectural legacy in the early Christian period, especially obvious in Byzantine vaulted churches. Hagia Sophia in

Istanbul and even St. Mark's in Venice are Nero's architectural progeny.

The dark ages in Western Europe precluded direct connection between Nero and the Western tradition of grand vaulted churches, but certainly Roman vaulted architecture provided some inspiration, for which Nero can validly claim a share of the credit. Nero's influence survived even into the Italian Renaissance, despite the preference for classical orders shown by architects such as Brunelleschi, Alberti, and Palladio. Although their designs are both harmonious and intellectual, they also serve most commonly as nonstructural decoration in the vast and sometimes exuberant vaulted interiors of Renaissance and Baroque churches. St. Peter's and San Carlino in Rome are salient examples, but by no means unique. They too are a continuation of the stylistic evolution begun in the Domus Aurea. Quite rightly, the Domus Aurea constitutes a true Neronian architectural revolution.

BIBL.: Larry F. Ball, *The Domus Aurea and the Roman Architectural Revolution* (Cambridge 2003). Laura Fabbrini, "Domus Aurea: Il palazzo sull'Esquilino," in *Lexicon topographicum urbis Romae,* ed. Eva Margareta Steinby, vol. D–G (Rome 1995). William L. MacDonald, *The Architecture of the Roman Empire,* rev. ed. (New Haven 1982). Clementina Panella, ed., *Meta Sudans I: Un'area sacra in Palatio e la valle del Colosseo prima e dopo Nerone* (Rome 1996). L.F.B.

Donation of Constantine

In the course of the 4th century CE the emperor Constantine and his family built numerous great churches in both the Western and Eastern parts of the Roman Empire. Four hundred years later the Roman popes, far poorer than their predecessors and hard-pressed by Lombards and other rivals for power, remembered these gifts and set out to make them the basis for still larger claims: claims, in fact, to secular dominion over the Western empire as a whole. An elaborate legend tied Constantine's decision to give the empire to the Church to his decision to move his own capital to Constantinople, and explained that he had done so to repay the holy Pope Sylvester for curing him of leprosy.

These documents may initially have been written as much to impress pilgrims to Rome with the sanctity and authority of the Church as to form the basis for claims to political power. But over time they came to serve as part of the underpinning for papal claims to temporal jurisdiction over the empire. In the 12th century they were incorporated into the basic corpus of documents for canon law, Gratian's *Canon of Discordant Canons.* Two hundred years later, as the papacy came under sharp criticism from those who saw it as corrupt and venal, the Donation of Constantine came to be seen not as a title of honor but as evidence of depravity: the point at which the Roman Church had lost its sense of mission as a purely spiritual organization and begun to strive for wealth and power.

In the 15th century, however, the Donation became the object of a new kind of criticism. Scholars challenging the political authority of the popes began to argue not only that Constantine's decision had been wrong from a theological and moral point of view, but also that it in fact had never taken place. Nicholas of Cusa, a supporter for much of his career of the Conciliarists' efforts to limit papal authority, noted in *De concordantia catholica* (1433) that history seemed to contradict the story of the Donation. If Constantine had really given the Western empire away, he reasoned, chronologers and historians would have recorded this radical break in the political history of the Roman world. In fact, however, no history mentioned it. The English theologian Reginald Pecock (d. ca. 1461) also subjected the document to destructive criticism.

The most radical—and in subsequent times the most celebrated—critique of the document came not from Nicholas, however, but from Lorenzo Valla, a gifted scholar then in the service of Alfonso of Aragon, the king of Naples, who was enmeshed in conflict with the papacy. In his searing *Declamatiuncula* (ca. 1440) Valla set out to show that Nicholas was right. The Donation could never have taken place, at least in the form the documents purported to record. Attacking rebarbative legal texts with the skill that befitted the son of a lawyer, Valla produced what may be history's greatest example of deconstruction.

Examination of the historical record showed, as Nicholas had already pointed out, no sign of the Donation. Close scrutiny of the text's wording—the part of Valla's argument that has remained most famous—made clear that it contained words and committed syntactical errors that could not have appeared in a genuine Latin work from the time of Lactantius. The text, in other words, violated the rule of decorum: the rhetorical principle that any utterance must fit its author and the context in which he spoke. Valla drove this point home by composing a series of more decorous utterances for the actors in the event: speeches in which the Senate, members of Constantine's family, and the pope himself urged him not to make the grossly inappropriate Donation. Valla, in other words, wrote not as a philologist but as an orator, as the title he chose made clear, and he drew on Aristotle and Quintilian as he attacked the document.

Yet Valla's work was more than an occasional piece, and his use of rhetorical methods reflected his belief in the central importance of formal persuasion. The work climaxed with a magnificent tirade against the Church's pervasive acceptance of spurious documents and relics, and it helped inspire new critical and polemical approaches to Christian antiquity. In the 16th century Ulrich von Hutten and Martin Luther made special efforts to reprint and publicize Valla's work, which became a fundamental work for Christian Humanists and Protestants. Catholic scholars—most notably Agostino Steuco (d. 1549)—mounted a formidable defense, using philological techniques more complex than Valla's to defend the Donation. So did the painter Giulio Romano, whose frescoes in the Sala di Costantino in the Vatican (1520s) used deep knowledge of Roman architecture and antiquities to bring the Donation compellingly back to life. By the end of the 16th century, however, even the Catholic Church historian Cesare Baronio accepted that the Donation was spurious, and the techniques that Valla wielded in the service of a local polemic were reconfigured into the methods of Catholic erudition, which transformed the study of early Christian and medieval history. Ironically, recent scholarship, which emphasizes the scale of the Constantinian donations to the Church and their transformation of Rome's topography, suggests that the imperfect collective memories Valla tore to shreds in fact recorded truths about the early Church that he and other critics did not wish to acknowledge.

BIBL.: G. Antonazzi, *Lorenzo Valla e la polemica sulla Donazione di Costantino* (Rome 1985). Salvatore Camporeale, "Lorenzo Valla's Oratio on the Pseudo-Donation of Constantine: Dissent and Innovation in Early Renaissance Humanism," *Journal of the History of Ideas* 57 (1996) 9–26. Ronald Delph, "Valla Grammaticus, Agostino Steuco, and the Donation of Constantine," *Journal of the History of Ideas* 57 (1996) 55–77. Riccardo Fubini, "Humanism and Truth: Valla Writes against the Donation of Constantine," *Journal of the History of Ideas* 57 (1996) 79–86. Carlo Ginzburg, *History, Rhetoric and Proof* (Hanover, N.H., 1999). N. Huyghebaert, "La Donation de Constantin ramenée à ses véritables dimensions," *Revue d'Histoire Écclesiastique* 71 (1976) 45–69, and "Une légende de fondation: Le Constitutum Constantini," *Moyen Âge* 85 (1979) 177–209. Joseph Levine, *Humanism and History: Origins of Modern English Historiography* (Ithaca 1987). Wolfram Setz, *Lorenzo Vallas Schrift gegen die Konstantinische Schenkung* (Tübingen 1975). Lorenzo Valla, *On the Donation of Constantine,* trans. G. Bowersock (Cambridge, Mass., 2007). A.G.

Donatus

Aelius Donatus (mid-4th cent.), Roman grammarian, possibly African by birth. It would be hard to overestimate his effect on the classical tradition, certainly on the shape and vitality of Latin studies on which that classical tradition depended for 1,500 years after his death. His influence extends far beyond his surviving texts, and most students of Latin today live in a Donatan world even if they have never read a word of his grammatical treatises.

One might well argue that Donatus exercised his greatest influence on Latin not through his writings on grammar and on two central Latin school authors (Virgil and Terence) but via one of the provincial students who came to study with him at Rome, a young man named Eusebius Hieronymus or, as we call him, Jerome. It is the Latin of Jerome's Bible translation that surely accounted for the lion's share of the Latin that was read—and, along with the Latin Mass that included it, heard—for more than a millennium. Jerome would not have been the student and interpreter of Hebrew or the master translator and stylist that he was, without Donatus (Holtz 1981, 46).

Like other Latin grammarians, Donatus adapted Greek grammatical concepts to Latin. He subsumed much of what preceded him, and although he had some competitors, grammatical instruction and thus all instruction in language arts in the West soon regularly began with the four-book *Ars Donati* (*Donatus' Art [of Grammar]*). By the time of Boethius (early 6th cent.), "Donatus" was the name of the *grammaticus par excellence* (Holtz 1981, 238). Priscian, whose *Institutiones grammaticales,* completed at Constantinople ca. 510, would eventually replace portions of the *Ars Donati* for more advanced students, which accorded Donatus the title *auctor latinitatis,* Author of Latinity (Holtz, 240), and the use of Donatus (and his commentators) in schools became nearly universal. For example, by the 7th century his work was the foundation for the study of Latin in Ireland, where a rich tradition of grammatical writings blossomed.

The widespread use of Donatus' textbook in schools, evidenced by its ubiquity in grammar anthologies, created the conditions for its own partial obsolescence through the cumulative effect of learning in the Carolingian renaissance and the centuries immediately following (Holtz 1981, 326, 340). Schoolmasters, though always employing at elementary levels the first book of Donatus' four-part course (already commonly referred to as the *ars minor*), increasingly turned to Priscian rather than to Donatus' more advanced books (*ars maior*) for instruction at higher levels.

In the 12th century Conrad of Hirsau classified Donatus among the "minor authors, . . . suitable for rudimentary instruction of the very young" (*minores,* [i.e.] *rudimentis parvulorum apti*), along with "Cato," Aesop, and Avianus (Curtius 1973, 466). Even as contemporary advanced texts were introduced in the 13th century, the *ars minor* remained standard for younger students, as did the third book of the *ars maior* (*Barbarismus,* covering vulgarisms, infelicities, and foreign borrowings) for university students. Martin Irvine, a Chaucerian scholar, has observed that "the treatments of *vox* [voice] in Donatus's *Ars maior* and Priscian's *Institutiones* remain the *loci classici* of the subject and were continually glossed by commentators and excerpted by compilers of encyclopedias," such that when Chaucer writes "a ful confus matere" in *The House of Fame* (3.1517) he refers to Donatus' *vox confusa* (1985, 854, 872). It was for his fundamental role in *grammatica,* the first of the *septem artes* or Seven Liberal Arts, that Dante praises him, having placed him (though a pagan) in Paradise (*quel Donato ch'alla prim' arte degnò por la mano, Paradiso* 12.137–138).

Donatus' grammar, especially the *ars minor,* was put to new and perhaps surprising uses. Jean Gerson (1363–1429) created a *Donatus moralisatus,* a version adapted to Christian values, which found its way into print by the end of the 15th century. Perhaps even more surprising was the role Donatus played in inspiring written grammars in several vernaculars. Between 1225 and 1245 Uc Faidit produced his *Donatz proensals* (*The Provençal Donatus*) for Italian users, "a grammar setting forth the rudiments of the [Provençal] language on a scale comparable with that of the *Ars minor* of Donatus" (Marshall

1969, 63). "Donatus' grammatical terminology had already been introduced in the second half of the 14th century" in Czech, in the *Vocabulař grammatický* of Claretus de Solentia (d. 1379), and "the first Czech grammar" in the 16th century was "modelled on Donatus" (Hüllen 2001, 215). Vernaculars were increasingly used in conjunction with the text of Donatus to teach students Latin. At least ten translations into French were effected between the 13th and 15th centuries with this end apparently in mind (Timelli 1996), and an early Augsburg incunable published the Latin text with an interlinear German trot (Henkel 1995, 213–215). Donatus most definitely held sway in the world of print. Indeed, the first book that Pannartz and Sweynheym printed after they brought Gutenberg's invention from Germany to Italy in 1464 and set up shop at Subiaco was Donatus. No copies of this *incunabulum* are extant, but we nonetheless still possess examples of well over 300 incunable printings of the *ars minor,* as well as "nine surviving blockbook editions" (Henkel, 212).

Although Donatus was virtually synonymous with grammar itself, remarks here would not be complete without reference to his work as a commentator. In his day the reading of the most fundamental Latin authors was very much the purview of grammarians. A student like Jerome would have read Terence and Virgil with Donatus, who commented on both poets. His commentary on Terence, mentioned by Jerome (*Contra Rufinum* 1.16), is extant in nearly complete form today (lacking only the commentary on *Heautontimoroumenos*), although the original is not faithfully preserved in the numerous 15th-century manuscripts (Reeve 1983, 153; there are a few earlier witnesses to portions of the commentary). Donatus' comment on *Eunuchus* 4.2.10 (where Phaedria wonders if he might at least view his beloved from a distance)—"There are five lines of love, that is, sight, speech, touch, the caress or kiss, and coitus" (*Quinque lineae sunt amoris, scilicet visus, allocutio, tactus, osculum sive suavium, coitus*)—made its way into commentaries on other authors' texts (e.g., Ovid) and also into vernacular literature (e.g., Clément Marot's "Des cinq points en amours"), and into common parlance. The Terence commentary was first printed in 1476.

Donatus' work on Virgil was originally more extensive—a variorum commentary (offering alternative readings) on the three major works—but what has been preserved more or less directly are only the dedicatory epistle, a life of Virgil (probably not entirely by Donatus), and the preface to his commentary on the *Eclogues.* More of Donatus' material is preserved in the Servian corpus of commentary on all Virgil's works, however, particularly in the tradition known as *Servius auctus* or *Servius Danielis.* Commentators are always conveyers of tralatitious material, and Donatus certainly passes along information from parts of Suetonius that we no longer possess, as well as material from other authors now lost to us. It is likely that his mapping of Virgil's three major works into the "tres modi . . . elocutionum" (Bayer 1987, 234)—that is, the *Eclogues* exemplifying the low style, the *Georgics* the middle style, and the *Aeneid* the high style—inspired both the *rota Virgilii* (Curtius 1973, 201), described, for example, in John of Garland's *Parisiana poetria* (book 2, ca. 1220) and the glorious picture, painted by Simone Martini, in Petrarch's own manuscript of Virgil (Milan, Biblioteca Ambrosiana Codex A.49.inf) with not only a shepherd, farmer, and soldier representing each of the three works, but the author himself and a figure that can only be the commentator. It is surely meant to be Servius, but we could also see Donatus in the figure, for Donatus too explicated Virgil, and if his explications are dissolved into those of his more famous successor, it is he who taught all future generations the language arts required to read Virgil, Terence, and other Latin authors.

BIBL.: Karl Bayer, ed., *Vergil-Viten,* in Vergil, *Landleben,* ed. J. Gotte and M. Gotte (Munich 1987). Ernst Robert Curtius, *European Literature and the Latin Middle Ages,* trans. Willard Trask (Princeton 1973, German 1948). Nikolaus Henkel, "Printed School Texts: Types of Bilingual Presentation in Incunabula." *Renaissance Studies* 9, no. 2 (1995) 212–227. Louis Holtz, "Donat et la tradition de l'enseignement grammatical," in *Étude sur L'Ars Donati et sa diffusion (IVe–IXe siècle) et édition critique* (Paris 1981). Werner Hüllen, "Reflections on Language in the Renaissance," in *Language Typology and Language Universals: An International Handbook,* ed. M. Haspelmath et al. (Berlin 2001) 210–222. Martin Irvine, "Medieval Grammatical Theory and Chaucer's House of Fame," *Speculum* 60 (1985) 850–876. J. H. Marshall, ed., *The Donatz Proensals of Uc Faidit* (Oxford 1969). P. K. Marshall, "Servius," in Reynolds 1983, 385–388, esp. 386. M. D. Reeve, "Aelius Donatus," in Reynolds 1983, 153–156. L. D. Reynolds, *Texts and Transmissions: A Survey of the Latin Classics* (Oxford 1983). Maria Colombo Timelli, *Traductions françaises de l'"Ars minor" de Donat au moyen âge (XIIIe–XVe siècles)* (Florence 1996).

R.H.

Doxography

The term *doxography* was invented in the late 19th century by the classical scholar Hermann Diels to refer to a group of ancient writings concerned primarily with the presentation of the *doxai* (or *areskonta,* or in Latin *placita*), that is, the "tenets" or "characteristic doctrines" held on specific issues by the main authorities in a particular subject or intellectual discipline such as natural philosophy, ethics, medicine, or mathematics. A number of such writings survive either directly (e.g., Theophrastus' *On the Senses,* pseudo-Plutarch's *On the Doctrines of the Philosophers,* pseudo-Galen's *History of Philosophy,* Anonymus Londinensis' doxography on medicine, Anonymus Parisinus' *On Acute and Chronic Diseases,* Anonymus Bruxellensis' *On the Seed*) or indirectly in later summaries or excerpts (e.g., Aëtius' *On Doctrines,* Arius Didymus' doxography on ethics). Because in many cases these texts attribute views to ancient thinkers whose own works are lost (such as the Presocratics, the Stoics, or Hellenistic medical writers), the classical tradition has primarily used these texts as sources for the reconstruction of ancient thought and culled the relevant sections for inclusion in collections of fragments such as Diels's *Fragmente der Vorsokratiker* (1903) or von Arnim's *Stoicorum veterum fragmenta* (1903–1905). Consequently, the influence of ancient doxography on 19th- and 20th-century perceptions of the history of ancient thought has been very considerable. Yet recent studies have highlighted the importance of analyzing doxographical writings in their own right and, in doing so, appreciating both the considerable variety they display in aims, methods, and intended usages and the ensuing difficulties involved in using these texts as sources. In its barest form doxographical discourse consists of a list of topics, often presented in the form of questions ("Is an embryo a living being?" "Is the world eternal?" and the like), each followed by the relevant views or answers as given by the main authorities—individual thinkers or "schools" of thought. These views are stated in a very concise format and usually arranged in systematic rather than chronological order. Often an element of comparison and contrast between the reported views seems envisaged, highlighting the variety and disagreement (*diaphōnia, dissensio*) among the authorities; and sometimes the arrangement follows the pattern of "division" (*diairesis*) according to logical categories (substance, properties, etc.). It has been argued that this method of presentation finds its origins in Aristotelian dialectics, for several of Aristotle's works (e.g., *On the Soul, Physics, Metaphysics*) begin with an elaborate but schematic and systematically structured evaluative discussion of the views of predecessors (*endoxa*, "reputable opinions") on the topic in question, which serves a philosophical rather than a historiographical purpose. In Aristotle's footsteps, the early Peripatetic school developed a number of projects outlining the historical development of the various sciences and intellectual disciplines of the time (Theophrastus' *Doctrines on Nature,* Eudemus' histories of mathematics and theology, Meno's history of medicine, etc.). Apart from recording the major "discoveries" (*heurēmata*) in a given subject, a major purpose of these collections was to serve as practice material for training in debating techniques (e.g., arguing *in utramque partem,* "on both sides" of a question) or for demonstration of the indeterminacy of specific issues (as in Neopyrrhonic Skepticism). But doxographical surveys clearly also served didactic purposes, the material often being presented in the easily memorizable form of question-and-answer (*erōtapokriseis, quaestiones*) or definitions (*horoi, definitiones*). This explains their usages as catechisms in late antiquity and the Middle Ages (e.g., pseudo-Soranus' *Medical Questions,* pseudo-Galen's *Medical Definitions*); it also explains how easily this petrified material could be recycled by later authors, thus forming doxographical traditions attested in several different authors, connected through chains or stemmatic ramifications of intellectual transmission, often spanning many centuries during which material was added, lost, or transformed (thus the influence of the doxographic handbook by the 1st-century CE author Aëtius stretches at least as far as the 11th century).

More elaborate narrative accounts of predecessors' views were developed from the 3rd century BCE onward in the "successions" literature (*diadokhai*), describing the development of thought within a particular philosophical or medical school, and in the literature on "schools of thought" (*haireseis* or *sectae*), a pattern reflected in (among other works) Diogenes Laertius' *Lives and Doctrines of the Philosophers,* which combines biographical anecdotes with information about doctrines arranged by philosophical school, and in Celsus' historiographical preface to his work *On Medicine,* which deals with the views of the medical sects of the Rationalists, Empiricists, and Methodists (a pattern followed also in Galen's *On the Sects* and in pseudo-Galen's *Introduction*). As such, these writings give us some idea of classical forms of intellectual historiography, though it is not always clear that the author's purpose is to provide an exhaustive, chronologically accurate, and explanatory account of the history of thought in a particular field. More often such accounts, like most ancient historiography, also serve literary, rhetorical, argumentative, or polemical purposes (e.g., self-definition or apologetics), and report and criticism are often mixed and handled with great literary virtuosity, as in Galen's *On the Medical Sects* and *On the Doctrines of Hippocrates and Plato,* in Caelius Aurelianus' *Acute and Chronic Diseases,* or in Christian writers such as Tertullian's *On the Soul,* Hippolytus' *Refutation of All Heresies,* and Epiphanius' *Cure of All Erroneous Doctines.* Yet for all its variety, ancient doxographical discourse testifies to the widespread tendency in classical thought to take explicit account of the doctrines of predecessors, often at a very early stage of one's own work. Thus engagement with the intellectual past became an established pattern (cognitive as well as literary) for the presentation of knowledge that was to have a long afterlife in the history and historiography of Western philosophy and science; and the technique of arguing *in utramque partem,* with the names of authoritative advocates attached as labels to either position, became a favorite style of reasoning in ancient and medieval rhetorical theory (e.g., in the distinction between a general or abstract question, *quaestio infinita* or *thesis,* and a specific or concrete one, *quaestio finita* or *hypothesis*), and in scholastic philosophy (*sic et non,* "pro and contra").

Classical doxographical traditions in philosophy and medicine persisted in late antique Christian authors such as Nemesius of Emesa, Theodoret of Cyrrhus, and Johannes Stobaeus, in Byzantine authors such as John of Damascus, Meletius of Sardes, Michael Psellus, and Photius, in the medieval canon of classical medical works (translated into Latin) known as the *Articella,* and in medieval Arabic philosophical and medical doxography, not least through Qusta Ibn Luca's translation of Aëtius' *Placita* and through the reception of Aristotle's and Galen's authoritative accounts of the views of their predecessors in Arabic authors such as al-Fārābī and Ibn Abi Usaibi'a.

In the Renaissance, Latin translations of (pseudo-)Plutarch's *On the Doctrines of the Philosophers* by Guillaume Budé in 1502 and of pseudo-Galen's *History of Philosophy* by Giulio Rota in 1541 gave rise to the first philological inquiries (by Konrad Gessner, Girolamo Mercuriale, René Chartier, and others) into the interdependence of these and other related texts, and the peculiar kind of historiography found in these writings attracted the attention of philosophers (Francis Bacon), historians of philosophy (e.g., Johann Jakob Brucker and Wilhelm Gottlieb Tennemann), and philologists such as Johannes Fabricius and David Ruhnkenius. But the study of ancient doxography was really revolutionized in the mid-19th century by the works of August Meineke, Richard Volkmann, and especially Hermann Diels, whose *Doxographi Graeci* (1879) not only provided a full critical edition of the most important surviving doxographical texts on natural and ethical philosophy but also presented a reconstruction of the lost work of the doxographer Aëtius, believed by Diels to be the archetypical source to which all other later texts could be stemmatically traced, and which in turn was believed ultimately to depend on Theophrastus' (lost) *Doctrines on Nature*. Diels's work has been of enormous influence on 20th-century classical scholarship but has recently been criticized from various angles, and new hypotheses regarding Aëtius and the *Placita* tradition have been presented. A further new development is the study of ancient medical doxography.

BIBL.: G. Cambiano, ed., *Storiografia e dossografia nella filosofia antica* (Turin 1986). H. Daiber, "Hellenistisch-kaiserzeitliche Doxographie und philosophischer Synkretismus in islamischer Zeit," *Aufstieg und Niedergang der römischen Welt* 2.36.7 (1994) 4974–4992. H. Diels, *Doxographi Graeci* (Berlin 1879). P. J. van der Eijk, ed., *Ancient Histories of Medicine: Essays in Medical Doxography and Historiography in Classical Antiquity* (Leiden 1999). A. Laks, ed., *Doxographie antique* (*Revue de métaphysique et de morale*) 97, no. 3 (1992) 311–325. J. Mansfeld, "Doxography and Dialectic: The *Sitz im Leben* of the *Placita*," *Aufstieg und Niedergang der römischen Welt* 2.36.4 (1990) 3056–3229, and *Studies in the Historiography of Greek Philosophy* (Assen–Maastricht 1990). J. Mansfeld and D. T. Runia, *Aëtiana: The Method and Intellectual Context of a Doxographer*, vol. 1, *The Sources* (Leiden 1996).

P.V.D.E.

Dramatic Unities

Also called the three unities. The dramatic unities of action, time, and place are, as a doctrine, a largely modern invention inspired by a classical lineage. Though they have some real basis in ancient Greek theatrical practice (particularly that of tragedy), the unities were first codified by 16th-century Humanist commentators on Aristotle's *Poetics* and by their French neoclassical descendants. Aristotle himself expounds only on the unity of action, defined as the organic coherence of a plot (with a "beginning, middle, and end") in which events are causally sequential and do not depend on outside happenstance or a deus ex machina (*Poetics*,. 7, 8, 15). In contrast, he refers only once to the unity of time, noting that works of tragedy, unlike epics, generally endeavor to contain the action depicted "within a single revolution of the sun" (*Poetics* 5); this phrase has been construed to mean anywhere from twelve to thirty hours, though twenty-four is the most common interpretation. As for the unity of place—that is, the limitation of a play's action to one, single defined space (such as a royal court or a street corner)—Aristotle makes no mention of it.

Although sensitive to the authority of the classical past, Humanists such as J. C. Scaliger (*Poetices libri septem*, 1561) and Castelvetro (*Poetica d'Aristotele*, 1570), as well as later French critics such as d'Aubignac (*La pratique du théâtre*, 1657), embraced the unities principally because of their own quite modern and rationalist concern with verisimilitude. The viewer's imagination supposedly took in the stage representation in an entirely literal fashion and thus expected it to conform to the conditions of the real world. In daily life one locality does not suddenly become another; the stage should obey the same rules. Likewise, time does not suddenly skip forward to the next day, much less the next year. Accordingly, the only way to maintain the believability of dramatic illusion is to scrupulously model the space and time of the representation (the stage) on that which it represents. Learned critics crafted elaborate rules to avoid even the appearance of a lack of unity: to guarantee, for example, that each act represented unbroken "real time" from beginning to end, the principle of the *liaison des scènes* prohibited the stage from ever being empty between characters' entries and exits (lest nervous spectators worry that the temporarily vacated stage signaled some break in time or location).

In practice, the dramatic unities took hold most firmly in France in the 17th century. Jean Mairet's *Sophonisbe* (1634) gained fame as the first French model of the perfectly "regular play." After the quarrel over Corneille's *Le Cid* (1637), which broke with the classical rules, the playwright's later tragedies largely adhered to the three unities, though his theoretical *Discours* (1660) frequently chafes at neo-Aristotelian precepts. Racine and Molière represent the apex of the dramatic unities.

On the English stage, in contrast, the three unities were largely ignored. Though Philip Sidney (*Apologie for Poetrie*, 1595) defended them and Ben Jonson put them to some practice, Shakespeare's famous neglect of the unities provided a powerful countermodel. Samuel Johnson most effectively condemned the literalism and impoverished view of the imagination implied by a strict adherence to the unities (*Preface to Shakespeare*, 1765). By the early 19th century, Romanticism had largely vanquished the sway of the unities, even in France.

Though their underpinnings in neo-Aristotelian poetics were exhausted, the dramatic unities nevertheless continued to provide a unique theatrical framework for physically and temporally concentrating action onstage, and the power of such 20th-century masterpieces as Sartre's *No Exit* and Beckett's *Endgame* testify to the continuing seductiveness of their principles.

BIBL.: René Bray, *La formation de la doctrine classique en France* (Lausanne 1931). Lodovico Castelvetro, *Castelvetro on the Art of Poetry,* trans. Andrew Bongiorno (Binghamton, N.Y., 1984). Stephen Halliwell, *The Poetics of Aristotle, Translation and Commentary* (Chapel Hill 1987). R. D. Stock, *Samuel Johnson and Neoclassical Dramatic Theory* (Lincoln, Nebr., 1973). L.NO.

Dream Interpretation

The views of Graeco-Roman antiquity on dreams and their interpretation are articulated in a wide variety of texts, including technical treatises (e.g., philosophical, medical) and works belonging to belles lettres and incorporating narratives of dreams (e.g., Greek and Latin epic poetry, the ancient novels, the orations of Aelius Aristides). Ancient authors discuss where dreams come from (possibilities include the gods, demons, the human soul or imagination), the process whereby they are formed, their practical function (e.g., as auxiliary tools in divining the future or providing a medical diagnosis), and in what circumstances, if at all, they can be considered truthful and reliable. The conclusions of the ancient authors are neither consistent nor always neatly placeable in a genealogical tree outlining direct connections between them. The triumph of Christianity significantly influenced the content but did not radically alter the scope of these discussions in subsequent centuries (Le Goff 1985). In general, the demonstrable penchant among Greek, Latin, and Arabic scholars of the Middle Ages for copying, studying, commenting on, and appropriating ancient texts on dream interpretation allowed for a certain continuity of ideas and practices into the Renaissance and later. Dream interpretation as a method for predicting the future remains a living tradition in Greece and the Middle East, though the advent of "modernity" stripped it of its highbrow associations and relegated it to the realm of "popular belief" or "folklore."

Among the earliest surviving ancient Greek texts that systematically treat the origin, function, and veracity of dreams are various instances in Plato's dialogues, especially the *Timaeus,* famously translated into Latin and commented on first by Cicero (in a version now lost) and later by Calcidius (in a surviving version) that became that work's main vehicle into the Latin Middle Ages. Further discussion is provided in Aristotle's two opuscules *On Dreams* (*De insomniis* in *Parva naturalia* 458a33–462b11) and *On Divination through Dreams* (*De divinatione per somnum* in *Parva naturalia* 462b12–464b18a). Both Plato and Aristotle are clearly informed by earlier approaches to this topic, of which no written trace survives. The use of dreams for medical diagnosis, also mentioned by Aristotle, is outlined in a text of the Hippocratic corpus (*Regimen* 4), possibly dating to the 5th or 4th century BCE; and in Galen's *On Diagnosis from Dreams* (ed. Kühn, 6:832–835; ed. Guidorizzi, *Bollettino del comitato per la preparazione dell'edizione nazionale dei classici greci e latini* 21, 1973, 81–105). Hippocratic and Galenic ideas about dreams are also repeated by medieval physicians.

None of the philosophical or medical discussions on dreams can compare in length and scope with the only manual on dream interpretation surviving from antiquity, Artemidorus' *Oneirocritica* (Greek, 2nd century BCE). Artemidorus aims to provide a practical guide for the systematic and accurate analysis of dreams as a technique for predicting the future. The work is based on his practical experience, his contemporary oral tradition, and a written tradition of considerable volume going back to the 5th century BCE (trans. White 1975, 11, 67; Mavroudi 2002, 128).

In the 9th century the *Oneirocritica* was translated from Greek into Arabic (Mavroudi 135–42). Soon thereafter its interpretations were incorporated into Arabic works on the same topic and continued to appear in manuals composed from the 11th through the 18th centuries, still printed and consulted in the Middle East today. In fact, the lore systematized by Artemidorus constitutes part of the present-day living tradition on dream interpretation throughout the Eastern Mediterranean.

The 10th-century *Oneirocriticon of Achmet,* the only surviving dream book of the Greek and Latin Middle Ages comparable in volume and ambition to the work of Artemidorus, was composed for Christian readers of Greek but repeats several interpretations offered by Artemidorus. A close comparison of the *Oneirocriticon of Achmet* with its medieval Arabic counterparts proves, however, that it is based exclusively on Muslim Arabic works. The similarities between the ancient and the Byzantine Greek texts are due to the influence of Artemidorus on the Arabic sources that the Byzantine author employed. Nevertheless, there can be no doubt that the work of Artemidorus was also known and read in Byzantium (Mavroudi 423).

In the 12th century excerpts of Artemidorus' work in Latin translation were included in the *Liber thesauri occulti* of Pascalis Romanus (Mavroudi 112–114). The earliest complete translation of Artemidorus' work from Greek into Latin, however, is possibly that by Janus Cornarius (1539), reprinted several times in the course of the 16th and 17th centuries. Translations of Artemidorus in Italian (1540), French (1555), English (1563), and German (1570) were printed and frequently reprinted during the same period. The Aldine edition of the original Greek had appeared in 1518.

The connection between dream interpretation and medicine is evident in the work of Artemidorus itself (Price 1986, 24–25) and in the contribution of physicians to its subsequent diffusion. The translators of Artemidorus into Arabic and Latin and an owner of its oldest surviving Greek manuscript were physicians. Two further Greek manuscripts combine Artemidorus with medical authors. Cornarius' Latin translation of 1539 is dedicated to two fellow doctors, Philipp Pucheymer and Johannes Megobacchus (Meckback). The translator of Artemidorus into German was the physician, mathematician, and Humanist Walter Hermann Ryff.

Thus, Freud must be viewed as part of a very long tradition of physicians interested in dream interpretation. In Freud's multiple reworkings of his *Interpretation of Dreams* (1st ed. 1899; 8th ed. 1930), Artemidorus is explicitly and increasingly mentioned. Freud became acquainted with the ancient work through B. Büchenschütz, *Traum und Traumdeutung im Altertum* (Berlin 1868), and Artemidorus' translation into German by F. S. Krauss, *Symbolik der Träume* (Vienna 1881) (Chryssanthopoulos 2005, 164). The correlation of Freud's theories with those of Artemidorus has been evaluated in various ways by scholars since the mid-20th century (outline, Chryssanthopoulos 150–181), clearly a result of changing perceptions, over the succeeding decades, not only of Freud's work but also of the role accorded to the classical tradition in modern culture. Briefly, the most salient and undeniable features of Freud's work that reveal his interaction with Artemidorus are his assertion that dreams can be interpreted by deciphering the symbolic significance of their content; that the dream interpreter ought to be informed about the personality and material circumstances of the dreamer in order to provide an accurate interpretation; and that dreams are language-specific and wordplay can be used in order to decipher them. The difference is that Artemidorus uses dreams to divine the future, whereas Freud uses them to understand the present and the past. The importance of mythology and literature for the decipherment of dreams, emphasized in the 20th century by Carl Jung (Freud's disciple and collaborator for a few years), is also explicitly mentioned by Artemidorus (2.66, 4.47).

BIBL.: Artemidorus, *Oneirocritica,* trans. Robert John White as *The Interpretation of Dreams* (Park Ridge, N.J., 1975). Michalis Chryssanthopoulos, *Freud and Artemidorus* (Athens 2005) (in Greek). Ludger Grenzmann, *Traumbuch Artemidori* (Baden-Baden 1980). John Lamoreaux, *The Early Muslim Tradition of Dream Interpretation* (Albany 2002). Jacques Le Goff, "Le christianisme et les rêves," in *I sogni nel medioevo,* ed. Tullio Gregory (Rome 1985) 171–218. R. G. A. van Lieshout, *Greeks on Dreams* (Utrecht 1980). Maria Mavroudi, *A Byzantine Book on Dream Interpretation: The Oneirocriticon of Achmet and Its Arabic Sources* (Leiden 2002). Simon R. F. Price, "The Future of Dreams: From Freud to Artemidorus," *Past and Present* 113 (1986) 3–37. M.M.

Dulce et decorum est pro patria mori

One of the most famous quotations from Roman literature: "Sweet and fitting it is to die for one's country" (Horace, *Odes* 3.2.13). The idea that a man must take up arms to defend his country is first found in Homer (e.g., *Iliad* 15.494–499). A fragment by the Spartan poet Tyrtaeus that derives from Homer is the direct predecessor of Horace: "For it is fine to die in the front line,/a brave man fighting for his fatherland" (fr. 10.1–2, trans. West). Simonides of Keos expressed a related idea in his epitaph on the 300 Spartans who died at Thermopylae (Herodotus 7.228). Uncritical acceptance of Horace's maxim, however, neglects its historical background. Horace had famously *not* died for his country in the battle of Philippi but ingloriously saved himself (*Odes* 2.7.9–14). By his time individual heroism had ceased to be a decisive factor in victory and become outdated. So his words should not be regarded as the straightforward exhortation that the patriotic-minded usually take them to be.

Numerous restatements attest to Horace's influence. Nathan Hale, an American spy aged 21, hanged by the British during the Revolutionary War, said under the gallows: "I only regret that I have but one life to lose for my country." His words derive from Joseph Addison's *Cato* (1713), a tragedy about Cato the Younger that was popular during and after the revolution: "What pity is it/That we can die but once to serve our country!" In England at the time of the Boer War, James Rhoades expressed the classical code of honor in a patriotic poem entitled "Dulce et Decorum Est":

> We, nursed in high traditions,
> And trained to nobler thought,
> Deem death to be less bitter
> Than life too dearly bought.

Devastating proof of the futility of traditional heroism in an age of mechanized warfare came with World War I, when patriotism turned to classical models and poems that took their titles from Horace justified self-sacrifice. Sydney Oswald, a major in the King's Royal Rifle Corps, commemorates heroic death in the Gallipoli campaign in "Dulce et Decorum est pro Patria Mori." The poem appeared in *Soldier Poets: Songs of the Fighting Men* (1916), and another one with the same title, by Cpl. Harold John Jarvis, was published in *More Songs by the Fighting Men* (1917). Disillusionment was voiced by several young poets who had experienced the horrors of modern war. Wilfred Owen, a recipient of the Military Cross, was killed one week before Armistice Day, at age 25. "Dulce et Decorum Est" (1918), his best-known poem, ends with an apostrophe to the reader:

> My friend, you would not tell with such high zest
> To children ardent for some desperate glory,
> The old Lie: Dulce et decorum est
> Pro patria mori.

Rudyard Kipling echoes Owen (and Simonides) in "Common Form" (1918), one of his *Epitaphs of the War,* written after the death of his son John: "If any question why we died,/Tell them, because our fathers lied." A memorable example of such a liar, although not a father, appears in the 1930 American film adaptation of Erich Maria Remarque's novel *All Quiet on the Western Front.* Euphoric at the outbreak of the war, a teacher in a German *Gymnasium* exhorts his students: "Let us remember the Latin phrase which must have come to the lips of many a Roman when he stood in battle in a foreign land: *dulce et decorum est pro patria mori*—'sweet and fitting it is to die for the fatherland.'"

Some of the "blood and soil" ideologies that became prominent in European totalitarianism after World War I also echoed Horace. A telling example from popular culture occurs in *Scipione l'Africano* (1937), a historical film financed by the government of Fascist Italy in which Scipio the Elder is modeled on Mussolini. Scipio exhorts his army: "Legionaries, Fortune offers you the most beautiful reward: to die for your country. Legionaries: Victory or Death!" Italians were already familiar with this kind of slogan—for example, from Mussolini's motto for his march on Rome ("Either Rome or death").

A pithy rejection of Horace opens the American film *Patton* (1970), when Patton addresses his soldiers: "I want you to remember that no bastard ever won a war by dying for his country. He won it by making the other poor dumb bastard die for *his* country." These words reflect the historical Patton's beliefs as reported by one of his daughters: "He was . . . fond of reminding us that 'any fool can die for his country because the band is playing and the flag is waving. It takes a real man to live for his country.'" The critical view of Horace continues with, for example, Tim O'Brien's *If I Die in a Combat Zone, Box Me Up and Ship Me Home* (1973), a fictionalized account of his service in the American infantry in Vietnam. Revealing chapter headings are "Pro Patria," "Mori," and "Dulce et Decorum." The American war correspondent Chris Hedges quotes the ending of Owen's poem as the epigraph for his meditations on war in *War Is a Force That Gives Us Meaning* (2002).

Horace's line also lends itself to witticism. In his edition of the fifth book of Manilius's *Astronomica* (1930), the poet and classical scholar A. E. Housman changes it to *Dulce et decorum est pro patria mentiri* (. . . to lie for your country). He ridicules the inadequacies and falsehoods that a German classicist, extolling the virtues of German scholarship over Housman's, had perpetrated in his review of an earlier volume of Housman's Manilius.

BIBL.: Modris Eksteins, "Memory and the Great War," in *World War I: A History,* ed. Hew Strachan (Oxford 1998) 305–317. Hermann Funke, "*Dulce et decorum,*" *Scripta Classica Israelica* 16 (1997) 77–90. Peter Parker, *The Old Lie: The Great War and the Public-School Ethos* (London 1987). Martin M. Winkler, "*Dulce et decorum est pro patria mori?* Classical Literature in the War Film," *International Journal of the Classical Tradition* 7 (2000) 177–214.

M.M.W.

E

East and West

When Socrates famously compared human habitation with that of "frogs and mice around a pond," the peri-Mediterranean community he had in mind stretched from "the river Phasis to the Straits of Gibraltar" (Plato, *Phaedo* 109B). A distance of nearly 2,500 miles is thereby implied, rather than the 400–500 miles between North Africa and southern France. But the entire Earth, said Socrates, is much larger than the part inhabited (*oikoumenē*), and in any case Socrates' implied geography invites no literal interpretation. Despite such qualifications, this passage suggests that the physical proportions of the Mediterranean add significance and context to the question of how East and West related in the classical tradition. That distance in part accounts for the fact that, at different times, the supposed division has been very differently mapped. This is not to downplay the historical importance of the north-south divide that has had much significance of its own. Rather, it is a reminder that the eastern Mediterranean is part of the Fertile Crescent, with traditions of urban settlement and writing much more ancient than anything to its west. Indeed, the vigor of urban traditions in western Asia remained significant throughout antiquity and beyond.

If the Mediterranean is central to this discussion, then the other larger physical unit to be considered is the Eurasian continent. In the absence of any natural boundaries running in a north-south direction, the division between Europe and Asia is not at all a given. In the case of certain countries such as Turkey and Russia, it has been a source of dispute accompanied by vast implications for international politics and social identities. In light of such questions, the division of East and West has been far too labile to constitute any inert fact of physical geography. Rather, East and West are considered here in relation to their changing cultural significance, with attention to the specifics of context, and not least to perspective: who determines the supposed division, and to what ends? If the intense debate around Edward Said's book *Orientalism* (1978) has reached any resolution whatever, there can be no longer any assumption of equality between East and West; indeed, elements of that debate will engage us at several points in what follows.

At least three paradigms for dividing East and West can be found in premodern thought. Though neither exhaustive nor mutually exclusive, these are worth canvassing, for both their ancient and later significance. A familiar theme in archaic and classical Greek texts is the idea of differences bordering on the Aegean coasts. The Lydians, known for their luxurious lifestyle, were distinctive in this respect, though the phenomenon at issue goes further back and stretches to the Levant. A good millennium later there would be a political division of the Mediterranean itself, most obviously under the Roman Empire after the death of Theodosius II in 395 CE, with the division into Greek-speaking Eastern and Latin-speaking Western empires. This would have massive implications for Christianity, for one thing, as Rome's Eastern heritage was focused on Russia. A third sense grew directly out of the second, adapted to the changed geopolitics after the 7th century. The rapid growth of Islam in the Levant marked it out as the East in ways that have had long-term effects. The division between East and West thus became one between Christianity and its rival, whereas previously it had been one within Christianity. Each of these three senses deserves more detailed consideration.

The Lydians of the eastern Aegean, who dominate the first part of Herodotus' *Histories* (1.6–92), controlled much of Asia Minor before the Persian advance. The wealth of their last king, Croesus, was legendary; it came from Pergamene mines, the Black Sea area, and even the

River Pactolus, mythically awash with King Midas's gold; it supported a far-flung kingdom (Herodotus 1.28). More than wealth itself, it was their luxurious living (*habrosunē*) that was distinctive, a theme that fascinated lyric poets. This was not initially a negative concept as expressed by eastern Greeks of their non-Greek neighbors, but it soon became one (Kurke 1992). It was here that coinage was first minted, around 600 BCE, using a natural alloy of gold and silver called electrum. Herodotus' Lydian *logos,* occupying such a prominent place at the beginnings of historiography, would provide a blueprint for Greek images of an Eastern people: despotism, grandeur, and commodities are central here.

As a native Ionian from Halicarnassus (Bodrum in Turkey), Herodotus would have regarded the Lydians as neighbors, but this image would gain new significance among the Athenians of the classical period. The westward campaign of Cyrus and the subsequent Persian Wars would cause those ethnographic features to be transferred to the Achaemenid Persians themselves, and this is after all the context of Herodotus' *Histories.* With Aeschylus' *Persians* (472 BCE) we have a clear discourse about an Eastern Other. The east-west divide it constructs is focused on the Aegean, but its implications would prove enormous. This Eastern mirage was central to Athens' conception of its own identity as a democratic polis, and perhaps even a perceived role of providing a model for other Greek city-states. By way of balancing an Athenian viewpoint, recent scholarship has sought to understand Persian culture through its own documents and material culture, and further shown that through the time of the Persian Wars the Athenians had a keen taste for Persian goods and styles. Nonetheless, Aeschylus and Herodotus, taken together, thus underline the importance of the Persian Wars as a key moment in the Greeks' sense of their own identity, viewed with increasing clarity against the mirror of an older Eastern society. And there can be no doubt that the war was central to the evolution of tragedy and historiography. It is no accident that in *Orientalism* Said uses Aeschylus as his earliest text, though merely in passing (e.g., 56–57). Of undoubted importance is Said's insistence, shared with the early Foucault, on the tight nexus of power and knowledge; likewise, his notion that texts themselves are a means of gaining power over the East has been by turns compelling and jarring. What is less clear, however, is to what extent we can compare the balance of international power between the 5th-century and 18th–19th-century Mediterranean worlds, given the difference in their technologies.

The Persian Wars, however important, need to be set in a context that is much wider, both in time and space. The century spanning the late dark age and early archaic period (roughly 720–620 BCE) has been seen as an "Orientalizing period" because of widespread Greek use of Eastern styles and media. Animals, both real and fantastic, and floral patterns are characteristic of the archaic period; like the designs of the earlier geometric period, these show strong affinities with Mesopotamian and other Near Eastern art. It is no accident that, in the archaic period, major innovations are seen in the vases of the Corinthians, some of the Mediterranean's most active traders. Further, Phoenician and Cypriot silverware seems to have left its mark on Etruscan metalwork. In such cases the greater age of the Eastern traditions in question has led to the view that Greeks and others farther to the west were influenced by Eastern models—in a word, subject to an Orientalizing dynamic (Morris 1992).

This is seen not only in the plastic arts but also in language, literature, and religious practices. Two philologists whose work in this respect has been influential are Walter Burkert and M. L. West (1997). Burkert, for example, has argued that alphabetic scripts of the 8th century BCE should be seen as part of a cultural "continuum of written culture . . . which stretches from the Euphrates to Italy" (1992, 31). Underlying such visions is the idea of the diffusion of human culture from east to west, something that is no surprise to world historians or evolutionary biologists, who adopt a very long view. This raises a related problem of methodology and parameters: how far back can the question of Eastern influence be traced? Some degree of this is inevitable for anyone who looks as far back as the Indo-Europeans. Sir William Jones in his 1786 lecture "The Sanscrit Language" pointed to similarities among Sanskrit, Greek, and Latin, and it was not long before philologists came to the conclusion that the Eastern language of Sanskrit was older than Greek or Latin. (Such a view would be at odds with those who, like James Mill in his *History of British India* of 1817, denigrated India as backward and corrupt.) The identity of the speakers of the Indo-European *Ursprache* remains hard to ascertain. To be sure, in the guise of Aryans these ancestors have been aggressively claimed for Western Europe, particularly German Romantic nationalism. Other scholars, looking at a somewhat later period of Greek culture, have identified Indian influence on Presocratic thought, not least the Pythagorean idea of the transmigration of the soul.

The Persian empire under the Achaemenids and Alexander's expedition (more briefly) brought an unprecedented degree of political and cultural unity to the eastern Mediterranean, linking it with areas as far as the Iranian plateau. Even though scholars have more recently questioned the depth and extent of such unities, the point remains that these empires facilitated the exchange of people, goods, and ideas within them. Yet it was the later ascendancy of Rome that was the first to create a polity spanning the Mediterranean. This unity was slow in coming, beginning with the unification of Italy in the 4th century BCE, though not concluded until 30 BCE, with the conquest of Egypt. The year 146 BCE is often considered the key point in the acquisition of this unity, for it saw the decisive conquest of both Carthaginians and Greeks. The cultural dynamics resulting from this included heightened Greek influence over Rome in the later Republic: as Horace memorably put it, "Captive Greece captured its savage victor and brought the arts to rustic Latium" (*Graecia capta ferum uictorem cepit et artes/intulit agresti Latio,* Epistles 2.155–156). Even as Greek literature provided the template for emerging Latin texts, Roman responses to the Greeks were mixed. The elder Cato was a notorious Hellenophobe.

Language provided a marked division between Latin West and Greek East of the high empire; the institutions of law and the army provided exceptions that proved the rule. In the 2nd and 3rd centuries the cultural movement known as the Second Sophistic provided a brilliant flowering of Greek oratory, to some degree in spite of the realities of Roman political power. By the late 4th century, East and West were destined for very different fates. The wealthier, more urbanized East was better able to withstand the military and economic threats linked to Germanic and other groups. Theodosius' successors Arcadius in the East and Honorius in the West were both puppet rulers, manipulated by powerful generals and courtiers. Only the Byzantine or Eastern empire would endure, whereas the Western empire fell in 476 CE to a Germanic alliance under Odoacer. The Byzantines, based in the new Rome that was Constantinople, would see themselves as true "Romans" (*Rhomaioi*), pointedly using that term without further qualification. In fact, when Byzantine Christians wrote polemics against the "Latins" of the West, they conflated ethnic and religious elements in their rhetoric, to the extent that those categories are not easily distinguished (Kolbaba 2000). Such conflict within Christianity was a source of anxiety, given the universal aspirations of the Christian Church and the claims of its leaders, Eastern and Western, to prime status. Certainly internal dissent and accusations of heresy were very much a part of Church history of the 4th and 5th centuries, but in this case the division (overlapping with a linguistic division) became institutionally entrenched. The fall of Constantinople in 1453 and the subsequent emergence of Russia as a center of Orthodox Christianity meant that Moscow became the "third Rome," the czar being the guardian of the Church. The phenomenon known as *translatio imperii* embraces both the political and religious aspects of empire, and in part posits a bridge between Western and Eastern empires.

The emergence of Islam in the 7th century brought a rival to Byzantine power, even though in some ways the new Islamic empire should be seen as the fulfillment of Roman imperial ambitions (Fowden 1993). Byzantine polemics against Islam largely relied on vague clichés, such as those written by the 8th-century theologian John of Damascus. Such polemics were made both within and outside Muslim-controlled lands and continued to the end of the Byzantine empire. An exception was Niketas Byzantios of the later 9th century, who studied the Qur'an (probably in Greek translation), engaged in a dialogue that centered on theological questions such as predestination versus free will, and also addressed political and social matters. Christian apologists presented Muhammad as a false prophet as part of their refutation of the authority of the Qur'an. They condemned Islam for sodomy, for polygamy, and, in its vision of paradise, for hedonism. Some of these themes we have already seen in archaic Greek literature, but the context is vastly different, and we cannot assume that there is direct continuity.

Western medieval authors were no less well disposed to Islam. To take an eminent case, Dante has Maometto suffer a gruesome fate in the ninth *Bolgia,* together with his first follower and son-in-law, Ali (*Inferno* 28). Muhammad's punishment is to be split open from chin to bowels, this severity resulting from the fact that he was a source of religious division. The medieval idea that Muhammad was originally a Christian cardinal seeking the papacy goes some way to explaining the luridness of the passage. Dante is part of Said's sweeping critique (68–70). There can be no doubt that this passage in its own right both expressed and encouraged a negative view of Islam.

Scholars on both the left (including Said) and on the right of the political spectrum have observed a hardening of the cleavage between Islam and Christianity. When the Western Civilization and Great Books curricula arose in U.S. universities in the first half of the 20th century, "the West" and its canon had no place for Islam—even though, from a purely cartographic point of view, Morocco is to the west of Britain (Lewis and Wigen 1997). Many scholars and politicians have presented Islam in terms of timeless, fundamental antithesis, so that events such as the 9/11 deaths have seemed an inevitable collision in the supposed "clash of civilizations." Such an approach overlooks the high degree of exchange between Islam and Christian cultures of the Middle Ages, for example in the philosophical and scientific domains.

The relation of East and West has been described here mostly in terms of supposed binaries in ancient thinking, with attention to the afterlife of those binaries. Though these are significant features of ancient and modern thought, there are certainly alternative ways of conceiving that relation. The issue of influence has already been seen in the "Orientalizing" styles of geometric- and archaic-period art. This is decided less in terms of manifest ancient perceptions than modern (scholarly) analysis. More broadly, however, the notion of intercultural exchange offers means of seeing the practices whereby East and West came into contact. If we are seeking to identify people whose lives defied the supposed binaries discussed here, then the Phoenicians come to the fore. Their trans-Mediterranean activity came at an early period of Greek history, and it overlapped with Roman ascendancy in the 3rd century BCE. They not only traversed the Mediterranean for centuries from their native Levant but around 800 BCE undertook a colonizing mission to the Maghreb (modern Tunisia). They left only a scant documentary record, and it was a Roman version of their story that became canonical: in Virgil's *Aeneid,* at an early and optimistic point (1.572), Dido presents their colonizing mission as parallel to and compatible with that of Aeneas's Trojans. In this version, the Trojan past is folded into a triumphal Roman present, characterized by victory not only over the Egyptians at Actium but also over the Carthaginians in the Punic Wars. Indeed, Virgil and Livy give the impression that the memory of the Phoenicians loomed large in Roman minds of the Augustan Age. The Carthaginians recounted here are, of course, not Eastern, in the narrow sense that they were based on the southwestern coast of the Mediterranean. Yet Virgil certainly suggests parallels between them and the undisputedly Eastern people of Cleopatra's Egypt. The Carthaginians were in this sense an Eastern people, in defiance of physical geography. A deep problem here is the near absence of their own perspective, and the pointed nature of the Roman views about them. Their shadowy case proves a rule: supposed ideological binaries are undermined in the exchange of people, goods, and ideas that so characterizes the history of Mediterranean premodernity. Ethnic stereotypes about the East may seem overdetermined at many points in history; it is only fairly recently that scholars have instead emphasized the dynamics of exchange within the Mediterranean, whether characterized as connectivity or communication.

BIBL.: W. Burkert, *Babylon, Memphis, Persepolis: Eastern Contexts of Greek culture* (Cambridge, Mass., 2004) and *The Orientalizing Revolution: Near Eastern Influence on Greek Culture in the Early Archaic Age* (Cambridge, Mass., 1992). G. Fowden, *Empire to Commonwealth: Consequences of Monotheism in Late Antiquity* (Princeton 1993). T. M. Kolbaba, *The Byzantine Lists: Errors of the Latins* (Urbana 2000). L. Kurke, "The Politics of *habrosunē* in Archaic Greece," *Classical Antiquity* 11 (1992) 91–120. M. W. Lewis and K. E. Wigen, *The Myth of Continents: A Critique of Metageography* (Berkeley 1997). S. P. Morris, *Daedalus and the Origins of Greek Art* (Princeton 1992). E. W. Said, *Orientalism* (New York 1978). M. L. West, *The East Face of Helicon: West Asiatic Elements in Greek Poetry and Myth* (Oxford 1997). G.PR.

Ecphrasis

For the ancient Greek rhetoricians who first used the term, *ecphrasis* was a type of speech or writing (*logos*) that appealed to the audience's visual imagination and made its members feel as if they could see the subject matter in their mind's eye. An ecphrasis could describe any type of subject and could even encompass vivid narrative. Works of art and architecture became a particularly popular subject for ecphrasis in later antiquity. In modem criticism, ecphrasis has come to be defined as the "description of a work of art," a category that may be restricted to the visual arts (painting and sculpture) or expanded to include architecture and other arts. Ecphrasis in this new guise is often used as the title of a genre or even as a distinct poetic mode or principle in which the relation of the verbal and the visual is explored.

The two distinct meanings of ecphrasis, ancient and modern, have many points of contact. The ancient definition of ecphrasis as a "speech that brings the thing shown vividly before the eyes" naturally included graphic descriptions of paintings, sculptures, and other artifacts. The Homeric Shield of Achilles was cited in an ancient handbook as an example of ecphrasis, and many Greek descriptions of paintings, sculptures, and buildings from the Roman and Byzantine period were referred to at the time as *ecphrases*. Examples are the *Imagines* of the Philostrati, Callistratus' descriptions of statues, and the 6th-century metrical ecphrasis of the church of Hagia Sophia by Paul the Silentiary. These works tend to emphasize the effect the sight has on the viewer, rather than dwelling on technical detail, often retelling the story depicted in the work in an attempt to create a similar effect in words.

There is no sign in antiquity or the Middle Ages that all descriptions of works of art were felt to belong to a single genre, though it is certainly possible to trace a direct relationship among certain examples. The descriptions of shields and other artifacts in later epic, such as the Virgilian Shield of Aeneas or the cloak of Jason in Apollonius of Rhodes' *Argonautika,* make reference to the Homeric Shield of Achilles, as do the descriptions of objects in pastoral poetry and in the prose ecphrasis of the Younger Philostratus (*Imagines* 10). Beyond the classical period, the Philostratean ecphrases inspired imitators in Byzantium and during the Renaissance.

The modern redefinition of ecphrasis resulted from a combination of factors. From the Renaissance onward, artists, patrons, and scholars sought out ancient descriptions of art objects as evidence for lost artifacts. Philosophers and critics of art and literature were also interested in these texts as evidence of the similarities and differences between art and literature (*ut pictura poiesis,* "as is painting so is poetry"). But even in these contexts the term ecphrasis was hardly used, and it was not until the mid-20th century that the modern definition was fully articulated by Leo Spitzer and then taken up and developed in various ways by other scholars and critics.

Whatever the nuances of their definitions, most studies of ecphrasis treat it as a phenomenon rooted in the classical Greek past. Spitzer's poetic ecphrasis, for example, encompasses Homer, Theocritus, Keats, the French Parnassians, and the German poet Rilke. But different assumptions about what ecphrasis means give rise to different versions of its ancestry. Studies of ecphrasis as art criticism suggest a lineage that runs from the Philostrati to Giorgio Vasari, Giambattista Marino, and Diderot, whereas a study of ecphrasis in its rhetorical sense would emphasize the continuity from imperial Greek rhetoric to the scholars and orators who maintained and developed that tradition throughout the Byzantine empire, a period that is often excluded from other traditions of ecphrasis.

Each of these proposed traditions is, of course, itself an interpretation and depends on the critics' understanding of cultural history and on their vision of the Western tradition. Svetlana Alpers's influential reading of Vasari as the heir to Philostratus, for example, sees ecphrasis as a mode of art criticism that was intimately linked to pictorial realism and thus reflected an aesthetic affinity between the classical period and the Renaissance. The poetic tradition of ecphrasis proposed by Leo Spitzer, a refugee writing in a world shattered by war, emphasized instead the unity of European poetry and its origins in Homer.

By contrast, the ancient rhetorical meaning of ecphrasis points to the discontinuities between ancient and modern attitudes to the word and to conceptions of literature. Though the modern definition treats subject matter as the defining characteristic of ecphrasis and focuses attention on the various interactions between art and text, the ancient definition emphasizes the effect of language on its audience, in particular the power of words to transport the reader or listener. This type of imaginative and emotional response to language, so valued in ancient criticism and education, with their rhetorical orientation, has been downplayed in a great deal of modern criticism (though it has reemerged in some recent reader-response criticism).

The borrowing of the classical term *ecphrasis* to designate the "genre" of descriptions of works of art has been fruitful in many ways for the study of literature both ancient and modern. As a convenient label it has facilitated a deeper exploration of the complexities of such texts, whether they are seen as evidence for certain cultures of viewing, as self-reflexive commentaries on the author and his art, as celebrations of the artifice of language by their reference to the art object, or as a means of exploring the very nature of the poetic though its relation to the "other" of the image. But the new use of the ancient term can also be deceptive: it can encourage an uncritical acceptance that all descriptions of works of art fall into a venerable "tradition" going back to Homer, masking the discontinuities and glossing over the different ways in which the term is used today.

The story of the definition of ecphrasis also illustrates the ways in which the history of the classical tradition is constantly being rewritten to fit the needs of the present and raises several important questions about the classical tradition itself. How much should we rely on ancient theories to elucidate ancient texts, and is it ever possible to reconstruct ancient readings? How are we to understand a "tradition" in literature? Is it enough to demonstrate a similarity between various texts (in which case many non-Western texts may be as much a part of the tradition of ecphrasis as Keats's "Ode" or the Shield of Achilles)? Or do we need to demonstrate the author's knowledge of the tradition in question? And, finally, why has it been so important for critics from Spitzer on to claim an ancient title and lineage for their own conceptions of ecphrasis?

BIBL.: Svetlana Alpers, "*Ekphrasis* and Aesthetic Attitudes in Vasari's *Lives*," *Journal of the Warburg and Courtauld Institutes* 23 (1960) 190–215. Jas Elsner, ed., *The Verbal and the Visual: Cultures of Ekphrasis in Antiquity* (special issue), *Ramus* 31, nos. 1–2 (2002). Paul Friedländer, *Johannes von Gaza and Paulus Silentiarius: Kunstbeschreibungen Justinianischer Zeit* (Leipzig 1912). Mario Klarer, ed., *Ekphrasis* (special issue), *Word and Image* 15, no.1 (1999). M. Krieger, *Ekphrasis: The Illusion of the Natural Sign* (Baltimore 1992). Leo Spitzer, "The Ode on a Grecian Urn, or Content vs. Metagrammar," *Comparative Literature* 7 (1955) 921–944.

R.W.

Education

At the most basic level, the survival of the classical tradition has been linked to what has been taught in the schools and universities, first in Europe, then in the places where Europeans exported their cultural and educational systems. The importance of this relationship is immediately apparent in the words used for "school," at least in its middle- and upper-class manifestations, in the various European languages. The German *Gymnasium* is the same word that the Greeks used for the place where athletic contests and philosophical lectures took place; the French *lycée* and the Italian *liceo* are named after the Lyceum, the Athenian *gymnasion* where Aristotle taught; and the English and American "grammar school" looks back to the time when boys began their education with the formal study of Latin grammar.

Because the classics exerted their greatest influence on secondary education, and because far more people learned what they knew about Greece and Rome from the schools than from universities, the discussion that follows devotes some attention to higher education but focuses on the schools. What was learned and how it was learned have undergone three major transformations since the fall of Rome, each of which is treated separately.

The Middle Ages. The Roman educational system, which was very similar to that of the Hellenistic world, had three stages. Beginning around age 7, children went to a primary school under the direction of a *magister ludi,* where they learned reading, writing, and some basic arithmetic. At age 11 or 12, they went to the school of the grammarian (*grammaticus*), where they learned how to speak correctly and interpret the poets, as Quintilian had put it (1.4.2ff.). Instruction focused on four key authors (the *quadriga*)—Virgil, Terence, Sallust, and Cicero—and involved a preliminary reading (*praelectio*), necessitated by the fact that written words were generally run together without punctuation, and then an exposition (*enarratio*) that critiqued both form (*methodice*) and substance (*historia*). Higher education was in the hands of the rhetorician (*rhetor*), who taught the Greek system of public speaking as preparation for a career in politics and the law.

The *Hermeneumata Pseudo-Dositheana* (3rd cent. CE), "interpretations" or perhaps "guidelines" in the present-day sense, suggest how students actually learned at the very end of antiquity. These are bilingual schoolbooks, composed of four parts: an alphabetical dictionary focused on verbs; a dictionary organized by topics (words about birds, magistrates, etc.); dramatizations of scenes from everyday life; and texts for reading practice, such as Aesopic fables, short mythological stories, and gnomic works. The *Hermeneumata* provide an interesting object lesson in the reception of classical texts, in that they survive because they were able to take on a new function in new educational environments: later, in the Middle Ages, they became an aid for the rare adult who wanted to try to learn Greek; during the Renaissance they attracted the attention of Humanists like Conrad Celtes, who thought they could be published as aids for an educational system that was returning more and more to its classical roots.

The educational system of late antiquity remained largely unchanged in the Byzantine East until the fall of Constantinople in 1453, but in the Latin West it was gradually transformed. Line-by-line commentary remained the norm for grammatical instruction, which dominated work in the medieval schools, but when Latin gradually became replaced by the vernacular as the native language of the students, the character of grammatical instruction changed: it became more and more an act of cultural recovery, which emphasized the role of the commentator to the extent that the commentary threatened to overwhelm the text. Rhetoric in turn was displaced from its position at the educational pinnacle by theology, after which its character slowly changed. Rhetorical theory was focused on two texts from antiquity, Cicero's *On Invention* and the pseudo-Ciceronian *Rhetoric to Herennius*, but practice evolved into three characteristically medieval forms that retained recognizable classical roots. Beginning with Alberic of Monte Cassino at the end of the 11th century, the six-part Roman scheme for constructing a speech was transposed into a five-part plan for composing the formal letter, giving rise to the term and practice of *ars dictaminis.* Between 1170 and 1280, six works on the arts of poetry (*artes poetriae*) appeared, in which the principles of grammar were adapted to guide the novice writer. And at the beginning of the 13th century the art of preaching (*ars praedicandi*) provided a rhetorical pattern for the sermon, beginning with the reading aloud of a scriptural "theme," followed by a division of the theme and an amplification of each part. The classical art of memory, which was also a part of rhetoric, underwent a similar transformation: the ancient system of mentally linking things to be remembered with architectural features was rather awkwardly married to a two-dimensional, diagrammatic grid system, similar to its classical prototype but different as well.

Medieval education also inherited from antiquity an approach to the liberal arts that identified seven disciplines and grouped them in a precise way, as the following couplet shows: "Grammar speaks; dialectic teaches the truth; rhetoric supplies the words; / Music sings; arithmetic counts; geometry weighs out; astronomy devotes itself to the stars." As Martianus Capella explained at the beginning of the 5th century, the first three, which are language-based, are associated in the *trivium* ("three roads"); the last four, which are numerically based, are called the *quadrivium* ("four roads"). Ancient practice emphasized the verbal arts at the expense of the *quadrivium,* as did medieval successors.

For medieval educators, the Bible offered two analogies for the absorption of pagan learning. As the Hebrew wanting to marry a heathen slave could do so only after cutting her hair and nails so that her virtue might be apparent to all (Deuteronomy 21:12), so the Christian should purge ancient wisdom of its errors and reveal its underlying truth. And as the Israelites had fled Egypt with their gold and silver vessels and left everything else behind (Exodus 3:22, 12:35), so Christians should leave behind the excesses and dangers of pagan learning and take only what is useful. The argument made in Cassiodorus' *Institutiones,* that pagan learning is necessary to understand Scripture, was repeated by Jerome, Augustine, and Isidore, until Bede argued that the Bible is actually superior to Greek and Roman writings in style. Hesitations about the content of the classical heritage resurfaced persistently through the early centuries of Christianity, the most famous being Jerome's dream that he would be denied entrance to heaven because he was more Ciceronian than Christian (Epistle 22), but by the 9th century Charlemagne succeeded in constructing a broadly disseminated educational system that was controlled by the Church but stood on a recognizable classical base.

Medieval education rested almost exclusively in Latin, which began with learning the language, then focused on reading the *auctores,* literally the authors or authorities who conveyed knowledge about the arts. Different writers proposed different authors for their ideal curricula, but most lists display a complete disregard for chronological order and arrangement by subject, pagan and Christian authors being intermixed: all *auctores* were seen as having the same value and as offering the same timeless truth. The *auctores* were technical authorities, but they were also sources of wisdom that encapsulated psychological insight or life experiences in concise, memorable form. Aristotle and Quintilian had focused attention on these *sententiae,* or apothegms, which were collected, memorized, and arranged in order for instant recall. Medieval teachers also focused attention on *exempla,* interpolated anecdotes or figures that exemplified virtues, as Cato represented virtuous restraint and Ripheus, a minor figure mentioned briefly in Virgil's *Aeneid,* vaulted up to heaven in Dante's *Paradise* (canto 20) because he represented the best of pagan values. Thus, medieval learning drew heavily from classical authors, but it fragmented them into shards that it found useful, so that Ovid and Lucan ended up reinforcing the values of medieval Christianity.

Sixteenth through Twentieth Centuries: A New Vision. Beginning in the second quarter of the 15th century, a group of Italian educators began an assault on the medieval system, which they found to be too narrow, too focused on technicalities at the expense of broader educational goals. First, teachers like Guarino da Verona and Vittorino da Feltre looked to Cicero and Quintilian for inspiration and changed the focus of secondary education, deemphasizing the *quadrivium* and modifying the *trivium* so that grammar, rhetoric, history, poetry, and moral philosophy—the disciplines that perfect a common humanity—structured the new learning. Then they refined the critical and historical approach to the curriculum, eliminating most post-classical authors in favor of classical ones, most commonly Cicero for rhetoric, Virgil for poetry, and Caesar, Valerius Maximus, or Sallust for history, on the argument that antiquity provided the best models for understanding people and their place in society. Latin language instruction was also reformed, the medieval interest in speculative or theoretical grammar being replaced by simplified rules derived from classical usage. Guarino, Vittorino, and their successors also insisted on the importance of Greek, which was virtually unknown in medieval Europe. Not all the recommended changes were fully implemented—only a minority of students actually learned much Greek, for example, and the Latin grammar books actually used in many schools retained a good deal from their medieval predecessors for several generations—but the reformers did introduce a revolution in the history of education.

The new Humanist approach prevailed in most parts of Italy by 1500 and in much of the rest of Europe by 1600, leading to a remarkable period in which education throughout the Westernized world was dominated for almost 400 years by the same basic canon of classical authors supported by similar goals, textbooks, and teaching methods. Children learned to read in Latin, then began to study grammar, so that schoolboys in Liège could make themselves understood in Latin as early as age seven. The world of the schools remained predominantly Latin from this point on for the upper and middle classes, with few real differences, so that in the 16th century we find the same curriculum in Brunswick that we find in Strasbourg; the English public school (in American terms, private school) curriculum that began at St. Paul's provided in turn the model for the Boston Latin School over a century later. Even well into the 19th century, Latin dominated the school day.

To be sure, there were some variations through the years: by the 18th century, for example, Latin was no longer being spoken "in hall" at Oxford and Cambridge. The 19th century, however, was a period of revival, and half to three-quarters of the day at the school level was still being spent on Latin; a general expansion of the educational system resulted in more students' passing through the Latin schools than ever before, even in czarist Russia, where Count Tolstoy set up a classical *Gymnasium.* Not every child, of course, was educated in a *Gymnasium,* a *lycée,* a *liceo,* or a public school: half the children in 16th-century Venice, for example, went to a vernacular school with a commercial curriculum, and similar "private" schools, run for profit and aimed toward the interests of the commercial class, flourished in 19th-century England as well. Yet even in the latter case, the prospectuses for these schools show that the classics were invoked to provide a veneer of respectability.

A close examination also reveals various nuances in different countries. Education in Spain, for example, was characterized by unusual chaos and lack of standardization. The English system, in which the emphasis on verse composition in Greek and Latin was striking, was structured so that it was unusually resistant to change: students passed from preparatory (grammar) school to public school to Oxford or Cambridge, then either returned to teach in the same school from which they had graduated or entered the ministry—or perhaps law or medicine. In Germany the classical seminar at the universities came to focus more on training schoolteachers than training ministers, with the politically marginalized upper middle classes hoping to transform their society into a modern nation-state with its roots in a romanticized Hellenism. In postrevolutionary France, by contrast, classical education was rooted in imperial Rome, supporting a state that was centralized, secular, and expansionist.

It is important to emphasize as well that some version of classical education accompanied European colonists wherever they went. In Latin America, for example, a number of native scholars learned Latin in the Franciscan colleges that had been set up in New Spain in the early 1500s. Students at these colleges produced grammars and dictionaries first, then translated classical authors like pseudo-Cato and Aesop into Nahuatl, the indigenous language of Mexico. By the 1560s one student at Santa Cruz de Tlatelolco in Mexico City was able not only to quote from Ovid's *Ars amatoria* (*Art of Love*) in a letter to Philip II of Spain, but also to write the letter itself in passable Latin. By the end of the 19th century, Miguel Antonio Caro could build on the proficiency he attained in a Jesuit school to combine a career in politics (he was president of Colombia from 1894–1898) with substantial contributions to literature and pedagogy. He co-authored a Latin grammar in 1867, wrote a treatise on the use of the participle three years later, and published a well-known translation of the complete works of Virgil into Spanish verse as well.

Something similar happened in North America. From the founding of Harvard College in 1636 until the 1880s, the classics stood at the center of college education in the United States. There, as in the grammar schools that prepared students for college, half the day was spent on Greek and Latin. A single professor would teach hundreds of boys something about the ancient world and its languages, as well as the educated public to whom he would address his lectures, pamphlets, and books. Instruction was not always inspired, but the classical roots of American morality, politics, rhetoric, and art are found in the schools of the day.

In sum, then, there were regional variations, but they were variations on the same theme. From 1600 to 1900, the Latin school was at the center of European education, wherever it was found.

Formal education in the classical tradition unfolded during this period on three levels. Instruction began in the elementary school, where boys at the age of 6 or 7 began to study reading, writing, arithmetic, and basic Christian doctrine. Latin was supposed to predominate, although the vernacular regularly crept in. Students remained here for three or four years, after which most quit to become servants, day laborers, or agricultural workers. The others went on to secondary school, whose curriculum was based in Latin grammar and the humanistic disciplines, although some work in other areas could be grafted on at the end. With this Latin base, students could proceed to a university, where they focused on the professional disciplines of theology, medicine, and law, though without completely leaving behind the classical world of the schools, as theology required a thorough knowledge of Aristotle, medicine looked to Galen and Hippocrates, and legal texts included the basic works of Roman law. A student's progress from one level to another could be recorded by the books he used. At the end of the 19th century, for example, various English editions of Virgil received "prize bindings" that marked distinguished achievement on key examinations, first on the one that allowed passage from the elementary school to secondary school, then on the "local examinations" at which scholarships to Oxford and Cambridge were awarded. An 1893 edition of Conington's translation of the *Aeneid,* for example, was awarded by Ripon Grammar School to Spencer H. Elliott, who went on to write several books published by the Society for Promoting Christian Knowledge.

The most thoroughly classical level was the second one, the grammar school, whose objectives emerged from *The Education of Boys* (*De librorum educatione,* 1450), a treatise written by Aeneas Sylvius Piccolomini, who later became Pope Pius II: "Thus a twofold advantage will accrue to you from reading ancient and modern authors who have written with practical wisdom. Through zeal for virtue you will make your life better, and you will acquire the art of grammar and skill in the use of the best and most elegant words, as well as a great store of maxims." The road to eloquence and virtue began with grammar, where the science of correct speech passed to the interpretation of model authors from antiquity, who provided the necessary examples of correct usage. In *A Program of Teaching and Learning* (*De ordine docendi et studendi,* 1459), Battista Guarino tells us which authors were taught by his father, the famous teacher Guarino da Verona: Valerius Maximus and Justin in history; Virgil, then Lucan, Statius, Ovid's *Metamorphoses,* Seneca's tragedies, Plautus, and Terence among the poets; Cicero for rhetoric, with Quintilian as a supporting text; and Cicero, Aristotle's *Ethics,* and Plato in moral philosophy. In 16th-century Brunswick, Cicero, Terence, and Virgil dominated. The reading list at St. Paul's in London at the end of the 17th century included Erasmus, Ovid, and Justin, then Martial, Sallust, Virgil, Cicero's speeches, Horace, Juvenal, and Persius in Latin, with more work in Greek than was customary on the Continent, beginning with the New Testament and an anthology of poets, then moving to Apollodorus on myth, Homer, Aratus, and "Dionysius." Instruction at the *collège* (i.e., secondary school) at Limoges was typical of the French curriculum around 1750: beginners studied Cicero's *Familiar Letters,* Ovid's *Tristia,* and Cato's *Distichs;* at the middle levels, one of Cicero's moral or philosophical treatises, Ovid's *Tristia* or *Metamorphoses,* Terence, and Virgil's *Eclogues* or *Georgics;* for the advanced students, one of Cicero's oratorical works, Livy (or sometimes Tacitus), Virgil's *Aeneid,* and Horace's *Odes.* There are, to be sure, some authors on one or two of these lists that are not on the others, but again, the similarities are more striking than the differences; indeed, most of the same texts were still being read in French schools at the end of the 1950s, Cicero and Virgil continuing to dominate.

How were the curriculum authors actually taught in the classroom? Basic instruction throughout this period relied on the paraphrase-commentary, as the teacher went through the text word for word. The procedure of Orazio Toscanella, who taught in Venice during the middle of the 16th century, was typical. First came translation: the words in the Latin text were rearranged into Italian word order, then translated, then revised into an elegant Italian version. Next came analysis, as Toscanella identified the genre of the work being read, explained the historical circumstances in which it was composed, provided biographical information about the author, divided it into parts, and identified exemplary aspects of its style. Each word generated what amounted to a dictionary entry, compensating for the fact that only a small amount of material was covered each day. The teacher dictated and the students copied his observations into their texts.

A modification of this system was worked out by the Jesuits and implemented throughout the areas ruled by Catholic Europe. Jerónimo Nadal drew features from the educational environment of Paris, where Ignatius Loyola and most of the other founders of the order had studied, and from the practice of the Dutch Brethren of the Common Life: students were divided into classes, where they stayed until they could pass a test to enter the next level, each class in turn being organized into groups of ten students (*decuriae*). Exposition of a set text was followed by questions from the master; the students defended various positions in formal disputations and strove to win prizes that recognized their accomplishments. Repetition, memorization, and review characterized this system, whose *Ratio studiorum* (definitive version, 1599) established the classes and their assigned reading. Heavily based in Cicero and Virgil, Jesuit education was more structured than its Italian predecessor and relied more on Greek than most other schools of the time, but its essential character remained that of the early modern Latin school.

Many early modern printed books contain handwritten "indexing notes," single words entered in the margin that refer either to a distinctive stylistic feature of the text (e.g., "simile") or to its content (e.g., "anger"). These notes reflect the educational practice of the period, in which students identified passages that were exemplary for verbal polish or moral value, then copied these passages into notebooks called commonplace books, where they were arranged under the headings reflected in the indexing notes. These notebooks in turn provided the student with material for his own "original" compositions in Latin, which reproduced the school exercises of such late antique authors as Aphthonius. Hugh Robinson, for example, provides a model for how Latin composition was managed at Winchester in the late 17th century. A student told to write on the theme *festina lente* ("make haste slowly") could begin by stating a proposition (excessive haste is to be condemned), followed in turn by an argument (nothing is so hostile to good counsel as excessive haste in conducting one's affairs), a proof (without good counsel, whatever is done cannot be done correctly), a comparison (as summer heat is to fruit, so time for deliberation is necessary for ripening one's affairs), an example (Quintus Fabius Maximus saved Rome by delaying), a reference to the Old Testament (everything comes to be done with sufficient speed if it is done well), and a conclusion ("make haste slowly" is therefore good advice), all supported with appropriate classical references.

The early modern Latin school offered a number of significant advantages to those who passed through it. On the most basic level, it marked a rite of passage, an initiation into the dominant social and economic group of the day. And the culture into which the student was initiated was truly international: when the British general John Whitelock negotiated surrender after a failed attack on Buenos Aires in 1807, he did so in Latin because no officer on either side understood the other's language. As this example suggests, those who had learned to speak extemporaneously in Latin in class and to write letters there in Ciceronian style could transfer these skills to careers in government service, law, education, and the church. Interestingly, the educational system survived long after Latin was used regularly as the medium of communication, when it came to be seen as the foundation for culture, a window, as the 19th-century British school inspector Thomas Arnold put it, through which one could see a better past as a way to ennoble the present. At the point when no one could claim any longer that being able to conjugate irregular Latin verbs was necessary to win cases in court, new support for the Latin schools came from "faculty psychology," the belief that certain mental faculties like the memory and logical reasoning could be exercised like a muscle and that the study of Greek and Latin provided the best all-around mental exercise. To an observer in the 21st century, the focus on language might appear narrow, but as Charles Nisbet, the president of Dickinson College at the end of the 18th century, noted, language and the literature written in that language were the key to understanding a people, their values, and their culture. The schoolmaster aimed to have a permanent effect on the character of his pupils, and there is abundant evidence that, in some cases at least, he succeeded. H. M. Butler, for example, continued the practice of composing verses in Greek and Latin from his school days as a way of helping him, "however imperfectly, to keep in touch with the thoughts of the wise, the pious, and the pure, and giving a kind of quiet unity to a life of some labours and many distractions."

The evidence also suggests, however, that Butler was the exception rather than the rule, and that what was actually accomplished throughout the early modern period fell far short of what was hoped for. In the French grammar school, for example, as few as 10 percent of the students attained any real facility in the Latin language; the vast majority remained unable, even after years of work, to read a classical Latin text accurately. How did the others manage to get through the system? The answer is simple: they cheated, as the following paean to the "pony" (an illicit translation) shows:

> And when leaving class, leave behind us
> *Ponies* for a lower class;
> *Ponies,* which perhaps another,
> Toiling up the College hill,
> A forlorn, a "younger brother,"
> "Riding," may rise higher still.

Even the publishers obliged, by producing translations "for young people beginning their study of the Latin language and for those who had, then lost, the language and wish to regain the ability to read Latin authors." The situation was still worse when Latin was spoken, even at the university level: at the beginning of the 17th century Isaac Casaubon, an accomplished Latinist himself, stormed out of a thesis defense at the Sorbonne, commenting, "I have never heard so much Latin without understanding it." In the universities of Pisa and Naples a couple of generations later, professors would lecture in Latin from the stage, then descend to the aisles or a courtyard to repeat the lesson in the vernacular.

Practice fell short of theory in other areas as well. The school of Guarino da Verona, which was one of the best of the new Humanist institutions, aimed at the formation of the whole man, whose character would be shaped by the ennobling sentiments of Virgil and Homer. The school day, however, consisted of copying, memorizing, repeating, and imitating; some moral observations certainly emerged in Guarino's lectures, but they tended to get lost amid grammatical and linguistic observations. The same thing happened later in England, as this limerick repeated by Balliol students suggests:

> There once were some lectures on Homer—
> But I think the name's a misnomer;
> Verbs, nouns and articles
> Verbs, nouns and particles
> But uncommonly little of Homer.

Students who managed to steer between the Scylla of deficient accomplishment and the Charybdis of excessive love of arcane detail still ended up the victims of an earlier, intensive style of reading in which breadth of knowledge was sacrificed to an intensive study of a few chosen authors: Cicero and Virgil, perhaps Horace and a little

Homer. It is true that even as late as the 19th century, Members of Parliament could quote the classics to one another and be confident that their point would be taken by colleagues who shared their upbringing—but in fact most of the quotations seem to be taglines like "voracious love, to what do you not drive the hearts of men" (*Aeneid* 4.412) or "be warned, learn justice and not to scorn the gods" (*Aeneid* 6.620), shards of ancient moral thought that served many generations as the residue of their classical education.

These traits became more pronounced when the classical school was viewed through the prism of vernacular culture. As is often the case, Shakespeare suggests the range of possibilities, from the country schoolmaster Holofernes, the pedant in the comedy *Love's Labor's Lost,* to Prospero in *The Tempest,* who devoted himself so exclusively to the "volumes that I prize above my dukedom" (1.2.167–168) that he lost the very political position he had been educated to hold. Rudyard Kipling, too, nuances his attitudes toward classical schooling in *Stalky & Co.* (1899), first presenting the masters as likeable enemies whose teaching is devoted primarily to good discipline, then filtering the ideals of translation and close reading through Horace's Regulus Ode. But the prevailing image is that of Robert Browning, whose "A Grammarian's Funeral" (1855) gives us a schoolteacher who is "dead from the waist down" (l. 132). This image reached its zenith in the popular imagination in George Eliot's *Middlemarch* (1872), where the passionless pedant Mr. Casaubon was widely understood to have been based on Mark Pattison, the rector of Lincoln College, Oxford, who was the author of the standard intellectual biography of the classical scholar Isaac Casaubon.

As is generally the case, the Latin schools supported the society that created them, reinforcing the basic values and other institutions of that society along with whatever limitations might be present there. The image of antiquity on which these schools rested was a conservative one, designed to produce citizens similarly resistant to change, citizens who were as comfortable taking orders and reproducing trite truisms from their commonplace books at court as they had been at school. Throughout the Ancien Régime there was an uncrossable divide that separated those who had absorbed the language and culture of antiquity (or at least some of it) from those who had not, and contrary to what might have been foreseen, this divide survived the revolutions that straddled the end of the 18th century. In its own day, as modern scholarship has emphasized, the literary culture of antiquity supported the political powers that nurtured it, and it continued to do so in its post-classical manifestations as well, where it served first to impart the linguistic skills and shared values on which worldly success depended, then as a means to initiate those who could afford to spend years learning something with little practical application into the world of privilege in which they were destined to live. Those who did not have it, like the hero in Thomas Hardy's *Jude the Obscure* (1895), recognized a Latin education as the key to advancement, whereas those who did have it regularly saw others' efforts to obtain it as a threat. When the Augustinians established a Latin school in Mexico City to train native scholars, Jeronimo Lopez complained in 1545 that they became insolent and refused to be treated as slaves. In 17th-century Spain, reformers known as *arbitristas* complained that a Latin education took the lower classes away from productive work in agriculture, artisanry, and commerce for nonproductive careers in church and government; the Spanish Crown limited the number of Latin schools in the kingdom, first in 1623 and again in 1743. It has often been noted that women as well as the lower classes were largely excluded from Latin schools until almost the end of the dominance of that tradition, and when women did find a way to enter that world, as they did in late Victorian England, they tended to move away from the authors canonized in the boys' schools, in this case toward Greek, which represented the exotic, instead of Latin, which represented the discipline and order of the status quo.

A classical education also supported the imperial enterprises of early modern Europe. As Sir Richard Livingstone's *Defence of Classical Education* (1917) put it in a sentence whose Ciceronian syntax would have made his teacher proud:

> We must go to Rome for our lessons. To govern peoples who differ in race, language, temper and civilization; to raise and distribute armies for their defence or subjection; to meet expences civil and military; to allow generals and governors sufficient independence without losing control at the centre; to know and supply the needs of provinces two thousand miles from the seat of government . . . Latin then stands in our education partly on linguistic grounds, partly on the heroic characters in its history, or the interest of its political and imperial problems, and on the capacities of its peoples for government.

The Humanists first entered universities in Italy around 1450, where they encountered relatively little opposition because the subjects they taught were not at the center of university education, which was focused on law and medicine. Representatives of the new learning were especially influential at Florence (Cristoforo Landino and Angelo Poliziano), Bologna (Filippo Beroaldo the Elder and Antonio Cortesi Urceo, called "Il Codro"), Rome (George of Trebizond, Lorenzo Valla, Pomponio Leto, and Antoine Muret), and Ferrara; professors at the smaller universities stayed largely with Virgil and Cicero, whereas the abler scholars at larger institutions branched off into other authors, supplementing basic instruction in style and moral wisdom with advanced lectures on textual problems and details of life in the ancient world that ultimately extended to an examination of the classical texts on which rested fields such as medicine and law. In Northern Europe the center of classical scholarship moved along with the famous professors, from the University of Paris in the middle of the 16th century (Jean Dorat, Adrien Turnèbe, and Denis Lambin) to the University of Leiden at the beginning of the 17th century (Joseph Justus Scaliger) to the universities of Göttingen and Halle after 1760 (C. G. Heyne and F. A. Wolf). In England classical studies were decidedly ancillary to the work in logic and moral philosophy that dominated the curriculum through the 17th century, but Latin was used to celebrate special occasions and to winnow out students for a series of special prizes, especially at Cambridge, which attracted considerable interest among the undergraduates. Britain's greatest classical scholar was undoubtedly Richard Bentley (1662–1742), although his chair at Cambridge was actually in theology. Around 1800 Oxford set a course of studies and a series of examinations leading to a degree in *litterae humaniores* (i.e., Greek and Latin), and Cambridge established the Classical Tripos (honors examination) in 1824 as an optional addition for those who qualified for a degree in mathematics; classics qualified for a degree on its own in 1857. By 1900 classics remained the second most popular tripos at Cambridge, and the School of Litterae Humaniores was the largest at Oxford.

The End of the Old Order. From the beginning, the strong emphasis on grammar evoked resistance on the part of some students—such as Winston Churchill, whose objection to how the vocative was explained to him ("it is used to address a table") elicited a threat of severe punishment if his impertinence ("but I never do so!") continued. In response to work they did not understand or found distasteful, other children cheated, relying surreptitiously on a dual-language edition to prepare their translations, then introducing a few mistakes to avoid getting caught by the teacher. Many suffered in silence—the grammar text used for many years at Eton has been accused of causing "more human suffering than Nero, Robespierre, or any other enemy of the human race" (Hill 1835)—while others searched in vain for simplified grammars like those of Melanchthon or the Port-Royal grammarians, which in the end failed to prevail because they replaced one overly complicated system with another. Many students refused to be content with the bowdlerized texts they were given and went in search of editions that contained the obscene words, anatomical details, and sexual episodes originally included in the works of Martial, Terence, Horace, and Juvenal.

Well-articulated challenges to the unified system of Latin education began to appear in the 18th century, when control of the language was not so obviously necessary as it had been, especially in the New World. Latin, it was argued, did not impart useful learning; the content of Latin literature was available in translation, and it impeded the development of a natural, clear style in the vernacular. Latin schools did not help people learn to reason but rather stifled their natural genius, turning out pretentious pedants, not civilized gentlemen; as Benjamin Rush put it shortly after the American Revolution, "Who are guilty of the greatest absurdity—the Chinese, who press the feet into deformity by small shoes, or the Europeans and Americans, who press the brain into obliquity by Greek and Latin?" Latin literature mixed the impurities of paganism into good Christian morality and encouraged ideas that were not appropriate to the democratic principles demanded by postrevolutionary societies. And classics suffered in the face of changing ideas about what constituted truth, which by the end of the 19th century was seen as tentative and progressive, not retainable in the form of permanently valid verities from the past. The defenders of the Latin schools did not remain silent, producing the same arguments for almost 400 years: Latin helps with vocabulary, especially in the Romance languages and the sciences; studying it helps develop the mind and the memory, and overcoming the concomitant difficulties produces a robust character fit to overcome the challenges of later life. It forms taste, counterbalances the growing threats of scientific and materialistic ideologies, and forms a free human being, aware of the past and ready to participate in the society of the day.

The final collapse of the traditional Latin school system took place dramatically, as part of the student revolts during the 1960s that changed the face of post-classical education a third time. In France, "Down with Latin" became one of the reformers' rallying cries, and it is important to note that the debates over the status of Latin at this time were fundamentally political: when the Italian parliament debated keeping Latin in the middle-class *liceo* but not in the socially inferior *scuola media* in 1962–1963, the argument proceeded along party lines: the Christian Democrats defended Latin and the Socialists and Communists opposed it. But if the values of the Latin school no longer seemed appropriate to an egalitarian, diverse modern society, it is also important to note that there were plenty of warning signs leading up to the final collapse. In the preceding century, the position of Latin in the elite schools of Europe and the United States had passed from virtual monopoly to dominance, then to one option among many, an option that was being chosen by fewer and fewer students in each generation. The student revolts simply accelerated this trend. In the United States, from 1960 to 1978 the number of secondary school students taking Latin fell from 7 percent to 1 percent, and the numbers at the university level declined from .7 percent to .2 percent; in 1994 only 600 of nearly 1 million bachelor's degrees were in the classics.

What will happen to the classical tradition in education? One possibility is what Britain's Joint Association of Classical Teachers has called a "new Latin for a new situation," a methodological shift that deemphasizes grammar and vocabulary drill in favor of more time spent on translation and reading, and a greater focus on history and aesthetics, targeted at all children, even if this means working entirely in English translation for those who cannot handle the original. At the university level, Latin is likely to be saved not by forcing many to learn it badly, as a recent Italian text puts it, but by having a few learn it well. Something a little different has been happening in American universities, where an admittedly small number of students continue to choose classics as a major but a considerably larger number receive some exposure to the ancient world through courses with readings in English. These measures appear to be having some success, in that in both the United States and the United Kingdom, the number of students studying Latin, and even Greek, has gone up noticeably over the last few years. The classics are still regularly brought into discussions of what makes a good humanistic education, and this has led to bracing efforts to reconcile the traditional elitism of the Latin schools with the egalitarian values of a democratic society. As long as these discussions continue, the classical tradition will retain a place, though undoubtedly an attenuated one, in education.

BIBL.: R. Black, *Humanism and Education in Medieval and Renaissance Italy: Tradition and Innovation in Latin Schools from the Twelfth to the Fifteenth Century* (Cambridge 2001). M. L. Clarke, *Classical Education in Britain, 1500–1900* (Cambridge 1959). R. Copeland, *Rhetoric, Hermeneutics, and Translation in the Middle Ages: Academic Traditions and Vernacular Texts* (Cambridge 1991). E. R. Curtius, *European Literature and the Latin Middle Ages,* trans. W. R. Trask (Princeton 1953). C. Dionisotti, "From Ausonius' Schooldays? A Schoolbook and Its Relatives," *Journal of Roman Studies* 72 (1982) 83–125. A. Grafton and L. Jardine, *From Humanism to the Humanities* (Cambridge, Mass., 1986); P. F. Grendler, *Schooling in Renaissance Italy: Literacy and Learning, 1300–1600* (Baltimore 1989). M. D. Hill, *Public Education* (1835). C. W. Kallendorf, ed. and trans., *Humanist Educational Treatises* (Cambridge, Mass., 2002). A. Laird, "Latin America," in C. Kallendorf, ed., *Companion to the Classical Tradition* (Oxford 2007). H. I. Marrou, *A History of Education in Antiquity,* trans. G. Lamb (New York 1956). A. D. Nuttall, *Dead from the Waist Down: Scholars and Scholarship in Literature and the Popular Imagination* (New Haven 2003). C. Stray, *Classics Transformed: Schools, Universities, and Society in England, 1830–1960* (Oxford 1998). F. Waquet, *Latin, or the Empire of a Sign: From the Sixteenth to the Twentieth Centuries,* trans. J. Howe (London 2001). C. Winterer, *The Culture of Classicism: Ancient Greece and Rome in American Intellectual Life, 1780–1910* (Baltimore 2002).

C.K.

Egypt

At the end of the fourth millennium BCE there emerged in the Nile Valley, out of several rival chiefdoms, what we call ancient Egypt. This process of cultural and political unification became, in ancient Egyptian and then especially in classical tradition, personified in Menes, the founder-king. After a formative period of 300 years, the Old Kingdom (2750–2160, dynasties 3 through 6) developed the centralized state whose cultural, political, and economic structures remained valid until late antiquity. After the collapse of the Old Kingdom, Egypt disintegrated again into various rival princedoms (2160–1940, dynasties 7 through 11). The ideal of the god-king was replaced by the figure of the patron, who assembled under his leadership a mass of loyal clients—a system whose ideology and rhetoric of loyalism were later adopted by the restored monocracy of the Middle Kingdom (1940–1750). With the rise of the Middle Kingdom a new form of literature developed that reflected in its narrative and didactic genres the fundamentals of civil society, political rule, morality, theology, and human destiny, including the ideas of judgment after death and salvation from death through moral perfection, that became canonized as a "great" or "classical" tradition in the later course of Egyptian history.

The expulsion of the Hyksos—Asiatic invaders (presumably western Semitic or Canaanite) who ruled Egypt between 1650 and 1540 (forming dynasty 15)—marked the beginning of the New Kingdom and Egypt's expansion into an empire that reached from Syria, where it joined boundaries with the Hittites, the Mitanni, Assyria, and Babylonia, to the Fourth Cataract, in what is today Sudan. Imperialist politics led to a universalist outlook that deeply changed the traditional world image of Egyptian religion and eventually culminated in the religious revolution brought about by King Akhenaten (1340–1324), who replaced traditional polytheism with the exclusive cult of the sun (Aten). After the death of Akhenaten, the "heretic king," his monuments were dismantled, his name erased from the king lists, and his religion forgotten, but the influence of this experience on Egyptian religious thought was enormous. It led, on the one hand, to the idea of a single, hidden world-god manifesting himself in the visible cosmos and in a plethora of other gods, and, on the other hand, to the rise of several forms of individual religiosity subsumed under the term *personal piety,* in which the idea of the patron is applied to theology.

After the collapse of the New Kingdom (1100 BCE) and after the ensuing Third Intermediate Period, when Egypt was again divided into a variety of (mostly Libyan) princedoms (Herodotus' dodekarchy: the "rule of the 12"), the 25th (Ethiopian) and the 26th (Saite) dynasties fostered, perhaps in reaction to the Assyrian invasions and destructions, strong restorative and archaizing or "classicist" tendencies, in which the idea of a classical tradition became very evident. Under conditions of political disempowerment and foreign domination, first by the Persians (525–332, interrupted by periods of Egyptian autonomy), then by the Ptolemies (332–330), and finally by the Romans, the temples became the centers of Egyptian civilization. Every religious center strived to develop its own highly complex theology, rituals, system of taboos and prescriptions, hieroglyphic font, and even grammar. Ritual and religion thus became mysteries demanding long periods of initiation, which some Greek visitors, such as Pythagoras, are said to have successfully undergone. Graeco-Egyptian contacts led to the rise of a body of Graeco-Egyptian religious, philosophical, and magical texts mostly attributed to Hermes Trismegistus, presenting themselves as a codification of esoteric wisdom. A selection of more philosophical texts survived through the Byzantine Middle Ages as the Corpus Hermeticum; other, more practically oriented magical and alchemical texts were transmitted to the West via Arabian sources.

The Greek encounter with and interest in ancient Egypt had two stages. During the first stage, which lasted until the Roman conquest, when Egypt, despite periods of foreign domination, figured as its own state, the country interested the Greeks as a full-fledged civilization in all its aspects, political, social, economic, geographic, religious, and so on. In the second stage, with Egypt under Roman rule, Greek and Latin authors concentrated on Egyptian religion and philosophy, hieroglyphs and mysteries. Texts belonging to the first period include Herodotus' book 2, Isocrates' *Busiris,* Plato's Egyptian excursuses, the lost Egyptian history by Hecataeus of Abdera (partly surviving in excerpts by Diodorus), the first book of Diodorus Siculus' *Bibliotheca historica,* and the 17th book of Strabo's *Geography.* To the second period belong Plutarch's *De Iside et Osiride,* Porphyry's *Vita Pythagorae,* Iamblichus' *De mysteriis Aegyptiorum,* the 11th book of Apuleius' *Golden Ass,* and Horapollo's *Hieroglyphica,* as well as some patristic texts, especially by Clemens and Cyril of Alexandria. For the earlier Greek authors, Egypt presented the unique case of a political system that, unlike both "oriental despotism" and Greek democracy, combined monarchy and law. This image of Egypt later became a model for the especially Masonic ideal of enlightened absolutism. Because of the archaizing conservatism and antiquarianism then prevailing in Egypt, this civilization preserved many features dating back to the highest antiquity, and Greek visitors such as Hecataeus of Miletus (after Herodotus 2.142f.) and Solon (after Plato, *Timaeus* and *Critias*) were deeply impressed by the enormous antiquity of Egyptian records and recorded history. For them a journey to Egypt was a voyage back in time to the origins of culture.

Another source of fascination for the Greeks was Egyptian writing: the coexistence of two or three seemingly unrelated writing systems. Herodotus, Diodorus, and many others agreed that the Egyptians used two forms, one called hieratic or hieroglyphic and the other called demotic or epistolic: "The Egyptians use two different scripts: one, called 'demotic,' is learned by all; the other one is called 'sacred.' This one is understood among the Egyptians exclusively by the priests who learn them from their fathers in the mysteries" (Diodorus 3.3, 4). The Greeks interpreted this situation of digraphia in terms of exoteric-profane and esoteric-sacred communication, the first open for use by all, the second restricted to the mysteries and the initiates. The same distinction was applied to Egyptian religion, which behind its polytheistic and often abstruse facade was believed to hide a deep esoteric wisdom. In the Hellenistic and Roman periods, the mysteries of Isis and Osiris/Sarapis spread the ritual experience of proximity to god and of the hope for immortality throughout the ancient world.

After the fall of ancient Egyptian civilization, it was exclusively on the testimony of Greek and Latin authors (and to a lesser degree also biblical, rabbinical, and Arabic writers) that later understanding of its history and way of life could be based. This history concentrates on three distinct but intersecting points of focus: hieroglyphs (or grammatology), Hermetism (or philosophy and theology), and mysteries (or ritual, initiation, and esotericism).

The discovery of a manuscript of Horapollo's *Hieroglyphica* on the island of Andros in 1419 led to a reopening of the ancient debate as to whether Egyptian words referred to things and concepts "by nature" (*physei*) or "by convention" (*thesei*). One of the main concerns of early modernity was the quest for a "scripture of nature," a writing that would refer not to the sounds of language but to the things of nature and to the concepts of the mind. Egyptian hieroglyphics were held to be such a script by many scholars from the 15th to the early 19th century. According to Ralph Cudworth (1617–1688), "The Egyptian hieroglyphicks were figures not answering to sounds or words, but immediately representing the objects and conceptions of the mind."

"For, using an alphabet of things and not of words," wrote Sir Thomas Browne in the first half of the 17th century, "through the image and pictures thereof they [the Egyptians] endeavoured to speak their hidden contents in the letters and language of nature," that is, of things. An alphabet of things and not of words, this was indeed "the best evasion of the confusion of Babel" (*Pseudodoxia epidemica* 3.148, quoted in Dieckmann 1970, 113). This interpretation explains the enormous interest that early modern Europe invested in ancient Egypt and its hieroglyphs.

The most interesting aspect of Egyptian literacy, however, was that it used the two different writing systems, one referring to things and concepts iconically and the other referring to concepts and sounds by arbitrary signs. This reconstruction of Egyptian grammatology, based on Herodotus, Diodorus, and other Greek accounts, became more complicated when Giordano Bruno and others introduced an evolutionary perspective. For Bruno (1548–1600), hieroglyphs were the original script, whereas alphabetic writing was a later invention: "The sacred letters used among the Egyptians were called hieroglyphs . . . which were images . . . taken from the things of nature, or their parts. By using such writings and voices, the Egyptians used to capture with marvellous skill the language of the gods. Afterwards when letters of the kind which we use now with another kind of industry were invented by Theuth or some other, this brought about a great rift both in memory and in the divine and magical sciences" (*De magia,* quoted in Yates 1964, 263). The connection between hieroglyphics and magic is provided by the church historian Rufinus, who reports that the temple at Canopus was destroyed by the Christians because a school of magic arts existed there under the pretext of teaching the "sacerdotal" characters of the Egyptians (*Historia ecclesiastica* 11.26).

Plato (*Phaedrus* 274C–275D, to which Bruno was referring) warns that writing will destroy memory because it makes people rely on external signs instead of interior insight and recollection. In Bruno's interpretation, the king is afraid that Theut's invention of phonographic letters will destroy the Hermetic knowledge stored in the hieroglyphic images. Not "memory" as a human faculty, but the *ars memoriae* of the hieroglyphic system would be destroyed by the invention of letters. Diodorus had already stressed the fact that the Egyptian method of figurative writing, by picturing "things" and using the properties of things to denote undepictable meanings, required a vast knowledge of natural history. This explains the striking analogies between Horapollo's interpretations of hieroglyphics and codifications of ancient natural sciences, such as those by Aelian, Pliny, and the *Physiologus:* "The relations between sign and meaning were according to Horapollo always of an allegorical nature, and it was always established by means of exactly the same sort of 'philosophical' reasoning which we find later in the Physiologus and the bestiaries of the Middle Ages" (Iversen 1993, 48).

According to William Warburton (1698–1779), who 150 years after Bruno gave the most detailed reconstruction of the evolution of the various Egyptian scripts, Egyptian writing became complex and developed into polygraphy because it did not take the common course from picture to letter. Unlike all other scripts, the Egyptian hieroglyphics remained a *Dingschrift*—a representational form—and thus a codification of cosmological and biological knowledge. Other writing systems lost this epistemological connection with the visible word and evolved into conventional codes. In the history of writing, the hieroglyphic system came first, then sacerdotal (hieratic), and finally epistolic (demotic) and symbolic (hieroglyphs used as cryptography for encoding esoteric theology). Warburton developed a theory of cultural evolution based on grammatology that became of utmost importance in the 18th century. Within this grammatological reconstruction of human evolution, the invention of alphabetic writing constituted a revolutionary step.

Though the grammatological discourse on hieroglyphs was triggered by the rediscovery of Horapollo, the rise of the Hermetic tradition was due to the rediscovery of the collection of the 17 Greek treatises known as the Corpus Hermeticum, which presented themselves as written by the divine Egyptian archsage Hermes Trismegistus. Among the various traditions and figures who kept images of ancient Egypt alive in Western cultural memory, Hermes Trismegistus is by far the most important. Since his writings were believed to date back to highest antiquity, alongside those of Zoroaster and Moses, and since they seemed to anticipate central Christian doctrines (as did the Chaldaean Oracles attributed to Zoroaster and some Orphic hymns), they gave rise to the idea of an "original theology" (*theologia prisca*) common to all humankind.

This paradigm lost much of its credit in 1614 when Isaac Casaubon proved that the texts dated not from primeval times but from late antiquity. The watershed character of this discovery, however, has been vastly overrated by Frances Yates, who held that it "shattered the basis of all attempts to build a natural theology on Hermetism." In fact, that was precisely what Ralph Cudworth, the most prominent of the Cambridge Platonists, attempted in his book *The True Intellectual System of the Universe: The First Part, wherein All the Reason and Philosophy of Atheism is Confuted and its Impossibility Demonstrated* (1678). Cudworth built a natural theology on the basis of the Hermetic writings, and he did so with tremendous success, helping the Hermetic ideas of cosmotheism and All-Oneness to perhaps an even more prominent position than they held in the Renaissance. There is no doubt that his book became one of the foundational texts of the Enlightenment.

Cudworth distinguishes between implicit, or secret, and explicit, or public, theology. The theological system that he presents as natural and common to all religions underlies or is implicit in the polytheistic religions of paganism and even atheism. In the context of this theory Egypt held a very prominent place. The Egyptian priests were the first to articulate the implicit theology in their sacred writings, but they kept it secret. The Hermetic writings are a late but authentic codification of this secret tradition. For Cudworth the decisive point was not the antiquity but the generality of this theology, its originality and naturalness, the fact that it was based on a set of assumptions shared by all human beings.

This esoteric "Egyptian" theology, which Cudworth extracts from a vast collection of quotations from Greek and Latin authors, among them the Hermetic texts, is based on the idea of "*A Perfect Conscious Understanding Being* (or Mind) *Existing of it self from Eternity, and the Cause of all other things*" (195). Its quintessential credo may be expressed by the formula "One and All," or *Hen kai Pan.* Cudworth was convinced that this doctrine of All-Oneness was also the most important part of Moses' Egyptian education. Cudworth's topic, however, was not the transmission of Egyptian wisdom to the Hebrews. He was interested in its transmission to the Greeks. In this respect, Orpheus played precisely the same role of mediator as Moses did in the biblical tradition. Orpheus was generally believed to have been initiated into the "greater" Egyptian mysteries. Egypt was thus connected to Europe in a double way: to Jerusalem via Moses and to Athens via Orpheus. The Moses connection informed European theology and religion, whereas the Orpheus connection influenced European philosophy. (This genealogy of philosophy goes back to Marsilio Ficino; cf. Yates 14 f.) Orpheus took the idea of *Hen kai Pan* to Greece, where it informed the philosophies of Pythagoras, Heraclitus, Parmenides, Plato, the Stoics, and others. *Hen kai Pan*—the conviction that one is all and all is one—was believed to be the nucleus of a great tradition that started in Egypt and was handed down to modernity. Cudworth prepared the way for the famous "pantheism debate" that held sway in Germany from 1785 onward and shattered the foundations of the Enlightenment with its slogan, One and All, triggering a new phase of Egyptomania that was characteristic of the last quarter of the 18th century and centered on the idea of mystery.

John Spencer, a contemporary of Ralph Cudworth and fellow "Christian Hebraist," published in 1685 a work on the ritual laws of the Hebrews, in which he held that Moses learned his religion in the Egyptian mysteries and that the laws that Moses instituted were just borrowed from Egyptian ritual and its hieroglyphs. Unlike Cudworth, however, Spencer did not deal with Egyptian theology. It is not the content but the structure of mystery religion that interested him, and he held that Moses copied the *structure* of the Egyptian religion, which Spencer reconstructed as double-faced, divided into inner and outer, esotericism and exotericism. Spencer believed that God chose Moses as his first prophet—a man "nourished with the hieroglyphic literature of Egypt"—to give the Jews a religion that was as double-faced as the Egyptian one, "carnal only in frontispiece, but divine and wonderful in its interior" (Assmann 1997, 79). He therefore attributes to the Israelite religion the character of a "double religion" after the model of ancient Egypt, quoting (among many other authorities) Eusebius of Caesarea: "Dividing the Jewish people into two classes, the Logos subjected the masses to the explicit commandments in their literal sense (*kata tēn rhētēn dianoian*), but liberated the other class, the experts, from this literal application, in order to attach themselves to a more divine philosophy, superior to the many, and to [pay attention] with a theoretical mind [*theoria*] to the higher meaning of the laws" (*Praeparatio evangelica* 8.10, 18).

Exactly 100 years later, this same quote was used, in Spencer's Latin translation, by the philosopher Karl Leonhard Reinhold for a motto in his book *The Hebrew Mysteries; or, the Oldest Religious Freemasonry.* To put it briefly, Reinhold holds that the Egyptian goddess Isis and the biblical Jehova (this is how he spells the Tetragrammaton) are one and the same deity, and that biblical monotheism is just a copy—and, moreover, a bad and reductive copy—of the Egyptian mysteries. The name Jehova means, according to Reinhold, "He who is" or "Essential Being," and God reveals himself as such to Moses, saying, "I am who I am," whereas Isis, in the famous inscription on the "veiled image" as rendered by Plutarch and Proclus, reveals herself to be "All that is, was, and will be," thus, again, as "Essential Being." Moses took everything from Egypt, whose wisdom he learned when he was educated as a prince at the pharaonic court, and created the monotheistic religion of the Hebrews, reducing the sublime deity of the mysteries, the All and One, to the national god of the Jews. Instead of revelation, Reinhold believed, we are dealing with translation.

Reinhold's book on the Hebrew mysteries was part of a far-reaching research project undertaken by the Viennese Masonic lodge Zur Wahren Eintracht in the years 1783–1787 and published in its *Journal für Freimaurer,* starting with a book-length treatise by Grand-Master Ignaz von Born, *Mysteries of the Egyptians,* and dealing in 14 studies with all possible other ancient mysteries. This project has to be seen, in turn, as part of a debate on the ancient mysteries that ranged across Europe, in the course of which appeared during the last quarter of the 18th century more than a dozen voluminous books, several bestselling novels, plays, and operas, among them the *Magic Flute.* This especially Masonic interest in the ancient mysteries, in which the Masons saw the origin and model of their own rituals and not a historical and archaeological interest in ancient Egyptian culture, was the central motive of the Egyptomania of the 18th century. Only the Napoleonic expedition to Egypt and the publication of its archaeological results in the much-celebrated volumes of the *Description de l'Egypte* from 1809 onward brought about a genuinely historical interest in Egyptian civilization. The difference between this new Egyptomania and the older one is best grasped by a comparison between Mozart's *Magic Flute* (which is situated not in ancient Egypt but in a utopia where the mysteries of Isis are still—or again—observed) and Verdi's *Aida,* in which the newly acquired historical knowledge of Egyptology—in fact, of Auguste Mariette, its first librettist and stage designer—is brought to bear for the decorations and costumes.

BIBL.: A. Assmann and J. Assmann, eds., *Hieroglyphen: Stationen einer anderen abendländischen Grammatologie* (Munich 2003). Jan Assmann, *The Mind of Egypt: History and Meaning in the Times of the Pharaohs,* 2nd ed. (Cambridge, Mass., 2003), *Moses the Egyptian: The Memory of Egypt in Western Monotheism* (Cambridge, Mass., 1997), and "Sapienza e mistero: L'immagine greca della cultura egiziana," in *I Greci: Storia Cultura Arte Società,* vol. 3: *I Greci oltre la Grecia,* ed. Salvatore Settis et al. (Turin 2001) 401–469. Liselotte Dieckmann, *Hieroglyphics: The History of a Literary Symbol* (St. Louis 1970). Florian Ebeling, *Das Geheimnis des Hermes Trismegistos: Eine Geschichte des Hermetismus von der Antike bis zur Neuzeit* (Munich 2005). Garth Fowden, *The Egyptian Hermes: A Historical Approach to the Late Pagan Mind* (Cambridge 1986). François Hartog, "Les Grecs égyptologues," *Annales ESC* 41 (1986) 953–967, and "Voyages d'Egypte," in *Mémoire d'Ulysse: Récits sur la frontière en Grèce ancienne* (Paris 1996). Erik Hornung, *Das esoterische Ägypten: Das geheime Wissen der Ägypter und sein Einfluß auf das Abendland* (Munich 1999). Erik Iversen, *The Myth of Egypt and Its Hieroglyphs,* 2nd ed. (Princeton 1993). Edgar Wind, *Pagan Mysteries in the Renaissance* (New Haven 1958). Frances Yates, *Giordano Bruno and the Hermetic Tradition* (Chicago 1964).

J.A.

Electra

Daughter of Agamemnon, sister of Orestes, chief mourner of her murdered father, and participant in efforts to avenge his death, Electra has enjoyed a rich afterlife in literature and the arts. She was especially appealing to dramatists: the tragedians Aeschylus (*The Libation Bearers*), Euripides (*Electra*), and Sophocles (*Electra*) each created a play around her plight. Though their representations differ considerably, each Electra is abused and embittered, capable either of a fine dramatic wrath or of eloquent mourning, superbly effective on the stage.

Her story remained popular in antiquity. Livius Andronicus (240–204 BCE) wrote a Latin *Aegisthus* (now lost) that may well have included Electra. So powerful is the character that although Seneca based his Latin *Agamemnon* on that of Aeschylus (in which she does not appear), he imported Electra into the play.

Plays about Electra have been written regularly since antiquity, often but not always with an author's political message embedded within. In the 17th and 18th centuries she appeared as a symbol for the nobility of a ruling house, but by the time of the French Revolution her suffering in the face of the dynastic strife in the house of Atreus could be read as a symbol of all that was wrong with monarchy. Writers of the 19th century tended to focus less on politics than on the melodramatic potential of the story. Modern writers and composers have generally presented an Electra pathologized, sexualized, and hysterical. Feminists read Electra as prey of the patriarchy, whereas Marxists construct her as victim of a degenerate royal house.

Thus, Electras vary; the original character can be interpreted in so many different ways that she almost demands to be appropriated. Royalist versions of her story were written by authors ranging from William Shirley, the British colonial governor of Massachusetts (*Electra,* 1765), to Vincente Antonio de la Huerta (*Agamenón Vengado,* 1779). In France versions were written by the revolutionary Marie-Joseph Chénier (an opera, *Élèctre,* unfinished at his death in 1811) and later by Alexandre Dumas *père* (in *Orestie,* 1856, a three-act drama). Marguerite Yourcenar's feminist *Élèctre, ou, La chute des masques* (1954) is the latest French-language treatment of the story.

Occasionally, Electra appears in disguise: T. S. Eliot uses her for Mary in *The Family Reunion* (1939). The links between the *Oresteia* and Eugene O'Neill's *Mourning Becomes Electra* (1931), however, are tenuous. O'Neill's Lavinia is far less an Electra figure than an allomorph of Hamlet, for the play is about the discovery and punishment of a hidden crime.

Electra has also been a poet's muse, perhaps most notably in *The Elektra Poems* (1982) of Alan Marshfield. Marshfield redrew Electra as a woman in control of her own life, though he described her as "fey and unoriginal."

Electra's notable appearances in the concert hall include the opera *Les Choéphores* (1915) by Darius Milhaud and the grandly operatic cantata *Élèctre* (1886) by Théodore Gouvy. A more recent addition is the concerto for cello and chamber orchestra *Electra Rising* (1995) by the Canadian composer Malcolm Forsyth.

A woman of intense passion, Electra naturally shines on the operatic stage. Mozart wrote her a dominant role in *Idomeneo* (1781). (Her presence on Crete, the opera's setting, is never explained satisfactorily.) She is at her most monumental in the *Elektra* (1909) of Richard Strauss. The libretto, by Hugo von Hofmannsthal, transforms her into a Freudian neurotic, implacably vengeful and unwholesomely incestuous. When the murders have taken place, she dances, Bacchante-like, then falls to the ground, dead. Once she has become a *fin de siècle* operatic heroine, however unconventional, she must suffer a conventional operatic fate.

BIBL.: E. M. Butler, "Hoffmannsthal's 'Elektra': A Graeco-Freudian Myth," *Journal of the Warburg Institute* 2, no. 2 (1938) 164–175. Martha C. Carpenter, "Orestes in the Drawing Room: Aeschylean Parallels in T. S. Eliot's *The Family Reunion,*" *Twentieth Century Literature* 35, no. 1 (1989) 17–42. Horst Frenz and Martin Mueller, "More Shakespeare and Less Aeschylus in Eugene O'Neill's *Mourning Becomes Electra,*" *American Literature* 38, no. 1 (1966) 85–100.

A.V.

Elegy

The term *elegy* and its cognates in other European languages refer to distinct (though intertwined) genres. Greek *elegos* and Latin *elegia* primarily denote elegiac (hexameter and pentameter) couplets, and in Renaissance literature *elegy* and its cognates often refer to imitations of classical poems in this meter, primarily Roman love complaints: for example, Christopher Marlowe's late 16th-century translation of Ovid's elegiac love poetry, the *Amores,* was published as *All Ovid's Elegies.* In antiquity, however, *elegi* were originally funerary laments (Ovid, *Amores* 3.9.3–4), and Roman love elegists' collections include funerary poems (e.g., Propertius 3.18, 4.11; Ovid, *Amores* 3.9). Over the course of the 16th century *elegy* and its European cognates also came to have the modern sense of funerary lament.

Composed in various metrical schemes and drawing motifs from diverse classical writings about death, and supplemented and modified by specifically Christian beliefs (such as heaven for the saved), post-classical funerary elegies normally move from lament to consolation; praise of the deceased emphasizes both the loss to the living and the deceased's enduring fame or heavenly reward. Though the classically influenced elegy flourished as a poetry of patronage, written to commemorate socially prominent personages, poets also composed elegies upon the deaths of other poets and those to whom they themselves were personally attached.

The most important classically influenced subgenre of funerary elegy from the Renaissance through the 18th century was the pastoral elegy, based on such major Hellenistic models as Theocritus's Idyll 1, the lament for Adonis attributed to Bion, the lament for Bion attributed to Moschus, and Latin models in Virgil's Eclogue 5 and Nemesianus's Eclogue 1. Nonfunerary pastorals, particularly Virgilian love laments, also furnished motifs. The pastoral elegy describes or enacts the ceremonial mourning of a shepherd—who exemplified various forms of excellence—by a fellow shepherd or (more often) group of shepherds. Much of the popularity of the genre lies in its representation of a close-knit community's response to the death of one of its members and in the diverse symbolic resonances of the shepherd figure. The highly imitative nature of pastoral elegy, its conventions recalled, reimagined, and sometimes subverted, allows poets to express or question the consolations inherent in a poetic tradition.

Virgil's Eclogue 5 provides the most imitated ancient model for the movement from lament to celebration. Virgil has two shepherd-poets, Mopsus and Menalcus, commemorate (and reveal themselves as poetic heirs of) the shepherd-poet Daphnis. Mopsus first laments Daphnis as a godlike figure whose death has caused all of nature to mourn (a pathetic fallacy that runs throughout the pastoral elegy tradition). Mopsus concludes his lament, however, with a triumphant panegyric, dictating the epitaph in which Daphnis declares from the grave his immortal fame, "known from here unto the stars" (line 43). Menalcus then describes the deceased's deification and nature's rejoicing and prays for Daphnis's beneficence as a tutelary deity for the pastoral world. Virgil provides hints that Daphnis represents not only an ur-poet but also Julius Caesar, an identification made explicit by the influential ancient commentator Servius. Christians also interpreted Daphnis's death and apotheosis as an allegory of Christ. Eclogue 5 thus became a model for elegies for public figures and for Christian celebrations of death and resurrection.

Biblical and patristic images of kings, ministers, and even Jesus himself as shepherds added new layers of meaning to medieval and Renaissance pastoral elegies. The Benedictine theologian Paschasius Radbertus's 9th-century imitation of Eclogue 5 features two nuns, personifications of Christian virtue, who mourn and praise the shepherd-monk Aldabertus and describe him in heaven. In the 14th century, Petrarch influentially imitated Virgil's Eclogue 5 in Latin elegies for both a public, state figure and the poet's personal beloved. Petrarch's Eclogue 2 echoes Virgil in lamenting the death of his patron King Robert of Naples as Argus, "king of shepherds," whose death has caused disorder for his flock (his subjects), and in celebrating his ascent to heaven. Petrarch, however, does not present heavenly Argus as posthumously guiding the pastoral world, a deviation from Virgil that conveys anxiety about the future. In Eclogue 11 Petrarch replaces Virgilian shepherds with allegorical mourners of his beloved "Galatea": Fusca (the dark one, i.e., despair), Fulgida (the bright one, i.e., Christian faith), and Niobe (enduring grief). Espousing a Christian theme adopted from Stoic philosophy (e.g., Seneca's *Consolation to Polybius* 9.3), in contrast to poetic tradition, Fulgida argues that bewailing the blessed dead betrays envy. Like Virgil's Mopsus, Fulgida concludes with a panegyric epitaph, describing Galatea's death as a liberation from the body's prison (a Platonic-Christian commonplace) and a flight to heaven, teaching both the vanity of mortal things and the immortal reward of virtue. Yet while Fulgida (unlike Mopsus) dismisses earthly fame, Petrarch gives the last word to Niobe, who declares that Galatea will be remembered as an inspiring example of female virtue and beauty. Petrarch "subjectivizes" the Virgilian pastoral by turning the shepherds into allegories of his divided feelings, yet he also asserts the public importance of the deceased by reimagining Daphnis's fame, and his posthumous oversight of his community, as Galatea's posthumous influence as a moral example.

Some later Italian pastorals convey the limits of poetic consolation. Baldassare Castiglione's Neo-Latin "Alcon" (1506), for example, lamenting his friend Matteo Falcone, initially asserts universal lamentation but then focuses on the solitary lament of Iolas (Castiglione), whose traditional assertions of nature's and the gods' and nymphs' mourning register as willful fantasy. The poem ends, like Mopsus's song, with an epitaph, but one that defies tradition by lamenting rather than proclaiming enduring achievement. Infusing a classical-humanist rhetoric of male friendship with Virgilian homoerotic longing, Castiglione emphasizes the isolation of intense grief by echoing Virgil's Eclogue 2, which depicts the shepherd Corydon's lonely lament for an unattainable boy.

Giovanni Pontano's Neo-Latin pastoral lament for his wife in "Meliseus" (1492) powerfully conveys the necessarily slow process of grief. Meliseus, Pontano's pastoral persona, describes himself weaving a basket (a Virgilian symbol for composing a pastoral), depicting, as the refrain puts it, "Orpheaque Eurydicenque sequentem" (Orpheus and Eurydice following). By evoking the myth of Orpheus, who temporarily triumphed over death by leading Eurydice from the underworld but ultimately failed to regain her because of his overpowering love, Meliseus acknowledges (and slowly comes to terms with) the failure of even the most powerful artistry to conquer death. Pontano evokes a sympathetic community by having his lament reported by two shepherd-friends, but they do not seek to overcome his temporary isolation: "Sadness has its limits," says one. Time—not art—will heal.

By contrast, Jacopo Sannazaro's *Arcadia* (1502; 1504), which influentially adapted classical pastoral to represent an elaborately imagined pastoral world in (mainly Petrarchan) Italian verse forms and style, is filled with laments that are primarily occasions for celebrations of poetic beauty and power. Eclogue 5 celebrates the poetic fame and heavenly bliss of a shepherd-poet (lines 14–23). Death poses little disruption because heaven, where Sannazaro's shepherd dwells with Daphnis and Meliboeus from Virgil's and Nemsianus's respective pastoral elegies, is another version of the idealized pastoral landscape. The final eclogue imitates Pontano's "Meliseus" eclogue, but Sannazaro's Meliseus triumphantly declares that through his poetic expression of grief the world "grows green again" (*rinverdesi*).

The pastoral elegy spread throughout Europe in the 16th century among royal and aristocratic patrons as well as poets. Clement Marot's influential pastoral elegy on the queen mother Louise of Savoy (1531) follows the general movement of Virgil's Eclogue 5 while also emphasizing the consolatory "sweetness" of artful lament with echoes of Theocritus's Idyll 1 (by way of Luigi Alamanni's 16th-century Italian imitations) and Sannazaro. Though Marot presents mourning as natural—"Plorons, Bergers, Nature nous dispense!" (Let us weep, shepherds, Nature excuses us; line 57)—and deploys the traditional pathetic fallacy in his description of Louise in the Elysian fields (heaven), he betrays the moral reservations expressed in Petrarch by presenting mourning as sadness that the deceased's happiness was based on false "humaines raisons" (human reasoning). The moral ambiguity of mourning also emerges in Marot's revision of the Virgilian pastoral value of "otium" (leisure, peace, tranquility), celebrated at the opening of the *Eclogues* (Eclogue 1, line 6) and restored to the pastoral world by the deified Daphnis (Eclogue 5, line 61). Marot commemorates Louise as a promoter of national "paix" (peace) (line 240) but recalls how she attacked a sinful "oisiveté" (laziness, leisure) (line 77) and commanded her entourage to perform virtuous labor, a labor that has temporarily ceased with mourning but must be eventually resumed. Edmund Spenser's pastoral elegy "November" (1579), written about the mysterious "Dido," contains various classicizing references but directly imitates Marot's French elegy rather than ancient models. He intensifies the condemnation of mourning as a false perspective, given the "trustlesse state of earthly thinges" and the deceased's blessed state as "a goddesse now emong the saintes" (line 175). The mixture of pagan and Christian elements here is characteristic of Spenser.

Renaissance poets also imitated classical nonpastoral funerary elegies and motifs. Pontano's *Tumuli* (1502) contains laments before the tombs of the dead. His lament for his wife (2.25) echoes Catullus's elegiac-metered lament at his brother's tomb (101); both poets perform funerary rites with an acknowledgment of their inadequacy. Angelo Poliziano's elegy on the death of Albiera degli Albizzi (d. 1473), the wife of Sigismondo della Stufa, follows the movement of Mopsus's song in Virgil's Eclogue 5 from mourning to a consolatory panegyric epitaph, but its combination of praise of the deceased with an extended description of the husband's sorrow imitates Statius's lengthy elegy on Priscilla (*Silvae* 5.1) in sympathetically depicting a "pious" widower's grief, which needs to be copiously indulged before it can be assuaged. Spenser's *Daphnaïda: An Elegie* (1591), by contrast, uses both pastoral and nonpastoral classical models to ironize its depiction of an inconsolable widower's grief. Though the poem's major model is Chaucer's *Book of the Duchess,* the widower's recounting of his wife's calm dying words, requesting that he not grieve (lines 263–293), echoes scenes from Statius (and Poliziano) in questioning the widower's refusal of consolation (lines 177–193). The ending, in which the widower spurns the pastoral narrator's hospitality by fleeing into the night, underscores the isolation of grief by recalling Tityrus's final invitation, at the end of Virgil's Eclogue 1, to the exiled Meliboeus to stay the night, a synecdoche for the consolations of pastoral community, here spurned by the mourner.

John Milton's "Lycidas" (1637), generally deemed the last great example of pastoral elegy, was composed on the death of Milton's Cambridge classmate Edward King (Lycidas), who drowned while sailing to Ireland to take up a ministerial position. Milton uses the pastoral shepherd's traditional association with both the poet and the minister to portray the loss of King as a symbol of high poetic and spiritual potential cut short. The poem's intensity springs from Milton's intense engagement with the pastoral tradition in working through the crisis he evidently felt as an aspiring poet with religious ambitions, confronted by the possibility of premature death. The poem contains bitter denunciations of a corrupt world (including a national church from which Milton was alienated), but it attains its hard-won consolation by both exploiting and revising pastoral themes. Declaring Lycidas to be in heaven, the poet compares him to the sun that sets but rises again (lines 168–171), thus rejecting the traditional pastoral lament, going back to the elegy for Bion (lines 99–104), that whereas nature follows cycles of death and rebirth, human beings die without awaking. Lycidas is able to rise again because of the "dear might" (line 173) of Christ: Christianity overturns pagan pessimism. Yet Milton also derives consolation from pastoral motifs. Though in Milton's Protestant milieu the deceased were generally thought to have no contact with the living, Milton imagines Lycidas, like Virgil's Daphnis, as a beneficent spirit: just as the deified Daphnis is expected to be "bonus . . . felixque" (good and propitious) to the pastoral world (Eclogue 5, line 65), so Lycidas is invoked as "the genius of the shore" (i.e., a pagan genius loci, or local spirit) who will be "good" to "all that wander in that perilous flood" (lines 184–185).

John Dryden's greatest elegiac poem, "To the Memory of Mr. Oldham" (1684), registers a personal sense of profound loss, as well as joy in glorious achievement, through epic rather than pastoral references. Allusions to the *Aeneid* generalize and claim public importance for Dryden's feelings as he pays tribute to a younger fellow satirist and kindred spirit, comparing himself and Oldham to the tragic Virgilian companions Nisus and Euryalus. The final couplets—"Once more, hail and farewell; farewell thou young,/But ah too short, Marcellus of our Tongue;/Thy Brows with Ivy, and with Laurels bound;/But Fate and gloomy Night encompass thee around" (lines 22–25)—evoke Roman mourning rituals and allude to the early death of Augustus's heir Marcellus (*Aeneid* 6.866). Dryden ignores Christian consolation for the secular, implying that both Oldham and Dryden represent Roman achievement: Dryden plays the role of both grieving Augustus and commemorating Virgil.

In the late 17th and the 18th century, the dominant form of classically inspired elegy, the pastoral elegy, lost its cultural centrality. Late 17th-century critics like René Rapin and Fontenelle influentially argued that pastoral provides an idealized depiction of "golden age" simplicity. In his *Pastorals* (1709), Alexander Pope sought to provide a definitive epitome of such self-consciously artificial pastoral. With echoes of Spenser and Milton, Pope's concluding elegy "Winter" follows Virgil's Eclogue 5 from lament to apotheosis, but then concludes by echoing the farewell to pastoral of Virgil's Eclogue 10. Death, for Pope, spells the end of pastoral artifice. In his "Milton" in *Lives of the English Poets* (1779–1781), Samuel Johnson condemned Milton's "Lycidas," and pastoral elegy in general, as "fiction" untrue to "nature" and betraying "little grief." In Salomon Gessner's idealizing pastoral *Idyllen* (1st ed. 1756), the harshness of elegiac lament is excised; death appears only as the peaceful exit of contented (and tranquilly remembered) old men.

Over the course of the 18th century the poetry of patronage also underwent a crisis and the celebration of the socially prominent came under attack. Thomas Gray's "Elegy in a Country Churchyard" (1751) proclaims the futility of the funerary "Flattery" of the social elite that was the basis of much earlier funerary poetry, while noting the desperate desire of all, high and low, to be posthumously remembered. The poem begins as a somber meditation on death that reveals a wider sense of "elegy" that developed in the 18th century out of both funeral elegy and the melancholic strain in Roman love elegy (especially Propertius and Tibullus): poetry devoted to what Gray's contemporary William Shenstone called "pensive contemplations." Gray's poem ends, however, as a kind of funerary elegy for the poet himself. Gray's classical model here is Propertius 2.1, which Gray translated, in which the Roman love poet imagines his own death and his patron Maecenas "forte" (perhaps) passing his tomb and pronouncing a commemorative line on the poet that serves as the poet's epitaph. But in place of Propertius's evident faith that a patron whom the poet has immortalized will in turn remember the poet, Gray's imagining of an unknown "kindred spirit" (line 95) who may "chance" to come upon and read his gravestone and "haply" (perhaps) hear a rustic "swain" describe his life (line 98) highlights the poet's (and, by implication, all persons') vulnerability: nobody is sure of finding the kindred spirit who will provide sympathetic mourning. Gray's evocation of a rural swain recalls the mourning shepherd of pastoral elegy, but Gray does not present himself as a shepherd who can naturally expect to be commemorated by other shepherds: the poem's deviation from pastoral elegy convention underscores the absence of an assured community of mourners for Gray or anyone else.

With the decline of classical imitation, changing beliefs about death (including skepticism about the afterlife), and the Romantic emphasis on the uniqueness rather than the universality of feelings, the modern elegy has had to find new modes of expression. In such poems as "The Two April Mornings" and "The Fountain," Wordsworth reinvents the pastoral elegy as Romantic lyric, grounded in the intensity of the poet's personal, not fully expressible grief. Pastoral elegies of the 19th and 20th centuries, such as Percy Shelley's "Adonais" (1821), Matthew Arnold's "Thyrsis" (1867), and William Butler Yeats's "Shepherd and Goatherd" (1918), self-consciously revive pastoral conventions that signify by their evident untimeliness. Thus "Adonais," presenting the death of John Keats as caused by hostile criticism, recalls Moschus and Bion, as well as Shelley's English pastoral predecessors Spenser and Milton, to pit an out-of-time poetic realm against the contemporary world. Nonpastoral elegies selectively reconceive traditional patterns going back to the classics; thus W. H. Auden's "In Memory of W. B. Yeats" explicitly rejects nature's mourning yet ends with an apostrophe to Yeats to "teach" the living that makes him potentially, like Daphnis and Lycidas, a beneficent spirit.

BIBL.: Thomas Perrin Harrison Jr., ed., and Harry Joshua Leon, trans., *The Pastoral Elegy: An Anthology* (Austin 1939). Ellen Zetzel Lambert, *Placing Sorrow: A Study of Pastoral Elegy Convention from Theocritus to Milton* (Chapel Hill 1976). G. W. Pigman III, *Grief and English Renaissance Elegy* (Cambridge 1985). Peter M. Sacks, *The English Elegy: Studies in the Genre from Spenser to Yeats* (Baltimore 1985). Joshua Scodel, *The English Poetic Epitaph: Commemoration and Conflict from Jonson to Wordsworth* (Ithaca 1991). J.S.

Elgin Marbles

Produced in the 5th century BCE for the Parthenon in Athens, the sculptures that came to be known as the Elgin Marbles were removed to England between 1802 and 1812 by Thomas Bruce, 7th Earl of Elgin (1766–1841) and acquired by the British Museum in 1816 at a cost of £35,000. Notwithstanding the protests of those—most notably, Lord Byron—who have viewed Elgin as an opportunistic looter, portions of the temple's two pediments, 15 of the 92 metopes, and 247 feet of the original 524-foot frieze have stood at the heart of the British Museum's collection for the past 200 years.

Access to the sculptures led 19th-century artists and connoisseurs to rethink the artistic heritage of the classical tradition, as the marbles challenged long-accepted stylistic expectations established by later Hellenistic and Roman statuary. In the wake of the Napoleonic Wars, the sculptures fueled Romantic engagements with Greek antiquity. Soon after the first shipment arrived in London, the pieces demonstrated their potential to stir debate—in terms of art theory, aesthetics, national ideology, politics, ethics, and international law.

Cyriac of Ancona had been impressed by the Parthenon and its sculptures as early as 1436, but as Athens fell under Ottoman control, some 250 years elapsed before Western Europeans addressed the Acropolis as an actual site. The earliest extensive drawings of the sculptures—crucially important because they predate the 1687 bombing of the Parthenon—were produced by Jacques Carrey in conjunction with a French envoy to Athens in 1674. More influential was the 1687 account of Jacob Spon and George Wheler, which introduced scholars across Europe to the marbles, though through verbal description rather than detailed illustrations (privileging Rome over Greece, Spon and Wheler mistakenly ascribed some of the sculptures to the reign of Hadrian). In the latter half of the 18th century the first prints of the marbles were made by Richard Dalton, Julien David Le Roy, and James Stuart and Nicholas Revett.

None of these sources, however, prepared viewers for seeing the marbles firsthand. Facilitated by the permission of the Turkish authorities (and the finances of his wife, Mary Nisbet), Elgin's relocation of the works to London caused a sensation. Shown first at Elgin's house at the corner of Picadilly and Park Lane (1807–1811) and then at Burlington House (1811–1816), the marbles finally settled in the British Museum (1817), where they remain today; they were celebrated as cultural evidence of Britain's geopolitical supremacy. Despite some initial reservations—most notably, those of Richard Payne Knight—the works won the praise of the period's leading artists, writers, and intellectuals, including Benjamin Haydon, Antonio Canova, Benjamin West, John Flaxman, Henry Fuseli, Thomas Lawrence, William Hazlitt, John Keats, Hegel, Chateaubriand, and Quatremère de Quincy.

In contrast to the freestanding sculptures that had anchored conceptions of classical art since the Renaissance, the Elgin Marbles were necessarily fragments of a larger whole. For 19th-century viewers, however, this only heightened their appeal; as traces and remnants of the early classical period, they evoked a historical moment that depended on discontinuity with the modern period and resonated with greater emotional significance as a result. At the same time, the stylistic restraint of the works led theorists to describe them as perfect expressions of Nature.

The marbles continued to inspire artists in the Victorian period. George Watts, Frederic Leighton, and Edward Burne-Jones all owned casts of the pedimental figures *Theseus* (Dionysus) and *Ilissus*. In his "Ten O'clock Lecture" of 1885, James McNeill Whistler judged that "the story of the beautiful is already complete—hewn in the marbles of the Parthenon." This comment signals the sculptures' importance even for the history of modern art, though the rest of Whistler's statement simultaneously demonstrates the eroding status of the classical tradition as the exclusive standard of taste: the painter found the completed story of beauty not only in the Elgin Marbles but also "broidered, with the birds, upon the fan of Hokusai—at the foot of Fusiyama."

BIBL.: Ian Jenkins, *Archaeologists and Aesthetes* (London 1992). Jennifer Neils, ed., *The Parthenon: From Antiquity to the Present* (Cambridge 2005). Alex Potts, "The Impossible Ideal: Romantic Conceptions of the Parthenon Sculptures in Early Nineteenth-century Britain and Germany," in *Art in Bourgeois Society, 1790–1850*, ed. Andrew Hemingway and William Vaughan (Cambridge 1998) 101–129. Jacob Rothenberg, *"Descensus ad Terram": The Acquisition and Reception of the Elgin Marbles* (New York 1977). Panyatis Tournikiotis, ed., *The Parthenon and Its Impact in Modern Times* (New York 1996). Timothy Webb, "Appropriating the Stones: The 'Elgin' Marbles and English National Taste," in *Claiming the Stones, Naming the Bones: Cultural Property and the Negotiation of National and Ethnic Identity*, ed. Elazar Barkan and Ronald Bush (Los Angeles 2002) 51–96.

C.H.

Emblem

Literary-artistic genre that flourished in Europe from the early 16th century into the 17th century and beyond. The emblem is one of the most characteristic forms of Renaissance classicizing culture. The term derives from the Greek *emblēma* (plural *emblēmata*), meaning "inserted part" or "inlaid work." During the Roman era the word was applied to any kind of ornament or insertion that was grafted onto a text or image, including legal or rhetorical compositions, which may help explain why a legal scholar (see below) applied the term to the first collection of emblems in the Renaissance tradition.

In its most familiar form the emblem comprises three basic parts: a short titular inscription or motto (called an *inscriptio* or *lemma*), a picture or representational image (*pictura*)—often a motif or subject derived from antiquity—and an explanatory text, usually in verse, called the *epigram* or *subscriptio*. But this three-part structure was not adhered to in all cases, and the term *emblem* came to be applied with a certain liberality to a wide range of image and text combinations as these were reshaped to suit the purposes of various authors and audiences. Indeed, it must be said that from the time of its invention, a certain flexibility or mutability was inherent to the emblem as both a genre and a concept.

The invention of the Renaissance emblem in the "canonical" form described above may be credited to the Milanese jurist and Humanist Andrea Alciato, also known as Alciati (1492–1550), whose *Emblematum liber* was composed in the 1520s. The first edition was printed without the author's permission in Augsburg (1531), and it may have been the decision of the printer, Heinrich Steiner, to provide woodcut illustrations (after designs by Jörg Breug) to the text. In 1534 an authorized edition was released in Paris. This was followed by many subsequent editions, as well as translations into French, German, Italian, and Spanish. In all, some 150 editions of Alciato's collection had appeared by the end of the 18th century, some illustrated, some not, although the definitive "final" count of 211 emblems was set in 1550. During the same period a host of imitations and variations on the theme were produced by presses in every corner of Europe.

The emblem as conceived by Alciato may be understood as part of the broader Renaissance project to renew and reinvent the culture of antiquity for modern usage. His initial inspiration seems to have come from the collection of ancient Greek epigrams known as the *Anthologia Graeca*, which was printed for the first time in Florence in 1494. During the period immediately preceding his work on the emblems, Alciato produced translations of these verses (published in 1529), 40 of which provided models for the epigrams in his first collection of emblems. Poets and scholars of the period were attracted to the poetic brevity of the epigrammatic form, which was linked in studies like Erasmus's *Adages* (*Adagia,* 1500–1508) to other literary and visual forms, including maxims, mottoes, *imprese,* rebuses, and hieroglyphs.

The fashion for devices and *imprese* (which may be defined as symbolic pictures accompanied by personal or philosophizing mottoes) spread from the French and Burgundian courts to their Italian counterparts during the course of the 15th century. In the process, they provided a general model and specific themes for the development of the emblem by Alciato and his successors. The intimate relation of the two forms is most evident in Paolo Giovio's influential *Dialogo dell'imprese* (1555), which drew on the older courtly traditions and provided rules and models that informed the works of later authors in the emblematic and other symbolic traditions. Another key source for both emblems and *imprese* was the Egyptian hieroglyph, which was understood in terms derived from Horapollo's *Hieroglyphica* (5th cent. CE, rediscovered in 1419) and other sources as a system of enigmatic but universally applicable allegorical image-signs. During the Renaissance, it was believed that the hieroglyphs had provided a model for the whole range of ancient symbolism and iconography produced by the Greeks, Romans, and virtually all other cultures. With notions like these informing their efforts, the inventors of emblems were able to frame their own inventions as contributions to an ageless and virtually limitless stream of symbolic discourse.

For a classic example of the migration and transformation of a single image and idea into emblematic, hieroglyphic, and other forms, we need only consider the fortunes of the celebrated printer's mark of Aldus Manutius (1449–1515), the dolphin and anchor. The origin of this device can be traced to the 1499 Aldine publication of Francesco Colonna's *Hypnerotomachia Poliphili,* where the dolphin and anchor, adapted from a Roman coin, appears as a "hieroglyph" for the ancient Augustan motto *semper festina tarde,* or *festina lente*—"Make haste slowly"—which expressed the notion of swift but careful planning in the successful completion of a project or scheme: "slow and steady wins the race," in effect. In 1501 Aldus adopted the dolphin and anchor as the printer's mark for the press's subsequent publications, including an expanded edition of Erasmus's *Adagia* (1508) that included the northern Humanist's elaborate explanation of Colonna's "hieroglyph," which he praised as the invention of a most learned scholar. Alciato was similarly impressed, so much so in fact that he adapted it in his own collection of emblems as the *pictura* for emblem number 10, where it denotes *maturandum,* "maturing." The release of the expanded Aldine edition of Alciato's collection in 1546 represents the culmination of these developments.

The sources for the many meanings assembled in early modern emblems ranged from classical and medieval compilations of all types to closely paralleled contemporary investigations into the fields of natural history, mythography, and epigraphy. The images in Cesare Ripa's *Iconologia* (Rome 1593, first illustrated edition Rome 1603) contain many details and ideas in harmony with contemporary emblematics. Among later 16th- and 17th-century collections, Guillaume de la Perrière's *Théâtre des bons engins* (the first French emblem book, Paris 1539), Johannes Sambucus's *Emblemata* (Antwerp 1564), Roemer Visscher's *Sinnepoppen* (Amsterdam 1614), and Filippo Picinelli's *Mondo simbolico* (Milan 1653–1654) represent the tip of an immense iceberg of publications. Among the many variations on the subject, scholars have identified genres of medical, political, religious, ethical, festive, amatory, and dynastic emblems, although the constant overlapping and cross-fertilization of forms make any clear distinction between the types seem elusive at best. In the religious sphere, collections were produced for both Protestant and Catholic readerships.

The emblem enjoyed a revival of sorts in the 19th century, especially in England, where the fashion was linked to renewed religious and artistic interest in medieval and early modern traditions. Gothic Revival designers and pre-Raphaelite painters were drawn to the form, as well as book collectors and illustrators. Scholarly revival of interest in emblems and other symbolic forms was indebted to the early 20th-century emergence of the discipline of iconology and has found perhaps its most sustained application in studies of Netherlandish art and in the ongoing efforts of John Manning, Peter M. Daly, Daniel S. Russell, and the scholars and editors associated with the journal *Emblematica: An Interdisciplinary Journal for Emblem Studies.*

BIBL.: Andreas Alciatus, *The Latin Emblems and Emblems in Translation,* ed. Peter M. Daly, Virginia W. Callahan, and Simon Cuttler, 2 vols. (Toronto 1985). Jochen Becker, "Emblem Book," *Grove Art Online* (Oxford University Press), www.groveart.com/. Peter M. Daly, John Manning, and Marc van Vaeck, eds., *Emblems from Alciato to the Tattoo,* 4th International Emblem Conference, 1996, Louvain, Belgium (Turnhout 2001). William S. Heckscher, *The Princeton Alciati Companion: A Glossary of Neo-Latin Words and Phrases Used by Andrea Alciati and the Emblem Book Writers of His Time* (New York 1989). John Manning, *The Emblem* (London 2002). Mario Praz, *Studies in Seventeenth-century Imagery* (London 1939; 2nd ed. St. Clair Shores, Mich., 1976). Daniel S. Russell, *The Emblem and Device in France* (Lexington, Ky., 1985); "Emblems and Hieroglyphics: Some Observations on the Beginnings and Nature of Emblematic Forms," *Emblematica* 1 (1986) 227–239; and *Emblematic Structures in Renaissance French Culture* (Toronto 1995). B.CU.

Empedocles

Putative author (ca. 492–432 BCE) of various writings, including tragedies that he is supposed to have destroyed; a Greek resident of Agrigentum, in Sicily. Two poems are certainly authentic: *On Nature* (probably not the original title) and *Purifications* (which some recent interpreters consider not an independent work). The poems, of which we possess numerous and in some cases lengthy fragments, were written (in the wake of Parmenides) following the metrics of Homer. The formal and verbal inventiveness they display explains why Aristotle accused Empedocles, whom he saw as the inventor of rhetoric (*Sophist*, fr. 1 Ross), of being too much of a poet, prone to metaphors, and not enough of a scientist (*Meteorologica*, 357a24–28), but also why Lucretius took him as a model for his poem *On the Nature of Things*.

Even in antiquity, two Empedocles existed side by side. Aristotle shaped the image of the naturalist-philosopher when he listed Empedocles among the "physicists" in the first book of the *Metaphysics*. Actually, Empedocles, for whom, unlike Parmenides, the world is the very manifestation of Being, developed a typically Presocratic cosmological system founded on the combined action of two forces, *Philotes* (Love) and *Neikos* (Hate), and on four "roots" that would become the four elements of the philosophical tradition (fire, earth, air, and water) but that also are divinities (Zeus, Hera, Aidoneus, and Nestis, fr. 6). With the expansion of Love, differences progressively disappear and fuse into a spherical god whose singular name (Sphairos) refers clearly to Parmenides' comparison of Being with a sphere. Sphairos shatters under the intervention of Hate, thus opening up a new process of reunification, of which the world as we know it is only one stage. The diversity and richness of the phenomena that caught Empedocles' attention (earth and sea, stars and seasons, and also blood, eyes, seashells, olives, and deers' antlers) explain Aristotle's interest, attested by the numerous citations in his biological and physiological treatises.

Plato also knew Empedocles the physicist. Thus, in the *Sophist* (242D), the doctrine of alternation between the one (under the power of Love) and the multiple (under the power of Hate) of the "Italic Muses" (Empedocles) is contrasted with the stricter doctrine of the "Ionian Muses" (Heraclitus). And the *Symposium* puts in Aristophanes' mouth a brilliant parody of Empedocles' physical system: the figure of the primitive spherical androgyne, which would later be divided into two different genders, strikingly presents the longing for a lost unity.

Nevertheless, what Plato bequeathed to posterity was not Empedocles the physicist-physiologist, but rather the author of an eschatological discourse on the fate of human souls, derived from an interpretation of the *Purifications*. In this ethical and religious poem Empedocles tells a story that, while displaying striking similarities with the story of the natural world, follows its own logic. In this case, too, the characters are divinities (*daimones* in Greek; hence the habit of calling them demons, but they are closer to traditional gods). When they commit murder, they are exiled for "thirty thousand seasons" (fr. 115) from the community of the blessed, an exile in which they pass through different embodiments, according to a scheme that, as early as antiquity, was seen as close to the (Orphico-) Pythagorian doctrine of metensomatosis ("For already have I once been a boy, and a girl, a bush and a bird, and a mute fish in the sea," fr. 117).

This particular aspect of Empedocles' doctrine, whose relationship to his physical doctrine has constantly been a topic of discussion among scholars (whether Empedocles wrote one or two poems is part of this), was exploited by Plato in the *Phaedrus* with the central myth of fallen souls, which explains, among other things, the birth of life (246D–249D). This is why, in the very influential Neoplatonist tradition, Empedoclean "demons" were interpreted as "souls," which they were not and could not have been in the original poem, where life preexisted the punishment of the gods.

Empedocles is, without any doubt, along with Heraclitus, the Presocratic philosopher who has held the greatest fascination for posterity. The tension between the scientist, on one hand, and the reformer of religion and charismatic thaumaturge, on the other, is a recurrent theme among Empedocles specialists and beyond: Ernest Renan saw in him a mix of Newton and Cagliostro; Romain Rolland considered him as bridging Greek reason and oriental mysticism. Empedocles' literary renown, however, is due less to his doctrines than to the biography preserved by Diogenes Laertius (8.51–74), which made Empedocles a legendary character. Three elements are fundamental for the construction of this legend: the practice of the thaumaturge who puts his knowledge at the service of humankind, stops the winds, and brings the dead back to life (59–63; cf. fr. 111); the democratic orientation of the citizen and his refusal to become a king (63–66); and above all, his own death, which, in the best-known version, happened when he jumped into the crater of Etna (67–74), symbolically interpreted as a return to the lost unity. Empedocles' reception was dominated by Hölderlin's dramatic versions in which he used him to illustrate the tension between the knowledge of nature and the human community, a tension that only voluntary death can overcome. Nietzsche planned to write a tragedy on this subject. The same theme is present in Matthew Arnold's poem "Empedocles on Etna" and in Bertolt Brecht's "Die Schuhe des Empedokles." Paul Celan's poem dedicated to Empedocles ("Ortswechsel") clearly falls outside this tradition.

Empedocles' reputation as a philosopher is less dazzling: Hegel treated him as a secondary figure, and Heidegger did not mention him. The contrast with Heraclitus is striking. Nietzsche, however, in *The Pre-Platonic Philosophers* presented Empedocles, for whom the order of the world is the result of a blind game between two opposite drives (*Trieb*), as the great harbinger of Darwin's biological evolutionism. And Freud considered the Love-Hate pair as a confirmation of his dualistic theory of two original drives, Eros and Thanatos ("Die endliche und die unendliche Analyse").

BIBL.: S. Bercovitch, "Empedocles in the English Renaissance," *Studies in Philology* 65 (1968) 67–80. K. Birkenhauer, *Legend und Dichtung: Der Tod des Philosophen und Hölderlins Empedocles* (Berlin 1996). J. Bollack, "Empedokles," in Bollack, *Dichtung gegen Dichtung: Paul Celan und die Literatur* (Göttingen 2006) 301–314. P. Kingsley, *Ancient Philosophy,*

Mystery, and Magic: Empedocles and Pythagorean Tradition (Oxford 1995). S. Kofman, "Freud et Empédocle," *Critique* 265 (1969) 525–550. W. Kranz, *Empedokles: Antike Gestalt und Romantische Neuschöpfung* (Zurich 1949). J. Söring, "Nietzsches Empedokles-Plan," *Nietzsche-Studien* 19 (1990) 176–211. A.L.

Translated by Elizabeth Trapnell Rawlings and Jeannine Routier-Pucci

Empire

Today the word *empire* is used to describe an extensive state made up of several ethnic groups but ruled by only one of them. It has, at least since the early 20th century, also carried the suggestion of tyranny and brutality, inherited from the practices of the modern European colonial powers. The European empires were all heavily influenced by the language, the institutional practices, and the ideology of ancient Rome. Although the leagues of the Greek city-states were frequently referred to as possible models for a federal state—for instance, by the founders of the United States—the Delian League or "Athenian empire" was rarely ever mentioned as something to be either emulated or avoided. *Empire,* as the very term implies, was a Roman, Latin creation.

The root sense of the word *imperium,* is "order" or "command," and it was originally used to describe the sphere of executive authority possessed first by the Roman kings and then, under the Republic, by consuls, military tribunes, praetors, dictators, and masters of the horse. After the establishment of the Principate, however, authority was limited to a group of army commanders whose *imperium* derived not, as had that of the republican magistrature, from the civil sphere (*domi*), but instead from the military (*militiae*). Augustus, although he paid due deference to the "empire of the Roman people," expected the honor owed to the people to be paid to him. And by the 2nd century the jurists Gaius and Ulpian had both come to insist that the *imperium* of the "prince emperor" had absorbed that of the *populus Romanus.* There was in law then only one imperator, who also by then bore the title Augustus. The origins of this title had been religious, and although it was less often used by Rome's imperial or would-be imperial successors, it remained throughout the Roman Principate the imperial title par excellence. (The Holy Roman emperors styled themselves "Augustus," but it would have been unthinkable for Queen Victoria, or even the Russian czars—or "caesars"—to have done so.)

For centuries after the collapse of the Roman empire in the West, however, the term *imperium* was used in civil law to mean little more than "sovereignty." This is the sense in which it is employed in the often-repeated phrase of French jurists, that, whatever the status of the emperor, each ruler is an "emperor in his own kingdom" (*rex imperator in regno suo*). And when, for instance, Sir Francis Bernard, the governor of Massachusetts Bay Colony, declared in 1774 that "the Kingdom of Great Britain is *imperial,*" he meant, as he explained, nothing other than "it is sovereign and not subordinate to or dependent upon any earthly power."

By the 1st century CE, however, the term was already being used in its more recognizable modern sense to describe a particular kind of state. As early as the 1st century BCE, the Roman historian Sallust had used the phrase *Imperium romanum* to describe not merely the power but also the geographical extent of the authority of the Roman people. And when, a century later, Tacitus spoke of the Roman world as an "immense body of empire," he was describing precisely the kind of political and cultural unity, created out of a diversity of different states widely separated in space, that Edmund Burke, in describing the Spanish and British empires in 1775, called "extensive and detached empire." "A nation extended over vast tracts of land and numbers of people," wrote the English statesman and essayist Sir William Temple in 1720, "arrives in time at that ancient name of kingdom or modern of empire."

Officially the Roman empire in the West came to an end in 476, when the German ruler Odoacer deposed the last Latin emperor, Romulus, contemptuously known as "Augustulus." (The Roman empire in the East, commonly called the Byzantine empire, survived until finally annihilated by the Ottomans in 1453.) In 800, however, Pope Leo III, in the name of the "people and the City of Rome," conferred the title of emperor on Charles I, king of the Lombards and the Franks and subsequently known as Charlemagne (742–814). Charlemagne's empire did not last long. But when in 1157 Frederick I added the word *sanctus* to his title, the empire became not only Roman but also holy. Throughout most of its existence, the Holy Roman Empire may have been, as Voltaire later said of it, "neither holy, nor Roman, nor an Empire," but it enjoyed immense prestige, if very little sovereign power, until it was finally dissolved by Napoleon in 1806.

The subsequent Western imperial powers, from Habsburg Spain in the 16th century to, some would say, the United States to this day, also inherited from Rome its universalism. Under the late Republic, and then more forcibly under the Principate, the legal formulation of *imperium* merged with a 2nd-century (BCE) Stoic notion of a single universal human race—to use Cicero's phrase, a "single joint community of gods and men." Just as the Roman empire had become the embodiment of the Stoic notion of the *koinos nomos,* the universal law for all mankind, so its heirs sought to impose their own legal and religious order on all the peoples they overran.

One thing all the various meanings of the word *imperium* have in common is the association between extended territorial dominion and military rule. The Roman emperors themselves, however, were not only generals. In time they also became judges, and although the famous phrase in the *Digest* (1.3.31) that the prince was an "unfettered legislator"—*princeps legibus solutus*—had originally simply exempted the emperor from certain rules, it came to imply the existence of a supreme legislative authority, and was interpreted in this way by the medieval glossators on the texts of Roman law. From at least the creation of the Principate, the concept of empire crucially involved both military power and the rule of law. "O Romans," Virgil has Anchises declare at the end of his famous exhortation to the new race, "to rule the nations with *imperium,* these shall be your arts—to crown peace with law, to spare the humbled, to tame the proud in war." "The imperial majesty," Justinian wrote at the beginning of his *Institutes,* "should be armed with laws as well as glorified with arms." The emperor may still have had a moral obligation, one that even the most absolute early modern monarchs retained, to observe his own commands, but there was also legal force that could compel him to do so. *Imperium,* therefore, came to denote supreme military and legislative power over widespread and diverse territories. This is why Augustus had considered taking the title Romulus, as the founder of the new Rome, although, according to his biographer, reverence for the ancestors prevented him from doing so. To claim to be an imperator was to claim a degree and eventually a kind of power denied to mere kings. It was in recognition of that meaning of the term that, from the moment he invaded the Duchy of Lorraine in 869, Charles the Bald, duke of Burgundy, styled himself "Emperor and Augustus." He may have ruled over only two territories, but to rule over more than one was, in effect, to be an emperor.

The transformation of the status of the Roman emperor from Augustus to Constantine the Great effectively involved the transformation of a Roman *princeps* into a theocratic Hellenistic monarch, no matter how far removed in historical origins the Roman court might have been from those of the Macedonian monarchy. In the 7th century this understanding of what it was to exercise *imperium* was identified by Saint Isidore of Seville with the Greek loanword *monarchy.* "Monarchies," he wrote, "are those in which the principate belongs to one alone, as Alexander was among the Greeks and Julius among the Romans." Thenceforth the term *monarchy* was frequently used as a synonym for empire, to describe a domain composed of a number of different states in which the legislative will of a single ruler was unquestioned, one in which the prince *legibus solutus* and the laws were the expression of the prince's will. In the terms of the *lex regia,* the body of Roman law that established the authority of the emperor, "that which pleases the prince has the force of law" (*quod principi placuit legis habet vigorem; Digest* 1.4.1.). In this context it is not insignificant that Dante should have chosen to call his defense of the role of the empire in 13th-century Europe *De monarchia,* "On Monarchy," rather than *De imperio.* For, he explained, "the temporal monarchy, commonly called 'Imperium,' is that sole principate which is above all other principates in the world, relating to all questions of the temporal order." *Imperium,* however, as Dante explained at greater length in *Il Convivio,* could also be exercised in spiritual affairs by the papacy. It was not, therefore, a fitting description for a purely temporal institution. For Dante, the term *monarchia* had none of these unfortunate papal associations, yet it still retained the crucial sense of a universal ruler. When in the 16th century the Spanish Habsburgs referred to their American domains as the "Kingdoms of the Indies," they were attempting to distinguish them as a separate part of a wider geopolitical community named the *Monarchy* of Spain.

It was this identification with empire understood as a diversity of territories under a single legislative authority and empire understood as monarchy that underpinned the medieval and early modern conflict between empire and republic. In principle, there was no reason a true republic—a *res publica*—could not also be an empire. Both Athens and Rome had, of course, been republican empires. Mere size, as Alexander Hamilton pointed out in 1788, was no impediment to true republican government, so long as the various parts of the state constituted "an association of states or a confederacy." Nor, as Hamilton stressed on more than one occasion, was the fact of its republican constitution any reason for preventing the United States from becoming a true empire, "able to dictate the terms of the connection between the old world and the new."

The conflict between the political visions of empire and republic is based on the assumption that because all empires are founded on conquests, none, in Hamilton's terms, is in fact ever able to achieve the transition from an extended assembly of states to a true confederacy. Eventually all are destined to be ruled by single individuals exercising supreme if not arbitrary power, and therefore all are ultimately destined to transform themselves into monarchies. The Roman Principate had been responsible for greatly enlarging the territorial limits of the Roman *imperium,* and it had also in the process conferred on it a new political identity, an identity that was a denial of precisely those political values—the participation of all the citizens in the governance of the state—that had been responsible for its creation. As many later commentators observed, only Sparta among the republics of the ancient world, and Venice among those of the modern, had managed to maintain their political integrity over an extended period, and both had achieved this by expressly forbidding all but the most restricted territorial expansion. As the English political and economic theorist Charles Davenant phrased it in 1701, "While Common wealths thus extend their limits, they are working their own Bane, for all big Empires determine in a single Person."

This association between empire and conquest made the early modern proponents of overseas expansion uneasy about claiming to be imperial, in particular after tales of Spanish atrocities in the Americas—the so-called Black Legend—received such prominence. By the early 17th century the English were already denying that their settlements in America (legally classified by the Crown as "conquests") constituted an empire in the commonly understood sense of the term. The tyrannous Spanish and the perfidious French had created overseas empires, but the English exercised what the republican political theorist James Harrington called—borrowing Cicero's description of the empire of the late Roman Republic—not *imperium* over its various dependencies, but *patrocinium* (a protectorate). From this irenic view of the Roman imperial project evolved the 18th-century concept of the "empire of liberty," used by Edmund Burke to describe the ideal (if not always the reality) of British rule in India, and then by Thomas Jefferson for the westward expansion of the United States.

But empires of liberty were based on a concept of universal citizenship, which allowed Burke to refer to the Indians as his "distressed fellow citizens." This created a paradox. If all the inhabitants of an empire were to be "fellow citizens," then a new kind of society, universal and cosmopolitan, would have to come into being to accommodate them. With hindsight it was possible to argue, as Edward Gibbon did, that in the 2nd century, when "the Roman Empire comprehended the fairest part of the earth and the most civilized portion of mankind," this is indeed what happened. But in the 18th century, despite attempts to portray Augustan England as the renaissance of the age of the Antonines, things did not look quite so harmonious. As the French political theorist the Marquis de Mirabeau claimed, what the British had created by the middle of the 18th century was an attempt to combine three entirely incompatible objectives—domination, commerce, and "population" (i.e., settlement)—to create "a new and . . . monstrous system."

Things looked even less rosy a century later, after Napoleon's attempt to re-create what he described as an "application" to Europe of "the American Congress or of the Amphictyons of Greece." To many of those who lived under it, it looked less like an empire of liberty than a nationalist tyranny. All such imperial projects, argued one of Napoleon's fiercest critics, the liberal Benjamin Constant, in 1813, were doomed because they belonged to a now-vanished phase in human history, one that was dominated by the "savage impulse" of war. Empire, Constant argued, belong to the ancient world. It had been the creation of societies that had been small and bellicose. Their customs were simple: they despised luxury and comfort and valued above all else generosity, hospitality, courage, and loyalty—loyalty to each other and loyalty to their leaders. Modern nations, by contrast, were large, amorphous, and individualistic. The only political goods the moderns required were the peace and security that would allow them to pursue their essentially private goals unhindered. In the ancient world a leader had only to point to the region of the world he wished to conquer and his warriors would follow him there. The objective was unimportant. In the modern world, now calculating and concerned to protect their own interests, the only response a people would give to a leader who urged them to follow him and conquer the world would be "to reply with one voice: 'We have no wish to conquer the world.'" Any modern government that "wished to goad a European people to war and conquest would be committing a gross and disastrous anachronism. It would labor to impose upon that nation an impulse contrary to nature."

Constant's optimism about the end of empire was short-lived. Less than two decades after Napoleon's defeat, Europeans were scrambling all over Africa and Asia to create what would become, if only briefly, the largest imperial network the world had ever seen. But in one sense he was right. The colonial settlements in Africa, and the indirect domination by the Western powers of much of Asia, owed far less to the older Roman models than the empires of the pre-Napoleonic era had. In their different ways, the imperial nations of early modern Europe had all sought to replicate the ancient Roman ideal of empire as a single *civitas,* a single civilization, governed from a metropolis bound by a common rule of law and embracing a common body of citizens. The assembly of dominions and colonies, mandates and protectorates, that emerged in the post-Napoleonic period had none of those ambitions. "I know of no example of it either in ancient or modern history," wrote the British prime minister Benjamin Disraeli in 1878, of the British Empire, whose public image he had largely created. "No Caesar or Charlemagne ever presided over a dominion so peculiar."

One thing that distinguished these new empires from their predecessors and effectively broke the chain of succession with the ancient world was precisely the conception of *imperium.* For the Romans, although there existed many semidependent states (such as Egypt under the Ptolemies), the true Roman province was fully dependent on the metropolis (something that became of great ideological significance during the American War of Independence). Sovereignty, in other words, was indivisible. In the new European overseas empires, with their notions of "indirect rule" and *politique des races* that conferred virtual independence on native rulers, sovereignty could only be divisible, as the jurist Henry Maine told a Cambridge audience in 1887. The notion of indivisible sovereignty, the *imperium* of one people over all others, which had been largely a Roman invention, could apply in the modern world only to nation-states. What Maine had not foreseen was that the end of indivisible sovereignty also marked the end of empire in any meaningful sense. Today the word survives only as a metaphor.

BIBL.: Brett Bowden, *The Empire of Civilization: The Evolution of an Imperial Idea* (Chicago 2009). Anthony Pagden, *Peoples and Empires: Europeans and the Rest of the World from Antiquity to the Present* (London 2002). A.P.

Endymion

A hunter or herdsman loved by the moon (Selene or Diana), he sleeps through her nightly visits; in some versions he sleeps forever, forever young. In late antiquity the two decorate sarcophagi: Selene wears a crescent (or her cloak arcs), and he is muscular and nude.

European art takes its popular Endymion from rediscovered Roman tombs; Il Guercino (1591–1666) sold five paintings of the boy. In Poussin's *Endymion* (1632) the youth is awake and kneeling to his goddess, perhaps a reference to an engraving for Jean Gombauld's *L'Endimion* (ca. 1613), where the Endymion pleads for the love of a goddess identified with Maria de' Medici.

In some 17th-century works (Daniel Seiter, ca. 1670–1688, and Pier Francesco Mola, ca. 1660), Endymion turns away from the goddess in his sleep. Others separate the two: in Fragonard's *Diana and Endymion* (ca. 1753–1755), a bare-breasted Diana leans back on her crescent moon away from Endymion. Girodet-Trioson's *Sleep of Endymion* (1792) notoriously replaces Diana with an ephebic Cupid hovering over an androgynous Endymion's luscious thigh; the light alone suggests the female moon. The 19th century, however, tends to show Diana swooping down for her kiss (e.g., John Wood, 1801; George Frederick Watts, 1892). Canova's Endymion (1819–1822) sleeps alone, as does the naked boy in Julia Margaret Cameron's silver-toned photograph *An Angel Unwinged (The Young Endymion)* (1872).

The shimmer is musical as well. Palestrina's lament "The Sweet Slumber" appeared ca. 1584, and serenades for Endymion were composed by Scarlatti (1705) and by J. C. Bach (1772), whose hunter would rather nap than love. Monteverdi wrote an intermezzo, *The Loves of Diana and Endymion* (1628), and Cavalli's *La Callisto* (1651), which braids Diana's love with Callisto's disgrace, has a bear ballet and a Jove in both bass and soprano. In Martín and da Ponte's opera *The Tree of Diana* (1797), Endymion's beauty defeats chastity. Samuel Coleridge-Taylor's 1910 *Endymion's Dream* features both emotional solos and a passionate duet.

Shakespeare cites Endymion only when Portia calls for quiet: "The moon sleeps with Endymion/And would not be awaked" (*Merchant of Venice* 5.1.109–110), but the myth was popular with other early-modern writers. John Lyly's *Endymion, the Man in the Moon* (1584–1586) makes Cynthia's (Diana's) kiss all that can awaken Endymion; Elizabeth I, often addressed by poets as Cynthia, is probably meant. Michael Drayton wrote two versions of the story (1595, 1606). Francis Bacon casts Endymion as a courtier in his *Endymion; or, A Favorite* (1609). Giambattista Marino names Galileo "the new Endymion" in his epic *Adonis* (1623).

In Keats's 4,000-line *Endymion: A Poetic Romance* (1818) the hero, trying to escape "dull mortality's harsh net" (3.907), rejuvenates all the lovers lost at sea. Though attracted by a more corporeal maiden, Endymion gains his Phoebe (Diana) and at last is "spiritualized" (4.993). Keats was identified with Endymion's desire for supernatural beauty in poems by Longfellow, Thomas Hood, and Countee Cullen.

Baudelaire ("The Offended Moon," 1857) tutoyers Endymion's lover; she in turn insults the poet's aging mother. Archibald MacLeish proclaims, "The moon . . . [who] Climbed through the woods of Latmos to the bed/Of the eternal sleeper—she is dead" ("Selene Afterwards," 1924), but Reginald Shepherd notes that "The moon outlasts Endymion, outlasts/the myths about the moon" ("The Moon with Its Cargo of Bullion," 1998). In C. P. Cavafy's "Before the Statue of Endymion" (1895), the mythic youth is a passive statue before which the poet performs secret rites of ancient days; Rilke instead sees the hunter, still hunting in the poet's dreams (1926). The final sonnet of Millay's *Fatal Interview* (1931) mourns a moon who "wanders mad, being all unfit/For mortal love, that might not die of it."

In biology, Endymion appears in names for English and Spanish bluebells, and for a butterfly with full- and crescent-moon–like spots. For astronomers the name denotes a sea on the moon; in the poetry of science, Endymion sleeps with the moon forever.

BIBL.: N. Agapiou, *Endymion au carrefour: La fortune littéraire et artistique du mythe d'Endymion à l'aube de l'ère moderne* (Berlin 2005). E.M.H.

Epic

The poetic materials (both Indo-European and Near Eastern) out of which the *Iliad* and the *Odyssey* evolved have all but vanished into the half light and the total darkness of Greece's early history. Nor is it much clearer how the matter and manner of generations of earlier oral poets eventually found their way into the two poems that became the basis for the classical tradition of epic. All we can be sure of is that somehow or other, somewhere, someone began to shape a structure and a technique to match it that permitted the selection from a dim, tangled batch of heroic figures a single individual, "the best of the Achaeans," whose life and death could be made to seem the quintessence of the heroic society that produced him and others like him. The singer who decided to focus this poem on the wrath of Achilles and to chart the course of that wrath with perfect clarity may be said to have invented the idea of classical epic for Western poetry. The focus on wrath turned godlike Achilles into a tragic figure, one whose grandeur moves unalterably past self-contradiction to what amounts to self-destruction. Achilles does not (in giving back to Priam the corpse of his son) become a better person, but he is revealed as a man who, having unwillingly begun to understand the dreadful consequences of his wrath, is forced to recognize the meaning of his choices and actions, is made to face what he has become, who he is: his anger, which fuels the entire poem, is described by Achilles himself as something far sweeter than honey, something that stifles the chest like smoke. This tragic worldview is at the core of the poet's dramatization of the heroic code. Viewed as a tragic hero, Achilles becomes not only the origin of classical epic, but also, as Aeschylus and his colleagues recognized, the model for tragic drama.

What happened after the Achilles-poet had discovered a way of eliciting a perfect form for heroic song from the welter of heroic lays inherited from earlier tradition is rather surprising. The only epic in the classical epic tradition to rival the story of Achilles and his wrath and to provide classical epic with an alternative model is the one that immediately followed it, the one that sought to challenge its worldview and its concept of the heroic. The *Odyssey*'s author creates a hero who is less a warrior than he is an adventurer, a seagoing explorer, something of a pirate, and something of a con man. The Odysseus-poet has taken the various legends that represented the return home of the Greek heroes who had survived the Trojan War and, focusing on one of those survivors, has shifted the business of epic from the celebration of splendid warriors to the celebration of sea merchants, of explorers, of colonizers. Odysseus, an essentially comic hero, is so much the antithesis of Achilles that he seems at times to parody him. He is much less interested in a brilliant demise on the battlefield than he is in richly flourishing in a dangerous, exciting, and finally pleasurable world of which he is, by hook or by crook, continually the master. His motto, as befits a clever contriver of lucky stratagems, is "Look, we have come through!"

The developments in epic composition immediately after the *Odyssey* are, save for some fragments, all but lost to us. The poems now known as the Epic Cycle treated mostly of what happened before and after the events of the war at Troy as those were represented in the *Iliad*. We have no sense that these poems made much use of what had been central to the work of the two Homeric poems: dynamic form, vitality of dramatic plots, and elegant design of characters. Nor is there any indication that these poems earned anything like the reverence that attended the reception of both the Homeric poems. By the time that classical Greek culture had reached its fullest blossoming in the 5th century BCE, Homer (by then regarded as the author of both epics) had become the consciousness and the voice of Greece, its teacher, its prophet, the repository of its values, the touchstone of its shared identities. It was during this period that Homer began making the move from the spoken to the written word, in the process becoming less theatrical as he becomes more textual. Though he continued, doubtless, to be enjoyed, he also became something (and something archetypal) to be pondered and judged, admired and analyzed.

But Homer's becoming textualized, his being preserved (and imprisoned) in libraries, was not the only thing that contributed to the crisis in the epic tradition that came about after the death in 323 BCE of Alexander the Great (who had carried the *Iliad* with him on his conquests, as an inspirational vade mecum). For those who understood what Homer's poems meant (among them, the librarian-poets who were now his guardians and interpreters) the idea of the heroic had become problematic. Their modern world was far more sophisticated (and knowing), far more given to habits of skeptical scrutiny than the poets and audiences who had once succumbed to the barbaric glamour of epic's original heroes. Thus, epics became abbreviated yet lavishly provided with high verbal gloss and with what Marguerite Yourcenar has called (in *Mémoires d'Hadrien*, 1951, referring to Lycophron) "an intricate system of echoes and mirrors"; they became rich in allusion, adorned with arcane lore, and for story material chose small segments, some of them minor or obscure, from a hero's entire repertoire of exploits. Epic became a poetry for "the happy few."

Much as we may regret the loss of Callimachus' *Hecale*, we cannot fail to be grateful for the survival of a single epic from the Hellenistic period, the relatively brief *Argonautica* of Apollonius Rhodius, which tells the story of Jason's voyage in his ship, the *Argo*, in quest of the Golden Fleece. This Alexandrian Jason (whatever he may earlier have been) is not specially suited to the role he is asked to play. His shipmates as often as not perform whatever clever or dangerous deed needs doing. He is, luckily for him, stupendously good-looking, and when the young witch Medea falls crazily in love with him, it is her passion for him that permits him to escape (along with her) back to Greece with the Golden Fleece. This abbreviated epic comes truly alive only when Medea has entered it, for she ignites the poet's imagination and sympathy, and she causes him to achieve something truly original. The *Argonautica* is a creative deformation of epic: it strips the adventure epic of what seriousness its comic core allowed it to possess and transforms it into an engaging romance that is centered on the transformation of Medea from a naive and memorably amorous maiden into a ruthless, formidable woman (a woman who will almost certainly find ways of losing her epic's pathetic hero at the first opportunity).

While these and other Hellenistic versions of epic were being written—we know that there were also historical, foundational, and panegyrical epics on leaders and cities—the idea of epic began to arrive in Rome. In the 3rd century BCE Livius Andronicus produced a Latin translation of the *Odyssey*, and Gnaeus Naevius wrote an epic on the Punic Wars; both were in saturnian verse. The versatile Quintus Ennius began writing a long epic in dactylic hexameters, the *Annals*, which survives in tantalizing fragments. Imagining himself as Homer reborn in Rome, Ennius nevertheless eschewed Homeric epic and busied himself in 18 books with the history of Rome from the fall of Troy down to the year 171 BCE. How much he borrowed from Homer besides his meter, how much he took of Homer's matter and manner, is unknowable, but his decision to survey the entire panorama of Rome's origins and her evolution toward empire suggests that he was not especially concerned with Homer's handling of plot or character.

In fact, it would be only a century later that a Roman poet would resist (almost) the pull of historical epic and feel emboldened to attempt to restore a genuinely Homeric epic form. The *Aeneid*'s peculiar achievement and yet more peculiar destiny combine to make it, after the Homeric originals it was modeled on, the greatest of classical epics and, through historical accident—the gradual disappearance of the Greek language and its literature from the culture of the West—the most influential. For more than a millennium it would be Virgil and not Homer who represented the idea of the epic in Western Europe. (Homer's recovery of his supremacy was a slow, uneven process that would not be complete until the Romantic era.) Had it been merely another honorable but bloodless effort to provide epic form with artificial respiration and Rome's rulers with the quantity of grandeur that only epic in its panegyric disguise can bestow, the *Aeneid* would have disappeared along with myriad mediocrities or would have maintained a feeble survival along with a few other Latin epics from the Flavian era that managed to imitate some of its virtues well enough to resist oblivion (Valerius Flaccus' *Argonautica,* Statius' *Thebaid,* Silius Italicus' *Punica*).

What gives Virgil some claim to be not Homer's rival but his rightful heir is his complete success, against all odds, in importing most of the letter and much of the spirit that make Homer's poems what they are. This miracle of ambition and tact is all the more remarkable because its odd purity coexists with a jumbled process of crossbreeding. Like Homer, he plots his epic around the deeds (and ethical and cultural significance) of a single hero, but he combines the comic hero of the *Odyssey* (in *Aeneid* books 1–6) with the tragic hero of the *Iliad* (in *Aeneid* books 7–12) and thus links the epic of adventure and exploration to the epic of war, its splendors and miseries. This oxymoronic pairing is further fused with the historical and political strains in Hellenistic epic. This aspect of the poem underscores a topic that had been unknown in Homer's poems: world history, here figured as the Destiny of Nations as directed by Divine Providence, the End of History in the Triumph of Roman Augustus. Finally, to this mixture, which should have been a total mess, Virgil added Apollonius: he took the Hellenistic poet's Medea and magnified her into his Dido, the woman who comes to dominate the first half of the *Aeneid* by luring its hero into a passionate romance that was fatal to her and was also (save for divine grace) nearly fatal to Aeneas as well. With the addition of this Alexandrian ingredient to the Homeric cocktail, the epic about Rome's (and Augustus') mission in the world takes on a subversive, emotional quality, a preference for lyrical strategies, from which it never quite recovers. The heroism of Aeneas tends to be baffled, tormented, uncertain; he moves unsteadily though a world governed not so much by iron fate and splendid yet capricious gods as by a mysterious spirit of historical progress that is often obstructed by inscrutable forces that are alien to it. The hero's devotion to his community (rather than to his personal glory) is admirable yet troubled and tainted; his victories are everywhere diminished by our sense of how much they cost him as well as those he abandons or conquers.

Hard on the heels of the *Aeneid* came another Latin poem that is sometimes (and probably mistakenly) accorded the epic label. Ovid's *Metamorphoses* is a long poem composed in dactylic hexameter, the classical epic meter, and it takes as its prime subject matter nothing less than the universal history of the world from Hesiod's Chaos down to the cosmos refashioned by Augustus Caesar. It chooses to imagine and to recount that process of the evolution of the early disorder of the world to the perfect order of the Roman Empire in a somewhat paradoxical manner: a series of seemingly random vignettes are ironically juxtaposed by a pattern of speciously logical transitions. The form of the poem, then, short narrative poems in the Alexandrian manner, gathered together into a broken unity, subverts the idea of epic by pretending to create an epic out of a carefully articulated farrago of brief counter-epics. Not least in its affectionate yet brutal parody of Virgil (in books 13–14) and its droll, ambiguous conclusion (a solemn-seeming, perfunctory glance at the Augustan triumph), this strange counter-epic is at once both inside and outside the classical epic tradition; yet its influence on Western culture (in literature, art, and music) has rivaled Virgil's and often surpassed it.

The last Roman epic to contribute to the development of the classical epic—some have thought to its destruction—was Lucan's *Bellum civile,* or *Pharsalia.* Like Ovid, Lucan finds his inspiration not in Homer but in historical epic in its Virgilian permutation. Abolishing divine machinery in favor of an expanded version of incomprehensible divine forces that govern (or misdirect) what happens in history, Lucan outdoes Virgil in transforming the clarity of Homeric warfare into an expressionistic nightmare, and he replaces Homeric conflict with a trio of cartoon figures (Caesar, Pompey, and Cato) who serve chiefly as allegories of, respectively, vice, failed virtue, and virtue, or as the purveyors or the subjects of epigrams, bitter and exquisitely wrought. This horrendously violent poem, a booming diatribe against the murder of freedom and the malevolence of history, is as unforgettable as it is frightening, and Dante was not alone in noticing its ferocious tensions and admiring them, warmly.

When the idea of classical epic entered into the medieval world in its Virgilian and post-Virgilian permutations, it faced obstacles that were difficult and, as it turned out, all but impossible to overcome. Virgil continued to be read and pondered and paraphrased (*Eneas,* a 12th-century French romance, is a prime example of this style of appropriating him), but Christian notions of heroism were permeated with habits of mind (e.g., guilt, humility, compassion, chivalry) that were powerfully in conflict with the pagan virtues that classical epic espouses. The figure of Aeneas may cast doubt on some of those virtues (and thus call Homer's celebration of glory into question as well), but he remains sufficiently in the Homeric mold to have made his naturalization in the medieval world problematic. He could be, and of course was, allegorized into a literary emblem suitable for the medieval imagination, he could be and was converted into a chivalric character; but the heroic spirit and the heroic form that he inherited from Homer and that he retained (sufficiently) for all his divergences from Achilles and Odysseus were untranslatable for the audiences that wanted and welcomed Beowulf, Roland, or the Cid. The author of the 10th-century *Waltharius* found it possible and advantageous to decorate his Latin "epic" about a Gothic warrior from the time of Attila with allusions to Virgilian themes and Virgilian language, but the breadth of classical epic and the shape that housed it were as unavailable to him as they were unknown and alien to his audiences.

With the rise of Humanism, hopes of recovering the spirit of the classical past kindled a belief that the forms and feelings of classical epic could also be revived. Sometime around 1338 Petrarch was inspired to begin work on a Latin epic, *Africa,* that would celebrate the career of Livy's supreme hero, Scipio Africanus, conqueror of Hannibal. Though he showed his manuscript in progress to a few enthusiastic readers, Petrarch continued revising his epic for the rest of his life, and it was released to the general public only posthumously. The poem is replete with Virgilian sights and sounds, but Petrarch avoided the problem of direct competition with his master in two ingenious ways: his Scipio, firmly rooted in Livy's historical narrative, shows little resemblance to Aeneas in character or behavior; and Petrarch claims as his model not Virgil but his precursor Ennius. In the ninth and final book of his epic, Petrarch imagines a dialogue between Ennius and Scipio, one in which they discuss the nature of epic. The climax of his conversation is Ennius's description to Scipio of a dream he has had: Homer had appeared to him, named him his equal and foretold to him that one day, in the far distant future, a young poet named Franciscus would compose another epic on Scipio's heroic warfare, a masterwork that would earn him a laureate's crown. With similar dexterity Petrarch evades the difficulty that awaited all writers of Renaissance classical epic: how to reconcile pagan heroics with Christian ethics and Christian spirituality. He simply constructs a double invocation, juxtaposing, without any effort to mediate between them, a pagan poet's prayer (1.1–6):

Muse, you will tell me of the man renowned
for his great deeds, redoubtable in war,
on whom first noble Africa, subdued
by Roman arms, bestowed a lasting name.
Fair sisters, ye who are my dearest care,
if I propose to sing of wondrous things,
may it be given me to quaff full deep
of the sweet sacred spring of Helicon

with a predictably Christian prayer for divine poetic help (1.10–14):

Thou too, Who art the world's
securest hope and glory of the heavens
. . . O come,
all-highest Father, bear me succor here.
(trans. Bergin and Wilson)

It was a valiant effort, and a landmark in the evolution of Humanism, but for all Petrarch's toil (or perhaps because of it), finding readers, much less admirers, of *Africa* is not easy. This epic, at once polished and correct, is soporific.

Just short of a century later (1428) Maffeo Vegio made another, very different attempt to accommodate classical (Latin) epic to Christian (now powerfully Humanist) culture. By this time readers were beginning to read more of books 7–12 of the *Aeneid* than the medieval allegorizers had been accustomed to do. The savage ending of Virgil's epic was fiercely resistant to Christian allegorizing, so Vegio supplied the poem with a comforting closure that could please Humanist and Christian alike. He furnished the poem with a 13th book, which took up precisely where Virgil had left off. Vegio allows Aeneas to celebrate his triumph over Turnus, to marry Lavinia, to ascend to the throne of Latinus, and, after a brief but virtuous reign, to undergo apotheosis. This Aeneas bears a decent resemblance to his pagan pattern, but in his chivalric decorum and his Christian temper (here the stamp of the allegorizers is much in evidence) and in his heavenly destination he provides precisely what his age demanded of Virgil. Vegio's *Supplement* was widely circulated in manuscript until it was published with Virgil's poem in 1471, an honor it would enjoy in other editions well into the 17th century.

As the Renaissance moved to its full flowering, the shift in the fortunes of classical epic was swift and dramatic. Among the complexities that clustered to create that sea change, the recovery and the gradual dissemination of Homer were not the least. Medieval versions of epic and its typical romances began to lose some of their popularity with the slow vanishing of the medieval world and the gradual fragmentation of Christian unity; new, urgent explorations of the heavens and of the world beyond Europe and a passionate interest in colonies and empire promoted a fervent taste for adventure and habits of uninhibited, even reckless self-assertion. This was a time and place in which both Achilles and Odysseus might have some hope of feeling at home. Nevertheless, the penchant for allegory did persist, as did a nostalgic hankering after chivalric glamour, and a central argument arose about the nature of epic, namely, whether romance and epic could be so fused as to create a viable hybrid, and whether Ariosto's *Orlando furioso* was a genuine epic or some species of mongrel. Purists, relying on the warrant they believed they found in Aristotle, insisted that it was not, whereas moderns, whom arguments from Aristotle did not intimidate, charitably opted for a more expanded and more flexible definition of epic than the ancient oracle had apparently prescribed. In his "Essay on Romance" (1824) Sir Walter Scott, who had a vested interest in the topic, decided that the distinction between epic and romance was a specious one and that "regularity of composition and poetical talent" could easily coexist with "extravagance of imagination and irregularity of detail" if "these properties are so equally balanced that it may be difficult to say to which class they belong." "Epopeia and Romance," he decides, can exist as "two distinct species of the same generic class." This is an equitable settlement to an argument that was fervent in the Renaissance and continues to offer food for speculation, and there are even now readers who think of both Ariosto's poem and *The Faerie Queene* as epics, but it is doubtful that romance and its transformations have much of a place in discussions about the classical tradition.

Though plenty of epics were attempted in the Renaissance, few of them, whatever their luck with their original audiences, managed, as the centuries passed, to endure outside the rare book collections. The major index of the continuation of the classical tradition in this period was the epic poet's habit of alluding to Virgil's (and sometimes to Homer's) language or type-scenes without attempting to recreate the heroic temper or the intricate narrative patterns and the dynamics of suspense and momentum that inform their models. It is a hard saying, but it will come as no surprise to readers of epics as diverse as Ronsard's *Franciade* (1572) or Abraham Cowley's *Davideis* (1656) or Agrippa d'Aubigné's (in some ways wonderful) *Les Tragiques* (1616–1623) that by and large the writers of inadequate epics have (as Mark Twain said to his wife when she tried to cure him of using swear words by using them herself) "the words but not the music." These writers tend to replace elegant plots with episodic narratives ("lays" stitched together, to recall the old slur against Homer as feckless, wandering minstrel); they have difficulty in focusing on a single hero (and even more difficulty in imagining someone ferocious enough or clever enough or complex enough to sustain the demands of a heroic plot); and they are prone, lacking both significant hero and coherent plot, to ornament their tales with allusions to the epic that they cannot accurately imitate. A glance at three epics from the 16th century may suffice to illustrate these problems: Girolamo Vida's *Christiad* (1535), Luís de Camões's *The Lusiads* (1572), and Tasso's *Gerusalemme liberata* (1581). Each of these poems can claim some degree of success as a classical epic, but each also shows the perils that accompany the enterprise of continuing the classical tradition.

In its own time widely esteemed as the product of "the Christian Virgil," the *Christiad* has seen its luster dwindle with most readers over the past few centuries, but if a present-day reader takes the trouble, glints of the epic's original charm can be recovered. Its hero is altogether lacking in the pagan vitality required, but he is the center of a story whose familiarity helps to pull the poem's episodic patterns, its developing plot, and its numerous flashbacks into a genuine if predictable unity. What benefits it most (and made it an attractive minor model for Milton) is its consummate handling of Virgilian type-scenes and, in particular, of Virgilian language: its verbal allusions are so pervasive and so seductive, their texture so dense and so delicate, that despite the poem's shortcomings it triumphs, against all odds, as a sort of artificial epic, one that can induce in the charitable reader the illusion of authenticity.

The 21st-century reader need not expend much critical generosity on taking up *The Lusiads* (the title refers to the sons of Lusus, founder of Portugal). Although the poem's formal hero, Vasco da Gama, is made of little more than cardboard and its form is essentially episodic, its gusto and fluid imagination earn it a secure place in world literature. Camões dismisses both Virgil and Homer as over-the-top fictioneers in a hilariously brazen and self-mocking riff on his own poetics: "Let us hear no more then of Ulysses and Aeneas and their long journeyings, no more of Alexander and Trajan and their famous victories. My theme is the daring and renown of the Portuguese, to whom Neptune and Mars alike give homage. The heroes and the poets of old have had their day; another and loftier conception of valour has arisen" (1.3, trans. Atkinson). In this opening invocation Camões goes on to invoke the nymphs of his native Tagus, whom he links with both Apollo and the pagan Muses (even as he manages to shade his prayers for poetic success into a properly Catholic zone of inspiration). But for all its nod to Rome and its fervent patriotism, this epic's manner is beautifully Virgilian, as are its type-scenes, its imperial themes, and its ironic manipulation of divine machinery. Furthermore, its matter and spirit are genuinely Homeric: it is the spirit of Odysseus that haunts this elaborate meditation on the meaning of exploration, adventure, trade, and colonization—in short, of empire in its Catholic and Portuguese incarnation. If too much of the poem seems involved in pageant and spectacle, what fuels it is its passionate understanding of this new heroic age (the modern world, the enlargement of Europe's knowledge and power and hunger) and its own nation's place in it. The poem is, in short, a rare and very satisfying encounter between some of the crucial ingredients of classical epic and a new and alien environment.

The *Christiad* succeeds by virtue of the near perfection of the mechanism that produces its apt Virgilian allusions; *The Lusiads* triumphs by imagining a new and powerful heroic spirit in a modern yet still classical epic form. Tasso's great poem on the liberation of Jerusalem, remote though it is from the modern temper, because of its firm control of its classical allusions is uniformly impressive, even as its grasp of narrative clarity and narrative momentum recalls, if it does not equal, that of the two Homeric epics and of Virgil's *Aeneid.* Despite these virtues, however, the poem is as much a product of Tasso's desire to unlock the secrets of the theory of epic as it is of his need to reimagine for his own age the heroic temper. His poem is a scholar's poem, both in the loving care he takes in choosing his allusions to classical epic and in his interest in re-creating the Crusades (that is to say, in representing what they should have been and were not). It is because his poem makes no attempt (like that of Camões) to discover what was heroic about the world he lived and wrote in that he ends up in a fantasy world straddling allegorical romance and epic, allowing allegory to interfere with epic and epic with allegory. This desperate compromise taints the ambition of a poet who was determined to resurrect the classical epic and purify its tradition, but if Tasso failed in that attempt, he nevertheless wrote a masterpiece, sui generis, beautiful and bizarre.

Poets continued to attempt imitation of classical epic poetry after the Renaissance and well into modern times, but the only poem that by nearly common consensus stands out preeminently among these efforts is the one that tested the limits of classical epic most ruthlessly and in the process broke its mold. *Paradise Lost* (1667, 1674) is suffused with many of the tensions (religious, political, and cultural) that wracked Europe's premodern consciousness and shaped it, and Milton's engagement with those tensions fuels his poem abundantly and violently with a unique heroic spirit. That spirit is strangely and unequally divided among three heroes (Satan, Christ, and Adam), and in their struggle to dominate the poem, Milton discovered a dynamic structure, its suspense and momentum beautifully arranged, that recalls its Homeric and Virgilian models. But Milton's copious classical imitations and allusions include Ovid and Lucan as well as Homer and Virgil. If Virgil reconfigures Homer, and Ovid and Lucan in their different ways challenge that reconfiguration, Milton avails himself of the three other poets in his attempt to reject Homeric glory while retaining the power of Homer's epic form. In doing so he succeeds in completing his "sad task" of representing an "argument/Not less but more heroic than the wrath/Of stern Achilles" or "the rage/Of Turnus disespoused' (9.13–17). That "sad task," the dramatization of the meaning of the fall of humankind, turns epic inside out and upside down. It enacts a rejection (however reluctant and conflicted) of the classical tradition, a rejection whose significance is best explicated by the small epic that followed it, *Paradise Regained* (1671).

Satan there tries tempting Jesus with mastery of the classical epic tradition if he agrees to visit Athens, where he promises his intended victim that he will

> hear and learn the secret power
> Of harmony in tones and numbers hit
> By voice or hand, and various measur'd verse,
> Aeolian charms and Dorian Lyric Odes,
> And his who gave them breath, but higher sung,
> Blind Melesigenes, thence Homer called. (4.254–259)

Jesus answers that if he wants to divert himself with "Music or with Poem" he can always turn to the Old Testament, from which Greece derived those poetic arts:

> Ill imitated, while they loudest sing
> The vices of their Deities, and their own,
> In Fable, Hymn or Song, so personating
> Their Gods ridiculous, and themselves past shame.
> Remove their swelling Epithetes thick laid
> As varnish on a Harlot's cheek. (4.339–344)

In these corrupt and corrupting poems the luckless reader will find little or nothing worth the trouble, certainly nothing in any way to compare with "Sion's song." This is the last and greatest poet in the classical epic tradition talking. So much, then, for classical epic.

The story does not quite end there. Milton's curse on classical epic did not discourage Alexander Pope from translating Homer magnificently, or avert the turn to mock epic that became fashionable in the Age of Prose and of Reason. After Paul Scarron's *Virgile travesti* (1648–1651) came both Pope's incomparable *Rape of the Lock* (1714) and his *Dunciad* (1743) and Henry Fielding's *Joseph Andrews* (1742) and *Tom Jones* (1749); then, as the Romantic age was reaching its zenith, came one of the greatest of English poems, Byron's bitter, hilarious satire on the Romantic hankering for "epic truth," *Don Juan* (1819–1824).

That need, fueled in part by Romantic Hellenism, is voiced by Percy Shelley (the phrase "epic truth" is his) in *A Defence of Poetry* (1821), in which, having summarily demoted Virgil from the place that Dryden had assigned him ("Three poets in three distant ages born"), he salutes Homer, Dante, and Milton as the first, second, and third of Europe's (authentic) epic poets. For Shelley poetic truth is the product of the sublime myths that humankind must have to live and that science and antimetaphysical reason had all but destroyed, and it is in what he called epic that it has been best found in the past and where it must be discovered in the present and the future. By the time Shelley was writing, the word *epic* had loosened most of its ties with the classical tradition and had multiplied its connotations: it was coming to denote "massive," "awesome," "profound," and "eternally true." This development presaged the current usage of the word, which lends itself to usurpation by journalists, advertisers, and movie publicists, by any wordsmith who feels in need of a pinch of vividness, a touch of glamour, something suggesting the stupendous, all of which a venerable if faded literary tradition readily bestows. (Bakhtin, who best taught us how literary genres evolve and decline, pronounced epic "antiquated.")

Romantic poets continued to try fabricating long poems on big classical subjects: Goethe wrote one canto of his epic on Achilles before abandoning the effort, and Keats labored bravely and in vain to write his epic on Hyperion; Robert Southey (one of Byron's chief targets) did manage to complete his *Joan of Arc* (1796), and Joel Barlow finished his final revision of his unreadable national epic for America, the *Columbiad,* in 1807. In contrast with these is Victor Hugo's splendid *La légende des siècles* (1859), an authentic (and nearly lonely) example of modern (semiclassical) epic.

Wordsworth, too, had been tempted to compose epic poetry, as he tells us in *The Prelude:*

> Sometimes, mistaking vainly, as I fear,
> Proud spring-tide swellings for a regular sea,
> I settle on some British theme, some old
> Romantic tale, by Milton left unsung. (1.166–169)

He goes on to ponder other epic topics, drawn from Gibbon and Plutarch, but none of them fastens on his imagination. Anguished, deeply troubled by writer's block, he takes refuge in his beloved, welcoming landscapes (the real ones he wanders through and those of his mind and spirit) from which he will learn to discover his proper, his fated poetic subject. Not entirely without reason, this poem has been called an epic. Its creation satisfied what its age (and Shelley) demanded of it. *The Prelude* is an "epic" exploration of modern humankind in search of itself in a new, unknown world, and its poet is nothing if not a maker of good myths. It is a brilliant and permanent contribution to world literature, but like other long, mythmaking poems (*Song of Myself, The Dynasts, Anabase, The Cantos, Notes toward a Supreme Fiction*), it has little or no connection with the classical tradition.

The heroic spirit in its Iliadic form seems to have been disappearing from Western poetry since the modern battlefield and its unheroic technological advances began to realize their capacity to baffle poetic representation. As Tolstoy saw (he whose grasp of Homer was impeccable), that moment of classical departure found its best incarnation in Fabrizio del Dongo, when he prudently withdrew himself from the battle of Waterloo in Stendhal's *La Chartreuse de Parme* (1839). Rupert Brooke might confidently slip the *Iliad* into his kitbag as he headed off to Skyros, but after Dresden, Auschwitz, and Hiroshima, after Primo Levi's *Se questo è un uomo* (1947), Achilles could hope for no better than the mordant representations offered him by Christa Wolf in *Kassandra* (1983) or Christopher Logue in *War Music* (1981, with later additions).

Odysseus, however, always partial to some degree of pastiche, could find it in his heart to enter into postmodern fun and games. Nikos Kazantzakis' *The Odyssey: A Modern Sequel* (1938, English translation 1958) found considerable approval from many of its initial readers, but a half century later it gives the impression of having been written by Zorba the Greek, after overdosing on sustained perusals of Madame Blavatsky and too many misreadings of Nietzsche. Kazantzakis begins his epic more or less where the *Odyssey*'s poet ended, then launches his version of Odysseus on a long series of contrived phantasmagorias, all drenched in predictable mystical allegory. Much more successful is Derek Walcott's *Omeros* (1990). Like Ennius and Petrarch before him, encountering his model in person, the poet receives his master's mantle. This Homer admits that praising war was a mistake, and he encourages his successor in his praise of peace and life and love and in his opposition to slavery and oppression. This elliptical, lyrical narrative is studded with classical ornament; it is charming, not least in the beauty of its imagery. But its links with the classical tradition are tenuous at best. Also firmly planted in its author's modern world, but triumphant in its classical retrievals, James Joyce's *Ulysses* was written with Homeric chapter headings, which were replaced with numerals when it appeared in book form in 1922. Nevertheless, its classical allusions and emphatic intertextualities are as ingenious as they are pervasive, and they illumine their original text as much as they are illumined by them. Here if anywhere in modern literature, the classical tradition is alive and well.

Finally, if the Iliadic Homer is to have any chance in the 21st century, it will probably be found in the path marked out for it by Vasily Aksyonov in his trilogy on Stalinist Russia, *Moskovskaya Saga* (1992, translated into English as *Generations of Winter*, 1994). In this frightening and noble work, all Tolstoy's Homeric power is recovered together with his skepticism about epic grandeur. But the novelist who imagines the sufferings and courage of the Gradov family makes us believe, while we are reading his book, that genuine heroism is still possible and that something like glory is not incompatible with it.

BIBL.: A. J. Boyle, ed., *Roman Epic* (London 1993). Colin Burrow, *Epic Romance* (Oxford 1993). Luís de Camões, *The Lusiads*, trans. William C. Atkinson (Harmondsworth 1962). Robert Fowler, ed., *A Companion to Homer* (Cambridge 2004). Thomas Greene, *The Descent from Heaven: A Study in Epic Continuity* (New Haven 1963). J. B. Hainsworth, *The Idea of Epic* (Berkeley 1991). Charles Martindale, *John Milton and the Transformation of Ancient Epic* (Totowa 1986). Petrarch, *Africa*, trans. Thomas G. Bergin and Alice S. Wilson (New Haven 1977). David Quint, *Epic and Empire* (Princeton 1993). Marguerite Yourcenar, *Mémoires d'Hadrien* (Paris 1951). W.R.J.

Epictetus

The slave-turned-Stoic philosopher Epictetus (ca. 50–130 CE) lectured at Nicopolis in western Greece around 100 CE. The *Discourses* that now circulate under his name are prefaced with a letter from Arrian of Nicomedia, who presents them as his lecture notes from Epictetus' classroom. The *Handbook* of Epictetus is Arrian's epitome of the *Discourses*.

Although Stoicism declined in influence in late antiquity, Epictetus still attracted readers. In the 6th century the Neoplatonist Simplicius devoted an entire commentary to the *Handbook*, and his compatriot Olympiodorus mentions Epictetus in a commentary on Plato's *Gorgias*. Their master Damascius refers to someone as being of the "school of Epictetus," which suggests that he still had his admirers.

Epictetus' works continued to circulate in the Eastern Mediterranean. In the 9th century Photius knew them, as did Arethas, archbishop of Caesarea. It is possible that the *Handbook* was one of the Greek philosophical texts translated into Arabic during this period; passages echoing Epictetus have been found in Al-Kindī's *On the Art of Dispelling Sorrows*.

Epictetus' practical exercises for a moral life also found their Christian admirers. Three adaptations of the *Handbook* were made for use in monasteries, and in one of these Epictetus' references to Socrates are replaced with references to Saint Paul.

The Renaissance brought Epictetus new readers. Niccolò Perotti translated Epictetus' *Handbook* into Latin ca. 1450, along with the preface from Simplicius' commentary. A little later, in 1479, Angelo Poliziano also translated the *Handbook,* and this version was published in 1497. His translation was accompanied by a prefatory letter to Lorenzo de' Medici and a letter to Bartolomeo Scala in defense of Epictetus, and in both of these he makes clear that he read Epictetus with the aid of Simplicius, drawing on that author's Neoplatonic interpretation of the *Handbook*. For instance, Poliziano attempted to make Epictetus more palatable to Scala by suggesting that "our Stoic fights boldly, using Platonic arguments as his shield."

In the late 16th century the Jesuit missionary Matteo Ricci produced a Chinese adaptation of the *Handbook* and argued that Epictetus' Stoicism was close in spirit to Confucianism. In Europe around the same time Justus Lipsius argued that Stoicism could profitably be combined with Christianity. And as Seneca shaped the Neostoicism of Lipsius, so Epictetus shaped the Neostoicism of Guillaume du Vair, who translated the *Handbook* into French and produced a number of treatises inspired by his reading of Epictetus. Vair indeed claimed that his *Moral Philosophy of the Stoics* was merely an attempt to rearrange Epictetus' *Handbook* into a more systematic form.

As Neostoicism exerted its influence, it soon found its critics. In his *Discussion with M. de Sacy* (published long after his death), Blaise Pascal objected that Epictetus' Stoicism assumed far too much power for the individual. Epictetus' claim that it is possible for us to have complete control over our happiness was, for Pascal, "wickedly proud." And although Epictetus might have done much to attack the vice of laziness, by denying the need for the grace of God he did not offer a genuine path to virtue.

In the next century Anthony Ashley Cooper, Third Earl of Shaftesbury, produced a series of notes inspired by Epictetus, posthumously published under the title *The Philosophical Regimen;* his scholarly annotations on the text of Epictetus were included by John Upton in his 1741 edition of Epictetus' works. Shaftesbury's own philosophy drew on his admiration of Epictetus, leading one commentator to proclaim him "the greatest Stoic of modern times."

As is true of the rest of Hellenistic philosophy, interest in Epictetus declined during the 19th century, although Nietzsche acknowledged him as one of the great moralists of antiquity, whose quiet slave nobility compared favorably with Christian slave morality. More recently Epictetus has benefited from a renewed scholarly interest in Hellenistic philosophy.

BIBL.: Gerard Boter, *The Encheiridion of Epictetus and Its Three Christian Adaptations* (Leiden 1999). A. A. Long, *Epictetus* (Oxford 2002) esp. 259–274. John Sellars, *Stoicism* (Berkeley 2006) esp. 135–157. Michel Spanneut, *Permanence du Stoïcisme* (Gembloux 1973).

J.SE.

Epicurus and Epicureanism

"Empty are the words of the philosopher who does not heal the suffering of man." As a pointer to the central concern of the Epicurean School, these words of its founder, Epicurus (341–270 BCE), serve as well as any. For while Epicurean teaching embraced all the established branches of philosophy, these were regarded as important only to the extent that they contributed to removing the obstacles standing in the way of personal happiness. In placing the needs of the individual front and center, Epicurus was at one with a general tendency at the close of the 4th century BCE to elevate the importance of private over public or corporate experience.

According to Epicurus, what stood most in the way of happiness was a nagging anxiety about the role of the gods in human affairs and a morbid fear of dying and punishment after death. The goal of Epicurean teaching was to liberate the individual from these concerns by fostering a true understanding of the natural origin and workings of the physical world and a proper appreciation of the nature of the human soul. Far from being the product of divine creation, the universe was formed through the chance combination of atomic particles. The gods, themselves atomic in structure, inhabit their own distinct realm, intent only on enjoying a truly "Epicurean" existence, unconcerned with and unmoved by the actions of humans. Death is nothing more than the scattering of that aggregate of extremely subtle atoms that we call the "soul" and which forms the seat of all consciousness. When these "soul" atoms are dispersed from their functional setting on the dissolution of the body, all present and future sensation is precluded. Once liberated from anxiety about the gods and about death, the individual is free to pursue a daily existence that affords the maximum degree of happiness—by cultivating friendships, by enjoying moderate pleasures, by maintaining a healthy regimen, and by avoiding all kinds of stressful activity.

To reduce Epicurean teaching to these fundamentals is to set aside a good deal of serious philosophical speculation in the areas of epistemology, psychology, physiology, the development of civilization, and others—speculation that both sparked controversy and elicited agreement during later periods. It is not a complete distortion, however. We may assume that what most appealed to Epicurus' immediate audience was not the philosophical niceties, important though they might be, but the simple prospect of a happy and carefree life.

From the beginning Epicurean teaching fired the popular imagination. Aided by the fact that its essentials were conveyed in the form of sayings both easy to memorize and convenient to transmit by word of mouth, it spread rapidly beyond the frontiers of Athens and the Greek mainland, gaining large numbers of converts in various places around the fringes of the Mediterranean world. By the first century BCE it had also gained a strong foothold in Italy, where the Roman poet Lucretius' *De rerum natura* (*On the Nature of the Universe*) provided the most comprehensive presentation of Epicurean philosophy since the founding of the school. Indeed, about the middle of the first century BCE the Roman orator and statesman Cicero, no admirer of Epicurean doctrines, declared that "the Epicureans have taken Italy by storm."

From this high point the popularity of Epicureanism

began to wane in the face of the growing strength of Stoicism, whose teachings were more in tune with traditional Roman values, as well as the spread of a popular movement that would eventually leave all the Greek philosophical schools in its wake: Christianity. Nonetheless, Epicureanism did continue to attract followers well into the imperial era (a lengthy inscription from Oenoanda in Asia Minor, ca. 200 CE, is eloquent witness), and the parent school at Athens remained open in the 3rd century when the other schools had closed. It was not until the beginning of the 5th century that Augustine could declare with only a little exaggeration that "its ashes are so cold that not a single spark can be struck from them."

However, by singling out Epicureanism Augustine emphasized the fact that of all the pagan creeds it was Epicureanism whose tenets stood most at variance with the fundamentals of Christian doctrine. After all, it postulated a material and mechanistic world whose origin and operation owe nothing to divine participation; it denied the gods a providential role in human affairs; it preached the mortality of the soul and the finality of death; and it advocated pleasure as the first goal of human existence. None of these positions escaped criticism from a long line of Christian apologists, including Justin Martyr and Athenagoras in the 2nd century, Tertullian and Clement in the 3rd, Arnobius and Lactantius in the 4th, and Jerome and Augustine in the 5th.

The fortunes of Epicureanism during the late antique and medieval periods are closely bound to the fortunes of antique culture generally. Some pagan writers, Plato and Aristotle in particular, enjoyed special status because they could be readily accommodated to Christian teaching. Epicurus' doctrines were the least adaptable to the Christian worldview. Hence, though knowledge of Epicurean teaching was possible through Lucretius' poem, which circulated in Germany in the 9th century and in France during the 12th, through Lucretian quotations in the standard Latin grammars of Probus, Nonius Marcellus, and Priscian, in florilegia, and in such encyclopedic works as Isidore of Seville's *Etymologies* (7th cent.) and Hrabanus Maurus' *De universo* (*On the Universe,* 9th cent.), there is no trace of any systematic study or comprehension of Epicurean philosophy as a whole.

If the role Epicurus played during this period was a decidedly minor one compared with other ancient writers, it did enjoy the distinction of being a double one: the Middle Ages knew not one Epicurus, but two. The first was the Epicurus who is found in the sources we have mentioned, Epicurus *philosophus* ("the philosopher"), proponent of a mechanistic universe and advocate of a corpuscular theory of matter. The second is the Epicurus of the popular imagination, gatekeeper of the *hortus deliciarum* ("garden of delights") and proprietor of the kitchen, the tavern, and the brothel. It is this Epicurus who plays cameo roles in notable works from Martianus Capella's *Marriage of Mercury and Philology* (5th cent.) to John of Salisbury's *Policraticus* (1159) and, in vernacular literatures, in John Gower's *Mirour de l'omme,* the songs of the *vagantes,* and Chaucer's *Canterbury Tales.*

Toward the close of the medieval period Epicurus also features in the Sixth Circle of Dante's *Inferno,* consigned to eternal punishment for believing that the soul perishes with the body. This entombment proved to be short-lived. In 1417 the manuscript hunter Poggio Bracciolini rescued from a monastery near Lake Constance a manuscript of Lucretius' *De rerum natura.* This discovery was greeted with excitement. At the very time when Italian Humanists were eager to expand their knowledge of the classical authors, the manuscript placed in their hands the most comprehensive Latin account of Epicurean teaching. But the influence of this find was not immediate. The copying process was slow, and the first extended Humanist treatment of Epicureanism, Lorenzo Valla's *De voluptate* (*On Pleasure*) of 1431, was written without reference to Lucretius' poem. It did, however, render to Epicureanism an important service. In structuring his examination of the nature of the highest good as a discussion among Christian, Stoic, and Epicurean spokesmen, Valla validated the place of Epicureanism in Humanist debate.

Valla's treatise cannot be taken as an endorsement of Epicurean views without serious misreading. Nor does Epicurean teaching receive a clear endorsement from any of the early Quattrocento Humanists. The most that can be said is that in the writings of Francesco Zabarella, Francesco Filelfo, Cristoforo Landino, and Leonardo Bruni we do find a more discriminating appraisal of Epicurean doctrine and a relaxing of the traditional prejudice against the person of Epicurus himself. Yet despite these encouraging signs, Epicureanism by no means shed its popular image of a philosophy that promoted unconditional surrender to sensual pleasures. When Giovan Battista Buoninsegni reported that "the Epicurean sect is growing daily," he was referring not to any dramatic shift in philosophical allegiance but simply to a trend in contemporary Italian society toward a life of indulgence. Indeed, it is fair to say that the general identification of Epicureanism with extreme hedonism was sufficient to discourage the orthodox from too open an interest in its teachings. The Italian fortunes of Lucretius' *De rerum natura* would seem to reflect this. Although 31 printings of the poem appeared between the *editio princeps* of 1473 and the end of the 16th century, only six of these were products of Italian presses, and there was no Italian printing at all between the second Aldine edition of 1515 and the Nardi edition at Florence in 1647. In short, we cannot truly speak of an Epicurean renaissance in Italy during the 15th and 16th centuries.

The same must be said for other parts of Europe. In England knowledge of some features of Epicurean teaching had filtered through, but for the most part the Epicurus most familiar to the general public was Epicurus the champion of sensual living. Nor did Epicureanism make any greater headway in France during the 16th century, even though Lucretius' poem was made available to the reading public in a variety of editions. *De rerum natura* was visited by representatives of *poésie scientifique,* but it was not their major source. Lucretius the artist was admired by poets, notably by members of the Pléiade, but he did not come close to rivaling Virgil, Horace, and Ovid as the Latin favorite. Writers of liberal temperament who might be expected to have been drawn to Lucretius' rationalism ignored him almost completely. His name appears just once, for example, in the writings of Étienne Dolet, and not at all in Rabelais. The one exception is Michel de Montaigne: no fewer than 450 lines from *De rerum natura* are cited in his *Essais*. Yet even Montaigne's admiration is reserved for Lucretius' poetic talents rather than his Epicurean message. Indeed, there are few aspects of Epicurean teaching that Montaigne does not soundly reject. Ultimately, in Germany and the Low Countries and especially in the context of the theological debate between Luther and Erasmus, the designation Epicurean was reduced once again to a *Schimpfwort,* a term of abuse to be hurled back and forth between opponents.

If during the 15th and 16th centuries Epicurean philosophy properly understood commanded only modest attention, in the 17th century its fortunes took a decidedly upward turn. The revival centered in France and was due in largest measure to the philosopher and scientist Pierre Gassendi. Initially, his promotion of Epicurean philosophy was motivated by strategic concerns, as part of a campaign to dislodge Aristotelianism from its position of authority. His first salvo against the enemy, book 1 of his *Exercitationes adversus Aristoteleos* (*Critiques of the Aristotelians*, 1624), was a frontal attack. By 1630 he had adopted a different approach, promoting the cause of a rival system. From this point onward he would no longer be simply an opponent of Aristotle; he would be the champion of Epicurus. It was a role that consumed his energies until his death in 1655. His work as an Epicurean commentator was painstakingly slow, revision following revision, and it was not until 1647 that the first installment of his *grand dessein* saw the light: *De vita et moribus Epicuri* (*On the Life and Morals of Epicurus*), a spirited defense of Epicurus against his detractors. This was followed in 1649 by his commentary on book 10 of Diogenes Laertius. His final grand synthesis of Epicurean doctrine, *Syntagma philosophicum* (*Philosophical Compendium*), was still in preparation at his death and was left to his editors to complete.

Gassendi was sufficiently astute to recognize that Epicureanism could not be revived without modification. He readily exposed and condemned features that were patently at variance with Christian teaching, replacing the notion, for example, that atoms are uncreated, eternal, and infinite in number and variety with the view that in the act of Creation, God brought atoms into being in sufficient number and variety to perform the motions necessary for the formation of the phenomenal world. By thus making God an efficient cause, Gassendi was able to satisfy the demands of orthodoxy. That his Epicurean commentary escaped the Church's *Index librorum prohibitorum* (*Index of Prohibited Books*) is a measure of his success in purging Epicurean doctrine of offending elements. In the process, however, Epicureanism underwent a radical sea change. From a purely materialist and mechanistic system it was transformed into one in which the immaterial is preserved and God placed at the very center.

Although Gassendi's ultimate synthesis of Epicurean teaching, finally published in 1658, was a lumbering work, his "purified" version came to exert considerable influence, especially in English scientific circles. In 1656 the diarist John Evelyn could fairly say that "little of the Epicurean philosophy was then known amongst us," even though the first half of the century had witnessed a lively interest in atomism on the part of members of the Northumberland Circle in the early decades and members of the Newcastle Circle in the 1640s. For those scientific theorists and experimenters, atomism on the Epicurean model was simply a starting point for their own idiosyncratic variations on the corpuscular theme, and their interest in it did not translate into a philosophical commitment to Epicureanism generally. And one has only to hear *De rerum natura*'s first English translator, Lucy Hutchinson, railing in 1635 against the "lunatic dog" Lucretius and his master's "ridiculous, impious, execrable doctrines" to be reminded that to the orthodox, Epicureanism was still a suspect creed.

What Epicureanism needed if it was to take hold in England was the support of someone of standing whose orthodoxy was beyond question, in short, a *Gassendi anglais*. This Epicurean benefactor materialized in the person of the respectable Dr. Walter Charleton, graduate of Magdalen Hall, Oxford, physician-in-ordinary to Charles I and future fellow of the Royal Society and the Royal College of Physicians. His first "Epicurean" publication, *The Darkness of Atheism Dispelled by the Light of Nature* (1652), set the stage for his promotional program by advertising that it was the "new" atomism that he was advocating, a point emphasized by the very title of his second publication: *Physiologia Epicuro-Gassendo-Charletoniana, or A Fabrick of Science Natural, upon a Hypothesis of Atoms, Founded by Epicurus, Repaired by Petrus Gassendus, and Augmented by Walter Charleton* (1654). The result of Charleton's efforts in behalf of Epicurean philosophy, and of his *Epicurus' Morals* of 1658, was twofold: it offered the English public ready access to ample detail concerning Epicurean physical and ethical theory, and it went some way toward assuring the orthodox that in its new guise Epicurean philosophy no longer posed a threat to Christian beliefs.

Much remained to be done, however, before the corpuscular hypothesis could gain the allegiance of the scientific community as a credible alternative to Aristotelian science. This work fell largely to the early members of the Royal Society, which was chartered in 1662. The task of answering the continuing theological objections of such opponents as Richard Baxter and Méric Casaubon was taken on by Thomas Sprat and Joseph Glanvill. As to demonstrating the usefulness of the corpuscular hypothesis, this was for the most part the goal of the Society's most active supporter of the new science, Robert Boyle, in such works as *The Origins of Forms and Qualities* (1666),

Experiments, Notes, etc. about the Mechanical Origin and Production of Divers Particular Qualities (1675), and *Of the Excellency and Grounds of the Mechanical Hypothesis* (1674). By the end of the 17th century the "atomical philosophy," as Boyle termed it, was generally taken to be the most fruitful starting point for the explanation of the physical world. Such had been the alterations and additions, however, that Epicurus was no longer recognizable as its first parent.

Tracing the fortunes of Epicureanism up to the beginning of the 18th century reveals the same cluster of associations eliciting repeated and ambivalent comment, and the interval from then to the present shows little modification of the pattern. In the area of moral philosophy, for example, in 1819 Thomas Jefferson could declare in the spirit of the Enlightenment, "I too am an Epicurean. I consider the genuine (not the imputed) doctrines of Epicurus as containing everything rational in moral philosophy which Greece and Rome have left us." But it was Bishop Joseph Butler's anti-Epicurean stance in his *Fifteen Sermons Preached at the Rolls Chapel* (1726) and in his *Analogy of Religion* (1736) that set the tone for the orthodox Christian attitude toward Epicurean ethics throughout the 18th and 19th centuries.

Meanwhile, Epicurus' primary spokesman, Lucretius, was largely ignored by the translators. It was not until 1650, with the French translation by Michel de Marolles, that he appeared in any language other than his own. And only three French translations ensued before the beginning of the 18th century. It was 1717 before Lucretius appeared in Italian dress, and German readers were kept waiting until 1788. *De rerum natura* did fare a little better in England. The diarist John Evelyn translated the first book of the poem into heroic couplets in 1656; the poet laureate John Dryden turned a few of his favorite Lucretian passages into verse in 1685; and Thomas Creech's complete verse translation of 1682 was a resounding success. The 18th century produced but two English translations (both anonymous) and the 19th century only six, one of these being the first American translation, by Charles Frederick Johnson, published in 1872.

In only a few areas do we meet a change in tone that is indicative of a more positive attitude toward Epicurean teaching generally, as we approach the modern era. One relates to the traditional association of Epicureanism with gluttony. It is an association that was as strong in the Middle Ages as it was in antiquity. But from around the middle of the 17th century there emerged a characterization much closer to the modern connotation of the word "epicure": not the unrestrained and indiscriminate devourer of food and drink, but rather one who cultivates a refined taste for the pleasures of the table. Thus, in his *Prototypes* of 1646 William Whately says, "such an epicure was Potiphar—to please his tooth and pamper his flesh with delicacies."

Another area of appreciative interest has to do with Epicurean praise of the unnoticed life. One of the charges that Cicero leveled against Epicurean philosophy was that it did harm to Rome by discouraging individuals of talent from devoting themselves to serving the state, a criticism voiced in later periods as well. In 1685 the English "Epicurean" Sir William Temple signaled a very different attitude by abandoning a promising early diplomatic career and retiring to his garden at Moor Park in Surrey, there to devote himself to writing moral essays (including "Upon the Gardens of Epicurus") and raising apricots. This was the same year in which Dryden translated the celebrated Lucretian lines that open book 2 of *De natura rerum:* "'Tis pleasant, safely to behold from shore/The rowling Ship, and hear the Tempest roar." In Temple's deliberate withdrawal from the active life can be seen the beginning of a more ready enjoyment of what Tennyson in his "Lucretius" of 1868 hails as "the sober majesties/of settled, sweet, Epicurean life" and an adumbration of the self-conscious quietism of Walter Pater and his fellow Victorian aesthetes.

A third area of increased positive attention is in epistemology, where through the agency of John Locke, influenced by Gassendi, that part of Epicurean canonics that insists on the primacy of sensation in the formation of ideas played an influential role in the development of British empiricism. Similarly, albeit in a less direct way, the Epicurean promotion of happiness as the chief end of living provided support for the Utilitarian movement in the 19th century.

What of Epicureanism at the beginning of the 21st century? As long as individuals are intent on attaining personal happiness, as long as the prospect of death instills fear, as long as there is an urge to escape the demands of a busy world, and as long as there is debate about the origins of the cosmos, it would be surprising if the basic teachings of Epicurus did not still exercise some appeal. How to gauge the breadth of that appeal is problematic. If it were a matter of academic interest in Epicurean philosophy, the answer would lie in the number of monographs, articles, conference papers, and abstracts devoted to the subject, which reveals that Epicureanism, along with the other Hellenistic schools, has been in vogue in recent years. In the matter of texts alone, promising new materials have come to light from the renewed excavations at Herculaneum, where the library of the first-century BCE Epicurean philosopher and teacher Philodemus of Gadara was discovered between 1750 and 1765 (during excavations sponsored by the Bourbon king Charles III of Naples), as well as from the ongoing work of scholars involved in the Philodemus Translation Project, funded by the U.S. National Endowment for the Humanities, and of members of the Centro per lo Studio dei Papiri Ercolanesi at Naples. Personal interest in Epicurus and his philosophy is another matter, more difficult to assess. But a starting point, at least, can be found in what has become a rough measure of the preoccupations of the popular mind: the World Wide Web. If we carry out a Google search, ignoring the academic and commercial stopping places, we discover a level of interest in things Epicurean that appears to be considerable. Indeed, in terms of numbers, Google fetches up 1.2 million sites that are devoted to or make reference to Epicurus or Epicureanism. What does this absolute number say about Epicurus' contemporary appeal? Relative numbers are possibly more instructive: Stoicism, Epicureanism's traditional rival, comes in at just under 2.0 million, Aristotle at 13.3 million, and Plato at 14.2 million.

BIBL.: J. Annas, *The Morality of Happiness* (Oxford 1993). G. Arrighetti, ed., *Epicuro: Opere* (Turin 1960, 2nd ed. 1973). C. B. Bailey, ed., *Epicurus: The Extant Remains* (Oxford 1926, repr. Hildesheim 1970). S. Fisher, *Gassendi's Philosophy and Science* (Leiden 2005). J. Gaskin, ed., *The Epicurean Philosophers* (London 1995). Dane R. Gordon and David B. Suits, eds., *Epicurus: His Continuing Influence and Contemporary Relevance* (Rochester, N.Y., 2003). B. Inwood and L. P. Gerson, eds., *The Epicurus Reader* (Indianapolis 1994). H. Jones, *The Epicurean Tradition* (London 1989) and *Pierre Gassendi: An Intellectual Biography* (Nieuwkoop 1980). A. A. Long and D. N. Sedley, *The Hellenistic Philosophers,* 2 vols. (Cambridge 1987). J. M. Rist, *Epicurus: An Introduction* (Cambridge 1972). M. A. Screech, *Montaigne's Annotated Copy of Lucretius: A Transcription and Study of the Manuscript, Notes and Pen-Marks* (Geneva 1998). Martin Ferguson Smith, ed., *The Epicurean Inscription: Diogenes of Oenoanda* (Naples 1993). Hermann Usener, *Epicurea* (Leipzig 1887, repr. Stuttgart 1966). J. Warren, *Facing Death: Epicurus and His Critics* (Oxford 2004).

H.J.

Epigram

The epigram (*epigramma,* or inscription) is a brief verse inscription or, more commonly, a poem written in an inscription's pithy style. Three major classical strands influenced the post-classical epigram. The Greek Anthology, composed of the Planudean Anthology, collected in 1301 and first published in Florence in 1494 and the major source of Greek epigram through the 18th century, and the Palatine Anthology, discovered in 1606/1607 and published near the end of the 18th century, includes Greek epigrams with highly diverse topics, tones, and meters (though elegiac couplets predominate), including panegyric, mournful, and comic epitaphs as well as erotic, descriptive, and admonitory epigrams. Writing in a variety of meters but again with the elegiac couplet predominating, the Latin epigrammatist Martial (ca. 40–103 CE) mixed conversational, sometimes obscene language and "pointed" antithetical rhetoric, often concluding with a witty surprise. In addition to comic epigrams on Roman social and sexual life, Martial wrote tender epitaphs (including some for beloved slaves) and sententious verse on contentment, friendship, and country life. The *Disticha Catonis,* probably dating from the 3rd century CE but often ascribed to Cato the Elder, provided moral advice in hexameter distichs.

Though the *Disticha* served as a Latin school text in the Middle Ages and the Renaissance, medieval epigrams were mainly indebted not to classical pagan authors directly but to early Christian epigrammatists (such as the 6th-century Venantius Fortunatus), who had themselves adapted classical forms and themes. Medieval epigrams occasionally echo Martial, but his work was largely known secondhand, from snippets in florilegia and encyclopedic works. In the first half of the 16th century, however, Humanist poets began translating and imitating Greek epigrams in Latin. Thomas More's representative 1518 collection of Latin epigrams includes many translations from the Planudean Anthology, including comic and satiric epigrams (on ugly women, tiny men, an astrologer) and sententious distichs on moderation and the inevitability of death. Somewhat later, vernacular poets also began translating and imitating Greek epigram (often by way of Humanist Latin versions). Cato's *Distichs* was also often translated and imitated in the vernaculars in the 16th and 17th centuries. After the 1501 Aldine edition of his *Epigrams,* Martial was often reprinted (though sometimes expurgated) in the 16th and 17th centuries. His panegyric epitaphs and comic and moralizing epigrams found a ready reception. Though imitators often toned down Martial's obscenity, some also imitated Martial's raciness in defiance of moralizing contemporaries. Vernacular short forms, such as sonnets and madrigals, were sometimes opposed to but often enriched by Greek epigrammatic motifs and Martial's antithetical wit.

English poets of the 1590s and early 1600s viewed themselves as Martial's heirs, turning his insulting distichs into heroic couplets: "I muse not your Dog turds oft doth eate,/To a tung that licks your lips, a turd's sweet meate" (Francis Davison, rendering *Epigrams* 1.83). John Harington's epigrams, posthumously published in 1615 and 1618, adapt Martial to contemporary (mainly court) life. Harington sometimes replicates Martial's terse antitheses, as in an epigram mocking a perfumed dandy (2.12): "Who smelleth ever well, smels never well." Hailed as Martial's heir and popular throughout learned Europe, the early 17th-century Welsh poet John Owen composed Latin epigrams in elegiac couplets (mainly distichs) with a witty concision indebted to the Roman poet. Owen's topics range from Martialesque humor (minus Martial's greatest obscenities) and satiric swipes at social types and sexual deviations to pithy admonitions concerning Christian doctrine, virtue, and vice. The 17th-century Spanish Baroque poets Francisco de Quevedo and Luis de Góngora composed Martialesque epigrams, and Martin Opitz's German epigrams imitated Martial (and Owen).

In the 17th century poets also mingled and played different epigrammatic strands against one another. Jonson's *Epigrammes* (1616) imitate Martial's antithetical wit and his moralizing vein but eschew the obscene and seek to condemn vice rather than poke fun. Though Martial rejected Cato the Censor as a suitable reader of his playful epigrams, Jonson declares his book suitable for "Cato," and his first epigram translates the conclusion of the moralizing *Disticha Catonis*'s preface. Robert Herrick in *Hesperides* (1648) includes some Martialesque comic epigrams and epitaphs on small or humble creatures (infants, a servant, a pet dog) that recall Martial's slave epitaphs, but he also writes moralizing distichs on contentment that echo the Greek Anthology and the *Disticha Catonis:* "Who with a little cannot be content,/Endures an everlasting punishment." Littleness is here both the medium and message.

The early 18th-century epigrammatist Antoine-Louis Le Brun, who translated Martial, also wrote urbane love epigrams in the Roman poet's spirit: "I don't play Tarquin [the rapist] with you/Don't play Lucrece [the chaste] with me." The ironic distance between modern epigrammatic mores and ancient legend recalls Martial's programmatic claim to write of humanity rather than myths (10.4). In the late 18th and the 19th century, however, taste shifted from Latin to Greek epigrams. The cult of rural retirement was expressed in inscriptions written on country bowers and other rural sites, evoking their charms with a brief simplicity. Such inscriptions recall the votive epigrams in the Greek Anthology describing objects and natural scenes, and they in turn inspired the nature poetry of William Wordsworth (e.g., "Lines Left upon a Seat in a Yew-Tree") and other Romantic poets. From the 19th century onward, the Greek epigram form was often "lyricized." Poets as different as Walter Savage Landor, Thomas Hardy, Edwin Arlington Robinson, and Walter de la Mare expanded Greek epigrammatic motifs through pathetic repetition and more emotional explicitness to create modern lyrics of feeling and self-revelation.

Poetic epitaphs alluding to the classical tradition remained a significant 20th-century genre. A. E. Housman, whose "For an Athlete Dying Young" (1896) recalls Greek epitaph's poignant brevity, composed a World War I epitaph that qualifies patriotic sentiment—like Simonides' in his famous epitaph on the Spartans who died at Thermopylae ("Go, stranger, tell the Spartans that here obedient to their laws we lie")—with understatement: "Life, to be sure, is nothing much to lose;/But young men think it is, and we were young." Transforming the common classical motif of the deceased's addressing the passerby with a self-identification designed to evoke admiration or pity, William Butler Yeats's final epitaph in "Under Ben Bulben" (1939), "Cast a cold eye/On life, on death./Horseman, pass by," substitutes an equestrian, evoking antiquated (Irish) nobility, for the classical pedestrian wayfarer and deploys classical pithiness to demand neither respect nor pity for the dead but heroic disdain for the merely mortal.

Some comic and ironic epigrams of the 20th century also draw from the Martial tradition. Hilaire Belloc's "When I am dead, I hope it may be said: 'His sins were scarlet, but his books were read' " playfully subverts Herrick's concluding lines in *Hesperides,* "To his Book's end this last line he'd have plac't,/*Jocond his Muse was; but his life was chast,*" which recall classical distinctions between poetry and life in Catullus, Ovid, and a programmatic Martial epigram (1.4.8). J. V. Cunningham, who translated Martial, writes epigrams with an ironic modern sensibility that reflects Martial's clear-eyed focus on the human rather than the mythological: "Jove courted Danäe with golden love,/But you're not Danäe, and I'm not Jove." The sententious advice found in all strands of the classical epigram also continues, but mainly in comic verse that tempers claims to wisdom with playfulness. Piet Hein's twenty volumes of epigrammatic verse, *Grooks* (published in Danish 1940–1963), which were popular and selectively translated into English in the countercultural 1960s, undercut their own didacticism: "Shun advice/At any price—/That's what I call/Good advice." More recently, Richard Wilbur delivers classical moral wisdom with humorous, disarming modesty: "The best thing's to avoid excess./Try to be temperate, more or less" (*More Opposites,* 1991).

BIBL.: Mary Thomas Crane, "*Intret Cato:* Authority and the Epigram in Sixteenth-century England," in *Renaissance Genres: Essays on Theory, History, and Interpretation,* ed. Barbara Kiefer Lewalski (Cambridge, Mass., 1986) 165–169. Geoffrey Hartman, "Wordsworth, Inscriptions, and Romantic Nature Poetry," in *Beyond Formalism: Literary Essays, 1958–1970* (New Haven 1970) 206–230. Henry Hoyt Hudson, *The Epigram in the English Renaissance* (Princeton 1947). James Hutton, *The Greek Anthology in France and in the Latin Writers of the Netherlands* (Ithaca 1946) and *The Greek Anthology in Italy to the Year 1800* (Ithaca 1935). T. K. Whipple, *Martial and the English Epigram* (Berkeley 1925).

J.S.

Epigraphy

Epigraphy is the study of texts written on durable materials, such as bronze, glass, and stone, with the exceptions of coins and gems, which have their own separate fields. Greeks, Romans, and those who fell under their sway avidly produced such inscribed objects, and although the vast majority of their output was reused or destroyed, thousands of examples have survived. They run from artists' signatures to records of decisions and laws, calendars to milestones, monuments for the living and the dead to name tags. From the Renaissance onward, they have fascinated classical scholars, who have collected, classified, and imitated inscriptions and used them as a means of understanding the ancient world.

Greek and Roman authors mention inscribed monuments, but rarely and usually in little detail. There are isolated examples of individuals in the medieval period referring to classical inscriptions, or copying them down, but it is only with the first stirrings of Humanism in Italy that we start to see a deeper interest in particular examples. In the early 15th century Poggio Bracciolini made a collection of inscriptions at Rome, which he used to identify particular buildings; his contemporary Cyriac of Ancona recorded examples across the Italian peninsula, but he also ventured eastward, along the Mediterranean trade routes, and brought back examples of Greek inscriptions. By the second half of the 15th century, scholars such as Felice Feliciano (who accompanied the painter Andrea Mantegna on an expedition to collect inscriptions around Lake Garda) and, most famous of all, Giovanni Giocondo could muster thousands of epigraphic records, taken either from inscribed monuments that they had seen or from existing sylloges (the term used for a collection of records) like those of Cyriac.

Classical scholars have continued to collect epigraphic material since. In the 16th century, as the collecting habit spread across central and western Europe, they started to think about classifying, editing, and representing what they had found. They experimented with arrangements by the contents of the inscription rather than where they were found—ordering them, for example, according to a particular emperor or deity—and worked out ways of representing letters that were unclear or that had been deliberately erased, and of showing broken monuments. They also were careful to reveal their source for individual examples, whether they had seen them in person or their information came from a correspondent or previous collection. The most visible example of their collective reach is the *Inscriptiones antiquae totius orbis Romanae,* edited primarily by a Low Countries Humanist, Jan Gruter, and printed in 1602–1603. The work included more than 12,000 inscriptions from 100 correspondents and sources. As the title of the work suggests, Gruter tried to cover the whole Roman world; in practice, however, scholars had limited access to Northern Africa and the areas of the Roman eastern provinces, and as a consequence they knew of relatively few inscriptions in Greek. Only in the late 17th century did that situation start to change, as a series of Western explorers started to gather material on the Greek peninsula and beyond. In the 19th century three great multivolume projects to survey all Greek and Roman inscriptions were initiated under the aegis of the Berlin Academy. Even before the index to the first, the *Corpus inscriptionum graecarum (CIG),* appeared, in 1877, the work was clearly outdated and was replaced by the *Inscriptiones graecae (IG),* of which Ulrich von Wilamowitz-Moellendorff became the director in 1902. For Latin inscriptions, Theodor Mommsen began the *Corpus inscriptionum latinarum (CIL)* in 1853. Members of the Berlin Academy continue to supervise revisions and supplements to *IG* and *CIL* today, and together the corpora represent two of the great achievements of modern classical scholarship.

Interpreters of the classical heritage have put inscriptions to a wide variety of purposes, and in many cases 15th- and 16th-century scholars paved the way. Roman inscriptions in particular have provided a model for the form and content of subsequent dedications and public records. Many Humanists advocated adapting Roman lettering as well as the ideas and style of Roman authors: Leon Battista Alberti, for example, advocated the use of classicizing inscriptions and included them in his design of the Malatesta Temple in Rimini. Feliciano created a pattern book demonstrating how to create epigraphic capitals, and in various works, such as the frescoes in the Church of the Eremitani at Padua, Mantegna showed how an artist might follow Feliciano's suggestions. Renaissance calligraphers adapted Roman capitals for their manuscripts, and they were mimicked in this, as in much else, by early printers. Many subsequent font designers have explicitly followed classical models.

Early Humanists also began to ask what the contents of inscriptions could reveal about the ancient world. They began by exploiting inscriptions as evidence for classical spelling. Inscriptions offered a route to ancient orthography unmediated by the incompetence and ignorance of medieval copyists, and they soon became a tool in the repertoire of any self-respecting textual critic. Legal scholars and historians of the late 15th century also started to ask what inscriptions could reveal about the institutions of the ancient world: unlike modern examples, ancient Roman funerary monuments tended to reveal full details of the deceased's public career, as did dedications to living patrons, and so both types of inscription reveal a lot about the structure of the Roman empire and its officers. But Roman inscriptions tended to employ abbreviations and formulae; to interpret these, scholars copied and expanded a guide that was attributed to the classical grammarian Marcus Valerius Probus, the manuscript of which Poggio had discovered in 1417. Once they were confident of the meaning of a particular set of letters, they were able to rely on the thematic organization of inscription collections to demonstrate the variety and spread of various aspects of Roman life, including many details that were not to be found in any other source. The work of these Renaissance scholars laid the foundations for the subsequent exploitation of inscriptions.

Beyond illuminating inscriptions, the insights of these epigraphers had a wider intellectual influence. Their research revealed that the interpretation of evidence from the ancient world was not simply a case of reading texts and taking them at face value. Studies of orthography turned up a variety of ways of spelling particular words. One explanation for these discrepancies was the historical development of classical languages; another, more problematic, was the potential fallibility of author or carver. From a historical point of view, inscriptions could challenge the evidence of classical authors. The most celebrated example was the difference between the chronology of the Capitoline Fasti (which included a list of the holders of annual consulships of the Roman Republic) and that of the historian Livy: 16th-century historians tended to prefer the former. And, perhaps most threatening of all, forgeries as well as imitations circulated freely, and they were known to do so, putting epigraphers on their mettle. Inscriptions, therefore, provoked comparative source criticism.

The scholars who looked at inscribed monuments also realized that there was more to them than simply a text. They saw that the actual shape and style of letters changed over time, and so, therefore, they could provide dates for inscriptions that did not contain any other chronological reference. Epigraphers had to become connoisseurs of style. They also saw that the decoration and form of the monument on which the inscription appeared could contribute to its interpretation: gravestones, say, could include representations of the deceased, or give some idea of the tools of his trade. These developments helped pave the way to the exploitation of nontextual evidence by historians of all periods. The limitations imposed, however, by the printing process—publishers from Gruter's to those of the *CIL* volumes have tended to exclude hundreds of expensive engravings or photographs, and have preferred straightforward text and maybe a description of the inscription's setting—have prevented armchair epigraphers from using the evidence of the inscribed monument as a whole.

Comprehensive manuals outlining epigraphic techniques have tended to lag behind the work of individuals in practice. Antonio Agustín's 1587 *Dialogos de medallas, inscriciones y otras antiguedades* was devoted mainly to coins, and it is only with Scipione Maffei's *Ars critica lapidaria,* first published in 1765, that a ready guide to the study of inscriptions became available. This delay occurred largely because narrative historians of antiquity did not see how to incorporate material evidence in their work. In the later 18th century, and then especially with the emergence of *CIL* and *IG,* that situation changed, and in the 20th century it was widely recognized that inscriptions were a vital resource for any historian of classical antiquity.

BIBL.: Wilhelm Larfeld, *Griechische epigraphik,* 3rd ed. (Munich 1914) 7–105. Ida Calabi Limentani, *Epigrafia latina,* 4th ed. (Milan 1991) 39–124. Armando Petrucci, *Public Lettering: Script, Power, and Culture* (Chicago 1993). William Stenhouse, *Reading Inscriptions, Writing Ancient History: Historical Scholarship in the Late Renaissance* (London 2005). W.S.

Epistolography. *See* Letters and Epistolography.

Erasmus, Desiderius

Dutch Humanist, scholar, and author (1466 or 1469–1536). Born in Rotterdam but determined to become a "citizen of the world," Erasmus earned that citizenship and with it a reputation as the chief intellectual of the European Renaissance. During three and a half decades he wrote as a scholar, advocate, and popularizer of ancient Greek and Latin. While focusing on the languages and literature of antiquity, however, he avoided the calling of the antiquarian, instead regarding the activity of reading the ancients, including the early Christians, as part of a fuller program of living the philosophy of Christ.

Erasmus was schooled too far to the north—at Deventer, then at Steyn, and finally at Paris—to benefit from the latest educational reforms in Italy that featured the classical tradition. As a teenager and a young man, he had to introduce himself to the new curriculum of Latin poets, orators, historians, and philosophers recently made available to larger audiences through the infant technology of printing. On more than one occasion he recalled in letters to friends the powerful early impression that these classical authors made on him, the contempt he felt, under their spell, for the literary deficiencies of more recent, especially Scholastic writing, and his growing sense of personal mission to bring Humanistic studies to Northern Europe (*Epistles* 152, 1110, 1183).

But returning to classical Latin was not enough. "For whereas we Latins have a few small streams, a few muddy pools," he pronounced with the overstatement of the enthusiast, "the Greeks possess crystal-clear springs and rivers that run with gold" (*Ep.* 149). Consequently, after repeated failures to find a suitable teacher, Erasmus undertook (when he was about 30) to teach himself Greek. From this undertaking came a few of his earliest publications and the start of an accomplished and eventually controversial career as a translator. "There is," he insisted, "no more daring feat than to try to make good Latin out of good Greek" (*Ep.* 197). In keeping with the translation theory of the Italian Humanists, Erasmus followed Ciceronian method in safeguarding the sense of the original at the expense of strict literality, even though he admitted to striving for greater accuracy.

In 1506 in Paris Erasmus published translations from two Greek authors: a couple of plays by Euripides and some dialogues by Lucian (in collaboration with his dear friend Thomas More). In 1514 in Basel he followed with selected essays from Plutarch's *Moralia.* This publication launched Erasmus' long and productive partnership with Johann Froben, whose plans for his printing house conveniently coincided with Erasmus' mission regarding the classics. (Before Froben, Erasmus had collaborated successfully with the other major publisher of ancient, especially Greek texts, Aldus Manutius.)

Over time, with all the energy of a missionary, Erasmus added Isocrates (1516), Galen (1526), and Xenophon (1530) to his list of published translations. But because "we can do nothing in any field of literature without a knowledge of Greek" and because "it is one thing to guess, another to judge; one thing to trust your own eyes, and another again to trust those of others" (*Ep.* 181), Erasmus also translated the best of the Greek grammars, that of the émigré Theodore Gaza (1516, 1518), to assist those who might be inspired, as he had been, to drink on their own from the "crystal-clear springs." And to what Greek literature he neither edited nor translated, such as Aristotle (1531), Demosthenes (1532), and Ptolemy (1533), he lent high-profile prefaces designed to increase sales and broaden readership. If at the turn of the century he had lamented the sorry state of Greek studies in Northern Europe, a generation later—and with no small thanks to his own efforts—he could "see Greek coming to life again everywhere" (*Ep.* 428).

Totally immersed after 1500 in reading, translating, and publishing Greek literature, Erasmus continued his scholarship on his favorite Latin authors. In 1501 he produced his first Latin edition, Cicero's *De officiis* (*On Du-*

ties), which he reedited in 1520. In 1515 and again, more carefully, in 1529, he joined with Froben to bring out his editions of Seneca. In these and other editorial efforts, Erasmus furthered the scholarly practices of his Italian predecessors, especially Lorenzo Valla. Very early in his career (1489) Erasmus prepared an epitome of Valla's groundbreaking study of the Roman language, which he later paraphrased. In 1504–1505 he found and saw through publication Valla's controversial notes on the New Testament. Under the influence of Italian scholarship, including Valla's, he advocated collating available manuscripts and grounding editorial conjectures on the elements of a writer's style. Even faulty manuscripts, he insisted, could provide valuable clues to an emended reading. In the interest of emendation, he pioneered a principle, still in use today, that directs the editor to prefer the more obscure reading (the *difficilior lectio*) on the grounds that it is less likely to represent a scribal alteration. In addition he inaugurated the practice in his own editions of separating out attributed works that he considered spurious.

In the meantime, Erasmus was also revolutionizing the training of young writers of classical Latin with a number of his most highly acclaimed works. Some of these, including *De ratione studii* (*On the Method of Study*) and *De recta pronuntiatione* (*The Right Way of Speaking Latin and Greek*), served as teaching manuals. Together they set the course in Northern Europe for what to teach, how to teach it, and even how to pronounce it. Other works were intended as aids for the student: among these, *De conscribendis epistolis* (*On the Writing of Letters*) and *De duplici copia verborum ac rerum* (*Copia: Foundations of Abundant Style*) were bestsellers and became standard textbooks, used widely by beginning and advanced students alike in the schools all over Europe dedicated to the revival of classical learning. No less successful were two other works designed as reading and writing aids: the *Adagiorum chiliades,* or *Adages,* a vast collection of more than 4,000 Greek and Latin proverbs that introduced its readers to the wisdom of the ancients, and the *Colloquies,* a collection of brief dialogues, often satiric in tone, at once illustrating good spoken (that is, Classical) Latin and exhorting good Christian living.

Although designed principally for pedagogy, these hugely popular works also served Erasmus' polemical aims. Targeting "prospective readers . . . who dislike the current jargon and are searching for greater elegance and a more refined style" (*Ep.* 126), they made the case for the ancients over the moderns. For guidance on method they recommended Aristotle, Cicero, and Quintilian. For stylistic models they featured Cicero, without taking the part of the more inflexible Ciceronians of the day (discussed below), who excluded altogether other writers of distinction. Indeed, Erasmus' own Latin style, a model throughout the next century for other writers not only in Latin but also in the vernaculars, intentionally avoided the flourishes of Ciceronian phrasing in favor of a more colloquial, appropriately Christian expression. Erasmus himself characterized this preferred style as "more genuine, more concise, more forceful, less ornate, and more masculine" (*Ep.* 1885). On both his own report and that of others, Erasmian Latin achieved distinction without the high polish of the Ciceronian.

But not all distinguished writing—not even all distinguished ancient writing—was suitable for teaching. "The Book of Psalms may be more holy than the Odes of Horace," argues one of the two principal interlocutors in Erasmus' dialogue on speaking proper Latin and Greek, "but for all that Horace is better to learn Latin from." Offered here as pedagogical advice, this comparison between the Horatian ode and the Hebrew psalm in the Vulgate's Latin signals Erasmus' investment in another major issue dividing Humanists of the 16th century: the relation between classical and Christian literature. (Unable to make much progress in Hebrew, Erasmus tended to exclude this ancient language from his discussions, sometimes even derogating both its literature and the "Pharisaical" types who read it.)

Taking on a religious establishment committed to the view that "the whole business of classical languages and the humanities . . . are the springs from which heresies flow" (*Ep.* 948), Erasmus rarely missed an opportunity to advance a position to the contrary. Throughout his writings, educational and otherwise, he did not merely encourage the good Christian's familiarity with the ancient world, he insisted on it. He believed that understanding the New Testament as the cornerstone of Christianity depended on an understanding of both ancient Greek and the cultures in which it flourished (*Ep.* 108, 149). To this end, he considered the writers of pagan Greece and Rome indispensable.

Thus in sacred no less than in secular literature Erasmus championed the priority of the original, the *fons et origo*. Indeed, his own motivation to master a difficult ancient language at a relatively late age was grounded in an intense desire not only to read for himself the words of Scripture as they were actually written but also, through his experience as editor, interpreter, and translator, to share his scriptural as well as his classical readings with the rest of Europe. He feared that the academic theology of the experts had become "too deeply sunk in the quibbling discussion of worthless minor problems" and needed to be recalled "to its sources" (*Ep.* 1183). Meanwhile, the general population, ignorant of Latin as well as Greek, was utterly denied access to the very texts that structured their lives and shaped their beliefs.

Addressing this ignorance head-on in *Paraclesis* (1516), a manifesto of popular religion appended to his first edition of the New Testament, Erasmus wondered pointedly if "he [could be] a theologian, let alone a Christian, who has not read the book of Christ?" As early as 1506, in fact, he had turned his attention to the scholarly project that would over the course of the rest of his life generate multiple editions of the New Testament (1516, 1519, 1522,

1527, 1535), including translation and annotations, as well as a running commentary in narrative form intended for easier reading, the so-called *Paraphrases* (1517–1524). All together this scholarly output, despite being written in Latin, supported a populist's vision of spirituality expressed most forcefully in the *Paraclesis:* a Christendom in which all men, women, and children go about their daily occupations reciting the words of a vernacular Scripture that they both comprehend fully and love wholeheartedly.

By his own account the centerpiece of his intellectual career, Erasmus' biblical scholarship, clearly modeled on his classical scholarship, plunged him into controversies with divines on both sides of the theological divide, from which he never disengaged. Although criticized and ultimately condemned by both parties, Erasmus nevertheless found confirmation for his views in the earliest Fathers of the Church, including Jerome, Augustine, Origen, Basil, and John Chrysostom, who, he assured his critics, not only were deeply learned in Greek and Latin literature but also recognized their debt to its cultural and linguistic richness.

In *The Antibarbarians* (1520), Erasmus' most extensive and outspoken defense of the classical tradition in the form of a dialogue, the principal spokesman, Jacob Batt, invokes the authority of Jerome and Augustine to justify "transfer[ring] heathen literature to the adornment of our faith." Passing lightly over the sensitive issue of the salvation of select classical authors, Batt makes no bones about Christianity's debt to them, saved or otherwise. "[We] Christians have nothing," he claims, "that we have not inherited from the pagans." And in his religious writings he softened but by no means retracted this position.

A handbook for the Christian soul in its battle against temptation, the *Enchiridion* (1503) recommends studying the classical tradition as a preparation for studying Scripture. The best preparation, moreover, is Plato and his followers, "because in much of their thinking as well as in their mode of expression, they are the closest to the spirit of the prophets and the Gospel." Indeed, Scripture itself resembles the Silenus that Alcibiades compares to Socrates in Plato's *Symposium:* crude and even ridiculous on the outside, but on the inside inexpressibly deep and holy. It stands to reason, then, that the Church Fathers most able to understand the mysteries of Scripture were those trained to read Plato.

Like the *Enchiridion* in this regard, the *Paraclesis* issues a call to reading Scripture that features the commonalities between the word of God and the classics. After all, how different from the teachings of Socrates, Diogenes, and Epictetus is the philosophy of Christ? "If there are things that belong particularly to Christianity in these ancient writers," Erasmus proclaims, "let us follow them"—a proclamation that also echoes loudly throughout his educational works.

In both the introduction to the *Adages* and in some of the explanatory essays accompanying individual adages, including "Silenus of Alcibiades," Erasmus singles out Christ and Plato as the two undisputed masters of proverbial wisdom. In the colloquy entitled *Convivium religiosum* (*Godly Feast*), modeled on Plato's *Phaedrus,* the group of friends assembled for a communal meal and a reading of Scripture not only invokes the prayers of "Saint Socrates" but also speculates playfully on the sanctification of several other pagan authors, including Virgil, Horace, and Cicero. So moving are the philosophical works of the Roman orator that those assembled agree that they would rather lose the whole of Duns Scotus than even a single Ciceronian fragment. Included in this treasured corpus is Cicero's *On Duties,* which Erasmus, as noted above, edited twice. In the preface to his second edition he contrasts Cicero with the "modern authors of our own country" (*Ep.* 1013). Though reading them leaves him cold, reading Cicero "fires my whole self with a zeal for honor and virtue." Here as elsewhere Erasmus holds to the view that reading literature, whether classical or Christian, is an ethical activity that culminates in virtuous action.

Also here as elsewhere he summons an esteemed Church Father to bolster his cause. "Never before," he admits, "have I more clearly felt the truth of what Augustine writes: that the virtuous acts of pagans are a sharper spur toward goodness in ourselves than those of our own people, when we reflect what a disgrace it is that a heart illuminated by the light of the Gospel should not see what was seen clearly by them with only nature's candle to show them the way." For Erasmus, in other words, Christians hold no monopoly on good "Christian" living. A classical tradition that embraces such worthies as Plato and Cicero, Plutarch and Seneca, provides invaluable models not only for eloquent expression but also for ethical action. And Erasmus routinely observes just how many Church Fathers appreciated this value.

But these frequently invoked patristic authorities do more than testify to an antiquity worthy of attention and even emulation. Like the New Testament, they belong to this antiquity, requiring no less than Cicero or Plutarch the efforts of the editor, translator, and interpreter. Erasmus began this effort with his monumental work on Jerome's letters, contemplated as early as 1500 (*Ep.* 139, 141) but not completed, like his New Testament, until 1516. Thereafter he added to his scholarly credits a long list of editions of other early Greek and Latin Fathers, including Cyprian (1520), Hilary (1523), Ambrose (1527), Augustine (1528–1529), Lactantius (1529), John Chrysostom (1530), Basil (1532), and Origen (1536). Freed from "the entanglements introduced by the modern school" and restored by Erasmus' best efforts to their original condition, these writings revealed "that ancient, true theology" (*Ep.* 108); at the same time they "cast light on the ancient world" (*Ep.* 1139).

Thus for nearly four decades Erasmus gave his considerable talents as a reader and a writer to explaining, promoting, and popularizing classical literature, especially the parts of it he deemed most compatible with Christianity. At regular intervals, moreover, he reaffirmed his service to the classical tradition as serving a higher calling to sacred literature. Compatibility, after all, differs from identity. Though sacred literature and classical literature share much, they are not the same. As a translator of Euripides, Erasmus explained, he could make a mistake "to the cost of my intellectual reputation alone," but as a translator of the New Testament, he could do real "harm to Holy Writ" (*Ep.* 188). Even those works, like his own *Paraclesis,* that advance the cause of classical literature consider it "wicked madness to wish to compare Christ with Zeno or Aristotle and His teaching with, to put it mildly, the paltry precepts of those men." Like the *Paraclesis,* these works address the dangers of idolizing secular writing and thereby substituting it for the only literature worthy of veneration. Most controversial among these works is Erasmus' *Ciceronian* (1528).

Responding to the excessive cultivation of Ciceronian style fashionable in Italy and France, Erasmus entered (inadvertently, it seems) a long-standing debate over the proper method of imitation. Before him, this debate had embroiled, among others, his favorite Italian Humanist, Lorenzo Valla. Afterward it would continue to exercise the argumentative skills of many others, including Peter Ramus in France and Gabriel Harvey in England.

In Erasmus' *Ciceronian* this debate takes the form of a satiric dialogue not unlike those of the *Colloquies.* The target of this satire, a strict Ciceronian named Nosoponus, labors to write like Cicero by copying the master to the letter, that is, by reproducing Cicero's vocabulary, his turns of phrase, his sentence structure. His partner in conversation, Bulephorus (presumably speaking for Erasmus), argues for a less rigid method, one that imitates the spirit, instead of the letter, of Ciceronian writing. This method, in contrast, is grounded in the fundamental rhetorical principle of decorum.

In keeping with all the best classical authorities, including Aristotle, Cicero, and Quintilian, Bulephorus understands decorum as the art of accommodating one's style to the subject matter, the speaker, and, most urgently, the audience. According to this principle, a writer like Nosoponus, who insists on imitating Cicero exactly, will inevitably fail to accommodate his audience—no longer the Romans of the late Republic but rather the Christians of early modern Europe—and therefore fail to qualify as Ciceronian in the true sense of the term. The real Ciceronian writing in Erasmus' day would thus handle Christian topics in a Christian way, even though Cicero himself never addressed these topics or used such language. Paradoxically, then, the writing that most exactly imitates Cicero is least Ciceronian. The real Ciceronian (i.e., Bulephorus rather than Nosoponus) is simultaneously a good Christian. Challenging at this point in his career not the anticlassical reader but rather the hyperclassical writer, Erasmus nevertheless upholds the fundamental compatibility between Christian and classical literature. Alive today, he insists, Cicero would surely not write as he did then but as the best writers do now. In his own writing, moreover, Erasmus practiced what he preached, regularly accommodating classical forms to a Christian agenda. His work best known to present-day readers, *The Praise of Folly* (1511), brilliantly adapts ancient sophistic encomium to Pauline theology.

As part of his case in *The Antibarbarians* against those defenders of ignorance who reject the study of classical literature, Erasmus offers an invidious (and provocative) comparison between scholarship and martyrdom, and he does so on the basis of influence. Whereas the martyr diminishes the number of the faithful by one, the scholar increases it by many. Indeed, the martyr's act of heroism remains unknown and inconsequential without the scholar to record it. For "where there is learned scholarship, nothing stops it from spreading out to all humanity." Without question, Erasmus entered the Renaissance world of classical scholarship intending to have such an effect. Arguably, he succeeded. At the very least, as one scholar of the Renaissance, Craig R. Thompson, puts it, "In [Erasmus'] lifetime no one did more to advance the intelligent study of classical languages and literatures and to explain their value for Christians."

BIBL.: Marjorie O'Rourke Boyle, *Christening Pagan Mysteries: Erasmus in Pursuit of Wisdom* (Toronto 1981). *Collected Works of Erasmus,* ed. R. A B. Mynors et al. (Toronto 1974–). Kathy Eden, *Friends Hold All Things in Common: Tradition, Intellectual Property, and the "Adages" of Erasmus* (New Haven 2001). Elaine Fantham, "Erasmus and the Latin Classics," in *Collected Works of Erasmus* (Toronto 1989) 29:xxxiv–l. John C. Olin, ed., *Christian Humanism and the Reformation: Selected Writings of Erasmus* (New York 1987). Rudolf Pfeiffer, *History of Classical Scholarship, 1300–1850* (Oxford 1976) 71–81. Margaret Mann Phillips, "Erasmus and the Classics," in *Erasmus,* ed. T. A. Dorey (Albuquerque 1970) 1–30. Erika Rummel, *Erasmus as a Translator of the Classics* (Toronto 1985).

K.E.

Eros. *See* Cupid.

Estienne, Henri II (Henricus Stephanus)

Henri II Estienne (1531–1598) is the best-known member of the distinguished Estienne (Stephanus) dynasty of French scholar-printers, founded in 1502 by his grandfather Henri I Estienne. Henri II was one of the foremost Humanists of the second half of the 16th century, owing to his wide-ranging and permanent contributions in the field of classical (especially Greek) philology.

Henri's father, Robert Estienne (1503–1559), also a prominent scholar, was the Royal Printer in Latin, Greek, and Hebrew. He is especially celebrated for his handsome Greek typography, used in the production of numerous noteworthy texts, several in *editio princeps* (first printing). Besides classical texts Robert Estienne also produced important critical editions of the Greek New Testament, of which the folio edition of 1550 was the first to contain a critical apparatus, recording variant readings from 15 manuscripts. This edition brought Estienne into conflict with the theologians of the Sorbonne, who viewed with suspicion any edition of the Scriptures questioning the authority of the Vulgate. That same year Robert Estienne was compelled to flee to Geneva, where he resumed his professional activities, which now included the printing of the writings of Calvin and Bèze.

It has been said that Robert Estienne's greatest contribution to the world of scholarship was to have been the father of Henri, who was brought up speaking Latin at home and learned Greek as a child. While still in his teens Henri was initiated to his life's work by assisting his father in correcting the Greek text of the *editio princeps* of Dionysius of Halicarnassus (1547).

In 1554 the young Henri burst on the scholarly and literary scene with his sensational publication of the *editio princeps* of the *Anacreontea* (a collection of Greek lyric poems then believed to be by the 6th-century BCE poet Anacreon but now established to be later imitations), which he had discovered in a manuscript in Louvain. Once Estienne made this collection known to the world, it became the most influential "ancient" Greek poetic text during the Renaissance, not only in France but throughout Europe. The *editio princeps* of "Anacreon," which has been termed "the starting-point of a new branch of modern literature," was greeted with unbounded enthusiasm by the members of the Pléiade, each of whom immediately translated and imitated some of these hitherto unknown Greek lyrics. Ronsard in particular was deeply influenced by the volume and immortalized Estienne and his discovery in one of his *Odes* (5.16: "Je vais boire à Henry Estienne/Qui des Enfers nous a rendu/Du vieil Anacreon perdu/La douce lyre Teïenne": I drink to Henri Estienne, who has retrieved from Hades the sweet Teian lyre of the old, long-lost Anacreon).

Soon thereafter Henri joined his father in Geneva, where he set up his own independent printing establishment, with eventual financial backing from Ulrich Fugger, a member of the wealthy Augsburg banking family. A prodigiously prolific scholar, Henri quickly gained a reputation as one of the dominant literary and scholarly figures of his time. He composed vernacular works that rank him among the greatest French prose writers of the Renaissance, in the company of Rabelais and Montaigne. These include the popular and notorious satire *Apologie pour Hérodote* (*Apology for Herodotus,* 1566) and the *Traité de la conformité du langage français avec le grec* (*Treatise on the Similarity of French to Greek,* 1565), which was the first in a trilogy on the defense and glorification of the French language.

Henri Estienne's most lasting contributions, however, were made in the field of Greek studies, through his numerous editions and translations of Greek authors. Among his Latin translations from the Greek, the most influential was that of Sextus Empiricus (1562). This translation was directly responsible for introducing the tradition of Pyrrhonian skepticism into French thought, notably through Montaigne: it was from Estienne's translation that Montaigne derived the Pyrrhonian maxims with which he adorned the beams of his library.

Henri Estienne's many Greek editions include revised and improved texts of those that his father had published, which Henri now enriched with his own important commentaries. He also added to his father's corpus by publishing the first complete editions of Aeschylus (1557), Diodorus (1559), and Plutarch (1572). In 1566 he produced a critical text of Homer that remained standard until the 19th century. It was Estienne's text that Chapman used for his famous English translations in the early decades of the 17th century, known to many readers today only from Keats's "On First Looking into Chapman's Homer" (1816).

Henri Estienne's most important Greek edition was his Plato of 1578, in three folio volumes. This edition has contributed considerably to immortalizing Henri's name, as to this day its pagination provides the universally accepted system of reference to Plato's text, which is traditionally cited according to the "Stephanus" numbers printed in the margins of all modern editions and translations.

By far Henri's greatest scholarly achievement was his truly monumental *Thesaurus graecae linguae* (*Thesaurus of the Greek Language,* 1572), whose publication in five folio volumes was the great event of his career, as well as a high point in the annals of European scholarship. This *Thesaurus* was a pioneering lexicographical work, following the scientific principle of arranging words not in the traditionally strict alphabetical order but rather in groups according to their etymological roots. To this day the *Thesaurus* has still not been replaced; its publication alone would have sufficed to ensure his everlasting scholarly fame.

Henri Estienne never fully recovered the enormous expense that went into the publication of this crowning work, and he continued to sink deeper and deeper into financial difficulties. He found himself more and more frequently on the road in search of new markets for his stock. During one of these trips, he died destitute in a hospital in Lyon.

BIBL.: Louis Clément, *Henri Estienne et son oeuvre française* (Paris 1899). J. Kecskeméti, B. Boudou, and H. Cazes, eds., *Henri II Estienne, éditeur et écrivain* (Turnhout 2003). John O'Brien, *Anacreon Redivivus: A Study of Anacreontic Translation in Mid-Sixteenth-Century France* (Ann Arbor, 1995). Antoine-Augustin Renouard, *Annales de l'imprimerie des Estienne,* 2nd ed. (Paris 1843). Fred Schreiber, *The Estiennes* (New York 1982) and "La tyrannie de Renouard sur Henri Estienne," in *Henri Estienne,* Cahiers V. L. Saulnier 5 (Paris 1988) 13–20.

F.S.

Ethics

The writings of ancient philosophers on ethics have been used by succeeding moral philosophers whenever they were available. For centuries, however, many of the texts of the ancient works were not available or could be read only in incomplete, corrupt, or translated form. A full history of uses of ancient ethics after antiquity would have to begin by tracing the work of recovering, editing, translating, disseminating, and explaining the original writings. Today most philosophers take for granted the results of these heroic labors. They also take for granted that by far the majority of students now are ignorant of Greek and Latin. Indeed, even teachers of ancient moral philosophy are often themselves not specialists in the subject and, like their students, must rely on translations. Many of them are thus less well equipped to use and teach the ancients than their predecessors, despite having more scholarly aids than ever before.

Ancient philosophical ethics has survived to the present day through three historical phases. In the first phase, Christian writers moved from contemptuously dismissing pagan thought to drawing on it in constructing their own ethical views. Lactantius (ca. 260–340 CE) disparaged the ancients as pretentious, useless, and (because uninformed by Christian Scriptures) hopelessly lacking in the wisdom they claimed to pursue. Later Christian apologists, from Augustine onward, took a more complex stance toward ancient moral philosophy. While emphasizing its defects (for example, its inability to come to agreement about the highest good), Augustine still found in it clear landmarks against which he could stake out a distinctive position for Christian morality. He also allowed that some pagan writers had come closer to the revealed truth about morality than others; and if the virtues that the pagans extolled were all hollow, because not inspired by Christian love, nonetheless for this world they had their uses. As the medieval Latin West recovered more of the work of Aristotle, often with the aid of Arabic and Jewish scholars, Christian thinkers began to see him as posing the greatest pagan challenge to their own attempts to systematize Christian doctrine. But he also provided tools for that systematization. From Augustine through Thomas Aquinas and on to Suarez, a major task of Western theologians was not so much the rejection of pagan thought as its absorption into Christian moral philosophy.

A second phase began toward the end of the 16th century, when the ancients became resources for thinking about how to broaden the Christian understanding of morality so that it would not be tied to the confessional particularities that had led to religious warfare. Eventually the ancients were used as aids for considering how to work out a wholly secular morality. The endeavor began strikingly in the *Essays* of Michel de Montaigne (1580, 1595); it remains the distinctive enterprise of current moral philosophy.

The third phase, which may be called neoclassicism in ethics, began in the latter part of the 20th century, when many philosophers had become deeply dissatisfied with utilitarianism and Kantianism, the positions that had dominated midcentury discussion. Critics often turned to the ancients to find ways of developing views that would remain secular while avoiding what they took to be the errors and omissions of the then-reigning alternatives. The reaction has been devoted especially to elaborating views of morality that give a preeminent place to virtue and the virtues and to their contribution to *eudaimonia,* or human flourishing. Some who have turned back from modern moral philosophy to antiquity have returned to the older way of using ancient moral philosophy to rework Christian views of morality. Aristotle in particular has been pressed into this service as well as into developing new secular positions.

From the 19th century onward, growing numbers of scholars worked on improving the texts of the ancient philosophers as well as on commentaries and translations. Philologically expert and philosophically acute scholars have made contributions both to our historical grasp of ancient moral philosophy and to an understanding of the continued pertinence of the ancients to current debates. Philosophers with no claims to expertise on antiquity have benefited considerably from their work. At the beginning of the 21st century more and better-informed use is being made of ancient moral philosophy than was or indeed could have been made previously.

Histories of philosophy usually scant the second and third phases of the uses of ancient philosophy. For our purposes, they are the focus.

Montaigne was the thinker who first raised the questions that have been central to modern moral philosophy. Plutarch, Cicero, and Seneca were his main sources for knowledge of Stoicism, Epicureanism, and Skepticism. He relied on those authors more than on Plato or Aristotle. Unlike many ancient readers, however, he did not seek a doctrine that he could wholly adopt or a teacher whose example he could try to imitate. He treated ancient moral philosophy critically, mainly by asking if he could actually follow any of the advice it gave about how to live. He concluded that he could not, and he thought almost no one else could, either. He also thought that the ancients had not succeeded in finding a highest good that would satisfy everyone. Rather, we must each find for ourselves what gives us the most satisfactory life. Luckily each of us has an inner voice—a version of the Socratic *daimōn*—that forbids some of our proposed actions and allows others. We must each be led by this ruling form to our own highest good, in our own way. Theories and universal principles are of no use in daily life. Montaigne learned much from ancient moral philosophy, but he rejected its central teachings.

Although he did not directly discuss the Thomist doctrine of natural law, Montaigne was as skeptical about it as he was about older views generally. His successors saw this aspect of skepticism as particularly threatening. In an era of endless warfare among Protestant states and between Protestant and Catholic regimes, and of trading ventures and battles with wholly non-Christian peoples, some basis in natural law seemed necessary if there were to be rules of war that all parties could accept. The first major presentation of a new theory of natural law was Hugo Grotius' *Law of War and Peace* (1625). Grotius was extraordinarily learned: his text is strewn with innumerable quotations and citations, and references to Christian Fathers, Talmudic treatises, jurisconsults, Roman law, and Scripture; Greek and Roman poets, tragedians, historians, and philosophers sprout all over his pages. Aristotle and Plato figure largely, still more so Plutarch, Cicero, and Seneca, and much less so Epicurus and Epictetus. But these flowers of learning are primarily Humanistic adornments. Grotius used the ancients as authorities only to support his claim that much of what he was saying has always and everywhere been known by the wise. Despite this, he was proposing a drastically new view of natural law. Like Montaigne, he set aside the search for a common highest good; unlike Montaigne, he undertook to show how natural laws might be justified without any appeal to it. In this departure from antiquity he was followed by many of the creators of modern moral philosophy.

The 17th century saw revivals of Stoicism and Epicureanism, both greatly aided by scholarly work of high quality. Justus Lipsius (1547–1606) went beyond Cicero and Seneca to recover the thought of the earlier Greek Stoics, creating the most advanced account of Stoic thought available at the time. He also defended Stoicism argumentatively in his widely read *On Constancy* (1584). Pierre Gassendi (1592–1655) defended Epicurus against what he called Stoic slanders (accusations of loose living) and devoted an immense treatise to expounding the logic, the physics, and the ethical thought of his hero—efforts that opened the way to modern understandings of Epicureanism. Like Lipsius, Gassendi aimed at more than accurate recovery of past thought. Each of these scholars tried to show that the ancient moral philosophy he favored was compatible with the basic elements of Christian belief. They each appealed to reason, not to revelation, and they avoided metaphysical issues as far as possible. They Christianized the ancient views to some extent, in the hope that a nonsectarian understanding of morality acceptable to Christians might help to bring an end to the religious persecutions and warfare of their times.

Scholastic moral theologians continued to use Aristotle as a source and guide, and his *Nicomachean Ethics* was widely taught (in Latin) at universities. But outside the Catholic Church Aristotle's position of authority declined as the prestige of the new science rose and as non-Aristotelian ways of understanding morality were created. In addition, during the golden age of modern moral philosophy the Humanistic habit of loading one's pages with citations of the ancients fell out of fashion. The moderns won the "battle of the books"; the ancients ceased to be universally accepted authorities. Themes and views from antiquity reappeared in new guises in the writings of many modern philosophers. But they were presented as deliverances of reason or experience, without reference to predecessors. Except for Catholic moral theologians, no important thinkers followed the model of Lipsius and Gassendi in presenting their own thought as reworking for modern times the views of earlier writers.

Hobbes found nothing but darkness in Aristotle and viewed the Roman philosophers as teaching a dangerous republicanism. He sought to put morality on a scientific basis and did not call on ancient predecessors to give authority to his work. Strong Stoic elements appear in Spinoza's ethics, but he makes no reference to any Stoic (or other) writings. Anti-Hobbesians at Cambridge found inspiration in Plato; but the more they relied on him, the less intelligible they were taken to be. Shaftesbury's thought was deeply shaped by his study of Greek philosophy as the Cambridge Platonists understood it, but he made few explicit references to it. Butler found Stoicism suggestive but obscure; his clarifications take him far from Stoic doctrine. Hume wrote essays portraying the character of the Stoic, the Epicurean, the Platonist, and the Skeptic. In his systematic work, however, he drew little from ancient moral philosophy and referred more often to ancient historians than to philosophers. Kant regularly gave his students potted histories of ethics at the start of his lectures on the subject. He thought that Stoicism and Epicureanism each contained half of the truth of which he was presenting the whole. But his point was not to show how much he owed to the ancients or to revitalize their views. It was, rather, to locate his own highly original position by contrasting it with theirs. Many of the British moralists worked out theories of virtue and discussed the virtues, as did Kant. But their views were strikingly different from anything Aristotle proposed. Bentham was so disgusted by the study of Cicero forced on him as a boy at Oxford that he dismissed ancient philosophy as rubbish. But he felt the same way about most of modern moral philosophy as well.

Hegel, who had a deep knowledge of ancient philosophy, made little use of its moral dimensions, but for a different reason. As a strong historicist he held that morality and politics in antiquity had not reached the level of development they had attained in modernity. Christianity had made a major advance in our understanding of how to live. Philosophers, he held, express abstractly the essence of their own times and cultures. No ancient thinker, therefore, could be simply taken over for use by moderns. It was Kant he needed to advance from, not Aristotle.

After the French Revolution, appeals to ancient philosophy were apt to remind readers of the dangerous uses the republican revolutionaries had made of it. Because the radicals had also tried to do away with Christianity, moral philosophy that did not appeal to religion was suspect. After midcentury these constraints lost strength, and philosophers again began to develop secular views and sometimes to make overt appeal to ancient sources. In 1834–1835 John Stuart Mill (1806–1873) published summaries of nine of the Platonic dialogues, so detailed as to be virtually full translations. (Jowett's translation of most of the dialogues, more accurate than Thomas Taylor's more complete version of 1804, was not published until 1871.) Mill's chief reason for admiring the Platonic dialogues was that they taught their readers how to think for themselves. The dialectical exercise of mind, not the doctrine, was what he took to be valuable. He thought that Aristotle's work, including the logical writings, could not serve the same purpose. In his *Utilitarianism* (1863), which outlines a wholly secular systematic ethics, he states that Socrates and Jesus taught versions of the moral view he has described. But though he refers to both of them with admiration, he does not appeal to either as an authority.

Nietzsche despised both utilitarianism and John Stuart Mill. Perhaps more than any other among modern philosophers, he knew and loved the Greeks and turned repeatedly to consideration of their writings. His views about Greek philosophy, however, are too complex to allow of any simple summary; and insofar as he can be said to have had a moral philosophy, it is not particularly indebted to antiquity.

William Whewell produced the most systematic British alternative to utilitarian ethics in the mid-19th century. He drew heavily on Platonism for his metaphysics but used his own original epistemology to show that moral knowledge could be as secure as scientific knowledge, though different in nature. He did not owe any of this line of argument to ancient moral philosophy. T. H. Green was opposed to utilitarianism; his contemporary Henry Sidgwick was a chief exponent of it. Each worked out views that started from modern rather than ancient predecessors. Both used their disagreements with ancient moral philosophy to locate their own views. Sidgwick's view of the major difference between ancient moral philosophy and modern has become classic.

The ancients, Sidgwick said, took the question "What is the highest good?" as central to moral philosophy. We moderns instead consider as central the question "What is duty, and what is its ground?" The ancients asked what would most attract and satisfy us; we moderns use a "quasi-jural notion" to ask what we are morally required to do. This way of drawing the distinction, though now contested, seemed correct to many philosophers for a long time. The third phase in the use of ancient moral philosophy resulted from refusal to take the central issue of moral philosophy to be what Sidgwick said it was for modernity.

The refusal began with expressions of dissatisfaction with the major views of morality that dominated modern moral philosophy. Critics took utilitarianism and neo-Kantian ethical theories to be unduly focused on finding formulations of universal principles with which any and all moral issues could be solved. Theories of these kinds concentrated on right acts, the critics thought, and neglected character and the virtues. They ignored or (as in Kantian views) condemned the emotions. Their moral psychology was at best thin and at worst derived from theories of knowledge or language that gave no special role to morality. They made no attempt to discuss the good life. And the morality that flowed from these views was itself, according to the critics, incomplete or shallow or even positively corrupt.

G. E. M. Anscombe's 1958 essay "Modern Moral Philosophy" added to these charges the claim that the moral vocabulary used, without examination, by utilitarian and Kantian thinkers was itself deeply flawed. Centering on obligation, moral law, and duty, it had originated when divinely ordained natural law was taken to be the core of morality. For an age when God was no longer supposed to be in charge of ethics, the vocabulary became meaningless, surviving owing only to habit. Anscombe suggested that it could not be profitable to carry on with moral philosophy until better views of moral psychology had been developed. Moderns, she said, would do well to look to Aristotle for guidance.

Without focusing on the need for an ethics of virtue, Iris Murdoch argued in 1967 that we should give up on Kant and utilitarianism and turn instead to Plato—not Aristotle—for ways to escape the thinness of modern moral philosophy. Plato could teach us, she said, the importance of looking carefully at the world in the light of the Idea of the Good. No explicit principles can help us toward solutions of moral problems. Only sensitive and cultivated perception can do so; but the perception would be that, not of scientists, but of those who understand that the Good is as real as the world scientists study. Reliable sensitivity was of course what Aristotle's virtuous agent would have, and recent exponents of virtue theory have all picked up on this theme.

Philippa Foot, G. H. von Wright, and Bernard Williams, whose work greatly stimulated interest in virtue ethics, drew more on Aristotle than on Plato. Like the many other exponents of virtue ethics, they are not interested primarily in exegesis, nor are later exponents of virtue ethics like Rosalind Hursthouse. Much of later 20th-century moral philosophy has been conducted by revising and arguing for, or against, older views. The proponents of virtue ethics have succeeded in bringing the moral philosophy of antiquity into the discussion. Not the least of their achievements is the reopening of the question of *eudaimonia*, the human good. After Montaigne and Grotius that had seemed a dead issue. It is now alive again, and the ancients are prime contributors to the discussion.

Most of those who have appealed to ancient moral philosophy in rethinking the virtues and *eudaimonia* have been secular thinkers. Anscombe, however, made her allegiance to Catholicism clear, as did Alasdair MacIntyre. In his *Short History of Ethics* (1966) and his widely read *After Virtue* (1981), he elaborated the argument, sketched by Anscombe, that morality is now a jumble of fragments left over from older, abandoned systematic ethical outlooks. He uses Aquinas as well as Aristotle, holding that only a return to a virtue ethic with religious commitments can help us out of our current morass.

Perhaps, as Sidgwick claimed, the main difference between the ancients' moral philosophy and ours is that theirs sought the highest good and ours the law that determines duty. But another distinction between ancients and moderns is at least as important. Ancient moral philosophy held that some men were superior to others in their ability to discover how to live and what to do. The few must know and lead; the many must follow. Distinctively modern moral philosophy rejects this idea. It has held, in varying ways, that all normal adults are able to determine by and for themselves what they ought to do. With its roots in the Protestant insistence on the unavoidable responsibility of each of us for his own behavior, this thesis makes for a striking difference between ancient and modern ethics. Moral elitism has no place in the ethics of democratic societies. Modern moral philosophy has given us ways of thinking through this central feature of modern morality.

BIBL.: Julia Annas, *The Morality of Happiness* (Oxford 1993). G. E. M. Anscombe, "Modern Moral Philosophy," in *Collected Philosophical Papers,* vol. 3, *Ethics, Religion and Politics* (Minneapolis 1981) 26–42. Henry Chadwick, *Early Christian Thought and the Classical Tradition* (New York 1966). John Cooper, "Justus Lipsius and the Revival of Stoicism in Late Sixteenth-century Europe," in *New Essays on the History of Autonomy,* ed. Natalie Brender and Larry Krasnoff (Cambridge 2004) 7–29, and *Reason and Emotion* (Princeton 1999). Roger Crisp and Michael Slote, eds., *Virtue Ethics* (Oxford 1997). Philippa Foot, "Virtues and Vices," in *Virtues and Vices* (Oxford 1978). R. A. Gauthier, *L'éthique à Nicomaque,* vol. 1, *Introduction* (Paris 1970). T. H. Green, *Prolegomena to Ethics* (Oxford 1883, 1929). Rosalind Hursthouse, *On Virtue Ethics* (Oxford 1999). Jill Kraye, *Classical Traditions in Renaissance Philosophy* (Aldershot 2002) and "The Legacy of Ancient Philosophy," in *The Cambridge Companion to Ancient Philosophy,* ed. David Sedley (Cambridge 2003). Alasdair MacIntyre, *After Virtue* (Notre Dame 1981, 2nd ed. 1984) and *A Short History of Ethics* (New York 1966). Iris Murdoch, *The Sovereignty of Good* (London 1970). Cary Nederman, *Medieval Aristotelianism and Its Limits* (Aldershot 1997). Frederick Rosen, "J. S. Mill on Socrates, Pericles and the Fragility of Truth," *Journal of Legal History* 25 (2004) 181–194. C. B. Schmitt et al., eds., *The Cambridge History of Renaissance Philosophy* (Cambridge 1988). David Sedley, ed., *The Cambridge Companion to Ancient Philosophy* (Cambridge 2003). Henry Sidgwick, *The Methods of Ethics* (London 1874, 1907). G. H. von Wright, *The Varieties of Goodness* (London 1963).

J.B.S.

Ethnography

The word *ethnography* (from Greek *ethnos,* "nation" or "people," and *graphia,* "writing") does not appear in ancient Greek and Latin sources; it first appears in German and English texts of the 1830s. *Ethnology* has a roughly similar history. The modern date is surely a reflection of the 19th century's interest in the perceived connections between language, race, and culture. But the concept of ethnography as theory and practice goes back at least to Herodotus (5th cent. BCE) if not to his intellectual predecessors. It was Herodotus' work, with its colorful descriptions of Egyptians, Scythians, Persians, and Greeks, that became established as an ethnographic and historical classic. Several of the categories through which he formulated his narrative exerted a lasting and profound influence on the ethnographic tradition. These include emphasis on autopsy, reliance on native informants, interest in oral tradition, use of polarity and analogy as an interpretive device, analysis of cultural signs in their social and political contexts, and apprehensions of cultural propriety. In a broad sense Herodotus' work also prefigured modern ethnographic concerns with health, education, science, material culture, communication, and deviance. Indeed, it is difficult now to perceive what an ethnography without Herodotus might look like, so intense and rigorous has been his influence on the field's founding moment. Certainly Herodotus is not the only ancient writer to leave a stamp on ethnographic theory and practice. There were already other contemporaries who wrote *ethnika,* as they styled their attempts to recount the customs and local histories of other groups, whether Greek or non-Greek. In the European Middle Ages and the Renaissance, would-be ethnographers found models and inspiration in Pliny the Elder, Tacitus (especially in the form of his *Germania*), Solinus (who, soon after 200 CE, wrote a *Collectanea rerum memorabilium* based largely on the work of Pliny and Pomponius Mela), and Isidore of Seville (7th century CE). But it is Herodotus who occupies a privileged place within the entire genealogy of ethnography, whether that genealogy is described in terms of institutions or more informally. Much of the 20th century's attempts to rethink the constitutive elements of the field can be understood as an effort to engage with his legacy.

As Herodotus' own example illustrates, ethnography has never been the sole province of the professional ethnographer, and the ancient ethnographer tended to don other hats as well. Among the earlier instances of ethnographic writing in the West are the texts of travelers, encyclopedists, explorers, traders, captives, and colonizers. Isidore, bishop of Seville and himself an encyclopedist, composed an *Etymologiae* between 622 and 632; his compendium was referred to as an authority by writers into the 13th century, until it was joined or supplanted by the *De proprietatibus rerum* (*On the Properties of Things*) of Bartholomaeus Anglicus. The Hebrew Bible and the classical Greek and Roman writers, as they were condensed into encyclopedias of this sort, were often the chief models for ethnographic writing in the Middle Ages. The Europeans who participated in the Crusades and made their way to Jerusalem responded to these earlier traditions in observations of their own. These overtly Christian accounts of the Near East record not just the writers' predilections for the fabulous and the marvelous but also their obsessions with nonbelievers. In the 13th and 14th centuries the accounts of Marco Polo (who returned from China in the 1290s) as well as John de Plano Carpini (who reached Mongolia in the 1240s) and William Rubruck (who traveled to the Tatars in central Asia in the 1250s) also show the influence of the classical writers and the Bible.

The Renaissance witnessed an explosion in the number of ethnographic narratives written by Europeans, who continued to draw on classical sources even when the latter were judged to be clearly incorrect or tendentious.

These narratives too were not self-consciously presented as ethnographic or anthropological writings but rather appeared in a number of different contexts. The major Spanish 16th-century authors to discuss human customs and behavior were Gonzalo Fernández de Oviedo Valdés, José de Acosta, Pedro de Cieza de Léon, Francisco López de Gómora, Bernal Díaz del Castillo, and Bartolomé de las Casas. Herodotus and Pliny were frequently invoked by Spanish writers of ethnographies, as were books of medieval lore and contemporary works of literature. The wider availability of classical authors in the Renaissance also affected these developments. Herodotus was translated into Latin by Lorenzo Valla and Mattia Palmieri in the 15th century, into German by Hieronymus Boner in the 16th century, and into English by Barnabe Rich also in the 16th century, and Latin writers such as Pliny and Tacitus could be readily consulted in printed editions. To this period belongs the magisterial work of Sebastian Münster, *Cosmographia* (ca. 1550), which took its information from scores of sources, ancient and modern. On the subject of monstrous races Münster both dismissed the unlikely stories of classical writers such as Megasthenes and Ctesias and yet recounted them in detail.

Some Renaissance writers also reframed the relationship between Herodotus and Thucydides as a debate over the participation of the observer in contemporary events. Many of these writers decided that contact with native inhabitants was not a necessary prerequisite for ethnographic exercises. Thus Joannes Boemus wrote *Customs of All Peoples* (*Omnium gentium mores,* 1520) but did not himself actually travel to the peoples and places he discussed in his collection. In 1673 Joannes Schefferus (Scheffer) published his *Lapponia,* about Lapland, which for some time was characterized as the first sustained ethnography of a tribal people. Scheffer did not himself visit the land he wrote of, though he claimed to have spoken with individuals who had had firsthand contact with the Lapps. But Díaz del Castillo, who had been with Hernán Cortés in Mexico, chastised López de Gómara on the grounds that López de Gómara had not journeyed to Mexico or spoken to the inhabitants before composing accounts (1551) of Cortés's travels that were based on reminiscences of Cortés himself. Jean de Léry, a Calvinist who had made the voyage to Brazil from Geneva, aggressively criticized André Thevet's *Singularités de la France Antarctique* (1557) for thoroughly misrepresenting the Tupinamba and their customs. Léry's work, *Histoire d'un voyage fait en la terre du Bresil* (1578), is rich in its references to classical authors and gives a sympathetic account of the Tupinamba; it was the only book that the anthropologist Claude Lévi-Strauss took with him to Brazil during his researches there in the first half of the 20th century. One common thread that runs through Renaissance accounts of other peoples—emphasis on the marvelous and the strange—also places these works squarely in the tradition inaugurated so vividly by Herodotus. Boemus, for example, places Herodotus first among the authorities he follows in his relatively short book. The influence of Greek and Roman writers, however, goes beyond issues of focus and theme. Renaissance writers used many of the same hermeneutic categories as Greek and Roman sources to describe the manners and customs of native peoples. Such transference led to fascinating instances of cross-cultural translation: the tropes developed by Herodotus in relation to Egypt, for instance, were applied to Renaissance accounts of the Americas.

Several Greek and Roman sources served the cause of colonialism and imperialism during the period of New World exploration. It became a matter of urgency for the conquerors to ascribe civilizing motives to themselves and to claim that their conquests were bringing progress and Christian values to savage populations who so resembled the archaic peoples described by the ancients. Another legitimating argument for the conquest of the Americas drew on a theory supposedly elaborated by Aristotle, that war against some human races was "just by nature." Such was the claim made by Juan Ginés de Sepúlveda in his response to the fiery allegations of brutality leveled by Bartolomé de las Casas against the Spanish colonizers. Las Casas replied to Sepúlveda with a denunciation that drew on many Greek and Latin sources; he reinterpreted Aristotle and Strabo to claim that the Spanish were the real barbarians, not the Aztec and Inca peoples they had obliterated. Nevertheless, Aristotle's statement that some human beings were slaves by nature continued to be quoted in discussions about the mass enslavements of men, women, and children. Many of the unfortunate clichés elaborated by the Greek and Roman sources were revived in the course of these debates, and indeed their currency is attested by the level to which they flourished in literature, philosophy, and the plastic arts as well as in the records of travel and conquest. The key texts are the works of William Shakespeare, who took his ethnographic material partly from Plutarch and Ovid, and the philosophical disquisitions of the early Renaissance. It was out of Greek and Roman texts that there developed the idea of Oriental despotism. If Herodotus and the Hippocratic corpus supplied the notion of environmental determinism, Aristotle provided a precisely calibrated statement on the nature of the despot, and the result was a widespread conception of Asia, seething and abject, as the elective breeding ground of despotism and tyranny. Thus, ethnographic and political philosophy combined to perpetuate a pernicious interpretation, which later came to serve the interests of European and North American Orientalism.

It would be misleading, however, to project modern demarcations between East and West on earlier epochs, or to claim that Greek and Roman authors found no audience in the traditions outside Europe. Some of the Arab geographers and historians reveal a clear if limited access to such sources as Ptolemy (2nd cent. CE), and they appropriated Aristotelian systems of classification in the treatment of Muslim and non-Muslim peoples. In his account of India, al-Bīrūnī of Ghazna gives a remarkably inspired and precise reading of cultural inversion in the 11th century: "Many Hindu customs differ from those of our country and of our times to such a degree as to appear to us simply monstrous. One might almost think that they had intentionally changed them into the opposite, for *our* customs do not resemble theirs, but are the very reverse; and if ever a custom of *theirs* resembles one of *ours,* it has certainly just the opposite meaning." There follows a series of descriptions of how the Hindus are different: eating, drinking, maintenance of body hair, and so on. This account is a striking reading of Herodotus' description of Egypt (*Histories,* book 2), in which the Egyptians are said to practice the opposite of many Greek customs. Renaissance men such as Roberto da Sanseverino, an Italian condottiere, and Pietro Martire d'Anghiera, Jean Palerne, and Francesco Suriano, all of whom wrote in the late 15th and the 16th centuries about their journeys to Egypt, drew on Herodotus in their works. But it is notable that Biruni, who wrote this narrative in Arabic, made a place for cultural pluralism and relativism in a manner that recalled Herodotus.

The discovery of the New World also contributed to a transformation in ethnographic thought. The Greeks and Romans were thenceforth not solely sources of intellectual inspiration; they were themselves assimilated, or at least compared, to the native peoples of the Americas. A suspicion had begun to take root that the American natives were similar to the Greeks and Romans insofar as both populations represented an early stage in the development of human civilizations. By the 1700s not only the European settlers and their descendants were being likened in some quarters to the ancient Greeks and Romans; the North American native peoples themselves also were commended for their display of Spartan virtues such as courage and justice. The willingness to treat the Greeks and Romans as one group among many took on a brilliant form in Bernard de Fontenelle's *De l'origine des fables* (1724), which laid the groundwork for the study of ancient myth. "Since the Greeks," he wrote, "with all their intelligence, did not, when they were still a new people, think more rationally than the barbarians of America who were also, according to all appearances, a new people when they were discovered by the Spanish, there is ground for thinking that the Americans would have, at last, come to think as rationally as the Greeks if they had had the leisure for it." The uniqueness of the Greeks was being called into question by a logic that would have been familiar to Herodotus if not to Socrates. The appeal for a broad-based comparative anthropology also found a sympathetic ear in Joseph-François Lafitau, the author of *Customs of the American Savages Compared to Customs of Earliest Times* (*Moeurs des sauvages amériquains comparées aux moeurs des premiers temps,* 1724), an essay based on a voyage to the Jesuit missions in French Canada. Lafitau used his detailed ethnographic study to prove that the existence of God could be established by comparing the beliefs and customs of different peoples. For him, the ancient Greek and Roman civilizations and the cultures of the New World could be justifiably compared, because each threw light on the other.

Fontenelle and Lafitau were not isolated in their ethnological projects, however. Giambattista Vico, whose acknowledged masters were Plato, Tacitus, and Machiavelli, published in 1725 his *Scienza nuova* (*New Science*), a treatise that is still considered a forerunner of modern ethnography and cultural anthropology; he postulated a common foundation for all history and argued for "a natural law of the peoples" that encompassed a movement from an age of gods, to an age of heroes, and thence to an age of human ascendancy, with the possibility of a return to an earlier stage. From Vico it was but a short step to William Robertson and Johann Gottfried von Herder. Herder wrote *A Treatise on the Origin of Language* (1772) and later undertook an (unfinished) *Outline of a Philosophical History of Humanity;* both works were influential in the development of several lines of German historical thought. Robertson's *History of America* (2 vols., 1777) accepted an original unity of all humankind, which had progressed successively through savagery, barbarism, and civilization. This publication, a product of the Scottish Enlightenment, prefigured the development of theories of cultural and biological evolution and the ideas of Lewis Morgan and Charles Darwin in the next century. Darwin treated biological evolution at length, of course. But Morgan's *Ancient Society* (1877) offered what was in many respects the first systematic discussion of social and cultural evolution; it also envisaged a progression of humanity through different stages, from the savage to the civilized, and placed the Greeks and Romans at an advanced stage of barbarism and in some cases at the ultimate stage of civilization itself. Theories of evolution, as they were refined over the course of the 19th century, suggested a more or less unbroken line of continuity from the primitive to the civilized and coincided with the detailed working out of the categories of kinship, property, and religion by such disparate individuals as Numa Fustel de Coulanges, Johann Jakob Bachofen, Karl Marx, and Friedrich Engels. In this context, James Frazer attempted to ascertain the origin of myths and indeed of all humankind by reliance on data from antiquity as well as from numerous other ethnographic works.

In the 20th century ethnography, conjoined with anthropology and other disciplines, flourished at the hands of a series of distinguished practitioners, most of whom were concerned less with the formulation of grand metahistories and more with the detailed scrutiny of discrete groups from a range of methodological approaches. With Claude Lévi-Strauss, however, the fields of ethnography and anthropology engaged with a highly original and sophisticated structuralism. Lévi-Strauss's output was wide-ranging and spanned several decades from midcentury onward, but one of its intellectual debts was to the study of ancient cultures; his own work in turn also had an influence on classical scholarship in the second half of the 20th century and beyond. If some of Lévi-Strauss's thinking about antiquity can be gleaned from his semi-autobiographical *Tristes tropiques* (1955), an elegant and fascinating meditation on the ethnographer's craft, that same book nonetheless also points to the problems that can arise in cross-cultural study. "I am only too well aware of the reasons for the uneasiness I felt on coming into contact with Islam: I rediscovered in Islam the world I myself had come from: Islam is the West of the East . . . I cannot easily forgive Islam for showing me our own image." For all his insight into the workings of colonialism, the uneasiness with Islam evinced by Lévi-Strauss spills over into an approach that seems dangerously reductionist, and his book refers to Muslims as "incapable of tolerating the existence of others as others." *Tristes tropiques* signals to the reader the brilliance of the ethnographer's insight and the limits of his encounter with alterity. But it would be wrong to hold up *Tristes tropiques* as an example of current thinking. In fact, the field of ethnography has subjected itself to several critiques over the past generation and has extensively interrogated its involvement with colonialism, ethnocentrism, and racism. No small part of that process has meant the rethinking of ethnography's relationship to the Greek and Roman sources that helped shape the modern field. A beneficiary of such self-scrutiny has been not only ethnography and its related disciplines but also the study of those traditions that have been handed down from antiquity to the present day.

BIBL.: P. Atkinson, A. Coffey, S. Delmont, J. Lofland, and L. Lofland, eds., *Handbook of Ethnography* (London 2001). M. Detienne, *L'invention de la mythologie* (Paris 1981). A. Grafton, with A. Shelford and N. Siraisi, *New Worlds, Ancient Texts: The Power of Tradition and the Shock of Discovery* (Cambridge, Mass., 1992). C. Lévi-Strauss, *Tristes tropiques* (Paris 1955). W. Nippel, *Griechen, Barbaren und "Wilde": Alte Geschichte und Sozialanthropologie* (Frankfurt am Main 1990). W. H. Oswalt, *Other Peoples, Other Customs: World Ethnography and Its History* (New York 1972). P.V.

Etruscans

Despite the nearly complete loss of all ancient literary sources on the Etruscan world, and especially of the treatises dedicated specifically to it—Aristotle's *Nomina Tyrrhenon,* Theophrastus' *Perì Tyrrhenon,* Sostratus of Nisa's *Tyrrhenika,* the work of Aulus Caecina, Verrius Flaccus's *Rerum Etruscarum libri,* the *Tyrrhenika* of the emperor Claudius—it nevertheless seems certain that Etruria constituted a solid benchmark in the ancient tradition. This was the case for its political and institutional, artistic and cultural, and especially its religious aspects, particularly because of the echo it had in Roman culture beginning in antiquity. The importance of this tradition before the late republican and imperial periods is not easily discernable; nevertheless, the little data available indicate that it was quite ample and varied.

Beyond the primacy that the ancient tradition granted to Etruria in various spheres, or to Etruscan culture's influence on political ideology and its related rituals in the Roman world, it is above all the magical-religious system of the Etruscans that left the greatest mark on the tradition of the ancients, who saw in the Etruscans "the most religious people" inasmuch as they "excelled everyone in religious observance" (Livy 5.1.6). Other topoi reappear several times in the tradition, such as the emblematic image of Etruscan piracy found in Syracusan and Athenian propaganda in the late classical period, or that of *tryphē,* dear to a certain moralistic and philosophical tradition from Theopompus to Poseidonius. In the realm of art history there is the recovery of "Etruscan" motifs, which, however, is limited to specialized treatises (e.g., Vitruvius' *Tuscanicae dispositiones*) or to the episodic revival of themes and motifs for the purpose of commemorating certain purchasers (e.g, the so-called Corsini throne from the villa of Plautius Lateranus). Nevertheless, it is this theme of religion that predominates.

If on the one hand imperial culture quite clearly emphasized the substantial otherness of the Etruscan world compared to the Graeco-Roman one (Seneca, *Naturales quaestiones* 2.32.2), on the other hand an uninterrupted tradition, running from Tarquitius Priscus to Justinian's Constantinople, is interested precisely in the *Etrusca disciplina,* or divination guide, thanks in part to the Roman custom of turning to Etruscan haruspices (diviners) in the case of *prodigia, ostenta,* and *portenta.* In the second half of the 3rd century, Cornelius Labeo turned his attention to clarifying certain aspects of it that at the time were still perfectly integrated into the religious practice of the Roman world. One century later, Macrobius in his *Saturnalia* explained not only the practical side of rites and divination, but also their doctrinal content. In the 5th century Proclus, the Neoplatonist product of Hellenistic culture, submitted the normative Etruscan myth of Tages, whom he compared to chthonic Hermes, to an allegorical interpretation. In the 6th century John the Lydian, in his treatise on prodigies, identified the *Etrusca disciplina* as the most perfect expression of the Roman *mos maiorum* (traditionalism). This line, however, was broken by the decisive establishment of Christianity and by the repeated condemnations, pronounced until the turn of the 7th century by the Church and by various political authorities, of the survival of the "haruspical superstitions of the Etruscans," which had been preserved through the years of the Empire and were in part continued in the barbarian kingdoms such as Visigothic Spain.

Not until the 14th century did the Etruscan world reappear in the tradition, especially in the culture of those regions that traced their own origins to the Etruscan past, Florence and Tuscany but also Rome, the area around Viterbo, and Umbria east of the Tiber. There are a few cases of the reuse of Etruscan monuments in the High Middle Ages, such as the late-classical urn used in the 12th century in Volterra as a reliquary for the remains of Saint Clement, as well as the possible (but not sufficiently substantiated) reappearance of iconographic motifs in the repertory of artists such as Nicola and Giovanni Pisano (13th and 14th cent.). For the most part, though, the Etruscan world (as opposed to that of imperial Rome, which had been dear to the entire medieval tradition) reappeared in an intellectual paradigm whose object was to identify the lines of an autochthonous and independent tradition. Thus, Giovanni Villani, taking a regional perspective rather than a specifically urban one, referred significantly to Etruria, not to Tuscia. This gradually seeped into the consciousness of important Humanists such as Coluccio Salutati and then Leonardo Bruni, who in his *Historiarum florentini populi libri XII* put the Etruscan myth of urban civilization to a cogent and significant use for the politics and ideology of his day.

With Humanism, then, literature, art, and culture embraced the "glorious people of Tages" (*glorioso popolo tageto*)—as Giovanni Gherardi da Prato referred to the Etruscans in his 1425 work, *Paradiso degli Alberti*—knowledge of whom was only then starting to be accumulated as artifacts were discovered. The influence of Etruscan and Roman remains can now be seen in the work of artists who turned ancient expressive forms to new creative ends, even inserting archaic elements into their work, as in the case of a clay bust of John the Baptist, preserved in San Matteo in Pisa, in which the lid of a Hellenistic chest is used as a halo. What is more, through the learned speculations of Alberti and Filarete, the period witnessed the recovery of ancient monuments, such as the tomb of Porsenna in Chiusi. It became an object of repeated exercises for architects, especially Antonio da Sangallo, and an undisputed landmark on the ideological panorama of the area, as can be seen in Vencenzo Fedeli's 1561 speech to the Venetian Senate. In early art history, the 1550 edition of Vasari's *Vite* emphasized Donatello's debt to the Etruscan past, or what was believed to be such. And an indication of the weighty significance which that past had for Humanistic culture is offered by the epitaph composed (perhaps) by Lorenzo Valla for the tomb of Beato Angelico in Santa Maria Sopra Minerva in Rome, where the painter is called *flos Etruriae* (flower of Etruria).

In Cosimo de' Medici's Florence, Ugolino Verino remarked on the city's roots in Sulla and the Etruscans. In Lorenzo the Magnificent's time, although Poliziano exalted the role of Octavianus in Florence's origins and identified the city as the successor to imperial Rome—much like what Sixtus IV was doing in Rome—Naldo Naldi celebrated *il Magnifico* as "Tyrrhenus Apollus," making recourse to a fanciful etymology for the name Lorenzo: *lauri dictus de nomine Daphnis/pastor ab Etruscis* (*Eclogues* 1). The view of the Etruscans as embodying a rural serenity and far-off wisdom was reinforced by several artifacts sent to Lorenzo, like the Venus with an Etruscan inscription found in Pistoia, or the supposed funerary urn of Porsenna offered by the Sienese.

It was nevertheless in the Rome of Alexander VI that the Etruscan world became an object of devoted interest, in the work of the Dominican Giovanni Nanni, better known as Annius of Viterbo (ca. 1432–1502). Drawing whimsically on a combination of classical, Old Testament, cabalistic, and astrological sources, he reconstructed a vision of Etruscan primacy in the history of the world, tracing the Etruscans' origin to Noah, and before him to Osiris, who came to Italy with the name of Janus (for the Latins) or Vertumnus (for the Etruscans). This figure supposedly acted as a bearer of civilization and founded, among others, the city of Viterbo, which thus took on the status of the ideal center of the entire region. Unlike previous attempts to exalt a city's most ancient past, such as Lorenzo Vitelli's (1454) in Corneto (Tarquinia), Annius's work, supported by documents and inscriptions often artfully invented by the author himself, found ultimate form in the publication of the *Antiquitates* (1498). Its popularity is attested not only by the subsequent Parisian editions of 1512 and 1515 and by Teodoro Siciliano's mid-16th-century use of it for his images in the Sala del Consiglio in Viterbo's Palazzo Comunale, but also by the extraordinary staying power that Annius's theory had, especially in Tuscan culture during the 16th century and beyond.

The increase of discoveries claimed the attention of scholars and artists, who then took up Etruscan themes. For example, in the 1510s Sansovino fashioned for Montepulciano a statue of Porsenna, the mythical founder of the city. Nevertheless, the Etruscan world's influence on art seems rather weak. If Leonardo sketched the tumulus in Castellina in Chianti, no such interest is found, contrary to what has been claimed several times, in Michelangelo, one of whose famous drawings seems to be based not on motifs of Etruscan demonology but rather on the *signiferi* of the Column of Trajan. Only in architecture would the recovery of an Etruscan style, revived through the reappropriation of Vitruvius, enjoy extraordinary popularity from the beginning of the Renaissance.

In smaller centers the Etruscan myth, through the filter of Annius's ideas, nourished the exaltation of the most ancient past, as can be seen, for example, in Raffaele Maffei in Volterra, Sigismondo Tizio in Siena, and Marco Attilio Alessi in Arezzo. It was above all Cosimo I's Florence, however, that used the Etruscan world to give a historical veneer to a ruling ideology. The Accademia Fiorentina, founded by the Duke in 1541, was where this political and cultural paradigm was forged. Giambattista Gelli in his *Dell'origine di Firenze* (ca. 1544) and Pier Francesco Giambullari with his *Gello* (1546) reconfirmed Annius's Noah myth with new information, and the Dominican Santi Marmocchini, in 1544, attempted to trace the Tuscan vernacular by way of Etruscan back to Hebrew. On the one hand, Marmocchini corroborated Annius's theory; on the other, he held up Tuscan as the language best suited to preserving the flavor of truth of the divine word passed down by the Bible. In this framework fits the Frenchman Guillaume Postel's *De Etruriae regionis originibus* (1551), with good reason printed in Florence and dedicated *Cosmo Medici illustrissimo Etruriae Occiduae Duci*. It supported the Medici family's dynastic exigencies with a mythical history that, through the Noah legend, firmly united Rome, Etruria, and France, projecting the roots of their identity into the pre-classical past, that is, into a time before the creation of the Holy Roman Empire. From there, however, Cosimo's orientation had to change only slightly to move in the direction of Roman classicism, as can be seen in the tastes of the prince's collections. For if, with Vasari, he put the Chimera of Arezzo in the Palazzo Vecchio, he kept the bronze statue of the Arringatore, discovered in 1566 and thought to be Scipio the Younger (although it was obviously Etruscan, as could be seen from its inscription), in his own apartment in the new ducal residence in Palazzo Pitti.

The refined and eclectic atmosphere of his successor, Francesco, continued the resuscitation of the Etruscan world through rhetoric and learning. Accordingly, when in 1578 Alessandro Allori finished his celebration of the Medici at the villa of Poggio a Caiano with the *Giardino delle Esperidi,* he paired Cosimo-as-Hercules with the image of Fortune-Providence. As a new goddess, Nortia, she drives in the tenth nail to mark the beginning of the tenth year since the Medici had gained possession of the grand-ducal crown, which she raises with a gesture of triumph. Similar erudition marked output in the minor arts, as seen in a small bronze by an unknown Florentine craftsman that depicts an Etruscan priest, once in Alfonso II's Antichario in Ferrara and today in the Museo Civico there (inv. 8462).

It is the years of Francesco's rule and then of Ferdinand I and of his successor (1574–1621) that witnessed the progressive assertion of a lay historiography, unfettered by the sacred Scriptures, beginning with the works of Vincenzo Borghini and Scipione Ammirato. This period also saw, regarding the Etruscan world, an abrupt shift in viewpoint to one that took its bearings from an Etruria of kings, of whom Porsenna was the most famous and the Grand Duke was the heir. Part of this effort was *De Etruria regali,* written between 1616 and 1618 by the Scot Thomas Dempster, a teacher at the Pisan Studio. Commissioned by Cosimo II himself, this work of ambitious but muddled scholarship uses a combination of classical sources and apocryphal literature of the 16th century to describe the cities of Tuscany and to reconstruct a legendary genealogy of kings; its obvious intention is to demonstrate an undisputed historical continuity between the Etruscans and the ruling family. This work was not printed at the time, however, in part because of a shift in the Grand Duke's viewpoint. It is no coincidence that in 1619 he had Zenobi Pignoni print the court poet Giovanni Domenico Peri's *Fiesole distrutta,* a work that took up the theme of the Caesarian origin of Florence, which had been dear to Giovanni Villani's medieval historiography, and exalted the Grand Duke as a new Caesar.

But it is not only the Florentine and Tuscan sphere that is interested in the Etruscans. The appearance and extraordinary success of Leandro Alberti's *Descrittione di tutta Italia,* first published in Bologna in 1550 and reprinted many times, spread knowledge of the Etruscan remains then known to a wider audience, attracting the attention of literati, scholars, and collectors to that world. Thus, in Bologna Ulisse Aldrovandi speculated on the Etruscan language and argued that it was derived from Aramaic in his *De linguis,* composed between 1579 and 1582 but never printed. And in Ferrara, among the *mirabilia* to be seen and admired in Alfonso II's collection, curated by Pirro Ligorio, was the famous Apollo of Ferrara, the *iuvenis laurea coronati signum aeneum pulcherrimum et vetustissimum* with an Etruscan inscription that the Dutchman Etienne Wijnants, better known as Pighius, noted in his diary during his tour of Italy in 1574.

The 17th century apparently took no interest in the Etruscans, apart from the attention of collectors or from a few lone and locally oriented writings, such as Felice Ciatti's work on Perugia (1638) and the reveries of Curzio Inghirami of Volterra (1637), which ignited a lively polemic even in the Roman sphere.

It was not until the beginning of the 18th century that the Etruscan world received a renewed interest. After Giusto Fontanini's parochial *De antiquitatibus Hortae* (1708) and the fleeting mentions in Montfaucon's *Antiquité expliquée et représentée en figure* (1719–1724), it was the publication of Dempster's work, promoted in Florence in the fall of 1719 by Filippo Buonarroti and financed by the Duke of Holkham, that directed and advanced the rediscovery of the Etruscans. This project thus came to be intertwined in the complex political picture of the end of the Medici dynasty and of the fate of the Granducato. These two volumes were introduced into circulation in 1726 by the grand-ducal printing office, and they were supplemented with a text by Buonarroti himself, which treated the principal issues of the Etruscan world with illustrations of well-known Etruscan artifacts (or those believed to be such at the time). Regarding politics and institutions, the publication contributed powerfully, on the ideological and cultural level, to the cohesiveness of a new identity being constructed for the region, where the primacy of Florence was dissolving into the more general dimension of Tuscany. On the other hand, it constituted a profound renewal of the tradition of archaeological studies, opening the way to the modern understanding of the Etruscan world, and the work enjoyed noteworthy success not only in Italy but also throughout Europe. In Rome Clement XII's elevation to the papal see was celebrated with Domenico Rolli's *Porsenna* (1731), and the anticipated revival of the papal state's centrality was exalted with the commemoration of the Roman-Etruscan alliance. At the same time academies were founded, such as the Etrusca in Cortona (1726) and the Colombaria in Florence (1735), and others, such as the Quirini in Rome, were renewed.

With the development of archaeological studies and the increase in discoveries, the first half of the 18th century witnessed a widespread Etruscomania that gripped the entire European intellectual world. Beside the work of Scipione Maffei, it is above all the Florentine Anton Francesco Gori and his *Museum Etruscum* (1737–1743) that dominated the cultural horizon—and not only in Italy, as can be seen by the echo his writings had in France, England, and German-speaking countries, where in 1770 a kind of *großer Querschnitt* of his *Museum Etruscum* was published for the use of students and collectors. As in the 16th century, issues of language and script were the privileged area in archaeological studies, in which a long-lasting reciprocal exchange of copies of inscriptions facilitated attempts at deciphering.

On the epigraphical side of things, a partial resolution of the difficulties in reading inscriptions came at the hands of the Swiss Louis Bourguet and the three essays he published in Geneva's *Bibliothèque Italique.* Regarding linguistic and lexical issues, however, it was not possible to go beyond a very elementary stage, and efforts at translation were limited to free and imaginative divinations that today seem embarrassing. Such were the conjectures of Giovan Battista Passeri of Pesaro in his *Lettere Roncagliesi* (1741), and of Giovanni Lami in his *Lettere Gualfondiane,* published under the name of Clemente Bini in the pages of *Novelle letterarie* in 1744.

With the passing of Gori and the intellectuals of his generation in the 1750s, a phase of rearguard positions of a purely parochial type neared its end, although it would continue on listlessly, with archaeologists all over Italy, until the turn of the next century. These were the years in which interest in the Etruscan world intensified on the part of non-Italian artists and archaeologists, such as the Englishman Thomas Jenkins, who in 1761 excavated the Monterozzi necropolis of Tarquinia, and the Scot James Byres, who a few years later began writing his *History of the Etrurians* (never finished), in which he reasserted the Etruscans' primacy over Rome in the fields of art, science, and literature. The observations and new aesthetic approach, first of Winckelmann and then of Ennio Quirino Visconti and Luigi Lanzi, soon had an effect on how the Etruscan world was viewed both in Italy and in the broader European sphere. The particular interest of the Pole Stanislaw Kostka Potocki in the Etruscans in Campania testified to this development.

In the language of melodrama we find an indication of the popular understanding of the Etruscan world: the term *Etruscan* is used as a synonym for excellence and originality, but also for "strange." And the activity of many craftsmen and artisans in various media, particularly ceramics, contributed in the decades around the turn of the 19th century to the diffusion throughout Europe of a very common "Etruscan style" of furniture and decoration. A more informed interpretation of painted ceramics evolved at this point. They had been considered Etruscan simply because of their discovery in Etruria, an idea confirmed in no uncertain terms in Giovan Battista Passeri's monumental work, the three-volume *Picturae Etruscorum in vasculis* (1767–1775), but they were actually Greek, as Winckelmann and Lanzi had already clarified. This fact gradually became widely accepted, thanks to Eduard Gerhard's 1831 essay on the Vulcian discoveries of Luciano Bonaparte, the Candelori brothers, and the Feoli.

In Italy the appearance of Giuseppe Micali's (1810) successful and oft-reprinted work, *Italia avanti il domonio dei romani* (1810), despite being steeped in the Enlightenment, provided nourishment for the neo-Guelph current of historiography throughout the entire 19th century, above all with Gino Capponi and Atto Vannucci. In Germany, philological *Altertumswissenschaft* (science of antiquity) took up the Etruscans with the first edition of Karl Otfried Müller's *Die Etrusker* (1828). In England the way was definitively opened for a more enduring interest in ancient Etruria and its culture by the exhibition organized in London in 1836 by the Campanari family, excavators and merchants of Tuscan art, as well as by Elizabeth Caroline Hamilton Gray's *History of Etruria* (1840) and George Dennis's *Cities and Cemeteries of Etruria* (1848), both reprinted many times. In France the *fascination des Etrusques* was echoed in the writings of Stendhal and Mérimée.

Starting in the second half of the 19th century, further discoveries, the parallel formation of the great European collections, and the development of philological studies and of research heedful of the historical evolution of Etruscan culture combined to lay the foundation for a more informed understanding of the Etruscan people and their world. Nevertheless, there remained irrational impulses toward a supposed "Etruscan mystery," which are still present today, especially at the level of popular culture. Be that as it may, interest in the Etruscans did not became a coherent and defined subject of historical knowledge until the 20th century. This civilization has continued to fascinate, a fact reflected in the art and literature of the Western world.

Regarding the figurative arts, even though it has been definitively shown that there was no Etruscan influence on the 20th-century sculptor Alberto Giacometti of Ticino, it is above all the Italian sphere that is most under the sway of the Etruscan heritage. On the one hand there are the more or less influence-free reinterpretations of certain sculptors, such as Marino Marini or Arturo Martini. On the other there is the proud insertion of Etruscan artifacts with symbolic meaning into pictures, such as Oscar Ghiglia's *Self-Portrait* (1919) in the Uffizi, where a famous boundary stone from Orvieto (held in the Museo Archeologico in Florence) depicted behind the painter emphasizes the Etruscan roots of his art. The fascination for the Etruscans can be discerned even more in literature. In Italy, Etruria is the land of tombs and underworld deities, as seen in D'Annunzio or Malaparte or Alberto Savinio. In France the same motif is tinged with further psychological and mediumistic elements, which characterize, for example, Daniel Rops's novella *Le Dieu de l'ombre du soir* (1935). The Anglo-Saxon world, however, has crafted a reinterpretation, as D. H. Lawrence (*Etruscan Places,* 1932) and Aldous Huxley (*Those Barren Leaves,* 1925, *Point Counter Point,* 1928) freely forged their own Etruria, lavishly and impulsively vital and happy, as part of their yearning for a lost world. Only the large traveling Etruscan exhibition of 1955–1956, which circulated to Zurich, Milan, Paris, the Hague, Oslo, and Cologne, made the Etruscan world properly known to the public and critics alike.

BIBL.: G. Baffioni and P. Mattiangeli, *Annio da Viterbo: Documenti e ricerche I* (Rome 1981). P. Barocchi, ed., *L'Ac-*

cademia Etrusca (Milan 1985). G. Bartoloni and P. Bocci Pacini, "The Importance of Etruscan Antiquity in the Tuscan Renaissance," *Acta Hyperborea* 10 (2003) 449–479. S. Bedford, *Aldous Huxley: A Biography* (London 1973–1974). C. Bendi and P. Rambelli, "Il mito della vittoria sugli Etruschi nel Porsenna di Domenico Rolli," *Studi Settecenteschi* 21 (2001) 43–51. L. Bonfante and N. Thomson de Grummond, "Wounded Souls: Etruscan Ghosts and Michelangelo's 'Slaves,'" *Analecta Romana* 17–18 (1989) 99–116. F. Borsi, ed., *Fortuna degli Etruschi* (Milan 1985). S. Bruni, "Anton Francesco Gori, Carlo Goldoni e 'la famiglia dell'antiquario,'" *Symbolae Antiquariae* 1 (2008) 11–69, and "L''ombra della sera': Uso e abuso di un'immagine," *Rassegna Volterrana* 84 (2007) 193–233. G. Camporeale, "La scoperta degli Etruschi nel Rinascimento," *Atene e Roma* 48, no. 4 (2002) 145–165. A. Chastel, "L'Etruscan revival du XVe siècle," *Revue Archéologique* 1 (1959) 165–180. G. Cipriani, *Il mito etrusco nel Rinascimento fiorentino* (Florence 1980) and Cipriani, ed., *G. Postel, De Etruriae regionis* (Rome 1986). M. Cristofani, *La scoperta degli Etruschi nel Settecento* (Rome 1983) and "Il *Von Kunst der Hetrurien* nelle due edizioni della *Geschichte,*" in *J. J. Winckelmann tra letteratura e archeologia,* ed. M. Fancelli (Venice 1993) 113–144. A. Dawson, *Masterpieces of Wedgwood in the British Museum* (London 1984). L. Deitz, "Die Scarith von Scornello: Fälschung und Methode in Curzio Inghiramis 'Ethruscarum antiquitatum fragmenta' (1637)," *Neulateineisches Jahrbuch* 5 (2003) 103–133. L. S. Fusco and G. Corti, *Lorenzo de' Medici: Collector and Antiquarian* (New York 2006). J. Heurgon, *La découverte des Etrusques au début du XIXe siècle* (Paris 1973). A. Hus, "Stendhal et les Etrusques," in *Mélanges offerts à Jacques Heurgon* (Rome 1976) 436–469. I. Jenkins, *Archaeologists and Aesthetes* (London 1992). M. Kunze, "Etruskische Kunst in Berlin," in *Die Welt der Etrusker: Archäologische Denkmäler aus Museen der sozialistisches Länder* (Berlin 1988) 397–420. R. Leighton and C. Castellino, "Thomas Dempster and Ancient Etruria," *Papers of the British School at Rome* 58 (1990) 337–352. E. Masci, "The Birth of Ancient Vase Collecting in Naples in the Early Eighteenth Century," *Journal of the History of Collections* 19 (2007) 215–224. M. Pallottino, *Les Etrusques et l'Europe* (Paris 1992). N. H. Ramage, "Sir William Hamilton as Collector," *American Journal of Archaeology* 94 (1990) 469–480. S. Reynolds and B. Gialluca, "Un documento inedito su 'De Etruria Regali': Novità e conferme," *Symbolae Antiquariae* 2 (2009). D. H. Rhodes, *Dennis of Etruria* (London 1973). A. Romualdi, "Etruschi nella Galleria d'Arte Moderna," in *Governare l'arte: Studi per A. Paolucci* (Bologna 2008) 11 ff. M. Rosa, "Dal 'primato fiorentino' alla cultura toscana: Uomini e idee nel Settecento," *Rassegna Volterrana* 79 (2002) 39–51. M. Rossi, *Le fila del tempo: Il sistema storico di luigi Lanzi* (Florence 2006). I. D. Rowland, *The Scarith of Scornello: A Tale of Renaissance Forgery* (Chicago 2004). K. Sagar, *D. H. Lawrence: Life into Art* (New York 1985). L. Saracco, "Un'apologia della 'Hebraica Veritas' nella Firenze di Cosimo I: Il 'Dialogo in defensione della lingua thoscana' di Santi Marmocchini," *Rivista di storia e letteratura religiosa* 42 (2006) 215–246. E. Schwarzenberg and B. Paolozzi Strozzi, "Norzia o la costante fortuna: La lunetta di Alessandro Allori a Poggio a Caiano," in *Kunst des Cinquecento in der Toskana,* ed. M. Cämmerer (Munich 1992) 197–206. K. Sloan and A. Burnett, eds., *Enlightenment: Discovering the World in the Eighteenth Century* (Washington, D.C., 2003). R. Weiss, *The Renaissance Discovery of Classical Antiquity* (Oxford 1969).

S.BR.

Translated by Patrick Baker

Etymology

In the first decades of the 7th century CE, Isidore, bishop of Seville, compiled a 20-book work in Latin called *Etymologiae sive origines* (*Etymologies or Origins*). Our knowledge of ancient and early medieval thought owes an enormous amount to this encyclopedia, a reflective catalogue of received wisdom, which the authors of the only complete translation into English introduce as "arguably the most influential book, after the Bible, in the learned world of the Latin West for nearly a thousand years" (Barney et al. 2006, 3). These days, of course, Isidore and his *Etymologies* are anything but household names—the translation dates only from 2006 and the heading of the Wikipedia entry "Etymology" warns, "Not to be confused with *Entomology,* the scientific study of insects"—but the Vatican is reportedly considering naming Isidore the patron saint of the Internet, which should make him and his greatest scholarly achievement known, if but dimly, to pretty much everyone.

People today are liable to confuse *etymology* with *entomology* because the words look and sound similar and, furthermore, because neither is so common, or describes so widespread a pursuit, as to be part of semantically transparent everyday discourse. Isidore himself would not have mixed them up: he knew Greek and understood that his subject was not "the study (*-logy*) of insects (*entomo-*)" but instead "the study of truth (*etymo-*)"—or, as he put it, "the origin of words, when the force of a verb or a noun is inferred through interpretation" (1.29.1, trans. Barney et al. 2006, 54). But it is not out of the question that he would nevertheless have believed them to be connected: perhaps there are *bees* in the *ABCs*? If it is of questionable judgment in a serious handbook to ascribe to Isidore, even in jest, an English-language–based case of wordplay (though I take comfort in knowing that the ardent wordsmith and lepidopterist Vladimir Nabokov shows himself scient in his 1969 novel *Ada* of the power potential in the anagrams *insect, incest,* and *nicest,* and also that the most Isidorean of contemporary Latinists, John Henderson, has recently written a pun-filled book on the *Etymologies*), it is nonetheless appropriately illustrative of the leading principle of ancient etymological practice, namely that things that sound even vaguely similar are the same in origin. For example, Isidore writes, "Fire [*ignis*] is so named because nothing can be born [*gignere*] from it, for it is an inviolable element, consuming everything that it seizes" (19.6.5, 376–377)—or, in Henderson's rendering, "'*Fire*' is so-called because *no* way to *sire* from it" (2007, 201). This is a case of an etymology *e contrario,* "from the opposite," a negative method that may well strike modern critics as peculiar. But it is noteworthy that Isidore's 1st-century BCE Roman forebear Varro took essentially the opposite tack in his etymology-filled work *De lingua Latina:* "Fire [*ignis*] is from being born [⟨*g*⟩*nascendo*] because from it there is birth, and fire sets alight everything that is born" (5.70).

Still, both Varro and Isidore employ the same basic etymological technique, deriving word *X* in language *L* from some other (like-sounding and either positively or negatively semantically connected, or at least connectable) word *Y* in the same *L*. Easily the best-known example of this method is *Lucus a non lucendo*—"A grove [*lucus*] is so called from [*a*] not [*non*] being light [*lucendo*]"—found as such in the commentary on Virgil (apropos of *Aeneid* 1.22) of the 4th-century CE grammarian Servius (and in various other guises through the ages: see, e.g., Isidore 1.29.3, 1.37.24, 14.8.30, and 17.6.7). This catchphrase is now infamous for expressing an absurd idea, as though "a grove is so called from not being grave." And this in turn has given rise to the waggish *Ludus a non ludendo:* "School [*ludus*] is so called because it's not cool [*ludendo,* literally 'playing']," a line whose first appearance in precisely this form only seems to be modern, though such major intellectual figures as Aelius Stilo (2nd–1st cent. BCE; fr. 59 Funaioli), Varro (according to Isidore 18.16.2), Quintilian (1st cent. CE; *Orator's Education* 1.6.34), and Festus (2nd cent. CE; ed. Lindsay 109, 23–24) report the essential idea (cf. Maltby 1991, 350). It was surely clear to many speakers of Latin, however, that *ludus* actually *does* in some sense come from *ludendo,* for the basic meaning of the noun *ludus* in classical times was "play," not (elementary or gladiatorial) school, a secondary sense that it probably acquired as a calque on Greek *skh*olē, "leisure → school." And as for *lucus,* some ancient sources report that it truly is *a lucendo* rather than *a non lucendo* (see Maltby 1991, 349–350), a view with which, as it happens, modern etymologists concur: a clearing (the original meaning of *lucus*) is called thus from being clear.

To return to fire, the language *L* to which Varro's and Isidore's etymologies of *ignis* are specific is Latin, and it should not come as a surprise that in the very first work in the Western tradition devoted to the origin of language and to etymology, Plato's 4th-century BCE dialogue *Cratylus,* Socrates engages in the same procedure for Greek. When, for instance, Hermogenes asks Socrates to account for the Greek word for fire, *pyr,* the philosopher says that it does not easily fit with the Greek language, suggests that it is originally a foreign ("barbarian") expression, and claims that one would therefore be making quite a mistake if one tried to use Greek to explain its etymology (409C10–410A8)—but he leads off by saying, *To "pyr" aporō,* "I have no idea about 'fire'" (409D1), a pithy phrase that deftly plays the usual linguistic game, as the verb *a-porō* ("I *fear* I don't know") looks to be the negation (in *a-*) of *pyr* itself.

The Varronian etymology of *ignis,* cited above, explicitly involves derivation and thus has at least an implicit diachronic dimension: that *X* comes from *Y* suggests that *Y* precedes *X*. But the ancient world also knew another technique, grounded in Epicurean and Lucretian atomism, that is today often referred to as etymological: likewise involving just a single language, it is above all playful (like, probably, Socrates' comment about *pyr*), though it frequently has a serious, scholarly purpose as well (see, e.g., Snyder 1980). In linguistic atomism, the smallest elements of language are the letters—known in Latin as *elementa* (a word whose etymology may well be the alphabetic sequence *LMN*)—and the complex arrangement of letters on the page is a major constituent feature of verse. When, therefore, the 1st-century BCE Roman poet Lucretius writes in his six-book hexametric poem *De rerum natura* (*On the Nature of Things*), *postremo in lignis cinerem fumumque videri,/cum perfracta forent, ignisque latere minutos* (finally, ash and smoke should be seen in wood when broken, and little fires should hide there, 1.891–892), he is describing with artistic iconicity a scientific belief about the makeup of the world: the material "element" fire is evidently connected with wood (*ligna*), and this fact is mirrored in the Latin language, in which the five linguistic "elements" of the word for fire, *IGNIS,* are literally "in pieces of wood," *in lIGNIS.* In fact (though this need not occupy us here), the precise nature of the analogy is disputed, and the philosophical situation is evidently very complicated. Although Lucretius repeatedly associates the two words in books 1 and 2 of his poem (on occasion he also associates *ignis* and the verb "be born," i.e., *gigni,* at 1.783–784), he mocks the 5th-century BCE Presocratic philosopher Anaxagoras for his belief that fire actually resides in wood (we might say in English, "in *firs*"): Lucretius 1.891–892, quoted earlier, is a counterfactual assertion (ash and smoke "should" be seen but actually are not), and the poet elsewhere says, *et non est lignis tamen insitus ignis* (and yet fire is *not* implanted in wood, 1.901).

It was only later—much later—that people began to etymologize across languages in a less scattershot way, in a way that would presumably be less likely to merit the scorn of such figures of the Enlightenment as Voltaire, to whom is attributed (perhaps incorrectly) the infamous remark that etymology is the science in which consonants count for little and vowels for nothing. True, in antiquity learned men and poets were already regularly comparing or translating between Greek and Latin, or playing on perceived connections (see, e.g., O'Hara 1996), and some etymological ideas were probably commonplace: for example, that the words for *god* in these two languages, respectively *theos* (more exactly, t^{h}eós) and *deus,* were somehow the same (see Maltby 1991, 185). (This view seems so evidently correct that people are always surprised to learn that modern linguistics has conclusively demonstrated it to be wrong: neither do the two words go back to a common source, nor does one derive from the other.) But *god* was a special case: early work from the Middle Ages and especially the Renaissance on linguistic kinship was generally intimately tied to one or another conception of the Tower of Babel and the relationships among languages and ethnic groups (see Borst 1957–1963). It is quite remarkable that Joseph Justus Scaliger in his *Diatriba de Europaeorum linguis* (*Diatribe on the Languages of the Europeans*), composed in 1599, went against the prevailing idea of immediately postlapsarian monolingualism by asserting that names of "god"—since they surely did not change over time—were a good way to determine linguistic relationship and that *theos* and *deus* were far enough apart in sound that Greek and Latin, two languages that we can now prove are related, had to belong to different *linguae matrices*, or "wombs of language." (Scaliger states elsewhere, however, that *theos* did give rise to *deus*.) The appearance of the following remark on "fire" in Erasmus's 1528 dialogue *De recta Latini Graecique sermonis pronuntiatione* (*On the Correct Pronunciation of Latin and Greek*) is thus striking for its reach beyond both words for *god* and the canonical trio of sacred tongues, Greek, Latin, and Hebrew: "*Pyr* is another word which . . . we [Dutch] pronounce wrong. The Germans, who have borrowed the word from Greek, pronounce it right except for changing the original smooth consonant for an aspirate [*Feuer*]. The Dutch change it to a *v* [*vuur*]" (947, trans. M. Pope). Erasmus had no theory of linguistic relationship, and in fact he made a significant mistake in deriving Dutch *vuur* (*X* in language *L*) from Greek *pyr* (*Y* in a *different* language *M*): the Germanic words for fire are cognate with *pyr*—that is, they all go back to the same source, a language now known as proto–Indo-European—rather than being borrowed from it. It was not until the end of the 18th century and the first half of the 19th that historical-comparative linguistics, in which whole sets of words are systematically compared, got off the ground. (The best, though idiosyncratic, book-length study of etymological practice over the past 200 years is by Yakov Malkiel [1993], who concentrates on the development of the Romance languages out of Latin.)

With the dawn of "scientific" etymology it became possible to compare *X* in language *L* and *Y* in language *M* and explain how both of them derive from **Z* in language *N*, where *N* is a reconstruction of something we know existed but for which there are no actual linguistic records (a proto-language) and where the asterisk indicates that *Z* is thus a reconstructed proto-form (see Watkins 2000). The name of fire—more exactly, names—is instructive in this regard. The evident similarities between Latin *ignis* and words for fire in the Indic, Baltic, and Slavic languages—e.g., Sanskrit *agní-*, Lithuanian *ugnìs*, and Old Church Slavic *ognĭ*—could finally be understood as pointing to the fact that about 6,000 years ago they were all one and the same thing, a proto–Indo-European noun that we would now reconstruct as something like ***$h_1og^{(w)}$*nis*. Similarly, Greek *pyr*, though bearing no resemblance to *ignis*, is almost the same as *pir*, the word for fire in Umbrian, a language very closely related to Latin; together with forms in many other Indo-European languages—e.g., English *fire* itself, Armenian *hur* (fire), and Czech *pýř* (ashes), as well as words for fire in two branches of the family that were not known until the 20th century, Hittite (Anatolian) *paḫḫur* and Tocharian B *puwar*/A *por*—they lead us to reconstruct a proto-form ***peh_2wr.

The Latin word *ignis* did not survive into the Romance languages, being replaced in proto-Romance by the accusative case form of Latin *focus* (hearth), whose meaning shifted metonymically to fire. Despite appearances, then, such words as Italian *fuoco*, Spanish *fuego*, and French *feu* have nothing etymological to do with English *fire*, German *Feuer*, and Dutch *vuur*—or for that matter with Greek *pyr*, which Joachim Périon in his 1555 treatise *De linguae Gallicae origine* (*On the Origin of the French Language*) explicitly claimed as the ancestor of *feu*. As for why the proto–Indo-Europeans would have spoken of fire in two different ways, it is noteworthy that the words in the former set (*ignis*, etc.) are masculine, while those in the latter (*pyr*, etc.) are neuter. This distinction has suggested to researchers in the past century, both grammarians and those with a broader interest in stories and myths, that the one is an active force, capable of personification (Agni is the Vedic god of fire), whereas the other represents fire as an "inactive" natural substance. It may be worth noting in this regard that a linguist who has contributed a rather different entry on etymology in another encyclopedia starts off his "History of Etymology" by citing textual (rather than reconstructed) support that the earliest Indo-European people of the Indian subcontinent regarded Agni as a specifically active force: in the *Rigveda*, forms of the verb *aj-* (drive), the Sanskrit cognate of the like-meaning Latin *agere* (from whose past participle, *actus*, comes English *active*), are occasionally used in connection with the god (cf. Hamp 2003, 7). Even if there is a real basis for the link between Agni and *aj-* (and it must be admitted that the evidence is not as robust as one might wish), it is folk-etymological rather than scientific, as there is no formal way to bring the noun ***$h_1og^{(w)}$*nis*, which may contain a root ***h_1eg^{w}*-* (shine), together with the root ***$h_2e\acute{g}$*-* (drive).

Now that a number of approaches to etymology have been mentioned that yield results that are difficult to reconcile with one another (e.g., that Latin *ignis* is related to *gignere* and also to *ligna* and also to Sanskrit *agní-*), it is appropriate to come back to the literal definition of *etymology* as "the study of truth" and ask what this means. Are some of these approaches and results "more true" than others? And (to return to Isidore's definition) through what sorts of "interpretation" is it sensible to "infer" the "force" of a word? As is so often the case with such questions, there are no simple answers: much depends on historical context and intellectual stance (see Del Bello 2007 on postmodern etymological allegoresis). From classical times until very recently the vast majority of etymologies, whether rooted in one language or more, rely in the first place on the story one tells about similarities in sound; these days, however, linguists interested in etymology mostly compare across languages while looking backward at some proto-language, and the vagaries of phonological change mean that just as forms that look similar are often historically unrelated (e.g., Greek *theos* and Latin *deus,* or French *feu* and German *Feuer*), so do forms often turn out to be related that do not at first glance seem to have much to do with each other (e.g., the Latin root-cognate of Greek *theos* is not *deus* but rather *festus,* festive). The linguist and classicist Roland G. Kent, editor of the standard Loeb Classical Library edition of *De lingua Latina,* comments in a terse footnote to Varro's claim that *ignis* is from ⟨*g*⟩*nascendo* that this etymology is "false"—by which he means that linguists today know that the proto–Indo-European root of "be born" is **ǵenh*$_1$- and unconnected to **h*$_1$*og*$^{(w)}$nis. This does not mean, however, that Varro's observation is worthless. Far from it: the Romans of Varro's time had no idea of proto–Indo-European; more than a few of them will have arrived, however, at the idea that "fire" and "birth" had something to do with each other, and thoughts of this kind have subtle linguistic and cultural consequences. A well-known example of such a consequence is the common spelling of the name Publius Vergilius Maro not as Vergil but rather as Virgil, a change due in part to the poet's reputation in the Middle Ages as a great magician or necromancer, someone who would have wielded a *uirga* (*virga*), or wand.

Broadly speaking, then, classical "etymology" in late antiquity (see Opelt 1966), the Middle Ages (see Klinck 1970), and beyond was largely a matter of what is today retronymically referred to as folk (or popular) etymology. But folk etymology, though often derided by those "in the know," remains an important linguistic force and must be taken seriously—for one reason, because the popular form often wins out. For example, the *mouse* in our word *dormouse* (plural *dormice*) reflects the influence of murine creatures on (probably) an Anglo-Norman word like *dormeus,* hibernating (see the sleepy Dormouse in *Alice's Adventures in Wonderland*); *rhyme* is hardly ever written *rime* any longer (as in "The Rime of the Ancient Mariner"), but the spelling with *rhy-,* which strongly suggests a borrowing of a rho-initial word in Greek (a language that, in the classical period, did not use rhyme as a poetic device), shows the influence of the (in fact unrelated, Greek-derived) word *rhythm;* and the Greek-derived word *asparagus* has since the 17th century often been called *sparrow-grass* (indeed, the *Oxford English Dictionary,* under "asparagus," notes that *sparrow-grass* "remained the polite name during the 18th c. [though] botanists still wrote *asparagus*").

Isidore wrote that "the knowledge of a word's etymology often has an indispensable usefulness for interpreting the word, for when you have seen whence a word has originated, you understand its force more quickly. Indeed, one's insight into anything is clearer when its etymology is known" (1.29.2, 55). Because language is an integral part of the human experience, the species-unique tool we use to describe and order our surroundings, it is understandable that people should wish to examine the tool itself: to take it apart, to play with it, to try to square the word with the world. Long may we continue to do so—and there are ample classical and post-classical models at our disposal.

BIBL.: Stephen A. Barney et al., *The Etymologies of Isidore of Seville* (Cambridge 2006). Arno Borst, *Der Turmbau von Babel: Geschichte der Meinungen über Ursprung und Vielfalt der Sprachen und Völker,* 4 vols. (Stuttgart 1957–1963). Davide Del Bello, *Forgotten Paths: Etymology and the Allegorical Mindset* (Washington, D.C., 2007). Eric P. Hamp, "Etymology," in *International Encyclopedia of Linguistics,* 2nd ed., ed. William J. Frawley, vol. 2 (Oxford 2003) 7–12. John Henderson, *The Medieval World of Isidore of Seville: Truth from Words* (Cambridge 2007). Roswitha Klinck, *Die lateinische Etymologie des Mittelalters* (Munich 1970). Yakov Malkiel, *Etymology* (Cambridge 1993). Robert Maltby, *A Lexicon of Ancient Latin Etymologies* (Leeds 1991). James J. O'Hara, *True Names: Vergil and the Alexandrian Tradition of Etymological Wordplay* (Ann Arbor 1996). I. Opelt, "Etymologie," in *Reallexikon für Antike und Christentum,* vol. 6, ed. Theodor Klauser (Stuttgart 1966) cols. 797–844. Jane McIntosh Snyder, *Puns and Poetry in Lucretius' De rerum natura* (Amsterdam 1980). Calvert Watkins, *The American Heritage Dictionary of Indo-European Roots,* 2nd ed. (Boston 2000).

J.T.K.

Euclid

Greek mathematician from the third century BCE. He is the author of the most famous book in the history of mathematics, the *Elements.* Yet we know nothing about where he came from or his family, nothing about his training. He probably taught in Alexandria, and ancient tradition suggests some connection with Ptolemy I.

Euclid composed a kind of encyclopedia that covered all the sciences that the ancients called mathematics, including the most abstract, such as geometry (*Elements* 1–4 and 10–13, *Data, On Divisions of Figures*) and arithmetic (*Elements* 7–9), as well as the sciences that applied to some aspects of the physical world (*Optics* and *Catoptrics,* dealing with the geometrical study of direct and reflected vision, respectively; *Phenomena,* a short treatise on spherical astronomy; *Elements of Music,* which explains the mathematical theory of musical intervals). These works are syntheses probably intended for teaching and organizing the mathematical corpus of the time. They all follow a deductive approach, and it is in geometry, particularly in the *Elements,* that this approach is best used.

At times Euclid was presented as the mere editor of textbooks. But taking into account his lost yet attested works (*Porisms, Surface Loci*), his successors, such as Apollonius of Perga and Pappus of Alexandria, drew a more nuanced portrait in their comments, that of a competent geometer, active in avant-garde research (conics, theory of geometric loci) and interested in the presentation of scientific demonstrations and the writing of reference texts. There is nothing here either contradictory or unique in the history of mathematics.

Euclid's fame is unquestionably attached to the success of the *Elements*. The number and relative antiquity of manuscript copies, the number of translations, abridged versions, and other adaptations, the variety of comments that have sprung from this text, which has enjoyed a large number of editions, prove the immense significance it has had in the history and teaching of mathematics. Its influence exceeds the limited field of mathematics, for it has had a dual function, serving as a mathematical monograph and, more important, providing a model for axiomatic deductive reasoning.

As early as Roman antiquity, then in late antiquity, and later during the Arabic and Latin Middle Ages, mastering the content of the *Elements* (the study of the simplest figures such as triangles, parallelograms, circles; the properties of equality and proportion among figures and solids or among numbers; the construction of polygons and regular polyhedrons; and so on) was fundamental for those who wanted to deepen their study. There are few fundamental objects in the *Elements*. We count essentially two: the number (whole natural and integers) and its different kinds, and the figure (plane or solid) and its elements (vertex, sides, faces, angles). The distinction between the different elements matches rather well the distinction introduced by Aristotle between two modes of composition, discrete (numbers) and continuous (geometrical magnitudes). Euclid thus proposed two different theories of proportion in books 5 (magnitudes) and 7 (numbers) that he used jointly when classifying irrational lines and surfaces (book 10).

These two themes, ratio and proportions on the one hand, and irrationality on the other, were among the most discussed in the Middle Ages. Scholars from Islamic countries wrote dozens of commentaries about these topics, and some were translated into Latin. The discussion was not limited to comparing Euclid's method to Aristotle's. The theory of proportions constituted the common language of mathematics used in natural philosophy; this situation went on at least until Galileo's time, when new calculations (algebraic, differential, and integral) were firmly established. The question of a numeric continuum would be solved only with the rigorous construction of the ensemble of real numbers in the second half of the 19th century.

Both writing style and reasoning method are implied by the title itself. An "element" is a fundamental result that is part of the demonstration of other, more complex results, following the pattern composing–composed. The intellectual structure is that of the alphabet and the composition of words from irreducible elements. Though this literary genre was not invented by Euclid (it goes back to the 5th century BCE), Euclid took it to a certain level of perfection. The narrative is deductive and synthetic, and it distinguishes on the one hand the primary principles as such, and on the other, the propositions demonstrated on the ground of these principles or previous demonstrations. Among the principles, Euclid distinguished definitions that established the meaning of the words, five geometrical postulates, and five common notions (for geometry and arithmetic), also called axioms. The authentic common notions deal with the property of equality and inequality. The fifth postulate is the most important one, indispensable for establishing the theory of parallels; as mathematicians of the 19th century would show, it characterizes one particular type of geometry among others, known ever since as "Euclidean geometry."

For ancient thinkers, a logical demand for minimalism, aesthetic considerations, and pedagogical efficiency based on concision and clarity went hand in hand. Editions from the Middle Ages and Renaissance did not always embody these characteristics; for instance, the Jesuit Clavius's edition favored thoroughness. Considerably enlarged, the *Elements* was then conceived as a *Summa* of elementary geometry. Yet Euclid's text remained a magnificent example of scientific account imitated by mathematicians as well as by philosophers and theologians proficient in the *more geometrico* style.

BIBL.: Thomas Little Heath, *The Thirteen Books of Euclid's Elements* (Cambridge 1926). Ian Mueller, *Philosophy of Mathematics and Deductive Structure of Euclid's Elements* (Cambridge, Mass., 1981). Sabind Rommevaux, Ahmed Djebbar, and Bernard Vitrac, "Remarques sur l'histoire du texte des Éléments d'Euclide," *Archive for History of Exact Sciences* 55 (2001) 221–295. Bernard Vitrac, "Euclide," in *Dictionnaire des philosophes antiques*, ed. R. Goulet (Paris 2000) 3:253–272, and "Euclid," in *New Dictionary of Scientific Bibliography*, ed. N. Koertge (Detroit 2008) 2:416–421. B.V.

Translated by Jeannine Router Pucci and Elizabeth Trapnell Rawlings

Euripides

Greek tragic dramatist, ca. 485–406 BCE. According to Aristotle, Sophocles said that he drew men as they ought to be, but Euripides drew them as they were. Euripides has always been a more controversial dramatist than Sophocles or Aeschylus. His plays take a more skeptical view of human, and specifically male, pretensions, at times bordering on black farce; the cosmos they portray is more savagely unpredictable; their aesthetic principles are at loggerheads with Aristotle's. No wonder that to later ages he has always seemed more "modern" than his rivals, though not necessarily more estimable. Nietzsche was not alone in deploring (with the exception of the *Bacchae*) the degenerate worldview that Euripides represented.

His plays appear more heterogeneous than those of his two peers partly because more of them have (accidentally) survived. Eighteen were published in Venice in 1503, and within a few years the great Humanist scholar Erasmus had produced Latin translations of *Hecuba* and *Iphigeneia in Aulis* that would find their way, along with the brief quotations included in his much-reprinted *Adages*, into schoolrooms and libraries throughout Europe. These two plays, together with *Medea* and *Alcestis*, also translated into Latin (by the Scots Humanist George Buchanan, mid-16th cent.), created the dominant image of Euripides at least up until the end of the 18th century, when, like Sophocles' and Aeschylus', his plays first became available to the Greekless reader in their entirety. Euripides was admired mainly for creating icons of female suffering, whether "good women" like Alcestis, Iphigeneia, and Polyxena (Hecuba's daughter) or "bad women" like Medea. The Phaedra of his *Hippolytus* was another significant figure, inflected by the later Senecan version in Latin, through which, along with the Roman dramatist's rewritings of *Medea, The Trojan Women,* and *Heracles,* Euripidean tragedy reached Shakespeare and Racine.

From 1660 onward Euripides was a major influence on the vogue for sentimental dramas known to British audiences as she-tragedies. Though *Creusa, Queen of Athens,* William Whitehead's adaptation of *Ion* (1754), has not stood the test of time, this phase of history did produce at least one masterpiece based on Euripides (and Seneca), Jean Racine's incomparable *Phèdre* (1677), itself the object of many subsequent rewritings, by Robert Lowell (1961), Tony Harrison (1975), and others. Euripides is also the source of two lesser but still magnificent tragedies by Racine, *Andromaque* (1667) and *Iphigénie* (1674). A hundred years later Euripides inspired another fine verse drama that marked a climax of the Enlightenment's faith in human reason and goodness, J. W. von Goethe's *Iphigenie auf Tauris* (1787). This is close in time and temper to two major works by the Viennese composer Christoph Willibald Gluck, whose *Iphigénie en Aulide* (1774) and *Iphigénie en Tauride* (1779) mark a turning point in the history of opera.

Alcestis, the wife and mother prepared to die for her husband, Admetus, has proved a particularly durable model of self-sacrifice, invoked by poets from Chaucer, Milton, and Wordsworth to Rainer Maria Rilke and Marguerite Yourcenar. Robert Browning gives her play a Christian turn and frames it within his narrative poem *Balaustion's Adventure* (1871), and it provides the basis for T. S. Eliot's verse drama *The Cocktail Party* (1950). Sacrificed at Aulis, sacrificer at Tauris, the virginal Iphigeneia also continues to appeal. But artists have been no less powerfully drawn to Medea and Phaedra, more insidiously passionate and dangerous to their nearest and dearest. Many divas, actors, and singers have been grateful for the chance to reincarnate them, in Luigi Cherubini's opera *Médée* (1797), in Martha Graham's dance dramas *Cave of the Heart* (1947) and *Phaedra* (1962), and in Benjamin Britten's cantata *Phaedra* (1975). Dramatists have been particularly attracted by the challenge of reimagining Phaedra's story in a modern setting. Prominent examples include Eugene O'Neill's *Desire under the Elms* (1924), Brian Friel's *Living Quarters* (1977), and Sarah Kane's *Phaedra's Love* (1996).

Euripides' tragedies attend closely to the passionate bond between mother and child and the violence unleashed by its rupture. For this reason Freud's Oedipal theories have less purchase on them than those developed by his successor, Melanie Klein (1882–1960). In addition to Medea, two further maddened and murderous mothers have proved significant, Hecuba and Agave (in the *Bacchae*). Through the 16th century the play to which Hecuba gives her name provided a memorable model of maternal revenge, but only in recent years has it begun to regain its potency, partly through its association with the other great war play dominated by Hecuba, *The Trojan Women.* Throughout the 20th century this latter has frequently been staged in times of war across the globe from Moscow to Brazil and Germany to Japan.

Before about 1900 no one paid much attention to the *Bacchae,* but it has come to seem one of the defining models of Greek tragedy and even of tragedy itself, rivaling Aeschylus' *Oresteia* and Sophocles' *Oedipus Tyrannus* and *Antigone.* For this Friedrich Nietzsche must take some of the credit. The idea of "the Dionysiac" propounded in his *Birth of Tragedy* (1872) has had a massive influence not only on understandings of tragedy but on theories of theatrical performance itself. Between them Nietzsche and Euripides sponsored the event that redefined the possibilities for Greek tragedy in the contemporary theater, Richard Schechner's *Dionysus in 69* (New York, 1968–1969). There has also been an upsurge in new works inspired by the *Bacchae,* including Hans Werner Henze's opera *The Bassarids* (1966), with libretto by W. H. Auden and Chester Kallman, and Wole Soyinka's *The Bacchae of Euripides: A Communion Rite* (1973), in which the Yoruba god Ogun merges with the Greek Dionysus.

Euripides' greatest legacy, however, has been his freedom from the precepts of the Aristotle (and Aristotelians) he never knew—his generic volatility, his nonconformity, his endless capacity to disconcert.

BIBL.: Peter Burian, "Tragedy Adapted for Stages and Screens: The Renaissance to the Present," in *Greek Tragedy,* ed. P. E. Easterling (Cambridge 1997) 228–283. Edith Hall and Fiona Macintosh, *Greek Tragedy and the British Theatre, 1660–1914* (Oxford 2005). Edith Hall, Fiona Macintosh, and Amanda Wrigley, *Dionysus since 69: Greek Tragedy at the Dawn of the Third Millennium* (Oxford 2004). A.PL.

Europe

First used to describe central Greece, by 500 BCE the word *Europe* had been extended to cover the whole of the Greek mainland. Geographically Europe was always described as if it were a continent, although it is also, significantly, a western peninsula of Asia. The traditional boundary between Europe and Asia was fixed, symbolically, at the Bosporus and, to the east, at the Don River. The first of these imaginary frontiers has remained unchanged, and will remain so, until and unless Turkey enters the European Union. The second began to shift at the end of the 15th century, first to the banks of the Volga, then to the Ob, then to the Ural River and Ural Mountains, until, in the 20th century, the boundary finally came to rest at the Emba River and the Kerch Strait.

Appropriately for so ambiguous a place, the origins of

Europe are to be found not in geography but in myth. Europa was a woman, "pale and golden-haired," the daughter of Agenor, king of the city of Tyre on the coast of Sidon, in what is now Lebanon. One day while she was sitting by the water, Zeus came out of the sea in the shape of a white bull, "his breath scented with saffron." He carried her out to sea and across the straits that separated two worlds, to Crete, where in the meadows of Gortyn they made love under a huge shady plane tree.

As Europa's home had been in Phoenicia, and the Phoenicians were a people of what later came to be called Asia, Europe had been born out of Asia. As is true of all myths, however, there is another, more mundane version of the story, this one first suggested by the Greek historian Herodotus in the 5th century BCE and attributed by him to the Persians. In this version, the Rape of Europa was an act of revenge for the seizure by Phoenician sailors of Io, the daughter of Inachus, king of Argos. Later on, wrote Herodotus, "some Greeks, whose name the Persians failed to record"—they were, in fact, Cretans—put into the Phoenician port of Tyre "and carried off the king's daughter Europa thus giving them tit for tat." The 3rd-century Christian theologian Lactantius provides the Cretans with a bull-shaped ship, to explain away Zeus, and says that Europa was intended as a present for the Cretan king Asterius. This version was taken up centuries later by the Italian poet Boccaccio, who added his own twist to an already overcomplicated story by renaming the Cretan ruler Jove.

These mythic abductions continued. The Cretans were "Europeans," and as Europa was an Asian woman, her rape was taken by all Asians to be an affront. Later the Trojans, a people from what we now call Asia Minor, seized a not wholly unwilling Helen, wife of the Spartan king Menelaus, in revenge, and carried her off to Troy. In turn, Menelaus' brother, Agamemnon, raised an army, crossed the sea, and laid siege to the great city of Troy for ten long years. The Persians, Herodotus tells us, found these tales of abduction puzzling. "We in Asia," they said, "regarded the rape of our women not at all, but the Greeks all for the sake of a Lacedaemonian woman mustered a great host, came to Asia, and destroyed the power of Priam. Ever since then we have regarded the Greeks as our enemies."

What in myth had been a divine appropriation becomes in mythopoeic history a tale of the hatred between two continents, a hatred that would burn steadily down the centuries as the Trojans were succeeded by the Phoenicians, the Phoenicians by the Parthians, the Parthians by the Arabs, the Arabs by the Ottoman Turks, and the Turks by the Russians.

It is, however, Rome—although the geographic extent of the Roman Empire reached well beyond the confines of Europe—that is the true creator of Europe as we understand it today. Rome also had its mythic origins, and these linked it inescapably to Asia as well. After the sack of Troy by the Greeks, Aeneas, a Trojan prince and son of the goddess Aphrodite, fled from the ruins of Troy and, after a series of westward journeys, arrived on the shores of Latium, in what is now central Italy. There he founded the city and the state of Rome.

Over time the association with Troy, however mythical, began to suggest potentially embarrassing racial, political, or cultural ties that later generations would have been happier to forget. By the 1st century BCE, the Romans had also developed a distrust of the peoples of the "East" and a strong desire to assert their own racial, linguistic, and cultural distinctiveness. In the 12th and final book of the *Aeneid,* Virgil therefore has the gods decide that the war between Aeneas' invading Trojans and the native Latins must finally be brought to an end. Juno, who has supported the Latins, agrees to allow the two peoples to intermarry and thereby create a new race. But she insists that this new race will look like the Latins, will dress like the Latins, will speak like the Latins, and their customs—their mores—will be Latin. All they will preserve of their oriental ancestors will be their gods, for those gods were also the gods of the Greeks and the common patrimony of all mankind.

Europe's always ambiguous relationship with its real or mythic Asian origins nevertheless survived even the collapse of the political structures of the Graeco-Roman world, for Christianity, which was to provide Europe with much of its subsequent sense of internal cohesion and its relationship with the rest of the world, was also in its beginnings an Asian religion. "Jesus Christ, who is the way the truth and the life," wrote the English propagandist for the settlement of America, Samuel Purchas, in 1625—in an attempt to secure the glory of Christ's apostolate, and of the overseas missions, exclusively for Europe—"has long since given the Bill of Divorce to ingrateful Asia where he was born and of Africa the place of his flight and refuge, and has become almost wholly European." Thus, an abducted Asian woman gave Europe her name; a vagrant Asian exile gave Europe its political and finally its cultural identity; and an Asian prophet gave Europe its religion.

But if this geographic uncertainty meant that the landmass of Europe could not be said to be at the center of the world, it could still be placed at the center of some other conceptualization of the environment. For the Greeks and their Roman heirs, the means of establishing a relationship with the rest of humanity frequently rested on a complex theory of climate and physical environment. According to this theory, the northern parts of the world were inhabited by peoples whose inhospitable climate had made them brave and warlike, but also uncouth, unthinking, and—to use the Latinized term that would become central to all modes of European self-fashioning—uncivilized. Those who lived in the south—the Asians—were, by contrast, quick-witted and intelligent, but also lethargic, slow to act, and ultimately corrupt—a claim that, in time, would become an enduring stereotype of the "Oriental." Europeans, which at this time meant only the peoples of the Mediterranean, living as they did midway between these extremes, represented the mean. This conception of Europe, much modified, it is true, but still insistent on the radical distinction between north and south, retained its imaginative force until at least the 19th century. Even the German philosopher Georg Wilhelm Friedrich Hegel, writing in 1830 from the viewpoint of an intellectually and culturally emergent north, could still (after having relegated America firmly to the domain of the future, "where in the ages that lie before us, the burden of the World's History shall reveal itself") speak confidently of the Mediterranean as the "uniting element" of "three quarters of the globe" and "the center of World-History."

It was not only climate and disposition, however, that distinguished the peoples of Europe from those of Asia. It was also culture. Herodotus, the first to attempt an explanation for the "perpetual enmity," as he called it, between Greeks and Persians—between Europe and Asia—put it down to a question of government. The Persians lived under tyrants. They were the slaves of their ruler. Such laws as they had reflected only his arbitrary will. The Greeks lived under what Herodotus called *isonomia,* "equality before the law." There lay their strength, their ability in the end to defeat the greatest military power in the ancient world. "Europe," wrote the 1st-century Greek geographer Strabo, "is both varied in form and admirably adapted by nature for the development of excellence in men and governments." The two instincts in man, the peaceable, which Strabo significantly called the "agricultural and the civilized," and the warlike, lived in Europe side by side, and "the one that is peace-loving is more numerous and thus keeps control over the whole body." The ability to harness the power of human aggressiveness rather than suppress it—freedom, but freedom contained and made strong through law—became and remains the defining distinction between Europe and Asia. The power of the Roman Republic, claimed Machiavelli in the 16th century, echoing the 1st-century BCE Roman historian Sallust, had derived, not as so many had supposed, from the exercise of a common will, but precisely from the opposition between the Senate and the Plebeians.

The rule of law, restraint through custom rather than will, was responsible for the fashioning of societies that provided a space for individual human action while at the same time ensuring that such action was rarely capable of reducing society to a state of simple anarchy. From this came the notion that all human improvement depends on conflict, that human beings are, by their nature, competitive creatures and only those societies that know how to harness what Immanuel Kant in the late 18th century called man's "unsocial sociability," instead of attempting to suppress it, will flourish. This assumption could have emerged only in a society or collection of societies that, while being in many significant respects very different from one another, shared the sense of a common identity. This combination of strength and dependency made the recognition of a shared political culture difficult to withhold. "The cities of Ancient Greece," wrote Edward Gibbon of the origins of modern Europe, "were cast in the happy mixture of union and interdependence which is repeated on a larger scale, but in a looser form, by the nations of modern Europe; the union of religion, language, and manners which renders them spectators and judges of each others' merits; the independence of government and interests, which asserts their separate freedoms, and excites them to strive for pre-eminence in the career of glory."

The various European societies that evolved out of this "union and interdependence" came to acquire many forms of government, some of them decidedly less liberal than others, but Gibbon's own contemporary Voltaire was echoing an enduring commonplace, at least among the educated elite of Europe, when he claimed that the Continent constituted a "kind of great republic divided into several states," all of which were united in having "the same principle of public law and politics, unknown in other parts of the world."

This political culture of a great republic was also centered on a unique form of life: the city. It was, of course, the case that the vast majority of the population in Europe, like that in most other civilizations, actually lived and worked in the countryside until well into the 19th century. It is also true that for most of the rural peoples of Europe, and for the illiterate majority in the cities, identity was a question of attachment to microcommunities: the parish, the village, the guild, sometimes the county, only rarely the nation, and never, one suspects, such an abstract cultural grouping as "Europe." In 1623 Francis Bacon could speak proudly of "we Europeans"—*nos Europaei.* But he did so in the awareness that he belonged to a small intellectual elite that shared a common language—Latin—and whose members had far more in common with similar groups from other nations than they did with their own peasantry.

Despite its dependence on agriculture, despite the real distribution of its populations, Europe, as a collection of social and political groups with a shared and historically determined culture, was conceived as overwhelmingly urban. The entire modern European political and social vocabulary derives from this fact. *Politics* and *polity* have their root in the Greek term *polis.* Similarly *civil, civility,* and *civilization* have their origins in the Latin word—*civis*—for the members of the same spatial, political, and cultural entity. Cities were, of course, by no means unique to Europe. Like all else that is defining of European culture, the walled, largely self-governing urban space had also originated in Asia. But it was only with the rise of Athens after the 6th century that an association in the European political imaginary began to form between an urban environment and a particular way of life.

This identification of a distinctive European communal life with a specific environment reached its peak with the effective domination of the whole of what we now call Europe, and much of Asia also, by the greatest city of them all: Rome. Like the Greek cities to which it was heir, Rome was the source of law, the place of custom, *mores,* which in the poet Virgil's punning vision was now encircled and protected by its massive walls (*moenia*): *Bellum ingens geret Italia, populosque feroces/contundet moresque viris et moenia ponet* ("In Italy he will fight a massive war,/Beat down fierce armies, then for the people there/Establish city walls and a way of life," *Aeneid* 1.263–264; trans. Fitzgerald). Unlike the Greek city-states, Rome, in particular after the collapse of the Republic, was heavily dependent for both its political identity and its continuing survival on the vast areas of Europe and Asia over which it exercised authority. Thus, to a far greater degree than its Greek antecedents, it welcomed outsiders within its walls, and at least during the periods when this particular civic community offered stability, security, and access to world power, it proved to be enormously attractive.

Rome was not only a political realm, but was also the embodiment of the Stoic belief in the possibility of a single law for all humanity. If the Greeks had given to Europe the philosophy and the mathematics that had made its subsequent scientific development possible, it was the Romans who gave it its legislative habits. And although, as we have seen, the concept of Europeans as law-governed peoples originated in Greece, it was the Romans who elevated the law to the place it still holds today—as the sole guarantor of the continuity of "civilization," however we choose to define that emotive term. Much of this was swept away during the Gothic invasions that followed the collapse of the Roman empire, and in the outer fringes of the empire Germanic customary law came to replace Roman law. But despite these changes, that law remained, and remains, the single most unifying feature of the Continent. Edmund Burke in the 18th century offered an image of a world of independent states united as a common culture, based on "the old Gothic customary [law] . . . digested into system and disciplined by the Roman law," in every part of which it would be possible for a European to feel at home. For this reason the creation of a single legislative order for the whole of Europe remained an ambition of the most powerful of Europe's rulers, from Emperor Justinian in the 6th century, through Philip II of Spain and Louis XIV, to Napoleon and, in somewhat muted form, the European Court of Justice.

After the triumph of Christianity, ancient Greek and Roman notions of exclusivity were further enforced by the Christian insistence on the uniqueness of the Gospels and the Church as the source of moral and scientific authority. Custom now, in Lactantius' words, had been "made congruent with religion." Christianity was thought of as spatially coextensive with the Roman empire. The world, the *orbis terrarum,* thus became, in terms of the translation effected by Pope Leo the Great in the 5th century, the *orbis Christianus,* or, as it would be called in the European vernaculars, simply "Christendom." As late as 1761 such a relatively hostile witness as Jean-Jacques Rousseau conceded that "Europe, even now, is indebted more to Christianity than to any other influence for the union . . . which survives among her members." It was a union Rousseau frequently abhorred, but from which he could never quite escape.

The scattered, diverse, and plural cultures that had grown up in the ancient world and constituted what we now call Europe shared, therefore, a single identity bound together by a common system of law. When they gradually converted to Christianity, they acquired a common religion and a common cult. They also shared a common language: Latin. Although, after the 4th century Roman institutions, Roman architecture, and Roman literature all gradually lost their power to unite Europe, and the concept of a single body of citizens vanished altogether, Latin remained as the language of the Church—it still is—and of the learned elites of Europe well into the 18th century. As the Italian republican Carlo Cattaneo noted in 1835, Europe possessed four unifying features: the power of the former imperial authority, the Roman law, Christianity, and the Latin language.

Today these no longer possess the force they had even in the middle of the 19th century. But the concept of Europe, despite the replacement of Latin first by French and now by English, and the steady disappearance of Christianity (along with the rise of other religions, particularly Islam), remains firmly centered on the idea of cultural unity grounded in the rule of law and a form of representative government—albeit one neither the Greeks nor the Romans would easily recognize—bequeathed to it by the Graeco-Roman world.

BIBL.: Anthony Pagden, ed., *The Idea of Europe: From Antiquity to the European Union* (Washington, D.C., 2002).

A.P.

Eustathius

Byzantine Humanist, Homeric scholar, and archbishop (ca. 1115–ca. 1199). Educated in Constantinople, he began his career as a scribe in the patriarchate, was ordained a deacon, and after 1166 was the appointed master of rhetors at the patriarchal school. This office placed him at the junction of classicizing rhetoric and contemporary politics; it entailed composing and performing encomiastic orations in honor of emperor and patriarch. He inspired a circle of gifted young intellectuals, including the Choniates brothers. His philological writings all fall into this Constantinopolitan period. In 1178 he was appointed to the important archbishopric of Thessalonica, where he seems to have spent the remaining two decades of his life. A series of homilies testifies to struggles with his unruly flock, especially the monks. His partly apologetic account of the city's sack by the Normans in 1185 offers some of the wittiest criticisms of 12th-century imperial politics.

Eustathius is best known for his commentaries on both the *Iliad* and the *Odyssey,* which drew on an enormous number of sources. Homeric ideals flourished at the chivalric court of the Comneni emperors (1118–1185), paving the way toward the "epic age" of Byzantine court culture and literature (manifest, e.g., in the *Alexiad,* ca.

1148). The increasing attention that Homer received in the curriculum culminated in Eustathius' monumental work. Unlike other writers of the 12th century, however, he was not prompted by imperial or aristocratic patronage to compile these gargantuan commentaries; he wrote them to equip his students of rhetoric for a public life at court or in the Church. Uniquely, the commentaries were clearly not intended for grammatical education only—as were the 14th-century commentaries on the dramatic triads—or to blow the author's own trumpet.

Eustathius argued for a moderately allegorical interpretation of the Homeric epics. This again ties the commentaries to the context of the aesthetics and rhetoric of his era, especially regarding the reemerging novel but also historiography. Eustathius clearly had access to some texts now lost (e.g., a complete version of Strabo's seventh book). He also quoted the "alphabetic plays" of Euripides, a copy of which he is likely to have brought from Constantinople to Thessalonica.

Additionally, his commentary on Dionysius Periegetes survives, again tailored to the needs of future rhetors. From a commentary on Pindar, only the preface is still extant. Internal references show that his work on all the commentaries continued in parallel. Those on the Homeric epics survive in autograph copies: for the *Iliad,* Biblioteca Laurentiana (Florence) 59.2–3, in which pieces of scrap paper inserted between the pages allow one to trace the compiler's ongoing rephrasing of the text; for the *Odyssey,* Bibliothèque Nationale (Paris), Parisin. graec. 2702, and Biblioteca Marciana (Venice) Marcian. graec. 460. A fifth autograph manuscript (Marcian. graec. 448) also contains a copy of the famous Suda lexicon.

These commentaries exerted considerable influence on Renaissance perceptions of Homer: Angelo Poliziano and Demetrius Chalcondyles excerpted them in Florence (Poliziano's notes survive in the Bavarian State Library, Munich, Monacens. graec. 182, and in Parisin. graec. 3069). So did Guillaume Budé and Janus Lascaris in Paris; Budé's annotated copy of the 1488 Florentine *editio princeps* of Homer is now at Princeton. Lascaris himself had brought a 13th-century codex of the commentary on books 1–9 of the *Iliad* from Crete (now Parisin. graec. 2695). In due course it became one of the exemplars of Nicolao Maiorano's *editio princeps* (Rome, 1542–1559), which (in Stallbaum's 1825–1826 reprint) is still relevant for commentary on the *Odyssey.*

Upon Eustathius' death his master pupil, Michael Choniates, remarked that Thessalonica mourned him as her virgin bridegroom and Constantinople as her son; his true *patris,* however, had been the heavenly Ithaca, to which he had now returned.

BIBL.: M. Angold, *Church and Society in Byzantium under the Comneni 1081–1261* (Cambridge 1995) 179–196. L. Silvano, "Estratti dal *commento all'Odissea* di Eustazio di Tessalonica in due zibaldoni autografi di Angelo Poliziano," in *Selecta colligere,* ed. M. R. Piccione and M. Perkams (Alexandria 2005) 2:403–433. N. G. Wilson, *Scholars of Byzantium,* rev. ed. (London 1996) 196–204, and "Three Byzantine Scribes," *Greek, Roman and Byzantine Studies* 14 (1973) 226–228.

N.G.

F

Fascism

This entry deals with the attitude of Italian Fascism and German National Socialism to ancient Greece and Rome from the 1920s through 1943–1945, the end of the Second World War. (Various concepts of antiquity have played a role, as yet scarcely investigated, in other Fascist movements and states such as *Action française,* Romania, Hungary, and the Franco dictatorship in Spain.)

The term *Fascism* itself embodies a specific connection between the Fascist movement and ancient Rome: "Rome is our point of departure and our point of reference, it is our symbol, or if you will"—as Mussolini pointed out in 1922—"our myth." The key word for this relationship is *romanità.* After Italian unification the cult of *romanità* emerged as a part of the secular religion of state and was transferred to "the Fascist cult of *romanità*" (Visser 1992), which created "a flexible Rome" (Stone 1999). From 1922 to 1943 this interest in *romanità* bred many images and allusions relating to ancient Rome, primarily to the imperial period and with special regard to Augustus.

In the 1920s classicists and classical archaeologists in particular found themselves involved in political service. In this context a school reform in 1923 initiated by the philosopher Giovanni Gentile (1875–1944) was supposed to confirm the sense of national identity ultimately with the myth of Rome. The Istituto di Studi Romani (ISR, founded in 1925) and its publications were supported by the Fascist regime and authorized the cult of *romanità.* From 1924 until 1938 Il Duce patronized well-known excavation and restoration programs.

The excavation of the imperial fora in Rome (more than 80 percent of the excavated area was filled in again later) led to the construction of the Via dell'Impero (1932)—a symbol of the imperial ambitions of the regime. This gigantic "reconstruction" of imperial Rome involved the uncompromising destruction of large areas of medieval and Baroque architecture.

Mussolini claimed the political heritage of the *princeps* Augustus in the field of foreign policy in the widest sense. Immediately after the annexation of Ethiopia, the reconstruction of the *impero,* or rather of the Augustan Empire, was proclaimed on 9 May 1936. Widespread Fascist "imperial" propaganda used all types of media, including monuments, postage stamps, and films. The film *Scipione l'Africano* (1937), for example, partially directed by Mussolini himself, illustrated "the racial reading of *romanità*" (Stone 1999) within the historical framework of the conflict between Rome and Carthage (and included anti-Semitic clichés).

Mussolini's modern "Augustan" propaganda culminated in celebrations of the Bimillennario Augusteo from 23 September 1937 onward (prepared by the ISR) and the opening of the great Augustan exhibition Mostra Augustea della Romanità (MAR). It had been preceded by commemorations of the 2,000th birthdays of Virgil (1930–1931) and Horace (1935–1936). Combined with the simultaneously reopened grand exhibition of the Fascist revolution, the MAR emphasized the symbiosis of Augustus and Mussolini or of Caesarism and Mussolinianism (Stone 1999).

Naturally, the academic field of classical studies in general and particularly the research efforts of historians of ancient Rome were supported by government and party, as can be seen in the *Storia di Roma* project, published by the ISR beginning in 1925. At the same time, prominent scholars became involved in Fascist propaganda and in the regime's ideological pressures on Roman history. The field of classical studies also saw a rising anti-Semitic climate (Cagnetta 1979), related to Italian race laws (1938).

Despite the manifest rise in expressions of *romanità,* the regime's cultural policy remained ambivalent. It is important to realize that in the debate between traditionalists and modernists in the 1930s, the "enlightened" Fascist Giuseppe Bottai (1895–1959), the former mayor of Rome who became Minister of National Education, supported concepts of nonhistoricist modernism, for example, in state art and architecture.

In the 1940s the "looking back" to imperial Rome and its civilizing mission—viewed as being continued in modern times with the Italian conquest of Ethiopia and Libya, and with Fascist "colonization" and the *mare nostro* ambitions—became more pronounced. In this sense the conflict between traditionalists and modernists was decided.

The most ambitious Fascist building project, the E42, now the Esposizione Universale Romana (EUR) in the south of Rome (planned primarily for a world's fair), presented in a union of architecture, painting, and sculpture an example of the "hyperbolic *romanità* of late Fascist culture" (Stone 1999). Through this concept, developed mainly by Marcello Piacentini (1881–1960), who was criticized as a "pseudo-Vitruvius," the regime attempted to embrace *romanità* as a "Fascist expression of the eternal idea of Rome" (Bottai). Because of World War II the E42 exposition never took place, and a marble ghost town stood unused until the postwar era.

Hitler's approach to the ancient world was based on his racial theories. Rome and Sparta were his favorite "distant models" (Nolte 1965). In *Mein Kampf* (1925–1927) he praised the political lessons offered by Roman history and the beauty of the Hellenic cultural ideal, at the same time asserting a significant racial community with "Germanity." From classical Greece he especially admired the building program of Pericles, but Sparta was much more important to him than Athens. For in Sparta he discovered the prototype of a minority ruling class in "the purest racial state." Sparta, like the early "peasant state Rome," exemplified for him the archaic condition of racial unity that he believed to be inherent in a (in some respects) utopian agrarian society.

After his seizure of power in 1933, Sparta and the Dorians became popular in Nazi Germany, as illustrated by the poet Gottfried Benn (1886–1956) in his famous essay "The World of the Dorians: On the Relationship between Art and Power" (*Dorische Welt: Eine Untersuchung über die Beziehung von Kunst und Macht,* 1934). Richard Walther Darré, the National Socialist Minister of Agriculture, saw in Sparta a model for the peasantlike character of Indo-Europeans and discussed the Spartan inheritance laws. The idealization of Sparta by the Nazis included an antidemocratic and conservative attitude.

The "laws" of race history shaped not only Hitler's ideas about the rise of Rome and the conflict with Carthage but also his concept of the decline and fall of Rome. He was convinced that Rome had been "broken" not by Germans or Jews but rather by Christians. And undoubtedly conflicts arose between Hitler's specific, positive assessment of ancient Rome and the extreme glorification of officially patronized Germanic prehistory by other leading Nazi ideologists, particularly Alfred Rosenberg (1893–1946) and Heinrich Himmler (1900–1944). For Rosenberg the ideology of Germanism, rooted as it was in the political Germanism of the 19th century, almost achieved the character of a state religion—and corresponded with a strong anti-Roman position. Closely connected with that attitude, the Italian and German Axis partners engaged in a dispute about the "level of German culture." Hitler himself held a more conservative, "Roman" view; like Mussolini, he admired primarily the architecture of the Roman state, which inspired his own program of rule.

Some leading German classicists welcomed Hitler's positive attitude toward ancient Greece and Rome. They found ways to integrate into their works National Socialist concepts that were far removed from ideas normally held by meticulous scholars— including even racial ideology. The example of Werner Jaeger (1888–1961), and his aristocratic and elitist *Paideia* concept, shows this clearly. His attempt to connect a "Third Humanism" with the program of "nationalist political education" developed by the National Socialist educator Ernst Krieck (1882–1942) was, however, a failure. Another consequence of Hitler's seizure of power was the prosecution and dismissal of numerous scholars for racial and political reasons—a substantial loss in the field of classical scholarship.

More conservative and antidemocratic concepts, like those of the "leader" (*Führer*) and the "empire" (*Reich*), in both ancient and modern forms, were taken up by scholars, as were such standard topics of racial history as "population decline" and "race mixture in the Roman empire." These ideas also found their way into the schools. Lessons in ancient history, Latin, and Greek were being conducted "with special attention to eugenics and racial development." During the Second World War, it was Hitler himself who connected the notion of the Roman empire as a "blueprint for world domination" (J. Thies) with the perspectives of race history and race laws.

During the war classicists also took part in the officially organized War Service of the Humanities, which they exploited to claim a renewal of the classics. One result of this activity was the collective volume *Rome and Carthage* (1943), which focused on the key question of the importance of the "racial conflict" in the wars between the two ancient powers. New fields were opened during the war for some activists who combined the ideas and plans of Himmler and Rosenberg with classical research. The goal was to prove the intellectual world leadership of Aryan Germanic culture. Another example of war-related work produced by classicists from various fields was a teaching manual for the Adolf Hitler Schools advocating a National Socialist elite education: *Sparta: The Fight for Life of a Nordic Master Race.* Representatives of classical academe and members of the National Socialist ruling class found some common ground here. Hans Oppermann (1895–1982), a recognized scholar with apparently sincere Socialist leaning, composed a brochure about the "ancient Jewish question," an example of unadulterated anti-Semitic propaganda.

Hitler's most important "distant" model was undoubtedly Sparta. The social structure of that ancient city-state looked to him like a proof of the social Darwinist principles of the "survival of the fittest" and "destruction of the weak," as well as seeming to provide a model for a modern "birth policy." The unconditional duty to self-sacrifice in the war was supported by the ideology of the battle of Thermopylae. In the context of Nazi European ideology, which was mobilized in the last years of the war, ancient Rome seemed to embody a kind of timeless advanced post in the struggle against Asia.

To the very end of his rule Hitler clung to the "Roman example." The Punic Wars were conjured up again in connection with racial ideology. Germany (Rome) was fighting against the "Semitic trading people of Carthage," and against "World Jewry." In this respect Jews and Carthaginians had somehow become merged. Between 1922 and 1943 imperial Rome and especially the age of Augustus, which was closely connected with the cult of *romanità,* were presented as a leitmotif of Fascist mass culture. Hitler's concepts of race and rule to a certain extent until his death were rooted in his "distant models," Sparta and Rome.

BIBL.: D. Britt, ed., *Art and Power: Europe under the Dictators 1930–45,* ed. D. Britt (exh. cat.) (Manchester 1995). M. Cagnetta, *Antichisti e impero fascista* (Bari 1979). C. Edwards, ed., *Roman Presences: Receptions of Rome in European Culture, 1789–1945* (Cambridge 1999). V. Losemann, *Nationalsozialismus und Antike: Studien zur Entwicklung des Faches Alte Geschichte 1933–1945* (Hamburg 1977). B. Näf, ed., *Antike und Altertumswissenschaft in der Zeit von Faschismus und Nationalsozialismus* (Mandelbachtal 2001). Ernst Nolte, *Three Faces of Fascism: Action Française, Italian Fascism, National Socialism* (London 1965). S. Pisani, "Faschismus," *Der Neue Pauly* 13 (1999) 1084–1096. L. Schumacher, "Augusteische Propaganda und faschistische Rezeption," *Zeitschrift für Religions- und Geistesgeschichte* 40 (1988) 307–330. F. Scriba, *Augustus im Schwarzhemd? Die Mostra Augustea della Romanità in Rom 1937/38* (Frankfurt am Main 1995). M. Stone, "A Flexible Rome: Fascism and the Cult of Romanità," in Edwards 1999, 205–220. R. Visser, "Fascist Doctrine and the Cult of the Romanità," *Journal of Contemporary History* 27, no. 1 (1992) 5–22.

V.L.

Fashion

Throughout history, fashion has turned to the ancient world and utilized Greek and Roman sources for inspiration. Impressions from antiquity echo throughout Western fashion history from Byzantium through the Middle Ages and into early modern times. The use of draped cloth in folds and layers has constantly reappeared in fashion and reveals close associations with the ancient world. The Greek draped peplos, chiton, and himation and the Roman tunic, stola, pallium, and toga have thus lived on and are continually revived in various forms. Even in the Church, many ancient styles of dress are mirrored in today's clerical robes.

Our richest source of knowledge about ancient fashion derives from findings made during excavations of Pompeii and Herculaneum, during the 18th century and onward. Through representations of the ideal body, murals, sculptures, and reliefs can often give minute information about dress, accessories, and hairstyles as well as the way in which clothes were worn. Written sources also provide unique insights into the fashions of their eras. Poets such as Cicero, Ovid, and Juvenal, for example, wrote letters and satires describing the vanity of modern times and the immoral fashions and customs of Rome.

In certain periods of the modern era, classical ideals have been particularly emphasized; during the 1600s and 1700s dress fashion was strongly influenced by ancient associations in all leading European nations. In portraiture during the 1600s both the use of drapery and inclusion of columns having clearly Roman origin conveyed an impression of stateliness and ease. Men could be portrayed as Roman commanders, but women's fashion revealed a more tangible inspiration from dress of ancient times. The informal *déshabillé* (a light nightgown worn over a smock) gave the impression of casually draped and folded attire that provided ease and freedom of movement, as it could be worn without stays. A quantity of richly flowing folds, allowing a relaxed natural body movement, had clear associations with fashion in the ancient world.

In the 1700s portraiture developed its own timeless fashion, distinct from the whims and variations dictated by contemporary modes. In England of the 1770s Sir Joshua Reynolds gave his female models an appearance of noble grace through use of the "Grand Style," as reflected by loosely draped gowns with clearly classical allusions. Throughout the rest of the 1700s ancient traditions strongly influenced women's fashion. France, which dictated international fashion trends of the time, saw during the 1780s the development of the chemise dress (derived from *déshabillé*), which employed the finest white muslin from India. This fashion, closely linked to the neoclassical movement of the late 1700s, was given a strong boost by the spectacular findings from the ancient Roman cities of Pompeii and Herculaneum. The chemise was a simple one-piece dress (without a bodice cut separately from the skirt), girdled with a sash at the waist.

Inspirations from the ancient world came to play an important role during the political upheavals of the late 1700s. During the French Revolution as well as the founding of the United States in North America, fashion was used to express and emphasize political ideas. Associations from the ancient world were employed both aesthetically and symbolically in the expression of concepts such as freedom, republic, and democracy. The high moral tone and strictness of the new political regimes encouraged their proponents to connect with the virtues and forms that they thought typified the classical world. Liberty and the luxury of the Ancien Régime were incompatible. But the symbolic significance of Liberty's red Phrygian cap was soon overcome by a tidal wave of modes *à l'antique,* which came to dominate fashionable society. Although prevailing ideologies envisioned how fashion might contribute to the new concept of equality, fashion itself quickly became instead an expression of the superiority of a social elite and reflected the norms of the new bourgeoisie.

By now the ideal of the marble-white simplicity of the classical world had been firmly established. Slim, lightly draped, high-waisted, and short-sleeved gowns, worn with shawls, flat shoes, and curls, represented the corresponding fashion. But this tailored and stitched silhouette bore little resemblance to the draped and pinned ancient dress forms; neither did the new, austerely classicized styles of adornment and color schemes (basically white, black, and red, derived from ancient statues and vases) match what would later become known of the bold colors and patterns of Greek and Roman art and fashion, or of the ancients' excessive use of jewelry, cosmetics, and artificial hair arrangements, including tinting the hair blond or red. (The full beard of Roman times, although customary during the Renaissance and occurring into the 17th century, did not come back into vogue until the second half of the 19th century.)

Early modern discoveries of ancient Greek and Roman art had placed nudity into immediate focus. The lightly draped bodies of ancient gods and Roman citizens alike inspired the revolutionizing fashion of the late 18th century. In France of the 1790s, the daring dressed *à la sauvage:* men wore tight-fitting pantaloons and women wore clinging, semitransparent muslin gowns over flesh-colored body stockings, to reveal naked breasts and bare arms and feet. Stories spread of French demimondaines clad in muslin dampened so as to cling to their naked bodies. Ancient dress, however, was actually often worn in several layers, with drapery held in place by girdles and fastened at the shoulders. During late Roman imperial times lavish tunics were made of Chinese silk, a fashion that provoked, among some contemporaries, disapproving comments about shameless exposure.

During the Napoleonic era, Egyptian themes were combined with classical styles after the emperor's campaigns in that land popularized knowledge of the rich ancient remains there. Luxury thus returned to fashion, and the high-waisted gowns were now made of thick silk and worn together with oriental-style turbans.

During the Romantic movement of the early decades of the 19th century, inspiration from ancient times again made a strong impression on fashion. By midcentury, in English Pre-Raphaelite circles the models wore long, loose "aesthetic" dresses without hoop skirt or corset. This more "natural" style of dress was directed at the "naturally" built woman and took inspiration from Greek statues such as Venus de Milo and Venus de' Medici. In the 1880s and 1890s "rational dress" associations, referring to the aesthetics of ancient Greece, protested against current fashions of tight lacing. Health and well-being constituted an important argument in this movement, and its recommendation of suspending clothing from the shoulders rather than the waist was derived from classical sculpture.

The early 1900s brought a new wave of classicism. The slim, pleated dresses of the 1920s, with low-cut backs, showed how bodily freedom was used to express emancipation and new thinking. For several decades thereafter, fashion designers such as Madeleine Vionnet, Mariano Fortuny, Madame Grès, and Bruce Weber continued to employ new materials and techniques in their classically inspired dresses to convey the same concepts of nobility, purity, and dignity that their predecessors had sought.

BIBL.: Anne Hollander, *Seeing through Clothes* (1978, rept. Berkeley 1993). Aileen Ribeiro, *Fashion in the French Revolution* (London 1988). C.B.

Fathers, Church

Since the 4th century, authoritative, nonbiblical witnesses to the orthodox Christian tradition of antiquity have been called Fathers of the Church. The distinction between orthodoxy and heresy, however, is highly complex, especially for Christianity's first three centuries. Therefore, today the Church Fathers are generally thought also to include certain Christian theologians from the beginning of the 2nd century CE until the early Middle Ages whose orthodoxy was doubted, such as Origen and Eusebius. In the Latin West the last authors of the patristic age were Isidore of Seville (d. 636) and Bede (d. 735), in the Greek East John Damascene (d. ca. 750). In addition, there were numerous Church Fathers who wrote in Armenian, Coptic, Syriac, and other languages.

The term *classical tradition* can have two meanings with reference to the Church Fathers. First, many Christian theologians of antiquity read and interpreted pagan authors. The Church Fathers were thus early representatives of the reception of antiquity. Second, the Church Fathers were themselves ancient authors: Justin Martyr, for example, wrote at about the same time as Lucian in the 2nd century; Origen was an older contemporary of Plotinus; and Ambrose lived around the time of Ammianus Marcellinus. Thus, the reception of the Church Fathers from the Middle Ages onward should be seen as a part of the reception of antiquity.

According to a classic simplification, the contribution of the Church Fathers consists in having combined the world of the Hebrew Bible with that of Greek philosophy and thereby having laid the intellectual foundation for Western civilization. The process, however, can be understood more precisely. Early Christianity certainly had its roots in Judaism, but it would be wrong to equate Judaism primarily with the Hebrew ancient Orient. Not only in the Greek-speaking Jewish diaspora around the Mediterranean, but also in Palestine, there had been an intense dialogue—partly critical, partly positive—between Judaism and Hellenism since the 3rd century BCE. A revolutionary project of this more than 300-year-long phase was the Greek translation of the Hebrew and Aramaic texts of the Bible. Several other writings, composed in Greek and heavily influenced by pagan Greek historiography and more popular Greek philosophy, also made their way into this Septuagint. This is also the case for numerous other

Jewish writings in Greek from the Hellenistic-Roman period that were not included in the Bible.

This is the context in which Christian literature began. All the writings of the New Testament, such as the letters of the Apostle Paul and the Gospels, were written in Greek. Whatever may seem to be a reminiscence of pagan Greek texts in the New Testament normally flows from the fusion of pagan Greek and Hebrew models in the writings of Greek-speaking Jews. The distinctive feature of Christianity, however—the universalization announced in Jesus' teaching—appears quite early. It can be seen most clearly in Paul. He wrote, perhaps around 55 CE, that not only the Jews but all those who had been baptized were the true descendants of Abraham: "There is neither Jew nor Greek, there is neither bond nor free, there is neither male nor female: for ye are all one in Christ Jesus" (Galatians 3:28). Decades later the Acts of the Apostles showed Paul, provoked by Epicureans and Stoics, speaking on the Areopagus in Athens. His speech contains the most important perspective through which the Church Fathers would later receive the classical tradition. "Who therefore ye ignorantly worship," Paul calls out to the Athenian pagans, "him declare I unto you" (17:23).

From the very beginning, patristic literature exhibited dissent regarding the value of the classical tradition. "What has Athens to do with Jerusalem? What the Academy with the Church?" But Tertullian, who posed this rhetorical question around 200 (*De praescriptione* 7.9), was, despite his radical critique of Greek education, thoroughly imbued with ancient pagan stylistics. His writings, which inaugurated Christian Latin literature, are the work of a master who obviously wants, and is able, to compete with pagan rhetoric. The contradiction became more pointed in Jerome. Around 384 he told how years before as a monk he had read his Cicero and Plautus right after doing penance. In a fever he had a dream. He is standing before the Last Judgment. Jerome says he is a Christian. But the judge (Christ) responds: "You lie. You are a Ciceronian, not a Christian. For where your treasure is, there too your heart." Christ exempts him from the punishment of a lashing on the condition that he no longer read the books of the pagans (Epistles 22.30). But this does nothing to change the fact that Jerome's works contain hundreds of citations of Terence, Cicero, Virgil, and others. Jerome's later claim that he had not had such authors in his hands for 15 years, and that citations of them are coincidental, vague reminiscences (preface to *Commentary on the Letter to the Galatians* 3), should not be taken completely seriously. Nearly all the Greek and Latin Church Fathers were deeply marked by their education in rhetoric, which until the very end of antiquity was based largely on the reading of the great pagan authors.

A similarly ambivalent approach to pagan culture can be found in the Greek apologists of the 2nd century. Some of them, like Theophilus (*Ad Autolycum*) and Tatian (*Oratio ad Graecos*), criticized pagan religion, science, and art. They saw the diversity of the Greek philosophical schools as proof of their invalidity. Nevertheless, these apologists felt the need, in the face of pagan criticism of Christianity, to think through their own faith in a form that would be acceptable to educated pagans. Thus, pagans could ask, for example, why a man in space and time, such as Jesus Christ in the prologue to the Gospel according to John, is identified with divine Logos. For his explanation, Theophilus used the distinction in the Stoic philosophy of language between *endiathetos logos*, a word thought in the human intellect, and *prophorikos logos*, a word spoken in space and time. In precisely this way, Christ exists in eternity as the Logos of God the father, and nevertheless he came into this world at a specific time and in a specific place (2.22).

Justin Martyr sketched in his *Apologies* a program for a positive relationship with the classical tradition. According to him, Plato's wisdom ultimately came from his knowledge of the writings of Moses. Justin also enunciated a Christian concept of history incorporating parallels between the crucified and resurrected Christ and "resurrected" pagan gods like Dionysus and Osiris. Of central importance is the notion of divine Logos, in which a righteous martyr like Socrates also had a part (*Apology* 1.46). Justin was one of those Christian "teachers" who, in imitation of pagan philosophers, offered private courses on Christian theology. Perhaps the most prominent feature of ancient Greek culture—the theoretical, argumentative, analytical inquiry into the universal origin of all things, into correct ethical principles, and into the rationality of given arguments—seeped into Christianity and fostered a religion more closely tied to rationality. Ancient Christianity understood itself as the "true philosophy," in contrast to the false or half-true philosophy of the pagans.

It was probably around the same time, the middle of the 2nd century, that Christian Gnosticism sprang up. It, too, grew out of the desire to rethink Christianity by means of a simplified form of Greek philosophy and wisdom, and thus to make it attractive to educated people. Men such as Basilides and Valentinus attempted to explain Christianity on the level of the average metropolitan citizen. Their students then gradually built up seemingly fantastic systems that, while still containing a great deal of vulgar Platonism, propagated a bleak view of the world. The Gnostics made a strict distinction between the supreme God and the divine powers that created the world. On this point they might have been following the connection between Greek cosmology and the biblical traditions already developed in the 1st century CE by the Jewish thinker Philo of Alexandria. But though Philo clearly identified the Creator-God of Abraham, Isaac, and Jacob with the supreme God, some of the Gnostics considered the God of the Old Testament to be one of the lesser divine powers. The crises of the 2nd and 3rd centuries around Gnosticism and related positions engendered in Christianity a wariness about pagan education. In a refutation of these heresies, Hippolytus attempted to trace Gnostic systems explicitly back to pagan philosophy. To carry out this task, however, he had to immerse himself in handbooks of philosophy and construe the heresies anew as if they were philosophies. Thus, Hipploytus helped to develop a kind of philosophical argumentation within theology, even when his intention lay elsewhere.

The Church Fathers did not turn away from the classical tradition. On the contrary, it was first in the theology of Clement of Alexandria and Origen that the method suggested by Philo was brought to bear: combining Old Testament exegesis with Middle Platonic *Prinzipienlehre,* pagan cosmology, and allegorical interpretation. In Alexandria, after Rome the great metropolis of the time, Christianity found in Clement a man who considered Greek wisdom a preparatory education (*propaideia*) for the correct understanding of Christianity. Clement artfully combined a hefty abundance of quotations from Greek poetry and philosophy with quotations from the Old and New Testaments, the point being to give the impression that the Bible was not a barbaric book but rather could rival the best writings of Greek civilization.

Clement also started the tradition of a scholarly theology: as the winemaker needs specialized knowledge, thus the Christian religion requires intellectual rigor and expert scholarship (*Stromata* 1.43.1 f.). His montage of pagan quotations might seem confused to modern eyes, but he justified it thus: eternal truth has been fragmented within philosophy, and one must prudently search out those things that are correct and belong together (*Stromata* 1.57.6). Clement, too, thought that Moses was ultimately the source for everything that is true in Homer, Orpheus, Hermes Trismegistus, the Sibyls, and the Greek mystery cults. But for this reason Greek culture provided possibilities for a more meaningful kind of preaching: "I want to show you the Logos and the mysteries of the Logos, and I want to explain them to you in pictures that are familiar to you" (*Protrepticus* 12.119.1).

With Origen (ca. 185–ca. 253), Christianity for the first time rose to the level of reflection, in all the complexity typical of contemporary philosophy and the philological commentary of texts. Like the Middle Platonist Atticus, who had described Plato's achievement as having molded philosophy into a "body" (*soma*), or integrated whole (quoted in Eusebius, *Praeparatio evangelica,* 11.2.2), Origen also wanted to provide a *soma* for theology, so that the truth could be ascertained in its various parts through clear and convincing arguments (*In Johannem* 13.46; *De principiis,* preface, 10). It is quite possible that Origen studied philosophy under Ammonius Saccas, who is considered the founder of Neoplatonism and was Plotinus' teacher. Origen, however, like Augustine later, was capable of transforming philosophy all on his own. Thus, for example, he appeared to use the Neoplatonic doctrine of emanation to describe how the Son of God proceeds from God the Father. But when it came to the divine trinity, he conceived of it not by way of analogy to the three highest hypostases of Neoplatonism but from biblical considerations.

Something of the freedom of thought so beloved to classical Greece also lived on in Origen. He loved to think an idea through to its logical conclusions, but without necessarily considering it on that account correct. Thus, he discusses the idea that eschatological salvation will lead humanity back to its freedom, but that freedom also implies the possibility of sinning anew. One consequence of this may be that history repeats itself. Such conclusions were later seen—perhaps wrongly—as signs of heresy in Origen, as a relapse into pagan notions of eternal return or reincarnation. Greater success was enjoyed for many centuries by Origen's reception of the allegorical method of interpretation, which he put to impressive use in detailed commentaries and many homilies on the Bible. As pagan allegorical interpretation of Homer had once done, allegorical exegesis of the Bible enabled its canonized, immutable text to be reconciled with the current needs of an intellectual culture, and at the same time to anchor these needs in holy writ.

With the "Constantinian turn" of the 4th century and the resulting convergence of the Roman Empire and Christianity, the context and character of the Christian reception of the classical tradition gradually shifted. Even into the 6th century, there was still great sympathy for ancient paganism at the highest tier of society. The schools and academies in no way modified their curricula in the Christian state. As always, proper Greek was learned in the Greek half of the empire by means of Homer and Herodotus, and in Latin areas Cicero, Virgil, and Horace remained standard authors for language instruction. Around 300 the Christian Lactantius published writings in exquisite, nearly classical Latin. As a matter of course, an aristocratic Christian like Basil of Caesarea did not only receive his training from Christians but studied first in Constantinople under the most famous rhetorician of his time, the pagan Libanius.

Basil, his brother Gregory of Nyssa, and his friend Gregory of Nazianzus, the three great theologians of Cappadocia in the mid- and late 4th century, themselves became Christian classics. Basil was a brilliant epistolographer and church politician, Gregory of Nyssa the thinker and philosopher among them. Gregory of Nazianzus became a celebrated orator and poet, and he was read and admired in the Byzantine period as a model for all Christian oratory. When in 362 the emperor Julian, who was devoted to reinvigorating paganism, decided to supervise the allocation of teaching posts, he noted that Christian teachers were using texts full of pagan mythology for grammar instruction. His conclusion, that only pagans should be allowed to teach, was forcefully rejected by Christian intellectuals, including the three Cappadocians. Julian's attempt was short-lived, but its unintentional result was probably to increase Christians' acknowledgment of the value of pagan learning.

Initially, the situation developed similarly in the Latin West. Upper-class Christians like Ambrose and Jerome were not inferior to their contemporaries in classical learning. Pope Damasus (r. 366–384) composed poems full of reminiscences of Virgil and Ovid and Christianized the aesthetic ideals of the pagan senatorial aristocracy. In contrast to these three contemporaries and to the three Cappadocian fathers, Augustine, a man from provincial North Africa, did not enjoy an upper class education. His knowledge of Greek was never adequate for the fluent reading of texts in that language. He was trained in rhetoric solely in North Africa. Only with his appointment to professorships, in Rome and Milan (384), did he come to know the world of a deeply intellectual Christianity heavily tinctured with Neoplatonism. In his *De doctrina Christiana* he articulates a theory of culture and cultural tradition in which he speaks about the jewelry that the Israelites stole from the Egyptians and took with them to put "to better use" (Exodus 3:22): Christians should use the classical tradition in the same way (2.40.60). Augustine's own works, however, go far beyond simple use. They confidently assimilate Platonic arguments, historical knowledge, and rhetorical and exegetical techniques, and they contain many quotations from Virgil as well as allusions to Sallust or Livy. When the North African city where he was bishop, Hippo Regius, was besieged by Vandals in 430, Augustine consoled himself with Psalms and a quotation from Plotinus.

In the Latin West a process began of collecting and salvaging the tradition that could include both its pagan and Christian aspects. The ideal monastic library, which Cassiodorus outlined ca. 551–562 in the *Institutiones divinarum et humanarum lectionum,* in many ways prefigured medieval monastic scriptoria and included, at least virtually, works of the Church Fathers as well as writings by Aristotle, Josephus, Porphyry (all in Latin translation) and Quintilian. When Boethius, jailed in 523 in the wake of late antique political intrigues, wrote his *Consolation of Philosophy,* he spoke on every page as a Christian poet and philosopher, but without one single specifically Christian word or quotation. It was as if he wanted to show one last time before his death that pagan learning and a deeply sophisticated Christianity were not in contradiction.

The Greek East took a different trajectory, as political continuity lasted there until the conquest of Constantinople by the Ottomans in 1453. At the beginning of the 6th century, the many writings that circulated under the name of the disciple of Paul, Dionysius the Areopagite, but whose true author is still unknown, transformed the metaphysics and cosmology elaborated in Neoplatonism (above all by Iamblichus and Proclus) into a Christian theology of the cosmos, the Church, and the liturgy. Nevertheless, the fact that the Athenian Academy, still under the leadership of brilliant pagan scholars, was in all likelihood closed by Justinian in 529 and may have emigrated to a Syriac-speaking area also shows how ambivalent ancient Christianity's relationship had always been to the classical tradition.

In the 4th century the Latin Christianity of the West and its Eastern counterpart began drifting further and further apart. This was also a matter of language. Many Greek patristic texts were translated into Latin beginning in antiquity, and in the Middle Ages and modern times as well, but only a few translations of Latin patristic texts were available in Greek. The same linguistic imbalance had previously existed in the pagan context. In addition, increasingly independent churches were emerging on the borders of Greek Christianity in an array of Near Eastern languages. Their reception of the classical tradition could take quite different paths: the Armenians, for example, translated much of Plato, but the Syriacs preferred Aristotle and the tradition of the Greek commentators on Aristotle; in this way Syriac Christians prepared the way for the later Arabic reception of Aristotle.

Important differences also emerged in the way the writings of the Church Fathers were received. In the Byzantine Church and its theology, not only did the Greek Church Fathers remain standard authorities, but their exegesis and theological method were carried forward and continue to be sustained, for example, in the present-day theology of the Greek Orthodox and Russian Orthodox traditions. In the Latin West, on the other hand, a new kind of theology developed beginning in the 11th century: the Scholastic method. In this context the writings of the Church Fathers, or rather their individual *sententiae,* were employed as authoritative testimonies of the tradition. But the hallmark of the Church Fathers—the combination of biblical exegesis, pagan rhetoric, spirituality, and independent philosophical-theological reflection—disappeared. In the Latin Middle Ages it gave way to a standardized, schoollike ("scholastic") method that produced shrewd conceptual distinctions but loosened its association with liturgy and spirituality. This tendency became stronger as familiarity with Aristotle increased in the Latin West during the High Middle Ages.

When the Humanists turned against Scholasticism and its (in their estimation) barbaric Latin, their rediscovery of ancient authors was in no way limited to pagans but also included the Church Fathers. Patristic texts were increasingly read as literature and not merely ransacked for dogmatic teachings. Petrarch counted Augustine among his favorite authors, and Erasmus published substantial editions of works of Cyprian, Ambrose, Jerome, and Augustine. The Humanists were happy to derive their combination of Christian faith and pagan learning from the Church Fathers. A programmatic text was provided particularly by Basil of Caesarea's *Ad adolescentes,* which Leonardo Bruni translated ca. 1400 into Latin. Mabillon still identified it in 1691 as the best patristic statement on the question of the place of classical studies in Christian education. Similarly important was Augustine's *De doctrina Christiana.* The Humanists read Fathers like Lactantius, Jerome, and Augustine as stylistic models for the combination of classical Latin and Christian thought.

The Humanists gladly celebrated their discoveries as a rebirth of antiquity. And yet the manuscripts of the ancient authors found by them lay in large part in the monastic and cathedral libraries of the West or in the libraries of Greek monks and bishops, where, in line with the intention of Church Fathers such as Basil and Augustine, nearly all of them had also been produced. Beginning ca. 1400 Greek manuscripts, containing both pagan and Christian texts, increasingly arrived in Italy from Constantinople. The home of Cardinal Bessarion became the treasury of Greek literature in Italy in the 15th century.

During the Reformation and the confessionalization of the 15th and 16th centuries, the Church Fathers became for Protestant theologians witnesses to a theology that, while perhaps not infallible, was nonetheless far more acceptable than that of the Church's Scholastic decadence. For their part, Catholics tried to demonstrate the correspondence between their theology and the testimony of the Church Fathers. Since the 19th century the interpretation of the Church Fathers has increasingly provided a foundation for ecumenical theology. In the mid-20th century a forceful return to the Church Fathers aided in overcoming Neoscholasticism, which had theretofore dominated Catholic theology. Leading Catholic theologians such as Jean Daniélou, Henri de Lubac, and Hans Urs von Balthasar were excellent patristic scholars. Today Christian theologians of all stripes are rediscovering the Church Fathers' scriptural hermeneutics in particular, which with its typological, allegorical, and mystical orientation stands in stark contrast to historical-critical exegesis.

Though philologists from the 16th to the 18th centuries frequently studied the pagan as well as the Jewish and Christian authors of antiquity, starting about 1800 classical scholars who had a tendency to classicism paid little attention to imperial authors and frequently ignored the Church Fathers utterly. Even some more recent descriptions of Greek and Latin literature, such as the *Cambridge History of Classical Literature* (Cambridge 1985), pass over the writings of the ancient Christians almost completely. Since the end of the 19th century, however, many philologists, such as Hermann Usener, Werner Jaeger, and Albrecht Dihle, have detached themselves from this kind of perspective, which to them seems ahistorical and narrow. Accordingly, they give equal consideration to the writings of pagans, Greek-speaking Jews, and Christians of the imperial period. Perhaps through their efforts a conception of the classical tradition can be recovered that comes closer to the complex reality of Antiquity.

BIBL.: Irena Backus, ed., *The Reception of the Church Fathers in the West,* 2nd ed., 2 vols. (Leiden 2001). Henry Chadwick, *Early Christian Thought and the Classical Tradition: Studies in Justin, Clement, and Origen* (Oxford 1966). Angelo Di Berardino and William C. H. Frend, eds., *Encyclopedia of the Early Church,* 2nd ed., 2 vols. (New York 1998). Albrecht Dihle, *Greek and Latin Literature of the Roman Empire: From Augustus to Justinian* (London 1995). Harald Hagendahl, *Augustine and the Latin Classics,* 2 vols. (Göteborg, 1967) and *Latin Fathers and the Classics* (Göteborg 1958). Werner Jaeger, *Early Christianity and Greek Paideia* (Cambridge, Mass., 1961). Theodor Klauser et al., eds., *Reallexikon für Antike und Christentum* (Stuttgart 1950–). Jaroslav Pelikan, *Christianity and Classical Culture: The Metamorphosis of Natural Theology in the Christian Encounter with Hellenism* (New Haven 1993). Guy Stroumsa, *Barbarian Philosophy: The Religious Revolution of Early Christianity* (Tübingen 1999). Frances A. Young et al., eds., *The Cambridge History of Early Christian Literature* (Cambridge 2004). R.K.

Translated by Patrick Baker

Faun

In Latin the word *faun* is synonymous with *satyr;* fauns or satyrs are demigod followers of Dionysus/Bacchus and have pointed ears and horses' tails. In Roman iconography, as in imagery since the 15th century and in modern linguistic usage, they are confused with other beings of the Dionysian sphere that have goats' legs and horns and whose specific Greek name was Pan. Roman relief sculpture (especially on sarcophagi), engraved gems, and statues have preserved the semiferal image of the faun from antiquity, which in the Middle Ages was considered diabolic. This figure of bestial, vigorous vitality has retained an uninterrupted fascination, in part through the medium of literature. Since the 15th century the faun has figured in Bacchus's retinue and in bucolic scenes, often absorbed in playing music and dancing, and often busy ambushing nymphs and hermaphrodites. Figurative representations are quite numerous and disparate. They range, for example, from painted caissons to Raphael's stuccos in the Vatican loggias; from panels by Botticelli (*Mars and Venus, Calumny*) and Piero di Cosimo (scenes of primitive life) to bacchanals by Titian and Poussin; from Rubens's allegory of peace to Sebastiano Ricci's and Fragonard's idyllic families of fauns; from engravings by Mantegna and Dürer to those of Picasso; from the small bronzes of Riccio and Antico to those of Rodin. A statue of a faun that comes to life and falls in love with a model is the protagonist of Febo Mari's film *Il Fauno* (1917), and Matthew Barney's video *Drawing Restraint 7* (1993) features two satyrs wrestling in the backseat of a moving limousine.

The faun has also made many appearances in literature throughout the centuries. Examples include the imaginary reliefs with seated nymphs that decorate the pages and the engravings of *Polifilo* (1490); the faun-rapist and *Aminta* (1590) of Tasso; Mallarmé's *L'Après-midi d'un faune* (1876), which was illustrated by Manet and then inspired a symphonic poem by Debussy (1894); and Hawthorne's *The Marble Faun* (1860), in which Donatello bears a mysterious resemblance to the Campidoglio's statue. This sculpture, thought by some to be a copy from Praxiteles, owes a great part of its notoriety to the novel; another replica of the same model, but in the act of playing the pan flute, belonged to the Giustiniani collection and appeared in the compilation of engravings of famous statues edited by Perrier (1638). The most famous statue of a faun, and the one most often reproduced and copied, is the *Dancing Faun* (with cymbals) that belonged to the Medici and was placed in the Tribuna room of the Uffizi in 1688. It was copied in marble by Foggini for Versailles in 1685–1686 and, at the turn of the 18th century, in bronze for the prince of Lichtenstein and for the Duke of Marlborough. It was also reproduced in porcelain by

Doccia's workshop, copied in small bronzes by Zoffoli and Righetti and in intaglio by Wedgwood, and adapted for a majolica composition of 18th century. The Florentine statue also owes its renown to its appearance in Maffei and De Rossi's *Raccolta di statue* (1704), which also features the Barberini *Faun,* now in the Glyptothek in Munich, and the *Faun with Kid* that belonged to Christine of Sweden, now in the Prado, both of which were very widely known and were also copied and adapted.

BIBL.: P. Pray Bober and R. Rubinstein, *Renaissance Artists and Antique Sculpture* (London 1986). F. Haskell and N. Penny, *Taste and the Antique* (New Haven 1981). L.F.

Translated by Patrick Baker

Ficino, Marsilio

Among the most learned and seminal thinkers of the Italian Renaissance, Marsilio Ficino, the Florentine Platonist and Humanist (1433–1499), was also its supreme translator and interpreter of Plato and Plotinus. Destined initially for a medical career (he in fact became a much-cited medical authority), he caught the eye of Cosimo de' Medici while still a Platonizing youth; it was Cosimo's patronage that enabled him to acquire a rare mastery of Greek and especially of the history, prehistory, and what he was to call the poetic theology of the Orphic and Platonic traditions and their recourse to myth. Over three decades he interpreted this theology through the eyes of the ancient Neoplatonists, most notably of Proclus and his pupil Dionysius the Areopagite (fl. ca. 500 CE), whom he and his contemporaries continued to misidentify with Saint Paul's Athenian convert in Acts 17:34—obviously with profound repercussions for their understanding of the history of later Platonism and its debts both to Johannine and Pauline theology and to a fully orchestrated 1st-century Christian Platonism. Two eminent Byzantine contemporaries, the controversial Pletho and Cardinal Bessarion, his pupil, also played a role, however: first, in shaping Ficino's understanding of Zoroaster as the first in the line of six "ancient theologians" culminating in Plato, and of the significance therefore of the *Chaldean Oracles* attributed to Zoroaster along with the interpretations of Pletho and his 11th-century predecessor Psellus; and, second, in alerting Ficino to the range of difficulties, ethical, political, and metaphysical, that Platonism posed for a Christian, and to its vexed relationship to Aristotelianism.

In 1463 Cosimo instructed Ficino to render into Latin the rediscovered canon of Plato's dialogues (largely unknown in the West for a millennium), though he ordered him to translate first the corpus of brief theological treatises attributed to the ancient Egyptian sage Hermes Trismegistus. In the summer of 1464 Ficino read to Cosimo on his deathbed from Plato's *Parmenides* and *Philebus*—an extraordinary witness to the notion of a holy Christian–Platonic dying. But it was not until 1484—a date selected surely for its planetary conjunctions—that Ficino finally published his complete translations of Plato, having selectively consulted renderings of a handful of the dialogues by his Humanist predecessors. He dedicated the translations to Lorenzo de' Medici, *pater patriae* (and his erstwhile pupil), and included *argumenta* (prefaces) for each dialogue along with an expansive commentary on the *Symposium,* which he had finished in 1469 and entitled *On Love.* This became the seminal text of Renaissance love theory and focused the age's attention on the dialogue.

Meanwhile, as he continually revised his Plato during the 1470s and published *On the Christian Religion* after he was ordained a priest in 1473, Ficino compiled an 18-book summa that he subtitled, with a bow to Plotinus and Augustine, *On the Immortality of Souls,* but formally entitled *Platonic Theology,* borrowing the appellation, significantly, from Proclus' magnum opus. Yet Proclus was an authority to whom he was often only silently indebted, even as he frequently referred by name to Plato, Plotinus, Augustine, the Areopagite, Averroes (by way of opposition), and Thomas Aquinas. Published in 1482, the work was the fruit of Ficino's conviction that Platonism—for us Neoplatonism, as he regarded Plotinus as Plato's most profound interpreter—was reconcilable with Christianity, above all on the pivotal question of the nature of the rational soul.

Though Plotinus had engaged him constantly since the 1460s, Ficino returned to him afresh in the 1480s and began to render into Latin for the first time the entire *Enneads,* again supplying extensive notes and commentaries. In 1489, and as an offshoot perhaps from the Plotinus project, he published a three-book treatise on prolonging health, *On Life,* which combined philosophical, magical, and psychiatric speculations and overflowed with pharmacological and astrological learning. The third book especially, which he subtitled "On Conforming One's Life to the Heavens," is one of the first studies of an occupational disease, namely scholarly melancholy, and it treats of amulets, talismans, star and demon magic, regimen, mood elevation, holistic medicine, and the occult. In response to the threat of a Curial investigation into its unorthodoxy, Ficino defended it and himself with the double-edged argument that he was expounding the views of the ancients, not his own; it remains, nonetheless, the pièce de résistance of Renaissance psychology and magic theory. The massive Plotinus edition itself was published in 1492, again with a dedication to Lorenzo.

In 1496 Ficino published six speculative Plato commentaries, some incomplete and some he had been working on for years, on a sestet of Plato's most difficult texts: the *Parmenides* (for him, as it had been for the later Neoplatonists, the master dialogue), *Sophist, Timaeus, Phaedrus, Philebus,* and the enigmatic passage on the Nuptial Number in book 8 of the *Republic.* He also published translations of Iamblichus, Porphyry, Proclus, and Synesius, translated and commented on the works of the Areopagite, and embarked on a commentary on Saint Paul's Epistle to the Romans.

Ficino was able to influence deeply the cultural and intellectual life of his own time and of two subsequent centuries, up to the mid–17th-century Cambridge Platonists and beyond, even to the Romantics. A revered teacher of the Florentine patricians and their sons, he cultivated a far-flung network of patrons, friends, and contacts, many of them, including Lorenzo and sundry prelates, in the highest offices of Church and state and constituting what has long been called—misleadingly, as it was never an institution of any kind—his Platonic Academy (a term he seems to have used variously to refer to Plato's works or to manuscripts of them or to his own pupils). His 12 books of Latin letters range from Ciceronian greetings and well-turned apologies to full-scale treatises. Many contemporaries were clearly fascinated by the novelty and force of his revival of Neoplatonism and his attempt to reunite theology and philosophy in the light of his commitment to the notion of an ancient theological Platonism stemming from Zoroaster, Hermes Trismegistus, and Orpheus. His ecumenical belief that worship is natural and inherently various, along with his psychological and syncretistic interests, would even today align him with the liberal wing of Catholicism. He was, furthermore, one of the first classicists whose scholarship enjoyed a Europe-wide dissemination because of printing, and his works are among the most splendid and valuable of the incunabula: indeed, *On Love* and *On Life,* along with the Hermes and Plato translations and a plague treatise, were often reprinted.

Though he was a Humanist who readily quoted the Roman poets, he was also a Scholastically trained philosopher-apologist who dedicated himself to inaugurating a Platonic revival and to spiritual renewal by way of redeploying the arguments and proofs both of the Schools and of the Platonists. But he was also the first of the Renaissance mages to reengage the *Timaeus'* notions of a World Soul and a World Spirit; and to this end he explored astrology, magic, harmonics, magical and figural numbers, demonology, the occult, music, and musical therapy—topics that he found in the later Platonists and thus saw as genuine aspects of the Platonic tradition. Although his technical understanding of Neoplatonic texts still impresses scholars, it is his original philosophical, theological, theosophical, amatory, and magical speculations that constitute his most enduring legacy, not least because they were widely and profoundly influential.

BIBL.: Michael J. B. Allen, *The Platonism of Marsilio Ficino* (Berkeley 1984), *Plato's Third Eye: Studies in Marsilio Ficino's Metaphysics and Its Sources* (Aldershot 1995), and *Synoptic Art: Marsilio Ficino on the History of Platonic Interpretation* (Florence 1998). Michael J. B. Allen and Valery Rees, eds., *Marsilio Ficino: His Theology, His Philosophy, His Legacy* (Leiden 2002). James Hankins, *Plato in the Italian Renaissance,* 2 vols. (Leiden 1990), and *Humanism and Platonism in the Italian Renaissance,* vol. 2, *Platonism* (Rome 2004). Paul O. Kristeller, *The Philosophy of Marsilio Ficino* (New York 1943). M.A.

Fin de Siècle Art

The phrase *fin de siècle* ("end of century") is first recorded in English in 1890, and as a significant term it seems to be not much older in France itself. It is the product of distinctively 19th-century circumstances. In 1898 the *Westminster Gazette* referred to the present age "which pessimists call *fin-de-siècle* with some sort of idea that the phrase indicates a weariness and weakening of purpose." The ancient world played some part in this idea, through the organic or biological metaphor so often favored by 19th-century thinkers for describing the development of civilization. On this account ancient Greece, blithe and athletic, represented the youth (or even the childhood) of the world, and the present time was seen by contrast as elderly. The decline of faith, the ravages of industrialism, and a sense that science had destroyed the magic and beauty of the world persuaded some people that the modern world was drab and dispiriting. Walter Pater's *Marius the Epicurean* (1882), set in Rome and Italy in the 2nd century CE, makes both explicit and implied comparisons between late antiquity and the "lateness" of 19th-century civilization. And it was as a fin de siècle aesthete that the young Yeats contrasted his own time with a lost classical idyll:

> The woods of Arcady are dead,
> And withered is their antique joy;
> Of old the world on dreaming fed;
> Grey truth is now her painted toy.
> ("The Song of the Happy Shepherd," 1889)

Fin de siècle was a term of vague application, floating among others that were perhaps not much more definite: decadence, aestheticism, the "fleshly school of poetry." On English-speaking lips the foreignness of the phrase added a note of Continental degeneracy, rather as decadence was sometimes written as *décadence,* in the French style. In the visual arts the term was especially fluid. Sometimes it was used as a label for trends, such as symbolism and the aesthetic movement, which can be seen as late Romantic, as precursors of modernism, or as both. But it has also been applied to the academic and salon styles of painting against which modernism decisively reacted. Such salon works as Lawrence Alma-Tadema's *The Roses of Heliogabalus* or J.-L. Gérôme's scenes of Roman slave markets seem to find a *fin-de-sièclisme* in the Roman world while enjoying the very decadence that they purport to reprehend.

BIBL.: Aleksa Celebonovic, *Some Call It Kitsch: Masterpieces of Bourgeois Realism* (New York 1974). Bram Dijkstra, *Idols of Perversity: Fantasies of Feminine Evil in Fin-de-Siècle Culture* (New York 1986). Richard Jenkyns, *Dignity and Decadence: Victorian Art and the Classical Inheritance* (Cambridge, Mass., 1991). R.J.

Florilegium. *See* Anthology and Florilegium

Forgery

In the late spring and summer of 1855, the Clarendon Press of Oxford University printed the first edition of a Greek text, news of which had aroused interest throughout the learned world: a history of the kings of Egypt, written in Greek by a historian named Uranios. The prolific Byzantinist Wilhelm Dindorf had obtained the manuscript that contained the work, a palimpsest, at great expense, and he supplied the edition with a Latin preface. Ancient Egypt appealed to readers who had marveled at the Napoleonic *Description de l'Egypte,* with its depiction of the country's ruins, and Champollion's deciphering of the hieroglyphs. The anticipation was great, and the consternation when the press withdrew it from publication even greater.

But the Oxford authorities could do nothing else when the Egyptologist Karl Richard Lepsius and the manuscript hunter Konstantin von Tischendorf both denounced the text of Uranios as a fake composed by the Greek who claimed to have discovered it, Constantine Simonides. When the British police arrested Simonides, they discovered in his rooms rusty nails, useful for faking aged paper, and technical books on Egyptian dynastic history and chronology—exactly the tools a forger would have needed to create such a work. In this case, and in others, Simonides convinced the authorities that he was innocent and regained his freedom. Eventually, however, the forger found himself forced to fake his own death. He retired to an obscure existence in Egypt.

Simonides drew on up-to-date information for his work, using recent studies of Egyptian chronology as sources and exploiting his own knowledge of Greek manuscripts, handwriting, and ink to craft the written text. But the two basic operations that he carried out were very old. To produce a convincing ancient history of Egypt, Simonides composed a Greek text that seemed, to some readers at least, like a genuine product of the ancient world, and he crafted a manuscript that seemed like a genuinely old and overwritten product of a medieval scriptorium. In making this double effort, he took his place in a long line of writers and artisans who produced documents and objects intended to deceive—a line that had its roots in the ancient world itself and that blossomed, with the revival of the classical literary heritage, in the Renaissance.

Forgery began as early as the 6th and 5th centuries BCE, both on the literary level (e.g., as when Athenians and others interpolated verses into Homer to prove the importance of their city in the earliest times) and on the public (e.g., when temple priests and public orators created records and cited laws that did not exist). But the real heyday of forgery came in the Hellenistic and imperial periods. Great collections—above all, the Alexandrian library—required texts by the greatest Greek writers, from the tragedians to the orator Lysias. Spurious supplies rapidly came into existence when the genuine works ran out—some of them, according to ancient reports, created by forgers, and others simply the result of literary imitation not intended to deceive. Latin collectors emulated the Greeks, with similar results. By the 1st century BCE, the Roman scholar Varro knew of 130 plays ascribed to Plautus. Of these, he declared, 109 were spurious. Meanwhile, religious and quasi-religious groups, from the Jews to the Egyptian followers of Hermes Trismegistus, produced revelations that claimed to be older and more full of marvels than they really were.

Ancient scholars developed tools for detecting these fakes. Each author, they noted, had a distinctive style, which made imitation difficult if not impossible. A true scholar should always be able to tell the difference, as Galen remarked one day when he watched a well-educated man in Rome pick up a text ascribed to Galen himself and reject it as unworthy of its supposed author. Callimachus, who drew up the first catalogues for the library at Alexandria, divided the works ascribed to each author into genuine and spurious, calling the former *gnesioi,* or legitimate, and the latter *nothoi,* or bastards. Others tallied the typical gestures that indicated a forger's effort to make his work appear genuine, and the more or less obvious inconsistencies that revealed these to the scrupulous reader. The philosopher Porphyry, for example, noted that though the author of the texts ascribed to Hermes Trismegistus claimed to be translating the alien wisdom of the Egyptian priests, in fact they were written in the technical language of Greek philosophy. The most extensive discussions of authenticity appeared in Christian literature, in which extensive efforts were made to distinguish between canonical and apocryphal works, some of them very elaborate, and formal lists were kept of the canonical ones. (Even the Gospels were misattributed to apostles who were not their true authors.)

Like the ancients, medieval forgers sometimes tried to create documents that would support the claims of a modern community or institution. Often such documents contained a measure of historical memory if not literal historical truth. In the 8th century, when members of the papal chancery in Rome drew up the documents that recorded how the emperor Constantine had been cured of leprosy by Pope Sylvester, and in return had given the papacy the entire Western Roman Empire, they imagined and recorded scenes that had never taken place. But they invented these records because they knew that Constantine and his family had in fact endowed the church with buildings and estates on a vast scale. A text that recorded these great events would have its uses for everyone from papal propagandists to pilgrims traveling to Rome.

Others forged documents precisely because they felt the historical distance that separated them from the ancient authors they loved most. The learned cleric who forged a substantial poem by Ovid, *De vetula,* in the 13th century composed a romantic story that turned the great Roman poet from a pagan lover into a faithful Christian. As early as the 14th and 15th centuries, readers like Petrarch and Pierre d'Ailly rejected the work because they thought it absurd to imagine that Ovid had used astrology to predict the coming of Jesus. Yet the author shaped the text as he did not out of naïveté but precisely because he wished to show that his beloved ancient poet had, in fact, believed in Christian doctrine. Many medieval commentators on Ovid took exactly this view, using hermeneutics, instead of original composition, as their tool of choice. Forgery was the tribute that learning paid to the difficulty of making the written record correspond to scholars' profound beliefs about the past. Many legends about travelers with rare manuscripts and distant libraries with sought-after treasures took shape in this period and would bedevil bibliographers and inspire forgers for centuries to come.

The Renaissance marched, as we know, under the banner of criticism. From the 14th century to the 17th, Humanists became increasingly self-conscious and articulate about the need to sort out the Latin and Greek traditions, distinguishing fakes from genuine works. In the 300 years that stretched between Petrarch, with his rejection of the *De vetula* and other fakes, and Richard Bentley, who demoted the monotheistic verses ascribed to Greek thinkers and the elegant letters ascribed to the tyrant Phalaris, scholars produced several demonstrations that particular works were forged. In the mid-15th century Lorenzo Valla reduced the Donation of Constantine to rubble by revealing its stylistic and substantive inconsistencies with genuine texts from the 3rd and 4th centuries; Erasmus denounced the Latin correspondence between Seneca and Saint Paul, another product of piety seeking salvation for the mighty dead; and Isaac Casaubon proved, phrase by phrase, that as Porphyry had suggested, the dialogues ascribed to Hermes Trismegistus had not been translated from Egyptian but composed in Greek, and late Greek at that.

Some of the arguments that underpinned these acts of higher criticism were novel—not surprising in an age that saw Humanists reconstruct Latin and Greek grammar, syntax, metrics, and prosody from firsthand study, philologists collect the fragments of lost works, and antiquaries juxtapose the material texts of coins and inscriptions to literary works. Valla reconstructed the history of the Latin language in the 15th century, Casaubon and Bentley that of Greek in the 17th, with such precision as to make clear that the texts they attacked simply could not have been written when they were claimed to have been. Yet other arguments were highly traditional, and some derived from the very scholarly traditions that had made the forgeries possible. In ancient times boys learned when studying rhetoric to put themselves in the place of others and to speak, or write, as those others would have: these innocent practices were responsible for the production of most spurious ancient texts. Valla drew on his mastery of this tradition when he imagined, in detail, what the Roman Senate, the family of Constantine, and the pope himself would have said had the emperor genuinely tried to give away his empire. In a sense, Valla composed forgeries of his own to trump the older, less satisfactory forgery that he denounced.

The period that saw the new tools of Humanism forged and honed also experienced a new flowering of fakes—some of them the work of the very scholars most qualified to detect the fakes of others. Erasmus evidently composed a work on martyrdom, a subject that mattered deeply to him, and ascribed it to Saint Cyprian, under whose name the treatise passed for a couple of centuries. Carlo Sigonio, master antiquary, definitely forged a text of the lost *Consolatio* of Cicero, which he defended fiercely against readers who rightly doubted its authenticity. Sigonio's work immediately provoked withering and accurate criticism, partly since it rested too obviously on the work that he and others had done in collecting the genuine fragments of the work. In this case, at least, the same new scholarship that enabled Sigonio to try his hand at fakery also made it impossible for him to succeed. Perhaps the most ingenious effort of this kind, however, was that of the anonymous forger who drew up a commentary in the style of Galen on the Hippocratic medical treatise *On Humors*. He inserted into this work a discussion, in Galen's own best style, of the prevalence of forged texts. No scholar showed a sharper consciousness of the ways in which ancient views on spurious and genuine texts still mattered in the Renaissance—though the artists and antiquaries who used their newly direct knowledge of genuine ancient statues and inscriptions to produce multiple fakes in both domains would have viewed the forger with the sympathy of skillful colleagues.

If some Humanists used their skills to create convincing fakes, others took a hypercritical attitude toward the transmitted texts. In these cases the new methods and forms of evidence that they brought to bear on supposed fakes provided no hedge against error and excess. When the *Cena Trimalchionis* was first printed in 1664, a number of scholars found it impossible to believe that an author regarded as the arbiter of what was elegant had included so many solecisms in his work. Close scrutiny revealed to some that it was actually the work of an Italian, its text full of idioms clearly derived from the modern language, and to others that it was actually the work of a Frenchman. The Jesuit Jean Hardouin, who did important work on the text of Pliny's *Natural History,* was also an expert antiquary. Like his colleagues, he preferred material evidence to that of texts, and he laid special weight on coins, since he saw them as contemporary witnesses to the events they recorded, hard to forge and easy to interpret. From this simple acorn of principle grew a vast oak of delusion. Over time, scrutiny of the numismatic evidence revealed to Hardouin that virtually the entire corpus of Greek and Latin literature was shot through with errors and contradictions—clear clues that the texts had mostly been composed not in the ancient world but in the 13th century.

Some Humanists set out to establish criteria for authenticating and evaluating texts. In the 1560s both François Baudouin and Jean Bodin wrote introductions to the study of history, and each of them discussed at length the problem of forged histories. Bodin even formulated precise rules for higher criticism. He argued that the critical modern reader should rely whenever possible on histories written by priests in their public capacity, rather than by individuals, such as the history of ancient Assyria and Babylon written by Berossus, and that of Egypt by Manetho. His rules, in turn, were often discussed and widely adopted. In fact, however, Bodin did not create them. The Dominican Giovanni Nanni, or Annius, of Viterbo had devised them, drawing his inspiration from the ancient polemical work of Josephus against Apion. He stated them in his massive commentary on the works of 24 ancient authors—most of them, including Berossus and Manetho, his own inventions—that he published in 1498, in order to convince readers that Berossus and Manetho, like the Bible, offered a more credible account of the past than mendacious Greek writers like Herodotus and Thucydides. An ingenious antiquary, Annius also forged and reconfigured stones and inscriptions to support his vision of ancient history in which Noah, otherwise known as Janus, landed his ark on the Gianicolo (Janiculum) in Rome. Some readers immediately saw that Annius was a forger. But many more, from Jewish commentators on the Bible to Protestant world historians and Bodin, did not. For the next century and more, most efforts to define which histories were genuine and credible rested on Annius's dangerous ideas.

Yet even Annius's forgeries had their slender core of factual content. He actually scored some successes in reading Etruscan script and identifying Etruscan words—just as his 17th-century successor Curzio Inghirami would combine real knowledge with exuberant fantasy and local polemic to devise the forged Etruscan texts and objects that he claimed to discover in 1634, only to run into a storm of criticism, not quite all of which was justified. When critics, such as Joseph Scaliger and Leone Allacci, tore down these forgers' webs, they demolished the true elements along with the false ones.

From the later 17th century on, a consensus gradually grew up about the signs, physical and textual, that marked a document as genuine or fake. Jean Mabillon and Bernard de Montfaucon transformed the study of manuscripts by treating the authentication of documents as a material process, akin to the barometric experiments carried out by 17th-century scientists. They printed elaborate facsimiles of different genuine scripts, giving scholars criteria for establishing the age and identity of writing forms. Jean Leclerc and others drew up fuller and more effective rules than their predecessors had for practitioners of high criticism. Later still, the discovery of actual papyri in Egypt vastly enriched scholars' understanding of the history of texts in antiquity, and it has since proved possible to authenticate the bulk of the new texts that have come to light in the past two centuries.

Yet for all the confidence with which scholars sometimes cite the results of modern stylistic and scientific tests, controversy—and forgery—persist. Each new set of real discoveries seems to inspire a companion set of more dubious ones. The Latin linguistics and Roman archaeology of the 19th century enabled gifted forgers to create the Praeneste fibula—a golden brooch bearing an archaic Latin inscription, supposedly from the 7th century BCE, that bore out once-influential theories about the development of the language. And the discovery of stores of genuine papyri at Oxyrhynchus and elsewhere made it possible for Simonides and other forgers to add a new kind of business alongside their efforts at faking parchment codices.

From the 18th century to the present, moreover, scholars and others have continued to argue that generally accepted ancient texts—from orations of Cicero to the *Histories* of Tacitus—are actually forged. In contemporary Russia, the followers of the mathematician and chronologer Anatoly Fomenko have revived and extended Hardouin's arguments in the hope of proving that the true center of political and cultural history lay not in the ancient Near East and Mediterranean but in the Eurasia of the second millennium CE. Their books sell by the thousands, and their ideas dominate much public discourse about the past. Meanwhile, Luciano Canfora and other notable scholars in Italy have argued, at length, that the illustrated Artemidorus papyrus is in fact a forgery, another work of the deft Simonides. The millennial contest between textual cops and robbers has continued into the age of modern *Wissenschaft* and the more recent one of modern chemistry. Only an optimist would believe that it is likely to reach an end in the near future.

BIBL.: Christian Gastgeber, ed., *Kopie und Fälschung* (Graz 2001). Anthony Grafton, *Forgers and Critics: Creativity and Duplicity in Western Scholarship* (Princeton 1990). Ingrid Rowland, *The Scarith of Scornello: A Tale of Renaissance Forgery* (Chicago 2004). Wolfgang Speyer, *Die literarische Fälschung im Altertum* (Munich 1971). Walter Stephens, *Giants in Those Days: Folklore, Ancient History, and Nationalism* (Lincoln, Nebr., 1989).

A.G.

Forma Urbis Romae

Colossal marble plan of Rome made under Septimius Severus between 203 and 211 CE. It measured 60 by 43 feet and was incised on 150 slabs clamped to the wall of a large hall in the Templum Pacis (Temple of Peace). Drawn to a scale of 1:240, it seems to have been a copy of the papyrus cadastral plans kept in the same hall. The latest building shown is the Septizodium of 203.

The plan suffered as the Templum Pacis fell into decay. Slabs were pried off by lime burners or fell into the rising swamp at its foot, until all memory was lost. There was thus great excitement in antiquarian circles in 1562 when an excavator working on Farnese property near the Basilica of Santi Cosma e Damiano came across a stone map "in a hundred thousand pieces." Four cartloads of fragments were transported to Palazzo Farnese, where Fulvio Orsini commissioned drawings from Giovanni Antonio Dosio (now in the Vatican, Vat. lat. 3439). Étienne Dupérac claimed to have studied the fragments when drafting his large plan of ancient Rome in 1574. But after Orsini's death in 1600 the fragments entered a cycle of prolonged neglect, followed by brief revival, then renewed neglect. Some were stored in the palace, and others were broken up and used in the construction of walls in the Farnese secret garden between Via Giulia and the Tiber.

The fragments in the palace were rediscovered in the 1660s by the architect Andrea Bufalini and the antiquarian Giovan Pietro Bellori, who published them as *Frag-*

menta vestigii veteris Romae ex lapidibus Farnesianis (1673). The fragments then slept for another half century until 1727, when Duke Francesco Farnese asked Francesco Bianchini, then excavating the Farnese gardens on the Palatine Hill, to reassemble them. Finally, in 1741–1742, the king of Spain, successor of the Farnese, donated them to the Roman people. The extant fragments were installed in 20 frames on the staircase of the Capitoline Museum, accompanied by a bronze scale affixed by the cartographer Giambattista Nolli. Authentic fragments were confusingly supplemented with copies of some of the lost fragments, made after the Bellori prints.

Giovanni Battista Piranesi (1720–1778) revived the idea first proposed by Bellori and Bufalini of publishing a map of ancient Rome based on the fragments. To this task he applied an extensive knowledge of ancient texts and of the surviving remains, but he also had a tool unavailable to previous topographers, Giambattista Nolli's extremely accurate map of the modern city, prepared 1736–1744 and published in 1748. In a print in his *Antichità romane* (vol. 1, 1756) Piranesi shows a version of the Nolli map with fragments of the Marble Plan crowded around its edges. Piranesi's famous *Ichnographia* of 1762, the fruit of this research, is an imaginative reconstruction of the ancient Campus Martius etched on six large sheets. A strange mixture of archaeological knowledge and baroque fancy, it is made to look as though the map were carved on a huge fragment clamped to a wall, thus giving it an air of marble authenticity.

Piranesi situated many fragments of the Marble Plan on his *Ichnographia*. These decisions were dictated sometimes by his knowledge of excavations and at other times by his extensive reading of Roman history. Except for his reconstruction of the Bustum Caesaris, the funeral pyre of the emperors, as a grand monument on the Pincian Hill, many of his identifications of the larger fragments held firm for more than a century and found their way into the reconstructions of ancient Rome by Luigi Canina (1825–1850), H. Jordan (1866–1873), and the great topographer Rodolfo Lanciani. Lanciani's monumental folio publication of 1893–1901, *Forma urbis Romae,* integrates the modern and ancient city plan and records countless archeological finds, but still retains some of Piranesi's identifications of the fragments.

A revolution in our understanding of ancient Rome was brought about by Guglielmo Gatti, shuffling fragments of the Marble Plan over a long career. In 1935 the young Gatti moved a fragment with the partial inscription [. . .]LIA from the Campus Martius to the Tiber bank in the distant harbor area; what Piranesi had read as *saepta iu*LIA (referring to a voting precinct) Gatti now read as *porticus aemi*LIA, the name of the large concrete portico of the late Republic that still partly exists in the Testaccio area. And in 1960, just days after the publication of the "definitive" edition of the fragments by a team of topographers including himself, Gatti moved two fragments and with them changed the location of two major monuments, the Circus Flaminius and the Crypta Balbi. Gatti placed the latter along the Via delle Botteghe Oscure; excavations carried out here in 1981–1990 proved its existence and led to the construction of the Museo Nazionale Romano Crypta Balbi, one of Rome's most appealing new museums.

The number of fragments has continued to grow. Four were found in the area of the Forum between 1813 and 1884. In 1888, when the secret garden of the Farnese was removed to make way for the Tiber embankment, 186 fragments came to light; an additional 451 were found here in 1899 and 14 more in 1902. Lanciani remounted the larger fragments on a wall in the garden of Palazzo dei Conservatori in 1903. But they began to suffer from exposure and were moved to the Antiquarium on the Caelian Hill in 1924, then back to the Capitoline in 1939, then to Museo di Roma in Palazzo Braschi in 1955, and finally in 1998 to the Museo della Civiltà Romana in the EUR district. At the time of the 1960 publication 712 fragments were known; today the total is 1,186, although these represent only 10 to 15 percent of the original plan.

The idea that ancient Rome could be reconstructed, first proposed by Raphael but given an inestimable boost by the ongoing study of the Marble Plan, also gave impetus to two large models, the famous *plastico* of ancient Rome at the time of Constantine in the Museo della Civiltà Romana, created by Italo Gismondi beginning in 1935, and the less well-known model by Paul Bigot in the Musées Royaux d'Art et d'Histoire in Brussels, done in 1911 and updated in 1937.

BIBL.: Gianfilippo Carettoni, Antonio M. Colini, Lucos Cozza, and Guglielmo Gatti, *La pianta marmorea di Roma antica (Forma urbis Romae),* 2 vols. (Rome 1960). John Pinto, "*Forma Urbis Romae:* Fragment and Fantasy," in *Architectural Studies in Memory of Richard Krautheimer,* ed. Cecil Striker (Mainz 1996) 143–146. Emilio Rodriguez-Almeida, *Forma urbis marmorea: Aggiornamento generale 1980,* 2 vols. (Rome 1981). Stanford Digital Forma Urbis Romae Project, *http://formaurbis.stanford.edu/.*

J.C.

Fortune

Fortuna was originally an archaic goddess of the Roman countryside, a bearer of abundance, a nurturing figure, and a provider of oracles. Once assimilated to the Hellenistic goddess Tyche, an abstract power that was both a protector and ruler over all things, she became the goddess of chance and was qualified as capricious and blind. The end of the Republic announced a personal Fortune ("Fortuna Caesaris"), who represented Caesar's divinity. During the imperial period, representations of Fortune were myriad, and her most frequent attributes were the cornucopia, the rudder on the globe, and the wheel.

The Christianization of the Roman Empire did not immediately bring pagan cults to an end. To eradicate Fortune, the Church Fathers (Lactantius, Augustine) denounced Fortune's diabolical character. They even sought to banish the very mention of "fortune" (a common word that meant chance, success, condition). The crucial linguistic fact is that the word worked its way into all the Romance languages. In France, for instance, by the end of the millennium, it meant a "find" or "a treasure discovered by chance."

Boethius's platonic and stoic *Consolation of Philosophy* was essential to the transmission of Fortune. In this work, Philosophy explains that the goods derived from Fortune (power, riches, glory) are to be shunned since they are external to man and transitory, and that the sole true good is the love of God. Fortune is also represented as having two sides, good and bad. She is also fearsome, for she takes pleasure in lowering what was elevated and in elevating what was low. She nevertheless reveals herself as helpless before the sage, and she gradually vanishes throughout the text.

From readings of *The Consolation of Philosophy* came the medieval Wheel of Fortune during the 11th century, depicting four characters: the first rises, the second sits enthroned, the third falls, and the fourth lies on the ground, fallen. This illustrates the four moments of a micro-narrative that aims to show the transitory, ephemeral, and almost illusory character of power. Sculpted on the facades of cathedrals, this image first appears during the Gregorian Reform, when the papacy sought to impose its autonomy vis-à-vis secular authorities. Though the image was scholarly at the outset, as it was disseminated throughout society its meaning changed. In some instances it became the wheel of life, illustrating the elementary cycle of biological processes, in others it was perverted as the figure of a world turned upside down, mocking the powers that be.

Following her wheel, Fortune became one of the stars of medieval iconography, along with Death and the Devil. In the 12th century her crown was her majesty and her sword was her justice. Thereafter, she was often represented blindfolded and in the striped robe of inconstancy. Whereas during the 12th century she was the denouncer of the vanity of worldly things, by the Renaissance Fortune had become denunciation incarnate: a courtesan.

During the same period the allegorical novel (*Roman de la Rose,* Dante) seized on Fortune to create a literary topos that remained an obsession until the end of the Middle Ages (Christine de Pizan). Reflection on the sorrows of the times also brought about an analysis of Fortune's nature and her power. This yielded Machiavelli's radical pragmatism, which sought to circumscribe the sphere of human action precisely, while going beyond the generalities of the stoic tradition (Petrarch), in which Virtue opposes Fortune (in the iconography, the cube is opposed to the sphere).

Fortune's popularity notwithstanding, theologians (Thomas Aquinas, Luther) wished to hear nothing of her since she recalled, at worst, the pagan divinity and, at best, a pretense masking the true, efficient cause that had to exist and had to be identified at the center of a divinely ordered universe.

As opposed to the theological repudiation of her existence, Fortune was perfectly integrated into medieval imagination: *fortune* was then a word, a figure, and even a power, the usage of which was of a practical nature since it could designate what is not usual, and which resists understanding without invoking divine intervention, whether in the form of punishment or of a miracle.

In 15th-century Italy a strictly positive image of Fortune arose as the distant heir of the male Greek figure Kairos ("propitious instant") that, in Rome, was transformed into the female figure Occasio ("seize the occasion"); the proverbial Latin expression belongs to the *Disticha Catonis,* the vernacular translation of which, in the 12th century, substituted fortune for *occasion,* the ancient meaning of which has been lost. In Chrétien de Troyes' *Perceval* (ca. 1190) it is Fortune who is seized by the hair and whose nape is bare.

The iconography of this new Fortune is complex. She is most often represented as a nude female figure, standing on a globe, deploying a flowing veil, her hair floating in the wind. As a capricious force, the sea is Fortune's natural place, where she can instantaneously unleash uncontrollable powers that menace the frail raft of human life. During the Middle Ages this storm on the sea was called *fortune.* Its herald is the dolphin, which was represented occasionally beneath the feet of Fortune.

The new image of Fortune was everywhere triumphant: in painted frescoes in the palace of a Florentine prince, where she represented "Fortuna Caesaris"; as a propitiatory figure sculpted above the rooftop of a Prague maritime insurance company; or as a weathervane suspended between sky and sea greeting incoming ships and guiding those departing from the Venetian lagoon. In each case, the image's function was personal and served to identify its owner: it represented an individual or a group, whereas Fortune spinning her wheel was impersonal and rhetorical. By then the image's function had changed, as had its form.

In the sphere of human activities, divination and games always have been linked to Fortune. Divination is strictly deterministic and, here, Fortune was another name for Destiny. As for games, the lotteries from which today's wheels of Fortune are derived arose during the 16th century. Public notices for these lotteries show a blindfolded Fortune along with her wheel and cornucopia. Like the medieval Fortune, she is blind. As she was during the Renaissance, however, she is also positive. Gamblers still believe in the power of Luck. Present-day thought has discovered the power inherent in randomness, which coincides with what exceeds computation, and thus rediscovers the "part of unintelligibility," as defined by Aristotle. Across the centuries, Fortune continues to smile.

BIBL.: Y. Foehr-Janssens and E. Métry, eds., *La Fortune* (Geneva 2003). H. R. Patch, *The Goddess Fortune in Medieval Literature* (Cambridge, Mass., 1927). L. Thomson, ed., *Fortune* (Washington, D.C., 2000).

O.V.C.

Forum

Not so much one type of building as clusters of buildings, early Roman fora had commercial, administrative, and political functions, like the Greek agora, but were also religiously defined spaces used for funerals and gladiatorial games. In the Forum Romanum the Via Sacra (Sacred Way) was aligned with the Alban Hills. The shape of the Forum Romanum was regularized in the 2nd century BCE with the introduction of basilicas along the sides, but then radically reformed by Julius Caesar and Augustus in the next century. Provincial fora were also regularized, and military planners often placed them at the crossing of streets. They were mostly rectangular, though curved examples can be seen at Jerash and Antinoöpolis. They were paved and commonly featured an inscription in applied gilded lettering. They tended to be focused on a principal edifice and bordered by administrative, religious, and commercial buildings.

The imperial fora of Caesar, Augustus, and Domitian (named for Nerva) in Rome, all organized around a dominant temple, were formal in design and judicial and ceremonial in function. Trajan's Forum varied this formula to include a transverse basilica, a commemorative column, and libraries; the inclusion of a temple is now doubted. The Forum Romanum similarly developed into a ceremonial and memorial space dominated by imperial monuments. It was emulated in late antiquity. In Constantinople several fora were linked in a sequence by continuous colonnades.

Although the Forum Romanum and many others effectively disappeared in the Middle Ages, some were preserved as public spaces, for example in Pisa (Piazza dei Cavalieri), Assisi, Spoleto, and Orvieto. By the 12th century some civic squares had comparable functions, notably Siena's Campo, but usually administrative and religious functions were clearly separated. Rival squares represented Church and state, and aristocrats also appropriated public space.

In the Renaissance the ancient forum was not widely imitated, in part because of misinterpretations of Vitruvius' "Greek" and "Latin" fora (*De architectura* 5.1.1–2) as a single building, the Palazzo della Ragione (completed 1219) in Padua. In the New World columnar monuments marked the central squares of Santa Fe and Mendoza (1563). In Rome ancient obelisks were reerected in four public spaces by Sixtus V (pope 1585–1590), particularly in the piazza of St. Peter's, which later was augmented with curved wings by Bernini (1656–1667). But these squares were more *theatra mundi* than fora in the classical sense. In the Plaza Mayor at Madrid, designed by Juan Gómes de Mora (1617–1619), administrative functions were less conspicuous than arrangements for spectacle, particularly bull-fighting.

The Roman style of forum was revived in Palladian form in Livorno, where the Piazza Grande (1600) is framed by arcades with a church as the focus, and in London, in the Covent Garden of Inigo Jones (17th cent.). Nicholas Hawksmoor's schemes for Oxford included a Forum Universitatis (ca. 1712) between the schools and the University Church of St. Mary's, and a Forum Civitatis at Carfax. The Forum Populi in Ripon emulated the Roman original with its obelisks.

The grandiose public squares of the absolutist monarchs evoked Roman fora. Examples are the Place Royale of Henri IV in Paris (now Place des Vosges) and the Place Louis le Grand (now Place Vendôme), with an equestrian statue and uniform facades (1690) by Jules Hardouin-Mansart. At Nancy the Place Royale (now Stanislas), focused on the town hall, with a statue of Louis XV; the Foro Carolino (1760) in Naples, commemorating Charles III Bourbon, was imposed by Vanvitelli on the disorder of the Largo del Mercatello. At Milan a circular Forum Bonaparte, 1,860 feet in diameter, was formed around Castello Sforzesco as an administrative center and commemorative plaza; its Neoclassical buildings included a "pantheon," baths, and theater. The culmination of this new wave of "imperial fora" was Gottfried Semper's Kaiserforum (1886), a development of the Habsburg Residenz on the Hofburg in Vienna. It sought to reproduce Trajan's Forum, excavated by Angelo Uggeri in 1833. To commemorate victory over Napoleon III, it integrated the Burgtor into a huge space with curved apses and a central equestrian statue.

The renewal of the forum idea by modern totalitarian regimes as a theater for mass performance and demonstration—Red Square in Moscow, Hitler's Congress Hall rally grounds in Nuremberg, and Mussolini's Foro Italico in Rome—has not discredited the form entirely. A more compact, postmodern version is the Piazza d'Italia in New Orleans (1978) designed by Charles Moore. The project for the 1992 Olympics at Barcelona, Spain, included a large "forum" and underwater aquarium.

BIBL.: F. A. Bauer, "Einige weniger bekannte Platzanlagen im spätantiken Rom," in *Pratum Romanum: Gedenkschrift Richard Krautheimer,* ed. M. Gill et al. (Wiesbaden 1997) 27–54. Richard Hewlings, "Ripon's Forum Populi," *Architectural History* 24 (1981) 39–52. Spiro Kostof, *The City Assembled: The Elements of Urban Form through History* (London 1992). Luisa Quartermaine, "Slouching towards Rome: Mussolini's Imperial Vision," in *Urban Society in Ancient Italy,* ed. Tim J. Cornell and Kathryn Lomas (London 1993), 203–216. J. B. Ward-Perkins, "From Republic to Empire: Reflections on the Early Provincial Architecture of the Roman West," *Journal of Roman Studies* 60 (1970) 1–19.

E.T.

Founding Fathers, American

The American Revolution was a Whig revolution, which made it also a neo-Roman revolution from the start. Americans petitioned, remonstrated, and eventually fought to preserve neo-Roman conceptions of mixed government, liberty, and the rule of law that had dominated British political discourse since the Glorious Revolution of 1688. When the patriot Josiah Quincy prepared his will in 1774, he left to his son, "when he shall arrive at the age of fifteen years," his copies of Algernon Sidney's works, John Locke's works, Gordon's *Tacitus,* and *Cato's Letters:* "May the Spirit of Liberty rest upon him!" These authors were all English partisans of liberty, but liberty with a Roman face, as their subject matter (Sidney), translations (Gordon), and pseudonyms (Cato) illustrate. But as the British king and his Parliament became more intrusive, Americans became less English and more Roman in the models they chose, until finally, by 1800, an American Senate sat on an American Capitol Hill, by the banks of an "American Tiber," making laws for an American republic. The Roman example gave Americans heroes the vocabulary, architecture, and constitution for their revolutionary experiment in government without a king.

John Adams, the most active political scientist and constitutional theorist of the American Revolution, set out in his *Defence of the Constitutions of Government of the United States of America* (1787–1788) the "reading and reasoning which produced the American constitutions." Adams identified three periods in English history that generated "useful" reflections on political science, beginning with the Reformation (especially the work of John Ponet), continuing with the Interregnum (particularly James Harrington and John Milton), and culminating with the Glorious Revolution in 1688 and the writers who developed and promoted Britain's balanced constitution, including Algernon Sidney, John Locke, Benjamin Hoadly, Marchamont Nedham, John Trenchard, and Thomas Gordon (the English "Cato"). But above all Adams recommended the Roman classics, beginning in his preface with Cornelius Tacitus and Marcus Tullius Cicero, whom he quoted at length and in detail on the "checks and balances of republican government." Adams translated the relevant passages of book 4 of Polybius' *Histories,* describing the perfection of the Roman Republic and incorporated them into his *Defence.* Advising Americans to cherish their British Whig predecessors as the "most precious relics of antiquity," Adams concluded that "as all the ages of the world have not produced a greater statesman and philosopher united than Cicero, his authority should have great weight."

Adams and the American revolutionaries saw themselves with Cicero and the Whigs as part of a 2,000-year-old tradition of liberty, pursuing (as Adams put it, following Aristotle and Livy) the "government of laws and not of men" against tyranny and corruption. They perceived the mixed and balanced "constitution of liberty" endorsed by Polybius and Cicero (and embraced by William III) as the central *palladium* of their freedoms, much improved by the use of elections and political representation to avoid direct democracy. Thus, Americans made a sharp distinction between the "turbulent" and imperfectly balanced democracies of Greece and the stable republics of America and Rome. Americans drew the vast majority of their classical models, as reflected in the pseudonyms they used in their newspaper debates, from the history of Rome's Republic, followed distantly by Greek lawgivers and resisters against tyranny, and more recent Whig heroes, such as "Sidney," "Hampden," "Harrington," and "John Wilkes."

In these debates Americans liked to refer to themselves as "Publius," "Publicola," "Junius," "Brutus," "Cato," "Cincinnatus," "Tullius," "Cicero," and the like because they saw their difficulties as being essentially the same as those that had threatened the justice and stability of Rome: how to protect law, liberty, and the balanced constitution against the twin incursions of monarchy (leading to tyranny) on the one hand, and democracy (leading to anarchy) on the other. The most energetic artist of the American Revolution, Charles Willson Peale, began his career in 1768 with a portrait of William Pitt, the earl of Chatham and a leading British advocate of American rights. Peale's portrait of Chatham illustrates the close association in American minds between British, Roman, and American liberty on the eve of the Revolution. Commissioned to commemorate Pitt's opposition to the Stamp Act, Peale's portrait shows him dressed as a Roman ("in a Consular Habit") speaking "in Defense of the claims of the AMERICAN colonies, on the Principles of the BRITISH Constitution" (broadside, *Allegory of William Pitt,* London, 1768). With the Magna Carta in his left hand, Pitt points his right toward the goddess of liberty, carrying the *pileus* (Phrygian cap) and *vindicta* (staff) of Roman *Libertas.* A flaming altar of liberty in the foreground carries busts of Algernon Sidney and John Hampden, martyrs for British liberty, while behind them stands Whitehall, where Parliament beheaded King Charles I for violating the liberty of his subjects.

American resistance to British corruption of their common constitutional heritage had as long and continuous a history as that of the colonies themselves, but the Stamp Act of 22 March 1765 initiated a new intensity of activity, which culminated in the war for independence. James Otis, the first great orator of the American Revolution, had already established two important prerevolutionary classical ideals in his *Rights of the British Colonies Asserted and Proved* (1764), which drew attention to Greek colonial policy and to Roman natural-law doctrine. Greeks were remembered for recognizing the full equality and independence of their colonies, Romans for the idea that "true law is right reason in accordance with nature" (Lactantius, *Divine Institutes* 6.8.6–9, quoting Cicero), and for the checks and balances that secure right reason in practice. Greek policy showed Americans how Britain ought to respect its colonies, Roman doctrine taught the limits of governmental power. Otis argued that Britain's balanced constitution gave Britons the world's best opportunity for honest prominence since the days of Julius Caesar, "destroyer of the Roman glory and grandeur," but that, like Caesar, British politicians were subverting their state by upsetting this balance.

The deepening conflicts that led to the American Revolution began when the British Parliament turned to America for revenue to offset its burgeoning national debt. Americans viewed the revenue and enforcement measures of the Sugar Act (1764), the Stamp Act (1765), the Declaratory Act (1766), and the Townshend Acts (1767) through the eyes of committed British Whigs, alert to the avarice and corruption of self-serving government ministers. Long before the final conflict, John Dickinson, the future "Pennsylvania Farmer," considered Hanoverian

London to be no better than Sallust's Rome: "Easy to be bought, if there were but a purchaser" (quoting Sallust, *Bellum Iugurthinum* 35.12–13). John Adams repeated the reference in his *Novanglus* essays (1774), as did numerous American visitors to Britain throughout the colonial period, who reported that "the people of England were depraved, the parliament venal, and the ministry corrupt," just as the Roman Republic had been when Jugurtha pronounced it "a venal city, ripe for corruption." The English "Cato" had long since made the same observation (Letter 18). British and American Whigs hoped to defend Britain's "mixed" constitution against the "luxury" and "corruption" of modern English life.

John Dickinson's *Letters from a Farmer in Pennsylvania* (1768) reminded Americans how this "decay of virtue" might lead to the loss of their liberty. Just as all England once united to defend John Hampden against improper requisitions, so Dickinson urged Americans to unite against the Townshend Acts. Recalling how "the Caesars had ruined Roman liberty" through subtle innovation, he wrote that "a FREE people . . . can never be too quick in observing, nor too firm in opposing, the beginnings of *alteration,* either in form or reality, respecting institutions formed for their security." The argument was conservative. No Parliament in 150 years had attempted to bypass the colonial assemblies to impose such taxes. Dickinson concluded his series as he had each of his letters by quoting and translating a Latin authority: "*Certe ego libertatem, quae mihi a parente meo tradita est, experiar: Verum id frustra an ob rem faciam, in vestra manu situm est, quirites":* "For my part I am resolved to contend for the liberty delivered down to me by my ancestors; but whether I shall do it effectually or not, depends on you, my countrymen" (quoting Sallust, *Bellum Iugurthinum* 31.5).

American confidence in Britain's mixed constitution made Dickinson willing, at first, to bypass Parliament to appeal to the king, as a check against his ministers' "avarice" and "ambition." Such complaints contributed to the repeal of the Stamp Act (18 March 1766), and patriots such as Dickinson ostentatiously eschewed the populism and violence of a Cleon or a Clodius. But British intransigence discredited this moderate approach. Soldiers sent to America to support the customs commissioners killed five Bostonians in the Boston Massacre of 5 March 1770. When Britain imposed further taxes on tea in 1773 and Americans resisted, the king and Parliament resorted in 1774 to the stronger Coercive Acts (also known as the Intolerable Acts) to strengthen their military occupation. Americans responded by convening a Constitutional Congress in Philadelphia, which declared that "the foundation of English liberty, and of all free government, is a right in the people to participate in their legislative council." Americans had repudiated their dependence on Parliament, and with it the necessity of respecting English precedents. They could turn from the quasi-Roman mixture of the British constitution to the unadulterated checks and balances of Cicero's republican Rome.

The British "Cato" had praised Britain's constitution as "the best Republick in the world, with a Prince at the Head of it" (Letter 37). Now Americans had the opportunity to create a true republic, without a king to corrupt them. The British attack on Lexington and Concord on 19 April 1775 confirmed the Americans' view of George III as a new Caesar, and themselves as beleaguered Catos, fighting to preserve liberty. John Hancock's widely circulated oration of March 1774 commemorating the Boston Massacre had compared the mercenary British garrison with Caesar's avaricious army, which "humbled mighty Rome" and "forced the mistress of the world to own a master in a traitor." Joseph Warren's massacre oration of 1775 (which he delivered wearing a toga) directed Americans to emulate the Roman people and "never to despair of the commonwealth," but to press forward, if need be through "fields of blood," until "tyranny is trodden under foot, and you have affixed your adored goddess Liberty . . . on the American throne." Warren's earlier massacre oration of 1772 had praised the free constitution of ancient Rome, "which guarded her liberties" and whose loss "plunged her . . . [into] infamy and slavery." Now Warren had to fight "for the salvation of [his] invaded country." By June he was dead, killed with many others at Bunker Hill while defending the "free constitution" of his native Massachusetts.

With the turn to arms, the Americans became true founding fathers for the first time, as they built new institutions to support their independent governments. Thomas Paine's pamphlet *Common Sense* heralded the change in February 1776, when he disparaged government by "king, lords and commons" as a "rotten constitution," and monarchy itself as unjust. England was no republic, Paine insisted (contradicting the British "Cato"), because "monarchy hath poisoned the republic" and "the crown hath engrossed the commons." Though in absolute governments "the king is law," in free countries, he wrote, "the law *ought* to be king." The Congress of the United States passed a Resolution for the Formation of Local Governments on May 10, 1776, calling on the colonies to establish new governments in which "every kind of authority under the . . . Crown shall be totally suppressed, and all the powers of government exerted, under the authority of the people." The Roman *imperium populi* was transported to America as the newly independent colonies established their own new republican constitutions, without the authority of the king.

The American Revolution was a dispute about government, and with the Declaration of Independence of 4 July 1776, Americans needed new models of government to replace the British institutions that had failed them. Rome supplied a name ("republic"), a goal ("liberty"), and a technique (checks and balances) in the structure of the Roman constitution that had endured for 500 years between the fall of the kings and the rise of the caesars. John Adams promoted this template for a new American constitution in a letter to Richard Henry Lee, published in 1776 as *Thoughts on Government,* in which Adams insisted that "there is no good government, but what is republican." Adams followed Livy in defining a republic as "an empire of laws, and not of men," arguing that whatever form of government secures just and impartial laws will be the best republic. Adams suggested a bicameral government with a popular assembly, as in Rome, controlled by a second legislative chamber and an elected executive. Lee and the Virginians took Adams's advice and created a new constitution, with a House of Delegates, a senate, an annually elected governor, and independent judges, serving during good behavior. Virginia also passed a bill of rights, declaring that "all power is . . . derived from the people."

Eleven of the newly independent American states would adopt new constitutions between 1776 and 1780, and each constitution was more elaborate and carefully thought out than the last. Among them, those of Virginia (29 June 1776), Maryland (18 November 1776), North Carolina (18 December 1776), New York (20 April 1777), South Carolina (19 March 1778), and Massachusetts (2 March 1780) established a senate, and the other state legislatures were bicameral, with the exception of Pennsylvania (28 September 1776) and Georgia (5 February 1777), which added senates later to bring them into line with the rest. The battle over Pennsylvania's anomalous constitution became particularly important, because it took place in Philadelphia and framed the discussion that would shape the U.S. Constitution soon afterward. Pennsylvania styled itself a commonwealth, recalling the unicameral commonwealth of Britain's Interregnum, and although Pennsylvania had a Council of Censors to oversee the legislative and executive branches, the Pennsylvania Republican Society denounced the unicameral constitution as "repugnant to the principles of liberty," because "all the most celebrated free governments of antiquity" had recognized the folly of resting the "whole legislative authority in a single body, without controul" ("To the Citizens of Pennsylvania," *Pennsylvania Packet,* 23 March 1779).

Some lessons of Rome were troubling, particularly as recorded by Tacitus and Sallust and mediated by recent European authors such as Jean-Jacques Rousseau (*Du contrat social,* 1762) and the baron de Montesquieu (*De l'esprit des lois,* 1758). Montesquieu and Rousseau both suggested that republics need exceptional virtue to survive, that such virtue is extremely hard to maintain, and that maintaining the requisite virtue will be almost impossible in large commercial states like late republican Rome. The history of Rome and of Britain seemed to confirm this diagnosis, both nations having become more corrupt as their empires became too large and too rich to sustain their primitive virtue.

Thomas Jefferson spoke for many Americans when he said that it was "the manners and spirit of a people which preserve a republic in vigour" and that "the mobs of great cities add just so much to the support of pure government, as sores do the strength of the human body" (*Notes on the State of Virginia,* 1784). John Adams and the drafters of the Constitution of Massachusetts felt it necessary to remind citizens that "piety, justice, moderation, temperance, industry, and frugality, are absolutely necessary to preserve the advantages of liberty and to maintain a free government" (Article 18), and that "the preservation of their rights and liberties" depends on "virtue [being] diffused generally among the body of the people" (chap. 5).

George Washington and the armies that fought beside him to protect the new American republics embraced this Roman image of simple rural virtue to sustain their sense of dignity in adversity. When Washington and his few remaining soldiers were confined, freezing and starving, at Valley Forge during the winter of 1777–1778, Washington arranged for the dramatic reenactment of Cato's last stand and death at Utica, fighting to save Rome's doomed Republic. These moving passages from Joseph Addison's play *Cato* also provided Patrick Henry with the best lines in his famous speech to the Virginia House of Burgesses: "Give me liberty or give me death." Washington and his officers modeled themselves on the Roman general Cincinnatus, who left his simple farm to save the Republic, then returned to his plow, despite the ingratitude of the citizens he had rescued. Washington himself ostentatiously resigned his commission and returned to his farm when the war was won, and he encouraged his officers, as the Society of the Cincinnati, to do the same. Their motto, *Omnia reliquit servare rem publicam* ("He gave up everything to serve the republic"), asserted their republican ideals, as did their commemorative medal, designed by the future architect of the District of Columbia, Pierre L'Enfant, which showed an American leaving his family to defend the republic and, on the reverse side, Cincinnatus returning to his plow.

Washington and his fellow soldiers supported the last and greatest achievement of the American Revolution when they helped secure a federal and thoroughly republican Constitution of the United States (1787). The battle for independence had been won despite the weak and inconstant leadership of a diplomatic Congress of thirteen sovereign states. The men who fought in the Continental Army and served the Continental Congress understood the need for efficient federal institutions better than the older local politicians who still dominated the state legislatures. As soldiers remained unpaid, and states failed to meet their financial obligations, the need for a stronger federal government became more apparent. But republican advocates of the new Constitution had to overcome the traditional fear of large states. John Adams insisted that if the federal government were to have more power, it should also have a fully republican structure, with a senate, an elected executive, the rule of law, and a fundamental basis in popular sovereignty, like the republican constitution of Rome.

Alexander Hamilton, James Madison, and John Jay, writing as "Publius" in defense of the Constitution of the United States, recognized the Constitution's greatest deviation from the Roman model, which was "*the total exclusion of the people in their collective capacity*" from any direct role in public life (*Federalist* No. 63). The "genius of republican liberty" required that "all power be derived from the people" (*Federalist* No. 37), but the Constitution was carefully controlled and balanced, to avoid an "*elective despotism*" (*Federalist* No. 48, quoting Jefferson, *Notes on the State of Virginia*). "Publius" and other proponents of the Roman model were careful to distinguish republican checks and balances from the "turbulent democracies" of ancient Greece and modern Italy (*Federalist* No. 14). Republics use "ambition . . . to counteract ambition" (*Federalist* No. 51), making government decisions "more consonant to the public good than if pronounced by the people themselves" (*Federalist* No. 10). The Americans' strong preference for Roman republicanism over Greek democracy made it easier to reject Rousseau's pessimistic conclusion that "a certain celestial virtue, more than human, has been necessary to preserve liberty" (Adams, *Defence*).

When George Washington gave his inaugural speech on April 30, 1789, as the first president of the United States under the new federal Constitution, he asserted that "the destiny of the republican model of government" was "*deeply,* perhaps . . . *finally* staked on the experiment entrusted to the hands of the American people." The most important of the many classical influences on the American founding fathers was the political history of the Roman Republic, because the American Revolution was political and could neither have taken place nor have succeeded as it did without classical learning to guide it. With the Revolution's triumph in the federal Constitution, the new American republic supplanted its ancient models. Subsequent revolutions would look to the United States and to its sister republic in France for political inspiration, just as Americans and their predecessors once imitated Rome.

BIBL.: John W. Eadie, ed., *Classical Traditions in Early America* (Ann Arbor 1976). Richard M. Gummere, *The American Colonial Mind and the Classical Tradition: Essays in Comparative Culture* (Cambridge, Mass., 1963). Paul A. Rahe, *Republics Ancient and Modern: Classical Republicanism and the American Revolution* (Chapel Hill 1992). Meyer Reinhold, *Classica Americana: The Greek and Roman Heritage in the United States* (Detroit 1984). Carl J. Richard, *The Founders and the Classics: Greece, Rome, and the American Enlightenment* (Cambridge, Mass., 1994). M. N. S. Sellers, *American Republicanism: Roman Ideology in the United States Constitution* (Basingstoke, 1994). Susan Ford Wiltshire, ed., *The Usefulness of Classical Learning in the Eighteenth Century* (Washington, D.C., 1977). M.N.S.S.

Fragments

Fragments are surviving parts of lost wholes. The fragments of Graeco-Roman antiquity are of two kinds: verbal (surviving parts of philosophical, literary, historical, epigraphic, and other kinds of texts that are lost as wholes) and material (surviving parts of marble, bronze, stone, ceramic, or other objects which are lost as wholes). In a larger sense, even the complete works that survive from antiquity may be considered fragments, inasmuch as the larger cultural context that produced and enjoyed them has been lost.

Verbal fragments survive because they are cited by later authors who themselves survive partially or completely (indirect transmission), because only some pieces of the material on which they were written (papyrus, parchment, clay, stone) have survived (direct transmission), or out of a combination of both reasons. Material fragments survive because they were, exceptionally, maintained continuously in their original usage, or, more often, because they were reused for some new purpose in later antiquity or in the Middle Ages or they were excavated by tomb robbers, professional archaeologists, or others, or out of a combination of the two. This article focuses on textual fragments (and among these primarily on those transmitted indirectly), but it begins with some observations about the relations between textual fragments and material ones.

In its first and primary sense, the word *fragment* is applied to material objects, not to verbal texts. Texts can be fragments, but only metaphorically. What we call a textual fragment is in fact an incomplete textual citation, incomplete either because it was intended to be complete but its material bearer has been damaged (for example, it is transmitted only on a papyrus fragment) or because it always was intended as an incomplete citation (for example, a quotation or an excerpt in a later author) and by chance there happen to have survived no other more complete citations of it. All of the Greek and Latin words for *fragment* are applied in antiquity only to physical objects, never to portions of written discourse: the Latin term *fragmentum,* and the corresponding Greek words *apospasmata, spasmata, apoklasmata,* and *klasmata*—etymologically, all these terms emphasize the violence that produced the fragment—refer to bits and pieces of material things like food or textiles and are never applied to broken-off bits of written texts otherwise lost. (The few passages cited in the lexica in a textual sense, such as Cicero, *Ad Atticum* 2.1.3, and Cornutus, *Theologia graeca* p. 26.16 Lang, are not in fact genuine exceptions, as they do not have this precise meaning.) The same applies to the earliest attestations for the word for *fragment* in the modern European languages as well. This is a metaphor that seems not to have been invented until relatively modern times (its history would be worth investigating).

And yet its foundation was partly laid in antiquity, by Plato in the *Phaedrus.* For what helps ground this usage is the Platonic notion of the complete, well-made text as being like a body, in particular a living human or animal body, all of the parts of which are subordinated to the organic unity of the whole and receive their meaning from their contribution to its total functionality (*Phaedrus* 264c; cf. Aristotle, *Poetics* 23.1459a20). Plato's concept raises the stakes in the definition of the interrelation between a text and its parts: only if the text as a whole is thought of as a body can its dissociated parts be conceived of not simply as segments or portions but as fragments—in Horace's phrase, speaking of the sublime poetry of Ennius as though he were the mutilated poet Orpheus, *disiecti membra poetae,* "the limbs of the dismembered poet" (*Satires* 1.4.62), where "limbs" means both the parts of the poet's body and the portions of his discourse. Without this premise, small parts of a larger text are not fragments but just quotations or excerpts.

Since antiquity, physical fragments and textual fragments have had different yet variously interrelated histories. At the risk of wildly oversimplifying, it might be tentatively suggested that beginning in the later Roman imperial period and continuing through late antiquity and the early Middle Ages, the prestige attributed to fragments of ancient sculptures and buildings had a rough equivalent with respect to fragments of ancient texts. Spolia, capitals, columns, and statues seem to have been not merely recycled as useful raw materials but (at least in the West) resuscitated as objects of great symbolic value, representative of Rome, the great political and cultural entity to which they once belonged and which they therefore connoted, and they were integrated into new artistic and architectural ensembles above all to enhance their prestige. During that same period there was a remarkable flourishing of excerpts, anthologies, and collections of proverbs, apothegms, philosophical and legal doctrines, and other brief texts, which were not intended as collections of fragments at the time but have served later ages in that function. In both the artistic and the textual domains we can see everywhere the effects of processes that led to fragmentation and the juxtaposition and correlation of these fragments. But with very few exceptions (if anywhere, then perhaps only among some early Christian scholars) we do not find procedures aiming at the systematic collection of fragments or the speculative reconstitution of lost wholes.

In the later Middle Ages and then especially in the Renaissance, the histories of artistic and of textual fragments coincide in a different way. In both cases, we can perceive the evident beginnings of an active search for fragments, though by and large (with the possible exception of such late medieval phenomena as the mendicant orders) the activity directed at fragmentary sculptural and architectural objects began earlier, received more attention, and was considered more prestigious than that directed to fragmentary texts. Both activities are often rather aesthetic and antihistorical in character, inasmuch as artists and scholars pay attention preferentially to finer fragments and do not hesitate to improve, supplement, correct, modify, or even invent fragments to make them seem more beautiful.

It was only in the 18th, but then especially in the 19th and 20th centuries that a taste developed, especially among scholars but even among some segments of the larger public as well, for appreciating both artistic and textual fragments in their purely fragmentary condition. Scholars took great pains to strip away the false accretions contributed by their well-meaning predecessors, in order to return the unadulterated fragment to its pristine state. This time it was the textual scholars who had shown the way, and the experts on fragmentary sculptures and vases had somewhat hesitantly agreed to follow their lead. No doubt they were motivated primarily by skepticism about earlier attempts to restore what was missing; and yet the very condition of fragmentariness could also come to exercise a compelling aesthetic and psychological fascination. As Rilke put it in his celebrated poem "Archaic Torso of Apollo" ("Archaïscher Torso Apollos," *Neue Gedichte,* 1907–1908), the statue is incomplete, damaged on its surface, mutilated in head and genitals—but for this very reason it has an overwhelming effect on the viewer, glittering with countless eyes like a candelabrum or like the pelt of a beast of prey, and expressing a vitality that can make us feel we must change our lives. Precisely by being incomplete it stimulates our imagination to try to complete it, and we end up admiring the creativity that would otherwise have languished within us.

Rilke's sonnet is characteristically modern in its celebration of an archaic primitivism; but the allure of ancient sculptural fragments that it expresses in a particularly memorable and intense way seems already to have been felt by at least some ancient viewers. In the case of textual fragments, on the other hand, matters appear to be very different. Post-classical scholars collect and study the verbal fragments of the ancients, but the ancients themselves seem never to have done so in any serious way. In the case of textual fragments, Jesus' injunction after feeding the multitude, "Gather up the fragments left over, that nothing may be lost" (John 6:12)—words cited regularly by editors of fragment collections from the 16th at least until the late 19th century—has come to ground a widespread scholarly practice that constitutes one of the most striking differences between antiquity and modernity.

For if we understand by the study of textual fragments the systematic search through the works by those authors who survive, in order to gather up as far as possible actual pieces from texts that have not survived and information about them and their authors, with the aim of reconstructing these latter as far as possible, we must acknowledge that there are virtually no traces of such a scholarly practice during antiquity. Of course, throughout antiquity many readers and speakers quoted and reused portions of other people's texts, thereby fragmenting them, and some went to the trouble of gathering together parts or wholes of such texts; but it was not until late antiquity that anything emerged that was even slightly similar to fragment collecting in the modern sense. Even in that period, however, neither the biographers and evangelists who collected oral anecdotes, apothegms, and stories, nor the metricians and grammarians who quoted snippets of verse of lexical or prosodical interest, nor the compilers of legal or philosophical or technical collections, nor the excerptors and anthologizers who prepared extracts and abridgments from one or more lengthy works or compiled florilegia of striking passages from a variety of works, were really collecting fragments in the modern sense—though of course their works have often gone on to function as a rich source of fragments for modern scholars.

And even in antiquity many texts vanished. One of the most important activities of ancient scholars was gathering, editing, and publishing unknown or little-known texts. But with very few exceptions (perhaps especially among early Christian scholars like Eusebius) they did so not by systematically scrutinizing all the texts they had at hand and excerpting from them the fragments of the authors or works that interested them. Instead, they brought to light manuscripts that had not been widely distributed, and if there turned out to be more than one of the same text, they compared them with one another in an attempt to establish a uniform text. In the ancient world the absence of printing, the lack of universally standardized cultural institutions, and the general difficulty of communications meant that not all texts were easily available in all places, that some places had many texts and other places very few, and that the version of a text available in one place might well vary from another elsewhere. The job of ancient scholars was to try to counteract cultural entropy by evening out the regional disparities between one place and another—that is, to make known more widely what had previously been known only locally.

What ancient scholars seem to have lacked, from the present-day point of view, was a sense that their object of study was radically discontinuous with respect to their own world, that the body of ancient texts that interested them was finite and remote. Even the philologists of Hellenistic Alexandria who gathered, edited, and studied the remnants of archaic and classical Greek literature appear to have felt that they were still connected by a viable cultural link to the preceding ages. It was not until the Byzantine period that someone like Photius could deal with the fragmentary texts available to him in a way that, for all its rootedness in ancient modes of thought, seems nonetheless in some ways to anticipate modern forms of scholarship. Perhaps only when a corpus of texts is limited because the culture that produced them has come undeniably to an end is it not merely practicable, but even conceivable, to undertake to gather all the remnants of whatever sort are contained within that corpus. That is why ancient scholars never collected fragments: they not only lacked the word for a textual fragment, they seem to have lacked the very concept. In reality, given the destructibility of manuscripts, the continuity of ancient culture did not in fact guarantee that there were no authors at all whose works had been destroyed in direct transmission but whose fragments could indeed have been collected from the indirect transmission consisting of the surviving manuscripts of other authors who quoted them. Yet it may never have occurred to the ancients to undertake such a collection: they seem for the most part to have believed, erroneously, that for any author they were interested in, they needed only to find the right surviving manuscript of his works—or, if they could not find it, to give up the search altogether. In short, ancient scholars were not collectors of fragments but hunters of manuscripts: they were the forerunners not of Schleiermacher and Diels, but of Petrarch and Poggio.

For a while, even after the end of antiquity, it was not unreasonable to hope that manuscripts of every single ancient author would one day turn up. But matters changed when the manuscript hunters started coming home with less, and less interesting, game. Eventually the law of diminishing returns began to suggest even to the most optimistic that there were not very many more manuscripts still lying around waiting to be discovered. With a shock whose intensity and pathos varied from individual to individual, certain Renaissance scholars began to realize in the meantime that the ancient world had died once and for all and was henceforth separated from their own by an unbridgeable historical caesura. It is this historical shock, the pained recognition that antiquity is dead and that the total stock of ancient manuscripts is therefore finite, that lies at the basis of the modern search for ancient fragments and endows the very term *fragment* with an emotional tone, connoting loss, injury, and deprivation, which is entirely lacking in such partial synonyms as *piece, excerpt,* and *citation.*

It was Petrarch who first extended the usage of the word *fragmentum* to encompass with deep pathos all that was left over from the fall of Rome. (He even used the term in the title of his collection of his vernacular lyrics.) A century later George Gemistus Pletho made a collection of the Chaldaean oracles, and by the end of the 15th century Politian could provide a remarkable anticipation of the methods of modern fragment collections in his work on Callimachus and Eupolis in his *Miscellanea*—and Annius of Viterbo could come up with the brilliant idea of forging those fragments whose genuine versions were no longer likely ever to turn up and thereby unmask his own inventions. Renaissance scholars could look back to such ancient authors as Aulus Gellius, Macrobius, and the Church Fathers (who had been collecting texts without thinking of them as fragments in the modern sense) and misunderstand their collections as having been intended to be exactly what historical chance had turned them into, collections of fragments. The advent of printing gave a further push to this activity, for the rapid and extensive succession of *editiones principes* tended to level the playing field of international scholarship by decreasing somewhat the differences between well-stocked and poorly stocked libraries. By the end of the 16th century almost all the classical works that we read today had been printed, and it was becoming clear that if one did not have a manuscript of Empedocles in Strasburg, no one in Paris or Venice did either: one had little recourse other than to search through the texts that had survived for the traces of the texts that had not.

Since the Renaissance there have been two phases of post-classical scholarship on the textual fragments of classical antiquity: first Humanist and early modern, then Romantic and contemporary. Each of these phases has sought, and sought to establish, fragments of a sort appropriate to the contemporary situation of the collectors' activity within their larger cultural context. Every culture that studies fragments tries to acquire the fragments it wishes it deserved.

The first phase began in the second half of the 16th century, once it had become clear that the sources of new manuscripts containing complete texts of the ancient authors had by and large dried up. It counted among its most prominent exponents such scholars as Antonio Agustin, who studied Varro and Festus; Fulvio Orsini, who worked on both textual and material fragments; and Henri Estienne, who published a corpus of Latin fragments and later edited the first collections of the fragments of Greek lyric poetry and of Greek philosophy. This first, Humanist phase was largely aesthetic in orientation: given on the one hand the unquestioned prestige and perfection of the ancient poets, historians, and philosophers and on the other hand the evident lack of sources for new complete texts of them, some scholar-entrepreneurs focused on bringing before the public the very best fragments of the most celebrated writers who were not transmitted directly, aiming neither for exhaustive coverage, nor for critical inspection, nor for wearisome documentation, but presenting them in as unencumbered and user-friendly a way as possible. Thus, Estienne justified his publication of the Greek philosophical fragments by reference to the beauty of Empedocles' poetry (as attested by Aristotle) and put Empedocles first in his collection "not because he is the oldest of them all, but because he is the most excellent"—and he goes on to add without embarrassment that he has not published all the fragments of Empedocles that he knows of but only those that consist of more than a few words and are free from gross corruption.

In general the Humanists' fragment collections are only rarely up to the level of their other scholarly achievements; Estienne's in particular were hasty, arbitrary, and hugely incomplete. Over the next two centuries there were a number of serious attempts to improve the first wave of Renaissance fragment collections—by Joseph Scaliger, Isaac Casaubon, G. J. Vossius, and others for the ancient historians, especially Polybius, but also for such lesser figures as Berossus, Manetho, and Nicholas of Damascus; by Pierre Gassendi, Thomas Stanley, Ralph Cudworth, J. J. Brucker, and others for the ancient philosophers; and by such very different figures as Pierre Bayle, Richard Bentley, and J. A. Fabricius for a large number of fragmentarily transmitted authors of different genres.

But it was not until the second half of the 18th century that the second phase of scholarship reformulated, on a new and more rigorous conceptual model, the collection of textual fragments as a central task of a newly conceived science of classical philology. This was the phase of German Romanticism, which represented the convergence of two fundamental factors.

First, there came a profound transformation in the self-understanding of the discipline of classical philology, from a fundamentally aesthetic admiration of the few surviving canonical masterworks of Greek and Latin literature to an increasingly historicist and anthropological attempt to understand the entire, complex totality of the ancient Greek and Roman cultures that had produced them. This change was a long time coming (and in some senses it has never fully arrived); but it was only after about the middle of the 18th century that for the first time a systematic and institutionalized effort was made to work against the canonical selection that the combination of chance, the ancients themselves, and the Middle Ages had imposed on modernity and instead to attempt to understand as fully as possible phenomena, authors, and texts that were interesting not because luck or other people's designs had chosen them to survive as classics, but simply because they had formed part of classical antiquity. Even tattered little fragments could come to seem classics, because they derived from a culture that as a whole had attained classic status. By the last decades of the 18th century progressive classicists such as Christian Gottlob Heyne and Friedrich August Wolf were already assigning to their brightest students the task of collecting the fragments of ancient authors, for such work was not only extremely challenging, but also, at least if done well, quite useful.

Second, in tandem with these developments in philology, a contemporaneous but differently oriented development in German literature and philosophy lent a new dignity to the fragment. For the German Romantics, such as Friedrich Schlegel and Novalis, the fragment was not necessarily a derivative form of literary communication to be dismissed as defective and incomplete in comparison with systematic treatises and extended narratives. Instead, it could be commended as the only appropriate vehicle for expressing revolutionary insights that went beyond established forms and genres. Not only did the Romantics entrust many of their most important ideas to the various collections of witty, provocative, and irritating fragments that they published, but by theorizing and philosophically justifying these fragments they helped train a generation of readers willing to take fragments seriously, to meditate on their implications and to seek out the hidden links between them. Now every good fragment was seen to contain within itself a whole system in a nutshell: as Schlegel wrote about fragments (in a celebrated fragment), "Just like a small work of art, a fragment must be completely separated off from the surrounding world and must be perfect in itself, like a hedgehog" (*Athenäums-Fragment* no. 206). Schlegel's own fragment does what it says all good fragments should do, and it ends with an amusing, but perfectly comprehensible surprise: for a hedgehog is a relatively small animal, in appearance has a jagged outline, and has the perfect organic unity required of a work of art. And it is no doubt also relevant that one of the most famous ancient fragments to survive from the Greek poet Archilochus (fr. 201 West) contrasted the cleverness of the fox, who knows many things, with that of the hedgehog, who knows only one (but that one is a big one).

These two contemporary developments, in philology and in literature and philosophy, contributed decisively to the general upsurge in collections of fragments of all kinds of ancient authors that began around the turn of the 19th century. The classicists and the Romantics certainly differed in important ways about what precisely fragments were, what was to be done with them, and what was so important about them—after all, the classicists were dealing with fragments from the past, whereas the Romantics were writing fragments for the future—but neither group had the slightest doubt that fragments were indeed enormously important, and together they contributed to conferring a new dignity on the status of the fragment. Friedrich Daniel Schleiermacher in particular embodied in his very person the convergence between these two explanatory contexts. He was both the close friend and associate of Friedrich Schlegel in the 1790s (he even contributed some of his own fragments anonymously to one of the collections of fragments that Schlegel published) and the colleague and, for a while at least, close friend of the philologist Friedrich August Wolf at Halle and at Berlin after 1804. And it was in Schleiermacher's edition and commentary on the fragments of Heraclitus, *Herakleitos der dunkle, von Ephesos, dargestellt aus den Trümmern seines Werkes und den Zeugnissen der Alten* (*Heraclitus the Obscure, of Ephesus, Depicted on the Basis of the Ruins of His Work and of the Testimonia of the Ancients*), as well as in his later articles on Diogenes of Apollonia and Anaximander, that the modern approach to the fragments of ancient Greek philosophy first achieved systematic coherence and philological rigor. Schleiermacher played a crucial role in this story, but he was not alone. For example, at the very same time, in the competing university of Heidelberg the Romantic classical philologist Georg Friedrich Creuzer was laying the foundations for the modern study of the fragments of the ancient Greek historians.

And yet despite the impetus provided by the collections of Schleiermacher, Creuzer, and their contemporaries, it was not until the middle and second half of the 19th century that this second phase of scholarship on ancient literary fragments really gained momentum, especially in the work of such scholars as August Meineke on the fragments of the Greek comic poets, Johann August Nauck on the fragments of the Greek tragic poets, and Hermann Diels and others on the fragments of ancient philosophy. By the end of the 19th century the systematic and rigorous study of fragments had come to be seen as one of the identifying marks that set German classical philology apart from, and higher than, that of competing nations. Why the delay? Perhaps it was necessary that two or three generations pass over the land before the challenge that Schleiermacher and his contemporaries had issued could finally be met, on the basis of more reliable texts, more abundant resources, and more highly organized research institutions that in 1807 could only have been dreamed of but that by midcentury were starting to become a massive reality.

In any event, modern fragment collecting has rested until today on four basic methodological pillars: (1) the priority given to the attempt to reconstitute, as far as possible, first of all the single identifiable works of individual authors, then the fragments that can be assigned to a specific author but not to a specific work of his, and only thereafter the fragments that can be determined to belong to a particular genre but not to a particular author or work; (2) the exhaustive investigation of all possible sources of information that can help establish the fragments in question, including not only the full range of the ancient literary evidence but also inscriptions, later sources in Greek (Byzantine) and translation (Syriac, Arabic, Hebrew, Armenian, Latin, etc.) where possible, and pictorial documentation where relevant; (3) the fundamental distinction between the actual words of the ancient author, so far as these can be established from the sources, and reports or paraphrases of the author's views by contemporary or later witnesses; and (4) *Quellenkritik* (source criticism), the systematic attempt, in evaluating the testimony of sources, to determine their relations of filiation in order better to assess their significance and reliability. The second of these four goals may be utopian and the last two have been exposed to various kinds of objections, especially during the past several decades; in recent years scholars have repeatedly reminded us that many later ancient authors are not just quarries of fragments in the pure state that can simply be extracted from them, but have their own qualities and intentions as authors and can creatively transform the fragments that they cite and transmit. Yet notwithstanding such limitations, these four principles have generated in the past century and a half numerous collections of the fragments of Greek and Latin poets, philosophers, historians, doctors, grammarians, and other writers that have undeniably enriched our knowledge of many domains of classical antiquity—and in doing so, at the same time largely abandoning, at least explicitly, the aesthetic dimension that had characterized parts of the earlier phase.

The history of the relations between artistic and textual fragments remains to be written; so too particular methodological problems arise in the supplementation and interpretation of intermediate cases in which there is both material loss and textual damage (especially in epigraphy and papyrology), problems that have interesting affinities to those encountered in dealing with ancient artworks. But even in the domain of textual fragments alone, there are many thorny methodological difficulties, not all of which have been adequately recognized, let alone resolved. For example, philologists sometimes seem to assume that all kinds of fragments are fragments of the same kind, raising the same kinds of questions and susceptible to treatment by the same kinds of methods. But is this in fact the case? What reason is there to think that poetic fragments, philosophical fragments, and historical fragments, to take only these three particularly prominent examples, are all fragments in the same way, pose the same kinds of problems, and can be edited and used along the same lines? Poetic fragments are usually cited because of their exact wording, at least by grammarians, metricians, and scholiasts (though some literary authors make it a point to demonstrate their own eloquence by varying the language of the passages they quote); and one may suppose, though without overconfidence, that they are probably transmitted fairly honestly (though of course their transmission is usually far more problematic than is that of complete works). Philosophical fragments are only rarely cited because of their exact wording, more usually because of their doctrine or argument; often they are cited by opponents, who disagree with the views expressed and may not be inclined to quote them too accurately. Historical fragments are usually cited because of the historical or geographical information they contain, and (unless they are cited by rhetoricians interested in the niceties of style) are perhaps least likely of all to respect the exact wording of the original. When philosophical fragments are treated as though they were poetic fragments (e.g., in some research on the Presocratics), various kinds of confusion are likely to ensue. Recently, scholars have begun to pay more explicit and public attention to the methodological issues involved in the collection and study of fragments; this will probably not help us discover new fragments, but it may aid us in achieving a better scholarly understanding of the fragments we already have.

In modern times fragment collections have become ever more scientific and reliable, but at the same time somewhat more recondite and rebarbative. And yet it is astonishing how many contemporary readers continue to be fascinated by ancient fragments, at least those of the Greek lyric poets and Presocratic philosophers, if not, to the same degree, of any other ancient authors. Beside the scholarly study of fragments, and underlying and enriching it, is a psychological fascination exercised on all of us by everything that is incomplete and suggestive of a lost plenitude. After all, even scholars are human beings, and in some cases their choice to dedicate a large part of their lives to the onerous and often frustrating study of fragments may be motivated by the satisfactions that imagining a whole on their basis can provide—satisfactions that may well be even deeper than the lost original real whole ever could have yielded, as the scholars themselves have helped to create that imagined one. This may be one reason why the discovery of papyri that have finally provided complete texts of ancient works that had previously been known only as fragments—Bacchylides' epinician poems, Aristotle's *Constitution of Athens,* Menander's comedies, the Latin poet Cornelius Gallus' elegiac couplets, the geographer Artemidorus' account of Spain—have often been greeted with expressions of disappointment and sometimes with accusations of forgery: some scholars seem to have found it difficult to forsake the author they had helped invent on the basis of his fragments, in favor of the one who really existed.

The preference for fragments may well be a typically modern (or postmodern, or rather post-Romantic) attitude, but it would not be difficult to find parallels in many other periods. In any case it is a feeling to which numerous works of 20th-century authors attest. Perhaps it is only since the beginning of that century that an Italian literary movement known as the Frammentisti could have flourished, or that Ezra Pound could have published a poem entitled "Papyrus" (1916), consisting entirely of the words "Spring . . . | Too long . . . | Gongula . . ." (cf. Sappho fr. 95.2–4 L.-P.), or that a sculptor like Rodin could not only collect sculptural fragments, but also produce them (though Michelangelo, whom Rodin so esteemed, may have anticipated him to some extent). The perfectly complete sonnet on the archaic torso of Apollo by Rodin's great admirer Rilke suggests that if the fragmentary statue has such extraordinary value for us, this is because of the lost wholeness it permits, indeed compels, us to imagine. So too, Proust's entire massive novel (itself an unfinished fragment) culminates in the discovery that a transcendental happiness and sense of unity can derive precisely from the repetition of mere fragments of existence, the most banal of experiences—the taste of a madeleine, the sound of a spoon clinking against a plate, the unevenness of two paving stones. And in what is perhaps his last surviving work, written probably in the spring of 1940, Walter Benjamin found in a painting by Paul Klee an idiosyncratic but deeply moving image for what he called the Angel of History (but we can also designate it as the patron saint of fragment collecting), conceived eschatologically, in the mode not of restoration and plenitude but of inconsolable anguish and irretrievable loss:

> A Klee painting named *Angelus Novus* shows an angel looking as though he is about to move away from something he is fixedly contemplating. His eyes are staring, his mouth is open, his wings are spread. This is how one pictures the angel of history. His face is turned towards the past. Where we perceive a chain of events, he sees one single catastrophe which keeps piling wreckage upon wreckage and hurls it in front of his feet. The angel would like to stay, awaken the dead, and make whole what has been smashed. But a storm is blowing from Paradise; it has got caught in his wings with such violence that the angel can no longer close them. This storm irresistibly propels him into the future to which his back is turned, while the pile of debris before him grows skyward. This storm is what we call progress. ("Theses on the Philosophy of History," no. 9)

BIBL.: Ernst Behler, *German Romantic Literary Theory* (New York 1993). Walter Benjamin, "On the Concept of History" (1940), in *Walter Benjamin: Selected Writings,* vol. 4, *1938–1940,* ed. Howard Eiland and Michael W. Jennings (Cambridge, Mass., 2003). Rudolf Kassel, "Fragmente und ihre Sammler," in *Fragmenta Dramatica: Beiträge zur Interpretation der griechischen Tragikerfragmente und ihrer Wirkungsgeschichte,* ed. Heinz Hofmann with Annette Harder (Göttingen 1991) 243–253. Glenn W. Most, ed., *Collecting Fragments—Fragmente sammeln,* Aporemata 1 (Göttingen 1997) and "À la recherche du texte perdu: On Collecting Philosophical Fragments," in *Fragmentsammlungen philosophischer Texte der*

Antike: Le raccolte dei frammenti di filosofi antichi, ed. W. Burkert, L. Gemelli Marciano, E. Matelli, and L. Orelli, Atti del Seminario Internazionale Ascona, Centro Stefano Fanscini 22–27 settembre 1996, Aporemata 3 (Göttingen 1998) 1–15. Eberhard Ostermann, *Das Fragment: Geschichte einer ästhetischen Idee* (Munich 1991). G.W.M.

Fraternities and Sororities

The system of collegiate and university student groups, often single-sex and usually bearing names consisting of two or three Greek letters, originating in the United States, as did the words *fraternity* and *sorority* when applied to these societies. Although some European higher education systems have student organizations that are roughly analogous to American fraternities and sororities, such as Cambridge and Oxford debating societies and the German *Verbindungen,* the American "Greek system" developed independently. The most common type of fraternity is the social fraternity, organized specifically to provide social events and to promote relations among its members. Such fraternities often maintain campus residences of their own. There are also honor fraternities such as Phi Beta Kappa (whose membership is restricted to students with demonstrated academic achievement), professional fraternities, ethnically based fraternities, and common-interest fraternities.

The first fraternities grew out of the literary and debating societies that were common in early American colleges and universities. The first recorded student organization was a "Society of pious and praying Youths" at Harvard, known through a single reference in the diary of the Puritan minister Cotton Mather in 1716. Eventually a large number of literary and debating societies developed in the colonial colleges and remained an important element of American university life well into the 19th century. The literary societies provided an opportunity for study and oratorical jousting in an age when the primary function of colleges was to train a male social elite of ministers, lawyers, and orators. A great deal of students' time in the formal curriculum of the college was spent in the acquisition of Greek and Latin and classical history, for the Graeco-Roman past was believed to supply an inexhaustible fund of noble exemplars of honor, virtue, and heroism. Many 19th-century students debated topics on explicitly classical themes ("Was Cicero greater as an orator than as a philosopher?" "Would Regulus have been justified in not returning to Carthage?"), and a good number of these early societies had vaguely classical names such as the Philomathesian (Kenyon College), Philologian (Williams College), and Cliosophic (Princeton University).

The first society to be known as a fraternity and the first society to take a Greek-letter name was Phi Beta Kappa, founded at the College of William and Mary in 1776. Greek-letter names in early American fraternities often stood for a Greek motto or phrase that represented the fraternity's official values. The name Phi Beta Kappa, for example, stands for *Philosophia Bious Kubernetes,* "Love of wisdom, the guide of life." Sometimes the Greek-letter name was used because the actual motto formed part of the fraternal bond of secrecy, but this was not true of all fraternities. Many modern fraternities have Greek-letter names that do not stand for anything in particular, understandable given that general knowledge of the ancient Greek alphabet and language has almost entirely vanished.

The first social organization for college women was the Adelphean Society, later Alpha Delta Pi, founded at Wesleyan Female College in 1851. All-female societies were at first called female fraternities; the word *sorority* did not enter into usage until the late 19th century.

The socially oriented "Greek system" in America flourished just as classicism began to fade from the academic core of American higher education. Most colleges and universities began to eliminate Greek and Latin requirements by the late 19th century, just as Greek-letter societies were perfecting their "classical" symbols and rituals: the Greek-letter names, mottoes in Latin and Greek, the occasional wearing of toga-like garments, and a tradition of revelry that recalls, if only indirectly, the banquet scene in Petronius' *Satyricon.*

BIBL.: Jack L. Anson and Robert F. Marchesani, Jr., eds., *Baird's Manual of American Fraternities,* 20th ed. (Indianapolis 1991). Helen Lefkowitz Horowitz, *Campus Life: Undergraduate Cultures from the Eighteenth Century to the Present* (New York 1987). J. McLachlan, "'The Choice of Hercules': American Student Societies in the Early 19th Century," in *The University in Society,* ed. Lawrence Stone, vol. 2, *Europe, Scotland, and the United States from the 16th to the 20th Century* (Princeton 1974). Diana Turk, *Bound by a Mighty Vow: Sisterhood and Women's Fraternities, 1870–1920* (New York 2004). C.W.

Freud, Sigmund

Though the Oedipus Complex is still not well understood, the idea that one *ought* to understand it pervaded American and Western European culture in the 20th century. Sigmund Freud purported to be telling us who we are—to be giving us insight into the human condition—and he did so by making essential reference to a play by Sophocles. In this way he transformed modernity's relation to classical antiquity. After Freud, *Oedipus Tyrannus* could no longer be treated as a great literary work from the past, a play about a bygone world in which oracles were still vibrant. The literary text became oracular for modern society: it would tell us who we are if only we could grasp its enigmatic meaning: "[Oedipus's] destiny moves us only because it might have been ours—because the oracle laid the same curse upon us before our birth as upon him . . . While the poet, as he unravels the past, brings to light the guilt of Oedipus, he is at the same time compelling us to recognize our own inner minds, in which those same impulses, though suppressed, are still to be found" (*Interpretation of Dreams, Standard Edition* [*SE*] 4.262–263).

Freud was an ardently secular European, but he showed how the most famous oracle of antiquity need not, ought not, be consigned to a pagan, religious past. It is not an exaggeration to say that he brought about a shift in the temporality with which modernity approached the classical world. One could no longer, as it were, visit it as though making a trip to a museum: one was rather *called upon to know it,* if one were to grasp one's own living present.

Freud also insisted on a grasp of the classical tradition as a scientific ideal. In general, scientific inquiry treats its own history as of no more than anecdotal interest. There is, for example, no reason for a contemporary physicist to learn Aristotelian physics as part of ongoing research. But Freud, who above all took himself to be a scientist, thought that the great minds of the ancient world could still provide invaluable insight into the workings of the human psyche. He was devoted to empirical research, but he used the classical tradition to locate the results of his research in a sufficiently broad context. He repeatedly discovered, for example, the (often hidden) significance of sexuality in human life, but he resisted the temptation simply to treat it as a biological force for reproduction. "What psychoanalysis calls sexuality," he wrote, "was by no means identical with the impulsion towards a union of the two sexes or towards producing a pleasurable sensation in the genitals; it had far more resemblance to the all-inclusive and all-preserving Eros of Plato's *Symposium*" (*Resistances to Psychoanalysis, SE* 19.218). This was not mere lip service. As his thinking developed, Freud eventually abandoned the idea that sexuality was the best way to conceptualize the impulsive force that holds sway over human life: "the libidinal, sexual or life instincts . . . are best comprised under the name Eros; their purpose would be to form living substance into ever greater unities, so that life may be prolonged and brought to higher development" (*Two Encyclopedia Articles, SE* 18.258). In his later theory sexuality remains important, but it can be properly understood only within the larger context of the human drive for development and differentiated complexity. The inspiration for this conceptual enlargement comes from Plato and the Presocratic philosopher Empedocles: "The philosopher [Empedocles] taught that two principles governed events in the life of the universe and the life of the mind, and that those principles were everlastingly at war with each other. He called them *philia* (love) and *neīkos* (strife) . . . The two fundamental principles . . . are, both in name and function, the same as our two primal instincts, *Eros* and *destructiveness,* the first of which endeavors to combine what exists into ever greater unities, while the second endeavors to dissolve those combinations and to destroy the structures to which they have given rise" (*Analysis Terminable and Interminable, SE* 23.2). At the present time the scientific study of the mind has to a large extent been taken over by empirical research on the brain. Freud would have been delighted. But he would have insisted that the great minds of the classical tradition are needed if new discoveries are to rise above the parochial understandings of the moment and achieve their true significance. As he put it, "no one can foresee in what guise the nucleus of truth contained in the theory of Empedocles will present itself to later understanding" (247).

Freud also used classical archaeology as a model for the psychoanalytic understanding of the mind. On explaining to a patient why unconscious ideas tend to be preserved in all their intensity, while conscious ideas diminish in importance over time and are often forgotten, he said, "I illustrated my remarks by pointing to the antiques standing about in my room. They were, in fact, I said, only objects found in a tomb, and their burial had been their preservation; the destruction of Pompeii was only beginning now that it had been dug up" (*Notes upon a Case of Obsessional Neurosis, SE* 10.176). And in an early essay he makes an analogy between a psychoanalyst first meeting a patient and an explorer who comes upon "an expanse of ruins, with remains of wall, fragments of columns, and tablets with half-effaced and unreadable inscriptions." If the explorer-analyst engages in a successful dig, "the discoveries are self-explanatory: the ruined walls are part of the ramparts of a palace or a treasure-house; the fragments of columns can be filled out into a temple; the numerous inscriptions which, by good luck, may be bilingual, reveal an alphabet and a language and, when they have been deciphered and translated, yield undreamed-of information about the events of the remote past." As he memorably put it, the stones speak (*The Aetiology of Hysteria, SE* 3.192).

Archaeology was already functioning in Western culture as a romantic ideal for how we might relate to the ancient world. Freud took that romance and transferred it onto the individual's journey of self-discovery. Three aspects of this archaeological metaphor are of enduring significance. First is the idea that symptoms present themselves to us as symptoms because they seem strange; and they seem strange because they have been cut off from a world of meaning in the context of which they would make sense. Symptoms should thus be seen as, say, inscriptions on the body, or surviving fragments from a lost ritual. Second, the explanatory ideal is holistic: if we could fit these symptoms into a larger (but as yet unknown) framework of meanings, the discoveries would be "self-explanatory." Like an ancient inscription, we understand a symptom when we grasp its place in a meaningful world. Third, classical archaeology provides the right kind of model for a distinctively psychoanalytic understanding of our relation to the past. Had Freud focused on cultural artifacts or literary works from the previous century, for example, it would have been natural to understand their exerting a normal historical influence of the past on the present. But Freud's point about unconscious ideas is not only that they are coming from the past, but that they are somehow "timeless." And their influence on us is not in terms of an ordinary historical chain of causation—in which past events affect the future—but as a "*directly* releasing cause." That is, the past is somehow directly intervening into the present much as an artifact from the ancient world suddenly protrudes into the contemporary world. (That artifact no doubt had its effects in the ancient world, which in turn had its effects, which in turn . . . ; but that is not how the artifact is affecting us now. It has directly come into our present and demands to be understood in the here and now.)

Freud bequeathed to the modern world the idea that for every individual the past was alive and functioning in the present—though not recognized as such. Each person was the site of primordial struggles whose intensity, complexity, and depth could be understood only by turning to the classical tradition. In this way he, more than anyone else, made the classical tradition a living necessity of the modern world.

BIBL.: Sigmund Freud, *The Standard Edition of the Complete Psychological Works of Sigmund Freud (SE)*, ed. James Strachey, 24 vols., (London 1953–1974). J.LE.

G

Galatea

Nereid living off the Sicilian coast who owes her fame to the love borne her by the Cyclops Polyphemus. Her myth has been known since classical times and probably has its origin in the poet Philoxenos. There are two versions of it: either the Cyclops manages to seduce Galatea by playing his flute (Nonnus 39.257–266; Propertius 3.2.7–8), or the sea nymph successfully resists his advances. The latter version is especially popular in the Hellenistic period (Theocritus, *Idyll* 11), and it provides the foundation for Ovid's dramatization of the myth (*Metamorphoses* 13.750–897) by introducing Acis as Galatea's lover and Polyphemus' rival. In his version jealousy drives the Cyclops to dash Acis to pieces with a boulder. Galatea, however, is able to revive her lover, transforming his blood into a spring spouting from under the rock and thereby turning him into a river god with whom she can be united in eternal love.

In all versions the confrontation between Galatea and Polyphemus, with its contrast between beauty and ugliness, sophistication and barbarism, and the irreconcilable habitats of sea and land, provides material for comedy, satire (Lucian, *Dialogi Marini* 1), and the grotesque. Ovid is the main source for the myth's post-antique reception. Another especially important one is Philostratus' ecphrasis of a painting (*Eikones* 2.18), in which he traces the ugly Cyclops' amorous gaze at Galatea in addition to idealizing the beauty of the naked nymph. This description had a direct effect on Raphael's influential *Triumph of Galatea* (ca. 1511) in the Villa Farnesina. Galatea stands in the middle of the painting, surrounded by love and its symbols, but the interaction between the love-arousing cupids in the upper portion of the painting and their targets, various couples of sea creatures, has an isolating effect on Galatea. For none of her possible amorous relationships are depicted, whereas Galatea's own *eros* might be symbolically viewing the whole scene as an idle cupid at the upper left corner of the picture. Instead of being portrayed as a lover or a beloved, Galatea becomes for the viewer a symbol of love, beauty, and longing. This stylization is conveyed not only in the painting itself and by the inclusion of a shell as a kind of sea chariot—the shell usually being reserved for Venus in Renaissance art—but also through the removal of the Cyclops to a painting on the opposite wall, which turns him into an external observer forced to behold the object of his desire from a distance. The triumphal motif of Galatea as a goddess of love driving a shell-chariot remained popular in art and literature into the late Baroque period—consider, for example, Francesco Trevisani's *Seaborne Galatea,* ca. 1717, or J. W. Goethe's depiction of the Triumph of Galatea in the "Classical Walpurgisnacht" scene in *Faust,* 2.8379–8478—but it competes with the dramatization of the myth in Ovidian reception. For example, Annibale Carracci depicted both of the central motifs of the story in a fresco cycle in the Palazzo Farnese (ca. 1597–1600), pairing the Cyclops' musical wooing of Galatea with his fit of jealousy and murder of Acis. The dramatic tension of the impending catastrophe is often maintained by depicting the Cyclops spying on the pair of lovers. Beginning with Nicolas Poussin, in his illustrations of Ovid's *Metamorphoses* (1620–1623), down to J. H. Tischbein the Elder, light is used as a metaphor for good and evil in such scenes, with the lovers in the bright foreground and the Cyclops in the dark background. The best-known musical adaptation of the Ovidian love drama is G. F. Handel's masque *Acis and Galatea* (1718), with a libretto by John Gay.

Ovid is also the source for an extensive literary reception. Since the 16th century the love drama has been staged in more than 400 plays of all kinds, often with a

Christian overtone, in which the Cyclops appears either as the devil or as a heavenly implement in the punishment of an immoral love affair between Galatea and Acis. Popularity is enjoyed by rhetorically polished orations and dirges of the Cyclops, in which courtship gives way to jealousy as a reflection of the soul. Cervantes' pastoral novel *Galatea* (1584) introduces this theme to pastoral poetry, a very popular genre in the 17th and 18th centuries. Cervantes uses the myth of Galatea to give concrete form to the name for bucolic beloveds already known from Virgil's *Eclogues*, and, probably following Jacopo Sannazaro's eclogue *Galatea* (1526), makes the sea nymph a focus of pastoral poetry. Cervantes uses the perception and the effect of Galatea's beauty in his novel to connect the Neoplatonic doctrine of Eros with Christian conceptions of love.

A special case is constituted by the remythologizing of Galatea within the reception of Pygmalion, which began with Rousseau's *Pygmalion* (1770). Rousseau gave the name of Galatea to the statue that Pygmalion creates and falls in love with, and in that sense he took up the tradition of Galatea's idealized beauty (inaugurated by Raphael) to fill a gap in the Pygmalion myth. On the other hand, as Pygmalion's mythological wife, Galatea is able to attain a human status that she possessed neither as an Ovidian nymph nor as an idealized Renaissance Venus.

BIBL.: H. Dörrie, *Die schöne Galatea: Eine Gestalt am Rande des griechischen Mythos in antiker und neuzeitlicher Sicht* (Munich 1968). M.BA.

Translated by Patrick Baker

Galen

Physician-philosopher from Pergamon (129–ca. 216 CE), the patron of a collection of writings that makes up about one-tenth of the entire corpus of Greek literature written before 350 CE, comprising the extensive work of an ancient physician. Of the approximately 430 writings that have been handed down under his name, some 350 are thought to be authentic. They include texts on anatomy, physiology, etiology, diagnostics, nosology, therapy, pharmacology, surgery, gynecology, neurology, psychiatry, ophthalmology, otorhinolaryngology, stomatology, philology, and logic. They aim to cover the entirety of human medicine and epitomize its unity. The restitution of this unity was one of the great goals of Renaissance medical reform (and numerous later forms of medical neohumanism); despite the 1,300 years that separated Galen and this new orientation, he was its most important focal point.

The Galenic writings represent the sum of ancient medicine and presuppose the idea of cumulative progress, which connects them with the present era. At the same time they are rooted in pre-Galenic intellectual history and offer a demonstration to today's readers of how tradition can be dealt with productively (intertextuality, reception theory), and hence the relevance of history for the future. Galen's broad education and experience formed the basis of a creative eclecticism that preserves what is presumed to be the best from the medical tradition, synthesizes it into a "Galenic" system, and incorporates it into the domain of *scientia aeterna*. Representatives of the dogmatic, empirical, methodist, and pneumatic schools of medicine supply the material for this eclecticism, the foundations of which can be found in the Hippocratic theory of humors (after the model of *De natura hominis*), Aristotelian physics, and the Platonic doctrine of the soul. Hence, it is not surprising that Symphorien Champier, a Galenist of the early 16th century, represented Hippocrates, Plato, Aristotle, and Galen as a string quartet in which Galen plays first violin.

Galen—perhaps the literary figure more than the historical one—has furthermore gone down in history as the paradigm of a successful (and thus reproducible) medical career, whose recipe for success consists in education and therapeutic achievements, a lifelong thirst for knowledge and delight in experiment, and self-assertiveness and self-dramatization in a highly competitive health-care market (although his relentless polemics against his unwelcome competition have probably done more harm than good to his later reputation). As a widely traveled physician-philosopher and world sage, Galen wrote autobi(bli)ographical works that served as models for others, such as Cardano's *De mirabilibus operibus in arte medica per ipsum factis* (1557, illustrated).

As an interpreter of Hippocrates, Galen brought the ancient Greek in line with his medical ideas and left to the world an idealized figure who dominated Hippocrates reception, in the form of Galenic Hippocratism, until about 1550. To medieval physicians Hippocrates stood for an era of inventions (*ordo inventionis*), whereas Galen stood for an era of interpretation (*ordo doctrinae*). The intertextual dialogue between the two (occasionally joined by Avicenna) has been recorded as a "live event" in numerous manuscripts and a famous fresco in the crypt of the Cathedral of Anagni; it can also be found in numerous title-page copper engravings in the age of the printed book.

As an anatomist for whom zootomy and the observation of surface human anatomy were an almost daily need throughout his life, Galen propagated anatomy as a basic medical science—as it remains today—although his own knowledge derived more from zootomy than dissection of the human body.

In his work Galen sketched a picture of the human being that remained unrivaled into the modern period. He assumed that there are three main areas of body function governed by special souls. The centers are the cardinal organs of the liver, heart, and brain, which are connected with the periphery by their own extensions (veins, arteries, nerves). The different parts of the body function by virtue of specific powers. The capacity for nourishment, growth, and reproduction (i.e., the vegetative faculty, *facultas naturalis*) is situated in the liver; life-giving innate heat (i.e., the vital faculty, *facultas vitalis*) is situated in the heart; the mental faculty (*facultas animalis*), which governs sensory and motor functions, is situated in the brain. The liver converts the nourishing pulp that is introduced through the portal system and prepared in the stomach into blood, understood as a dynamic equilibrium of the four humors with their attendant qualities, which the veins carry to all parts of the body and tissues. Thanks to specific capacities (attraction, retention, transformation, excretion), the organs absorb the most suitable elements of the nourishment. Pneuma, the product of inhalation and absorption of air through the pores of the body, flows to the right heart. Through pores in the cardiac semptum it penetrates to the left heart, where it is mixed with blood and distributed through the arteries. A part of this *pneuma zotikon* (*spiritus vitales*) is transformed in a network of vessels at the base of the brain (*rete mirabile*) into psychic pneuma (*spiritus animales*), which mediates nerve activity.

The philosophical grounding of medicine suggested in this anthropology was decisively furthered by Galen in an epistemological, ethical, and logical sense. *Logos* and *peira,* reason and (qualified) experience, are the cornerstones of his theory of medicine, in which observation and experiment illustrate or confirm insights achieved through speculation. In the field of pharmacology this process bore fruit into the 19th century (the term *galenics* is still in use today for pharmaceutical technology, i.e., the preparation of medicines). It was initially replaced only *ex nihilo* by the therapeutic nihilism of the second Viennese school of medicine. Galen's consciously deductive method, which had no serious competition until Francis Bacon (1561–1626) developed his inductive scientific model, is grounded on the model of geometry. His ethics can be described as a compromise among the ethics of responsibility, conviction, inclination to good, and deontology and belies the modern view that medical ethics based on rationality is a new phenomenon. His logic corresponds to the formal logic founded by Aristotle, and the surviving writings on the subject suggest that Galen made important contributions to its teachings on terms, propositions, and inferences.

Galen's anthropology further includes a concept of health that, under the heading *sex res non naturales,* covers the environment, diet, sleeping and waking, rest and movement, filling and voiding, and the emotions. These are the areas of good and bad habits and behavior that influence good health, illness, or the neutral gray zone in between. Galenic medicine has a useful reminder for modern practitioners, namely the insight that medicine consists not only of teachings on disease, but also on health —not only therapy but also prophylaxis, not only crisis management but also the art of living (and dying).

When physicians thought about human beings' physical makeup, the relationship between body and mind, concepts of health and sickness, dietetics, pharmacology and surgery, medical theory and practice, and clinical and experimental medicine, it was almost heretical not to be a Galenist in the post-Galenic period, at least up to the 17th century. Whatever the custodians of the Catholic, Orthodox, or Muslim religions or post-Galenic philosophers taught about human beings and their physical and mental makeup was on the whole Galenic. The same holds for physicians who absorbed and passed on Galenic medicine in the systematized form of Galenism from 350 CE onward. The Galenic harvest of what Hippocrates had sowed dominated *in rebus medicinalibus* throughout the age of the three cultures of the Middle Ages: Byzantine, Arabic, and, from the 12th century, Latin. The hellenization of medicine, which commenced at the end of the 15th century, focused attention on versions of Greek texts preserved in Byzantine manuscripts and expanded the basis of Galenic medicine as new texts were discovered. In the course of a Galenic renaissance the entire corpus was edited in Greek (the Aldine edition of 1525 made 106 texts available, 46 of which were printed for the first time), translated into Latin, provided with commentary in Latin, depicted in diagrams, analyzed lexically, summarized in handbooks, and gradually translated into modern languages. In the process of clarifying problems of transmissions or variant readings, Galen proved to be fallible, especially when it emerged—to the surprise of many—that his understanding of human anatomy was based on zootomy and not on dissection of human bodies. Galen's prestige suffered especially in the second half of the 16th century, after men such as Andreas Vesalius had introduced reforms to the field of anatomy; physicians learned more and more to distinguish between Hippocrates' teachings and Galen's, even if a number of proponents of the reform accelerated by Vesalius regarded him as more of a *Galenus redivivus* than an anti-Galenist. The teachings of Plato and Aristotle became more sharply differentiated from Galenism, so that criticism of Galenism arose from this quarter as well. Unitarian doctrines of the soul, which cast doubt on Galen's tenet of three souls that he had adopted from Plato; William Harvey's discovery of the circulation of blood, which rocked the foundations of Galen's physiology; the crisis into which humoral pathology was thrown by the concepts of iatrochemistry (after Paracelsus), iatrophysics, and iatromechanics; the triumphant advance of inductive methodology (Bacon)—all these tendencies of the early modern period hastened the demise of Galenism as an anthropology penetrating the higher faculties of medicine, philosophy, and theology. Critics attacked many of his views, including his agnostic standpoint on the materiality or immateriality and mortality or immortality of the soul; his conceptions of space, time, and causality; his theory of vision; his neglect of hypothetical and mixed syllogisms; his postulation of pores in the cardiac septum and of the *rete mirabile;* his distinction between cosmic heat and the heat of the body; his boasting, his inconsistency, his models for reasoning. Galen drew the criticism of scholars such as Simeon Seth (11th cent.), Gómez Pereira (1500–ca. 1558), Ioannes Argenterius (1513–1572), Bernardino Telesio (1509–1588), Tommaso Campanella (1568–1639), and—to name one reader from the modern period—Ulrich von Wilamowitz-Moellendorff (1848–1931). Nevertheless, despite all this criticism, Galen and the Corpus Galenicum remained a dynamic source of inspiration for all kinds of Neohumanist movements in medicine. They were initiated by physicians such as Karl-Gottlob Kühn (1754–1840) and Arthur Brock (1879–1947), who conceived his neo-Galenism as a cure for the neurasthenic effects of modern life. Remnants of Galenic medicine as handed down in the translations and commentaries of scholars writing in Syriac and Arabic are still in use today in Unani medicine, which is taught in Islamic schools in India.

BIBL.: J. Barnes and J. Jouanna, eds., *Galien et la philosophie* (Geneva 2003). V. Boudon-Millot, *Galien: Texte établi et traduit,* vol. 1 (Paris 2007). A. J. Brock, ed. and trans., *Greek Medicine* (New York 1972). D. Cantor, "Between Galen, Geddes, and the Gael: Arthur Brock, Modernity, and Medical Humanism in Early-Twentieth-century Scotland," *Journal of the History of Medicine and Allied Sciences* 60 (2005) 1–41. A. Cunningham, *The Anatomical Renaissance* (Aldershot 1997). A. Debru, ed., *Galen on Pharmacology* (Leiden 1997). G. Fichtner, *Corpus Galenicum* (Tübingen 1985). S. Fortuna, "Aspetti della tradizione del 'De locis affectis' di Galeno nel Rinascimento," in *Studi di storia della medicine antica e medievale,* ed. M. Vegetti et al. (Florence 1996) 101–111; "Edizioni e traduzioni del 'De locis affectis' di Galeno tra Cinquecento e Seicento," *Bollettino dei classici* 14 (1993) 3–30; "Galen's 'De constitutione artis medicae' in the Renaissance," *Classical Quarterly* 42 (1993) 302–319; "I 'Procedimenti anatomici' di Galeno e la traduzione latina di Demetrio Calcondila," *Medicina nei secoli* 11 (1999) 9–28; "A proposito dei manoscritti di Galeno nella biblioteca di Nicolò Leoniceno," *Italia Medioevale e Umanistica* 35 (1992) 431–438; and "Sulla tradizione e sul testo del commento di Galeno al Prognostico di Ippocrate," *AION* 23 (2001) 233–249. R. K. French, *Dissection and Vivisection in the European Renaissance* (Aldershot 1999). Galen, *Opera omnia,* ed. C. G. Kühn (1821–1833; repr. 1998). I. Garofalo and A. Roselli, *Galenismo e medicina tardoantica* (Naples 2003). A. Garzya, ed., *Tradizione e ecdotica dei testi medici tardoantichi e bizantini* (Naples 1992). A. Garzya and J. Jouanna, eds., *Storia e ecdotica dei testi medici greci* (Naples 1996); *I testi medici greci: Tradizione e ecdotica* (Naples 1999); and *Transmission et ecdotique des textes médicaux grecs* (Paris 1997). N. H. Keswani, ed., *The Science of Medicine and Physiological Concepts in Ancient and Medieval India* (New Delhi 1974). J. Kollesch and D. Nickel, "Bibliographia Galeniana," *ANRW* 37, no. 2 (1994) 1351–1420, 2063–2070, and Kollesch and Nickel, eds., *Galen und das hellenistische Erbe* (Stuttgart 1993). F. Kudlien and R. Durling, eds., *Galen's Method of Healing* (Leiden 1991). J. A. López Férez, ed., *Galeno: Obra, pensamiento e influencia* (Madrid 1991). P. Manuli and M. Vegetti, eds., *Le opere psicologiche di Galeno* (Naples 1988). V. Nutton, *From Democedes to Harvey* (London 1988) and *Karl Gottlob Kühn and His Edition of Galenic Works* (Oxford 1976). V. Nutton, ed., *Galen: Problems and Prospects* (London 1981) and *The Unknown Galen* (London 2002). P.-G. Ottoson, *Scholastic Medicine and Philosophy* (Naples 1984). P. E. Pormann and E. Savage-Smith, *Medieval Islamic Medicine* (Georgetown 2007). H. Schlange-Schöningen, *Die römische Gesellschaft bei Galen: Biographie und Sozialgeschichte* (Berlin 2003). P. N. Singer, ed., *Galen: Selected Works* (New York 1997). O. Temkin, *Galenism* (Ithaca 1973). T. L. Tieleman, *Galen and Chrysippus on the Soul* (Leiden 1996). T.R.

Translated by Deborah Lucas Schneider

Galileo Galilei

The scientist Galileo (1564–1642) enjoyed a lifelong engagement with the classical tradition. Though best known for his excessively persuasive promotion of Copernicanism in his *Dialogue concerning the Two Chief World Systems* (1632) and for his condemnation and recantation in Rome a year later, Galileo offered less a thoroughgoing rejection of the works of Aristotle and Ptolemy than an objection to the intellectual practices of their early modern heirs. Though scarcely sympathetic to Aristotle's relative neglect of geometry throughout his natural philosophy—and in this particular much closer in spirit to Plato—Galileo revered the Stagyrite as an extraordinary logician and as one who prized sensory observation over the authoritative weight of tradition. Galileo frequently derided the early modern Peripatetics, attributing to them an impression that Aristotle alone had seen all phenomena for all eternity, and mocking their crabbed habit of reading nothing but him and his commentators and suturing together such passages, sometimes alongside Holy Scripture, in response to any query. He extended a special dispensation to both Aristotle and Ptolemy—both of whom were popularly credited with possession of an ancient version of the telescope—maintaining that, had these philosophers had access to his instruments and data, neither would have been in disagreement with the Copernican position.

Galileo's most speculative arguments drew on classical literature; around 1602, for instance, he offered a quantitative approach to the mythical "creation point" mentioned in *Timaeus* 37, that place or places from which the Divine Architect originally dropped the planets, and soon thereafter took up a neo-Stoic view of the Nova of 1604, basing his discussions of the phenomenon on Seneca's *Natural Questions* and Cicero's *On the Nature of Gods.* These texts promoted a cosmos characterized by a single medium and animated by endless cycles of condensation and rarefaction. Though consonant with a Copernican world system and sometimes associated with it, these features were most noteworthy for their sharp departure from the Aristotelian model. It is significant that Galileo's early and erroneous explanation of the aurora borealis also emerged in the context of neo-Stoic physics; in 1600 his friend Bernardo Davanzati offered a detailed summary of this hypothesis in the course of his translation of Tacitus' *Annals.*

Galileo's first astronomical publication, *Starry Messenger* (*Sidereus nuncius,* 1610), offered in its address to Cosimo II de' Medici a variant of, or rather an improvement on, the bold claims of Propertius' *Elegy* 3.2 and Horace's *Ode* 3.30 that their poetic works would outlast the earth's brazen monuments: his Medicean stars, the newly discovered satellites of Jupiter, will survive longer still. As if to clothe another novel assertion with the patina of the antique, Galileo recalled the Pythagorean impression of an Earth-like moon in the midst of his detailed discussion of the terrestrial features of that body. And even as he stated that he would, in time, present extensive arguments in support of a Copernican world system, Galileo referred to the mistaken impression of Earth as a lowly sinkhole not in terms of the powerful Aristotelian tradition, but as an offshoot of the decidedly less decorous theory of *faex caeli*.

The vigor with which Galileo and his supporters reacted to his rival Christoph Scheiner's ill-advised adoption of the pseudonym Apelles during the debates over sunspots suggests a close familiarity with Pliny's description of that ancient artist and his sometime rival Protogenes in *Natural History* 35, as well as with the influential account offered by Lucian of Samosata in his treatise on slander. Scheiner also had fused together, in a single line of verse, two brief allusions to sunspots in *Georgics* I, because, he suggested, in the course of revising an embarrassing error, his own method of composition was not unlike that popularly associated with the Mantuan poet—a stream of genius afterward licked into shape like bear cubs "after the ursine fashion"—and because his supporters included those who considered their Virgilian centos an improvement on their source material. Thus, Galileo would eventually compare the typical Peripatetic thinker, busily ransacking the Aristotelian corpus for the appropriate response to every query in natural philosophy, to those who so brazenly borrowed from and tampered with Virgil's works.

Though familiar with the work of ancient Democritus and Epicurus, subscribing at times, as in *Discourse on Bodies That Float* (*Discorso . . . intorno alle cose che stanno in su l'acqua,* 1612) and *The Assayer* (*Il saggiatore,* 1623), to a theory of minimum particles, and openly engaging with questions of voids and interstitial *vacua* directly after his condemnation and in *Two New Sciences* (*Discorsi e dimostrazioni matematiche, intorno a due nuove scienze,* 1634), Galileo was at most a sometime disciple of the atomists. Both because atomism was associated with theories of a plurality of worlds, and because he had been denounced in 1626 by Orazio Grassi as a follower of Epicurus, who in that Jesuit's view "had denied Divine Providence," Galileo's fellows in the Academy of the Lynxes, the first scientific society, took particular care to mute any connections between their natural philosophy and this useful but curiously suspect doctrine.

Vincenzo Viviani, Galileo's last student and one of his earliest biographers, wrote that his mentor's love for Latin poetry was so great that he knew by heart much of Virgil, Ovid, Horace, and Seneca. The corpus of Galileo's literary works, though largely dispersed, reveals other and more surprising enthusiasms; among them are a glossary of words and phrases found in the works of Plautus and a project to translate the Homeric *Battle of the Mice and the Frogs* into Italian, apparently unrealized (though it is in keeping with the scientist's composition of burlesque verse). It is, finally, Viviani's description of Galileo's impatience with those who, like him, had been bred on classical authors but were unable to accept any authorities that best captures his complex relationship to antiquity; such people, he said, "when old consider it infamy to admit as false/what they learned when young," a rough paraphrase of Horace, *Epistle* 2.1.84–85.

BIBL.: Peter Barker, "Stoic Contributions to Early Modern Science," in *Atoms, Pneuma, and Tranquility,* ed. Margaret Osler (Cambridge 1991) 135–154. Jochem Büttner, "Galileo's Cosmogony," in *Largo Campo di Filosofare: Eurosymposium Galileo 2001,* ed. José Montesinos and Carlos Solís (La Orotava 2001) 391–402. Stillman Drake, *Galileo at Work: His Intellectual Biography* (Chicago 1978). Galileo Galilei, *Sidereus Nuncius,* Italian trans. Maria Timpanaro Cardini, ed. Andrea Battistini (Venice 1993). Paolo Ponzio, "À propos de l'atomisme de Galilée: Questions cosmologiques et problèmes théologiques," *Revue d'histoire des sciences* 55, no. 2 (2002) 199–214. E.R.

Gandhara

The ancient kingdom of Gandhara was situated in the northwestern corner of the Indian subcontinent, in what is today northwestern Pakistan and adjacent parts of eastern Afghanistan, south of the Hindu Kush mountains. Its geographical location included it within the Indian cultural sphere and at the same time linked it to regions to the west: Iran, central Asia, west Asia, and, for some centuries, the Hellenistic and Roman worlds of the eastern Mediterranean. The contact with the classical West, and the confluence that followed with Indian traditions, was culturally the most significant. This began with Alexander's conquest of the Achaemenid Persian empire, which brought him to Gandhara, the easternmost Persian satrapy, in 327–326 BCE. Alexander's generals were left behind to control Gandhara and neighboring Bactria, across the Hindu Kush (present-day northern Afghanistan). Bactria remained under the Greeks for the next two centuries (until the mid-2nd century BCE, when it fell to nomad groups from central Asia), but the history of Gandhara shifted between Greek and Indian rulers. Within two decades Alexander's general Seleucus Nicator was forced to cede Gandhara to Indian control. Later, when Indian power weakened, Greeks from Bactria ruled Gandhara for a century (2nd century BCE) as the Indo-Greek kings. They were overthrown, once again by central Asian nomads, in the beginning of the 1st century BCE, but pockets of Greek control continued, in Hadda until 50 BCE, and in Taxila until 10 CE.

Magnificent series of coins have survived from the period of Greek rule in Bactria and Gandhara, which technically and aesthetically rival, and even excel, their counterparts from the eastern Mediterranean. Other material of this period (architectural remains, sculptures, carved ivories, terra-cottas, mosaics, inscriptions) has been found in Bactria, from the Hellenistic settlement sites of Ai

Khanum (northeastern Afghanistan) and Takht-i Sangin (southern Tajikistan), and from a hoard containing objects in gold, found recently, believed to be from Mir Zakah (near Gardez).

Very little has been found in Gandhara of the Greek period (apart from coins), mainly because the Greek levels have not been fully excavated, but it is generally held that Greek civilization, evident in Bactria, existed in Gandhara also. The strongest testimony for this position is the persistence of Greek traditions, even a century after the end of Greek rule, in the pronounced classical style of Buddhist sculptures associated with the efflorescence of Buddhist monasteries in Gandhara between the 1st and 5th centuries CE. The rise of Buddhism in Gandhara and other parts of India at this time is linked to the long-distance trade in luxury goods for the elite between Rome, India, and China that developed from the early 1st century CE onward, as the monasteries were patronized largely by merchants who had grown wealthy on the lucrative trade. Exquisite Roman glassware, bronze statuettes, and plaster molds for making silver vessels (together with Chinese lacquer and Indian ivories), were found in Begram (northwestern Gandhara). The lure of trade led the nomad Yuezhi-Kushanas in Bactria to take control of Gandhara, strategically as important as Bactria in the network of trade routes that linked east and west; it led also to the creation of the Kushana empire, which included Bactria, Gandhara, and Mathura (near Delhi).

The decoration of monasteries during the Kushana period (sculptures in gray and green schist, stucco, clay, terra-cotta, and paintings, of which only a few fragments have survived), the result of the intermingling of Greek and Roman with indigenous Indian traditions, led to the emergence of the distinctive and important Gandharan school of Buddhist art and iconography. The Hellenistic-Roman presence clearly acted as a catalyst to changes taking place in the Buddhist order. The most significant development was the worship of the Buddha in human form, in Gandhara and Mathura, a major shift from the earlier practice of using symbols (aniconic forms) to signify his presence. The Gandharan image was created in the mold of Apollo, the Buddha's robes depicted with classical folds, whereas Mathura used indigenous Indian prototypes. Another significant development, which began in Gandhara, was the chronological depiction of the historical life of the Buddha (a classical Hercules appearing as Vajrapani, his constant companion), following Hellenistic-Roman methods of narration, a departure from earlier indigenous Indian practice devoted largely to representations (generally in continuous narrative form) of the Buddha's former lives before he attained Enlightenment. Hellenistic and Roman motifs and mythological figures occurred freely in the reliefs: Corinthian pilasters, acanthus foliage, bead and reel, dentils, vine creeper, rinceau, garland and putti, atlantes, tritons, and sea monsters. Dionysian scenes appeared (popular in Bactria also), with figures, occasionally in classical attire, engaged in music, dance, and drunken revelry. Hellenistic traditions laid down during the Greek period were reinforced by the Roman presence from the 1st century CE, in the form of Roman artifacts (at Begram), and also, as the remarkably fresh treatment of classical forms in some monasteries (at Hadda) suggests, by the arrival of artisans from the eastern Mediterranean.

The Gandharan school influenced centers of Buddhist art elsewhere in India, whereas the Rome-China-India trade of the early centuries CE carried Buddhism, mainly in its Gandharan form, into central Asia and China.

BIBL.: Osmund Bopearachchi, *Monnaies Gréco-bactriennes et indo-grecques: Catalogue raisonné* (Paris 1991). Alfred Foucher, *L'art gréco-bouddhique du Gandhâra,* 2 vols. (Paris 1905–1951). J. Hackin et al., *Nouvelles recherches archéologiques à Begram, ancienne Kâpicî, 1939–1940 (Mémoires de la Delegation Archéologique Française en Afghanistan),* 2 vols. (Paris 1954). John Marshall, *Taxila,* 3 vols. (Cambridge 1951), and *The Buddhist Art of Gandhara* (Cambridge 1960). Lolita Nehru, *Origins of the Gandharan Style* (Delhi 1989). Benjamin Rowland, *The Art and Architecture of India,* 2nd ed. (Harmondsworth 1956) chap. 9. Z. Tarzi, "Hadda à la lumière des trois dernières campagnes de fouilles de Tapa-e-Shotor (1974–1976)," *Comptes rendus des séances de l'Académie des Inscriptions et Belles-Lettres* (1976) 381–410. Francine Tissot, *Gandhâra* (Paris 1985). R. E. Mortimer Wheeler, *Flames over Persepolis* (London 1968). Wladimir Zwalf, *A Catalogue of the Gandhāra Sculpture in the British Museum,* 2 vols. (London 1996). L.NE.

Ganymede

Son of Tros, eponymous king of Troy; because he was a divinely beautiful mortal, the gods transported him to heaven to become Zeus's cupbearer. Homer recounts the story (*Iliad* 20.231–235) without any direct implication that sex was involved, or indeed that the king of the gods was himself responsible for the abduction. It is Ovid who establishes the canonical narrative: Jupiter falls in love with Ganymede, who had been hunting on Mount Ida, and transforms himself into an eagle so as to bring him forever to Olympus. In subsequent tradition the story tends to be grouped (sometimes uneasily) with such metamorphic but heterosexual loves of Jupiter as Europa, Leda, and Danaë, even though it appears in quite a separate part of Ovid's poem. It would go on to be interpreted in ways that were as problematic and paradoxical as everything else in the classical tradition that is concerned with the performance of same-sex desire.

For Plato in the *Laws* (1.636D), the story is a fiction wickedly invented by the Cretans to justify their practice of pederasty; in his *Phaedrus* (255C), on the other hand, it is put forward as an example of the loftiest spiritual attainment, though not without a frisson of sexuality (when the lover and beloved embrace, they experience "the fountain of that stream, which Zeus when he was in love with Ganymede named Desire"). No opprobrium attaches itself to the tale in the *Metamorphoses:* Ovid tells us that this is the only occasion when Jupiter found something he would rather be than himself, and it is further characterized as the sole instance in which he brought his beloved to heaven rather than enjoying him on earth and leaving him there. Nor does Virgil (who pictures the scene of the abduction as stitched in gold on a beautiful cloak) disapprove, though he does suggest that the appointment of the boy as cupbearer, in preference to Hebe, helped produce the rage of Juno that in turn caused the Trojan War.

One might expect a negative view of the story from medieval Christianity, given its hostility to pagan eroticism and its anxiety regarding the homosocial world of monasticism. This attitude is borne out by a 12th-century column capital at Vézélay Cathedral, which shows the boy terrified, upside-down in the beak of an eagle, and menaced by a hellish demon. On the other hand, there is a considerable, generally covert, medieval literature of same-sex love, in which Jupiter and Ganymede are celebrated as heroes; and Dante—with, presumably, no pederastic axe to grind—borrows the Ganymede abduction story for a prophetic dream in the *Purgatorio*. It was the revival of Platonism, beginning in 15th-century Florence, that enshrined Ganymede as the perfect exemplar of the ladder of love, making the transit from earthbound carnality to ecstatic spiritual union with the divine—though the story never quite loses its associations with erotic heterodoxy. Thus Michelangelo produced a drawing (1533) of Ganymede floating serenely heavenward in the embrace of the eagle, but the accompanying message when he gave the drawing to his beautiful young friend Tommaso Cavalieri appears nervously cryptic. Less problematic is the version by Correggio (ca. 1531–1532), in which the ascent of the Trojan boy is paired with the descent of Jupiter in a cloud to make love to Io. From the Renaissance onward, if Ganymede often appears in contexts where homosexual desire is the text or subtext (from Cellini to Thorvaldsen, from Christopher Marlowe to W. H. Auden), many other versions of the subject are more difficult to classify, including the boy's astral appearance as the constellation Aquarius in Baldassare Peruzzi's Villa Farnesina fresco (ca. 1510), Rembrandt's terrified and urinating baby (1635), or Goethe's lyric of ecstatic pantheism, subsequently set to vertiginously modulating music by Schubert. The myth, along with its characteristic iconography, survives in the Eagle and Child pub in Oxford; its famous habitués J. R. R. Tolkien and C. S. Lewis always referred to it, however, as the Bird and Baby, perhaps to distance themselves from the story.

BIBL.: Leonard Barkan, *Transuming Passion: Ganymede and the Erotics of Humanism* (Stanford 1991). Vittorio Lingiardi, *Men in Love: Male Homosexualities from Ganymede to Batman* (Chicago 2002). James Saslow, *Ganymede in the Renaissance: Homosexuality in Art and Society* (New Haven 1986).

L.B.

Gellius, Aulus

Latin author (ca. 125–180 CE or later) whose miscellany *Noctes Atticae* (*Attic Nights*) ranges from literature to law, from wondrous tales to moral philosophy; one of his favorite topics is the Latin language, and he has a strong preference for authors of the Republican era. The exposition, in a mildly archaizing but never difficult Latin, often takes the form of dialogues with or between culturally eminent persons whom Gellius had known, or of reminiscences about them.

Although Gellius never counted as a major author in antiquity, in both matter and manner his writings were exploited by pagan as well as Christian authors. After the 6th century there is little trace of him until the 9th, when our oldest surviving manuscript copies of his works were made, containing either the preface and books 1–7 or books 9–20, and leading scholars sought him out and quoted him. The second part was known to Einhard, Servatus Lupus, and Hrabanus Maurus in the 830s; knowledge of the first part can be demonstrated for Eriugena and the school of Laon by scientific and literary quotations. In the same circles, a chapter explaining that palms were awarded to athletic victors because palm wood resists pressure was combined with patristric extracts on the tree (which had numerous Christian associations); the complex was much expanded in later manuscripts.

From the late 11th century, knowledge of Gellius can be demonstrated for France and England through florilegia, from the 12th through manuscripts and direct quotations; besides piquant tales and moral sentiments (not always cited at firsthand), he is quoted for ancient theories of sound and exploited for technical vocabulary. Manuscripts of his work are known to have existed in Germany; in late 13th- and early 14th-century Italy there are echoes in Jacobus de Cessolis' allegory of chess and quotations in Bartolomeo da San Corcordio's bilingual *Documenta antiquorum/Ammaestramenti degli antichi* (*Instructive Texts of the Ancients*), though direct use is hard to prove. Stories from Gellius were also retold in the *Gesta Romanorum*. By the 14th century a work on Alexander the Great's battles in Armenia had been concocted in Gellius' name.

From Petrarch onward Gellius became a favorite author of the Renaissance. More than 100 manuscripts were copied; in some he is portrayed in his study, and in one the great men he had known are seated together in front of his house. On the one hand, he was a valuable source of information, not least on the Latin language, and had preserved numerous quotations from lost authors; on the other, he presented that information with grace and elegance, sometimes in reports of discoveries in old manuscripts such as Renaissance scholars themselves were constantly making, sometimes in courteous debates among the learned that could serve as models to the cultured courtier, sometimes in demolitions of the narrow professional and the presumptuous ignoramus that delighted Humanists pursuing their own intellectual feuds—but always in handy installments with constant changes of topic to prevent the reader's interest from flagging. And his language afforded unusual words and idioms for writers seeking to enrich their style.

Not only scholars appreciated Gellius: he is quoted by Castiglione, More, Rabelais, Montaigne, and many other important writers; his reference to the philosopher Archytas' invention of an aerodynamic wooden dove led in the 17th century to attempted reconstructions. In the 18th century, however, new canons of elegance caused his style to seem less attractive, and compilation sank to a minor merit; nevertheless, the first translations were made then, beginning with one of ca. 1760 by the Quaker schoolmaster William Massey (Edinburgh University Library MS Dc 4.81). By the late 19th century Gellius was widely written off as a naive pedant valuable only as a field for source-critical speculation, though he still found devoted readers outside the academy; in the late 20th century scholarly interest revived.

BIBL.: Leofranc Holford-Strevens, *Aulus Gellius: An Antonine Scholar and His Achievement,* rev. ed. (Oxford 2003). Leofranc Holford-Strevens and Amiel D. Vardi, *The Worlds of Aulus Gellius* (Oxford 2004). L.H.-S.

Gems. *See* Cameos and Gems.

Genius

The idea that extraordinary creative achievement is the product of genius has a long and complex history whose roots go back to classical antiquity. From Homer onward poets attributed their gift to the Muses, and the inexplicable nature of the creative process was highlighted in Plato's influential account of poetic inspiration as a form of enthusiasm or divine frenzy (see *Ion* and *Phaedrus*). But it was also recognized that poetry depended on inborn talent, a theme that received its fullest expression in Pindar, who asserted the superiority of nature over learning. These two models, of divine *afflatus* and natural talent (Latin *ingenium*), remained standard for centuries to come; they were combined in Longinus' treatise *On the Sublime* to produce a theory of natural greatness that was instrumental in the formation of the modern idea of genius.

The Latin word *genius* designated a kind of tutelary spirit embodied in each man, not quite identical with him but intimately connected with his personality. Like the Greek *daimōn,* the Roman *genius* was born with each man and accompanied him throughout his life (see Horace, *Epistles* 2.2.187–189), the female equivalent being the *iuno. Genius* in this sense, as guardian spirit, was attributed not only to individuals but also to groups of people and to places, as in the celebrated *genius loci,* "spirit of the place," still familiar today. The notion of genius as an attendant spirit, allotted to every man at birth and more or less responsible for his character, was central throughout the Latin Middle Ages and remained one of the dominant meanings of the word until the 18th century. But during the course of that century a fundamental change occurred: until that time, genius as a personal, protective spirit had been something every man possessed; but now genius as an extraordinary creative power became the prerogative of a highly selected and privileged few.

This conception had been to some extent anticipated in the Renaissance veneration of artists such as Leonardo da Vinci and Michelangelo, supremely gifted individuals who were seen as having achieved near-immortal status through their transcendent talents (M. Kemp in Murray 1989). The vocabulary of "genius" (*ingenium, ingegno*) that had previously been reserved for poets was now applied also to practitioners of the visual arts, and the creative powers of painters, no less than those of poets, were likened to those of God himself. The belief in the divine capabilities of the artist is reflected in the epithet *divino,* which came to be applied increasingly to artists during the 16th century, most memorably in connection with Michelangelo, whom Pietro Aretino addresses in a famous pun as *Michel più che mortal/Angel divino* (Michael more than mortal/Angel divine). But though the Renaissance image of the *divino artista* prefigures the genius of later ages, praise of the inborn talent of the artist is always accompanied by an emphasis on the importance of discipline and learning for the production of great works of art.

By contrast, modern conceptions of genius oppose creativity and hard work. We see this opposition emerging primarily in discussions of poetry in which the neoclassical concern with rules and techniques was gradually replaced by an interest in the inexplicable factors in poetic composition and the effects that poets could achieve without the aid of rules. With the cult of primitivism and the explosion of interest in the sublime, sparked by Nicolas Boileau's translation of Longinus (1674), the traditional combination of natural talent and the imitation of canonical authors of the past could no longer explain the primitive naturalness of Homer or the apparently artless inspiration of Shakespeare, the poet of nature par excellence. Original genius came to be regarded as the essence of poetry, and what earlier ages had attributed to divine inspiration was now seen as emanating from the creative imagination of the poet himself. Aesthetic theory of the 18th century, with its emphasis on imagination, originality, and creativity as opposed to the mechanical imitation of rules, contrasted genius with talent and elevated the two great exemplars, Homer and Shakespeare, to quasi-divine status. Pindar too was seen as a paradigm of wild, untutored genius, together with the Old Testament prophets and the newly invented Gaelic bard Ossian. Key texts in the development of this new concept include Joseph Addison's *Spectator* essay no. 160 (3 September 1711), William Duff's *Essay on Original Genius* (1767), and Alexander Gerard's *An Essay on Genius* (1774). The most influential was Edward Young's *Conjectures on Original Composition* (1759), in which the mysterious processes of genius were likened to the hidden growth of plants: "An Original may be said to be of a vegetable nature; it rises spontaneously from the vital root of Genius; it grows, it is not made." Young's treatise had an enormous influence on the cult of natural genius among the German writers of the Sturm und Drang (Storm and Stress) era, also known as the *Genieperiode* (Period of Genius), and subsequently on the English Romantic movement.

Genius soon came to denote not only a prodigious capacity for imaginative creation but also the individual in whom that capacity was embodied. The accolade, at first bestowed on poets, rapidly spread to other areas of achievement, as Newton joined the ranks of Homer and Shakespeare as the first scientific genius, despite Kant's argument in the *Critique of Judgment* that genius should be limited strictly to the aesthetic sphere. Genius has remained a highly contested term, and its meaning continues to change with the changing values of society: it is hardly accidental that the archetypal image of genius for the 20th century was Albert Einstein, a reflection of the prestige of science in modern society and the quasi-religious awe accorded to its outstanding practitioners.

One surprisingly tenacious myth is that of the mad genius. Authority for this view is sometimes sought in Plato's metaphorical image of inspiration as a form of divine madness (*furor poeticus*) and in Aristotle's alleged statement in *Poetics* chapter 17 (the text is disputed) that poetry is produced either by a man of great natural ability or by a madman. The Renaissance conception of creative melancholy, derived from a passage in the pseudo-Aristotelian *Problems* 30 and epitomized in Albrecht Dürer's famous engraving *Melencolia I,* contributed to the development of the notion, also expressed in Seneca's much quoted formulation that "there never has been any great *ingenium* without a touch of madness" (*On Tranquility of Mind* 17.10). A belief in the alienation and otherness of the creative individual was a hallmark of Romantic ideologies of genius, but the connection between genius and madness took a more literal turn among 19th-century proponents of degeneration theory, such as Cesare Lombroso, who described genius as a degenerative psychosis of the epileptoid group and traced that idea back to antiquity.

The scientific analysis of genius, which began with Francis Galton's *Hereditary Genius* (1869), continues to flourish today among behavioral scientists and psychologists, but the concept has been severely criticized elsewhere as being both sexist and elitist. It nevertheless remains deeply embedded in our culture as a means of explaining the sources of human creativity.

BIBL.: Jonathan Bate, *The Genius of Shakespeare* (London 1997). Christine Battersby, *Gender and Genius: Towards a Feminist Aesthetics* (London 1989). Patricia Fara, *Newton: The Making of Genius* (London 2002). Penelope Murray, ed., *Genius: The History of an Idea* (Oxford 1989). P.MU.

Genre

The term *genre* is applied in classical scholarship to the literature of antiquity in two senses. The first covers major classifications of literature: epic, lyric, elegy, epistolography, historiography, and so forth. Each of these literary types has its own distinct conventions and history, and they often share little of either and hence cannot easily be aggregated or analyzed as a group. They are not the subject of this entry, however, which deals rather with genre in its second sense, genre of content. To this category belong genres such as the *propemptikon* (the address to a departing traveler), the epithalamium (a work celebratory of a marriage), the *prosphonetikon* (the address of welcome), and *komos/paraklausithyron* (the account of the activities and experiences of a lover in quest of sexual fulfillment). Genres of content entail the existence of certain flexible expectations about subject matter and tone on the part of the audience, and further expectations about audience response on the part of the writer. The ancient writer could, through generic writing, manipulate his audience by fulfilling or frustrating their expectations in numerous ways; thus, he might achieve a more economic, more subtle, and more satisfying communication with his audience than can be achieved when an audience has no (or few) predictable expectations.

Since genres of content originate in typical human experiences and social situations, it is no surprise that they are already present in the earliest classical literature. Homer, whose epics are full of "typical scenes," including specialized descriptions, speeches, and narratives, was regarded by later Greeks of the Second Sophistic period as "the inventor of the genres," and certain Homeric passages were later identified as generic prototypes. The dissemination of rhetoric in the Greek world over the 5th century BCE through the teachings and writings of peripatetic Sophists and rhetoricians eventually had an effect on Greek generic writing. An instance is the late 5th-century "Ode to Man" in Sophocles' *Antigone,* which embodies a more formalized encomiastic framework than do, for example, Pindar's earlier encomia and *epinikia* (victory poems): Sophocles was clearly aware of and responsive to contemporary rhetorical prescriptions enjoining the four cardinal virtues as the basis of praise. But only in the Hellenistic era (4th century BCE on) did generic poems start to look more frequently to rhetorical models. Thus, Callimachus' *Epigram* 1 Pf. is a straightforward example of the rhetorical *progymnasma* (elementary exercise), the *chreia*—an anecdote, pithy saying, or both; and Theocritus' *Idyll* 17 is a thoroughgoing rhetorical encomium of the subtype later designated *basilikos logos*—encomium of a ruler. Theocritus was drawing on the theory and practice of ruler eulogies in prose as composed earlier by Isocrates. These developments reflect contemporary teaching of the *progymnasmata* and of the three major divisions of rhetoric: dicanic (oratory of the courts), symbouleutic (oratory of the public assembly), and epideictic (oratory of praise and blame). The influence of earlier poetic models remained predominant throughout this period, however, as indeed it did throughout the whole of antiquity.

It is unclear when prescriptions and models for differentiated epideictic genres such as the *propemptikon,* epithalamium, and *syntaktikon* (the speech of a departing traveler) began to form part of rhetorical instruction. Convincing evidence emerges in the 1st century BCE: one strand concerns the poet-instructor Parthenius of Nicaea, who composed in Rome and introduced several major epideictic genres: the *propemptikon* and *epikedion* (mourning poem), which were taken up by Parthenius' Roman pupils Helvius Cinna and Licinius Calvus, respectively, and probably also the epithalamium, of which Catullus wrote two. The other strand revolves around the teaching of rhetoric at Rome from at least 100 BCE by "grammarians" and teachers of rhetoric proper. By the third quarter of the 1st century BCE, young Romans must routinely have been receiving formal instruction in the differentiated epideictic genres. Octavian's *syntaktikon* to the citizens of Apollonia in 44 BCE attests to this (one of his entourage was his teacher of rhetoric, Apollodorus of Pergamum). Many Augustan poets, including Virgil, Horace, and Ovid, exploited in their generic writings the synthesis of poetic and rhetorical stimuli to which Roman literature now had full access. In the reign of Augustus, Roman rhetorical interest began to move toward prose declamations—oral performances of highly sophisticated *progymnasmata* (*controversiae* and *suasoriae*). This naturally affected subsequent Roman poetry, which became more overtly rhetorical in style and content but remained in part concerned with genres associated with the higher branches of rhetoric, and which continued to emphasize literary precedents. In the 1st and 2nd centuries CE, Lucan, Statius, Martial, and Juvenal are notable exponents of this kind of writing.

Relatively little Latin poetry has survived from the years between 150 and 350 CE, but Latin prose (especially the *Panegyrici Latini,* formal laudations of Roman emperors) testifies to the continuing power of rhetoric. Similar testimony comes from Greek rhetorical handbooks from this time, the period known as the Second Sophistic: treatises on epideictic genres by pseudo-Dionysius of Halicarnassus and Menander (Rhetor) of Laodicea, and a work on *progymnasmata* attributed to the latter. They and authors of the Greek generic literature of the Second Sophistic and its aftermath (rhetoricians such as Choricius, Himerius, and Themistius) refer to and cite earlier Greek poetry and prose, particularly of the archaic and classical periods. A similar fusion of rhetorical and poetical influences lies behind the rich outpouring of Latin literature in Christian late antiquity: Claudian, Ausonius, Paulinus of Nola, Sidonius Apollinaris, Fulgentius, and Venantius Fortunatus are all examples. Paulinus' *propemptikon* (Poem 11) is paradigmatic of the quality and scope of this late Latin writing: of considerable length (340 lines of sapphics), it exemplifies the ethos and some of the precepts of Menander's handbook on epideictic genres but is clearly a work that has also absorbed and redefined the entire Latin poetic tradition of the genre.

Though the Byzantines retained—and from the 8th century on revived—knowledge of ancient rhetoric, and so were able to produce almost up to the fall of Constantinople generic writings, both in prose and poetry, that reflected the same combination of rhetoric and poetry as had characterized the generic practices of earlier centuries, the same cannot be said of the Latin West. The barbarian invasions and settlements in continental Europe, even when mitigated by the reimportation of Latin and Christianity from Ireland and Britain, obliterated many aspects of the culture of antiquity after 600.

One possible result of this in the generic sphere is conceptual discontinuity: it is symptomatic of this cultural break that the term *epithalamium* could come to be used in the Middle Ages to mean a poem in honor of the Virgin. Nevertheless, at least into the late 9th century some Latin versifiers were making conscious efforts to write within genres they recognized as ancient, so that some (especially Carolingian) writings can give an initial impression of continuing the traditions of an ancient genre. But this impression is, to a greater or lesser extent, delusory. Carolingian genre poems rely purely on literary antecedents, they show scant understanding of the associated rhetorical dimensions of their ancient forebears, and they have lost the lexical sensitivity of their predecessors and so employ a generalized poetic vocabulary that is rooted in classical Latin but is willing to draw indiscriminately on any Latin. The *propemptikon* of the Irish monk Colmanus to a homonymous Irish fellow monk planning to return to his native land (*Carmina varia aevi Karolini* II Suppl.) is a good example of all this, since in appearance it comes as close to an ancient genre as such poems do. It exemplifies a number of the standard propemptic topoi—for example, the departing monk is abandoning the speaker, he is urged to remember the speaker, and the speaker wishes him safe arrival. Such commonplaces, along with certain turns of language, show that the writer was familiar with older *propemptika.* But because the writer was unaware of the rhetorical prescription for the *propemptikon* and was not well enough read in the genre, his poem contravenes generic practice in naive ways. He combines excuses for not accompanying the departing monk (this is rhetorically inappropriate, since he is the elder monk and therefore in the superior position) with advice to the intended traveler (which is rhetorically appropriate from a superior). Linguistically, too, Colmanus' *propemptikon* is out of keeping with the ancient propemptic tradition. Like most Carolingian poetry, it draws heavily on Virgil—indeed, one line is lifted in its entirety from the *Aeneid*—but it is quite undiscriminating about the Virgilian contexts of its borrowings. Moreover, it supplements Virgil with a ragbag of phrases from other classical, late Latin, and near-contemporary authors, again with no thought about their original contexts. There must be a strong suspicion that what look at first sight like quotations of Lucan, Avitus, Hrabanus Maurus, and so forth in this poem are actually nothing more than plunderings of florilegia. In any event, the poem reads out of register from beginning to end.

Because of the cultural break with antiquity that took place in the West, the medieval Latin and vernacular literatures of the post-Carolingian Middle Ages make no pretense of continuing the classical generic tradition. They admittedly share numerous commonplaces, usually context-free, with the literature of antiquity, but they developed their own exclusively medieval genres of content

—the fabliau, alba/*aube, pastourelle, Märchen,* romance, chanson de geste, sermon, *adventus,* and so forth. Some of these new medieval genres might on the surface seem similar to ancient genres, but closer examination reveals little or no shared content or cultural contiguity. Dawn poems are a case in point. There are Greek and Latin poems with dawn as one of their themes—not all, it seems, members of the same ancient genre, although their precise classification has yet to be resolved. Similarly, the alba/*aube* is a well-enough exemplified medieval genre for which there even exists a brief prose prescription, albeit a puzzling and seemingly inaccurate one. The two traditions, however, are not comparable, and one did not develop out of the other. Dawn, love, and (often) a wish that dawn had not come are (naturally enough) frequent themes of both. But other concepts are more specific to one or the other: there is no trace in the classical tradition of the watchman who often gives the wake-up call in the Provençal and Old French pieces. The crowing of the cock or the song of another bird is the classical equivalent (and a lark sometimes features in alba/*aube*). Moreover, in their general ethos and overall layout and details, the ancient and medieval dawn poems are no closer to each other than either is to "dawn songs" in many unrelated languages and from completely unconnected cultures. Similarly, there is little to connect the *adventus* tradition of the Middle Ages with the classical *prosphonetikon* except that both celebrate an arrival. The classical genre was often employed to welcome loved ones; hence it concentrates to a larger extent on the warm feelings of the welcomer(s) for the person arriving, even when, as in Horace, *Odes* 3.14, that person happens to be someone of political importance, in this case the emperor Augustus. The medieval genre has a different pattern and feel: because it started as *Herrscher-Adventus* (marking the ceremonial entrance of a ruler) its essence is the eulogistic description of the arrivals of great men (or their equivalent). It therefore concentrates on those aspects of an arrival that dramatically confirm the power of the person being welcomed, such as the large crowds participating in the welcome and escorting the ruler into the city or monastery, the playing of musical instruments, and the people's vocal expressions of joy. From *Carmen* 20 of Froumund of Tegernsee, addressed to the emperor Henry II, to the Saint Gall lyric welcoming the relics of Saint Magnus to Walter of Châtillon's imagined account of the entry of Alexander the Great into Babylon, the focus of this medieval *Herrscher-Adventus* is always the status and general popularity of the arriving leader.

It was only in the early Renaissance that poets and orators again started to acquire the broader and deeper knowledge of classical Latin literature that enabled them to perceive the existence and workings of some ancient genres of content and so to imitate them in their own writings. Initially this process involved the influence of ancient poetry and prose more than that of ancient rhetorical prescriptions for genres of content. Parts of the writings of the late Greek rhetoricians were certainly available in Latin to the Humanists. By 1443 Theodore of Gaza had translated into Latin the portions of pseudo-Dionysius of Halicarnassus' treatise dealing with wedding and birthday speeches, and translations of Menander of Laodicea's account of the monody were also current in the 15th century. These translations (along with the titles given in manuscripts to some ancient poems) certainly helped the Humanists understand and use these categories. But, for example, in the wedding orations and epithalamia named as such that were being written and delivered from the later 14th century to the middle of the 16th century, poets were still looking mainly to epithalamic models in classical Latin poetry. An examination of some of the more distinguished of the numerous Latin epithalamia of the late 15th century—specifically those by Pontano, Naldi, Altilio, Bonomo, and Gigli—confirms this pattern. These writers were all Italian, but some commissions were coming from other European countries: thus, Bonomo composed his epithalamium to celebrate the marriage of the future Emperor Maximilian I and Bianca Maria Sforza, and Gigli wrote his for the marriage of Henry VII of England and Elisabeth Woodville. Among a number of classical and late Latin precedents for the wedding poems of these and other contemporaries, the Latin epithalamia of Catullus, Statius, and Claudian were the most influential; exceptionally, in Altilio's case a Greek antecedent, Theocritus' *Idyll* 18, the "Marriage of Helen," also contributed. To eke out the epithalamic exemplars available to them—and to make further display of their Humanist learning—these poets supplemented those models with copious allusions to and quotations from other classical Latin poets, most of which operate on a purely verbal level. Minor versifiers display the same limited generic understanding and background. For example, the numerous, mainly brief Latin compositions of the northern Italian poet Nicolò D'Arco (ca. 1492–1547) all have titles that he personally gave them (his manuscript, which survives, is an autograph). But only a few of the titles of Nicolò's 412 known poems go so far as to even evoke an ancient genre; rather, each of his poems links itself with classical antiquity by recalling either an ancient work or the style of an ancient author. The poet most often laid under contribution is Catullus.

The failure of late Greek rhetoric to have an early influence on Latin Humanism is striking but explicable. Manuscripts of both pseudo-Dionysius of Halicarnassus and Menander Rhetor were in circulation in the West even before the 1508 Aldine edition, but many Humanists either could not read Greek or could not read it easily. Even Angelo Poliziano, a Humanist competent in Greek and interested in Greek rhetoric, was not able to propagate his concerns. Poliziano in his autograph lectures on Statius' *Silvae,* unpublished until 1978, translates passages from Menander and pseudo-Dionysius (on rhetoric in general and on the *paramythetikos*) and he quotes in Greek from both authors' accounts of marriage speeches. But this aspect of Poliziano's lectures had, it seems, no noticeable effect on his contemporaries. Natale Conti's complete

Latin translation of Menander Rhetor of 1558 did have its desired effect, but it was J. C. Scaliger's *Poetices libri septem* of 1561 that fully reintroduced the Renaissance world to the rhetorical aspects of the genres of content. Scaliger drew much of his generic material without acknowledgment from Menander Rhetor, whom he read in the 1508 Aldine edition of the *Rhetores Graeci.* Scaliger's reworking of Menander relaunched into the Humanist world a series of ancient rhetorical genres, together with some new genres of his own invention. No one at the time seems to have been aware of the true origin of this material (it has been demonstrated only recently). But the *Poetice* launched a tidal wave of generic writing, mainly in Latin but also in various vernaculars. The information retrieved and recycled by Scaliger was disseminated by his own *Poetice,* but it reached a pan-European audience even more effectively via lower-level, derivative works. A highly efficient agent in this process was the frequently published *Sacrarum profanarumque phrasium poeticarum thesaurus* of Johann Buchler. This manual contained as an appendix a condensed version of the Jesuit Jacopo Pontano's *Reformata poeseos institutio,* in which Scaliger's entire gamut of genres of content was set out. As a result of the widespread circulation of Scaliger's ideas, the later 16th century and the 17th century were the post-classical high point of such rhetorico-poetical compositions. In Britain alone hundreds of books were published in this period whose titles announce that their authors were attempting to write within the categories recommended by Scaliger and his successors. The genres naturally continued to include those, like the epithalamium and *genethliakon* (a poem for a birth or a birthday), that had been composed earlier solely on the basis of poetic models; but these genres too were now prescribed in the handbooks. In addition, poems began to be composed in the genres newly revealed by Scaliger and his followers, and in the more specialized variants of genres known earlier, which the *Poetice* described. Richard Wills's *Poematum liber* of 1573 offered examples of no fewer than six death genres (some known pre-Scaliger, but now all neatly named and distinguished). Even in a peripheral area of Europe like the British Isles, the genres (including genres misnamed through misunderstanding) written and published in Latin from this time are impressively numerous: panegyrics, *eucharistika, apobateria,* protreptics, *proseuctica, soteria, hodoeporica, epinicia, prosphonetika,* prosopopoeia, to name only a few. Vernacular literatures also took up such genres, but not to the same degree: for example, in Elizabethan England Edmund Spenser wrote various poems to which he gave the generic titles "Prosopopoia," "Epithalamion," and "Prothalamion." But they are not particularly close to the classical models to which their titles point. By the 17th century such terms, when applied to English poems, as in the work of Robert Herrick—hymn, canticle, prayer, panegyric, "paraenetical," thanksgiving, vow—were mere formalities; they affected to attach a poem to the general tradition but did not follow through in their details.

By the 18th century the classical generic tradition was becoming moribund, and the Romantic revival of the late 18th century, along with the consequent decline in the teaching of ancient rhetoric in universities, meant that this sort of generic writing finally petered out.

BIBL.: J. W. Binns, *Intellectual Culture in Elizabethan and Jacobean England: The Latin Writings of the Age* (Leeds 1990). F. Cairns, *Generic Composition in Greek and Roman Poetry* (Edinburgh 1972) and "The *Poetices libri septem* of Julius Caesar Scaliger: An Unexplored Source," *Res Publica Litterarum* 9 (1986) 49–57. J.-L. Charlet, "L'épithalame de G. Altitio pour les noces de Jean Galéaz Sforza et Isabelle d'Aragon, dans ses rapports avec la tradition et la culture classiques," *Res Publica Litterarum* 6 (1983) 91–112. P. Harsting, "The Discovery of Late-Classical Epideictic Theory in the Italian Renaissance," in *Ten Nordic Studies in the History of Rhetoric,* ed. P. Harsting and S. Ekman, Nordic Studies in the History of Rhetoric 1 (Copenhagen 2002) 39–53. A. T. Hatto, ed., *Eos: An Enquiry into the Theme of Lovers' Meetings and Partings at Dawn in Poetry* (The Hague 1965). L. Cesarini Martinelli, ed., *Angelo Poliziano: Commento inedito alle Selve di Stazio,* Istituto nazionale di studi sul Rinascimento: Studi e testi 5 (Florence 1978). D. A. Russell and N. G. Wilson, eds., *Menander Rhetor* (Oxford 1981). G. Tournoy and G. Tournoy-Thoen, "Giovanni Gigli and the Renaissance of the Classical Epithalamium in England," in *Myricae: Essays on Neo-Latin Literature in Memory of Jozef IJsewijn,* ed. D. Sacré and G. Tournoy. F.C.

Geography

The contrasting fortunes of Pliny's *Natural History* and Ptolemy's *Geography* make those texts instructive points of departure in considering the classical tradition of geography, and they point to the limits of talking about that tradition. Both draw deeply on writers of the Hellenistic period, while reflecting concerns that go back to the earliest Greek thinkers; both draw (albeit less obviously) on the experiences of those traveling for military or commercial purposes. Geography of a descriptive kind is merely part of Pliny's wide-ranging Latin encyclopedia, whereas it embraces all of Ptolemy's technical and mathematical Greek work. Unlike the *Geography,* the *Natural History* was well known in the Western Middle Ages. But in the Age of Exploration both were read with renewed intensity and became intimately entwined with changing geographic and cartographic enterprises.

The elder Pliny (ca. 23–79 CE) held various civilian and military offices, culminating in his command of the fleet at Misenum at the time of an eruption of Vesuvius. His death, caused by respiratory problems exacerbated while trying to observe the volcano, marked him out as a tireless researcher, as his adoptive son admiringly recounts (Pliny the Younger, *Letters* 6.16, 20). Only 4 of the 37 books (nos. 3–6) of his *Natural History* are devoted to geographical matters, yet these would prove hugely influential in later antiquity and beyond. The *Natural History* reveals Pliny's extensive use of earlier scholars, both

Greek and Roman, including the lost "map" (or perhaps treatise) of Augustus' general Marcus Vipsanius Agrippa (e.g., 3.16–17). Pliny goes to great lengths to cite his authorities in the first book of the *Natural History,* Agrippa and Augustus himself looming large. The *Natural History,* not least its geographical section, closely reflects the sweep of Roman power under the *pax Romana.*

The life of Claudius Ptolemy, by contrast, is very little known: from his name at least it is assumed that he was of mixed Roman and Greek descent. It is for his astronomical work that Ptolemy is best known: originally named the *Mathematikē suntaxis* (*Mathematical Arrangement*), it was translated first into Arabic and then into Latin in the Middle Ages. For many centuries his *Guide to Geography,* or *Geographikē huphēgesis,* did not enjoy the same level of popularity; it was not translated into Latin until the early 15th century. This work offers both an extensive theoretical discussion and then a lengthy series of locations identified by latitude and longitude, together with brief commentary. Some 8,000 locations are "mapped" in the *Geography:* though it is unclear whether the original text contained illustrations, the coordinates themselves provide a means by which the entire known world could be set out. The technical difficulties involved in such a text, including the ease with which numbers become corrupted in transmission, have led to a situation in which the first critical edition of the *Geography,* prepared from a text made under the direction of Alfred Stückelberger at the University of Bern, did not appear until 2006.

Both works are unimaginable without the considerable body of earlier speculation about the Earth and its proportions and elements. By the 4th century BCE the notion of a spherical earth was well established (e.g., Aristotle, *Meteorologica* 354b). One of Pythagoras' earliest followers, Philolaus (ca. 470–390 BCE), even held that the Earth revolved around a central fire. Such examples warn us against any linear view of geographical thought.

The vast enterprise of Hellenistic science, more than anything, underpins both the *Natural History* and Ptolemy's *Geography.* What distinguishes these scholars from earlier ones is that there is a much greater degree of disciplinary division and specialization than there had been, say, in the time of the Presocratics. One figure stands out, yet is known only from fragments, mostly in Strabo's *Geography:* Eratosthenes of Cyrene. His insistence on a framework of measurement, calibrated by latitude and longitude, would prove to be of lasting importance and would make him in this sense Ptolemy's direct forerunner. In calculating the Earth's circumference at 250,000 stades, Eratosthenes compared the lengths of the sun's noontime shadow at two points, Syene (Aswan) and Alexandria. Strabo and others criticized Eratosthenes' calculation as an exaggeration.

The *Geography* of Strabo of Amasia is by far the major work of descriptive geography to survive from antiquity. He begins with a discussion about the size of the Earth and other theoretical matters (books 1–2), ahead of his detailed treatment of particular areas, their settlements, and natural features. Strabo moves around the Mediterranean in a clockwise direction, beginning with the Iberian peninsula (3.1.2 C137). The western and southern parts of the Asian continent receive detailed treatment, to some degree through the lens of Alexander's expedition. As recent scholars have pointed out, Strabo's geographical enterprise should be considered in close relation to his historical one, even if the latter work is now lost. It is also evident that the *pax Romana* saw an upsurge of interest in universal history among both Greek and Latin authors.

Pomponius Mela, writing around 44 CE and thus a generation younger than Strabo, composed his Latin *Chorographia* on a much smaller scale than Strabo's. Mela proceeded as a traveler, starting at the Pillars of Hercules (Straits of Gibraltar) and traversing the African coast first and moving in a counter-clockwise direction (note 1.24; 2.1). The terminus of the work is in Spain, Mela's apparent origin (2.96).

Pliny and Mela were destined to have a vigorous afterlife in late antiquity. This was in part through the *Collectanea rerum memorabilium* (*Compendium of Noteworthy Information*) of Julius Solinus (fl. ca. 200 CE). Even if his modern designation as "Pliny's ape" is exaggerated, there is no doubt that Pliny and Mela were his direct sources, though unacknowledged. Solinus was the first to use the term *mare Mediterraneum* (18.1, though in the plural) in preference to the older *mare nostrum.* The work is a series of highly derivative geographic texts, put together, often with pedagogical intent, in keeping with a late ancient penchant for epitomes and abridgments.

Such dynamics are more clearly visible in later texts, notably those of Orosius and Isidore. Some of these texts are part of a Christian milieu, and in many cases their geography reflects this. It was in the 4th century, following Constantine's adoption of Christianity, that a Christian Holy Land came into being, a status established and reaffirmed by pilgrimages. An overall consequence of such religious travel was the integration of Christian elements into Graeco-Roman geographies, even if some Christian texts owe little to classical learning beyond the use of Latin, and a distinctively colloquial Latin at that. Other itineraries are much more jejune, some restricted merely to places and distances in the style of the milestones that were their likely origin.

When, in the 5th century CE, Orosius begins his *History against the Pagans* with a survey of the space covered in it, he was providing a prefatory geographic setting in the mold of Sallust, whose *Jugurthine War* (17–18) he certainly knew; but by sketching a Mediterranean framework he far exceeded Sallust in scale. Orosius effectively added a spatial dimension to the universalist vision of his teacher Augustine's *City of God.* This is the frame for the successive human calamities that constitute Orosius' world history. Itself a summa of classical geography, Orosius' scheme would provide the shape of medieval *mappae mundi.*

Isidore's *Origines*, or *Etymologiae*, brought together vast amounts of classical learning in a compendium that would be central to Western medieval thought, in geography as in other fields. In contrast to Pliny's *Natural History* (one of his major sources), there is not even lip service paid to the critical evaluation of information or authorities, nor does his own experience play any part in the geographical section.

Standing far outside the Latin tradition of Pliny's geography is the *Christian Topography* of Cosmas Indicopleustes (fl. 545). The work of a merchant-turned-monk with Nestorian leanings, Cosmas's unwieldy Greek text presents an altogether different world, one in which classical learning is largely rejected in favor of a literal interpretation of the Hebrew Bible's cosmology. The illustrations, which were part of Cosmas's original text, depict his view of the universe (shaped like the Tabernacle) as well as of the flora and fauna he supposedly encountered in Sri Lanka.

The texts of the *mappae mundi* contain extensive extracts from what might well be called the Plinian tradition of the Middle Ages, which coexists with such explicitly Christian features as detailed coverage of the Holy Land, the centrality of Jerusalem, and the presence of Christ himself. Thus, in the 13th-century Hereford Mappa Mundi Christ is depicted sitting above the world, at the apex of the frame, his right hand raised in a gesture suggesting the Day of Judgment, whereas in the contemporary Ebstorf map (destroyed during World War II) Christ's head, outstretched hands, and feet frame the world at its four cardinal points. Other geographical texts, such as those of the Ravenna Cosmographer (7th cent.) or the shadowy "Aethicus Ister" (probably 8th cent.), also show the force of Plinian tradition.

But world maps constituted merely one facet of medieval geography. Dating also to the 13th century is Peutinger's map, which is unique in that it is enormously elongated (6.82m x 34cm) and emphasizes multiple land routes between Britain and India, marking settlements, changing stations, and the distances between them. The choice of toponyms points to prototypes and sources from the Augustan age (perhaps linked with Agrippa himself) up to the 4th century. Other features reflect a Christian milieu. This complex map is linked to no one time, as is clear from the fact that both Pompeii (destroyed in 79 CE) and Constantinople (founded in 324) are marked.

Whereas many types of medieval map were deeply classicizing, one category leaves questions: the portolani, with their detailed sketches of the coast and wind directions, have a practical aspect that evokes the periplus tradition of ancient seafaring. But in the absence of any surviving illustrations of periplus texts, such a connection remains somewhat speculative. It is undoubtedly true that these portolan maps both attested and facilitated an invigorated degree of trans-Mediterranean travel in the later Middle Ages.

Medieval Islam plays a major part in the classical tradition of geography, not least via the translation activity that took place at 8th- and 9th-century Baghdad, the newly founded Abbasid capital. There Greek treatises competed for authority with Iranian and Indian. Ptolemy's *Geography* was translated several times, most influentially by al-Kwārizmī. When al-Muqaddasi sought to provide a systematic basis for Arab geography, Ptolemy was a cornerstone of his work. Some, such as al-Mas'ūdī (d. 956), combined travel accounts with descriptive geography, though not necessarily in an explicit manner. Among later writers, al-Bīrūnī (d. 1048) wrote extensive regional geographies and also theoretical treatises. The work of al-Idrisi at the 12th-century Norman court in Sicily offered further adaptations to Ptolemy's scheme. Arabic scholars generally showed reverence for Ptolemy as an authority, even as their own theories and travels caused his information to be revised and expanded. The work of Ibn Battuta (ca. 1304–ca. 1369) culminates an active Ptolemaic tradition. Though the *Geography* received much attention from Muslim scientists and travelers, little of this filtered into western Europe: the Ptolemy they would eventually inherit showed few signs of his Islamic career.

Whereas both Arabic and Latin versions of Ptolemy's astronomy were well known in the Middle Ages, his *Guide to Geography* did not enjoy the same level of popularity. It was not until 1406 that Jacopo d'Angelo translated it into Latin. The 15th century saw not only the diffusion of Ptolemy's geography in the West but also, in its second half, the invention of printing and several major voyages of exploration. It is in this period that the ancient texts became better known, only to undergo more rigorous criticism than ever before. They were, after all, being asked to make sense of two continents of which their authors had no notion. It is in this spirit that Pliny and Mela received direct critique from Ermolao Barbaro (1454–1493) in his *Castigationes Plinianae et in Pomponium Melam*. Isaac Casaubon's edition of the entire Strabo (1587), though his first effort as an editor, would long set the standard for this text. The same ancient texts would continue to be subjected to scholarly exegesis and critique in the 17th century: thus Claude Saumaise's lengthy commentary on Solinus, more precisely of its Plinian intertext, in his *Plinianae exercitationes* (1629). The authority of Ptolemy received a fatal blow with the publication in 1543 of *De revolutionibus orbium coelestium* by Nicolaus Copernicus, who proved that the Earth was merely one of the planets encircling the sun, an approach that would be modified by Kepler. Yet Ptolemy's principle of mapping by coordinates would persevere.

The basis for geographical thought, including the Earth's dimensions, its relation to other heavenly bodies, and surface divisions, would receive definitive treatment in the *Geographia generalis* of Bernhard Varen (1650). Significantly, Varen's geography was not merely theoretical; his *Descriptio regni Japoniae* (1649) reveals a full range of ethnographic interests.

The concept of environmental determinism—the idea that climate and other environmental features deeply affect human culture—was common throughout antiquity, beginning with early Ionian prose. Both Herodotus ("custom is the law of all things": 3.98, quoting Pindar) and Hippocrates (*Airs, Waters, Places*) state this principle explicitly and reveal its deep influence, as do Plato and Aristotle. It was enthusiastically taken up in the Enlightenment, for example by Montesquieu in *Spirit of the Laws* (1748, esp. books 14–19). This idea was still debated by early 20th-century anthropologists such as A. L. Kroeber, who by contrast emphasized human agency; today the issue of environmental determinism is discussed in any course on human geography.

Alexander von Humboldt's journeys to South America and elsewhere around 1800 mark the point when it becomes less meaningful to talk about a classical tradition in geography. The many journeys in the second half of the 18th century, involving such people as James Cook and Georg Forster, produced a flood of new information. After 1800 the various activities subsumed under the blanket rubric of geography fast became so specialized that ancient writers ceased to be the sources of authority they had been. For one thing, Ptolemy's geocentric thinking was overturned by Copernicus's approach in the 18th century.

The changing relation of word and image is an important question to trace through any historical consideration of geography, though not an easy one when so few actual maps have survived. It is worth asking just how map-minded the ancients were in the sense that they—like users of Mapquest today—could have used either verbal or visual cues in tracing routes. The question and the analogy, further, make it necessary to consider the use to which geographic information is put—practical or scholarly, small or large in scale. Perhaps the greatest difficulty in working with the concept of tradition in ancient geography is the inevitable variety of spatial thinking and practices. It has always been tempting for later readers and scholars to retroject their own interests onto the complexities and silences of ancient geography. Arguably, it is in the mathematical system of latitude and longitude—initiated by Eratosthenes, developed by Ptolemy, and the basis of contemporary geography and geographic information systems—that Greek and Roman geography would leave their greatest mark.

BIBL.: J. L. Berggren and A. Jones, eds., *Ptolemy's Geography: An Annotated Translation of the Theoretical Chapters* (Princeton 2001). J. B. Harley and D. Woodward, eds., *The History of Cartography,* 3 vols. (Chicago 1987–2003). C. Jacob, *The Sovereign Map: Theoretical Approaches in Cartography throughout History* (Chicago 2006). D. N. Livingstone, *The Geographical Tradition: Episodes in the History of a Contested Enterprise* (Oxford 1992).

G.PR.

Gesture and Dance

A classical tradition of gesture and dance implies that the ancient civilizations of Greece and Rome attached particular values to bodily movement that ensuing European civilizations wished to preserve and integrate into an evolved moral and aesthetic conceptualization of order for the movement of the body. Any such sense of order entails some measure of gestural codification. But the ancient civilizations left behind no clear system for assessing the expressive value of bodily movements. The perception of a classical order for regulating bodily expression therefore derives from codifications ascribed to the ancient civilizations rather than articulated by them. The values that formed the classical tradition in gesture and dance were, rather, inferred from manifold images of the ancient world.

Surviving texts describing the expressive value of gestures and dance were and have remained scant. In his extensive and popular treatise on oratorical technique, Quintilian devoted only a few paragraphs to gesture, and it is by no means evident that he refers to commonplace gestural practices. Cicero, in *De oratore,* devoted even less space to gesture. The lack of commentary probably encouraged a belief in the idea that the ancients, cultivating decorum, modesty, and civilized self-control, placed a high aesthetic value on restraint of physical expression. In *De saltatione,* Lucian described a strange form of dance theater unique to Roman civilization, the pantomime, which was a kind of ballet most often featuring a solo performer who enacted scenes from myths. Lucian's essay was a defense of the pantomime against those who viewed it as a superficial entertainment. As such, the essay focuses largely on the subject matter of the pantomimes and on the theatrical qualities of the genre; it provides very little detail about the movements of the dancers or about the expressive values attributed to particular choreographic devices. Later, Libanius wrote another treatise defending the pantomimes, but he said even less about the nature of pantomime movement than Lucian. Nevertheless, the pantomime aesthetic constituted a performance tradition that lasted well beyond the fall of the Roman Empire in 410 CE and deep into the Romanesque era, when, as a component of aristocratic castle and manor entertainments, it fused with the Scandinavian skaldic tradition to tell, through dance, stories of heroes and mythic adventures.

Much scholarship on Roman theater has focused on the efforts of governments to regulate and even proscribe the performances of actors and dancers, and this focus has strengthened the perception that the Roman world placed a high value on physical restraint and gestural economy. Embedded in this perception was the assumption that the expressive freedom of the performers, combined with their low social status, produced a corresponding and perhaps infectious lack of moral virtue in them, especially in regard to sexual behavior. The poses of statues and certain figures in ancient paintings perhaps reinforced the assumption that one could discern "laws" or principles for disciplining the body to produce optimum, virtuous, transparent signification with no excess of movements, although such laws applied mainly to images of aristocrats or high-level officials, for in reality ancient art teemed with images of extravagant but inscrutable gestures and movements. The rise of the Christian religion was largely responsible for the disappearance of much evidence for ancient performance and for predisposing even intellectual elites to construct a classical tradition of stoic restraint, virtuous self-control, and symbolic efficiency of kinetic signification.

Thirteenth-century manuscripts of Terence's plays contain miniature illustrations of scenes from the texts; it is possible that these images are copies of long-lost originals, because of the way they display masks in a manner that was extinct centuries before. The pictures are remarkable for the dullness and monotony of the gestures displayed by the actors. Perhaps the religious authorities who employed the illustrators urged restraint in the representation of bodily expression, if, indeed, as some have conjectured, the illustrators based their images on attempts to perform the texts in theaters, which nevertheless seems doubtful, considering the lack of evidence for such performance. Rather, the point of the illustrations may have been to link the study of the texts and the ancient language to a rhetorical-oratorical disciplining of bodily movement, not to the text's power to animate the body toward a theatrical or dancelike enthusiasm for improvised display of freedom from a "higher" regulating principle.

The need to copy the plays at all and then to illustrate them suggests that the medieval world preserved an awareness of the power of the plays to inspire a performance style that required definition if it was to be suitable for Christian audiences. Such awareness was already evident in the seven plays dealing with Christian martyrs by the German nun Roswitha von Gandersheim (ca. 930–1002). These took Terence's plays as their model, but the strange organization of action and the turbulently emotional speech of the characters entailed a unique, "ecstatic" performance style. Hrosvitha probably wrote the plays for performance by the nuns in her convent.

The advent of the Renaissance at the end of the 15th century awakened a monumental ambition to align gestural signification with textual authority. The "Terence stages" that emerged in German universities around 1495 attempted to stage Terence's plays under conditions that the professors believed resembled the original performance environment: lecture rooms were given a proscenium frame and a *scenae frons,* before which students spoke the dialogue. The desire to revive other ancient dramatic texts led to a vast transformation of theater architecture and performance that was guided by a profound respect for the civic importance of theatre in ancient times. As scholars analyzed the texts, they discerned complex metrical patterns, intricate literary tropes, and elaborate manipulations of signs and symbols, all somehow rooted in the archaeological debris of a mighty but vanished civilization. The emerging Humanist consciousness sought to align the rational organization of language with a rational organization of physical expression. The body's signifying power, the Humanists proposed, would intensify if it submitted to universal laws of kinetic communication revealed through mystical or mechanistic theories of universal order. A civilization was great because it recognized the authority of universal laws to bring humanity closer to the realization of ideal forms. The notion of "regulating" physical expression by integrating the body into a cosmic system of signification governed by the rationality of texts was necessary to counteract the tenacious authority of the Church to discredit the ancient, pagan idealization of the body.

Perhaps the most ambitious effort to "regulate" physical expression on behalf of an idealized image of the body was the invention of ballet in the late 16th century. In 1581 Catherine de Medici introduced at the court of Paris an elaborate form of spectacle that combined dancing with music and spoken text. At about the same time the English court of Elizabeth I devised a similar entertainment called the masque, for which John Lily, Ben Jonson, John Milton, and other prominent writers wrote scenarios supervised by the master scenographer Inigo Jones (1573–1652). Originally only aristocrats could perform in these spectacles. Severely weakened by her failures and miscalculations in trying to resolve the conflict between Catholics and Protestants, Catherine de Medici saw the ballet as an instrument for establishing the power of the court to unify a chronically divided and undisciplined nobility. It was under Louis XIV (1638–1715), however, that ballet succeeded in achieving this political objective. Under him the ballet became more opulent and refined at the same time that it became professionalized; performers from different sectors of society were recruited on the basis of their capacity to charm aristocratic audiences. The king aimed to consolidate state power through a network of academies and bureaucratic procedures that regulated all aspects of culture to create a powerful national cultural identity. Ballet became rigidly codified, so that it could be systematically taught and institutionalized.

Acting underwent similar codification of gesture. The Comédie-Française, established by the king in 1680, became the model throughout Europe for proscenium-oriented state and municipal theaters, wherein the education of actors became a component of a larger government system for regulating the production and consumption of theatrical representations. In the *Hamburg Dramaturgy* (1769), Gotthold Ephraim Lessing described in abundant detail some of the strengths and many of the limitations defining the neoclassical theater aesthetic. He complained that the gestures employed by actors were too often cold, mechanically pantomimic, overly choreographed, and far removed from the ancient "perfection" of gesture they tried to emulate. "Of this whole [ancient gestural] language we seem to have retained nothing but an inarticulate cry, nothing but the power to make movements without knowing how to give these movements an accurately determined meaning." In effect, however, Lessing advocated that actors become more restrained, economical, and purposeful in the use of gesture than the neoclassical code allowed. The true classical ideal lay in the symbolic resonance of a gesture, not in its pictorial "grace."

Far more scholarly was the monumental treatise *Gesture in Naples and Gesture in Classical Antiquity* (1832) by the Neapolitan canon Andrea de Jorio (1769–1851), who compiled a comprehensive encyclopedia of physical expressions that he saw performed by people of all classes in Naples. These expressions he compared with gestures recorded in ancient Roman and Etruscan artifacts and images, and he discovered that, even though Neapolitans retained much of the ancient gestural language, this language was so localized, enigmatic, and lacking a clear relation to idealized beauty or virtue, that a great dictionary, based on extensive anthropological-archaeological investigation, was necessary to decipher it. But de Jorio's superb scholarship scarcely undermined the neoclassical fixation on a unifying ideal, for which the ancients functioned as proof of its eternal universality. The Romantic movement did not subvert the neoclassical aesthetic to nearly the extent that its proponents intended. Though major actors made highly idiosyncratic use of their bodies to fashion characters around their personalities, the codification of gesture continued to intensify until the end of the 19th century, sometimes justified with a veneer of "scientific" authority. Only then, when realism, as theorized especially by Konstantin Stanislavsky (1863–1938), began to replace neoclassicism in acting, was the theater prepared to break down the "fourth wall" separating itself from the audience and present "life itself," without by now enervating "eternal" ideals.

Neoclassicism, however, accommodated "life" more comfortably than the advocates of realism supposed. Middle-class culture found immensely appealing the idea that mastering codes of deportment, poise, and "attitudes"(understood to prevail in "life") enhanced upward class mobility. The teaching of these codes to people with ambitions outside the theater precipitated a new institutional apparatus. François Delsarte (1811–1871) introduced a hugely popular pedagogical method (Delsartism) that associated a presumed universal system of bodily communication with the revelation of moral character and a divine moral order. Students in Delsartean schools learned how to "read" bodies and then how to emulate the movement and gestures attributed to persons of a higher social class, who were presumed to perpetuate the ancient ideal of restraint, economy, and commanding symbolic resonance of bodily signification. Delsartism attracted numerous female followers, who saw in the pedagogy the acquisition of skills that improved their chances at economic opportunities or at finding a husband from a higher social class. Genevieve Stebbins (1857–after 1915), an American disciple, downplayed the idea that Delsarte's system was the manifestation of a divine will; she proposed instead that it perfected the reconciliation of voluptuous beauty with virtue, a theme of great significance for her many female students. She introduced "harmonic gymnastics," which fused the study of movement, gesture, and posing to create a refined physical identity that evoked an idealized "Grecian" femininity—uncorseted, diaphanously draped, luminous, bold, and yet elegant, decorous, modest. Her student Bess Mensendieck (1864–1957), a physician, produced her own code of movement based on scientific principles, which proposed that the signification of ideal femininity depended on equating beautiful movement with superior health. A more radical thinker than either Delsarte or Stebbins, Mensendieck used photographs of nude women to contrast the "correct" and "incorrect" performance of simple movements, such as bending and lifting, but, as she observed repeatedly, the idealized prototypes for such movements could always be found in ancient classical art.

The Romantic era (ca. 1790–1840) proved unexpectedly rewarding for the neoclassical aesthetic of ballet. The strict movement vocabulary of ballet expanded only slightly throughout the 19th century, yet it was astonishingly successful at constructing huge, extravagant narratives using Romantic, rather than classical, subject matter, and it was more than compatible with music that avoided neoclassical formal controls in favor of intensely emotional tonal structures. The Romantic world created by ballet was completely artificial, inhabited by exotic medieval or folkloric creatures: sylphs, goblins, exotic peasants, erotically inflamed princes, and fantastically ethereal women, who, as modeled by the great ballerinas Marie Taglioni (1804–1884) and Fanny Elssler (1810–1884), seemed to float and flutter across the stage like elusive phantoms of unearthly purity. But by appropriating Romantic subject matter, ballet not only exaggerated even further the neoclassical distinction between art and life, it also compromised the moral clarity offered by neoclassical principles.

By the end of the 19th century, however, a virulent reaction to the stagnation of ballet culture emerged. In Germany the gymnastics movement, guided especially by the great pedagogue Friedrich Ludwig Jahn (1778–1852), invoked ancient, Olympian examples of physical discipline to build an educational system that integrated intellectual development with muscularity, athletic prowess, bodily strength, and a healthy, "natural" cultivation of self-awareness. The gymnastics movement tended to follow scientific rather than classical principles of truth-seeking, but by the 1890s it began to absorb dance culture when pioneer figures of modern dance looked to the ancient world from a perspective different from the one that shaped the neoclassical aesthetic of ballet. Early in the 20th century the American Isadora Duncan (1878–1927) awakened tremendous excitement throughout Europe and then America by proclaiming that her style of solo dancing better achieved the "Grecian" ideal of dance than anything in ballet culture. For her, dance was the glorification of bodily freedom, of release from constraints and rules imposed on the body. She improvised her dances; she moved when the music stirred her and not according to any script or score; she emphasized the expressive power of her upper body rather than the agility of her legs; and she danced barefoot, with free-flowing garments and swirling hair. In 1903 she dramatized her affinity with an ancient ideal by dancing in the ruins of the Theatre of Dionysos in Athens, although she never linked her dancing to any serious study of the evidence for movement aesthetics in the ancient world. The invocation of ancient images of dance actually had little to do with recovering some lost or eternal ideal of kinetic expression; rather, the point was to establish the power of dance to reinterpret the past from a "modern" perspective, so that dance, like ancient art, functioned as an emblem of social and cultural transformation.

About the same time as Duncan achieved her fame, the Swiss pedagogue Émile Jaques-Dalcroze (1865–1950) introduced a pedagogic method, "rhythmic gymnastics," that attempted to reconcile the neoclassical spirit with the modernist spirit of improvisation. For him, images from the ancient world revealed the beauty and freedom bodies possess when they are not constrained by the determination of Christian morality to regulate and stifle them. He was hostile to ballet and indeed to any separation of performer and audience. Rhythmic gymnastics perfected physical coordination by strengthening the ability to listen to music, especially rhythmic patterns. Learning always took place in groups, so that a major aim of rhythmic gymnastics was to synchronize movements unique to the individual with movements forming a group, a task of considerable complexity.

The fortunes of neoclassicism in dance reached perhaps their lowest point in the 1920s and revived somewhat in the 1930s, when Igor Stravinsky (1881–1971) began composing ballets that glorified the "old" unity of restraint and freedom (agility) over the voluptuous excesses of the previous decades. In Nazi Germany the neoclassical aesthetic inspired a respect from theater culture that had been lacking in a nation familiar with Lessing's complaints about it. But this respect did not translate into work that established neoclassicism as a relevant or credible response to modernity. A happier pursuit of the neoclassical aesthetic appeared in the United States, with the prodigious choreographic work of George Balanchine (1904–1983), a Russian émigré and veteran of the Romantic extravagances of the Russian ballet. Balanchine made few, if any, additions to the movement vocabulary of ballet; his approach to performance was abstract, intellectual, almost geometrical, yet rich in affection for the formal tensions, the complex calculation of restraint and impulse, binding pairs and groups together. What made his choreography modern was his skill at creating a mood of majesty, elegance, even grandeur, without depending on the spectacular theatrical decor that had propped up the Romantic ballet. His control over his creations extended even to the physiognomic regulation of his dancers' bodies, including their diets, so that they perfected the image of women who embodied "the power to disrupt self-control." Balanchine greatly benefited from his collaborations with Igor Stravinsky, which began in 1928 and continued into the 1960s, but he was comfortable with a wide range of music and thereby showed that neoclassicism did not depend on its association with modern harmonies (or, for that matter, decor) to sustain its modernity. The neoclassical ideal that Balanchine perfected with the formation of the New York City Ballet (1948) allowed New York to dominate American ballet until after his death, and by the 1950s it had made America a dominant market for international ballet culture.

The 1940s also witnessed the extraordinary competing ambition to preserve the classical tradition in dance offered by the turbulent American modern dancer Martha Graham (1894–1991), the leader of the most prominent modern dance company in the United States since 1930. In previous decades Graham, though always preoccupied with "primordial" manifestations of humanity, had not found much inspiration in the classical heritage of the ancient world, which perhaps she had associated with an oppressive, decadent fabrication of femininity in ballet. Beginning with *Herodiade* in 1944, she produced for the next 20 years a highly dramatic, violently emotional series of complex group dances in which she cast ancient myths in her severely modernist idiom. For Graham, classical mythology was not the foundation for an idealistic civilization, but the articulation of primal, conflicting drives buried within the body because of their capacity to destroy the unity of the self and the unity of civilization. She revealed how demonic, archaic pressures, archetypes of tormented femininity, lived on in modern bodies, as manifested through an expressionistic movement aesthetic that stressed the contraction and release of inner tensions. By appropriating classical mythology when she reached the age of 50, Graham freed dance from its perpetual identification with youth and ethereal idealizations of a timeless but fundamentally immature femininity that failed to embody any serious historical consciousness: modernity for Graham was no longer about the glorification of youthful or emergent energies, but about the transformation of old, dormant powers into a new condition of freedom and openness to the future.

BIBL.: Gregory S. Aldrete, *Gestures and Acclamations in Ancient Rome* (Baltimore 1999). Marie-Laure Bachmann, *Dalcroze Today: An Education through and into Music,* trans. David Parlett, ed. Ruth Stewart (Oxford 1991). Pierre Louis Ducharte, *The Italian Comedy* (London 1929). Lynn Garafola, ed., *Rethinking the Sylph: New Perspectives on the Romantic Ballet* (Hanover, N.H., 1997). Andrea de Jorio, *Gesture in Naples and Gesture in Classical Antiquity,* trans. Adam Kendon (Bloomington 2000). Deborah Jowitt, *Time and the Dancing Image* (New York 1988). Gotthold Ephraim Lessing, *The Hamburg Dramaturgy,* trans. Helen Zimmern (1962, repr. London 1890). Nancy Lee Chalfa Ruyter and Thomas Leabhart, eds., "Essays on François Delsarte," special issue of *Mime Journal* 23 (2004–2005). Karl Toepfer, *Empire of Ecstasy: Nudity and Movement in German Body Culture, 1910–1935* (Berkeley 1997).

K.T.

Giants

Mythical ancient races of savage hominids. In Greek and Roman mythology, Giants were born of the Earth, fertilized by spilled blood (Hesiod, *Theogony* 51, 185; Ovid, *Metamorphoses* 1.152). Giants symbolize the forces of nature hostile to human life and civilization, always ready to devour or swallow it (Stewart 1984).

Early Christian writers interpreted Graeco-Roman myths in light of Genesis 6:4, which declared that "there were Giants in the earth in those days." The ancient Jewish myth attributed the birth of Giants to miscegenation between the "sons of God" and the "daughters of men." Later literature, especially the apocryphal Book of Enoch, interpreted this passage to mean that certain angels, attracted by the beauty of human women, had married them and produced monstrous offspring. Genesis 6:5–7 implies that when God "saw the wickedness of man" and decided to destroy all life in a universal flood, the Giants were somehow responsible for the enormity of human wickedness. Some authors decided that the Flood was sent expressly to destroy the Giants. After Saint Augustine (d. 430 CE), the great majority of Christian Bible commentators rejected the interpretation of "sons of God" as angels, since it implied a second fall of angels after the fall of Adam and Eve. Instead, Augustine and others declared that the "sons of God" had been descendants of Adam's good son Seth, and the "daughters of men" descendants of Cain.

This interpretation still implied a deterministic origin of evil, one based on race. Moreover, since all Cain's progeny perished in the Flood, Giants should not have reappeared afterward; yet the Bible speaks of Goliath (1 Sam. 17:4) and Og of Bashan (Deut. 3:11). Augustine minimized the problem by declaring that Genesis 6:4 means that Giants also existed before the "sons of God" and were thus merely outsized people, otherwise normal. Yet the problem persisted throughout medieval Christian historiography. Nicholas of Lyra (d. 1349), a widely read Christian commentator, derided rabbinical legends about Og, but he offered no solution.

In 1498 Annius of Viterbo solved the problem by radically redefining the Giant in forged ancient chronicles bearing his own elaborate commentaries. Annius's pseudo-author Berossus of Chaldea declared that Noah had been a renegade Giant, whose goodness and piety contravened the savage norm. Noah founded an Etruscan empire and established the Etruscan priesthood, becoming its first *pontifex maximus* and prefiguring the papacy. Thanks to Annius's Noah, Giants symbolized magnanimity and virtue for the first time; Annius probably intended them to inspire Pope Alexander VI and his son Cesare Borgia to unify Italy.

Annius's good Giants inspired more patriots outside Italy than in it. Jean Lemaire de Belges, writing in French, distorted Annius's forgeries (1512–1513), claiming that Noah, the first Gaul, founded the French monarchy, giving Louis XII right of empire. Writers in other countries followed suit, flooding European print shops with patriotic pseudo-histories. François Rabelais parodied Lemaire's pseudo-history in *Pantagruel* (1532), but in later novels he gradually succumbed to the charm of magnanimous, erudite Giants, transforming them into an enduring symbol of Renaissance achievement.

Since Rabelais, gentle Giants have peopled fiction as often as their evil cousins from ancient mythologies. Not until 1911 did the *Encyclopaedia Britannica* opine that Giants were probably mere myth, and fundamentalist Christians still defend the antediluvian Giants of Genesis.

BIBL.: Don Cameron Allen, *The Legend of Noah: Renaissance Rationalism in Art, Science, and Letters* (Urbana 1963). John Block Friedman, *The Monstrous Races in Medieval Art and Thought* (Cambridge, Mass., 1981). Walter Stephens, *Giants in Those Days: Folklore, Ancient History, and Nationalism* (Lincoln 1989). Susan Stewart, *On Longing: Narratives of the Miniature, the Gigantic, the Souvenir, the Collection* (Baltimore 1984).

W.ST.

Gibbon, Edward

British historian (1737–1794). His fame rests on his monumental *History of the Decline and Fall of the Roman Empire,* which covers the period from the middle of the 2nd century CE to the capture of Constantinople by the Turks in 1453. During his studies at Oxford Gibbon read works on theological controversy and risked all his chances for a successful career by converting to Catholicism in 1753. His father thereupon sent him to a Calvinist pastor in Lausanne for "re-education," which ultimately brought about his return to Protestantism. Gibbon made a delayed Grand Tour of the Continent in 1763–1765, which included long stays in Paris, Lausanne, and Italy. Inheritance of a fortune in 1770 enabled him to acquire a house in London and an extensive private library. From 1774 to 1780 Gibbon served as a member of Parliament. A memorandum he composed in French defending the British response to its rebellious American colonies was rewarded by the government with a well-paid sinecure and a new seat in Parliament (1781–1783).

In the meantime he had begun publishing his history of the Roman Empire. The first volume appeared in February 1776; a second edition followed later the same year and a third in 1777. In 1779 he responded to criticism of his interpretation of early Christianity with *A Vindication of Some Passages in the Fifteenth and Sixteenth Chapters of the History of the Decline and Fall of the Roman Empire.* The second and third volumes of his history were published together in 1781, bringing his account up to the end of the Western Roman Empire in 476.

The fall of Lord North's government in 1782 soon brought about the loss of Gibbon's government post. For financial reasons, among others, he settled in Lausanne in autumn 1783. There he completed his history, and the last three volumes were published together in 1788. The title of the work had not specified the period to be covered, and the great success of the early volumes encouraged Gibbon to include the history of the Byzantine Empire.

After a long search for a suitable topic Gibbon had settled on the history of the Roman Empire; because he had few predecessors it gave him an opportunity to present himself as a historian of great originality. He wanted to fulfill the expectations of his contemporaries for a "philosophical history," but at the same time he strove to present the results of his antiquarian research in a work of high literary quality. Gibbon was not the "English Voltaire" for which he has often been taken. This can be seen in his treatment of Christianity, which has often been read one-sidedly as a demonstration that the religion's success contributed decisively to the downfall of the Roman Empire. Taking the Protestant church historian Mosheim as a model, Gibbon asserted that the task of the impartial historian is not to take a stand on questions of theological truth but rather to analyze the factors that led to the success of Christianity in Roman society. He stressed the voluntary social isolation of Christians on the one hand and the development of their highly effective organization on the other to account for the Roman authorities' abandonment of their traditional policy of tolerance. Since this view had given rise to considerable controversy, Gibbon's assessment of the emperor Julian, the great hero of Enlightenment critics of Christianity, proved all the more surprising, for Gibbon charged him with having aroused religious conflict that endangered the stability of the empire. The historian's continuing account emphasized two points: first, that the Church diverted valuable resources from the empire (above all through its monasteries); and, second, that the Church became a last refuge of freedom in an increasingly despotic political system. Gibbon saw the seeds of this development toward despotism as having already been sown in the principate of Augustus, which offered only the "image of a free constitution" without effective controls on the exercise of power. Hence, the principate represented "an absolute monarchy disguised by the forms of a commonwealth." This criticism applies to the era of the Antonines in the 2nd century as well. When Gibbon stated that "the condition of the human race" had been "most happy and prosperous," he was playing on quotations from Francis Bacon and William Robertson; he did not intend it as unqualified praise. The "virtues" of a Marcus Aurelius and "monstrous vices" of his son Commodus are two sides of the same coin.

The significance of Gibbon's work rests on his new approach to sources and secondary literature. Even though he did not practice *Quellenforschung* (source investigation) in the 19th-century sense of the term, he possessed both a high degree of sensitivity to differences between different genres in the sources and also the ability to recognize the perspectives and particular interests they represented. Gibbon himself documented his source materials in more than 8,000 footnotes that amount to almost a quarter of the total text. They provide extended commentary on the secondary literature he consulted in a wide range of disciplines, including archaeology, history, geography, jurisprudence, theology, economics, and the natural sciences. Gibbon's pointed and sometimes mocking comments make for entertaining reading at the same time.

Decline and Fall is the only 18th-century work of history whose literary and scholarly qualities still attract readers in large numbers, as countless editions and modern translations attest. Scholars today continue to debate various theories of his as well, including Gibbon's interpretation of early Christian history.

BIBL.: Patricia B. Craddock, *Young Edward Gibbon, Gentleman of Letters* (Baltimore 1982) and *Edward Gibbon, Luminous Historian, 1772–1794* (Baltimore 1989). John G. A. Pocock, *Barbarism and Religion,* 4 vols. (thus far) (Cambridge 1999–2005). David Womersley, *Gibbon and the "Watchmen of the Holy City": The Historian and His Reputation, 1776–1815* (Oxford 2002) and Womersley, ed., *Edward Gibbon: Bicentenary Essays* (Oxford 1997). W.N.

Translated by Deborah Lucas Schneider

Glass

Glass, a mysterious material, ductile but impermeable like metal, transparent like air and water, colorful like precious stones, retained its age-old fascination even for the "barbarian" invaders of the Roman Empire. Isidore of Seville's *Etymologies* (mid-7th cent.), the last encyclopedia of late antiquity or the first of the Middle Ages, opens the chapter on glass (16.16) with the legend (gleaned from Pliny's *Natural History* 35.65) of its invention by the Phoenicians. In fact, it was the movement of skilled glassworkers from the Near East to the West in the first centuries BCE and CE that spread the appreciation for glass, which became a symbol of resplendent brightness (*NH* 14.3). Pliny speaks of its first use on a monumental scale on the theater of the aedile M. Scaurus, where the socles of the walls were decorated with plates of colored glass as well as marble and gilt wood, all ranked in a scale of preciousness (*NH* 36.114).

Thereafter, aside from the glass vessels, which were an indispensable ornament to the dinner table, plate glass and glass tesserae were employed in mosaic techniques, along with colored stones, in luxury pavements or wall revetments. The invention of free blowing in Palestine in the second century BCE, using hollow iron tubes, greatly accelerated production, especially of glass vessels and window panes. Late imperial legislation mentions highly specialized workmen such as *musivarii,* who made tesserae for mosaics, and *diatretarii,* experts in vases of cut or engraved glass. Under Constantine in the 4th century, glassmakers were assigned to corporations of artisans in precious materials, a status that they maintained throughout late antiquity. This changed in the Dark Ages, when they were forced into rural and extra-urban areas to assure supplies of fuel and sand. Their importance rose once more in the Middle Ages. Between the 11th and 13th centuries colored and painted glass became the emblem of the Christian cathedral.

Semitransparent colored glass had been employed on a massive scale in windows in private houses and in bath architecture since antiquity, from the early Empire onward, and successively in buildings dedicated to Christian practices. Early glass windows, with geometrically shaped panes from the 1st to 6th centuries and with pieces cut to form images of people, animals, and vegetal motifs in the 8th and 9th centuries, took on a role of increasing importance in the decoration of Western sacred space. The production of glass painted in grisaille (for tonal effects) began in the Carolingian period, but the first technical description of the procedure dates from the 11th century, in the treatise of the German monk Theophilus, who offers instruction on the manufacture of grisaille and the processes for making it adhere to colored glass.

By the late 4th century glass windows had invested the Basilica of St. Paul Outside the Walls in Rome with an air of preciousness and mystery. Prudentius compared their sparkling colors to fields carpeted with spring blossoms. Venantius Fortunatus mentions the colored glass of major churches in 6th-century Gaul and implies that in that province glass and other Roman decorative norms were still in use. In Britain, Bede tells how the aristocratic monk Benedict Biscop, at the close of the 7th century, called in glass workers to decorate "according to the custom of the Romans" the two monasteries he had founded in the north of England, summoning them "from beyond the sea," presumably from Gaul, to produce fine tableware and windows. It was then that the art of glass, almost lost when the Romans withdrew, was reintroduced into the British Isles.

The new overlords of the Middle East, the Umayyads, were not immune to the fascination of glass; excavations of their 7th- and 8th-century villas in the deserts of present-day Syria and Jordan have shown the influence of late antique decorative traditions such as modeled stucco and glazed windows. The Eastern Mediterranean was destined to remain the center of glass technology, especially of the production of precious vessels, through the Middle Ages. Here Roman decorative forms and techniques evolved into a whole new spectrum of precious wares. Some of these objects, of superb craftsmanship, have deceived the Western eye for centuries, such as the green glass plate (known as Sacro Catino) which came to the Cathedral of Genoa at the time of the Crusades; it was misidentified as emerald and taken to be the Holy Grail, the chalice from which Christ drank at the Last Supper.

The most famous glass vessel from the Roman past is certainly the Portland Vase (1st cent. CE), a dark blue vase with a white outer layer that was cut like a cameo to represent mythological scenes related to love and marriage. First recorded in Rome during the 17th century in the Del Monte and Barberini collections, it was acquired in 1778 by the English ambassador at Naples, Sir William Hamilton, and in 1786 by the Duke of Portland, who lent it to Josiah Wedgwood, who drew inspiration from it for the classical tablewares still produced today by the family firm.

Among the glass production techniques of antiquity, millefiori glass was revived at Murano in the latter half of the 19th century; the ever-popular round paperweights of transparent glass encasing a layer of multicolored rods encapsulate the magic of glass and of the city of Venice itself.

BIBL.: Francesca Dell'Acqua, *"Illuminando colorat": La vetrata tra la tarda Antichità e l'alto Medioevo attraverso le fonti e l'archeologia,* Studi e ricerche di archeologia e storia dell'arte 4 (Spoleto 2003). David Whitehouse, *Roman Glass in the Corning Museum of Glass,* 3 vols. (Corning, N.Y., 1997–2003). F.D.

Goethe, Johann Wolfgang von

Eminent German intellectual and writer (1749–1832). In the English-speaking world he is frequently identified as a Romantic. But in the German tradition he is regarded as the quintessential representative of German classicism, the embodiment of a fruitful—and some would say fateful—synthesis of German and classical, particularly Greek, culture. From the beginning to the end of his long and extraordinarily productive career, Goethe's involvement with the classical past was profound, idiosyncratic, and inseparable from his conception of himself as artist and human being.

He grew up surrounded by reminders of antiquity. As a child born to a patrician family in the Free Imperial City of Frankfurt, he was taught Latin as a matter of course, and as a boy he read the canonical classical texts. In 1740 his father had made the requisite Grand Tour to Italy, bringing back engravings of the principal sights of Rome that hung in the family home, a map that traced the route of his journey, and fragments of marble and ancient stone. His father also produced a narrative of his travels, written in Italian, called *Viaggio in Italia,* which not only instilled an unquenchable desire in his son to see Italy as well, but also inspired the much more famous *Italienische Reise,* documenting the two years the younger Goethe spent there in 1786–1788.

The experience transformed both Goethe and German letters as a whole in immeasurable ways. But Goethe had gone to Italy in search of Greece. At the time, firsthand knowledge about Greece was virtually nonexistent: until well after midcentury there were few examples of Greek sculpture in Germany; it was impossible to learn the ancient Greek language except by self-instruction; and most accounts of antiquity made no distinction between its Greek and Roman constituents. With the appearance in 1755 of Johann Joachim Winckelmann's *Thoughts on the Imitation of the Greeks in Painting and Sculpture* and, eight years later, of his *History of Art in Antiquity,* interest in Greece became fashionable. In 1769 Goethe viewed the most important product of that interest in Germany: the recently completed collection in Mannheim of more than 20 plaster copies of ancient statues, including the famed Laocoön group, which particularly impressed him. Indeed, the words Winckelmann had used to describe the expression on the dying Trojan priest's face—that they signified a "noble simplicity and quiet grandeur"—were to shape Goethe's conception of the Greeks forever after.

The work that brought Goethe European fame, *The Sorrows of Young Werther* (1774), offers, among other things, testimony to his intensifying preoccupation with Greek literature. The epistolary form of the novel allows the protagonist to speak in his own words, and the repeated phrase "I am reading my Homer" is one of the most familiar leitmotifs of the novel. Inspired by Thomas Blackwell's *Life and Writings of Homer* (1736) and encouraged by his friend Johann Gottfried Herder, Goethe understood Homer's world as an immediate and direct reflection of the world around him: as Blackwell wrote, "Homer took his Plan from *Nature.*"

But it was not until his play *Iphigenie in Tauris,* which he completed in prose form in 1779 and in its final form in 1787, that Goethe managed to fuse his perception of nature with a Winckelmannian conception of the Greeks, creating a work that was meant to be timeless by virtue of its indebtedness to that particular model. Friedrich Schiller obligingly understood *Iphigenie* in this way as well, writing in a review of it in 1789: "One cannot read this play without feeling a certain spirit of antiquity, which is much too true, much too vital to be a mere imitation, however successful. One finds here the impressive grand serenity that makes all antiquity so unattainable, its dignity and beautiful seriousness, even in the highest eruptions of passion—this alone lifts this product out of its contemporary epoch."

Increasingly, Goethe's view not just of nature, but also of humanity at its greatest potential, became identical with his view of the Greeks. Just as he thought that "the ultimate product of nature, which constantly heightens and intensifies itself, is the beautiful human being," so too did the Greeks stand at the pinnacle of humanity. Idealized portrait it might have been, but for Goethe this view of the Greeks as the highest representatives of humanity served as both an inspiration and a reproach. Perhaps his most ambitious attempt to meet that challenge, and perhaps for that reason destined to fail, was his dramatic fragment *Helena,* on which he worked for the better part of 50 years, between 1775 and 1825. One commentator has rather optimistically written that it is "no copy of the Greek spirit, but the complete evocation of it by one who has made himself a Greek and has only to speak with his proper voice, falsifying nothing, abating nothing, to make Hellas live again as it lived of old" (Fairley 114). Few would concur with this assessment, and even Goethe probably realized that if it really had been his intention to turn himself into a Greek, it was an aim that could never be realized.

Thus, like so much else in his later years, Goethe relinquished or resigned the hopeful dream of reanimating the classical past and in particular ancient Greece. Or rather, as symbolized by the appearance of Helen in the "Classical Walpurgis Night" in the second part of *Faust,* which was published in 1830, two years before Goethe's death, Greece finally stood as an eternal reminder of what had once been achieved and to what we should always continue to aspire.

BIBL.: Barker Fairley, *Goethe as Revealed in His Poetry* (London 1932). Henry Hatfield, *Aesthetic Paganism in German Literature: From Winckelmann to the Death of Goethe* (Cambridge, Mass., 1964). Walther Rehm, *Griechentum und Goethezeit: Geschichte eines Glaubens* (Munich 1936). Humphrey Trevelyan, *Goethe and the Greeks* (Cambridge 1941).

R.NO.

Grammar

According to Martianus Capella (*The Marriage of Mercury and Philology,* 5th cent. CE), Grammar was the first of the Seven Liberal Arts that the god Mercury offered as wedding presents to his fiancée, Philology. Yet despite the prominent position given to her, Lady Grammar's self-presentation, including a lengthy description of phonetics, morphology, and so on, was briskly interrupted by Minerva "because the council of the gods and Jove were bored" (3.326). This wry but acute perspective has persisted through the centuries. An important and wide-ranging discipline, grammar had in the classical era become the essential requirement for a deeper knowledge of literature. In later antiquity it also came to serve as the common cultural basis of both the lay and the ecclesiastical governing classes. A few centuries later, Martianus' medieval commentator Remigius of Auxerre (d. 908) could still maintain that "grammar is older than the other arts, since it was invented before them, and it is through grammar that we deal with other arts" (ed. Lutz, p. 3). But grammar was also perceived as a "first step," a "preparation" for something better and more important, especially for the two other arts of the Trivium, rhetoric and dialectic. Thus it was generally viewed as a necessary but ultimately unsatisfying (and tedious) technical knowledge, more suitable to be taught to schoolboys than to be appreciated as an art in its own right. Grammarians themselves, though highly praised as the "guardians of language" and guarantors of cultural continuity, were also a favorite object of satire on account of their pedantry, social awkwardness, and narrow-minded attitude toward life—a tradition stretching from Horace and the Greek epigrammatists down to the 12th-century vernacular Greek Ptochoprodromos poems ("Cursed Be Learning," for instance) and the comedies of Molière in the 17th. The study of Greek grammar, first developed by the Stoics, reached its golden age between the *Technē grammatikē* (*Art of Grammar*) by Dionysius Thrax (ca. 100 BCE) and the 2nd-century CE treatises on syntax and the parts of speech by Apollonius Dyscolus and on prosody and orthography by Herodian. In the Greek tradition, throughout the ancient and medieval eras, morphology and the analysis of single words were preferred to the study of syntax, an inclination mirrored in the bulky early Byzantine commentaries on Dionysius Thrax and on the

Canones of the 4th-century grammarian Theodosius of Alexandria, a systematic collection of regular and irregular noun and verb forms.

Classical Latin writings on grammar, from Varro (d. 27 BCE) to the (lost) *Ars grammatica* (*Art of Grammar*) of Remmius Palaemon (1st cent. CE), mainly followed Greek models. The most influential works in this field, however, were from later antiquity: two by Aelius Donatus (mid-4th cent.), usually termed the *Ars minor* and *Ars maior* (*Lesser Art* and *Greater Art*), were short grammars of the schoolbook variety, cast in the question-and-answer format; a far more significant third was Priscian's *Institutio grammatica* (*Grammatical Instruction*), in 18 books, written in Constantinople in 526–527 and originally aimed at a Greek-speaking educated elite that wished to study Latin. Priscian's treatise soon acquired (and maintained throughout the entire Middle Ages) the status of a reference work, copied and excerpted in hundreds of manuscripts, both for private study and for public teaching. Because it was both an exhaustive compilation of everything achieved in the mainstream tradition of Graeco-Roman scholarship and a starting point for all further teaching and research, Priscian's treatise also became a bridge between ancient and medieval grammar.

Of the basic subjects taught in the schools of antiquity, grammar—"the art (or science) of interpreting poets and other writers and the principles for speaking and writing correctly," as a medieval definition put it—was the only one to survive the barbarian invasions intact. The quality of Latin manuals, mostly bad reworkings of Donatus' *Ars maior* with some incoherent Christian additions, sank abruptly to a low level, and it was only in Carolingian times, thanks mainly to the efforts of Alcuin, that teachers returned to ancient treatises such as the "true" Donatus and Priscian. Yet even in the Dark Ages the "art of grammar" (as an inclusive term embracing anything from elementary literacy to advanced scholarly study of Latin language and literature) continued to enjoy a distinguished role in learning. This can be gathered from Isidore of Seville's encyclopedic *Etymologies* (mid-7th cent.), the first book of which is entitled "On Grammar," and from writings of the Insular teachers of the 8th century who held that "those who are not philosophers are not grammarians" and vice versa.

As a key to understanding the central writings of Christian culture, grammar became not just a descriptive discipline but a model of learning and interpretation that was itself productive of knowledge. Grammar acquired this status in the Christianized world owing chiefly to Saint Augustine, who described it as reason's tool for solving all problems of signification. Augustine also conceived of an ideal intellectual, devoted to biblical (literal and allegorical) interpretation and to a new secularizing and demythologizing hermeneutic of classical texts—an ideal later embodied by scholars such as Cassiodorus, Isidore, and Alcuin. Of these notable figures Cassiodorus in particular expressed an awareness of the ideological function of the discipline as the distinctive mark of Roman and Western civilization: "Grammar is the mistress of words, the outfitter of the human race, which, through the exercise of the finest readings from the ancients, is known to assist us with their wisdom. The barbarian kings do not employ this art; it is acknowledged that it remains only among rulers living by law" (*Variae* 9.21.4). The spread of interest in grammar is witnessed by the hundreds of grammatical manuscripts (manuals, commentaries, encyclopedias, lexicons, catalogues, etc.) that were copied throughout Europe from the very early Middle Ages down to the Renaissance. Donatus and Priscian came to represent for the West an incredibly powerful and influential canon: Priscian was even included, with his *Institutio grammatica*, in the series of sculptures of the Seven Liberal Arts at the cathedral of Chartres.

No comparably strong canon ever emerged in the Greek tradition. Byzantine grammarians generally were more inclined than their Latin counterparts to quote examples from Christian and pagan authors side by side (Homer and Demosthenes being consistently the most popular among the latter). Focusing, however, on the teaching duties of professors and schoolteachers, who regarded themselves as defenders of the pure language of the "Romans" (i.e., the Greek of the Eastern Roman Empire), they devoted most of their attention to the pedantic exercise of allocating single words to specific grammatical classes: hence the "epimerism," in which a line of verse was parsed to death, and the closely related but more elaborate "schedography," a dictation exercise concentrating on words and grammatical constructions that sounded similar but had different meanings and so were written or spelled differently. Epimerisms were usually presented in question-and-answer format, and their aim was to analyze important and widely read texts (e.g., Homer, the Psalms, Philostratus' *Imagines*) by posing every possible question concerning the morphology of a specific word. In the 12th century Anna Comnena (*Alexiad* 15.7) sharply condemned this practice because it threatened to destroy the study of rhetoric and philosophy (the *enkyklios paideia,* "comprehensive educational curriculum") and to undermine the deeper understanding of texts minutely dissected in this way. Syntax continued to be neglected in favor of word-by-word analysis, leaving little room for thorough study of the reciprocal relationships of the parts of speech within the sentence. Consequently, even the most distinguished representatives of Byzantine grammar (Michael Syncellus, Gregory of Corinth, John Glykys, Maximus Planudes) failed to produce the theoretical development and independent treatment of syntactical categories on the basis of logic (e.g., the distinction between syntactic and logical subject and object) that came to characterize "speculative grammar" in the Latin West during the 12th and 13th centuries.

This development, a great leap forward, occurred when the categories of Aristotelian logic were introduced into the study of grammar, leading to the creation of completely new theoretical principles. This can be seen first in the work of William of Conches and his pupil Petrus Helias (mid-12th cent. author of a monumental and systematic *Summa* of Priscian) and, later on, during the late 13th and early 14th centuries, in a Scholastic science of linguistic analysis based on the modes of signification (*modi significandi*). Grammar, for the *modistae,* became the autonomous foundation for a grand account of universal knowledge and was no longer attached to other disciplines such as criticism or language learning. Though they based their science on a reworking of Priscian's grammatical categories, the *modistae* assumed that the study of sentences led directly to an understanding of the nature of reality. Grammar thus acquired a far-reaching theoretical prestige on the grounds that it was universal (i.e., not limited to one particular language) and could be understood theoretically through the adoption of Aristotelian categories—not to mention more ambitious and pedantic claims, such as the notion that the first, second, and third persons of the verb mirrored the three divine persons of the Trinity.

Although speculative grammar produced remarkable achievements in the later Middle Ages (including a treatise on the subject written by John Duns Scotus in the late 13th century), it did not supersede normative grammar. Quite the contrary: in the early 1200s two fundamental tools for the teaching of Latin were written: the versified grammars of Alexander of Villedieu (*Doctrinale,* in 2,465 hexameters) and Évrard de Béthune (*Grecismus,* in 440 leonine hexameters). Both texts were heavily influenced by Donatus and Priscian, especially the *Doctrinale,* which aimed to cover all possible aspects of linguistic teaching, from orthography to syntax and meter. And ca. 1280 Giovanni Balbi's *Catholicon*—the third Latin glossary of the Middle Ages after Papias' *Vocabolarium* (1053) and Uguccione of Pisa's *Derivationes* (late 12th cent.)—included an introductory manual that began with the usual medieval division of grammar into "orthography, etymology, syntax, and prosody."

Latin grammatical studies of the medieval era show various interesting features. For instance, terms such as *res agens* and *res patiens* were used to designate that which "acts" (active) and that which "undergoes" an action (passive) respectively, and terms such as *suppositum* ("subject") and *appositum* ("predicate") referred to the position of words within the strict order of subject–verb–object, taken as the standard against which all sentences should be measured. Verbs, moreover, were classified according to their syntactical behavior rather than their morphology. And, notably, rules and principles were illustrated by examples from invented sentences rather than by quotations from ancient sources.

One of the earliest methodological criticisms of such works came from John of Garland (13th cent.), himself the author of a manual and, to a certain extent, the precursor of the new Humanistic grammar of the Renaissance. His fellow countryman Roger Bacon was also critical of this approach to grammar and, in addition, deserves special mention because he was the first Western scholar to write a Greek grammar (1267), based on the epimerisms and schedographies of the mature Byzantine age but also informed by the Latin tradition of Isidore of Seville and the Venerable Bede.

A renewal of interest in Latin grammar occurred in 15th-century Italy. It consisted in the partial rejection of medieval terminology, the reassertion of the primacy of ancient usage, and the gradual rediscovery of previously unknown classical texts such as Varro's *On the Latin Language* and Quintilian's *Education of an Orator* (esp. book 1). Quintilian's treatise gave a particular impulse to revisiting the connections between grammar and rhetoric, and the ties between grammatical and logical analysis simultaneously loosened. Nevertheless, the grammatical method of Italian Humanists was an expurgated version of late medieval grammatical theory rather than a radical departure from it: earlier works such as Donatus, Priscian, the *Doctrinale,* and the *Grecismus* still formed an essential background for scholars such as Petrarch and Guarino of Verona, and some of these works continued to be popular in European schools as late as the 18th century. Guarino's *Regulae grammaticales* (*Grammatical Rules*) (1414–1418), a very short, partially versified manual, was the first that dared to discard most medieval terminology and to adopt concepts such as concordance and regimen: it is Humanistic more in what it excludes than in what it includes. In the medieval fashion, Niccolò Perotti's *Rudimenta grammatices* (*Basics of Grammar,* 1468) resorted to invented examples, and the texts provided for student practice included the *Ave Maria, Pater Noster,* and other familiar material. Perotti's verbal system and his concluding treatise on epistolary style, however, introduced genuinely new elements. Some 25 years later, Aldus Manutius' *Institutiones grammaticae* (*Grammatical Instructions*), despite employing the traditional question-and-answer format, referred directly to the ancient grammarians and to ancient Greek and Latin texts.

In the same period Lorenzo Valla's *Elegantiae linguae Latinae* (*The Fine Points of the Latin Language,* issued in various versions from 1441 to 1449) marked the triumph of stylistic sensibility and the refined analysis of ancient Latin prose (following the practice of Cicero and the theory of Quintilian) over preoccupation with minute grammatical points—in a word, the triumph of rhetoric. Valla expressly disparaged medieval grammarians and lexicons as "barbaric" and described Priscian as a sun at times obscured by eclipses. The *Elegantiae* were widely quoted or exploited by later grammarians down to Francisco Sanchez de las Brozas's *Minerva* (1587).

The first visiting scholar to take to his homeland the new grammatical methods developed in Italy was the Spaniard Antonio de Nebrija (later 15th cent.), who had studied in Bologna; an extremely learned and versatile scholar, he wrote both (in Latin) a standard grammar of the Latin language—in which, among other achievements, he anticipated Erasmus's reformed pronunciation of Latin and Peter Ramus's distinction between *u* and *v*—and (in Spanish) the first grammar of Castilian Spanish. In these endeavors Nebrija was a harbinger of the increasingly close interconnection between Latin and vernacular grammars that was to become prevalent in the 16th and 17th centuries. After the Humanist debate about the value of Latin and Neo-Latin—in which "grammar" was often used as a synonym for "Latin" as opposed to the vernacular—the efforts of many grammarians were devoted to normative description of modern idioms, using the framework of the old Roman system (chiefly Priscian) with some medieval syntactic elements.

The first grammar of demotic Greek was composed by Nikolaos Sophianos in Venice in the mid-16th century, when Greece was under Turkish rule. Long before that, however, ancient Greek grammar had played a decisive role in Italian Humanism. Manuel Chrysoloras, the first Byzantine teacher to be called to Florence (in 1397), was an outstanding grammarian and the author of an influential textbook entitled *Erōtēmata* (*Questions*), published first in 1475 in an abridged form edited by Guarino (a rough Latin translation had appeared as early as 1471), then in its original, unabridged form in 1496. Though written in the usual question-and-answer format of the Byzantine tradition, *Erōtēmata* had the great merit of radically simplifying the field of nominal declensions, and it paved the way to a fundamentally new manner of writing and teaching Greek grammar in Humanist Italy. Along with other manuals of Greek scholars who had migrated to Italy, such as those by Constantine Lascaris (published in Milan in 1476, one of the first Greek books to be printed in Italy, and later the first book published by the Aldine Press in 1495), Demetrius Chalcondyles, and Theodore Gaza (the book from which Angelo Poliziano studied Greek), Chrysoloras' *Erōtēmata* enjoyed a success proportional to the ever-growing importance of studying the language. It also influenced the most successful Greek grammar of Latin Humanism, written by Urbano Bolzanio and first printed by Aldus Manutius in 1497. In the following century this phenomenon acquired an international dimension, and many other works on Greek grammar were published, including those of Philipp Melanchthon, Erasmus, and Guillaume Budé.

Both Greek and Latin grammar flourished at the beginning of the 16th century: by 1540 Greek was taught throughout Europe, Villedieu's traditionalist *Doctrinale* had been banished from the schools of Paris, and the ideal of the "trilingual man" (with mastery of Greek, Latin, and Hebrew) had spread throughout Europe, from Oxford to Alcalá and from Louvain to Paris. Some of the leading grammarians of this period (Thomas Linacre, Julius Caesar Scaliger, Jean Despautère, Peter Ramus, and Francisco Sanchez, among others) were educated in Italy. It would be impossible to trace the many different paths taken by grammar and grammarians from the Renaissance until our own times, but it is worth emphasizing that the distance between theoretical and prescriptive grammar (or, in Tommaso Campanella's words, between "philosophical" and "civic" grammar) grew wider and wider. Although the prescriptive approach, directed toward the teaching of ancient and modern languages, followed quite closely in the footsteps of Priscian and of the old Roman theory (no radical change in this respect can be detected down to 19th-century Prussian colleges and ultimately to our own schools), the theoretical approach was progressively enriched by themes and approaches with no roots in the classical world. Among the most significant stages in this diverse process were the grammar of Port-Royal in 1660 (treating living languages rather than literature and searching for elements common to the grammars of different languages); the 18th-century debates on the origin and formation of languages; the comparative method that gave birth to modern glottology (the scientific study of the history of languages based on a detailed analysis of their relations) in the 19th century; and more recent trends such as structuralism (Saussure) and generative grammar (Chomsky).

The classical tradition played virtually no role in these theoretical developments. By 1672 not only was traditional grammar, "which rules even kings and makes them, with a high hand, obey her laws" (Molière, *The Learned Ladies* 2.6), the object of satire, as it had often been in the past, but *grammaire* had now become a *grand-mère:* a "grandmother" whose descendants were to grow up and live in a different world.

BIBL.: M. Arrivé and J.-C. Chevalier, *La grammaire: Lectures* (Paris 1970). B. Colombat, *La grammaire latine en France à la Renaissance et à l'âge classique* (Grenoble 1999). M. Irvine, *The Making of Textual Culture* (Cambridge 1994). R. Kaster, *Guardians of Language: The Grammarian and Society in Late Antiquity* (Berkeley 1988). W. K. Percival, *Studies in Renaissance Grammar* (Aldershot 2004). A. Pertusi, "*Erōtēmata:* Per la storia e le fonti delle prime grammatiche greche a stampa," *Italia medioevale e umanistica* 5 (1962) 321–351. R. H. Robins, *The Byzantine Grammarians: Their Place in History* (Berlin 1993).

F.M.P.

Grand Tour

Travel on the European Continent, the Grand Tour was undertaken during the 18th century mainly by British patricians and particularly by the young, for whom it was an essential part of their education. A tour of Italy, which was the prime source of Roman antiquity, was the main objective. During the second half of the 18th century, artists, architects, designers, and scholars increasingly made the journey for professional enhancement.

The 18th-century Grand Tour was to be of major consequence for the development of classical archaeology. It was also to prove of major significance in the diffusion of the classical tradition throughout the visual arts and literature. British collectors, patrons, and artists (notably the architect Inigo Jones with the First Earl of Arundel, the first great collector of antique sculpture in Britain) had traveled abroad during the 17th century in search of classical antiquity, but the golden age of the Grand Tour (a term first used in 1670) was bounded chronologically by the treaty of Utrecht in 1713 and the start of the French revolutionary wars in 1793. At its highest level the tour was not only the climax to a classical education (as described by Gibbon in his *Autobiography,* 1796) but frequently led to the formation of important collections, the design of country houses and their parklands, and the promotion of archaeological inquiry. For example, Thomas Coke, later First Earl of Leicester, made an exceptionally long tour, from 1712 to 1718, which resulted in the creation of the monumental neo-Palladian mansion Holkham Hall, Norfolk, together with its gallery of outstanding classical sculpture and its consciously Arcadian landscape, and in the publication of Thomas Dempster's key Etruscan research, *De Etruria regali* (1723–1726). Other tours, such as the Earl of Burlington's two in 1715 and 1727, introduced the complex forms of Roman thermal planning into contemporary architecture and led to the sponsorship of Robert Castell's reconstruction of Roman gardens in his *Villas of the Ancients Illustrated* (1728). The artist William Kent, who collaborated with Burlington, created a range of informal landscape gardens with ornamental buildings, inspired by classical literature and mythology (epitomized by those at Rousham, Oxfordshire, ca. 1738, and Stowe House, Buckinghamshire, ca. 1735), which eventually had a profound influence on garden design throughout the European Continent and the colonies in North America.

The Society of Dilettanti, originally founded in the 1730s as a dining club for former Grand Tourists, was transformed later in the century into a learned body that played a key role in inspiring the Greek Revival movement in art and architecture, mainly through the promotion of significant archaeological expeditions and publications. The activities of leading members ranged from acquiring classical sculpture to be displayed in specially designed galleries (such as those of Charles Townley and William Weddell, whose collections remain largely intact, in the British Museum and Newby Hall, Yorkshire, respectively), accumulating and publishing painted vases (the diplomat Sir William Hamilton became a notable authority), and surveying and illustrating important Greek architecture (as did the architects James Stuart and Nicholas Revett, through their *Antiquities of Athens,* 2 vols., 1762, 1789).

Meanwhile, archaeological studies on the tour continued to stimulate contemporary design. Stuart, on returning to London in 1759, created the first neoclassical interior in Europe with the Painted Room *all'antica* at Spencer House, involving wall decorations derived from Herculaneum and integrated furniture based on a fusion of Greek and Roman prototypes. His rival, Robert Adam, after four years traveling in Italy and Dalmatia, fashioned a highly eclectic language of design, drawn from a wide range of archaeological sources and applied in an unprecedented range of media. Notable examples are to be seen at Kedleston Hall, Derbyshire (1760–1777); Syon House, Middlesex (1760–1767); and Osterley Park, Middlesex (the Etruscan Dressing Room, 1775). In turn, the Earl of Aylesford, aided by Joseph Bonomi, used the results of accounts of new excavations in Southern Italy (as delivered to the Society of Antiquaries of London) to design the first ever Pompeian Revival interior at Packington Hall, Warwickshire (1785–1788).

Given the increasingly professional nature of the later Grand Tour, the most significant artists and designers found study in Italy an essential part of their training. The artist Joshua Reynolds, as a result of his Italian tour (1749–1752), acquired a lifelong dedication to the classical tradition, which he consciously introduced into his paintings and teaching as president of the Royal Academy of Arts, founded in 1768. The sculptor John Flaxman was sent to study in Italy by the great ceramic innovator Josiah Wedgwood, who opened his factory Etruria in Staffordshire in 1769 to promote his earthenware products based on Etruscan, Roman, and Greek artifacts.

During the same era women (initially accompanying husbands and brothers on their travels) were beginning to make distinctive contributions to the world of the tour. The portrait painter Angelica Kauffmann was internationally recognized as a leading figure of the Roman art scene (as recorded in Goethe's incomparable travel journal devoted to the influence of the classical tradition, *Italienische Reise,* 1816–1817). Emma Hamilton (wife of Sir William, the famed collector of vases) devised while in Naples a pioneering form of mimed dance based on classical images; these became widely known as her "attitudes" and were published by Frederick Rehberg in 1794. Prominent among widely used books of travel correspondence were Anna Miller's *Letters from Italy* (London 1776–1777) and Marianna Starke's *Letters from Italy between the Years 1792 and 1798* (London 1800).

By the turn of the century, apart from restricted travel on the Continent during wartime, the gradual decline of the Grand Tour with the shift of taste from Rome to Greece was symbolized by the arrival of Lord Elgin's marbles in London in 1812, amid fierce aesthetic controversy, and their eventual purchase for the British Museum in 1817. Nevertheless, Italy continued to provide inspiration for architects and designers in the classical tradition as a result of major new excavations of the Forum in Rome, and at Pompeii. The increasing democratization of the Grand Tour continued apace, and by 1821, six years after the Battle of Waterloo, a regular steamship service was crossing the English Channel. Twenty years later, a network of railways was spreading throughout Europe, and the Grand Tour had been replaced by "A Great Tour of the Continent" advertised by the father of all travel agents, Thomas Cook.

BIBL.: Jeremy Black, *The British Abroad: The Grand Tour in the Eighteenth Century* (New York 1992). Brian Dolan, *Ladies of the Grand Tour* (London 2001). Jonathan Scott, *The Pleasures of Antiquity: British Collectors of Greece and Rome* (New Haven 2003). Andrew Wilton and Ilaria Bignamini, *Grand Tour: The Lure of Italy in the Eighteenth Century,* exhibition catalogue (London 1996). J.W.-E.

Greek, Ancient

"Rome withdrew its legions, Greece withdrew its language, and the Middle Ages began." The apodictic naiveté of this sentence, uttered in 1848 by the young Ernest Renan, can nevertheless serve as an introduction to one of the most relevant cultural changes between late antiquity and the early Middle Ages, namely the disappearance of Greek from both scholastic curricula and the common knowledge of the cultural elites.

After the decline of the cosmopolitan aristocracy of 5th-century Rome (the milieu of such distinguished philhellenes as Macrobius and Symmachus), the barbarian invasions put an end to the teaching of Greek in most regions of the former Roman Empire. Italy benefited to some extent from the cultural openness of Theodoricus and the Ostrogoths: the 6th century witnessed the work of both Boethius and Cassiodorus, chiefly translations of Greek philosophical and historical (and, in the latter case, technical) texts, but by 600 Romans had virtually no more knowledge of ancient Greek, nor did the Byzantine domination in Italy alter significantly this state of affairs. The more Greek studies were delegated to monastic centers, the more Greek acquired the "sacral" dimension of a holy language (from Augustine through Isidore of Seville), the more the gap between pagan and Christian culture widened. Knowledge of Greek, already (though rather hypocritically) deemed worthless by Jerome, became increasingly rare, and what remained was a fading interest in Christian exegesis, liturgy, and ecclesiastical rite. An interesting case in point is Dionysius the Small, who translated Greek hagiographies and conciliar canons and in 532 introduced—on the basis of his knowledge of ancient chronology—the system of dating *post Christum natum,* which we still use today.

During the early Middle Ages, Western scholars were acquainted with scattered Greek glossaries and rare bilingual manuscripts, chiefly of religious content. In some cities, parts of the Mass were read or sung in Greek, and the Greek alphabet was often endowed with the mystic value that pertains to things exotic. No systematic study of the language was possible, given the lack of grammars or teaching tools designed for the needs of Latin-speaking students. Latin lexicography, although it did provide medieval writers with some attractive Greek-sounding gems, embraced mistakes and fanciful etymologies, as can be seen in the dictionary of Papias, and later in Eberhard of Béthune's *Grecismus* and in Hugutio's *Derivationes.* From the late 7th to the 9th century an elementary practice of the language is attested in Ireland, and the emigration of Irish scholars to Carolingian monasteries elicited on the Continent a sporadic interest in Greek in the field of testamentary and patristic erudition. The most relevant case was represented by John Scotus Eriugena, who in the second half of the 9th century translated pseudo-Dionysius the Areopagite's *Heavenly Hierarchy* and also gave a Greek title to one of his theological works. In Italy, despite the persistence of some contact with Greek, no great achievements were recorded apart from Anastasius Bibliothecarius' translations of ecclesiastical literature, whereas the only remarkable cultural output of the growing diplomatic and political exchange with the Byzantine empire (from Charlemagne to Ottonian times and beyond) was the work of Liutprand of Cremona (mid-10th cent.), whose *Antapodosis* is full of Greek words and phrases designed to embellish the Latin style.

A renewed interest in ancient Greek arose in Italy during the 12th century: men such as Moses of Bergamo, Jacobus Venetus, Burgundio of Pisa, and Leo Tuscus traveled to Constantinople for diplomatic or commercial reasons and became familiar with ancient Greek to the point of engaging in important translations of philosophical, ecclesiastical, and technical texts, from Aristotle to Galen to the Church Fathers. Yet this cannot be considered a "humanistic" approach (the language did not carry any content relating to classical culture in the proper sense), nor did any organic change in favor of Greek studies take place. Even in the 13th century (an age when most of the Greek-speaking world was under Latin rule, 1204–1261), knowledge of the ancient language remained the privilege of single individuals: very few scholars embarked on translations (notably William of Moerbeke, who settled in the Peloponnese and translated Aristotle's *Politics*) and no schools were created—even such an innovative work as Roger Bacon's Greek grammar (1268) remained largely ignored. When the Council of Vienne (1311) recommended that the major European universities introduce the study of Greek (along with Hebrew, Arabic, and Syriac), it was in vain.

The first real (albeit unsuccessful) attempt to restore Greek studies in the West originated in 14th-century Italy, and this time it was indeed in response to a "protohumanistic" attitude. Prompted by the innumerable references to Greek literature scattered in the classical Latin authors he loved to unearth and peruse, Petrarch wished to read Homer, which had remained a closed book for the Latin Middle Ages. In 1360, with Boccaccio's help, he engaged a Greek-speaking Calabrian named Leonzio Pilato to teach Greek in Florence and to translate for him both the *Iliad* and *Odyssey.* Not only were Pilato's character and doctrine rather disappointing in Petrarch's eyes, and not only was his word-for-word translation anything but satisfying on the literary and stylistic levels, but this seed did not fructify at all in contemporary Italy: Pilato left in 1363, by which time he had not held regular courses, and his only Italian pupil, Boccaccio, had proved an unpromising Hellenist. More generally, the venture's failure is an example of the scarce effect produced on rising Humanism by the tradition of classical Greek studies in southern Italy, a tradition that had produced one of its best fruits in the 12th century with Henricus Aristippus' translations of some Platonic dialogues.

Thirty years after Pilato, the first chair of Greek in the West was held by a distinguished Byzantine scholar. When Manuel Chrysoloras, invited by the Florentine chancellor Coluccio Salutati, was appointed in Florence in 1397, few could have foreseen that his influence would reach far beyond the years of his stay. Chrysoloras (who later taught in Pavia and Rome) gave much-attended lectures, produced the first Greek grammar in the West, and above all succeeded in developing an interest in ancient Greek in a wider circle of young Italian scholars, who in their turn promoted Greek as one of the main components of Humanism.

This step was of the utmost importance: Greek became the first language in the Christian West to be taught as a purely scholarly language. Virtually all Chrysoloras' successors in the 15th century—and particularly after the fall of the Byzantine empire in 1453—were Greek refugees fleeing their troubled fatherland (and often willing to incite Westerners to a crusade against the Turks): among others, Demetrius Chalcondylas, Theodore Gaza, John Argyropoulos, and Constantine Lascaris. These scholars followed a traditional pedagogic method, leading from alphabet and morphology to grammatical and stylistic commentary on a text, yet they had to face the fact that in Italy, from the very beginning, Greek was taught in Latin, and Greek language and literature were not studied per se but rather as adjuncts to Latin. All orators praising Greek letters, from Gaza to Pietro Bembo (with the remarkable exception of the Cretan Michael Apostolis, who in 1472 pleaded for a monolingual approach), insisted precisely on this filiation of Latin from Greek—in the field of grammar as well as in all domains of wisdom—as one of the main reasons for studying the language in the first place. This is why a teacher's syllabus had to include a further essential step, namely translation, which became immediately—from Leonardo Bruni to Lorenzo Valla and beyond—both a subsidiary means of practicing the language and a literary activity in its own right. And sometimes the teachers were actually Italian: the most well-known being Guarino of Verona, who taught Greek to an international audience in Ferrara, and Vittorino da Feltre, who gave Greek a place of honor in the curriculum of his innovative school at Mantua.

The multiplication of Greek manuscripts brought from the Levant and collected in the new libraries of Italy, the new interest in hitherto unknown classical texts, the philosophical weight of Plato and Platonism, an enhanced sensibility for the historical evolution of ancient Greek, a new philological approach based on textual criticism and on more direct contact with ancient writings (some Humanists, from Francesco Filelfo to Angelo Poliziano, even tried their hand at composing epistles and epigrams in Greek): all these elements contributed to a gradual reshaping of the teaching of Greek during the later 15th century. The old Byzantine style was slowly replaced by new grammars (carrying examples from classical authors), new working tools (e.g., the Greek-Latin dictionary produced at the end of the century by the Carmelite monk Giovanni Crastone), and the first printed editions of ancient Greek literature. In the last field, the main achievement was that of Aldus Manutius in Venice (1495–1515): besides publishing the first and most relevant series of Greek texts in Europe, following a wonderful if utopian project of Hellenocentric culture that was ultimately deemed a failure, Aldus was also the host in the early 1500s of a club of Greek scholars called the New Academy, whose members were compelled to speak to each other exclusively in Greek.

That Erasmus of Rotterdam was for a while a member of this club testifies to the fact that the time was ripe for an international diffusion of Greek studies. Certainly many German, French, and English scholars had come to Italy to learn Greek during the 15th century, and Greek Humanism had already borne its first fruits in central Europe; but it was thanks to Erasmus that the Greek language became a fundamental element of the European intellectual identity. This happened not only because in his travels and in his correspondence with other scholars Erasmus unceasingly propagated the idea that Greek had brought Europe out of the Middle Ages and should therefore be learned by all, but also because—in the wake of Lorenzo Valla's example—he dared apply his knowledge of the language to the study of the New Testament, of which he provided the *editio princeps* in 1516. By restoring a reliable text on the authority of the manuscripts, and by correcting the Vulgate Latin translation that had become standard in Western liturgy and culture, Erasmus used Greek to challenge the authority of the Church. The importance of the language was no longer confined to small intellectual circles or Humanistic debates: Greek had bearings on matters of interest for every single Christian. Erasmus's free attitude toward the Holy Writ inevitably led his contemporaries to detect in him (as well as in the German Johannes Reuchlin, who had done a similar job with Hebrew) a proto-Lutheran stand, all the more so when Martin Luther used Erasmus's text for his German translation of the Gospels. As a matter of fact—despite Erasmus's orthodox appeal for the separation of Humanism from the Reformation in his *On Free Will* (1524)—the paths of Greek scholarship and Protestantism were converging in that they answered the same need for a purer and sounder approach to the Bible.

Hostility toward Greek studies, which had been kept to a minimum in 15th-century Italy, now shifted on the ideological level: for many intellectuals (even former members of Aldus's New Academy, such as Hieronymus Aleander and Alberto Pio da Carpi), learning Greek was heresy. This shift took place at a moment when all European universities were concerned with the institution of chairs of Greek: Pope Leo X had opened the short-lived Collegio Greco in Rome in 1514; Reuchlin, Celtis, Melanchthon, and others had been appointed in various German universities; Erasmus himself was involved in the foundation of the Collegium Trilingue at Louvain (1518). The inaugural lecture there was delivered by the Erasmian Petrus Mosellanus, who argued for the superiority of Pentecost over Babel and insisted that theology could not be properly studied without a deep and wide linguistic knowledge; still more clearly, Philipp Melanchthon proclaimed in Wittenberg in 1518 that "it is impossible that, if Greek is despised, the care for sacred matters should not disappear" (again in 1549: "The Greek language is the teacher and, so to speak, the fountainhead not only of the celestial doctrine but of all learning").

Anti-Erasmians proliferated, however, particularly in France, before and after the institution of a prominent chair of Greek at the Collège Royal, founded by Francis I in 1529 under the guidance of the great Hellenist Guillaume Budé. These opponents attacked Greek as the impious language of Homer and Lucian, extolled linguistic ignorance as the most genuine form of faith, and praised the non-Hellenized Augustine for his spontaneous understanding of the Holy Writ; in a word, they did not accept the limitation of heresy to the *res* rather than to the *lingua,* proposed by the Spaniard Juan Luis Vives in 1531. The eyewitness Nicolas Bobadilla (later a founder of the Jesuit order) reported that among the scholars burned at the stake at Maubert in Paris in 1534, "the Greek-speaking ones were Lutherans."

Yet the success of "Grecomania" in 16th-century France, from Francis I to the Valois dynasty, is shown by the study and reception of Greek language and literature from Budé to Ronsard, from Dorat to Rabelais (Budé's bulky *Commentaries of the Greek Language,* published in 1529, is the first comprehensive attempt to describe syntactical and stylistic features on the basis of quotations from ancient sources), and also by the political value attached to Greek by the ruling dynasties. On the strictly linguistic level, one need only think of the numerous scholarly works postulating derivation of French from Greek, building on the old story that the Druids used Greek characters (this is the theory of "Celt-Hellenism" espoused by Léon Trippault and the distinguished editor Henri Estienne), or of Greek from Old Gaul (Jean Picard, Guillaume Postel, Pierre de la Ramée). These fanciful genealogies originated in a time when the quest for the origin of vernacular French reflected the need for a noble descent of the French population, which many, from Jean Lemaire de Belges to the poet Ronsard, traced back to the (Greek-speaking) Trojans; no wonder, then, that the Trojan Paris could be regarded by some as the eponymous hero of the French capital.

Similar genealogical claims were made for other languages as well: affinities between Greek and Italian words were detected by Raffaele Maffei as early as 1506; a Greek origin was argued for Welsh by John Price in 1573, and for Old British by the Oxford linguist Robert Sheringham in 1670 (this recalls Geoffrey of Monmouth's idea that London was founded by Aeneas' son Brutus); a special link between Greek and German (again via the Druids) was postulated by Konrad Celtis in 1497, and then by Luther himself. The derivation of Greek from Hebrew remained for centuries a very popular idea.

The battle for the survival of Greek studies fought in France, Germany, and the Low Countries in the years around 1520 resulted eventually in a partial victory in Protestant Europe and a defeat in the Catholic one. Especially after the Council of Trent, studies of classical Greek—little practiced even in Jesuit schools—disappeared almost entirely from Italy and Spain, where scholars devoted their efforts to a new kind of Christian Latin Humanism. (The last great Italian Hellenist was Pier Vettori, 1499–1585.) The same climate of the Counter-Reformation also abated the interest of the French, where Greek came to be identified with Aristotelian doctrine and Christian apologetic texts. In France, however, this negative trend was enhanced by other factors: the wars of religion forced many philologists to leave the country (among them Joseph Justus Scaliger, Isaac Casaubon, and Henri Estienne, the compiler in 1572 of the invaluable *Thesaurus graecae linguae,* the first complete dictionary of all classical and post-classical Greek); in the cultural revolution of the Grand Siècle, erudition and philology were considered pedantic and were superseded in the salons by wit and brilliant conversation; and the quarrel of the ancients and moderns called into question the very authority of classical texts and doctrines. All this did not prevent single philologists from achieving outstanding results (most important of all, the *Glossary of Middle and Late Greek* by Charles Du Cange, 1688, and Bernard de Montfaucon's *Greek Palaeography,* 1708). In the 17th and 18th centuries, classical studies were cultivated more intensely in England and the Low Countries, though with a special stress on Latin philology. Perhaps the most brilliant result of this age was Richard Bentley's speculative restoration of the digamma in the archaic Greek alphabet (1732), an idea that later discoveries confirmed in full.

Yet the genealogical status of Greek with respect to other languages remained fluid. Some scholars insisted on Greek's nature as a holy language. Comenius in 1648 described Hebrew as "prophetic," Greek as "apostolic," and Latin as "ecclesiastical," but more profane functional descriptions of Greek's poetic and descriptive power were common from Casaubon to André Chénier and Franz Grillparzer. Others took up the old theories of Greek's special relationship with the Semitic languages or with German: in 1794 Friedrich G. Klopstock argued the latter thesis, against the sneering objections of Frederick the Great, and compiled long lists of allegedly related words from the two languages; the philosopher Johann Gottlieb Fichte was still convinced of the supremacy of both German and Greek over all other languages.

All this speculation came to an end with the sensational development of Indo-European studies at the beginning of the 19th century. The discovery that Greek, Latin, Sanskrit, and the Germanic languages share a common origin was the result of research inaugurated by Sir William Jones in 1786, continued by Friedrich von Schlegel (*On the Language and Wisdom of the Indians,* 1808), and culminated in two generations of German linguists (from Bopp, Grimm, and Schleicher to Osthoff, Brugmann, and Wackernagel) who shaped the modern Indo-European theory. This theory has been variously amended and enlarged, but in its general frame it still holds true today.

The revolution in the linguistic description of Greek had its root in the romantic passion for history and the unveiling of the past, but it also overlapped with the beginning of German Neo-Hellenism—namely, with the large movement of renewed interest in classical antiquity inaugurated by Johann Winckelmann's artistic theories and soon developed into the *Altertumswissenschaft* (science of antiquity) in the early 19th century by the generation of Friedrich August Wolf, Wilhelm von Humboldt, and August Böckh. Greek language then became part of a larger unity that included Greek (and Latin) archaeology, history, epigraphy, religion, anthropology, and so on. It was precisely the study of this world—a study that presupposed a thorough linguistic knowledge—that was regarded in 19th-century Europe (and in the United States) as the cornerstone of the moral and intellectual formation of every cultivated man.

It would be hard to describe how a century later Greek was driven from its prominent status in education and society, and gradually transformed into a dead language taught by frustrated and sadistic pedants (both George Eliot's Casaubon in *Middlemarch,* 1871, and the title character in Heinrich Mann's *Professor Unrat,* 1905, are Hellenists). It would also be hard to tell how the renewed popularity of Greek myth and culture in the second half of the 20th century was not matched by a similar enthusiasm for the language. No longer perceived as a holy tongue, too difficult to be popular (Heinrich Heine once described Greek as "an invention of the Devil"), and yet not remote enough to sound really mystic and exotic, Greek struggles against its alleged "unknowability" and waits for an answer to the crucial questions asked by Virginia Woolf in the 20th century: "Are we not reading into Greek poetry not what they have but what we lack? Does not the whole of Greece heap itself behind every line of its literature?" (*On Not Knowing Greek,* 1925).

BIBL.: W. Berschin, *Greek Letters and the Latin Middle Ages: From Jerome to Nicholas of Cusa,* trans. Jerold C. Frakes (Washington, D.C., 1988). A. Borst, *Der Turmbau von Babel,* 5 vols. (Stuttgart 1957–1963). P. Cohen, "La Tour de Babel, le sac de Troie et la recherche des origines des langues: Philologie, histoire et illustration des langues vernaculaires en France et en Angleterre aux XVIe–XVIIe siècles," *Études Épistémè* 7 (2005) 31–53. S. Goldhill, *Who Needs Greek?* (Cambridge 2002). M. W. Herren, ed., *The Sacred Nectar of the Greeks: The Study of Greek in the West in the Early Middle Ages* (London 1988). W. K. Percival, "Greek Pedagogy in the Renaissance," in *Heilige und profane Sprachen/Holy and Profane Languages,* ed. W. Hüllen and F. Klippel (Wiesbaden 2002) 93–109. R. Pfeiffer, *History of Classical Scholarship from 1300 to 1850* (Oxford 1976). E. Rummel, *The Humanist-Scholastic Debate in the Renaissance and Reformation* (Cambridge, Mass., 1995). N. G. Wilson, *From Byzantium to Italy: Greek Studies in the Italian Renaissance* (London 1992).

F.M.P.

Greek, Modern

Greek is the official language of the Republic of Greece and (with Turkish) one of the official languages of the Republic of Cyprus.

The relationship between ancient Greek and the language spoken and written today is complex. Most of the sound changes that differentiate modern from Classical Greek had taken place by the beginning of the Byzantine period (4th cent. CE). Unlike Latin, however, Greek did not split into separate languages in the medieval and modern periods, and the continuity of its development has remained unbroken. Greek today still uses three genders; the case system is only slightly different from that of Classical Greek (employing four cases instead of the ancient five); and the verb system, despite the loss of the infinitive, the optative, and the single-word future and perfect tenses, is still close to that of the ancient language. In vocabulary, most of the basic items, as well as most of the less frequently used words, either remain unchanged from ancient Greek or are derived from ancient Greek stems.

Yet, ever since the end of the Classical period, writers of Greek have tended to use a variety of the language that is markedly different from the spoken Greek of their time, including some archaic vocabulary and grammatical features. During and after the Byzantine period, the chief models for Greek writing were the literary Attic of Classical antiquity and the Koine of the New Testament and other early Christian texts. Thus, though the spoken language of the uneducated developed naturally, the written language tended to ignore the changes that had taken place in the mother tongue.

From the 12th century CE, however, some verse writers used a literary language based on the spoken tongue, though it still contained some archaic features. This tradition culminated in the radical experiments of Cretan writers during the Venetian occupation of the island in the 16th and 17th centuries, in which poems based on Western Renaissance genres were written in a sophisticated language based almost entirely on the vocabulary and morphology of the local spoken dialect. These texts in turn provided a model for poets who emerged during and after the Greek war of independence in the 1820s.

During the Greek Enlightenment, in the decades leading up to independence, writers needed to decide on the form of language to be used in educational works and ultimately by the Greek state. Around 1800 at least three alternative versions of written Greek were proposed. The archaists claimed that only Classical Greek was capable of expressing philosophical and other cultural concepts. The vernacularists argued for the use of the spoken language in writing. In between were Korais and his followers, who argued that modern Greek should be the starting point for the written language, but that it should be "corrected" through the replacement of loanwords by words of ancient Greek origin and through the restitution of ancient morphology.

By the late 19th century the language controversy had become polarized between those who supported the use of the spoken language (by then known as demotic) for written purposes and the proponents of the "corrected" language (known as *katharevousa*). Although most literary texts were being written in demotic by 1900, *katharevousa* continued to be the official language of Greece and Cyprus until it was formally abolished in 1976.

Since the 1970s the language debate has focused on whether ancient Greek should be a compulsory subject in Greek high schools, some arguing that modern Greek should be presented to pupils as the most recent phase of a timeless Greek language and others that it should be treated as an autonomous language in its own right.

BIBL.: Geoffrey Horrocks, *Greek: A History of the Language and Its Speakers* (London 1997). Peter Mackridge, *The Modern Greek Language* (Oxford 1985). P.MA.

Greek, Modern Uses of Ancient

The use of the ancient Greek language has been a battleground in modern education, politics, and literature.

In 19th-century Europe philhellenism was a major cultural and intellectual movement, which developed the Romantic and Renaissance passion for all things Greek in new directions. In Germany, the educational reforms of Wilhelm von Humboldt made the classical languages central to the state system: "In the Greeks alone," he wrote, "we find the ideal of that which we ourselves should like to be and to produce." To that end, 80 percent of the school curriculum could be taken up with the study of Greek and Latin. This had a huge effect on the imagination of those educated in such a system, as is reflected in the all-pervasive turn to Greece among artists and thinkers from Hegel to Wagner and Nietzsche. In particular, the sublimity and perfection of the Greek language itself was an artistic credo that justified its educational privilege. Greek was perceived a language of supreme beauty and expressiveness. Similar levels of commitment to the study of Greek and Latin were seen in England and elsewhere. The study of Greek became a sign of elite culture and literary sensibility and consequently acted as a mark of social exclusion and class affiliation. Women were often prevented from studying Greek, and in the U.S. Senate it was discussed whether Howard University, established for black students, should teach Greek or merely agriculture.

Because of the place Greek held in the educational system and in the maintenance of social privilege it became the object of aggressive attempts at reform, particularly from the middle of the 19th century onward. The reformers had several agendas: some were educationalists who wished to broaden the curriculum, others were liberals who desired social change, still others supported an increased place for science and technology as essential for progress. Each argument also became tied up with burgeoning nationalist ideologies, as education was viewed as the production of citizens. Thus it was that Kaiser Wilhelm II at the end of the 19th century declared, "We should raise young Germans, not young Greeks and Romans." Henry Sidgwick, founder of Newnham College, Cambridge, proposed simply "to exclude Greek from the regular curriculum" as being of no use. The British government minister Robert Lowe caused a furor when he suggested that it was more important "to know where the liver is situated . . . than to know . . .it is called *hēpar* in Greek." The multiform attacks on learning Greek prompted many defenses, especially from a religious perspective. T. S. Eliot in the 20th century stated that "readers who wish to see a Christian civilization survive" would support the continuing study of Greek: because the Gospels are written in Greek, not to know Greek is to be cut off from the original words of God and Western tradition. Yet modernism could also link a love of Greek with a rejection of Christianity. Virginia Woolf's famous essay "On Not Knowing Greek" ends by suggesting that we need Greece especially "when we are sick of the vagueness, of the confusion, of the Christianity and its consolations, of our own age." Learning ancient Greek was, in the eyes of its supporters, an idealist look toward a lost and perfect past and a proper education for a modern citizen; but in the eyes of its opponents it represented a religious and political conservatism, resistant to the rise of science and modern materialism.

It was only after World War II that Greek could be properly said to have lost this conflicted cultural status, when it also finally lost its privileged place in the school systems of the West and its political and cultural role in society.

BIBL.: Simon Goldhill, *Who Needs Greek? Contests in the Cultural History of Hellenism* (Cambridge 2002). Artemis Leontis, *Topographies of Hellenism: Mapping the Homeland* (Ithaca 1995). Carl Richard, *The Founders and Classics: Greece, Rome, and the American Enlightenment* (Cambridge, Mass., 1994). Christopher Stray, *Classics Transformed: Schools, Universities, and Society in England, 1830–1960* (Oxford 1998). Caroline Winterer, *The Culture of Classicism: Ancient Greece and Rome in American Intellectual Life* (Baltimore 2002). S.GO.

Greek Anthology

Although the term *anthologion* (lit. "a collection of flowers"; compare Latin *florilegium*) was applied to literary collections perhaps by the time of Hadrian (1st–2nd cents. CE), the name Greek Anthology is a term coined by modern scholars for the surviving corpus of several thousand short poems, or epigrams, by classical and Byzantine Greek poets found in two manuscript collections (Anthologia Palatina and Anthologia Planudea) of partially overlapping content.

The origin of the epigram lies in archaic Greece, where short poems of two or more lines were inscribed on funerary and other monuments to serve as mementos or dedications. In the 5th century BCE epigrams further developed into a literary form of occasional poetry, often intended for public recital at banquets. A wide variety of themes could be addressed: death, drinking, love (for women and young men), praise of soldiers or athletes, descriptions of buildings, and riddles. The most common metrical form was the elegiac distich, a hexameter verse followed by a pentameter. This form of poetry continued to be produced by the Greek poets in ancient, Hellenistic, and Byzantine times—after the 4th century CE with the addition of Christian themes.

The popularity of epigrams is evident in the repeated efforts to gather them into collections. The first written collection, entitled *Stephanos* (*Garland*) and undertaken by Meleager in the early 1st century BCE, was arranged alphabetically by author and perhaps based on preexisting collections available in Alexandria. Another *Stephanos* was produced by Philippus of Thessalonica, during the golden age of Augustan poetry. During the Justinianic renaissance of the 6th century, Agathias gathered together his own poems and those of his literary friends into a collection of epigrams that he titled *The Circle* (*Kyklos*). This and all later collections were arranged thematically.

The Macedonian renaissance of the 10th century was a watershed in the history of epigrammatic poetry. During that era Constantine Cephalas, attested as a high ecclesiastical dignitary (*protopapas*) of the imperial palace in 917, compiled an anthology of several thousand epigrams. Based on the earlier collections of Meleager, Philippus, and Agathias (complete with their original prefaces) and others, Cephalas' anthology sometimes retained the sequence of his sources (e.g., the description by Christodorus of Coptus of the baths of Zeuxippus in Constantinople in book 2, or the homoerotic poems of Strato's *Mousa paidiki* or *Musa puerilis,* produced during the reign of Hadrian, in book 12), and sometimes placed epigrams under different thematic headings. For all his interest in retaining the classical tradition of epigrammatic poetry, Cephalas dedicated book 1 to Christian themes, defiantly announcing: "Let the pious and godly Christian epigrams take precedence, even if the pagans [*Hellēnes*] are displeased." He also included his own poems and those of his contemporaries, such as Arethas of Caesarea and Ignatius the Deacon, as well as epigrams copied directly from monuments.

The reconstruction of the content of all earlier epigram collections depends on two main manuscripts known as the Anthologia Palatina and the Anthologia Planudea. The Palatine Anthology is a collection of 3,700 epigrams, based on but not identical to Cephalas' anthology, largely preserved in the Codex Palatinus 23, which was copied around 980. The manuscript was in Heidelberg in the early 17th century but was taken to the Vatican Library in Rome, under the directorship of Leo Allatius, as a consequence of the Thirty Years' War and there was bound in two volumes. Both were taken to Paris in 1797 by arrangement between Napoleon and Pope Pius VI, but only the larger part was eventually returned to Heidelberg, whereas the smaller part (Codex Parisianus gr. suppl. 384) remains in Paris.

The first complete edition of the epigrams contained in the Anthologia Palatina was made by R. F. P. Brunck (Strasburg 1772–1776). Rather than retaining the thematic sequence of the manuscript, he arranged the poems by author. This edition provided the basis for the recognized scholarly edition by Friedrich Jacobs (Leipzig 1794–1814), which showed significant improvements in its second edition (Leipzig 1813–1817), adding 388 poems from the Anthologia Planudea as well as 394 poems from ancient authors and metric inscriptions.

The Anthologia Planudea is contained in an autograph manuscript composed in 1299 by Maximus Planudes, the great scholar of the Palaeologan renaissance; the document was part of Cardinal Bessarion's original bequest to the library of Saint Mark's Cathedral in Venice (Codex Marcianus 481). Planudes drew on Cephalas' collection, but not the manuscript of the Palatine Anthology, and added 395 further epigrams. Until the early 17th century this was the only collection of Greek epigrams known to European scholars, and it enjoyed great popularity as a source of easily accessible Greek poetry on a large variety of themes through the centuries. Eleven manuscript copies of this text were made from the 16th through the 18th centuries. The Anthologia Planudea formed the basis of the numerous early printed editions, beginning with the *editio princeps* by John Lascaris (Florence 1494). The edition by Aldus Manutius (Venice 1503) was reprinted in 1521 and in 1530. Especially noteworthy are the scholarly edition by Henri Estienne (Paris 1566), the partial French verse translation of 1589, and the Latin verse translation by Hugo Grotius included in the Utrecht edition (1795–1822).

It was through the Greek Anthology that the German poets of the 18th and 19th centuries gained access to ancient Greek poetry. Lessing and Herder wrote treatises on epigrams, which soon inspired Goethe to adapt ancient Greek meters for his own poetry. Many, such as Kleist, Herder, Goethe, Schlegel, Schiller, Humboldt, Rückert, Mörike, and Hofmannsthal, also attempted translations of selected epigrams from the collection, in the original meter.

Since the revival of Greek learning in the Germany of the late 18th century, classical philologists have taken a great interest in these collections, mainly with the aim of reconstructing the oeuvre of ancient Greek poets. Recent scholarship has also turned to questions of codicology and palaeography raised by the two significant manuscript collections.

BIBL.: H. Beckby, *Anthologia Graeca, Griechisch-Deutsch* (Munich 1957?) 10–116. A. Cameron, *The Greek Anthology from Meleager to Planudes* (Oxford 1993). J. G. Herder, *Sämtliche Werke,* ed. B. Suphan (Berlin 1882) vol. 26. J. Hutton, *The Greek Anthology in France and in the Latin Writers of the Netherlands to the Year 1800,* rev. ed. (New York 1967), and *The Greek Anthology in Italy to the Year 1800* (Ithaca 1935). E. M. Jeffreys, "Greek Anthology," in *Oxford Dictionary of Byzantium* (Oxford 1991) 2:872–873. K. Krumbacher, *Geschichte der byzantinischen Literatur* (1897, repr. New York 1970) 2:725–730. L. Schmidt (rev. by R. Reitzenstein), "Anthologie," Pauly-Wissowa, *Realencyclopädie der classischen Altertumswissenschaft* (*RE*) (Stuttgart and Weimar 1894, repr. 1998) 1.2:2380–2391. P. Waltz, *Anthologie Grecque* (Paris 1960) 1:iii–lxxxviii.

C.R.

Greek Revival

Although the Roman author Vitruvius underlines the important contribution made by the Greeks to architectural theory and composition, his Renaissance interpreters did not investigate these references, and it was not until the 18th century that a substantial interest in Greek buildings emerged in European architectural discourse. With the publication of the first reasonably accurate images of Greek temples in the 1740s and 1750s, and further researches in the eastern Mediterranean funded by the London-based Society of Dilettanti, a fascination with Greek antiquity gripped European architects, transforming the way that the classical orders, and architecture in general, were understood.

Compared with the more complex and profusely ornamented architecture of imperial Rome, the simple, bulky forms of 6th- and 5th-century BCE temples in Greece, Turkey, Sicily, and southern Italy were disturbing; it would be difficult to maintain that all ancient monuments were manifestations of a transcendental beauty grounded in Platonic notions of number and proportion. In 1753 the French critic Marc-Antoine Laugier stated in his *Essai sur l'architecture* that architecture reached a point of perfection under the Greeks. The German scholar Johann Joachim Winckelmann likewise positioned the Greeks at the pinnacle of artistic achievement, advancing an influential theory of historical development in his *Geschichte der Kunst des Alterthums* (*The History of Ancient Art among the Greeks*) of 1764. Having traveled to Greece in 1754–1755, the French architect Julien-David LeRoy suggested that the effects of Greek architecture resided in the play of light and shadow over massive, minimally articulated forms. These ideas were part of a larger debate that pitted LeRoy against the British antiquary James Stuart and the Italian engraver Giovanni Battista Piranesi in a battle of the books that was played out between 1758 and 1770. Both lashed out at LeRoy's hastily prepared but magnificently illustrated *Les ruines des plus beaux monuments de la Grèce* (1758), but whereas Stuart asserted the superior accuracy of his monumental *Antiquities of Athens* (1762–1816), Piranesi in his *Della magnificenza ed architettura de'Romani* (1761) contrasted the barrenness of Greek forms with the fertility of Roman invention.

As an architectural style, Greek Revival was a current within late 18th-century Neoclassicism and 19th-century Historicism, adopted with varying degrees of creativity and literalism in Europe and North America. Stuart and his colleague Nicholas Revett were among the first to apply their researches in Greece directly to domestic projects for British aristocrats, and Greek temples and baseless Doric columns quickly found their places in picturesque gardens. In public architecture the Greek Doric order appeared before the French Revolution in Claude-Nicolas Ledoux's *barrières* around Paris (1785–1789) and in Carl Gotthard Langhans's Brandenburg Gate in Berlin (1788–1791). In the first half of the 19th century the Greek orders were deployed around Great Britain to signal the altruistic goals of public institutions, such as Robert Smirke's British Museum in London (1823–1848) and William Henry Playfair's Royal Institution in Edinburgh (1822–1835). French architects were as keenly interested in Greek archaeology as their English colleagues. Such fads as the mid-18th-century *goût grecque* and the rigorous *néo-grecque* architecture of the 19th century, however, were less literal in their imitation of antique forms. Henri Labrouste derived compositional principles from his study of the Greek temples at Paestum, and Jacques Ignace Hittorff's research in Sicily and Charles Garnier's work on the temple of Athena Aphaia at Aegina reveal a fascination with the Greeks' use of color. In early 19th-century Prussia, public architecture was marshaled to underline national ideals, the Greek orders being associated with virtue and heroism. In the United States, freedom and democracy were thought to be most fittingly expressed through Greek Revival state capitols and courthouses, but all building types, from insane asylums to plantation houses, were susceptible to Greek detailing.

BIBL.: David Constantine, *Early Greek Travellers and the Hellenic Ideal* (Cambridge 1984). Joseph Mordaunt Crook, *The Greek Revival: Neo-Classical Attitudes in British Architecture, 1760–1870* (London 1972). Robert K. Sutton, *Americans Interpret the Parthenon: The Progress of Greek Revival Architecture from the East Coast to Oregon, 1800–1860* (Niwot, Colo., 1992). Dora Wiebenson, *Sources of Greek Revival Architecture* (University Park, Pa., 1969).

C.D.A.

Grotto

Either a natural cave in a landscape or an artificial cave in a garden (the word, from Italian, is related to Latin *crypta* and Greek *kryptē*). In Greek religion caves were consecrated to a number of divinities, particularly Dionysus, Pan, and the Nymphs. These natural sanctuaries allowed contact with the divinity outside the urban framework; they were a mythic residence of the deity, its "homeless home" (Sophocles, *Philoctetes* 534). The grotto of Calypso (*Odyssey* 5.55–77), a metaphor of the harmony of the cosmos and the vitality of the *physis,* stirred all who glimpsed it to amazement. It became the archetype of the *locus amoenus* (charming locale), a commonplace in landscape description. In literature the cave is a synecdoche for wilderness. Virgil explores the possibilities: either as a refuge of happiness in a primitive world (*Eclogues* 1.75); or as the entrance to the netherworld, exciting terror in the face of the sacred and of the chthonian powers (*Aeneid* 7.563–571). The former image is widespread in pastoral poetry, and the second found its afterlife in Baroque opera, in stage sets representing Hell.

Such ambivalence is enriched by a complex exegetical tradition, epitomized in a short tract by Porphyry (*De antro nympharum*, ca. 260–280 CE), which turns the cave into a symbol of the material, sensible world, as in the philosophy of Plato (*Republic* 7.514A–517B). In his *Discorsi del poema eroico* (1594) Torquato Tasso would sum it up by saying, "The grotto allows a wide range of allegory."

Artificial grottoes appeared in the Hellenistic period and underwent further development in Roman gardens, designated by different terms such as *musaeum* or *nymphaeum.* They sometimes imitated natural caves and were lined with spongy stone (Pliny, *Natural History* 36.154). They could contain jets of water turned on for entertainment, but also sculptures and inscriptions. They were one of the foremost types of *opera topiaria,* the representation of real or fictive landscapes within gardens. At Sperlonga, Tiberius outfitted a natural grotto at sea level as a banqueting chamber (*triclinium*) containing a sculpture group representing the Polyphemus episode in the *Odyssey.* The *amaltheum,* which Cicero devised on the basis of a model by Atticus, alluding to Amalthea, the goat who nursed the infant Zeus, was taken up by the painter Hubert Robert in the grotto of the dairy designed for Marie-Antoinette at Rambouillet, built in 1783–1784.

From the 16th through the 18th centuries, artificial grottoes were restored to a place of honor in the gardens of Italy and then throughout Europe, where they served as places of rest refreshed by shade and water, and as one of the principal contemporary allusions to the antique world. In a letter from Rome in 1543 Claudio Tolomei praised "the ingenious skill newly rediscovered to make fountains, in which mixing art with nature, one cannot judge if it [the fountain] is the work of the former or the latter." Such grottoes were decorated with embedded minerals, shells, and mosaics; none are finer than those by Galeazzo Alessi (1512–1572) in Genoa and by Bernardo Buontalenti (1523–1608) in Florence. As in the Roman models, the decor was often given a mythical theme imbued with a poetical and at times fairylike atmosphere, all enhanced by its setting in a grotto. All this recalls in a metaphorical way the ancient cave viewed as sanctuary or as the dwelling of the divinity. For example, at Versailles the grotto of Thetis, built in 1665, alludes to the undersea resting place of Apollo (Ovid, *Metamorphoses* 2.67–69), the divinity who returns reincarnate as Louis XIV, the Sun King. The topos was continuously rewritten, and the typology was susceptible to innumerable nuances of content. Alexander Pope's grotto at Twickenham was dedicated to solitary retreat and thus combined the tradition of classical *otium* (ease) with the image of a desert refuge for the Christian hermit. The fashion for grottoes remained undimmed even in the 19th century: at Linderhof, Louis II of Bavaria built a grotto of Venus inspired by Wagner's *Tannhäuser,* illuminated by electric lights.

BIBL.: Isabella Lapi Ballerini and Litta Maria Medri, eds., *Artifici d'acque e giardini: La cultura delle grotte e dei ninfei in Italia e in Europa* (Florence 1999). Henri Lavagne, *Operosa Antra: Recherches sur la grotte à Rome de Sylla à Hadrien* (Rome 1988). Naomi Miller, *Heavenly Caves: Reflections on the Garden Grotto* (New York 1982).

H.B.

Guidebooks to Ancient Rome

Petrarch's oft-quoted letter to Giovanni Colonna di San Vito, recalling their ambulations through Rome in 1337, conjures an image of the city encapsulated in classical times (*Epistolae familiares* 6.2). His itinerary loosely parallels the trajectory of Roman history, beginning at the old Porta Carmentalis and ending at the Baths of Diocletian. Its inspiration comes from Virgil's *Aeneid,* in which Evander recounts his journey from Arcadia to Latium, accompanied by the priestess Carmenta, and sets eyes on the future site of Rome.

Such literary reconstructions were followed by more empirical attempts to correlate the topography of the early city with the physical layout of contemporary Rome. The anonymous author of the *Tractatus de rebus antiquis et situ urbis Romae* (ca. 1410) relied on the Constantinian regionary catalogues to situate monuments with respect to the boundaries of the 13 *rioni.* Niccolò Signorili, a *caporione* from the Monti neighborhood from 1423 to 1425, used the regionaries more systematically in his *Descriptio urbis Romae,* supported by evidence from ancient inscriptions. In 1429 came Poggio Bracciolini's critical discovery of Frontinus' *De aquaeductis* in the scriptorium at Monte Cassino. Having earlier toured Rome with Cosimo de' Medici and Niccolò Niccoli, Poggio set to writing his own *Descriptio* as the first book of a larger historical work, *De varietate fortunae* (begun in 1431, not published until 1448). Poggio and his companion Antonio Loschi muse about how the vicissitudes of fortune have ravaged some monuments and spared others. Beginning on the Capitoline, Loschi comments on the squalid state to which it had fallen since the days of Virgil. Poggio refers to an epigraphic corpus devoted solely to Rome (subsequently lost), while frequently adducing inscriptions as evidence of renovations by later emperors (namely, at the Aqua Claudia, Baths of Constantine, and Temple of Saturn). Poggio looks at the city from a stratigraphic vantage, demonstrating how variations in brick technique or masonry coursing reveal distinct phases in the formation of the Servian and Aurelian walls. In the case of the pyramid of Gaius Cestius, long held to be the tomb of Remus, he notes how even the learned Petrarch had missed the prominent inscription on its travertine revetment. Leon Battista Alberti, like Poggio a *scriptor* in the curia of Eugenius IV and Nicholas V, gave primacy to the Capitoline as the symbolic nexus of the city. To create his disk-like map of Rome, of which all that survives are the table of coordinates and a drawing of the mariner's compass used to record orientation, Alberti stood on the Capitoline and calculated the radial distance to monuments using triangulation.

The *De Roma instaurata* of Flavio Biondo was already acclaimed by its completion in 1446 as a groundbreaking work for the study of Roman archaeology. Basing the structure of his guide on the regionaries (ascribed erroneously to Sextus Rufus), Biondo divides monuments by type into three books. Book 1 proceeds from the walls to the gates—with a brief excursus on the Trastevere—then to bridges and thermae, the catacombs, and the Vatican. Biondo cites Festus on the derivation of the name from the *vaticinia,* or prophecies of the seers who plied their trade on this hill, and alternately Varro, who traced it to the primordial crying of babies (*vagire*) as an invocation of the *deus Vaticanus.* Biondo disproves the widely held theory that a *palatium Neronis* had stood on the site. From Tacitus, a portion of whose *Annales* had recently come to light, Biondo identifies the location of Peter's grave near the Naumachia of Nero, and he corrects the reading of his crucifixion *inter duas metas* as between the two goalposts of the Circus of Gaius and Nero, though he too was convinced that the orb atop the obelisk erected in the circus's center held the ashes of Julius Caesar. Moving from general to specific, Biondo opens his second book with a definition of the thermae, then turns to those of Alexander Severus, Agrippa, Caracalla, Gordianus, and Constantine. Similarly, he prefaces a discussion of the Temple of Iove Stator with a discussion of the sacred rituals of ancient Romans and their altars. His reputation as a historian and philologist notwithstanding, Biondo's reasoning at times leads him astray: he mistakes the Temple of Portunus in the Forum Boarium (rededicated to Santa Maria Egiziaca) as the former site of the Asylum Romuli, given that it served as a refuge for prostitutes and orphans, and the nearby Janus Quadrifrons is confused with Numa's Temple of Janus, long since destroyed. After exonerating the Goths, and particularly Theodoric, for the destruction of Rome's aqueducts, Biondo closes book 2 with the theaters and *ludi spectaculi.* Much of book 3 is taken up with the Colosseum, erected on the site of the *stagnum* from Nero's Domus Aurea, as well as the Christian basilicas.

From 1480 to 1483 Pomponio Leto mesmerized audiences at the university with his lectures on Varro, Florus, and Virgil. The work that gained him greatest fame was an interpolated edition of the regionary catalogues, first published under the authorship of Publius Victor by Giano Parrasio in 1503. Shortly after 1484 Leto composed a guide, only fragments of which survive. The *Excerpta,* a miscellany of notes from his forays through the city, starts out from the Colosseum (*in media Urbe Amphitheatrum*). On the northern rim of the Campus Martius, Leto reports the recent discovery of an obelisk Augustus had reerected as a gnomon beside his mausoleum, with the names of the winds still visible in the mosaic floor. Leto clarifies the topography of the Quirinal and Esquiline, in particular the siting of the Domus Aurea. Biondo had mistaken the vestiges of the Temple of Serapis below Monte Cavallo as the infamous tower from which Nero had watched Rome burn, arguing that the modern toponym Tor di Mesa was a vulgarization of Turris Moecenatis. It so happened that Biondo's own Maecenas, Cardinal Prospero Colonna, occupied the palace just below this promontory beside Santi Apostoli. Leto correctly placed the tower's ruins on the Esquiline beside the cisterns known as the Sette Sale. He also witnessed the spectacular trove from the Ara Maxima behind the Church of Santa Maria in Cosmedin, adding that the round Temple of Hercules Invictus had been demolished during the pontificate of Sixtus IV.

Francesco Albertini's *Opusculum de mirabilibus nouae & ueteris urbis Romae,* composed at the behest of Cardinal Galeotto della Rovere, was published by Jacopo Mazzocchi in 1510. A Florentine member of the Academia Pomponiana, his text draws heavily on the spurious *Antiquitates* of Annius of Viterbo (1498). Andrea Fulvio, who had assisted Albertini in culling epigraphic material, composed his own poetic encomium, the *Antiquaria urbis* (1513), dedicated to the newly elected Medici pope, Leo X, and auguring the arrival of a new golden age. Fulvio was the principal contributor to Mazzocchi's *Epigrammata urbis* (1521). In the preface to his expanded guide, the *Antiquitates urbis* (1527), he recalls accompanying Raphael around Rome (*per regiones explorans*), pointing out sites as the artist sketched their remains. Raphael's death in 1520 cut short his project to graphically reconstruct the imperial city. In a memorandum addressed to Leo X, Raphael names his principal source as Publius Victor; his *diségno* would have comprised an album or composite of drawings of the individual regions, but only the first of these was actually completed. Some glimpse of this project saw light in the *Antiquae urbis Romae cum regionibus simulachrum* (1527) of Fabio Calvo, a scholar of Hippocrates who had collaborated with Raphael to translate Vitruvius. Its author perished in the ensuing Sack of Rome. Schematic representations of the city under Romulus, Servius, Augustus, and Pliny—the woodcuts by Tolomeo Egnazio da Fossombrone—derive from ancient gromatical treatises (the Codex Arcerianus, brought from Bobbio to the Vatican Library), while crude reconstructions of monuments are cribbed from the reverses of imperial coins (e.g., Circus Maximus, Temple of Apollo).

Whereas Fulvio had focused on toponomastics rather than the physical configuration of ancient Rome (*non modo geographice, sed ethymologice cum rerum causis*), the small handbook of Giovanni Bartolomeo Marliani, *Antiquae Romae topographia* (1534), was more ambitious in scope. François Rabelais, then a guest of Cardinal Jean du Bellay in Rome, prepared a second printing of the *Topographia* that same year in Lyons. Trained in law, Marliani relied on the assistance of Antonio Alegreto and Annibale Caro for inscriptions, but the book was harshly criticized for its numerous errata. The amplified edition, *Urbis Romae topographia,* dedicated to Francis I, appeared in 1544 and proved an instant commercial success. Ludovico Lucena and Orazio Nucleo produced the large folio illustrations in plan, elevation, and section—many lifted straight from Sebastiano Serlio's *Terzo libro dell'architettura,* published in Venice in 1540.

The indefatigable antiquarian Pirro Ligorio was outspoken in denouncing Marliani, particularly on the early formation of Rome. Ligorio argued his case in the *Paradosse,* first published by Michele Tramezzino as an addendum to the *Libro delle antichità di Roma, nel quale si tratta de' circhi, theatri, amphitheatri* in 1553. Ligorio made extensive use of the recent commentary by Benedetto Egio and Gabriele Faerno to the interpolated regionaries, as well as the *editio princeps* of the *Notitia dignitatum* by Sigismund Gelenius and Andrea Alciati, which also provided the basis for his archaeological map of Rome issued that same year.

In 1562 fragments of the 3rd-century Severan plan were unearthed behind the Church of Santi Cosma e Damiano off the Roman Forum. Giovanni Antonio Dosio recorded the fragments before they were moved to the Palazzo Farnese, where Onofrio Panvinio set to reassembling them. Bernardo Gamucci first announced the discovery in his *Libri quattro dell'antichità della città di Roma* (1565), conjecturing from the siting of various monuments—the Mole Hadriana, in particular—that the imperial city had already been in decline. Dosio executed the illustrations, including the Frontispizio di Nerone, Bagni di Paolo Emilio (Markets of Trajan), and Septizonium. These panoramic *vedute* appealed to tourists, as did the earlier handbook of Lucio Mauro, *Le antichità della città di Roma,* bound with Ulisse Aldrovandi's *Tutte le statue antiche* (1558).

Few new guides to antiquities appeared in the latter half of the 16th century, a result of the intensified focus on paleo-Christian Rome, as well as the interest among a small circle of professionals—Ligorio, Panvinio, Jacques Boissard, Martin de Smet, Antonio Agustín, and Fulvio Orsini—in systematizing and classifying the entire *antiquitates* into a single corpus. Pompeo Ugonio's *Historia delle stationi di Roma,* published in 1588 and dedicated to Camilla Peretti, was the presage to a much larger work that would consume Ugonio up to his death in 1614. The *Theatrum urbis Romae,* a compendium of notes so vast in scope that it never saw publication, survives in two voluminous manuscripts (Cod. Vat. Barb. Lat. 1994, and Ms. I, 161, Biblioteca Ariostea, Ferrara). In a series of diagrammatic maps, Ugonio attempted to trace a continuum in the evolution of Rome from its origins through its transformation into a Christian capital, culminating in his own time with the master plan envisioned and partly realized by Sixtus V.

BIBL.: Cesare d'Onofrio, *Visitiamo Roma nel quattrocento: La città degli Umanisti* (Rome 1989). Philip Jacks, *The Antiquarian and the Myth of Antiquity: The Origins of Rome in Renaissance Thought* (Cambridge 1993). Peter Murray, *Five Early Guides to Rome and Florence* (Farnborough, U.K., 1972). Ludwig Schudt, *Le guide di Roma: Materialien zu einer Geschichte der römischen Topographie* (Vienna 1930). Roberto Valentini and Giuseppe Zucchetti, *Codice topografico della città di Roma,* 4 vols. (Rome 1940–1953). Roberto Weiss, *The Renaissance Discovery of Classical Antiquity,* 2nd ed. (Oxford 1988).

P.J.

Gymnasium

Latin term (from Greek *gymnasion,* originally referring to exercise by naked athletes, as seen, e.g., on ancient vase paintings) applied to a school or, later, to a university. Its use goes back at least to the 11th century, but it increasingly was applied, from the 15th century onward, to schools that were founded to teach the Humanistic curriculum of Latin, Greek, and, to a lesser extent, Hebrew. By the late 16th century the word had entered vernacular usage, although it could apply equally to a school or to a university. When used of a school, the Greek root alluded to training the mind (rather than athletics) and, often, to the school's role in preparing students for a university (which, in consequence, might be termed *archigymnasium*). The relationship between gymnasium and university might be very close. Often attendance at university was restricted to those who had attended a gymnasium. In the 18th century at St. Petersburg, gymnasium and university had the same rector, and cooperation between the two was substantial.

Physical exercise (whether or not in a specially constructed building, a gymnasium), had little role in education until the 19th century, and the early advocacy of gymnastics by the English schoolmaster William Mulcaster (fl. 1586) fell on deaf ears. Mulcaster drew heavily on the *De arte gymnastica* of Girolamo Mercuriale (1559), one of a series of Renaissance medical writers who wished to reintroduce physical activities into their health regimens, following the example of Galen. They favored running and ball games and left gymnastics, in the sense of leaping, vaulting, and tumbling, to lower-class acrobats or trainers, presumably because it was more spectacle than exercise. Later editions of Mercuriale's work were illustrated with ancient coins and monuments, not all of them authentic, and included a detailed plan of an ancient gymnasium. The abundance of information in *De arte gymnastica,* and the elegance of its illustrations, kept ancient gymnastics before the eyes of antiquarians long after Mercuriale's death. They led Winckelmann in the 18th century, for instance, to consider naked exercise as one of the hallmarks of the Greeks. The organizers of the 1896 Olympic Games also depended on Mercuriale's illustrations for their recreation of Graeco-Roman wrestling, in which participants were not allowed to use their legs to throw or hold. Ordinary freestyle wrestling had to wait longer for inclusion.

Whereas almost all medical authors praised the benefits of exercise, it was the Swede P. H. Ling who at last argued successfully for a specific role in medicine for gymnastic exercise. Ling, who opened his Gymnastic Institute in 1818, used weights and balancing as part of therapy, and such exercise has continued to play a major role in medical rehabilitation. At the same time in Germany, F. L. Jahn, a Berlin schoolmaster, introduced gymnastics into education in 1811 for patriotic as well as pedagogical reasons, wishing to encourage healthy recruits for the forthcoming struggle with Napoleon. His example was widely followed both in Germany and elsewhere. In Britain many public and grammar schools in the 19th century built large gymnasia as part of their mission to produce hearty and healthy leaders of society. Although school gymnastics has declined, physical exercise, whether as jogging or aerobics, in pursuit of health and the body beautiful, became important again in the later 20th century, and many now have recourse to a gymnasium, a place with machines and facilities for exercise.

By contrast, the educational meaning of the word has become less common. Particularly in Germany, the notion was narrowed to one particular type of school, the Humanistic Gymnasium (*Humanistisches Gymnasium*). Devised in Prussia in 1809–1810 as part of the educational reforms of Wilhelm von Humboldt, this type of *Gymnasium* bridged the gap between elementary school and university with a curriculum heavily skewed toward Greek and Latin. Some 40 percent of all lessons were devoted to classical studies, and the percentage increased in the higher forms. Access to Prussian universities was confined to those who had studied at a *Gymnasium*, and this model was soon followed by other German states (e.g., Bavaria in 1830). Other countries adopted the same type of education, although not necessarily with the same title or the same level of professional expertise among the teachers: for instance, the curricula of English grammar schools and public schools (private schools, in U.S. parlance), and the Italian *licei*. Humboldt's original emphasis on the educational and moral value (*Bildung*) of Greek, however, was soon eroded toward a concentration on Latin language, and his aesthetic and moral preferences for the classics came up against the hard realities of an increasingly industrialized world. By 1900, even in Germany some *Realgymnasien* taught only a moderate amount of Latin alongside modern languages and science, enough to pass the university entrance examination, and there were some schools that did not do even that. Satirists throughout Europe poked fun at the *Gymnasium* teacher for his pedantry, chauvinism, and irrelevance to the modern world. (Few schools for girls adopted the curricula of the *Gymnasium*.) Some of this criticism was well deserved, but that should not hide the important commitment to classical scholarship on the part of these schoolteachers, or the considerable contribution made by them particularly to the editing of texts: examples include Peter's *Historicorum Romanorum reliquiae*, the *Corpus commentariorum Aristotelicorum*, and the *Corpus medicorum*.

During the 20th century the decline in the prestige of the *Gymnasium* continued further still, not least with the abolition of a Latin requirement for university entrance. Claims for the *Gymnasium*'s superiority of sensibility or morality disappeared with the Third Reich and the demise of Jaeger's Third Humanism, even if the high level of academic expertise continued among its teachers. In many German towns the *Gymnasium* still retains a certain degree of preeminence among schools, as well as continued teaching of the classical languages, albeit to only a fraction of the school population.

BIBL.: H. J. Apel, "Humanistisches Gymnasium," in *Der Neue Pauly* (1999) 14:563–567. A. Arcangeli, *Recreation in the Renaissance* (London 2003). J. Céard, M. M. Fontaine, and J. C. Margolin, *Le Corps à la Renaissance* (Paris 1990). K. E. Jeismann, *Das preussische Gymnasium in Staat und Geschichte*, 2 vols. (Stuttgart 1974–1996). M. Landfester, *Humanismus und Gesellschaft im 19. Jahrhundert* (Darmstadt 1988). R. L. De Molen, *Richard Mulcaster's Positions* (New York 1971).

V.N.

Gynecology

Until the 19th century, medical treatment of women's diseases depended on ideas derived from a range of classical sources that offered conflicting images of the female body. Although authorities disagreed over the hotter sex, and the roles of the sexes in generation, they agreed that women were by nature "wet." They relied on observation of the body's external changes, although briefly in 3rd-century BCE Alexandria Herophilus and Erasistratus performed human dissection and described the ovaries (though not understanding their role).

The earliest texts, from the 5th-century BCE Hippocratic corpus, include two volumes called *Gynaikeia* (literally "Women's Things" but usually translated as *Diseases of Women*), one on conditions of barren women and the other on the nature of woman. These treatises share many theories and therapies, and their lists of remedies using plant and animal substances may in part derive from female oral tradition. They focus almost exclusively on promoting conception, enabling a woman to fulfill her role in producing the next generation. Abortion is mentioned in the Hippocratic Oath and recommended in *Nature of the Child* for a slave entertainer; but because conception was seen as a very gradual process in which the seed "set" and was slowly "cooked" in the womb, little distinction was generally made in the ancient world between contraception and abortion. "Bringing on a late period" could, in practice, be an early abortion, whereas infanticide could be seen as a particularly late abortion.

Historically, however, the most influential ancient author on gynecology is Aristotle (e.g., *Parts of Animals* 650a8ff.; *Generation of Animals* 774a1), whose description of women as colder than men, and thus unable to "cook" their blood into semen, dominated medieval medical accounts of the female body. His ideas were developed by Galen, who envisaged women's bodies as being controlled by two fluids, menstrual blood and female seed. In his *On the Usefulness of Parts of the Body* he stated that retention of seed was even more dangerous than suppression of menstruation, as the seed could rot and become poisonous, causing the symptoms of "hysterical suffocation." Women's health thus depended on sexual intercourse. In women of childbearing age, if blood was not expelled each month, illness would automatically follow; menstruation was a "useful excrement." Galen also discussed the womb; the functions of this organ extended beyond childbirth to affect all women, pregnant or not. Although ancient gynecological texts were not translated, the Arabic medical tradition preserved Hippocratic ideas about female wetness and the dangers of retained menstrual blood.

Alongside Galen and Aristotle, who remained the main

authorities in medieval and early Renaissance medicine, writings associated with Soranus of Ephesus (fl. 120 CE) were also highly influential. In his *Gynecology* Soranus insisted, as had Herophilus, that male and female bodies were made of the same materials and subject to the same conditions. His work was used in later antiquity by the Byzantine encyclopedists Oribasius, Aëtius, and Paul of Aegina and formed the basis of the Latin *Gynecology* of Caelius Aurelianus (ca. 5th cent.). An influential abridgement for midwives was first written in Latin by Muscio ca. 600 and later translated into Greek. For Soranus menstruation, although needed to produce a child, was not essential to health; perpetual virginity was a healthy state.

By the 16th century, with the publication of the entire Hippocratic corpus in Latin (Calvo's translation of 1525, Cornarius' edition of 1546), there was a movement back to Hippocrates. Although treatises on obstetrics had existed since the Middle Ages, the 16th century saw an explosion of texts devoted to gynecology that acknowledged Hippocrates as their ancestor and agreed with the statement in *Diseases of Women* (1.62) that "the cure of the diseases of women differs greatly from that of men." For example, the Galenist Giambattista da Monte, professor at Padua ca. 1540–1551, in his *De uterinis affectibus* (1554) presented Hippocrates rather than Galen as the fullest authority and the most careful of all ancient doctors in addressing the problems raised by disorders of the womb. Many writers cited the Hippocratic *Places in Man* 47: "The womb is the origin of all diseases of women."

By the 1580s Hippocrates was firmly established as the supreme gynecological expert. Galen had devoted several treatises to the topics of the nature of seed, fetal formation, and uterine anatomy but had written no comprehensive work on gynecology. In Galen's model men and women essentially shared the same body, except that men's greater heat enabled their genital organs to be outside the body whereas a woman's organs were inside. The shift of scientific interest to Hippocrates revived the perspective that a woman was neither a man with a womb nor a reverse male but instead differed in every part of her body, her spongy flesh being like wool, absorbing more fluid from her diet and making her "wet." Social factors also came into play; women were believed to take less exercise than men and thus could not use up any accumulated excess fluid. Hence the idea arose that women were specifically designed to live sedentary lives at home whereas men were constituted to deal with the "things outside," a view also found among ancient writers in pseudo-Xenophon (*Oeconomicus* 7.22–23). Renaissance and early modern writers debated the nature of menstrual blood, disagreeing on whether it differed from other blood. Following Galen, many argued that, like other blood, it was produced by the liver but came from an earlier "concoction," thus being similar but not identical, and formed the raw material of the fetus.

Writers in the 16th century insisted that only Hippocrates had understood the complexity of women's disorders and the difficulty of diagnosing them. They used their concern about the prevalence of sterility as a way of becoming more involved in the general disorders of women, which were also the province of midwives. Proclaiming Hippocrates as a founding figure for gynecology and, indeed, for midwifery allowed them to argue for greater male involvement in that field. Hippocratic gynecology remained central to medicine until the 19th century, when in debates about women's education it supported claims that excessive use of the brain would divert blood away from the genital organs, thus leading to their atrophy.

BIBL.: G. R. Dunstan, *The Human Embryo: Aristotle and the Arabic and European Traditions* (Exeter 1990). M. H. Green, *The Trotula: A Medieval Compendium of Women's Medicine* (Philadelphia 2001). A. E. Hanson and M. H. Green, "Soranus of Ephesus: *Methodicorum princeps*," *Aufstieg und Niedergang der Römischen Welt* 37, no. 2 (1994) 968–1075. H. King, *Hippocrates' Woman: Reading the Female Body in Ancient Greece* (London 1998) and *Midwifery, Obstetrics, and the Rise of Gynaecology: Uses of a Sixteenth-century Compendium* (Aldershot 2007). I. Maclean, *The Renaissance Notion of Woman: A Study in the Fortunes of Scholasticism and Medical Science in European Intellectual Life* (Cambridge 1980).

H.K.

H

Hadrian's Villa

Hadrian's Villa, constructed between 118 and 134 CE, surpasses all other ancient villas in its scale, architectural originality, and resonance. A passage in the 4th-century *Historia Augusta* relates that the emperor intended portions of the villa to recall famous places and provinces of the Roman Empire. Thus his villa came to be seen as a paradigm of what might be termed the landscape of allusion, in which gardens and parks are seeded with references to famous and exotic sites. The villa's site near Tivoli, covering a greater area than Pompeii, contains more than 60 distinct buildings, constituting an extended landscape enlivened by the play of water and enriched by the display of sculpture.

The earliest post-classical descriptions of the building's remains, by the Humanist Flavio Biondo and his patron Pope Pius II in 1461, affirmed the connection between the passage in the *Historia Augusta* and the site below Tivoli, identifying it as Hadrian's Villa. Following close upon the Humanists, Renaissance artists and architects began to visit the ruins. Francesco di Giorgio Martini made measured drawings of site's structures, and during the first decades of the 16th century Bramante, Raphael, and other High Renaissance architects are known to have visited the villa and the surrounding buildings. By the middle of the century references to Hadrian's Villa began to appear in guidebooks and architectural treatises, such as those of Palladio and Philibert de l'Orme.

In the 1550s Pirro Ligorio began excavations at the villa, recording his findings in the first systematic description of the site. There is evidence that Ligorio may also have prepared a general plan of the villa; but his drawings were never published, and credit for the first comprehensive survey of the site belongs to Francesco Contini. Long before its publication in 1668, Contini's plan was available for study by Francesco Borromini and other Baroque architects. Attracted by the numerous departures from Vitruvian classicism on display at the villa, Borromini drew inspiration for some of his greatest works, especially the Oratory of the Filippini and the Church of Sant'Ivo alla Sapienza, both in Rome.

The influence of Hadrian's Villa became more diffuse in the course of the 18th century. A great many distinguished artists from throughout Europe were drawn to the site, including Charles-Louis Clérisseau, Robert Adam, Jean-Honoré Fragonard, and Hubert Robert. Giovanni Battista Piranesi emerged in midcentury as its most inspired interpreter, issuing ten printed views of villa structures in his series known as *Vedute di Roma,* as well as a great annotated plan of the entire site, issued posthumously by his son Francesco in 1781. Over the course of the 18th century, statues excavated at the villa found their way into every major European collection, and today its contents are scattered from Malibu in California to St. Petersburg in Russia. The influence of the villa's pavement, mural, and vault decorations may be discerned in countless interiors ranging from Charles Cameron's Agate Rooms (also called Agate Pavilion) at Tsarskoye Selo (for Catherine II) to Robert Adam's Syon House in London.

In the 19th century Hadrian's Villa came to be viewed through the twin lenses of beaux-arts classicism and Romanticism. In 1870 most of the site was acquired by the Italian state, effectively preserving it from further depredation. Much as Piranesi had used the villa to highlight the creative dimension of Roman architecture and its relevance to architects in his day, Le Corbusier, one of the heroic figures of modernism in the 20th century, invoked it as a stimulus to designers engaged in the creative transformation of the past. Architects, scholars, artists, and writers continue to draw and study the relics of Hadrian's extraordinary retreat, proving that its affective and instructive potential remains undiminished.

BIBL.: Jacques Charles-Gaffiot and Henri Lavagne, eds., *Hadrien: Trésors d'une villa impériale* (Milan 1999). William L. MacDonald and John Pinto, *Hadrian's Villa and Its Legacy* (New Haven 1995). Eugenia Salza Prina Ricotti, *Villa Adriana: Il sogno di un imperatore* (Rome 2001). J.PI.

Hagia Sophia

Cathedral church of Constantinople (6th cent. CE). When the old cathedral church of Constantinople, known as Megale Ecclesia (Great Church) or Hagia Sophia (Holy Wisdom), was destroyed by a fire consequent to a major riot in 532, the emperor Justinian (527–565) immediately summoned two renowned architects to reconstruct it. Over a five-year period, Anthemius of Tralles and Isidore of Miletus created their breathtaking masterpiece: a basilica surmounted by a huge dome (100 Byzantine feet, or 31 m, in diameter), flooded with light entering through its many windows to illuminate the golden mosaics and shiny marbles of the interior. The dome had to be rebuilt after an earthquake in 558, but since then, despite some later alterations and additions, the original lines have remained substantially unchanged.

Contemporaries highly praised the artistic and technical achievement both in prose (Procopius, *Buildings,* 1.1.20–66) and in verse (Paul Silentiarius, *Description of Hagia Sophia*), emphasizing the role of the emperor himself, both as a Maecenas and also as a technical adviser directly inspired by God. The logistical skills and the material resources that had permitted the creation of the Great Church vanished soon after the death of Justinian, and for almost a millennium Hagia Sophia remained an unrivaled architectural marvel in the Mediterranean world, viewed with awe and even with superstition. In a Byzantine treatise *About the Building of Hagia Sophia* (9th cent.), the construction of the cathedral is described in a mythical manner: the walls and the dome are raised with the help of angels and of innumerable relics embedded in the brickwork; the wondrous serpentine columns (undisputedly dating back to Justinian's time), considered too fine to be a "recent" production, are supposed to have been retrieved from old pagan buildings.

With the development of Humanism, however, Hagia Sophia began to be mainly appreciated as a fundamental part of the monumental legacy of antiquity. In his *Comparison of Old and New Rome,* Manuel Chrysoloras, professor of Greek in Florence 1397–1400, states (38–57) that "the most powerful and most intelligent peoples," the Greeks and the Romans, mingled to build Constantinople, whose supreme monument was the church of Hagia Sophia, unique in the whole world, a prodigy of technical skillfulness, the ultimate achievement of the reason and intelligence of the human race. In the middle of the 15th century the Humanist and traveler Cyriac of Ancona brought to Italy accurate sketches depicting Hagia Sophia (along with those of the Parthenon and other classical monuments), which aroused the interest of antiquarians and architects. His drawings of the Great Church survive in the copy made by Giuliano da Sangallo (1443–1516), now to be found in the Vatican Library (Barberin. lat. 4424). It has even been suggested that Hagia Sophia, with its huge dome overlooking the imperial capital of the East, could be associated, at least in an ideological way, with the development of the great domed basilicas of Renaissance Italy, such as the cathedral of Florence and maybe even Saint Peter's in Rome.

On the other hand, its influence in the East is indisputable, as the Great Church (converted into a mosque after 1453) is professedly the prototype for the great Ottoman mosques of the 15th and 16th centuries. Scientific investigation of the monument began in 1934, when it was declared a museum, and has never stopped since then.

BIBL.: G. Dagron, *Constantinople imaginaire: Études sur le recueil des "Patria"* (Paris 1984) 191–314. R. Mainstone, *Hagia Sophia: Architecture, Structure and Liturgy of Justinian's Great Church* (London 1988). R. Mark and A. H. Çakmak, eds., *Hagia Sophia from the Age of Justinian to the Present* (Cambridge 1992). T.B.

Hannibal

Carthaginian commander (ca. 247–ca. 183 BCE). He led an enormous army over the Alps at the beginning of the Second Punic War in the late autumn of 218. He beat the Romans in the same year in northern Italy at the Ticino and the Trebia, the next year at Lake Trasimene, and finally in 216 near Cannae in southern Italy. Rome had sent 80,000 men onto the field; 50,000 are supposed to have fallen. Never before had the Romans experienced such a catastrophe. Rome seemed lost.

But most of its allies in Italy did not defect to Hannibal. The Romans saved themselves in the toughest phase of the war with a consistently defensive strategy. They obstinately tried to cut Hannibal off from his supplies. Ultimately the fortunes of the war shifted: Scipio defeated the Carthaginians in Sicily and in Spain, and then he and his army crossed over to North Africa. Near the city of Zama, Hannibal, who had won so many battles, lost the war in 202. The beaten general returned home after his defeat. His subsequent attempt to reform the constitution of Carthage was thwarted by domestic political enemies who accused him of the anti-Roman conspiracy, and thereafter he found himself constantly on the run from the Romans. When threatened with extradition in 183, he committed suicide by poison in Libyssa, on the northern coast of the Gulf of Izmit (Turkey).

From the early modern period on, Hannibal's tragic fate provided inspiration for poets and artists. In the work of Thomas Corneille and Pierre de Marivaux, his demise became a symbol for human transience. Historical and political treatises, on the other hand, were initially heavily influenced by the anti-Carthaginian perspective of the Roman tradition, and they idealized the Roman *res publica* and its representative Scipio Africanus. But by the 18th century the perception of Carthage and its commander was gradually changing. Machiavelli had already glorified Hannibal's military accomplishments in the 16th chapter of *Il principe*. A more expansive study of the ancient sources and the discourse on constitutional theory in the 18th century gave new impetus to research into Carthaginian history. Hannibal became a positive model. Montesquieu and Chateaubriand compared France and England with Rome and Carthage, and Marlborough became Hannibal's successor. Napoleon not only canonized his military accomplishments, but also identified himself during his Italian campaigns with the ancient general and had himself lionized by writers and painters as a "second Hannibal."

Gustave Flaubert's historical novel *Salammbô* reflected his French audience's interest in Carthaginian history, which was heightened by the political vision of French hegemony in North Africa. Hannibal's deeds were consistently given contemporary relevance in political, military, and philosophical contexts. In Germany, Hegel acclaimed the "great Hannibal," who had brought Rome to the brink of destruction. On the eve of the First World War, Hannibal was considered a model for the modern strategist: after Count Schlieffen's study, it was not only the German general staff who regarded Cannae as the paradigm for a perfect encirclement battle, in which even a numerically inferior army could gain the victory. After 1918 and 1945 interest intensified especially in the Second Punic War and the "war guilt question." Meanwhile, fascination with the figure of the general consumed not only military officers but also numerous novelists and filmmakers; to Sigmund Freud, Hannibal, who had avenged himself on his father for the many indignities he had suffered, was a "favorite hero" from his school days.

Beginning in the second half of the 19th century, scholarly research, with the help of historical-critical method, relativized the traditional, Rome-centered view of antiquity, integrated Carthage's history into a universal-historical context, and inquired into "Hannibal's legacy" (Arnold Toynbee), that is, into the manifold consequences of the war for Roman history. Scholars nevertheless remain biased in their discussions of Hannibal's political and military accomplishments and goals, and no common judgment has yet emerged on his person and his actions. For some he is the last and greatest of the Hellenistic *condottieri* (Arnaldo Momigliano), for others he is a lawfully appointed army commander, loyally supported by his government (Serge Lancel).

BIBL.: *Carthage: L'histoire, sa trace et son écho* (Paris 1995). Karl Christ, *Hannibal* (Darmstadt 2003) 153–186. Hans Georg Niemeyer and Alexandra Kopka, "Karthago," *DNP* 14 (2000) 836–854. Jakob Seibert, *Forschungen zu Hannibal* (Darmstadt 1993) 57–82.

S.R.

Translated by Patrick Baker

Harmony of the Spheres

For a number of ancient, medieval, and early modern thinkers, *harmonia* ("joining," "fastening," "attunement," "agreement") has cosmic significance, providing order in the universe. The origin of the idea is usually credited to early Pythagoreans; several fragments of Philolaus (ca. 470–390 BCE) attest to the importance of harmony. In a passage referring to the Pythagoreans, Aristotle (*On the Heavens* 290b12–291a27) argues against the notion that the celestial motions produce a harmony, a musical sound. He explains that its advocates believed that large bodies must inevitably produce sound while moving and, furthermore, that the speeds of the motions of the heavenly bodies and their distances are in the same mathematical relationships as concordant musical sounds. Though Aristotle commends the idea itself as elegant, he nevertheless rejects it, claiming that such a loud noise as would be caused by the motion of large bodies would surely be destructive.

Aristotle's denial of celestial sound highlights one sense of *harmonia,* the musical; the fragments of Philolaus suggest that harmony had a more general meaning. The earliest surviving account of an idea of the harmony of the spheres is in Plato's recounting of the myth of Er, in which the Sirens sing a harmony while the Fates, also singing, turn the spheres as on a spindle (*Republic* 10.616B–617D). For Ptolemy (*Harmonics* 3.13–15) mathematical relations underlie the structures of audible music; these have analogues in the heavens and the soul and are manifest in beauty, celestial geometry, and virtuous character. The harmony of the celestial spheres is related to musical concordance and human virtue.

During the medieval and early modern periods the harmony of the spheres was discussed by many writers, reflecting diverse interests and backgrounds, including philosophy, cosmology, music, and literature. Authors such as Macrobius (fl. 400 CE), Marsilio Ficino (1433–1499), Franchino Gaffurio (1451–1522), Heinrich Cornelius Agrippa (1486–1535), Robert Fludd (1574–1637), Giovanni Battista Riccioli (1598–1671), and Benedict Spinoza (1632–1677) all made reference to the idea, which they understood and interpreted variously. For Boethius (ca. 480–524 or 525) celestial harmony, bodily harmony, and aural harmony were linked; the healthy body imitates the harmony of the heavens, and music is an imitation of the harmony of human life. Some authors were particularly interested in the relevance of the idea of the harmony of the spheres for cosmological and astronomical problems, such as the order and distances of the planets and the periods of their revolutions. For Johannes Kepler (1571–1630) harmony describes the fundamental mathematical reality of the universe, divinely ordained. The mathematical harmony present in movement and arrangement of the heavenly bodies is analogous to that of heard music. Regarding himself as in some ways completing the work of Ptolemy, in *Harmonices mundi* (1619) Kepler described planetary motions using musical notation. Others, the Jesuit Athanasius Kircher (1602–1680) for example, regarded the mathematical relationships as less important than the teleologically and harmoniously ordered arrangement of the cosmos.

For some interpreters the harmony of the spheres was understood metaphorically, or in terms of analogy. The idea of cosmic harmony was represented in visual culture and pervaded many works of literature during the early modern period. Some of the authors mentioned above, including Kircher and Fludd, included images to illustrate their ideas on harmony; the harmony of the spheres was the theme of one of the scene designs, by Bernardo Buontalenti (1536?–1608), planned for the Florentine *intermezzi* to celebrate the Medici wedding of 1589. A number of English poets, including Edmund Spenser (1552–1599), incorporated ideas and images of cosmic harmony into their work; Philip Sidney (1554–1586) referred to "the Planet-like Musicke of Poetrie."

At the beginning of the 21st century the idea of the harmony of the spheres continues to attract many, including artists and musicians. In their theoretical work astronomers and cosmologists often incorporate ideas of pattern, regularity, and harmony. Some have described the "sounds of the universe," referring to pulsars (whole stars spinning at up to 800 revolutions per second, more than an octave above middle C) and the ultra–low-frequency sound waves that are understood to be the precursors of galaxies and clusters.

BIBL.: Andrew Barker, *Greek Musical Writings,* vol. 2, *Harmonic and Acoustic Theory* (Cambridge 1989). Gretchen Ludke Finney, "Harmony or Rapture in Music," in *Dictionary of the History of Ideas,* ed. Philip P. Wiener (New York 1973). James Haar, "Pythagorean Harmony of the Universe," in *Dictionary of the History of Ideas,* ed. Philip P. Wiener (New York 1973). Fernand Hallyn, *The Poetic Structure of the World: Copernicus and Kepler,* trans. Donald M. Leslie (New York 1993). S. K. Heninger Jr., *Renaissance Diagrams of the Universe* (San Marino, Calif., 1977) and *Touches of Sweet Harmony: Pythagorean Cosmology and Renaissance Poetics* (San Marino, Calif., 1974). James Laver, "Stage Designs for the Florentine Intermezzi of 1589," *Burlington Magazine* 16 (1932). Bruce Stephenson, *The Music of the Heavens: Kepler's Harmonic Astronomy* (Princeton 1994).

L.T.

Heidegger, Martin

Widely acknowledged to be one of the most original and important philosophers of the 20th century, Heidegger was born in Messkirch, Germany, in 1889; he spent his early years as a student and later as an instructor at the University of Freiburg, where he was influenced by Edmund Husserl. Except for an interval on the faculty of the University of Marburg (1923–1928), he remained at Freiburg until his death in 1976.

In 1927 he published his fundamental, but also unfinished, treatise, *Being and Time.* Within a few years this book was recognized as an epoch-making philosophical work. Heidegger's main concern was ontology, or the study of Being. He endeavored to initiate a totally different approach from that of the prevailing philosophical tradition. In *Being and Time* he attempted to access Being (*Sein*) by means of phenomenological analysis of human existence (*Dasein*) in respect to its temporal and historical character. After his thinking took a new direction (*die Kehre,* "the turn"), he placed an emphasis on language as the vehicle through which the question of Being could be unfolded. He turned to the exegesis of historical philosophical texts, especially of the Presocratics, but also of Kant, Hegel, Nietzsche, and Hölderlin. He addressed various subjects, such as poetry, architecture, and technology. Instead of looking for a full clarification of the meaning of Being, he tried to pursue the kind of thinking that was no longer "metaphysical." He criticized the tradition of Western philosophy, which he regarded as nihilistic, for, as he claimed, the question of Being as such was obliterated in it.

In his later works, beginning with *An Introduction to Metaphysics* (1935), he referred frequently to ancient Greek thought. He attempted to open a space for thinking outside the traditional metaphysics of Western philosophy by turning his attention to the fragments of Presocratics: Anaximander, Heraclitus, and Parmenides. He also discussed selected texts of Homer, Sophocles, and other early Greek poets. Yet he never became a classical scholar. He carefully distinguished his own philosophical project from a historical exegesis that would satisfy the criteria of classical scholarship. His study of the Greeks gave him a lever with which he tried to dislodge modernity. By going to the Greek beginnings of Western thought, he wanted to "repeat" the early Greek experience of reality or, as he would describe it, the experience of "beings in Being," so that the West could turn away from the dead end of nihilism and begin anew.

The Presocratics were for Heidegger the thinkers who had reflected on the question of Being. Their task was to bring reality as a whole to its first recognition and simplest interpretation. He believed that their thought had become falsified in the tradition of Western philosophy, which, he claimed, from its beginnings with Plato and Aristotle had brought about forgetfulness of Being. Consequently, he did not undertake his "thoughtful repetition" of the Greek experience of beings in Being for the sake of the Presocratics themselves. His work is neither a mere antiquarian, scholarly study of early Greek thinking nor an affirmation of a long-lost Greek way of life. Rather, it is set within the perspective of nihilism and the oblivion of Being, both unknown to the Greeks, and has as its goal the future possibilities for human existence. Heidegger's interpretations of early Greek thinkers take place in the "echo" of the Presocratics. His inquiry into Presocratic thought brings him beyond the early Greek experience of beings to his concept of the openness of Being.

BIBL.: Charles Guigon, ed., *The Cambridge Companion to*

Heidegger (Cambridge 1993). Michael Inwood, *Heidegger* (Oxford 1997). W. J. Korab-Karpowicz, "Heidegger, the Presocratics, and the History of Being," *Existentia* 11, no. 3–4 (2001) 491–502. Glenn W. Most, "Heidegger's Greeks," *Arion* 10, no. 1 (2002) 83–98. W.J.K.-K.

Helen of Troy

Daughter of Zeus and Leda, sister of Clytemnestra and of Castor and Pollux. She makes her first literary appearance in the *Iliad,* which by interrogating her responsibility for causing the Trojan War establishes her doubleness, which became explicit in the tradition of the two Helens: was she a willing partner in elopement with Paris, or did he abduct her? In his *Phaedrus* Plato alludes to Stesichorus' *Palinodia,* in which the poet begs Helen's pardon for singing of her elopement with Paris. Herodotus too states that Helen was not abducted by Paris but eloped with him willingly, and that the Greeks should not have launched a war to reclaim her: a woman would not be carried away unless she wished to be. (But he also maintains that she never went to Troy and remained in Egypt.) In *The Trojan Women* Euripides puts Helen on trial, as it were: while she defends herself by blaming Aphrodite, Hecuba and the chorus blame Helen for the destruction of Troy and for the pitiable fate of the Trojan women. In the palinodic *Helen,* Euripides follows Stesichorus, claiming that Helen never went to Troy but remained in Egypt with Proteus, and that it was over her *eidolon,* a phantom created by Hera, that the Trojan War was fought: the *eidolon* taunted the warriors for their folly, while Helen, like Penelope in the *Odyssey,* waited chastely at home for Menelaus to reclaim her. Gorgias' *Encomium* exonerates Helen by claiming that his power to tell the truth will set her free from the bondage of the lying testimony of the poets; he assumes that she went to Troy but excuses her because (in his view) she acted for one of three reasons, coercion, persuasion, or being in love.

The contrasting representations by Virgil and Ovid, in Latin literature, further exemplify this doubleness of Helen. In book 6 of the *Aeneid* Deiphobus depicts Helen as a perfidious murderer. In Ovid's *Heroides* 17 her letter to Paris reveals a woman careful of her honor and good name, possessed of a clear-eyed and skeptical intelligence superior to Paris's naive assurance. The letter nevertheless records her gradual acceptance of her love for Paris despite her many misgivings concerning its consequences, including her premonition of the Trojan War.

In canto 5 of Dante's *Inferno* (1308–1321) Helen appears in the catalogue of lovers (following Dido and Cleopatra) as the one responsible for the ills of the Trojan War. Similarly, Boccaccio in his *Famous Women* (*De claris mulieribus,* 1359) calls her "notorious" for her "lustfulness." Although he follows Virgil in excoriating Helen for aiding the Greek warriors on the night of Troy's fall, he also mentions "other sources" that relate Helen's abduction against her will. Christine de Pizan's *Book of the City of Ladies* (1405) includes Helen in a catalogue of beautiful women and accepts the account that Troy was destroyed as the result of her rape by Paris, concluding thereby that she was the most beautiful of all, without blaming her in any way for the destruction.

Ronsard addressed his *Sonets pour Hélène* (1578) to Hélène Surgères, a lady-in-waiting to Catherine de Médicis. He likens the fire of love that consumes him to the fire that destroyed Troy (2.16). The best known sonnet in the collection, "Quand vous serez bien vieille" (2.24), was translated by W. B. Yeats ("When You Are Old," 1893).

In *The Faerie Queene* (1590) Edmund Spenser features (3.9) the seduction of Hellenore by Paridell, latter-day versions of Helen and Paris. His Helen-whore or Helen-ore (now) is the naive wife of Malbecco, a jealous, one-eyed husband, and she easily succumbs to Paridell's use of seduction techniques derived from Ovid's *Amores.* Soon (3.10), already abandoned by Paridell, she chooses satyrs as her lovers.

Shakespeare appears to follow Spenser's lead in *Troilus and Cressida* (1601–1602), a bitterly cynical and satiric debunking of the heroic claims made for the Trojan War. The Trojans debate whether to keep or return Helen; they ultimately decide that they must keep the woman extolled by Troilus as the "theme of honour and renown." Yet Shakespeare's characterization of Helen calls attention to the gap between this high-minded abstraction and the disillusioning reality—a shallow and decadent woman obsessed with love. In *A Midsummer Night's Dream* (1595–1596) and *All's Well That Ends Well* (1602–1603), however, Shakespeare represents characters named Helen positively as active, desiring subjects rather than as passive objects of contention; their character ironically contradicts that of their prototype and namesake.

Christopher Marlowe's well-known praise of Helen in *Doctor Faustus* (1604) for having "the face that launched a thousand ships" informs Goethe's celebration two centuries later in *Faust,* Part 2 (1832), of Helen as emblematic of the ideal form of beauty.

Jean Giraudoux's *La Guerre de Troie n'aura pas lieu* (1935)—*The Trojan War Will Not Take Place*—is centered on the question whether the Trojans will be able to avoid the war by returning Helen to the Greeks. Though declining to exonerate Helen, Giraudoux's play, like the *Iliad* and Shakespeare's *Troilus,* shows Helen to be ultimately beside the point. Though this idea recalls Euripides' *Helen,* in its negative representation of Helen and her juxtaposition with Trojan Andromache and Cassandra, *La Guerre* harks back to *The Trojan Women.*

The poet H.D.'s visionary epic *Helen in Egypt* (1954) follows Stesichorus and Euripides in defending Helen, "hated of the Greeks"; it expands on the tradition of the meeting between Helen and Achilles in the underworld, to focus on their equivalences and to imagine their enduring relationship.

In Derek Walcott's *Omeros* (1990), set on the Caribbean island of St. Lucia, Helen is a beautiful black woman loved by both Achille and Hector—an allusion not only to the conflict between Menelaus and Paris but also to that between Agamemnon and Achilles over Briseis in the *Iliad*—and is the occasion for Major Plunkett's writing of the history of St. Lucia, the "Helen of the West Indies."

Notable visual representations of Helen include Maarten van Heemskerck's *Panoramic Landscape with the Abduction of Helen* (1535) and Guido Reni's *Abduction of Helen* (1631). Both depict Helen willingly departing with Paris, rather than being abducted. Jacques-Louis David's *Paris and Helen* (1788) depicts the two lovers languidly dallying in a Trojan interior, with no sign of Helen's contempt toward Paris that marks their exchange in *Iliad* book 6.

BIBL.: Norman Austin, *Helen of Troy and Her Shameless Phantom* (Ithaca 1994). Matthew Gumpert, *Grafting Helen: The Abduction of the Classical Past* (Madison 2001). Susan Snyder, "*All's Well That Ends Well* and Shakespeare's Helens: Text and Subtext, Subject and Object," *English Literary Renaissance* 18 (1988) 66–77. Mihoko Suzuki, *Metamorphoses of Helen: Authority, Difference, and the Epic* (Ithaca 1989).

M.SU.

Hellenes

Hellēnes is the generic ethnic name for all Greeks during classical, Hellenistic, and Roman times. In the Christian era the name underwent considerable changes of meaning. The Christians identified polytheistic religion in all its expressions as Greek. Therefore, in their polemic against pagan beliefs and rites they labeled collectively as *Hellēnes* all their non-Christian enemies. In this sense the Saracens in the Arab desert and the Scythians of the north in the late antique period were conveniently called *Hellēnes,* and the Russians before their conversion at the end of the 10th century were charged as being followers of the "Hellenic and godless faith." Even the Chinese in the 11th century were given the attribute "religiously *Hellēnes.*" Consequently, *hellēnismos* as a system is applied to all non-Christian religions. This categorical attitude faced educated Christians with the dilemma of rejecting or following the classical Greek *paideia,* the cultural tradition in language, philosophy, rhetoric, and art as well as the educational system that produced them. With the substantial contribution of the Church Fathers who had studied in the Greek rhetorical and philosophical schools in Athens, Alexandria, and many other cities of the Eastern Roman Empire, still flourishing in the 4th century, this cultural tradition was maintained while disconnected from its religious implications. Even after the collapse of the Western empire in the 5th century, residents of the Eastern branch of the empire (which became Byzantium) continued to term themselves Roman (*Rhōmaioi*) citizens, until the fall of the Byzantine Empire a millennium later; their cultural and ethnic self-perceptions were more complicated.

In the 10th century and later, during what has been called the first era of Byzantine humanism, which saw a conscious turn to the past and a revival of classical culture in language, historiography, rhetoric, and art, Constantine Porphyrogenitus (r. 908–945) distinguished Hellenic culture, which he identified as the culture of his ancestors, from the non-Christian beliefs of the pagans (*paganoi*). In accordance with this new attitude, in the 11th century the great scholar Michael Psellus would provide a positive application of *hellēnismos* as the definition of all Greek cultural tradition. Thenceforth Byzantines who had enjoyed proper education could be called *Hellēnes* despite their Christian faith. But the term still bore no connotation of ethnic affiliation. Thus, for the citizens of Maina in the Peloponnese, who are attested to have been called *Hellēnes* by the local inhabitants, Constantine Porphyrogenitus provided the explanation that "though they are from the ancient Romans . . . in very ancient times they were idolaters and worshipers of images after the fashion of the ancient *Hellēnes.*"

In the 12th century, when many Westerners began to appear in the East either as merchants of the Italian cities—Venice, Genoa, and Pisa—or as crusaders, all usually labeled by the Byzantines as Latins (*latinoi*), it was no longer possible to claim exclusive use of the term *Romans* for citizens of the Byzantine Empire. Especially after the sack of Constantinople in 1204 (during the Fourth Crusade) and the foundation of a Latin empire and patriarchate in the Byzantine capital in the name of Rome, the Byzantines, Greek-speaking in their vast majority and consistently termed *Gr(a)eci* by their new Latin-speaking rulers, rediscovered in the term *Hellēnes* their ethnic name and identity as an attribution alternative to *Roman.* With the empire's decline in the 14th and 15th centuries this trend received additional impetus. The Byzantines' dogmatic opposition to the Catholic Church permitted a terminological shift such that the Orthodox rite and faith were now distinguished as Hellenic. The common feeling was that the people of the Eastern empire were Hellenes by birth, culture, *and* religion. Even the clothes they wore were said to be of the Hellenic style. A dramatic climax was reached during the fall of Constantinople to the Turks in 1453, when the attacked Byzantines proclaimed that "we are Hellenes from birth, as proven by our language and culture."

BIBL.: A. Garzya, "Visages de l'Hellénisme dans le monde byzantin," *Byzantion* 55 (1985) 463–482. K. Lechner, *Hellenen und Barbaren im Weltbild der Byzantiner* (Munich 1954).

E.C.

Hellenistic Age

The legacy of Alexander is considered the focal point of the Hellenistic age, emerging with the conquest of the Achaemenid empire in 330 BCE. The integration of the territories ruled by Alexander and his successors in either the Parthian or the Roman Empire, a process ending with the Roman capture of Alexandria in 30 BCE, marked the end of the political existence of a sovereign Hellenistic world. But Hellenistic culture maintained its influence in imperial Rome and the East until late antiquity and the early epoch of Arab expansion.

The underlying concept of Hellenism has a certain background in Hellenistic antiquity itself, since it is related to the Greek verb *hellēnizein* and the noun *Hellēnismós,* both referring in the strictest sense to the correct use of the Greek language and, in a wider sense, to an acculturation of different aspects of Greek lifestyle, including religious beliefs. In 2 Maccabees (4:13) *Hellēnismós* is considered to be a mortal threat to Jewish identity through acculturation. The role of the *Hellēnistai* in Acts (6:1) reflects a first glimpse of the future separation of a Christian community from the Orthodox Jewish traditions. In late antiquity *Hellēnismós* came to mean a respect for classical philosophy and pagan religion and was used in a positive way by the emperor Julian (*Epistulae* 84a Bidez–Cumont) but also in a critical, distancing way by a variety of Christian writers. In Renaissance Humanistic scholarship a debate developed concerning the character of the *lingua hellenistica* used in the Septuagint and the New Testament. Early 19th-century scholars also discussed the Greek language used in the Near Eastern kingdoms of Alexander's successors as being Hellenistic in nature. The general sense of *Hellenism* among scholars of that era implied acculturation to a superior Greek tradition, as seen in opposition to *Orientalism* (referring to the Near East).

It was at this time that the Prussian historian J. G. Droysen developed the concept of Hellenism as a progressive principle in world history, and of Alexander as its instrument (*Geschichte Alexanders des Grossen,* 1833; *Geschichte des Hellenismus,* 2 vols., 1836, 1843). Greek philosophical rationalism, and religious anthropomorphism as well, were viewed as undermined by their confrontation and amalgamation with the traditions of the Near East, a process that made way for the birth of Christianity and later for Islam. Such ideas reflect Hegelian influence. But Droysen restricted the historian's view to assiduous research in original sources. Thus, great parts of his work deal with realities: with warfare and diplomacy, politics and economics. In this way he was able to define the Hellenistic world with its balanced system of states as a modern one. With the successful second edition of his work in 1877–1878 the concept of a Hellenistic age became generally accepted. At that time and for the next generations, the rather romantic idea of a real synthesis of Greek and Eastern traditions gave way to a concept of *hellenization* in the sense of political and cultural superiority: on the one hand, the dynamic forces of the Greek spirit transformed the Ancient Near East into a modern world of Hellenistic culture; on the other hand, the "melting" of civilizations—and in the racist form of that concept, the mixing of blood—was seen to undermine the pure Greek identity in a dangerous way.

The most recent decades of intensive scientific work have tended to take a very different approach: the idea of the Near East as a cultural unit, along with simplistic models of a cultural synthesis or acculturation, has been fundamentally criticized. The concept of Greek culture itself has been reconceived as being widely differentiated, as were the many forms of cultural contacts and types of lifestyle in the Hellenistic world. Nevertheless, Droysen's perception that the Hellenistic world in some way mirrors the modern, present-day world, is still a fascinating one, all the more so as the confrontation of Hellenism with the expanding Roman Empire invites speculation about analogies in contemporary public debates.

BIBL.: Andrew Erskine, ed., *A Companion to the Hellenistic World* (Oxford 2003). Bernd Funck, ed., *Hellenismus: Beiträge zur Erforschung von Akkulturation und politischer Ordnung in den Staaten des hellenistischen Zeitalters,* Akten des Internationalen Hellenismus-Kolloquiums Berlin 1994 (Tübingen 1996). Susanne Said, ed., *Hellenismos: Quelques jalons pour une histoire de l'identité grecque,* Actes du Colloque de Strasbourg 25–27 October 1989 (Leiden 1991). R.B.

Heraclitus

As great as the gap has often been between original productions of archaic philosophy and their subsequent presentation by later philosophers, the reception of Heraclitus of Ephesus (late 6th–early 5th cent. BCE) in antiquity stands as a unique case. There is a Platonic Heraclitus and an Aristotelian one, a Stoic Heraclitus and even a Skeptical one. These different reappropriations were by and large detached from the original text and subsequently acquired their own life, according to a process we encounter often in doxography. The reason for this lay with Heraclitus' striking pronouncements expressed in sentences or groups of sentences (in aphoristic form) with particularly cryptic meanings (hence Heraclitus the Obscure). Heraclitus' texts easily produce arbitrary readings. Starting with Plato, two main interpretations were common, of which different variants dominated the modern and antique history of reception: either Heraclitus was the thinker of universal flux (*Theatetus* 160B, *Cratylus* 402A) and therefore denied the principle of contradiction (Aristotle, *Metaphysics* 1005b23a), or he was the thinker of the coincidence of the opposites (Plato, *Sophist* 242E, *Symposium* 187AB), and therefore of reason (*logos*), which is the paradoxical unity of all things. Following Aristotle, who in the first book of *Metaphysics* (984a) presented Heraclitus as a "physicist" whose principle is fire, the Stoics recognized him as the author of a cosmotheological system very similar to their own, in which universal reason was identified as a demiurgic fire. The different interpretative planes rested on certain selected statements. The doctrine of flux hinged on one fragment: you cannot step into the same river twice (fr. 12). This fragment was the source of a philosophy that Plato characterized as "afflicted with catarrh" (*Cratylus* 440C) because it implied that "everything flows" (*pantha rhei*). The cosmological interpretation drew from a series of fragments in which fire played a crucial role (fr. 30), although, in the original text, fire functioned probably as the symbol for contradictory *logos* rather than as a material principle. The interpretation that least betrayed Heraclitus is one that emphasized the paradoxical identity of all things, an identity that can be perceived only through its opposite (fr. 66, 67, 88).

Of all these interpretations, "everything flows" has become the most well known and has granted Heraclitus extraphilosophical survival. It is linked, through a tradition that began as early as the imperial period (Seneca, *On Anger* 2.10; Lucian, *Philosophies for Sale* 13s) and that was richly illustrated later in literature (Montaigne, *Essays* 1.50) and art (Jacob Jordaens in the Metropolitan Museum), to the pessimistic figure of Heraclitus in tears, embodiment of all melancholy, in contrast to Democritus, who laughed at human stupidity. The Hegelian interpretation, based on the notion of "becoming" and "contradiction," viewed Heraclitus as the father of dialectic; Hegel claimed in his *History of Philosophy,* "Hier sehen wir Land; es ist kein Satz des Heraklit, den ich nicht in meine Logik aufgenommen" ("Here we see land; there is no proposition of Heraclitus which I have not adopted in my *Logic*"). Nietzsche, who initially praised all the Preplatonic philosophers, eventually recognized in Heraclitus his master (*Ecce Homo* 3). Since Nietzsche, Heraclitus has been given a radically antidialectical interpretation. His preconceptual discourse easily served Heideggerian phenomenology, which saw in Heraclitus' prophetic flashes the original unveiling of Being.

BIBL.: J. P. Herschbell and S. A. Nimis, "Nietzsche and Heraclitus," *Nietzsche-Studien* 8 (1979) 17–38. U. Hölscher, "Die Wiedergewinnung des antiken Bodens: Nietzsches Rückgriff auf Heraklit," *Neue Hefte für Philosophie* 15/16 (1978) 156–182. G. W. Most, "*Polemos panton pater:* Die Vorsokratiker in der Forschung der Zwanziger Jahre,"in *Altertumswissenschaft in den 20er Jahren,* ed. H. Flashar (Stuttgart 1995) 87–114. N. Walcker, *Heraklit und die deutsche Romantik* (diss., Tübingen 1923). W. Weisbach, "Der sogenannte Geograph von Velasquez und die Darstellungen des Demokrits und Heraklits," *Jahrbuch der Preussischen Kunstsammlungen* 49 (Berlin 1928) 151–158.

A.L.

Translated by Elizabeth Trapnell Rawlings and Jeannine Routier-Pucci

Herculaneum

According to the Greek historian Dionysius of Halicarnassus (1.44), this town was named after its founder, Heracles (Latin Hercules). The ancient geographer Strabo tells us that it originally was settled by Oscans, Tyrrheneans, Pelasgians, and finally by the Samnites. After more than 250 years of independence, Herculaneum fell to the Romans in 80 BCE and became a Latin municipality. Facing Neapolis (Naples), right on the coast of the bay, Herculaneum from the late 1st century BCE became one of the best-known summer resorts or residencies for local as well as for Roman aristocrats. In 79 CE neighboring Mount Vesuvius buried it under enormous surges of pyroclastic flow.

The first modern finds (marble sculpture) emerged incidentally at the beginning of the 18th century. In 1738 the young Don Carlos (the first Bourbon king of Naples, later Charles III of Spain) initiated excavations under the guidance of militarily trained engineers, notably Rocca de Alcubierre and Karl Weber. Deep tunnels dug into the petrified lava fortuitously hit remains of the theater and led to immediate identification of the site. In the following years more than 200 sculptures were found, more than 90 of them belonging to the famous Villa of the Papyri, named after finds there of ancient papyri, mostly of Epicurean content. (The building itself has now been replicated at the Getty Museum in Malibu, California.) Precious objects from Herculaneum, housed today at the National Museum in Naples, were at first transferred to the newly built royal museum in neighboring Portici. The finds at Herculaneum caused an immense sensation among European intellectuals, and the site and its nearby museum soon became one of the most highly appreciated destinations of the Grand Tour.

Because of easier excavating conditions at Pompeii, Herculaneum lost its status as favored site after 1761. Further excavations that for the first time dispensed with the tunnels and cleared an open area occurred only after 1855 but did not last long. What is visible today covers only some 4.5 hectares and is attributable mainly to the "new" excavations undertaken by A. Maiuri between 1927 and 1958. It is believed that only one-third of the ancient town is currently known. The site of Herculaneum is overlain by modern Resina (renamed Ercolano in 1969), which dates to medieval times.

The excavated ruins of Herculaneum belong to the last decades before 79 CE. Compared to Pompeii (of which 44 hectares have been excavated), little is known of the town's urban infrastructure. No forum or basilica or any main religious sanctuaries have been found. Instead, a "town quarter" has been excavated that includes the ancient coastline with sections of a harbor, a sanctuary for Venus, and a bath complex (labeled the Suburban Baths in modern guides and maps). On the northwestern outskirts of the town lie the excavated areas of the Villa dei Papiri, first discovered by the 18th-century tunneling. The richness of the villa's remains and artifacts suggests that it must have belonged to one of the leading aristocrats of its time. The hillside overlooking the Bay of Naples was occupied by villa-like houses with long terraces directly facing the sea, from which could be viewed a magnificent panorama. A bit farther from shore were smaller houses and apartment buildings whose upper floors were the dominant facades along narrow lanes. The conditions of the volcanic flow led to the preservation of a remarkable quantity of architectural and interior furnishings (doors, cupboards, beds, balconies, roofing, etc.) that have offered valuable insights into the lifestyles of Roman families of that era.

Toward the town center a stretch of one of the main ancient throughfares, the *decumanus maximus,* has been excavated. In addition to rows of shops, the avenue revealed a large building complex, obviously dedicated to the worship of the Roman emperor and his family. The famous equestrian statues of two citizens, Marcus Nonius

Balbus senior and junior, are found at this location; it was probably their family who financed the spectacular training ground (*campus*) for young men nearby (the palaestra). This complex also contained a large, columned courtyard with a cross-shaped water basin, a ceremonial hall, and at least two sanctuaries for Egyptian deities and the goddess Cybele. Shops and apartments with at least three floors, along the adjoining street, were rented out to generate income for the town itself.

BIBL.: J. J. Deiss, *The Town of Hercules: A Buried Treasure Trove,* rev. ed. (Malibu, Calif., 1995). M. Pagano, ed., *Gli antichi ercolanesi: Antropologia, società, economia,* exhibition catalogue, Ercolano 2000 (Naples 2000), and *Herculaneum: A Reasoned Archaeological Itinerary* (Torre del Greco 2000). M. E. A. Pirozzi, *Herculaneum: The Excavations, Local History and Surroundings* (Naples 2003). J.-A.D.

Hercules

Hercules—Herakles in Greek—was probably the most adaptable, and adapted, mythological hero in Graeco-Roman antiquity. The range of his qualities, from prodigious strength to moral and intellectual wisdom, was extraordinary. So was the range of his exploits, and their geographical compass—and in fact the range of his very existence: he was the only Greek hero (in the cultic sense) who also was a god, and he could become, at the same time, the very incarnation of human suffering, endurance, and triumph.

Subsequent ages therefore found a plethora of material to work with in the Hercules myth. Just as in antiquity, no one comprehensive treatment emerged either in literature or in the arts. Instead, one could freely pick and choose, and some aspects of the hero were clearly more congenial than others, depending on factors such as the adaptor's time, locale, and personal or public agenda. The resulting contradictions have mattered little (being important only to academics, for whom the demonstration of dichotomies and ambiguities is part of making a living). As is true of any multifaceted figure, what was merely Hercules' baggage to some was a glorious burden or asset to others. It has been left to the reader or viewer to consider any individual portrait of Hercules within the context of all the others. But because viewing him against the entire spectrum of his characterizations would have required a great deal of knowledge, compartmentalization ruled the reception of the Hercules character, and compartmentalization, as we know from complex and contradictory figures in our own times, can be an essential ingredient of survival.

Survive Hercules did, and handsomely at that. In literature, his heyday came in the Middle Ages and the Renaissance, whereas the moderns generally found the more unequivocally cerebral and psychologically complex Ulysses more to their liking. As for art, the statistics from *The Oxford Guide to Classical Mythology in the Arts, 1300–1990s* (1993) are enlightening: the list of representations of Hercules is substantially longer (45 pages) than for any other character from Greek and Roman mythology save Aphrodite/Venus (48); by comparison, Odysseus gets 30, followed by Aeneas with 27, whereas Hercules' father, Zeus, winds up with 12 and Achilles with 15. There is an unquestionable concentration of images from the 15th to the 17th century, due to heraldic and genealogical factors as well as simple moralizing, which then fell out of vogue until it was revived by modern interpreters of Virgil's *Aeneid;* Aeneas, in many ways, is a Hercules-like character. But Hercules was not to be denied in the 20th century, when the new medium of film eagerly seized on an action hero who could travel far and across time: witness Arnold Schwarzenegger's film debut in *Hercules in New York* (1970), which launched a trajectory that now includes Herculean tasks of a different kind.

Like other mythological heroes and deities, Hercules was able to escape the brunt of the Christian attack by way of allegory. This tradition had taken root with the Hercules myth before the onset of patristic chastising by Augustine and others, who reduced him to a strongman who clubbed his way around: far from being the exemplar of physical strength, Hercules was seen as a wise man, a philosopher, an initiate of "the celestial science," and as "most skilled in logic" (so wrote Plutarch), qualities summed up by Servius' uncharacteristically pithy phrase describing Hercules as *mente magis quam corpore fortis* (stronger in mind than in body). Some of his exploits, too, had been conveniently allegorized—the Hydra, for example, stood for envy and even sophistry—and this *modus interpretandi* reached new heights in Fulgentius' *Mythologiae* (late 5th cent.), which was much read in the Middle Ages. Fulgentius was a Christian and opened the path for others, such as Isidore of Seville. When Hercules fully emerged in works of the 13th century, the mantle of respectability was draped securely around his formerly bare shoulders, and he was portrayed in modes both courtly and Christian. What is more, to use a distinction made by Benedetto Croce, the best of these works and those of later periods genuinely enriched the life of the myth, rather than that of its interpretation.

One such work was Raoul Le Fèvre's *Recuyell des hystoires de Troyes* (1464; for further works, see Galinsky 1972). Both Le Fèvre's original and Caxton's English version (1474), which happens to be the first book printed in English, were republished more than 20 times over the next two and a half centuries. Le Fèvre freed Hercules from his allegorical cage and, with cheerful liveliness and narrative aplomb, presented his fortunes as a medieval knight while not changing the ancient Greek locale; the illustrations enhance this *aggiornamento* by presenting the hero in proper medieval costume, parallel to Gentile da Fabriano's and others' paintings of biblical subjects. At the cusp of the Renaissance, Le Fèvre was one of the few writers in the entire tradition to try his hand at portraying Hercules' wide range of exploits and abilities. Hercules is a medieval knight through and through: a practitioner of courtly love, a competitor in the tournament of the Olympic Games, a selfless, chivalrous protector of others from all kinds of evil (the contemporary version of the Greek *alexikakos*), and his opponents, instead of being river gods like Achelous, now are malignant knights; accordingly, Hercules lays siege to Achelous' castle. But there is more: the tradition of Hercules' being *mente fortis* is worked into a spirited presentation of him as a paragon of academic pursuits: instructed by Atlas, whose burden now is a huge pile of books, Hercules goes on to teach philosophy in Athens, investigates the mystery of Cacus' smoke, and founds a school at Salamanca, which he ingeniously staffs (as the students were "rude and dulle") with a double of himself while he goes on an indefinite leave of absence. In addition to all its other qualities, the *Recueil*'s combination of entertainment and deeper meaning makes it one of the unique works in the history of Hercules' reception.

Most others, as might be expected, display a narrower scope and, quite often, less creativity. Whatever life they have is the life of the myth's interpretation. Typical examples are the Florentine chancellor and Humanist Coluccio Salutati's *De laboribus Herculis* (ca. 1406) and, in Spain, Enrique de Villena's *Los doze trabajos de Hercules* (1417). They are compendia that offer diligent categorizations and taxonomies of Hercules' actual exploits and of the way one should look at them: *ad litteram, moraliter, naturaliter,* in terms of *verdad,* and so on. One dimension is added: the instruction of nobles. In keeping with this function as *Fürstenspiegel,* the coarser, more lifelike, and carnal features of the hero are transmuted, not only by sublimation but also by making him into the representation (*incarnation* might be the wrong term) of an abstract idea. Hercules is not just *homo virtuosus* but "a higher state of virtue" and "both virtue and reason"; the action hero of Greek mythology is not only a practitioner of the contemplative life but also the very "light of explored truth." Though he is a guide to virtuous action, this Hercules ceases to live and breathe and becomes an abstraction, a type.

This approach helped elide, of course, his more problematic aspects. Another factor in the choice of Hercules as an exemplar was genealogical. Regal and noble families all across Europe claimed descent from the paragon—just as the Dorians had, once upon a time—including the courts of Burgundy (Le Fèvre's patron), Castile, Navarre, and Habsburg, and the d'Este and Farnese families. Hercules' unceasing efforts at having progeny bore fruit beyond all expectations. The list of Renaissance and Baroque painters who chose Hercules as a subject for their patrons also contains prominent names: Mantegna, Pollaiuolo, Correggio, Annibale Carracci, Giulio Romano, Guido Reni, Veronese, Tiepolo, and Rubens, among others. There was room for originality: Pollaiuolo's splendidly dynamic small-scale group *Hercules and Antaeus* (ca. 1475) exhibits a three-dimensional combination of centrifugality and perfect balance for which "there is no precedent . . . among earlier statuary groups of any size, ancient or Renaissance" (Janson 1986, 427). Would it be compatible with the moralizing interpretation, such as de Villena's, that Antaeus symbolized the desires of the flesh, fostered constantly by contact with carnal Earth? According to a reception aesthetic that advocates viewer-response criticism, everything is possible.

The meaning of Hercules is more tightly defined in such works as Carracci's in the Farnese Gallery in Rome (1597–1601). In the small room called the Camerino, the ensemble of representations of the hero, anchored by the iconic *Choice of Hercules,* centers on the idea of the rejection of the sensual life in both *vita activa* and *vita comtemplativa.* While Hercules is shown in action, such as bearing the (real) globe, we see a mature Hercules with a philosopher's beard, a seeker of wisdom. The labors depicted in the four roundels represent the triumph of virtue over the elements. Similar themes are shown on the ceiling of the gallery, including an adaptation of the Farnese Hercules. But besides all the allegorizing and moralizing directed at his patron, Cardinal Odoardo Farnese, who was invoked as Hercules, Carracci made an addition for his own cause. It is the rare scene of Hercules freeing Prometheus; Prometheus, at the time, had become the archetype of the creative artist.

Similarly, in Carracci's *Choice,* which became determinative for the subsequent tradition (after earlier attempts by Cranach and others), a *poeta laureatus* and the figure of Pegasus hint at Hercules' poetic fame. In the fable of the Sophist Prodicus, the emphasis had been not on Hercules choosing virtue per se but on his ability to deliberate and use his mind. There are some traces of that in Carracci's portrait, but it is but the visual culmination of a 16th-century tradition that, so far even from de Villena's compendious view of the hero's character and exploits, narrowed him down to a mere exemplar of virtue as opposed to vice. Ironically, that tendency flourished in the very compendia of myth, such as Natale Conti's *Mythologiae libri decem* (1551) and Vicenzo Cartari's *Images of the Gods* (1556), which were highly influential, as were Cesare Ripa's *Iconologia* (1593) and emblem books like Andrea Alciato's (1531) and Geoffrey Whitney's (1586).

Being virtuous meant being Christian, and therefore it was not a big step to identify Hercules with Christ. Besides Chrétien le Gouays, who single-mindedly pursued such goals in his *Ovide moralisé* (early 14th cent.), Dante compared Hercules' descent into Hell with Christ's, reprising a theme that had already occurred in catacomb painting. Further, in a canzone ascribed to him, he invoked Hercules in terms similar to those used for Christ and Mary. The most methodical proponent of the Christ-Hercules equation was Ronsard, who, in his *Hymne de l'Hercule Chrestien* (1564), listed 18 parallels between the two—far fewer, it should be added, than biblical scholars in the 20th century, one of whom postulated that the three synoptic Gospels ultimately were based on a Cynic-Stoic biography of Hercules. More allusively, Milton used Hercules as a suggestive symbol of Christ at some significant junctures of *Paradise Lost.* Even more pervasive was Spenser's use of Hercules as a heroic matrix for some of his heroes in the *Faerie Queene,* which reflected the Renaissance ethos of virtue guiding action.

In a different way, Hercules became an emblem of Renaissance Humanists, especially in France. Guillaume Budé and others rediscovered Lucian's description of a curious image, which he claimed to have seen in Gaul. It represented a wizened Hercules, who led his joyous followers by a golden chain that was fastened to his tongue and to their ears. The real Hercules, Lucian's mentor explains, was a wise man who achieved everything by eloquence and persuasion—*eloquentia fortitudine praestantior,* read the caption in Alciato's design that was duly parodied by Dürer. The French, however, took their Hercules seriously; by comparison, the Greek hero became "le petit Hercule Grec," and Joachim du Bellay's plea in the *Defence and Ennoblement of the French Language* (1549) culminates with a reference to the Gallic Hercules.

In contrast, the post-Renaissance tradition of Hercules lacks any defining focus. It is scattered rather than diverse, as different aspects of the hero tend to become vignettes. They can be intensely personal; Goethe, in his period of Sturm und Drang, provides a good example in his farce *Gods, Heroes and Wieland,* where he reasserts naturalness (*Natürlichkeit*), unshackled by conventions, in the face of bookish modes of life and literature, and simplistic moralizations. Later, in the second part of Goethe's *Faust,* it is Hercules who approximates most closely the idea of the *Urmensch,* God's idea of man, precisely because of the unequaled range of his qualities. With this comes the realization that it is impossible to express Hercules' full complexity (7395–7396): "Though men may strive in stone and story / Never has he appeared in all his glory." Goethe's own complexity and contradictions of character led him to a sympathetic understanding of Hercules' same qualities that is rare in the tradition; Jung's assigning to Hercules only a minor and schematic role in his theory of archetypes provides an illustrative and somewhat unexpected contrast.

Even more than Goethe's, Hölderlin's self-identification with Hercules stands out for its intensity and because it lasted almost his entire poetic life. Unlike most writers, he was not concerned with adapting the Greek hero to contemporary taste (let alone mores), but Herakles became his "brother" and a means of constant self-expression for all phases of his poetic thematics and life, right up to the madness they both shared: primal stage of development, conflict, man conquering nature, struggle, achievement, divine infinity and human limitation, cool-headed thinking, dynamic life force, and much more. The result is one of the most consummately ethereal (Hölderlin's Herakles has no rough edges) and original symbioses of a poet and a mythological figure in the entire tradition.

Most of the literary tradition of Hercules, however, was a great deal more humdrum. He reappeared unmemorably on the tragic stage in France (Rotrou, La Tuillerie), England (Thomas Heywood), and in numerous operatic versions of the Alcestis story, including Handel's and Lully's. Among 20th-century dramatists, Wedekind cast him in a profoundly pessimistic vein, whereas Pound, eschewing much of the bombast of previous dramatizations of Hercules (not entirely Seneca's fault) in *The Women of Trachis* (1954), did everything to ennoble him: Deianeira's role is diminished and, also quite in contrast to Sophocles' play, Hercules reaches apotheosis—not on faraway Olympus, but by being able to see the meaning of his life ("Splendour, it all coheres").

There were some other brave attempts to bring Hercules back onto the stage (e.g., Archibald MacLeish's verse drama *Herakles,* 1967) and even into epic (Carl Spitteler's *Olympian Spring,* 1900–1906, rev. 1910), in addition to Émile Verhaeren's powerful but bleak vision of him as a loner (*Hercule,* 1910). More successful was Dürrenmatt's revival of the most difficult Hercules, the comic one, in his poignantly modern adaptation *Herakles and the Stables of Augias* (1954). The medium, however, was one of limited duration: a radio play. Instead, it was cinema that triumphed in the second half of the 20th century and became Hercules' favorite venue.

Even more decisively than in art (and there were some notable representations of Hercules after the Renaissance and the Baroque, including works by De Chirico, Dalí, Bourdelle, and Paul Manship), Hercules outdistanced any other mythological figure in film: there are more than 40 movies about him. Easily the most popular and entertaining Greek hero, he is ideally suited for the requisite fare of escapism, entertainment, adventure, romance, and, here and there, an underlying note of seriousness that smartly stayed away from the *Tiefsinn,* profundity or pensiveness, that had weighed down some of his earlier portrayals in the tradition. The path breaker of the sword-and-sandal genre was *Hercules* (1959), with its earlier incarnation as *Le fatiche di Ercole* (1957). Against a background of other films on Greece and Rome that pretended to strive for some kind of authenticity and serious character exploration, *Hercules* was pure action and entertainment, all personified by the exquisitely muscular bodybuilder Steve Reeves. Spurred on by one of the greatest box office successes ever (a $120,000 investment played out into ticket receipts of some $18 million), it fixed the matrix for Hercules and his image in popular culture: prodigious strength, *alexikakos* against all sorts of villains and monsters, and romance without nuance, but also glimpses of loneliness—even an un-Shakespearean audience understands that heroes stand apart from their society. If the Hercules movies are one dimensional, so was much of his characterization in the Renaissance, and the emphasis on his sheer physicality reverberated beyond the screen: in the 1950s the U.S. Air Force named both its largest cargo plane, the C-130, which has had the longest continuous production run of any military aircraft in history, and a powerful booster rocket after him—so much for modern-day patronage of the hero of the d'Este, Habsburg, and Gonzaga families. Similarly, the reach of the cinematic Hercules was not limited to Greece; besides Rome, we find him fighting in Troy, Atlantis, and New York City, and against Genghis Khan, Moon men, and Incas. To be sure, none of these movies was ever nominated for an Oscar (except for the song "Go the Distance" from the delightful and clever animated version by Disney, 1997), but they are undeniable testimony to the hero's enduring appeal.

BIBL.: G. K. Galinsky, *The Herakles Theme: The Adaptations of the Hero in Literature from Homer to the Twentieth Century* (Oxford 1972). H. W. Janson, *History of Art,* 3rd ed. (New York 1986). M.-R. Jung, *Hercule dans la littérature française du XVIe siècle* (Geneva 1966). E. Panofsky, *Hercules am Scheidewege* (Leipzig 1930; new ed. Berlin 1997). M. Simon, *Hercule et le Christianisme* (Paris 1955). Jon Solomon, *The Ancient World in the Cinema* (New Haven, 2001). K.G.

Herm

A freestanding rectangular pillar (often slightly tapering), roughly human height, topped with a bust, especially of Hermes (according to folk etymology, though in fact "herm" comes from the Greek *herma,* cairn). A "term" (originally said to be topped with the Roman god Terminus) differs in having a carved torso, waist, or arms.

The original Greek herms displayed erect phalluses and were used as apotropaic guardians of entrances and boundaries. The mutilation of the herms was one of the omens marking the disastrous Sicilian expedition (415 BCE, Thucydides 6.27). The Greeks quickly created portrait herms (Themistocles, ca. 460, and Pericles, ca. 425, survive in Roman copies). These, and double herms pairing Aristophanes and Menander, for example, or Herodotus and Thucydides, became popular decorations for the libraries and villas of wealthy and learned Romans.

Ancient collections of herms first started to come to light around 1488 near Hadrian's Villa in Tivoli. Other rich strikes were made through the 1700s. The pioneering archaeologist Stephanus Pighius while in Rome (ca. 1548–1556) persuaded Julius III to collect them in the papal villa (now the Villa Giulia National Museum). Fulvio Orsini (1529–1600) gathered other discoveries for the Farnese, whose collection passed to the National Archaeological Museum in Naples. His publication of ancient portraits, *Imagines et elogia virorum illustrium* (Rome 1570), and *Inlustrium virorum ut extant in urbe expressi vultus* (Rome 1569) by Achille Estaço (1524–1581) popularized the images.

Thus herms came to denote the ancient countryside in such works as Tintoretto's *Miracle of the Slave* (1548), Domenico Fetti's *Vertumnus and Pomona* (ca. 1621–1623), and Nicolas Poussin's *A Bacchanalian Revel before a Term* (1632–1633). They feature in sketches by Filippino Lippi, *Two Draped Women Standing on Either Side of a Herm* (1488/1493), Parmigianino (1503–1540), and Michelangelo, *Archers Shooting at a Herm* (1530–1533).

The freestanding herm was quickly returned to its original stance in the gardens of the learned; thus Jacopo Vignola at the Palazzo Farnese at Caprarola (1547–1549), Bartolomeo Ammannati for the Villa Medici (1574–1587), Pietro and Gian Lorenzo Bernini for the Borghese Gardens (1606–1621), Poussin for Vaux-le-Vicomte (ca. 1644), Simon Hurtrelle for Versailles (1686–1688), William Kent for Chiswick House (before 1733), Luigi Vanvitelli for Caserta, 1752–1774. Thomas Hope championed herms as archaic and "Grecian" in his influential *Household Furniture and Interior Decoration* (1807). Neoclassical sculptors, such as Johan Tobias Sergel (1740–1814) and François Jouffroy (*Premier secret confié à Vénus,* 1839), played with the form.

Architecturally, herms were fused with pilasters to form (mostly male) caryatids as supporting units (hermetic columns). Some of the earliest uses were by Sangallo for the Villa Medici at Poggio a Caiano (1490), and by Michelangelo for the Tomb of Julius II (1505 and later versions). Popularized in architectural treatises such as Serlio's (1537, 1551), herms became common decorative elements used, for example, by Sansovino in the entrance to the Zecca (Mint) in Venice (1554–1556) and by Prospero Spani (il Clemente) for the Tomb of Girolamo Fossa (1566) in the cathedral in Reggio Emilia. Borromini created new falcon herms for the Palazzo Falconieri (1638–1641). Christopher Wren built a fence of them for the Sheldonian Theater at Oxford (1664–1667). Johann Bernhard Fischer von Erlach wittily incorporated them into the entrance to the archbishop of Salzburg's stables (1693). Two monumental herms of Puget and Poussin by Louis Mercier guard the entrance to the École des Beaux-Arts in Paris (1838). The use of herms to invoke classical architecture can be seen in the work of Georg Wenzeslaus von Knobelsdorff (Park Sanssouci, Potsdam, 1745–1747), Edward Middleton Barry (Victoria Embankment, London, 1878–1879), Emil Wikström (Main Railway Station, Helsinki, 1914), and Julia Morgan (Hearst Castle, San Simeon, California, 1920–1948).

Hugues Sambin's *L'oeuvre de la diversité des termes dont on use en architecture* (1572) created herms for each of the five orders and popularized them for decorative work. His success roused Joseph Boillot, in *Nouveaux pourtraitz et figures de termes pour user en l'architecture* (1592), to create a new set of supporting "termes" of animals paired according to "antipathies" supposedly found in Pliny's *Natural History.* Herms were used in the decoration of fireplaces (Piranesi, *Diverse maniere d'adornare i cammini,* 1769), andirons, cassoni, candlesticks, and virtually any object with a columnar shape.

BIBL.: Claudia Echinger-Maurach, *Studien zu Michelangelos Juliusgrabmal* (Hildesheim 1991) 1:206–219. Eugene J. Johnson, "Portal of Empire and Wealth: Jacopo Sansovino's Entrance to the Venetian Mint," *Art Bulletin* 86 (2004) 430–458. B. Palma Venetucci, ed., *Pirro Ligorio e le erme di Roma* (Rome 1998). Henning Wrede, *Die antike Herme* (Mainz 1985).

H.PA.

Hermaphroditus

The nymph Salmacis fell in love with the beautiful son of Hermes and Aphrodite. The gods granted her prayer that she might be joined with him forever and so fused their bodies (Ovid, *Metamorphoses* 4.285–388; 15.319).

A human body combining both set of genitals or female breasts with a penis is an enduring symbol of the unity of opposites. The classical myth has given the figure its usual name in the West, but the tale itself is not very common. Thus, Antonio Beccadelli (Il Panormita) named his collection of (mostly) erotic and transgressive epigrams *Hermaphroditus* (ca. 1425) not from the myth but as an allusion to the content: half *mentula* ("cock"), half *cunnus* ("cunt").

The story was retold by Christine de Pizan in *L'epistre d'Othea à Hector* (ca. 1400, ch. 82); Abraham Fraunce, *Aminta's Dale* (1592, in ghastly English "hexameters" with astrological and biological explanations of the birth of hermaphrodites); Francis Beaumont's charmingly digressive *Salmacis and Hermaphroditus* (1602; "I hope my Poem is so lively writ,/That thou wilt turn half-maid with reading it"); Girolamo Preti, *Salmace* (1608), translated by Edward Sherburne as *Salmacis, Lyrian & Sylvia* (1651); Charles Hopkins, *The History of Love* (1695); and John Hopkins, *Amasia* (1700). Newer transformations include Gabriele D'Annunzio, "L'androgine" (1885; in *La chimera,* "Idilli"), and his novel *Il piacere* (*The Child of Pleasure,* 1889); Andrea Sperelli, "Favola d'ermafrodito" (in imitation of the "Favola di Orfeo" of Poliziano); Kenneth Hare, "Salmacis" (1923); and Ted Hughes, *Tales from Ovid* (1994; adapted for the stage by Tim Supple and Simon Reade, 2000). Julia Older's epic poem, *Hermaphroditus in America* (2000), follows the adventures of two halves, Herman and Hermione, until they can rejoin.

Ovid's version was moralized as a warning against the effeminizing effects of luxury and idleness, and especially love or sex itself: *Ovide Moralisé* 4.2224–2389; Évrart de Conty, *Le livre des Eschez amoureux* (ca. 1400), 646–648; Golding's "Epistle" to this section of his translation of Ovid (1567); Peend in his (1565; "that filthy loathsome lake/Of lust, the strength from lusty men/by hidden force to take"); and Lodovico Dolce allegorized Hermaphroditus as the union of the soul with God through contemplation (*Le transformationi,* 1568, 48).

Swinburne's "Hermaphroditus," signed "Au Musée du Louvre, Mars 1863," envisions the famous Borghese *Sleeping Hermaphroditus* (discovered 1608 in Rome). Giovanni Francesco Susini's copies in bronze miniature (1639, Metropolitan Museum, N.Y.) added the warning: *Duplex cor uno in pectore/Saepe invenies/Cave insidias* (You will often find a double heart in one breast. Beware of treachery). Other statues were known from antiquity: Ghiberti had seen a version of the Borghese type; the Villa Doria Pamphili has a statue to which extra disambiguating drapery was added. François Bosio sculpted *La nymphe Salmacis* (Louvre, 1826; now used as the statuette for the Festival de Télévision de Monaco). A painting of Salmacis and Hermaphroditus in the background of Paulus Moreelse's "Girl with a Mirror" (1627, Fitzwiliam, Cambridge) warns us against lust.

The myth has given artists the opportunity to contrast (or unite) male and female beauty. Representations include Mabuse (ca. 1516, Boymans–van Beuningen, Rotterdam); Annibale Carracci (in the mythological frescoes of the Palazzo Farnese, 1597–1600); Carlo Saraceni (Capodimonte, ca. 1608); Francesco Albani (ca. 1630–1640, Louvre); Johannes Glauber (Polidoro) (*Arcadisch landschap met Salmacis en Hermaphroditus,* before 1726, Rijksmuseum), François-Joseph Navez (1829, Museum voor Schone Kunsten, Ghent).

BIBL.: Jane Davidson Reid, ed., "Hermaphroditus," in *The Oxford Guide to Classical Mythology in the Arts, 1300–1990s* (New York 1993) 1:561–562. H.PA.

Hermes Trismegistus and Hermeticism

A Graeco-Egyptian god and the theosophy named for him. The pioneers who came to Egypt from Hellas in the 7th century BCE needed Greek names for the gods of that ancient land, which some later Greeks would regard as the ancestral home of the Olympians themselves. Egypt's Amon became Zeus, Imhotep became Asclepius, and Thoth became Hermes the Thrice-Greatest—Trismegistus—when mutual responsibilities for messages, magic, technology, and death linked the Greek god of communication and guidance with his Egyptian cousin. Under the Ptolemies, Egypt's hellenized population grew rapidly after the 4th century BCE, creating a readership for Hermetica, texts written in Greek but ascribed to the Egyptian Hermes and revered because of the god's great age and wisdom. Evidence of Trismegistus as the god's title survives from the 2nd century BCE, but reliable signs of the literature itself—mainly astrological, alchemical, and magical—are later by several centuries.

By the 2nd century CE, Christians had started to canonize the Gospels as their own sacred books, just as the successors of Plotinus would revere the alien, non-Attic wisdom of the *Chaldaean Oracles,* the Orphic poems, and the Sibylline verses. But the saving truth as Christians saw it was an exclusive property, their true and only heaven, and so Christians became orthodox or "right-believing" by battling the competing mythologies of those other Christians and semi-Christians whom we now call Gnostic. The Mediterranean basin of late antiquity, a hothouse of those proliferating religions, was where the Hermetica grew and thrived. Lactantius, Augustine, and other Christian sages knew them well.

The texts named for Hermes, a god of many faces, sometimes scandalized the Christians, and they have puzzled modern scholars by their variety. Are they popular or learned, technical or theoretical, magical or philosophical? Is their morality optimist or pessimist? Is their metaphysics monist or dualist? The best answers will constrain our categories, not the texts, which all evolved alike from Graeco-Roman Egypt and should not be impaled on our later and remote dilemmas.

In many of the Hermetic writings, philosophical problems of metaphysics and morals do not arise: their content is technical, not theoretical. Like Thoth himself, such texts offer practical guidance to people who need various kinds of lore: magical, medical, astrological, alchemical, botanical, mineralogical, and so on. The theoretical Hermetica do not lack practicality, but their main practical aim is the larger one of salvation. In the Gnostic way, these theoretical texts tell people what they need to know in order to be saved, disclosing anthropological, cosmological, theological, and metaphysical secrets: secret theories of redemption, in other words. Today I may need to be saved by moral guidance or metaphysical consolation, tomorrow to be healed by a medical recipe or a magic spell: Trismegistus has answers of both kinds—theoretical and practical, speculative and technical—spoken originally to Tat, Asclepius, and other disciples and then written down in the many Hermetic texts.

The surviving theoretical Hermetica, composed in the 2nd and 3rd centuries CE, are preserved in various formats and languages: the 17 Greek treatises of the Corpus Hermeticum; the 40 related texts and fragments collected by John of Stobi (Stobaeus) around 500 CE; the Latin *Asclepius;* the three Coptic Hermetic texts in the Nag Hammadi codices; the Armenian *Definitions;* and a few others. The technical Hermetic writings, which left traces as early as the 3rd century BCE, deal with astrology, magic, divination, meteorology, medicine, zoology, botany, mineralogy, alchemy, and other topics, a miscellany that found its way into even more literary forms and languages than the theoretical material.

One astrological manual, a Latin *Liber Hermetis,* appeared in the 4th or 5th century CE. Hermetic prophecies circulated in Syriac by around 600, shortly before the Sabians began to celebrate the Hermes whom they identified with Enoch or Idris. A little later, Arabic became a common medium for astrological, alchemical, magical, and other technical Hermetica. This Arabic (and Hebrew) genre kept growing through the 13th century, and some of the same texts were Latinized by the 12th century, when Western interest in the Hermetica revived for the first time since Augustine's day. After this revival, before which the only theoretical text known in the Latin West had been the *Asclepius,* the Trismegistus recognized by most Western readers was the magus, astrologer, and alchemist of the technical treatises.

The 17 theoretical treatises in Greek now called the Corpus Hermeticum were transmitted as a group by medieval scholars of Byzantium, beginning in the 11th century; it may be that this collection was a Christian construct meant to segregate Hermetic piety from magic. That was the result, in any case, since there are no magical recipes or spells in these theoretical texts, and not even much evidence of theoretical interest in magic.

When Cosimo de' Medici acquired a Byzantine manuscript that preserves most of this collection, he was so taken with it that he asked the young Marsilio Ficino to interrupt the great project of translating Plato that he had just begun under Cosimo's patronage. Ficino finished his translation of the first 14 treatises of the Greek Corpus Hermeticum in 1463, shortly after Cosimo gave him the job, and the result was soon printed under a single title, *Pimander,* in 1471. The three treatises omitted by Ficino were then Latinized by Lodovico Lazzarelli and also printed, after Lazzarelli produced the first of many original Renaissance Hermetica, his *Crater Hermetis,* in 1492 or shortly after. Lazzarelli's successors in this long labor of interpretation and emulation include Jacques Lefèvre d'Étaples, Agostino Steuco, Francesco Giorgi, Francesco Patrizi, Giordano Bruno, Robert Fludd, Michael Meier, Athanasius Kircher, and many, many others. With new editions of the Greek text, the first by Adrian Turnebus in 1554, Humanist philology at first fed the Hermetic fever, before starving it.

An efflorescence of Hermetic theosophy in the dazzling volumes produced by Fludd, Meier, and Kircher was contemporary with the Rosicrucian craze, but also with the Thirty Years' War and the early career of one of its soldiers, René Descartes. Like Pierre Gassendi and Gabriel Naudé, Descartes was one of those correspondents of the indefatigable Marin Mersenne, who went to war against what Henry Cornelius Agrippa von Nettesheim had called "the occult philosophy" in the title of another famous book. Mersenne was Fludd's bête noire, and one of Fludd's heroes, of course, was Hermes Trismegistus, who by this time came armed not only with Ficino's theoretical wisdom and the older Hermetic technical lore but also with newer devices of the "Hermetic art," the alchemy that Europe's ruling class found so alluring in this age of religious war.

Isaac Casaubon, a fierce religious controversialist and a skilled philologist, published linguistic evidence in 1614 that proved the Hermetica to have been written in the late Greek of the New Testament and patristic period, ruling out the authorship of anyone as ancient as Moses—as Ficino believed Hermes to have been. Ficino, a student of the Church Fathers, had extracted from their apologetic writings a theory of history, the "ancient theology," that posited a pagan channel of sacred learning running from the Persian Zoroaster and the Egyptian Hermes to Greece and Plato, parallel to the holier and revealed stream of wisdom that flowed from Sinai and Moses. Casaubon debunked all that.

Or not quite. Half a century after Casaubon demoted the venerable Hermes, the mighty Newton was still interested in the ancient theology, not to speak of such lesser lights as the Chevalier Ramsay and P. E. Jablonski in the Age of Enlightenment. Casaubon's real heirs, however, were the scholars who inaugurated the modern era of Hermetic studies, Dietrich Tiedemann in 1781 and Gustavus Parthey in 1854, after whose work the learned debate has never stopped, while the theosophy has also gone on and on. G. R. S. Meade produced his excellent translation, *Thrice-Greatest Hermes,* for the Theosophical Society in 1906; Clement Salaman and others associated with the School of Economic Science in London were still at work on the texts 100 years later.

The Hermetica made their largest mark on the contemporary world of learning through the writings of Dame Frances Yates of the Warburg Institute, starting with her enormously influential *Giordano Bruno and the Hermetic Tradition* (1964). Very briefly, Yates found the roots of modern science in the magic of the ancient Hermetica, as interpreted by Ficino and other Renaissance thinkers. Very briefly again, the major defect of this much-controverted view is that in the Hermetica translated and disseminated by Ficino, there is no magic to speak of. Moreover, Wouter Hanegraaff has recently shown that Lazzarelli has a better claim to the label "Hermetic" than Ficino or Pico, two of Yates's heroes. Whatever the merits of the Yates thesis, in any case there is no doubt that its brilliant author, through assiduous research and eloquent writing on the Hermetica in the Renaissance, made the occultist tradition a legitimate object of contemporary scholarship.

BIBL.: Brian Copenhaver, "A Grand End for a Grand Narrative," *Magic, Ritual and Witchcraft* 4 (2009), and "Natural Magic, Hermetism, and Occultism in Early Modern Science," in *Reappraisals of the Scientific Revolution,* ed. D. C. Lindberg and R. S. Westman (Cambridge 1990) 261–301. Garth Fowden, *The Egyptian Hermes: A Historical Approach to the Late Pagan Mind* (Cambridge 1986). Anthony Grafton, *Defenders of the Text: The Traditions of Scholarship in an Age of Science* (Cambridge, Mass., 1991) chaps. 5, 6. Wouter J. Hanegraaff and Ruud M. Bouthoorn, *Lodovico Lazzarelli (1447–1500): The Hermetic Writings and Related Documents* (Tempe, Ariz., 2005). *Hermetica: The Greek Corpus Hermeticum and the Latin Asclepius in a New English Translation with Notes and Introduction,* ed. and trans. B. Copenhaver (Cambridge 1992).

B.C.

Hero

The hero played a leading role in the social practices, spiritual beliefs, and artistic creations of the ancient world, establishing a cultural repertoire that has profoundly shaped representations of the heroic ever since. The hero was a man who performed great deeds in the service of the community, attaining a status between god and human in polytheistic Greek religion. Most heroic cults expressed local allegiances, but the stories of a select few, such as Heracles and Jason, were retold throughout the ancient world. This classical tradition was distinguished by a number of features that remain familiar today: the use of the hero to promote civic or national pride; the narrative structure of the heroic quest; and the position of women as auxiliaries to male heroes, as mothers, wives, daughters, lovers, and foes.

Homer's *Iliad* emphasized three tensions characteristic of the heroic mode. First, "war is the medium of human existence and achievement" (Schein 1984, 68) in the world of the poem: Achilles confirms his status as the supreme warrior-hero by killing Hector. Yet his victory leads to the destruction of Troy, as the triumph of the hero exacts a heavy price. Second, although Greek religion offered a vision of the hero as a demigod intervening in human affairs after his death, Homer presented a mortal hero, forced to choose either the shame of a long life of anonymity or death and glory. This confrontation with mortality lends the hero a grandeur denied even to the gods. Finally, the ambiguous position of Homer's mortal hero, neither ordinary man nor divine, foreshadows a tension in later heroic narratives: should the hero be worshiped and obeyed, or admired and emulated?

It is tempting to claim that classical heroic ideals subsided under the assault of Christian theologians in the medieval period, before reviving during the Renaissance. Religious writers certainly questioned the violence and thirst for glory at the heart of the classical tradition. Orosius' 5th-century attack on Alexander the Great's abominable pride, for example, proved highly influential. But the complex cultural legacy of antiquity defies such simple periodization. Long before the fall of Rome, Stoics and Neoplatonists had been troubled by the warlike culture described by Homer. George Cary has exposed the astonishing variety of medieval representations of Alexander—moralistic, theological, anecdotal, and exemplary—which include the German poet Ulrich von Eschenbach's depiction of a knight driven not by glory but by his courtly love for Candace, queen of Nubia. Martial prowess and moral virtue could be reconciled in the medieval figure of the chivalric knight, servant of Church and royal authority.

Misgivings about classical heroic ideals persisted after the revival of interest in antiquity during the 15th century. Humanist writers such as Erasmus fiercely denounced the glamorization of war, and Jansenists later condemned the pursuit of glory as the false ideal of a fallen humanity. The Italian poet Ariosto criticized the legend of Troy as Greek political propaganda: "Aeneas was not as devoted, nor Achilles as strong as is rumored, nor was Hector so fierce. There have been thousands upon thousands upon thousands of men who could, in truth, supersede these men" (*Orlando Furioso* canto 35.25). Rather than simply rejuvenating the classical hero, the Renaissance inspired an efflorescence of meditations on human virtue, which critically engaged with heroic narratives from Greece and Rome. Shakespeare followed Ariosto by interrogating the legend of Troy in *Troilus and Cressida,* and Milton's epic poems ultimately positioned the classical hero in the shadow of the divine.

The classical heroic tradition arguably reached its apogee not during the Renaissance but through the 19th century, with the rise of the nation-state. The ancient world offered a rich resource for nation builders, as the invocation of antiquity bestowed legitimacy on new formations. Classical, chivalric, and Christian influences were woven into a cult of patriotic sacrifice. When Captain Lawrence Oates died in the Antarctic in 1912, for example, pupils at his old school, Eton College, composed tributes in Greek, comparing the dead explorer's quest for the South Pole with the voyages of Odysseus. The First World War offered a stage for the performance of such heroic fantasies. Classical allusions were invoked most explicitly by the Gallipoli campaign (February 1915–January 1916), the allied assault on the Dardanelles Straits to divert Turkish resources from the Russian front. Soldier-poets such as Rupert Brooke romanticized the campaign as a recreation of the Trojan War. But the initiative proved disastrous, and the allies were forced to withdraw. Brooke himself died of blood poisoning and was buried on the island of Skyros, whence Achilles was said to have sailed to Troy.

Many have argued that this moment marked the death of heroic ideals amid the carnage of modern industrial warfare. The most famous English soldier-poet, Wilfred Owen, chose to express his disillusionment by condemning Horace's proclamation *Dulce et decorum est pro patria mori* (It is sweet and noble to die for one's country) as "the old lie." Yet it is misleading to suggest that the classical heroic tradition perished amid the slaughter of the First World War. Many scholars now argue that the war breathed new life into traditional forms, as the legions of the bereaved found consolation in classical texts and images. Artists continued to engage with classical models when contemplating the horrors of the 20th century. Tim Rood has recently shown how modernist writers have been fascinated by Xenophon's *Anabasis,* in which 10,000 Greek mercenaries, trapped in the heart of the Persian Empire and surrounded by hostile tribes, marched across formidable terrain to safety. Italo Calvino even claimed the Ten Thousand as "an appropriate symbol of the modern condition," in which there "are no victories, but there is endurance" (Rood 2004, 192–193).

The classical hero, however, remains a contested figure. The German writer Christa Wolf's *Kassandra* (1983), for example, a powerful feminist work that tells the story of the Trojan War through the eyes of Hector's sister, attacks the nexus of patriarchy and violence that characterizes both the ancient and the modern world. Again and again "heroism" is exposed as a facade to compensate for male inadequacy: Agamemnon's cruelty in battle results from his impotence, and Achilles is a brute, guilty of grotesque atrocities.

Interest in the classical hero has flourished in the 21st century, nourished both by the malleability of the original narratives and by their centrality within the literary canon. The 2004 movie *Troy,* starring the male icon Brad Pitt as Achilles, testifies to the strength of this interest in popular culture. The film exposes how the 20th century deepened contradictions in the classical heroic ideal: contempt for ordinary lives sits uncomfortably alongside current conceptions of citizenship, by which all are encouraged to achieve their potential. But Hollywood offers a very different interpretation of the Trojan War from Wolf's *Kassandra.* Although Hector lectures Paris on the brutality of face-to-face killing in an early scene, much of the rest of the film presents sculpted male bodies locked in glamorous struggle for death and glory. Women, as ever, remain on the margins.

BIBL.: N. T. Burns and C. J. Reagan, eds., *Concepts of the Hero in the Middle Ages and Renaissance* (New York 1975). G. Cary, *The Medieval Alexander* (Cambridge 1956). T. Rood, *The Sea! The Sea! The Shout of the Ten Thousand in the Modern Imagination* (London 2004). S. L. Schein, *The Mortal Hero: An Introduction to Homer's Iliad* (Berkeley 1984). M.J.

Hero and Leander

Love drove Leander, a youth of Abydos, to swim the Hellespont to tryst with Hero, a Sestian priestess of Aphrodite. When he drowned, she died of grief. Virgil makes them the archetype of love, "the same for all" (*Georgics* 3.244–263). Ovid's *Heroides* (18–19) has Leander ask Hero for a beacon, a motif that dominates the only full classical narrative, a Greek text by Musaeus (ca. late 5th century CE). Musaeus' lamp witnesses and symbolizes illicit love; a storm blows it out, and Leander's battered body makes Hero throw herself from her tower. They die together, love the same for both.

An early Aldine edition and Latin translation of Musaeus (ca. 1494) influenced vernacular adaptations like Bernardo Tasso's (1537), which supported Juan Boscán Almogáver's poem of 2,793 lines (1541). In these renditions Leander swims because "to go in a boat would be to lose time"; Hero worries about her honor. Cupid strikes Clément Marot's French sophisticates with the same arrow; but "after death, which separates lovers, the two are always again found together."

The most famous version is Christopher Marlowe's unfinished poem (ca. 1593), with its hapless innocents. His Leander "as a brother with his sister toyed." Exposed to Neptune's desires, Leander argues, "'I am no woman, I.'/Thereat smiled Neptune." Leander safely reaches Hero, but after the pair somehow couple, Marlowe breaks off. George Chapman, who also translated Musaeus, completed Marlowe's poem in 1598. Shakespeare most memorably includes Leander in Rosalind's false myths about love: "He went but forth to wash him in the Hellespont . . . and the foolish coroners of that age found it [the cause of his death] was 'Hero of Sestos'" (*As You Like It* 4.1.95–99).

Skepticism becomes scatology in Góngora's burlesque (1589–1610): his Leander is a "great pisser in corners." Thomas Nashe's Hero (*Lenten Stuffe*, 1599) tries to kiss the dead Leander "on his blue-jellied sturgeon lips"; the gods make her a herring, him a ling, and her maid their mustard. For Jonson's *Bartholomew Fair* puppets (1614), Leander has sexy legs, and Love's arrow comes in a pint of sherry. William Wycherley's parody goes furthest: his drunken Leander cannot consummate the first night.

The "degenerate modern wretch" Byron swam the Hellespont in 1810, but Romanticism preferred mournfulness. Schiller's 1810 ballad traces Hero's guilt. In the Austrian dramatist Franz Grillparzer's greatest tragedy, *The Waves of the Sea and of Love* (1813), friends encourage Leander to love Hero to cure depression. He loves too much, and falls into a fatal trap when Hero's uncle, a priest, puts out her lamp. Lovers in life, their two bodies fill one grave, where Milorad Pavić's *Inner Side of the Wind* (1993) gives his disconnected Hero and Leander only death in common: even their stories are separated by two opposed front covers.

In musical treatments of the story, Nicholas Lanier's lament (ca. 1628) is probably the first instance of recitative in English. A libretto by Boito was set by both Bottesini and Manicelli in the late 19th century, and Victor Herbert composed a symphonic poem on the couple (op. 33, 1900). Eric Speiss adapted Grillparzer and Musaeus for a work by Günter Bialas (1965), and Christopher Burns made an eight-channel tape composition (2003) inspired by a Cy Twombly triptych (1981–1984). Antiquity depicts Leander swimming; Rubens shows him dead in the arms of pale nereids against a dark sea (ca. 1605); Regnier (ca. 1626) and Taillasson (1798) show him lying ashore beside a clothed Hero; Etty (1828–1829) paints her half-nude body prostrate on Leander. The 20th-century sculptor Edward Bramwell hides Hero's face in Leander's corpse (1908); by 2002 the story encodes the separation of cyberspace in Jamiesen, Ptacek, Saarinen, and Smith's performance piece "swim."

Musaeus described Hero as everywhere rosy; today a David Austin rose (1982) bears her name.

BIBL.: Gordon Braden, *The Classics and English Renaissance Poetry* (New Haven 1978). E.M.H.

Herodotus

Author of *Histories* (written before 425 BCE), among the most controversial ancient works on history. Some modern scholars insist that he was a romancer, who freely invented facts, citations, and even descriptions. Others treat him as a gifted and imaginative writer who did not derive his representations of Egyptians, Scythians, and other non-Greeks from independent, personal inquiry, as he claimed, but spun them from his own assumptions about the various nations. Still others argue that he proceeded by the most rigorous empirical and analytical standards of his time (standards that he shared, as he shared many interests, with the Hippocratic medical writers) and should be regarded, along with Thucydides, as one of the first creators of written history—even if Thucydides himself would have disagreed.

In this respect at least, Herodotus' present position in the classical tradition does not mark a radical change with the past. Even in antiquity he and his *Histories* provoked sharp criticism. Thucydides rejected his wide-ranging model of historical writing, with its interest in Greek and barbarian customs and beliefs and its curiosity about much earlier times, for one that concentrated on recent politics and battles. The medical author Ctesias, who lived and worked in Persia, insisted that Herodotus' account of that great land bristled with errors, which Ctesias himself claimed to correct from archival documents (in fact, he was often wildly wrong). Plutarch in his essay *The Malignity of Herodotus* (1st cent. CE) accused his predecessor of Athenian favoritism, of listening to barbarians, and many other offenses; this work is the only surviving representative of a substantial literature of this type. Yet throughout the Hellenistic age and later, writers like Megasthenes followed Herodotus' lead, treating the early history and present customs of the barbarians as part of the historian's legitimate range of concerns. Geohistorians like Strabo also clearly reflected the influence of Herodotus.

Little discussed in the Middle Ages, Herodotus nonetheless offered a powerful framework for medieval and later Christian thinkers who needed to understand and describe the confrontation between the Christian and Islamic worlds. The last great Byzantine historian, Laonicus Chalcondyles (1423–1490), modeled his wide-ranging treatment of the long wars between Byzantium and the Ottoman Turks on the *Histories,* even adorning his work with Herodotean descriptions of London and other European cities. The first Western Humanists to master Greek—notably Guarino of Verona, who translated a substantial part of book 1 of the *Histories,* and Lorenzo Valla, who produced the first Latin version of the whole text—read his work with a fascination natural in men who had seen Constantinople first menaced, then conquered in 1453 by what they regarded as a powerful barbarian empire.

For all the utility of the Herodotean model, its creator's ill repute shadowed, and even preceded, his reappearance in the West. Petrarch, who could not read Herodotus in Greek, was puzzled that Cicero described him both as a liar and as the father of history. Later Humanist scholars, from Giovanni Pontano, who drew up a preface for an edition of Herodotus that did not materialize, to Juan Luis Vives, both referred explicitly to his problematic reputation. The marvels that dotted the text, giving it a curious resemblance to the *Travels* of Sir John Mandeville and other medieval works about the marvels of the East, did nothing to make the *Histories* more credible.

Yet even in the 15th century Herodotus found warm advocates, notably Valla, and eager readers, notably Leon Battista Alberti, who played with Herodotean stories in his literary works and drew a vast amount of information about ancient buildings and builders, barbarian and Greek alike, from the *Histories.* As European horizons expanded, the Herodotean model became more and more attractive and valuable, and the wonders that Herodotus described came to seem no more implausible than the marvels of modern India or Mexico. Aldus Manutius and Joachim Camerarius defended Herodotus in the prefaces to their editions of 1502 and 1541. Henri Estienne edited the fragments of Ctesias before he printed Herodotus; but he insisted in his edition of 1570 that Herodotus' digressions on past times and present barbarians, for all their reliance on oral tradition, were delightful, credible, and no closer to fiction than the partly imaginary speeches in Thucydides. As the Jesuit Antonio Possevino—who himself traveled both in Scandinavia and in Muscovy—explained, "As to the fabulous things that Herodotus is accused of inventing, first, I say that those who have never set foot in foreign lands find many things incredible. Once they have traveled in Asia, Africa, and India, they will change their opinion" (*Apparatus,* Rome 1597, 39r.).

Cosmographers and writers of *relazioni* (diplomatic reports) not only used Herodotus as a model, but drew a surprising amount of what they had to say about distant peoples and places from his work, often without revising it substantially. Learned chronologers such as David Chytraeus, Paulus Crusius, and Joseph Scaliger, recognizing that Herodotus' work supplemented, and largely matched, the accounts of Persian and Egyptian history given in the Old Testament, insisted on his basic accuracy. By the end of the 16th century Isaac Casaubon found eager listeners in Paris when he argued that Herodotus had been a hard-working, self-critical inquirer who willingly drew information from non-Greeks and did his best to establish by personal inspection the facts that he narrated. A few decades later, the Inca Garcilaso de la Vega would model his great account of Spanish and Indian history in the New World on Herodotus' epic tale of Greeks and barbarians in combat.

Yet neither then nor later did Herodotus occupy a single, firm niche in the classical pantheon. Parts of his work, such as his brilliant account of the Battle of Thermopylae, found special favor when they fitted contemporary needs—as during the First World War, when both British and German schoolboys imagined themselves as the Spartans who died with Leonidas. His complex and problematic accounts of non-Greeks could serve many purposes, including those of German "racial scientists," who tried to show that the Spartans must have been Nordic. But even in the great age of German philology, his work received both warm admiration from Wilamowitz, who thought students should read Herodotus as an introduction to Greek culture, and sharp criticism from Eduard Meyer and Felix Jacoby, who denied him the standing of a true, critical historian even as they recreated, with a new level of precision and authority, the contexts within which he had written. To this day, scholars find it impossible to agree on how much Herodotus actually knew about the places, peoples, and events he described. And to this day, his wider influence remains complex and paradoxical. Shortly before his death, the Polish journalist and historian Ryszard Kapuściński told the story of how a translation of Herodotus' work was suppressed as subversive for a time in Poland's postwar years. Reading the *Histories,* he made clear, had inspired his own career as a traveler and travel writer, in which he produced brilliantly written reportage. Like Herodotus, Kapuściński has had a troubled afterlife. Some have sharply criticized his work as unreliable, and others have powerfully defended its fundamental profundity and truth. Herodotus somehow manages to remain, as he has been for centuries, at once the father of history and the father of lies.

BIBL.: Stefan Kipf, *Herodot als Schulautor* (Cologne 1999). Arnaldo Momigliano, "Erodoto e la storiografia moderna," *Aevum* 31 (1957) 74–84, and "The Place of Herodotus in the History of Historiography," *History* 43 (1958) 1–13, repr. in *Studies in Historiography* (London 1966) 127–142. Oswyn Murray, "Herodotus and Hellenistic Culture," *Classical Quarterly* 22 (1972) 200–213. Achille Olivieri, *Erodoto nel Rinascimento: L'umano e la storia* (Rome 2004). A.G.

Hesiod

Archaic Greek poet of Boeotia, ca. 775–660 BCE, to whom the poems *Theogony* and *Works and Days* are attributed. Hesiod's reception has been chiefly confined to the myths and motifs that he provides, rather than to his poems as complex wholes. These motifs include a codification of the Greek gods; a cosmology; the Muses who encounter the shepherd Hesiod on Mount Helicon and initiate him into poetry; the gods' complex, violent, bloody familial politics; the intercourse of earth (Gaia) and sky (Ouranous); Kronos' castration of Ouranos and Aphrodite's subsequent birth from Ouranos' severed genitals, which had been cast into the sea; battle among gigantic primal beings, including monsters of many limbs, many heads, and voracious appetites; the intertwined stories of Pandora and Prometheus; the labors of the agricultural year; and the Five Ages of the World. These myths and motifs were staples of mythological encyclopedias by the late 15th century, when the earliest printed versions of Hesiod appeared.

Hesiod's poems were known across the Aegean world by 600 BCE; they have been well preserved and disseminated by rhapsodes, scribes, editors, grammarians, commentators, philosophers, mythographic encyclopedists, and other poets. Extensive allegorical scholia derived from grammarians' commentaries on Hesiod were used to explain Hesiod to Byzantine schoolboys. There were editions out of Basel throughout the mid-16th century, usually with parallel Latin translation; in 1566 Henri Estienne published Hesiod in his large folio edition of the major Greek poets, *Poetae graeci principes heroici carminis.*

Hesiodic details of myth saturate European epic and mythopoeic writing, perhaps most spectacularly in Dante, Milton, Blake, and Keats, who make much of Hesiod's infernal regions, his Titans and primordial monsters, his giant battles. In the 20th century Charles Olson juxtaposed Hesiod with the local lore of his New World epic in *Maximus, from Dogtown,* I and IV. Women writers have countered the ill fortunes and bad characters of Hesiod's female beings; perhaps most remarkable of these efforts is the Korean American feminist poet Theresa Hak Kyung Cha's *Dictée* (1982), which profoundly reworks and challenges Hesiod on the Muses and the *Catalogue of Women* long attributed to him, and focuses the gender politics represented in Hesiod's works.

Artists have never abandoned a fascination with Hesiod on the Muses. In the 19th century the artist Gustave Moreau created many visual representations of their initiation of the poet. Both Rubens and Goya painted famous and harrowing pictures of Kronos (Saturn) devouring one of his children, a motif from the *Theogony;* William Blake engraved a series after drawings by his friend John Flaxman called *The Theogony, Works and Days, and the Days of Hesiod* (1816–1817); Georges Braque chose the *Theogony* as the subject of 20 etchings.

Recently the rising global poetry movement has looked to Hesiod as spokesman for the laborer and the harsh but life-giving locality. He figures thus for the Irish poet Seamus Heaney, for the Australian Les Murray (whose polemical contrast between an urbane country of the mind called Athens and a rugged native land called Boeotia sparked significant discussion of white Australian culture), and memorably for the Australian-born British poet Peter Porter, in his influential poem "On First Looking into Chapman's Hesiod":

> Long storms have blanched the million bones
> Of the Aegean, and as many hurricanes
> Will abrade the headstones of my native land:
> Sparrows acclimatize but I still seek
> The permanently upright city where
> Speech is nature and plants conceive in pots,
> Where one escapes from what one is and who
> One was, where home is just a postmark
> And country wisdom clings to calendars,
> The opposite of a sunburned truth-teller's
> World, haunted by precepts and the Pleiades. (68–78)

BIBL.: Hesiod, *Theogony, Works and Days, Testimonia;* and *The Shield, Catalogue of Women, Other Fragments,* ed. and trans. Glenn W. Most, Loeb Classical Library (Cambridge, Mass., 2006, 2007). T.KR.

Heyne, Christian Gottlob

German classical scholar (1729–1812). His career marked the transition from an older style of Humanistic scholarship, rooted in the encyclopedic learned traditions of late Humanism and the Baroque university, to the more professional form of classical philology that flourished in the 19th-century German university. Born in Chemnitz, the son of a weaver, he overcame great difficulties to study at Leipzig, where he received an M.A. in 1752. He first found work as a copyist in the library of Count Brühl at Dresden, where he met Winckelmann and began to develop an interest in ancient art. One of his early publications, an edition of Epictetus, won him appointment as professor of eloquence and poetry at the University of Göttingen in 1763.

Founded only 30 years before, the university in Göttingen was designed to form a new class of administrators and aristocrats. Its founder, Gerlach Adolph von Münchhausen, hired professors for their publications, endowed the library with a large yearly acquisitions budget, and fostered new institutions, such as a historical seminar designed to train students in the critical study and writing of history. Heyne flourished in this rich environment. In some ways he brought the university the skills—and the encyclopedic knowledge—of Baroque scholarship. His erudition made him the natural supervisor for the university library. He not only ordered and catalogued books but also reviewed some 8,000 of them in the journal *Göttingische Gelehrte Anzeigen* (*Göttingen Scholarly Notes*).

At the same time, he rapidly acclimated to Göttingen's bracing, up-to-date atmosphere and learned from colleagues like Johann Christoph Gatterer to approach his own subject in a new, interdisciplinary way. Like his old friend Winckelmann, he saw the study of ancient art as fundamental for anyone seeking to grasp ancient culture as a whole. He taught his students not only to read ancient texts but also to look at casts of ancient sculptures, with which he illustrated his expensive and fashionable private lectures on the history of ancient art. In addition to innovative editions of Virgil (1767–1775), Pindar (1773, 1798–1799), and Apollodorus (1782–1783, 1802), he produced a stream of innovative dissertations, mostly in Latin, on a vast range of questions in ancient literature and history. In one of the most original and influential of these, "The Genius of the Age of the Ptolemies," an interdisciplinary analysis and reconstruction of Hellenistic culture, he put scholarly muscle and flesh on the skeletal concept of the national spirit, or *Geist.* In others he argued, in the spirit of Enlightenment conjectural history, that primitive peoples of that time came far closer in their habits of thought and expression than modern Europeans could to the Greeks of the heroic age. To understand early Greek culture one should thus draw on modern travel literature, as Robert Wood had done in his *Essay on the Original Genius and Writings of Homer* (1775), which Heyne eagerly publicized in Germany.

In yet another famous series of studies, devoted to ancient mythology, Heyne tried to show that the ancient myths had taken shape before the poems that preserved them. Only a close historical analysis, one that began by abandoning modern assumptions, could retrace their development: "The fundamental principle of interpretation is that once you have heard another's words, you feel what the other person, who uttered those words, felt. We cannot interpret an ancient writer correctly unless we rid our mind of all our common notions and feel and think what the writer could and should have felt when he uttered those words" (*Apollodorus* vii). Heyne's effort to recover the history buried in myth resembled the projects of such Baroque polyhistors as Gerardus Joannes Vossius and Athanasius Kircher. But he framed his work in characteristically modern analytical terms, and his rigorously historical approach also set him off from older traditions of learning.

Though he was not an eloquent lecturer—so one expert witness, Friedrich Gedike, reported—Heyne's teaching presented his hearers with a "wealth of new ideas and new applications of old ideas." Both of the Schlegels and both of the Humboldts made a point of studying with him, and Wilhelm von Humboldt took extensive notes on his characteristically rich lectures on Homer. Heyne's editions and commentaries integrated line-by-line grammatical and historical exposition with a keen sensibility. At the same time, his seminar produced a stream of well-trained *Gymnasium* teachers, and many of his pupils turned out original dissertations and journal articles in his interdisciplinary mode. By the time Heyne died in 1812, his articulate and ungrateful pupil F. A. Wolf had put his achievements somewhat in the shade. In the 18th century, however, no one did more than Heyne to transform and modernize the traditions of classical learning, and Wolf built his own achievements in part on foundations Heyne had laid.

BIBL.: William Clark, *Academic Charisma and the Origins of the Research University* (Chicago 2006). Christian Gottlob Heyne, ed., *Apollodori Atheniensis Bibliothecae libri tres et fragmenta,* 2nd ed. (Göttingen 1803). Robert Leventhal, "The Emergence of Philological Discourse in the German States, 1770–1810," *Isis* 77 (1986) 243–260. Clemens Menze, *Wilhelm von Humboldt und Christian Gottlob Heyne* (Ratingen 1966). Werner Mettler, *Der junge Friedrich Schlegel und die griechische Literatur* (Zurich 1955). Martin Vöhler, "Christian Gottlob Heyne und das Studium des Altertums in Deutschland," in *Disciplining Classics—Altertumswissenschaft als Beruf,* ed. Glenn Most (Göttingen 2002) 39–54. *Der Vormann der Georgia Augusta: Christian Gottlob Heyne zum 250. Geburtstag: Sechs akademische Reden* (Göttingen 1980).

A.G.

Hieroglyphs

Ancient Egyptian script using pictorial image-signs. Renaissance and later conceptions of hieroglyphs were inspired by classical explanations of this script as a system of allegorical communication and concealment. The term was also applied to Mesoamerican writing systems by European observers.

The Greeks applied the term (from *hieros,* "sacred," and *glyphein,* "to carve, inscribe") to the pharaonic picture-script, the Egyptian term for which may be translated as "words of god." The earliest manifestations of the script appeared at the beginning of the Dynastic period (3200–2900 BCE). From about 2600 BCE onward the system remained in relatively stable use, until the end of the 4th century CE, when it passed into extinction. In their mature phase hieroglyphs were primarily associated with religious and funerary texts and with inscriptions on monuments. They were supplemented for more practical and secular use by cursive forms known to the Greeks and also today as hieratic ("sacred," ca. 2700–665 BCE) and demotic ("popular" or "common," ca. 665 BCE–452 CE).

The Egyptians believed that in addition to their communicative function, hieroglyphs had religious or magical powers. In some cases hieroglyphs in tombs, especially those representing dangerous animals, were drawn in "mutilated" form so that they would not be able to harm the deceased. Greek and Roman commentators such as Diodorus Siculus, Clement of Alexandria, and Ammianus Marcellinus explained hieroglyphs as an allegorical system invented by Egyptian priests (or, in some accounts, by the Egyptian sage Hermes Trismegistus) to preserve the records of their kings and encode their sacred doctrines so that these would be inaccessible to the multitude but available to the wise and enlightened. In later antiquity Neoplatonic writers like Plotinus associated hieroglyphs more explicitly with the enigmatic expression of sacred wisdom. These late antique developments are epitomized by the *Hieroglyphica* of Horapollo (ca. 450–500), which provides allegorical explanations for each of its 189 hieroglyphic images. A number of these images and their meanings have been shown to derive from authentic Egyptian tradition, but the text provides no indication of how they could be joined to form sentences or compound thoughts—a reflection, perhaps, of the fading memory of the original system.

Horapollo's book would prove influential when a copy was discovered on the island of Andros and taken to Florence at the beginning of the 15th century. Armed with this and other ancient sources, early Humanists such as Niccolò Niccoli, Poggio Bracciolini, and Cyriacus of Ancona began to think, write about, and even copy hieroglyphic inscriptions in an attempt to understand their meanings. The Humanist and architect Leon Battista Alberti described hieroglyphs as being ideal for the decoration of commemorative monuments, as they had the ability to communicate in a "universal language" whose meanings could survive the extinction of alphabetic scripts. In this spirit, from the 1430s onward invented "hieroglyphic" devices and compositions began to be produced by artists and writers, a trend that helped fuel the broader development of Renaissance symbolic forms such as emblems. From the 1460s onward writers like Marsilio Ficino and Pico della Mirandola associated hieroglyphs with a revived Neoplatonism and with "wisdom texts" of Hermes Trismegistus in particular. The specimens in Francesco Colonna's *Hypnerotomachia Poliphili* (1499) represent a high point in the Renaissance tradition of "invented" hieroglyphs, but exercises of this sort continued throughout the early modern period, and even into the post-decipherment era.

From the Renaissance into the 18th century, scholarly study of hieroglyphs proceeded somewhat erratically, as relatively restrained efforts at epigraphical or philological study alternated with bolder claims regarding their decipherment. In the 1490s Giovanni Nanni (Annius of Viterbo) claimed to have deciphered a hieroglyphic inscription recording the exploits of Osiris in Italy—but his source was a medieval tablet. Epigraphical copies of hieroglyphic inscriptions were being made by the 1480s, and by the mid-16th century, compilations were assembled by Fulvio Orsini and others. At the same time, an ambitious interpretive effort was inaugurated by the Italian scholar Pierio Valeriano, whose *Hieroglyphica* (1556) claimed to reconstruct a transcultural system of hieroglyphic symbolism. Later commentators such as Michele Mercati and Lorenzo Pignoria were more skeptical in their approach to the subject, but during the 17th century the Jesuit polymath Athanasius Kircher authored a series of monumental studies that claimed to reveal, in copious detail, the mysteries of hieroglyphs. Kircher also recognized Coptic as the original Egyptian language and presciently postulated that hieroglyphs functioned phonetically as well as allegorically.

In the wake of the Napoleonic campaign in Egypt (1788–1801) the discovery of the Rosetta Stone, which preserved an inscription of the Egyptian king Ptolemy V in hieroglyphs, demotic, and Greek, provided the impetus for the decipherment of the script. Following preliminary work by Thomas Young (1773–1829), decipherment was achieved by Jean-François Champollion (1790–1832) in 1822–1824. It is at this point that the "classical tradition" of hieroglyphs ends and the modern Egyptological one begins. Yet notions of Egyptian wisdom and enigmatic codes have proven remarkably durable, and the mixed character of hieroglyphs as both a speech- and an image-based system has continued to attract the attention of scholars of language and culture, Jacques Derrida prominent among them, in the modern and postmodern eras.

BIBL.: George Boas, trans., *The Hieroglyphics of Horapollo* (New York 1950), repr. with foreword by Anthony Grafton (Princeton 1993). Brian Curran, "The Renaissance Afterlife of Ancient Egypt (1400–1650)," in *The Wisdom of Egypt: Changing Visions through the Ages,* ed. Tim Champion and John Tait (London 2003) 101–131. Karl Giehlow, "Die Hieroglyphenkunde des Humanismus in der Allegorie der Renaissance," *Jahrbuch der Kunsthistorischen Sammlungen des Allerhöchsten Kaiserhauses* 32 (1915) 1–229. Erik Iversen, *The Myth of Egypt and Its Hieroglyphs in European Tradition* (Copenhagen 1961). Maurice Pope, *The Story of Archaeological Decipherment, from Egyptian Hieroglyphs to Maya Script,* 2nd ed. (London 1999). Penelope Wilson, *Hieroglyphs: A Very Short Introduction* (Oxford 2003).

B.CU.

Hippocrates

"The history of Hippocratism is the history of medicine itself" (Henry E. Sigerist, 1931). The name Hippocrates (ca. 460–ca. 370 BCE) thus stands metonymically not only for the works passed down under his name (Corpus Hippocraticum), but also for the history of medicine in all its scientific, humanistic, social scientific, political, religious, philosophical, legal, and artistic manifestations. The reception of Hippocrates provides a unique guide for tracking the metamorphosis of Western medicine without interruption from the classical period to the present.

The sparse information available on the historical Hippocrates (Plato, *Protagoras* 311B–C, *Phaedrus* 270C–D; Aristotle, *Politics* 7.1326a14–16) stands in contrast to a legendary profile whose development has thrived since antiquity and that offsets the lack of any distinct historical profile of the physician from Cos. Such constructions can still be grasped in the following core sources: in a *Vita Hippocratis* ascribed to Soranus of Ephesus (1st–2nd cent. CE; Ilberg, *Corpus medicorum Graecorum* 4.175–178), in the information about Hippocrates in the *Ethnica* of Stephen of Byzantium (6th cent.; Meineke, ed., 1849, 402–403), in the biographical entry on him in the Suda, the most substantial Byzantine lexicon, of the 10th cent. (Adler, ed., 662–663), in the biography of Hippocrates by the Byzantine scholar Tzetzes (*Historiarum variarum Chiliades* 7.155), and in the *Vita Bruxellensis,* the fragment of an anonymous biography of Hippocrates in Latin that presumably derives from a Greek model (Schöne, ed., *Rheinisches Museum* 58, 1903, 56–66). These sources, relying implicitly on the Hippocratic Corpus, condense information about Hippocrates and direct quotations from the writings transmitted under his name into a life history that is constructed according to the classic loci of birthplace, descent, class, ability, education, teachings, deeds, death, and reputation in posterity. Behind the information about what Hippocrates, as the founder of medicine, experienced and learned, thought and wrote, tested and rejected, lurks information about the vicissitudes of medicine itself, its hopes and errors, temptations and achievements. Whoever talks about Hippocrates—and this is the case even in modern times—is usually not indulging any purely historical interest, but is rather choosing a biographical-narrative context with which to give concrete form to the concerns of professional politics and religion, to theoretical concepts, and to ethical-moral claims. Thus, the theoretical understanding, ideals, worldviews, states of discourse, and conflicts of interest prevailing at any given time shape and assimilate the heterogeneous information handed down by the tradition, arranging it into a consistent history that in turn seems to attest to the sources' homogeneity. This applies to all biographies of Hippocrates from the Latin Middle Ages (Isidore of Seville, Vincent of Beauvais, Walter Burley, Lorscher Arzneibuch, Lübeck) and the Renaissance (Symphorien Champier, Pierre Verney, Otto Brunfels, Johannes Cuspinian, Konrad Gesner, Philipp Melanchthon) to entries on Hippocrates in modern encyclopedias, and even to the numerous 20th-century novels about Hippocrates. In the genre of biography we witness the triumph of a bimillenary image campaign that stylized Hippocrates as the founder of medicine (Celsus, *De medicina, prooemium* 8, 66), the ideal physician (Cicero, *De natura deorum* 3.91; Seneca, *Epistulae* 95.20; pseudo-Galen, *Definitiones medicae,* prooemium 19.347K), a model human being (Scribonius Largus, prooemium 5.2; Pliny, *Naturalis historia* 7.123, 171; 26.2; Quintilian, *Institutio oratoria* 3.6.64; Plutarch, *De profectu in virtute* 11.82d), and a hero to be imitated or worshiped (Hippocrates, *Epistulae* 2; Gellius 19.2.8; Macrobius 161.1; Athenaeus, *Deipnosophistae* 9.399b). All this placed him in a semi-mythological genealogy, beginning with Apollo and continuing through human history over the Asclepiads, including Hippocrates and his countless followers, down to our own day. As nature become flesh, he was even likened to the Son of God become man. Thus, Hippocrates became the guarantor of medicine's principles of succession (including ancestry, allegiance, and representation) and seniority, which are as important there as in the history of religion and politics. Hippocrates' enduring authority lies in the greatness that has accrued to him over such a long history of reception and influence. The meaning of such an epithet can be illustrated with interchangeable, related ones: "the Divine," "the Good," "the True," "the Wise." The all-encompassing form "the Great" contains within itself the certainty that what is good and right is Hippocratic. Hippocrates is the projection screen for all the medicinal utopias that since the Roman Republic have taken him and his writings in tow. In him resides the hope that greatness will come to all those who prove themselves as his successors, whether as the "second" Hippocrates, Diocles of Carystus (4th cent. BCE); the "Italian" Hippocrates, Giovanni Filippo Ingrassia (1510–1580); the "Dutch" Hippocrates, Pieter van Foreest (1523–1597); the "English" Hippocrates, Thomas Sydenham (1624–1689); the "German" Hippocrates, Samuel Thomas Soemmering (1755–1830); or simply as a follower of Hippocrates without representing any specific nation.

In this impressive reception history, anecdotes about Hippocrates were generally accepted as true: that he burned down the library of his native island of Cos; used fire to deliver Athens from a plague; healed the Macedonian Perdiccas of an incestuous love for his mother; pronounced healthy his contemporary Democritus, whom the Abderans thought crazy on account of his permanent laughter; and refused his aid to the Persians in their fight with the plague. With these "deeds," Hippocrates won a lasting connection to the histories of pestilence, of lovesickness, of anatomy and philosophy, and of nationalism, and he provided material for didactic poems, plays, *Meisterlieder,* frontispieces, satires, paintings, and bronze clocks. His "pervasive presence in Western medicine and culture" (Cantor 2002) has proven itself across countless media. Hippocrates won a firm place in legal history, down to the Nuremberg Doctors' Trial and the legendary case *Roe v. Wade.* His incessantly changing likeness is emblazoned on postage stamps, postcards, title pages, and advertisements. His portrait bust graces institutes of medical history, offices of deans of medicine, and university buildings, and it haunts novels like Thomas Mann's *Magic Mountain* as a fixture of medical examination rooms. Unexpectedly, Hippocrates long ago conquered the media worlds of the 20th century and has done the same for the virtual one of the 21st.

These incarnations of the ancient Coan can sometimes eclipse the work to which he has given his name. The latter represents the evolutionarily most ancient attempt to secularize medicine in an age marked by belief in the power of the divine. It strives for the objectification of medicinal discourse, deploying in this task numerous rhetorical aids and a broad variety of textual genres. It aims at empirically validating the speculation of natural philosophy, theoretically justifying medical intervention, securing the retention and transmission of medical know-how, interpreting illnesses, finding their causes, and charting their course, naming and classifying diseases, and developing confidence-building measures, by means of cultivating the image of a competent, humble, disinterested group of authors who, as physicians, act as a moral censor of their own activity in a highly competitive, unregulated health-care market with no medical law. It is true that a good two-thirds of the writings collected in the Corpus Hippocraticum fall within Hippocrates' supposed lifetime, but this proves nothing about their authorship. The "Hippocratic" question about the authenticity of texts bearing his name remains as contested as ever. Indeed, precisely this uncertainty, as well as the fact that the texts of the Corpus Hippocraticum ultimately constitute a cross-section of all ancient, pre-Galenic medicine, has always encouraged readers to approach them selectively and to rediscover—or reinvent—"their" Hippocrates. He became a figurehead for dogmatics and pneumatics, for empiricists and vitalists, for Muslims, Catholics, Lutherans, Philippists, and Calvinists, Spinozists and atheists, for humanists and national socialists. He was the inspiration for humoral pathology, solidary pathology, homeopathy, iatrotheology, iatromechanics, iatrochemistry, and iatrodemonology, and he prompted all possible forms of Neohumanism and Neohippocratism in the history of Western medicine. He withstood the anti-Hippocratism of Nicholas of Poland (ca. 1300), the decline of Galenic Hippocratism in the 16th century, the crisis of humoral pathology beginning in the 17th century, the debate over his possible atheism in the 18th century, the textual criticism of the 19th and 20th centuries, the scientification of medicine beginning in the second half of the 19th century, and the proclamation of a post-Hippocratic age at the turn of the 21st century. He was part of the medical curriculum at all centers for the training of physicians from late antique Alexandria to 19th-century Vienna, and he called forth thousands of translators, commentators, interpreters, and editors, who have amalgamated the reconstruction of Hippocratic medicine inextricably and for all time with its reception. That Hippocrates is still a household name today is a cultural rarity of the first order.

BIBL.: D. Cantor, ed., *Reinventing Hippocrates* (Aldershot 2002). J. Jouanna, *Hippocrates,* trans. M. B. DeBevoise (Baltimore 1999). J. R. Pinault, *Hippocratic Lives and Legends* (Leiden 1992). T. Rütten, *Demokrit—lachender Philosoph und sanguinischer Melancholiker: Eine pseudohippokratische Geschichte* (Leiden 1992). O. Temkin, *Hippocrates in a World of Pagans and Christians* (Baltimore 1991). T.R.

Translated by Patrick Baker

Hippocratic Oath

Ethical oath generally attributed to the Greek physician Hippocrates (ca. 460–ca. 370 BCE). Evidence for its use in late antiquity is unclear. Gregory of Nazianzus (*Orations* 7.10) claims that his brother Caesarius did not swear the oath as a medical student at Alexandria, thus implying that others did. But there is no proof of formal compulsion to swear in Byzantium or in the Muslim world, although the oath was well known. But it took second place in practice to the Galenic concept that equated ethical medicine with effective treatment and that looked back to the Hippocratic legends and the so-called Testament of Hippocrates for guidance on behavior. Although translations and modifications of the Hippocratic Oath exist in many medieval languages, most medical oaths took the form of expressions of loyalty to a ruler or university allied to specific instructions on practice and fees.

Some of the wording of the oath appears in Renaissance university oaths (e.g., at Wittenberg in 1508 and at Basel in 1570). At Heidelberg in 1558 the dean of medicine had to affirm it publicly within one month of taking office; at Jena, from 1558 until the 19th century, graduates had to agree to do everything that Hippocrates had demanded in the oath and in his *On the Physician.* At Leiden in the 17th century, and at Edinburgh between 1705 and 1731, assent was made to a Latin version of the oath, which was thereafter replaced by a briefer and much vaguer redaction. At Montpellier from 1804 onward each medical graduate had to recite the oath on graduation, standing before a bust of Hippocrates donated by the French government. Demand for the taking of the Hippocratic Oath was particularly intense in the United States after 1840, especially as its ban on abortion would serve to distinguish the true doctor from the quack, though a new ethical code was thought by some to be more suited to a new country.

By 1880 this zeal for the oath had waned, and schools where it was taken, such as McGill University, were seen as old-fashioned. Where medical oaths were sworn, they tended to be of the loyalty form (e.g., the Prussian medical oath of 1810, devised by C. W. Hufeland, affirming obligations to both state and patients). The Second World War marked a big change; a renewal of interest in medical oaths and codes followed the revelations at the Nuremberg trials. The Geneva Declaration of 1948 transmuted the oath into a modern context, and in the United States and Canada the number of medical schools using the Hippocratic Oath, or something resembling it, rose from 20 in 1928 to 69 in 1965, 108 in 1977, and 119 in 1989. A similar trend can be seen in Britain, where in 1996 the British Medical Association issued a revised version of the oath for the 20th and 21st century.

From late antiquity onward clauses in the oath have been changed or dropped to suit the circumstances of society (e.g., the religious proem or, in the 1960s, the abortion clause), but without removing its symbolic function. Some medical ethicists, especially the more conservative, continue to appeal to the principles thought to be enshrined therein—although the broader the principles, the less specifically Hippocratic their content—while others see the oath only as an outmoded stage in the creation of a modern medical ethic.

BIBL.: David Cantor, ed., *Reinventing Hippocrates* (Aldershot 2002). *The Hippocratic Oath,* special issue, *Journal of the History of Medicine* 51, no. 4 (1996) 401–500. Vivian Nutton, "Hippocratic Medicine and Modern Morality," in *Médecine et morale dans l'antiquité,* Entretiens sur l'antiquité classique (Fondation Hardt) 43 (Geneva 1997) 31–63. Thomas Rütten, *Hippokrates im Gespräch* (Münster 1993).

V.N.

Historicism

Term denoting a central paradigm of modern scholarship. Scholarly discussion has arrived at no consensus over the meaning of the concept. Not only do various disciplines have their own specific understandings of historicism, but different definitions have been, and continue to be, proposed even within disciplines. In Germany historians often connect historicism with Friedrich Meinecke and the attempt, beginning around 1800, to raise history to the level of a systematic science (*Wissenschaft*). This scholarly paradigm led to the historicization of the *Kulturwissenschaften,* but it then underwent a crisis in the late 19th and early 20th centuries.

This concept is found starting at the turn of the 19th century. Of decisive importance for its further development was the theory of historical knowledge developed within the discipline of history over the next 100 years. On the basis of a thorough survey of the sources, the interpretation of their transmission came to be portrayed as the decisive means of producing knowledge within the context of historical research whose aim was objectivity. In the realm of method a connection was made to critical philology; J. G. Fichte, F. D. E. Schleiermacher, and G. W. F. Hegel provided manifold theoretical stimulus. A deeply rooted belief in the intrinsic meaning of historical events was accompanied by an accentuation on the historical importance of the individual and his role in the progressive manifestation of reason.

In classical studies, which contributed definitively to historicism's ascent, efforts toward developing a scientific theory of scholarship and a universal methodology did not continue after the 1840s. Research was increasingly confined to the highly specialized techniques of source criticism and hermeneutics. This produced tremendous achievements. Enormous cooperative projects made the legacy of the ancient world available and set the trend for other disciplines. An analytical-historical empiricism self-confidently raised its head. Faith in progress and optimism about the power of scholarship marked the professionalized and diversified study of antiquity in universities and academies. Classical studies became a big industry that spectacularly confirmed the effectiveness of historical-critical method, but one in which heuristics and interpretation diverged and the scholar turned into a worker and valet.

At the end of the 19th century and the beginning of the 20th, the explosive increase in knowledge and the pluralization of ideals led to a profound sense of insecurity. Criticism was increasingly expressed for a self-absorbed empirical research into facts (*Tatsachenforschung*), as well as for the relativism of an analytical-empirical scholarship that historicized indiscriminately and that undermined the normative function of antiquity. Historicism became equated with the sterile, enervating zeal for objectivity characteristic of antiquarian research. First Jacob Burckhardt and Friedrich Nietzsche and then Ernst Troeltsch and Max Weber raised the question of the correlation between historical research and the exigencies of real life, and it became a central problem of the philosophy of history and epistemology that also occupied classical scholarship. But this discourse had only a slight effect on scholarly practice: meticulous work on the ancient sources continued to receive the loudest acclaim from the scholarly community.

World War I intensified the identity crisis of historicist classical studies. Not only the adepts of Stefan George's circle (*George-Kreis*), but also scholars like Werner Jaeger, sought to bridge the divide between scholarship and life and to rehabilitate antiquity as a meaningful historical parameter. Criticism for a supposedly degenerate historicism grew louder in the 1920s and 1930s in Europe. The competition of leading scholarly and political systems, antidemocratic and antiparliamentary convictions, the dwindling public importance of antiquity, and—last but not least—an antihistoricist reflex led particular Italian and German scholars to find the ideological components of Fascism and National Socialism in their search for a new image of antiquity. But historicist-minded classical scholarship and the strict objectivity and rationality it at least verbally demanded were ultimately not compatible with the theory of history of National Socialism, characterized as it was by irrationalism and the criticism of high culture (*Kulturkritik*).

Since 1945 classical scholarship in Europe and North America has taken pains to find its place between "historicist" factual research and poststructuralist models of interpretation. The second half of the 20th century witnessed the defense and the damnation of historicism. The overhaul of historicism from the perspective of classical studies is necessary for the self-understanding and self-assurance of the discipline. It is a desideratum.

BIBL.: Glenn W. Most, *Historicization = Historisierung* (Göttingen 2001). Otto Gerhard Oexle, *Geschichtswissenschaft im Zeichen des Historismus* (Göttingen 1996). Stefan Rebenich, "Historismus I: Allgemein," *DNP* 14 (2000) 469–485. Annette Wittkau, *Historismus: Zur Geschichte des Begriffs und des Problems*, 2nd ed. (Göttingen 1994). S.R.

Translated by Patrick Baker

Historiography

Early in the 19th century, an Oxford undergraduate read aloud passages from his diary of a trip to Venice. "Painted beauty, six shillings," he noted, presumably with a smirk. One of his audience immediately rose and said, "*Philokaloumen met'euteleias,*" and then left the room, to general applause. None of those present ever forgot the event. None of them needed an explanation, either. For they knew at once that the young man had condemned his college mate's vulgar, prurient words in the most crushing possible way, by quoting a slightly abridged phrase from Pericles' funeral oration for the Athenian dead in the first year of the Peloponnesian War: *Philokaloumen gar met'euteleias kai philosophoumen aneu malakias,* "We are lovers of beauty without extravagance and lovers of wisdom without effeminacy." They knew the phrase from Thucydides' history of the war. This included Pericles' speech (2.40) and many others, in versions that, so the author claimed, reflected both what the statesmen and generals should have said and, in general terms, what they did say.

In the first decades of the 19th century Oxford scholars and students still shared a classical training that formed them to rule, one that had an influence far outside the universities. Its results were manifest everywhere, from the House of Commons, where the clerk had to keep classical reference books handy in order to settle bets between MPs who accused one another of misquotations, to the world of literature. For the study of classics was designed not to imprison Wissenschaftler in an iron cage of lexica and footnotes but to sculpt active men who could succeed in the public realm: men who were prudent enough to know the right course and eloquent enough to persuade their fellow citizens to follow it. And the ancient historians held out the key to two connected kingdoms: civil and military prudence and political and juridical eloquence.

None of these ideas was new: that was part of their power. Historians and rhetorical theorists—Thucydides and Polybius, Isocrates and Cicero—had never tired of proclaiming that history should form the core of an education for public life, that it offered examples of right and wrong speech and action. When studied intensively, histories revealed the principles that a statesman or general needed to apply in real life, adapting them to circumstances. The continuity of human affairs and human nature—"in the course of human things," Thucydides assured his readers, the future must "more or less resemble" the present (1.22.4)—guaranteed that past examples would still offer usable lessons centuries, or millennia, later. Historians cast these lessons, moreover, in the most effective possible way, not as abstract, off-putting statements but as crisp, emotionally effective, memorable examples and speeches—exactly what teachers and practitioners of oratory needed most. History, as Cicero explained in sustained and much-quoted discussions, was "oratorical above all" (*De legibus* 1.5); the power of speech made history "the witness to the past, the torch of truth, the light of memory, the teacher of life" (*testis temporum, lux veritatis, vita memoriae, magistra vitae; De oratore* 2.9.36). No wonder then that gleaming passages from the Greek historians stuck in alert students' minds. These views were still alive in the later 19th century. When innovators demanded that Oxford and Cambridge introduce courses in modern history, which would teach a critical method and the comparative study of sources, conservatives complained that such a study could not be rigorous or valuable, since students had no single set text to master.

The actual legacy of ancient historiography—the body of Greek and Latin historical texts and commentary on them—was far more complex than these traditional evaluations suggest. Ancient historiography included epic narratives of great events and peoples—the wars of the

Greeks and the Persians, the rise of Rome—and short, quirkily detailed biographies of emperors, grammarians, and theologians; extended, complex battle scenes and speeches, embedded in rich contextual discussions and designed to provoke debate, and simple anecdotes torn from time and space and arranged to teach simple lessons; world chronicles, austere in form but studded with fascinating details, and local antiquarian monographs, with detailed information on local religious life and political institutions; accounts of wars, in the first person and the third; late antique narratives and republican ethnographies; and much more. Many of these forms were unlikely sources for the sort of pragmatic and moral instruction for which pedagogues looked to history. Cicero insisted that history had laws, one of which required that the historian tell the truth. Yet he himself admitted that "there are countless fables in Herodotus, the father of history, and in Theopompus" (*De legibus* 1.5). The prudent reader must sort histories into their proper categories before trying to use them.

More important, many of the historical texts that medieval and early modern readers liked most do not appear in today's canon of great ancient writers. Ancient historians preferred, when possible, to write about events that they had witnessed themselves—even if some, like Herodotus and Livy, had to extend their inquiries into the distant past. Isidore of Seville, the 7th-century bishop and encyclopedist, seems to echo this canonical principle when he argues, "None of the ancients would write history unless he had been present and had seen what he narrated" (*Etymologies* 1.41.1). But he probably drew his thesis not from Caesar or Sallust but from the writer whom he described as the first historian among the Gentiles, as Moses had been first "among us": "Dares the Phrygian, who published the history of the Greeks and Trojans, which he supposedly recorded on palm leaves" (1.42.1). The narratives of Dares and his fellow historian of the Trojan War, Dictys of Crete, purported to be older than Homer. Elaborate, implausible prefaces signed by Cornelius Nepos and Lucius Septimius described the conditions in which the Greek originals had turned up and been translated into Latin. Though genuinely derived from Greek originals, as they claimed, these texts look trivial now beside Livy—to say nothing of Tacitus. To an erudite bishop, however, they were older than the texts that would now be classified as classical histories, and no less instructive. Throughout the centuries, from the fall of the Roman Empire to very recent times, Dictys and Dares—and Josephus, in Latin translation, and Eusebius, in the Latin adaptation by Jerome—helped frame many intellectuals' vision of both history writing and the past.

The Christians who reconfigured the classical heritage, moreover, made choices that strongly affected the reception of the historians. Some, like Eusebius, believed they could descry God working in particular events; others, like Augustine, insisted that such judgments were not for men to make. Yet all of them saw history, ultimately, as the work of a providential hand. All of them sought to incorporate the histories of ancient Greece and Rome into larger schemes that traced human history from Adam and Eve—or at least from Nimrod and Abraham—to the present. And all of them agreed that secular history, when torn from the theological framework that gave human life meaning, degenerated into a meaningless chronicle. The ancient historians, accordingly, did not find a place in the Christian vision of learning comparable to that accorded those Greeks and Romans whose works expounded the Trivium and Quadrivium arts.

Still, the ancient historians were studied, especially during periods of classical revival such as the 8th and 9th centuries, which saw the Greek historians transliterated into minuscule script and the main Latin historians, from Livy and Tacitus to Suetonius and the *Scriptores historiae Augustae,* actively copied and imitated in the great monastic centers like Lorsch. They had attracted little formal commentary in the ancient world—essays by Dionysius of Halicarnassus and Plutarch and some witty short works by Lucian are among the lonely exceptions to this rule. At some point in late antiquity, however, scholia crystallized like diamonds around the troubling names and technical terms in Thucydides. And though the Latin historians survived the heyday of glossing with their texts still unbarnacled, they did not escape another process of interpretation that had a much more radical effect on them. From the imperial period onward, long histories like those of Livy circulated not only in their original form but as epitomes. In the 4th century members of new elites, both pagan and Christian, needed rapid access to the outlines of Roman history and some account of its relation to that of the larger world. The anonymous author of the *Periochae* of Livy, Eutropius, the Christian Sulpicius Severus, and others met this need with short, accessible works that were widely copied and read, and that may have helped drive the full original texts of Livy and Tacitus out of circulation. Others, from Isidore to Vincent of Beauvais half a millennium later, recycled the historians' texts in encyclopedic compilations. Only in the 14th century, however, did erudite Mendicants like the English Dominican Nicholas Trevet begin to collate Livy's history of early Rome with the parallel accounts in authoritative texts that ranged from Eusebius's *Chronicle* to Augustine's *City of God,* and to compile rich explanatory commentaries.

Both in Byzantium and in the West, nonetheless, ancient historians offered readers and writers much that could not be found in extracanonical books and compilations or in other disciplines. Throughout the Middle Ages, ancient historians offered a powerful model for writing on a vital range of topics. Einhard, writing in early 9th-century Gaul, used the *Lives* of Suetonius as the last on which he cobbled his own impressive life of Charlemagne, which detailed not only his political and military accomplishments, but also his habits at table and his favorite sayings—though not his sexual foibles, which Suetonius would certainly have recorded. Michael Psellus, a century later, used Plutarch as a central model for his own lives of

Byzantine rulers. Appropriate subjects and acceptable models varied quite widely. Laonicus Chalcondyles, writing his history of the fall of Byzantium to the Turks in the late 15th century, emulated Herodotus as he laid out his wide-ranging ethnography, which included both the empire's barbarian enemies in Asia and its supposed allies in Western Europe. Medieval historians created genres of their own: genealogical histories of peoples, saints' lives, histories of monasteries and other religious institutions. When they set out to write the history of a nation or that of its rulers, however, the ancient models remained supreme—even if those models actually caused much confusion (for example, by supplying anachronistic names that classicizing historians like Chalcondyles applied, regardless of plausibility, to the peoples of their own day who lived and worshipped differently from Christians).

In the same centuries, moreover, some of the most impressive protagonists of ancient historiography—Alexander the Great and Julius Caesar, Augustus and Hadrian—escaped the texts that recounted their lives. Suitably dressed and armored as medieval knights, their exploits updated and dramatized to include feats of chivalrous courage, they became the heroes of romances in French and Italian. Images of them adorned the illuminated pages of vernacular literature, the stained-glass windows that lit great halls in the palaces of cultivated men, and the tapestries that warmed their bedchambers. Kings and aristocrats envisioned themselves as the successors of these worthies of antiquity.

Ancient history was thus widely present in medieval culture, clerical and courtly. And yet something changed, in the 14th century, in Western scholars' approach to reading and writing history. Giovanni de Matociis, mansionary of the cathedral in Verona and a habitué of its great library, noticed that even ancient historical sources disagreed. He drew up his own history of the Roman Empire, in the margins of which he inserted neat drawings of the coins that his protagonists had minted. Petrarch, a few decades later, made clear that he brought a new viewpoint to the study of the ancient historians. Like Trevet, he knew and prized the great compendia of Eusebius-Jerome and Augustine as well as the ancient historians. But it was Livy and Suetonius—as well as Virgil and Ovid—whose works he designated his "favorite books" in a programmatic list, made up almost entirely of pagan authors. "What else," Petrarch asked, "is history but the praise of Rome?" Though the question was rhetorical, Petrarch's answer was extremely substantive. He gathered 30 of the 35 surviving books of Livy's history into a single manuscript—the first time in centuries that any single reader had confronted so much Livy at once—and worked through it, making emendations and comments that are still impressive. He read as many other histories as he could. When Petrarch and his friend Giovanni Colonna walked the streets and explored the ruins of Rome, Giovanni described the Christian sites—and Petrarch, as his expertise allowed, the pagan ones. And he put this rich material to use again and again: in an epic of Rome's wars against Carthage, the *Africa;* in a massive set of lives of famous men, which Petrarch wrote and rewrote; and in his letters to Livy and other ancient writers, in which he made clear his sense of the distance, temporal and cultural, that separated them. Ancient history had been revived, in a distinctive and consequential way. Yet Petrarch never declared allegiance to the alien code of values that Latin historiography embodied. He found worthies in the biblical as well as the classical narratives, and he worried—as Jerome had worried about his love of Cicero—about the fact that his favorite historians and histories had not belonged to the Christian tradition. His disciple Boccaccio followed in Petrarch's footsteps: the heroines of his massive historical compendium on the fates of famous women were mostly, but not entirely, ancient Greeks and Romans.

The two generations of Humanists that came after Petrarch followed his lead in many ways, sometimes literally. Lorenzo Valla, who made brilliant emendations of his own to the text of Livy, entered them in the margins of the same manuscript that Petrarch had brought together. Coluccio Salutati and Leonardo Bruni, Poggio Bracciolini and Guarino of Verona, also collected and corrected the manuscripts of ancient historians. Guarino, who served and taught the Estensi of Ferrara, loved Livy and put his own stamp on the text of Caesar's *Commentaries,* which he not only taught but also corrected. Three-decker copies of Livy, as redacted in Florence and handsomely produced in the atelier of the bookseller Vespasiano da Bisticci, circulated through the libraries of Italy and beyond. At Ferrara, educated courtiers even used them in games of *sortes Livianae,* opening the text at random to see if the episode they happened on revealed the special qualities of their favorite historical characters. Humanists also composed histories of their own, in classical style and on the ancient scale. Bruni and Poggio both wrote histories of the Florentine people, in the style of Livy—but, in Bruni's case, with a mischievous sense that the true heroes of the early centuries of Rome had been the Etruscan ancestors of the modern Tuscans, whose virtues had to be excavated from Livy by reading against the grain.

But Petrarch's followers also studied and used the ancient historians in new ways. As skilled antiquaries, Poggio, Leon Battista Alberti, and Flavio Biondo examined Rome's pagan ruins. They found that even Petrarch had sometimes accepted local legends that an energetic inspection of the sites in question would have dispelled, and they realized that the monuments sometimes confirmed and often contradicted or complemented the narratives in their ancient texts. As pioneering Hellenists, both Bruni and Guarino translated Greek histories—Procopius and Plutarch, among others—into Latin. As teachers, the members of this generation created new secular schools in courts and cities, in which they offered a version of the ancient rhetorical training to the sons of royal and noble families and urban patricians. In the school of the most influential Humanist teacher, Guarino, and in those of his rivals, history enjoyed a central place in the curriculum.

Even an elementary writer like Valerius Maximus, Guarino's son Battista explained, afforded "actual illustrations of virtuous precepts couched in attractive style." The other Roman historians would help the schoolboy "to understand the manners, laws, and institutions of different types of nations, and to examine the varying fortunes of individuals and states, the sources of their success and failure, their strength and their weakness. Not only is such knowledge of interest in daily intercourse, but it is of practical value in the ordering of affairs" (*De ordine docendi et studendi,* 1459). The full Ciceronian set of claims for the value of history was not only revived but also made a cornerstone of the curriculum. Soon, as in the Middle Ages, ancient heroes and heroines escaped the classroom and the scholar's study to appear in manuscript illuminations, panel paintings, and massive frescoes. In the hands of Mantegna, Botticelli and others, the most instructive and dramatic ancient histories became prime subjects for the elaborate, multi-character paintings known as "histories." But then—and for centuries to come—the ancient heroes who struck attitudes, took oaths, or stole brides from their Sabine neighbors were dressed in Roman clothing and armor, and acted their scenes before Roman buildings.

No one did more than Lorenzo Valla to open up new realms of ancient history. He not only corrected Livy but also rendered both Herodotus and Thucydides into Latin—the latter with a selection of the scholia. He argued, in his own history of Alfonso of Aragon, that Aristotle had been wrong: history of the classical kind was actually more profound and instructive than poetry. And in his famous attack on the Donation of Constantine and other works, he suggested—more forcefully than anyone had before him—that the scholar must not only find moral lessons in the ancient histories, but also subject them to critical examination. Valla dedicated a short work to showing that Livy had gone wrong on a point of Roman genealogy, and some of his fellow Humanists went further toward showing that the great ancient narratives were not identical to the history they recounted. Pomponio Leto and other antiquaries scoured the city's antiquities and lectured on them. Pomponio also lectured on Sallust and other Roman historians, drawing on the detailed antiquarian material assembled by Dionysius of Halicarnassus to make clear that the ancients had already disagreed about the early history of Rome.

At first, these new questions did little to delay the spread of interest in these writers. Across Italy and beyond, a new, secular history, based on study and emulation of an ever-increasing range of texts, became part of the common definition of learning. New texts continually came into play. Tacitus's *Germania,* for example, returned to circulation in the 15th century. It gave both German and Italian scholars a model for discussing a realm that had never been comfortably integrated into Roman culture. Diodorus Siculus, translated in part by Poggio, offered rich mythological material on ancient Egypt, Chaldaea, and Greece to chroniclers and artists. However rich and complex this new material proved, it did not pose any clear challenge to the central position the ancient historians now occupied: as a central part of the education of young men destined to live the public life. To Giovanni Gioviano Pontano, composing his discourses on the study of history in Naples, to Leto in Rome, and to Bembo in Venice, it must have seemed that ancient history, studied in the traditional, rhetorical way, held an impregnable position in culture and in pedagogy. *Historia* was once again *magistra vitae.*

The ancient histories, read in the light of contemporary events, now served many purposes, some of them quite unexpected. As European knowledge of Asia and the Americas grew, what had seemed tall tales in Herodotus gained a new plausibility, and he offered a powerful model for writers who set out to describe the peoples that conquistadores and missionaries met in Mexico and the Andes, China, and India. As the Spanish empire expanded into territories around the globe, Livy's history of the Roman people took on a new function. It became the model for a heroic history of national growth, as Virgil's epic version of Roman history served the Portuguese. Diodorus's account of how humanity was generated as the Earth dried out offered what seemed a pagan counterpart to the story of human origins in Genesis. Translated and incorporated into the world chronicles of Jacopo Foresti and Hartmann Schedel, Diodorus inspired a miller in Friuli—one Menocchio—to spin his own new theories about the cosmos and its origin.

Traditional approaches to ancient history remained dominant for a time. Guarino's patron, Leonello d'Este, was a highly trained Humanist in his own right who wrote clean, lucid Latin prose and loved his Livy. He could read critically as well. Angelo Decembrio, a Humanist who knew the Este court well, portrayed Leonello as dissecting Quintus Curtius's history of Alexander the Great, showing that it was drawn from earlier writers and lacked credibility, and denouncing the historical errors so common on the Flemish tapestries that depicted ancient heroes. Yet Leonello was very fond of Flemish tapestries, anachronisms and all, and he collected them actively. Many of the manuscripts of ancient historians produced for courtly patrons were illuminated, unlike those made for scholars, and the illustrations often represented Greek statesmen and Roman emperors as medieval knights and kings. This anachronistic but effective way of making ancient history seem up-to-date survived for decades. Ben Jonson took his Roman tragedies from the best sources, which he read in the original, and footnoted them to show how faithfully he had worked. But Shakespeare, who drew his Roman tales from Livy and Plutarch in translation, did not hesitate to have Brutus and Cassius hear a clock strike three as they waited out the night before they murdered Caesar.

But in the last decade of the 15th and the first two decades of the 16th century, the foundations of *historia magistra vitae* shook as multiple crises struck. In 1494 the French invasion and the expulsion of the Medici from

Florence threw Italian affairs—including the status of ancient history—into chaos. A Dominican of vast learning, Giovanni Nanni (or Annius) of Viterbo, though steeped in the new texts that the Humanists had made available, felt nothing but disgust for the pagan learning of *Graecia mendax*. He produced a set of rival texts designed to challenge the ancient historians. Several of them he ascribed to authors mentioned by Josephus and Eusebius: Berossus the Chaldean, Manetho the Egyptian, Metasthenes (not Megasthenes) the Persian. Others supposedly came from better-known figures like Cato and Philo. Almost all of them were in fact his own forgeries (one was real: Propertius' poem on Vertumnus, 4.2). Faked inscriptions, whose discoveries Annius staged in Viterbo, confirmed these new accounts of everything from the life of Osiris in Egypt to that of Desiderius, king of the Lombards. Taken together and strewn like fragments of spicy meat in the vast stew of Annius's commentaries, which appeared in a magnificent volume at Rome in 1498, the forged texts offered a rich and cogent account of history—one according to which all men had been giants until the Flood, which Noah had prophesied by astrological means, and one that gave the ancestors of all the modern nations—not to mention those of the reigning Borgia pope, Alexander VI—a prominent place in the past.

Both the writers Annius published and their commentator pointed out, again and again, how well this collective narrative correlated to that of the Old Testament, and how much more trust the collective, public histories of priests deserved than those scribbled down by individual Greeks who had had no public position. When Annius's collection appeared, a few expert scholars condemned it. Beatus Rhenanus, Erasmus's friend and assistant, noticed immediately that the same man had written the purportedly ancient texts and the modern commentary. "One of them," he remarked, dourly quoting Erasmus, "milks the he-goat, while the other holds out the sieve." But texts and commentaries alike were reprinted again and again, and many learned readers accepted them. The erudite Cardinal Egidio da Viterbo, a polyglot who knew Hebrew as well as Greek, filled his copy with approving marginalia. When Annius rebutted Flavio Biondo's assertion that Viterbo had been founded in fairly recent times, Egidio took sides with great simplicity, scribbling "Blondus blondellus" (Biondo is a ditsy blonde) in his book. The colorful material that Annius had assembled soon came to form the core narrative of ancient history in the most popular chronicles and introductions to world history.

In the 1510s and 1520s, moreover, as Philipp Melanchthon and other Protestant intellectuals began to write and teach history, they looked back to the early Christian world of chronologies and epitomes for their models. Annius's texts closely followed the biblical account of early history and rejected pagan wisdom for sacred narrative. These qualities gave them a special appeal for Protestant world historians, notably Luther and Melanchthon. But Catholic printers and historians also accepted the Annian texts, reprinting them many times and working them into the structure of short textbooks on world history. Many young readers wondered, as they worked through some version of the Dominican's patter about deceptive Greeks, whether it was licit at all to study the ancient historians—or whether, like Egidio, they should look for other sources of wisdom, prophetic rather than pragmatic.

The second challenge came from within the Humanist tradition. The Florentine Niccolò Machiavelli grew up with a solid classical education and worked for Piero Soderini, who ran the government of the Florentine republic from 1494 until the Medici returned in 1512. He served as an ambassador and tried to build up a native army, since he considered the professional mercenaries who dominated warfare in Italy unreliable and incompetent. After Soderini fell and Machiavelli himself was arrested and tortured, he made a second career as a political commentator, supported by the Rucellai family, in whose gardens he lectured on Livy's Roman history. Where Annius had found the ancients untrustworthy, Machiavelli found them incomparably grave, honest, and profound. What pained and annoyed him were the moderns, who, he argued, claimed to love the ancients and collected every fragment of an ancient statue or plinth, but refused to learn the political lessons that were the true core of the classical tradition. Reading Livy and Polybius—notably book 6—Machiavelli saw that Christianity had done more harm than good to Italy. A pagan religion of the sort that Numa had invented for the Romans—as Livy made clear—helped forge a strong, martial people, whereas Christianity merely softened the people and deluded their "unarmed prophets," such as Savonarola. Annius challenged the study of the classical historians as an enterprise, but Machiavelli insisted that it could survive only by becoming truly historical. Moderns had to learn to read the ancients as the alien pagans they were and still take advice from them. Many learned statesmen agreed. Lazarus Schwendi, a ruthless soldier and politician who served Charles V, carefully read and annotated his copy of Machiavelli's *Discourses on Livy* in the 1540s, noting the similarity between the Florentine's vision of politics and that expressed by Thucydides in the *Melian Dialogue*.

Through the 16th century and beyond, the schools continued to teach history, and the scholars to edit and comment on it. The presses of Basel and Geneva poured out massive editions of Greek and Roman historians alike, accompanied in the former case with Latin translations, and in both with commentaries that grew longer and denser. From the 1530s onward, Juan Luis Vives and other writers began to reflect on the twin challenges of Annius and Machiavelli. A literature of *artes historicae* (arts of history) took shape. Learned philosophers and jurists—Francesco Patrizi, François Baudouin, Jean Bodin, and others—instructed readers on how to decide which ancient historians to trust and then how to wring the proper lessons from them. Gradually Livy lost credit, and Polybius and Tacitus gained special prestige as teachers of military wisdom and courtly survival tactics. Other scholars filled in the corpus of preserved texts and began to collect the fragments of what had been lost. Antonio Riccobono brought together everything he could salvage of Cato and the other lost Latin writers, Fulvio Orsini edited the fragments of Polybius, and Joseph Scaliger assembled the genuine bits of Berossus and Manetho in the hope—which proved vain—of dealing a death blow to the forgeries of Annius.

Scholars came to appreciate the acuity and learning that had gone into ancient historical enterprises attested only in fragments: for example, the work of ancient antiquaries such as Varro, who had not composed elegant narratives, but instead had drawn on texts and other forms of evidence to re-create past beliefs and institutions. Yet challenges remained—and in some ways the activities of the critics exacerbated them. From Jacopo Mazzocchi, Jean Matal, and Antonio Agustín to Carlo Sigonio and Onofrio Panvinio, antiquaries expanded their collections of inscriptions—some of which, like the Roman *fasti,* called basic data in the historians into question. Baudouin insisted that the availability of new evidence on this scale made the historian's task more rewarding than it had ever been. Yet he himself noted that banquet songs rather than official records had preserved early Roman tradition—though he claimed to find this fact encouraging, since it suggested that one could use the songs of New World peoples to reconstruct their histories as well. Within a few decades, however, more radical scholars such as Jean du Temps and Philip Cluverius were drawing very different inferences from the banquet songs. They insisted that Romulus and Numa had never lived at all, and that the early history of Rome must be set on a completely different foundation—theories that would be revived more than once and always provoke sharp debate.

The choice of the best historians to follow and the proper way to interpret them remained especially contentious. Even those who partly accepted Machiavelli's pragmatic way of reading felt it necessary to conceal their sympathy for the devil. The most influential single teacher of and writer on history, Justus Lipsius, was a brilliantly successful teacher of history at Calvinist Leiden and Catholic Louvain alike. He drew from Polybius a rich account of the reasons the Roman army had been so successful, which helped Maurice of Nassau and other military leaders create the first modern armies on what they saw as a Roman model. And he drew from Tacitus, whose works he edited and commented on, a powerful, chiaroscuro account of life under absolute rule. This, he argued, was simply more relevant than Livy's account of the virtuous early Republic to moderns who lived, as Tacitus's friends and ancestors had, under the thumb of autocratic rulers. Machiavelli thus took on a new life in the guise of the Roman historian, whom he had greatly admired. Lipsius attracted dozens of students, and his books found thousands of readers. Tacitism, in his version and many others—notably the subversive, republican form espoused by Isaac Dorislaus, first professor of history at Cambridge, who was allowed to give only two lectures before being silenced—came into vogue. Yet Lipsius's Tacitism was parodied by Traiano Boccalini and rejected by his one-time friend Isaac Casaubon, who insisted that Polybius provided *the* model of a history at once pragmatically useful and morally virtuous. Most still agreed that ancient history offered precious, practical help with the life of affairs. Kings and aristocrats paid scholars to read and explicate the ancient histories to them: great men held debates at country houses about whether Scipio was superior to Hannibal, or vice versa. The Duke of Essex even blamed his abortive rebellion against Queen Elizabeth on the Humanist Henry Cuffe, who had read Lucan—often seen as a historian—with him. But the status of ancient history was becoming ever more problematic.

The problems grew all the more serious in the 17th century. More and more thinkers—not only prophets of innovation like Bacon and Descartes, but more traditional intellectuals like the Danzig scholar Bartholomew Keckermann—were arguing that ancient history deserved no special priority. After all, as both Keckermann and Descartes noted, one could learn by traveling, more efficiently and pleasantly than by reading, that things were done differently in other countries. The antiquarian enterprise continued to expand. As physical collections and printed corpora of inscriptions and coins swelled, the ancient texts lost more and more of their centrality to the specialized study of antiquity. Influenced by the new philosophy, with its strong emphasis on empirical evidence that could be weighed and measured, some began to see the material remains of the ancient world as more central than any written evidence—even that of the historians—to its reconstruction. One skilled antiquary, the Jesuit Jean Hardouin, went so far as to argue that the coins and inscriptions showed that the corpus of ancient historians—like almost all other ancient texts—were actually forgeries from the 13th century. Not long after, Isaac Newton set out to revise the history of all ancient civilizations in an equally radical way, using astronomical evidence. Meanwhile, Francesco Bianchini and Giambattista Vico, among others, were setting out to replace ancient narratives of the history of Greece and Rome with new ones based, in the former case, on material remains, and in the latter, on a conjectural theory of social development.

At the same time, older arguments about the ancient historians continued to be recycled. Deeply erudite moderates such as the Leiden professor of ancient history Jacob Perizonius did their best to show that parts of the traditional narrative still deserved credence, drawing on the older scholarship. But Perizonius worked in the narrow, Latinate world of the Dutch universities. The critics who became famous knew far less than he: often they simply did not realize that earlier scholars had made the same points. But they published their theses in the accessible modern languages rather than in Latin, and they discussed them in the accessible social setting of the academies rather than the old universities. The traditional narratives of early Greek and Roman history, which du Temps and Cluverius had shredded long before, came in for renewed criticism and defense in the Paris Academy of

Inscriptions after its reorganization as a learned society in 1701. Boivin noted sarcastically that historians credited no fewer than ten different groups with the founding of Rome; Étienne Fourmont argued that the Trojan War had lasted only one year. In December 1722 Louis Jean Lévesque de Pouilly read a paper in which he dismissed the traditional narrative of Roman history as mere legends, transmitted by late sources. The Abbé Sailly defended the tradition, arguing that the priestly annals and other credible witnesses had transmitted at least part of the story. Eventually the two men agreed that a critical method would eliminate parts of Roman tradition and support others. Their colleague Nicolas Fréret argued that all ancient historians had seen it as their task to connect great events with omens: a critical historian could neither accept their reports in toto nor simply reject them as contaminated with error. But in 1738 Louis de Beaufort transposed older criticisms of Roman tradition into a sharper key. He showed that the Romans themselves, from Livy onward, had acknowledged the total uncertainty of their early history. Though more than one of these writers argued that early Roman tradition had been as sacrosanct as the Bible when they set to work, in fact they acquainted a large reading public with the most radical arguments of Humanist philology. But that was enough to inflict lasting damage on the cultural status of the tradition.

The ancient narratives continued to enjoy pride of place in schools and universities. Great translation projects—such as Hobbes's rendering of Thucydides into English from the Greek original—made almost all ancient historians more widely accessible than ever before. Young men still grew up imagining themselves as reenacting the great scenes of Roman history—an effort that helped shape both the English civil war and the French Revolution, in rather different ways. But the separation between scholars' increasingly critical and detached view of the ancient historians and teachers' and general readers' continued love of the traditional heroic stories grew wider and wider—especially in such institutions as the new universities of Göttingen and Halle, where influential professors like Christian Gottlob Heyne and Friedrich August Wolf made clear to their students that the ancient historians had worked in a way that no modern, critical reader could find fully acceptable. New histories of Greece and Rome appeared: Gibbon's history of the Roman Empire, which consisted of a text and a separate apparatus that weighed the sources against one another; Stanyan and Rollin's histories of Greece, with their acute political judgments and their awareness that not only many Greek cities, but Persia as well, formed organic parts of the story; Niebuhr's history of the Roman Republic, which alchemically transformed ancient narratives into a forgotten social history; Grote's history of Greece, which took the Sophists as the ancestors of modern liberal politicians; Mommsen's history of Rome, which made a hero of Caesar and dismissed Cicero, master orator, as a pathetic, powerless journalist like those of Mommsen's own day. Radically different from one another, all of them clearly departed from the classic models. Over and over, new models of inquiry into the economy and society—from the historical theories of Marx and Engels to the sociology of Weber—raised questions about the Greek and Roman worlds that their inhabitants would have found profoundly strange. Ancient historiography came to seem more and more antiquated, part of the past rather than an authoritative record of it.

The new methods of 19th-century scholarship opened the gap between ancient and modern historiography even further. The great compilations of inscriptions and the new archaeology of Greece, Rome, and Magna Graecia revealed more and more gaps and errors in the ancient writers. Mommsen, as brilliant an organizer of scholarly enterprises as he was a writer of history, helped ignite the explosion of new evidence and hone the new technical methods that made it impossible for later historians to emulate the literary coherence and power of his Roman history. The new source criticism developed by Jakob Bernays, Hermann Diels, and others working on the tradition of ancient philosophy found a counterpart in the realm of historiography in the work of Heinrich Nissen. Later famous as a master archaeologist, epigrapher, and student of the Italian landscape, always known as a daring spinner of wild theories, Nissen began his career in 1863 with a dissertation on Livy. He argued that the Roman historian—and, by extension, all his ancient colleagues—had worked not like modern critical scholars but like modern journalists. They simply copied existing sources, and they resorted to comparison not as a systematic tool but when two sources clearly and sharply disagreed.

Inspired by the belief that the extant histories could reveal their secrets if subjected to analysis on principles like this, great scholars such as Ulrich von Wilamowitz-Moellendorff and the younger Felix Jacoby set out to turn Greek historiography itself into part of history. They reconstructed from fragmentary and sometimes contradictory evidence the history of the various genres that had existed before Herodotus and Thucydides, and sifted the shattered remains of these texts for information that might be of actual historical worth. The greatest single historiographical enterprise of the 20th century—the massive collection *Die Fragmente der griechischen Historiker,* which occupied Jacoby for most of his life, and which remained unfinished at his death (a team of ancient historians is continuing it)—was dedicated to this enterprise. Many of the most substantial ancient histories—not only the work of Diodorus Siculus, but the histories of Herodotus and Livy—were, if not dismissed, at least relegated to the status of collections of useful fragments of the more profound and accurate sources that had perished.

Yet even as Jacoby began to quarry his fragments, a countervailing scholarly tendency appeared—one that emphasized, in Homeric studies, the unity of the poems that Wolf and other analysts had sought to analyze into their lost component lays, and that highlighted, in historiography, the coherence and power of the ancient texts that survive. The focus of debate shifted, in some quarters, from the events narrated by a given historical text and the sources from which it was drawn to the history itself, as a text. New debates arose over larger questions: for example, whether Thucydides saw himself as pursuing a rigorous inquiry, comparable to those of the philosophers who were his contemporaries, or creating a work of art, more comparable to those of the tragedians. New intellectual concerns—for example, the rise of anthropology—have brought with them a new appreciation, and a new criticism, of the ethnographic accomplishments of Herodotus.

Through the 20th century, the reputations of the ancient historians have fluctuated as widely as the Dow Jones Industrial Average—and sometimes with as little relation to the underlying value of the texts in question. Scholars continue trying to re-create the stages of historiography that preceded the composition of the texts we have, and to understand what sources of information ancient historians drew on, and how they did so. Some continue to denounce individual ancient historians—Herodotus, in particular—as especially given to fantasy and mendacity, or to argue that the entire tradition was colored by its authors' commitment to the art of rhetoric that enabled them to compose their protagonists' speeches and aim not at truth but at an attractive and moving narrative. On the whole, however, contemporary scholarship has come to appreciate the intellectual enterprise and the literary mastery of the ancient historians.

For all the metamorphoses and demotions they have undergone inside the cobwebby castles of professional learning, in the world outside the Greek and Roman historians continue to find a wide and attentive audience. New translations of the major ancient historians continue to appear and to sell thousands of copies. Generation after generation, new readers discover the ancient historians and are transformed by what they read. The brilliant Polish journalist Ryszard Kapuściński credited his ability to think his way into foreign cultures from Ethiopia to Iran in part to his reading of Herodotus, whom he called "the first globalist," in the Polish translation of the *Histories* that came out in 1955. In Michael Ondaatje's 1992 novel *The English Patient* and the film made from it in 1996, the protagonist has survived a plane crash in North Africa with only one possession, his annotated Herodotus, which records his exploration of the Sahara. Sales of Herodotus boomed—perhaps inspired by the tender, sexy scene in which Kristin Scott Thomas tells the story of Gyges and Candaules from book 1.

Despite everything, students of the ancient historians—including professional scholars—still go back to them in the hope of extracting lessons of immediate relevance and power. As this book goes to press, the Yale historian Donald Kagan, a preeminent student of the Peloponnesian War who has used every resource known to scholarship to verify and qualify Thucydides' account of events, is publishing a book that argues—as many have before him—that Thucydides created "the first modern work of political history," a work that still holds vital lessons for statesmen. Evidently Thucydides and Herodotus, the predecessor he learned from and disliked, were not wrong to suggest, each in his own way, that their works would be read with deep interest for a very long time to come.

BIBL.: H. J. Erasmus, *The Origins of Rome in Historiography from Petrarch to Perizonius* (Assen 1962). Anthony Grafton, *The Footnote* (Cambridge, Mass., 1997) and *What Was History?* (Cambridge 2007). Chantal Grell, *Le dix-huitième siècle et l'antiquité en France, 1680–1789,* 2 vols. (Oxford 1995). Ryszard Kapuściński, *Travels with Herodotus,* trans. Klara Glowczewska (New York 2007). Joseph Levine, *Humanism and History* (Ithaca 1987). David Lupher, *Romans in a New World* (Ann Arbor 2003). Rosamund McKitterick, *History and Memory in the Carolingian World* (Cambridge 2004). Arnaldo Momigliano, *The Classical Foundations of Modern Historiography* (Berkeley 1990) and *Studies in Historiography* (London 1966). Wilfried Nippel, *Griechen, Barbaren und "Wilde": Alte Geschichte und Sozialanthropologie* (Frankfurt 1990). J. G. A. Pocock, *Barbarism and Religion,* 4 vols. to date (Cambridge 1999–). Mouza Raskolnikoff, *Histoire romaine et critique historique dans l'Europe des Lumières: La naissance de l'hypercritique dans l'historiographie de la Rome antique* (Rome 1992). Beryl Smalley, *Historians in the Middle Ages* (New York 1974). Gerrit Walther, *Niebuhrs Forschung* (Stuttgart 1993).

A.G.

History Painting

A genre of painting that focuses on the representation of historical, mythological, or biblical scenes often based on ancient sources. The content of history paintings is almost always heroic, providing the viewer with a morally instructive *exemplum virtutis.* The form or style is grand, usually designed with life-size figures in classical poses inspired by ancient statues or based on close studies of live models. History paintings derive their subject matter from the great artworks and literary texts of the past, but they are also structured around the Aristotelian principle of the unity of plot and action as outlined in the *Poetics.* The episode chosen for representation should portray an intense dramatic moment in which the protagonists of the scene perform their moral exemplarity in an unambiguous manner. Secondary figures should be positioned to elaborate the heroic qualities of the main characters of the narrative; the overall composition should be purged of any incidental details and extraneous figures. In Benjamin West's *Death of General Wolfe* (1770), for example, the Christlike general is juxtaposed on the left by a contemplative American Indian who serves as a "local" witness to Wolfe's "universal" virtue and heroism. In this regard, history paintings are fundamentally ideological constructions.

To be sure, the concept of history painting can be discussed under two rubrics: the *tradition* and the *category* of history painting. The former embraces a more generalized definition of narrative paintings based on classical and religious texts. The latter refers to an art form that belongs to a specific historical moment that began in the 17th century and reached its apex in the late 18th century, as well as to the particular institutional context of the academy and salon in early modern Europe.

The rise of a tradition of history painting is connected with the Humanist project of recuperating and interpreting the classical tradition. In book 2 of *De pictura* (1436), Leon Battista Alberti defined *istoria* as the representation of persuasive, dynamic figural compositions, and he identified this narrative form as the highest goal of painting. Though *istoria* can, roughly speaking, be compared to the idea of history painting, it was by no means the only term used to describe pictures illustrating scenes from identifiable classical texts. Titian, for example, referred to his own mythological paintings for Philip II as poems (*poesie*), whereas Pietro Aretino spoke of Tintoretto's *Apollo and Marsyas* as a fable (*favola*) and the painter's *Argus and Mercury* as a short story (*novella*). Religious narrative paintings, in contrast, were often called devotional images (*devozioni*).

Although there has always been a tradition of paintings of stories, history painting as a category is associated with two specific moments: first, with the establishment of a hierarchy of genres in painting in early modern academies of art; second, with the interconnected development of the salon as a cultural institution and of the idea of the "public" in pre- and post-Revolutionary France. One of the key figures in the first period was Nicolas Poussin. With Raphael in the 16th century, Poussin is identified as the leading representative of the classical tradition in the history of art. Poussin's paintings and writings, moreover, helped construct the classical ideal for modern history painting both in practice and in theory. For instance, influenced by the Counter-Reformation's interest in sacred antiquarianism and archaeology, Poussin was among the first artists to portray Christ and the disciples reclining at a historically accurate ancient Roman triclinium in *The Eucharist* (ca. 1640). In the mid-17th century a great debate occurred in the French Academy when one of the academicians pointed out that in the well-known painting *Rebecca and Eliezer at the Well* (ca. 1648), Poussin had failed to represent the camels that were mentioned in the passage from Genesis 26. Such close attention to detail reflected a desire to promote painting as a liberal art on a par with poetry and with history as well. The academic system in early modern Rome and Paris did much to raise the status of history painting. Under the directorship of Charles Le Brun and André Félibien, the French Academy of Painting and Sculpture established history painting as the most important genre, followed by landscape, portraiture, and still-life.

This leads us to the second historical moment of history painting, during which it came to be aligned with the intertwined contexts of the salon and the "public." The academic codification of a hierarchy of genres was closely tied to the trajectory of the art student. History painting was considered the culmination of the painter's formation in the academy (comprising copying from drawings and prints, copying from statues and Renaissance masterpieces, figure drawing). In the 18th century large-scale history paintings were destined for public commissions or salon exhibitions rather than for royal patrons, as had been the tradition. In the conflict between revolutionary forces and the Ancien Régime, between the nascent liberal bourgeois order and the socially bankrupt system of aristocratic privilege, between the political differentiation of public and private spheres, history painting repositioned itself as an instrument for a newfound civic humanism. In the fervor of the French Revolution, painting drew on the stories of the ancient Greeks and Romans in order to envision a new progressive order for the future. In light of such works as David's *Death of Marat* (1793), contemporary events came to take on the urgency of historical narrative. With the ascendancy of Napoleon and the increasing conservatism of the salons, the genre would come to be associated negatively with blatant political propaganda on the one hand, and with retrograde academic costume dramas on the other, and the historical "moment" of history painting had passed.

BIBL.: Michael Baxandall, *Giotto and the Orators: Humanist Observers of Painting in Italy and the Discovery of Pictorial Composition, 1350–1450* (Oxford 1971). Thomas E. Crow, *Painters and Public Life in Eighteenth-century Paris* (New Haven 1985). David Solkin, *Painting for Money: The Visual Arts and the Public Sphere in Eighteenth-century England* (New Haven 1993). M.H.L.

Homer

Legendary founder of the major tradition of Greek epic; undatable. The most recent consensus puts him in the 8th century BCE.

Herodotus, the earliest author to propose a context for Homer, was explicitly conservative in placing the author of the *Iliad* and *Odyssey* "no more" than 400 years before his own time. Along with Hesiod, Herodotus claimed (2.53), Homer invented the theology of the Greeks, providing the gods with their genealogies, their names, their other attributes, and their stories, and he did this roughly in the middle of the 9th century. From the perspective of classical Athens, Homer was credited not only with the two epics at the core of the tradition but also with a number of other epics, most of them belonging to a cycle that began with a *Theogony,* included the legends of Thebes and the Troy tale, and ended within a *Telegony,* a sequel to the *Odyssey.* Added to this was a considerable collection of hymns and two mock epics (the *Battle of Frogs and Mice* [*Batrachomyomachia*] and the *Margites*), both manifestly derivative of the epic tradition but utterly different from each other. The story of the reception of Homer, which is also the story of his invention, is vast, and the most important developments took place before the end of antiquity.

The notion that a single creative individual was the author of (at least) the two major epics has had a long and odd history. Josephus, in the 1st century CE, doubted whether Homer in fact had *written* the poems. He claimed, rather, that Homer had composed and performed them, thus founding the oral tradition by way of which they were eventually written down, attendant contradictions and all (*Contra Apionem* 1.12). Cicero (*De oratore* 3.34.137) had said much the same thing a century earlier, attributing the two epics as we know them to the tyrant Pisistratus, late in the 6th century BCE. This opinion was often repeated and found a place in two of the ancient biographies of Homer, one of which (Allen's *Vita* 4) quotes three elegiac couplets, supposedly—if improbably—inscribed by the Athenians on a statue of Pisistratus, where the honoree boasts of precisely this accomplishment.

In 1795 F. A. Wolf influentially returned to this evidence for an oral Homer (*Prolegomena* 1, chaps. 33–35; Wolf 1985), and thanks to him, Homer the oral bard was reinstated in the scholarship of a period drawn to the notion that the voice of nature (or more often of the *Volk* or *ethnos*) was to be heard in "primitive" poetry. All these developments, however, Wolf's contribution included, still found room for a Homer who—at least potentially—had a biography. It was only in the 20th century that the field of oral poetics, stimulated by the work of Milman Parry on Homer and on Serbo-Croatian epic, placed scare quotes around the name "Homer" and seriously and systematically explored the notion that what we have in the *Iliad* and *Odyssey* is not in any meaningful sense the creation of a single individual but instead represents traditions of oral composition in which the creative contribution of any single individual—or any generation—is lost without hope of recovery.

In retrospect, the early biographical traditions, with their poetic elaborations of a life and identity out of pitifully sparse internal evidence and a host of peripheral anecdotes, can best be seen as attempts to accommodate to a familiar model of text generation a body of poetry for which that model was and is quite foreign.

The trajectory of the *Iliad* and *Odyssey* through the Western tradition, along with the oscillating and mutually incompatible notions of their authorship, has been quite an exceptional one, marked by improbable contradictions and reassessments. Contemporary scholarly opinion remains divided, as do positions on what we are to do with the material before us. Some "oralists" take the position that the poems *have* no definitive form, that no edition of the traditional sort could possibly represent the true *Iliad* or *Odyssey.* If we take seriously the notion that the primary task of philology is to restore the received text to the form it had when it issued from the pen of the author, then clearly Homer (along with a few other corpora of early Greek poetry) must constitute an exception, requiring a new definition of the enterprise.

The emergence in the 2nd century BCE of a conservative, normative text, a "Hellenistic vulgate" of sufficient authority to dominate the subsequent manuscript tradition, marks an important step in the long process of accommodation. This was the Homer of the Roman Empire, and it formed the basis of all modern editions: a fixed, no longer variable text, and one that was already well on its way toward generating its author.

The impulse to provide the *Iliad* and *Odyssey* with an author was expressed visually from at least the 5th century BCE, when a dedicatory statue of Homer, along with one of Hesiod, was placed in the shrine at Olympia (Pausanias, 5.26.25). There arose over the following centuries various "types" of Homer portraits, dated stylistically on the basis of their extant copies and each departing from some group of visual hints in the poetry itself—most conspicuously the verse in the *Hymn to Apollo* long identified as the bard's unique description of himself: "A blind man from rocky Chios" (*Hymn to Apollo,* line 172). Though the roots of this iconography are classical, the vast majority of ancient images of Homer that we hear of, along with the extant portrayals, are Hellenistic or Roman. Rome and Byzantium likewise are responsible for the flowering of the biographical tradition, which fleshed out those same hints into a constellation of mutually contradictory tales of the life of the poet. These in turn became part of the mushrooming interpretive literature on Homer. The ancient portraits of Homer are echoed in modern representations, though the latter respond to the paradoxical status of the "ideal portrait" in a variety of ways. Perhaps the most striking is the frontispiece of Joshua Barnes's 1711 edition of Homer, where Homer is depicted as Tiresias ("solus sapit hic homo") while Time as the grim reaper tries unsuccessfully to smash the *Iliad* and *Odyssey.*

From the first evidence regarding Homer's readers, we see that his language and narrative required mediation. The earliest preserved comments on Homer are denunciations of his representation of the gods, and as soon as we hear of hostile critics (Xenophanes and others in 6th-century Ionia) we are told that there were also defenders—"first" among them the obscure allegorist Theagenes of Rhegium.

Used as school texts for millennia, the *Iliad* and *Odyssey* have attracted a body of commentary that has its roots in the classroom. The earliest collection of such material is attributed to Aristotle, and some plausibly identified fragments survive, but the culmination of the ancient tradition of commentary, in the work of Eustathius, the 12th-century bishop of Thessalonica, runs to nearly 4,000 oversize pages in its 20th-century edition (Van der Valk, 1971–1987)—and that is just the *Iliad:* his commentary on the *Odyssey* raises the total to nearly 6,000 pages. The numbers are indicative of both the sheer bulk of accumulated commentary from antiquity and the Middle Ages, and the higher status (as a school text) of the *Iliad,* about which twice as many questions were asked—and twice as many solutions offered—as was the case for the *Odyssey.*

From collections such as this, along with the marginal notes of medieval manuscripts, we can recover a range of ancient discourse on Homer, critical or defensive, self-serving or aspiring to philological (or other) objectivity. The Stoics, in particular, were repeatedly denounced for claiming to find Stoic doctrine in early poetry. If their intent was (as represented, e.g., in Cicero's *De natura deo-*

rum) to appropriate Homer—the very core of the pedagogic canon—as an authoritative witness to the truth of their cosmology, then however questionable the tactic, its strategic attractiveness is clear. The Stoics, at any rate, emerge as the principal ancient practitioners, if not the inventors, of the sort of reading that is commonly called "allegorical." Since interpretation as such commonly takes the form of claims that a text means something other than what it might seem to say, virtually all interpretation is, in this sense, allegorical. The curricular status of the two epics resulted in the interrogation of these texts with an intensity and range that give to the tradition of Homeric interpretation a distant resemblance to biblical exegesis. The resemblance is deceptive. The poems in fact never had, in a polytheist context, an authority resembling the authority of Scripture in the monotheisms, but by dint of addressing such an odd variety of questions to them, the ancients accumulated a body of interpretive material that blurs the distinction. No question was too small or too large.

Broadly speaking, a range of Homers emerges from this interrogation. Right from the beginning, Xenophanes questioned Homeric theology and found it wanting. This Homer—Homer the theologian, both in Aristotle's sense (as a mythic poet who talked about gods) and in that of the later Platonists (who were exceptional in taking seriously the idea of Homer's theological authority)—probably generated more sheer bulk of commentary than any other Homer. But there was also Homer the educator, born of the conviction that Homer's goal was instruction, a widely held position, doubtless arising from educational practice reflecting back on the text. A few Epicureans thumb their noses at this orthodoxy, but they are a decided minority. There was also a Homer who passed for a philosopher—an interpretive tradition of which we get a single distant echo in Aristotle's catalogue of earlier philosophers on first causes (*Metaphysics* A, 983b–984a), but one that was taken seriously by some Platonists, who proposed to expound that philosophy.

It is tempting to see the emergence of an all-wise Homer —and sometimes even a visionary Homer, his blindness the conventional metaphor for spiritual sight—as a function of all those centuries of interrogation. This is indeed the sort of Homer we encounter near the end of the polytheist tradition. It is also the Homer of the Middle Ages, although (as happened more effortlessly than one might think) theological authority has been withdrawn from the scope of his wisdom.

The Renaissance, and especially the 16th century, was heir to this vast literature of commentary and the florid and hyperbolic eulogies of the poet that went with it, but the Renaissance already represented a turning point. This is visible in a very immediate way in the history of the early printed editions of the *Iliad* and *Odyssey*, and the ancillary material the Renaissance and early modern editors chose to include. The *editio princeps* of Homer (by Demetrius Chalcondyles, Florence, 1488) offered the reader, first, the introduction attributed to Plutarch, with its generous claims for the vastness of Homer's wisdom, a good bit of it stashed away in allegories and things "hinted at," and, after that, the related *Life* narrated through the persona of Herodotus, and finally Dio Chrysostom 53, an encomium of the poet along with a review of other eulogists (Plato, Zeno, and so on) building to a laudatory portrait of Homer himself as a self-effacing and itinerant performer, clearly anticipating the life of the Cynic philosopher, embraced for a time by Dio himself.

This interpretive triad became standard fare, notably in the Aldine and other 16th-century editions. An important rival in shaping the reader's expectations in Renaissance editions was the Neoplatonist Porphyry, whose elaborate allegory of the *Cave of the Nymphs* in *Odyssey* 13 appeared as a preface in a 1541 Basel edition. The 17th century delivered to its Homeric public leaner and more streamlined editions, gradually relegating the ancient eulogies and allegories to the back and eventually dispensing with them entirely. There were exceptions, however. Joshua Barnes published in 1711 in Cambridge (at the expense of his pious wife, having convinced her that the true author of the poems was Solomon) a truly lavish and, for its date, eccentric edition of Homer, in which he put between the reader and the text perhaps the largest collection of ancillary texts—encomia, lives, and allegorical exposition—ever assembled around the *Iliad* and *Odyssey*.

The overall picture, however, remains clear. The Renaissance inherited from the Roman Empire, and then expanded, the various forms of allegorical reading. Though this was in fact the golden age of allegory, the Renaissance also discredited allegory. The earliest editions of the Greek text of Homer were printed with the writings of the ancient allegorists as introductory matter. The mysteries and secret meanings on which Porphyry was so eloquent, and which "Plutarch" put in perspective but likewise took as given, were presented to the first readers of a printed Homer as a characteristic mode of his poetry. The epics were puzzles to decipher, and it was in that spirit that influential teachers like the Hellenist Jean Dorat, who led the Pléiade to Homer, expounded the text. But instead it was the contemporary skepticism of a Rabelais that was to prevail. The ancient ancillary texts were pared away and lost their status as the privileged interpreters of Homer. Contemporary commentary on Homer likewise changed. From texts that were to be read as encoded revelations, the *Iliad* and *Odyssey* became, gradually, aesthetic objects, and in a new context again took on their ancient role as models of eloquence and narrative.

The 16th century saw a peak in the wave of translations of Homer. In the Greek East, where the *Iliad* and *Odyssey* retained their curricular prestige, John Tzetzes' 12th-century paraphrase, undertaken for the education of a nonnative speaker unfamiliar with Homeric Greek, had been further modernized and demoticized two centuries later for what was clearly a growing public unable or unwilling to read either Homer or Tzetzes' classicizing substitute. The early 1st-century *Ilias latina* in 1,070 verses showed up in medieval curricula, but a new Latin translation of Homer's Greek had to wait until the early 15th century, when Leonardo Bruni and, later, Lorenzo Valla put much of the *Iliad* into Latin prose. Some early editions of the Greek text of Homer were accompanied by Latin translations, including a lavish 1567 Basel edition of both epics, the *Hymns,* and the *Batrachomyomachia* (whose popularity in the Renaissance rivaled that of the *Iliad* and *Odyssey*), accompanied by ancillary texts, including "Plutarch," also translated into Latin.

The first vernacular paraphrases and translations appeared in the 15th century in Spain, then throughout Europe in the 16th. By 1600 the *Iliad* and *Odyssey* could be read in Italian, the *Iliad* and part of the *Odyssey* in French, parts of both poems in German, and nearly half of the *Iliad* in English. George Chapman completed his *Iliad,* the first complete English translation, in 1611 and his *Odyssey* in 1614.

The famous quarrel of ancients and moderns, which loomed large in the aesthetic life of the late 17th and early 18th centuries in Europe from the salons to the Académie Française, saw Homer trotted out by both sides, and not always in the roles one might expect. Before the Académie in 1668, Charles Perrault, the great advocate of the moderns, praised Homer in language that belonged to the previous century ("Épitre sur le génie"): in "the palace of Beauty," Perrault told them, Homer "discovered the most sacred mysteries of his art." But then Perrault turned on those who "Pretend that in our time one must be content/To contemplate the ancients and to imitate them." That, finally, was the crux of this odd episode in early modern intellectual history: the status of the ancients as model. The battle raged around the *Iliad* with the publication of Madame Dacier's translation (1699), which presented itself as a manifesto for the ancients, but the question of the *Iliad* as exemplary was unlikely to find resolution. The dispute itself is simplistic in its presentation, particularly in the form in which Perrault took it to the public (*Parallèles des anciens et des modernes*), but its aftermath is nevertheless interesting, and in a sense it is still with us.

The issue comes down to the nature of imitation rather than to the viability of specific models. The *Iliad* and *Odyssey* had been exemplary from our earliest evidence of them, but even in the tightly knit epic tradition the "imitations" departed radically from the original. The *Iliad* and *Odyssey* together had generated the *Aeneid* (with some help from Apollonius Rhodius, Lucretius, and, of course, Virgil). Prudentius (around the year 400) used Virgil as his primary model in creating a new kind of epic based on personification allegory. But the next great adaptation is the *Divine Comedy,* in which epic is radically rethought and antiquity ever present; the principal representative of both epic and antiquity, Virgil, is the guide only to the realm of the damned and those far removed from salvation.

Are the 20th-century epics that have aspired to extend the tradition imitations of Homer? In the sense embraced by the most sophisticated debaters on both sides of the quarrel, such as Fontenelle, the answer must be affirmative. What these authors imitate is much larger than the content of the *Iliad* and *Odyssey,* and sometimes far divorced from that content. But by invoking Homer as the source of their narrative, they assert the continuing immediacy of this first voice in European literature. In the great monument of modernism, Ezra Pound's *Cantos,* Odysseus repeatedly joins the chorus of voices from the past, mediated, translated (mostly), competing for space. In the most striking postmodernist revision, *The Changing Light at Sandover,* James Merrill follows Dante and Pound in taking the *Odyssey's nekuia* (visit to the dead) as a model, substituting for Virgil and Dante (or Pound and Plotinus) a gay couple with a Ouija board.

These 20th-century "imitations" of Homer are, to a greater or lesser extent, ironic. The epic tradition is the most self-consciously, self-referentially coherent sequence in Western literature, but each step, from Virgil to Merrill, represents a distancing as well as an embracing of models. This is what Harold Bloom calls "the anxiety of influence," and (though present from the start) it is increasingly important as a factor in every 19th- and 20th-century "adaptation" of Homer, in poetry, in prose (Joyce's *Ulysses*), and ultimately in cinema. In Virgil's footsteps, Joyce, Pound, and others embrace Homer in order to make space for their own voices, for their own stories—that is, both to acknowledge and to supersede him.

One last irony is visible, however, only from a distance. The 20th century, outstanding for its mindless brutality and genocidal wars, embraced the *Odyssey* in preference to the *Iliad*—as all the works referred to above attest. The military epic, which clearly had more prestige than the *Odyssey* in the ancient pedagogical canon, has been eclipsed, as an object of imitation, by the story of the man who "saw the cities of many men and knew their minds." The explanation no doubt lies in the evolution of Western literature, which has conferred a curious modernity on Homer's intellectual hero while, at the same time, the athletic and military heroism of Achilles has lost its aura. It seems, on the whole, an encouraging development.

BIBL.: T. W. Allen, *Homer, the Origins and the Transmission* (Oxford 1924). Jean Dorat, *Mythologicum, ou, L'interprétation allégorique de l'Odyssée x–xii et de l'hymne à Aphrodite* (Paris 2000). Luigi Ferreri, *La questione omerica dal Cinquecento al Settecento* (Rome 2007). Otto Finsler, *Homer in der Neuzeit von Dante bis Goethe: Italien, Frankreich, England, Deutschland* (Leipzig 1912). Noémi Hepp, *Homère en France au xviième siècle* (Paris 1968). R. Lamberton and J. J. Keaney, eds., *Homer's Ancient Readers* (Princeton 1992). Adam Parry, ed., *The Making of Homeric Verse: The Collected Papers of Milman Parry* (Oxford 1971). Plutarch, *Essay on the Life and Poetry of Homer,* ed. and trans. J. J. Keaney and R. Lamberton (Atlanta 1996). Kirsti Simonsuuri, *Homer's Original Genius: Eighteenth-century Notions of the Early Greek Epic* (Cambridge 1976). M. Van der Valk, ed., *Eustathii Commentarii ad Homeri Iliadem pertinentes* (Leiden 1971–1987). F. A. Wolf, *Prolegomena to Homer,* ed. and trans. A. Grafton, G. W. Most, and J. E. G. Zetzel (Princeton 1985).

R.L.

Homosexuality

From the Renaissance onward, classical forms and myths have provided a means by which homosexual themes and emotions could be overtly explored, whether in literature or in visual art. For centuries their classical reading provided the young of the elite with much of their sex education. In *Don Juan* Byron made fun of the paradox that pious tutors pressed so much shocking stuff on their charges (2.45):

> Ovid's a rake, as half his verses show him,
> Anacreon's morals are a still worse sample,
> Catullus scarcely has a decent poem,
> I don't think Sappho's Ode a good example,
> Although Longinus tells us there is no hymn
> Where the sublime soars forth on wings more ample;
> But Virgil's songs are pure, except that horrid one
> Beginning with "*Formosum pastor Corydon.*"

Ovid was unequivocally heterosexual; Anacreon's morals are worse because he wrote about youths as well as women. Sappho's ode is a bad example because the passion it depicts is lesbian. Virgil's second Eclogue ("that horrid one") is an exception not because it takes an erotic theme but because the love in question is for a male.

Most young gentlemen read about homosexuality first in Latin poetry. Virgil depicts the love of Nisus and Euryalus in the ninth book of the *Aeneid* (though the notion that the poet himself was a homosexual according to modern understanding—that is, a person wholly or principally attracted to his own sex—should be rejected). Horace represents himself as a highly susceptible bisexual ("a thousand passions for girls, a thousand for boys," *Satires* 2.3.325); Tibullus claims the boy Marathus as well as women among his love objects; Catullus' poems include a few addressed to the youth Juventius. It was often supposed, however, that the homoeroticism in Latin poetry was in most cases a literary exercise, one more example of the Romans imitating Greek forms. "We should be glad to believe it to be wholly imaginary," the Victorian scholar John Conington wrote of the second Eclogue, "though even then it is sufficiently degrading to Virgil." People were aware of the *pueri delicati* kept in wealthy households, but these could be taken to exemplify the decadence of the Roman Empire, in contrast to an earlier austerity. Juvenal excoriates homosexuals in his second and ninth satires; essentially the first of these mocks effeminacy and vulgarity, while the second is an attack on prostitution and on self-pity. But the position, now discredited, that Juvenal was a deep and passionate moralist seemed to confirm the belief that the Romans condemned homosexuality as sinful. Though pathics and effeminates were despised throughout antiquity, the Romans did not commonly regard love for youths as perverse or shocking.

In Plato's *Symposium* Aristophanes tells a fable. Originally, human beings were spherical creatures with two sets of genital organs. Some of them had two male sets of genitals, some two female sets, and some one set of each kind. Zeus then split these creatures in two, and since then human beings have been looking for their other half: love is accordingly "the desire and pursuit of the whole." The implication of this is that people are either homosexual or heterosexual innately. But such a view was rare. Notoriously, neither Greek nor Latin has a word for *homosexual.* (The German word *Homosexualität* was coined in 1869; *homosexuality* is first found in English in 1890.) Usually the Greeks seem to have conceived homosexual emotion as an overflow of heterosexuality: a strongly sexed man would naturally feel many attractions, to youths as well as to women.

Love poetry is inspired by the lover's vulnerability; the fact that the best Greek love poetry is homosexual and the best in Latin is heterosexual does seem to reflect differences between Greek and Roman society. Greek sculpture could supply an opportunity for half-hidden homoerotic musings: this can be seen in Winckelmann in the 18th century, and in Pater in the 19th. But the greatest importance of Greece to homosexual apologists has been as a culture in which homosexuality was openly discussed, and where it was even admired and idealized. Here Plato's *Phaedrus* and *Symposium* were supremely significant. One of the speeches in the *Symposium* introduces the idea that there are two Aphrodites and two Loves: one is common and is physical rather than spiritual; the other is heavenly (*Ouranios*). And Socrates' revelation of the final truth about love represents it as an ascent from the physical and the particular to an abstract realization of the highest beauty.

Aristophanes' fable both showed homosexuality as a natural, unalterable condition and made it seem romantic: one of Baron Corvo's homoerotic novels is entitled *The Desire and Pursuit of the Whole.* It also represents homosexuals as actually more masculine than other men. The rest of the *Symposium* licenses the notion that homosexuality is especially pure and high-minded. In the 1860s Karl Heinrich Ulrichs began defending Uranian love (the word having been taken from Plato's Aphrodite Ourania), and *Uranian* soon became a term for homosexual in the English-speaking world also. There was a good deal of insincerity, unconscious and conscious, in this. Pederasts could persuade themselves that their yearnings, unacted upon, were nobler than carnal love; this was far from what Plato had meant by a philosophical love transcending the physical. Oscar Wilde's defense of his relations with rent boys in terms of a pure, perfect, and intellectual love, "such as Plato made the very basis of his philosophy," was in the kindest interpretation self-deceived. On the other hand, E. M. Forster in *Maurice* (written 1913–1914) describes serious-minded young homosexuals taking Plato as their guide to a love denied physical expression, "the love that Socrates bore Phaedo . . . love passionate but temperate, such as only finer natures can understand." This seems to reflect reality; as a young man, John Addington Symonds, for instance, attempted chastely romantic friendships inspired by Plato. Whether in fiction or in life, however, so difficult a balance was seldom maintained. Symonds's essay *A Problem in Greek Ethics* also illustrates how Greece could offer a way of discussing matters that were otherwise hardly mentionable. Later generations would not need to be so oblique.

BIBL.: K. J. Dover, *Greek Homosexuality* (London 1978). Linda Dowling, *Hellenism and Homosexuality in Victorian Oxford* (Ithaca 1994). Richard Jenkyns, *The Victorians and Ancient Greece* (Cambridge, Mass., 1980). Craig Williams, *Roman Homosexuality* (New York 1999). R.J.

Horace

Quintus Horatius Flaccus (65–8 BCE), Roman poet, author of verse *Satires* (*Sermones*) and *Epistles* (including the *Ars poetica, The Art of Poetry*) in dactylic hexameters, and of lyric *Epodes, Odes* (*Carmina*), and a *Centennial Hymn* (*Carmen saeculare*).

Horace himself, with his characteristic mixture of complacent self-deprecation and unembarrassed recognition of the value of his achievements, foretold in his *Epistles* (1.20.17–18) that his poetry would someday end up "teaching children the alphabet." Unlike most such predictions, his turned out to be true. His commonsense morality, moderate political engagement, exquisite language, impeccable form, and (for the most part) short texts have made him seem the ideal school author, capable of teaching the young not only how to write well but also how to live well, and for millennia they have induced teachers to condone or veil his favorite lyric themes, wine and love (indifferently heterosexual and homosexual)—a welcome stimulation and consolation for young adults and aging ones, but perhaps not ideal instructional material for children or adolescents. Horace's uninterrupted centrality in educational curricula until well into the 20th century has made him a continuous presence in European culture, whom few other ancient authors can rival. His *Satires* and *Epistles* have been taken as a model for courteous civility in dealing with equals and superiors (especially with patrons), for a highly refined conversational tone recognizably close to a version of ordinary speech, and for unphilosophical, pragmatic moral reflection. His *Art of Poetry* has been mined for precepts not only of literary but more generally of aesthetic theory and has even been interpreted and applied as a systematic textbook. His *Odes* (and to a lesser degree his *Epodes*) have provided poets with a high standard for formal finish, elegant meter, and lexical purity, have conveyed an idea (largely erroneous) of the nature of Greek lyric poetry, and have transmitted a variety of codes of comportment ranging from Stoic self-control to Epicurean delight in modest pleasures, and from participation in affairs of state to withdrawal into private entertainments. Beyond the effect of his literary compositions taken as wholes, Horace has been a central figure in the Western tradition as a historical individual with an immediately recognizable voice and character, affable, self-ironic, congenial, sociable, commonsensical, who has inspired affection in many generations of (mostly male) readers, providing them with companionship, inspiration, and solace: "Horace . . ./Will, like a friend, familiarly convey/The truest notions in the easiest way" (Pope, *Essay on Criticism,* 654–656). His gift for memorable phrases has made him the most quotable, and the most quoted, ancient author. Horace's influence on Western culture has been so predominantly linguistic, textual, and moral in character that visual traces of his influence are very scarce indeed: a handful of fictitious portraits (including, perhaps, one in Raphael's *Parnaso* of 1511); a monumental statue of the poet in the Piazza Orazio at his hometown of Venosa (the town's football team is called Horatiana Venosa, and a local wine is labeled Terre di Orazio); an impressive villa, located near Licenza, northeast of Rome, identified as early as the 18th century as having been the one he owned and described in his poetry (in recent decades extensively excavated); and a crater (characteristically, modestly sized) on the planet Mercury that bears his name. A passage in Shakespeare's *Titus Andronicus* (4.2.18–23) shows with particular clarity the connections that for many centuries linked schoolwork, texts, language study, moral maxims, quotation, and memory:

> *Demetrius.* What's here? A scroll, and written round about?
> Let's see:
> Integer vitae scelerisque purus,
> Non eget Mauri jaculis, nec arcu.
> *Chiron.* O, 'tis a verse in Horace, I know it well,
> I read it in the grammar long ago.

The passage is *Odes* 1.22.1–2: "The man who is pure of life, and free of sin,/has no need for Moorish javelins/nor a bow and a quiver" (trans. Kline 2003).

Horace claims in the fourth book of his *Odes* (4.3.22–23) that passersby pointed to him as the man who played the Roman lyre, a fame certainly augmented by his appointment to compose the *Carmen saeculare* to be sung at the official celebration of Augustus' rule on 3 June 17 BCE—at the third hour, in the temple of Apollo near the palace (Zosimus 2.4). A commemorative inscription, still extant, includes the statement CARMEN COMPOSUIT Q. HOR[ATI]US FLACCUS, "Q. Horatius Flaccus composed the poem" (*CIL* 6:32323.149). By sometime in the 1st century CE a papyrus (P. Hawara 24) that contains two lines of Virgil's *Aeneid,* one written seven times and the other five times, includes a line of Horace's *Ars poetica* (78) copied seven times. Writing later in that century, Quintilian (1.8.6) refers to Horace as belonging self-evidently to the canon of school authors, though he complains of lewd passages that he would be embarrassed to explain to schoolchildren. In the first decades of the 2nd century Juvenal (7.225–227) provides a gritty picture of early morning at a Roman school, where the teacher's editions of Horace and Virgil are blackened by the soot of the pupils' oil lamps. Horace's works were edited by the Neronian scholar M. Valerius Probus and by the Hadrianic scholar Q. Terentius Scaurus, and they were explained in two, possibly three, surviving commentaries:

one by Pomponius Porphyrio (3rd cent.), the oldest and most important, published first with a text of the poems and then separately; another by pseudo-Acro, an anonymous collection, attributed during the Renaissance to Helenius Acro (2nd cent.) but certainly postdating Porphyrio and Servius, in later antiquity; perhaps a third by the *commentator Cruquianus* (though suspicion surrounds these notes, purportedly transcribed by the Dutch scholar Jacobus Cruquius [Jacob van Cruucke] from manuscripts now lost).

All of Horace's works were widely studied in ancient schools, but even in antiquity his reception became divided into a hexametric branch and a lyric one: as an author of verse epistles Horace had no followers, as a satirist he had rivals, as a lyric poet he had imitators. Horace's success as a satirist helped condemn to oblivion the writings of Republican satirists like Ennius, Lucilius, and Varro: for Western literature Horace is effectively the founder of the genre of verse satire. Yet his good-natured, self-ironizing, and indirect satires differ in tone, language, mode of argument, and content from Persius' (more philosophical) and Juvenal's (more furious), even if Persius does cite Horace as his model (1.116–118) and is followed in this by Juvenal (1.51). (Juvenal was fond of Horace's Roman odes and of the more abrasive epodes.) As for lyric poetry, it is only in the 1st century CE, with the choruses of Seneca's tragedies, and then again in Statius' *Silvae,* that the effect of Horace's odes can be measured. But occasional references to his odes demonstrate the continuity of the school tradition. Petronius (*Satyricon* 118) has Eumolpius cite *Odes* 3.1.1 with approval, and it is perhaps to the lyric poems that Petronius is referring when he speaks (118.5) of Horace's *curiosa felicitas,* artless simplicity achieved at the cost of unremitting toil. Quintilian (10.1.96) says that Horace is the only Roman lyric poet worth reading, though he also praises some minor contemporaries. The Younger Pliny (*Letters* 9.22.2) writes about a sick friend who earlier had imitated Propertius' elegies but now has switched to Horace's lyrics. Horace (*Epistles* 1.6.45–46) is the only Latin poet quoted by Plutarch, in his *Life of Lucullus* (39.5). One might expect the high finish of Horace's verbal artistry and the individuality of his poetic voice to have discouraged imitators and forgers; yet in his biography of Horace, Suetonius reports that he owns some elegies attributed to him and a letter in prose recommending himself to Maecenas: he repudiates both as inauthentic, the former as being vulgar, the latter as being also obscure (not, according to him, one of Horace's faults).

In later antiquity Horace continued to find readers, though less predictably and less consistently. The emperor Alexander Severus (r. 222–235) is said to have devoted his leisure hours to Plato's *Republic,* to Cicero's *De officiis* (*On Duties*) and *De re publica,* and to Horace—presumably the *Satires,* perhaps also the *Epistles* (*Scriptores historiae Augustae,* Severus Alexander 30.1–2). Horace was much studied by poets like Ausonius (4th cent.), whose poems contain many verbal citations and reminiscences and sometimes use Horatian poems as models or Horatian situations as starting points, and Claudian (late 4th cent., mostly the *Odes*). Servius (5th cent.), always attentive to school conditions, cites Horace in his Virgil commentary more than any other author; but other literary scholars in late antiquity, such as Aulus Gellius (2nd cent.) and Macrobius (5th cent.), scarcely mention him. Christian prose authors, when they refer to Horace at all, view him as a moralist and emphasize his hexametric over his lyric production. Most of Lactantius' citations from and allusions to Horace appear in his *Divinae institutiones* (ca. 310) (e.g., 2.4.3, as *satirici carminis scriptor,* "writer of satiric poetry") and furnish arguments against pagan polytheism. By contrast, Horace is second only to Virgil among the favorite authors of Jerome, who quotes the *Satires* and *Epistles* frequently; he ranks third, after Virgil and Terence, for Augustine (especially the hexametric poems; citations from the *Odes* are found in *De musica*). Ambrose, Boethius (in his prose works), and Cassiodorus refer to him hardly ever; Minucius Felix, Tertullian, and Cyprian not at all. It is among the Christian poets that Horace's lyric finds its greatest admirers in late antiquity. Prudentius (termed a Christian Horace by Sidonius Apollinaris, *Epistles* 2.4.9) imitates Horace's *Odes* in diction, meter, and themes, applies the language of Horace's praise of Augustus to Jesus, and transforms the *Carmen saeculare* into a hymn for the good shepherd Jesus. The *Carmina* (odes) of Paulinus of Nola contain many quotations and allusions to Horace. Sidonius Apollinaris (*Epistles* 8.11.3.22–25) says Horace is greater than Alcaeus and (8.11.7) comparable only to Pindar, though the poem of Horace's he cites most often is the *Ars poetica.* Venantius Fortunatus takes Horace as a model for a poem in minor sapphic strophes and frequently quotes or adapts Horace's language and varies his images and *sententiae.* As late as the 6th century, according to a subscription found in a number of manuscripts, the *consul ordinarius* for the year 527, Vettius Agorius Basilius Mavortius, aided by his assistant Felix, revised the text of the *Odes* and *Epodes,* and perhaps of the other poems as well. But after that there are virtually no traces of familiarity with Horace's writings for several centuries.

And yet so widespread had Horace's poems been as school texts that they managed to survive the Dark Ages in two, perhaps three codices, from which the medieval manuscripts are derived. Knowledge of the poet and manuscripts of his works began to reappear in the 7th century with Isidore of Seville (8.7.7, listing him with Persius and Juvenal as an author of satires), and then, more massively, in the 8th century: Bede cited him several times; Alcuin took the pen name Flaccus and knew the *Ars poetica* and perhaps the *Satires;* Paul the Deacon composed a poem in the sapphic meter, which he learned from Horace; a surviving Carolingian commentary to the *Ars poetica* was sometimes attributed to Alcuin himself. Though Horace never reached the degree of popularity during the Middle Ages that Virgil achieved (Horace is missing, for example, from the catalogues of St. Gallen, Reichenau, and Bobbio, and only Nevers and Lorsch seem to have possessed his complete works) he nonetheless became one of the most important school authors after Virgil: his poems (especially the *Epistles*) were excerpted frequently by anthologies for their philosophical maxims and are transmitted in around 300 medieval manuscripts; the best and the oldest ones come from France, and secondarily from Germany, rather than from Italy.

For the Middle Ages, Horace was above all the writer of the *Epistles* (especially the *Ars poetica*) and *Satires* rather than a lyric poet, not only for reasons of content but also because the language and meter of his hexametric poems posed fewer difficulties. Dante calls him "Orazio satiro" (*Inferno* 4.89) and attributes to him the honorific Latin title *magister* (master, teacher), otherwise reserved for Virgil among classical authors (*De vulgari eloquentia* 2.4.4). In the 10th-century epic *Ecbasis captivi* (*Escape of a Captive*), a beast epic in which one-fifth of the verses are taken from Horace, the preponderance of his hexametric poems is overwhelming (213 lines versus 20 from his lyrics). Writing at about the same time, Roswitha of Gandersheim inserted moralizing Horatian material into the Christian dramas she created from the plays of Terence; a century later, Horace inspired the satirist Amarcius. But starting in the 10th century, Horace's lyric production slowly began to gain in popularity as well: the Ode to Phyllis (*Odes* 4.11) is set to music in a 10th-century manuscript from Montpellier, and in the early 12th century Metellus of Tegernsee imitated a number of Horace's odes and epodes in his polymetric praise of Saint Quirinus.

With Petrarch, for the first time the lyric Horace triumphed over the hexametric one. Horace was Petrarch's favorite author after Virgil, one of the few he claimed to have read not once but thousands of times (*Epistolae ad familiares* 22.2.12–13); he listed him among his favorite books (*libri . . peculiares*), and indeed four manuscripts of Horace that he possessed are still extant; the most important one, with pseudo-Acro's commentary and with autograph notes by Petrarch, is now in Florence (Biblioteca Medicea Laurenziana, XXXIV.1). Petrarch was of course familiar with Horace's hexametric poems—he wrote three books of hexametric *Epystole metrice* in imitation of Horace's *Epistles*—yet his preference for the *Odes* seems unmistakable: the verse letter he addressed to Horace (*Ad familiares* 24.10) is written in minor asclepiads, in homage to one of Horace's favorite lyric meters, and it begins *Regem te lyrici carminis,* "Thou, king of the lyric poem." Boccaccio too seems to have studied Horace's *Odes* even more closely than the rest of his poems, at least to judge from his citations and from the list of names of famous poets and philosophers and of noteworthy historical, geographical, and mythological matters, derived from Horace's poetry and written in Boccaccio's hand, found in his *Zibaldone Magliabechiano* (Florence, Biblioteca Nazionale, Banco rari 50, fols. 300r, 302v–303r).

The Italian Renaissance made up for the relative lack of Italian medieval manuscripts of Horace by producing a flood of printed editions of his works: the *editio princeps* appeared in 1470, pseudo-Acro's notes in 1474, a text with the notes of pseudo-Acro and Porphyrio in 1476, Landinus' commentary (the first one by a modern Humanist) in 1482; 44 editions were published in Italy between 1470 and 1500, 13 in Venice alone between 1490 and 1500; the first Aldine edition was printed in 1501. Petrarch's preference for the *Odes* was continued and reinforced by such Italian Humanists as Filelfo, Landinus, and Politian and expanded together with Humanism itself throughout Europe, to Salmonius Macrinus in France, Anthony Alsop in England, Conrad Celtis in Germany, Jan Kochanowski in Poland, and many others. During the Renaissance Horace's fame as a lyric poet came to overshadow his *Satires* and *Epistles* (with the exception of the *Ars poetica*). For Neo-Latin poetry until modern times, and for all the vernacular literatures of Europe from the 16th through the 18th centuries, Horace provided the dominant model both for private lyrics celebrating wine and love and for public lyrics celebrating affairs of state: in Italy, Spain, France, and Germany especially, in such 16th- and 17th-century poets as Bernardo Bembo and Fulvio Testi, Garcilaso de la Vega and Luis de León, Ronsard and the other poets of the Pléiade, and Martin Opitz and his followers; and in England from Ben Jonson through Herrick, Marvell ("Upon Cromwell's Return from Ireland"), Milton (whose translation of the Pyrrha Ode, *Odes* 1.5, is generally regarded as the worst rendition in English), Pope ("Ode on Solitude"), and Swift (who imitated *Odes* 1.14, 2.1, 3.2, and 4.9), to later poets like Gray, Collins ("To Evening," "To Simplicity"), and Cowper (who translated *Odes* 2.10, 1.9, 1.38, and 2.16). The formal polish, linguistic precision, and concision of Horace's lyrics made them an ideal object for vernacular verse translation, by means of which young poets could learn their trade and experienced ones could practice their skills. In 1906 Stemplinger counted 90 translations of the four books of *Odes* into English since the Renaissance, 70 into German, 100 into French, and 48 into Italian. Latin imitations in Horatian meters were also frequently composed, especially in the 17th century (Maciej Kazimierz Sarbiewski, Jacob Balde, Simon Rettenbacher) but even down to the present day. During the Renaissance, Horace's odes were also set to music (P. Tritonius in 1507, L. Senfl in 1534, P. Hofhaimer in 1537), apparently to help pupils memorize their complicated metrics; and it has been suggested that the stanzas of some German Lutheran church hymns go back to Horatian alcaics and sapphics. In general, lyric in the Horatian mode, even at its most inspired, remains cool and detached, aiming at moderation and self-control; those who preferred their poetry hot could always turn to Pindar (misunderstood through the filter of Horace's own *Odes* 4.2).

Though the *Ars poetica* had decisively influenced Renaissance poetics through its paraphrase by Robortello (published in 1548 with Aristotle's *Poetics*) and continued to shape literary theory through the 16th century (Dionysius Lambinus inserted a programmatic discussion and partial Latin translation of Ronsard's *Franciade* into his commentary on the *Ars poetica,* 1561), though Ariosto's satires are sometimes reminiscent of Horace's, and though Horace's hexameters were the ancient texts cited most often by Montaigne (80 citations in the first edition of his *Essais,* almost 150 in the last, published posthumously in 1595), it was the 17th and early 18th centuries that saw the high point in the fortunes of Horace's *Satires* and *Epistles.* Boileau composed Horatian *Satires, Epistles,* and an *Art poétique* (1674) that became manifestos of classicism (the notorious rules of French Neoclassical drama derive far more from Horace than from Aristotle). In England a wave of translations and imitations of Horace's *Satires* and *Epistles* was theorized by Cowley in the preface to his *Pindarique Odes* (1656) and initiated by Cowley's and Thomas Sprat's imitation of *Satires* 2.6 (1662), which went on to inspire poets great and small, including Rochester, Matthew Prior, Dryden, and Congreve. Pope, in response to Bolingbroke's proposal that he revive satire by adapting Horace, published his celebrated *Imitations of Horace* (1733), comprising six satires and six epistles; Swift wrote imitations of *Epistles* 1.5 and 1.7 and of *Satires* 2.6; Cowper translated *Satires* 1.5 and imitated *Satires* 1.9.

Horace's elegant rationalism and moral wisdom, and also his disabused and tolerant tone, made his poems favorite reading during the Enlightenment. "The eighteenth century breathed Horace" (Ogilvie 1964)—and not only in parsonages, universities, and schools (every week, pupils at Westminster had to put an ode of Horace into Latin elegiac couplets, and pupils at Eton had to compose six or seven Horatian lyric stanzas): Lord Chesterfield wrote to his son on 11 December 1747 about "a gentleman, who was so good a manager of his time that he would not even lose that small portion of it which the calls of nature obliged to pass in the necessary house . . . he bought a common edition of Horace, of which he tore off gradually a couple of pages, carried them with him to that necessary place, read them first and then sent them down as a sacrifice to Cloacina." The 18th century saw at least 20 different editions of Horace's complete works or of his *Odes;* the most popular was Desprez's text (1694, in the Delphin series), of which a 12th edition appeared as late as 1799. In England, Bentley published in 1711 an edition both celebrated and notorious, in which he altered more than 700 passages, often against the consensus of the manuscripts (one John Underwood requested in his will that he be buried with "*Bentley's Horace* under his Arse"). In Germany, Wieland translated Horace and Kant quoted him, Gottsched revered his authority and Lessing defended his character, Herder studied him ("that fine echo of the Greeks") in an attempt to recover the spirit of his lost Greek originals and Friedrich von Hagedorn wrote a long didactic verse epistle, "Horaz," with footnotes indicating the exact lines in Horace's works that the poet had in mind. In France, Diderot translated the beginning of *Satire* 1.1 and published quasi-Horatian satires of his own, each with a Horatian motto (in *Le neveu de Rameau* the parasite Rameau is a descendant of Davus in *Satire* 2.7), and Voltaire regarded Horace as his model and alter ego, addressing to him his *Épître* 114, in which he presented a balance of his whole life and personality; to the south, Horace massively influenced the Italian satirist Giuseppe Parini ("Alla Musa," 1795), while farther east, Gavrila Derzhavin, the greatest Russian poet of the century, began his career by translating Horace's odes and writing his own Horatian odes.

Horace's position in the school curriculum helped him survive the advent of Romanticism longer than many other Latin authors, and through the 19th century he continued to fascinate classically trained and oriented poets and to provide a recognizable mark of gentlemanly breeding and taste. Even among the English Romantic poets he had his admirers, especially Wordsworth, whose love for the poet is reported by various contemporaries: what appealed to him most was Horace's sense of place, his fondness for rural simplicity, the moments "As a chance-sunbeam from his memory fell/Upon the Sabine farm he loved so well;/Or when the prattle of Bandusia's spring/Haunted his ear—he only listening" ("Liberty" 102–105, 1829). Coleridge studied the *Ars poetica* closely; Keats displays very few traces of familiarity with or even much interest in Horace's poetry, yet the opening lines of "Ode to a Nightingale" are unmistakably indebted to *Epodes* 14.1–4. Byron claimed to have developed such a loathing for Horace at Harrow that he refused to quote Horace's Soracte Ode, *Odes* 1.9, when he first saw the mountain during his travels in Italy ("Childe Harold's Pilgrimage" 4.74–77); yet his celebrated "Then farewell, Horace—whom I hated so," continues, "Not for thy faults, but mine." And he deeply admired Horace's hexametric works (his *Hints from Horace* is a satire built around the *Ars poetica*) and translated and imitated a number of the *Odes* (including 3.30 into Italian, while he was learning the language).

Odes 3.30 was also imitated by Pushkin, in a poem entitled "Exegi monumentum," later translated by Nabokov (there are at least 21 Russian translations of the same ode). Hölderlin translated two poems of Horace; August von Platen composed Horatian odes honoring Napoleon and King Ludwig; Eduard Mörike (whom contemporaries called "the son of Horace and a refined Swabian woman") sought a Horatian ideal of simplicity in idyllic scenes of rustic life (which he also sometimes parodied). Among the Romantics it was probably Leopardi whose relation to Horace was most complex and subtle. In his youth he translated a number of the *Odes* (1809), wrote a parody of the *Ars poetica* (1811), and composed a rather strange essay, "Della fama di Orazio presso gli antichi" ("On the Fame of Horace among the Ancients") in which he argued that Horace was less highly regarded in ancient than in modern times. As a mature poet he admired in Horace's *Odes* a kind of politically engaged poetry lacking in Italy; he defended Horace against the Romantics who found him too lifeless and artificial (yet he also criticized Horace's formal perfection for sometimes suffocating any genuine emotion) and echoed him in his *Canzoni* (1820–

1823), often noting the echoes explicitly himself. Leopardi admired Horace's poetic qualities (though insisting that Petrarch's were greater) but never overcame his coolness toward an ethos the very opposite of his own ideal of sublime heroic pessimism.

Throughout the 19th century, school curricula, gentlemanly class, and unphilosophical moralism combined to make Horace (especially the *Odes*) a favorite of writers, especially in England. Kipling's experience of his school classics teacher—"C. taught me to loathe Horace for two years, to forget him for twenty, and to love him for the rest of my days and through many sleepless nights" (*Something of Myself,* 1939)—must have echoed that of many other Englishmen of his century. A scene in Kipling's *Stalky & Co.* (1899) memorably shows a classics master teaching the Romulus Ode (*Odes* 3.3) at a school for future military officers and Indian civil servants. Together with A. D. Godley and C. Graves, Kipling contributed to a fifth book of Horace's odes in Latin, *Q. Horati Flacci carminum liber quintus* (1920). Robert Browning's father thought Horace superior to Homer, Virgil, Shakespeare, and Milton and required Browning as a child to memorize all the odes of Horace (and *Iliad* 1 for good measure); his Uncle Reuben gave him for his 12th birthday a copy of Christopher Smart's 1767 prose translation of Horace's works; notwithstanding all this Browning remained fond of Horace throughout his life. Austin Dobson wrote in "To Q.H.F." (1873) that the modern world contains many of Horace's characters but no one quite like Horace himself; Oliver Wendell Holmes wrote to Dobson to express admiration for the Horatian, gentlemanly style of his poems, and the aged Tennyson advised him (unnecessarily) to read Horace every day of his life. Tennyson's own affinities with Horace were noted by contemporaries (C. S. Calverley translated *Odes* 1.24 into English in the quatrain style of Tennyson's *In Memoriam,* and *In Memoriam* into Latin in Horatian alcaic stanzas), although their importance was denied by Tennyson himself. Gladstone published a verse translation of Horace's *Odes* in 1894. Thomas Hardy's private library contained at least four volumes of Horace's poetry, annotated, underlined, and supplied with marginalia by Hardy himself, and quotations occur in many of his novels (in *Jude the Obscure,* the impoverished young autodidact Jude sees the sun setting and the moon rising, falls to his knees, and declaims the *Carmen saeculare*). The 19th century in England saw more travesties and parodies of Horace's works published than of any other classical author, from James and Horace Smith's *Horace in London* (1813) through G. O. Trevelyan's *Horace at the University of Athens* (1861) to Charles Graves's *Hawarden Horace* (1891). Thackeray's version of Horace's *Odes* 1.38 humorously transforms Roman simplicity into British plain fare and Persian luxury into French frippery:

> Dear Lucy, you know what my wish is,—
> I hate all your Frenchified fuss:
> Your silly entrees and made dishes
> Were never intended for us.
> No footman in lace and in ruffles
> Need dangle behind my arm-chair;
> And never mind seeking for truffles,
> Although they be ever so rare.
> But a plain leg of mutton, my Lucy,
> I prithee get ready at three;
> Have it smoking, and tender and juicy,
> And what better meat can there be?

On the Continent in the same century Horace influenced Giosue Carducci only superficially (Carducci borrowed some proper names, especially of women, some titles, and some meters), but his influence on Giovanni Pascoli was second only to Virgil's. François Ponsard tried to turn Horace into a romantic lover in *Horace et Lydie* (1850), and Jean-Pierre Béranger, "the French Horace," propagated a vague aesthetic Epicureanism. But for the later 19th century Friedrich Nietzsche signally deserves special mention in even a short account of Horace's influence. Nietzsche's works are filled with testimonies to his affection for Horace. In his 19th year he sent a letter to his mother and sister in December 1862 listing what he wanted for his birthday, namely the complete Byron and a sumptuous edition of Horace; 19 years later, on 29 January 1882, he wrote from Genoa to Heinrich Köselitz (Peter Gast) in Venice, "If I were with you, I would introduce you to Horace's *Satires* and *Epistles*—I think that we are both finally mature enough for them. When I glanced at them today I found all the phrases enchanting, like a warm day in winter." In his unpublished notebooks (summer 1875) he writes that Horace has provided him with much-needed relaxation and restoration, just as Montaigne did for Shakespeare. In his very last works Nietzsche returned repeatedly to Horace. In the chapter "What I Owe the Ancients" ("Was ich den Alten verdanke") in *Twilight of the Idols* (*Götzendämmerung,* 1888) he declares, provocatively, that his poetic tastes were formed not by Greek authors but by Latin ones, Sallust and Horace, and he leaves a moving testimony to the latter:

> The reader will notice in my style, as late as my *Zarathustra,* a very serious ambition for a Roman style, for the "aere perennius" ("more lasting than bronze," *Car.* 3.30.1).—The same thing (scil. as with Sallust) happened the first time I encountered Horace. Until this day I have never felt the same artistic delight in any other poet that Horace's odes gave me from the very beginning. What is achieved here cannot even be hoped for in certain languages. This mosaic of words, where every word as sound, as place, as concept radiates its power right and left and throughout the whole, this minimum in the size and number of signs, this maximum in the energy of the signs achieved thereby—all that is Roman and, if you are willing to believe me, dignified *par excellence.* By contrast, all

the rest of poetry becomes too popular—a mere emotional blabber.

And in "Why I Write Such Good Books" ("Warum ich so gute Bücher schreibe") in *Ecce Homo* (1888) he expressed the hope that he would someday find an adequate reader, one who would read him as carefully as good philologists used to read their Horace—a hope that, like Horace's at *Epistles* 1.20.17–18, was fulfilled.

Since the beginning of the 20th century Horace's most fervent admirers have been lyric poets, who make up in intensity for what they lack in numbers. In Germany this may be due partly to Nietzsche's influence, partly to the temporary continuation of the same educational practices that had shaped him. Rudolf Alexander Schröder imitated a number of Horace's odes in the first third of the century; Durs Grünbein has continued that tradition more recently. It is above all in Bertolt Brecht that Horace lived on in 20th-century German literature. Horace was a favorite poet of Brecht's from his schooldays, when he got into trouble for polemicizing against the poet's *dulce et decorum est pro patria mori* (*Odes* 3.2.13, "it is a sweet and decorous thing to die for one's fatherland"). Brecht attempted to revivify the verse epistle and frequently argued against the *Ars poetica;* his late *Buckower Elegien* (1953) contains the short and moving poem "Beim Lesen des Horaz" ("While Reading Horace"), six verses in Horatian meters on the passing of time and the resistance of poetry to oblivion.

Horace was a frequent target of English antiwar polemics during World War I (Wilfred Owen, "Dulce et decorum est," 1917), and in a certain sense the whole world of Bloomsbury represented a rejection of Horatian values. But thereafter he flourished in 20th-century English and American poetry, in such poets as Ezra Pound (who wrote ambivalent essays about him in his early years but toward the end of his life produced memorable translations of *Odes* 1.11, 1.31, and 3.30), Robert Frost ("The Lesson for Today," 1942), J. V. Cunningham (*The Helmsman,* 1942), Louis MacNeice (who published translations and adaptations of Horace and wrote *Carpe diem,* a radio play, in 1956), Robert Lowell (*Notebook 1967–68*), Robert Pinsky (*An Explanation of America,* 1979), C. H. Sisson (who translated the *Ars poetica* and, more unusually, *Carmen saeculare*), Donald Davie ("Wombwell on Strike," 1990), Richard Wilbur—and especially W. H. Auden, whose *Nones* (1951) was celebrated (by Robert Fitzgerald) as marking a new Horatian style in his development and who himself acknowledged Horace as a crucial influence, teaching him formal control, mental sobriety, a withdrawal from politics, and a distrust of Romantic extravagance. Most recently, in his "Letter to Horace" (1995) the Russian-born poet Joseph Brodsky composed a moving reflection on Horace's meaning as a master of lyric meters for one latter-day Hyperborean poet. Addressing a poetic epistle to Horace (as Petrarch and Andrew Lang had done before him) in homage to the poet who invented the genre, Brodsky balances memories of a personal past of youthful ardor in the Roman neighborhood of Suburra (a red-light district in ancient times) with the less remote cultural past of Latin poetry (especially love poetry). He begins with an erotic dream in which the body with which he is trying to grapple turns out to be the corpus of Latin poetry, and ends with an anticipation of the conversation with Horace he expects that he will soon be having in the Underworld: "Worse comes to worse, we can communicate through meters. I can tap the First Asclepiadic stanza easily, for all its dactyls. The second one also, not to mention the Sapphics. That might work; you know, like inmates in an institution. After all, meters are meters even in the netherworld, since they are time units. For this reason they are perhaps better known now in Elysium than in the asinine world above. That's why using them feels more like communicating with the likes of you than with reality."

Brodsky died a year later, in 1996. Whatever else he and Horace are discussing in the Underworld now, they are certainly swapping favorite quotations. Memorable lines are the small change of poetic commerce and of cultural economies. Consider the opening line of the last poem of Horace's first collection, *exegi monumentum aere perennius,* "I have completed a monument more lasting than bronze" (*Odes* 3.30.1)—a strikingly expressed poetic vaunt combining hyperbolic aspirations with the allures and limitations of sensuous materiality in a paradoxical and surprising way, a memorable tag quoted innumerable times on more and less appropriate occasions. No other ancient poet had a greater gift for coining unforgettable phrases than Horace, and no other has been quoted so often. Issues 252–321 of the *Spectator* are headed by more quotations from Horace than from Virgil, Ovid, and Cicero combined; 140 of the approximately 200 Latin quotations in the works of Thackeray and more than half of those in Trollope's novels come from Horace. Any dictionary of quotations contains pages and pages of familiar citations from Horace: *in medias res,* "into the midst of things" (*Ars poetica* 148), *laudator temporis acti,* "a praiser of past time," (*Ars poetica* 173), *ut pictura poesis,* "a poem like a picture" (*Ars poetica* 361), *sapere aude,* "dare to be wise" (*Epistles* 1.2.40), *concordia discors,* "a discordant harmony" (*Epistles* 1.12.19), *silvas Academi,* "the groves of Academe" (*Epistles* 2.2.45), *beatus ille,* "happy the man" (*Epodes* 2.1), *carpe diem,* "seize the day" (*Odes* 1.11.8), *auream . . . mediocritatem,* "golden mean" (*Odes* 2.10.5), *post equitem sedet atra cura,* "behind the horseman sits black care" (*Odes* 3.1.40), *dulce et decorum est pro patria mori,* "it is a sweet and decorous thing to die for one's fatherland" (*Odes* 3.2.13), *disiecti membra poetae,* "the limbs of the dismembered poet" (*Satires* 1.4.62)—the list could be extended at will. Other poets are quoted too, of course, but Horace's tags are different: they are almost always quoted out of context, indeed with no regard whatever for their original context. Peter Weir's award-winning film *Dead Poets So-*

ciety (1989) is centered movingly on the phrase *carpe diem* but does not mention Horace even once by name, let alone refer to *Odes* 1.11. The whole to which such quotations refer us by synecdoche is not the specific poem from which they happen to be derived but the general ethos of classicism for which Horace functions as a privileged paradigm. Citations from Horace are fragments valued precisely as fragments, glittering chunks of marble, remnants of the classical tradition redolent of antiquity and suggestive of permanence. They gleam in our night and remind us of who we never were. They are lapidary enough not only to be like marble but also, often, to have been inscribed on marble. Horace's vaunt in *Odes* 3.30.1 linked the survival of his poetry to the continuity of the institutions of Roman religion; but in fact his work long outlasted them, and the hope expressed in this tag turned out to be truer than even he could have imagined. In this sense, Horace's tags are not only an example of the classical tradition, but also a symbol of it.

BIBL.: E. D. Armour, *Echoes from Horace in English Verse* (Toronto 1922). *The Cambridge Companion to Horace,* ed. Stephen Harrison (Cambridge 2007). D. S. Carne-Ross and Kenneth Haynes, eds., *Horace in English* (Harmondsworth 1996). Frederick B. Clifford, *Horace in the Imitations of Alexander Pope* (Lexington 1954). Caroline Goad, *Horace in the English Literature of the Eighteenth Century* (New Haven 1918). S. J. Harrison, ed., *Homage to Horace: A Bimillenary Celebration* (Oxford 1995). Walther Killy, ed., *Geschichte des Textverständnisses am Beispiel von Pindar und Horaz* (Munich 1981). Helmut Krasser and Ernst A. Schmidt, eds., *Zeitgenosse Horaz: Der Dichter und seine Leser seit zwei Jahrtausenden* (Tübingen 1996). B. Kytzler, *Horaz, Eine Einführung* (Stuttgart 1996) 161–184. Walther Ludwig, "Horazrezeption in der Renaissance, oder Die Renaissance des Horaz," in *Horace: L'Œuvre et les imitations, un siècle d'interprétation,* ed. O. Reverdin and B. Grange, Entretiens sur l'antiquité classique 39 (Geneva 1992) 305–379. C. Maddison, *Apollo and the Nine: A History of the Ode* (London 1960). Charles Martindale and David Hopkins, eds., *Horace Made New: Horatian Influences on British Writing from the Renaissance to the Twentieth Century* (Cambridge 1993). Robert M. Ogilvie, "Horace and the Eighteenth Century," in *Latin and Greek: A History of the Influence of the Classics on English Life from 1600 to 1918* (London 1964) 34–73. *Orazio: Enciclopedia Oraziana,* vol. 3, *La fortuna, l'esegesi, l'attualità* (Rome 1998). *Orazio nella letteratura mondiale* (Rome 1936). Ezra Pound, "Horace," *Criterion* 9 (1930) 217–227. M.-B. Quint, *Untersuchungen zur mittelalterlichen Horaz-Rezeption* (Frankfurt 1988). N. Rudd, ed., *Horace 2000, A Celebration: Essays for the Bimillenium* (Ann Arbor 1993). P. F. Saitonge, G. Burgevin, and H. Griffith, *Horace: Three Phases of His Influence* (Chicago 1936). E. Schaefer, *Deutscher Horaz: Conrad Celtis, Georg Fabricius, Paul Melissus, Jacob Balde; Die Nachwirkung des Horaz in der neulateinischen Dichtung Deutschlands* (Wiesbaden 1976). Grant Showerman, *Horace and His Influence* (Boston 1922). Eduard Stemplinger, *Das Fortleben der horazischen Lyrik seit der Renaissance* (Leipzig 1906) and *Horaz im Urteil der Jahrhunderte* (Leipzig 1921). Mary Rebecca Thayer, *The Influence of Horace on the Chief English Poets of the Nineteenth Century* (1916, repr. New York 1968).

G.W.M.

Households and Householding

The ancient household (Greek *oikos,* Latin *familia*) typically consisted of a nuclear family and its possessions, including slaves. Advice on managing a household or estate dates as far back as Hesiod's *Works and Days* (ca. 700 BCE), but the systematic discussion of domestic economy emerged only with the rise of the sophists in Athens ca. 400 BCE, and even then the crucial topic of estate planning and inheritance is lacking from writings in the classical and later Western tradition.

Xenophon, a pupil of Socrates, couched his *Oeconomicus* as a dialogue in which Socrates asks the wealthy Athenian Critobulus about estate management, and another interlocutor, Ischomachus, about the role of a wife and the fundamentals of sound farming. Xenophon observes that "a wife who is a good partner in the estate carries just as much weight as her husband in attaining prosperity" (*Oec.* 3.15): within the patriarchal framework of Greek society, the husband managed affairs outside the home, while the wife managed what was within. Drawing on his experience as a soldier, Xenophon repeatedly compares householding to military and government administration, stressing the need for orderly allocation of things to their proper place, as in an army or aboard a ship (*Oec.* 8). A parallel between farming and empire is drawn by citing the accomplishments of Cyrus the Great. In a similar spirit Xenophon discusses ideal macroeconomic management in other works: his *Education of Cyrus* (on the Persian Empire) and *Ways and Means* (on the Athenian economy). The *Oeconomicus* was later translated into Latin by Cicero, but that version survives only in fragments.

Aristotle in his treatises on ethics and politics regards the household as the building block of society, and economics as a sphere between private ethics and public politics; hence his term for managing the home (Greek *oikonomia*) acquired the sense of "economy" in a wider sense. The *Economics* attributed to Aristotle is spurious, but it reflects the patriarchal nature of Greek households, which pseudo-Aristotle characterizes as a form of monarchy. (The first book repeats several of Xenophon's observations, and the second consists of a series of anecdotes about governmental policies. A third book, on marriage, survives only in a Latin translation.) The extant writings of the Greek essayist Plutarch (2nd century CE) include two essays with household precepts: *De liberis educandis* (*The Education of Children*) and *Praecepta coniugalia* (*Advice to the Bride and Groom*). Although the former is not authentic, both works enjoyed considerable fortune in the Renaissance.

The 13th century witnessed an outpouring of treatises on the education of children in noble families: Vincent of

Beauvais's *De eruditione filiorum nobilium* (*On the Education of Noble Children,* 1245), William Perrault's *De eruditione principum* (*On the Education of Princes,* ca. 1265), and Giles of Rome's *De regimine principum* (*On the Governance of Princes,* ca. 1281). Giles's work includes a discussion of household administration. In addition to his work on child rearing, Vincent of Beauvais (ca. 1190–1264) treated the "economic art" in book 6 of his massive florilegium, *Speculum doctrinale* (*Mirror of Learning*). He divides the subject into two parts. The first concerns the family and its members—the choice of a wife, the education of children, the management of servants, and the cultivation of friends—topics that are elucidated by classical citations. The second part, the science of estate management, involves extensive and detailed precepts about farm buildings, livestock, and produce, most of it derived from the Roman agriculturalist Palladius (4th cent. CE).

In 14th-century Europe the devastation of the Black Death may have influenced attitudes toward the family, highlighting the need to marry and produce offspring as a survival strategy. The most celebrated treatise of the Quattrocento, Leon Battista Alberti's Italian *Libri della famiglia* (*Books on the Family,* 1434–1437), opens with a reflection on the decline and disappearance of ancient families. Although Alberti's dialogue generally follows the Ciceronian model, his third book, titled *Economicus,* acknowledges a debt to "that sweet and suave Greek author Xenophon." In fact, the subsequent discussion of training a wife as a partner in household affairs imitates and cites Socrates' conversation with Ischomachus in Xenophon's *Oeconomicus.* In his discussion of *masserizia.* estate management, Alberti further adopts Xenophon's notion that wealth consists in the proper use of one's assets. In the early 20th century the German economists Max Weber and Werner Sombart would use Alberti to develop their theories of bourgeois culture and capitalism. Yet as is typical of the Humanist movement, Alberti's treatise devotes more attention to personal education and ethics than to corporate finances.

The topic of marriage was especially important to early Humanists. In 1416 the Venetian Humanist Francesco Barbaro composed a marriage tract called *De re uxoria* (*On Wifely Duties*), which draws on various works by Plutarch, including his *Advice to the Bride and Groom.* Twenty years later Leonardo Bruni composed an Italian *Life of Dante,* in which he defended the poet's marriage against the praise of celibacy and solitude common in Christian teaching. Bruni also contributed to the discussion of householding by translating the pseudo-Aristotelian *Economics* into Latin.

While celebrating the rediscovery of classical learning, such Humanist treatises may also reflect the needs of an urban society whose growing mercantile class required a firm grounding in reading, writing, and arithmetic. The Milanese Humanist Lampus Biragus dedicated a Latin version of Xenophon's *Oeconomicus* to Pope Nicholas V (r. 1447–1455), but it was never published. In the next century Xenophon's dialogue enjoyed immense popularity. It was printed at least 18 times between 1506 and 1603 in the Latin version of Raphael Maffeius; it was also translated into Latin by Bernardinus Donatus, Joachim Camerarius, Jacobus Lodoicus Strebaeus, and Johannes Levvenklaius. A Tuscan version of the *Oeconomicus* by the Sienese archbishop Alessandro Piccolomini (1508–1578) appeared in 1540; Montaigne aided in the 1571 posthumous publication of *La Mesnagerie,* a French version made by his friend Étienne de la Boétie.

The 16th century witnessed an explosion of treatises on householding both in Latin and in vernacular languages, most of them heavily reliant on classical themes and structures. The Spanish Humanist Juan Luis Vives cited Xenophon approvingly in his treatises *De institutione foeminae christianae* (*On the Education of a Christian Woman,* 1523) and *De officio mariti* (*On a Husband's Duty,* 1529). His contemporary Erasmus treated marriage both humorously in his 1523 colloquy *Coniugium* (*Marriage*) and seriously in his 1526 tract *Institutio christiani matrimonii* (*The Institution of Christian Marriage*), dedicated to Catherine of Aragon.

The print culture of the Cinquecento accelerated the production of marriage manuals. In 1533 the Paduan Humanist Sperone Speroni wrote a *Dialogo della cura familiare* (*Dialogue on Householding*) in which he drew freely from Plutarch's *Advice to the Bride and Groom.* In 1560 the Italian military engineer Giacomo Lanteri published a two-part dialogue titled *Della economica* in which men debate the fine points of managing a villa and women discuss their household duties and decorum. In the late 16th century authors such as Torquato Tasso and Francesco Tommasi wrote about the duties of the *padre di famiglia* or household father.

Writers of the Enlightenment continued to cite classical views on householding. Even the iconoclastic Jean-Jacques Rousseau, in *Émile, ou de l'éducation,* lauds Plato's *Republic* as the finest educational treatise ever written and contrasts it to the severe education of ancient Sparta. Yet the emergence of the industrial age witnessed a revolution in economic thought, as thinkers like Adam Smith analyzed the concepts of labor, production, and consumption in the context of national and international markets. The economic thought of antiquity, with its emphasis on the household, was supplanted by what is known paradoxically as "classical economics."

As industrialization accelerated, the purported benefits of ever-widening market economies seemed to pale beside their dehumanizing effect on the family and the individual. Dissident voices were inevitably raised to protest the encroachments of so-called progress. In the 1860s the art critic John Ruskin turned his attention to the Industrial Revolution and its effects on the individual and society in Victorian England. He attacked the exponents of "political economy," notably John Stuart Mill and his follower Henry Fawcett, as contributing to the dehumanization of modern life and sought to develop his own theory of householding based on ancient sources, especially Xenophon's *Oeconomicus,* which he read and annotated. (In 1876 Ruskin published a translation of the work, by his Oxford students W. G. Collingwood and A. D. Wedderburn, that constituted the first volume of his *Bibliotheca Pastorum,* which he conceived as a "library for British peasants.") His essays on political economy appeared in the volumes *Unto This Last* (1863) and *Munera Pulveris* (1871). "Xenophon's theory of management or of economic agency within the context of *oikos,* taken to be a household estate organized along Athenian lines, is worked out in the context of the military and then applied to the management of the estate" (Henderson 2000, 72).

As social reformers began to analyze the household as a microcosm of sexual politics, the home became a symbolic battleground for proponents of feminism. Although Ruskin took exception to the economics of John Stuart Mill, the latter struck a blow for women's emancipation in his essay *The Subjection of Women* (1869), in which he challenged the "classical" notion that women are naturally subject to men: "There was a time when the division of mankind into two classes, a small one of masters and a numerous one of slaves, appeared, even to the most cultivated minds, to be a natural, and the only natural, condition of the human race. No less an intellect . . . than Aristotle, held this opinion without doubt or misgiving; and rested it on the same premises on which the same assertion in regard to the dominion of men over women is usually based, namely that there are different natures among mankind, free natures, and slave natures."

Postmodern views of ancient householding reflect Mill's vision of the home in terms of sexual polarity. In his *History of Sexuality* (1976–1984) the social historian Michel Foucault interprets Xenophon's depiction of Ischomachus and his wife as the *locus classicus* for the Greek ideology of power, according to which a man's control of his emotions was externally reflected in his control of his wife, his slaves, and his political subordinates. Sarah Pomeroy, a Xenophon scholar and an expert on women and antiquity, maintains that Xenophon gave due recognition to the value of female labor and management within the home. By contrast, Foucault cites Plutarch's *Advice to the Bride and Groom* as evidence for a more egalitarian partnership that was emerging in ancient marriages under the Second Sophistic. The debate will no doubt continue as long as the classics are read.

BIBL.: L. B. Alberti, *The Family in Renaissance Florence,* trans. R. N. Watkins (Columbia, S.C., 1969). R. E. Backhouse, *The Ordinary Business of Life: A History of Economics from the Ancient World to the Twenty-first Century* (Princeton 2002). Willie Henderson, *John Ruskin's Political Economy* (London 2000). David Herlihy, *Medieval Households* (Cambridge, Mass., 1985). S. B. Pomeroy, *Xenophon's Oeconomicus: A Social and Historical Commentary* (Oxford 1994). D.M.

Humanism

The word *humanism* was first used in a fully theorized way in 1808, when the German educator Friedrich Immanuel Niethammer employed it to argue for the importance of a secondary educational system based on the Greek and Roman classics (Niethammer 1808; Campana 1946; Kristeller 1956). A contemporary and colleague of Johann Gottlieb Fichte at Jena, Niethammer was later appointed minister for education for the Protestant confession in Bavaria. It was the demands of this role that led him to write a short, polemical book that pitted what was termed *Philanthropismus* against *Humanismus.* Philanthropism was a style of education developed in the middle of the 18th century in the German-speaking world that emphasized freedom in children's education, with a focus on sports and seemingly practical subjects. Humanism, for Niethammer, stood in contrast to this notion. It reflected a love for classical languages, especially Greek, and a belief that the ancient, classical world was the most useful reference point for bringing the minds of young learners to their fullest human potential (Schauer 2005). Niethammer's use of the term *humanism* has a complicated history, rooted as it is in the educational politics of the fast-changing world of Napoleonic Europe. Still, his adoption of the term and his defense of the ideals he believed implicit in it invite us to return to its ancient roots, and to two Latin words, *humanitas* (humanity) and *humanus* (human).

Writing in the late 2nd century CE, toward the end of the classical age, Aulus Gellius discussed *humanitas* in his miscellany *Attic Nights* (*Noctes Atticae* 13.17), noting that those who use Latin correctly (as opposed to the common crowd) distinguish *humanitas* from Greek *philanthropia,* which means a benevolent love toward all people. The truer meaning of the Latin word, he suggests, is closer to the Greek *paideia,* "what we call learning and education in the liberal arts . . . In fact, the devotion to this kind of knowledge and the method that results from it has been given to man alone, out of all living creatures." He then offers an example from Varro (1st cent. BCE), who had written that the famous Greek sculptor Praxiteles "is unknown to no one who is in the least bit humane." Gellius then comments that "humane" here means someone who is well instructed and learned, who knows who Praxiteles was through books and through history. Thus, one principal meaning of *humanitas* in antiquity was bound up with learning, a sphere proper to human beings but not one in which all human beings partook. To be humane (*humanus*) meant not only to be a human being but also to have exercised one's capacity as a human being to the fullest through learning.

Humanism, then, with reference to the classical tradition, can be thought of as a respect for the authoritative and exemplary status of the classical, Graeco-Roman world. It is in these senses, the authoritative and the exemplary, that the classical world is conceived of as worthy of imitation, exegesis, and, most important, constant reinterpretation. The rise of Christianity, many of whose early patristic architects were steeped in classical culture, did nothing to change the fundamentally exegetical nature of reading; but the range of texts did change, and the messages thought to lie behind them changed in focus.

During the Middle Ages monasteries did the vital work of copying and transmitting both Christian and classical texts, and major centers emerged in the era of Charlemagne (king of the Franks from 768, emperor of the Holy Roman Empire 800–814). During the early Middle Ages, much of Greek literature and philosophy had been lost, and the number of thinkers who were skilled in both classical languages had declined dramatically. The 11th through 13th centuries saw the translation into Latin of the majority of Aristotle's works (Minio-Paluello 1953–). The rise of medieval cathedral schools and eventually universities, along with the communities of intellectuals that naturally gathered around those institutions, produced in Western Europe a rediscovery and increase in knowledge of the *auctores*, the authors of the canon of surviving classical Latin works. Certain intellectuals of this period, most notably John of Salisbury (d. 1176), demonstrated a lively interest in these classical texts. But another feature of humanism, one that would later become particularly important in 15th-century Italy, began to emerge: a tendency to question established canons of texts and to add to them in the service of a notionally better human life. Human life could be, and in most cases was, conceived as Christian in outlook, but during this period the ability to theorize aspects particular to humanity as being good in themselves began to flourish.

Evolving humanism lacked a key element, however, until intellectuals began to be conscious of the language they used for their major works, Latin. In the late 13th century a group of thinkers, centered in northern Italy, especially in Padua, consciously began attempting to imitate classical Latin (Witt 2000). Spurred on by the enthusiasm for classical texts present in the world of the French schools and universities, they opened contact with that world both through travel to the University of Paris and through connections with traveling poets. These early humanists were the direct precursors of those more commonly considered as Renaissance Humanists. Comparatively little known today, thinkers such as Lovato dei Lovati in the 13th and Albertino Mussato in the early 14th centuries wrote poetic works in Latin in which they consciously attempted to reproduce ancient Latin style. They focused their enthusiasms largely on secular matters: for example, Lovato "discovered" the location of the tomb of the ancient Trojan hero Antenor in Padua, mining classical sources as he did so. These thinkers and their immediate intellectual heirs provided the background for the person who made Humanism a European phenomenon in the 14th century: Francesco Petrarca (1304–1374).

Petrarch united two passions without which no contemporary intellectual movement could hope to thrive, given prevailing social norms; and he added a third, which became a hallmark of the best Renaissance Humanists. First, he engaged without reservation the growing contemporary fascination with classical antiquity. He became an excellent Latinist, and in doing so he saw distinctly that the Latin then in use, in the Church and in universities, did not seem to match in style the Latin he found in classical Roman sources. As he did pioneering philological work (on the text of Livy, for example), he also allowed this passion for antiquity to fuel a new historical sense. He realized the great distance between himself and the ancients, sometimes lamented it, but never allowed that distance to go unrecognized.

The second factor that fueled Petrarch's Humanism was his preoccupation with religion. The two intellectual generations immediately before Petrarch had been fascinated with the classical world; they had embraced a precise and classicizing Latinity, and they had shared in the evolving historical sense that grew along with this love of classical sources. Petrarch, however, took these engagements and redirected them. Drawing inspiration from classical sources, he used these sources and others in his self-directed quest to become a better person and a better Christian. He derided contemporary Scholastic philosophers (with the rhetorical exaggeration characteristic of his age) not only for their unclassical Latin style but also because in focusing (he claimed) too exclusively on non-Christian sources of philosophy, they actually veered close to rejecting Christianity.

Petrarch's religiosity was related to his historical sense, and it teaches an important lesson to anyone who might unhistorically equate humanism with antireligiosity. If there is anything permanent and enduring about humanism, it is this: its leading figures, in whatever epoch, have always had the ability to situate themselves in the present, however much they admire and draw inspiration from the exemplary classical past. In Petrarch's day an integral part of the present was, in the West, Christianity. This is not to say that Petrarch necessarily supported institutional Christianity or its various epiphenomena, such as the papal court—which he lambasted in a letter collection entitled *Sine nomine* (*Without a Name*) as having abandoned its true mission—or certain segments of contemporary universities that supported the teaching of theology, "Queen of the Sciences."

This anti- or extrainstitutional bent represents the third formative aspect of Petrarch's Humanism, a tendency that lasted most durably throughout the history of Humanism. His life was marked by itinerancy. He tended to travel where patronage was available, working at different times for a cardinal, for the Visconti despots of Milan, for the Carrara family of Padua, and for the Republic of Venice; clearly he had various institutional affiliations, and yet he still managed to express his own viewpoints in his writings. He also expressed his identity as an intellectual from a deliberately extrainstitutional vantage point. He served as the first Humanist in Renaissance Europe to point out the dangerous sterility of intellectual orthodoxies, the way that intellectuals, gathered in groups and institutionally enfranchised, allowed themselves to reproduce in a social sense, stifling creativity. Renaissance Humanists after Petrarch did not, by and large, cause by their writings great changes in institutional structures, such as the methods of elementary and secondary education, those of university learning, or the morality of the papal court, but they did serve as a voice advocating critique of fixed ideas.

In one important respect Humanists did make an inroad into established conventions of learning: their reform of the official language of education, Latin, was a reform whose consequences for the life of Humanism thereafter were momentous. In the five intellectual generations after Petrarch in Italy, Humanists succeeded in fundamentally changing the way Latin was employed (Celenza 2005a). First, from Petrarch's era into that of Coluccio Salutati (d. 1406), in recognizing that the Latin then in use did not match ancient Latin, Humanists developed some of the toolkit that we today associate with historical thinking. By the middle of the 15th century Humanists successfully imitated ancient Ciceronian Latin to such an extent that it became the gold standard of elite education. In their dialogues, histories, orations, and letters, authors such as Leonardo Bruni and Poggio Bracciolini turned Humanism's sharp critical eye on contemporary society and made Latin an acceptable vehicle for a new kind of literature.

Italian Humanism took a turn toward the philological in the mid- to late 15th century, as its two most brilliant exponents in that era, Lorenzo Valla and Angelo Poliziano, moved beyond the now achieved objective of successful imitation of classical Latin. Both wrote creative philosophical literature in Latin, Valla concentrating much of his energy on what he perceived to be a Christianity gone astray. His penetrating dialogues, like his *On Free Will* and *On the Profession of the Religious* (1440) ask some of early modern Christianity's most penetrating questions: How can it be that a supremely good being, God, seems to allow people, His creations, freely to choose to perform evil acts, when with His omnipotence He could easily prevent them from doing so? What is the nature of the status of those who have taken religious vows? Does their vow count as a meritorious work and therefore bring them ipso facto closer to heaven, or are Christians who have not taken a vow equally rewarded if they have lived a just life? Because these works are true dialogues and thus at points strategically ambiguous, Valla's messages, his powerful and controversial questioning, come through in a fashion that is more subtle than direct (Celenza 2004, 85–100). Poliziano, an accomplished Tuscan poet, taught at the University of Florence, and at the same time he enjoyed Medici patronage. As he taught, he wrote some of his most scintillating Latin works to accompany or to aid his teaching: sometimes these took the form of poetic introductions to the texts he was to teach in his courses, at other times he posed small but erudite solutions to textual problems in classical works (which he then collected into his masterpiece of scholarship, the *Miscellanies*, 1489), and at still other times he offered *praelectiones*, lengthier introductions to the texts for a course, written in precise, elegant, and highly individualistic Latin.

By the late 15th century the ability to write acceptably classical Latin had become routine among educated elites in Italy. Thereafter their sense of history, of irony, their propensity to take the (sometimes imagined) position of the outsider in relation to existing intellectual institutions—all these made their way beyond Italy even as, within Italy, many of those inherently Humanistic traits were being transferred to the vernacular language and literature.

Part of the success of Italian Renaissance Humanists had also to do with a factor that was, loosely speaking, curricular. In 1440, in a suggested library acquisitions list prepared for Cosimo de' Medici, for the first time we see mentioned together a group of five verbally oriented academic subjects. These subjects (grammar, rhetoric, history, poetry, and moral philosophy, known together as the *studia humanitatis* or "the Humanities") had been at the unarticulated center of the Humanist movement since Petrarch (Kristeller 1956; Kohl 1992). They were at the center in the sense that it was these subjects that Humanists cared about most, the ones in which and through which they discovered, learned, and employed their new Latin style. These were the subjects to which Humanists referred obliquely when they talked about "these studies of ours" (*haec nostra studia*), as so many did in correspondence with one another. Humanists, especially in the early phases of the movement, were not always able to implement this new curricular and stylistic ideal in their day-to-day work as educators, secretaries to princes or cardinals, or governmental bureaucrats. Still, these classically grounded verbal arts represented an important thread that remained woven deep within Humanism's genetic texture from this point onward.

Humanism as a movement for stylistic reform of Latin succeeded completely on the level of education. From the era of Pietro Bembo, who wrote a definitive work on the Italian vernacular in 1525, Latin and the vernacular came to have clearly defined places, both within Italy and beyond. The vernacular, evaluated on classicizing lines, became a language suitable for serious intellectual work, in a way that only Latin previously had been. Nevertheless at the same time Latin remained the basic language of Western education, and the Latin in use from the early 16th century onward in education was basically Ciceronian. It is an easy, relatively uncontroversial matter to trace the progress of certain subjects, the *studia humanitatis*, for example. It is more difficult but no less useful to attempt to delineate how this verbal turn among certain intellectuals adumbrated what would turn out to be one of Humanism's greatest triumphs: the definition and celebration of the human individual, as a being in whom certain rights inhere precisely by virtue of being human. The full realization of this complex group of factors would not come to fruition until the 18th century.

In the meantime Italian Humanism's main scholarly thrusts—a purified Latinity, a delight in the recovery of ancient classical texts, a concern for source criticism, a dialogical, sometimes ambiguous irony fueled by history, and an occasional propensity to take the posture of the iconoclastic outsider—took hold throughout early modern Europe in different ways. The most famous Humanist of the early 16th century, Erasmus (1466–1536), performed numerous works of scholarship, not least the editing of the New Testament in Greek and providing, quite controversially, a new Latin translation, a corrective to the Vulgate then in use, on which his Italian forbear Lorenzo Valla had earlier worked with acuity. In his own Latin writings Erasmus provided beautifully written short works, including his *Colloquies,* designed to help schoolboys learn their Latin. He combined creativity and scholarship in one of his best-selling works, the *Adages*—a collection, first published in 1500 and which grew with every new edition, of proverbs annotated and explained by Erasmus with scholarly virtuosity. His fame was diffused throughout the learned world by constant correspondence, as he wrote letters that today illuminate invaluably the intellectual world of Renaissance Humanism. His most lasting work, the *Praise of Folly* (1511), served as a summing up of earlier Renaissance Humanism. In it he recapitulated Italian Humanism's penchant for a deliberately dialogical type of philosophizing, whereby the reader is made into a silent but powerful interlocutor. The narrator, Folly herself, is as such inherently unreliable, but she mercilessly and humorously skewers institutionalized learning and religion in a way that would have been familiar to Erasmus' 15th-century Italian forebears. The work looks forward as well, in the sense that its boldness highlights a freedom of thought and expression soon to be extinguished by the forces of religious ideology. Erasmus' entire oeuvre was placed on the 1559 *Index of Prohibited Books;* though that complete ban was soon mitigated, his name on the *Index* signals that the broader intellectual underpinnings of Italian Humanism would be transformed decisively.

Vernacular early modern literature took up some of the tendencies of Italian Humanism and made them more broadly available. Michel de Montaigne, who "never saw a greater monster or miracle" than himself, wrote his *Essays* (1580–1595) to express his innermost feelings and predilections. His self-scrutiny represented one result of the occasional focus on the individual person that reached back to the days of Petrarch. Montaigne, too, was steeped in classical sources, later claiming that his father had hired a tutor to speak nothing but Latin to him for the first five years of his life. He never tired of reading about exemplary ancient figures from the translated *Parallel Lives* of Plutarch, and though many of his essays have little to do with the classical world, his focus on the legitimacy of the human individual remained at least part of Humanism for its duration.

Another result of the growth of Humanism was continued interest in the kind of philological scholarship at which Poliziano had been adept. Figures such as Isaac Casaubon and Joseph Scaliger (later 16th and early 17th cents.) brought their erudition to bear on a variety of Greek and Latin texts and produced definitive, lasting critical editions of them. In doing so they and others like them laid the groundwork for the encyclopedic scholarship characteristic of the Enlightenment. In turn, Enlightenment thinkers of various stripes, informed by ancient sources and having fully assimilated what was then available, went on to provide the foundations of modern humanism by coming to certain conclusions about the nature of the human individual.

The late 18th century saw the theory of the integral individual take shape. This individual was conceived of as a being in whom certain rights reside and of whom certain obligations, conditioned by learning and culture, are expected. Humanistically inclined thinkers like Petrarch and Montaigne had earlier foregrounded individual identity by making themselves the subject of their art. Still, it was only in the 18th century that the concept of the individual was buttressed in practice by being developed in rights-based theories suitable for inclusion in law. One can add that although thinkers such as John Locke (d. 1704), Voltaire (d. 1778), and Jean-Jacques Rousseau (d. 1778) differed in many respects, on one issue they were united: they agreed that many of the social structures that evolve as people gather into groups can become stultifying, intellectually sterile, and even patently immoral in their effects. Because there are limits to human understanding, it was important to arrive at a notion of what those limits might be and then base one's theories and actions on the limits of that sphere.

These notions tended naturally to prompt a lack of respect for traditional religion and a corresponding fear that the place of the transcendent would be erased from human life. In response to the seemingly antireligious tendencies of British empiricism and to French Enlightenment antireligiosity, German thinkers of the 18th and early decades of the 19th century, such as Johann Joachim Winckelmann, Gotthold Ephraim Lessing, Johann Wolfgang von Goethe, and Friedrich Schiller, variously stressed the importance of the human individual but in a larger context. Disenchanted with traditional religion (in most cases Lutheranism), these thinkers drew inspiration from the ancient Greek world, finding there a love of harmony and beauty that they idealized. Other early 19th-century thinkers such as Wilhelm von Humboldt and Johann Gottlieb Fichte helped to translate these predispositions into a pedagogical program, and it was in this environment that the word *humanism,*in German *Humanismus,* has its origin.

The centrality of the classical Hellenic world meant

largely an idealization of Plato and the creation of Plato as predominantly a metaphysical rather than a dialogical thinker. Secure in the knowledge of the eternal transcendent Forms, humankind could dedicate itself to the pursuit of beauty and virtue without the structures of organized religion but grounded in the knowledge that transcendence existed. Another way to put this, and one from which many German thinkers drew inspiration, was related to the philosophy of the Infinite, represented by Immanuel Kant (d. 1804). Humankind could be logically sure that infinity existed but could never fully know it in this world, even as the existence of the Infinite provided mystery and inspiration to those pursuing truth. It was on this trajectory that the modern research university was set in the early 19th century, with the reform of the University of Berlin in 1810.

At the same time, there occurred a radical change in the discipline of philosophy—so implicated in the question of humanism. Philosophy became professionalized in university settings, and as the first modern histories of philosophy began to be written, it was the metaphysical style of philosophy, associated with the idealization of Platonism, that received most emphasis (Celenza 2005b). Late 18th- and early 19th-century humanism, or what is sometimes known as Neohumanism (*Neuhumanismus*) became, in effect, idealism. Yet the encyclopedic, canon-expanding, and philological style of Renaissance Humanist thinking never died. One saw this style of thought in Valla and Poliziano, in the great early modern philologists, and even in the propensity toward encyclopedism that so entranced Enlightenment thinkers of all philosophical bents. Detail-oriented, this type of scholarship was inherently antimetaphysical, suspicious of large, umbrella-like theories that tend to obscure individual counterexamples, and is best seen in its modern form in the thought of Friedrich Nietzsche. With respect to the classical tradition, Nietzsche presented the beginnings of a problem that would bedevil humanist thinking in the 20th century. Before writing his *Birth of Tragedy* (1872) Nietzsche had received one of the best classical educations available in the Neohumanist mode, at a classically oriented high school known as the Schulpforta in Naumburg, relatively near Leipzig and Halle. From his graduation onward he began publishing precise philological articles, and though the *Birth of Tragedy* signaled a departure in style, in substance he remained throughout his career a devotee of classical philology (Porter 2000). For example, in his *Genealogy of Morality* (1887) he demolishes the notion that the ancient, Presocratic Greeks believed in an idealized, transcendent world. For Homeric Greeks, he suggests, an action that they might have designated with the word *good* (*agathos*) did *not* mean that they believed that action somehow corresponded to a transcendent realm of "goodness" (a staple of the Platonic tradition, especially as this was refracted through Neohumanist German idealist interpretations). Instead, the Good, Nietzsche argued, represented no more than this: what the "good people," the *agathoi*—in effect, the power-wielding nobility—did or deemed acceptable (1887, 1).

The case of Nietzsche indicates the twin face of classically influenced humanism and the propensity its proponents have often shown to veer off into extremes. On the one hand, the dignity of humankind can sometimes be raised, rhetorically, to such a metaphysical level that it becomes antihistorical. Celebratory humanists of this orientation idealize humanity to such an extent that they are forced to find and ultimately bow before transcendent realms unable to be accessed in the world of day-to-day life. The danger is that one forgets the power of culture and history to shape events and becomes instead enamored of absolute ideas. One leaves people out. On the other hand, the philological side of humanism—the side whose representatives want to count every example and counterexample, to leave no text unconsidered, and to expand canons ever outward—tends when taken to extremes to set no limits and to veer off into nihilistic destructiveness. Here the danger is that, with no idealism of any sort, nothing is left unscathed, so that there is no persuasive way to make a case for any rules whatsoever: socially reproduced power rules all, and one realizes one has arrived at this point only after it is too late.

Medieval thinkers took what classical texts they knew and applied them to Christian concerns, even as Renaissance and early modern thinkers later made classically influenced humanism the basis for an entire culture, diversely expressed and oriented as that culture was, from century to century and place to place. In the Enlightenment and even well into the early 20th century, to be "educated" meant, at least in one's relatively early years, to learn classical languages. The relationship of the modern world to classically influenced humanism is difficult to gauge, because during the 20th century the centrality of classical learning and languages (in elementary and secondary schools) passed decisively out of fashion in Western culture.

BIBL.: August Buck, ed., *Humanismus: Seine europäische Entwicklung in Dokumenten und Darstellungen* (Freiburg 1987). A. Campana, "The Origin of the Word 'Humanist,'" *Journal of the Warburg and Courtauld Insititutes* 9 (1946) 60–73. Christopher S. Celenza, *The Lost Italian Renaissance: Humanists, Historians, and Latin's Legacy* (Baltimore 2004), "Petrarch, Latin, and Italian Renaissance Latinity," *Journal of Medieval and Early Modern Studies* 35 (2005a) 509–536, and "Lorenzo Valla and the Traditions and Transmissions of Philosophy," *Journal of the History of Ideas* (2005b) 483–506. Vito Giustiniani, "Homo, Humanus, and the Meanings of 'Humanism,'" *Journal of the History of Ideas* 46 (1985) 167–195. Benjamin Kohl, "The Changing Concept of the *Studia Humanitatis* in the Early Renaissance," *Renaissance Studies* 6 (1992) 185–209. Paul O. Kristeller, "Humanism and Scholasticism in Renaissance Italy," *Byzantion* 17 (1944–1945) 346–374, repr. in his *Studies in Renaissance Thought and Letters* (Rome 1956) 1:553–583. Lorenzo Minio-Paluello, ed., *Aristoteles Latinus* (Bruges 1953–). Friedrich I. Niethammer, *Der Streit des Philan-*

thropinismus und Humanismus in der Theorie des Erziehungs-Unterrichts Unserer Zeit (Jena 1808). James I. Porter, *Nietzsche and the Philology of the Future* (Palo Alto 2000). Markus Schauer, "Friedrich Immanuel Niethammer und der bildungspolitische Streit des Philanthropinismus und Humanismus um 1800," *Pegasus-Onlinezeitschrift* 5, no. 1 (2005) 28–45. Ronald G. Witt, *In the Footsteps of the Ancients: The Origins of Humanism from Lovato to Bruni* (Leiden 2000). C.C.

Humors

Fluids, saps, and juices, whose imbalance or blockage was thought by many Greeks and Romans to be responsible for illness. The theory that there were only four humors in the body—blood, phlegm, bile, and black bile—was first formulated around 400 BCE and well before the second century CE was ascribed to Hippocrates of Cos. Galen's authority, buttressed by his logical and rhetorical skills, ensured that it became for centuries the dominant theory in Western medicine and in its Eastern siblings. It was expounded in short (often pseudonymous) tracts like the Greek pseudo-Galenic *De humoribus* (*On Humors*) and the Latin *Epistula Yppocratis de quattuor humoribus* (*Letter of Hippocrates on the Four Humors*), in medical lectures as well as in large compendia, like the *Canon* of Avicenna.

Its foundations were part empirical, based on the human body's tendency to homoeostasis, and part theoretical. Its combination of Hippocratic and Aristotelian doctrines (e.g., Melancholy) made it particularly attractive to an intellectual community used to explaining the universe in terms of elements and qualities. Its cyclical nature, as the balance of humors changed with the seasons in an orderly manner, could be easily adapted to explain, for example, the colors of urine on a medieval urine chart.

Galen's insistence on the interaction between body and soul was developed in late antiquity and the Middle Ages into a theory of temperament that divided human beings into four main psychological as well as physical types. Visual representations stressed the psychological aspect of the four temperaments at least as much as they did the physical. Poets, playwrights, and essayists based characterizations of their heroes and villains on this understanding of the four humors.

This classification system was extended in the Middle Ages to cover far more than the elements, qualities, and seasons of Galen. The link with the mind explained the physical effects of the four main musical tonalities; the seasonal rhythm fitted easily with the constellations of astrology. Organs that were thought to be under the influence of a particular sign could thus be assigned to one of the four humors. Other tetrads, like the four Evangelists, could also be adapted to this scheme.

Until the Paracelsian revolution of the 16th century the doctrine of humors was unchallenged. Academic debate refined the categories, such as the different types of melancholy or phlegm, rather than rejecting them. Even academic Paracelsians, at Basel and Montpellier, accepted humors, explaining their differences in terms of their chemistry.

William Harvey's *On the Motion of the Heart and Blood* (*De motu cordis et sanguinis,* 1628) challenged but did not overthrow this humoralism. While asserting the primacy of blood, circulating throughout the body, Harvey in his therapeutics continued to talk in terms of the four humors, which he viewed as constituents of his supreme blood. Other, more radical, doctors saw temperaments and humors as at best secondary features of developments elsewhere in the body. By 1850 humors and temperaments had largely disappeared from formal Western medicine, although in many Muslim countries today there are officially backed attempts to relate these traditional concepts of Yunani (Greek) medicine to the findings of modern medical science. In the West, lay perceptions of disease often involve explanations inherited from humoralism; the resurgence of alternative medicine after 1970 has seen a return to notions of holistic balance and imbalance that go back, sometimes overtly, to ancient humoral theories. Humoralism is a long time dying.

BIBL.: Guy Attewell, *Refining Unani Tibb* (London 2007). Chandler McC. Brooks et al., *Humors, Hormones, and Neurosecretions* (Albany 1962). Zirka Z. Filipczak, *Hot Dry Men, Cold Wet Women: The Theory of Humors in Western Art, 1575–1700* (New York 1997). Cecil G. Helman, "Stuff a Cold, Starve a Fever," *Culture, Medicine and Psychiatry* 2 (1978) 107–137. Erich Schöner, *Das Viererschema in der antiken Humoralpathologie* (Wiesbaden 1964). V.N.

Hunayn ibn-Ishāq

Christian Arab translator, physician, and scholar (808–873), active during the height of the Graeco-Arabic translation movement in Baghdad. He came from a Nestorian Arab family in al-Hīra, a city in the south of Iraq close to the Euphrates, where his father was an apothecary. Though al-Hīra, which had been the capital of the pre-Islamic Arab dynasty of the Lakhmids (a tribe in federation with the Sasanian Persians against the Byzantines), had lost much of its former splendor at the time Hunayn was born, the schools of the Nestorian community there must have been good enough to have provided the basic education and attitude to learning that we can witness in his works. We have no reliable details about his early education, though it is clear that he must have been trilingual, speaking Arabic at home and studying Syriac and Greek at school, the latter two being the languages of Nestorian and Orthodox Christianity.

He moved to Baghdad by the time he was 16 and entered the employ of the powerful Bakhtishūʿ family of Nestorian court physicians. So great was the need in Baghdad for translators from Greek into Syriac and Arabic that even a provincial youth of 17 could find commissions from the highest echelons of society. But his first translations of Galen, he tells us, were clumsy and inaccurate, and he felt the need for more training. He went to study medicine with Yūhannā ibn-Māsawayh, another renowned court physician, but apparently had to interrupt his studies when Yūhannā rebuffed him for his insufficient knowledge of Greek. He left Baghdad, then reappeared more than two years later, with such a command of Greek as to be able to recite Homer by heart, as one anecdotal source informs us. Upon this return, in 827, he was reconciled with Yūhannā and resumed his studies.

He soon made a name for himself as a translator of Greek works into both Syriac and Arabic and found powerful sponsors and patrons in Baghdad among the members of the ruling family, various high-standing government officials, and numerous scholars and professionals. The intellectual culture in Baghdad, fostered by the Graeco-Arabic translation movement, which was already more than half a century old by the time of Hunayn's youth, set high store by the talents of translators.

As the major translator and transmitter of the classical heritage into Arabic and thus to Islamic civilization, Hunayn can be credited with two achievements. From what we can judge by his extant translations and his own admission, he gained expertise primarily in scientific (and especially medical) Greek; he was thus able to make faithful and accurate translations while honestly informing the reader of areas of inferior competence. In a translator's note to Galen's work *De nominibus medicinalibus* he says,

> In the following passage Galen quotes Aristophanes. However, the Greek manuscript, from which I translated this work into Syriac, contained such a large number of mistakes that it would have been impossible for me to understand the meaning of the text had I not been so familiar with and accustomed to Galen's Greek and acquainted with most of his ideas from his other works. But I am not familiar with the language of Aristophanes, nor am I accustomed to it. Hence, it was not easy for me to understand the quotation, and I have, therefore, omitted it. (Rosenthal 1975, 19)

Hunayn's extant Arabic translations in fact evince an unparalleled expertise in the comprehension of scientific Greek and a masterly Arabic style that is distinctive for its clarity and precision. His Syriac must have been equally good—he made many more translations into Syriac than into Arabic, it seems, though apart from a few fragments his Syriac translations have not survived.

He also developed a philological method for establishing a critical text before translating it, which is best described in his own words in an essay he wrote on his own translations of Galen:

> When I was a young man of twenty or a little older, I translated [Galen's *On the Sects*] . . . from a very faulty Greek manuscript. Later, when I was about forty, my pupil Hubaysh asked me to correct the translation. Meanwhile a number of Greek manuscripts had accumulated in my possession. I collated these manuscripts and thereby produced a single correct copy. Next, I collated the Syriac text with it and corrected it. I am in the habit of doing this with everything I translate. (Rosenthal 1975, 20)

The scrupulousness and philological exactitude with which he approached his work of translation enabled him, among other translators who shared his methods and goals, to create an Arabic scientific vocabulary and expository style that by and large has remained standard to this day.

His own scientific activities were mostly in the area of medicine and especially ophthalmology. In general medicine he composed an introductory handbook in the form of questions and answers, *Questions on Medicine,* which met with great popularity both in Arabic and, in its Latin version (*Isagoge Johannitii*), in the medieval West. His scholarly interests were broad, and he wrote treatises on sundry subjects, including philosophy, meteorology, Christian theology, and the maxims of Greek philosophers, some of which are extant. But his great contribution was doubtless in his capacity as translator of classical Greek works into Syriac and Arabic.

In addition to translating the works of Galen, he is credited with numerous translations of works by many other authors, including the Septuagint. He and his colleagues and students were responsible for accurate Arabic and Syriac versions of hundreds of scientific and philosophical texts, thus generating a classical renaissance within Islamic civilization and opening the way for the European Renaissance.

BIBL.: G. Bergsträsser, *Hunain ibn Ishāq über die Syrischen und Arabischen Galen-Übersetzungen* (1925, repr. Liechtenstein 1966) and *Hunain ibn Ishāq und seine Schule* (Leiden 1913). M. Cooperson, "The Autobiography of Hunayn ibn Ishāq," in *Interpreting the Self: Autobiography in the Arabic Literary Tradition,* ed. D. W. Reynolds et al. (Berkeley 2001) 107–118. F. Rosenthal, *The Classical Heritage in Islam* (Berkeley 1975). G. Strohmaier, "Hunayn b. Ishāk," *Encyclopaedia of Islam* 3:578–581.

D.G.

Hydra

A mythic water snake inhabiting the marshes of Lerna, south of Argos in Greece. The Hydra had multiple heads, from 9 to 100 in various sources, though Pausanias (2.37.4) was sure that there had really been only one; if severed, these heads could regenerate in multiple form. Slaying the Hydra was Heracles' second canonical labor, which he accomplished after much difficulty with the aid of Iolaus; the trophy of his victory was a set of arrows poisoned with the creature's blood. That poison eventually dyed the shirt of Nessus and occasioned Heracles' own death. Both the Hydra and the Crab (Cancer), which Hera sent to help it in the fight, became constellations.

The battle with the Hydra, usually as part of a series on

Heracles' labors but sometimes treated on its own, became a standard subject for artists from the late 15th century onward. Antonio del Pollaiuolo painted it for the Palazzo Medici (ca. 1460); now lost, it is known through other sources. John Singer Sargent included it in his murals for the Boston Museum of Fine Arts (1921–1925). An ancient statue of Heracles unearthed at Rome ca. 1620 was restored by Alessandro Algardi, perhaps correctly, as a depiction of the hero with the defeated monster. From 1738 until 1817 the Hydra gave its name to the Stanza d'Ercole in the Capitoline Museum and was one of the prime exhibits until moved elsewhere. There are modern sculptures as early as Alfonso Lombardi (ca. 1525), as recent as Mathias Gasteiger (1930); reliefs adorn a bronze roundel from the 1490s by the Mantuan artist known as Antico, and a popular line of silver vases designed by John Flaxman (1805–1806).

In literature there are no important narrations of the story as such; its main life is as a vehicle for metaphor. Medieval and Renaissance mythographers, citing the etymological connection with *hydōr* ("water"), often treat the myth as an allegory of the difficulties of swamp reclamation. In *The Hydra Head* (*La cabeza de la Hidra,* 1978), Carlos Fuentes's novel about late 20th-century Mexico, the treacherous fluid is petroleum. Plato, in a much noted passage (*Euthydemus* 297C), likens Heracles' labor against the Hydra to that of arguing with Sophists; the motif later became a commonplace figure for single-minded truth struggling with endlessly resourceful error. In *The Faerie Queene* (1590–1596) Edmund Spenser uses the Hydra for similes about the creature attendant on the giant Orgoglio, a brutal champion of the Roman Catholic Church (1.7.17), and about the Blatant Beast, the noisy slanderer of courtly virtue (6.12.32, the head count here rising to 1,000). On the other side of the Channel, the slaughter of Protestants on and following Saint Bartholomew's Day 1572 was celebrated with a medal likening the event to the killing of the Hydra. Horace, to different effect, had cheerfully used the Hydra as an image of Rome's imperial success in the 1st century BCE (*Odes* 4.4.61–68), and Christopher Marlowe's Tamburlaine (ca. 1587) makes the same celebratory identification:

> as the heads of Hydra, so my power,
> Subdued, shall stand as mighty as before.
> If they should yield their necks unto the sword,
> Thy soldiers' arms could not endure to strike
> So many blows as I have heads for thee.
> (*1 Tamburlaine* 3.3.140–144)

Paul Valéry imagines the adversaries mingled in blessed repose and release after their struggle:

> Beneath the footsteps of the stars
> Sleep, victor, slowly decomposed,
> For the Hydra latent in the hero
> Unfolds out to infinity.
> ("Ode secrète," in *Charmes,* 1922)

In 1756 Carolus Linnaeus appropriated the name *Hydra* for a class of freshwater organisms, related to jellyfish, with impressive regenerative powers; the largest is an inch long. G.B.

Hypnerotomachia Poliphili

A philosophical, erotic, archaeological, and architectural romance printed in Venice, 1499. In *Hypnerotomachia Poliphili* (*Poliphilo's Strife of Love in a Dream*) the protagonist (whose name is variously interpreted) tells how, being in love, he journeys in sleep through an Arcadian land of wildernesses and cultivated gardens, observing the natural history, artworks, and resident nymphs, and is united with his beloved Polia; her image vanishes when he awakes.

Noted for its extravagantly Latinized Italian prose, the book has been called both the consummation of 15th-century Humanism and the caricature of it. On the question of what type of Latin, or of Italian, should be the medium of literature in Italy, some, like Bembo, proposed transferring to Trecento Tuscan prose the elegance of Ciceronian Latin; this book instead generates, in a Boccaccian literary vernacular, an equivalent to the eclectic and inventive Latin of Poliziano, embracing early and late ancient sources from Plautus to Apuleius; it abounds in lexical novelties and rhetorical conceits, playing on etymology, the archaeology of language.

The author is usually identified as Francesco Colonna, a friar from the Veneto, though candidates are proposed from elsewhere in Italy. If Venetian, the work belongs to a world without the physical presence of Roman remains, where classical antiquity was a recreative fantasy. Poliphilo romantically enjoys ruins as ruins and contemplates ancient tombs with melancholy, while recording measurements and inscriptions as a scientific connoisseur. Most of the buildings, however, are in pristine condition; they house song, dance, and ceremonial, recalling contemporary professionals who exploited the scenic possibilities of antique themes. All the buildings combine, in their original designs, diverse ancient exemplars, drawn from both ancient books and modern sources like Cyriac of Ancona, and are described not impressionistically but as projected by a draftsman. Polemical passages deplore a lost inheritance of architectural craftsmanship and terminology. Thus the author combines a variety of ways of making antiquity contemporary.

He extensively borrows architectural theory from Alberti, correlating new technical terms with those of Vitruvius. He finds erotic feeling in the embodied forms of classical columns and entablatures. At the same time, he insists on the composition of building plans using mathematically proportioned grids. These, as subsequently presented with the first translation of Vitruvius (1521, by Cesariano, also influenced by his language), came to shape the canon of classical architecture. Analogously disciplined patterns may be regarded as a defining factor of classicism across all the arts.

Christian ideas paganized as the cult of Venus, and encyclopedic references to Greek and Roman mythology and history, generalize the story of the lovers, whose timeless heritage comprehends universal wisdom and primeval practice, in Egyptian hieroglyphs and Etruscan rites. Material from realms of medieval romance is given a philosophical aura, the sensuousness of Ovid being combined with the elation of Platonism.

The detailed descriptions of works of art, reviving an ancient genre of writing, and of landscapes and their occupants in similar terms, have since inspired painters of humanist dreamlands. Particular images from the book include Giorgione's sleeping Venus and Bernini's elephant-supported obelisk in Rome.

The aggregative prose composition and graphic layout of the text integrate linguistic and pictorial representation, for which drawings must have figured in the manuscript. It was the first vernacular publication by Aldus Manutius, a masterpiece of typography and woodcut illustration, and a pioneer in communicating the visual culture of classicism through the printed book.

Publication of the first French translation (1545) helped establish the Renaissance in France. In the 17th century French authorities still recommended it as capturing the spirit of ancient architecture. The sublime scale of its monuments appealed to French architects of the late 18th century. Later, in England too, its emphasis on archaeologically informed design was congenial to Grecian neoclassicism, as it had been to the Roman classicism of the Renaissance.

Scholars in the 20th century supplied philological commentaries, and critics compared its learnedly creative writing to moderns such as Joyce. Though the beautiful illustrations have been admired, the difficult language has been relatively neglected, yet the images would not have had such influence without the visible presence of the text, supplying imaginative comprehensiveness in an idea of a classical world.

BIBL.: Francesco Colonna, *Hypnerotomachia Poliphili,* ed. Giovanni Pozzi and Lucia A. Ciapponi, 2 vols., rev. ed. (Padua 1980), and CD-ROM facsimile of the 1499 Aldine edition (Oakland, Calif., 2004). Patricia Fortini Brown, *Venice and Antiquity* (New Haven 1997) esp. 207–222. Michael Leslie and John Dixon Hunt, eds., "Garden and Architectural Dreamscapes in the *Hypnerotomachia Poliphili,*" *Word and Image* 14, no. 1/2 (January–June 1998). John Onians, *Bearers of Meaning* (Princeton 1988) esp. 207–215.

I.W.

I

Iconoclasm

A modern term designating the period between roughly 730 and 843 in the Eastern Roman Empire (Byzantium), when members of the Church and court debated the status of religious portraits. Such portraits (often called icons) had served as honorific commemorations from at least the 4th century, but toward the end of the 7th century they became absorbed into the cult of saints and relics. Around the year 680 people came to believe that sacred portraits were able to channel prayers directly to the person pictured. For this reason, icons at the time became, like relics, objects of veneration honored with candles, incense, and curtains.

For many years it was confidently asserted that the emperor Leo III (r. 717–741) initiated iconoclasm in 726 or 730. Recently, however, this view has been called into question as scholars have realized that the evidence for Leo's involvement—and, indeed, most of the data for the whole movement—was written in the 9th and 10th centuries by the promoters of icons (iconophiles, or friends of images). Contemporary documents provide little evidence for Leo's beliefs about icons one way or the other but instead make it clear that during his reign a group of churchmen began to question the growing cult of images. Official policy, imperial and ecclesiastic, did not appear until 754, during the reign of Leo's son Constantine V (r. 741–775), when the veneration of icons was declared heretical by a Church council held at Hieria. The council forbade the destruction of images that already existed without imperial consent but allowed them to be covered over. In exceptional circumstances images were replaced: in the 760s, for example, portraits of saints were replaced by crosses in the reception room of the church of Hagia Sophia in Constantinople. Iconoclasm—a term derived from the Greek word *eikonoklastēs*, or image breaker—is thus somewhat of a misnomer, and the Byzantines themselves preferred the term iconomachy (image struggle), though their opponents called those against the veneration of images iconoclasts as a term of condemnation.

The first phase of the iconomachy ended in 787, when the seventh ecumenical council, held at Nicaea during the reign of Constantine VI and his mother, the regent Eirene, declared that the veneration of sacred portraits was orthodox. The situation was reversed in 815 by Leo V, apparently in emulation of Constantine V, whose military and political success he aspired to equal. The era finally ended in 843 with what has been called the triumph of orthodoxy, engineered by the patriarch Methodius during the reign of Michael III and his mother, the regent Theodora.

Early arguments against image veneration invoked the biblical Second Commandment and charged the iconophiles with idolatry; increasingly, however, the main accusation against the venerators of images was that icons could portray only the human nature of Christ and thus denied his divinity. The proponents of image veneration countered with arguments that the coming of Christ overturned the laws of the Old Testament, and they accordingly accused the iconoclasts of denying the incarnation: Christ appeared on Earth, was seen by humans, and could therefore be depicted—to say otherwise was to deny his humanity. Major spokesmen for the iconoclast position were Constantine V and John the Grammarian, patriarch of Constantinople from ca. 837 until 843; notable iconophiles included John of Damascus (ca. 675–ca. 750) and the patriarchs Tarasius (784–806) and Nicephorus (806–815).

Across the roughly 120-year period of debate there was little destruction, and persecutions of image venerators were limited to brief periods under Constantine V (apparently in response to an attempt at a coup unrelated to iconoclasm) and Theophilus (r. 829–842). The most significant result of the struggle was the development of a theology of icons, still a mainstay of the Orthodox Church. Its other enduring legacy is terminological: modern scholarship labels as iconoclasm all periods of image destruction—from the Reformation to the French Revolution to the Taliban uprising.

BIBL.: M.-F. Auzepy, M. Kaplan, and B. Martin-Hisard, *La chrétienté orientale du début du VIIe siècle au milieu du XIe siècle* (Paris 1996). L. Brubaker and J. F. Haldon, *Byzantium in the Iconoclast Era (ca 680–850): A History* (Cambridge 2006) and *Byzantium in the Iconoclast Era (ca. 680–850): The Sources,* Birmingham Byzantine and Ottoman Monographs 7 (Aldershot 2001). A. A. M. Bryer and J. Herrin, eds., *Iconoclasm* (Birmingham 1977). S. Gero, *Byzantine Iconoclasm during the Reign of Constantine V, with Particular Attention to the Oriental Sources,* Corpus Scriptorum Christianorum Orientalium 384, Subsidia 52 (Louvain 1977), and *Byzantine Iconoclasm during the Reign of Leo III, with Particular Attention to the Oriental Sources,* Corpus Scriptorum Christianorum Orientalium 346, Subsidia 41 (Louvain 1973). L.BR.

Imitation and Mimesis

Greek *mimesis* and Latin *imitatio,* most often translated as "imitation" or "representation," refer to classical conceptions of the representation of the world and the imitation of previous art. These notions have been central to the Western theory and practice of literature, the visual arts, and, intermittently, music, especially during the periods in which classical texts were considered most authoritative, the Renaissance through the 18th century. Throughout their history, however, *mimesis* and *imitatio* have had ambiguities and tensions and have been adapted to diverse, contradictory understandings of artistic methods and goals.

Successive defenders of poetry and art have responded to Plato's influential attack, in *Republic* 10, on Homeric and Greek tragic mimesis. As is frequently done throughout the tradition, he compares poetry to painting: both copy mere appearances. Plato condemns as false and pernicious the powerful illusionism of imitations of human beings and gods enthralled by illusory passions that arouse similar passions in audiences.

Indirectly rebutting Plato, Aristotle's *Poetics* offers the most sophisticated ancient discussion of mimesis. Aristotle argues that men naturally enjoy recognizing what is represented in art. He treats poetry (primarily tragedy and epic) not as copying appearances but as instructively representing general features of human action. Chapter 9 of *Poetics* claims that poetry is more universal than history because it imitates not the real actions of particular persons but the necessary or probable actions of kinds of persons in certain situations. Yet Aristotle tempers his emphasis on mimetic plausibility in various ways. He influentially argues that plots should not only be mimetically plausible but also include wonder-inducing surprise. Generic constraints partially determine characters' resemblance to ordinary life: comedies depict men worse than "us"; tragedies, men who are "better" (in heroic dignity, presumably, though this remains a debated point).

Roman discussions of visual mimesis balance verisimilitude and idealization. Quintilian praises Zeuxis for figures nobler than reality, other painters for lifelike "truth" (*Institutes* 10.12). Pliny the Elder's *Natural History* celebrates lifelike portraiture (35.88) but also recounts an anecdote recycled throughout the 15th through 18th centuries, about Zeuxis's combining of different women's beauties to depict an ideal (35.64).

Another idealizing strand in Roman and late Greek thought counters Plato's attack on mimesis of appearances by locating the perfect object of imitation in the mind. Cicero describes as an inspiring exemplar a perfect orator who, like a painter's similitude of perfect beauty, corresponds not to anything existent but to a perfect Neoplatonic "idea" (*Orator* 1.7). Plotinus describes the artist imitating a metaphysical beauty envisioned by the mind (*Ennead* 5.8.1).

Finally, Roman and late Greek writers often subordinate verisimilar mimesis to moral instruction. Horace's *Ars poetica,* whose comparison of poetry to painting, *ut pictura poesis* (line 361), taken out of context, became the licensing tag for countless Renaissance and neoclassical parallels between poetic and painterly imitation, advises using traditional myths or pleasant fictions "near to the truth" (line 338) that ideally combine pleasure with moral instruction (lines 343–344). Horace advises poets both to observe life and manners (lines 156–178, 317–318) and to read Platonic dialogues on the duties of different social roles (lines 309–316). Horace's *Epistle* 1.2 praises Homer for presenting good and bad through examples, more clearly than philosophers. Influential late-classical treatments of comedy (Evanthius, Donatus, Servius) treat comedy as fictitious imitations of ordinary life, depicting virtues to follow and foibles to shun.

Ancient writers also recommend the imitation of illustrious predecessors (while warning against servile copying). Horace's *Ars poetica* advises the would-be poet constantly to study Greek models (lines 73–90, 131–135, 268–269). Seneca (*Epistle* 84) and Quintilian (*Institutes* 10.2) insist that the imitator must transform his models into something that is his own and, ideally, superior. Longinus argues that emulative struggle with a predecessor engenders sublime thought and expression (*On Sublimity* 13.2–4).

Medieval treatises promoted the didactic mimesis found in Roman sources and such works as Averroës's commentary on the *Poetics* (translated into Latin in 1256), which assimilated Aristotelian imitation to didactic praise and blame of virtue and vice. Medieval authors like John of Salisbury (*Metalogicon* 1.24) and Geoffrey of Vinsauf (*Poetica nova* 1705–1709) advised stylistic imitation of excellent models. In the Renaissance, the rich range of classical theories of imitation were encountered and transformed. Theorists of painting of the 15th and 16th centuries, such as L. B. Alberti and G. Vasari, celebrated the accurate representation of human beings and their emotions, and the progress of Renaissance painting was partially conceived along the lines of Greek art's increasing "truth" to nature as described by classical writers. Verisimilitude was balanced, as in classical discussions, by a form of idealization, such as compositional "dignity" (Alberti).

Aristotle's *Poetics* was published and translated into Latin and the Continental vernaculars beginning in the mid-16th century. Numerous commentaries appeared, often reading Aristotle through the prism of Horace's *Ars poetica,* which was treated as wholly compatible with Aristotle's *Poetics* (which Horace knew only at secondhand). Against the Platonic suspicion of poetic lies, numerous authors celebrated verisimilar poetic fictions. *Imitatio* and its vernacular cognates, though the dominant terms, were used interchangeably with such terms as *finzione* and *feigning.* Authors often associated such fictions with pleasurable didacticism, conceiving the Aristotelian universal as examples of virtue and vice for imitation and avoidance, often reached by way of Neoplatonic "ideas." Such theory coalesced in the treatment of the epic as the highest genre, representing the perfect aristocratic hero. In his posthumously published *Defence of Poesy* (1595), Philip Sidney rebuts Plato's attack on poetic mimesis in the *Republic* with an eclectic mixture of Aristotelian, Horatian, and Neoplatonic theorizing. Poetry is "an art of imitation" that seeks "to teach and delight" with "feigned" or made-up "perfect pattern[s]" of what is to be imitated or shunned. Sidney posits Virgil's Aeneas as a model "excellent" in "every way." J. C. Scaliger's *Poetice* (1561), to which Sidney is indebted, similarly hymns Aeneas as the Platonic "idea" above all imperfect individuals. Scaliger also treats Virgil as the perfect author, surpassing nature itself as a model for literary imitation.

Scaliger was one voice in a debate throughout the 16th century between those who advocated primarily imitating a single literary model of perfection, Virgil in poetry and Cicero in prose, and those who urged an eclecticism closer to that which was followed by the ancient authors themselves. Desiderius Erasmus's *Ciceronianus* (1528) argued, against advocates of Ciceronian imitation like Pietro Bembo, that writers could not slavishly imitate Cicero because of the vast differences between Roman and modern Christian culture. The tension between imitation of ancient predecessors and imitation of one's own world, largely unaddressed in classical criticism, is indirectly suggested in Girolamo Vida's *De arte poetica* (1527), which influentially advocated (and exemplified) primarily imitating Virgil. Vida echoes Horace's advice to the would-be poet to observe human manners and study literary models, but Vida explicitly subordinates the former to the latter, warning that because life is short, one must study ancient literary models rather than indulge in overextensive real-life observation (Book 1, lines 391–414).

The gap between ancient and modern was also central to the literary debates in which critics adapted or countered ancient theory to attack or defend modern vernacular works that did not fit classical accounts of mimesis. Giraldi Cinthio's 1554 defense of romance (primarily Ludovico Ariosto's popular *Orlando furioso*) argues that romance legitimately differs from ancient norms by providing more pleasurable variety, such that "nothing" escapes its imitative scope. Yet Cinthio's celebration of mimetic inclusivity builds on classical conceptions: while criticizing ancient epic's lesser unity compared with tragedy, Aristotle concedes that epic episodes provide grandeur and pleasurable variety (chap. 24); Quintilian praises Homer as an "ocean" that contains every type of eloquence and emotion (*Institutes* 10.46–48); Cinthio suggests that the baggier modern romance outdoes ancient epic. Noting the ancient emulative ideal, Cinthio claims elsewhere that Ariosto surpassed predecessors to become himself a new model for imitation. Cinthio also defends the romance in terms of the Aristotelian mimetic criteria of probability, wonder, and (as Renaissance readers often interpreted *Poetics* 9) imitating what ought to be. With an Aristotelian, Horatian, and Neoplatonic eclecticism characteristic of his age, Torquato Tasso's *Discourses on the Heroic Poem* (published in 1594) justifies his own melding of ancient epic and modern romance in *Gerusalemme liberata* (1580–1581) and its revision, *Gerusalemme conquistata* (1593). Seeking to show how to live through the pleasant imitation of the universal and what ought to be, the poet should depict a perfect knight inspiring of imitation. Combining ancient unity with romance variety, the heroic poem is a "little world" resembling the "discordant concord" of God's marvelous creation. Tasso here adapts the late-Latin author Macrobius's comparison of Virgil's mastery of all styles with the world's concord of discords (*Saturnalia* 5.1.7) to glorify the modern poem's mimetic ambition.

Tasso justifies departures from ancient models in response to modern beliefs. To combine the marvelous with the verisimilar, Tasso argues for Christian supernatural elements that, unlike the discredited gods of ancient epic, will seem credible to Christians, a theme that would resound in 17th- and 18th-century polemics for the distinctively modern, and true, "Christian marvelous." In another influential move, Tasso defends the modern poet's representation of an ennobling love unknown to the ancients.

Seventeenth-century French neoclassical theory systematizes and expands on 16th-century Italian criticism, constructing strict rules of verisimilitude and decorum out of Aristotle and Horace. Various English critics, in contrast, qualify such norms to promote a distinctive English mimetic tradition. John Dryden's *Essay of Dramatic Poesy* and *Defense of the Essay* (1668) defend English drama by examining how different objects and modes of mimesis suit diverse cultures and different times. Modern drama depicts a love unknown to the ancients, Dryden says. French drama's moral seriousness and Aristotelian unities nicely counterbalance the French people's "airy" temperament, but English drama's comedies, native tragicomedies, and plot variety suit a more "sullen" people seeking entertainment. Like this flexible, culture-specific inflexion of Horatian "pleasure and instruction," Dryden's description of drama as the "just and lively image of human nature, representing its passions and humors," reveals his distance from Renaissance conceptions of the didactic imitation of virtues and vices. Dryden celebrates vivid representations of passion, qualifying verisimilitude less with moral strictures than with formal techniques (like rhyme) that represent human nature at a "higher pitch" to arouse Aristotelian "admiration" (wonder).

The *Essay* brings out the tension between imitation of human nature and the imitation of predecessors by celebrating Shakespeare, who had no need of books to imitate human nature, a claim echoed by 18th-century writers like Edward Young (*Conjectures on Original Genius,* 1759) and Samuel Johnson (*Preface to Shakespeare,* 1765). Yet though admiring such mimetic originality, Dryden figures himself as the eclectic, improving imitator of ancient theory, denying that Shakespeare and his classicizing foil, Ben Jonson, provide "a perfect pattern for imitation." Throughout his career, Dryden recalls Horace's claim that his satiric predecessor Lucilius would have revised more carefully had he lived in Horace's day (*Satire* 1.10.68–71) to justify emulatively rewriting his English predecessors, however great, to conform to the decorum of his more "correct" neoclassical age.

Writing in the wake of the quarrel of the ancients and moderns regarding the relative merits of classical and modern culture that erupted in 1690s France and continued in France and England through the early 18th century, Joseph Addison warmly praises ancient writing but celebrates modern English literature, particularly Shakespeare and Milton, for surpassing the ancients in original imitation of things beyond "nature." His *Spectator* papers canonizing *Paradise Lost* (1712) assert its excellence in terms of Aristotle's account of the major elements imitated in tragedy: plot, character, thought (chap. 6). Although 16th- and 17th-century critics normally harness Aristotelian imitation to moral instruction, Addison (like many other 18th-century critics) emphasizes pleasure. *Paradise Lost's* plot contains "everything great . . . within the verge of nature or outside of it," as well as "surprising incidents" of Milton's "own invention." While noting Milton's imitations of Homer and Virgil, Addison claims Milton's perfect, unfallen Adam and Eve are "more new" than ancient epic characters and indeed "lie out of nature."

In his influential, wide-ranging *Spectator* papers on the pleasures of the imagination (1712), Addison notes, like Aristotle, the cognitive pleasure of recognizing represented things in mimetic arts such as sculpture and painting. He argues, however, that poetry in particular conjures ideas "more great, strange, or beautiful" than the actual world, "perfecting nature" and "adding greater beauties." Addison anticipates Charles Batteux's *Fine Arts Reduced to a Single Principle* (1746), the first systematic account of the interrelations among the *beaux-arts,* or fine arts. Batteux claims that such arts provide pleasure by imitating what he influentially calls (following late 17th-century French critics) *la belle nature,* a beautiful nature identified by Batteux both with Aristotle's things that could happen, imitated by poetry (*Poetics* 9), and with Zeuxis's ideal beauty obtained through judicious selection. Yet while Batteux insists that art "imitates nature" (ideally defined), Addison celebrates an "imagination" that goes beyond nature, praising Shakespeare's nonclassical, distinctively English "extravagance of fancy" when depicting "ghosts, fairies, witches." Nevertheless, Addison still appeals to Aristotelian mimetic probability: Shakespeare was able to make "imaginary" creatures like Caliban appear so "natural" that it seems "highly probable they should talk and act" as they do (if they existed).

Addison equates and celebrates the "new," the "uncommon," and the "strange," but the novel was a self-consciously modern genre (as the gradually stabilized term *novel* suggests) staked on the imitation of the ordinary contemporary world. Eighteenth-century defenders of this modern genre combined the traditional notion that fictional examples provided powerful instruction with the claim that its resemblance to contemporary readers' everyday experience made it more credible and therefore more affecting than pagan epic, with its discarded—and, as many felt, brutal—customs and beliefs, or unbelievable modern romance.

Henry Fielding's prefaces to *Tom Jones* (1749) mediate between ancients and moderns by applying, with an assured, light touch, neoclassical criteria to his version of the new form. Fielding defends his restricting of his work to "human nature" and morally mixed characters in terms of verisimilitude. He rejects the "marvelous" of pagan gods and English fairies but retains the wonder-inducing plot twists commended by Aristotle. He points out the tension between imitation of life and of predecessors: only through "experience" with "every kind of character" can a writer accurately represent current "manners" (preface to Book 13), which cannot be learned from "imitation" of earlier, no longer up-to-date works (preface to Book 14). Not all, of course, were happy with the new form. Like Fielding, Samuel Johnson, in *Rambler* 4 (1750), favorably contrasts the novel's "accurate observation of the living world" with romance "incredibilities." Johnson, however, wishes to combine (somehow) novelistic verisimilitude with a didactic idealization recalling Renaissance poetics: he rejects mixed characters in favor of representations of a "perfect idea of virtue" that is yet not "above probability, for what we cannot credit we shall never imitate." Johnson's ambivalent response to Shakespeare in his preface—whom he lauds for providing "a faithful mirror of manners and of life," yet criticizes for writing "without moral purpose"—arises from Johnson's competing desires for mimetic verisimilitude and moral instruction.

Describing his work as "prosai-comi-epic," Fielding associates his modern novel with the classical genre long associated with the verisimilar representation of everyday life, comedy. Numerous authors of the mid- to late 18th century, by contrast, including Bernard de Fontenelle, Denis Diderot, Pierre de Beaumarchais, and Gotthold Lessing, celebrated genres like domestic tragedies or sentimental comedies that directly challenged classical tragic-comic hierarchies with serious representations of middle-class life. Yet Fielding's claim to be writing "comi-epic," evoking his mock-heroic measuring of modern life's distance from ancient heroics, is also a serious claim that his work is an up-to-date version of the highest literary genre because of its distinctively modern form of mimetic inclusiveness: in place of Tasso's or Milton's cosmos, Fielding depicts the panorama of contemporary social life. Such "sociological" mimetic ambition remains a central aspect of the novelistic enterprise today.

With the weakening of classical authority and decline of classical education among a growing middle-class reading public, classical and neoclassical conceptions of imitation lost centrality beginning in the late 18th and early 19th centuries. In spite of the antimimetic movements in modern literature and art, the conception of the novel as a mimetic mirror of its time and place endures, but new modes of understanding mimesis (e.g., realism, naturalism) have largely replaced classically derived conceptions. In other areas of artistic theory and practice, as Abrams demonstrated, during the late 18th and early 19th centuries—intensifying strands evident in earlier celebrations of Shakespeare and Milton—the artist's creative imagination and self-expression displaced "imitation" as the defining concept in poetry and the fine arts. The term *imitation,* when still used, took on new inflections: William Hazlitt's "Of Poetry in General" (1818) reinterpreted the traditional claim that poetry is "an imitation of nature," with the proviso that the poet's "imagination" and "passions" were the crucial aspects of "nature." Lyric became poetry's defining instance, and literature's links to expressive music rather than mimetic visual arts were emphasized. In the 20th and 21st centuries, formalist notions of the self-reflexive or abstract work of art have in turn challenged the classical emphasis of mimesis. In contemporary discussions of literary and artistic representation, critics may allude to Aristotle, but they generally get their bearings from modern and postmodern explorations of linguistic, artistic, and political modes of representation.

Imitation of predecessors, which from the time of the Renaissance had come into increasing tension with glorifications of originality and imitation of the modern world, also lost centrality with the aggressive cult of originality from the Romantics onward. The imitation of predecessors did not of course disappear, but it took on new oblique or tortured or ironic shapes. The unavowed anxiety of influence that Harold Bloom argues is central to Romantic and post-Romantic poetry; modernist bricolage of fragments and postmodernist pastiche; and the poststructuralist notion, most notably propounded by Julia Kristeva, of inescapable intertextuality, according to which all texts are perforce mosaics of quotations from other texts—these are all very different from classical theories of imitation and emulation.

BIBL.: M. A. Abrams, *The Mirror and the Lamp: Romantic Theory and Critical Tradition* (New York 1953). Thomas M. Greene, *The Light in Troy: Imitation and Discovery in Renaissance Poetry* (New Haven 1982). Stephen Halliwell, *The Aesthetics of Mimesis: Ancient Texts and Modern Problems* (Princeton 2002). Barbara Hathaway, *The Age of Criticism: The Late Renaissance in Italy* (Ithaca 1962). Erwin Panofsky, *Idea: A Concept in Art Theory,* trans. Joseph S. Peake (New York 1968). Bernard Weinberg, *The History of Literary Criticism in the Italian Renaissance,* 2 vols. (Chicago 1961). J.S.

Immortality of the Soul

Classical ideas of the soul's survival after bodily death in relation to accounts of the afterlife in the three Abrahamic religions.

Plato and Aristotle have dominated discussion of the soul's immortality. For Plato the soul, unlike the body, is immortal. Liberated from the body, it retains its conscious activities and can apprehend directly the intelligible realities, that is, the Platonic Ideas, underlying the flux of sensibilia. Aristotle's comments are ambiguous. In *On the Soul* (2.2.413b25–27) he observes that the intellect (*nous*) "seems to be a distinct species of soul," which, unlike the other parts of the soul, "alone admits of being separated, as the eternal from the perishable." How do this and other remarks about a separable intellect fit his insistence that the soul is a unity and that (pace Plato) soul and body are inseparable? The soul is like an impression made on wax (2.1.412b7). The obvious inference is that, just as an impression vanishes when wax melts, so too, the soul perishes with the body. Aristotle's Greek commentators interpreted his remarks variously. Alexander of Aphrodisias' solution proved the most important for post-classical authors. The individual soul derives from (rather than, as Pythagoreans had claimed, is equivalent to) the mixture and proportions of the four elements constituting the body and, as such, is perishable. It has the potential to think but only when illuminated by the agent intellect. The latter, said Alexander, is the intellect that Aristotle (*De anima* 3.5.430a23) called "eternal and immortal." Alexander's agent intellect, however, far from being a power of the soul, is Aristotle's first mover, God.

In Jewish writings, Greek ideas of the soul's immortality first occur unambiguously during the Hellenistic period. References appear in the pseudepigraphal 4 Maccabees (18:23), written in the 1st century BCE, and conspicuously in the apocryphal Wisdom of Solomon, written in the same century or, according to some scholars, ca. 40 CE. The author of the latter, a Jewish Alexandrian familiar with Hellenistic philosophy, particularly Platonism, describes the corruptible body as weighing down the soul (9:15). The souls (*psuchai*) of the righteous have "hope full of immortality" (3:1–4). The wicked believe that righteous souls die "at their departure," that is, with the death of the body; in fact, they find themselves "at peace" (3:3).

The Greek notion of an immortal soul seems to have encouraged Hellenistic Jewish authors to interpret the afterlife, more emphatically than before, as the preservation of the individual after death. The Hebrew Bible had described the spirits in Sheol enduring a bleak, incomplete existence, similar to that experienced by the shades in Hades, and had spoken, in ways variously interpreted, of the resurrection of righteous Israelites, all Israelites, or the righteous collectively. Conversely, Jewish concepts of the afterlife, at least in certain instances, undermined the Greek idea that the soul was intrinsically immortal. God intended man "for incorruption" (Wisdom of Solomon 2:23); he did not endow him with immortality. Wicked souls would suffer the annihilation that they themselves predicted for the righteous (3:10).

In the 1st century CE Philo of Alexandria, writing in Greek, gave philosophical arguments for the soul's immortality. God created man "in his own image" (Genesis 1:26–27). God is not corporeal or mortal; nor, then, is "his image." The phrase refers to man's incorruptible superior soul, the thinking subject, as defined by Greek philosophers, especially Plato. At death, the soul, if perfected intellectually during bodily life, returns to its "source," the world of Platonic Ideas. The body is "a plotter against the soul," "a corpse and always a dead thing" (*Allegorical Interpretation* 3.69–76). Platonic notions of the soul's immortality and yearning to escape bodily incarceration also featured in Gnostic works attributed to the Egyptian philosopher-king Hermes Trismegistus, purportedly a near contemporary of Moses. Written in Egypt between the late 1st and late 3rd century CE, they drew on Jewish and Greek thought, possibly on Philo too, or a tradition common to Hermes and Philo. References of a poetical kind (e.g., Berakhot 60b) to the soul's survival and bodily resurrection also occur in Rabbinic texts of the Talmudic period (2nd to 6th century CE).

The New Testament sometimes distinguishes the inner and outer man as "soul" and "body," respectively. But, notwithstanding later interpretations, notably scholastic, it neither stated nor implied that they are intrinsically antagonistic. Soul and body constitute, as in the Hebrew Bible (Genesis 2:7; Psalm 104:29–30), a divinely created whole. The Christian body is "the temple of the Holy Spirit" (*to hagion pneuma*) (1 Corinthians 6:19), created by God, not a prison impeding the soul from reaching its home, the intelligible realm of truth and beauty. The conflict is instead between "spirit" and "flesh," the power of life and death, struggling for dominion over body and soul. "May your whole spirit (*pneuma*), soul (*psychē*), and body (*sōma*) be kept blameless at the coming of our Lord Jesus Christ" (1 Thessalonians 5:23). This and similar passages, to follow a standard interpretation, declare the revival of the individual—body and soul—through the Holy Spirit. Without the spirit, man remains "flesh" (*sarx*), unregenerated and incapable of attaining "immortality," "incorruptibility," and "eternal life" (1 Corinthians 15:53–54; Romans 2:7) at the Second Coming. Paul recognized that his anthropology was distinctive. The Corinthians whom he chastised for denying "the resurrection of the dead" (1 Corinthians 15:12) probably adhered to views of the soul's disembodied immortality inspired by Philo. Many modern scholars have concluded from this kind of evidence that early Christianity did not draw on Greek or Hellenistic doctrines of the soul's immortality. This view ignores the fact that, even before Christ's ministry, Jewish anthropology and eschatology had become, at least in part, Hellenized. Paul's distinction of soul and spirit was not Jewish. His notion of soul drew on the Greek dichotomy of body and soul, whereas his interpretation of spirit drew on the Jewish idea of *ruach,* which he recognized as a divine gift and power rather than a life principle.

The Church Fathers—Tatian being a rare exception—held that the souls of the good and the evil alike survive bodily death. The soul's immortality, wrote Athanasius of Alexandria (*Against the Heathen* 33), was "in the Church's teaching." The story of Lazarus and the rich man (Luke 16:19–31) shows that the soul survives and receives retribution (Augustine, *On the Soul and Its Origin* 2.4.8). Many Fathers cited arguments derived from Plato or Middle Platonic and Neoplatonic intermediaries. Notable in this respect, among the Latin Fathers, was Augustine in *On the Immortality of the Soul,* written shortly after his conversion, and, among the Greek Fathers, the Alexandrians Origen and Athanasius. The soul is immortal because it is a spontaneous principle of motion, is unlike the body, which is mortal, and deliberates continually on immortal things, even when the body is "as if dead," asleep (Athanasius, *Against the Heathen* 32–33). These interpretations, said the Fathers, conformed with Scripture. Origen interpreted Genesis 1:26 Platonically, in much the same way as Philo. God created man in his own image. Since God is not corporeal and not mortal, neither is man. Therefore man must be an immortal soul. Hellenisms in the Book of Wisdom, Enoch, the Apocalypse of Saint Paul, and other Jewish and Christian apocrypha or pseudepigrapha that the Fathers believed canonical encouraged Platonic interpretations. The Fathers ignored Aristotle's ambivalent comments. Origen mentioned Aristotle's views only to accuse him of treachery for having belittled the doctrine of his master, Plato (*Contra Celsum* 2.12).

Platonic arguments, the Fathers contended, served several purposes. They corroborated scriptural accounts of the afterlife, disproved wayward interpretations of the afterlife proposed by Christians in Arabia and elsewhere, and enticed pagans to accept Christian doctrines. Pagans ridiculed Christian resurrection, exclaimed Origen (*Contra Celsum* 2.16). Yet what were they to make of the myth of Er (*Republic* 10.614B–621)? Comments on the afterlife by Hermes Trismegistus and the Sibyls served the same purpose. Nevertheless, the Fathers were circumspect. Some Platonic arguments were fallacious. Arnobius (*Against the Heathen* 2.24) distrusted, for example, Plato's argument from reminiscence in the *Meno.* The young slave whom Socrates questioned must have already had a good everyday understanding of mathematics. Further, Platonic doctrines (e.g., transmigration) were, the Fathers held, no more than garbled versions of what Pythagoras, Plato, and other Greeks had learned, while in Egypt, of truths revealed to Jewish prophets (Minucius Felix, *Octavius* ch. 34; Origen, *Contra Celsum* 7.28–30). More disconcerting still was ancient philosophers' ignorance of the body's resurrection. Man's fulfillment must accommodate both aspects of his nature, body and soul. Even Platonizing Fathers such as Origen (*Contra Celsum* 5.22) insisted that the body is resurrected, albeit in a spiritualized, ethereal form.

The Fathers' teaching depended on an unstated premise: the soul's survival does not require divine intervention of the same order as that entailed in bodily resurrection. In this sense, with few exceptions, they implicitly agreed that the soul is naturally immortal. Yet its survival is, like all Creation, contingent on God's will. It depends on God, who alone—following the Greek conception of divine attributes—is absolutely immortal. Or, to invert the argument, since nature is the greatest miracle, the soul's survival, though natural, is miraculous. Yet even this quintessentially patristic subordination of Greek philosophy drew partly on Platonism. Plato and Middle Platonists had, as Irenaeus, Justin Martyr, Athanasius, and other Fathers observed, made a similar point. The Platonic Demiurge had created the gods—the planets and Earth—and sustained them, though mortal, by his will (*Timaeus* 41A–B). Immortality in the sense of survival is, anyway, not what Christians desired. Evil souls punished posthumously long to perish. The soul desires immortal "Life," that is, everlasting union with God, who is Life—salvation. Immortality in this sense is not natural.

Greek philosophy also led Islamic theologians and philosophers to interpret the soul (*nafs* or *rūh*) as an intelligible and immortal substance. Al-Ghazālī, writing in the late 11th to early 12th century, made this view acceptable theologically. The Qur'an allegedly implies that the soul survives death: "Allah takes to Himself souls at the time of their death, and those that do not die, in their sleep" (39.42). Comments in the Qur'an and Hadith concerning the soul's condition between death and the day of judgment are, however, enigmatic and variously interpreted. Some claimed, for example, that the soul "slept," others that it remains conscious. Islamic philosophers, citing the Qur'an (e.g., 16.125) to prove that they were authoritative interpreters of revelation, exploited this diversity of interpretation. Qur'anic promises that soul and body would be resurrected encouraged the uneducated to observe Islam. Philosophers, on the other hand, could interpret these passages figuratively in accordance with Greek philosophy to mean that posthumously the soul remains disembodied.

Three Aristotelian ideas proved formative for Islamic thinkers. First, the agent intellect is distinct from the soul. It is a unique, separate, incorruptible intelligence. It is not, however, God, contrary to what Alexander of Aphrodisias had argued. Rather, it is an intelligence akin to the intelligences guiding the celestial spheres. Second, in the act of intellection, the soul identifies with the agent intellect. Actual knowledge is identical to the intelligible object of knowledge. If it were not, then to know something would, contradictorily, be to know something other than that object. Third, the soul's *telos* is contemplation. Adaptations of these three points also featured in pagan Neoplatonic works studied by Islamic authors. Hence Islamic philosophers identified the soul's fulfillment in this and the next life with intellection. During bodily existence, wrote Avicenna, the soul develops its faculty to think. Since objects of thought are incorporeal, this faculty too must be incorporeal and so incorruptible. The faculty of sight, following Aristotle (*De anima* 1.4), is not the organ of sight. An old man whose eyes have become enfeebled would see clearly again if given new eyes. Likewise, the soul does not cease activity with the demise of its organ, the body. At death, those faculties of the soul that require a body to function become inoperative, leaving the soul, with its acquired perfections, imperfections, and individuality, to persist as a thinking substance. Its happiness is commensurate with what it has achieved intellectually through its endeavors while embodied. Al-Fārābī expressed similar views in his surviving works. According to Averroës and others, however, al-Fārābī denied in his lost *Nicomachean Ethics* commentary that the soul is immortal and dismissed all talk about the afterlife as "an old wives' tale." Whatever is generated, said an Aristotelian axiom, is corruptible.

Al-Ghazālī and others condemned these ideas as heretical and philosophically inconsistent. Revelation alone proves the soul's immortality. Averroës' position, though disputed, can be read, at least partly, as a reply to al-Ghazālī. In treatises on reason and revelation he espoused bodily resurrection and retribution for conduct in mortal life. The Qur'an is a true body of revelation, superior to philosophy, but philosophers are better exegetes than theologians. Aristotelian philosophy, for instance, clarifies Qu'ran 39.42, quoted above. The verse states that, with respect to the soul's activity, sleep and death are the same. Since sleep does not entail the soul's annihilation, neither does death. On bodily death the soul becomes inactive, but it continues to exist, a point clarified by Aristotle's analogy between the faculties of sight and thought. This fitted Averroës' interpretation of Aristotle's agent intellect. The agent and material intellect are two aspects of the unique intellect separate from the soul. The soul, via the imagination, memory, and the semirational power of cogitation, thinks by conjoining with this intellect. In so doing, the soul supplies the separate intellect with the objects of thought that it requires for actualization. The soul's posthumous happiness depends on its fulfillment of this task. A corollary is that the unique, separate intellect cannot think—that is, exist—without individual souls actively thinking. The human race collectively ensures that it continues to think and therefore exist.

The Jewish thinker Moses Maimonides, writing in Arabic in the 12th century, drew on Islamic philosophy, especially Avicenna, to prove that the intellectual soul is immortal by nature. When grasping an intelligible object deriving from the agent intellect, the soul, as mentioned above, becomes identical with that object. The objects of thought are either corporeal or incorporeal "forms" (in the Aristotelian sense of "form"). The "forms" of incorporeal things are timeless and imperishable; hence souls apprehending them must be, at least potentially, imperishable. The soul achieves immortality by perfecting itself, that is, by acquiring knowledge of incorporeal forms. Maimonides interpreted Rabbinic comments concerning the "world to come" to refer to the perfected soul. His insistence that the perfected soul survives bodily death led to accusations that he denied bodily resurrection. Aristotelian approaches also prevailed in later medieval Jewish philosophical considerations. Gersonides (Levi ben Gershom), for example, drew on classical ideas through the medium of Islamic philosophy, as Maimonides had done. Unlike Maimonides, however, he knew some of Averroës' Aristotle commentaries, in Hebrew translation, and hence Averroës' quotations from, and considerations of, Aristotle's, Alexander of Aphrodisias', and Themistius' views concerning the soul's immortality. He concluded that the material intellect is, as Alexander had said, a disposition for knowledge inherent in the soul understood as the form of the body. As such it is mortal. By acquiring knowledge of eternal verities in the transcendental agent intellect, however, it can become immortal. This "acquired intellect" is, moreover, individual, in that it is the sum of knowledge that an individual soul accrues in mortal existence. Gersonides disagreed, however, with Alexander on some points, notably his idea that the agent intellect is God. It is, Gersonides wrote, a divine emanation.

In the Latin West, the Church Fathers' views, including their recourse to Platonic doctrines, prevailed well into the 12th century. Alain de Lille invoked Hermes Trismegistus and Plato as authorities for the soul's immortality in a treatise, *On the Catholic Faith* 1.30 (ca. 1185–1200), refuting the Cathars, who, he claimed, believed in transmigration. By the early 13th century, however, Aristotelian interpretations could no longer be ignored. Latin translations of almost the entire Aristotelian corpus, together with some Greek commentaries, and, more or less simultaneously, Latin translations of works written in Arabic by Islamic and Jewish authors (notably Avicenna, Averroës, Avicebron, and Maimonides), made Aristotelian philosophy, in its several Greek and Islamic variations, the most comprehensive body of non-Christian learning available to Latin authors. *On the Immortality of the Soul,* attributed by some scholars to Dominicus Gundissalinus (d. after 1190) and by others to William of Auvergne (d. 1249), marked the turning point. The treatise, the first dedicated to the subject since Augustine's work of the same title, drew on "Aristotle and his followers." Among the latter were Avicenna and Avicebron. The author used, for example, Avicenna's argument that since the soul's distinctive operation of intellection does not depend on the body, the soul is incorruptible. He discounted Plato's proofs because, he declared, they did not corroborate faith in the soul's immortality. Moreover, they would, if true, lead to the conclusion that all souls, animal and vegetal alike, were immortal. The author was thinking, presumably, of Plato's argument (originally Alcmaeon of Croton's), recorded by Cicero in his *Somnium Scipionis* (27–28) and Macrobius's commentary on Cicero's work (2.13), that since the soul is a principle that moves itself continuously, it is immortal. He was unaware, it seems, of his own debt to Platonism. An instance is an argument inspired by Avicenna's explanation that prophecy and ecstasy are the embodied soul's most exalted and powerful intellectual conditions. They occur, the author continues, when the body's influence is at its most tenuous. So, when the body's influence completely disappears, at death, the soul flourishes completely.

The soul's immortality thereafter became one of the most debated subjects in Scholastic theology and philosophy. Was it true that the soul, since it is a continuously self-moving principle, must be immortal? William of Auvergne argued that it was; Alexander of Hales concurred with the author of *On the Immortality of the Soul* that it was not. Was the entire soul immortal or just the intellect? Platonic concepts and arguments continued to be cited—Augustine had ensured as much. But it was Aristotle's axiom that the soul was the body's form that provided the point of departure. It appeared admirably suited to Christian anthropology. Before the Fall Adam and Eve had bodies that, through God's agency, did not suffer corruption. After the Fall their bodies and those of their progeny decayed and died. At the resurrection God will, miraculously, restore them to the embodied condition that he had originally envisaged. Man is, as Aristotle said, a body and a soul. He is not a soul, observed Thomas Aquinas, not the "ego," a "thinking self" using, as Plato had suggested, the body like an instrument.

Aristotle's axiom, however, presented a problem. If the soul is the form of the body, it must perish with the body. This conclusion would contradict revelation (for instance, the story of Lazarus and the rich man) and the unanimous opinion of Christian theologians from the Church Fathers onward. It would also disprove the existence of Purgatory, the efficacy of intercessionary prayers to the Virgin Mary and the saints, and the validity of indulgences and other Christian beliefs and practices. And it was, according to Thomas Aquinas and Dominican theologians generally, false philosophically. "The form of Man is his rational soul, which is in itself immortal" (Thomas, *Summa theologiae,* 2a.2ae.164.1, ad 1m). If the soul is intrinsically (i.e., by nature) immortal, then this can be demonstrated by philosophy. Aristotle had himself taught that it is. Further, revelation brings out the full significance of this philosophical truth. The soul's distinctive operation is thought, and thought is incorporeal. Given that a distinct operation implies a distinct substance, the soul is incorporeal and incorruptible. When the body dies, the soul survives as a thinking substance, albeit in an unnatural condition, since it can no longer abstract intelligible objects from sense data. Its essence, nevertheless, remains identical, just as, analogously, the essence of a light object remains identical whether or not it is in its natural place, that is, the air or fire sphere. True, in this unnatural condition, it can grasp only purely abstract truths, in the manner of angels, and so cannot understand particulars as it did while embodied. But this unnatural state of affairs will cease with the resurrection. Nothing in nature, as Aristotle had taught, stays forever in an unnatural condition.

Not all theologians were so convinced of philosophy's merits. John Duns Scotus, arguing against Thomas, held that philosophy provides probable but not conclusive reasons for the soul's immortality. William of Ockham, a Franciscan like Duns Scotus, was more forthright. Neither argument nor experience proved the soul immortal. The soul's immortality was an object of faith. What Aristotle had thought, both Duns Scotus and Ockham agreed, was unclear. Theologians adopting these and similar views were, perhaps, taking a controversial stance, but not a heretical one. More delicate, however, was the position of philosophy lecturers at universities. Philosophers in arts faculties were not qualified theologians and, though they often introduced into their lectures ideas based on Scripture and other sources of revelation, they did not pretend to teach theology. This was the prerogative of theologians, whose first principles were the objects of faith, ultimately, the articles of the Creeds. A philosophy lecturer's main task was, instead, to explain, say, Aristotle's comments concerning the soul's immortality and to elaborate on them with the help of his ancient Greek and Arabic commentators.

Philosophical discussion in this vein sometimes raised suspicions. Were philosophers sincere when they claimed to be doing no more than presenting a philosophical argument? Was it wise to publicize ideas that might mislead students? Ecclesiastical authorities sometimes responded by forbidding philosophers from teaching that the soul was mortal or that the intellect was separate from the soul and unique. In 1277 the bishop of Paris, Étienne Tempier, proscribed 219 theological and philosophical propositions discussed by scholars of the university's arts faculty, over which he had jurisdiction. Among several banned propositions concerning the soul's immortality were ones claiming that (1) a philosopher should not accept the doctrine of the resurrection since it could not be analyzed rationally; (2) the form of man—that is, his intellectual soul—"was educed from the potentiality of matter"; and (3) the soul corrupted with the corruption of the body's harmony. Ecclesiastical proscription of this kind proved effective in northern universities such as Paris and Oxford, with their powerful theology faculties. But Italian university philosophers, institutionally attuned to natural philosophical rather than theological concerns, continued to venture opinions about the soul that disconcerted ecclesiastical authorities. In 1489 Pietro Barozzi, bishop of Padua and chancellor of the university there, forbade public disputations (but not university lectures) on the Averroist doctrine that the intellect is separate and unique; the following year he accused Nicoletto Vernia, the leading philosopher at the university, of popularizing the doctrine throughout Italy. In 1492 Vernia obligingly wrote a treatise refuting Averroës' doctrine, in which he claimed that philosophy, understood as a consensus of arguments proposed by Greek, Roman, Arabic, and scholastic philosophers, could prove the individual soul immortal. Later in life he claimed, possibly disingenuously, that he had proposed the Averroist doctrine only in academic disputation, not as his personal view.

Disillusioned by scholastic disputes and indiscretions, some 15th-century thinkers turned to Platonism. Plato, after all, had unambiguously taught that the soul is separate from the body and incorruptible. Sometime between October 1404 and March 1405, Leonardo Bruni completed a translation of Plato's *Phaedo* or, as he called Plato's work, *On the Immortality of the Soul,* dedicating it to the recently elected Pope Innocent VII. When people read that the wisest of pagan philosophers held the same views about the soul's immortality as Christian theologians, they would be fortified in the true faith. Two sources of authority supported this revival of Platonic ideas of the soul's immortality: Byzantine thinkers, notably Pletho and Bessarion, who had came to Italy as a result of the rapprochement between the Eastern and Western Churches; and the Church Fathers, notably Augustine and Origen. Marsilio Ficino, who received patronage, first from Cosimo and then from Lorenzo de' Medici, gave the fullest Renaissance Platonic account of the soul's immortality. His *Platonic Theology concerning the Immortality of the Soul* (1474) was driven chiefly by his desire to refute Alexander of Aphrodisias' and Averroës' doctrines of the soul. That Plato himself had, as Aristotle's supporters pointed out, taught transmigration was not an insuperable objection. Ficino found one of his several solutions in Augustine. Plato's comments on transmigration illustrate allegorically what happens in this life to those who, forsaking reason, abase themselves to the level of brute animals. Like Origen, and possibly influenced by him, Ficino proposed that the glorified resurrected body is made of a lightlike ether or *spiritus* (*Platonic Theology* 18.9), an idea rejected by Augustine and by Ficino's most important Scholastic source, Thomas Aquinas.

Ficino's Platonic interpretation may well have contributed to the Church's response to the Averroist and Alexandrian interpretations circulating in Italian universities. On 19 December 1513, the Fifth Lateran Council, presided over by Pope Leo X, Lorenzo de' Medici's son and a former pupil of Ficino's disciple Francesco da Diacceto, promulgated the bull *Apostolici regiminis.* The bull, it is often claimed, declared that the soul is immortal and that, contrary to what many philosophers claimed, philosophy can prove this. In its dogmatic statement, however, the bull did no more than "define" and "resolve" that all philosophical doctrines contradicting the truth of faith are false and that anyone proposing them as true commits heresy. To prove the soul immortal, the bull quoted Matthew 10:28 and John 12:25 and referred, among other scriptural proofs, to Christ's assurances of reward and punishment in the afterlife. There are not two standards of truth: "truth cannot in any way contradict truth." Examples of false philosophical propositions were those stating that the intellectual soul is mortal, that the intellectual soul is common to all mankind, and that the world is eternal. When lecturing at universities and elsewhere, philosophers were permitted to discuss propositions of this kind provided that they explain to their audiences why they contradict revealed truth and, to the best of their ability, refute them philosophically. The bull, in short, did no more than restate, in the light of contemporary debates, the position, held by the Church Fathers and generations of Christian theologians, that philosophy is subordinate to revelation.

Misinterpretation of *Apostolici regiminis* has a long history. In 1516 Pietro Pomponazzi, who taught philosophy at Bologna University, published *On the Immortality of the Soul.* Philosophically speaking, the intellectual soul is mortal. Its distinctive operation of intellection invariably depends, contrary to what Thomas Aquinas and many others claimed, on sense data. This operation ceases, as Alexander of Aphrodisias had said, at bodily death, and hence the soul as a whole expires. Pomponazzi rehearsed and rejected many other traditional arguments for the soul's immortality. It was said, for instance, that if the soul is mortal and therefore not rewarded or punished posthumously, people have no incentive to act virtuously in this life. Pomponazzi disagreed. People who act virtuously only out of self-interest are less virtuous than those, such as some pagan philosophers, who do so because they hold that virtue is its own reward. In the final chapter Pomponazzi stated his position—whether sincerely or not is contested. First, philosophy cannot prove or disprove immortality. Second, revelation and Scripture alone prove the soul is immortal. The soul's immortality is "an article of faith," as indicated in the Apostles' and Athanasian Creeds. Nor was his interpretation of Aristotle's teaching theologically exceptionable. He reached the same conclusion as Cardinal Cajetan, who had helped formulate *Apostolici regiminis.* Cajetan, good Dominican and Thomist though he was, had concluded, contradicting Thomas Aquinas, that Aristotle had taught that the soul is mortal.

The treatise nevertheless provoked outrage in some quarters. Treatises written in reply attacked it for stating that the soul is mortal. The Venetian Senate banned the book's sale. Friars denounced it and its author from the pulpit as heretical. The Dominican theologian Bartolomeo della Spina, Pomponazzi's most determined and perceptive critic, declared that Pomponazzi had flouted the Lateran bull's decree. Leo X initially warned Pomponazzi that if he did not retract, he would instigate proceedings against him. A more considered line of response prevailed. Cardinal Pietro Bembo, secretary to Leo X and a former student of Pomponazzi, assured the pope that *On the Immortality of the Soul* was not heretical and quashed moves to proceed against Pomponazzi. When Pomponazzi replied to his critics in 1518 and 1519, he restated his original position. In 1519 his contract to teach at Bologna University, the most important university of the Papal States, was renewed. Nor was *On the Immortality of the Soul* ever placed on the *Index of Forbidden Books.* It remained, nonetheless, notorious well into the next century, detractors and admirers alike interpreting it as a declaration of the soul's materiality and mortality.

The decisive factor, however, in the long-standing misinterpretation of the papal bull was Luther. On several occasions, Luther mentioned contemptuously that the Council Fathers had decreed the soul immortal. The pope's entourage, he wrote in his *Address to the Christian Nobility of the German Nation* (1520), had become so obsessed with courtly extravagance that the Fifth Lateran Council had had to remind them, "among many other childishly trivial matters," that man's soul is immortal and that priests must pray once a month. How could these men be taken seriously when they had only now decided that the soul was immortal? Luther's interpretation inspired similar comments among other Protestants and established the idea, repeated by many theologians thereafter, that Roman Catholic theology sought to combine two incompatible ideas of the afterlife, the Christian belief in bodily resurrection and the Greek doctrine of the soul's innate immortality. In his controversy with Thomas More, who supported the Roman Catholic view, William Tyndale observed that "heathen philosophers"—that is, ancient Greek and Roman philosophers—denied bodily resurrection and claimed that "souls did ever live." The pope, perverting the sense of Scripture, "joins the spiritual doctrine of Christ and the fleshly doctrine of philosophers together, things so contrary that they cannot agree" (*An Answer unto Sir Thomas More's Dialogue,* bk. 4).

The soul, for Luther, was immortal, but philosophers could not prove this. Aristotle shrewdly had not stated his opinion. Plato had merely reported the views of others, an allusion presumably to Socrates in the *Phaedo.* Not even Augustine's arguments were conclusive. Scripture was the only proof. And Scripture showed, Luther said in sermons and other writings from 1522 onward, that the soul survived asleep until the resurrection. Death was no more than being laid, like a child, in a cradle to sleep. Luther's interpretation was inspired by his revulsion at the Roman Catholic Church's exploitation of the fear of death, evident above all in practices connected with the fiction of Purgatory, such as the invocation of saints and prayers and indulgences for the dead. One scriptural proof was Ecclesiastes 9:10: "for there is no work, nor device, nor knowledge, nor wisdom, in the grave." Few mainstream Reformers agreed with Luther. Heinrich Bullinger, a follower of Ulrich Zwingli, and John Calvin in his first theological treatise, the *Psychopannychia* (ca. 1534), both rejected the doctrine of soul-sleep.

New theological and philosophical ideas ensured that the immortality of the soul remained a significant issue in the following centuries. In the *Meditations* or, to follow the full title of the first edition (1641), *Meditations concerning First Philosophy, in Which Is Proved the Existence of God and the Immortality of the Soul,* René Descartes explained that the soul, or rather mind, is a person's identity or ego, distinct from corruptible matter and therefore incorruptible. After death, however, it remains without memory, a conclusion that irritated G. W. F. Leibniz because it undermined the ethical sanctions of reward and retribution in the afterlife. John Locke, influenced possibly by the German Socinian Ernst Soner, believed in psychopannychism. Thomas Hobbes professed thnetopsychism (*Leviathan,* chs. 38, 44), if inconsistently. Philosophy—his materialist philosophy—proved that the soul is mortal, but Scripture proves that body and soul will be resurrected. The notion that the soul is conscious after death is the "window" through which passed Purgatory, ghosts, indulgences, exorcism, and other superstitions (ch. 44). Hobbes's profession of faith, like those of Maimonides and Pomponazzi, provoked accusations of insincerity from contemporaries and continues to do so to this day. No doubts were or have been raised about the piety of John Milton, whose thnetopsychism was based solely on scriptural references. David Hume's brief essay on the subject unpicked many traditional philosophical arguments for the soul's immortality. If, as souls, we do not die, why does nature, which makes nothing in vain, fill us with horror of death?

Speculation on the soul's immortality remained equally vibrant in Jewish and Islamic thought. Debates within the Jewish community of Amsterdam in the 1630s led rabbis and laymen to write on the subject. Rabbi Menasseh ben Israel directed his *On the Resurrection of the Dead,* published in 1636 in both Latin and Spanish, against "Sadducees" and other "atheists" who denied the resurrection of the body and soul. Menasseh drew mainly on Jewish, classical, and Christian sources. At one point he cast his net even wider. Not only did Scripture and the prophets, as well as Greek and Roman philosophers and poets, assert the immortality of the soul, but also, as various 16th- and 17th-century accounts had confirmed, did the Chinese, Peruvians, Mexicans, and other newly discovered peoples. The use of this criterion—the *consensus gentium*—to prove the soul immortal derived, ultimately, from Cicero (*Tusculan Disputations* 1.36). In his first Hebrew work, *The Breath of Life* (1651), or, according to its additional Latin title, *On the Immortality of the Soul,* Menasseh reverted to a familiar line of Jewish thinking. The soul is immortal—Alexander of Aphrodisias' materialistic doctrine of the soul was wrong—and transmigrated. This could be proved by natural reason and by Scripture. It was also the doctrine of the Kabbalah. Objections to transmigration proposed by Aristotelians, Tertullian, and others were unfounded. Abraham had first introduced the doctrine. From him it had spread to India and eventually to Greece via Pythagoras, who had adopted the Jewish religion. The excommunication of Menasseh's former pupil Baruch Spinoza from the Amsterdam community in 1656 may have been connected to these debates and writings. The pantheistic philosophy of his published works excluded personal immortality. Post-medieval Islamic discussions, for instance those of the 17th-century Persian thinker Mulla Sadrā, were less open to classical, Jewish, and Christian influence—or so the few studies to date seem to suggest.

The debate continued but its connection with the classical tradition became increasingly tenuous. Plato, Aristotle, and their ancient commentators were inspiring thinkers, no doubt, but they were no longer authorities. The demise of Aristotelian philosophy during the 17th century eliminated the contribution of the Peripatetic tradition to innovative philosophical debate about the soul's immortality, at least among Christian and Jewish thinkers. Platonic notions, it is true, proved more resilient. In *The Immortality of the Soul* (1659) the Cambridge Platonist Henry More drew on Platonism, adapting it to new currents of thought, including Cartesianism. Moses Mendelssohn gave a final Platonic flourish in his popular *Phaedon* (1767), subtitled *On the Immortality of the Soul,* modeled, as its title suggests, in content and style on Plato's work of the same title. But with Immanuel Kant, a contemporary of Mendelssohn, although the resonances are Platonic, the arguments are not. The soul cannot be proved immortal theoretically because it is impossible to determine the constitution of the self theoretically and as an object of pure reason. But it must be assumed to be immortal and have the possibility of continuing to perfect itself morally on the grounds of pure practical reason. Without this assumption, it is impossible to pursue the ends imposed by morality. A corollary, stated in his *Religion within the Boundaries of Mere Reason* (1793), is that physical resurrection is not required for personal immortality. In "Theism," the third of his *Three Essays on Religion,* published posthumously in 1874, John Stuart Mill denied that either the soul's immortality or mortality can be proved. He dismissed the many philosophical theories that had been proposed over the ages: "those in the *Phaedon* of Plato are an example; but they are for the most part such as have no adherents, and need not be seriously refuted, now."

BIBL.: Norman T. Burns, *Christian Mortalism from Tyndale to Milton* (Cambridge, Mass., 1972). Eric A. Constant, "A Reinterpretation of the Fifth Lateran Council Decree *Apostolici regiminis* (1513)," *Sixteenth Century Journal* 33 (2002) 353–379. Herbert A. Davidson, *Alfarabi, Avicenna, and Averroes on Intellect: Their Cosmologies, Theories of the Active Intellect, and Theories of Human Intellect* (Oxford 1992). Jill Kraye, "The Immortality of the Soul in the Renaissance: Between Natural Philosophy and Theology," *Signatures* 1 (2000) 1–24. Steven Nadler, *Spinoza's Heresy: Immortality and the Jewish Mind* (Oxford 2001). Émile Puech, *La croyance des Esséniens en la vie future,* 2 vols. (Paris 1993). Krister Stendahl, ed., *Immortality and Resurrection: Four Essays by Oscar Cullmann, Harry A. Wolfson, Werner Jaeger, and Henry J. Cadbury* (New York 1965).

D.K..

India

In essence, the expedition of Alexander the Great in 326 BCE exceeded any other source of Greek and Roman knowledge about India. The earliest extensive accounts of

India were written by the historians, geographers, and scientists he commissioned—a phenomenon matched in Napoleon's Egyptian campaign in 1798, some 21 centuries later. This conventional wisdom carries much truth but needs qualification on two counts. First, the Achaemenid empire and particularly its court had been a source of Greek Indography long before Alexander. This much is clear not only from Scylax of Caryanda, Hecataeus, and Ctesias of Cnidos, all of whose works survive only in fragments, but also in Herodotus' *Histories* (3.98–106). For these writers India was a resource-rich satrapy of the Achaemenid emperor (termed the King of Kings), and with them there is already a hint of the marvels that would dominate later, fuller accounts of India. Many Greeks were active in the Achaemenid world. Second, accounts of Alexander's expedition survive most fully in Roman versions, mostly of the early imperial period, and inevitably intersect with the concerns of later writers conscious of Rome's ascendancy. On both these counts, Graeco-Roman Indography is thus a matter of reception from the start.

The most plentiful sources on India are from the Roman era (1st cent. BCE–1st cent. CE): in Greek, Diodorus Siculus and Strabo's *Geography;* in Latin, Pliny's *Natural History.* In these compendious works, much authority hinges on the figure of Megasthenes (later 4th cent. BCE), the Seleucid ambassador at Chandragupta Maurya's court in Pataliputra (Palibothra), whose *Indika* is known via the later works. Indeed, there is substantial overlap in the accounts from the Roman era. Much of Megasthenes' information rehearses the standard questionnaire of classical ethnography, addressing topics such as gender and other social divisions, domestic arrangements, and topography. But a major feature is also the kind of marvel that is typical in Hellenistic literature and would live long in Western literature and visual arts. The "shade-footed," "one-eyed," "backward-footed" (*antipodes*) and others in the Nuremberg Chronicle of 1493 are direct descendants of Hellenistic marvel-literature, as is the content of medieval *mappae mundi.* In Pliny and Strabo, marvels are frequently subjected to critique and discussion regarding the relative reliability of Hellenistic sources.

Concurrent with the scholarly enterprises of Strabo and Pliny there was commerce between the Mediterranean and the Indian subcontinent, involving a combination of land and sea routes. The anonymous *Periplus of the Erythraean Sea* (ca. 40–70 CE), written in artless *koinē* Greek, leads readers through ports from the Egyptian Red Sea coast and thence, with the southwest monsoon, past the Arabian Peninsula to the west coast of India. Such information, exchanged between humble persons making such journeys, can be glimpsed in Strabo and Pliny; but they explicitly relegate this kind of autopsy (eyewitness account) below the authority of texts. As a result, Roman ideas about India are largely those of Alexander's expedition and the generation immediately following. The addition of new knowledge, including information on the Bay of Bengal (described in Claudius Ptolemy's *Geography,* 2nd cent. CE) makes no impression on the literary idea of India.

In the medieval West, Pliny's geographical information was transmitted not only through excerpts and epitomes but also through intervening texts by authors such as Solinus, Orosius, and Isidore. The last two, particularly, would become sources of information for *mappae mundi,* medieval maps of the world. One late antique inflection of India, linked with the *Alexander Romance,* is the subcontinent's geographical proximity to possible sites of Eden, the biblical earthly paradise, an attribute that would leave a mark on medieval geographies such as the Hereford Mappa Mundi. Alexander's eastward expedition sometimes seemed like a pilgrimage. India thus remained an "oneiric horizon" (LeGoff 1980), teetering on the edge of geographic knowledge, and journeys such as Marco Polo's in the later 13th century did little to change that status.

The *Christian Topography* of Cosmas Indicopleustes (fl. 550) substantiated the classical tradition in different ways. Surviving in just three manuscripts (9th–11th cents.), this text conceives of Earth in the shape of the tabernacle, in keeping with a literal interpretation of Genesis. The author's earlier experience as a trader accounts, however, for some apparently eyewitness knowledge of Sri Lanka, with particular attention to its fauna. The manuscripts provide some telling miniatures that appear to point back to the original text and are qualitatively different from the (Western) tradition of marvels. It is hard to assign Cosmas to any place in the classical tradition: he does cite some polytheist works (the shadowy Ephorus) alongside the Scriptures, but this eccentric work has remained on the edges of tradition.

Among medieval accounts the fantastic tales of John Mandeville (14th cent.) were more widely read than the sober one of Marco Polo, which was based on autopsy. Mandeville's account, closer to ancient texts than Polo's, had many features in common with the Romance tradition and also with the *Letter of Prester John* (12th cent.), invented during the Crusades but purportedly the work of a Christian king in a marvelous, remote land, which would for some five centuries serve as a pretext for colonial enterprises. Some of these texts also mention the Christian legend of Thomas, the apostle who according to Syrian tradition (late 2nd cent. CE) had preached in India and was martyred there.

With the voyages of Columbus and Vespucci to the New World, a new "India" entered European consciousness. The error stemmed from Ptolemy's underestimation of the Earth's circumference, such that the (eastern) Indies mistakenly seemed accessible via a transatlantic voyage. This misperception was compounded by the fact that early accounts of the Americas deployed ancient geographic discourse about India, certainly drawing on Plinian language. Terms still in common use today—for example, West Indies and Indians (for indigenous North Americans)—reflect the long-term influence of this misunderstanding.

Meanwhile, Vasco da Gama became the first European of the modern period to reach India by sea, arriving at Calicut (Kozhikode) in 1498—a Portuguese overseas enterprise that had been spearheaded by Prince Henry the Navigator. Like Bartholomew Dias's rounding of the Cape in 1488, da Gama's voyage necessitated a rethinking of Ptolemy's world map, as it was now empirically proven that the Indian Ocean was not an inland sea.

Orientalist scholarly enterprises reached a landmark with Christian Lassen's *Ancient Sources on India* (*Indische Alterthumskunde,* 1858–1874). This massive attempt to measure Graeco-Roman sources against South Asian ones would lay the foundations for the historical study of ancient India. The Raj brought to India a number of British officers and functionaries steeped in Greek and Latin texts, many educated at Balliol College, Oxford. Translations of Graeco-Latin Indography made by John Watson McCrindle, a sometime Calcutta school principal, appeared in the 1880s and though outdated are still in print.

In all, peninsular India has played a small part in the classical tradition, in large measure because of the low social status of ancient traders. By contrast, Alexander's overland route has been a topic of continued interest, reaching even into contemporary Hindi and American cinema. In another way, ancient Indography has appealed to more antiquarian tastes: from Lassen to the present day, moderns have not tired of trying to identify Herodotus' gold-digging ants (3.102) with local fauna.

BIBL.: A. Dihle, "The Conception of India in Hellenistic and Roman Literature," *Proceedings of the Cambridge Philological Society* 190, n.s. 10 (1964) 15–23, repr. in his *Antike und Orient. Gesammelte Aufsätze,* ed. V. Pöschl and H. Petersmann (Heidelberg 1984). A. T. Grafton, *New Worlds, Ancient Texts: The Power of Tradition and the Shock of Discovery* (Cambridge, Mass., 1992). K. Karttunen, *India and the Hellenistic World* (Helsinki 1997). J. LeGoff, "The Medieval West and the Indian Ocean: An Oneiric Horizon," in his *Time, Work, and Culture in the Middle Ages,* trans. A. Goldhammer (Chicago 1980). G. R. Parker, *The Making of Roman India* (New York 2008).

G.PR.

Inscriptions, Greek and Latin

In a public oration held in San Giovanni in Laterano in May 1347, the self-proclaimed tribune of the Roman people Cola di Rienzo tried to persuade his audience to struggle to regain their heritage of pristine glory and power. He supported this claim by reading aloud and commenting on an inscription he himself had found and translated a few days before, the famous *lex de imperio Vespasiani* (1st cent. CE), which determined the authority and prerogatives delegated by the Romans to their emperor.

Cola could make political use of an ancient inscription because of his deep acquaintance with ancient monuments (69 epigraphs are collected in his *Descriptio Urbis Romae,* ca. 1344–1347), but this was indeed a rare occurrence in his time. The Latin Middle Ages had lost almost every contact with Roman epigraphs: leaving aside isolated *syllogae* (collections) such as the Codex Einsidlensis 236 (mid-9th cent.) and information scattered in the *Mirabilia Urbis Romae* (12th cent.), we gather the impression that ancient inscriptions had become unintelligible, mainly because of their script and abbreviations. In the 14th century, exceptions to this rule are Boccaccio's awkward transcripts of a couple of Greek and Latin inscriptions, and the translation of a Greek epigraph on the temple of the Dioskouroi (now San Paolo Maggiore) in Naples by the learned doctor Nicholas of Reggio. In the Byzantine world, after Cosmas Indicopleustes' accurate copy and analysis of two very old Greek inscriptions from Ethiopia (*Topographia Christiana* 2.54–65, ca. 520 CE), even men of letters paid hardly any attention to the written monuments of their glorious predecessors. An exception is the learned archbishop Arethas of Caesarea (10th cent.), in whose scholia to Pausanias' *Periēgēsis* we find a reference to a classical inscription he had seen in Patras years before.

The man who dramatically changed this state of affairs was an Italian merchant from Ancona named Ciriaco de' Pizzicolli (1391–ca. 1453; known as Cyriac of Ancona): he traveled in Italy and Africa and in the territories of the (former) Byzantine empire, copying in his notebooks all sorts of inscriptions he found on his way. We owe to Ciriaco a number of transcriptions of epigraphs that have now been lost; but what is more important is that his activity excited among Italian Humanists a huge interest for this hitherto almost entirely neglected aspect of the classical heritage. The resulting enthusiasm for classical inscriptions both as historical documents and as works of art affected architecture, painting, book production, and other fields of endeavor; it explains, for instance, the growing interest in epigraphs as architectural elements (Leon Battista Alberti), the appearance of classical inscriptions in paintings and frescoes (such as Mantegna's frescoes in Padua, destroyed during World War II), and the use of capital letters by Janus Lascaris in the first edition (Florence 1494) of the Planudean Anthology, the widest collection of Greek epigrams then known. (Epigrams themselves, as the noun itself reveals, were originally written on stone.) It is pleasant to recall in this context that in September 1464 Mantegna, together with other outstanding scholars such as Giovanni Marcanova and Felice Feliciano, embarked on a two-day excursion to Lake Garda in search of inscriptions.

The enthusiasm also led to less desirable consequences: along with the growing number of *syllogae* recording lapidary (stone) inscriptions, there developed forgeries as well. Among the most remarkable were those of Annius of Viterbo, who used fake epigraphs to demonstrate the deep antiquity of his hometown and to shed light on the history of the Lombard kingdom in Italy; and of the famous architect Pirro Ligorio, an indefatigable if sometimes dishonest compiler of 30 manuscript volumes titled *Antichità,* still preserved in Italian libraries.

Epigraphy soon became an international phenomenon:

symptoms of this are the flourishing editorial activity in books about inscriptions (by Konrad Peutinger, Antonio Agustín, and Nicolas de Peiresc, among others) and of epigraphical collections of ever growing size, most notably a compilation of more than 4,000 items by Justus Lipsius and Martin Smet (1588) and the enormous compendium of more than 12,000 inspired by Joseph Scaliger and edited by Janus Gruter as *Inscriptiones antiquae totius orbis Romani in corpus absolutissimum redactae* (Heidelberg 1603). A few sensational discoveries also date from this period, notably the famous bronze tablets displaying the *Res gestae divi Augusti* (*Deeds of the Divine* [*Emperor*] *Augustus*) found in Ankara in 1555 by the Flemish ambassador Augier Ghislain de Busbecq, and the Marmor Parium or Parian Marble (from the island of Paros, although the first fragment was found in Smyrna in 1627), a stele whose inscription would change the study of ancient Greek chronology.

By the middle of the 17th century antiquarians preferred to turn to "easier" ancient objects such as strange artifacts and different sorts of curiosities. Especially after Winckelmann's revolutionary publications in the mid-18th century, it was classical archaeology that gained a more prominent position in the consciousness of European culture. Epigraphy, having lost its initial impetus, slowly grew into a more and more specialized discipline. Thus, when they visited the beautiful museum set up in Verona by the ambitious and farsighted antiquarian Scipione Maffei (1675–1755), who also had written the important manual *Ars critica lapidaria* (1765), neither Winckelmann himself (in 1768) nor Goethe (in 1786) paid any special attention to the inscriptions but rather concentrated on ancient stelae and reliefs. Michel Fourmont's spectacular forgeries (1729–1730) were a byproduct of French academic interests rather than a matter of art and artists, as had been the case with Ligorio some two centuries before. And when Lord Nelson managed to seize the Rosetta Stone from the hands of the French army after the battle of Aboukir, the Greek section of the inscription was for some while appreciated merely as the key to the deciphering of another alphabet, namely Egyptian hieroglyphs.

Partial collections and integrations to Gruter's corpus of 1603 continued to be published for decades, but it was only in the course of the 19th century that scholars felt that the time was ripe to establish epigraphy as a modern science in its own right. This was made possible by the publication of the integral corpora of ancient Greek and Latin inscriptions. Both projects were undertaken in Berlin. The Greek collection was begun under the auspices of the classicist August Böckh, whose interest in inscriptions had originally been aroused by his desire to write a comprehensive essay on Greek civilization called *Hellen*. The resulting *Corpus inscriptionum Graecarum* of 1828–1859 was eventually replaced by *Inscriptiones Graecae*, in print since 1873 with 15 volumes completed as of this writing. It should be emphasized here that Böckh's innovative approach to ancient epigraphy, as an autonomous discipline whose scope was broader and whose tools were different from what had hitherto been customary for classical philology on literary texts, initially enjoyed a far from warm reception, as the fierce controversies between Böckh and Gottfried Hermann abundantly show.

The *Corpus inscriptionum Latinarum*, begun in 1863 and with 17 volumes published thus far, originated as an enormously ambitious project of the historian Theodor Mommsen, prompted and inspired by the Italian scholar Bartolomeo Borghesi, an eccentric man who in a sense mediated to Mommsen the old Italian antiquarian tradition. (Besides writing important essays on Latin epigraphy, Borghesi had also ruled for 39 years the independent state of San Marino.)

Apart from these and other scientific editions, directly or indirectly Greek and Latin inscriptions also continued to influence and inspire artists and architects around the world, as can be verified by the ideological evolution of public epigraphs over the centuries from Sixtus V to the Bauhaus, by the inscriptions on many tombstones in our graveyards, and by the mottoes engraved on 19th- and 20th-century public and private buildings in Europe and the United States. It comes as no surprise, then, that political use of inscriptions was attempted by the Italian Fascist regime, both through imitating the magniloquent sans-serif lettering of Roman public epigraphs and by appropriating such significant ancient epigraphical monuments as the bronze *Res gestae divi Augusti*, which was reproduced in its entirety at the Mostra Augustea (Augustan Exhibition) organized in Rome by Mussolini in 1937 and later became a substantial part of the new arrangement of the square designed to host the monumental stone Ara Pacis Augustae (Altar of the Peace of Augustus), which had been reconstructed with many of its original ancient components.

This political use of ancient inscriptions, 600 years after Cola di Rienzo, brings us back to where we began: it was perhaps no coincidence that in 1912 the poet Gabriele d'Annunzio, later one of the leading intellectuals of early Fascism, had written an enthusiastic biography of Cola. Almost simultaneously (1914), in a totally different cultural climate, Claude Debussy's *Six épigraphes antiques* (piano, four hands) represented one of the last imperishable monuments of the Symbolistic taste for the ancient world.

BIBL.: I. Calabi Limentani, *Epigrafia latina* (Milan 1974) 39–124. A. Cooley, ed., *The Afterlife of Inscriptions* (London 2000). W. Larfeld, *Handbuch der griechischen Epigraphik*, vol. 1 (Leipzig 1907) 16–171. S. Morison, *Politics and Script* (Oxford 1972). W. Stenhouse, *Reading Inscriptions and Writing Ancient History* (London 2005). R. Weiss, *The Renaissance Discovery of Classical Antiquity*, 2nd ed. (Oxford 1988) esp. 1–58, 131–166.

F.M.P.

Interpretatio Christiana

Latin, meaning "Christian interpretation." The term has the advantage, over its English equivalent, of designating a broader field of hermeneutic activity, which ranges from exposition to translation. It seems to have been coined early in the 20th century and has been used widely since (Hagendahl 1967, 440).

In the narrow sense, Christian *interpretatio* of the Graeco-Roman tradition refers to its appropriation by interpretation, or simply by citation, of literary and philosophical texts, a process as old as Christianity itself (Acts 17:28) and one proclaimed as a right and a priority by Justin Martyr: "Whatever things have been said rightly among all men are the property of us, the Christians" (*Apologia* 2.13).

Justin's shrill, divisive, and confrontational tone is typical of the 2nd-century apologists, but that tone was soon replaced by a more thoughtful and hermeneutically sophisticated discourse, perhaps the most impressive example of which is to be found in Basil the Great's homily in the form of a letter to his siblings' children, bearing the traditional title "To the Young, How they might profit from polytheist literature," or *Ad adulescentes.* Basil works toward his goal by a combination of selection of texts and manipulation of the young readers' expectations, predisposing them to look for messages of value for Christian education while sidelining and largely ignoring the polytheist trappings of the texts. In Basil's essay (in all probability written in response to Julian the Apostate's ineffectual prohibition, in 362, of the teaching of polytheist texts by Christians), we see the process of appropriation already at an advanced stage, the polytheism of the literary texts in question apparently no longer a threat.

The process was far from uniform over time and space, however, and in Augustine (who was no more than a child when Basil wrote) we find abundant evidence that in early Latin Christianity the polytheist texts were tamed and appropriated less easily, and over a greater span of time. There was in fact little alternative to such appropriation, because the models of eloquence that had formed the core of Graeco-Roman education could not be replaced. Rather, those aspects of the ancient literature offensive to Christians had to be neutralized, and the polytheism of the texts stripped of theological authority and translated to the realm of the aesthetic. This process was long and complex and not complete before the Renaissance, when new manuals of mythology explicated the complex symbolism of the resurgent ancient imagery, now entirely the property of the artists. In the interim a few monuments, such as the 13th-century *Ovide moralisé* (later to be ridiculed by Rabelais), allow us to observe the process at work, while documenting the imaginative and aesthetic power and status of Ovid's stories in the alien cultural environment of the Christian Middle Ages.

The term *interpretatio christiana* has been usefully applied in a much broader or more extended sense, to designate the entire process by which all the intellectual accomplishments of polytheist antiquity were absorbed by the Christian later Roman Empire (Inglebert 2001). So configured, the field is vast, including the rethinking of history (itself an evolving process) and of science, including cosmology. Most of the intellectual disciplines of antiquity made relatively smooth transitions into the increasingly Christian environment of the schools of the later empire. The principal exception was the study of philosophy in the tradition of Plato, whose practitioners in 5th- and 6th-century Athens and Alexandria were, after Julian, the most conspicuous among the opponents of the *interpretatio* of the Christians, to whom they referred as "those in power" (*hoi en telei*), clearly clinging to the hope that they would eventually go away. A comparable cell of resistance in Rome is evoked in Macrobius' *Saturnalia.* These diehard polytheist intellectuals of the late 4th, 5th, and 6th centuries represented a shrinking interpretive community whose voices gradually faded away behind the dominant Christian discourse.

BIBL.: David Dawson, *Allegorical Readers and Cultural Revision in Ancient Alexandria* (Berkeley 1992). Harald Hagendahl, *Augustine and the Classics* (Stockholm 1967). Hervé Inglebert, *Interpretatio Christiana: Les mutations des savoirs (cosmographie, géographie, ethnographie, histoire) dans l'antiquité chrétienne 30–630 après J.-C.* (Paris 2001). H.-I. Marrou, *Saint Augustin et la fin de la culture antique,* 4th ed. (Paris 1958).

R.L.

Iphigenia

Iphigenia is the heroine of two tragedies by Euripides: *Iphigenia in Tauris* (or *Iphigenia among the Taurians*) (ca. 413 BCE) and *Iphigenia in Aulis* (ca. 405 BCE).

In the latter the Greek fleet is becalmed at Aulis, where it has assembled to sail for Troy. An oracle demands that Agamemnon sacrifice his daughter Iphigenia, in order that the winds may blow. Agamemnon vacillates; Clytemnestra protests; Achilles defends Iphigenia; Iphigenia goes willingly to the altar. Artemis carries Iphigenia off at the last minute, leaving a deer in her place. (This ending may not be by Euripides.) In the earlier work Iphigenia is a priestess at the temple of Diana in the remote barbarian kingdom of Tauris (the Crimea), having been transported there by Artemis after her supposed sacrifice in Aulis. Her brother Orestes arrives in Tauris with his faithful friend Pylades. He is being pursued by the Furies for having killed his mother, Clytemnestra, and must do penance by finding the statue of Artemis in Tauris and returning it to Greece. They are captured and the tyrant Thoas demands that they be sacrificed. There is a recognition scene between Iphigenia and Orestes, an attempt to escape, and a final dea ex machina (Athena), who allows them to escape. Both plays use human sacrifice (by Greeks and barbarians) to explore the clash between political expediency and individual choice.

The plays were extremely popular in the ancient world and continued to be central to European culture. *Aulis* was translated into Latin by Erasmus (1507), and it was the first Greek tragedy translated into English (by Lady Jane Lumley, 1558). Racine's *Iphigénie* (1674) is the most important retelling of *Aulis.* Racine could not accept the death of a character as "virtuous and lovable" as Iphigenia. He introduces a second, rather unpleasant Iphigenia known as Ériphile. At the last moment the priest realizes that Ériphile is the Iphigenia whose sacrifice is demanded by the gods; Ériphile kills herself, and Iphigenia and Achilles marry. Here virtue is rewarded and evil punished; the gods are no longer arbitrary and unjust.

Both Iphigenia stories became very important sources for opera libretti in the 18th century. Zeno's *Ifigenia in Aulide* (1718), based on Racine, was the most popular Iphigenia libretto of the century, set by seven different composers. Influential advocates of reform opera such as Algarotti and Diderot proposed *Aulis* as an appropriate subject in the 1750s. Gluck brought some of these suggestions to fruition in his *Iphigénie en Aulide* (Paris 1774; rev. 1775). It was *Tauris,* however, that became the dominant subject for reform libretti. The moral clarity of the plot, the lack of a love interest, and the noble friendship of Orestes and Pylades appealed to neoclassical sensibilities. Guimond de la Touche's spoken tragedy, *Iphigénie en Tauride* (Paris 1757) was highly influential and inspired reform operas on the subject composed by Traetta (Vienna 1763) and de Majo (Mannheim 1764). Both these operas would influence Gluck's masterpiece, *Iphigénie en Tauride* (Paris 1779); Piccinni's opera of the same title (1781) led to the "Querelle des Gluckistes et des Piccinnistes." Gluck's Iphigenia operas were revived and revised in the 19th century by Wagner (*Aulide,* Dresden 1847) and Strauss (*Tauride,* Weimar 1889).

In Goethe's *Iphigenie auf Tauris* (prose version 1779; final version in blank verse, 1787), Iphigenia has reformed the barbarian tyrant Thoas, who has given up the practice of human sacrifice. He falls in love with Iphigenia; when she rejects him he regresses and demands that the Greek prisoners, Orestes and Pylades, be sacrificed. They plan a secret escape, and Iphigenia is faced with the moral dilemma of lying to Thoas or risking her brother's life. She ultimately chooses to do the right thing and reveal all. Thoas relents and allows them to leave unharmed. Here the gods have no role: Iphigenia becomes the model of a moral being. The play became a standard text in German schools.

Early 20th-century revivals of Greek tragedies by Gilbert Murray and others led to a new image of Iphigenia as a feminist pacifist that has been taken up by recent science fiction writers, such as Sherri Tepper. Iphigenia—the innocent victim sacrificed for political goals, and the unwilling executor of barbaric laws—remains tragically relevant.

BIBL.: S. Aretz, *Die Opferung der Iphigeneia in Aulis: Die Rezeption des Mythos in antiken und modernen Dramen* (Stuttgart 1999). J.-M. Gliksohn, *Iphigénie: De la Grèce antique à l'Europe des lumières* (Paris 1985). C. Hermann, *Iphigenie: Metamorphosen eines Mythos im 20. Jahrhundert* (Munich 2005). L. Secci, ed., *Il mito di Ifigenia: Da Euripide al Novecento* (Rome 2008).

J.E.C.

Iranian Hellenism

The influence of Greek culture in Iranian, especially Persian, tradition. Hellenism did not become a major force in Iran until after the conquests of Alexander the Great. Under the Seleucids, immigrant Greek populations flourished in the former Achaemenian Persian Empire in colonies built on the model of the Greek polis, some enjoying gymnasia and theaters and participating in Panhellenic games. Evidence of this Iranian Greek culture includes fragments of a Greek philosophical dialogue discovered as far away as Ai Khanoum, in present-day Afghanistan, where Aristotle's student Clearchus of Soli left an inscription. Aristocratic Iranians assimilated to their rulers' way of life, and some learned Greek. The lasting prestige of Greek culture is visible in the use of Greek language by the Parthian kings in inscriptions and on coins. Mithridates I (ca. 171–138 BCE) proclaimed himself "Philhellenic." Members of this dynasty as well as a number of their subjects are reported to have composed literature in Greek.

In their wars against the Roman Empire, the Sasanid kings (r. 224–661) used a pro-Iranian, outwardly anti–Graeco-Roman cultural policy that portrayed Alexander as an accursed destroyer and a thief of ancient Iranian science. This allowed the translation of Greek works into Middle Persian (the Sasanian court language) on the implied grounds that this was really in effect a restoration of what was originally Iranian but had been stolen by Alexander. Later reports in Zoroastrian Pahlavi and Arabic traditions indicate that Persian translations were made from Greek according to this ideology as early as the 3rd century CE, but there is no sure contemporary evidence for this. Though none of this literature survives in Middle Persian (indeed, most Middle Persian literature is now lost), Arabic and Syriac translations of some of these Middle Persian versions do survive, proving that a Sasanian Persian literature translated from Greek did in fact exist. Information about this Middle Persian tradition remains scanty, however, and much work remains to be done in reconstructing it.

The Persian emperor Chosroes Anushiraven (r. 531–579) was famous for his interest in Greek philosophy. Agathias reports that the last persecuted philosophers of Athens found refuge in his court before eventually returning to the Byzantine Empire. At least two works of Hellenistic philosophy addressed to Chosroes survive (by Priscianus of Lydia and Paul the Persian).

Alongside the tradition of Alexander the Great as accursed was another tradition, derived partly through a Middle Persian translation of the *Alexander Romance,* making Alexander into an Iranian model for world rulers. Later the Arabic *Sirr al-asrar* (known in Latin as *Secretum secretorum*) was composed in Arabic but based on Iranian traditions, putting Iranian political wisdom into the mouth of Aristotle addressing Alexander. This work was extremely popular in the Middle Ages in many languages as a handbook for royal conduct, an example of old Iranian traditions surviving under the cover of Hellenism.

In the 8th century, under Muslim rulers Arabic became the principal language of scholarly discourse in Iran, and Iranian scholars who spoke Persian as a first language were nevertheless very active in the creation of the new Arabic literature. Middle Persian versions of Ptolemy's

Almagest, Cassianus Bassus Scholasticus' *Geoponica,* and astrological works of Dorotheus, Vettius Valens, Teucer of Babylon, and Hermes were translated in turn into Arabic. The preservation of these works in Arabic translation (made ca. 750–850) is due to the interest in astrology among members of the early 'Abbasid court in Baghdad, where Iranian astrologers found lucrative employment. It is quite likely that other Greek works were available in Middle Persian versions now lost.

The earlier reception of Greek thought in Iran and its Iranian tradition were important factors leading to the formation of Arabic Philhellenism, a separate but related subject. From about 750 onward, traditions of Greek scholarship continued to be imported into Iran through the comprehensive translation and naturalization of Greek sciences in Arabic. Greek wisdom enjoyed such high prestige in early Islamic Iran that originally Persian sayings might be falsely ascribed to Aristotle or other ancient Greek figures.

When Persian (or New Persian), now written in Arabic script, regained its prestige as a language of literature and scholarship from the late 10th century onward, it continued to absorb Hellenistic traditions through translations from Arabic, which always remained in use alongside Persian. This phase of Persian Hellenism is still not well known; originally Greek works translated into Persian by way of Arabic exist but have scarcely been studied. Hellenism in Persian tradition, as in Arabic, predominantly meant Greek science, philosophy, medicine, and wisdom traditions. Along with Arabic but to a lesser degree, Persian tradition must be regarded as one of the important heirs of ancient Hellenistic learning.

BIBL.: "Greece" (various authors), *Encyclopaedia Iranica,* vol. 11 (2001) 292–363. H. W. Bailey, *Zoroastrian Problems in the Ninth-century Books* (Oxford 1943). Laurianne Martinez-Seàve, "Hellenism," *Encyclopaedia Iranica,* vol. 12 (2001) 156–164. Kevin van Bladel, "The Iranian Characteristics and Forged Greek Attributions in the Arabic *Sirr al-asrar (Secret of Secrets),*" *Mélanges de l'Université Saint-Joseph* 57 (2004 [2005]) 151–172.

K.V.B.

Irony

In Classical Greek *eirōneia* had three overlapping senses: dissimulation, self-depreciation, and (as a rhetorical trope or figure of speech) the opposite of the intended meaning. Deception was common to all three; but whereas in dissimulation, at one extreme, the deception was intentional, in the trope, at the other extreme, it usually was not. To call an evil person "good" was jest or sarcasm, not deceit. Gesture, intonation, context, or other signs disclosed the real meaning. Classical authors deemed Socrates the great master of *eirōneia.* His humorous, self-deprecatory manner shows how the three meanings overlapped in practical application. The term was current in Latin (as *ironia*) by the time of Cicero and Quintilian.

Latin Church Fathers and (even more so) medieval authors confined the word to the third, rhetorical sense. They followed definitions in classical grammatical and rhetorical works, notably Donatus' *Ars maior* and the pseudo-Ciceronian *Rhetorica ad Herennium,* and noted occurrences in classical literature (such as Lucan's praise of Nero) and in Scripture (such as Jesus' words to Judas: "My friend, on what errand have you come?" Matthew 26:50). They often used irony in their own writings, sometimes composing entire works in an ironic vein. Renaissance authors followed medieval precedent. Giordano Bruno ridiculed scriptural exegesis for identifying examples of irony opportunistically; Jewish, Islamic, and Christian commentators interpreted *yes* and *no* to mean ironically *no* and *yes* as they pleased, thereby arriving at contradictory interpretations of the same passage. The most common occasion for irony, according to medieval and Renaissance authors, was satire and mockery, whether gentle or caustic. Yet contrary to what is often assumed, irony had other purposes besides. Classical and contemporary mock encomia of fleas, gout, baldness, and the like were, for instance, appreciated for their own sake as virtuoso displays of extended irony.

Scholasticism introduced two innovations. First, Scholastics discovered and, with customary zeal for fine distinctions, explored Aristotle's definition, in his *Nicomachean Ethics,* of *eirōneia* as self-depreciation. Was it deceitful? Why was *eirōneia,* for Aristotle, a less reprehensible departure from veracity than boastfulness? Second, Scholastics applied Aristotle's doctrine of the four contraries to irony as a trope. For instance, *genius* in the ironic comment "He's a genius" meant, they claimed, its contrary, *idiot,* rather than *not a genius* in the sense of having only average intelligence. But *trustworthy* in the ironic comment "He's trustworthy" meant its contradictory, *untrustworthy.* Their analyses overlooked the nuance that irony is explicitly or implicitly propositional and that gesture, intonation, or other signs disclosing the true meaning marked a suppressed *not.* This explains how irony works in questions, exclamations, and other nonpropositional sentences. "O death, where is thy victory? O death, where is thy sting?" (1 Cor. 15:55), a commonly cited example, depends for its effect on the implied propositions "Death, you have victory, you have a sting" and their intended contradictions "Death, you do *not* have victory, you do *not* have a sting."

Latin medieval authors ignored Socrates' irony (as indeed did Arabic and Jewish authors, for similar reasons). No classical account or example of it circulated widely. The only significant exception occurred in the *Nicomachean Ethics*—an exception proving the rule. Here the word *eirōneia,* Scholastics concluded, denoted outright dissimulation, not the trope of meaning the opposite of what is said. Accidents of textual transmission are not, however, the sole explanation. Byzantine authors, many of whom were familiar with Plato's dialogues, also ignored Socrates' irony. To flourish it needed, like other features of the dialogues (such as philosophical use of myth and allegory), a favorable intellectual climate. The metaphysical and spiritual concerns of pagan Neoplatonism and more emphatically those of its heirs, Greek and Latin theology, proved inhospitable. Plotinus, faithful interpreter of Plato though he claimed to be, does not mention Socrates' irony at all.

The Renaissance revival of ancient learning satisfied both conditions. Cicero's *On the Orator,* Quintilian's *On the Education of Orators,* and other classical texts favored by Humanists discussed Socrates' irony. Plato's dialogues showed Socrates using irony to ridicule sophists and other pretentious contemporaries and as a maieutic device for eliciting the truth from, above all, the young. Renaissance authors found irony especially useful for explaining away perceived blemishes in the dialogues, such as homosexuality, communism, and Socrates' lack of interest in metaphysics and natural philosophy. During the 16th century the intellectual climate became less clement; some Reformation thinkers, among them Philipp Melanchthon, deemed Socrates' irony a distraction. Nevertheless, like the trope, it continued to be appreciated in later centuries for these virtues. For G. W. F. Hegel, Socrates' irony was maieutic or a form of mockery.

"Irony of fate," "dramatic irony," "tragic irony," "situational irony," and similar expressions denote predicaments, created by a literary or supernatural author, that chasten unwitting victims for unwarranted assumptions. A standard example is Sophocles' Oedipus, betrayed by his own honorable intentions. The sense of mockery, whether playful or remorseless, justifies, it is argued, assimilating irony of these kinds to rhetorical irony (though the latter, to repeat, is not necessarily derisive). Like rhetorical forms of irony, too, they can be said to depend on a contrast between a proposition (Oedipus: "I am not my father's murderer"), implied or stated, and a partially concealed contradiction apparent, if sometimes only retrospectively, to the onlooker. In other respects, however, the connection with rhetorical irony is tenuous. We might equally insist, and to no greater advantage, on a concept of *question* that embraces both grammatical questions and existential challenges presented in life or onstage.

Closer to classical *eirōneia* and *ironia* is "Romantic irony," originating with Friedrich Schlegel and inspired by 18th-century German doctrines of subjectivity. Here at least, though amid diverging interpretations, Socrates (as depicted by Plato) remained conspicuous. His intellectual agility, his quest for self-knowledge, humor, and enthusiasm for the absolute, tempered by a recognition that it was unattainable, anticipated the conscious detachment characteristic, according to Romantic authors, of art and life at their most sublime. Together these features constituted a "finer" or "higher" irony, distinct from rhetorical irony—an interpretation that disregarded the rhetorical interpretation of Socrates' irony prevalent from the mid-14th century onward. His profession of ignorance, rather than being an ironic affectation assumed for the sake of eliciting truth or exposing false pretensions, was an acknowledgment that the soul, while unable to attain the absolute, could aspire to higher levels of subjective freedom through negation of the particular. Søren Kierkegaard discussed these "modern" ideas of irony in his doctoral thesis, *The Concept of Irony with Continual Reference to Socrates* (1841), the first book-length study devoted to the subject. Irony in its dynamic, "Greek" form, wrote Kierkegaard, summarizing Socrates' irony, was "ironic *ataraxia*," "the infinite, nonchalant freedom of subjectivity" (65–66). It offered a degree of self-understanding and hence existential fulfillment of the kind achieved by Socrates, quite unlike the contemplative lethargy of "Oriental mysticism" (211, 213).

Hegel, Kierkegaard's chief source, had been less enthusiastic. He contemptuously dismissed the "modern" irony beloved by Friedrich Schlegel and other "apostles of irony" (*Werke,* 12:106, 221) and denied its Socratic pedigree. It was, he thought, an amoral superciliousness leading to *ennui* and, metaphysically, to an endless vortex of negation. Schlegel's "modern irony" riled Hegel above all because, or so he believed, it claimed that self-conscious subjective thought could transcend and master contemporary morality and truth. Self-conscious thought, axiomatically for Hegel, was itself part of the dialectic of history through which the *Geist* progressively fulfilled itself as self-reflexively conscious being. Socrates, and other great men chafing at the limitations imposed by contemporary morality and the state, may have believed that they were subjectively autonomous, but they were deluded. They were part of the dialectic between the individual and contemporary morality, in which both parties, as moments in the outward development of the *Geist,* were in different senses justifiable. This had been the "tragic irony" (*Werke,* 18:64) of Socrates.

Hegel notwithstanding, Romantic irony, as it subsequently came to be known, found many literary and philosophical applications, some indiscriminate. Thomas Mann confessed that he was "bored" with the critical pigeon-holing of his novels as ironic. More attention, he commented, drawing perhaps on a distinction made by Hegel, Kierkegaard, and others, needed to be paid to their humor, which was the affective complement to the aloof, Apolline, stance created by irony. This and other modern interpretations of irony as artistic or existential detachment mention Socrates only incidentally, if at all, thereby losing touch entirely with the rhetorical notions of irony that had prevailed in the classical tradition.

BIBL.: E. Behler, *Klassische Ironie, romantische Ironie, tragische Ironie* (Darmstadt 1972); "Ironie," in *Historisches Wörterbuch der Rhetorik,* ed. G. Ueding et al. (Tübingen 1992–) 1:cols. 599–624; and *Ironie und literarische Moderne* (Paderborn 1997). G. W. F. Hegel, *Sämtliche Werke,* 20 vols. (Stuttgart 1927–30). S. Kierkegaard, *The Concept of Irony with Continual Reference to Socrates,* trans. H. V. and E. H. Hong (Princeton 1989). D. Knox, *Irony: Medieval and Renaissance Ideas of Irony* (Leiden 1989). N. Knox, *The Word Irony and Its Context, 1500–1755* (Durham 1961). H. Prang, *Die romantische Ironie* (Darmstadt 1972). D.K.

Isagoge

Latin, an introductory manual to a subject, deriving from the Greek word *eisagōgē,* "bringing in(to)." Introductory texts to a discipline were a staple of classical literature. Corax of Sicily's *Technē* or "Art" (Latin *Ars*) of rhetoric, written ca. 465 BCE, is the earliest known Greek manual. The popularity of the term *eisagōgē* in titles for such works may derive from its adoption by the Stoics in the 3rd century BCE, if we are to judge by writings with this title ascribed to Chrysippus (ca. 282–206 BCE) among others, and by a scornful later reference by Aulus Gellius (2nd cent. CE), in Latin, to their "puerile *isagoges*" (*Attic Nights* 1.2.6). Certainly from the Stoics onward, *eisagōgē* became an established title, for example, in medicine (pseudo-Galen, *Isagoge, or the Doctor*), mathematics (Nicomachus' *Isagoge to Mathematics*), music (Cleonides' *Isagoge to Music*), philosophy (Albinus' *Isagoge to Plato's Dialogues*), and Christian theology (Eusebius' *Basic General Isagoge*). Indeed, as we know from Galen in medicine and from Eusebius in theology, beginners in a discipline were commonly referred to as *eisagōmenoi*, "those being introduced to." Greek introductory manuals, whether titled with *eisagōgē*, "art of," or some similar term (such as Alcinous' *Handbook of Platonism* or Proclus' *Elements of Theology* and *Elements of Physics*) followed no single method of organization.

Latin writers also provided a wide range of disciplinary manuals, covering everything from agriculture and warfare to rhetoric and theology, usually with a title consisting simply of the name of the subject preceded by the preposition *de* ("concerning," "about"). Occasionally one finds the word *institutio* ("principle," "training," "education"), as in Quintilian's *Institutio oratoria* (*Education of an Orator*), Gaius' *Institutiones* (*Principles* [of Roman law]), or Lactantius' theological *Divinae institutiones* (*Divine Principles*); but these were quite substantial works and hardly manuals for juvenile beginners. Although Gellius tells us (14.7) that Varro in the first century BCE wrote an *Eisagōgikos* (*Introduction*) to senatorial procedure, it appears that only in later antiquity did Latin authors publish beginners' manuals with *isagoge* in the title: for instance, pseudo-Soranus' medical *Isagoge* and Boethius' translation of Porphyry's *Eisagōgē*, on logic, which cemented the form *Isagoge* in the Latin Western tradition.

The Latin Middle Ages teemed with introductory manuals, but they usually went by the name of *Ars* (*Art*) or *Summulae* (*Summary Handbook*) or *Compendium*, if they had a generic name at all. The odd exceptions—the Arabic introduction to Galenic medicine, translated into Latin as *Johannitius' Isagoge*, and the Catalan Scholastic Ramon Llull's *Isagoge to Rhetoric*—only proved the rule. The Renaissance infusion of Greeks and Greek learning into 15th-century Italy resulted in the publication of some new *isagoges*, starting with George of Trebizond's *Isagoge to Dialectics* (ca. 1440) and continuing on to Iacopo Berengario da Carpi's medical *Pithy Isagoges* of the 1530s and Peder Palladius' *Isagoge to the Prophetic and Apostolic Books* (1561). But in the Renaissance the fashionable word for introductory manuals eventually became *methodus*. Early Humanists had refused to transliterate this common Greek word, opting instead to translate it as *via* ("way"). But the issue of pedagogical and scientific method was in the air, and Erasmus used the term in the title of his *Ratio seu methodus compendio perveniendi ad veram theologiam* (*Plan or Compendious Method for Arriving at True Theology*) of 1519. The leading Lutheran pedagogue, Philipp Melanchthon, discussed method and praised Aristotle as the true *artifex methodi* ("master of method"). In the second half of the century Peter Ramus popularized epitomes, each called *Methodus*, which promised to give readers mastery of a subject through a series of dichotomous divisions of its elements. The use of the word *isagoge* in the sense of introduction to a subject survived this Renaissance fad and has remained in use until this day in titles such as George Heffernan's *Isagoge to Phenomenological Declaration* (1989), an introduction to the philosophy of Edmund Husserl.

BIBL.: Manfred Fuhrmann, *Das systematische Lehrbuch: Ein Beitrag zur Geschichte der Wissenschaften in der Antike* (Göttingen 1960) and "Isagogische Literatur," in *Der Kleine Pauly*, ed. Konrat Ziegler and Walther Sontheimer (Stuttgart 1962) 2:1453–1456. Neal W. Gilbert, *Renaissance Concepts of Method* (New York 1960). Eduard Norden, "Die Composition und Litteraturgattung der Horazischen Epistula ad Pisones," *Hermes* 40 (1905) 481–528. Porphyry, *Introduction*, trans. Jonathan Barnes (Oxford 2003). J.MO.

Isidore of Seville

Bishop and scholar (ca. 560–636). He joins the two Senecas, Lucan, Martial, and Quintilian in any list of prominent Latin authors hailing from Spain. Though the earlier men made their way to Rome for their careers, this would have made no sense in the 6th century, by which time the traditional center—Rome, and Italy more widely—no longer held, and regional exceptionalism had become the norm. Isidore's achievements, above all the compilation of his encyclopedic *Etymologiae* (also known as *Origines*) can only be understood in the context of Visigothic Spain.

In 6th-century Spain most Roman families would have been Catholic, and Isidore's was no exception. He succeeded his older brother Leander as bishop of Seville, a position yet more powerful once Rekkared, king of the West Goths, converted from Arianism to Catholicism in 589. Whatever influence Isidore had on the Spanish Church and state, however, was wiped away in 711, when Visigothic dominion was abruptly terminated by the Islamic conquest. Indeed, it is uncanny to reflect that the Prophet Muhammad, whose dates are traditionally given as 570–632, was Isidore's contemporary.

Isidore's widely circulating writings constitute his lasting legacy. Of his many works—*Chronicon, Contra Judaeos, De fide catholica, De haeresibus, De natura rerum, De nominibus legis et evangeliorum* [= *Allegoriae*], *De numeris, De origine Gothorum, De ortu et obitu patrum, De viris illustribus, Differentiae, Epistulae, Officia, Origines* [= *Etymologiae*], *Prooemia, Quaestiones, Regula monachorum, Sententiae, Synonyma, Versus in bibliotheca* (to list only those now considered genuine)—several stand out. In *De viris illustribus* (*On Great Men*) he continues the work of Jerome and Gennadius but with a significantly more elaborated chronological framework that enables "a Christian theory of literature" and claims "the primacy . . . of Israel in philosophy, science, and poetry" (Curtius 1973, 451, 452; the chronicle of great men was in turn continued by Ildefonsus, bishop of Toledo). What came to be known as the "Isidorean style," a chiming and often rhyming prose style of exalted emotion (which also had been employed by Augustine in his *Soliloquies*) takes its name from Isidore's *Synonyma.* His *Versus in bibliotheca* (*Verses in a Library*), however they were assembled, open a window onto the texts available in Isidore's Spain and, when combined with careful analysis of his other works, convey an idea of the learning accessible to the scholar-bishop. His *De natura rerum* (*On the Nature of Things*) makes use of some of the same "natural historical" material that finds its ways into the *Etymologiae,* but here he offers extensive allegorical interpretations.

Such interpretations are by and large absent from Isidore's largest and massively influential work, the *Etymologiae* or *Origines,* on which he was still at work at the time of his death. Though certain details, including some book divisions, are due to Isidore's literary executor, his own architecture for the whole is relatively clear (if somewhat arbitrary). He begins with the seven *artes liberales* (books 1–3, with disproportionate emphasis on *grammatica*), proceeds to medicine (4), laws and books of the Scripture (5–6), and then to the universe itself, moving from God and divine hierarchies (7) to religions and languages (8–10); he next surveys humans and other living creatures (11–12) and inanimate elements (13–17) and concludes with three complexes of miscellanies that cover military, nautical, and transport terminology (18–20).

At the deepest level Isidore's encyclopedia is rooted in the dream that language can capture the universe and that if we but parse it correctly, it can lead us to the proper understanding of God's creation. His word derivations are not based on principles of historical linguistics but follow their own logic, serving as the basis for assertions and linkages of all sorts, often multiple and unresolved. "Human being" (*homo*) is so called from "soil" (*humus*), the material origin of the body (7.6.4); *Mercurius* is related to speech because speech is a "go-between" (*medius currens*), but the god's name is also linked to "commerce" (*merx*) (8.11.45–46); and poetry (*carmen*) derives either from the metrical and thus choppy way (*carptim*) it is recited or from poets' madness (*carere mente*) (1.39.4).

The *Etymologiae* displays all the late antique techniques of abbreviation, abridgment, selection, (re)ordering, and harmonizing, and Isidore is the master of bricolage. Jacques Fontaine aptly describes one passage as a "rhapsody" (1959, 1:520), and Ludwig Traube described the work as "a mosaic" (Curtius 1973, 455). His reductions and compilations did indeed transmit ancient learning, but Isidore, who often relied on scholia and earlier compilations, is often simplistic scientifically and philosophically, especially compared to 4th- and 5th-century figures such as Ambrose and Augustine. The *Etymologiae* frequently preserved for later generations some of the least helpful theories (from a scientific point of view) that were rooted in philosophy, not observation—for example, the notion of the fixed "sphere" of stars that derives from Plato's *Timaeus.* It also passed along, willy-nilly and however much its author as a Christian bishop may have regretted it, a universe filled with mythological references. If Isidore, like Augustine (from whom he adopts much), wished to banish the pagan gods, he nonetheless keeps them alive in his writings via euhemerist and other rationalizing explanations of pagan names and stories, just as he cites as authorities the very Latin poets whose works he asserts are "fables" and "fictions" (*Etymologiae* 1.40.1).

The influence of Isidore's varied corpus can be traced over most of the subsequent millennium, with early influence in Ireland, Gaul, and England. He is cited (with others) in discussions of *grammatica* and the *septem artes,* and in the 9th century Aurelian of Réôme in his *Musica disciplina* expanded on Isidore's musical doctrines. Although it is important not to underestimate the importance of Isidore's theological writings, the *Etymologiae* define him. The work itself provided the stuff of medieval word lists and encyclopedias (e.g., by Papias, Hugucio, Bartholomaeus Anglicus, and Vincent of Beauvais) as well as "lexical poetry" (Curtius 1973, 135, 183–184). Individual tidbits are used as building blocks ubiquitously and without end, in Latin texts and in vernacular as early as Anglo-Saxon literature. His definitions of tragedy and comedy (*Etymologiae* 8.7.6) were often the source of medieval knowledge about those two ancient genres (including Dante's letter to Can Grande; Curtius, 357). "As a *terminus technicus* the *locus amoenus* appears in Book XIV of Isidore's encyclopedia" (Curtius, 192), and details from the *Etymologiae* (13.13.10) are taken into the description of a pleasance in Berceo's *Milagros de Nuestra Señora* (Curtius, 202n). And even if the *Etymologiae* was not always the immediate source, Isidore's name was invoked by Boccaccio, Petrarch, and Gower, among others. He is quoted but not named in Chaucer (Barney et al. 2006, 26). The *Etymologiae* was among the earliest printed books (first in Augsburg, 1472).

Isidore is given a place in Dante's vision of Paradise (*Paradiso* 10.130–131), and he was officially canonized in 1598. As a saint, he is venerated (on 4 April, the date of his death in 636) and frequently depicted in manuscript illuminations, paintings (including one by Murillo), and statues. He wears a bishop's miter and is usually shown holding a book. Quite recently he has been proposed to become the patron saint of the Internet, but this has not yet happened.

BIBL.: Stephen A. Barney, W. J. Lewis, J. A. Beach, and Oliver Berghof, trans., *The Etymologies of Isidore of Seville* (Cambridge 2006). Franz Brunhölzl, *Geschichte der lateinischen Literatur des Mittelalters* (Munich, 1975) 1:74–91. Ernst Robert Curtius, *European Literature and the Latin Middle Ages,* trans. Willard Trask (Princeton 1973, German 1948). Jacques Fontaine, *Isidore de Séville et la culture classique dans l'Espagne wisigothique,* 2 vols. (Paris 1959, 1983). R.H.

Islam

The Near East and Central Asia—from Egypt to Bactria—were hellenized after Alexander the Great, but at different levels and with varied intensity. Different aspects of the classical tradition survived and even flourished at various times and places during the millennium between Alexander the Great and the rise of Islam, but by and large the living tradition already lay moribund when Arab armies conquered the territories that had fallen to Alexander. Current scholarship is investigating with intensity the late-antique transition from the Eastern Roman Empire to Islam, and there is increasing evidence that elements of the classical tradition in this part of the world had already disappeared by the time of the Prophet Muhammad.

Most significantly, the ancient city structure and administration, and the citizenry that had upheld a classical worldview, social mores, and culture, had ceased to exist. There was no longer a living tradition of such classical features as, say, athletic games or theater. This clearly explains why scholars and philosophers in the Islamic world, when later engaged with a translation of Aristotle's *Poetics,* failed to grasp the very concepts of comedy and tragedy and rendered these terms as satirical and panegyric poetry, respectively. Certain other features of city organization in the early Islamic world, such as the office of the market inspector (*muhtasib*) and the land tax (*kharaj*), which may have been modeled on Byzantine precedents (the office of *agoranomos* and the *choregia,* respectively), were nevertheless so drastically redefined and integrated into the new Islamic order of things as to be practically unrecognizable. The same is true of Islamic law, in which some scholars have seen certain features of Roman law, though this is an issue that is highly contested.

In matters of religion, paganism, though not quite extinct, was very much on the decline in the cities. It may have survived a few centuries more in the villages, though no written testimonies to that effect seem to have survived. In any case, whatever pagan communities had survived the persecutions by the Christians could not be expected to retain for long their old beliefs under another emphatically monotheistic system, Islam. The major exception is the city of Harran, the ancient Carrhae in southeastern Asia Minor, which had a very active pagan citizenry well into the 10th century. Although the significance of Harran has been exaggerated in the past two decades (the theory that the last pagan philosophers in the 6th century, upon their return from the Persian court of Chosroes, continued the Platonic academy there is completely unfounded and has been debunked), the fact remains that Harran was the one center of living Hellenism that provided the Islamic world, from the 8th to the 10th century, during the period of the Graeco-Arabic translations, both information on scientific and philosophical subjects and educated personnel with a sound knowledge of Greek.

In matters of higher education, the classical tradition survived in the Near East relatively indirectly. The school in Athens had already been rendered inoperative by Justinian a century before Islam, whereas that of Alexandria expired, it seems, by attrition and under the relentless pressure from Christians. According to the current interpretation of the relatively flimsy evidence, the last scholarch ("philosopher" may be too presumptuous in his case), Stephanus, is said to have been invited to Constantinople by the Byzantine emperor Heraclius. He went to Constantinople, and apparently there was no one left in Alexandria to continue the teaching of philosophy; Stephanus himself would appear to have gone to pasture in Constantinople—short of some astrological texts ascribed to him (if it is the same Stephanus), no philosophical production in Constantinople is known by his hand. When the Muslim Arab armies entered Alexandria in 642, what they most likely found still operating was the medical college, whose curriculum, which had been recently restructured, included the study of the first four books of Aristotle's Organon, four treatises by Hippocrates, and abridgments of 16 treatises by Galen, called *Summaria Alexandrinorum* in the Arabic sources, which alone report these activities.

The Greek method of teaching philosophy and medicine, through logic, together with a knowledge of the respective curricula of those two disciplines, attenuated though it may have been, survived to a certain extent in the Syriac schools. The living tradition of Greek science and philosophy may have died by the beginning of the 7th century, even before the Greek-speaking Chalcedonian populations in Byzantium and the Near East were engulfed in the Iconoclastic controversy, but the non-Chalcedonian Syriac-speaking communities (Nestorians and Monophysites) preserved the pedagogy of Greek *paideia,* a fair command of its language and many of its manuscripts, and a Scholastic knowledge of its bibliography. The great translator Hunayn ibn-Ishāq (d. 873) tells us about the activities of such medical schools two and a half centuries after Stephanus, and from the revival of Aristotelian studies by the Nestorian scholar Abū-Bishr Mattā ibn-Yūnus (d. 940) at the beginning of the 10th century we can infer the knowledge about, if not the actual teaching of, a similar philosophical curriculum in his hometown, Dayr Qunnā, on the Tigris south of Baghdad.

Not only Syriac speakers preserved remnants of a living tradition of some sciences. Hellenistic mathematics and astronomy traveled to India relatively early—apparently in Hellenistic times—and they were cultivated in that milieu until well after the rise of Islam. From India they also traveled west to Sasanian Persia, where, in addition, astrology, agriculture, and apparently some Aristotelian physics and logic were translated into Middle Persian. It appears that translations from Greek into Middle Persian under the Sasanids were encouraged as part of an effort to "recover" the ancient Zoroastrian wisdom (including all knowledge), which was allegedly stolen for the Greeks by Alexander the Great, "translated" into Greek and Coptic, and subsequently dispersed around the world. Also in Persia, in Gondeshapur, there appears to have been a medical school that continued the curricular practices of Alexandria; although the significance of this school (if not its very existence) is being contested, the fact remains that several families of Nestorian Christian physicians that served the early Abbasid caliphs came from there.

These relatively few elements of a living classical tradition at the time of the rise of Islam would have eventually died out (and with them classical tradition itself in the East) had it not been for the energetic prosecution of a vigorous Graeco-Arabic translation movement by the rulers and elites of the new Arab dynasty, the Abbasids, who came to power in 750. Circumstances generated by their seizing power at the end of a civil war (against the preceding Islamic dynasty, their distant cousins the Umayyads) necessitated that they adopt an ideological stand that included promoting themselves as the defenders of multicultural science and learning and, accordingly, sponsoring the translation movement, during the course of which almost all nonliterary and nonhistorical secular Greek works on science and philosophy were translated on demand into Arabic. Once thus introduced and sponsored from the top, the translation movement found further support from below, through the incipient scientific tradition in Arabic that was developing at the hands of scholars and scientists actively recruited to the newly founded capital of Baghdad (762) by the same elites who were commissioning the translations. The dialectic between scientific thinking and research, on the one hand, and the translation activity, on the other, was responsible for the amazingly rapid development of the sciences in Arabic in the second half of the 8th century and their establishment as a major cultural force in early Abbasid society. As a result, not only were the surviving elements of the classical tradition in scientific pedagogy reinvigorated but also, through their help and mediation, many of the extinct aspects of Greek learning of a similar universalistic application were resurrected. The classical tradition that we find in Islam is an amalgam of its remnants in late antiquity and a resuscitated bookish and scholarly enterprise.

The subjects that were translated and studied in Baghdad included the entire secular classical Greek production, with the exception of history (other than Christian chronographies) and high literature (in particular drama and poetry). A relatively full inventory of the subjects concerned would be, in alphabetical order: agriculture, alchemy, astrology, astrometeorology, astronomy, biography, botany, geography, grammar, literature (in the form of literary theory—poetics—and popular literature, which included gnomic and paraenetic works, fables and Aesopica, novels, and the Alexander romance), magic, mathematics (all branches, including new fields: algebra, arithmetic, geometry, trigonometry), mechanics, medicine, meteorology, military manuals (*tactica*), mineralogy, music, oneiromancy, optics, pharmacology (*materia medica*), philosophy (all branches: logic, physics, metaphysics, ethics, *oeconomica,* politics), physiognomy, veterinary science, and zoology (including *cynegetica* and falconry).

In all these subjects the basic texts were translated—in a number of instances more than once (as in the case of the more essential texts, such as Aristotle's *Physics* and *Topics*)—frequently accompanied with late-antique commentaries, and further elaborated in original Arabic compositions that went beyond the translated material. The massive infusion of this material into the Islamic world helped shape classical Islamic civilization, which was formed during the period of the translation movement, and made it the successor civilization to classical antiquity.

Each of these subjects was organized in Arabic into a curriculum of studies that was presented to the student as a rationalized and unified field. The curriculum, in other words, presented not only what was to be learned but also how and in what order: it determined the agenda of learning. This Scholastic reorganization of Greek learning and its enrichment through the addition of new research constituted one of the greatest contributions of Islamic civilization to the survival of the classical tradition, both in Islam and in its eventual adoption and acceptance in medieval Christendom, East and West, through translations (back) into Greek and Latin. The medical teachings of Hippocrates and Galen, for example, were integrated anew in Arabic, with much new information, into medical textbooks and encyclopedias that presented medical knowledge as a rationalized and systematic field, thus relieving the student of the need to resort to the usually garrulous and frequently repetitive individual works by Galen. This system was appreciated by the Byzantines who, in their medical literature, preferred reading translations of Galenic material from the Arabic to consulting Galen in the original, thereby sparing themselves the trouble of translation. The same applies to the translations from Greek and Arabic into Latin. Although medieval scholars had access in many cases to Latin translations made directly from the Greek, they frequently preferred the translations made from an Arabic intermediary or works that were composed originally in Arabic: the curriculum was better represented by the Arabic sources, and it mirrored the agenda of learning in a way more suitable to the needs and views of medieval societies.

Among all the subjects translated, philosophy needs to be singled out because its resurrection in Arabic in the early 9th century was, by all accounts, a revolutionary event. Throughout antiquity and until the death of Greek philosophy early in the 7th century, all creative philosophizing was done in Greek. It is true that there was some philosophical activity first in Latin, and later in Syriac, and even in Middle Persian, as mentioned, but all such activity was derivative from, and dependent on, the main philosophizing going on simultaneously in Greek. The efforts in these other languages were aimed at popularizing Greek philosophy in the target languages and had an educational character, whereas anybody pursuing philosophy creatively, regardless of his linguistic or ethnic background in multicultural late antiquity, did it in Greek. The situation was completely different when Arabic philosophy emerged: it was from the very beginning independent, it chose its own paths, and it had no contemporary and living Greek philosophy either to imitate or to seek inspiration from. Arabic philosophy was the same enterprise as Greek philosophy, but this time in Arabic: Arabic philosophy internationalized Greek philosophy, and through its success demonstrated that philosophy is a supranational enterprise.

Arabic philosophy was revolutionary in another way as well. Although Greek philosophy in its later stages in late antiquity may be thought to have yielded to religion—Christianity—and indeed in many ways imitated it, Arabic philosophy developed in a social context in which a dominant monotheistic religion was the ideology par excellence. Because of this, Arabic philosophy developed as an ideology not in opposition to religion but independent from religion—indeed from all religions—as a methodologically unassailable system that rationally explained all reality, including religion. This aspect of Arabic philosophy, which reasserted the original function of Greek philosophy on its first appearance in classical antiquity, influenced decisively intellectual developments in both Christianity and Islam. In the former, the translation after the 12th century of Arabic philosophy into Latin generated numerous confrontations with religion in the universities of Europe and started the long process toward the Enlightenment. In the latter, it permeated all higher intellectual discourse, to the point that theology and mysticism became heavily philosophical, and caused the distinctions among the three disciplines to be blurred; thus, largely bereft of its independence as a discipline in the Islamic world in the later premodern centuries, philosophy failed to raise its distinctive voice in the period of retrenchment and economic decline attendant on the 17th-century expansion of Europe into traditionally Islamic areas and its eventual colonization of most of the Islamic world after Napoleon.

The significance of these developments in the first two centuries of Abbasid rule in Baghdad (ca. 750 to 950) is manifold. On a technical level, the translations and scientific work conducted in these two centuries generated a highly sophisticated scientific language and a massive amount of source material based on the classical tradition that would feed scientific research for the following centuries, not only in the Islamic world but beyond, in Greek and Latin Christendom and, within it, among the Jewish populations as well. On a social level, they created a cultural attitude—a fashion, one could say—that scientific work based on the Greek pattern was something socially valuable and prestigious; the massive amounts of money that were spent on translations and original Arabic works on scientific subjects during the first two centuries of the Abbasids are sufficient proof of this. The continuum of translation and science—the practice, the study, and the sponsoring of it—defined a large percentage of public culture in the first two Abbasid centuries and created a precedent that could never be ignored throughout the medieval period, in either the East or the West. Early Abbasid Baghdad became both a symbol of the highest achievement of Islamic civilization and an example to be imitated; Baghdad, as the capital of a world empire, exercised what would today be called cultural hegemony over not only the rest of the Islamic world but also the entire Western world, as the subsequent translations from Arabic into Latin, Hebrew, and Byzantine Greek indicate.

Thus, in the course of the 10th century, with the breakdown of the authority of the Abbasids and the attendant decentralization of political power, numerous provincial capitals, from Córdoba in Spain to Bukhara in Central Asia, vied to reproduce the glory of early Baghdad through their patronage of scientists and scholars and the amassing of huge library collections. This pattern continued throughout the premodern period in all Islamic states that were politically stable, militarily strong, and economically robust: from the earlier Umayyads in Spain and Ayyubids and Mamluks in Egypt and Syria to the later Safavids in Iran, the Ottomans in Asia Minor, and the Mughals in India. The ideal Islamic ruler became the one who, like the early Abbasid caliphs, promoted classical science and learning, now heavily domesticated in Islamic civilization. The cultivation of each of the translated fields listed above and the new developments in them in Arabic and (later) in Persian, as documented in the various entries of this volume, sustained the vitality of the classical tradition in the Islamic world well into premodern times.

Outside the Islamic world, the Graeco-Arabic translation movement had historical consequences for the Greek classical tradition. In a way, it can be maintained that the movement helped the classical tradition survive, at least to the large extent to which it has. The demand by the Arabic translators for manuscripts of Greek scientific and philosophical texts, many of which were at that time available only in uncials dating from the 6th century, was a contributing factor in the transcription of these texts by Greek scribes into minuscule writing, thus generating the minuscule archetypes of the copies extant today. The same demand for classical learning in Baghdad, and the high prestige among intellectuals there that it enjoyed, directly occasioned, it would seem out of a desire for emulation, the 9th-century "first Byzantine humanism." Further, the Greek texts in Arabic translation, and the original Arabic compositions based on them, constituted the sources of the translations back into Byzantine Greek, into Hebrew, and into Latin, where they were directly responsible for the 12th-century renaissance. Finally, the Graeco-Arabic translation movement demonstrated for the first time in history that scientific and philosophical thought is international and universal, not bound to a specific language or culture. And the classical tradition, about which we write books and encyclopedias today, *became* the classical tradition first in Abbasid Baghdad.

BIBL.: A. Al-Azmeh, *Muslim Kingship: Power and the Sacred in Muslim, Christian and Pagan Polities* (New York 1996). S. Brock, *Syriac Perspectives on Late Antiquity* (London 1984). C. D'Ancona, ed., *The Libraries of the Neoplatonists* (Leiden 2007). J.-F. Duneau, "Quelques aspects de la pénétration de l'hellénisme dans l'empire perse sassanide (IVe–VIIe siècles)," in *Mélanges offerts à René Crozet,* ed. P. Gallais and Y.-J. Riou

(Poitiers 1966) 1.13–22. D. Gutas, "The 'Alexandria to Baghdad' Complex of Narratives: A Contribution to the Study of Philosophical and Medical Historiography among the Arabs," *Documenti e Studi sulla Tradizione Filosofica Medievale* 10 (1999) 155–193; "Geometry and the Rebirth of Philosophy in Arabic with al-Kindī," in *Words, Texts and Concepts Cruising the Mediterranean Sea,* ed. R. Arnzen and J. Thielmann (Leuven 2004) 195–209; and *Greek Thought, Arabic Culture* (London 1998). J. F. Haldon, *Byzantium in the Seventh Century: The Transformation of a Culture* (Cambridge 1990). H. Hugonnard-Roche, *La logique d'Aristote du grec au syriaque* (Paris 2004). R. MacMullen, *Christianity and Paganism in the Fourth to Eighth Centuries* (New Haven 1997). F. E. Peters, *Aristotle and the Arabs: The Aristotelian Tradition in Islam* (New York 1967). R. Rashed, ed., *Encyclopedia of the History of Arabic Science,* 3 vols. (London 1996). F. Rosenthal, *The Classical Heritage in Islam* (Berkeley 1975) and *Knowledge Triumphant: The Concept of Knowledge in Medieval Islam* (Leiden 2007). G. Saliba, *Islamic Science and the Making of the European Renaissance* (Cambridge, Mass., 2007). S. Shaked, "Paymān: An Iranian Idea in Contact with Greek Thought and Islam," in *Transition Periods in Iranian History* (Paris 1987) 217–240. A. Speer, ed., *Wissen über Grenzen: Arabisches Wissen und lateinisches Mittelalter* (Berlin 2006). J. van Ess, *Theologie und Gesellschaft im 2. und 3. Jahrhundert Hidschra: Eine Geschichte des religiösen Denkens im frühen Islam,* 6 vols. (New York 1991–1997). R. Walzer, *Greek into Arabic* (Oxford 1962). Edward Watts, "Where to Live the Philosophical Life in the Sixth Century? Damascius, Simplicius, and the Return from Persia," *Greek, Roman, and Byzantine Studies* 45 (2005) 285–315.

D.G.

J

Janus

A distinctively Roman god with no ancient Greek equivalent, two-faced Janus presided over doors (in Latin, *janua;* an ancient Roman doorman was a *janitor*) and more generally over openings and closings; his month, January, opened the year. His main temple in the Roman Forum stood with its doors wide open except on the rare occasions when the city was at peace, a reminder that this ancient deity had presided over a Golden Age when gods and mortals lived in concord with the world's creatures and with one another, long before that tale of progressive decline known to us as history. The Romans themselves identified Janus as an Etruscan divinity who had given his name to the city's "eighth hill" across the Tiber, the Janiculum, and whose double face featured on Etruscan coins from Volterra and early Roman coins from Rome. The reverses of these coins often showed a ship's prow; perhaps this was what inspired the *Graphia aurea urbis Romae,* a 12th-century guidebook for pilgrims to Rome, to report that Janus was really the Hebrew patriarch Noah, who had come to Italy after the Flood. This peculiar local legend took on a new urgency in the late 15th century when a Dominican friar, Annius of Viterbo, revived it in several publications, most notably his *Commentaries on the Works of Divers Authors Who Speak about Antiquities* (*Commentaria super opera diversorum auctorum de antiquitatibus loquentium,* 1498). An eloquent orator, a deft courtier, and a shameless forger, Annius bolstered his *Commentaries* with archaeological artifacts, most of them (but not all) his own creations. According to Annius, Noah had come to Italy 100 years after leaving the Ark on Mount Ararat. After changing his name to Janus, he introduced the natives to the cultivation of grapevines, established laws, founded Etruscan cities, and fostered Etruscan religion; the Etruscan language, Annius declared, was descended from Hebrew by way of Aramaic. Janus/Noah, in his account, also created the ancient Roman priestly office of Pontifex Maximus, lending this title (Supreme Pontiff) and his attributes to the papacy. Like Noah's Ark in the Old Testament, the ship on ancient coins of Janus was held by Christians to foreshadow the symbolic ship of the Christian Church. And Janus/Noah's choice to settle opposite Rome on the left bank of the Tiber prefigured Saint Peter's association with the Vatican; because Janus was the first Pontifex Maximus, he was also, in effect, the first pope, and Peter his successor. Peter's keys preserved Janus/Noah's ancient association with doors.

Popes of his era believed in Annius and his forgeries; Alexander VI Borgia appointed him Master of the Sacred Palace in 1493, an office in which Annius served until his death in 1502. The legend of Janus and Noah also inspired important works of Renaissance art in Rome, including Michelangelo's Sistine Chapel ceiling (1508–1512), Donato Bramante's round Doric Tempietto (1502)—an attempt to re-create Etruscan architecture—Pinturicchio's Borgia Apartments (1503), and Raphael's Loggia of Cupid and Psyche (1518), and lent its imagery to papal oratory under Popes Julius II (1503–1513) and Leo X (1513–1521). Within a generation of Annius' death, his forgeries had largely lost their appeal, although the Dominican philosopher Tommaso Campanella could still say of Rome in the 17th century: "The inventor of wine founded his kingdom in you/The first Pope." The ideas of Annius survive today in the proverbial image of Saint Peter standing guard, Janus-like, at the Pearly Gates—an image given indelible force by Erasmus in his satirical dialogue about Julius II, *Julius Excluded from Heaven* (1512). The double face of Janus also has a long history as an image of prudence, the embodiment of foresight and hindsight, although Titian's *Allegory of Prudence* (1543) gives him a third face to command the present as well. I.D.R.

Jesuits

Founded by Ignatius of Loyola (1491–1556) and approved in 1540 by Pope Paul III (r. 1534–1549), the Society of Jesus was an order of priests and lay brothers that answered directly to the Father General (*praepositus generalis*) and ultimately to the papacy. In addition to the more traditional vows of poverty, chastity, and obedience, the Jesuits made a unique vow to undertake ministry anywhere in the world.

The Jesuits' contribution to classical studies derived primarily from their role as teachers and rhetoricians. They were the first religious order to operate educational institutions as a principal and distinct ministry. They founded their first college in Messina in 1547, and by 1773 the Society ran more than 800 schools around the world. Most were secondary schools, but beginning with the Roman College (Collegio Romano, 1551), several were raised to the status of university. The Jesuit curriculum was modeled on the Renaissance *studia humanitatis,* a reading list of Greek and Latin works of poetry, rhetoric, drama, and history meant to instill basic civic values into boys and young men about to enter public service. This approach was first mentioned in a 1547 letter from Juan de Polanco (1517–1576), Ignatius' secretary, in which he exhorts Jesuits to study *cosas de humanidad* to help them acquire the rhetorical skills necessary for ministry and for a better understanding of Scripture and philosophy. The following year Jerónimo Nadal (1507–1580) set up a Humanistic curriculum as the foundation for the college at Messina.

The Jesuit school curriculum was codified with the *Ratio studiorum* (*Plan of Studies,* 1599), a compilation of important texts and detailed teaching methods. The *Ratio* was designed primarily as a guide for training Jesuits, and its hierarchical structure placed humanities subjects among the "lowest" disciplines (rhetoric and grammar), as a first stage in acquiring knowledge in the "higher faculties" of Scripture, Scholastic theology, cases of conscience, and ethics. Nevertheless, the text was unique in also being directed to lay students, and nearly all Jesuit schools focused exclusively on those "lower" disciplines, making them and their reading list of Latin and Greek writers (Homer, Pliny, Virgil, Cicero, and Terence) the *Ratio*'s most widely influential legacy in Catholic Europe.

Individual Jesuits, most of them teachers at Jesuit schools, made important contributions to classical studies and to Latin poetry, prose, and theater. Like the Society itself, these efforts were international, with an unusually strong contribution from France. René Rapin (1621–1687), known as the "second Theocritus" after the publication of his *Eclogae sacrae* (1659), was a Latin poet who also wrote important studies of Horace, Virgil, and Aristotle, including *Observations sur les poèmes d'Horace et de Virgile* (1669) and *Réflexions sur la poétique d'Aristote et sur les ouvrages des poètes anciens et modernes* (1676). Classical dance was the focus of the work of Claude Ménestrier (1631–1705), a collector of antiquities who composed ballets and plays for the Jesuit college in Lyon (including one later performed for Louis XIV's visit in 1758), and in 1682 he published an important history of ancient and modern ballet. Charles de la Rue (1643–1725), a professor at the Jesuit college of Louis-le-Grand in Paris, was a great orator favored by Louis XIV and published Latin poetry and an edition of Virgil.

No study of Jesuit classicists can omit the strange personality of Jean Hardouin (1646–1729), librarian at Louis-le-Grand from 1683 until his death. Hardouin wrote editions of Themistius (1684) and of the *Natural History* of Pliny, as well as several works devoted to numismatics. But he is best known for his extravagant claim, in his *Chronologiae ex nummis antiquis restitutae* (1696) and *Prolegomena ad censuram veterum scriptorum,* that all of classical literature except for Homer, Herodotus, Cicero, and selected works of Pliny, Virgil, and Horace had been fabricated by late medieval monks. Later French Jesuit classicists include Noël Sanadon (1676–1733), who wrote Latin poetry and an edition and translation of the *Odes* and *Epodes* of Horace, and François Desbillons (1711–1789), a Latinist and poet whose principal works were a collection of Aesopian fables and a Latin text of the *Imitation of Christ.* Pierre Brumoy (1688–1742) wrote a number of sacred tragedies to be performed in colleges, as well as Latin poetry such as his celebrated work on the passions called *De motibus animi* (*On the Passions*). His greatest contribution to the history of classical theater is his *Théâtre des Grecs* (1730), an edition and translation of Greek tragedies.

The Jesuits also produced exceptional classicists elsewhere around the world. The German Jacob Balde (1604–1668), known during his time as the "second Quintilian," was a Latin poet and court preacher in Munich and elsewhere in southern Germany who wrote music and theater pieces for Jesuit schools. Not to be outdone, Poland produced its "Christian Horace" in Maciej Sarbiewski (1595–1640), an extraordinarily popular Latin poet whose work was translated into numerous European languages within decades of his death. Rafael Landivar (1731–1793), a Spanish Jesuit resident in Guatemala, wrote an astonishing 15-book description of the indigenous customs of Mexico and Guatemala in Latin hexameters entitled *Rusticatio mexicana* (1782); he is now considered one of Guatemala's greatest poets.

The "Old Society" Jesuits were suppressed by Pope Clement XIV in 1773, the result of court intrigue and international political pressure, especially from Portugal, Spain, and France. The Society of Jesus reemerged in 1814 in what is known as the "New Society" and has continued to enjoy a leading role in Catholic education ever since.

BIBL.: Luce Giard and Louis de Vaucelles, *Les Jésuites à l'âge baroque* (Grenoble 1996). John O'Malley, *The First Jesuits*

(Cambridge, Mass., 1993). John O'Malley et al., *The Jesuits: Cultures, Sciences, and the Arts,* 2 vols. (Toronto 1999, 2006).

G.A.B.

Judaism

Contacts between Jews and the Greek world and culture seem to have begun rather late, in the days of Alexander the Great. In 333–331 BCE Alexander conquered the Near East (including Palestine) and, according to a Jewish legend, went to Jerusalem to meet the head of the Jewish religion, the High Priest Yaddus. In the Hellenistic period, Jews lived not only in Palestine but also in Mesopotamia—as a consequence of the 586 BCE exile from Jerusalem ordered by the Babylonian king Nebuchadnezzar—and in Egypt—Alexandria, the capital of Hellenistic Egypt, was populated by a great number of Jews—and were subjects of the successors of Alexander, the Seleucids and the Ptolemies. Jewish attitudes toward these two dynasties and the Greek culture connected to them appear to have varied.

In Egypt Jews apparently cooperated with the Hellenistic rulers and absorbed most of Greek culture. They adopted Greek as their language; after 250 BCE they translated first the Pentateuch and then the rest of the Hebrew Bible into Greek, thereby creating the *Translation of the Seventy;* and a Judeo-Hellenistic literature in Greek developed, of which only few texts (or fragments of them) are extant. One should mention the well-known *Letter of Aristea,* a Greek defense and description of Judaism, probably written in the second half of the 2nd century BCE. The list of minor Judeo-Hellenistic texts probably written in Ptolemaic Egypt includes also a set of letters falsely ascribed to the Greek philosopher Heraclitus, a poem of 250 hexameters falsely ascribed to Phocylides, a tragedy on Moses (the *Exagoge*) written by a certain Ezechiel, and even an epic poem by a certain Theodotus, describing the legendary massacre of Sichem by the patriarchs Simeon and Levi in vengeance of their sister, according to *Genesis* 34. In this way, methods and even ideas taken from Greek philosophy and literature were explicitely applied to the interpretation of Jewish religious doctrines and texts, including the Bible.

Things appear to have been different in Seleucidic Palestine. The effort to impose Greek culture, education, and even religion on the local Jewish people by Antioch IV (r. 175–164 BCE) instigated a rebellion led by the Maccabean family, and Palestinian Jews gained political autonomy after 135 BCE. This fact, however, did not hinder the absorption of elements probably (although not declaredly) taken from or inspired by the classical tradition. According to a number of scholars, an implicit influence of Greek culture, thought, and literature results in some texts of the Hebrew Bible: Giovanni Garbini has found in the *Song of Songs,* which he has suggested as dating only to 68 BCE, stylistic manners and contents possibly taken from Theocritus' love poetry; in the *Ecclesiastes* there are themes and doctrines very similar to those of some Hellenistic philosophical schools, in particular of Epicureanism, Cynicism. and Stoicism—for example, the alternation of goods and evils in human life, and the value and the vanity of human knowledge; also in the *Fourth Book of the Maccabees,* an apocryphal text probably written at the end of the 1st century CE, there are implicit traces of Platonic and Stoic ethical doctrines, such as the resistance to injustices and the control over human passions.

The influence of the classical tradition on Judaism before 70 CE culminated in two major authors: Philo and Flavius Josephus. Both were characterized not only by their deep knowledge of Greek culture and literature, but also by their direct personal contacts with the new Roman rulers, who dominated the Near East from the mid-1st century BCE onward. Philo, living in Alexandria ca. 20 BCE–45 CE, is well known for his interpretation of the Pentateuch, written in Greek and reflecting many doctrines of Platonism and Stoicism: the concept of God as a Platonic demiurge, creating the world through angelic "ideas"; the identification of the "Word of God" with the Stoic *Logos spermatikos;* and the doctrine of the Stoic *apatheia* as a way for conjoining the human soul to God. Flavius Josephus, living in Palestine 37–ca. 100 CE, saw himself as the defender of the Jewish tradition in front of his non-Jewish Greek and Roman audience. True, he appears to have followed the objective methods of Thucydides and Polybius in writing the history of the 66–70 rebellion of Palestinian Jews against the Romans in his *Bellum Iudaicum;* but this is not the case of his other historical Greek work, *Antiquitates Iudaicae,* which he probably wrote to defend Jews' sacred history and to show that Jewish tradition was as ancient and trustworthy as the Egyptian and Mesopotamian traditions and surely preceded Greek culture.

The events of 70 CE, in particular the destruction of the Jerusalem Temple by the Roman army, opened a crisis in the relationship between Judaism and the classical tradition in the Near East. Egyptian Jewish culture, which had been strictly connected to Hellenism, lost importance, and the stewardship of Judaism was assumed by the rabbis of Palestine and Mesopotamia. They saw the Roman world as the enemy of Israel, and this idea was explicitly expressed in their main works, in which they refounded Judaism as religion: the Mishnah (dating back to the Palestinian period before 220 CE) and the Talmud (written down in Palestine and in Mesopotamia during the 6th century). In these texts they explicitly condemned the main aspects of classical culture (which they called *hokmah zarah,* "alien wisdom"): Greek education (the *paideia*)—they wished to replace it with the study of the Jewish law (the Torah); Greek language—according to them, Jews must speak and write either in Hebrew or in Aramaic; Greek literature—Jews should not give any importance to it; Roman law—the Talmud appears to have been compiled as a Jewish response to the *Corpus iuris civilis;* Greek philosophy—Epicurus became, in the Mishnah, the damned atheist through antonomasia, and the permission to study philosophy was denied to Jews younger than 25.

Notwithstanding these rejections, many aspects of the Greek and Roman cultures, even if officially condemned, influenced rabbinic Judaism.

First of all, Palestinian and Mesopotamian rabbis created new academies that imitated some characteristics of the Greek schools of rhetoric, law, and philosophy found in the Near East during late antiquity at Gaza, Alexandria, and elsewhere: for example, the method of questions and answers typical of rabbinical academies seems to reflect an identical approach, the *aporiai kai luseis,* applied in the Alexandrian school. The Greek language influenced the creation of a number of new technical terms of Jewish law in the Mishnah and the Talmud. Even Greek philology, if not Greek literature proper, might have left consistent traces in the rabbinic interpretation of the Bible: according to the Mishnah, Homer's works could be read by Jews if they did not take into consideration their religious and ethical ideas; and the ways and rules followed by the Alexandrinian Homeric scholars might have influenced the creation of what is regarded as the canon of the Hebrew Bible (24 books, the same number of the books of the *Iliad* and of the *Odyssey*), as well as the hermeneutic rules applied by the rabbis to their legal interpretations of the Pentateuch. Finally, a number of possible, mainly implicit traces of the knowledge of Greek Hellenistic philosophy have been detected in the Talmud. Talmudic rabbis explicitly praised the Cynic philosopher Oenomaus of Gadara (2nd century CE), possibly because he wrote a treatise against pagan oracles; they condemned the doctrines of "Sadoq and Baytos," possibly an allusion to Boetus of Sidon (1st century BCE), who denied Plato's doctrine of the immortality of the human soul; even the Talmudic tale about the existence of a dangerous "garden" that misled three famous rabbis might allude to the Epicurean school, the Garden (Greek *kēpos*). As a matter of fact, in condemning Epicurus the Talmud followed a tendency found in another Greek philosophical school, Stoicism. Flavius Josephus had already identified the Pharisees (the ancestors of the rabbis) with the Stoics; both the Talmudic rabbis and the Stoics of late antiquity agreed on some doctrines: monotheism, cosmopolitanism, indifference to Roman power, asceticism, and the exaltation of the "ethical suicide." Both of them agreed in their attitudes to some Greek sciences or pseudo-sciences (astrology, magic, medicine) and expressed their ideas in the same ways, through ethical sentences and public diatribes. Research into the relationship between rabbinic Judaism and the classical tradition, however, is still in its infancy: it should be continued by overcoming some ideological and religious obstacles to its full comprehension.

Things are different in the case of medieval Judaism. The extent of the knowledge of Greek culture (although often indirect and limited to philosophy and sciences) among Jews in the Mediterranean area (the Near East, Spain, Provence, and Italy) ca. 800–1500 is better understood and has been studied in detail. Medieval Jews generally did not have an immediate knowledge of Greek and Latin literatures, at least not before the age of Humanism (from 1400 onward): only a very few texts pertaining to them appear to have been read, quoted, or translated into Hebrew in the Middle Ages. They knew the classical tradition through medieval Arabo-Islamic literature and thought, and, especially after 1300, through medieval literature in Europe (in Latin and in vernacular languages).

In the period 800–1200, medieval Mediterranean Jews knew ancient philosophy and science mostly through their interpretations in Arabic texts. A very significant case of this relationship to the classical tradition is found in the most well-known medieval Jewish author, Moses Maimonides (1138–1204). As Shlomo Pines and Herbert A. Davidson both point out, most of Maimonides' explicit references to Aristotle (whom he calls "the prince of philosophers") in his major philosophical and theological work, the *Guide of the Perplexed,* are in reality taken from medieval Arabic authors, in particular from al-Fārābī and Avicenna. Of course, this does not prevent other early-medieval Jewish authors, such as Saadia Gaon (882–942) in Mesopotamia, Isaac Israeli (ca. 850–950) in Egypt and Tunisia, and Solomon ibn Gabirol (1021–1058) and Moses ibn Ezra (ca. 1055–1138) in Spain, from making implicit or explicit references to ancient Greek philosophy and science in their works. In some passages of his main theological work, *The Book of the Beliefs and Convictions,* Saadia mentions and discusses the opinions of several philosophers (probably Plato, Aristotle, Hippocrates, the Sophists, the Skeptics) about the origin of the world, as well as the ideas of other authors (probably Pythagoras, Dicaearchus, Asclepiades of Prusa, Empedocles, Heraclitus) about the nature of the human soul, without any explicit reference to them. As a matter of fact, he apparently knew these doctrines through an Arabic compendium of pseudo-Plutarch's *Placita philosophorum* or through the Arabic translation of patristic Greek works. (Some traces of the knowledge of Philo's works and doctrines have also been recently detected in the Jewish Kalam, of which Saadia himself was a practitioner; but no translation of Philo's texts into Arabic or Hebrew has yet been found.) Isaac Israeli devoted one of his philosophical works, *The Book of the Elements,* to defend Aristotle's doctrine on the quality and quantity of the elements; however, his knowledge of this doctrine and of the ideas of other Greek authors explicitly mentioned (e.g., Galen) might have come to him from Arabo-Islamic philosophy—in particular from al-Kindi. A more direct relationship to Greek sources is found in a work by Moses ibn Ezra, the *Treatise of the Garden,* wherein a relevant number of explicit references to Greek philosophers and to their authentic works (among them Plato's *Timaeus* and Aristotle's *De caelo* and *De partibus animalium*) have been found. This is also the case in Solomon ibn Gabirol's ethical treatise, *The Correction of the Moral Characters,* which quotes Galen's writings on ethics from their medieval Arabic translations. As a matter of fact, other quotations of Greek authors found in early-medieval Jewish thinkers might have been taken from Arabic collections of ancient philosophical maxims, for example from Hunayn ibn-Ishāq's *Moral Sayings of the Philosophers.*

A more direct relationship to the classical tradition might have been found in 12th-century Christian Spain, where Jewish authors were probably able to read and employ Latin sources. For example, traces of a direct knowledge of the contents of Orosius' *Adversus Paganos*—a well-known work in early-medieval Spain, probably the only Latin text translated into Arabic in the Middle Ages—are found in a history of the Jewish people, *The Book of Tradition* by Abraham ibn Daud, a Jewish philosopher active in Toledo ca. 1145–1180; and possible traces of Isidore of Seville's doctrines on Christian sacred history have been pointed out in a work of Abraham bar Hiyya (d. 1136), a Jewish author active in Barcelona.

From 1200 onward the knowledge and absorption of some elements of the classical tradition by European Jews became more important through the new phenomenon of translations of philosophical and scientific works into Hebrew, which was widely and deeply studied by Moritz Steinschneider in the second half of the 19th century. This phenomenon was stimulated by a famous 1199 letter of Maimonides to Samuel ibn Tibbon, in which he affirmed that Aristotle's books were "the roots of scientific works" and should have been studied as recommended by Alexander of Aphrodisias and Themistius. (Maimonides apparently regarded Plato's works, on the other hand, as abstruse and useless.) In reality, in the late Middle Ages Aristotle was read by Jews less through his Greek interpretations than through his main Arabic interpreter: Averroës. After Samuel ibn Tibbon's Hebrew translation of Aristotle's *Meteorologica* (1210), only a few Greek philosophical texts were rendered into Hebrew, and those mostly from Arabic: in the mid-13th century, in Provence, Moses ibn Tibbon translated Themistius' paraphrase of book *Lambda* of Aristotle's *Metaphysica* and pseudo-Aristotle's *Problemata physica;* in Rome ca. 1284 Zerahyah Hen translated Aristotle's *De generatione et corruptione* and *De anima,* as well as Themistius' paraphrase of Aristotle's *De caelo* (the Hebrew translation is noticeably the only extant witness of this work); in northern France, before 1300, an anonymous author translated most of Aristotle's zoological books from a Latin version of the medieval Arabic translation of them; in 1314 Qalonymos ben Qalonymos of Arles translated Nicolaus Damascenus' *De plantis;* between 1323 and 1340 Samuel of Marseilles translated book 1 of Alexander of Aphrodisias' *De anima;* around 1375 David ibn Yaish of Seville translated a lost Greek work, Bryson's *Oeconomicum.* Other main texts of the *Corpus Aristotelicum,* such as the *Analytica posteriora,* the *Physica,* and the *Metaphysica,* were read by European Jews in the Hebrew translations of Averroes' "long commentaries" on them.

A limited number of Greek scientific works also were rendered into Hebrew from their medieval Arabic translations in the 13th and 14th centuries. In medicine one should mention Hippocrates' *Aphorismi* and *Prognostica* (according to Galen's commentary on them), and his treatises *De diaeta in morbis acutis, De aere aquis et locis,* and *De superfoetatione,* as well as Galen's *Ars parva, Katagenos, De crisibus, De venae sectione,* and *De puero epileptico consilium.* (Galen was read mostly by medieval Jewish doctors, however, according to the Arabic-to-Hebrew translations of the *Summaria Alexandrinorum,* a compendium of his main works.) A greater number of fundamental Greek scientific texts were translated into Hebrew, since they concerned mathematical sciences (arithmetic, geometry, astronomy): Nicomachus of Gerasa's *Introductio arithmetica;* Euclid's *Elementa* (translated into Hebrew four times in the period 1230–1300) and *Optica;* some geometrical works by Archimedes (*De mensura circuli, De sphaera et cylindro*) and by minor Greek mathematicians, such as Autolycus of Pitane, Menelaus of Alexandria, and Theodosius of Tripoli; Ptolemy's *Almagest* and other astronomical works, as well as Geminus of Rhodes' *Introductio ad phaenomena.* This interest in classical mathematical texts was probably due to the professional interest of a number of medieval Jews, as some of them were employed as astronomers and astrologers in princely courts. Apart from this practical use of the classical tradition, the knowledge of Greek and Latin nonscientific literature among late-medieval European Jews was scant: only such works as Aesop and a Latin medieval reelaboration of pseudo-Callistenes' romance of Alexander the Great, *Historia de proeliis,* were rendered into Hebrew in various ways.

A short, final flush of interest in the classical tradition appeared among the cultural Jewish elite in Spain and Italy during the age of Humanism. In these countries, learned Jews tried to emulate and even surpass the recent cultural tendencies of their Christian countrymen; some of them elaborated and propagated a legend according to which Aristotle was of Jewish origin. In Spain such works as Aristotle's *Ethica Nicomachea* and *Metaphysica,* pseudo-Aristotle's *Oeconomica,* and Boethius' *De consolatione philosophiae* were translated once or twice into Hebrew during the 15th century, usually from their Latin medieval or Humanistic versions. In Italy one of the chief figures of Jewish Humanism, the philosopher and author Judah Messer Leon (living in northern Italy and in Naples 1425–1498), not only translated from Latin into Hebrew the first three books of Aristotle's *Physica,* but also wrote a treatise of Hebrew rhetoric, *The Book of the Honeycomb's Flow,* applying to the interpretation of the Hebrew Bible the rules found in Latin rhetorical works: Cicero's *De inventione,* pseudo-Cicero's *Rhetorica ad Herennium,* Quintilian's *Institutio oratoria,* and Victorinus' commentary on Cicero. In the same period, the interpretation of Plato and of the Hermetic tradition promoted by the Platonic Academy in Florence had a Jewish follower: Yohanan Alemanno, a collaborator of Giovanni Pico della Mirandola. Jewish Humanism—probably the last example of a direct involvement of Judaism in the study and interpretation of the classical tradition—still left some traces in Italy in the first half of the 16th century, owing to the works of Isaac Abravanel as a Neoplatonic interpreter of the Hebrew Bible, and of his son Judah Abravanel, better known as Leone Ebreo, the author of the *Dialoghi d'amore* (ca. 1502; publ. 1535).

BIBL.: Elias J. Bickerman, *The Jews in the Greek Age* (Cambridge, Mass., 1988). H. A. L. Fischel, *Rabbinic Literature and Greco-Roman Philosophy* (Leiden 1973). Emil Schürer, *Geschichte des jüdischen Volkes im Zeitalter Jesu Christi*, 4th ed., 3 vols. + index (Leipzig 1901–1911). Moritz Steinschneider, *Die hebraeischen Übersetzungen des Mittelalters und die Juden als Dolmetscher* (1893; repr. Graz 1956). Mauro Zonta, *La filosofia antica nel Medioevo ebraico* (Brescia 1996). M.Z.

Julian

Julian (331–363), universally known as the Apostate, is the best documented and the most enigmatic of the emperors of late antiquity. His father was a half brother of Constantine the Great, who had imposed Christianity on the government of the Mediterranean world. Soon after Constantine's death in 337 the empire was divided among his three sons. The family of Julian was largely wiped out in a massacre that eliminated his father and eight relatives. Only Julian and his half brother, Gallus, were spared, presumably because they were so young. The two boys were sent into exile for six years on a royal estate in central Asia Minor, not far from Kayseri in modern Turkey. The trauma incurred by the massacre and long years in isolation is incalculable, but there is no doubt that during the time of his exile the eunuchs who guarded him made every effort to raise Julian as a Christian. Nonetheless, he had access to a library containing the classical works of paganism, and when he emerged from exile at the age of 18, he was ready for a covert conversion to Neoplatonic polytheism at the hands of charismatic teachers in Pergamum and Ephesus. At Pergamum his teacher was Aedesius, a pupil of the great Iamblichus, after whose instruction Julian fell under the spell of the wonder-working "theurgist" Maximus of Ephesus.

The emperor Constantius II named Julian his Caesar (junior partner), and in that capacity the young man proved himself a successful general in Gaul, where his troops proclaimed him emperor at Paris in an act of usurpation in 360. The death of Constantius in 361 averted a civil war and allowed Julian to espouse openly the paganism he had long concealed: hence the epithet Apostate, by which he is generally known. Julian was content to let the Christians quarrel among themselves as he endeavored vigorously to restore blood sacrifice and austere worship of the old gods. In this cause he promoted without success the restoration of the temple at Jerusalem, the only place where Jews could offer sacrifice. He notoriously forbade Christians to teach the pagan classics. His death in a war against the Persians in 363 ended his rule, and a Christian, Jovian, succeeded him.

Inspired perhaps by a series of eloquent hymns directed against Julian and composed in Syriac by his contemporary Saint Ephrem, a lavishly ornamented account of Julian's exploits began to circulate among Syriac-speaking Christians in the form of a narrative conventionally called the *Julian Romance*. This work had a great influence on apocalyptic literature in the later 7th century among Christians living under Muslim rule.

Julian's disposition was ascetic and demanding. Many pagans together with comfortably assimilated Christians found that the life they had enjoyed in Antioch and other centers of Hellenism was severely curtailed. Julian's voice can be heard memorably in his surviving writings, particularly in his letters, in a fierce denunciation of the people of Antioch (*Misopogon*, "Beard-Hater"), and in a satire on his imperial predecessors (*Caesars*), which ends with a vicious portrait of Christ.

The view that Julian "turned the clock back" and restored a world of pagan libertinism could not be more inaccurate. Yet in later tradition he was often assigned this role. In the 18th century the Abbé de la Bletterie audaciously published translations of Julian's work and wrote a subversive biography of Julian (from which the Abbé felt obliged to omit his name). Ibsen's *Emperor and Galilaean* (1873) and Merezhkovsky's *Christ and Antichrist* (3 vols., 1896–1905) represent a romantic nostalgia for a pagan hero that never existed. Gore Vidal's *Julian* (1964) is much closer to historical reality.

The mystical aura of Julian the Apostate appeared early in the ecclesiastical tradition, where his dying words, "Thou hast won, pale Galilaean," first appeared. Curiously, the pagan tradition, represented by the late antique historians Ammianus Marcellinus and Zosimus, was far from unconditionally eulogistic. Following Ammianus, Gibbon faulted Julian for an excess of "enthusiasm." Gibbon's portrait was an important inspiration for the modern Greek poet C. P. Cavafy (1863–1933), who wrote no fewer than 12 poems about Julian. Cavafy, who was certainly a sensualist if there ever was one, despised Julian for his asceticism. His repudiation of this emperor's idiosyncratic polytheism does Cavafy credit and Julian justice.

BIBL.: Polymnia Athanassiadi, *Julian: An Intellectual Biography*, 2nd ed. (London 1992). G. W. Bowersock, *Julian the Apostate* (Cambridge, Mass., 1978) and "The Julian Poems of C. P. Cavafy," *Byzantine and Modern Greek Studies* 7 (1981) 89–104. René Braun and Jean Richer, eds., *L'Empereur Julien: Études*, vol. 1, *De l'histoire à la légende (331–1715)*; vol. 2, *De la légende au mythe (de Voltaire à nos jours)*(Paris 1978–1981). A. Muravyov, "The Syriac Julian Romance and Its Place in the Literary History," *Khristianskii Vostok*, n.s. 1 (1999) 194–206. Kate Philip, *Julianus Apostata in der deutschen Literatur* (Berlin 1929). G.W.B.

Juvenal

Decimus Iunius Iuvenalis, ca. 55–140 CE, Roman satiric poet from Aquinum (modern Aquino). The last and most influential of the Roman satirists, he wrote 16 satires published approximately between the years 110 and 130.

Very little is known about his life. His reputation rested largely on an ancient report that the emperor Domitian, who appears as a tyrant in *Satire* 4, banished him to Egypt. Thus Juvenal, exemplifying the perils inherent in the exercise of free speech in a closed imperial society, became "a Zealous Vindicator of *Roman* Liberty" (Dryden).

In his satires Juvenal uses names and examples from the past as protective covers for his exposés of contemporary vice and folly. The republican satirist Lucilius was his model (1.19–20, 165–166). Juvenal's main theme is the dissolution of the social fabric, exemplified in the most famous satires by the evils of the city of Rome (3, foreshadowing the problems of the modern megalopolis), monarchical government (4), the plight of intellectuals (7), the corruption of nobility (8), and the futility of prayer (10; "The Vanity of Human Wishes" has been its unofficial title since Samuel Johnson). In the notorious *Satires* 2 (against hypocrisy as evinced by homosexuals), 6 (on women and marriage), and 9 (a male prostitute's lament), Juvenal links his condemnation of society to deviations from traditional sexual norms.

Juvenal's satires are written in the grand style of epic, the first consistent instance of the use of that style in satire, which set the standard for much of modern verse satire. In particular, hyperbole and incongruous juxtapositions of incompatibles for the sake of satiric inflation and subsequent deflation reinforce Juvenal's indictments. Pithy expressions of universal applicability point out obvious morals: "It is difficult not to write satire" (1.30), "indignation makes my verse" (1.79, programmatic for the early satires), "who'll guard the guardians?" (6.347–348 = Oxford fragment 31–32), "bread and circuses" (10.81), and "a sound mind in a sound body" (9.356) are the most famous instances. Juvenal even more than Virgil became a source of aperçus. *The Tatler* and *The Spectator* frequently used tags from Juvenal as their mottoes. Pope's *Dunciad* (1728–1743), a mock-heroic epic on the Juvenalian theme of bad contemporary poetry (and itself the progenitor of numerous other mock-epics) illustrates how effectively Juvenal's style may be brought to bear on English.

Juvenal seems to have been popular neither in his own day nor for the next 250 years. Editions and commentaries began to appear in the late 4th century. The Church Fathers referred to him or quoted him. He was revered as a moral teacher (*Juvenalis ethicus*) and eventually became an author studied in the schools. Sebastian Brant based a section of *The Ship of Fools* (1494) on *Satire* 10 and helped establish it as a major instance of popular moralizing. Christian ethicists could also appropriate Juvenal's memorable description of a guilty conscience in *Satire* 13. The general view of Juvenal as a committed moralist continued until the 20th century. Longfellow, for example, visited Monte Cassino near Aquino and commented on the town's two famous sons, Juvenal and Thomas Aquinas ("Monte Cassino: Terra di Lavoro").

Since the Tudor age Juvenal has been well established in British literature. There have been few decades in which he was not translated, imitated, or mentioned. Shakespeare's Polonius asks Hamlet what he is reading; in reply, Hamlet mentions "the satirical rogue" and summarizes part of *Satire* 10, the best reading matter for a melancholic (*Hamlet* 2.2). Hall, Marston, and Jonson, among other poets, prepared the way for the firm establishment of Juvenal in English literature during the 17th century, by Chapman, Vaughn, Oldham, and Prior. The greatest impulse, however, came with the 1693 translation by John Dryden and his collaborators. Dryden's lengthy *Discourse concerning the Original and Progress of Satire,* which precedes the translation, proved highly influential in perpetuating a view of Juvenal's satires (as contrasted to those of Horace) that had originated in the Middle Ages:

> I wou'd willingly divide the Palm betwixt them; upon the two Heads of Profit and Delight, which are the two Ends of Poetry in general . . . I am profited by both, I am pleas'd with both; but I owe more to *Horace* for my Instruction; and more to *Juvenal,* for my Pleasure . . . *Juvenal* is of a more vigorous and Masculine Wit, he gives me as much Pleasure as I can bear: He fully satisfies my Expectation, he Treats his Subject home: His Spleen is rais'd, and he raises mine: I have the Pleasure of Concernment in all he says; He drives his Reader along with him; and when he is at the end of his way, I willingly stop with him . . . When he gives over, 'tis a sign the Subject is exhausted; and the Wit of Man can carry it no farther.

Samuel Johnson's two imitations of Juvenal, "London: A Poem in Imitation of the Third Satire of Juvenal" (1738, later revisions) and "The Vanity of Human Wishes: The Tenth Satire of Juvenal Imitated" (1749, revised 1755), have been called "the greatest verse satires of the English or any other language" (T. S. Eliot). Boswell called Johnson "the English Juvenal." Prominent British poets who in various ways translated or imitated Juvenal in the 18th and 19th centuries include Defoe, Fielding, Wordsworth, and Shelley. The American tradition of translation and adaptation of Juvenal began with John Quincy Adams. Boileau, the most important French satirist, imitated both Horace and Juvenal and in turn influenced English satire. In 1970 the German-American scholar and translator Harry C. Schnur published, under his Latinate name C. Arrius Nurus, a witty hoax: a Latin continuation of Juvenal's incomplete *Satire* 16 from a manuscript of Juvenal said to have been discovered in Schnur's home. The award-winning German poet and essayist Durs Grünbein (b. 1962) frequently takes recourse to antiquity, especially to Juvenal (*Nach den Satiren,* 1999; *Antike Dispositionen: Aufsätze,* 2005).

Aphra Behn's 1687 poem commending a new version of *Satire* 10 elegantly summarizes Juvenal's status in English:

Great *Juvenal* in every Line,
True *Roman* still o're all does shine;
But in the *Brittish* Garb appears most fine.

BIBL.: R. M. Alden, *The Rise of Formal Satire in England under Classical Influence* (Philadelphia 1902). R. M. Colton, *Juvenal and Boileau: A Study of Literary Influence* (Hildesheim 1987). Gilbert Highet, *Juvenal the Satirist* (Oxford 1954). William Kupersmith, *Roman Satirists in Seventeenth-century England* (Lincoln 1985). Howard D. Weinbrot, *Alexander Pope and the Traditions of Formal Verse Satire* (Princeton 1982). Martin M. Winkler, ed., *Juvenal in English* (London 2001).

M.M.W.

K

Knossos

Knossos is renowned in Greek mythology as the palace of the legendary Cretan King Minos, at the heart of which lurked the Labyrinth, a prison for the Minotaur, monstrous fruit of Queen Pasiphae's adulterous coupling with a white bull. In the passage on Achilles' shield in Homer's *Iliad,* the Labyrinth appears in a more gentle guise as a mazy dancing floor, installed at Knossos by Daedalus for the princess Ariadne.

A few kilometers south of Crete's capital, Hērákleion, lies a low mound surrounded by olive trees, among which it used to be possible to find coins of the 5th century BCE, bearing the name Knosos and featuring labyrinth designs or images of the Minotaur, relics of the classical settlement built here on what was supposed to be the site of the Palace of Minos. In 1878, after Heinrich Schliemann had astounded the world with his archaeological exploits at the legendary cities of Troy and Mycenae, a Cretan antiquarian named Minos Kalokairinos made a preliminary excavation of the mound, uncovering the stones of what promised to be a huge building, and a row of clay storage jars that were large enough for a person to climb inside.

Many people, including Schliemann himself, petitioned Crete's government for the chance to finish what Kalokairinos had started, but it was only after the island had won its independence from the Ottomans in 1898 that the excavation became feasible. Permission to dig was awarded to Arthur Evans, an autocratic Englishman, heir to an industrial fortune, who had already bought a substantial share of the site from its Turkish owners, and who would spend the rest of his life and a large share of his father's money digging the mound. Under a thin layer of soil and wildflowers, Evans and his team uncovered the remains of a vast, rather shoddily built palace or temple complex, decorated with bright frescoes and containing hundreds of fragments of inscribed clay tablets. This, Evans announced, was the true Labyrinth of legend, and in 1905 he dubbed Europe's oldest civilization "Minoan" in honor of its mythical ruler.

The Labyrinth turned out to be more dance floor than monster's prison. According to Evans's interpretation, Knossos was the site of a series of Bronze Age temple-palaces built between about 2000 and 1400 BCE, the domain of a dynasty of priest-kings who ruled over a literate, unwarlike, and rather decadent court, in which wasp-waisted ladies worshipped the Great Cretan Mother Goddess, enjoyed high social status, took frequent baths, and used the world's first flush lavatory. Whether hailed by feminists as a center of the ancient matriarchy, shuddered at by novelists and journalists as a vision of cultural degeneration, or celebrated by pacifists as a symbol of the very possibility of peace, Evans's Palace of Minos became one of the sensations of the fin de siècle.

The excavation of Knossos presented great technical challenges. Many walls were discovered held together by debris, even though the wooden beams that had originally supported them had rotted away. Evans's solution was to rebuild parts of the palace, inserting columns whose red color and downward-tapering shape were based on paintings of architectural forms on fresco fragments. The most impressive result of this strategy was the Grand Staircase, which rises and descends through no fewer than five levels.

Starting in 1910 Evans switched to reinforced concrete for the reconstruction work. Inspired by the strength, cheapness, and plasticity of this material, he became more speculative and extravagant in his rebuilding, and 1930 saw the reconstruction of the entire throne-room complex in reinforced concrete, including the addition of two completely conjectural upper floors. Postwar Minoan archaeology has involved the revision of much of Evans's interpretations, including, recently, a reassessment of the pacific character of ancient Cretan society, but his concrete labyrinth has withstood wars and earthquakes, has been lovingly restored, and remains Crete's principal tourist attraction.

BIBL.: Arthur Evans, *The Palace of Minos,* 4 vols. (London 1921–1936). Joan Evans, *Time and Chance: The Story of Arthur Evans and His Forebears* (London 1943). J. Wilson Myers, Eleanor Emlen Myers, and Gerald Cadogan, *Aerial Atlas of Ancient Crete* (Berkeley 1992). C.G.

Korais, Adamantios

The leading classical scholar of the Greek Enlightenment, Korais was born in Smyrna in 1748 to a family of Chiot origin. He was educated locally and learned Latin from the chaplain of the Dutch consulate, Bernard Keun. He spent the years 1772–1778 in Amsterdam. After a short period back in Smyrna (1779–1782), he left for Montpellier in France with the intention of studying medicine. He graduated with a dissertation dealing with fevers entitled *Pyretologiae Synopsis.* In 1787 he defended his doctoral thesis, *Medicus hippocraticus,* on the medical doctor's ethical duties according to Hippocrates' first aphorism. These early works bore the influence of the Neohippocratic revival in 18th-century French medicine. To pursue further research on the Hippocratic corpus Korais moved in May 1788 to Paris, where he lived until his death in 1833.

In his correspondence during the 1790s he commented on the French Revolution, indicting Jacobinism as a modern form of tyranny and barbarism. He remained equally skeptical toward Bonapartism and reflected on the preconditions of liberty and on the virtues of moderation, following Montesquieu and Condorcet.

In 1799 he inaugurated his philological career with the publication of a French translation of Theophrastus. The following year he published his monumental two-volume edition of Hippocrates' *Of Airs, Waters, Places,* with extensive prolegomena that synthesized classical scholarship with late Enlightenment social theory. This work established his reputation as an authoritative editor of classical texts and secured him a pension from the Institut de France that enabled him to prepare an edition of Strabo. Shortly thereafter he joined the Société des observateurs de l'homme and espoused the anthropological and ethical theory prevailing among its members. These views are evident in his prolegomena and commentary to his Greek translation of works by the Italian economist and jurist Cesare Beccaria (1802) and in his edition of Heliodorus' *Ethiopics* (1804).

The major milestone in his work as a classicist came in 1805, when he founded his Hellenic Library, with funding from the Zosima brothers, wealthy Greek merchants in Russia. This project was designed to produce editions of major classical texts with extensive prolegomena for the instruction of his compatriots in the moral culture of the classics. The successive volumes of the Hellenic Library were published in Paris, and owing to generous sponsorship from the Zosima brothers they were distributed free of charge to school libraries and to scholars in the Ottoman-held Greek territories and in diaspora. The publication and circulation of these volumes contributed to the culture of rising expectations that preceded the Greek Revolution of 1821.

Between 1805 and 1827 the Hellenic Library produced 17 volumes, including Aelian, Isocrates, Plutarch's *Parallel Lives* (6 vols.), the *Iliad* (books 1–4), Strabo, Marcus Aurelius, Aristotle's *Politics* and *Nicomachean Ethics,* Xenophon's *Memorabilia,* and Plato's *Gorgias.* What is particularly notable is Korais's judgment of the political relevance of the texts selected for publication in the 1820s as his contribution to the Greek struggle for liberation.

Korais commanded an outstanding knowledge of the manuscript tradition, which contributed to his fame among classicists. On the basis of his expertise in the history and structure of the Greek language, he often proposed quite daring corrections to the texts he edited. He was deeply interested in the Greek language as a cultural and historical phenomenon and collected considerable textual and lexicographic material, which he published in the four volumes of his *Miscellany* (*Atakta,* 1828–1832). His familiarity with the evolution of the Greek language, including phases he considered periods of decline and corruption that had removed the language from its Attic authenticity, prompted him to propose a program of linguistic reform that entailed purification of the contemporary vernacular from extensive lexical loans from foreign languages and partial correction of its grammar so as to make plainer its lineage from Classical Greek. This involved him in many controversies over the "language question" in pre-independence Greek cultural politics.

Korais opted for a middle ground between the archaists, who wanted to revive Attic Greek as the language of Greek education and philosophy, and the proponents of what at the time was described as the "vulgar style," that is, the unconditional use of vernacular Greek as a language of culture. Korais supported the use of Modern Greek, but in the purified form he proposed. This purified form came to be called *Katharevousa* (literally, "the purified one"), but Korais's linguistic theory and practice was quite moderate and restrained in comparison to the excesses to which learned Greek would be taken by the zeal of purifiers later in the 19th century.

Besides his imposing works in the fields of classics and language, Korais wrote extensively on politics and elaborated a theory of cultural and political change as a blueprint for the reconstruction of his homeland. Throughout his writings he remained consistently within the Enlightenment tradition, and his voice in classical studies as well as in politics resounds with the principles and values of early 19th-century liberalism.

BIBL.: C. Th. Dimaras, *Istorika Phrontismata,* vol. 2, *Adamantios Korais,* ed. P. Polemi (Athens 1996). P. M. Kitromilides, *Neoellinikos Diaphotismos* (Athens 1996). A. Korais, *Prolegomena stous archaious Ellines syggrapheis,* 4 vols. (Athens 1984–1995). V. Rotolo, *A. Korais e la questione della lingua in Grecia* (Palermo 1965). D. Thereianos, *Adamantios Korais,* 3 vols. (Trieste 1889–1890, repr. Athens 1977). P.M.K.

L

Labyrinth

Polyvalent symbol. Neither the etymology nor the origin of the labyrinth has been fully explained. The most ancient representation that can be dated with certainty is on a Mycenaean clay tablet from Pylos of 1200 BCE. Similar motifs can be found from earliest times in non-Western cultures, such as India, or among the Hopi of North America, which suggests that it is an archetypal structure of the sort dear to anthropologists, a symbol that can be interpreted in various ways over the course of history.

Originally the labyrinth may have been the materialization of choreographic movement. One finds this tradition in Homer's description of the shield of Achilles (*Iliad* 18.590–606); in the crane dance (*geranos*) executed by Theseus and his companions in Delos after their victory (Plutarch, *Theseus* 21), which the 4th-century grammarian Marius Victorinus interpreted as the movement of the celestial bodies; and even in the equestrian game of Troy (*Lusus Troiae*) associated with funeral rites and the foundation of cities (*Aeneid* 5.545–603). Recent research has called attention to later revivals of this tradition, for example, in 16th-century French court ballet or in the labyrinthine dance of the angels in Milton's *Paradise Lost* (5.618–627).

Virgil put the image of Daedalus' labyrinth near the entrance to the underworld (*Aeneid* 6.27). The myth of the Minotaur recalls initiation rites seen as a journey through the underworld and the kingdom of death, ending in rebirth. Medieval culture Christianized the symbol with the aid of the Church Fathers: the path that leads via turnings and detours to the center represents the circumambulations of human existence in a world of sin, where the "thread of Christ" (Jerome) leads to redemption. Labyrinths abound in the interiors of churches, especially the large-scale labyrinths on the pavements of French cathedrals from the 13th century onward, where they are associated with the liturgical dances performed at Easter (documented from 1396 at Auxerre); sometimes the music is even preserved. On the other hand, it was only from the 18th century onward that the labyrinths in churches came to be used in rituals of penance, traversed by pilgrims on their knees as substitutes for pilgrimage to the Holy Land.

The more secular image of Daedalus as the personification of human skill and of the genius of the architect gained momentum with the Renaissance. The labyrinth was often selected as a personal emblem, and it was the heraldic device of the Gonzaga family in Mantua. The apotropaic function that the labyrinth assumed in antiquity, for example in mosaics placed in the entryways of Roman houses, is based on the notion that wicked spirits can move only in straight lines, an idea that continues in the fortification projects of Filarete and Francesco de' Marchi and in the maze that surrounds and protects the garden of Armida in Torquato Tasso's *Gerusalemme liberata* (16.1–9).

Here we see a decisive shift in form reflecting a change in meaning. In antiquity and the Middle Ages all representations show a unicursal labyrinth, which offers a single possible route to the center that is slowly traversed through a succession of concentric circuits: seven in the Cretan spiral-form labyrinth, eleven in the so-called Chartres type, which made its first appearance in the 10th century. On the other hand, the multicursal maze, where the path is determined by the choices made at intersections, with the risk of going astray at any point and sometimes with multiple centers, was only a literary motif in antiquity, for example in Ovid (*Metamorphoses* 8.157–168). Before the drawings of the engineer Giovanni Fontana (ca. 1420–1440), there is no known figure showing this alternative tradition, but it became frequent in the modern world. Hundreds of mazes were realized for amusement in the gardens of Europe in the 16th through the 18th centuries. Some scholars have tried to link this evolution with a new vision of the place of humanity in the world, where the notion of free choice came into play, especially in theological discussions of salvation (Santarcangeli 1967).

Finally, the labyrinth has come to represent the complexity of reality and of human experience, where life and thought are likened to physical movement. This metaphorical dimension, though already present in Plato (*Euthidemus* 291B), is generally associated with Jorge Luis Borges, in whose work the image of the maze merges with that of the library to signify the totality and the infinity of the universe.

BIBL.: *Caerdroia: The Journal of Mazes and Labyrinths* (1980–). Penelope Reed Dobb, *The Idea of the Labyrinth from Classical Antiquity to the Middle Ages* (Ithaca 1990). Hermann Kern, *Through the Labyrinth: Designs and Meanings over 5,000 Years* (Munich 2000). Pietro Santarcangeli, *Il libro dei labirinti: Storia di un mito e un simbolo* (Florence 1967). Craig Wright, *The Maze and the Warrior: Symbols in Architecture, Theology, and Music* (Cambridge, Mass., 2001). H.B.

Lachmann, Karl

Eminent German philologist (1793–1851). He holds the unique distinction of having produced work of fundamental importance in three separate areas of textual scholarship: the Greek and Latin classics, Middle High German poetry, and the Greek New Testament. The focus here is on his contributions to classical scholarship.

The first decades of the 19th century witnessed the greatest single advance in the history of classical editing. Most of the first printed editions of classical texts were based on manuscripts of no outstanding merit with a modicum of editorial correction. Those early texts had remained the point of departure for subsequent editions; new manuscript readings or conjectures were unsystematically patched onto the received text (*textus receptus*), but the underlying fabric escaped scrutiny. A new approach, which attempted to sort manuscripts into groups or families based on shared errors, was first articulated by New Testament critics toward the end of the 18th century and took root in classical circles between about 1815 and 1840. Significant figures in this development include J. A. Ernesti, J. N. Madvig, K. G. Zumpt, Hermann Sauppe, J. C. Orelli, and Friedrich Ritschl. Uncovering the genealogical relationships among manuscripts would show which textual "witnesses" (versions) possessed independent authority and which were purely derivative; furthermore, agreements observed in the main families of manuscripts of a text could be used to infer the readings of their lost common source, or archetype. (This type of analysis is sometimes referred to as "stemmatic," since the genetic affiliations of the witnesses can be graphically depicted by a family tree, or *stemma;* examples sometimes appear in present-day classical editions.)

Lachmann's main theoretical contribution to this new critical method was his division of the editorial process into two distinct phases: *recensio* (recension), analysis of the manuscript evidence to select the most authoritative witnesses; and *emendatio* (emendation), the examination of those manuscripts' testimony—variant readings, evidence of additions or omissions, perhaps comments from ancient and modern sources, and other relevant documentation—and, thus informed, the correction of these best witnesses where they are judged to have departed from older and more reliable texts closer to the first writing (which is virtually always no longer extant). The aim is to produce a single master edition of the entire text, meticulously annotated, that is the closest possible approximation of the author's original words.

Lachmann's own editorial practice varied according to the nature of the texts he dealt with and the resources available to him. In his edition of Propertius (1816), an astonishing achievement for a 23-year-old, he correctly identified a manuscript in Wolfenbüttel as one of the principal witnesses, but in his editions of Catullus and Tibullus (both 1829) he relied on inferior manuscripts and made correspondingly less progress. Several of the classical texts he edited were preserved in unique manuscripts, where there was no scope for *recensio,* whereas in some of his editions of medieval German texts he renounced a genealogical approach and based the text on a single manuscript that he judged closest to the original. In his edition of Lucretius' *De rerum natura* (1850), completed late in his career, he encountered a text of which the oldest and best manuscripts had already been identified and their stemmatic affiliation mapped. By noting lacunae and other dislocations of text shared by the oldest witnesses, he was able to determine the precise physical layout (pagination, columns, etc.) of the Lucretian archetype, a manuscript that had been lost for a millennium.

Although he had played a relatively modest part in the evolution of the stemmatic method, his application of that approach to the text of Lucretius, and in particular his reconstruction of its archetype, had a profound influence on his contemporaries, an effect deepened by his relatively early death one year later. In Germany, Lachmann became what A. E. Housman (himself a master of textual criticism) would later call a "deified hero." His biographer Martin Hertz hailed him as a Prometheus of scholarship, bringing the fire of critical method to benighted mortals. Lachmann's edition of Lucretius attained an iconic status as "the book from which we have all learned critical method," an often-quoted phrase of Wilamowitz, who wrote 70 years later.

The consequences of Lachmann's exalted standing were not uniformly benign. Critics professing to follow his example often narrowly focused their attention on a group of allegedly "pure" witnesses and dismissed the remaining majority as "interpolated." In some cases a single manuscript was identified as the *codex optimus* and its readings adopted wherever possible, a practice that has often been discredited but that has yet to disappear. In dealing with manuscripts, Lachmann had shown no interest in their historical context or cultural significance; greater knowledge of and access to manuscript material, together with new intellectual stimuli, would be needed before the study of manuscript transmission as a historical discipline could come of age.

Textual scholarship in the 20th century posed further challenges to the stemmatic method. The most serious was the recognition that many manuscript traditions do not permit the plotting of genetic relationships among the witnesses, primarily because of the blurring of lines of descent caused when a manuscript incorporates readings drawn from more than one source (a process usually known as contamination). In some cases the result is effectively to foil all efforts at stemmatic analysis.

Lachmann's enduring influence is felt indirectly through the basic principles of recension that he championed, which in a more refined and restricted form remain the starting point for all classical editing. His gifts as a philologist are more clearly visible in his many conjectures that remain accepted by modern editors, most especially in his Lucretius commentary, a work of prodigious learning and acumen that is still, as H. A. J. Munro in 1864 predicted it would be, "a landmark for scholars as long as the Latin language continues to be studied." R.T.

Laocoön

Laocoön was the priest of Apollo who spoke the famous words "I fear the Greeks, even when bearing gifts" (*timeo danaos et dona ferentis;* Virgil, *Aeneid* 2.49), counseling the Trojans against admitting the enormous wooden horse to their city. Because it was the will of the gods that Troy should fall, his words went unheeded by his countrymen, especially after he and his two sons were strangled by sea serpents, which the Trojans construed as a sign that his advice was blasphemous.

His career as one of the most famous icons of the classical tradition derives in part from Virgil (*Aeneid* 2.201–249). But it is equally due to the fortunes of a statue of Laocoön and his sons, of uncertain date but extant by the mid-1st century CE, when Pliny the Elder (*Natural History* 36.37) described it as superior to all other works of painting and sculpture; he declared it miraculous in particular for the fact that three sculptors worked together to produce it out of a single piece of marble. On 14 January 1506—or so a letter written several decades later by Francesco da Sangallo attests—the statue was accidentally discovered in a vineyard on the Esquiline Hill in Rome. Michelangelo himself was said to have been summoned to the scene and to have identified the statue as the masterpiece described by Pliny. Whatever the particles of truth in all of this, the Laocoön became almost immediately an object of historical, aesthetic, and political fascination. A competition was staged to restore the principal figure's right arm (Raphael, as judge, awarded the prize to Jacopo Sansovino); motifs from the statue turned up promptly throughout the oeuvres of Michelangelo and Titian, among others; and when representatives of Francis I suggested that the king should be honored by a gift of the statue, Giulio de' Medici, the future Pope Clement VII, commissioned Baccio Bandinelli to make a replica. That work never made it out of Italy, and the French had to content themselves with plaster replicas made from castings executed by Primaticcio and Cellini. Only with the victories of Napoleon did the Vatican Laocoön, along with hundreds of other famous artworks, make its way to Paris in 1797, where it remained until the Council of Vienna restored it, as well as most of the other booty, to its original location.

For centuries artists from El Greco to Rubens to Géricault to Max Ernst, Jean Arp, Salvador Dalí, and Alexander Calder have been inspired by the story and the sculpture. So widely familiar is the composition that it has also had a noteworthy history as a caricature. Titian produced a parody Laocoön, consisting of three apes, possibly mocking Michelangelo's style of depicting human bodies or possibly wishing to assert that "art is the ape of nature." William Blake rendered the statue in an etching which he entitled *Jehovah and His Two Sons Satan and Adam* (ca. 1820); he surrounded the figures with mottoes celebrating, among other things, art and nakedness. In the European popular press the image has been used to criticize the high cost of living in Berlin (1872), the expense of installing a cable system for television (1995), and the woes of an Austrian transport minister beset with telecommunication and railroad difficulties (2001). In the United States, a Christmas-season *New Yorker* cover staged the familiar composition with three individuals atop their boxes of presents, entangled in gift wrapping (1990).

As important to the tradition as the statue itself is the essay by Gotthold Ephraim Lessing entitled *Laokoon oder Über die Grenzen der Malerei und Poesie* (*Laocoön; or, The Limits of Painting and Poetry,* 1766), in which he compares Virgil's verbal account of the priest's suffering to the means that the visual artists had at their disposal to express that same pain. Through the influence of this text, along with writings by Winckelmann and Goethe, the statue became a touchstone in theorizing the relationship between words and pictures as well as between ancient and modern theories and practices of art. Later responses, by authors including Matthew Arnold, Irving Babbitt, and Clement Greenberg, have confirmed the centrality of Laocoön in formulating modern aesthetics.

BIBL.: Leonard Barkan, *Unearthing the Past: Architecture and Aesthetics in the Making of Renaissance Culture* (New Haven 1999). Phyllis Bober and Ruth Rubenstein, *Renaissance Artists and Antique Sculpture* (London 1986). Francis Haskell and Nicholas Penny, *Taste and the Antique: The Lure of Classi-*

cal Sculpture, 1500–1900 (New Haven 1981). Gotthold Ephraim Lessing, *Laocoön: An Essay on the Limits of Painting and Poetry,* trans. Edward Allen McCormick (Indianapolis 1962). L.B.

Latin and the Professions

The uses of Latin since it became a "dead" language, without native speakers, early in the Middle Ages, have been many and various. The language survived and was transformed owing to its use in major institutions such as the Church, the state, and the universities. Latin was for a long time the professional language of the clergy, lawyers, doctors, and university teachers and for a shorter period was the language of diplomats.

Latin was the language of the Catholic Church from the 360s until the 1960s, employed in the liturgy and to a lesser extent in Church administration. The clergy were therefore supposed to be able to read, write, and speak Latin, and many did so, although it is clear from the records of episcopal visitations in the late Middle Ages that some parish priests lacked that skill. It was only in the later 16th century that seminaries were founded to give priests a formal training for their profession. In other words, at the very time that the Protestants were insisting on a vernacular liturgy, the Catholic Church was becoming more Latinized. Even sermons were sometimes delivered in Latin in the Europe of the Counter-Reformation, and attempts were made to teach the language to Catholic converts in other continents, from Mexico to Japan. Latin is still used for papal encyclicals, and there is an office at the Vatican for translating neologisms into Latin, from *atomic bomb* (*globus atomicus vi explodans*) to miniskirt (*tunicula minima*) to *computer* (*instrumentum computatorium*).

Latin was also the language of Europe's universities, from their rise in the 12th century until the 18th century or even later. In the Middle Ages, when most of the students as well as the teachers were clergy, the use of Latin in the academic world posed few problems. But serious criticisms of this practice emerged, from England to Germany, in the 17th century, and a shift to lecturing in vernacular languages, at least in some subjects, came in the 18th century. By the 19th century, use of the vernacular had become the norm, although in some places (such as The Netherlands, France, and Germany) Latin remained the language of inaugural lectures—to the embarrassment of some professors—and also that of doctoral dissertations, forcing some scholars to seek professional translators. A last vestige of the system, which survived into the second half of the 20th century, was the elementary Latin required for entry to Oxford and Cambridge, irrespective of the subject the student wished to study. At Heidelberg some knowledge of Latin is still required of doctoral candidates in oriental studies.

In medieval and early modern universities it was possible, after gaining a general education by following the "arts" course, to acquire a professional training in one of three subjects: theology, law, or medicine. In Catholic Europe, theology was studied from Latin texts, such as the writings of Thomas Aquinas, and the Bible was cited in its Latin translation, known as the Vulgate. Even in the Protestant world, theologians (including Luther and Calvin) often wrote in Latin. As for the two secular professions, "law" generally meant either civil or canon law, studied from Latin texts, and medicine was based on Greek texts (especially those of Hippocrates and Galen) in Latin translation. To this day, the jargon of lawyers (*cui bono, habeas corpus,* etc.) draws heavily on Latin, and that of the medical professions draws on Greek. It was only from the 18th century onward that vernacular languages were regularly used in the training of lawyers and physicians.

Beginning in the Middle Ages, university graduates were employed in government, and much government business was conducted in Latin or at least recorded in that language. In the 16th century the use of Latin as a language of administration declined in France, England, and some other states, though it remained the norm in the Habsburg Empire until the 1790s. Latin was also the language most used by diplomats until the rise of French at the end of the reign of Louis XIV. It remained the language of the learned world (the *respublica litterarum,* or republic of letters) until the 18th century. Both the advantages and disadvantages of the employment of Latin in all these domains are clear enough. Speaking and writing Latin excluded the majority of the population, from peasants to upper-class women (with a few famous exceptions, from the Italian Isotta Nogarola to Queen Elizabeth I). Some early modern reformers claimed that the clergy, the lawyers, and the physicians did this deliberately, to drum up trade—that is, to make a mystery of the ordinary and so create a need for their professions. On the other hand, given the number and variety of European languages, the use of Latin as a lingua franca was convenient, to say the least. In the academic world students and teachers were able to move from one country to another and still communicate. Diplomats did not need to learn one another's languages, as they possessed a common, neutral medium of negotiation. Again, it is no accident that it was in the multilingual Habsburg Empire that Latin survived the longest as the language of administration. The Latin sermons of the Counter-Reformation Church may also have been a kind of lingua franca through which speakers of one Romance language could communicate with speakers of others.

The kind of Latin that was used in all these domains and over all these centuries naturally varied a great deal. In the universities, thanks to the importance of Aristotle, Plato, and Hippocrates, many Greek technical terms were current in a lightly Latinized form, from *entitas* to *democratia.* In writing, and probably in speaking as well, it was common to mix languages. In composing formal documents, the scribe who could not think of an appropriate Latin term might lapse into the vernacular, as can be seen in contracts with painters in Renaissance Italy. Conversely, the record of Luther's conversations during meals shows him speaking German most of the time but introducing Latin phrases when speaking about philosophy. Some Renaissance Humanists criticized post-classical Latin as a kind of corruption and tried to speak and write like Cicero, despite the problem of discussing, in the language of ancient Rome, post-classical topics such as cannonry or institutions such as the papacy or the Ottoman Empire. It might be argued that they nearly killed the language they loved, because the continuing vitality of Latin depended on its adaptation to the purposes of different professions, in other words, to the production of jargons. One of these jargons, the slang of 15th-century students, a mix of Latin and Italian, was modeled on—or parodied—the hybrid Latin of lawyers and notaries.

BIBL.: Peter Burke, "*Heu Domine, adsunt Turcae:* A Sketch for a Social History of Post-medieval Latin," in *Language, Self and Society,* ed. Peter Burke and Roy Porter (Cambridge 1991) 23–50. U.P.B.

Latin Language

In 1819 Joseph de Maistre considered Latin the "European sign." This brief formula accurately conveys the scope of Latin in the Western world at that time, and it was still true into the 20th century. It is important to clarify how the phrase should be understood.

The *Latin sign* did not refer to Latin or Neo-Latin (the term for literary works in Latin since the Humanist restoration) literature. There were a great many works produced in Latin beginning around 1400 that demonstrated the highest level of mastery of the ancient language and the adoption of a repertory of genres, styles, and forms that had flourished in antiquity. With the second half of the 17th century, however, Neo-Latin production declined markedly; there were fewer Latin writers, and, although signs of virtuosity remained, the era of masterpieces had passed. Thenceforth the great genres were abandoned in favor of schools of drama, university rhetoric, and, especially, short forms of poetry; a vast amount of Latin verse continued to be produced until the beginning of the 20th century. But despite their technical virtuosity, the best of these were not of high quality, and they reached a very limited readership. Moreover, doubts grew early on about the possibility of a true resurrection of literature in Latin. Even Boileau (1636–1711), who was partial to the ancients, denounced those poets of Latin verse who were simply "stitching together old scraps" to fashion poems and mockingly charged that "if Terence and Cicero were to come back to earth, they would laugh out loud at the Latin works of all the Fernals, Sannazars, and Murets."

Moreover, when we designate Latin the sign of the Western world, we are not referring to the vitality of Latin civilization since antiquity or to the influence it exercised through the growing emphasis on classical knowledge. Throughout the modern period philologists, historians, and archaeologists studied and explored the classical past just as thinkers and artists maintained a rich relationship with works from antiquity. But the "nonspecialists," the laymen who dealt, even on a daily basis, with Latin, did not have more than a vague notion of antiquity, as these lines from a very good student, Vittorio Alfieri (1749–1803), attest: "We translated lines from the lives of Cornelius Nepos, but none of us, and probably not even the teacher, knew who these men were whose lives we were translating, nor where they came from, nor in what period, under what government they lived." Ernest Lavisse (1842–1922) had an equally abstract view from his years in high school: "None of the writers was presented to us in the context of his times, living among and speaking with others. They seemed like shadows gliding through a colorless and silent environment. We hardly knew who were the first speakers, Greeks or Romans, and we were left to think that Pericles and Cicero were contemporaries."

The Latin sign actually referred to a precise linguistic reality. In the modern era, historiography has stressed the emergence of vernaculars, and, in terms of political order, it has celebrated the progress and victory of modern languages. In some cases progress and victory have been based on Latin and at the same time opposed to it. The monumental *History of the French Language* by Ferdinand Brunot (21 vols., 1905–1953) is not only a summary of philological erudition but also an ideological work that traces changes over several centuries and an affirmation of French over Latin. Still, the triumph of vernacular languages and national differences did not harm the long European tradition of teaching, reading, and praying in Latin.

The schoolroom expression "Latin country" is an indication of the place Latin held in education. In the 16th to 18th centuries it had a near monopoly. In France and Italy children learned to read from Latin books. Students in Jesuit schools everywhere were fed a massive amount of Latin, as both primary material and as a pathway to other knowledge. The expression "Latin school," heard in England and Germanic countries to designate what today we would call secondary education, confirms the major role that Latin held in pedagogy. The Reformation did not challenge this monopoly of Latin in schools. All schoolchildren, Catholic and Protestant, learned Latin and, often, only Latin. Latin was taught in the Orthodox world as well. Under Peter the Great Russian schools were established on the Jesuit model, and in 1750 there were 26 colleges in the Russian empire offering an education founded on the Latin curriculum. Even in the New World Latin was the norm for students. The school system established in the American colonies was modeled on that of England: the Boston Latin School (1635), the first secondary school established in the colonies, was based on the pedagogical tenets of English grammar schools.

Although by the 1750s Latin's monopoly was being challenged and weakened in secondary schools, it continued to be almost total in universities. Professors taught and students argued in Latin. The majority of universities did not move to vernacular education until the 19th century. Latin continued to put up some resistance here and there: in France the requirement for the second thesis in Latin did not disappear until 1903.

The challenge to Latin in the 18th century on the part of philosophers and their friends might have led one to expect it to decline in secondary education during the following century. That did not happen. On the contrary, there was a widespread humanist revival everywhere, ancient languages were revered everywhere, and they always distinguished institutions for the elite. The life of a high school student was marked entirely by Latin; the only difference from the past was that teaching was not done in Latin, although there were a few exceptions. Latin was king everywhere. Greek was dominant in the Prussian *gymnasium* at the time it was founded in 1810, but Latin played an increasingly larger role, and by 1837 it had become the major discipline. In England the cult of the classics reached its peak in education, and ancient languages amounted to half, if not three-fourths, of the schedule in some public schools. In tsarist Russia "classicism" peaked under the ministry of Count Tolstoy, who reformed the education system copying the Prussian model; in 1871 classical subjects, and Latin particularly, represented 41 percent of the curriculum in the classic *gymnasia.*

Until the beginning of the 20th century, the college world remained heavily tinged with Latin. In the first half of the century, Latin gave up more and more ground, and the 1960s and 1970s marked a major break: Latin, which had been mandatory, became an option. In France, following the events of May 1968, Latin ceased to be required in middle school, a move that marked the beginning of its disappearance from secondary schools. In some places the evolution came earlier; in Soviet Russia, following the first Bolshevik reforms of 1920, Latin was suppressed in all programs as a symbol of the pedagogical ancien régime. In some places it came later; in Fascist Italy the worship of Roman culture aroused a true "pan-Latinism" in the schools that outlasted the regime. Latin continued to be important in secondary school as long as it remained a requirement for higher education; in the United States the 1931 decision by Yale University (followed by other institutions) to drop the Latin requirement for admission had a major effect on the study of classics in high schools: the number of Latin students fell precipitously.

From the Renaissance until the middle of the 20th century, Latin was dominant in schools extending from the Old to the New World. Not only did it unify the landscape of Western schools, it also brought with it a common practice. Students learned a lot of Latin, and, despite minor national differences in the pedagogy, they learned it in the same way. They struggled over the same store of authors and especially of texts elevated to the rank of Classics. The teaching was primarily of grammar, a trend that grew in the 19th century under the influence of German philology to a point that could be called "grammatical hypertrophy." This Latin training always had a moral dimension. Not only did students work from expurgated texts, some specially prepared for them, such as the famous *De viris illustribus* by Abbé Lhomond, but teachers stressed the moral content of the texts. This practice soon led to questions about the proper place of pagan authors in a Christian world, and about how much emphasis to place on the adventures of ancient gods. Efforts were made to develop more reliable "resources." One example was a proposal, in England around 1582, to replace ancient writers such as Ovid, taught in grammar schools throughout the kingdom, with a modern poem by Christopher Ocland. Taking a more direct approach, teachers in Jesuit colleges used classical texts to denounce the errors of the ancients, and as apologies for Christianity. Hence, the pagan text, judiciously chosen and commented on, became a source of wisdom and morality in the classroom. That role continued in the secular and republican French high school; Cicero's and Seneca's tirades on the vices and virtues of man, the duties of friendship, forgiveness, and so on, all obligatory fragments of Latin texts, were also the basis for lessons on personal and civic morality.

Latin's reign was not limited to schools. It also dominated the religious life of large numbers of people. Up until Vatican II and the *Sacrosanctum concilium,* Latin was the liturgical language of the Catholic Church, particularly the liturgy for the celebration of Mass and administration of the sacraments. This was the legacy of an old custom, consecrated at the Council of Trent in September 1562. Prompted by the advances of the Reformation and in light of the prevailing definition of the Mass as sacrifice, the Tridentine Fathers agreed on a text that made no rule about celebrating Mass solely in Latin but stated: "Anyone who says that Mass must be said only in vernacular languages . . . shall be anathema." Those Fathers made it clear that, while they did not think it would be beneficial to celebrate Mass in the vernacular, the lessons contained in the Mass ought to be explained to the faithful in their languages. The same principle was adopted for the sacraments: the administration of the sacrament in Latin would be followed by explanation in the vernacular. The decisions made at Trent remained in force until Vatican II. As for the liturgy, in practice it was celebrated in Latin exclusively and the vernacular explanations were not given. Moreover, every attempt to make the slightest room for the vernacular failed—Rome considering any attempt to be the seed of schism—and became another item for building a case and reinforcing an apology for Latin, which came to be regarded by the faithful as a sacred tongue (which from a theological point of view it had never been). Until 1963 the Catholic Church remained, in the words of Ferdinand Brunot, a "Latin fortress." We should add that the constitution of 1963 did not, as is often said, repudiate Latin; rather, it welcomed the use of vernacular languages in the liturgy.

We ought to remember that the Protestant world, contrary to another commonly held opinion, was not without Latin. Protestant rituals were observed in vernacular languages, and the faithful read the Bible in their own tongues. Nevertheless, Protestant theologians, beginning with the Reformers, used Latin widely in their writings on doctrine; pastors were trained in ancient languages and they were often better Latinists than the Catholic priests.

For quite a long time Latin was also the shared language of European scholars. Though it soon represented a minor share of published works overall, it remained very common throughout the 17th and 18th centuries in theology and in scholarly and scientific works. Its appearance was most lasting in Germanic countries and in central and eastern Europe. Three practices are particularly revealing of the persistence of Latin: the publication of scholarly journals in Latin; the translation of works originally written in vernacular languages (Descartes's *Discourse on Method* enjoyed a wider circulation in Latin than in the original French); bilingual editions of illustrated scientific works that, for economic reasons, were intended for European diffusion, such as Albert Seba's *Locupletissimi rerum naturalium thesauri accurata descriptio et iconibus artificiosissimis expressio* (1734–1765), published in Latin-French and Latin-Dutch editions. During the modern period we can cite numerous works that undermine the simplistic equation often posited between Latin and ancient, modern and vernacular, including, from the 18th century, the works of Newton, Bernoulli, Euler, Linnaeus, and Galvani. Latin may, over the course of time, have lost ground in publications, but it does not follow that it disappeared from the realm of knowledge. Specialized vocabularies developed in the vernaculars were often Latin-based; one science that developed entirely from Latin in the 18th century and has remained Latin-based to this day is botany.

Latin long retained its place in government and administration in some modern European states, as in Poland and the Habsburg monarchy. It was still being used at the end of the 17th and beginning of the 18th century as the language of diplomacy.

With its wide influence, Latin constituted a familiar universe, one that lasted until quite recently for believers who followed the Mass in Latin and for students who were given a steady dose of Latin. This familiarity appeared in a variety of forms, among them the case of Italian political journalism that, at the end of the 19th century, made use of a large number of words and expressions from Latin itself or derived from it. This use has not entirely disappeared: a few years ago, during an ongoing debate about equitable access to television for all political parties, the expression *par condicio* ("equal time") was used in Parliament and the press.

Despite its omnipresence, Latin was not commonly spoken or read as easily as one might think. Although up until the 18th century we find some accomplished Latinists, in the realm of letters as well as the highest levels of the Catholic Church, Latin proficiency was not great, and comprehension of spoken Latin encountered serious difficulties owing to national pronunciations; many scholars wrote in their own languages as soon as they could. The faithful who prayed in Latin were far from understanding all the words they heard or said, and they sometimes understood them in their own way. Tuscan peasants transformed *santificetur* and *da nobis hodie* into Santo Ficè and Donna Bisodia. Schoolchildren were far from satisfying the demands of their teachers, and though it would be naive to expect results to match goals, there was always a large gap between reality and the ideal; but this was not for a lack of a multitude of pedagogical methods introduced over the course of time to make Latin easy.

Since these performances were so mediocre overall and Latin was losing its practical utility, there came a point, around the middle of the 18th century, when instruction in Latin was questioned, and this in turn led to finding justifications. One such rationale was based less on linguistic competence or access to the classical corpus than on the inherently useful intellectual and moral discipline that Latin, or at least the study of it, instilled. This argument—never proven—has hardly changed over the course of time; it was still heard far and wide in the middle of the 20th century.

The success of the passionate discourse that went on was due in part to the social cachet of Latin. Ever since the 17th century, at least, Latin served as a mark of distinction that helped to determine social class and to reproduce and reinforce the structural model of contemporary society, with its elite and those who are excluded from it (inferior classes and women). In the hands of the elite, competence mattered little—a liberal education was not meant to train specialists—since Latin represented symbolic capital and constituted a credential-supporting social status.

Latin was thus an expression of the power one group exercised over another. Embedded in an extremely hierarchical system, it reinforced the status of those who knew it and was the basis for the trust, respect, and submission of those who did not. Theater, notably the famous comedies of Molière, *The Imaginary Invalid* and *The Doctor in Spite of Himself*, satirized the power that doctors had over their patients through their use of Latin or, rather, Latinate rubbish. Yet some doctors used Latin not simply to impress their patients, but to conceal harsh or even frightening realities, and thus to protect them. In this euphemistic function, Latin was widely used in the area of sexuality to designate things that propriety prevented one from saying or writing in fields that were neither pornographic, obscene, nor even erotic—for example, in forensic medicine. Though such use could appear to be a means of censure and thus of power, it was also, clearly, a way for an author to spare the embarrassment of others and sometimes himself.

In yet another example of its modern uses, Latin seems to have been a resource when vernacular languages created a new Babel in the Occident. Many scholars, beginning with D'Alembert and up to the 20th century, saw in Latin "the universal and efficient language" to facilitate communication. Although it was not reestablished, Latin provided a goldmine for inventors of artificial international languages who were especially active from 1880 to 1914.

Between the 16th and 20th centuries Latin wielded immense authority. In its many uses it was invested with numerous and contradictory virtues, and it constituted a value system closely linked with the prevailing ideals and norms of Western civilization. Once such ideals changed, however, an era ended, an era during which Latin was more than the language of the classical tradition, but also the expression of the realities and passions of the modern West.

BIBL.: Peter Burke, "Heu domine, adsunt Turcae," in *Language, Self and Society,* ed. Peter Burke and Roy Porter (Cambridge 1991). Jozef IJsewijn, *Companion to Neo-Latin Literature: Part I, History and Diffusion of Neo-Latin Literature* (Leuven 1990). Meyer Reinhold, *Classica Americana: The Greek and Roman Heritage in the United States* (Detroit 1984). Christopher Stray, *Classics Transformed: Schools, Universities and Society in England, 1830–1960* (Oxford 1998). Françoise Waquet, *Latin: The Empire of a Sign* (London 2001; French ed. Paris 1998).

F.W.

Translated by Jeannine Routier Pucci and Elizabeth Trapnell Rawlings

Law, Roman

The history of Roman law is a story of ideas and power that has shaped the entire development of the West, one that begins toward the middle of the 8th century BCE and in some sense has never really ended. Roman law is importantly present along the whole lengthy parabola of the history of ancient Rome and its empire. But starting in the 4th century CE that empire was divided into two distinct parts; and though the Western part was extinguished in the course of the following century, the Eastern part managed to reorganize itself, and during the 6th century one of its emperors, Justinian, succeeded in systematizing within a single unified corpus, to be applied in the tribunals, an enormous mass of Roman legal norms deriving from a distant past. Hence, the legal system that he codified is called by his name. The law of Justinian has always been considered as the final manifestation of historical Roman law, inasmuch as the norms that Justinian accepted in his compilations (*Digest, Institutions, Codex, Novellae:* all together, the celebrated *Corpus iuris civilis*) were Roman. From that time on, in the East as in the West, the survival of Roman law, both as a valid norm and as legal culture, remained indissolubly linked to but also, to a certain extent, constrained by the definitive form that Justinian had decided to give it; and even when, during the period of legal Humanism, attempts were made to reconstruct the genuine form of historical Roman law, that is, that of the ancient Romans, the principal source, indeed almost the exclusive one, always was none other than the *Corpus iuris.*

Even after Justinian's death, his compilations retained their validity for more than three centuries as official law in the East: they went on to constitute the constant foundation and reference for Byzantine law during the whole course of its historical development. Nonetheless, precisely in the East, which in fact had generated it, the *Corpus iuris* was perceived from the very beginning as a foreign body, especially in legal practice. For it made prescriptions in one language, Latin, within a context in which the most widely diffused language was a different one, Greek; moreover it was full of purely historical elements, expressions of Western Roman values and ideas, and for this reason it was hard to understand in a cultural context that tended toward Orientalism, Christianity, and Hellenism. Hence, it was inevitable that, even during the lifetime of Justinian himself, the texts of his compilation were reelaborated in several ways. They were translated and simplified, in ways designed above all to make it easier to find for any particular case the relevant texts, most of which could be discovered only with considerable difficulty within the boundless panorama of the *Corpus iuris.* And they were explicated with references to parallel texts pertaining to the same subject.

This initiative and other ones succeeded only partially in easing the difficulties; but it was not until the end of the 9th century, in a climate of general cultural renewal, that the Macedonian dynasty dared to replace Justinian's compilations with a single compilation in the Greek language, commonly called *Ta basilika* (imperial matters or laws). But the compilations that had to be abrogated were the very same ones that constituted the almost exclusive source of the new collection; in fact, *Ta basilika* contains summaries of the texts of Justinian, deriving from each of the compilations and from their various Greek elaborations, organized by subject matter. This was certainly a help for Byzantine judges and lawyers: for the first time they had access to a reasoned selection of the sources of Justinian's codification, purged *inter alia* of irrelevant historical elements and of those norms that had been abrogated after Justinian.

Later Byzantine legal production continued to make reference to *Ta basilika;* but this work too turned out to be disproportionately large compared with the needs of practical users, and for this reason further simplifications were sought by preparing repertories and compendia. It is to one of these works, the *Hexabiblos,* a manual composed ca. 1345 by the judge Konstantinos Armenopoulos, that Greek populations continued to make reference even after the end of Byzantine law, following the conquest of Constantinople by the Turks in 1453; indeed, this work went on to become an official source in Greece from the end of the Turkish domination until the codification of 1946. In this perspective, Byzantine (or Graeco-Roman) law can be considered the starting point for further lines of research, which can only be indicated here: in particular there are the questions of its influence on the systems of Christian law of the Eastern Mediterranean and of Eastern Europe and (a hotly disputed question) on Islamic law.

In Italy the force of Justinian's compilations had been extended by the military reconquests he made in the West in 554; but this was destined to last only a short time, since by 568 the Longobards succeeded in conquering the

Italian peninsula. But Roman law did not disappear in the West, even though the legal systems of the occupying Germanic peoples prevailed there: its ideas and concepts were kept alive by study in the schools and by the Church, which adopted many of them within its own legal system (canon law).

Then, starting in the 11th century, something quite extraordinary happened. In Italy the first university came into being, in Bologna; and here a teacher of rhetoric, Irnerius, rescued Justinian's *Digest* from oblivion so that he could extract questions about law from it to pose to students who were being trained in argumentation. The *Digest* was a collection of excerpts (*iura*) taken from the works of the Roman jurists who had lived during the end of the Republic and the first three centuries of the empire: it was a vast repertory of normative solutions that they had ingeniously elaborated regarding the discipline of controversial cases, sometimes deriving from real-life experience, sometimes invented for the purposes of legal instruction. It is from Irnerius and the "School of Glossators" he created that the rediscovery of Roman law began. The glossators thoroughly examined Justinian's compilations, creating an ever more closely woven network among the Roman texts, explicating their every possible meaning, reconciling contradictions. The final goal of this intense work of interpretation was not only to supply future operators with a professional preparation adequate for the circumstances of the age, but also to create norms, schemes, criteria, and modes of resolution that could be applied immediately in the tribunals. Many of the *doctores iuris* who received a degree at Bologna and the other universities that were founded later in northern Italy (the first was at Padua) came from the farthest countries of Europe; and they returned home carrying the *Corpus iuris* with them as a vademecum to which they continued to make reference in the exercise of their legal practice. This educational formation, shared by the programs of study of all the universities, prepared the grand return of Roman law, such as it was interpreted by the glossators and the Italian teachers of the following age (Bartolus de Saxoferrato above all among the commentators), to its positive force in late medieval and modern Europe.

This was an event of truly extraordinary importance, which began in the 13th century in Italy and elsewhere—in Spain, in France, and especially in Holland. But the penetration of the *ius commune* in Germany is a story in itself. To understand how strange it is, we must bear in mind that, starting in the second half of the 10th century, the title of emperor belonged to a German king who on the basis of the theory of the *translatio imperii* could consider himself to be the legitimate successor of the Roman emperors and as such could recognize as official law precisely the *ius commune,* inasmuch as it was imperial law. Nonetheless, a strong movement of opposition to Roman law arose in Germany, and it was only with difficulty that the *ius commune* managed to prevail over local legal systems—and it did not succeed finally in doing so until the end of the 15th century. The considerable political fragmentation of Germany, which consisted of myriad autonomous principates and free cities, was the first obstacle; this was reflected on the level of law, as is demonstrated by the very large number of local and personal legal systems in force within the confines of no fewer than 300 territorial entities. But precisely this extreme particularism prevented the formation of a unified German legal system and consequently of a class of jurists who could be the bearers of an autochthonous legal culture, and in the end this absence turned out to contribute decisively to the final victory of Roman law.

More generally, the *ius commune* was constructed for the protection of the interests of property and commerce; this individualism did not find the favor of those lower classes (peasants, miners, urban workers) who, inspired by vaguely socialist ideas and appealing to the Bible, wanted to create a Christian community of equals with communal ownership of goods, and for this reason rose up in revolt during the Protestant Reformation. This created many a problem for Luther himself, who ended up condemning them ("with great wickedness they have robbed and looted convents and castles that did not belong to them") and even advocating their extermination. In this context it was certain aristocratic circles and above all the rural classes that rebelled against the prospect of the extension of the *ius commune* into German lands. The mass of peasants demonstrated a strong attachment to local customs, not out of nationalism but out of pure self-interest: for those customs (the *usus terrae*) guaranteed that farmers could not be removed from the lands they cultivated, whereas the Roman scheme of *locatio rei* required that they be considered as tenant farmers and granted the owner the possibility of evicting them. Indeed, it was by appealing to Roman law that the feudal lords had reclaimed the exclusive property of waters, forests, and pastures, instead of the common property guaranteed by custom that gave every peasant the right to fish, cut firewood, and graze his animals. But the peasant troops and the ideas professed by their prophets were defeated over and over in 1525 and 1526; the egalitarian and communitarian model faded away, and Roman law no longer encountered significant opposition.

Besides, the newly dynamic economy that changed Europe starting in the 14th century came to affect Germany as well, which began to perceive the need for a legal system that could use general schemes and categories to organize a reality that was engaged in a process of transformation for which local customs and judges could not provide an adequate legal form. The decisive factor in this context was precisely the strong tendency toward the *ius commune* felt by the *doctores iuris* who had gotten degrees in the Italian universities and also, starting in the middle of the 14th century, in the German ones, in which regular courses on Roman law began in the 15th century. In this way a very powerful class of jurists was formed who were inserted into the ganglia of power, from the imperial court to the urban administrations, from the bureaucracy to the tribunals. All this prepared the way for the understanding and acceptance of the *ius commune* in Germany and in the end made it seem natural: this process took place en bloc, for whatever party could invoke in support of its thesis any Roman norm was considered the bearer of *fundata intentio,* that is, a claim with a presumption of legitimacy. This process of assimilation culminated at the Diet of Worms in 1495 in the creation of the *Reichskammergericht,* the supreme tribunal of the empire, with its headquarters at Frankfurt; its judges, all of them experts on Roman law, swore that they had made their judgments *nach des Reichs unde gemeinen Rechten* (according to the common law of the empire). Thus it was that the *ius commune* became the official German law—a choice that had long-term consequences and that continued to be confirmed until the beginning of the 20th century.

These, then, were the paths by which Roman law was revived or, better, received the chance of having a new life, thanks to the work of glossators and commentators. In consequence, the term *Roman law* has at least two meanings: the system of legal experience that developed starting from the foundation of the city and that lasted until the death of Justinian (565 CE); and the whole subsequent legal tradition formed as a consequence of the Bolognese rediscovery of the *Corpus iuris.* The new Roman law that began from this rediscovery was regenerated by a study that was not at all interested in past history, since it aimed entirely at resolving the problems of the present: this was a professorial law, and yet it was one that was conceived and constructed for the sake of practice, enriched by the contributions of canon law, able to obtain force in the countries of the Catholic world (and then also introduced by the conquistadors into the lands of the New World). For this reason it was usually termed *ius commune* and applied in the territories of the Holy Roman Empire of the West, where the particular legal systems of the various places (*iura propria*) were unavailable or incomplete. But because only the *ius Romanum commune* was able to supply the indispensable framework of the system and its fundamental concepts, it was much more than a set of norms from which one could always argue the solution of a case: the *ius commune* embodied the entire legal culture of the West, which could understand social and institutional life only on the basis of the Roman categories and schemes, and indeed embodied its very soul, since it was in the juridical tradition established in Roman law that the West found the values that inspired it in its daily action trying to fulfill justice in this world. Thus, the mission of the law remained exactly the same as what the Roman jurist Celsus had delineated as early as the 2nd century BCE, a definition of law that was to be found, and not by chance, on the very first page of the *Digest:* law (*ius*) is "the art of the good and the just."

This system of *ius commune* succeeded in assuring the legal unity of continental Europe for centuries; and it makes us feel admiration, and even astonishment, when we consider that, within that supranational system, a judge in Frankfurt could apply the very same norm that would have been applied by his colleague in Florence or Barcelona or Amsterdam. Notwithstanding the many normative varieties that existed on a local level, the basic language, concepts, and ideas were really shared; in a word, a European legal civilization was created whose traces are visible, indeed evident, even in our own time.

But despite its indubitable merits, the study of the texts of the *Corpus iuris* conducted by glossators and commentators, with the only goal of deriving valid rules from it, encountered the severe criticism of the Humanists during the 16th century. Even in the somewhat remote world of the science of law, the Renaissance burst in, with its proposals of cultural renewal and with its basically civic project to put man into the center of reality and to make him independent of any kind of authority different from his own faculty of reason. This required that all the activities of study, including that whose object was *ius,* be animated by a vigorous critical spirit using the contributions of all the forms of knowledge available (*pansofia*) in order to discover or reestablish the truth of any phenomenon whatsoever, be it natural or historical. So we can understand how it came about that the partisans of legal Humanism were obliged to distinguish themselves from the Italian and foreign experts in the *ius commune,* thereby inaugurating a completely new method of approach to the Roman texts of the *Corpus iuris.*

In this way the *mos gallicus* ("French style") arose in declared opposition to the *mos italicus* ("Italian style") that was professed by the glossators and commentators. It was called *mos gallicus* because it was cultivated especially in France, where it had its center in the University of Bourges, in which Jacques Cujas taught, the most illustrious teacher in the "School of the Cultured Men" who developed this new methodological approach. The attack of the Cultured Men against the Bartolists, who adhered to the *mos italicus,* was harsh and full of the most colorful insults: the Bartolists were not forgiven for having worked on the *Corpus iuris* without any historical sensitivity and for having employed fantastic textual interpretations in order arbitrarily to manipulate a work that should instead have been recognized for what it really was, a monument of classical antiquity. Indeed, the *Corpus iuris* had to be purified even of the alterations that Justinian's collaborators themselves had performed on the originals of the texts that they had assembled into the anthology to update them: the help of philology and of general history was indispensable for this research, which set out to rediscover Roman juridical wisdom, according to a scholarly protocol of virtuous interaction among different disciplines. In this way an activity of textual reconstruction began that aimed to recover the genuine version of the individual passages collected in Justinian's anthologies, especially in the *Digest;* this activity continued with intensity until the first half of the 20th century, sometimes resulting in exaggeration (texts were condemned as interpolated that in reality were not), but sometimes giving an important contribution to the reestablishment of the historical truth and to a better understanding of the past—

for example, toward the end of the 19th century in the palingenetic studies of Otto Lenel, who succeeded in recomposing the jurisprudential texts collected in the *Digest* in what was presumably the original order of the individual works.

But in the 16th and 17th centuries legal Humanism also introduced a further instance of renewal that was quite fertile in future developments: it sought to give the newly born national legal systems of the common Roman matrix a new expository order, new with respect both to the chaos in which the legal material was arranged in the *Corpus iuris* and to the overly analytic and dispersive schemes used by the jurists of the *mos italicus* in their publications and teaching. A long season of studies with this goal began, culminating in the German school of *Pandektistik,* to which we will return. Here the contribution of the Cultured Men was of crucial importance from the practical point of view as well: for even if in the short term it remained unusable for practice, which continued to adapt itself to the results of the *mos italicus,* in a longer perspective it formed the basis for that change in European legal thought that nourished the movement toward codification. For the Humanists, the new legal orders had to be constructed following perfect symmetries and proportions, just like the ones that can be immediately observed in the monumental edifices built by the great Renaissance architects: they had to be systems organized according to a rational project in which every part would find its natural place and there would be a complete harmony among the individual elements and with respect to the whole. In this perspective the Cultured Men admired the tripartite systematic order (*personae, res, actiones*) invented by the Romans and made famous by Gaius, a jurist of the 2nd century CE: this was not a new order, but it was one that had the virtue of placing the *persona,* the human being, in the center of the legal system, in conformity with Renaissance postulates that were then adopted by a theory of natural law inclined to conceive law above all as a system of rights naturally pertaining to every *persona.*

The Humanists' criticisms eroded the authority that the *Corpus iuris* had enjoyed until then and made clear that it was obsolete. They thereby accelerated the crisis that the *ius commune* gradually underwent during the 17th century, whose outcome was the dissolution of legal unity, at least with regard to the positive force of that legal system. But other important factors besides Humanism pushed the system into crisis. One of these was internal: the developmental capacity of the *ius commune* was entrusted to the wisdom of the jurists, and this dried up. The interpretation of law became manneristic, in effect reducing itself to distasteful discussions of the opinions of the various jurisconsults and thereby in the end losing its direct contact with the normative source represented by the texts of Justinian. So there was a constant whirl of opinions upon opinions; and the system became unreliable because it was intrinsically contradictory, and the chaos inevitably affected the administration of justice, which no longer succeeded in fulfilling its institutional obligations. Voltaire described this situation vividly in his *Dictionnaire philosophique:* less than two decades before the French Revolution, he could suggest only a single remedy: burn the existing laws and make new ones.

But the juridical unity guaranteed by Roman and canon law had already been compromised by two external factors of crisis, the Protestant Reformation and, especially, the rise of modern states, absolute and national. It is not by chance that Hobbes had already insisted that the Leviathan state he theorized could not afford to entrust the production of the law to a class of jurists independent of the will of the absolute monarch; and in his *Dialogue between a Philosopher and a Student of the Common Laws of England* (ca. 1668) he expressed the hope that English common law would be replaced by general and abstract law, the expression of the supreme will of the state. If in England common law was not dethroned, in continental Europe a debate opened up in the 17th and 18th centuries concerning the desirability of overcoming once and for all the system of Roman and canon *ius commune.* This was an exciting debate in which the greatest intellectuals of Europe participated: from Grotius to Leibniz, from Bentham to Savigny. Leibniz, in particular, in his *Ratio corporis iuris reconcinnandi* (1668), campaigned for reducing all of the *ius commune* "to a single page" of first postulates: his idea was that of a sort of code understood in the modern sense, but constructed, as always, on the basis of Roman law. And this was the direction in which history actually went. In 1804 Napoleon declared the force of the first civil code, his own, the *code Napoléon;* as was only to be expected, it abrogated every earlier source and decreed that all future cases be decided by the exclusive application of the dispositions it contemplated. Was this the end of Roman law? No, even if the area of its positive force began to decline. For the *code Napoléon* did not arise out of nothing, and its redaction was made possible only by the work conducted by legal scholarship for more than a century of preparation. In France the two greatest jurists, Jean Domat and Robert Joseph Pothier, were both convinced that the new arrangement still had to be founded on Roman law; and since their treatises largely determined the order and contents of the code, they assured the conservation of the categories, principles, and institutes of Roman law within the new normative system.

In the course of the 19th century the French model was adopted by various countries of Europe (Holland, Italy, Spain, and Portugal) and of Latin America. But Germany preferred to resist the codification movement: its most illustrious jurist, Friedrich Carl von Savigny, was convinced that a legal system must evolve spontaneously by means of the jurists' interpretation and must not be crystallized within a law or a code. The system elaborated by the ancient Roman jurists had to be elevated to become an unsurpassable model of legal rationality, and their solutions were considered to be the result of a mathematical operation since, as Savigny wrote, "they calculate with their concepts." Now this legal system could be called "classical" in comparison not only with that of the preceding ("pre-classical") and successive ("post-classical") ages, but even with any other system whatsoever: those jurists had discovered the secret of law, and their work was thereby accepted as representing the legal classicism of the West. It was in this atmosphere that the last great season of the common Roman law began in Germany: as always, the range of the construction was that of the patrimonial relations among private persons. G. F. Puchta, Rudolf von Jhering, Bernhard Windscheid, and the German school of *Pandektistik* performed mighty labors to bring the tradition of common law up to date; and the outcome was a logically perfect, pyramidal normative system, expressed in categories, classes, and concepts of proportionally increasing inclusiveness, intimately coordinated among themselves and able to guarantee by deduction an almost infinite production of norms to apply to practice. But in 1900 Germany too capitulated to codification, and on 1 January of that year the *Bürgerliches Gesetzbuch* (*B.G.B.*), the German civil code, came into force. In this way Roman law left the ranks of positive legal systems (with the exception of a few marginal survivals, to which we will return); and yet, looked at more closely, this turns out to have been yet one more of its great victories. As others have noted, the *B.G.B.* is nothing other than the division into paragraphs of the laws of the *Pandekten* (*Pandectae* was the other title, derived from the Greek, for Justinian's *Digest*) published by Windscheid, a professor of Roman law in various German universities and a member of the government commission charged with editing the code.

Thus, the German model was added to the French one: these models were different in various regards, yet nonetheless they had in common that they both derived from the Roman matrix. They have guided the civilizing movement of codification in Europe and elsewhere in the 20th century, and even today the two archetypes, the *code Napoléon* and the *B.G.B.*, are still in effect. So one can say that Roman law is still alive today: it is on the basis of the tradition founded on it that jurists in many parts of the world recognize, sometimes unconsciously, their own legal culture. This tradition makes it possible to consider all the legal systems that originate from it or are prevalently influenced by it—the legal systems of continental Europe and Latin America, of many countries of Africa and Asia—as belonging to the same genus. And common Roman law continues to be the valid legal system in San Marino, in South Africa, in Scotland, in Sri Lanka, in Andorra. All these legal systems that germinated from the Roman tradition are as a whole termed civil law, and they form one of the great legal systems of the West. The other great system, Anglo-Saxon common law, has a different history and hence different characteristics (its normative evolution is entrusted to judicial opinions rather than to the law, as is the case for civil law); and yet at the beginning of its development common law too was influenced by Roman law via the famous *Tractatus* of Henry Bracton, an English judge of the 14th century, who not only accepted Roman solutions but in his exposition of English law also made use of the tripartition found in the *Institutions* of the Roman jurist Gaius.

Thus, painting with very broad strokes, we have arrived at the present day; and now the question arises of the reason for the extraordinary influence that has been exerted by Roman law, for its extraordinary duration of almost 2,800 years, longer perhaps even than that of the grand philosophy of the Greeks.

The first reason resides in history itself. Around 1140 a teacher from Bologna, the glossator Vacarius, landed in England; he founded a school in Oxford, wrote a handy compendium drawn from Justinian's *Digest* and *Codex*, and enjoyed considerable success. But in 1151 King Stephen I closed the school and Vacarius changed his profession, in 1234 Henry III forbade the teaching of Roman law in England, and in the 15th century all authority was denied to Bracton's treatise. Roman law simply did not manage to penetrate into English practice and into the English courts: there was no room for it, since at the time when Vacarius made his attempt an embryo of common law already existed, and the king and his judicial jurists wanted to transform it from what it was at its origin, a heap of local customs, into English national law, the first in all of Europe.

Instead, on the European continent, when Irnerius began to give his courses on the *Digest*, a society existed that was ready to free itself from customs that were riveted to the morphology of the individual territories, in order to accept juridical forms capable of satisfying the new possibilities that were opening up once the narrow feudal dimension had been overcome. Professional merchants became the protagonists of a newly dynamic society and economy; monetary intermediation, and the recourse to credit, came into force in a climate of reciprocal trust between parties in often quite complex transactions. A legal system composed of categories and principles that could support the needs of exchange was needed, one that would be full of contractual figures, would facilitate credit and at the same time could protect the creditor, would favor private property but on the basis of a number of titles that could be acquired pacifically, and would be equipped with an efficient judicial procedure. These were elements that emerged clearly from the reading of the Roman texts proposed by Irnerius; but his own reading remained difficult, because in order to permit the juridical measurement of the new social relations, these texts required a work of reciprocal coordination and of updating such as could be performed only by professional interpreters. But in this regard too the times were propitious: intellectual activity had been reawakened and new energies were released in the fields of science, philosophy, and theology; and then there was the miracle of the rapid diffusion of the institution of universities in so many European cities.

Hence, the renewal of Roman law that was sought by Irnerius and his four *doctores,* Bulgaro, Martino, Ugo, and Jacopo, was possible in continental Europe, in contrast with England, because on the Continent there was a normative space to occupy; everything seemed to come together in favor of the way pointed out by the Bolognese scholars—a way that originated, in all probability, in the chance circumstance that Irnerius stumbled one day on an almost complete copy of the *Digest,* the so-called *Vulgata* or *littera Bononiensis.* This *Vulgata* was almost certainly derived from the most ancient manuscript of Justinian's collection, the *littera Pisana* or *Florentina,* a mysterious manuscript going back to the 6th century, almost a religious relic, which perhaps originated in the Constantinople of Justinian, then reappeared in Amalfi, where it was seized as war booty by the Pisans, and then wrested from them by the victorious Florentines, who took it from Pisa to Florence, where it is now in the Laurentian Library. The Bolognese scholars needed only a link with a power capable of sanctioning the entrance of Roman law into the usage of the tribunals; and so the doctrine of *unum imperium, unum ius* was invented. From the time of Charlemagne the figure of an *imperator Romanorum* had reappeared; he was crowned at Rome by the pope, of whom he declared himself to be the defender in the whole Catholic world; and so the conclusion followed that only Roman law could be the legal system common to all the territories reached by the Holy Roman Emperor's general power—a power that was in reality largely formal, given the rebellious tendencies of various national monarchies whose rulers refused to recognize any authority superior to themselves. But the Bolognese needed only a formal titulature for their operation of legitimation to succeed.

The last glossators, Odofred and Accursius, died in the second half of the 13th century. Accursius himself had collected in the *Magna glossa,* an immense anthology destined to become the almost exclusive source of reference for judges and lawyers, the results of the interpretative work performed on the texts of Justinian by that school, which had restored Roman law to the legal theory and practice of the time. This work, as we know, was continued by the post-glossators or commentators, and it culminated in the triumph of the *ius commune Europaeum.* The heritage of this rediscovery is still very far from being exhausted; the positive force of Roman law lasted, at least in Germany, until the end of the 19th century, whereas the study of the subject has never ceased, given that even today there are chairs and courses in Roman law in many universities in Europe (including England) and elsewhere. For centuries Europe has demonstrated its trust in the ordering capacity of the *Corpus iuris.* This was made possible by the fact that Justinian's texts permitted much more than the mere interpretation of the law: in fact, they also opened the road to the creation of law and at the same time legitimated this process by appeal to the authority of the source. To be sure, very little embarrassment was felt if the text was assigned a meaning that was the exact opposite of what its words seemed to require; but even more, it was the wealth of contradictions internal to the *Corpus iuris* that permitted legal scholars to argue for a plurality of solutions, thereby creating a means for updating the law in force. We can well believe the traditional anecdote according to which the great Bartolus, when set a question, first worked out by an analysis of the facts the solution that seemed most adequate to him, and then searched in the *Corpus iuris* for the text or texts that could lend themselves to supporting that solution normatively.

In the 18th century the tribunals became exposed to much criticism because their interpretations were too various and mutable; and in his pamphlet *Dei delitti e delle pene* (*On Crimes and Punishments,* 1764) Cesare Beccaria accused the judges of having made themselves into legislators. The "torrent of opinions" Beccaria stigmatized was a consequence of the degeneration of the *ius commune;* but it was also a result of the very mode of being of the *ius commune* and of the *Corpus iuris.* In short, Roman law was felt to be a tangled skein that legitimated judicial caprice; and we should not be surprised that in 1793 the revolutionaries in France went so far as to suppress the law faculties. The new myth was that of the popular law, simple and clear, and for this reason immediately comprehensible to everyone, including the least well educated. But this was not how the lawyer Robespierre saw matters; and he often appealed to Justinian and to his prohibition forbidding judges to interpret the laws, together with his requirement that they refer to the legislators when faced by anything ambiguous in the law (*Codex Iustinianus* 1.1.7.2.21). Thus, the "radically" new found its inspiration and norm in the antiquity of the *Corpus iuris;* and with the *référé législatif* the revolutionaries introduced the obligation that the judges direct to the legislative assembly every more complicated question pertaining to the interpretation of the law.

Tocqueville wrote that in the Middle Ages the old institutions were transformed and abolished by means of Roman law. Now we must ask ourselves whether the same thing happened in the legal laboratory of modernity. In order to answer, we must distinguish between public institutions and private ones or, technically, between *ius publicum,* law concerning the organization of the state, and *ius privatum,* law that disciplines the competing interests of men with regard to the title to goods and resources (*Digest* 1.1.1.2).

In the 17th and 18th centuries, cutting-edge research in public law was performed by the great philosophers of natural law: Grotius, Hobbes, Montesquieu, Locke, Rousseau, Kant. To establish the modern state, as is well known, they made use of the category of the social contract, which they elaborated in different ways. In itself this is a Roman category: it was invented by the jurists of the Severan period to support the emperor's claim of legislative power, which he exercised de facto. The formula is still found in Justinian's *Institutes* (1.2.6: *cum de lege regia, quae de imperio eius lata est, populus ei et in eum omne suum imperium et potestatem conferat,* "by the royal law that has been made concerning the emperor's authority, the people have conferred on him all their own sovereignty and power"), a location that has doubtless contributed to its diffusion and generalization. This is a construction that the medieval jurists had already rediscovered in order to justify the emperor's general power in all the territories of the Holy Roman Empire. Now the philosophers of natural law took up the medieval construction again and relocated it within the national sphere; but a thread of continuity connects the modern social contract with the *lex regia* of the Roman jurists, even if the concept has been remodeled many times (most recently in the 20th century by Rawls in *A Theory of Justice*).

In the age of the construction of the state based on the rule of law (*Rechtsstaat*), Roman public institutions fulfilled a further important function, that of supplying the constructors with positive or even mythical examples to which they could appeal in their persuasive texts. This is a line of research that was cultivated for a long time, from Machiavelli to Montesquieu: the Roman *res publica*—the "admirable" or even "perfect" republic—became a model for the patriotic sense that animated all the citizens, from the very last one to the consul in charge, and for the balance between the fundamental powers (senate and people) that was able to prevent the supremacy of the one at the expense of the other; in this regard it provided an illustrious precedent for maintaining the advantages of the separation of powers, and the downfall of this balance during the imperial age was taken to have been the cause for the origin of Roman decadence. This idea influenced the French revolutionaries and above all the Founding Fathers of the United States, who made use of it symbolically (and, probably, not only so), as the names of places (Capitol) and institutions (Senate) demonstrate; and even today, in the debate on the new forms that Western democracy might take on, the model of the Roman Republic can still arouse interest.

The fate that post-classical history has reserved for the categories of Roman private law has been different. Some of these have gradually lost all meaning: this is the case of the institution of slavery. But the majority have lasted until our own times, either completely or partially; the different socioeconomic contexts have not deprived them of all meaning, and it is not an exaggeration in their case to speak of a continuity between ancient, modern, and contemporary. To see this, it is enough to take a look at any of the European civil codes. The reason for this is surprising only in appearance, and to explain it, it is not enough to appeal to the fact that the *ius privatum* was characterized by a less political character (and, hence, of ability to change) than the *ius publicum*. The real reason is different: social relations, and in particular relations between private persons, are not infinite, and thus they do not produce infinite legal forms; or, more precisely, even if new contexts can generate new relations and new forms, the preceding forms do not consequently cease, since the old relations continue to exist and very often to fulfill the same functions. And it can also happen that forms that once fell into disuse are taken up again at a later time. For this reason, in civil law we continue to talk about predial servitude, usufruct, mortgage, society, and so on, using words, concepts, even values that a Roman could have used 2,000 years ago. The number of institutional models, as has just been said, is not infinite; and this is true, with the necessary qualifications, in the realm of public law as well, where instead we see infinite variations within the forms of government transmitted to us by ancient thought.

To return to the subject of private law, it must be emphasized that the fundamental categories, persons and things, are still the same ones established by the Romans; and perhaps matters could not be otherwise, since law always serves to discipline the relations among persons regarding the title to things. Studies of Roman law continue without interruption throughout almost the entire world to our own day, with the goal of deepening our historical knowledge and at the same time of making today's jurists aware that civil law is sustained by a long and illustrious tradition.

It is to be hoped that those who study this tradition will continue to reveal themselves capable of contributing to the construction of future legal arrangements: for in fact the scientific and technological progress of the last several decades has made it urgent to rethink the Roman categories. The Romans had delineated the categories of persons and things with providential elasticity. *Personae* were all *homines,* "human beings," including slaves; hence, the affirmation of the principle of equality has not impaired this fundamental category. *Res* were not only the things that can be touched (*corporales*) but also those that cannot be touched (*incorporales*): the Romans ascribed to this latter category all rights, obligations, and heredity. This is an extension that has been particularly appreciated in modern times, when literary works and inventions have come to be classified as *res incorporales.* But today we are no longer certain that only human beings (or their associations) should be persons, and not also animals; above all, we wonder whether an embryo or a human being in a permanent vegetative state can be considered a person. And we have trouble locating the whole new space of the Internet within the traditional regime of *res.* We urgently need new categories, or renovated ones; but these can be constructed, at least within civil law, only by rethinking Roman law and its tradition once again.

We must emphasize in conclusion that this is a legal system that has the great merit of always having been absolutely secular. In all history, only German Nazism tried to eliminate it because it "served the materialistic world order," decreeing that it be replaced "by a common German law" (§19 of the Party Program of 24 February 1920). Perhaps there is no better confirmation of the strength of Roman law, and we may count ourselves very lucky that it is still alive.

BIBL.: A. J. Arnaud, *Les origines doctrinales du code civil français* (Paris 1969). M. Ascheri, I. Baumgärtner, and J. Kirshner, eds., *Legal Consulting in the Civil Law Tradition* (Berkeley 1999). A. Cavanna, *Storia del diritto moderno in Europa: Le fonti e il pensiero giuridico* (Milan 1979). J. P. Dawson, *The*

Oracles of the Law (Westport, Conn., 1968). P. Grossi, *L'Europa del diritto* (Rome 2007). J. L. Halpérin, *Le code civil* (Paris 2003). H. F. Jolowicz and B. Nicholas, *Historical Introduction to the Study of Roman Law* (Cambridge 2008). H. Kantorowicz, *Studies in the Glossators of the Roman Law* (Cambridge 1938). D. Kelley, *François Hotman: A Revolutionary's Ordeal* (Princeton 1973). P. Koschaker, *Europa und das Römische Recht* (Berlin 1947). W. Kunkel, *An Introduction to Roman Legal and Constitutional History,* trans. J. M. Kelly (Oxford 1973). A. E. Laiou and D. Simon, *Law and Society in Byzantium: Ninth–Twelfth Centuries* (Washington, D.C., 1994). R. Lesaffer, *European Legal History: A Cultural and Political Perspective,* trans. J. Arriens (Cambridge 2009). J. H. Merryman, *The Civil Law Tradition: An Introduction to the Legal Systems of Western Europe and Latin America* (Stanford 1985). B. Nicholas, *An Introduction to Roman Law* (Oxford 1976). A. Schiavone, *Ius: L'invenzione del diritto in Occidente* (Turin 2005). F. Schulz, *History of Roman Legal Science* (Oxford 1953). P. Stein, *Roman Law in European History* (Cambridge 1999). R. C. van Caenegem, *The Birth of the English Common Law* (Cambridge 1988) and *European Law in the Past and the Future* (Cambridge 2002). U. Vincenti, *Diritto senza identità: La crisi delle categorie giuridiche tradizionali* (Rome 2007). J. Whitman, *The Legacy of Roman Law in the German Romantic Era: Historical Vision and Legal Change* (Princeton 1990). U.V.

Translated by Glenn W. Most

Leda

Wife of Tyndareus, king of Sparta; mother of Helen, Clytemnestra, Castor, and Polydeuces (Pollux). All these children were believed to have hatched from two eggs, which she produced after a union with Zeus, who had transformed himself into a swan. The eggs contained both Zeus's and Tyndareus' progeny. The female children brought destruction, respectively, to the city (Troy) and to a family (Agamemnon's). In contrast, the male children became symbols of fraternal love. Appropriately, the motif of Leda and the Swan came to symbolize harmony in discord (*discordia concors*). Readers of Horace's *Art of Poetry* (*Ars poetica* 147–148) are familiar with the poet's recommendation to follow Homer's example in his recounting of the War of Troy by placing the listener *in medias res,* "in the midst of things," rather than by starting the story *ab ovo,* "from the egg"—that is, from the egg from which Helen hatched.

In antiquity the myth of Leda was a subject of the visual arts, not poetry. Recumbent or upright, she was often represented as struggling with the bird, whose quasi-phallic neck is arched aggressively. Later representations of Leda, particularly those that show her in a recumbent position as expressive of her submission, captured viewers in the post-classical era. Churchmen of the 12th century (who encountered mythical images on antique Roman gems that were used as seals by prelates in high office) saw engraved depictions of Leda and the Swan as prefiguring the meeting of the Virgin and the Holy Ghost (Reinach 1895; Heckscher 1938). Reliefs of recumbent Leda were carved on numerous ancient sarcophagi, and the funerary contexts of this depiction intrigued Renaissance Neoplatonists (Wind 1993).

The motif of Leda and the Swan depicts the union of an earthbound creature (a woman) with a creature that descends from the heavens (a bird). Because the swan was sacred to Apollo, its presence often evoked the musical harmony of the universe; an example of this can be found in Correggio's painting of the scene (ca. 1531–1532), which includes cupids playing musical instruments. When interpreted positively, the motif conveys the idea of love as a cosmic force, embracing the earthly and spiritual, or female and male, components of the cosmos. Leda might express happiness at being chosen by Zeus (as shown in Leonardo's rendering, ca. 1504, which emphasizes her smile as she returns the Swan's embrace) or gloom, due to an awareness of the inevitable collision of the opposite forces reigning in the world (as in Michelangelo's painting, post-1530, which sets her arm in the same pose as the arm of Christ in his *Pietà*). Because the Swan was a form assumed by the king of the gods, works such as these were commissioned by rulers—of Mantua (Correggio's), Milan (Leonardo's), and Ferrara (Michelangelo's).

The woman's royal stature and the bird's association with Apollo and Zeus elevate the representation of the procreative act to an emblem of universal creation. At the same time, it was precisely because Leda was often rendered in works of Greek and Roman art as a participant in a very sexual act that such depictions of her were also viewed misogynistically, as a reflection of a woman's insatiable sexuality. Several early modern depictions, mainly in prints and on tin-glazed earthenware (majolica), expressed the sensuous, intimate embrace between the woman and the bird. The erotic overtone of the scene's depiction sparked accusations that the works provoked libidinous thoughts, leading, for example, to an actual assault on Correggio's painting in the 18th century. Nevertheless, the numerous replicas produced by Leonardo's and Michelangelo's followers and later depictions in the visual arts and poetry all testify to the irresistible appeal of Leda's mysterious union with the Swan from Olympus.

BIBL.: W. S. Heckscher, "Relics of Pagan Antiquity in Medieval Settings," *Journal of the Warburg Institute* 1, no. 3 (1938) 204–220. Salomon Reinach, *Pierres gravées des collections Marlborough et d'Orléans, des recueils d'Eckhel, Gori, Lévesque de Gravelle, Mariette, Millin, Stosch, réunies et rééditées avec un texte nouveau* (Paris 1895). Edgar Wind, *The Eloquence of Symbols: Studies in Humanist Art* (Oxford 1993).

L.FR.

Lessing, Gotthold Ephraim

German writer and representative of the Enlightenment (1729–1781). Throughout the course of his life, Lessing fought for the emancipation of intellectuals from court patronage: thus, on the issue of aesthetics he waged an unending polemic against classicizing court tastes inspired by French models, as promoted by Johann Christoph Gottsched. The imitation of the ancients made sense for Lessing only as it was fruitful for contemporary art; he labored for the development of a German bourgeois culture through the creation of a national theater whose models, in addition to English and Spanish authors, were above all supposed to be the ancient dramatists. The characters in Greek tragedies, according to Lessing, are not fixed and rigid like those of French tragedies, but instead display their "natural" humanity and their closeness to reality. Lessing's chief aesthetic problem was, as a matter of fact, the proper relationship between the "fiction" (or "illusion") of art and reality.

Latin was the central focus of his education in Meissen (1741–1746), and it is on Latin authors (Plautus, Terence, Horace, Seneca) that he made his first attempts at criticism. Later, however, Lessing came to see the relationship between Latin and Greek authors as one of imitation to original. As a theology student in Leipzig (1746–1748), he attended the lectures of the leading exponent of "neohumanism," Johann August Ernesti (1707–1781), and assimilated his principles: ancient authors had to be read in their entirety, not as anthologized fragments, and historical understanding was more important than grammatical. Lessing's experience with concrete theatrical practice began in lively Leipzig (working with Caroline Neuber's company, an exception in the disastrous world of German theater, which staged his comedy *The Young Scholar,* 1748). After moving to Berlin in 1749, he edited with Christlob Mylius the *Contributions to the History and Improvement of the Theater,* whose pages announced his program for creating a distinctly German theater through the imitation of the ancients. His later exchange of letters (1756–1757) with Moses Mendelssohn and Christoph Friedrich Nicolai centered on the passions that drama aroused in the audience; the problem of reception became central. For Lessing the purpose of tragedy is to move the audience to compassion (*Mitleid*), which is the feeling that characterizes us as human beings. Models had to be found in the Greek tragedians: "to rouse compassion, Alcestis and Oedipus were stripped of all heroism" (to Mendelssohn, 28 Nov. 1756). To Sophocles, the model par excellence of modern dramaturgy, Lessing dedicated in 1760 a critico-biographical essay that far exceeds the Enlightenment genre of the "rehabilitation."

Lessing took up the specific problem of catharsis in his *Hamburg Dramaturgy,* (1767), which he wrote while superintendent of the Hamburg theater, basing his work on the French theorists Rapin, Dacier, and Batteux. He began his argument with the translation of the term *phobos* in Aristotle's *Poetics* (read in light of the *Rhetoric* and the *Politics*). By *phobos* Aristotle means "fear" (*Furcht*), not sudden or momentary, but lasting: it is not provoked by someone else's misfortune; it is, rather, fear for ourselves, as it is based on the analogy that we establish between ourselves and the person suffering. Aristotelian catharsis, Lessing explains, "consists in nothing other than the transformation of the passions into virtuous dispositions" (*Hamburg Dramaturgy,* 78). The purpose of tragedy is therefore not to stir up violent passions, as Nicolai and Mendelssohn thought, or a moralistic and Christian extirpation of them, as it seemed to Corneille, but rather a rational mediation of the passions, a process in which reason purifies their excesses and reduces them to the just measure in which (Aristotelian) virtue consists.

His *Laocoön; or, The Limits of Poetry and Painting* (1766) is directed against rationalistic poetics, according to which the same standards should be used for judging poetry and the figurative arts (*ut pictura poesis*). The central argument of the work, which begins with a polemic against Winckelmann, is that although they both imitate nature, poetry and the figurative arts nevertheless use different media: painting uses figures and colors in space, poetry sounds articulated in time. Therefore, figurative art has bodies as its object, poetry actions. The argument unfolds by way of a commentary, with philological observations, on ancient texts. Drafts of the work, contained in the *Nachlaß* (published in 1788), demonstrate with what intensity Lessing had worked to improve his "knowledge of Greek" since 1763. Lessing used philology as an autonomous science with its own techniques (textual and conjectural criticism). His *Laocoön* contributed substantially to the age's knowledge and interpretation of Homer. Among other things, Lessing identified in Thersites a peak in Homer's art for the portrayal of the comic (ch. 23 ff.): this gave rise to the stubborn reaction of the archaeology establishment, represented by Christian Adolf Klotz (1738–1771), upon which followed a violent controversy (*Letters on Archaeology; How the Ancients Depicted Death,* 1769).

BIBL.: Wilfried Barner, "Lessing und die griechische Tragödie," *Tragödie: Idee und Transformation,* ed. H. Flashar (Stuttgart 1997) 161–198. Ignace Kont, *Lessing et l'antiquité: Étude sur l'hellénisme et la critique dogmatique en Allemagne au 18e siècle,* 2 vols. (Paris 1894–1899). Uta Korzeniewski, *Sophokles! Die Alten! Philoktet! Lessing und die antiken Dramatiker* (Konstanz 2003).

S.F.

Translated by Patrick Baker

Letters and Epistolography

The theory and practice of the art of letter writing. The letter has always been one of the most difficult forms of literature to grasp theoretically as a genre. Depending on the intention with which a letter was composed and the use to which it was put, numerous classifications have been made, each with its own stylistic and structural requirements. In antiquity laws and other legal documents took the form of letters. Private individuals wrote open letters or private letters. Letters also functioned in literary contexts: authors selected and edited their letters for publication (often posthumous), but they also wrote poetry and didactic treatises in epistolary form, or composed letters addressed to or written by imaginary or historical figures. The private letter had no independent place in the literary theory of antiquity: the letter was treated in the periphery of rhetoric or as part of school exercises (progymnasmata). There existed two independent treatises on the art of letter writing, but they were in Greek and unknown during the Middle Ages: pseudo-Demetrius, who identified 21 different types of letters (and who should not be confused with the better-known pseudo-Demetrius, who dedicated paragraphs 223–235 of his treatise *On Style* to letters), and pseudo-Libanius' Greek *Epistolici characteres,* published in 1504 in a Latin translation by Pontico Virunio. Also unknown were important collections of published letters from antiquity, such as the correspondence of Cicero and of Pliny the Younger.

In the late Roman Empire, Christian communities used the letter as a means to unify and codify religious doctrines and practices, the apostolic letters (either original or not) by Saint Paul being one example. Church Fathers corresponded with each other in Latin and addressed a wider public by means of epistles. Many letters from Jerome and Augustine are in fact treatises in epistolary form. Papal letters developed into decrees for the entire body of the Church. After the fall of the Western Roman Empire, letter writing became a monopoly of the clergy. Rulers were dependent on clerks for drafting letters for official use. The letter as a genre became almost identical with the official document, exemplified in Cassiodorus' *Variae epistolae* (537). Throughout the Middle Ages, the letter was used primarily for ecclesiastical, political, and legal purposes.

Letters grew more important still with increasing centralization in the 11th century, the growing complexity of the legal system, and expanding commercial interests following the rise of the Italian city-state and the bourgeoisie. Professional scribes had the task of composing letters and had to be trained in the art of letter writing by manuals. Like other instructive literature, these manuals were modeled on examples from antiquity. As letters primarily served public affairs, it is not surprising that the theorists did not look at the two-page appendix about letters at the end of Julius Victor's *Ars rhetorica* (known to Alcuin, but not printed until 1823), or at the isolated remarks scattered throughout the correspondence of Seneca, but instead took their lead from ancient theories of rhetoric, which offered guidelines to the composition of texts for legal and political affairs. Hence, underlying the medieval manuals were the fundamental rhetorical division into the demonstrative, deliberative, and judicial genres and a focus on those structural requirements that were relatively independent of the narrative content of the body of the letter and that had limited and therefore manageable possibilities for variation.

Thus, Alberico of Montecassino (fl. 1170) applied rules from Cicero's *De inventione* and the *Rhetorica ad Herennium* to letters in his *Rationes dictandi:* letters should be divided into *salutatio, exordium, narratio, petitio,* and *conclusio.* Much emphasis was put on the proper use of titles and epithets in addressing the recipient. The typical medieval treatise on the art of letter writing consisted of rules for style and structure, followed by model letters. The formal theory of epistolography thus conceived, known as the *ars dictandi* or the *ars dictaminis,* was applied above all in the chancery, where a formal style, known as the *cursus,* was developed. For letters of personal communication, Seneca's letters were considered the model: letters were seen primarily as a vehicle for instruction in moral philosophy.

In the 14th century the discovery of new letters from antiquity gave rise to the "familiar" letter. Petrarch knew the letters of Pliny the Younger, discovered a generation earlier, and he also gleaned from Seneca that Cicero had written letters that had been published in antiquity. In 1345 Petrarch uncovered Cicero's letters to Atticus (which contained several remarks on the style and character of letters) and to his brother Quintus. Although he proclaimed to be shocked that Cicero, whom he knew mainly as a writer of philosophical dialogues in a highly literary style, turned out to be a politician who was entangled in the prosaic daily affairs of his time, the discovery inspired him to make a selection of his own letters and publish them after a thorough editing. Although any stylistic influence of Pliny the Younger's letters is hardly perceptible, Petrarch's project in itself is entirely imitative of Pliny's *Epistulae.* The letters were completely rewritten, sometimes redated, and in some instances completely fictitious. Like Cicero, he used proverbs and quotations, but imitation of Cicero's style seems limited to opening and closing formulas and occasional turns of phrases. The publication of a corpus of letters as a literary genre in which the author presented himself in a particular fashion marked the beginning of a new era for the art of letter writing.

A new impulse to the development of the letter was given when Coluccio Salutati discovered Cicero's *Ad familiares* in 1392. When Petrarch was in the process of editing his own correspondence, he read Quintilian for the first time, which may have led him to realize how much the letter was connected to the lower of the three modes of style in antiquity, the *sermo* or colloquial style (Quintilian 9.4.19). Cicero's *Ad familiares* provided new evidence that the letter in antiquity was primarily seen as part of a conversation with absent friends and hence required a colloquial style (*Ad familiares* 9.21.1, 2.4.1, 4.13.1). The principal distinction between the plain style of a letter to a friend and the high style required for letters for political or legal purposes posed a problem for the definition of the letter as a genre. The discovery of Cicero's *Ad familiares* led Salutati to leave it to posterity to edit his own letters (just as Cicero had left the task to Tiro). The influence of the medieval *cursus* is still dominant in Salutati's letters, not in the least because most of his letters were written in his capacity as chancellor to the city of Florence. The prescriptions of medieval theories of rhetoric continued to be echoed in other 15th-century letters, such as those of Leonardo Bruni. The distinction between official letters (congratulatory letters to highly positioned officials, dedicatory letters, letters of moral philosophical instruction, or political epistles) and letters addressed to friends is clearly discernable in the collections of the papal secretaries Pietro Bembo and Jacopo Sadoleto. Increasingly, however, Humanists modeled their letters on those of Cicero. The *Ad familiares* provided an especially attractive model, for the letters in that collection are addressed to different people and treat a variety of subjects, which gave the Renaissance letter writer a variety of examples.

New Humanist theories of epistolography incorporated much of their medieval predecessors but struggled to define the appropriate style. The *Libellus de conficiendis epistolis* attributed to Lorenzo Valla, who himself never cared to collect and organize his own letters for publication, still prescribed the five parts of letters. Niccolò Perotti (*Rudimenta grammatices,* 1486) tried to tackle the problem of style by positioning the letter below oratory and historiography, while ascribing to the letter three levels of style of its own. According to him, the middle style in the general literary system posed as the highest style in epistolography; likewise, the lower style for literature counted as middle style for letters. This implied, however, that the colloquial style of a letter corresponded with a subcolloquial style on the general level, placing the letter on a par with barbarity. Angelo Poliziano in his commentary on Statius' *Silvae* (1480–1481, publ. 1978) positioned the letter between a dialogue and an oration: as a written text, it differed from the spontaneity that characterized the dialogue proper and hence required higher stylistic criteria. But as letters needed to be brief and lively, they did not qualify for the treatment of philosophical or political themes, which were proper to the oration. Francesco Nigri (*De modo epistolandi,* 1490) defined the nature and function of the letter and subsequently offered a list with 20 different types of letters, following the structure of the medieval *ars dictandi.*

The invention of the printing press accelerated the success of published letter collections, especially in Italy in the 1470s (Cardinal Bessarion 1471; Leonardo Bruni 1472; Francesco Filelfo 1472–1473, 18 reprints; Enea Silvio Piccolomini 1473, 20 reprints; followed later by Giannantonio Campano, Marsilio Ficino, Pico della Mirandola, Angelo Poliziano, and Robert Gaguin). Carefully selected, edited, and published, these collections fulfilled a need for self-presentation in a system of patronage. Letter collections became so popular that some of the authors published letters that had never actually been sent. Petrarch had already addressed letters to Cicero and Seneca in the underworld, but less obviously fictitious are many of the letters in the correspondence of Antonio Beccadelli (Il Panormita).

Following Horace and Ovid, the letter in verse became a subgenre of its own (Petrarch, *Epistolae metricae,* spanning 40 years of his lifetime, first publ. 1501; Michel de l'Hôpital, *Epistolarum seu sermonum libri sex,* 1585). Ovid's *Heroides,* moreover, inspired authors to write fictitious letters that concealed their own identity. The epistolary form was used for other fictional prose, such as Piccolomini's *Historia de duobus amantibus* and, on the other hand, for treatises, allowing the author to present a text as written at the request of the addressee. Thus, Erasmus's *Enchiridion militis Christiani* and *De virtute amplectanda* were styled as letters, disregarding one of the most important requirements of the letter: brevity. Travel accounts also often appeared in the form of long letters, such as those of the imperial ambassador at Constantinople, Augier de Busbecq (1589).

Ciceronianism having established itself in the course of the 15th century, the question of style became paramount. The Humanists universally condemned the formalistic style of the *ars dictandi,* identifying it with the style of Scholastic philosophy. Never was this contempt made clearer than in the fictitious *Epistolae obscurorum virorum* (1515). The pseudonymous work, presumably written by Ulrich von Hutten, parodied the Scholastic style of medieval philosophers and was favorably received by Erasmus. As the critique of Scholastic style increasingly came to be associated with Lutheranism, however, Erasmus published a carefully ordered and modified selection of his own letters, in which he distanced himself from the book.

It is in this light that one must see his *Opus de conscribendis epistolis* of 1522. The work was still very much directed against the *ars dictandi,* but it was also aimed at the strict Ciceronians. Erasmus maintained the rhetorical division into three genres (juridical, epideictic, and deliberative), but he added the "familiar letter" as a fourth genre; he admitted that many letters shared the characteristics of several different types of letters. Erasmus's manual was bulky and lacked structure, but it proved to be a lasting success, not in the least because he had included numerous examples and long lists of stylistic variations on the same opening or closing lines. With Erasmus's rich collection of proverbs in his *Adagia* it formed a treasure trove of commonplaces and a gold mine for *copia verborum.* The manual was meant primarily for teachers of Latin, but it was used by students as well. After all, emulation of letters from Pliny the Younger and Cicero had become a standard exercise in secondary Latin education. Cicero's *Ad familiares,* for example, was one of the basic texts in the school of Guarino da Verona (ca. 1360–1460). Latin letters from the Renaissance consistently echo phrases from these authors, but they often also include moral sententiae and idiomatic expressions from Horace's *Epistulae* and Ovid's *Epistulae ex Ponto.*

The popularity of Erasmus's manual overshadowed the publication by Juan Luis Vives of a much more concise and well-structured manual, *De conscribendis epistolis* (1534). Vives abandoned the three rhetorical genres and emphasized the role of the letter as part of a conversation with absent friends. He was especially keen on addressing the recipient in the correct way, taking into account both the author's and the recipient's social positions and personal characters. Significantly, he pointed out that the rules set forth in his manual applied not only to Latin letters but also to letters written in the vernacular, which in

Italy became dominant in the second half of the 16th century.

In the course of the 16th and 17th centuries, because of the religious wars and the rise of Protestantism, the letter tended to become more personal and private in character. The Protestant Church called on the believer to look into his own soul and study the Bible in private. When one reflected on free will, predestination, and grace, confession became less mechanical. As a consequence of the religious wars, Stoicism became more widespread and the influence of Ciceronianism decreased. These developments meant that rhetorical rules were less strictly followed to allow more space for individual expression. This is reflected by a third important 16th-century letter manual.

Like Vives, Justus Lipsius in his *Institutio epistolica* (1591) abandoned the tripartite rhetorical scheme. He distinguished between conventional aspects such as salutation, valediction, and subscription, on the one hand, and the varying content of the body of the letter on the other. There were three types of letters: serious, learned, and familiar. Lipsius was concerned primarily with this last type, which functions, as Seneca and Erasmus had also maintained, as a "message of the mind" (*animi nuntium*). The aim of the letter is to make the absent person present, and hence an informal and colloquial style is required. The letter writer should employ what one editor of the text called calculated disorder, or a stylish lack of style. Paradoxically, one can have an original and personal style only by imitating a lot of different classical authors. A letter must be clear, simple, elegant, and fitting, but above all short. This last requirement applies not only to the length of the letter, but also to the sentences: Lipsius favored the concise style of Tacitus and Seneca. According to Francis Bacon, Seneca's philosophical letters were in fact essays. As Lipsius' treatise was published at a time when Ciceronianism was in retreat and the essay became more popular, it occupies a niche in the history of modern prose.

The increasingly private character of the letter is mirrored by the fact that most scholarly letter collections published in the 17th century, at least in Northern Europe, were published posthumously, whereas in the preceding centuries the letter writers themselves usually—but not always, as is clear from the examples of Salutati and Valla—oversaw the publication. The 17th century has been seen as the Golden Age of the publication of correspondence. Most of the collections appeared in the United Provinces and Germany. Of course, it was not possible to edit and publish everything. So there appeared *Epistolae quotquot reperiri potuerunt, Epistolae mutuae* and *Epistolae ad Gallos* or *ad Germanos, Epistolae medicinales, Epistolae philologicae-criticae,* or, in the vernacular, *Lettres choisis.* Nevertheless, such printed collections contained letters that had been modified not by the author but by the editor. If certain remarks in letters were deemed harmful to the reputations of scholars still alive or of their descendants, editors took care to omit passages or replace with asterisks proper names or other information that could reveal the identity of a person mentioned in an unfavorable light.

After the rise of the scholarly journal halfway through the 17th century, and with the increasing popularity of commercial newspapers and pamphlets in the 18th century, epistolography became even more private in character and less dependent on classical examples. The learned letter still functioned as an important medium for the gathering and exchange of knowledge (the 17th-century scholar Johannes Georgius Graevius claimed to have spent 20 percent of his salary on postage), but Latin gradually gave way to the use of French and other vernaculars. The hope for a united Christendom was lost and nation-states were increasingly politically defined and confessionally divided. With the reorientation of science in the 17th century, which favored newly gathered knowledge about the world over classical scholarship, Latin as a universal language of communication for a unitarian and international Republic of Letters became more and more a remote ideal. Hence, the influence of classical models in epistolography slowly dwindled. Paradoxically, it was only then that the letter could approach more closely than ever before the ancient ideal of a spontaneous conversation with absent friends in colloquial language.

BIBL.: Cecil H. Clough, "The Cult of Antiquity: Letters and Letter Collections," in *Cultural Aspects of the Italian Renaissance: Essays in Honour of Paul Oskar Kristeller,* ed. Clough (Manchester 1976) 33–87. *La correspondance d'Érasme et l'épistolographie humaniste: Colloque international tenu en novembre 1983* (Brussels 1985). *L'épistolaire au XVIe siècle* (Paris 2001). Marc Fumaroli, "Genèse de l'épistolographie classique: Rhétorique humaniste de la lettre, de Pétrarque à Juste Lipse," *Revue d'Histoire Littéraire de la France* 78 (1978) 886–905. Toon van Houdt et al., eds., *Self-Presentation and Social Identification: The Rhetoric and Pragmatics of Letter Writing in Early Modern Times* (Leuven 2002). Jozef IJsewijn, with Dirk Sacré, *Companion to Neo-Latin Studies,* 2nd ed. (Louvain, 1998) 218–228. Abraham J. Malherbe, ed., *Ancient Epistolary Theorists* (Atlanta 1988). Frans Jozef Worstbrock, ed., *Der Brief im Zeitalter der Renaissance,* Mitteilung 9 der Kommission für Humanismusforschung (Weinheim 1983).

D.V.M.

Liberal Arts

The Liberal Arts are a canon of disciplines for acquiring education (*litterae,* "letters") that took shape in the Hellenistic era. The name originally indicated that such disciplines were regarded as suitable for a free man, in contrast to those which were not, known as the *artes illiberales* or *sordidae* ("illiberal" or "lowly arts"). Under the influence of Christianity this legalistic definition was abandoned, and the liberating effect of studying these subjects was recognized. At the outset the number of disciplines included in the canon varied considerably, from as many as nine (Varro) to fewer than seven. The classic group of the Seven Liberal Arts was created by Boethius, who also introduced the term Quadrivium for the four "calculating" arts (arithmetic, music, geometry, and astronomy), which later on were sometimes referred to as *mathēsis*. The three philological arts (grammar, rhetoric, and dialectic) began to be called the Trivium in Carolingian times. In the early Middle Ages the term Liberal Arts was applied both to theoretical knowledge and to the curriculum in the schools. Although these arts were believed to represent the foundation of all learning, physics and mechanics could only partly be deduced from them, and the biological sciences, as developed by Aristotle, not at all. Moreover, the arts of the Quadrivium did not encompass the entirety of the mathematical and astronomical knowledge of the late antiquity.

With the translation of Greek and Arabic writings into Latin starting in the 12th century, new disciplines appeared outside the canon of Liberal Arts (such as theology, law, and medicine, but also sciences, including biology, physics, chemistry), and with them emerged a new system of classifying knowledge. The arts themselves also changed to some extent. At the universities, which began to become established at this time, the Liberal Arts were taught in the lower or arts faculty as preparatory instruction, before a student was allowed to study law, medicine, or theology in one of the higher faculties. The changes that occurred in some disciplines, for example rhetoric and grammar, were partly brought about and accompanied by changes in politics, law, and society that were taking place at the time in northern Italian towns.

The idea of the Greek and Egyptian origin of the disciplines was introduced in the 5th century by Martianus Capella, the last non-Christian compiler of a classical syllabus grounded in the canon of the Liberal Arts. This view, although repeated by Hugh of St. Victor at the beginning of the 12th century, was based on mere anecdotal evidence. In reality the Liberal Arts continued the tradition of the Sophists, who had established a canon of subjects for study in the schools. This was, however, an ideal canon, not one that existed as a textbook or manual, either in classical antiquity or in the Hellenistic era.

It was the Roman scholar Varro who first collected all the contents of this canon in his *Disciplinarum libri IV* (*Four Books of the Disciplines*) in the 1st century BCE. This work, which was probably lost in antiquity, dealt not only with the classic seven arts but also with architecture and medicine. Moreover, quite different compilations of knowledge also existed, as for example the *Natural History* of Pliny the Elder (1st cent. CE), which, with the exception of astronomy, bears no relation to the Liberal Arts. The only texts connected to the Liberal Arts that have survived from antiquity are works on specific problems within a discipline or compendia of individual disciplines.

Although some Romans, like Cato the Elder, were culturally conservative and rejected all Greek influences completely, by the late Republic every educated Roman learned Greek and usually traveled to Greece for the purpose of study, thus acquiring direct access to Greek texts. Long after the fall of the Roman Empire in the West, there was still an upper class with a good command of the Greek language. Latin, however, gained ground only slowly among the German conquerors as the new lingua franca—thanks largely to the Church. Greek texts, including scientific writings, were not only directly accessible to Romans but also transmitted by them. Countless allusions and citations in literary works show how widespread classical Greek education was among the Romans; these quotations were not only understood but also highly esteemed. Translations of Greek texts were made only later, especially in the 5th century, when knowledge of the language gradually vanished in the West.

It was largely due to five scholars that the Liberal Arts survived the Dark Ages, when standards of education plummeted. The first of these, Martianus Capella, about whom we know very little, produced a survey of the Seven Liberal Arts in his work *De nuptiis Philologiae et Mercurii* (*The Marriage of Philology and Mercury*). In this treatise the god Mercury gives his bride, Lady Philology, who is made into a divinity, seven handmaidens, each of whom represents one of the Liberal Arts. The second notable scholar was Cassiodorus, who founded a monastery, called Vivarium (Fishpond), on his country estate at Squilace after retiring from politics in the mid-6th century; there he enjoined the monks to study not only the Bible but also the Liberal Arts and to copy the books of ancient authors. The monastery did not survive after Cassiodorus' death, but Saint Benedict, the founder of the Benedictine Order, continued this tradition. Third is Boethius, who, instead of retiring from politics in a civilized manner like Cassiodorus, was imprisoned and finally executed (ca. 525). Both before and during his incarceration, Boethius translated and commented on parts of Aristotle's logic and the most important Greek writings on the Quadrivium. These were the only texts based on Greek originals that were available during the early Middle Ages. Fourth, Isidore, bishop of Seville (d. 636), made a short compilation of the Liberal Arts and the *Natural History* of Pliny. Although precise details were scarce in Isidore's book, it became one of the most studied works of the Middle Ages. Last but not least, there is Saint Augustine of Hippo, who is significant in this context not so much for his writings on grammar or music, but for his positive attitude toward the Quadrivium (he intended to write on each of the four arts), which had an important influence on subsequent centuries.

Gerbert of Aurillac, who was elevated to the papacy in 999 as Sylvester II, was the first medieval scholar to be well versed in all the Liberal Arts. He also drew the attention of the Latin-speaking West to the Greek texts—dealing not only with sciences but also with mathematics, medicine, and philosophy—which Muslim scholars had translated on a large scale into Arabic and then used as the basis for further studies. It was almost another century before Western scholars began to travel to the areas of the Iberian Peninsula under Muslim rule, where the translation of these Arabic texts into Latin was promoted. Around the beginning of the 12th century Hugh of St. Victor in Paris wrote his *Didascalicon,* an introduction to knowledge with the ultimate aim of attaining wisdom in

51 Biagio d'Antonio, *Allegory of the Liberal Arts,* second half of the 15th century.

52 A cover for Richard Strauss's *Elektra.* Sketch by Lovis Corinth, 1908.

Donatus (51)

Aelius Donatus, a roman grammarian of the mid-4th century CE, played a major role in shaping the Latin studies on which the classical tradition depended for many centuries. In his *Allegory of the Liberal Arts,* the **Renaissance** painter Biagio d'Antonio da Firenze depicted Priscian or Donatus with **Grammar** to the left of the gate of Wisdom, **Cicero** with **Rhetoric, Aristotle** with **Logic,** Tubalcain with **Music, Ptolemy** with **Astronomy, Euclid** with Geometry, and **Pythagoras** with Mathematics.

Electra (52)

Daughter of Agamemnon, sister of Orestes, and participant in efforts to avenge her father's murder, Electra has enjoyed a rich afterlife in literature and the arts. Her story and the violence of her passions made Electra a favorite subject for opera, resulting in complex reinterpretations of her character. The libretto for Richard Strauss's *Elektra* (1909), for example, transforms her into a Freudian neurotic, implacably vengeful and unwholesomely incestuous.

53 Standing horseman, Parthenon, west frieze, ca. 438–432 BCE.

54 Paul Gaugin, *Man with an Adze,* 1891.

Elgin Marbles (53, 54)

The British Museum acquired the pediments and frieze of the Athenian **Parthenon** in 1816. For those who viewed the Marbles in the 19th century, their appeal was magnified by their stark contrast with the freestanding sculptures that had shaped popular taste for ancient art until then. Stylistic restraint, dignity, and naturalness are the visual marks of Paul Gaugin's Polynesian woodcutter (1891), whose pose is based on a figure from the west frieze of the Parthenon, **plaster casts** of which circulated at that time.

Endymion (55)

A hunter or herdsman loved by the moon, Endymion slept through her nightly visits, in some versions for eternity, forever young. Eroticism becomes a central theme in Anne Louis Girodet de Roussy-Trioson's painting as the androgynous Endymion, attended by a **cupid,** revolves toward the viewer in his voluptuous sleep and exposes his sensual nudity.

Epictetus (56)

According to the **Stoic** philosopher Epictetus, all external events are determined by fate and are thus beyond our control; from his perspective, happiness is closely connected with a calm and dispassionate acceptance of stern fortune. His most famous adage, "bear and forbear," is vividly illustrated by this image from Alciato's *Book of Emblems,* in which a bull, fettered by his right knee, endures his master's rules and meekly abstains from pregnant cows.

55 Anne Louis Girodet de Roussy-Trioson, *The Sleep of Endymion,* 1793.

56 Andrea Alciato, *Book of Emblems,* no. 34, "Bear and Forbear."

57 Leon Battista Alberti, Facade of the Temple of the Holy Sepulcher, 1464–1467.

Epigraphy (57)

Since the **Renaissance,** ancient epigraphy has fascinated classical scholars who have collected, classified, and imitated Greek and Latin inscriptions. **Leon Battista Alberti** decorated his Holy Sepulcher in the Cappella Rucellai in San Pancrazio, Florence, with an inscribed frieze like those on ancient **temples** such as the **Pantheon** and the Temple of Antoninus and Faustina in the Roman Forum. Such authentic looking antique Roman lettering was still unusual in Italy shortly after the mid-15th century.

Faun (58)

The figure of this bestial, vigorous member of Bacchus' retinue has been a subject of continual fascination throughout modernity. From the Renaissance onward, fauns have appeared regularly in literature and art, often absorbed in playing music, dancing, and ambushing nymphs. In Roman as well as in modern imagery, fauns are a symbol of drunken revelry, joyful mischievousness, and the pleasures of nature.

Fin de Siècle (end of the century) Art (59)

Alma-Tadema's *The Roses of Heliogabalus* is based on a presumably fictional episode in the life of the Roman emperor Heliogabalus as related by the *Historia Augusta* (a collection of biographies of emperors probably written between 390 and 420 CE). The guests at one of his luxurious banquets are covered in rose petals released from false panels in the ceiling. Alma-Tadema's canvas vividly reflects the tastes and general attitudes peculiar to this trend in painting, which came to be identified with the academic and salon style during the last decades of the 19th century.

58 Arnold Boecklin, *Faun and Blackbird,* 1866.

59 Lawrence Alma-Tadema, *The Roses of Heliogabalus,* 1888.

60 Charles Willson Peale, *George Washington (1732–1799),* 1784.

Founding Fathers, American (60)

The circumstances, places, and heroes of Roman **republican** history provided American revolutionaries with a rich vocabulary of symbols, references, and images. These Roman models played a central role in shaping the rhetoric, self-presentation, and expectations of the young American republic and of its founders. One of the most popular heroic figures from Roman history was **Cato the Younger,** who refused to submit to the tyranny of **Julius Caesar** and gave his life for freedom. George Washington was so stirred by Cato's fate that he had Joseph Addison's play *Cato* performed for his troops at Valley Forge during the winter of 1777–1778.

61 The cast of *National Lampoon's Animal House,* 1978.

62 Raphael, *The Triumph of Galatea,* 1512.

Fraternities (61)

The American system of collegiate and university student groups, which usually bear names consisting of two or three Greek letters, has long been a common subject in various expressions of popular culture. *National Lampoon's Animal House* is probably one of the most famous films inspired by college life and the world of fraternities. The 1978 comedy revolves around the antics of a misfit group of fraternity men who challenge their college's administrators who, in turn, are determined to expel Delta Tau Chi and its troublemakers from the campus.

Galatea (62)

As a counterpart to Sebastiano del Piombo's fresco of the **Cyclops** Polyphemus in the Villa Farnesina (see 34), **Raphael** painted a panel depicting the Nereid Galatea, the other protagonist of their myth. References to any events of the story are replaced by the image of her apotheosis as a symbol of love, beauty, and longing, surrounded by love-arousing **cupids** and couples of various sea creatures.

63 Standing image of the Buddha. Gray schist, 2nd–3rd century.

Gandhara (63, 64)

The strongest evidence of the links this region had with the Hellenistic world, following **Alexander's** conquest of the Achaemenid **Persian** empire, is the persistence of Greek traditions in its Buddhist sculptural production between the 1st and 5th centuries CE. The Graeco-Roman influence can be easily detected in the classical folds of Buddha's robes, as well as in the prevalence of scenes drawn from the Greek repertoire such as **Dionysian** feasts with figures engaged in music, dance, and drunken revelry.

64 Scene of Dionysian revelry, from Hadda. Limestone, 1st–2nd century.

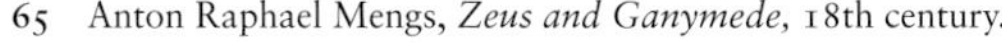

65 Anton Raphael Mengs, *Zeus and Ganymede,* 18th century.

66 Giulio Romano, Detail from the Chamber of the Giants.

Ganymede (65)

Because he was a divinely beautiful mortal, the young Ganymede was transported to heaven to become Jupiter's cupbearer. In a fake imitating the frescoes then recently uncovered at **Herculaneum** and **Pompeii** which he created to cheat art historian **Johann Joachim Winckelmann,** the 18th century painter Anton Raphael Mengs depicted with striking frankness an enthroned Jupiter in tender embrace with a nude Ganymede.

Giants (66)

Giulio Romano's Chamber of the Giants is the most famous and most arresting room in the Palazzo Te, Mantua. The room is conceived as an illusionistic space where decoration and reality overlap. The story of the wild earthly inhabitants who planned to overthrow the gods, taken from **Ovid's** *Metamorphoses,* unwinds across the walls. On the vault, the crowd of Olympian gods watches the ruinous fall of the assailants, under whose bodies buildings and temples collapse.

67 Giambologna, *Appennino*, ca. 1570–1580.

Grotto (67)

From the 16th through 18th centuries, artificial grottoes were restored to a place of honor in garden architecture where they served as places of rest, refreshed by shade and water, and as one of the principal allusions to the antique world. In the magnificent park of the Medicean Villa in Pratolino near Florence (later Villa Demidoff), art challenged nature through a profusion of artificial caves and water-driven **automata.** All that remains today of the original Renaissance structure is the colossal statue-fountain of the *Appennino* by Giambologna, along with the adjacent lake.

Hadrian's Villa (68, 69)

The villa built by the emperor Hadrian at Tivoli, outside Rome, hosted an exceptionally rich collection of art. It included numerous copies of ancient Greek sculpture, such as the marble statue of **Hercules** with club and lion skin, found in 1790–1791. Later purchased by Lord Lansdowne, the statute is now at the Getty Villa in Malibu, California. The series of prints issued by **Giovanni Battista Piranesi** is among the most suggestive evidence of the interest piqued by the first explorations of Hadrian's Villa during the latter half of the 18th century.

Harmony of Spheres (70)

For a number of ancient, medieval, and early modern thinkers, harmony has cosmic significance, providing order in the universe. With his model of the solar system, Johannes Kepler proposed that the distance relationships between the six planets known at his time could be understood in terms of the five **Platonic** solids: each geometric solid would fit between a pair of planetary spheres, thus demonstrating that harmony governed the universal order.

68 Giovanni Battista Piranesi, *Ruins of a Gallery with Statues at Hadrian's Villa.*

69 Statue of Hercules (*Lansdowne Herakles*), Roman, ca. 125 CE.

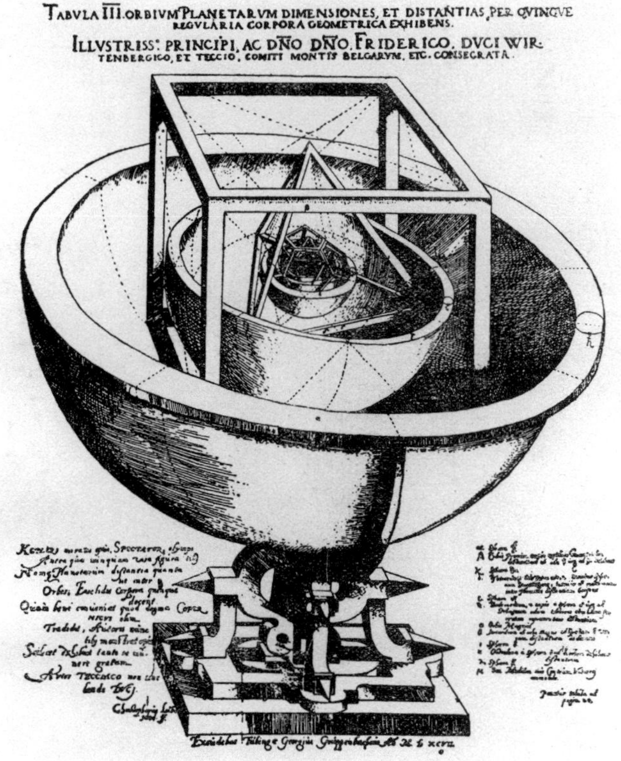

70 Johannes Kepler, Regular Polyhedra, from *Harmonices Mundi,* 1619.

71 Antonio Canova, *Helen of Troy,* early 19th century.

72 *Paris Wearing a Phrygian Cap,* copy of a 4th century Hellenistic statue.

73 The garden at the Getty Villa, Malibu, California, opened in 1974.

74 Louis Valadier, *Herm of Bacchus,* 1773.

75 Bartholomeus Spranger, *Hermaphroditus and the Nymph Salmacis,* 1580–1582.

Helen of Troy (71, 72)

The story of the beautiful yet troubled couple of Helen and Paris has inspired countless artists from antiquity through modern times. For his bust of Helen, Antonio Canova chose as a model the ancient images of her lover, Paris, which traditionally combined effeminate looks and the conical Phrygian cap of Eastern youths.

Herculaneum (73)

In the 1970s, J. Paul Getty constructed a replica of the famous Villa of the Papyri at the Getty Museum (now Getty Villa) in Malibu, California, as the ideal setting for his remarkable collection of antiquities. The gardens are furnished with modern **replicas** of the bronze statuary on display in the original villa in Herculaneum.

Herm (74)

Ancient collections of herms first came to light during the late 15th century near **Hadrian's Villa** in Tivoli. As knowledge about herms increased, particularly with additional discoveries through the 1700s, new freestanding herms like Valadier's *Herm of Bacchus* were created following the ancient models and used to decorate luxurious palaces and gardens.

Hermaphroditus (75)

In **Ovid's** account, Hermaphroditus, the beautiful son of Hermes and **Aphrodite,** encountered the nymph Salmacis in her pool near the town of Halicarnassus. Bartholomeus Spranger's painting depicts the moment when Salmacis first sees the boy, from behind the foliage of a tree, and falls in love with him. Unable to control her feelings, she will soon jump into the water and wrap herself around Hermaphroditus, praying the gods that they might never be parted.

76 Francisco Goya, *Saturn Devouring One of His Sons* (detail), ca. 1819–1823.

77 Anonymous, *The Hercules of the Union,* 1861.

Hesiod (76)

Hesiod's reception has been confined chiefly to the myths that he provides. In this picture of Kronos (Saturn) devouring one of his children, a motif from Hesiod's *Theogony,* Goya exploits the whole emotional potential of the story, stressing both the unseemliness and the dimmed ferocity of the old god, who emerges from a pitch-black background.

Hydra (77)

The second labor of **Hercules** was slaying the Hydra, a water snake with multiple heads that could regenerate if severed. In modern times, the Hydra has come to symbolize a treacherous threat created by a multitude of circumstances, factors, or rivals. In this anonymous 19th century print, *The Hercules of the Union,* Winfield Scott uses a club to battle a Hydra composed of his political opponents.

Hypnerotamachia Poliphili (78)

Detailed descriptions of art and architecture occupy a significant portion of this philosophical and erotic romance, printed in Venice in 1499. The main character, Poliphilo, contemplates ruins and ancient buildings with romantic melancholy, while carefully recording particular architectural features such as measurements and inscriptions as a scientific connoisseur.

Knossos (79)

According to Greek mythology Knossos, on the Greek island of Crete, was the **palace** of the legendary King Minos, and in its heart was hidden the **Labyrinth,** a prison for the Minotaur. Early in the 20th century, Arthur Evans unearthed an intricate collection of interlocking rooms used for religious, administrative, and ceremonial purposes, as well as workrooms, storage areas, and food processing centers. The structures and artifacts found at Knossos not only became instantly famous at the time of their discovery but also contributed centrally to the modern understanding of Minoan civilization. Evans has been severely criticized for rebuilding substantial parts of the complex with contemporary materials, following his own vision of Minoan architecture and customs.

78 Francesco Colonna, *Hypnerotomachia Poliphili,* fol. 93.

79 Reconstruction of Knossos Palace.

80 Nicholas Beatrizet the Younger, *Laocoön,* 16th century.

Laocoön (80–83)

The iconic status of Laocoön derives in part from the *Aeneid* of **Virgil** but also from **Pliny the Elder's** writings about a marble statue of Laocoön and his sons which he described as being superior to any other work of art. In 1506, the statue was accidentally discovered in Rome and almost immediately became an object of great historical, aesthetic, and political interest. Countless artists, including Nicholas Beatrizet the Younger, have drawn inspiration from the myth of Laocoön and from the statue for centuries. The composition became so well known that it developed an exceptional history as the basis for a wide variety of caricatures and **parodies,** as well as for many new creations purposely different from the antique, such as El Greco's painting.

81 El Greco, *Laocoön,* ca. 1610/1614.

82 Honoré-Victorin Daumier, *Imitation of the Laocoön,* 1868.

83 Charles Addams, *Laocoön Sausage,* 1975.

84 Edouard Manet, *Le dejeuner sur l'herbe,* 1863.

Locus Amoenus (84)

In Greek and Roman imagery, the pastoral world was a privileged setting for tales of erotic seduction. The sensual delights of the country landscape are the subject of a famous painting by Manet, *Le déjeuner sur l'herbe* (The Lunch on the Grass), which plays on the shocking effect of a nude woman casually lunching with two fully dressed men. Manet's composition reveals his study of the old masters: the disposition of the characters is derived from Marcantonio Raimondi's engraving *The Judgment of Paris* after a lost drawing by **Raphael,** inspired by a Roman **sarcophagus** relief in the Villa Medici.

Lucan (85)

Lucan's **epic** *The Civil War* (*De bello civili,* often called *Pharsalia*) had an important afterlife both as a model for composing epics about comparatively recent historical events and as a rich repertoire of stories from the Roman past. Giovanni Antonio Pellegrini's *The Head of Pompey* is inspired by one of the most tragically crude episodes of the poem, when **Caesar** parades a gesture of grief at being offered the head of his enemy.

Lucretius (86)

The opening verses of Lucretius' *De rerum natura,* which tell of Venus' seductive power over **Mars,** are probably the best known passage of this poem. Sandro Botticelli drew the inspiration for his *Venus and Mars* from these lines. In this painting, the god of war has taken off his armor and is lying asleep on his red cloak, while his clothed companion keeps an attentive watch over him. The boisterous little satyrs in the background, who are playing mischievously with Mars' helmet, lance, and cuirass, were probably suggested by an **ecphrasis** by the Greek writer **Lucian.** According to Lucian, the famous painting of the wedding of **Alexander the Great** and Roxane featured **cupids** playing with the king's spear and armor.

85 Giovanni Antonio Pellegrini, *The Head of Pompey Presented to Caesar.*

86 Sandro Botticelli, *Venus and Mars,* ca. 1485.

87 Giambattista Tiepolo, *Maecenas Presenting the Liberal Arts to the Emperor Augustus*, ca. 1745.

88 Niccolò dell'Arca, *Lamentation over the Corpse of Christ*, ca. 1460–1480.

89 Map of the area known as Magna Graecia.

Maecenas (87)

Gaius Maecenas was not only one of the richest men in Rome and an advisor to **Augustus;** he was also a connoisseur and an enthusiastic patron of poets and artists. In Tiepolo's painting *Maecenas Presenting the Liberal Arts to the Emperor Augustus,* the **Liberal Arts,** dressed as elegant ladies, curtsy low before the enthroned emperor while Maecenas introduces them. The painting was commissioned by Count Francesco Algarotti, who presented it to Count Heinrich von Brühl, a contemporary Maecenas and the powerful minister of another Augustus, King Augustus III of Saxony and Poland.

Maenads (88)

The female followers of **Dionysus** have always had a prominent role in the history of classical reception. Their frenzied and unruly behavior, the celebration of drunkenness their image implied, and the opportunity they provided to display wild women in various states of undress has always appealed to artists. In Niccolò dell'Arca's terracotta *Lamentation over the Corpse of Christ,* Mary Magdalen rushes toward Jesus' body with the exaggerated gestures, the expressive hands, and the wailing mouth of a maenad. In her horrified and explosive sorrow, her sexual power is still apparent, as her shapely body presses against her flying robe.

Magna Graecia (89)

In modern scholarship, the name Magna Graecia refers to the area of southern Italy where the Greeks established **colonies** as early as the 8th century BCE. The rediscovery of **Paestum's** Doric **temples** in the mid-18th century sparked a revival of interest in Magna Graecia, and knowledge of the area began to spread among the learned, along with a new curiosity about the name Magna Graecia itself, its origin, and the geographical boundaries it defined.

90 Poster of the Maison Carrée, advertising Nîmes, "the French Rome," ca. 1930.

91 Diego Rodriguez Velazquez, *Mars,* 1640–1642.

Maison Carrée (90)

This ancient building in Nîmes, in southern France, is one of the best preserved Roman **temples** and owes its survival to the fact that it was rededicated as a Christian church in the 4th century. Subsequently, the Maison Carrée became a meeting hall for the city's consuls, a canon's house, a stable for government owned horses during the **French Revolution,** a storehouse for the city archives, and after 1823, a museum. The international importance of the Maison Carrée derives from its significance as a model for **Neoclassical** architecture.

Mars (91)

In this painting, Velazquez depicts the dual nature of Mars, the god of war and Venus' lover, by employing clearly different treatments for his head and body. While the face is obscured and the helmet remains as the sole instrument of war, the body, stripped of its armor, is resplendently naked, lazy in the aftermath of love.

92 Titian, *The Flaying of Marsyas,* 1570–1575.

93 Martianus Capella, *Satyricon: Grammar, Dialectic, and Rhetoric,* ca. 1200.

Marsyas (92)

The myth of Marsyas was endlessly fascinating for ancient and modern artists, owing to its tragic conclusion as much as to the manifold forms of opposition symbolized by the contest between the reckless satyr and the god **Apollo.** In 16th century art, the flaying of Marsyas was depicted with even greater crudity than in Roman sculpture, with the victim shown helplessly hanged upside-down.

Martianus Capella (93)

Martianus Capella's encyclopedic work, *De Nuptiis Philologiae et Mercurii* (On the Marriage of Philology and Mercury), sometimes called *De septem disciplinis* (On the seven disciplines) or the *Satyricon,* is an elaborate didactic **allegory** written in a mixture of prose and verse. The book was of great importance in defining the standard formula of academic learning and in developing the system of the Seven **Liberal Arts** that structured early medieval education.

94 Swearing-in ceremony for Israeli soldiers, Masada, 2007.

Masada (94)

This cliff-top fortress in the Judean Desert was the last stronghold against the Romans during the Jewish Great Revolt (66–73 CE). According to Flavius Josephus, Masada's defenders chose suicide over captivity when they sensed imminent defeat. In modern Israeli culture, the site of Masada has become a powerful national symbol and the venue of the swearing-in ceremony for soldiers who have completed their basic training.

95 Ceremony at the Lenin Mausoleum in Red Square, Moscow, November 2006.

96 Maria Callas in her film role as Medea, 1970.

Mausoleum (95)

The Mausoleum was a tomb built at Halicarnassus (present-day Bodrum, Turkey) for Mausolus, a satrap in the **Persian** Empire. Each of its four sides was adorned with sculptures created by a famous Greek sculptor: Bryaxis, Leochares, Scopas of Paros, and Timotheos. The finished structure, with its impressive size and magnificent decoration, was considered one of the **Seven Wonders of the World.** Today, any colossal sepulcher built in perpetual glorification of the deceased can be called a mausoleum.

Medea (96)

The story of Medea, the sorceress, poisoner, adventuress, abandoned wife who takes revenge on her younger rival, and the mother who kills her own children has long been a staple in literature, in art, and on the stage. The role of Medea has often been associated with famous divas, notably Maria Callas. She first played the title role in 1953 in Cherubini's 1797 opera *Medea* and later in a 1970 film by Pier Paolo Pasolini based on the plot of Euripides' *Medea.*

97 Albrecht Dürer, *Melancholia I,* 1514.

98 Giorgio de Chirico, *The Melancholy of the Politician,* 1913.

Melancholy (97, 98)

The pose in which one hand supports the head commonly signified deep thought in ancient sculpture. It became the pathognomonic gesture of melancholy from the time of Albrecht Dürer's *Melancholia I,* a complex allegorical composition that has been the subject of many interpretations. But in De Chirico's *Melancholy of the Politician,* the image of absorbed contemplation as indicative of melancholy has been replaced by a palpable sense of anguish and desolation.

Michelangelo (99, 100)

With his virtuoso *Bacchus,* Michelangelo created an image that surpassed all ancient antecedents in the striking novelty of its staggering, intoxicated **Dionysus.** The statue was commissioned for Cardinal Raffaele Riario, who intended for it to complement the classical sculptures displayed in his garden. After being rejected by Cardinal Riario, the *Bacchus* found its way to the collection of Jacopo Galli, where it stood among a rich collection of antiquities in Galli's garden.

Midas (101)

Botticelli's theme for *The Calumny of Apelles* was drawn from a famous lost painting by the Greek master Apelles, which had been extensively described by **Lucian.** An innocent man is dragged before the throne of King Midas by the personifications of Calumny, Malice, Fraud, and Envy, followed by Remorse as an old woman gazing downcast at the naked Truth, who is pointing toward heaven. The judge is surrounded by Suspicion and Deceit, who whisper false accusations in his ear.

99 Michelangelo, *Bacchus*, 1496–1497.

100 Maarten van Heemskerck, *The Garden in the Casa Galli*, ca. 1532–1536.

101 Sandro Botticelli, *The Calumny of Apelles*, ca. 1490–1495.

Monsters (102)

In the Greek and Roman world, anomalous births were considered a portent or a prodigy. In **Pliny the Elder's** *Natural History,* the topic is discussed at length as a manifestation of nature's variety. To accounts of monstrous births, Pliny added the tradition, well rooted in Greek writings on geography, of the monstrous races that were thought to inhabit the far margins of Africa and Asia. Classical ideas about monsters also had a rich afterlife during the Middle Ages, as demonstrated by this folio from the late 15th century encyclopedic treatise by Hartmann Schedel, *The Nuremberg Chronicle,* showing an illustrated list of exotic monsters.

Secunda etas mundi — Folium XII

De hominib⁹ diuersaꝝ formaꝝ dicit Pli.li.vij.ca.ij. Et Aug.li.xvi.de ci.dei.ca.viij. Et Isidorus Ethi.li.xi.ca.iij. oĩa q̃ sequũtur in india. Cenocephali homines sunt canina capita habẽtes cũ latratu loquũtur aucupio viuũt. vt dicit Pli. qui omnes vesciũtur pellibus animaliũ.
Cicoples in India vnũ oculum hñt in fronte sup nasum hij solas ferarũ carnes comedũt. Ideo agriofagite vocãtur supra nasomonas confinesq3 illorũ homines esse: vtriusq3 nature inter se vicibus coeũtes.
Calliphanes tradit Arestotiles adijcit dextram mãmam ijs virilem leuam muliebrem esse quo hermofroditas appellãmus.
Ferunt certi ab oriẽtis pte intima esse homines sine naribus: facie plana eq̃li totius corpis planicie. Alios supiore labro orbas. alios sine linguis ⁊ alijs cõcreta ora esse modico foramine calamis auenaꝝ potũ hauriẽtes.
Item homines habentes labiũ inferius. ita magnũ vt totam faciem contegant labio dormientes.
Item alij sine linguis nutu loq̃ntes siue motu vt monachi.
Pannothi in scithia aures tam magnas hñt. vt contegant totum corpus.
Artabrite in ethiopia pni ambulãt vt pecora. ⁊ aliqui viuũt p annos. xl. quẽ nullus supgreditur.
Satiri homũciones sunt aduncis naribus cornua ĩ frontibus hñt ⁊ capraꝝ pedibus similes qualẽ in solitudine sanctus Antonius abbas vidit.
In ethiopia occidentali sunt vnipedes vno pede latissimo tam veloces vt bestias insequantur.
In Scithia Ipopedes sunt humana formaꝫ eq̃nos pedes habentes.
In affrica familias quasdã effascinãtiũ Isigonus ⁊ Memphodorus tradũt quaꝝ laudatõne intereãt pbata. arescãt arbores: emoriãtur infantes. esse eiusdem generis in tribalis et illirijs adijcit Isogon⁹ q̃ visu quoq3 effastinent iratis pcipue oculis: quod eorũ malũ facilius sentire puberes notabili⁹ esse q̃ pupillas binas in oculis singulis habeant.
Item hoĩes. v. cubitoꝝ nũq3 infirmi vsq3 ad morteꝫ Hec oĩa scribũt Pli. Aug. Isi. Preterea legit̃ ĩ gestis Alexãdri q̃ ĩ india sunt aliq̃ hoĩes sex man⁹ hñtes.
Itẽ hoĩes nudi ⁊ pilosi in flumine morãtes.
Itẽ hoĩes manib⁹ ⁊ pedib⁹ sex digitos habentes.
Itẽ apothami ĩ aq̃s morantes medij hoĩes ⁊ medij caballi.
Item mulieres cũ barbis vsq3 ad pect⁹ s3 capite plano sine crinibus.
In ethiopia occidẽtali sũt ethiopes. iiij. oclos hñtes
In Eripia sunt hoĩes formosi ⁊ collo gruino cũ rostris aĩalium hoĩmq3 effigies mõstriferas circa extremitates gigni mĩme mirũ. Artifici ad formanda corpora effigiesq3 celandas mobilitate ignea.
Antipodes ãt eẽ. i. hoĩes a 9tria pte terre vbi sol orit̃ qñ occidit nob aduersa pedib⁹ nr̃is calcare vestigia nulla rõe credẽdũ ẽ vt ait Aug. 16. de ci. dei. c. 9. Ingẽs tñ h pug̃ lraꝝ 9traq3 vulgi opĩoeꝫ circũfundi terre hoĩes vndiq3 cõuersisq3 ĩter se pedib⁹ stare et cũctis silẽm eẽ celi vtice. Ac sili mõ ex q̃cũq3 pte mediã calcari. Cur ãt ñ decidãt: mireẽt ⁊ illi nos ñ decidere: nã eĩn repugnãte: ⁊ quo cadãt negãte vt possint cadere. Nã sic ignis sedes nõ ẽ nisi ĩ ignib⁹: aq̃rũ nisi ĩ aq̃s. spũs nisi in spũ. Ita terre arcentibus cũctis nisi in se locus non est.

102 Hartmann Schedel, *The Nuremberg Chronicle,* fol. XIIr, 1493.

103 Detail of *The Good Shepherd,* mosaic, 5th century.

104 Raphael, *Parnassus,* detail of Apollo and the Muses, 1510–1511.

105 Raphael, *Parnassus,* detail of the Muses, 1510–1511.

Mosaic (103)

During the 5th century CE **Ravenna,** the capital of the Western Roman **Empire,** became the center of late Roman mosaic art. Churches and imperial buildings were decorated with sumptuous mosaics that exploited the Roman technique and iconographic repertoire to create compositions inspired by Christian themes. In the **Mausoleum** of Galla Placidia, the lunette over the north entrance displays a mosaic of the Good Shepherd tending his flock, which lavishly uses the type of vivid blue glass mosaic traditionally associated with fountains and garden decoration in Roman architecture.

Musical Instruments (104, 105)

The linkage between classical musical instruments and their successors is mostly etymological, with Greek terms persisting throughout later cultures but applied to completely different items. Figural arts played a central role in handing down the shapes and types of ancient instruments. **Raphael's *Parnassus,*** based on the iconography of Roman **sarcophagi** with **muses,** became a main source of information on Greek lyra and cithara. (For the whole fresco, see 123.)

106 Heinrich Schliemann's wife Sophia wearing ornaments excavated at Mycenae, 1877.

Mycenae (106)

The **Homeric epics** refer to Mycenae as the capital city of King Agamemnon, leader of the Greek army during the Trojan War. Mycenae languished in obscurity for many centuries until 1876 when the merchant-turned-archaeologist Heinrich Schliemann made a discovery that immediately provoked great excitement: a series of graves containing corpses covered with jewelry and precious ornaments, which he identified as King Agamemnon and his retinue.

Mystery Religions (107)

Popular interest in mystery religions, their rites of initiation, and their promise of a secret wisdom has never waned. Masonic rituals, for instance, incorporated a number of features supposedly drawn from antiquity. The opera *The Magic Flute* by Wolfgang Amadeus Mozart is noted for its prominent Masonic elements. The trials of Papageno and Tamino are clearly reminiscent of a Mason's initiation, a fact that must have been well known to Mozart and to the librettist, Emanuel Schikaneder, both of whom were Freemasons and lodge brothers.

107 Unknown, Scene from Mozart's *The Magic Flute*.

Narcissus (108)

According to **Ovid's** *Metamorphoses*, Narcissus was a famously beautiful boy who fell in love with his own reflection in the water, becoming engrossed to his death in this passion. The story was particularly appealing to artists because of the obvious opportunity it provided to reflect on art itself and the concepts of imitation, resemblance, and truthfulness. In his interpretation of the subject, Caravaggio concentrated on the virtuoso depiction of the relationship between the image and its double in the mirror.

Neptune (109)

The Fountain of Neptune in Piazza della Signoria, Florence, was commissioned from Bartolomeo Ammannati on the occasion of the wedding of Francesco I de Medici. The colossal god of water, carved in Apuan marble and imposingly dominant over the wildest creatures of the sea (Scylla and Charybdis as portrayed on his pedestal), was meant to be an allusion to the dominion of the Florentines over the sea.

108 Caravaggio, *Narcissus*, ca. 1599.

109 Bartolomeo Ammannati, *The Fountain of Neptune*, 1560–1565.

51. Musée Condé, Chantilly, France. Réunion des Musées Nationaux/Art Resource, NY.

52. Getty Images.

53. Charles Yriate, *Les frises du Parthénon par Phidias* (Paris, 1868). Courtesy of Special Collections, Fine Arts Library, Harvard College Library.

54. Private collection. Snark/Art Resource, NY.

55. Louvre, Paris, France. Erich Lessing/Art Resource, NY.

56. Andrea Alciati, *Emblemata* (1621), Typ 625.21.132, Houghton Library, Harvard University.

57. S. Pancrazio, Florence, Italy. Scala/Art Resource, NY.

58. Neue Pinakothek, Munich, Germany. Bildarchiv Preussischer Kulturbesitz/Art Resource, NY.

59. Private collection. Visual Arts Library/Art Resource, NY.

60. Harvard Art Museum, Fogg Art Museum, Bequest of Grenville L. Winthrop, 1943.144. Photo: Katya Kallsen © President and Fellows of Harvard College.

61. Universal Studios/mptvimages.com.

62. Villa Farnesina, Rome, Italy. Scala/Art Resource, NY.

63. British Museum, London. Registration no. 1880.73. © The Trustees of The British Museum.

64. Musée des Arts Asiatiques-Guimet, Paris, France. Borromeo/Art Resource, NY.

65. Galleria Nazionale d'Arte Antica, Rome, Italy. Alinari/Art Resource, NY.

66. Palazzo del Te, Mantua, Italy. Erich Lessing/Art Resource, NY.

67. Villa Demidoff, Pratolino, Italy. Alinari/Art Resource, NY.

68. Staatliche Museen, Berlin, Germany. Bildarchiv Preussischer Kulturbesitz/Art Resource, NY.

69. The J. Paul Getty Museum, Villa Collection, Malibu, California.

70. Bildarchiv Preussischer Kulturbesitz/Art Resource, NY.

71. V&A Images/Victoria and Albert Museum.

72. Musei Capitolini, Rome, Italy. Vanni/Art Resource, NY.

73. Gabriel Bouys/AFP/Getty Images.

74. Galleria Borghese, Rome, Italy. Scala/Art Resource, NY.

75. Kunsthistorisches Museum, Vienna, Austria. Erich Lessing/Art Resource, NY.

76. Museo del Prado, Madrid, Spain. Erich Lessing/Art Resource, NY.

77. National Portrait Gallery, Smithsonian Institution/Art Resource, NY.

78. Francesco Colonna, *Hypnerotomachia Poliphili* (Venice, 1499), WKR 3.5.4, Houghton Library, Harvard University.

79. © DeA Picture Library/ Art Resource, NY.

80. Harvard Art Museum, Fogg Art Museum, John Witt Randall Fund, R835NA. Photo: Imaging Department © President and Fellows of Harvard College.

81. Samuel H. Kress Collection. Image courtesy of the Board of Trustees, National Gallery of Art, Washington, DC.

82. Harvard Art Museum, Fogg Art Museum, Bequest of Frances L. Hofer, M20976. Photo: Imaging Department © President and Fellows of Harvard College.

83. © Charles Addams. With permission Tee and Charles Addams Foundation.

84. Musée d'Orsay, Paris, France. Réunion des Musées Nationaux/ Art Resource, NY.

85. © Musée des Beaux-Arts, Caen, France/ Giraudon/ The Bridgeman Art Library.

86. National Gallery, London, England. Art Resource, NY.

87. Hermitage, St. Petersburg, Russia/ The Bridgeman Art Library.

88. S. Maria della Vita, Bologna, Italy. Scala/Art Resource, NY.

89. Engraving after Guillaume Delisle. Private Collection/ Ken Welsh/ The Bridgeman Art Library.

90. After a painting by Hubert Robert. Bibliothèque des Arts Decoratifs, Paris, France/Archives Charmet/ The Bridgeman Art Library.

91. Museo del Prado, Madrid, Spain. Erich Lessing/Art Resource, NY.

92. Archbishop's Palace, Kromeriz, Czech Republic. Erich Lessing/ Art Resource, NY.

93. Bibliothèque Sainte-Geneviève, Paris, France. Erich Lessing/Art Resource, NY.

94. Menahem Kahana/AFP/Getty Images.

95. Denis Sinyakov/AFP/Getty Images.

96. Keystone/Getty Images.

97. Victoria and Albert Museum, London, England. Art Resource, NY.

98. Kunstmuseum, Basel, Switzerland. Erich Lessing/Art Resource, NY. © 2010 Artists Rights Society (ARS), New York/SIAE, Rome.

99. Museo Nazionale del Bargello, Florence, Italy. Alinari/Art Resource, NY.

100. Staatliche Museen, Berlin, Germany. Bildarchiv Preussischer Kulturbesitz/Art Resource, NY.

101. Uffizi Gallery, Florence, Italy. Scala/Ministero per i Beni e le Attività Culturali/Art Resource, NY.

102. Courtesy of William H. Scheide, Princeton, New Jersey.

103. Mausoleum of Galla Placidia, Ravenna, Italy. Erich Lessing/ Art Resource, NY.

104. Vatican Palace. Scala/Art Resource, NY.

105. Vatican Palace. Scala/Art Resource, NY.

106. Time Life Pictures/Getty Images.

107. Getty Images.

108. Galleria Nazionale d'Arte Antica, Rome, Italy. Alinari/Art Resource, NY.

109. Piazza della Signoria, Florence, Italy. Timothy McCarthy/Art Resource, NY.

the Pythagorean sense. He included the disciplines of theology, medicine, and the mechanical arts in his new system. In the 13th century Thomas Aquinas stated: *Septem artes non sufficienter dividunt philosophiam theoricam,* "The seven arts do not sufficiently divide up theoretical philosophy." In a Latin translation of Avicenna, he had discovered the term *scientia naturalis* ("natural knowledge" or "natural science"), which he introduced into his philosophical system.

During the late Middle Ages the division of the disciplines changed with the reception of Greek and Arabic texts; moreover, the Liberal Arts no longer had the same importance after the foundation of universities that they had enjoyed during the early Middle Ages. At most universities the study of mathematics and the sciences remained limited to the lower, arts faculties. Oxford, Vienna, and St. Andrews were the exceptions: beginning in the 14th century, *scientia naturalis* was taught in these universities as part of the main program, which was based on the Liberal Arts.

Grammar. The first discipline of the Trivium, grammar, had involved the study, originally, of the Greek language and, later, of Latin, which in the aftermath of the barbarian invasions increasingly became a foreign tongue. Grammar as a discipline consisted of a theoretical part (language teaching, which was based on the writings of classical authors) and a practical part (the reading of ancient poets). Preliminary courses where students learned to read and write prepared the ground for grammatical instruction. Starting in the early Middle Ages, grammar teaching became separated from other disciplines: it was often the only one of the Liberal Arts taught in monastery schools at a time when education had generally declined to a low level.

The discipline of grammar was transmitted to the Middle Ages by Isidore of Seville, drawing on Varro's *On the Latin Language* (*De lingua latina*) and on Augustine's *On Dialectic* (*De dialectica*). The Greek system of syntax, as represented by the first (and only) work on the subject in antiquity, a treatise written in the 2nd century CE by Apollonius Dyscolus in Alexandria, had been adopted by Roman grammarians; via Donatus and Priscian, whose writings served as manuals throughout the Middle Ages and beyond, it influenced grammars until the 20th century.

The foundation of the first universities in the 12th century and the increase in knowledge of ancient Greek authors affected the individual Liberal Arts in different ways. With grammar the result was its exclusion from the classical teaching canon of the universities and its relegation instead to schools, which began to spring up in every sizable town. To meet the need of these schools for easier learning tools, grammar treatises were written in verse: for example, the widely disseminated *Doctrinale* by Alexander of Villedieu and the *Graecismus* by Eberhard of Béthune. Students were now older and better prepared when they started their university studies; and by the end of the 14th century the amount of time devoted to the Liberal Arts was generally reduced.

New grammatical requirements emerged with the rise of national languages. There were efforts at the court of the emperor Frederick II to make Occitan, the language of the troubadours, comprehensible to foreigners with the help of an adapted Donatus. The first French grammars, such as the *Orthographia gallica,* appeared around 1300 in the Anglo-Norman region as manuals for English speakers. Poetry, formerly the "handmaiden of grammar" (*famula grammaticae*), acquired independence as a subject in its own right.

Grammar and poetry both enjoyed a temporary revival during the Renaissance because of the renewed interest in classical literature: in Toulouse and Perpignan, for instance, there was a faculty of grammar and poetry during the 15th century. These subjects were eventually replaced by disciplines such as philosophy, medicine, law, and theology and partly even by mathematics and natural science.

Rhetoric. The second branch of the Trivium, rhetoric, was in the Roman world strongly indebted to the Greeks as well as to Cicero. In Cicero's day rhetoric was not considered an appropriate subject for a young Roman to study, so he had gone to Greece for his education; later on, Greek teachers of rhetoric came to Rome. Ciceronian rhetoric was, however, fundamentally different from the Hellenistic discipline that had been shaped by Aristotle. An important difference was that Cicero introduced instruction in law, a subject that had not been included in Greek rhetoric but now became an integral part of the young orator's training. Cicero's polemic against Aristotle with regard to ethics reveals Stoic influence: though Aristotle had never lost sight of usefulness as the uppermost aim of rhetoric, what mattered to Cicero was the *honestum,* that which is morally honorable. Distancing himself from Plato's rejection of rhetoric, Cicero instead gave it a specific purpose—the common good—which later on would permit Christians to adopt the discipline in a slightly modified form.

The connection between rhetoric and law established by Cicero also appears in the work of Cassiodorus and Isidore of Seville. By the 10th century rhetoric had gained new importance in the northern Italian schools, which trained notaries, among others, and preceded the first universities. Of all the three arts of the Trivium, rhetoric was the one that underwent the most important changes in the Middle Ages. It also became useful for commerce and trade: Hugh of St. Victor regarded foreign trade as a kind of sister of rhetoric, because Mercury, the god of rhetoric, was also considered the patron of the merchants. In the 13th century, rhetoric and the specializations that developed out of it—the *ars dictandi* and *ars notaria,* which dealt with the composition of documents—served the business community because notaries' offices dealt with important matters of private and public law; and the privileges of merchants became a fundamental element in town constitutions, known as the "freedom of the towns."

Particular attention was paid to rhetoric at the universities of Bologna and Orléans, where there is evidence that law had been taught since the 9th century. From the

12th century onward law schools brought prestige to northern Italian towns, which competed for the most famous teachers. In his *Rhetorica antiqua* (early 13th century) Boncompagno, one of the most influential rhetoric teachers in Bologna, stressed the importance of his profession by describing rhetoric as *artium liberalium imperatrix et utriusque iuris alumna,* "empress of the Liberal Arts and pupil of both laws," that is, both civil law and canon law. In the *Rhetorica ecclesiastica* (ca. 1160–1180) an anonymous author described and explained the ecclesiastical judicial process.

Dialectic. The third and most abstract of the arts of the Trivium, dialectic taught a logical method of thought based on the model established by Plato, originally through conversation (or dialogue) but increasingly, as the Middle Ages progressed, through written texts. In this sense Plato was present in the medieval period as the "inventor" of dialectic, even though he did not write down his method in a manual or develop a theory. Aristotle, on the other hand, had laid the theoretical foundations of philosophy in his writings on logic and had made dialectic into a formal art. Compilers of authors on the Liberal Arts condensed his logical writings into a single work, containing an incomplete version of the Organon. The terms *dialectic* and *logic* became synonymous in late antiquity and the Middle Ages.

Some of the logical or dialectical writings of Aristotle and his commentator Porphyry were available in the early Middle Ages in Latin translations made by Boethius. It was not until the 12th century, however, that the complete texts of Aristotle's logical treatises and some of his scientific writings were translated into Latin. Although this generated considerable excitement, some of Aristotle's doctrines were perceived as a threat by Christian theologians because they contradicted certain fundamental truths of Christianity: Creation, Providence, redemption, and the individual immortality of the soul were incompatible with the Aristotelian image of the world. It looked, for a time, as if Christian theology could not be brought into line with experience and reason, as embodied in Aristotle. It was forbidden to read Aristotle at the University of Paris from 1210 to 1231, and a little later also in Toulouse; yet a lecture list of 1255 shows that this directive was not observed. In the meantime, Albertus Magnus, in his fundamental writings on theology (*Summae,* ca. 1246), used Aristotelian philosophy to substantiate and defend the Christian faith; following in Albertus' footsteps, his student Thomas Aquinas created a Christian Aristotelianism. This did not prevent a second wave of prohibitions at the University of Paris in the years 1270–1277: indeed, among the forbidden texts were works by Albertus and Thomas. It was the English theologian and philosopher William of Ockham who finally succeeded in bringing about a reconciliation and integration of Aristotelian philosophy and Christian theology—to the benefit of both—around 1300.

Arithmetic. Of the four arts constituting the Quadrivium, arithmetic, together with music, originated with the Pythagoreans, who developed a coherent theory of numbers and numerical ratios. According to Aristotle:

> The so-called Pythagoreans applied themselves to mathematics and were the first to develop this science; and through studying it they came to believe that its principles are the principles of everything . . . And since they saw further that the properties and ratios of the musical scales are based on numbers, and since it seemed clear that all other things have their whole nature modelled upon numbers, and that numbers are the ultimate things in the whole physical universe, they assumed the elements of numbers to be the elements of everything, and the whole universe to be a proportion or number. (*Metaphysics* 1.5.1)

A systematic account of the basic principles of arithmetic is found in book 5 of the *Elements* of Euclid. Boethius translated the arithmetic of Nicomachus of Gerasa into Latin, making it a standard work that was used until modern times.

Arithmetic had no practical purpose; but the Romans developed their own methods of calculating, which they employed on abacuses using unmarked stones. Roman numerals—still in use today—were more suitable for this counting method than the Greek system based on letters of the alphabet. The *Calculus* of Victorius of Aquitaine (ca. 450 CE) complemented the abacus, making it possible to find the positional value after a multiplication, and also introduced the reader to the Roman system of fractions (with the denominator 12).

An outgrowth of Boethius' number theory was the development of number symbolism, including themes such as holy numbers, which attracted wide interest. Isidore of Seville was the first in a long line of authors who composed treatises entitled *De numeris.*

Rithmomachia, a kind of numerical tournament, was based on Pythagorean number theory, with its special relationship to the Boethian theory of proportions. This game, invented before 1030, enjoyed great popularity throughout the Middle Ages and did not fall into oblivion until the 17th century. Two players sat on opposite sides of an oblong board, a little bigger than a chessboard, with black and white squares. Each player had 24 different stones, which represented the Pythagorean number ratios. The game, whose rules varied considerably, enabled players to engage in a lively competition while simultaneously acquiring experience in dealing with numbers and numerical ratios. Although numerical tables were available, players were supposed to know this information by rote. Increasingly, the *rithmomachia* provided training in music, geometry, and astronomy, as well as in arithmetic; and from the 13th century onward anonymous treatises presented the game as a guide to all realms of life. Comprehending the world with the help of numbers—something very much in the Platonic tradition—was now practiced on a broad social scale.

Indo-Arabic numerals first arrived in the West in the 10th century, together with the type of abacus written about by Gerbert of Aurillac; but it took some time for them to become generally accepted. Similarly, the arithmetic of al-Khwārizmī spread slowly at the beginning of the 12th century. It was the many treatises on elementary algorism, derived from the arithmetic of al-Khwārizmī and produced for the use of students, that helped to propagate the new methods of calculating as well as the new numerals. The most successful algorism treatises were written by Johannes de Sacrobosco and Alexander de Villa Dei. These works did not deal with commercial counting methods, which were instead taught by *maestri di abaco*, "abacus masters," who emerged in Italy in the 13th century and by their German counterparts, known as *Rechenmeister*, who emerged in the 14th.

Long before such masters appeared, collections of mathematical problems had been employed in the education of children and had also served as a form of social entertainment. These problems can be partly traced back to ancient Eastern societies. In the early Middle Ages, Alcuin was the first to collect them for the court of Charlemagne, under the title *Propositiones ad acuendos iuvenes* (*Propositions to Sharpen the Minds of Young People*). Although it is possible to discern from these collections what sort of problems were to be solved, they do not contain mathematical rules.

Music. Like arithmetic, music had its roots in Pythagorean number theory; it was the doctrine of the numerical ratios, which were the basis of harmonic sounds. A work of crucial importance for the Middle Ages in this field was Boethius' *De institutione musica* (*On Musical Education*) in five books, which was based on various Greek sources. Boethius divided music into three categories, according to the Platonic model: *musica mundana* originated from the perfect harmony of the celestial spheres; it was reflected as *musica humana* in human harmony; but it was only *musica instrumentalis* that could be heard by the human ear as sounds (*cantus*).

Musica speculativa played a central role in music theory until the early Middle Ages and found its expression in the practice of ecclesiastical music. In this way, music became a bridge between theology and the Liberal Arts; and from the end of the 15th century it was closely linked to poetry. As for instrument making, *musica mensurabilis* or *musica figurativa* continued to be based on harmonic theory; but the creation of melodies departed from this foundation. In the late Middle Ages music was de facto dropped from the curriculum of the Liberal Arts.

Geometry. In the Greek tradition geometry reached its culmination in Euclid's *Elements* (ca. 300 BCE), which incorporates older material from the 5th century BCE that is no longer extant. Euclid's great merit was to compile into one unified compendium all the knowledge available in his time concerning the problems of plane geometry. It was decisive for the development of Western mathematics that he confirmed his mathematical statements by proofs. Over the ensuing centuries Euclid's proofs were modified, first by his Greek commentators, then by Arabic and medieval translators and compilers, who not only altered but also amplified them and even replaced his proofs with others.

There are points of contact between Euclidean geometry and some of the writings of the Roman *agrimensores* or *gromatici* (land surveyors), although the simple geometrical problems dealt with by the latter were not really of scientific importance. Some of their writings concerned juridical problems of land surveying, while others concerned mechanics, waterworks, agriculture, architecture, and military issues. Among the Roman authors who wrote about geometrical problems the most significant are Varro, Hyginus, Epaphroditus, Vitruvius Rufus, and Balbus, whose *Expositio et ratio omnium formarum* (*Exposition and Account of All Forms*), a manual of geometry for land surveyors, was influential in the Middle Ages.

Boethius translated Euclid's *Elements* into Latin, but only excerpts and citations from the first five books survived to have an influence on early medieval geometry. During the Middle Ages two different treatises, ascribed to Boethius, were in circulation: the *Geometria I*, which was compiled in the monastery of Corbie during the 8th or 9th century and achieved its greatest importance before the availability of translations from Arabic (about 1120); and the *Geometria II*, a compilation of poor quality that can be dated to after 1025 and, on stylistic grounds, can perhaps be attributed to Franco of Liège. Another work, known as the *Geometria incerti auctoris* (*Anonymous Geometry*) and based mainly on the corpus of texts by the *agrimensores*, was written in the 9th or 10th century—at any rate, before Gerbert of Aurillac, who himself composed a geometry that is regarded as one of the most outstanding contributions to the field before the 12th century. These early medieval geometries did not become obsolete when a Latin translation (made from the Arabic) of the complete *Elements* of Euclid appeared about 1120; on the contrary, they continued to be copied and used, above all because of their relevance to practical geometry.

The medieval building trade was the first technical sector to make explicit use of geometrical knowledge, especially in relation to the construction of cathedrals. Both Vitruvius and his 13th-century counterpart, Villard de Honnecourt, recommended that architects study geometry. Doubts have often been expressed whether they actually did so, given the lack of evidence. In recent years, however, records of medieval architects and of those for whom the work was done have been systematically collected and published (Binding and Linscheid-Burdich 2002). In these records occur phrases such as *secundum formam* or *secundum figuram*, which in the Middle Ages were technical terms: the former meant "according to the geometry of the *agrimensores*," the latter "according to Euclid's *Elements*." Medieval architects thus justified their procedure by the application of practical geometry (*forma*) or the *Elements* (*figura*). Cicero's translation of Plato's term *idea* as *forma* ("These patterns [*formas*] of things called *ideai* or ideas by Plato . . . exist forever and depend on intellect and reason," *Orator* 3.9.10) established a bridge from Pythagorean thinking to Thomas Aquinas, who wrote in his *Summa theologiae* I (1265) that "*idea* in Greek means *forma* in Latin . . . So it is possible to speak of the idea of a house, since the architect intends to construct a house similar to the geometrical pattern that he conceived in his mind." We find this notion visualized in illustrations depicting *Deus Creator* (God the Creator), which show either God or Christ holding a compass.

Astronomy. Advances in higher mathematics, the leading science both in antiquity and in the Middle Ages, were necessary to understand the problems dealt with in astronomy. In archaic cosmology—in the works of Homer and Hesiod, for example, but also as transmitted by Aristotle—astronomical knowledge was expressed in terms of the myths of gods and heroes (von Dechend and Santillana 1969). Greek cosmology, however, eventually developed into a scientifically grounded discipline, whose principles were laid down by Ptolemy in the first manual of astronomy, the *Syntaxis mathēmatikē* (2nd cent. CE), which since ca. 800 has been known by its Arabic title, *The Almagest.*

In antiquity as well as in the Middle Ages interest was focused on planetary motion, which could be calculated with the help of the rules set out by Ptolemy in tabular form. Knowledge of the constellations and planets had a fundamental significance in astrology, a discipline that had come down from the Babylonians and that was used for predicting and interpreting human destiny. Astrology therefore acted as a potent spur to astronomical research from antiquity down to the 17th century, when the renowned astronomer Johannes Kepler provided astrological advice to General Albrecht von Wallenstein and Emperor Rudolf II.

Plato had stressed the importance of achieving a mathematical understanding of the celestial orbits, maintaining that mere observation should be left aside because it diverted the mind to no purpose. He realized that it might be difficult to comprehend motion and especially time by using mathematical methods and therefore considered it necessary to study, first of all, stereometry, that is, the geometry of space (*Republic* 528B–530B). Although Plato's recommendations were not followed, mathematics nonetheless played a vital role in classical astronomy, as can be judged from the crude instruments employed for observation—an application of mathematics to astronomy that would not have found favor with Plato. Celestial globes and armillary spheres were in use as early as the time of Anaximander and Hipparchus, but they served only the purpose of visualization. Archimedes constructed a famous movable armillary sphere, which was still admired by Cicero. Ptolemy employed a quadrant provided with a scale of degrees for the purpose of observations, as well as the planisphere, a precursor to the astrolabe. To determine the height of the sun, a gnomon was used, that is, a vertical rod placed in a round cup inscribed with a scale. Sundials and clepsydras (water clocks) indicated the time of the day. Hero of Alexandria invented a complicated tool, the dioptra, which he described as two circular disks, one horizontal and the other vertical, mounted on a rodlike base and able both to move and to tilt. The two disks had scales and a sighting device, known as a diopter. Although it is highly unlikely that this invention was used at all as an instrument in antiquity, its description reappeared in the 15th century; and under the name theodolite, it became the most important surveying instrument of modern times. In the 16th century the diopter was replaced by a sighting tube and in the 17th by the telescope.

Astronomy established the basis for two new sciences that became independent disciplines: geography (with cartography) and computus, the computation of the Christian calendar. The term *geographia* originally meant the graphic representation of the earth's surface. It applied the same coordinates used to measure the heavens, based on the polestar and the equator. Latitudinal positions were located by determining the height of the polestar; longitudes were deduced by calculating the time difference of lunar eclipses in different places. According to Pliny, this phenomenon was of some antiquity in his own time, having attracted the attention of Alexander the Great. In the 9th century Muslim astronomers developed a new method, using the distance between the moon and a star near the ecliptic, which allowed them to measure longitudes irrespective of lunar eclipses. Instead of determining the coordinates of longitudes ancient cartographers contented themselves with using distances measured on the surface of the earth between two or more places. Latitudes alone were employed to determine the "climatic zones," in which geographical places were provisionally located until exact measurements of their positions could be made. In the early Middle Ages, Gerbert of Aurillac taught his pupils to calculate the height of the polestar. His treatise *De utilitatibus astrolabii* (*On the Uses of the Astrolabe*) contains—unlike contemporary Arabic models—two chapters on climatic zones, including the geographical places within these zones. The portolans (sea charts) of the late Middle Ages were the first maps to be based on astronomically determined coordinates of longitudes and latitudes.

The computus gained importance for determining the calendar of the Christian year, with its movable date for Easter, dependent on the spring equinox and the phases of the moon. The Venerable Bede, an English monk of the 8th century, noted that the correction of the length of the year in the Julian calendar was not sufficient, so that the calendar no longer accurately reflected the true dates of Christ's life and death. This was a cause of much complaint throughout the Middle Ages because it made it impossible to celebrate religious feasts on the correct day; nevertheless, a thorough reform did not take place until the introduction of the Gregorian calendar in 1582. Independently of this long-term calendrical problem, it was necessary to ensure that the Christian feast days were observed on the same calendar days across Christendom; thus, clergymen had to be able to compute the date on which Easter fell in each year. Although this was essentially an astronomical problem, computus, which was taught in universities as a subject within the Liberal Arts, reduced it in practice to an exercise in calculation.

For instruction in the fundamental principles of astronomy the main textbook was Sacrobosco's *De sphera*, a work based on the second book of Pliny's *Natural History.* Although there were special courses on *theoria planetarum* (theory of the planets), these were very rare.

Far from dying out at the end of the Middle Ages, the Liberal Arts continued to be the mainstay of secondary education until modern times. The canon of the Liberal Arts also remained a stable component of university arts faculties, which survived in France and the United States until the 19th century and in some cases even until the 20th.

BIBL.: *Arts libéraux et philosophie au moyen âge,* Actes du IVe Congrès international de philosophie médiévale (Montreal 1969). G. Beaujouan, "The Transformation of the Quadrivium," in *Renaissance and Renewal in the Twelfth Century,* ed. R. L. Benson, G. Constable, and C. D. Lanham (Cambridge, Mass., 1982). Günther Binding and Susanne Linscheid-Burdich, *Planen und Bauen im frühen und hohen Mittelalter nach den Schriftquellen bis 1250* (Darmstadt 2002). Arno Borst, *Computus: Zeit und Zahl in der Geschichte Europas* (Berlin 1990). Menso Folkerts, *"Boethius" Geometrie II: Ein mathematisches Lehrbuch des Mittelalters* (Wiesbaden 1970) and *Essays on Early Medieval Mathematics: The Latin Tradition* (Aldershot 2003). Josef Koch, ed., *Artes liberales: Von der antiken Bildung zur Wissenschaft des Mittelalters* (Leiden 1959). Uta Lindgren, *Die Artes liberales in Antike und Mittelalter: Bildungs- und wissenschaftsgeschichtliche Entwicklungslinien,* 2nd rev. ed. (Augsburg 2004). *Maß, Zahl und Gewicht: Mathematik als Schlüssel zu Weltverständnis und Weltbeherrschung,* ed. Menso Folkerts et al., 2nd rev. ed. (Wiesbaden 2001). William H. Stahl, *Roman Science: Origins, Development and Influence to the Later Middle Ages* (Madison 1962). Michael Stolz, *Artes-liberales-Zyklen: Formationen des Wissens in Mittelalter,* 2 vols. (Tübingen 2004). Jutta Tezmen-Siegel, *Die Darstellungen der septem artes liberales in der Bildenden Kunst als Rezeption der Lehrplangeschichte* (Munich 1985). Hertha von Dechend and Giorgio de Santillana, *Hamlet's Mill: An Essay on Myth and the Frame of Time* (Boston 1969). U.L.

Liberty

The most lasting legacy of classical democracy, exemplified especially in Athens of the 5th and 4th centuries BCE, is the definition and practice of freedom (*eleutheria*) as civic political participation in the processes of self-government. If, as Giambattista Vico (1668–1744) thought, the history of politics is largely the history of the embodiments of changing popular imaginaries of the political order and its elements, then freedom as the salient principle of ancient Athenian democracy has a foundational place in the development and transformations of Western and, in many respects, world politics. Vico characteristically attributed the rise of democratic politics to a historic shift in the popular political imagination toward the delegitimation of hierarchical government. "It was Solon" (640–558 BCE), he wrote, "who urged the plebeians to reflect on themselves and to conclude that they were equal to the nobles in their human nature and consequently should be equal in human rights. . . ; the plebeians of all ancient peoples took Solon's reflection literally, and also changed the commonwealths from aristocracies to democracies" (*New Science,* 1744, 414–415).

Inasmuch as the Athenian example of democracy and freedom became a potent rhetorical and political resource for subsequent generations, it has been a continually contested legacy. As such, far from providing a linear narrative of continuities, the life of ancient Greek democracy in the Western political imagination and its correlate political practices consist of a series of relentless struggles and debates on the nature and place of liberty in a legitimate political order. The memory and projections of the Greek experience of freedom in the discourse and practice of Western politics have been shaped by the myths and scattered historical accounts of classical democracy, as well as by the logic of their political applications in constantly changing contexts.

Despite reciprocal influences between the popular political imagination and the tradition of political philosophy, they have produced two dominant, often opposite, responses to the problem of political liberty that have evolved into distinct, albeit occasionally converging, traditions. The first, embodied in the Athenian democratic experience, advanced participatory civic politics, the practices of self-government, as a measure against tyranny and other forms of citizens' subordination to arbitrary rule. The second, associated mostly with Plato and his followers in the Western tradition, opted for government directed and legitimated by knowledge rather than by citizens' participation from below. Direct popular participation secured freedom from domination, though not from error or tragic consequences, but government guided by knowledge appeared to constitute a measure against errors and flawed decisions, though at the cost of being compatible with hierarchical rule. As long as the philosopher-king was seen to be guided by knowledge, not caprice or vested interest, however, the hierarchical principle was mitigated by the depersonalization of authority.

In the Age of the Enlightenment, leading thinkers like Leibniz, Locke, Condorcet, Kant, and later J. S. Mill and Dewey tried to weld the two traditions through the democratization of knowledge. The cultural movements of the Enlightenment devised numerous encyclopedias, dictionaries, science museums, and programs of public instruction aimed at a universal dissemination of knowledge that would render almost any citizen a philosopher-king. These efforts to fuse knowledge with participation were bound to have only limited success because they failed to appreciate the initial insights of classical rhetoricians that political persuasion is actually a performing art, that politics is irreducible to knowledge, and that knowledge itself and its applications cannot escape inherent uncertainties.

More recently, classical scholars working in diverse disciplines (such as anthropology, archaeology, literary studies, and legal-political history) have been uncovering new evidence in support of a view contrary to the entrenched image of Athens as a culturally homogeneous society that built participatory civic politics on common ethnic and cultural foundations. Recent research suggests that it was actually much more a multicultural and multiethnic society, whose polity rested on thin rather than thick cultural coherence. This picture seems more compatible with a liberal rather than republican, nationalist, or communitarian perception and appropriation of Athens as a polity held together by civic politics rather than by common roots. This line of thought has insisted that the great innovation of the Greek *polis* was the invention of politics, of participatory civic culture, as a universal human option based on recognizing humans as political animals capable of self-government. Seen as an increasingly general turn away from hierarchical and toward egalitarian imaginaries of legitimate political order, this development has been associated with the emergence of the common person as the principal political actor, the source of political authority and binding judgments on the direction and management of the common life. The Greek invention of participatory civic culture has implied a dramatic shift toward the temporalization of politics and a view of law as the result of specific voluntary human (and therefore alterable) acts, rather than timeless customs or imperatives sanctioned by mythologized ancestors.

Classical historians note a close affinity between the early genealogy of the Greek idea of freedom and the experience of slavery. From its very beginning free persons were defined and recognized as not slaves, as individuals whose bodies, actions, and utterances were not owned by other individuals. Aristotle, though not particularly sympathetic to democracy, provided a very succinct and influential formulation when he wrote that a free citizen is an individual who both rules and is being ruled. In Sophocles' *Antigone,* Creon says he would trust only an obedient citizen to be "ruler or ruled" (660). In the course of time the idea of being ruled evolved mostly as the duty to obey laws, and the idea of ruling found its most common expression in the freedom to influence the process of government, particularly the making of laws and policies. Rousseau's famous formulation linked obedience, legislation, and liberty: he wrote that if citizens, as sovereign, participate in making the laws that they must obey as subjects, they actually are obeying only themselves. The implication of this view was, of course, that for noncitizens obedience to the law does not correspond to freedom. Politically this recognition underlay centuries of struggle over the boundaries of obedience and citizenship. In the modern period, and particularly during the Enlightenment, liberal thinkers like Kant attempted to reconcile the authority of the law with the citizen's freedom as an autonomous individual on an even more universal basis by voluntarizing obedience, describing it as following certain imperatives of one's own reason.

The Greek juxtaposition of free persons and slaves has had powerful resonance for later centuries, especially in countries such as the United States and South Africa, which practiced slavery; in states where native peoples rose against colonial rule; and in societies where the political order rested on hierarchical structures where lower classes experienced repression by and dependence on the upper class. Images of Athenian direct democracy and the Spartan martial-republican democracy inspired the modern English, American, French, and other revolutionaries, who framed their struggles as liberation from enslaving monarchs and aristocracies. Monarchists, other antidemocrats, and even republicans like the American Federalists, however, had no difficulty contesting this classical political legacy, sometimes employing the same historical examples from ancient Greece and later Rome to make opposing claims, equating democracy with anarchy, disorder, instability, or the tyranny of the masses.

The Athenian idea of freedom as political participation and government by and for the people indeed had a revolutionary and deterrent potential that has been expressed over the centuries in rhetoric, political movements, successful and unsuccessful attempts of tyrannicide, and frequent explosions of rebellious violence against aristocratic and authoritarian governments. The fear of critics such as Plato, Aristotle, Cicero, Machiavelli, Montesquieu, Burke, and Madison regarding the fragility of a responsible participatory citizenry, which can easily degenerate into mob rule by mass violence, has had enough foundation in experience to warrant repeated attempts to constitutionalize (that is, to channel and restrain) the breadth and freedom of citizens' participation. This ground for setting limits on public participation, which has increasingly been restricted to periodic elections and other temporally limited vehicles for expression of public feelings and opinions, was further supported by the limitations deriving from the large size of the populations of modern states. These pressures have led to the passing of laws and the institutionalization of customs that have increasingly transformed what in Athens was direct political participation into mediated, ritualized, and symbolic participation. Such transformations have correspondingly changed the historic meanings of democratic political freedom and its practices. Trying to moderate and mediate the actual politics of direct citizen participation while retaining the political imaginary of popular sovereignty, Western political tradition gave rise to diverse alternative or supportive symbolic and institutional instruments such as social contract and natural law theories, constitutions often considered impartial regulatory mechanisms, the market as an impersonal instrument for the distribution of wealth, and later such constructed political agencies as public opinion.

Rome during the late Republic and early Principate, though heavily drawing on Greek ideas and experience, already exemplified this historic shift away from Greek democratic practices and the meanings of political freedom. Like the Athenian *eleutheria*, the Roman *libertas* embodied in the *res publica* connoted the principle of the people's sovereignty in contradistinction to tyranny and kingship. Both implied equal citizens' political rights and a fair share in the common weal. But the Roman Republic was much more minimally democratic. It was actually an aristocratic republic in which citizens were more likely to be invited to listen to their governors and representatives than to speak to the assembly. Republican government came to be identified more with a commitment to serve the public good than to a practice of government by the people. The Roman constitution treated the Assembly as the embodiment of the people and provided protection of individual freedom, property, and equality before the law. Though empowering the Senate in relation to the chief executive, in the long run it could not effectively constrain the destructive imbalances produced by ruthless factional competition for hegemony and the eventual centralization of power necessitated by Rome's imperial expansion. Moreover, preoccupation with war and pursuit of imperial greatness stifled the cultivation of domestic political freedoms. Despite the facade of serving the "public good" and the rule of law, still reasonably respected in the Republic under Augustus, the regime eventually degenerated into tyranny and despotism.

The Roman path from republicanism to tyranny, buttressed by the glorification of the virtues of military valor, the pursuit of greatness, and a rhetoric of "serving the people" cultivated by monarchic and aristocratic regimes, made domestic individual freedoms, understood as the legally protected right of unconstrained individual action, more dependent on the benevolence of the leader than on actual political participation or constitutional guarantees. Such deterioration of republican political norms and institutions has not been less a part of the classical legacy to the modern world than the Greek city-state concept of freedom as civic political participation, its lasting power in the theories legitimating modern states, and its early institutional expressions in antiquity. This lesson was very much on the minds of Montesquieu and Madison, among many other modern political and constitutional thinkers, who, skeptical about the reliability of an enduring virtuous citizenry, searched for the best structural formula to secure domestic institutional and class balance.

The Graeco-Roman legacies of civic virtue and individual freedom faced another formidable challenge with the rise of Christian monotheism, its novel vocabulary linking human virtues to the individual as a sinner driven by a personal spiritual quest and moral development, its preoccupation with individual salvation, and the spread of a radically new vision of order resting on otherworldly transpolitical sources of meaning. In some respects the Christian imagination has reinforced and deepened such classical themes as individualism and universalism. The later conflicts between Protestants and Catholics can be seen as something of a replay of the classical clash between participatory and hierarchical government. Throughout the Middle Ages these themes were subordinate to Christian ideals focusing on personal repentance and redemption, religious structures of authority, and the Christian drive for world expansion.

These themes were destined to erupt again in a new guise with the emergence of early Renaissance Humanism and neorepublicanism, which laid down the grounds for modern liberal and democratic conceptions and practices of freedom. Despite its theological aims, a work like Saint Augustine's *Confessions* (4th century) and its echoes, reflected nearly a millennium later in such works as the lyrical poetry of Petrarch and Dante's *Divine Comedy*, contributed heavily to the development of modern imaginaries of human interiority and its associated notions of individual human personality and subjectivity. Such developments created radically novel frames for the discourse and practices of freedom, according to which political freedoms are unsustainable without the legal-political protection of freedoms of thought, culture, religion, economic transactions, science, the arts, and so on. Although modern individualism thus expanded the classical conception of freedom beyond the civic context, these modern spheres of individual freedom have had to struggle continually to protect their autonomy in relation to the state and to assert their role in reinforcing and articulating the power of the citizens and their voluntary associations in relation to the government. Along those lines, the post-classical distinction between state and society emerged as a liberal imaginary, supporting diverse strategies for limiting the powers of the state. Each of these emergent spheres concomitantly became an arena of contest between those who sought to depoliticize religion, culture, science, and the market as social spheres protected from the divisions and struggles of politics, and those who sought to politicize religion, culture, science, and the market as resources influencing the course of public affairs.

Perhaps the Roman synthesis of ancient Greek political freedom with republican virtues and institutions (revived and variously modified in the early modern period by such thinkers as Machiavelli, Harrington, Montesquieu, and Rousseau) faced its greatest challenge in the rise respectively of market and commercial values and of modern nationalism. The former encouraged powerful processes of privatizing the consciousness and practices of the public regarding citizenry, whereas the latter enlisted the individual's service and sacrifices for the nation-state, subordinating individual freedoms to the supposed collective needs of the nation. Privileging group solidarity over the freedom to criticize and challenge the government, the repression of forms of political participation that make government dependent on people has inevitably made the people increasingly dependent on the government. Many modern nation-states have proved by negation the classical legacy that the freedom to participate politically in the making and unmaking of governments is the best guarantee of freedom from government interference in the private lives of the citizens.

Classical democratic and republican values of participatory, free, and egalitarian citizenry have persisted throughout the modern history of Western politics and its global extensions as a powerful resource for political criticism and delegitimation of authoritarian regimes. Modern ideas of the social contract and constitutional government (intended to balance citizens' freedoms with social stability) have combined with the 17th-century scientific revolution (culturally augmented by the European Enlightenment) to reinvoke and sustain the Platonic vision of overcoming arbitrary power by founding politics on reason and knowledge, rather than on popular opinion. To its detriment, this vision has ignored another resilient Athenian legacy, that of the Athenian tragedians. If one considers the texts of the tragedies of Sophocles, Aeschylus, and Euripides as an integral part of embedded Athenian political theory, the tension between the image of the citizen as a purposeful and responsible rational agent and the theatrical enactment of the individual as a tragic actor is salient. Tragedies like *Oresteia, Oedipus Rex,* and *Antigone,* whose performance before thousands of Athenians constituted major civic-political events, conveyed the harsh message that political freedom to act is usually combined with the actor's own ineluctable ignorance of the causal chains that determine his actions' consequences; both as individuals and in groups, human agents are unknowing yet volitional agents. Classical tragedians taught their democratic citizens lower expectations and humility in the face of the uncertainties inherent in politics as a human enterprise. Political participation emancipates citizens from subordination to the arbitrary powers of tyrannical rulers and legitimates the decisions of the state and their consequences. But it does not protect the public from the uncertainties and unknowns that produce tragic results. Knowledge is better than opinion and ignorance as guidance for government. But even at the cost of limiting participation to a knowledgeable few, it does not guarantee sufficient control over uncertainties. This political message was echoed in the neorepublicanism of Machiavelli, who appreciated the crucial role of *Fortuna* (chance) in political history; in Rousseau's preference for guidance by the common sense of lay people over the knowledge claims of philosophers and scientists; and in Nietzsche's political pessimism. There is obviously great continuity between our contemporary declining faith in the role of scientists and other experts in producing rational politics and the Greek commitment to the view that though participation can at least secure freedom, knowledge cannot fully control *Fortuna.* Similarly, there is great continuity between Sophocles' view of the individual as a tragic actor and the postmodern view of the individual as a riddle even to herself, and an agent who must conduct himself in a basically unintelligible world.

Since late modernity, however, the Greek equation of liberty and participatory civic culture seems increasingly challenged by the emergence of the camera, or the electronic mass media, as the principal medium of democratic politics. Contrary to initial expectations that documentary photography would introduce new clarity to political discourse, the political difficulties caused by the ambiguities inherent in human linguistic communications have only been compounded by the commensurate difficulties of fixing the meanings and interpretations of pictures. The importance of photographs in our mass media seems to reflect more of the logic of rhetoric than philosophical or scientific persuasion. The old political philosopher's vision of the role of knowledge in fixing the meanings of public discourse appears as unrealizable as ever. This severely constrains the ambition of contemporary media experts, our current rhetoricians, to claim sufficient knowledge to control and manipulate the public effects of mass communications. Postmodern public opinion appears just as shifty and contradictory an embodiment of the common sense of the *Demos* as it was 2,500 years ago. But together with periodic elections, and despite lingering skepticism, the indirect and delayed effects of public opinion on democratic governments, as projected daily by the mass media, apparently produce a sufficient sense of public participation to sustain the system. If this state of affairs can be described as the post-Enlightenment triumph of the people's common knowledge over philosophy or science in public affairs, it may also be regarded as merely a partial and thoroughly modified version of the classical Athenian civic ideal of government by the people, of liberty not free from tragedy.

Classical democratic and republican imaginaries of politics, like almost all those that followed, could never be fully realized. But as inspiration for governments for and especially by the people, offering powerful resources for political critique of authoritarian governments, its legacy is likely to endure.

BIBL.: J. P. Euben, John R. Wallach, and Josiah Ober, eds., *Athenian Political Thought and the Reconstruction of American Democracy* (Ithaca 1994). C. Meier, *The Greek Discovery of Politics* (Cambridge, Mass., 1990). J. Ober, *Athenian Legacies: Essays on the Politics of Going On Together* (Princeton 2005). M. Ostwald, *From Popular Sovereignty to the Sovereignty of Law: Law, Society, and Politics in Fifth-century Athens* (Berkeley 1986). Q. Skinner, *Liberty before Liberalism* (Cambridge 1998). C. Wirszubski, *Libertas as a Political Idea at Rome during the Late Republic and the Early Principate* (Cambridge 1950).

Y.E.

Libraries

Since antiquity, libraries have served as important conduits for the material preservation and transmission of classical texts. Representative of wealth and power—books and their production remained an expensive business well into modern times—libraries also reflect the cultural and ideological priorities of their age. In the long journey classical texts have made from antiquity to the present, large institutional libraries and small private collections alike have played important roles: the former for the size and permanence of their collections, the latter for their ubiquity.

Though the first major book collections appeared late in the Greek world, not before the early 4th century BCE, for Aristotle at the end of that century a sizable working library had become essential. By the early 3rd century it was possible for the Ptolemies to contemplate the wholesale importation of Greek culture into Egypt by establishing a library at Alexandria. The Alexandrian library would become the foremost research library of the ancient world. Its resident scholars invented what would remain the fundamental tools of scholarship down to the Renaissance: the authoritative textual edition, the commentary, the glossary, and the grammar. They also devised library catalogues and bibliographies, keys to managing a large working library. This model of the research library spread elsewhere in the Hellenic world: to Antioch, Caesarea, and, by the 4th century CE, Constantinople, where foundations were laid for the selective preservation—amid bouts of persecution—of the classical Greek textual heritage within the Byzantine empire.

No public libraries existed in Rome until the very last days of the Republic, but by the 4th century CE more than two dozen public libraries had been established, largely under imperial patronage, in the city of Rome itself. Indicative of the great Roman debt to the Greek intellectual heritage, Roman libraries contained both Latin and Greek texts and many Greek authors in translation.

In late antiquity libraries underwent significant material and intellectual changes that fundamentally affected the transmission of the classical tradition. The 4th century witnessed the rejection of the fragile papyrus roll in favor of the more durable codex. The literary tastes and intellectual needs of the libraries of late antiquity likely exercised considerable influence in the choice of which authors were copied to codex. With few exceptions, if not transferred to the codex form, Latin texts simply did not survive.

The Christianization of the Roman world initiated a process of selection of a different order on the classical heritage. In the East, scholarly Christian libraries modeled on the pagan libraries of antiquity were established at Jerusalem, Caesarea, and Alexandria. Pagan and Christian literatures existed side by side in these libraries. Yet though the study of Scripture and of the Judeo-Christian tradition was informed by the philological methods and habits of scholarship borrowed from the study of classical texts, pagan authors occupied a position of second rank on the library shelves. This would remain true until the late Renaissance.

Nonetheless, over the course of the 5th century Christianity's definitive adoption of secular learning had enormous consequences for the ultimate survival of classical literature. Christian and pagan men of letters read the same books, used the same centers of book production, and had a shared if unequal attachment to classical culture. Reading and collecting works by classical authors constituted an essential element of the aristocratic ethos, a mentality fundamental for the material survival of the classical tradition in the centuries to come. In the face of the mounting social and political crisis presented by the barbarian invasions, a concerted effort was made to gather together a corpus of texts felt to be "classics"—that is, emblematic of a traditional culture then in need of protection and conservation by Christianized Roman elites. Extant manuscripts from the late 4th to the early 6th centuries reveal a library culture in which classical learning still played a fundamental role.

With the end of antiquity came the rise of monastic libraries. Though eventually they played a crucial role in the preservation of classical texts, their beginnings were highly inauspicious. Monastic libraries were fundamentally different from the great public and private libraries of late antiquity. Indeed, early monasticism espoused an ideal of the religious life that envisioned a complete break with profane culture. The internal book needs of early monastic communities were relatively meager: liturgical works and a modicum of additional texts, predominantly Scripture, intended for intensive reading and memorization. Until the 6th century, monasteries were furnished with only a handful of such books, barely a collection and hardly a library. Yet the intellectual potential of the monastic library was very soon exploited by figures such as Benedict at Montecassino. Its most tangible expression is to be found in the library at Vivarium established by Cassiodorus in the mid-6th century. Espousing an ideal of Christian learning that combined sacred and profane studies, Cassiodorus established an ambitious plan for monastic education in the seven liberal arts, complete with a catalogue of classical authors to be mastered and guidelines on copying and preserving books. His *Institutions* was later used as a manual of library economy by medieval institutions intent on reassembling the textual legacy of the ancient world.

Neither Montecassino nor Vivarium survived the social and political devastation of the period from 550 to 750. The final collapse of the Roman Empire in the West proved fatal to institutional support for classical learning. Active interest in classical texts for the most part was restricted to technical treatises in education, law, and medicine; it seems that few if any literary works were copied in these centuries.

What is clear is that classical works of all kinds survived. Their recovery in the late 8th and 9th centuries was largely the work of the network of monastic libraries in France, Germany, and Switzerland established under first Irish and later Anglo-Saxon influence. Most of these monasteries followed the rule of Benedict, in which reading and the books dispensed from the abbey library were integral parts of the rhythm of monastic life. Importing new ideals of monastic learning from the northern fringes of the former empire, the monasteries replaced older ascetic forms of monasticism with an educational culture that sought to return to the literary heritage of the Graeco-Roman tradition.

Monasteries were isolated and financially autonomous, and book copying—considered a manual rather than an intellectual task—became an important source of earned income. With the collapse of the secular commercial book trade in the early Middle Ages, monastic collections only increased in importance, providing a nucleus for the great medieval scriptoria. The frequently close ties of the monasteries with secular elites, who depended on the monk-scribes for stocking their own libraries, provided yet another vector of influence on the copying and conservation of classical texts within the monasteries. Monasteries in this period did not have reading rooms; books were stored in chests or cupboards and distributed for reading and copying in individual cells. From the late 8th century, the task of copying was organized in a space specifically designated for the purpose, the scriptorium. This model would be enshrined in Benedictine monasticism and the scriptoria of the great abbeys of the Middle Ages: Bobbio, Tours, Corbie, St. Gall, Lorsch, Fulda, and Montecassino (once firmly reestablished in the 10th century), among a host of others.

The new monastic foundations were well equipped to play a key role in the cultural renewal initiated by Charlemagne. Though the monasteries had long had schools for the education of monks, Charlemagne looked to monastic and cathedral schools for training the secular and ecclesiastical administrators of empire. Many of the monasteries became important educational and, in time, literary centers. Classical texts were essential to this endeavor. Modeled on the pagan schools of late antiquity, the Carolingian schools established a curriculum that relied heavily on a handful of classical authors, mostly poets, for instruction in the rudiments of Latin language and grammar. The court library of Charlemagne actively collected works by many classical authors for both pedagogical and intellectual purposes—Charlemagne enjoyed having the works of the ancient historians read aloud—but its role as a center for the diffusion of classical literature has perhaps been exaggerated. Certainly of far greater importance to the long-term survival of classical texts was the social and political support ecclesiastical libraries received for the new learning during the Carolingian period. Thus, with the Carolingian Renaissance of the 8th and 9th centuries, the classics, though greatly restricted in number and studied mostly for linguistic reasons, once again occupied a central place on library shelves. Though the number of classical authors in widespread circulation was small, this core stimulated the search for more obscure and recondite authors. With very few exceptions, all Latin authors available today can be traced to Carolingian libraries.

Where did these books come from? The Carolingian thirst for books is indisputably rooted in the Anglo-Saxon world. Nonetheless, the classical resources in the British Isles were meager, and the same was true of Spain, France, and Germany. Texts appear to have migrated north from Italy: from Rome, from the area around Naples, and particularly from Ravenna, captured by Charlemagne's armies. The wholesale transfer of classical texts from Italian collections to northern libraries is one of the key features of the Carolingian renaissance.

The monastic orders were international organizations, and books were regularly loaned for copying purposes both locally and more globally: monastic libraries in Ireland, England, France, Switzerland, Germany, and Italy all exchanged texts for copying (though they were not always returned). Many classical texts continued to be added to the core monastic collections—in the 11th century Tacitus and Apuleius were copied at Montecassino, for example, and at the end of the century Jerome, the abbot of Pomposa, searched high and low for the text of Livy. After the 12th century the cultural importance of the monasteries would decline, but their book collections—jealously guarded as valuable property—would remain. In later centuries the Humanists ransacked these libraries in search of classical texts.

The rise of the universities in the 12th century brought a new library type. University libraries were in fact a rarity. But the study houses of the new monastic orders, particularly of the Dominicans and the Franciscans, and the colleges that clustered around the universities of Paris, Oxford, Bologna, and elsewhere gradually came to be furnished with sizable collections used by both teachers and students. The library of the Collège de Sorbonne in Paris, for example, became one of the largest libraries of the Middle Ages. The new intellectual orientation of the universities meant that the contents of libraries shifted dramatically: though Scripture and works of theology dominated, there was a marked increase in classical texts, particularly those important for the study of logic, mathematics, and philosophy. For the first time since the 6th century, Greek authors—in Latin translation from Greek or Arabic—returned to the bookshelves of men of learning in significant numbers. Although these medieval translations would later be decried by the Humanists as replete with linguistic and technical inaccuracies, an institutional home for Greek philosophical, scientific, and medical authors was established nonetheless. Later, under Humanist influence, the search for manuscripts of the original Greek texts would commence.

The universities had many indirect effects on the library culture of the High Middle Ages. Unlike the older monastic libraries, the new conventual and college libraries that came to maturity in the late 13th and 14th centuries were consulting libraries, intended for professional training in the university faculties of theology, law, and medicine. The libraries were furnished with reading rooms and books were set out, chained to desks or lecterns, to enable ready consultation. Thus, multiple texts and authors could be studied together rather than borrowed and read separately, and books could be returned to again and again as the need arose. This change in library culture is reflected in the growing tendency in this period to gather together the works of an author into a single corpus. Perhaps the greatest testimony to the classical resources of these libraries lies in the collections of excerpts from classical texts, drawn from multiple authors, subjects, and genres, that began to circulate in large numbers in the 12th and 13th centuries. The new libraries, well stocked and readily accessible, were crucial for this newfound familiarity with classical authors.

The universities created a large literate urban elite, both lay and religious, for whom books were both a professional necessity and an intellectual comfort. It is thus no coincidence that from the mid-13th century onward private libraries once again began to play a significant role in the book life of the West. For the most part classical texts were represented by works of law and medicine, but private libraries occasionally contained classical authors, which indicated a broader interest in the classical world.

Early Humanism was born of this milieu. Centered first in Padua and then in Florence in the 14th century, subsequent generations of lawyers, notaries, secretaries, and chancellors turned to Latin texts of antiquity for both professional and intellectual purposes. Professionally, this group sought to develop new rhetorical models based on classical ideals of eloquence; many also penned poems in imitation of ancient authors. Petrarch exemplifies this trend well. Nurtured in the early Humanist circles of the Veneto, Petrarch spent his early career at the papal court at Avignon, where he was exposed not only to the enormous papal library but also to the great French libraries of Carolingian foundation, in which he foraged for manuscripts by classical authors. He spent the end of his career in Venice, where he was informally associated with the ducal chancery. In between, Petrarch amassed a private library of classical texts that was without parallel in his day. He was followed by Humanist collectors, such as Collucio Salutati, Poggio Bracciolini, among many others, who rifled through early medieval Italian collections in search of ancient authors. And, like Petrarch, later Humanists repeatedly traveled to northern libraries in search of classical booty. With their ties to ruling elites—Salutati was chancellor of the Florentine Republic, Poggio was papal secretary—the lasting influence of such Humanist collectors is seen in the libraries founded on Humanist principles at the courts of Milan, Ferrara, Urbino, and Naples, at the Vatican, and in the Medici-supported libraries of San Marco and San Lorenzo in Florence. These libraries programmatically acquired classical texts, dispatching agents to search for new texts in northern and Italian libraries, commanding copies of known exemplars, commissioning translations of Greek authors into elegant Humanist Latin, and frequently absorbing the private libraries of Humanist collectors.

The acquisition of Greek manuscripts remains the enduring legacy of the libraries of the Renaissance. In the middle of the 14th century only a handful of manuscripts of classical Greek texts were to be found at the papal library at Avignon; by the end of the following century the collection, now ensconced in the Vatican, comprised hundreds of classical Greek titles. Individual scholars also possessed sometimes astonishing collections of Greek literary, philosophical, and scientific texts. In the late 15th century Pico della Mirandola owned more than 80 Greek manuscripts bearing on the classical world; in 1525 the library of the Ferrara physician Niccolò Leoniceno contained some 117 volumes of Greek manuscripts, including virtually every Greek scientific text now known. Though some Greek texts had survived the Middle Ages in libraries in southern Italy and Sicily, for the most part texts came into Renaissance libraries via Byzantine scholars resident in Italy who were in contact with the Greek book trade in Crete, Constantinople, and elsewhere in Byzantium. With the collapse of the Byzantine empire in 1453, the recovery of the classical Greek textual heritage in Italy began in earnest; Bessarion, the Greek Orthodox archbishop turned Latin cardinal, attempted to establish a complete library of Greek texts for the use of Byzantine émigrés in Italy. His collection, bequeathed to the city of Venice for the common use of scholars, served as the core of the Marciana Library, the National Library of Saint Mark.

This symbiotic relationship between Humanist collectors and large state collections was played out repeatedly over the following centuries. The El Escorial library in Spain, the Bibliothèque du Roi (King's Library) in France, numerous court libraries in Germany, and the omnipresent Vatican Library vied with one another in acquiring Greek and a dwindling supply of Latin manuscripts until the end of the 18th century. But the advent of print meant that manuscript collections, though vital for editorial scholarship, would decline in cultural importance. These collections, nationalized over the course of the late 18th and 19th centuries, form the basis of the great manuscript research collections of today.

Libraries nonetheless played an important role in the diffusion of classical learning in the age of the printed book. In the 16th century Francis I of France and Cosimo I of Florence made a great show of publishing the manuscript riches of their libraries, engaging top scholars as librarians, editors, and printers to oversee the task. The renowned Venetian printer of classical texts, Aldus Manutius, believed that his invention of the cheap pocket book meant that a "portable library" of classical authors would become available to a wider reading public. As books became more affordable, the dream of assembling a complete library of classical texts came to be more and more a reality. Classical texts occupied pride of place in Konrad Gesner's bibliography of all known texts (both those that had survived from antiquity and those that had perished owing to the vagaries of fire, war, and negligence) in Hebrew, Greek, and Latin in 1545. Gesner's list of some 3,000 authors and perhaps 10,000 to 12,000 texts was appropriately enough entitled *Bibliotheca universalis*—"universal library." With the firm establishment of the classical curriculum in European schools over the course of the early modern period, classical texts formed the backbone of libraries from the Jesuit colleges in Catholic lands to the great universities of the north. The result was that any Enlightenment "gentleman's library" had at its core—whether for show or for real, whether in the original languages or in translation—a collection that included Cicero and Plutarch, Virgil and Horace, Polybius and Tacitus. This classicizing ideal of the library found architectural expression in the 19th century in the round reading rooms, reminiscent of the Roman Pantheon, in the British Museum Library in London, the National Library in Paris, and the Library of Congress in Washington. Today the close association of the classical world with the cultural ideal of the library endures in the editions of ancient works published in the series titled Bibliotheca Teubneriana and Loeb Classical Library.

BIBL.: Bernhard Bischoff, *Manuscripts and Libraries in the Age of Charlemagne,* trans. M. Gorman (Cambridge 1994). Donald A. Bullough, "Charlemagne's Court Library Revisited," *Early Medieval Europe* 12 (2003) 339–363. Lionel Casson, *Libraries in the Ancient World* (New Haven 2001). Guglielmo Cavallo, *Dalla parte del libro: Storie di trasmissione dei classici* (Urbino 2000). Luce Giard and Christian Jacob, eds., *Des Alexandries,* vol.1, *Du livre au texte* (Paris 2001). Anthony Grafton, ed., *Rome Reborn: The Vatican Library and Renaissance Culture* (London 1993). Armando Petrucci, "Le biblioteche antiche," in *Letteratura italiana,* ed. Alberto Asor Rosa (Turin 1983) 2:527–554. L. D. Reynolds and N. G. Wilson, *Scribes and Scholars: A Guide to the Transmission of Greek and Latin Literature* (Oxford 1991). P.N.

Ligorio, Pirro

Painter, architect, and antiquarian (Naples 1513–Ferrara 1583). During the 1540s and 1550s, as he sought membership in Roman academies and artistic patronage from the Este and Farnese families, he began composing an immense corpus of work on antiquities, of which he published only a slim, pugnacious volume (1553) and several remarkable maps reconstructing ancient Rome. The bulk of his work—including writings on such topics as ancient ships, images of the gods, coins, inscriptions, temples, villas, herms, rivers and fountains, sepulchral monuments and customs, weights and measures, and clothing, as well as a vast alphabetical encyclopedia of antiquities—survived the ensuing centuries in the form of daunting folio-sized manuscripts that came to tantalize scholars of Greek and Roman archaeology.

Ligorio designed the garden fountains of the Villa d'Este at Tivoli and the casino (villa) of Pius IV and was architect of St. Peter's in 1564–1566. Yet he is remembered chiefly as an antiquarian, locating, recognizing, interpreting, and reemploying the material remains of ancient Rome for the beautification of the villas and palaces of cardinals, popes, and aristocrats. Other artists participated in this trade, but most produced sketchbooks rather than illustrated scholarly treatises. Ligorio drew damaged and lost artifacts, described their precise discovery locations and sequences of collectors, and analyzed their iconography and textual sources. Although these methods bear an uncanny resemblance to present-day archaeological cataloguing techniques, his surviving work often infuriated the first modern archaeologists, who in the late 19th century flocked to Rome to investigate the manuscripts documenting Renaissance discoveries of the objects that were of interest to them. He was accused during his lifetime of forging coins, yet he also wrote a technical treatise on how to detect such forgeries. When publishing on antiquities he declared his "amateur" status, saying he was an artist—but he considered that his "artist's eye" gave him a specialized visual knowledge that rivaled the philological superiority of the Humanist. And he apparently forged countless inscriptions that had found their way into the published collections of G. B. Doni, Janus Gruter, Thomas Reinesius, and L. A. Muratori and thus eventually into the *Corpus inscriptionum graecarum* (1828–1859) and *Corpus inscriptionum latinarum* (1863–), whose editors had allegedly managed to sort the authentic wheat from the Ligorian chaff. More generally, a negative view of Ligorio's antiquarian research passed from his contemporary Antonio Agustín through Ezechiel Spanheim in the 17th century to Giuseppe Volpi in the 20th; and Ligorio's original manuscripts were seldom consulted before the 1860s. An exception was Scipione Maffei, who wrote a thoughtful critique (sometime after 1711) of the scholarly value of Ligorio's Turin manuscripts, noting the importance of the architectural drawings. If the first compilers of the monumental series of inscriptions still consulted today thought that they had silenced Ligorio, they were mistaken. Since the 1950s research into Renaissance antiquarianism has blossomed, and art and architectural historians have painstakingly investigated Ligorio's manuscript drawings as evidence of his eyewitness experience of Roman excavations. Archaeologists began to take a fresh look at alleged forgeries in the Ligorian corpus, realizing that a case-by-case assessment was necessary. As historians have lately turned increasingly to the visual records of material culture, antiquarianism itself has been judged more worthy of scholarly investigation than midcentury luminaries such as Arnaldo Momigliano considered it to be. Ligorio, like it or not, was one of the founders of modern archaeological method. That he attempted this without Humanist credentials still troubles some scholars today, and his writings remain a contested site, mirroring the paradigms, strengths, and weaknesses of the modern university disciplines.

BIBL.: Isabella Barisi, Marcello Fagiolo, and Maria Luisa Madonna, *Villa d'Este* (Rome 2003). David Coffin, *Pirro Ligorio: The Renaissance Artist, Architect, and Antiquarian* (University Park, Pa., 2004). Robert W. Gaston, "Merely Antiquarian: Pirro Ligorio and the Critical Tradition of Antiquarian Scholarship," in *The Italian Renaissance in the Twentieth Century,* ed. Allen Grieco and Fiorella Superbi Gioffredi (Florence 2002) 355–373. Robert W. Gaston, ed., *Pirro Ligorio, Artist and Antiquarian* (Milan 1988). Erna Mandowsky and Charles Mitchell, *Pirro Ligorio's Roman Antiquities* (London 1963). Anna Schreurs, *Antikenbild und Kunstanschauungen des Pirro Ligorio (1513–1583)* (Cologne 2000). R.W.G.

Livy

Titus Livius, 59 BCE–17 CE, Roman historian, a native of Patavium (Padua). He was the author of the greatest historical undertaking of classical antiquity, the history of Rome from its foundation (traditionally held to have occurred in 753 BCE) to 9 BCE, in 142 books, of which books 1–10 and 21–45 survive.

This surviving text is almost entirely owed to Petrarch, who in the 14th century assembled the first, third, and fourth decades of the books under one cover (Brit. Lib. Harley MS 2493). Books 41–45 were found at Lorsch by Simon Grynaeus in 1527. The hope of finding the lost books has never dimmed: they were claimed to be in Germany (14th cent.), England (15th), Norway, Tunisia, or on Iona (16th), in Constantinople or on Mount Athos (17th), in the Escorial, on Malta, or in the French monasteries after their dissolution (18th), in Padua (19th), in Naples (1924), and even now at Herculaneum. Leonardo Bruni (d. 1444) wrote a history of the First Punic War to compensate for the lost second decade, and the Swede Johannes Freinsheim composed replacements for 60 lost books (Strasbourg 1654). The earliest translation was an anonymous rendering into Italian (1476); the most famous early translation to English, by Philemon Holland, appeared in London in 1600.

Parallel to the search for the lost books was the medieval fascination with Livy's physical remains. His supposed tombstone was discovered in the early 14th century at Padua; what is now accepted as his epitaph (*Corpus inscriptionum latinarum* 5:2975) is preserved in the Palazzo Capodilista in Padua. In 1413 bones were discovered at the Basilica of Santa Giustina in Padua and were placed in the wall of the Palazzo della Giustizia. Various rulers begged for samples, which they treated as holy relics.

Livy has been used as a source by a host of classical and later writers: Lucan, *Civil Wars;* Silius Italicus, *Punica;* Florus; Plutarch; Dio Cassius; Eutropius; Orosius; Augustine; William of Malmesbury, *History of the English Kings* (ca. 1120); Petrarch, *Africa* (1338–1343); Boccaccio, *On Illustrious Women* (1360s); Chaucer, *Book of the Duchess* (ca. 1370), the *Doctor's Tale* (1380s); Guicciardini, *History of Italy* (published 1561); Aretino, *Orazia* (1546); William Painter, *The Palace of Pleasure* (1566); Shakespeare, *The Rape of Lucrece* (1594); Montaigne, *Essais* (1595); Hugo de Groot, *The Rights of War and Peace* (1625); Jean Mairet, *Sophonisbe* (1634); Pierre Corneille, *Horace* (1640), *Nicomède* (1651), *Sophonisbe* (1663); Vittorio Alfieri, *Verginia* (1777); Thomas Macaulay, *Lays of Ancient Rome* (1842); and Emile Augier, *Ciguë* (1844).

It is Livy's more general influence, however, that has been enormous. Tacitus declared him "brilliant for eloquence and credibility" (*Annals* 4.43). Einhard's biography of Charlemagne (819–831) imitated Livy. Dante described him as "Livio che non erra" (*Inferno* 28.12) and the "outstanding historian" (*De monarchia* 2.3.33). Of great consequence was Cola di Rienzo's reading of Livy, which produced revolution in 14th-century Rome. Petrarch wrote a letter of thanks to Livy (*Epistolae familiares* 24.8). Boccaccio compiled a short biography. Lorenzo Valla's essay on the Tarquins (1442) was written precisely to demolish Livy's account of the Etruscan kings. Other 15th-century Humanists wrote histories of their states to equal what Livy had done for Rome—Leonardo Bruni on Florence, Marc Antonio Coccio (Sabellicus, d. 1506) on Venice—and Flavio Biondo's *History from the Fall of the Roman Empire* (1453) imitated the scheme of a comprehensive history. Livy also served as a model in his attention to political institutions, foreign policy, and style. The earliest great example of this influence in the early modern era was Machiavelli's *Discourses on the First Decade of Livy* (1510s), using Livy's depiction of republican Rome and the citizen soldier as a model for reform in contemporary Florence.

In the 16th century, after the sack of Rome (1527), interest turned more to Tacitus, for his lessons on how to live under tyrants, as Beat Bild (Beatus Rhenanus) asserted in the preface to his edition of Tacitus (1532). Outside Italy, on the other hand, Livy retained his preeminence as a historian in France, Switzerland, and Germany. Francis Bacon declared Livy the best historian, who provided models for behavior (*Advancement of Learning,* 1605), and English republicans such as Milton were likewise inspired by him. Significantly, Clarendon quotes Livy only once, on political flexibility (24.25), in his *History of the Rebellion and Civil Wars in England* (book 7).

Special studies began to appear in the wake of the first editions and translations. René Rapin's *Comparison de Thoucydide et de Tite-Live* (1683) found the former more exact, but Livy more "ornate." John Toland defended Livy from a charge of credulity and superstition (*Adeisidaemon sive Titus Livius a superstitione vindicatus,* 1709). Jacob Perizonius in his fundamental *Observationes historicae* (1684) used Livy in support of his famous ballad theory for early historical sources.

By the early 18th century the teaching of Livy's republican ideals in universities may be accounted one of the stimuli to revolution. Pietro Giannone, the greatest Italian historian of the century, composed in prison his *Discourses on the Annals of Titus Livius* (1736–1739) as an education for his son and for the heir to the Piedmontese throne. Giannone was the bridge for Livy between Machiavelli and the Enlightenment. He saw Livy as critical of both legend and superstition and politically honest regarding Augustus. Diderot and d'Alembert's *Encyclopédie* (1751, 4:658) described Livy as the "greatest of Roman historians" despite his bias and what the authors continued to call his "puerility" over prodigies. Even Edward Gibbon, as he records in his *Memoirs,* could be distracted from his own history of the Roman Empire long enough to offer an emendation on Livy 30.44. The orators in the French parliament during the Revolution took as their main source, both for examples and for rhetorical patterns, a collection of Livy's speeches translated by Rousseau; Saint-Just especially liked the "tall poppies" story (1.54), in which the ancient tyrant Tarquin slashed away the topmost blooms in his garden to indicate to his son that to retain power once achieved, the most prominent persons among a subject populace should be executed. Livy, indeed, was the bible for the French cult of antiquity.

A critical reaction set in early in the 19th century. A crucial figure was Barthold Niebuhr, who was scathing in his contempt of Livy as a source for early Roman history. That view continued well into the 20th century (one thinks of Ettore Pais, among others), alongside a German-orchestrated diversion in search of Livy's lost sources. Livy is now the subject of a more balanced understanding of the enormous range of his history and the difficulty of his sources, toward which he was indeed highly critical. This has been accompanied by increased appreciation of his brilliant characterization and narrative skills, a spirited debate over his religious and philosophical views, and a clearer realization of his unique position as hymnist of the lost Republic.

BIBL.: Giuseppe Billanovich, "Petrarch and the Textual Tradition of Livy," *Journal of the Warburg and Courtauld Institutes* (1951) 137–208. L. A. Jardine and A. T. Grafton, "'Studied for Action': How Gabriel Harvey Read His Livy," *Past & Present* 129 (1990) 30–78. M. D. Reeve, "'The Vetus Carnotensis' of Livy Unmasked," in *Studies in Latin Literature and Its Tradition: In Honour of C. O. Brink*, ed J. Diggle et al. (Cambridge 1989). Berthold Ullman, "The Posthumous Adventures of Livy," in his *Studies in the Italian Renaissance* (Rome 1955).

R.T.R.

Locus Amoenus

A Latin phrase meaning "a pleasant place." The term is often identified with the physical landscape of the pastoral world, but ancient bucolic poetry is actually rather spare in its description of the environment and focuses more on the subjective reactions of (usually alienated) characters to the pleasance, as in Theocritus, *Idylls* 7.131–146 or Virgil, *Eclogues* 1.51–58. The shady setting of pastoral contests may provide the precedent for the extended landscape descriptions found in so many medieval debate poems, such as the *De Ganymede et Helena* or the *Altercatio Phyllidis et Florae.*

Evocative descriptions of especially serene or alluring places of repose occur in a variety of ancient genres, including epic, drama, lyric, and the prose dialogue. In all these, such special places appeal to the full range of human senses and at the same time hint at the presence of the divine. Stereotypical characteristics include cool shade, flowing water, sweet scents, and the audible song of birds, cicadas, or even country folk; caves or other forms of bounded enclosure are common.

The *locus amoenus* sometimes forms a point of contact with the divine, either before or after life: in ancient tradition, an Isle of the Blest (Pindar, *Olympian* 2.61–80; Lucian, *True History* 2.14–16) or the Elysian Fields within the underworld (Virgil, *Aeneid* 6.637–659); in Christian tradition, the Earthly Paradise as a gateway to Heaven (Dante, *Purgatorio* 28–33) or the primeval Garden of Eden (as in Milton, *Paradise Lost* 4.131–285)—often reimagined as the virgin territory of the New World (as in Drayton's "To the Virginian Voyage" or Marvell's "Bermudas").

The sensual delights of the pleasant landscape can make it a locus of erotic seduction (Hesiod, *Works and Days* 582–596; Plato, *Phaedrus* 230B–C), particularly associated with temples of Aphrodite (Sappho, fr. 2v.) or the distraction of heroes from their manly duties (as at Calypso's island in *Odyssey* 5.55–74). In ancient epic the *locus amoenus* often conceals latent threats, as on the Cyclops' island (*Odyssey* 9.105–141) and the Laestrygonians' (10.81–99). Ovid's *Metamorphoses* programmatically combines erotic and threatening qualities: beautiful landscapes are full of sexual allure but captivate their victims into scenes of rape, madness, or violent death, as we see in the setting of Actaeon and the bath of Diana (3.155–178), Narcissus' self-rapture (3.407–412), Salmacis' rape of Hermaphroditus (4.297–315), or Pluto's of Proserpina (5.385–395; elaborated in Claudian, *De raptu Proserpinae* 2.71–112).

The House of Venus was a paradigmatic *locus amoenus* in the Middle Ages too, as in Boccaccio's *Teseida* (7.51–53) or Chaucer's *Parlement of Fowles* (169–210); some later *loci amoeni,* such as that in Saint-Amant's notorious "La Jouissance" (1629), are explicit and celebratory in their sexual content. Renaissance epic renewed the classical tendency to cast the erotic pleasance as a locus of the hero's captivity and emasculation, as in the enchanted gardens of Alcina (Ariosto, *Orlando furioso,* canto 6) and Armida (Tasso, *Jerusalem Delivered,* cantos 14–16). The topos influenced Spenser's *Faerie Queene,* especially Phaedria's island (2.6.11–18) and Acrasia's Bower of Bliss (2.5.27–36, 2.12.42–80); the Garden of Adonis (3.6.29–50) provides a more positive sensual paradise, and the pleasant setting of the Temple of Venus (4.10.21–29) leads to an allegory of true love. This positive fusion of the erotic landscape with prefiguration of eternal afterlife also characterizes the Isle of Venus in Camões' Portuguese epic *Os Lusíadas* (canto 9).

BIBL.: E. R. Curtius, *European Literature and the Latin Middle Ages,* trans. W. R. Trask (Princeton 1973) 183–202. A. B. Giamatti, *The Earthly Paradise and the Renaissance Epic* (Princeton 1966). N. B. Hansen, *That Pleasant Place: The Representation of Ideal Landscape in English Literature from the 14th to the 17th Century* (Copenhagen 1973). Petra Hass, *Der locus amoenus in der antiken Literatur: Zu Theorie und Geschichte eines literarischen Motivs* (Bamberg 1998).

T.HU.

Lodging

Wayfarers in the classical Mediterranean world, as in later periods, shared a common need for lodging while they were on the road, whether this was the house of friends, a public hostelry, a religious guesthouse, a tent, a cave, or some other place to sleep. Although hospitality was deemed a virtue in many classical cultures, travelers often stayed at established hostels rather than in private houses. As Joseph discovered when he arrived in Bethlehem with his pregnant wife (Luke 2:7), one sometimes had to put up with whatever lodging was available. The classical world boasted a number of different types of organized accommodation, some of them providing rooms and food for free, usually for the love of God, whereas others charged a fee for such services. Some were well kept and respectable; others were dirty and disreputable, often doubling as taverns and brothels.

These establishments went by various names. The famous inn in Bethlehem, in Luke's gospel, was *katalyma* in Greek (a place for "loosening," as a harness is undone after a day's journey), a word that never found a cognate in later western European languages. The tale of the Good Samaritan (Luke 10:34) refers to another type of hostelry, the *pandocheion* to which the injured man was taken by the Samaritan. This word (meaning "accepting all comers") would take on other forms not only in Latin and Romance languages, but also in Arabic, as will be seen below. In general, a classical *pandocheion* was likely to have been a rougher sort of place than a *katalyma*. Strabo, for instance, writes of a pimp who set up business in a *pandocheion,* and Philostratus tells of travelers disturbed by drunkenness in such a place. Two other Greek terms, *xenon* and *xenodocheion* ("accepting strangers"), do not appear in the Bible, but they would become by far the most common terms in Christian Greek. They refer particularly to religious hostelries, often attached to a church or monastery, offering lodging to pilgrims and other travelers. Many were founded by charitable patrons, including a *xenon* established in Constantinople in the 6th century by the emperor Justinian and his wife, Theodora. Versions of *xenodocheion* would later appear in medieval Latin, although the cognate died out in modern European languages. For example, the Rule of the Hospitallers (a military order during the Crusades), written in 1113, describes the founding of their *xenodocheum* in Jerusalem to provide *hospitalitas.* Here the sense of *hospitalitas* is closer to the modern English word *hospital* than to its close cousin *hospitality,* but the context indicates the intimate relationship then prevailing among lodging, medical care, and charity.

Both *hospital* and *hospitality* derive from Latin rather than Greek, coming from the family of related words *hospes* (which, curiously, can mean both "guest" and "host"), *hospitalis* (a guest, guesthouse, relating to a guest or host), and *hospitium* (hospitality or a guesthouse). This group would become prolific in spawning cognates in later languages, but there were also other Classical Latin words for hostelries. When Saint Jerome (d. 420) undertook his Latin translation of the Bible, he chose the classical terms *stabulum* for the story of the Good Samaritan, and *diversorium* for the inn in Bethlehem. Both words survived into medieval Latin, but neither emerged in modern languages with the same meaning. *Stabulum* retained its implication of shelter—though for horses, not people. It was already drifting in this direction by the 13th century, as we can see in the stained-glass windows at Chartres Cathedral, which show the Good Samaritan taking the sick man to a stable, presumably following contemporary interpretation of Jerome's text.

The most enduring classical terms for lodging were those derived from the family of words related to *hospitium* (including, in English, *hospitality, hospice, hospital, hostel,* and *hotel*) and *pandocheion.* In the latter case, there is no English cognate, but traces survive in modern Italian (*fondaco*) and Spanish (*alhóndigo*) as warehouses—places for goods rather than guests. In modern Arabic, however, *funduq* (a cognate of *pandocheion*) remains the predominant word for a hotel or lodging house. The word had come into Arabic by the 9th century, and *funduq*s soon appeared throughout the Muslim world. This is only one example of the degree to which the Islamic world, as well as Europe, can trace the roots of many cultural institutions to classical Mediterranean tradition. In contrast to their seedy classical counterparts, however, *funduq*s were often charitable or mercantile hostelries where respectable travelers could stay.

Hotel, along with French *hôtel* and variants in other European languages, is the most common of the modern terms derived from the Latin *hospitium.* The most modern derivative of this group is the characteristically American conflation *motel* (motor + hotel), a word that reflects our passion for travel by automobile. This group of cognate words overcame its competitors during the Middle Ages, when increasing numbers of traveling merchants, pilgrims, diplomats, and other wayfarers intensified demand for hostelries. Medieval town records often cite large numbers of *otels, hostals,* and the like, mostly designated by individual names. When Chaucer's pilgrims set out for Canterbury in the 14th century, their journey began at a "gentil hostelrye" called the Tabard. The tradition of naming hotels continues today, even though many now affiliate their individual names with that of a chain, such as Hyatt or Marriott.

It is worth noting that the translators of the King James Bible chose to render both *katalyma* and *pandocheion* as "inn," a word of Old English origin that has no roots in classical tradition. Nevertheless, it was the most common English word for a lodging house in the early modern period. Shakespeare, for instance, uses the word "inn" a number of times but never mentions a "hostelry" or any Latin cognates. Today "inn" retains a quaint and rustic connotation in modern English, which links it to its Anglo-Saxon heritage rather than to classical tradition and the idea of the "grand hotel." O.R.C.

Loeb Classical Library

An ongoing series of small, uniform volumes that aims to present, with facing English translations, all the most important literary, historical, philosophical, and scientific writings of the classical Greek and Roman world. Introductions to each work and notes on the text and translation are provided by the individual editor-translators. Greek writings are bound in green, Latin in red.

Founding of the series was jointly announced in November 1911 by the London publisher William Heinemann and by James Loeb, an American banker who had retired in 1902 at age 35 and in 1905 moved permanently to Bavaria. The death of his parents in 1902 and 1903 provided him with a very large fortune, which he proceeded to devote primarily to philanthropy and the collection of ancient art.

The purpose of the new project was eloquently stated in an essay, "The Loeb Classical Library: A Word about Its Purpose and Its Scope," which was printed at the beginning of all early volumes. As a student at Harvard, Loeb had studied mainly the classics and had found as his mentor Charles Eliot Norton, the historian of art and wide-ranging humanist. Loeb was convinced that even for men of affairs the humanities represented the best education, and he lamented the declining knowledge of Latin and Greek. The guiding principle of Loeb's plan was to make all of Greek and Latin literature easily accessible—in presentation, in format, and in price.

The initial grandiose proposal to include writings up to the fall of Constantinople (in 1453) was silently abandoned, and the series ends with the late Roman Empire in the West, in the 5th century, including only a few Christian authors with strong classical affinities. Some anomalies represent predilections of earlier editors.

In the early decades of the series the printing of obscenities was punishable under English and American law of the time by fines and imprisonment, and by confiscation of the offending volumes. Loeb gave instructions to follow the customary course of paraphrase or omission or of reprinting the original language. Since the laws were changed in 1959, a systematic debowdlerization of the series has proceeded, which has made full and accurate translations available.

Loeb worked feverishly on preparations before the inaugural announcement, and within two years some 30 volumes were published. He appointed as general editor T. E. Page, who continued until his death in 1936. Despite disruptions of the First World War and Loeb's periods of crippling depression, the series survived and prospered. Upon his death in 1933, Loeb bequeathed the Library series to Harvard University, with which it had had no previous connection. He gave instruction for the appointment of trustees to a foundation to supervise its functioning, and provided supporting funds.

Harvard took over financial accounts and management and transferred American distribution from G. P. Putnam's Sons to the Harvard University Press but otherwise left editorial and publishing operations with Heinemann, an arrangement that continued until 1989, when Heinemann withdrew completely from participation in the series. Succeeding editors have continued the work routinely. Over the years higher standards of scholarship in the introductions, notes, and texts became the norm, and a program of revision and replacement of earlier volumes was introduced, especially under the editorship of G. P. Goold (1974–1999) and his present successor, Jeffrey Henderson. When computerized printing replaced moveable type, new fonts (ZephText and ZephGreek) were developed, which elegantly matched the original Loeb typeface.

In his will Loeb also instructed that any profits generated by the Library be used toward grants for individual scholarly projects in classical studies, including archaeology. The financial stability of the series allowed this provision to be activated on a regular annual basis beginning in 2003.

The 500th volume of the series was published in 2006. The influence and importance of the Loeb Classical Library can be attributed in part to the dominance of English as a second language in recent times and to the shrinking of the Teubner publishing house in Leipzig after the Second World War, which has left the Loeb series as the most easily available large collection of Greek and Latin texts in print. Its heightened scholarly standards have given it far greater authority than it enjoyed in its earlier years. In its breadth and effectiveness it is reminiscent of the vast translation projects of Pope Nicholas V in the 15th century, which introduced Greek literature and learning to the Latin West.

BIBL.: Brigitte Salmen, ed., *James Loeb 1867–1933: Kunstsammler und Mäzen* (Murnau 2000). Z.S.

Logic

In 1787 Kant praised Aristotle's logic, writing that it was "to all appearance a closed and completed body of doctrine" (*Critique of Pure Reason,* B viii). His words capture the reality that for most of Western educational history, Aristotle's logic has been an essential part of the curriculum. Even today undergraduates taking elementary logic courses are told something about the nonmodal categorical syllogism. Nonetheless, Kant failed to realize that the way in which Aristotle was presented varied from period to period, both because of the changing availability of texts and because of different educational contexts. Nor has there ever been complete agreement about what Aristotle's logic amounts to. The syllogism itself, which is at the heart of Aristotle's system, has been interpreted in a number of ways, and logicians have disagreed about the very number of valid nonmodal categorical syllogisms: are there fourteen, or fifteen, or nineteen, or twenty-four?

First we must ask: "Why Aristotle?" After all, he was not the only ancient logician. Stoic logicians, especially Chrysippus (ca. 280–ca. 206 BCE), seem to have been brilliant and dedicated thinkers who developed areas of logic virtually untouched by Aristotle. They are noteworthy for their semantics, especially the doctrine of the *lekton* or propositional content; for their study of paradoxes, including the Liar ("What I am now saying is false"); and for their propositional logic. Their study of the relations between unanalyzed propositions, captured in the five "indemonstrables" or basic propositional argument forms, and their sophisticated analyses of the conditional proposition have no parallel in Aristotle's logic. Moreover, their works were prolific; Chrysippus alone produced 311 logical writings, according to Diogenes Laertius. But all these works were lost, and today Stoic logic survives only in fragmentary form, largely through the much later reports of Sextus Empiricus (2nd cent. CE) and Diogenes Laertius (3rd cent. CE). Nor were matters much different in late antiquity. At the beginning of the 6th century the Greek commentator Simplicius reported that he could find hardly any works by Stoics. His contemporary Boethius did have some access to Stoic material, but in his commentary on Aristotle's *De interpretatione* he twice remarks that he is deliberately omitting that material because it is of no interest. During the Middle Ages there were very interesting developments in semantics and in propositional logic that are closely parallel to Stoic theories, but no direct relationship can be traced. The Renaissance recovered the full texts of both Diogenes Laertius and Sextus Empiricus, and as a result the Stoic indemonstrables do reappear as a package of argument forms in 16th- and early 17th-century textbooks. Stoic presentations of semantic paradoxes also reappear, replacing medieval examples, but there was no detailed examination of Stoic views. It is only in recent years that serious consideration has been given to Stoic logic, largely because modern developments in logical theory have enabled researchers such as Benson Mates to see, even from the fragmentary evidence available, just how original the Stoic logicians were.

One reason for the disappearance of Stoic logic was the revival of Aristotle's logic. His logical works, called collectively the Organon ("Instrument" [of thought or knowledge]) by late Greek commentators, were first arranged by Andronicus of Rhodes (1st cent. BCE) in a way that had little to do with Aristotle's own order of composition, but even more important is the work of the Neoplatonic philosopher Porphyry (ca. 232–305), who saw the Organon as providing a comprehensive logic syllabus: The basis is provided by the *Categories,* which, if we ignore its metaphysical implications, classifies simple expressions, the terms that serve as the subjects and predicates of propositions. Next comes *De interpretatione,* which deals with propositions and simple logical relationships, such as contradiction and subordination, between pairs of propositions. The *Prior Analytics* takes up the nature of valid arguments, that is, those whose premises will, if true, lead us to true conclusions. It is here that we find the study of categorical syllogisms, so-called to differentiate them from hypothetical syllogisms whose premises contain such connectives as *if–then* and *or.* The categorical syllogism itself was of two types, assertoric (or nonmodal) and modal, the latter containing such logical operators as *necessarily* and *possibly.* The *Posterior Analytics* presents a model for scientific reasoning and discusses the demonstrative syllogism, which has necessarily true premises. The *Topics* tells us how to find and organize the material for arguments whose premises are not necessarily true. Finally, *Sophistical Refutations* tells us how to deal with fallacies, invalid arguments that will mislead us into accepting false conclusions. Some late Greek commentators belonging to the School of Alexandria also added Aristotle's *Rhetoric* and *Poetics* to the Organon and were followed in this by Islamic logicians; but although some medieval philosophers, including Thomas Aquinas and Albertus Magnus, paid lip service to these additions, they were never popular in the Latin-speaking West. In any case, the *Poetics* was largely unknown in the West until the Renaissance. What did become popular was Porphyry's own addition to the curriculum, his *Isagoge,* or introduction, to Aristotle's *Categories,* in which he organized the terms that could serve as predicates under five headings.

Porphyry's *Isagoge* and the Organon offered a complete logic syllabus to students at Neoplatonic schools, but they were in Greek, and many educated people in the Western part of the Roman Empire did not read Greek. Boethius (ca. 475–ca. 524) set out to remedy this situation by translating all of Plato and Aristotle into Latin, though he succeeded only in translating the Organon and Porphyry's *Isagoge.* He also wrote logic commentaries that relied heavily on the works of Greek commentators, as well as some free-standing logical works. For much of the Dark Ages, even this was lost to the Latin-speaking West, and logic was taught from small compendia and encyclopedias. But by the end of the 10th century, Porphyry's *Isagoge,* the *Categories,* and *De interpretatione* were being taught in the Latin-speaking West, forming the core of what came to be known as the *logica vetus.* By 1159 the *logica nova,* comprising the *Prior* and *Posterior Analytics,* the *Topics,* and the *Sophistical Refutations,* had been recovered. Only the *Posterior Analytics* needed a new translation, as Boethius' rendition had been lost (if indeed it ever existed). The central logic curriculum for the medieval and post-medieval university was now firmly in place, supplemented by commentaries. Works by Ammonius and Simplicius were translated in the 13th century, as were works by such Islamic logicians as Averroës, who had made much use of the rich classical material still available in the Muslim world.

The next wave of translation came during the Renaissance, when the study of Greek was once again important. Greek commentators, namely Alexander of Aphrodisias, Themistius, Ammonius, Philoponus, and Simplicius, were published and were said to be "excellent interpreters" of Aristotle by the Jesuit authors of the popular Coimbra commentary of 1606. There were some new translations of Aristotle, but most important of all, the second part of the 16th century saw bilingual Latin–Greek editions of the Organon together with commentaries, including the Coimbra commentary, that paid careful attention to philological and historical questions. This activity died out during the 17th century, and the 19th-century revival of Aristotelian studies was motivated by an interest in the history of philosophy rather than by Aristotle's place in the logic curriculum.

To understand these changes, we need to consider the historical context. In the medieval university, where logic prepared students (at least the small proportion who proceeded beyond the early undergraduate program) for sophisticated work in natural philosophy and theology, logic had a highly technical orientation, and Aristotle's logic was supplemented by a range of new developments. Logicians agreed that the categorical syllogism provided the model of good argumentation, but this view was not necessarily reflected in the time devoted to syllogistic, especially at northern universities. At Italian universities, the syllogism's use in scientific reasoning was emphasized, and the *Posterior Analytics* served as a basic logic text well into the 16th century. Renaissance Humanism brought about significant changes in the type of logic teaching. Logic was still central to the undergraduate curriculum, but the most sophisticated medieval developments were explicitly rejected. There was a new emphasis on the logic of the *Topics* as a means of organizing discourse and presenting informal argumentative strategies; the formal logic that a student should know was largely reduced to the Square of Opposition and the nonmodal categorical syllogism as summarized by the new textbooks. Indeed, despite attacks by such authors as Pierre de la Ramée (Peter Ramus), Aristotle was in a sense more central to logic teaching than he had been during the Middle Ages, given that the new textbooks concentrated on giving an overview of the Organon, supplemented by Porphyry's *Isagoge,* and nothing else.

By the end of the 17th century a radical change had occurred. New scientific developments meant that the *Posterior Analytics* was no longer seen as offering the model of scientific thought, and new philosophical developments, through the work of Descartes and Locke, led to the rise of facultative logic, which emphasizes the study of the faculties of the human mind as a guide to clear thinking. In the 18th century abbreviated forms of Locke's *Essay* were used as logic textbooks, despite the absence of syllogistic; and while the equally popular *Port-Royal Logic* (1662) did contain an account of the syllogism, this material was more and more frequently omitted by its 18th-century French followers.

The place of Aristotle in logic altered yet again in the 19th century. Some logicians, such as George Boole, saw logic as something that could be treated mathematically, as a kind of algebra, and offered a purely formal treatment of the syllogism. Others, notably Gottlob Frege, thought of logic as the foundation of mathematics, and in order to carry out their program they produced an analysis of propositions that was radically different from Aristotle's. The powerful formal system that grew out of Frege's work, first-order quantificational logic, included the syllogism as a very minor part, to be mentioned only for historical reasons. But in recent years logicians have come once more to pay serious attention to Aristotle and to read his work in the light of modern developments. Thus in 1957 Jan Łukasiewicz presented syllogistic as an axiomatic theory in which syllogisms are conditional sentences; more recently John Corcoran (1974) has presented syllogistic as a natural deduction system, which gives rules for the construction of sentence sequences. Journal discussions of these issues present Aristotle as a living logician, rather than as of purely antiquarian interest.

The study of the assertoric categorical syllogism has been the one constant through all the changes in the reception of Aristotle's logic: but what is it, and why has it been subject to different interpretations? We have to start with the notion of the categorical proposition, which is a simple affirmation or negation composed of a subject term and a predicate term together with a copula that brings them together. If we add the logical words *all, no, not,* and *some,* we get four standard categorical propositions: "All A is B" (universal affirmative, A-form), "No A is B" (universal negative, E-form), "Some A is B" (particular affirmative, I-form), and "Some A is not B" (particular negative, O-form). These stand in various logical relations captured by the Square of Opposition, whose corners are the A-, E-, I-, and O-forms. For example, by subalternation one can infer an I-form from an A-form and an O-form from an E-form. If we take two categorical propositions that have exactly one term in common, as in "All A is B" and "All C is A," we have the premises for a categorical syllogism. The term in common is called the middle term, and of the remaining terms, one will be the subject of the conclusion and the other will be the predicate of the conclusion. If we consider the position of the middle term in two undifferentiated premises, we get three figures: the middle term is subject of one premise and predicate of the other, or it is the subject of both premises, or it is the predicate of both. If we then pay attention to whether the premises are A, E, I, or O propositions, we can work out the number of combinations (moods) possible for each figure and then decide which of the possible moods is valid. Thus from "All A is B" and "All C is A" we can infer "All C is B." According to Aristotle's explicit discussion, there are fourteen valid syllogisms.

One problem that immediately arises concerns the possibility of particular conclusions. From the premises given above and the rules of subalternation, we can also infer "Some C is B," and overall there are five cases in which a syllogism with a universal conclusion can also produce a particular conclusion. This fact was recognized by later Greek logicians and also by such medieval logicians as William of Ockham, but only a few later logicians, notably Henry Aldrich (1691), insist on the presence of the five subalternate modes, for reasons of formal completeness.

If we accept the subalternate modes and consider them together with those syllogisms (four in all) that produce only a particular conclusion from universal premises, we run into a further problem. Many logic textbooks written today will say that these nine syllogisms are not valid, because a universal proposition can be true when the corresponding particular proposition is false. The issues here are, first of all, whether we should admit propositions about nonexistent objects such as chimeras and, if we do, how we are to find a uniform way of ascribing truth or falsity to such propositions? It seems that Aristotle and his immediate successors did not think of logic as being about nonexistent objects; but the issue came to be of concern in the later Middle Ages, and such logicians as John Buridan decided that affirmative claims (the A- and I-forms) about chimeras would be false, and negative claims (the E- and O-forms) would be true. On this interpretation, subalternation and the nine problematic syllogisms are all valid. Modern logicians, on the other hand, have deliberately symbolized categorical propositions in such a way that universal claims, whether affirmative or negative, will come out true and particular claims will come out false. This does indeed mean that only fifteen of a possible twenty-four syllogisms can be captured by the first-order quantificational calculus.

The mention of a possible twenty-four syllogisms raises two other important questions: are there indirect modes, and are there three or four figures? To understand the problem, we need to consider the relation of the terms in the premises to the terms in the conclusion. In standard examples, the subject of the conclusion appears in the second premise and is called the minor term, and the predicate of the conclusion appears in the first premise and is called the major term. But can there be nonstandard examples? That depends on how one defines the major and minor terms. John Philoponus (ca. 490–ca. 570), in a definition that became popular during the Renaissance, defined the major term as the predicate of the conclusion. Given this definition, one can easily differentiate syllogisms in which the middle term is the subject of the major premise but predicate of the minor premise (first figure) from syllogisms in which the middle term is the predicate of the major premise and subject of the minor premise (fourth figure). Moreover, there can be no conclusion that is indirect in the sense that the major term is subject and the minor term is predicate. During the Middle Ages, however, logicians tended to define the major term as that which appeared in the first premise and the minor term as that which appeared in the second premise. This definition allows indirect conclusions, and it also leaves open the possibility of acknowledging the fourth figure, though this possibility was rarely recognized. Many logicians from Theophrastus onward added five indirect modes to the first figure, giving a standard listing of nineteen syllogisms (or twenty-four, if one adds the subalternate modes). Insofar as a fourth figure was mentioned, logicians took it to be just the first indirect figure with transposed premises, and they did not count this as involving a genuinely different disposition of the middle term. Nor did they add the indirect modes of the second and third figures to their list of valid syllogisms. Ockham, for instance, noted their existence but said that they were not worth discussion. When the alternative definition of the major and minor terms was adopted in the 16th and 17th centuries, a very few logicians, especially Henry Aldrich at the end of the 17th century, insisted on the legitimacy of the fourth figure and the exclusion of indirect modes; but others, especially Jacopo Zabarella in the 16th century, argued at length that although a fourth figure was possible, it represented an unnatural form of reasoning and should be rejected.

In short, whether one recognizes fourteen or fifteen or nineteen or twenty-four valid syllogisms depends partly on one's basic definitions, partly on one's semantics, and partly on whether one sees syllogistic as a formal system or as a system designed to produce arguments acceptable in ordinary language.

BIBL.: William Kneale and Martha Kneale, *The Development of Logic* (Oxford 1962). Norman Kretzmann, Anthony Kenny, and Jan Pinborg, eds., *The Cambridge History of Later Medieval Philosophy* (Cambridge 1982). John Marenbon, *Boethius* (Oxford 2003). John M. Rist, ed., *The Stoics* (Berkeley 1978). Charles B. Schmitt et al., eds., *The Cambridge History of Renaissance Philosophy* (Cambridge 1988). Robin Smith, introduction, notes, and commentary in *Aristotle: Prior Analytics,* trans. Robin Smith (Indianapolis 1989). E.J.A.

Lucan

Marcus Annaeus Lucanus (39–65 CE), Roman poet, nephew to the philosopher Seneca the Younger. Implicated in a conspiracy against the emperor Nero, he and his uncle were both forced to commit suicide.

Much of Lucan's work is lost, but his epic *The Civil War* (*De bello civili,* often called *Pharsalia*) had an important afterlife. A violent and despairing vision of the end of the Roman Republic, it covers action between Julius Caesar's crossing of the Rubicon up to his peril in Alexandria, when it breaks off abruptly. Three of its ten books were published during Lucan's life. It is parodied in Petronius' *Satyricon* (119–124)—scholars disagree on the point of the joke—and strongly influenced the style of Statius (who celebrates Lucan's birthday in his *Sylvae*). Lucan was one of the most popular pagan writers throughout the Western Middle Ages, as both poet and historian. As a school text his work accumulated a tradition of scholia; a prose rendering in Middle Irish (*In Cath Catharda*) survives in several manuscripts. Dante placed Lucan with Homer, Horace, and Ovid (*Inferno* 4.88–90); the laughter with which Lucan's Pompey views from heaven the degrading of his corpse (9.14) is echoed in *Paradiso* (22.135), and in Chaucer's *Troilus and Criseyde* (5.1821). Lucan's epic was first printed in 1469; in 1493 Johannus Sulpitius published 11 new lines in Latin to bring the action to a slightly more satisfactory stopping point, and these became an established feature of the text. They are mimicked by Ariosto at the end of the *Cinque canti* (ca. 1519), his abortive continuation of *Orlando furioso.* Thomas May composed a longer *Continuation,* in English (1630) and in Latin (1640), taking the action down to Caesar's assassination; this Latin addendum appeared in editions of Lucan for another two centuries.

For the Renaissance, Lucan provided an important precedent for composing epics about comparatively recent historical events, and, more remarkably, with its clear admiration for Cato, for epics whose sympathies favor the losing side. In both regards Lucan assisted the conception and execution of Alonso de Ercilla's *Araucana* (1569–1589), about the Spanish conquest of the Mapuche of Chile (a conquest still incomplete when Ercilla wrote), and Agrippa d'Aubigné's *Tragiques* (1616–1623), even more partisan in dramatizing the persecution of the Huguenots. D'Aubigné assembled a cento from Lucan's first book to create a history of the French religious wars; in a prefatory poem he casts himself as a defiant improvement on his predecessor: "Lucan died unarmed; I will not die as a willing victim without a fight." The situation in England gave Lucan particular relevance. Thomas May's *Continuation* was an adjunct to his translation from the original Latin (1627, with Lucan's suicide depicted on the title page)—itself one in a series of efforts at rendering the poem into English, preceded by Christopher Marlowe's version of book 1 (published posthumously in 1600) and Arthur Gorges's translation of the complete poem (1614). Lucan's opening was recited in Parliament at a dire moment in 1642. One especially provocative line (1.128, *victrix causa deis placuit sed victa Catoni,* "The victor's cause pleased the gods, but that of the vanquished pleased Cato"), inscribed in honor of Bacon's Rebellion of 1676, still presides (unattributed) over the Virginia House of Delegates. (There have been calls for its removal.) Most admirers of the poem were drawn to it by its republicanism, though not all; the troubles of his time were cast into epic form by the royalist Abraham Cowley, who wrote his versified *Civil War* with Lucanian inspiration and guidance even as the events it relates were unfolding in the early 1640s. The poem was abandoned after three books when the parallel with Lucan became too strong: Cowley was writing in behalf of a lost cause.

In later centuries Lucan has found fewer literary imitators; his reputation has fluctuated. Some Romantics treasured him—the poet Shelley includes him in *Adonais* (1821) in a list of admirable poets who died young—but for many he came to seem a poet of rhetorical excess and narrative inelegance. Critical respect revived significantly in the later 20th century, in part because of fresh appreciation for the realities of imperial derangement.

BIBL.: David Norbrook, *Writing the English Republic* (Cambridge 1999). David Quint, *Epic and Empire* (Princeton 1993).

G.B.

Lucian

Author of Greek prose satires and dialogues. Born ca. 125 CE in Samosata on the Euphrates River in eastern Syria, Lucian studied Greek as a young man and soon pursued a career as an itinerant lecturer, touring provinces of the Roman Empire as far as Gaul. What little is known about his chronology must be deduced from allusions in his works, many of which can be dated to the reign of Marcus Aurelius (161–180). By 156 he had settled in Athens and regularly attended the Olympic Games. In 162 he traveled to Antioch, and between 171 and 175 he served as a Roman official in Alexandria. Because the last historical fact mentioned in his writings (*Alexander* 48) is the death of Marcus Aurelius, most scholars believe that Lucian died during the early years of Commodus' reign (180–192).

Lucian's extant works, numbering about 80, consist principally of short essays and dialogues that were declaimed before the learned audiences of his day. These display the themes and concerns of the period now known as the Second Sophistic. His popularity waned soon after his death, but he was eventually rediscovered by Byzantine readers, beginning with the scholarly patriarch Photius (ca. 810–895), who praised Lucian's prose style—a taste shared by successive generations of Byzantine scholars and authors, including Arethas of Caesarea (ca. 860–944) and John Tzetzes (ca. 1110–1185). The 12th century in particular produced Lucianic imitations, by Theodore Prodromus (ca. 1100–1170) and Eugenius of Palermo (1130–1203), as well as the anonymous dialogue *Timarion* (before 1150).

At the turn of the 15th century the Lucianic revival in Constantinople left its mark on the early Italian Renaissance. In 1397, when the Byzantine scholar Manuel Chrysoloras (ca. 1350–1415) began to teach Greek in Florence, Lucian was the first author taught in the Renaissance classroom; Latin versions of the dialogues *Charon* and *Timon,* found in a manuscript dated 1403, can be attributed to Chrysoloras' pupils. One of these, Guarino of Verona, soon traveled to Constantinople, where as a guest in the Chrysoloras household he translated Lucian's essays *Slander* and *The Fly;* a decade later he translated *The Parasite.* Other Humanists followed suit, and by 1440 Latin versions of Lucian in Italy were as numerous as those of Plato and Plutarch. It is not difficult to understand the Humanists' enthusiasm for the Syrian rhetorician. Students of Greek found his colloquial style congenial, and Renaissance wits strove to imitate his humorous vision of the world. Lucian's vocabulary is Attic and idiomatic, and his style supple and limpid. That Lucian furnished varied examples of rhetorical set pieces warmly commended him to Renaissance secretaries and orators whose careers depended on their verbal facility. Renaissance students of Greek found in his dialogues a pleasant introduction to conversational Attic, one rich in lively proverbs and vivid figures of speech.

Lucian's satirical works, which were his most popular, rely heavily on striking paradoxes, which readily lend themselves to rhetorical imitation. Four particular genres constitute the Lucianic tradition in European literature: the dialogue of the dead, the dialogue of the gods, the paradoxical encomium, and the fantastic voyage. In the dialogue of the dead, such as *Charon,* souls who meet in the underworld offer curious insights into human behavior among the living. In the dialogue of the gods, the Olympian deities prove to be as petty and conceited as the mortals who worship them. In the paradoxical encomium, the rhetoric of eulogy is applied to lowly or unpleasant objects, as is the case in *The Fly* and *The Parasite.* The fantastic voyage narrated in Lucian's paradoxically titled *True Story* parodies the incredibly exotic tales of mariners and explorers in strange regions of the globe.

Some Humanists preferred emulating Lucian to translating him. In his Latin *Dinner Pieces* and his satirical novel *Momus,* Leon Battista Alberti imitated Lucian's dialogues of the dead and of the gods, just as his comic orations *The Fly* and *My Dog* (1441) adapt the Lucianic rhetoric of paradox. In the early 16th century the Dutch scholar Erasmus praised Lucian as a "relentless persecutor of all superstition," and many of his Latin *Colloquia,* such as *Charon* (1529), draw inspiration from Lucianic dialogue. He also published a Latin selection of Lucian's works together with his friend Sir Thomas More, whose *Utopia* (1515) is indebted to the fantastic voyage of the *True Story.* But the 4th-century Church Father Lactantius in his *Divine Institutions* (1.9.8) had labeled Lucian a writer "who spared neither the gods nor men," and this reputation for impiety moved many to brand Lucian an atheist. In the wake of the Council of Trent (1545–1563) the Roman Church put Lucian's works on its *Index of Prohibited Books,* and the Jesuits banished Lucian from their schools.

Two of Lucian's works, *Menippus* and the *True Story,* inspired an astonishing variety of literary imitations. *Menippus,* a dialogue of the dead, offered a rich repertory of Lucianic motifs that could be used to comment on the human condition. In this dialogue the Cynic philosopher Menippus descends into the underworld, where he surveys the workings of infernal justice and mocks the transience of worldly glory by comparing the world to a stage. At the end of the dialogue Menippus encounters the seer Tiresias, who observes that wisdom consists in laughing at one's own folly and in living a simple life.

Renaissance readers clearly appreciated the secular common sense of Lucian's Tiresias in commending laughter as the best medicine for the world's woes. Menippus' cynical quest for true wisdom inspired such writers as Alberti, Giovanni Pontano, Erasmus, and Rabelais. In Alberti's *Momus* the title character, who is the Greek god of mockery, is sent to earth to discover how Jupiter should change human society. In Pontano's *Charon,* the legendary boatman of the Styx seeks to understand the upper world of the living. In the *Third Book* of Rabelais' series of novels on Gargantua and Pantagruel, Panurge conducts a comical search to learn whether he should take a wife. After the picaresque peregrinations of Renaissance narratives, the Lucianic quest culminated in the philosophical *conte* of the Enlightenment, of which Voltaire's *Candide* (1759) is the most celebrated and influential example.

Lucian's *True Story,* a fantastic voyage narrated with parodic irony, is both one of the simplest and one of the most influential prose fictions of classical antiquity. It consists merely of a brief preface and two books, narrated in the first person, which describe an incredible journey into the unknown. The comic effect of Lucian's mock odyssey derives in large part from his outlandish descriptions and verbal inventiveness. But it also depends on the pervasive irony of the narrative voice, for Lucian promises his reader only one truth, namely, that he is lying. This combination of the incredible and the ironic spawned numerous literary progeny, including Cyrano de Bergerac's *Comic History of the Moon and the Sun* (1650), Jonathan Swift's *Gulliver's Travels* (1726), and Edgar Allan Poe's *Narrative of Arthur Gordon Pym* (1838).

During the Enlightenment the dialogue of the dead enjoyed a particular vogue. In France authors like Fénelon, Voltaire, and d'Alembert were inspired by Bernard de Fontenelle (1657–1757), whose *New Dialogues of the Dead* (1683) was dedicated to Lucian and featured illustrious figures both ancient and modern. In England, *Dialogues of the Dead* was written by Matthew Prior (1721, publ. 1907) and Lord Lyttleton (1760), and in Germany the prolific Christoph Martin Wieland (1733–1813) published *Dialogues of the Gods* (1791), *Dialogues in Elysium* (1796), and the dialogue-novel *Peregrinus Proteus* (1789), as well as a complete translation of Lucian's works (1788–1789).

Lucian's influence continued even after the classical heritage was shaken by Romanticism. In the 1850s Gustave Flaubert was reading and annotating Lucian's *Menippus* as he planned the "philosophical novel" that would eventually become the ironic and incomplete *Bouvard et Pécuchet.* In the conclusion of the novel as Flaubert planned it, the title characters were to emulate Lucian's *Menippus* as well as Voltaire's *Candide:* discovering the vanity of philosophy, they would embrace the ordinary life and return to their humble trade of copying.

By contrast, classical philologists of the 19th century generally dismissed Lucian as a journalist or hack. Such censures were most often expressed by German scholars, who implicitly derided "the Syrian" as a venial Semitic hireling. Only in the 20th century did classicists recognize Lucian as one of the most vital and original of the Greek authors during the Second Sophistic. Despite the waning of his influence after the Enlightenment, Lucian continues to find readers even today.

Most notably, several prominent Italian authors have experimented with Lucianic themes. In the 19th century Giacomo Leopardi imitated Lucian in several dialogues published as part of his *Short Moral Works* (1827), and a complete translation of Lucian's works was made by the patriot Luigi Settembrini (1813–1876) during five years of imprisonment after the 1848 revolution. In the second half of the 20th century Italo Calvino returned to the tradition of Lucian's *True Story* in works such as *Cosmicomics* (1965), which cast its fantastic narratives in the futuristic world of science fiction. The Lucianic tradition also inspired the Italian poet and novelist Cesare Pavese (1908–1950) to compose his *Dialogues with Leucothea* (1947), a series of 27 brief dialogues that evoke both Lucian and his imitator Leopardi. In poetic exchanges, pairs of figures such as Oedipus and Tiresias or Circe and Leucothea examine the meaning of mythological events in a sort of lyrical existentialism that, while grounded in ancient myth, holds implications for the contemporary human condition.

BIBL.: Manuel Baumbach, *Lukian in Deutschland. Eine Forschungs- und Rezeptionsgeschichtliche Analyse, vom Humanismus bis zur Gegenwart* (Munich 2002). Christopher Ligota and Letizia Panizza, eds., *Lucian of Samosata vivus et redivivus* (London 2007). David Marsh, *Lucian and the Latins: Humor and Humanism in the Early Renaissance* (Ann Arbor 1998). Christopher Robinson, *Lucian and His Influence in Eu-*

rope (London 1979). M. O. Zappala, *Lucian of Samosata in the Two Hesperias* (Potomac, Md., 1990). D.M.

Lucretius

In his didactic epic *De rerum natura* (*On the Nature of the Universe,* in six books) Titus Lucretius Carus, the Roman scientific poet of the 1st century BCE, used the image of a honeyed cup of wormwood to encapsulate his philosophico-poetic mission: with his sweet verses he would make palatable to his readers the "medicine" of Epicurean physics. Roman poets, notably Virgil, Ovid, and Manilius, swallowed this medicine with relish; but a work that rejected divine creation and providence and set out to eradicate our fear of death and posthumous punishment was not destined to become a classic of the Christian Middle Ages.

When a text of Lucretius was recovered in 1418 by the Humanist manuscript hunter Poggio Bracciolini, a flurry of editorial and poetic activity ensued. The creative reception of Lucretius in the Italian Renaissance is associated with some controversial names. The Greek exile Michael Marullus (d. 1500), an early editor of the text, combined Neoplatonism and Lucretian materialism in his Latin *Hymni naturales* (*Natural Hymns*), a rather *unnatural* marriage as the work celebrates the gods of the ancient pantheon. "Palingenius'" *Zodiacus vitae* (*The Zodiac of Life,* Venice 1535?), read by Shakespeare, contained earthy satire of Church abuses and an unorthodox cosmology of infinite worlds derived from Lucretius. In a trilogy of Latin poems expounding his own heretical natural philosophy, Giordano Bruno struck a defiantly Lucretian pose, exploiting to the full the irony and iconoclasm of his model. One suspects that Bruno's bad Lucretian "attitude," perhaps more than his philosophical sympathies with ancient atomism, contributed to the unhappy outcome of his trial by the Roman Inquisition. *De rerum natura* was safely ingested by other Cinquecento poets, notably Torquato Tasso, who memorably adapted the image of the "honeyed cup" in the proem to his *Gerusalemme liberata,* ca. 1575 (Prosperi 2004), as well as by medical scientists such as Girolamo Fracastoro, who drew on Lucretius' treatment of the plague of Athens in his didactic poem on syphilis (1530).

Lucretius' dissemination in Renaissance France was facilitated by his great French editor, Denis Lambin. Although it was not the first, Lambin's edition (1563) provided a superior text, notes, and index and an influential preface confronting the issue of Lucretius' nonconformity with Christianity. Lambin pleaded: "Are we to pass over a poet who not only delights our minds, but also unravels the most obscure problems in natural philosophy in the most beautiful verses?" Those beautiful verses were appreciated and imitated by the leader of the Pléiade, Pierre Ronsard, but, paradoxically, were relatively absent from contemporary French *scientific* poetry (Ford 2007). Montaigne quotes readily from Lucretius in the *Essais,* and readers may now consult his annotated edition of *De rerum natura* (ed. Screech). The Catholic priest and mathematician Pierre Gassendi (d. 1655) attempted to reconcile Epicurean atomism and ethics with Christianity, expending as much philological as philosophical energy on that pious project. But not much later, in libertine and Enlightenment France, Lucretius was instead admired for being "skeptical" (Théophile de Viau), "voluptuary" (Cyrano de Bergerac), and "atheist" (Denis Diderot)—though in fact none of those tags is entirely true of the Epicurean poet. In his *D'Alembert's Dream* (1769) Diderot put a delightfully anarchic spin on Lucretian atomic biology.

A taste for Lucretius persisted in the Italian south into the 17th century, where the freethinking Investigantes (Academy of the Investigators) alluded in their motto, *Vestigia lustrat,* "He surveys the tracks," to a Lucretian passage on the "hunt" for truth, and Alessandro Marchetti's Italian translation circulated in manuscript amid great demand. Lucretius was associated with the penetration into Italy of the suspect physical systems of Gassendi and Descartes: that unholy trinity was attacked in a subversively Lucretian poem by the Milanese Jesuit and geometer Tommaso Ceva in his *New-Ancient Philosophy* (1704). The 18th century saw the publication of an ambitious Lucretian poem aimed at giving Lucretius and his modern materialist acolytes a dose of their own medicine: *Anti-Lucretius, or, On God and Nature* (1747) by Cardinal Melchior de Polignac. Scientific poets in 18th-century Rome, mostly Jesuits, assumed a sublime Lucretian manner in long Latin poems about subjects from Cartesian to Newtonian physics, and astronomy to electricity (Haskell 2003).

The first English translation came from the hand of the Puritan poet Lucy Hutchinson, who was attracted by Lucretius' intellectual radicalism but later regretted her youthful flirtation with the impious philosopher. Composed in the 1650s, Hutchinson's translation remained in manuscript until recently (ed. de Quehen). Although the standard 17th-century English translation was Thomas Creech's (1682), Dryden's partial versions shine by comparison. English writers responded to the political Lucretius, from Hutchinson and Hobbes to Richard Payne Knight, poet of *The Progress of Civil Society* (1796), and Wordsworth, e.g., in "Salisbury Plain" (Priestman 2007). Erasmus Darwin (grandfather of Charles) donned the Lucretian mantle of evolutionary biologist and scientific educator in his *Temple of Nature* (1803), and Lucretius was much invoked in Victorian debates about religion and science (Turner 1993). A more melancholy vision haunted Tennyson, whose "Lucretius" (1868) was inspired by Saint Jerome's mischievous report that the poet was driven mad by a philter. Matthew Arnold recycled material from his abandoned play on Lucretius in *Empedocles on Etna* (1852) (Culler 1966).

Whether Brecht's projected poem on the Communist Manifesto would have been particularly Lucretian we cannot say—although Marx, who wrote his doctoral dissertation on the ancient atomists, might have appreciated that. It is a measure of the power of Lucretius' poem that it continues to command attention in its own right—not just as a source for Epicureanism—from the most original, and even postmodern, thinkers. Michel Serres, a contemporary philosopher of science, has written poetically about the birth of chaos theory in Lucretius.

BIBL.: A. Dwight Culler, *Imaginative Reason: The Poetry of Matthew Arnold* (New Haven 1966). Philip Ford, "Lucretius in Early Modern France," in *The Cambridge Companion to Lucretius,* ed. Philip Hardie and Stuart Gillespie (Cambridge 2007). Yasmin Haskell, *Loyola's Bees: Ideology and Industry in Jesuit Latin Didactic Poetry* (Oxford 2003). Martin Priestman, "Lucretius in Britain, 1790–1890," in *The Cambridge Companion to Lucretius*, ed. Hardie and Gillespie (Cambridge 2007). Valentina Prosperi, *Di soavi licor gli orli del vaso: La fortuna di Lucrezio dall'Umanesimo alla Controriforma* (Turin 2004). Hugh de Quehen, ed., *Lucy Hutchinson's Translation of Lucretius, "De rerum natura"* (Ann Arbor 1996). M. A. Screech, *Montaigne's Annotated Copy of Lucretius* (Geneva 1998). Michel Serres, *La naissance de la physique dans le texte de Lucrèce: Fleuves et turbulences* (Paris 1977). Frank M. Turner, "Ancient Materialism and Modern Science: Lucretius among the Victorians," in *Contesting Cultural Authority: Essays in Victorian Intellectual Life* (Cambridge 1993) 262–283.

Y.H.

Lyceum

A gymnasium near Athens that was the site of a philosophical school founded by Aristotle, *lyceum* is also a term used for later educational institutions in Europe and America. Located outside Athens' eastern city walls amid shady groves, the Lyceum provided facilities for athletics, military drills and muster, meetings of the assembly, and religious cults from at least the 6th century BCE onward. During the intellectual ferment of the 5th century BCE, the Lyceum attracted Sophists and philosophers such as Socrates, Protagoras, and Plato's rival Isocrates to engage in argument, debate, and teaching. In 335 BCE Aristotle rented buildings in the Lyceum and established a school where for nearly the remainder of his life he lectured, wrote philosophical treatises, and collected Europe's first library.

After Aristotle's death in 322 the Peripatetic School (the name probably derived from the Lyceum's *peripatoi,* or walkways) continued to flourish. The library's quality declined with the apparent loss of many of Aristotle's works, but the Lyceum's fame continued to attract philosophers and students. The sack of Athens by Sulla in 86 BCE destroyed much of the Lyceum, but Andronicus of Rhodes may have reestablished the school by the century's end. The destruction of Athens in 267 CE by the Herulians ended this renaissance, and when the emperor Justinian closed the Athenian philosophical schools in 529, study in the Lyceum probably had ended centuries earlier.

The Lyceum has remained a powerful and evocative symbol of learning in the Western tradition. One of the most famous paintings of the Italian Renaissance, Raphael's *School of Athens* (1510), presents Plato and Aristotle, along with a constellation of Greek, Roman, Persian, Arabic, and contemporary European scholars, walking and debating together in an imagined Lyceum. In a more pedestrian way, a connection with the ancient Lyceum resides in the name for modern European secondary schools, such as the French *lycée* created by the Napoleonic educational reforms of 1801 as preparatory training for university admission. Originally, students at *lycées* followed courses of study for seven years and specialized either in the Greek and Latin classics or modern studies, or in science and technology. During the late 1960s the *lycée* was reorganized into shorter, three-year curricula focused either in the *lycée d'enseignement général et technologique,* in which students specialize either in the humanities or in science or technology; or in the *lycée d'enseignement professionel,* which has more than thirty vocational or technical studies from which students may choose. This system has been the model for other secondary educational systems like the Italian *liceo,* where the term is used for a broad range of schools. For example, the Italian *liceo classico* focuses on the Greek and Latin classics, but the *liceo linguistico* offers courses in modern languages such as French and English, the *liceo artistico* provides instruction both in art history and in studio art, and the *liceo scientifico* concentrates on chemistry, physics, and other sciences.

In 19th-century America the idea of Aristotle's school inspired the Lyceum Movement, which sought to bring education and ideas of social reform to the masses and involved luminaries such as Ralph Waldo Emerson, Henry David Thoreau, Frederick Douglass, and Susan B. Anthony. The Lyceum Movement was a catalyst for public education, the abolition of slavery, and the enfranchisement of women—none of which Aristotle would have approved.

BIBL.: Carl Bode, *The American Lyceum: Town Meeting of the Mind* (Oxford 1956). Jean Delorme, *Gymnasion* (Paris 1960). John Patrick Lynch, *Aristotle's School: A Study of a Greek Educational Institution* (Berkeley 1972). John Travlos, *Pictorial Dictionary of Ancient Athens* (Athens 1971). R. E. Wycherley, *The Stones of Athens* (Princeton 1978). W.S.M.

Lyric Poetry

In his 1842 essay "The Poetic Principle," Edgar Allan Poe—America's most lyrical champion of "the glory that was Greece,/And the grandeur that was Rome" ("To Helen," 1831)—attacked a literary orthodoxy that privileged epic over "minor" (that is, shorter), supposedly less rigorous and culturally significant kinds of poetry. Far from emulating extended narrative works like the *Iliad,* he asserted, writers and their readers needed to recognize that "the phrase, 'the long poem,' is simply a flat contradiction in terms." The best he could say in behalf of epic was that "we have, if not positive proof, at least very good reason for believing it [was] intended as a series of lyrics," and he concluded that "if, at any time, any very long poem *were* popular in reality, which I doubt, it is at least clear that no very long poem will ever be popular again."

Even to an audience that had long since come to appreciate the genre distinguished and promoted by Wordsworth and Coleridge's *Lyrical Ballads* (1798), Poe's claims may have sounded extravagant. Yet in its confrontational pose, his polemic itself displays a chief characteristic that had, since antiquity, come to typify the ideal "lyric" manner. Conspicuously rejecting or at least retiring from an arena of public expectation, the lyric poet would often cultivate a self-consciously "private" demeanor that willfully opposes prevailing generic conventions. Whatever other features may characterize this mercurial poetic form, notoriously difficult to pin down, lyric marks off an authorial space that paradoxically struggles to distance the very audience it aims to invite.

What lyric has traditionally lacked in prestige it has made up for in primacy and longevity. The poet and critic Allen Grossman calls lyric "the most continuously practiced of all poetic kinds in the history of Western representation" (1990, 6). From antiquity to the present, moreover, lyric has enjoyed recognition as the poetic form most capable of traversing class boundaries, finding voice in the songs of the illiterate and sophisticated alike. Rustic laborers' field chants, the drinking songs composed by and for the more privileged attendants at urbane symposia, and the most highly ritualized metrical celebrations of public figures or events are all encompassed by the term, as are both the unassuming verses of current popular tunes and the demanding complexities of modern "high art" practice. Yet the category's very inclusiveness presents serious difficulty for anyone attempting to define lyric's characteristics beyond its relatively abbreviated length. Elegy, iambus, hymn, ode, and epigram, along with many other subcategories, cluster beneath the umbrella of "lyric," and scholarly efforts to align them quickly lose focus within the vast generic field. In one of our language's earliest extended works of literary criticism, *The Arte of English Poesie* (1589), George Puttenham—for all his deep investment in the Humanist rage for generic specificity—could still do no better than to locate lyric somewhere between the epic and dramatic modes he more confidently determined. Though he singled out elegy as the metrical style adopted by those who specifically "sought the favor of faire Ladies, and coveted to bemone their estates at large, and the perplexities of love in a certain piteous verse," he corralled "*Lirique* Poets" together gregariously as those "others who more delighted to write songs or ballads of pleasure, to be song with the voice, and to the harpe, lute, or citheron." Over the centuries, commentators have improved little on his generalization. We are still left, as Daniel Albright has remarked, with a frustrating impression that "the lyric genre consists of what is left over when all other genres are subtracted from the corpus of literature" (1985, ix).

If this is the case, however, lyric capitalizes wonderfully on its residual, subsidiary status. The lyric artist has conventionally drawn profound strength from the sense of freedom that the practice's generic indeterminacy and eccentricity impart. So consistently does an independent, highly subjective manner imprint the lyric performance that many readers have come to identify the form's distinguishing feature as the voice of "one speaking person, who is nameless or to whom we assign the name of the author," a speaker Grossman deftly identifies as "the hero of private space who both keeps and breaks central rules" (1990, 6, 39). As such, lyric gains a reputation as the literary vehicle best suited to psychological self-exposition, often set against the larger social orthodoxies from which the speaker in the poem stands apart. In Paul Allen Miller's words, lyric in its purest manifestation offers "the representation not simply of a 'strong personality,' but of a particular mode of being a subject, in which the self exists not as part of a continuum with the community and its ideological commitments, but folded back against itself; and only from this space of interiority does it relate to 'the world' at large" (1994, 4).

Lyric disruption of a social "continuum," and the subjectivity that this removal characteristically reinforces, are of course themselves often part of an elaborately crafted fiction. Despite their formal and substantial idiosyncrasies, for instance, Pindar's odes remain commissioned, sponsored performances in honor of very public athletic triumphs. Likewise, much of the vital tension animating Horace's expression, Miller again notes, traces its roots to the writer's simultaneous "rejection of a traditional Roman political career and his necessary attachment to the most powerful people in Rome" (1994, 152). Nor does the oppositional stance on which lyric thrives necessarily divorce it from a firm sense of civic purpose. Lyric poetry's "public" function originates in the dual impulses of praise and blame, formally cast in terms of elegiac and iambic meters, as Aristotle observes in the *Poetics*. And, as W. R. Johnson has pointed out, in archaic Greek poetry "the business of the lyric poet is to provide a criticism of human passion that will indicate which passions are to be embraced and which are to be shunned: the purpose of this demonstration is the education of the hearer, a process of education that functions not by the poet's stating what must be done or learned but rather by showing what sorts of behavior, what configurations of identity, are possible or preferable" (1982, 31). In other words, lyric subjectivity reorients the larger analytic or didactic drives of literary art. What ultimately counts is the poet's willingness to adopt a more individuated perspective to unsettle and interrogate the communally established orthodoxies that have come to determine the audience's viewpoint. This is what largely keeps lyric poets' relationship with their readers so complex and interesting: they must maintain their distance from the very subjects they wish to inspire, if not change.

The immediacy that lyric's "personalizing" tone typically conveys has long prompted audiences to suppose an intimate connection between poet and speaker, often much to the author's consternation. Critical presumption that the lyricist speaks in his or her own person notably inspires the kind of exasperated anger that Catullus displays in his *carmen* (poem) 16, where he proposes that those who fail to understand the distance separating a writer from his lyric speaker deserve to be forcibly sodomized. Less aggressively (but with no less conviction), modern practitioners still insist that lyric poetry affords "a fiction of a self seen from within" (Grossman 1990, 34). However much the sentiments expressed within a lyric may agree with the author's own point of view, we collapse the two only at serious risk to our critical understanding of the poem. The autobiography that lyric appears to lay open for the reader remains at best highly stylized, if not altogether fictional. Ovid's Corinna, like Petrarch's Laura or Shakespeare's Dark Lady, may or may not correspond to an actual historical figure; we need not ascribe to the authors the infatuations expressed in the poems, any more than we identify, say, Robert Browning with the speakers of his dramatic monologues, or T. S. Eliot with the title character of his "The Love Song of J. Alfred Prufrock." In short, lyric poets retain the right to craft personae as one of their most valued, if frequently misconstrued, generic privileges.

Sensitivity to an artist's disengagement from his or her lyric persona further enhances our appreciation of the unique way that lyric's archly subjective voice invites or even obliges its audience to inhabit the intensely personal perspectives it articulates. It is this capacity "to superpose the subjectivity of the scripted speaker on the reader" that Roland Greene associates with lyric's "ritual dimension," wherein the reader of the poem "might be said to shed his or her all-too-specific person, and to take on the speaking self of the poem" (1991, 5–6). In a richly complex maneuver, the lyric poem simultaneously excludes the reader as one who merely overhears or intrudes on the speaker's private utterance, and ironically absorbs the reader into that very subjectivity. This "democratizing" capacity perhaps finds its most overt expression in the striking opening passage of Walt Whitman's *Leaves of Grass:* "I celebrate myself/And what I assume you shall assume,/For every atom belonging to me as good belongs to you." Revolutionary in its candor, Whitman's statement nonetheless only epitomizes a sentiment germane to lyric since its classical inception.

To illustrate the contraventional stance that has from the outset characterized lyric poetry, literary historians have routinely cited the way that such a manner colors even the few shards of Sappho's work that survive. Her fragmentary poem on Anaktoria affords a particularly beautiful instance of epic's martial emphasis displaced by lyric eroticism, when the speaker reflects on how much more appealing she finds the face of her beloved than the grand spectacle of war chariots and soldiers in battle. More recent scholars such as Miller, citing the oral character of archaic lyric's performance and transmission, have questioned whether the genre originally intended to oppose public values or norms quite so radically as it might now appear; but even subscribers to this revisionary reading affirm that the distinctive oppositional voice of lyric became a conspicuously self-conscious affair during the Hellenistic period. By then lyric had lost its oral, civic context and transformed into a chiefly textual medium, crafted and collected by artists and scholars who had migrated to the new seat of imperial patronage at Alexandria. The poetry that grew from this altered political and cultural setting appears "introspective and subjective to a degree previously unknown in the West, as the conjunction of writing and an alienating social environment combined to create a sense of distance from the self" (Miller 1994, 123). Thus, in a more confrontational vein than we find in the earlier poets, the Hellenistic writer Callimachus snipes boldly from the sidelines, offering in the preface to his *Aetia* (*Causes*) a candid dismissal of those who fault him "because I have not consummated a continuous epic/of thousands of lines on heroes and lords/but turn out minor texts as if I were a child," with the retort that "a few subtle lines" of lyric outweigh the grandiose pretensions of contemporary epic (trans. Stanley Lombardo and Diane Raynor). In this manner, ideological challenge comes ever more expressly to inform generic identity.

As it gradually emerged in the post-Hellenistic world, Latin lyric of the republican and imperial eras inherited Alexandria's textual legacy. With the work of the neoteric poets—Catullus chief among them—the lyric collection or anthology enabled an even more sustained prospect for the formulation of a distinctive poetic "self." Now recorded in a form that permitted comparative rereading of individual poems within the larger context of a lyric sequence, the poet's voice potentially betrays even greater occasion for intensive self-exploration. This professed literary orientation toward the private self and away from epic and tragic conventions crystallized, eventually, into the Latin trope of lyric *recusatio,* or open refusal to address more politically sanctioned topics. Horace would adopt this pose most influentially. In a poem like *Odes* 1.6, the speaker polishes his lyric expression with a self-effacing urbanity, disclaiming his skill to celebrate Agrippa's great deeds: parties are the only battlefields, and lovers' assignations the only contests for which the poet's lyric muse enables him. Reverence for his patron's broader civic milieu, on which his own privileged security relies, subtends the deliberate disavowal of any interest in political topicality but never cancels the speaker's unambiguous preference for the less opulent luxuries enjoyed by the "unwarlike" lyre.

It remained for Ovid, however, to animate this stance in what would prove the most witty and enduring manner. The great synthesizer of Graeco-Roman myth in effect mythologizes lyric practice itself in the poems introducing each of his *Amores*' three books. In the first, Cupid hobbles the poet's planned epic by removing one foot from alternating hexameter lines, thereby reducing his heroic measures to those of erotic elegy. In the second, the poet's amorous obsession with a mistress again preempts the ambitious *Gigantomachia* (*Battle of the Giants*) he has undertaken. In the final book the goddesses Tragedy and Elegy themselves face off to assert dominion over the poet's allegiance: as highly as the author respects the "scepter and buskins" that Tragedy puts at his artistic disposal, he nonetheless opts for Elegy, the form that "offers my passions undying glory" (trans. Peter Green). Ovid's eventual exile from Rome, purportedly for the moral offensiveness and political insubordination of his verses, isolated him in the popular imagination as an exemplar of the price such a subversive stance might occasion. It also lent further romance to the lyric artist's oppositional character. While the elegiac laments that Ovid composed from exile turned ultimately to attempts at currying favor with the new regime, they never relinquish the disarming subjectivity he had so powerfully fashioned throughout his career.

Lyric's relatively diminutive form has, over the centuries, rendered it more vulnerable to time's ravages; amid the attrition that earlier Greek and Latin texts suffered generally in the era following the Roman empire's decline, lyric experienced the highest casualty rate. Thus, for instance, even an author as allegedly prolific and indisputably popular as Sappho has come down to us only in the slightest handful of fragmentary passages. By the time that early modern Humanists had undertaken a concerted effort to salvage what little survived of classical lyric, European vernacular literatures had already begun independently to develop lyric practice anew. Moreover, the form's peculiar resurgence at the dawn of the early modern period, when the very idea of "selfhood" was undergoing a radical and determinate reconceptualization, argues further for the distinctive allure of lyric's individuated speaking voice. It would fall to a single figure, Petrarch, to revitalize the vernacular lyric at this juncture in a way that relocated it from the margins of respectability to the defining literary mode of the next several centuries. Despite the poet's professed indifference to his vernacular lyric output (in deference to his unsuccessful "classical" ambitions to forge a larger Latin epic), Petrarch single-handedly popularized and gave the form a credibility with his sequence known as the *Canzoniere* (literally, *Songbook;* i.e., *A Book of Poems*) or *Rime sparse* (*Scattered Verses*). The 366-poem collection, originating in the 1320s and ending near the time of his death in 1374, unfolds the tormented emotional odyssey of the poet, torn between his obsession for the elusive Laura (who dies two-thirds of the way through the sequence) and his higher awareness of the vanity of all earthly attachments. Not since antiquity had a lyric persona uncased himself in such a profoundly resonant and moving way. Petrarch's accomplishment would go on to inspire a golden age of lyric productivity, best represented in English by the likes of Sir Philip Sidney, Edmund Spenser, and Shakespeare himself, whose *Sonnets* (1609) stand among the best-known exercises in the genre.

Even the thrust of Petrarchan influence and the remarkable accomplishments it inspired across the Continent could not ensure the genre against subsequent uneven fortunes. Lyric declined in prevalence over the course of the 18th century, edged out (along with tragedy and epic, significantly) as prose narrative evolved into what we know as the modern novel. It would, however, suffer this brief remission only to return with a fresh dynamism at the hands of the next century's Romantic reawakening, which effectively valorized the poet as the primary subject of literary artistry, over both the audience and the external world they ostensibly inhabit. Sponsored largely by the Hellenizing proclivities of 19th-century German scholarship, and then by the 20th century's retreat inward under the auspices of modern psychoanalysis, the form has never since flagged, down to our own postmodern moment.

For better or for worse, modern lyric practice has borne out Poe's assertions, and Grossman's claim that lyric endures as the literary form "most endemic to the present post-modern situation" rings true (1990, 6). As epic has undergone extraordinary novelistic reinvention in works like James Joyce's *Ulysses,* and tragedy shifts focus and form under artists as various as Brecht, Beckett, and Pinter, lyric has by comparison stayed a remarkably steady course. While we may easily imagine Homer's or Virgil's posed (if impressed) reaction to the mythic flow of *Finnegans Wake,* we can just as readily envision Sappho, Catullus, or Ovid altogether at home with Dickinson, Baudelaire, or Pound. If anything, the once-privileged forms have come to adopt the more subversive antiheroic ironies endemic to their older but historically lesser generic sibling. It seems no accident that we know and celebrate contemporary reworkings of classical material in poems such as Derek Walcott's *Omeros* (1990) or Ted Hughes's *Tales from Ovid* (1997) especially for the distinctive lyric intensity and immediacy of their component movements. So long as audiences maintain interest in pronouncedly individuated perspectives, and our imagination remains stimulated by the idiosyncratic and unfamiliar, lyric as a form promises to retain its artistic efficacy and appeal.

BIBL.: Daniel Albright, *Lyricality in English Literature* (Lincoln 1985). Roland Greene, *Post-Petrarchism: Origins and Innovations of the Western Lyric Sequence* (Princeton 1991). Allen Grossman, "*Summa Lyrica:* A Primer of the Commonplaces in Speculative Poetics," *Western Humanities Review* 44 (1990) 1–138. W. R. Johnson, *The Idea of Lyric: Lyric Modes in Ancient and Modern Poetry* (Berkeley 1982). Paul Allen Miller, *Lyric Texts and Lyric Consciousness: The Birth of a Genre from Archaic Greece to Augustan Rome* (London 1994).

C.M.

M

Macaulay, Thomas Babington

English historian, essayist, and politician, 1800–1859. Macaulay's father, a Scot, was a leading slavery abolitionist; both parents were devoutly Evangelical. Macaulay was a child prodigy; at Cambridge (1818–1822) he won several university prizes in English and Classics. He served four times as a Member of Parliament and held various government posts; in 1834 he went to India as a member of the Council of the East India Company, and in the same year, while reading Latin and Greek for several hours each day, he began to compose his *Lays of Ancient Rome* (Letters 3:129). In 1835 he lost his two youngest sisters, to whom he was passionately attached, one to scarlet fever, the other to marriage. "That I have not utterly sunk under this blow," he wrote, "I owe chiefly to literature" (3:158–160). The reading that saved him was almost all classical (3:199–202). After returning to England, he traveled in Italy in 1838–1839, visiting the sites of the events he commemorated in the *Lays* and following Gibbon's celebrated example (from 1764) of experiencing the ruins of ancient Rome.

After its publication in 1842, Macaulay's *Lays of Ancient Rome* became—and remained for decades—one of the best sellers of Victorian poetry (23,000 copies in 12 years; 63 editions by 1939). The *Lays* were inspired by the theory of the German historian Barthold Niebuhr (drawing on the work of the 17th-century Dutch scholar Jacob Perizonius) that the narrative of the first few books of Livy's *History of Rome* had been based on early Roman ballads. Another exemplar was the work of Ossian, the alleged (but nonexistent) author of poems published in the 1760s by James Macpherson. Macaulay's aim was to put the stories back into ballad form for English readers. Each of the four lays ("Horatius," "The Battle of Lake Regillus," "Virginia," and "The Prophecy of Capys") was prefaced by a prose introduction, on the model of Thomas Percy's *Reliques of English Poetry* (1765). Each was assigned to an imagined author, a Roman bard who drew on earlier legends: here Thomas Gray's Pindaric ode "The Bard" (1757) provided a model. Macaulay himself drew on Homeric phrases and technique, and on Walter Scott's reconstruction of Scottish minstrelsy, to create a picture of early Rome in vivid and swinging ballad meter. The *Lays* resonate both with Macaulay's personal and family life (hence the stress on parallels between Roman and Scottish bards) and with contemporary politics. The Licinio-Sextian laws of 367 BCE, which opened the consulship to plebeians, and which are the central focus of the third lay, "Virginia," he saw as a parallel to the Reform Bill of 1832, which extended the franchise in Britain. The *Lays* have in fact been called "the Philistine epic of the political class which was created by the political reforms of 1832" (McKelvy 2000, 293).

Macaulay was encouraged to publish by the favorable response of Thomas Arnold, who heard two of the *Lays* recited on his deathbed. Arnold's son Matthew, however, later initiated a chorus of highbrow depreciation in his *On Translating Homer* ([1861] 1960, 211), referring to the "ring of false metal" in Macaulay's text—which he misquoted—as did later the eponymous hero of *Buck Rogers in the Twentieth Century* (O. D. Edwards 1988, 54–55). Several school editions were published from the 1880s onward, when compulsory elementary education was established in England and the *Lays,* especially "Horatius," remained widely read, memorized, and quoted in England until World War II. Some lines persist still, especially these from "Horatius": "Lars Porsena of Clusium/By the nine gods he swore" (1.1–2); "'And how can man die better/Than facing fearful odds./For the ashes of his fathers./And the temples of his Gods?'" (27.4–8); "Was none who could be foremost/To lead such dire attack;/But those behind cried 'Forward!',/While those before cried 'Back!'" (50.1–4); "Even the ranks of Tuscany/Could scarce forbear to cheer" (60.9–10). The style, as these lines suggest, is in some ways reminiscent (or rather prescient) of Kipling, whose fame and fate Macaulay anticipated: the echoes of empire, the scorn of the academic literati, and the persistence in popular memory. Though the *Lays* fade from memory, paradoxically the idea of Roman myth transmission through song has recently been (controversially) revived (Habinek 1998).

BIBL.: Matthew Arnold, *Complete Prose Works,* vol. 1, *On the Classical Tradition,* ed. R. H. Super (Ann Arbor 1960). Catharine Edwards, "Translating Empire? Macaulay's Rome," in *Roman Presences: Receptions of Rome in European Culture, 1789–1945,* ed. C. Edwards (Cambridge 1999), 70–87. Owen Dudley Edwards, *Macaulay* (London 1988). Thomas Habinek, *The Politics of Latin Literature* (Princeton 1998). Thomas Macaulay, *The Letters of Thomas Babington Macaulay,* 6 vols., ed. T. Pinney (Cambridge 1974–1981). William R. McKelvy, "Primitive Ballads, Modern Criticism, Ancient Skepticism: Macaulay's *Lays of Ancient Rome,*" *Victorian Literature and Culture* 28 (2000) 287–309. W. Williams, "Reading Greek Like a Man of the World: Macaulay and the Classical Languages," *Greece and Rome* 40 (1993) 201–216.

C.A.S.

Machiavelli, Niccolò

Florentine political thinker (1469–1527). In his major political works, *The Prince* and *Discourses on the First Decade of Titus Livy,* he called for imitation of classical virtue yet originated the tradition of modern political thought that condemns classical political philosophy as utopian or impractical.

In his dedicatory letter to *The Prince* Machiavelli wrote that he got the knowledge of the actions of great men that the book conveys from "long experience with modern things and a continuous reading of ancient ones." The book refers to only two classical authors by name: Xenophon, a Greek historian writing about the Persian emperor Cyrus (chap. 14), and Virgil, a Roman poet writing about the Carthaginian queen Dido (17). Nonetheless, the book frequently holds up for modern imitation Greek and Roman rulers and republics, whose wisdom and success generally contrast with the folly and failure of modern counterparts; for example, the wisdom of the Romans in conquering Greece is contrasted to the errors of Louis XII in attempting to conquer Italy (3). (Unnamed classical sources for these examples include Livy, Plutarch, Suetonius, Cicero, Diodorus Siculus, Justin, Herodian, and Polybius.) His greatest examples of new princes who founded new principalities through their own arms and virtue are all premodern, though not all classical: Moses, Cyrus, Romulus, and Theseus (6).

Machiavelli urges princes to read histories and "do as some excellent man has done in the past who found someone to imitate who had been praised and glorified before him" (14). Modern imitators are at three removes from classic originals: imitating predecessors who imitated more distant predecessors as described by poetic, historical, or philosophic writers such as Homer, Xenophon, or Plutarch. Machiavelli immediately makes clear, however, that these writers cannot be trusted: they have imagined republics and principalities that have never been seen or known to exist in truth (15). They admire the actions of great men without understanding their causes; thus, Livy condemned Hannibal's inhuman cruelty, little considering that it was the principal cause of his accomplishments (17)—though Machiavelli also suggests that ancient writers "taught covertly" what he teaches openly and takes to the extreme (18). He departs from previous writers by writing not about "imagined republics and principalities" but about the "effectual truth" that takes its bearings not by what ought to be done but by what is done, by the goals men actually pursue, wealth and glory (25). His conception of *virtù* shares with its classical archetypes an emphasis on manly courage but departs from them in its focus on worldly effectiveness to the exclusion of concern with the perfection or salvation of the soul. Machiavelli's invocations of classical (and biblical) rulers and republics in *The Prince* reveal a critique of classical (and biblical) writers and an aspiration to replace them as the authoritative interpreter of those examples.

The dual themes of radical innovation and return to classical antiquity mark the *Discourses on the First Decade of Titus Livy* as well. Machiavelli's preface to book 1 claims both that he has found new modes and orders by a taking a path yet untrodden by anyone and that he writes to turn men from the error of judging imitation of the ancients to be impossible. He coyly suggests that this error is due to Christianity, which denies that "men are born, live, and die always in one and the same order" in ancient and modern times through its doctrines of being born again and life after death (1.11). The work is therefore not simply a commentary on Livy but includes reflections on modern times and original interpretations of antiquity. Machiavelli praises pagan antiquity at the expense of Christian modernity (2.2) but also criticizes classical writers and even Rome itself. Unlike Livy in his praise of concord, he praises the discord between the plebs and patricians as the source of Roman liberty (1.3–6); explicitly disagreeing with Livy and Plutarch, he attributes the Romans' empire more to virtue than to fortune (2.1). The neoclassical republicanism that he inspires differs from classical and Humanist conceptions in its emphasis on the political utility of class conflict, individual ambition, and extralegal violence at moments of founding and renewal. The model he offers is not the Rome of the classical writers but Rome as he reinterprets and even improves on it.

His chief military and historical works display a similar pattern. The chief speaker in his *Art of War,* Fabrizio Colonna, emphatically presents the Romans as his military models but then freely departs from them in his incorporation of modern pikes, harquebuses, and artillery and in his assumption that soldiers fight from necessity, not patriotism. Machiavelli's *Florentine Histories* follows classical models such as Livy and Thucydides in its free invention of suitable speeches, while pursuing its modern agenda of dissecting the differences between the pernicious internal divisions of Florence and the salutary ones of ancient republics. Though delicately and dryly eschewing open criticism of the ruling Medici family, the work avoids the patriotic glorification of Florence found in its Humanist predecessors.

Machiavelli's letter of 10 December 1513 to Francesco Vettori includes a beautiful description of his communing with the ancients: "I enter the ancient courts of ancient men, where, received by them lovingly, I feed on the food that alone is mine and that I was born for. There I am not ashamed to speak with them and to ask them the reason for their actions; and they in their humanity reply to me." His new understanding of the actions of ancient rulers led him to break with the thoughts of ancient thinkers.

BIBL.: Gérald Allard, "Machiavel, lecteur des anciens," *Laval théologique et philosophique* 46 (February 1990) 43–63. Felix Gilbert, *Machiavelli and Guicciardini: Politics and History in Sixteenth-century Florence* (Princeton 1965). Victoria Kahn, *Machiavellian Rhetoric: From the Counter-Reformation to Milton* (Princeton 1994). Niccolò Machiavelli, *The Prince,* trans. Harvey C. Mansfield (Chicago 1985, 1998), and *Discourses on Livy,* trans. Harvey C. Mansfield and Nathan Tarcov (Chicago 1996). Quentin Skinner, *The Foundations of Modern Political Thought,* vol. 1, *The Renaissance* (Cambridge 1978). Leo Strauss, "Machiavelli and Classical Literature," *Review of National Literatures* 1 (Spring 1970) 7–25.

N.T.

Macrobius

A late classical scholar of the early 5th century CE, Macrobius was a notable link between the cultures of antiquity and the Middle Ages. A Roman senator and high-ranking administrator, he represented an aristocratic tradition of amateur erudition that had Cicero and the elder Pliny as its most distinguished avatars. Though he lived in a highly Christianized empire, there is no sign of Christianity in his writings, which instead suggest (at the very least) an informed interest in the traditional beliefs commonly called "pagan."

Macrobius is represented by two substantial works. His *Saturnalia,* a learned compilation in seven books cast in dialogue form, recreates and idealizes the cultural life of an earlier generation, in the manner of Cicero's *On the Orator* and *On the Commonwealth.* Set during the Saturnalia in 383, it gathers several (conspicuously non-Christian) members of the aristocracy and their entourage to discuss matters ridiculous (e.g., a number of rather good jokes) and sublime (e.g., the divinity of the sun), and above all the poetry of Virgil. Quarried from mostly unnamed sources—including Gellius, Seneca, Plutarch, and the tradition of scholastic commentary today known from Servius—the discussion presents Virgil as the master of all human knowledge, from diction and rhetoric through philosophy and religion. In this respect it makes explicit a view of Virgil long implied by the scholarship gathered around the poems and anticipates the miraculous figure of "Virgil the magician" known to the Middle Ages. Though less influential as a source of ancient lore than Martianus Capella's allegory of the Seven Liberal Arts (later 5th cent.), Macrobius' *Saturnalia* was used (perhaps) by Isidore of Seville in the 7th century and (certainly) by John of Salisbury and William of Conches in the 12th. Like the latter scholars, we know the work only because a single manuscript lacking the end of book 7 survived into the 9th century. Now lost itself, that defective copy begat a series of copies extending from the 9th century into the 15th, when the *Saturnalia* reached the height of its popularity (over 60 known manuscripts, which is more than half of the total extant).

More consequential was Macrobius' other major work, a commentary on the "Dream of Scipio" passage that concluded book 6 of Cicero's *On the Commonwealth.* (It is thanks to Macrobius that we have a complete text of the "Dream," for the rest of book 6 is lost.) Like the myth of Er in Plato's *Republic* that inspired it, the "Dream" presents a view of the soul and the afterlife meant to support the arguments that have preceded, in Cicero's case urging just and vigorous participation in civic life. Placing his emphasis elsewhere, Macrobius uses Cicero's text as the starting point for a thoroughly Neoplatonic treatment of (especially) cosmology and the soul's ascent to the One, with direct debts to Porphyry and Plotinus. A copy of the *Commentary* corrected in 485 by Aurelius Memmius Symmachus, Boethius' father-in-law, played an important role in the text's transmission, the early stages of which are otherwise unclear: after weathering the 6th through 8th centuries, aided in the latter stages by the work of Irish scholars active on the Continent, the text emerged in 9th-century France, where most of the earliest surviving manuscripts were written. By the end of the 11th century copies were widely diffused, from England to southern Italy; but the true efflorescence came in the 12th century, which has left us more than 100 manuscripts (not quite half of all extant). From the 12th century onward Macrobius enjoyed a reputation as a major Platonist: praised as a philosopher by Abelard (d. 1142) and used extensively by Vincent of Beauvais (d. 1264) and Albertus Magnus (d. 1280), he continued to be influential into the Renaissance and beyond, when the cosmological views of the "Dream" and his *Commentary* left their traces in writings as diverse as those of Dante (d. 1321), Chaucer (d. 1400), Juan Luis Vives (d. 1540), and Edmund Spenser (d. 1599).

In modern scholarship Macrobius has sometimes been depicted as participating in the "pagan revival" of the 380s and 390s, but that view cannot survive the demonstration that he wrote at least one and more likely two generations later. We know too little of his immediate milieu to draw reliable inferences concerning his motives.

BIBL.: B. C. Barker-Benfield and P. K. Marshall, "Macrobius," in *Texts and Transmission,* ed. L. D. Reynolds (Oxford 1983) 222–235. H. Bloch, "The Pagan Revival in the West at the End of the Fourth Century," in *The Conflict between Paganism and Christianity in the Fourth Century,* ed. A. Momigliano (Oxford 1963) 192–218. Alan Cameron, "The Date and Identity of Macrobius," *Journal of Roman Studies* 56 (1966) 25–38. Jacques Flamant, *Macrobe et le néo-platonisme latin, à la fin du IVe siècle* (Leiden 1977). Macrobius, *Commentary on the Dream of Scipio,* trans. W. H. Stahl (1952, repr. New York 1990), and *The Saturnalia,* trans. P. V. Davies (New York 1969). F. J. E. Raby, "Some Notes on Dante and Macrobius," *Medium Aevum* 35 (1966) 117–121. R.A.K.

Maecenas

Gaius Maecenas (d. 8 BCE), one of the richest men in Rome and said to be a descendant of Etruscan kings, was Augustus' agent and adviser, but he remained in the equestrian rank and never held an official position. He supported Octavian from the time of the battle of Philippi, served him on diplomatic missions, and between 36 and 29 governed both Italy and Rome for years at a time in his absence. He was notorious for his extravagant love of luxury and his scandalous sexual affairs. He also wrote poetry (some fragments survive) and was the patron of three major Augustan poets: Virgil, Horace, and Propertius. He seems to have been closest to Horace, who frequently mentions his gifts (including the famous Sabine farm) and muses on the affectionate but also delicate relationship between client and patron. In his *Life of Horace* Suetonius says that in his will Maecenas appealed to Augustus to look after Horace: "Be mindful of Horatius Flaccus as you are of me." (The request was unnecessary, for Horace died within a few months of Maecenas. He was buried near his tomb.)

Maecenas' name has become synonymous with artistic or literary patron, but it also suggests a patron like him. Maecenas was rich, politically important, a connoisseur of beauty (a euphemistic but not inaccurate way to describe his hedonism), and a poet in his own right. He had an eye for talent and supported his favorite poets, Virgil and Horace, for many years, treating them as friends and companions. He undoubtedly discussed their work with them (although modern scholarship is skeptical of the old claim that the poets wrote to order or that Maecenas was "Augustus' Minister of Propaganda").

The term Maecenas was used relatively little in the Renaissance, perhaps because it was not grand enough for the greatest patrons. Maecenas, for all his wealth and power, was subordinate to the emperor, but the popes and princes of the Italian Renaissance considered themselves preeminent—Augustuses, we could say, not Maecenases. The name might also have suggested too much familiarity between dependent and patron. Artists, however talented, were deemed intellectual and social inferiors. Humanists and poets, higher on the scale, sometimes referred to a patron as "my Maecenas." The optimistic title was sometimes justified, but most patronage was briefer, more businesslike, and less advantageous for the client than the relationship between the ancient Maecenas and his poets had been.

In the 17th and 18th centuries the term was used more frequently, perhaps because of an increasing number of patrons in secondary political positions. Patrons who were nobles but not heads of state could see themselves as a Maecenas to someone else's Augustus and embrace the name as a way to promote their own magnificence. The idea is neatly expressed in Tiepolo's painting *Maecenas Presenting the Liberal Arts to Augustus* (1743). In it the Arts, dressed as elegant ladies, curtsy low before the emperor enthroned on his dais, while *Maecenas,* every inch the refined courtier, introduces them. The painting was commissioned by Count Francesco Algarotti, who presented it to Count Heinrich von Brühl, a contemporary Maecenas and the powerful minister of another Augustus, King Augustus III of Saxony and Poland.

In contemporary usage *Maecenas* has lost some of its specificity, meaning little more than "generous patron of the arts."

BIBL.: Werner L. Gundersheimer, "Patronage in the Renaissance: An Exploratory Approach," in *Patronage in the Renaissance,* ed. G. F. Lytle and S. Orgel (Princeton 1981) 3–23. Kenneth Reckford, "Horace and Maecenas," *Transactions and Proceedings of the American Philological Association* 90 (1959) 195–208. Peter White, *Promised Verse: Poets in the Society of Augustan Rome* (Cambridge, Mass., 1993). J.H.G.

Maenads

Female followers of Dionysus. Also called Bacchae, Bacchantes, Bacchanales, Bassarae, and Bassarides. Literally "madwomen," they became possessed by the god, and in their ecstasy tore up small animals (*sparagmos*) and ate the flesh raw (*ōmophagia*); yet they were famed for their sexual appeal.

Many works survived from antiquity to supply Renaissance artists and scholars with a basic iconography, especially the bacchic sarcophagi: examples are held today by the Accademia Etrusca in Cortona, the British Museum, the Museo Capitolino and Villa Medici in Rome, the Uffizi in Florence, the Metropolitan Museum in New York, Blenheim Palace Garden in Oxfordshire (splendidly over the top), and in the Museo Nazionale in Naples (stunningly obscene). Other notable antiquities showing maenads include the Borghese Vase from the ancient Horti Sallustini in Rome (now in the Louvre in Paris) and the Torlonia Vase (Museo Torlonia, Rome).

The combination of a metaphor for creative frenzy, a celebration of drunkenness, and a chance to display wild women in various states of undress has always been appealing. From among thousands of works of art one might single out:

The illustrations (perhaps by Benedetto Bordone) to Francesco Colonna, *Hypnerotomachia Poliphili* (1499)

Andrea Mantegna, *Bacchanal with a Wine Vat* (1470s), Metropolitan Museum, New York

Titian, *Bacchus and Ariadne* (1520–1523), for the camerino of Alfonso I d'Este in Ferrara; National Gallery, London
Dosso and Battista Dossi, *Bacchanalia* (ca. 1520), National Gallery, London
Baldassare Peruzzi, frescoes (1518–1519), Villa Farnesina, Rome
Annibale Carracci, frescoes (1597–1601), Palazzo Farnese, Rome
Nicolas Poussin, *Bacchanal: The Andrians* (ca. 1630), Louvre, Paris; *Bacchanal before a Herm of Pan* (1630s), National Gallery, London
Hendrick ter Brugghen, *Bacchanal with an Ape* (1627), Getty Museum, Los Angeles
Giulio Carpioni, *Bacchanal* (1638), Columbia Museum of Art, Columbia, S.C.
Charles Joseph Natoire, *Le Triomphe de Bacchus* (1747), Louvre (formerly attributed to Le Moyne or Fragonard)
Jean-Baptiste Greuze, *Bacchante* (1780s), Wallace Collection, London
Emma Hamilton was painted as a Bacchante several times: twice by Marie Louise Élisabeth Vigée-Lebrun (1785), Clark Art Institute, Williamstown, Mass., and (1790–1791), Lady Lever Gallery, Liverpool; also by George Romney (ca. 1786), Tate Britain, London; and by Sir Joshua Reynolds (1784), private collection
Angelica Kauffmann, *Bacchante* (before 1786), Gemäldegalerie, Berlin (possibly a self-portrait)
William Etty, *Bacchante with Tambourine* (before 1849), Louvre, Paris
Jean-Léon Gérôme, *Bacchante* (1853), Musée des Beaux-Arts, Nantes (bizarre, with ram's horns)
Léon Riesener, *Bacchante (with Leopard)* (1855), Louvre, Paris
Jean-Baptiste-Camille Corot, *Bacchante with a Panther* (1860), Shelburne Museum, Vermont; *Bacchante by the Sea* and *Bacchante in a Landscape* (1865), Metropolitan Museum, New York
William Adolphe Bouguereau, *Bacchante* (1862), Musée des Beaux-Arts, Bordeaux
Mary Cassatt, *Bacchante* (1872), Pennsylvania Academy of Fine Arts, Philadelphia (a student work)
Lawrence Alma-Tadema, *The Women of Amphissa* (1880s), Clark Institute, Williamstown, Mass. (one of the few representations of a historical event).

In the 20th century Pablo Picasso returned to the figure of the bacchante in etchings and other works. Sculptural renderings include numerous works by Clodion, Albert-Ernest Carrier-Belleuse, Rodin, and Bertel Thorvaldsen. The figure of the maenad seemed particularly to pique Victorian sensibilities, perhaps because it permitted an open display of female sensuality (however tasteful the renderings might seem to us today); noteworthy if unsettling examples include Prosper d'Épinay's *Bacchante* (1866), Hermitage Museum, St. Petersburg; Aimé Jules Dalou's *Bacchanal* (1879), Victoria and Albert Museum, London; and Frederick William MacMonnies's *Bacchante and Infant Faun* (1893–1894), Metropolitan Museum, New York.

Euripides' *Bacchae* (405 BCE) has exerted a powerful effect in theater. A landmark year for 20th-century postwar productions was 1969, with Richard Schechner's *Dionysus in '69*, John Bowen's *The Disorderly Women*, and Maureen Duffy's *Rites*. Subsequent years brought Wole Soyinka's *The Bacchae of Euripides: A Communion Rite* (1973) and Caryl Churchill's *A Mouthful of Birds* (1986). Modern operatic works include Karol Szymanowski's *King Roger* (1926), Egon Wellesz's *Die Bakchantinnen* (1931), Giorgio Federico Ghedini's *Le baccanti* (1948), Harry Partch's *Revelation in the Courthouse Park* (1961, Dionysus as Elvis), Hans Werner Henze's *The Bassarids* (1966, libretto by W. H. Auden), Roy Travis's *The Black Bacchants* (1982), Daniel Börtz's *Backanterna* (1991, directed by Ingmar Bergman), and John Buller's *The Bacchae/Bakxai* (1992). Jean-Philippe Rameau's *Platée* (1745) features a happier chorus of bacchantes.

Maenads provide similes (Shelley, "Ode to the West Wind"), serve as attributes of Bacchus (André Chénier, "Bacchus"), or are actors in the death of Orpheus (Rilke, *Sonette an Orpheus* 1.26). They have furnished subjects of their own, for example, in Pierre Louÿs's "Les ménades" in *Chansons de Bilitis* (1894), Albert Samain's "Bacchante" (before 1900); Renée Vivien's "Bacchante triste" (1903), and Sylvia Plath's "Maenad" (1960). They have also inspired a contender for the worst couplet in English poetry, from Francis Thompson's "A Corymbus for Autumn" (1893): "Hearken my chant, 'tis/As a Bacchante's."

BIBL.: Jane Davidson Reid, ed., "Bacchanalia," in *The Oxford Guide to Classical Mythology in the Arts, 1300–1990s* (New York 1993) 1:258–271. H.PA.

Magic

Beliefs and practices often, but problematically, compared with religion and science. Among the large concepts that people have used to sort their ideas and actions—economics, politics, religion, science, art, magic, and so on—magic has a very strange history. The ancient Greeks first used the word *magic* to describe the religion of the Persians, their worst enemies. More than two millennia later, Europeans educated in the classics were still using it, applying it not to enemies, however, but to colonial subjects. When they called this modern magic "primitive," the theory that they relied on was most famously expressed by an eminent classicist, J. G. Frazer, who maintained that magic was related to religion and science as a lower stage of evolution is to higher stages. What was Frazer thinking about—or the anthropologist E. B. Tylor before him? What could a religion of ancient Iran have to do with the Anahuac or Papua of their day? To answer that question, let us ask another that Frazer knew well: "How old were you when the Mede came?"

Xenophanes of Colophon, an Ionian poet and philosopher, asked that question sometime after 546 BCE, roughly half a century before the massive Persian invasions of the Greek mainland reported by Herodotus. Since the question is a fragment, its point is uncertain, like that of other fragmentary evidence suggesting that Xenophanes was a monotheist—or a henotheist—who tried to understand the cosmos by investigating its material elements. Long before Herodotus invented history, Xenophanes may have had notions about religion and science that foreshadowed our own. But when the Mede finally came in force, it was Herodotus who gave one of their tribes, the Magoi, the name from which later Greeks derived the word *mageia*. Herodotus described the Magi as rebels and conspirators who also sacrificed horses, poured libations at funerals, sang chants at sacrificial rites, and cast spells to quell storms. Xenophon characterized them as members of an official state priesthood, and it seems—though our knowledge is fragmentary—that they practiced a religion both creedal and reforming, a faith whose two supreme deities were locked in cosmic combat, and whose priests tended sacred fires, never letting them die, and burned the flesh of animals in the flames.

In Greek, Roman, and Christian tradition, however, the Magi were celebrated and remembered, blamed and praised, as experts on mysterious and exotic arts. Over time, the Greeks came to identify magic as bad behavior characteristic of "barbarians"—foreigners, Persian or other—and eventually to condemn it as evil. The early Romans, as pragmatic in this domain as in others, outlawed practices of the same kind, but their descendants called the practices "magic" only after Cicero, Catullus, and other learned writers had imported information about the Magi from Greek sources. And in both Greece and Rome the same magic whose dark spells and secret recipes horrified some poets and philosophers proved popular with other people, from the top of society to the bottom.

Naturally, the new Christian Church insisted that its true miracles were not the magic, known by other names, that was reviled in the Hebrew Bible, where Moses defeats Pharaoh's wizards and a donkey gets the best of Balaam, a heathen seer. Yet Balaam is a wise pagan who predicts that "a star will come out of Jacob," the same star that shines on the Magi of Matthew's Gospel. And how did Moses overcome Pharaoh's tricksters? The author of Acts says that he knew "all the wisdom of the Egyptians and was powerful in his words and actions": that reputation linked the name of Moses with Greek pseudepigrapha on magic and led Pliny to list him after Zoroaster as the founder of "another sect of magic."

That Jews, Christians, and pagans were confused about magic and religion is not surprising, since magic at its core is just a reflex of religion: having no essence, it is an evil attributed to someone else's religion, one of those defects that the religious subject attributes to its other. As theology needs heresy in the domain of theory, in order to define what it claims not to be, piety needs magic in the domain of practice, and for that reason religion can never eliminate magic.

Yet magic—the strange work of Persian priests transformed into Graeco-Roman conjurers—gradually won a place in the reverend annals of ancient learning. Pliny the Elder opened book 30 of his *Natural History* with the most influential account of magic written in Latin before the Renaissance, inserting it into a long discussion of natural substances used in medicine. *Magia* for Pliny is fake medicine that claims religious authority and divinatory power, since healers often need to prognosticate. It is a corruption of astrology, religion, and medicine traced to Persia and Zoroaster—not to the historical prophet, however, but to the arch-magus whose primordial age alone was enough to make him exotic. By extension, the same arcana belong to the witches of Thessaly, the Druids of Gaul, the stargazers of Chaldaea, and all the other magicians. Their unpronounceable names evoke faraway places and unintelligible languages that contain unutterable words of power—*arrheta,* ancestors of the "occult" powers of later magical theory that would be unseeable rather than unsayable. When exile drove sages like Pythagoras and Democritus to the remote regions where such speech was heard, even those wise philosophers were befuddled by it.

But if Pliny and Apuleius—a well-born philosopher who defended himself against charges of practicing magic—regarded the art with scorn or suspicion, other highly educated authors treated it with respect and transformed its status, especially in relation to philosophy.

Plotinus, born in Egypt ca. 205, a few decades after Apuleius died, was a better philosopher than the Roman Platonist. He established the tradition—Neoplatonism—that first explained the philosophical basis for belief in magic that Apuleius only mentioned. Although Plotinus himself was once attacked by a magic spell, which he swiftly deflected back to his assailant, he had no interest in magical technique, dismissing it as a distraction from philosophy. But he thought of nature itself as magical, filled with divine powers that are always already there, ready to be activated by the magus who knows how to switch them on. Porphyry, a student of Plotinus, had similar reservations about practicing magic, though he never doubted its reality.

It was Iamblichus, the next Neoplatonic successor, who turned his full attention to theurgy—literally, "god-making"—as a way to ascend to the divine by first calling a god down into a material receptacle here below. The metaphysics behind this technology is intricate and subtle. A key idea is that the cosmic and hypercosmic hierarchies are arranged in *taxeis* or "series" so that, for example, the material image of a scorpion made on earth will belong to a series that includes the actual arachnid and also rises far beyond it to a supercelestial divine Scorpion and many others in the grades of being in between, one of them the Scorpio that we see among the constellations. The magus who understands the nature of the celestial and supercelestial Scorpions will also know which earthly elements are like them and which are not. Such a magus can then call down the gods, or fend them off, by manipulating the physical things—stones, plants, colors, odors, tastes, sounds, and so on—that resonate sympathetically with the divine or drive it away with antipathies. Proclus, the last of the great Neoplatonists who wrote in Greek, produced the best summary of this ancient magical theory, *On the Priestly Art according to the Greeks,* though it survives only in a digest.

By the time Proclus died, in 485, the pagan gods had all but succumbed to the new Christian deity, and Christians despised the old gods as demons. They also promoted the inconspicuous Adversary of the Hebrew Bible to the lordship of Hell, empowering their Satan to command hosts of unclean spirits and, eventually, unleash them on the poor and powerless people who were the main victims of witchcraft persecutions. Thus, in the nightmares of Christians, the magus had finally turned into the *maleficus.* Sadly, all this was compatible not only with the theology that educated Christians professed but also with the science and philosophy that they inherited from classical authorities.

The universe of Aristotle and Ptolemy is a nested set of concentric spheres through which causality moves from outside to inside—or above to below, from a terrestrial point of view. The heavens in between God and the lowest reaches of the cosmos, where humans live, transmit this power through planets and constellations that not only resemble living things but actually have souls and minds. Although the stars that Aristotle calls gods were obviously a problem for Christians, the discomfort was not harsh enough to discredit the larger cosmology, which provided physical and metaphysical foundations both for astrological divination and for the magic that manipulates celestial influence.

The Christian authorities were always anxious about magic, some of them going as far as Augustine when he condemned any use of amulets—even if they were undecorated—as invitations to demons. But no one could replace the cosmology that sustained belief in magic, not even a hero of orthodoxy like Thomas Aquinas. Even the Angelic Doctor, who had to believe in angels, also believed in demons as their hellish counterparts. Aquinas also agreed that the stars were ensouled, and he wrote a little treatise to explain why natural magic operates in the world. The basis of his convictions was Aristotelian and philosophical, including such technical metaphysical doctrines as the hylemorphic theory of qualities and substantial forms.

As philosophers and theologians, almost all the Scholastics—even those who disagreed with Aquinas—shared his reliance on Aristotle's capacious and tightly structured system. Hence, the philosophical authority that ratified key items of Christian dogma and ritual was the same Scholastic Aristotelianism whose physics and metaphysics now underwrote magic as well. Demons who tempt the faithful with magic and turn them into witches are angels gone to Hell. At the other end of Aristotle's cosmos, the providential Christian God is a Creator and First Mover who acts through the stellar and planetary spheres to cause motion, generation, and corruption below on earth, which explains how astrology works without calling on demons, thus allowing for a natural magic reinforced by astrology. In light of such features of the prevailing cosmology, and of their consecration as Christian doctrine, educated Europeans accepted magic, astrology, witchcraft, demonology, divination, and so on as normal beliefs in the Middle Ages, and long afterward.

At this point in magic's strange history, we should note two things: first, we have come a long way from Persian fire worship; second, we are even further from anything that might be called primitive. What justified magic for medieval thinkers was a sophisticated intellectual construct built on classical precedent in late antiquity. This is not to say that "popular magic," or folk magic, was unknown or unimportant, then or ever, but it does mean that the "magic" in such phrases can only be our own etic, or observer term—not, for example, the emic, or agent use of "magic" by Roger Bacon or Pietro d'Abano.

Etic magic might be anybody's, in principle, including the people that Tylor and Frazer called primitive. Why not study them to shed light on the beliefs and practices of still other people—the Greeks, for example? That was Jane Harrison's thought when she wrote that "in primitive days in Greece, as in Persia, magic had to do, if not with divinities (*θεοί*), yet at least with things divine, with sanctities (*τὰ θεῖα*), and . . . magic was assuredly part of the necessary equipment of a king (*τὰ βασιλικὰ*) . . . We [also] have to deal with the manipulation of sanctities by the tribe or . . . the medicine-man . . . The attitude towards *mana* is a two-fold one, the positive attitude which is magic, the negative which is *tabu*" (Harrison 1912).

According to Harrison, "We know that certain 'magical practices' survived among the Greeks" of later periods. It remains only to link *mageia,* the loanword applied to those practices, with the native evidence from "primitive days in Greece" that will then lead us to magic's true nature. From ancient Thessaly to the modern Trobriand Islands, magic of the etic kind will be all around us, across the millennia. The term *magic* will then join art, science, religion, and other universals of the human condition. And the same term will now be exalted by association with classical Greece. It will no longer belong to the "ignorant old women, hole and corner charlatans, or lovers insane through passion" listed by Harrison to contrast with the archaic Greek magic that was something nobler, something regal and sanctified, and yet primitive. And the primitive itself will have been ennobled.

Hearing this attractive story, now a century old or more, it is hard to exaggerate the moral force of the classical ideal that guided Harrison and Frazer. It was Frazer, after all, who tried to resign his Cambridge fellowship when a reader discovered a single error in his translation of Ovid. Despite the ethical imperative, however, and even though no account of magic has had more readers than Frazer's *Golden Bough,* the story breaks down if we apply the etic magic of Tylor, Frazer, and Harrison—which is still the standard model for educated nonspecialists—to Avicenna, Albertus Magnus, or Marsilio Ficino. In practice, given the slim evidence, it is hard to say what magic the chiefs and shamans of archaic Greece may have had in common with "primitive" people studied by Malinowski, Evans-Pritchard, and other early anthropologists. What they could not possibly have had in common is clear enough, however: the philosophical and other remains of classical antiquity that gave medieval and early modern intellectuals reason to believe in magic.

During the Renaissance, the philosophy that sustained belief in magic grew even more refined than it had been in the Middle Ages. Ficino, who first put all of Plato into a language that Western Europeans could read, was also a theoretician of magic. The third book in his *Three Books on Life,* "On Arranging Life by the Heavens," was the most influential account of magic of its day, perhaps of all Western history: between 1489 and 1647 the book went through nearly 30 editions. In his philosophical account of magic, Ficino confirms the Aristotelian cosmology and much of the physics and metaphysics that the Scholastics had accepted, but he also adds new notions from the ancient Neoplatonists, especially the metaphysics of Plotinus and Proclus and the theurgy of Iamblichus.

Although Ficino was nervous about his new philosophical magic, fearing what the Church might say, he was too dazzled by his discoveries to suppress them. Instead, he worked hard to distinguish a legitimate natural magic from the demonic kind. Since some magic was thought to work by invoking demons, which would always be sinful, the crux of a theory of natural magic was to exclude them, which Ficino thought possible if he used only natural things found everywhere on earth—stones, plants, vapors, and sounds—to make sympathetic connections with (or antipathetic defenses against) higher levels of the cosmos.

Ficino surely realized that his theory was flawed. The same Neoplatonic sages who convinced him that magic was real, Iamblichus especially, also showed that it was always divine. Magic could never really avoid the personal spiritual beings—gods for Iamblichus, demons for Christians—that Ficino needed to banish to keep magic natural. His anxiety on this point is evident when he mentions the *Asclepius,* a text ascribed to Hermes Trismegistus, in order to condemn its account of statue making in the temples of ancient Egypt. Although the objects used to make statues fit for the gods were natural, the images themselves were plainly idols animated by demons.

Hermes was a key figure in the mythic cultural history—the ancient theology—that Ficino derived from the Church Fathers. God had provided not only the sacred revelation given to Moses on Sinai but also a profane yet pious wisdom inaugurated by Zoroaster and Hermes, culminating in Plato and continued by the Neoplatonists. The place of Hermes in this lineage was clearer to no one than Ficino. One of his earliest works was the first Latin version of the Greek Corpus Hermeticum, previously unknown in the West. Ficino cites it nowhere in the *Three Books on Life,* probably because its subject is theology and spirituality, not magic. In fact, he gives serious though brief attention only to the Latin *Asclepius,* a Hermetic text that he did not need to translate; outside the single chapter that condemns the *Asclepius* for demonolatry, he mentions Hermes as an author of Hermetic texts only four times in passing—once to link him with Plotinus, who was disdainfully critical of magical practice.

While Ficino was reviving Neoplatonic magic and fitting it into his ancient theology, Giovanni Pico della Mirandola was adding Kabbalah as yet another piece of this syncretizing puzzle. Learned Jews had taught Pico that Kabbalah was part of the oral law. Besides the written law known to Christians as the Pentateuch, God had also given Moses an unwritten law passed down as "kabbalah," a transliteration of *reception* in Hebrew. Pico adapted Kabbalah to the theurgic magic of ascent that Ficino had discovered and made it part of a mystical discipline that rises to *henosis*—union with God and annihilation of the self.

Pico died in 1494, Ficino in 1499, 11 years before Heinrich Cornelius Agrippa von Nettesheim finished the first version of his large manual, *On Occult Philosophy.* Like Ficino's *Three Books on Life,* Agrippa's *Occult Philosophy* was still being printed in the 17th century, after Descartes had died and long after its first edition of 1533. Agrippa's big book is a compendium of the many beliefs, practices, and phenomena thought at the time to be based on or explained by theories like those that Ficino and Pico had proposed. After summarizing the theory, Agrippa catalogs the results: astrology, including astral and talismanic magic and medical magic; theurgy, sorcery, necromancy, and the evil eye; oracles, prophecy, divination in its many varieties, including oneiromancy, or dream interpretation, and also lots; the magic of names, words, letters, charms, spells, chants, and curses; numerology and the magic of numbers, figures, signs, seals, characters, and images, including the letters of Latin, Greek, and Hebrew; the magic of music and sound; demonology, angelology, and the magic based on them; and Kabbalah.

Between the covers of this one large volume Agrippa put whatever had come to seem magical, sometimes in the etic sense, to educated people of his day. But because Agrippa also inherited an emic magic with a classical pedigree from the Middle Ages and the Renaissance, the reader of his book encounters thousands of Greek and Roman people, places, ideas, and words—the fragments of an ancient lexicon of magic. Agrippa's magic had been classicized, in other words, at a time when Humanist culture tried to classicize everything that it respected and much that it feared. And Agrippa gave it a new name, the "occult philosophy" that would eventually become "occultism" in the 19th century, the seedtime of so many -isms.

During the 16th and 17th centuries Pietro Pomponazzi,

Girolamo Cardano, Giambattista della Porta, Giordano Bruno, Tommaso Campanella, Robert Fludd, Athanasius Kircher, Henry More, and many others kept searching the ancient ruins for traces of magic. But the same curiosity that tempted Ficino (or his patron, Cosimo de' Medici) to suspend work on Plato for a few months in order to translate the Greek Hermetica led others toward a more critical philology that, by the early 17th century, put new weapons in the hands of debunking scholars whose target was credulity about the classics. In 1614 Isaac Casaubon concluded from linguistic data that the Hermetica could not be records of anything as old as Ficino's ancient theology.

Breakthroughs like Casaubon's did not stop the literate public from believing—or wanting to believe—in magic. Far from it. During the century of Galileo, Descartes, and Newton, the market for magic books continued to boom, and it still thrives today. Nonetheless, in the age of the new science, and a new philology, magic became so disreputable for intellectuals that ambitious scholars avoided it or attacked it more than ever before. The key change was the collapse of another classical creation—Aristotelianism. Without the cosmological framework and metaphysical foundations of that comprehensive system, magic became incredible to critics, who mostly ignored its debts to Neoplatonism. Since the ideas that meant so much to Ficino's magic had no secure place in the universities where Aristotle ruled, Neoplatonism mattered little to the professional philosophers whom Descartes opposed.

After the 17th century, when philosophy and philology turned Europe's high culture decisively against magic, the ancient classical tradition had little left to give to the modern occultist tradition—as Agrippa understood it. But more was to be heard from the specialized study of the classics that evolved from the work of Casaubon and his Humanist predecessors.

Even as magic was being ejected from normative natural philosophy and metaphysics, it popped up again in the new fields of classical philology and the history of religion. One of the demons that drove the acolytes of *Altertumswissenschaft* was a compulsion to cover the classics exhaustively. Every scrap of ancient evidence, on every topic, had to be recovered, preserved, and studied—even magic. Scholars who held magic in contempt as a primitive delusion still insisted on tracking it down. To some extent, this was just the logic of textual recovery playing itself out: for every Plato, there was a Proclus; for every Aristotle, an Apuleius; what was good for the Younger Pliny must be good for the Elder.

Those had been names to conjure with for centuries, but experts on classical philology also added new items to the library of Western arcana, especially by finding and deciphering papyri and archaeological deposits. The *Catalogus codicum astrologorum graecorum,* the *Collection des alchimistes grecs,* the *Papyri graecae magicae,* and other such projects uncovered whole corpora that had been unknown when learned magic last seemed respectable, during the Renaissance. Much of the scholarship that went into this period of gathering, hunting, and collecting was dry and positivist in its inspiration: scholars like Auguste Bouché-Leclercq and A. E. Housman loathed the magical texts that they read and interpreted so skillfully.

And no wonder, for it was hard at first to reconcile the magic uncovered by modern archaeology and papyrology with the refined magical cosmologies preserved in the older philosophical tradition. The spirit of the newly recovered documents, whatever the style of their language, was distinctly demotic: the spells and recipes that Albrecht Dieterich studied and Karl Preisendanz collected in the *Greek Magical Papyri* seemed not to come from the same ancient world where Ficino had found his elegant Neoplatonic metaphysics. But in 1922, just two years before Preisendanz published his first volume of magical papyri, Bronisław Malinowski made his name with the *Argonauts of the Western Pacific,* his classic account of the Trobriand Islanders, followed in 1925 by his influential study, *Magic, Science and Religion.* Here was more evidence that if modern primitives made etic magic function effectively as part of a complex cultural system, the same analysis might apply to the emic magic of the papyri and other ancient texts.

The subsequent influence of anthropology on the study of magic as part of the classical tradition has been deep and enduring: contemporary authorities like Walter Burkert still think and express themselves in anthropological terms. But the outstanding case of mutuality between the classics and anthropology remains Frazer's *Golden Bough,* first published in 1890 and still growing when the author added a supplement to its 12 volumes in 1937.

Frazer opens his interminable story with a tale from the classics, about "a line of priests known as Kings of the Wood," doomed to be assassinated but kept safe by a sacred tree so long as the tree stays intact. "In early society," Frazer explains, "the king is frequently a magician as well as a priest; indeed he appears to have often attained to power by virtue of his supposed proficiency in the black or white art." For the kings of the sacred grove, the most vital magic was the kind that Frazer calls "sympathetic," while declaring it "essential to have some acquaintance with the principles of magic . . . in all ages and all countries." To that end, he constructs a taxonomy of magic empirically, beginning with "homoeopathic or imitative magic" as a species of the sympathetic kind.

"Thousands of years ago," Frazer continues, this type of magic "was known to the sorcerers of ancient India, Babylon, and Egypt, as well as of Greece and Rome, and . . . is still resorted to by cunning and malignant savages in Australia, Africa, and Scotland." He then piles case history upon case history from North and South America, Sumatra, New Guinea, Malaysia, Borneo, the Torres Strait Islands, central Celebes, the East Indian islands of Saparoea, Haroekoe, and Noessa Laut, from the Warramunga and Arunta of Central Australia, from a Cambodian hunter, from people closer to hand in Bulgaria and among the Bosnian Turks, and even from "our Scottish

Highlands." Part and parcel of the same barrage of data are reports from Diodorus Siculus, Plutarch, and Pliny.

Not surprisingly, with so much information on the table, students of Graeco-Roman magic could make what they liked of it, and so they did. Primitive magic might be either appreciated as popular religion (or science) or condemned as degenerate religion (or science). If it was a product of syncretism, the forces in play might be either creative, leading to new horizons of the spirit, or corrupt, ending in miscegenation. In any case, if magic was primitive in its essence, it ought to be a terminus from which evolution advances to something better, leaving scholars to quarrel about where that something might be located, whether inside ancient culture or outside it. The primitive as exotic belongs to someone else by definition, and as arcane it is someone else's secret.

Any such option that survived had to be placed not only within a taxonomy of magic, like Frazer's, but also within a larger taxonomy of culture, wherein magic usually is related antithetically to religion or science, or both. The ghosts of Hegel and Comte must have applauded as the debate raged. Was magic marked by the opposition between heteronomy and autonomy? Or between the irrational and the rational? Supernature versus nature? Manipulation versus submission? Performative versus assertoric? Perhaps theory versus practice, the last resort of the taxidermy of ideas. While deciding these undecidable questions, modern students of ancient magic produced not only scholarly monuments, like the *Greek Magical Papyri,* but also masterpieces of interpretation. The most memorable was the work of Aby Warburg, the eponymous hero of the Warburg Institute and therefore a patron saint of the modern study of the classical tradition.

When the *Golden Bough* was still a new book, Warburg read Franz Boll's *Sphaera* (1903), a notable application of advanced philology to the new evidence about ancient astrology. Boll's book inspired Warburg to decode the decan images invented by ancient Egyptian priests, mixed with zodiacal signs by Hellenistic astrologers, and transmitted to medieval and Renaissance readers in grotesquely mutated forms. The spherical geometry of the Egyptians was clear, but the associated imagery became opaque as the night sky shifted over the centuries. Passing time and failed memory distorted the decan images in very odd ways.

Warburg thought that Giovanni Pico must have seen a striking record of the old images painted on the walls of a palace in Ferrara, Palazzo Schifanoia, near Pico's estates and owned by a family friend, Borso d'Este. Warburg also knew for certain that in his late and unfinished attack on judicial astrology, Pico had denounced "the absurd Arabian doctrine of the decans. It is understandable that a Renaissance man, on finding these astrological specters, . . . should have taken up arms against so barbaric a combination of idolatry and fatalism." On the other hand, he also understood that Pico had written in praise of magic and Kabbalah only a few years earlier.

Genius in the service of magic was not so much a paradox for Warburg as a predictable betrayal—treason all too human in what Jacob Burckhardt had called "the warfare which the clear Italian spirit waged against this army of delusions," a campaign conducted despite "the great monumental glorification of astrology . . . in Borso's summer palace" (Burckhardt 1990). It was from Burckhardt that Warburg inherited the capacity to see historical agents as merely inconsistent or irresolute where others saw contradiction. Since the Burckhardt who hailed Pico as author of "the loftiest conceptions . . . on the dignity of man" also saw occultism as a debasement, however, full appreciation of Pico's magic might have strained even his forbearance.

Warburg, who wanted a humanism purged of superstition but doubted that possibility, ends his famous essay on the murals of Schifanoia with the claim that "the grandeur of the new art, as given to us by the genius of Italy, had its roots in a shared determination to strip the humanist heritage of Greece of all its accretions of traditional 'practice,' whether medieval, Oriental or Latin. It was with this desire to restore the ancient world that 'the good European' began his battle for enlightenment, in that age . . . that we—a shade too mystically—call the Age of the Renaissance" (Warburg 1988). Enlightenment requires not just a rebirth of ancient humanism but also a catharsis. Yet Warburg's ironic use of Nietzsche's phrase suggests a darker conviction: that history always thwarts the good European's desire for disenchantment.

Ernst Cassirer summarized Warburg's thinking about magic and astrology in a few dense lines: "Warburg has shown from its history," he wrote, "that astrology . . . presents a double intellectual front. As a theory, it seeks to place before us the eternal laws of the universe in clear outline; whereas its practice stands under the sign of the fear of demons" (Cassirer 1963). What Warburg called the "de-demonizing process" was the great step taken by the Renaissance toward the modern world, which meant turning away from an older, magical worldview grounded in the classics.

Warburg had studied psychology, anthropology, and evolutionary biology as they were taught in the late 19th century. His project was a grand theory of social memory to explain the persistence and transformation of images since antiquity. Although he respected Burckhardt, he despised Burckhardt's vulgarizers, especially those who beatified the free Renaissance individual and gave the impression that mankind's escape from the primitive was simple or easy. Warburg saw the task as always incomplete: the civilizing process was never a linear advance but a perpetual oscillation between magic and logic in which "Athens constantly needs to be won back again from Alexandria."

In a "phobic reflex," primitive people had suppressed their terrors by making concrete images of them, surrogates to manipulate and replicas to overcome in ritual: thus, "celestial bodies were visualized in human form in order to limit their daemonic power." His fascination with the primitive caused Warburg to travel in 1905 to "prehistoric and 'wild' America," going all the way to New Mexico in the hope (disappointed) of seeing a Native American snake dance. But it is the menace of Europe's old gods that haunts his prose:

> The astral deities were faithfully transmitted . . . from the Hellenistic world by way of Arabia, Spain and Italy to Germany . . . They lived on as time gods, . . . beings of sinister, ambivalent, and indeed contradictory powers: as star signs they expanded space, marking the way for the soul's flight through the universe; as constellations they were also idols, with whom . . . the mere creature might aspire to mystic union through devotional practices. The astrologer . . . accepted these opposite poles of mathematical abstraction and devout self-association . . . as the pivots of one vibrant, primordial psychic state. Logic sets a mental space between man and object by applying a conceptual label; magic destroys that space by creating a superstitious . . . association between man and object. In . . . the astrologer's mind, these two processes act as a single primitive tool that he can use both to make measurements and to work magic.

Ideal humans would have marched straight from reflex to reason, but real people always shuttle between magic and logic, concrete and abstract, personal and conventional, rising from embodiment to detachment and sinking again from mathematics to religion, never finally securing the scientist's desired distance or the artist's poise.

The role of images in this work is mediating and bivalent; they are channels of energy that can illuminate or obscure; they externalize and sublimate fear in artistic conventions or immerse and concentrate it in human persons. The magical images to which Warburg returned again and again were those of the pagan gods, which, reflecting Burckhardt's view of late antiquity, he saw as deformed and degraded in that age, having lost their noble Hellenic forms and reverted to clumsy fetishes. Two of Warburg's major works describe the liberation of the older gods during the Renaissance, their escape from the bad dreams of medieval astrology and their return to Olympian serenity. "In the transitional age of the early Renaissance," he argued, "pagan-cosmological causality was defined in classicizing terms through the symbols of the gods, . . . approached in due proportion to their degree of saturation with human quality; from a religious daemon-worship at one extreme to a purely artistic and intellectual representation at the other."

Warburg saw this struggle recorded in Borso's palace and in the pamphlets of the Reformation, especially the woodcut propaganda that fueled debate about the date of Luther's birth and its purported coincidence with the great celestial conjunction of 1494. He regarded astrology—with its images of astral gods—as a shifting weight on the delicate scales of culture: even horoscopic figuring and fanciful celestial geometry need rational calculation to free the mind from the star-demons and their terrors, or the reverse. Hence, "in astrology two entirely antithetical mental forces . . . combine to form a single 'method.' On one side is mathematics, the subtlest operation of the abstract intellect; on the other is the fear of daemons, the most primitive causative force in religion. The astrologer . . . is gripped, as he pores over his mathematical tables, by an atavistic and superstitious awe of those very star names that he wields like algebraic formulas; to him, they are daemons, of which he lives in fear."

If some scholars took the high road to reason, others lost the true path. The learned Melanchthon is a dupe in Warburg's drama, whereas the cruder Luther knew absolutely that astrology was the devil's tool and unrighteous. It was Raphael and Dürer who saved the old gods aesthetically—especially Dürer, who engraved the reflective genius who stares from his magical *Melencolia I* (1514).

> Its consoling, humanistic message of liberation from the fear of Saturn . . . can be understood only if we recognize that the artist has taken a magical and mythical logic and made it spiritual and intellectual. The malignant, child-devouring planetary god . . . is humanized and metamorphosed . . . into the image of the thinking, working human being . . . Debased, repellent planetary spirits contending for the control of human destiny . . . are reborn into a classical language of form; and yet their Hellenistic-Arabic travels have left them bearing the marks of subjection to fate.

Dürer's age, according to Warburg, was also Faust's, when "the modern scientist . . . was trying to insert the *conceptual space* of rationality between himself and the subject." But science and art always leave this quest for reason unfinished, moving Warburg to describe the objects of his research as the "unread records of the tragic history of freedom of thought," which he tries to explain by deciphering magical images passed down from antiquity. His abhorrence of magic as primitive and of astrology as fatalist reflects a Kantian wish to free the moral agent from an unfree state of nature—the strongest conceptual bond between Warburg and Cassirer.

Frances Yates, who spent her whole splendid career at the Warburg Institute, was no more philosophical than Warburg, but her work also shows traces of Cassirer's Kantian morality. Near the end of her celebrated study of Ficino, Pico, and Bruno, Yates claims that modern science emerged after the Renaissance from "a new direction of the will towards the world." "The real function of the Renaissance Magus," she declares, "is that he changed the will. It was now dignified and important for man to operate . . . and not contrary to the will of God that man, the great miracle, should exert his powers." The world-engaging will finally prevailed in "that momentous hour . . . [when man] first began to tread securely in the paths which have since led him unerringly onwards to that mastery over nature in modern science which has been the astonishing achievement of modern European man" (Yates 1964).

Yates, Cassirer, and Warburg could all have agreed that "mastery over nature in modern science" was a great civilizing force, but for Warburg the course of civilization was far from unerring, as we learn from the fortunes of ancient magic. In Warburg's view, culture always wavers between reason and unreason, between disciplined will and emotional panic. Although Yates shared Warburg's goal of understanding the afterlife of the classical tradition, even finishing projects (such as the interpretation of the Valois Tapestries) that he had started, her best-known book—which contains the best-known account of the ancient magic revived in the Renaissance—departed from Warburg's tragic sense of history in two ways: first, her story is a melodrama that ends happily in the bright dawn of science; second, Man the Magus is a conquering hero in her tale, conjuring up the modern world in a way less opposed to Warburg's dread of magic than oblivious to it. She cites Warburg only once in her *Giordano Bruno and the Hermetic Tradition* and nowhere confronts his ideas about magic, so unlike her own.

BIBL.: Robert Ackerman, *J. G. Frazer: His Life and Work* (Cambridge 1987). Jacob Burckhardt, *The Civilization of the Renaissance in Italy,* trans. S. G. C. Middlemore (1878; London 1990). Ernst Cassirer, *The Individual and the Cosmos in Renaissance Philosophy,* trans. Mario Domandi (New York 1963). Brian Copenhaver, "Astrology and Magic," in *The Cambridge History of Renaissance Philosophy,* ed. Charles Schmitt and Quentin Skinner (Cambridge 1987) 264–300; "Hermes Trismegistus, Proclus and the Question of a Philosophy of Magic in the Renaissance," in *Hermeticism and the Renaissance: Intellectual History and the Occult in Early Modern Europe,* ed. I. Merkel and A. Debus (Washington, D.C., 1988) 79–111; "How to Do Magic, and Why: Philosophical Prescriptions," in *The Cambridge Companion to Renaissance Philosophy,* ed. James Hankins (Cambridge 2007); "Magic," in *The Cambridge History of Early Modern Science,* ed. L. Daston and K. Park (Cambridge 2006) 518–540; "Magic and the Dignity of Man: De-Kanting Pico's Oration," in *The Italian Renaissance in the Twentieth Century: Acts of an International Conference, Florence, Villa I Tatti, June 9–11, 1999,* ed. Allen J. Grieco et al. (Florence 2002) 295–320; "Natural Magic, Hermetism and Occultism in Early Modern Science," in *Reappraisals of the Scientific Revolution,* ed. D. Lindberg and R. Westman (Cambridge 1990) 261–301; and "The Occultist Tradition and Its Critics in Seventeenth-century Philosophy," in *The Cambridge History of Seventeenth-century Philosophy,* ed. D. Garber and M. Ayers (Cambridge 1998) 454–512. Matthew W. Dickie, *Magic and Magicians in the Greco-Roman World* (London 2001). E. R. Dodds, *Pagan and Christian in an Age of Anxiety: Some Aspects of Religious Experience from Marcus Aurelius to Constantine* (Cambridge 1965). Valerie Flint, *The Rise of Magic in Early Medieval Europe* (Princeton 1991). J. G. Frazer, *The Golden Bough: A Study in Magic and Religion* (London 1925). Fritz Graf, *Magic in the Ancient World,* trans. F. Philip (Cambridge 1997). Anthony Grafton, *Defenders of the Text: The Traditions of Scholarship in an Age of Science* (Cambridge, Mass., 1991), chaps. 5 and 6. Jane Harrison, *Themis: A Study in the Social Origins of Greek Religion* (Cambridge 1912). Richard Kieckhefer, *Magic in the Middle Ages* (Cambridge 1990). G. E. R. Lloyd, *Magic, Reason and Experience: Studies in the Origin and Development of Greek Science* (Cambridge 1979). Gregory Shaw, *Theurgy and the Soul: The Neoplatonism of Iamblichus* (University Park, Pa., 1995). Aby Warburg, "Italian Art and International Astrology in the Palazzo Schifanoia in Ferrara," in *German Essays in Art History,* ed. Gert Schiff (New York 1988), and *The Renewal of Pagan Antiquity,* trans. D. Britt (Los Angeles 1999). Frances Yates, *Giordano Bruno and the Hermetic Tradition* (London 1964).

B.C.

Magna Graecia

Area of southern Italy where Greeks established settlements as early as the 8th century BCE. The peculiar name Magna Graecia—Great Greece—refers in modern scholarship specifically to the area of southern Italy where the Greeks established colonies between ca. 740 and 433 BCE. These coastal settlements flourished and put Greeks in contact with native Italian populations. The wealth of the city of Sybaris was proverbial. The philosophers Parmenides and Zeno from Elea, and Pythagoras, who founded his school in Croton, exercised great influence. Magna Graecia's cities progressively lost power, either to native populations—for example, Lucanians took over Paestum ca. 420 BCE—or through internecine wars—Siris was destroyed ca. 530 BCE by Sybaris, which was routed in turn by Croton in 510 BCE. After various vicissitudes under the leadership of Taras (Taranto), Magna Graecia finally entered the Roman sphere in the 3rd century BCE.

Magna Graecia's rich history and crucial role in introducing the Romans to Greek culture contrast with a paucity of ancient written sources. Its odd place in the classical tradition is reflected in the peculiarity of the name itself. Magna Graecia first appears only in the 2nd century BCE in Polybius, and today there is no agreement on the origins of the name or the area it denominates—for example, Strabo seems to include even Sicily. The recently coined term *Western Greeks* elides some of the issues such as the inclusion of Sicily and implies a peripheral role in relation to mainland Greece.

A. Galateo and G. Barrio—writing in the Renaissance tradition of historical-topographical survey—invoked the Greek past and the glory of Magna Graecia in, respectively, *De situ Iapygiae* (1558), a description of Puglia, and *De antiquitate et situ Calabriae* (1571), on Calabria. Yet the first book specifically on Magna Graecia was the Dutch antiquarian Goltzius's 1576 study of its coins. In the mid-18th century interest in Magna Graecia revived with the discovery of the inscriptions of Heraclea and the rediscovery of Paestum's Doric temples. The 1758 lavish publication of the inscriptions by the Neapolitan A. S. Mazzocchi included an extended discussion of the name Magna Graecia and of all its cities. Paestum became a favorite travelers' destination and a crucial site for modern Hellenism and the Doric revival. Winckelmann, who never traveled to Greece, visited Paestum with enthusiasm; his pupil Baron Riedesel ventured further, to Sicily, Calabria, and even Greece, to claim in his 1771 travel account that in Italy ancient Greekness was better preserved than in Greece itself.

As Greece became more accessible in the 19th century, interest in Greek southern Italy declined. In the 1880s the Frenchman Lenormant's travelogues on Magna Graecia were successes precisely because the area was by then not well known. This shift was also conceptual, as Magna Graecia came to be seen as a periphery. Painted vases—mostly excavated in southern Italy—were analyzed primarily for their style. Southern Italian varieties of art and architecture were judged against the Athenocentric canon and considered contaminated by native influences. In British historiography this colonial approach can be detected even as late as Dunbabin's 1948 *The Western Greeks.* Italian studies followed a different route. Extensive state-sponsored archaeology began after unification with the identification of many lost sites and the exploration of both indigenous and Greek sites, thus pioneering modern acculturation studies. Yet tensions of regional identity, often linked to Italy's Southern Question (the issue of southern Italy's alleged difference from or inferiority to northern Italy), long remained. For example, the major 1972 discovery of the Riace classical bronzes initiated a protracted battle about where the statues should be displayed, in one of the capital cities of Italy, or in Reggio Calabria, where they now stand.

BIBL.: Franco De Angelis, "Ancient Past, Imperial Present: The British Empire in T. J. Dunbabin's *The Western Greeks,*" *Antiquity* 72 (1998) 539–549. *Eredità della Magna Grecia* (Taranto 1998). S. Settis, "Idea dell'arte greca d'Occidente tra Otto e Novecento: Germania e Italia," in *Un secolo di ricerche in Magna Grecia* (Taranto 1989) 135–176. S. Settis and M. C. Parra, eds., *Magna Graecia: Archeologia di un sapere* (Milan 2005).

G.CE.

Maison Carrée

The Maison Carrée (or Quarrée) in Nîmes is as much admired for the beauty of its architectural ornament as for its volumetric and structural clarity. The motifs are from the Ara Pacis Augustae in Rome, and the temple was built by Augustus' son-in-law Agrippa in memory of the emperor's deceased sons Caius and Lucius, as stated in the dedication formerly in the entablature of the pediment above the pronaos. Although this would suggest a dating to the first decade of the 1st century CE, some think the temple belongs to the final decades of the previous century. The source of the ornament makes it probable that the craftsmanship was Roman, but the stone is a fine-grained limestone from the local Bois des Lens quarry.

Joseph Spence described it succinctly in 1733: "'Tis 120f. long. 60f. high and 60f. broad—a double cube, all surrounded with fluted Corinthian columns, six at the front and eleven at the sides, thirty in all." An equally concise description was offered by the Neoclassical theorist Marc-Antoine Laugier 20 years later: "A rectangle where thirty columns support an entablature and a roof which is closed at both ends by a pediment—that is all; the combination of a simplicity and a nobility which strikes everybody." The use of the phrase "noble simplicity and quiet grandeur" by J. J. Winckelmann to characterize the quality of Greek architecture made the Maison Carrée as acceptable to the architects of the Greek Revival as it had been to Palladio, who included it in his *Quattro Libri,* first published in 1570.

The international importance of the Maison Carrée is due to its fame as a model for Neoclassical architecture. It was described as "the most perfect model existing of what may be called cubic architecture" by Thomas Jefferson, who adapted it for the design of the State Capitol of Virginia in Richmond, the first example of classical revival themes in monumental architecture in America. His contemporaries shared his enthusiasm for the building, a survey of which was published by Jefferson's collaborator C.-L. Clérisseau in 1778. In England an earlier adaptation of it had been the Temple of Concord and Victory at Stowe Gardens in Buckinghamshire, begun in the late 1740s but not completed until the late 1760s. Like the State Capitol of Virginia, it is Ionic rather than Corinthian and has ten columns on each side rather than eleven. Michael Bevington has proposed that as Jefferson visited Stowe in 1786, the Capitol building in Richmond may be read as a conflation of the Stowe temple with the Maison Carrée.

The interior of the Maison Carrée derives its only light from the entrance door. The current door is part of alterations to the building (previously in use as a church) made in 1824, when it was adapted to serve as a repository of the town museum. The most recent restoration of the interior was in 1988, when the ceiling and the walls were colored Pompeian red. Statuary of the Roman period is displayed within, but the temple's sculptural distinction derives rather from the carving of its Corinthian capitals and the acanthus scroll frieze, which make it one of the best extant examples of architectural ornament from the Roman world.

The temple was originally surrounded by an oval portico, the fragments of which enabled the original location of the former portico to be marked in the layout of the area completed by Norman Foster in 1993, intended to establish spatial continuity with the multipurpose art complex, the Carrée d'Art, built to his design across from the temple. The roof of the temple was restored at the same time with handcrafted tiles faithful to the originals.

BIBL.: Jean Ch. Balty, *Études sur la Maison Carrée de Nîmes* (Brussels 1960). Michael Bevington, "The Development of the Classical Revival at Stowe," *Architectura* (1992) 136–163. Desmond Guinness and Julius Trousdale Sadler, *Mr. Jefferson, Architect* (New York 1973). Wolfgang Herrmann, *Laugier and Eighteenth Century French Theory* (London 1962). Thomas J. McCormick, *Charles-Louis Clérisseau and the Genesis of Neo-Classicism* (New York 1990).

M.MC.

Mars

Roman god of war, thus symbol of a society that for centuries was thought of as essentially belligerent. Mars was identical with Greek Ares, although Ares never had a notorious position in the Greek pantheon. One of the most prominent and worshiped gods of Rome, Mars lent his name to a Roman district, the Campus Martius (Field of Mars), which announces even today his status as the city's protector and as father of the Roman people. Romulus, one of his twin sons born to the Vestal virgin Rhea Silvia, legendarily founded the city.

In the post-classical era Servius's commentary on Virgil's *Aeneid* (1.292) was the major source of knowledge of Mars's dual role as a keeper both of war and of peace. Servius refers to two temples of Mars: one outside the city that served as a temple for warriors, dedicated to Mars Gradivus, the god "that walks in battle"; the other inside the city, charged with guarding tranquility and dedicated to Mars Quirinus. (Originally, in old Italian beliefs, Mars had been associated with fertility, vegetation, and the protection of cattle; he became fused with Quirinus, previously the Sabine god of war.) Vitruvius (2.8.11), writing in the 1st century BCE, mentions a colossal acrolithic statue of Mars (a draped or gilded wooden body with marble head and extremities) that stood in a temple atop a hill in Halicarnassus.

During the revival of classical values and customs in 16th-century Venice, a colossal marble statue of Mars as a nude warrior was set next to one of Neptune in the inner court of the Doge's palace. Several ancient coins inscribed MARTE PACATORE (Mars the Peacemaker) display a nude, helmeted Mars holding an olive branch. His nudity is not merely a sign of his divinity, as was the case with artistic images of other Olympian gods; in the Renaissance it was also interpreted as a sign that he lacked fear in the face of danger—for example, in Sebastiano Erizzo's *On Ancient Medallions* (*Discorso sopra le medaglie antiche,* 1559, 120). Ancient coins also depict him wearing armor; an inscription that often accompanies this image aids in distinguishing Mars from a cuirassed emperor.

Mars is usually associated with a brutal, vigorous energy, driven by instincts rather than by reason. (He has none of the complexity attributed to his stepbrothers Apollo and Mercury.) As Marsilio Ficino notes in a passage that mingles the characteristics of planets with the roles of their homonymous gods in the ancient beliefs, only Venus dominates Mars, and he never dominates her (*On Love,* speech 5, chap. 8). Whether humorously portrayed as being caught in jealous Vulcan's net, or merely presented as a contented couple, depictions of the divine lovers were popular in art and literature during antiquity and in the Renaissance. Their images can be interpreted as signifying a union of opposites, of Love and Strife. The positive aspect of their union is alluded to in the name of their daughter Harmonia. Peaceful repose is symbolized by a disarmed, often sleeping Mars. But his sleep can be interrupted, as is evoked in the ritual incantation of the ancient Romans, *Mars vigila!*—"Mars, awaken!" The juxtaposition of Mars and Venus in a pictorial or literary work, regardless of their represented attitudes toward each other, is an expression of the brief, temporary nature of love and peace. At the same time, depending on the figure's posture and appearance, a depiction of Mars in the company of Venus can convey the destructive effect of love and of prolonged peace on a soldier and how it can lead to the loss of warlike spirit.

BIBL.: V. Brinkmann, ed., *Die Launen des Olymp: Der Mythos von Athena, Marsyas und Apoll* (Frankfurt 2008). K. Marano, *Apoll und Marsyas: Ikonologische Studien zu einem Mythos in der italienischen Renaissance* (Frankfurt 1998). U. Renner and M. Schneider, eds., *Häutung: Lesarten des Marsyas-Mythos* (Munich 2006). E. Wyss, *The Myth of Apollo and Marsyas in the Art of the Italian Renaissance* (Newark, Del. 1996).

L.FR.

Marsyas

Mythical Phrygian musician; with a pipe discarded by Minerva, he risked severe punishment to challenge Apollo and, when he lost, was flayed alive. The contest between the two musicians came to symbolize opposition: between two creatures, one a satyr (a man with a goat's legs, nose, and ears) and the other the anthropomorphic god of harmony; between the two types of composition, music spontaneously and intuitively created, and that which is tested against the metrical configurations of sound; between the effects of music on its listeners, either exciting and orgiastic or soothing and melodic; between two kinds of instruments, woodwinds played by blowing, using the body's strength, and strings played by striking while keeping the body and face still; between the two uses of the voice, for heavy breathing or for singing or reciting words; and between opposed participants in a contest to the death, one a victim condemned to martyrdom, the other a victor who will be glorified for eternity (Apuleius, *Florida* 3). When viewed sociopolitically, the contest between Marsyas and Apollo can be interpreted as a caveat to those who would dare to challenge authority. Pliny the Elder (35.66) refers to the painter Zeuxis' *Bound Marsyas* (5th cent. BCE), which hung in Rome's Temple of Concordia, probably placed there as a warning to those who might disturb the peace. This image was a powerful one: any representation of Marsyas as a bound satyr would instill an unavoidable feeling of tension to those viewing it, because a bound satyr is the very opposite of the typical image—frolicking creatures unrestrained both psychologically and physically, so often pictured dancing, playing music, and living by their instincts. Pliny's mention of Zeuxis' picture, along with the scenes from Marsyas' story in various classical statues, reliefs on sarcophagi, and gems, all had a strong influence on later visual renditions of the subject.

The myth also was seen as one that conveyed the edifying message manifested in Plato's comparison of Socrates and Marsyas in terms of external similarities and the enchantment of listeners. The difference between them was that the philosopher searched for the underlying hidden truth, while the flute player was satisfied by the effect produced by his music (*Symposium* 215). Apollo's excoriation of Marsyas became a metaphor for the freeing of the soul from its fleshy prison. Didactically, however, Apollo's action was used as an analogy for an anatomist's research to obtain knowledge of the structure of the human body. The skinless Marsyas became an artistic model for *écorché* (anatomical illustration), as seen in woodcut renderings published from the 16th century onward.

As an account of a musical contest, the myth was used to reflect on the artist's aspirations and the nature of art. Dante's verses (*Paradiso* 1.19–21) have him begging Apollo for inspiration, so that he too might be able to sing songs similar to those that the god had sung on the day when Marsyas was punished. Illustrations for this scene in Dante's poem, the first post-classical depictions of Marsyas, were done independently of antique images or artistic interpretations of Ovid's version of the story (*Metamorphoses* 6.382–400) and thus in retrospect today appear clearly dissimilar to subsequent representations that turned to ancient models with the revival of classical learning in the Renaissance. In 16th-century art Marsyas is often shown upside-down, occasionally with King Midas present at the contest, thus departing from the way the myth was recounted and depicted in antiquity while retaining the sculpturally shaped figures characteristic of ancient art. Most of these works explore the philosophical aspects of learning and artistic creativity.

BIBL.: V. Brinkmann, ed., *Die Launen des Olymp: Der Mythos von Athena, Marsyas und Apoll* (Frankfurt 2008). K. Marano, *Apoll und Marsyas: Ikonologische Studien zu einem Mythos in der italienischen Renaissance* (Frankfurt 1998). U. Renner and M. Schneider, eds., *Häutung: Lesarten des Marsyas-Mythos* (Munich 2006). E. Wyss, *The Myth of Apollo and Marsyas in the Art of the Italian Renaissance* (Newark, Del., 1996). L.FR.

Martial

Marcus Valerius Martialis (ca. 41–104 CE), Roman epigrammatist. His 14 books of epigrams embraced many topics: flattery of social superiors, satire of man's foibles, eroticism, and devotion to his Spanish heritage. Born in Bilbilis, a provincial city in ancient Hispania, he left for Rome after receiving a standard Roman education in Greek and rhetoric. Once in Rome, he wrote epigrams praising many patrons, most prominently the emperor Domitian. After Domitian's fall, Martial retired to Bilbilis, where he lived until his death.

Contemporary Romans valued Martial's work highly for its concentrated wit, bitterness, and frankness. His influence can be seen in the satires of Juvenal, a near contemporary. Many patristic writers (including Jerome) and grammarians of the 4th, 5th, and 6th centuries mined Martial's epigrams for adages. During the Middle Ages, however, knowledge of his work was limited to the highly educated, such as the circle around Charlemagne's court.

As the Renaissance moved through Europe, Martial became both a canonical and a controversial author. From the 13th through 17th centuries Humanists in Italy, France, Germany, Spain, and England rediscovered, edited, and printed Martial's texts, which sparked a resurgence of Neo-Latin and vernacular epigrams throughout Europe. In England, John Owen published three volumes of Neo-Latin epigrams between 1606 and 1612, earning the title "the British Martial." Martial's witty, satiric epigrams provided an alternative to the didactic and descriptive epigram based on the Greek Anthology. The pointed brevity of his epigrams made their style a popular form for taking sides in literary and scholarly debates, satirizing contemporary morals, or addressing social, religious, and political upheavals like the Reformation. Meanwhile, his epideictic (praise) poems illustrated how the epigram could cultivate literary patronage, especially at courts. Ben Jonson outdoes Martial in epideixis (if not sycophancy) in his Epigram 36, "To the Ghost of Martial":

> Martial, thou gav'st far nobler epigrams
> To thy Domitian, than I can my James;
> But in my royal subject I pass thee:
> Thou flattered'st thine, mine cannot flattered be.

Renaissance writers emulated the condensed wit of Martial in a number of movements: the pasquinade in Italy, the Baroque and Mannerist styles in France, metaphysical poetry in England, and *conceptismo* in Spain. Martial's admirers included some of the most famous Renaissance writers: Clement Marot, Joachim du Bellay, and Ben Jonson.

At the same time, Martial's obscenity created a dilemma for scholars. Humanists in Italy and France, the earliest modern groups to encounter his works, worried about their effect on young minds and criticized his eroticism. Catholic censors banned the poems, and editors throughout Europe expurgated, bowdlerized, or failed to annotate the more obscene items, although Martial himself, anticipating this practice, had warned, "Don't try to emasculate my little books" (1.35.14–15). Others solved this quandary by publishing only anthologies of Martial's more acceptable poems, rather than his complete works. Meanwhile, contemporary translators either censored objectionable material or Christianized it. In combination with the literary vogue for epigrams, these measures gave Martial a double reputation as an approved literary model and an obscene moral danger.

His status began to decline during the 18th century. Although Goethe and Schiller collaborated in writing a collection of "Xenia" in imitation of Martial, published in 1796, tastes were changing. As Romanticism privileged Greek literature, and literary critics condemned the epigram as spiteful or expository rather than witty, Martial became less influential. Robert Burns fused both spite and wit in his scathingly critical epigram "On Elphinstone's Translation of Martial's Epigrams" (1782):

> O Thou whom Poetry abhors,
> Whom Prose has turnèd out of doors,
> Heard'st thou yon groan?—proceed no further,
> 'Twas laurel'd Martial calling murther.

Although epigrams continued to be written after the 17th century, Martial himself generally became available only in expurgated or bowdlerized editions. Even as late as the 1960s, the Loeb Classical Library edition by E. H. Warmington translated the most obscene epigrams into Italian rather than English. For the past two centuries, Spain, however, has celebrated Martial as the first in a long line of illustrious Spanish writers. Interest in Martial increased greatly during the 20th century. As contemporary poets have translated and imitated his epigrams, critical inquiry has advanced steadily. Early 20th-century discussions of Martial's immorality have been superseded by explications of Martial's eroticism (Watson 2005), use of Epicurean philosophy, and his construction of a literary persona. More broadly, critics have debated his status as a classic (Mason 1988), the seriousness of his works, and his literary influence (Hartle 1995).

BIBL.: Paul Hartle, "'Quaint Epigrammatist': Martial in Late Seventeenth-Century England," *Neophilologus* 79, no. 2 (1995) 329–351. H. A. Mason, "Is Martial a Classic?" *Cambridge Quarterly* 17 (1988) 297–368. J. P. Sullivan, ed., *Martial* (New York 1993). Patricia Watson, "*Non Tristis Torus et Tamen Pudicus:* The Sexuality of the *Matrona* in Martial," *Mnemosyne* 58, no. 1 (2005) 62–87.

M.T.C. and J.GO.

Martianus Capella

Virtually nothing is certain about the author Martianus Capella beyond his name. His single work, *De nuptiis Mercurii et Philologiae,* bespeaks a North African origin, and although it has been dated as early as the end of the 3rd century and as late as the first third of the 6th century, its completion and publication are likely to have fallen between 410 and 429. (In light of comments Martianus makes, one might imagine his birth falling between 360 and 380. For comparison, Augustine was born in 354, Macrobius in 360, and Servius in 370. Martianus Capella lived possibly until the early or mid-5th century.) His activity at Carthage, the region's cultural center, is entirely likely.

Formally, *De nuptiis* belongs to the tradition of Menippean satire, a combination of alternating prose and verse sections (in multiple meters) to which Petronius' *Satyricon,* Seneca's *Apocolocyntosis,* and Boethius' *Consolation of Philosophy* also belong. Varro likewise wrote a *prosimetrum,* and Martianus also follows Varro in his focus on the encyclopedic arts.

The story of the marriage of Mercury (the "mind" of Jupiter and thus divine knowledge) with Philology (human knowledge) occupies the first two of the work's nine books. The remaining seven are devoted to the canonical *septem artes*—grammar, dialectic, rhetoric, geometry, arithmetic, astronomy, and music—all of which appear (along with other figures) as personification allegories. The whole is framed as instruction for Martianus' son (who is not merely addressed but also speaks; cf. Augustine's *De magistro*) and plays out on an elaborate two-tiered stage. "The *fabula,* the play on the upper stage, is a vision—a work which has come during the time of dreams and has awakened the poet" (Lemoine 1972, 39).

To judge from the work, Martianus would appear to be pagan, but "he does not believe any more than the Christians in the ancient conception of Greek mythology" (Courcelle 1969, 214). Rather, "combin[ing] Stoic, Neoplatonic, Hermetic, Neopythagorean and Orphic elements in the construction of his own philosophic and religious world-view," Martianus creates his own complex philosophical allegory to make *De nuptiis* "a cosmic myth . . . in which wisdom and the divine gift of intellect join to raise mankind to the stars" (Lemoine 1972, 68, 70). How much Martianus drew directly on Greek sources is open to debate.

Many over the following millennium found irresistible Martianus' eclectic mixture of exotic allegorical fantasy and esoteric learning with a pedagogical theme, but the work's challenging style and content begged for commentary. The 5th-century mythographer Fulgentius, who certainly knew it, may well have written a commentary (now lost) on the first two books. In the 6th century Gregory of Tours cites him, the first to refer to the author as Martianus. It was with the "third generation" of Carolingian scholars (mid-9th century) that *De nuptiis* took a significant place in Carolingian school culture. Over the years, commentators included Martin of Laon and Remigius of Auxerre. In the early 11th century Notker Labeo translated the first two books (interwoven with commentary) into Old High German. Ratherius of Verona called the book *mirabile,* and Wibald of Corvey (in a letter dated to 1149) calls it *illo Marciani Capellae multiplici et enigmatico epithalamio* (Lemoine 1972, 3).

De nuptiis was prized for its enigmas as well as for its learning, its first two books attracting the most attention. In the High Middle Ages many manuscripts offered only books 1 and 2 (Lutz 1971, 369; of the later books, sometimes book 8, on astronomy, circulated independently, but there was no lack of manuscripts for all nine books), and some commentators—Alexander Neckam, for example—also restricted their attention to the first two books. Of Bernardus Sylvester's commentary we have only portions on the first book. Indeed, it is impossible to separate medieval reception of *De nuptiis* from the commentaries to which it gave rise. It is in some of these that we find full enunciation of the influential doctrine of the integument (*integumentum*), a myth or philosophical fiction "covering" a true meaning. (*Integumentum* is distinguished from *allegoria,* which *stricto sensu* presents historical [that is, scriptural] truth via a figured narration; both are species of *involucrum.* Westra translates *integumentum* as "secular allegory"; Westra 1986, 23.)

Study of *De nuptiis* as *integumentum* proved richly productive of mythographic literature first in Latin—notably the highly influential prosimetrical allegories of Chartians such as Bernard and Alan of Lille—and subsequently in various vernaculars. Even if Macrobius and Boethius were more frequently named, the more esoteric Martianus contributed to a literary culture and tradition that included Dante, the *Roman de la rose,* Chaucer, and

Spenser (not to mention a host of lesser-known allegories such as *Le mariage des sept arts*). One must not forget Martianus' influence within the separate traditions of each of the individual *artes,* for example, music or astronomy. It was as an authority on the constellations that the character "Chaucer" thinks of him as he is borne aloft into the high heavens by the eagle in *The House of Fame* (2.985). Later in his career Chaucer amusingly has his Merchant—one of the many Canterbury pilgrims debating the good of marriage—apostrophize "thou poete Marcian,/That writest us that ilke weddyng murie/of hire Philologie and hym Mercurie,/And of the songes that the Muses songe!/To smal is bothe thy penne, and eek thy tonge,/For to descryven" the nuptials of January and May in "The Merchant's Tale" (*Canterbury Tales,* "The Merchant's Tale," 520–525).

Alfonso de la Torre combined material drawn from Martianus and the very Latin traditions in which he worked (encyclopedic: Isidore; allegorical: Alan of Lille) with material from different traditions (e.g., Maimonides' *Guide of the Perplexed,* al-Ghazālī) to create his *Visión deleytable de la filosofía y artes liberales* (ca. 1440; published ca. 1485), a remarkable late-medieval blossoming of Marcianic eclecticism. Martianus' detailed descriptions had long inspired not just visions but visual representations, from figures gracing French cathedrals to Botticelli's *Young Man Being Introduced to the Seven Liberal Arts* (1484–1486, now in the Louvre). Martianus also inspired a rich vein of Renaissance mythography, as evidenced in well-known image collections like those of Lilio Gregorio Giraldi and Cesare Ripa. The allegorical ceremony described in *De nuptiis* also inspired court pageants, including magnificent weddings of nobility (Virginia de' Medici and Cesare d'Este, in Florence, 1586) and even royalty (Margaret of Austria and Philip III of Spain, in Mantua, 1598), when scenes from *De nuptiis* were interpolated into a performance of Guarini's *Pastor fido.* It was in these contexts that the first Italian translations of the first two books of *De nuptiis* were effected (Moretti 1995).

The Latin text of *De nuptiis* received its *editio princeps* in 1499 and was reprinted with some frequency. In the 16th century Copernicus praised Martianus for observing that Mercury and Venus revolve around the Sun, and at the end of the next century, no less a critic than Hugo Grotius published an edition of Martianus (1599). Leibniz contemplated undertaking a new edition, a task that, despite his admiration of Martianus, he never fulfilled. It may be a stretch—and is certainly a leap—but it is tempting to read Roberto Calasso's *Le nozze di Cadmo e Armonia* (1988; English trans., *The Marriage of Cadmus and Harmony,* 1993) as a contemporary reflection of Martianus.

BIBL.: Pierre Courcelle, *Late Latin Writers and Their Greek Sources,* trans. H. E. Wedeck (Cambridge, Mass., 1969). Fanny Lemoine, *Martianus Capella: A Literary Re-evaluation,* Münchener Beiträge zur Mediävistik und Renaissance-Forschung 10 (Munich 1972). Cora E. Lutz, "Martianus Capella," in *Catalogus Translationum et Commentariorum* [*CTC*], ed. P. O. Kristeller and F. E. Cranz, vol. 2 (Washington, D.C., 1971) 367–381 (especially "Fortuna," 367–369); see also "Addenda et Corrigenda," in *CTC* 3 (1976) 449–451, and H. J. Westra, in *CTC* 6 (1986) 185–186. Gabriella Moretti, ed., *I primi volgarizzamenti italiani delle "Nozze di Mercurio e Filologia"* (Trent 1995). Bernhard Pabst, *Prosimetrum: Tradition und Wandel einer Literaturform zwischen Spätantike und Spätmittelalter,* 2 vols. (Cologne 1994) 1:105–133, 211–222, 229–249. William Harris Stahl et al., *Martianus Capella and the Seven Liberal Arts,* 2 vols. (London 1971). Haijo Jan Westra, ed., *The Commentary on Martianus Capella's De Nuptiis Philologiae et Mercurii Attributed to Bernardus Silvestris* (Toronto 1986). James Alfred Willis, ed., *De nuptiis Philologiae et Mercurii* (Leipzig 1983). R.H.

Marxism

Karl Marx (1818–1883) and Friedrich Engels (1820–1895) were well acquainted with antiquity. A thorough grounding in the classics was a fundamental part of 19th-century German secondary education. Marx obtained a doctoral degree in ancient philosophy; Engels was an inspired autodidact. With some exceptions they offer in their writings no coherent treatment of antiquity, but scattered remarks appear in a number of texts of diverse sorts, from great scholarly works like *Capital* (*Das Kapital,* 1864–1894) down to political pamphlets, newspaper articles, and letters.

In *The Communist Manifesto* (1848), Marx and Engels counted the fight of slaves against free men as one of the class struggles that had determined the course of history. But they did not seriously believe in a class struggle carried out by slaves. In *Capital* Marx stresses that in antiquity class struggle had taken place between creditors and debtors, with the result that in ancient Rome plebeian debtors were replaced by slaves as a workforce. Statements of systematic importance occur where Marx and Engels attempt to integrate classical antiquity into a model of human history. This likewise holds true for *German Ideology* (*Die deutsche Ideologie*), written in 1845–1846 but not published during the authors' lifetimes; here early Roman history is understood as revealing the step from collective to individual property, which implied the emergence of chattel slavery.

Most famous in this vein are some pages of Engels's *Anti-Dühring* (late 1870s). Here he declares slavery a necessary step for the course of human progress: "Without slavery, no Greek state, no Greek art and science; without slavery, no Roman Empire. But without the basis laid by Hellenism and the Roman Empire, no modern Europe either . . . Without the slavery of antiquity, no modern socialism . . . We are compelled to say . . . that the introduction of slavery under the then prevailing conditions was a great step forward." According to Engels, this development did not apply to the realms of "oriental despotism" (e.g., the Persian empires), which knew neither private property nor chattel slavery. In his famous statement in the preface to *A Contribution to the Critique of Political Economy* (1859), he had written: "At a certain stage of their development, the material productive forces of society come in conflict with the existing relations of production . . . From forms of development of the productive forces these relations turn into their fetters. Then begins an epoch of social revolution . . . In broad outlines Asiatic, ancient, feudal, and modern bourgeois modes of production can be designated as progressive epochs in the economic formation of society." Marx himself did not develop a theory of ancient economy according to this concept. Engels's hastily written *Origin of the Family, Private Property and the State* (1884) could not fill this gap. It showed a shift of interest toward the primordial stages of social organization that allegedly could be reconstructed by the ethnological evidence collected by Lewis Henry Morgan. Engels also seemed to accept the enormous estimate of the number of slaves in Athens that had been reported by Athenaeus (272c). This is not so surprising, as Hume's correction of this famous figure (*Of the Populousness of Ancient Nations,* 1752) had not been generally accepted. But Engels does not speak of 400,000 (Athenaeus' figure) but of 365,000 slaves. He simply followed the rounding off that August Böckh had suggested in his *Staatshaushaltung der Athener* (1817).

As for the lasting influence of Marxian ideas concerning antiquity, one must differentiate between their considerable influence with respect to a realistic view of ancient society that takes seriously its material basis, and the development of (party-official) dogmas formulating indisputable laws of history. The latter attempts were based on combining paragraphs of Marx's and Engels's writings from different times and with diverse intentions, often quoted without considering (or even while suppressing) the respective contexts, as, for example, when statements concerning slavery in North America were applied to ancient slavery as well. Discussion of the Stalinist doctrine of an "epoch of slave revolution" and the accompanying theory of economic formations, as well as debate on the place of the "Asiatic mode of production" in respect to universal history have proved fertile only in the sense that in the long run even scholars in Communist regimes realized their doubtfulness. But it was the challenge of Marxism that led scholars of (almost) all ideological stances to abandon an idealistic picture of classical antiquity and undertake research on the material foundations of ancient cultures, and to investigate thoroughly all implications of slavery and other forms of forced labor.

BIBL.: Special issues, *Arethusa* 8 (1975) and *Helios* 26 (1999). Wilhelm Backhaus, *Marx, Engels und die Sklaverei* (Düsseldorf 1974). Heinz Heinen, ed., *Die Geschichte des Altertums im Spiegel der sowjetischen Forschung* (Darmstadt 1980). Lawrence Krader, *The Asiatic Mode of Production: Sources, Development and Critique in the Writings of Karl Marx* (Assen 1975). Wilfried Nippel, "Marx, Weber und die Sklaverei," in *Unfreie Arbeits- und Lebensverhältnisse von der Antike bis in die Gegenwart,* ed. Elisabeth Herrmann-Otto (Hildesheim 2005) 317–356, French trans. *Anabases* 2 (2005) 11–52. Geoffrey E. M. de Ste. Croix, *The Class Struggle in the Ancient Greek World* (London 1981).

W.N.

Masada

Cliff-top fortress in the Judean Desert. Masada was the last fortress to hold out against the Romans during the Jewish Great Revolt (66–73 CE). According to Josephus, our only source, Masada's defenders chose death over captivity and committed mass suicide as they sensed imminent defeat. In modern Israeli culture the story and the site of Masada became powerful national symbols.

Masada (Hebrew *metzadāh*) is located in Israel on the southeastern edge of the Judean Desert (N31°18′48.6″ E35°21′09.9″), on the flat top of an arrestingly beautiful, steep rock near the Dead Sea. Masada is mentioned by Strabo (16.2.44), Pliny the Elder (5.15.73), and, following him, Solinus (*Collectanea* 35.9–12). The history of the site, however, is known to us only from the writings of Flavius Josephus (ca. 38–ca. 100 CE), mainly *The Jewish War* (7). According to Josephus, Masada was first fortified in the Hasmonean period (140–37 BCE) and further developed by Herod (d. 4 BCE) into a lavish royal shelter. In the final stages of the revolt, the Romans laid siege to Masada, held at that time by the Sicarii (Dagger Bearers), a violent group led by Eleazar, son of Jair. When the Roman army breached the wall of the fortress, Eleazar, in two polished speeches, persuaded his followers, 960 people including women and children, to commit collective suicide and torch the compound rather than fall captive. Only a few survivors remained to tell the story to the astounded Romans.

Josephus, a Jewish commander captured in the early stages of the revolt, shifted allegiance and spent the rest of his life as a Flavian client in Rome. There he wrote *The Jewish War* in Aramaic (now lost) and Greek versions, and other works of Jewish apologetics. From late antiquity onward the Church saw in Josephus a necessary complement to Scripture, and his works were widely circulated in Byzantium and Europe. Josephus appeared very early in print and was translated into several vernacular languages. It is not surprising therefore that Masada is regularly mentioned by medieval and early modern Europeans (sometimes as Masara or Mezira) and that it appears on maps of the Holy Land from those eras. But the site never assumed a symbolic significance comparable to that of the destruction of the Temple as God's punishment to the Jews. Similarly, the Holy Maccabees (4 Mac.) provided Christians with a fitter example of pious martyrdom than the rebels of Masada. For some radical thinkers of the Enlightenment, Masada represented the barbarity of Judaism (and hence of Christianity). Rabbinic literature is silent about Masada, which is perhaps a sign of disapproval of the militant Sicarii. Although Josephus' books were largely unknown to medieval Jews, a variation on the story of Masada was accessible through the *Josippon,* a 10th-century Hebrew text based on *Hegesippus,* a 4th-century Latin adaptation of Josephus. Still, Masada did not play a meaningful role in premodern Jewish memory.

All this changed with the emergence of Jewish nationalism and secular historiography in the 19th century. Josephus' tale, translated into modern Hebrew (1923) and read as a factual account of a sober historian of the nation, inspired youth movements in the early 20th century to take the strenuous and risky pilgrimage to Masada (the site was first identified in 1838 by the Americans Edward Robertson and Eli Smith). Yitzhak Lamdan's poem "Masada" (1927), especially his words "never again shall Masada fall!" had a major influence on the perception of Masada as a metaphor for the determined yet frail Jewish community in Palestine. After the Holocaust and the establishment of the State of Israel, Masada represented heroic resistance and activism, as the bloody suicide was played down. The last warriors of the Second Temple period seemed now the direct predecessors of the new Jews, who negated the exilic curse of repeated persecution. The construction of the myth of Masada intensified in the mid-1960s, when comprehensive Israeli excavations, led by Yigael Yadin and supported by an international volunteer corps, uncovered a wealth of archaeological finds (including a synagogue), which partly confirmed Josephus' descriptions, although not the collective suicide. Masada's defenders were now officially honored as national heroes, and the site was gradually incorporated into civic and military ritual, with, for example, nightlong marches ending in ceremonies atop the rock. Following the excavation and restoration of the site, it became a hugely popular tourist destination. Increased visibility brought alternative interpretations of the story in its wake. Critics, particularly after the 1973 war, referred to the "Masada complex" that gripped the Israeli psyche, questioned the educational value of the murderous Sicarii, and reexamined the legality of the ancient mass suicide. Masada became a contested political symbol, adopted by right-wing hardliners and rejected just as strongly by their opponents. Scholars pointed to discrepancies between the newly spun myth and Josephus' account. Others analyzed his literary tactics in view of his pro-Roman ideology, for after all, it is Josephus who is the real father of the myth of Masada.

In 2001 UNESCO declared Masada a World Heritage Site, referring to its archaeological significance, its meaning for Jewish identity, and, refreshingly, its value as a universal symbol of the human struggle for liberty.

BIBL.: Nachman Ben-Yehuda, *Sacrificing Truth: Archaeology and the Myth of Masada* (Amherst, N.Y., 2002). Flavius Josephus, *The Jewish War,* trans. H. St. J. Thackeray, 3 vols. (Cambridge, Mass., 1997). Pierre Vidal-Naquet, "Flavius Josephus and Masada," in *The Jews: History, Memory, and the Present* (New York 1996) 20–36. Yigael Yadin, *Masada: Herod's Fortress and the Zealots' Last Stand* (London 1966). Yael Zerubavel, *Recovered Roots: Collective Memory and the Making of Israeli National Tradition* (Chicago 1995). Z.SH.

Matriarchy

The idea of societies ruled by women is found in classical literature in the legends of the Amazons and the celebrated account of the Lycians in Herodotus (*Histories* 1.173). Early terms for such societies in English were *gunarchy* (i.e., gynarchy)—used by Holinshed in 1587 in his *Chronicles of England, Scotland and Ireland* to describe the rule of King Lear's daughter, "Queen Cordeilla"—or *gynaeococracy* (Coke 1660, 100).

Reports of female-dominated peoples in ancient literature and in contemporary travelers' tales became the object of renewed attention in the 18th century, especially from scholars trained in the classics and in law. Inspired by the example of Montesquieu, the "Newton" of the social universe, to seek the "spirit of the laws" governing the vast range of human societies, Enlightenment scholars collected and compared data about the laws and customs of historically or geographically remote and exotic peoples. In section 2 of his pioneering *Origin of the Distinction of Ranks* (1771), John Millar, a student and colleague of Adam Smith at Glasgow, where he was professor of law, drew on both classical literature and travelers' accounts of contemporary peoples—such as the inhabitants of the Malabar coast of India, the island of Formosa (Taiwan), and the native Americans of the Jesuit missionary Father Lafitau's popular *Moeurs des sauvages américains* (1724)—to review the phenomena of matriliny (determination of identity, position, and inheritance rights by descent through the female line) and matrilocality (residence of the male in the house of his mother's family and, after marriage, in that of his wife's family). For their part, classical scholars, responding to the redefinition of their discipline as *Altertumswissenschaft* rather than traditional philology, began to study ancient myths as residual evidence of prehistoric conditions. In a 10-page appendix—"On the Historical Basis of the Legend of the Killing of Their Menfolk by the Women of Lemnos"—to his *Die Aeschylische Trilogie Prometheus* (1824), Friedrich Welcker gathered together much of the classical and some of the modern literature concerning primitive societies in which mothers rather than fathers allegedly played the dominant role. No one, however, distinguished between a matrilineal or matrilocal form of social organization and a gynaeococracy, or society in which women wield supreme power. Nor did anyone suggest that supposedly women-dominated societies were anything but exceptional, deviations from the norm.

The introduction of the term *matriarchy* in the second half of the 19th century coincided with the emergence of anthropology as a distinct discipline, the object of which is a general science of ancient societies; it reflected a new evolutionist view of the social world, according to which the pattern of development of *all* human societies was said to be from a prehistoric, primitive condition, sometimes described as "promiscuity" (though this term was questioned by some evolutionists), by way of a period of relatively stable relations between the sexes in which women are dominant and kinship and inheritance are determined by the mother (matriarchy), to the form of social organization characteristic of all advanced or civilized societies, in which fathers are predominant (patriarchy). In 19th-century usage, *matriarchy* could refer to matriliny, matrilocality, or gynaeococracy. It was still generally assumed, however, that all three occurred together. Only later was it observed that they do not necessarily coincide. "Matriliny," Robert Briffault pointed out, "is compatible with a very depressed status for women, as, for example, among the majority of Australian tribes" (1927, 70; see also Stagl 1990, 7).

The evolutionary process itself was usually defined in materialist terms. Shifts from one form of social organization to another were attributed to changes in the way society provides for its needs. One major figure, however, the Swiss jurist and classical scholar Johann Jacob Bachofen, working from an extensive study of ancient myth and guided by Neoplatonic philosophical speculations rather than the empirical tradition of Montesquieu and Smith, presented the history of society as, above all, a development from lower to higher forms of religion and spirituality (*Das Mutterrecht*, 1861). The three-stage account of social evolution that Bachofen was the first to articulate was accepted nevertheless, thanks in part to Alexis Giraud-Teulon's elegant French summary of the massive German original (*Les Origines de la famille,* 1874), even by those who, like J. F. McLennan, L. H. Morgan, Marx, and Engels, supported a materialist explanation of how the evolution occurred and what it meant.

As Bachofen understood it, the social evolution of humanity was the consequence of a religious development from primitive fertility cults, through the worship of mother goddesses, to the emergence of purely spiritual divinities such as Athena and Apollo; it was manifested politically as a movement from anarchy to the highest realization of ethical humanity in Roman law and the state. As understood by Engels, in contrast, social evolution was a movement from primitive communism to an oppressive patriarchal regime determined by exclusive property rights and relations. Even though he regarded the third, patriarchal stage of development as the highest, however, Bachofen painted the second, matriarchal stage in glowing colors and considered it vital that it be remembered with love and respect, not repressed and denied. By rebelling against the violence of primitive promiscuity and establishing the first laws, women, Bachofen insisted, had been the founders of human civilization.

The theory of matriarchy historicized the institution of marriage as it is known in all Western societies, along with the power and property relations associated with it, and challenged the common view that the prevailing patriarchal order is the only natural one, so that any deviation from it is an anomaly or a perversion. Marx read Morgan and Bachofen attentively, and the Marxist canon soon included Engels's *Origins of the Family* (1884), in which the violent subjection and exploitation of the female by the male appears as the opening move in a process leading ultimately to modern capitalist society and the exploitation of the working class by the property-owning class. In *Aeschylus and Athens* (1941) the Marxist classical scholar George Thomson gave Bachofen's interpretation of Aeschylean tragedy in terms of the struggle between martriarchy and patriarchy an appropriately materialist turn. Though Freud himself remained reserved, the implications of Bachofen's matriarchy hypothesis for the new field of psychoanalysis were eagerly explored by those outside the orthodox Freudian mainstream—C. G. Jung, Erich Fromm, Wilhelm Reich, and Otto Gross. For obvious reasons, the theory of matriarchy was taken up with special fervor by feminist scholars. Jane Harrison, the first important female classical scholar in England and the founder of the influential Cambridge Ritualist School, was one of its most ardent advocates at the turn of the 20th century. She shared Bachofen's view of the fundamental role of religion in the evolution of social organization (*Prolegomena to the Study of Greek Religion,* 1903; *Themis,* 1912).

From the beginning, the absence of hard empirical evidence for the evolutionist thesis was one of the chief arguments of those who—like Sir Henry Maine, the author of *Ancient Law* (1861)—continued to hold that the patriarchal organization of society was the norm and the matriarchal the exception (*Dissertations on Early Law and Custom,* 1883). Whatever ideological motives inspired the critics of matriarchy, in other words, their position did not lack scholarly justification. In the early 20th century the evolutionist thesis was further undermined by developments in the discipline of anthropology itself. Along with other disciplines in the humanities and social sciences, anthropology turned its back on inquiries into historical evolution, regarded as speculative and unscientific, and committed itself instead to empirical functional and structural studies of observable societies. The few who remained true to the theory of matriarchy tended to be marginal or nonprofessional (e.g., Robert Briffault, Robert Graves); others tried to extricate it from its evolutionist framework (e.g., Wilhelm Schmidt). With some exceptions (Evelyn Reed, Françoise d'Eaubonne), even feminists gave up on the idea that there were once societies in which women played a dominant, governing role. A few argued, not implausibly, that the whole evolutionist theory of matriarchy, especially in the form it took in the influential writings of Bachofen, was in fact ideologically weighted against women (Janssen-Jurreit 1976; Eller 2000).

BIBL.: Joan Bamberger, "The Myth of Matriarchy: Why Men Rule in Primitive Society," in *Women, Culture and Society,* ed. Michelle Zimbalist Rosaldo and Louise Lamphere (Stanford 1974) 263–280. Robert Briffault, *The Mothers* (London 1927). Roger Coke, *Elements of Power and Subjection, wherein is demonstrated the cause of all humane, Christian and legal society* (London 1660). Johannes Dörmann: "War Johann Jakob Bachofen Evolutionist?" *Anthropos* 60 (1985) 1–48. Margaret Ehrenberg, *Women in Prehistory* (London 1989). Cynthia Eller, *The Myth of Matriarchal Prehistory* (Boston 2000). Marie-Luise Janssen-Jurreit, *Sexismus: Über die Abtreibung der Frauenfrage* (Munich 1976). Karl Meuli, "Entstehung, Wesen und Nachwirkung des 'Mutterrechts,'" in J. J. Bachofen, *Gesammelte Werke,* vol. 3 (Basel 1948) 1079–1117. David Schneider and Kathleen Gough, eds., *Matrilineal Kinship* (Berkeley 1961). Justin Stagl, "Johann Jakob Bachofen, 'Das Mutterrecht' und die Folgen," *Anthropos* 85 (1990) 11–37. L.G.

Mausoleum

A vast tomb in Halicarnassus (present-day Bodrum, Turkey), commemorating Mausolus, satrap of Caria 377–353 BCE. Artemisia, sister and wife of Mausolus, commissioned the Mausoleum as his tomb, his memorial, and the focus of extensive funerary rituals. According to Pliny, writing in the first century CE, the architect was Pytheos of Priene. His design, 140 feet high, combined a rectangular podium with an Ionic colonnade and a pyramidal roof, supporting a statue of Mausolus in a quadriga. Four of the most skilled sculptors of the time, Scopas, Bryaxis, Timotheos, and Leochares, were engaged to embellish its surfaces. The Mausoleum quickly achieved its own fame, earning a place in Antipater's list (2nd cent. BCE) of seven great "sights" or wonders of the world.

Of the tomb, little survives in situ beyond the reconstructed burial chamber and access staircase, foundations, and a scattering of architectural fragments (sufficient to indicate the extraordinary quality of workmanship). The upper sections probably collapsed in an earthquake, and from 1494 through 1522 the Knights of St. John of Malta dismantled what remained to fortify their castle at Bodrum. Charles Newton led excavations at the site beginning in 1857, sending much of the surviving sculpture to the British Museum. Kristian Jeppesen conducted more systematic excavations from 1966 to 1977.

Conceptually, the Mausoleum was not unique. During the 1st millennium BCE, rulers around the Mediterranean had erected grand tombs; Mausolus' was simply the grandest of its time, and it came to be synonymous with the concept. When the first Roman emperor, Augustus, built a massive tomb for his dynasty, it quickly became known as his mausoleum, despite its circular ground plan. Thereafter the term could be applied to any large-scale tomb, especially, though not exclusively, to those of the imperial family. Implicit in the word was grandeur, and something akin to heroization of those buried within. A popular form soon crystallized for the ruling elite, not the rectangular design of Mausolus' tomb but a conflation of Augustus' circular plan with the domed interior of the Pantheon, itself a descendant of Hellenic ruler-cult buildings.

Form and concept passed together into the early Christian world as martyria (martyries), like the Church of the Holy Sepulcher in Jerusalem and the Mausoleum of Santa Costanza in Rome. In the medieval period, however, they diverged. The centralized plan survives in medieval and Renaissance church architecture, sometimes with specifically funerary associations, as at Torres del Rio, Navarre, in Spain, where the 12th-century funerary Church of the Holy Sepulcher is octagonal in plan. Similarly, Bramante's round Tempietto at San Pietro in Montorio in Rome (ca. 1505) commemorates the site of Saint Peter's crucifixion. The centralized plan of antique mausolea even inspired the Islamic Dome of the Rock in Jerusalem (687–692). As a concept, however, mausolea were less prevalent in the medieval and Renaissance periods. Believing that the living could intercede on behalf of the dead, the elite generally buried their dead in churches, so that the church, in a sense, became a mausoleum. A renowned example is the early Gothic Church of St. Denis in Paris, burial place of Carolingian and early Capetian royalty. Most early burials of this sort were in wall niches known as arcosolia, but tombs quickly took on grand dimensions and architectonic form. Often burials were in chapels within or adjoining the church; King Henry VII's Chapel at Westminster, of the early 16th century, is among the most lavish.

The notion of building freestanding monumental sepulchers reemerged among post-Reformation Protestants, whose liturgy did not include prayers in behalf of the dead. Beginning in Scotland, the trend spread to England, where a renowned mausoleum was built on the grounds of Castle Howard for Charles Howard, Earl of Carlisle, in 1726. Nicholas Hawksmoor's design, probably based on reconstructions of ancient ruins by the antiquarians Palladio and Bartoli, spawned numerous imitators. As religious attitudes relaxed with the Enlightenment, monumental tombs inspired by classical prototypes became features of English and subsequently of Continental gardens, where they served as evocations of classical landscapes, as cenotaphs or as genuine mausolea. Meanwhile architects from Sir Christopher Wren to Étienne-Louis Boullée and George Dance concocted magnificent mausolea on paper that were based on classical prototypes. The attraction of the concept, as Pytheos had discovered in the 4th century BCE, was the freedoms it offered the architect to fantasize over and experiment with form without excessive regard for practical necessities.

BIBL.: Howard Colvin, *Architecture and the After-Life* (New Haven 1991). K. Jeppesen, F. Hojlund, and K. Aaris-Sorensen, *The Maussolleion at Halikarnassos,* vol. 1, *The Sacrificial Deposit* (Aarhus 1981). K. Jeppesen and A. Luttrell, *The Maussolleion at Halikarnassos,* vol. 2, *The Written Sources and Their Archaeological Background* (Aarhus 1986). G. B. Waywell, *The Free-Standing Sculptures of the Mausoleum at Halicarnassus* (London 1978). P.J.D.

Maxims

The maxim (originally *maxima propositio,* "a very general statement") is a short comment on human affairs, often but not always from a moralizing point of view, expressed in an elegantly laconic form. In Greek maxims were known as *aphorismoi* (originally "definitions") or *apophthegmata* ("sayings"), in Latin as *gnomologiae* or *sententiae* (from which we derive the term "sententious"). They were often collected independently (a literary genre in itself), as in the case of the *Aphorisms* of Hippocrates and the *Apophthegmata* of Plutarch, but also featured in works of philosophy and history, such as the writings of Seneca and Tacitus. Jurists also collected rules in order to simplify decision making.

These traditions continued during the Middle Ages, becoming fused or confused with the popular wisdom of the proverb. The aphorisms of Hippocrates were taught at Chartres and elsewhere. The maxim was consciously revived during the Renaissance, when Seneca and Tacitus became fashionable authors. Erasmus made his reputation as a scholar with his *Adagia,* a collection of maxims with commentaries (which swelled into an essay in such instances as *dulce bellum inexpertis,* "War is sweet to those who have never experienced it"). Machiavelli and Guicciardini offer famous examples of the trend. Despite his criticism of Machiavelli for generalizing too easily and neglecting local circumstances, the explanations Guicciardini offers in his *Storia d'Italia* (ca. 1540) are often couched in the form of aphorisms.

The tradition of the maxim reached its peak in the 17th century, despite or because of increasing divergence from the classical model. Writers on medicine still followed Hippocrates, including Herman Boerhaave with Latin aphorisms "on the recognition and cure of diseases" (1709) and Thomas Tryon, whose *Aphorisms* (1691) was subtitled "rules, physical, moral, and, divine, for preserving the health of the body, and the peace of the mind." But the domain of the maxim was greatly extended at this time. Both following and diverging from Seneca, Francis Bacon employed the aphoristic mode in his legal, moral, and scientific writings. Published collections of aphorisms ranged from law to botany, from theology to chemistry, and from happiness (John Stearne) to warfare (Raimondo Montecuccoli). The traditional analogy between the human body and the state or "body politic" encouraged political writers in particular to employ this genre, as in the case of the *Aphorismi Politici* (1635) of Tommaso Campanella, the *Aphorisms Political* (1656) of James Harrington, and the *Aphorisms of State* (1661) attributed to Sir Walter Raleigh.

This extension of domain was not the only divergence from the classical model. In an age in which geometry was believed by many to offer a model of good intellectual method, the tradition of the maxim was influenced by that of the axiom. Even more important was the shift from morals to psychology, exemplified in three masterpieces. The first was Baltasar Gracián's *Oráculo manual* (1647), a collection of 300 brief *aforismos* such as *saber olvidar,* "Know how to forget," with a paragraph of commentary unpacking each one. The second was the Duc de La Rochefoucauld's *Maximes* (1665), which was closer to the oral tradition of the *bon mot,* the witty remark made in public (this was the age of the *salon*), and aimed at producing an impression of spontaneity: for example, "Hypocrisy is the homage that vice pays to virtue." The third was Blaise Pascal's posthumously published *Pensées* (1670), which includes the famous maxim "The heart has its reasons that reason does not know." Besides these collections, aphorisms continued to appear in other works, notably works of history.

The maxim was not only a mode of writing, it was also a mode of reading, linked to the tradition of "commonplaces." Students were taught at school to make excerpts from their reading in a notebook under various headings, so as to be able to draw on this material if they needed to make a speech or write a report. Maxims obviously lent themselves to this kind of treatment, and publishers often drew attention to them by means of references or pointing figures in the margins of books in which they occurred (a practice that goes back to medieval manuscripts). That the works of theologians, philosophers, historians, and others were often read with eyes on the lookout for these generalizations is suggested by the publication of anthologies of maxims from particular writers, most notably Tacitus, whose histories (like the writings of Machiavelli) were reduced to maxims, inspiring thousands of pages of commentary and application. This tendency is confirmed by the custom of providing editions of classical and occasionally modern texts with indexes of maxims (often described as *gnomologiae*). Among the ancient authors who received this treatment were Homer, Plato, Demosthenes, and among historians Curtius, Dionysius of Halicarnassus, and Herodian. Modern authors whose maxims have been anthologized or indexed range from Calvin to Guicciardini.

The interest in Guicciardini's maxims is a paradoxical one, for the author criticized his friend Machiavelli for believing in the possibility of formulating general rules of human behavior. It was only very gradually and for the most part after 1750 that this faith in generalization declined, and the maxim with it. In the 18th century, collections of maxims (notably those of Georg Christoph Lichtenberg) acquired a more personal tone, suggesting that they were no more than the expressions of individual points of view. The epigrams of Friedrich Nietzsche and Oscar Wilde belong to this later tradition, like the *Aphorisms* of John Morley (1887) and of the philosopher F. H. Bradley (1930). For Nietzsche, at least, the choice of this literary form expressed not only his personal predilection but also his vision of philosophy. But a split in the later 19th century between what C. P. Snow famously called the "two cultures" was virtually fatal to the traditional maxim. On one side, historians, philosophers, and writers now emphasized the uniqueness of each event, person, or culture and became increasingly suspicious of generalization. On the other side, sociologists, psychologists, and others who still believed in general statements about human behavior preferred to present them in a scientific rather than a literary manner.

BIBL.: Sydney Anglo, *Machiavelli: The First Century* (Oxford 2005) 630–670. Peter Burke, "Tacitism," in *Tacitus,* ed. T. A. Dorey (London 1969) 149–171. Ann Moss, *Printed Commonplace Books and the Structuring of Renaissance Thought* (Oxford 1996). Gerhard Neumann, ed., *Der Aphorismus: Zur Geschichte, zu den Formen und Möglichkeiten einer literarischen*

Gattung (Darmstadt 1976). Peter Stein, *Regulae juris* (Edinburgh 1966). U.P.B.

Medals. *See* Coins and Medals

Medea

In myth, daughter of King Aeëtes of Colchis, in the western Caucasus (thus niece to Circe and granddaughter of Helios, from whom she received a golden chariot drawn by dragons); wife of Jason, prince of Iolcus in Thessaly, to whom she bore two children; a powerful sorceress, poisoner, and adventuress. She has many aspects: the passionate princess who helps Jason steal the Golden Fleece, dismembering her own brother to halt the pursuers; the magical stranger who can restore or destroy waning manhood; the fugitive who flees from her home in Colchis to Jason's Iolcus, to Corinth, to Athens, and back to the East; the abandoned wife who takes revenge on her younger rival (and her rival's father); and the mother who kills her own children. Medea is a dream and a nightmare, the romance heroine who becomes the murderous mother.

The most influential sources of her story are the tragedies bearing her name by Euripides (431 BCE) and Seneca (mid-1st century CE), Pindar's Fourth Pythian Ode (462 BCE), the epic *Argonautica* by Apollonius Rhodius (3rd century BCE), and Ovid's *Heroides* and *Metamorphoses* (early 1st century CE). The Ovidian Medeas were particularly important in the Middle Ages, most prominently in the works of Boccaccio, Chaucer, and Christine de Pizan. English Renaissance writers were fascinated by the adolescent queen's bold sexuality, her fratricide, and her rejuvenation of Jason's father, Aeson. There are traces of the young Medea in Shakespeare's Jessica (*The Merchant of Venice*), and of the mature murderess in Lady Macbeth. From the 16th century onward the Senecan and Euripidean Medeas reached the stage in adaptations by Pierre Corneille (1635), Richard Glover (1767), and others. Francesco Cavalli's opera *Giasone* (1649) began a long tradition of musically eloquent Medeas, from Marc-Antoine Charpentier's opera (1694) and Luigi Cherubini's (1797) to Darius Milhaud's (1938) and Gavin Bryars's (1984, revised 1995). These roles have often been associated with famous divas, notably Maria Callas, who also played the title role in a film version by Pier Paolo Pasolini (1970). Other great actresses have made the role their own, including Adelaide Ristori, Judith Anderson, and Diana Rigg. Medea has inspired memorable dance renditions, including Martha Graham's *Cave of the Heart* (1946), to music by Samuel Barber. Euripides' tragedy has been widely performed in translation and has served (with Medea's other classical sources) as the basis for dramatic versions by Franz Grillparzer (*Das Goldene Vliess*, 1822), Ernest Legouvé (1856), Robinson Jeffers (1947), Heiner Müller (*Medeaspiel*, 1974; *Medeamaterial*, 1982), Tony Harrison (*Medea: A Sex-War Opera*, 1985), and John Fisher (*Medea: The Musical*, 1996). Leading theater directors who have created arresting new *Medea*s include Robert Wilson (notably 1970, 1981), Andrei Şerban (1972), and Yukio Ninagawa (1983). Medea has also attracted treatments from visual artists, who often depict the moment just before she kills the children, as in the dramatic painting by Eugène Delacroix (1838).

Over the past two centuries Medea has provided a focus for debates about gender politics, women's rights, motherhood, colonialism, and racial difference. There was an outburst of Medeas on the London stage around the time of the 1857 Divorce Act, and post-apartheid South Africa has seen some striking productions with multiracial casts. Recent writers who have been inspired by Medea's story include Adrienne Rich (*Of Woman Born*, 1977), Toni Morrison (*Beloved*, 1987), Margaret Atwood ("Hairball," in *Wilderness Tips*, 1991), and Christa Wolf (*Medea-Stimmen*, 1996).

Does Medea really kill her two boys? In some early versions it is the people of Corinth who do so. But if she does, what drives her to it? She may seem trapped and accused of terrible crimes, but artists from Euripides to the present day have freed her to speak, and sing, for herself.

BIBL.: James J. Clauss and Sarah Iles Johnston, eds., *Medea: Essays on Medea in Myth, Literature, Philosophy, and Art* (Princeton 1997). Edith Hall, Fiona Macintosh, and Oliver Taplin, eds., *Medea in Performance, 1500–2000* (Oxford 2000). John Kerrigan, *Revenge Tragedy: Aeschylus to Armageddon* (Oxford 1996) 88–110, 315–342. Ruth Morse, *The Medieval Medea* (Cambridge 1996). A.PL.

Medicine

The history of classical medicine developed in different ways in the three distinctive cultures of Byzantium, Islam, and Latin Christianity. The first two shared a heritage of late antique Galenism, which was far less pervasive in Western Europe and North Africa than in the Greek world and among the Syriac Christians of the Near East. From the 11th century onward Western Europe rediscovered Galenism largely through Arabic-language intermediaries. During the Renaissance the proponents of medical Humanism advocated a direct acquaintance with Greek medicine in the original language, bringing about a new Galenism. From the 1550s onward this was superseded by a revived Hippocratism, which in its stress on the individual, holism, and natural cures based on sound clinical observation still resonates in modern debates on medicine.

Byzantium. The Galenic system of medicine as defined in 5th- and 6th-century Alexandria dominated Byzantine medicine. Official medical education was based on a series of lectures on set texts from Galen and Hippocrates. These provided both theoretical discussion and advice on clinical practice: anatomical dissection was at best extremely rare and may never have been performed. Manuscripts of the major classical authors seem to have been widely available in the 9th century, although Hunayn ibn Ishāq (d. 873) in his search for Greek manuscripts of Galen remarks that many of Galen's books were becoming rare and some had been lost entirely. By 1200, however, the number had shrunk considerably, almost to our present Galenic corpus. Whereas copies of the commentary on the Hippocratic *Aphorisms* were widespread, some of them written away from Constantinople, works outside the main syllabus were now rare. Some texts, like *De partibus artis medicae* or *De causis contentivis,* which were still available in 1300, have since disappeared in Greek but survive in translations. The fate of the manuscripts of Rufus of Ephesus (fl. 100 CE) was similar, the major losses occurring after the 9th century. Earlier writers not in the Galenic tradition may, however, already have been lost except where, as is the case with Soranus' *Gynaecology,* they described material not already in Galen or, like the *Introduction,* happened to have been ascribed to Galen.

The classical heritage was dealt with in a variety of ways. Material scattered across the Galenic corpus was brought into shorter handbooks, such as Philaretus' *On Pulses* (ca. 8th cent.), and Theophilus' (7th cent.) *On Urine,* or formed the basis for larger syntheses incorporating more recent material, for example, by Johannes Actuarius (fl. 1320) and treating both theoretical and practical issues. Some of Galen's writings were summarized in the form of consecutive excerpts (as in Paris, Bibliothèque Nationale MS gr. 2332), whereas others existed only as quotations in larger handbooks, like those of Paul of Aegina (7th cent.) or John the Archiatros (14th cent.). In this process the encyclopedia of Aëtius of Amida (ca. 500) arguably played a more important role than the Galenic originals themselves. The introduction of material from Arabic or Persian sources, as, for example, by Simeon Seth (fl. 1075), enriched but did not fundamentally change the character of this learned medicine.

Medical practice continued the classical tradition. Doctors in Constantinople were organized within a college, with a variety of grades, and under the supervision of a number of doctors. An examination system, with certificates, was in existence by 1140 that tested both theory and practice. Evidence of tension between religious and nonreligious healing is lacking, and doctors were in attendance (and often teaching) at the great metropolitan hospitals such as the Pantokrator or the Kral.

In the 15th century Greek medical men like John Argyropoulos went to Italy, and the library collections of the Medici, Cardinal Bessarion, and, especially, Niccolò Leoniceno (1428–1524) included copies of almost all the medical texts surviving in Greek. Venetian doctors serving in colonies or trading posts, like Alessandro Benedetti (d. 1512), also helped to disseminate knowledge of Byzantine Galenism before any genuine work of Galen became available in the West in printed form (*Methodus medendi,* 1500; *Opera omnia,* 1525).

The Islamic world. The earliest medical translations from Greek into the vernacular languages of the Middle East were made by the priest-doctor Sergius of Resaina (d. 536), who translated at least 37 works of Galen into Syriac, 5 of them twice, as well as other non-Galenic medical tracts. Other Greek medical writings may also have been translated into Pahlavi at about the same time, while David Anhacht (ca. 500), who had studied in Alexandria, conveyed Galenic medical ideas in his Armenian philosophical writings. Syriac authors also developed Galen's medicine in specific tracts, such as that by Sergius on dropsy, or in large compendia of general medicine, such as the *Pandects* of Ahrun (fl. ca. 600). This medicine was far more sophisticated and wide-ranging than that practiced by the Muslim Arab conquerors themselves in the 7th century, and it is not surprising that Christian physicians and a Christianized Galenic medicine continued to hold sway for several centuries.

The age of Hunayn. Information is scanty, however, before the 9th century. Then, with the strong encouragement of caliphs like al-Mā'mūn (d. 833) and wealthy courtiers, like Djibril ibn Bakhtishu' (d. 827), himself a doctor and a (weak) translator, a massive wave of translations occurred, usually first into Syriac and then into Arabic. The leading spirit in this was Hunayn ibn Ishāq, assisted by his son Ishāq (d. 910) and his nephew Hubaish (d. ca. 900), working in Baghdad, but there were others, like Theophilus of Edessa (d. 785) and Job of Edessa (Ayyub al-Ruhawi, d. ca. 832), who were active elsewhere, especially in the largely Christian frontier region of northern Syria. By 900 more than 129 treatises of Galen were available in Arabic, some of them in several different versions, including works on logic and philosophy as well as medicine. A smaller proportion of the Hippocratic corpus was translated into Syriac or Arabic, sometimes indirectly as the lemmata to Galen's commentaries, but the Arabs possessed more works by Rufus of Ephesus than survive today, as well as the late antique encyclopedists, Dioscorides, and the physiognomical writers. The Alexandrian *Summaries of Galen* was also translated into Syriac and Arabic (and, much later, into Hebrew, by Shimshon ben Shlomo in 1322). From Arabic were made translations into Armenian (9th–10th cents.), Pahlavi, and Hebrew (e.g., by Samuel ibn Tibbon, fl. 1200), and, from the late 11th century onward, into Latin. There is even a report that some of Galen was translated, or at least transcribed, from Arabic into Chinese.

The quality of the versions by Hunayn and his school is remarkably high. Hunayn himself in his *Risala* detailed his own careful methods of collation and translation, preferring to keep the sense of a passage rather than the exact word order, and at times he confessed to his inability to translate a word because of its rarity and its lack of context. He followed the Greek closely, making occasional modifications to avoid offending religious sensibilities or to omit some of Galen's etymological comments. How far others followed the same methods is unclear, but one should not necessarily believe Hunayn's dismissive descriptions of his competitors' abilities.

Modern historians of ancient medicine depend on these versions in a variety of ways. Some ancient treatises survive only in Arabic or Hebrew, such as Galen's *On Examining the Physician* and his *Commentary on the Hippocratic Airs, Waters, and Places.* Others, no longer extant in full, are cited in part by Arabic or Jewish authors, such as Rufus of Ephesus' *On Melancholy,* by Ishāq ibn 'Imrān (d. 907), or Galen's *On the Avoidance of Grief,* by ibn Aknin (fl. 1300). Other works, like Galen's treatises *On the Eye,* formed the basis for subsequent development in Arabic authors, although what is development and what represents the Greek original is not clear. Even when the Greek survives, the Arabic often permits a view of the text at an earlier and often less corrupt stage in the process of transmission.

Arabic Galenism. Most significant is the overall Galenic nature of formal Arabic medicine. Galen's perspective dominated all others, and its monotheistic ideas on causation and purpose made it attractive to Jews, Christians, and Muslims alike, even if they rejected some of Galen's own doubts about the nature of God or Creation. Learned doctors studied Galen with their masters, following the Alexandrian syllabus, and it is no coincidence that many of the great names in Arabic and Jewish medicine, such as Avicenna (Ibn Sīnā, ca. 980–1037) and Maimonides (Moses ben Maimon, 1138–1204), were, like Galen, famous as philosophers as much as doctors. But the sheer size of the Galenic corpus, even in translation, was daunting. Ibn Ridwan (d. ca. 1068) was unusual in his day for the breadth of his knowledge of Galen, and few followed him in his insistence that an acquaintance with Galen's own writings was far more beneficial to the practitioner than any reading in subsequent handbooks. His opponent in a celebrated controversy, Ibn Butlan (d. ca. 1068), took a more pragmatic line, relying on contemporary writings in the Galenic tradition.

Both sides had a point. Summaries and handbooks were effective in presenting the main outlines of Galen's theories, but the process of abridgment inevitably left out Galen's hesitations and much of his empirical evidence. Authors like Haly Abbas (al-Majusi, d. ca. 999) and Avicenna, above all in his *Canon,* provided logically constructed syntheses that took Galen's ideas (e.g., on the three spirits) far beyond what he had written. Pharmacological and dietetic writers, such as Ibn Butlan in his *Treasury of Health,* applied Galen's incomplete theory of grades of drug action systematically to a wide range of substances. But impressive as they were in their organization and clarity, these handbooks lost some of the energy and immediacy of Galen's original.

The best Arabic medicine often begins with a Galenic or Hippocratic model but goes far beyond it. Ibn Ridwan's *On the Prevention of Bodily Ills in Egypt* develops ideas from the Hippocratic *Airs, Waters, and Places,* and the treatise *On Smallpox and Measles* of Rhazes (al-Rāzī, 865–925) refines Galen's nosology; Rhazes' experiments on animals recall those of Galen. The surgeon Albucasis (al-Zahrawi, ca. 936–ca. 1013) constantly proclaims his debt to Galen, while describing many new operations and techniques.

The Arabic authors saw themselves as building on solid foundations. Criticism of the Greeks in medical matters took the form of adding new information rather than abandoning the old. The discovery by Abd al-Latif al-Baghdadi (d 1231), from examining skulls, that Galen had wrongly described the human jaw did not lead to widespread distrust of Galenic anatomy—and dissection of humans was almost impossible. Ibn al-Nafis (d. 1288) discovered the passage of blood from one side of the heart to the other via the lungs by a mixture of observation (presumably of an animal heart) and meditation on the words of Galen in a thought experiment. Although his discovery was often reported in later texts, it was merely placed without further comment alongside Galen's alternative theory, and Ibn al-Nafis himself did not draw further conclusions from it.

Yunani medicine. Greek humoralism in Arab dress, Yunani or Unani (i.e., Ionian or "Greek") medicine came under attack from religious fundamentalists from the 10th century onward who sought to impose on Muslims the Medicine of the Prophet, but it was never entirely replaced as the primary medicine of the educated doctor. Western Renaissance discoveries in anatomy, physiology, and Paracelsian medical chemistry were assimilated where necessary. Only with the advent of colonialism and the imposition of modern Western medicine did Yunani medicine come to be seen, at least by the ruling classes, as inferior and ineffective. Nonetheless, as mediated through the *Canon* of Avicenna, it remains today an important medical tradition in Pakistan and elsewhere in the Muslim world (including Western Europe).

Western Europe before 1100. Early medieval Western Europe knew little of the Greek classical authors. Traces of the late antique syllabus of Galen and Hippocrates can be found in the Ravenna region and in some Latin translations available in the libraries of a few large Benedictine monasteries. Brevity and practicality predominated, so that drug books like that of pseudo-Apuleius or small handbooks of rules and recipes, sometimes ascribed to Hippocrates, were copied more often than lengthy books in Latin such as Cornelius Celsus or Caelius Aurelianus. In the 9th century the medical poem of Q. Serenus became popular again, but evidence of theoretical discussions on the Galenic model is missing until the 11th century.

Southern Italy and Sicily, however, continued to retain links with Byzantium, and manuscripts of Greek medicine continued to be copied there at least into the 13th century in this bi- or trilingual area. The Jewish physician Shabbetai ben Donnolo (913–ca. 982), who was active in Apulia, combined Greek anatomy and pharmacology with Jewish mysticism and astrology in his *Book of Wisdom.*

Medieval translations and translators. In 1063 Alfanus, bishop of Salerno, traveled on an embassy to Constantinople, where he became acquainted with Greek medical texts. He translated into Latin Nemesius' *On the Nature of Man,* and his own writings reflect Byzantine works on pulses and the four humors. Greek influence is also visible in the *Salernitan Questions* (ca. 1200). Shortly thereafter Constantine the African, a monk of Montecassino, began a series of translations from the Arabic, including Galen's *Art of Healing* and his commentaries on the Hippocratic *Aphorisms* and *Prognostic.* His adaptation of Hunayn's *Medical Questions*, the *Isagoge,* provided an elegant summary of Galenic medicine. By 1200 these texts had been joined by Latin versions of Theophilus and Philaretus to form the *Articella,* the *Little Art,* which along with the Hippocratic *Regimen in Acute Diseases* formed the staple of learned medicine for the next 300 years.

From the 1140s onward, a group of translators working in Spain, principally Gerard of Cremona (fl. 1150–1187), worked on medical, philosophical, and scientific texts. Gerard translated only a few Galenic texts, including the *Method of Healing,* but he was concerned mainly with turning into Latin the major Arabic syntheses of Galenic medicine, notably Avicenna's *Canon* and the *Liber ad Almansorem* of Rhazes. At the same time, working in Constantinople and with the aid of the Italian Greek copyist Iohannikios, the judge and merchant Burgundio of Pisa (1110–1193) was amassing a collection of Galenic Greek manuscripts (now in the Laurentian Library, Florence), from which he made versions of several important treatises, including *On Crises* and *On the Natural Faculties.*

Toward the end of the 13th century there ensued another burst of medical translations. Some were of Arabic authors, such as Rhazes' *Continens,* translated by Abulfaragius in Sicily in 1282; others were of Greek authors via the Arabic, like the 1282 version of Galen's *On Rigor* by Arnold of Villanova (d. 1311); still others were directly from the Greek. Hebrew translations also began to be made of Galenic works in Arabic. The Spanish Jewish philosopher Shem Tob ibn Falaquera (ca. 1225–after 1290) cites several philosophical works of Galen that are now lost in Greek. Of prime significance were the translations made by the Paduan professor Pietro d'Abano (1257–ca. 1315), which were based on Greek manuscripts he had brought back from Constantinople. Among them were the final books of Galen's *Method of Healing,* which was more accurate than Gerard's earlier version, and some of *On the Use of Parts.* The final translator of significance was Niccolò Deoprepio da Reggio (fl. 1308–1345), who was employed at the Angevin court of Naples as a doctor, diplomat, and translator. In a career spanning almost 40 years he turned into Latin more than 50 Galenic treatises, ranging from a complete version of *On the Use of Parts* to smaller tracts, such as *On Prognosis.*

Galen, directly or indirectly via the Arabic syntheses, was the main beneficiary of these translations. A few works by Hippocrates were available in Latin, principally those commented on or singled out by Galen, but most of the writings circulating under his name did not form part of the Greek Hippocratic corpus. Some gynecological material from Soranus appeared in the Latin version of Muscio; Rufus was known largely through fragments in Rhazes' *Continens;* a Latin version by Niccolò of his *On Jaundice* circulated under the name of Galen.

Vernacular translations of classical works were much rarer; parts of the *Articella* appear in French, English, and even Gaelic, and there is an English redaction of Galen's *Method of Healing.* The London surgeon who commissioned the English version of an *Anatomia Galeni* that appears in Wellcome MS 290 (London) believed he was reading a genuine work of Galen, although the work is Lanfranc's *Anatomy of the Pig.*

The influence of medieval translations. Each stage in the arrival of translations of ancient medicine, with one exception, changed ideas on medicine substantially. The contrast between the sophisticated Salernitan commentaries on medicine from the mid-12th century and medical learning a century earlier is marked. The Salernitans expounded medical theory and set medicine against the wider background of the natural world. They raised questions, rather than simply repeating recipes, and used the commentary format to explore arguments. The *Isagoge,* with its ultimately Galenic division of medicine into the natural (the body, its functions, and its parts), the pathological (diseases, causes, and consequences), and the nonnatural (food, environment, sleep, evacuation, exercise, and emotions), provided a way of structuring medical discourse that lasted for centuries. By 1120 the Salernitans had also introduced animal dissection into their teaching.

The 12th-century translators from the Arabic also established a wider vocabulary for learned medicine and provided the basis for the development of university-taught medicine as a series of lectures on set texts. A century later this intensely Arabized medicine was in part superseded by a new Galenism that was based on a more direct acquaintance with Galen's own work. So, for instance, at Montpellier Arnold of Villanova used his knowledge of Galen's writings to criticize Arabic interpretations of fever. Pietro d'Abano's *Conciliator,* as its title implies, attempted a new synthesis of the art of medicine on the basis of his new translations and the older Avicenna. The appearance of new translations may also have stimulated new investigations into marasmus (a form of malnutrition), or into the workings of drugs. In Italy, Taddeo Alderotti (teaching at Bologna 1260–1295) was prompted to formulate new ideas on diseases and internal medicine. His pupils were equally keen on their Galen, and it is no coincidence that it was the example of Galen that was followed by Mondino dei Liuzzi when (ca. 1315) he introduced the dissection of a human corpse into university teaching at Bologna. (Dissections did not, however, become common until the 16th century.) The new Galenism provoked new debates, not least on the relationship between medicine and philosophy.

By contrast, Niccolò's translations were little read: the famous Avignon surgeon Guy de Chauliac (ca. 1300–1368), who drew heavily on Niccolò's work in his *Chirurgia magna,* is an exception. His word-for-word translation technique, although maintaining a remarkably high standard of accuracy, leads often to unintelligibility, and many of his renditions were often irrelevant to medical practice and teaching, especially as the syllabus of set texts for lectures had by the 1340s become standard across Europe. Only the committed and the wealthy, like Giovanni di Marco (d. 1474), doctor to the Malatesta family of Cesena, could afford to devote themselves to such small and medically marginal treatises.

Three other late medieval medical innovations derive ultimately from classical and late antique precedents. The new hospitals of 13th- and 14th-century Europe were larger and more complex than their Western predecessors, and were based on ideas brought back from the Crusades, either from Byzantium or from the Near East. The institution of civic physicians, first recorded at Reggio and Bologna in the early 13th century, may have been inspired by knowledge of the recently revived Roman law texts on the subject. By the 15th century many medical guilds and colleges acknowledged precedents from classical antiquity. The London College of Physicians, founded in 1518, had a very stiff entrance examination in the works of Galen and Hippocrates.

The Renaissance return of Greek. The influence of the Latin Humanism of the 14th and 15th centuries on contemporary medicine was slight. Although a manuscript Cornelius Celsus' *De medicina* was rediscovered in 1426, it was little studied by medical practitioners. Pliny and (briefly, at the end of the 15th century) Q. Serenus were cited for pharmacology, and among medical writers a more classical Latin style gradually took over from the Arabicized technical language. But the medieval authors and translations remained the basis for medical teaching and practice well into the 1530s, despite the presence of several Greek manuscripts in Italy from the 1460s onward and calls for a return to their Greek sources by medical Humanists.

In 1492 Niccolò Leoniceno, professor of medicine at Ferrara and the owner of the finest contemporary library of Greek medical and scientific writings in the West, showed in his *De Plinii et plurium aliorum erroribus* (*On the Errors in Pliny and Many Others*) that confusion abounded through ignorance or misunderstanding of the Greek of Galen, Dioscorides, Hippocrates, and other ancient medical writers. His prescription was a return directly to the Greek texts or, since only a very few scholars knew both Greek and medicine and had access to Greek manuscripts, to new Latin translations based on the Greek. These were slow in coming, and except for those by Thomas Linacre (ca. 1460–1524), were at first confined to the handful of texts already studied at universities.

Greek medical texts were rarely printed. The plans by Zacharias Kallierges and Nicolaos Vlastos for a complete edition of Galen in Greek came to a premature end in 1500 with the publication of the two works comprising *On the Method of Healing.* Aldus, who printed Dioscorides in 1499, obtained manuscripts for an edition of Galen but failed to follow through with a prompt publication. The value of Greek for medicine was thus asserted rather than widely accepted, for readers of Greek were few, certainly beyond Italy, until the 1520s. But the importance of Greek for clarifying and creating a new technical vocabulary was shown in works on botany and anatomy, particularly those coming from Leoniceno and his pupil Giovanni Manardi (1462–1536).

The situation altered drastically in 1525, with the publication of the Aldine edition of Galen and the first Latin translation of the Hippocratic corpus, by M. F. Calvo, followed in 1526 by the Aldine Hippocrates in Greek. Paul of Aegina followed in 1528, but the Aldine series ended abruptly (probably on grounds of cost) halfway through the edition of Aëtius in 1534. The Greek text of Rufus had to wait until 1554, and Oribasius until 1556 (books 24 and 25 of his *Synopses*), although they had been available earlier in Latin translation. With a few exceptions, notably Galen's *On Bones* (Latin, 1535; Greek, 1543), all the medically significant writings of Galen and Hippocrates were available by 1526 in the original Greek.

Their appearance was followed by a flood of translations into Latin, and occasionally into the vernacular. In the 1530s and 1540s, an average of 15 editions and translations of Galen were published annually; there were 20 in 1538, 32 in 1549. Numbers of editions and translations of Hippocrates were fewer, reaching a maximum of 11 in 1545 and 1552, but they did not suffer the massive decline in numbers seen for Galen from 1555 onward, averaging 5 editions a year and comfortably outstripping Galenic printings. These translations were made by medical men rather than by Humanists, from all parts of Europe. Special mention must be made of the Italians M. F. Calvo (d. 1527), G. B. Rasario (1517–1578), and G. P. Crassi (d. 1574), the Swiss Guillaume Copp (1460–1532), the Frenchman Jacobus Sylvius (1478–1555), the Germans Janus Cornarius (1500–1558) and Johann Guinther von Andernach (1505–1574), and the Englishman John Caius (1510–1573).

Most of these versions were based on either the Aldine editions or the better Basel editions of the Greek (Galen, 1538; Hippocrates, 1538). But some translators, most notably Linacre, Caius, and the Italian editors of the 1541–1545 Venice *Opera omnia Galeni,* A. Ricci (1512–1564) and Vittorio Trincavella (1496–1568), also inspected Greek manuscripts. A few Latin authors were also rediscovered (Scribonius Largus in 1528, Caelius Aurelianus in 1529), but it was Greek medicine, albeit mainly in Latin translation, that held sway. Lexica, summaries, commentaries, and guides to reading all helped make the material accessible to contemporary doctors.

Renaissance Galenism. The revived Galen differed from the medieval Galen in many ways. His image, and that of his Renaissance followers, was that of a doctor with wide cultural and philosophical interests. His polemics helped define acceptable practice, pushing astrology and uroscopy to the margins of medicine and the province of the quack. At the same time, his emphasis on academic learning, books, and authority, to say nothing of his belief in a purposeful Creator, allowed his writings to dominate in Renaissance universities and medical colleges.

Two areas of study revived in part because of classical precedent. Leoniceno's attack on Latin and medieval authors for misunderstanding Greek pharmacology and botany provoked a vigorous controversy that resulted in a new methodology for investigating and identifying herbs that incorporated both visual and written evidence, such as *On the History of Plants* and *Five Books on Medical History and Materials* (L. Fuchs, *De historia stirpium,* 1542; P. A. Matthioli, *Libri cinque della historia e materia medicinale,* 1544), and the creation from the 1540s onward of botanical gardens (at Pisa, Ferrara, Padua, and Bologna) and of university chairs in botany. It also encouraged doctors to travel in search of drugs that had been forgotten since antiquity or were entirely unknown in Europe.

The central role given by Galen to anatomy led to a massive renewal of interest in the subject. At first concerned with correcting anatomical nomenclature (A. Benedetti, G. Valla), medical Humanists supported the introduction of dissection into university teaching (M. Corti, J. Sylvius, J. Caius). Most acknowledged mistakes in Galen's descriptions of the body but explained them as the result of errors by copyists or translators. Galen's injunctions to dissect and examine personally were welcomed, although it was generally realized that he had largely relied on animal specimens, not human cadavers.

The new Galenism also stressed the importance of proper method in diagnosis and treatment. Giovanni Battista da Monte (1498–1551) at Padua was famous for his clinical observations. The recovery of classical techniques also extended to surgery, where Vidus Vidius introduced in his *Chirurgia* (1544) drawings of instruments and bandaging taken from the Nicetas Codex, a 10th-century Byzantine surgical work. Girolamo Mercuriale, who edited Hippocrates, brought together ancient writings on gymnastics to produce his own *De arte gymnastica* (1569).

The attack on Galenism. By 1550 most leading doctors in Europe were Galenists. But their position was coming under attack from three sides. Galenic method in clinical medicine was cumbersome and beyond the capacity of most doctors to carry out properly. The followers of Paracelsus (1493–1541), still few in number but with powerful lay allies, asserted that Galenic herbal remedies were useless compared with their own chemical preparations. Galen's anatomy was further challenged by the findings of Andreas Vesalius (1514–1564), who had revised versions of Galen's anatomical works for the 1541–1542 Juntine edition of the Latin *Opera omnia.* His *De humani corporis fabrica* (1543, 2nd ed. 1555) exploited a Galenic methodology and a Galenic rhetoric to claim that Galen had never dissected a human corpse and that in consequence his anatomy was seriously flawed. These exaggerations aroused the anger of Galenists like Janus Cornarius and Franciscus Sylvius, but many others, such as Philipp Melanchthon (1497–1560), saw Vesalius as a fellow Galenist modifying Galen's discoveries, albeit in many details. By 1560 Vesalian human anatomy had largely replaced that of Galen: dissectors like Fabricius of Aquapendente (1533–1619) and Volcher Coiter (1534–1576), who concentrated, like Aristotle, on animal dissection, became more sophisticated in their comparative studies.

Galen's physiology, with its belief in three largely independent bodily systems, based on three organs—liver, heart, and brain—was generally accepted in the 16th century by all except a few philosophers who favored Aristotle's centralizing theory of the heart as the seat of the soul. It was the committed Galenist and Aristotelian William Harvey (1578–1657) who, in his *Motion of the Heart and Blood in Animals* (*De motu cordis et sanguinis in animalibus,* 1628), demonstrated the unity of the venous and arterial systems in a single circulation as well as their separation from the nervous system, a physiological dichotomy that was further strengthened by the philosophical arguments of Descartes (1596–1650).

The return to Hippocrates. The attack on Galen and Galenism was almost totally successful. Thereafter, Galen became seen as the archpedant, a windbag, an anatomical bungler—a reputation that lasted at least until the 1970s. Defenders of traditional medicine turned to Hippocrates, the father of medicine, whose precepts were capable of flexible interpretation and development. Particularly in Paris, teaching by means of commentary on Hippocratic texts, including the *Coan Prognoses,* led to new ideas about environmental medicine, surgery, and treatment. Clinical medicine continued to be based on the principle of the four humors, but respect was paid to individual response to illness. Great stress was placed on Hippocrates' role as an observer of individual illness, whose course was in part determined by Nature. Great observers, like Pieter van Foreest, who wrote 41 books (*Observationes et curationes,* 1584–1610), and Thomas Sydenham, whose *Observationes medicae* (1676) gave masterly descriptions of fevers, were respectively called the Dutch and the English Hippocrates.

The doctrines found within the Hippocratic corpus could be reinterpreted in line with new thinking. J. A. van der Linden (1609–1664) showed, to general satisfaction, that Hippocrates had anticipated Harvey in his discovery of the circulation of the blood. F. W. Hoffmann (1660–1742), by contrast, used a variety of Hippocratic texts to support his very different theories of iatromechanism.

In Holland, Hippocrates came to be seen as the fount of clinical knowledge, the most faithful collector of facts. Herman Boerhaave (1668–1738) spread this message worldwide through his numerous pupils. At the end of the 18th century academic medicine, particularly in Germany, rejected medical systems of causation in favor of a careful observation of signs and symptoms, which were then to be treated by whatever remedies had worked in the past. Ancient texts, properly edited and understood, offered as much valuable information as more recent case histories, and the neutral Hippocratic observer was thought more likely to cure than partisan supporters of Brunonianism or homoeopathy. This was the context for the reprinting of many classical authors, including Hippocrates, Galen, and Aretaeus, by K. G. Kühn (1754–1842). Many ancient Hippocratic commentaries were also edited for the first time in Greek by F. R. Dietz in 1834.

From medicine to history. That classical authors were still seen as sources of valuable therapeutic information can be seen in the prefaces to Francis Adams's English translation of Paul of Aegina (1844–1847) and to Émile Littré's monumental edition and French translation of Hippocrates (1839–1861). But within the time span of Littré's edition the change toward a historical-philological approach can be clearly seen. With rare exceptions, such as J. P. E. Pétrequin's *Chirurgie d'Hippocrate* (1877–1878), mention was no longer made of the value for contemporary medicine of ancient theories or therapeutics, although many ancient remedies themselves survived in pharmacopoeias until the 20th century.

Hippocrates instead became the symbol of an ideal, most notably in the constant reference in contemporary debates to what is presumed to be the message of the Hippocratic Oath. Littré's Hippocrates is a 19th-century anticlerical rationalist, a skilled observer and believer in environmental medicine. In the 1920s and 1930s across Europe, Hippocrates was held up as the model clinician, who alone could interpret the varied data provided by each individual patient. In a world increasingly dominated by technology, the modern Hippocratic doctor alone retained the personal touch and the holistic approach. Indeed, ancient Greek medicine is still cited today by writers and practitioners of complementary medicine as proof of the virtues of medical holism. Traces of classical medicine are also found in modern Tibetan medicine and in Yunani medicine within Islam, where modern laboratory and clinical sciences are being used to demonstrate the value of statements in Avicenna or Galen.

The significance of classical medicine has also changed among students of the classics. An emphasis on ancient medical texts, properly edited and interpreted, as examples of Greek and Latin or as repositories of earlier and more valuable Greek learning has been succeeded by a wider interest in healing practices and ideas themselves and in their different contexts. New discoveries from papyri, archaeology, and later versions of texts lost in their original Greek have permitted scholars in the 21st century a broader vision of ancient medicine than was possible for any of their predecessors since the 6th century.

BIBL.: Guy Attewell, *Refining Unani Tibb* (London 2007). Augusto Beccaria, *I codici di medicina del periodo presalernitano (secoli IX, X e XI)* (Rome 1956). Véronique Boudon-Millot and Guy Cobolet, eds., *Lire les médecins grecs à la Renaissance: Aux origines de l'édition médicale* (Paris 2004). Thomas H. Broman, *The Transformation of German Academic Medicine, 1750–1820* (Cambridge 1996). David Cantor, ed., *Reinventing Hippocrates* (Aldershot 2002). Lawrence I. Conrad, Michael Neve, Vivian Nutton, and Roy Porter, *The Western Medical Tradition 800 BC to AD 1800* (Cambridge 1995). Andrew Cunningham, *The Anatomical Renaissance of the Sixteenth Century* (Aldershot 1997) 88–142. Richard J. Durling, "A Chronological Census of Renaissance Editions and Translations of Galen," *Journal of the Warburg and Courtauld Institutes* 24 (1961) 230–305. Roger French, *Medicine before Science: The Business of Medicine from the Middle Ages to the Enlightenment* (Cambridge 2003). Roger French, Jon Arrizabalaga, Andrew Cunningham, and Luis García Ballester, eds., *Medicine from the Black Death to the French Disease* (Aldershot 1998). Roger French and Andrew Wear, eds., *The Medical Revolution of the Seventeenth Century* (Cambridge 1989). Frank Huisman, *Locating Medical History: The Stories and Their Meanings* (Baltimore 2004). Danielle Jacquart, *La science médicale occidentale entre deux renaissances (XIIe s.–XVe s.)* (Aldershot 1997). Anna Manfron, *La biblioteca di un medico del Quattrocento* (Cesena 1998). Michael R. McVaugh and Nancy G. Siraisi, eds., *Renaissance Medical Learning: Evolution of a Tradition, Osiris,* 2nd ser., 6 (1990). Vivian Nutton, *From Democedes to Harvey* (Aldershot 1988). John Scarborough, ed., *Byzantine Medicine, Dumbarton Oaks Papers* 38 (1984). Nancy G. Siraisi, *Taddeo Alderotti and His Pupils* (Princeton 1981). Wesley D. Smith, *The Hippocratic Tradition* (Ithaca 1979). Manfred Ullmann, *Islamic Medicine* (Edinburgh 1978). Andrew Wear, Roger K. French, and Iain M. Lonie, eds., *The Medical Renaissance of the Sixteenth Century* (Cambridge 1985). Mauro Zonta, *Un interprete ebraico della filosofia di Galeno* (Turin 1995).

V.N.

Melancholy

Melancholy bears its legacy from antiquity in its name, which literally means "black bile" or "black bile disease." It originated in the context of ancient pathology and the doctrine of "humors," or basic bodily fluids.

Historically black bile was the last of the fluids to be identified. It appears to have developed from thinking on the humors and their pathology in the second of the Hippocratic books on epidemics, around 400 BCE. Further refinement of the four-humor formula led to the association of black bile not only with the qualities "dry" and "cold" and the element earth, but also with the season of autumn, the life phase of maturity, the organ of the spleen, the color black, the planet Saturn, and the mixolydian mode in music. Black bile thus was part of a universal formula that connected the microcosm of the human organism with the macrocosm through analogies. This web of relationships in which conditions governed by black bile had a place lives on in poetic imagery and common expressions.

Though black bile was held to have its place in a well-balanced, healthy mixture of the humors, at the same time the word *melancholy* denoted a condition in which an excess of black bile was present in the body as a result of poor diet or seasonal, climatic, or planetary influences. According to the logic of humorism, this type of *dyscrasia* or imbalance caused the organism to dry out and lowered its temperature, leading to physical and mental symptoms.

The mental symptoms seem to have dominated: "If fear and sadness last for a long time, this is a sign of melancholy" (Hippocrates, *Aphorisms* 6.23), or "Melancholy is a (chronic) despondency with regard to a specific fancy, without fever" (Aretaeus, *Corpus medicorum Graecorum* 2.3.3.39.27 Hüde). The term *melancholy* thus became associated with psychopathology and has remained so to the present day, when it is often used as a synonym for depression. Treatment was also influenced by the "psychotherapeutic" approaches of ancient physicians like Archigenes of Apamea, Aretaeus of Cappadocia, and Soranus of Ephesus.

Rufus of Ephesus and Galen taught that the various forms of melancholy were based on residues left after bodily humors have been burnt (*melancholia adusta*), an idea that was later systematized by Avicenna (11th cent.). He distinguished four forms of melancholy according to whether the disease resulted from combustion of yellow bile, blood, phlegm, or black bile. The psychopathological symptoms are linked to the specific characteristics of each humor, insofar as they have a bearing on the formations of a man's character. Hence, sanguine melancholy (prototype: Democritus) is more cheerful and less dangerous than the completely melancholic kind (prototype: Bellerophon) or raging choleric melancholy (prototype: Ajax). Melancholy thus became a category of various forms of psychopathological conditions and constructs, including lovesickness, the mortal sins of *acedia* and *tristitia* in Christian doctrine, lycanthropy, hypochondria, hydrophobia, and Saint Vitus' dance. Even the sharp line drawn in antiquity between frenzy or mania and melancholy can occasionally disappear altogether.

The understanding of melancholy was significantly broadened early on—with significant consequences—by the pseudo-Aristotelian problem 30.1, which is attributed by some modern-day researchers to Theophrastus. The author asserts that black bile can be heated as well as cooled. With this "thermodynamic amphiboly" (Klibansky et al. 2002) he declares melancholy to be a bipolar phenomenon that can be accompanied by two types of symptoms: either rigidity, moodiness, and anxiety or euphoria and ecstasy (Aristotle, *Problematica* 954a23, 25). In individuals who by nature possess normal levels of black bile such variations in temperature and the resulting symptoms are temporary, but in those whose constitutions tend to an excess of cold or warm black bile, they affect the psyche. Persons with cold bile become sluggish and indifferent, whereas individuals with warm bile may become "manic, docile, lustful, excitable, and sometimes garrulous" (Aristotle, *Problematica* 954a30, 31) before they develop a manifest and exacerbated form of melancholic disease. With this bipolarity melancholy not only maintained its claim on the terrain of cold, dry, earthbound, and depressive elements but also annexed the area traditionally associated with yellow bile: heat, fire, mania, and divination. It almost appears as if ancient authors recognized melancholy as a cyclothymic process, a bipolar affective disturbance or manic-depressive illness in the sense of modern psychopathology.

Chiefly, however, problem 30.1 forms the overture to the symphonic development of the philosophical and psychological concept of genius, whose never-ending melody can be traced to the present day. The author is concerned namely with the question of why the best men (*perittoi*) in politics, art, and science are melancholics. His answer is that such leaders are men of moderation, able to temper their excess of natural black bile and to maintain it in balance (if only in unstable equilibrium). Pseudo-Aristotle thus distinguishes the pathological forms of melancholy from an ennobled form characteristic of the most gifted. Cicero (*Tusculanae disputationes* 1.80) translates the term *perittoi* of problem 30.1 as *ingeniosi,* a usage that marks the beginning of the history of the term *genius.* From Cicero the thread leads to the Platonic discourse and genius and madness, through which it is passed on to the modern era via Ficino's description of the melancholic character in *De vita triplici,* Melanchthon's *De anima,* and Burton's *Anatomy of Melancholy* as well as Dürer's "image of images" (Peter-Klaus Schuster 1991), the copper engraving *Melencolia I* (1514). In this process the *Regimen sanitatis Salernitanum* (late 13th cent.) and Albertus Magnus served as a bridge in a certain sense, since they contributed to a positive or ennobled view of the melancholic, who was portrayed in a negative light throughout the Middle Ages. They take up the idea disseminated by Rufus and his commentator Constantinus Africanus that scholars are particularly susceptible to melancholic illnesses and modify it by declaring melancholy to be the prerequisite for intellectual achievement.

The position in which one hand supports the head, which occurs as early as ancient sculpture to signify deep thought, became the pathognomonic gesture of melancholy from the time of Dürer's *Melencolia I* at the latest, and an architectural ruin became the emblematic background. Ficino's *De vita triplici* again strengthened the links between melancholy and Saturn and between humoral and astrological medicine. Since that time melancholics, as children of Saturn, have been life's problem children and putative geniuses. The ancient conceptions of melancholy are also deeply engraved in modern literary history: Hamlet, Faust, Don Quixote, Werther, and William Lovell are among the best known. The Romantic movement, with its depictions of extreme states of mind, owes much to ancient traditions of melancholy, particularly pseudo-Aristotelian amphiboly. In modern psychopathology the ennobled form of melancholy from problem 30.1 is resurrected with approval or disapproval in the works of Arthur Schopenhauer, Friedrich Nietzsche, Cesare Lombroso, Max Nordau, Paul Julius Möbius, William Hirsch, Wilhelm Lange-Eichbaum, and many others. Modern psychiatrists such as Hubertus Tellenbach, who understand the term *melancholy* as a diagnostic entity in the framework of psychosis, have kept the premodern semantics of this long-lived medical term in the awareness of modern psychopathology, and they interpret premodern representations of melancholy in the light of current medical research on melancholy.

BIBL.: Robert Burton, *Robert Burton's The Anatomy of Melancholy*, ed. T. C. Faulkner et al., 6 vols. (Oxford 1989–2000). J. Clair, ed., *Melancholie: Genie und Wahnsinn in der Kunst* (exhibition catalogue) (Ostfildern-Ruit 2005). A. Gowland, *The Worlds of Renaissance Melancholy: Robert Burton in Context* (Cambridge 2006). S. W. Jackson, *Melancholia and Depression: From Hippocratic Times to Modern Times* (New Haven 1986). R. Klibansky, E. Panofsky, and F. Saxl, *Saturno e la melanconia: Studi su storia della filosofia naturale, medicina, religione e arte*, rev. ed. (Turin 2002). S. Krämer, "Melancholie: Skizze zur epistemologischen Deutung eines Topos," *Zeitschrift für philosophische Forschung* 48 (1994) 397–419. F. Loquai, *Künstler und Melancholie in der Romantik* (Frankfurt 1984). H. J. Schings, *Melancholie und Aufklärung: Melancholiker und ihre Kritiker in Erfahrungsseelenkunde und Literatur des 18. Jahrhunderts* (Stuttgart 1977). P.-K. Schuster, *Melencolia I: Dürers Denkbild*, 2 vols. (Berlin 1991). H. Tellenbach, *Melancholie: Problemgeschichte, Endogenität, Typologie, Pathogenese, Klinik*, 4th ed. (Berlin 1983). W. Weber, "Im Kampf mit Saturn: Zur Bedeutung der Melancholie im anthropologischen Modernisierungsprozess des 16. und 17. Jahrhunderts," *Zeitschrift für Historische Forschung* 17 (1990) 155–192. T.R.

Translated by Deborah Lucas Schneider

Melanchthon, Philipp

Humanist, Lutheran, educational reformer, 1497–1560. His surname, originally Schwarzerdt, was hellenized to Melanchthon by a relative, Johannes Reuchlin, because of Philipp's early proficiency in the classics. In 1518 Melanchthon was appointed professor of Greek at the University of Wittenberg, where he quickly became a colleague and ally of Martin Luther. He composed the first exposition of evangelical doctrine, *Loci communes rerum theologicarum* (*Theological Commonplaces*, first published in 1521 and revised successively), a new kind of theological tract using a topical method recommended by Desiderius Erasmus. Melanchthon maintained a cordial if somewhat strained correspondence with Erasmus; each had respect for the other's classical scholarship, but they disagreed on points of theology. Melanchthon was further instrumental in penning statements for the evangelical cause, such as the *Augsburg Confession* (1530), its *Apologia*, and the *Saxon Confession* (1552). His last years, however, were dogged by controversy with those (such as Matthias Flacius Illyricus) who accused him of diverging from Luther's original teachings.

If Melanchthon's posthumous reputation as a Lutheran remains ambiguous, his legacy as the Praeceptor Germaniae (Teacher of Germany) is indisputable. Through curricular reforms in schools and universities and by the promotion of classical studies in person and in print, Melanchthon established Humanism at the core of Protestant learning in the German lands. He reorganized the traditional *Trivialschule* to focus on mastery of Latin (using the works of Erasmus, Cicero, Terence, and Aesop), in addition to music and the rudiments of Christian doctrine. He also spearheaded curricular reforms at the universities of Wittenberg, Leipzig, Heidelberg, Tübingen, and Jena. He believed that in addition to knowledge of Greek and Hebrew, the rules of classical rhetoric and dialectic were necessary for reading the Bible. These subjects thus became the foundation of the arts curriculum alongside mathematics, natural philosophy, and moral philosophy. Although metaphysics was later to return to Protestant universities, Melanchthon rejected that discipline on the basis that study of the mode of divine being was pointless.

Melanchthon wrote textbooks on Latin grammar, Greek grammar, rhetoric, and dialectics that were published frequently and used extensively across Europe. He composed short commentaries on the works of Hesiod, Homer, Ovid, Terence, Virgil, and Cicero and extolled the importance of many others—Aratus, Aristophanes, Demosthenes, Plutarch, and Sallust—by writing prefaces to their texts and delivering orations on their educational value. In person he lectured on the works of, among others, Aristotle, Ptolemy, Cicero, Demosthenes, Thucydides, Quintilian, Pindar, Theocritus, and Nicander.

Melanchthon also promoted a version of Aristotelian natural philosophy and moral philosophy that was based on the fundamental Lutheran distinction between Law and Gospel. The saving message of Christ could be understood only through reading the Bible, not through philosophizing, which belonged to the category of Law. Philosophy was nevertheless useful for understanding and regulating this life on earth. His commentaries on parts of Aristotle's *Nicomachean Ethics* and *Politics* and on Cicero's *De officiis* (*On Duties*), as well as his own topical manuals on moral philosophy (*Philosophiae moralis epitome*, 1538; *Ethicae doctrinae elementa*, 1550), consistently emphasize civic virtue and order, a point that became increasingly important for the Magisterial Reformers. Melanchthon's two textbooks on natural philosophy (*Liber de anima*, 1549; *Initia doctrinae physicae*, 1549), which clearly drew on Aristotle's *libri naturales*, with eclectic incorporations from Galenic anatomy (and Andreas Vesalius' *De humani corporis fabrica*, of 1543), the works of Ptolemy, and Nicolas Copernicus' *De revolutionibus orbium coelestium* (1543)—though denying Copernicus' heliocentrism on scriptural grounds—showed God's providential design of the physical universe. His belief in God's providence underpinned his belief in planetary influences as well as divine chronology: he promoted astrology as part of natural philosophy in numerous orations and continued to compile and update the world history (*Chronicon*) begun by Johannes Carion.

Melanchthon's students became well trained in Humanist values and skills, and several were inspired to develop their teacher's interests further (e.g., Kaspar Peucer on astrology and history), or into new fields such as the study of plants (e.g., Valerius Cordus on Dioscorides). Others engaged with his work more critically or even turned against him (e.g., Flacius Illyricus) while retaining their Humanist training. Ultimately Melanchthon became an authority whose views many other European and Protestant thinkers engaged with seriously as well, and sometimes critically. His institutional reforms endured, providing generations of students with the study of the classical tradition in German gymnasia and universities.

BIBL.: Claudia Brosseder, *In Bann der Sterne* (Berlin 2004). Ralph Keen, *A Checklist of Melanchthon Imprints through 1560* (Saint Louis 1988). Philipp Melanchthon, *Orations on Philosophy and Education,* ed. Sachiko Kusukawa, trans. Christine Salazar (Cambridge 1999). Heinz Scheible, ed., *Melanchthon in seine Schülern* (Wiesbaden 1997). S.K.

Menander

Greek playwright (ca. 343–292 BCE). Each time he read a verse fragment of Menander's, Sainte-Beuve thought he heard—or so he claimed in his famous essay on Terence—his ghost whisper to him: "For the love of me love Terence." There is no better image for portraying the paradox that underlies Menander's reception from late antiquity to the 21st century. In fact, although Menander can be considered the most influential representative of ancient theater on the subsequent history of Western comedy, the truth is that his importance is of the secondhand variety. Until the discovery of papyri in the 20th century that restored one of his plays (the *Dyskolos*) almost fully and fragments of the rest, the comic genius of Menander wandered like a ghost over the scripts of modern dramatists. From the Renaissance on he lived through his Latin imitators, Plautus and especially Terence, through fragments preserved in other texts, which Molière avidly studied, and through anecdote. His plots (forbidden loves between youths of good stock and prostitutes, adventures with happy endings revolving around the abandonment of children and their later recognition) and his characters (the surly old father, the enamored youth, the shrewd servant) have had an extraordinary influence on all modern theater (think only of Shakespeare, Molière, and Goldoni) and melodrama (not to mention modern soap operas). Indeed, it can be said that he has been so thoroughly imitated as to be unknowable, since for a long time now his identity has been lost in that of his imitators.

A premature textual "death" was suffered by this poet, whom the Alexandrian philologist Aristophanes of Byzantium considered second only to Homer for having portrayed life on the stage. Four of his comedies (*Dyskolos, Epitrepontes, Samia, Aspis*) were still being read in the 6th and 7th centuries, but thereafter all the texts of Menander were lost. It was his great popularity outside the theater that led to the disappearance of his corpus.

If only 8 of the 109 plays staged by Menander were prizewinners, many were successfully copied after his death. This performance practice was continued, above all—but not only—by his Latin imitators in the republican period, with a few reprises in the imperial age (attested by the mosaics of Mytilene). Menander's afterlife continued in two other forms as well: the recitation of individual passages at symposia, and reading. Menander offered not only a dramatic and literary model, but a rhetorical and ethical one as well. Because of the simplicity of his style, which would enrapture Racine, Quintilian included him in the perfect orator's canon of *auctores,* and Plutarch preferred him to Aristophanes for his superior moral dignity. It was, however, the characteristic sententiousness of Menander's plays that made them an object of particular interest in the imperial and Byzantine periods: the *gnomai* that studded their verbal fabric made Menander an undeniable *maître de vérité*, a source of pithy phrases about everyday morality to be used in any context, rather than a product of effective comic potential. Precisely this quotidian, utilitarian contact with Menander's verse inhibited the formation of the kind of erudite distance that ended up assisting in the preservation of other textual corpora, and it transformed Menander's original dramatic dimension into a ghost, to which it was up to the Renaissance to attempt to give a second life.

But we are periodically offered precious signs of the first life of Menander's comedy by the discovery of new papyri and codices, which have followed one another nearly without interruption from the end of the 19th century to our own day. In addition to numerous fragments, they have restored to us a rather substantial textual corpus of seven plays, preserved, if not whole, then in large or quite sizable excerpts: *Aspis* (*The Shield*), *Dyskolos* (*Old Cantankerous*), *Epitrepontes* (*Men at Arbitration*), *Misoumenos* (*The Man She Hated*), *Perikeiromene* (*The Girl Who Has Her Hair Cropped*), *Samia* (*The Girl from Samos*), *Sikionios* (*Sicyonian*). The most important recent finds have been the Bodmer papyrus, which between 1959 and 1969 returned the *Dyskolos* to us nearly whole; a papyrus at the Sorbonne, which in 1964 brought to light a sizable portion of the *Sikionios* from the cartonnage of a mummy; finally, a Syriac palimpsest of the 9th century, found in the fall of 2003 in the Vatican library, which promises the resurrection of about 200 verses of another, unknown comedy, and which, when published, will certainly hold more surprises. The ghost of Menander still haunts the most hidden corners of archives and libraries, waiting to be brought out into the open.

BIBL.: Pat Easterling, "Menander: Loss and Survival," in *Stage Directions: Essays in Ancient Drama in Honour of E. W. Handley,* ed. Alan Griffiths (London 1995) 153–160. Elaine Fantham, "Roman Experience of Menander in the Late Republic and Early Empire," *Transactions of the American Philological Association* 114 (1984) 299–309. E. J. H. Greene, *Menander to Marivaux: The History of a Comic Structure* (Alberta 1977). M.T.

Translated by Patrick Baker

Mercuriale, Girolamo

In Latin, Hieronymus Mercurialis (1530–1606); physician, editor, antiquarian, and professor of medicine successively at Padua, Bologna, and Pisa. He oversaw editions of both Galen and Hippocrates, in part based on manuscripts in his own possession, and published in successive editions of his *Variant Readings* (*Variae lectiones,* 1570–1598) emendations and explanations of classical authors. His most innovative medical writings drew on passages from a wide range of ancient texts, not all of them medical, to classify and elucidate modern diseases. His *De arte gymnastica* (1562) was written with the aim of reintroducing ancient physical exercises into medicine (and into education, where he was followed by the Englishman Richard Muncaster). He went further than earlier proponents of physical activities as part of the education of a gentleman, such as Vittorino da Feltre, by reconstructing ancient practice on the basis of medical and nonmedical texts. The second edition (1573) was enriched with many illustrations allegedly based on ancient coins, sculptures, and inscriptions, the fruit of his friendship with Pirro Ligorio and others in the Farnese circle in Rome. That almost all this material can now be shown to be the result of imaginative reconstruction, or straightforward forgery, was unknown to his readers, who assumed that the images confirmed the truth of what Mercuriale had deduced from the evidence of texts. Subsequent printings added further new archaeological material. In a major appendix to book 1, chapter 11, he used the evidence of Ramusio's relief to support his original theory that Christ and the disciples reclined at the Last Supper on couches and did not sit upright, as artists such as Leonardo had previously portrayed them. The argument and illustrations in *De arte gymnastica* demonstrated the prime place of gymnastics in Greece and Rome and, later, convinced Winckelmann of the importance of nudity in Greek civilization and art.

In the middle years of the 19th century interest in *De arte gymnastica* revived among medical writers. (It had never disappeared among antiquarians and scholars.) Giovanni Rinaldi's Italian version of 1856 and John Blundell's English version of 1864 were in part manifestos for a new medical gymnastics that would, as Mercuriale himself had wished, contribute to the wider health of society. Ligorio's inventive illustration of wrestling holds was also influential in the definition (or even invention) of Graeco-Roman wrestling as an appropriate sport for inclusion in the revived Olympic Games of 1896, as it suggested a distinction between a cultured form of exercise, in which holds below the waist were excluded, and ordinary free-style wrestling.

BIBL.: Jean Michel Agasse, ed., *Girolamo Mercuriale: De arte gymnastica* (Paris 2006–). Alessandro Arcangeli and Vivian Nutton, eds., *Girolamo Mercuriale* (Florence 2007).

V.N.

Metaphrasis

An alteration of the manner in which a text is expressed—from Greek *meta-,* "change," and *phrasis,* "way of speaking" or "text"—metaphrasis in antiquity described the practice of changing a text into a different language (translation) or of reformulating it within the same language ("intralingual translation," Høgel 2002, 95; i.e., paraphrase).

The classical authors can speak for themselves. Plutarch uses the cognate verb *metaphrazein* to introduce a translation from Latin into Greek ("one might translate the inscription [in this way]," *Marcus Cato* 19.3) and also describes Demosthenes as privately devising paraphrases (*metaphraseis*) of speeches he had heard in order to refine his oratorical skills (*Demosthenes* 8.2). A passage from the Roman rhetor Quintilian neatly illustrates different levels of intervention that paraphrase might involve. He advises a schoolteacher that his students should "relate the narrative in a pure and restrained diction . . . then explain it in different words, and finally change it more drastically with a paraphrase in which both abbreviation and rhetorical amplification of the poet's ideas are allowed" (*Institutio oratoria* 1.9.2). Quintilian's predecessor Seneca the Elder used *metaphrasis* in Latin (*Suasoriae* 1.12) to describe radical stylistic revision of a passage, complaining that the Greek orator Dorion produced a notorious piece of bombast in his reformulation (*in metaphrasi*) of Homer's Cyclops episode.

In the scholarly and literary sense of "stylistic revision," metaphrasis never gained currency in the Latin tradition. The practice persisted in Greek literature, however, where a dynamic tension with classical models led to continual stylistic evaluation and revision of texts. Around 400 CE Nonnus versified the Gospel of John, and pseudo-Apollinaris of Laodicea rewrote the Psalms in hexameters and the New Testament in Platonic dialogue form. Their desire to raise Christian writings to the status of classical literature endured in Byzantium.

In Byzantine hagiography the practice of metaphrasis gained its greatest significance. Many contemporaneous *vitae* of saints and martyrs composed in simple style during late antiquity were rewritten in an elevated, encomiastic form during the 9th-century post-iconoclastic period. Shortly before 1000 CE this trend reached a remarkable climax with the production of a 10-volume collection of traditional saints' lives intended for liturgical use, arranged in order of the feast days (a *menologion*) and rewritten in consistently elevated style. The scholar supervising the project became known as Symeon Metaphrastes (the Metaphraser). Symeon's *menologion* was a smash success in Byzantium; the survival of some 700 extant manuscripts indicates that it responded to a real need. What was that need? Høgel suggests (2002, 157) that the Metaphrastic enterprise promoted a standard canon of saints' lives and of saints for a society lacking a formal process of canonization. Ironically, the polymath Michael Psellus subsequently elevated Symeon himself to the status of saint in a hagiographical encomium. Symeon's reputation remained so high that Constantine Akropolites, rewriter of 29 saints' lives in the early 14th century, earned the title The Second Metaphrastes.

Metaphrasis affected literature other than hagiographical texts in low style, however. The 9th-century patriarch Nicephorus I rewrote a few pages of his own *Breviarium* in the classicizing style favored for historical works, a style later carried to breathtaking extremes by authors like Manasses, Choniates, Anna Comnena, Blemmydes, and Pachymeres. Later generations, eager for historical content but baffled by the style of these authors, turned gratefully to skillful metaphraseis produced in the Palaeologan period and written in the more accessible "writers' *koinē*" that offered straightforward vocabulary, familiar morphological forms and syntax, logical word arrangement, and streamlined imagery and allusions. Even scholars preferred it for their private reading; Nicephorus Gregoras (14th cent.), for example, owned the metaphrasis of Blemmydes' convoluted princes' mirror *Imperial Statue* but not the original.

Metaphrasis provided a useful means of exploring and clarifying difficult or obscure texts. The 10th-century writer on siegecraft Heron of Byzantium justified simplifying and expanding his classical source text "lest with the obscurity that predominates . . . the [reader's] mind . . . be too exhausted for comprehension even of what is clear" (*Parangelmat Poliorceta* 1, trans. Denis Sullivan). Medieval scribes consciously or unconsciously altered texts in a process now considered corruption but then regarded as modest metaphrasis meant to improve a work. Even in this modern age of scientific textual criticism, the poems of Cavafy could not escape what amounts to editorial metaphrasis through standardization and modernization (Mullett 2004, 9, noting Hirst on p. 296).

In the Latin West regard for paraphrase as a pedagogical tool continued from the classical period into the Renaissance. Saint Augustine recalls his schoolboy triumph paraphrasing in prose Juno's hexameter tirade from *Aeneid* book 1 (*Confessions* 1.17), and Jesuit education in the Renaissance retained strict paraphrase in the *praelectio* of an author. Direct evidence of paraphrase in the classroom survives in pamphlets published in Paris for a 16th-century college lecture series. Notes and a summary in Latin accompany the full text of each classical work to be discussed, which was then glossed by the student with an interlinear Latin paraphrase dictated by the lecturer.

In the late 17th century the elegant collection of 39 classical Latin authors published in Paris, *Ad usum Delphini,* that is, for instruction of the dauphin, provided on each page an original Latin text accompanied by notes and paraphrase in Latin. Designed to build competence in Latin by immersing the reader in varying stylistic levels of the language, these luxury texts failed to engage the affable but incurious son of Louis XIV for whom they were intended. Others did not share the Dauphin's indifference. The complete collection was reissued in London by Valpy (1819–1830), and collectors and bibliophiles today treasure volumes of the original royal edition.

BIBL.: Anthony Grafton, "Teacher, Text and Pupil in the Renaissance Class-Room: A Case Study from a Parisian College," *History of Universities* 1 (1981) 37–70. Christian Høgel, *Symeon Metaphrastes: Rewriting and Canonization* (Copenhagen 2002). Margaret Mullett, ed., *Metaphrastes, or Gained in Translation: Essays and Translations in Honour of Robert H. Jordan* (Belfast 2004). Ihor Sevcenko, "Levels of Style in Byzantine Literature," *Jahrbuch der Österreichischen Byzantinistik* 32, no. 1 (1982) 289–312, and "Additional Remarks to the Report on Levels of Style," *Jahrbuch der Österreichischen Byzantinistik* 32, no. 2 (1982) 220–238. Catherine Volpilhac-Auger, *La Collection ad usum Delphini: L'antiquité au miroir du Grand Siècle* (Grenoble 2000). E.F.

Metaphysics

The most central discipline in philosophy, which investigates fundamental and general problems, such as the nature of being, substances and attributes, individuals and universals, identity, act and potency, and causation. The name *ta meta ta physika* was first used as the title for a group of Aristotle's texts dealing with problems that go "beyond" physics. Aristotle himself never used this term for his novel philosophical project. He instead called it "first philosophy," because it is a science about the first causes of whatever exists. It also investigates the first principles of all rational discourse, that is, the law of noncontradiction, which states that "it is impossible to hold the same thing to be and not to be."

In some texts Aristotle defines this philosophy as a general discipline, a science that investigates being qua being and its essential properties. "This science is not the same as any of the particular sciences, for none of them investigates being qua being in general; they divide off some portion of it and study its attributes, as do, for example, the mathematical sciences" (*Metaphysics* 4.1003a21–26). When taken in this general sense, metaphysics is a science of being, or *ontology* (a term created in the early 17th century).

The possibility and method of such a discipline was from the beginning problematic. How is a general knowledge of being possible, if being itself is not one specific "genus" (as nature, which is the object of physics or number, is the object of arithmetic)? But, as Aristotle argues, although the verb *is* is said in many different senses, it is not as a purely equivocal term, for in all usages there is a reference to one focal meaning. The primary sense of *being,* to which all other meanings are related, is what a thing is, its *ousia. Ousia* can be understood as "essence" because a thing owes its being to what makes it this specific being, whereas the other categories of being, such as quantity, quality, and relation, only point to accidental modes of being. *Ousia* may also be translated as "substance" because it is what remains permanent through change and supports the accidental forms of beings.

It is a difficult question to determine what kinds of beings are substances: only material things, such as animals and plants? or also spiritual beings such as minds, or numbers, or universal forms (as the Platonists thought)? Although Aristotle rejected the Platonic forms, he accepted that there are forms beyond matter and motion, such as the immobile movers of the celestial spheres and the first immobile mover of the cosmos, the divine intellect. In its search for the first principles of whatever exists, metaphysics ultimately seeks to investigate these divine essences and thus becomes a "theology" (a term first created by Aristotle). Thus, in the celebrated book 12 (or *lambda*) of the *Metaphysics* Aristotle describes the first mover of the universe as a self-thinking intellect, which moves "as an object of love and striving." But how can first philosophy still be of universal range if it is about a particular sphere of beings, the divine essences? It is *universal,* Aristotle answers, because the divine natures it is dealing with are the *first* causes of whatever exists.

From its start the metaphysical project is thus characterized by a fundamental ambivalence: it is both an ontology and a theology. According to Martin Heidegger, an influential 20th-century philosopher, this is the original sin of the metaphysical project: instead of revealing the meaning of being as being, the project ends as a study of the supreme forms of being, the god(s). This ambivalent project of onto-theology set the agenda for centuries of metaphysical speculation, whereby the original question, the wonder about being and its disclosure, was eclipsed (*Seinsvergessenheit,* "oblivion of being").

In late antiquity metaphysics was indeed understood as a theological science. The Neoplatonic commentators even used the term *theology* to refer to Aristotle's metaphysics. In their interpretation metaphysics is a science of being qua being, because it investigates what truly exists, the transcendent intellectual forms. The sensible things, which are in permanent change, never fully are what they are and exist only insofar as they have some share in being. Metaphysics thus became the study of the suprasensible world.

It was only in medieval philosophy that metaphysics was rediscovered as an ontology: some present-day scholars even speak of this development as the "second start" of metaphysics. The credit for this new understanding of Aristotle's metaphysics goes to Avicenna (11th cent.). In his view metaphysics cannot be defined as a theology, because the existence of God is demonstrated in this science, and no science can be about an object that is to be demonstrated in it. First philosophy is an investigation of being in general and of its properties, which transcend all categories, such as one, good, true, necessity, and contingency. As Thomas Aquinas says in the prologue to his commentary on the *Metaphysics,* "The subject matter of a science is the genus whose causes and properties we seek, and not the causes themselves of the particular genus studied; for a knowledge of the causes of some genus is the goal to which the investigation of a science attains." Hence, the subject matter of metaphysics is being in general (*ens commune*), considered in separation from matter and motion. That is, it examines all things that are—natural objects, mathematical objects, spiritual beings such as minds—under the aspect of being, making abstraction from the fact that they exist or do not exist in matter and motion. This science also studies God insofar as God is the first cause of all being. According to Duns Scotus, metaphysics is a transcendental science because it primarily investigates the properties of being that "transcend" the distinction between finite and infinite beings.

This scholastic conception of metaphysics as a study both of being and its properties, and of the divine cause, was continually refined throughout the early modern period, as is witnessed in the vast synthesis of Francisco Suárez (*Disputationes metaphysicae,* 1597). But the tension within its object led eventually, at the beginning of the 17th century, to the division of metaphysics into two different disciplines, namely *metaphysica generalis* (dealing with general notions of being) and *metaphysica particularis* (dealing with spiritual substances, such as god and the soul). This modern tradition dominated central European thought until Kant in the 18th century.

There was, however, a growing disillusionment among modern thinkers about "this abstruse philosophy and metaphysical jargon" (David Hume, *An Enquiry concerning Human Understanding,* 1748). For Thomas Hobbes and other empiricist thinkers metaphysics was the coronation of the "vain philosophy" of Aristotle, the scholasticism still dominating the universities. What is written in handbooks of metaphysics, Hobbes says, "is so far from the possibility of being understood, and so repugnant to natural reason, that whosoever thinketh there is any thing to be understood by it, must needs think it supernatural," for those people talk about essences separated from bodies and substantial forms, which are "names of nothing . . . not names of things" (*Leviathan,* 1651, chap. 46). Of course, Hobbes and his cohorts attempted to develop a first philosophy themselves, explaining our most fundamental notions concerning the nature and generation of all things, but they refused the sort of first philosophy taught in the schools.

An interesting example of the increasingly negative connotation of the term *metaphysics* in that era is that at the end of the 17th century a group of English poets with a love of elaborate style and abstractions came to be called "metaphysical." In his *Discourse concerning Satire* (1693) John Dryden criticized the poetry of John Donne for being so: "He affects the Metaphysics . . . in his amorous verses, where nature only should reign; and perplexes the minds of the fair sex with nice speculations of philosophy, when he should engage their hearts." Other authors in England still adhered to the Neoplatonic metaphysical view. Henry More, one of the Cambridge Platonists, in his "handbook" on the topic defined metaphysics as "the art of the right contemplation of the incorporeal things in so far as they are evident in the natural light of reason" (*Enchiridium metaphysicum,* 1679).

The critique of traditional metaphysics as a subtle speculation floating above reality among abstract entities did not prevent the development of some of our most admirable metaphysical systems during the 17th and 18th centuries, most notably Descartes in his *Meditations on First Philosophy* (in Latin, 1641; translated as *Méditations métaphysiques touchant la première philosophie,* 1647), Spinoza in his *Ethics* (which starts with the definition of substance and its properties), and Leibniz's *Discours de la métaphysique* (1686). Leibniz is a typical representative of rational metaphysics. In his *Principles of Nature and Grace* (1718) he exhorts us "to move up to the metaphysical level," on the great principle that "nothing comes about without a sufficient cause." Whoever understands a phenomenon well enough must be capable of giving a sufficient reason why this is the case rather than its opposite. Given that principle, the first question we have to ask is why there is something rather than nothing. Having admitted that things must exist, we must be able to give a reason why they have to exist as they are, and not in another way. This sufficient cause cannot be found in the series of contingent things (the bodies and their representations in the souls) but has to be outside the series of contingent causes, in a substance, which is a necessary being, having in itself the cause of its own existence (what is called God) (§§ 7–10).

In his early philosophical education Immanuel Kant had been fully exposed to this type of rationalistic metaphysics, but his reading of Hume had made him skeptical about the possibility of such a project. As he writes in the first preface of his celebrated *Critique of Pure Reason* (*Kritik der reinen Vernunft,* 1781), "Human reason has the peculiar fate that it is burdened with questions which it cannot dismiss, since they are given to it as problems by the nature of reason itself, but which it also cannot answer, since they transcend every capacity of human reason." Such are questions about the eternity of the world or its creation in time, the existence of a first cause beyond the physical world, the eternity of the soul (topics traditionally studied in *metaphysica specialis* as distinguished from *metaphysica generalis* or ontology). As Kant explains, metaphysics "begins from principles whose use is unavoidable in the course of experience, but then is required to take refuge in principles that overstep all possible use in experience." That is what Leibniz was doing in applying the principle of sufficient reason beyond the series of contingent things. But when we try to surpass the bounds of experience in an attempt to find an ultimate explanation, we "fall into obscurity and contradictions" because we no longer recognize "any touchstone of experience"—hence "the battlefield of these endless controversies in metaphysics." We are far from the time that metaphysics was called the "queen of all sciences" because of the sublimity of its subject, offering an ultimate explanation going beyond nature. Therefore, we should suspend all metaphysical projects until we have solved the critical question about the possibility and bounds of pure knowledge. Kant aims at the "rebirth" of metaphysics as a science through the fundamental critique of reason. Transcendental philosophy, which investigates the a priori structures of human reason, replaces the general metaphysics or ontology. The metaphysics of nature is a critical analysis of the fundamental concepts of the empirical sciences; the metaphysics of morals is a nonempirical study of the concepts and postulates of a pure free will.

Kant's critique of traditional realistic metaphysics was so overwhelming that no return to traditional metaphysics was possible. "That which, prior to this period, was called metaphysics, has been, so to speak, extirpated root and branch and has vanished from the rank of sciences . . . The fact is that there no longer exists any interest either in form or in the content of metaphysics or in both together" (Hegel, in the first introduction to his *Science of Logic,* 1812, trans. A. V. Miller). Hegel observes how in the aftermath of Kant "philosophy and the ordinary common sense cooperated to bring about the downfall of metaphysics": "There was seen the strange spectacle of a cultured nation without metaphysics—like a temple richly ornamented in other respects but without a holy of holies"; "If it is remarkable when a nation has become indifferent to its constitutional theory, to its national sentiments, its ethical customs and virtues, it is certainly no less remarkable when a nation loses its metaphysics, when the spirit which contemplates its own pure essence is no longer a present reality in the life of a nation."

It all sounds nostalgic, but Hegel was just as much as Kant convinced that the traditional metaphysics was finished. It was no longer possible to take the determinations of thought in a naive realism as the determinations of being itself (as ontology—a pretentious term—aims to do). In Hegel's view the "science of logic," which examines the concepts of the spirit by itself, should replace the traditional metaphysics of being. Those concepts, however, are not just a priori forms of reason, as Kant thought, but constitute the essences of things themselves. Hegel's metaphysical logic comes close to what Platonists call "dialectic." Interestingly, he does not consider Plato or Aristotle as "metaphysicians." As with Kant, his critique on metaphysics is directed mainly against the modern development of metaphysics, as one can find in the writings of Christian Wolff (1679–1754).

Kant's idea that the metaphysical project is founded in the nature of human reason was radicalized by Arthur Schopenhauer, who notably defined a human being as an *animal metaphysicum.* Among all other animals humans are the only ones that wonder about their own existence, because they are aware of their own death. Only humans have a "metaphysical need." The fundamental unrest, the awareness that the world can as well be and not be, the wonder not only that the world is, but that it is such a miserable, depressing world, "that is the *punctum pruriens* [burning issue] of all metaphysics." For the rest Schopenhauer holds a rather traditional definition of metaphysics, as a knowledge going beyond the possibilities of experience, beyond nature, to grasp the fundamental ground of all phenomena, the *Ding an Sich* ("Thing in itself"), which is for him the Will. Not only metaphysics but also music expresses what the Thing is in itself. Melodies are somehow analogous to universal concepts. In fact, they are better than concepts, because in concepts we have only the most abstract external shells of things, whereas in music we hear the inner heart vibrate. Music thus becomes an unconscious exercise in metaphysics in which the mind does not know it is philosophizing.

For Friedrich Nietzsche the metaphysical need is not the origin of religion, as Schopenhauer thought, but an offspring of it. Metaphysical thinkers attempt to find absolute truth, foundations, certainty, and meaning, and are thus driven to postulate a world beyond appearances.

What they in fact do is to continue a rationalized form of religion in concepts and with rational demonstration, which can lead only to a greater disillusionment. "How one would like to exchange the [false assertions of the priests] for truths that would be as salutary, pacifying, and beneficial as those errors are! yet such truths do not exist!" The most philosophers can do is set against these religious errors metaphysical plausibilities, but those are at bottom likewise untrue. "The tragedy lies in the fact that one cannot believe these dogmas of religion and metaphysics if one has in one's heart and head the rigorous methods of acquiring truth, while on the other hand one has, through the development of humanity, grown so tender, sensitive and afflicted one has need of means of cure and comfort of the most potent description" (*Human, All Too Human,* 109, trans. R. J. Hollingdale).

Kant's critique of metaphysics becomes more radical with the empiricism and logical positivism of the early 20th century, exemplified in a celebrated paper by Rudolf Carnap, "The Overcoming of Metaphysics through the Logical Analysis of Language" (1931). For Ludwig Wittgenstein metaphysical statements are nonsensical and due to linguistic confusion. But later developments in analytical philosophy, starting with Willard Quine and Peter Strawson, have led to a renewed interest in ontological questions. According to Strawson (*Individuals: An Essay in Descriptive Metaphysics,* 1959) metaphysics is an inquiry into the framework of our discourse and thought about the world, analyzing its ontological presuppositions. Quine (*Word and Objects,* 1960) investigates the "ontological commitments" of a given body of discourse, in particular a scientific theory as physics.

The most recent decades have witnessed a remarkable revival of studies in metaphysics in the Aristotelian tradition of ontology—as one may learn from browsing, for example, through the *Oxford Handbook of Metaphysics* (2003). Philosophers discuss substances (what kinds of things there are, in what ways they exist), individuals, categories, identity, modality and possible worlds, space and time, events and causation, persons and minds, freedom, realism and idealism. But this academic discussion is worlds removed from what one may find when browsing through the Internet on the search word *metaphysics:* an amazing spectrum of sites devoted to metaphysical poetry and painting, metaphysical health care and alternative medicine, metaphysical spiritual publications, metaphysical fairs with community celebrations of personal growth, planetary consciousness and holistic lifestyle. Metaphysical Painting is an Italian art movement, founded in 1917 by Carlo Carrà and Giorgio de Chirico. In their paintings they aimed to give a picture of a reality beyond the surface of the physical world, a "higher, more hidden state of being" to which simple ordinary objects point. All these examples show, as Nietzsche once said, that the traditional concept of metaphysics as an attempt to go beyond experience surprisingly survives the critique of Kant and the more radical forms of critique after him. Having been separated from "rigorous methods of acquiring the truth," however, this metaphysics is more and more relegated to the margin of philosophy, in various forms of music and art and, alas, in various esoteric pseudo-religions.

What at the beginning was only a certain ambivalence in a new philosophical project seems, after more than 20 centuries, to have led to a real split—which we may deplore—between metaphysics as ontology in an analytical tradition and metaphysics as a kind of theo-philosophy in the Continental tradition. But all this is the astonishing heritage of a rather technical work by Aristotle, which never had the title *Metaphysics* and maybe never was planned as a unitary philosophical project.

BIBL.: H. Burkhardt, B. Smith, et al., eds., *Handbook of Metaphysics and Ontology,* 2 vols. (Munich 1991). T. Crane and K. Farkar, eds., *Metaphysics: A Guide and Anthology* (Oxford 2004). "Metaphysics," in *Encyclopedia of Philosophy,* 2nd ed., ed. D. Borchert (Detroit 2006) 169–212. "Metaphysik" and "Metaphysikkritik" in *Historisches Wörterbuch der Philosophie* (Darmstadt 1980) 5:1286–1294. *The Oxford Handbook of Metaphysics,* ed. Michael J. Loux and Dean W. Zimmermann (Oxford 2003). P. Porro, ed., *Metaphysica, sapientia, scientia divina: The Subject and Status of First Philosophy in the Middle Ages,* Quaestio: Yearbook of the History of Metaphysics 5 (Turnhout 2005).

C.S.

Meteorology

The modern term *meteorology* derives from the ancient Greek word *meteorologia,* referring to the study of the *meteora,* the "things high up." Aristotle, in his natural philosophical work *Meteorology* (ca. 350 BCE), defines the subject as "everything that happens naturally, but with a regularity less than that of the primary element of bodies, in the region which borders most nearly on the movements of the stars." To some extent, meteorology is defined by the location in which meteorological phenomena occur, that is, below the region of celestial motion. Its study is concerned also with "all phenomena that may be regarded as common to air and water, and the various kinds and parts of the earth and their characteristics." Accordingly, Aristotle discusses a wide range of topics: shooting stars, colorful nighttime phenomena (possibly the aurora borealis), comets, rain, clouds, mist, dew, snow, hail, rivers and springs, coastal erosion and silting, the origin and saltiness of the sea, thunder and lightning, hurricanes, typhoons, whirlwinds and thunderbolts, haloes, rainbows, "rods" and *parhēlia* ("mock suns"), as well as winds and earthquakes. From the modern vantage point, these are not all meteorological, and not all atmospheric. For Aristotle, they can all be understood as being the products of exhalations, involving changes from one terrestrial "element" to another. Meteorological processes serve a mediating role in the natural world: meteorological phenomena are caused by motions in the celestial region and, in turn, affect the terrestrial region, including life on earth.

Several of the Presocratic natural philosophers, including Anaximander and Anaximenes, were concerned with explaining the *meteora*. Aristotle's treatise is the earliest extant; his *Meteorology* and Seneca's *Natural Questions* (1st cent. CE) are the two most complete surviving ancient natural philosophical texts on the subject. A number of other ancient philosophers addressed the subject, including Theophrastus and Epicurus, and others also wrote on meteorology, including the Roman Epicurean poet Lucretius in book 6 of *De rerum natura* (mid-1st cent. BCE) and Pliny the Elder in his *Natural History* (ca. 77 CE).

Commentaries on Aristotle's *Meteorology* were produced not only in Greek, but also, in the medieval period, in Hebrew, Arabic, and Latin; it was the first of his writings to be translated into Hebrew. Pliny served as a source (perhaps secondhand) for Isidore of Seville's encyclopedic *Etymologies* (early 7th cent.), in which he explains the nature of air and clouds (13.7), thunder and lightning (13.8), and rainbows and rain (13.10). Lucretius' poem found many readers during the Renaissance and modern periods, attracted in part to the rational explanations offered for alarming phenomena. Unusual meteorological events can be frightening and fascinating, and there are numerous examples of publications from the early modern period alerting people to particular phenomena, including comets, and their portents.

For the ancients, *meteorologia* was concerned with the explanation, not prediction, of phenomena. Pliny is unusual in that he discusses prediction (in book 18), as well as explanation (in book 2). A number of other ancient texts offer help in predicting meteorological phenomena, using traditional methods that relate, for example, to the observation of animal behavior or celestial occurrences. Aratus's Greek poem *Phaenomena* (3rd cent. BCE) and its various ancient Latin translations, as well as the written texts and stone inscriptions known as *parapegmata* (relating celestial phenomena to weather), offer insights into ancient Greek and Roman techniques of weather prediction. Similar approaches to weather prognostication can be found in medieval and modern weather calendars and almanacs.

BIBL.: Resi Fontaine, "The Reception of Aristotle's *Meteorology* in Hebrew Scientific Writings of the Thirteenth Century," *Aleph* 1 (2001) 101–139. Vladimir Janković, *Reading the Skies: A Cultural History of English Weather* (Chicago 2000). Paul Lettinck, *Aristotle's Meteorology and Its Reception in the Arab World* (Leiden 1999). Liba Taub, *Ancient Meteorology* (London 2003).

L.T.

Michelangelo

Born in 1475, Michelangelo came of age in the 1490s in Florence, in the garden of Lorenzo de' Medici, where, according to the poetically embellished accounts of his 16th-century biographers, Vasari and Condivi, he made his first essay in the classical style by carving in marble a smiling faun that was based on an ancient sculpture. At the suggestion of the distinguished classicist and poet Angelo Poliziano, who was part of Lorenzo's circle, he next executed the *Battle of Lapiths and Centaurs.* Seemingly unfinished, the figures of this relief create an Ovidian effect, since they appear to be, as if in a metamorphosis, emerging from stone. Such ambitious, boldly animated, and complexly interwoven figures in Michelangelo's virtuoso piece demonstrate the artist's goal to surpass ancient relief statuary. His ambition is especially evident in the figure of the bearded old man, at the left of the relief, holding a large stone with two hands, who is an allusion to Plutarch's description of Phidias' self-portrait in a relief sculpture. This conceit, probably provided to him by Poliziano, suggests Michelangelo's persona as a modern Phidias.

Classical antiquity dominated Michelangelo's early work. Lorenzo di Pierfrancesco de' Medici, il Magnifico's cousin, persuaded Michelangelo to present his *Cupid* (ca. 1495) as an ancient work, a forgery that created a scandal when it was discovered to be modern. The artist next went to Rome, where he made the virtuoso *Bacchus* (ca. 1497), which, in its bold, playful representation of the staggering, intoxicated deity, surpassed all ancient antecedents in its novelty. Even in his most devotional work, Michelangelo's classical roots are evident; above all, the Apollonian beauty of Jesus in his beloved Rome *Pietà* (ca. 1498). Carving his epoch-making, colossal *David* in Florence several years later (1501–1504), Michelangelo surpassed, Vasari writes, all previous sculptors, both ancient and modern. When Michelangelo was called on in 1505 to design the tomb of Pope Julius II, his first monumental work of architecture and sculpture, the artist was inspired by the form of the classical triumphal arch—a type of structure that later influenced his design for the ultimately unrealized facade for the church of San Lorenzo in Florence (ca. 1517).

The artist's original design for the tomb of Julius, realized in diminished form years later in San Pietro in Vincoli (1545), stands behind the scheme of his great Sistine ceiling decoration (1508–1512), in which the beautiful, aggrandized nudes are informed by the aesthetic ideals of the recently rediscovered ancient Laocoön and Torso Belvedere, statues that similarly influenced the even more monumental figures of his *Last Judgment* (1536–1541), also in the Sistine Chapel.

Between the two Sistine projects, Michelangelo worked for the Medici at San Lorenzo, during the 1520s and early 1530s, primarily on their burial chapel and library, projects carried out in the classical idiom with extraordinary poetic license and fantasy: for example, in the frieze of the chapel, grotesque, monstrous heads, worthy of Horace's *Ars poetica,* have prominent pairs of teeth that jokingly play on the classical dentils nearby.

Michelangelo's design for the buildings and space of the Campidoglio on the Capitoline Hill, where he had the ancient statue of Marcus Aurelius placed for Pope Paul III in 1538, was conceived in a grand classical manner, appropriate to the original site of important Roman shrines. Inspired by the modern classicism of Brunelleschi and Bramante, Michelangelo also gave final form to the dome of St. Peter's (1547–1564), a great cupola that ultimately harked back to the vast vaulted spaces of ancient Rome, and in his last years he designed the grandiose church of Santa Maria degli Angeli (1561–1564), built on the colossal ruins of the baths of Diocletian.

In the period before his death in 1564, however, Michelangelo wrote penitential poetry that, reflecting an increasingly zealous Counter-Reformation piety, rejected the Neoplatonic vision of beauty absorbed from Marsilio Ficino during his early years in the Medici milieu. As his badly battered and broken Rondanini *Pietà* (ca. 1554–1564) makes manifest (especially when compared with his first *Pietà*), Michelangelo was no longer able to reconcile his Christian aspirations to spiritual perfection with the aesthetic ideals inherited from the classical tradition.

P.B.

Midas

Mythical king of Phrygia, possibly identifiable with a historical figure whose tomb has been excavated at Gordium (Yass Höyük) in modern Turkey.

Ovid tells two stories of Midas's *pingue ingenium* (thick-wittedness; *Metamorphoses* 11.148). Because of a kindness to Silenus, Bacchus offers Midas his choice of gifts; the king's wish to have everything that he touches turn to gold leads to near starvation, and he is allowed to wash away his power in the Pactolus. The phrase "Midas touch" has its own life as a term of praise, but the story itself is cautionary, even satiric; Ovid's 17th-century translator George Sandys calls Midas "the image of a covetous man, who while he seeks to augment his riches denies himself the use of his own and starves in abundance" (1632). In the 1620s Nicolas Poussin at least three times painted the scene of the king divesting himself of his gift. In *Les fleurs du mal* (1857) Charles Baudelaire claims that he is "the equal of Midas" for being able to "change gold into iron" with his sadness ("Alchimie de la douleur"). Nathaniel Hawthorne gives the story an influential twist in *A Wonder Book for Girls and Boys* (1852) by adding a daughter, Marygold, transformed when her father kisses her. This version has become popular in retellings for young readers; Mary Zimmerman uses it as the frame for her stage version of the *Metamorphoses* (2001). A villainous Dr. Midas and his embittered daughter, Oubliette, figure in Grant Morrison's comic book *Marvel Boy* (2000–2001).

In a further folly, Midas prefers Pan to Apollo in a music contest and acquires a pair of ass's ears for his bad taste. A headdress conceals them, but his barber knows the truth and tells it to a hole in the ground; the reeds that grow there sing the news to the world. The Judgment of Midas, often conflated with the competition between Apollo and Marsyas, is a subject in visual art from the early 16th century; a painting from a design by Rubens (1636–1638) has a triple presence in the Prado: in its original execution by Jacob Jordaens, in a copy by Juan Bautista Martínez del Mazo, and seen on the back wall of Velázquez's *Las Meninas*. Thomas Campion composed a song on the subject (1617), J. S. Bach a cantata (BWV 201, 1729). Kane O'Hara's burlesque (1760) has had a lively career in Ireland, Britain, and America; there have been several operas, including one in Turkish by Ferit Tüzün (1969). Plays encompassing both parts of Midas's story have been written by the Elizabethan John Lyly (1589; perhaps inspiring the "large, fair ears" that Shakespeare's Bottom acquires a few years later in *A Midsummer Night's Dream*) and by Mary Shelley (1820; including two lyrics by her husband, Percy). Tüzün's opera takes its text from the first part of a Midas trilogy (1959–1970) by the Turkish playwright Güngör Dilmen.

In addition to a daughter, Midas occasionally acquires a wife. Geoffrey Chaucer's Wife of Bath tells the story about the ass's ears with the wife taking the part of the barber, as testimony that "we wommen konne nothyng hele [hide]" (*The Wife of Bath's Tale* l.950). Alexander Pope endorses this version in defending the craft of satire: "The truth once told (and wherefore should we lie?),/The queen of Midas slept, and so may I" ("Epistle to Dr. Arbuthnot" 1735, ll.81–82). More recently, Carol Ann Duffy's poem "Mrs. Midas" (*The World's Wife,* 2001) is a vignette of conjugal wariness: "I made him sit/on the other side of the room and keep his hands to himself./I locked the cat in the cellar."

G.B.

Milton, John

English poet and political pamphleteer, 1608–1674. Milton is the most learned English poet, and classical literature and history influenced every aspect of his poetic and political career. He was taught Greek and Latin from an early age, both by private tutors and at St. Paul's School. After attending Christ's College Cambridge (1625–1632), he devoted six years (1632–1638) to private study. In a Latin letter addressed to his boyhood friend Charles Diodati, he says that his reading has traced "the affairs of the Greeks to the time when they ceased to be Greeks" (1637). He toured Italy in 1638–1639, impressing his Italian hosts with the quality of his Italian and Latin poems. Many of his early poems, including *Arcades* and *A Mask* (commonly known as *Comus*), bear the stamp of Greek and Roman pastoral. "Lycidas," written in 1637 to commemorate the death by drowning of Milton's Cambridge classmate Edward King, is widely regarded as the best pastoral elegy (even the best short poem) in English. Milton also wrote a Latin pastoral elegy, *Epitaphium Damonis,* commemorating Diodati's untimely death in 1638. Like Petrarch and Mantuan before him, he makes pastoral a vehicle for anti-ecclesiastical satire by incorporating a biblical contrast between good and bad shepherds.

Milton played no active role in the English Civil War, but he defended the execution of King Charles I in several prose pamphlets (both Latin and English), beginning with *The Tenure of Kings and Magistrates* (1649). These pamphlets evoke biblical and classical precedents to justify regicide and advocate a republican form of government. Milton's most celebrated pamphlet, *Areopagitica* (1644), is an argument against prepublication censorship, modeled on Isocrates' *Areopagiticus* (355 BCE). The relation of Milton's tract to its Isocratic precedent has puzzled many, since Isocrates contrasts the degenerate democracy of his own time with the old Athenian court of the Areopagus, which had acted as a censor of public morals. Many have thought it strange that Milton should model his speech against censorship on a speech that had advocated censorship. But the truth is more complicated than this. Both Milton and Isocrates argue that it is futile to legislate virtue, and Isocrates praises the Areopagus for *not* imposing laws. Milton directly echoes this part of *Areopagiticus* in *Areopagitica.*

Milton frequently refers to ancient history in both his poetry and his prose. A favorite source is Plutarch's *Parallel Lives,* which is beautifully evoked in Sonnet 8, as well as in *Paradise Lost* (9.509) and *Paradise Regained* (2.196). All of the poems (and much of the prose) are rich in mythological allusions, and *Paradise Lost* and *Paradise Regained* are steeped in the memory of Homer and Virgil. Critics differ on the question of how, and how often, Milton alludes to specific, identifiable poetic passages. Harding (1962) sees almost all the intertextual moments in *Paradise Lost* as literary allusions, calculated to invite comparison and contrast with their classical target texts. Martindale (1985) and Porter (1993) are more skeptical, dismissing most of Harding's "allusions" as epic commonplaces or topoi. They conclude that the number of literary allusions in *Paradise Lost* has been exaggerated. The question is still debated.

Paradise Lost (1st publ. 1667, rev. 1674) is the culmination of Milton's lifelong ambition to write a great epic. More than this, it is the culmination of Renaissance Europe's numerous attempts to create a new epic based on classical models. Milton's is one of very few such epics (Tasso's *Gerusalemme liberata,* 1580–1581, is another) to have achieved the status of a permanent classic in its own right, and so to have made the Renaissance epic enterprise worthwhile. Milton's relation to classical epic precedent is nevertheless a matter of some dispute. There has been much debate as to whether *Paradise Lost* is an epic or an anti-epic. The poem's action (unusually for epic) presents not a triumph but a defeat: the Fall of Man. Early critics, including John Dryden (1631–1700), were troubled by the unhappy ending and spent much energy on the task of identifying the poem's hero. A common Renaissance and neoclassical assumption was that epic heroes should prosper and that epic poems should move readers to virtue by depicting virtuous acts. Milton's Adam does not prosper, and his main action (eating an apple) is neither heroic nor virtuous. Despite this difficulty, Joseph Addison praised *Paradise Lost* for its supposed conformity with epic precedent, and his 18 *Spectator* papers (1712) helped establish the poem as a classic of the same kind as Homer's *Iliad* and Virgil's *Aeneid.* A reaction to this view occurred in the 20th century, when many critics saw *Paradise Lost* as an anti-epic that disparages traditional epic virtues by conferring them on Satan. Whatever Milton thought of martial heroism, he certainly loved Homer and Virgil (he is reputed to have been able to recite the former from memory). Norbrook (1999) and others have recently argued that Lucan's *Pharsalia* is a significant influence on *Paradise Lost,* providing epic precedent for both republican politics and a triumphant hero-villain.

An ambivalent attitude to classical literature is also found in *Paradise Regained* (1671), wherein Jesus, tempted by Satan in the wilderness, notoriously rejects Athenian philosophy and poetry as unworthy of comparison with Hebrew culture. Some have interpreted this as evidence of Milton's own renunciation of the classical learning to which he had devoted so much of his life. Others have emphasized that Athenian culture is not part of Satan's formal temptation and so is implicitly not his to give.

Samson Agonistes, published in the same volume as *Paradise Regained,* is a closet drama modeled on Greek tragedy, and Milton in his preface praises Aeschylus, Sophocles, and Euripides as "three tragic poets unequaled yet by any." This enthusiasm was unusual for its time, when the Greek tragedians were barely known in England (the first English edition of Aeschylus dates from 1663). *Samson Agonistes* is the first important work of English literature to bear the stamp of the Greek tragic poets. Critics still debate whether the presiding spirit of Milton's play is Hellenic, Hebraic, or Christian. In recent years critics have been much exercised by the question whether Milton's Samson is a "terrorist." Both defenders and disparagers of Samson have tended to use the word "terror" as if it had no place in great literature–even though Milton's preface explicitly endorses Aristotle's theory (in his *Poetics*) that tragedy should both excite and purge "pity and fear, or terror." The influence of Greek tragedy on *Samson Agonistes* has still to be fully explored.

The effect of the classics on Milton is also felt on a minutely local scale, most famously in his use of Latinate English, especially in *Paradise Lost.* Many readers have seen this aspect of Milton's style as a blemish, and it provoked much adverse criticism in the first half of the 20th century, when Milton was faulted for his supposed idiomatic remoteness and insensitivity to English as a living language. Such complaints are still sometimes voiced, but Milton's poetic reputation has enjoyed a revival since 1963, when Ricks demonstrated that the Latinisms in *Paradise Lost* are not the result of mere antiquarian pedantry. Where earlier critics had chided Milton for writing English as if it were Latin, Ricks credits Milton with verbal wit and imaginative precision in playing English and Latin senses against each other. A famous example is the newly created river that moves "with serpent error wand'ring" (7.302). Here "serpent" and "error" have Latin senses (*serpere,* "to creep"; *errare,* "to wander"), but both words are also ominously proleptic in a poem where the serpent Satan will indeed lead man into error. After Ricks, critics have given Milton more credit for his Latinisms, and Fowler ([1971] 1998) has taken the defense a step further by demonstrating that many supposed

Latinisms (e.g., "admire" for "wonder") are normal 17th-century English.

BIBL.: Alastair Fowler, ed., *Paradise Lost* (1971, rev. ed. New York 1998). Davis P. Harding, *The Club of Hercules: Studies in the Classical Background of "Paradise Lost"* (Urbana 1962). Charles Martindale, *John Milton and the Transformation of Ancient Epic* (Totowa, N.J., 1985). David Norbrook, *Writing the English Republic: Poetry, Rhetoric, and Politics, 1627–1660* (Cambridge 1999). William Porter, *Reading the Classics and "Paradise Lost"* (Lincoln 1993). Christopher Ricks, *Milton's Grand Style* (Oxford 1963).

J.LN.

Mime and Pantomime

In ancient Greece and Rome, mime referred to a wide range of imitative dramatic performances involving stock situations and characters, performed by actors without masks. Mime was presented on the streets, in homes, and in other impromptu theatrical venues. Often of a farcical or even sexually explicit nature, mime—despite its influence on comedy and satire—was regarded as the antithesis of formal theatrical genres. Pantomime, on the other hand, which was particularly popular in 1st-century Rome, lacked the coarseness of mime. Pantomime featured a solo dancer, wearing a mask showing closed lips, who enacted scenes from mythology through body and gesture, accompanied by chorus and instruments.

In modern usage, however, the differences between *mime* and *pantomime* have been obscured; the terms are often used synonymously to denote any dramatic action presented entirely through movement and gesture, although numerous works that are called pantomimes include dialogue and song (such as the English pantomimes that are still popular at Christmastime). The conflation of these distinctive ancient practices renders all but invisible the fact that the most direct descendants of Greek and Roman mime are all the sorts of farcical, politically or sexually charged improvisational dramas that stand in opposition to elite theater. These might include the commedia dell'arte (with its stock scenarios and characters) and its numerous legatees—harlequinades, burlesques, vaudeville, puppet theater, and even television skits, such as those on NBC's *Saturday Night Live.*

In post-classical times, the term *pantomime* is perhaps best understood as a central element in the history of dance; it has been used to describe any number of entertainments that rely heavily, if not exclusively, on body, gesture, and facial expression as the primary expressive media. The continued influence of the ancients is apparent in the treatises by such writers as Giovanni Doni (1632), Andrea Perrucci (1699), John Weaver (1712), and Gasparo Angiolini (1765), which testify to a perennial, self-conscious desire among dance practitioners and theorists to move the passions of the viewers by invoking classical precedents.

Pantomimic dance, featuring specific actions—battles, games, contests, and the like—was a primary feature in early modern Italian theater, such as the *moresche* praised by Isabella d'Este in the late 15th century, or the *giuoco della cieca* in Guarini's *Il Pastor Fido.* Athletic and acrobatic pantomimic dance—featuring dancing Turks, Moors, madmen, philosophers, statues, clowns, lions, and bears, as amply illustrated by Giorgio Lambranzi (1716)—was the central element that differentiated 17th-century Italian theatrical dance from its more restrained French counterpart. Silent dramas, or "dumb shows," were also an essential feature of the English masque in the 16th and 17th centuries; 18th-century London was swept away by a dizzying array of classically influenced harlequinades, including John Rich's *Jupiter and Europa; or, The Intrigues of Harlequin* performed at Drury Lane, and they spread to the American colonies in, for example, *Columbus; or, the Discovery of America, with Harlequin's Revels,* staged in New York in 1782.

In mid-18th century Europe the neoclassic impulse that led to the opera reforms of Gluck and Calzabigi championed narrative dance with a strong pantomimic component over divertissements, and writers would continue to argue over the relative aesthetic merits of abstract dance and silent drama. Both the *ballet d'actions* of the 18th century (by such choreographers as Jean-Georges Noverre, Gasparo Angiolini, and Gennaro Magri) and the *ballet pantomime* of early 19th-century France (such as *Giselle* or *La Sylphide*) enjoyed close and complex relationships with opera: narrative ballets served as entertainment in the intervals of operas, competed with opera as an independent theatrical genre, borrowed plots from popular opera librettos, and, through the use of well-known tunes or the highly expressive *musique parlant,* created the illusion that dancers sang or conversed with one another. In France restrictions on spoken theater inspired generations of French mimic actors, such as Jean Gaspard Deburau (1798–1846), who created the mute Pierrot character to great acclaim at the Théâtre des Funambules.

Though 20th-century choreographers have tended to reject the broad pantomimic facial expressions and gestures favored by their predecessors, the continuation of the tradition might well be seen in the French mimic immortalized in Marcel Carné's film *Les enfants du paradis* (1945) and made popular by Marcel Marceau, Charlie Chaplin, the silent comedy of Harpo Marx, and—perhaps unexpectedly—in Looney Tunes cartoons (Warner Bros.), which preserve one of the most perfect marriages of gesture and music.

BIBL.: Irene Alm, "Pantomime in Seventeenth-century Venetian Theatrical Dance," in *Creature di Prometeo: Il ballo teatrale: Dal divertimento al drama: Studi offerti a Aurel M. Milloss,* ed. Giovanni Morelli (Florence 1996) 87–102. Etienne Decroux, *Words on Mime,* trans. Mark Piper (Claremont, Calif., 1985). Pat Easterling and Edith Hall, eds., *Greek and Roman Actors: Aspects of an Ancient Profession* (Cambridge 2002). Elaine Fantham, "Mime: The Missing Link in Roman Literary History," *Classical World* 82 (1989) 158–163. Kathleen Hansell, "Theatrical Ballet and Italian Opera," in *The History of Italian Opera, Part 2: Systems,* vol. 5, *Opera on Stage,* ed. Lorenzo Bianconi and Giorgio Pestelli, trans. Kate Singleton (Chicago 2002) 178–287. Nino Pirrotta, "Classical Theatre, *Intermedi* and *Frottola* Music," in *Music and Theatre from Poliziano to Monteverdi,* by Nino Pirrotta and Elena Povoledo, trans. Karen Eales (Cambridge 1982) 37–75. Marian Smith, *Ballet and Opera in the Age of Giselle* (Princeton 2000). W.H.

Mimesis. *See* Imitation and Mimesis.

Mirabilia Urbis

"The city's wonders." *Mirabile,* like *miraculum,* is that which causes admiration, astonishment, surprise. The word and the concept were known in antiquity, and a list of the Seven Wonders of the World, still well known today, was transmitted to the Middle Ages. It is worth noting that five of these are constructions or monuments located in just as many cities; the hanging gardens of Semiramis are not buildings, but they are also found in a city, Babylon.

For Western Christianity, the city of wonders is above all Rome. Ammianus Marcellinus reported that in 357 the emperor Constantius II was dumbfounded by the stateliness and beauty of its countless wonders (*miracula*), and that the Forum of Trajan seemed to him especially *mirabile.* But this was classical Rome. It was followed by Christianized Rome, which began repurposing pagan buildings, assigning them Christian functions, and the Rome of the popes, who reused antiquity but also destroyed its monuments, quarrying them for precious materials.

By the High Middle Ages it had become a widespread practice to make pilgrimages to the ancient capital of the empire, now the capital of Christianity, the place of martyrs and saints, Peter and Paul foremost among them. Itineraries sprung up to guide pilgrims toward the holy city, but also, inevitably, toward the stunning visible signs of its ancient might: buildings, sculptures, inscriptions, often misunderstood (like the equestrian statue of Marcus Aurelius, taken for Constantine), but always admired. The wonders of the two Romes, pagan and Christian, lived on in the written records of those who either came from afar to visit them (such as the English *magister* Gregorius at the turn of the 13th century) or were born there (like Cencio Savelli, later pope Honorius III, d. 1227).

Another literary genre had its place alongside the *itineraria* and the *mirabilia urbis:* that of the *laudes civitatum.* In classical antiquity, praises of cities were a typical rhetorical exercise. The rules, preserved in a Lombard manuscript of the 8th century, entailed praise of the city's founder (a famous man or even a divinity) and descriptions of its site and walls, the beauty of its buildings, the fertility of its surrounding fields, the abundance of its waters, the customs of its inhabitants, and everything that could instill glory and pride, from conquests obtained through military valor to the presence of famous personages. Comparisons with other cities were also possible.

These norms were adhered to, more or less faithfully, by all the *laudes civitatum* we know, starting with the *Ordo urbium nobilium* of the Bordeaux poet and rhetorician Ausonius (310–395). The first of these "noble cities" is, of course, "golden Rome, home of the gods," touchstone for all the others, like Carthage, Milan—full of *mirabilia*—Capua, once the second Rome, and Arles, "the little Rome of Gaul."

Beginning in the 8th century *laudes civitatum* multiplied, especially in Italy, transcending the boundaries of Scholastic exercises to take on different tones, mostly political, but always maintaining their reference to classical, especially Roman, antiquity. This is the case with praises of Milan and Verona (8th cent.), Bergamo (12th), Lodi (13th), and Pavia (14th). Sometimes the epithet of second Rome was repeated verbatim, "in war stronger than Thebes, in thought stronger than Athens."

Mirabilia of Rome, but also of other cities, are found in the *Otia imperialia,* a work written around 1214 for the emperor Otto IV by Gervase of Tilbury, an important member of the Anglo-Norman aristocracy. Gervase distinguishes between (natural) *mirabilia* and (supernatural) *miracula.* In addition to references to the monuments of antiquity, we find here the medieval transformation of the classical author par excellence: Virgil has become a scientist and magician, and he supposedly effected extraordinary prodigies in Naples, such as the construction of a bronze fly capable of magically driving all the flies out of the city.

Bonvesin de la Riva's *De magnalibus urbis Mediolani* (*On the Marvels of Milan,* 1288) corresponds to the new social, cultural, and political aspects that characterized Western Christianity in the 13th century: here *grandeurs* accompany *wonders.* This Milan abounds in *mirabilia* because it abounds in all things: shops, food, men, military glory (it defeated Frederick Barbarossa), such that it should be called not *Milan* but *Miran,* from the Latin verb *mirari,* "to wonder." Indeed, this "second Rome" could even become the first: one need only move the papacy and its entire court there.

At the end of the 13th century Western Christianity was already heading toward Humanism and the Renaissance. With Dante, Virgil would return to being only (no small thing) a great Latin poet; and the praise of cities, the protagonists of the shift from the middle to the modern age, would be supplanted by their history.

BIBL.: Gina Fasoli, "La coscienza civica nelle *laudes civitatum,*" in *La coscienza cittadina nei comuni italiani del Duecento* (Toti 1972). Gervase of Tilbury, *Otia imperialia: Recreation for an Emperor,* ed. and trans. S. E. Banks and J. W. Binns (Oxford 2002). Jacques Le Goff, "Merveilleux," in *Dictionnaire raisonné de l'Occident médiéval,* by J. Le Goff and J.-C. Schmitt (Paris 1999). Cristina Nardella, *Il fascino di Roma nel Medioevo: Le "Meraviglie di Roma" di maestro Gregorio* (Rome 1997). Christine Smith, *Architecture in the Cul-*

ture of Early Humanism: Ethics, Aesthetics, and Eloquence, 1400–1470 (New York 1992). D.RM.

Translated by Patrick Baker

Mithras

"The origins of the public cult, and the secret cult, or mysteries of Mithra is one of those hard questions for which the savants of Europe have been seeking a solution about as long as their attention, more or less, found itself absorbed in esoteric study of the antiquities of Judea or Palestine, of Egypt, of Greece, and of Italy." So wrote Félix Lajard (1867, 1) in a manuscript devoted to the origins of the cult of Mithras, which lay still unfinished at his death in 1858.

Lajard's original treatment of the problem had won the prize offered by the Académie des Inscriptions in 1823; he had invoked Greek authorities, such as Herodotus, who mistakenly made "Mithra" a foremother of Aphrodite (1.131), as well as Persian texts (most notably the *Zend Avesta*). In his later work he added newly discovered cuneiform cylinder seals to the well-known Roman-era reliefs depicting the god. But how reliable these authorities were—and how relevant the later material evidence might be—was a question Lajard knew had not yet been answered. Nor did he underline the central reason for so much esoteric interest in Mithras: the god and the ritual practices that grew up around him bear more than a superficial resemblance to Christ and the cults of the early Christians. Lajard was hesitant to commit his speculations to print. Others have not been so cautious.

The history of reflections on Mithras and Mithraism is one of combat between two types of scholars, who may be caricatured as hasty, Orientophilic, and often iconoclastic "lumpers," pitched against skeptical, West-oriented and often orthodoxy-defending "splitters." Briefly, a "Mitra" shows up in the *Rig-Veda* as the god who, together with Varuna, is responsible for upholding order in the cosmos. A similar god is known from ancient Persian texts—and identified with the sun. But here the textual trail goes cold, and though Porphyry much later heard claims that Zoroaster himself dedicated a natural cave in honor of Mithras, there are no contemporary accounts of the worship of the god in the Hellenistic Mediterranean (a 1st-century BCE stele from Commagene, however, shows Antiochus I shaking hands with Mithra). The first inscriptions and monuments testifying to a Mithraic cult in the West date to the post-Christian era, 100–150 CE; the cult flourished thereafter. As a result, it was widely denounced by numerous Church Fathers, some of whom attributed similarities between Mithraism and Christianity to Satan's attempts to discredit the true faith by prefiguring it. The abundance of artifacts and sites, ranging from Anatolia to Scotland, demonstrate the Roman-era cult's widespread appeal and its longevity; it was finally suppressed, along with other non-Christian cults, by Theodosius' decree of 394.

A battery of early modern antiquarians reproduced images of Mithras and his ritual sacrifice of the bull (the tauroctony). Montfaucon, in particular, emphasized the centrality of astrological symbols in the depictions. But the period of deepest interest in the origins of the cult arrived as decipherments of Avestan, cuneiform, and Sanskrit got under way, and etymological and mythographic evidence was compiled to connect the Roman-era cults back to Indo-Aryan roots. Creuzer was just one of the Romantics to concern himself with Mithraism's ur-origins—which he thought lay in a primitive doctrine common to Brahmanism and Magism. And it would be fair to say that Creuzer's vision—inspired by an esoteric desire to find traces of a universal revelation—was reborn and given scientific credibility by the Belgian scholar Franz Cumont. The self-proclaimed apostate Ernest Renan once remarked, ruefully, "If Christianity had been stopped at its birth by some moral illness, the world would have become Mithraic" (quoted in Ulansey 1989, 4), but it was Cumont who raised Mithraic rivalry, and prefiguration, to a higher and more sympathetic status. Cumont's publications on Mithraism were both a sign of and a spur to a revival of interest in the cult at the fin de siècle that prompted Freud to make his own interpretation of the tauroctony (as an allegory for humankind's suppression of its animal instincts). Freud's rival, Carl Jung, devoted more attention to the subject (he may even have fancied himself an initiate). Already well versed in late-antique esoterica, James George Frazer and Madame Blavatsky predictably saw Mithras as confirmation of their own theories.

Cumont's *The Mysteries of Mithra* appeared in 1900, and the long trajectory it sketched, based on the skillful weaving together of ancient Persian texts and more recent Western monuments, held sway for nearly three-quarters of a century. More recently, however, scholars such as R. L. Gordon and David Ulansey have suggested that links between the Vedic or Iranian Mithra and the Roman god are tenuous, and perhaps not very useful in explaining the practices, iconography, and popularity of the cult. A brief survey of the online literature, however, suggests that if the skeptics are making inroads in academic circles, for many the function of Mithras as the predecessor to Christ—whether with pious, iconoclastic, or impish intent—remains alive and well.

BIBL.: Corinne Bonnet, *Le "grand atelier de la science": Franz Cumont et l'Altertumswissenschaft,* 2 vols. (Brussels 2005). Georg Friedrich Creuzer, *Symbolik und Mythologie der alten Völker, besonders der Griechen* (Leipzig 1810–1812). Franz Cumont, *Textes et monuments figurés relatifs aux mystères de Mithra* (Brussels 1896–1999). R. L. Gordon, "Franz Cumont and the Doctrines of Mithraism," in *Mithraic Studies: Proceedings of the First International Congress of Mithraic Studies,* vol. 1, ed. John R. Hinnells (Manchester 1971) 215–247. Félix Lajard, *Recherches sur le culte public et les mystères de Mithra en Orient et en Occident* (Paris 1867). Bernard de Montfaucon, *Antiquity Explained and Represented in Sculptures,* trans. David Humphreys (London 1721–1722).

Richard Noll, *The Aryan Christ: The Secret Life of Carl Jung* (New York 1997). David Ulansey, *The Origins of the Mithraic Mysteries* (New York 1989). S.M.

Mnemonics

The core texts that transmitted the classical tradition of the art of memory to the Middle Ages and the Renaissance are of several kinds. First are the rhetorical texts, since the orator must count on a well-trained memory both during the phase of *inventio,* the creation of his discourse, and in that of *actio,* its recitation in public. Cicero's *De oratore* (2.86–88), the *Rhetorica ad Herennium* (3.16–24), which was long attributed to Cicero, and Quintilian's *De institutione oratoria* (11.2) (which also expresses doubts and reservations about traditional mnemonic practices) handed down the basic components of a technique that had been developed in Greece: the idea is to fix in one's mind an ordered course marked by places in which to put images (*imagines agentes*) that are associated with the things and words to be remembered. Later, one retraces one's steps through these places, which call to mind the images and thereby activate the memory.

Aristotelian texts were also essential, especially the *De anima* (3.3.427b–432a) and the *De memoria et reminiscentia* (451b–452a), which emphasize the link between memory and imagination and describe the processes underlying the associations that facilitate recollection: similarity, opposition, contiguity. To these must be added medical texts. In particular, Avicenna takes up the task of reconciling the various traditions regarding the location of the faculties of the soul; the faculty of memory is usually placed in the lower part of the brain, and diets and therapies are prescribed for improving the physical conditions that underlie memory.

With the establishment of Christianity, and then in the Middle Ages, memory took on a strong ethical connotation. Aristotelian psychology and the precepts of Cicero and of *Rhetorica ad Herennium* were taken up and commented on by the great Dominican writers Albert the Great and Thomas Aquinas. In addition to the classical tradition, an important role was played by the techniques of monastic meditation, which called for temples, tabernacles, palaces, gardens, and itineraries to be constructed in the mind and traversed in a process of spiritual improvement. In this way the memory becomes an archive stocked with the Bible, or rather with certain biblical passages that are imprinted on the mind so as to construct a grid of *loci,* back to which everything leads, and from which everything flows. It is a memory that has as its object the heavenly Jerusalem and the eternal world of the Beyond; it is a memory that marshals the passions and strongly ties reading to writing, retention to invention. Hugo of St. Victor's *Ark of Noah* constitutes a telling example.

The logical procedures of Scholastic philosophy and the rhetorical schemes of the *artes praedicandi* also played an important role. An ordered division of the material to be treated facilitates both teaching and memorization.

It must be emphasized that what changed was the very meaning of memory: Christianity is a religion of recollection, and the liturgy arranges individual and collective time so as to call to mind the story of the Passion and the Resurrection of Christ. Furthermore, it is essential for each Christian to remember things that aid in the salvation of the soul: basic prayers, articles of faith, sins to be confessed (and thus the vices and the virtues, with examples of each), the punishments of Hell and the joys of Paradise. The techniques of memory have been indispensable tools for preachers, especially Franciscans and Dominicans, who used them to compose and to remember the texts of theirs sermons, as well as to make them more memorable, that is, to imprint them forcefully on the minds of their listeners, who were for the most part illiterate. The *Divina Commedia* can thus be considered an extraordinary example of this new stage in the art of memory.

In the 15th and 16th centuries mnemonic techniques were the object of criticism and satire for literati and philosophers such as Erasmus, Melanchthon, Agrippa, and Rabelais. The teachers of memory were criticized for the useless labors they inflicted on their students, for the purely passive and repetitive nature of their skills, and for their claims of quickly communicating a kind of knowledge based on words instead of on things. The spread of printing, moreover, helped create a situation in which the art of memory seemed to lose importance: the book, the dictionary, and the index furnished readers with fundamental tools both for their own personal enrichment and for the writing of new works. Yet in this period of crisis and polemics, the art of memory got a new lease on life and enjoyed its heyday in European universities, courts, and print shops. The key to this paradoxical situation lay in the felicitous coincidence between the primary aspects of the new culture of the 16th century and the art of memory. In fact, the latter was intertwined in the flourishing of the arts and letters, in the sense that it promised to commit to memory the models that, according to the classicizing canon, it was necessary to imitate. Furthermore, it received a new impulse from various philosophical and religious currents—such as Neoplatonism, hermeticism, cabala—that exalted the powers of the imagination and of the human mind. An example is provided by Giulio Camillo's (ca. 1480–1544) theater of memory. On the one hand it is a kind of gadget for literary memory, providing the tools for remembering and imitating exemplary texts; on the other it is a guide for assimilating knowledge and the powers of the mind, understood in its universal dimension.

Images seem capable of epitomizing secret knowledge: hence the cults of hieroglyphics, of emblems and devices, and of iconology. The *imagines agentes* of the memory became magical images, almost talismans, capable of capturing the power of the stars and of establishing contact with the hidden structures of the cosmos. The universal communicative capacity of images was also used by missionaries as an intermediary between different cultures, in Mexico as well as in China.

The work of Raymond Lull (ca. 1235–1315) enjoyed renewed popularity, inasmuch as it was thought capable of supplying the universal key, the letters of that fundamental alphabet that one can combine in such a way as to know and remember everything. It was the inspiration for Giordano Bruno's (1548–1600) art of memory, which is proffered as both a universally applicable tool (an inventive and imaginative logic) and one particularly accommodated to magic and reform. For Bruno the *compositio imaginum* belonged equally to the master memory and to the philosopher, to the painter and to the poet, permitting them to act on the "shadows," on the "seals" of ideas, and was thus tied to metaphysics and cosmology.

In the 16th and 17th centuries a movement grew up especially in Protestant lands around Pierre de la Ramée (Peter Ramus), a Huguenot killed in 1572 in the St. Bartholomew's Day Massacre in France. Ramism sought to free the memory from all ties with rhetoric: memory became instead a part of logic, since it was closely connected to the problem of the method to be followed in the search for and transmission of knowledge. It became typical of Ramism to use diagrams in which the pursued logical course is visualized and which facilitate memory and exposition. Printing—which contributes to the conception of the text as a totality of objects arranged in space, and which assures the technical reproducibility of images—interacted positively with Ramism: illustrated books, especially large folio works, lent themselves well to the reproduction of diagrams and synoptic tables, based on the principle of dichotomy, that placed knowledge under the eye of the reader in a manner that was ordered and easily assimilated.

In the 16th and 17th centuries, then, the problem of memory was tied to the search for universal knowledge, and therefore also to the problem of organizing the encyclopedia, of constructing effective classifications for a body of knowledge that continued to expand and change. The paths followed could vary (for example, for all the 17th century there was a magical and occultist strand that linked the techniques of memory to analogies and mysterious correspondences among different levels of reality), and they could be intertwined with one another, according to a widespread syncretistic practice. For example, Johann Heinrich Alsted (1588–1638) tried to construct an *ars generalis* that drew on both Lullism and Ramism. In a Europe rent by wars, the search for a path to universal knowledge could take on the sense—which it already had in Lull—of a search for general pacification. The techniques of memory thus came to be enmeshed with pedagogy, as in the case of Amos Komensky (1592–1670), with utopia, as in Tommaso Campanella's *City of the Sun* (1602), and with the search for a universal language, as in England in the second half of the 17th century.

The rejection of magic, the growth and specialization of knowledge, and the dissatisfaction with a unitary conception of the world and of knowledge led to a radical crisis in the tradition of the art of memory. It would not be rediscovered until the mid-20th century, as an important part of the European cultural experience.

In the modern world the evolution of computer technology and the new realm of the Internet have cast attention back to what seems like a kind of prehistory of "artificial memory"; Camillo's theater, for example, has piqued the interest of those working to develop search engines based on a logic that can be controlled by the user. Certain artists have felt themselves inspired by a tradition in which theaters and images are constructed in such a way as to control, almost to incorporate, the reaction of the spectators; video art in particular has used modern technology to expand and explore this possibility.

Among the reasons for the renewed interest in the tradition of the art of memory is the central role that it tends to attribute to images. This has led to crossovers with modern techniques of advertising and of political propaganda, in addition to prompting the interest of psychoanalysts, especially of the Jungian school.

Furthermore, from the beginning the techniques of memory have been based on the observation of how the mind works naturally, according to the principle that art imitates nature. Today some neuroscientists look to the age-old experience of the art of memory as an observation post for helping them learn something about the brain's functioning. In so doing they have opened up a fascinating and rocky terrain for the meeting of, and negotiation between, different disciplines and points of view. Something similar has happened in the field of anthropology, where the basic schemes of the European art of memory have been used—and at the same time have been subjected to debate—to study the shamanic rituals of the peoples of Central America and Africa.

Surely a comparison between ancient mnemonic practices on the one hand and neuroscience and anthropology on the other could help us better understand how much has changed over the course of time in the way we remember.

BIBL.: Lina Bolzoni, *The Gallery of Memory: Literary and Iconographic Models in the Age of the Printing Press* (Toronto 2001). Mary J. Carruthers, *The Craft of Thought: Meditation, Rhetoric, and the Making of Images* (Cambridge 1998). Paolo Rossi, *Logic and the Art of Memory: The Quest for a Universal Language* (London 2000). Frances A. Yates, *The Art of Memory* (London 1966). L.BO.

Translated by Patrick Baker

Modernism in Art

Among the many impulses that animated the modern movement in the arts, none was stronger than the yearning for essentials, which was in many respects a classical impulse. This passionate desire to identify the origins of form—to penetrate to the essence of form—had already been articulated in the neoclassical doctrines of the early 19th century, and was an animating force in the Post-Impressionist paintings of Seurat, Degas, and Cézanne. The works of these artists, though frequently grounded in close observation of nature, also announced, through their severe stylizations and classical allusions, that nature was not enough, or that the truth of art had to be found in a natural order that lay beyond mere appearances. The classical viewpoint, which modern artists tended to identify with what Otto Brendel has referred to as "an autonomous world of form," helped shape the skeletal geometries of Cubism and the astringencies of abstract art, which was sometimes seen as Platonic in its search for essentials. But if classicism offered an antidote to the anarchic and nihilistic strains in modern experience, the ancient world had nearly as much to teach artists about the unruly unconscious, for classical dramas and myths and legends were full of monstrous figures and disquieting or terrifying situations, which Giorgio de Chirico and Pablo Picasso and the Surrealists drew on in their work. Whether the ancient world was invoked as an ideal of order or as a myth of disorder, modern artists saw in the classical past a key that could unlock the reality beyond or beneath everyday reality.

The period in modern art that is most often associated with a classical impulse converges on World War I, when figures ranging from Jean Cocteau to the painter André Lhote called for a return to order in the arts. Many artists wanted to see if the radical, near-abstract or abstract experiments of the years 1910–1915 could be reintegrated with ideas of form, structure, and meaning that were lodged deep in the Western tradition. The renewed interest in the classical past, which remained strong all through the 1920s, built on a utopian vision of the Mediterranean world and a celebration of the ideals of French classicism, both of which had already been themes in the late 19th-century canvases and murals of Puvis de Chavannes. In Catalonia, in Provence, and in Italy artists and writers spoke of reviving what they imagined to be the lost simplicity of Mediterranean culture. This revival included an interest in traditions of popular entertainment, ranging from the circus to the commedia dell'arte, which could be seen as quotidian survivals of ancient theatrical conventions. By the beginning of World War I, Aristide Maillol's massively modeled female figures were already well known, de Chirico's metaphysical visions, with their classical colonnades and statues, were beginning to appear, and André Derain was moving from Cubist simplifications to a monumental figure style that echoed Byzantine icons and other late classical models. Pretty soon, in the work of Picasso, Georges Braque, Derain, Juan Gris, and Henri Matisse, there was an emphasis on the figure as a self-contained, irreducible volume. Artists were finding their way, almost intuitively, back to a classical method. And surely they would have agreed with Cocteau, who in *Cock and Harlequin* (1918) announced that "instinct needs to be trained by method; but instinct alone helps us to discover a method which will suit us, and thanks to which our instinct may be trained."

The involvement of many artists—and of Cocteau and Igor Stravinsky as well—in the work of Serge Diaghilev and the Ballets Russes tended to encourage a new approach to the figure, for at the core of the classical ballet was a recognition of the human figure as the fundamental measure, the basic unit of creation. Fauvism and Cubism, those lightning bolts of the early years of the new century, had confounded the old Western idea of the painting as a theatrical illusion, and the fascination that the theater now exerted for the artists of the School of Paris had to do, paradoxically, with the extent to which actually working within the proscenium arch suggested a way of reviving the very conventions they had only recently called into question. Matisse, Picasso, Braque, and Derain, who had all been involved in the breakup of traditional pictorial space, found themselves celebrating classical structure not as a representational technique but as a poetic meditation on illusionism. When Picasso drew a series of female heads in pastel in 1921, the forms became so vehemently, so insistently three-dimensional as to feel almost unreal, as if he were abstracting the third dimension. Thinking of Picasso's work—and of the relationship between classicism and modernity in general—Brendel has written that Picasso "established the independence of the image as a formal configuration which is capable of infinite variations and thereby, with each new pattern, may create new connotations of meaning." Once the artists had embraced this modern classicism, they could see that it had been foreshadowed in Poussin's architectonic compositions, in Corot's figures and cityscapes (many of which were homages to Rome's classical past), in Ingres's furiously stylized society portraits, in Renoir's late, monumental nudes, and in Cézanne's bathers and landscapes, which were hewn from hundreds of overlapping brushstrokes. No less an observer than Picasso's friend André Salmon wrote in 1918 that Picasso's admiration for Ingres might have had something to do with the development of Cubism, because Ingres "was a great draughtsman, that is to say, a great deformer, that is to say, a great constructor."

The reimagining of representation in the wake of abstraction, with classical ideas of form and structure as the mediating force, affected a wide range of works: Derain's Provençal landscapes, with their bright light and sculpted perspectives; Gris's crisply modeled, silver-toned harlequins and pierrots; Fernand Léger's massive figures, like machine-age goddesses; Matisse's sensuous odalisques set in dazzlingly patterned settings; Braque's brooding illustrations for Hesiod's *Theogony,* with their attenuated Etruscan stylizations. When Italians such as Carlo Carrà and Mario Sironi took up classical ideas, they tended to filter them through the narrative conventions of Giotto and various other Florentine and Sienese masters; and in Germany the Neue Sachlichkeit movement, which could be said to be more realist than classicist in orientation, at times saluted the northern Renaissance principles of Dürer and others. It was Gris who said that "the 'quality' of an artist derives from the quantity of the past that he carries in him—from his artistic atavism. The more of this heritage he has, the more 'quality' he has." In the 1920s classical ideals tended to be rather broadly conceived, so as to describe a grand tradition in the visual arts that included Watteau, Rubens, and Titian as well as Ingres, Poussin, and Michelangelo, and reflected not so much a particular standard of beauty as the idea of a standard, pure and simple.

"In the great classical epochs," Paul Dermée wrote in *Nord-Sud* in 1918, "the independence and autonomy of each art was carefully safeguarded. Neither overlapping nor penetration: purity!" The belief that the most concentrated expression was the most powerful—and that form must follow function, and that art was about essences—evoked a group of ancient images, from the Doric columns of the temples at Paestum, to the distilled contours of the Parthenon frieze, to the beautifully succinct shape of a Greek amphora. Constantin Brancusi's sculpture was grounded not only in Romanian folk styles and in primitive art, but also in the classical world, which he evoked in the *Torso of a Young Man* (1916) and in the delicately angled tilt of many of his female heads. The extraordinary refinement with which Brancusi shaped and polished marble and bronze suggests the artisanal traditions of the Mediterranean, even as the startling boldness of his forms reinstates the sense of a sculpture as an idol. In the case of Hans Arp, a Dadaist in his early years, the classical forms that were increasingly a factor in his work from the 1930s onward evoked the liquid profiles of ancient sculptures as well as their startling eroticism. The search for a vision that was pared down yet intensified informed abstract painting as well as sculpture, and certainly there were echoes of the gravely expressive balance of Greek architecture in Piet Mondrian's paintings of the 1920s, where all visual experience was reduced to a few vertical and horizontal black lines and a few rectangles of red, yellow, and blue. It's no wonder that the 1920s are often referred to as Mondrian's classical period. The ancient world was also a theme in the work of Paul Klee, who was fascinated by Greek and Roman architecture and by certain mask-like antique heads, and who drew inspiration from the tiny units of color in ancient mosaics. Klee's *Classical Coast* (1931), with its cool colors, is an Attic dreamscape. The idea that classical forms were primal forms also had a fascination for some of the Abstract Expressionists; one thinks of Barnett Newman's decision to title what is perhaps his greatest painting, the vast red composition from 1951, *Vir Heroicus Sublimis.*

The exploration of ancient themes by painters and sculptors can in turn be related to broader currents in the arts. Some of the giants of modern architecture had been neoclassicists in their youth. Ludwig Mies van der Rohe and Alvar Aalto both found in a rather severe, pared-down, sometimes Doric variety of classicism an antidote to the overelaborated sensibility of Beaux-Arts classicism, and the reverence in their mature work for the value of an I-beam or a brick wall can be seen as related to the essentialism of Greek design. Le Corbusier, before turning most of his attention to architecture—and villas that had their own white-on-white Attic elegance—had been involved with Amédée Ozenfant in the Purist movement and the magazine *L'Esprit Nouveau,* which in 1920, in a feature on good and bad art, placed an archaic Greek statue and classicizing paintings by Seurat and Gris on the list of approved works. The graphic and typographic arts of the early 20th century often favored a classicizing severity; there was an interest in lettering based on Roman carved inscriptions; and even the sans-serif typeface, that icon of the modern age, has its classical roots. The austerity of the Bauhaus's machine-age aesthetic can be traced back to a neoclassical forthrightness, and the decorative work of the Wiener Werkstätte, which can at times be positively rococo, also evinces elements of architectonic severity that recapitulate the Biedermeier taste of the 19th century, with its domestication of classical values.

The significance of classical themes and ideals in modern art has been subject to widely varying interpretations. From the beginning, some commentators were inclined to see any avant-garde artist who embraced traditional models as capitulating to the philistinism of an audience that might prefer a classicizing figure or landscape to a Cubist still life or an abstraction. The immense popularity of Derain's neoclassical work and the increasing sales that Matisse garnered with his figure paintings in the 1920s could fuel such speculations, although it is not clear that Picasso's rather ferocious neoclassical images sold that well. There can be no question that after World War I Matisse and Picasso were moving from an interest in certain forms of disorder to an interest in certain forms of order, but whatever economic or psychological or political motives can be ascribed to such moves is another question entirely, one that preoccupied people at the time and that has preoccupied historians a good deal in the past quarter century. In 20th-century Europe, where democratic and socialist and communist and conservative and fascist political parties and movements vied for attention and power, certain types of abstraction and expressionism came to be associated with left-wing feeling, and certain types of classicism, rightly or wrongly, came to be associated with the right. In France neoclassicism was sometimes linked to a conservative and nationalistic strain in French culture during and after World War I. And by the 1930s the Nazis and the Fascists both had a taste for neoclassical forms. The fact that Derain and some other artists associated with classical pictorial values visited Germany during World War II has sometimes been presented as proof that classicism equals conservatism if not fascism, but the circumstances of those visits were complex, and there is little reason to accept Picasso's view, offered right after the Liberation, that Derain was a collaborationist; there is, in fact, evidence to the contrary.

Some of the great literary modernists, T. S. Eliot and Ezra Pound especially, believed that their embrace of classical artistic values reflected a rejection of liberal culture, and even, at certain times, a celebration of violently anti-liberal ideas. Yet among the visual artists, classicism could often be seen as reflecting leftist as easily as rightist ideas; certainly no one could accuse either Picasso or Léger of tilting in any direction except to the left. And though Pierre Bonnard was strongly supportive of the Vichy government, Matisse was surely not. Nevertheless, by now there are certainly a great many historians who would agree with Yve-Alain Bois, who in a recent textbook on the history of modern art identifies the return to order as a "conservative backlash" and "a reactionary trend." Elizabeth Cowling, however, in her pioneering 1990 exhibition, On Classic Ground, argued strenuously and convincingly against this linkage. "There is the suspicion," she observed, "that [the work] is at worst authoritarian and oppressive, at best rhetorical and sham. Indeed because of its presumed *arrière-garde* nature, the post-war classical revival has received scant attention until quite recently, and the work produced has often been treated with contempt. Yet that work is often of the highest quality, and the accusation of conservatism (in the pejorative sense of reaction against innovation and invention) does not stand up." Though Kenneth E. Silver, in his influential *Esprit de Corps* (1989), located avant-garde encounters with classicism within the increasingly nationalistic tendencies of French culture during and after World War I, he did not make the linkages quite as tightly as some have imagined, and in Silver's more recent *Making Paradise: Art, Modernity, and the Myth of the French Riviera* (2001), neoclassicism is often celebrated as having its own freestanding value. There is no reason to believe that classicism in art should necessarily be fueled by conservative political or social views. Classicism, which is an attempt to penetrate to the core of things, can as easily be viewed as inherently radical, which was surely what Jacques-Louis David was thinking around the time of the French Revolution, when he dramatized the emergence of republican values in figure compositions that evoked Greek and Roman ideals through the very severity of the forms.

What classicism offered to 20th-century artists, no matter what their political orientation, was an alternative to the present, the immediate, the quotidian. Utopian ideals could be cast in the image of a Golden Age, whether by Matisse in *Luxe, calme et volupté* (1904–1905) and *Le bonheur de vivre* (1905–1906), by Picasso in the *Joy of Life*, or *Antipolis* (painted in Antibes in 1946), or by Bonnard in any number of canvases. For modern artists, who tended to shy away from elaborate narrative or literary schemes, certain classical images took on an immediate metaphoric power. Although it was not necessarily Freud who taught the artists to recognize in Greek myths and legends the abstraction or essentialization of empirical experience, painters and sculptors certainly used classical sources in this way. Odilon Redon's many studies of Apollo and his chariot were meditations on the heroism of art and the creative spirit's lofty ambitions. Through Picasso's explorations of the legend of the minotaur, he celebrated his own violently erotic nature even as he saw in the figure that was only half human an emblem of man's poignantly divided nature. Some of Matisse's most erotically charged images are not to be found in his studies of the model in his studio but in his less frequent reflections on classical themes. De Chirico used the chilly image of a classical statue in an empty piazza to suggest the anomie of urban life. And Picasso and André Masson saw in classical images of rape and violence a language that would enable them to respond to the unfolding political horrors of the 1930s and World War II. The classical world was a parallel universe from which artists drew images and ideas that reflected their own inclinations and attitudes and moods.

The classical impulse suffused the arts of the modern period, not only the visual arts but also Joyce's *Ulysses* (which Matisse illustrated), the writings of Valéry and Gide, the spare sonorities of Satie's and Stravinsky's music, and Balanchine's plotless ballets. This impulse or cluster of impulses was not so much idealist as it was essentialist—a belief in basics, in basic emotions, basic materials, basic experiences. Renaissance thinkers had sought to present the artists of the classical period as learned men, but it was probably closer to the truth to regard the ancient painters and sculptors as extraordinarily sophisticated craftsmen, and it was this essentially artisanal aspect of their nature that 20th-century artists held most dear. In the Doric temples and the kouros figures and the black figure vases, Picasso and Brancusi and Matisse and Mies van der Rohe and a great many other artists saw a vision that was heroic precisely because it was so fundamentally simple, so miraculously succinct. It is that primal eloquence that Braque had in mind when, late in his life, he modeled a series of horses that might have emerged from a Cypriot tomb. These images have the haunting power of classical playthings recovered from the beginnings of time. For modern artists, who had been bewitched by primitivism in the years before World War I, classicism turned out to be the primitivism of their own tradition—an elemental truth to which they looked back even as they were moving forward.

BIBL.: Otto Brendel, "The Classical Style in Modern Art," in *From Sophocles to Picasso*, ed. Whitney Oates (Bloomington 1962). Elizabeth Cowling and Jennifer Mundy, eds., *On Classic Ground* (London 1990). Christopher Green, *Cubism and Its Enemies* (New Haven 1987). Jed Perl, *Paris without End* (San Francisco 1988). Kenneth Silver, *Esprit de Corps* (Princeton 1989).

J.PE.

Mommsen, Theodor

German historian of antiquity (1817–1903). The son of a Protestant minister, he is one of the most important ancient historians of modern times. Although he abandoned his paternal faith as a young man, he was deeply marked by modern liberal Protestantism's worship of education.

After attending the Royal Christianeum, an elite school in Altona, Mommsen studied law at the University of Kiel (1838–1843). His primary subject was Roman law, but the greatest influence on him was exercised by the classical philologist Otto Jahn, only four years his senior. After a brilliant exam and a successful doctorate on a topic in Roman law, a fellowship from the Danish king allowed him to travel to Italy (1844–1847). There he laid the foundation for a comprehensive collection of Latin inscriptions, the *Corpus inscriptionum Latinarum*.

During the revolution of 1848 Mommsen became committed to a united and liberal Germany. In the autumn of that year he left his work as a journalist in Rendsburg for an associate professorship in Roman law in Leipzig. Let go in 1851 for political reasons, he was appointed in 1852 to a full professorship in legal history in Zurich, which he followed with a move to Breslau in 1854. In 1858 he was appointed to a research professorship at the Berlin Academy as the editor of the *Corpus inscriptionum Latinarum.*

In Berlin, especially through his work there at the Academy of Sciences, Mommsen placed classical scholarship on a new foundation. He organized the archives by combining a new method—authenticity and conjectural criticism—with a new agenda—the ideal of totality—for the purpose of constructing a new vision of antiquity and of Roman history especially. No longer the textual witnesses alone but the entire legacy of Greek and Roman antiquity was now taken into consideration. Here it stood Mommsen in good stead that he was not only an ingenious researcher but also a brilliant organizer who succeeded in implementing the principle of a factory-like division of labor. Thus, several long-term editorial projects were organized at the Berlin Academy of Sciences, some of which are still ongoing.

Mommsen became famous thanks to his brilliantly written three-volume *Roman History* (1854–1856), for which in 1902 he became the first German to win the Nobel Prize for Literature. The third volume ends with Caesar's victory against his adversaries in 46 BCE. The focus of the account is the crisis of the late Republic. This work put the historical material into a modern context, offset the failure of the 1848 revolution historiographically, and gave voice to a power politics for uniting the nation. A fourth volume, which was to treat the Roman imperial period, was never written. A fifth volume containing the history of the Roman provinces appeared in 1885.

Mommsen's principal work of scholarship is his *Roman Constitutional Law* (3 vols., 1871–1888). In it he provided a new account of the constitutional law applicable to the republican and imperial periods of Roman history, interpreting the broad literary and nonliterary tradition according to the rules of the hermeneutics of classical philology and analyzing its statements about "constitutional history" with the aid of strictly legal concepts. The engagement with this product of 19th-century legal research methods has had a sustained influence on views of ancient history.

Scholarship and politics were for the liberal Mommsen inseparable. Up to the end of his life he believed in the political responsibility of intellectuals. The severing of the idea of national unity from the liberal ideal of freedom, a process initiated by the foundation of the German Reich in 1871, was something that Mommsen perceived over thirty years later as a painful political process. In advanced age he advocated friendship between Germany and England and called for an alliance between the Liberals and the Social Democrats.

BIBL.: Alexander Demandt et al., eds., *Theodor Mommsen: Wissenschaft und Politik im 19. Jahrhundert* (New York 2005). Alfred Heuss, *Theodor Mommsen* (Kiel 1956). Stefan Rebenich, *Theodor Mommsen: Eine Biographie,* 2nd ed. (Munich 2007) and *Theodor Mommsen und Adolf Harnack* (Berlin 1997). Lothar Wickert, *Theodor Mommsen: Eine Biographie,* 4 vols. (Frankfurt 1959–1980). Josef Wiesehöfer, ed., *Theodor Mommsen: Gelehrter, Politiker und Literat* (Stuttgart 2005). Karl Zangemeister, *Theodor Mommsen als Schriftsteller,* 3rd ed. (Hildesheim 2000). S.R.

Translated by Patrick Baker

Monsters

In the ancient world monstrous births, such as conjoined twins, hermaphrodites, or human children with apparently animal features, were an important type of portent or prodigy—a category of anomalies in the natural order that also included comets, earthquakes, and unusual meteorological phenomena. In *On the Nature of the Gods* (*De natura deorum,* 45 BCE) Cicero noted that their name (derived from *monstrare,* "to show") reflected their commonly accepted function as signs by which the gods revealed future events, including famines, plagues, and wars. Pliny also discussed monsters in his *Natural History* (ca. 77–79 CE), although he emphasized their origin as manifestations of nature's infinite variety, rather than as signs of coming misfortune. To anomalous individual births he added (from a separate tradition rooted in Greek writing about India, which went back to Herodotus) whole races of apparently monstrous human beings who were reported to inhabit the far margins of Africa and Asia, among them peoples with enormous ears, dog's heads, or no heads at all.

Both types of monsters, the individual birth and the monstrous race, attracted the attention of early Christian writers, of whom Augustine of Hippo (d. 430) and Isidore of Seville (d. 636) were the most influential. Over the course of the Middle Ages, however, the two traditions had somewhat different histories. The monstrous races populated the pages of cosmographies, encyclopedias, and travel narratives; individual monsters, as terrifying signs of divine wrath, appeared in local chronicles and histories. The fear of future misfortune did not exhaust ancient and medieval reactions to monstrous births, however. Aristotle had laid out the natural causes of monsters in *On the Generation of Animals* (*De generatione animalium,* 4th cent. BCE), attributing them to the presence of too little or too much matter in the mother's uterus (e.g., conjoined twins or babies with missing limbs) and to the resistance of maternal matter to paternal form (e.g., daughters or children who looked like animals born to human mothers). Beginning in the 13th century, these ideas were elaborated by medieval commentators, such as Albertus Magnus and Nicole Oresme, whose acceptance that many monsters resulted from natural causes, rather than divine wrath, implied that not all creatures of anomalous appearance need inspire terror and dread.

In the 16th century new attention to ancient texts concerning monsters enriched these diverse traditions. The Italian physician Girolamo Cardano celebrated natural diversity in the Plinian vein, whereas scholars such as the German Protestant Conrad Lycosthenes scoured the works of late antique writers on prodigies and embraced the portentous meanings of monstrous births—an idea that gained new intensity during the religious conflicts of the Reformation. In the meantime, surgeons and anatomists began to dissect humans with unusual bodily characteristics and reflected, following Aristotle, on the natural causes that produced them.

By the end of the 17th century, however, these intellectual traditions had lost their force, at least among learned writers. Travelers to the far reaches of Africa, Asia, and the newly discovered Americas found peoples who differed only superficially from Europeans, and natural philosophers and medical writers increasingly emphasized monsters as expressions of natural law rather than divine messages and elaborated new theories of generation, such as preformationism and epigenesis, that departed from ancient models. At the same time, however, monsters retained their popular fascination, as in the freak shows that flourished until well into the 20th century; juxtaposing representatives of exotic peoples (real or purported) with midgets and giants, the armless and legless, and conjoined twins, these commercial spectacles were a dying, disturbing echo of Pliny's celebration of human diversity.

BIBL.: J. Céard, *La nature et les prodiges: L'insolite au XVIe siècle, en France* (Geneva 1977). L. Daston and K. Park, *Wonders and the Order of Nature* (New York 1998). J. B. Friedman, *The Monstrous Races in Medieval Art and Thought* (Cambridge, Mass., 1981). R. Wittkower, "Marvels of the East: A Study in the History of Monsters," *Journal of the Warburg and Courtauld Institutes* 5 (1942) 159–197. K.P.

Montaigne, Michel de

French author and philosopher (1533–1592), known primarily for his work *Essais,* first published in 1580, which established the essay as a mode of thought and expression. As precursor to Descartes and Rousseau, he is celebrated as one of the sources of the modern, skeptical self, and as an apostle of modernity's concern with human contingency. An inspiration for poets and anthropologists alike—Shakespeare's *Tempest* lifts passages more or less verbatim from Florio's 1603 translation of "Des Cannibales," and Claude Lévi-Strauss founded structural anthropology in part in response to the same essay—Montaigne is often (mis)read as the inventor of such ostensibly "modern" philosophical modes as, for instance, cultural relativism.

In truth, he is only an accidental philosopher, and he is as engaged in a dialogue with the ancients as he is with establishing the coordinates of contemporary experience. His unusual education—he was taught to speak Latin before French—and his reading of the more than 1,000 volumes in his library bear witness to a sustained reverence for Greek and Latin texts. He stands as a powerful mediating figure between the legacy of antiquity and the vernacular cultures of the Renaissance. The *Essais,* at once object and process, emerge out of commentaries on classical texts and commonplaces: witness, for instance, his busily annotated copy of Lucretius. But in time, and as if by accidental response to his own times, Montaigne's writing modulates into an original form of narrative, philosophizing in the vernacular. Had his great friend La Boétie survived, Montaigne might have written him letters in the manner of a Pliny, a Seneca, or, indeed, a Cicero (1:40). Montaigne might also have followed Le Roy in his translation—or Castiglione in his transposition—of the Platonic dialogue into the vernacular (3:8, 3:9). Instead, he mixes the composite genres of the miscellany, the commonplace book, and the commentary to forge the *essai:* a test, or trial of judgment; the term derives from *essayer,* "to test, try out, taste." For Montaigne, then, the new form constitutes an experiment in the connection of close, if often cursory and unsystematic, reading, imitation, and revision of the ancients—Plutarch, in Amyot's French translation, most happily; Sextus Empiricus, in Estienne's Latin edition, most anxiously—with the recounting of the details of daily life.

Thanks to his father's insistence, Latin was Montaigne's mother tongue. Ovid was his secret first love: "The first taste of feeling I had of books was of the pleasure I took in reading the fables of Ovid's *Metamorphoses;* for being but seven or eight years old, I would steal and sequester myself from all other delights only to read them" (1:25). Ovid introduced Montaigne to the pleasures of the changing shapes of narrative, and the Latin poets gave him a taste for emblems and metaphors—the Danaides and the Cornucopia, for instance—around which his own writing would turn. The young boy's habit of hiding himself away to read became a daily practice for the man: in 1571 he officially retired from public life as counselor to the Bordeaux Parliament, to sequester himself, to read, and to write. In practice, this self-styled *otium*—"leisure," or *oisiveté* as he terms it in the essay of that name (1:8), a putative preface that then developed into a full-fledged chapter—was only intermittent. Montaigne continued to act as a mediator between the warring parties in the religious civil strife that tore France apart through the 1570s and 1580s. But the ancient idea of *otium* was instrumental in clearing a space in which Montaigne could write, read, and rewrite his books. And that early glimpse of the boy stealing away to read Ovid, escaping into what he would later call his *arrière boutique*—at once the storeroom at home and the back room of the more public print shop—recurs time and again in his volumes as the accumulating essays make their way through their many changes, shapes, and forms.

The experiment that is the *Essais* occupied Montaigne for the last 20 or so years of his life, from the book's conception in the early 1570s through to publication of the first two volumes in 1580, followed by a third in 1588. He was in the process of revising all three volumes when he died in 1592. No new essays were written in the last four years of his life; rather, he continued the process of rewriting his own work, revising his thoughts and the rhythm of his phrases in the light of new reading or new events. The surviving annotations, more than 1,000 in number, are handwritten in the margins and on loose pages inserted into his own printed copy of the *Essais*. These formed the basis of a posthumous edition, brought out by his adopted daughter and literary executor, Marie de Gournay, in 1595.

Most modern editions of the *Essais* signal the three stages of composition (1580, 1588, 1595), not least since scholarship for many years followed Pierre Villey in tracing an evolutionary perspective in the work, particularly in its relation to the ancient philosophical ideal of preparing for death. Montaigne was held to have passed from an early stoic stage (grounded in readings of Seneca), through to a skeptical crisis occasioned by his reading of Sextus Empiricus, which animated the inquiry into faith, doubt, and *nostre humaine condition* that structures the longest of all the essays, the "Apology for Raymond Sebond" (2:12). The skeptical crisis was then said to have given way to a final, more settled Epicurean stage, characterized by a kind of Lucretian coming to terms with change, mutability, and flux. Such an account of the development of Montaigne's thought is sustainable only if we ignore the particularities of his style. It pays scant heed to the ways in which the essayist is not so much rehearsing ancient roles and replaying ancient themes as drawing out, in the process of rewriting and revision, the implications of his own thinking, challenging as he does so the limits not only of his own endeavors but also of those of his age. Recent scholarship has been concerned to show how the variety of subjects about which Montaigne writes —cruelty, friendship, sadness, virtue, names, presumption, vanity, thumbs, three fine women, horse riding, lines in Virgil, and so on—all resolve themselves into the theme of writing itself, or, alternatively, writing the self. Neither the evolutionary nor the proto-postmodernist approach is fully alive to the challenge of Montaigne's writing, however. For each, in its efforts at systematization, runs counter to the programmatically prefatory and provisional nature of the *Essais* as form, and as a mode of thought.

BIBL.: Terence Cave, *The Cornucopian Text: Problems of Writing in the French Renaissance* (Oxford 1979). Mary McKinley, *Words in a Corner: Studies in Montaigne's Latin Quotations* (Lexington, Ky., 1981). Ann Moss, *Printed Commonplace-Books and the Structuring of Renaissance Thought* (Oxford 1996). Michael Screech, *Montaigne and Melancholy: The Wisdom of the Essays* (London 1983) and *Montaigne's Annotated Copy of Lucretius: A Transcription and Study of the Manuscript, Notes and Pen-Marks* (Geneva 1998). Pierre Villey, *Les sources et l'évolution des idées de Montaigne*, 2 vols. (Paris 1908).

W.W.

Mosaic

An agglomerate of many small pieces of material (tesserae) of stone, glass, earthenware, and sometimes mother of pearl, used singly or in combination, set into a bed of mortar. The origin of the word is controversial, but the most attractive explanation was offered by the 18th-century lexicographer Egidio Forcellini, who associated the term with the nimble fingers of the Muses and the meeting place of scholars and philosophers (*mouseion, musaeum*, or museum). In the guise of the name of a profession, it appears in Diocletian's *Edict of Prices* (301 CE), which distinguishes between artisans who laid pavements (*tesselarii*) and *museiarii* the makers of wall and vault mosaics.

By the end of the 4th century BCE, multicolored pavements of stone tesserae had superseded monochromatic pebbled floors, and by the 2nd century CE some contained colored glass otherwise too brittle for large-scale use. The invention of glassblowing during the 1st century BCE (Pliny, *Natural History* 36.189, 193) facilitated the production of metallic tesserae: foil was sandwiched between a thicker poured-glass base and a thin blown-glass covering layer (*cartellina*). Egypt paid part of its annual tribute to Rome with this material, and by the 3rd century CE glass tesserae were available in great abundance, as shown by the 17,000 square meters of mosaic on the vaults of the Baths of Caracalla.

As a moisture-resistant revetment, glass mosaics were also used in Roman garden architecture, such as the fountains and grottoes in and around Rome and Herculaneum, which include a vivid blue glass also found in early Christian churches in Ravenna (Mausoleum of Galla Placidia), Naples (Naples Cathedral baptistery), and Rome (Santi Cosma e Damiano). The brilliance of other colored tesserae (orange and yellow) was due to the high lead content innate to their pigments. Occasionally lead was added to enhance opaque red, and possibly to other colors as well. But we know that during the Middle Ages lead was forgotten in the coloration of glass tesserae, and it did not reappear until 15th-century Venice. Ever since, tesserae with a high lead content have been described as enamels (*smalti*), as distinct from glass paste (*paste vitree*), which contains either no lead oxide or much lower amounts of it. Between the 7th and 11th centuries brilliantly colored tesserae evidently became so rare that they were taken as spoils. Charlemagne stripped mosaics from the walls of churches in Ravenna for his palace chapel in Aachen. Orange, yellow, and turquoise tesserae from late antique monuments were inserted into mosaics at Santa Cecilia in Trastevere and in other early 9th-century churches.

Until Palaeologan times (1259–ca. 1390), Byzantine mosaics seem to have had a narrower color range than contemporary Western examples. Although technology may have been a contributing factor, there is a noticeable preference for shimmer rather than hue in Byzantium that may go back to ancient Greek ideas concerning nature and the supernatural. Gold mosaic grounds, so characteristic of Byzantium, deliberately exploited light refraction as a means of materializing divine illumination. To enhance glitter and refraction the wall surfaces were not flat, and the golden grounds, as well as details of garments and other objects, included tilted tesserae, a technique occasionally used in the West as well.

The ancient taste for naturalism, illusion, bucolic subjects, heroic scenes, and monumental figures occasionally emerged in early Christian and medieval mosaics as well as in Islamic buildings from Damascus to Córdoba. Mosaic pictures, or *emblemata,* the centerpieces so often embedded in ancient Roman pavements, eventually expanded to become surrogate paintings on facades, such as Giotto's lost *Navicella* in the atrium of Old St. Peter's Basilica and, later in the 14th century, the mosaics on the front of Orvieto Cathedral. These, together with the Baroque interior of Rome's St. Peter's, represent the use of mosaic as a means of making murals eternal.

Some of the subjects of ancient pavements persisted, such as the famous *Unswept Floor* of Pergamum (*Natural History* 36, 184), repeated in Rome and Pompeii. Then there are the small scenes of everyday life that inhabit the borders of pavements in Antioch, Rome, and North Africa and turn up in the 4th-century CE vault of Santa Costanza in Rome, on the floor of Aquileia Cathedral, and later amid the scrolling acanthus in the apse of San Clemente in Rome (ca. 1123). Heroic Greek and Roman statuary inspired Galla Placidia's *Good Shepherd,* and *Christ and the Apostles* in the apse of Rome's Santi Cosma e Damiano (526–530). The latter, however, was carried out in a painterly style closely resembling allegorical figures in pagan classical pavements at Antioch (House of the Calendar and the Constantinian Villa). Antioch was destroyed by an earthquake in 526, and it has been suggested that the Roman apse mosaic could have been made by refugee artisans from that Syrian city. In fact, throughout the centuries mosaicists tended to be itinerant artisans.

Because mosaics were so labor intensive and expensive (about four times more costly than wall paintings), few church interiors were entirely covered with them. Those in Ravenna, Norman Sicily, and San Marco in Venice are exceptional. Usually mosaics were reserved for facades, apses, and vaults.

After the 6th century the classical heritage is visible less in the forms represented than in the ideas mosaics evoke, as in light metaphysics, rhetoric, and allegory, which contributed to their brilliance and compositional eloquence. During the 19th century mosaic enjoyed revivals under the aegis of King Ludwig of Bavaria and the Hohenzollerns in Prussia, as well as in England (the Albert Memorial in London and Frogmore in Windsor). Early Christian mosaics from Ravenna were sent for study to Berlin, mosaic schools were established in Innsbruck, and Venetian mosaic makers were sent to England. Today mosaic tesserae are made in Ravenna, Spilimbergo, Venice, and the Vatican.

BIBL.: E. Borsook, "Rhetoric or Reality: Mosaics as Expressions of a Metaphysical Idea," *Mitteilungen des Kunsthistorischen Institutes in Florenz* 44 (2000) 2–18. E. Borsook, F. Superbi, and G. Pagliarulo, eds., *Medieval Mosaics: Light, Color, Materials* (Cinisello Balsamo 2000). C. Harding, "The Production of Medieval Mosaics: The Orvieto Evidence," *Dumbarton Oaks Papers* 43 (1989) 73–102. H. P. L'Orange and P. J. Nordhagen, *Mosaics* (London 1966). E. Marianne Stern, "Roman Glassblowing in a Cultural Context," *American Journal of Archaeology* 103 (1999) 441–484. M. Verità, "Mosaico vitreo e smalti," in *I colori della luce,* ed. C. Moldi Ravenna with English trans. (Venice 1996) 184–191. M. Verità, B. Profilo, and M. Vallotto, "I mosaici della Basilica dei Santi Cosma e Damiano a Roma: Studio analitico delle tessere vitree," *Rivista della Stazione Sperimentale del Vetro* 32, no. 5 (2002) 13–24.

E.B.

Moschopoulos, Manuel

Byzantine schoolmaster and humanist, and an innovator in the teaching of grammar in late Byzantium (ca. 1280–ca. 1316). His books remained exceedingly popular throughout the Palaeologan period and the Italian Renaissance, well into the early modern period.

Little is known about Moschopoulos. He studied in the circle of Maximus Planudes (presumably at the Akataleptos monastery), who referred to young Manuel in a letter addressed to the boy's bibliophile uncle, Nicephorus Moschopoulos, the titular metropolitan of Crete. The nephew was not always wise in his choice of friends, allegedly having been betrayed by a "scoundrel" of foreign origin, for whom he had pledged himself. He was duly charged with treason and imprisoned in the winter of 1306–1307 (one may think of his teacher Planudes' own alliance with Alexios Philanthropenos). From prison Moschopoulos addressed a pointed treatise to Andronicus II, discussing the rights of sovereign and subject. At one time his term in prison prevented him from meeting the "philosopher" John, a major figure of early 14th-century intellectual life and a link between the scholars of Constantinople and Thessalonica. Like Planudes, Moschopoulos became involved with the theological quarrels of his age; an anti-unionist treatise on the Holy Spirit can be inferred from the angry reply it evoked. An essay on magical squares deserves to be mentioned as an intellectual curiosity.

Moschopoulos' philological oeuvre consists of four main components. First, there are works of reference: he composed a grammar, entitled *Questions,* and revised a collection of 21 bulky schedographical essays expounding simple phrases of biblical and epic content. Second, he compiled the so-called Scholastic Anthology, a collection that represented the first prose texts introduced into grammatical instruction in Byzantium; it included excerpts from Philostratus, Marcus Aurelius, Aelian, the "Planudean Anthology," and a poem titled "On the Bathhouse in Pythia," by the 10th-century Byzantine poet Leo Choerospactes. Third, there is some evidence that Moschopoulos also cared for the more traditional elements of the Byzantine curriculum. In another canonical collection, his *Sylloge,* he provided full commentaries on the triads of Euripides and Sophocles, on the Olympic hymns of

Pindar, Hesiod's *Works and Days,* and the *Idylls* of Theocritus. He also paraphrased the first two books of the *Iliad,* up to the catalogue of ships. Nonetheless, his innovations diminished, to say the least, the traditional role of the triads, especially of Aeschylus. The fourth component—not, strictly speaking, Moschopoulos' own work but compiled from his commentaries—is the *Collection of Attic Words,* an Atticizing guide on grammar and style, that also enjoyed considerable success.

Moschopoulos must be considered innovative in two important respects: besides his introduction of prose texts to the grammarian's school, the consistent insertion of a schedographical methodology into commentaries, even of a supposedly higher level, clearly sets his work apart. Other contemporary commentaries were often heavily interpolated within decades, but Moschopoulos' compositions survived in a remarkably pure condition. Clearly they were widely considered canonic.

His innovations were contested early by his contemporaries; in an apology from his pen directed against the students of a rival schoolmaster, he tried hard to play down his innovation in teaching. More than a hundred years later, in the mid-15th century, Constantine Laskaris, an émigré teacher of Greek in Syracuse, Sicily, still complained about Moschopoulos' "destructive" influence.

BIBL.: H.-C. Günther, *The Manuscripts and the Transmission of the Paleologan Scholia on the Euripidean Triad* (Stuttgart 1995) 25–91. J. J. Keaney, "Moschopulea," *Byzantinische Zeitschrift* 64 (1971) 303–321. I. Ševčenko, "The Imprisonment of Manuel Moschopulos in the Year 1305 or 1306," *Speculum* 27 (1952) 133–157. R. Webb, "A Slavish Art? Language and Grammar in Late Byzantine Education and Society," *Dialogos* 1 (1994) 81–103.

N.G.

Muses

Goddesses of poetry, music, and song, who came to preside over intellectual life as a whole. Originally they appear to have been nature deities of the same stock as the nymphs, like the Graces and the Seasons, with whom they are often linked. In the divine world they form the archetypal chorus, singing and dancing for the pleasure of the gods, often with Apollo as their leader; in the human world they inspire poets and bestow on mortals the divine gift of song. But the myth of Thamyris, the legendary Thracian bard who challenged the Muses' superiority, shows that they punish those who misuse their gifts. Traditions about their number and parentage vary, but the standard conception is that of Hesiod's *Theogony* (later 8th cent. BCE): born in Pieria near Mount Olympus, they are the daughters of Zeus and Mnemosyne (Memory), nine in number, with individual names, though at this stage they do not have specialized functions. Mount Helicon, with its sacred springs Hippocrene and Aganippe, is their special haunt, and it was here that they singled Hesiod out to be a poet as he was tending his sheep, plucking for him a branch of laurel and breathing into him a divine voice so that he could sing of past and future and celebrate the immortal gods. This canonical and much imitated account provides the pattern for many initiation scenes in later poetry, from Callimachus and Ennius to Virgil, Propertius, and Horace and their many medieval and Renaissance imitators (Ziolkowski 1990, 16–17; Revard 2001, 70–77).

Poets from Homer onward invoked the Muses, either singly or as a group, and depicted themselves in elaborate imagery as servants, priests, or prophets of the goddesses (see esp. Pindar). But the Muses were far more than goddesses of poetry: in the oral culture of early Greece, in which all ideas, whether religious, political, moral, or social, were expressed through the medium of song, the Muses effectively encompassed all human wisdom. *Mousikē,* that combination of poetry, music, song, and dance over which they presided, formed the basis of education (*paideia*); hence, the Muses became firmly associated with *paideia* and were subsequently used as symbols of learning in a wide variety of contexts (Murray 2004). At the same time, Plato's use of Muse imagery and his designation of philosophy as the highest form of *mousikē* (*Phaedo* 61A) established a connection between the Muses and prose. Both Plato's Academy and Aristotle's Lyceum contained *mouseia,* sanctuaries with statues of the Muses, and the Hellenistic world saw a development of their role as goddesses who preside over education, scholarship, and learning, exemplified in the founding of the Museum (Greek *mouseion,* literally a place connected with the Muses) at Alexandria. This was also the period when the functions of the nine Muses began to be differentiated one from another, on the basis of the Hesiodic names. Despite considerable variations, these eventually stabilized as Calliope (epic), Clio (history), Euterpe (lyric and flute playing), Terpsichore (lyric and dance), Erato (lyric and love poetry), Melpomene (tragedy), Thalia (comedy), Polyhymnia (hymns and pantomime), and Urania (astronomy). The iconography of the individual Muses, though not firmly fixed until the Roman imperial era, clearly derives from Hellenistic art, and Hellenistic traditions lie behind the important discussion of the Muses and their functions in Diodorus, *Historical Library* (*Bibliotheca historica,* 4.7), written in the 30s BCE. In Rome the Muses continued as patrons of intellectual life; Cicero declared that "to live with the Muses is to live humanistically" (*cum Musis, id est, cum humanitate et doctrina, Tusculan Disputations* 5.66). They were a favorite theme in sculpture, especially on sarcophagi, and in mosaics (Zanker 1995, 267–287).

In the medieval period poets continued to invoke the Muses, though the conventions of Latin poetry were adapted to bring them into line with Christian doctrine; some Christian poets rejected the pagan deities altogether, appealing to Christ or the Holy Spirit for inspiration (Ziolkowski 1990). Knowledge of the Muses was preserved in mythological handbooks (such as Fulgentius', late 5th or early 6th cent.), but they more or less disappear from the visual record: in place of the nine Muses we find the Seven Liberal Arts. Key texts for this transition are Boethius' *Consolation of Philosophy* (ca. 524) and Martianus Capella's *Marriage of Philology and Mercury* (before 429).

The revival of the pagan goddesses began with the early Humanists, notably Petrarch and Boccaccio, and Muses are ubiquitous in Renaissance poetry, both as decorative figures and as spiritual forces who bestow their inspiration on the poet (Revard 2001, 50–119). Representations of Muses in the visual arts are equally prevalent, culminating in Raphael's *Parnassus* (1510–1511): Apollo plays the lyre, seated beneath a laurel grove and surrounded by the nine Muses representing different types of poetry. The great poets of classical antiquity are depicted, together with their modern counterparts, the whole scene suggestive of musical harmony and the timelessness of inspiration. Poetic inspiration was also an important theme in the work of the French classical painter Nicolas Poussin, whose paintings include an *Apollo and the Muses on Parnassus* (1631–1632), modeled on Raphael's fresco, as well as *The Inspiration of the Lyric Poet* and *The Inspiration of the Epic Poet* (ca. 1630). In the latter picture Apollo sits in the center with his lyre, imparting inspiration to an unnamed epic poet, while the Muse Calliope looks on; the *Iliad,* the *Odyssey,* and the *Aeneid* lie at Apollo's feet. The canvas as a whole sums up in visual terms the epic tradition and mythology of inspiration so characteristic of pagan antiquity. Epic had always been the most elevated of genres, and the invocation to the Muse played an essential part in its composition; but poetic commonplace is transformed into a deeply expressive symbol of the divine nature of inspiration in Milton's great invocations to the Christianized Muse, Urania, in *Paradise Lost* (Gregory 1989).

In the 18th century a new issue emerged, that of the Muses' femininity. As women began to participate actively in the public sphere as patrons, producers, and consumers of literature and the fine arts, Muse imagery becomes increasingly popular as a way of celebrating feminine achievement, epitomized in Richard Samuel's painting *The Nine Living Muses of Great Britain,* exhibited at the Royal Academy in 1779 (Eger 2001). The novelty of Samuel's painting is that it depicts living women as Muses, at the same time evoking the ethereal mythological figures of earlier famous portrayals of the Muses such as those of Raphael and Poussin. By the 20th century the descent of the Muses from Parnassus was complete, and the most popular image of the Muse, still current today, is of a real, flesh-and-blood woman who inspires an (invariably male) artist. But the Muse is a figure with multiple meanings that can be adapted to suit changing historical circumstances; at the same time it gives metaphorical expression to a nexus of attitudes toward human creativity that, from their roots in classical antiquity through the Renaissance to the present day, have played an essential part in the shaping of Western culture.

BIBL.: Elizabeth Eger, "Representing Culture: *The Nine Living Muses of Great Britain,*" in *Women, Writing and the Public Sphere,* ed. E. Eger, C. Grant, C. Ó Gallchoir, and P. Warburton (Cambridge 2001) 104–132. E. R. Gregory, *Milton and the Muses* (Tuscaloosa 1989). Penelope Murray, "The Muses and Their Arts," in *Music and the Muses: The Culture of Mousike in the Classical Athenian City,* ed. Penelope Murray and Peter Wilson (Oxford 2004) 364–389. Stella P. Revard, *Pindar and the Renaissance Hymn-Ode: 1450–1700* (Tempe 2001). Paul Zanker, *The Mask of Socrates: The Image of the Intellectual in Antiquity* (Berkeley 1995). Jan M. Ziolkowski, "Classical Influences on Medieval Latin Views of Inspiration," in *Latin Poetry and the Classical Tradition: Essays in Medieval and Renaissance Literature,* ed. Peter Godman and Oswyn Murray (Oxford 1990) 15–38.

P.MU.

Museum

The language, idea, and even architecture of many modern museums owe a distinct debt to their classical origins. The word *museum* derives most immediately from the Greek *mouseion* and the Latin *musaeum,* which referred initially to an ideal—the sanctuary of the Muses (*Mousai*), the mythological setting inhabited by the nine goddesses of literature, poetry, history, art, music, and astronomy, who were most often considered to be the offspring of Zeus and Mnemosyne. The idea of worshipping the Muses led to the creation of *mouseia,* sites of retreat and contemplation associated with the cult of the Muses. In his *Description of Greece* (ca. 150–170 CE) Pausanias famously wrote of finding the "grove of the Muses" at the base of Mount Helicon (29.5).

During the Hellenistic era the term *museum* became associated with a new kind of institution, closely associated with the idea of the library, designed to store and to generate many different kinds of knowledge. Before the 16th century people spoke primarily not of museums in general, even though there were many libraries and other kinds of collections in the ancient world, but of *the* museum—the great library and research institute (*mouseion*) of Alexandria that was the wonder of the ancient world. Reportedly founded in the 3rd century BCE by Ptolemy I Soter (r. 305–283), at the encouragement of Demetrius of Phaleron, a student of Theophrastus and therefore an indirect disciple of Aristotle, it drew inspiration from Aristotle's Lyceum as a model for a community of scholarly research and instruction. Under Ptolemy II Philadelphus (r. ca. 283–246), the Alexandrian museum expanded to become a full-fledged research complex, including a library estimated to contain, as a result of the aggressive book-collecting policies of Ptolemy III Euergetes (r. 246–222), more than 500,000 scrolls, though such numbers are imprecise and unverifiable. We do know, however, that Callimachus of Cyrene (310–240) left behind a catalogue, *Pinakes,* of some 120,000 scrolls housed in this fabled library, providing subsequent generations with an invaluable record of the literary legacy of antiquity.

Strabo (63/64 BCE–24 CE) offered the most complete eyewitness account of the mature phase of the Alexandrian museum in his *Geography* (17.1.8), in which he described the complex associated with the royal palace as containing scholars' lodgings, a common dining hall, public meeting rooms, and covered walkways. He also noted that a priest was "in charge of the Museum," reminding his readers that this royal think tank was, in its origins, yet another sacred grove of the Muses. Reportedly the museum also included a garden, dissecting rooms, and an observatory. Its professors and librarians were among the most distinguished minds of the ancient world; scholars came from all over the Mediterranean from the 3rd century BCE through the 3rd century CE to enjoy learned conversation and instruction, and to read and copy precious scrolls in its facilities. The museum became a nexus of all disciplines, not simply a repository of written knowledge but a place from which to generate new ideas. There are many conflicting accounts of the destruction of the Alexandrian museum, but the current consensus is that the primary destruction of the library occurred during the war between the Roman emperor Aurelian (r. 270–275 CE) and Zenobia of Palmyra in 272.

Before the disappearance of the Alexandrian museum, the idea of the *mouseion* had already made its way into the Roman world. In imitation of Alexandria, institutions of advanced learning as well as temples filled with objects occasionally bore the name *musaeum*. And the term came to describe not only sites of "religious dedication and public benefaction" (Strong 1994, 13) but also ones devoted to private contemplation and study. Though there are just a handful of references to this Latin word in Roman texts that do not invoke the Alexandrian museum, they are nonetheless illuminating in understanding the transformation of the museum from a sacred and public setting into one equally devoted to a more private and solitary engagement with words and things. Marcus Terentius Varro (116–27 BCE), for example, mentioned the *musaeum* he created in proximity to his country villa (*De re rustica* 3.5.9), perhaps somewhat similar to the painted room surviving in the House of the Muses in Ostia Antica, ca. 128 CE, or the idealized Roman gallery described by Philostratus the Elder in his *Imagines* (ca. 3rd century CE). In his *Natural History,* Pliny the Elder (23–79 CE) called stone grottoes made for the pleasure of Roman nobles *musaea* (36.154), suggesting the ways in which the original idea of *musaeum* had become, to some degree, desacralized to include more profane pleasures. Pliny's famous description of Rome—filled with so many monuments and wonders that, in his opinion, no other city could compete with it as a treasury of the world—implicitly completed the process of making Rome the first city-museum. Both Varro's and Pliny's accounts of Roman museums would become important ingredients in subsequent reinventions of this idea between the Renaissance and the French Revolution.

Scholars of the Middle Ages seem to have been largely uninterested either in this idea or in its institutional expression. When the 17th-century French philologist Dominique du Cange published his dictionary of medieval Latin, *Glossarium ad scriptores mediae et infimae Latinitatis* (1678), his entry on *musaeum* referred primarily to the institution of ancient Alexandria, offering no new definitions of this word that reflected its use in medieval society and culture. Vernacular terms such as *musée* and *museo* did not appear in dictionaries until the 16th century. For the Middle Ages, the museum was a historical entity that had vanished; in the Renaissance its revival and reconstitution signaled the rebirth of the liberal arts and the renewal of the encyclopedic ideal of knowledge that the Muses patronized.

Temples of the Muses, so popular in the ancient world, first made their reappearance in 15th-century Italy. When the Florentine architect Antonio di Pietro Averlino (ca. 1400–ca. 1469), commonly known as Filarete, included a temple of the Muses, filled with portraits of famous men and their trophies, on the highest level of the imaginary Palace of Virtue described in his *Trattato di architettura* (ca. 1464), he reflected a renewed engagement with the idea of the *musaeum* in an era in which many rulers—among them, Cosimo de' Medici in Florence, Leonello d'Este in Ferrara, Federigo da Montefeltro in Urbino, and Isabella d'Este in Mantua—created rooms dedicated to the Muses. None of these spaces, however, was called a "museum," though perhaps Duke Federigo came closest to this by describing one of his creations as a *Tempietto delle Muse*. By the 16th century the presence of "little rooms" (*camerino, studio,* and *studiolo*) in Renaissance palaces, designed for display, study, and contemplation, was indelibly associated with the idea of the *musaeum*. The Renaissance revival of the Muses, in other words, found its most concrete expression not only in the literary and artistic production of this period but in the creation of spaces dedicated to this purpose.

Renaissance museums were created not only by princes, however, but also by a wide range of individuals who believed in several things: the value of specifically reinventing ancient rooms of the Muses in classically inspired Renaissance buildings such as palaces and villas; the importance of collecting as a form of social, political, and economic power; and the project of reconstituting the ideal of the Alexandrian museum through the creation of great libraries and academies, designating the museum as the supreme site of knowledge. The *musaeum* of the Humanist writer and bishop Paolo Giovio (1483–1552)—the most prominent building to bear this name in 16th-century Italy—offers an early and important example of the interconnections between these three models. Built between 1537 and 1543 on the shores of Lake Como on the alleged site of the ruins of the villa that Pliny the Younger had described in his letters, Giovio's *musaeum* was a memorial both to the past and the present, a kind of archaeological fantasy built to house his portrait gallery of famous Renaissance men and women, his collection of arms and armor, and other objects he deemed worthy of commemoration. Successfully persuading patrons to help fund this villa and encouraging them to visit it regularly, he presented his building and its collections not simply as a private endeavor but as a monument to his times.

Giovio was perhaps the first person since antiquity to imagine the *musaeum* as a specific kind of building. Inspired by his reading of the Roman architect Vitruvius, he created an edifice made by and for his patrons, and certainly to the glory of himself, to house noteworthy objects for purposes of public display. He called both the great hall and the entire villa his *musaeum*. Yet it was also a "temple of virtue," with a library, armory, garden, porticos, and a room dedicated to Minerva. Its ingredients cleverly combined elements of the Alexandrian museum with Pliny the Younger's account of his villa. When Giovio described his museum in print at the beginning of his project to compose elegies of famous men whose portraits adorned the walls of his villa, he not only underscored the idea that a *musaeum* was a place to see the past through its images but also emphasized the power of a history that was literally constructed on the ruins of antiquity. His was a far more elaborate project than the Roman antiquarian Pirro Ligorio's equally interesting reconstruction of Varro's *musaeum* on paper in 1558.

Giovio belonged to an early generation of Renaissance collectors who increasingly felt that museums should be eternal monuments of culture. When he died in 1552, his will specified not only that his heirs had to keep and maintain his villa with its objects intact but also that his eldest nephew, Giulio, was obliged to live in the museum in order to show it to visitors, acting as its custodian. By the 1590s successive floods had ruined the villa, leading heirs to remove and divide up the family patrimony. In 1613 the family sold what was left of Giovio's villa to Marco Gallio, who tore it down a year later to build his own country estate.

In the decades between the creation and the destruction of Giovio's museum, collections of all kinds proliferated throughout Western Europe. Creating, describing, and visiting early modern cabinets of curiosities breathed new life into the ancient idea of the museum, transforming it in the process. Though many collections initially focused on antiquities, especially in Rome, where nobles and clerics competed with each other to lay claim to the ancient city's heritage, others juxtaposed them to modern, scientific, and exotic artifacts (as Giovio himself had). Alexandria remained the site of the original *musaeum*, but late 16th- and 17th-century collectors understood their task to be driven by the quest for erudition as well as an expansive curiosity about the world in general. They thought carefully about how to arrange their objects and began to publicize them in print.

The first ideal description of a museum—the Belgian physician and librarian Samuel Quiccheberg's *Inscriptiones vel tituli theatri amplissimi*—appeared in 1565. The first catalogue—the physician Giovan Battista Olivi's *De reconditis et praecipuis collectaneis ab honestissimo et solertissimo Francisco Calceolari Veronensi in Musaeo adservatis*, describing the apothecary Francesco Calzolari's collection in Verona—was published in 1584. Increasingly the term *museum* became virtually synonymous not only with words to connote public repositories of valuable things, such as *treasury* (from Pliny the Elder's *thesaurus*), but also with a vocabulary used interchangeably to describe the study of those things and the furniture used for storing them (*studio, scrittoio, cabinet, kunstschrank*) as well as collections of specific kinds of things, such as the *Wunderkammer* and the *Kunstschrank*. As Cardinal Federico Borromeo, founder of the Bibliotheca and Pinacotheca Ambrosiana, reminded readers of his *Musaeum Bibliothecae Ambrosianae* (Milan 1625), collecting and writing about paintings was a natural outcome of his decision to transform his personal art collection into a public museum in 1618. He also considered his catalogue, the first published guide to an art gallery, an explicit homage to those chapters in Pliny the Elder's *Natural History* concerned with the history of ancient art.

By the early 17th century the idea of the "paper museum" (*museo cartaceo*)—made especially famous by the Roman collector Cassiano dal Pozzo (1588–1657), who began his collection of approximately 7,000 drawings around 1615—envisioned an encyclopedia of drawings that would visually represent all kinds of knowledge. As the term *museum* became increasingly associated with encyclopedic collections of any kind, growing numbers of books used the term to denote a comprehensive work of reference, such as Claude Clement's *Musei, sive bibliothecae tam privatae quam publicae extructio, instructio, cura, usus* (Leiden 1635), the anonymous collection of alchemical texts entitled *Museum Hermeticum reformatum et amplificatum* (Frankfurt 1678), and Jean Mabillon and Michel Germain's classic guide to manuscripts in Italian libraries, the *Museum italicum, seu collectio veterum scriptorum ex bibliothecis italicis* (Paris 1724). In this sense, a museum was defined by its ability to complete knowledge—an idea that harkened back to the notion of the Library of Alexandria as the first universal repository. It also could be a place of rediscovery, as Thomas Browne reminded readers of his *Musaeum clausum, or Bibliotheca abscondita* (1683), in which he satirized the penchant for strange, marvelous, and ancient things by creating an imaginary catalogue of lost books and objects.

Growing interest in the history of the Alexandrian museum produced a series of publications attempting to reconstruct it for early modern readers. Justus Lipsius' account of Alexandria in his *De bibliothecis syntagma* (1602) described the museum in relationship to the library. But later works, such as Johannes Fredericus Gronovius' *De Museo Alexandrino exercitationes academicae* (1667) and Ludolf Küster's *De Museo Alexandrino diatribe*, both published in volume 8 of Jacobus Gronovius' *Thesaurus graecarum antiquitatum* (Leiden 1697–1702); Adam Rechberg's *Dissertatio de Museo Alexandrino* (Leipzig 1698); and Carl Friedrich Gerischer's *De Museo Alexandrino* (Leipzig 1752) focused on the museum itself. Building on several centuries of antiquarian scholarship and textual rediscovery, they created the first modern histories of this ancient institution.

The philological and antiquarian scholarship of late 17th- and 18th-century Europe created the intellectual framework in which a new kind of public and state museum emerged. In the case of the British Museum (established 1753), its combination of Sir Hans Sloane's collection with two of Britain's most famous libraries (the Cottonian and Harleian), and subsequently with the Royal Library in 1757, underscored its role in the British Empire's claim to have bested Alexandria. By contrast, both the Capitoline Museums (1734) and the Museo Pio-Clementino (1771)—the progenitor of the Vatican Museum—in Rome established their relationship with antiquity by displaying their considerable and important holdings of ancient sculpture, as was also the case with the Dresden Art Gallery. No national museum could truly claim to be a museum by the mid-18th century if it did not have some substantial investment in antiquity—a point underscored by Napoleon's decision to loot the treasures of Italy as an essential component of the opening of the Louvre as France's first public art museum in 1793. And yet critics argued that a *musée* (a place for displaying objects to the public) was not ultimately the same thing as a *muséum* (a site of research and knowledge production), insisting that any institution belonging in the second category continue to retain its Latin name, *musaeum,* to make the specific connection to Alexandria explicit.

In 1779 the Académie Royale d'Architecture in Paris offered a grand prize for the best design for a museum, as part of a growing interest in the museum as a design problem. The emergence of a neoclassical architecture in the design of many new museums in Europe and North America in the late 18th and 19th centuries made the importance of the past even more visible, perhaps reaching its culmination in the stark aesthetic of the Pergamon Museum in Berlin, completed in 1930, which created a virtual antiquity through its reconstruction of large archaeological treasures such as the Pergamon Altar and Ishtar Gate. It was only with the advent of a new kind of "modern" museum, such as the Museum of Modern Art in New York (1929), explicitly committed to an architecture and art that denied the power of antiquity and movements imitative of it, such as the Renaissance and neoclassicism, to dictate what counted as aesthetics, that the museum in a certain sense ceased to be a sort of classical palimpsest. Museums devoted to entirely contemporary subjects with social resonance—such as Jane Addams's Labor Museum, which she and Ellen Gates created at Chicago's Hull House in 1900, inspired by the arts and crafts movement spearheaded by William Morris—are further examples of this erasure of the past. Frank Gehry's titanium geometric jungle, the Guggenheim Museum Bilbao (1997), stands in marked contrast to the Metropolitan Museum of Art in New York or the National Gallery of Art in Washington, D.C., in proclaiming the museum as something utterly new and confounding and radically modern rather than a legacy of a distant past.

BIBL.: Ken Arnold, *Cabinets for the Curious: Looking Back at Early English Museums* (London 2006). Norman Bryson, "Philostratus and the Imaginary Museum," in *Art and Taste in Ancient Greek Culture,* ed. Simon Goldhill and Robin Osborne (Cambridge 1994) 255–283, 312–314. Stephen J. Campbell, *The Cabinet of Eros: Renaissance Mythological Painting and the Studiolo of Isabella d'Este* (New Haven 2004). Luciano Canfora, *The Vanished Library: A Wonder of the Ancient World,* trans. Martin Ryle (Berkeley 1990). John R. Clarke, *The Houses of Roman Italy 100 B.C.–A.D. 250: Ritual, Space, and Decoration* (Berkeley 1991). Steven Conn, *Museums and American Intellectual Life, 1876–1926* (Chicago 1998). Susan A. Crane, *Collecting and Historical Consciousness in Early Nineteenth-century Germany* (Ithaca, N.Y., 2000). Carol Duncan, *Civilizing Rituals: Inside Public Art Museums* (New York 1995). Marcin Fabianski, "Iconography of the Architecture of Ideal *Musaea* in the Fifteenth through Eighteenth Centuries," *Journal of the History of Collections* 2 (1990) 95–134, and "*Musaea* in Written Sources of the Fifteenth to Eighteenth Centuries," *Universitas Iagellonica, Acta Scientiarum Litterarumque* 948, *Opuscula Musealia,* fasc. 4 (1990) 7–40. Paula Findlen, "The Museum: Its Classical Etymology and Renaissance Genealogy," *Journal of the History of Collections* 1 (1989) 59–78. Oliver Impey and Arthur MacGregor, eds., *The Origins of Museums: The Cabinet of Curiosities in Sixteenth- and Seventeenth-century Europe* (Oxford 1985). Pamela M. Jones, *Federico Borromeo and the Ambrosiana: Art Patronage and Reform in Seventeenth-century Milan* (Cambridge 1993). Bent Juel-Jensen, "Musaeum Clausum or Bibliotheca Abscondita: Some Thoughts on Curiosity Cabinets and Imaginary Books," *Journal of the History of Collections* 4 (1992) 127–140. Linda Susan Klinger, *"The Portrait Collection of Paolo Giovio"* (PhD diss., Princeton University, 1991). Paula Young Lee, "The Museum of Alexandria and the Formation of the Muséum in Eighteenth-century France," *Art Bulletin* 79 (1997) 385–412. Paolo Liverani, "The Museo Pio-Clementino at the Time of the Grand Tour," *Journal of the History of Collections* 12 (2000) 151–159. Roy Macleod, ed., *The Library of Alexandria: Centre of Learning in the Ancient World* (London 2004). Suzanne Marchand, *Down from Olympus: Archeology and Philhellenism in Germany, 1750–1970* (Princeton 1996). Andrew McClellan, *Inventing the Louvre: Art, Politics, and the Origins of the Modern Museum* (Berkeley 1999). Paul Nelles, "Juste Lipse et Alexandrie: Les origines antiquaires de l'histoire des bibliothèques," in *Le pouvoir des bibliothèques: La mémoire des livres dans la culture occidentale,* ed. Christian Jacob and Marc Baratin (Paris 1996) 224–242. Giovanni di Pasquale, "The Museum of Alexandria: Myth and Model," in *From Private to Public: Natural Collections and Museums,* ed. Marco Beretta (Sagamore Beach, Mass., 2005) 1–12. James J. Sheehan, *Museums in the German Art World: From the End of the Old Regime to the Rise of Modernism* (Oxford 2000). Donald Strong, *Roman Museums: Selected Papers on Roman Art and Architecture* (London 1994) 13–30. Geneviève Warwick, *The Arts of Collecting: Padre Sebastiano Resta and the Market for Drawings in Early Modern Europe* (Cambridge 2000). P.E.F.

Music

The powers attributed to music by Greek and Roman poets, playwrights, and philosophers, not to mention the complex systems of music theory developed in the Pythagorean and Aristotelian traditions, intrigued writers of late antiquity and have remained objects of fascination to the present day. Whether or not these writings accurately reflect the actual music of classical Greece and Rome, this classical tradition has exerted a pervasive influence in Western, Islamic, and Byzantine culture, from the music theory of the Middle Ages through the modern music of Olivier Messiaen, Harry Partch, and Iannis Xenakis; in observations about the effect of music on behavior, ranging from the Church Fathers through today's music therapists; in concepts of a harmonic ordering of the universe, extending from Ptolemy's *Harmonica* (2nd cent. CE) through Kepler's *Harmonices mundi* (1619), the law of planetary distances formulated in the 18th century by Johann Titius and Johann Bode, Viktor Goldschmidt's work on the structure of crystals (*Über Harmonie und Complication,* 1931), and on to the Stephen Hawking–Roger Penrose debates on space and time; in acoustics and tuning systems; and in philosophical considerations of music and aesthetics.

Traces of classical and Hellenistic musical styles may have survived in the active musical life of late antiquity, but by the 6th century CE and most probably long before, the classical tradition in music had become in essence a literary tradition. Although a Greek notational system existed and was preserved to a greater or lesser extent by several Greek authors and by Boethius (*De institutione arithmetica* and *De institutione musica,* early 6th cent. CE), by the early decades of the 7th century even the polymath Isidore of Seville (d. 636) was either unaware of it or knew of no notated music: "Unless sounds are held by human memory, they perish because they cannot be written down" (*Etymologiarum sive originum libri xx,* 3.15) In any case, until the notated hymns of the Cretan Mesomedes (fl. 141 CE) were published for the first time by Vincenzo Galilei in his *Dialogo della musica antica, et della moderna* (1581), writers of late antiquity, the Middle Ages, and the Renaissance seem not to have known any actual music of classical Greece and Rome and never comment on specific compositions, beyond references to titles or text.

The literary tradition, on the other hand, is extremely rich, represented in Greek by the musical allusions and descriptions that appear in the *Iliad* and the *Odyssey,* lyric poetry, and dramatic works; in the writings of Plato, Aristotle, Plutarch, Sextus Empiricus, and many other representatives of various philosophical schools who wrote in considerable detail about the use, character, and value of music; and in historical, anecdotal, and encyclopedic works such as Pausanias' *Graeciae descriptio,* Athenaeus' *Deipnosophistae,* Plutarch's *Quaestiones convivales,* and Pollux's *Onomasticon.* Beyond these general works in which music is not normally the primary focus, the classical tradition also includes a systematic theory of music, formulated in a group of treatises ranging from the 4th century BCE to the 4th or 5th century CE.

A few of these are elaborate, extended books that treat scientific problems (such as the *Elementa harmonica* and *Rhythmica* of Aristoxenus, 4th cent. BCE, and the *Harmonica* of Ptolemy, 2nd cent. CE) or show the way in which the science of music reveals universal patterns of order, thereby leading to the highest levels of knowledge (such as the *De musica* of Aristides Quintilianus, late 3rd–mid-4th cent. CE, and, again, Ptolemy's *Harmonica*). Other, shorter technical treatises fall within the Pythagorean or Aristotelian traditions, or sometimes bridge the two. Pythagorean treatises typically concentrate on the musical ratios; their application to the *canon,* an instrument with one or more strings on which notes and intervals can be precisely measured and compared; and other aspects of Pythagorean mathematics or lore, including the story of Pythagoras' discovery of the musical ratios (2:1, 3:2, 4:3, 3:1, and 4:1, equivalent to the consonant intervals of an octave, 5th, 4th, 12th, and 15th) in the hammers of a blacksmith's shop. The Aristotelian tradition, represented especially in the treatises of Aristoxenus and his followers, concentrates on systematic classification of musical phenomena, including such subjects as the identification of notes as fundamental elements in music; the function and placement of notes within various types of intervals (especially the tetrachord, a characteristic group of four consecutive notes) and scales, further classified as consonant or dissonant; the arrangement of different sizes of intervals to create six shadings of three basic musical genera (enharmonic, chromatic, and diatonic); the mapping of potential musical space by various locations of scales, or *tonoi* (Dorian, Phrygian, Lydian, and so on); the possibility of shifting among the various options, that is, modulation; the patterns used in composition; and musical ethos. A similar set of classificatory elements is identified for rhythm and meter.

In the West this Greek tradition was carried forward into late antiquity and beyond by a varied group of writers who made use of Greek material in books more suited to the needs of their time, such as manuals on the nine traditional disciplines and commentaries on the complex works of the past, making them accessible while also perhaps reinterpreting them to accord with such contemporary philosophical or theological movements as Neoplatonism and Christianity. Moreover, with the waning of the Roman Empire, writers responded to an interest in magic and the supernatural that developed as individuals lost confidence in society and in the value of reason, turning instead to supernatural determinism. Modern distinctions among science, technology, magic, and religion did not apply: the works of Censorinus (*De die natali,* 238 CE) in the 3rd century and of Macrobius (*In somnium Scipionis commentarium*) and Martianus Capella (*De nuptiis Philologiae et Mercurii*) early in the 5th century, for example, present scientific and technical discussions of the Greek musical tradition in decidedly supernatural contexts. Music's ostensibly magical power both to reflect and to influence individual behavior—and perhaps even nature itself—ensured a continuing fascination with the tradition.

In the Carolingian and post-Carolingian eras, Martianus Capella's *De nuptiis* and especially Boethius' *De institutione musica* were the preferred sources for knowledge of the classical tradition in music because of their technical content. Medieval readers did not know that these books relied heavily on earlier Greek sources, but they did recognize that the treatises, taken together, provided a wealth of information about Pythagoras' discovery of the mathematical nature of music, its gradual development by later musicians, and its individual parts: notes, intervals, genera, scales, modes or tonoi, and so on. Of course, the writings of the other authors continued to be studied as well: some indication of their relative popularity is provided by the number of surviving manuscripts, dating from the 8th through the 15th centuries, that preserve the musical treatises of Calcidius (133 MSS of his commentary on Plato's *Timaeus,* from ca. 321 CE), Macrobius (250), Martianus Capella (242), Augustine (82 for *De musica,* of 389 CE, including those containing only *De musica,* 6), Boethius (150), Cassiodorus (27 for *Institutiones divinarum et saecularium litterarum,* mid-6th cent., not including those containing only *Institutiones,* 1), and Isidore (152).

Reception of the treatises of Martianus Capella and Boethius is partially revealed in the extended glosses and commentaries that accompany the original texts in many manuscripts. Much of this material was eventually absorbed into the first stages of a new tradition of specialized music theory, represented by Aurelian of Réôme's *Musica disciplina* (mid- to late 9th cent.), Hucbald's *De harmonica institutione* (late 9th cent.), and Regino of Prüm's *De harmonica institutione* (ca. 900), all of which exhibit a conscious adaptation of the tradition to the new problems of conceptualizing and organizing a theoretical framework for the tones or modes of liturgical chant. Moreover, both Aurelian and Regino preserve the story of Pythagoras' discovery (as transmitted by Boethius), accepting the centrality of Pythagorean ratios as the basis of music theory; Hucbald and Regino also provide systematic discussions of the Greek note and scale systems.

By contrast, the anonymous *Musica* and *Scholica enchiriadis* (late 9th cent.) adapted tradition to the practical exigencies of singing chant, whether as a single musical line (monophony) or in the parallel lines of organum, while drawing as necessary on earlier authorities for content, definitions, and structure. The treatises' unique notational system is constructed around a set of four basic figures, inverted and rotated to indicate higher and lower positions, clearly derived from the Greek notational system. Likewise, the traditional Greek 18-note tetrachordal scalar system was reorganized so that the second tetrachord is aligned with the initial pitches (the finals) of the four authentic tones of chant (D, E, F, and G). This requires a different species of tetrachord and a number of further modifications in the scalar system, which nevertheless still retains recognizable traces of the classical tradition. Practice and theory are brought into an uneasy alliance here, and it is perhaps no coincidence that the story of Pythagoras and the smithy is absent from the *enchiriadis* tradition.

For the next several centuries theorists pursued the basic tasks of preserving the valued heritage of the intellectual literary tradition while also adapting it to the very real needs of musical practice: the definition and classification of notes, intervals, scales, modes or tones, the repertory of chant, notation, tuning, and pedagogical methods. The balance between preservation and adaptation varied from writer to writer, but even a theorist such as Guido of Arezzo, who largely ignores the classical tradition, still closes his *Micrologus* (ca. 1025) with the story of Pythagoras and praises Boethius as the "expositor of this art" (*panditor huius artis,* 20). The conceptualizations of medieval music theorists were strongly influenced by the classical tradition even as the tradition itself came to be understood in terms of current practice.

Toward the end of the Middle Ages music theory was increasingly concerned with measuring time in order to coordinate the multiple lines of polyphony. Thus, the rhythmic theory of Augustine's *De musica* and the binary and ternary multiples inherent in the cosmogony of Plato's *Timaeus* (as described by Calcidius) play a substantial, if unacknowledged, role in the 13th- and 14th-century tradition of *musica mensurabilis* (measurable music). Likewise, from the 14th century onward Pythagorean ratios were regularly applied to large-scale temporal relationships.

While Latin authors in the West were busy appropriating the classical tradition through translation and adaptation, Arabic scholars in the 8th and 9th centuries were active in the translation of Greek technical, scientific, and philosophical literature. With the growth of the Islamic empire in North Africa and Spain, the newly translated literature traveled to regions where the original texts had never been known or had long since been forgotten. The *Kitāb al-fihrist* (*Index to Arabic Books,* ca. 987) of Ibn al-Nadīm indicates that Arabic translations of the *Sectio canonis* and treatises by Aristoxenus, Nicomachus, and Euclid (probably the treatise of Cleonides) were in circulation; shortly thereafter, commentaries, now lost, on both the *Sectio canonis* and Cleonides' *Harmonica introductio* were written by the 11th-century Egyptian physicist Ibn al-Haitham (also known as Alhazan). Internal evidence in the treatises of al-Kindī (d. ca. 874) and al-Fārābī (d. ca. 950) makes it clear that Ptolemy's *Harmonica* and perhaps Aristides Quintilianus' *De musica* were known at this time, and both Arabic authors adapted the theory to the music of their own era. Arabic theorists of the 9th and 10th centuries were equally interested in the Platonic view of music as a paradigm for the larger harmony of the universe, in the physics of sound, and in the scientific classification of melodic and rhythmic elements. Some engaged in pure speculation about musical phenomena, adapted from the Aristoxenian and Pythagorean traditions, but al-Fārābī advocated that theory be based on musical practice. In fact, following the tradition of Ptolemy's *Harmonica,* much Arabic music theory emphasizes that theory and practice must complement one another for the perfection of music.

In contrast to the activity of the Latin West and the Islamic empire, the Greek East seems to have been content to continue the tradition of the *tetraktys* (the Quadrivium in the West), with arithmetic based on Nicomachus and John Philoponus's commentary, geometry on Euclid, astronomy on Ptolemy, and music on Ptolemy, Cleonides, Aristoxenus, and Aristides Quintilianus. Byzantine scholarship paid little attention to expanding its store of musical literature in the period between the last decades of the 5th century and the establishment of a new university at Constantinople in the 11th century, although Photius' *Bibliotheca* (mid-9th cent.) and the *Etymologicon magnum* and the *Suda* (both 10th cent.) reflect important activity in the preservation of the classical literary tradition in music, including much that no longer exists today. The importance of the rebirth of scholarly activity beginning with Michael Psellus in the 11th century and extending through George Pachymeres, Maximus Planudes, Theodorus Metochites, and Manuel Bryennius in the 13th and early 14th centuries can hardly be exaggerated: this period also saw the production of the most important surviving Greek manuscripts containing the corpus of music theory, which eventually found their way to the West and into the hands of the Renaissance Humanists, many of them through the collection of Cardinal Bessarion.

Music did not find a place in the *studia humanitatis* of the earliest generations of Western Humanists, but it did not take long for Humanism to embrace rediscoveries in the disciplines of the Quadrivium. A second generation of Humanists, Vittorino da Feltre, Marsilio Ficino, Angelo Poliziano, and Giorgio Valla, began to study Greek texts pertaining to music, known, if at all, only through Latin intermediaries; they soon recognized the extent to which the classical tradition in music had been misunderstood, misappropriated, or simply forgotten by the writers of late antiquity and the Middle Ages. In the 15th century the establishment of centers for the Humanistic study of music at Mantua, Parma, Bologna, Padua, and eventually Milan—not to mention developments in printing—encouraged a veritable explosion of musical treatises over the next two centuries, almost all of which addressed the classical tradition and imitated classical models in one way or another.

Treatises of the 15th and 16th centuries are commonly classed as *musica theorica* or *musica practica,* but some of them combine the two. *Musica theorica* typically concentrates on the more speculative aspects, especially such matters as the "history" of music, Pythagorean mathematics and its relationship to musical intervals, musical metaphysics, and the general principles of harmonics, rhythmics, and metrics. *Musica practica,* on the other hand, is occupied with notation and other elements of mensural music, counterpoint, and principles of composition. Insofar as possible, the theorists try to rationalize practice so that it will reflect the principles of *musica theorica.* Complementing these two traditions is a tradition of musical poetics, in which principles of classical rhetoric are applied to create music that will be clear and powerful, embracing Plato's dictum (*Republic* 3.10.398C–D) that extols text as the basis and foundation for rhythm and melody.

The tradition of musical ethos in the writings of Plato, Aristotle, and the Greek music theorists, its ostensible connection with the various genera and modes or *tonoi,* and its vaunted effect on behavior and on the human spirit encouraged Humanistic writers (many also composers) to concentrate on these subjects. The ancient sources, however, were contradictory and in any case difficult to apply to the polyphonic style of the Renaissance. Composers experimented with various ways of employing ancient genera and modes in their compositions, which sometimes required new types of instruments—as specified, for example, in Nicola Vicentino's *L'Antica musica ridotta alla moderna prattica* (1555).

Notions of ethos rely to some degree on the relationship between music and the universal order of the cosmos, whether or not it is reflected in an audible harmony of the spheres. Ficino's translation and discussion of Plato's *Timaeus* as well as the musical cosmologies in the rediscovered treatises of Aristides Quintilianus and Ptolemy provided Renaissance theorists with alternatives to the commentaries of Calcidius and Macrobius. On this new basis, elaborate complexes of universal relationships among seasons, the four elements, signs of the zodiac, planets, muses, modes, and so on could be developed. (A good example appears in the famous illustration on f. 94v of Gaffurio's *De harmonia musicorum instrumentorum opus,* 1518.)

A continuing problem for the Renaissance theorists was the limitation imposed on tuning and acceptable consonant intervals by the tradition of the Pythagorean hammers, which could not accommodate intervals regularly employed in polyphonic music. The solution was either to demonstrate that these limitations were invalid, as Fogliano did in *Musica theorica* (1529), or to preserve the basic tradition of Pythagorean mathematics while expanding it beyond the limitations of the first four numbers, as Zarlino did with his harmonic theory embodied in the first six numbers (*Le istitutioni harmoniche,* 1558). But even a theorist such as Vincenzo Galilei, who rejected the traditional Pythagorean limits, still employed Pythagorean mathematics in his *Dialogo* to demonstrate his premises, including the assertion that consonance and dissonance were not based in nature or number but rather in context and taste. "This emancipation of harmony from numerical theory . . . is one of the achievements that can be traced directly to the revival of ancient learning" (Palisca 1985, 21).

In the later 16th century, early Greek and Roman treatments of music, which had become more widely accessible in the West through the work of the Humanists, formed a regular topic of discussion in various academies in Florence, Ferrara, and elsewhere. In particular the Florentine Camerata, an informal group hosted by Count Giovanni Bardi, regularly discussed correspondence with the Florentine Humanist Girolamo Mei (working in Rome), who believed that much of the earlier scholarship on ancient music was erroneous. Mei condemned counterpoint as antithetical to the classical tradition, a view adopted by Bardi and promulgated by Galilei in his *Dialogo*. Considerable attention was devoted to the role of music and type of singing in classical tragedy. Inspired by such discussions, Giulio Caccini published a set of monodies (solo vocal lines with light chordal accompaniment) in his *Nuove musiche* (1601–1602), stating in the preface that this music attempted to conform to "Plato and other philosophers (who declared that music is naught but speech, with rhythm and tone coming after; not vice versa) with the aim that it enter into the minds of men and have those wonderful effects admired by the great writers." Jacopo Peri employed a similar style in his setting of Ottavio Rinuccini's dramatic *L'Euridice* (1600), and many other composers experimented with this "new music," quite often in dramatic contexts based on classical subjects.

In the 17th and 18th centuries more of the literary sources pertaining to ancient Greek music began to be circulated in published form, including Marcus Meibom's *Seven Authors on Ancient Music* (*Antiquae musicae auctores septem,* 1652), intended in part as a corrective to the numerous errors Meibom detected in Athanasius Kircher's famous *Musurgia universalis* (1650). Both books influenced John Wallis's 1682 and 1699 editions of two treatises that Meibom had not included in his collection: Ptolemy's *Harmonica* and Porphyry's commentary on it (3rd cent.). These substantial publications supplied 18th-century scholars with material that appealed to their antiquarian and historical interests, providing fodder as well for arguments about the purpose and meaning of music. Lorenz Christoph Mizler and Johann Mattheson, for example, drew on ostensibly divergent trends in the Greek sources to bolster their own aesthetic differences; historians such as F. W. Marpurg, G. B. Martini, and Sir John Hawkins tried to develop coherent historical surveys.

In the 19th century a great deal of scholarship was devoted to ancient music. A fair amount of Greek music notated on stone and papyrus and in manuscripts was discovered, heightening enthusiasm for the subject and in some cases influencing musical style. For example, Friedrich Nietzsche's Basel lecture "Das griechische Musikdrama" (18 January 1870), read to Richard Wagner during a visit to his home on 11 June 1870, enlarged Wagner's understanding of Greek *Musikdrama* and enhanced its application in *Der Ring des Nibelungen.*

Interest in the classical tradition of music, which continued unabated throughout the 20th century, is reflected in the enormous amount of secondary literature devoted to the topic, especially in dictionaries and encyclopedias of music and in specialized monographs. Most of this scholarship was a continuation of the literary tradition, but some of it found its way into compositions that tried to apply ancient Greek theories of harmonics and rhythmics. Influenced by Maurice Emmanuel's articles on ancient and oriental music in the *Encyclopédie de la musique et dictionnaire du Conservatoire* (ca. 1913–1931), Olivier Messiaen incorporated principles of Greek modality and meter in many of his compositions. Harry Partch, fascinated by Pythagorean musical mathematics and the scales described by Kathleen Schlesinger in *The Greek Aulos* (1939), developed his own unique microtonal tuning system and explored Greek scales in compositions such as *Two Studies on Ancient Greek Scales* (1946) and *Oedipus* (1952/1967). Iannis Xenakis, interested like Wagner in the synthesis of the arts represented by ancient Greek drama, composed his own *Oresteïa* (1965–1966), followed later by *Kassandra* (1987) and *La déesse Athéna* (1992).

The period between 1990 and 2005 saw the publication of four full-scale monographs on ancient Greek music, a new edition and at least half a dozen recordings of the surviving fragments, four substantial volumes of musical archaeology, a number of Web sites, and more than 100 new editions, translations, scholarly articles, and monographs. Fascination with the classical tradition in music remains undiminished.

BIBL.: R. R. Bolgar, *The Classical Heritage and Its Beneficiaries* (Cambridge 1954). Thomas Christensen, ed., *The Cambridge History of Western Music Theory* (Cambridge 2002). Michel Huglo, "The Study of Ancient Sources of Music Theory in the Medieval Universities," in *Music Theory and Its Sources: Antiquity and the Middle Ages,* ed. André Barbera (Notre Dame 1990) 150–172. Kenneth Levy, "Music," in *Late Antiquity: A Guide to the Postclassical World,* ed. G. W. Bowersock, Peter Brown, and Oleg Grabar (Cambridge, Mass., 1999) 598–599. T. J. Mathiesen, *Apollo's Lyre: Greek Music and Music Theory in Antiquity and the Middle Ages* (Lincoln 1999) esp. chs. 1 and 4–7. C. V. Palisca, *Humanism in Italian Renaissance Musical Thought* (New Haven 1985) and *Music and Ideas in the Sixteenth and Seventeenth Centuries* (Urbana 2006).

T.J.M.

Musical Instruments

Music was omnipresent in Greek antiquity: in religious festivals, in athletic games and competitions for musicians, in private *symposia,* at war, in lyric poetry (songs accompanied by a lyre), and, of course, in drama both tragic and comic. Typical musical instruments of that time, such as the *auloi* (pipes) and stringed *kithara* and *lyra,* were not Greek inventions and did not give rise to specific musical instruments in the Western Middle Ages. The Romans easily assimilated Greek musical culture and used Greek instruments, to which they sometimes gave Latin names (e.g., *tibiae* for *auloi*). Under Etruscan influence, Romans used trumpets and horns on a much larger scale than did the Greeks, not only in military situations but also for sounding alarms of all kinds. They called these *tuba, lituus, bucina,* and *cornu.*

The best-known classical influence on the music of the West—if not the emblematic function of Orpheus and his lyre—is an etymological one; the most intriguing influence is a theoretical one, which left as its concrete remainder the organ and the keyboard.

Linkage between classical musical instruments and their successors in later cultures is mostly etymological. Greek terms persisted throughout the Roman, Byzantine, and Arab worlds, even if, in the end, they were applied to completely different items. The Greek term *kithara* refers to a lyre, but only the Ethiopian *kissar* is a true one. Other instrument names derived from *kithara,* such as *guitarra, quwaytara,* and *chitarrone,* as well as the modern *guitar,* actually designate different forms of a lute: *guitarra* (Eng. *gittern*) is a small medieval lute, *quwaytara* a small unfretted short-necked lute of the Maghrib, and *chitarrone* a large Renaissance lute with supplementary bass strings. In the same way, Western *liras* have nothing to do with the antique *lyra:* the *lira da braccio* and *lira da gamba* are Renaissance viols, with two off-board drone strings, and a *lira* is a folk fiddle in Crete, Greece, and Bulgaria. Although the Roman *tuba* was originally a straight trumpet, today tubas are low-pitched horns with a large conical bore, comparable to or identical with large saxhorns. *Bucina,* in Rome a curved or natural (animal) horn, got a new life as *buccin* during the French Revolution and became very popular in the first half of the 19th century as a trombone with a dragon's mouth. The *cornu,* a narrow-bored Roman horn 6 or 7 feet in length but curved into a circle and held with a rod fixed diagonally across the loop, was used by the Romans in the amphitheater together with the *hydraulos* (water organ). Like the *bucina,* the *cornu* reappeared during the French Revolution, under the name of *tuba curva,* in marches and symphonies by Gossec and Catel and in an opera by Méhul.

When scholars in the Western Middle Ages discussed music, they relied on the theoretical heritage of the Greeks through Boethius' Latin treatise *De institutione musica.* As a liberal art, *musica* constituted an acoustical and mathematical discipline, in the Pythagorean tradition, rather than a musical practice. As a consequence, the monochord, a sound box with one string that served to illustrate theoretical discussions, survived from Graeco-Roman antiquity. In the 12th century a mechanically bowed monochord with a key mechanism was developed, probably in monastic circles, to serve the same pedagogical purposes. It was called *organistrum* or *symphonia,* from Greek *organon* (musical instrument), or *symphōnia* (chord, harmony). This *organistrum* is essentially the hurdy-gurdy, but its relationship with Greek music is more than an etymological one: the use of a keyboard, i.e., a mechanical interface to make harmony and to concretize scales and intervals, is derived directly from the Greek *hydraulos* or water organ. Keyboards have determined a kind of harmonic thinking that became characteristic of Western music. The *hydraulos,* which once served in Roman amphitheaters and the palaces of the Byzantine emperors, became the Western organ of the Christian churches.

BIBL.: John G. Landels, *Music in Ancient Greece and Rome* (New York 2001). Christopher Page, *Music and Instruments of the Middle Ages: Studies on Texts and Performance,* Variorum Collected Studies Series CS562 (Aldershot 1997). Peter Williams, "How Did the Organ Become a Church Instrument? A Sequel of Further Questions," in *Studia Organologica: Festschrift für John Henry van der Meer zu seinem fünfundsechzigsten Geburtstag,* ed. Friedemann Hellwig (Tutzing 1987) 523–533.

I.D.K.

Mycenae

Mycenae appears in the Homeric epics as the capital city of King Agamemnon, leader of the Greek army during the Trojan War. The ruins still stand in a remote corner of the northeastern Peloponnese. Walls constructed of vast stones rear up from a rocky outcrop. Above the entrance to the citadel sits the oldest piece of monumental sculpture in all of Europe that can still be viewed in situ—a relief carving of two lions flanking a downward-tapering column. Outside the citadel walls, the steep dome of the underground tomb known as the Treasury of Atreus rises 40 feet overhead. Such is Mycenae's legendary predominance that its name has been bestowed on the whole of the age in which it prospered; the Bronze Age civilization that flourished in Greece between 1600 and 1200 BCE is known as Mycenaean.

Ever since the Homeric poems began to circulate in the 8th century BCE, the remains of Mycenae have been venerated as a tangible connection to Homer's Age of Heroes. Iron Age Greeks built a shrine to King Agamemnon in the ruins. Aeschylus, Sophocles, and Euripides all rewrote the city's grisly legends to reflect on the dangers of the heroic ethic. Thucydides opened his *History of the Peloponnesian Wars* with some reflections on Mycenae's role in the Trojan conflict. The 2nd century CE topographer Pausanias made a pilgrimage to the city and was shown the spot where Agamemnon was supposedly buried. If *The Iliad* and *The Odyssey* are the closest thing to a Bible possessed by pagan Greece, then Mycenae is its Jerusalem.

Mycenae languished in obscurity through the Byzantine and Ottoman empires, neither of which had much use for pagan heroes, but in the early years of the 19th century, as Ottoman power began to wane, a steady trickle of Grand Tourists from England and France made their way to the ruins. After the Greek War of Independence in the 1820s, the Lion Gate was cleared down to its threshold by the Greek Archaeological Society. In 1876 the merchant-turned-archaeologist Heinrich Schliemann (fresh from the triumph of having identified and excavated Troy) discovered a series of deep, rock-cut graves inside the citadel containing 17 treasure-laden corpses, which he identified as King Agamemnon and his retinue. The British politician William Gladstone wrote a preface to the archaeologist's excavation report; the Italian poet Gabriele d'Annunzio penned a neo-Greek tragedy pivoting on the discovery of Agamemnon's corpse; scholarly patriots from various nations claimed the heroes as their ancestors; the trickle of tourists swelled to a stream.

Meanwhile, the systematic excavation of the site began under the supervision of the Greek archaeologist Christos Tsountas, who dug for 18 years at Mycenae and laid the foundations for the current understanding of the Mycenaean Age. He also gently pointed out that the gold-smothered burials discovered by Schliemann were 400 years too early to have anything to do with the heroes of the Trojan War. As the archaeological discoveries began to mount up, allowing Mycenaean civilization to be understood on its own terms, the Homeric epics (composed at least four centuries after the city was abandoned) became progressively less important for any understanding of the site. In 1952 the script that the Mycenaeans used to keep their records was deciphered by the British architect Michael Ventris, who identified the language as an archaic form of Greek. Mycenae now stands as the perfect example of a Bronze Age city, one of the regional centers of a bureaucratic, centralized, literate civilization whose downfall ushered in the Greek dark ages.

BIBL.: John Chadwick, *The Decipherment of Linear B* (Cambridge 1967). Elizabeth French, *Mycenae: Agamemnon's Capital, the Site in Its Setting* (Stroud, U.K., 2002). Christos Tsountas and J. Irving Mannat, *The Mycenaean Age: A Study of the Monuments and Culture of Pre-Homeric Greece* (London 1897). Emily Vermeule, *Greece in the Bronze Age* (Chicago 1964). C.G.

Mystery Religions

Secret rites of initiation practiced in the Mediterranean world from the 7th century BCE to the 5th century CE. They differed widely but shared common features: they were voluntarily entered by men and women seeking a significant change of status; initiates engaged the power of a god or goddess and entered a profound and transformative religious experience. The term "mystery" derives from the Greek *mystēria,* used to describe the initiation rites of Eleusis, from which the terms and images associated with such mysteries are derived. Originally, mystery rites in Greece and elsewhere were tied to the vegetation cycle, but social and political changes in the Mediterranean world after the time of Alexander the Great (4th century BCE) transformed the function of the rites, giving them heightened psychological significance. Eleusinian and Dionysian mysteries were Greek; mysteries of Isis and Osiris, Mithras, Cybele, and Attis came from the East. Common to all mysteries was the prohibition against disclosing secrets, "spoken," "performed," or "revealed." This prohibition reflected the perception that the mysteries were, in any case, indescribable. As Aristotle put it, "those who enter initiations do not learn anything (*ou mathein ti*) but experience (*pathein*) something" (fr. 15); they are put into a changed state of awareness. It was not knowledge that the mysteries brought, but rather a transformation of mind realized through the performance of an initiatory rite.

It is precisely the mysteries understood as dramas of transformation that became the legacy transmitted to us by philosophers. Specifically, the Neoplatonists, following Plato, believed themselves to be mystagogues, leading initiates into the transformation and deification they associated with the mysteries. Whatever the ancient Eleusinian rites may have been, in the view of the Platonists of late antiquity—as Wind (1958) has rightly observed—the mysteries had become indistinguishable from the metaphorical meanings these philosophers gave to them, meanings that were more than simply conceptual. Underlying the complexity and subtlety seen in the writings of the later Neoplatonists such as Iamblichus and Proclus was their longing to experience a profound change in perception: to move into an awareness of their identity in the World Soul, to experience divinity. This experience could not be taught. It was not accessible to rational formulation, which explains the remark of the Renaissance philosopher Giovanni Pico della Mirandola that the words of a true mystagogue must simultaneously reveal and veil the mysteries ("Oration on the Dignity of Man" 250). Renaissance thinkers belonging to this tradition aimed, through their hieroglyphs, discourse, and art, to lead readers through images and concepts into an experience that the imagery both reveals (for the experienced) and conceals (from the uninitiated). This paradox reflected the structure of the Neoplatonic cosmos, in which the utterly ineffable One was similarly revealed and veiled: in nature, in the gods, and in ourselves.

Much early 20th-century scholarship dismissed the mysteries and the practice of mystagogy as irrational, as misguided philosophy. Wind (1958), for example, valued the figurative use of ritual but decried its actual practice, on the ground that ritual practices had no place alongside rational philosophy. According to him, the Platonists and Renaissance thinkers who embraced mystagogic rites betrayed their philosophical tradition and succumbed to hocus-pocus. Yet this rational critique, one that Wind shared with many scholars of his generation, disregards Aristotle's observation that initiates in the mysteries do not learn anything but instead have an experience that changes their perception.

Hadot (2006) has recently reopened this theme. In his view Pico's veiled discourse, far from being the contrivance that struck Wind as unnecessarily obscure, was his way of enacting and revealing the mysteries in the only way they could be: covered in veils. Hadot has drawn attention to the subtle insights of profound ancient philosophers such as Proclus, Renaissance thinkers like Pico, and German poets from Schiller in the 18th century to Rilke in the 20th.

Even if mystagogic Platonists and poets were reading their own intuitions and insights into cultic imagery, to dismiss the validity of their ritual practices simply reveals our own bias and tells us little about the existential meaning of their rites. The sustaining theme throughout the history of mystery cults and mystery literature is self-transformation. From antiquity to the Renaissance, to modern poets and even to contemporary mystery initiates (among others) who believe that a hallucinogenic fungus, ergot, was used at Eleusis, the constant element associated with the mysteries is self-transformation. To be initiated, Plutarch said, is to die (fr. 178); yet from this ritual death initiates enter a more fulfilling and universal existence. Mystery religions are an enduring testament to the fundamental human need for this experience.

BIBL.: Aristotle, *The Works,* trans. D. Ross, vol. 12, *The Fragments* (Oxford 1952). Walter Burkert, *Ancient Mystery Cults* (Cambridge, Mass., 1987). Pierre Hadot, *The Veil of Isis: An Essay on the History of the Idea of Nature,* trans. Michael Chase (Cambridge, Mass., 2006). Marvin Meyer, ed., *The Ancient Mysteries: A Sourcebook* (San Francisco 1987). Giovanni Pico della Mirandola, "Oration on the Dignity of Man," in *The Renaissance Philosophy of Man,* ed. E. Cassirer et al. (Chicago 1948) 223–254. Plutarch, *Moralia,* vol. 15, *Fragments,* trans. F. H. Sandbach, Loeb Classical Library (Cambridge, Mass., 1969). Jean Seznec, *The Survival of the Pagan Gods,* trans. Barbara Sessions (New York 1953). R. Gordon Wasson, Carl. A. P. Ruck, and Albert Hoffman, *The Road to Eleusis: Unveiling the Secret of the Mysteries* (New York 1978). Edgar Wind, *Pagan Mysteries in the Renaissance* (New York 1958). G.S.

Mythology

Along with philosophy and politics, mythology is one of the major areas of influence of ancient culture on our own. In the most common sense of the word, mythology belongs to the classical tradition. Among ancient societies, it was the Greeks who spoke and wrote in words and categories that we continue to use, often unwittingly. From Homer's time to our own day, mythology and myths have been Greek. Moreover, mythology, both as a category and as a field, belongs to what we call the Western tradition. It is a very particular tradition, one that has used writing to establish the "past" as both historical object and tradition, and one that, early on, cultivated the art of judging its own tradition as well as that of other cultures. Among some Greek thinkers, and other British ones, such as Locke, Western tradition took it upon itself to question its own validity. Therefore, critical thinking about mythology and the nature of myth is intrinsically part of the classical tradition. Many of our theories on myths and mythology as ways of thinking are inscribed in that tradition. We must be aware of that if we want a better understanding of the efficiency and persuasiveness held by "the" mythology, specifically Greek mythology, in Western societies.

For more than two centuries, mythology and the nature of myths have constituted one of the most important objects of reflection for anthropologists and philosophers, even though the latter are often oblivious to anthropology, whether contemporary or ancient.

With some irony, the word *mythologeuein,* "mythologizing," appeared as early as in the *Odyssey,* in a scene of dialogue between Nausicaa (princess of the Phaeacians) and the bard Demodocus, at a moment when the epic multiplies the stagings of its own representation. At some point the bard and his Muses give the floor to Odysseus, who begins to narrate his adventures; the impossible return from Troy, navigating between Charybdis and Scylla; the visit to the Land of the Dead; the unfortunate sacrifice of the Oxen of the Sun; love and pleasure in the arms of Calypso; and, toward the very end, Odysseus's melancholy and the evocation of his wife in Ithaca. The whole story is told in great detail, and without the presence of any Muse. This story is called *mythos* in the Greek, a name given to many other tales and narratives in the epic.

Once he reaches the end of his adventures, at the point where he had started his narrative, Odysseus stops, and puts an end to his "performance" with the following formula: "Why recount? Why tell (*mythologeuein*) what I was saying last night (*mytheisthai*)? I dislike retelling (*mythologeuien*) once more a story already told and known." Here Odysseus winks, as it were, at the best bards among the oral performers, who left the pleasure of repeating old stories to poets incapable of inventing new ones. Odysseus, presenting himself as a rival to Demodocus, the inspired blind poet, lets us know that he is not about to rattle off the same old stories.

In recent decades scholars have studied the polysemy of the word *myth.* From the archaic period until the 5th century BCE *mythos* meant authoritative speech, efficient discourse, or "argumentative" narration. In a large part of archaic poetry, the term *logos,* which for us evokes "reason," was commonly used to mean *mythos,* as account, discourse, speech, without any clear distinction between the content and the effect of a speech or a narrative. Thus, the phrase "From myth to reason," or "From *mythos* to *logos,*" that seemed so clear in the European tradition of the 20th century had to be reconsidered. For the ancient Greeks, "myths" did not coincide with the Oedipus story or Cronus's cannibalism. In his *Inquiries* (*Historiai,* mid-5th cent.), today called his *Histories,* Herodotus tells us about some particularly "holy traditions" or "discourses" (*hieroi logoi*) that he encountered during his travels. Although we would be tempted to interpret these famous "holy discourses" as myths, because they often refer to traditions mixed with ritual gestures or acts, they are not actually "myths" as we might like them to be. On the contrary, "myth" for Herodotus was the effort by some "scholars" to explain the flooding of the Nile by alleging the immensity of the river Ocean that ran around the Earth. This was a "myth," says Herodotus, pure fiction based on no empirical observation and no argumentation. Similarly, he avers, the Greeks' claim that Busiris, the legendary king of Egypt, wanted to offer Heracles as a sacrifice to the gods was a "myth," an absurd and silly story—for how could the Egyptians, the most pious of all people, even imagine such sacrilege?

There is another example: a contemporary of Herodotus, the philosopher Empedocles, presents in his poems theories about the origin of the world and the coming into existence of life, terming these a "myth," a tale coming from divinities, an efficient and knowledgeable narrative, a well-reasoned and richly ramified discourse. During the same century, but in another field, the historian Thucydides created a model for political action by analyzing the history of his own time—the Peloponnesian

War—and designated as "mythical" (*mythōdes*) or "mythicized" everything that circulated by word of mouth: conventional ideas, fabulous stories, in a word the whole tradition handed down by the poets and circulated by what the Greeks called "logographers"—"tale writers."

But where is the beginning of what would become "mythology" in the present sense, construed as a collection of extensive traditional narratives involving gods and heroes? There is a distinction to be made here between exegesis and interpretation: exegesis could be construed as developing and spreading from the inside outward. It is speech that accompanies and feeds the tradition it belongs to. Interpretation, in turn, begins as soon as there is an external perspective, when in a society, for instance, some individuals begin to discuss, to critique the tradition, and to step back from the "tribal histories."

Using the gaze of the "other" to look at what is known and accepted by everyone can take at least two forms. The minimalist form began in the 6th century BCE with the prose accounts of the logographers, who used the new graphic space of handwritten text on a prepared surface freely to treat tales and histories of the tradition, from divine genealogies to great heroic poems. Parallel with this sober and silent distancing, produced by the very act of writing, appeared another strong and assertive form, also closely related to writing; this occurred in new fields of knowledge such as philosophy, as presented by Xenophanes of Colophon, or historical thinking, as conceptualized by Hecataeus of Miletus, both in the 6th century BCE, well before Herodotus and Thucydides. These new fields of knowledge often brutally questioned a tradition, denouncing it as inadmissible or incredible, whether for its immediate meaning or its whole signification.

Among the first philosophers, Xenophanes, who left Asia Minor for Magna Graecia, violently condemned a whole part of the tradition: the tales about Titans, giants, and centaurs, including Homer's poems and Hesiod's songs. Why? Because in his eyes and to his ears these were scandalous stories using gods and superhuman characters to stage what was insulting and wicked in the world of men: thievery, adultery, cheating of all sorts. Xenophanes dismissed such tales; he wanted to banish them from banquets and poetic competitions. They were, he said, forgeries, pure fictions, *plasmata.*

Xenophanes' critique aimed at the content of traditional stories sung and transmitted by poets, quite a large group at the time, one to which Xenophanes himself belonged, as he wrote in verse. In the second half of the 6th century the disciples of Pythagoras, who had himself left Samos for Croton, took upon themselves to compose anthologies of passages of Homer and Hesiod. With this, we detect the beginning of a debate about education (*paideia*) that would last until Plato and Isocrates, a debate over how to give citizens the best education for life in the city, or if not the best, the fairest. We must recall that public schools (in the present-day American sense) did not exist in Greek cities. The teaching of literature and other knowledge was in the hands of "grammarians," teachers paid by families rich enough to offer their children an education to ensure them some success in the very competitive world of the Greek cities—all this arising probably long before the beginning of the 6th century. The question was raised by thinkers and counselors, before the Sophists and philosophers entered the picture: which poets, which poems to select, both to memorize and to interpret, that is, which were to be taken as objects of commentaries that would become the center of the educational system, the way to attain new knowledge and transmit accepted values, chosen by the families and citizens most motivated to think about "common administration," or even "the common good"? This was a major problem for Solon and Theognis of Megara, for Socrates and his adversaries, the Sophists, even before Plato put it at the center of the *Republic,* on the art of fashioning the best citizens. It has remained a problem ever since.

Yet anyone is free to call a "myth" the sacrifice of Heracles in Egypt or the awful victory of Odysseus against Ajax, the most courageous of the Greeks. There are some "deceptive tales" that are called "myths" by poets like Pindar, who grounded each book on a narrative he called *logos,* be it the story of the Telchines, at the origins of Rhodes, or the adventures of the son of Achilles in Apollo's sanctuary.

A near contemporary of Pythagoras and Xenophanes, an "investigator" and logographer sometimes known as a "historian," presented himself as follows: "Hecataeus of Miletus speaks in this way (*mytheisthai*). I write (*graphein*) these tales as they seem to be true to me. The tales (*logoi*) of the Greeks, as I see them, are many and laughable." Later, Herodotus made fun of the naiveté of his "colleague" Hecataeus, an "inventor of tales" (*logopoios*). Nevertheless, this "inventor" attests for us that some people took it upon themselves to put into perspective the many versions of the same story and to criticize the prevailing tradition, to question it instead of simply transmitting it with the variations that each performance entailed for the greatest pleasure of the audience.

Things were more complex than this, of course, and of the debates on tradition, the interpretations, and the education of citizens we know too little to measure Socrates' and Plato's debt to their predecessors. We can agree on the following: for us, as Hellenists, the totalizing science of Platonic philosophy is most rigorous in its frontal critique of the entire "tradition" that Plato and his contemporaries called "archaeology" and "mythology." The texts were collected sometimes to exclude, sometimes to criticize, and sometimes to suggest a substitute for traditional "mythology." Plato gathered all this material and analyzed it. In the *Laws,* in particular, he makes an intuitive analysis of what constitutes a *tradition:* rumor, whether malicious words circulating orally or a discourse inspired by the gods; oracles or words of praise that fashioned great fame; ever-changing genealogies; the founding narratives of terrestrial cities; the good old stories beginning with Deucalion or Phoroneus; and nurses' stories, proverbs, and maxims—whatever is constantly repeated and accepted by all. The radical critique that the *Republic* makes of the whole tradition, through the poets and craftsmen of "discourse" or "tales" (*logoi*), is aimed mostly at the mimetic nature of what Plato often called "mythology," that is to say ways of expression with the formulaic, rhythmic, and musical aspects needed to satisfy the demands of memorization and oral communication. For the philosopher of ideas, however, these aspects were the irrefutable sign that the "mythology" belonged to the polymorphic and gaudy world of all that delighted the inferior part of the soul, the solitary realm of overwhelming passions and desires. Not only was the discourse of "mythology" scandalous—and the *Republic* makes a complete catalogue of obscene, absurd, and wild stories—it was also dangerous and harmful because of the illusions produced whenever communication by word of mouth is not severely controlled.

If in Plato's ideal city it was easy to forbid ancient recollections by censoring traditional narratives and driving out the poets, the very Platonic project of reforming the Athenian city, and others, required the fabrication, the invention of a new "mythology," of another "mythologem." Even a society pondered and governed by philosophers needed something that only cohesion could provide: a collective and implicit knowledge that gave the impression that the community shared a single opinion, throughout its existence, in its songs, narratives, and stories. Plato called this new "mythology" the "useful and beautiful lie" that would make everyone willing to do what was just.

In short, we can say that toward the end of the 4th century BCE a new landscape appeared, a "mythology" beginning with Homer and Hesiod, whom Plato called "the gatherers." Under the direction of the "mythographers," collections, known as "libraries," of traditional tales were written in the very fragile shadow of the Library of Alexandria.

Since the 18th century, and particularly during the 19th century, "our" approach to mythology has followed the steps of "our" Greeks. Sociologists, historians of religions, philosophers, and anthropologists kept talking and thinking Greek. A debate about "fable" began in the 16th century with the discovery of the Native American peoples. Two books were published in France in 1724, one by Bernard de Fontenelle entitled *The Origin of Fables,* the other by J.-F. Lafitau, *Customs of American Savages Compared with Those of Earliest Times.* These comprise the first comparative ethnology: through their respective and very similar fables and mythologies, the new discipline studied the intellectual activity of the ancient Greeks and Romans on one hand and that of the New World peoples on the other. Lafitau's conclusion was radically different from Fontenelle's. For the former, fables and myths attested to the existence of an early "civil religion" of Adamic origin. American natives (perceived as savages) and ancient Greeks shared the same "religious thinking," independent of the Bible and Christianity. For Fontenelle, the extraordinary similarities between the fables of ancient times and the mythology of the New World proved that in primitive times, when the language of reason was unknown, men invented fables because they wanted to explain phenomena and the world that surrounded them. A Jesuit, Lafitau wanted to place religion at the origin, even if fables and myths were going to degrade it, as Plato had observed. A philosopher with a critical mind, Fontenelle saw in these absurd and insensate narratives the first drafts of what would become religion for savages and barbarians, in prehistory and in the present. From this perspective it would seem that we should read and interpret myth and mythology in relation to something that would increasingly attract everyone's attention: religion, the first thought of humankind and the origin of language.

Mythology, language, and the idea of God or of gods: the problematic was born with the Western discovery of Sanskrit, the Vedas and Gathas, the creation of a comparative grammar of Indo-European languages from very early times in India up to Western languages, and, with Max Müller (1823–1900), the establishment of a science of mythology fully based on the science of language. Earliest humanity, he wrote, knew a "mythopoetic" age, when grammatical structures silently took form in the abyss of language and when the first myths appeared as bubbles exploding at the surface in the words issuing from the mouth of the first people. Soon human beings would be the victims of the illusions that words produced. The mythology of the ancients would quickly become a disease of language. It was up to the linguist, the interpreter of mythology in its different layers, to detect traces of the grand displays of nature that so violently shook the beginnings of humanity.

A "science of language" thus self-assured would put an end to the scandal of "savage and insane" stories that had seemed to blemish Greek beauty and mythology, the closest to the ideal educated man of the West. Between 1850 and 1890, from Oxford to Berlin, London to Paris, the "science of myths" fed itself on the general understanding that mythologies were always filled with the fantasy of a "revolting immorality." The nascent science of anthropology, which Edward Burnett Tylor (1832–1917) would call "the science of civilization," was intrigued by the strange conformity existing between Greek fables and the fables of the first Americans. This "science of civilization" shared the impression of scandal felt by ministers, priests, and university clergymen, both in Europe and in the New World. The novelty of this science came from the breadth of its field of observation and comparison. The "myths" or large narratives that the ethnologists brought back in large quantity from their missions in Australia, their visits to American natives made accessible by conquest, or the thousand "nations" of the African continent, could not be explained by Müller's linguistic method.

Then came a new approach, once more attached to ever-powerful language. It considered the primordial state of humanity that ethnologists luckily were able to observe and analyze in people usually termed primitive. It was the only way to understand that in the beginning, all languages were subject to the "same intellectual art," as Tylor said. Language and myth do coincide everywhere in the world. Thus, what was to be seen in mythology was the primordial state of human mind. The "savages" who were contemporaries of Jefferson and Tylor were still in a period of mythical creativity. Myth was a natural byproduct of the human mind confronting certain events. A human mind "in its childhood," along with the evolution of humanity, would reach maturity in societies where "civilization" is discovered and reason is invented under the double form of philosophy and science. Neither the Indians of the Vedas nor the Egyptians of the Pyramids were good candidates for this fundamental passage from "myth to reason." It seemed that only the Greeks offered all the qualities and guaranties necessary to go beyond mythic thought.

The concept of mythic thought appeared in intellectual discourse between the time of Friedrich Schelling and that of Ernst Cassirer. In the *Historical-Critical Introduction to the Philosophy of Mythology* (1856) Schelling, the philosopher of "speculative idealism," showed that an original orientation of the mind appeared in mythology. Conscience was put on trial. Under his influence, Cassirer and Marcel Mauss, both writing in the first half of the 20th century, thought that the just interpretation of mythology must follow the "tautegoric" path: the meaning of the myth lay in what it said, and nowhere else. With Emile Durkheim's *Elementary Forms of Religious Life* (1910), mythology identified as religion became the thought of thoughts, the whole that included every element that, by being dissociated and infinitely reorganized, would produce the different manifestations of collective life. Mythical thought held the power of producing the main forms of culture and the fundamental notions of science. Along those lines, but with a more philosophical project, Cassirer claimed in 1924 that mythical consciousness represented a particular mode of the spiritual formation of humankind. As the original form of the mind, mythical thought was fascinated by the sensible presence and "concrescence" of the world, and it was alien to conceptual action. As a form of symbolic thought, mythology holds in itself the original virtues of speech and belief. Religion was already fully present in the mythical experience. In the same way, all forms of culture were somehow dressed and wrapped within figures emerging from the myths.

Obviously, the Greeks, who alone would seem to have invented mythology and philosophy, were at the very center of the debates that sprang up around concepts of mythical mind, rational mind, savage mind, and philosophical thinking, as well as scientific thinking. These debates began in 1958 with Claude Lévi-Strauss's *Structural Anthropology,* which described his structuralist methods of analyzing the myths, his propositions about *savage mind,* and the vast voyage recounted in his *Mythologiques* (4 vols., 1964–1971). For the classical tradition, it is interesting to notice that Lévi-Strauss was convinced that "a myth is perceived as a myth by any reader of the world": that myths constantly think about each other; that mythical thought, at one point, began moving toward abstraction; and that all by itself, myth is able to contemplate a "world of concepts whose relationships are freely established." People say it was in Greece that "mythology stepped aside in favor of a philosophy that came about as preliminary to any scientific thinking."

The Greek paradigm seemed so rich that Lévi-Strauss spoke of the ancient Greeks as those who "seemed to have perceived their mythology within a problematic that is similar to the one contemporary ethnologists use in order to decipher the intention and the meaning of the myths of people 'without writing.'" Of course, this did not stop other anthropologists, and even some classicists, from raising a series of questions in return, regarding such issues as the meaning of terms such as "tradition," "traditional narrative," the writing of "mythological narratives," and "perspective views of literary and narrative forms or traditional tales," when compared among ancient China, Japan, Melanesia, and, of course, ancient Greeks and modern and first Americans.

BIBL.: W. Burkert, *Structure and History in Greek Mythology and Ritual* (Berkeley 1979). C. Calame, ed., *Métamorphoses du mythe en Grèce antique* (Geneva 1988); *Mythe et histoire dans l'Antiquité grecque* (Lausanne 1996); and "Mythos, logos et histoire: Usages du passé héroïque dans la rhétorique grecque," *L'homme* 147 (1998) 127–149. M. Detienne, *L'invention de la mythologie* (Paris 1981), in English as *The Creation of Mythology,* trans. M. Cook (Chicago 1986), and *The Writing of Orpheus: Greek Myth in Cultural Contexts* (Baltimore 2003). L. Edmonds, ed., *Approaches to Greek Myth* (Baltimore 1990). R. L. Gordon, ed., *Myth, Religion, and Society* (Cambridge 1981). F. Graf, *Greek Mythology* (Baltimore 1993). C. Jacob, "L'ordre généalogique entre le mythe et l'histoire," in *Transcire les mythologies,* ed. M. Detienne (Paris 1994). C. Lévi-Strauss, *Anthropologie structurale* (Paris 1958); "De la fidélité au texte," *L'homme* 101 (1987) 117–140; *Myth and Meaning* (New York 1979); and *Mythologiques,* 4 vols. (Paris 1964–1971). G. Nagy, *Greek Mythology and Poetics* (Ithaca 1990). P. Veyne, *Les Grecs ont-ils cru à leurs mythes? Essai sur l'imagination constituante* (Paris 1983). M.DT.

Translated by Jeannine Routier Pucci and Elizabeth Trapnell Rawlings

N

Names

To discover the attitudes and values of individuals and groups beyond relatively narrow circles of elites, scholars have sometimes studied the distribution of personal names according to regions, periods, and social classes. This concern with "name culture" is potentially valuable for historians of the classical tradition. The work of collecting and counting has not yet been carried out as systematically as it might be, but the following examples of personal names (and more rarely the names of ships, inns, clubs, theaters, newspapers, cities, etc.) may be sufficient to suggest some provisional conclusions about the appeal of certain Greek and Roman heroes in certain places, times, and social groups in later centuries up to the present.

Generally speaking, classical names were for a long time the property of the upper classes, a sign of distinction that was open to criticism (notably by the satirist Jean de La Bruyère). There were exceptions to this rule, however. The 16th-century craftsman-poet Giulio Cesare Croce was the son of a blacksmith, and early modern villagers in Buckinghamshire, in Provence, and also in Minas Gerais in Brazil often rejoiced in Greek and Roman names. (In these cases one may suspect the influence of classically educated parish priests.)

In the Middle Ages children were usually named after saints, thus excluding the ancients. One of the rare exceptions, the bishop Caesarius of Arles, comes from the 5th century, when many elements of classical culture still survived. Another, Ptolemy of Lucca, assistant to Thomas Aquinas, may not be an exception at all, as the Italian version of his name, Tolomeo, may be no more than an abbreviation of Bartolomeo, after Saint Bartholomew. A third, Phoebus, for a 14th-century count of Foix, was in fact a nickname (his given name was Gaston).

Predictably, it was in Renaissance Italy that the revival of classical names occurred, in the first half of the 15th century. In his famous study of the Italian Renaissance, Jacob Burckhardt noted the spread of names such as Agamemnon and Minerva. Other female examples include Lucrezia Borgia, the poet Olimpia Morata, the artists Properzia de' Rossi, Sofonisba Anguisciola, Lavinia Fontana, the learned lady Cassandra Fedele, and the courtesan Tullia d'Aragona. Boys might be named after Aeneas (Enea Piccolomini, later Pope Pius II), Aristotle (the engineer Aristotele Fioravanti), Hercules (Ercole d'Este, the ruler of Ferrara), Caesar (Cesare Borgia), or Romulus (the Humanist Romulo Amaseo).

These choices tell us something about the interests and ideals of some fathers, or possibly mothers, of the time. Cardinal Rodrigo Borja, a Valencian living in Rome, not only called his children Cesare and Lucrezia but called himself Alexander upon his election as pope. His successor, Cardinal Giuliano de' Rovere, chose the name Julius. It is touching as well as significant that the artist Giovanni Sodoma should have called his son, who died young, after the ancient Greek painter Apelles; the architect Vincenzo Seregni, equally hopeful but more successful, named his son after the Roman architect Vitruvius. Greek and Roman names account for most of the examples, but Hannibal also occurs, as in the case of the artist Annibale Carracci. The tradition has continued into our own time; there has been a distinct rise from the mid-19th century onward. An identification between modern Italy and ancient Rome was part of the ideology of the Risorgimento, as it was of Fascism.

The Italian example was followed in many parts of early modern Europe, though with distinctly less enthusiasm. In France, for instance, there was Diane de Poitiers, the mistress of King Henri II, who was constantly compared to the goddess Diana. One distinguished family of

French lawyers, the Harlays, had a predilection for the name Achille (borne by five family members of the 16th and 17th centuries who are distinguished enough to appear in the *Dictionnaire de biographie française*). The revolutionary we know as Gracchus Babeuf was actually christened François-Noel, but after 1789 Gracchus became a fashionable name; Brutus was even more common.

In Northern Europe examples of classical personal names were relatively rare, with a few exceptions such as Pompeius Occo, an Amsterdam banker, and Wespajzan Kochowski, a Polish poet and historian. In early modern England, among the classical names that come first to mind are those of Sir Julius Caesar, a 17th-century Chancellor of the Exchequer (the son of an Italian) and of the Isham family, where boys were regularly christened Justinian, originally in honor of an uncle, Sir Justinian Lewyn, the son of a judge. One of the most unusual 18th-century names, that of the Prussian noble revolutionary Anacharsis Cloots, was chosen by himself in honor of the Greek or Scythian philosopher. To his parents he was simply Jean-Baptiste.

The Renaissance was also a time of the classicization of surnames, at least those of Humanists. In the Middle Ages it had been normal to add a Latin ending to one's name; in the 16th and 17th centuries some scholars went further. Peter Bierewitz, for example, called himself Apianus, Georg Bauer became Agricola, Bonaventura de Smet became Vulcanius, and a number of Febvres, Lefevres, and Smiths became Faber. More ingenious choices were made by Philipp Melanchthon (originally Schwarzerde) and Johannes Oecolampadius (formerly Hausschein).

Cities, on the other hand, illustrate both the survival and the revival of the classical tradition. The continuity of certain names is a reminder of the contribution of the Romans to European urban life. In Britain one thinks of Chester, derived from Latin *castrum,* "fort," and in Wales Caerleon or Caerllion, "fort of the legions," a term also traceable in compound names such as Gloucester, Leicester, and Winchester. The name Augsburg preserves something of Augusta Vindelicorum, as Lyon does of Lugdunum. Other names are Renaissance inventions, such as Lugdunum Batavorum for Leiden or Leopolis for Ukrainian L'viv (Czech Lvov).

The names of institutions drew attention to or continued the classical tradition. In Amsterdam a school founded in the 17th century was called the Athenaeum in honor of an academy founded at Rome by the emperor Hadrian, itself named in homage to Athene. In Britain inns were sometimes given classical names, notably the Andromache and the Bacchanals, apparently known locally as the Andrew Mac and the Bag of Nails respectively (incidentally, there still exists a London wine bar named Bacchus' Bin). In similar fashion the ship *Bellerophon,* which was launched in 1786 and took Napoleon to Britain before his exile to St. Helena, was rechristened the *Billy Ruffian* by the sailors. French and Italian ships were also given classical names such as *Giove Fulminante, Hercule, Neptune, Triton,* or for more obscure reasons *Eurydice* (the vessel from which Garibaldi deserted in 1834).

Places of entertainment or performance were often given classical names, perhaps because they were in need of legitimation. Athenaeum also became the name of a number of literary clubs, from Venice to London. The Odeon, originally a theater in Athens, became the name of a theater in Padua (1524), a theater in Paris (1795), and a concert hall in Munich (1828) before it was adopted by innumerable cinemas in the 20th century. The London Palladium (1871)—another reference to Athene—was successively a circus, a music hall, and a theater. New York's Apollo, in Harlem, was a music theater. The London Coliseum (the spelling is from Medieval Latin) was a theater before it became a cinema. The Copenhagen Tivoli (1843) was named in homage to Hadrian's villa.

Two early 19th-century literary journals, one in Germany and the other in Britain, were titled *Athenaeum. Argus* and *Mercury* were among the favorite names for newspapers and journals, some of which still survive in a world in which the meaning of the names has been virtually forgotten. Two early 20th-century political parties were given classical names, the Spanish Falange (from Greek *phalanx*) and the Italian Fascists (from Latin for the lictor's *fasces*). The code breaker installed at Bletchley Park in 1943 was christened Colossus.

Commodities are often given classical names to make them seem chic and perhaps to suggest that they are timeless classics. Lux was introduced as a toilet soap in 1925, as if advertisers were still confident in the power of classical associations to sell products. On the other hand, the choice of Medusa as the name of an American cement company or Argus as the name of a security system may be no more than a reminder that workers in the advertising industry have often had a literary education. Hermes is probably better known today as a Webmail service and as a kind of perfume than as the name of a classical god.

In the 20th century examples of classical personal names could still be found in many places, from the Daphnes, Helens, and Penelopes of Britain to the translator Achilles Fang in China. Names of this kind clustered most thickly in Italy (Cesare, Flavia, Fulvia, Mario, Massimo, etc.), in Eastern Europe, and in the New World. It is of course no surprise to find classical names in modern Greece, from the linguist Dionysis Goutsos to the shipowner Aristotle Onassis or the politicians Themistocles Sophoulis and Xenophon Zolotas. These are cases of revival rather than survival, the collective wish being to present modern Greece as the heir of ancient Greece rather than just another Balkan country.

Romanians have followed a similar strategy, using names as a way of emphasizing their Roman roots. Among the best-known Romanians of the last century were the economist Virgil Madgearu, the lawyer Virgil Potârcă, the biologist Traian Săvulescu, the novelist Traian Filip, the poet Ovidiu Genaru, the politicians Ovidiu Beldeanu and Lucreţiu Pătrăşcanu, and, appropriately enough, the philologist Cicerone Poghirc. (The names

Ovid and Trajan were chosen for local reasons, the former because he was exiled to the Black Sea coast and the latter because he conquered Dacia, a region roughly corresponding with present-day Romania.) By contrast, Hungarian parents preferred to call their sons after the barbarian Attila, though there was also a certain predilection for Tiberius (Tíbor).

In the New World classical names have had the function of establishing continuity with the European past. This is particularly clear in the case of cities. Following the American Revolution, when names like New York savored of colonialism, new foundations were given ancient Greek and Roman names such as Cincinnati (Ohio, 1790), Ithaca (New York, 1795), Utica (New York, 1798), Athens (Ohio, 1800; Georgia, 1801), and so on. In the Caribbean, slaves were not infrequently given classical names such as Adonis, Apollo, Brutus, Cato, Caesar, Hercules, Nero, or Pompey for men and Cleopatra, Daphne, Diana, Juno, or Phoebe for women. Some of these may be explained by similarities between classical and African names (Phoebe and Phiba, Cato and Keta, etc.), others by the fantasies of the slave owners.

In both North and South America in the 19th and 20th centuries, the custom of naming children after heroes or heroines was stronger than it was in Europe. In the United States, for instance, alongside the Washingtons and Jeffersons one finds General Ulysses Grant, for instance, the baseball player Homer Thompson, and the boxer Cassius Clay. In Venezuela two heads of state have been named after Romulus: Rómulo Betencourt and Rómulo Gallego. In Argentina parents seem to have a predilection for Nestor; witness the sociologist Néstor Canclini and the politician Néstor Kirchner. Among the intellectuals with classical names in early 20th-century Brazil were the painter Cícero Dias, the doctor Ulisses Pernambucano, the politician Plínio Salgado, and the writers Euclides da Cunha, Aníbal Machado, Otávio Tarquínio de Sousa, and Caio Prado Júnior. More recent examples include Sócrates de Oliveira, who played for Brazil in the World Cup for 1982 and 1986, the politician Ulysses Guimarães and, most appropriately of all, the popular poet from the northeast named Homero do Rêgo Barros.

In short, classical names remind us of the continuing appeal of antiquity in different places and times. They also express a variety of attitudes, from national pride to specific aspirations for children. Research of a comparative, quantitative kind is still needed to identify the chronology, geography, and sociology of certain patterns of choice: collective preferences for Greek or for Roman names, for instance, or for mythology rather than history or for philosophers rather than political leaders. All the same, it might be unwise to assume much knowledge of the classical tradition among the choosers of classical names. Greek girls are still named Medea or Clytemnestra, despite the unfortunate careers of the prototypes. The flight magazine of the Brazilian airline Varig is called *Icaro*.

BIBL.: David Cordingly, *The Billy Ruffian: The Bellerophon and the Downfall of Napoleon* (London 2003). Eric R. Delderfield, *British Inn Signs and Their Stories* (Dawlish 1965). Stephen Wilson, *The Means of Naming: A Cultural and Social History of Personal Naming in Western Europe* (London 1998) esp. 199, 202–204, 309.

U.P.B.

Narcissus

A famously beautiful boy who fell in love with his own reflection in the water, Narcissus died of this enamorment and became the flower of the same name. The oldest and most influential telling is Ovid's (*Metamorphoses* 3.339–510), where the character's infatuation with himself is punishment for his indifference to the passion that his beauty inspires in others; his rejection of the nymph Echo reduces her to a disembodied voice. Explicit moralizations of the story from the Middle Ages onward draw a cautionary lesson, either about mistaking image for reality or, more seriously, about the dangers of pride, the most insidious of sins for a Christian. In art and literature the moralistic tradition can be felt, but it contends with the character's suave allure, often implicitly but unmistakably homoerotic. Paintings generally emphasize Narcissus' languor and the landscape around him, sometimes including a distraught Echo; one intense exception, plausibly attributed to Caravaggio (ca. 1600, now in the Palazzo Barberini), focuses tightly on the young man and his mirror image, jointly surrounded by darkness. One of the few surviving works of Benvenuto Cellini is a marble Narcissus (ca. 1548, in the Bargello Museum in Florence). The myth has a particular presence in love poetry. The lover in the 13th-century *Roman de la Rose* comes early in his allegorical journey to *la fontaine de Narcissus;* lyric poets from Bernard de Ventadour ("Can vei la lauzeta mover," mid-12th cent.) to Maurice Scève (*Délie* 60, 1544) compare themselves to Narcissus in their hopeless love for their ladies. Petrarch, in a pair of widely imitated sonnets (*Canzoniere* 45–46), complains that the unattainable Laura risks the fate of Narcissus; his rival for her heart is her mirror, and it is her pride in her beauty that makes her refuse him. Milton's Eve, upon her creation, sees her own image in a pool and is enthralled; God and Adam must summon her to a different love object and destiny (*Paradise Lost* 4.449–491). A religious drama by the Mexican nun Juana Inés de la Cruz, *El divino Narciso* (ca. 1688), effects a theological reconfiguration of the myth into celebratory terms; the title character is Christ, who gazes into a well and falls in love with the face of Human Nature that he sees there. For André Gide, Narcissus is a figure of the modern artist ("Le traité du Narcisse," 1891). The very name, writes Paul Valéry, "is a tender perfume/To the gentle heart" ("Narcisse parle," 1891).

The story's prominence in the 20th century receives significant enhancement from being appropriated as the second classical myth to embody a key concept of psychoanalysis. The term *Narzissmus* was coined in 1899; Freud's essay "On Narcissism: An Introduction" (1914) sets out the basic theory, distinguishing between an infantile primary narcissism and a later, secondary narcissism. The latter is associated with behaviors that Freud considers aberrant—he links it overtly to male homosexuality and to the style of female narcissism that Petrarch attributes to Laura—but the underlying disposition is inescapable and central to the creation of adult identity: "The development of the ego consists in a departure from primary narcissism and gives rise to a vigorous attempt to recover that state." In later psychoanalytic theory the myth reappears as Jacques Lacan's *le stade du miroir,* the mirror stage, a primal experience of unsatisfiable desire. In less specialized senses, *narcissism* and *narcissistic* have become common currency, often invoked with regard to society at large (e.g., Christopher Lasch, *The Culture of Narcissism,* 1978).

BIBL.: Louise Vinge, *The Narcissus Theme in Western European Literature up to the Early 19th Century* (Lund 1967). Paul Zweig, *The Heresy of Self-Love* (Princeton 1980).

G.B.

Natural History

Up until the middle of the 17th century, and, less formally, beyond that time, natural history was essentially based in the classics. In contrast to the fields of astronomy and physics, which broke from the classifications and factual data of the classical period, the knowledge held by the Greeks and Romans was considered essential for describing the natural world, and that knowledge was transmitted with little modification up to the end of the modern period. Still, the classical legacy was never applied in a univocal or static manner.

In the first place, the corpus inherited from the ancients was rich and varied enough to offer numerous perspectives on natural history in vastly different styles. Theophrastus' reflections on plants (4th cent. BCE) were entirely different, for example, from the *Histories* of Aelian (3rd cent. CE), who framed the animal world in apologetic and moral terms. Moreover, ancient texts were not always available: some of the most important ones were missing throughout the medieval period. Classical works that were available during the Middle Ages were used as references for describing a natural world that was not always observed carefully and attentively.

What became of this approach later, when, after an epistemological breakthrough, direct observation came to be regarded as the principal means of acquiring knowledge of the natural world? During the Renaissance, texts of the ancient naturalists were not invalidated by the return to close observation; rather, they provided the intellectual framework that made observation possible. As a result, modern natural history incorporates many approaches, concepts, and plant and animal names whose origins can be traced to remote antiquity.

The long-standing importance accorded to ancient natural history stems primarily from its technical aspect. One-third of the known works of Aristotle (4th cent. BCE) dealt with zoology and provided an enormous amount of reliable and coherent information about animals and about the anatomical and physiological mechanics that constitute them. The description of the chameleon's anatomy illustrates the precision that could sometimes be attained:

> With regard to the position of the oesophagus and the windpipe it resembles the lizards. It has no flesh anywhere except some tiny portions on the head and jaws and the root of the tail. It has blood only round the heart, the eyes, and the region above the heart, and in the small blood-vessels ramifying from them, though even in these parts there is a very small quantity . . . It actually goes on functioning with its breath for a long time after being cut open completely, there being still a very slight movement in the breath around the heart, and while contraction takes place particularly round the ribs, it affects the remaining parts of the body as well. It has no spleen that is visible. It lives in holes like the lizards. (*Historia animalium* 2.11–503a15, trans. Peck)

Such a precise description was the product of serious study involving vivisection and depending on a highly specific anatomical vocabulary for analyzing organs in terms of their functions. Aristotle's work is actually extremely important for its technical vocabulary and its classifications: many of the concepts that today structure our perceptions of the natural world derived from it. A similar kind of philosophical and taxonomical thought is found in Theophrastus' studies of plants, from the same era. These two Greek authors were not accessible to medieval Western readers, however, and for a long time were known only through Pliny the Elder's later compilations (1st cent. CE).

Another important classical work on the subject, Pliny's *Natural History,* was in large part a resumption of the Greek legacy. This work, fascinating for its breadth, cites hundreds of names of plants and animals, accompanied by their medicinal properties, histories, and anecdotal wonders. Pliny proclaimed his epistemological departure from his Greek predecessors when he wrote, "But our purpose is to point out the manifest properties of objects, not to search for doubtful causes" (*Natural History* 11.2.8, trans. Rackham). In fact, the search for causes was eclipsed by an emphasis on the marvelous, set in a geographical expansion of the flora and fauna he described.

The diversity of classical approaches to the natural world expanded further in the early centuries CE. Works have come down from that time with more strictly utilitarian purposes, such as the *Halieutica* (*On Fishing*) of the Cilician poet Oppian (2nd cent.), the *Cynegetica* (*On Hunting*) of the other Oppian (3rd cent.), and some practical agricultural treatises. Dioscorides' *De materia medica* (1st cent.) constituted the major botanical reference work until the end of the 16th century, despite its medical orientation. More literary approaches that appeared in the 3rd century, such as Aelian's *De natura animalium,* which developed a moral approach to the animal kingdom, met with great success during the medieval period. Thus, classical natural history was a multifaceted corpus from which specialists in later centuries would choose whatever best suited their own conceptions of the world.

Two important works that touched on natural history marked the transition from late antiquity to the Middle Ages and offered original approaches to the natural world that were widely adopted later. The *Etymologies* of Isidore of Seville (636) may be seen as a general study of the names of things and their meanings. The work took up natural history in book 12, devoted to animals, and in book 27, dedicated to plants, which in the general organization of the work follows the section devoted to agriculture. The entries on names of natural things provided information about their deep nature that needed to be decoded from a utilitarian point of view: the presentation of animals began, significantly, with cattle, whereas grains and legumes were presented first among plants. The researching of names that typified Isidore's methodology was an early indication of a certain departure from the legacy of the ancients and also revealed the difficulties of identifying in a later era the natural objects that were named in classical texts. Another major component of medieval natural history followed the *Physiologus* (3rd cent. CE and perhaps later), a collection of Greek allegorical texts with a moral purpose in the tradition of Aelian. Of pagan origin, the *Physiologus* was Christianized and soon translated into Latin over the course of successive versions and finally became a sort of edifying commentary on the animals of the Bible. The animals were presented on three levels: the real, the allegorical, and the moral. Elements of classical knowledge were thus superimposed with a Christian interpretation that gave them new meaning. The *Physiologus* mentioned just a very few animals, only twelve in some versions of the work, and favored those that lent themselves most easily to symbolic and moral interpretation (the lion, the ant, the swallow, the snake, etc.). Thus, the collection stands at the origin of the great tradition of moral bestiaries, the most beautiful examples of which came out of England during the 12th century.

Like the *Physiologus,* numerous ancient texts were subject to revisions during the medieval period. Dioscorides' *De materia medica,* initially organized by medicinal type beginning with ointments and oils, was rearranged alphabetically by plant names. This new discursive arrangement, following the example of Galen (2nd–3rd cents.), is first evident in a 6th-century manuscript now in the National Library in Vienna. Alphabetical order became the norm for medieval herbals, collections that described the medicinal properties of plants. Through illustrations in Dioscorides' treatise the ancient iconography was passed on throughout the medieval period in the Byzantine world. But copying the ancient forms from manuscript to manuscript rapidly led to stylized representations, so that the plants depicted became almost unrecognizable. Herbals that issued from the tradition of Apuleius Platonicus (5th cent.), for example, with highly stylized illustrations and indications of medicinal properties of plants that are not described, have only a tenuous link with nature as observed: the words are for the most part unrelated to the things they describe.

In the 13th century Latin translations of Arabic versions of previously inaccessible Greek works opened up entirely new perspectives. The *De vegetalibus* of the Dominican Albert the Great (Albertus Magnus, d. 1280) was based on a Greek treatise, not, as he thought, from Aristotle, but rather from Nicolaus Damascenus (1st cent.), who followed the tradition of Theophrastus. Albert broke away from traditional herbals: the first five books of his treatise show a philosophical and physiological approach to the vegetable world, for example, in a consideration of plant *pneuma* (spirit or soul); the sixth book is a list of plants useful for medicine; the seventh is directed toward agriculture and horticulture. His classification of plants was inspired by that of Theophrastus, who accorded the highest place to the trees, considered to be the most noble and developed of plants. Equally important was his work in zoology: his *De animalibus* constituted a synthesis of the findings of Pliny and Aristotle. The Arabic version of Aristotle that he used sometimes led to difficulties with nomenclature and identification: the Arabic-sounding names he used for some plants or animals earned him the scorn of Renaissance authors despite his original contributions based on firsthand observation.

The Middle Ages also produced works of natural history closer to the Bible than to treatises from classical antiquity. For example, the *De proprietatibus rerum* (*On the Properties of Things*) of Bartholomaeus Anglicus, a contemporary of Albert the Great in the 13th century, was a sweeping synthesis of the natural world organized according to the book of Genesis. In these works too, different intellectual lineages were superimposed, and the tradition of herbals and bestiaries continued to be vibrant, as is apparent in German herbals printed at the end of the 15th century. The publisher of *The Garden of Health* (*Gart der Gesundheit,* 1485) set out to combine in a single book "the virtue and nature of many herbs out of the acknowledged masters of physic, Galen, Avicenna, Serapio, Dioscorides, Pandectarius, Platearius, and others." This work was soon expanded to include the rest of the natural world, with the addition of chapters on animals and minerals, in a Latin version (*Hortus sanitatis,* 1490). This Latin edition was presented as a medical treatise for those who could not afford a doctor, but the structure of the book revealed its naturalist ambitions: it offered a complete and richly illustrated account of the natural world. The subsequent dozens of editions, in Latin and in vernacular languages as well, attest to the success of this formulation. Ancient texts were cited alongside medieval texts, including some Arabic ones, but the references were often imprecise: the secondhand nature of the work and the process of compilation meant that ancient texts endured merely as references of authority.

The return to direct observation that characterized the

middle of the 16th century did not in the least diminish the importance accorded to ancient texts. In his illustrated treatise on unusual sea fish (*Histoire naturelle des estranges poissons marins,* 1551) Pierre Belon said of antiquity: "There has never been a law, no matter how strict, which says that one could not add . . . a reasonable thing to something that had already been discovered."

A traveler and a keen observer who wrote in French because of his poor mastery of Latin, Belon displayed a profound respect for classical knowledge. He considered it a corpus that needed to be updated and completed in certain details, but one that was not easily refuted. When he wondered whether dolphins were really able to jump over the masts of ships, Belon remarked that it must be true, for otherwise Aristotle would not have written about it, though he himself had never observed it. This respect for the ancient texts was such that certain historians of science (Sarton 1953) have described the Renaissance naturalists as slaves of antiquity who valued the books of men more than the book of nature. That distinction is inaccurate, however: the mastery of ancient knowledge also served as the basis for direct observation, stimulating the accumulation of knowledge and exchange of information about natural objects.

In the history of printed books the influence of classical natural history is evidenced from the very beginning, in the large-scale publication of texts on related subjects. Aristotle's zoology was printed in Latin in 1476, under the title *De animalibus,* and reprinted seven times before the middle of the 16th century. Between 1504 and 1552 six editions were published in tandem with the botanical treatises of Theophrastus. The successive productions of such a compendium of Greek natural history show the existence of a specialized, trained readership. Yet these publications came to an abrupt halt in midcentury (we shall return to the reasons for this below). Pliny was not neglected, however: almost 100 editions of his *Natural History* appeared in the 15th and 16th centuries. A few Humanists set out to illustrate Pliny's encyclopedia with scientific drawings. In a letter dating from 1528 Andrea Alciato expressed his hope to produce an edition of the *Natural History* with engravings: "I wish to see, chapter by chapter, the addition of painted images of animals, landscapes, fish, plants . . . This not only would serve to teach about natural things, which Pliny does, but would reveal them even to the uneducated." He was optimistic, believing the task would be an easy one and even expecting to be able to apply his knowledge of Dioscorides; but this hope was never realized. One version of *Natural History,* printed in Parma in 1481, also shows signs of a vast iconographic project, with marginal cues (*tituli*) calling for pictures (Walter 1990). Some 70 illustrations were indeed made, but more than 500 were intended, solely for the books on animals and plants. The whole set would have constituted a vast illustrated encyclopedia of natural history. This project was never completed owing primarily to the lexical difficulty: many of the plants and animals cited by Pliny had not been clearly identified in terms known to Renaissance observers. Illustration of his text depended on the capacity to connect most of the Latin names to recognizable plants and animals.

As these efforts show, the scientific updating of natural history was difficult. The first obstacle arose from differences between the natural world described by the ancients (basically the Mediterranean region, with some eastward extensions) and the world in which the naturalists of the Renaissance lived (the northern or Atlantic regions of Europe): many species found in one region were not present in the other. This geographical gap grew greater with the discovery of the New World. A second difficulty was the problem of identifying correctly the natural objects described in ancient texts. Although readers in the Renaissance wished to find a unified and coherent portrayal of the natural world in the classical works, that was not always the case. Beyond their differences in style and tone, ancient authors often used different names to describe the same species, which required finding equivalencies of nomenclature. Shifting from Greek to Latin renewed and magnified this difficulty. Even Pliny, who summarized in Latin the naturalist works of Aristotle and several other Greek physicians, was guilty of some inaccuracies and mistakes. The problem persisted right into the early modern period: in the middle of the 15th century Theodore Gaza, a translator of the treatises of Aristotle and Theophrastus, often paraphrased descriptions of natural objects that he was unable to identify. Early modern naturalists were sometimes obliged to refer to the Greek text and propose new matches for names, depending on the extent of their knowledge of the subjects. Thus, though ancient treatises fed and irrigated the modern practice of natural history, their study was not free of problems. Most of these eventually would be resolved by Humanist naturalists, but other problems proved insurmountable: vestiges are found today in classical editions that include many untranslatable plant and animal names.

A process that might be termed the "domestication" of classical texts began toward the end of the 15th century and ended a century later when most of the reading difficulties were resolved. First and foremost, it required establishing fixed versions of the texts. It also required that they be understood and translated in modern terms; that became the role of the commentaries. Once fixed and understood, ancient texts were integrated into the large natural science publications that characterized the middle of the 15th century, first in botany and then in zoology. The printing of books greatly enhanced this work of domestication. It gave essential support to the establishment of fixed versions of ancient texts, a vulgate from which naturalists in succeeding generations would work.

It is possible to follow the steps of the process of domestication with the example of Pliny's *Natural History.* This work remained available throughout the medieval period and was the object, at the end of the 15th century, of an immense philological study accompanied by vigorous debates. Pliny's first great commentator was Ermolao Barbaro, a philosophy professor at Padua, who proposed nearly 5,000 corrections in his *Castigationes Plinianae* (1492–1493). Many of them were incorporated into later editions of the *Natural History.* Working from two printed editions, Barbaro combed Pliny's text for errors that had accumulated over the centuries. He distinguished between corrections he considered as definitive and those suggesting mere pathways for later philologists. When he corrected the text, he usually relied on ancient manuscripts. But he also followed the authority of other authors at times, such as Aristotle, Athenaeus (2nd–3rd cents. CE), and Solinus (mid-4th cent. CE), and ultimately offered some guesses suggested by context. Theodore Gaza's recent translation allowed him to restore the names of plants and animals that had been altered. Barbaro himself relied at times on vernacular languages: writing about garlic to prevent an unidentified animal from biting (*Natural History* 20.6), he restored the name *mus araneus,* noting that the common shrew had preserved its Latin name in several modern languages. Thus, by using Italian dialects and natural objects to compare with the classical sources and rediscover Pliny's meaning, Barbaro showed the philological breadth that led him to sources beyond classical texts. The *Corollarium* to his translation of the works of Dioscorides (posthumously published in 1517), dedicated to a medical and botanical interpretation of the text, was even more focused on understanding the natural world. He did not hesitate to say that Pliny was wrong about the plant called wild nard (spikenard), whereas in his *Castigationes* he had restored the text without mentioning the botanical error.

Niccolò Leoniceno, professor of medicine at Ferrara, faulted Pliny for having misunderstood certain Greek sources and for seriously confusing certain botanical data. He published only one small work on medicinal plants (*De Plinii et aliorum in medicina erroribus liber,* 1492) but stated that he could fill a whole volume with Pliny's mistakes. He was clearly less interested in restoring an altered text than in discovering useful medical recipes. The jurist Pandolfo Collenuccio, equally knowledgeable in natural sources, criticized in his *Pliniana defensio* (1493) Leoniceno's arrogance in attacking Pliny's authority and showed that many of the errors attributed to Pliny had in fact resulted from mistakes made by later copyists. In this controversy we may discern two conceptions of Humanist commentary, one that resided in the philological arena and one that sought practical information. These two possible approaches to antiquity stayed closely related in the 16th century but diverged thereafter.

Francesco Massari's *In nonum Plinii De naturali historia librum castigationes et annotationes* (1532) illustrates the methodology used in the Renaissance to make technical texts from antiquity clear. In this detailed commentary focused entirely on book 9 of Pliny's *Natural History,* Massari sought to tighten the link between ancient nomenclature and modern aquatic animals. In his remarks on *Natural History* 9.15.17, for example, he sought to identify the Nile *silurus,* a large fluvial fish, with the *isox* native to the Rhine and the *attilus* found in the Po. The difficulty arose in that no one was able to compare fish living in such widely dispersed habitats, which had resulted in contradictions among ancient descriptions, making associations with known fish difficult. Massari, for example, used Aristotle's description of *glanis* (*Historia animalium* 9.37.621a21) to analyze Pliny's *silurus.* The problem was resolved at the end of the 1550s when Ippolito Salviani understood that Pliny, followed by Theodore Gaza, had attributed to the *silurus* the features of two different fish, Aristotle's *glanis* (which seems to be the real *silurus*) and the *silouros* of other Greek authors (a sturgeon). This shows the shift that had occurred since Barbaro's *Castigationes* in the 1490s: the investigation involved only a small fragment of Pliny's text but gave rise to a systematic reading of ancient sources available and to a zoological analysis of modern fauna in order to rediscover the origin of Pliny's notes. At the beginning of the 16th century the debate about the botanical and zoological books of *Natural History* was a lexicographical one.

In the 1540s several lexicons of plants and animals were published. The *Avium praecipuarum quarum apud Plinium et Aristotelium mentio est historia* (1544) by William Turner was a lexical study of birds, comparable to Massari's work on fish, providing short descriptions and the English and German names of the birds mentioned by Pliny and Aristotle. Also in 1544 appeared Charles Estienne's lexicon of plants and animals, *De latinis et graecis nominibus arborum, fruticum, herbarum, piscium et avium liber,* which matched French names of trees, fruits, plants, fish, and birds to the Latin and Greek. The *Appelationes volucrum et piscium* (1549) of Paul Eber and Kaspar Peucer gave the Greek and German equivalents of Latin names for animals, particularly birds and fish. This lexicon was issued as an annex to a compilation on classical coins and measures: it was clearly meant to facilitate the technical reading of treatises from antiquity, as well as to update the information they contained. Expanding to include botany, the *Appellationes* was enriched with each edition until it constituted the core of the volume. Such publications would merit closer study: they make it possible to track the progressive intelligibility of technical treatises from antiquity. Republished 10 times in the 16th century, the *Appellationes* came to be used as a manual of the ancient world by students at Wittenberg. Beginning in the 1540s, early treatises could be read correctly and good translations were available. The identification of the natural objects they described was important for medicine but also for literary works that referred to the natural world, such as poetry and symbolic treatises. The readership of these technical philological treatises went well beyond the small circle of natural history specialists.

This philological work was also a powerful auxiliary to field observation. Renaissance scholars viewed the inventory of objects of the natural world as a collective undertaking for which classical treatises constituted the epistemological foundation. It is important to realize that all observation had to be conducted in a particular geographical context, beginning with local vernacular names.

Anyone who discovered the value of a particular plant, for example, and wished to share that knowledge, had to know what Pliny or Dioscorides called it. That enabled someone who observed a comparable plant elsewhere to determine whether it belonged to the same species. Mastery of the technical vocabulary of the ancient works not only helped with reading those texts, it also helped with organizing newly collected data about the natural world. At the beginning of the 16th century the discovery of plants or animals missing from the ancient treatises sometimes created utter confusion for the observers. This was the case for Otto Brunfels, whose collection of illustrations made from live plants, *Herbarum vivae eicones* (1532), represented plants identified by their classical names and linked to the properties referred to by the early writers. A small anemone unknown to the ancients perplexed him: he provided a beautiful illustration and specified its German name and medicinal usage, but he did not know what else to say about it and called it the naked herb (*herba nuda*), as if the German name were insufficient to clothe the plant; he inserted the entry for it discreetly, as though ashamed of it, between two chapters of his book.

Once the main difficulties of nomenclature were resolved, classical knowledge could spread into the great syntheses of natural history that marked the second half of the 16th century. Ippolito Salviani's *Aquatilium animalium historia* (1557–1558) shows the continuing importance of the intellectual framework of the ancients. The book begins with a 112-page table summarizing all the ancient textual references to fish. The first three columns give names in Latin, Greek, and Italian, and the fourth identifies the organ or feature described; the remainder of the table is a summary, author by author, of all known references to the subject. Five nominative columns were attributed to Aristotle, Oppian, Pliny, Athenaeus, and Aelianus. A final column referred to other authors: Dioscorides, Galen, Strabo, and Herodotus appeared frequently in the list. The rare citations to works by Salviani's contemporaries are for the most part to treatments of ancient texts, such as Pierre Gilles's translation of Aelian, and Barbaro's and Massari's studies of Pliny (described above). The table offers eloquent testimony to the importance of antiquity in the mid-16th century: five ancient authors were responsible for 4,315 of 5,640 citations. This vast compendium of classical references preceded the author's remarks on the direct observation of fish.

An important Humanist and author of the famous *Universal Library* (*Bibliotheca universalis,* 1545), Konrad Gesner accorded equal importance to classical sources in his monumental *Historia animalium* (1551–1558). This compilation was intended to bring together all knowledge on each animal, so that it would no longer be necessary to refer to earlier sources. The first volume began with a list of 251 authors whose works had been scrupulously examined. Nearly all the ancients appeared in this list: 68 Greek authors and 49 Latin ones. The list was organized according to the hierarchy of languages and the antiquity of the knowledge: Hebrew, Greek, Classical Latin, and Medieval Latin preceded modern works in Latin and then those in vernacular languages. Gesner thus implicitly traced the degradation of language from the beginning of the world, and a tendency for knowledge to be lost that it at last seemed possible to reverse. By going back to biblical Hebrew and to early Greek antiquity, to Homer and Hesiod, he hoped to rediscover original names that might contain an essential element of the designated plants and animals. Like Salviani, Gesner provided a number of updated images taken from nature to illustrate the knowledge of the ancients. He also described every animal that had been mentioned before him, even those that were not identified. In this respect, the *Historia animalium,* a multivolume work arranged alphabetically, was a vast dictionary. This was claimed in the subtitle of the first volume, which called the book "as useful as it is enjoyable for philosophers, physicians, grammarians, philologists, and all those who study different languages." Accompanying each animal, alongside the zoological descriptions, were all the Humanist trappings that stated every possible use of the animal as well as its poetic and symbolic significances. Exceptions were the East Asian and American animals (sloth, armadillo, bird of paradise), which began to appear in the inventories, distinguished by the absence of any cultural layering from antiquity.

One might think that ancient works had been made obsolete by the exploration of the New World. In fact, the American natural world was approached through the conceptual framework of antiquity, which led to underestimating its novelty. In his *Historia general y natural de las Indias* (1526) Gonzalo Fernández de Oviedo described the species of the New World with enthusiasm, emphasizing their nutritional usefulness. He classified plants according to their utility and made multiple comparisons with the flora of Castile. In describing the jaguar he adopted the name "tiger," which previous European voyagers had given it by analogy, but he questioned the validity of that identification. He noted that the ancients considered the tiger to be the fastest of all animals, whereas the American animal seemed to him slow and lazy. Never having seen a tiger, Fernández de Oviedo studied the large American cat by way of Greek authors. There was in this an attempt to make the American world conform to familiar flora and fauna, stressing the unity of Creation. Some years later, the physician Francisco Hernández explored New Spain with his own manuscript translation of Pliny's *Natural History* into Castilian. Thus, Pliny would serve as his guide in understanding the unfamiliar in this new natural environment. Paradoxically, the mastery of ancient sources seemed to be the best way of describing the New World. Conversely, knowledge of America helped complete the work of the ancients: notes on Gerónimo de Huerta's Spanish translation of the *Natural History* (1624–1629) supplied the "missing" chapters to Pliny's work. Huerta described, for example, the armadillo and the turkey, which were illustrated in his book. He did the same for the "monsters" that appeared in the

16th century: at the end of book 9 he describes several aquatic monsters, such as the leonine monster captured near Rome shortly before the death of Pope Paul III in 1549. Instead of devaluing Pliny's work, the discovery of the Americas and of such recent monsters gave his material even greater interest. Pliny's *Natural History* continued to be as helpful in understanding the American world as it had been for decoding the wonders of the Renaissance.

The project to illustrate Pliny's botanical and zoological books, something that had proved in Alciato's time to be a utopian dream, became possible beginning around 1560. Ironically though, by the time the work became feasible, it had lost some of its importance: there was little reason to illustrate Pliny's zoology once it had been incorporated into the volumes of Gesner's *Historia universalis,* with pictures and additional descriptions. This is why Pliny's work was never scientifically illustrated. Once the old names of plants and animals were matched with well-identified modern species, however, translation of the treatises of ancient naturalists became possible. It was precisely in the 1560s that vernacular translations of the *Natural History* were first published. The French translation by Antoine du Pinet (1562), which relied on the zoological treatises of the 1550s as dictionaries, would have been inconceivable a decade earlier. Likewise, German adaptations of *Natural History* books 7 through 9 flourished after 1565. Translators relied on Gesner's polyglot index. Francisco Hernández's Castilian translation also appeared in the 1560s. The only translation to appear earlier (in 1476) had been in Italian. Even there, in his dedication, the translator had defended the right of vernacular languages to use the technical words of antiquity—and so, for the most part, dodged the issue by Italianizing the names of plants and animals.

The assimilation of ancient knowledge in specialized botanical and zoological works, the final phase of the domesticating process referred to earlier, explains the abrupt halt, in the 1550s, of publication of the naturalist volumes of Theophrastus and Aristotle. They were replaced by new illustrated encyclopedias, which took most of their substance from the classics. Once the particular problems they posed were resolved, the technical texts from antiquity were no longer the object of research and were read as part of the category of *opera omnia.* The study of the natural world was no longer based on Aristotle and Pliny but on the illustrated works of the Renaissance.

In the second half of the 16th century the work of the ancients was still considered a model, but one that could be surpassed. Ulisse Aldrovandi, for example, compared himself with Aristotle and Pliny on the title page of his first book, but he remarked that the 18,000 natural objects collected in his museum in Bologna were far more numerous than the species described by the ancients. Similarly, Gaspard Bauhin offered his *Illustrated Exposition of Plants* (*Pinax theatri botanici,* 1623) as an "index of the plants described by Theophrastes, Dioscorides, Pliny, and the botanists who wrote across several centuries," but he also noted that he described nearly 6,000 plants, far more than the ancient authors.

The innovation of the microscope in natural history in the 17th century revealed the complex organization of the very smallest of living things and led to the discovery of many more, even smaller ones, but it did not lead to the rejection of ancient works any more than had the discovery of America. In Rome the Accademia dei Lincei developed a sweeping project of observation and representation in natural history but adhered closely to 16th-century practices and did not mark a break with antiquity (for a contrasting view see Freedberg 2002). The new century also saw emerging and important debates concerning, for example, the mechanisms of generation and the definition of vital principles. Once again, traditional interpretations and ancient concepts, particularly those of Greek origin, were called upon in modern controversies.

The gradual distancing that occurred over the 17th century from natural science as it had been understood by the ancients and their Humanist successors might best be explained as a rejection of the idea of natural history as a "totality," following Aldrovandi's final attempt. The explosion of the number of identified species and the heterogeneity of available data about each one made it impossible to attempt a complete description of all forms of natural life. Jan Jonston's *Natural History* (1650–1657), relying on that of Aldrovandi, still attempted to describe all species of known animals but abandoned the Humanist bent in natural history and focused the study on the animals themselves. This break cast off an important part of classical knowledge, which constituted the "history" of plants and animals. Ancient knowledge became less central after that time, although it remained important for naming and classifying. The explosion in the number of species to be counted led naturalists to favor inventories and reflections on the organization of Nature: general "systems" were sought that would categorize every living being.

The persistence of ancient categories in taxonomy was striking: the names of animal groups (quadrupeds, amphibians, cetaceans, ostracoderms, etc.) in Linnaeus's *Systema naturae* adopted the vocabulary of Aristotle. The words of the ancients and the categories they covered were still the tools with which the natural world was viewed and were difficult to escape. In the 10th edition of his *Systema naturae* (1758) Linnaeus followed internal organization rather than external appearance to classify animals. Thus, for example, he separated cetaceans from fish and put them closer to quadrupeds. In doing so, he went back to the anatomical definition of the term "fish," following Aristotle's example. He could not consider cetaceans, aquatic animals with two fins, to be quadrupeds, however. He freed himself from that Aristotelian concept by inventing the term *Mammalia*—though the innovation earned him the mockery of French naturalists who considered that an artificial convention.

The ancient terms are still present today in the standard international binomial nomenclature in Latin. Many names of actual genera and species are based on interpretations, sometimes erroneous, from ancient sources dating from the Renaissance. The current scientific name for silurid (*Silurus glanis*), for example, retains Pliny's confusion between two different fish. This 2,000-year-old hereditary line illustrates perfectly the profound influence of classical natural history on the modern natural sciences and civilizations of today. It has in turn affected our reading of ancient works: the names of plants and animals that have passed into modern scientific nomenclature have forced translation in ways that do not always represent the authors' thinking. Our understanding of the technical vocabulary in ancient natural history is an open question and probably always will be.

BIBL.: Agnes Arber, *Herbals, Their Origin and Evolution: A Chapter in the History of Botany, 1470–1670* (Cambridge 1986). Aristotle, *Historia animalium*, trans. A. L. Peck. (Cambridge, Mass., 1965). Ann Blair, *The Theater of Nature: Jean Bodin and Renaissance Science* (Princeton 1997). Minta Collins, *Medieval Herbals: The Illustrative Traditions* (London 2000). Paul Delaunay, *La zoologie au XVIe siècle* (Paris 1962). Paula Findlen, *Possessing Nature: Museums, Collecting, and Scientific Culture in Early Modern Italy* (Berkeley 1994). David Freedberg, *The Eye of the Lynx: Galileo, His Friends, and the Beginnings of Modern Natural History* (Chicago 2002). Brian Ogilvie, *The Science of Describing: Natural History in Renaissance Europe* (Chicago 2006). Anna Pavord, *The Naming of Names: The Search for Order in the World of Plants* (London 2005). Pliny the Elder, *Natural History*, trans. H. Rackham. (Cambridge, Mass., 1991). George Sarton, *The Appreciation of Ancient and Medieval Science during the Renaissance (1450–1600)* (Philadelphia 1953). Nancy G. Siraisi, "Life Sciences and Medicine in the Renaissance World," in *Rome Reborn: The Vatican Library and Renaissance Culture*, ed. Anthony Grafton (New Haven 1993). Hermann Walter, "An Illustrated Incunable of Pliny's *Natural History* in the Biblioteca Palatina, Parma," *Journal of the Warburg and Courtauld Institutes* 53 (1990) 208–216.

L.P.

Translated by Jeannine Routier Pucci and Elizabeth Trapnell Rawlings

Neo-Latin

The term *Neo-Latin* refers to postmedieval Latin. This designation represents a set of events, definitions, and categories that requires explanation. During the early Middle Ages, as the Romance languages took shape in Western Europe, Latin ceased to be a language that was "native," that is, spoken naturally, without conscious reflection, in the home from childhood onward. Thereafter, in the high and late Middle Ages, Latin became a language of culture, one employed in a pedagogical context: in elementary schools, cathedral schools (from approximately 1000 onward), and eventually universities, which began formally to exist in the early 13th century. This pedagogical context represented the foundation on which medieval theories regarding Latin were built.

To compress a set of developments that lasted four centuries into one moment: during this period a principal designation emerged to refer to Latin. Many high and late medieval thinkers termed Latin a *lingua artificialis*, an "artificial language" or, more precisely, a "language of craft." The majority of educated medieval European thinkers assumed Latin was a language that was permanent: an ordered, logically consistent mode of expression that possessed its own set of inherently unchanging rules, which needed to be learned through repeated practice. The assumed fact that Latin possessed permanently valid rules implied that there should be schools, rules, and institutions to teach, foster, and propagate this language of culture.

The 14th century saw the beginnings of a challenge to this conception, specifically in the lifetime of Francesco Petrarca, or Petrarch (1304–1374). Petrarch called Latin "the mother of all our arts" and in medieval fashion considered Latin an artificial language. Still, he was distinguished by his historical sense. He saw that the Latin in schools, universities, and the Church did not match the more natural and authentic Latin found in the ancient, classical sources he revered, conditioned as he was by the ever more popular vogue for studying the classics. Petrarch's classical orientation impelled him to write Latin in a fashion that accorded more with the syntax, norms, and lexicon of ancient Latin. Though there had been two generations of northern Italian thinkers before him who attempted to imitate ancient Latin in their poetry, Petrarch was the first to weave all these historicizing strands together. It is with Petrarch, in short, that "Neo-Latin" begins.

The 15th century in Italy witnessed a lively debate that allowed participants to express their positions on the kind of Latin spoken in ancient Rome. Did the revered ancients possess two modes of expression, a vernacular and a more formal, rule-bound style (like "us moderns," so the implication went)? Or did they write in the language in which they spoke, occasionally adjusting the tenor of what they said, perhaps committing the more informal things they had spoken publicly to a more structured written form?

A luminary like Leonardo Bruni (1370–1444) favored the former opinion, believing that the ancients employed both a vernacular and a more polished speech. Like medieval thinkers, Bruni considered Latin an artificial language. Bruni was the last major thinker in 15th-century Italy to consider Latin in such an idealized fashion. After him, most 15th-century Italian thinkers deemed ancient Latin a "natural" language, one that had its own trajectory of historically conditioned birth, growth, and decline. By the end of that century, Humanist Latin education, begun in Italy, had become the norm for Europe's educated elites, and Neo-Latin had assumed a definitive, lasting character.

This character can be described as moderately Ciceronian, and its formation can be best understood by three Renaissance examples. First, in 1470, a Sienese Augustinian scholar named Agostino Dati wrote a short textbook entitled *The Little Elegances* (*Elegantiolae*). In its early printed form, it took up only 20 pages and, immensely popular, went through more than 110 printings before 1501. Dati taught his readers how to sound like Cicero by means of short examples, stock phrases, and typically Ciceronian word order. The fact that Ciceronian style was being distilled into a best-selling book for students tells us that Humanist and Ciceronian education had gone mainstream.

Second, the late 1480s saw an interesting debate between Angelo Poliziano (1454–1494) and Paolo Cortesi (1465–1510) that encapsulated the possible contrasting opinions on Neo-Latin. Cortesi had collected his own letters for publication, as was customary, and sent them before publication to Poliziano, whom he admired, hoping for an evaluation. In his reply Poliziano criticized Cortesi, arguing that Cortesi had tried too hard to imitate Cicero, a practice that could only impede creative thinking and writing. In the same letter Poliziano made an important statement. Should a hypothetical critic take Poliziano to task for not sounding enough like Cicero, Poliziano responds that he would reply: "What then? I am not Cicero. Still, I am expressing my own viewpoint, I believe." Poliziano's statement can stand for one side of the debate regarding Neo-Latin: though he does not use the word, it is really authenticity that he seeks, and he wants to express himself in a way that is classically appropriate but not tied to any one single author.

Cortesi's much longer, somewhat surprised but very civil reply is noteworthy, both because it expressed the opposing viewpoint and, more important, because in the teaching of Latin prose thenceforth, Cortesi's opinion became, in pedagogical practice, the majority opinion. Cortesi contended that those who use Latin in the modern era are like strangers in a strange land, who need a guide. When traveling in a foreign land, one always picks the best possible guide; Cicero is universally recognized as the best guide to writing ancient Latin prose; therefore, imitating Cicero is appropriate, provided it is done in the way "a son imitates a father," meaning devotedly but not slavishly and in a fashion in which something original will inevitably shine through.

Cortesi's overall position frankly recognized that Latin was no longer a native language (which all medieval thinkers had also known); but he recapitulated over half a century's thinking concerning the historical nature of the problem. Cortesi came from a family with long ties to the papal court, and he himself held curial offices. As someone intimately familiar with Europe's most intense place of "international" exchange, he could see the problem with a clear-sightedness that the avant-garde philologist Poliziano could not. Latin had, and would continue to have for some time to come, an important role in society: in the Church, in education, and in the bureaucracies of the newly emerging order of European sovereign states. Given his "international" perspective coupled with the frank recognition of ancient Latin's historical nature as a natural language, Cortesi intuited the direction in which Neo-Latin prose would go: a moderately Ciceronian one in which the basic periodic structure of a Ciceronian sentence became the stylistic norm.

Third, the Dutch Humanist Erasmus, alarmed by what he saw as an uncritical overreliance on Cicero's style, vocabulary, and textual corpus, published a satirical dialogue on the topic in 1528 entitled *The Ciceronian.* The dialogue's two interlocutors discuss matters of literary style. One of them, an ardent Ciceronian, insists that he has consulted only books of Cicero for the last seven years, and that there are no exceptions: if a word or phrase does not appear in Cicero, it should not be used. He is compelled to admit that in conversation he restricts himself to short phrases that he has memorized. As the dialogue progresses, Erasmus's position becomes clear: Cicero's preeminence is undoubted, but for culture to live, a modern Latin writer must use many approved ancient authors as models and admit that, since times have changed, the need for neologisms will occasionally arise. Yet by this point in Italy, the 1520s, the early plantings of the avant-garde, authenticity-seeking mentality seen in Poliziano had borne fruit in emerging treatises on the vernacular. In Neo-Latin's place of origin, Italy, the same sorts of avant-garde Humanists who had used (for five intellectual generations since Petrarch) progressively more classical Latin to examine the day's pressing questions began to use the vernacular. Erasmus, himself moderately Ciceronian in style, wrote truly creative philosophical literature in Latin in that earlier Humanist mold; and he began a Low Countries tradition that had issue later in the 16th century in the writings of the Neostoic Justus Lipsius.

Another important strand in Neo-Latin's complex tapestry can be seen in poetry. From the late 13th century onward, Neo-Latinists wrote Latin poetry in all the genres known from antiquity. Petrarch's attempt at epic, his *Africa,* remained uncompleted at his death and came to be considered unsuccessful; but later poets employed Neo-Latin in a variety of ways. Bawdy, erotic poetry, such as the *Hermaphrodite* of Antonio Beccadelli (1394–1471, alias *Panormita*) competed with funeral poetry, eclogues, and metrical theater pieces. Witty Latin epigrams led to the development of a new genre, the "emblem." The combination of a short, often mysterious Latin epigram with an at times equally enigmatic image caught the imaginations of 16th-century Europe's learned elites, as they used these emblems to delineate insiders and outsiders in their own intellectual communities.

Perhaps the most interesting form of Neo-Latin poetry was what one might loosely call academic poetry, of various sorts, in which one observes Renaissance thinkers reading antiquity through poetic evocations of their own. One example is that of Maffeo Vegio (1407–1458), who was so entranced by Virgil's 12-book *Aeneid* that he added a beautifully written 13th book, in which he detailed Aeneas's wedding to Lavinia, among other things. Another example is represented by certain academic *praelectiones* of Angelo Poliziano. It was customary in late medieval and early modern universities for professors to begin the course they were to teach during the academic year with an opening oration, or a *praelectio*, that would describe the upcoming course's subject matter and importance. Poliziano, a professor at the Florentine university (and innovator that he was), offered poetic *praelectiones* when he taught certain poets in the 1480s, as his four *Silvae* demonstrate. The *Manto* concerned Virgil's *Aeneid;* the *Ambra* preceded a course on Homer; the *Rusticus* had to do with Virgil's *Georgics* and Hesiod's *Works and Days;* and the *Nutricia* represented nothing less than a poetic survey of the history of poetry from ancient through modern times. Both examples, Vegio's supplement to the *Aeneid* and Poliziano's poetic *praelectiones,* show us a predominant passion of Renaissance Neo-Latinists: to read by writing, and to write by reading. The result was that *imitatio* (the learning of stylistic perfection by careful imitation) occasionally graduated to *aemulatio* (the attempt to go beyond imitation and to rival the ancient models one revered, to present them in a new idiom and a different key).

After the 1520s Neo-Latin served a series of important functions. It became a language of (often quite creative and brilliant) scholarship, the arena in which international scholarly contests were waged in Europe's increasingly and self-consciously international Republic of Letters. Early modern Europe's great philologists, numismatists, and paleographers all used Neo-Latin in their works, as did the natural scientists Galileo, Francis Bacon, William Harvey, Andreas Vesalius, and Isaac Newton, all of whom wrote important scientific works in Latin.

The 18th century saw Neo-Latin become somewhat displaced. Many Enlightenment thinkers came to believe that native languages represented true and authentic culture (as a glance at the *Encyclopédie*'s entry on "langage" confirms). French became the West's international language of diplomacy, and, finally, European nationalisms led to pride in a culture's presumed "national" characteristics, one of which was language.

Still, Neo-Latin continued to be employed throughout the world in different contexts and, sometimes, in striking ways. The longest Latin novel ever published, the Hungarian András Dugonics's *Argonautica sive de vellere aureo libri XXIV,* came out in the height of the Enlightenment, in the year 1778. The great German Romantic folklorist and collector of fairy tales, Jacob Grimm (1785–1863), delivered an inaugural oration in 1830 at the University of Göttingen, where he had become a librarian. Its subject was the greatness of the German language and the manner in which it had finally reached parity with French and English. Tellingly, he delivered the oration in Latin. Croatia maintained Latin as its language of Parliament until 1847. In Poland throughout the 20th century it was common for classical scholars to deliver their talks in scholarly venues in Latin.

The use of Neo-Latin could also serve as a form of resistance. A German scholar, Hermann Weller (1878–1956), wrote a poem in 1937 that served as a critique of anti-Semitism. Entitled "Y," it won the Gold Medal in the 1938 iteration of the annual Amsterdam Latin poetry competition, the *Certamen Hoeufftianum* (which lasted from 1844 until 1978). There were other times in Neo-Latin's long history when resistance might have seemed appropriate, but when the weight of tradition impelled just the opposite. Jacobus Capitein (1717–1747) serves as a case in point: a freed African slave who attended the University of Leiden, Capitein wrote an academic dissertation in the form of a treatise in 1742; he argued there was nothing in the biblical or classical traditions that could serve as an effective argument against slavery.

Throughout the modern era, many Western universities encouraged their students to submit dissertations in Latin, well into the early 20th century. Notable figures who wrote some sort of academic thesis in Latin include Friedrich Nietzsche, Jean Jaurès, and Maurice Blondel. Today there is a Finnish radio station that broadcasts the news once a week in Latin; the bank machines in Vatican City still offer Latin as a language option; and one can even find Latin translations of various modern children's classics: *Winnie ille Pu* (*Winnie the Pooh*) and *Harrius Potter et Philosophi Lapis* (*Harry Potter and the Philosopher's Stone*) are only two from among a vast sea of entries.

BIBL.: Josef IJsewijn with Dirk Sacré, *Companion to Neo-Latin Studies,* 2 vols. (Louvain 1990–1998). Françoise Wacquet, *Latin; or, The Empire of a Sign* (New York 2001).

C.C.

Neoclassicism

Eighteenth-century architects, artists, and designers did not describe their work as "neoclassical" but did view it as an attempt to recreate "the true style of the ancients." Their aim was thus scarcely different from that of Leon Battista Alberti (1404–1472) and his followers during the Renaissance. Thus the term *neoclassicism* can hardly denote a new intellectual concept, though it may help identify what we today see as a visual link between, say, a vase by Josiah Wedgwood (1730–1795), a painting by Jacques-Louis David (1748–1825), a sculpture by Bertel Thorvaldsen (1768–1844), and a building by Karl Friedrich Schinkel (1781–1841). These share a taut and crisp elegance that their creators perceived, rightly or wrongly, to be of Grecian origin. But immediately we encounter a difficulty, for Wedgwood, Thorvaldsen, Schinkel, and the whole Empire style were excluded from Hugh Honour's *Neo-Classicism* (1968), a pioneering study of the subject, reprinted unchanged in 1991. Despite this exclusion, it is now widely agreed that neoclassicism covers the period from about 1750 until at least 1830 and includes architecture, painting, sculpture, and—of equal note—the decorative arts.

Neoclassicism, with or without a hyphen and capital letters, is not included in the *Concise Oxford Dictionary,* though it has acquired many overtones in discourse on art history. Although the term means simply "new classicism," its meaning remains imprecise because every age from ancient Greece to the present has interpreted "classical" language and culture anew. Though neoclassicism has been a continuous factor in Western civilization, the style currently identified as such by art historians is rooted in the 18th-century Enlightenment and its search for a return to first principles and origins in all fields of human endeavor. It can also be seen as a perhaps understandable rationalist reaction, beginning ca. 1750, against the elaborate Baroque and Rococo ornament that had prevailed in the first half of the century. To justify their reaction against such styles of design, artists and architects claimed to find in ancient architecture and sculpture a model for the purity and simplicity they sought. In particular they pointed to ancient Greece as a guide, though virtually none of them had visited Greece or knew any Greek art firsthand.

In art-historical contexts, the word *neoclassicism* was invented in the mid-19th century to criticize what was by then felt to be the frigid character of the white, neo-antique sculpture of artists such as Antonio Canova (1757–1822). Thus, like the terms *Gothic* and *Baroque*, it initially had pejorative implications but was subsequently adopted as a neutral descriptive term. The rehabilitation of neoclassicism, initiated by German art historians ca. 1900, took place in the first half of the 20th century during the dominance of modernist aesthetics, which had reacted against tradition and the classical language in particular. Those defending neoclassicism thus chose to present it as essentially "modern," even a precursor of modernism, seeing it as separate from other revivals, for revivalism was a concept condemned by the modernists.

Because "neoclassicism" was interpreted in light of contemporary issues, writers in the 1930s such as Sigfried Giedion (1888–1968) and Emil Kaufmann (1891–1953) valued architects like Étienne-Louis Boullée (1728–1799) and Claude-Nicolas Ledoux (1736–1806) as anticipating the aesthetics of the 20th century: according to Kaufmann, they "restored the elementary forms to their rightful place in architecture . . . The effects which Ledoux proposed were almost the same which are being used by the architects of today . . . simplicity, sincerity and dignity."

Nikolaus Pevsner (1902–1983) brought this concept to England in *An Outline of European Architecture* (1942), in which he discussed the 18th-century classical revival in a chapter titled "The Romantic Movement, Historicism, and the Beginning of the Modern Movement, 1760–1914." Because the program defined by this title enabled him to hail John Soane (1753–1837) and Friedrich Gilly (1772–1800) as proto-modernists, he asked, "Why is it then that a hundred years had to pass before an original 'modern' style was really accepted? How can it be that the 19th century forgot about Soane and Gilly and remained smugly satisfied with the imitation of the past?" This interpretation neglected to note that Soane himself was so rooted in the classical orders that he believed that "art cannot go beyond the Corinthian."

The exhibition The Age of Neo-Classicism held in London in 1972 was based on a far wider interpretation of neoclassicism than Pevsner's or Honour's. It was now defined in its own terms, not those of the 20th century. David Irwin's admirable *Neo-Classicism* (1997) takes a similarly broad view. The prewar, modernist interpretation, however, still colors the entry on neoclassicism in Grove's authoritative *Dictionary of Art* (34 vols., 1996), where it is described as creating "consciously new and contemporary forms of expression" and thus establishing a "concept of modernity [that] set Neo-classicism apart from past revivals of antiquity."

Yet if neoclassicism simply means new classicism, then it is surely a phenomenon we would expect to discover in the ancient world where, in the Hellenistic period from 323 to 27 BCE, and especially from the 2nd century BCE, we find new styles that have recently been summarized as neoclassical, archaic, Neo-Attic, and Pergamene Baroque; architecture, too, appears to have experienced a baroque phase (Lyttelton 1974). Imitation of past styles and monuments characterized the 1st century BCE, when Neo-Attic sculptors produced copies and imitations of earlier exemplars, adding the descriptor "the Athenian" after their signatures.

The essentially neoclassical character of Hellenistic art heralded the Roman veneration of Greek art, as is demonstrated by Hadrian's Villa at Tivoli (118–134 CE). This landscaped theater of memory included a temple of Aphrodite inspired by that at Cnidus in Asia Minor, from the 3rd or 2nd century BCE. Inside his temple of Aphrodite, Hadrian even reproduced the 4th-century BCE statue of Venus by Praxiteles that had been at Cnidus. Hadrian's temple of Aphrodite occupied a site at Tivoli overlooking what he called the Vale of Tempe in honor of the celebrated valley of that name in Thessaly. The closest parallel to Hadrian's program in recent centuries would be 18th-century Picturesque landscaped parks such as Shugborough, in Staffordshire, scattered with numerous neo-antique monuments.

By contrast, Pevsner found the buildings of ancient Greece and Rome alien and irrelevant to the modern world of which "neoclassicism" was a fundamental part because of its supposed role as a harbinger of modernism. He went so far as to assert that "the Greek temple, most readers would probably agree, and the Roman Forum, belong to the civilization of Antiquity, not what we usually mean when we speak of European civilisation." As a result, he explained, the works of the Greeks and Romans would "appear only very briefly" in the exposition that he nonetheless titled *An Outline of European Architecture*.

The situation has changed markedly since then with the publication of books such as Pierre du Prey's *Villas of Pliny from Antiquity to Posterity* (1994) and William MacDonald and John Pinto's *Hadrian's Villa and Its Legacy* (1995). Studies of this kind reveal a new awareness of the diversity and, in a way, "modernity" of ancient architecture and design, and of its continuing relevance in the modern world. A key statement enabling us to understand what we call "neoclassicism" might actually have meant in the 18th century, as opposed to the 20th, occurs in a letter of advice sent in 1774 by the architect William Chambers (1723–1796) to a pupil visiting Rome (and also given, four years later, to the young John Soane, who treasured it for the rest of his life): "Always see with Your own eyes. Work in the same quarry with M. Angelo, Vignola, Peruzzi, and Palladio . . . Observe well the works of the celebrated Bernini, at once an able architect, painter and sculptor; see how well they are conducted . . . Converse much with artists of all Countrys, particularly foreigners, that you may get rid of national prejudices." Chambers went on to urge his students to meet the engraver and architect Giovanni Battista Piranesi (1720–1778), and to admire the Trevi Fountain in Rome by Nicola Salvi (1697–1751), inspired by ancient Roman triumphal arches. They were also told to draw accurately the ancient "fragments which lie scattered in all the villas about Rome, and in the environs of Naples."

Chambers's advice encapsulated the spirit of the Enlightenment as a pan-European, not a nationalist, project whose protagonists aimed to return to first principles by relying on their own eyes and experience, rather than by unquestioningly accepting received opinion. His pupils had thus to be open to all aspects of the classical tradition from antiquity to Salvi and Piranesi. This is in contrast to modern art historians who would bracket Chambers as "neoclassical," in opposition to the "Baroque" Bernini, though neither architect saw himself as thus confined: indeed, had Chambers regarded Bernini as Baroque, he would hardly have recommended him to his pupils.

As a captivating vision of Italy, and of ancient and modern Rome, Piranesi's engravings were a catalyst for the imagination of countless 18th-century architects and artists, including Chambers, Adam, Dance, Mylne, and Soane in England, and Clérisseau, Hubert Robert, Peyre, LeGeay, Le Lorrain, De Wailly, Boullée, Ledoux, and Valadier in France. In his *Prima parte di architettura e prospettive* (*Part One of Architecture and Perspectives,* 1743) Piranesi explained that his heady evocations of grandiose public buildings and awesome ruined structures were intended to reprove contemporary architects for their mediocrity. Believing that he had a mission to reform modern architecture, he explained that "these living, speaking ruins have filled my spirit with images that accurate drawings, even such as those of the immortal Palladio, could never have succeeded in conveying . . . New pieces are daily dug out of the ruins and new things present themselves to us capable of fertilizing and improving the ideas of an artist who thinks and reflects. Rome is certainly the most fruitful magazine of this kind." This seems no different from Raphael's concern to preserve ancient Roman monuments, expressed in his report to Pope Leo X in 1519.

The art historian and archaeologist Johann Joachim Winckelmann (1717–1768) praised the supposed simplicity of the Greeks and condemned its decline under the Romans, as proved by their greater use of ornament. This threat to Piranesi's vision and livelihood as a purveyor of views of Rome may partly explain the latter's devotion to Robert Adam (1728–1792), whom he saw as a brilliant designer sympathetic to his Roman cause, as well as a representative of the richest nation on earth. While Adam was in Rome (1755–1757) he discussed architecture with Piranesi, by whom he confessed he was captivated. It was in his lovely neo-antique interiors at Syon House, Middlesex (1762–1769), that Adam first achieved the rich ornamental synthesis, the "novelty and variety," as he termed it, for which Piranesi had called.

The eight Etruscan rooms that Adam designed, including that of 1775–1777 at Osterley Park, Middlesex, owed something to Piranesi's stress on the role of the Etruscans. In reality these rooms were more indebted to ancient Roman interiors such as those at the Golden House of Nero, as recreated in the 16th century by Raphael and Giovanni da Udine in stuccoed and painted interiors at the Villa Madame and elsewhere. Chambers himself, Adam's rival, had lived with Piranesi in Rome in the 1750s when he designed a mausoleum for Frederick, Prince of Wales. In his drawings for that circular classical temple, Chambers showed it set romantically in a landscaped garden, in one instance even as a ruin, thus evoking the 18th-century theme of the vanity of human wishes.

In his influential *Essai sur l'architecture* (1753), Marc-Antoine Laugier (1713–1769) urged that since the primitive hut was the origin of Doric architecture, modern architects should retain the image of the hut at all times. Jacques-Germain Soufflot (1713–1780), after seeing the Greek Doric temples at Paestum, designed the church of Ste-Geneviève, Paris (1757–1790), now the Panthéon; in the crypt there he did not copy Greek detail but invented a simplified Grecianizing order. In 1758 James ("Athenian") Stuart produced the first Greek Revival building since antiquity, a garden temple at Hagley Park, Worcestershire. Larger and more inventive was the Radcliffe Observatory, Oxford (1776–1794), by James Wyatt (1746–1813), possibly the first public building since antiquity based on a Greek model, albeit of a late Hellenistic type, the Tower of the Winds in Athens.

A parallel in painting was Gavin Hamilton (1723–1798), who turned to Homeric subjects in the 1760s; also an archaeologist, Gavin provided newly excavated antique sculpture to English collectors. The American-born artist Benjamin West (1738–1820) began an Italian Grand Tour in 1760, becoming a friend to Hamilton and taking up history painting on arriving in London in 1763. For his *Agrippina Landing at the Port of Brindisi with the Ashes of Her Husband* (1768), he drew on the monuments of ancient Rome as well as on the plates in Robert Adam's *Ruins of the Palace of the Emperor Diocletian at Spalatro* (1764). Jacques-Louis David, in Italy 1775–1780 and 1784, also echoed Hamilton's stern moral themes in his famous *Oath of the Horatii* (1784) and *Death of Marat* (1793).

Josiah Wedgwood influenced public taste from the 1760s onward through his pottery and other manufactures, imitating Greek vases in his "black basalt" ware, on which he painted in the red and black of the originals. On jasperware he put white decoration on a colored ground such as green, lilac, or often the color that came to be known as Wedgwood blue. The sculptor Antonio Canova (1757–1822), who settled in Rome in 1780, was also influenced by Hamilton and Winckelmann, as can be seen in his stern *Theseus and the Dead Minotaur* (1781–1782). His *Hercules and Lichas* (1795–1802) had the more dynamic flavor of Pergamene Baroque, the sensuous grace of his *Cupid and Psyche* (1787–1793) being echoed in his famous *Three Graces,* commissioned in 1812 by Empress Josephine.

An early masterpiece by Canova's successor, Bertel Thorvaldsen, was a heroic *Jason,* begun in 1802 for the designer and collector Thomas Hope, who created a room in his London mansion for the sculpture *Aurora Visiting Cephalus* by John Flaxman (1755–1826). The event portrayed took place, according to Ovid's *Metamorphoses,* at dawn—an effect that Hope evoked by lining the walls of the room with mirrors edged in black velvet, over which were hung curtains of black and orange satin.

Such poetic effects were rooted in the new philosophy of the sensations, including the Sublime, variously promoted by authors such as Condillac, Burke, and even Rousseau. Nicolas Le Camus de Mézières, in *Le Génie de l'architecture; ou, L'analogie de cet art avec nos sensations* (1780), recommended manipulating light and shadow to create interiors that could move the soul as well as express different emotions and sensations. Such effects were paralleled in the work of Boullée, Ledoux, and Soane. Ledoux's dynamic Hôtel de Thélusson, in Paris (1778–1783), boasted a theatrical approach through a seemingly half-buried arch, as though strayed from an engraving of ancient Rome by Piranesi. The Greek Doric gateway to Ledoux's Saltworks at Chaux (1779) shelters a grotto recalling underground salt chambers—an arresting conjunction suggesting the parallel powers of architecture and nature.

Soane's interiors at the Bank of England, in London (1788–1833), with their floating vaults and domes, exemplified what he, like Boullée, called "the poetry of architecture." Soane's study of Le Camus de Mézières was reflected in his house and museum in Lincoln's Inn Fields, built between 1792 and 1824 with a unique deployment of colored light and mirrors.

Neoclassicism was exported as the expression of democracy to the United States, notably by Benjamin Latrobe (1764–1820), an English architect who settled there in 1796; his career was promoted by Thomas Jefferson. Latrobe's works include the Supreme Court Chamber (1815–1817) in the Capitol Building in Washington, D.C., with Paestum Doric columns supporting a lobed vault echoing that of the Serapaeum at Hadrian's Villa at Tivoli. The Grecian-inspired urban contributions to Berlin from 1816 to 1823 by Karl Friedrich Schinkel, including the Royal Guard House, Theater, and Altes Museum, were a modern essay in the exercise of antique civic virtue. More visionary was the Walhalla (1830–1842) by Leo von Klenze (1784–1864), towering above the Danube near Regensburg. This Greek Doric symbol of pan-German national unity, with its sumptuously polychromatic interior lined with portrait busts, is perhaps the greatest masterpiece of neoclassicism.

Used to express the ideals of many different regimes, neoclassicism was adopted later in Germany by Paul Troost (1878–1934) for his twin Temples of Honor on the Königsplatz in Munich (1933–1937). These were open pavilions in the language of Gilly and Schinkel but lacked the megalomania sometimes visible in the work of Albert Speer (1905–1981), who described as "neoclassical" his Zeppelin Field in Nuremberg (1937–1940), which drew on ancient Egyptian architecture and the Great Altar of Pergamon (2nd cent. BCE).

Vincent Scully's belief that "since civilisation is based largely on the capacity to remember, the architect builds visible history" lies behind the extensive Queen's Gallery at Buckingham Palace (2002) by John Simpson (b. 1954). Here, an entrance portico in the Paestum Doric order leads to a top-lit, two-storied hall, its side walls lined with long, sculptural friezes on Homeric themes, adapted to the history of Britain in the 20th century. These are the work of Alexander Stoddart (b. 1959), a sculptor whose work draws frequently on the legends and art of ancient Greece and Rome.

Though the vision of Greece lay behind much of the movement we call neoclassical, the physical reality of Rome was vitally important. The description of Rome by the novelist George Eliot in *Middlemarch* (1871–1872), which could have been inspired by Piranesi, evokes the enduring power and resonances of "the city of visible history, where the past of a whole hemisphere seems moving in funereal procession with strange ancestral images and trophies gathered from afar."

BIBL.: Arts Council of Great Britain, *The Age of Neo-Classicism* (London 1972). Hugh Honour, *Neo-Classicism* (Harmondsworth 1968). David Irwin, *Neoclassicism* (London 1997). Margaret Lyttelton, *Baroque Architecture in Classical Antiquity* (Ithaca 1974). Mario Praz, *On Neoclassicism* (London 1969). David Watkin, *Thomas Hope (1769–1831) and the Neo-Classical Idea* (London 1968). J. J. Winckelmann, *Writings on Art,* ed. David Irwin (London 1972). D.W.

Neoplatonism

The term was first used in the 19th century to designate a period stretching from the career of Plotinus (204–270 CE) to the closing of the Athenian Academy by the emperor Justinian in 529. Those who partook in this trend thought of themselves as Platonists, adhering to the notion that Plato was the philosopher who had come closest to the truth; they believed that it was their responsibility to draw that truth out by exegesis, teaching, and rational argumentation.

According to his student and editor Porphyry (ca. 234–305), Plotinus's last words were "Try to lead the god in you up to the divine in the universe" (*Life of Plotinus* 2.26–27). Embedded in this sentence are some key notions that after Plotinus became recognizable parts of the armature of Neoplatonism: emanation, ascent, and mentalism.

For Plotinus the metaphysical universe is structured hierarchically, and at the top of the hierarchy sits an absolute first principle (*archē*), which is also a goal (*telos*): the One. The One, a combination of Plato's Form of the Good and Aristotle's prime mover, is everywhere, "filling all things," yet it is also nowhere, as it must be distinct from the world it creates (*Enneads* 3.9.4). The One exists ineffably beyond being, and from its powerful, generative thought emanates the rest of the levels of the universe, in succession: Mind, Soul, and a fourth realm that includes Nature, Matter, and Sensation. Human beings occupy by choice an intermediate rank (3.2.9). We are embodied, and so we have within us a part of the lowest level of the universe, matter, which Plotinus conceives of as antisubstantial and evil (1.8.10). We also partake of soul, and we possess an inborn desire to ascend the hierarchy, which we can do by purifying our souls from material corruption, in order to unify ourselves with the One after our ascent. This we do by disciplining our minds by meditation. We do not, in Plotinus's view, need many external rituals to accomplish this unification. We have instead within us the mental power to do it alone. Odysseus, Plotinus says (1.6.8, 18–28), was not satisfied to remain among the sensual delights of Calypso. As he set back out to sea to reach his true goal, so too should we strive for the vision of the One using the power within us. To ascend upward, we must reach inward.

Plotinus's Platonism established factors that remained part of the Western classical heritage: a hierarchical ordering of reality with immaterial divinity at the top and matter and the everyday world we inhabit at the bottom; a propensity toward monotheism; and the belief that one must turn within oneself to communicate with the divine. Through his students, his influence became extensive. Porphyry wrote a philosophical introduction to Aristotle's logical work that became (after being translated from Greek into Latin by Boethius in the early 6th century) a standard part of Western secondary education. In his *Cave of the Nymphs,* a Platonizing reflection on a Homeric passage (*Odyssey* 13.102–112), he took a tendency toward allegory in Plotinus (cf. *Enneads* 1.6.8, 19) much further than others had done before him. Homer's Cave, with one opening reserved for mortals, another for the gods, here becomes an allegory signifying Neoplatonic ascent, along with a vigorous defense at the outset of the technique and practice of allegory. Porphyry dealt in other treatises with behaviors and rituals, writing a treatise on vegetarianism, a *Life* of Pythagoras, and various works dealing with aspects of ritual piety.

This latter problem, ritual, proved a turning point in the history of Neoplatonism, specifically in the thought of Porphyry's student and eventual antagonist Iamblichus (ca. 245–ca. 325). Plotinus's mentalism had enabled him to define the lifestyle of a philosopher as that of a person who by the use of spiritual exercise could successfully ascend the hierarchy of the universe. Yet even as Plotinus was writing, a sea change was occurring in the late antique world, among pagans as well as Christians. This change had to do precisely with the power and importance of ritual. Iamblichus embraced the notion that all people, philosophers included, should engage in rituals to assist them in the process of Neoplatonic ascent. For him these rituals could be classified as *theourgia,* or theurgy (from *theion,* "divine" and *ergon,* "work"), whereby the petitioner attempts to persuade the divinity toward or away from some kind of action. These rituals could include chants, the use of "signed" objects (like certain stones, plants, and herbs), and sun worship. These and other techniques exploited the hidden "sympathies," or links that were believed to exist in the cosmos between the earthly and the celestial. Iamblichus in his *De mysteriis* (*On the Mysteries*) defines *theourgia* as "the accomplishment of acts not to be divulged and beyond all conception" (2.11.96; Clarke et al. trans., 115). The literal meaning of *theurgy,* divine work, suggests that someone engaging in theurgy is "doing divine work," or even "working the divine," the latter suggesting that the human operator has a certain measure of efficacy. This efficacy could be assured only if the rituals were done correctly, so that outward human action, rather than Plotinian inwardness, became thereafter another key element of Neoplatonic tradition.

Iamblichus also expanded the canon of texts thought appropriate to the mission of Platonism. He was the first, for example, to endorse the dignity of the Hermetic Corpus, a body of writings in Greek dating mostly to the 2nd century CE. He believed, however, that these writings were authored by an ancient Egyptian, pre-Platonic sage, thought to be roughly contemporary with Moses. This author, Hermes Trismegistus, served symbolically as a fountainhead of ancient, mysterious, "Egyptian" wisdom. Iamblichus' appropriation of this and other extra-Platonic material broadened the base of texts that could be used in the process of exegesis necessary to find Plato's "true meaning"; it meant that, from Iamblichus' day onward, Neoplatonism as a philosophical approach would be intentionally eclectic, its representatives seeking out the one unitary truth believed to be contained in many philosophical and religious systems; and it led to a connection with Christianity that lasted until modern times.

Some late antique Neoplatonists were anti-Christian in outlook. Still, we can observe consistencies in both pagan and Christian approaches to ritual, as well as other similarities in approach to the world. Their vitriolic polemics show us in hindsight that pagan and Christian antagonists were often fighting over the same things. Saint Augustine (354–430) did much to incorporate Neoplatonism into Christianity. He believed that of all the pagan philosophers, the Platonists (by which he meant those who shared the Neoplatonic interpretation of Plato and Platonism) represented "the closest approximation to our

Christian position" (*City of God* 8.9). His *Confessions* (7.9.3, 8.2.3) describes the influence that "books of the Platonists" (probably Marius Victorinus' translations of Plotinus as well as other works) had on him. He reports that he learned from these books that the doctrine of the Word as set out in the Gospel of John (chap. 10) was shared by the Platonists, even if the doctrine of the Incarnation was not. Finally, in one of his polemical works, the *Treatises against the Donatists,* he sets forth the Christian view of the power and efficacy of sacraments, which function *ex opere operato,* or "from the work having been worked." Provided that the ritual of the sacrament was performed correctly, the sacrament would function efficaciously and serve to channel toward the divine whatever moral condition the individual operator exerted. This notion possesses obvious affinities with theurgy.

There existed one more affinity between Neoplatonism and early Christianity: the tendency to focus on the omnipotence of the supreme being, which was conceived to be so great that it could scarcely be known by human beings. This tendency had a long history, reaching back to the motif of Plato's Cave (*Republic* 7.515) and to Saint Paul's memorable description of the manner in which we now see "through a glass, darkly" but someday will see "face to face" (1 Corinthians 13:12). Plotinus's ineffable, reserved One inaugurated a new era in thinking about the one supreme being. From a secularized standpoint, this move betokens the human tendency to project a unitary, absolute principle into logical space, and it carries with it all of those allegiances to absolute ideas that are its consequence. In the later history of Neoplatonism this logical tendency came to the fore. In the early Christian era the seeming ineffability of the one supreme being led to a type of theologizing known as "negative theology," whose guiding idea is that because we can never, in our finite human capacity, know what God is, we can at least approach God through saying, in a prayerful ritualized fashion, what God is not.

A key thinker in this regard was pseudo-Dionysius the Areopagite, believed to be the Dionysius mentioned in Acts 17:34, the first Athenian gentile convert to Christianity (sometimes also confused with Saint Denis, the French patron saint). In fact, he was a contemporary of the Neoplatonist Proclus (411–485), who was head of the Athenian Academy for 50 years. Pseudo-Dionysius' work was translated into Latin, first by Hilduinus (775–855), prior of the abbey church of St. Denis, and then in a better, more widely diffused version by John Scotus Eriugena (810–877), an exemplar of the flowering of Greek studies in early medieval Ireland. Pseudo-Dionysius' work exercised continuous influence throughout the Middle Ages because he mediated some of the dangerous aspects of Neoplatonism from a Christian point of view (the difficulty of reconciling absolute logical monotheism with the Trinity) while still retaining the mystery of the One, hidden god. In his work *On Divine Names* he set out the program for negative theology. In his work *On Mystical Theology* he put it into practice: as he writes there, the more his argument rises from the lower realm to the higher, transcendent realm, the more language becomes inadequate; at a certain point, "it will become entirely silent, since it will finally be at one with Him who is indescribable" (ed. Heil and Ritter, 1033C).

By the end of the early Middle Ages most elements were in place to create the foundations for lively medieval interest in Neoplatonism: an association between Platonism and Christianity; belief in an immaterial, notionally superior world that superintended our mundane material one and whose majesty could be accessed sacramentally; the conception of the human soul as an immortal, individual entity subject to rewards and punishments after death; and a stance toward ascetic meditation that suggested that through it human beings could have ecstatic contact with the divine.

Great energy and dynamism in philosophical speculation occurred in the Islamic and Byzantine worlds from the 9th through the 11th centuries. A number of Islamic thinkers considered Aristotle the fountainhead of philosophical wisdom. Still, much of their interpretation of Aristotle was guided by fundamentally Neoplatonic late antique commentaries on Aristotle, as well as by certain works such as the *Liber de causis* (attributed to Aristotle but actually an epitome of Proclus's *Elements of Theology*). Neoplatonic concepts of emanation pervade the thought of al-Fārābī (d. 950) and Avicenna (d. 1037); the works of both had significant diffusion in the West in the high Middle Ages. In the Byzantine world, Michael Psellus (1018–1081), to give just one example, drew criticism for his study of Plato, which it was feared would challenge Byzantine Christian orthodoxy. His study of Plato was fundamentally Neoplatonic, and he reintroduced his contemporaries to later Platonic thinkers like Plotinus, Porphyry, Iamblichus, and Proclus. His work would likewise later be influential in the West, during the 15th century in Italy.

During the 12th century thinkers in the environment of the cathedral school at Chartres became interested in Platonism, spurred by the availability of a partial translation of Plato's *Timaeus* that had been made in the 4th century by Calcidius. This work gave thinkers such as Bernard of Chartres (fl. 1120) and, a generation later, in the 1140s, Thierry of Chartres, Bernard of Tours, and William of Conches, among others, a springboard for exploring philosophical themes in a loosely Neoplatonic mode.

It is heuristically useful to separate Neoplatonism from Platonism. Still, two factors should be recalled: first, most thinkers commonly identified as Neoplatonists considered themselves followers of Pythagoras as much as of Plato; second, most premodern thinkers interested in Plato and "Platonic" wisdom did not categorically separate those thinkers whom we now term Neoplatonists from the larger treasury of wisdom they thought Plato represented. To an extent this configuration changed in the 15th century: by the end of that century most of what we now consider Neoplatonic texts, from Plotinus to Proclus, were recovered and translated from Greek into Latin. Yet the notion that these texts belonged to a larger trove of wisdom to which Plato and others had contributed grew stronger. Thus, the 15th century is crucial to tracing the fortunes of Neoplatonism. But to imagine that 15th-century thinkers were engaged in historicizing reconstruction of Neoplatonism would be misguided (Hankins 1989).

Marsilio Ficino (1433–1499) was the key thinker behind 15th-century Neoplatonism. Before him, at the outset of the century, thinkers like Leonardo Bruni (ca. 1370–1444), one of Plato's early Renaissance translators, rediscovered the aporetic Plato—the Plato whose dialogues delighted with wit, left important questions sometimes open to interpretation, and, in effect, made the reader into another interlocutor, stimulating thought by means of dialogue rather than didacticism. By the 1460s a number of Plato's dialogues had been translated into Latin. But it was only with Ficino, who began translating a series of texts deemed "Platonic" (from Plato's dialogues to the Hermetic Corpus, Plotinus to Proclus), that a new impetus was given to the Neoplatonic interpretation of Plato. Ficino not only made Plato available to European elites, but also provided Neoplatonic commentaries and summaries to those works that became part of reading Plato for centuries thereafter. He also translated Plotinus's *Enneads* into Latin, and he wrote, as his own major philosophical work, *Platonic Theology* (1489), which begins with a lengthy statement of a fundamentally Neoplatonic ontological hierarchy, God at the top and nature at the bottom. In his *Three Books on Life* (1489), a work that had wide European diffusion, Ficino also made available (and to an extent respectable) to his contemporaries the late antique propensity to theorize the universe in terms of "sympathies" between the earthly and the divine. His translations, commentaries, and works of synthesis provided early modern Europe with all the tools needed to renew the Neoplatonic approach to Plato that had crystallized in late antiquity.

Ficino's friendly rival in the Florentine Republic of Letters, Giovanni Pico della Mirandola (1463–1494), was Neoplatonic in his broad ambition to synthesize all philosophies. When it came to metaphysics, however, he was more of an Aristotelian, believing that the One and Being were coextensive, rather than hierarchically ordered. Pico's deep Aristotelianism reflected something important about the Renaissance and its ordering and organizing of knowledge: Neoplatonism as a philosophical stance was something that remained extrainstitutional, as philosophy faculties in universities, despite Ficino's influence, continued to teach fundamentally Aristotelian philosophy.

In the 16th century Ficinian Neoplatonism became diffused in a variety of ways. Ficino's Neoplatonic theory of love, which drew on the notion of sympathies and natural attractions, found expression in Baldassare Castiglione's *Courtier* (1528), one of whose interlocutors, Pietro Bembo, expounded Ficinian love theory at court. In the sciences the sense of the operator's power, so much a part of the post-Plotinian Neoplatonic tradition, manifested itself in the birth and growth of the new science. By the end of the century, Ficino's Neoplatonism was so well diffused that the Dominican philosopher Giordano Bruno was accused of plagiarizing Ficino in a public lecture that he gave at Oxford.

The early 17th century saw the beginnings of the decline of Neoplatonism as an interpretive stance toward Plato. Isaac Casaubon (1559–1614) proved that the Hermetic Corpus, linked to the broad version of Neoplatonism so popular since Ficino's revival, was inauthentic, that is, that it could not be as old as its adherents claimed. Meanwhile the new science evolved, seeking gradually to eliminate occult entities such as "sympathies" from accounts of how the natural world worked. Along with this evolution there occurred a gradual severance of natural philosophy (what became natural science) from philosophy as a whole, so that metaphysical questions ceased to matter as much as they previously had done. Still, even thinkers who followed the new science's empiricism in natural matters retained Neoplatonic inspiration. The Cambridge Platonists, such as Henry More (1614–1687) and Ralph Cudworth (1617–1688), reacted to the austerity of Calvinism, with its presupposition of an inaccessible "hidden God." They also believed that the door needed to be left open for spirituality and meditation alongside the study of natural science.

In the 18th century a death blow was dealt to the Neoplatonic interpretation of Plato, and hence to Neoplatonism as a viable form of academic philosophy, when Johann Jakob Brucker stigmatized it as unphilosophical and unsystematic in his influential *Critical History of Philosophy* (1742–1744). From that point on, the rise of historicism meant that interpreting Plato signified stripping away later Neoplatonic accretions from the traditions of Platonic interpretation. This historicizing tendency also meant that new interest arose in individuating the thought of the different Neoplatonic thinkers from Plotinus onward. In the early 19th century the antireligiosity of the French Enlightenment sparked a renewed interest in Neoplatonism in England and Germany. In England, Romantic poets like Samuel Taylor Coleridge drew inspiration from the almost cult-like Neoplatonism of Thomas Taylor (1758–1835), a private scholar who devoted his life to translating Aristotle, Plato, and the Neoplatonists into English. In the German-speaking world, both Friedrich Wilhelm Josef von Schelling (1775–1854) and Novalis (Georg Philipp Friedrich von Hardenberg, 1772–1801) became interested in Plotinus; Novalis averred in a letter that Plotinus was "the first to step truly into holiness" (*Schriften*, ed. R. Samuel, 4:276). Georg Wilhelm Friedrich Hegel (1770–1831) saw the new forces being discovered and retheorized by natural science, such as magnetism, as part of a Neoplatonic cosmological unity, unfolding itself in the worldly realm, even as Plotinus's One emanated down the hierarchy. This interest laid the groundwork for the first modern scholarly edition of Plotinus's work (by Georg Friedrich Creuzer in 1835).

In the 20th century Martin Heidegger (1889–1976)

was attracted by Plotinus's notion that the One was literally beyond being, drawing on Plotinus to interpret Plato's *Sophist* in a lecture course in 1924–1925. Two years later the fundamentally antimetaphysical philosopher would publish *Sein und Zeit* (*Being and Time*), suggesting that *Dasein,* or "being-in-the-world," was the only realm of being to which we had access. *Sein,* pure Being, was inaccessible to humans and for all practical purposes nonexistent. Yet in its *impossibility* of access, Heidegger's Being reminds one of the *difficulty* of access of Plotinus's One. Plotinus reached unification with the One only a few times during his life, Porphyry tells us. After the death of God, the prophet of postmodernity could not find grounds to conceive of a suprahuman entity, even as he was haunted by the imagined trace of a transcendent unity above the world we inhabit.

BIBL.: Lloyd Gerson, ed., *The Cambridge Companion to Plotinus* (Cambridge 1996). Pierre Hadot, *Plotinus, or the Simplicity of Vision,* trans. M. Chase (Chicago 1993). James Hankins, *Plato in the Italian Renaissance,* 2 vols. (Leiden 1989). Iamblicchus, *De mysteriis,* ed. and trans. Emma Clarke, John Dillon, and Jackson Hershbell (Boston 2004). Dominic J. O'Meara, *Plotinus: An Introduction to the Enneads* (Oxford 1993). Plotinus, *Enneads,* 7 vols., ed. and trans. A. H. Armstrong (Cambridge, Mass., 1966–1988). Pseudo-Dionysius, *De mystica theologia,* in *Corpus Dionysiacum,* ed. G. Heil and A. M. Ritter (Berlin 1991) 2:139–150. Lucas Siorvanes, *Proclus: Neo-Platonic Philosophy and Science* (New Haven 1996). Eugène N. Tigerstedt, *The Decline and Fall of the Neoplatonic Interpretation of Plato* (Helsinki 1974). C.C.

Neptune

Neptune was the Roman god of fresh and salt water, a conflation of the Etruscan god of wells (Nethuns) and the Greek god of the sea (Poseidon).

Though in antiquity Neptune was often pictured similarly to his brother Jupiter, as a vigorous man with copious locks and a wavy beard, images of him differed from those of his brother in several respects. Neptune was never shown seated on a throne (as Jupiter was), but always in an upright position. In contrast to Jupiter, who was never represented with his foot set on the eagle, Neptune was frequently depicted with his foot on a dolphin or a ship's bow. He held a trident (a three-pronged staff), symbolic, according to Servius (1.138), of the three types of water: sea, river, and spring. The trident's origins are subject to debate. Guillaume du Choul argued in 1559 that it sprang from an "instrument very necessary to seamen."

Two contradictory aspects of the Roman image of Neptune influenced the subsequent depiction of this god. One is his quintessential association with water. On the one hand he is seen as controlling the irrational forces of the ever-changing marine world, but on the other hand he personifies the uncontrollable passions signified by flowing water. Both sides of his persona manifest themselves in the art created in the post-classical era. Neptune is depicted triumphantly, standing in a chariot drawn by richly crested *hippocampi* (seahorses), either holding his trident still or shaking it aggressively. Several depictions of the god show a dolphin under his foot (not a nautical bow, as on antique coins) to convey his sovereignty over the marine domain, where every creature is subservient to him. (He is occasionally accompanied by either his wife, Amphitrite the Nereid, or their son Triton, a merman, who blows a conch shell to proclaim the end of a storm.)

Another aspect of the Roman image of Neptune is important to understanding the reasons for erecting his statues from the 16th century onward, although this aspect is barely visible in portrayals of the god. It concerns his distinction from Jupiter, who is always pictured regally (Ovid, *Metamorphoses* 6.74), as befits the supreme ruler of the gods. Neptune was believed to have his own palace on the ocean floor, not on Olympus among the other gods who surrounded his brother. In response to the needs of local propaganda, his subordination, albeit not his total obedience, to Jupiter is stressed. An analogy was drawn in works of art and literature between Neptune's relationship to Jupiter and local dukes' service to the Holy Roman Emperor Charles V.

The Greek custom of erecting statues of the god of the sea in cities that were important seaports was revived during the Renaissance. A statue of Neptune was set in the central square of Messina and on the impressive staircase of the Doge's Palace in Venice. Bologna and Florence also featured statues of this god, designed to celebrate not only an exit to the sea but also the finding of a source of fresh water. As a declaration of intent for preserving antique values in more recent times, his statues have been erected in such cities as Gdansk, Berlin, and Bristol. Most of the images of Neptune provoke a recollection of the god's truncated exclamation, *Quos ego!* (literally, "You whom I!"), wrathfully addressed to Aeolus, the Keeper of the Winds, who created a tempest (Virgil, *Aeneid* 1.135). In most European cities there is only one statue of Neptune, but Rome has several of them in notable locations, including the Piazza Navona, the Piazza del Popolo, and the *rione* Trevi. L.FR.

Nero

Roman emperor (37–68 CE). One of the relatively few figures of antiquity still known today, at least in name, to a broad public. Today he evokes above all matricide, the persecution of Christians—and artistry. His full name as emperor was Nero Claudius Caesar Drusus Germanicus. He was born on 15 December 37 to Gnaeus Domitius Ahenobarbus and Agrippina, a great-granddaughter of Augustus. The mother's burning ambition to play a leading role in Rome supposedly shaped the son's development. The young man's prospects for the principate—and indirectly those of his mother—were initially slight. But Agrippina was exceptionally determined. Seneca was given the task as Nero's educator of preparing him for his future duty. The emperor Claudius, married to Agrippina in 49, was induced to wed Nero to his daughter Octavia, and, against the interests of his own son Britannicus, he adopted Nero in 50. When the emperor died a possibly violent death in October 54, everything was prepared for the succession.

The young *princeps*'s affinity for literature, creative art, and the attractions of the big city was, to the detriment of his political duties, uncommonly intense. But his two most important advisers, the Praetorian Prefect Sextus Afranius Burrus and Seneca, long provided for the orderly management of affairs in both domestic politics (especially vis-à-vis the Senate) and in all questions of imperial administration. On that account later tradition considered the first five years of Nero's reign to be exemplary, a *quinquennium Neronis*.

Agrippina's struggle for political influence was adroitly checked by Seneca, but Nero was so unsettled by his mother's constant meddling in questions of politics and even in his own personal life that in 59 he decided to have her killed. Only after his mother's death did his desire intensify for the stage appearances that would end up giving such firm shape to his memory. He initially performed in small circles, and then for the first time before a general audience in Naples in 64. Against the growing opposition of the Senate, Nero stuck to his dramatic performances and even increased their number. Starting in 65 he performed regularly in the capital itself and paid less and less attention to the conventions of the upper class. Should the frequency of Nero's artistic appearances have been more than vanity and exhibitionism, then they may have been intended to offend his senatorial critics and to win the *plebs urbana* entirely over to his side in a bid to retain power.

Nero bore no personal responsibility for the great fire of Rome in 64, but public opinion turned against him and his intimate circle. Christians were convicted of arson and offered up as culprits to appease the public's rage. It was only after the destruction of a central section of Rome in this catastrophe that Nero was able to plan the Domus Aurea, a vast palace and park complex. The Domus Aurea was not yet completed at the time of Nero's death, but its remains reveal that he was an imaginative builder who engaged the most talented men of his time for the job.

Nero's admiration for Greek culture was extraordinarily intense. In September 66, despite a freshly discovered conspiracy and difficult political problems in the capital and in the dissatisfied western part of the empire, he traveled to Greece for several months. As a participant in all the festivals, which in his honor were held outside their regular calendar, he had himself awarded many prizes. In a speech that is still extant as an inscription, Nero granted freedom to the enthusiastic Greeks of the province of Achaea. His attempt to dig a canal through the Isthmus of Corinth was a continuation of earlier projects. It is difficult to say whether these are cases of delusional vanity or of a genuine philhellenism that in a certain way anticipates developments of later decades.

Unrest in the western provinces forced Nero to return home early. Trusting in his irreplaceability as the last direct descendant of Augustus, he reacted too late and too carelessly. When even the Praetorian Guard deserted him and the Senate declared him a public enemy, the only resort left him was suicide, which he committed in June 68. His last words are supposed to have been *Qualis artifex pereo* ("What an artist dies with me!"). If this tradition is true, then he really did see himself at the end of his life more as an artist than as *princeps*.

Nero's condemnation by the senatorial tradition (Tacitus) was not the only form of his reception in antiquity. His grave site continued to be decorated with flowers for a long time, and his portraiture style was imitated by private citizens again and again. A characteristic witness to Nero's later—pagan—memory in Rome as a builder, a provident ruler, and a host of festivals are the contorniate medallions of the 4th and 5th centuries.

The nebulous circumstances surrounding Nero's death led to the belief that he was not really dead, but rather would return one day from the east. A result of this belief was the appearance in Greece and Asia Minor of false Neros who tried to take advantage of the enthusiasm of a part of the Greek people for the emperor's philhellenic politics. The Christian reception of Nero can be seen through his importance for the history of the early Church. The burning of Rome and the subsequent punishment of Christians made him a persecutor in the eyes of Christian authors (starting with Tertullian). At the end of the 1st century Nero became for the Christian tradition a harbinger or a servant of the Antichrist, or even the Antichrist himself. The dreadful beast of the Apocalypse (chap. 13) is perhaps meant to be Nero.

In the Middle Ages there was also a certain amount of theological speculation about Nero as the Antichrist. Yet actual historical knowledge was paltry, confined to the burning of Rome and the murder of his mother. Nero's memory gained in political importance from the occasional use of his name as a fighting word in the controversy between the pope and secular rulers.

As familiarity with the ancient sources (Suetonius, Tacitus) grew, Humanists started seeing Nero again as a tyrant in accordance with the senatorial tradition. A distinctive exception is the *Encomium Neronis* of Girolamo Cardano (1501–1576), a comprehensive defense of Nero that clashes with the prevailing opinions of his contemporaries and is meant as a personal criticism of the politics of the Milanese "Senate" of his time.

The most important aspect of the modern reception of Nero is its sense of him as an artist and builder. The rediscovered remains of the Domus Aurea had a great influence on artists of the time (e.g., Raphael). The modern term *grotesque* derives from the ornate murals that were discovered in the underground grottoes of the Domus Aurea and then imitated. In the Baroque period Nero appears in drama (e.g., Lohenstein, *Agrippina,* 1665) and opera (e.g., Monteverdi, *L'incoronazione di Poppaea,* 1643), above all as an example of tyranny and egocentrism.

Nero's self-portrayal as a *princeps* who simultaneously wanted to be an artist could find no purchase among his senatorial contemporaries, who always oriented themselves by Augustus' model. Recent research no longer accepts the image passed down from antiquity of the eccentric artist incapable of coping with his duties as a ruler. Nero's stage performances are reinterpreted as a calculated act of self-promotion in the face of an oppositional Senate; the creative elements of his building policy are given greater recognition; and his philhellenic political program—which recurs later in no uncertain terms, for example in Hadrian—is evaluated as a conscious, untimely innovation.

The perception of Nero in recent times has, however, not been shaped by research but by Henryk Sienkiewicz's 1894 novel, *Quo Vadis,* which was filmed in 1951 with Peter Ustinov in the leading role. It is therefore no accident that in the Caesar's Palace hotel complex in Las Vegas, Nero is portrayed not as a ruler on the model of Augustus, but as a singer with a cithara.

BIBL.: Edward Champlin, *Nero* (Cambridge, Mass., 2003). Nikolaus Eberi, *Cardanos Encomium Neroni* (Frankfurt 1994). Margaret Malamud, "Living Like Romans in Las Vegas: The Roman World at Caesar's Palace," in Sandra R. Joshel, Margaret Malamud, and Donald T. McGuire, eds., *Imperial Projections: Ancient Rome in Modern Popular Culture* (Baltimore 2001) 249–270. Maria Wyke, "Make Like Nero! The Appeal of a Cinematic Emperor," in Jas Elsner and Jamie Masters, eds., *Reflections of Nero: Culture, History and Representation* (London 1994) 11–28. J.M.

Translated by Patrick Baker

Nicetas Codex

Illustrated manuscripts on ancient medicine and surgery are extremely rare, even though many procedures are best explained visually. The most important survivor is the Nicetas codex, written in Constantinople in the first half of the 10th century for a surgeon, Nicetas, and now in Florence in the Biblioteca Medicea Laurenziana. The codex was included in the library of the Orphanage of Alexius Comnenus, and later in that of the Hospital of the Forty Martyrs. It contains the commentary on Hippocrates, *On Joints,* by Apollonius of Citium (fl. 100 BCE) and a section on bandaging from Soranus of Ephesus (fl. 120 CE), both illustrated with drawings that in essence, although not in detail, go back to their authors. Brought from Crete to Florence by Lascaris in 1492, the Nicetas codex was in 1530 in the hands of Giulio de' Medici, Pope Clement V, who loaned it back to Lascaris for a proposed and never completed edition of the medical and surgical texts it contained. From a copy made by Lascaris, now in Paris in the Bibliothèque Nationale, Ferdinando Balami produced the first Latin translation of Galen's *On Bones* (1535). This copy, illuminated by Santorinos of Rhodes, entered the library of Cardinal Ridolfi, who arranged for yet a third copy to be prepared by Christoph Auer and sent as a present to Francis I in 1542. This volume, now also in the Bibliothèque Nationale, was taken to Paris by a young Florentine doctor, Guido Guidi (Vidus Vidius), who had prepared a Latin translation of the surgical texts. Guidi was appointed royal physician and the first reader in medicine at the Collège de France. His translation, titled *Chirurgia,* was published in 1544 in Paris, by P. Gaultier, with illustrations by artists of the school of Salutati and Primaticcio, who were working for the king. The book was an instant success, prized as much for its beauty as for its medical information. The illustrations continued to be reproduced and to influence later depictions of surgery, as well as to emphasize the lost elegance of classical surgery. The original manuscript shows both patients and doctors naked, but the later copies, and the book, show the doctor clothed and the patient in full vigor.

BIBL.: M. D. Grmek, "Vestigia della chirurgia greca: Il codice di Niceta e i suoi discendenti," *Cos* 1 (1984) 48–60. V.N.

Niebuhr, Barthold Georg

German historian (1776–1831). Niebuhr was the son of the Danish explorer Carsten Niebuhr, who was famous for his travels in Arabia, Persia, and India. Barthold was considered a child prodigy with an extraordinary talent for languages. At the age of 15 he was already corresponding with the classical scholar Christian Gottlob Heyne about a Pindar manuscript in the Royal Library in Copenhagen. After being educated privately and attending the University of Kiel (1794–1796), he entered the Danish civil service, but he was first permitted to spend a year and a half studying in London and Edinburgh. Upon his return, he occupied several administrative positions in finance, becoming director of the National Bank of Denmark in 1804. At the same time he developed an interest in the history of the Roman Republic, which he saw as having balanced the interests of patricians and plebeians while protecting an agrarian economy. Prompted by contemporary controversies over the liberation of peasants, Niebuhr produced numerous manuscripts on the agrarian reforms of the Gracchi (first published in 1981 by A. Heuss)—reforms that he did not regard as having been revolutionary alterations of the property laws. Niebuhr's views were in part a reaction to the failed attempt by François-Noël "Gracchus" Babeuf to instigate an uprising in France in 1796 that was intended to bring about a redistribution of land; Babeuf had cited the Roman agrarian laws to legitimate his aims.

Despite the uncertain future of the Prussian state, Niebuhr accepted an offer to join the Prussian civil service; on his arrival in Berlin in 1806, however, he was forced to flee with the government to Königsberg (Kaliningrad, in Russia). He contributed greatly to financing Prussia's war debts (and reparation payments) and consolidating the currency. Throughout his life Niebuhr was uncertain whether he should devote himself primarily to scholarship or government service. After various conflicts, he resigned his official post in June 1810. Having just been elected a member of the Prussian Academy of Sciences, he began giving lectures on Roman history at the newly founded University of Berlin in November 1810.

Niebuhr's lectures created a stir because he voiced doubts about the reliability of ancient historiography (doubts that had been expressed by earlier scholars, such as Perizonius, although neither Niebuhr nor the public was aware of this) and presented a reconstruction of historical events based on a critical analysis of the source material. In taking this approach, he became the founder of a new field, the critical historiography of antiquity.

Though Niebuhr is recognized as the founding father of the modern study of ancient history, many of his conclusions, based on analogies and "divination" as well as his expertise as a political economist and man of affairs, have not stood the test of time. His work was accompanied by rapidly swelling criticism of his treatment of the sources and his reconstructions of the history and constitution of the Roman Republic. When his *Römische Geschichte* (*Roman History*) was published in its first two volumes in 1811–1812, covering the period up to the end of the struggle between the orders of patricians and plebeians in the later 4th century BCE, contemporary critics found fault with his style, which did not meet the literary standards associated with historiography.

The resumption of war against Napoleon in 1813 required Niebuhr to reenter active government service as an expert on finance. From 1816 to 1823 he served as Prussian envoy in Rome; the territorial changes required negotiations with the Vatican on Prussian law concerning the Catholic Church, and Niebuhr achieved a favorable settlement for Prussia. He used his journeys to and from Rome to search for unknown texts; in Verona he made the sensational discovery of the *Institutes* of Gaius, and on his return he discovered Merobaudes' *Panegyricus* to Aetius.

Niebuhr then settled in Bonn. From 1825 until his death in 1831 he lectured on many aspects of Roman history at the University of Bonn, revised his *Roman History* (a third volume was published posthumously in 1832), and was active in organizing various projects, such as the founding of the *Rheinisches Museum für Philologie* (a scholarly periodical) and an edition of Byzantine sources.

BIBL.: Alfred Heuss, *Barthold Georg Niebuhrs wissenschaftliche Anfänge* (Göttingen 1981). Arnaldo D. Momigliano, "Perizonius, Niebuhr and the Character of Early Roman Tradition," *Journal of Roman Studies* 47, no. 1/2 (1957) 104–114. Ronald T. Ridley, "*Leges agrariae:* Myths, Ancient and Modern," *Classical Philology* 95, no. 4 (2000) 459–467. Gerrit Walther, *Niebuhrs Forschung* (Stuttgart 1993). Barthold C. Witte, *Der preussische Tacitus* (Düsseldorf 1979). W.N.

Translated by Deborah Lucas Schneider

Nietzsche, Friedrich

Classical philologist and philosopher (1844–1900). He conceived of the relationship between antiquity and modernity as a "rebirth" or a (partial) "continuation" or as a rupture. The "abiding bond of love between German and Greek culture" leads, according to the early Nietzsche (*Birth of Tragedy,* 1872), to a "rebirth" of tragedy, of German myth, even of Greek antiquity. The history of Europe, writes Nietzsche the critic in his most lucid book (*Human, All Too Human*, 1878), must be made "into a continuation of that of Greece." The concepts of Nature and Reason and the criticism of myth make up that "ring of culture that now links us with the enlightenment of Graeco-Roman antiquity." Other equally central concepts for this connection, such as (Roman) Law, Freedom, and Equality, were omitted by Nietzsche, no doubt deliberately.

In addition to the paradigms of "rebirth" and "continuity," Nietzsche also uses—and simultaneously, at that—the paradigm of "rupture." The foundation of ancient cultures, particularly in the realms of religion and myth, is for us "unsound"; the world of Greece is "irretrievable"; the "death" of ancient culture is "unavoidable" ("We Philologists," 1875, *KSA* 8.83–84). The consequence—or the root—of this paradigm is the end of Christianity, which Nietzsche understood utterly as an ancient religion: "With Christianity antiquity will be swept away" (*KSA* 7.80).

Nietzsche plays an important role in the persistent presence of Greek antiquity, whether positively or negatively received, outside scholarship and schools and among the educated classes and the intelligentsia, whose circles are generally marked by a modern outlook and unconcern for Christianity. Nietzsche modernized and contorted the German tradition of philhellenism, for which he stood as a new witness. Contemporaries saw a direct line from Johann J. Winckelmann—murdered in Trieste in 1768—and Friedrich Hölderlin—from 1805 unhinged in a tower in Tübingen—to Friedrich Nietzsche, who from 1889 to 1900 lived in "mental derangement" in Jena, Naumberg, and even in Goethe's Weimar. His secondary education at the elite Schulpforta school (1858–1864), his studies in Bonn and Leipzig (1864–1869), and his career as a teacher and professor in Basel (1869–1879) profoundly connected Nietzsche to this tradition. Hölderlin was the darling of his time at Schulpforta. Richard Wagner's (1813–1883) reception of antiquity—Wagner being for a time an admired father figure and friend—strengthened his faith in the fruitfulness and relevance of the ancients for the moderns: "Schopenhauer and Goethe, Aeschylus and Pindar live yet, believe me" (Nietzsche to Erwin Rohde, 3 September 1869). Humanistic education, classical literature, and the temporary enthusiasm for the renewal of ancient drama in Wagner's Bayreuth Festival were, needless to say, complemented and contrasted by other strong influences that shaped his life and work: birth into a long line of Protestant ministers; fascination with the flourishing natural sciences, especially biology; dread of democracy, mass society, and the strengthening of the fourth estate.

The most important of Nietzsche's writings on antiquity and its reception are, in chronological order: (1) texts dating to his secondary schooling (essays on Theognis) and university education (comments and glosses on lectures), his own lectures (on Aeschylus, Sophocles, Euripides' *Bacchae*) and publications (on Diogenes Laertius, Theognis, the *Certamen Homeri et Hesiodi*); and (2) popular and philosophical writings, "The Greek State" (1872), *The Birth of Tragedy from the Spirit of Music* (1872), an unfinished tragedy entitled "Empedocles" (1870–1872), *Philosophy in the Tragic Age of the Greeks* (1873), "On the Uses and Disadvantages of History for Life" (1874), drafts of "We Philologists" (1875), *Human, All Too Human* (1878), *The Antichrist* (1888, on ancient Judaism and Christianity, among other things), "What I Owe the Ancients" (1888), and "Dionysus-Dithyrambs" (1889).

In these texts Nietzsche presents antiquity as an archaic (antimodern), aristocratic (antidemocratic, antisocialist), and anti-Christian (alternative) utopia. Nietzsche's antiquity is an academic, heuristic construct useful for scholarship and the critique of culture and religion. The most popular of these texts, widely diffused as a programmatic statement for the Bayreuth movement, was that on the birth of tragedy: sprung from music, Nietzsche argues, its "Dionysian" essence was forced by an "Apollonian" power into a new form. Philologists criticized this writing for certain details of literary and religious history as well as for the intrusion of Schopenhauer's philosophy and Wagner's sacralizing reform of opera. Nietzsche himself criticized its clumsiness and frantic imagery. The most important things for Nietzsche the philosopher were the free-thinking impulse of ancient materialism (Democritus, Epicurus, Lucretius, Diogenes Laertius) and the ancient evidence from the Presocratics and the Stoics. From these sources he developed his doctrine of eternal return, thus winning for himself an argument, legitimated in antiquity, against the doctrine of salvation and eschatology.

Nietzsche's most fruitful contribution to classical scholarship was his elucidation of what would later be called the archaic period (8th–6th cents. BCE). He highlighted the autonomy of the polis, the decentralized structure of Hellenic culture, and the agonal, manly, aggressive characteristics of the Greek world, and he recognized the meaning of the Panhellenic cults and festivals for this competitive society, composed of so many small, independent parts. Accordingly, archaic and archaizing authors (Theognis, Pindar), the Presocratics, and early drama all rise in value. Most dangerous for scholarship is Nietzsche's inclusion of teachings about race and breeding into his historical discourse, his antithesis between Judaism-Christianity and Hellenism ("Dionysus against the crucified"), and his interpretation of the history of ancient Israel "as a typical history of the denaturalizing of all natural values" (*Antichrist,* chap. 25). For this, too, he had guidelines from antiquity: the anti-Semitic tradition in Tacitus' excursus on the Jews (*Histories* 5), which in 1880 Nietzsche had excerpted (*KSA* 9.270–277).

Nietzsche's image of antiquity made its effect felt through his friends (Erwin Rohde), pupils (Jacob Wackernagel), and students (Karl Reinhardt the elder). Ernst Holzer, Otto Crusius, and Wilhelm Nestle later oversaw the collection of his philological writings, and classical philologists participated in assembling the Nietzsche Archive. Nietzsche's influence on classical scholarship, however, was and is slight. The sarcastic criticism that Ulrich von Wilamowitz-Moellendorff, his fellow student from Schulpforta, heaped on his first work (1872) destroyed his philological prestige. The majority of classicists, who tended to be liberal or conservative, nationalist or Christian, were uneasy with the free-thinking, ultraconservative, European, anti-Christian teachings of their erstwhile colleague who was slowly becoming famous. Nevertheless, a considerable number of contacts with classical philologists and historians can be traced in the Nietzsche Archive in Weimar, which houses his scholarly and personal *Nachlass* as well as evidence of a cult of Nietzsche once tended in ancient style—to mention a few names: Franz Altheim, Hans Blüher, Ernst Bickel, Ludwig Gurlitt, Richard Heinze, Werner Jaeger, Walther Kranz, Walter F. Otto, Karl Reinhardt (elder and younger), and Gilbert Murray. Nietzsche's antiquity remained known beyond academic philology and philosophy (Walter Benjamin, Martin Heidegger), particularly through the efforts of W. F. Otto (1874–1958), a classical philologist in Frankfurt, Königsberg (Kaliningrad), and Tübingen. Otto, occasionally mocked as "Nietzsche redivivus," was one of the directors of the Nietzsche Archive (from 1933). He outdid Nietzsche's criticism of Christianity (1923) and broadly expanded on his statements and aphorisms regarding inebriation, masks, tragedy, and the mysticism of life in an informative monograph on religion and contemporary history (*Dionysus,* 1933).

BIBL.: S. Aschheim, *The Nietzsche Legacy in Germany, 1890–1990* (Berkeley 1992). H. Cancik, *Nietzsches Antike: Vorlesung,* 2nd ed. (Stuttgart 2000). H. Cancik and H. Cancik-Lindemaier, *Philolog und Kultfigur: Friedrich Nietzsche und seine Antike in Deutschland* (Stuttgart 1999). *Friedrich Nietzsche, Sämtliche Werke: Kritische Studienausgabe (KSA),* ed. Giorgio Colli and Mazzino Montinari (Berlin 1980). J. C. O'Flaherty, T. F. Sellner, and R. M. Helm, eds., *Studies in Nietzsche and the Classical Tradition* (Chapel Hill 1976) and *Studies in Nietzsche and the Judaeo-Christian Tradition* (Chapel Hill 1985). J. Porter, *Nietzsche and the Philology of the Future* (Stanford 2000). M. S. Silk and J. P. Stern, *Nietzsche on Tragedy* (Cambridge 1981). B. von Reibnitz, *Ein Kommentar zu Friedrich Nietzsche: "Die Geburt der Tragödie aus dem Geiste der Musik"* (Stuttgart 1992), chaps. 1–12. H.C.

Translated by Patrick Baker

Notitia Dignitatum

The *Notitia omnium dignitatum et amministrationum tam ciuilium quam militarium* is, as its full title implies, "a list of all ranks and administrative posts both military and civil." This bureaucratic conspectus of Roman government and military resources was first compiled sometime in the 4th century CE (and no doubt regularly updated) by a trusted court official, the *primicerius no-*

tariorum, the most senior of the *notarii,* a secretariat closely associated with the emperor. The surviving copy of the *Notitia* is a composite document. It offers a fairly comprehensive view of the administrative and military establishments in the eastern half of the empire at the end of the 4th century, and, somewhat later and more haphazardly, in the West.

The *Notitia* consists principally of a series of lists: an outline catalogue of civil positions and the staff serving each administrative department, and a list of military commands and the troops under each high-ranking officer's disposition. Detailed illustrations were an integral part of each entry; those for the praetorian prefects, the most powerful civil officials in the empire, showed their documents of appointment (*codicilli*), exhibited between burning tapers on a blue cloth-covered table, a sumptuous state carriage sheathed in silver, and a large golden ceremonial inkwell (*theca*) more than three feet high and decorated in relief with images of the emperor.

The text and illustrations of the *Notitia* were preserved in a codex (now lost save for a single unillustrated bifolium) in the cathedral library at Speyer. Count Palatine Ottheinrich (1502–1559) was presented with a copy by the cathedral chapter in 1550. Ottheinrich was dissatisfied with the copy's illustrations, whose modernizing, Gothic style he disliked, and had the originals traced on oiled paper and bound together with the first set. It is likely that these offer a more reliable guide to the illustrations in the original 5th-century manuscript than the versions by the French miniaturist Peronet Lamy that illustrate two earlier copies of the Speyer codex, one made in 1436 for Pietro Donato, bishop of Padua, and a second, produced around the same time, for Francesco Pizolpasso, archbishop of Milan. Whatever the deficiencies of Lamy's illustrations as copies, they are good examples of an early Humanist engagement with antique art, and in a manner later to influence Andrea Mantegna and the Paduan school.

The Speyer codex and its exemplar were probably written in insular script, and it is tempting to speculate (in part, also based on the other works collected together in the codex) that the *Notitia* may originally have been transmitted to the Continent by Alcuin, perhaps through one of his pupils. It has also been suggested that some 9th-century Carolingian miniatures show clear allusions to the *Notitia*'s illustrations. Whatever the precise details, Carolingian interest in the *Notitia* reflects part of a wider claim by Charlemagne and his successors to the political and cultural authority of a reestablished Roman Empire. Along with copies of other texts included in the Speyer codex—such as *De rebus bellicis* (an illustrated 4th-century treatise containing innovative designs for war machines) and a number of topographical and geographical works—the *Notitia dignitatum* offered an attractive image of administrative sophistication and imperial stability: an image that was already largely illusory in the West when the archetype was revised for the last time in the 5th century CE.

BIBL.: Pamela Berger, *The Insignia of the Notitia Dignitatum* (New York 1981). Peter Brennan, "The Notitia Dignitatum," in *Les littératures techniques dans l'antiquité romaine: Statut, public et destination, tradition,* ed. Claude Nicolet (Geneva 1996) 147–178. Roger Goodburn and Philip Bartholomew, eds., *Aspects of the Notitia Dignitatum* (Oxford 1976). Robert Grigg, "Illustrations and Text in the Lost Codex Spirensis," *Latomus* 46 (1987) 204–210.

C.KE.

Novel

The literature of the classical world included significant genres of prose fiction, including the Heliodorian romance and the Menippean satire, but it is generally considered that the novel, which arose in the 18th century with Richardson and Fielding in England, with Prévost and Rousseau in France, and with Goethe in the German lands, and which was eventually to dominate Western literary art, was, as these writers themselves saw it, "a new kind of writing" that owed very little to classical precursors. Most of that little involved the prose fiction satire of Lucian, Apuleius, and Petronius, whose influence can be clearly seen in *Don Quixote,* in *Gargantua et Pantagruel,* and in *Tristram Shandy;* even later echoes of Menippean satire can be located in postmodern contemporary writers such as Thomas Pynchon and Don DeLillo. The romance, both Greek and Latin, was more long-winded and more short-lived. Only the most tenuous connections link the classical romances of Chariton, Longus, and Heliodorus with the medieval romances that were based on national sagas, such as the Arthurian legends, the French songs of Charlemagne and his paladins, and the saga of the Volsungs. Nor is the medieval flowering of romance implicated in the growth of the realistic novel, which grew from roots in journalism, history, travel literature, and other factual narrative. (A counterclaim has been made by Margaret Doody in *The True Story of the Novel,* 1996.)

This is not to say that the modern novel entirely neglected the classical world. Those who created the new art form in the 18th century looked to the literary criticism of classical antiquity for rules to govern texts whose like Aristotle and Horace had never seen. And for literary theorists up until our own day, the novel has defined itself in contrast to the epic, the form of narrative at the zenith of the ordering of the arts in the ancient world. Finally, beginning in the mid-19th century, the classical erudition that had long immersed serious readers in the poetry and prose of the ancient world began to lose its hold on the educational system, and it was just then, perhaps not accidentally, that the historical novel began to create for the reading public a vision of antiquity, one that changed according to the needs of the dominant forces of the period, from the era of Bulwer-Lytton to that of Gore Vidal and Mary Renault.

In his preface to *Joseph Andrews* (1742), Henry Fielding appealed to Aristotle and Homer to define his undertaking, which he called "a comic epic-poem in prose," based on the lost *Margites* of Homer and suitably different from serious epic by including light and ridiculous actions, characters of inferior rank and manners, and language that included parodies and burlesque imitations of serious literary forms. In doing so, Fielding defined his shapely comic forms against a literary scene that included rambling, episodic fictional autobiographies, like Defoe's *Moll Flanders* (1722) and the 1741 continuation of *Pamela* by Samuel Richardson. In Aristotelian fashion, Fielding argued that a novel must recount a single, unified action from beginning through middle to end, that a comic novel must substitute ridicule for the tragic catharsis, and that the representation of affectation and hypocrisy should replace pity and fear as the means to that end. Before Fielding, a poetics of the novel would have been an impertinence; after Fielding, the novel had its place in the neoclassical Augustan world.

Naturally, once it had a place, the novel tended to sit down in someone else's place, or to stand on its head. The narrator of Laurence Sterne's *Tristram Shandy* (1760) begins his shaggy dog autobiography at the moment of his own conception, and plans, he says in chapter 4, "to go on, tracing every thing in it, as Horace says, *ab Ovo*" (lit., "from the egg," *Ars poetica* 147). Sterne's learned reader is expected to remember that in the *Ars poetica* (also known as the Epistle to the Pisos) Horace had praised Homer for beginning the *Iliad* with the anger of Achilles, rather than going all the way back to the egg from which Helen of Troy had hatched (Zeus had come to her mother, Leda, in the form of a swan). And Tristram goes on, "Horace, I know, does not recommend this fashion altogether: But that gentleman is speaking only of an epic poem or a tragedy;—(I forget which,) besides, if it was not so, I should beg Mr. Horace's pardon;—for in writing what I have set about, I shall confine myself neither to his rules, nor to any man's rules that ever lived."

By the 20th century the opposition between epic and novel had become a commonplace of literary theory, although each major theorist set up the opposition in his own way. Georg Lukács, writing *The Theory of the Novel* as a young Hegelian in 1914–1915, before his Marxist phase, viewed the novel as having taken the place of the epic, which it transcended but also destroyed in the process. The epic hero is representative of his society; the epic narrative is the story not of an individual but of his community, a community that is known in its totality. In the novel, on the other hand, the community cannot be known in that way, for it is still—always—in the process of coming into being. The hero of the novel too is an individual whose destiny is problematic, something that he or she must discover in the course of events.

Mikhail M. Bakhtin in "Epic and Novel" (1941) regarded the distinction as primarily one of discourse. Whereas the epic has a single voice, that of the epic narrator, restricted to a single tone, the carnivalesque novel revels in its plurality of competing voices, its "stylistic three-dimensionality," along with its "multi-languaged consciousness," lustily incorporating into itself any genre with which it comes into contact. The novel's time is characteristically the present, fraught with forces of change, whereas the epic is always set deep within the past, a past that holds the present in its grip. The epic is about memory, the novel about coming to learn.

Erich Auerbach, in *Mimesis* (1946), took a somewhat different tack. For him the epic mode of representation is directly opposed not to the novelistic, but to the biblical. Homer presents reality as schematic, lying on the surface, accessible through the selection of details used to sketch characters and events. In Homer past events not only shape the present situation, they also can be represented as present memory through the narrative vision. In the Bible, on the other hand, reality is implicit rather than explicit; the figural representation of the patriarchs and kings suggests that the interior truth of their histories is contained in a vision too vast and deep to be expressed in words. This figural vision therefore demands interpretation and exegesis, in which the individual event becomes iconic for a reality that recurs in later history. Auerbach views both the schematic and the figural modes of representation as vectors within the history of narrative, arguing that both of them shaped the novel throughout its history, which he traces from Cervantes to Marcel Proust and Virginia Woolf.

Even if the novel stands opposed to the classical epic, it engulfed the ancient world, as it engulfed the other exotic eras of the past, through historical fiction, which gave access to an exotic past for those unwilling to travel the path of scholarly history. As early as the late 18th century, German novelists such as Wieland and Heinse had experimented with various novelistic forms set in an idealized ancient Greece, and Hölderlin's *Hyperion* (1797–1799) had embedded a story of the doomed revolutionary aspirations of modern Greece in profound philosophical reflections on ancient Greece and modern times. A few decades later, with the same refulgent prose that has made his name a synonym for bad writing, Edward Bulwer-Lytton pioneered the genre in his romance of the classical world entitled *The Last Days of Pompeii* (1834), set just before the eruption of Vesuvius in 79 CE. Despite the lovingly reproduced antique decor, his Rome and Pompeii are peopled by the usual inhabitants of Victorian melodrama: pert servants, grasping shopkeepers, wicked debauchees, tender maidens, and the occasional gentleman of principle. But one can tell that we are not in England because Christianity is a religion taken with desperate seriousness by those few who profess it. Many of *Pompeii*'s successors in the 19th century also focused on the confrontation between earnest Christians and dissolute pagans. Not only Lew Wallace's *Ben Hur* (1880) and Henryk Sienkiewicz's *Quo Vadis* (1896), but even Walter Pater's philosophical novel *Marius the Epicurean* (1885) fits this pattern: Pater's pagan hero, moving through Epicureanism to Stoicism, contemplates the end of his life as a Christian. Charles Kingsley reversed the formula by making Hypatia a central figure in a heavily researched, sharply anti-Catholic novel, *Hypatia, or the New Foes with an Old Face* (1853). He represents her death, depicted in a vividly erotic way, as the murder of Hellenism and Reason by a mob of wild Christians, many of them monks—the end of antiquity, embodied. To similar effect, Gore Vidal's *Julian* (1964) portrays a virtuous pagan struggling tragically against bigoted and hypocritical Christian leaders in the generation after Constantine.

Since the 20th century, as totalitarianisms of various kinds have threatened democratic polities, the Roman novel has tended to be concerned with political change in the century after the death of Julius Caesar, the gradual replacement of republican institutions with imperial military tyranny. Thornton Wilder's *The Ides of March* (1948) views with an ironic eye the social and sexual chaos that preceded the anarchy of 44 BCE, much as Robert Graves's *I, Claudius* and *Claudius the God* (1934–1935) observe the destruction of residual republican ways and values from the perspective of the most improbable of the early emperors. The attraction of that era may also have to do with the availability of historians like Tacitus and Suetonius on whom to draw for detail.

Historical novels set in ancient Greece have tended to be less presentist than novels about Rome, perhaps because there was no unified nation-state onto which one could project contemporary politics. The best-known have instead retold in prose the legends that the Greeks had originally woven into epic and poetic drama: Robert Graves's *Homer's Daughter* (1955) adapts the story of the *Odyssey* to a female protagonist, and his *Hercules, My Shipmate* (1944) recounts the *Argonautica* of Apollonius of Rhodes. André Gide's last novel was *Thesée* (1946), a rendering of the myths about Theseus. Mary Renault is perhaps the historical novelist most celebrated for rendering the land and people of ancient Greece in various periods from the archaic era of the Theseus legend (*The King Must Die,* 1958) through the aftermath of Alexander's conquests (*Funeral Games,* 1981). The love lives of her protagonists, always in search of a stable sexual identity, mirrored Renault's own polymorphous relationships. The notion that those who wrote about Rome were often writing about their nations while those who wrote about Greece were writing about themselves is supported by the first novel to be set in ancient Greece, Christoph Wieland's *Agathon* (1766–1767), a thinly veiled spiritual autobiography that influenced the young Goethe.

Today, with some striking exceptions, the literary historical novel, seldom prized throughout its history, does not flourish in England and America (though it continues to survive on the European Continent), and the media that convey to the masses the glory of Greece, the grandeur of Rome, and countless other fantasies as well are the cinema and television. Wolfgang Petersen's *Troy* and Oliver Stone's *Alexander* (both films 2004) have given contemporary viewers a taste of Greek legend and history, in however distorted a form; Michael Apted's television series *Rome* (2005), supported by entire teams of classical specialists, has represented the chaotic era of the First Triumvirate and the Civil Wars from the plebeian perspective of two soldiers whose names were drawn directly from Caesar's *Gallic Wars.* Meanwhile, narrative theory, long concerned with epic and novel, is only beginning to work out the rules and conventions of stories told onscreen, and the relation of the ephemeral flickering image to the eternal epic.

BIBL.: Erich Auerbach, *Mimesis* (Bern 1946). Mikhail M. Bakhtin, "Epic and Novel" (1941), in *The Dialogic Imagination,* ed. and trans. Michael Holquist (Austin 1981) 3–40. Margaret A. Doody, *The True Story of the Novel* (New Brunswick 1996). Georg Lukács, *The Theory of the Novel,* trans. Anna Bostock (Cambridge, Mass., 1971). D.R.

Nudity

Representation of the nude human body on the model of Greek statuary. Since the Middle Ages the nude statue has been considered a distinctive mark of classical antiquity, and rightly so: beginning in archaic Greece, artists, purchasers, and viewers believed that showing the body in full was suited to the celebration of divinity and the commemoration of individual human beings. But the meaning of "ideal nudity" is still debated, and there is a division between those who think it directly reflects the role of the nude body in Greek culture and those who see it substantially as an artistic device.

The Greeks practiced nudity specifically in athletic competitions—which for their part pertained to the religious sphere—and in gymnasia (from *gymnos,* "nude"), institutions common to very many *poleis.* At the center of the gymnasium—a space devoted to athletic and educational activity, and to social and, in particular, homoerotic relations—was the precisely groomed and trained male body. The relationship that Winckelmann many times identified between gymnastic activity and the nudity of statuary is thus anything but baseless. He did not see in the latter a mere illustration of the life of the gymnasia, but rather believed that the admiring familiarity with the nude male body was the foundation of a purely artistic expression. It was along these lines that Canova defended his decision to depict Napoleon nude, claiming that "like the poets, we, too, have our language."

A passage in Pliny (*Natural History* 34.17–18) shows that "heroic nudity" was received by the world of Roman art as a fundamentally Greek element: "In old days the statues dedicated were simply clad in the toga. Also, naked figures holding spears, made from models of Greek young men from gymnasiums—what are called figures of Achilles—became popular. The Greek practice is to leave the figure entirely nude, whereas Roman and military statuary adds a breastplate" (trans. H. Rackham). The case of Gaius Hostilius Mancinus, depicted as a prisoner, nude and with his hands behind his back (Velleius Paterculus 2.1; Pliny, *Natural History* 34.18), reminds us, however, that in the Roman world not all cases of artistic nudity imply the reception of Greek models.

Such is particularly true with the advent of Christianity, which brought about a total redefinition of the body (and of its nudity). The Scriptures, in various situations and personages, drape meanings previously given to nudity with a new sense: innocence and guilt (Adam and Eve before and after the Fall), shame (Noah), obeisance (Job), chastity (Susannah), humiliation (Jesus on the cross). Therefore, images of the baptismal nudity of men (or women: Chapel of St. Isidore in San Marco, Venice), and of Jesus himself, should not be considered per se a reflection of classical "heroic" nudity (even though Winckelmann in his *Gedanken* connects the two). The same goes for other figures in Christian history: Saint Jerome, who proclaims to want to follow "the naked Cross naked" (e.g., the wooden statue of Bertoldo di Giovanni, Faenza), or Saint Francis, who divests himself of his clothing and inherited goods. Even in scenes that depict the resurrections of bodies, nudity derives more from the discussion on the state of the risen that we find in Augustine (*Enarrationes in Psalmos* 51.14) or in Peter Chrysologus (*Sermons* 72). Therefore, there exists in Christian thought an autonomous reflection on the sense of nudity, as can be seen in Petrus Berchorius' quadripartite distinction of *nuditas naturalis* (state of Adam), *temporalis* (voluntary poverty), *virtualis* (innocence achieved through religious practice), and *criminalis* (lechery and vanity).

Despite the cultural revolution effected by Christianity, the Middle Ages did not wipe out "heroic" nudity and even used it polemically against paganism: "idols," against which the Old Testament had already raged, were now by definition naked. In fact, a miniature in the *Vita et passio sancti Killiani* (10th cent., Niedersächsische Landesbibliotek, Hannover), uses an idol, a masculine figure standing naked on a column, to describe the religious practice of the ancients. Other than nudity, these idols have no characteristic traits; they are always slumping on columns while the Holy Family rises, ubiquitous iconography derived from the Gospel of pseudo-Matthew.

And yet it was a column on which, during the Middle Ages and right next to the Lateran palace of the popes, sat the ancient statue of the Spinario, a completely naked child picking a thorn out of his foot (Museo Capitolini). Also in Rome were erected the colossal Dioscuri of Montecavallo: according to the *Mirabilia,* they were naked because all knowledge was "naked and open" to their eyes. Furthermore, in late antiquity and the entire Middle Ages, especially in the East, the apparition of mythological figures almost always coincided with classical nudity: we see it, for example, in the silver plates of the *Byzantinische Antike* of the 6th and 7th centuries, and later ivory caskets. A special case is that of the image of the soul as a small naked body (e.g., in scenes of the *Dormitio Virginis* or in the *Creation of Adam*); it does not derive from the "heroic" nude at all, but from the figurative tradition of the *eidola* attested as early as archaic Greece.

Nude figures, predominantly male, also appear in ornamentation, in the peopled scrolls around the portals of churches or in rarer contexts such as marble candelabra (e.g., Salerno, cathedral); for the most part these are most likely evocations of antiquity rather than precise citations; in fact, nude figures probably acted in and of themselves as references to classical antiquity in the visual memory of medieval man (Himmelmann 1985), in a process that also extends to literary space. Boccaccio, who certainly knew ancient iconography (e.g., *Amor*), attributed nudity to the Muses, who in ancient art were usually dressed. This "hieroglyphic" interpretation of the nude, in itself a mark of classical antiquity, continued through to the Renaissance, for example in Signorelli's *Sacra famiglia* and Michelangelo's *Tondo Doni* (both Uffizi, Florence).

As it was in Byzantine art, personification was used frequently in the art of the medieval West. In this context nudity could be said to act as a signal for the distinctiveness of certain images, an idea typical in classical thought. Thus, personifications of landscape elements are nude or seminude: the Jordan in the 5th-century *Battesimo di Cristo* (Battistero Neoniano, Ravenna); the Earth and the Sea, or natural forces like the Winds, Night, and Day, the Seasons, and the Four Elements; and astrological images. A naked man standing in a frontal position appears in certain depictions of the Microcosm (e.g., *Glossarium Salomonis,* ca. 1165, Bayerische Staatsbibliotek, Munich). Some of these personifications disappeared, whereas others survived in the Renaissance, side by side with creations that perhaps recast ancient models, like Time, Chance, and Fortune. Still others lent themselves to the depiction of fully modern values, as in Delacroix's *Liberty Leading the People* (1830).

A special case is that of Truth. Whereas in the ancient world *Aletheia-Veritas* was nearly absent, its iconographical developments from the 15th century onward are owed to Horace (*Odes* 1.24.6–7: *nuda Veritas,* "naked Truth") and to his medieval reception. If Leon Battista Alberti described the personification of Truth in the *Calumny of Apelles* only as "shameful and demure," it was Botticelli who painted her totally nude, following Horace's expression. Thus began the theme's popularity (with the variant *Veritas filia Temporis*): Andrea Alciato (*Emblemata,* 1531), Cesare Ripa (1593), Gian Lorenzo Bernini (1646–1652), P.-J. Cavalier (1849–1853), down to Gustav Klimt's *Nuda Veritas* (1899) and Wilhelm Wandschneider's statue *The Naked Truth* (1914).

The iconography of *Eros-Amor* developed without parallel. Beginning in classical Greece, the god had been depicted as a nude winged youth. In Rome—when he was increasingly considered less like a god and more like a personification—we witness the attempt to interpret his attributes symbolically: for Philostratus (*Epistulae* 7.1) he was nude because he was frank and open. This iconography of *erotes* and *amores* remained intact until late antiquity and—nearly without interruption—reappeared in medieval *angioletti,* in Renaissance *putti,* and in Caravaggio's *Amor Victorious.* In the Romanesque period the variant of Eros with a torch is documented—*Welfenkreuz* (11th cent., Kustgewerbemuseum, Berlin), Wiligelmo in the cathedral of Modena (12th cent.)—which perhaps preserves the original funerary meaning.

Of the original medieval personifications, two bear on the history of artistic nudity: Nicola Pisano's *Fortitude* (pulpit of the baptistery, Pisa, ca. 1260) and his son Giovanni's *Temperance* (or *Castitas*) (pulpit of the cathedral, Pisa, 1302–1310). In each nudity is embraced as a value within a fully Christian program. It is this road that would be taken definitively in the 15th century, and Donatello's bronze *David* (ca. 1432), which also has many other iconographical implications, is one of the most noteworthy manifestations of it. It shows the grafting, typical of Humanism, of classical models onto a new structure of Christian thought, although it must be observed that the parallel between the athlete and the Christian ascetic appeared as early as St. Paul and continued through the Middle Ages, culminating in the verse in which Dante describes Saint Dominic as a "holy athlete" (*Paradiso* 12.56).

The obverse of a medal by Andrea Guazzalotti for Niccolò Palmieri shows the bishop of Orte (d. 1467) barechested; its caption reads, *Nudus egre[s]sus, sic redibo,* which summarizes Job 1:21 ("Naked came I out of my mother's womb, and naked shall I return thither"). On the reverse is a male nude with a lance and an hourglass (Time?). The nakedness of man before God and "heroic" nudity show themselves to be fully compatible on a medal by Zuan Boldù (1458): one side has the nude bust of a crowned self-portrait, the other an allegory of Death, with a seated man, naked and forsaken, which anticipates the central figure in *An Allegory of the Old and New Testaments* by Hans Holbein the Younger, ca. 1532 (National Galleries of Scotland, Edinburgh).

A unique case is the *Hypnerotomachia Poliphili* (1499), in which ancient nudity is repeatedly encountered. The marble statue of a sleeping nymph, for one, excites whoever happens to find himself before it. Here Francesco Colonna's text takes its theme, love with a nude female statue, from Pliny (*Natural History* 36.21), whereas the woodcut uses Dionysiac sarcophagi as its model to depict the scene of the sleeping Arianna surprised by a satyr.

Michelangelo—who beginning with his *Battaglia dei centauri* and later in his *Bacco* had shown evidence of having understood the "Dionysiac" side of the ancient nude—was the Renaissance artist who most richly joined the two poles of "humanistic" nudity: the ennobling and triumphal forms of ancient statuary and the tragic sentiment of the Christian vision. Representative of this tension are the *David,* the *Ignudi* of the Sistine Chapel ceiling, the *Schiavi* for the tomb of Julius II, and the *Giudizio universale.* But his *Cristo della Minerva* (1519–1521) is perhaps the work in which this dialectic appears with the greatest clarity. The contract itself stipulated that Christ should be "of natural size, naked." Nakedness is in line with the account of the Crucifixion; heroic nudity is perfectly in tune with a risen Christ, triumphing over death. Regarding Jesus' nudity—a theme already treated in certain 15th-century crucifixes—a letter of Lorenzo Pignoria to Peiresc (1606) is worthy of note, in which the scholar declares that "nudity doesn't offend me, considering that even Our Lord was crucified thus, and that the Painters add a loincloth of their own accord."

The Renaissance also concentrated on the nudity of the body by way of the reception—through Vitruvius—of the theory of its proportions formulated in classical Greece, as seen in Leonardo's *Uomo Vitruviano* or in a treatise such as Dürer's *Vier Bücher von menschlicher Proportion* (1528). But concentrating on the body's proportions also meant measuring all its parts and respecting their forms and dimensions, as was noted by Leon Battista Alberti (*On Painting*). The artist must thus know how to draw nudes to be able to paint the human figure in every situation. This relationship between artistic technique and anatomical observation forms the basis of the "nude study" that would become common practice, and it remains so today in many art academies. That the models often assumed, at least up until the 19th century, poses of classical statues is the confirmation of this practice's inseparability from the history of the classical tradition. The artist must know the human body perfectly and, in a certain sense, go beyond the nude. Accounts of artists dissecting cadavers derive directly from this idea of the nude's necessary "transparency"; and in this case, too, it is no surprise that ancient statues end up being used for anatomical research (e.g., Jean-Galbert Salvage's *écorché* of the Borghese *Gladiator,* 1804) and appear in medical iconography up to the 19th century.

The harsh reactions to the nudes of the Sistine Chapel's *Giudizio* indicate a challenge to the ideas that had informed "humanistic" nudity. From its unveiling (1541), the fresco was judged indecent in curial circles, even among ecclesiastics who were friends of Michelangelo. Although points of emphasis differ, the indecency of the nudes is the central argument of the numerous attacks on the *Giudizio*—from Ambrogio Politi (who equated them with heresy) to Aretino (who wished that the popes would take up the model of Gregory the Great, destroyer of the idols), from Gilio to antiquarians like Antonio Agustín and Pirro Ligorio, even to Federico Borromeo and Salvator Rosa. These attacks culminated in Daniele da Volterra's censorship of the fresco (1564), but the fact that Paolo Veronese cited Michelangelo's nudes in his Inquisition trial (1573) shows the effect this discussion had.

The polemic against the nude also animated treatises of the post-Tridentine era. According to Gabriele Paleotti, Satan "sees to it that a painter, instead of giving shape to a Christ, gives shape to an Apollo," and Rinaldo Corso even posited the equivalences God : clothing :: Demon : nudity. Bartolomeo Ammannati (1582) abjured his own nude sculptures and affirmed that, by doing away with its nudes, Florence would no longer be a "nest of idols." After the end of the 16th century, religious sites eradicated the nude when it was not expressly called for by the Bible or authorized by tradition.

The heroic nude, on the other hand, did not stop being used in profane settings. There it remained almost compulsory, from the Baroque period until the beginning of the 20th century, for the depiction of mythological figures (one thinks of the *Tre Grazie*) or personages from ancient history. The genre of the portrait in mythological dress—whose precedents reach back to the Roman era, in the apotheoses of men of state and of private individuals, which is also attested in the Renaissance (Bronzino, *Cosimo I come Orfeo; Andrea Doria come Nettuno,* ca. 1540)—enjoyed great success in the Neoclassical period, boosted by Winckelmann's writings. Goethe even added that a nude statue like the *Agrippa* of Venice raised man to the divine level. And Hegel abundantly explained why in Greece "a great number of artistic creations are intentionally nude" (*Aesthetics* 3.2b). Quatremère de Quincy said that the ancients had used "ideal nudity" to transport people "dans une région poétique et imaginaire" (1834), an idea that is also found in Schopenhauer (1851). Canova had claimed that nudity, "when it is pure and adorned with exquisite beauty," could appear "like a spiritual and intellectual thing" and raise "the spirit to the contemplation of the divine." Thus, Anne-Louis Girodet painted *Élizabeth Lange as Danae* (1799), and Francesco Hayez *Carlotta Chabert as Venus* (1830). Canova sculpted Paolina Borghese as *Venus victrix* (1804) and Napoleon as Mars the Peacemaker (1803–1806).

Napoleon's rejection of Canova's work is only one episode in the rocky reception that the "ideal" nude had even in the Neoclassical period. A few years earlier, the exhibition of David's *Intervention of the Sabine Women* (1799) had given rise to a heated debate (involving the painter himself) on the topic of male and female nudity and on the *à la grecque* style. Pierre-Louis Roederer proclaimed: "Painters of talent! It is in virtues, and not in the license of nudity, that there are treasures for you," and Louis-Sébastien Mercier concluded, "Morality and statues are two incompatible things."

Polemics and attacks against the artistic nude began in the High Middle Ages and have continued to our own time. Theodoretus argued in the 5th century that statues of Venus were even more scandalous than prostitutes. Much later, in the 15th century, Savonarola's preaching drove the Florentines to destroy a "vast quantity of nude figures, both in painting and sculpture" (Vasari, *Lives* 1:538). Again in Florence, the city council decided to commission a metal "garland" (*ghirlanda*) to cover Michelangelo's *David.* In 1549, when Baccio Bandinelli's *Adam* and *Eve* were uncovered in Santa Maria del Fiore, an anonymous voice judged them "filthy and gross" (*lorde et porche*). Adrian VI's disgust for the Sistine Chapel ceiling is well known; he compared it to a *stufa,* a bathroom with licentious decorations. Montaigne (*Essais* 3.5) condemned a pope for "castrating so many beautiful ancient statues . . . so that they would not corrupt the eyes." Ingres (1835) complained that the Capitoline Venus in Rome had been "shut up in a room like women of bad reputation," a report confirmed by Jacob Burckhardt (1855), who also saw the Vatican copy of the Cnidian Aphrodite "covered with a modern tin drape." And even in a half-serious context, Mark Twain's reaction to Titian's *Venus of Urbino* is noteworthy: it seemed to him "the obscenest picture the world possesses," as much for its nudity as for its attitude (*A Tramp Abroad,* 1880).

The connection between sexuality and classical art exists in our own day, even if it is female students in Edinburgh in the 1930s whom Muriel Spark (*The Prime of Miss Jean Brodie,* 1961) portrays deciding to visit the museum where "there's a Greek god . . . standing up with nothing on" and escaping their chaperones to examine its parts more closely.

When the *all'antica* nude does not give rise to scandal, it can still provoke bewilderment. Pondering a personification at the base of Pigalle's monument to Louis XV in Reims, Friedrich Melchior Grimm (1765) wondered at the presence of "une grande figure toute nue," since such was sensible only in warmer countries like Greece and Italy. And looking at David's *Sabine Women,* someone thought it impossible that ancient warriors fought without any clothes. In short, what escaped these viewers is that nudity for the ancients was not meant literally but was rather a means for avoiding the incidental and the individual. This idea was quite clear to the artists who continued to use it for public commemorative monuments from the 18th to the 20th centuries: Pigalle for Voltaire (1776) and Max Klinger for Beethoven (1902).

In 19th-century art, the *all'antica* nude becomes merely a chapter in the history of artistic nudes. Instead of countless Venuses, nymphs, and naiads, we find its original capacity for exalting the human figure in rather less conspicuous scenes, like the female nude of Manet's *Déjeuner sur l'herbe,* related to antiquity by way of Raphael. When, however, its sensual side is shown off, as in Jean-Léon Gérôme, it degenerates into picturesque superficiality, which also characterizes sculptures like his *Tanagra* and *Corinthienne.* Accusing him of pornography, Degas justly scorned the pose of his *Phryne before the Areopagus* (1861): the courtesan does not attempt to hide herself, but exults in her body. Degas himself interpreted ancient nudity altogether differently, focusing on its austerity, in his *Young Spartans* (1860).

BIBL.: Larissa Bonfante, "Nudity as a Costume in Classical Art," *American Journal of Archaeology* 93 (1989) 85–106. Kenneth Clark, *The Nude: A Study in Ideal Form* (London 1956). Colin Eisler, "The Athlete of Christ," in *De artibus opuscula XL: Essays in Honor of E. Panofsky,* ed. Millard Meiss (New York 1961) 82–97. G. Fossi, ed., *Il Nudo: Eros, Natura, Artificio* (Florence 1999). Darcy Grimaldo Grigsby, "Nudity *à la grecque* in 1799," *Art Bulletin* 80, no. 2 (1998) 311–335. C. H. Hallett, *The Roman Nude: Heroic Portrait Statuary, 200 B.C.–A.D. 300* (Oxford 2005). Nikolaus Himmelmann, *Ideale Nacktheit in der griechischen Kunst* (Berlin 1990) and "Nudità ideale," in *Memoria dell'antico nell'arte italiana,* ed. Salvatore Settis, 3 vols. (Turin 1985) 2:201–278. Berthold Hinz, "Nacktheit," in *Der Neue Pauly: Enzyklopädie der Antikek: Rezeptions- und Wissenschaftsgeschichte,* ed. H. Cancik, H.

Schneider, and M. Landfester, 15 vols. (Stuttgart 2001) 1:650–656. Ralf Konersmann, "Implikationen der nackten Wahrheit," *Scholion* 5 (2008) 21–55. Victor Schmidt, "Statues, Idols and Nudity: Changing Attitudes to Sculpture from the Early Christian Period to the Counter-Reformation," in *Antiquity Renewed,* ed. Z. von Martels and V. M. Schmidt (Leuven 2003) 211–229. C.F.

Translated by Patrick Baker

Numbers, Numerals, Notation

Western Europe inherited the Classical Latin system of notation—roman numerals—and was exposed in different ways to the ancient Greek system of alphanumerical notation. In roman notation integers (whole numbers) follow a decimal system. Originally nonalphabetical symbols, they became assimilated to letters of the alphabet in classical times, I, V, X, L, D, and M, and later could be written as lowercase letters as well. Numbers were written additively (L + X + X + X = 80) or subtractively (X taken from L = 40). Strokes above the numerals indicated a multiplication by 1,000 ($\overline{\text{II}}$ = 2,000), a double stroke, a multiplication by 1 million. There is no higher limit to numeration, and concepts of the generative potential of numbers and their infinite growth were powerful in philosophy and theology as well as in arithmetic. The lower limit, however, is one. Neither a negative number nor a fraction can be expressed with a roman numeral. The duodecimal divisions of the unit (now called by the Latin word *as*) were expressed with special symbols that gradually fell out of use during the Middle Ages. Roman numerals are notoriously difficult to calculate with but remained a clear and convenient way to express the results of calculations on the fingers and the abacus until early modern times, and even now are widely used for dates, as an alternative notation to Hindu-Arabic numerals (e.g., in pagination of prefaces to books) and in official documents.

Greek alphanumerical notation also followed the decimal system for integers. Units, tens, and hundreds were expressed by taking the letters in alphabetical order (so that α = 1, ι = 10) and adding some extra symbols at the end to reach 999. The sequence began again with 1,000, a subscript tick being added to indicate the higher order. In astronomical contexts the same notation was used for successive 60th-parts of integers. Moreover, a special sign was used to indicate the absence of a number. Thus, ιδ.ō.κι would mean 14 integers (minutes), 0 60th-parts (seconds), and 21 60th-parts of 60th-parts. This notation remained in use wherever the Greek language was used; it was taken over in other scripts adapted from the Greek, such as Coptic and Cyrillic. The Greek and Coptic numerals, in turn, became the notation most commonly used by merchants and notaries throughout the Islamic Mediterranean.

The idea of alphanumerical notation probably arose in the ancient Near East and was used not only in Greek, but also in Hebrew and Arabic script where it was the norm in mathematical contexts. Occasional attempts were made to model a Latin alphanumerical system on that of these other languages, especially in the mid-12th century, but these did not catch on, partly, one may suppose, because of the advent of a totally new system of notation, that known by its origin as Hindu-Arabic numerals. Their distinctive elements are that each numeral derives its value from its decimal place and that zeros are used to indicate "empty" places. The Brahmi symbols from northwest India became known in the Near East in the early 7th century and in Christian northern Spain by the end of the 10th century, but it was only in the 12th century that they began to threaten the hegemony of classical notation in Greek and Latin (they had impinged on Arabic mathematics from the early 10th century onward). In reaction to their seemingly barbarous shapes other, more familiar-looking systems were experimented with in Latin, such as the alphanumerical notation referred to above, streamlined roman numerals (in which the longer notation for 4, 8, and 9 was replaced by the initial letters of the respective numbers *q, o,* and *n,* and the Greek zero was used), or the first nine roman numerals were used as numerals with place value. But the convenience of Hindu-Arabic numerals, especially in calculating with pen and paper (algorism), was widely recognized, and its use was canonized by the mid-13th century both in university curricula, where John of Sacrobosco's *Algorismus vulgaris* joined Boethius' *De institutione arithmetica* in the arithmetical division of the Quadrivium, and in the business schools (*scuole d'abbaco*) in Italy.

The main rival to algorism was the abacus, which had been used in antiquity, and which was revived in the Middle Ages in the form of a board with lines for different denominations (units, tens, hundreds; pennies, shillings, pounds, etc.) on which counters were placed. Such a board was used from the early 12th century onward in the English royal chancery, which derived its name Exchequer from the gridlike appearance of the abacus. The continuing rivalry of these two methods of calculation into the early modern period is nicely illustrated by a depiction of an abacist and an algorist making calculations under the aegis of Lady Arithmetica in Gregor Reisch's *Margarita philosophica* (Freiburg 1503). The bead or frame abacus, having been introduced to Western Europe from Russia in the early 17th century, has retained the principle of the classical abacus until the present day. And although the binary numeral system, first fully documented by Leibniz in his *Explication de l'arithmétique binaire* (1705), is used by virtually all computers, ordinary mortals still universally use the decimal system of numeration that began with the ancients.

BIBL.: C. Burnett, "Indian Numerals in the Mediterranean Basin in the Twelfth Century, with Special Reference to the 'Eastern Forms,'" in *From China to Paris: 2000 Years Transmission of Mathematical Ideas,* ed. Y. Dold-Samplonius et al. (Stuttgart 2002) 237–288. Georges Ifrah, *The Universal*

History of Numbers, trans. David Bellos (London 1998). Paul Kunitzsch, "The Transmission of Hindu-Arabic Numerals Reconsidered," in *The Scientific Enterprise in Islam,* ed. J. P. Hogendijk and A. I. Sabra (Cambridge, Mass., 2003) 3–21. J. M. Pullan, *The History of the Abacus* (London 1968). C.BR.

Numismatics

It has been said of the emperor Augustus that he made presents of old coins to his friends; antiquarian writers such as Festus discuss the significance of coin types; and there are records from antiquity of the discovery of hoards of coins (e.g., Horace, *Satires* 2.6, 10; HERODES ATTICUS). In fact, hoards are both the principal source of the coins in modern collections and the major tool used by modern scholars in attributing and dating individual issues of coins. The Romans indeed legislated on the rights of the emperor with respect to hoards. The coinage itself also provides evidence of awareness of earlier issues of coins, such as the choice under Augustus, Vespasian, and Trajan to release coin types from issues that were no longer in normal circulation.

With the end of the Roman Empire in the West, the successor kingdoms deliberately imitated Roman coins and coin types. It is hard to see the collection of coins in the Tomb of Chilperic as other than a claim to be the successor to the emperors whose coins they were. A similar claim is implicit in the augustalis coin issued by Frederick II.

Early in the 14th century Giovanni Mansionario copied the heads of emperors from coins to illustrate his *Historia imperialis,* and a manuscript by Suetonius, for instance, of about 1350, uses a coin image of Galba to portray the emperor. In 1354 Petrarch presented a few coins of Roman emperors to Charles IV, urging him to imitate his predecessors. By the time we get to the middle of the 15th century, there are substantial coin collections in existence, such as those of the Venetian Pietro Barbo (later Paul II), of Domenico Grimani, and, somewhat later, of Andrea della Valle. The 15th century also saw the widespread use of Roman coin types as models for the decoration of monumental buildings, for instance the Colleoni Chapel in Bergamo and the Certosa di Pavia.

Perhaps the first to publish on the values of the coins mentioned in classical sources was Giannantonio Pandoni, whose *De talento* dates to 1459; in 1464 A. Santacroce wrote about the abbreviations and numerals on Roman coins. There followed, around the turn of the century, a flurry of works on these themes: by F. Redditi (1492); by G. A. Questenberg (1499), referring to earlier work by Johann von Dalberg, bishop of Worms, his dedicatee; and Alfonso de Portugal's *Tractatus de numismate* (1510), Guillaume Budé's *De asse et partibus* (1514), and Leonardo Porzio's *De sestertio* (1515–1520). G. B. Egnazio claimed in 1516 to have seen Porzio's work in manuscript in 1511; the question of whether either knew of and used the other has been much, but inconclusively, discussed. G. Biel's *Tractatus de potestate et utilitate monetarum* appeared in 1516.

The pattern for publishing in the 16th century was set by Andrea Fulvio's *Illustrium imagines* of 1517, with its portraits of endlessly fascinating figures, such as Cleopatra, and surrounding legends, mostly improving on rather than faithfully representing the coins on which the plates were modeled. Picture books of coins were in fact the coffee-table books of the late Renaissance, appearing throughout the century in vast numbers and frequently in several editions. In contrast, it was extremely hard to interest publishers in volumes of inscriptions.

Although attempts were made to improve the level of faithfulness in reproduction, and of scholarship in interpretation, few authors could resist the sensational. A medal of 1537 honoring the assassin of Alessandro, Duke of Florence, is accurately modeled on the EID MAR (Ides of March) denarius of Brutus, but a coin type that even a passing familiarity with Livy would have revealed as an oath-taking scene was interpreted by J. Huttich in 1534 as a representation of soldiers seizing a baby from its mother, and hence of the Slaughter of the Innocents. The high point in 16th-century publishing in both the reproduction and the interpretation of coin types is represented by the work of Enea Vico and Sebastiano Erizzo. Vico made, in particular, a serious attempt to portray and understand the reverse types of Roman imperial coins with his *Le imagini con tutti i riversi* (1548); he worked as well on ancient gems and published a general account of what would now be called numismatics, his *Discorsi* (1555). Erizzo's *Discorso sopra le medaglie degli antichi* (1559) dealt with the types of both republican and imperial coins, including what would now be called Roman Provincial coinage.

The *Vivae omnium fere imperatorum imagines* of Hubert Goltz (1557), although based on an extensive autopsy of coins in collections across Europe, is marked by its inclusion of the most audacious forgeries; the lists of collectors, indeed, serves more to help us understand the scale of interest in ancient coins, and hence the market for coin books, than to authenticate the pictures. In the case of one great 16th-century collection, that of the Este family, an image of its scale and quality survives: the gold coins in it were stamped with a tiny silver eagle, and although the collection was dispersed, many of its more spectacular coins can be identified in the collections of today.

The alleged coin portraits of Adam and Eve, and of Jesus Christ, offered by Guillaume Rouillé in 1577 can hardly be said to represent progress, and it was the posthumous publication in 1587 of Antonio Agustín's *Dialogos de medallas, iscriciones y otras antiguedades* that set the agenda in the study of ancient coins for the next two centuries. Like much of the rest of his work on pagan antiquity, this book was a product of the 1540s and 1550s, before ecclesiastical administration and Counter-Reformation publishing took his activities elsewhere; his letters of those years refer regularly to the discovery of coin hoards and hitherto unknown coins.

Meanwhile, Agustín's protégé, Pedro Chacón, had devoted his careful and scholarly attention to the problem attacked by Budé and Porzio, the values to be attributed to ancient coins, and although his *Imagines* was in the tradition of the coffee-table books mentioned above, Fulvio Orsini undoubtedly knew and learned much from Agustín, with whom he was in regular contact. The book by Agustín, when it finally appeared, was remarkable for its systematic discussion of the identification of forgeries and the attribution and dating of coin issues. It was not until the career of Bartolomeo Borghesi, around 1800, that the discovery and recording of coin hoards allowed his sharp intellect to formulate the principle on which all subsequent work on the chronology of ancient coinage has been based: namely, that if there are two hoards, one of which contains, say, 20 issues that are not in the other hoard and are also less worn, those 20 issues are later than the rest. But that is another story. M.CR.

Obelisk

In 10 BCE the emperor Augustus imported to Rome an obelisk from Heliopolis in Egypt, where it had honored the 19th-dynasty pharaohs Sethos I and Ramses II. Its new Roman location was at the center (*spina*) of the Circus Maximus; its new base added a Latin dedication to the sun (*Corpus inscriptionum latinarum* 6.701). There it stood into medieval times. The Middle Egyptian inscription on its flanks so fascinated Ammianus Marcellinus (4th cent.) that he included a translation, made into Greek by a certain Hermapion (17.4). At an unknown point in the Middle Ages the obelisk collapsed and broke. Though seen by Leon Battista Alberti in 1471, it was not excavated until 1587, following a lengthy search. In 1589 Domenico Fontana, acting at the behest of Pope Sixtus V, oversaw its reerection at its current location in Piazza de Popolo. Giuseppe Valadier added the two Egyptian-style lions in 1818, as part of a neoclassical design.

The eventful career of this obelisk may be taken as an invitation to see Rome's 13 major obelisks in quasi-biographical terms, and in particular to recognize the different needs and interests with which their histories have intersected. They were all imported between the reigns of Augustus (27 BCE–14 CE) and Theodosius (379–397), with the result that today more large obelisks stand in the city of Rome than in Egypt itself. In many respects, modern interests in obelisks were prefigured in antiquity, not least the phenomenon of Egyptomania. As the Elder Pliny shows (*Natural History* 36.64–74), Romans regarded obelisks as symbols of imperial power, and their transportation as achievements in engineering. The mystery of ancient Egypt and its hieroglyphic script underpinned the concerns of Romans, just as they would do for others subsequently.

The award among moderns for obelizing zeal must surely go to Sixtus V (r. 1585–1590): in just five years as pope he oversaw the excavation, restoration, and redeployment of four of Rome's grandest obelisks. Just as Augustus had used them to realign the ancient city's public spaces, so Sixtus would use them to change the face of Renaissance Rome. Their most industrious and imaginative scholar was the Jesuit polymath Athanasius Kircher. Among his various writings on Aegyptiaca, his *Obeliscus Pamphilius* (1650) focuses on the obelisk now at Piazza Navona, expounding the supposed metaphysical meaning of its Middle Egyptian inscription. The cartouches on that obelisk formed part of Champollion's decipherment of Egyptian hieroglyphics in 1822.

The obelisks imported to Constantinople (390), Paris (1833), London (1878), and New York (1881) have articulated those cities' metropolitan and imperial credentials; compare the prominent uses of the obelisk form, for example, in Sydney (1857), Washington (1848–1884), and Buenos Aires (1936). On varying but usually smaller scales, obelisks have also marked private gravestones, notably in Civil War cemeteries (e.g., at Arlington, Virginia).

Romans regarded obelisks as symbols of distant antiquity, but ironically they have sometimes been pressed into service to celebrate high modernity; the one that Mussolini dedicated to Marconi (1939–1959) is one example. Looking beyond Rome, there is the metal structure at Moscow's Museum of Space: tapering like an Egyptian obelisk, its swerve denotes a space voyage. By the same token, one may point to postmodern versions of the form, such as Barnett Newman's *Broken Obelisk* (1963), in which the top part of an obelisk is suspended upside-down above a pyramid. Such instances suggest that the obelisk form is distinctive enough to allow creative kinds of adaptation. The Axum obelisk—to use that term loosely for the 4th-century CE monolith imported by Mussolini from Ethiopia to Rome in 1937—shows how, in the postwar period, prominent antiquities have become part of international debates over cultural property.

BIBL.: B. Curran et al., *Obelisk: A History* (Cambridge, Mass., 2009). E. Iversen, *Obelisks in Exile* (Copenhagen 1968–1980).

G.PR.

Ode

Though the term *ode* (song) has been applied to diverse lyrics, it often refers to lyrics in the Pindaric, Anacreontic, or Horatian traditions. Composed in triads of strophes and antistrophes with identical metrical patterns and a final, distinctive epode, Pindar's odes celebrated athletic victories. Their exalted tone, brilliant but obscure images, myths linking victors to gods, sententious pronouncements, abrupt transitions, and celebrations of the poet's inspired artistry projected a sublimity that subsequent lyric poets sought to emulate. The *Anacreontea,* composed from the Hellenistic period to the 5th or 6th century CE but ascribed during their period of greatest influence to the archaic poet Anacreon, are short celebrations of love and wine and the eschewal of larger, anxiety-producing concerns. Horace's *carmina (Odes),* the most influential European lyric collection, adapt a range of Greek lyrics and meters to Latin and Roman concerns. Enlivening familiar themes with surprising images and turns of thought, Horace wrote high-style poems celebrating political order that included Pindaric echoes, sententious celebrations of rural contentment and moderation, and convivial and erotic poetry recalling archaic Greek personal lyrics and the *Anacreontea.* Yet Horace's diverse lyrics consistently emphasize decorous attunement to particular occasions, public or private.

Italian Humanists imitated Horace and Pindar in Latin and Italian. The 15th-century Neo-Latin poets Giovanni Pontano and Michael Marullus deployed Horatian meters and style on new themes, as in Pontano's "Hymn to Night," on night's solace and erotic joys, and Marullus's May Day ode, which adapts Horace's erotic carpe diem to exhort a friend to participate in springtime festivity. After the 1513 Aldine edition of Pindar, Italian poets sought Pindaric sublimity (often combined with motifs from classical hymns) to praise rulers' and aristocrats' achievements as well as the Christian God, saints, and martyrs.

In 1554 Robert Estienne's *Anacreontea,* with partial Latin translation, and Elie André's complete Latin translation appeared, followed in 1556 by Remy Belleau's French version. Pierre de Ronsard imitated Horace and Pindar in his *Odes* (1550) as well as the *Anacreontea.* Ronsard intensified Horace's evocations of rural life with a pantheistic embrace of nature. Making use of Pindaric enjambments and mythopoesis, Ronsard's triadic Pindarics eulogize royal and aristocratic exploits, including military victories and peacemaking. (Ronsard hymns peace as cosmic harmony.) "À Michel de l'Hôpital," whose 24 triads outdo Pindar in sheer length (Pindar's longest, *Pythian* 4, has 13), celebrates poets' Neoplatonic inspiration. Yet in a paradox that runs through Pindaric imitations from Horace's Ode 4.2 onward (which imitates Pindar while declaring him inimitable), Ronsard suggests that the modern poet is perforce not the inspired Pindaric bard but the learned imitator. In contrast, François de Malherbe's early 17th-century monostrophic odes celebrating French monarchical and military power replace Ronsard's Pindaric extravagance with neoclassical formal control.

In early 17th-century English odes, Ben Jonson mingled Horatian and Pindaric elements with Stoic didacticism. His triadic Cary-Morison ode celebrates an aristocrat's death as a Pindaric victory by which he "leap'd the present age" (line 79). John Milton's "Nativity Ode" (1629) depicting the infant Jesus as Hercules recalls Pindar's Hercules (*Nemean Odes* 1) and turns Pindaric victory into Christ's defeat of paganism.

The Polish Jesuit Maciej Kazimierz Sarbiewski's Neo-Latin Horatian odes (1625, 1628) preach Christian Stoic retirement in the face of European war. In war-torn England of the mid-17th century, Sarbiewski's odes were translated and imitated, and Horace and Anacreontics were polemically adapted. Richard Lovelace's "The Grasse-hopper" of the late 1640s recalls an Anacreontic ode and Horace's call to answer winter chill with wine and fire (Ode 1.9) to celebrate drunken defiance after Charles I's defeat. Anacreontic drinking poets challenge killjoy Puritan "Earthly Powers" (Robert Herrick) and (coarsening their models) eschew "thinking" for "freedom of drinking" (Alexander Brome). By contrast, Andrew Marvell's "Horatian Ode" (1650) recalls Horace's decorous responses to occasion, to urge "'tis time" to support Oliver Cromwell's Puritan victory. Marvell's implicit comparison of Charles I's dignified acceptance of execution and the Horatian Cleopatra's defiant suicide (Ode 1.37.21–32) humanizes the defeated but suggests the wisdom of assent to the new order. In two convivial sonnet-odes of the 1650s, John Milton echoes Horace to celebrate a temperate pleasure compatible with the Puritan-parliamentary cause, as opposed to contemporary poets' Anacreontic-Horatian celebrations of drunken defiance.

In 1656 Abraham Cowley, under arrest as a Royalist spy, published escapist Anacreontic odes. He also followed Horace's characterization of Pindar as "free" like a river torrent (Ode 4.2) by composing influential Pindaric odes in stanzas of irregular line lengths and rhyme schemes. Cowley spurns Pindaric warnings against hubris to celebrate modernity: reversing Pindar's figurative warning not to sail beyond the "pillars of Hercules" (*Olympian Odes* 3.42–45, *Isthmian Odes* 4.10–13), for example, Cowley praises Hobbes for discovering a "vast Ocean" beyond the ancients' "slender-limb'ed" Mediterranean. Cowley's Pindarics in *Essays* (1668) treat Horatian retirement as sublime; adapting Pindar's self-representation as a soaring eagle, Cowley compares his retired freedom to the eagle's flight. Several of John Dryden's Cowleyan Pindarics celebrate and exemplify poetic power. A tour de force of imitative metrics, Dryden's

"Alexander's Feast" (1698) renders a bard's use of shifting melodies to arouse contrasting passions in the world's supposed master, Alexander the Great.

Heavily echoing earlier English poetry, William Collins's *Odes* (1746) nativizes both Horatian and Pindaric modes. Monostrophic odes recalling Horace, "Ode to Simplicity" and "Ode to Evening," celebrate a "temperate" retirement and a "modest" evening both Horatian and English; the triadic Pindaric "Ode on Liberty" celebrates liberty's progress from Greece to Britain. Collins's free Cowleyan Pindaric "Poetical Character" celebrates the godlike creativity of England's Spenserian-Miltonic vatic line, though denying that such inspiration is still available. Thomas Gray's triadic Pindarics of the 1750s, "The Progress of Poetry" and "The Bard," similarly trace poetic power's transfer from Greece to England but despair that contemporary poetry can recapture Pindaric sublimity.

In their Pindarics, 18th-century Russian court poets such as Mikhail Lomonosov and Gavrila Derzhavin combined the French neoclassical ode's structure with sublime style and rhetoric to celebrate Russian imperial might. In mid- to late18th-century Germany, Friedrich Gottlieb Klopstock adapted Horatian meters and wrote exclamatory free Pindarics. Employing free metrics and deploying Pindaric images as well as coinages, bold enjambments, and a tortured syntax evoking sublimity, Goethe's "Wanderers Sturmlied" (1772), "Mahomets Gesang," and "Prometheus" (1773) celebrated the original genius. Horace's Pindar as torrent informs these poems, but Goethe also admits the gap between the ancient genius and the modern imitator. Friedrich Hölderlin's turn-of-the-century free Pindarics melded classical and Christian elements for unique mythopoetic mediations. Also recalling Pindar as river, "Der Rhein" associates the Rhine with various heroic figures mediating between the earthly and divine.

English Romantic odes, in contrast, generally recall English poetic predecessors more than classical poetic models. Yet with their high-style seriousness and amplitude and their classical generic designation, the great Romantic odes of William Wordsworth, Percy Bysshe Shelley, and John Keats evoke the vatic status and public character of the Pindaric and grand-style Horatian ode. Keats explicitly engages with Greek art and myth-making in "Ode to Psyche" and "Ode on a Grecian Urn" (written in 1819).

Modernist odes often have an ironic or revisionist relation to classical tradition. In his pessimistic free-verse "Horseshoe Finder: A Pindaric Fragment" (1923), Osip Mandelstam concedes the anachronism of Pindaric celebrations of the new Soviet state. Allen Tate's "Ode to the Confederate Dead" (1928) is, on his own accounting, a Cowleyan Pindaric ode in form but ironically related to the classical ode in its "solipsism" and replacement of "public" pronouncement with personal, elegiac reflection. Pablo Neruda's *Odas elementales* and its sequels (1954–1957) evoke the lyric grandeur of the classical and Romantic ode to celebrate ordinary, everyday things as wondrous: not only wine (like classical odes) but tomatoes, bicycles, salt. Yet 20th-century poets such as Basil Bunting, W. H. Auden, Donald Davie, J. V. Cunningham, and Donald Hall have also directly imitated the form and adapted some of the values of the Horatian ode. Auden's late odes in Horatian meters, for example, self-consciously measure modernity against Horatian values, both in grand-style odes on modern ambitions ("Moon Landing," "Ode to Terminus") and in his deft updating of the convivial ode as a depiction of contemporary life ("The Garrison"). Geoffrey Hill's 21 triadic "Pindarics: After Cesare Pavese" (2006) revive the Pindaric structure not for celebration but for harsh explorations of the relationship of poetry and the poet to modern culture.

BIBL.: William Fitzgerald, *Agonistic Poetry: The Pindaric Mode in Pindar, Horace, Hölderlin, and the English Ode* (Berkeley 1952). John T. Hamilton, *Soliciting Darkness: Pindar, Obscurity, and the Classical Tradition* (Cambridge, Mass., 2003). Carol Maddison, *Apollo and the Muse: A History of the Ode* (Baltimore 1960). Charles Martindale and David Hopkins, eds., *Horace Made New: Horatian Influences on British Writing from the Renaissance to the Twentieth Century* (Cambridge 1993). Stella Revard, *Pindar and the Renaissance Hymn-Ode, 1450–1700* (Tempe 2001).

J.S.

Odysseus

A mythical ruler of Ithaca and a Greek general at the siege of Troy, Odysseus (Ulysses in Latin) is celebrated for his intelligence and resourcefulness in the Homeric epics, though he appears to mixed effect on the Athenian stage as a sometimes unscrupulous schemer. In Virgil's *Aeneid* the surviving Trojans remember him bitterly for the criminally deceitful way in which he won the war for the Greeks. This mixed heritage initiates a vigorous and diverse afterlife and has attracted a remarkable roster of talent.

Dante, guided by Virgil and with no direct recourse to Homer, assigns the character to the penultimate circle of hell (*Inferno* 26). In the pit of the evil counselors because of his offenses against Troy, Ulysses tells the story of the fatal voyage that he undertakes when, still longing "to become experienced in the world, and in human vice and valor," he decides not to return to Ithaca; eternal damnation is joined to an open-ended restlessness for adventure and knowledge. Shakespeare, in *Troilus and Cressida* (1603), makes Ulysses both the eloquent theorist of a vision of cosmic order ("The heavens themselves, the planets, and this center/Observe degree, priority, and place," 1.3.85–86) and the voice of a resourceful cynicism about human motivation ("One touch of nature makes the whole world kin," 3.3.175). The conceit of a post-Homeric voyage is given a particularly idealistic development by Alfred Tennyson in his famous monologue "Ulysses" (1833), where the speaker's endless discontent is presented as exemplary and unambiguously heroic. In the 20th century Nikos Kazantzakis celebrated these new adventures in great and tumultuous detail in a 24-book poem in modern Greek that he boldly entitled *Odyssey* (1938); the English edition of 1958 is more modestly subtitled *A Modern Sequel.* The character's most momentous avatar, however—and the focus of one of the most important works of 20th-century Modernist literature—manifests a drastic and inventive curtailing of epic scope into the constraints of the ordinary and familiar. James Joyce's novel *Ulysses* (1922) tells of a day (specifically 16 June 1904) in the life of Leopold Bloom, a Jewish advertising canvasser in Dublin; by a scheme nowhere explicit except in the book's title, Bloom's movements about town are seen to restage in elaborate particulars the actions of Homer's *Odyssey.* Contemporary life is in complicated ways both mocked and ennobled in these parallels.

The character Odysseus has appeared in musical treatments (songs, cantatas, quite a few operas), and various episodes from his adventures have been repeatedly represented in the visual arts; his encounters with Polyphemus, Circe, and Nausicaa have been particularly favored. No other work of classical literature has been of greater interest to filmmakers; the character's recent cinematic career has been both overt and allusive. Odysseus makes an especially strong impression in *Troy* (2004), a big-budget redaction of the *Iliad.* Homer receives screen credit (and appears briefly as a character) in Ethan and Joel Coen's *O Brother, Where Art Thou?* (2000), the saga of a chain-gang fugitive named Ulysses Everett McGill who is trying to return to his ex-wife, Penny. The hero of Park Chan-wook's Korean thriller *Oldboy* (2003), seeking to reclaim his former life after 15 years in prison, has the name Oh Dae-su. *To vlemma tou Odyssea* (*Ulysses' Gaze,* 1997) by Theo Angelopoulos, a contemporary filmmaker's search through the history of the 20th-century Balkans, metaphorically identifies the Greek hero's gaze with the cinematic art itself.

BIBL.: W. B. Stanford, *The Ulysses Theme,* 2nd ed. (Oxford 1963). G.B.

Oedipus

A preeminent Greek tragic hero. Sophocles' *Oedipus the King* had long exercised an impressive power of cultural renewal in Europe when, at the end of the 19th century, Sigmund Freud explained its universal success—every male spectator saw in it his hostility to his father and love for his mother—taking from it the decisive confirmation of his nascent psychoanalysis. Actually, the double violation of taboos in Sophocles' tragedy pertains solely to the realm of facts and does not tap into that of intentions. Yet the dramatic action, according to a widespread interpretation, given voice by Jean Cocteau in *The Infernal Machine* (1934), is not reduced to fatalism. For the action does not consist in the crimes but in their discovery, and for this Sophocles' Oedipus is responsible. In him innocence is associated with a positive display of social virtues: the power that Oedipus exercises in the interests of all, and the intellect that, through the solution to the Sphinx's riddle, is at the base of that same power and necessarily requires the search for virtue.

Such idealization would not be found again in the Oedipal tradition. It is definitively clouded, on the threshold of the common era, in Seneca's *Oedipus,* where the representation of power is inverted from a positive to a negative value, from a remedy to a malady of society. It places on Oedipus the stamp of subjective culpability, undefined and unmotivated, but as undeniable as the oracle.

The story of Oedipus finds in Seneca an essential subarchetype that was passed down to later ages together with Sophocles, and which perhaps even prevails over him. It is Jesuit drama—in particular the *Oedipus* plays of Emanuele Tesauro (1661) and Melchior Folard (1722)—that rationalizes the Senecan sense of guilt, giving man the responsibility (at least for a criminal thoughtlessness) so as to avoid riskily charging the divinity with having punished the innocent. In many other texts, encounters with the father, Laius, or the mother, Jocasta, are infused with guilt, in their reminiscence, by forebodings and the call of blood's voice.

But above all, treatments of the Oedipus myth became litmus tests for epochal political conceptions. Corneille's *Oedipe* (1658) is a paradoxical manifesto of legitimism. It portrays an Oedipus who behaves as a usurper, fragile, fear-ridden, and suspicious, who finds peace in the discovery that he is of royal blood, even if he has spilled that blood in homicide and spills it again by blinding himself. In a different vein, the *Oedipus* of Dryden and Lee (1678) sketches a heroic and sovereign figure of the protagonist, taking up Sophocles' exaltation of human reason. But Oedipus' social figure is gutted by his mysterious and destructive love for Jocasta, which he somehow always sensed was incestuous (the same thing would happen in Pier Paolo Pasolini's film *Edipo Re,* 1967), and which, with an outcome that scandalizes despite punishment in the form of Jocasta's insanity, continues even after its discovery. In Voltaire's *Oedipe* (1718), itself destined to become a classic, the incest is exorcised by the passion that Jocasta never felt either for Laius or for Oedipus, but instead always felt chastely for a third man with the unlikely name of Philoctetes. Meanwhile, Oedipus once again takes on the guise of the good sovereign, solicitous only of the good of his people.

Twentieth-century versions invariably depend on Freud. The first and greatest, Hofmannstahl's *Oidipus und die Sphynx* (1904), has the incest revealed not by the oracle but by a dream that stages the latent desire, while the oracle is limited to the role of interpreter. Some more recent treatments, like Testori's *Edipus* (1977) and Steven Berkoff's *Greek* (1980), have gone beyond Freud, representing the incest without any anxiety, as the highest pleasure and at the same time as the key to destroying patriarchal society. Alberto Moravia's *Dio Kurt* (1968), on the other hand, is motivated by a criticism of Freud, namely that he limited himself to diagnosing the taboo without destroying it.

A separate place is occupied by André Gide's *Oedipe* (1931), where the incest is simply a symbol of familial belonging, understood as an obstacle to human creativity from which Oedipus is called, at a high price, to free himself. G.P.

Translated by Patrick Baker

Olympia

Some say that in mythical times Heracles regularized the already ancient games held in honor of Zeus at Olympia, on the banks of the Alpheus River. But the Delphic oracle played its part too, insisting that a sacred truce be established, ensuring strangers safe conduct to the games. A continuous list of the victors, begun in 776 BCE, was kept for every four years down to the abolition of the ancient games by the emperor Theodosius I in 393 CE. The sacred precinct in which the festival was celebrated was renowned throughout the Greek world for its overstuffed treasuries and for Phidias' gigantic gold and ivory statue of Zeus (now lost).

After 393 Olympia was largely left to return to nature. In the 18th century Montfaucon and Winckelmann surmised from the remains that the site had once been "teeming with ancient monuments and inscriptions" (Montfaucon, in Weil 1897, 102), but they were unable to rouse their patrons' interest in extensive excavations. A string of English and French antiquaries visited the site, beginning with Richard Chandler in 1766, but their presence had little effect on the pastoral landscape—so little, in fact, that in 1813 the Académie des Inscriptions was still debating where exactly the ancient city center had been sited. Ernst Curtius found the ruins overgrown and the bandits rife on his visit in 1838—but he recited Pindaric odes on the Hill of Cronus nonetheless.

Schemes abounded for uncovering Olympia's treasures but were largely squelched by political uncertainties and by lack of investors, as was Hermann von Pückler Muskau's plan to restore the Altis and surround it with the Edenic garden that he imagined had existed in ancient times. The French managed to make a quick trawl for treasures in 1829, but formal excavations did not begin until 1875, under the direction of the newly formed Deutsches Archäologisches Institut. The Greek-German excavation treaty is notable for having been the first in which the excavators agreed to leave all original artifacts (except duplicates) to the host country, and even to build an on-site museum to house them. The German team, which included Ernst Curtius, Wilhelm Dörpfeld, and Adolf Furtwängler, dug through layers of lime but found neither an Eden nor, to their minds, sufficient numbers of Phidean sculptures—though they did locate the pieces now known as the Hermes of Praxiteles and the Nike of Paionios, and the pediment sculptures of the Zeus Temple, whose iconography and even arrangement have proved frustratingly difficult to reconstruct. Disillusionment, and the growing prospects at the time for finding and acquiring Greek monuments in Asia Minor, led to the closing of these excavations—perhaps the first truly modern archaeological campaign—in 1881. New excavations at the site have been conducted periodically ever since.

If the Germans prized Olympia chiefly for its art, for the French educator Pierre de Coubertin, Olympia was the birthplace of peaceful, hygienic athletic competition—and since his revival of the ancient games in 1896, this is what Olympia has meant to most nonspecialists. But Coubertin was not sufficiently concerned about the authenticity of the spectacle to hold it at Olympia (the 1896 games were held in Athens), and ever since, popular books and sportscasters have been satisfied with a casual glimpse of the original site. This is true even of Leni Riefenstahl's movie about the 1936 Berlin Olympics, *Olympia,* which is famous now chiefly for its innovative images of the athletic competitions (and for its warm and fuzzy images of Hitler).

BIBL.: Helmut Kyreleis, ed., *Olympia 1875–2000: 125 Jahre deutsche Ausgrabungen* (Mainz 2002). John J. MacAloon, *This Great Symbol: Pierre de Coubertin and the Origins of the Modern Olympic Games* (Chicago 1981). Suzanne L. Marchand, *Down from Olympus: Archaeology and Philhellenism in Germany, 1750–1970* (Princeton 1996) and "The Excavations at Olympia: An Episode in German-Greek Cultural Relations," in *Greek Society in the Making, 1863–1913,* ed. Philip Carabott (London 1997) 73–85. Rudolf Weil, "Geschichte der Ausgrabung von Olympia," in *Olympia: Die Ergebnisse der von dem deutschen Reich veranstalteten Ausgrabung,* vol. 1, ed. E. Curtius and F. Adler (Berlin 1897) 101–154. S.M.

Olympic Games

Of the many influences from ancient Greece, the Olympic Games are perhaps the best known today. What probably began as a spontaneous, ritual gathering in the sanctuary (*Altis*) has evolved into one of the largest mega-events and cultural phenomena of modern times. The founding myths, including those of Pelops and Heracles, are unclear, bewildering even Strabo (8.3.30). The traditional dates of 776 BCE to 393 (or 426) CE are controversial, but it is evident that the ancient games lasted a millennium or more.

This festival in honor of Zeus became the supreme expression of competition (*agōn*) in Greece, where winning, not participation, was important. It was held every four years at the time of a full moon at some point in the summer (July or August). A single city, Elis (occasionally Pisa), ran the festival, being accountable to Rome for the last 500 years. The games were officially only for Greeks (but there were exceptions). They were Panhellenic, although Panhellenism was probably not a founding ideal. The sacred truce guaranteed safe passage for competitors, but Olympia was associated as much with war (dedication of weapons) as with peace. Aspiring contestants endured a rigorous, thirty-day training period at Elis. After the procession from Elis to Olympia (symbolically linking city and sanctuary), athletes competed naked on sacred ground. They were whipped, fined, or excluded for infringements of the rules. The victor alone received the olive wreath and could be materially rewarded by his home city.

Of the 23 ancient events, variations on the stade (200-meter race), diaulus (400 meters), dolichus (perhaps 5,000 meters), pentathlon, boxing, and wrestling have passed into the modern games, but the ancients would not recognize modern equestrian events. There were no team events or women competitors, although unmarried girls competed in the Heraia. At the peak perhaps 300 athletes (including boys) competed over five days. About 40,000 spectators willingly endured the pilgrimage and harsh conditions. Contrary to modern romanticizing, the games were bloody and violent. They had commercialism, political interference, and corruption (although no recorded examples of drugs). Their insignificant location in the northwest Peloponnese, and the oracle and seers (associated with colonization to the West), may explain in part their popularity.

Romantic accounts of the Olympics are found in European literature, frescoes, opera, and opera-ballets, especially in the 18th and 19th centuries. The Expédition Scientifique de Morée began excavations at Olympia in 1829, as did the German School under Curtius in 1875. The Olympics of Robert Dover in the Cotswolds, England (1612), are the earliest known revival. Those of William Penny Brookes held nearby at Much Wenlock (1849 onward) had prizes in sport and, unlike Olympia, in culture. Of the many other Olympic revivals in Europe and North America in the 18th and 19th centuries, the national Games of Zappas in Athens (1859) are especially significant.

The Frenchman Baron Pierre de Coubertin is the major figure in the modern Olympic movement, although the Greeks Soutsos, Zappas, and Vikelas, all played roles. The 1896 games followed only partly the ancient games, for Coubertin's own ideals, 19th-century beliefs, earlier modern Olympics, and the European romantic tradition were strong influences. Coubertin's major achievements were to introduce Olympism (a philosophy of life) and internationalism. Neither ideal was found in the ancient games. In 2004, after more than 1,500 years, the Olympic stadium again hosted an athletic event (shot put).

BIBL.: N. B. Crowther, *Athletika: Studies on the Olympic Games and Greek Athletics* (Hildesheim 2004). J. O. Segrave and D. Chu, eds., *The Olympic Games in Transition* (Champaign 1988). D. C. Young, *A Brief History of the Olympic Games* (Malden, Mass., 2004). N.C.

Olympus

Name of many mountains and mountain ranges in Greece and Asia Minor; particularly well known is the massif in central Greece, which in ancient Greek mythology was considered the residence of the gods. Many-peaked Olympus is Greece's highest mountain range. Measuring 20 km in diameter, the massif rises near Greece's east coast, 50 km north of the city of Larissa. Its summit is Mytikas, at 2,918 meters. The first ascent was made in 1862 by H. Barth; C. Kakalos was the first to reach the summit (1913). Owing to the peculiarity of its flora, fauna, and geological formations, the densely wooded massif was declared a nature conservancy in 1938, and in 1981 a biosphere reserve.

The Greek notion of "Olympus, abode of the gods" has analogues all over the world; tall mountains seem to reach into the sky and to tower over the everyday level of human beings. At any rate, "sacred" mountains and those associated with "divine revelation" are frequently considered symbols of divine power: in Shintoism Mount Fuji is considered a wonder, a residence of the gods, and a symbol of immortality; the Canaanite deity Baal is connected to Mount Zaphon; Jahwe has his dwelling on Mount Zion. The cloud-encased summits are often associated with conceptions of weather divinities, in which capacity Zeus was initially lord of Olympus. It was imagined that there the "Olympian" gathered clouds from which to send forth rain, snow, lightning, and thunder onto the Earth. That indeed not only he but also other Olympian gods (a designation for individual gods such as Hera, but also for groups of gods like the Muses) inhabited Olympus is first voiced neither in lyric poetry (Pindar, fr. 30.3–4; *Paean* 6.92–95 fr. 52–53) nor in drama (Sophocles, *Antigone* 604–610; Euripides, *Hippolytus* 64–72). Homer had already sung of the presence and the dwellings of the gods (*Iliad* 1.595–604; 11.75–77; 18.369–379). He vividly portrays their high, steeply rising residence, snowy and dotted with chasms, as furnished with gates, veiled in clouds, and entrusted to the Horae (*Iliad* 1.420; 5.395–402; 5.867; 13.523; 20.5). The idea of Olympus transcending the human world comes to the fore especially in the idealization of its climate (*Odyssey* 6.42–46): "Neither is it shaken by winds nor ever wet with rain, nor does snow fall upon it, but the air is outspread clear and cloudless, and over it hovers a radiant whiteness; here the blessed gods are happy all their days." The appellation "Olympian," which Aristophanes, parodying Homer, assigns as an honorary name to Pericles in his *Acharnians,* is often bestowed today on poet laureates as masters of their art. Such a one, ahead of all the rest, is Goethe.

Homer's description of Olympus can be read as an image of the Greeks' mythological concept of the sky, based on the notion in their religious worldview that Olympus and the sky—the heavens—were once able to merge into one another. The equation of the two, which is also well documented in Latin literature (such as *Hercules Oetatus* 1907; Valerius Flaccus, *Argonautica* 1.4), has also inscribed itself in our culture (heaven and Olympus as synonyms). Poets especially—in particular the German classical poets (Goethe, Hölderlin, Jean Paul, Schiller)—return again and again to Olympus and its "mythical Pantheon" (Goethe, *Aus meinem Leben, Dichtung und Wahrheit,* 6.1811–1822). The metaphor is used in quite exemplary fashion by the protagonist of Grabbe's *Don Juan and Faust,* in a dialogue with Donna Anna:

> Only now do I grasp what death is—
> It closes life and opens Olympus!
> In the sight of your joyous glance,
> angel of death, the past [. . .] passes away,
> And a new Eden takes its place!

The concept of Olympus can also be used in all sorts of ironic, disrespectful ways that tend to bring the gods down to Earth, as can be seen in everyday, humorous phrases such as the playful nickname for the uppermost seats in a theater—in German "Olymp" and in British English "the gods" (and thus the German title *Kinder des Olymp* for the 1945 cult film *Les Enfants du Paradis*). Only one of the very many examples of ironic, critical plays on the metaphor is *Joachim Ringelnatzens Turngedichte* (1920), which pokes fun at the German "people of gymnasts and thinkers" along with "Turnvater" Jahn, the father of gymnastics:

Clamber valiantly,
Old codger!
Clamberissimus
to Olympus! Higher up! Good luck!

The German phrase "to sit on Olympus" (*Auf dem Olymp sitzen*) means that someone's too high opinion of himself is causing him to be condescending to others. A.-B.R.

Translated by Patrick Baker

Opera

The invention of opera around 1600 was one outcome of the most pressing theoretical musical debates of the day, which concerned the right relationship between word and music in public song; these debates were disputed in the contexts of the two major centers of power, the court and the Church. Vocal music of the late Renaissance was richly polyphonic, so that text was very often obscured by the sensuous intertwining of multiple vocal lines in both liturgical text and secular madrigal. The Counter-Reformation, as codified by the Council of Trent (1545–1563), demanded a music that made clear the words of the Catholic liturgy. On the secular side, scholars of music, including Girolamo Mei in Rome and Vincenzo Galilei, father of the astronomer, in Florence, were concluding that the confluence of word and music in ancient tragedy had an affective power lacking in their contemporary drama and music, and they urged a reinvention of musical style that would support the words of a text rather than drown it out in polyphonic splendor. Experiments with monodic styles of singing made by a group in Florence known as the Camerata, associated with the polymath Giovanni de' Bardi, were put to use in Medici court celebrations. Believing that Greek tragedy had been sung throughout, Giulio Caccini and Jacopo Peri wrote music for the first operas to Italian poetic texts by Ottavio Rinuccini: Peri for *Dafne* (1598) and both of them for versions of *Euridice* (1600–1601). During the next decade Claudio Monteverdi, working in Mantua, put the new genre on solid footing with his *Orfeo* (1607) and *Arianna* (*Ariadne,* 1608). Ariadne's lament from the latter, with sources in Catullus's Poem 64 and Ovid's *Heroides,* set a fashion for women's laments that became a locus for reflection on female roles in contemporary society. The lament was also where composers of the new dramatic recitative style might indulge in the more lyrical music that became the center of opera, and its heritage is still to be found in the grieving heroines of Verdi and Puccini.

The new genre called *dramma per musica* spread first to the palaces of Rome, where lives of saints and martyrs were depicted, and then to Venice, where the first commercial opera theaters were established to provide Carnival entertainment on pagan subjects. From that point, classically inspired plots proliferated to an extent not seen on the stage since antiquity. Monteverdi, who became principal composer of liturgical music for the Cathedral of St. Mark, also wrote for Venetian opera houses: *Il Ritorno d'Ulisse in Patria* (1640), *Le Nozze d'Enea e Lavinia* (1641; music lost), and *L'incoronazione di Poppea* (1643). *Poppea* established history as a legitimate subject for opera; thereafter Monteverdi's student Cavalli, to pick but one example, composed operas that included not only mythical subjects like Jason, Orion, and Callisto, but also Xerxes, Antiochus, Coriolanus, Scipio Africanus, and Heliogabalus. Opera flourished in Venice and spread thence to all the European centers of culture and power. It was largely the Italian *dramma per musica* that held sway: Italian artists found their way to Vienna, Dresden, London, and St. Petersburg. They went to Paris, too: Jean-Baptiste Lully, the inventor of French *tragédie en musique,* was born Giovanni Battista Lulli in Florence. But the French favored a form that incorporated chorus and ballet and stories from Ovidian mythology (Lully's operas included *Acis and Galatea, Proserpina, Perseus,* and *Phaeton*), in contrast to the soloist-driven operas of Italy, where historical subjects became increasingly the fashion.

Between opera's invention by Caccini, Peri, and Monteverdi and its maturation as public entertainment, however, there occurred a shift in the discussion of the genre's debt to the classical world. The Florentine scholars had been interested in affect and narrative music in relation to what they thought they knew of the Greek, and they set out to imitate the rhetorical techniques described in Plato and the musical treatises. What they produced of course was modern music: one need only listen to Monteverdi's stage piece for three singers titled "The Combat of Tancred and Clorinda" (1624) to get a sense of the experimentation that was going on, even as Monteverdi insisted he was trying to imitate the Dorian mode described in Plato's *Republic* (399A; Strunk 1998, 4:158). Operatic composition was never antiquarian, but determinedly in the latest style, at first in an effort to subordinate it to the words of the text, and then to satisfy the public with innovative, beautiful music. Consequently, it is the librettists as playwrights rather than the composers who must be examined for classical influence. This was to remain true for the rest of operatic history, with a few exceptions, such as Gluck and Wagner, who deliberately composed their music in consonance with what they perceived to be Greek ideals of dramaturgy.

A theoretical precedent had nevertheless been set from the start: opera was meant to reflect the ancient Greek model, and this expectation increasingly governed critical expectations about operatic dramaturgy. But neoclassical theory and the actual production of opera very quickly went their separate ways. The dramatic form that came naturally to writers of the Italian Baroque had little to do with the structure and sensibilities of the drama of the Greek polis, and instead with the mix of Senecan tragedy, Roman New Comedy, and Virgilian and Ovidian pastoral that informed the pastoral tragicomedies of Torquato Tasso and Giambattista Guarini. Drama in the Baroque necessarily included an important element of romantic love, which had no place in ancient tragedy, and an instinctive preference for happy endings. This, after all, was the age when Nahum Tate rewrote *King Lear* to eliminate the deaths of Cordelia and Lear. The agonies of operatic characters, however tragic their plights might have been in the original sources, were set in a New Comic structure in which society is endangered and then renewed. Whatever the vicissitudes suffered along the way, in the final scene the dominant male celebrates victory, magnanimously forgives malefactors, and unites lovers. Dido marries Iarbas, and Scipio forgives and reunites Sophonisba and Syphax. This was to remain a standard feature of serious opera to the end of the 18th century, as may be observed in Mozart's *Idomeneo* and *La Clemenza di Tito*.

Moreover, scholarly obsessions with Aristotelian rules about tragic structure, as they were perceived in the late Renaissance, made little impression on writers of librettos, despite what they might say in their prefaces. If Monteverdi's *Return of Ulysses* or *Coronation of Poppea* may be judged to observe the unity of action suggested by their titles, and, with some goodwill, the unity of time, they in no way play out in a single location. Busenello's libretto *La Prosperità infelice di Giulio Cesare dittatore* (1646) or Cicognini's *Giasone* (1649) continues the epic ambitions of *The Return of Ulysses,* Busenello depicting landscapes from Lucan and Plutarch and Cicognini from Apollonius of Rhodes. Cicognini and his contemporaries were further affected by a fashion for the expansive, non-Aristotelian messiness of Spanish drama, itself an inheritance from early Italian experiments in Plautine-style comedy. *Giasone* was a popular and influential libretto that finally separated aria from recitative and freely mixed tragic-heroic and low comic elements, combining plots from the Jason legend as told by Euripides, Apollonius, and Ovid. Characters called Jason, Medea, Hypsipyle, Hercules, Orestes, and Aegeus come together on the island of Colchis and at the mouth of the Danube to undergo a complicated series of romantic entanglements and rub shoulders with servants, a stuttering hunchback, gods, winds, and spirits. And though Cicognini and his composer Cavalli kept all this pretty well under control, his successors in the second half of the 17th century were not always so conscientious or talented. "Opera," as Piero Weiss has said, "flourished in Italy with the abandon of an uncultivated vegetation, its constituent parts barely, if at all, held together" (1988, 25). During its first century, opera, only very distantly related in structure to Greek tragedy and born of the mistaken belief that tragedy was sung through, was almost entirely unlike the source of its inspiration.

In the later 17th century there was a reaction. Credit for the reform of the Italian opera libretto that occurred in the decades around 1700 is generally given to the Arcadian Academy, a group of artists and intellectuals devoted to reforming Italian literature and poetry who called themselves by pastoral nicknames reminiscent of the shepherds and nymphs in Theocritus and Virgil. Beginning in the 1690s, a series of Italian poets produced librettos that attempted to eliminate the nondramatic excesses and generic impurities of the later 16th century and bring opera back to the ideals espoused by the Florentines a century earlier. The Arcadian poets Silvio Stampiglia, Apostolo Zeno, and finally and most definitively Pietro Metastasio, all of whom began their careers in Italy and ended them as court poets to the Habsburgs in Vienna, worked to refine *dramma per musica* into what we now call *opera seria,* or heroic opera, although that term did not actually come into vogue until later in the 18th century.

The improvements consisted of as much tightening of dramatic structure as was practical, given that all the singers had to have their arias, and an elimination of the overtly comic elements and characters that had been included in earlier librettos, thus eliminating, too, the satiric tone that had permeated many of the Carnival operas of the Italian 17th century. Metastasian-style opera took on the solemnity and didacticism of the French neoclassical tragedy of Corneille and Racine, including its 17th-century Neostoic philosophy. But the happy ending and erotic subplots were left intact. Romantic passion, derived ultimately from Roman comedy and Ovidian elegy, served as a foil for the nobility of the characters and the Neostoic generosity and clemency of the ruler. The genre celebrated the legitimacy of the ancien régime, whether Holy Roman emperor, Neapolitan viceroy, English monarch, or Venetian republican aristocracy. This fundamentally Baroque form of serious opera, melded together from a mélange of classical influences, was then fitted to subjects that were nonclassical as well as classical, and resonated with the spirit of its age in a way that opera on these themes has not done since. Almost all the composers we popularly think of as in the mainstream of the Baroque—Handel, Vivaldi, Albinoni, Telemann, and Alessandro Scarlatti—wrote music for these texts.

Overtly comic elements in opera were in the meantime left to go their own way. Comic opera emerged from Venice and Naples as spin-offs from *opera seria.* The comic lowlifes and servants that had been part of the 17th-century libretto were separated out into intermezzi; these offshoots were first performed between acts of the *seria* performances and then achieved an independent life of their own. They, even more directly than *opera seria,* are heirs of Roman New Comedy, involving erotic complications among ordinary people that result in the overthrow and then reestablishment of domestic authority in the interest of marriage and social stability: the pattern is as obvious in one of the earliest of these intermezzi, Pergolesi's very successful *La serva padrona* (*The Maid as Mistress,* 1733) as it is in late examples such as Mozart's

Marriage of Figaro and Rossini's *Barber of Seville.* Ironically, these comic operas are perhaps the most successful fulfillment of the Florentine Camerata's desire to support speech with music. For humor to succeed, the meaning must be clear, and the composers working in Naples and Venice—often the same ones writing music for serious opera—developed a flexible and lively style to enhance the comic dialogue they were setting.

While comic opera was emerging in the mid-18th century, the first seeds of doubt were being sown about the relevance of the classical material to effective opera, even in the context of a renewed attempt to reestablish Metastasian and Aristotelian ideals. In 1755 Francesco Algarotti asserted in his *Saggio sopra l'opera in musica* (*Essay on Opera*): "The intent of our poets was to revive Greek tragedy in all its lustre and introduce Melpomene on our stage, attended by music, dancing, and all that imperial pomp with which, at the brilliant period of a Sophocles and Euripides, she was wont to be escorted." At the same time he wondered if "the trillings of an [aria] flow so justifiably from the mouth of a Julius Caesar or a Cato as from the lips of Venus or Apollo." He therefore recommended myth and remote legend as subjects more suitable as sources for plots and vehicles for song.

The best-known results of Algarotti's suggestions are the reform operas of Gluck and his librettist Calzabigi, *Alceste* and *Orfeo ed Euridice,* influenced directly by Algarotti's essay and including French elements of chorus and dramaturgy that supposedly reflected Greek drama. Algarotti's and Gluck's preference for more remote, mythic stories proved to be an accurate reading of contemporary taste. Perennial interest in myth and the increasing use of choruses, combined with the appearance of genuinely tragic librettos, produced operas that are more in the spirit of Greek tragedy than had been achieved to that point. And though the French Revolution produced a temporary revival of interest in the patriots and tyrannicides of ancient history, such as Domenico Cimarosa's *Giunio Bruto* (1788), the newer ideas were taking hold. Cimarosa's 1797 *Gli Orazi e i Curiazi* (*The Horatii and the Curiatti*) is a fine synthesis of all these late-century trends, an episode from Roman legend that concludes with the victorious Horatius murdering his sister and pitching her down a flight of stairs, to the horror of the onstage chorus.

At the same time a series of literary and political influences originating in northern Europe drew opera away from classical stories. Enlightenment ideas began to focus on the common man rather than the aristocratic hero. Shakespearean tragedy, the Scottish pseudo-epics ascribed to Ossian, and gothic literature were coming into vogue in southern Europe, and operas on these subjects began to appear. Even operas based on classical history show an increasing abstraction and retreat into the woods of the north. Giuseppe Sarti's popular *Giulio Sabino* (1781), based on an episode in Gaul reported by Tacitus and Plutarch, was a full-blooded, melodramatic celebration of conjugal love of the kind to be made famous by Beethoven's *Fidelio;* Vincenzo Bellini's *Norma* (1831) is a freely invented story that owes more to *Medea* than to Roman or Druidic history.

In fact, the bonds that had connected both theory and subject of opera in the first century of its existence with the social realities of its age had been severed. Although *opera seria* on classical topics was still composed well into the 1820s by the very popular Luigi Cherubini, Giovanni Pacini, and Saverio Mercadante, Bellini declared the traditional Metastasian topics "as old as Noah," and literati such as Alessandro Manzoni and Jean Paul concluded that classicism was opposed to the spirit of romanticism. In 1854 the critic Adolph Bernhard Marx wrote, "Perished is that unparalleled national drama of Aeschylus, and every attempt to restore it to life (like those made formerly by Caccini and his associates, and of late by Mendelssohn) has proved a mockery, a caricature devoid of all those elements . . . which imparted life and reality to the original . . . That rich existence had lived its time; and terminated after it had fully satisfied the youthful spirit of mankind" (Strunk 1998, 6:73). Even Richard Wagner, whose *Ring* cycle owed much to Aeschylus' trilogic *Oresteia,* regarded the Greeks as a primitive model to be superseded rather than directly imitated. Classical subjects became a form of exoticism, and the remoteness recommended by Algarotti finally achieved a distancing effect rather than a reaffirmation of the world order as the operatic audience lived it.

Nevertheless, the combination of inherited tradition and exoticism provided by the classical world, especially as expressed in its mythology and legend, proved impossible to resist. French opera, for its part, maintained an unbroken tradition of classical subjects: Berlioz's *Les Troyens* is the most famous example, but from the 1850s to the 1920s, Gounod, Hervé, Saint-Saëns, Massenet, and Milhaud each wrote three or more operas on mythological subjects. French comic operas like Offenbach's *Orphée aux Enfers* (1858) and Poulenc's *Les Mamelles de Tirésias* (1947) are mythological travesties that address contemporary social issues. Wagner's encounter with Aeschylus in 1847 affected his production of the *Ring* at every level, literary and musical, and influenced the musical dramaturgy of generations of subsequent composers. Most notably, Richard Strauss worked with classically themed material until 1952, including the bitter *Elektra* and the more cheerful *Ariadne auf Naxos.* Wagner's legacy was also indirectly responsible for Stravinsky's reactionary *Oedipus Rex,* written to a text partially in Latin, as a neoclassical response to late romanticism. Marianne McDonald (2001, 195) has noted a marked increase of new operas written on classical subjects in the 20th century as compared to the 19th, suggesting that the old stories have again provided vital sources for musical and psychological experimentation.

The baroque revival of the 20th century also has brought the earlier operas with their Graeco-Roman heritage back into public view, to the point where one critic suggested that we might regard Handel as the latest "new" opera composer. But the degree to which the aristocratic assumptions of the originals differed from what is palatable in the democratic West is often visible in the way in which productions deconstruct and finally mock their subjects. In such presentations, it is Plautus after all, and not Aeschylus or Aristotle, whose influence remains most visible.

BIBL.: Michael Ewans, *Wagner and Aeschylus: The* Ring *and the* Oresteia (London 1982). Wendy B. Heller, *Emblems of Eloquence: Opera and Women's Voices in Seventeenth-century Venice* (Berkeley 2003). Robert Ketterer, "Why Early Opera Is Roman and Not Greek," *Cambridge Opera Journal* 15, no. 1 (2003) 1–14. Marianne McDonald, *Sing Sorrow: Classics, History, and Heroines in Opera* (Westport 2001). Oliver Strunk, *Source Readings in Music History,* 5 vols. (1965); rev. ed., 7 vols., ed. Leo Treitler (New York 1998). Piero Weiss, "Opera and Neoclassical Dramatic Criticism in the Seventeenth Century," *Studies in the History of Music* 2 (1988) 1–30.

R.C.K.

Optics

Optics is the mathematical science of light, which from antiquity has usually been divided into optics proper (concerning direct vision) and catoptrics (concerning mirrors). Many writers in antiquity and in the Renaissance added a third division: scenography (concerning illusory painting), or dioptrics (concerning refracted vision).

The principal ancient optical texts known in the Renaissance were Euclid's *Optics* and *Catoptrics* (ca. 300 BCE). Ptolemy's much more sophisticated *Optics* (mid-2nd cent. CE), which covered optics proper, catoptrics, and dioptrics, was little known and, indeed, survives only in a fragmentary Latin translation from Arabic. The works of the 13th-century Perspectivists, John Pecham, Roger Bacon, and Witelo, were of the greatest importance for Renaissance opticians, surpassing the ancient texts. Friedrich Risner's *Opticae thesaurus* (*Compendium of Optics,* 1572) consisted of Witelo's *Optics,* together with a translation of the *Optics* of the 11th-century scientist Alhazan (ibn al-Haytham). Two of the most important optical theorists of the Renaissance—Thomas Harriot and Johannes Kepler—began their optical studies with this volume.

Euclid, Ptolemy, and other ancient opticians postulated the existence of a "visual ray," sent out from the eye, which was responsible for vision ("extramission"). So too did Galen and other writers on the physiology of the eye. Though there were important philosophical theories of vision in which the eye received something from the visual object ("intromission"), there was no apparent way to subject such theories to mathematical treatment. Even Aristotle, the proponent of the most important intromissive theory, assumed extramission when accounting for particular visual phenomena.

Alhazan attempted to reconcile the teachings of the opticians with those of the philosophers. While absorbing and extending Euclid's and Ptolemy's observations concerning direct and indirect vision, he essentially inverted their theories of vision, postulating that the eye experienced vision through the reception of light. The primary problem with earlier intromissive theories had been the apparent incoherence of the light that fell on the eye: even a single point on an object might send its image to every point on the pupil. Alhazan made the crucial observation that the eye is constructed from optical materials of different densities, so that any ray that is not perpendicular to the cornea will suffer refraction. By assuming that only perpendicular, unrefracted rays are actually *seen* (that is, a single ray from a single point in the visual field) he came to understand the eye as a sort of filter, constructing a coherent picture from the chaotic light impinging on it.

The teachings of the medieval opticians closely resembled Alhazan's, although they put somewhat less emphasis on light itself and more on the immaterial species that supposedly carried the appearance of the visual object. Kepler in his *Paralipomena in Vitellionem* (*Remarks on Witelo,* 1604) transformed the medieval theory of vision into the modern account of the formation of the retinal image. One unlikely source of inspiration for him was Giambattista della Porta's *Magia naturalis* (*Natural Magic,* 1558–1589), which popularized the use of the camera obscura.

It is debatable whether the discovery of linear perspective by Florentine artists of the 15th century can be attributed to the rediscovery of ancient optical texts. Ancient artists certainly employed the illusion of depth (and this is one of the problems addressed in Euclid's *Optics*), but the single-point perspective of Brunelleschi and Masaccio seems to have been a Renaissance invention. Nevertheless, the first treatise to explain perspective in detail—Alberti's *Della pittura* (*On Painting,* 1436)—drew extensively on Euclid's theory of vision to explain the mathematical basis of the new technique.

The phenomenon of refraction presented particular problems to optical theorists. Ptolemy had included in his *Optics* some results of refractive experiments, but he was unable to state a general mathematical rule for the deviation of refracted rays. Witelo reproduced Ptolemy's tables in a slightly garbled form, but, like Alhazen and Ptolemy himself, he devoted more attention to phenomena of reflection, which had a complete mathematical description. Medieval perspectivists completely ignored the contemporary invention of eyeglasses, no doubt in part because of the difficulties of refraction. The modern sine law of refraction was discovered (but not published) by Thomas Harriot around 1601; Willebrord Snell rediscovered it independently in 1621, and it was first published in 1637 by Descartes.

Theoretical optical knowledge played little role in the development of the telescope in 1608–1609. Despite his occasional claims to the contrary, Galileo seems to have developed and improved his instrument by trial and error. The first optical analysis of the telescope was due to Kepler, who added several modifications and improvements to Galileo's design in his *Dioptrice* (*Dioptrics,* 1611).

BIBL.: S. T. Edgerton, *The Renaissance Rediscovery of Linear Perspective* (New York 1975). M. Kemp, *The Science of Art* (New Haven 1990). D. Lindberg, *Theories of Vision from al-Kindi to Kepler* (Chicago 1976). A. I. Sabra, *Theories of Light: From Descartes to Newton* (London 1967). A. M. Smith, *Ptolemy and the Foundations of Ancient Mathematical Optics* (Philadelphia 1999). A. van Helden, *The Invention of the Telescope* (Philadelphia 1977). R.G.

Oracles

An ancient form of divination by which individuals received answers to questions about the future. Because finding out about the future has been a human desire throughout history, a description of oracles as part of the "classical tradition" runs the risk of including instances that do not belong to that tradition but may well have existed independently. It also runs the risk of not doing justice to the ongoing scholarly debate regarding the "rationality" of dreams and oracles that effectively started with the 25th Sather Lectures, "The Greeks and the Irrational," delivered by E. R. Dodds in 1949.

Classical evidence for oracles suggests that they were received in a variety of ways. There were, for instance, institutional oracles located at sacred places that one had to visit in order to receive a prediction; in the Graeco-Roman world these were governed by a god, most frequently Apollo (e.g., Delphi, Claros, Didyma) or his father, Zeus (e.g., Olympia, Dodona; also at the Siwa oasis in the Egyptian desert, consulted by Alexander the Great). Additionally, there were individuals capable of finding and interpreting signs that predicted future events, such as the flight of birds, the shape of sacrificial victims' entrails, images seen in a dream, or a text like the (lost) Sibylline Oracles. And there were oracles available to the individual without an intermediary, some of which allowed the user to receive a ready-made answer, consisting of a verse from Homer or some other source, selected by lot, dice, or some other divinely inspired form of chance: for example, the oracle in Boura in Achaia was consulted by casting dice in front of a statue of Hercules; for every throw an answer was written on a board (Pausanias 7.25.10). Others required the seeker to select, from a list of possible questions, the one nearest to his or her request and then to receive, by lot or inspiration, one of a number of prefabricated replies: a significant example is the *Sortes Astrampsychi* (attributed to Astrampsychus, a Persian magician), attested starting from the 2nd or 3rd century and continuing throughout antiquity and well beyond.

Although the Old Testament refers to ancient Near Eastern oracular methods such as asking a god for an oracle (Exodus 33.7) or throwing lots (1 Samuel 14.41–45), the rise of Christianity brought about the inevitable decline of pagan oracular institutions. In the early 390s the emperor Theodosius closed down all pagan cults, including institutional oracles, as a consequence of the First Ecumenical Council of Constantinople in 381. Nevertheless, the fame of Delphi, in particular, survived, as it was frequently referred to in classical literature and described in detail by Pausanias (10.5.1–10.32.7). Cyriac of Ancona visited Delphi in 1436, and after the foundation of the modern Greek state, excavations were begun there in 1837 by Greek, German, and French groups, which culminated in the Grande Fouille undertaken by the École Française d'Athènes, 1892–1903. The aim of these archaeological endeavors was to recover the Delphi known to Pausanias; they focused on the site's art and architecture, and any interest in the oracle was purely antiquarian.

Apart from the *Oneirocritica* (*Dream Book*) of Artemidorus (2nd cent. CE), which was repeatedly copied and adapted, the knowledge of individuals capable of finding and interpreting signs that predicted future events remained secret and therefore unexplained in the ancient evidence. Consequently, it did not play a significant part in the classical tradition.

Written oracles available to individuals without an intermediary, on the other hand, not only became part of the classical tradition but were adapted and actively put into practice. The most remarkable of these, the *Sortes Astrampsychi,* did not have a fixed text; instead, the text was altered to suit contemporary needs. Thus, a late version transposes some of the 92 questions from pagan forms such as "Will I become an *agoranomos* [market overseer]?" or "Will I marry the woman I want?" into Christian ones such as "Will I become a *presbyteros* [church elder]?" or "Will I become a monk?" Other versions specify in the preface that the "inspiration" behind the individual's choice of answer is the Christian God, or add the names of prophets and saints as guides to the groups of ten ready-made answers, or (as in the *Sortes Sangallenses*) change the number and nature of the potential answers. The text of the *Sortes Astrampsychi* was copied throughout the Middle Ages and into the early modern period. The version in the Codex Erlangensis A4, for example, was transcribed by the astronomer and scholar Regiomontanus (Johannes Mueller, 1436–1476); the condition of this manuscript, with the list of questions marked and the pages torn from frequent use, shows just how relevant it was perceived to be. A modernized version of Astrampsychus is marketed as *Napoleon's Oracle.*

BIBL.: Anonymous, "The Oracles of Astrampsychus," trans. R. Stewart and K. Morrell, in *Anthology of Ancient Greek Popular Literature,* ed. W. Hansen (Bloomington 1985) 285–326. K. Brodersen, *Astrampsychos: Das Pythagoras-Orakel* (Darmstadt 2006). W. Burkert, *Greek Religion* (Oxford 1985) 109–118. T. Curnow, *The Oracles of the Ancient World* (London 2004). E. R. Dodds, *The Greeks and the Irrational* (Berkeley 1951). J. Hall, *Napoleon's Oracle* (New York 2003). H. W. Parke, *Greek Oracles* (London 1967). K.B.

Ornament

Greek and Roman architects and builders have given the world one of its major and most widely deployed systems of ornament. The principal features of this classical tradition are architectural elements: bases, columns, capitals, arches and frames for doors, windows, and pediments. This fundamental vocabulary is supplemented by borders of egg and dart patterns and dentils and by floral and leaf scrolls, the subject of a large body of scholarship. In addition, wreaths, key fret, figural representations, animal heads, and other creatures rendered in sculpture, paintings, mosaics, and other materials enrich the classical tradition of ornament. As in any well-developed system of design, these components are assembled and varied according to rules that have changed over time. Originally, the rules of the classical tradition derived from the architectural conventions of early Greek buildings, especially temples, and of their Hellenistic and Roman successors.

In early and classical Greek buildings, such as the Temple of Apollo at Corinth and the Parthenon at Athens, the simplicity and integrity of Doric columns, on a stepped base supporting the architrave, frieze, and cornice, draw attention away from the strongly ornamental potential of these structural features. Yet as the classical orders developed, they emerged as essentially ornamental variants of a simple column and capital, while at the same time retaining a large measure of mechanical function. In such structures as the 4th-century BCE Choragic Monument of Lysicrates at Athens, however, the Corinthian order is entirely decorative; fine ribbing on the engaged columns with intricate capitals leads the eye to read them as structural elements, but their primary role is to add rhythm to the drum and to persuade the viewer to understand them as part of the support of the roof. Other buildings produced dramatic effects through manipulation of the proportions of columns. Some might be doubled in size, as in the Temple of Jupiter at Baalbek; others might be reproduced simply on painted surfaces, as in houses in Roman Italy. Rectilinear boxes were particularly suited for the miniaturization of architectural design, as seen in the gilded silver Casket of Projecta in the Esquiline treasure, and the 4th-century sarcophagus for Junius Bassus, which exploits the framing potential of columns and arches to present figures of Christ and the Apostles and biblical stories such as those of Adam and Eve, Job, and Daniel.

Moldings, universal in the classical system of the orders and employed to articulate facades and interiors of buildings, were scarcely mentioned by Vitruvius (1st cent. BCE) and given only limited attention by his 15th-century follower, Leon Battista Alberti. Yet they are perhaps the most fundamental basic components of the system. Moldings occupy much of the first five books of Sebastiano Serlio's illustrated work on architecture, and they have preoccupied masons and joiners ever since. They were essential elements of the ornament of furniture and utensils in the classical period itself, as well as in all later centuries.

Roman methods of building, with concrete and rubble faced by stone or brick on the exterior and stone, marble, plaster, and mosaic on the interior, allowed increased attention to ornament, as surface was in part disengaged from support. The use of the arch also stimulated variants in moldings, as did the development of domes and barrel vaults. The coffering of the Pantheon and the triumphal arches in the Roman Forum reproduced earlier embellished wooden forms of construction, giving them instead an ornamental function.

The longevity of the classical system was in large measure ensured by the survival of massive ruins that were copied and revived over two millennia. Geographical expansion through the conquests of Alexander the Great and, later, the Romans carried classical forms of public buildings east to the Indus and north and west to Hadrian's Wall. Such resilience in an ornamental system derived from architecture is rare and remarkable. Radically different systems of ornament have prevailed in other cultures. For example, the most enduring ornamental system in China is based not on architecture but on floral and zoomorphic motifs organized according to a system of linguistically determined puns, metaphors, and allusions.

In Europe the classical system was so effective that it supplanted or marginalized others, such as the geometric pottery style in Greece and Celtic and Viking traditions from later periods in the north. These disappeared or were assimilated into the classical system, as in the geometric ornament in Norman and Romanesque buildings. Over the centuries, the classical system proved able to adopt and adapt features from the Islamic world and even the Far East, incorporating borrowed sculptural figures, geometric patterns, and floral elements.

The later history of architectural style in Europe and the Mediterranean basin is one in which structural support functioned simultaneously as ornament. Reuse of columns, capitals, and marble facings in early Christian Rome facilitated the great basilicas of the 4th and 5th centuries, such as Santa Maria Maggiore. In these churches figural embellishment originating in sculpture or relief was reduced to pictorial design in brilliantly colored mosaic. In the Middle East as well, the Great Mosque at Damascus and the Dome of the Rock at Jerusalem combine spoliate columns and capitals with brilliantly colored surfaces.

A new dialogue between imposing structure and intriguing surface is seen in Romanesque and Gothic architecture. The balance varied from territory to territory and period to period. In central France, at Saint-Savin-sur-Gartempe in the Vienne, heavy columns were painted to give the appearance of ancient marble; at Saint-Lazare at Autun square-sectioned piers reproduced the engaged piers of the Roman era. The multiplication of colonnettes on piers and of ribbing in arches and in vaults created rippling surfaces, often in geometric configurations, as in the vaults of Exeter Cathedral, the Chapel of Kings College in Cambridge, and the Vladislav Hall in the Hradčany Castle in Prague. Similar attention to surface appeared on the exterior, as in the choir of the Cathedral of Monreale in Sicily, and in the ecclesiastical furnishings of the Cosmati school, with their spiraling columns inlaid with mosaic. Leaves and figures reshaped the Corinthian capital beyond recognition. In the Byzantine East and in Islamic

Spain trapezoidal, block-shaped capitals were pierced to transform the leaf-covered capitals of the ancient world.

Just as columns, arches, and vaults are both structure and embellishment, so too friezes of figures, found in major public buildings from the Parthenon to the present, play a dual role. On the one hand they are part of a unified program in which figures and architectural elements cannot legitimately be separated. They were meant to clothe otherwise plain buildings and define them as temples of classical deities or, in the Christian era, as the House of God. Transformation is indeed a function of all ornament, whether it is added to a building or to a garment. But friezes also carried religious and political messages and recounted narratives that were incorporated into the ornament of complex buildings. Columns, arches, and niches with figures on or in them reinforced the presence of God and the prophets in churches as varied as the former abbey church (now basilica) of Sainte-Marie-Madeleine at Vézelay, the Cathedral of Notre-Dame at Chartres, and the Cathedral of Santiago at Compostella.

Much Western figural representation in both painting and sculpture was integral to the decorative schemes of major buildings, to their furnishings, and to the books and altarpieces inside them. Whereas a classical temple or a Gothic cathedral might house life-size or monumental images, miniaturized images and architectural ornament were created for altars, chapels, pulpits, and reliquaries, as in the Reliquary of the Three Kings at Cologne (13th cent.) and in Andrea del Castagno's polyptych in the altar of the chapel of San Tarasio in the Church of San Zaccaria in Venice (1442). Frames, executed with moldings and scrolls of the classical system, continued to dominate the presentation of religious figures over the next four or five centuries. The frames painted around Michelangelo's figures in the Sistine Chapel are among the most accomplished and visually baffling representations of molded architectural elements; in the Scuola Grande in San Rocco, Venice, Tintoretto's cycle of paintings is presented in elaborate and highly decorated frames.

In the same vein, manuscript illumination from the Byzantine, Romanesque, and Gothic periods, such as that in the Gospel Book of Saint Augustine in Corpus Christi College, Cambridge, exploited the representation of columns, capitals, and arches to frame and focus visual attention on the Evangelists. Manuscript illumination of the 15th century and later, more closely based on classical forms, was equally sensitive to the role of architectural features to present the major figures and narratives of the Bible.

The Renaissance-era retrieval of the ornamental styles of the classical past was achieved by Brunelleschi, Leon Battista Alberti, Raphael, and Bramante through careful study and drawing of surviving fragments, especially in Rome. Alberti, who followed the ideas of Vitruvius where possible, exerted wide influence on European architecture through his treatise *De re aedificatoria* (*On the Art of Building,* 1452) more than through his few built works, such as the facade and interior of Sant'Andrea at Mantua. In the elaborate geometrical ornament of the loggia of the Villa Madama in Rome, designed for Cardinal Giulio de' Medici, Raphael benefited from the recently discovered Golden House of Nero. Michelangelo exploited a similar play of surfaces and, at the same time, subverted classical conventions in the interiors of the Laurentian Library and the Medici Chapel.

Illustrations in manuals and treatises on architecture published in the 16th through 18th centuries (by Serlio, Vignola, Palladio, Scamozzi, Pozzo, Guarini, and Vittone in Italy, and others in France, Germany, and England) accelerated attention to surface, that is, to transformation. Their influence is felt on facades ranging from the simple to the complex, such as Borromini's facade of the Church of San Carlo alle Quattro Fontane in Rome (1667) and Perrault's east facade of the Louvre in Paris (1670). The basic elements could be infinitely varied in number, form, and proportion. The classical system was also exploited for political display, notably in the palaces of Fontainebleau and Versailles, the Hermitage at St. Petersburg, and the Capitol in Washington, D.C. Perhaps the most fascinating creations occur in the etchings and drawings of Piranesi (mid-18th cent.). His imaginary buildings were concocted from elements of surviving ancient buildings with fantastical combinations of bases, columns, capitals, and larger elements to create fanciful and dramatic theatrical effects. As in earlier periods, the revived classical system was engaged to decorate prized miniature buildings of precious metal, in the form of caskets and jewel cases, household altars and reliquaries.

In the 18th and 19th centuries the bond between architecture and ornament was theorized in the writings of Gottfried Semper and Alois Riegl. Semper's determination to justify styles of buildings on technological grounds, in *Der Stil in den technischen und tektonischen Künsten* (1860), provoked a response in Riegl's *Stilfragen* (1893), which countered the view that technique played a defining role and argued instead that ornament had a spontaneous life of its own, a *Kunstwollen.* He was especially engaged with exploring the origin of the palmette and acanthus in Egyptian lotus motifs. Semper's contemporary Owen Jones, working at the Victoria and Albert Museum, had noted the close link between ornament and architecture and also the dependence on ornament of what we term "style." Jones's *Grammar of Ornament* (1856) is particularly remembered for its wide-ranging approach that embraces ancient Egyptian, Indian, Chinese, and even Pacific Island designs along with a wide spectrum of classical ornament. The intricate link between ornament and artifact was broken, however, as all Jones's examples were rendered as flat, colored patterns in small rectangular segments printed several to a page, which diminished the role of the actual building in the ultimate effect. This practice of separating pattern from context was perpetuated by others, who reproduced ornaments for use in the industrialized production of wallpaper, textiles, and terra-cotta.

The privileging of pattern divorced from its origins contributed to the assumption that ornament could be separated from structure, and this, paradoxically, supported a claim of modernist theorists that ornament should be rejected as artificial and superfluous. Adolf Loos ("Ornament is crime") is usually seen as a key figure here. Although his condemnation of ornament has been exaggerated, he did indeed expound the view that materials and structure, not embellishment, should define good building. The bond between structure and ornament also changed with the development of structural engineering, in particular in the great 19th-century sheds of glass and iron, such as London's Crystal Palace (1851) and the many railway stations built in Victorian England and elsewhere. The ever upward-stretching skyscrapers of the late 19th and early 20th centuries inserted many repetitive stories between the colonnaded or arched entrance and the highly embellished cornice line, as in Louis Sullivan's masterpieces. Attempts during the 20th century to strip the classical system from buildings altogether finally provoked a reaction in postmodern architectural works by Robert Venturi, Michael Graves, and others.

Ornament theorists at the turn of the 20th century, primarily Alois Riegl and Howard Goodyear, correctly noted that elements of Western ornament, especially the palmette and acanthus, had close connections with Egypt. They realized that the study of classical ornament would eventually lead eastward: Egypt had numerous colonnaded structures, as did Western Asia and Iran. These same regions also contributed the lotus scroll and the palmette, the lion, and the winged beast to the ornamental system.

The conquests of Alexander the Great and the successor states of the Seleucids took a classical vocabulary eastward to sites on the Oxus. Reinforced by contact with the Romans, the Kushans of Gandhara (in present-day Pakistan), and the Matura dynasty in India employed decorative plinths, piers, attached columns, and capitals that are easily recognized as variants of the Corinthian order. In addition, Buddhist art incorporated and adapted the classical combinations of figure and frame. In cave chapels and rock-cut temples at Ajanta, Vihara, and Allora, columns with capitals and embellished ceilings elaborated the ornament taken over from the classical tradition. At Sanchi and Amaravati religious narratives were presented within friezes and between columns, often surrounded by frames derived from classical moldings and the palmette motif. Figures also appeared with classical architectural frames on small artifacts such as the Bimran reliquary. These adaptations in the service of Buddhism ensured the spread of the classical system of ornament throughout the Indian subcontinent, Sri Lanka, and Indonesia, where it was also adapted for Hindu and Jain temples, as at Luna Vasahi Temple at Mount Abu in Rajasthan.

Buddhism was also responsible for the transmission of classical ornament to the Far East. Buddhist proselytizers moved from Gandhara eastward along the Silk Road in the early centuries CE. Meanwhile, Chinese Buddhists in search of sacred texts traveled in the opposite direction. Traces of these movements are seen in images and texts but most notably in the wooden fragments of pseudo-Ionic columns and undulating palmette scrolls at Loulan at the eastern end of the Silk Road. At Yungang, a cave complex hollowed out and decorated in the 5th century CE, near the modern Chinese city of Datong, the walls of several caves are rendered as if they were the facades of buildings. The plinths, columns, and entablatures employed as frames represent a newly formed vocabulary of Buddhist architecture that had absorbed Iranian, Roman, and Kushan versions of the classical system. Arched openings with pointed tops and, most especially, scroll designs at Yungang are characteristic of this transcultural style of architecture and ornament.

In Asia classical scrolls took on an entirely new life. Running scrolls were most usually employed for the lotus, the symbol of rebirth in Buddhist contexts, as in the cave temples at Dunhuang, or for the peony, the emblem of wealth and power, on elaborate stone carvings and silverwork found at the Tang capital of Chang'an; many other flowers appeared on Chinese ceramics, metalwork, and textiles. The Silk Road was one way such designs made their way westward. Movements of peoples fleeing the Mongols in the 13th century, and eventually the Mongols themselves, also introduced Chinese versions of these flower patterns to Iran, whence they found their way to Turkey and later to Venice, to appear in manuscripts and on the textiles and carpets reproduced in European paintings, especially scenes of the Virgin and Child. Furthermore, with the export of Chinese porcelain, adaptations of classical scrolls spread to all areas of the world where imitations of these ceramics were produced locally.

Beginning in the 16th century, trade and colonization continued the spread of the classical ornamental system around the world. In areas previously unaffected by the classical tradition, especially the New World, cathedrals, churches, and mansions based on classical forms were constructed, as in the Mexican Baroque churches of Our Lady of Ocotlán Sanctuary at Tlaxcala, or the Church of Santa María Tonantzintla. In Asia incursions of Europeans resulted in a new wave of classical influence, evident in the design and ornamentation of Victorian imperial buildings in Delhi and in the commercial and government buildings on the Bund in Shanghai.

BIBL.: Brent C. Brolin, *Architectural Ornament: Banishment and Return* (New York 1985). Bernd Evers (preface) and Christof Thoenes (intro.) in *Architectural Theory, from the Renaissance to the Present: 89 Essays on 117 Treatises,* ed. V. Biermann et al. (Cologne 2003). E. H. Gombrich, *The Sense of Order: A Study in the Psychology of Decorative Art* (Oxford 1979). Owen Jones, *The Grammar of Ornament* (London 1856). Adolf Loos, *Spoken into the Void: Collected Essays, 1897–1900,* trans. Jane Newman and John H. Smith (Cambridge, Mass., 1982). Harry Francis Mallgrave, *Gottfried Semper, Architect of the Nineteenth Century* (New Haven 1996). John Onians, *Bearers of Meaning: The Classical Orders in Antiquity, the Middle Ages, and the Renaissance* (Princeton 1988). Jessica Rawson, *Chinese Ornament: The Lotus and the Dragon* (London 1984). Alois Riegl, *Problems of Style: Foundations for a History of Ornament,* trans. Evelyn Kain (Princeton 1992). Joseph Rykwert, *The Dancing Column: On Order in Architecture* (Cambridge, Mass., 1996). Debra Schafter, *The Order of Ornament, the Structure of Style: Theoretical Foundations of Modern Art and Architecture* (Cambridge 2003). Gottfried Semper, *Style in the Technical and Tectonic Arts; or, Practical Aesthetics,* trans. Harry Mallgrave (Los Angeles 2004). John Summerson, *The Classical Language of Architecture* (London 1980). Peter Thornton, *Form and Decoration, Innovation in the Decorative Arts, 1470–1870* (London 1998).

J.R.

Orpheus

Hero of Greek myth, poet and musician, supposed founder of a mystery religion and writer of "Orphic" verse. Wild Thrace was home to Orpheus, a figure of distinguished lineage. His mother was said to be the Muse Calliope and his father, the local river god Oeagrus or Olympian Apollo himself. Singer, lover, priest, and prophet, a mortal man who had journeyed to the underworld, Orpheus was renowned in antiquity for having composed songs about the origins of things and for having prescribed an ascetic way of life. His story, rich in drama, demonstrating the strange powers of music, has had extraordinary resonance over the centuries.

Two Latin texts stand behind most retellings of the myth in the European tradition: the poignant narrative in Virgil's *Georgics,* book 4, and the detail-rich account in Ovid's *Metamorphoses,* books 10 and 11. No comprehensive account of Orpheus' tale survives in Greek, although allusions to the myth are many, and these imply the coexistence of competing versions. In the earliest surviving literary witness, a line of verse attributed to the lyric poet Ibycus (mid-6th cent. BCE), he is already referred to as "famous Orpheus."

Orpheus' deeds set him apart from other Greek heroes. An Argonaut, one of Jason's fellow travelers on the quest for the Golden Fleece, he was a hero who bore no arms, his weapon being the enchanting sound of his voice and lyre: through his music he overcame even the Sirens' song (Apollonius, *Argonautica* 4.905). A devout lover, he was stricken with grief at the death of his wife, Eurydice, who had been killed by a serpent's bite when fleeing the amorous attentions of the shepherd Aristaeus. To win her back, Orpheus crossed over into the realm of the dead. With his music he held spellbound the denizens of the land of Dis: Cerberus, the Furies, Tantalus, Ixion, Sisyphus. Pluto gave him leave to lead Eurydice to the upper world; Proserpina set a single condition, that during the journey he not look back at his bride. But love can abide no law: Orpheus' backward glance lost him Eurydice forever. His anguish great, he inhabited the untamed forests of Thrace singing mournful songs that drew beasts, trees, and stones to him.

A gruesome death awaited the hero. Frenzied maenads, drowning out his song with their clamor and ululations, tore him limb from limb. Why such punishment? Various reasons were supplied: because Orpheus favored the cult of Apollo over that of Dionysus (Aeschylus, *Bassarids*), because he passed on calumnies about the gods (Isocrates, *Busiris* 39), because he lacked the courage to die with Eurydice (Plato, *Symposium* 179D), because in his mourning he shunned women (Virgil, *Georgics* 4.520), because he turned to the love of boys, first among the Thracians to do so (Phanocles, fragments; Ovid, *Metamorphoses* 10.83–84). After his violent dismemberment, the river Hebrus gently wafted Orpheus' lyre, still sounding, and his severed head, still speaking, to the island of Lesbos, where his head pronounced oracles until Apollo jealously demanded it cease. The Muses placed Orpheus' lyre in the heavens.

Decisively separating Orpheus from other heroes of myth is the existence of a corpus of works that he was believed to have written. For the ancient Greeks Orpheus was a historical figure: a religious poet who composed cosmogonic verse and a priest who studied the mysteries in Egypt and founded a religious sect. Orphic texts surviving intact to the present are pseudepigraphic and late. They include a collection of 87 Orphic hymns (2nd–3rd cents. CE) and the *Orphic Argonautica* (probably later 5th cent. CE), the latter an account of the voyage of the Argo told in the boastful voice of Orpheus. The Greek Neoplatonists were drawn to Orphic writings: Proclus (d. 485 CE) is said to have studied Orphic hymns and to have practiced Orphic ritual (Marinus, *Life of Proclus*).

From Hellenistic Jewish circles in Alexandria came the invented *Testament of Orpheus* (first redaction possibly 3rd or 2nd cent. BCE), premised on the idea that Orpheus, when in Egypt, became a student of Moses: the text professes to be Orpheus' last words to his disciple Musaeus, urging him to renounce the pagan gods and to worship the one true God. Christian apologists of the 3rd and 4th centuries seized on this pagan recantation of polytheism; indeed the *Testament* survives only because Clement of Alexandria, pseudo-Justin, Eusebius of Caesarea, and others cited it at length in their own polemical writings. Augustine could blame Orpheus for not having acted on the truth revealed to him (*Against Faustus* 13.15).

The hero found a place in Christian art and thought through analogies drawn to David and to Christ. Jewish tradition first linked the Thracian singer and the Psalmist: Orpheus, wearing Phrygian costume, holding a lyre, appears in the synagogue frescoes of Dura-Europos (ca. 245) and Orpheus/David appears on early medieval synagogue pavements. Early Christians assimilated Orpheus to Christ on the grounds that both had descended to the underworld to lead souls to salvation. Late antique images of Orpheus surrounded by animals are to be found in the catacombs, on sarcophagi, and on church pavements, alluding to the motif of Christ as Good Shepherd and evoking paradisiacal harmony.

In the early 6th century Orpheus' story was submitted to influential exegesis, both allegorical and etymological. Boethius (*Consolation of Philosophy* 3.12) interpreted Orpheus' backward glance as applying to those who strive for the good but lose that excellence when they yield to earthly desires. Fulgentius (*Mythologies* 3.10) observed that the name Orpheus signifies *oraia phōnē,* that is, *optima vox,* "best voice," whereas Eurydice means "broad judgment." Medieval schoolmen would draw on both as they searched for the moralizing messages hidden in the pagan myth. The 12th-century Platonist William of Conches, commenting on Boethius, interpreted Orpheus ("best voice") as a wise and eloquent man who loved and then grieved for Eurydice, a symbol of the natural desire that not even the wise can conquer; representing virtue, she had fled from Aristaeus, and thus descended to the underworld, which signified earthly delights. In the 1360s Boccaccio prepared a synthesis of ancient myth and its post-classical moralizations in his encyclopedic *Genealogy of the Gods,* including, in the entry on Orpheus (5.12), the notion that the hero taming the beasts signifies eloquence recalling rapacious men to humanity—an echo of the ancient portrayal of Orpheus as a civilizing force (Horace, *Art of Poetry* 391–393).

Moral allegory and romance readily intermeshed. In the influential *Ovide moralisé* (*Ovid Moralized,* ca. 1300), Orpheus is reason and Eurydice is sensuality of the soul: she is plunged into the hell of bad conscience when bitten by the serpent of mortal vice. Illustrations in early manuscripts, however, show Eurydice as a lady of fashion threatened by a small dragon, while Orpheus is a minstrel, harp in hand. The classic lovers had become courtly lovers. In the mid-14th century Guillaume de Machaut, drawing heavily on the *Ovide moralisé,* introduced "the good poet Orpheus" as an exemplary, persevering lover in his *Confort d'ami* (*Comfort for a Friend,* 2277ff.); Petrarch refers to the hero in the first of his six *Trionfi,* the "Triumph of Love" (4.13–15). Sometime before 1330 an anonymous Middle English poet composed a full-verse romance, *Sir Orfeo,* drawing on material generically related to the Breton *lai.* Here King Orfeo, a skilled harpist, retreats to the wilderness after Queen Heurodis has been abducted and taken to fairyland. As a poor minstrel, he gains entrance to the fairy castle. The blissful notes of his harping win him a boon from the fairy king, and he is able to claim Heurodis and lead her back to his kingdom for a happy ending. In the later 15th century the Middle Scots poet Robert Henryson stayed closer to the Virgilian story line: King Orpheus journeys to Pluto's domain, wins back his queen with his harp playing, but loses her with a backward glance; Henryson then completes his romance with a moralization drawn from Nicholas Trivet's commentary on Boethius (ca. 1300).

The Orphic texts became again an object of study among the Italian Humanists, notably the Neoplatonist Marsilio Ficino, who drafted a Latin translation of the Greek hymns for personal use as early as 1462. For Ficino, Orpheus was the pagan theologian who best understood divine rapture and mystical ascent. Believing, with others of his time, that music was a means to ready the spirit for contemplation, he himself performed Orphic hymns "in the ancient manner," accompanying himself on a lyre that is said to have borne an image of Orpheus. Naldo Naldi claimed that Orpheus' soul had been reborn in Ficino; Angelo Poliziano praised Ficino and his lyre for having successfully retrieved Eurydice—that is, Platonic wisdom, with its "broad judgment."

Orpheus' tale seemed made for musical dramatization. As opera emerged, innovators turned repeatedly to the myth about the power of song. Sometime in the 1470s, Angelo Poliziano composed a pastoral drama, *La Fabula d'Orfeo,* as an attempt to recuperate ancient theater: his verse text, part spoken, part sung, ending with the death of Orpheus, was performed in Mantua and other northern Italian courts with full visual effects. In 1600 Jacopo Peri created the earliest extant *dramma per musica* when he prepared a musical setting for Ottavio Rinuccini's *Euridice.* With others of the Florentine Camerata, he sought to imitate the ancients by using monodic settings that allowed singers to "speak while singing." In 1607 Claudio Monteverdi staged his *Orfeo* in Mantua (libretto by Alessandro Striggio), influentially employing a greater range of musical and instrumental effects. Undoubtedly the greatest of operatic treatments of the theme is Christoph Willibald von Gluck's *Orfeo ed Euridice* (libretto by Ranieri de' Calzabigi), first performed in the Burgtheater in Vienna in 1762: a landmark "reform" opera, elegantly spare, psychologically intense, it had great influence on subsequent interpretations of the myth. When in 1858 Jacques Offenbach first staged his comic opera *Orphée aux enfers* (*Orpheus in the Underworld*), a send-up of classical mythology and Second Empire politics, the nobility of the works of his predecessors made the satire all the more pointed.

Orpheus' passion-rich tale inspired myriad works of painting and sculpture. Scenes favored in Renaissance interiors, on walls and on domestic furnishings, included the Death of Eurydice, Orpheus in the Underworld, and Orpheus Taming the Animals—the last a bucolic scene in which the hero typically plays a contemporary viol, the *lira da braccio,* rather than the lyre of antiquity. The desire to recuperate ancient visual forms is seen in Albrecht Dürer's much-discussed drawing *The Death of Orpheus* (1494), adapted from a print by a follower of Mantegna. Here Orpheus is shown set upon by wild women with clubs: he falls to his knees with hand raised in a posture of defeat drawn from ancient sculpture; a scroll on a tree beside him reads *Orfeus der erst puseran* (Orpheus the First Sodomite)—an Ovidian idea alluded to by Poliziano in his *Fabula d'Orfeo.*

Artists visualized a wide range of episodes. Pieter Brueghel the Elder painted *Orpheus before Pluto and Proserpina* (1604), and Hendrick de Keyser cast an *Orpheus and Cerberus* in bronze relief (1611). Nicholas Poussin, in his *Landscape with Orpheus and Eurydice* (ca. 1650), focused on Fortune's cruel trick: Orpheus plays his lyre, unaware that a serpent threatens Eurydice. Antonio Canova sculpted Orpheus at the fateful moment of the backward glance (1775–1777); Lord Leighton, in the painting that inspired Robert Browning's "Eurydice to

Orpheus," showed Eurydice pleading for her husband's glance (1864); Auguste Rodin depicted Orpheus, hand over his eyes, emerging from Hell with Eurydice at the moment before he gives way (1893). Broader themes were broached: Eugène Delacroix painted *Orpheus Civilizing the Greeks* (1838–1847) for the library in the Palais Bourbon in Paris as a pendant to *Attila and His Hordes Overrunning Italy and the Arts*; J.-B. Camille Corot, who often turned to the myth, painted *Orpheus Greeting the Dawn* as a pendant to *The Sleep of Diana* (1865).

Orpheus appealed to poets and artists as a model of the heroic creator, the enraptured singer of truth-revealing song. Goethe in his "Urworte: Orphisch" (Primaeval Words: Orphic, 1817) explored the sources of poetic inspiration. Stéphane Mallarmé described the task of the poet as "the Orphic explanation of the world" (letter to Paul Verlaine, 1885). The Symbolist painter Gustave Moreau assigned the Silver Age of the world to Orpheus in his nine-paneled polyptych, *La vie de l'humanité* (*The Life of Humanity,* 1886), where images of the hero are entitled "Inspiration," "Song," and "Tears." In his earlier *Orphée* (1865), Moreau had depicted a scene unattested in myth: an exotically clad Thracian girl holds and gazes reverently on Orpheus' lyre and severed head. To give to myths "all the intensity they can have," Moreau was willing to abandon classical formulae and to draw on inner vision. In 1912 the poet and critic Guillaume Apollinaire coined the term *Orphism* to describe a pure art generated from within the artist, drawing on the inner "voice of light." František Kupka and Robert and Sonia Delaunay, who followed Apollinaire in correlating color and music, are sometimes referred to as Orphic Cubists. Allusions to Orphic themes are explicit in the works of heroic Modernists, including Franz Marc, Oskar Kokoshka, Paul Klee, Jacques Lipchitz, Barnett Newman, and Barbara Hepworth. Isamu Noguchi designed sets and costumes, and Igor Stravinksy supplied the music for George Balanchine's ballet *Orpheus* (1948).

Twentieth-century writers seized on the myth in noteworthy numbers, valuing it as a parable of the violation of boundaries, the presence of death in life, and the interior journey of the poet. Most powerful of the evocations, perhaps, is Rainer Maria Rilke's poetic cycle *Sonette an Orpheus* (*Sonnets to Orpheus,* 1922)—a meditation on death and life and Orpheus' creative song, composed, its author maintained, in a state of near rapture. Random factors converged in its making. Rilke was residing at the Château de Muzot in the Swiss Valais preparing to complete his *Duino Elegies.* He had been reading Ovid and translating Michelangelo's sonnets, his mistress had pinned on the wall opposite his desk a reproduction of a Renaissance drawing of Orpheus Taming the Animals, and he had been given to read the last diaries of the 19-year-old Vera Ouckama Knoop, who had died of leukemia. "In a few thrillingly impassioned days" he composed 25 of the 26 poems in Part I; a few weeks later, he wrote 29 more: "the most enigmatic dictation I have ever endured and performed."

Dramatists including Jean Cocteau (*Orphée,* 1926), Jean Anouilh (*Eurydice,* 1941), and Tennessee Williams (*Orpheus Descending,* 1957) recast the story in contemporary terms. In Cocteau's film version of the play (1950), the Princess in a Rolls Royce, representing Death, loves the poet Orphée and kills Eurydice, causing Orphée to embark on surreal journeys in the zone behind the mirror. Inspired by Cocteau, the French filmmaker Marcel Camus created his *Orfeu Negro* (*Black Orpheus,* 1959), a film adaptation of Vinicius de Moraes' play *Orfeu da Conceiçao* (1954). Set in Rio de Janeiro against the backdrop of Brazilian Carnaval, it tells the story of the tram driver Orfeu, who awakens the sun by playing his guitar; he loses Eurydice to Death and pursues her even to a rite of spirit possession. The desire to transpose the Greek myth into an exotic New World setting had a political aspect. The title refers to an essay by Jean-Paul Sartre ("Orphée noir," 1949), in which the Existentialist championed the work of black francophone poets of Africa and the Caribbean: former colonials, they were able, through a reversal of the gaze, to make France seem exotic.

Creative reworkings of the myth of Orpheus have inevitably been inflected by current understandings of the nature, limits, and function of myth. Nineteenth-century efforts to demonstrate the unity of world myth have resulted in enduring shifts in the perception of Orpheus. Folklorists have found Orphic motifs (underworld journeys in search of the beloved, taboos against looking back) embedded in the mythologies of far-flung peoples: the Maori, the Central Siberian Tungus folk, indigenous North American tribes. Comparative anthropologists have recognized in Orpheus the figure of the shaman, borrowing the Tungus word for a magician who has power over nature, who, in a trance, can travel outside the body and mediate between the realms of the living and the dead. Early 20th-century efforts to link myth and ritual made it possible to see Orpheus' journey and his dismemberment as rationalized, Hellenized descriptions of intrusive (non-Greek) shamanistic ritual. Early Orphism continues to be studied as a site of the convergence of religious traditions and as a movement distinctive for its emphasis on the written word. W. K. C. Guthrie (*Orpheus and Greek Religion,* 1935; *The Greeks and Their Gods,* 1950) saw Orpheus' story as providing evidence of the movement of Apollonian ideas into Dionysian Thrace. The discovery in 1962 of the Derveni Papyrus (340–320 BCE)—the oldest extant Greek book—in a tomb in Macedonia has thrown welcome new light on early Orphism and its initiatory rites, for the fragmentary text comprises a theogony in archaic hexameters with an allegorical explanation of its contents.

BIBL.: Anna Maria Babbi, ed., *Le metamorfosi di Orfeo* (Verona 1999). Judith Bernstock, *Under the Spell of Orpheus: The Persistence of a Myth in Twentieth-century Art* (Carbondale 1991). J. B. Friedman, *Orpheus in the Middle Ages* (Cambridge, Mass., 1970). Elisabeth Henry, *Orpheus with His Lute: Poetry and the Renewal of Life* (Bristol 1992). Laurence Vieillefon, *La figure d'Orphée dans l'antiquité tardive* (Paris 2003). John Warden, ed., *Orpheus: The Metamorphoses of a Myth* (Toronto 1982).

E.SE.

Ovid

Roman poet (43 BCE–16 or 17 CE). Although he lacks the perceived gravitas of Homer, Sophocles, or his fellow Roman Virgil, Ovid is perhaps the most consistently influential and popular writer of the classical tradition. His central position is suggested by the many surviving manuscripts of his works and their early publication in printed editions. *Editiones principes* of all his works were published in 1471 in Rome and Bologna. Most would agree that it is his *Metamorphoses* that has had the greatest influence, but his other major poems, the *Heroides, Tristia, Fasti,* and particularly his racier works, the *Amores, Ars amatoria,* and *Remedia amoris*, have played their part in maintaining his reputation as a writer of enduring importance and appeal.

His first significant work is thought to have been his *Amores* (ca. 1 CE), a sequence of witty verses about the poet-narrator's liaison with Corinna, generally assumed to be a fictional or composite figure. She is represented either as a challenge to be conquered or as a dominating mistress to whom the poet is in thrall, rather than as an equal partner. The *Amores,* not surprisingly, left its mark on the love poems of many later writers. Its influence is perhaps most apparent in the Renaissance. "To His Mistress Going to Bed," an erotic elegy by the Metaphysical poet John Donne (1572–1631), begins with a bawdy and typically Ovidian invocation of love as a military campaign. *Militat omnis amans,* "Every lover is a soldier," wrote Ovid (*Amores* 1.9.1), and Donne offers a lewd elaboration of the conceit: "The foe oft-times having the foe in sight,/Is tired with standing though they never fight" (3–4). The poem ends with an equally Ovidian equation between his mistress and a text:

> Like pictures, or like books' gay coverings made
> For laymen, are all women thus arrayed;
> Themselves are mystic books, which only we
> Whom their imputed grace will dignify
> Must see revealed. (39–43)

The concept of the *scripta puella,* the "written girl," has been the subject of much recent commentary on Ovid and other Roman elegists. Critics such as Maria Wyke and Alison Sharrock have identified the peculiarly textual quality of the poets' mistresses, the way in which the poetry calls attention to its constructed quality and probable fictionality. The elegiac mistress is a work of art, brought into being by the poet's stylus just as Pygmalion's statue is a product of the sculptor's skill. This motif is particularly evident in *Amores* 1.12. Here Ovid creates a clever identification between his mistress and the wax writing tablets on which she sends him her messages. Because the wax has a naturally reddish tinge, the angry narrator claims that it is blushing and goes on bitterly to assert that the tablets deserve to be neglected and, like a forsaken woman, lose their color. Although the wax and stylus were displaced in later centuries by pen and ink, the *scripta puella* remained a popular trope. Another striking Renaissance example is Philip Sidney's Stella, the unattainable heroine of his sonnet sequence *Astrophil and Stella,* written in the 1570s. In sonnet 67 Astrophil explicitly describes his beloved as a book—and one over whose meaning he has ultimate control: "Look on again, the fair text better try;/What blushing notes dost thou in margin see?"

These lines describe the narrator's attempt to "read" Stella's face. The comparison between her blushing cheeks and "notes" is ingeniously apt because the notes on the margins of early books were characteristically printed in red. But there is a further point to the simile. At this period a text's notes were usually written by a commentator rather than the original author, perhaps someone who sought to impose his own reading on the original just as Sidney, with a nearly postmodern scorn for authorial intention, explicitly chooses to read in Stella's ambiguous silence a message favorable to his own desires:

> Well, how so thou [i.e., Hope] interpret the contents
> I am resolved thy error to maintain,
> Rather than by more truth to get more pain.

A further variation on the *scripta puella* theme can be found in the *Roman Elegies* (1795) of Johann Wolfgang von Goethe, when he describes how the classical surroundings of Rome, and particularly its women, encourage a spirit of artistic emulation.

> Also, am I not learning when at the shape of her bosom,
> Graceful lines, I can glance, guide a light hand down her hips?
> Only thus I appreciate marble; reflecting, comparing . . .
> Often too in her arms I've lain composing a poem,
> Gently with fingering hand count the hexameter's beat
> Out on her back. (no. 5, trans. Michael Hamburger)

In a sense Goethe caps Ovid by his double objectification of the woman with her "graceful lines" (*lieblichen . . . Formen*) as both statue and poem.

The *Amores*' influence was not confined to love poetry. John Milton incongruously ends his Latin "Elegia Tertia" (1626) on the death of the bishop of Winchester with an allusion to the end of *Amores* 1.5. The poem's climax is a vision of the bishop in Paradise, and Milton exclaims, *Talia contingant somnia saepe mihi,* "May I often be lucky enough to have dreams like this," thus echoing Ovid's own reflection after an impassioned daytime encounter with Corinna, *Proveniant medii sic mihi saepe dies!* "May my lot bring many a midday like to this!" In Marlowe's *Dr. Faustus* (1604) the doomed Faustus repeats a line from the *Amores* (1.13.40) in a still more poignantly contrasting context: *O lente, lente currite, noctis equi,* "Oh, run slowly, slowly, you horses of the night," pleads the narrator, desirous to prolong a night of pleasure with his mistress. Faustus's anguished exclamation, on the other hand, although he repeats Ovid's line word for word, is a response to the knowledge that when day breaks he will be damned forever.

The spirit of the *Amores* is still very much alive today. Even where there is perhaps no evidence for a direct influence at work, the sexual freedom and frankness of modern Western society encourages writers to follow in the footsteps of Ovid's real or apparent self-revelations. Western culture has a long tradition of setting first-person love lyrics to music—the troubadours' songs of 12th-century France and the productions of the Tudor court are typical—so it is not surprising that the atmosphere of the *Amores* is particularly apparent in the lyrics of modern pop songs. Pulp's "Pencil Skirt," for example, shares Ovid's coolly lubricious attitude toward sexual encounters as well as the vivid specificity of poems such as *Amores* 1.5:

> Lo! Corinna comes, draped in tunic girded round, with divided hair falling over fair, white neck—such as 'tis said was famed Semiramis when passing to her bridal chamber, and Lais loved of many men. I tore away the tunic—and yet 'twas fine, and scarcely marred her charms; but still she struggled to have the tunic shelter her. Even while she struggled, as one who would not overcome, was she overcome—and 'twas not hard—by her own betrayal. (1.5.9–16)

> When you raise your pencil skirt,
> like a veil before my eyes,
> like the look upon his face as he's zipping up his flies.
> Oh, I know that you're engaged to him.
> Oh, but I know that you want something to play with, baby.
>
> I'll be around when he's not in town,
> I'll show you how you're doing it wrong,
> I really love it when you tell me to stop.
> Oh, it's turning me on.
> ("Pencil Skirt," *Different Class*, 1995)

On one level any similarities between the two poems could be described as chance or generic. Yet many of the conventions of love poetry that we tend to take for granted and assume to be universal can be traced to the Roman elegists, and in particular to Ovid. His influence on most of today's writers and lyricists may be mediated through several degrees of separation, but that does not detract from the continuing importance of his love poetry.

Published ca. 1 BCE, the *Ars amatoria* was a mock-didactic poem in three books. The first two contain instructions for male seducers, the third, addressed to women, offers tips on how to entice men. The shorter *Remedia amoris* (ca. 1 CE) provides advice on how to overcome inappropriate or unrequited love. The solutions offered include travel, teetotalism, bucolic pursuits, and (ironically) avoidance of love poets. The *Ars amatoria* was apparently partly responsible for Ovid's exile to Tomis (modern Constanţa), on the Black Sea coast, and continued to attract controversy centuries after the poet's death. The 14th-century Latin *Antiovidianus,* written in Italy, asserted that Ovid, together with his books, deserved to burn in the fires of Hell.

Christine de Pizan (ca. 1400) was equally hostile toward Ovid, accusing him of misogyny. The equivocal status of the *Ars amatoria* is suggested by its presence in Chaucer's *Troilus and Criseyde,* written in the late 14th century. Here it is the ambiguous though engaging go-between Pandarus who functions as the Ovidian *praeceptor amoris,* or teacher of love. His fluent mastery of the advice contained in the *Ars amatoria* is impressive, yet his teaching ultimately fails when Criseyde abandons Troilus. Pandarus is equally at home with the teachings of the *Remedia amoris,* yet here too Ovid proves wanting, for Troilus is not to be comforted by any of the recommended remedies.

Despite (or because of) the *Ars amatoria*'s notoriety, its influence remained strong. It was translated several times in the early modern centuries, most notably by Thomas Heywood (1600) and John Dryden (1709). Shakespeare's Juliet has apparently read the *Ars amatoria,* for she cautions Romeo that "at lovers' perjuries/They say Jove laughs" (2.2.92–93), a near translation of *Ars amatoria* 1.633, and in *The Taming of the Shrew* Bianca's suitor Lucentio has also made a special study of the poem. Like the *Amores,* the *Ars amatoria* has penetrated popular as well as literary culture. In Stanley Kubrick's film *Eyes Wide Shut* (1999) the heroine is accosted by a middle-aged admirer who asks whether she has read Ovid. He then demonstrates his own familiarity with the poet's works by drinking out of her wineglass, an intimate gesture that Ovid recommends in the *Ars amatoria* as a surefire seduction technique.

In some ways the modern discourse that most resembles Ovid's pick-up manual is the magazine agony column. Only in some ways of course, for such columns are not noted for their wit or allusive subtlety, and Ovid's tips seem rather tame compared to those of today's publications, even those aimed at teenage girls. But in "Void," a short story by Philip Terry, in his story collection *Ovid Metamorphosed* (2001), the central character is a journalist who has been instructed to make his copy sexier. His column, "Void's Sex Tips," is an updated version of the *Ars amatoria.* Here he adapts Ovid's own remarks about the value of sport as a dating tool: "In the case of golf, don't neglect the nineteenth hole. Like the swimming pool, it's a good place for talent-spotting, especially if older women appeal. Avoid snooker, however, darts too, and above all avoid going to the gym" (40). The Ovidian persona, urbane and opportunistic, smoothly accommodates itself to the idiom of the modern metrosexual male.

The *Heroides* (ca. 4–8 CE), a collection of letters from mythical women such as Dido and Briseis to their lovers and husbands, some of them paired with replies from their correspondents, has spawned many imitations. An early example is a further pair of letters between Paris and Helen written by Baudri, Abbot of Bourgeuil (1045–1130). Many of Ovid's letter writers—Dido, Ariadne, and Hypsipile, for example—also feature in Chaucer's *Legend of Good Women,* which, like Ovid's poem, treats its heroines with a blend of sympathy and detachment that can prove difficult to disentangle. But Chaucer's brief tales are neither first-person nor epistolary in presentation, and we see a closer imitation of the *Heroides* in *England's Heroicall Epistles,* composed by Michael Drayton at the end of the 16th century. As the title suggests, this is an updated adaptation of Ovid rather than a translation, and the classical heroines have been replaced with English noblewomen, including Lady Jane Grey and Rosamund Clifford (Fair Rosamund, mistress of Henry II). Drayton's work is typical of Christian literary culture's love-hate relationship with Ovid. Closely modeled on the *Heroides,* the poems can yet be read as a rejection of Ovidian frivolity and immorality. Their Ovidian spirit can be seen in the following lines, taken from Rosamund's epistle:

> If yet thine eyes (Great Henry) may endure
> Those tainted Lines, drawn with a Hand impure,
> (Which faine would blush, but Feare keeps Blushes backe,
> And therefore suted in despairing Blacke)

She goes on to elaborate the typically Ovidian comparison between herself and her letter by drawing an analogy between her reputation and the paper, once pure white, now stained and blotted. But in another epistle, penned by Matilda (daughter of Henry I and for a short while in 1141 ruler of England), Ovid is explicitly rejected:

> Lascivious Poets, which abuse the Truth,
> Which oft teach Age to sinne, infecting Youth,
> For the unchaste, make Trees and Stones to mourne,
> Or as they please, to other shapes doe turne.

Perhaps closer to the spirit of Ovid than Drayton or even Chaucer is Pope, in his verse epistle *Eloisa to Abelard* (1717). Here, as in the *Heroides* itself, the poem's real pathos is undermined by our heightened awareness of the male poet's presence in the text. In the third letter of Ovid's *Heroides* Briseis' complaint that her language is barbaric and her text blotted with tears is at odds with the smooth Latin elegiacs we are reading. Similarly, Pope's Eloisa's wistful conclusion to her epistle becomes knowing and complacent when we remember who has really composed "her" letter:

> Such if there be, who loves so long, so well;
> Let him our sad, our tender story tell;
> The well-sung woes will soothe my pensive ghost;
> He best can paint 'em, who shall feel 'em most. (363–366)

The jaunty epigrammatic quality of the last line would seem to ensure that the mourning Eloisa is subsumed by her male creator. Other important examples of the female voice ventriloquized by a male writer within an epistolary context include the Vicomte de Gilleragues's *Letters of a Portuguese Nun* (1699) and Samuel Richardson's celebrated novel *Clarissa* (1748).

Responses to the *Heroides* have been composed by women as well as men. Aphra Behn contributed the translation of Oenone's letter to Paris in Dryden's 1688 edition of the poem translated by several hands. Although her lively, witty rendition demonstrates a thoroughly Ovidian spirit, the poem is lent a new edge by the translator's sex. Now that the forsaken nymph is voiced by a woman rather than ventriloquized by a man, we are encouraged to wonder whether Behn is importing her own experiences and feelings into the epistle. The freedom of the translation—it is by far the freest in the volume—contributes to such a possibility, particularly as Behn chooses to heighten Ovid's eroticism. No longer is there a knowing complicity between the male poet and his implied male readers. Instead, we are encouraged to assume an identification between Behn, a woman with an equivocal reputation attempting to make her way in a man's world, and the passionate, unfortunate Oenone.

The influence of the *Fasti* (ca. 8 CE), Ovid's poem based on the Roman calendar, has perhaps been limited by its cultural specificity, and the reception of the poem as a whole has been less than the sum of its parts. It was not translated into English until 1640, when a minor poet, John Gower, produced a version. One of the most significant episodes in the poem for later writers was the narrative of Tarquin's rape of Lucretia. Ovid's version of this story, the foundation myth of the Roman Republic, was a major source for Shakespeare's *Rape of Lucrece* (1594), although Shakespeare also seems to have been familiar with the rather different version offered by Livy. It is indicative of Ovid's massive importance for Shakespeare that *The Rape of Lucrece* also alludes to a parallel rape narrative from the *Metamorphoses,* the tale of Philomela, and draws on the tradition of female complaint exemplified in Ovid's *Heroides.* (Like Ovid's letter-writing heroines, Lucrece is disconcertingly and unconvincingly eloquent and rhetorically artful despite her appalling predicament.) Perhaps Shakespeare's oddly detached, even critical stance toward the wronged Lucrece also owes more to the *Heroides* than to the *Fasti.*

The anthropologist Sir James Frazer, whose *Golden Bough* (1890) exerted such an influence on T. S. Eliot, emphasized the importance of the *Fasti,* as did Eliot's fellow Modernist Ezra Pound. Yet few have imitated Ovid's calendar format. Spenser's *Shepheardes Calender* (1579) is a notable exception, although it owes more to Virgil's *Eclogues* than to the *Fasti.* A more clearly Ovidian calendar work is Durs Grünbein's *Das erste Jahr,* published in 2001. In this unusual response to Ovid's poem Grunbein takes the *Fasti*'s calendar format and bases his own parallel project on personal and public events in the year 2000.

Most would agree that the *Metamorphoses* (ca. 8 CE) is

Ovid's masterpiece. Ovid called it a *carmen perpetuum,* a continuous song. This is a reference to its seamless and unbroken quality but might also function as a description of its *Nachleben,* or afterlife. Ovid's reputation may have had its ups and downs, but the *Metamorphoses* has been a persistent presence in post-classical Western culture. Its central position is reflected in the quality of its many important translations, in particular those of Arthur Golding (1567), George Sandys (1632), and Samuel Garth, whose edition of the poem, prepared by several hands (including those of Dryden and Gay), appeared in 1717. The *Metamorphoses*' combination of strong, memorable narratives and striking visual appeal lent itself to a huge variety of adaptations and reinventions. Music, painting, sculpture, film, and literature are all in its debt. The poem has also had a significant influence on landscape gardening—the Villa d'Este in Italy, Nonsuch Palace in England, and Sophievka in Ukraine all allude to the distinctive settings of the *Metamorphoses.* In Sophievka we can trace a re-creation of the *Metamorphoses*' topography in miniature, for the park contains imitations of numerous Ovidian sites, including Diana's grotto, the scene of Actaeon's tragic end. Here we can also follow the path of Orpheus from his descent into the underworld to the final journey of his severed head to Lesbos.

In some ways the *Metamorphoses* was more amenable to Christianization than Ovid's other works. In the 8th century the venerable Bede's commentary on Genesis drew an implicitly approving parallel between the biblical account of the Creation and Ovid's own description of the first men in *Metamorphoses* 1. Bede's willingness to spot affinities between Ovid and the Bible was typical of a wider commentary tradition in the Middle Ages. This tradition strikes many modern readers as alien, particularly when it attempts to reconcile myths less amenable to Christianization than Ovid's account of the Creation with the teachings of Scripture. In making Ovid's often salacious stories into allegorizations of Christian doctrine, the exegetes frequently seem to be reading perversely against the grain of the original. There is often an implicit misogyny in the readings—for example, it was claimed that Jupiter's rape of Europa prefigured Christ's salvation of Mankind. Still more counterintuitive is the equation made between Myrrha, whose son Adonis was born following an incestuous liaison with her own father, and Mary, whose "father," God, is also the father of her child. But there is a paradox at work here. In their ingenious absurdity, their blatant anachronism, they may distort Ovid's original text but they do so with the effect, if not necessarily the intention, of a decidedly Ovidian *ingenium.* This commentary tradition continued to exert a powerful influence well into the 17th century. Two of the best-known examples were produced in the 14th century: the French verse treatment *Ovide moralisé* and the Latin prose *Ovidius moralizatus.*

Other responses show that it was possible for Christian writers to engage with the irreverent stories of the *Metamorphoses* without this allegorical whitewashing as long as they did so in a properly corrective spirit. For example, in the *Metamorphoses* Ovid describes the weaving competition between Minerva and Arachne: the goddess's tapestry gloried in the power and majesty of the Olympian gods, but Arachne portrayed their cruel and rapacious treatment of mortal girls (she lost the contest and was transformed into a spider). A similar *agon* is depicted by Baudri of Bourgueil in a poem (composed around 1100) addressed to William the Conqueror's daughter Adela. The poem describes the wonderful tapestries woven by Adela and her maids. On one side of her bedroom is a depiction of Old Testament heroes, on the other is a tapestry of characters from the *Metamorphoses.* Ovid's contest between gods and mortals is here reinvented as a contest between the Bible and the *Metamorphoses.* In a paradox typical of Christian Ovidianism the ecphrasis is simultaneously an homage to Ovid—the parallel is highlighted when Baudri describes Adela's tapestry as subtler than a spider's web—and a veiled reproof whose implicit message is an assertion of Christianity's triumph over Ovidian paganism. At least, that seems a reasonable assumption to make of a poem by a bishop, although perhaps Baudri (whose bisexual poetic persona suggests a certain unorthodoxy) wanted the implicit contest between his own two tapestries to retain the ambiguity of Ovid's original.

As the Middle Ages drew to a close, Neo-Latin increasingly gave way to strong vernacular traditions. But the influence of the *Metamorphoses* continued unabated. Dante's *Divina Commedia* is another telling example of a poem torn between Christianity and Ovidianism. Although the poet appears to privilege the proto-Christian shades of Virgil and Statius, it is Ovid whose more subversive presence makes itself felt in the poetic, structural, and imaginative texture of the *Commedia.* In *Inferno* 25 Dante bids Ovid be silent, asserting that the transformations of Hell are more startling than any in the *Metamorphoses;* but the poem as a whole is clearly reliant on Ovid's masterpiece, even at apparently inappropriate moments. In *Paradiso* 1 the poet compares the grace lent him to communicate his divine vision with the macabre transformation wrought on Marsyas when his skin was flayed from his body, a complex and startling moment of counterintuitive allusion.

The poems to Laura written by Dante's fellow countryman Petrarch (14th cent.) are still more Ovidian. Their form, the first-person love poem, might suggest that their biggest debt is to the *Amores,* but in fact it is the *Metamorphoses* to which Petrarch repeatedly turns for inspiration, in particular the story of Daphne, who, as the laurel, *laurus,* has a special affinity with Laura. Yet again, an absorption in an Ovidian aesthetic of transformation is countered by a sense of difference from Ovid, a consciousness of the gulf between the pagan past and the Christian present. Laura's association with a tree recalls not only Daphne but also Eve, and thus serves as a reminder of the fallen state of both poet and reader.

As we have already seen, Petrarch's younger contemporary Chaucer is typical of his age in combining a clear admiration for Ovid with an apparent wish to distance himself from the pagan poet. Chaucer's debts to Ovid are apparent in numerous individual allusions but also in the trajectory of Chaucer's entire oeuvre, which can be seen as a kind of recasting of Ovid's own checkered career. Chaucer rejected his own earlier love poems in favor of Christian morality, a repentant move exemplified in *The Parson's Tale* and the *Retraction.* This sequence simultaneously mirrors the development of Ovid's poetry and constitutes at least a partial rejection of his predecessor. Ovid had cause to regret his earlier licentious poetry when he composed the *Tristia* (*Sorrows*) in exile; in these poems he begged his friends to intercede with Augustus on his behalf and hoped for immortality through his poetry. Chaucer's position, although superficially similar, is transformed by his own Christian context. His repentance is presented as sincere, whereas Ovid is more concerned to persuade the reader that his verse should not be taken as a true reflection of the poet's character or life: "I assure you, my character differs from my verse (my life is moral, my muse is gay), and most of my work, unreal and fictitious, has allowed itself more licence than its author has had" (*Tristia* 2.353–356).

Although Ovid, politic for once, paints in his *Letters from the Black Sea* (ca. 10 CE) a picture of an Augustus who resembles the Christian God, "slow to punish, quick to reward, who sorrows whenever he is forced to be severe" (*Epistulae ex Ponto* 1.2.121–122), his situation is quite different from that of Chaucer. The medieval poet seeks forgiveness from a heavenly rather than an earthly ruler, and hopes for eternal salvation rather than mere literary fame. At a more local level the same kind of tension can be seen in Chaucer's frequent omissions of the climactic moment of metamorphosis from his retellings—for example, in *The Book of the Duchess* the dead King Ceyx is not revived as a bird to be reunited with his mourning wife Alcyone but remains drowned. Because the internal listener (John of Gaunt) and the poem's actual readers or audience would have known the myth, the abrupt and unexpected ending, the refusal to offer easy and indeed unchristian consolation, acts as a potent reproof. A similar dynamic is at play in the works of a later Christian Ovidian; Milton's *Paradise Lost* is full of classical allusions, especially to the *Metamorphoses,* but again and again these are undercut. A typical dismissal follows his enthralling description of the fall of Mulciber: "Thus they relate,/Erring" (1.746–747).

Central to the *Metamorphoses*' reception are the works of Shakespeare. Ovid's poem lends a decorative eroticism to Shakespeare's epyllion *Venus and Adonis* (1592–1593), brings a comic entanglement of tragedy and mirth to the Pyramus and Thisbe interlude in *A Midsummer Night's Dream,* and imparts a far more disturbing hybrid of beauty, violence, pain, and laughter to *Titus Andronicus.* This grotesque revenge play is underpinned by one of Ovid's most gruesome tales, that of Tereus and Philomela, but Shakespeare "improves" on the horrors of the original on several counts. Whereas Ovid's Tereus had cut out his victim's tongue to prevent her revealing her rapist's identity, Lavinia's rapists go one better and cut off her hands to stop her from sewing her story into a tapestry, as Philomela had done. (For barbarians—they are the sons of Tamora, defeated queen of the Goths—they are remarkably up on their Ovid.) By making Ovid such an explicit presence in the play—Lavinia actually brings the text onstage to help explain what has happened to her—Shakespeare compromises the tragedy of *Titus* because the audience is constantly reminded of its fictional status. Another appearance of Ovid's poem (in *Cymbeline*) has a similarly distancing effect. The unscrupulous Iachimo, spying on the sleeping Imogen, notes that she has been reading the tale of Tereus. Although he is a voyeur rather than a rapist, Iachimo's situation, his predatory role in relation to a vulnerable woman, is very similar to that of Tereus. Imogen's choice of book is almost too appropriate, and the prop functions as a kind of secret message from playwright to audience, a bridge, like a chorus, between the play world and the real world that reminds us that *Cymbeline* is itself only a story.

Some of Shakespeare's most memorable borrowings can be found in two of his very last plays. In *The Winter's Tale* Ovid's miraculous story of Pygmalion's statue is reanimated in the figure of Hermione, whose "statue" is revealed to be a real woman, kept hidden from her jealous husband for 15 years. This startling explanation cannot quite dispel a suspicion of necromancy, although the mistress of ceremonies, Hermione's lady-in-waiting Paulina, assures us that this is "art/Lawful as eating" (5.3.110–111). Necromancy also lies behind a still more obtrusive use of Ovid, Prospero's description of his magic arts in *The Tempest* (5.1.33–57), a near translation of words originally spoken by Ovid's Medea in book 7 of the *Metamorphoses.* Critics are divided as to why Shakespeare thus hints at a bond between Prospero and the notorious witch who killed her own brother and children. Is he suggesting that Prospero is a sinister or evil figure? Or is he highlighting the differences rather than the similarities between the two powerful practitioners of magic? He may of course simply have been drawn to the effectiveness of Ovid's language and not have intended his audience to import the source into *The Tempest* at all.

Although the *Metamorphoses* never completely lost its hold on Western culture, its influence declined in the 18th and 19th centuries before being revived at the beginning of the 20th century with the advent of Modernism. In Europe and America writers as different as Kafka, Rilke, T. S. Eliot, and Virginia Woolf all found inspiration once again in the *Metamorphoses,* combining sometimes startling formal innovation with a renewed enthusiasm for the classical tradition. It has been suggested that Ovid's influence has been strongest at times of transition and uncertainty, and it may thus be significant that this revival of the *Metamorphoses,* Ovid's great poem of change, synchronized with a series of radical and disruptive discoveries in science (Einstein) and human behavior (Freud). The

20th century, like the Middle Ages, was inclined to adapt Ovidian material to fit its own preoccupations, although these tended to be secular rather than religious. Freud coopted the story of Narcissus to illustrate an aspect of his psychoanalytic theory, and Hélène Cixous used Medusa as a sign of female sexuality, simultaneously threatening and desirable. Recent literary responses to the poem are similarly marked by their readiness to update the tales of the *Metamorphoses.* In Mary Zimmerman's 1998 adaptation of the poem a very modern Phaethon, like one of Bret Easton Ellis's more vacuous heroes, floats on a yellow raft wearing sunglasses while he tells his therapist about his troubled relationship with his father. Cotta, the hero of Christoph Ransmayr's *The Last World* (1996), searches for the exiled Ovid in a Tomis that is simultaneously mythical—it is inhabited by oddly altered characters from the *Metamorphoses*—and postindustrial—its amenities include a bus station and a cinema. Ted Hughes's widely admired *Tales from Ovid* (1999) is less audaciously, programmatically modern but includes many startling contemporary details. Some of these are immediately obvious, as when Zeus is described as launching a "nuclear blast." Others are more subtle and Ovidian, such as Hughes's comparison between the swimming Hermaphroditus and "a lily in a bulb of crystal." "Bulb" translates Ovid's *vitro,* "glass" (4.355) and also functions as a metamorphic pun, invoking simultaneously the organic stem of the lily and the anachronistic technology of a light bulb. It thus yokes together two apparently unrelated substances—flowers and glass—in an elaboration of the original Latin that is thoroughly Ovidian; for Ovid too revels in ingenious, linguistic links between apparently unrelated elements, as when he points out that Myrrha's bone marrow remained the same even after her metamorphosis into a tree—the Latin *medulla* (10.492) can mean both marrow and pith.

We have seen how pagan mythology was grafted onto the quite different traditions of Judaeo-Christian teaching by medieval commentators. Perhaps today we can identify another fusion at work in the increasing interplay between Western and Japanese culture. In particular, anime, with its emphasis on the boundaries between fantasy and reality, human and nonhuman, is a medium with strong Ovidian potential; as early as 1979 Takashi's film *Hoshi No Orpheus* presented animated versions of five tales from the *Metamorphoses.* More recently Ovid has been cited as an influence on two of Hayao Miyazaki's films, *Spirited Away* (2001) and *Howl's Moving Castle* (2004). The recent novels of David Mitchell are embedded in oriental traditions, and in his highly successful *Cloud Atlas* (2004) we can perhaps see a natural interpenetration between this new idiom and Ovidianism. This book, like the *Metamorphoses,* is a complexly circular collection that might lay claim to Ovid's epithet *perpetuum.* Particularly Ovidian are the ingenious links between each story, the countless odd echoes and parallels which alert us to the curious bonds between Mitchell's six protagonists, apparently reincarnations of the same person, all of whom have a comet-shaped birthmark on the shoulder. In the chronologically penultimate tale, set in a future Korea where cloning is commonplace, we encounter Madam Ovid, a plastic surgeon with the power to completely alter one's appearance. She is in a sense an avatar of the novel's creator, who has himself refashioned his hero(ine) six times over the course of this playful and haunting fiction. Mitchell's attraction to a characteristically Ovidian aesthetic of repetition and fragmentation is shared by another contemporary novelist, Kate Atkinson, whose mythical yet very modern story collection *Not the End of the World* (2004) is still more overtly indebted to the *Metamorphoses.*

Ovid's poems from exile are attracting an increasing amount of critical attention, which reflects both their own subtle power and their ability to inspire a striking variety of creative responses. Just as Ovid's great poem of change invited aptly metamorphic treatments, his poems of exile have been in turn displaced in various ways. Ovid was writing at the height of Rome's glory, but as the power of the empire declined, the *Tristia* took on a new resonance. Rutilius Namatianus, writing in the 5th century shortly after the sack of Rome by Alaric, shared Ovid's wistful sense of distance from Rome's splendor, but as an exile in time rather than space. A few centuries later, when Rome's heyday was still more remote, poets responded to Ovid's exile poetry in the knowledge that their situation, however favorable by the debased standards of their own day, was more akin to that of Tomis than Augustan Rome. We find a different kind of misprision at work in the poems of Joachim du Bellay (1522–1560), who draws on the *Tristia* (in an ingeniously Ovidian reversal) to describe exile not *from* Rome but *to* Rome:

> France, oh France, answer me mercifully!
> But the echo only brings back my own words.
> I am left to wander among hungry wolves.
> Winter approaches, I feel its breath is cold
> —It rasps, and sends a shiver down my back.
> (Sonnet 9, trans. C. H. Sisson)

Du Bellay is somewhat uncharacteristic of *Tristia* imitators in that he presents Rome itself as cold and unwelcoming. Far more typical is a kind of barbarism anxiety whereby later poets are uneasily conscious of their failure to measure up to Ovid's standards of refined urbanity. Although Pushkin's own exile to the Black Sea was conspicuously similar to Ovid's, he was struck not by the landscape's harshness but by its softness, beauty, and warmth. In "To Ovid" (1821) he contrasts the mildness of its winters with the rigors of the Russian climate to which he is accustomed.

The *Tristia* were popular teaching texts in the Renaissance, and early translations into English were composed by Thomas Churchyard in 1572 and Wye Saltonstall in 1639. We know that Shakespeare was conscious of Ovid's exile because in *As You Like It* the clown Touchstone punningly compares his own exile in the forest of Arden with that of Ovid: "I am here with thee and thy goats, as the most capricious poet, honest Ovid, was among the Goths" (3.3.6–9). David Slavitt ingeniously encourages us to see another, more covert allusion to the exile poetry in Shakespeare's works when, in his creative translation of the *Tristia* (1986) he makes Ovid describe his metamorphosis in a line adapted from *The Tempest:*

Tasting my own
Medicine of metamorphosis, I change
Into something poor and strange.

Might Prospero, exiled on his island as Shakespeare would soon withdraw to Stratford, alienated by the uncouth barbarism of Caliban and on the point of renouncing his metamorphic power, represent the aging Ovid as well as his own aging creator? This is not the only occasion on which Slavitt seems to enrich the *Tristia*'s long *Nachleben* retrospectively, as it were. His translation of 3.8, in which Ovid describes his longing to soar up into the air on some chariot of the gods and bemoans his transformed appearance, is subtly tweaked to transform slight chance affinities with Keats's "Ode to a Nightingale"—the wish to fly, the evocation of physical decline, and the sense of death's allure—into far stronger parallels. For example, Ovid's expression of a longing for wings beginning "Oh, for" is echoed in the same construction in Keats's Ode "Oh, for a draught of vintage"; and Slavitt's Ovid (unlike the original) compares his imagined flying self with "a huge gangly bird."

Recent responses to the *Tristia* may have largely put barbarism anxiety behind them, but still they exploit the interesting effects made possible when a poem of displacement is further displaced. George McWhirter, for example, transplants the poem to the bleak Canadian prairies in *Ovid in Saskatchewan* (1998) and in "The Hotel Normandie Pool" (1981). Derek Walcott draws analogies between his own legacy of displacement and Ovid's exile from Rome. Perhaps part of Ovid's enduring appeal is the way his poetry combines themes that we sense are universal and unchanging with a dynamic of change and dislocation that reflects the geographical, temporal, and cultural distance between our world and his own.

BIBL.: Jonathan Bate, *Shakespeare and Ovid* (Oxford 1993). Barbara Weiden Boyd, ed., *Brill's Companion to Ovid* (Leiden 2002). Sarah Annes Brown, *The Metamorphosis of Ovid* (London 1999). Michael Calabrese, *Chaucer's Ovidian Arts of Love* (Gainesville, Fla., 1994). Philip Hardie, ed., *The Cambridge Companion to Ovid* (Cambridge 2002). Genevieve Liveley, *Ovid: Love Songs* (Bristol 2005). Raphael Lyne, *Ovid's Changing Worlds* (Oxford 2001). Charles Martindale, *Ovid Renewed: Ovidian Influences on Art and Literature from the Middle Ages to the Twentieth Century* (Cambridge 1988). Charles Martindale and Michelle Martindale, *Shakespeare and the Uses of Antiquity* (London 1990). Alison Sharrock, "Womanufacture," *Journal of Roman Studies* 81 (1991) 36–49. Madison U. Sowell, *Dante and Ovid: Studies in Intertextuality* (New York 1991). Maria Wyke, *The Roman Mistress* (Oxford 2002). Theodore Ziolkowski, *Ovid and the Moderns* (Ithaca 2004).

S.A.B.

P

Paestum

Roman name of Poseidonia, the site of a Greek colony 50 miles south of Naples. Founded on the coastal plain by Greek colonists in the 7th century BCE, Poseidonia flourished in the 6th and 5th centuries. Its fame comes principally from three spectacular Doric-style temples of local limestone and sandstone completed by 460 BCE. Around 400, Samnite Lucanians occupied the city and renamed it Paistom, later transformed into Paestum when it became a Roman colony in 273. The city remained prosperous until malaria caused its abandonment in the 5th century CE. The temple colonnades remained standing, roofless, throughout the Middle Ages. In the 18th century they began to attract great attention, making Paestum a crucial site for modern Hellenism.

The ancient sources never refer to Paestum's temples, and for many centuries they went unappreciated. As late as 1740, a Neapolitan architect considered using their columns to decorate the Capodimonte residence, and local antiquarians mistakenly spoke of the temples as gymnasia or porticos. Around 1750, with their "rediscovery," the site became a favorite destination for travelers on the Grand Tour. By the end of the century eight illustrated books had been dedicated to Paestum.

One of the first modern encounters with archaic Doric architecture, Paestum and its unexpected proportions elicited strong reactions, ranging from open rejection to passionate praise for its original simplicity, often in the context of 18th-century primitivism. The temples played a significant role in architects' debates over the traditional Vitruvian canon and inspired the neo-Doric revival: prominent examples include London's Euston Station, the crypt of the Church of Ste. Geneviève (now the Panthéon) in Paris, and Philadelphia's Second Bank.

The topos of sudden discovery after centuries of neglect fascinated travelers, who repeatedly described the difficult journey to Paestum's imposing ruins, isolated in a marshland, long after a new road had been built. Winckelmann, who never traveled to Greece, visited Paestum in 1758 and published an enthusiastic early description of the temples, judging them more ancient than anything in Greece itself.

As Athens' classical architecture became better known and accessible, however, Paestum was marginalized as an expression of the colonial periphery of the ancient Greek world. By the time Goethe wrote about his visit to Paestum (1787), he judged the temples strangely primitive and appreciated them as an early step leading to later, classical developments. Italian interpretations differed. Piranesi, for example, who had long opposed Greek architecture, visited Paestum only at the end of his life (1778) but produced haunting images of the temples, highlighting their Italic character. Similarly, in Micali's early 19th-century nationalist interpretation of Italian ancient history, the temples figured as an inspiring expression of the pre-Roman Italic past.

Paestum's Lucanian painted tombs, discovered in the early 19th century, were first excavated mainly for their Greek vases and other objects. In the early 20th century official excavations began to explore the full layout of the Greek and Roman city. In the late 1930s P. Zancani Montuoro and P. Zanotti Bianco, interned in the region by the Fascist regime, located and excavated the famous and long-lost extramural sanctuary of the Sele with its archaic metopes. This discovery marked the so-called militant archaeology of the site and its project to use the local past to revitalize modern South Italy's cultural backwardness. Since then, research has focused on Paestum's urban plan and territorial organization and the cultural interactions between locals and Greeks. The famous painted Tomb of the Diver, discovered in 1968, well embodies this acculturation process as it combines Greek painting technique with the Italic custom of tomb painting.

BIBL.: Joselita Raspi Serra, ed., *Paestum and the Doric Revival, 1750–1830* (Florence 1986) and *Paestum: Idea e immagine: antologia di testi critici e di immagini di Paestum, 1750–1836* (Modena 1990). John Wilton-Ely, *Piranesi, Paestum and Soane* (London 2002). G.CE.

Paganism

The polytheistic religions of the classical world organized the political, religious, and cultural life of a succession of peoples around the Mediterranean. But they were not *paganism*. Paganism did not exist in the ancient world. The word *pagan* was simply not a religious term in antiquity. The meaning and the description of an entire religious and political worldview as paganism emerged not from the classical world but from its dissolution. It was the product of early Christian efforts to break away from the peoples that it despised.

Although the Jews had long rejected the "gods of the nations" (2 Kings 18:33), Christianity dedicated itself from very early onward to both the description and the eradication of its divine competition. The new faith originated in the hostile Roman empire, whose imperial cult forced early Christians to justify themselves against polytheistic practices. Yet its universalizing mission also compelled Christianity to engage with local religious practices. When Saint Paul insisted that "what gentiles [i.e., non-Christians] sacrifice they offer to demons and not to God" (1 Cor. 10:20), he had already begun to distinguish the conceptual complex that we now know as paganism. Through history the notion of paganism has never lost the strong marks of this originally polemical origin. It can never, in Leonard Barkan's terms, "be a thing in itself." Rather, in Europe, paganism has always stood in a bitter conjugal relationship with the religion that so successfully conceptualized and abolished it.

And yet it was the very proximity of polytheism to the religion that superseded it that made the polytheistic practices of Greek and Rome such potent cultural and intellectual forces in the post-classical period. From the apostolic period well into late antiquity, the Church Fathers devoted enormous intellectual resources to the problem of pagan religions. These resources were, at the same time, defenses of Christian piety and scorching attacks on pagan rites. Notable Fathers such as Tertullian and Arnobius bolstered their piety by contrasting it with what they saw as, alternately, demonic foulness and human fancies that formed the bulk of pagan religions. The gods were, at the same time, devilish manifestations on earth and mere products of a deluded imagination. This latter, euhemeristic argument—the insistence that the gentile gods were noble and powerful men raised to divine status by the passage of time—was among the most durable and powerful weapons in the hands of Christian polemicists. It was all the more effective because it was drawn from the armory of Greek and Latin writers themselves.

The vitriol that early Christian fathers poured on paganism was, however, only one part of the story. Patristic fathers were, at times literally, the archive that preserved knowledge of polytheism in the years after its real decline. Nor could the Church Fathers wholly forswear their pagan environment. At the very least, the revealed universal history that Christianity endorsed meant that paganism must have originally derived from God's peoples. Apologetic fathers like Eusebius were thus forced to account for the growth of pagan error from revealed truth. Pagan errors, they insisted, were not unique fabrications of a corrupt human mind but instead preserved original kernels of the scriptural story. The wisest of the pagans must have had direct contact with Scripture itself. When the Latin Father Lactantius (d. ca. 320) discovered traces of Genesis in the myth of Prometheus' creation of man from dust, he performed an apologetic analysis that became a cornerstone in the Christian imagination of paganism.

This effort to integrate paganism into Christianity was not motivated just by dogma. It was also crucially motivated by that most Christian enterprise, conversion. Lactantius wanted both to dispel the pagan gods and to convert their devotees. "Recalling men from evil paths" meant, for him, showing both the mistakes gentiles were making and the ease with which they might rectify them. In this sense paganism and Judaism were closely linked. The typological exegesis that integrated Old and New Testaments was mirrored by an allegorical or historical exegesis that linked pagan theology with Christianity. In both cases Christians were motivated both to distinguish themselves from the errors of the religions they spurned and to integrate these religions, and their practitioners, into their universal creed.

Paganism thus emerged from the late antique world with a variety of ambivalent attributions. The medieval period accepted all of these. Certainly as Christianity expanded into northern Europe, it found a variety of religious practices that it classified, once more, as pagan. In the 8th and 9th centuries, for example, penitential books condemned soothsaying, vows made by springs, the use of amulets, sacrifices to Mercury and Jupiter, idols made of dough and rags, and so on. Four hundred years after the fall of Rome, Christians were still trying to describe and uproot the indigenous religions they encountered in Europe and elsewhere.

Even as folk religions were sturdily rejected, however, the gods of classical antiquity very quickly found secure homes in medieval intellectual and cultural life. Medieval Christianity had at least two major textual approaches to the ancient gods. First, and most important, it rendered them into allegorical fable. The mythologies of Homer, Virgil, and Ovid, for example, had already begun to be remade into moral allegories in the twilight of the antique world. By the 5th century Macrobius' *Saturnalia* and Martianus Capella's *Marriage of Mercury and Philology* combined mythographic information about the pagan gods with symbolic interpretation of their virtues and attributes. In the 6th century the Christian author Fulgentius used pagan fertilizer to grow tales of moral edification. In his *Mythologiae* the gods of Olympus were tamed, their scandalous behavior given didactic form: when the rending of Actaeon by Diana's dogs offered nothing more than a cautionary tale against curiosity, it had lost much of its ferocious power. By the 12th century, allegory had become a cornerstone of interpretive literature, used as an expository device for Scripture, nature, and myth alike. All of these came together—as Curtius (1953) convincingly showed—in poets like Bernard Silvestris and Alan of Lille. Bernard's *De universitate mundi* (*On the Universe*) has the goddess Natura describe the formation of the cosmos and mankind in concert with both God and the gods. Mercury, Urania, Natura: all are linked in a nominally Christian but ultimately syncretic vision. More clearly allegorical is Alan's *De planctu Naturae* (*Nature's Lament*), whose visionary prose has Natura again standing in subordinate relation to God, yet creative herself, birthing the world in concert with Venus and Cupid (sexual love), Hercules (strength), Helen (beauty), and others. Allegory bound the spiritual and material world in webs of equivalences, generating an abundant imaginative energy that kept the gods of Greece and Rome active within the European imagination.

Second, Christianity organized the materials of paganism into encyclopedias of world history. Isidore of Seville's 7th-century *Etymologies*, for example, served as a clearinghouse for the pagan gods: he created genealogies of myth, presented the heroic creators of ancient civilizations under various divine forms, and grounded it all in histories of the ancient Mediterranean. Euhemerism was again a main conceptual device. In the third age of man, Isidore explained, between Abraham and Samuel, Atlas invented astrology and Apollo invented medicine. Similarly, ancient kings were later made into idols and objects of devotion: the Assyrian king Belus was worshiped under the guise of Saturn and found his deification in the Babylonian idol Bel. After Isidore, the inclusion of the pagan gods in the universal histories and chronicles of the Middle Ages became commonplace. Peter Comestor in the 12th century and Vincent of Beauvais and Guido delle Colonne in the 13th were just a few of the chroniclers who incorporated the euhemeristic encyclopedia of classical gods into their works. Comestor wrote a *Historia scholastica*, a sacred history that included a synopsis of mythological fables in which, for example, Isis is said to be the inventor of the alphabet; Minerva, inventor of weaving; and Zoroaster, inventor of magic. This text was only one of many medieval encyclopedias that preserved the pagan gods as historical figures, with fundamental connection to the chronologies described in Scripture.

These two textual traditions, allegorical and euhemeristic, both preserved the memory of pagan gods and were exercises in demystification. Collecting the tales of antiquity and transforming them, whether by allegorical or historical reason, cast doubt on the gods and the credulous masses who believed in them. Jupiter's lechery—his repeated seductions of Antiope, Mnemosyne, Proserpina, Leda, and others—not only gave the lie to his divinity but also reflected badly on his worshipers. Yet here again Christians found themselves in an ambivalent relationship to paganism. They worked both as guardians of cultural and religious memory and aggressors against it. The very form of aggression was itself a kind of preservation.

This ambivalence extended to other zones of pagan presence in medieval Christian culture. The figure of the wise pagan survived from late antiquity into the Middle Ages, mediated by writers like Boethius, whose *Consolation of Philosophy* (ca. 525 CE) helped to transmit to the Latin West a vision of Homer as a poet of profound authority. Homer's writings were themselves effectively unknown, but the sense of his wisdom, and that of an also largely unknown Plato, was firmly established by the High Middle Ages in the School of Chartres. An altogether less comforting aspect of the Olympian gods could be found in judicial astrology, where the demonic powers of Jupiter and Saturn irresistibly touched the fortunes of mortals. The treatises of Roger Bacon and Thomas Aquinas, the poetry of Dante, Arabic astrological manuscripts brought back by crusading Europeans, protective amulets inscribed with the figures of Jupiter and Minerva: all insisted on the portentous effects of the planets on nature and man. By the dawn of the Renaissance, paganism existed in the form of what Warburg (1999) has called a "Janus-faced herm," showing both a "daemonic scowl" and a visage "Olympian and serene."

The Olympian face of the pagan gods is undoubtedly the more familiar today. It is found in the cheerful aestheticism of the painters, sculptors, writers, and scholars who in the 14th and 15th centuries began to take up the materials of Roman and Greek antiquity and reinvest them with enormous cultural energy. At its most basic, the Renaissance supplied its contemporaries with a corpus of literature unavailable for millennia. It is hard to imagine a world without Homer, but the *Iliad* and the *Odyssey* were first made widely available in 1488 by a Greek scholar and then, more famously, reissued in 1517 by the Venetian printer Aldus Manutius. As for Plato, it was only after the Florentine philosopher Marsilio Ficino translated and published his works (1484), along with those of his major early interpreters (Proclus, Porphyry), that a serious engagement between Christianity and Platonic tradition was even possible. The Neoplatonism of late antiquity may have persisted in a crude form into the Middle Ages, but its revival reached maturity late in the 15th century, when the cosmologies and mystery religions of ancient Greece were again mined for their hidden Christian topoi. Between Orpheus and Ovid, Renaissance interpreters had an abundance of mythological material that they refashioned to suit a Christian sensibility. The gods of antiquity helped Italians like Ficino, Pico della Mirandola, and many others break through the orthodox crust of Christian doctrine to penetrate its mystical essence.

With the rise of the Renaissance, pagans and Christians thus began to walk comfortably together for the first time.

As a metaphor for the sympathetic relations between the two we may look to the Vatican Palace itself, which under the aegis of Pope Alexander VI became a monument to Christian-pagan syncretism. At a time when Rome was making itself once again an Eternal City, this syncretism wedded Christian and imperial ambitions. The Borgia apartments, for example, painted by Pinturicchio between 1493 and 1495, featured a complex set of allegorical figures drawn from the Egyptian, Greek, Roman, and Christian religions. In its Hall of the Saints, Apis, Osiris, and Isis are ranged next to Mercury, Jupiter, Saint Catherine, and Saint Anthony in a complex visual presentation of *prisca theologia,* the Christian wisdom hidden within the aberrations of the gentiles. Twenty years later, when Raphael painted the Stanza della Segnatura for Pope Julius II, he juxtaposed the Holy Spirit and the dwelling of Apollo on Parnassus and paired the Judgment of Solomon with the Flaying of Marsyas. Viewers would find here a complex set of visual analogies between Christian virtue and pagan wisdom. From Boccaccio to Michelangelo, Jerusalem and Athens were set into productive conversation. Nor was this restricted solely to the fine arts. Pagan pageantry was a mainstay of patrician weddings, for example, where plays featured Orpheus, Apollo, the Three Graces, and other classical figures. In 1565, when Francesco de' Medici married Joanna of Austria, Vincenzo Borghini and Giorgio Vasari designed a procession of 21 chariots, each bearing a god and a set of painted mythological reliefs with the deeds of the gods rendered in exquisite allegorical detail.

This pageantry and its eclectic allegories were paralleled in the scholarly world by the emerging science of mythology. Between 1532 and 1556 Germans and Italians alike began to publish comprehensive treatises on pagan mythology, which blended Greek, Roman, and other Near Eastern traditions into a symbolic stew that nourished the syncretic impulses of the age. The German Georg Pictor set the tone with *Mythological Theology* (1532), which offered both descriptions and moral readings of the gods, drawn from a familiar series of texts, including (among others) Fulgentius and Martianus Capella. By the time Vincenzo Cartari published his vernacular treatise *The Images of the Gods* (1556), the concept of paganism had expanded widely. The origins of the Renaissance fascination with the Orient can be discerned here. From the familiar Egyptian pantheon (Isis, Osiris, Horus, Anubis, etc.) to the more obscure Syrian gods, Cartari combined all into an eclectic set of iconographical vignettes drawn from across the literary spectrum. His Apollo of Elephantinopolis, for example, has the god bearing, on his human torso, a shrunken hawk's head; standing next to him is a Diana sporting the heads of a horse, a boar, and a dog.

Moral edification was never far from the scene. Natale Conti's *Mythology* (1551), for example, organized its myths according to the secret teachings contained in each, arguing that "all philosophical doctrines are contained in fables." This sentiment would echo throughout the century, finding expression even in unlikely authors such as Francis Bacon. Widespread interests in paganism, iconology, and moral teaching converged, finally, in the emblem books of the period. The most famous of these, Andrea Alciato's *Emblematum liber* (1531), offered a series of imagistic vignettes drawn from (among other places) pagan mythology, each underwritten by a short, edifying poem. Thus, on the subject of the difficulty of eloquence, Alciato has Mercury bringing to a drowsy Odysseus the antidote to the wine of Circe, an antidote made from the stubbornly rooted plant *moly.* Though it looks easy, Alciato means to say, eloquence demands labor.

The new synthesis between Christianity and paganism did not stop with moral teaching. Indeed, even the more ostensibly barbaric aspects of paganism were brought into the Christian fold and, at times, embraced. There were hints of this, for example, in the Borgia apartments, where the bloody murder of Marsyas seemed an emblematical double of the cool decisions of Solomon. More dramatic were the explicit parallels of Christ's sacrifice on the Cross and the pagan slaughter of animals on the altar. As Fritz Saxl (1939) has noted, Giovanni Bellini's *Redeemer* (ca. 1460–1465) has at its center a devotional image of the Man of Sorrows whose sacred blood redeems the world, and, in the background, a series of pagan sacrificial motifs: an altar, a sacrificial vessel, the double flutes of a satyr. The woodcuts that portray the erotic and graphic sacrifices to Priapus in the *Hypnerotomachia Poliphili* (1499) may be seen as an even more extreme effort to bring the spirit of pagan antiquity back to life in the Renaissance.

This syncretic amalgamation of the "gods of the nations" and Christianity was not wholly welcome, however, even for those who generally promoted the embrace of pagan antiquity. Erasmus, for one, was made anxious by Renaissance paganophilia. Truly to emulate such an eminent pagan as Cicero, he argued in his *Ciceronianus* (1528), one would have to rebuild Rome itself, with its temples, shrines, and rites. We must "destroy this paganism," the great Latinist and lover of classical antiquity exclaimed, for although "we have Jesus on our lips . . . it is Jupiter Optimus Maximus . . . that we have in our hearts." The "daemonic scowl" that Warburg described was, in other words, not wholly effaced from Jupiter and Apollo, let alone Osiris and Typhon.

The darkest sides of paganism were revealed, unsurprisingly, in the religious polemics of the period. The epithet *pagano-papism* stands as a key marker of this darker side. As early as the mid-16th century, Protestants began to use the pagan gods to scourge their Catholic opponents. In the words of the Anglican theologian Richard Hooker (1598), "Papists are to us as the [Gentile] nations were unto Israel." Calvinists and Anglicans, like the ancient Israelites, needed to describe, detect, and eradicate the errors of the Gentiles and thus devoted enormous exegetical resources to detecting the similarities between pagan excess and the rituals of the Catholic Church.

Although this logic was widely applied, two areas attracted particular attention. The first was sacrifice, where

Protestants labored to prove that the Catholic Mass repeated the bloody rituals of dark and ancient deities. Calvin, in his *Institutes of the Christian Religion* (1536), insisted that any effort to understand the Eucharist in sacrificial terms—as if the presentation and consumption of the Host were materially effective in changing God's attitude toward man—was a form of false sacrifice. It had more in common with the children sacrificed to Saturn or Moloch than with real worship. This polemical point would continue for more than a century as critics of Catholicism used the sacrifices of the ancients to score theological points against their adversaries. Second, Protestants detected, in the Catholic cult of images, the pagan idols so well described by late antique critics like Arnobius. Even the pagans knew better than Catholics, Edward Stillingfleet argued in 1671: wise men like Plato and Zeno "condemned the Worship of *God* by Images, as . . . a disparagement to the *Deity*," which was better than Catholic apologists such as Cardinal Robert Bellarmine could claim. Theophilus Gale's windy arguments in his *Court of the Gentiles* (1672), that pagan practices were no more than corrupted Jewish rites, encoded an anti-Catholic argument as well. Just as paganism was "nothing else than Judaism degenerated," in Gale's words, so too was Catholicism the deformed ape of true Christianity.

Thus, like their late antique predecessors, early modern Protestants found in paganism the diabolical hand of error that threatened the integrity and purity of Christianity. And yet, as in earlier centuries, their diatribes also served as a preservative, keeping paganism on the front burner of European culture. Enormous treatises like Gerardus Vossius' *Theology of the Gentiles* (1641) traced the history of solar worship across dozens of antique cultures, laying out in excruciating detail the histories of false religion for an educated Christian audience. Travel books carried a similarly dual message. Samuel Purchas's *Pilgrimage* (1613), a geography modeled on Richard Hakluyt's *Principal Navigations . . . of the English Nation* (1598–1600), included long discussions of Near Eastern religions and their gods. And Thomas Fuller's *Pisgah Sight of Palestine* (1650) offered a marvelous plate illustrating the Gentile idols that had seduced the ancient Jews. Even relatively lowbrow and popular books like Thomas Goodwin's *Moses and Aaron* (1625) set their Christian protagonists into dialogue with the heathen gods, arguing for the close cultural connections between ancient peoples.

Long the product of Christian polemics, paganism began to wither when these polemics faded. The end of the European wars of religion had profound consequences for the cultural, political, and religious fortunes of the Olympian gods. The ancient and theologically significant division of religions into Christianity, Judaism, Islam, and paganism was superseded by a more generic "religions of the world," of which the gods of Greece and Rome were just one pantheon, and perhaps not even the most important. Thus, Bernard Picart's illustrated *Ceremonies and Customs of All the World* (1723) left the Olympian gods behind, preferring to focus on the history of living religions rather than dead ones. Only then could what Warburg (1999) describes as the "classically rarefied version of the ancient gods" become possible (he was referring specifically to the 18th-century German aesthete Johann Winckelmann). As the theological power of paganism waned, aesthetics and scholarship were free to take up the slack, producing the peculiar Enlightenment and 19th-century cultures of classicism. A science of mythology and an unabashed philhellenism in matters literary and artistic joined forces as the power of the gods began to diffuse into the realms of art and pedagogy.

The gods did not necessarily go easily. The early 19th century witnessed fierce conflicts between, on the one side, philological purists and classicist aesthetes and, on the other, Romantic fans of pagan mythology seeking a revitalized Christianity for the modern world. The philosopher Friedrich Schelling and the poet Friedrich Hölderlin, for example, summoned up the pagan gods to reanimate an essentially religious spirit for the modern world. And when the scholar Friedrich Creuzer published his monumental *Symbolism and Mythology of the Ancients* (1810), it was in the service of religious invigoration. His goal was to enliven Christianity by linking it to the vital paganism that had permeated the ancient Near East. The power of human sensuality, the celebration of the divine, the mysteries of the priests: all were praised by the Romantic mythographers. Here too, as earlier, paganism's power depended on Christianity. Creuzer's eulogies to ancient gods were, for his Protestant critics, a barely disguised mystical Catholicism, and the intensity of the controversy over his work hinged on the threat that his pagans seem to have posed to contemporary Christians.

In the end, however, this enthusiastic mythography succumbed to more sober scholarly appreciations. As the discipline of comparative religion took shape in European universities, the pagan gods were integrated into the wider classical world. Paganism became just one of many localized religions, all rooted in specific times and places. The power of paganism as a conceptual partner and challenge to Christianity evaporated in the sunshine of scholarship and aesthetics. It was this sunny vision of the ancients that Friedrich Nietzsche rejected in *The Birth of Tragedy* (1872). The "artistic structure of Apollonian culture" and the subsequent loss of Dionysian violence and joy both depended on the theological deflation of paganism and its elevation into the realm of culture.

This history does have an interesting final twist, however. In recent years paganism has made a self-styled form of resurgence. The Internet abounds with sites dedicated to neo-paganism, neo-druidism, shamanism, Wicca, and related interests. Neo-pagan journals, conferences, and advocacy groups are everywhere, as new devotees attempt to synthesize New Age sensibilities (environmentalism, feminism, holism, and so on) with the gods and values of antiquity. Seen as an anodyne for an overly mechanistic, hypertechnological, and too strictly Christianized world, neo-paganism cheerfully blends as many traditions as it can fit together, revisiting the pantheons of the ancients and discovering there allegorical or real manifestations of the God and Goddess. Greek gods are favored, but not all of them. Diana has a legion of fans, but few devote themselves to the services of Zeus or Poseidon. In a sense, neo-paganism perfectly expresses the death of paganism. No longer do the pagan gods wear anything like a demonic scowl, nor do they exercise the authoritative claim over their worshipers that they once were believed to do. Instead, their worshipers approach them selectively, reserving the option to annex or turn to other powers. The ineluctible gods of classical antiquity are truly gone.

BIBL.: Don Cameron Allen, *Mysteriously Meant: The Rediscovery of Pagan Symbolism and Allegorical Interpretation in the Renaissance* (Baltimore 1970). Leonard Barkan, *Gods Made Flesh: Metamorphosis and the Pursuit of Paganism* (New Haven 1986). Ernst Curtius, *European Literature and the Latin Middle Ages,* trans. Willard Trask (New York 1953). Ralph Häfner, *Die Götter im Exil: Frühneuzeitliches Dichtungsverständnis im Spannungsfeld christlicher Apologetik und philogischer Kritik (ca. 1590–1736)* (Tübingen 2003). Fritz Saxl, "Pagan Sacrifice in the Italian Renaissance," *Journal of the Warburg Institute* 2 (April 1939) 346–367. Jean Seznec, *The Survival of the Pagan Gods: The Mythological Tradition and Its Place in Renaissance Humanism and Art* (New York 1953). D. P. Walker, *The Ancient Theology: Studies in Christian Platonism from the Fifteenth to the Eighteenth Century* (Ithaca 1972). Aby Warburg, "Pagan-Antique Prophecy in Words and Images in the Age of Luther," in *The Renewal of Pagan Antiquity,* trans. David Britt (Los Angeles 1999). J.SH.

Palace

Wary of comparisons with Persian palaces or Greek *basileia,* the emperor Augustus reportedly adopted the word *palace* for his residence from the place where it stood, the Palatine Hill in Rome (Cassius Dio 53.16.5; Ovid, *Metamorphoses* 1.176). His house occupied only part of the hill, however, and the name primarily reflected Augustus's creation of a new administrative and religious center within his house—and thus a notion of religious legitimacy rather than regal sumptuousness. As the hill filled with buildings erected by Nero, Domitian, and the Severan emperors, the concept of a palace as an extravagant residence emerged. The hill became wholly identified with the imperial residence, producing an opposition and interdependence between the city (*urbs*) and the palace (*palatium*).

Although emperors such as Trajan Decius, Claudius Gothicus, and Julian created palaces of their own elsewhere in the city, most subsequent palaces were inspired by the Palatine buildings, especially those of Domitian, and, outside Rome, by Hadrian's Villa at Tivoli. Although not a palace as such, Hadrian's Villa served the same political functions and featured sumptuous decoration. Diocletian's palace at Split in Dalmatia had a regular plan of courtyards, arcades, and a mausoleum. In late antiquity, not only imperial residences but also public buildings (e.g., Trajan's and Diocletian's baths) were known as "palaces," as were the late-antique houses of senators (Chromatius, Pilatus, Sallustius), because of their owners' power as much as the buildings' sumptuousness. The new Sessorium and Lateran palaces became centers of imperial and pontifical power, respectively, but were less important for the development of the concept. It was to the Palatine complex that the Germanic rulers of the Western empire looked as a model. Otho's palace was probably not there (as traditionally believed) but on the Aventine, but Theodoric's residence is labeled a *palatium* on a mosaic in Ravenna.

Of the two hundred episcopal and royal medieval palaces in England deserving the name because of their royal ownership, regular residence, and administrative and ceremonial uses, the Palace of Westminster in London stands out. Its juxtaposition of administrative center and church recalls Charlemagne's palace at Aachen, itself shaped by late-Roman villa and mausoleum complexes. In the 12th century Henry of Blois built *palatia sumptuosissima* (Giraldus Cambrensis): the Winchester Annals for 1238 called his East Hall at Wolvesey in Winchester a *domum quasi palatium.* Slightly later, William Fitzstephen called the Tower of London an *Arx Palatina.* Royal palaces increased in number under John, now used as pleasure grounds for hunting, tournaments, and spectacles, and almost doubled under Henry VIII, concentrated in southeastern England (Thurley 1993).

In Germany the imperial palace at Goslar, rebuilt after 1132, had an *aula regia* for summer use. In Italy the Venetian Doge's Palace was for a long time unique, distinguished in nomenclature until 1797 from the aristocratic Venetian "house" (*ca'*). An alternative tradition of "civic palaces" (*palazzi pubblici*) emerged, notably in Siena. Among Renaissance aristocratic rulers reviving the classical notion, Federico da Montefeltro planned his Palazzo Ducale at Urbino as "a city in the form of a palace" (Castiglione, *Il cortegiano* 1.2). Luca Pitti's Florentine palace, with its famous rusticated front, was later purchased by Eleanora di Toledo, the wife of Duke Cosimo de' Medici, and became the grand-ducal residence. Alberti's design for the Palazzo Rucellai used Vitruvius' prescription for tragic stage sets representing royal buildings (*De architectura* 5.6.8). Other new palaces directly evoked those of imperial Rome: the Cancelleria and Conservatori palaces and the Vatican palace of Julius II in Rome, where Bramante's Belvedere was inspired by literary descriptions of ancient porticoes; Sangallo's Palazzo Farnese, reproducing the classical combination of public square, courtyard palace, and ornamental garden; and later, Palazzo Barberini. "Palace streets" or "parade streets" developed, like the Via Alessandrina (Borgo Nuovo) in Rome and the Strada Nuova in Genoa, spacious thoroughfares along which elite residences were clustered. In northern Italy Giulio Romano's Palazzo del Te in Mantua enlivened the concept, and the villas of Palladio were shaped by the concept of the classical house. In Genoa the classical association between villa and mausoleum was reproduced in the relation of the Palazzo Doria with the church of San Matteo.

The classicizing palace spread across Europe: one might think of Francis I's Fontainebleau, Pierre Lescot's rebuilding of the Louvre (1545–1551), Henry VIII's Nonsuch and Hampton Court, and Charles V's palace in Córdoba. Philip II's palatial monastery, the Escorial, has proportions derived from Vitruvius and Solomon's Temple, and a "Pantheon" of royal tombs under the church. The palace reached its most extravagant phase in the age of absolutism, with Inigo Jones's Queen's House at Greenwich, remodeled as a hospital by Christopher Wren and Nicholas Hawksmoor; the Banqueting House within the Whitehall complex; and Louis XIV's Versailles. Wren was also employed to redesign Hampton Court to rival Versailles. The royal palace at Caserta took inspiration from the excavations starting at Herculaneum in 1738; and the bishops' palace at Würzburg borrowed trophy motifs from Roman triumphal arches and had a *Kaisersaal* (Imperial Hall) as its principal focus. The tradition was extended by Leo von Klenze's Munich Residence and the palaces of King Ludwig of Bavaria, such as Linderhof.

In the late 20th century the palace concept was much discredited by the presidential palaces of dictators such as Nicolae Ceauşescu in Romania and Saddam Hussein in Iraq. The notion of the public palace, by contrast, has reappeared in elaborate casino halls, such as Caesar's Palace in Las Vegas, and in the Italian labeling of cavernous sports halls as *palazzi dello sport.*

BIBL.: Charles Burroughs, *The Italian Renaissance Palace Façade: Structures of Authority, Surfaces of Sense* (Cambridge 2002). Inge Nielsen, ed., *The Royal Palace Institution in the First Millennium* BC*: Regional Development and Cultural Interchange between East and West* (Athens 2001). Pasquale Rotondi, *The Ducal Palace of Urbino: Its Architecture and Decoration* (London 1969). M. Royo, *Domus imperatoriae: Topographie, formation et imaginaire des palais impériaux du Palatin* (Rome 1999). Simon Thurley, *The Tudor Palaces of England* (New Haven 1993). E.T.

Palimpsest

A manuscript whose parchment has been used more than once (usually twice, perhaps three times); from the Greek *palin* and *psēn,* to scrape clean, to smooth. The initial writing is erased with a pumice stone or a knife, and a new text is written in its place. Depending on the relative positions of the first and second texts, and depending as well on the thoroughness of the erasure, it is sometimes possible to decipher the first text.

The reuse of parchment is attested since antiquity and also became a matter of conciliar provisions; instructions for removing the first text date to the Middle Ages.

The reading of the erased text is a matter of interest, as the contents of the original texts are of great importance for the cultural history of the Middle Ages. A codex in the Vatican Library (Vat. lat. 5757), for example, contains a textual witness of Cicero's *De re publica* (1st cent. BCE). Under a biography of the patriarch John Chrysostom in the Austrian National Library (Cod. Hist. gr. 10) lies a handbook of the Greek language by Aelius Herodianus (*General Prosody,* 3rd cent. CE), which was otherwise handed down only in excerpts; in the same library is a Greek biography of the martyr George (Cod. 954), erased probably in the 8th century in the monastery of Bobbio to make way for a letter of the Church Father Jerome. The Codex Carolinus in Wolfenbüttel (Cod. Guelf. 64 Weißenburgensis) contains a copy of Isidore of Seville's *Etymologiae* (7th cent.) over Greek fragments from the Bible and from the works of Galen, a medical authority of the 2nd century CE. The upshot for Galen, thanks to the dating of the later text to the 8th century, is above all that we have a textual witness for him that is much older than all previously known copies.

Manuscripts in the British Library in London (Add. 7210) lead to the East: fragments of the Greek poet Homer are under a Syriac text; the earlier layer dates to the turn of the 6th century and is therefore of central importance for the textual history of Homer.

A parchment in the Vatican Library (Cod. Vat. gr. 2061 A) was written on three times. In the 5th century the work of the geographer Strabo was copied; over it are fragments from a legal text of the late 7th century; then in the 10th century a collection of sermons of the Church Father Gregory of Nazianzus was placed over the other layers.

The allure of the riddle of the original texts led, beginning in the late 18th and early 19th centuries, to attempts to bring these writings back to light. Thus, Cardinal Angelo Mai (1782–1854) made use of reagents that, in the short term, caused the earlier text to emerge but that, over time, damaged the parchment. Therefore, since the end of the 19th century only photographic methods have been used to study palimpsests; for the most part these involve infrared and ultraviolet exposures. A center for the study of palimpsests, led by Alban Dold in Beuron Archabbey, has succeeded in producing impressive results with these means.

Methods of electronic data processing can also be useful in deciphering erased writings. Multispectral photography can be combined with electronic manipulation to bring out the original text without harming the manuscript. The goal of Rinascimento Virtuale, a project of the European Union and countries of Eastern and Central Europe, was to apply new methods of this kind to the study of Greek palimpsests and at the same time to assemble a more precise inventory of extant palimpsests. It was concluded in the autumn of 2004 with exhibitions in Athens, Rome, Saragossa, and Vienna. The image produced of Herodianus' treatise *General Prosody* not only resulted in better readability of that text, but also brought an 11th-century statute collection to light that is of central importance for the reconstruction of Byzantine legal history.

BIBL.: A. Dold, ed., *Palimpsest-Studien* (Beuron 1955). A. Escobar, ed., *Palimpsestos: News from Rinascimento Virtuale—*

Digitale Palimpsestforschung: Rediscovering Written Records of a Hidden European Cultural Heritage (Zaragoza 2004). D. Harlfinger, ed., *Rinascimento virtuale—digitale Palimpsestforschung: Rediscovering Written Records of a Hidden European Cultural Heritage: Perspektiven des Netzwerks* (Bratislava 2002). Projekt Rinascimento Virtuale, www.rrz.uni-hamburg.de/RV/. E.G.

Translated by Patrick Baker

Palladio, Andrea

Italian Renaissance architect (1508–1580). Thanks to his own study of Roman antiquities, Palladio achieved a profound understanding of the legacy of the classical tradition, which he transmitted to future architects through his highly influential treatise as well as his own buildings.

Born in Padua, Palladio was apprenticed to a stonemason's workshop in Vicenza. His real name was Andrea di Pietro della Gondola, but he was given the classical name Palladio by the Vicentine Humanist Gian Giorgio Trissino, who took him to Rome for the first time, probably in 1541. Vicenza was to prove the ideal center in which the young architect could develop his talents. Although a subject city of the Venetian Republic, the town was administered by a fiercely independent local elite, proud of its strong cultural identity.

Palladio made a total of five visits to Rome during his career. A profusion of surviving drawings demonstrate how carefully he observed and measured the remains of Roman antiquity. Although he had learned of the theory of the orders in classical architecture from the writings of Vitruvius and Alberti, he sought to penetrate the underlying principles of ancient design through discriminating firsthand observation of Roman archaeological sites. His drawings show how he often reconstructed ruined buildings graphically, seeking a regularity and harmony of proportion that was not always present in the original. In 1554 he published his own guidebook to the antiquities of Rome, as well as a pilgrim's guide to the Holy City. Two years later, he provided illustrations for Daniele Barbaro's authoritative translation and commentary on Vitruvius.

In his built architecture, Palladio began to develop his own system of design, emulating what he felt to be the true spirit of ancient Rome. He eschewed pedantic antiquarianism in favor of a distillation of the essence of the remains he had observed. For example, his Basilica, an arcaded structure, begun in 1549, surrounding the medieval communal palace of Vicenza, achieves its grandeur through the simplicity and proportion of its superimposed Doric and Ionic orders. In his designs for Vicentine palaces and country villas, Palladio tried to recreate the character of the ancient Roman *domus*. Later in his life he turned to religious architecture, obtaining a series of prominent commissions in Venice, notably the monastery of the Lateran canons known as the Convento della Carità, the facade of the Church of San Francesco della Vigna, and the churches San Giorgio Maggiore and Il Redentore. The unprecedented monumentality of these later works was to transform Venetian architectural tradition.

Palladio's treatise on architecture, *I quattro libri dell'architettura,* published in Venice in 1570, presented his principles of design to the public across Europe. The text, written in Italian and illustrated by woodcut plates, is both lucid and practical. The four books discuss, respectively, the classical orders of architecture, domestic building, public building, and temples. Whereas the last two books concentrate on known Roman antiquities, the second book focuses on Palladio's own designs for villas and palaces. In 1574–1575 he published a translation of Caesar's *Commentaries* with illustrations by his sons, both recently deceased. This enterprise reflected his lifelong interest in ancient Roman fortification, and especially in the *castramentatio* of Polybius.

Over the five centuries since his birth, Palladio has had many followers and imitators, from Vincenzo Scamozzi onward. The English architect Inigo Jones used Palladio's *Quattro libri* as his principal guide to the antiquities of Rome. In the 18th century a more dogmatic form of Palladianism flourished in England, where Whig aristocrats modeled their country houses on Palladio's villas. The classical authority of the Palladian villa has proved an enduring symbol of landownership, as is also evident in the houses of plantation owners in America and the West Indies. The interpretation of Palladio's use of harmonic proportion in Rudolf Wittkower's *Architectural Principles in the Age of Humanism* (1949) influenced many postwar Modernist architects, though some Postmodernists have emulated the more superficial elements of Palladian classicism.

BIBL.: James S. Ackerman, *Palladio* (Harmondsworth 1966). Bruce Boucher, *Andrea Palladio* (New York 1994). Howard Burns et al., *Andrea Palladio 1508–1580: The Portico and the Farmyard* (London 1973). André Chastel and Renato Cevese, eds., *Andrea Palladio: Nuovi contributi* (Milan 1988). Andrea Palladio, *I quattro libri dell'architettura* (Venice 1570) and *The Four Books on Architecture,* trans. Robert Tavernor and Richard Schofield (Cambridge, Mass., 1997). Lionello Puppi, *Andrea Palladio: Complete Works* (London 1989). Giangiorgio Zorzi, *I disegni delle antichità di Andrea Palladio* (Venice 1959). D.H.

Palmyra

The rise to power in the Roman East of the kingdom of Palmyra in the late 260s and early 270s CE has prompted continuous academic fascination with the ruins of the city of that name since the mid-18th century. Zenobia, widow of the Palmyrene leader Odaenathus and regent for their infant son, Vaballathus, briefly ruled large parts of the Roman empire. In post-classical traditions she appeared early in Renaissance literature as a chaste warrior-queen in Boccaccio's *On Famous Women* (1360–1374) and in Chaucer's *Canterbury Tales* (1380s–1390s).

An oasis city in the Syrian steppe, Palmyra was first visited by Europeans when British merchants based at

Aleppo traveled to the site in the late 17th century. When the explorer Lady Hester Stanhope arrived at the ruins in 1813, dressed in local style and followed by her own caravan of camels, she was heralded as the new queen of the Arabs, thus living up to her own perceived destiny. The first half of the 19th century saw the publication of a series of "Letters of Lucius M. Piso, from Palmyra, to his friend Marcus Curtius, at Rome," written by the American romancer William Ware (1797–1852), republished in midcentury under the title *Zenobia, or the Fall of Palmyra.* More recently, another fictitious Roman, detective Marcus Didius Falco, visited the oasis in Lindsey Davis's *Last Act in Palmyra* (1994). Much debated, though little known, is the assembly of intellectual figures (some historical, others legendary) at Zenobia's court, a welcome topic of speculation for ancient and modern authors alike (Charles-Gaffiot et al. 2001; Stoneman 1992). Over the years the queen's image has spearheaded Arab nationalism, and most recently her life and legend were revisited by Yasmine Zahran (2003).

When the first proper modern expeditions began in the mid-18th century, inscriptions were copied and brought back to the West. The Aramaic dialect of Palmyra was the first of the "forgotten scripts" to be discovered. It was deciphered in 1754 by the Englishman John Swinton and the French abbot J. J. Barthélemy, working independently (Daniels 1988). Swinton worked from inscriptions collected in a newly published illustrated folio by Robert Wood (1753), communicating his findings in a series of letters published in the *Philosophical Transactions* of the Royal Society. Palmyra's riches were soon understood to have been based on the city's location at a crossroads of the main trade routes of its day. Later dubbed "the Venice of the sands" (Will 1992), as a center of caravan trade Palmyra was seen by Sir Moses Finley as the main exception to his agricultural and self-sufficient model of the ancient economy—although intriguingly the most famous "evidence" for this, the bilingual (Greek-Aramaic) tariff inscription now on display in the Hermitage in St. Petersburg, Russia, has since been exposed as a law dealing with local trade only.

Among museum visitors worldwide the best-known artifacts from Palmyra are no doubt the funerary reliefs (their subjects typically staring proudly outward), found in abundance in underground burial chambers, and the evocative tower tombs surrounding the ruins. Designs used in Palmyrene architecture, a classical baroque drenched with indigenous peculiarities, influenced the decoration of many an 18th-century British country house.

BIBL.: Jacques Charles-Gaffiot, Henri Lavagne, and Jean-Marc Hofman, eds., *Moi, Zénobie reine de Palmyre* (Paris 2001). P. T. Daniels, "'Shewing of Hard Sentences and Dissolving of Doubts': The First Decipherment," *Journal of the American Oriental Society* 108 (1988) 419–436. Richard Stoneman, *Palmyra and Its Empire: Zenobia's Revolt against Rome* (Ann Arbor 1992). Ernest Will, *Les Palmyréniens: La Venise des sables* (Paris 1992). Robert Wood, *The Ruins of Palmyra, Otherwise Tedmor, in the Desart* (London 1753). Yasmine Zahran, *Zenobia: Between Reality and Legend* (Oxford 2003). T.K.

Pan

Deity of the mountainous and remote region of Arcadia in ancient Greece, where he was worshiped as a god of fertility and protector of shepherds and flocks. Half-human and half-animal, he had the upper body of a man and the horns, ears, legs, and hooves of a goat. Shepherds worshiped and feared him, but hunters would scourge the statue of the god if a hunt was unsuccessful. Nobody was allowed to disturb him when he slept in the hottest hours of midday (Theocritus, *Idylls* 1.15–18, 7.106–108). The sleeping goat-god is the image of the menacing silence of nature. The Romans attributed similar physical features and powers to their gods Faunus and Silvanus.

The two most important myths associated with Pan emphasize his musical talent and lecherous temperament. Both suggest a symbolic link between the soundscape of nature and the irrational power of music. In one myth, Pan pursued the nymph Syrinx, whose sisters, to aid her escape, transformed her into marsh reeds. Pan heard the nymph's lamenting voice as the wind stirred the reeds; he cut some stems and bound them together into the musical instrument known as a syrinx, or panpipes (Ovid, *Metamorphoses* 1.689–713). In one version of the second myth, Pan incited shepherds to kill and dismember the nymph Echo, because he was jealous of her ability to sing and imitate both human and natural sounds (Longus, *Daphnis and Chloe* 3.23). Like Marsyas, he was eventually defeated by Apollo in a musical contest (Ovid, *Metamorphoses* 11.146–180). He was also believed to be the source of sudden and mysterious sounds that induced uncontrollable fear in men and animals (Pausanias, *Guide to Greece* 10.23.7; Flaccus, *Argonautica* 3.46–57). His terrifying voice survives in the English term *panic.*

Despite his somewhat ambiguous identity as a creature at once bestial, human, and divine, or perhaps because of it, Pan has continued to exert an extraordinary influence on the Western imagination. Throughout the centuries, his half-animal and half-human body has served as a symbol of shifting and at times competing ideas about man and nature, reason and the senses, and good and evil. Part of his fame and allure overlapped with the dissemination of pastoral poetry and the iconographic apparatus associated with it, following the Humanistic revival of the genre. He was usually depicted as intent on playing his seven-reed pipe, tending his flock, or chasing nymphs in the woods. But even after the decline in popularity of pastoral lyric and drama, the figure of Pan continued to be used to evoke the existential and affective universe of Arcadia, especially in connection with ideas of primitivism, naturalism, unbridled sexuality, and the instinctual pursuit of artistic creativity.

As early as the 7th or 6th century BCE (in Homeric Hymn 19) Pan's name appears to have been linked to the Greek word *pan* ("all"). Capitalizing on the suggestive power of language, later commentators made Pan into an image of the totality of all that exists, the universal god. "They call him Pan," wrote Isidore of Seville (7th cent. CE), "as if to say everything." He reinterpreted Pan's anatomical traits from a cosmological perspective:

> For he has horns in the shape of the rays of the sun and the moon. He has skin marked with spots because of the stars of the sky. His face is red, in the likeness of the upper air. He carries a pipe with seven reeds, because of the harmony of heaven in which there are seven notes and seven distinctions of tones. He is hairy, since the earth is clothed and is stirred by the winds. His lower part is filthy, because of trees, wild beasts, and herds. He has goat hoofs to show forth the solidity of the earth. (*Etymologies* 8.11.82–83, trans. Merivale)

Modern scholars have rejected this etymology in favor of a root *pa-*, meaning herdsman, guardian of flocks (cf. English *pasture*). The Pan–universe identification has, however, found fertile terrain, whether in an implicit or explicit form, in pantheistic views of the world, as well as in idealized representations of a prelapsarian existence in perfect harmony with nature. A supernatural episode recounted by Plutarch in which a mysterious voice announced that the great Pan was dead (*Moralia* 419c, ca. 100 CE) also fostered a symbolic association of the pagan god of nature with Christ.

The animalistic and lascivious side of Pan's character has generated an equally enduring and widespread view of the goat-god as embodying the negative and dark forces of nature. His horns, hairy legs, and hooves reappeared in Christian iconography as attributes of the devil (an identification probably encouraged by the anatomical similarities and sexual prowess he shared with satyrs). For Augustine, the sylvan deities and Pan, "who are commonly called incubi, had often made wicked assaults upon women and satisfied their lust upon them" (*City of God* 15.23, trans. Dodds). As incubus, Pan was sometimes adopted as an archetypical figure for the psychological status associated with nightmares. In this context Jungian approaches to the study of mythology have stressed the link between Pan-like animal demons and the repression of violent and negative impulses. The sinister Pan, in Patricia Merivale's words, seems to have enjoyed a renewed popularity in English fiction of the late 19th and early 20th centuries. His legacy is still visible in the prototypical image of horned and goat-faced gods and demons in neopagan movements.

BIBL.: John Boardman, *The Great God Pan: The Survival of an Image* (New York 1998). Philippe Borgeaud, *The Cult of Pan in Ancient Greece,* trans. Kathleen Atlass and James Redfield (Chicago 1988). James Hillman, *Pan and the Nightmare* (Woodstock, Conn., 2000). Patricia Merivale, *Pan, the Goat-God: His Myth in Modern Times* (Cambridge, Mass., 1969).

G.G.

Pandora

Mythological figure from the cycle of stories about Prometheus' strife with Zeus; she was taken as a wife by Prometheus' brother Epimetheus. She first appeared in literature in the works of Hesiod. The Greek poet relates how Zeus commissioned from Hephaestus, god of the forge, "the semblance of a reverend maiden" to be given as an "evil" "in exchange for the fire" stolen by Prometheus (*Theogony* 570–572; *Works and Days* 57, 71). After being beguilingly furnished with divine gifts, this "beautiful evil" received the name Pandora. The creation is considered "a steep deception, intractable for human beings" (*Theogony* 585, 589; *Works and Days* 83). Once introduced to mankind—Epimetheus accepts the "gift"—Pandora opens a massive jar (Greek *pithos*), and fatal consequences ensue: mankind is now exposed to illness and want; only hope or expectation (Greek *elpis*) stayed in the jar.

Hesiod's dark formulation of the Pandora myth opens up countless possibilities for appropriation. Certain motifs condensed in the myth—such as *elpis,* Pandora's similarity to the biblical Eve, her double nature as evil and good (Renger and Musäus 2002, 93–140)—took on independent life and have remained operative, usually decontextualized, in various media to the present day. The motif that separated itself most enduringly from the reception of the original work is that of the opening of the jar. After Erasmus scaled the container down to a box (Latin *pyxis*) in 1508 (*Adagia* 1.1.31)—the first echo in pictorial art is found ca. 1535 (pen drawing by Giovanni Battista di Jacopo, known as Rosso Fiorentino)—the ominous opening of "Pandora's box" became a figure of speech. Since then artists and litterateurs have been changing the form and size of the container at will (carton, chest, cabinet; can, vase, tureen; safe, music box, room, and the like; see Panofsky and Panofsky 1956; Renger and Musäus 2002, 21–41).

In the course of the very many appropriations in pictorial art, poetry, and theory, Pandora's jar was also equated with the human body, especially Pandora's own, so that attribute and character coincided. Thus, in his *Prometheus* (1773), Goethe eulogizes Pandora as "sacred vessel of all gifts." Just as Boccaccio had 300 years earlier in *Genealogie* 45, Goethe makes Prometheus the creator of Pandora; in his *Pandora* (1808) he associates the reception of good, culture-inspiring gifts with her character. The reference to the body can be traced to, among other things, the everyday human experience of the body as a vessel, and moreover to the fact that the vessel is concretely connected to the feminine symbolism of the state of containing. This is made clear in Erich Neumann's depth-psychology interpretation of Pandora as a symbol for "the feminine as a fascinating and yet deadly vessel." In *The Great Mother* (1956, 168), a Jungian account of the world of the Great Feminine, the vessel is the core symbol of the feminine. The Earth also belongs to the typology of the vessel: as a belly and living space, underworld and place of the dead. Here the enduring tradition of *pandora ge* ("Earth, giver of all things") can be felt, which has lived an active, independent life alongside Hesiod's Pandora since antiquity, as attested by, for example, Philo of Alexandria (*On the Creation of the World* 133, *On the Imperishability of the World* 63). An exemplary conflation of the Earth goddess with Hesiod's negative image can be found in the dark netherworld goddess Pandora of the *Orphic Argonautica* (977–985), an anonymous composition of the 4th or 5th century CE.

Ambivalent representations of Pandora culminate in fin de siècle femme-fatale depictions. The best known of these is Frank Wedekind's Lulu in *Earth Spirit* (1895) and *The Box of Pandora* (1904). In 1929 G. W. Pabst summarized both plays in a cinematic refiguration of the myth's history, in which feminine beauty, erotic charisma, and childlike coquetry take on lethal form in the dancer Lulu. The inversion of character (Pandora-Lulu) and attribute (jar-box) in Wedekind's film title—*The Box of Pandora*—once again makes reference to the equation of (beautiful female) body and (ominous) vessel.

In the 21st century Pandora has finally become an attribute of the vessel. In the jargon of journalism, "Pandora's box" has been used ad infinitum as a kindred formula for the criticism of technology. At the same time it is a virtual box in cyberspace whose purpose is to pique the curiosity of Web surfers, induce them to open the box, and thus seduce them to linger on a specific Web site.

BIBL.: Immanuel Musäus, *Der Pandoramythos bei Hesiod und seine Rezeption bis Erasmus von Rotterdam* (Göttingen 2004). Dora Panofsky and Erwin Panofsky, *Pandora's Box: The Changing Aspects of a Mythical Symbol* (New York 1956). Almut-Barbara Renger and Immanuel Musäus, *Mythos Pandora* (Leipzig 2002). A.-B.R.

Translated by Patrick Baker

Panegyric

Elaborate, formal, set-piece orations in praise of emperors or high dignitaries; an integral part of the ceremony of politics in the Roman empire. Very few of the thousands of panegyrics that must have been delivered survive. The most influential was given in 100 CE by Pliny the Younger before the emperor Trajan and the Senate in Rome. This speech mapped out a powerful version of the autocrat as imagined by a loyal member of the privileged elite: above all, a praiseworthy ruler who, for all his self-evident power, remembered that he was still a citizen among citizens, collectively bound by the rule of law and a mutual respect for social status. The text of Pliny's speech was well known in late antiquity. It is preserved as the leading example in a late 4th-century collection of 11 speeches delivered between 289 and 389 CE, known collectively as the Panegyrici Latini. There is no good evidence of the knowledge of either Pliny or the Panegyrici Latini in the Middle Ages, until their rediscovery in 1433 by Giovanni Aurispa in a manuscript (now lost) in Mainz.

Pliny provided his restorers with a useful model for the praise of kings. His most famous imitator was Erasmus, who delivered his *Panegyricus* in January 1504 before Philip the Handsome, Archduke of Burgundy. For Erasmus (*Epistles* 180) the panegyric offered "men of good judgment" (among whom he counted Pliny) the opportunity to place "an image of virtue" before even a bad prince. That claim to a combination of praise and didactic instruction was a common justification for such orations in the 16th and 17th centuries. In 1686 White Kennett, offering an English translation of Pliny's *Panegyric* to James II of England, suggested that this monarch had finally fulfilled the ideal that Pliny had presented as "a kind of winning Lecture to future Princes."

Alongside the few surviving examples of antique Latin panegyrics flourished a rich tradition of rhetorical handbooks. The fullest discussion of how a speech in praise of an emperor might be constructed is contained in a late 3rd-century CE treatise conventionally attributed to Menander of Laodicea. The treatise offers a schematic set of categories (family, birth, upbringing, virtues, military successes, physical appearance, and so on) that could form the basic building blocks of such a speech. But formal training in panegyric remained at the margins of early modern rhetorical education. Indeed, by the 18th century (and until revisionist approaches in the late 20th) panegyric was treated with suspicion. That reflected a nervousness—especially among those advocating the intellectual or moral benefits of rhetoric—of the easy slide from praise into flattery. Hugh Blair, Regius Professor of Rhetoric and Belles Lettres at the University of Edinburgh, regarded panegyric as "quaint and affected," marked by a clear deficiency "in nature and ease" (*Lectures on Rhetoric and Belles Lettres,* no. 26, 1783). For Edward Gibbon, the Panegyrici Latini were indicators that by the late 4th century Roman government had become a dazzling, theatrical sham, "filled with players of every character and degree who repeated the language, and imitated the passions of their original model" (*Decline and Fall of the Roman Empire,* 2:1781). For Enlightenment critics, panegyrics were not to be seen as part of a vital political culture; rather, they were a sure index of the constriction of personal liberty and the inevitable bankruptcy of language under autocracy.

BIBL.: James Garrison, *Dryden and the Tradition of Panegyric* (Berkeley 1975). C. E. V. Nixon and B. S. Rogers, *In Praise of Later Roman Emperors: The Panegyrici Latini* (Berkeley 1994). D. A. Russell and N. G. Wilson, *Menander Rhetor* (Oxford 1981). Andrew Wallace-Hadrill, "*Civilis princeps:* Between Citizen and King," *Journal of Roman Studies* 72 (1982) 32–48. C.KE.

Pantheon

Constructed during the reign of the emperor Hadrian between 118 and 125 CE in the Campus Martius district of ancient Rome, the imposing Pantheon still dominates its surroundings today. Ammianus Marcellinus, writing in the mid-4th century, likened the building to "a self-contained district." Dio Cassius (early 3rd cent.) reports that the temple was dedicated to many gods and attributes its name to the way in which its soaring dome resembles the heavens. Although he appears to have confused the Hadrianic Pantheon with an older temple on the same site constructed by Marcus Agrippa, whose name is recorded by an inscription on the facade, Dio's description remains apt.

The Pantheon is composed of two principal elements—a columnar porch supporting a pediment, and a domed rotunda—joined by a rectangular transitional block. Structurally it represents a brilliant integration of the trabeated systems of the Hellenistic tradition with the space-molding forms of arch and vault perfected by the Romans. In scale and structural audacity the Pantheon commands respect; at 142 feet (43 meters), the span of its dome has never been surpassed in masonry. The proportions of the rotunda, generated by the basic geometry of circle and square, contribute to the cosmic associations noted by Dio. The interaction of architecture and nature, particularly evident in the view of the celestial vault framed by its oculus and the constantly changing effects of illumination, suggests a potent linkage between empire and cosmos, between the human and the divine.

The Pantheon's excellent state of preservation is due to its transformation into a church (Sancta Maria ad Martyres) early in the 7th century. The Byzantine Emperor Constans II removed its gilded roof tiles in 663, but the building's structural fabric was maintained in its essentials throughout the Middle Ages. Stamps on the lead sheathing of the dome record the intervention of Pope Nicholas V (1447–1455) and his successors. The most noteworthy alterations to the fabric took place under Pope Urban VIII (1623–1644): the removal of bronze from the trusses of the portico and the addition of two bell towers, which were eventually removed in the 1880s. Within the rotunda, the attic zone was altered following designs of Paolo Posi in 1756–1757.

Over the past five centuries the Pantheon's reception has been characterized by both praise and criticism. Raphael admired the spatial qualities of the interior, and Michelangelo described its design as "angelic, not human." Gian Lorenzo Bernini resisted the efforts of Alexander VII to alter the attic, claiming that he lacked the talent to improve on the original scheme. Ironically, the ideal proportions of the Pantheon caused the building's anomalies and imperfections to stand out. Francesco di Giorgio Martini, perceiving a discordant relationship between the coffering of the dome and the attic pilasters, sought to correct this defect in his drawings. Another anomaly, the double pediment, prompted Andrea Palladio's imaginative solution for the facade of the Redentore in Venice.

Variations on the theme of Hadrian's Pantheon have repeatedly enriched the history of Western architecture. The stepped exterior profile of the Pantheon's dome was echoed by Bramante in his design for a new St. Peter's, by Borromini in Sant'Ivo alla Sapienza, and by John Russell Pope in the National Gallery of Art in Washington. The paradigmatic image of a domed rotunda rising behind a temple front has proven remarkably flexible through the ages, recognizable in Palladio's Villa Rotonda, Jefferson's library rotunda at the University of Virginia, and a host of other examples. The Pantheon's legacy, together with its distinguished progeny, reveals the enduring vitality of its artistic potential.

BIBL.: Tilmann Buddensieg, "Criticism and Praise of the Pantheon in the Middle Ages and the Renaissance," in *Classical Influences on European Culture, A.D. 500–1500,* ed. R. R. Bolgar (Cambridge 1971) 259–267. William L. MacDonald, *The Pantheon: Design, Meaning, and Progeny* (Cambridge, Mass., 1976). Susanna Pasquali, *Il Pantheon: Architettura e antiquaria nel Settecento a Roma* (Modena 1996). J.PI.

Pantomime. *See* Mime and Pantomime.

Paper Museum

Paper Museum (Museo Cartaceo) was the title that Cassiano dal Pozzo (1588–1657) gave to the collection of drawings that he assembled with his brother Carlo Antonio (1606–1689). The drawings included representations of a variety of antiquities and of a range of natural historical phenomena. Artists, scholars, and travelers observed them in situ; after Carlo Antonio's death the drawings began a tortuous journey through a variety of hands. Most that survive today are divided between the Royal Collection in Windsor and the British Museum in London.

Cassiano was born in Turin and moved to Rome in 1612, where he soon became acquainted with prominent scholars and churchmen. In 1622 he became a member of the Accademia dei Lincei, whose members included Galileo and Maffeo Barberini (elected Pope Urban VIII in 1623). By that time Carlo Antonio had joined him, and the two moved into a palazzo in the Via dei Chiavari in 1626. Like other 17th-century dignitaries, they collected antiquities, paintings, and books; they supplemented these with drawings of objects that they could not obtain for the collection. They bought some of the drawings, but most they commissioned from artists in Rome, among the best known of whom was Nicolas Poussin. Nearly 7,000 survive today. The brothers complemented the drawings with a collection of prints, to comprise a visual archive of unprecedented size. By including images of *naturalia*—from fossils to fungi and citrus fruit to birds—alongside those of human creations, the dal Pozzo brothers paralleled the macrocosmic ambitions of contemporary museums and *Wunderkammern* (cabinets of curiosities).

Around 4,200 of the drawings show classical and early Christian antiquities. Because of the complicated afterlife of the collection, it is impossible to reconstruct exactly how the brothers arranged it, but their basic organizing principle was thematic. Drawings of classical Roman reliefs and architectural features make up a large part of the collection. There are also significant numbers of illustrations of Christian and pagan wall paintings and mosaics; of small objects like lamps and seals; and of particular antiquarian treasures, both ancient, such as the 5th-century Vatican Virgil manuscript, and modern, such as the work of Pirro Ligorio (d. 1583). The strengths of the collection reflect the achievements of previous antiquarian scholars and the interests of the scholars with whom Cassiano was in contact. There are virtually no drawings of coins and few commissions of inscriptions, probably because large compilations with records of both types of evidence had been printed by the early 17th century. On the other hand, the drawings of relief sculpture and small objects provided evidence for ancient religious practice and daily life that fascinated the dal Pozzos' contemporaries.

Cassiano received thousands of letters from across Europe; he and Carlo Antonio were the dedicatees of numerous books; and there is evidence for many travelers' visits to the palazzo. Direct references by contemporary scholars and artists to the Paper Museum, however, are frustratingly few, and it is probably better to see the dal Pozzos as patrons of a learned salon, for which their drawings and other objects provided inspirations for discussion, rather than as directors of a utilitarian research center.

Carlo Antonio's son sold the Paper Museum to Pope Clement XI, who in turn sold it to his nephew Cardinal Alessandro Albani in 1714. In the Albani family collection it was reordered and combined with other drawings. Agents of George III of England bought the entire Albani collection in 1762. Once in England, this larger collection was subdivided. The Paper Museum was not forgotten, but it was certainly neglected until the late 20th century, when scholars recognized its value as a visual record of archaeological remains extant in the 17th century (many of which have subsequently disappeared or been damaged), and of 17th-century learned culture.

BIBL.: Ingo Herklotz, *Cassiano dal Pozzo und die Archäologie des 17. Jahrhunderts* (Munich 1999). Dirk Jacob Jansen, "Antiquarian Drawings and Prints as Collector's Items," *Journal of the History of Collections* 6 (1994) 181–188. *The Paper Museum of Cassiano dal Pozzo: A Catalogue Raisonné,* Series A, *Antiquities and Architecture,* 10 vols. (London 1996–).

W.S.

Papyrology

Over the course of the 20th century, papyri became the acknowledged source not only of literary works that the manuscript traditions had not absorbed but also of unique documents that offer details about ancient lives as they were being lived. The nearly 60,000 papyri now published, many in Greek and Egyptian, fewer in Latin and other languages of the eastern Mediterranean, have opened up direct and immediate contacts with the ancient world in ways unimaginable before the final decades of the 19th century.

Papyrus rolls of Greek literature, unseen and unread for centuries, arrived at the British Museum in the 1890s: Aristotle's *Constitution of the Athenians,* victory odes by the 5th-century poet Bacchylides, orations by the 4th-century Athenian Hyperides, and mimes by the Hellenistic poet Herodas. Bernard P. Grenfell and Arthur S. Hunt took the search for papyri to Egypt and eventually Oxyrhynchus, a regional capital, where its rubbish heaps yielded boxes of papyri, now published in 72 volumes, with more to come.

Papyri were not always prized for their contributions to knowledge of the literature and society of the ancient world. Prosperous Greeks and Romans left behind luxury items, abandoned in tombs and buildings, that were more immediately attractive: bronze and marble statues; emblemata cut from mosaic floors; gold and silver cups, bronze mirrors, jewelry. These were ripped from their ancient contexts when discovered because peasants recognized them for the valuable objects they were. Papyri were slow to attract collectors, antiquarians, and scholars, and stories abound of rolls carelessly treated or deliberately destroyed. Recent years, however, have seen the employment of new technologies, a renewed enthusiasm, and a dramatic flow of publications.

The tunnels dug beneath early 18th-century Herculaneum in the hunt for Roman treasures in that seaside town on the Bay of Naples, buried by the eruption of Vesuvius in 79 CE, eventually reached the Villa of the Papyri. More than 200 rolls of papyrus, first mistaken for wooden logs, were brought to the surface between 1752 and 1754; they were fragile and difficult to unroll and read, for the eruption had carbonized them. Father Antonio Piaggio soon arrived from the Vatican with a machine he had devised to facilitate unrolling ancient papyri, but the work went slowly. Publication of the rolls—many contained treatises by the Epicurean philosopher and poet Philodemus of Gadara—remained sporadic for the next two centuries. Toward the end of the same century, peasants at the site of Giza and the pyramids offered an Italian merchant a wooden chest containing 40 papyrus rolls. He bought one that had 13 columns of Greek text, and the peasants supposedly burned the remainder. The merchant gave the roll to Cardinal Stefano Borgia upon his return to Italy, where it graced the cardinal's collection of antiquities. When the Danish classicist Niels Iversen Schow published an edition of the text in 1788, it proved to be not a long-lost work of literature but a list of the names of peasants who repaired the dikes at Ptolemais Hormou in February 193 CE.

Scholars' knowledge about papyrus as the writing material of antiquity continued to depend on the account of its manufacture in Pliny's *Natural History* (13.74–82), rather than on the examples brought home in increasing quantities by travelers. This is evident not only in Melchior Guilandinus's *Papyrus,* published in Venice in 1572, but also in Friedrich August Wolf's *Prolegomena to Homer,* published some 200 years later, in 1795. Guilandinus, a medical botanist and prefect of the University of Padua's gardens, saw papyrus plants while in Egypt, but his rambling commentary on Pliny depends far more on other authors than on personal experience. Wolf's imaginative and creative intellect heightened his desire to inspect copies of Homer's *Iliad* that antedated the surviving Byzantine manuscripts, and to read the works of Hellenistic critics on Homer's text. It did not occur to Wolf that papyri might someday aid him and others in this quest. Rather, his hopes for reading Alexandrian criticism lay in finding "a book . . . in its pristine form . . . in some library." Even small papyrus fragments of literary works read in Byzantine manuscripts since the Renaissance exhibit a Greek text a thousand years older, and the preponderance of Homer's *Iliad* among papyri demonstrates that this was the most widely read piece of Greek literature throughout antiquity.

Thanks to a century of attention given to papyri in Europe and America by specialists from many disciplines, papyrologists are now better equipped to read and interpret fragmentary specimens passed over by previous generations. A papyrus documenting everyday matters, such as Schow's text on the dike corvée, is of little historical import in isolation, since it captures only an ancient moment. When a number of documents involve the same subject, or derive from archives covering the same institution or the same individuals, however, a more coherent picture of social interactions and shared interests emerges. We know how town councils in the district capitals Oxyrhynchus and Hermopolis Magna functioned after their institution at the beginning of the 3rd century CE, run by wealthier citizens who were responsible to the central government for collecting taxes and requisitions, as well as for internal administration. Individuals are known with a familiarity otherwise lacking until relatively modern times, from Zenon, an estate manager in the Fayum village of Philadelphia in the 3rd century BCE, to the bilingual Greek and Coptic Flavius Dioscorus of Aphrodito, a gentleman farmer, lawyer, and poet in the 6th century CE. The archive of Nemesion, a collector of taxes in Philadelphia under Julio-Claudian emperors, demonstrates that he had as his partner in agricultural activities for some ten years the Roman centurion Lucius Cattius Catullus; Cattius supplied Nemesion with soldiers to facilitate Nemesion's collection of private debts and to help him settle disputes with shepherds in his employ, while Nemesion served as owner of record for the land and animals whose profits they shared, as Roman law prevented Cattius from owning property in the province in which he was serving.

Most recently, the past decades have witnessed fruitful probing in the oases of the western desert and the quarries of the eastern desert, such as those at Mons Claudianus, whence derived the gray marble columns on the porch of the Pantheon. Provisioning the small Roman forts that guarded the route from Coptus on the Nile to Myos Hormou on the Red Sea required transporting water, wine, and foodstuffs into desert settlements. Papyrus was scarce, so accounts and private letters are often written on pieces of broken pots, or ostraca. The usefulness of gathering, analyzing, and synthesizing data from related documents was amply demonstrated in 1994, when census declarations, submitted by heads of households in Egypt to authorities for the Roman census between 11–12 and 257–258 CE, were gathered and subjected to modern demographic methods. Plausible patterns of mortality, marriage, fertility, and migration emerged. Greek papyri and ostraca detailing quotidian matters, very similar to those from Egypt, have been found in most regions of the eastern Mediterranean. Private letters from areas outside Egypt, for example, replicate the Egyptian habit of rehearsing the contents of a package to be dispatched, as a check on the honesty of the courier, a social practice that sometimes had economic implications. The plentiful information from Roman Egypt and neighboring provinces about the agrarian and urban economies or social behaviors have the potential to provide more sophisticated and reliable models for the world of the ancient Mediterranean.

Like documents, literary rolls tend to have been written without division of individual words, although their calligraphy has usually been written more slowly, with articulation of individual letters. The only papyrus from the Greek mainland, and currently the earliest (copied in the late 4th century BCE), was discovered in 1962 in a tomb at Derveni, a mountain pass near Thessalonica. It was carbonized when the funeral pyre and corpse were burned. The final 21 columns of text present an allegorical exegesis of a hexameter poem that the unnamed author of the prose commentary attributes to Orpheus. Parts of the *Physica* by the Sicilian Presocratic Empedocles were cut into 52 strips and fashioned into a wreath to adorn a mummy in a cemetery of Panopolis, in Upper Egypt. A roll containing 119 epigrams of Posidippus, a poet of the earlier 3rd century BCE, was recycled as a cartonnage breastplate for a mummy about a century after the poet's lifetime. Still, Posidippus was neither unpopular nor unread, for some 20 of his epigrams were subsumed into Meleager's *Garland* and subsequently into the Greek Anthology. Perhaps also interred with a mummy is the roll containing a description of the Mediterranean and Atlantic coasts of Spain that may be by the geographer Artemidorus of Ephesus.

Fragments in boxes dispatched from Oxyrhynchus also remain an important source of new discoveries. The elegiac poems of the versatile poet Simonides, whose long life spanned the tyrants at Athens, the transition to democracy, and the wars against the Persians, were unknown until fragments were published in 1992; these fragments not only overlap another papyrus published in 1954, its author then unknown, but also include lines assigned to Simonides by Plutarch and Stobaeus. The result is nearly 100 lines, some 50 of which celebrate the battle of Plataea (479 BCE), composed a generation earlier than Herodotus' account of the same campaign. Poems of Archilochus emerge from a roll copied in the 2nd century CE, found at Oxyrhynchus in February 1897 and published in 2005—elegiac couplets narrating the wounding of Telephus by Achilles. The poetess Sappho also benefited in similar fashion when a 12-line poem, sometimes called "Tithonus," was added to her largely fragmentary corpus by combining two papyri, one from mummy cartonnage and the other copied centuries later and from an Oxyrhynchus box. Latin epigrams attributable to the first prefect of Egypt, Cornelius Gallus, because one mentions his mistress Lycoris, were found near a Roman fort at Qasr Ibrim in ancient Nubia. The papyrus was probably copied not long after Gallus's disgrace and suicide (26 BCE); his name was effaced from an obelisk he set up in Egypt that was subsequently transported to Rome. It now stands in front of St. Peter's.

Nothing has proved so revolutionary as the sectarian literature written by outliers and eventual heretics, for these writings permit the losers in the religious struggles to speak in their own voices. The early life of Mani is recounted through dialogues in the some 130 surviving pages of a miniature parchment codex (4.5 by 3.5 cm), copied in the 5th century CE. Previously the Manichaean sect was known mainly from its Christian enemies, including Saint Augustine, who followed Mani for nine years. Shortly after World War II, papyri in Hebrew, Aramaic, and Greek were found in caves near Qumran along the western shores of the Dead Sea, perhaps hidden before Titus' sack of Jerusalem. About the same time Greek and Coptic texts from the Gnostic Christian community were discovered at Nag Hamadi in Upper Egypt, apparently secreted away in the later 4th century as notions of orthodox Christianity began to harden. Both sets of texts complicate our understanding of the religious milieus from which Christianity emerged and challenge the winners' positivist narratives. The Coptic version of the *Gospel of Thomas* from Nag Hamadi, attributed to Didymus Judas Thomas, "twin brother" of Jesus, presents 114 sayings of Jesus, some of which appear in canonical Gospels. If moderns express surprise at Jesus' pronouncement that "every woman who shall make herself male will enter the kingdom of heaven," the Coptic *Gospel of Judas* is equally startling. This portion of the papyrus codex Tchacos was published in 2006, to considerable fanfare, for it begins, "The secret account Jesus spoke with Judas Iscariot before the Passover." Judas is no longer the betrayer and archvillain but rather the beloved disciple, the only one privy to the true knowledge (gnosis) of Jesus' message: Judas betrays because Jesus commands him to do so.

BIBL.: Roger S. Bagnall and Bruce W. Frier, *The Demography of Roman Egypt* (Cambridge 1994). Alan K. Bowman et al., eds., *Oxyrhynchus: A City and Its Texts* (London 2007). Mario Capasso, ed., *Hermae: Scholars and Scholarship in Papyrology* (Pisa 2007). Kathleen McNamee, *Annotations in Greek and Latin Texts from Egypt* (Oxford 2007). Jane Rowlandson, ed., *Women and Society in Greek and Roman Egypt: A Sourcebook* (Cambridge 1998). David Sider, *The Library of the Villa dei Papiri at Herculaneum* (Los Angeles 2005). Eric G. Turner, *Greek Papyri: An Introduction,* enlarged ed. (Oxford 1980).

A.E.H.

Parasite

Greek *parasitos* (Latin *parasitus*), "fellow diner." It was a respectable title for religious officials whose meals were provided by the state, but it came to be casually used for people who attached themselves to persons of substance, flattering them and running errands in hopes of being asked to stay for dinner. As a comic character, renowned for shamelessness and wiliness, the parasite may have appeared in works as early as Epicharmus' in the 5th century BCE; the role became standard in New Comedy and its avatars, often as an important agent in the plot's connivances. Sometimes he has no other name than Parasite; in Plautus's *Curculio* (*The Weevil*) and Terence's *Phormio* he is the title character. A mock Platonic dialogue attributed to Lucian (2nd cent. CE) sets out a comprehensive theory of "the Parasitic" as "the art (*technē*) concerned with food and drink and what must be said and done to obtain them"—a downscale Epicureanism: "its end (*telos*) is pleasure" (*The Parasite* 9).

Italian writers reinventing Roman comedy for the 16th-century stage explicitly revived the classical character. Ligurio, who "used to be a marriage-broker, but is now busy cadging dinners and lunches," has a role in the sexual intrigue of Niccolò Machiavelli's *The Mandrake* (*La mandragola,* 1518); Pasifilo's hungry willingness to be of service aids the intricate plot of Lodovico Ariosto's *I suppositi* (1509, sometimes translated as *The Pretenders*) work itself out. In England the figure made early appearances as Matthew Merrygreek in Nicholas Udall's *Ralph Roister Doister* (ca. 1540) and as a slightly more cynical Pasiphilo in George Gascoigne's *The Supposes* (1566), and proceeded to mingle with the growing and diverse crowd of tricksters and lowlifes on the Elizabethan stage. Shakespeare omitted a parasite from the plot of Plautus's *Menaechmi* when he adapted it as *The Comedy of Errors* (ca. 1594), only to insert one, incongruously and momentously, into English history in the two parts of *Henry IV* (1596–1597): Sir John Falstaff. In Falstaff the classic parasite becomes merged with another stock figure, the braggart soldier; the parasite dominates, acquiring a new eloquence in self-justification regarding his appetites and capacity for fraud: "I lie, I am no counterfeit. To die is to be a counterfeit, for he is but the counterfeit of a man who hath not the life of a man. But to counterfeit dying when a man thereby liveth is to be no counterfeit, but the true and perfect image of life indeed" (*1 Henry IV* 5.4.113–118). Later examples of the type can be notably malicious (Molière's Tartuffe), comically annoying (Horace Skimpole in Charles Dickens's *Bleak House*), or wholly benign (the hamburger-seeking Wimpy of the *Popeye* cartoons, after whom a restaurant chain was named).

Beginning in the 18th century *parasite* came to be used in the technical, biological sense, for an organism deriving its nourishment from another organism, a host that may or may not be harmed. The less technical overtones of the word become harsher, often with a social dimension. In the early modern period it was often applied to courtiers and royal favorites. Later on, Marxist polemics regularly used the term for unproductive members of society, and *parasitism* was the name of a crime in the Soviet Union. The metaphor was satirically literalized in Vladimir Mayakovsky's *The Bedbug* (*Klop,* 1929): a proletarian opportunist who dies while trying to exploit the limited capitalism of Lenin's New Economic Plan is resurrected in a Communist utopia of 1979 and exhibited to the public along with the parasitic insect that makes the trip with him. Theoretically their ways should find no purchase in the new order, but when obsolete tastes for alcohol and love begin to spread among the populace, the authorities must take action. G.B.

Parmenides

Greek philosopher from Elea, in Italy (fl. early 5th cent. BCE). He wrote only a single work, a poem, of which only fragments survive. He has always been perceived, at least since Plato, as holding a foundational position within the history of philosophy. In the *Sophist* Plato calls him the "father" (241D3) for having raised the question "what is being?"—the question that has been central to philosophy ever since, from Aristotle (*Metaphysics Zeta,* 1028b2–4) to Heidegger, who took the epigraph of *Being and Time* from this passage of the *Sophist.*

We have firsthand access to Parmenides' main argument thanks to the extensive quotes made by Simplicius from the first part of the poem, aware as he was in his own time of the rarity of a text that deserved to be passed on to posterity (see his commentary on Aristotle, *Physics* 144.28 Diels). Given the impossibility of conceiving nonbeing, Parmenides made impossible any doctrine of being that would deny its essential predicates, such as eternity, immobility, impassibility, and unicity (this last predicate may result from an interpretation as old as Parmenides' disciple Melissus, but which was then taken up and popularized through Plato's *Sophist*); therefore, engendering and destroying, and any form of "becoming," were deprived of philosophical legitimacy. They could survive only at the level of the "opinions (*doxai*) of the mortals" (fr. 1.30 and 8.51 DK), treated in the second, cosmological part of the poem. One of the most important lines of development of post-Parmenidean thinking was to find a solution to the obstacle presented by a doctrine that ontologically prohibited conceptualizing the world. This is what Plato's *Sophist* called the "parricide" (241D5). In the *Republic* Plato had distinguished, in a Parmenidean vein, the domain of truth (*aletheia*) dealing with separate Forms, from the domain of opinion (*doxa*) dealing with sensible objects, and proposed a theory of participation (*methexis*) to fill the gap between them. The *Sophist* went further by developing an analysis according to which "not being" does not mean "not being, absolutely speaking," but rather, and foremost, "not being *something,*" which is of course compatible with "being something" (258A). By distinguishing among different meanings of being ("being is said in a plurality of senses"), Aristotle too could escape the constraint of Parmenides' ontology. The semantic perspective has systematically been pursued in modern times by interpreters directly or indirectly inspired by Gottlob Frege; they wondered how to read the word "being" in Parmenides: was it "to exist," "to be such" (predicative meaning), "to be the case" (veridical meaning)? Parmenides will not yield an answer to the question. His enormous importance lies, rather, in the fact that by *not* distinguishing between the different meanings of the verb "to be," he prompted later thinkers to do so.

There is more to Parmenides than the true ontology exposed in the first part of the poem. In its second part he developed a cosmology of which we know much less, but which has nevertheless been influential. In antiquity Empedocles derived much from it; and it may be the elaboration of a system of the world, more than the ontology, that allowed Parmenides to be seen as a "natural philosopher" (*physikos*), as attested by the inscription on a statue from the 1st century discovered at Elea in 1962, although the term *phusis* also serves, in some of its occurrences, to refer to "being." For the moderns, the cosmology was less interesting for itself than for the problem raised by its relationship, from a philosophical perspective, with the first part of the poem—"one of the most difficult and obscure questions, one of the most discussed in the history of Greek philosophy," according to Ernst Cassirer. Was it simply a dialectical game (as proposed by the influential interpretation of Diels) or a hypothetical construction, as is the case for scientific practices, or, despite appearances, was the continuity between the two parts of the poem more profound (K. Reinhardt and the phenomenological tradition after him)? Once more, the question is not easy to settle. But what really matters here is probably the challenge itself. It was taken up by Zeno, Parmenides' most important disciple and the one designated by Aristotle as the founder of dialectic (hence Diels's interpretation of Parmenides). Parmenides' original paradox consisted in juxtaposing an "untrustworthy" cosmological discourse in the second part of his poem to the true ontological discourse of the first part; Zeno deepened the gap by building a series of arguments to the effect that neither plurality nor motion can be logically thought (Achilles will never catch up with the tortoise, the thrown arrow cannot advance). Zeno's paradoxes have teased everyone who has dealt with the issue of infinite division, from Aristotle in book 6 of *Physics* to Bergson. Paul Valéry's famous poem "Le cimetière marin" ("The Cemetery by the Sea") is an anti-Eleatic ode to life that directly apostrophizes Zeno ("Zeno! Cruel Zeno!").

Parmenides' poem as a whole presents itself as the revelation of an anonymous goddess to an exceptional mortal. The introduction, or "proem," explains the circumstances of this encounter. After a cosmic trip, a "young man" (*kouros*), "keen" and "knowledgeable," reaches the dwelling of a benevolent goddess who instructs him in "all things." Philosophers in antiquity were intrigued by this fantastic cavalcade, which made sense to them only if taken as an allegory (see Sextus Empiricus, who transmitted the whole of the proem, *Adversus mathematicos* 7.111–114). The relationship between this "mystical" introduction and the "rationalism" that manifests itself in the poem is as interesting as the relationship between the two parts of the poem. Taken as a trace of the passage from one type of discourse to another, it played an important role for the development of an anthropological perspective on the origins of Greek philosophy, first for Louis Gernet, and later for his disciple Jean-Pierre Vernant.

BIBL.: C. Kahn, "A Return to the Theory of the Verb *Be* and the Concept of Being," *Ancient Philosophy* 24 (2004) 381–407. A. Laks, "Gadamer et les Présocratiques," in *Gadamer et les Grecs,* ed. J.-C. Gens, P. Kontos, and P. Rodrigo (Paris 2004) 13–29. C. Mugler, "Der Schatten des Parmenides," *Hermes* 103 (1975) 144–154. J. A. Palmer, *Plato's Reception of Parmenides* (Oxford 1999). M. Riedel, ed., *Hegel und die antike Dialektik* (Frankfurt 1990). A.L.

Translated by Jeannine Routier Pucci and Elizabeth Trapnell Rawlings

Parnassus

Many-peaked central massif (Greek *Parnassos*) in the vicinity of Delphi in Greece. Considered to be the residence of Apollo and the Muses, in figurative usage it stands for the realm of poetry. It is one of the highest mountains in Greece (2,457 m.). Since Homer (*Odyssey* 19.430–433) it has often been the object of allusions and fitting epithets ("inaccessible," "steep"; Euripides, *Phoenician Women* 207; Strabo 8.379; Virgil, *Georgics* 3.291), and it is associated with numerous myths and cults. It derives special fame from the Apollo of Delphi (the name "Parnassus" sometimes stands for Delphi itself, particularly among the Roman poets). But Dionysus also has his cult here. In the eyes of the Greek tragedians of the 5th century, Parnassus appeared as his dominion alone; the Augustan poets, however, push Apollo into the foreground (Virgil, *Georgics* 2.18, *Eclogues* 6.29; Propertius 3.13.54). The prevailing view—as seen in the epithet "two-peaked," which refers to the Phaedriades above Delphi—is that one god inhabits each peak. It is expanded by Servius' commentary on Virgil (7.641, 10.163), which specifies that Bacchus's peak is called Cithaeron, Apollo's Helicon. This tradition was continued by medieval commentaries and encyclopedias.

In the history of ideas, the Renaissance is the decisive moment for the transformation of the ancient understanding of Parnassus. Thus, in the *Purgatorio* of his *Divina commedia,* Dante uses the term *Parnassus* for ancient poetry (28.65, 31.141) and as a comparison for the earthly paradise atop the mountain of Purgatory (28.149), and in *Paradiso* he entreats Apollo to make him a vessel of divine wisdom (1.13–36). He also solicits the laurel wreath, which Petrarch received in 1341; on the capitol in Rome it was the first poetic crowning there since antiquity. Petrarch constructed his acceptance speech on the Virgilian motto of the arduous climb to the "steep," "deserted" peaks of Parnassus (Virgil, *Georgics* 3.291–293). That Parnassus is, so to speak, a defining term of the Renaissance is ultimately shown by Raphael's fresco *Parnassus* (1510–1511, Vatican). It portrays a single-peaked mountain on which Apollo sits under laurels, playing the lira da braccio amid the nine Muses, surrounded by eighteen poet laureates of all times (Homer, Virgil, Dante, Ovid, Sappho, and other ancient and modern lyric poets). The great resonance of this depiction was formative for the modern iconography of Parnassus. A famous example is provided by *Apollo and the Muses* by Nicolas Poussin (1630–1632, Madrid, Prado), in which Apollo, in the presence of the Muses (representing the various kinds of poetry) and famous bards, consecrates a poet. A further example—it, too, influential—is Anton Raphael Mengs's ceiling fresco *Parnassus* (1761, Rome, Villa Albani), which inaugurated the age of anti-Baroque classicism and which, according to Winckelmann, surpassed Raphael's fresco. It portrays Apollo, surrounded by Muses, on the ancient model of the standing Apollo Citharoedus; among the Muses, enthroned to Apollo's left, sits their mother, Mnemosyne, goddess of memory. This classicizing depiction was a major influence on Italian and German painters until the turn of the 19th century. The concept also found a place in theory. A famous example is the treatise on counterpoint, *Gradus ad Parnassum* (1725), which brought worldwide fame to its author, Johann Joseph Fux, perhaps the most important late-Baroque composer in Austria.

Parnassus' figurative meaning as a symbol for or embodiment of lyric poetry also inspired poets, particularly those of German classicism. As a locus of poetic inspiration and the undying fame of "noble" spirits, the mountain served their self-portrayal as a group of elite poets (Goethe, *Deutscher Parnass,* 1798: "All of whom he [Apollo] is fond/are to him mightily drawn,/And one noble being follows another"). This applies to the Parnassiens as well, although their lyric poetry obeyed different maxims. A group of French poets dedicated to "art for art's sake" (second half of the 19th century), they named themselves after Alphonse Lemerre's anthology *Le Parnasse contemporain* (*The Contemporary Parnassus,* 1866); their leaders were Leconte de Lisle and Théophile Gautier, their most important exponents Verlaine and Mallarmé. Whether a *Deutsch-jüdischer Parnass* (*German-Jewish Parnassus*), in the sense of a true cultural synthesis, has ever existed is discussed by Willi Jasper in his 2004 homonymous study of the contradictory history of German-Jewish literature. Montparnasse in Paris takes its name from Mount Parnassus. Today the massif is a well-known ski region.

BIBL.: Françoise Bader, "Mont Parnasse," in *Hédiston logodeipnon: Logopédies: Mélanges de philologie et de linguistique grecques offerts à Jean Taillardat* (Paris 1988) 1–23. Laurence Campa, *Parnasse, symbolisme, esprit nouveau* (Paris 1998). Elisabeth Schröter, *Die Ikonographie des Themas Parnass vor Raffael: Die Schrift- und Bildtraditionen von der Spätantike bis zum 15. Jahrhundert* (Hildesheim 1977). A.-B.R.

Translated by Patrick Baker

Parody and Burlesque

The terms imply mockery of a serious or "high" literary genre (usually epic or tragedy, sometimes lyric), or of a specific writer or work. In general, *parody* suggests a more detailed engagement with the model that is being mocked; parodies are not funny unless one knows the author or genre to which the parody alludes. *Burlesque* (from Italian *burla,* "joke") also suggests mocking literary imitation but may engage less directly with any particular source. Both terms entered the English language in the 17th century, along with *travesty* and *mock-heroic*—a mark of the sudden swell of interest in classical parody in that period. The ancient Greek term *parodia* did not necessarily imply mockery of the source text, only close imitation; related ancient critical terms include Greek *mimēsis* and Latin *imitatio,* although neither of these necessarily suggests any satirical intention.

Send-ups of serious literature have, of course, appeared whenever serious literature itself has been produced. One can trace the tradition of literary mockery back to antiquity. Hipponax (fl. mid-6th cent. BCE), whose work survives only in fragments, was supposedly the inventor of mock-heroic poetry (Athenaeus 698b). The *Margites,* long attributed to Homer but probably from the 5th century BCE, was composed in the same meter and style as the *Iliad* and the *Odyssey;* it tells the story of an idiotic man called Margos, who "knew many things, but misunderstood them all" (fr. 3). Another supposedly Homeric poem, *The Battle of the Mice and the Frogs,* tells the story of a one-day battle between these tiny creatures—perhaps mocking the pretensions of Homeric epic. Aristophanes' *Frogs* (performed in 405 BCE) parodies both the bombast of Aeschylus and the sophistic rhetoric of Euripides. Panegyrical rhetoric is parodied in a long-running tradition of mock encomia (of tyrants, insects, baldness, etc.). Lucian's *True History* (2nd cent. CE), a fantasy story about a journey to the moon, parodies history writers (especially Herodotus) who tell tall tales and claim that they are true. The classical parodist who was perhaps best known in later times was Ovid (43 BCE–17 CE), who engaged in complex literary parody of Virgilian epic in the *Metamorphoses,* and of Latin love elegy in his *Ars amatoria* and *Amores.*

Many of these classical examples, like later parodies of classical literature, poke fun at "high" literary genres. Parody is a form of literary sabotage, which may be inspired by a sense of cultural oppression or deprivation. Send-ups of classical literature written in postantiquity often respond to a cultural suspicion that elevated classical genres, such as epic or tragedy, are no longer appropriate in the modern age.

In the European tradition, serious study and imitation of classical literature inescapably brought parody with it. Erasmus's *Praise of Folly* (1509), one of the most enduring works of Renaissance Humanism, is a mock encomium elevated to an inclusive vision of life on earth. Direct mockery of classical literature itself flourishes most widely in periods when that literature has been most zealously crammed down the throats of schoolchildren and undergraduates. The history of such parody is intimately connected with the development of vernacular national literatures, which were defined by contrast with classical literature. The single classical poem that has inspired the most parodies is the *Aeneid,* a work featured in school curricula almost since the time of its composition. Romance, that quintessentially "modern" genre that arose with the Renaissance, was deliberately developed (especially by the Italian poets Boiardo and Ariosto) as a parodic counterpart to Virgilian epic.

In many cases, it is difficult to distinguish clearly between parody and more serious kinds of literary imitation. Christopher Marlowe's *Dido Queen of Carthage* (1594) adapts the content of book 4 of the *Aeneid* as a "tragedy" of Dido; but a parodic element is added to the work by the opening scene, in which Jupiter dandles his boy toy, Ganymede. Shakespeare's *Troilus and Cressida* (1602), for which the main source was Chaucer's *Troilus and Criseyde,* is an example of "mock-heroic" literature in which the mockery seems aimed directly at the notion that there ever were heroes: the great, lost civilizations of Greece and Troy were actually riddled with corruption, bribery, and venereal disease.

The great age of classical parody was the "long 18th century" (from the mid-17th to early 19th). One can trace the beginnings of mock epic, and the death of epic itself as a viable modern genre, to Milton's *Paradise Lost* (1674), in which Satan seems at times to be most ridiculous when he tries hardest to resemble a classical epic or tragic hero. Milton treads a fine line between homage and parody of the classical texts he adapts. The Christian emphasis on "the better fight" (*Paradise Lost* 6.30), that is, to keep faith, may make the military subjects of Homer and Virgil seem relatively unimportant, or even wrongheaded.

Important 17th-century examples of mock-heroic classical parody include a notorious attempt to take Virgil down a peg or two, *Le Virgile Travesti* by Paul Scarron (published in installments between 1648 and 1649). Another, much more dignified parody of the *Aeneid,* entitled *The Lectern* (*Le Lutrin,* 1674–1683), by the neoclassical theorist Nicolas Boileau, uses the language of classical epic to mock the pretensions of ecclesiastical politics. An influential English example was Samuel Butler's *Hudibras* (1663–1678), a mock epic about the English Civil War.

Parodies are often inspired by the suspicion that a classical genre is irrelevant to contemporary concerns. Although epic has been the most important genre in the history of classical parody, there have also been parodies of lyric, classical oratory, and history writing. John Wilmot, Second Earl of Rochester (1647–1680), parodied both the classical pastoral and its contemporary imitators in poems such as "Fair Chloris in the Pigsty Lay," which describes a country girl masturbating in the mud.

In some cases of classical parody—as, arguably, in Milton's account of the War in Heaven (*Paradise Lost,* book 6)—the target of the parody may be classical literature itself. But in other cases allusion to classical literature is used to point up the shortcomings of the unheroic modern age. The works of John Dryden and Alexander Pope offer several examples. Dryden's *MacFlecknoe* (1678) uses the idiom of the *Aeneid* to mock a rival contemporary poet, Thomas Shadwell, for his dullness:

At his right hand our young Ascanius sat
Rome's other hope, and pillar of the state.
His brows thick fogs, instead of glories, grace,
And lambent dullness played around his face. (100–103)

Similarly, Pope's *Dunciad* (1726) makes Dullness the goddess who presides, in mock-Homeric or mock-Miltonic fashion, over all his tedious fellow writers' efforts. Pope's *Rape of the Lock* (1714) tells the entirely unheroic story of a flirtation at a tea party. The great Virgilian question *tantaene animis caelestibus irae?* (*Aeneid* 1.11), "Can heavn'ly minds such high resentments show?" (as Dryden phrases it), becomes "In tasks so bold, can little men engage,/And in soft bosoms dwells such mighty rage?" (*Rape of the Lock* 1.11–12). The language of heroes is applied to a world of pygmies, women, and teacups.

Jonathan Swift's "Battle of the Ancients and Moderns" (in *A Tale of a Tub,* 1704) differs importantly from these works by Dryden and Pope. It is in prose, not verse, and it uses the tropes of classical epic to mock all those who favored ancient learning over modernity. Swift parodies the apparatus of classical scholarship, as well as classical authors themselves. Eighteenth-century novelists (most notably Henry Fielding) used parodic versions of the Homeric simile to mark the difference between the world of classical epic and the world of the novel.

After the 18th century, parody—in the sense of imitation aimed at a specific author, text, or genre—often seems to have given way to burlesque and other forms of comic imitation. In Byron's *Don Juan,* a sprawling comic masterpiece in ottava rima that was unfinished at the time of his death in 1824, the narrator breezily mocks all the old classical conventions: the third canto begins, with characteristic nonchalance, "Hail Muse! et cetera." This is not exactly a parody of Homer or Virgil; it is as if Byron does not take his classical antecedents seriously enough even to parody them.

In the theater classical burlesques became increasingly popular in the 19th century. The appeal of these performances seems to have lain largely in the costumes (women in tights), and lavish set designs. The performances included sub-Byronic rhyme schemes, dreadful puns, songs and dancing, fancy lighting, and adapted motifs from Greek mythology, epic, and tragedy in a fairly indiscriminate way. The result was a style of performance that could appeal both to those who had very little previous knowledge of antiquity and to those who were bored stiff from too much schoolroom Latin. As Theseus remarks in one burlesque (*Ariadne; Or, The Bull! The Bull!* by Vincent Amcott, 1870), after his friend Mentor falls "overboard": "Away with Latin, Greek, and all such stuff,/For I've been *over bored* with them enough."

By contrast, A. E. Housman's "Fragment of a Greek tragedy" (1883) aimed for a much more literate, educated readership. The piece brilliantly mocks the absurd tropes of Attic drama by echoing them in detail. "Fragment" begins with an Aeschylean compound epithet—"O suitably-attired-in-leather-boots"—and includes, among other glories, a wonderfully digressive Euripidean chorus ("Why should I mention Io? Why indeed?/I have no notion why"), and a parodic version of Attic conventions for representing violence offstage: "He splits my skull, not in a friendly way!"

Books and films of the 20th century include many parodic or semiparodic allusions to classical literature, often combined with more serious literary or political intentions. James Joyce's *Ulysses* (1922) reimagines the journeys of Homer's Odysseus as a single day in the life of a modern Jew in Dublin. Parody is too simple a term for Joyce's relationship to his classical sources, but there are certainly parodic moments in the novel.

In recent years comic and semicomic allusions to classical literature in popular culture have been plentiful. The third episode in the *Simpsons* television series, "Homer's Odyssey" (1990), parodies the ancient Homer's epic in the story of Homer Simpson's journey after being fired from Mr. Burns's dangerous nuclear power plant. Homer temporarily becomes a passionate advocate for environmental safety, but he finally accepts a new job as a wage slave and returns home. The real target of the satire is not, of course, the Homeric poems themselves, and the episode requires no knowledge of anything classical. Like many other parodies, this episode uses literary allusion in the service of political satire.

BIBL.: Reuben Arthur Brower, *Mirror on Mirror: Translation, Imitation, Parody* (Cambridge, Mass., 1974). Edith Hall and Fiona Macintosh, *Greek Tragedy and the British Theatre, 1660–1914* (Oxford 2005). Ralph Rosen, *Making Mockery: The Poetics of Ancient Satire* (Oxford 2007). E.W.

Parthenon

Over the past two and a half millennia the Parthenon has been temple, church, mosque, ruin, reconstruction, and icon. Built as a temple to the goddess Athena between 447 and 432 BCE, it was converted into a Christian church probably sometime in the 5th century CE and into a mosque, under the Ottoman rulers of Greece, in the mid-15th century. The essential form of the ancient building survived these conversions, as did most of the architectural sculpture. In fact, despite some intentional defacement by Christians and possibly Muslims, the reuse of the building was a crucial factor in its preservation.

The main changes in the Parthenon's conversions were in its orientation (the principal entrance was moved to the west from the east) and its internal decoration. Numerous fragments of medieval marble fittings and inscriptions survive, Christian frescoes could still be made out in the 19th century, and tesserae from a Christian mosaic of the Virgin Mary could still be picked up on the Acropolis in the 20th century. Contemporary descriptions of both church and mosque praise its beauty and venerable history (not always accurately: the Ottoman traveler Evliya Çelebi, who visited Athens in the 1630s and 1640s, believed that the building had originally been the Academy of Plato and that its doors had been the gates of the city of Troy). For the Englishman George Wheler, writing in 1682, it was simply "the finest mosque in the world."

In 1687, during the wars between Venice and the Ottoman Empire, the Parthenon was catastrophically damaged. Put to use by the Ottoman garrison as a gunpowder store and then hit by Venetian cannonballs, it exploded, causing some 300 fatalities—and was left beyond repair. Although a small mosque was rebuilt within its shell, for the next century and a half the Parthenon was left as a ruin within a military base. It was looted for building material and for what remained of any value. Most notoriously, in the early years of the 19th century much of the Parthenon's surviving sculpture was removed by the diplomat Lord Elgin and taken to Britain. The controversy around his actions remains intense. Was Elgin a destructive, self-interested vandal, or did he save masterpieces that would almost certainly have been destroyed? There have been prominent partisans on either side—from Lord Byron on—and their loudly discordant voices have certainly contributed to the Parthenon's present fame.

Following the Greek War of Independence (1821–1832), Athens became the capital of Greece under a Bavarian monarchy. The Acropolis was converted into an archaeological site: excavation work removed almost all traces of later structures, leaving the ruins of the Parthenon isolated on bare rock, along with the other buildings erected in the 5th century BCE. Major restoration work in the 1920s (directed by N. Balanos) reerected many of the dispersed columns and gave the ruin its now familiar silhouette. But the iron clamps used in the reconstruction gradually expanded, causing such damage to the marble that a further complete restoration was begun in 1986 and is ongoing.

Since the late 18th century the Parthenon has been a model for architects and designers, from Neoclassicists to such prophets of Modernism as Le Corbusier. New Parthenons have been built across the Western world, from Bavaria (where Leo von Klenze's Valhalla is a more-or-less exact copy) to Nashville (where the full-size replica erected for the Tennessee Exposition of 1897 still stands)—not to mention the thousands of miniatures sold as ouzo bottles, key rings, even toasters. The Parthenon has also become an icon of classical culture. Its image is the official symbol of the United Nations Educational, Scientific, and Cultural Organization (UNESCO), and it is often taken to stand for all we owe to ancient Greek civilization. Though most have admired it, for some its mythic status has proved oppressive. Sigmund Freud was famously reluctant to visit. When he finally did, he claimed that the experience was rather like discovering that the Loch Ness monster really did exist after all.

BIBL.: M. Beard, *The Parthenon* (Cambridge, Mass., 2003). A. Kaldellis, *The Christian Parthenon* (Cambridge 2009). J. Neils, ed., *The Parthenon: From Antiquity to the Present* (Cambridge 2005). P. Tournikiotis, ed., *The Parthenon and Its Impact in Modern Times* (Athens 1994). M.B.

Pasquino

Pasquino, a mutilated ancient statue set up on a Roman street corner, became the repository for anonymous and usually satiric comments (pasquinades) on contemporary events and persons. It was one of several "talking statues" in early 16th-century Rome. Its most important counterparts were Marforio (a statue of a reclining river god, now in the Capitoline Museum) and Madonna Lucrezia (a statue of Isis in Piazza Venezia sometimes characterized as Pasquino's wife).

Pasquino was discovered near the end of the 15th century, probably near the palace of Cardinal Oliviero Carafa, between Piazza Navona and Via dell'Anima. The statue, which consists of the mutilated portions of two figures—one little more than a head and torso with its hand on the other, a piece of a second torso—was generally identified at the time as Hercules, but probably represents Menelaus holding the body of Patroclus. In 1501 Cardinal Carafa had it placed on a pedestal outside his palace near the eponymous Piazza del Pasquino, where it resides today. The origin of Pasquino's name is unknown; in the 16th century it was said to have been named after various "real" people, including a local schoolmaster and a tailor of antiestablishment views.

The earliest attested pasquinade attached to the statue is a squib on Pope Alexander VI from August 1501. Soon Pasquino's comments became institutionalized under the patronage of Cardinal Carafa, who inaugurated an annual celebration of Pasquino on Saint Mark's day (April 25). As the religious procession passed the cardinal's palace, everyone could see Pasquino, painted and costumed in a different guise each year, and covered with scores of Latin or Italian verses. Beginning in 1509 selections of these verses were collected and published. In 1509 Pasquino was garbed as Janus, and a small "temple of Janus" was set up nearby, its doors open to signify that Rome (the papacy) was at war with Venice. Many of the verses celebrated both the war and its author, Pope Julius II. In 1513 Pasquino became Apollo, to celebrate the election of the Medici pope, Leo X, who was expected to be a great patron of the arts. In one verse Pasquino/Apollo proclaims:

> I used to be an exile, but I'm back in Leo's reign.
> So burn your midnight oil, boys, and follow in my
> train.
> For no one leaves my Leo without a handsome gain.
> Bards will sing for prizes, and they'll not sing in vain.

Many verses were written by Humanists associated with the Curia, who often viciously criticized the prelates they served. During the conclave of 1522 that elected Leo's successor, Pope Adrian VI, Pasquino satirized Leo, the cardinals, and Adrian with equal venom. Although Pasquino's comments were officially anonymous, their authors were sometimes known. (In the 1520s and 1530s Pasquino was often the mouthpiece for Pietro Aretino.) Church authorities generally tolerated Pasquino (although Adrian threatened to throw him into the Tiber); but as Pasquino became more satirical and strident, publication became less frequent. It ceased altogether in 1566, less than three years after the Council of Trent.

Pasquino began as a demonstration of a cardinal's magnificence and became a literary game and outlet for the Roman Humanists—often subversive, but not a voice of the people. Pasquinades, however, did not require Pasquino or Rome. The term and the practice, like so much else from the Italian Renaissance, soon crossed the Alps. Pasquinades became a regular means of public propaganda from Reformation Germany until at least the time of the French Revolution. Pasquino himself is sometimes still adorned with satirical comments.

BIBL.: Leonard Barkan, *Unearthing the Past* (New Haven 1999) 209–231. Valerio Marucci, Antonio Marzo, and Angelo Romano, eds., *Pasquinate romane del Cinquecento* (Rome 1983). Anne Reynolds, "Cardinal Oliviero Carafa and the Early Cinquecento Tradition of the Feast of Pasquino," *Humanistica Lovaniensia* 34 (1985) 178–208. J.H.G.

Pastoral

Literary subgenre involving shepherds and their songs. Although usually classified as a genre, pastoral is just as much a theme and set of conventions that transcend traditional generic boundaries, with manifestations in lyric, drama, mime, and prose romance. In the formal sense of short mimes involving the loves, laments, songs, and rivalries of shepherds, the genre began to take form as a subset of Theocritus' *Idylls* in the 3rd century BCE and remained popular in European literature until the 18th century.

Many critics have tended to read the pastoral metaphor as an Epicurean retreat from urban civilization and its discontents, a form of nostalgia for a simpler, prelapsarian existence. Others, however, have regarded this sentimentalization of the genre as a relatively late and oblique development; rather, what we see from the very beginning is use of the rustic community to provide an allegorical mask for personas and concerns of the author's own political or literary environment. Perhaps the broadest definition of the pastoral tendency is William Empson's "process of putting the complex into the simple."

Theocritus probably did not see himself as inventing a new genre but rather, in typical Alexandrian fashion, importing into the familiar genre of mime a landscape and set of thematic associations drawn from various other generic traditions. The elegist Philetas, a slightly earlier contemporary, was likely his most immediate source for poetry situated in a pleasant rural milieu, but to judge from the extant fragments, little in Philetas' work resembled what we would today call pastoral. Critics have sought more distant ancestors in the choral lyric of Alcman and Stesichorus, the pastoral similes of the *Iliad,* the Dionysiac mystery cults, Near Eastern epic and hymnic imagery, and even actual herdsmen's songs.

Sentimentalization of the countryside as a locale of innocence and plenitude is largely absent from Theocritus' work and these other sources. Indeed, the predominating tone of Theocritus is one of ironic detachment and allusive cleverness; the country setting figures mainly as an element of coarse realism and occasional barnyard vulgarity, never as an ideal of lost innocence. Theocritus, of course, never called what he was doing "pastoral" (the word derives from a Latin term first used as a generic designation by the grammarian Terentianus Maurus in the late 2nd century CE) but used the verb *boukoliasdein* (7.36, "sing bucolic songs") as an embedded description of the songs his characters perform. The distinction of turning this subject matter, favored among Theocritus' mimes, into a genre may actually belong to the now anonymous imitator who composed the post-Theocritean Idyll 8, in which we see the traditional shepherd-hero Daphnis (whose death was lamented in Idyll 1) win a contest with Menalcas (a character from the elegy of Hermesianax) in what is presented as the juxtaposition of two competing generic forms.

It is in the work of Theocritus' Roman imitator, the young Virgil, that we find an element of nostalgic sentimentalization of an ideal landscape, sometimes but not always represented as "Arcadia." This pastoral Eden, however, is elusive and problematic in Virgil's *Eclogues:* subject to political confiscation (*Eclogues* 1 and 9), the dream of a returned golden age in the future (4), or the fantasy of an alienated outsider (10). The most impressive landscape description (1.46–58) is, not uncharacteristically, put into the mouth of a shepherd who has lost everything and can only admire with envy what his cohort Tityrus has been allowed to keep.

Although the exact dating of these various eclogues is controversial, most scholars agree that they are unlikely to have been composed earlier than 45 or later than 35 BCE. Accordingly, they are Virgil's first major literary effort, and several passages suggest that Virgil from the beginning planned a career trajectory that would ascend from the lowly genre of bucolic, to didactic, and then culminate in a grand epic (see esp. *Eclogues* 4.1–3, 6.1–5; *Georgics* 3.1–48, 4.559–566). This career pattern became an influential model for future generations of poets, who chose pastoral as a work of their youth: among others, we can name Modoin of Autun, Sannazaro, Mantuan, Spenser, Milton, and the 16-year-old Alexander Pope.

What Virgil saw in the bucolic idylls of Theocritus and his Greek successors was a vehicle for poets to articulate their interrelationships of rivalry, mentorship, emulation, reverence, and succession, cloaked in the guise of shepherds exchanging songs or praising those of others. Many of Theocritus' idylls do appear to be structured as confrontations or contests between a young, aspiring shepherd and a seemingly more experienced one—Corydon and Battus (probably a figure for Callimachus) in Idyll 4, Lacon and Comatas in Idyll 5, Simichidas (Theocritus himself) and Lycidas (probably Philetas) in Idyll 7. By sustained allusive engagement with the work of one Alexandrian predecessor, the young Virgil hoped to present himself to his Roman public as an emerging voice conversant with the niceties of Alexandrian technique and erudition, but at the same time able to transcend the limitations of his models by creating something distinctive and new.

For Latin poetry of the imperial age, Virgil understandably became a dominating precursor; an author's choice of pastoral as a generic form during that era seems to be a deliberate technique of self-positioning relative to Virgil's authority. Virgil's best Latin successor, Calpurnius Siculus, likely dates to the early 3rd century. Calpurnius also invokes the Neronian epic poet Lucan in a spirit of trying to invent an encomiastic rhetoric that supersedes that of his primary model. Like Virgil, Calpurnius arranges his poems in a significant order, self-fashioning a stylized poetic autobiography in the persona of Corydon. In contrast to the linear progression of Virgil's collection and career, however, he presents a parabolic movement from timidity to ambition to resignation, from expectant hope in the future (Faunus's prophecy of a golden age under the new emperor in Eclogue 1) to concerted effort in the present (a duet in praise of the emperor sung together with Corydon's younger brother in Eclogue 4) to bitter memory of the past (as a frustrated Corydon returns home to the country from Rome, aware of his own insignificance to the emperor, in Eclogue 7). Corydon's disappointed expectations are metonymic for Calpurnius's own; just as Corydon cannot rival Tityrus, Calpurnius is only too aware of his belatedness and inadequacy in Virgil's shadow.

Perhaps the most successful post-Virgilian rendition of pastoral for the next thousand years is Longus's transposition of pastoral themes, characters, and setting into the genre of prose romance in the 3rd century. Self-consciously drawing on both Theocritus and Virgil, his *Daphnis and Chloe* presents a highly sentimentalized narrative in which the pastoral world becomes a metaphor for childhood innocence. Although various external threats intrude into that world, a benevolent Providence protects the young lovers, as in other Greek romances, and in the end both Daphnis and Chloe are revealed to be the abandoned children of wealthy families from the city. Here more than anywhere else in ancient tradition does Arcadia take form as a tangible ambience in the here and now.

The currency of the shepherd-and-flock metaphor in Jewish and early Christian literature, as well as the widespread interpretation of Virgil's Eclogue 4 as a prophecy of the coming Messiah, made pastoral an attractive theme and generic form for some early Christian authors. This Christian appropriation is seen as early as Endelechius' *De mortibus boum* (*On the Death of Cattle*), from the 4th century. Amid this massive shift of cultural and religious paradigms, Virgil was no longer an overweening and oppressive precursor but a vital link to an increasingly remote past. The Carolingian poet Modoin of Autun was able to appeal to Virgil's *Eclogues* as a model for his hopes of a renewed Augustanism under Charlemagne; classical precedents provided him with a foil against the complacency and self-satisfaction of the immediate past. From the same general period, Alcuin and Theodulus invoked the eclogue form to stage allegories of Christian truth, although the latter relegates all allusions to pagan myth to the speech of the goatherd Pseustis (Liar), defeated by the Scripture-quoting shepherdess Alithia (Truth).

Erotic subjects were generally avoided in medieval Latin pastoral, which was mainly a product of the monasteries. But in the four eclogues of the little-known Martius Valerius, perhaps of the 12th century, we do see, without any pretense of Christian allegory, imitation of the full range of classical subject matter on the part of a poet who was familiar not only with Virgil but with Calpurnius as well. The amatory side of ancient pastoral was largely displaced into the vernacular traditions of the troubadours, who elaborated a variant known as *pastourelle,* where not-so-courtly knights seduce buxom shepherdesses.

Dante experimented with pastoral at the end of his life (1319) in an epistolary exchange with Giovanni del Virgilio, the professor of Latin at Bologna; Dante invokes the humble style of Virgil's *Eclogues* to justify his preference for writing in the vernacular. Similarly, Petrarch appeals to Virgil's Eclogue 1 in his own first eclogue, to articulate a positive vision of classical aestheticism against the narrower strictures of his day, embedded in the person of Monicus (based on Petrarch's brother Gherardo, a Carthusian monk), who was uniquely devoted to the sacred music of the biblical shepherd-king David. Under the cover of an intricately allegorical style, which he considered central to the genre on the basis of his reading in late antique Virgilian commentaries, Petrarch added to pastoral an element of satire against the papal court and secular authorities. In this development he was followed by his friend Boccaccio (1313–1375) and more especially in the highly influential work of Mantuan (1447–1516) a century later.

The late 15th century was a period of great pastoral

creativity and innovation in both Latin and Italian, as Greek bucolic came to be familiar along with classical Latin models. Like Dante, the Neapolitan Humanist Giovanni Pontano (1424–1503) turned to pastoral at the end of his career, using the form as a meditation on his own posterity and influence as he imagined other shepherd-poets reciting his verse. His younger colleague Jacopo Sannazaro (ca. 1458–1530), on the other hand, was perhaps the first self-consciously to model his career path on Virgil's by starting with pastoral as the prologue to undertaking a great national epic. Sannazaro followed Dante's notion that the humble genre of pastoral was linked to the popular and vernacular: the result was *Arcadia* (1480s; 1st publ. 1502), a prosimetric romance in Italian (following the precedent of Boccaccio's *Ameto* of 1341–1342). Plot is minimal, but the interwoven songs and prose do constitute a complex autobiographical program, as the *Arcadia* takes on a progressively more narrative form and alludes more and more to epic texts as well as pastoral models.

The Virgilian career model became even more powerfully resonant for Edmund Spenser, who seems from the first to have conceived the *Shepheardes Calender* (1579) as a meditation on his readiness and his time's suitability to produce the kind of great national epic he was undertaking with the *Faerie Queene.* In the *Calender* we see in the persona of Colin Clout the self-doubting ephebe-poet progressing through the seasons as through an entire life span. In the mode of Virgil's and Calpurnius's Corydons, romantic rejection is emblematic for fears that his song will be rejected: unhappy in love, Colin feels inadequate and threatens to stop singing. On another level, he moves through a long literary history of influences, starting with clear classical subtexts in *January* through *April,* progressing through Mantuan's antierotic, anticlassical pastoral of ecclesiastical satire in the middle eclogues (*May* through *September*), and at the end imitating a pastoral poet closer in time to himself, Clément Marot (1496–1544), who introduced the genre into France, particularly in the service of royal encomia.

Milton's two pastoral elegies, *Lycidas* (1637) and the Latin *Epitaphium Damonis* (1640), present themselves as affirmations of Christian vision and certitude, in response to the ambiguities and doubts expressed by Spenser's *Shepheardes Calender.* Milton converted the apotheosis of classical pastoral laments like Virgil's Eclogue 5 into a triumphant vision of Christian afterlife and beatitude. The speaker's anguished struggle to rationalize the experience of death in *Lycidas* recapitulates the entire history of the genre, moving from pagan divinities, imagery, and allusions to Mantuanesque ecclesiastical satire to Christian revelation at the end, from worldly pursuits to objects of eternal value.

This period may legitimately be considered the high point of the genre's diffusion into vernacular literatures throughout Europe. Drayton's *Idea, The Shepheardes Garland* (1593) consciously imitated the countrified diction, names, and other appurtenances of Spenser's book. In contrast, Marvell (1621–1678) avoided the eclogue form but Christianized classical themes to create engaging lyric meditations on the part of various rustic characters. In Italy, particularly in Ferrara, pastoral drama began to take form, partly as an extension of the dialogic aspects of the eclogue and partly as an outgrowth of attempts to revive the classical satyr play, which typically featured sylvan settings. *Il sacrifizio* (1554) by Agostino Beccari counts as the first real effort in this vein, but the two most influential examples were Tasso's *Aminta* (1573) and Guarini's *Il pastor fido* (1590). With romantic plots and happy endings, they were a subspecies of comedy and probably influenced Shakespeare in his choice of comic settings.

A parallel development was the courtier Sir Philip Sidney's *Lady of May* (1578), a pastoral masque, which anticipated his greatest achievement, the prosimetric *Arcadia* (1590). Unlike Sannazaro's, this Arcadia appears as a historical place situated in the Hellenistic period, populated by royalty and nobles for whom the shepherds are largely entertainment and diversion, a move also evident in Jorge de Montemayor's Spanish romance *Diana* (ca. 1560) and later in Honoré d'Urfé's *Astraea* (1607). Influenced by the Greek romances, which were by then better known, all of these works featured far more plot development than Sannazaro's.

This period also made pastoral the focus of literary theory, beginning with Julius Caesar Scaliger (1561) and culminating in the treatises of René Rapin (1659) and Fontenelle (1688), who are often seen as valorizing the authority of the Ancients and the Moderns respectively, though actually they shared a distaste for both excessive coarseness and excessive refinement in depiction of the pastoral life.

Influenced by these, the young Alexander Pope composed a theoretical *Discourse* and four illustrative eclogues (1704), named after the seasons; although models of erudition, their strict adherence to Neoclassical strictures of propriety leaves them somewhat lifeless and uninspired. The 18th century saw other pastoral efforts as well, such as Ambrose Philips's archaizing Spenserian eclogues (1709) and John Gay's satirical parodies of this style (1714). But by this time pastoral had become more a mannerism than a vibrant, self-reinventing tradition.

One offshoot of the pastoral tradition that did remain vital well into the 18th century was the piscatory pastoral, fishermen's idylls. This vogue began with the five Latin piscatory eclogues of Sannazaro, most of which were written during the period of his exile from Naples (1501–1504). Inspired in part by Idyll 21 in the Theocritean corpus, Sannazaro aimed to transfer the themes of death, amatory estrangement, and political loss to a new landscape more familiar to the maritime orientation of his city and age. But his original conception of the piscatory form was as a counterpoint to Arcadia, not a relocation of Arcadian ideals to a watery setting: like Idyll 21, these poems convey a consciousness of labor and physical danger that seems quite alien to the shepherd's domain. We also find within Sannazaro's piscatory eclogues a thread of allusion to passages and topoi of ancient epic, as if the author conceived these poems as an intermediate, "georgic" stage on his path from the pastoral *Arcadia* to his epic *De partu Virginis,* which he was already conceiving at that time.

Despite Sannazaro's original intent for his innovation on the form, it rapidly caught on as merely a variant of pastoral with different setting and scenery. Beginning with his younger Neapolitan contemporary Bernardino Rota, who composed a full book of piscatories in Italian, Sannazaro's experiment rapidly spawned a school of imitators. As early as 1546 the great Portuguese poet Luíz de Camões wrote a song contest between a shepherd and a fisherman, juxtaposing the pastoral and piscatory as competing genres. Similarly, Remy Belleau's pastoral romance *La Bergerie* (1572), inspired by Sannazaro's *Arcadia,* devoted a substantial section to songs of a fisherman. Christophe de Gamon composed two books of *Pescheries* (1598), which combined Sannazaro's themes with a renewed interest in their Theocritean subtext. The popularity of Tasso's and Guarini's pastoral dramas in this period inspired corresponding piscatory dramas in Italy, Antonio Ongaro's *Alceo* (1581) and Lodovico Moro's *Il pescatore infido* (1621). In England, Phineas Fletcher exploited the New Testament resonance of Christ and his fishermen disciples to compose a Mantuanesque religious satire in piscatory guise (1633), directly modeled on the structure and style of Spenser's *Shepheardes Calender.* Although the piscatory vogue was attacked by Addison in the early 18th century, it found a stalwart defender in the Reverend Moses Browne, who composed a lengthy treatise on the form along with nine illustrative eclogues (1729).

The artificiality of the pastoral form, particularly as practiced in the Neoclassical period, left it unpopular with the Romantics, although Wordsworth subtitles a few of the *Lyrical Ballads* (1800) "Pastoral," most notably his long meditative monody "Michael," a work that seems only too aware of the obsolescence of the pastoral way of life. Matthew Arnold's "Thyrsis" (1866) clearly evokes Milton's *Lycidas,* to lament the death of a close friend, but it takes its title character and diction from Theocritus. Mallarmé appropriates the eclogue form for "L'après-midi d'un faune" (1887): here, pastoral becomes a trope for fantasies of sexual liberation and fulfillment, as also in the evocative tone poem of Debussy (1894) and the adolescent nostalgia of Ravel's *Daphnis and Chloé* (1912). But for all these artists, pastoral was an experimental foray and even a curiosity, and what they created bears little resemblance to its classical form.

BIBL.: Paul Alpers, *What Is Pastoral?* (Chicago 1996). David M. Halperin, *Before Pastoral: Theocritus and the Ancient Tradition of Bucolic Poetry* (New Haven 1983). Thomas K. Hubbard, *The Pipes of Pan: Intertextuality and Literary Filiation in the Pastoral Tradition from Theocritus to Milton* (Ann Arbor 1998). E. Kegel-Brinkgreve, *The Echoing Woods: Bucolic and Pastoral from Theocritus to Wordsworth* (Amsterdam 1990). Renato Poggioli, *The Oaten Flute: Essays on Pastoral Poetry and the Pastoral Ideal* (Cambridge, Mass., 1975). Thomas G. Rosenmeyer, *The Green Cabinet: Theocritus and the European Pastoral Lyric* (Berkeley 1969).

T.HU.

Pausanias

An educated traveler, born in Asia Minor, almost certainly of an elite and wealthy background, Pausanias spent much of the third quarter of the 2nd century CE traveling around mainland Greece (the Roman province of Achaea). He wrote a remarkable description of his journeys in 10 books, paying very close attention to issues of antiquarian and religious interest with relatively little discussion of contemporary matters or people. His account of Greece is the only extended example of what appears to have been the relatively popular ancient genre of *periēgēsis* (a description or sketch) to survive into the Renaissance. It seems to have had some reception in antiquity and in Byzantium (where at least his manuscript was copied) but became hugely significant after its rediscovery in the modern era. Pausanias gives us not only our most extensive ancient account of the lost masterpieces, cities, and sites of ancient Greece (admittedly in the Roman era, although this has not stopped scholars from using his text to reconstruct the 5th century BCE), but also the richest and most precise description of ancient Greek religion and ritual (also of course from the Roman period, though here again scholars have systematically used his work to envision archaic and classical religion).

Despite Pausanias' dismissal by positivists and high-stylist scholars (such as Ulrich von Wilamowitz-Möllendorff, 1848–1931) in the 19th and for much of the 20th centuries, his influence on classical archaeology, anthropology, and religious studies and on romantic engagements with Greece can hardly be overstated. Not only is J. J. Winckelmann's *History of the Art of Antiquity* (1764), the foundational text of both modern archaeology and modern art history, indebted to Pausanian references on virtually every page, but much of its structure of periods in Greek art is dependent on the implicit art history offered by Pausanias (as well as other ancient sources, like Pliny). More telling still, some of Winckelmann's most important conceptual contributions—such as his vision of Greek artistic naturalism as promulgating an ideal of freedom (a crucial ideological theme, one of his great legacies to many significant art historians, not least Ernst Gombrich)—are effectively lifted from Pausanias' narrative. J. G. Frazer's *Golden Bough* (1890), a seminal text for modern cultural anthropology, may not be explicitly indebted to Pausanias page by page, but many of its reflections and insights are the result of Frazer's monumental translation of Pausanias, with commentary (eventually published in 6 vols., 1898). Similarly, 20th- and 21st-century understanding of Greek religion (which is to say of pre-Christian polytheism in Greece), developed in the work of some of its most formative scholars, such as Jane Ellen Harrison and L. R. Farnell, has its roots in a long and creative interrogation of Pausanias' discussions of ritual and monuments.

Travelers to Greece, meanwhile, including topographers and archaeologists, have used Pausanias since the 19th century as their key guide, the result being that his choices of what to see and his descriptions have largely defined the ancient landscape as we now know it. This is true not only of actual travel, travel writing, and archaeological survey and digging, but also of the idealization of Greece as an imaginary topography that is ancestral. The visionary architect and draftsman J. M. Gandy (1771–1843), long the perspectivist employed by the great English Neoclassical architect Sir John Soane, exhibited numerous architectural fantasies based on a close reading of the Neoplatonically inflected translation of Pausanias made by his contemporary Thomas Taylor (1757–1835), sometimes called the English Platonist.

Modern discussion has begun to acknowledge the importance of the history of the reception of Pausanias, as well as to revise views on the accuracy and reliability of his text, which is now seen as remarkably trustworthy. As new subjects have emerged—such as the study of pilgrimage in antiquity (in the 1990s) and interest in antiquity's own forms of educated antiquarianism—it is striking how Pausanias remains a central source and arena of debate.

BIBL.: S. E. Alcock, J. F. Cherry, and J. Elsner, eds., *Pausanias: Travel and Memory in Roman Greece* (Oxford 2001). K. Arafat, *Pausanias' Greece* (Cambridge 1996). C. Habicht, *Pausanias' Guide to Ancient Greece* (Berkeley 1985). W. Hutton, *Describing Greece: Landscape and Literature in the Periegesis of Pausanias* (Cambridge 2005).

J.E.

Pederasty

Modern dictionaries usually define pederasty as an act—sexual relations with a boy—but to the Greeks *paiderastia* was an emotion: desire for a youth, gratified or not. In modern societies we can distinguish between men who are attracted to masculine men and men who are attracted to those males who are most like women in appearance, commonly those who are not yet old enough to have developed full masculine characteristics. It is this second, pederastic type of homosexuality that was widely accepted and sometimes idealized in ancient societies. The object of *paiderastia* was commonly somewhat older than seems usually to be implied by English *pederasty.* Conventionally, a youth was supposed to be most beautiful when the first down was on his cheeks.

Pederastic desire was conceived not as a fixed condition but as one expression of normal sexuality. The relationship was accepted as being asymmetrical: the olderzman was the *erastes* (lover), while the youth was the *eromenos* (beloved). But it was consensual; indeed, one reason most of the best Greek love poetry is homosexual is that the youth could say no, whereas most of the women with whom Greek men had sexual relations, wives and prostitutes, either had no choice or were paid. From the Greek root *paid-* come words meaning education (*paideia, paideusis*). This helped support the pederastic ideal, most eloquently developed in Plato's *Phaedrus* and *Symposium,* according to which each party benefits: the *erastes* gains the acceptance of his love, while the *eromenos* is educated by his lover in courage or virtue. Plato has Pausanias in the *Symposium* insist that *paiderastai* in fact love not *paides* (boys) but youths old enough to have minds.

Plato's Pausanias also claims that the love of youths is at best more spiritual than the love of women; and the authoritative doctrine of Platonic love, expounded later in the dialogue, sees the highest love as transcending the physical altogether. This nexus of ideas was attractive to the half-covert defenders of pederastic feeling who began to appear in the latter part of the 19th century; it may be detected especially in their verses, of small aesthetic merit but considerable sociological interest. One approach was to claim that the unrealizable emotions of the modern pederast made him superior to the ancients: "Is Boy-Love Greek?" asked E. E. Bradford, who answered, "Our yearning tenderness for boys like these/Has more in it of Christ than Socrates." Another approach used Hellenism as a purifying tincture; thus, S. E. Cottam, hymning the beauty of young swimmers, saw in "English boyhood" the "thews of Grecian limbs," and E. C. Lefroy included sonnets about modern lads at their sports in a volume entitled *Echoes from Theocritus.*

Theocritus and Sicily indeed became code words for pederastic sentiment. "How wonderful to be at school!" says one of the characters in Compton Mackenzie's *Sinister Street* (1913). "How Sicilian! Strange youth, you should have been sung by Theocritus." When the German photographer Baron Gloeden settled in Taormina ca. 1880, his portraits of local youths, nude or classically draped, became much sought after. Sicily was thus a usefully ambiguous term: it might allude both to ancient idyll and to modern reality. But the charm of Greece as a whole was indeed ambiguous: it could seem an inspiration both to those who sought to sublimate their pederastic desires and to those who hoped to enact them.

BIBL.: K. J. Dover, *Greek Homosexuality* (London 1978). Timothy D'Arch Smith, *Love in Earnest* (London 1970).

R.J.

Pegasus

Winged horse that, along with Chrysaor, sprang forth from Medusa when she was beheaded by Perseus; Poseidon is considered their father (Hesiod, *Theogony* 278–286). In mythology Pegasus is associated in particular with the Corinthian hero Bellerophon, who either tamed him with Athena's help (Pindar, *Olympian Odes* 13.66–86) or received him as a gift from Poseidon; together they won a series of battles against the Chimera or Amazons (Apollodorus, *Bibliotheca* 2.3.1–2). After Bellerophon's deadly fall during his attempt to explore the heavens, Pegasus flew to Olympus alone, where he served Zeus by carrying lightning and thunder. Later he appeared as a constellation between Andromeda and Aquarius.

Pegasus's reception has been divided into two strands since antiquity: his role in the Perseus and Bellerophon myths, and an allegorical-symbolic interpretation that is largely independent of these myths. The former is found intact from the Greek archaic period down to modern times, although its precise form depends on the popularity and interpretation of Perseus and Bellerophon prevailing at any given time. Many paintings show Perseus with Pegasus when the former frees Andromeda (Peter Paul Rubens, *Perseus Liberating Andromeda,* ca. 1622; Giovanni Battista Tiepolo's *Perseus and Andromeda,* ca. 1730). In music Pegasus had a firm place in the numerous Bellerophon operas of the 18th century (Jean-Baptiste Lully, *Bellerophon,* 1679; Christoph Graupner, *Bellerophon,* 1708; R. Keiser, *Iobates and Bellerophon,* 1717; J. F. Binder von Krieglstein, *Bellerophon,* 1785). Beginning in Byzantine times Pegasus was also placed in the service of the Christian imagination—in analogy to the ancient myth—as a war horse, such as when the Archangels Michael and Gabriel fight atop a winged horse. In Ariosto's *Orlando furioso* (34.51–59) Pegasus serves the knight Astolfo, who survives adventures similar to those of Bellerophon. Unlike the ancient hero, however, he manages to return safely to the Earth after his moon flight precisely because he was on a Christian mission and was not motivated by hubris.

The allegorical-symbolic interpretation of Pegasus' myth is based on two specific deeds and is encouraged by the possible etymology of his name from the Greek *pegē,* meaning "spring": by stomping his hoof, Pegasus is supposed to have tapped both the Peirene spring at Corinth and the Hippocrene in Boeotia (Strabo 8.379). Because of the Hippocrene's proximity to Helicon, the mountain of the Muses, the latter deed provided the foundation for Pegasus' symbolism as a poet-horse, which was a popular motif in art and literature starting in the Hellenistic period. As a source for inspiration and wisdom, Pegasus symbolizes the flight of thoughts as well as the way to truth, and in allegorizing depictions he was placed in direct proximity to Apollo and the Muses. Andrea Mantegna's *Parnassus* (1495–1497) portrays Pegasus next to the nine Muses, accompanied by Hermes. Other important artistic portrayals of this allegorizing interpretation include Andrea Schiavone's *Pegasus Crowned by a Muse* (1543–1546), Luca Cambiaso's *Apollo, the Muses and Pegasus* (mid-16th cent.), Gustave Moreau's *A Muse and Pegasus* (ca. 1871), Albert Pinkham Ryder's *The Poet on Pegasus Entering the Realm of the Muses* (1883–1887), and Giorgio de Chirico's *Apollo with Pegasus* (1958). In literature this motif is employed especially in Neo-Latin didactic poems and educational texts as an image of the human striving for knowledge. Giordano Bruno put it to satirical use in his dialogue *The Cabala of Pegasus* (1585): not only does the ass Onorio tell of his ancient transformation into the famous Pegasus, but in various metamorphoses (into the philosopher Aristotle, among others) he also exposes the "asininity" of ancient philosophy and the Christian religion, and in dialogue with Bruno's other speaker, Saulino, he preaches his own naturalistic worldview. Equally satirical is Friedrich Schiller's treatment of the motif in his ballad "Pegasus in Harness" (1795): he reduces Pegasus from a poet-steed to an everyday horse that falls into the wrong hands and loses his inspirational power by eating earthly food; only in the care of a poet is he able to be revitalized.

Owing to his swiftness and ability to fly, a second allegorical interpretation associates Pegasus with "winged" *Fama,* that is, poetic "fame" or, more simply, "rumor." Based on Fulgentius (1.26), this interpretation recurs in, among others, Boccaccio (*Genealogy of the Gods of the Gentiles* 10.26) and the *Ovidius moralizatus* (5808–5811), both of the 14th century, and posits a strict connection between a heroic deed and its fame in poetry.

Today the name Pegasus lends itself concretely to products from the world of horses. It is also used just as often as a symbol: for every form of flying (airlines, satellites), as well as for the speed and universal reach of online magazines, e-mail programs, and oil companies.

BIBL.: M. Shapiro, "Perseus and Bellerophon in 'Orlando Furioso,'" *Modern Philology* 81 (1983) 109–130. N. Yalours, *Pegasus: The Art of the Legend* (Athens 1975). M.BA.

Translated by Patrick Baker

Penelope

Wife of Odysseus and mother of Telemachus, in Homer's *Odyssey.* She is a central figure in Odysseus' homecoming to Ithaca. Preserving her chastity and remaining loyal to her husband (by contrast to Clytemnestra and Helen), she successfully holds off the suitors through weaving by day and unraveling by night the shroud of Odysseus' elderly father, Laertes. The veil she wears suggests her opacity and indecipherability. In Hellenistic and later Roman times Penelope's ambiguity became split and reified: in popular literature she was reduced to the cliché of a virtuous wife, whereas the poet and tragedian Lycophron (3rd cent. BCE) portrayed her as a shameless prostitute who dissipated Odysseus' goods with her suitors and enjoyed the spectacle of his humiliation. Douris of Amos and Theocritus made her the mother of Pan, fathered by all the suitors.

Penelope's letter to Ulysses (Odysseus) constitutes the first chapter of Ovid's *Heroides.* It is an impassioned complaint addressed to a long-absent husband by an anguished and fiercely loyal wife impatient for his return. In Boccaccio's *Famous Women* (*De claris mulieribus,* 1375) Penelope is celebrated for her "untarnished honor and undefiled purity" and her "feminine cunning" in deceiving the suitors. His praise of Penelope, however, is predicated on the belief that her steadfast resistance is a rarity among women. Christine de Pizan devotes an entire chapter of *The Book of the City of Ladies* (*Le livre de la cité des dames,* 1405) to Penelope as a "chaste, good, and honest" woman, praising her wisdom and prudence during her husband's absence. For Christine, Penelope refutes male assertions that women cannot be both beautiful and chaste.

Juan Luis Vives, in *The Education of a Christian Woman* (*De institutione feminae Christianae,* 1523), written for the young Mary Tudor, mentions Penelope a number of times as a chaste and exemplary wife. In 1540

Cosimo de' Medici and Eleonora of Toledo commissioned from Giorgio Vasari a number of rooms in the Palazzo Vecchio depicting the politics of female virtue, which featured the Sabine women, Queen Esther, and Penelope. The central tondo in the ceiling of the Sala di Penelope depicts Penelope at her loom surrounded by her women, who spin and engage in other work. At Hardwick Hall in Derbyshire tapestries created by Elizabeth of Shrewsbury and Mary Stuart (d. 1587) depict Penelope as one of the female worthies.

In Robert Greene's *Penelope's Web* (1587) Penelope tells stories while she weaves, thus making explicit the relationship between weaving and narration that is implicit in the Homeric epics (as, for example, when Helen weaves the story of the Trojan War). The stories that Penelope tells both impress on women the qualities of obedience, chastity, and silence and dramatize women's agency.

By contrast, Margaret Cavendish represents Penelope as an "Indifferent Wife" in *The World's Olio* (1655), faulting her for "g[iving] herself leave to be Courted, which is a degree to Unchastity . . . she loved to have her Ears filled with her own Praises." Similarly, in Cavendish's play *Bell in Campo* (1662) the protagonist, Lady Victoria, criticizes Penelope for allowing the suitors to decimate Odysseus' property.

Notable pictorial representations of Penelope include Joseph Wright of Derby's *Penelope Unravelling Her Web* (1783–1784) and J. W. Waterhouse's *Penelope and the Suitors* (1912). Both represent her as a loyal wife, though Wright of Derby characteristically shines a dramatic light on her, whereas Waterhouse depicts her as a Pre-Raphaelite beauty turning away from the suitors to work on her loom.

Derek Walcott's *Omeros* (1990), which refashions both the Homeric epics and sets them on the present-day Caribbean island of St. Lucia, includes Maud Plunkett, the Irish wife of an English colonial, as a latter-day Penelope who weaves a tapestry that becomes her own shroud; her husband becomes infatuated with Helen, a beautiful black woman who works as their servant. In *The Odyssey: A Stage Version* (1993) Walcott makes explicit what was left implicit regarding Penelope's subjectivity in Homer by dramatizing her impassioned protest against Odysseus' slaughter of the suitors.

The Austrian writer Inge Merkel's novel *Odysseus and Penelope: An Ordinary Marriage* (*Eine ganze gewöhnliche Ehe*, 2000) revises the *Odyssey* from Penelope's perspective, questioning the value of the war and Odysseus' adventures and instead calling attention to Penelope's heroism. In Margaret Atwood's *Penelopiad: The Myth of Odysseus and Penelope* (2005) Penelope speaks from the underworld and demystifies Odysseus' adventures with monsters and beautiful witches as encounters with innkeepers and whores. Emphasizing her cleverness, she discloses that she immediately recognized Odysseus in disguise and orchestrated the contest of the bow (here Atwood's account is congruent with recent feminist criticism of the *Odyssey*). For Atwood a significant focus of Penelope's narrative is the fate of the maids who were executed by Telemachus for their disloyalty. Penelope explains that they were her allies in spying on the suitors; she claims that they, not the suitors, were the twelve geese in her famous dream, and she expresses regret and accepts responsibility for their deaths. Mary Zimmerman's *Odyssey* (2006), a dramatic adaptation of the ancient original, also participates in the feminist reassessment of the epic, by introducing the play as a woman reader's re-creation of Homer. Making explicit what was implicit in the epic, Zimmerman has Penelope actively plan and administer the contest of the bow.

The figure of Penelope has emerged as an evocative critical paradigm for feminist theorists such as Peggy Kamuf (1982), who likens Penelope's weaving and unweaving to the work of the poet and the critic; Penelope, a "shuttling figure," mediates between "the work of history and the unworking of fiction" and thus can embody "the place of woman's art."

BIBL.: Peggy Kamuf, "Penelope at Work: Interruptions in *A Room of One's Own*," *Novel* 16, no. 1 (1982) 5–18. Marie-Madeleine Mactoux, *Pénélope: Légende et mythe* (Paris 1975). Mihoko Suzuki, *Metamorphoses of Helen: Authority, Difference, and the Epic* (Ithaca 1989) and "Rewriting the *Odyssey* in the Twenty-first Century: Mary Zimmerman's *Odyssey* and Margaret Atwood's *Penelopiad*," *College Literature* 34.2 (2007) 263–278. Georgianna Ziegler, "Penelope and the Politics of Women's Place in the Renaissance," in *Gloriana's Face: Women, Public and Private in the English Renaissance*, ed. S. P. Cerasano and M. Wynne-Davies (Detroit 1992) 47–62.

M.SU.

Pergamon

Ancient Thracian city near the Aegean seacoast in what is now Turkey, north and west of present-day Bergama; capital of the Kingdom of Pergamon under the Attalids (281–133 BCE); after 133 in the possession of Rome (the Latin form of the name is Pergamum). Augustus allowed a temple to be built in his honor here in 29 BCE, but even in Roman times Pergamon was much more famous for the Greek gods worshiped there: Zeus, and especially Asclepius. Like all good spa towns, however, it offered a diverse range of spiritual and physical goods, including an early Christian sanctuary, a gymnasium, a 15,000-seat theater, and a renowned library. The Great Altar (begun by Eumenes II and completed ca. 160 BCE), a commemoration of the triumph of the Attalids over the Galatians in the 230s, seems to have been pulled down in Byzantine times, perhaps to build fortifications against the Arabs, who nonetheless took the city in 716. The once-thriving Roman town disappeared for a few centuries but revived under Byzantine rule in the 12th century; it was conquered by the Ottomans ca. 1315.

The Frenchman Charles Texier visited the site during his state-sponsored antiquities trawl in Asia Minor in the 1830s but did not find much. The German engineer Karl Humann thought the site promising as early as 1871, but only in 1878 did Berlin officialdom take notice. By then Humann had begun to excavate large slabs of the Altar (including well-preserved pieces of the major frieze, the Gigantomachia), as well as other items; his first year's haul filled 462 crates. By 1880 two large fragments of the Gigantomachia were on view in the German Royal Museums. In 1886 an enormous panorama of the (reconstructed) acropolis at Pergamon was the hit at the Berlin Art Academy's Centennial Exhibition. Excavations continued, uncovering the theater, Asclepion, and many other Hellenistic and Roman buildings, but it was the Altar that then shaped, and has shaped since, European perception of the site.

It should not be thought, however, that this was a uniformly positive perception. Many of the Gigantomachia's first viewers found the sculptures depicting the battle between the gods and the giants (as described in Hesiod's *Theogony*) baroque and grotesque, or at the very least overwrought; they did not fit the ideals of serenity and silent grandeur described by Winckelmann and reflected in the Elgin Marbles (these latter, however, had also initially seemed shocking to connoisseurs). The Swiss art and cultural historian Jacob Burckhardt liked them, though his comments—"The narrow aesthetic is shaken at its roots, everything that had been written about the pathos of the Laocoön is wastepaper"—suggest he was also savoring a little *Schadenfreude* at the expense of the German classicists he despised.

As it happens, the Altar's bigness, Greekness, and (now) Germanness ultimately have helped to sustain German classicism, even though it has been on view in its entirety for nearly half of the 130 years since its excavation (and during much of that era the Academy was virtually out of reach in East Berlin). Many 20th-century writers, artists, and architects claim to have been moved by it; Peter Weiss's three-part novel *The Aesthetics of Resistance* (1957–1981) is perhaps the best-known literary enrollment of the monument. The Altar may have been the model for Lenin's tomb in Red Square as well as for Albert Speer's Zeppelin Grandstand in Nuremberg. Now the centerpiece of the newly refurbished Pergamon Museum in Berlin, it is again accessible to enthusiastic Western visitors—though the Turkish citizens of Bergama still hope to retrieve it.

BIBL.: Suzanne L. Marchand, *Down from Olympus: Archaeology and Philhellenism in Germany, 1750–1970* (Princeton 1996). Renate Petras, *Die Bauten der Berliner Museumsinsel* (Berlin 1987). Arnold von Salis, *Der Altar von Pergamon* (Berlin 1912). H. J. Schalles, *Der Pergamonaltar: Zwischen Bewertung und Verwertbarkeit* (Frankfurt 1988). S.M.

Persephone. *See* Demeter and Persephone.

Persia

God gave all knowledge in the form of the Avesta to Zarathushtra (Zoroaster, ca. 628–ca. 551 BCE), who then passed this on to the Persians. When Alexander of Macedon conquered Persia (331 BCE), the Greeks came into contact with Persian texts and translated them into their own language, and so the knowledge of the Persians was disseminated far and wide across the world. Later the Sasanian kings promoted Zoroastrianism, and they ordered that the materials then scattered throughout the Earth be brought together and translated back into Persian. And later still, at the direction of the ʿAbbasid caliphs in Baghdad, the Persian texts were translated into Arabic and once again distributed to the world at large. The circle that began with God and Zarathushtra was thus closed with the return of knowledge to Persia, but it was also supplemented with the translation into Arabic and the transfer of learning to the Islamic peoples at large. This account, which largely derives from two early Arabic sources and the Pahlavi (Middle Persian) *Denkard,* points to some of the factors that need to be understood in discussions of the encounter between Greek and Persian cultures: the importance of religion, translation, conquest, and appropriation for cultural traditions; the pivotal place occupied by Alexander and his conquests; and the historical closeness of Persian and Greek as well as Persian and Arabic cultures.

The story of relations between the Greeks, Romans, and Persians is not just of borrowing by one side at one time, but rather of an ongoing process of interactions and exchanges. Contact between the Greeks and Persians, and later between the Romans and Persians, facilitated the exchange of cultural traditions that occurred between these peoples, and such contact goes back at least to the Achaemenid era (550–330 BCE). The widespread notion of implacable conflict between Greeks and Persians in this period needs to be understood in light of profound cross-cultural interaction between the two groups; *mutatis mutandis,* the same also holds for relations between the Persians, on the one hand, and the Macedonians, Seleucids, Parthians, or Romans, on the other. Aristocratic and elite groups often turned to each other on both sides, as is indicated by the example of Pharnabazus (4th cent. BCE), who was the satrap of Daskyleion; the ancient sources note his homosexual behavior, his time in his gymnasium, and his friendship with Agesilaus, the king of Sparta. Greek artists and sculptors worked in Susa for rulers such as Darius I and Artaxerxes II, and the influence of Hellenic motifs and styles can be discerned in Asia Minor as well as in the far-flung satrapies of the empire. The presence of numerous Greeks is also well attested in a range of roles, from doctor (Ctesias) to mercenary (Clearchus) to political adviser (Themistocles). The details of Persian Hellenism are now becoming better known, and the picture is emerging of a long-term phenomenon whereby Persians remained open, with varying degrees of adaptability, to Greek beliefs and practices throughout the ancient period.

Without a doubt, the Greek name that dominates the record in Persia is that of Alexander, who is eulogized, commemorated, and reviled (he is the "accursed" one in Pahlavi texts) in the literature for centuries. His exploits were recounted in Greek romance as well as in the Greek histories; it is the former, based initially on the account given by pseudo-Callisthenes and perhaps subsequently on an intermediate Syriac version, that enters the Persian tradition as the *Eskandar-nama.* There are numerous renditions, in verse (*mathnawi*) and prose, of the romance in Persian, which vary, often considerably, from the early Greek recensions. A striking feature of the Persian tales is Alexander's birth from Darab (a possible surrogate for Darius II) and the daughter of Philip; no less striking is the association between him and Dhu'-l Qarnayn, the prophet of Surah 18 in the Koran. Two of the earliest verse treatments are also among the most influential, notably those of Ferdowsi, who portrays Alexander in his epic *Shahnama* (ca. 1010), and Nezāmi, whose account is given in the *Sharaf-nama* and *Eqbal-nama* or *Kherad-nama* (ca. 1202). Other major verse tellings of the Alexander romance in Persia are the *A'-ina-ye eskandari* (ca. 1300) by Amīr Khusrow Dehlawī and the *Kherad-nama-ye eskandari* (ca. 1485) by ʿAbd al-Rahman Jami. Among prose versions, the most widely renowned appear to be the *Iskandar-namah,* composed at some time between the 12th and 14th centuries, and the story narrated in the 12th century by Abu Taher Tarsusi in the second half of his *Darab-nama.* These multifarious accounts of Alexander remain fascinating sources for the study of the classical tradition in Persian culture, and they are still relatively understudied by historians of reception.

The *Eskandar-nama* is not the only literary example to show the influence of Greek culture; nor is the traffic in one direction only, though claims of literary priority are less interesting than analysis of the hybridity within the texts. *Metiochus and Parthenope,* an early work of Greek prose fiction, bears remarkable resemblances in theme and content to ʿUnsuri's poem *Vameq o ʿAdhra.* The core story of the two lovers who are separated by misfortune and subjected to further travail is widely known, largely through the story of Layla and Majnun, celebrated by Nezami and scores of others. There are startling parallels as well between Greek prose fictions and such medieval Persian romances as ʿAyyūqī's *Varqa o Golshah* and Gorgani's tragic *Vis o Ramin.* The interpretive context for these works encompasses Arabic and Indian narratives as well as Greek, and the Persian romance offers evidence of a rich cross-fertilization of disparate but connected literary traditions.

Along with literature and material culture, there are numerous spheres of activity in which Persian traditions interact with the ancient Greek and Roman. Philosophy, ethics, astronomy, physics, mathematics, medicine, geography, politics, meteorology, social custom, and religion are all among the areas in which the sway of Greece and, to a smaller extent, Rome, can be discerned. In connection with these fields, scholars have documented the circulation of ideas and influences in the Achaemenid, Seleucid, Parthian, and Sasanian periods at a level of detail that cannot be provided in the brief compass of this essay. To be sure, contact with the Greeks should be interpreted within the wider context of relations with other cultures, for example, with Arab and Indian cultures, which formed profound and meaningful relationships with the Persians. Even as the handling of Greek materials and concepts continues into the Islamic centuries, for instance, the Persian language begins to be written in Arabic script, and educated Persians show a command of both Arabic and Persian. It is the closeness (religious, political) of Persian and Arabic cultures that facilitates the translation movement into Arabic and provides a sociopolitical framework for the transfer of Greek knowledge into Islamic thought and learning.

If the content and status of Greek accomplishments were articulated forcefully, the question of Rome was not always answered clearly in Persian or Arabic writings. Rome was the focus of intermittent aggression throughout the Parthian and Sasanian times, and the history of the wars between these groups is as long and bloodstained as any, a point made by contemporary chronicles on all sides. But in the later texts of Persian and Arabic authors, the city and empire of Rome provoke relatively little comment. For Arab and, afterward, for Persian and Turkish writers, *Rum* meant Byzantium rather than Rome, especially since Byzantium styled itself as a Roman Empire and its inhabitants as Romans. (The usage has continued into the present: in Islamic cultures, Greece and the Greeks are known as *Rum,* and the Greek language is called *Rumi.*) At times *Rum* might even refer to Central and Western Europe. The confusion and marginalizing of Rome extended to the translation movement as well. In contrast to the scores of works translated from Greek into Persian and Arabic, only one work appears to have been translated from Latin at the close of the first millennium CE. Orosius' *Historiae adversum paganos* (*History against the Pagans*), dedicated to Augustine and composed in the 5th century, was translated into Arabic in southern Spain. This work, which also enjoyed a widespread popularity in medieval Europe, disseminated an awareness of ancient Rome among Muslim audiences. There are few if any developed treatments of Rome among the Persian and Arabic writers, however, and the surviving literature seems to be oriented more toward Byzantium than Rome. Ibn Khurradadhbeh, one of the earliest Muslim geographers, was a Persian who composed his work in Arabic in the 9th century. He devotes some space to the Byzantine Empire, which for him was part of a world divided into four sections, Europe, Libya, Ethiopia, and Scythia. In the 14th century Rashīd al-Dīn, who converted from Judaism to Islam, wrote *Tarikh-e Afranj* (*History of the Franks*); this work is said to constitute an innovative step in Persian writings about Europe, and it has much of interest on contemporary Europeans ("the Franks") but only a little on the ancients.

Beginning in the Renaissance, if not earlier, European writers for their part also lay the groundwork for the idea of Oriental despotism, a stereotype that is significantly based on the ancient Persian monarchy as it appears in Greek and Latin sources. Thus, Persia is triangulated by European intellectuals through ancient Greek and Roman materials, which are often unsympathetic to the Eastern culture. It is important to see the dialectical relationship between the European texts and the Graeco-Roman representations of Persia (especially of the Achaemenid Empire), and to understand how they map onto each other. The European tradition concerning Darius III, say, or Cambyses, is based heavily on Greek and Roman rather than Persian sources, and it is therefore hardly surprising that the early representations of these Persians offer images of avarice, decadence, effeminacy, and luxury.

It is also through Greek and Latin sources that Europeans attempt to study Zoroastrianism. Thomas Hyde notes the centrality of the Greek and Latin texts to his Zoroastrian studies in 1700, and he gives these more credence than the writings of Muslim authors. Abraham-Hyacinthe Anquetil du Perron, later in the 18th century, is unable entirely to set aside the Greek and Latin materials after his breakthrough publications on Avestan and Pahlavi texts, and he continues to use them in his treatises. Even after the decipherment of Avestan texts in Europe, then, the Greek and Latin sources are seen as necessary aids for an understanding of Zoroastrianism; they are a check on the Persian sources and a means to complement these materials when they are thought to be imperfect, inaccurate, or defective in some respect. Such an attitude about the primacy of Greek and Latin sources lasts through the 19th century, through the decipherment of Old Persian by Henry Rawlinson, among others, and spills over into the 20th. Significantly, Persian writers in the 19th century themselves also respond to European texts about Persia and repeat, rework, and transform the treatments of non-Persian sources. So a complex dialectical phenomenon continues whereby Persian, Greek, Roman, and other traditions interact with and engage each other, with consequences that continue into the modern period and beyond.

BIBL.: P. Briant, *Darius dans l'ombre d'Alexandre* (Paris 2003). J. Duchesne-Guillemin, *The Western Response to Zoroaster* (Oxford 1958). D. Gutas, *Greek Thought, Arabic Culture: The Graeco-Arabic Translation Movement in Baghdad and Early ʿAbbāsid Society (2nd–4th/8th–10th Centuries)* (London 1998). T. Hägg and B. Utas, *The Virgin and Her Lover: Fragments of an Ancient Greek Novel and a Persian Epic Poem* (Leiden 2003). B. Lewis, *The Muslim Discovery of Europe* (London 1982). F. Pfister, *Alexander der Grosse in den Offenbarungen der Griechen, Juden, Mohammedaner und Christen* (Berlin 1956). E. W. Said, *Orientalism* (New York 1978). M. Stausberg, *Faszination Zarathustra: Zoroaster und die Europäische Religionsgeschichte der Frühen Neuzeit,* 2 vols. (Berlin 1998). See also *Encyclopaedia Iranica,* esp. "Byzantine-Iranian Relations," "Diaspora, Iranian," "Eskandar-Nama," "Europe, Persian Image of," "Falsafa, Philosophy," "Greece," and "Hellenism."

P.V.

Petrarch

Francesco Petrarca (1304–1374); the most celebrated and influential man of letters of the Trecento. He was born in the Tuscan town of Arezzo, where his father had settled after being exiled from his native Florence in 1302. His father, Ser Petracco, was a notary and soon found employment in the papal Curia, which had recently been transferred from Rome to Avignon; the young Francesco grew up in nearby Carpentras. At his father's urging, he studied law in Montpellier and Bologna and then took minor orders. But his main ambitions were literary, and he sought fame as a poet. Over the course of his lifetime he carefully assembled the Italian love poems of his youth into what would become known as the *Songbook* (*Canzoniere*), and later he undertook a series of historical and allegorical poems written in Italian *terzine* (tercets) and called *Triumphs* (*Triumphi*).

Yet his public fame rested principally on his Latin works. For his Latin epic *Africa,* a Virgilian account of the Roman general Scipio Africanus that he never finished, he was crowned poet laureate on the Capitoline Hill in Rome in 1341 by Robert, King of Naples. His prose works in turn reflected and reinforced his social ascent as Europe's foremost man of letters. He recorded his relations with scholars and potentates in his correspondence, which in later life he revised and published as *Letters to Friends* (*Epistolae ad familiares*) and *Letters of Old Age* (*Seniles*). And his various treatises and dialogues on historical and moral topics—including *On Illustrious Men* (*De viris illustribus*), *On Religious Leisure* (*De otio religioso*), *On the Solitary Life* (*De vita solitaria*), and *Remedies for Good and Ill Fortune* (*Remedia utriusque fortune*)—are dedicated to eminent contemporaries. As Petrarch's fame grew, he came under attack from various quarters, and he replied in four invectives, in which he assailed the prominent bastions of late medieval authority: the practice of medicine in *Against a Physician* (*Contra medicum*), ecclesiastical dignity in *Against a Man of High Rank* (*Contra quendam magni status*), Scholastic philosophy in *On His Own Ignorance and That of Many Others* (*De sui ipsius et multorum ignorantia*), and French nationalism in *Against a Detractor of Italy* (*Contra eum qui maledixit Italie*). In his later years he was lionized by great cities such as Milan and Venice; but he constantly yearned for the more congenial setting of the countryside and spent his final years near the village of Arquà outside Padua, where he died in 1374.

The influence of Petrarch's Italian poetry on the European lyric is immeasurable. The sonnet cycle unified by a single love object and the conflicting extremes of amorous passion are just two of the hallmarks of vernacular poetry that Petrarch made canonical. His influence on vernacular poetry over the next three centuries was so pervasive that Petrarchism—now an established discipline in Western literary studies—can be traced even in the Latin poets of the Renaissance. The poet's lyric genius was not based on erudition; and unlike the *Songbook,* his *Triumphs,* with their dense allusions to ancient history and mythology, found few imitators.

By contrast, the study of the classics that inspired his Latin writings gave impetus to the epoch-making cultural movement known as Renaissance Humanism. Rejecting the abstract medieval teaching of medicine, law, and theology, Petrarch called for the personal study of the disciplines known as the liberal arts or humanities: grammar, rhetoric, history, poetry, and moral philosophy. In his view these disciplines contributed to the formation of an individual's character and, unlike the medieval professions, had the power to shape the inner self. Paradoxically, in promoting such introspective self-betterment Petrarch had recourse to the extrovert arsenal of rhetoric—treatises, invectives, and especially epistles—and his process of inner self-fashioning entailed changing the outward form of his name, from the rough Petracco to the graceful Petrarca. By studiously cultivating the role of a prominent citizen in the Republic of Letters—a private arbiter of learning and morals with a public voice—he set an example for generations of Humanists.

After his death his legacy was initially preserved in two cities, Padua and Florence. In Padua his literary ideals paved the way for the Ciceronian teaching of Gasparino Barzizza, whose Paduan school was attended by such notable Humanists as Vittorino da Feltre, Francesco Filelfo, and Leon Battista Alberti. His *On Illustrious Men* inspired the frescoes in the Sala dei Giganti in the city's Palazzo Liviano. In Florence the chancellor Coluccio Salutati not only emulated Petrarch in his moral treatises but also promoted the study of Greek, which Petrarch had attempted to learn without success. One of Salutati's young protégés, among the first Italians to master Greek, was Leonardo Bruni, who later became the chancellor and historian of the Florentine Republic. While in his teens Bruni had greatly admired a portrait of Petrarch that he saw in his native Arezzo; in his Latin *Dialogues to Pier Paolo Vergerio* (1402–1405), which portrays Salutati's circle in Florence, Bruni asserted that Petrarch had "opened the way" to Humanist studies. In 1436 he composed Italian lives of Dante and Petrarch, thus elevating the two poets to the dignity of the great men immortalized in ancient biographies. Bruni also wrote a Latin *History of the Florentine People* (1442), in which he borrowed elements of style and organization from Livy, the Roman historian whose text Petrarch had so carefully assembled.

The never-completed *Africa,* the Latin epic in nine books about the Roman general Scipio Africanus that had earned Petrarch his laureate in 1341, inspired numerous Italian Humanists to compose poetry in Latin hexameters. In the early Quattrocento, Maffeo Vegio wrote a 13th book to supplement Virgil's *Aeneid,* as well as various short epics on mythological themes. He also wrote the *Life of Saint Anthony* (*Antonias*), the first Christian epic of the Renaissance, a work possibly inspired by Petrarch's *Bucolic Poem* (*Bucolicum carmen*), a set of 12 Latin eclogues laden with the sort of Christian allegory that medieval readers found in Virgil's eclogues. In the next century the tradition culminated in Jacopo Sannazaro's *On the Virgin Birth* (*De partu virginis*) and Girolamo Vida's *Life of Christ* (*Christias*).

Petrarch's emphasis in his prose works on the social and historical context of moral debate promoted the Renaissance burgeoning of the epistle and the dialogue. His role as a pioneer in Humanist epistolography is clear. As a young man he apparently saved his letters, conceived of as descendants of Seneca's *Epistulae morales,* with a view to future revision and publication. When he discovered a manuscript of Cicero's *Letters to Atticus* in Verona in 1345, he was at first shocked to read about his idol's vacillating moods. But the record of Cicero's private experience in this epistolary collection proved a revelation; as he revised his own correspondence, Petrarch often mingled private experience with public moralizing. The most notable instance of this self-fashioning, which characterizes much of Renaissance literature, is found in *Letters to Friends* 4.1, addressed to the Augustinian monk Dionigi of Sansepolcro, in which Petrarch describes how he climbed Mount Ventoux in Provence in 1336. Yet subsequently, as if to contrast his friend's Christian piety to Cicero's instability, he rewrote the experience as an allegory of spiritual ascent.

Eventually Petrarch bequeathed five collections of Latin epistles to posterity, including an unfinished missive addressed to Posterity itself. These comprise 350 *Letters to Friends* in 24 books; 125 *Letters of Old Age* in 17 books; a "nameless" (*sine nomine*) book of 19 letters denouncing the Avignon papacy; 67 "verse epistles" (*Epystole metrice*) in 3 books; and 76 "miscellaneous letters" (*Varie*). The style of his letters marks a clear break with the medieval tradition of *ars dictaminis,* the formulaic repertoire employed by chancellors and secretaries in their official correspondence.

After his death Petrarch's example would inspire Salutati, who in 1392 obtained a copy of Cicero's *Letters to Friends.* Not surprisingly, Salutati's successors as chancellor, Leonardo Bruni and Poggio Bracciolini, also collected their private correspondence, an example followed throughout Italy by Humanists like Francesco Barbaro, Pier Candido Decembrio, Enea Silvio Piccolomini, Antonio Beccadelli (Panormita), Francesco Filelfo, and Giannantonio Campano. The writing of letters was soon established as an important component of Humanism. The educator Gasparino Barzizza, who wrote a brief treatise on letter writing, composed a series of exemplary letters as a didactic tool and collected his own correspondence. In the next generation Niccolò Perotti included a short discussion of epistolography in his *Elements of Grammar* (*Rudimenta grammatices,* 1468). Later theoreticians of the genre compiled lengthy treatises on letter writing—Juan Luis Vives and Erasmus, two of the most prominent, both wrote works titled *De conscribendis epistolis.*

In the years following his laureate in 1341 Petrarch suffered a spiritual crisis that caused him to question his pursuit of love and fame. He dramatized this inner struggle in a revolutionary dialogue entitled *Secretum* (*My Secret*), in which he portrays himself as Franciscus, in conversation with Saint Augustine, who challenges him to renounce his vain ambitions and turn to pious worship of God. His dramatic portrayal of this discussion marks a sharp break with medieval styles of dialogue, which tended to take the form of formulaic disputation or catechism. Instead, Franciscus holds his own against the revered authority of his favorite Church Father, and the *Secret* ends with the unresolved opposition of views that once characterized the Academic dialogues of Cicero. Thus, even though Petrarch does not strictly adhere to a classical model of debate, his work points the way toward the revival of Ciceronian dialogue in the Quattrocento, when the genre became a favorite forum of literary discussion for Humanists like Leonardo Bruni, Poggio Bracciolini, Lorenzo Valla, Leon Battista Alberti, and Giovanni Pontano.

In his epistolary invective *On His Own Ignorance* Petrarch denounced the sterility of Aristotelian science and dialectic. He used arguments that had already been employed by Scholastic thinkers like Saint Bonaventure but clearly situated himself outside the schools and universities and proposed no method of teaching. Instead, he advanced a new way of reading and studying texts. His denunciation of dialectic, natural science, and metaphysics was taken up by Humanists of the Quattrocento. Thus, in Bruni's *Dialogues with Pier Paolo Vergerio,* the interlocutor Niccolò Niccoli attacks the empty disputations of the Schoolmen, for which Bruni's work itself offers the alternative of debate along Cicero's rhetorical model.

In contrast to the Aristotle of the Schoolmen, Petrarch praises Plato as a sublime thinker. Except for a Latin translation of the *Timaeus,* he could not read Plato, but he embraced the judgment of Cicero and Augustine, who celebrated the philosopher for urging humankind to contemplate the eternal order of the universe and the providence of its Creator. In the next century the study and translation of Plato would transform the course of Western philosophy, leading to the "Platonic theology" of Marsilio Ficino and others who devoted themselves to recuperating the heritage of Plato and the Neoplatonists.

According to Cicero, Aristotle was an eloquent writer; Petrarch blamed the inelegance of the Latin corpus of Aristotle on the ineptitude of medieval translators. When the study of ancient Greek was revived in Florence around 1400, Petrarch's animadversions moved Humanists like Leonardo Bruni to retranslate Aristotle despite opposition from traditionalists. The new translations did much to expand the philosophical perspective of Italian Humanists. But a more conservative style of Aristotelian instruction remained firmly ensconced in the universities, and Humanists continued the Petrarchan polemics as late as Vives, whose 1520 *Against the Pseudo-Dialecticians* (*In pseudodialecticos*) excoriated the Scholastic professors whose instruction he had suffered at the University of Paris.

Despite his use of rhetorical persuasion, Petrarch's call for cultural reform was rejected by more conservative thinkers with a vested interest in established hierarchies. Hence, as part of the price of his literary and social success, he came under attack from various quarters. He responded by using the most formidable weapon in his arsenal, the rhetoric of invective. His invectives constitute a primary source for his intellectual program, offering a negative counterpart to the more positive reflections of his epistles and treatises. His combative attitude found imitators in the next century as Humanists engaged in literary quarrels of their own. For example, the *Antidotes* (*Antidota*) of Lorenzo Valla against Bartolomeo Facio and Poggio Bracciolini are filled with Petrarchan touches.

In the field of historiography, Petrarch viewed antiquity more from the perspective of biography and anecdote than did the Renaissance historians who succeeded him. His *On Illustrious Men* originally comprised 23 biographies of great Romans from Romulus to Cato the Censor; later he added a dozen biblical and mythological figures, including Adam, Jason, and Hercules. (In the next century Humanists' enthusiasm for ancient biography would be heightened by the rediscovery and translation of Plutarch's *Lives of the Greeks and Romans.*) Petrarch's title echoes that of biographies written by Suetonius (now lost) and Saint Jerome, and his work was soon imitated by Boccaccio, who in homage to his learned friend composed a set of female biographies, *On Famous Women* (*De claris mulieribus*). Petrarch also began, but never finished, *Memorable Events* (*Rerum memorandarum libri*), a compilation of *exempla* whose title and format evoke the *Memorable Deeds and Sayings* of the Roman historian Valerius Maximus.

Although Petrarch's own approach to history seems more personal than political, his sense of the gap between Roman antiquity and his own age laid the basis for the Renaissance division of Western history into three periods: a classical period, its decline into "barbarity," and its rebirth in the new cultural ideals of Humanism. He also provided an invaluable model of methodology in historical studies. His interpretation of ancient historians, and of Livy in particular, applied keen philological tools—comparing different sources and textual variants, and even drawing on the evidence of Roman coins and inscriptions—an example that inspired later Humanists like Lorenzo Valla and Flavio Biondo.

Indeed, Petrarch's insatiable curiosity for antiquity led him to assemble a vast library of classical works, including a Greek codex of Homer that he never learned to read. The extent of his library has been brilliantly reconstructed by Berthold L. Ullman (1955), and Pierre de Nolhac's magisterial study (1907) of his wide reading fills two large volumes.

The moral essays by Petrarch that were most influential soon after his death now seem decidedly medieval in outlook. His *On the Solitary Life* and *On Religious Leisure* inspired similar tracts by Coluccio Salutati, *On Fate and Fortune* (*De fato et fortuna*) and *On Religion and the Flight from This World* (*De religione et fuga saeculi*). Yet even in these works Petrarch often draws on classical ethicists in pointing out the lessons of Christian morality, as when, in his treatise on solitude, he twice alludes to the Choice of Hercules. Before 1600 his most popular work was *Remedies for Good and Ill Fortune,* a massive collection of short debates on moral topics argued by Joy, Grief, Reason, and Hope. Today the work is often dismissed as a series of artificial declamations, but in fact it contains a vast array of classical learning and many passages of heartfelt introspection.

Petrarch's role in laying the foundations of modern classical archaeology and philology has been clear since the Renaissance. Quattrocento Humanists like Poggio Bracciolini took up Petrarch's critical survey of Roman ruins; both men are immortalized in chapter 71 of Edward Gibbon's monumental *Decline and Fall of the Roman Empire* (1776). More important, the Renaissance recovery of neglected ancient texts begins with Petrarch, who during a visit to Liège in 1338 discovered a codex containing unknown orations by Cicero, including *Pro Archia*, a speech notable for its defense of poetry. (As noted above, his discovery in 1345 of Cicero's letters would inaugurate a new age in epistolography.) His philological care in assembling and correcting the text of Livy's history of Rome was continued by Lorenzo Valla, who acquired Petrarch's codex and composed a treatise, *Emendations of Livy's Six Books about the Second Punic War* (*Emendationes sex librorum Titi Livii de secundo bello punico*). Inspired by Petrarch, Valla went on to examine the Greek text of the New Testament; in turn, Valla's Petrarchan philology eventually inspired the biblical philology of Erasmus and others.

The career of Erasmus reminds us how Petrarch's Humanism shaped the Renaissance in Northern Europe. In 1474, the centenary of Petrarch's death, Rudolph Agricola wrote the first trans-Alpine biography of Petrarch. But when Erasmus published *The Ciceronian* (*Ciceronianus*, 1528), a dialogue that reviewed the merits of Latin prose writers from antiquity to his own time, he called Petrarch "a keen intellect who had spurred the revival of eloquence, but who today is read by few." By the same token, Petrarch's Latin poetry was by the 16th century considered so awkward that Julius Caesar Scaliger omitted it from the survey of Neo-Latin verse found in book 6 of his *Poetics* (1561). Nevertheless, the advent of printing brought a new wave of popularity for Petrarch's works, especially for his Italian poetry, which was published in numerous incunable editions; his Latin works appeared more sporadically until the Basel publisher Sebastian Henric Petri issued the four-volume *Opera omnia* (1555).

Petrarchism dominated Renaissance and Baroque vernacular poetry, and even Romantic poets paid their tribute: witness Shelley's *Triumph of Life* (1822). In the 1820s Ugo Foscolo, living in London, published English essays on Petrarch with translations by the celebrated Lady Dacre. Petrarch the philologist was rediscovered only in 1859–1860, when Georg Voigt and Jacob Burckhardt published massive studies of the Italian Renaissance that recognized Petrarch's central role in the Humanist movement.

As 20th-century Renaissance studies emerged in Western scholarship, Petrarch's remarkable self-fashioning, coupled with his mastery of persuasive rhetoric, assured him a central place in the pantheon of the Humanist movement. Recent scholarship has challenged this monolithic interpretation, and the historian Ronald Witt (2000) has redefined Petrarch's role in the emergence of Humanism as simply the most prominent figure in a sequence of five generations of cultural innovators.

BIBL.: Leonard Forster, *The Icy Fire: Five Studies in European Petrarchism* (Cambridge 1969). Pierre de Nolhac, *Pétrarque et l'Humanisme* (Paris 1907). J. B. Trapp, *Studies of Petrarch and His Influence* (London 2003). B. L. Ullman, *Studies in the Italian Renaissance* (Rome 1955). J. H. Whitfield, *Petrarch and the Renascence* (New York 1943). E. H. Wilkins, *Life of Petrarch* (Chicago 1961). R. G. Witt, *In the Footsteps of the Ancients: The Origins of Humanism from Lovato to Bruni* (Leiden 2000).

D.M.

Petronius

Titus or Gaius Petronius Arbiter, high-ranking magistrate of the 1st century CE (consul ca. 62) and "arbiter of elegance" (*elegantiae arbiter*) under Nero, who ordered him to commit suicide in 66. Author of the comic novel *Satyrica*.

Three interconnected factors have dominated the transmission and reception of Petronius' *Satyricon* (as it was, and is, predominantly known): the fragmentary nature of the text, its linguistic and generic characteristics, and the sexually explicit episodes in the story. The identity of the author (see Tacitus, *Annals* 16, 17–20) and the extent to which his characters and plot relate to the society in which he lived have proved a further puzzle. The text was lacerated early on: homoerotic scenes had been eliminated by Carolingian times. Late Latin and medieval authors preserve fragments or poems attributed to Petronius that are not found elsewhere. The most extensive fragment, the *Cena Trimalchionis* (Trimalchio's Feast), was known to the 15th-century Humanist Poggio Bracciolini but not rediscovered until the mid-17th century. Meanwhile, other passages (the intercalated tale of the Widow of Ephesus and the poem on the civil war) sparked traditions of their own. Almost 400 years after the *editio princeps* (Milan ca. 1482), the first reliable edition of Petronius was established by Franz Bücheler in 1862. The maze of the text's transmission and its interpolation, however, has not yielded all its secrets yet.

The French Humanists of the 16th century were particularly intrigued by the *Satyricon:* the legal scholar Jacques Cujas (d. 1590) owned the most complete manuscript available to that point, a version of which survives in the copy made by his student lodger Joseph Scaliger; this was also used by Pierre Pithou for his revised edition of Petronius (1583). Nevertheless, the Flemish Humanist Justus Lipsius (d. 1606) famously branded Petronius an *auctor purissimae impuritatis*, "author of the purest impurity," and the Jesuit François Vavasseur warned that the *Satyricon* was unsuitable reading for young Christians (1658). Censorship continued well into the 19th century, while others tapped the market for subversive and prurient novelties. The most successful hoax was a "complete" version of the *Satyricon* published by François Nodot in 1691, supposedly based on a newly discovered manuscript from Belgrade. In 1979 death interrupted the 20th-century Latin author Harry Schnur in his own rewriting of the *Satyricon,* titled *Supplementum Petronianum.*

The rediscovery of the *Cena Trimalchionis* in 1650 (first published 1664) lent a significant impetus to the study of the *Satyricon,* leading for instance to a recognition of the author's deliberate use of vulgar Latin as a means of social characterization and mockery; some, however, drew from it crass (historically unacceptable) inferences about life in ancient Rome. Gradually the parodic and allusive nature of the text has become better understood. The title *Satyricon* itself is now regarded as a neuter genitive plural (a Greek form, *satyricōn*) dependent on an absent but understood *libri,* that is, *[Libri] Satyricōn,* "[Books of] satyr-like tales," somewhat in the style of titles of ancient Greek romances such as Heliodorus' *Aethiopica, Ethiopian Tales* (on which it draws)—hence the more recent preference among some scholars for the neuter nominative plural *Satyrica.* In the early modern period, however, the title was mostly understood as a nominative neuter singular (Greek *satyricon,* with a short o), thus *A Satyr Tale,* and associated with satire, above all Menippean satire, because of the text's mixture of prose with verse. The *Satyricon* thus gave rise to a string of satirical narratives, such as John Barclay's *Euphormionis Lusinini Satyricon* (ca. 1605), which criticized contemporary society under pseudonyms, just as Petronius was thought to have satirized the excesses of Nero's court. As a boisterous, episodic narrative, with a traveling narrator and several low-life characters, the literary texture of Petronius' work can also be discerned in the Spanish picaresque novels, the French *histoires comiques,* and their German and English counterparts and successors. Petronius' unruly jocularity was hailed by Nietzsche (in *The Antichrist*), and the text's "realism" was explored and developed in Federico Fellini's film *Satyricon* (1969). Petronius' life (insofar as it is known) has been an inspiration too: the French essayist Michel de Montaigne, writing in the later 16th century, mused on Petronius' imposed suicide (as described by Tacitus) in his "De la vanité" (*Essais,* 3.9). Petronius as "arbiter of elegance" appears as a character in the best-selling novel *Quo vadis?* (1896) by the Polish author Henryk Sienkiewicz, who went on to win the Nobel Prize for literature. The first English translation of Petronius' work was W. Burnaby's *The Satyr of Titus Petronius Arbiter* (London 1694). A Paris edition of 1902 (repr. Chicago 1927) includes an English translation questionably attributed to Oscar Wilde.

BIBL.: Ingrid A. R. De Smet, *Menippean Satire and the Republic of Letters 1581–1655* (Geneva 1996). Donato Gagliardi, *Petronio e il romanzo moderno: La fortuna del Satyricon attraverso i secoli,* Biblioteca di cultura 185 (Florence 1993). P Senay, ed., *La matrone d'Ephese: Histoire d'un conte mythique,* 2 vols. (Quebec 2003). A. Fred Sochatoff, "Petronius Arbiter," *Catalogus Translationum et Commentariorum* (Washington, D.C., 1976) 3:313–340. J. P. Sullivan, "The Social Ambience of Petronius' *Satyricon* and Fellini's *Satyricon,*" in Martin M. Winkler, ed., *Classical Myth and Culture in the Cinema* (Oxford 2001) 258–271. P. G. Walsh, "'Nachleben' and the Rebirth of the Picaresque," chapter 8 in *The Roman Novel* (Cambridge 1970) (dated, but still useful as an introduction). *The Petronian Society Newsletter,* 1970– (since 2000 online): www.ancientnarrative.com/PSN/.

I.D.S.

Phaedra

Daughter of Minos and Pasiphaë, sister of Ariadne, wife of Theseus, king of Athens; through divine connivance or human error she fell in love with Hippolytus, her husband's son from another marriage, which wrought his doom. Euripides' *Hippolytus* is the second of his two plays on her story (the first is lost, as is Sophocles' treatment). In the first, Phaedra was apparently aggressive in pursuing Hippolytus; in the second, exonerated as the victim of Aphrodite, she virtuously resists her passion. This doubleness characterizes Phaedra's representation throughout the tradition.

Ovid's *Heroides* 4 consists of a letter from Phaedra exhorting Hippolytus to answer her love. Rather than experiencing guilt over her passion or attempting to suppress it, she justifies it as deriving from her family—which includes Europa and Pasiphaë, as well as her sister Ariadne (who in turn pined for Theseus). Moreover, far from considering her kinship with Hippolytus as potentially incestuous, she dismisses such scruples as outdated and invokes Jupiter's marriage to his sister Juno. Seneca, like Ovid, shifts the attention from Hippolytus to Phaedra—a shift that would become even more pronounced in Racine. Seneca's Phaedra, unlike Euripides', is strong-willed and clear-sighted, displaying a great self-awareness and purposefulness. Her audacious eloquence contributes to a heroic stature that exceeds her persona in Euripides' version.

In his *Novelle* (1554–1573), no. 37, Matteo Bandello makes explicit reference to Phaedra in recounting the story of Niccolò d'Este, who had his wife and son executed upon discovering their adultery. Bandello's version renders the young lovers more sympathetic than the philandering husband, father of numerous bastards. Lope de Vega knew Bandello's story in a Spanish translation, but he also based Casandra, the heroine of *El Castigo sin Venganza* (1631), on Seneca's Phaedra. He follows Bandello in having Federico accept Casandra's advances, yet these lovers display more self-awareness than Bandello's, rendering the play closer in this respect to Seneca's version.

Because Racine's *Phèdre* (1677) became the paradigmatic and exemplary work in French literature, the character Phaedra has also attained an iconic status. Her contradictory lineage—exemplified in the famous line "La fille de Minos et de Pasiphaë," which traces her descent from the judge of the underworld and the lascivious woman who desired a bull and became mother to the Minotaur—encapsulates Phaedra's overwhelming passion for Hippolytus, which coexists with her own severe self-judgment on her passion.

Swinburne's *Phaedra* (1866) is a dialogue between Hippolytus and Phaedra, attended by a chorus of Troezenian women, at the point when Phaedra seeks to have Hippolytus slay her. She represents herself as a hybrid and speaks passionately of her love for her "son" and eloquently of her love as "a god about me like as fire." Inflected by Nietzsche, D'Annunzio's *Fedra* (performed 1908, published 1909) transforms the figure of Phaedra into an aggressively passionate, at times violent, and ultimately defiant superwoman who claims Hippolytus as her own even after his death and who dies unrepentantly celebrating her passion.

The story of Phaedra has proven resonant for modernist women writers seeking to reimagine classical myths. In *Hippolytus Temporizes* (1927), a verse play based on an earlier series of Phaedra poems about Artemis and Aphrodite, H.D.'s Phaedra, like D'Annunzio's, actively pursues the fulfillment of her passion. She succeeds in seducing Hippolytus, who is tricked by her disguise as Artemis, the tutelary goddess of his mother, the Amazon Hippolyta. Marina Tsvetaeva's *Ariadna* (1927) and *Fedra* (1928) represent the first two parts of an unfinished trilogy about Theseus. While challenging the patriarchal authority of the tradition of Phaedra's story by positing the importance of feminine and maternal language, Tsvetaeva nevertheless dramatizes how Fedra's speech and writing (confessing her love in her letter to Hippolytus) are rejected (by Hippolytus) or misunderstood (by Theseus). Marguerite Yourcenar's "Phaedra, or Despair" is the first lyrical prose piece in *Feux* (1936), which consists of new interpretations of classical protagonists and their stories. Yourcenar reimagines Phaedra as a Haitian, "permeated with the odor of the ranch and of the fish from Haiti, unsuspectingly carrying the leprosy contracted in a torrid-heart Tropic." In the satiric play *Qui n'a pas son Minotaure?* (1963; published in English as *Who Doesn't Have His Minotaur?*), based on an earlier version, *Ariane et l'aventurier* (1939), Yourcenar focuses on the rivalry between Ariadne and Phaedra over Theseus, representing Phaedra as a destructive force seeking her own doom and contrasting her with Ariadne as a figure of transcendence.

Characteristically exploring the vexed relation between a father and a son, Eugene O'Neill's *Desire under the Elms* (1924) translates the Phaedra story to a New England farm in the 1850s. Robinson Jeffers's *The Cretan Woman* (1954), based on Euripides' *Hippolytus,* emphasizes Phaedra's struggle with her passion for a homosexual Hippolytus. Like O'Neill, Jeffers explores throughout his play the issue of human agency and the ascendancy of the female protagonist over the hitherto powerful but now emasculated patriarchal figure of Theseus.

Racine's *Phèdre* has been translated into English by some of the most distinguished poets of the 20th century: Robert Lowell (1961), Richard Wilbur (1962), C. H. Sisson (1989), Derek Mahon (1999), and Ted Hughes (2000). Benjamin Britten composed music for a dramatic cantata, *Phaedra* (opus 93), based on Lowell's translation.

Jules Dassin's film *Phaedra* (1962), set in contemporary Greece, where the latter-day Theseus is a shipping magnate, features Melina Mercouri as Phaedra, who engages in an affair with Alexis (Hippolytus), played by Anthony Perkins. Tony Harrison's *Phaedra Britannica* (1975) sets the play in the India of the Raj, where the Hindu deities take the place of the Greek gods. In Brian Friel's *Living Quarters: After Hippolytus* (1977), set in Ballybeg, a small Donegal town, Anna, the latter-day Phaedra, and Ben (Hippolytus) engage in an affair; rather than Phaedra, the Theseus-figure, Commandant Frank Butler, commits suicide. Sarah Kane's *Phaedra's Love* (performed 1996, published 1998) is a postmodernist play of graphic sex and violence.

BIBL.: Marta Stadler Fox, *The Troubling Play of Gender: The Phaedra Dramas of Tsvetaeva, Yourcenar, and H.D.* (Selinsgrove, Pa., 2001). Richard Goodkin, *The Tragic Middle: Racine, Aristotle, Euripides* (Madison 1991). M.SU.

Phaethon

Son of Helios (Phoebus), the sun god. He insisted on proving his divine lineage by driving his father's chariot. He lost control but was prevented from destroying the earth by Zeus (Jupiter), who struck him down with a thunderbolt. The only important source for this mythical story is Ovid's *Metamorphoses,* where Phaethon's initial crisis and journey are introduced near the end of book 1. The main part of the story, positioned prominently at the beginning of book 2, unfolds in lavish detail.

Recent allusions to the myth in contemporary contexts suggest its many themes: high aspirations and willingness to take risks (the Web site *Phaeton Descending: A Memorial to the Crew of the Space Shuttle Columbia,* 2003); out-of-control failure in the American economic arena (McDonald 1974); an artist's rendition of punishment for self-indulgence (Gerald Pas, *Phaethon's Faux Pas,* an autobiographical triptych, 1996–1998); protection of the environment from destructive human behavior (Phaethon 2004, a race for solar-powered cars at the Olympics in Athens); a powerful and ultimately indestructible vehicle (a luxury sedan by Volkswagen); the recklessness of adolescence (Ted Hughes's Phaethon allegory, cited in Winstanley 2004; a teenager borrows his father's Ferrari to impress his date, then crashes it); and the parent-child relationship (Winstanley 2004, on her own emulation of her high-achieving absentee father).

Medieval glosses on Ovid's *Metamorphoses* present Phaethon as a Christian sinner, punished for his hubris and imprudent ambition. He is one figure in *The Four Disgracers* engraved by Hendrik Goltzius (1588). The preferred Renaissance allegory was political: Phaethon as the immature prince who attempts to rule before he is ready. Shakespeare's Richard II, who refuses advice and cannot control his subjects, identifies his own fall with Phaethon's (*Richard II,* 3.3.178–179; Merrix 1987). Phoebus is of course a central figure. In a woodcut for *La métamorphose d'Ovide figurée* (Lyon 1557) Bernard Salomon couples the actual sun, its equidistant rays forming a soothing backdrop to Phaethon's dramatic fall, with Jupiter throwing the fatal thunderbolt. Together these images reflect heaven as a place of Christian redemption as well as Jupiter's punishment (Marechaux 1996). Medieval and Renaissance illustrations of Phaethon presenting himself at his father's splendid palace often show the body language of a vassal pledging fealty to his lord. In contrast, 18th-century imagery shows that era's sentimental father-son relationship. In Giambattista Tiepolo's *The Harnessing of the Horses of the Sun* (ca. 1731; Bowes Museum, Co. Durham, UK), Phoebus bids a tender farewell to his son as Father Time pushes Phaethon toward the chariot. In Carl Ditters von Dittersdorf's symphony *The Fall of Phaethon* (*Symphonies after Ovid's Metamorphoses,* no. 2, ca. 1781) the Andante is an orchestral conversation for a gentle father and a fretful son; the Minuet is a poignant soliloquy for Phoebus.

The spectacular image of tumbling horses, chariot, and head-over-heels boy has been a topos of Western art since the Renaissance, when illustrated editions of *Metamorphoses* became common. Even Pablo Picasso's etching (1931)—a line drawing that condenses horses and boy "into an utter tangle of limbs" (Florman 2000)—can be shown to descend from Salomon's influential woodcut by way of Peter Paul Rubens. (It is ironic that John Singer Sargent's mural at the Boston Museum of Fine Arts, 1922–1925, in which Phaethon does not tumble but hurls forward in flames, is truer to Ovid.) The ride itself is also a favorite topic. Christopher Rouse's *Phaethon* (1986) comprises an extended orchestral crescendo, blaring syncopated trombones representing the horses, a percussion thunderbolt, then chaotic falling figures in the strings. The opera *Phaëton* (1683) by Jean-Baptiste Lully and Philippe Quinault, though largely a human drama about the effect of Phaethon's ambition on the people around him, reaches a climax with his spectacular appearance on the chariot (a Baroque stage machine) while the chorus calls for Jupiter's intervention.

BIBL.: Lisa Florman, *Myth and Metamorphosis: Picasso's Classical Prints of the 1930s* (Cambridge, Mass., 2000). Pierre Marechaux, "La fable morte: La chute de Phaéton à travers l'essor de l'iconographie et de l'herméneutique ovidiennes aux XVe et XVIe siècles," in *Antiquités imaginaires: La référence antique dans l'art moderne de la Renaissance à nos jours* (Paris 1996) 159–183. Forrest McDonald, *The Phaeton Ride: The Crisis of American Success* (Garden City, N.Y., 1974). Robert P. Merrix, "The Phaeton Allusion in Richard II: The Search for Identity," *English Literary Renaissance* 17 (1987) 277–287. Diana Winstanley, "Phaethon: Seizing the Reins of Power," in *Myths, Stories, and Organizations: Premodern Narratives for Our Times,* ed. Yiannis Gabriel (Oxford 2004) 176–191. *Phaeton Descending: A Memorial to the Crew of the Space Shuttle Columbia,* 2003, www.datamanos2.com/phaeton_descending.htm.

L.R.

Pharmacology

The theory that there were substances from the natural world (sometimes hardly distinguishable from poisons or simply food) that contributed to the cure of diseases by helping to restore the balance of humors (fluids that constituted the body, whose imbalance produced illness) goes back to Hippocrates and his contemporaries. According to the Hippocratic Corpus, plant, animal, and mineral substances (*pharmaka*) operated by their *dynamis* through broad categories known as purgatives, caustics, emollients, and so on, on the basis of an attractive and gravitative kinetics that was, not least, due to a supposed qualitative analogy between them and humors. Where those first trends in pharmacological speculation came from is a question still open to debate.

Theoretical pharmacological innovations are expounded in the most prominent drug treatise of the ancient world by Dioscorides of Anazarba, compiled around the 1st century CE. Dioscorides adds to the *dynamis* theory the need for empiric wisdom as the most prominent source of knowledge, to see how drugs really worked. In his treatise known by the textual tradition as the *De materia medica* (*On the Materials of Medicine*), drugs are grouped according to their activity, and within each group they are ranked by their intensity. Properties of drugs are thought to be transmitted to the *materia medica* and thus to the body by the *kosmos.* Not by chance does the plant called *Yris* (identified as the gods' messenger in Greek mythology) open the treatise.

Galen's authority ensured that the pharmacological wisdom from Hippocrates to Dioscorides, including a body of writers on pharmacology active in the previous century, along with his own 2nd-century CE contribution, became for about 16 centuries the dominant theory in Western medicine and its Oriental siblings. He built up a theory that he expounded in tracts such as *De compositione medicamentorum per genera, De compositione medicamentorum secundum locos* (*On the Composition of Drugs*), and *De simplicium medicamentorum temperamentis et facultatibus* (*On the Properties of Simples*). Galen's therapeutic method assumed that the action of a particular drug was to be explained through a physiological understanding of bodily processes. He asserted the existence of 12 categories of drug action, which he adopted in his studies of simples and which formed the basis for later Galenic pharmacology, particularly in the Islamic world.

The predominance of the Greek and Roman tradition, after the fall of the Roman Empire, through the Arab Middle Ages was due largely to the hellenized Christians, Jews, and Persians who made up the bulk of the population in the newly established empire and to the persistence of their centers of learning. Arab pharmacologists acculturated and simplified Galen's theories on drug action when they became available in Arabic translation by Hunayn ibn-Ishāq (809–873) and others. A well-documented area of pharmacology concerns the recognition and accurate naming of drugs through a correct knowledge of the Greek and Arabic languages. Volumes such as those of Abulcasis (d. ca. 1013) and Maimonides (1135–1204) were devoted to providing synonyms and explanations for the names of drugs in various languages (Persian, Berber, "Spanish" Arab, etc.).

Galen's insistence on the correlation between the 12 categories of drug intensity and the patient's condition was subsequently developed in the Islamic world. Authors such as al-Kindī (ca. 801–873) categorized drugs by their efficacy: a geometric progression of drugs' dosages produces an arithmetic increase in their effects.

As that process was being accomplished in the East, North Africa, and southern Spain, Europeans of the Dark Ages were able to preserve empirical knowledge of plants, animals, and minerals as therapeutic tools thanks to compilations of ancient drug lore made at monasteries or commissioned and prized in court circles; these were known to historians as the Latin herbals. One of the most important texts of this period is the *Herbarius* of pseudo-Apuleius, thought to have been compiled in Latin in the 4th century from Greek and Latin sources, in particular Pliny and *Medicina Plinii,* but containing also Dioscoridean interpolations. Almost 130 illustrated chapters, each devoted to one plant, including its synonyms in most languages, are accompanied by a list of complaints enumerated *a capite ad calcem* (from head to toe). There are few surviving copies of most of those herbals, and to what extent they were used at a practical level is a question not yet answered. By the end of the 13th century the herbarium was no longer useful for the translations of Arabic medical treatises; the ascendance of theoretically oriented medical literature rendered these outmoded texts of little use to the educated physician.

By 1056, as Arab power decreased, the southern Italian city of Salerno had became an active center of translation of scientific books from Arabic to Latin. It is at this time that figures such as Constantine the African translated Galenic theories into Latin; it was precisely the theory of interaction of properties that soon found an application in pharmacology. A Constantinian translation, *De gradibus,* gave a clear definition of Galen's notion of degree, one of the four elements into which the ancients divided the temperament. The facts provided by this work were integrated in the *Circa instans* by Mattheus Platearius (12th cent.), a member of an important Salernitan family of doctors, which became one of the most well-used medieval and Renaissance pharmacopoeias; together with other contemporary pharmacological texts, such as the *Antidotarium nicolai,* it formed a handbook for the pharmacist and medical man, including those from Salerno whose task was to control the making of medicines by pharmacists.

At the beginning of the 16th century pharmacological works by Galen still competed with Arab works such as the second book of Avicenna's 11th-century *Canon of Medicine.* But soon the Humanists gave preeminence to the liberal Greek tradition, and Galen's works were followed by teachers and students of medicine. At the same time the *Materia medica* of Dioscorides gave rise to the emergence of botany as a discipline separate from pharmacology. The discovery of the New World and the introduction of chemical remedies, courtesy of the Paracelsian revolution, did not challenge the validity of Galenic medicine until the beginning of modern pharmacology, during the first half of the 19th century, when alkaloids were isolated and the first laboratory for experimental pharmacology was created.

Graeco-Roman botanical terminologies still illustrate the general principles of the formation of modern words. Our *dandelion,* for example, is an anglicized form of the medieval French *den de lion* (tooth of a lion), from the medieval Latin *dens leonis.* Additionally, ancient practices and pharmacological information still survive, ready to be mined when current medical practices come under question.

BIBL.: Minta Collins, *Medieval Herbals: The Illustrative Tradition* (London 2000). Albert Dietrich, "Islamic Sciences and the Medieval West: Pharmacology," in *Islam and the Medieval West: Aspects of Intercultural Relations,* ed. Khalil I. Semaan (Albany 1980) 50–63. Galen, *Galen on Pharmacology: Philosophy, History and Medicine,* ed. Armelle Debru (New York 1997). Vivian Nutton, *Ancient Medicine* (London 2004).

T.H.-T.

Philhellenism

The terms *Hellenism* and *philhellenism* have been used by some authors almost interchangeably. *The Oxford English Dictionary,* however, carefully distinguishes the two. Hellenism is defined as an ardent admiration for the cultural and intellectual tradition of the ancient Greeks. Philhellenism, on the other hand, is said to be a devotion to the political cause of the Greeks, especially during the Greek War of Independence (1821–1828). Confusion of the two terms results from the fact that philhellenes' devotion to Greek freedom stemmed, in most cases, from the same ardent admiration of ancient Greece that inspired Hellenists. The difference is that Hellenists tended to see the Greek tradition as a path to personal salvation by pursuing, or withdrawing, into contemplative musing about its storied past. Philhellenes sought a more millenarian solution to contemporary malaise; they wanted a physical revival of the ancient Greeks as a spur to the formation of a whole new world. Although the immediate goal of philhellenism in the late 18th and early 19th centuries was to free Greeks from oppression, the ultimate purpose was for the revived Greeks to lead the world to new political and aesthetic achievements. The independence of modern Greece was never an end in itself but rather a prelude to the regeneration of "Greece," an artistic, spiritual, and political ideal. Philhellenism, then, was always something more than a chapter in the story of 19th-century nationalism.

Several factors contributed to the idea that the freedom of the Greeks would lead to a rebirth of Greek culture. One was the notion that ancient Greece, and specifically 5th-century Athens, embodied the pinnacle of human artistic and cultural achievement, an idea shared by both Hellenists and philhellenes that was largely founded on the work of the art historian Johann Joachim Winckelmann (1717–1768). Another was that the increase of travelers to Greece during this period, and their drawings and descriptions of the ancient monuments, put Greece on the map of Europe with new prominence. Also significantly influential were Enlightenment ideas about how landscape and climate influenced populations. Greece, it was thought, physically had changed little from ancient times. By this logic, Greece could still produce "Greeks" if the one crucial missing element was supplied. As Sydney Owenson (Lady Morgan) put it in her novel *Woman; or, Ida of Athens* (1809), the contemporary Greeks "are only debased because they are no longer free." If that deficiency were corrected, a new Greek miracle could occur.

Because of the link between the ancient Greeks and liberty, philhellenism was more subversive politically and intellectually than Hellenism. For example, many of those who spoke fondly of a rebirth of the Greeks hoped that it would bring an end to the burdensome strictures of Christian morality. Percy Bysshe Shelley lamented: "O, but for that series of wretched wars which terminated in the Roman conquest of the world; but for the Christian religion, which put a finishing stroke on the ancient system; but for those changes that conducted Athens to its ruin, to what an eminence might not humanity have arrived!" (Shelley to T. L. Peacock, 26 January 1819).

Although the idea of Greek freedom captured the imagination of many Europeans, particularly writers and intellectuals, it also posed a challenge to the existing governments of Europe, most of whom were unenthusiastic about the prospect of Greek freedom and offered the movement no official support. In his preface to his verse play *Hellas* (1822) Shelley remarked of European monarchs: "Well do these destroyers of mankind know their enemy, when they impute the insurrection of Greece to the same spirit before which they tremble throughout the rest of Europe, and that enemy well knows the power and cunning of its opponents, and watches the moment of their approaching weakness and inevitable division to wrest the bloody scepters from their grasp." From an intra-European perspective, philhellenism appeared to some as revolutionary and subversive despite the foundation of philhellenic ideology in the idea of the superiority of the European culture transmitted from ancient Greece. Philhellenism, like Hellenism, celebrated the ancient Greeks partly because they were ancestors of a great European past, one that was viewed as culturally superior to the Muslim and Asian traditions. It is interesting to note that the idea of the regeneration of Greece arose ca. 1771, the date that Raymond Schwab (*La renaissance orientale,* 1950) uses for the Oriental Renaissance, a movement that looked to the texts and beliefs from India, China, and other parts of Asia as an inspiration for Western culture. Philhellenism and Hellenism can be viewed as countervailing developments that found cultural inspiration in a return to Western roots, not Eastern influences.

Philhellenism was an important literary and cultural phenomenon from 1770 into the 19th century, whose influence can be seen in the literature of every major European language: examples include Friedrich Hölderlin's novel *Hyperion* (1799), Voltaire's "Ode Pindarique à propos de la guerre présente en Grèce" (1768), and Thomas Hope's *Anastasius* (1819). The greatest influence came from the writings of Lord Byron, who first traveled in Greece from 1809 until 1811. In the years after his return to England, he published the second canto of *Childe Harold's Pilgrimage* and his Turkish Tales ("The Giaour," "The Corsair," "The Bride of Abydos," and "The Siege of Corinth"), which became enormously popular in England, continental Europe, and America. Byron did not create philhellenism, but his writings created far more philhellenes than anything else did. Indeed, when Victor Hugo addressed ancient and modern Greece together he called them "Grèces de Byron et d'Homère." Byron's stirring verse provided a canonical text, almost a scripture, which voiced the hope for Greek regeneration. Every philhellene in Europe or America was able to quote the more famous lines, such as

> Fair Greece! sad relic of departed worth!
> Immortal, though no more! though fallen, great!
> Who now shall lead the scatter'd children forth,
> And long accustom'd bondage uncreate?
> (*Childe Harold's Pilgrimage,* 2)

and

> The mountains look on Marathon—
> And Marathon looks on the sea;
> And musing there an hour alone,
> I dreamed that Greece might still be free.
> (*Don Juan,* 3.94)

Byron himself voiced doubts about the prospects of Greek regeneration, especially in a note to *Childe Harold* 2 and in some of his letters, yet in 1823 he decided to enlist actively in the fight for Greek freedom. He also recognized that many of those who went to fight for Greek freedom when the Greek War of Independence began in 1821 did so because they were inspired by his verse. More than 1,000 philhellenes participated in the Greek War of Independence, and estimates are that one-third died of wounds or disease. The remainder returned home disillusioned by the gap between their idealistic notions of the Greeks and the reality they encountered. Yet the dream "that Greece might still be free" survived their reports about conditions in Greece.

Byron's death from fever in 1824 in the Greek town of Missolonghi marks the high point of philhellenic feeling. The philhellene and historian George Finlay (1799–1875) aptly noted that the enthusiasm aroused by the news of the poet's death "perhaps served Greece more than his personal exertions would have done." The connection to Byron kept philhellenism alive as a symbolic force long after the conditions that had led to its appearance had disappeared. For much of the 19th century the cause of the Greeks remained, as one author put it, "a bastard sister of Liberty" and was a test of a person's radical or liberal credentials.

Finlay, reflecting in his history on his personal contact with philhellenes during the Greek War of Independence, noted: "The interference of foreigners in the affairs of Greece was generally unfortunate, often injudicious, and sometimes dishonest" (*A History of Greece* 4.3). Philhellenism was indeed guilty on all these counts, because it sought to impose on the Greek people foreign ideas about the Greek past. What most Greeks acknowledge, and what Finlay has left out, is that philhellenism aided the country in its initial struggle for independence and in subsequent conflicts with the Ottomans aimed at extending Greece's national boundaries.

The renewed interest in the Hellenic past in Western Europe, coupled with the increase of European travelers to Greece in the late 18th century, encouraged Greek intellectuals of the era to refer to themselves as Hellenes and to embrace a connection with ancient Greek heritage as a means of fostering a national identity. One of the most prominent leaders of this movement was Adamantios Korais (1748–1833), a native of Smyrna who lived most of his adult life in Paris. Korais, a classical scholar in his own right, believed that education was the key to a national revival and in 1805 began the publication of a Greek Library, texts of ancient Greek authors in a version of Greek called *katharevousa* or "purified," which included some of the grammatical structure and vocabulary of ancient Greek but was still accessible to those who knew the contemporary (demotic) language. Korais promoted *katharevousa* as a means of returning Greeks to their roots but, influenced by the Enlightenment, deliberately chose to avoid the clerical language of the Orthodox Church. By this effort he bequeathed to the Greek nation the "language question," whether Greeks should write, and be taught, his purified version of Greek or the Greek that they spoke every day. The controversy continued for nearly two centuries until in 1976 demotic Greek officially became the language of culture as well as the people.

The effects of employing the classical Greek past in the formation of the modern country is ubiquitous throughout Greece today in such things as architecture, names (for example, Kerkyra for Corfu), and street signs. This revival certainly contributed to but was not solely responsible for the patriotic Great Idea to expand the Greek state to incorporate all regions where Greeks were numerous. The main goal of the Great Idea was to recover the city of Constantinople, which had religious rather than classical significance. But the idealized Greek past that the Greeks borrowed from Europe certainly complicated the country's negotiation of its place in the Balkans, the Eastern Mediterranean, and Europe.

BIBL.: Nina Athanassoglou-Kallmyer, *French Images from the Greek War of Independence (1821–1830)* (New Haven 1989). Loukia Droulia, *Philhellénisme: Ouvrages inspirés par la guerre de l'indépendance grecque, 1821–1833: Répertoire bibliographique* (Athens 1974). Regine Quack-Eustathiades, *Der Deutsche Philhellenismus des griechischen Freiheitskampf, 1821–1827* (Munich 1984). David Roessel, *In Byron's Shadow: Modern Greece in the English and American Imagination* (New York 2001). William St. Clair, *That Greece Might Still Be Free: The Philhellenes in the Greek War of Independence* (Oxford 1972). C. M. Woodhouse, *The Philhellenes* (London 1969).

D.RO.

Philo

The most important representative of the Greek-speaking Jewish community that flourished in Alexandria from about 200 BCE until the devastating Jewish revolt of 115–117 CE. Born in 15 BCE into a wealthy and distinguished Alexandrian family, even during his lifetime Philo gained a high reputation for learning and wisdom, as witnessed by Josephus, who tells us that Philo was "held in the highest honor" in the Jewish community and was "not unskilled in philosophy" (*Antiquities* 18.259). He died in 50 CE.

Philo wrote at least 75 treatises, of which about 50 are still extant, making him one of the more prolific writers from the ancient world to survive. Most of these engage in exposition of Mosaic law, that is, the first five books of the Bible in the Greek translation of the Septuagint. Their most distinctive feature is the extensive use of allegorical interpretation, which allows him to employ Greek philosophical doctrines in explaining Scripture. He also wrote a number of works on contemporary Jewish life in Alexandria, including *On the Contemplative Life,* which gives a famous description of the Therapeutae, a group of ascetic men and women living in a community outside the city. (Eusebius in his *Church History,* ca. 325, erroneously identified them with early Christian converts in Alexandria, and they figure prominently in later accounts of the origins of Egyptian monasticism.) There are also five treatises discussing Greek philosophical topics.

Judaism as it developed after Philo's death either ignored or rejected his legacy, presumably because it was too Hellenized. He is never named by the Rabbis; Maimonides, who would surely have been intrigued by his thought, never knew of his existence. He was rediscovered for Judaism by the Italian Jew Azariah de' Rossi, who discusses him critically in *The Light of the Eyes* (1573). Even today Philo is not part of mainstream Judaism, although since the 19th century many Jewish scholars have contributed to the scholarly investigation of his writings and thought.

Philo's writings survived because they were preserved by the early Christian church. The first Christian writer to mention him is Clement of Alexandria (d. ca. 215), who quotes extensively from his writing almost to the point of plagiarism. It is likely that his works were preserved in the Alexandrian catechetical school headed by Clement's teacher Pantaenus. Origen took copies to Caesarea when he moved there from Alexandria in 233. The manuscript tradition of Philo's works derives from their presence in the episcopal library of Caesarea, where they were transferred to parchment codices by Bishop Euzoius (376–379) (Jerome, *On Illustrious Men* 113). In the 4th century Didymus the Blind continued the Alexandrian tradition, and in the West, Ambrose and Augustine made good use of his writings in their interpretations of the Old Testament. After the 4th century his influence waned, partly because his thought was seen as having affinity to heretical doctrines, partly because by then many of his ideas had been absorbed into the Christian tradition.

In the 6th century a slavishly literal Armenian translation was made of a substantial number of his writings, many of which were subsequently lost in the Greek original; thus, modern scholarship can gain access to them only through the Armenian. A notice is devoted to Philo in the Suda (10th cent.), and he is mentioned by Byzantine authors such as Psellus (11th cent.) and Theodore Metochites (d. 1332). In the West during the Middle Ages he was for a considerable time known only through the *Liber Philonis,* an inferior Latin translation of two of his works, and through the erroneous idea, reported by Jerome, that Philo was the author of the Wisdom of Solomon and thus prophesied the death of Christ.

His original Greek writings were rediscovered in the 16th century and first published in the *editio princeps* of Adrian Turnebus (Paris 1553). They were soon translated into Latin, and Philo's doctrines became a talking point in the theological controversies of the 17th century. Modern Philonic scholarship commences with the dissertation of J. A. Fabricius and the notice in his famous *Bibliotheca Graeca* (1705–1728). Since then more than 5,000 books and articles have been devoted to Philo's writings and thought. Evidence in his writings has proved invaluable for a number of disciplines, including classics, ancient history, ancient philosophy, Jewish studies, and New Testament and patristic studies.

BIBL.: A. Kamesar, *The Cambridge Companion to Philo* (Cambridge 2009). Philo, complete writings in 10 volumes and 2 supplements, ed. and trans. F. H. Colson, G. H. Whitaker, and R. Marcus, Loeb Classical Library (Cambridge, Mass., 1929–1962), and *Philo of Alexandria: The Contemplative Life; The Giants; and, Selections,* trans. D. Winston, Classics of Western Spirituality (New York 1981). D. T. Runia, *Philo in Early Christian Literature* (Assen 1993). Annotated bibliographies appear annually in *The Studia Philonica Annual,* where references to earlier bibliographies can be found. D.T.R.

Philosophy

The last of the great Neoplatonic philosophers who wrote in Greek was Proclus Diadochus. The word Diadochus, "Successor"—a title, not a proper name—signifies that Proclus, as head of an Athenian philosophical school in the 5th century CE, belonged to a sometimes interrupted line that reached back eight centuries to Plato and his Academy. More than three centuries before Proclus died, the Roman emperor Marcus Aurelius, a philosopher himself, had founded chairs in Athens for Platonic, Aristotelian, Stoic, and Epicurean philosophy, calling their occupants Successors and thus institutionalizing an even earlier Hellenistic conception: that the cultural present inherits an authoritative past that is to be imitated, emulated, or perhaps contested and even repudiated. A rhythm both mimetic and antiphonal—conjectures inspire refutations; theses elicit antitheses; from the weary paradigm the revolution erupts—is a still older feature of philosophy as a classical tradition.

By the 2nd century CE, Latin critics were using the word *classicus* to praise literary authorities deemed worthy of imitation, linking merit not just with class but also with the bare fact of antiquity: words worth repeating will have been said by "one of that band of ancients, . . . a well-endowed writer of the highest class and no mere commoner." When we think of philosophy as *classical,* then, as a Graeco-Roman heritage, we employ a notion that itself has classical roots, roots that grew deeper for millennia until Descartes cut them off and tried to kill the tree in order to grow a better one.

The classical philosophy renounced by Descartes insisted on more distinctions than age and class, however: most particularly language and ethnicity, and gender as well. And yet the Greeks themselves were ambivalent on the former point. By the time there were enough philosophical views to be compiled in doxographies, the main entries were about Greek texts written by Greeks. But before Diogenes Laertius assures us that philosophy arose "from the Hellenes, and that the very word resists being turned into a barbarian name," the first sages he mentions are Persians, Babylonians, Assyrians, Indians, Celts, Gauls, Phoenicians, Thracians, Libyans, and Egyptians (*Lives and Opinions of Eminent Philosophers* 1.1, ca. 3rd cent. CE). After all, Plato himself had cited the Hyperborean Abaris, the Egyptian Theuth, and the Thracians Zalmoxis and Orpheus, though sometimes only to disagree with them.

Philosophy is not and never was anyone's ethnic property, of course, inasmuch as the core philosophical questions about reality, reason, and value are universal and perennial. And yet a distinctive way of posing such questions and seeking answers to them arose in ancient Greece and persists today as a characteristic feature of Western culture. When eminent philosophers say that "Plato invented the subject of philosophy as we know it" or that philosophy is "a series of footnotes to Plato," this is usually what they mean. But the inventing started before Plato, and speakers of Greek continued it, in varied forms, for a thousand years and more after his time.

In the Roman imperial period and after, intellectuals with assumptions, values, and methods quite unlike those of the ancient Greeks and their successors in republican Rome were still trying to solve the old metaphysical and moral puzzles, which required them to come to terms with a philosophical tradition that had already become classical. When Tertullian—inviting the negative—asked, "What has Athens to do with Jerusalem?" (*The Prescription against Heretics* 7), he was thinking of the Greek city as the site of philosophical schools and of Jerusalem as God's own real estate. From his early Christian point of view, the secular pursuit of philosophy not only profaned the sacred; it also missed the point epistemically. In the light of faith, the outrages in the Gospel stories that scandalized the heathens confirmed the Gospel for Tertullian. Why would God—or even a god—put on corruptible human flesh, die the death of a criminal, and then rise again? Because the very thought is shameful, Tertullian is not ashamed to think it; because it is absurd, he believes it; he is certain *because* it is impossible. This conception of faith, and the strange treatment of the word *because,* takes Christianity to its limits as a repudiation of philosophy—of principled deliberation, grounded in evidence, guided by reason, and always open to questions.

Tertullian, obviously not timid about paradoxes, was himself actually sensitive to philosophical issues and helped adapt the Latin philosophical vocabulary to Christian theology. Many early Christians were even better-schooled in philosophy, which some of them attacked not reflexively but because they were well informed: Justin Martyr, Irenaeus, and Lactantius stand out among Latin writers; Athanasius of Alexandria, Basil of Caesarea, Clement of Alexandria, Eusebius, Gregory Nazianzen, and Gregory of Nyssa among the Greeks. Origen, with whom this first age of Christian philosophizing reached its peak in the East, died around 254 CE, a full century before Augustine was born to write his timeless Latin works in Italy and North Africa.

Augustine, though he stayed within the confines of a strict Christian faith, is still read as one of the greatest of all philosophers for magnificent achievements in metaphysics, moral philosophy, and philosophical psychology. The *Confessions,* his autobiography, is in no small part a philosopher's story, the biography of a Christian who found faith after searching "the books of the Platonists" in vain for it. The Platonic succession, thinned or broken several times since the original Academy, had been restarted by Plotinus, a Hellenized Egyptian who taught in Rome; he was Origen's contemporary and the first of the Neoplatonists. The immense labor of Latinizing all of Plato and all of Aristotle was eventually undertaken by Boethius, who was executed around 524, a century after Augustine's death. He is sometimes regarded as the last ancient Roman writer of Latin, but his grand project failed. The outcome of his death sentence was *The Consolation of Philosophy.*

Most of the other works by Boethius that Christians read in the medieval West were the technical treatises, commentaries, and translations that grew out of his work on Aristotle's logic and on the enormously influential *Introduction* (*Isagoge,* ca. 270) to philosophy by Porphyry, a Syrian student of Plotinus. After the Roman Empire fell and its civilization collapsed, these writings by Boethius—the Old Logic—and the much larger body of Augustine's books were the core philosophical texts of an impoverished, depopulated, and uneducated Europe. Rome's disintegration hurt the West more than the East, where a richer philosophical curriculum soon stabilized and continued in more or less that state until the Turks took Constantinople in 1453.

First formally organized in the late 2nd century CE, this Greek curriculum began with Aristotle on logic, ethics, and metaphysics, and also Euclid's mathematics, before moving on to Plato in an ascent through selected dialogues to the *Parmenides.* Though some of the bones of this *paideia* were Aristotelian, its soul was Neoplatonic, the term customarily used to describe Plotinus, Porphyry, Iamblichus, Proclus, and lesser figures of that tradition. The Neoplatonists not only respected Aristotle—and the Stoics, with their zeal for coherence—they also hoped to harmonize his thought with Plato's. Although Aristotle's works had not recently been read much, even by his followers, the project of harmonization was made plausible by a new edition of the texts begun in the 1st century BCE by Andronicus of Rhodes. We should therefore think of the Neoplatonists, Plotinus and Porphyry especially, as contributors to another tradition that was not really separate, the long line of Greek Commentators, meaning commentators on Aristotle, even though most of them were Platonists. The most important commentators—Alexander of Aphrodisias, Themistius, Ammonius, Philoponus, and Simplicius—taught from the beginning of the 3rd century through the end of the 6th in Athens, Alexandria, Constantinople, and perhaps Harran, though others were still teaching in Byzantium in the 12th century.

Harran (Roman Carrhae) was where the Emperor Julian had stopped in 363 to sacrifice to the Moon before a Persian army killed him. Julian, a pagan recidivist whom Christians called the Apostate, had studied philosophy with Maximus of Ephesus, a Neoplatonist theurge. But the Byzantine Empire was soon so thoroughly Christianized that it took no courage for a later emperor, Justinian, to close the Athenian school in 529. Philosophy's pagan heritage had become heavy baggage. Hypatia, a woman who taught philosophy, mathematics, and astronomy brilliantly in Alexandria, was lynched as a pagan witch by a Christian mob in 415. Philosophical teaching continued there, however, until the city fell to the Muslims in 640, just eight years after the death of the Prophet Muhammad. From that time onward the only future for classical philosophy was in a world that despised the gods of Plato and Socrates.

Once the Latin West was also converted, no more cocks were owed to Asclepius (the dying Socrates' famous pledge to the god of healing), and in Europe prayers were offered lawfully only to the God of Christians and of the few Jews settled there in that era. The most efficient engines of prayer were monks who abandoned the world, the flesh, and the pagan devil-gods, especially monks who lived communally and not as hermits. Justinian may have shut down the school in Athens in the very year when Benedict of Nursia led his friends out of the solitary life to a new community of prayer in Monte Cassino, some 80 miles southeast of Rome. Prayer is the work of monks, and he gave them a "rule"—now known as the *Rule of Saint Benedict*—to regulate it, prescribing not only the observation of liturgical hours by day and night but also the "divine reading" of sacred books. Because monks had to have books, and because there were few places left to buy them, the scriptorium or writing-room became a fixture of monastic architecture.

The *Instructions,* a compendium and bibliography of what monks ought to read and therefore copy, was composed by Cassiodorus, a relative of Boethius', in the middle of the 6th century. His book is a manual of Christian education in the new institutional framework of monasticism, but Cassiodorus was a learned man who salted his new curriculum with bits of the old classical *paideia,* suitably sanitized. Of this fragile remnant, the largest philosophical part was rudimentary Aristotelian logic. But many books on many subjects, not just missals and hymnals, were eventually copied by the diligent and (sometimes) meticulous monks to whom we owe the survival of Latin literature, including the philosophical kind.

All that monastic labor notwithstanding, until the 13th century Western Christians had little direct knowledge of classical philosophy, even in translation: not much Aristotle, less Plato, and nothing Stoic, Epicurean, or Skeptical except what Cicero, Seneca, the Church Fathers, and a few others had passed on indirectly—to Abelard (12th cent.), for example, who made creative use of Stoic ideas. The available Aristotelian material was only what was translated or interpreted in the Old Logic. Of Plato there was only part of the *Timaeus,* though in two different translations. When the *Meno* and *Phaedo* were Latinized in the 12th century, almost no one read them, despite growing interest in the *Timaeus.*

As classical philosophy withered away in the Latin West, it found fresh voices in the East in tongues once called barbarian. Even before the Greek schools closed, translators were putting Aristotle into Syriac, but much more extensive and lasting in their influence were the many Arabic translations of Greek works—and not just philosophy—that followed the swift and stunning victories of militant Islam. For two centuries after 750, the Abbasid caliphate of Baghdad financed a mammoth project of translation that took advantage of the many Greek texts acquired over the centuries by scholars in Alexandria and other conquered cities of the East.

In the early 9th century, at the height of the Abbasid project, the most powerful philosophical mind behind it was al-Kindī's. His most enduring work was not translation, however; still felt today are the effects of his fateful ideological accommodation between Islam and Greek philosophy—fateful because of the pattern that it set not only for Muslims but also for Jews and Christians. If a Muslim sage could untie such knots as Aristotle's perplexing view of the eternity of the world, and still leave an Aristotle fit for the godly, then surely others could do likewise for other faiths. In fact, Jews who lived in the Muslim world and wrote in Arabic, like Isaac Israeli and Saadia Gaon in the 9th and 10th centuries, would soon adapt al-Kindī's strategy to the needs of Judaism.

The achievements of these philosophical Jews and Muslims are far more impressive than the meager products of Christendom at that time. Even with a seat in Charlemagne's court at the opening of the 9th century, Alcuin could do little more than secure a place for rudimentary logic in Christian schools. The most original Latin writer of the period, John Scotus Eriugena, had channels to Byzantium as well as the patronage of Charles the Bald. But even if Eriugena had heard of the Muslim thinkers who paved the way for al-Fārābī, he could never have equaled them with the material and cultural resources available to him.

Although al-Fārābī got his start in the Baghdad project of the late 9th century, he distanced himself from al-Kindī in order to make his own mark, and he made it quite convincingly by creating an Arabic terminology for logic. Even bigger and bolder was his conviction that philosophy is not just a catechetical tool. He taught that philosophy by itself shows a way to happiness, even Islamic beatitude, through a Neoplatonized Aristotelian cosmology and psychology in which logic itself becomes a rigorous path of ascent to a divine Active Intellect, an entity that al-Fārābī derived from Aristotle's treatise *On the Soul* as read by the Greek Commentators.

In 980, a generation after al-Fārābī died, Avicenna, the greatest philosopher to write in Arabic, was born at the eastern edge of the Muslim lands. His ambitions were encyclopedic and centered on Aristotelian philosophy, though he was expert in Neoplatonism and also one of the great Muslim physicians. He claimed to have read Aristotle's *Metaphysics* 40 times before understanding it, and only then after having read al-Fārābī. Then he set out to surpass both the philosopher and his interpreter with new and interlocking theories of prophecy, the immortal soul, and the soul's dependence on the Agent Intellect for genuine intellectual thought.

As in the past, Avicenna's contemporaries in the West were not his philosophical peers, though Gerbert of Aurillac and Abbo of Fleury kept up the debate about logic, and Peter Damian later had some original thoughts about it. Eventually, however, Anselm and others created in the 11th and 12th centuries a new tradition of formal debate about theology. Though Anselm himself paid strikingly little attention to ancient authorities, pagan or Christian, the normal method of the time was to compile authoritative statements, locate conflicts, and use the tools of logic to resolve them.

Gradually Abelard and others created forms of instruction founded on those tools, and it was in this context that the study of ancient philosophy revived, in a new form, in the Latin West. In principle, the "arts" that undergraduates in the schools of the era studied were all the ancient liberal arts but in practice the requirements were mainly philosophical. For some students the arts course was preliminary to advanced study in theology, law, or medicine, where philosophy might also be involved. In the schools that eventually coalesced into universities, medieval Christians created an institutional vehicle for philosophy and other disciplines that turned out to be more robust than anything known in antiquity. The medieval university, modernized or even postcontemporary, has been going strong ever since, for more than eight centuries, and for half that time it was thoroughly Aristotelian. Almost all primary texts read in the arts faculties of medieval universities in northern Europe were from the Aristotelian corpus, and most of the corpus was studied by arts masters.

Later, in the 14th century, when this revived classical philosophy provoked a different kind of classicism, the challenge from Petrarch and other Humanists was not a reaction from within the universities. Aristotelian Scholasticism continued to rule those institutions as they matured into the 17th century, when Galileo and Descartes detached their new science and philosophy not just from Aristotle but from authority as such. Mimesis and tradition, built into European culture from the start, yielded to inventiveness, creativity, autonomy, and free critical judgment. The bitterest philosophical opponents of these new attitudes in Descartes, Galileo, and their followers were university Aristotelians.

The cultural and linguistic roots of Aristotelianism in the universities were not just Greek and Latin, however, but also Hebrew and Arabic. During Anselm's lifetime, in fact, the last great wave of wisdom to pour over the West from Muslim and Jewish philosophy was building strength. Al-Ghazālī, who died in 1111, was born in Persia but taught in Baghdad, intent on crushing the threat to Islamic orthodoxy that he saw in Avicenna's Aristotelianism. Accordingly, he called his great book *The Incoherence of the Philosophers.* In the same period or shortly afterward, the Iberian Peninsula far to the west was remarkably hospitable to philosophy, to Jews, like Solomon ibn Gabirol and Judah Halevi, and to Muslims as well, such as Ibn Bajja and Ibn Tufayl.

Two towering figures of this period were born in Cordoba, Averroës in 1128 and Moses ben Maimon in 1135. Both were Aristotelians who wrote in Arabic, and both lived to see the turn of the new century, or almost. Gentiles came to know Maimonides not for his authoritative rabbinical and legal works but for his *Guide for the Perplexed,* which applies Aristotelian philosophy to puzzles of faith and Scripture. Averroës, whose talents were also manifold, came to be called the Commentator (as Aristotle was the Philosopher) for his explications of essentially the whole Aristotelian corpus in short and mid-size commentaries, and of five of Aristotle's works in exceedingly detailed and precise long commentaries. Largely ignored by Muslims, Averroës is second only to Aristotle in his influence on later medieval Christian philosophy.

Because Averroës and Maimonides lived until the end of the 12th century and beyond, Latin versions of their works became available only later, though not much later in the case of Averroës. Michael Scot and others were soon at work on his commentaries in the third phase of a long era of philosophical translation that had begun around 1130 in Constantinople, Toledo, Sicily, and other places where students of Latin could make contact with Greek, Arabic, and Hebrew. The job was done, as much as it would be, when William of Moerbeke died in 1286. He was a Dominican from Flanders who collaborated on projects of translation with Thomas Aquinas and other scholars. After 1260 he either translated or revised all the Aristotle then available, except the logic, as well as texts by Greek Commentators and some Proclus (including lemmata from the *Parmenides*).

The main effect of the new translations from Arabic, Hebrew, and Greek came after 1200, and it was stunning. Aristotle's nonlogical works—nearly nine-tenths of the corpus—flooded the new universities with treatises designed to be taught and conceived as parts of a grand system. In these circumstances, especially as little had been added to the Plato or the secondhand Stoicism long known to medieval readers, it is no surprise that the university became a near monopoly for the Christian Aristotelians who adapted the Stagirite's thought to their faith and made it compatible with the Neoplatonism transmitted by Augustine and a few others. Although Henricus Aristippus, who worked in Sicily and traveled to Constantinople, translated Plato's *Meno* and *Phaedo* in the mid-12th century, hardly anyone read them, or the Latin translation of Sextus Empiricus that appeared more than 100 years later. There was plenty of Averroës and Avicenna in Latin, however, and a good many of the other Muslim and Jewish philosophers could be read. Not much Proclus made it into Latin, no Plotinus, and little of the Greek Commentators. Access to the Hellenistic schools remained as it had been, coming only at second hand through Cicero, Seneca, the Fathers, and a few other authorities.

Whatever the calendar says, 1200 was surely a millennial year for philosophy. Until then, the only Aristotle in the schools was logic. Afterward, as Aristotle's nonlogical works competed with logic for curricular space, his many treatises on natural philosophy and science proved especially attractive. But as temptations to naturalism they were also risky. In 1210 the *Notebooks* of David of Dinant were burned in Paris as a danger to the faith, an early warning of controversies about Aristotle and his commentators, Averroës especially, that would go on for centuries, until the post-Cartesian age in which Aristotle was no longer the Philosopher and hence no longer a threat.

For some Christians philosophy had always been a cause of religious anxiety. The earliest regional and ecumenical assemblies of institutionalized Christendom were Church Councils that condemned theological positions of philosophical interest. Philosophers themselves became victims. Abelard was twice declared a heretic, once by the pope himself. After David of Dinant's troubles in 1210, the authorities were still worried enough to order an expurgation of Aristotelian texts in 1231. And yet within a quarter century the Paris arts curriculum was thoroughly Aristotelian. In the broadest sense, the fight was over and Aristotle had taken charge, even though some of his positions remained contentious and some of his expositors found themselves in deep trouble.

The first of the great Aristotelian Scholastics were William of Auvergne, Robert Grosseteste, and Roger Bacon, then Albert the Great, Bonaventure, and Thomas Aquinas. Thomas's commitment to Aristotle was particularly strong, leading him to write many commentaries not strictly required by his teaching. In that way he and his colleagues authenticated Aristotle for other Christians, endowing the ancient pagan sage with authority not just in philosophy but also in rational or philosophical theology. Once Aristotle gained this theological purchase, especially given the systematic character of his thought, the study of theology in the universities, along with the great prestige of that field, had the effect of confirming the Aristotelian system as a whole. The cycle was hard to break, and only Descartes and Galileo were able to break it.

But there was always plenty of controversy. The arts masters, for example, lacking formal obligations to theology, were open to naturalist readings of Aristotle that some of them discovered with the help of Averroës, who contradicted key tenets of faith on the immortality of the individual soul and the creation of the world. In 1270, when Thomas wrote against the Averroist view of the soul and intellect, the bishop of Paris also condemned several propositions of a leading arts master, Siger of Brabant. In 1277 another condemnation by the same bishop included 219 propositions in a broad indictment of naturalism and the whole project of Aristotelian philosophy, seen as an overweening intrusion into theology.

Scholasticism is the broader and commoner word for the way that medieval thinkers philosophized, though the term is not entirely accurate, as some medieval philosophers were not Scholastics; some medieval Scholastics were not philosophers; and many Scholastic philosophers were not (and are not) medieval. Although modern experts on medieval philosophy have defined Scholasticism as obligated, in part, to ancient pagan authorities—mainly, but not only, Aristotle—the Scholastic method became so distinctively unclassical, especially in its spoken and written language, that Humanist critics in the Renaissance would condemn it not just as a violation of classical linguistic norms but also as a cause of cultural decadence. Humanists who saw the *aetas media,* the middle age, as a chasm between themselves and the ancient sages were seldom disposed, or equipped by education, actually to read the new philosophical Latin, especially in its logical uses, which they condemned as barbaric.

Yet ancient texts and forms of argument continued to play a prominent role in Scholastic thought, and often an unpredictable one. Thomas Bradwardine, who became archbishop of Canterbury, was also the best—or in some quarters the most notorious—of the Oxford philosophers called Calculators because of their efforts to connect philosophy with mathematics, an unusual move for Aristotelians. Bradwardine also studied divine foreknowledge as a constraint on human freedom until his own was ended by the plague in 1349. The same dread disease killed Robert Holkot, a Dominican with an unusually broad conception of classical authority; he and Nicholas Trivet, also a Dominican and a commentator on Seneca, have been termed "classicizing friars." Holkot thought that the wisest of the pagans had access to a special channel of sacred wisdom outside the Mosaic and Christian revelations—in effect, an ancient theology of the kind that Marsilio Ficino would lodge in the Platonic tradition. In the most general sense Holkot's notion was unusual but not unique among medieval philosophers. Abelard had found evidence for the Trinity in the ancients, whom he therefore treated as all but Christian, thus elevating the status of philosophy.

The language used for teaching and writing by all the Scholastics was an aggressively unclassical Latin, meant to serve a philosophy and theology much unlike what the ancients taught. That this Latin developed its own vocabulary and its own manner was inevitable, especially in the environment of the emerging vernaculars. In fact, philosophy had always needed a discourse and a terminology of its own. Plato was exceptional in his mastery of the literary Greek that he helped create. Closer to the philosophical norm was Aristotle's Greek, plain at best, often terse to the point of obscurity, and not shy of lexical and syntactic novelties. In Latin the pattern is similar. Cicero, even though he occasionally neologized in philosophy, was a great stylist but not a great philosopher. Boethius wrote more stylish Latin in the *Consolation of Philosophy* than in his dense technical works.

By the time the New Logic was being read, effects of the Aristotelian ideal of scientific knowledge began to be felt. Scientific conclusions, including those about language, had to be necessary and universal propositions derived deductively from first principles. But the best account of Latin available to medieval grammarians was the descriptive grammar of Priscian, whose empirically derived rules spoke only for contingencies of that one natural language, which in its classical form had died. The solution was a speculative grammar for language in general, but no one invented a formalism that could detach it from Latin, which as a consequence served awkwardly as its own metalanguage.

Where the grammarians entered, logicians did not fear to tread. To take just one example: they devised *sophismata,* problem-sentences deliberately contrived to display difficulties of logical interest—ambiguity, for instance. But the language in which such sophisms were constructed was the same Latin used for all learned communication, much to the dismay of Petrarch, Lorenzo Valla, and a long line of Humanist critics. The Humanists worked hard at correcting the Latin that they saw as having been corrupted once there were no ancient Romans left to speak it. They took their norms not from abstract logic but from the concrete (and now always written) evidence of ancient usage.

Much of their criticism was cultural, literary, or even belletristic and thus of no great interest to philosophers, whatever its value for other learned people. Even before Petrarch and Boccaccio in the 14th century, students of poetry, rhetoric, grammar, and history had begun to see differences between their own Latinity and that of the ancients. The perception became a movement and a slogan—"back to the sources"—that expanded to include the founding documents of religion itself, both Greek and Hebrew. The grave sin against culture committed in the middle age—seen more and more as a disastrous and protracted interval between the ancient past and a present that recovered it—was to have lost the sources that had to be refound, including philosophical sources. Philosophy thus entered the ambit of Renaissance Humanism—a 19th-century label for the project of recovering antiquity that started before Petrarch and has never really stopped.

The first task was to make philosophy readable in a *Latin* culture—despite increased attention to Greek—whose newly reclassicized norms of Latinity were taken from Cicero, Livy, Virgil, Quintilian, and other eminent authors or *auctores,* the "authorities." Although an essentially complete Latin Aristotle (more than 80 different texts by two dozen translators) had been available since Moerbeke's time, Leonardo Bruni and others—tutored by Manuel Chrysoloras, an émigré from the Greek East—began to translate the whole Aristotelian corpus again into a more classical Latin around 1400, a long job by many hands that was finished, more or less, by the end of the century.

A very long line of Renaissance scholars (about 70) made many, many translations (about 250) of Aristotelian and pseudo-Aristotelian treatises, not only replacing the medieval versions but also creating demand for new commentaries and interpretations keyed to this immense and influential product of the new Humanist philology. But Humanist commentaries, sometimes only in manuscript, did not make all the medieval commentaries obsolete. Some medieval works (Albertus Magnus, Thomas Aquinas, Duns Scotus, and Giles of Rome were especially popular) were regularly printed for Renaissance philosophers to use, including the growing number who could now read Aristotle in Greek alongside his earlier interpreters. Commentaries themselves also became bilingual.

Philosophy, even Aristotelian philosophy, had been philologized, rebuilt on its ancient textual foundations. The indispensable basis of Aristotelian scholarship in the 16th century was the complete Greek text in five volumes that Aldus Manutius published in the closing years of the Quattrocento (1495–1498). Nine other complete Greek editions appeared in the new century—three times as many as Greek editions of Plato. The new Greek and Latin Aristotle also inspired a good many vernacular versions of individual works—though none of the refractory logic.

Although the original Aldine Aristotle included Greek works by Aristotle's student Theophrastus, an *Opera omnia* for Theophrastus had to wait until the bilingual edition (Greek and Latin) by Daniel Heinsius, which appeared in 1605, though his collection was preceded by many Latin translations of individual and partial treatises. In 1473 Ermolao Barbaro and others had begun to put the huge fund of Greek commentaries (the standard edition now fills 23 volumes) into print in Latin versions (sometimes from Hebrew) and Greek texts. Although Moerbeke's translation of Simplicius' commentary on Aristotle's *De caelo* was also printed, the far more momentous publication was the massive Giunta edition of Averroës printed 1562–1574, thus keeping the troublesome commentator in circulation.

Meanwhile, Bruni and the other translators who began the new Latin Aristotle had also started on Plato (and pseudo-Plato), finishing 10 of the genuine dialogues by 1435 before the next generation of scholars, including Francesco Filelfo from Milan and George of Trebizond from Crete, took over. But it was a Florentine, Marsilio Ficino, who would complete that massive task in 1484 with a complete Latin Plato of his own, a job that he had suspended for a few months to put most of the Greek Corpus Hermeticum into Latin in 1463. Aldus followed up Ficino's Latin Plato with the first complete Greek text, but not until 1513, 14 years after Ficino died.

The great Platonist had also translated Plotinus as well as various works by other Neoplatonists, including Porphyry's *Life of Plotinus,* Iamblichus' *On the Mysteries,* and Proclus' *On Sacrifice and Magic.* The first complete Plotinus in Greek appeared in 1580, long after the Greek Porphyry in the 1495 Aldine Aristotle. In fact, Porphyry was much better known than Plotinus—in a conventional Aristotelian context, because his *Introduction* was part of the Old Logic. For the same reason, at the close of the 16th century new Humanist versions of Porphyry had failed to drive the Latin of Boethius out of the market, and publishers still sold medieval commentaries by Scotus and Buridan.

Ficino saw the theology of pseudo-Dionysius, which was actually contemporary with Proclus (5th cent.) and not Saint Paul, as part of the Platonic tradition, which is why he translated and commented on two of the Dionysian works in the early 1490s. Doubts about their authenticity, posed since the early Middle Ages, did not prevent their being revered and therefore translated several times before the Renaissance. Although Valla and other Humanists had made their sharper criticisms known by the middle of the 15th century, Catholics attributed apostolic authority to Dionysius for two centuries more, and meanwhile other Latin versions by Ambrogio Traversari, Jacques Lefèvre d'Étaples, and Joachim Périon were also printed, alongside medieval versions and commentaries and one vernacular translation, in French.

Ficino translated a commentary by Proclus, on the *First*

Alcibiades, and partial Greek texts of Proclus' commentaries on the *Republic* and *Timaeus* were available by 1534. Moerbeke's old translation of the *Parmenides* commentary was still read, but not published, in the 16th century, even though Nicolaus Scutellius made a new Latin version in 1521. Nicholas of Cusa, who knew Moerbeke's Latin *Parmenides* commentary and his rendition of Proclus' *Elements of Theology*, brought a Greek manuscript of Proclus' immense *Platonic Theology* from Constantinople, which enabled Pietro Balbi to put it into Latin and supply his employer, the Greek Cardinal Bessarion, with material for his polemic *Against Plato's Calumniator* (1469), the cardinal's target being a fellow Hellene, the testy George of Trebizond. Greek editions of the *Platonic Theology* and the *Elements of Theology* appeared in 1618, but these difficult metaphysical works were much less popular than *On the Sphere*, a treatise that was falsely attributed to Proclus.

The long philological labor of recovering, editing, translating, and publishing the many other Greek texts that Humanists studied, even when their philosophical value was small, could still be philosophically productive; for example, when the shallow and unreliable *Lives of the Philosophers* by Diogenes Laertius was fully translated by Traversari around 1433, a large piece of Epicurean material was put into circulation and attracted attention to the ancient atomist philosophy that was all but unknown in the Middle Ages. Atomism might have been known sooner and better if Henricus Aristippus had been luckier with his 12th-century readership; like his Latin translations of Plato's *Meno* and *Phaedo*, however, his complete Diogenes fell stillborn from the scriptorium, producing only the condensation (probably not by Walter Burley) that was copied hundreds of times after 1326, printed in 11 incunabular editions and seven more times in the 16th century. There were also vernacular versions of this digest of philosophical doxography, which had many more readers than the *Lives of the Sophists* by Philostratus, the work of the same title by Eunapius, or the *Lives of the Learned* by Hesychius.

Like the *Lives* by Diogenes Laertius, the long didactic poem *On Nature* by Lucretius certainly had a previous life in medieval scriptoria before it was studied closely in the Renaissance. There was little real interest in it before 1417, however, when Poggio Bracciolini, one of the great book hunters of his day, found a manuscript. Forty years later, the young Ficino wrote notes on Lucretius, but atomism was still a scandal to Christians, and the author eventually burned them.

Epictetus, the Stoic slave exiled for philosophizing by the Emperor Domitian, could be read in Latin by 1450, long before the Stoic Emperor Marcus Aurelius, whose *Meditations* was not Latinized until 1570. Its Stoicism was late and derivative, in any case, like the Latin material preserved in works of Cicero and Seneca, both of them favorites of Renaissance readers and teachers. Classical Greek Stoicism had long been reduced to fragments, larger and smaller, but more and more of the pieces could now be put together from Plutarch, Galen, Dio Chrysostom, Diogenes, Sextus, and other Greek authors, including the much later Greek Commentators and Greek Fathers. The same tale about finding fragments and fitting them together can be told about the Presocratics, the Sophists, and the Cynics, whereas the non-Platonic Socrates was also visible in complete texts by famous contemporaries, Aristophanes and Xenophon. Because Plutarch (1st–2nd cent. CE) was both prolific and eclectic, his *Essays* (or *Moralia*) were especially rich in fragments, as were the two (or three) big books by Sextus. Thirty-two of Plutarch's *Essays* were translated between 1373 and 1500, a complete Greek text following in 1509 and a complete Latin translation in 1526. All the *Moralia* were published in English, French, and Spanish between 1548 and 1603.

Montaigne, the most important vernacular writer of his time—unless Shakespeare counts as a contemporary—read Plutarch and vastly improved the essay form as he found it in the *Moralia*. Like the dialogue, another classical genre, the essay became one of the characteristic vehicles of modern philosophy, loosening the constraints of medieval questions and propositions and turning contemplation inward upon itself. Like the medieval disputation, however, the dialogue required a number of voices and was thus less private than the essay. The essay came into its own with Bishop Berkeley as a neoclassical form, before David Hume used it not so much to clarify as to camouflage his skepticism about religion.

The ancient sources of Skepticism were available to Hume in the 18th century because Humanists had recovered and translated them in the Renaissance, enabling Montaigne in the 16th century to read Sextus Empiricus and transform his pedestrian Greek into the long and seductive *Apology for Raymond Sebond*, which, along with other expressions of doubt by Francisco Sanchez and Pierre Charron, transmitted Skepticism to the 17th century and to Descartes, who would make lastingly effective use of it.

Scholars had started to translate the works of Sextus in the 1480s, though Filelfo had already owned them in Greek by 1427. Henri II Estienne printed a Latin Sextus between 1562 and 1569, but there was no Greek edition until 1621. By that time the Skeptical tropes and questions had long been doing their corrosive work. Poliziano and both Picos had made use of Sextus, especially the younger Pico, Gianfrancesco, whose fideist Christianity embraced Skepticism as a prophylactic against rationalist philosophizing and its treacherous testing of Christian belief. By the 18th century, Skepticism would be seen as a danger to religion—notoriously so in Hume—but just before and during the Reformation the ancient Skeptical texts entered philosophical conversation from the opposite direction, as bulwarks to faith.

When Humanists interpreted the classical philosophy that they revived and translated, the results could not always equal Montaigne's, but the new philology added a great deal to philosophy's understanding of itself and its past. In the 1440s Giannozzo Manetti made an early contribution to a nascent genre, the history of philosophy, with his *Life of Socrates.* Ficino's seven large studies of works by Plato and shorter treatments of all the dialogues belong to a classical genre, the commentary, and his *Platonic Theology* (1474), echoing the title used by Proclus, is an extended philosophical treatise that also imitates an ancient form. The audacious Giordano Bruno absorbed both the monism of the Eleatics and the atomism of the Epicureans into his disorderly but fascinating books, some of them dialogues. When Justus Lipsius explained Stoicism in the early 17th century, and when Pierre Gassendi studied Epicurus a little later to construct his own atomism, they too were extracting futures for philosophy from its classical past.

Montaigne was still alive when Lipsius started to write about the Stoics, but Lipsius' most influential works, the *Digest of Stoic Philosophy* and the *Physics of the Stoics,* appeared only in 1604, which was soon enough to influence Descartes, especially his study of the passions. In his earlier work Lipsius had seen Stoic moral philosophy as a refuge from the calamitous wars of religion that followed the Reformation, wars in which Descartes himself would enlist in their later phase that started in 1618. The more comprehensive approach to Stoic thought in Lipsius' *Digest* and *Physics* was invaluable because, despite the Stoic desire for rigorous coherence, accidents of survival had left that ancient system in fragments.

Although the Humanists had made Lucretius a literary classic, the older Greek atomism behind his Latin poem was preserved only a little better than the works of the early Stoics. Gassendi, a skilled and industrious philologist who started as a Skeptical critic of Aristotle, worked for the rest of his life to extract a modern philosophy from the remains of Democritus, Epicurus, and their followers. Philosophers read Gassendi today mainly as an objector to Descartes's *Meditations,* seldom examining the larger posthumous product of his labors, the massive Latin *Syntagma* (1658), which thoroughly grounds Gassendi's thought—broadly, an empiricist atomism—in its classical and post-classical sources, which are varied enough to qualify his system as eclectic.

The stricter standards of the new philology, both Greek and Latin, and sustained study of the remains of antiquity greatly enriched the practice of philosophy for Gassendi and many others. Although it is hard to think of an earlier figure like Erasmus (d. 1536)—eloquent in Latin, expert at Greek, a pioneering Patristic scholar and an icon of the new classicism—as a philosopher, he and many lesser scholars after him surely helped make Europe a better place to do philosophy. His contemporary and imitator Juan Luis Vives actually knew more about philosophy, but Vives also recycled the facile and contemptuous slanders—"barbarian," "ignorant," "unlettered," "captious"—that had been circulating since Petrarch had railed against the Scholastics.

It was Giovanni Pico, with his exquisite skill in Latin, who made the best argument against this reflexive calumny in an epistolary essay of 1485: philosophy needs its own kind of speech, he insisted, even if the speech is Scholastic. Having read the Scholastics at Padua and Paris, he went on to write both in the Humanist manner and in what he called the "Parisian style." He was also the first Christian since antiquity to work hard at understanding the Jewish mystics and philosophers whom he introduced to Christian Europe. Although Pico called himself a philosopher, his most original thinking was about the Kabbalah, an antiphilosophy. He worked throughout his adult life with Jews who translated and explicated Hebrew and Aramaic texts for him, not just the Kabbalists but also Averroës.

Lorenzo Valla, who died in 1457, a few years before Pico was born, was the Humanist who had the most to say philosophically about the failures of his Scholastic contemporaries. Like many of the Humanists, Valla wrote about ethics, boldly and creatively, but his most important philosophical work was the *Dialectical Disputations*, which he drafted around 1430 and constantly revised over three decades. His hero in this book on language and logic is a Roman orator, Quintilian, and on the surface his main targets are Aristotle, Porphyry, and Boethius, the mainstays of the outmoded Old Logic. But these ancients seem to stand in both for followers of Ockham, Burley, and Buridan (who, in Valla's own day and by his lights, were corrupting the classical language with their phantasmagoric logical inventions) and for a somewhat earlier figure, Peter of Spain, whose logic text had dominated the universities since the 13th century. Although Valla's attack on the Scholastic logicians was genuinely philosophical, not just a screed against bad taste and bad style, it had little effect on the subsequent practice of philosophy.

Valla, Ficino, and Pico—the leading philosophical minds of the Humanist movement—worked against the grain of Scholasticism and, in Pico's case, far outside its received traditions. The same is true of their greatest successors, Machiavelli, Montaigne, and Bruno, all of them vernacular writers of the first rank. None of these thinkers, except Valla briefly, had professorial careers, and in that respect they were a tiny minority among Renaissance philosophers, most of whom continued to teach Aristotle in universities: Achillini, Cremonini, Nifo, Pomponazzi, Suárez, Vernia, Vitoria, and Zabarella are only a few of the more prominent names from the long list of Renaissance philosophers who taught and wrote in the Scholastic tradition. The last large collection of Scholastic commentaries on Aristotle (before the later Neoscholastic movement) was written by Portuguese Jesuits and published in Descartes's lifetime.

And yet Renaissance philosophy, a revival of the classical tradition, was distinct from medieval philosophy even when it was still Scholastic. Scholasticism had always been Aristotelian, but Aristotle himself had now been reclassicized, in new Greek texts and in a commentary literature that attended to the Greek. The Humanists achieved something never attempted by medieval scholars and, to some extent, impossible for them: recovering not just the philosophy written in classical Greek and Latin, but also its context; looking for all the ancient evidence; and then studying the languages of the old texts with great care in order to stabilize works written in those languages before disseminating new editions and translations widely, through the new medium of print.

Renaissance philosophy was distinctive, then, but was it effective? To some degree it was not, evidently, for until recently the history of philosophy canonized in the Anglo-American tradition has ignored it. Ancient philosophy has always been part of that canon, however, because modern and contemporary philosophers have always looked there for the roots of their own ideas. But it was Renaissance philosophers, not their medieval predecessors, who began to conduct that search in a modern way by grounding philosophy in philology. In that sense the new classicism of the Renaissance was effective and enduring. So why has its philosophy not been studied more by philosophers? Was anything else achieved in the Renaissance?

By recovering so many ancient texts, Renaissance philosophers not only preserved them for posterity but also provoked a productive crisis of authority. To say that all philosophical authority in the Middle Ages had been Aristotelian would be wrong, but not entirely off the mark. Aristotle ruled the universities, and philosophy was a university enterprise—for the most part. Then the Humanists and philosophers of the Renaissance looked beyond Aristotle to the Presocratics, Socrates, and Plato, and to Stoics, Epicureans, Cynics, Skeptics, and anyone else who had left records of philosophical thought in classical Greek and Latin. These Renaissance scholars and thinkers were so intent on the past, just because of its revered antiquity, that its preservation was a paramount concern. What was long past was best just because it was very old. Whatever was venerable was authoritative. But before long there were too many antique authorities making too many incompatible claims, too much confusion to sustain the veneration. In the vatic dreamspeak of James Joyce (*Finnegans Wake* 1.1), "clashes here of wills gen wonts, oystrygods gaggin fishygods! Brekkek Kekkek Kekkek!"

How to resolve the confusion? One old answer, a classical answer, was to suspend judgment, on the advice of the ancient Skeptics, and then, in a distinctly modern voice, on Montaigne's advice. Eventually, in his *Discourse on Method* (1637), Descartes would make Skepticism a philosophically productive tool, not a surrender to tranquility but a step along the way to certainty—or so he thought. In that same work he explains that he will use his doubts constructively to destroy the old house that philosophers had built but then replace it with a new one. He had seen the books in the library of that old house when he studied with the Jesuits at La Flèche: they were a medley of Latin Scholasticism and Humanist philology. Descartes found the old books—including the *new* old books of the Renaissance—useless and deceptive, so he claimed to have stopped reading them in order to look to himself, to other people, and the world.

Modern philosophy arrived with Descartes and his repudiation of mimesis, his disavowal of tradition and authority: he had hoped to find a single authority to trust, but he never could. Even in post-Cartesian philosophy, however, even after Spinoza's austere ethical geometry carried it even further from tradition; after Locke turned the tabula rasa of Aristotle and Aquinas into a blank slate of a different sort, to register data received by open minds; after Kant declared himself as much a revolutionary in philosophy as Copernicus had been in astronomy; even after all that, philosophy could never call off its old engagement with the classical tradition. A persistent challenge to the classics came from language itself, however, as learned and creative people in Western Europe turned away from Latin to the many regional and local forms of speech that had emerged to compete with it during the Middle Ages.

In the 16th century philosophers of the first rank began to use the vernaculars that had gradually attracted thinkers in other fields after Dante wrote the *Divine Comedy* in Italian in the early 14th century. More than two centuries later, Machiavelli and Bruno were the first to write enduring philosophy in Dante's tongue. Montaigne and Descartes did the same for French, Hobbes and Locke for English, and Kant for German. But it took a long time for Latin to lose its monopoly as Europe's medium of learned communication. Leibniz and Wolff wrote mainly in Latin, as Kant did until the *Critique of Pure Reason* of 1781. One of Kant's aims was to bring philosophy up to date with Newtonian science, but Isaac Newton had also written the *Principia* in Latin.

But now that the special sciences—especially the natural sciences—were being vernacularized by such widely read publications as the *Journal des scavans, Philosophical Transactions,* and the *Encyclopédie,* philosophy had to follow suit in order to maintain its role as public critic and explicator of the sciences. If science, as a "career open to the talented" (the phrase is Napoleon's, "la carrière ouverte aux talents"), was now open to people like Benjamin Franklin, John Dalton, and Michael Faraday, who had no traditional schooling in the classics, there was less reason for the larger educational apparatus, with philosophy at its summit, to keep the classics obligatory. And because historical consciousness in general was so strongly linked to Graeco-Roman antiquity, once the ancient authorities lost their grip on culture, the withdrawal from history itself that Descartes had recommended to philosophers became more plausible.

The cultural vortex in which philosophy was vernacularized, romanticized, and slowly liberated from the classics has attracted little attention from Anglophone philosophers—with the eminent exception of Isaiah Berlin. Instead, and not inaccurately, philosophers in England and North America have focused on the three moments when canonical heroes of their discipline took decisive steps to detach it from the past and thus from the classical ideal: when Descartes repudiated Renaissance Humanism and its historicism; when Kant discarded all of metaphysics since Plato as unproductive squabbling; and when

Gottlob Frege replaced the old Aristotelian logic with a new logic expressed not in Latin, Greek, or any other natural language but in an abstract, artificial notation.

For Anglophone philosophers this last revolution in logic was the most momentous, though it is the least familiar of the three changes to nonphilosophers. Even in broad cultural terms, however, the displacement of Aristotelian logic from schools and universities was an immense transformation. Until Frege invented his logic and passed it on to Bertrand Russell and others, Aristotle's Organon had been the official roadmap of the Western mind for more than 2,000 years. No other product of antiquity, except perhaps the idea of politics itself, had had more influence, and few have been more enduring. That philosophers were especially impressed by its sudden end is no surprise, nor is their lasting memory of the other great changes wrought by Descartes and Kant.

Less easily explained is Francis Bacon's excision from the story of modern philosophy as now told to students in the English-speaking world. Philosophers still write good books about him, to be sure, but he no longer stars in the curriculum—unlike Descartes, his contemporary. Whereas Descartes settled his divorce from history in public and made it part of his legend, Bacon respected the Humanism that Descartes repudiated, which may be why Anglophone philosophy has lost interest in him, a figure who was once one of its culture heroes, as a pioneering empiricist and inventor of what we now call the scientific method.

Bacon, a ferocious critic of almost everything, acknowledged the successes of Humanism, especially the progress that it made in morals and politics through critical study of the ancients. His project of finding a method for the sciences grew out of his Humanist education at Cambridge, when ambitious undergraduates debated the new philology along with the methodological innovations of Pierre de la Ramée (Peter Ramus). On those foundations Bacon constructed his grand project of reforming the sciences, which was actually a way of historicizing natural philosophy—organizing information about the natural world in order to adapt it to the new critical methods that philologists had developed from their studies of antiquity.

Bacon thus found the history of Greece and Rome worth learning, but not their poetry. Ancient rhetoric could also be useful, but not the bombastic kind. Disputatious philosophy was no use at all, because its method was unproductive. Aristotle was worthless, but not Democritus. Bacon was no more prepared to dismiss all the ancients than ready to accept all the moderns: Paracelsus, Cardano, and Fernel got the same rough treatment as Plato, Cicero, and Galen. Authority itself, whether new or old, he called an Idol of the Theatre, and his wish to topple it undercut the classical habit of mimesis. Because progressive knowledge is cumulative, however, something would have accumulated from the deep past, even though moderns had the benefit of experience unknown to the ancients—from the "industry of artificers," for example, even if the printing press, the compass, and the cannon were accidental discoveries.

Pitting the old against the less old had started in antiquity, of course: why else did Horace remind us (*Art of Poetry* 359) that "good Homer sometimes nods"? The self-presentation of the Humanists who worked so hard to imitate Horace's Latin—but not Aristotle's Greek—was emulation as well as mimesis, and thus a prelude to the modern quarrel of the ancients and moderns that Bacon inaugurated, in his own muddled way. In later generations, when the French phase of the quarrel became mainly literary, Bacon's countrymen were still fighting about natural philosophy and history. William Wotton's shocking insight about history was that philology had equipped the moderns to understand the ancients better than the ancients had understood themselves.

This was a license not so much for the antiquarianism of the 18th century as for the *Altertumswissenschaft* that grew out of it. In that context, the philosophical corollary of Wotton's insight was that philology enables philosophers to know Aristotle better than Aristotle had known himself. Meanwhile, the sheer bulk of the surviving literature—especially the texts of Plato, Aristotle, and Cicero—assured a large place for ancient philosophers in the modern study of the classics. Part of this project from early on was the history of philosophy that emerged in the 17th century as a distinct and autonomous genre. At first only the oldest philosophy was studied in this new way, as in the *History of Philosophy* that Thomas Stanley published in England around 1660. Eighty-two years later Johann Jakob Brucker's *Critical History* brought the post-Cartesian period within the limits of philosophy's history, though most of the multivolume work was still about the Greeks and Romans.

From a history of philosophy equipped by philology to study its own past, it was a short step to reflection on the nature of philosophy itself. And insofar as philosophy had the ambitions of a metadiscipline, reflection of that kind came naturally to it—with or without historical stimulation. When Kant suggested that he knew more than Plato knew about Plato, for example, his perspective was philosophical, not historical. Even now, on the other hand, more than two centuries after Kant declared himself the Copernicus of his field, philosophy is still much more interested in its deep history, its classical past, than most other disciplines are in their own ancient annals. Why should this be? Are very old philosophical problems still problematic—still classics—just because they are so hard? Or is any reflection on any human endeavor inevitably historical, and all the more so for an enterprise as old, as contemplative, and as well documented as philosophy?

Although Hegel offered profound answers to such questions in his *Phenomenology of Spirit* (1807) and later works, the *Phenomenology* is now read in English more often as a monument of culture than as a statement of philosophy to philosophers. Hegel taught that philosophy's first object, in the order of knowing, is the philosophical experience itself and therefore the history of that experience. History itself is the history of the Spirit or Mind, of reason progressively realizing itself in communal human action. Since history is at the core of Hegel's conception of philosophy, the historical phenomenon of change and the historical construct of periodization—the transition from ancient to medieval to modern, for example—are key items of the Hegelian philosopher's repertoire. Change understood philosophically is dialectical, according to Hegel, and the logic of history is its dialectical rhythm.

Hegel's rich but obscure ideas, which provoked a great deal of action once Marx and Engels reinterpreted them, nonetheless lost the attention of Anglophone philosophers at the start of the 20th century. Hegel's voluminous *Lectures on the History of Philosophy*—which are mainly about the classics—no longer appear in the core curriculum. And the very idea of a philosophy of history, of which Hegel was also an original architect, has come to seem implausible, if not far-fetched. It seems unlikely, for example, that the movement from ancient to medieval to modern is just built into things in a way that could be accessible to philosophy as an a priori discipline.

Still, despite the unhappy fate of Hegelian idealism in the Anglophone world, the classical philosophy that Hegel idealized was also studied empirically and critically in the 19th century, to become the philological basis of analytical readings of the philosophical classics in the 20th century and later, when the ancient canon has expanded to include Hellenistic and even later texts, like the many that survive from the Greek Commentators. That ancient philosophy in this extended form is still an object of expert study and teaching by analytic philosophers is evident, for example, in the collections of articles by Bernard Williams published in 2006, three years after his death. The titles of those books, *The Sense of the Past* and *Philosophy as a Humanistic Discipline,* proclaim their traditional motives. At roughly the same time, English translations of works by Pierre Hadot, *Philosophy as a Way of Life* and *What Is Ancient Philosophy?* have given readers of English access to a distinctive Continental view of the field and of its ancient origins.

Hadot's key idea is that the philosophy that was a way of life in antiquity is now not that but merely a way of talking: "Philosophy is obviously no longer a way of life or form of life—unless it be the form of life of a professor of philosophy . . . [in] the state educational institution, . . . a discourse developed in the classroom and then consigned to books" (1995, 271). He notes an earlier version of this complaint by Schopenhauer, and he recognizes Schopenhauer and Nietzsche as exceptions to philosophy's professionalization, and confinement, by the university.

Nietzsche, who was a university classicist before he was a vagrant philosopher, started his mad career in 1872 with a book about Greek drama, *The Birth of Tragedy out of the Spirit of Music.* Where Winckelmann had frozen the Greek spirit in the serene rationalism of its marble statuary, Nietzsche made it rage in the dithyrambs of choral song. His god of the chorus was the crazed Dionysus, not the Apollo who in the body of an actor stood apart from the chorus, speaking in reasoned words. Rational dialogue, in Nietzsche's view, was Euripidean and a crime against art, but it was also Platonic and, worst of all, Socratic.

The Socrates who argues his way through Plato's dramatic dialogues put both philosophy and art on the road to ruin, according to Nietzsche. The right path leads back to the primitive Dionysus, to the pre-Socratic as anti-Socratic, which Nietzsche prescribes as the best purge for the sickness of reason that turns humans into self-deluded slaves. The sermon that Nietzsche preaches against philosophy in *The Birth of Tragedy* is impassioned and more concrete than the related message of his *Genealogy of Morals* (1887). The scandal disclosed by this later book is just that morality itself—the very notion of good or evil as a moral primitive—has a genealogy rather than a ground.

Without a hook in the sky from which to hang our morals or any stable soil in which to plant them, we should search instead for their history, says Nietzsche, and for the motives of that history, which will show that Christian morality is a self-deception arising unconsciously from resentment. Thus, not so much enlightened as deprived of false consolation, a critical, indeed cynical historicism and a reckoning of perspectives will disclose, as he puts it in *The Gay Science* (1882), that "God is dead. God stays dead. And we have killed him." Nietzsche's bitter meditations, starting with Dionysus and Socrates, end by moving God inside history, within it as its doomed victim, no longer outside it as a providential Creator.

Since Nietzsche's influence—as a philosopher on other philosophers—has been stronger on the Continent than in England or North America, it was natural for Gadamer, Foucault, and other Continental thinkers to take up the classical themes that they found in Nietzsche and Hegel. The most influential of those philosophers, for better or worse, was Martin Heidegger. After his early period that culminated in *Being and Time* (1927), Heidegger turned more and more to the view, somewhat like Nietzsche's, that philosophy had been on the wrong track almost since it began in ancient Greece.

Heidegger charged that Plato and Aristotle had turned philosophy away from its real purpose by burying it under metaphysics, which they invented and used to cover up the Being that the Presocratics knew better how to disclose by not making an object of it. Accordingly, to find evidence of how philosophers had known more before the eventual disaster, the later Heidegger studied the gnomic fragments of the Presocratics, often turning to etymology as a philosophical method. Etymology had known little success among philosophers since Plato wrote the *Cratylus,* but now philosophy had come full circle, back to its immemorial beginnings. And meanwhile, because Heidegger also returned to the classical poetic texts, like *Antigone,* that Hegel and Hölderlin had found so important, modern classicism was given another way to reconnect with modern philosophy.

BIBL.: Brian Copenhaver, "Translation, Terminology and Style in Philosophical Discourse," in *The Cambridge History of Renaissance Philosophy,* ed. C. Schmitt and Q. Skinner (Cambridge 1988) 77–110. Brian Copenhaver and Charles Schmitt, *A History of Western Philosophy,* vol. 3, *Renaissance Philosophy* (Oxford 1992). Stephen Gaukroger, *Francis Bacon and the Transformation of Early-Modern Philosophy* (Cambridge 2001). Pierre Hadot, *Philosophy as a Way of Life: Spiritual Exercises from Socrates to Foucault,* ed. A. I. Davidson, trans. M. Chase (Oxford 1995), and *What Is Ancient Philosophy?* trans. M. Chase (Cambridge, Mass., 2002). James Hankins and Ada Palmer, *The Recovery of Ancient Philosophy in the Renaissance: A Brief Guide,* Quaderni di Rinascimento 44 (Florence 2008). R. J. Hollingdale, *Nietzsche: The Man and His Philosophy* (Cambridge 2001). William Jordan, *Ancient Concepts of Philosophy* (London 1990). Joseph M. Levine, *Humanism and History: Origins of Modern English Historiography* (Ithaca 1987). John Marenbon, *Medieval Philosophy: An Historical and Philosophical Introduction* (London 2007). Joseph McCarney, *The Routledge Philosophy Guidebook to Hegel on History* (London 2000). Arnaldo Momigliano, *The Classical Foundations of Modern Historiography* (Berkeley 1990) and *Studies in Historiography* (New York 1966). Riccardo Quinto, *Scholastica: Storia di un concetto* (Padua 2001). Giovanni Santinello, ed., *Storia delle storie generali della filosofia* (Brescia 1972–). Christopher Stead, *Philosophy in Christian Antiquity* (Cambridge 1994). Bernard Williams, *Philosophy as a Humanistic Discipline,* ed. A. W. Moore (Princeton 2006), and *The Sense of the Past: Essays in the History of Philosophy,* ed. Miles Burnyeat (Princeton 2007). B.C.

Photius

Byzantine humanist and patriarch of Constantinople, ca. 810–ca. 893. Without his monumental compilation, conventionally called the *Bibliotheca* or *Myriobiblion,* our knowledge of ancient Greek literature outside the canon would be much more fragmentary and uncertain. This collection of reviews, epitomes, and excerpts covers both pagan and Christian literature in almost equal proportions, from Herodotus in the 5th century BCE to a certain Sergius the Confessor in Photius' own 9th century; it is also an important source of Byzantine literary criticism and biography. Besides his literary works, which also include a *Lexicon,* a theological-philosophical treatise (*Amphilochia*), homilies, and about 300 extant letters, Photius had a distinguished career as a civil servant and was an influential and controversial patriarch during two periods (858–867, 877–886). His name is connected with such epoch-defining events in world history as the first schism between the Orthodox Church and the pope in Rome (867) and the Christianization of the Slavs.

Photius' life is so full of active involvement in the politics of church and state that it seems almost incredible that he was also the most prolific and influential representative of the humanistic revival of the 9th century. Some scholars assign the learned studies that are reported in the *Bibliotheca* to Photius' early youth; others believe the enormous collection to be the work of his old age, after his second deposition from the patriarchal throne. Both opinions may well partake of the truth. But the letter to his brother Tarasius that serves as a preface to the compilation rather situates its genesis in the midst of his active political service: appointed a member of a diplomatic mission to Baghdad, he professes to give his brother, as a consolation for their separation, a written account of all the 279 books that "were read when you were not present" (in fact, the *Bibliotheca* contains notices on no fewer than 386 works, discussed in 280 chapters usually cited as codices).

We are thus presented with the alluring picture of a reading group led by Photius, consisting of some promising young men of Constantinople intensely occupied with rediscovering the cultural heritage of antiquity. In an almost Renaissance spirit (we may presume) they hunt out, in archives and libraries, all kinds of ancient and early Byzantine literature, from history to medicine, from novels to apologetics, in order to read and discuss their findings together. The only criteria for inclusion are novelty and obscurity: the great literature they all know from school is excluded. Thus, the *Bibliotheca* has nothing to say on epic and drama, little on poetry on the whole; and Plato and Aristotle, of whom Photius shows intimate knowledge elsewhere, are also absent.

New historical knowledge, be it of "unclassical" periods and non-Greek peoples, is particularly sought after, as are accounts of the paradoxical and grotesque, preferably in oriental surroundings. We thus owe to Photius and his circle most of what we possess of Ctesias, the Greek historian at the Persian court (ca. 400 BCE), and of Olympiodorus of Thebes (ca. 400 CE), as well as substantial epitomes of the 2nd-century CE novels of Iamblichus and Antonius Diogenes.

Much else, of course, is what one would expect from the future (or retired) patriarch: a keen interest in Christian dogmatics and exegesis, an outspoken disgust at heresies and theological nonsense, and reverence for the great patristic writers (Gregory of Nazianzus is absent, probably because he had achieved canonic status and was read at school). Hagiography is not one of Photius' favorite Christian genres, but he reviews some works concerned with the lives of great church leaders, such as Athanasius, though he largely avoids legendary saints' lives of more popular appeal (again, perhaps because of their banality and easy access). He looks for historical facts, not for edification or aesthetic pleasure. Yet, as always, he is a stern judge of style and openly tells us when a work is worth reading for its contents only. Inversely, a pagan novel like Achilles Tatius' *Leucippe and Clitophon* (ca. 2nd cent. CE) may be praised for its composition and language while condemned for its indecency.

The *Bibliotheca* itself, as a work of literature, is difficult to assign to any one genre, no doubt because it came into being through such a mixed and presumably lengthy process. It certainly had no predecessor in ancient or Byzantine book culture. It may be described as a huge annotated bibliography, sometimes concentrating on the actual codex and the contemporary availability of the work(s) it contains, sometimes rather taking on the character of a generous anthology of textual extracts. But the most typical kind of chapter may be best described as a book review, offering biographical facts about the author, a synopsis of the work itself, and finally the reviewer's own comments on its contents, style, and significance. George Saintsbury, in his *History of Criticism* (1900), dubs Photius the first in European tradition to have "dealt practically with literature from the reviewer's point of view" (from Wilson 1994, 2). This is an accurate observation: whereas the critical essays produced in antiquity discussed Thucydides or Demosthenes as old texts that had always been available in an unbroken tradition, Photius typically approaches his subjects as previously unknown and describes them as such to their prospective readers, sometimes adding a personal recommendation—or the opposite, if the book has proved a disappointment.

No fewer than 211 of the works that Photius reviewed have not reached us in their complete form by direct textual transmission; some 110 are entirely lost, and 81 would be entirely unknown if not included in the *Bibliotheca* (Treadgold 1980, 9). Photius obviously had a well-developed sense for a book's rarity. His own reviews, however, seem to have been largely ignored in later centuries, even during the Renaissance; it was not until 1601 that the *Bibliotheca* was first printed (it was translated into Latin in 1606). Since then classicists have used it mainly as a quarry for information about lost works, more seldom regarding it as a whole and assessing Photius' personal achievement.

BIBL.: Paul Lemerle, *Byzantine Humanism: The First Phase,* trans. Helen Lindsay and Ann Moffatt (Canberra 1986). Photius, *Bibliothèque,* ed. and trans. René Henry, vols. 1–8, Budé series (Paris 1959–1977), vol. 9, index by Jacques Schamp (1991). Warren T. Treadgold, *The Nature of the Bibliotheca of Photius* (Washington, D.C., 1980). N. G. Wilson, *Photius, The Bibliotheca: A Selection Translated with Notes* (London 1994).

T.H.

Physiognomy

The study of an individual's character from the external form of his body. Physiognomy existed as a set of popular beliefs and as a realm of technical knowledge before its first systematic treatment, found in a Peripatetic treatise dating to the 3rd century BCE (*Physiognomica*). Subsequent known treatises are those of Polemo (2nd cent. CE), Adamantius, and Anonymus Latinus (4th cent. CE). The Peripatetic treatise describes three methods of physiognomy in particular: zoological analogy (if a man has traits similar to a lion's, he will have an irascible character, like a lion), ethnological analogy (if a man has bristly hair like Nordic peoples, he will be similarly courageous), and pathognomonic analogy (if a man's permanent skin shade is like that of one who is angry, he will have, by analogy, an ill-tempered character).

Implicit theoretical premises include the general Aristotelian notion that every external part of the body (*compositio*) has a certain configuration because it expresses a form or finality of the soul and, later, the Galenic notion that the soul is influenced by the mixture (*temperamentum* or *complexio*) of the body's fluids (elements, qualities, or humors).

A knowledge of physiognomy seems to be at work in Hellenistic art, which, stressing psychosomatic individualities in portraiture, transcends the rigid norms of *kalokagathia* (perfect moral and physical beauty) in favor a greater expressiveness and individual characterization. Portrait galleries of famous men sprang up that, continuing well into Roman times, responded to the question "What did someone look like?" (*Qualis fuit aliquis,* Pliny, *Naturalis historia* 35.10–11).

In the 9th and 10th centuries, Arab authors took up the classical notions of physiognomy based on Aristotle and Galen and developed practical uses from them. Some related to medical semiotics (external, psychosomatic signs connected to internal organs; e.g., Rhazes, *Liber ad Almansorem,* and Avicenna, *Canon*), others to "politics" (recognizing a prince's true counselors; e.g., *Secretum secretorum*).

Arab medicine was the vehicle for classical physiognomy's reemergence in the 13th century, when it once again took on a more philosophical dimension. Michael Scot translated Aristotle's zoological texts from Arabic into Latin and composed a treatise on physiognomy (*Liber physionomie*). Albertus Magnus combined concepts of physiognomy, anatomy, and philosophy in his *Liber de animalibus.* The unitary character of the classical and Aristotelian conception inspired the grand Scholastic synthesis. Thanks to the development of Aristotelian and Galenic notions, physiognomy received a scientific justification that integrated it into the philosophical, biological, and medical knowledge of the time. Not only the notion of *complexio,* but also craniology (the study of the natural and nonnatural forms of the cranium) and embryology (a more or less effective action of the soul's *virtus formativa* that gives shape to the form of the body in the course of embryogenesis) permitted this integration.

The Renaissance articulated a physiognomic iconography. At first it accepted physiognomy (Leonardo; Johannes de Indagine, *Introductiones apotelesmaticae,* 1522) and, in the spirit of Humanism, considered it a useful tool for reconstructing the physical appearance of great personages of the past on the basis of written descriptions of their characters (Pomponio Gaurico, *De sculptura,* 1504). Nevertheless, it was once again the unitary character of the classical conception of physiognomy that was responsible for its chief influence. If the Middle Ages achieved a perfect philosophical and scientific synthesis, the Italian Renaissance achieved a synthesis of science and art. Physiognomy entered into artistic theory and practice. It was associated with the correct representation of character and emotions in the human figure, and with the general conception of art as the radical imitation of nature. The representation of corporeal forms implied an understanding on the part of the artist of the natural laws behind those forms. Leonardo planned and collected notes for a treatise entitled *De figura umana,* in which he included physiognomy, anatomy, anthropometry, embryology, and more. As the title indicates, the treatise aimed at the comprehension of the natural laws or internal causes behind the *figura,* or external form, of the human body, which became the shared subject of scientific investigation and artistic creation.

This is the last grand synthesis inspired by classical physiognomic thought. Giovan Battista della Porta's treatise *De humana physiognomonia* (1586) also points to a continuing relationship among physiognomic depiction, behavior, and the rhetoric of the emotions, but in this case the synthesis consisted of a simple collection of previously known ideas, characteristic of the inventorial tendency of late 16th-century science. A corresponding phenomenon in art was the interest (also present in Hellenistic art) in fantastic faces and caricatures (Arcimboldo, Carracci), which continued into the 18th century and beyond (Hogarth, Daumier). In the 17th century Descartes served as the inspiration for Le Brun's academic synthesis of physiognomy and art, undertaken in the spirit of a rationalist classicism (geometric analysis of faces and expressions). From the point of view of Cartesian philosophy, however, the clear separation of soul and body, thought of as a machine, constituted a moment of abrupt rupture in the unitary conception that had been characteristic of classical physiognomic thought. This rupture rendered subsequent reemergences of classical physiognomy partial and problematic.

At the end of the 18th century Johann Lavater's revival of physiognomy doubtlessly influenced Franz Gall's conception of phrenology (the relationship between the form of the skull and psychic functions). Along the same lines was Pieter Camper's craniometry, which mentions classical authors. These reemergences were nevertheless met with violent polemics (Lichtenberg, Buffon, Kant), but their conception of the body continued into the 19th and 20th centuries (Bell, Lombroso, Kretschmer).

On a more general level, this body-focused conception is followed by the psychologically tilted conceptions of Freud, and then by the eclectic and ambiguous positions of modern psychiatry and psychology, where Freud's ideas collided with new, prevailingly somatic paradigms (genetics, psychopharmacology).

Today, with the eclipse of Descartes and the loss of the metaphysical and philosophical dimension, considerations on the relationship between soul and body are, from an epistemological point of view, unsettled, fragmentary, and conflicted, far indeed from that classical and Aristotelian synthesis of which physiognomy was one of the most interesting manifestations.

BIBL.: T. S. Barton, *Power and Knowledge: Astrology, Physiognomics and Medicine under the Roman Empire* (Ann Arbor 1994). Jean-Jacques Courtine and Claudine Haroche, *Histoire du visage* (Lausanne 1994). E. C. Evans, "Physiognomics in the Ancient World," *Transactions of the American Philosophical Society* 59 (1969) 5–97. Domenico Laurenza, *De figura umana: Fisiognomica, anatomia e arte in Leonardo* (Florence 2001). M. M. Sassi, *The Science of Man in Ancient Greece* (Chicago 2001). Claudia Schmölders, *Das Vorurteil im Leibe: Eine Einführung in die Physiognomik* (Berlin 1995). Ellis Shookman, ed., *The Faces of Physiognomy: Interdisciplinary Approaches to Johann Caspar Lavater* (Columbia, S.C., 1993).

D.L.

Translated by Patrick Baker

Physiologus

Late antique collection of moralizing, Christianized animal and natural allegories. The precise origins of the *Physiologus,* meaning the "Naturalist" or "Natural Scientist," are unclear. It was originally written in Greek between the 2nd and 4th centuries CE and contained up to 50 chapters describing the allegorical significance of various animals, along with a few plants and stones. The author is not known, although it was attributed at various times to any number of early Christian worthies, including Epiphanius, Ambrose, Basil, and Peter of Alexandria. The place of composition is also disputed, Alexandria and Syria being the most commonly favored. No manuscripts of the original Greek version survive (there were, however, some retranslations into Greek), but Latin translations are attested as early as the later 4th century. It was translated and adapted into many languages, including Armenian, Arabic, and the vernacular languages of Europe, and it provided the foundation for the medieval bestiaries. Like them, it appeared in a bewildering variety of abridgments, expansions, and editions (some of them in verse).

In its standard form, the individual chapters of the *Physiologus* are introduced with a quote from the Old Testament that is relevant to the animal being described. This is followed by a description of the animal's characteristic nature and behavior, after which is an allegorical explanation of these features as symbolizing one or more aspects of Christ or Christian doctrine. Thus, the lion (chap. 1) is a symbol of Christ's divine nature, because, as the lion covers its tracks as it walks in the desert, so Christ concealed his divine nature in his incarnation as a man. And the pelican (chap. 6), who becomes annoyed by the pecking of its children and kills them, but, feeling remorse after a period of three days, revives them by feeding them with its own blood, symbolizes the redemption of sinners by the blood of Christ.

The animal symbolism in the *Physiologus* has its roots in a rich classical tradition of natural history and animal stories. Other manifestations of this tradition include Aristotle's *De natura animalium,* Pliny the Elder's *Natural History,* Aelian's *De natura animalium,* and Horapollo's *Hieroglyphica.* What distinguishes the *Physiologus,* however, is its transformation of this tradition into explicitly

Christian terms and its emphasis on the world of creation as a kind of sacred text in its own right. This idea, which has roots in later antique Neoplatonism, had a significant effect on Renaissance ideas about hieroglyphs and symbolism in general.

BIBL.: Patricia Cox, "The Physiologus: A Poesis of Nature," *Church History* 52, no. 4 (1983) 433–443. Nikolaus Henkel, *Studien zum Physiologus im Mittelalter* (Tübingen 1976). *Physiologus: The Very Ancient Book of Beasts, Plants and Animals,* trans. F. J. Carmody (San Francisco 1953). *Physiologus,* trans. Michael J. Curley (Austin 1979). F. Sbordone, ed., *Physiologus* (Rome 1936). Alan Scott, "The Date of the Physiologus," *Vigiliae Christianae* 52, no. 4 (November 1998) 430–441. Michael Burney Trapp, "Physiologus," in *The Oxford Classical Dictionary,* ed. Simon Hornblower and Antony Spawforth, 3rd ed. (Oxford 2003) 1181. B.CU.

Picasso, Pablo

Picasso (1881–1973), the most omnivorous of modern artists, embraced the classical world in nearly all its divergent and even dissonant forms. This Spaniard, who came of age in Barcelona and spent the last quarter century of his life in the south of France, regarded the classical culture of the Mediterranean as a birthright, a dreamscape, and a storehouse packed with images and ideas. In the Barcelona of the early 20th century, the Noucentisme movement had replaced the smoky Symbolist yearnings of the fin de siècle with a sunlit vision of a Spanish-Hellenistic Golden Age, and Picasso would over the years reflect on this lost utopia in works ranging from *Boy Leading a Horse* (1906), in which the youth has the powerful yet delicate proportions of a kouros figure, to the laurel-crowned child, a self-portrait, in a print from *Suite 347* (1968).

Though it was in the work of the decade 1915–1925, when he had abandoned his bohemian beginnings and was moving in the glittery circles around Diaghilev's Ballets Russes, that Picasso was most unabashedly a classicist, there was hardly a time in his life when classicism was not a force that he reckoned with. Fifth-century Greek sculpture informed the massive female figures in the paintings of 1906, and there were classical references mixed into the primitivism of *Les Demoiselles d'Avigon* (1907). Cubism itself has been said to be Platonic in that it involved an investigation of the essential nature of things. The myth of the Minotaur and his violent world was at the very heart of Picasso's Surrealist phase. The political rhetoric of *Guernica* (1937) was fueled by numerous references to the classical tradition in European history painting. The ceramics that Picasso produced in Vallauris in the 1940s and 1950s were an extended homage to one of the great industries of the ancient world. And the work of his later decades had its share of centaurs, pipers, nymphs, and shepherds. Picasso was as interested in the European artists who absorbed the classical tradition as he was in the ancient world; he responded to Giotto, Masaccio, the School of Fontainebleau, Poussin, David, Ingres, and Corot. He even took an interest in the sugary-kitsch interpretations of classical style that were common in the 19th century, and he incorporated their porcelain-brilliant colors and ultrasmooth surfaces in compositions such as *Sleeping Peasants* (1919).

For Picasso, whose essential artistic impulse was graphic rather than painterly, the revelatory power of line was something that could be traced back, through Degas and Ingres and Leonardo, to Greek vase painting, Etruscan engraved mirrors, and the drawings on marble uncovered in Pompeii. Though his passionate embrace of such sources placed him firmly on the classical side of the great split in European art—the split between classicism and romanticism, *disegno* and *colore,* Michelangelo and Titian—Picasso nevertheless saw classicism itself as unstable and changeable, as dynamic and unruly, as a matter of abnormalities as well as norms. In 1931 he drew on the attenuated forms of Etruscan figures for a series of spectral wooden images, even as he experimented with Hellenistic idealism in some of his monumental plaster heads. Picasso's classicism was at times Cycladic or Iberian or Pompeian—a classicism not so much of norms but of endless variations on norms. And as much as he was fascinated by ancient images, he was also obsessed with ancient myths and legends and modes of conduct. He celebrated the irrationality as well as the rationality of the Greeks. The Minotaur, alternatively ferocious and poignant, became a sort of alter ego. And Picasso reimagined his own tangled feelings about love, lust, friendship, children, growing old, and remembering his own youth through his study of pagan images of gods, goddesses, nymphs, shepherds, parents, children, young men, and old men. His drawings and graphic work, including prints for Ovid's *Metamorphoses* (1930) and countless other projects, took him through many of the highways and byways of classical experience. In a group of etchings from 1933, Picasso turned himself into a bearded sculptor in an Attic atelier, at ease with his beautiful model-mistress, contemplating the magical power of his own creations.

If there was a guiding principle behind the kaleidoscopic variety with which Picasso embraced the classical past, it was Nietzsche's vision of Greek experience as an incendiary combination of the Apollonian and the Dionysian spirits, an idea that was much discussed in the avant-garde circles where Picasso moved as a young man. Picasso exulted in the extent to which the Apollonian and Dionysian principles were always at war in his perfervid imagination; he was a master of transformation who constantly moved between these dazzling extremes. This artist—who in his personal life was surely far more pagan than Christian—may have sometimes imagined himself as mingling with the immortals on Mount Olympus. He was, like the ancient gods, superhuman and all-too-human, immensely wise and hopelessly reckless, forever changing one thing into another, forever breaking and remaking the world.

BIBL.: Jean Clair, ed., *Picasso: The Italian Journey* (New York 1998). Elizabeth Cowling, *Picasso: Style and Meaning* (New York 2002) esp. 390–451. Lisa Florman, *Myth and Metamorphosis* (Cambridge, Mass., 2000). Kyriakos Koutsomallis et al., *Picasso and Greece* (Andros 2004). Susan Mayer, *Ancient Mediterranean Sources in the Works of Picasso* (New York 1980). Gary Tinterow, ed., *Picasso Clasico* (Málaga 1993). Ulrich Weisner, ed., *Picassos Klassizismus* (Bonn 1988).

J.PE.

Pico della Mirandola, Giovanni

Italian philosopher and inventor of Christian Kabbalah (1463–1494). Pico is famous mainly for a speech that he never gave, his *Oration on the Dignity of Man,* which got its title decades after he died. Three centuries then passed before the work began to be read as most people still read it today: as a proclamation of human freedom and dignity by a Humanist of the Renaissance, one of those pioneers who restored the classical tradition and made it foundational for modern culture.

Pico wrote the *Oration* in 1486 to introduce his *900 Conclusions,* a stunningly ambitious collection of philosophical propositions—many attached to the names of Graeco-Roman authorities—that he declared he would defend against all challengers, even offering to pay the way to Rome for anyone who would come there to debate him publicly. This brash young man chose the capital of Christendom as just the place to dispute outrageous theological novelties, including the claim that magic and Kabbalah were the best proofs of Christ's divinity. In fact, the strongest sense of tradition in all of Pico's thinking—in contrast to the views of Marsilio Ficino, his contemporary—is Hebrew and Kabbalist, not Graeco-Latin and classical.

The pope quashed Pico's rash project, but not before the learned count had already published the *Conclusions,* which he then defended in his unsubmissive *Apology.* Pico never delivered or published the less inflammatory *Oration,* which first appeared in the collection of his works published by his nephew Gianfrancesco Pico in 1496. Gianfrancesco, the main source of biographical information about Pico, tells us that his uncle thought little of the *Oration,* regarding it as a piece of juvenilia.

For several centuries, few of Pico's learned readers were moved to challenge this verdict, despite the author's enormous fame. Until post-Kantian historians of philosophy were charmed by it, the *Oration* was largely ignored. Pico had been a celebrity in his own lifetime, and he remained famous as a critic of astrology, as a promoter of Christian Kabbalah, and as Pico—as the phoenix who blazed through a brief life in the triple glare of an old aristocratic society, a new mandarin culture of classical scholarship, and, in his last years, the millenarian fantasies of Savonarola's Florence. Noble origins, fashionable friends, physical beauty, prodigious learning, capacious memory, scholarly journeys, youthful sins, a collision with the Church, eventual repentance, and a pious death: these are the motifs in the family hagiography by his nephew that have over the centuries kept Giovanni Pico famous for being famous.

Having died young, Pico finished very little and published less: his vernacular *Commento* on a love poem was neither completed nor published by him; the *900 Conclusions* are just bare statements of theses that are often enigmatic; half of the hastily written *Apology* is lifted from the unpublished *Oration; On Being and the One* is a small part of a larger effort to harmonize Plato and Aristotle; and Gianfrancesco found the unfinished *Disputations against Astrology* bundled with his dead uncle's papers. Unless we count two epistolary essays on poetry and philosophical language, the only substantial and completed work that Pico gave to the world in his lifetime was the *Heptaplus* (1489), a Kabbalist commentary on the first verses of Genesis.

That topic was a favorite of Menahem Recanati, Abraham Abulafia, and other medieval Kabbalists to whom Pico had been introduced by contemporary Italian Jews, including Elia del Medigo, Flavius Mithridates, and Yohanan Alemanno. Kabbalah, which Pico saw as the holier Hebrew analogue of the Gentile "ancient theology" studied by Ficino, is the most prominent topic of the *900 Conclusions:* 119 of the conclusions, including the final 72, are Kabbalist theses—outlandishly Kabbalist from a Christian point of view. Pico's project, part of a search for harmonies that would connect all the world's wisdom traditions, was to ground primary doctrines of Christology and Trinitarian theology in Kabbalah, which he traced to the oral Torah confided to Moses and passed on in secret. Pico was the first Christian who could claim the expertise, including knowledge of a little Hebrew and Aramaic, to back up such astonishing claims. In the *Heptaplus* we hear the Kabbalist voice of the *Conclusions,* but it is quieter, muffled by the Church's rage at the events of 1486.

It was the extravagant Kabbalah of the *Conclusions,* framed posthumously by the *Oration,* that made Pico the patriarch of Christian Kabbalah. German theologians and biblical scholars were still debating Pico's theses when the young Immanuel Kant began teaching in Königsberg. By the end of the 18th century Kant had so thoroughly revolutionized philosophy that its history had to be reformulated in Kantian terms. In practice, the task was to update the huge *Critical History of Philosophy* produced by Johann Jakob Brucker in 1742, where the eclectic Brucker describes Pico as that worst of all monsters, a Platonizing, Judaizing syncretist. Half a century later, Wilhelm Tennemann began writing his revisionist *History of Philosophy* (1798–1819), in which Pico made his first appearance as herald of a key Kantian principle: human freedom and dignity.

In the first few pages of the *Oration,* pages read more often than any other product of Renaissance classicism, God tells Adam that he, alone of all creatures, can make himself what he wants to be. Fascinated by this stirring prelude to a longer speech, Tennemann, and many readers after him, have taken Pico's oratorical prelude as evidence of a morality grounded, like Kant's, in human freedom and dignity. Having grown stronger during the 19th century and acquired a romantic patina, this view of Pico—and, by implication, of Renaissance Humanism—reached its peak with the great neo-Kantian of his age, Ernst Cassirer. When Cassirer and Paul Kristeller, also a Kantian, went to the United States, they took their Kantian Pico with them, launching his long career in post–World War II university textbooks on Western civilization.

Those alluring pages of the *Oration,* however, are just the first few. Assured by them that we *can* be what we want to be, we are then told that what we *must* be is not human at all but angelic—bodiless, sexless, and, ultimately, that most unromantic of all conditions, *selfless* in the strict sense. Cherubim, the next-to-highest angels, are the first stage of unhumanity that we must reach, and to achieve that lofty state we must shed not only the body that imprisons us but also the identity and personality that distinguish us from all other persons and from God. Union with God is Pico's goal, and extinguishing the self is a necessary consequence of achieving it. At the lowest level of a self-annihilating *paideia,* the mystic starts as a philosopher—with logic, ethics, natural philosophy, and theology—before ascending through the arcana of magic and finally Kabbalah to drown the self in the abyss of divinity. This is not a Kantian project, and the *Oration on the Dignity of Man* that centers the human condition on human freedom and dignity is a text created by us post-Kantians, not by Giovanni Pico.

BIBL.: Crofton Black, *Pico's Heptaplus and Biblical Hermeneutics* (Leiden 2006). Brian Copenhaver, "Magic and the Dignity of Man: De-Kanting Pico's *Oration,*" in *The Italian Renaissance in the Twentieth Century,* ed. A. J. Griego et al. (Florence 2002) 295–320, and "The Secret of Pico's *Oration:* Cabala and Renaissance Philosophy," *Midwest Studies in Philosophy* 26 (2002) 56–81. Eugenio Garin, *Giovanni Pico della Mirandola: Vita e dottrina* (Florence 1937). Chaim Wirszubski, *Pico della Mirandola's Encounter with Jewish Mysticism* (Cambridge, Mass., 1989). Brian Copenhaver, "Giovanni Pico della Mirandola," *Stanford Encyclopedia of Philosophy* (2008) http://stanford.library.usyd.edu.au/entries/pico-della-mirandola.

B.C.

Pindar

Greek lyric poet, ca. 518–ca. 438 BCE. Pindar's reception has never been unproblematic. Whereas Isocrates turns to the Theban bard for persuasive models of encomium, Aristophanes mockingly presents the Pindarizing poet as an embarrassing fool, pretentious and irrelevant (*Birds* 921–930). By the following century the comic poet Eupolis can only bemoan Pindar's general unpopularity, whereas Callimachus and Theocritus reveal his potential to enliven Hellenistic literature. For Horace, Pindar is, with or without irony, the epitome of lyric art—a rushing river, crashing down from the mountaintop, overflowing the banks of convention (*Carminum* 4.2). Horace's ode thereby lays out the terms of the sublime style that will define and sometimes mar the "greater" ode tradition across Europe. It becomes a genre capable of transmitting the loftiest strains of poetry: brilliant in presentation and ambitious in scope, but also, frequently enough, in hands less competent, liable to put forth ridiculous lines, fraught with affectation or indecorous bombast. The tradition therefore causes Voltaire to quip that Pindar has left us verses that demand admiration and always frustrate comprehension. If he remains the paradigm of fiery genius for Goethe and Hölderlin, he is also, in Ezra Pound's estimation, "the prize wind-bag of all ages."

Modernity's means for judging Pindar are significantly limited. Of the 17 papyrus rolls of poems collected in the 2nd century BCE by Alexandrian editors, only the four books of *epinicia,* or victory songs, composed for athletes in the Panhellenic games, survive more or less intact. In celebrating the victor, his family, and his native city, each ode draws from a variety of historical, cultural, and mythological sources. The highly allusive manner by which this material is presented is complemented by an equally rich repertoire of metrical patterns from epic, Doric, and Aeolic systems. So complex are the rhythmic forms that centuries of readers—indeed until August Böckh's discoveries in the early 19th century—were convinced that Pindar's verses were altogether free. Extended similes and difficult metaphors, intricate syntax and rapid narration, far-reaching digressions and bold disruptions: all contribute to the impression that here is a poetic genius too inspired to be restrained by rational control, too grandiose to be held by the occasion at hand. For this reason, although Pindar's praise for the great colonizers Theron and Hiero could be viewed as a model for political encomium, from Francesco Filelfo and Giovanni Pontano to Abraham Cowley and John Dryden, it nonetheless persistently furnished examples in which poetry might enjoy unfettered freedom from the commission assigned, as in lyrics of Pierre de Ronsard, which pay but oblique homage to Henri II, or in the odes of Écouchard-Lebrun, dubbed "Lebrun-Pindare," the fanatical poet of the Terror.

The gnomic statements that tersely punctuate the *epinicia* invite decontextualized citation and were frequently collected in anthologies of *sententiae.* The practice, best represented by Erasmus's *Adagiorum Chiliades* (1508) and later by Michael Neander's *Aristologia Pindarica Graecolatina* (1556), coincides with the first printed books of Pindar's works: the *editio princeps* by Aldus of Venice (1513) and the first full Latin translation by Johannes Lonicerus (Basel 1528), which indexed all the gnomes according to moral lessons. The sententious Pindar, so different from the expansive, dithyrambic portrayal, provided the Humanists of the Reformation with pithy statements of moral instruction and worldly advice, which ensured the poet's place in pedagogical circles. Moreover, as a source of proverbial wisdom, Pindar was elevated nearly to the status of biblical Solomon. This honor would only confirm the poet's importance for the religious hymn tradition, which Friedrich Klopstock developed in the mid-18th century.

In England the fundamentally religious quality of the Pindaric ode, also explicit in Cowley's conflation of the genre with the Psalms, nourished a long tradition of the personal and confessional Pindaric. It is manifest in the so-called Progress Poems of Thomas Gray and William Collins, in which Horace's depiction of Pindar's inspired flood declines into metaphors of fluidity, which may fertilize a desiccate modernity with the vitalizing, excessive waters of the ancient source: "From Helicon's harmonious springs/A thousand rills their mazy progress take" (Gray, "Progress of Poesy," 1757). On the Continent, the young Goethe appropriated similar imagery for the genius poetry that defined the Sturm und Drang, as in *Wandrers Sturmlied* (1772) and *Mahomets Gesang* (1777). Goethe adopted a good deal of Klopstock's hymnal style, especially in the striking composita that so readily pointed to Pindar's innovations in lexical compounds. Together with the free verse described by Horace (*numeris lege solutis*), Goethe established Pindar as the sponsor for a fervid version of German Philhellenism, whose tropes of unrestrained, irrational passion directly contradicted Winckelmann's stoic ideals of nobility, simplicity, and calm. Instead of preaching a program of imitation, the tradition represented here posited Pindar, however paradoxically, as the model for breaking all models. To imitate Pindar was to imitate a posture of originality that, by definition, must renounce all imitation.

Along similar lines, Friedrich Hölderlin placed Pindar at the center of his engagement with Greek poetry, which was not to be copied as much as used to rekindle modern verse. His obsessively literal translations of the *epinicia* and fragments, produced on the eve of his fall into madness, seem to confirm the veracity of Cowley's warning: "If a man should undertake to translate Pindar word for word, it would be thought that one Mad man had translated another." But this madness, especially in the fragment translations, resounds in a different key from the frenzied irrationalism of the Sturm und Drang. It is not so much the digressive expansiveness of Pindar's art but rather his concision that occasions prolonged reflection and patient unfolding. For each of the fragment translations Hölderlin appends an enigmatic, philosophical *poème en prose,* which anticipates later appropriations of Pindaric verses, for example in Paul Valéry's *Cimetière marin* (1920) and Albert Camus' *Mythe de Sisyphe* (1943).

The sheer variety of Pindarically influenced traditions —the political ode and the personal, the religious hymn and the song of genius, the freely aimless and the rigorously concise—all serve as a testament not only to Pindar's versatility, but also to his rich potential to inspire. A large measure of that potential is perhaps grounded in a fundamental idea of displacement. A Theban in a culture newly centered on Athens, an aristocrat in an age of burgeoning democracy, Pindar readily serves as an allegory for that which is always out of place and already outmoded. What better poet, then, to introduce a utopian vision or an untimely meditation—a critique of the present that would allow new legitimization, passion, or vitality, however banally, however sublimely.

BIBL.: William Fitzgerald, *Agonistic Poetry: The Pindaric Mode in Pindar, Horace, Hölderlin, and the English Ode* (Berkeley 1987). John Hamilton, *Soliciting Darkness: Pindar, Obscurity, and the Classical Tradition* (Cambridge, Mass., 2003). Stella Revard, *Pindar and the Renaissance Hymn-Ode: 1450–1700* (Tempe 2001). Steven Shankman, *In Search of the Classic: Reconsidering the Greco-Roman Tradition* (University Park 1994).

J.T.H.

Piranesi, Giovanni Battista

A Venetian architect, designer, and graphic artist, 1720–1778, Piranesi remains among the greatest interpreters of Roman antiquity through an output of well over 1,000 etchings, ranging from souvenir views to technical illustrations and architectural fantasies, which he disseminated by means of the European Grand Tour. As an architect, he extended the range of archaeological investigation as a source of inspiration and played a leading role in the debate in the second half of the 18th century over the comparative virtues of Greek versus Roman styles of architecture. Through a series of polemical publications he advocated a highly original style of composition in architecture and the decorative arts, one based on a wide-ranging study of the classical past, which had a considerable influence on Neoclassical designers such as the Adam brothers, Bélanger, Ledoux, and Soane.

Architecture was to be the controlling discipline of Piranesi's multifaceted career. Born at Mogliano, near Venice, the son of a master builder, he trained under Lucchesi and Scalfurotto, architects and hydraulic engineers in the service of the Venetian Republic. He was influenced by the radical ideas of the architectural theorist Carlo Lodoli, who challenged the conventional authority of Vitruvian design, particularly with reference to Etruscan civilization. In 1740 Piranesi achieved his aspirations when he arrived in Rome as a draftsman in Marco Foscarini's embassy. Frustrated by a lack of professional opportunities, he acquired skills as an engraver of souvenir views (*vedute*) for visiting Grand Tourists while sublimating his architectural ideas in composing elaborate fantasy designs.

Shortly after publishing a collection of these epic compositions as a stimulus for contemporary architects in 1743, he visited the recently discovered site at Herculaneum, where he became convinced of the critical need for more effective archaeological illustrations. After further stays in Venice beginning ca. 1744, his final return to Rome was marked by the issue in 1750 of 14 prints of imaginary prisons (*Carceri*), a highly experimental series of architectural compositions, laced with Venetian fantasy, on the theme of the vaulted Roman interior. Meanwhile, he began to transform the conventional engraved view into a vehicle for combining powerful emotive imagery with a wealth of technical information, as exemplified by the 135 prints in his magisterial *Vedute di Roma,* issued individually from about 1748 onwards. This influential series heightened his contemporaries' awareness of the engineering achievements of classical antiquity (exemplified by an aerial view of the Colosseum's structural system) and of how classical antiquity had powerfully conditioned the development of the modern city of Rome and its environs.

Topography rapidly developed into archaeological enquiry. A modest publication on tomb chambers (ca. 1750) and a folio on the Trophies of Marius on the Capitol (1753) were followed by a four-volume comprehensive survey of ancient Rome (*Le Antichità Romane,* 1756), which was to prove a landmark in the history of classical archaeology, not only for its innovative illustrative techniques (comparable to Leonardo's revolution in anatomical drawing) but also for revealing applications that combined a specialized understanding of architecture and engineering with reconstructive faculties of the highest order. The work's 250 plates fulfilled a crucial and coordinated role: the 315 monuments they depicted were cross-indexed and related to surviving inscriptions and to the known fragments of the Severan Marble Plan (a huge map of Rome incised in marble, 203–211 CE), which had been gradually accumulating since the first rediscoveries in the 16th century. As never before, their full significance was conveyed through the topographical context of a master plan that showed the complex integration of the aqueduct and defensive systems. In addition to his concentration on the ornamental riches of surviving funerary monuments, his exaggerated emphasis on the scale and complexity of the Roman past reflected Piranesi's initial response to the provocative claims made by the protagonists of Greek originality, such as Julien-David Le Roy and Marc-Antoine Laugier, in the emerging debate over Greek or Roman ascendancy in style and architecture.

Academic recognition was swift—Piranesi was elected an Honorary Fellow of the Society of Antiquaries of London in 1757—but these scholarly pursuits were soon transformed into intense archaeological polemics represented in a series of elaborate illustrated folios. *Della magnificenza ed architettura de' Romani* (1761) established the foundations of his defense, based on the Etruscans as the sole founders of Roman civilization; the *Acqua Giulia* (1761) explored the public water system of Rome, and the *Lapides capitolini* (1762) featured a lengthy inscription from the Forum Romanum stressing the long and complex history of Rome. A highly technical treatise on the hydraulic mastery of the emissarium, or drainage outlet, to Lake Albano, also followed in 1762, and further publications recorded the antiquities of the Albano and Castelgandolfo area as well as the ancient city of Cori. Most significant of all, the *Campo Marzio dell'antica Roma* (*The Campus Martius of Ancient Rome,* 1762), which was dedicated to Robert Adam, countered Winckelmann's accusation of decadence in the Late Roman Empire by tracing the evolution of a densely monumental townscape of unprecedented complexity. The culminating plan (*Ichnographia*) was an apotheosis of Roman urban design, principally intended as an exhortation to contemporary designers, which provided a veritable anthology of ingenious planning concepts that would be used by architects well into the 19th century.

The reissue of the heavily reworked *Carceri* prints in 1761 marked the climactic point in Piranesi's career. Through Pope Clement XIII and the Rezzonico family, he finally obtained a series of commissions for decorative interior schemes as well as two architectural works: a new tribune (dais) for the Lateran (unexecuted), and the reconstruction of Santa Maria del Priorato. These were all expressed in terms of a novel system of eclectic design, incorporating a wide range of antique motifs, which were justified theoretically in a fictional debate between opposing architects in his *Parere su l'architettura* (*Opinions on Architecture,* 1765). By the close of the decade, the folio volume *Diverse maniere d'adornare i cammini ed ogni altra parte degli edifizi . . .* (*Diverse Ways of Decorating Chimneypieces and Every Other Part of a Building . . . ,* 1769)—his final statement in the Graeco-Roman quarrel—illustrated his new system of design in action. The essay, which introduced etchings of his compositions for interior embellishments and furnishings, reiterated the inventive genius of the Etruscans and also advanced a remarkable pioneering analysis of Egyptian art (featured in several of the etched designs).

After the end of Rezzonico patronage with Clement XIII's death in 1769, Piranesi developed a prosperous business in the highly imaginative restoration of marble antiquities for the Grand Tour market, including chimneypieces and other works composed of classical fragments. Many of these complex objects found their way into British collections, such as the giant Warwick Vase (Burrell Collection, Glasgow), the two Newdigate Candelabra (Ashmolean Museum, Oxford), and the Piranesi Vase (or Boyd Vase) in the British Museum. Disseminated by a series of striking plates in his *Vasi, candelabri, cippi, sarcofagi* (1778)—*cippi* are short, usually squared signposts or funerary pillars—this application of fantasy to classical forms influenced a new generation of designers in the British Regency and French Empire.

By now, Piranesi's collaborators included his son Francesco (1758–1810), who helped prepare a folio meticulously depicting the three monumental relief columns in Rome and another on the three Greek Doric temples of Paestum. The latter work, in which Piranesi was won over by the sheer grandeur of these monuments, received the papal imprimatur shortly before his death in November 1778 and was ironically to play a decisive part in promoting the heavyweight aesthetic of the later Greek Revival. Francesco completed and published posthumously several more of his father's archaeological works, such as the first fully comprehensive plan of Hadrian's Villa and views of Pompeii, which were later included in a reissue of Piranesi's works in a 27-volume edition between 1800 and 1807.

As archaeological science developed from the early 19th century onward, Piranesi's potent images of classical antiquity were superseded by more clinical illustrations, although they still deeply affected topographical perceptions of Rome. The ultimate legacy of his unique vision of the classical world, however, is represented above all by the perennial appeal of the *Carceri* prints—visual metaphors for the endlessly creative inspiration of the classical past, which have continued to inspire writers, poets, and musicians as much as artists, designers, and film directors.

BIBL.: John Wilton-Ely, *Giovanni Battista Piranesi: The Complete Etchings,* 2 vols. (San Francisco 1994), and *The Mind and Art of Piranesi* (New York 1978). J.W.-E.

Plague

Descriptions of large-scale epidemic disease, loosely termed plague, are rare in ancient medical writings. Plagues were attributed to a combination of bad air and individual susceptibility, a theory that lasted until the 19th century. "New" epidemic diseases were also examined through ancient lenses. Galen provided the inspiration for *On Measles and Smallpox* by al-Rāzi (865–925) and *On the Prevention of Bodily Ills in Egypt* by Ibn Ridwan (d. 1068). Guillaume de Baillou's pioneering study of meteorogical medicine, *Epidemiorum et ephemeridum libri* (ca. 1580, publ. 1640), owed much to the *Constitutions* (summary accounts) in the Hippocratic *Epidemics.* Niccolò Leoniceno (1428–1524) claimed to have found ancient precedents for syphilis. Even the most apparently novel contribution to early modern epidemiology, Girolamo Fracastoro's *De morbis contagiosis* (1546), combined Galenic medicine with a notion of contagion based partly on Lucretian theories of seeds of disease.

Far more extensive and informative are the ancient literary descriptions of plagues, first introduced into medical debates by Girolamo Mercuriale in *De peste* (1577) to justify his belief in the corrupting power of bad air. Chief among these ancient sources were the accounts in Thucydides (*Histories* 2) and Procopius (*Wars* 2) and, in Latin, in Lucretius (6) and Virgil (*Georgics* 3). But their vagueness, already condemned by Galen in antiquity, challenged scientifically trained doctors from the mid-19th century onward to offer modern identifications for ancient epidemics. Whether the archaeological discovery in 2006 of a 5th-century BCE pit in Athens filled with victims of typhus will resolve the identity of the plague mentioned in Thucydides remains to be seen.

Ancient literary descriptions of plague fostered imitations in a variety of genres. In the 14th century John Cantacuzenos and Nicephoros Gregoras described the Black Death in Byzantium on the models of Thucydides and Procopius, whose powerful narratives also inspired doctors like Petrus Forestus, who witnessed plague at Alkmaar in 1557 and at Delft in 1573, to depict signs of civic as well as medical disintegration (*Observationes medicinales* 6, 1588). Conversely, Agrippa d'Aubigné in *Les tragiques* (1616), his epic treatment of France's religious wars, was not alone in using metaphors of plague to evoke civil chaos. Early Christian narratives of plague survival were used by Jesuit missionaries in New Spain to persuade converts of the power of the Christian god to cure their epidemics.

Virgil's imitation of Lucretius in including the devastation of plague in poetry was directly imitated in the Renaissance, notably by Fracastoro in his *Syphilis* (1530), and also specifically noted by Julius Caesar Scaliger in his *Poetics* 5.10–11 (1561). Conscious echoes of classical literary descriptions, emphasizing the loathsome nature of the disease and its pitiful effects on sufferers and survivors, appear in many authors. Some, like Georges Scudéry (*Alaric,* 1654), incorporate a section on plague into a longer epic; others, like Thomas Dekker (*Newes from Graves-ende,* 1604), take it as the main theme. The 19th-century Polish Romantic poet Juliusz Słowacki's long *Ojciec zadzumionych* (*Father of the Plague-Stricken*) weaves Virgilian and Lucretian reminiscences into his own experiences of the plague at El-Arish in Palestine in 1836. Other authors, from Boccaccio (*Decameron,* mid-14th cent.) to Manzoni (*I promessi sposi,* 1822), structure their stories around a background of plague, following the precedent of the *Iliad,* Sophocles' *Oedipus Rex,* and Seneca's *Oedipus.* Albert Camus goes further in *La Peste* (1947), alluding to Thucydides and using the onset of plague to discuss wider ethical and social questions.

BIBL.: René Girard, "*To Double Business Bound*": *Essays on Literature, Mimesis, and Anthropology* (Baltimore 1978). Jürgen Grimm, *Die literarische Darstellung der Pest in der Antike und in der Romania* (Munich 1965). Alessandro Pastore and Enrico Reruzzi, eds., *Gerolamo Fracastoro fra medicina, filosofia e scienze della natura* (Florence 2006). Daniel T. Reff, *Plagues, Priests, Demons: Sacred Narratives and the Rise of Christianity in the Old World and the New* (Cambridge 2005).
V.N.

Planudes, Maximus

Byzantine humanist and politician (ca. 1250–ca. 1305). He was the most versatile scholar of the Palaeologan renaissance. He showed interest in all subjects of the Quadrivium and—an exception among his colleagues—proved to be a prolific translator from Latin. Planudes' letters, of which a considerable number survive, grant interesting insights into the modalities of late Byzantine scholarly activity.

Born in Bithynian Nicomedia (as Manuel) in the days of exile, Planudes moved to Constantinople shortly after the Byzantine reconquest (1261), perhaps in imperial service. He seemingly supported the union of churches under Michael VIII Palaeologus, in all likelihood translating the 15 books of St. Augustine's *De trinitate* for that purpose. After 1282, under Michael's son Andronicus II, however, he joined the anti-unionist party. It remains unclear whether he joined out of conviction or fear: his *Life of Saints Peter and Paul* seems to hint at Roman tendencies; but George Metochites and, in later times, Demetrios Kydones and Cardinal Bessarion refuted his *Treatise on the Holy Spirit.*

Assuming monastic status around 1283 (as Maximus),

Planudes was a resident in the monastery of Christ Akataleptos in Constantinople from about that time. There he seems to have presided over a scholarly circle, possibly succeeding Gregory of Cyprus, who was then appointed patriarch. Manuel Moschopoulos and the Zarides brothers Andronicus and John reckon among his most prominent students. Planudes' frequent and intimate correspondence with the unfortunate general Alexios Strategopoulos testifies to his being involved with high, and potentially insurgent, aristocrats. He served as an imperial ambassador to Cilician Armenia in 1294, and to Venice the year following. He composed a quite overtly critical mirror for princes upon the coronation of co-emperor Michael IX in May 1294, urging the emperors to take military action.

His letters and surviving manuscripts testify to his manifold activities. His scientific interests ranged from the *Geography* both of Ptolemy and of Strabo to astronomical and mathematical sciences (Cleomedes, Aratus, Diophantus, Euclid). He took part in copying a manuscript of Plato and showed interest in classical rhetoric and historiography. His interest in political panegyric is reflected in an extensive commentary on Hermogenes' rhetorical writings.

Planudes is best known, however, for his recensions of two seminal corpora of classical texts, a somewhat purified and otherwise enlarged recension of the Greek Anthology duly dubbed Anthologia Planudea, and the compilation of the "collected works" of Plutarch, raising the number of moral essays from a mere 31 to 69 and collecting most, if not all, of the latter's *Lives*.

Throughout his career, Planudes composed a number of translations from Latin, attending to both secular and theological texts. It remains unclear where he gained his excellent command of that language, as do the exact circumstances of his efforts. Though it might be tempting to link his version of Boethius' *De consolatione philosophiae* to the calamity of Planudes' equally imprisoned friend Alexios Philanthropenos, his translation of Ovid's *Heroides* and *Metamorphoses* may have satisfied the court's literary tastes and should possibly be seen in the context of the roughly contemporary "vernacular romances of love." After all, Planudes also found the leisure to compose a bucolic poem of 270 hexameters, a dialogue between the yeomen Cleodemus and Thamyras about a bewitched ox.

BIBL.: C. Constantinides, *Higher Education in Byzantium in the Thirteenth and Early Fourteenth Centuries, 1204–ca. 1310* (Nicosia 1982) 66–89. E. A. Fisher, "Planoudes' Technique and Competence as a Translator of Ovid's *Metamorphoses*," *Byzantinoslavica* 61 (2004) 143–160. A. Laiou, "Observations on Alexios Strategopoulos and Maximus Planoudes," *Byzantine and Modern Greek Studies* 4 (1978) 89–99. N. G. Wilson, *Scholars of Byzantium*, rev. ed. (London 1996) 230–241.

N.G.

Plaster Casts

Casting in plaster is a commonly employed technique for producing copies of sculpture. Casts of famous classical sculptures have been made since antiquity. More than 400 fragments of Roman casts have been found at Baiae in southern Italy, taken from (among other pieces) Polyclitus' *Doryphoros* (*Spear Bearer*) and the Apollo Belvedere. They are assumed to have come from a workshop of Roman copyists that produced replicas or versions of famous masterpieces.

The modern history of casts taken from classical antiquities (not only from sculpture, but also from coins and gems) dates from the early 15th century, when the Paduan artist Francesco Squarcione, the teacher of Andrea Mantegna, assembled a collection of casts for instructing his pupils. From then on, plaster casts of the ancient sculptures that were discovered in increasing numbers throughout the Renaissance played an important role both as art objects in their own right and as a tool of artistic instruction. Across Europe the houses of the elite and the earliest museums were adorned with casts of "the most beautiful statues." In some cases, as at the French royal palace at Fontainebleau, plaster molds were used to create copies in bronze. A central element in the training of young artists was drawing "from the antique," which meant producing accurate sketches of plaster casts of ancient sculpture.

Plaster casts remained extremely expensive until the 19th century, when mass production spread them more cheaply and so more widely through Europe and North America. Napoleon established a cast workshop (*atelier du moulage*) in Paris, originally to disseminate copies of famous sculptures he had brought from Italy to the Louvre (though it remained in operation long after most of the sculptures had been returned). In England the British Museum supplied casts of the Elgin Marbles to purchasers at home and abroad (the British government sometimes used them as diplomatic gifts). The prevalence of plaster casts in the mid-19th century is best captured by the displays at the Great Exhibition in London in 1851 (which continued on permanent display until destroyed by fire in 1936): it included several thousand casts of ancient and other sculpture.

During this period plaster casts also came to be seen as an essential resource in the new academic study of classical art history. Cast collections primarily for teaching university students were established first in Germany and soon afterward in the rest of Europe and the United States. At the University of Cambridge, for example, almost 600 casts were acquired in the early 1870s and established in a purpose-designed cast museum.

This heyday of plaster casts was followed in the 1930s by a violent reaction, in which many collections were smashed or removed from public display, which often amounted to much the same thing: in Boston, for example, in the early 20th century a large collection of casts was demoted to damp storage conditions and crumbled. In art schools drawing "from the antique" became associated with frigid classicism. In universities photographs superseded casts as the prime medium of instruction. In museums modern reverence for the "original" in artistic expression relegated casts to the status of "mere copies." In the 1930s, for example, the British Museum removed the casts (which had been used to stand in place of sculptural elements that remained in Athens) from its display of the Elgin Marbles.

With postmodernism (and renewed interest in the contested boundary between original and copy) plaster casts have recaptured some of their past fame. Casts have always raised important questions about the status of the art object. This is reflected in the apparently contradictory phrase "original cast," traditionally used to describe a cast made from a mold taken directly from the original sculpture. Most vividly of all, the boundary between life, art, and replica is questioned in an 18th-century example from the collection of the Royal Academy (London): a cast of the dead body of a criminal, arranged in the pose of the famous Hellenistic *Dying Gaul.*

BIBL.: P. Connor, "Cast-Collecting in the Nineteenth Century," in *Rediscovering Hellenism,* ed. G. W. Clarke (Cambridge 1989) 187–235. F. Haskell and N. Penny, *Taste and the Antique: The Lure of Classical Sculpture, 1500–1900* (New Haven 1981). A. Hughes and E. Ranfft, eds., *Sculpture and Its Reproductions* (Chicago 1997). M.B.

Plato and Platonism

The Greek philosopher Plato (428 or 427–348 or 347 BCE) and the intellectual tradition ultimately derived from him have been highly influential not only in philosophy and theology but also in the visual arts, music, and literature. With respect to their influence in cultural history, neither Plato nor Platonism can be characterized easily. On the most basic level, he has been considered from ancient times to the present day to be the defining figure, together with his former student Aristotle, in the development of Greek philosophy. This was undoubtedly the reason his writings have for the most part survived the ravages of time, whereas those of important predecessors and contemporaries like Empedocles and the Atomists had disappeared by the end of antiquity. Complications arise, however, in that the historical reality of Plato and his writings has been submerged by the activity of later thinkers who claimed his legacy throughout the premodern period. Attempts by historians of philosophy since the 18th century to separate his original insights from these later elaborations have had limited success, some of them—for example, the recent preoccupation with the "unwritten doctrines"—being partially a return to the premodern style of reading Plato in terms of a theory of first principles.

The term *Platonism* is essentially modern. It indicates either the philosophy that a particular interpreter extracts from Plato's works or the collective viewpoint of later thinkers influenced by Plato. In the second sense Platonism most often signifies the lengthy and complex evolution in which the philosophical views of "those around Plato" (the most ancient term for Plato's own students) became merged with those of the wider tradition of Platonists (the *Platōnikoi* or *Platonici* of late antiquity), and subsequently with those of the still wider tradition of Platonism (denoting where a tradition in the real sense turns into a hermeneutic category). In this article the second sense predominates.

The historical phenomenon of Platonism can be approached in the first instance by invoking the usual historical and geographical criteria. Thus, fundamental differences in form and content can be detected when the history of Platonism is considered as it occurred in the ancient world (from ca. 347 BCE to 529 CE); during the Middle Ages, for which it is necessary to distinguish the separate but interacting linguistic and cultural traditions of Western Europe, the Byzantine East (ending in 1453), and the Islamic world; in the Renaissance (roughly the 15th and 16th centuries); and in the modern period (from the 17th century until the present). Obviously Platonism was conceived in radically different ways by its advocates depending on whether it had to be accommodated to monotheistic religion and, if so, whether that monotheism was Christian or Islamic. Moreover, in each community where Platonic philosophy was being developed, the level of Greek study attainable and the availability of translations from the Greek into the prevailing Latin, Arabic, or vernacular were factors influencing the understanding of doctrine.

During the ancient period of Platonism, Plato's writings were available in Greek and occasionally also in Latin translation (as shown by the extant translations of his *Timaeus* by Cicero, 106–43 BCE, and Calcidius, late 4th–early 5th cent. CE). Following a classification made in the original sources, historians are accustomed to dividing Platonism after its founder's death into two phases: the Old Academy (347–267 BCE), comprising the official heads and other members of the philosophical school established by Plato himself, and the New Academy (267–80 BCE), representing a continuation of the former marked by a radical change of doctrine from a more Platonic to a more Socratic style. Pagan Platonism remained influential in the centuries during which Christianity rose to prominence, and historians have applied a modern terminology to the two phases in the history of this development: Middle Platonism (80 BCE to ca. 250 CE), in which the older Platonic style of philosophy was restored, together with new features drawn from various sources; and Neoplatonism (ca. 250–529), in which the doctrine underwent such radical transformations of a systematic and religious nature that it might reasonably be considered a new phenomenon. The rise to prominence of Christianity is associated with a notable Platonizing of Christian philosophy, and here historians either speak more generally of Christian or Patristic Platonism (so named for the Fathers of the Church) or else, taking account of doctrinal links with contemporary non-Christian thought, of Christian Middle Platonism or Christian Neoplatonism. This article is concerned primarily with influences stemming from this late antique phase and to a lesser extent with those deriving from the Old Academy and Middle Platonism and will deal with both pagan and Christian material. Although influences stemming from Middle Platonism are also of historical importance, they are perhaps more effectively treated in connection with Skepticism than with Platonism.

Medieval Platonism is characterized textually by a severe reduction in the range of Plato's own writings available in milieus where the official language of learning was either Latin or Arabic, and doctrinally by the displacement of Plato himself by the later ancient Platonisms and especially by Neoplatonism. In the Latin cultural sphere between ca. 550 and 1150, the only work of Plato known was the *Timaeus* in Latin translation. Although fresh Latin versions of the *Meno* and *Phaedo* were produced in the 12th century, and a section of the *Parmenides* embedded in a translation of a late ancient commentary on that text became available in the 13th century, the *Timaeus* virtually held the stage alone until the end of the medieval period. However, the nonavailability of Plato's own texts was offset by the enormous influence of Christian Neoplatonism contained in patristic biblical commentaries and doctrinal treatises, and of pagan Neoplatonism in liberal arts handbooks and commentaries on classical poets like Virgil. The medieval Platonism of the Islamic and Byzantine worlds is equally distant from Plato himself and the early Academy. Under the Umayyad and Abbasid caliphs at Baghdad, various works of Plato were translated into Arabic. The dominant philosophical tradition, however, was one in which the Neoplatonism of late antiquity was disseminated as a higher exegesis of Aristotelian texts—a practice initiated by Greek commentators in Alexandria. At Constantinople and especially in the time of the Comneni (ca. 1081–1185) Plato's works continued to be read in Greek. But here the dominant traditions were Greek Patristic Neoplatonism in theology and the Neoplatonism of Aristotelian commentary in philosophy.

From the textual standpoint the Renaissance constitutes a major change in the history of Platonism. Following the inspiration of Petrarch (1304–1374), who elevated Plato as a counterweight to the Averroism that he despised, Italian Humanists of the 15th century embarked on a program of translating Plato into Latin from newly acquired Byzantine manuscripts. This development reached its climax with Marsilio Ficino (1433–1499), who published the first complete non-Greek version of Plato in 1484. From the doctrinal viewpoint, however, things did not change very much. Despite its hermeneutical sensitivity, the reading of Plato and Platonism transmitted by Ficino to later Renaissance and modern thinkers rests firmly within the tradition of pagan and Christian Neoplatonism, important examples of which he also translated. Nevertheless, somewhat tentatively in Giovanni Pico della Mirandola (1463–1494) and more overtly in Gottfried Wilhelm Leibniz (1646–1716), we see the beginnings of the characteristically modern tendency of attempting to distinguish between the doctrines of Plato and of later (Neo-)Platonists.

Because it has had as much effect on literature, music, and visual art as it has in theoretical or practical philosophy, Platonism is arguably the most influential intellectual tradition in European culture. Within the sphere of theoretical philosophy, we find the response to Plato's legacy by later thinkers as being really directed to a comprehensive system rather than simply to individual teachings. Although it is difficult to express this comprehensive system in a few words, one might provisionally characterize Platonism as maintaining that there is a contrast between a realm of being that is not liable to change and is the object of knowledge or reasoning and a realm of becoming that is liable to change and is the object of opinion or sensation. The first realm is identified with the world of universal Forms or Ideas and the second with the world of particular or individual things, the Forms being described as "participated in" or "imitated by" the particulars. Platonism also maintains that the soul, which exists indestructibly, also before and after the period of its association with the body, provides a special link between the realms of being and of becoming, in treating the former as an object not only of its knowledge but also of its aspiration.

Plato's doctrinal influence on European philosophy can perhaps be divided into various broad historical phases initiated by dramatic turning points, these phases embodying some chronological overlap and being independent of the question of Christianization. The first historical phase consists of the encounter between Platonism and Aristotelianism. In the sense that philosophical disagreements had arisen between Plato and his student within the Academy itself, one can obviously date the beginning of this controversy to the lifetime of the master. The notion of a dialectical relation between two fundamental systems of thought, however, could not be fully grasped until their respective proponents had achieved their preeminent status as philosophical authorities. By the end of antiquity the debate between the rival philosophies—which perhaps hinged on Aristotle's rejection of the Ideas' status as separately existing causes of particular things—had achieved a resolution long to be thought definitive. Thus, for Neoplatonic thinkers like Plotinus (205–269 or 270 CE) and Porphyry (233–ca. 304 CE), Aristotle's logical and physical teachings were valid in relation to the lower sphere of sensory becoming, although with respect to the higher sphere of intelligible being only the dialectical and theological doctrines of Plato could apply. In the medieval Latin world, the university or Scholastic philosophers of the 13th and 14th centuries, who had little access to Plato's own writings or to the late ancient commentaries on them but much exposure—via translations recently made from Greek or Arabic into Latin—to the anti-Platonic critique in Aristotle's *Metaphysics* and *Physics,* were compelled to understand the relation between the two Greek philosophers as a completely adversarial one. The reconciliatory strategy mentioned above, however, which was not forgotten at Byzantium and left some traces in the West, came to characterize the Platonist side of the extremely virulent debate that erupted in the 15th century when Byzantine thinkers were forced to react against the Aristotle of Latin Scholastic theology. On the Platonic side were George Gemistus Pletho (ca. 1355–1452) and Cardinal Bessarion (ca. 1403–1472), and on the Aristotelian side was George of Trebizond (1395–1484). The other historical phases and turning points in Plato's influence on European thought—the encounters with the empiricism and mathematics of modern science, with the Kantian critique of traditional metaphysics, and with Heidegger's "destruction" of metaphysics—mostly engaged isolated Platonic doctrines rather than Platonism as a coherent tradition. They have been left outside the main argument of this article but retained for brief comments in the conclusion.

But with respect to the first historical phase, how did Platonic doctrine—the complex of notions summarized above—evolve during the history of European thought? Amid the enormous variety of additions, subtractions, and modifications to the basic set of assumptions made between antiquity and the 16th century, there arose a few notions of such overwhelming philosophical importance that Platonism as a tradition cannot be understood without them.

A first notable transformation of the basic tenets of Platonism was the theory of *hypostaseis* (beings, existents) that, with the advent of Neoplatonism especially, came to replace the original dualism of the intelligible and the sensible mediated by soul. This new theory was an attempt to account for the many aspects of the human encounter with reality by postulating a descending series of levels of experience, each less unitary, less worthy, less powerful, and—with the exception of the second level, which is peculiar in this respect—less real than the previous. Given that the descending series of levels was defined in the first instance by the property of unity, the precise number of levels being assumed even within the thought of a single philosopher became more difficult to determine at the end than at the beginning of the sequence. The theory appeared in two forms, which might be termed the purely Platonic and the Platonic-Aristotelian.

Plotinus provided a statement of the purely Platonic theory of hypostases that would become decisive for the ancient world when he postulated the One or Good, which is the unknowable cause of all things; followed by Intellect, which timelessly thinks itself, is equivalent to Being or the first determinate thing, and contains the totality of the Forms or Ideas; followed by Soul, which generates time and receives the Forms into itself as *logoi*—this threefold structure being supplemented by a division of Soul into a higher Soul and a lower Soul called Nature, and by the placement after Soul of Body, divisible into Form and Matter. For Plotinus, Intellect and Soul were unities of which the pluralities of intellects and souls were essentially modalities. Ficino provided the statement of the Platonic theory of hypostases, which plays an equally determinative role for the modern world. Employing an essentially fivefold structure apparently designed to give prominence to its central or mediating term, he postulated the One or Good, followed by Angel, followed by Soul, followed by Quality, and followed by Body, the first, second, third, and fifth hypostases having properties similar to those possessed by the equivalent terms in the ancient scheme, the fourth hypostasis having properties not previously associated with a single term. For Ficino, Angel and Soul were pluralities of intellects and souls that were not essentially the modalities of a unity.

The Platonic-Aristotelian theory of hypostases, which combined the Plotinian scheme with Aristotle's cosmology, was typical of medieval Islamic philosophy. Thus, in the *Book of the Pure Good,* or *Book of Causes* (before 892) and in the writings of al-Fārābī (Latin Alfarabius; ca. 870–950) and Ibn Sīnā (Latin Avicenna; 980–1037), the hypostasis of Intellect became the series of 10 intelligences, and the hypostasis of Soul the series of 10 souls that moved the fixed stars, planets, and sublunary sphere.

An important aspect of the theory of hypostases is the manner in which each term in the descending series was derived from the previous, a process usually labeled *emanation* in modern historical scholarship if not in the ancient sources themselves. As formulated most clearly by Proclus (ca. 411–485 CE), every process of hierarchical causation could be viewed, first, as containing three moments (that of *remaining,* where the effect is identical with its cause; that of *procession,* where the effect does not maintain identity with its cause; and that of *reversion,* where the effect strives to regain identity with its cause) and, second, as comprising a kind of transition whereby the effect achieves sufficient identity through reversion to become in its turn the cause of a further process. Since remaining, procession, and reversion are sometimes aspects of the derivation of one hypostasis from another (for example, of Soul from Intellect) but are sometimes hypostases themselves whose derivation must be explained (for example, Being, Life, and Intellect), there results an internal multiplication of the levels of being, which is considered to be the defining characteristic of Proclus' philosophical system.

The alterations to which the theory of hypostases was subjected in order to accommodate Christian doctrine are worthy of note. One modification identified the One with God, and Intellect with Angel, but also identified both the One and Intellect with God, obviously on the assumption that intellect has a "created" sense in the former case and a "creative" sense in the latter. This arrangement, which was necessary in order to reconcile God's freedom from the multiple character of Intellect as the Forms with the paradigmatic character of intelligible Form, was worked out by Augustine (354–430) and adopted from him by Ficino. Another modification involving the identification in some manner of the One, Intellect, and Soul with the Father, Son, and Holy Spirit can be found in the writings of Thierry of Chartres (fl. 1121–1148). Because a series of subordinated terms was being assimilated with a set of nonsubordinated terms, Thierry had to explain that the pagan triad constituted merely an exterior reflection of the inner truth represented by the Christian Trinity.

A second transformation of what we have termed the basic doctrine of Platonism, in this case with only a flimsy basis in the original teaching of Plato, involved an increasing emphasis on a superior kind of thinking that is nondiscursive. If discursive thinking is a cognitive activity formulated in propositions or groups of propositions and necessarily temporal in nature—here assuming that the logical formulation of propositions is inseparable from the psychological process of judging—then nondiscursive thinking is a cognitive activity not formulated in propositions or groups of propositions and not requiring temporal articulation. Plato was clearly talking about discursive thinking in the *Phaedo* when he argued that the hypothesis that Forms exist provided a better account of natural processes than did the mechanistic explanation of Anaxagoras, and also in the *Republic* when he described how the rulers of the perfect state ascend to knowledge of the Good by formulating a series of increasingly powerful hypotheses. According to the Neoplatonists, although Plato in the *Sophist* was obviously providing an analysis of propositional form in explaining the utterance "Theaetetus flies," his account of the relations among the "greatest kinds" (*megista genē*)—being, sameness, otherness, motion, and rest—in the same dialogue does not necessarily imply that these terms are linked in a propositional structure.

For Plotinus, the hypostasis of Intellect was characterized especially by a nondiscursive thinking, the existence of which was justified textually by applying to that hypostasis not only a dialectical process of the "greatest kinds" with respect to Intellect derived from Plato's *Sophist* but also the intuitive identity of mind and object with respect to the Unmoved Mover implied in Aristotle's *Metaphysics,* whereas the hypostasis of Soul was especially characterized by the discursive mode of thought. Although the problematic nature of nondiscursive thought often leads to its marginalization in practice, all subsequent Neoplatonists exploited the notion to some degree. A particularly self-confident application occurs in the work of Nicholas of Cusa (1401–1464), who habitually distinguishes the discursive reason (*ratio*) that judges that something is *x,* and that it is both *x* and non-*x,* and that it is non-*x,* and that it is neither *x* nor non-*x,* from nondiscursive intellect (*intellectus*) in which such distinctions do not apply. In the latter case, because the logical subject does not expand in order to receive the alternative predicates, the distinction between subject and predicate and therefore the formal structure of the proposition collapses into what Nicholas famously calls the "coincidence of opposites" (*coincidentia oppositorum*).

A third notable transformation of the basic tenets of Platonism, again with only a flimsy basis in the original writings of Plato, consisted of the tendency toward idealism found in many writers. If we take as a definition of idealism the notion that reality is to some extent mind-dependent—a definition which would encompass not only all the modern philosophical positions usually classified as idealisms but also any premodern anticipations of those positions—it is possible to argue that the theory of hypostases harbors a certain inclination to idealism. But it is important to speak precisely about this tendency, which varied during the history of Platonism. In Neoplatonic writers of late antiquity such as Plotinus and Proclus, the theory of hypostases predominated over the tendency toward idealism, as the notion of mind-dependent objects was applied only within the hypostasis of Intellect. During the medieval period the traditional theory of hypostases was largely eclipsed by the notion of a God who produces the world as his own mind-dependent object. This represents the position of pseudo-Dionysius the Areopagite (late 5th cent.) and John Scotus Eriugena (ca. 815–ca. 877). In Neoplatonic writers of the Renaissance such as Nicholas of Cusa and Giordano Bruno (1548–1600), the theory of hypostases and the tendency toward idealism achieved equilibrium, as the notion of mind-dependent objects was seen as grounding the distinction between the hypostases themselves.

To chart this historical evolution more precisely, it is also necessary to distinguish the various ways in which the mind-dependence of the objects—or alternatively the relation between the mental and the real—in the presence or absence of the hypostases was conceived. Here we should at least contrast the notions (A1) that reality constitutes a single cycle of procession and reversion through several stages and (A2) that reality consists of a series of cycles of procession and reversion connected to one another; and (B1) that the cycle(s) of procession and reversion are simultaneously real and mental, (B2) that there are distinct real cycles of procession and reversion and mental cycles of procession and reversion, and (B3) that the cycle(s) consist of a real procession and a mental reversion. On this basis we should predominantly assign the single cycle of procession and reversion through several stages that are simultaneously real and mental (A1 + B1) to Augustine, pseudo-Dionysius the Areopagite, John Scotus Eriugena, Thierry of Chartres, Nicholas of Cusa, and Giordano Bruno; a series of cycles of procession and reversion connected to one another that are simultaneously real and mental (A2 + B1) to the anonymous *Book of Avicenna on the First and Second Causes* (early 13th cent.); a series of cycles connected to one another, each of which has a real procession and a mental reversion (A2 + B3) to Plotinus, Proclus, and the *Book of Causes;* and a series of cycles connected to one another that is real and a series of cycles connected to one another that is mental (A2 + B2) to Dietrich of Freiberg (ca. 1240–1318 or 1320) and Berthold of Moosburg (fl. before 1361)—although we must sometimes assign several of these patterns to the same writer. With respect to the various ways in which the mind-dependence of the objects was conceived, it may be necessary also to contrast mental in the sense of what is both mental and real with mental in the sense of what is mental but not real. The first sense clearly applies to cyclic causality in all the authors mentioned above, whereas the second has been attributed to one case of cyclic causality in Meister Eckhart (ca. 1260–1327).

Because this attribution probably depends on misreading, it seems better to conclude that application of the notion of something that is mental but not real in such a context is really post-Kantian.

The necessity of accommodating Christian doctrine was responsible not only for increasing the tendency toward idealism but also for determining the precise form in which the latter occurred. It is because Christian theism requires that any priority of the One to Intellect be replaced by the identification of God with both the One and Intellect that the traditional theory of hypostases was eclipsed by the notion of a God who produces the world as his own mind-dependent object. Moreover, because this theism tends to distinguish creation out of nothing from other types of causality and to assign the former to God exclusively, the single cycle of procession and reversion through several stages (A1 + *n*) came to be preferred over the series of cycles of procession and reversion connected to one another (A2 + *n*). The effects of this Christianization can be seen most readily by comparing various Christian formulations with their specific pagan models. Thus, Augustine's theory may be compared with that of Plotinus, pseudo-Dionysius the Areopagite's theory with that of Proclus, and so forth.

These three transformations of what we have termed the basic doctrine of Platonism had an obvious influence on the interpretation of the theory of Forms. In addition to the fact that Plato's original teaching regarding the dichotomy between the world of universal Forms or Ideas and the world of particular or individual things, in which the former is participated in or imitated by the latter, had been combined with Aristotle's teaching that the universal forms have subsistence only within particular things or only through mental abstraction from particulars, we have to consider what this double doctrine of separated Platonic and not really separated Aristotelian forms became when subjected to the theory of hypostases, the emphasis on nondiscursive thinking, and the tendency toward idealism. In connection with the theory of hypostases, we should note that the accommodation of this theory to Christian dogma, whereby the identification of the One with God, and Intellect with Angel, was supplemented by the identification of both the One and Intellect with God, led to difficulties regarding the location of the Forms. The solution favored by Augustine, Anselm of Canterbury (1033–1109), Ficino, and others was to divide the world of Forms into two distinct groups: moral Forms like goodness and truth together with logical Forms like sameness and difference, and mathematical Forms like unity and equality together with cosmological forms like fire and man, and then to identify the first group with divine attributes or names and the second group with thoughts in the divine mind. As for the effect on the theory of Forms of the emphasis on nondiscursive thinking, the most important point is that the Forms acquired a status of nontemporal dynamism. The paradoxical nature of the latter was certainly not evaded by such writers as John Scotus Eriugena, Thierry of Chartres, and Nicholas of Cusa. Finally, in connection with the tendency toward idealism we should note that the identification of God with both the One and Intellect and the attendant notion of a God who produces the world as his own mind-dependent object resulted in a theory of Forms that was both strengthened and weakened. The theory was strengthened in that the Forms no longer had an unspecified status but a status specified as intellectual and intelligible, weakened in that the Forms were no longer universal existents clearly demarcated from particular existents but a single emanation with both universal and particular modalities.

When we turn from theoretical philosophy to practical philosophy and specifically to the field of ethics, we find the response to Plato's legacy by later thinkers as being directed to individual teachings rather than to a comprehensive system. In this area it is undoubtedly the doctrine attributed to Plato regarding the nature of love that has surpassed all others in terms of the intensity and longevity of the discussion it has engendered.

The starting points for consideration of the theme of love are Plato's *Symposium,* where heavenly and vulgar kinds of love are distinguished and love is ascribed a mediating function, and his *Phaedrus,* in which love is associated specifically with the soul's ascent and with the sense of vision. These ideas formed the nucleus of very complex developments in later Platonism. According to Plotinus' *Enneads* 1.6 and 3.5, love is identified on the one hand with the hypostasis of Soul in its relation to the Good as source of beauty and to Intellect and Matter as source and recipient of *logoi* respectively, and on the other with the movement of reversion toward a higher term. In the context of Christian Neoplatonism—for example, that of Augustine, pseudo-Dionysius, and Boethius (ca. 476–ca. 524)—love is identified not only with the souls that replace the hypostasis of Soul but also with God, who represents the combination of the hypostases of the One and Intellect, and not only with the movement of reversion toward a higher term but also with the movement of procession to a lower.

These transformations of Plato's original doctrine regarding love formed the backdrop of important discussions during the Middle Ages and the Renaissance. The medieval debate—which might be described as the "mystical" discussion of love—was conducted not on the basis of Plato's own writings but on those of pseudo-Dionysius and concerned the nature of the higher or spiritual type of love as a modality of the relation between man and God. According to pseudo-Dionysius' *On Mystical Theology,* our final approach to God is something that surpasses the uttering or thinking of both affirmations and negations regarding the deity, although the nature of this something is nowhere specified by the writer. During the Middle Ages one school of interpreters, including John Scotus Eriugena, Meister Eckhart, and Nicholas of Cusa, argued that this transcending approach was a supra-intellectual intellection, whereas for interpreters in the tradition of Hugh of St. Victor (1096–1141), Thomas Gallus (d.

1246), and the author of the *Cloud of Unknowing* (14th cent.) the transcending approach was a supra-intellectual love. The Renaissance debate—which might be termed the "Humanistic" discussion of love—was conducted on the basis of Plato's own dialogues and concerned the natures of both the higher or spiritual and the lower or carnal loves as modalities of the relations between man and God and man (or woman) and man. After George of Trebizond's *Comparison of Aristotle and Plato* had employed as its primary weapon in a polemic against Platonism the alleged recommendation of sexual intimacy between man and boy in the *Symposium,* it was necessary for the rival faction to respond by maintaining the primacy of spiritual love and clarifying the relation between carnal and spiritual loves. We therefore find in the Renaissance a series of Platonic discussions of love, beginning with *Against the Calumniator of Plato* by Cardinal Bessarion, in which the higher love was interpreted in terms of the scriptural love of the *Song of Solomon* and Saint Paul, and continuing with Ficino's *Commentary on the Symposium,* in which a love between males of a chaste variety was accepted as a stimulus to their pursuit of spiritual love, and with *The Book of the Courtier* by Baldassare Castiglione (1478–1529), in which a similar argument was made with respect to a love between male and female, and with many other works. That the Renaissance debate also repeated certain features of its medieval antecedent is documented by another important work in the same genre, the *Commentary on the Canzone of Girolamo Benivieni* by Giovanni Pico della Mirandola.

Although the doctrine attributed to Plato regarding the nature of love has been perhaps his most influential contribution to the history of ethical discourse, it must be admitted that a kind of general Platonic morality pervaded the thinking of many Humanists and especially the Humanists of northern Europe. For example, Desiderius Erasmus (1466 or 1469–1536) contrasted the higher folly of the spiritual life with the lower folly of everyday existence in works like the *Praise of Folly,* and Sir Thomas More (1478–1535) in his celebrated *Utopia* obviously took from Plato's *Republic* his project of discussing the best kind of state as well as many specific features of that state.

We also find the response to Plato's legacy by later thinkers as being directed to individual teachings, rather than to a comprehensive system, when we again turn from theoretical philosophy to practical philosophy but specifically to the field of aesthetics. In this area it is perhaps the doctrines derived from Plato regarding the nature and function of light, proportion, and analogy that have exerted the greatest influence on European thought. Here it is the Pythagorean rather than the Socratic side of Plato's philosophy that is prominent.

Consideration of the theme of light must begin with the analogy of the sun in Plato's *Republic.* Plato there attempts to explain that greatest knowledge that the rulers of his ideal state must possess by comparing the sun's production and illumination of all visible things with the Good's production and illumination of the intelligible world. Having combined this powerful image with the notion of transparency in Aristotle's *On the Soul,* the principle of the double movement of procession and reversion, and various developments in the theory of vision, Platonically inspired writers of late antiquity, in the Middle Ages, and in the Renaissance achieved a conception of solar light as an expression of universal causality that contained perhaps as its most important features the notions of emanation, instantaneity, and mediation. It was undoubtedly Augustine's explanation of human knowledge as an illumination by God and pseudo-Dionysius' evocation of mystical experience as the paradoxical fusion of light and darkness that provided the twin stimuli for the medieval tradition of reflection on the nature of light. Within the philosophical tradition, Robert Grosseteste (ca. 1175–1253) explained the cosmological function of light in producing the nine celestial spheres by emphasizing light's function of extending matter into three dimensions through its tendency to self-multiplication. Within the artistic tradition, Suger of St. Denis (ca. 1081–1151) in explaining the symbolic significance of light in the architecture and artifacts of his abbey church emphasized sensible light's function as mediating the observer's spiritual ascent from the corporeal to the incorporeal realm. The philosophical and artistic traditions come together in a striking comparison—between the stability of God's vision with respect to each person's actions and the painted Christ in Brussels, whose eyes seem to follow the movements of its observers—on which the entire argument of Nicholas of Cusa's *On the Vision of God* is based.

The themes of proportion in the mathematical and analogy in the semantic sphere have a close interrelation, which Plato was among the first to reveal through his geometrical theory of solids in the *Timaeus* and his simile of the divided line in the *Republic.* Here *proportion* represents an equivalence of ratios between terms distinguished in a quantitative manner, and *analogy* likewise represents an equivalence of relations between terms distinguished in a qualitative manner. In musical theory and in the philosophical application of musical paradigms during the Middle Ages, ratio and proportion with respect to the sense of hearing provided the basis for the elaboration of modes and rhythms by a succession of theorists beginning with Aurelian of Réôme (fl. ca. 850) and culminating with James of Liège (ca. 1260–1330). Most of this reflected the influence of Platonic thought transmitted particularly through Augustine's *On Music* and through the *On Arithmetic* and *On Music* of Boethius. During the Middle Ages and Renaissance in the literary sphere it was the genre of allegory—the narrative and temporal extension of analogy that had first risen to prominence among the Stoics of the Hellenistic era and was further elaborated in late antiquity in connection with the exegesis of both sacred and secular texts—that provided the vehicle for Platonism. There is something of a historical irony in the rise of a Platonic allegorical tradition, given that Plato's own *Republic* had argued that allegorical writing in anything other than a deliberately circumscribed form was to be excluded from the ideal society along with its poetical practitioners. Among the most extensive literary works that might be held to represent allegorical Platonism are the *Complaint of Nature* by Alan of Lille (ca. 1128–1202 or 1203) and the *Mutabilitie Cantos* of Edmund Spenser (ca. 1552–1599), both of which contain narrative personifications of the Neoplatonic hypostases of the One, Intellect, and Soul. In architectural theory and in the philosophical application of architectural paradigms during the Renaissance, ratio and proportion with respect to sight provided the basis for the measurement of walls and columns by such theorists and practitioners as Leon Battista Alberti (1404–1472) and Andrea Palladio (1508–1580). In these instances the influence of the Platonic tradition was legitimately combined with that of the Roman architectural writer Vitruvius (fl. 50–26 BCE) because of a shared indebtedness to Pythagorean mathematics.

The preceding discussion has argued that there occurred a coherent albeit evolving intellectual structure in Platonism between late antiquity and the early 16th century. During the subsequent period down to the present day the same label can be applied only to a more disparate collection of phenomena. Some of the main features of the modern reception, however, may perhaps be noted briefly.

In particular, the tendency of attempting to distinguish between the doctrines of Plato himself and of later (Neo-) Platonists—which had perhaps first appeared clearly in Leibniz—continued to gain ground throughout the 18th century. Evidence of this is provided by such reference books as J. J. Brucker's *Historia critica philosophiae* (1742–1744) and Denis Diderot's *Encyclopédie* (1751–1765). The attempt to distinguish between the doctrines of Plato himself and of later (Neo-)Platonists was generally combined with an assumption of the philosophical superiority of the former, for example in the introduction to F. D. E. Schleiermacher's German translation of the writings of Plato published in 1804–1809.

During the late 16th and early 17th centuries the residue of the Platonic tradition encountered the empiricism and mathematics of modern science. Of the two main components of traditional mathematical Platonism—the notions of the a priori validity of numbers and of the symbolic power of numbers—the first alone can be found in Galileo Galilei (1564–1642) and both the first and the second in Johannes Kepler (1571–1630). The variegated Platonism of the period between the early 17th and the early 18th centuries represents an interesting mixture of tradition and innovation. As an example of the older ways of thought, one might mention the philosophy of inner spirituality advocated by the Cambridge Platonists Henry More (1614–1687) and Ralph Cudworth (1617–1688); as an example of a newer perspective, the notion of reality as a system of spiritual monads, each of which reflects the entire universe from its own viewpoint, elaborated by Leibniz. During the late 18th and early 19th centuries the remnants of the Platonic tradition encountered the critical philosophy of Immanuel Kant (1724–1804). In consequence such doctrines of traditional theological Platonism as the notion of a universal intellect and of its nondiscursive thinking would be transferred from a substantial to a subjective form in the Absolute Idealism of G. W. F. Hegel (1770–1831).

It was perhaps historical rather than philosophical studies of Platonism that made the greatest advances during the 20th century. Of special note is the establishment particularly by Willy Theiler and Heinrich Dörrie of the names Middle Platonism (occasionally Pre-Neoplatonism) and Neoplatonism as standard terms to characterize distinct phases in the evolution of late ancient Platonism. (These terms have been used throughout the present article.) Also noteworthy is the thesis of Hans-Joachim Krämer and Konrad Geiser that certain important doctrines were taught orally by Plato but not included in the dialogues, and that these doctrines elucidated the meaning of ideas expressed obscurely in the dialogues.

BIBL.: John M. Dillon, *The Middle Platonists: A Study of Platonism 80 B.C. to A.D. 220* (London 1977). Stephen Gersh, *Middle Platonism and Neoplatonism: The Latin Tradition*, 2 vols. (Notre Dame, Ind., 1986). James Hankins, *Plato in the Italian Renaissance*, 2 vols. (Leiden 1990). Raymond Klibansky, *The Continuity of the Platonic Tradition during the Middle Ages*, 2nd ed. (Munich 1981). P. O. Kristeller, *Renaissance Thought and Its Sources*, ed. M. Mooney (New York 1979), chaps. 3 and 8. E. A. Tigerstedt, *The Decline and Fall of the Neoplatonic Interpretation of Plato* (Helsinki 1974). Richard Wallis, *Neoplatonism* (London 1972).

S.G.

Plautus

Titus Maccius Plautus (ca. 254–184 BCE), Roman comic playwright. Some 21 of his plays and fragments, along with the plays of his later, more sober contemporary Terence, constitute most of surviving Roman New Comedy. This kind of comedy features stock situations from everyday life: a young man, for example, falls in love with a flute girl or courtesan, encounters opposition from a blocking character, but ultimately gets the girl through the tricks of a clever slave. It also features stock character types—the soldier, youth, old man, pimp, and wife—each with a costume and mask. Plautine comedy is inventive, exuberant, varied, full of rollicking eavesdropping scenes, lyrical meters, slapstick, and verbal fireworks. The texts are preserved in two closely related manuscript forms, one as a palimpsest in the Ambrosian Library in Milan, the other in three 10th- or 11th-century manuscripts written in Germany. In 1429 Nicholas of Cusa discovered in Germany an 11th-century manuscript (now Vat. lat. 3870) that contained, among others, 12 previously unknown plays. The *editio princeps* appeared in 1472. Early editors, commentators, and translators ransacked the plays for rhetorical and moral examples.

Though earlier generations tended to depreciate Plautus in comparison with the more elegant Terence, he has always found life in the theater. Pomponius Laetus (1425–1498) and his academy staged the first post-classical performances of the plays in Rome. At the end of the 15th century the court of Ercole I at Ferrara encouraged production and translation; the wedding festivities for Lucrezia Borgia that took place there in 1502 featured the staging of five Plautine comedies on five successive days. Such productions often treated audiences to various entr'acte entertainments—dancing, music, pantomime—as did Italian translations of classical plays, which were likewise beginning to flourish. Latin adaptations of Plautus and Terence, often commingled with elements of medieval drama, appeared in the 15th century from such writers as Leon Battista Alberti, Leonardo Bruni Aretino, and Enea Silvio Piccolomini (later Pope Pius II).

The learned Italian comedy of the 16th century, *commedia erudita,* developed largely through imitation of Roman New Comedy. Ariosto, a pioneer of this genre, transposed Plautine situations and characters into Italian settings. His *I suppositi* (1509, first produced 1528–1531) reworked *Menaechmi,* Plautus' comedy about identical twins, and found its way into English literature through Gascoigne's adaptation, *The Supposes* (1566), the first English prose comedy. Bibbiena's *La calandria* (1513) changed one of the twins to a girl and added a pedant, a necromancer, and a character from the *novelle,* the foolish husband. The introduction of the girl twin, Lidio *femmina,* and that of Fulvia, a female love interest, began a great and fertile innovation to Plautine comedy. There the *virgo,* often a girl of unknown parentage in the power of a slave dealer, is usually a secondary character, distinctly subordinate to the men. Italians moved female figures front and center and placed them in complicated plots and amatory intrigues. Granted ever more audible voices and increasing stage presence, the Plautine *virgo* became in some Italian plays a *donna angelica,* a wondrous figure of healing mercy and love who miraculously appears after reported death—for example, Oddi's Erminia (*Prigione d'amore,* 1590) and Alessandra (*I morti vivi,* 1576), Borghini's Elfenice (*La donna costante,* 1578), Bargagli's Drusilla (*La pellegrina,* 1589), and Della Porta's Carizia (*Gli duo fratelli rivali,* 1601). Plautine adaptations were also written by Lodovico Dolce (1508–1568) and Giovanni Maria Cecchi (1518–1587).

Apart from comedy for learned audiences, Plautus influenced the popular, improvisatory *commedia dell'arte* (14th-18th cents.). In these the *senex* became Pantalone; the *miles gloriosus,* Capitano; the *servus,* Zanni, Brighella, or Arlecchino; the *adulescens* and *virgo,* variously named young lovers; and the *ancilla* or maidservant, Columbine. Rebelling against *commedia dell'arte* traditions, Carlo Goldoni eventually staged a dark adaptation of *Menaechmi* entitled *The Venetian Twins* (*I due gemelli veneziani,* 1748), which ended not in joyful discovery of identity but in poisoning and suicide.

Medieval Spain saw the rise of *comedias elegíacas,* Latin verse that incorporated Plautine passages into dialogue. In the Siglo de Oro, the golden age of literature in Spain (early 16th through 17th cents.), translations began to appear, notably *Amphitryon* by López de Villalobos (1517) and F. Pérez d'Oliva (1530). In 1559 Juan de Timoneda published *Tres comedias,* which included two lively, free versions of Plautine plays, *Amphitrión* and *Los Menemnos.* In the first the slave, renamed Sosia Tardia, speaks Spanish proverbs, delights in olives and rice, and alludes to local customs; in the second, the doctor becomes a necromancer. The Seville native Lope de Rueda (1510–1565) wrote five plays in imitation of Plautus and the Italians, as well as many short farces (*pasos*) that showed the influence of the *commedia dell'arte.* Although Lope de Vega self-consciously proclaimed independence from classical models, he used Plautine traditions innovatively. *The Gardner's Dog* (*El perro del hortelano,* first published 1618), for example, subverts the standard errors and restoration of identity by having the low-born Teodoro fake the discovery of a noble father. Plautus and Terence deeply influenced the *comedia de figurón,* starring a ridiculous figure who personifies a flaw or vice; they also influenced the enormously popular *comedia de capa y espada* (the cloak-and-sword comedies), composed of romantic plots, intrigues, and deceits. Calderón wrote many of these, including *A House with Two Doors Is Difficult to Guard* (*Casa con dos puertas mala es de guarder,* 1629), which adopted New Comedic stage conventions and inflected the visit to the lady's home with the highly inflammable Spanish sense of honor.

Across the Rhine, Hans Sachs, burgher, playwright, and Meistersinger, produced a *Menaechmi* in 1548. Andreas Gryphius, the greatest dramatist of 17th-century Germany, adapted *Miles Gloriosus* into a play (1663) featuring two braggart soldiers with jaw-breaking names, Horribilicribrifax (also the title of the play) and Daradiridatumtarides. Like the Plautine original Pyrgopolynices in *Miles Gloriosus,* these soldiers boast, court women ridiculously, and keep flattering servants who secretly mock them. In France Jacques Grévin imitated the form of New Comedy while adapting the language, setting, and character. He refashioned the Plautine lockout, for example, in *The Treasurer* (*La Trésorière,* 1558), wherein the husband and rival lover suffer exclusion from the home while a third party within makes love to the wife, ironically named Constante. A similar variation on the Plautine *matrona* or wife, Agnes in Grévin's *Taken by Surprise* (*Les Esbahis,* 1560) plays mistress to three men, including an aged husband. Jean Rotrou also wrote Plautine variations, including *Les captifs* (1638, based on *Captivi*) and a *Les ménechmes* (1631) that endows the shrewish Plautine *matrona* with a name, jealousy, and comic pathos. The greatest comic playwright of his age, Molière, imitated Plautus directly in *Amphitryon* (1668) and in the darker comedy *L'avare* (later in 1668), based on *Aulularia.* Molière's Harpagon differs from Plautus's Euclio in his cruelty, pathological loneliness, and, perhaps, insanity. Harpagon plays the *senex amans* who rivals his son for a lady and, simultaneously, the *senex iratus* who blocks his daughter's romance.

Early modern drama in England also drew on New Comedy and especially on Plautus. The prolific Thomas Heywood turned *Mostellaria* into a diverting subplot of *The English Traveller* (1633) and expressed some of the darker potential of *Amphitryon* in *The Silver Age* (1613), wherein the husband beats a servant and Alcmena yearns for death. *The Captives* (1624) refigures the Plautine romance *Rudens,* emphasizing the virtue of the heroine and setting the final scenes not in the Temple of Venus but in a monastery. Ben Jonson started his dramatic career under the tutelage of Plautus, whose *Captivi* and *Aulularia* furnish *The Case Is Altered,* Jonson's earliest surviving play (published in 1609, it apparently was in circulation at least a decade earlier). The exchange of identities between master and servant in *Aulularia* recurs in the persons of the French general Chamont and Camillo Ferneze; Euclio of *Aulularia* gets new life as Jaques, who hides his gold under a dung heap and frets over his daughter Rachel. Jonson returned to Plautus, this time to *Mostellaria,* for his masterpiece *The Alchemist* (first performed in 1610). Here Jonson expands Plautine intrigue into dazzling trickery as two con artists, Subtle and Face, stage their scams in the house of the absent master, Lovewit.

Plautine comedy provided Shakespeare with character and action throughout his career, beginning with the direct imitation of *Menaechmi* and *Amphitryon* in *The Comedy of Errors* (ca. 1594). Shakespeare multiplies the twins and the confusion, increases the love interest, expands the female roles, and emphasizes the elements of romance. *Twelfth Night* (1601) presents further exploration of errors, this time with a gender change, as one of the twins is female (in the style of the Italian *commedia erudita*). Plautine originals inspired some of Shakespeare's great comic creations: Pyrgopolynices swaggers into his plays as Parolles and Falstaff; Euclio and his daughter live on in Shylock and Jessica. Plautine dramatic devices like the lockout, eavesdropping, and disguise appear in strange new forms throughout the Shakespearean canon, as does the standard New Comedic configuration—the blocking father, nubile *virgo,* and yearning lover. This triangle motivates the action of *A Midsummer Night's Dream* (ca. 1596) and undergoes a transformation in *The Taming of the Shrew* (ca. 1594), wherein Baptista has two daughters, and Katherine, no less than Petruchio, plays against the traditional masks and roles. Mothers get into the act in *The Merry Wives of Windsor* (before 1597), and Prospero only pretends to block Miranda and Ferdinand's budding love in *The Tempest* (ca. 1610). The New Comedic configuration recurs poignantly in the tragedies, there turned to dark and deadly ends—the senior Capulets, Juliet, and Romeo; Polonius, Ophelia, and Hamlet; Lear, Cordelia, and Burgundy.

Directly and indirectly Plautus provided later generations with comic models and prototypes. Filtered through Molière, his works inspired Henry Fielding's *The Miser* (1733) as well as *The Intriguing Chambermaid* (1733), wherein the witty French maid, a variation of the Plautine *callidus servus,* is reborn as the delightfully impudent Lettice. She tells an old suitor of three obstacles to his success with a lady: his age, for which half his fortune may compensate; his terrible manners, for which the other half may compensate; and, finally, "that horrible face of yours, which it is impossible for anyone to see without being frightened" (1750, sig. C1v). Accommodations more oblique include the "anti-romantic comedy" of George Bernard Shaw, *Arms and the Man* (1894), which mocks military and amorous ideals; and Bertolt Brecht's *The Caucasian Chalk Circle* (*Der kaukasische Kreiderkreis* 1944), which turns the quest for identity into a scathing critique of modern selfishness.

Amphitryon, the story of the amorous Jupiter's visit to Alcmena, disguised as her husband, has enjoyed many transformations. John Dryden reworked the play in 1690 to emphasize marital discord, providing each Sosia with a wife who gets angry not because her supposed husband (Mercury) makes love to her but because he fails to. Heinrich von Kleist's serious German retelling (1807) explores the doubts, emotions, and pain of the duped wife. Jean Giraudoux playfully recognized the extent of the tradition in the title of his recasting, *Amphitryon 38* (1929). (Modern scholars put the number of previous versions much higher.) Providing comic twists and turns, Giraudoux amusingly discomfits Jupiter, as Alcmène recalls better nights of love with her real husband. Instead of a god's coming in disguise to the unsuspecting wife, Harold Pinter's *The Lover* (1963) has the boring suburban husband transform himself in name and appearance into the passionate lover of his wife, herself changed likewise from prim housewife to erotic mistress. As the couple enacts a shared sexual fantasy, the play explores the attractions and dangers of role-playing and the difficulty of integrating desire into conventional social structures.

Plautus has enjoyed new life on the modern stage and in modern film. Richard Rodgers and Lorenz Hart created the music for one famous descendant of *Menaechmi,* via Shakespeare, *The Boys from Syracuse* (1938). The opening number, "Dear Old Syracuse," playfully rejects classical locality (and authority):

> It is no metropolis,
> It has no big Acropolis,
> And yet there is a quorum
> Of cuties in the forum
> Though the boys wear tunics that are out of style
> They will always greet me with a friendly smile.
> I wanna go back, go back
> To dear old Syracuse.

Menaechmi more remotely inspired the film *Big Business* (1988), wherein Bette Midler and Lily Tomlin play two sets of identical female twins, born in the small town of Jupiter Hollow and accidentally separated at birth. The siblings all cross paths riotously in the Manhattan Plaza Hotel.

The Plautine *servus* Pseudolus appears *in propria persona* in Burt Shevelove and Larry Gelbart's hilarious musical *A Funny Thing Happened on the Way to the Forum* (1962, music and lyrics by Stephen Sondheim), based on

Pseudolus and *Miles Gloriosus*. In the film version (1966) Zero Mostel, a fat, lazy, pop-eyed Pseudolus, schemes to get his freedom by purchasing a young virgin from the house of the sharp slave trader Lycus, played by Phil Silvers, reprising his role as Sergeant Bilko, the fast-talking con man in a popular 1950s television series. Buster Keaton appears as a sad-eyed Erronius. The adaptation catches something of the inventive exuberance and musicality of the original, as the opening number (added later) witnesses:

> Something familiar,
> Something peculiar,
> Something for everyone:
> A comedy tonight!
> Something appealing,
> Something appalling,
> Something for everyone:
> A comedy tonight!
> Nothing with kings, nothing with crowns;
> Bring on the lovers, liars and clowns!

The play enjoyed an award-winning revival on Broadway in 1972 with Phil Silvers as Pseudolus and in 1996 with Nathan Lane and then Whoopi Goldberg in that role. Jason Alexander (*Seinfeld*'s George Costanza) also played Pseudolus, among other roles, in the revue *Jerome Robbins' Broadway* (1989); Desmond Barrit played that tricky slave most recently at the Royal National Theatre in 2004.

The vitality of Plautus in the theater ultimately, in the 20th century, drew critical appreciation away from demeaning comparisons with Terence toward overdue recognition of Plautus's excellence as a playwright. Eduard Fraenkel's *Plautinisches im Plautus* (1922) demonstrated the dramatist's originality in handling Greek originals; W. Beare (1950) illuminated the context of the Roman stage; G. Duckworth (1952) analyzed the plays as popular entertainment; Erich Segal (1968) argued that Plautus provided a Saturnalian inversion of Roman values to evoke Roman laughter. Niall Slater (1985) and Timothy Moore (1998) have studied the power of Plautus in performance. Revivals now proliferate on college campuses and in the professional theater: Peter Oswald's *The Storm,* for example, from *Rudens* (*The Rope*), had a good run at Shakespeare's Globe in 2005. The team of Deena Berg and Douglass Parker (1999) and also Amy Richlin (2005) have produced notably energetic and witty translations of the plays into contemporary English idiom.

BIBL.: W. Beare, *The Roman Stage: A Short History of Latin Drama in the Time of the Republic* (London 1950). Deena Berg and Douglass Parker, trans., *Five Comedies: Miles Gloriosus, Menaechmi, Bacchides, Hecyra and Adelphoe* (Indianapolis 1999). George E. Duckworth, *The Nature of Roman Comedy* (Princeton 1952). Marvin T. Herrick, *Italian Comedy in the Renaissance* (Urbana 1960). Timothy J. Moore, *The Theater of Plautus: Playing to the Audience* (Austin 1998). Gilbert Norwood, *Plautus and Terence* (New York 1932). Karl von Reinhardstoettner, *Plautus: Spätere Bearbeitungen plautinischer Lustspiele* (Leipzig 1886). Amy Richlin, trans., *Rome and the Mysterious Orient: Three Plays by Plautus* [*Curculio, Persa, Poenulus*] (Berkeley 2005). Erich Segal, *Roman Laughter: The Comedy of Plautus* (Cambridge 1968). L. R. Shero, "Alcmena and Amphitryon in Drama," *Transactions of the American Philological Association* 87 (1956) 192–238. Niall W. Slater, *Plautus in Performance* (Princeton 1985).

R.MI.

Pléiade

A group of seven French Renaissance poets whose poetic principles were based on the imitation of the ancients. Known originally as the Brigade, the group of poets that formed the kernel of what has become known as the Pléiade was centered on Jean Dorat (1508–1588), employed as tutor to Jean-Antoine de Baïf (1532–1589) and Pierre de Ronsard (1524–1585) from 1544 to 1547. Teaching subsequently at the Collège de Coqueret in Paris, where he numbered Joachim du Bellay (ca. 1522–1560) as one of his pupils, Dorat instilled in his students an admiration for classical, particularly Greek, poetry, and a deeply syncretist view of the ancient world. To this group of four may be added Remy Belleau (1528–1577), Étienne Jodelle (1532–1573), and Pontus de Tyard (ca. 1521–1605), though other poets such as Jacques Peletier (1517–1582) and Guillaume des Autels (1529–ca. 1581) have also been associated with the Pléiade, a term used by 19th-century critics on the basis of a couple of allusions by Ronsard to the Alexandrian Pleiad.

Although the term itself is now disputed, the poets who aligned themselves with Ronsard shared a common set of values, set out in the enormously influential manifesto published in 1549 by Du Bellay, *Deffence et Illustration de la langue françoyse.* Starting with the proposition that French poetry has previously achieved little of any note, the author puts forward a program for a radically new kind of poetry, with roots in the Graeco-Roman tradition, but avoiding mere translation or servile imitation. To achieve this, writers were exhorted to read the whole corpus of ancient literature so that it became part of their makeup—the principle of *innutrition*—and to draw on this rich vein of writing to form the basis of their own works. Medieval forms of poetry (e.g., the rondeau and the ballade) were to be replaced by classical or Italian forms (the ode, the elegy, the eclogue, the sonnet, the epic), and a suitably lofty diction was to be developed, where necessary, by creating neologisms or making use of archaic terms. Above all, writing was to be governed by the principle of poetic decorum, so that vocabulary, meter, and subject were all appropriate.

After some initial resistance in court circles, Ronsard and his followers achieved considerable success, particularly in the area of love poetry, where sonnet cycles, inspired not only by Petrarchism but also by Neoplatonism, became all the vogue. Du Bellay and Tyard both published collections in 1549 (*L'olive* and *Erreurs amoureuses,* respectively), and many others followed. All the poets associated with the group composed in a wide range of genres, however, including tragedy in the case of Jodelle, and their works are characterized by a highly allusive, frequently allegorical style, in which interpretation often depends on finding precisely the right intertext in a classical author. In addition, they had learned from Dorat that ancient writers such as Homer and Hesiod had, through divine inspiration, acted rather like the psalmist David in revealing universal truths to the human world, albeit in a veiled, mythological form. This colored profoundly their view of ancient texts, in addition to their own poetic goals.

Despite their initial success, literary tastes changed in the final decades of the 16th century, and a reaction set in against the multilayered, sensual, but frequently obscure poetry of the group. In particular, Julius Caesar Scaliger in his *Poetices libri septem* of 1561 and the poetic theories of Malherbe (1555–1628) turned the tide against them by advocating a more straightforwardly elegant style of writing, inspired by Virgilian rather than Greek models. Their reputation did not recover until the 19th century.

BIBL.: Grahame Castor, *Pléiade Poetics: A Study in Sixteenth-century Thought and Terminology* (Cambridge 1964). Henri Chamard, *Histoire de la Pléiade,* 4 vols. (Paris 1939). Dorothy Gabe Coleman, *The Gallo-Roman Muse: Aspects of Roman Literary Tradition in Sixteenth-century France* (Cambridge 1979). Claude Faisant, *Mort et résurrection de la Pléiade* (Paris 1998).

P.J.F.

Pliny the Elder

First-century CE Roman polymath, imperial administrator, and author of the encyclopedic *Historia naturalis.* He died investigating the eruption of Vesuvius in August 79.

"Learned, comprehensive, as full of variety as nature herself": his nephew's critique (*Letters* 3.5) of Pliny's *Historia naturalis* largely explains the survival and enduring popularity of a text that, more than any other, encapsulated for later ages the accumulated knowledge of antiquity. Unlike other ancient encyclopedic works that were lost in antiquity, and the large number of their medieval successors (many of them indebted to Pliny), which did not survive the advent of printing, Pliny's was one of the first ancient texts to be printed (1469). By the early 20th century, there had been more than 200 editions and more than 100 partial editions and criticisms. Tracing its influence is complicated by its very size, which led early on to abridgments, such as the early 4th-century *Medicina Plinii;* the early 3rd-century *Collectanea rerum memorabilium* of Solinus, although not strictly an epitome, was drawn largely, uncritically, and without acknowledgment from the *Historia naturalis.* Judging who has read Pliny firsthand can therefore be difficult, especially if the citations in question are brief and factual. In addition, some readers may have possessed only partial copies of the original. Bede, for instance, seems to have known about half of the 37 books, and there is considerable controversy whether Isidore of Seville knew Pliny firsthand or through Solinus.

For two millennia after its author's death, the *Historia naturalis* has exercised an influence that has changed in accordance with the shifting cultural emphases of successive ages. For medieval readers, it was a repository of information on the natural world; it was embedded in monastic culture, where it was consulted for practical information, especially on medicine, and raided for natural allegories for biblical commentaries. Pliny's factual authority was largely unquestioned, although his information might be edited in accordance with Christian theology, as in the 12th-century précis of Robert of Crichlade.

The advent of Humanism was critical to the reputation and influence of Pliny's work. There was a more holistic appreciation of ancient texts, Pliny's included, as aids to a historically aware understanding and appreciation of classical culture. This interest encouraged successive recensions of a text that, because of an unfamiliar scientific vocabulary, had become increasingly corrupt, as Petrarch had noted when he purchased a manuscript in 1350. The emergence of printing was an added impetus, and most of the early printed editions rested on the textual efforts of Humanist scholars. Petrarch had admired Pliny's inquiring mind, and it was the *curiositas* of Renaissance scholars in the field of natural science, together with greater appreciation of rediscovered Greek texts, that led to increasing calls for works such as the *Historia naturalis* to be evaluated in terms of factual as well as textual errors. The controversy, initiated in 1492, between Ferrara's professor of medicine, Niccolò Leoniceno, who attributed a number of errors not to textual corruption but to Pliny himself, and the jurist Pandolfo Collenuccio, who sprang to Pliny's defense, was symptomatic of an increasing tendency to question Pliny's authority as a scientific source.

This tendency had penetrated beyond specialist scholarship by the 16th century, if Montaigne's complaint (*Essays* 1.26) that mere schoolboys were convicting the author of error and lecturing him on the progression of nature's handiwork is not an exaggeration. That Montaigne attacked such detractors, however, is indicative of the extent to which Pliny was still embedded in the educated culture of the period. That he did so in the context of stressing the possibilities of nature and the danger of mistaking the unusual for the impossible (an unmistakable echo of Pliny himself in *Historia naturalis* 7.7–8) is a reminder that the expansion of geographical and other knowledge could open as well as close minds to the possible truth of Pliny's more extraordinary statements. This phenomenon was mirrored in the enduring popular interest in natural *mirabilia,* many of which originated in the *Historia naturalis.* Enshrined in medieval encyclopedias, popular wonder culture continued until the late 16th century and beyond. The accessibility of the *Historia naturalis* itself was also enhanced by translations into the vernacular; the first English translation, by Philemon Holland (1605), was used by Shakespeare, among others.

The century following Montaigne's defense of Pliny produced the scholar who was perhaps the most sympathetic and perceptive of the *Historia naturalis*'s readers. The physician Sir Thomas Browne (1605–1682), whose explorations of his own, god-centered universe were frequently couched in language reminiscent of Pliny's divine natural pantheism, shared Pliny's tireless curiosity, most notably in his examination of popular conceptions and misconceptions, *Pseudodoxia epidemica* (1650). That many of these originated with Pliny was due in Browne's opinion to the carelessness of readers who failed to note that Pliny did not vouch for his stories, "wherein the credulity of the reader is more condemnable than the curiosity of the Author" (1.8.5).

But Browne's era was also that of Galileo, Vesalius, and Harvey, and Pliny's authority as a natural scientist declined inexorably over the next two centuries. Scholars of the 19th century dismantled the coherence of Montaigne's and Browne's *Historia naturalis* as they mined the text, not in the manner of their medieval predecessors, but in the furtherance of source criticism. Pliny had boasted that he had collected over 20,000 facts from more than 100 authors (*Historia naturalis* praef. 17), an underestimate. Yet those who derided him as a mere compiler were missing an important point: the *Historia naturalis*'s status as a tour de force of collecting, cataloguing, and arranging had directly inspired the developments that led to the modern museum. Federico Borromeo (1564–1631), founder of the Ambrosiana library and picture gallery, mentioned Pliny as his inspiration in his *Musaeum* (1625), whereas Ulisse Aldrovandi (1522–1606) strove to surpass Pliny's total, expanding his notable collection to more than 18,000 specimens by 1595. The *Historia naturalis*'s classification of material into a universal system foreshadowed the great classificatory systems of the 18th-century naturalists such as Buffon and Linnaeus. Finally, although largely superseded, Pliny's work was not forgotten by natural scientists: the early 19th-century Lemaire edition of *Historia naturalis* 7–11 included notes by Georges Cuvier (1769–1832), who had read Pliny in his youth.

Today the *Historia naturalis* has regained its status to a greater extent than at any time since the advent of Humanism. Work by those with scientific as well as philological expertise has resulted in improvements both to Pliny's text and to his reputation as a scientist. The essential coherence of his enterprise has also been rediscovered, and his ambitious portrayal, in all its manifestations, of "nature, that is, life" (*Historia naturalis* praef. 13) is recognized as a unique cultural record of its time.

BIBL.: Marjorie Chibnall, "Pliny's *Natural History* and the Middle Ages," in *Empire and Aftermath: Silver Latin II*, ed. T. A. Dorey (London 1975) 57–78. Paula Findlen, *Possessing Nature: Museums, Collecting, and Scientific Culture in Early Modern Italy* (Berkeley 1994) 61–70. Roger French and Frank Greenaway, *Science in the Early Roman Empire: Pliny the Elder, His Sources and Influence* (London 1986). Charles G. Nauert Jr., "Humanists, Scientists, and Pliny: Changing Approaches to a Classical Author," *American Historical Review* 84 (1979) 71–85.

M.A.B.

Pliny the Younger

I. The Politician and Author

Caius Plinius Caecilius Secundus (ca. 61–ca. 113 CE), nephew of the Roman naturalist Pliny the Elder, had interests that were much less encyclopedic and vastly more influential on later centuries than his illustrious uncle's. Yet his own mark remains conspicuous on several literary genres and a crucial set of architectural questions, and it is fitting that both Plinys are represented together in Renaissance statues on the Cathedral of Como, their native town.

The younger Pliny's speech of thanks to Trajan for his election to the consulship served as a model for rhetoricians in late antiquity, when such public eulogies became a favorite literary genre in Gaul (*Panegyrici Latini*), and after its rediscovery in 1433 it went on to teach many Renaissance and Baroque ceremonial orators how to address supreme political authorities in public speeches that aimed at being eulogistic without servility and at providing advice without rudeness. But above all it was his collection of 247 letters that inspired many later authors. Pliny's letters to his friends and relatives tell of events he witnessed, lawsuits new and old, marvels of nature, his literary and poetic efforts, and services he rendered. They portray noteworthy contemporaries (describing for example the elder Pliny's methods of composition and his death while investigating the eruption of Vesuvius), give descriptions of villas, and recommend up-and-coming talents, such as the young Suetonius. Pliny's correspondence with Trajan offers both a model of how a man of standing and culture should write to a superior—a matter of deep interest to Renaissance Humanists, who offered to teach young men exactly that skill—and a rich source of information about how the Roman Empire had functioned at its height. Pliny's and Trajan's views on how to deal with Christians seemed highly relevant to scholars living through Europe's 16th- and 17th-century religious wars. No wonder, then, that such erudite scholars as Isaac Casaubon and Conrad Rittershusius devoted attention to Pliny's correspondence, or that the letters have continued to play a central role in recent times in assessments of Roman imperial government.

Personal letters worthy of being published as models of style and content are known from Cicero. But in Pliny the addressee often seems no more than an excuse for what follows: in effect a public essay, which at that time had not yet been established as a literary genre. This new form of the epistolary essay was taken up 250 years later by Apollinaris Sidonius, later bishop of Clermont, and by the orator Q. Aurelius Symmachus. Without a doubt the learned correspondence of Christian late antiquity, of Jerome and Augustine, and also of the Renaissance (Petrarch, Aeneas Sylvius Piccolomini, Thomas More) and the age of Humanism (Desiderius Erasmus, Justus Lipsius) is composed of literary letters conceived of as artistic productions. But the model falls just as much into the tradition of the didactic letter, begun by Plato and used to great effect by Seneca and especially the apostle Paul. Though the corpus of Pliny's letters was indeed extant throughout late antiquity and, with little notice, the Middle Ages, it first began to have widespread influence as the literary letter evolved definitively into the essay and shed the epistolary form altogether—one striking example is the bulky collection of essays by the British journalist Gilbert Keith Chesterton (1874–1936). In addition, various phenomena typical of our modern culture, like the newspaper column and the short story, also grew out of the Plinian tradition.

BIBL.: Edward Champlin, "Pliny the Younger (ca. 61–ca. 112)," in *Ancient Writers: Greece and Rome,* ed. T. J. Luce (New York 1982) 1035–1047. Pliny the Younger, *Epistularum libri decem,* ed. R. A. B. Mynors (Oxford 1963), and *Letters and Panegyricus of Pliny,* 2 vols., trans. Betty Radice (Cambridge, Mass., 1969). A. N. Sherwin-White, *The Letters of Pliny: A Historical and Social Commentary* (Oxford 1966).

K.S.

Translated by Patrick Baker

II. Pliny's Villas

It is particularly for Pliny's descriptions of his two country houses that his letters have continued to fascinate later generations. Among his extant letters are one purportedly sent to a certain Gallus (book 2, no. 17) and another to Domitius Apollinaris (book 5, no. 6) that conduct carefully crafted house-and-garden tours, each devoted to a different one of Pliny's villas. Such ancient descriptions extolling the architectural and horticultural charms of country estates are rare in the classical tradition. Later architects, especially, have found the glowing accounts in these epistolary texts to be perennial sources of inspiration for imaginary reconstructions.

Various corrupt Pliny manuscripts circulated in the centuries after his death, until a complete set of the letters reemerged in 1419, paving the way for the *editio princeps* in 1471. As early as the 1430s such Humanists as Francesco Pizolpasso and Guarino da Verona were comparing villas—their own and those of their patrons— to those of Pliny. By midcentury *De re aedificatoria* by the Humanist architect Leon Battista Alberti had already recommended a design solution that Pliny describes in his letter to Gallus. In 1518 the bibliophile Pope Leo X commissioned from Raphael the first documented example of a country house in emulation of Pliny's villas. Raphael described his ideal design for the Villa Madama outside Rome in a letter of his own that conflates passages from Pliny. The Madama's hilltop situation recalls the mountainous locale that Pliny mentions in describing his Tuscan villa to Apollinaris. The Madama's large, circular courtyard, if completed, would have evoked Pliny's seaside villa, supposedly located at Laurentinum, near Rome. Around 1536 Pliny's countryman Paolo Giovio had his own villa built near Como (Museo Gioviano) in imitation of those described by Pliny.

No modern excavation has conclusively identified the site of either of Pliny's villas, despite claims that the Laurentine one was unearthed near Ostia in 1984 and the discovery at a recent Tuscan dig of bricks stamped with Pliny's insignia. This dearth of physical remains suggests that Pliny's sprawling seasonal habitations—summer in the mountains, winter by the sea—may have been largely literary figments. At last count, 72 known imaginative restitutions of the Laurentine and Tuscan villas have resulted from the dreamlike quality of Pliny's prose, coupled with freedom from the constraints of actual ruins to emulate. Some of that number, like Giovanni Ambrogio Magenta's Laurentine plan of ca. 1620 (recently brought to light at Windsor Castle), are architectural drawings; others have exerted more lasting influence by appearing in books. Each designer firmly claims to have provided the definitive interpretation, yet each design reflects the stylistic preferences of its age. Vincenzo Scamozzi began the process by printing his Laurentine scheme in 1615. Published landscape plans by Latinists such as Jean-François Félibien des Avaux (1699) and Robert Castell (1728) show Pliny's villas surrounded by regimented allées of trees reminiscent of Versailles, or with English-style naturalistic gardens like those at Chiswick, home of Lord Burlington (the dedicatee of Castell's book).

Despite their authors' assurances of uniqueness, many of these villa designs resemble one another. For instance, the Frenchman Jules Bouchet's 1852 publication beautifully but derivatively reproduces Louis-Pierre Haudebourt's 1838 design, allegedly inspired by a romantic dream. The Neoclassicist Karl Friedrich Schinkel's sensuous Tuscan and Laurentine designs of 1840 excel at the garden layouts but take into account earlier proposals by the obscure Dresden architect Friedrich August Krubsacius (1760–1762) and the Mexican archaeologist Pedro José Márquez (1796). In the 20th century Clifford Pember, an architect turned movie-set designer, produced a scale model of Pliny's seaside villa (1947) that continues to delight visitors to the Ashmolean Museum at Oxford and also inspired the villa plan included in the Loeb Classical Library edition of Pliny's letters.

In 1981 an international design competition and exhibition on the theme of Pliny's villas generated a wealth of imaginative projects: archaeological in character, like that of Jean-Pierre Adam; Marxist-leaning, like that of Fernando Montes; tongue-in-cheek, like that of Fraisse & Braun; sublimely ethereal, like that of Léon Krier. The theme's seemingly endless possibilities continue to challenge students of architecture and to inspire young practitioners such as Erik Marosi and Thomas Gordon Smith, both of whom have attempted Laurentine restitutions of their own.

This kaleidoscopic and by no means all-encompassing overview conveys only a basic impression of the influential vitality and richness of Pliny's Tuscan and Laurentine villas. In the pantheon of architectural projects that have survived in the classical tradition, these villas continue to occupy a prominent place after 1,900 years.

BIBL.: Barbara Agosti, *Paolo Giovio: Uno storico lombardo nella cultura artistica del Cinquecento* (Florence 2008). Pierre de la Ruffinière du Prey, *The Villas of Pliny from Antiquity to Posterity* (Chicago 1994). Reinhard Förtsch, *Archäologischer Kommentar zu den Villenbrefen des jüngeren Plinius* (Mainz 1993). Pierre Pinon and Maurice Culot, *La Laurentine et l'invention de la villa romaine* (Paris 1982). Pliny the Younger, *Lettere scelte,* ed. Karl Lehmann-Hartleben, intro. by Paul Zanker (Pisa 2007). Helen Tanzer, *The Villas of Pliny the Younger* (New York 1924).

P.D.P.

Plutarch

L. Mestrius Plutarchus (ca. 45–after 120 CE), Greek philosopher, biographer, statesman, and educator. He was born during the reign of the emperor Claudius into an affluent and well-connected family in Chaeronea in Boeotia, a small, remote city nearer to Delphi than to Athens. He came of age within a few years of the fall of Nero and died, after an exceptionally long and productive life, in the early years of the reign of Hadrian. By that time his reputation as the preeminent Greek intellectual of his time was firmly established, and he became an instant classic, cited with deferential respect within a few years of his death, and thereafter constantly at the core of the canon of Graeco-Roman authors. To be educated, throughout much of the history of European culture, has meant having at least some knowledge of the "noble Greeks and Romans," knowledge acquired by way of Plutarch's biographies.

In part because of his hybrid status—an emphatically Greek intellectual in a world dominated in every way by Rome—and in part because the most influential portion of his voluminous works concerns events and personalities ranging over many remote centuries, there is a timeless quality about Plutarch. To think of him as a younger contemporary of the Roman historian Tacitus is difficult; he was not embroiled in the events he wrote about, but viewed them from a scholarly distance. The facts that he took such an interest in the phenomena of religion and the symbolism of myth and cult, and that he viewed these things, as well, across an abyss of time, fascinated by the decline of oracles and the "death" of the god Pan—all contribute to a sense that he somehow belongs to a time several centuries later than his own, more at home in the later, declining Roman Empire than the time of its greatest expansion.

In fact, however, he too, like Tacitus, lived in difficult times for intellectuals in the Rome of the Flavian emperors and had associates who fell victim to Domitian's lethal combination of paranoia and power. As a highly educated and prominent man in Chaeronea, Plutarch performed political and ambassadorial duties, visiting Rome, probably repeatedly, and finding time while there to lecture on philosophy (but not to master Latin, at least not to his own standard). Still, we associate him more with Athens, where he was a student (and where education had replaced other sectors in a much diminished economy), with bucolic Chaeronea, where he lived much of his life, and with Delphi, where he served late in life as a priest of Apollo's oracular shrine. Even in old age, his status attracted duties and honors, first from Trajan and then from Hadrian, who made him Procurator of Achaea, an office that (if not wholly honorific) carried with it administrative duties and the oversight of the imperial property in the province. Along with all this, he at various times in his life concerned himself with education, probably including rhetorical education.

The corpus of Plutarch's works is huge and divided into two quite disparate parts. First is the *Parallel Lives,* which have gone under many collective titles, perhaps most colorfully *The Worthies of the World; or, The Lives of the Most Heroick Greeks and Romans Compared* (London 1665). This enormous project, with its overdetermined and rhetorical symmetry, numbered, when complete, 23 pairs of biographies, each presenting a Greek and a Roman (in one case two of each) as foils to each other. A single pair—the first in order of composition, *Epaminondas and Scipio*—has unaccountably been lost, but the minor lacunae occurring everywhere in ancient texts aside, the project has reached us otherwise intact. This is unquestionably due to the fact that it has been one of the most frequently and continuously read books of the Western tradition. A few other Plutarchan biographies that do not fit into this bilateral symmetry are known, some surviving and some (including most of a series of emperor biographies) lost.

The *Lives* seem to have been a project of Plutarch's mature years, begun when he was about fifty and continued into the early decades of the 2nd century. He mentions the sequence of composition of a few of the pairs, but modern editions have in general arranged the *Lives* more or less in the chronological order of the Greek biographies, so that the *Parallel Lives* are usually presented as beginning with *Theseus and Romulus,* the founders of Athens and of Rome, and concluding with the relatively obscure *Philopoemen and Flamininus,* both statesman-generals of the last quarter of the 3rd and first quarter of the 2nd centuries BCE. This procrustean solution to an insolvable problem—we have no evidence how Plutarch himself would have arranged a complete edition—obscures the fact that many of Plutarch's noble Romans are concentrated in the late Republic. Thus, on the Roman side, the *Parallel Lives* end chronologically with the deaths of Antony and then of Cleopatra in 30 BCE.

The rest of his corpus, given collectively the traditional title *Moralia,* is just that: the rest. It is a huge grab bag of nearly 100 items of various lengths, including essays (some "moral"), dialogues, rhetorical display pieces, and collections of anecdotes and stories (probably compiled for the use of students and practitioners of rhetoric). Not surprisingly, given his prestige and the large size of the authentic corpus, there are a considerable number of works of questionable or clearly un-Plutarchan provenance as well.

In the decades after Plutarch's death, his literary status and reputation were maintained by his friends and then by *their* younger friends. This burst of eulogy of Plutarch in the 2nd century was no doubt instrumental in laying the foundation for the extraordinary reputation he was to enjoy later. Aulus Gellius, the 2nd-century author of a rambling but elegant and scholarly intellectual miscellany entitled *Attic Nights,* cites Plutarch frequently. One of Gellius's teachers in Athens was L. Calvenus Taurus, himself once a pupil—or at least a young friend—of Plutarch. Favorinus, a colorful figure and prolific writer to whom the much younger Gellius attached himself, appears in Plutarch's *Table Talk* and forms a bridge between Plutarch's generation and Gellius's. In *Attic Nights* ignorance of Plutarch is one of the defining characteristics of a "boor" (*opicus,* 11.16.7), and Plutarch himself is evoked by Taurus as "a man of the greatest learning and wisdom" (1.26.4). Gellius even contrived to make *Plutarch* the first word in *Attic Nights,* and Gellius's contemporary Apuleius has the protagonist of his novel *The Golden Ass* proclaim himself a descendant of "the famous Plutarch" (1.2) (Holford-Strevens 2003, esp. 283–285). *Attic Nights* was a favorite with the Renaissance Humanists, in part for qualities it shares with Gellius's model, Plutarch.

The key to Plutarch's tremendous prestige during the centuries following his death is his preeminence in rhetoric, in eloquence as much as thought. Intellectually, he has been found wanting by modern scholarship. He is a tremendously valuable witness for the intellectual life of the half century between Nero and Hadrian, but he gets little credit for original ideas. He opens a window on contemporary issues in Platonic, Stoic, and Epicurean thought, but his presentation of the arguments is often questionable, and not only because he gives them to us in a context of polemic. These deficiencies bothered his admirers in the later Roman Empire not a bit. It was Plutarch's eloquence they praised, and in an age in which philosophy and rhetoric were in large part reconciled (or better, when eloquence broadly usurped the prestige of philosophy), flowery praise of Plutarch was frequent.

Eunapius of Sardis, whose *Lives of the Sophists* is our principal guide to the rhetorical and intellectual revival of the 2nd and 3rd centuries known as the Second Sophistic, calls Plutarch "oracular" and "the grace and lyre of all philosophy" (454). Many of Plutarch's interests—the symbolism of religion, hermeneutics, the souls of animals, and more—had little precedent in earlier Greek literature, so Plutarch appeared to introduce into literature and serious discussion generally matters that surfaced again and again in the literature of the later empire. His status among later Platonist thinkers was remarkable, as was the frequency with which he emerged as a figure of importance in the history of a given intellectual problem. For all his unexpected philosophical status, however, the same Eunapius provided the evidence that around the year 400 the *Lives* were still considered "the finest of his writings" (454).

The Athenian and Alexandrian practitioners of Platonic philosophy dug in their heels against the growing force of Christianity, and from the 4th to the 6th centuries they were, as a result, increasingly marginalized and isolated. But Plutarch had died before the existence of Christianity needed to be acknowledged in his intellectual landscape. Since Augustine and other Christians had identified Platonism, among the varieties of pagan wisdom, as the one ripest for appropriation, Plutarch, one of the last Platonists of the Roman Empire who was not explicitly anti-Christian, looked more than congenial. The rather simple, unexceptionable ethical messages of the essays that gave the *Moralia* its title likewise lent themselves to reuse in sermons and other edifying genres, and so Plutarch came effortlessly to have his place in Christian rhetoric.

A few generations after Plutarch's death, as Christianity began to take on intellectual respectability, Clement of Alexandria was making very extensive use of the corpus, including some of the pseudepigrapha. The absorption of Plutarch into Christian education encountered few obstacles. A little over a century after Eunapius offered his elegant tribute, the classicizing Christian Agathias, at the court of Justinian, composed this epigram on a statue of the biographer:

> The sons of the great Ausonians, Chaeronean
> Plutarch, set up your renowned image,
> because in your parallel lives you fitted the
> noblest Greeks to the warlike Romans.
> But a life parallel to your own, not even you
> could write, for you have no equal.
> (Palatine Anthology 16.331)

The Byzantines inherited from the Church Fathers an already assimilated, immediately available Plutarch, whose fortunes inevitably varied with the times and with the contraction and regrowth of the Byzantine world of learning. Aside from the Lamprias Catalogue (a tantalizing list of 227 works allegedly by Plutarch, perhaps a library list from as early as the 3rd century), little is known of the state of Plutarch's corpus before the late 13th century. Then, not long before 1300, a Byzantine monk named Maximus Planudes (himself a lover of rhetoric and learning) devoted himself to assembling everything that survived. His project had several stages (Russell 2001, 147), but the result was—some undoubted pseudepigrapha aside—very close to what we now think of as the extant works of Plutarch. Against all odds, Planudes' editorial accomplishment is represented by three important surviving manuscripts, apparently dating to his lifetime, that found their way to Milan and Paris.

Plutarch all but disappeared from the consciousness of Greekless Western Europe after the 5th century, but he rode the wave of the return, figuring in the curricula of the first schools of Greek in Italy in the 15th century. Among Greek prose authors, he, Plato, and Aristotle were the best represented in the libraries of 15th-century Italy. Translations into Latin and the vernaculars began in the 14th century; the *Parallel Lives* could be read in their entirety in Latin by 1470. Jacques Amyot's much-retranslated French version of the complete works was finished just over a century later (1572), and in 1579 Thomas North published his complete English *Lives* (often referred to as "Shakespeare's Plutarch," after its most famous reader and imitator). By that time, both the *Moralia* and the *Lives* could be read in their entirety in German, Italian, and Spanish as well.

It is no exaggeration to say that Renaissance and early modern Europe discovered Greece and Rome through Plutarch's eyes. This meant, first and foremost, that Western Europe was introduced to Alexander the Great, Julius Caesar, Antony and Cleopatra, Pericles, and all the other *capitanes valerosos* (as Cervantes called them, with a nod to Plutarch) as Plutarch portrayed them. If the tales of their daring and their superhuman accomplishments gripped the imaginations of many in 15th- and 16th-century Europe, this was because Plutarch's rhetorically and imaginatively charged portraits were their first introductions to the noble Greeks and Romans. The success of Plutarch, in his own time, in the Renaissance, and today lies in his accessibility and in the organization of his portraits. What could have been more appealing to Renaissance readers, at a time when individualism—or better, "self-fashioning," to borrow Stephen Greenblatt's term—was taking on a new meaning, and a new breed of princes of unprecedented ambition, ruthlessness, and culture was emerging.

There is in fact a complex relationship between Plutarch and self-fashioning. Now that Greenblatt has turned our attention to its role in the mentality and the social relationships of the Renaissance, we tend to look for other periods in which self-fashioning has played a special part. If we direct this inquiry to the Graeco-Roman world, the periods that stand out—5th-century Athens, Alexander and his successors, and the late Republic—are precisely those in which Plutarch's biographies are concentrated. Plutarch's reinvention of that past has a part in our own perceptions of it, no less than it did for Renaissance readers, and in the English-speaking world this fact is inseparable from Shakespeare's *Julius Caesar, Antony and Cleopatra,* and *Coriolanus.* The language of North's Plutarch is repeatedly audible behind Shakespeare's own, and the biographies' role in shaping these three plays is pervasive. If Caesar and Cleopatra have come to be the major exemplary figures of antiquity in the English tradition, the reasons are easily found. In both instances, Plutarch had before him sources that were both vivid and (for political reasons) contradictory, and in each instance he created a synthesis that was already rhetorical and theatrical. Of Cleopatra, in particular, it is fair to say that it was Plutarch who invented her for the subsequent tradition, later receiving more than a little help from Shakespeare.

Another among the many Renaissance readers of Plutarch who deserves special mention is Montaigne. For him, Plutarch—the Plutarch of the essays and dialogues—was a stylistic model in a unique sense. Few modern readers of Plutarch, however enthusiastic, have not been frustrated by the essayist's insistent pluralism, his diffuseness, his utter lack of commitment to pursuing an argument to a unique and necessary conclusion. The skeptical Montaigne—whose invention of the essay for the modern tradition was in multiple ways indebted to Plutarch—praised precisely that diffuseness, that timeless willingness to view the matter at hand from every perspective, embracing even the attendant contradictions. As he saw it, the alternative was dogmatism, and Plutarch was the author who could teach us to avoid it.

Admirers like Shakespeare and Montaigne are the strongest witnesses to the significance of Plutarch in what was surely his moment of greatest prestige and influence. It is important to realize, however, that when Plutarch was praised by medieval and Renaissance authors, it was not always *our* Plutarch who was meant. Both Rabelais and Montaigne, among many others, referred to Plutarch as an authority on Homer, but that authority was in fact vested in a widely known and often reprinted introduction to the *Iliad* and *Odyssey,* usually called *De Homero,* no longer thought to be an authentic work of Plutarch. Similarly, the medieval notion of Plutarch the adviser of emperors—though, like "Plutarch"'s claims to Homeric expertise, it had some historical validity—rested in large part on a forgery known as the *Institutio Traiani,* which entered on the stage of literary history quite improbably with John of Salisbury in the 12th century.

Plutarch's stature was so great in the Renaissance that a decline was perhaps inevitable, but it was long in coming. In the 18th century the same texts that had fueled a cult of personal ambition and accomplishment in the Renaissance were continually repoliticized in new and different ways. The *Lives* provided models for the whole political spectrum, and the ebullient classicism that went hand in hand with the anticlericalism of the French Revolution greatly privileged Plutarch's exemplary Greeks and Romans, particularly the latter. At the time, however, it was the opponents of Caesar and of tyranny who were invoked as models, especially Cato and Cicero. The founders of American democracy were avid readers of Plutarch as well, and some laced their prose with evidence of that fact. Franklin and Hamilton, in particular, proclaimed their admiration for the *Lives.*

It was not until the 19th century that historians began to distance themselves from a Plutarch who—though he himself emphatically differentiated between his biographies and the writing of history—had become de facto the most popular historian of Greece and Rome. This rejection, along with a decline in the taste both for his grand, rhetorical antitheses and for his diffuse, expansive style as an essayist, marginalized him in an age when his noble Greeks and Romans had themselves lost some of their aura. There were still admirers—notably Emerson, the main link between Plutarch and the remarkable Platonist revival in 19th-century American intellectual life—but the chorus of praise was distinctly less enthusiastic.

On the whole, Plutarch has been the hero of a popularizing mode of classicism since the Renaissance, and it has been primarily in contexts where such an interest has flourished that he has been read and admired. Professional historians now tend to cite him reluctantly and disparagingly, and only when he is a source of last resort, but the story in the classroom is a different one. Their elegant, rhetorical symmetries stripped away, Plutarch's biographies are the texts of preference of many if not most undergraduate courses in ancient history. They thus have the extraordinary privilege, among ancient texts, of serving today much the same purpose for which they were apparently written. With their vividness and theatricality, they provide an alternative to narrative history that has a durable appeal, keeping them among the most-read books about Greece and Rome. Given that we seem still to glean satisfaction from using the Greeks and Romans as a foil and point of comparison for ourselves, they may well have a long future in that role.

BIBL.: Tim Duff, *Plutarch's Lives: Exploring Virtue and Vice* (Oxford 1999). Rudolf Hirzel, *Plutarch* (Das Erbe der Alten, 4) (Leipzig 1912). Leofranc Holford-Strevens, *Aulus Gellius: An Antonine Scholar and His Achievement,* rev. ed. (Oxford 2003). C. P. Jones, *Plutarch and Rome* (Oxford 1971). Robert Lamberton, *Plutarch* (New Haven 2001). D. A. Russell, *Plutarch,* 2nd ed. (London 2001). R.L.

Poetics

The phenomenon of poetry, understood as measured speech, was dealt with by a number of classical authors, either on its own or in connection with rhetoric, which teaches the appropriate way of expressing oneself in any given circumstance. The boundaries between the two were anything but impermeable.

Classical Greek works. On the Greek side, Hesiod (7th cent. BCE) was probably the first to opine that most poetry belonged to the realm of fiction and to state that poets were likely to be liars, though he also conceded that they could speak the truth when they chose to do so (*Theogony* 27–28). But serious discussion of the nature of poetry started, as did so many other things, with Plato (428–348/7). An eminent man of letters himself, Plato was very skeptical of the moral effects of poetry on the soul, and he strenuously denied its usefulness in the quest for truth, which he considered to be the philosopher's sole aim. Though allowing the divine origin of poetry (in *Phaedrus* 245A, the canonical formulation of what would later be known as *furor Platonicus,* "Platonic frenzy"), he ridiculed rhapsodists (professional interpreters of poetry) in the *Ion.* He notoriously banned the poetry of Homer (whom he revered), as well as dramatic representations, from his ideal republic because of their deleterious effects on public mores (*Republic* 2–3, 10) and even stated in *Laws* (700A–701B) that poets are the real "ring-leaders of lawlessness, because they are ignorant of that kind of justice and law that is a fruit of the true Muse." For these and other similar pronouncements, the philosopher K. R. Popper would famously call Plato an "enemy" of any "open society."

Aristotle in his *Poetics* (the first work exclusively devoted to the topic to survive) was more historically minded and less judgmental than Plato. The *Poetics* has not survived in its entirety; its second part, which would have dealt with comedy, is lost. (That loss has been a source of inspiration for many writers: Umberto Eco colorfully imagines how and why it might have come about in his novel *The Name of the Rose,* 1980; and J. L. Borges, in "Averroës' Search," in the collection *The Aleph,* 1949, describes, with greater sobriety, Averroës' despair at being unable to understand and translate the notions of "tragedy" and "comedy" into Arabic.) Setting out to discuss poetry in general—its origin, its genres, and their development, plot, construction, etc.—Aristotle held that the key notion for its understanding is *mimēsis,* a word variously translated as "imitation" or "representation." *Mimēsis,* he maintained, is accessible to rational discourse and conceptual interpretation—a conviction that "has elicited admiration in some readers, and discomfort in others" (Halliwell 1998), since it sets exacting intellectual standards for would-be literary critics.

Unlike Hesiod and especially Plato, Aristotle insisted that poetry is "more philosophical and of greater ethical import than history, since poetry is more closely related to the universal, whereas history relates particulars." The "universal" here invoked is "the kinds of things which it suits a certain kind of person to say or do, in terms of probability or necessity" (*Poetics* 9.1451b). This was an extraordinarily felicitous observation, a healthy antidote against irrational subjectivism and any sort of vaguely felt empathy, but it did not have the kind of later influence that it deserved.

Another notion first formulated in Aristotle's *Poetics* that did (and still *does*) have an influence quite out of proportion to its real importance is that tragedy, "through the arousal of pity and fear, brings about the catharsis of such emotions" (6.1449b). The German classicist Jakob Bernays (1824–1881), in a monograph of 1858, was the first to point out that the "cathartic," or "purgatory," function of tragedy was apparently rooted in archaic orgiastic cults, an interpretation that seems to have deeply influenced Friedrich Nietzsche's first major work, *The Birth of Tragedy out of the Spirit of Music* (1872; later editions bear the subtitle *Hellenism and Pessimism*), which split the German intelligentsia of the day into two opposing camps. (It also may have helped Sigmund Freud, who was married to a niece of Bernays, to formulate his "cathartic method," most notably in his *Studies on Hysteria,* 1895.) It must be said, however, that in the absence of any explanation of the meaning of "catharsis" by Aristotle himself, its exact significance may never be conclusively established.

Besides texts such as the ones just mentioned that deal with the nature and essence of poetry, one finds in antiquity treatises devoted to applied literary criticism and practical craftsmanship. One of the oldest to survive is the extraordinarily useful *On Style,* of uncertain date but conventionally ascribed to Demetrius of Phaleron (ca. 360–280 BCE), who was a pupil of Aristotle and a friend of Theophrastus. Demetrius distinguishes the grand, the elegant, the plain, and the forceful styles and describes the means to be sought or avoided in order to achieve each of them. A 13th-century Latin paraphrase of the treatise (preserved at the University of Illinois) significantly omits all mention of the fourth style, since its presence conflicted with the medieval theory of three styles (see below). The scribe of this manuscript patently thought that *On Style* was part of the pseudo-Aristotelian *Rhetoric to Alexander,* for it follows immediately after that text and ends with the words "here concludes Aristotle's *Rhetoric.*"

Issues similar to the ones found in *On Style* are dealt with in the works of Dionysius of Halicarnassus (1st cent. BCE), whose *On Literary Composition,* a treatise on how to choose and to arrange words, is the most important in the present context. They feature as well in the five works ascribed to Hermogenes (d. ca. 225 CE), which were introduced to the Latin West by the generous use the Byzantine émigré George of Trebizond made of them in his Latin treatise *Five Books on Rhetoric* (ca. 1433; publ. 1471).

If Hermogenes' *On Ideas* contains the most comprehensive treatment of the issue of style in Greek, the anonymous *On the Sublime* (early 1st cent. CE), usually ascribed to an otherwise unknown Longinus, contains perhaps the most original. Although this treatise, first printed in 1554, had little influence in the 16th century, it became immensely popular after 1674, when Nicolas Boileau published a French translation, establishing it as a central text in European literary criticism throughout the 18th century until the beginning of Romanticism, which finally took for granted the freedom from rules advocated by its ancient author.

Many other Greek treatises taught how to write and appreciate both verse and prose, of which the *Progymnasmata (Preparatory Exercises)* of Aphthonius (4th–5th cent. CE) were perhaps the most popular until recent times. These exercises contain 14 definitions of key rhetorical notions such as "fiction," "praise and blame," "comparison," and *ekphrasis,* each illustrated by at least one example. This made the work particularly well suited for beginners, and it was virtually omnipresent in the Renaissance, after the Marburg professor Reinhardus Lorichius (d. 1556 or 1564) had trimmed down, rearranged, and translated the 14 categories into Latin to produce a 400-page octavo that was universally used as a quarry for *loci communes* (commonplaces) of ancient poetry, history, and eloquence (more than 100 printings in at least 25 cities are known before 1700).

Classical Latin works. Although poetics and rhetoric are properly Greek inventions, we must turn to Latin antiquity for the two texts that were read and referred to more often than all others until very recent times. Pride of place undoubtedly belongs to the anonymous manual addressed to C. Herennius, the *Rhetorica ad Herennium* (1st cent. BCE). This rather dry and technical compendium would probably not have achieved the signal success of becoming a textbook for well over a millennium, starting from the time of Saint Jerome (347–420), had it not been transmitted in the corpus of Cicero's rhetorical writings, following after *On Invention.* Because of its position in the manuscripts it was referred to, at least from the 12th century onward, as the *Second* or *New Rhetoric,* in the mistaken belief that Cicero himself had written it to replace his juvenile *On Invention* (known as the *First* or *Old Rhetoric*). Book 4 of the *Rhetorica ad Herennium* comprises the oldest systematic treatment of style in Latin, in fact the oldest extant inquiry into the subject after Aristotle. Although it depends in that respect on Greek models, it further offers the oldest extant division of the kinds of style into three, as well as the first formal study of figures to survive in its entirety. The division of style into grand (or high), middle, and simple (or low), and of figures into figures of speech (such as alliteration or repetition) and figures of thought (such as metaphor or metonymy), remained unquestioned throughout the Middle Ages and the Renaissance and is still partly adhered to today. More than 100 surviving manuscripts, as well as translations or adaptations into Italian (Guidotto da Bologna and Bono Giamboni, *Fiore di rettorica,* before 1266), French (by Jean d'Antioche de Harens, 1282), Castilian (by Enrique de Villena, 1427), and Greek (by Maximus Planudes, 14th cent., and by Theodore Gaza, 15th cent.), testify to the enormous diffusion and popularity of this pseudo-Ciceronian text.

Of equal importance, though for entirely different reasons, was Horace's *On the Art of Poetry* (*Ars poetica,* 18 BCE). Far from a systematic treatise on poetry, it consists of various precepts and analyses that Horace, himself a poet, thought important. Two of these proved to be especially influential. The first, an explicit summons to imitate Greek models (268–269), was echoed and adapted to his own time and circumstances by Joachim du Bellay in his *Defense and Illustration of the French Language* (1549), which advised the future poet to "read and reread, above all, give your nights and days to Greek and Latin models" (2, chap. 4). The second, a statement that the main aim and purpose of poetry was "to combine the useful with the pleasant" (343), though perhaps an aside in the overall architecture of Horace's poem, became one of the crucial elements for defining the nature of poetry and its place in society, right up until Friedrich Schiller's *Letters on the Aesthetic Education of Man* (1795), where the *Sittengesetz* (moral law) corresponds to the useful and the *Schöne* (the beautiful) to the pleasant.

Other works from Latin antiquity noteworthy for their subsequent influence include Cicero's *On Invention* (84 BCE), which was nearly as popular as the *Rhetorica ad Herennium* (165 surviving medieval manuscripts have been identified); his *Topics* (44), which deals with the question of how to find and formulate arguments pro and con; and his twin treatises *On the Orator* (55) and *The Orator* (46), which, although primarily concerned with public speech, gave aspiring poets and theorists precise notions of how to order and present complex material. Quintilian's *Education of an Orator* (*Institutio oratoria,* late 1st cent. CE) would become famous for its detailed presentation of the five canonical parts of a speech —proem, narration, proof, refutation, and peroration— which would reappear, for example, in French guise in Brunetto Latini's encyclopedic *Treasure Books* (*Li livres dou trésor,* ca. 1260) as *prologue, fait, confermement, deffermement,* and *conclusion. Education of an Orator* would also be remembered for Quintilian's insistence on the necessary ethical foundation of speech in general and for his portrait of the elder Cato as "a man of flawless character, skilled in speech" (12.1.1), generally taken to imply that a blameless life of high virtue was the necessary prerequisite for skillful, that is, morally irreproachable, use of language.

Late antiquity. Moving forward in time, we should note especially Diomedes' *Art of Grammar* (4th cent.), the third book of which is entirely devoted to poetics and metrics. Diomedes is chiefly recognized as the first to formulate a comprehensive theory of poetical genres. His first genre, dramatic or active poetry, consisted solely of actors playing, without any addition of the poet's voice: "in Greece, tragedy, comedy, satyr [play], and mime; in Rome, the *praetextata* or tragedy with a Roman subject, low comedy, popular farce, and pantomime." The second genre, narrative or exegetical poetry (with a number of subdivisions, including historical and didactic poetry), consisted solely of the poet speaking in his own voice: "Hesiod's *Catalogue of Women* . . . the philosophical poems of Empedocles and Lucretius . . . the *Georgics* of Virgil, and suchlike poems." In the third genre, mixed or common poetry, the poet both spoke in his own voice and introduced other characters speaking: "heroic poetry such as the *Iliad* and the *Aeneid,* and lyric poetry like that of Archilochus and Horace." Distinction of these three genres of poetry became a topos of all medieval reflections on the subject, by virtue of its inclusion in the *Etymologies* (8.7, On Poets) of Isidore of Seville (d. 636), as well as in Bede's *On Prosody* (*De arte metrica,* ca. 700), although the latter replaced the classical examples with biblical ones. In fact, the division of poetry into dramatic, lyric, and epic, still commonly accepted today, goes straight back to Diomedes.

The Middle Ages. Building on the legacy of antiquity, the Latin Middle Ages witnessed a number of specific though not independent developments in poetics, of which four are especially noteworthy.

(1) The *accessus ad auctores* (ways of approaching [i.e., interpreting] authors) method was widely applied to texts in general and to poetry in particular. These devices would almost certainly not have gained the prominence that they achieved from the 8th century onward as the main hermeneutical toolbox of the Middle Ages if they had not been deployed at the very beginning of one of the most universally read texts besides the Bible, Servius' *Commentary* (ca. 400 CE) on Virgil's *Aeneid:* "When explaining an author, the following points should be carefully studied: the poet's life (*poetae vita*), the title of the work (*titulus operis*), the generic quality of the poem (*qualitas carminis*), the author's aim (*scribentis intentio*), the number of books (*numerus librorum*), the order of the books (*ordo librorum*), [and] the meaning (*explanatio*)." The explanation of the author's aim and of the poem's meaning required exegetical (grammatical, lexicographical, rhetorical, metrical, historical, and antiquarian) skills, and the whole approach rested on the assumption that each and every text had one clearly identifiable meaning and purpose. (Servius understood the purpose of the *Aeneid* was "to imitate Homer, and to praise Augustus through the praise of his ancestors.")

Closely akin to but apparently independent of Servius' recommendations for the proper understanding of literature was another interpretative framework distilled into a list of seven *circumstantiae* or *periochae,* concomitant qualities of every text. Summarized in the less than perfect hexameter *Quis, quid, ubi, quibus auxiliis, cur, quomodo, quando?* these were supposed to answer the questions Who? (the author, the main character), What? (the title of the work, its main plot), Where? (the setting of the story), By what means? (human or divine), For what purpose? (praise, blame, edification), How? (by simple narration, or ornate speech), and When? (mythical times, or a historical era). Here again it was assumed that these questions admitted of one and only one answer—a patently absurd assumption for minds with some degree of sophistication.

(2) Such minds turned readily to the intellectually more challenging idea that literary texts cannot, as a rule, be reduced exclusively to one single meaning, and would have chosen the rival option that texts can, and often do, have a three- or fourfold sense. This approach had originated in Greece with what was known as the allegorical explanation of the Homeric poems: *allēgorein* means "to signify something else besides that which is obvious at surface level." Gods gladly committing adultery, for example, could not mean just that, and stories depicting them as such had to have a different (some would say, a deeper) meaning besides. Allegory was mainly developed in the context of scriptural exegesis by the Jewish Neoplatonist Philo of Alexandria (1st cent. CE) and especially by the Greek Church Father Origen (185–253).

It was in the West, however, that the most systematic accounts of allegory were elaborated; these normally extended the number of meanings to be reckoned with to four, which were eventually summarized in two shaky hexameters ascribed to Augustine of Denmark (d. 1285): *Littera gesta docet; quid credas, allegoria;/moralis, quid agas; quo tendas, anagogia* (The literal sense teaches what happened; allegory teaches what one should believe;/the moral sense teaches what to do; the anagogical sense teaches whither to strive). The stock example used to illustrate this fourfold division, from the *Conferences* of John Cassian (ca. 360–ca. 430), a monk of the Eastern Church who wrote in Latin, refers to the city of Jerusalem: in the literal (historical) sense, it means the ancient capital city of the Jews; as an allegory (interpreted from a doctrinal point of view), it can be understood as the Church; morally, or tropologically (concerning the lessons to be learned for one's life), it stands for the human soul; and anagogically (lifting the mind to the contemplation of ultimate reality), it can be identified with the celestial Jerusalem. In general, the Old Testament lent itself more easily to being read and interpreted along these lines (especially its more enigmatic books, such as the openly erotic *Song of Solomon*) than did the New Testament.

	High style	Middle style	Low style
Title	*Aeneid*	*Georgics*	*Bucolics*
Social class	warrior	farmer	shepherd
Name	Hector, Ajax	Coelius, Triptolemus	Tityrus, Meliboeus
Animal	horse	ox	sheep
Tool	sword	plough	staff
Place of action	town	field	pasture
Tree	laurel tree	fruit tree	beech tree

Thus, it was mainly to the former that this theory of four senses was applied as an interpretative strategy, though with notable exceptions, such as Augustine's *On the Literal Interpretation of Genesis,* which served in turn as a model for the widely read *Commentaries* of the Spanish theologian Alfonso Tostado ([1400–1455). There are also a number of famous instances of the fourfold theory being applied to profane texts: the interpretation of Virgil's Fourth Eclogue as a Messianic poem announcing the Virgin Birth of Christ; the *Commentary* on *Aeneid* 1–6 ascribed to Bernardus Silvestris (12th cent.), which sees in the wanderings of Aeneas the course of human life from birth to manhood; Pierre Bersuire's (14th cent.) *Ovidius moralizatus* and book 15 of his encyclopedic *Reductorium morale;* and Cristoforo Landino's Neoplatonic interpretation of *Aeneid* 1–6 in his *Camaldulensian Disputations* (ca. 1474)—a work not altogether different in outlook from that of Bernardus Silvestris—and his commentary (1481) on Dante's *Divine Comedy,* itself a massive allegory on a truly cosmic scale.

(3) Very different in outlook from these first two approaches but no less influential in application was the *rota Vergilii* (Virgil's wheel), whose canonical formulation is ascribed to John of Garland (d. 1272). The name derives from its representation as a series of concentric circles, schematized here in tabular form.

The notion that the three main works of Virgil could serve to illustrate the three kinds of style set out in the *Rhetorica ad Herennium* (4.8.11) had already occurred to the ancient commentators on the poet. They, however, reduced it to an issue of *elocutio* (manner of expression): solemn, smooth, and ornate language in the high register; correct but unadorned language in the middle register; everyday, perhaps even sloppy, language in the low register. But from an issue of style, it became one of social status: for John of Garland, the main criterion was the quality of the actors rather than the sophistication of the language. This parallelism between the manner of expression and a very specific social rank had two momentous consequences. It established a hierarchy among the genres that mirrored the hierarchy of medieval society. (This effect manifestly was not intended by the *Rhetorica ad Herennium,* which saw expression as subservient to appropriateness; different circumstances simply require different ways of expressing oneself, which are in no way intrinsically superior or inferior to one another.) It also allowed epic poetry, supposedly featuring kings, queens, and heroes, to be likened to tragedy, mostly with the same cast of characters. This notion was pursued to such a degree that parts of the *Aeneid* (mainly book 4) were rewritten as tragedies, on the premise that they contained "characters of high rank," as Nicodemus Frischlin explained in the preface to his *Dido: A New Tragedy, . . . Portraying the Passionate Love of Dido and Aeneas, and Its Tragic Outcome* (1581). His fellow German Humanist J. J. Volfius similarly argued, in the preface to his *Two Tragedies Taken over from Virgil's Aeneid: The First about Dido, the Second about Turnus* (1591), that it was perfectly legitimate to make book 4 of the *Aeneid* into a tragedy because its main characters were "famous heroes, princely characters, kings, queens, and generals." The misguided poetics of the *rota Vergilii* thus paved the way for the theoretical underpinning of one of the more interesting 16th-century developments in the confrontation between genres, establishing for centuries to come the primacy of tragedy and of epic poetry over all other poetic genres.

(4) A final word needs to be said about the medieval treatises exclusively devoted to poetics. They deal chiefly with questions of how to structure and to present the subject matter: directly or indirectly? by way of amplification or of understatement? with the help of figures of speech and thought, or without? etc. But without entering into the complexities of their frequently daunting technical expositions of such matters, we should remember that these treatises were written with the dual purpose of (descriptively) explaining how the texts of the classical authors were crafted, and (prescriptively) teaching how one should write decent Latin poetry by imitating, emulating, and even surpassing the artifices used by the classical models. Matthew of Vendôme (12th cent.), Galfridus de Vino Salvo (13th cent.), and a host of less well-known authors wrote manuals on the art of versifying, entitled *Artes versificatoriae* or *Poetriae,* informed by the convictions that metrical speech can be explained, understood, and taught by means of rhetorical analysis and that only a perfect mastery of the tools of the trade enables one to write poetry worthy of that name.

The Renaissance. It is helpful to begin discussion of poetics in the Renaissance by dispelling a number of errors that have crept into reference works and other sources. It is, first, a mistake to believe that "Renaissance poetics" can be defined by any sort of unity of content or intent. That is simply not true, although it is often repeated that Renaissance treatises on poetics are "in general" indebted to one of the three canonical positions (Plato, Aristotle, or Horace) inherited from antiquity, and that these can be reduced to more or less subtle musings on *furor* (frenzy), *mimēsis* (imitation), or *utilitas* (usefulness). It is also wrong to claim that some of the larger treatises on poetics (e.g., J. C. Scaliger's *Seven Books of Poetics,* 1561) attempted anything like the impossible task of synthesizing these three, along with other, ultimately irreconcilable positions. Further, it should be borne in mind that the extraordinarily large quantity of works on poetics produced during the Renaissance, whether commentaries on specific texts or independent works, makes any sort of generalization highly implausible. No reliable figures exist, but a conservative estimate is that in Italy alone at least 260 *Poetics* were published in the 50 years between 1535 and 1585. And some of the more interesting treatises on poetics were issued under titles that would not immediately lead one to suspect the true nature of their content. For instance, Alberico Gentili, an Italian jurist who taught at Oxford, cast his defense of poetry and drama in the form of a learned work on Roman law: *Commentary on the Third Law of the Title of* [Justinian's] *Code "On Teachers and Doctors"* (1593). Clearly, it would be invidious and misleading to try to do full justice to a highly complex and often contradictory phenomenon by singling out a handful of texts and applying to them such terms as "pioneering," "important," or "influential." That said, a few spotlights focused on a handful of core issues will have to do, with the proviso that they do not exhaust the topic under discussion.

Much, probably too much, has been made of the supposed influence of Aristotle's *Poetics* in the Renaissance. As with the dialogues of Plato, the Latin translation of Aristotle's text (by the Italian Humanist Giorgio Valla in 1498) preceded the first edition of the Greek original. The *Poetics* was not included in the five-volume complete works of Aristotle in Greek published by Aldus Manutius from 1495 to 1498; not until 1508 did it appear in the sizable folio volume of Greek rhetoricians edited by the Byzantine scholar Demetrios Doukas and issued by the Aldine press. It is crucial to remember that more than the rediscovery of Aristotle's treatise as such, it was the publication of this volume as a whole that marked the rebirth of ancient rhetoric and poetics. The table of contents is worth reproducing in full:

(i) Aphthonius (4th cent. CE), *Progymnasmata*
(ii) Hermogenes (2nd cent. CE), *Rhetoric*
(iii) Aristotle (4th cent. BCE), *Rhetoric*
(iv) Pseudo-Aristotle, *Rhetoric to Alexander*
(v) Aristotle, *Poetics*
(vi) Sopatrus (4th cent. CE), *Treatise on Progymnasmata*
(vii) Cyrus the Sophist (of unknown date), *On the Difference between Statuses*
(viii) Dionysius of Halicarnassus (1st cent. BCE), *Rhetoric*
(ix) Demetrius of Phaleron (4th cent. BCE), *On Style*
(x) Alexander the Sophist (1st/2nd cent. CE), *On Figures of Thought and Speech*
(xi) [Anonymous], *On Figures*
(xii) Menander Rhetor (3rd cent. CE), *On Epideictic Speeches*
(xiii) Aelius Aristides (2nd cent. CE), *On Political Speech*
(xiv) Aelius Aristides, *On Simple Speech*
(xv) Apsines (3rd cent. CE), *Rhetoric*
(xvi) Minucianus the Younger (3rd cent. CE), *On Methods of Proof*

It is obvious at first glance that the volume contains texts of widely different provenance, content, and scope. Writers on poetics had to make choices, and the overwhelming richness of material transmitted in these texts was further supplemented by a host of other, less technical, but no less important sources that had become newly (and comparatively widely) available in the West during the century following the fall of Constantinople (1453) and the invention of printing (1454). Thus, the few lines devoted to the prehistory and origins of poetry in Aristotle's *Poetics* could be richly interlarded with details about the characters acting onstage derived from the *Onomasticon* (1502) of Pollux (2nd cent. CE); by information regarding the musical instruments, songs, and dances accompanying dramatic performances found in the *Deipnosophistae* (*Professors at Dinner*) of Athenaeus (2nd cent. CE) (1514); by the detailed discussions of the origin of Greek comedy contained in the anonymous *Introductions to Comedy,* heading almost all editions of Aristophanes published in the 16th century; or by similar analyses concerning Latin comedy set out in the treatises *On Fable* and *On Comedy* attributed to Euanthius (4th cent. CE) that were universally prefaced to Terence. Scholia (on Pindar, on the Greek tragedians, on Theocritus, on Lycophron, and on many other authors) would also be used, not to mention the works of lexicographers and antiquarians such as the *Attic Nights* of Aulus Gellius (2nd cent. CE) (1469), *On the Meaning of Words* by Sextus Pompeius Festus (2nd cent. CE) (1500), the *Dictionary of Republican Latin* by Nonius Marcellus (1471), and the Byzantine lexicon known as the Suda (10th cent. CE) (1499).

A similar embarrassment of riches would confront any author trying to come to grips with the classical theories of poetical genres. Though Diomedes was omnipresent, his threefold classification could not account for the many minor genres of occasional verse, the *Silvae* (literally *Forests* but meaning *Raw Material*), a title already given by Statius (1st cent. CE) to his collection of (broadly speaking) lyric verse and later taken up by Angelo Poliziano (1454–1494) to describe his own poetical introductory lectures to classical authors. Here, Menander of Laodicea's treatise *On Epideictic Speeches* (ca. 3rd cent. CE), which gave precise indications of how to write poems for birthdays, marriages, funerals, etc., would come to the rescue. Interestingly, some authors thought that even Menander's comprehensive survey was not nearly complete enough: Scaliger, after discussing Menander's *epibaterion* (a speech delivered by someone returning home after a long absence abroad), remarked that people leaving home could equally well deliver a public speech of farewell, and that this might be called an *apobaterion* (*Poetics* 3.106). This innovation was to become an indispensable feature of some of the most widely read 17th-century works on poetics (see, for example, Johann Buchler's *Treasury of Sacred and Profane Expressions*, printed at least 18 times between 1621 and 1679), and it even gave rise to real verse compositions, such as the "Apobaterion to His Aberdeen," published by the Scottish Neo-Latin poet and physician William Barclay in his *Poemata* of 1637. This is but one example of the undeniable fruitfulness of theoretical poetics for the practice of writing polished verse.

Similarly oriented toward practical usefulness were manuals of poetics that gave advice on metrical matters. This may seem a very technical issue, but Latin poets, as well as readers of Latin poetry, needed to be aware that *levis* with a short first syllable means "light," whereas the same word means "smooth" when the first syllable is long. Because classical poetry consists, formally speaking, of alternations of short and long syllables according to sets of well-defined patterns, it was absolutely mandatory to know what quantity was allowed in what part of the verse—and what was considered to be a verse, or a stanza, in the first place. Here again, classical treatises came to the rescue: most prominently, but not exclusively, Servius' *On One Hundred Meters* for Latin poetry, and the *Handbook* of Hephaestion (2nd cent. CE) for the various forms of Greek meter. In practice, the dactylic hexameter carried the day for Neo-Latin epic (e.g., Petrarch's *Africa*) and for didactic poetry (e.g., Girolamo Fracastoro's *Syphilis*, 1530), whereas the sapphic stanza, introduced into Latin poetry by Horace, was one of the preferred lyrical meters (and was also used for a large number of hymns sung in the Catholic Church). The Netherlandish schoolmaster Johannes Murmellius (1480–1517) composed what was probably the most widely read Renaissance treatise on metrics, *Tables Presenting the Rudiments of the Art of Verse Composition*, which went through 64 editions between 1515 and 1658. The various manuals entitled *Gradus ad Parnassum* (*Steps to Parnassus*) still in use today for Latin verse composition do not greatly differ from the textbooks used 500 years ago.

Many other issues inherited from antiquity were debated (more often than not controversially) in Renaissance poetics. Examples include: Should the three levels of style be abandoned, since they were unable to accommodate the minor genres, and replaced by the 21 qualities of style distinguished by Hermogenes? How could the mind-boggling contradictions inherent in the various treatises devoted to the figures of style and of thought be dealt with? Who should be imitated, and why: Greeks or Romans, Homer or Virgil, many authors or just one? What was the place of poetry in society, and in relation to the other arts? Were the rules that applied to religious poetry different from those to be observed in secular poetry? What was the relationship between Latin and vernacular poetry? Should the action of a tragedy take place within the span of 24 hours, or not?

No facile generalization is ever likely to do justice to these questions, and the only way to find out what individual authors thought about them is to read their works against the background of the whole of the classical tradition accessible to them. Full critical editions of the major Renaissance treatises on poetics therefore remain an urgent desideratum.

As was the case with so many other aspects of the ancient world, the Renaissance marked the real heyday of the rediscovery and reappropriation of classical poetics. Although some treatises (probably Scaliger's more than most) continued to be quarried, often indirectly, until well into the 18th century, the rise of vernacular literature and the "quarrel of the ancients and the moderns" (which was decided in favor of the latter) meant that some of the categories specifically developed for Greek and Latin poetry had to be abandoned, or at least supplemented by others. Furthermore, the high value assigned, in the wake of the Romantic movement, to subjective aesthetic assessments based on the individual's own mood or whim to the detriment of objective criteria of judgment meant that any sort of poetics claiming to establish a set of rules for creation, appreciation, and criticism was likely to be frowned on.

For these and other reasons, both the art and the science of poetics, as presented here, seem to have spent their vital force. Like so many other words, *poetics* has lost its precise meaning in recent decades. Its increasingly inflationary use is a sure sign that it no longer has any clearly identifiable contours: books are now being published about the poetics of "critical space and postmodernity," of the "in-between," of "technoscience" and the "chronotope," even of "soccer" and "village politics," with subgenres including "destructive," "disembodied," "transcultural," "visionary," and many other "poetics"—with no end in sight.

BIBL.: E. Faral, *Les arts poétiques du XIIe et du XIIIe siècle* (Paris 1924). C. C. Greenfield, *Humanist and Scholastic Poetics, 1250–1500* (Lewisburg, Pa., 1981). S. Halliwell, *Aristotle's Poetics* (Chicago 1998). G. A. Kennedy, *The Art of Persuasion in Greece* (London 1963) and *The Art of Rhetoric in the Roman World, 300 B.C.–A.D. 300* (Princeton 1972). H. Lausberg, *Handbook of Literary Rhetoric* (Leiden 1998). J. C. Scaliger, *Poetices libri septem: Sieben Bücher über die Dichtkunst*, ed. and trans. L. Deitz (books 1–4, 7) and G. Vogt-Spira (books 5–6) (Stuttgart 1994–2003).

L.D.

Political Theory

Although the term *political theory* has only recently come to stand for a distinct field of intellectual inquiry, theorizing about political life is an activity in which ancient Greek and Roman writers certainly excelled. The depth and originality of their reflections on politics, as well as the prestige of their names, would no doubt have gained them considerable attention from later generations. But two additional factors have made the classical legacy especially important in the history of Western political thought.

First, there is the unique combination of familiarity and distance associated with our classical inheritance. Classical traditions typically provide their heirs with exemplary cultural models. But in the Western tradition the "classical" authors are untimely as well as exemplary. They call out to us from the far side of some of the deepest divides in our historical self-consciousness: pagan-Christian, ancient-modern, and so on. Heeding their call thus compels us to take some distance from ourselves and ask what is keeping us from living up to the classical models that we admire. This is especially true in a field like politics, where these models challenge basic structures of authority and social organization, not just the tastes and beliefs of individuals. As a result, the classical tradition in political theory is much richer and more diverse than one might expect. Political theorists have, ironically, developed many of their most original ideas in response to the appeal of classical political ideals and institutions.

The second factor that gives the classical legacy special significance for modern political theorists is the revival of republican and democratic forms of governance in the last two centuries. In politics, unlike most other areas of modern life, the classical tradition seems to becoming more, not less, timely, because Greek and Roman writings are grounded in a familiarity with everyday democratic politics that is completely lacking in most of the great works of political theory between our age and theirs. Of course, it takes considerable effort to uncover their insights into the nature and value of democratic institutions, given the distaste for democracy expressed by most ancient writers. But that has not stopped political theorists from mining classical sources for alternative visions of democratic theory and practice.

Given their extraordinary influence on later political thinking, a chronological account of the afterlife of classical political ideas could easily turn into a breathless rush through the history of Western political thought. Thus, rather than tracing the influence of classical political theorists on their successors, this article focuses on some of the most original and influential ideas that the former have inspired among the latter. From a brief summary of the contents and character of the classical heritage in political theory we may distinguish and illustrate five ways in which later political theorists made use of that heritage. What this thematic approach lacks in comprehensiveness it should make up for by highlighting the depth and diversity of the significance of classical ideas in the development of Western political thought.

The classical legacy in political theory consists of historical and dramatic writing, as well as philosophical texts. The philosophical legacy begins, of course, with the writings of Plato and Aristotle and their followers. Plato's most important political works are his two longest dialogues, the *Republic* and the *Laws*. Aristotle's key works in this area include the *Rhetoric* and the *Nicomachean Ethics*—whose fifth book presents his seminal analysis of the concept of justice—as well as the *Politics*. Next in importance to Platonic and Aristotelian texts are probably Cicero's political writings, though more for the ideas that they transmit than for the original insights of their author. Cicero's version of the *Laws*, for example, contains the most complete extant account of the Stoic view of natural law; his *On Duties* presents an effective synthesis of Roman and Stoic views of public morality. Epicurean political philosophy is much less developed and influential on the subject of politics, as should be expected from a sect that advises us to retire with our friends to the privacy of our gardens. Nevertheless, Lucretius' ideas about the social contract and the state of nature sparked considerable interest in early modern Europe, particularly with Rousseau, whose story about the evolution of civil society (in his *Discourse on the Origins of Inequality*) is clearly modeled on the one that he found in book 5 of Lucretius' *Nature of Things*.

Although classical philosophic analyses of politics have had the deepest effect on the ideas of later political theorists, the works of Greek and, especially, Roman historians have at times rivaled the works of ancient philosophers as bearers of the classical legacy in political theory. For example, the idea of the mixed regime, one of the most influential of classical political concepts, has been disseminated primarily in the fairly mechanical version presented by Polybius in book 6 of his Roman history, rather than in the much subtler version developed by Aristotle in book 4 of the *Politics*. Similarly, the image of republican virtue that inspired so many later thinkers owes its origins more to such historians as Sallust, Livy, and Plutarch than to the writings of the classical philosophers. The most influential classical study of political corruption, the obsession of so many modern republicans, is undoubtedly Tacitus' account of the first Roman emperors in his *Annals*. And Thucydides' history of the Peloponnesian Wars is the first and perhaps the most inspiring of all analyses of international politics and its influence on domestic political life. His devastating account of the consequences of civil war is probably the inspiration for modern political theory's most famous single image: the portrait of the state of nature as a war of all against all, painted by his early English translator, Thomas Hobbes.

Greek dramatic writing has, in contrast, only recently begun to draw the attention of political theorists—although Hegel did base a crucial argument in his *Phenomenology of Spirit* on an extended analysis of Sophocles' *Antigone*. The main objects of attention have been Aeschylus' *Oresteia* trilogy, the seven extant plays of Sophocles, and a few of Euripides' plays, such as *The Bacchae* and *Medea*. Interestingly, Aristophanes' comedies have also begun to be seen as a source of political insight. Valuable work is now being done, for example, on his parody of Socrates in *The Clouds,* his ridicule of communism and equality in *The Assemblywomen,* and his utopian satire, *The Birds.*

Generalizations about the character of the classical legacy in political thought require considerable caution. One of the most common fallacies in the classical tradition is the celebration of the "ancient" view of liberty or some other value, when it is really a Greek—or rather an Athenian, or rather an Aristotelian, Platonic, or Periclean—view that one has in mind. Nevertheless, these materials do tend to share a number of characteristics that help explain their influence on later thinkers.

The first of these common features of the classical legacy in political theory is probably the most obvious: its republicanism. The Greek and Roman writers, as Thomas Hobbes complained, taught that "no man is free" in any other than a republican government—a fact that led Hobbes to lament that "there was never anything so dearly bought, as these Western parts have bought the learning of the Greek and Latin tongues" (*Leviathan* chap. 21). The great classical political texts were written for citizens who took turns ruling and being ruled, rather than for the subjects of monarchs. And those that were written after the collapse of republican institutions, like the histories of Livy and Tacitus, were clearly inspired by republican ideals as well. The one great exception is Plato's *Republic,* which, with its invocation of a philosopher-king, gave powerful ammunition to those who idealized monarchic rule, despite its utopian character.

A second common feature is an emphasis on the priority of the community in political life. With the important exception of the Epicureans, who, as already noted, developed a contractarian view of political society, the classical writers generally began by asking about the place of individuals within communities rather than by asking how individuals go about constructing political institutions to meet their needs and solve their problems. (The contractarian view is explicitly presented and rejected in both Plato's *Republic* and Aristotle's *Politics.*) They tend to treat the bonds of justice and friendship as manifestations, rather than corrections, of human nature. This tendency in classical political thought is often characterized as a disdain for the value of private life. But that characterization is not quite accurate. All the classical schools, Platonists, Aristotelians, and Stoics, not just Epicureans, expressed doubts about the ultimate value of politics and a commitment to a public life. What they denied was that we can or should construct public institutions in ways that would best serve the private interests of individuals. For them, to engage in public life was to accept the priority of communal concerns and obligations. The pursuit of private needs entailed the individual's withdrawal from politics, usually to a life of philosophic contemplation, rather than a program of political reform.

A third shared feature of classical political thought follows naturally from the second: its association of politics with morality. The classical writers that have come down to us—again excepting the Epicureans—treat politics as an activity that perfects our character and judgment, rather than as a means to private ends. But the political morality that they celebrate is the kind exercised by people who share in the making and execution of laws, rather than the kind sought after by people who need to figure out which laws they ought to obey. Classical political morality thus focuses more on the development of virtues, such as equity, prudence, liberality, magnanimity, and good judgment, than on the identification of morally correct political standards to follow. For this reason, later political thinkers have often turned to classical political thought to challenge political moralism as well as reliance on self-interest.

Finally, there is the decidedly aristocratic or oligarchic strain in the classical legacy as it has come down to us. Apart from a few historians like Herodotus and Sallust, the disdain for democracy is almost universal in our sources. (Here, at last, is one opinion that the Epicureans share with their rivals.) From Plato and Aristotle to Livy and Tacitus our sources make it quite clear that the wealthy and well-born have a stronger claim to rule than the people, an opinion that follows from the demands that the political virtues make on the time and resources of individual citizens.

Those who draw more positive insights into democratic ideals and institutions from classical sources do so in a variety of ways. Some focus attention on advocates of democracy whose voices are preserved within our sources—Protagoras in the Platonic dialogues or Pericles in Thucydides' history, for example. Others generalize claims that in our sources are made about elites, such as the celebration of the liberty and dignity of Roman grandees. Still others work through the broader implications of alternative analyses of the functioning of democratic institutions that can be found in their work, as many political theorists have done with Aristotle's account of democracy in the *Politics.* That said, it is important to remember that when political theorists draw insights into the nature and value of democracy from their classical sources, they are almost always reading them against the grain.

Appeals to classical political ideals and institutions have been a constant in Western political thought since the collapse of the Roman Republic, let alone the fall of the Roman Empire. But theorists making these appeals have used the classical legacy in very different ways for very different purposes. To appreciate the breadth and depth of the classical tradition in political theory, we need to distinguish these different ways of invoking the ideas of ancient Greek and Roman political thinkers.

Many later thinkers have been inspired by the classical legacy to call for the recovery or renewal of the sound approach to politics that they discovered in ancient Greek and Roman texts. But others, like Thomas Aquinas, have tried to work out some kind of synthesis of the best of classical and post-classical moral and political ideals. Still others, like Machiavelli and Montesquieu, have invoked classical political ideals to help emancipate people from moral and religious authorities empowered by such syntheses. The most radical devotees of classical political ideals, like Rousseau and some of his German heirs, have demanded a revolutionary transformation of modern individuals and society in order to correct the flaws that keep us from living up to ancient models. And their critics, such as Benjamin Constant, have sometimes used our inability to live up to classical ideals to help us identify and become reconciled to our distinctive political strengths, as well as our limitations. Renewal, synthesis, emancipation, revolution, therapy—the classical legacy in political theory has served its heirs as a means to all these ends and has thus inspired an extraordinary range of political insights.

The simplest and most direct response to the appeal of the classical legacy in political theory is to call for the recovery of its most admired ideals and institutions, as do so many republican admirers of classical politics. Medieval and early modern Europe may have been dominated by monarchs and emperors. But because the classical education connected their subjects to a glorified republican heritage, the assertion of republican political ideals has usually been seen as a return, rather than as an innovation, in Western political history.

The call for the renewal of classical republican ideals first took shape among the Humanists of the Italian Renaissance, heirs in their city-states to republican institutions as well as to classical texts and ruins. Drawing on Cicero and Aristotle, among others, they strove to articulate and popularize the sense of communal engagement that they believed the modern world had lost. They sought, in particular, to recover from classical authors the spirit as well as the practice of republicanism, the sense of what it means to be a citizen rather than a subject. In doing so, they gave birth to a tradition of discourse about politics that has come to be described as civic humanism, a tradition that spread from Renaissance Italy to Reformation Europe and then to revolutionary England, France, and America. Interestingly, this discourse persisted even after the recovery of republican political institutions, as its advocates sought to recover the spirit of republican citizenship, not just the end of monarchy and empire.

Political virtue and its corruption are the special focus of civic humanist discourse, a focus that it owes largely to the Roman writers of the late Republic and early Empire. For Cicero, Tacitus, Livy, and most other writers of this period, the collapse of republican institutions was the primary fact of political life. They bequeathed to their heirs an image of republicanism in danger, an image that highlights the corrosive effect of wealth and power on the virtues of character upon which republican institutions were founded. Civic humanists have eagerly exploited this image in their efforts to recover the spirit of republican citizenship, a tactic that eventually set them at odds with modern thinkers who celebrated the civilizing effects of the growth of luxury and commerce.

Nevertheless, there is at least one important sense in which civic humanist discourse tends to depart from its classical sources: its democratization of the concept of political virtue. Virtue retains its classical sternness in civic humanist rhetoric, but not its aristocratic hauteur. Increasingly, it came to be seen as the expression of the honest citizen's devotion to duty, rather than the excellence or perfection of human qualities that we expect from those endowed with substance and position. Rousseau completed this democratization of classical political virtue in his *Discourse on the Arts and Sciences,* where, inspired by Montesquieu's conceptualization of republican virtue as the passionate love of one's country, he celebrated virtue as "the sublime science of simple souls"—a description that must have made Cicero and Tacitus, let alone Plato and Aristotle, turn in their graves. Modern republicans are inclined to democratize classical political virtue because they tend to invoke it as part of an effort to recover the meaning of citizenship, something that, unlike excellence or perfection, is shared by great and small within republics.

The civic humanist tradition is notable more for its rhetoric and breadth of influence than for the creativity of its theorizing. Most civic humanists are studied today for what they can teach us about their time and place rather than about the nature of republicanism. The most original thinkers associated with their tradition of discourse—Machiavelli, Montesquieu, and Rousseau, for example—all burst the boundaries of its appeal to classical sources, as described below. It is not surprising, then, that the most notable present-day scholarly works associated with this appeal to classical politics, such as J. G. A. Pocock's indispensable *Machiavellian Moment* (1975), are more historical than theoretical in their approach.

Recently, however, there have emerged some very interesting attempts to develop a distinctly republican conception of liberty, one drawn quite self-consciously from Roman political theory and practice. This neorepublican theory of liberty, developed most systematically by Philip Pettit (1997), tries to recover and articulate the resistance to personal domination expressed so strongly by Roman republicans. It contrasts liberty as nondomination with the civic humanist conception of liberty as collective self-rule, not just with the liberal conception of liberty as noninterference. Nevertheless, like the civic humanist concepts of political freedom and virtue, it tends to democratize its classical inspiration, turning something that the Romans saw as an achievement of the great into a right for all.

Attempts at synthesizing classical political ideals with the best of their contemporary counterparts are common in the history of Western political thought. Christian Spartas and socialist re-creations of Athens fill some of the more curious corners of the modern political imagination. But the most profound and influential examples of the synthetic response in the classical tradition in political theory are undoubtedly those provided by the religious thinkers, Muslim, Jewish, and Christian, of the Middle Ages.

Augustine's *City of God* provides an early and especially powerful example. It is clearly inspired by Plato's sharp contrast, in the *Republic,* between the ordinary city and the ideal "city in speech," that "pattern laid up in heaven" for the edification of our souls. Ordinary political justice, from these authors' shared point of view, is tainted. It is the justice that allows a gang of thieves to cooperate—a Platonic image that figures prominently in the *City of God.* Like the Platonic philosopher, Augustine's true Christians need to keep the limitations of political justice in mind, especially when they participate in political life. But whereas Plato merely acknowledges the need for the philosopher to return to the cave of the ordinary city, Augustine gives an extensive account of how members of the City of God should conduct themselves within the imperfect institutions of the city of man. In doing so, he goes well beyond Plato to develop a unique and influential synthesis of political realism and idealism.

But the most important and influential example of the synthesis of classical and post-classical political ideals is surely Thomas Aquinas's idea of natural law. The classical legacy here is twofold: the Aristotelian idea of natural right, which refers to a kind of justice that does not derive its force from changing human opinions; and the Stoic idea of natural law, which refers to a universal law of reason by which the wise should live. Aquinas gives these ideas new meaning by reconceptualizing them as part of a world governed by an omnipotent Creator God. Natural law, in this schema, becomes that part of God's government of creation, the eternal law, that is knowable by means of unaided human reason. It is a law built into the nature of things, into the structure of our needs and faculties, because God's purpose structures all of Creation. Yet its dictates are accessible to, and therefore incumbent upon, all rational beings. Aquinas's synthesis effectively answers doubts about the existence and goodness of natural ends by deriving them from God's creative will. But he leaves reason free to discover those ends by means of the kind of self-examination that Stoic and Aristotelian philosophers favored.

The influence of this synthesis of classical and Christian thinking is hard to exaggerate. The great speculative systems of natural law, those constructed by rationalist as well as Catholic philosophers, are its fruits. There is nothing like these speculative systems in the works of classical philosophers, no weighty tomes outlining the dictates of natural as opposed to conventional law. The classical philosophers thought of natural right and natural law as a guide for the wise, rather than as the ultimate standard by which human societies should be governed. As a political weapon, this synthesis of classical and Christian understandings of law has been a two-edged sword. On the one hand, it legitimizes resistance to established authority in the name of a higher, natural law. On the other hand, it opens up any number of ways of deepening the hold of established authority by grounding its legitimacy in the higher standards prescribed by natural law.

In addition to calling for the recovery of classical political ideals or their synthesis with the best of post-classical thinking, there are subtler ways of invoking the classical legacy in political theory. Some participants in the classical tradition in political theory have invoked these ideals more as a means of loosening the grip of later religious and moral ideals than as models for imitation. By drawing our attention to how the ancient Greeks and Romans surpassed the political achievements of more recent eras without the imposition of moral and religious dogma, these thinkers have invoked the classical legacy to promote civil emancipation from religious authority. This subtler appeal to the classics helps explain why some of the most influential thinkers in the classical tradition in political theory, such as Montesquieu and Machiavelli, seem at times to reject many of the ancient political ideals that they so powerfully invoke.

The best example of such an appeal to classical political ideals is probably Montesquieu's celebration of virtue (in *The Spirit of the Laws*) as the principle of republican government. This famous argument is clearly derived from his careful analysis of Roman political theory and practice, much of which is presented in his *Considerations on the Causes of the Grandeur and Decline of the Romans.* Yet his celebration of virtue seems to run contrary to the defense of individual liberty that stands at the center of his work. This tension leads his interpreters to wonder whether Montesquieu is a confused civic humanist or instead the promoter of an especially subtle synthesis of ancient and modern political ideals. But a better solution to this puzzle emerges once we learn to recognize the emancipatory use of the appeal to classical political ideals and institutions. Montesquieu emphasizes at the beginning of *The Spirit of the Laws* that the virtue that makes republics work is a distinctly "political" virtue, the passionate love of one's country, rather than any kind of moral virtue. He thereby implies that the great achievements of classical republicanism were the product of human passions, rather than their suppression by religious and moral authorities. His aim, it seems, is not to promote the imitation of ancient republican virtue, which he associates with cruelty and violence. (In a particularly powerful aphorism from his notebooks, he suggests that the ancients "conquered without reason, without utility. They ravaged the earth in order to exercise their virtue and demonstrate their excellence.") It is, rather, to encourage us to free ourselves from the futile and self-destructive quest to suppress the passions that has so preoccupied modern moral and religious authorities.

Machiavelli's *Discourses on Livy* provides an even more complex example of this emancipatory invocation of classical republican virtue. This work clearly stands at the center of civic humanist rhetoric about the recovery of classical republican ideals. Yet the substance of his teaching often seems to run counter to the classical models he invokes, so much so that his *Discourses* sometimes appears to be written against, rather than about, the first 10 books of Livy's history of Rome. Virtue stands at the center of Machiavelli's understanding of political success, as it does for Livy. But Machiavelli's virtue is amoral in a way that Livy's never was. Its distinctive characteristics are energy, courage, and resourcefulness, rather than anything approaching moral rectitude. And in an even more radical departure from Livy, Machiavelli treats the endless struggle between patricians and plebeians as one of the sources of Rome's greatness, rather than as its fatal flaw. He invokes the classical republicans to teach us that we need virtue, but does so in a way that both demoralizes our understanding of virtue and liberates us from demands for the imposition of moral consensus. No doubt he seeks, to a certain extent, the recovery and renewal of classical republican institutions. But at the same time he is also interested in using the appeal of classical republicanism to challenge the way we think about the relationship between morality and politics, even if it means undermining many of the political ideals celebrated by his sources.

The most radical responses to the classical legacy in political theory have come from those who focused their attention on what keeps us from reproducing the ancient achievements that they so admire. They broadened and deepened the discontent inspired by the admiration of classical political ideals and institutions, thereby feeding the demands for the wholesale transformation of modern individuals and society that emerged among European social critics in the 19th and 20th centuries.

Rousseau is the first, and still the most influential, political thinker to invoke ancient political theory and practice in this way. He certainly wanted to recover classical models of citizenship and republican virtue. But he feared that modern societies have been rendered incapable of even understanding the meaning of the word *citizen* by the inflated needs that our socialization has made second nature to us. Before we can truly appreciate the meaning of citizenship, let alone practice it, he suggests, there must be a transformation of human character that will turn us—bourgeois subjects, good neither for ourselves nor for others—into something whole again. Without this deeper transformation, the direct pursuit of republican political ideals is bound to fail, which is one reason Rousseau never endorsed the kind of political revolution that his French followers made in his name.

This way of invoking classical political ideals clearly involves a call for their recovery or renewal. But it shifts the focus of change to the more fundamental social and psychological transformations needed to remove the obstacles to the recovery of these ideals. Some of the most prominent 20th-century proponents of classical political theory and practice clearly proceeded in this way. Take, for example, Hannah Arendt, probably the most influential of the postwar celebrators of the political wisdom of the ancients. She was clearly an admirer of classical republicanism, especially as dressed in the rhetoric of Pericles' famous funeral oration commemorating Athenians who had perished in war. But the focus of her most important theoretical work, *The Human Condition* (1958), is the identification and elimination of the primary obstacle to its revival: our loss of the sense of what it means to live an "active" life, as opposed to the life of production and consumption we now enjoy. Like Rousseau, Arendt saw little hope for the recovery of what she called the "lost treasure" of republican politics, until we can transform the moral psychology produced by some of the most powerful and productive forces in the modern world.

Interestingly, in the hands of some of Rousseau's German heirs, such as Schiller, Hölderlin, and the young Hegel, analysis of the obstacle to our living up to classical ideals came to be attached to an even grander project of synthesis. These philosophers and social critics wanted to reproduce the communal warmth of ancient citizenship without losing the moral autonomy that Kant had taught them was the source of human dignity. Their longing for the communal life of the ancients thus inspired them to attack what the young Hegel called the modern spirit of dichotomy, the pervasive sense that in the modern world we must choose between freedom and community, duty and inclination, reason and nature. As Schiller put it near the beginning of *On Naïve and Sentimental Poetry,* the Greeks, like all youthful things, "are what we were. They are what we should become again. We were nature, just as they, and our culture, by means of reason and freedom, should lead us back to nature again." Schiller sought a "total revolution" in human character that would recover the ancient ties of political community, but as a freely chosen expression of our moral reason. By inspiring such broad demands for the transformation of modern individuals and society, the appeal to classical political ideals played a crucial role in the extraordinary expansion of the idea of social revolution that occurred in 19th- and 20th-century political thought.

Perhaps the subtlest way of invoking classical political ideals is their therapeutic use as a means of identifying and reconciling us to the special virtues of modern political life. The most influential example of this use of the classical legacy in political theory is probably Benjamin Constant's famous essay "On the Liberty of the Ancients Compared to That of the Moderns." This lecture, the inspiration for Isaiah Berlin's distinction between negative and positive liberty, seeks to undermine Rousseauian appeals to the glories of classical republicanism. But it does so by pointing out the disastrous consequences of trying to reproduce ancient participatory freedoms in modern circumstances, rather than by denying their intrinsic value. Ancient freedom, Constant argues, may have been good for ancient citizens. But the increased size and complexity of modern commercial societies have diminished its value and vastly inflated its cost for modern individuals. Attempts to reproduce ancient freedom are bound, like the Jacobin dictatorship, to fall back on force and terror in order to compel lip-service to ideals that run against our deepest inclinations. They take from us the distinctive forms of freedom nurtured by modern society, independence from external authority and freedom from personal domination, without being able to offer the ancient forms of freedom in return. In this argument Constant uses the appeal of classical political ideals to promote understanding and appreciation of their distinctively modern counterparts.

A more recent example of this therapeutic use of the

appeal of the classical legacy in political theory can be seen in Bernard Manin's pathbreaking *Principles of Representative Government* (1997). Manin builds his reinterpretation of representative government on an Aristotelian insight that reflected a commonplace of ancient politics. Election, Aristotle suggested, is an aristocratic or oligarchic way of selecting people for political office—since it compels us to seek the best or most distinguished individuals for the job. Lottery, that ubiquitous feature of Athenian politics, is, in contrast, the democratic method of selecting officials. By taking this insight seriously and asking why modern societies have abandoned lottery as a way of selecting officeholders, Manin evokes the peculiarity of the representative form of democracy that prevails in the modern world. He argues that it is not so much that we have replaced the direct rule of the people with their indirect rule through their representatives. It is, rather, that we have replaced the sharing and rotation of political office with the consent of the governed as the primary principle of political legitimacy. Lottery guarantees equal opportunity to share power, but it does so at the cost of denying the opportunity to choose or consent to our leaders. Taking seriously the insight of classical democratic theory and practice leads him to a better appreciation of the strengths as well as the limitations of modern democracy.

The work of Leo Strauss and his followers provides another, more idiosyncratic example of this therapeutic invocation of the classical legacy in political theory. Strauss is famous for his appeal to the political wisdom of the ancients—by whom he means primarily Aristotle and Plato—as a corrective to modern political theory and practice. But he invokes them for their alternative understanding of the limits of political rationality and justice, rather than as a guide to the transformation of modern political institutions. Modern political philosophers, he believes, have been seduced by the Enlightenment's dream of conquering nature and relieving the suffering that has hitherto defined the human condition. The reading of ancient political philosophers, and especially Plato, can cure us of these delusions, which he believes lead to tyrannical and self-destructive intellectual ambitions. And unlike most modern proponents of political restraint, the ancients do not ask us, in abandoning these delusions, to abandon rationalism in the name of skepticism or conventionalism. The Straussian appeal to ancient political wisdom thus seeks to transform our understanding of politics while reconciling us to the limitations of our own political life.

What will happen to the classical tradition in political theory now that Greek and Roman texts no longer provide the foundation of a liberal education? Inevitably, it must lose a great deal of its breadth and vitality. Few thinkers are likely to measure themselves and their institutions against ancient political ideals that they do not recognize, let alone treat as exemplary or classic. In this light, the great postwar burst of theorizing about ancients versus moderns that marked the mid-20th century begins to look like something of a last gasp of the tradition, a late harvest of the superb classical education that the German gymnasia provided to political philosophers such as Hannah Arendt and Leo Strauss. Their work has had some broader influence on American intellectual life, Arendt's with the radical democrats of the New Left, Strauss's with the neoconservatives of the Reagan and Bush eras. But their heirs are primarily academic specialists in the field of political philosophy.

Nevertheless, the classical tradition may weather the demise of classical humanism better in political theory than it will in many other fields. For the revival of republican and democratic politics lends it some relevance to make up for its loss of exemplary status. Fewer and fewer intellectuals may, as time passes, treat the Greek and Roman classics as a measure of their humanity. But many more will probably consider them as the source of alternative ways of conceiving of democratic ideals and institutions, alternatives that challenge us to reform either our practices or our self-understanding. It is in this somewhat more limited form that the classical tradition in political theory is likely to survive the death of classical education.

BIBL.: Hannah Arendt, *The Human Condition* (Chicago 1958). Bernard Manin, *Principles of Representative Government* (Cambridge 1997). Philip Pettit, *Republicanism: A Theory of Freedom and Government* (Oxford 1997). J. G. A. Pocock, *The Machiavellian Moment* (Princeton 1975). Leo Strauss, *Natural Right and History* (Chicago 1953). B.Y.

Poliziano, Angelo

Florentine Humanist (1454–1494), called Politian in older English-language scholarship. Born Agnolo Ambrogini in the Tuscan hill town of Montepulciano, from whose Latin name, *Mons politianus,* he acquired his adopted surname, he came to prefer the more easily Latinized spelling Angelo (Angelus). When Poliziano was 10 years old, his father, who practiced some kind of legal profession, was brutally murdered by a man he had convicted. Soon thereafter Poliziano was sent to Florence, where he was destined to become one of the leading protagonists of the Italian Renaissance.

His earliest years in Florence remain somewhat obscure, but eventually he came under the protection of Lorenzo de' Medici (the Magnificent), from whose side he would seldom depart, save for a brief period of estrangement in 1479–1480. Poliziano was tutor to Lorenzo's three children (the youngest of whom would later become Pope Leo X), and in 1492 he was present at Lorenzo's bedside to witness his final hours. Adrift in the aftermath of his patron's death, Poliziano himself died two years later of an illness that detractors attributed to unbridled passion for a boy.

A tireless and omnivorous reader of classical literature, Poliziano achieved a mastery of what he read that was, and remains, astonishing. Though well versed in antiquity's most imposing literary monuments, he often explored works (such as those of the Latin Silver Age) that contemporaries dismissed as secondary, venturing even beyond, into technical literature, commentaries, and medieval sources that preserved classical fragments. Even the slenderest remains of the most obscure authors could command his extended attention and also provide models for imitation. Such priorities (or lack thereof) eventually brought him into sometimes ferocious conflict with contemporary Ciceronians (most notably Paolo Cortesi and Bartolomeo Scala), whose insistence on Cicero as the principal or even exclusive model for Latin prose left him cold. His wider reading enabled him to achieve, as a writer, what has been called *docta varietas* (erudite variation), a feature that lends his style not only color, through a more extended palette of words and figures than reliance on a single model would permit, but also depth, through a complex and often quite abstruse allusiveness.

His access to fame originated with his translation, into Latin hexameters, of the second book of Homer's *Iliad,* a project begun in 1470 and dedicated to Lorenzo de' Medici. For his pains he earned the nickname *Homericus adulescens* (Homeric youth) from Marsilio Ficino, whose lectures Poliziano attended and whose reputation as Florence's leading scholar he would eventually eclipse. Three years later Poliziano was officially a Medici protégé, with access to Lorenzo's library; 1473 also saw the composition of two original Latin poems: *Elegy for Bartolomeo Fonzio,* which, among other things, describes his own early studies; and *Epicedion for Albiera degli Albizi,* a dirge on the death of a young Florentine bride of noble birth. Both demonstrate his talent as an assembler of phrases borrowed from classical precedents, sometimes to make pointed allusions but more often fusing his models into something new.

In 1475 Lorenzo's brother Giuliano won a jousting tournament in Piazza Santa Croce in Florence; Poliziano celebrated the victory in an extended poem in vernacular octaves, *Stanze per la giostra di Giuliano de' Medici,* which gives Italian expression to classical motifs drawn from, among other sources, Latin pastoral and the late-antique poet Claudian. In 1478 Florence was rocked by an anti-Medici plot that saw Giuliano murdered and Lorenzo wounded while at Mass in the cathedral. Poliziano's response, the succinct and moving (but also propagandistic) *Commentary on the Pazzi Conspiracy,* in Latin prose, was modeled on Sallust's account of the conspiracy of Catiline. In 1479, during a long and melancholic absence from a plague-stricken Florence, Poliziano produced a Latin translation of the *Manual* of the Greek Stoic philosopher Epictetus. His strange but virtuosic poem *On Scabies,* discovered in the 20th century, probably also dates to the late 1470s. Perhaps in the same decade, or in any case before 1483, came his most sophisticated work in the vernacular, *Orfeo,* a short play in verse written for the Gonzaga court in Mantua. Based on accounts of the myth of Orpheus in Vergil and Ovid, the play embellishes these ancient sources with a vast panoply of extraneous allusions and borrowings. *Orfeo* is a major monument in the history of the Italian stage, and to it may also be connected, a century later, Monteverdi's *Orfeo* and other early operas.

In 1480 Poliziano was made professor of poetry and rhetoric in the Florentine Studium (the city's small university), in which role he would offer, over the years, courses on, among others, Aesop, Aristotle, Cicero, Hesiod, Homer, Horace, Juvenal, Ovid, Persius, Porphyry, Quintilian, Terence, Theocritus, and Vergil. In an often-cited published version of a *praelectio* (introductory lecture) delivered in his very first year, on Quintilian's *Education of an Orator* and the *Silvae* of Statius, he cleverly argues that these two authors' evident inferiority to Cicero and Vergil does not preclude the utility of studying them, for by scaling these lesser rungs on the literary ladder young students may arrive more easily at its summit. (More cogent, however, is the lecture's air of electric excitement over straying from the beaten path, as well as the steady development of an argument that the Latin of antiquity cannot be reconstructed on the basis of a mere handful of canonical authors.)

Among Poliziano's greatest works are four *praelectiones* in verse: *Manto* (1482), on Vergil and the texts now known as the Appendix Vergiliana; *Rusticus* (1483), on Hesiod's *Works and Days* and the *Georgics* of Vergil; *Ambra* (1485), on Homer; and *Nutricia* (1486, publ. 1491), a history of poetry from its origins. Collectively the four are known as his *Silvae.* In 1489 he completed and published the work for which he was most celebrated (including by himself) in his own lifetime: his *First Century of Miscellanies,* a collection of 100 mostly philological essays that vary in length from a paragraph to several pages, on subjects that range from the ridiculous to the sublime. (Poliziano's stated model was the equally miscellaneous *Attic Nights* of Aulus Gellius.) The lack of a continuous narrative and the seemingly random choice and arrangement of topics initially convey a sense of the fragmentation of antiquity; yet the final effect is analogous to that of a Renaissance *studiolo,* where a small library or collection of antiquities becomes metonymic for the whole vast achievement of the ancient world and, at the same time, a monument to the collector's own discrimination, taste, and elegance. The *Miscellanies* was also prized for its specific content, that is, the discoveries and opinions of someone already regarded as one of Italy's leading scholars. (Here, for example, he defends the spelling *Vergil* against the traditional *Virgil.*) Contemporary accounts describe avid readers sharing copies hot off the presses.

The most enduring impact of the *Miscellanies* arose from the intelligence, consistency, and rigor with which Poliziano united an array of critical practices into something like a method for the study of ancient texts. Perhaps his greatest accomplishment in this regard lay in his understanding of how texts become corrupt through copying. In particular, his efforts to piece together stemmatic relationships between manuscripts (determining which manuscripts or manuscript families descend from which) anticipated principles of textual criticism not fully codified until the 19th century.

In his final years, Poliziano began but did not finish *Second Century* (a draft was discovered and first published in the 20th century). In the 1490s he lectured frequently on Aristotle, but he found himself, along with others, under increasing attack from Girolamo Savonarola, who in 1492 published *Apologia de ratione poeticae artis,* an offensive against the study and imitation of pagan poetry; although it did not mention Poliziano by name, it had him fairly clearly in its sights. An avid correspondent throughout his career, Poliziano late in life assembled a collection of his Latin letters; these were published only posthumously. Among them the most famous are his long account of the death of Lorenzo de' Medici in 1492 (4.2) and a diatribe against Paolo Cortesi and other "apes" of Cicero (8.16) that includes the stunningly modern rejoinder, "Someone says to me, 'You don't express Cicero.' So what? I'm not Cicero! All the same, as I see it, so I express myself."

BIBL.: Vittore Branca, *Poliziano e l'umanesimo della parola* (Turin 1983). Anthony Grafton, "Angelo Poliziano and the Reorientation of Philology," in his *Joseph Scaliger: A Study in the History of Classical Scholarship,* vol. 1 (Oxford 1983). Thomas M. Greene, "Poliziano: The Past Dismembered," in his *The Light in Troy: Imitation and Discovery in Renaissance Poetry* (New Haven 1982). Martin L. McLaughlin, "The Dispute between Poliziano and Cortesi," in his *Literary Imitation in the Italian Renaissance: The Theory and Practice of Literary Imitation in Italy from Dante to Bembo* (Oxford 1995). William Roscoe, *Life of Lorenzo de' Medici, Called the Magnificent* (London 1796, often reprinted).

S.B.

Pompeii

Within the communications networks of 18th-century Europe the discovery and excavation of the Campanian cities Herculaneum (1738) and Pompeii (1748), buried by the Vesuvian eruption of 79 CE, commanded international attention. Eventual dissemination of information and images from the sites sparked imitative design and interior decoration. Fiction and film have elaborated the mystique of the destroyed city; and classical pedagogy, seizing on Pompeii as the closest possible approach to everyday life in the Roman world, has enlivened Latin teaching with documented Pompeian personalities.

One reason that Campanian discoveries appeared to bring classically educated Europe into vital contact with its cultural heritage was the sites' apparent corroboration of information long familiar from literary texts. The Swiss engineer Karl Weber, the first authority placed in charge of excavations, identified the spatial configurations of domestic interiors with reference to terminology employed by the Augustan architectural writer Vitruvius. The well-preserved wall paintings, especially large-figured mythological panel paintings, were hailed as evidence of the lost masterworks of Apelles and other celebrated Greek artists known vicariously through such testimony as the art-historical chapters of the elder Pliny's *Natural History.* Such literary testimony formed the written component of Campania's first official excavation reports, *Le Antichità di Ercolano esposte con qualche spiegazione* (9 vols., 1755–1792), which published a selection of choice statues and paintings accompanied by commentary prepared by the 14 scholars appointed to the Herculanean Royal Academy. Sponsors of the publication were the jealously possessive Bourbon rulers of Naples, who had for many years granted only a few visitors access to the Royal Museum at Portici, until external pressure drove them finally to commission the publication as a species of traveling museum to be sent to universities, royal courts, and certain influential personages. Its chief defect was an unrealistic separation of images from their contexts; among the critics, the contemporary art historian J. J. Winckelmann, in keeping with his characteristically negative opinion of Roman artistic production, denigrated the paintings as copies inferior to their putatively great originals. Yet with its declared purpose of "creating desire for the objects," *Le Antichità di Ercolano* evoked from antiquity a more intimate accessibility than all the statues of Rome's Vatican collections had previously achieved.

Though its focus on the isolated object gave scant grounds for the reconstruction of ancient life, the publication provided abundant models of the material culture to imitate in answer to the craving to reexperience ancient life that the discoveries at Pompeii had generated. First to adapt the antique style into interior decoration was the French architect Charles-Louis Clérisseau, who studied and worked in Italy from ca. 1750 until the 1770s. His English friend and counterpart Robert Adam, who visited Italy but may never have seen Pompeii, created interior designs for English country houses that featured distinctive Neoclassical adaptations in stucco and paint; he often employed the artist Angelica Kauffmann and her husband to complement his garlands and arabesques with mythological vignettes.

Eventually new publications with fuller representations of Pompeian walls (by Wilhelm Zahn, publ. 1827–1859, and by the Niccolinis in 1854), as well as the reconstructive illustrations in books by Sir William Gell (publ. 1817–1832), provided models for more comprehensively imitative wall schemes that especially emulated the most abundant and flamboyant decorations of Pompeii's final decades, commonly known as Fourth Style. Although many 19th-century intellectuals were given to constructing these representations in imagination, and some even included a "Pompeian room" in their houses, actual large-scale realization was reserved for regal resources. Three notable examples were produced by rulers in France, Germany, and England—Prince Louis Napoleon, King Ludwig I of Bavaria, and Queen Victoria—each creation bearing a conspicuously self-conscious expression of its commissioner's ideology. Victoria's decorative production survives only in the publicity volume produced by Mrs. Anna Jameson, but two panels of the Parisian installation can be seen in the Musée d'Orsay, and recent restoration has opened Ludwig's Pompeianum, positioned above the River Maine at Aschaffenburg, to public access. Constructed over a period of two decades in consultation with scholars and architects, this project epitomizes the serious

German scholarship of its era in its replication of the spaces and decorative features of its principal model, the Pompeian Casa dei Dioscuri.

Likewise still visible, in the Senate wing of the U.S. Capitol Building in Washington, D.C., is the decorative program conceived and executed in the mid-19th century by Constantino Brumidi, which comprises one of the most creative modern combinations of Pompeian compositional style with images of national import. Beginning in 1856, Brumidi, an Italian painter well versed in the classical tradition, engaged a large workforce of decorative fresco painters to execute along the corridors and in the committee chambers of the Senate wing his designs combining illusionistic architecture and intricate ornamentation in Fourth Style format to frame significant scenes from American history often modeled upon the work of such Neoclassical painters as Benjamin West. Although some critics have characterized the installation's heavy-duty Victorian classicism as retrograde, it does appear symbolically reflective of the eminence of the senior American legislative body.

Perhaps no single written work has given Pompeii so great a hold on imagination as Edward Bulwer-Lytton's fictive romance *The Last Days of Pompeii* (1834), many of whose vividly drawn characters were inspired by the discovered remains of victims seen by the author when visiting the site. Aligning his firsthand observations with Gell's scholarship, he portrayed householders whose choice of artworks revealed their personalities. Like the aesthetically prejudiced Winckelmann, Bulwer-Lytton brought a philhellenic bias into his descriptive characterizations, and his scenes of self-indulgent banquets and gambling parties, especially as they involved Romans, colored Pompeii as a hedonistic, even decadent society—although the thriving, commercially active town in ancient actuality would have been no more decadent than any other Roman municipality of the late 1st century CE. A later visitor, the Victorian painter Sir Lawrence Alma-Tadema, created his own versions of the Pompeian domestic picture gallery, incorporating replications of paintings seen in the Naples Museum into the backgrounds of his own popular renditions of scenes of Roman life. His fancy was especially captured by the large figure painting of a feminized Hercules in bondage to Omphale (from the House of Marcus Lucretius), which he introduced into several pictorial settings as an overt reflection of Roman decadence. Among the earliest cinematic exploitations of Roman antiquity, films derived from Bulwer-Lytton's novel similarly capitalized on the allure of decadence, although, as Wyke (1997) has pointed out, their sensationalism redressed itself by moralistic plotting whereby natural cataclysm brought deserved punishment on the evils emanating from the seamy, oriental side of imperial culture.

Without engaging in full-scale interior decoration, present-day enthusiasts nevertheless have abundant opportunities to own a small bit of Pompeiana. Museum gift shops market scarves and neckties featuring motifs derived from Pompeian wall paintings, and the Metropolitan Museum offers a color print of the *cubiculum* (bedchamber) of the museum's Villa Boscoreale. In the Cambridge Latin Series, the Pompeian banker L. Caecilius Jucundus and his fictionalized household introduce many youthful Latin learners to ancient culture; the Poppidii, a fictional family of freedmen, own the Casa del Citharista figures, unjustifiably vulgarized, in Robert Harris's novel *Pompeii* (2003). Although debate continues within the Italian cultural ministry concerning appropriate measures of preservation and the desirability of exposing still uncovered parts of the city, Pompeii continues to be among the world's most visited tourist sites.

BIBL.: I. C. McIlwaine, *Herculaneum: A Guide to Printed Sources,* 2 vols. (Naples 1988). Christopher Parslow, *Rediscovering Antiquity: Karl Weber and the Excavation of Herculaneum, Pompeii, and Stabiae* (Cambridge 1995). Barbara A. Wolanin, *Constantino Brumidi: Artist of the Capitol* (Washington, D.C., 1998). Maria Wyke, *Projecting the Past: Ancient Rome, Cinema and History* (London 1997). E.LE.

Pope, Alexander

The greatest English poet of the 18th century, Pope (1688–1744) consistently drew inspiration from Greek and Roman poetry and literary criticism.

Pope's poetic career began in 1709 with his publication of *Pastorals,* which is lovely but conventional. As a poet in the classical tradition, Pope truly hit his stride with his *Essay on Criticism* (1711), a stylistic masterpiece that brilliantly recreates and displays the wit and restrained ease of Horace's *sermones* (conversation poems). The *Essay on Criticism* also offers (lines 645–680) a concise and profound summary—at times through exemplifying the very stylistic qualities the poet-critic is extolling—of the contributions of some of the greatest figures of Greek and Roman literary criticism (Aristotle, Horace, Dionysius of Halicarnassus, Petronius, Quintilian, and Longinus).

Pope translated and imitated a number of classical poets, including Horace (odes and conversation poems), Ovid (*Metamorphoses* and *Heroides*), Statius, Tibullus, and Martial. Echoes of classical poetry can be heard in virtually all Pope's verse. In *Eloisa to Abelard* (1717), for example, Pope's depiction of Eloisa's hopelessly conflicted suffering is indebted to Ovid's *Heroides.* The ancient poet with whom Pope spent the most time and over whom he expended the most labor, however, was Homer.

In 1715 Pope published the first volume of his complete translation of the *Iliad.* The final volume of the first edition was published in 1720. The great 18th-century critic Samuel Johnson justly referred to Pope's *Iliad* as "the noblest version [translation] of poetry that the world has ever seen." More recently, George Steiner aptly remarked that "Pope's *Iliad* is a masterpiece in its own right and an epic which, as far as English goes, comes second only to Milton." Pope recreates Homer's poetic fire and the ancient poet's unflagging formal power. The *Odyssey* translation began appearing in 1725 and was completed the following year. Thus the poet spent 16 years, beginning when he was 21, translating and commenting on Homer.

Much of Pope's original poetry bears the traces of his long and loving, if often taxing, engagement with Homer. The notes that Pope published with his translations of the *Iliad* and *Odyssey* contain some of the finest reflections on the classical tradition available in the English language, as readers are privy to the insights of one poetic genius drawing on all of Graeco-Roman literary criticism to illuminate the works of the very poetic genius whose works are the font of that tradition.

An Essay on Criticism is a paean to Homer. "Be *Homer's* Works your *Study* and *Delight,*" Pope writes; "Read them by Day, and meditate by Night" (lines 124–125). The other great early success of Pope, the mock-heroic *Rape of the Lock,* would probably never have been written had Pope not been reading Homer by day and meditating on him by night. The first version (consisting of two cantos) appeared in 1712, and the final five-canto version in 1717, the same year that Pope published the third volume of his ultimately six-volume complete translation. Pope echoes his own *Iliad* translation in *The Rape of the Lock,* as he invites his audience to read his poem through a Homeric prism.

Both *Eloisa to Abelard* and the *Elegy to the Memory of an Unfortunate Lady* were published in 1717, a year that falls roughly midway between the appearance of the first (1715) and last (1720) volumes of his *Iliad.* The passionate natures of the unfortunate lady and of Eloisa recall Pope's passionate Achilles, a portrait that is freed of the moralizing distortions of Achilles' character found in the George Chapman's version, Pope's great Renaissance predecessor in the field of Homeric translation.

The final volume of Pope's *Odyssey* appeared in 1726. Seven years later Pope published the first of his Horatian imitations, *The First Satire of the Second Book of Horace,* later subtitled *To Mr. Fortescue.* Though Pope's Homer has had its detractors, no one has doubted the stylistic brilliance of Pope's imitations of Horace. As Pope observes in the postscript to his *Odyssey,* what drove him to distraction when translating that work was the challenge of rendering—with the dignity required by Augustan epic style—the more domestic, everyday, and hence less elevated portions of that work that, as Longinus observed, lack the consistently elevated intensity of the *Iliad.* In contrast with the rigorous demands of translating Homeric epic with the requisite decorum, it was with considerable relief that Pope began to turn the witty, conversational style of Horace's *sermones* into English heroic couplets.

Pope's final poem, the *Dunciad,* was published in its first version in 1728, just two years after the final volumes of the *Odyssey* translation. In the *Dunciad* Pope was able to make full use of his eye for the sort of sharply rendered particulars that would have been deemed too low for an Augustan version of Homeric epic, and he could place these particulars within a framework that allowed him to make the kind of generalized major statement about the reasons for the decline of a civilization that is worthy of Homer's *Iliad.* The *Dunciad* is indebted for its structure to the *Aeneid* rather than to the *Iliad,* but it possesses Iliadic fire rather than Virgilian pathos. The *Dunciad* is characterized, moreover, by the kind of rugged excellence and disdain for careful mediocrity that Pope's admired Longinus associated with the Homer of the *Iliad.*

In the *Iliad* Homer sings of Achilles' wrath. Pope's wrath animates his final version of the work, the often ruggedly (if comically) sublime *Dunciad in Four Books* of 1743, a year before his death. What motivates Pope's anger in the *Dunciad* is in part the arrogant and ignorant hostility, as he perceived it, of the contemporary literary establishment toward the classics and the classical tradition. Pope concludes the *Dunciad* with the phrase "Universal Darkness buries All" (4.656). Pope's apocalyptic vision of the demise of the classical tradition is not necessarily hyperbolic. Most of today's reading public in the West—including university professors and their students in the humanities—inhabit the very darkness in regard to classical languages and learning that Pope prophesied.

BIBL.: Reuben Brower, *Alexander Pope: The Poetry of Allusion* (Oxford 1959). Maynard Mack, *Alexander Pope: A Life* (New York 1985). Felicity Rosslyn, *Alexander Pope: A Literary Life* (Houndmills, U.K., 1990). Steven Shankman, *Pope's Iliad: Homer in the Age of Passion* (Princeton 1983). Frank Stack, *Pope and Horace: Studies in Imitation* (Cambridge 1985).

S.SH.

Popular Culture

At first sight, the classical tradition might appear to have nothing to do with popular culture. The classics were long considered part of the Great Tradition transmitted via elite grammar schools and universities, institutions that excluded the majority of the population. Ordinary people were presumed to have their Little Tradition, the artifacts and practices that expressed their own view of the world. Historians and other students of popular culture have learned in recent decades not to distinguish these two cultures too sharply but to recognize interactions between them. Some scholars go so far as to renounce the concept of popular culture altogether. But it is difficult to speak of some kinds of cultural interaction without adverting to the term. Certainly among the items from high culture that have passed into popular culture are elements from the classical tradition.

The list of such items might begin with the language. Latin words and phrases have been used over the centuries by people who do not know Latin: *memento mori, compos mentis, nosce teipsum, tu quoque,* and so on. In Italian, such words and phrases (taken from the Vulgate and the Catholic liturgy but deriving ultimately from ancient Rome) can still be found in a number of dialects. Thus, a person who complains too much may be nicknamed a *sequerio,* quoting the antiphon to Saint Anthony of Padua, *Si quaeris miracula;* and the phrase "It is always the same story" becomes *é semper sicuteratinprinzipio* (Beccaria 2001).

Some stories about figures from classical antiquity were widespread. In the Middle Ages minstrels and preachers introduced them to a public that was socially and culturally mixed. Minstrels sang about Helen of Troy, for instance, and Odysseus and Orpheus. A study of the themes of medieval exempla notes stories about more than 30 classical gods, heroes, and emperors. Alexander the Great was the most popular figure, followed by Socrates, Aristotle, and Nero. Similar themes appear in medieval churches, in stone capitals and wooden misericords.

In the Renaissance some of the renewed interest in classical antiquity percolated down to ordinary people, especially in cities. One medium that brought the classical tradition to many ordinary people from the 15th century onward was of course print. A number of cheap booklets or chapbooks took their themes from ancient history or mythology. Among the most popular figures were (once again) Alexander the Great, Apollonius of Tyre, the emperor Octavian—whose adventures seem to have had a special appeal in Central and Eastern Europe (Kośny 1967)—and Virgil (the hero or antihero of texts in English, French, German, Dutch, and Spanish). Chapbook versions of classical themes seem to have been particularly popular in 16th-century Italy, including *Ammaestramenti di Seneca Morale, Cerbero, Orfeo, Lucrezi,* and *Perseo.* These stories sometimes recorded performances by minstrels, the "singers of tales" (*cantastorie*).

Public performance was the second important medium of dissemination. Public festivals often included representations of classical figures. The Fête-Dieu at Aix-en-Provence in 1462 included Diana, Mercury, Pan, Bacchus, Pluto, and Proserpine. In Rome the pageants presented during Carnival included the triumphs of Julius Caesar (1500) and of the consul Paulus Aemilius (1536, a compliment to Pope Paul III). In Nuremberg in the late 15th and early 16th centuries, Carnival plays (*Fastnachtspiele*) portrayed Apollo, Aristotle, Caesar, Fabius, and Lucretia; one was titled *The History of the Roman Empire.* In 17th-century London the annual Lord Mayor's Show introduced (among other classical figures) Astraea, Apollo, Mercury, Neptune, Orpheus, Scylla and Charybdis, Thetis, and Ulysses (the emphasis on maritime themes should be noted). In Naples in the 1770s one Carnival was organized around the siege of Troy, which led a patronizing foreign visitor to comment that she found it "admirable that in a public entertainment the lowest class of society . . . should know that there was a siege of Troy."

These pageants might be described as official street theater. There were also unofficial forms of street theater, notably the Italian *commedia dell'arte,* which was seen by ordinary people as well as by elites and is linked to the ancient world, whether as a form of survival or of revival. It is possible that these performances, first documented in the 16th century, were part of a continuous underground tradition stretching back to the Atellan farces of republican Rome—at any rate, the masks were similar. In any case the plots of the *commedia,* like the written comedies of the same period, drew heavily on the classical comedic dramatists Terence and Plautus.

In the more indoor culture of Northern Europe, some theaters were open to a wide public. In London around 1600, the public theaters cost a penny per performance, a price within the range of artisans, shopkeepers, and their apprentices, who had the opportunity to see Shakespeare's Roman plays. Shakespeare and his friend Ben Jonson mocked ordinary people who took an uninformed interest in Tarquin and Lucretia, Hero and Leander, or Pyramus and Thisbe (an interest confirmed by a few references to village plays in Italy and the Netherlands). After the English Restoration in 1660, when theaters became too expensive for ordinary people, it remained possible to see plays such as *The Siege of Troy* at fairs and inns. In similar fashion the audiences in the theaters at the fairs in Paris or at the operas in Venice and Naples were able to become familiar with the stories of Theseus and Ariadne, Dido and Aeneas, or Poppaea and Nero.

Performances had the advantage of reaching the illiterate as well as the literate. So did printed images. An anonymous early 16th-century print shows Martin Luther as the German Hercules, striking down Aristotle. Paintings and sculptures with classical subjects were usually confined to the private houses of elites, but prints were cheap and by the 18th century they could be viewed in the windows of print shops as well as purchased from itinerant peddlers. Again, motifs from classical architecture, especially after its revival in the Renaissance, passed from churches and palaces to ordinary houses, transmitted by prints and pattern books such as Moxon's *Mechanick Exercises* (1682). Ceramics, such as Italian majolica of the Renaissance, often represented classical themes. The larger, more complex and more expensive pieces were intended for elites, but smaller, simpler, and cheaper pieces have survived that also represent figures and scenes from classical antiquity. Popular paintings (inn signs, for instance, or murals inside and outside houses) also displayed and transmitted such images. Ships with classical names such as *Neptune* and *Jupiter* displayed images of their namesakes. In similar fashion, in the 20th century, the British Royal Corps of Signals adopted Mercury as its emblem, which figured on cap badges and elsewhere (though the soldiers themselves referred to the figure as Jimmy). From the 19th century onward the names of certain products, from soap to jewelry, have made many people familiar with some classical names.

The geography, chronology, and sociology of these popularizations of the classical tradition have yet to be investigated systematically. Such an investigation would inevitably encounter a number of problems.

First, there is the importance of mediation and of different kinds of mediator. Among these mediators were the clergy, especially the friars, who regularly preached to a broad public from the late Middle Ages onward; professional entertainers such as minstrels, who often performed for an illiterate audience but might well have been literate themselves; and even the artists of the Renaissance—Botticelli, for instance—who recreated scenes from classical mythology and ancient history for patrons from the elite but participated themselves in artisan culture, socializing with other craftsmen.

It should be added that popular contact with the classical tradition was not so much second-hand as third- or fourth-hand. It was derived not directly from, say, Livy but from a minstrel who had read a Renaissance writer such as Boccaccio, often in translation. In the course of this complex chain of transmission, all sorts of changes naturally occurred. In a few cases it is possible to observe classical material being appropriated and consciously adapted to new circumstances. That Virgil should have been transformed into a necromancer (Spargo 1934) speaks volumes about the cultural distance of some medieval people from the author of the *Aeneid.*

It might also be useful to speak of unconscious adaptation. What did all these items from the classical tradition mean to the different groups (male and female, young and old, urban and rural) who went to plays, observed processions, read chapbooks or inn signs, and the like? References to classical heroes and heroines tended to be stereotyped and might even be described as moral ideograms; Venus or Helen as an ideogram for beauty, Lucretia for chastity, Nero for cruelty, and so on. Such stereotypes may be clues to the choice of certain classical names for the children of artisans or peasants, not only in Italy and Greece but in parts of rural England and France as well (though the possible influence of the parish clergy as mediators should not be ignored). Everyday references to someone enduring pain with "stoicism" or making a "laconic" comment provide further examples of stereotyping.

Another problem concerns meaning: understanding or misunderstanding. How important and how common were misunderstandings of the classical tradition? Like the Frenchwoman in Naples quoted above, scholars used to take a rather condescending view of popular misunderstandings of classical names, like the transformation of HMS *Bellerophon* by its crew into *Billy Ruffian* or *Billy Rough-un.* Today they are more open to the possibility that such transformations were examples of conscious mockery. Some Italian scholars have likewise interpreted popular distortions of Latin phrases as cases of irony rather than of ignorance. In similar fashion the folktales about the amorous misadventures of Aristotle (who was ridden by Phyllis) and Virgil (who was exposed to public ridicule stuck in a basket halfway up the tower in which he hoped to visit a lover) might be interpreted in terms of popular anti-intellectualism, as a put-down of great men.

In the 19th century popular historical novels helped to spread some knowledge of ancient Rome, particularly in the time of the early Christians: those most remembered today include Edward Bulwer-Lytton's *The Last Days of Pompeii* (1834), Lew Wallace's *Ben-Hur* (1880), and *Quo Vadis* (1896) by Henryk Sienkiewicz. Gustave Flaubert situated his less popular novel *Salammbô* (1862) in ancient Carthage during a siege of the city. In the 20th century new media brought antiquity to an even wider public, global rather than merely Western. One of these new media was film. At the beginning of the century, classical themes were a specialty of the Italian cinema—*Spartaco* (1911), for example, *Nerone e Agrippina* (1913), and *Caligula* (1916). Hollywood followed, with *Ben-Hur* (1925, 1959), *Caesar and Cleopatra* (1946), *Quo Vadis* (1951), *Spartacus* (1960), and *Gladiator* (2000) as successful high-budget epics; more recently *Alexander the Great* (2005) and *Troy* (2005), made with high expectations, fared less well at the box office.

Another new medium is the comic strip. René Goscinny and Albert Uderzo's *Astérix,* set in Gaul at the time of Caesar and appearing in print from 1959 onward, has sold more than 18 million copies and been translated into at least 15 languages. In Japan the heroine of a comic strip by Hayao Miyazaki is called Nausicaa. In France, Philippe Druillet turned *Salammbô* into a comic strip, and it has since been adapted as a video game.

The significance of these recent examples should not be exaggerated. It is likely that the relative importance of the classical tradition for popular culture has been declining over the last two centuries, even if a little knowledge has become more widespread than before. In any case, we need to ask whether elements of the classical tradition were perceived—by different groups in different regions and periods—as classical, or exotic, or whether they had become domesticated. We can of course ask the same questions about the elites.

BIBL.: Gian Luigi Beccaria, *Sicuterat: Il Latino di chi non lo sa,* 2nd ed. (Milan 2001). David G. Bergeron, *English Civic Pageantry, 1558–1642* (London 1971). A. Borgeld, *Aristotles en Phyllis* (Groningen 1902). Peter Burke, "The Classical Tradition and Popular Culture," in *Les intermédiaires culturels,* ed. Michel Vovelle (Paris 1981) 237–244. George Cary, *The Medieval Alexander* (Cambridge 1956). W. Kośny, *Das deutsche Volksbuch vom Kaiser Octavian in Polen und Russland* (Berlin 1967). Salvatore Settis, *Futuro del "classico"* (Turin 2004). J. W. Spargo, *Virgil the Necromancer* (Cambridge 1934).

U.P.B.

Pornography

All discussions of pornography demand a prologue, either to explain the necessity of bringing up the subject or to define what is meant by the term. Given the widespread diffusion of works from antiquity that have been viewed and labeled pornographic by later ages, we can dispense with an apologia for the discussion. The hundreds of definitions attributed to the term, and the constant need to redefine its parameters, however, lie at the very core of its function, from the time the word was first given widespread application in the 19th century right up until the present day. As is well known, although the term is Greek in origin it was never used in ancient Greece with the significance it has assumed today. The classical erudition that marked European culture in the late 18th and 19th centuries unearthed the bookish, and therefore nonoffensive, term for writing about prostitutes and adopted it for academic discourse on sexual matters. Introduced for disparate reasons by writers in German, French, and English, through extrapolation the word quickly came to stand for objectionable or obscene material in art and literature. As early as 1864 *Webster's Dictionary* defined the word with latitude but little nuance as "licentious painting." Given the widespread intolerance in Victorian times for cultural discourse that involved the erotic, the term found massive application in English.

As a conceptual tool pornography is a deeply flawed category, beginning with its pseudo-connection to the classical world. Yet the pervasiveness of its deployment, and the degree of comforting subjectivity it provides the user, has firmly entrenched the word within the modern discourse of the erotic. The more inclusive term from the ancient vocabulary, *erotica,* is far easier to define, derived from *erōs,* pertaining to sexual love and lust. Pornography is a subdivision of the larger realm of the erotic and functions as the expression reserved for pejorative assessment of texts, images, and objects that are deemed offensive, illicit, or obscene. Thus, contrary to many explanations that aspire to universality, pornography is defined not by the artistry of the form or by the intention of the maker but by the judgment of the perceiver. For this reason the pornographic is a fluid category, which changes from one time to another and from one place to another. Indeed, the pornographic designation is unstable even within a single society; because it is designated by its reception, the label "pornographic" is always contentious.

There are generally two systems that are invoked against material classified as pornographic: social controls marshaled under the strictures of decorum, and religious taboos linked to proscribed practices. The obvious mutability of the standards of decorum over time and the variety of taboos across religious sects further ensure that classifications of the pornographic will vacillate widely. It is important to acknowledge, however, that every culture has established boundaries in its reception of erotic art and the use of sexual vocabulary. The classical world was no different in this, although we understand its demarcations only imperfectly. Distinctions have always been made between the licit and illicit; they have been insisted on, argued about, and enforced, despite their shifting parameters.

A result of the subjectivity of the term is that texts and objects seen as acceptably erotic in classical culture were later defined as unacceptably pornographic. A reversed mechanism sometimes operates whereby cultural products once regarded as pornographic later receive approbation. An example from recent history readily illustrates this point. James Joyce's *Ulysses* (1922), now a part of the literary canon, was classified as pornographic writing by the United States court system and not legally obtainable in that country until 1933. The initial ban functioned despite the book's impressive claim to the status of "high art," with its patent allusions to classical literature and literary characters. Not only in its title but in the very structure of its narrative, *Ulysses* abounds with episodes that refer directly to Homer's *Odyssey* and references that make its artistic credentials clear. Joyce's sophisticated, mock-heroic makeover of the Greek epic was a 20th-century continuation of a long tradition in Western culture that looked to classical sources for, among other things, treatments of the erotic—and sometimes succeeded, like Joyce, in conjuring eroticism from the vapors rather than the substance of the models.

The extant corpus of Greek and Roman literature did provide many explicit models for later erotica of all varieties, in written texts as well as visual images. A potent mixture of obscenity in language and costume, put to the use of satire, was performed in Athenian comedy and the satyr plays, written in the 5th century BCE as part of the Dionysian festivals. These spectacles, supported and sanctioned by the state, featured vulgar language, flaunted inflated phalluses, and delighted in sexual situations. Although never approximated in later dramaturgy—and certainly not with governmental funding—such revels provided a model of the subversive use of sexual elements in performances that are calculated by their creators to express disregard for established mores, to poke fun at authority, and to provide release from societal constraints.

The Latin poems of Catullus, Martial, and Juvenal have proved an abundant source of sexualized imagery as an instrument of castigation. Witty, ferociously pointed invective targets society's customs and sacralities, as well as the indecent behavior of individuals. Not many authors have been as fearless in their repartee, or cultures as tolerant of poetry's excoriating potential; yet a few authors have explicitly trod the path of the Latin bards of barbs. During the 16th century Pietro Aretino forged a poetics of obscenity that both titillated and disturbed his contemporaries. He was individually responsible for the transmission throughout Europe of models of obscene texts that were as highly influential as they were clandestine, which became part of the definition of the genre. Aretino's licentious writings, which self-avowedly took their license from classical models, were thrillingly disreputable among the Elizabethans and had major bearing on the development of the English libertine tradition.

The poetry of Ovid that deals with sexual themes configures a distinctive twist. In his *Art of Love* (1 BCE) Ovid sets himself up as the master of the erotic and enumerates explicit positions of heterosexual congress. During his lifetime his contribution was retrospectively singled out by the emperor Augustus as a corrupting influence; there is, however, every indication that this was a political maneuver, a convincing excuse—or contributory factor—in an underlying, egregious, and top-secret crime against the emperor. Ovid's disgrace points to another use of the pornographic (and its cognates of different names). Throughout history allegations of pornographic creations or illicit behavior have been leveled against individuals when it is desirable to cover the real motive for condemnation.

A genuine outrage against the "educational" aspect of Ovid's poem apparently did operate among his contemporaries. The explicatory and cataloguing nature of Ovid's list of sexual positions was linked to an earlier genre of Hellenistic literature, the sex manual. Although no examples have survived, references are made to them and their authors in several texts. The handbooks were condemned for their immodesty, more in the sense of overindulgence than in our sense of modesty as chasteness. Immoderation is one of the qualities that in the Greek mentality came closest to our concepts of the gross and lewd. The iteration, through a mixture of word and image, of sexual cavorting found in the manuals may have really been a type of classical "pornography." Etymologically it is indeed linked, as the supposed origin of these texts was in the writings of women who would presumably have been prostitutes of some sort, in order to gain the required experience; and, uniquely, the handbooks merited an ancient classification as a genre of objectionably licentious literature. A name associated with illustrated books of sexual instruction was Elephantis, cited by Suetonius and Martial and in the *Priapea.* It is remarkable to consider that when a similar combination of image and accompanying text cataloguing sexual positions was fabricated during the Renaissance, when there was access to the sources mentioned, the result was equally condemned and forcibly banned. Giulio Romano's 16 drawings of men and women in various postures of intercourse were matched with sonnets that Pietro Aretino wrote to explicate them, bound together into a volume. The book's combination of illustration and text became a template for an entire genre of erotic literature, avidly read and energetically prohibited, for centuries to come.

Romano's original impetus was intimately connected to his knowledge of antique erotica, particularly as a collector of medals termed *spintriae* in the late 16th century, which feature similarly configured couples on their obverse. When prints were independently made of the drawings in the circle of Raphael's collaborators in papal Rome, the engraver Marcantonio Raimondi was imprisoned and the plates were confiscated, which made this an early instance of systematic state censorship of art. Many examples survived, however, and traversed Europe to ensure the lasting influence of this classically derived, outlawed group of images.

Although we have no definitive explanation as to the exact function of the *spintriae,* they point to an important aspect of ancient erotica: an entire class of objects embellished with sexual images passed from hand to hand in quotidian activities. Starting with archaic decoration of drinking vessels, the tradition continued through time in other household trappings such as lamps and metalwork, in the specialized production of Arretine pottery, and apotropaic votives, which also took the form of personal talismans. Later cultures, while passionately collecting these ornaments, have never replicated their usage or completely understood their function. This class of antiquities has consistently received the unequivocal label of pornography. In particular the apotropaic objects shaped as phalluses, which variously are crowned with eyes, have sprouted wings, or have evolved into fantasy creatures, occasioned locked cases, uncatalogued stashes, and barely concealed sniggering in the earliest "scholarly" acknowledgments of their existence. Discussions were usually banished to footnotes written in Greek or Latin, thus exclusively addressed to erudite readers.

A more democratic jeu d'esprit infuses an etching attributed to Parmigianino (1503–1540). The tradition of the animated phallus informs a massive, tailed monster mounted by a witch as she prepares to ride off to her nocturnal mischief. We may conclude that the artist purposely used the motif in an obscene way, unable within the premises of 16th-century Italian culture to conjure a less sensational role for a detached penis, perhaps the most proscribed image it would be possible to flaunt in postpagan cultures. It should be noted that the phallic figure par excellence, Priapus, whose name is invoked regularly in self-styled pornographic traditions, was originally a figure called on to protect gardens and orchards. His oversized phallus indicated potency connected to fertility, and its power warned off potential thieves of the harvest. Robbed of that context, later priapic appropriations are generally limited to celebration of the male sexual organ.

Among the few examples of ancient licentiousness whose original context was reproduced along with its imagery, one has a singularly fascinating pedigree. Pliny records with strong language a fashion for chalices engraved with erotic scenes:

"It has pleased us to engrave scenes of license upon our goblets, and to drink through the midst of obscenities" (*Natural History* 33.2.5, trans. H. Rackham). An extant example of such a silver drinking vessel, known as the Warren Cup (now in the British Museum), has an exterior surface embellished with vignettes of homosexual couplings. The convention of placing libidinous imagery on cups ultimately goes back to archaic vase painting; that the Renaissance was cognizant of the later variation mentioned by Pliny is made clear in a story recorded by Brantôme (1540–1614) in *Les dames galantes.* His extended, leering description recounts the game a noble lord played while dining. A young female guest would be invited to sip unknowingly from a chalice decorated with figures in dissolute activities. Engraved on the interior, these scenes were revealed only gradually as the targeted guest drank. Perhaps the real obscenity was that the rest of the company, in on the joke, eagerly watched for the victim's reaction and made sport of her discomfiture.

If texts and Renaissance interpretations were the main channels for the transmission of classical erotica in early modern Europe, a spectacular discovery changed this at the dawn of the Neoclassical era. Direct exposure to Roman paintings and artifacts with erotic themes was gained from the treasures unearthed during the recovery of the Vesuvian sites at Herculaneum and Pompeii, tentatively begun in the 18th century and gaining momentum as excavation intensified during the 19th century. Archaeologists, connoisseurs, collectors, and scholars of every stamp were stunned by the material that emerged. The erotica in particular caused amazement and much consternation to the well-bred viewer, at a loss to assimilate the imagery into an idealized view of classical civilization. One way of doing this was to roundly misinterpret the finds, as when Pierre-Sylvain Maréchal referred to the small household objects as "the accomplices of their libertinism" in his 1780 register of Pompeian finds. Another reaction was to ruthlessly extract all the erotic images from their sites and contexts and segregate them into a special pornographic collection in the National Museum of Naples, access being restricted to curious males of a certain social class. The open secret of the existence of the pornographic collection did much to consolidate the atmosphere of stealth and prohibition that has enveloped erotic imagery in modern history.

Perhaps greater societal ease with the naked body, from the gymnasia and athletic competitions in Greece to the public baths in Roman culture, allowed for extensive ease with the representation of the nude in classical art, where its idealized form and symbolic potential were freely explored. The divergent norms and religious creeds of the later societies that rediscovered classical representations of the nude body resulted in an anachronistic assessment of the imagery as indecent and illicit, which did not tally with the original situation of the art in question. The belief system of the ancients exploited the fundamental human component of sexuality to suggest answers for the deep mysteries of existence.

Classical mythology, where sexual union was a metaphor that explicated phenomena found in nature and societal constructs, was a major source of erotic themes explored by ancient artists and by their emulators in the Renaissance; their vestiges occasionally seep into modern culture. In addition to dependence on readings of Ovid's *Metamorphoses,* later artists looked to a corpus of classical sculpture for imaginative and in certain instances highly eroticized presentations of mythological stories. A case in point is the many versions of Leda and the Swan in Renaissance art based on Graeco-Roman models that survived in sculpture and gems. One Roman relief, based on a Hellenistic prototype, shows a slightly stooping Leda actively engaging the Swan as her head bends under the protracted beak nibbling her neck. Adaptations were made in drawings by several artists, while an exact copy exists in the Fossombrone Sketchbook, from Raphael's workshop. The mystique endured in the best circles; another version of the relief that passed through a London dealer inspired William Butler Yeats to compose his own evocative verses on the subject.

The most influential treatment, however, of Leda's sexual union with a feathered Zeus was hatched from a sarcophagus on the Quirinal, known and frequently copied throughout the 15th and 16th centuries. This composition shows Leda recumbent on voluminous fabric draped over the ground, supported on her elbow, with one knee raised to receive the Swan that swoops upon her with wings outstretched. The figure also underlies Titian's portrayal of *Danaë,* the artist cleverly substituting one instance of Zeus's visits-in-disguise for another while retaining the graphic posture of the heroine. But the most significant version in painting is now lost. Michelangelo's large-scale copy is known only through the several examples that record it, perhaps most faithfully in the replica attributed to Rosso Fiorentino. The procession of copies, adaptations, and variations is typical of the afterlife of ancient erotica. Most often the initial exemplar sparks a sequence of copies, eventually evolving at second or third hand—and beyond—from the prototype, gradually assuming a type of reverential distance from it. Often this occurs from necessity, owing to the disappearance of the original, whether from censorship or overuse, or its being secreted away in a closed collection.

The nude figure was neither covert nor censored in its representation in a variety of media and contexts in classical art. Yet despite the openness with which erotic situations were presented and body parts displayed, there were zones of reserve in ancient art that are, ironically, contrary to the traditions that grew in its wake and under its influence. There was a reticence with regard to nudity in sculpted female figures until the second half of the 4th century BCE. Establishment of the canon for the female nude is traditionally ascribed to Praxiteles in the carving of his Venus of Cnidus. The scandalous novelty of the statue is attested by the story that it was first offered to the people of Kos and rejected; its compelling sexual effect is told in the legend that a young man stained the sculpture after engaging in sexual activity with it. The convention of the female nude conceived as a work of art and object of lust thus was propagated at one and the same time, and the tradition has continued unabated. The gesture of the Venus of Cnidus, one hand attempting to cover—at the same time that it indicates—her genitals became a convention much used in art that followed. It was employed to great effect by Giorgione in his *Sleeping Venus* (ca. 1510) and expertly by Titian in the *Venus of Urbino* (1538), with the added flirtation of the woman's direct gaze forthrightly confronting the viewer. These two paintings continue to provoke arguments about the nature and effect of their eroticism, extending debates variously and creatively engaged during the 19th century. Mark Twain (*A Tramp Abroad,* 1880) sermonized, in his usual entertaining but pointed manner, about the figure's obscenity, whereas Edouard Manet shocked the bourgeoisie by portraying a well-known Parisian prostitute in the position of Titian's Venus in his painting *Olympia* (1863).

If Venus was from the start the preferred female vehicle for eroticism, Bacchus developed into the male equivalent from the mythical canon. Just as the physical perfection of Venus and her rule as the goddess of love are commanding vehicles for erotic representation, Bacchus's presiding over wine and orgiastic rites proved an irresistible spur to highly charged art. Michelangelo's handsome, youthful Bacchus of ca. 1496 weaves unsteadily in a drunken stupor with heavy-lidded eyes and a lustful lurch. The figure, carved in open competition with the achievement of the ancients, was placed in a garden with the patron's classical collection. A century later Caravaggio painted a boy from the streets of Rome as Bacchus, whose proffered glass of wine and loosely draped sheet cleverly allow him to play the role of the deity, while the motion to untie his costume indicates that more than a drink is on offer.

Only isolated examples of knowledgeable adaptations from classical erotica appear in late 20th-century and contemporary art, in large part because the classical corpus is no longer the basis of our educational systems. When skillfully appropriated, however, classical elements can add unexpected conceptual force and visual splendor to the most daring and accomplished contemporary works. The enduring force of the tradition in the hands of Robert Mapplethorpe was recently revealed in an exhibition where the photographer's unarguable submersion in the forms and ethos of classical sculpture served as a conceptual basis for his aestheticizing the erotic nude body. Mapplethorpe's work revitalizes approaches to the erotic that have their roots in the classical past, incorporating representational strategies that, after centuries of exploration, will continue to inform the discourse around issues of legitimacy and prohibition in literature and art.

BIBL.: Otto J. Brendel, "The Scope and Temperament of Erotic Art in the Greco-Roman World," in *Studies in Erotic Art,* ed. Theodore Bowie and Cornelia V. Christenson (New York 1970) 3–107. Germano Celant et al., eds., *Robert Mapplethorpe and the Classical Tradition: Photographs and Mannerist Prints* (New York 2004). Walter Kendrick, *The Secret Museum* (New York 1988). Ian Moulton, *Before Pornography: Erotic Writing in Early Modern England* (Oxford 2000). Holt N. Parker, "Love's Body Anatomized," in *Pornography and Representation in Greece and Rome,* ed. Amy Richlin (Oxford 1992) 90–111. Bette Talvacchia, "The Art of Courting Women's Laughter," in *New Perspectives on Women and Comedy,* ed. Regina Barreca (Philadelphia 1992) 213–222, and *Taking Positions: On the Erotic in Renaissance Culture* (Princeton 1999).

B.T.

Porphyry

An Egyptian stone quarried in antiquity and later reused to exploit its associations with empire, sacredness, and permanence. Porphyry is a type of igneous rock, hard and compact by virtue of its fiery geological origin but varied in color depending on its local constituents. The white-flecked reddish-purple porphyry taken in antiquity from Mons Porphyrites in Egypt's Eastern Desert is of interest here because of the powerful meanings associated with it in imperial Rome, in Byzantium, and in post-classical Western Europe by those who appreciated its illustrious associations. After the 4th or 5th century CE the exact location of the quarries was no longer known; that all works in porphyry now had to be made from stone previously extracted or deployed added rarity to the qualities that made porphyry prestigious.

Porphyry's extreme hardness suggested a durability that countered the fugacity of human life, dynasties, and regimes. Popes and secular rulers, such as Sicily's Norman kings, emulated Roman and Byzantine emperors by commissioning tombs for themselves in porphyry; the Medici dukes used it for dynastic portraits. Because it resisted the attack of ordinary steel chisels, intricate carvings in porphyry attracted particular attention, especially during the Italian Renaissance. Tuscan writers such as Vasari wondered how the Romans had been able to execute ornate foliage and finely modeled figures in a stone so impervious to the sculptor's tools of the time. That the process was a mystery to the ancients themselves is suggested by the legend of the Passion of the Four Crowned Saints (Passio Sanctorum Quattuor Coronatorum), attributed to the late 3rd century: Christian porphyry carvers who refused to produce pagan images for the emperor Diocletian were executed; but the tools used by their pagan colleagues broke on porphyry, whereas theirs had worked marvelously, because tempered by Christ himself. When the 16th-century Florentine stoneworker Francesco Ferrucci del Tadda began cutting porphyry with steel tools, their efficacy was attributed, misguidedly, to the tempering process used to harden them. Admiration for the appearance and technical virtuosity of ancient works in porphyry inspired Tadda's figurative works in the hard purple stone, but softer white marbles were preferred by contemporary sculptors, unsympathetic to the ancient Roman taste for colored stone figures and averse to the mechanical toil involved in working porphyry (Tadda took a month to carve one porphyry eye, and twelve years to execute a large statue of Justice). Most early modern patrons and Grand Tourists preferred the appearance and cost of porphyry shaped by abrasion into vessels, veneers, and components for *pietre dure* inlays, which still bore precious classical associations.

Porphyry's purple color offered powerful symbolic potential. In ancient Rome and Byzantium the purple stone, like the dye *porpora,* had been reserved for those of imperial rank; "born to the purple" literally described Byzantine princes born in Constantinople's porphyry-clad imperial birth chamber. Porphyry also recalled the blood shed by Jesus and the Christian martyrs, on altar tables or in sculptures such as Tadda's heads of Christ and of the controversial Dominican priest Savonarola. It was used to mark strategic points in church pavements and was exploited liturgically to reinforce sacred hierarchies on ceremonial occasions, including imperial coronations. Because most prestigious materials were vulnerable (gold and bronze could be melted down, and marble reduced to lime), porphyry's durability and fire-resistance offered patrons opportunities to proclaim their invincibility. That the stone could be quarried to produce monolithic columns, uniform rather than composite, was valued aesthetically and technically by classicizing architects and, by their patrons, as another flattering allusion. Ancient porphyry columns were plundered by Western rulers to display as military trophies (e.g., at St. Mark's in Venice and at the Baptistery in Florence) and accumulated for a dynastic mausoleum (the Medici Chapel of the Princes), but they were also appreciated as beautiful objects by collectors of antiquities. Surviving porphyry figures and receptacles were displayed in public squares, palaces, and gardens, or adapted to new purposes. Set with a golden head, wings, tail, and talons, an ancient porphyry vase became an eagle's body in a vessel for Suger's abbey at St.-Denis. The lid of "Hadrian's" tomb was recut in the 17th century as a baptismal basin for St. Peter's in Rome, and an ancient bath urn was reshaped into the tomb of Pope Clement XII. The lack of freshly quarried porphyry encouraged the development of ingenious uses and display situations for surviving fragments, and thus to the invention of new imagery and layers of symbolism.

Today, with the Mons Porphyrites again accessible for the first time since antiquity, a sculptor like Stephen Cox can quarry porphyry directly and so reassert links with classical sculpture in natural stone, its geology, scale, shape, texture, color, and significance. That many of Cox's porphyry works explore familiar themes of sacredness and permanence reconfirms the cultural logic that guaranteed this ancient purple stone a major role in the classical tradition.

BIBL.: G. Baldwin Brown, ed., *Vasari on Technique,* trans. L. S. Maclehose (New York 1960) 26–34, 108–116. Suzanne B. Butters, *The Triumph of Vulcan: Sculptors' Tools, Porphyry, and the Prince in Ducal Florence* (Florence 1996). József Deér, *The Dynastic Porphyry Tombs of the Norman Period in Sicily* (Cambridge, Mass., 1959). Richard Delbrück, *Antike Porphyrwerke* (Berlin 1932). Raniero Gnoli, *Marmora Romana* (Rome 1988) 14–15, 81–96, 122–144. S.B.B.

Portico

The Roman *porticus* originated in the early 2nd century BCE as a ground-level, open colonnade, like the Greek stoa, longer than wide, with sloping roof and one, two, or three aisles separated by rows of columns. Early examples met commercial needs, like the Porticus Aemilia (194 BCE), and commemorative purposes, like the Porticus Octavia (168 BCE), with its double colonnade (Pliny, *Natural History* 34.13). But the portico quickly became a versatile form. It could be added to public or private buildings for ornament or used to create enclosed, colonnaded spaces for display and ceremony. Fascinating viewers with perspectival effects (Lucretius, *On the Nature of Things* 4.426–431) and favored in domestic architecture for their *dignitas* (Cicero, *Letters to His Brother Quintus* 3.1), porticoes became an archetype in public architecture, notably in Rome's imperial fora and in provincial fora. They are sometimes constructed on vaulted cryptoporticoes.

The portico's most lasting legacy is the street-side arcade. The ground-level wooden arcades of republican Rome brought rhythmical order to urban space, which was elaborated after 64 CE by the brick and stone porticoes of Nero's "new city." These included the Golden House's mile-long triple porticoes, Gallienus' Flaminia colonnade, and Constantine's Porticus Maximae. In the Eastern Empire, broad avenues (*plateae*) with continuous porticoes roofing the space between the roadside and the building frontage, as at Ephesus, Antioch, Palmyra, and Alexandria, found their inheritance in the colonnaded streets of Constantinople (Byzantium). In the West street-side porticoes were preserved in medieval cities, often doubling as facades for public buildings. Some owed their survival to building laws. At Bern elevated arcades above street-level cellars belonged to the municipality, which maintained their proportions from the 13th to the 19th century. Bologna's famous porticoes, initially wooden but rebuilt in brick or stone, were regulated in height by statute in 1249, so that horses could pass beneath. Uniting private houses and public loggias for 21 miles, they became a signature metaphor for the city (Miller 1989). But Rome's porticoes had become so cluttered with refuse in 1475 that Ferrante (Ferdinand I), king of Naples, urged Pope Sixtus IV to demolish them. To Alberti, porticoes served "the common use of the citizens," offering both shelter and noble frontages for aristocratic houses, where the young could wait for their elders by enjoying "all manner of exercise" (*The Art of Building, in Ten Books* 2.8). Even where there was no room for projecting porticoes, he noted, the engaged orders on the facade of the Palazzo Rucellai in Florence recreated a "portico for the highest citizens" (9.4). Domestic porticoes and loggias were regarded as a privilege, used for family ceremonies; as families became more inward-looking, they were replaced by inner courtyards.

Fixed within the vocabulary of classical architecture by Serlio and Vignola, porticoes became widely dispersed during the Renaissance and after. Beginning in the 16th century, the *Laws of the Indies* governing Spanish colonies overseas introduced arcaded streets to the New World as "of considerable convenience to the merchants who generally gather there," and Carlo Borromeo's *Lessons on Building* (1577) gave church porticoes a liturgical function. Major European cities acquired grand colonnaded areas: in Turin, Carlo di Castellamonte's Piazza San Carlo (1640–1650); in London, John Nash's Quadrant (1813); in Paris, the rue des Colonnes (1795), symbol of republican idealism, and rue de Rivoli (1800–1835). In Rome the semicircular arcades of Gaetano Koch's Piazza della Repubblica (1886) were built over the porticoes of the Baths of Diocletian (early 4th cent. CE). Friedrich Nietzsche and Walter Benjamin lauded the arcades of Italy and France, but their Anglo-Saxon contemporaries saw them as dark and narrow.

Although churches from Justinian's Hagia Sophia (6th cent.) onward maintained the portico front of Roman temples, the portico as temple front had greatest influence on domestic architecture, particularly in English Palladianism. Wilton House (ca. 1633) in Wiltshire was designed with an elevated portico fronting a great room of state, which was no longer needed after its owner, the Earl of Pembroke, fell out with Charles I. In the Earl of Burlington's Chiswick House (1727) in London, the Corinthian portico, with only a passage behind it, reflected taste and style, rather than ceremonial function (Riddell 1995). By 1800 entrance porticoes were smaller and placed at ground level, where the main rooms now were, following the Greek model. In the 19th century, though they might symbolize owners' authority and taste, porticoes were often rejected as sham, authoritarian, and un-English, to be replaced by smaller porches in the Gothic style. Meanwhile, in North America, the front porch or verandah was becoming "an American institution of high civic and moral value" in cities as well as the countryside, and "a sign that the people who sit on it are ready and willing to share the community life of their block with their neighbors" (Ford 2000, 46, quoting a 1952 article in *House and Garden*).

BIBL.: Larry Ford, *The Spaces between Buildings* (Baltimore 2000). J. F. Geist, *Arcades,* trans. J. O. Newmann and J. H. Smith (Cambridge, Mass., 1983). Naomi Miller, *Renaissance Bologna: A Study in Architectural Form and Content* (New York 1989). Björn Olinder, *Porticus Octavia in Circo Flaminio: Topographical Studies in the Campus Region of Rome* (Stockholm 1974). Richard J. Riddell, "The Entrance-Portico in the Architecture of Great Britain, 1630–1850" (D.Phil. thesis, Oxford University, 1995). E.T.

Portraits, Reception of Ancient

The study, identification, and misidentification of Greek and Roman portraits has followed a fascinating and unpredictable path from the Renaissance to the present. There has been, on the one hand, a steadily improved understanding based on ever more and better-studied evidence. On the other hand, pulling against empirical scholarship and often mixed in with it, there have been other forces—above all, the need to find faces for the great figures of antiquity and the desire to provide precise names for often striking and individual images that seem otherwise difficult to understand. These forces have often defeated and can still defeat even the best documentary evidence when that evidence points in an unwelcome direction. The modern world has often found in ancient portraits only what it wanted to find.

The willful practice of reinterpreting undocumented Roman images in contemporary terms began early, for example, in the medieval reception of the great imperial cameos that had remained in circulation, moving from treasure cabinets in Rome and Constantinople to church collections in Europe. One of the grandest, the Gemma Augustea (now in Vienna), which shows Tiberius before Augustus, was for a long time interpreted as Joseph at the court of the Egyptian pharaoh.

Large public monuments above ground since antiquity naturally acquired the greatest accretion of local and scholarly interpretation. The gilded bronze equestrian statue of Marcus Aurelius, moved from before the Lateran basilica to the Campidoglio in 1538, had popularly been thought for many centuries to represent a peasant, a warrior, or Constantine. In scholarly circles, it had at the same time been identified as an understandably wide range of 2nd-century emperors, all of whom wore more or less similar long beards on their coins. Hadrian, Antoninus Pius, Marcus Aurelius, Lucius Verus, Septimius Severus were all in play. The typologically correct identification as Marcus Aurelius had been proposed by the later 14th century, but it did not impose itself as the single correct identification for at least another century. The popular interpretations were of course unaffected by the early realization that the statue was certainly one of the 2nd-century Roman emperors.

The discovery, unearthing, and collecting of Roman portraits (mostly marble busts and heads) had a major influence on 15th-century art—for example, in the works of Donatello and Mantegna. And in the 16th century the scholarly pursuit of identifying ancient portraits began in earnest, with proper publications to collect and disseminate results. Several different volumes of *Imagines illustrium* appeared through the 16th and 17th centuries. The most authoritative was that of F. Ursinus (Fulvio Orsini) of 1570. The focus was naturally not art but history. The steady flow of new pieces, helped out by coins, both stimulated and fed the need for portraits of the powerful and the learned of antiquity to set beside and illustrate the writers and rulers known from classical literature.

The twelve Caesars were early in demand, one that could be satisfied only with willing imagination. It was easy to find busts and heads that would conveniently and sometimes correctly represent the bland youthful figures of the Julio-Claudian dynasty, but the short-lived and gnarled old emperors of 68 CE, such as Galba and Vitellius, attested to on their highly specific coin images, were nowhere to be found. The immediate success of the Grimani *Vitellius* found in Rome in 1505 (now in Venice) was thus understandable. The bust combines the age, corpulence, and vigor of the Vitellius on coins, and it was much copied. The vivid lifelikeness of the original (rare in imperial portraits) has caused more than one scholar to declare the Grimani bust itself post-antique too. It is clearly ancient and so good as a Vitellius that it was difficult to give up. Only since 1927 has it been recognized correctly as a portrait of a private, or nonimperial, figure of the Hadrianic period.

Many early portrait identifications were not even of portraits at all. The Belevedere *Cleopatra* or the Capitoline *Antinous,* for example, are statues respectively of Ariadne and Mercury. One of the greatest of such ancient portrait creations was the Borghese *Seneca.* There was no special pressure to find Seneca's face, as there was for Vitellius, admired Stoic moralist though he was. The impetus came, as it did with the others, from the ground, from an astonishing black marble statue discovered on the Esquiline in Rome in 1594. The arresting figure (in the Louvre since Napoleon) clearly contained a narrative of pain and suffering, and it was quickly connected with the unforgettable account of Seneca committing suicide in his bath given by the Roman historian Tacitus (*Annals* 15.63–64). The identification, though incorrect, is still immediately convincing. The figure wears a loincloth—bath wear. Veins stand out, as they do in Tacitus. And above all, the figure represents the climax of Tacitus' report, which describes how Seneca, frustrated by the slowness of merely opening his wrist veins, finally cut the tendons behind his knees, which as the historian emphasizes is excruciatingly painful. The knees of the statue are indeed bent as though cut behind, and the head looks up in agony.

The tight connection between statue and text was consolidated and made permanent by the brilliant restoration of the statue, standing in this pose in a gray bath basin, its lower legs emerging from blood-red marble "water" inside it. The restoration was incorrect, but from a badly fragmented figure it created a new image that represented Seneca. The statue was influential: it inspired, for example, Rubens's grand canvas of Seneca's suicide (now in Munich).

It was the sharp eye and writing of J. J. Winckelmann in the mid-18th century that first shot down such fantastic interpretations. He had noted the *Seneca*'s similarity to Roman genre figures carrying baskets and suggested that it might instead be not a dying philosopher at all, but a toiling slave. The interpretation was essentially correct. Later scholarship and other versions soon showed it was in fact a peasant fisherman. The subsequent discovery of a real, inscribed Seneca portrait in 1813 (now in Berlin) aroused little interest. The Berlin portrait shows a bald, jowly, clean-shaven, and self-satisfied patrician and stood no chance of capturing the imagination, in contrast to the agonizing power of the Borghese statue. Here, from one perspective, fiction was more interesting than truth.

Meanwhile, scholarly understanding and even aesthetic appreciation continued apace. The monumental Albani relief of Antinous, for example, was both correctly identified and lovingly art-historicized by Winckelmann. Chance discoveries were now supplemented increasingly by large, targeted excavations in and around Rome and the Bay of Naples that produced an abundance of new pieces. Where heads and busts could be matched with clearly defined portraits on coins or other inscribed versions, all went well. Where, however, no external documents were available to secure verifiable identifications, the "biographical" method, encountered in brilliant form in the naming of the *Seneca,* was deployed with less brilliant results.

Since it was agreed that ancient portraits depicted the real inner character and life of the subject, then literary accounts of character, deeds, and biographical peculiarities should enable identification of unnamed portraits. This practice, though obviously fallacious and subjective, was pursued in scholarly works and produced a dense undergrowth of confidently asserted identifications, based on pure guesswork, that were mixed in the published record with well-founded identifications. The guesses seemed convincing because they were erudite and backed by detailed knowledge of often obscure classical texts.

Many of the approximately 40 unknown bronze and marble portraits tunneled out of the Villa dei Papiri at Herculaneum in 1750–1761 were given spurious names of this kind. Two busts, for example, though neither laughs or cries, were named Democritus, the laughing philosopher, and Heraclitus, the weeping philosopher. Though entirely baseless, the Democritus remained an accepted identification until recently. The bust was a nationalist emblem on 10 drachma coins and 100 drachma notes of the modern Greek state until the introduction of the euro in 2002.

The accumulated results of this antiquarian tradition, which mixed willful biographical identifications with genuinely verifiable ones were collected in the great 19th-century works of E. Q. Visconti, *Iconographie Grecque* (1811) and *Iconographie Romaine* (1817–1829). They were replaced by a more scientific and scholarly evaluation in J. J. Bernoulli's *Griechische Ikonographie* (1901) and *Römische Ikonographie* I–II (1882–1894).

The 20th century saw a more or less steady advance in the right direction, especially in defining and refining a scientific method for understanding the operation of the Roman imperial portrait system. This culminated in the work of K. Fittschen and P. Zanker, most notably in their great catalogue of the Roman portraits in the Capitoline collections: *Katalog der römischen Porträts in den Capitolinischen Museen und den anderen Kommunalen Sammlungen der Stadt Rom* I, III (1983–1985). The Capitoline contains many of the key pieces of Roman imperial portraiture, and this work has had a big and beneficial effect on the study of the subject in the last 25 years.

Fallacious biographical interpretation and identification have remained alive and well alongside more rigorous methods. Ancient portraits still seem to demand a name, a life, and an attested character before sense can be made of them. Some figures are so potent in the modern imagination—Hannibal, Sulla, Brutus—that major portraits must be found even when they are not available. A spurious portrait of Hannibal still decorates the cover of his many modern biographies.

One of the strangest, most interesting examples of this phenomenon, which exemplifies many aspects of ancient portrait reception, is the portrait of Virgil. The case is all the more curious for having been pursued entirely within the highest scholarly circles. Authorized portraits of Roman emperors and Greek writers survive in multiple ancient copies and versions, and their numbers are rightly thought to indicate something about the significance and popularity of the subject in the Roman period. For example, many portraits survive of Euripides (about 30), Demosthenes (about 50), and Augustus (about 215). One such portrait of an attractive, clean-shaven, mature individual, "Roman"-looking but not an emperor, is known in so many Roman marbles (around 70 are known today) that it was thought it might, should, indeed must represent the most significant figure of Roman culture known to us—the incomparable Virgil. His portrait was badly wanted, and here one had been found.

The idea gained considerable ground in respectable scholarship in the mid-20th century. There was not only nothing solid in favor of the Virgil identification, there was also much clearly against it. There had always been good evidence for the identity of this portrait type that indicated a quite different and unwelcome direction. A lost version of the portrait known in a 16th-century drawing as well as a version formerly in Marbury Hall, England, both carried clearly inscribed labels and agreed in naming the subject not Virgil but Menander, the Athenian playwright. It was, however, not until 1971 when a third, sharper version of the portrait, also inscribed "Menander" (now in the J. P. Getty Museum, Malibu) was published that the correct identification of the whole series was finally and generally accepted: Menander not Virgil, a Greek not a Roman, a superstar of light comic drama, not much to 20th-century taste, but, by the measure of his portrait remains alone, a towering cultural force in antiquity.

Today the chastening lesson of the Virgil-Menander case has mostly been learned, and archaeological and art-historical study of ancient portraits generally stays close to the evidence and to verifiability. In other areas and in popular culture, however, the need to find by imaginative intuition faces for famous names, such as Hannibal, and names for unidentifiable portraits, such as the Grimani *Vitellius,* remains as strong as ever. It is because we still receive these potent images as part of our culture and visual language that we feel able to know and interpet them with such ease.

BIBL.: S. Bailey, "Metamorphoses of the Grimani 'Vitellius,'" *J. Paul Getty Museum Journal* 5 (1977) 105–122. K. Fittschen, "Zur Rekonstruktion griechischer Dichterstatuen. 1. Teil: Die Statue des Menander," *Athenische Mitteilungen* 106 (1991) 243–279. F. Haskell and N. Penny, *Taste and the Antique* (New Haven 1981) 303–305. D. C. Kurtz, ed., *The Reception of Classical Art* (Oxford 2004). Parisi Presicce, *The Equestrian Statue of Marcus Aurelius in Campidoglio* (Milan 1990). R. Weiss, *The Renaissance Discovery of Classical Antiquity,* 2nd ed. (Oxford 1988).
R.R.R.S.

Poseidon. *See* Neptune.

Praeneste

Town in Latium, now called Palestrina, 40 km southeast of Rome. Praeneste is famous for its sanctuary dedicated to Primordial Fortune (Fortuna Primigenia), built ca. 100 BCE on the slope of Mount Ginestro. A highly sophisticated structure based on Hellenistic prototypes, it consists of several terraces arranged on an axis and connected with stairs and ramps, which are topped with an exedra to which is attached a circular temple. In the lower part is a vaulted hall with an apse, where a large mosaic with magnificent Nilotic scenes (2nd cent. BCE) was discovered in the 17th century (it is now in the Museo Nazionale Archeologica Prenestino).

During the Middle Ages the town spread over the terraces of the sanctuary, while the upper part was rebuilt as a palace of the princely Colonna family. During the Renaissance the rediscovery of the sanctuary was initiated by Giuliano da Sangallo (d. 1516), who identified the apsidal hall as a temple of Fortuna. In the mid-1540s Pirro Ligorio and Andrea Palladio made elaborate reconstruction drawings in which the whole site was regarded as the forum of the ancient town. The hillside composition became the prototype for Donato Bramante's Cortile di Belvedere in the Vatican (completed 1565), from which numerous Renaissance and Baroque villas and gardens derived, such as the Villa d'Este in Tivoli and the Villa Aldobrandini in Frascati. And in a reversal of influence the sophisticated circular staircase invented by Bramante for the Belvedere and published by Serlio was used in reconstructing the exedra staircase of the sanctuary.

In Pietro da Cortona's reconstruction, published in 1655, the entire area of the medieval town was drawn into a single scheme of the sanctuary. Cortona's patrons, the papal family of Barberini, who had bought Palestrina from the Colonna family in 1630, appear to have intended to rebuild part of the sanctuary as a villa. Cortona's reconstruction was frequently republished, and its monumental appearance was an inspiration for many Baroque buildings and projects, ranging from Cortona's own designs for the Boboli Gardens behind the Pitti Palace in Florence to Johann Bernhard Fischer von Erlach's first project for the castle at Schönbrunn near Vienna.

More detailed studies of the sanctuary were not made until the late 18th century, when Pierre-Adrien Paris began to investigate the site and George Hadfield executed a set of views and monumental reconstructions (1792). The most accurate study and an imaginative reconstruction were undertaken by Jean-Nicolas Huyot in 1807–1812, whereas Konstantin Thon (1825) and Luigi Canina (1830) published reconstructions in which the sanctuary was still seen as a unified monument. These images of the sanctuary and others deriving from them were widely published and used as references in two different ways. Though the unified vision of the sanctuary with its emphasis on the ramps and terraces was regarded as a prototype for national monuments, such as the Monument to Vittorio Emanuele II in Rome, the more detailed idea of the sanctuary proper became a source of inspiration for major public buildings, for instance the Union Building, the seat of the national government in Pretoria, South Africa.

Although further studies of the sanctuary appeared in the 19th and early 20th centuries, its true dimensions were not discovered until excavations following the bombing of the town during World War II. Postmodern architecture again shows affinities with the repertoire of forms—terraces, ramps, exedra—displayed in the Sanctuary of Fortune.

BIBL.: Filippo Coarelli, *I santuari del Lazio in età repubblicana* (Rome 1997). Furio Fasolo and Giorgio Gullini, *Il Santuario della Fortuna Primigenia a Palestrina,* 2 vols. (Rome

1953). J. M. Merz, *Das Heiligtum der Fortuna in Palestrina und die Architektur der Neuzeit* (Munich 2001). P. G. P. Meyboom, *The Nile Mosaic of Palestrina* (Leiden 1995). J.M.M.

Presocratics

The first known use of the term *Presocratic* appeared in a handbook on the history of philosophy published by J.-A. Eberhard in 1788. The idea that there existed a sharp break between Socrates and what preceded him, however, goes back to antiquity. The manner in which ancient thinkers conceived the relationship between Socrates and his predecessors explains the modern fate of the Presocratics. Two separate patterns are apparent in this regard: one emphasizes the break between Socrates and his predecessors and the other the continuity between them.

The first was a tradition that we might call the Socratic-Ciceronian. This was closely linked, from the beginning, to the trial of Socrates and to the necessity for him, in order to answer the charges of impiety brought against him, to distance himself from an enterprise known generally as early as 430 BCE as the "inquiry into natural phenomena." The inquiry amounted to a general history of the universe and its constituent parts from creation to destruction. The account included a certain number of more or less obligatory elements. From Anaximander to Philolaos and Democritus, by way of Anaximenes, Parmenides (in the second part of his poem), Empedocles, Anaxagoras, and Diogenes of Apollonia, all the major accounts "on nature" included an explanation of the way in which, beginning from a greater or lesser number of elementary principles, the universe, the stars, and the Earth were formed, as well as, very early on, a treatment of more technical or specialized problems, such as the limits of the celestial and terrestrial spheres, the inclination of the poles, meteorological and terrestrial phenomena, the emergence of living beings and their reproduction, the mechanisms of physiological and intellectual life, and even the development of life in society. In ancient texts the *meteora* (literally phenomena of the heavens) often represented, by synecdoche, the inquiry into nature as a whole.

The inquiry into natural phenomena, which began in Ionia, particularly in Miletus, in the 6th century BCE, came under suspicion in Athens, where it was introduced in the middle of the 5th century. A decree of 438–437 BCE authorized bringing charges of impiety against anyone involved in examining the heavens. Anaxagoras was the first victim, in an attack aimed at his protector Pericles, for having held that stars were simply igneous rock. Diogenes of Apollonia also appears to have been at risk. It may now seem very curious, given how inconsistent it is with the image we have based on Plato's *Apology* and Xenophon's *Memorabilia,* that Socrates himself was suspected of sharing the naturalists' curiosity about the mechanisms of the universe, and thus their impiety. The key text in this regard is Aristophanes' *Clouds,* presented in 423, explicitly denounced by Plato in his *Apology* (18A–B, 19A–C) as the first formal attack on his master some 25 years before the trial in 399. In *Clouds* Socrates is seen suspended in a basket spouting phrases that parody the doctrine of Diogenes of Apollonia, who believed that the higher air was more intelligent for being dryer (*Clouds* 225–236). According to Plato, no one ever heard Socrates discuss "what was under the earth and in the sky" (19C; cf. *Clouds,* 180–195). Xenophon's *Memorabilia* (1.1.1) repeats Plato's claim: far from involving himself in "divine things" like the naturalists, Socrates turned his attention exclusively to "human things" (*ta anthropina*), the good of mankind and the practice of virtue. In both Xenophon and Plato's *Apology,* Socrates figures as the first "humanist."

The simple and rhetorically useful opposition of Presocratic "naturalism" with Socratic humanism was primarily intended to show a typological difference between two kinds of intellectual orientation. It also lent itself to a historiographical interpretation, however, in that one orientation followed another. The *Phaedo,* which, compared to the *Apology* or the *Memorabilia,* developed a more complex picture of the relationship between Socrates and the old physics, quite clearly favored this interpretation; it recalled what both the *Apology* and the *Memorabilia,* for reasons that are understandable, refrained from mentioning, namely that Socrates himself experienced a phase as a naturalist in his early years (96B1–C1). The doxographic tradition gives greater relevance to this assertion when it makes Socrates the disciple of Archelaus, a naturalist who himself was within Anaxagoras's circle (Diogenes Laertius 2.16). The two epochs in the history of thought, before and after Socrates, that histories of philosophy would later distinguish, were first of all two epochs in the life of one and the same Socrates, who had been a naturalist before he was himself.

The prologue to book 5 of Cicero's *Tusculan Disputations,* which enjoyed wide distribution, was no doubt the historical text with the greatest influence in the process of constructing a Presocratic "era." According to Cicero, the time of the first "wise men" (those who served human civilization and its practical development) was followed by a period that began with Pythagoras, who advocated a new approach called "philosophy." Its distinctive characteristic was observation for observation's sake, guided by no other motivation than the satisfaction that such observation would offer. This was the birth of "theory" or contemplation, whose favorite object of study was the sky (Cicero, *Tusculan Disputations,* 5.3, cf. Diogenes Laertius 1.12). Cicero would look again to Socrates to steer philosophy in his famous phrase, "from the sky back to the Earth," where it had first taken root but had since been neglected, refocusing on the question of how mankind ought to live.

The Socratic-Ciceronian tradition is thus characterized by the fact that it situated the break between Socrates and his predecessors in the context of a particular *object*—man versus the heavens. The Platonic-Aristotelian tradition, on the other hand, considered Socrates' importance to be basically the introduction of a new *method,* one that questioned the concepts being used before trying to explain phenomena. This shift toward epistemological questions was first presented in Plato's *Phaedo,* which paved the way to a much more homogeneous vision in the history of philosophy. Although the method was different, the object was the same: the *Phaedo* held that a demonstration of the immortality of the soul (the subject of the dialogue), called for "deep research into the cause of birth and decay," which corresponded to the program, if not the realization (from Plato's perspective), of the old "inquiries on nature."

Aristotle, for his part, reasserted the idea that the Presocratics and Socrates were engaged in the same effort, whose objective, generally speaking, was to find primary causes. This was what earned them the name "first philosophers" in the first book of *Metaphysics* (983b6), which, directly, and through subsequent commentaries, is the ultimate source of much of our information about the earliest Greek thinkers. Beginning in chapter 3, Aristotle endeavors to draw out, from among all his predecessors, the progressive appearance of the four causes that are at the base of his own theory of physics: first, concerning the material cause, Aristotle asks whether it might be attributed to the "theologians" (Hesiod and the Orphics), and he states that it clearly was a major theme of Thales, Anaximenes, and Heraclitus. Next he considers the attribution of the efficient cause to Hesiod and Parmenides, the final cause to Anaxagoras and Empedocles, and the formal cause to the Pythagoricians and Plato (chaps. 5 and 6). In every case the question is one less of discovery than of anticipation. For Empedocles, the final cause is called "friendship." For Anaxagoras, it was implied by the guiding function of the intellect; the efficient cause, once again, is called "love" by Hesiod and Parmenides. "Bodies" themselves, which the physicists take as principles, are only the prefiguration of the Aristotelian's notion of substrate and potentiality. From this perspective, there is no gap from Thales to Aristotle, and Socrates is but one step, albeit an important one, on the path that leads to truth. The price of this interpretation is a teleological view of the history of philosophy whose influence has extended at least as far as Hegel. Thus, we see that the anti-Peripatetic movements from the early modern period went along with a reevaluation of the Presocratics (G. Bruno). The same was true for the ancients as well, Epicurus finding his real inspiration from Democritus, the Stoics finding theirs in Heraclitus, and the Platonists (supposedly) in Pythagoras.

Although the neologism *Presocratic* appeared at the end of the 18th century, it was not immediately adopted; rather, it launched a debate because of the difficulties encountered by people who tried to use it in a rigorous, historical manner. Eberhard's handbook is an early example of the problem, since he began the period he called "Socratic" with a series of paragraphs devoted not to Socrates himself but to the Sophists—and understandably so, since they too were interested in human affairs. In view of the difficulty, would it not have been more judicious to reserve the honor of beginning a second period in the history of philosophy for Plato, and move the Sophists and Socrates back to the end of the preceding period? Throughout the 19th century we can trace a hesitation, notably through the opposing views of Schleiermacher (a partisan of the Socratic revolution) and Hegel (one of the first to rehabilitate the Sophists as the initial thinkers of subjectivity). It was Eduard Zeller, the founder of modern historiography of ancient philosophy, who, relying on the Aristotelian tradition, finally established Socrates as the true dividing line in his *History of Greek Philosophy,* first published between 1844 and 1852. The fact that Socrates was the earliest representative of a philosophy of concepts (*eidos*) was sufficient to recognize him as marking a new beginning. As for the Sophists, they could easily be placed with the Presocratics, since, with their practical interests, they proposed the dissolution of a philosophy, rather than a truly new philosophy. The periods delimited by Zeller prevailed for being both more plausible and easier to handle. These were the basis, in particular, of Diels's collection *Fragmente der Vorsokratiker* (1st ed. 1903), which remains to this day the referential edition and which encompasses, beside the "natural philosophers" (the Eleatics included), all the figures of the Sophistic movement.

It is Nietzsche, however, not Zeller and Diels, who has been credited with being the (modern) "inventor" of the Presocratics. This is because of the decisive role he played in the extraordinary intellectual reputation that the Presocratics enjoyed in the 20th century, accounting for the special role they came to play in the Continental philosophical tradition.

Nietzsche at one time preferred to speak of pre-Platonics, or more precisely, according to the lectures delivered in Basel in 1872, the "pre-Platonic philosophers." The dividing line passed then between two types of philosophers: on the one hand, those, including Socrates, characterized, in a new categorical division, by the originality and "purity" of their approach, immune to the logic of compromise, and on the other, those, beginning with Plato, characterized by the "hybrid" and dialectical nature of their philosophy, which for Nietzsche also meant democratic. (The idea of the syncretic character of Plato's philosophy, which ultimately derives from Aristotle's presentation in *Metaphysics* A, had been strongly emphasized in the 18th century by J. J. Brucker in his very influential *Critical History of Philosophy.*) It is only when the construct that made Socrates the first promoter of an optimistic modernity, as opposed to a philosophy that was still designated as "tragic," prevailed in the years 1875–1876, that Socrates was made again the proper dividing line. The Presocratics were thenceforth considered the only authentic "tyrants of the mind" (*Human, All Too Human* 261).

Like Schopenhauer, who had inspired him, Nietzsche

saw in most of the pre-Platonic philosophers potential allies in the fight led by contemporary science against finalisms of any kind. Nietzsche insisted on the fact that Greek philosophers had developed certain intuitions in which contemporary science might recognize itself. The lectures on pre-Platonic philosophers are regularly interrupted by scientific digressions. Thus, the theory of Kant-Laplace about the states of matter is invoked to justify the theory of Thales, according to which water is the source of everything: "Astronomical facts prove it. A state of less dense aggregation must have preceded present conditions." Heraclitus' "everything flows" is interpreted in light of the concept of "energy" (*Kraft*) developed by Helmholtz in his "Interaction of Natural Forces": "Nowhere is there fixed permanence because ultimately it always comes down to forces whose action contains the loss of force." This interpretation gives way to a long comparison with the biological relativism of Karl von Baer, a theory that Nietzsche shared: "His conception of living nature is the right one." As for Empedocles, he anticipated Darwin's evolutionary biology: the order of the world, far from being the product of an intention (as for Anaxagoras), results from the random interplay of two opposing forces (*Trieb*). The hero of the series is unquestionably Democritus, the materialist and antiteleologist philosopher.

Like Aristotle, Nietzsche saw the pre-Platonics as precursors. Nietzsche, however, rejected the teleological model that viewed each pre-Platonic as one "step" along the path to truth. By directly linking Thales and Kant-Laplace, Heraclitus and Helmholz, Empedocles and Darwin, Nietzsche shattered the notion of progress as a continuum in which the meaning of each protagonist resided in its being surpassed. The pre-Platonic philosophers anticipated what came after them, but in no way did they prepare it. Their scientific accomplishments were only one aspect of their singular "personalities," of the way each one lived in his social milieu. This is why Nietzsche was interested in the biographical material conveyed by Diogenes Laertius, an author whom Hegel, fully happy with Aristotle, dismissed as lacking the philosophical spirit.

In fact, while the Presocratics might have been men of science, that was not an end in itself. Science served a "corrective" role at the heart of a culture that, as Nietzsche conceived it, was fundamentally tragic. It followed that, as great as the Presocratics were, they could not serve directly as a model. It is true that the dangers weighing on German culture were in some way the same as those that, according to Nietzsche, confronted Greek culture: social conformity and the prominence of the collectivity are important in both. Facts being different, however, what Nietzsche credited the Presocratic thinkers with was more of a liability for German culture. This was particularly so in the case of faith in science to combat myth, something Nietzsche would denounce more and more forcefully.

From this we see that Nietzsche's criticism of Presocratic philosophers was germinating as early as the Basel lectures. He emphasized that though the Presocratics may in fact have launched a movement of cultural reform, that movement remained unfinished. Socrates interrupted it before it came to term; he severed something that was merely a hope: "The sixth and fifth centuries always seemed to promise more than they produced; they never got beyond a promise, and an announcement" (*Human, All Too Human* 261). In "Science and Wisdom in Conflict" he wrote, more generously, "There are many more possibilities, that have not yet been discovered; that is because the Greeks did not discover them. There are others that the Greeks discovered and later rediscovered" (ed. Colli-Montinari, 6.6). Here we might discern the very structure of unveiling-veiling, which Heidegger, Nietzsche's greatest heir in terms of Presocratic philosophy (although he never used that term), would promote under the names of *physis, logos,* and *aletheia.* In any case, the pathos of truth, in which Nietzsche had once seen an element of Presocratic grandeur, soon became for him the name for a problem, and a favorite expression of a detested ascetic ideal. His preference for *The Gay Science* necessarily led to a decline in the importance of a Democritus. Empedocles himself no longer offered to the mature Nietzsche the appeal he once had; he was both too scientific and too democratic, not to mention pessimistic, which put him on the side of Schopenhauer. The only Presocratic ultimately to be saved, in *Ecce Homo* (3), would be Heraclitus.

If the Nietzschean problematic evolved, the fundamental insight that had been the vector for it was preserved, beyond Nietzsche, in the phenomenological tradition, and particularly in Heidegger. Representatives of the "tragic" epoch, the first philosophers had become for Nietzsche a glimpse of hoped-for postmodernity, once modernity had been opened up by the victory of theoretical optimism and the primacy of morals (a reversal of the Ciceronian schema). After Nietzsche, the Presocratics would continue to figure, with other parameters of course—in this case, re-ontologized—within a modernity that worried about its crisis and its failings. In this sense, Nietzsche was not only the true "inventor of the Presocratics," but also Heidegger's great source of inspiration for understanding the Greeks. It is remarkable that we can contrast these "Continental" Presocratics, distant heirs of the model of the radical break between the time before and the time after Socrates, to a tradition of analytical interpretation that, in the tradition of Aristotle, simply thought of the Greek thinkers as "the first philosophers," already speaking, in their own way, the language of philosophy that issued from it. Thus, when turning to the origins of philosophy, the two main trends in modern philosophy stand in opposition to each other, reflecting the same contrasting models formulated in antiquity in totally different contexts.

BIBL.: T. Borsche, "Nietzsches Erfindung der Vorsokratiker," in *Nietzsche und die philosophische Tradition,* ed. J. Simon (Würzburg 1985) 62–87. A. Laks, *Introduction à la "philosophie présocratique"* (Paris 2006). A. Long, ed., *The Cambridge Companion to Early Greek Philosophy* (Cambridge 1999). E.

Zeller, *History of Greek Philosophy to the Time of Socrates*, trans. S. F. Alleyne (London 1881). A.L.

Translated by Jeannine Routier Pucci and Elizabeth Trapnell Rawlings

Professionalization of Classics

It used to be relatively easy to sing the heroic tale of professionalization, which was thought to begin with F. A. Wolf's insistence on registering for a degree in philology rather than theology at the University of Göttingen in 1777. But in recent years histories of scholarship have moved both backward and forward from this founding moment, locating on the one hand individuals endowed with critical tools and minds unclouded by theological or antiquarian fogs who lived and worked much earlier than Wolf and, on the other, paid-up members of the guild who sacrificed pure erudition for politics, religion, or simple self-interest long after Wolf departed the scene. A rich literature, especially for the early modern period, has looked beyond the Germanies to show how much the Italians, French, Dutch, English, Scandinavians, and Americans have contributed to the study of the ancient past, demonstrating that in each case classical learning was put to particular, culturally conditioned ends. But a consensus still holds that major features of what was universally recognized as "professional" classical scholarship came together in Hanover and Prussia sometime between about 1750 and 1810 and then diffused outward, blending with local institutions and traditions. Not only the founding moments but this process of diffusion can be called professionalization; it is a process that classical scholarship shares, of course, with many other fields of human activity and one that characterizes, in many ways, our modern way of work as a whole.

It must be understood that professionalization means practicing classical scholarship not just for oneself but for its own sake and, usually, belonging to a particular kind of learned institution: a university, a "higher" secondary school, or in some cases a museum. Being a "professional" is also a form of self-identification, as one who has a degree in classics or "does classics" for a living; in adopting such an identity, one does not (necessarily) claim greater intelligence, linguistic proficiency, or originality of thought. Much less, of course, does the era of professionalization signify the beginning of classical scholarship per se, which, most historians and practitioners agree, dates back to antiquity itself. Nor does professionalization mean the abandonment of personal delight in classical texts: it would be a poor scholar who did not love the subject, even if obliged to take it up as work, not purely for the purposes of self-cultivation, or to pursue it for extra-disciplinary ends, such as the study of right reading of the New Testament for purposes of religious instruction.

In fact, "doing classics" for a living was more or less what many clergymen and gentlemen (and gentlewomen) have done, from Roman times forward. But after Christianity's consolidation of cultural hegemony, one usually studied classics in the context of Christian history, and within institutions (monasteries, universities) operated by the Church. Of course, well-educated princes also found antiquity (and antiquities) interesting; and as, in the wake of the Renaissance and Reformation, they grew bolder, richer, and more desirous of attracting intellectuals to their courts, their patronage laid the foundations for new forms of scholarly inquiry. Whereas clerics wanted to know more about the contexts in which Christian ideas were formed, princes were interested in what the ancients had to teach them about rhetoric, governance, artistic ideals, and ethics—so that the classics in the early modern era came to be pursued both as a means to deepen Europeans' understanding of their past and as a pathway to self-improvement.

There were already scholars who specialized in classical rhetoric or Roman antiquities before the 18th century, but by the time that century ended, these specialties had become more pronounced, loftier peaks in an increasingly dense range of other specialized summits of learning. But what really removed classics from the more general public sphere was the emerging sense that the present was distinctively unlike the past. A combination of cultural, economic, and political changes suggested to elite Europeans that their world was, quite literally, breaking with that of their fathers and grandfathers. Global commerce was making Europeans, for the first time, richer than their Asian neighbors, and rich enough to afford to produce and consume a large number of books, musical compositions, and exotic foods. The battle of the ancients and moderns was over, and classical authorities (and biblical texts) were increasingly treated with critical suspicion rather than reverence. Poets, painters, and playwrights broke "classical" rules; scholars largely ceased publishing and lecturing in Latin. Though the political theory of Thomas Jefferson and Jean-Jacques Rousseau drew heavily on the ancients, that of the post-1789 generation, from Edmund Burke to Charles Fourier, felt a necessity to concern itself more centrally with current events, rather than ancient and ideal types. Ultimately the wave of revolutions that commenced in North America, then swept, with Napoleon's army, the European continent, and recrossed the Atlantic to transform Latin America, convinced observers that a new world had come into being—at least, it was said after 1815, in the realm of the mind, if not in Metternich's Europe.

It was in the context of these social and political changes that the study of classical antiquity became an autonomous scholarly field, or, in German terms, a *Wissenschaft,* separate from theology and philosophy, and that antiquity itself became a period that could be torn from the pageant of universal history and scrutinized, even admired, more exclusively. Indeed, classics became *the* proper *Wissenschaft* for the noncommercial middle as well as upper classes, people, that is, who were not entirely enraptured by the modern world and yet comfortable enough to be able to invest some time and money in nonutilitarian educations. In some senses, then, classicism became scientific precisely when its relevance to the living culture of Europe was waning. Born in the world of Friedrich Schiller and Edward Gibbon, the new science would take on the deep-dyed Romantic longing to live in a world it knew to be irretrievably lost.

The study of the classics had always had a strong scholarly component, though up until the later 18th century this had usually been subordinated to other ends—the understanding of Scripture, the training of well-spoken, ethically sound individuals, the adaptation of past texts to present purposes (such as determining the proper date for Easter or simply filling up empty hours). What made classical studies *wissenschaftlich* was the conviction on the part of a few members of the scholarly elite that classics, like philosophy, should not be subordinated to any other endeavor or driven out of learned curricula by the more "useful" arts (as Rousseau would have wished), but rather should be studied for its own sake, a process that involved putting the ancient texts through a modern philological wringer. Philology, the exacting study of words, and of texts in their original languages, was increasingly seen as the means to free important texts from corruptions, rather than simply continuing to contribute additional explications to available renditions. The application of philology to secular texts, especially to poetry and drama, made it *the* defining method of professionalized classical scholarship.

Of course, serious textual criticism had been practiced since at least the days of Lorenzo Valla in the 15th century, but the arena in which it was practiced and the purposes to which it was put made the new, professional era different. Other new factors were the enormous changes in the scale, scope, and public accessibility of the endeavor. A brief contrast of the days of Valla with those of C. G. Heyne is instructive. Valla was trained as a priest and worked for a prince; he had to appear before the Inquisition twice, lost his job at the University of Pavia as the result of attacking the writing of an important jurist, and at one point had to flee Rome to evade being killed for ridiculing the Latin of the Vulgate. Whether aimed at Christian asceticism or Scholastic jurisprudence, Valla's work was polemical, and his polemics related directly to contemporary issues and individuals. Heyne, by contrast, though he began as a court copyist, spent most of his career in a state-funded university (Göttingen) and suffered relatively little interference in his teaching and publishing from Church officials. From this position he began the transformation of the teaching of classics, emphasizing the need to understand the past in its own terms while also maintaining the view that classical antiquity provided the best models for cultural production and civic virtue in the present. F. A. Wolf, his student, would prove even more insistent on the centrality of language training to the appreciation of the classics; together with Gottfried Hermann, professor of eloquence at the University of Leipzig, he formulated a model of stringent and disinterested attention to the reconstruction of classical texts that was widely imitated in Europe and in the United States. Neither Wolf nor Hermann was made to serve under the aegis of the theological faculty or to defend (probably quite unorthodox) personal religious beliefs; their contemporary in England, Richard Porson, lost his fellowship at Trinity College, Cambridge, because he refused to take holy orders. From time to time thereafter, German faculty members were dismissed for political or religious reasons —in the wake of the 1830 and 1848 revolutions, for example; but that was more reflection than abuse of the model going forward. In exchange for the university bureaucracy's protection of the staff from market forces and overt manipulation by Church interests, professional classicists were not supposed to trifle in outside affairs.

The model was shaped not only by this bargain but also by the segregation of three fields that both Heyne and Valla had practiced as a group: Greek studies, Latin studies, and "oriental" studies (the last referring at that time chiefly to what once had been the Eastern Roman Empire, or the Near East). Special literatures already existed in each field, but the rising cultural and aesthetic value accorded to the Greeks in particular increasingly inclined scholars to specialize. The emergence of Greek as a language of equivalent or even (aesthetically) of surpassing importance in relation to Latin was a product of the Romantic and revolutionary eras; in the wake of J. J. Winckelmann's art-historical paeans to the beauties of pure, universally appealing Greek sculpture, and after Lord Byron's death at Missolonghi, it became highly fashionable to immerse oneself in the faraway world of the Greeks. Though Latin continued to be studied, by far more students, in fact, than were enrolled in Greek courses, especially in the Germanies, Britain, and the United States, the study of Greek seemed, as one wag put it, to resemble the taste of the purest wines, while reading Latin was rather like drinking (déclassé) schnapps. After the 1820s it became, professionally speaking, almost insupportable to combine the study of classical languages with the study of the world of the Orient; not only were skills and literatures now too specialized, but the highly speculative Romantic discussions about the oriental origins of the cults of classical antiquity were vigorously criticized by those who preferred narrower, and in some cases racially segregated, histories.

After the initial period of classicizing school reform, museum building, and the strengthening of the (secular) philosophical faculty over and against the more utilitarian faculties (the career paths for those who studied theology, law, or medicine were quite clear), the most important moments in the story of professionalization of the classics came in the 1830s and the 1890s. In the 1830s two passionate intradisciplinary battles were concluded, and the winning factions—headed respectively by the Greek philologist Gottfried Hermann and the historian K. O. Müller—established what would be core principles for 19th-century classical scholarship. Language studies, rather than the study of state forms, artifacts, or mythological meanings, would be paramount; indeed, linguistic virtuosity would be the sine qua non of the successful classicist. And the focus of study would be on individual, nationally (or, better, linguistically) defined groups, and cross-linguistic comparisons or etymological derivations would be viewed suspiciously as smacking of dilettantism. After this point there were some who still tried to traffic across the bridges between, for example, Greece and Persia, or Rome and Egypt, but most of these ventures started from the oriental rather than the classical side. Of course, the more contributors emerged within each field, and the thicker the pile of publications mounted, the higher rose the barriers to entry in each subject area. In the Germanies, in particular, not only competition between universities for faculty members and faculty members' competition with one another contributed to the swift growth of laborers in the field; but perhaps even more important was the expectation that teachers at the higher schools would participate in the culture of *Wissenschaft* as well. For many years they did, which had the positive effect of keeping their skills well-honed and their interest in new research high. But the problematic effect was to make some yearn for university posts that they never received or neglect the duty to suit their lessons to the needs and interests of their students.

Perhaps it was precisely this unintended consequence of deep professionalization that set the stage for the powerful anticlassical movements that shattered classicism's cultural hegemony in late 19th-century Germany. But elsewhere too, in America and Britain, in the Netherlands, and in Greece itself, by the 1890s a series of profound critiques had been mounted against classical scholarship and the school systems that supported it. Criticisms came from all manner of outsiders—proponents of national, "modern," and utilitarian forms of education, socialists, feminists, natural scientists, and orientalists all complained about the narrowness of classical education and the pedantry of the philologists who overloaded students with useless studies of irregular Greek verbs. These criticisms were of course threatening to classicists, at both the university and the high school level, for the more such objections were aired and heard by state ministries, publishers, and parents, the more the supporting infrastructure of classical studies was scaled down or dismantled to build other professions. But perhaps even more distressing to the old guard was what one might call an oedipal revolt, begun by a generation trained in the classics but now repulsed by sickly sweet neoclassicism and dry-as-dust Prussian *Wissenschaft*. The Basel triumvirate of J. J. Bachofen, Jacob Burckhardt, and Friedrich Nietzsche was, of course, the pioneer force here, but the next generation too began to reach across the oriental divide; to abandon the secular and rational antiquity upon which the midcentury had for the most part focused, for the darker and earlier undersides of ancient culture; and to challenge philology as the means for understanding the truth of the Greeks. In Britain, Cambridge Ritualists like Jane Harrison adopted anthropological perspectives and, though outsiders at first, gradually attracted students and, even more gradually perhaps, acquired professional respectability.

Everywhere that professionalization took hold there were gains in the quantity and quality of specialized knowledge about the ancient world. There were, however, also losses, which will be suggested below. Over the course of the 19th century the entire infrastructure supporting professionalization—lower schools, libraries, publishing houses, university seminars, academic positions—expanded, creating new possibilities for even more intensive research and more extensive penetration of the cultural world as a whole. Students, faculty, and their work could be held to higher standards and expected, as time went on, to achieve greater levels of accuracy, complexity, and coverage. There were also profoundly important ways in which classical learning contributed to the secularization of school systems (especially at the secondary level), university appointments, and the humanities as a whole; it is no coincidence that the neoclassical school reform movement saw as its primary rivals (at least at first) the clergymen who dominated both lower education and the university theological faculties—whose appointments were usually vetted by the Church consistories. In most places the reformers, with state backing, won these battles. The professionalization of classics, and the accompanying conviction that classical antiquity represented an inheritance about which every educated European (male) should know, contributed greatly to a deistic broadening of the realm of the spiritual and laid the foundations for a secular patrimony that we would probably call Western Civilization.

The list of 19th-century classicist achievements is long: it was this world that produced great multivolume works like Barthold Georg Niebuhr's *History of Rome* and George Grote's *History of Greece,* enormous text-editing projects like the *Corpus vasorum antiquorum* and the Pauly-Wissowa *Realencyclopädie für classischen Altertumswissenschaft;* major journals were begun, and grand archaeological projects launched. Charismatic and influential mid-19th-century teachers like Benjamin Jowett, Ernst Curtius, and Numa Denis Fustel de Coulanges and important bureaucrat-scholars like Edward Everett and Wilhelm von Humboldt made major contributions to the cultural worlds in which they operated. Numerous writers and artists, as well as natural scientists, were inspired by these scholars and often acknowledged that their training in classical studies gave them the intellectual discipline, the historical perspective, and the cosmopolitan erudition on which their achievements were based.

But there were also costs. Classics, as a specialized science, was almost exclusively a male affair, and one that often suffered from the distance it put between itself and poetry, politics, religious sentiment, and humor, not to mention its self-imposed isolation from oriental and European vernacular philology. The field often looked to the past to avoid present-day conflicts and definitely preferred debating the foundations of ancient Greek democracy to working to create one at home. From our historical viewpoint, we can, and should, celebrate professional scholarship's achievements, but we must likewise deplore its blind spots and exclusionary practices. Professionalization is not something we can undo; nor is its history something we can unproblematically admire.

BIBL.: M. L. Clarke, *Greek Studies in England, 1700–1830* (Cambridge 1945). Anthony Grafton, *Defenders of the Text: The Traditions of Scholarship in an Age of Science, 1450–1800* (Cambridge, Mass., 1991). Suzanne Marchand, *Down from Olympus: Archaeology and Cultural Politics in Germany, 1750–1970* (Princeton 1996). Arnaldo Momigliano, *Essays in Ancient and Modern Historiography* (Oxford 1977). Glenn W. Most, ed., *Disciplining Classics—Altertumswissenschaft als Beruf* (Göttingen 2002). Christopher Stray, *Classics Transformed: Schools, Universities, and Society in England, 1830–1960* (Oxford 1998). Caroline Winterer, *The Culture of Classicism: Ancient Greece and Rome in American Intellectual Life, 1780–1910* (Baltimore 2002). S.M.

Progress and Decline

From the ancient world, medieval and modern historians and moralists inherited a rich vocabulary for describing and analyzing decline, as well as a more limited repertoire for discussing progress. The Greek terms for progress were *epidosis,* "increase," or *prokopē,* translated into Latin as *progressus.* With these terms Aristotle, Plato, Polybius, Cicero, Lucretius, and Pliny the Elder discuss past progress in knowledge, warfare, rhetoric, technology, and the arts.

They were, however, less sure of progress in the future. A common view of history was cyclical rather than linear, which meant that sooner or later a rise would turn into its opposite. Analogies between human bodies and states, languages, arts, and even the cosmos were often drawn, implying that birth and youth would inevitably be followed by maturity, old age, and death. The idea of four ages, those of gold, silver, bronze, and iron, each worse than the preceding one, was a literary topos (sometimes inaccurately attributed to Hesiod). Aristotle and the Stoics believed in cycles of cosmic destruction and renewal. The language of "decline" was common in historians such as Sallust, Tacitus, and—in the case of art and literature—Velleius Paterculus. States were viewed by Polybius and others as subject to corruption. Decline was viewed as fundamentally moral and associated with softness and effeminacy. It was the inevitable effect of the rise of civilization. Vivid and recurrent metaphors of decline included corruption and disease ("contagion" or "pestilence" in Sallust, for instance). Cycles of progress and decline were compared to the waxing and waning of the moon and the ebb and flow of the tides; even in antiquity the goddess Fortune was represented with a wheel. All the same, it was widely believed that decline might be arrested, at least for a time, thanks to efforts at reform, renovation, restoration, restitution, or regeneration (*reformatio, renovatio, restauratio, restitutio, regeneratio*). Virgil's Fourth Eclogue expresses contemporary ideas of cosmic renewal, the return of Astraea, the virgin goddess of justice, and the revival of the kingdom of Saturn—in other words, the golden age.

This rich tradition of concepts, metaphors, and associations continued to work powerfully in the post-classical world. Virgil's eclogue was reinterpreted to refer to the birth of Christ from the Virgin Mary and to the coming of the Christian millennium. In this way classical ideas became mixed or fused with ideas of progress and decline derived from both the Old and the New Testament, including the succession of four empires described in the Book of Daniel. Christianity might be said to have implied an idea of progress, for Christians claimed that the world had been changed for the better by the birth of Christ and that the New Testament went beyond the Old. All the same, in a work that would become one of the most influential works of the Middle Ages, *The City of God* (426 CE), Saint Augustine, though not against progress itself, wrote against preconceived notions of progress. He believed that change took place in a linear fashion, as God's plans for the world gradually unfolded, and indeed he sometimes used the verb *progredi,* but it was in the sense of "to proceed" rather than "to improve," because he did not think that life was getting better.

In the Middle Ages and in early modern times, decline was a more central idea than progress, whether in the case of the Church or that of states, the arts, or what we call the economy. There was, for example, a long tradition of writing about the decline of the Church, viewed as corrupted by its increasing wealth. As early as the 5th century, Caesarius, bishop of Arles, hoped that the Church would return to its former health (*ad sanitatem pristinam*). In the late Middle Ages, a chorus of ecclesiastical writers developed this theme. In an image reminiscent of Sallust, the Czech reformer Jan Hus (d. 1415) described the Church as "afflicted with leprosy." The theologian Nicholas de Clémanges (d. ca. 1435) wrote that "riches, luxury, and pride conquered the Church." The historian Dietrich von Nieheim (d. 1418) noted the increase among the pope and cardinals of what he called "intolerable pomp, avarice, and ambition." All these men were reformers, believing that it was possible to return to the poverty, humility, and virtue of what they called the *ecclesia primitiva,* in other words, the Church of the first centuries after Christ. Protestant reformers such as Martin Luther (d. 1546) and John Calvin (d. 1564) stand in this tradition, viewing themselves not as the founders of a new form of Christianity but as re-formers of an old one, rescuing the Church from decline. The more radical the reformer, the earlier the decline would be dated. For Luther, for instance, it began in the 6th century with Pope Gregory the Great, whereas the Anabaptists dated it to the conversion of Constantine at the beginning of the 4th century, in other words, to the official establishment of the Church. Some writers referred to the "fall" of the Church, on the analogy of the fall of Adam and Eve from grace. In the 17th century the decline of the Church was the organizing principle of two major works of history, Paolo Sarpi's

Treatise on Benefices and Gottfried Arnold's *Impartial History of the Church and Heretics* (1699). In the 18th century, reformers such as the German Pietists and the British Methodists still viewed themselves as arresting the decline of the Church rather than introducing new forms of Christianity.

The decline of Rome, both the Republic and the Empire, became a paradigm for interpreting the decline of other states. Sallust was read in the Middle Ages; Tacitus and Polybius were rediscovered in the Renaissance. The works of Tacitus in particular provoked or offered opportunities for numerous political commentaries. The Humanist Leonardo Bruni (d. 1444), for instance, followed Tacitus in attributing the decline of the Roman Empire to the loss of liberty following the end of the Republic. Amalgamating classical and biblical schemata, the German Humanist Johann Sleidan (d. 1556) wrote about the decline of four successive ancient empires: the Medes, Persians, Greeks, and Romans. From the historian Orosius in the 5th century to Bishop George Berkeley in the 18th, it was sometimes suggested that empire had a tendency to move westward (it is for this reason that a campus of the University of California is named after the bishop). Closer to classical models was Claude Duret's comparative *Discours des causes et effets des décadences, mutations, conversions et mines des monarchies, empires, royaumes et républiques* (1595).

Some authors believed that decline could be resisted. Developing an idea most closely associated with Polybius, the Venetians claimed that their state was not subject to decline because it was a mixture of the three basic forms of government: monarchy, aristocracy, and democracy. Niccolò Machiavelli believed that the Florentine state had become corrupt, but he also believed in the possibility of reform. He thought that all states would decline eventually, but he was impressed by the way in which the Romans had been able to resist decline for centuries. He hoped that the Florentines would imitate the Roman example rather than the Venetian one. Montesquieu's *Considérations* (1734), on both the rise and the decline (*décadence*) of Rome, follows Sallust in stressing "corruption" but also innovates by discussing economic reasons for decline, implying a parallel with the decline of Spain in the 17th century, on which the author had already written. As late as Edward Gibbon's *Decline and Fall of the Roman Empire* (1776–1788), the causes of the decline of the Roman Empire were still being discussed in terms that the ancients would have recognized.

Like the Reformation, the Renaissance was perceived by participants not as an innovating movement but as a revival, restoration, or "rebirth" of classical antiquity. The astronomer Nicolaus Copernicus (d. 1543) and the anatomist Andreas Vesalius (d. 1564), now famous for their innovations, believed that they were rediscovering ancient knowledge. Even the scientific revolution of the 17th century was presented by a major player, Francis Bacon (d. 1626), within a cyclical framework, as the recovery of wisdom lost at the time of Adam's fall. Ancient debates on the rise and decline of the arts furnished models for later writers on this theme. Bruni, for instance, followed Tacitus and linked the decline of Latin literature to the decline of liberty: "After the Republic had been subjected to the power of one man, these brilliant minds vanished." In similar fashion the 18th-century philosopher Lord Shaftesbury associated the flourishing of rhetoric with periods of political freedom.

Diverging from ancient writers but continuing to reflect on ancient history, the Italian Humanist Lorenzo Valla (d. 1457) argued that the Latin language declined together with the Roman Empire at the time of the invasions of the barbarians. Other Humanists suggested that the history of Latin followed a cyclical pattern, rising to perfection in the age of Cicero and then declining into the "silver age" of Seneca. Joseph Scaliger (d. 1609) viewed the history of Greek hexameters in a similar way, dividing it into four ages. Following Valla's model, some Humanists linked the progress and decline of other languages, notably Spanish, to the rise and fall of empires.

In his lives of Italian artists, first published in 1550, Giorgio Vasari drew on classical texts (notably the history of rhetoric sketched in Cicero's *Brutus*) to present the three main stages of progress in painting, sculpture, and architecture against a background of possible decline. It was only in the 18th century that Johann Joachim Winckelmann gave a similar account of stages in the development of ancient Greek art, which had been viewed in the Renaissance as a timeless model.

Some writers were still more ambitious and wrote about decline on a cosmic scale. Writing world history in a comparative manner, the French Humanist Louis Le Roy (d. 1577) discussed what he called the "vicissitudes" of empires, languages, and other human creations. In the 17th century the possible decline of the cosmos, or old age of the world, was debated by scholars such as Godfrey Goodman, who supported the proposition, and George Hakewill and Secondo Lancellotti, who both rejected it, Lancellotti claiming in his *Hoggidì* (1623) that "the world was not worse or fuller of calamities than in the past." The 17th century was also the era of the great debate between the "ancients" and the "moderns," the question being whether modern writers and thinkers such as Racine or Newton had equaled or could equal the achievements of antiquity. It should be said that the two sides were closer in attitude than they were later portrayed to be (especially in the 19th century), for the leading moderns, including the great classical scholar Richard Bentley, continued to venerate antiquity (Levine 1999).

From the 18th century onward discussions of decline and progress reveal a gradual emancipation from ancient models. As early as 1600, Spanish writers began to analyze what they called the *declination* of their country, supplementing classical models with discussions of economic and demographic trends. By the 18th century the decline of the Roman Empire was being discussed in terms derived from the debate on the decline of Spain, as well as the other way round. Joseph de Guignes (d. 1800) was the first scholar to explain the fall of Rome through events in Central Asia that had triggered the westward barbarian invasions of late antiquity. Moralists discussed corruption in new ways, exemplifying it by the bribery associated with the English prime minister Sir Robert Walpole (d. 1745) and explaining it by "the cancer of commerce" and the rise of paper money and public debt. Others saw commerce and even luxury as beneficial to the human race.

It was only very slowly that the belief in unlimited progress spread. A fundamentally cyclical view of human history was put forward by Giambattista Vico in his *New Science* (*Scienza nuova,* 1725–1744). David Hume (d. 1776) also remained within the cyclical framework when describing the historian's task as "to remark the rise, progress, declension, and final extinction of the most flourishing empires," as well as "the rise, progress and decline of art and science" ("On the Study of History"). He seems to have used the term "progress" in the same limited sense as Augustine when writing about "commerce in its progress through Tyre, Athens, Syracuse, Carthage, Venice, Florence, Genoa, Antwerp, Holland, England" ("Of Civil Liberty"). The critique of contemporary society and praise of the primitive introduced by the highly popular works of Jean-Jacques Rousseau (d. 1778) gave a new twist to the ideas of classical moralists. On the other hand, some people now wrote about tendencies to "improvement," a term used in agricultural discussions before becoming more general. The political economists A. R. J. Turgot (d. 1781) and Adam Smith (d. 1790), among others, viewed the human past as a sequence of four stages (hunters, shepherds, farmers, merchants), a development seen as both positive and irreversible. Without necessarily accepting the idea of four stages, Gibbon wrote of "the gradual progress of society from the lowest ebb of primitive barbarism to the full tide of modern civilization" and argued that a modern empire could not fall victim to barbarian invasions as Rome had, because the barbarians could not adopt the technology necessary for conquest without becoming civilized themselves. Voltaire (d. 1778) and Condorcet (d. 1794) were among those who believed in the progress of the human mind, or *esprit.* In the history of the ideas of change over time, as in that of other key concepts, the late 18th century was a moment of change, the sense of irreversible progress being marked by the change in the meaning of the word "revolution," originally linked to historical cycles.

In the 19th century the distance from classical ideas of progress and decline increased still further. Auguste Comte (d. 1857) and Thomas Macaulay (d. 1859) are two of the thinkers who expressed almost unqualified belief in progress, which was built into the Grand Narrative of Modernity, in which the Renaissance was followed by the Reformation, the Scientific Revolution, and the Enlightenment. The accumulation of data and the refinement of methods in the natural sciences were taken as a paradigm for intellectual and even social improvement or "reform." The latter term, originally religious, as we have seen, was now secularized, as the Reform Bill of 1832, designed to change the structure of the British Parliament, reminds us. There was increasing interest in processes of "development," a word that John Henry Newman (d. 1890) dared to apply to religious doctrine, and also in "evolution," a word that goes back a century before Darwin but was widely applied to society and culture after his *Origin of Species* (1859), notably by the English sociologist Herbert Spencer (d. 1903).

There was some dissent from the assumption of progress, by writers in particular. Théophile Gautier described himself and the poet Baudelaire as *décadent,* a term that came to apply, a generation later, to a movement exemplified by the hero of J.-K. Huysmans's novel *À rebours* (1884), who was both refined and perverse. By the end of the 19th century the idea of progress was powerfully challenged. A popular fin-de-siècle word was *degeneration,* a term originally signifying structural change, then pathological changes in organisms, and finally social and cultural decline explained in physiological or psychological terms, as it was by Max Nordau in his best-selling book with that title (*Entartung,* 1892). Cyclical theories of rise and decline began to be reasserted, notably in Oswald Spengler's study of the decline of the West (*Der Untergang des Abendlandes,* 1918–1922). It is interesting to note that major contributions to discussions of decline were made by two ex-classicists, Friedrich Nietzsche, who revived the idea of eternal return, and Arnold Toynbee, whose *Study of History* (1934–1961) interpreted world history in terms of a model originally derived from ancient Greek and Roman experience.

To sum up a long and complex process, a conceptual apparatus created by the ancients to interpret their own culture was appropriated by the moderns to distinguish their own time from antiquity. It was modified over the years, so much so as to become virtually unrecognizable, with an occasional return, like that of Nietzsche, to the original fount of inspiration.

BIBL.: Peter Burke, "The Idea of Decline from Bruni to Gibbon," *Daedalus* (1976) 137–152. Ludwig Edelstein, *The Idea of Progress in Classical Antiquity* (Baltimore 1967). John Elliott, "Self-Perception and Decline in Early 17th-Century Spain," *Past & Present* 74 (1977) 41–61. Ernst H. Gombrich, "The Renaissance Conception of Artistic Progress and Its Consequences," repr. in Gombrich, *Norm and Form* (London 1966) 1–10. Reinhart Koselleck and Paul Widmer, eds., *Niedergang* (Stuttgart 1980). Gerhart B. Ladner, *The Idea of Reform: Its Impact on Christian Thought and Action in the Age of the Fathers* (Cambridge, Mass., 1959). Joseph Levine, *Between the Ancients and the Moderns: Baroque Culture in Restoration England* (New Haven 1999). Arthur Lovejoy and George Boas, *Primitivism and Related Ideas in Antiquity* (Baltimore 1935). Ronald Meek, *Social Science and the Ignoble Savage* (Cambridge 1976). Glenn W. Most, "Hesiod's Myth of the Five Races," *Proceedings of the Cambridge Philological Society* 43 (1997) 104–127. Robert Nisbet, *History of the Idea of Progress* (London 1980). J. G. A. Pocock, *Barbarism and Religion,* vol. 3, *The First Decline and Fall* (Cambridge 2003). Koenraad W. Swart, *The Sense of Decadence in Nineteenth-century France* (The Hague 1959). Henry Vyverberg, *Historical Pessimism in the French Enlightenment* (Cambridge, Mass., 1958).

U.P.B.

Prometheus

Son of the Titan Iapetus; for giving fire to mankind, his cousin Zeus condemned him to be bound to a rock and perpetually tortured by an eagle. In Hesiod's *Theogony* (ca. 700 BCE) Prometheus is a trickster competing above his weight; Zeus's victory over him is appropriate and satisfying. Two centuries later he was the hero of a tragedy, *Prometheus Bound,* attributed to Aeschylus; here his gift to humanity is of the whole range of civilized skill, and Zeus is a tyrant and agent of injustice. (Fragmentary evidence indicates that this play was the first of a trilogy, whose remaining titles have been generally hypothesized as *Prometheus Unbound* and *Prometheus the Fire-Bringer.*) Ovid in the *Metamorphoses* (8 CE) makes Prometheus responsible for the creation of mankind by imparting the spark of rational life to inanimate matter (1.76–88); there is no reference to his punishment, and the scene has a remarkable similarity to that in Genesis. The mythographer Fulgentius (5th cent. CE) reports the collaboration of Athena. A Christianized allegory, incorporating the etymology of Prometheus' name, dominated through the Middle Ages and into the Renaissance; in George Sandys's summary (1632), "Prometheus signifies Providence, and Minerva heavenly wisdom; by God's providence therefore and wisdom man was created." Phrases like "Promethean fire" and "Promethean heat" came to designate vital spirits generally, both intellectual and physical. Francis Bacon in *On the Wisdom of the Ancients* (*De sapientia veterum,* 1609) reads the myth as affirming that "all things are subservient to man, and he receives use and benefit from them all." The king of heaven, he adds, fully approved of the technological benefit that Prometheus bestowed on humanity, and the torment to which man's benefactor was sentenced merely wards off complacency about the status quo. Bacon's mythography of Prometheus is offered in behalf of the great enterprise of scientific research that he accurately foresaw; its contemporary embodiment is Paul Manship's statue of an airborne, torch-bearing Prometheus (1934) presiding over the skating rink at Rockefeller Center.

In the 18th century less benign interpretations of the myth flourished. In Voltaire's *Pandore* (1740), the libretto for an unperformed opera, Prometheus is assimilated to his brother Epimetheus as both creator and lover of Pandora, and Jupiter's refusal to allow their happiness prompts the rebellion of all the Titans and causes the gods to be denounced as "jealous tyrants" and their king as the "eternal persecutor." The provocative sense in the ancient *Prometheus Bound* that the divine order of things is itself being judged comes again into its own. The young Goethe, even as he was creating the first drafts of *Faust,* wrote two acts of a *Prometheus* (1773) that is an early manifesto of Romantic defiance; "I refuse!" (*Ich will nicht!*), it opens.

The 19th century manifested particular interest in the lost parts of the Greek trilogy. Sections of Johann Gottfried Herder's *Der entfesselte Prometheus* (1802) were set to music by Franz Liszt (1850). Friedrich Nietzsche put a woodcut of the newly freed Prometheus on the title page of his *Birth of Tragedy* (*Die Geburt der Tragödie,* 1872). Perhaps most notably, Percy Bysshe Shelley's *Prometheus Unbound* (1820) involves a significant expansion of the mythological apparatus and an uncompromising adaptation of the story to the revolutionary hopes of the time: the eventual freeing of Prometheus is not, as in ancient tellings, a reconciliation with Olympus, but the decisive and welcome end to that supposedly omnipotent regime. Shelley's wife, Mary Wollstonecraft, had already given the myth a mordantly skeptical turn by embellishing her novel *Frankenstein* (1816) with the title *The Modern Prometheus.* (In homage to the book, now an icon in the history of Western popular culture, the American television series *The X-Files* in 1997 titled an episode on genetic engineering *The Post-Modern Prometheus.*)

On the brink of the 20th century André Gide satirized the new age in *Prométhée mal-enchaîné* (1899), in which the "ill-bound" hero exchanges his rock for the boulevards of Paris. He gives a public lecture explaining that the eagle that has been feeding on him is the human belief in progress; after a prison term for the illegal manufacture of safety matches, he announces that he has killed the eagle and invites his friends to dine on it at his favorite restaurant.

BIBL.: Louis Awad, *The Theme of Prometheus in English and French Literature* (Cairo 1963). Raymond Trousson, *Le thème de Prométhée dans la littérature européenne* (Geneva 1964).

G.B.

Pronunciation of Greek and Latin

The sound of sheep and the wickedness of sailors—such is the amusing but often fiercely contested stuff of Classical Greek and Latin pronunciation in the millennia since the heyday of those languages. We know thanks to the comic poet Cratinus (5th cent. BCE) that the sheep of Attica said *bē bē* (pronounced *bay bay*), which none too surprisingly resembles our *baa baa.* But when the study of ancient Greek language and literature began its ascent in Western Europe during the early Renaissance, it was the current Byzantine pronunciation of the language that was projected back to classical times, with the result that *bē bē* was spoken as *vee vee* rather than *bay bay* (to say nothing of the shift from pitch accent to stress). Credit for pointing out this particular anachronism goes to the Italian printer Aldus Manutius, but the Dutch Humanist Erasmus was the man whose detailed researches, presented in his dialogue *On the Correct Pronunciation of Latin and*

Greek (*De recta Latini Graecique sermonis pronuntiatione,* 1528), have led to 500 years of debate. Never since have the consequences of choosing whether to adopt what is today usually called the "Erasmian pronunciation" been as grave as they were in mid-16th-century England, when religious tensions became conjoined with scholarly ones. The University of Cambridge was genuinely shaken by the battles between its chancellor, Stephen Gardiner (also bishop of Winchester and, under Mary Tudor, Lord Chancellor of England), who in 1542 banned the "new" style of Greek, and the Erasmians (and Protestants) John Cheke, the first Regius Professor of Greek, and Thomas Smith, the first Regius Professor of Civil Law. Cheke's treatise *On the Pronunciation of the Greek Language* (*De pronuntiatione Graecae linguae,* 1555) reproduces his correspondence with Gardiner. The Erasmians won—and it is not an exaggeration to suggest that the wider study of phonetics, a branch of linguistics in which the British would later come to excel, owes much to their efforts.

This is not to say that the British (or any other nation) have held to a strict form of Erasmian pronunciation—or to the "restored pronunciation" that is its modern scholarly successor. For Latin in particular it was only in the 20th century that dons began to abandon, often under protest, the idiosyncratic English manner of Latin pronunciation (a result, in part, of the Great Vowel Shift in early modern English) that allowed Roman sheep to say *bee bee;* that led Lord Byron (*Don Juan* 6.17) to rhyme a couplet as "In short, the maxim for the amorous tribe is/Horatian, '*Medio tu tutissimus ibis*'" (i.e., *eye-bis* rather than *ee-bis*); and ensured that educated English people knew that the answer to the question "Why were Roman sailors wicked?" was "Because they were *nautae*"—that is, "sailors," the Latin pronounced *naughty* rather than *now-tie*.

Every country in which Greek and Latin are taught has its own peculiar traditions. There are, in brief, two reasons for this. First, Greek and Latin are, paradoxically, dead and alive at the same time: Cratinus' Greek is no more, but the Greek language today is the direct living continuation of a language whose documentation goes back to the second millennium BCE; similarly, Latin is alive and well in the Romance languages (e.g., Italian, French, and Portuguese). It is thus not strange that Greeks tend to pronounce Plato *à la moderne* or that Italians—many of whom grew up with a regular dose of Italianate "Church Latin"—do not make all their *c*'s and *g*'s "hard," as they would have been for Cicero (*Kikero*) or Gellius (*Ghellius*). And, second, when people pronounce a foreign tongue, they invariably put their own accent in it—and all the more so when there are no native speakers around to correct them: Germans, especially older ones, pronounce Caesar as *tsay-zar* (rather than *ky-sar*), and *nautae* as *now-tay,* because in German the digraph *ae* is another way of writing *a* with an umlaut (*ä*).

In conclusion, it is worth remembering that there is not just one classical tradition. Teaching the restored pronunciation of Greek and Latin has much to recommend it: we should want to hear and understand the cadences of Homer and Virgil. But it would be a mistake to dismiss the traditions that have sprung up over the ages, be they national, religious, or artistic (for example, the use of Latin in song), for we should obviously want to hear and understand the cadences of Cavafy and Poulenc, too.

BIBL.: William Sidney Allen, *Vox Graeca: A Guide to the Pronunciation of Classical Greek,* 3rd ed. (Cambridge 1987) esp. Appendix A, and *Vox Latina: A Guide to the Pronunciation of Classical Latin,* 2nd ed. (Cambridge 1978) esp. Appendix B. Harold Copeman, *Singing in Latin, or Pronunciation Explor'd,* 2nd ed. (Oxford 1996). Engelbert Drerup, *Die Schulaussprache des Griechischen von der Renaissance bis zur Gegenwart im Rahmen einer allgemeinen Geschichte des griechischen Unterrichts,* 2 vols. (Paderborn 1930–1932). Christopher Stray, *Classics Transformed: Schools, Universities, and Society in England, 1830–1960* (Oxford 1998) 126–132, 196–199. Françoise Waquet, *Latin; or, The Empire of a Sign from the Sixteenth to the Twentieth Centuries,* trans. John Howe (London 2001, French 1998) esp. chap. 6. J.T.K.

Propertius

Roman elegiac poet (ca. 50–45 BCE–after 15 CE). A generation younger than Catullus, about a decade older than Ovid, he published four books of poems, most of them about the narrator-poet's tumultuous affair with a woman called Cynthia. She is the most exacting of the mistresses in classical love poetry. The poems mention infidelity and abuse on both sides, and in book 3 the poet seems, somewhat ambiguously, to make a final break with her; in book 4 she returns terrifyingly from the grave to denounce him and the insufficiency of his grief. She is also *docta puella,* a cultivated woman capable of appreciating her lover's poetry, and emotional violence mixes with antiquity's most elevated claims for heterosexual love, not to be outdone until the songs of the troubadours in a later age. Cynthia is the center of the poet's life and his art, and to die from that love would win him great praise.

Propertius' elegies were overshadowed by the greater urbanity of Ovid's *Amores,* though as Quintilian observes, "There are those who prefer Propertius" (*sunt qui malint Propertium,* 10.1.93). From the Renaissance onward Propertius has often been printed with Catullus and Tibullus: the "triumvirs of love" Joseph Scaliger calls them (he himself translated two Propertian elegies into Greek). Much of Propertius' influence on post-classical poets, beginning with Petrarch—who owned an important manuscript, now lost, and would have recognized an especially kindred spirit in elegy 1.18—has been as part of the corpus of Roman love poetry generally, rather than through his particular manner. Goethe pronounced himself "inspired by Propertius," whom he cites by name in his *Römische Elegien* (1795); but the mistress in that sequence is faithful and compliant, and the nostalgic idealization of clandestine sensuality is relatively untroubled. Goethe's *Euphrosyne* (1798), in the same elegiac meter, is shaped in certain ways by the poem about Cynthia's ghost; but the returning spirit is muted in any reproach against the poet, and her general tone is kind and sorrowful.

A closer match is provided by the *Elegies* that John Donne composed at the end of the 16th century. Their proximate inspiration is Ovidian (Christopher Marlowe's scandalous translation of the *Amores* was newly in print), but the personality on view looks more Propertian: "neurotic; intelligent; witty but eccentric; learned but difficult in his learning; cold and sensual at the same time; forever defining and redefining his feelings and those of his mistress" (Revard 1986, 70–71). The affinity shows in other poems of Donne's, often with a twist; in "The Apparition" the male speaker imagines returning after his own death to make a faithless woman break into a cold sweat.

The most famous recent development in Propertius' legacy is Ezra Pound's *Homage to Sextus Propertius* (1917), a sequence of translations from the first three books, arranged to emphasize the poet's effort to define his own vocation within the triumphalist propaganda of Augustan Rome. Pound's sense of a wary sarcasm toward the civic references in Propertius suffuses the love story as well ("It is noble to die of love, and honourable to remain/uncuckolded for a season"); his aim, he later wrote, was to present "certain emotions as vital to men faced with the infinite and ineffable imbecility of the British Empire as they were to Propertius . . . faced with the infinite and ineffable imbecility of the Roman Empire." The work provoked outrage from some classicists—for Gilbert Highet (1961) it "degraded the sensitive thoughts of another poet" and constituted "a fundamental failure of taste"—but it made a durable mark both on modern poetry and on the reading and translation of Propertius. In his own act of homage, Robert Lowell included in *Lord Weary's Castle* (1946) a memorably brutal version, inconceivable without Pound's example, of the visitation from Cynthia's ghost.

BIBL.: Stella Revard, "Donne and Propertius," in *The Eagle and the Dove: Reassessing John Donne,* ed. Claude J. Summers and Ted-Larry Pebworth (Columbia, Mo., 1986) 69–79. J. P. Sullivan, *Ezra Pound and Sextus Propertius* (Austin 1964).

G.B.

Prosody

Most metrical study in antiquity centered on the foot, an imaginary unit that remains, in practice, as durable as its detractors' criticisms have been heartfelt. The extant treatises in Greek and Latin evidently addressed two interlocking needs: the textual correction of poems, and their explication to pupils and inquisitive readers. Some meters were more satisfactorily explained via feet than others, however. Thus, for the Homeric epics exceptions and special rules proliferated, whereas for the meters of tragedy and comedy no completely workable explanation survives. A few writers ventilated an alternative account of the sound patterns of poetry, centering not on the foot but on a category called rhythm. But as the sound of spoken Greek and Latin changed in late antiquity, the foot reestablished total dominance. Word accent was now pronounced while quantity was not; under these conditions, the foot system was the only guide to what had effectively become a foreign poetic language, both in Byzantium and in the Latin West until the 15th century and beyond.

In the 16th century Humanists aimed first to extend the scope and accuracy of the foot system, especially for meters on which ancient guidebooks were reticent. For example, following the discovery, made famous by Erasmus, that the comedies of Terence and Plautus were written in meter—many manuscripts presented the texts as prose—debate ensued over permissible feet and the degrees of ancient poets' metrical *licentia.* Meter also helped scholars discover and emend poetic fragments embedded in prose treatises by Varro, Cicero, Athenaeus, and others, and in dictionaries. Some contemporaries explored a speculative historical approach, as when Julius Caesar Scaliger, following Aristotle, pointed to the trochee as the originary foot of Greek poetry; others attempted to discover Greek and Latin quantitative meters in the Hebrew Bible, a project that superimposed debates about classical meters onto a supremely resistant corpus of material.

In the late 17th century, when urgent debates about the foot system had faded, Isaac Vossius' bold theoretical approach reanimated meter as a topic for the shrewd and the ambitious. According to Vossius, "accent" and "rhythm"—not quantitative meter per se—were the true formal principles of classical verse, obscured until then by the fallacious system of written accents devised by late-antique grammarians. His theory turned on two overt confrontations between classical poetry and the 17th-century world. The early opera, first, had been explained by its theorists as a comprehensive attempt to reconstruct the classical tragedy as text and performance. Vossius, however, derided contemporary vocal compositions for their disregard of natural sentence rhythm and word accent, demanding a return to what he characterized as ancient exactitude on these points. Second, and more momentously, Vossius argued that when we read classical poetry aloud in such a way that we "hear the meter"—effectively, placing a stress accent on each long syllable and ignoring word accent, a practice sternly forbidden to pupils then as now—far from perverting the true ancient sound, we are accurately recreating it. Although Vossius restricted this incendiary claim to "sung poetry," he set no historical boundaries for that category; indeed, in his view, the Homeric epics clearly belonged to it. Under Vossius' influence, combined with that of H. C. Hennin, many classicists through the late 18th century declined to use accents when writing ancient Greek. The relation among meter, accent, and music has provoked controversy for even longer.

Richard Bentley first applied his magnificent expertise in meter to Greek poetic fragments, emending Callimachus, Menander, Aristophanes, and others. His first publication elucidated the forgotten rule that in anapestic lines the final syllable is not indifferent and synaphea takes place between one line and the next. But Bentley's Terence (1726) exerted a more transforming influence, showing for the first time how Vossius' proposals could be persuasively applied. Illustrating his suggestions about the poetic form of iambics and trochaics with lines from contemporary British songs, Bentley advocated both the term *rhythm* and the further categories of *ictus* and *arsis*, imagining that Terence's comedies were entirely sung to instrumental accompaniment with well-defined beats. Accordingly, his Terence text displayed accent marks on the three or four *ictus* of every line. Bentley's unpublished project to insert the digamma in the Homeric epics formed a similar experiment in systematically regularizing the meter of ancient poems.

Like Bentley, Richard Porson preferred to educe metrical arguments from individual poems; Porson concentrated on the textual study of the Athenian comedy and tragedy, appealing to manuscripts but also to metrical considerations, scholia, and lexica. His posthumous *Adversaria* and notes on Aristophanes reveal a mind drawn irresistibly to the most concrete, localized problems. In the preface to his second edition of Euripides' *Hecuba*, Porson also surveyed systematic generic rules for the iambic, trochaic, and anapestic meters of Greek tragedy. His discussion of caesuras and bridges in the iambic trimeter was important; more famous is the prohibition he identified against resolving a fifth-foot spondee into a dactyl or anapest (Porson's Law). At once a brilliant conjectural critic and a pessimist about the propensity of conjecturers to commit grave mistakes, Porson saw meter as a vital curb for controlling textual emendation.

During the same years, Gottfried Hermann's metrical study captured the expansive confidence, both conceptual and disciplinary, of German classical study around 1800. He attacked individual texts with alacrity, especially Plautus, Photius, and the poems attributed to Orpheus (which, Hermann pointed out, display neither lengthening before the caesura nor hiatus like the allegedly coeval epics of Homer and Hesiod). Years of debate with colleagues—and years of teaching, as one of Germany's most favored professors—culminated in Hermann's massive textbook, the *Elementa doctrinae metricae* (1816). On the formal plane, Hermann extended Bentley's emphasis on rhythm, with his terms *ictus* and *arsis*, to the entirety of ancient verse. Hermann also articulated a general doctrine of *anacrusis*, or pickup syllables, that worked both as a hallmark for Ionic lyric verse and, more generally, as a powerful device for turning one meter into another—an addictive game Hermann learned from Bentley and from the ancient grammarian Marius Victorinus. Indeed, this technique apparently underlay Hermann's comprehensive structural account of ancient meters: he placed these in two major groups, the trochaic and the dactylic, whose members could readily be transformed into one another in both Greek and Latin. Whether and how such transformations had happened in history was not Hermann's concern in this book, however, despite the wealth of his examples and his own keen, lifelong interest in historical change in poetry. Rather, the outlines of his system were static and formal, a decision he emphasized through Kantian methodological language that served some contemporaries as an easy butt. The relentlessly formalist Hermann of the subsequent *Philologenstreit*, then, was in large part a creature of circumstance, squeezed into a new shape by the imposing experiment in metrical systematization that he was the first to take on since late antiquity.

The ensuing decades saw extremely bold speculation about ancient meter, based particularly on its presumptive relationships with music; these developments are invaluably surveyed, though with polemical intent, in the *Griechische Verskunst* (1921) of Ulrich von Wilamowitz-Moellendorff. Wilamowitz's own approach presupposed the thoroughgoing model of national and cultural genealogy that dominated classical study, like other fields, in the later 19th century. Concentrating purely on Greek verse, Wilamowitz proposed to seek and reconstruct its ur-forms; he believed, indeed, that a prosody of "Indo-Germanic" might be described by future scholars, a project undertaken in the 20th century by M. L. West, among others. For Greek, by way of hundreds of examples, Wilamowitz himself identified an originary eight-syllable verse with four accents, an originary six-syllable verse with three accents, and a "short verse" usually appearing with five syllables. Not only did these categories provide fresh, if hypothetical, evidence for the bankruptcy of the foot as a meaningful unit, but they also generated between them all comic and lyric meters (given the options of anacrusis, catalexis, and hypercatalexis) and even the complex lines of the tragic chorus and of Pindar. Meanwhile, two additional narratives integrated Wilamowitz's argument about the origins of form with a broader literary history. First, Wilamowitz discovered the ur-verses exclusively in sung forms of poetry, which he took to mean only dramatic and lyric genres: the epic hexameter did not figure in his book, and he took every opportunity to consider the ritual and social settings of performance for the forms he did treat. He also traced an evaluative story of Greek versification, from great formal subtlety in Archilochus and Anacreon to a loosening of standards when their forms traveled to Athens, to a renewed sophistication among the scholarly Alexandrians.

On the plane of methodological debate, which he relished here as elsewhere, Wilamowitz described himself and his favorite predecessors, Hermann and Bentley, as empiricists. The term amply captures their massive erudition, as well as their drive to show how their arguments changed the understanding of individual lines. Yet we have also seen that their empiricism was profitable only in their respective climates of scholarly debate—indeed, of theory. The means of finding answers becomes a genuinely interesting matter above all when some large question is at hand. As to the conditions under which prosody might again become a central and prestigious field in classical literary study, it is open to anyone to speculate.

K.H.

Psellus, Michael

Psellus (1018–after 1081 CE) enjoyed the status of an intellectual supernova in the political and cultural life of 11th-century Byzantium. Court functionary, prolific writer, and complete polymath, he confided immodestly, "People tug and pull at me, loving to hear my voice above all others, because I know more than anyone else" (Wilson 1996, 161).

His remarkable intellectual abilities emerged early. In his native Constantinople he mastered the recitation, explication, and interpretation of Homer before reaching the age of ten. After completing the traditional Byzantine liberal arts curriculum, he entered the provincial bureaucracy before he was twenty, proceeded to rise at the imperial court among the advisers of Constantine IX Monomachus (1042–1055), and became "Consul of the Philosophers," a sort of imperial dean of liberal arts who coordinated teaching in Constantinople, delivered scholarly lectures, and composed numerous orations for important public figures and events. When a power struggle arose between emperor and patriarch, Psellus lost influence and withdrew reluctantly in 1054 to a repressive provincial monastery. He joyfully returned to the court as prime minister for Isaac I Comnenus (1057–1059), served as private imperial tutor under Isaac's successors, and observed court life firsthand until his second eclipse, around the time that Byzantine power collapsed at the Battle of Manzikert (1071). Some of his writings postdate 1081; the date of his death is unattested.

Psellus left a prodigious literary legacy of approximately 1,100 heterogeneous works surviving in nearly 1,800 manuscripts. Chief among them is the *Chronographia,* a masterly account of imperial rule 976–1078 invigorated by adept psychological observations. Consistently the consummate rhetorician, here and throughout his writings Psellus expresses himself artfully and obliquely, eluding censure for his unorthodox religious views and Platonic political ideals by dazzling the audience with his stylistic fluency and displays of immense classical learning. For this reason, and because much of Psellus' huge and multifaceted oeuvre remains untranslated and is available only in manuscript or in outdated editions, his towering personality and legacy have escaped satisfactory definition or appreciation. Among his most familiar works are his literary assessments of classical and patristic authors, his essay on Symeon the Metaphrast, his encomium of his mother (proclaimed by the 12th-cent. scholar Gregory of Corinth to be one of the four all-time best orations), his miscellaneous essays based on Plutarch and entitled *De omnifaria doctrina,* and two occult texts, the *Chaldean Oracles* and *On the Workings of Demons* (probably spurious).

Prominent Byzantine and international students alike studied with Psellus, whose stellar reputation persisted into modern times, approximating in the East Virgil's influence in the West. For example, he appears in the anonymous 12th-century satire *Timarion* enthroned in Hades among the revered sophist-rhetors of antiquity; his lectures on Aristotle served as a textbook until the 14th century; and he influenced the 15th-century Platonist George Gemistus Pletho (1360–1452), a participant in the development of Italian Humanism. Marsilio Ficino (1433–1499) translated some of Psellus' philosophical texts into Latin, and Xylander his treatise on the mathematical disciplines (1556). Psellus' enduring reputation as an authority on the occult even prompted Samuel Taylor Coleridge (1772–1834) to recommend consulting "the Platonic Constantinopolitan, Michael Psellus" (annotation to "Rime of the Ancient Mariner" 2.12). A comprehensive edition of Psellus' works is currently in progress, published as part of the Teubner series (formerly of Leipzig, now produced through Saur Verlag in Munich).

Psellus' scholarly career typifies the Byzantine intellectual tradition, which simultaneously promoted the survival and prestige of ancient literature and retarded the development of a Greek vernacular literature able to compete with the entrenched classical paradigm.

BIBL.: Charles Barber, David Jenkins, et al., *Reading Michael Psellos* (Leiden 2006). Anthony Kaldellis, *The Argument of Psellos' Chronographia* (Leiden 1999). Jeffrey Walker, "These Things I Have Not Betrayed: Michael Psellos' Encomium of His Mother as a Defense of Rhetoric," *Rhetorica* 22 (2004) 49–101. Nigel Wilson, *Scholars of Byzantium,* rev. ed. (London 1996) 156–179.

E.F.

Ptolemy

Claudius Ptolemaeus, mathematician, astronomer, and geographer (ca. 90–ca. 168 CE). In 1600 the mathematician François Viète found an effective way to express his contempt for Copernicus. He called the astronomer "Ptolemaei paraphrastes," the paraphraser of Ptolemy. Copernicus, Viète insisted, had depended on an ancient authority for the central elements of his planetary theory. He had thus revealed a damning lack of both intellectual independence and mathematical insight. Viète's striking phrase attracted the interest of such alert contemporaries as Johannes Kepler, who hoped that he might find help from the Frenchman in establishing the paths of the planets. But the factual statement that Copernicus depended on Ptolemy for the basic elements of his system caused no scandal in the years after 1600. Every well-trained astronomer knew that Copernicus, for all the daring that had enabled him to refound planetary theory on a heliocentric basis, had drawn his methods and the bulk of his data from the ancient master of geocentric astronomy. A couple of years before Viète's remark reached print, Kepler's teacher of astronomy, Michael Mästlin, had shown him in detail that Copernicus's models for the motions of the planets basically replicated Ptolemy's models.

As late as the end of the 16th century, in fact, astronomers and geographers, students of optics and of musical theory continued to draw on, and to struggle against, the authoritative works of Ptolemy. And no wonder. Ptolemy, an Alexandrian Greek who flourished in the years after

140 CE, was a supremely energetic, skillful, and widely read student of the mathematical branches of natural philosophy. Aristotelian in his general viewpoint and in his systematic method of presenting material, subject by subject, he was also, like most philosophers of his time, willing to draw eclectically on other traditions, especially Platonic and Stoic. Though he carried out astronomical observations and optical and musical experiments of his own, his chief gift was for the synthesis of large bodies of existing information. Ptolemy took brilliant advantage of his position in Alexandria, the catchment area for information pouring in from many parts of the Mediterranean world.

The corpus of Ptolemy's works has many components. His most influential single work was the *Mathematikē syntaxis* (*Mathematical Treatise*). In it he brought together, in many cases for the first time, empirical data that had been collected and parameters that had been established by the astronomers of Mesopotamia with the geometrical models created by earlier Greek mathematicians and astronomers. He derived and explained geocentric models for the motion of the moon, the sun, and the five known planets, together with tables for predicting their motions and a catalogue of 1,028 stars in 48 constellations. He also drew up tables for predicting planetary motions, a work on stereometric projection, and a calendar of the appearance and disappearance of the fixed stars during the year. And where his *Treatise* offered purely mathematical models that predicted the positions and movements of the planets, in his *Planetary Hypotheses* he laid out what he regarded as a true physical picture of the cosmos. To produce this he assumed that there was no empty space between the sets of nested spheres that accounted for each planet's motion. Ptolemy set out both a theory of the order of the planets and dimensions for them. His *Tetrabiblos,* a treatise on astrology, stood out from his other works on the heavens for the absence of a mathematical approach. Instead, he drew up a rigorous account, as Aristotelian in form as he could make it, of the influence of the heavenly bodies and their movements on events on earth.

Ptolemy's *Geography,* a systematic manual of cartography, synthesized a vast amount of information about the Earth's surface, including longitudes and latitudes for some 8,000 places, and offered technical instruction in how to map the known world, both as a whole and then in 26 smaller areas. His *Optics,* only parts of which are preserved, offered a geometrical account of vision and light. The *Harmonics*, finally, dealt with the nature of the musical intervals, a subject of deep interest from the Pythagoreans onward. In several distinct traditions, Ptolemy's works dominated theory and practice for almost a millennium and a half. The great prestige that he enjoyed on this account may help explain a common error: the belief that he was one of the Ptolemies who ruled Egypt. Though any astronomer would have known that chronology made this impossible, the identification survived until the 16th century; in Raphael's *School of Athens* Ptolemy still wears his inappropriate crown.

Ptolemy's astronomy had an almost continuous afterlife. The Alexandrian mathematicians Pappus and Theon, and Theon's brilliant daughter Hypatia, all redacted and explicated the *Mathematical Treatise,* and the late Neoplatonist Proclus, in his *Hypotyposis,* raised philosophical questions about what he saw as inconsistencies in Ptolemy's planetary theory. The *Handy Tables* were widely copied, commented on, and studied, not only by practicing astronomers, but also by the 5th-century historians Annianus and Panodorus. They tried to use Ptolemy's astronomical information to establish a firm foundation for the chronology of the world. Boethius, who translated other Greek works, did not produce a full version of the *Harmonics,* but he incorporated much of Ptolemy's doctrine into his own *De musica* (early 6th cent.), with its influential treatment of celestial harmony. Ptolemy, accordingly, remained a vital presence in the musical tradition, Eastern and Western. The *Geography* and the *Optics,* by contrast, both continued to be read, but seem to have stimulated less full-scale commentary—perhaps, in the former case, because text and maps presented formidable difficulties for copyists, and in both cases because the subject did not have a firm place in the curriculum.

References to Ptolemy, and systematic efforts to use and emulate his work, declined in frequency in the Greek world after the Alexandrian tradition in science came to an end in the 5th century. But in Persia and the Greek and Syrian Christian communities under Islamic rule, his work continued to be studied. In the 8th and early 9th centuries, however, he became a powerful—but also a controversial—presence in the Islamic world. As bureaucrats struggled for position in the new empire of the Abbasids, mastery of the ancient sciences came to be a prized possession. The *Mathematical Treatise* was translated into Arabic—a process that gave it the name by which it is still normally referred to, *Almagest*—around 800 and epitomized half a century later by al-Farghānī, who included the *Planetary Hypotheses* with it. By the late 9th century Muslim astronomers were beginning a long process of creative engagement with Ptolemy's astronomy. They corrected his parameters, improved on his observations, and emended his theory in many details—but never fundamentally abandoned his geocentric model of the universe or his vision of what astronomy should be.

What made Ptolemy's astronomy uniquely stimulating for his Muslim readers were the apparent contradictions that ran through his work. In theory he held that all planetary motions were generated by spheres, which themselves turned uniformly, as spheres logically must. But the kinematic models of planetary motion that Ptolemy laid out in the *Almagest* achieved accuracy by making some spheres turn with a linear velocity that was uniform as seen not from their centers but from another point, the equant. Did empirical accuracy matter enough to justify compromises on basic philosophical principles? Debate raged, often at a very sophisticated level. The 13th-century astronomer Naṣīr al-Dīn al-Ṭūsī and other members of the Maragha school took a special interest in what they saw as philosophical objections to Ptolemy's work—

above all his use of the equant—and devised an alternative way of producing the same effects, the "Ṭūsī couple," in which the planet in question turned on a small sphere that itself rolled inside another, which revolved around the center of the world. Ptolemy's *Tetrabiblos* also found extensive use in the Islamic world, in which astrology was widely practiced. It attracted multiple commentaries and inspired the creation of a very popular astrological work falsely ascribed to Ptolemy, the *Centiloquium*. The *Geography*, translated in part in the 9th century, provided the core techniques for several Muslim schools of cartography, whose members, unlike the astronomers, improved on certain details in Ptolemy's work without transforming its main structure. The *Optics* inspired the greatest medieval specialist in optics, the 11th-century scientist Ibn al-Haytham, who modeled his work on Ptolemy's and emulated his great predecessor in designing systematic experiments.

Even in the early Middle Ages, Ptolemy's star charts circulated in the Latin world: the famous Leiden manuscript of the *Aratea*, an astronomical and meteorological treatise by Aratus, translated into Latin by Germanicus and copied and splendidly illuminated early in the 9th century, incorporates material from them. And the great wave of translation that began with the work of Gerard of Cremona and others in Sicily and Iberia brought much more of Ptolemy's work into the medieval West. In Europe as in the Islamic world, astronomers used Ptolemy's models and methods even when they adapted Arabic astronomical tables more up-to-date than his. And astronomers and engineers constructed miniature working models of the Ptolemaic universe in a fantastic variety of forms—from the equatoria, or solar, lunar, and planetary models, made of wood, paper, or metal, created by Campanus of Novara in the 13th century and Petrus Apianus—in his case, as a printed book—in the 16th, to the great astronomical clocks crafted by Giovanni de' Dondi, Richard of Wallingford, and Conrad Dasypodius. The Ptolemaic universe was omnipresent, embodied in elaborate models whose parts were in constant, regular motion, in monastic communities, city squares, and cathedrals as well as in the university faculties of arts and medicine where the texts were read and studied. The most skillful Western astronomers knew of the Islamic critique of Ptolemy. A few Scholastics—above all the Viennese Henry of Langenstein—criticized Ptolemaic astronomy for its apparent conflict with Aristotelian cosmology. For the most part, though, Ptolemy's geocentric cosmology and kinematics retained their authority.

From the 13th century, the *Tetrabiblos* became a standard work as well, used by everyone interested in showing that the widely practiced and widely criticized art of astrology in fact rested on sound Aristotelian principles. Multiple commentaries explicated the text and used illustrative horoscopes to show the application of its principles. Though the *Optics* was not preserved as a whole, Ibn al-Haytham transmitted Ptolemy's ideas and methods to Roger Bacon and Witelo, and through them to the Western optical tradition. No wonder, then, that Ptolemy not only maintained his position as a curriculum author, but won admiration and literary adaptation from Dante and Chaucer. Both credited him with creating the models of the cosmos that they accepted and described. It is even possible that Chaucer composed an English description of a Ptolemaic equatorie.

Between the 15th and the early 17th centuries, Ptolemaic science was finally and definitively superseded. Like so many other premodern revolutions, this one began as an effort at restoration. And like many such enterprises, it moved to the tempo of two steps forward, one step back. Around 1300 the Byzantine scholar Maximus Planudes redacted the text of the *Geography* and brought back into circulation the corpus of maps that went with it. The new text—at once fascinating, beautiful, and full of errors—provoked multiple efforts at explication and emendation. Ptolemy's methods proved vital for the new cartography that took shape in the 15th and 16th centuries. His work even helped inspire Columbus to undertake his expedition, since it provided him with the information that Ptolemy's predecessor Marinus had thought Asia much closer to Europe than Ptolemy himself did. The *Geography*, in other words, provided many of the tools needed to show that Ptolemy's own picture of the surface of the earth was radically flawed. Yet the work itself remained in place, more coherent and substantial than any rival, and it continued to be reproduced for decades after every literate person knew that the Indian Ocean was open to the south and that the Americas existed. In cartography, Ptolemy played two roles at the same time: his work both supported the exploration and mapping of the earth's surface and hindered the coherent, systematic presentation of this new knowledge to a wide public.

In astronomy Ptolemy met a similar fate: revival led to supersession. George of Trebizond, an erudite Humanist, made a new translation of the *Almagest* from the Greek. More important, the Viennese scholar Georg Peurbach and his brilliant pupil Joannes Regiomontanus, who subjected George's work to withering criticism, drew up a systematic *Epitome* of the text. They clarified Ptolemy's methods and models, step by step, and compared his results with the work of later Islamic astronomers. The Greek text of Ptolemy's work appeared in 1533. For decades, however, every serious astronomer—including Copernicus—gained mastery of Ptolemaic planetary theory by working through the *Epitome*.

When Copernicus set out to show that the sun, not the Earth, was the center of the universe, he based his work, in structure and in substance, on Ptolemy's, sometimes chapter by chapter and table by table, for want of an alternative source of data and models. To that extent, Viète was right: Copernicus, the great innovator, depended at every turn on the work of Ptolemy that he set out to replace. Yet his reading included later texts. Presumably, one or more of these were Islamic works, now unknown, that showed him how to replace the equant and its nonuniform motion with the Ṭūsī couple, which achieved the same ends but did not cause philosophical offense. Most important, Copernicus managed—as his predecessors had not—to combine the enterprises that Ptolemy had held separate. He insisted that astronomy provide both the sort of models and tables that had filled the *Almagest* and an account of the real physical universe comparable to that offered by the *Planetary Hypotheses*. Only a heliocentric model of the universe, he claimed, could do this demanding job.

Copernicus's work found readers, and his theory supporters and critics, almost at once. Still, through the 16th century and beyond, Ptolemy retained immense authority. When the Italian mathematician and astrologer Girolamo Cardano (1501–1576) set out to develop a truly scientific astrology, he cast his major work in the form of a commentary on the *Tetrabiblos*. Though Johannes Kepler (1571–1630) came to maturity as a convinced Copernican, he devoted elaborate studies to Ptolemy's astronomy and astrology, his optics and his musical theory. Kepler even planned a translation of and commentary on the *Harmonics,* though in the event he offered his account of Ptolemy's work in his own *Harmonice mundi.*

Officially, the Ptolemaic system remained the one accepted and taught at universities across Europe—even as Tycho, Galileo, and Kepler offered more and more cogent evidence that the Copernican system was superior. Galileo's sharp attack on it eventually provoked full-scale censorship—to the dismay of the Jesuits who generally accepted the Copernican theory in the 17th century—and reassertion of Ptolemy's status. For decades astronomical textbooks and lectures treated the Ptolemaic, Copernican, and Tychonic systems as comparable in value and profundity, and compared them at length. In 1651, when Giambattista Riccioli produced what became, for the next half century, the standard survey of astronomy, he entitled it *Almagestum novum.*

For many 17th-century thinkers, however, as Viète's disdainful language suggests, Ptolemy's failings, from individual mistakes to the grand error of his geographical system, bulked larger than his virtues. Mention of his work came to evoke the limitations of ancient philosophy and science as a whole, which such prophets of the New Science as Francis Bacon stressed in their manifestos. Historians of geography and astronomy in the 18th and 19th centuries often dismissed Ptolemy as a talentless hack who had stolen his best ideas from Marinus, Hipparchus, and nameless Chaldaeans and imposed his authority on men who should have devoted themselves instead to empirical observation.

Despite the efforts of Nicholas Halma and J. L. Heiberg, who made the *Almagest* accessible in modern editions, Ptolemy's reputation has never been quite stable. Throughout the 20th century accusations of plagiarism and fraud continued to be made. Yet from the 1920s onward historians of ancient science, led by Otto Neugebauer, examined Ptolemy's work with a new precision. They have shown how much he—and all other Greek astronomers—owed to their colleagues in Mesopotamia. They have established that he fudged observations in order to establish the parameters that he wanted. But they have also come to appreciate the extraordinary technical innovations that enabled him to synthesize his own and others' work in a form that proved durably useful. The equant model, for example, stayed in use until the time of Copernicus and after because it replicated, almost exactly, the actual movements of planets on the elliptical orbits that they actually trace. And they have shown that he had a passion for information of every kind that made him, in profound ways, an empirical thinker. Similarly, historians of cartography have taught us that Ptolemy himself—not his later readers and commentators—drew up the corpus of maps that accompanied the *Geography* in the ancient world, and thus created what may have been the ancient world's most complex and coherent illustrated scientific text. Now that we know that Ptolemy's picture of the world was false in almost every respect, we can better understand the brilliance and utility of the approximations that he crafted for everything from the surface of the Earth to the sphere of the fixed stars.

BIBL.: Patrick Gautier Dalché, *La Géographie de Ptolémée en Occident (IVe–XVIe siècle)* (Turnhout 2009). Florian Mittenhuber, *Text- und Kartentradition in der Geographie des Klaudios Ptolemaios* (Bern 2009). O. Neugebauer, *The Exact Sciences in Antiquity,* 2nd ed. (New York 1962). Emmanuel Poulle, *Les instruments de la théorie des planètes selon Ptolémée: Équatoires et horlogerie planétaire du XIIIe au XVIe siècle* (Geneva 1980). George Saliba, *Islamic Science and the Making of the European Renaissance* (Cambridge, Mass., 2007). Noel Swerdlow, "The Recovery of the Exact Sciences of Antiquity: Mathematics, Astronomy, Geography," in *Rome Reborn: The Vatican Library and Renaissance Culture,* ed. Anthony Grafton (New Haven 1993) 125–167. N. Swerdlow and O. Neugebauer, *Mathematical Astronomy in Copernicus's De revolutionibus* (New York 1984).

A.G.

Purple

The most prestigious color in antiquity, purple is still a potent metaphor for nobility. But what color was it?

As early as Alcman (7th cent. BCE) and Pindar (5th cent. BCE) the purple shellfish dye was seen as the finest color, but it was not considered a specifically royal hue before Cicero (1st cent. BCE). By the late Empire it had become exclusive to the imperial family; yet many restrictive edicts, from Gratian to Justinian, suggest that this prerogative was seldom honored. The royal, even divine, aura of purple was magnified during the Middle Ages: the mantle of the Virgin Mary disinterred at Byzantium in the 7th century was of a perfectly preserved purple wool; and Christ was allegedly robed from childhood in a purple garment, preserved at Argenteuil, which miraculously grew as he grew.

Purple's royal connotations have persisted: William Perkin in 1857 called the first synthetic purple dye Tyrian purple, until marketing imperatives led him to rename it mauve, made fashionable in the 1850s by the French Empress Eugénie. Queen Victoria soon copied her French model, and fashion made Perkin's fortune, bringing purple to a wide public. Although still the British royal ceremonial color, by the late 20th century it had largely lost its exclusive resonance, in the age of Purple Hearts, Alice Walker's novel and Steven Spielberg's film, *The Color Purple* (1982, 1985), and Prince's film and album, *Purple Rain* (1984).

The ancient prestige of shellfish purple depended largely on its permanence, celebrated by Lucretius, and on the very high cost of processing the dye. The vast shell middens of the eastern Mediterranean testify to the enormous consumption of animals; Carl Friedlaender, who first analyzed shellfish purple in 1906, used 12,000 specimens, which yielded only 1.4 grams of dye. Pliny described how the application of a mulch of raw *purpura* was followed by steeping in a vat of *buccinum,* which was fugitive if used alone, but in this combination gave the blackish *purpura* the "crimson-like sheen which is in fashion." The imperial edicts emphasized that it was the animal origin of true purple that was crucial; many cheap imitations were made from fugitive vegetable dyes.

Recipes for purple substitutes usually involved mixtures, and the belief that it was indeed a mixture led a number of 15th-century heraldic writers to downgrade purple to the lowest of the tinctures in heraldry, where its place as a royal color was already being usurped by blue. Chemically, the coloring matter of the shellfish gland is very close to the blue vegetable dye indigo; and, conversely, the dye produced from the plant *indigofera* has, chemically, a red tinge of *indirubin,* so the borderline between these purple and blue pigments is very ill defined. Vitruvius held that the dye from shellfish in colder waters was bluish, and that from those in warmer waters reddish, a suggestion that sits uneasily with the Venerable Bede's admiration of the beautiful red dye derived from shellfish gathered on the Northumbrian coast of England in the 8th century. The purple regulations of the emperors Diocletian and Theodosius distinguished between reddish, *blatta,* and bluish, *hyacinthina,* varieties; and modern chemical experiments have produced shellfish purples in a range from reddish to blue.

Linguistic evidence suggests that ancient purple owed its esteem to its being classed with reds, which connoted light and divinity. The 3rd-century legal code of the Emperor Ulpian defined *purpura* as all red cloths except those dyed with the insect-derived *coccum,* and in some 15th-century Spanish and Italian texts, dying with *purpura* was seen to produce "crimson." On the other hand, late medieval *purpura* referred to any precious textile (usually silk) , which might well be dyed red or green, or remain undyed.

Aristotle's term *phoinikoun* (Latin *puniceus*) referred not, as we might expect, to the renowned Phoenician purple, but to the red of the rainbow, and so the term was generally understood in the Middle Ages. Yet in his 14th-century encyclopedia, *On the Properties of Things,* Bartholomaeus Anglicus asserted that *puniceus* was indeed shellfish purple. The confusion may derive from the mistaken belief that it was the blood of the shellfish that produced the dye.

Certainly purple and red seem to have been interchangeable: when the Turkish conquest of Byzantium in 1453 stopped European trade in purple cloth, the Church substituted crimson for the cardinals' dress. Goethe found a color he called blue-red disturbingly unstable: "It unceasingly aspires to the cardinal's red through the restless degrees of a still-impatient progression." Goethe's own highest color was a red that he believed embraced all colors, which he called *Purpur,* "although we are quite aware that the purple of the ancients inclined more to blue." It is astonishing that, although Goethe knew of the photochemical color sequence, from yellow to green to blue and finally to amethyst during the shellfish dyeing process, he saw the final product as "bright red."

Perhaps it was not hue that gave purple its peculiar allure but rather, as Pliny had suggested, its sheen.

Democritus included white in his analysis of purple, to give it brilliance or luster (*lampron*), and Pliny stated that purple "brightens (*illuminat*) every garment." This emphasis persisted into late antiquity and the Middle Ages: the Greek *Stockholm Papyrus* (3rd century CE) includes recipes for substitute purple dyes that gave "an extremely beautiful luster" to the cloth; and a 12th-century treatise on tempera describes a glossy red surface as giving "almost the effect of the most prized purple." In his influential *Etymologies* Isidore of Seville (7th century CE) derived *purpura* from *puritate lucis* (purity of light), an idea amplified by the 15th-century Netherlandish herald Jehan Courtois: "It grows naturally in those countries of the world which the sun illuminates most."

BIBL.: Philip Ball, *Bright Earth: Art and the Invention of Color* (New York 2001). J. Doumet, *Étude sur la couleur pourpre ancienne* (Beirut 1980). R. J. Edgeworth, "Does 'Purpureus' mean 'Bright'?" *Glotta* 57 (1979) 281. George Henderson, "The Colour Purple: A Late Antique Phenomenon and Its Anglo-Saxon Reflexes," in *Vision and Image in Early Christian England* (Cambridge 1999). J.G.

Pygmalion

Legendary sculptor. Disgusted by the shameless behavior of real women, he carved an ivory statue of an ideal woman, miraculously lifelike; he fell in love with her and wooed her. Venus understood the real wish that lay behind his prayer for a wife like the statue; at his touch, the ivory softened into flesh, art turned into life, and Pygmalion was able to marry his own creation. The story is an invention of Ovid (*Metamorphoses* 10.243–297), based on a Cypriot legend of a king who fell in love with a statue of Aphrodite. One of a number of ancient tales about sexual desire for statues, it is also a fantasy on the dominant ancient aesthetic of verisimilitude. By making Pygmalion both sculptor and desiring beholder of the statue, Ovid comments on the psychology of both the creation and the reception of art; it was left to later centuries to explore the psychology of the statue.

Since the later Middle Ages Ovid's tale has prompted, in literature and in the visual and performing arts, numerous responses that examine variously the relationship between art and reality, the power of artistic illusion, desire, and subjectivity. In Jean de Meun's *Roman de la Rose* (lines 20,817–21,191) a Christian disapproval of idolatry condemns Pygmalion's love for the statue, animated by Venus's bad magic, as being contrary to nature. Petrarch, well aware of the idolatrous temptations of his love for Laura, praises Simone Martini's portrait of her as lacking only voice and intellect to be real (*Rime sparse* 78). She seems to listen, but her failure to reply is the point at which Petrarch realizes that he can only envy Pygmalion. The soundlessness of the image is also the moment of realization for Ovid's Narcissus (*Metamorphoses* 3.462–3): the stories of Pygmalion and Narcissus are profoundly connected, both in their Ovidian tellings and in their reception. Desire also converts representation into presence in the "lawful" magic of the statue scene at the end of Shakespeare's *The Winter's Tale,* when what Leontes is persuaded is a statue of Hermione made by "Nature's ape," Julio Romano, walks off its pedestal into his arms. The scene is a vertiginous exploration of the illusionist power not just of the visual arts, but of Shakespeare's own verbal and dramatic fictions.

An implicit contest with the powers of the legendary Pygmalion enlivens the numerous paintings (and some sculptures) of Pygmalion and his statue (particularly frequent in 18th-century France), in which the artist tests his own ability to persuade the viewer of the reality and desirability of a work of art at two removes from life. An artistic narcissism is pronounced in the works of Jean-Léon Gérôme (1824–1904), whose serial paintings of the subject are also illustrations of his own sculpture *Pygmalion and Galatea.* Gérôme was a noted exponent of a 19th-century craze for sculptural polychromy, creating uncannily lifelike works.

A tradition of plays, operas, and ballets on Pygmalion started in the 17th century. Jean-Jacques Rousseau introduced a new style of melodrama with his highly successful *scène lyrique, Pygmalion,* first performed in 1770 but composed in 1763, the year in which Maurice Falconet's sculpture of Pygmalion and his statue was the sensation of the Salon. Rousseau, who first christened the statue Galathée (Galatea), dramatized the artist's intense identification with his creation.

The subjectivity of the statue, rather than the artist, is the focus of a series of writings by 18th-century philosophes who used the myth both to speculate on the transmutability of matter into spirit and to imagine the sensations and pedagogy of a mature human first coming to consciousness. The education of the former statue is also the theme of later stage works, among them W. S. Gilbert's comedy *Pygmalion and Galatea* (1871), and G. B. Shaw's *Pygmalion* (1912), which was adapted as the musical production *My Fair Lady* (Broadway 1956, film 1964), the most recent in a long line of rationalizing retellings of the story.

BIBL.: Andreas Blühm, *Pygmalion: Die Ikonographie eines Künstlermythos zwischen 1500 und 1900* (Frankfurt 1988). J. K. L. Carr, "Pygmalion and the Philosophes: The Animated Statue in Eighteenth-century France," *Journal of the Warburg and Courtauld Institutes* 23 (1960) 239–255. Annegret Dinter, *Pygmalion-Stoff in der europäischen Literatur. Rezeptionsgeschichte einer Ovid-Fabel* (Heidelberg 1979). Kenneth Gross, *The Dream of the Moving Statue* (Ithaca 1992). Mathias Mayer and Gerhard Neumann, eds., *Pygmalion: Die Geschichte des Mythos in der abendländischen Kultur* (Freiburg 1997).

P.R.H.

Pyramid

Architectural form consisting of a square or trapezoidal base with four triangular sides meeting at a central point or apex. The pyramid achieved its characteristic form in pharaonic Egypt, where edifices of this type were employed as sepulchral monuments. The largest and most celebrated examples were constructed ca. 2500 BCE from great masses of stone masonry and were the focal points of enormous funerary complexes constructed for the burials of Egyptian kings. In the classical tradition, pyramids have been constructed primarily as tombs, often in conscious emulation of Egyptian precedent. The pyramidal temples of Mesoamerica represent a separate tradition whose nomenclature is a product of European interpretation.

The word derives from the Greek *pyramis,* meaning "wheat cake," although some commentators in antiquity associated the form with the *pyr,* or "flame," that consumed the body and transformed it into spirit, according to later Graeco-Roman thinking. The Egyptian word for pyramid was *mer,* represented by a hieroglyph in the shape of its sides, Δ. Like its cousin the obelisk, the pyramid seems to have derived its shape from the *benben,* a sacred stone that symbolized the mound of creation, where the rays of the life-giving sun first touched the earth. Inscriptions in the burial chambers of some later pyramids suggest that the pyramids were conceived as monumental stairways to heaven which the spirit of the king could ascend to take his place among the stars. The Egyptian name of Khufu's pyramid, "Khufu belongs to Horizon," neatly invokes the solar and celestial aspect of the pyramids' meaning.

As enduring symbols of pharaonic power and the afterlife, pyramids were sometimes imitated by tomb builders in the Hellenistic and Roman periods. Among the Greeks the most notable case was the stepped pyramid on the upper part of the Mausoleum at Halicarnassus (ca. 350s BCE). In Rome several pyramid tombs were erected during the imperial era. The best-preserved of these is the tomb of the Augustan official Gaius Cestius in Rome (built after ca. 12 BCE). During the Middle Ages a new explanation of the Giza pyramids, as being the granaries built by Joseph that are mentioned in Genesis, emerged in the European pilgrim literature, but writers in Arabic continued to recognize them as tombs and associated their conception with the mystical doctrines of Hermes Trismegistus.

During the Renaissance the Roman pyramids were recognized as imitations of those in Egypt, and travelers to Egypt like Cyriacus of Ancona (d. ca. 1455) explored the Giza monuments with the explanations of ancient writers like Herodotus and Pliny the Elder as their guides. The classical authors did not really approve of the Egyptian pyramids, which they saw as impressive but ultimately useless monuments to vainglorious luxury and tyranny. But this did not prevent later and modern artists from designing, and patrons from ordering, versions of pyramids. The gold- and jewel-encrusted pyramids of Osiris in Pinturicchio's frescoes in the Borgia Apartment (Vatican Palace, 1492–1494) were inspired by the remains of the so-called Meta Romuli Pyramid in the Vatican. In contrast, the huge, imaginary pyramid temple that appears in Francesco Colonna's 1499 romance, the *Hypnerotomachia Poliphili,* seems to draw from both classical and contemporary accounts of Egyptian pyramids. Some years later the pyramid was transformed from a freestanding to a wall-mounted monument in the tombs of the Chigi Chapel in Santa Maria del Popolo in Rome (designed ca. 1518–1519 by Raphael).

During the 17th and 18th centuries printed descriptions and travel accounts helped to sustain and renew European interest in the pyramids. In the 18th century architects like Johann Bernhard Fischer von Erlach, Nicholas Hawksmoor, Étienne-Louis Boullée, and Claude-Nicolas Ledoux produced designs for, and in some cases actually built, pyramidal monuments for gardens, mausolea, and even industrial structures. In 1782 the Masonic image of a pyramid topped by the all-seeing Eye of Providence was adopted for the obverse side of the Great Seal of the United States, and it is in that context that it appears today on the back of the dollar bill.

The publications released in the wake of the Napoleonic Egyptian campaign of 1798–1801 continued to fuel the taste for pyramids and for Egyptianizing designs in general, and variants of the form became familiar elements in cemeteries. The taste for pyramids has erupted periodically ever since, most recently and visibly with I. M. Pei's glass pyramid at the Louvre in Paris (1989) and the glamorized splendor of the Luxor Hotel in Las Vegas (1992).

BIBL.: Peter Berg and Michael Jones, eds., *Pyramidal Influence in Art* (Dayton 1980). James Stevens Curl, *The Egyptian Revival: Ancient Egypt as an Inspiration for Design Motifs in the West,* 3rd ed. (London 2005). Brian A. Curran, "The *Hypnerotomachia Poliphili* and Renaissance Egyptology," *Word and Image* 14 (1998) 156–185. I. E. S. Edwards, *The Pyramids of Egypt* (1947; 5th ed. London 1993). N. Pevsner and S. Lang, "The Egyptian Revival," *Architectural Review* 119 (1956) 242–254, revised in *Studies in Art, Architecture and Design,* ed. N. Pevsner, 2 vols. (London 1968) 1:213–248. B.CU.

Pyramus and Thisbe

In Roman legend, two young lovers from feuding families in Babylon. Ovid (*Metamorphoses* 4.55–166) tells how their attempt to meet outside the walls of the city led to their mutual suicide. Through Ovid their fate became a popular story of tragic young love, their devotion to each other being interpreted as either heroic or foolish. Dante (ca. 1265–1321) twice compares himself to Pyramus as he draws closer to Beatrice in the *Purgatorio.* Boccaccio tells the story in *Famous Women* (1374) and in *The Elegy of Lady Fiammetta* (1343–1344), as does Christine de Pizan in *The Epistle of Othea to Hector* (1399–1400) and *The City of Ladies* (1405). The first notable use in England was in the late 14th century: John Gower moralized the story in *Confessio amantis* (1390). His treatment is not unsympathetic, but it is reductive, dispensing with mythic, heroic dimensions. Driven by "hote" love, the lovers make a "hole" in the partition-wall between their two houses; Thisbe hides from the "Leoun in a buisshe"; there is no royal trysting place, no mulberry tree, no double urn; and they die because of their "folhaste." Writing for the court, Chaucer afforded the myth more sophisticated treatment in *The Legend of Good Women* (1385). Outwardly blaming their parents for the tragedy, he implicitly mocked the lovers and Ovid with sly humor; he also laced the story with bawdy trimmings, having them kiss the wall's "lyme" and "stoon," euphemisms for penis and testicles. Where Gower and Chaucer led, others followed.

In the premier Elizabethan translation of Ovid's poem (1567), Arthur Golding moralized the myth as a warning against "the headdie force of frentick love." But in translating, as always, emotional involvement and a naive sense of wonder take over, in a Pietà-like scene in which Thisbe discovers the dying boy and "taking him betweene hir armes did wash his wounds with teares"—an exceptional moment that Shakespeare adopted for a couplet among Juliet's loveliest lines, "Wash they his [Tybalt's] wounds with tears: mine shall be spent,/When theirs are dry, for Romeo's banishment" (*Romeo and Juliet* 3.2.130–131). In George Sandys's translation (1632), controlled couplets aim at emulating the wit of Ovid's verse; in his commentary the parents are blamed, but moral implications are of secondary interest compared to scientific and historical considerations.

Chaucer's sly mockery led to Shakespeare's more robust send-up in *A Midsummer Night's Dream,* and particularly to its bawdy aspects—as when "Thisbe" kisses "Wall's" "stones with lime and hair knit up." But sexuality is never far below the surface in Ovid himself: *rima,* the word he uses for the crack in the wall, is used elsewhere in Latin poetry for the vulva; the simile of the broken pipe is now recognized as a grotesque parody of ejaculation. And there is also what has been called "the rape of the veil": it is immediately after discovering her veil "Stain'd with blood" that Bottom's "Pyramus" concludes that "Thisbe" has been "deflower'd" (5.1.271, 281). At one level Bottom is again mangling Quince's script, but at another Shakespeare is acknowledging Ovid's symbolic use of the virginal girl's veil for the hymen. Notwithstanding the burlesque, Shakespeare basically viewed the myth as romantic, as is shown by his use of it elsewhere in the *Dream* and his inclusion of it in Lorenzo and Jessica's beautiful duet, "In such a night" (*Merchant of Venice* 5.1.7–10).

After Shakespeare the myth virtually disappeared from

general use. When English writers refer to tragic young lovers, they turn instead to Romeo and Juliet; Ovid's myth is confined to translations of the *Metamorphoses.* This situation reached its nadir in England in a thoroughly undistinguished version of the *Metamorphoses* composed by various hands under the aegis of Sir Samuel Garth (1717). The translator of this particular story, Laurence Eusden (whom Pope featured in *The Dunciad*) refers to Pyramus and Thisbe as "lifeless lumps" in death; they are scarcely more lively in his lines.

Of an entirely different order is the powerful, primitive version of Ted Hughes's *Tales from Ovid* (1997): Babylon is a "mud-brick city," the crack in the wall is caused by an "earth tremor," and the lioness is predictably impressive —"rippling shoulders," "bloody jaws," "hanging belly." Both lovers are repeatedly identified with the lioness. Myth, Hughes says in introducing his work, touches the supernatural; the love depicted in the story of Pyramus and Thisbe is "absolute," making them, like animal life, an illustration of the powerful creative core at the center of all life. Becoming a nature myth in his hands, the myth moves full circle; originally, before its relocation to Babylon, it had been a myth about the love of the river Pyramus for the goddess of a fountain, Thisbe.

BIBL.: D. Fowler, "Pyramus, Thisbe, King Kong: Ovid and the Presence of Poetry," in *Roman Constructions: Readings in Postmodern Latin* (Oxford 2000) 156–167. P. E. Knox, "Pyramus and Thisbe in Cyprus," *Harvard Studies in Classical Philology* 92 (1989) 315–328. C. Newlands, "The Simile of the Fractured Pipe in Ovid's *Metamorphoses,*" *Ramus* 15 (1986) 143–153. A. B. Taylor, "'When Everything Seems Double': Peter Quince, the Other Playwright, in *A Midsummer Night's Dream,*" *Shakespeare Survey* 56 (2003) 55–66. A.B.T.

Pythagoras and Pythagoreanism

Pythagoras (who lived from approximately 570 to 475 BCE and was born on the island of Samos) was a political, religious, philosophical, and scientific reformer whose fame in his own lifetime rested as much with his learning as it did with his mores. What gave the Pythagorean tradition such a long-lived reputation was the tendency of its adherents to seek, to define, and—for some—to practice a suitable *bios,* or "way of life" (cf. Plato, *Republic* 600B). Pythagoras is said to have traveled to the East and gained wisdom there; he eventually returned, settling in southern Italy, in what is now Calabria, in the city Croton. He served as the organizer of political life, a cult leader, and a figure who left behind a body of thought and social practices unified enough to be considered a *bios* that existed in social memory for a long time thereafter (Burkert 1972).

As is true of many early Greek philosophers, we have few contemporary sources concerning Pythagoras and no writings directly attributable to him. It is probable that Plato adopted a number of Pythagorean doctrines and in so doing transformed them, even as he also assured their continuance. From Plato onward it becomes impossible to separate the Platonic from the Pythagorean. Themes of transmigration, rewards and punishments after death, veneration for mathematics, and a propensity to idealize unity all became linked to Pythagoreanism after Plato.

Still, it was only in late antiquity that certain key features coalesced. Two Neopythagorean Platonists, Porphyry and Iamblichus, wrote biographies of Pythagoras that show to the modern scholar how interlinked Platonism and Pythagoreanism had become by that time. Porphyry (234–305 CE) was a student of Plotinus (205–270), and Iamblichus (245–325) a student and eventual antagonist of Porphyry. In both biographies Pythagoras' doctrines are presented alongside copious, personality-revealing anecdotes, the presence of which indicates the authors' search for a style of life commensurate with elevated philosophical doctrines.

Pythagoras is presented in these biographies as a wonder-working holy man whose soul was sent by Apollo to humanity. As a child his aspect was so appealing that he was revered and believed divine. Upon reaching early adulthood he had already learned proper diet, abstaining from meat because it compels one to sleep more. His Eastern travels are highlighted, until his return to Greece in his 56th year, when he unfolded the secrets to living well: "The best constitution, concord among people, communion of goods among allies, worship of the gods, pious respect for the dead, legislative activity and education, silence, respect for other living things, self-control and temperance, intelligence, affinity toward the divine, in short whatever is desired by lovers of learning, he brought to light" (Iamblichus, *Life of Pythagoras* 6). In sum, by this point Pythagoras had become what he has been ever since: a canvas on which can be depicted doctrines, behaviors, and attitudes considered characteristic of wisdom in the painter's own time and place.

An important part of the Pythagorean way of life had to do with secrecy. Secret teachings represented a means of designating insiders even as they helped define the boundaries of the community. Foremost among these teachings was that of the transmigration of souls. An individual soul, conceived as immortal, remained alive despite the dissolution of the body. It would then pass into another body as its animating force. In later Pythagorean tradition the soul represented a means by which one might suggest affinities with other living beings. For example, Pythagoras is reputed to have said that he had in an earlier life been Euphorbus, a Homeric hero who himself told of the fates of souls in Hades (Heraclides Ponticus, at Diogenes Laertius 8.4). This notion suggests that the historical Pythagoras was seen as a shamanic figure, one who practiced dormition in dark places such as caves and underground sites, coming back to the light to lead his comrades and to tell the divinely inspired truths he learned during his time away from the day-to-day world. Another early Greek philosopher who was considered a Pythagorean, Empedocles, is known to have done the same (Kingsley 1995). In one sense, this practice represents a visionary side to Pythagoras; in another, a way to gain perceived sanctity, status, and leadership by seeming close to the divine. Naturally associated with the belief in transmigration was vegetarianism, as one could never be sure if the animal one was eating was a former associate. Some ancient sources speak of this vegetarianism among Pythagoreans as complete, others as partial.

Many early Greek philosophers sought to locate an element of the universe that could be deemed essential, something without which the phenomenological world could not exist. For Pythagoras this element was number. Since the time of Aristotle himself (*Metaphysics* 1), many interpreters have been puzzled by the Pythagorean fascination with number. If "all things are number," difficulty arises in deciding just how this is the case. Do things as we see them "imitate" number? Are numbers somehow themselves physical things? Are "all things numbers" only in the sense that physical objects are subject to measurement and hence possess properties that can be reduced to numbers? Is number somehow divine, and did numbers actually (mysteriously) generate the natural world?

It is likely that over time self-identified Pythagoreans could and did give affirmative answers to all these questions depending on context. Pythagoras himself came from a merchant society, so that all things at one level (that of trade) could be reduced to number. Yet number possessed a mysterious significance, and the phenomena of the natural world were secondary to this significance. Justice was represented by the number 4, a square number that symbolized perfectly the reciprocity for which justice stood. Number also played a role in the birthing of the universe, when the two opposing numerical principles, "limit" and "the unlimited," came together. Not unlike the cosmogonic myths of the Orphics, Pythagorean cosmogony melded the mythic with the observable. Pythagoras is credited with the discovery of the harmonic ratios in music, and here too one sees an admixture of various areas often considered separately. The entire range of musical notes is unlimited; harmony is created when limits are placed at certain points within that range. This harmony can be heard, many Pythagoreans believed, in the movements of the celestial spheres, proceeding in regular intervals and patterns. Here natural philosophy, cosmology, and cosmogony are linked.

Pythagoras' reputation as more than human was apparently acquired even during his lifetime. Some considered him a manifestation of the god Apollo, venerated by the mythical northern Greeks inhabiting Hyperborea. Others believed he possessed a golden thigh, also proof of divinity. After his death his suprahuman reputation led some self-identified Pythagoreans to attribute any doctrine of significance to him. He became the archetypal sage, and if something was discovered that seemed wise, it stood to reason that he was its original source, even in the absence of direct testimony.

As Christianity developed side by side with late antique Pythagoreanism, so too did Pythagorean Platonists fashion the story of their founder in similar terms. Pythagoras, they said, had performed wonders. For example, Iamblichus tells us that once, on the way to Croton, Pythagoras astounded local fishermen by guessing the number of fish they had caught. He then ordered them to return the fish to the sea, which they did, after which he paid them the price that their catch would have garnered. The fishermen spread the word of this incident, and all who heard were seized with the desire to see the stranger; when they did, his countenance revealed his true, divine nature. It was then, again according to Iamblichus, that Pythagoras began teaching at the gymnasium, revealing truths about the gods, conduct, and erudition. Pythagoras was also said to have promulgated certain sayings, known later as the *akousmata* (things heard) or as the "symbols" of Pythagoras. Though in his own lifetime these sayings represented cultic precepts, commands that made sense precisely because of the authority of the person promulgating them, a later tradition of interpretation developed within which authors sought to unveil the esoteric meaning thought to lie behind the sayings.

Late antique Pythagorean Platonists also developed two cultural characteristics that were similar to emerging Christian practices. First, like Christians they developed a mistrust of the body and a tendency to subject it to tests, in order to purify it and allow the mind to function undisturbed. *Askēsis* (the word originally meant training or exercise) became spiritual training and in certain circles denoted what we now mean by *asceticism:* the denial of bodily pleasures, the better to achieve the goal of self-mastery and ritual purity. Pythagoras was said in some accounts to enjoin his prospective disciples, after they had passed through a regimen of strenuous mental exercise, to five years of silence. Only if they successfully learned his teaching were they then permitted into the inner circles of the *mathēmatikoi,* or the "learned." Second, Pythagorean Platonists developed rituals thought to serve the purpose of channeling divinity. Especially with Iamblichus these rituals became prominent, and some practices grew to be called collectively *theourgia,* "theurgy," a word whose Greek etymology suggests "doing divine work" or even "working the divine." Iamblichus' theurgy was believed to function because of the ritual. These rituals might involve singing, chanting, vestments, the arrangement of garments, or the use of other such physical means to gain contact with the divine. (Saint Augustine, 354–430, would argue similarly that Christian sacraments functioned *ex opere operato,* or "from the work having been worked.")

By this stage it is impossible to separate Pythagoreanism from Platonism. The temptation to do so has more to do with the passions of modern classificatory scholarship than it does with the intentions of thinkers who considered themselves Pythagoreans. This unity, in practice, of strains of thought that later thinkers have tried to keep separate also reflects a notion that from late antiquity onward became the common property of Pythagorean Platonists: the unity of all wisdom. All great thinkers had something to teach us. Pythagoras had traveled far and wide for a reason; Plato had written a set of dialogues that represented a treasury of wisdom; Aristotle had taught basic rules of reasoning and systematic thought; in short, one could not afford to ignore any one school of thought. It was up to the interpreter to bring the truth out of even seemingly contradictory thinkers. When the modern history of ancient philosophy took shape in the late 18th and 19th centuries, Plato and Aristotle came to be seen as representatives of rival systems of thought. No late ancient thinker saw them in that way. They were separate in many respects, of course, and they might indeed disagree on specific issues, but it was assumed that the truly wise interpreter could bring out their agreement on central issues (Gerson 2005). This idea of the unity of truth is essentially a canon-expanding idea. It was with Iamblichus that reputedly ancient texts that belonged to "Eastern" wisdom (the *Corpus Hermeticum,* for example) were adopted into the Pythagorean Platonic tradition.

The notion that there existed a unity of truth that could be accessed in various ways eventually served to separate Christians from Pythagorean Platonists, though it resurfaced in the 15th century. Christianity remained strongly tied to notions of bodily purity, sacramentally efficacious rituals, disdain for worldly fame, and other staples of the Pythagorean way of life, but on this issue they disagreed. The Judeo-Christian God was the god who said, "I am Who am," and his believers were to have no other gods but him. Though most intellectuals in late antiquity, pagan or Judeo-Christian, believed in the existence of one supreme being, translatability divided the two groups. A number of the Platonizing Pythagoreans of late antiquity were anti-Christian. This fact, together with the general loss of much Greek literature, served to prevent the Pythagorean-inflected texts of Porphyry, Iamblichus, and others from entering into Western medieval canons.

Pythagoras was remembered, however, during the Middle Ages, as the father of two of the Seven Liberal Arts: arithmetic and music. Numerous artistic representations attest to this status, from illuminated manuscripts to the relief sculptures on the portal of the Cathedral of Chartres. Boethius (480–ca. 525) had authored the key texts, *On Arithmetic* and *On Music,* through which Pythagoras was known as perhaps the greatest ancient authority in those fields. The *Timaeus,* the only Platonic dialogue to survive (via Latin translation) into Western medieval thought, was often interpreted as Pythagorean owing to its explanations of harmonies and numerical ratios. William of Conches (ca. 1080–1160), a member of the Platonizing school of Chartres, even went so far as to say that Plato was a Pythagorean (Joost-Gaugier 2006).

It was not until the 15th century that a fuller range of sources could be appreciated. All the principal sources used by modern scholars to reconstruct Pythagorean thought were available in Latin translations by the end of that century. Diogenes Laertius' *Lives of the Philosophers,* an important late antique biographical compilation, was translated in the 1430s by the Camaldolese friar Ambrogio Traversari. Book 8 of that work presents a lengthy life of Pythagoras. The 1460s saw the philosopher Marsilio Ficino (1433–1499) commence his monumental task of translating Greek sources into Latin, among which figure certain texts by Porphyry and Iamblichus. Ficino helped revive the idea of the unity of truth that the late ancient Platonizing Pythagoreans had done so much to animate, even as he placed blame on Pythagoras for certain ideas, like the transmigration of souls, that Ficino believed had been mistakenly attributed to Plato (Celenza 1999). During the 15th and 16th centuries a minor tradition arose of interpreting the sayings of Pythagoras, in which thinkers such as Leon Battista Alberti took part (Celenza 2001). The revival of the idea of the unity of truth also led to Pythagoras' assimilation into early modern and eventually modern esotericism.

The attractions of Pythagoreanism to early modern thinkers, like those of Hermes Trismegistus, the Magi, and other semimythical ancient figures for whom no authentic writings survived, lay in its mystery and in the manner in which it represented a wisdom always superior to contemporary norms. After the recovery of ancient sources that especially marked the early Renaissance, the fascination with mathematics, mystery, hidden wisdom, and a culture for initiates continued to manifest itself in later evocations of Pythagoreanism, mixed as it had been since late antiquity with Platonism.

Copernicus cited in the preface to his *On the Revolution of the Heavenly Spheres* (1543), as influences upon his thinking, various Pythagoreans known to have speculated about the physical structure of the universe; he also cited (as an explanation for his reluctance to publish) the Pythagorean tradition of keeping certain things secret. Johannes Kepler saw his mathematical laws for the motions of the planets as fundamentally Pythagorean, as can be observed even in the title of his most famous book, the *Harmonics of the World* (1619), a work in which he hoped to restore knowledge of the "universal music" that permeated the universe (Kahn 2001, 161–172).

Beyond the natural sciences, early modern European esotericism drew on the figure of Pythagoras. Rosicrucian writings of the early 17th century used Pythagorean imagery, as did thinkers such as Robert Fludd (1574–1637), who considered his own musical writings to have Pythagorean inspiration. Early modern examples could be multiplied, but it should be remembered that Pythagoras by then was considered one of many sages who had contributed to the provenance of authentic, yet often hidden, pathways to knowledge. Any number of modern secret societies and self-styled wise men, too, credited Pythagoras as an inspiration. It would remain for modern scholarship, from the late 18th century onward, to disentangle Pythagoras and Pythagoreanism from the many legends and achievements that had accrued over time.

BIBL.: Walter Burkert, *Lore and Science in Ancient Pythago-*

reanism, trans. Edwin Minar (Cambridge, Mass., 1972). Christopher S. Celenza, *Piety and Pythagoras in Renaissance Florence: The Symbolum Nesianum* (Leiden 2001) and "Pythagoras in the Renaissance: The Case of Marsilio Ficino," *Renaissance Quarterly* 52 (1999) 667–711. Lloyd P. Gerson, *Aristotle and Other Platonists* (Ithaca 2005). William K. C. Guthrie, *A History of Greek Philosophy,* 6 vols. (Cambridge 1962–1981), vol. 1. S. K. Heninger, Jr., *Touches of Sweet Harmony: Pythagorean Cosmology and Renaissance Poetics* (San Marino 1974). Christiane L. Joost-Gaugier, *Measuring Heaven: Pythagoras and His Influence on Thought and Art in Antiquity and the Middle Ages* (Ithaca 2006) and *Pythagoras and Renaissance Europe: Finding Heaven* (Cambridge 2009). Charles H. Kahn, *Pythagoras and the Pythagoreans: A Brief History* (Indianapolis 2001). Peter Kingsley, *Ancient Philosophy, Mystery, and Magic: Empedocles and Pythagorean Tradition* (Oxford 1995).

C.C.

R

Rabelais, François

French Humanist and physician (ca. 1483–1494 to 1553); the author of *Gargantua* and *Pantagruel.* He was born near Chinon, where Joan of Arc in 1429 had identified the future king Charles VII disguised among a crowd of courtiers. The lime-rich tufa soil there still produces fine white wine. Rabelais may have studied law before he joined the Franciscans around 1510, becoming a friar in 1520. He began to learn Greek, which was forbidden by French theologians: his books were confiscated. Guillaume Budé, a contemporary, wrote a letter (in Greek) about the absurdity of Rabelais's being persecuted for his great love of the Greek language. Rabelais matriculated in medicine at Montpellier in 1530, lecturing on Greek texts of Hippocrates and Galen. In 1532 he published a pocket edition of Hippocrates' *Aphorisms* and Galen's *Art of Raising Children* and, pseudonymously, his *Pantagruel.* He corresponded with Erasmus and was a protégé of the Du Bellays and Marguerite de Navarre; he also read and admired Teofilo Folengo's cheesy macaronic mock epic *Baldus* (1517–1540), which offered a partial precedent for his own work. Rabelais's excoriation of Scholastic theology and his support for Catholic reform and French independence from papal authority provoked edicts of censorship (1543, 1544), although the *Third Book* (*Tiers livre,* 1546) was published by royal privilege.

Rabelais's fictional world of giants has two touchstones: the Scholastic measures ignorance; the classical measures sophistication and wisdom. In *Pantagruel,* Scholasticism becomes an intolerable confinement: the giant cannot burst the chains of his cradle but must carry the burden on his back until freed by his father, who realizes that Pantagruel has been given nothing to feed on and thus recommends that he learn Greek. In *Gargantua* (ca. 1534), a prequel to *Pantagruel,* the prologue's first sentence cites Plato's *Symposium,* the archetype of the intoxicated philosophy that Rabelais, like Plato in that dialogue, self-mockingly creates. *Gargantua,* like the *Symposium,* is a Silenus box, a figurine of the tipsy god used as a container for treasures, in this case arguments of unparalleled sobriety.

For Rabelais, Greek is the foundation. *Pantagruel*'s first paragraph cites the Greeks even before the Bible. Pantagruel's father writes a letter (chap. 8) defining the Humanist program: first Greek, then Latin (with Plutarch and Plato, then Cicero as models) and the biblical languages. The Greeks first made law, though it cannot be properly understood without Ciceronian Latin. A character possibly modeled on Thomas More cites Plato before Solomon when he requests a debate. The Elysian Fields, not Hell, hold the dead, nearly all of them from classical history and literature. In those fields, a characteristic Rabelaisian *bouleversement* makes Dido (queen of Carthage) and Penthesilea (a tragic Amazon) into shopgirls. The first library at the utopian Abbey of Thélème contains books in Greek, followed by libraries for Latin and the modern languages (*Gargantua,* chap. 53).

Whereas *Pantagruel* was like Plato's Silenus box, the *Third Book* is characterized in its prologue as being like Diogenes' barrel, from which he observes France's bellicose activities. This book's debate over whether Pantagruel's companion Panurge should marry sparks hundreds of classical allusions, culminating in a proposal to discover his destiny through the *sortes Vergilianae,* the traditional practice of casting one's lot by selecting lines from the *Aeneid.* Pantagruel's authority for using Virgil comes from Plato's *Crito* (44B), where the imprisoned Socrates foresees his death when a dream figure alludes to the passage in Homer's *Iliad* concerning Achilles' threatened departure from the siege of Troy. Pantagruel also cites ancient

Romans who used Homer and Virgil. Each line drawn from Virgil predicts a hellish marriage for Panurge, who perversely construes them all as predicting such hyperbolic glory that he will wind up castrating the randy Jupiter.

Rabelais began to use his own name in the *Third Book,* and the dedicatory letter and prologue of the second edition of the *Fourth Book* (*Quart livre,* 1552) begin with his old friends Galen and Hippocrates. These most authoritative doctors recommend moderation and encourage making the patient happy; Rabelais himself suggests having three drinks. Pantagruel's survey of strange deaths tells stories about Alexander and Anacreon before he takes up the Roman who fatally held in his wind in the presence of the emperor (chap. 17). Slapstick becomes mourning, as his moving account of Guillaume du Bellay's death merges seamlessly into a Christianized version of Plutarch's reference to a mysterious voice announcing the death of Pan (chaps. 27–28).

The authenticity of the *Fifth Book* (*Quint livre*) has been debated ever since its publication 11 years after Rabelais's death in 1553. Its classical allusions are characteristically rich, however: the first island adventure alone draws on Plato, Ovid, Homer, Pythagoras, Aesop, Anaxagoras, and Democritus to satirize corruption in the Church. Pantagruel's company soon meets Aristotle's 1,800-year-old goddaughter and eventually reaches the classically built Temple of the Holy Bottle: the Greek for the maxim "In Wine, Truth" (Latin *In vino veritas*) is inscribed on its door, and the walls depict Bacchus at war. Leading their advance guard is Silenus (recalling the prologue to *Pantagruel*), and bringing up the rear is Pan, from the *Fourth Book.* Calling on Bacchus and Noah, Panurge finally gets the answer to his question about marrying: Drink! It is explained that Greek *oinos,* wine, is like Latin *vis,* force. Like Odysseus, the travelers are given bags of wind (not, for once, Rabelaisian flatulence); in the end, they pass through a land more temperate than Tempe, greener than Thermischyra, more fertile than Hyperborea, and, ultimately, as delightful as Rabelais's own native Touraine.

Rabelais's attitude toward his classical patrimony is complex: he plunders it for similes, parodies it, and venerates it. *Gargantua* alludes to the *Symposium*'s Androgyne, but where Aristophanes' halved humans' faces turn in opposite directions as they seek their missing counterparts (189E–190A), Gargantua's emblem shows "two heads, one turned towards the other, four arms, four feet, and two asses, just as Plato says" (chap. 8). Plato, of course, does not exactly say this; Rabelais renders graphic Aristophanes' idea that intercourse substitutes for psychic wholeness. The emblem reaches Christian transcendence with the phrase (in Greek) "Charity seeketh not her own" (1 Corinthians 13:5). The *Fourth Book* gives an equally complex metaphor for Rabelais's relationship to antiquity. When words come out of thin air, the Pythagorean travelers expect to see the floating head of Orpheus, but it is instead the thawing sounds of a battle on the frozen sea (chaps. 55–56). Disembodied words seem to speak to them from the past, as do the words of classical authors frozen in place in writing, often about ancient battles. Modern science, however, explains that they hear the sound of cannon fire: the new learning is not Diogenes' tub; rather, it serves the wars of the new nations. Yet Rabelais himself seems to be thawing antiquity into warm new life: the dizain by Hugues Salel (a noted translator of Homer) that is an epigraph to the author's prologue to book 2 of *Pantagruel* praises him as a new Democritus; Joachim du Bellay compares him to Lucian and writes, "He . . . has made Aristophanes be born again" (*Défense et illustration de la langue française,* 2.12).

BIBL.: M. A. Screech, *Rabelais* (Ithaca 1979). Florence M. Weinberg, *The Wine and the Will: Rabelais's Bacchic Christianity* (Detroit 1972). E.M.H.

Racine, Jean Baptiste

Preeminent French tragedian (1639–1699). Unlike Shakespeare, about whose training in the classics little is known, Racine had extensive schooling in Latin and Greek. Orphaned in 1643 at the age of three, he was educated at the Jansenist convent school of Port-Royal and the Collège de Beauvais. In addition to Latin, Port-Royal placed great emphasis on Greek, which was unusual for the time, and Racine developed into a competent Hellenist.

Scholarship on Racine's classical influences draws on several types of evidence. He wrote marginal notes—translations, summaries, and commentary—in his Greek and Latin books. He also translated several Greek texts into French, including approximately the first quarter of Plato's *Symposium,* part of Diogenes Laertius' *Life of Diogenes the Cynic,* and passages of Aristotle's *Poetics.* He also mentions in the preface to each of his tragedies the classical sources for the play, although these claims are not necessarily to be taken at face value.

Greek writers with whom Racine was most familiar include Homer, Sophocles, Euripides, Aristotle, Plato, Plutarch, and Heliodorus. Important Latin influences are Seneca, Ovid, Horace, Cicero, and Virgil—at school Racine probably memorized entire books of the *Aeneid.* For his historical tragedies he consulted a wide array of Greek and Latin historians, including Appian of Alexandria, Cassius Dio, Plutarch, Tacitus, Livy, Suetonius, Quintus Curtius, Justinus, and Florus.

During his short and concentrated career as a playwright (1664–1677) he composed nine tragedies, of which all but one, *Bajazet* (1672), have Greek or Latin sources. The four mythological plays are principally Greek in inspiration: *La Thébaïde, ou Les frères ennemis* (1664), based mainly on Euripides' *Phoenissae* (with a possible debt, denied in Racine's preface, to Seneca's version); *Andromaque* (1667), inspired by the *Iliad,* the *Aeneid,* and Euripides' *Andromache; Iphigénie* (1674), drawn mainly from Euripides' *Iphigenia at Aulis;* and *Phèdre* (1677), which relies heavily on Euripides' and to a lesser extent on Seneca's *Hippolytus.* Racine also wrote notes for the first act of a planned *Iphigénie en Tauride,* a play he never composed. As for his four historical tragedies, three of them—*Britannicus* (1669), *Bérénice* (1670), and *Mithridate* (1673)—dramatize events from Roman history, whereas only one—*Alexandre le Grand* (1665)—deals with Greek material. Thus, the distinction between his mythological and historical tragedies coincides largely with that between Greek myth and Roman history. Although his tragedies have been described as Senecan, Racine himself downplayed a connection to the Latin tragedian. He also wrote one comedy, *Les plaideurs* (1668), partly inspired by Aristophanes' *Wasps.* Later in life he composed two sacred tragedies drawn from the Bible, *Esther* (1689) and *Athalie* (1691).

Although Racine sometimes observes differences that separate the classical world from his own, he also voices his belief in universal values that they share. His preface to *Andromaque* characterizes his decision to make Andromaque's threatened child be the son of Hector rather than of Pyrrhus (Greek Neoptolemos), as "conforming to the idea that we now hold of that princess." And yet the fundamental similarity of the classical world and his own is expressed by his preface to *Iphigénie:* "I have recognized with pleasure, by the effect produced on our theater by everything I have imitated from Homer or Euripides, that good sense and reason are the same in all centuries. The tastes of Paris conform to those of Athens. My public has been moved by the same things that once brought tears to the eyes of the wisest people in Greece and inspired Euripides' reputation as extremely tragic, *tragikotatos,* that is, able to excite great compassion and terror, which are the true effects of tragedy."

Indeed, while he held Homer and Sophocles in particularly high esteem, his greatest Greek influence is Euripides. The opposition between Racine's unstable protagonists and the resolute characters associated with his most important predecessor and rival, Pierre Corneille (1606–1684), is somewhat analogous to the contrast often drawn between Euripides' volatile heroes and the more steadfast figures of earlier Greek tragedy. If classical tragedy stages—and questions—the heroic values of the rising nation-state, the idealism of Corneille's early tragedies was undermined a generation later by Racine quite as dramatically as Aeschylean and Sophoclean characters and plots were deconstructed by Euripides. Exemplifying what Paul Bénichou (1948) terms the "demolition of the hero," Racine, like Euripides, regularly challenges the good faith, constancy, and validity of his characters' moral stances.

His universalizing tendency may also be seen both in his relationship to Aristotle's *Poetics* and his creation of a tragic universe of ill-defined cultural contours. He was more interested in Aristotle's discussion of the effects that tragedies produce on the audience than in the specific formal considerations that preoccupied most French theoreticians of the period, who had transformed Aristotle's descriptive observations about drama into a prescriptive aesthetic and ethical code overseen by the Académie Française, founded four years before Racine's birth. Unlike Corneille, whose career was launched before the founding of the Académie, he is known for his effortless conformity to the rules of theater, what George Steiner (1961) calls "Racine's unworried, persuasive use of the unities" of time, place, and action. Indeed, this streamlining effect of Racinian as opposed to Corneillian tragedy is a major factor that distinguishes Racine from Euripides, whose often unwieldy tragedies tend toward complicated and disjointed plots. Nevertheless, although Racine takes great care in choosing the moments and places at which the action of his plays begins, what makes his tragedies into seamless expressions of classical perfection is not the concentrated re-creation of a specific time and place but rather the forgoing of a sense of time and place altogether, the transcendence of the particularities of an individual culture. Thus, despite the strong influence exerted on Racine by models from classical antiquity, he can be seen as the consummate French classical tragedian less because he returns to classical sources—he is certainly not alone in that—than because he embodies one of the principal paradoxes of the period: he appropriates classical myths that are not French in origin and transforms them into stories unanchored in time and place, all the while illustrating the superiority of the French classical aesthetic.

BIBL.: Paul Bénichou, *Morales du grand siècle* (Paris 1948). Richard E. Goodkin, *The Tragic Middle: Racine, Aristotle, Euripides* (Madison 1991). R. C. Knight, *Racine et la Grèce* (Paris 1951). Georges May, *D'Ovide à Racine* (Paris 1949). George Steiner, *The Death of Tragedy* (New York 1961). Ronald Tobin, *Racine and Seneca* (Chapel Hill 1971). R.E.G.

Raphael

Italian painter and architect (1483–1520), more fully Raphael Sanzio, Italian Raffaello Santi, of Urbino. In his *Gedanken über die Nachahmung der griechischen Werke in der Malerei und Bildhauerkunst* (1755), Johann J. Winckelmann states, "The noble simplicity and quiet grandeur of Greek statues constitute the true, characteristic sign of the Greek writings of better times . . . ; and these are also the qualities that mark Raphael's particular grandeur, which he obtained by imitating the ancients." In this passage, one of many dedicated to the Italian artist by the author of the *Geschichte der Kunst des Altertums,* Winckelmann confirms the classical essence of Raphael's language by linking it directly to the art and literature of 5th-century BCE Greece. The idea that Raphael had established a special relationship with the art of the ancient world was developed well before the 18th century. Indeed, we can find the first signs of it in the proem to book 3 of Pietro Bembo's *Prose della volgar lingua* (1525), in a passage very probably written around 1515. There Michelangelo and Raphael are identified as the artists who have profited most from the study of Roman antiquity, so much so that it would be easier to say how close they are to the ancient masters than to establish a hierarchy between the two. The parallel that Bembo posits between these artists who investigated "beautiful ancient figures," "arches and baths and theaters," and the literati who studied the writings of the ancients is of a decisively humanistic stamp and can help explain the interest for ancient literature, and especially for Vitruvius, that we find in Raphael himself. There is nothing accidental about Giorgio Vasari's observation (ed. Milanesi 4.359) that in the *Fire in the Borgo* in the Vatican *Stanze*, "a sick old man is depicted, just like Virgil describes Anchises being carried by Aeneas."

Acknowledgments of Raphael's "classicism" increased, with different emphases, right after the artist's death. In his *De inventoribus rerum* (1521), Polydore Vergil, after mentioning some great painters of antiquity, praises Raphael for having "in all respects, as it were, restored (*restituit*) for the present the art of painting." In the epitaph that Pietro Bembo (if not Antonio Tebaldeo) composed for Raphael's tomb in the Pantheon, the painter is called *veterum aemulus* ("disciple of the ancients"). Vasari (4.335) notes that "the most famous ancient and modern poets" depicted in the *Parnassus* (*Stanza della Segnatura*) "were derived partly from statues, partly from medals, and many from ancient paintings," and that in *The Council of the Gods* in the Farnesina, "the forms of many lineaments and articles of clothing were clearly derived from antiquity." Attempts to find precise ancient sources for individual works of the painter also began early. According to Paolo Giovio, *The Council of the Gods* portrayed a figure of Mercury that was "similar to" (*a similitudine*) the Belvedere Antinous. According to Giovan Pietro Bellori (*Descrizzione delle imagini dipinte da Rafaelle d'Urbino*, 1695), this same ancient statue, along with the Belvedere Torso, was the model for the Jupiter and suppliant Venus in the vault of the Farnesina's loggia. And according to Stendhal (*Promenades dans Rome*, 1829), the Belvedere Torso was an object of special admiration for Raphael, "qui l'a reproduit dans le torse du Père éternel de la *Vision d'Ézéchiel*." The 19th century, first with F.-A. Gruyer's grand synthesis (1864) and then with the essay by Emanuel Loewy (1896), significantly an archaeologist, methodically confronted the problem of the ancient models at Raphael's disposal. In the course of the 20th century this question became an object of further, detailed analyses for both painting and architecture.

Beginning with *The Borghese Deposition* (1507) and building in a crescendo to the works of his final years, Raphael took the classical artistic patrimony available at the beginning of the 16th century as an object of study and of dialectical integration with the efforts of other artists of his time. On no occasion, among the countless derivations from classical art present in his works (and in those of his workshop), did Raphael see antiquity as a static repertory, but rather as a "generative grammar" that allowed, in every context, the assimilation and reelaboration of acquired forms. This is what happened in the drawing of his that was used for Marcantonio Raimondi's engraving of *The Judgment of Paris* (ca. 1513): figures from Roman sarcophagi depicting the same subject, in particular the one at the Villa Medici, are variously replicated, modified, and substituted according to a process that acquired, within a fully modern landscape, the corporeal plasticity of the ancient reliefs (and it was naturally in turn a model for Edouard Manet's *Dejeuner sur l'herbe*). This freedom in the face of models persisted even where the reflection on antiquity became programmatic and informed the general decorative system as well as the detail, as in Cardinal Bibbiena's *stufetta* and *loggetta* in the Vatican. The models come from the Domus Aurea, which was visited by Raphael and Giovanni da Udine, who, as Vasari notes (6.551–552), "were both left stupefied by the freshness, the beauty, and the excellence of the work." In the *Logge vaticane* (1519), the Domus Aurea is again the principal point of reference for Raphael and his workshop for the compositional structure, the individual decorative partitions, and even the recovery of ancient techniques (stucco); but even in this undertaking we witness the free combination of patterns and motifs taken from different sources (sarcophagi—especially Dionysiac ones—basreliefs, gems, coins, statues).

No less complex was Raphael's attitude toward classical subjects—from the *Stanza della Segnatura* to the Farnesina—since the clarity of the design and the limpidity of the forms always hid a program that was anything but conventional in its meanings. On one wall of the *Segnatura*, one lone space, Mount Parnassus with the Castalian Spring, accommodates the meeting of the Muses, Apollo with his lyre, the great poets of antiquity and the Middle Ages, and even some living poets. On the adjacent wall, the *School of Athens*, a grandiose ancient building with niches sheltering colossal statues (Apollo and Athena), hosts a full gathering of ancient thinkers, of whom only a few are recognizable with certainty: Plato, Aristotle, Diogenes, Pythagoras, Ptolemy, Socrates (the last with the silenic appearance described by ancient authors). Certainly advised by an intellectual close to Julius II (perhaps Giles of Viterbo), the painter constructed a synthesis of Greek philosophy based on the centrality of Plato and Aristotle, but at the same time he went much further, translating "into numerous acts of lively demonstration and ardent listening," as Jacob Burckhardt argued, "the thought and the knowledge of classical antiquity." Raphael's intention was not therefore to give form to a simple list of wise men, but rather to restore visually the process of philosophical understanding as conceived by the ancients: reflection and study, conjecture and demonstration, interrogation and explanation, teaching and learning. Not for nothing did Laurence Sterne precisely admire "the particular manner of the reasoning" (*Tristram Shandy*, 4.7) in the figure of Socrates, that is, the gestures of dialectic and of argumentation.

It is peculiar that, in light of this universally recognized practice of emulation, only a few drawings of ancient monuments have come down to us that can be attributed to Raphael with certainty. Standing out among these are the relief of the Trajanic frieze on side E of the attic of the Arch of Constantine (Munich, Staatliche Graphische

Sammlung 2460), dated to around 1512, and the drawing of the horse of the *opus Praxitelis* on the Quirinal (Chatsworth, Devonshire Collection 657), which contains some measurements, leading to the hypothesis that it might have been a preliminary study for a restoration project. Regarding architecture, there is an autograph drawing of the interior and the pronaos of the Pantheon (Florence, Uffizi 164A), quite probably datable to about 1506 and thus evidence that Raphael was in Rome around that time. The Pantheon is the subject of another, later drawing in which certain architectural details are accompanied by notes and measurements (London, Royal Institute of British Architects 13.1). Much better documented is the activity of Raphael's workshop, as seen especially in the Fossombrone Sketchbook (Biblioteca Passionei, Disegni 3), which for the most part contains drawings of ancient architecture and sculpture. Vasari's claim (4.361) that Raphael "kept draftsmen all over Italy, in Pozzuoli, and even in Greece" is supported by an engraving by Agostino Veneziano of the base of the Column of Marcianus in Constantinople, which bears the caption "The base of the column in Constantinople/sent to Rafelo [*sic*] of Urbino" ("Basamente d[e] la colona d[e] Costantinopolo/mandato a Rafelo da Urbino").

An episode around 1510 nicely illustrates the reputation that Raphael had acquired as an expert on antiquity a few years after having arrived in Rome. Vasari relates (7.489) that at the invitation of Bramante four sculptors had made wax copies of the Laocoön, the sculpture group discovered only a few years earlier, and that Raphael was summoned to judge and that he awarded the victory to the young Jacopo Sansovino. It was certainly thanks to this authoritativeness that in 1515 a brief of Leo X granted the artist the task of superintending the antiquities of the city of Rome as *praefectus,* a job whose significance and duties have often been misunderstood. Raphael was not asked to conserve the ancient monuments but rather, in his capacity as chief architect (an appointment that dates to 1514), to supervise the provisioning of materials for constructing St. Peter's. The *praefectus,* then, would have had to collect information, potentially useful for the construction of the new basilica, on the excavations in Rome (and within ten miles of the city). The papal brief specified that Raphael had to be consulted if any ancient monuments bearing inscriptions came to light, "the preservation of which would be worthwhile for the cultivation of literature and for improving the elegance of the Roman language" (trans. J. Shearman). Indeed, for several decades inscriptions had enjoyed a special status over other antiquities, and Fra Giocondo himself, who worked side by side with Raphael on the building site of St. Peter's, had compiled a collection of more than 2,000 of them. That the job of *praefectus* did not bring with it the duty of presiding over the city's antiquities is further demonstrated by a 1517 letter from Beltrando Costabili to Alfonso I d'Este in which he assures the lord of Ferrara that Raphael would look for "medals, heads, and figures" for the Este collection and check on the possibility of acquiring the so-called *Letto di Policleto,* a bas-relief that would also be cited in the *stucchi* of the *Logge vaticane.* An isolated piece of evidence, but not to be underestimated, also gives us a glimpse of the possibility that Raphael, too, possessed a collection of antiquities: Pierio Valeriano (*Hieroglyphica,* 1556) describes a statue seen in Raphael's house, identifiable, thanks to its Greek inscription, as an image of Philemon, the New Comedy poet.

A hazy episode has been incorrectly connected with Raphael's appointment as *praefectus.* Gabriele de' Rossi, in the will drawn up in the year of his death (1517), asked that his personal collection of antiquities remain intact and with his heirs in the family residence. He had, however, inserted a clause providing, in case a powerful individual tried to take possession of his collection "by force or by excessive [use of] favor," that it be transferred to the Palazzo dei Conservatori on the Campidoglio. In July 1518 a conflict arose between the conservators and Raphael over the possession of de' Rossi's collection. According to a notarial document, "Raphael of Urbino claims that he had received orders from the pope (*commissionem a sanctissimo domino nostro*) to take and remove these antiquities against the will and command of the aforementioned testator" (trans. K. W. Christian). Raphael's role in this affair, as well as the pope's, is unclear. The artist's involvement cannot be due to the position he received from the 1515 brief, since his bailiwick did not include fine sculptures like those in de' Rossi's collection, which, by the way, were well known to Raphael and to the artists in his workshop. Ultimately the collection was scattered and the sculptures went neither to the pope nor (except one statue) to the conservators.

Closer to the role of *praefectus* is instead an endeavor that was never realized. A report from Rome to the Venetian Senate (1519) describes the ruinous state of the mausoleum of Augustus and refers to the discovery of one of the two obelisks that had flanked it, and it refers as well to Raphael's idea to set the obelisk up in St. Peter's Square after a restoration (it was in three pieces). It is no coincidence that it was Baldassarre Peruzzi, an artist in Raphael's inner circle, who made a few drawings of the obelisk, accompanied by measurements.

It has been noted many times that Raphael's interest in architecture manifested itself even in his youthful paintings, and that in the Vatican *Stanze* and in the cartoons for the tapestries in the Sistine Chapel the painter dedicated ever greater attention to the historical plausibility of the edifices providing the background for his scenes. The passage of Pietro Bembo cited above vividly illustrates the notion that the classical world acts as a teacher to the moderns, on the one hand by way of its texts, on the other by way of its artifacts, including statues and reliefs as well as "arches and baths and theaters." It is no surprise, then, that in 1516 a troupe of literati (Pietro Bembo, Andrea Navagero, Agostino Beazzano, Baldassare Castiglione) accompanied none other than Raphael on a visit to Tivoli and Hadrian's Villa, as a letter by Bembo tells us. Architectural drawings—like those of the

Pantheon noted above—thus naturally take their place beside sketches dedicated to statuary and bas-reliefs, and both prompt the consultation of literary texts, in line with an integral approach to antiquity that Raphael had been able to observe in Fra Giocondo, who was an architect, the editor of Vitruvius (Venice, 1511), and an expert on epigraphy. Into this context fits the vernacular translation of Vitruvius that Raphael requested around 1519 from Marco Fabio Calvo, who had already translated the *Corpus Hippocraticum*. Both the manuscript (Bayerische Staatsbibliothek, Munich, It. 37)—from which it emerges that the text was translated "in Raphael's house . . . and at his request"—and a letter of Celio Calcagnini to Jakob Ziegler testify to the intimacy and the collaboration between the two; perhaps they had an illustrated edition of the ancient treatise in mind (Shearman 2003), as is also suggested by certain drawings in the Fossombrone Sketchbook (Nesselrath 1986). As for Vitruvius, Calcagnini maintains that "he not only expounds, but with the surest arguments either defends or rebukes, but so charmingly that no ill-will attaches to the rebuke" (trans. Shearman 2003).

The idea of verifying classical authors starting from surviving buildings comes up again in the letter to Leo X ("comparing works with their [the ancients'] writings"). The artist's use of Latin literature also receives confirmation, around 1519, in a letter to Castiglione in which he talks about the project for Villa Madama, the Medici residence under construction in the Roman suburbs. Here we find references not only to Vitruvius but also to the letters of Pliny the Younger in which the Laurentine and Tuscan villas are described. For its part, the project consisted in the attempt to restore the typology of the ancient suburban villa, complete with *diaetae*, hippodrome, baths, theater, *xystus*, and *cryptoporticus*.

The letter to Leo X has come down to us in three manuscript versions—the first in the archive of the counts of Castiglione (Mantova), a second belonging to Scipione Maffei and published in 1733, and a third in Munich (Bayerische Staatsbibliothek It. 37b)—which differ in many passages and which, since the 18th century, have provoked an intense discussion over the identity of its author. Today the consensus is that the text, conceived as a dedicatory letter, is the fruit of close collaboration between Raphael and Baldassare Castiglione. Disregarding the variants between the Mantova manuscript and the other two, which seem to derive from it independently, the content of the letter is articulated in two parts. The first records the destruction wrought for centuries on the body of the ancient city, by that time reduced to "bones . . . without flesh," which was caused by the barbarians but also tolerated by preceding popes, so that "much pity" is caused by the memory of demolitions that occurred only a few years earlier. Therefore, the pope is exhorted to take care of "the little that remains of this ancient mother of Italian glory and greatness," to exalt culture and the arts, in a continuous comparison with the ancients ("keeping the comparison with the ancients alive"), and to favor peace. The job given by the pope to Raphael of putting "ancient Rome into a drawing" would be able to be completed thanks to a direct study of its buildings in light of literary sources and a critical analysis of the style of the monuments. (It is here that Raphael proposed his chronological differentiation of the reliefs reused on the Arch of Constantine, which is still to a large degree accepted today.) The second part of the letter, which is much more technical, explains the tools and the graphic method—with the distinction of plan, elevation, and section—useful for precisely reconstructing the form of ancient buildings ("infallibly to re-create exactly how they stood"). A third part, which exists only in the Munich manuscript, returns to the methods of architectural relief and design and discusses, using Vitruvius and Pliny the Elder, the topic of the classical orders.

Contemporaries were struck by Raphael's rare capacity to combine artistic creativity and scholarship with the direct knowledge of antiquities. Though the poems composed upon his death (Calcagnini, Castiglione, Evangelista Maddaleni Capodiferro, Lilio Gregorio Giraldi, Francesco Maria Molza) exalt the unfinished project's complexity, they seem to regret the loss more of the scholar than of the artist. A Latin poem by Girolamo Aleandro insists on his cleverness in investigating and measuring ruins hidden underground, rescuing them from obscurity; Marcantonio Michiel, when recording his death in his personal diary (1520), connects his "description and painting of ancient Rome" with the brief of 1515, thus suggesting that the examination of excavations was undertaken for the plan of Rome. From this idea of Raphael as an archaeologist springs the hypothesis of Crowe and Cavalcaselle (1882), earlier put forth by J. D. Passavant (1839), that the sudden fevers that caused his death were brought on by "excavations in the refuse of old Rome."

BIBL.: Giovanni Becatti, "Raffaello e l'antico," in *Raffaello: L'opera, le fonti, la fortuna* (Novara 1968) 2:493–569. P. Pray Bober and Ruth Rubinstein, *Renaissance Artists and Antique Sculpture: A Handbook of Sources* (London 1986). Howard Burns, "Raffaello e 'quell'antiqua architectura,'" in C. L. Frommel, S. Ray, and M. Tafuri, eds., *Raffaello architetto* (Milan 1984) 381–404. Ferdinando Castagnoli, "Raffaello e le antichità di Roma," in *Raffaello: L'opera, le fonti, la fortuna* (Novara 1968) 2:571–586. Kathleen Wren Christian, "The De' Rossi Collection of Ancient Sculptures, Leo X and Raphael," *Journal of the Warburg and Courtauld Institutes* 65 (2002) 132–200, and "Raphael's *Philemon* and the Collecting of Antiquities in Rome," *Burlington Magazine* 146 (November 2004) 760–763. Nicole Dacos, *Le logge di Raffaello: Maestro e bottega di fronte all'antico* (Rome 1986). Francesco P. Di Teodoro, *Raffaello, Baldassar Castiglione e la lettera a Leone X* (Bologna 2003). François-Anatole Gruyer, *Raphaël et l'antiquité*, 2 vols. (Paris 1864). Rodolfo Lanciani, "Le piante di Roma antica e i disegni archeologici di Raffaello," *Rendiconti della Reale Accademia dei Lincei*, 4th ser., 3 (1894) 797ff. Emanuel Loewy, "Di alcune composizioni di Raffaello ispirate ai monumenti antichi," *Archivio Storico dell'Arte*, 2nd ser., 4 (1896)

241 ff. Glenn W. Most, *Raffael: Die Schule von Athen* (Frankfurt 1999). Arnold Nesselrath, "Raphael's Archaeological Method," in C. L. Frommel and M. Winner, eds., *Raffaello a Roma* (Rome 1986) 357–369, and "Raffaello e lo studio dell'antico nel Rinascimento," in C. L. Frommel, S. Ray, and M. Tafuri, eds., *Raffaello architetto* (Milan 1984) 405–408. John Shearman, "Raphael . . . 'fa il Bramante,'" in *Studies in Renaissance & Baroque Art Presented to Anthony Blunt* (New York 1967) 12–17, and *Raphael in Early Modern Sources (1483–1602)*, 2 vols. (New Haven 2003). C.F.

Translated by Patrick Baker

Ravenna

City in the southeastern Po Valley, close to the Adriatic coast; today capital of the Italian province of Ravenna. It was a primary political and cultural arena from late antiquity into the early Middle Ages (5th through 8th cents.). During that time the city also played a major role in mediating the relationship between the Latin West and the Greek East of Mediterranean Europe. For these reasons art and literature in recent centuries (beginning with the 19th) have often envisaged the city as a favorite, if largely conjectural, exotic location.

A Roman town since the beginning of the 2nd century BCE, Ravenna came to the foreground only ca. 402 CE, when the court of the Western Roman Empire settled there, as the city was deemed to be unconquerable by invasion via land owing to marshy surroundings, while the suburban harbor of Classe enabled connections with Constantinople, the Eastern imperial capital. Transformations and enlargements in urban planning took place; architecture and art became monumental, with the erection of religious buildings such as the Basilica of Saint John the Evangelist, the Mausoleum of Galla Placidia, the Orthodox Baptistery, and important civil enterprises such as the building of an encircling wall and the large palace area. A major event, the deposition of the emperor Romulus Augustulus, occurred there in September 476. The Western Roman Empire had come to its end.

The ensuing political and military upheavals led to success for the Ostrogoths and their king, Theodoric, who from Ravenna ruled his kingdom of Italy (*regnum Italiae*), subject to and (after 497) acknowledged by Anastasius, the Byzantine and sole "Roman" emperor in Constantinople. Theodoric, sensitive to cultural traditions, tried until his death in 526 to accommodate the city's Roman populace, the prevailing Greek-Eastern influences, and his native German element in a political program of mutual reconciliation, whose main visual expression was his mausoleum. Religious buildings—the palace church, known as Sant'Apollinare Nuovo, and the Arian Baptistery—introduced monumental figures against a continuous gold background, a style of Eastern origin.

There were some fruitful developments in art and literature: Theodoric's daughter Amalasuntha was considered as fluent in Latin and in Greek as in her native language, and a disciple of hers, Cassiodorus—a scion of the old Roman elite and an officer at the Gothic court himself—wrote a *History of the Goths* (ca. 530) in which his "barbarian" rulers were depicted with an archaizing veneer. This matched Theodoric's program of reconciliation as well as a wider trend at that time toward agreement and synthesis, as can be seen in the rise of Boethius, a noted scholar and a scion of the old Roman nobility, to high office at the Gothic court. Yet Boethius' brief experience of Ravenna (522–524) was short and ill-fated: he was suspected of treason and executed with a number of others thought to be too loyal to Byzantine political and religious interests. Yet Cassiodorus—who was probably Boethius' successor in office—mentions none of this.

During the last Roman imperial decades as well as Theodoric's reign Ravenna hosted social and cultural elites who required suppliers of arts and other luxury items. The city has thus been considered a possible seat for the production of famous masterpieces of manuscript illumination such as the Vergilius Romanus (codex Vat. lat. 3867)—perhaps a late antique revival of an idealized classical past—and the Codex Argenteus, a Gothic translation of the Gospels (now in Uppsala, Bibl. Univ. DG 1).

The war between the Goths and Byzantium (535–553) led to the Byzantine conquest of Ravenna (540), after which the city increasingly served as the empire's main Western outpost. This was true of politics as well as of art and architecture. New decoration in Sant'Apollinare Nuovo canceled the former Gothic styles; the Basilica of San Vitale, with its circular plan and mosaics representing the Byzantine emperors Justinian and Theodora, emphasizes the universal primacy of Constantinople. Yet the craftsmanship may have been local, as it occurs in other buildings of the same era, both religious (Basilica of Sant'Apollinare in Classe) and civil (the recently discovered House of the Stone Carpets, with elaborate mosaic floors).

From 585 Ravenna was the capital of the anti-Lombard Byzantine exarchate, slowly declining until it fell to the Lombards (751). A series of political developments then led the area of the former Ravenna exarchate to identify largely with the Roman Church's Patrimonium Petri (lands and estates controlled from Rome).

The quality of education in the schools of Ravenna can be inferred from the literary achievement of Venantius Fortunatus (later 6th cent.), but schools were especially needed for training civil officers. Political-administrative business generated mountains of texts connected to land surveys, bureaucracy, law, and even medicine. The illuminated Greek medical manuscript Dioscurides Neapolitanus may be a 6th-century production from Ravenna. Yet the political links with Byzantium did not seem much to widen the ambit of Greek language, for it was employed only for official uses.

Ravenna's archbishopric, established in 549, contributed to the survival of acceptable standards in written Latin, as in Agnellus' *Liber pontificalis Ecclesiae Ravennatis* (830–846), a biographical history of the Church and of churches in Ravenna. The city's celebrated craftsmanship in ivory, epigraphy, and mosaic also influenced the Carolingian renaissance in the 9th century. Some ancient arts and crafts traditions remain alive in Ravenna today.

BIBL.: A. Carile, ed., *Storia di Ravenna: Dall'età bizantina all'età ottoniana,* 2 vols. (Venice 1991–1992). P. Cesaretti, *Ravenna: Gli splendori di un impero* (Bologna 2005). F. W. Deichmann, *Ravenna: Hauptstadt des spätantiken Abendlandes,* 3 vols. in 4 (Wiesbaden 1969–1976). P.CE.

Renaissance

I. Byzantium

Byzantium did not experience a rebirth of the classical tradition after an intermediate period of obscurity, in the way the Italian Renaissance self-consciously revived the art, literature, and thought of Roman (and, to some extent, Greek) antiquity after what had been declared a "middle" age. The Byzantine Empire, by contrast, prided itself on having maintained its classical Greek heritage in a continuous, living tradition. Its cultural slogan was not "renewal" but *mimēsis* (imitation) of Greek antiquity.

There were, however, periods in Byzantine history when heightened literary and artistic activity followed a time of political instability that had brought a lull in cultural production, and when social and economic conditions facilitated elite or imperial patronage of the arts. At such times, artists often sought inspiration in models from late antiquity that provided mitigated, indirect access to pagan imagery. Authors and textual scholars, on the other hand, made direct use of ancient models. The only mitigation that was necessary to justify their interest in classical, pagan literature within a Christian intellectual framework was the concept of *chrēsis* (proper use) that the Church Fathers had formulated in the 4th century.

Most prominent are the Macedonian and Palaeologan renaissances. Some scholars have also suggested Theodosian, Justinianic, and Comnenian renaissances. Several of these renaissances have close chronological parallels in the West. The criteria that distinguish these periods from others are not merely the quantity of cultural production, but the conscious effort of gathering and commenting on materials from the past, which is reappropriated and actualized for use in the present.

The Theodosian renaissance signaled the solidification of a firmly Christianized empire that increasingly lacked a rival in the West. The period from 380 to 450, much more so than the reign of the emperor Constantine, saw several imperial projects on a grand scale: the use of world maps, the foundation of a university in Constantinople, the collecting and compiling of laws into the Theodosian Code. This was accompanied by the concerted effort to preserve the written heritage of the past by transferring it to a new medium, from papyrus to parchment.

Private initiative and patronage showed an interest in maintaining a link with the classical past: Proclus (ca. 410–485), head of the Academy in Athens, composed commentaries on several works of Plato that continued to be popular throughout Byzantine history. Lausus, the pious eunuch, would-be monk, and imperial chamberlain of the emperor Arcadius and empress Eudoxia, was famous for the collection of ancient statues he had assembled in his palace in Constantinople, including a statue of Zeus made by Phidias which had originally stood in the sanctuary at Olympia, and the Aphrodite of Cnidus by Praxiteles. At the end of the Theodosian period the work of a female patron, Anicia Juliana, especially her church of Saint Polyeuctus in Constantinople, with its fine sculptural relief decorated with an epigram, would define ecclesiastical architecture in the capital until it was outdone by Justinian. Anicia was also the recipient of a beautifully illuminated manuscript of the *Materia medica* of Dioscorides, a handbook of medicinal plants and additional texts on animals and birds (now in Vienna, Österreichische Nationalbibliothek, cod. med. gr. 1). Not too dissimilar from the taste of collectors, the repertoire of artists, whether book illuminators or silversmiths, borrowed heavily from the motifs and style of the early Roman Empire.

The concept of a Justinianic renaissance in the 6th century owes its origin to Procopius of Caesarea's effusive praise in his treatise *On Buildings* (*De aedificiis*) of the many civic, religious, and military building projects that were carried out as a result of the emperor's successful military campaigns in North Africa, in Persia, and in Italy. At Justinian's behest, the church of Hagia Sophia in Constantinople was rebuilt on a grand scale after a violent riot had burnt down one-third of the inner city. The spectacular churches in Ravenna (San Vitale, Sant'Apollinare in Classe, Sant'Apollinare Nuovo) constructed after the end of two decades of warfare, however, owed their existence not to the emperor but to the powerful local clergy, both Arian and Orthodox.

It was the Theodosian period that provided inspiration for these efforts. In Constantinople, the lavishly decorated mosaic floor of a large peristyle building in the palace area picked up motifs that were common in villa decoration in late Roman North Africa and Antioch. The decoration of luxury objects, including manuscript illumination, often employed themes from classical mythology that were depicted in a style reminiscent of the first centuries of the Roman Empire and its Theodosian reprise. Next to Justinian's building of Hagia Sophia, the greatest impetus of imperial initiative was the creation of several works for the study and administration of law, which became known as the *Corpus iuris civilis;* it included a new standardized law code compiled from existing laws, the Codex Iustinianus. In this regard Justinian's efforts may be seen as an attempt to reach back to the Theodosian project of legal codification.

The 6th century was also a period of intense literary activity. Most authors, however, did not enjoy imperial patronage. Agathias compiled a *Kyklos* of epigrams by ancient authors that he had collected, augmented by those from his own pen and those by his friends among the literati. Contemporary histories were written by Procopius and Agathias, who modeled themselves on Thucydides and Herodotus to such an extent that modern scholars have called their Christian beliefs into question, although their reluctance to employ specific Christian terms was probably only a reflection of their mimetic literary posture. Philosophy was another area of interest, and many commentaries on Plato and Aristotle were composed in the 6th century, before Justininan's order for the closure of the Academy in Athens in 529. The imperial decree to end this institution, which had been founded by Plato himself many centuries before, is a further reason why the notion of a Justinianic renaissance is problematic.

The Macedonian renaissance is still a convenient term for the flourishing cultural conditions that marked the 9th and 10th centuries. The beginning of this period is associated with the founder of the Macedonian dynasty, Basil I (r. 867–886), although the earliest stirrings of this renaissance can be pushed back to the 780s. This was the first renaissance in Byzantium that can be seen as a rebirth in the literal sense, following as it did upon the loss of one-third of Byzantine territory to Arab invasions and subsequent religious soul-searching and polemic during Iconoclasm (726–843). From the visual and written sources that survive, it appears that during this period of crisis aristocratic patronage and artistic production had been confined to the construction of local churches and monasteries (although there is some evidence for the allocation of imperial resources to the rebuilding of infrastructure), and literary production was limited to the composition of religious treatises. The beginnings of the Macedonian renaissance coincided with similar intellectual developments in the Carolingian kingdom in the West and at the court in Baghdad. It has been reported that Caliph al-Māʾmūn (r. 813–833) invited to his court Leo the Philosopher (ca. 790–ca. 869), who was widely famous for his expertise in science, mathematics, and philosophy and who owned several manuscripts of Ptolemy, Euclid, and Archimedes—an invitation that was politely declined.

The Macedonian renaissance was an intensive time of collecting, both in the imperial chancery and in the patriarchate, but what was being gathered and assembled were not artifacts of Greek antiquity in isolation, but rather precedent-setting materials of the Byzantine past since the 4th century, which had already absorbed and internalized Greek culture into a Christian framework.

The debate over the value of icons and their proper use in private and public worship that occupied the Church councils in the 8th and 9th centuries sent iconoclast and iconophile scholars searching for old manuscripts of texts of Church Fathers in the libraries of monasteries and of the patriarchate. The authenticity of these ancient proof texts was often questioned by the opposing side on the basis of text-critical or codicological arguments, such as cut-out pages, erasures, or changes in script. Religious and liturgical poetry experienced something of a revival during this time, including the works of the poetess Kassia.

In the imperial chancery, during the reign of Constantine VII Porphyrogenitus (r. 945–959), a large staff was employed to sift through existing, but probably increasingly deteriorating, records of administrative importance. This resulted in the production of several large compilations of extracts from older texts that addressed issues of provincial administration (*De thematibus*), diplomacy (*De legationibus*), military matters (*De insidiis*), foreign relations (*De administrando imperio*), and imperial ceremonies (*De ceremoniis*). As in the Theodosian renaissance, transfer to a new medium also played a role, in that older documents written in uncial letters were now transferred to minuscule script, which had gained acceptance in the second half of the 9th century, in a process referred to as *metacharactērismos* (transposition to a different script).

During the Macedonian renaissance collecting was closely connected to antiquarianism, the acknowledgment that a period had ended and that particular efforts were needed to ensure its preservation for the future. In this spirit Symeon Metaphrastes was commissioned by Constantine VII Porphyrogenitus to assemble a collection of all the saints' lives that circulated throughout the empire, and to tone down or spruce up their literary style in order to achieve a uniformity that was pleasing to contemporary tastes. The resulting *Lives* was a compilation of the biographies of 117 saints, arranged into 10 volumes in calendrical order, that became the standard reading material for the cult of saints throughout the empire.

The greatest antiquarian collector of literature was Photius (ca. 810–ca. 893), the erudite patriarch of Constantinople who engaged in a temporary schism with the papacy in Rome and sent Cyril and Methodius as missionaries to the Slavs. Like many other learned men, Photius held an appointment in the Church hierarchy that provided for his upkeep. For the benefit of his brother Tarasius he compiled his *Bibliothēkē* (*Library*), collecting short summaries of books that he knew, but not necessarily owned, describing their content, evaluating their style, and providing biographical details about their authors. This compilation is a major source of information for much of ancient literature that is now lost. Of the total of 280 chapters in the *Bibliothēkē,* the majority (158 versus 122) concern Christian rather than pagan authors.

Occupation with classical authors is also reflected in the Suda, an encyclopedic lexicon compiled probably in the second half of the 10th century that enjoyed great popularity in subsequent centuries. The work provides explanations of words, grammatical forms, persons, and concepts that occur in ancient authors (Aristophanes and Homer in particular) as well as in biblical writing, with additional mention of some more recent Byzantine authors.

The Macedonian renaissance produced the earliest extant manuscripts of Aristotle and Plato, many of them connected to Arethas, the learned bishop of Caesarea (d. after 932) who spent most of his life in Constantinople. He not only commissioned many manuscripts but also wrote annotations and scholia himself. It is possible to trace to Arethas two manuscripts of Aristotle and four of Plato as well as manuscripts of Aelius Aristides, Athenaeus, Dio Chrysostom, Euclid, Lucian, Marcus Aurelius, and perhaps a few others. In comparison to the 20 or so manuscripts of classical content that are connected to Arethas, only three manuscripts in his collection would have been relevant to his role as a bishop: a commentary on the Apocalypse by Andrew of Caesarea, a codex containing various writings of Church Fathers, and a copy of the Nomocanon of Fourteen Titles (a compilation of canon law).

In art and manuscript decoration the Macedonian renaissance picked up on Roman imperial styles and employed motifs from pagan mythology as well as from the Bible. By this time the pagan aspect of the Graeco-Roman heritage no longer presented a challenge to Byzantium's religious and cultural identity but was appreciated for its historical value and the aesthetic pleasure it could provide. Works produced during this period sought to imitate the styles developed under the Theodosian emperors. The Paris Psalter (Paris, Bibliothèque Nationale, MS gr. 139), for example, resembles the Vienna Dioscurides in its page layout. A colorful painted glass bowl now in the Museum of San Marco in Venice shows mythological scenes and portraits set in small roundels influenced by the style of ancient cameos, which had continued to be appreciated well into the 10th century, as were the ancient epigrams on buildings and other objects collected by the emperor Constantine VII during the heyday of this encyclopedic age. The revival of a number of artistic media, such as intarsia (mosaic), in this period also suggests an interest in building decoration and artistic forms that characterized luxury art and architecture in the period before Iconoclasm.

The Comnenian period (1081–1185) may not deserve the designation of a renaissance, but it coincides neatly with a parallel cultural revival in the 12th-century West. In Byzantium this renewed flourishing of literature and the arts was preceded by the securing of the northern frontier of the empire against the threat of the First Bulgarian Kingdom, in the time of Basil II, the Bulgar-Slayer (r. 976–1025). It ended abruptly with the capture of Constantinople by the Fourth Crusade in 1204. This cultural revival was marked by an affirmative use of and engagement with classical authors by a large number of literati in the orbit of the imperial court at Constantinople. Many of them also held offices in the Church that provided them with a source of income. The main classical authors to elicit interest were Aristotle and Plato, along with Homer.

One of the most colorful figures of this era was Michael Psellus (1018–ca. 1081), a true polymath who worked in close proximity to the imperial court. Originally trained in jurisprudence, he also had a lively interest in medicine, alchemy, and magic. Today he is best known for his historical work (*Chronographia*), although in his own time he was famous for his appreciation of ancient philosophy. John Italus (ca. 1025–ca. 1082), Psellus's pupil and successor as professor of philosophy who held a special appreciation for Aristotle, was excommunicated for being an unbeliever and a follower of the "foolish and empty wisdom of the pagans."

The only woman historian of Byzantium, Anna Comnena (1083–ca. 1153), wrote a history of the reign of her father and the dynasty's founder, Alexios I Komnenos, and also instigated the production of several commentaries on Aristotle. The ease with which intellectuals of this period claimed the classical and the Christian heritage as their own is reflected in the advice to future rhetoricians offered by Gregory Pardus (ca. 1070–1156), a teacher in the capital and later bishop of Corinth, who also wrote a treatise on ancient Greek dialects: "If you wish to get a good reputation nowadays you must write works that are a blend of rhetorical and philosophical notions . . . As an example . . . take works by the great Gregory the theologian, Basil the Great, (Gregory) the bishop of Nyssa, Psellos' orations and letters, Synesius, Themistius, Plutarch and many others who to our knowledge follow their lead" (trans. Wilson 1983, 186). The most prolific commentator of ancient authors, from Homer and Thucydides to Euripides and Pindar, was John Tzetzes (d. ca. 1180), who is credited with the composition of 60 books. His letters give insight into the fate of Byzantine literati of this time who had no other source of income than their intellectual credentials, rhetorical skills, and connections to the court and aristocrats. An equally prolific commentator on Homer was Eustathius, who later in life became bishop of Thessalonica (ca. 1115–1195 or 1196)—thus beginning a trend for the decentralization of instruction in the classics that would become even more prominent in the last centuries of Byzantium. Not long before the Latin conquest of Constantinople, the fearful populace of the capital attacked and destroyed the 30-foot-high statue of Athena outside the Senate house, believing that her outstretched arm was beckoning the Crusaders. At least 100 ancient statues adorned the city at this time, historical remnants of the past that no longer were believed to represent powerful pagan deities but were still regarded as inhabited by demonic forces.

The Palaeologan renaissance of the 13th and 14th centuries was a triumph of the aristocratic elite in the face of ineffectual imperial leadership and against the backdrop of continuous threat that the Ottomans posed to the very existence of the capital itself. The period began with the reconquest of Constantinople in 1261 by Michael VIII Palaeologus after 57 years of Crusader rule and ended with the capture of the city by the Ottomans in 1453. This was a fragmented empire, as Greek despots ruled semi-independently in Epirus, Mistra, and Thessalonica, and Latin lords remained in power in Achaea, Athens, and Cyprus; Crete served as a major commercial hub, administered by Italian city-states. The only kingdom that was independent was Trebizond. At this time, when the political and cultural dominance of Constantinople and its court was fading, several regional cultural centers emerged alongside it, but without questioning its political dominance: rhetors gave performances in the style of the ancient

Greeks before local aristocrats in Thessalonica, while philosophers debated and commented on Plato and Aristotle in Mistras. Aristocratic women in Constantinople, many of them living in convents, played an important role as patronesses of literature and art.

For the first time Byzantine scholars produced Greek translations of ancient and Christian Latin texts on a significant scale. It was also at this time that scholars like Demetrius Triclinius rediscovered ancient poetic meters and employed this knowledge of prosody in their editions and annotations of Greek tragedies and comedies. It became standard to focus on only three tragedies of Aeschylus, Sophocles, and Euripides, and an equal number of comedies of Aristophanes, with the result that what is now called the Byzantine Triad of each of these authors dominates the manuscript tradition. Many autograph copies of the works of these scholars survive in the major libraries of Europe, their identification being facilitated by the increasing habit of Byzantine scribes to identify themselves by name.

The first Greek translations from the Latin of Ovid, Cicero, Augustine, and Boethius were the work of Maximus Planudes (ca. 1250–ca. 1305), an influential scholar, translator, and commentator who lived most of his adult life as a monk and teacher in Constantinople. He was renowned for his commenting and editorial work on the texts of Homer, Hesiod, and Plutarch and for his collection of 395 epigrams, which were added to the Greek Anthology. His interest in Greek antiquity extended to its tangible remains as well: in his letters he mentions his visits to temples of Zeus near Miletus and in Cyzicus. The next notable translator after Planudes was Demetrius Cydones or Cydonius (ca. 1324–ca. 1398), who rendered into Greek not only Thomas Aquinas but also Augustine of Hippo and Anselm of Canterbury.

A different career was that of Theodore Metochites (1270–1332), prime minister (*mesazōn*) of the emperor Andronicus II, who devoted himself to the study of literature, manuscript collecting, and patronage of the arts. He acknowledged with some misgivings the overwhelming heritage of Greek writing that had accumulated over the centuries: "Practically every topic has been taken by others already, nothing is now left as our share at this late date; we cannot write either about matters divine, which one should expect to attend to as a first duty, or about the other subjects of secular learning" (trans. Wilson 1983, 259). Yet he assumes an unbroken continuity in this heritage, when he says: "The Greeks quite naturally recorded in writing all their own achievements, thinking it right to give them every attention, so transmitting them to the future, that is to us, partners and successors in their race and language" (264). Metochites paid for the restoration of a chapel in the Chora Monastery in Constantinople, which was adorned with a mosaic portrait that shows him wearing a tall headdress in the fashion of the day. This monastery also received his collection of manuscripts, which must have been extensive, judging from the fact that he refers to more than 80 ancient authors in his writings. In the period preceding the collapse of the Byzantine Empire, intellectuals such as Georgius Gemistus Pletho (ca. 1360–1452), who attracted pupils to the Peloponnesian city of Mistra, and his disciple Bessarion (ca. 1400–1472), who ended his life as a Catholic cardinal in Rome, fostered a renewed interest in Platonism both through their own writings and—in the case of Bessarion—through an extensive collection of manuscripts of ancient Greek authors.

In the realm of artistic production, the Palaeologi made reference to older Byzantine works as well as to ancient works. We know of two Palaeologan adaptations of the 10th-century Paris Psalter (in the Vatican Library and at Sinai). Church decoration, too, demonstrates a remarkable ability to include images from ancient periods—carved sarcophagi, echoes of ancient statues such as the *Spinario* (*Boy with Thorn*), and masks. These details, incorporated into sacred iconography, demonstrate an awareness and interest in the classical past on which Byzantium was built.

Byzantium had its own renaissances, but it also contributed to the Renaissance in Italy in various ways. Many scholars fled the Byzantine Empire in the 14th and 15th centuries and settled in Italy, where they taught ancient Greek and produced the first Greek grammar in print. The learned theologians who attended the Council of Ferrara (later Florence) in 1438–1439 brought with them manuscripts of classical texts that were much admired. The printing press of Aldus Manutius in Venice, the first to publish the works of ancient Greek authors, employed Greeks from the Byzantine Empire on its staff. In the 1470s printing presses in Italy began to issue Greek grammar books that had been composed by Byzantine authors based on late antique models.

BIBL.: H. Hunger, *Die hochsprachliche profane Literatur der Byzantiner* (Munich 1978) 1:4–62, 2:3–83. A. Kazhdan and A. Wharton Epstein, *Change in Byzantine Culture in the Eleventh and Twelfth Centuries* (Berkeley 1985). P. Lemerle, *Byzantine Humanism* (Canberra 1986; French ed. 1971). W. Treadgold, *Renaissances before the Renaissance: Cultural Revivals of Late Antiquity and the Middle Ages* (Stanford 1984). N. G. Wilson, *Scholars of Byzantium* (London 1983). C.R.

II. The West

In the West the term Renaissance, with a capital R, is inseparably associated with the period of Italian history from the 14th through 16th centuries and its cultural aftermath in the rest of Europe during the 16th and early 17th centuries. Although it was not until the 19th century that the Renaissance began to be thought of as a historical epoch, the idea that these centuries witnessed a rebirth, in which the revival of classical antiquity played a significant part, was proclaimed from the first by those engaged in recovering what they regarded as their lost heritage. Although they did not hesitate to blame their medieval predecessors for neglecting or even destroying this inheritance, modern scholarship has identified various earlier movements, similar to those in Byzantium, in which a renewed interest in the classical tradition featured prominently. It now seems that practically every medieval century after the end of the Dark Ages can claim a renaissance of its own.

The first of these—variously referred to as the Carolingian renaissance, revival, or *renovatio*—was an offshoot of Charlemagne's political and religious reform of his empire in the late 8th and early 9th centuries. Although the intellectual flowering and surge of scholarship that characterized this period was a crucial factor in the survival of the greater part of classical Latin literature, these pagan texts occupied only a limited space within the wider context of Carolingian studies, which were primarily focused on Christian learning: the Latin Bible, above all, and the Church Fathers, especially Gregory the Great and Augustine. Charlemagne's program of establishing schools at all monasteries and cathedrals in his realm, with the aim of improving the educational level of monks and clerics, had the side effect of producing scribes and scholars who engaged in the copying and editing of texts on a previously unimaginable scale. Only a small proportion of these works were classical, but the end result was that the canon of Latin literature as we know it was preserved and transmitted to future generations—securely in the case of some authors (Virgil, Horace, Lucan, Juvenal, Terence, Persius, Statius, Cicero, Sallust, Pliny the Elder, and Vitruvius), less so for others (Seneca, Martial, Quintilian, Plautus, Lucretius, Pliny the Younger, Ovid, Columella, Petronius, and Ammianus Marcellinus), and by the slenderest of threads for a few (Tibullus, Catullus, Propertius, and certain works of Tacitus and Livy). In the palace scriptorium of Charlemagne and his successor, Louis the Pious, and in those located in monasteries (such as Fulda, Hersfeld, Corvey, Lorsch, Reichenau, St. Gall, Tours, and Fleury), manuscript exemplars, many of them ancient and written in majuscule scripts, were carefully copied in the elegant minuscule hand that was universally adopted in the Carolingian empire and on which the Humanists of the 15th century modeled their own script.

Charlemagne's masterstroke was to recruit from far-off York the brilliant scholar Alcuin (ca. 735–804) as the director of educational reform within the empire. Through this position Alcuin helped shape Carolingian attitudes toward classical antiquity: although learning was intended to serve God and his Church, there was nevertheless a place for pagan texts, which could be tolerated, even when not amenable to Christian glossing, on the grounds of utility, both moral and political. One of Alcuin's students, Hrabanus Maurus (ca. 780–856), himself became an influential educator, earning the title Praeceptor Germaniae (Teacher of Germany) and including among his pupils the greatest scholar of the age, Lupus of Ferrières (ca. 805–862). An avid manuscript hunter, Lupus attempted not only to fill gaps in the holdings of the library at Ferrières but also to acquire exemplars of works already in his possession so that he could use them to correct and supplement his own copies. Moreover, in collating these manuscripts he worked out sophisticated methods of textual criticism—leaving spaces for lacunae, marking corruptions, and recording variants—that anticipated practices developed centuries later by classical philologists. His student Heiric of Auxerre (ca. 841–876) is notable for compiling collections of excerpts from Latin authors such as Valerius Maximus, Suetonius, Pomponius Mela, and Petronius. It was mainly from such anthologies (called *florilegia,* from the notion of gathering flowers of eloquence) that most Carolingian—and, indeed, later medieval—scholars gained access to classical texts.

Another Carolingian compiler and student of Hrabanus Maurus was known as Walafrid the Squinter (Walafrid Strabo, ca. 808–849). A poet, biblical exegete, and abbot of Reichenau, he included only a small amount of pagan material in his famous commonplace book (now St. Gall MS 878) but was sufficiently interested in classical Latin poetry to emend the oldest surviving manuscript of Horace (now Vat. Reg. lat. 1703). He also provides eloquent testimony, in his prologue to Einhard's *Life of Charlemagne,* that he was aware of living in a time that was "radiant with the blaze of new learning, previously unknown to our barbarism," though the precariousness of this shining moment of cultural rebirth was equally apparent to Walafrid, who went on to lament that this "light of wisdom" was now dying out.

Walafrid's pessimism was to a large extent justified, as the political disintegration of Charlemagne's empire inevitably led to a general decline in the level of education and culture in the second half of the 9th century. Nonetheless, the Carolingian tradition was not entirely extinguished, and it served as the basis for the Ottonian renaissance, which took place in the 10th century during the reigns of Otto I, Otto II, and Otto III. The era is particularly noted for the lavish manuscripts of Christian texts that were produced in monasteries such as Corvey, Hildesheim, and Reichenau, their magnificent illuminations inspired by late ancient, Byzantine, Carolingian, and Insular (i.e., British) art. Characteristic of the revival of classical antiquity in this period are the six Latin dramas in rhymed prose by the Benedictine canoness Roswitha of Gandersheim (ca. 935–ca. 975): presented as a reworking (*retractatio*) of the plays of Terence, they highlight the chastity, steadfastness, and asceticism of Christian heroines. The central intellectual figure of the Ottonian renaissance was Gerbert of Aurillac (ca. 940–1003), whose rise from abbot of Bobbio to archbishop of Reims and then of Ravenna and finally to the papacy as Sylvester II was not the result of a pact with the devil, as a later legend would have it, but was due instead to the support he received from Otto III, whom he served as tutor and counselor. A keen collector of manuscripts—a 10th-century codex of Cicero's *De oratore* (now Erlangen 380) was made for him—Gerbert helped Otto to expand the imperial library, which acquired from Italy copies of Livy's fourth decade, pseudo-Quintilian's *Declamationes maiores,* and a collection containing Florus, Festus, and Eutropius. Valuable as Gerbert's contribution to the preservation of ancient Latin texts was, it was his technical knowledge of music, mathematics, and science that earned him renown and notoriety.

Although referred to as the 12th-century renaissance, the next resurgence of interest in classical antiquity began around the mid-11th century and lasted until the early 13th. Unlike the Carolingian and Ottonian renaissances, it was not fostered by a particular court or dynasty; its geographical scope, moreover, was much broader, encompassing Sicily, Salerno, Bologna, Toledo, Montpellier, Chartres, Paris, Canterbury, and Oxford. The cultural advances of this "long 12th century" were also wide-ranging, involving literature, art, law, medicine, science, philosophy, and education; and the influence of the classical tradition was felt in all these spheres. Vernacular romances such as the *Roman de Thèbes, Eneas,* and the *Roman de Troie* drew on material and themes from the Latin literature of antiquity. Illuminated manuscripts of classical or pseudo-classical texts depicted figures from pagan mythology and history, and the sculptural decoration of Romanesque cathedrals and churches abounded in motifs borrowed from ancient art. The Digest of Justinian was rescued from neglect and became the foundation of the discipline of Roman law. Greek medical, scientific, astronomical, and mathematical works were recovered, sometimes via Arabic versions, and rendered into Latin. Previously unavailable treatises of Aristotle were translated, commented on, and taught in the universities, which began to be founded in this period. The strengths and weaknesses of 12th-century classical scholarship are exemplified by John of Salisbury (ca. 1115–1180). He was a fine Latin stylist, intimately familiar with a broad range of ancient Latin literature, which he was able to adapt and apply to the concerns of his own time; yet much of his effort still went into compiling collections of related classical texts, and his knowledge of certain authors was dependent on earlier anthologies, which continued to be the mainstay of his less accomplished contemporaries.

The existence of the Carolingian, Ottonian, and 12th-century renaissances was uncovered through the research conducted by medieval historians over the course of the 20th century. Scholars had begun to hint in this direction as early as the 19th century: Jean-Jacques Ampère, for instance, suggested in his *Literary History of France before the Twelfth Century* (*Histoire littéraire de la France avant le douzième siècle*, 1840) that the intellectual movement at the end of the 11th century "presented all the characteristics of a veritable renaissance." But it was Charles Homer Haskins, with his groundbreaking volume *The Renaissance of the Twelfth Century* (1927), who initiated what has been described as "the revolt of the medievalists." Haskins and his followers were determined to refute the idea that the cultural and intellectual revival that occurred from the 14th through the early 17th centuries, first in Italy and then spreading throughout Europe, was a distinctive and singular event that merited exclusive ownership of the term *renaissance.* In contrast, however, to their novel idea of medieval renaissances, the concept of the Renaissance that they set out to undermine had a long history, going back to the founders of the movement.

For Petrarch (1304–1374), the first Renaissance man, the thousand years between the collapse of the Roman Empire and his own day was a *medium tempus,* a "middle period" of unrelieved darkness and ignorance, a "sleep of forgetfulness" (as he portrayed it in his unfinished epic, *Africa*) from which he earnestly hoped future generations would awaken, enabling them to return to "the pure, pristine radiance." No stranger to the art of self-publicity, Petrarch associated himself with this return through his participation in the revival of the ancient ceremony of poetic laureation. His devoted admirer Giovanni Boccaccio (1313–1375) reinforced this association in a letter of around 1370, in which he praised Petrarch for bringing back "to his own age the laurel wreath that had not been seen for perhaps a thousand years or more," for "cleansing the fountain of Helicon, clogged with mud and rushes, and restoring its waters to their former purity," and for "returning the Muses, sullied by rustic uncouthness, to their pristine beauty." Coluccio Salutati (1331–1406), first in a distinguished line of Humanist chancellors of Florence, expanded on the closely related ideas that classical culture had entirely died out after the fall of Rome and was undergoing a rebirth, or renaissance, in his own time. In a letter of 1395 he lists the leading lights of the 12th century, including John of Salisbury, maintaining that they were unworthy of being compared to ancient authors, from whom they were "more remote in style than in time." Salutati then goes on to chronicle the reemergence of literature in the 14th century, at the hands of Dante in the vernacular and of Petrarch and Boccaccio in Latin.

The next Humanist chancellor of Florence, Leonardo Bruni (ca. 1370–1444), gave voice in his dialogues dedicated to Pier Paolo Vergerio (*Dialogi ad Petrum Histrum,* ca. 1405–1406) to what had by his day become a conventional lament for the lost patrimony of classical antiquity: "even the few books that do exist are so corrupt in their texts that they cannot teach us anything." The work nevertheless ends on a cautiously optimistic note, with the hope that Florence, inspired by the example of her three glorious poets—Dante, Petrarch, and Boccaccio—will soon lead the way out of darkness into the light. In the biographies of Dante and Petrarch which he wrote in 1436 Bruni gave a rather grudging assessment of their contributions to the revival of classical culture. Though Dante excelled in vernacular rhyme, in Latin verse and prose "he barely comes up to average"; and while Petrarch was the first "to call back to light the antique elegance of the lost and extinguished style," he did not himself achieve the elegant perfection of Ciceronian Latin but instead "opened the way" for those who followed him—Bruni no doubt had himself in mind—to attain it.

In his *Commentary on the Events of His Time* (*Rerum suo tempore gestarum commentarius,* 1440) Bruni recalled his life-changing decision in 1398 to abandon the study of law and to attend instead the Greek classes given by the Byzantine scholar and diplomat Manuel Chrysoloras (ca. 1349–1415), noting that "for 700 years now, no one in Italy has been able to read Greek, and yet we admit that is from the Greeks that we get all our systems of knowledge." The Humanist educator Guarino da Verona (1374–1460), who in the first decade of the 15th century had followed Chrysoloras back to Constantinople in order to learn Greek, shared Bruni's conviction that the renewed study of Greek was an essential factor (alongside the recovery of lost works by Cicero) in the revival of antiquity going on in their time. So, too, did the historian Flavio Biondo (1392–1463). In his *Italy Illustrated* (*Italia illustrata,* 1453), after celebrating his own role in the rediscovery of Cicero's *Brutus*—he was the first to make a copy from the manuscript found in Lodi in 1421—he claims that although Chrysoloras taught in Italy for only a few years, this had the effect of making those who did not know Greek appear to be ignorant of Latin. Learning Greek, according to Biondo, not only provided access to a "massive supply of historical and moral matter," which stimulated the acquisition of eloquence, but also improved the writing skill of those who translated Greek works into Latin. By the time Paolo Giovio (1486–1552) published his *Brief Lives of Illustrious Men of Letters* (*Elogia virorum litteris illustrium,* 1546), Chrysoloras—"the first to bring back to Italy after 700 years Greek literature which had been driven out by the barbarian invasions"—and a host of other Byzantine émigrés had become a staple feature in accounts of the rebirth of classical culture.

The revival of ancient art also became a standard element in such narratives. In his *Decameron* (1348–1351) Boccaccio had praised Giotto for "restoring to light" the art of painting, "which for many centuries had been buried under the errors of those who painted for the sake of pleasing the eyes of the ignorant rather than satisfying the intelligence of the knowledgeable." In his chronicle of 1382 Filippo Villani (1325–1407), while placing Cimabue among the "first to recall ancient painting to life," maintained that Giotto had not merely equaled but surpassed ancient painters and had "restored painting to its ancient dignity." The sculptor and goldsmith Lorenzo Ghiberti (1378–1455) spoke with the professional authority of a renowned artist when he stated in his *Commentaries* (*I commentarii,* begun 1447) that after Constantine "art was dead, and the temples remained white for some 600 years." Paralleling his Humanist contemporaries' dismissive attitude toward medieval Latin literature and learning, Ghiberti looked with disdain on medieval Byzantine painting: "The Greeks began painting and produced some works of great crudity; as the ancients had been highly skilled, so the men of those times were rough and crude." It was Giotto who had abandoned the "crude manner of the Greeks" and brought in "the new art" by inventing or discovering doctrines that "had lain buried for about 600 years."

A link between the Humanist revival of classical Latin and the artistic revival of ancient art was postulated by Lorenzo Valla (1406–1457) in the preface to his *Fine Points of the Latin Language* (*Elegantiae linguae Latinae,* 1441–1449). "Is there anyone," he asked, "who does not know that when the Latin language flourishes, all studies and disciplines thrive, just as they fall to ruin when it perishes?" Similarly, "the arts of painting, sculpture, modeling, and architecture," which had degenerated and almost died along with the liberal arts during the Middle Ages, were now reawakened and brought to life again. In an inaugural lecture delivered in 1455 to the University of Rome, Valla explained that it was the ability of ancient artists to communicate in a single language—classical Latin—and therefore to compete with one another for fame and glory that had driven the flourishing of art in antiquity. And when that capacity was lost, art too declined, just as the men constructing the Tower of Babel "stopped building it precisely because they did not fully comprehend each other's speech."

In a letter of 1489 the Dutch Humanist Erasmus (1466 or 1469–1536), picking up Valla's account in the *Elegantiae,* discusses the connection between the "fortunes of literature" and those of art. After the blossoming of all disciplines in ancient times, Erasmus writes, a period ensued "when men turned their backs on the precepts of the ancients," and there was such a "stubborn growth of barbarism" that eloquence completely disappeared, so that no trace of it remained. In like manner, an inspection of reliefs, paintings, sculptures, buildings, or any other works of art that were more than two or three hundred years old would provoke astonishment and laughter at the "artists' extreme crudity." And just as, in his own age, artists had once again "achieved every effect of art," Lorenzo Valla had rescued "Latin from death when it had almost expired" and had zealously fought in his *Elegantiae* "to refute the foolish notions of the barbarians" and to bring back the practices of ancient prose and verse authors that had "long been buried and forgotten."

The painter and art historian Giorgio Vasari (1511–1574) in his *Lives of the Most Eminent Architects, Painters, and Sculptors* (*Vite de' più eccellenti architetti, pittori e scultori,* 1550; 2nd ed. 1568) describes how art was "reborn" in Italy in the late 13th century with Cimabue and Giotto and "reached perfection" in the 16th with Leonardo da Vinci and Michelangelo. In the prologue to the first edition he portrays the surviving art of antiquity as the midwife in this rebirth. During the Middle Ages, he explains, Italians had copied Byzantine artists, whose style he, like Ghiberti, regarded as "clumsy" and "awkward"; even though they had before their eyes "the remains of arches and colossi, statues, pillars, and carved columns," they had "no idea how to make use of or profit from this excellent work." The artists who came later, however, "abandoned the old manner of doing things and began once again to imitate the works of antiquity as skillfully and carefully as they could."

In the mid-1490s the Dominican friar, apocalyptic preacher, and self-proclaimed prophet Girolamo Savonarola (1452–1498) waged a campaign of radical religious reform in Florence, urging its citizens to abandon, among other worldly "vanities," the revival of classical art, literature, and culture that had reached such heights under Lorenzo the Magnificent de' Medici (1449–1492) and encouraging them instead to transform their city into a New Jerusalem, a holy republic that would serve as a shining example of Christ-centered spirituality and asceticism. For all its notoriety, this was a short-lived and localized episode; in direct contrast to Savonarola's program, the notion of cultural rebirth became closely associated in the 16th century with the idea of religious reform, the recovery of classical learning paving the way for a return to the true Church of early Christianity. Erasmus—here too following the lead of Valla, who had championed the eloquent theology of the Church Fathers, schooled in the best traditions of ancient literature and rhetoric, while condemning the illiterate, jargon-ridden philosophical theology of the medieval Scholastics—in his *Against the Barbarians* (*Anti-Barbari,* 1520) railed against the "unlearned learning" of the Middle Ages, which had corrupted not only literature but religion too, and argued for a return to the theology of Jerome (his personal hero), Augustine, and other patristic authors who had been well versed in the classics. Two years earlier, in his inaugural address to the University of Wittenberg, Philipp Melanchthon (1497–1560), the German Humanist who would become Luther's closest ally in the battle to establish the Reformation, had put forward a program of secular and sacred educational reform in which Greek and Hebrew, alongside classical Latin, took center stage. In explaining the need for this Humanist reform, Melanchthon narrated the history of learning from antiquity onward, observing that Charlemagne, by putting Alcuin in charge of education within the empire, had managed to revive the ancient disciplines that had perished after the barbarian invasions and that would soon die out again owing to the neglect of the medieval Schoolmen. Melanchthon's description of this brief, shining moment in the otherwise pervasive darkness of the Middle Ages hints at an awareness of the Carolingian renaissance—also found in other German scholars of the time, such as Johannes Trithemius (1462–1516), as an expression of their patriotic attachment to the empire of Charlemagne—which would not become fully developed until modern times.

The belief that the rebirth of ancient learning in the 14th and 15th centuries was a divinely ordained precursor of the Reformation in the 16th became enshrined in Protestant historiography. Although this often entailed a greater emphasis on the part played by northern Humanists who had thrown in their lot with the Reform movement, the earlier Italian phase of the classical revival was not forgotten, nor was the contribution of Byzantine scholars. In his *Ecclesiastical History of the Reformed Churches of the Kingdom of France* (*Histoire ecclésiastique des Églises Réformées au royaume de France,* 1580), Theodore Beza (1519–1605), Calvin's right-hand man and successor in Geneva, attributed particular importance to the refugees from Byzantium who had promoted the study of Greek in the universities of Italy. This idea was repeated by a later French Calvinist, Pierre Bayle (1647–1706), who noted in his *Historical and Critical Dictionary* (*Dictionnaire historique et critique,* 1695–1697; 2nd ed. 1702) that although interest in the classics did not revive in France until the time of Francis I (r. 1515–1547), "belles lettres" had started to be reborn in Italy after the fall of Constantinople. This inaccurate theory, which ignored the role of Chrysoloras and other émigrés from before 1453, nevertheless caught on, presumably because it was handy to have a precise date and dramatic event to mark the rebirth of classical studies. Bayle gave due credit to the Italian Humanists as well but portrayed them as having "little religion" in contrast to their northern counterparts, who had served the cause of the Reformation.

Both the irreligion of the Italian Humanists and the fall of Constantinople as the pivotal moment in "the renaissance of literature and the fine arts" feature in the *Essay on the Manners and the Spirit of Nations* (*Essai sur les moeurs et l'esprit des nations,* 1756), a pioneering work of cultural history in which Voltaire (1694–1778) charts the "extinction, renaissance, and progress of the human mind" from the barbaric and ignorant Middle Ages to the enlightened Age of Reason presided over by Louis XIV (r. 1643–1715). Voltaire gave a new twist to the story of the revival of antiquity by linking the material prosperity of Italy to its advanced civilization: the wealthy Medici rulers of Florence had not only patronized the arts but also welcomed the scholars who fled Byzantium in 1453. This brilliant culture—"the glory of genius belonged then to Italy alone, just as it had once been the possession of Greece"—was, however, suffused with immorality: no other period in history, he maintained, was "so prolific in assassinations, poisonings, treason, and monstrous debauchery." Having left religion behind but not yet reached the safe shores of rationalism, the Italians of the 15th and 16th centuries had lost their moral compass.

The moral failings and religious shortcomings of the early Italian Humanists in particular were given a thorough airing by the German historian Georg Voigt (1827–1891) in his *Revival of Classical Antiquity, or the First Century of Humanism* (*Die Wiederbelebung des classischen Altherthums, oder das erste Jahrhundert des Humanismus,* 1859). Although he regarded Petrarch as "the prophet of the new age, the ancestor of the modern world" and respected the early Humanists for their philological and historical studies of classical texts, as well as for their frontal attack on Scholastic obscurantism, he felt that their excessive reverence for antiquity had inhibited independent and critical thought: "What they called philosophy was little more than the rehearsal and variation of classical commonplaces." With the exception of Petrarch, moreover, their religious thought was shallow and frivolous. And the self-conscious individualism that had stood forth "strong and free" in Petrarch had degenerated into shameless egoism in his followers.

Four years earlier, in 1855, the French historian Jules Michelet (1798–1874) had published *La Renaissance,* the seventh in his 17-volume *Histoire de France* (1833–1862). This was the first time that the Renaissance was treated as a historical period. He applied the term, however, to 16th-century Europe, not to 14th- and 15th-century Italy; and, for him, the renewed study of antiquity was only one facet of a much wider phenomenon, which also embraced geographical exploration (Columbus), scientific discovery (Copernicus and Galileo), the Reformation (Luther and Calvin), and the rise of national literatures (Montaigne, Shakespeare, and Cervantes).

For the Swiss historian Jacob Burckhardt (1818–1897), by contrast, the Renaissance was a period in the history not of Europe as a whole, but specifically of Italy: an expression of both the *Zeitgeist,* the spirit of the times, of the 15th and 16th centuries and the *Volksgeist* of the Italian people. Like Michelet, nonetheless, Burckhardt in *The Civilization of the Renaissance in Italy* (*Die Cultur der Renaissance in Italien,* 1860) presented the revival of antiquity as merely one element—and by no means the most essential—in the larger picture of cultural rebirth. And like Voigt, he had a low opinion of Italian Humanists, whom he portrayed as amoral pens for hire, ready to put their literary skills at the service of ruthless monsters such as Sigismondo Malatesta of Rimini. Voigt, in later editions of his work, would revise his view of Humanists downward in light of Burckhardt's compelling picture of their rootless and licentious lifestyle.

Since its publication, Burckhardt's enormously influential book has set the agenda for debates about the Renaissance. It was against his widely adopted view of the distinctiveness of the Renaissance that Haskins and other medievalists revolted, putting forward claims for the Carolingian, Ottonian, and 12th-century renaissances. In his *Renaissance and Renascences in Western Art* (1960) the art historian Erwin Panofsky (1892–1968) attempted to explain the difference between these medieval "renascences," which were "limited and transitory," and the Renaissance, which was "total and permanent." Invoking his "principle of disjunction," Panofsky maintained that medieval art exhibited either classical form or classical content, but never both together; it was only in the Renaissance that the two were reintegrated. For his fellow art historian Ernst Gombrich (1909–2001), however, Burckhardt's Hegelian interpretation of the Renaissance was fundamentally misguided: it was not an "age" but a "movement." Paul Oskar Kristeller (1905–1999), who devoted his life to the study of Renaissance philosophy and Humanism, downgraded the concept even further: the Renaissance for him was nothing more than a "historian's construct." For Hans Baron (1900–1988), like Kristeller a German refugee scholar who made an academic career for himself in America, the Renaissance was, above all, an ideological struggle between the liberty of republican governments such as Florence and the despotism of princely regimes such as Milan—an interpretation that was strongly colored by his perception of the political situation in Europe during the 1930s and its aftermath in World War II. These debates will no doubt continue into the future; yet however much the significance of the term is questioned and however many earlier renaissances are identified, it seems likely that the Renaissance will remain part of our historiographical vocabulary.

BIBL.: R. L. Benson and G. Constable, eds., *Renaissance and Renewal in the Twelfth Century* (Oxford 1982). J. B. Bullen, *The Myth of the Renaissance in Nineteenth-century Writing* (Oxford 1994). W. K. Ferguson, *The Renaissance in Historical Thought: Five Centuries of Interpretation* (Boston 1948). E. H. Gombrich, "The Renaissance—Period or Movement?" in *Background to the English Renaissance: Introductory Lectures,* ed. J. B. Trapp (London 1974) 9–30. D. Hay, ed., *The Renaissance Debate* (New York 1965). W. Kerrigan and G. Braden, *The Idea of the Renaissance* (Baltimore 1989). P. O. Kristeller, "The Renaissance in the History of Philosophical Thought," in *The Renaissance: Essays in Interpretation* (London 1982) 127–152. R. McKitterick, ed., *Carolingian Culture: Emulation and Innovation* (Cambridge 1994). M. L. McLaughlin, "Humanist Concepts of Renaissance and Middle Ages in the Tre- and Quattrocento," *Renaissance Studies* 2 (1988) 131–142. R. Ragghianti and A. Savorelli, eds., *Rinascimento: Mito e concetto* (Pisa 2005). L. D. Reynolds and N. G. Wilson, *Scribes and Scholars: A Guide to the Transmission of Greek and Latin Literature,* 3rd ed. (Oxford 1991) chap. 3. E. Rudolph, ed., *Die Renaissance als erste Aufklärung,* vol. 3, *Die Renaissance und ihr Bild in der Geschichte* (Tübingen 1998). J.K.

Replicas

Guided by the Modernist demand for artistic originality, art critics, scholars, and lay viewers alike usually dismiss replicas of classical works of art as mechanical copies of their models and regard them as distinctly inferior to the originals in quality and creativity. Yet without replicas of works of Greek and Roman art, in particular replicas of antique marble sculptures, the development of a classical tradition would not have been possible. Whether reproduced in two or three dimensions, in various sizes and media, replicas of classical artworks were, and arguably still are, ubiquitous emblems of classical knowledge and powerful instruments for transmitting and reformulating that knowledge in visual and intellectual terms. Replicas have thus been central participants in dynamic, contested arenas of cultural and political change from antiquity to the 20th century. At various times they have been valued as works of art in their own right and admired as much as the ancient works on which they are modeled, and even in postmodern times replicas of classical artworks have given rise to artistic, critical, and political response.

Ancient attitudes toward the practice of replication prefigured those of post-classical times. Modern audiences customarily regard Roman art as copied from original works by famous Greek masters, unaware that the classical Greeks themselves produced replicas in large numbers, often for cultic purposes. Small-scale bronzes and terra-cotta figurines were turned out from molds by the score, to serve as offerings to the gods or as images for household shrines. But even large-scale marble and bronze sculptures were produced in multiples. Striking examples include famous sculptures on the Acropolis of Periclean Athens. The six nearly identical caryatids on the Porch of the Maidens on the Erechtheion differ from one another only in subtle details of hairstyle, drapery, attribute, and, for reasons of architectural symmetry, ponderation. The splendid bronze warriors, discovered in 1972 in the sea off the coast of southern Italy near Riace, offer a vivid example of the serial production of monumental bronze statues. Extensive computer-generated measurements indicate that the torsos of the two figures were most likely made from the same mold and that only the limbs and heads were manipulated to create slightly different postures and facial types. Though scholars disagree on the dating of these bronzes, most favor the period of Phidias in the mid-5th century BCE. The colossal chryselephantine statue of Athena Parthenos, created by Phidias for the Parthenon in 438 BCE, was itself reproduced countless times at a reduced scale on red-figure vases, on votive reliefs, and in three-dimensional sculptures. A colossal copy was made for the Attalids of Pergamon in the 2nd century BCE, and small-scale sculptural replicas continued to be made in the Roman era well into the late empire.

In Roman times the replication of statues of both Greek and Roman creation was carried out on an industrial scale. In addition to thousands of idealized images of Greek and Roman gods, heroes, and personifications, there were equally large numbers of portrait busts and statues of Greek and Roman notables that once populated public and private spaces across the empire. In the case of replicas of idealized subjects the prototypes are rarely known, but modern scholars have usually presumed that they were masterpieces by famous Greek artists—a presumption based largely on 18th-century and later reconstructions of ancient events.

Though Greek and Roman society did not place as high a value on personal creativity as the art world does today, technical skill and the innovations of famous artists were certainly admired. More common in the classical world, however, was the use of accepted, recognizable models from an established iconographic repertory, either repeated straightforwardly or used as the basis of invention. Within the ancient cultural frame, replicas were essential for preserving, transposing, and broadcasting political, cultic, philosophical, and social concepts that were central to maintaining social order and cultural cohesion. The practice of replication itself, whether visual or verbal, was crucial to the mimetic system of education that stressed acquiring cultural knowledge from approved models and using them to hone one's skills.

During the Roman Empire sculptors, painters, and architects, many of whom were Greek at least in name, would have regarded their predecessors as models to learn from and to surpass. The Augustan architect Vitruvius says as much in his *Ten Books on Architecture.* Moreover, ancient rhetorical manuals, such as the *Institutio* of Quintilian, abound in citations of famous exempla and recommendations to cull the best features of the works of the old masters in the quest to emulate them. Basic to Roman elite education, the teaching of rhetoric encouraged a conservative classicizing aesthetic that was considered socially appropriate. Replicas not only reinforced elite status by advertising an owner's cultural awareness but also served personal political ends.

Ancient attitudes and practices were transmitted via rhetorical manuals, which were studied with renewed intensity beginning in the 15th century in Italy, along with other writings of Greek and Roman authors. But it was the growing knowledge of the antiquities themselves that directly inspired the production and acquisition of replicas. In the 15th century antiquities that had long remained visible began to be recorded in sketchbooks, the earliest known of which is by Cyriacus of Ancona (1391–1455), who recorded the monuments he saw on his travels in Italy, Greece, and the Levant. Shortly thereafter in Rome an old collection of antiquities at the Lateran Palace, in existence since the 8th century, received renewed attention when in 1472 Pope Sixtus IV created the first municipal museum in the Conservators' Palace on the Campidoglio, in part from sculptures that had been in the Lateran collection. Among them were the boy pulling a thorn from his foot (the *Spinario*) and the *She-Wolf,* which was later augmented with suckling twins—Romulus and Remus. As fresh discoveries were made, an enlarged but still limited corpus of antique works became widely known among the educated elite in Italy and abroad through the agency of replication, and the replicas themselves became engines of change in the rapid evolution of the new standards of classical taste.

The earliest recorded full-scale replicas of classical sculptures made in the Renaissance, however, were not of these famous works. They were plaster casts of reliefs, very likely from Roman sarcophagi, made for Francesco Squarcione, who established an art school in Padua. His use of the casts for teaching is recorded as of 1455, at a time when the young Andrea Mantegna received his early training by drawing from them. The plaster cast would later come into prominence for replicating three-dimensional sculptures, but in the 15th century the first known sculptural replica of an ancient statue was more modest in size and degree of accuracy—a small-scale bronze statuette by Filarete of the monumental equestrian statue of Marcus Aurelius. At the time that Filarete made his statuette, the ancient original still stood outside the Lateran Palace, where it had been set up by Pope Clement III in 1187. (It was not taken to the Campidoglio until 1538.) Filarete's statuette bears a 1465 inscription to Piero de' Medici, perhaps a flattering attempt to liken him to a great Roman emperor. In any case, it was not long before other Italian nobles began to collect such small images after the antique. In 1497 the Gonzagas of Mantua sent Pier Jacopo Alari Bonacolsi, known as L'Antico, to Rome to make the first known set of small bronze copies of the most famous ancient marble and bronze statues there, and other Italian nobles followed suit. Such small replicas, luxuries in themselves, gained great popularity in Italy and abroad during the following centuries.

The 16th century saw the full-scale replication of antique sculptures, sometimes carried out in a spirit of artistic rivalry. Vasari reports that a few years after the discovery of the Laocoön in 1506, Bramante encouraged four of the best sculptors in Rome to make large wax models of it and arranged for Raphael to assess their artistic merits.

The prize went to the young Jacopo Sansovino; his model was cast in bronze and given to Cardinal Grimani, who is said to have prized it as much as the ancient sculpture. But political rivalry as much as the new taste for the antique drove the making of replicas of famous statues. The earliest full-scale replica of the Laocoön in marble—the first marble copy made since antiquity—was carved in the 1520s by the Florentine sculptor Baccio Bandinelli. According to one story, his copy was intended as a gift from Pope Leo X to Francis I of France as a substitute for a bronze cast of the original, which, following his victories in Italy, the king had requested in 1520 for his hunting lodge at Fontainebleau. Leo X's successor, Clement VII, admired Bandinelli's copy so much, however, that he decided to keep it for himself, and a bronze cast of it was sent to Fontainebleau instead.

Francis I set the pace for other European monarchs when, between 1532 and 1540, he sent the Florentine artist Primaticcio to Rome (apparently at the artist's suggestion) to acquire artworks and make the first molds of the most famous antique statues, bronze casts of which were to be displayed at the king's newly refurbished hunting lodge. Primaticcio's molds were almost exclusively of the statues that filled the niches in the Belvedere Courtyard. Destined to become the central icons of the classical tradition, these statues included the Apollo Belvedere, the Laocoön, and the Ariadne-Cleopatra, among others. The resulting ensemble at Fontainebleau was so impressive that Vasari praised the king's estate as "almost a new Rome in France." Cardinal Grimaldi's esteem for his replica of the Laocoön suggests that replicas could be admired as much as their antique models. Only the very rich could afford large-scale bronze casts and marble replicas of the already canonical antique sculptures, and they were among the most highly prized possessions of those who acquired them. The reception of sculptural replicas of the antique, however, was sometimes mixed. For instance, artists who were Bandinelli's contemporaries found little other than technical skill to admire in his marble Laocoön. In Renaissance Italy, as in classical antiquity, proper imitation needed to involve the addition of something new to the ancient model, not simply replicating it.

The importance of replicas to European culture of this period went beyond their ability to fulfill cultural and monarchical ambitions. They were the touchstones of what would emerge in the 17th century as codified classical aesthetic criteria, nowhere more programmatically than in France under Louis XIV. The French Academy in Rome, founded in 1666 at the order of the king, focused on acquiring antiquities and training artists to produce replicas of the famous works in Italy solely for the French court. The Academy strictly enforced aesthetic standards, and by the last quarter of the century French academic classicism was firmly in place as public doctrine and official court style. At Versailles alone some 200 replicas of ancient statues and strongly imitative classicizing works by well-known artists were installed in the gardens, and smaller-scale replicas ornamented the palace interior. Soon other châteaux gardens, such as those of Marly, Chantilly, and Seaux, were furnished with marble replicas as well. In general, however, bronze was the medium of choice among European aristocrats. The discriminating collector Prince Johann Adam of Liechtenstein (1666–1712) notably insisted on the highest quality of casting and surface finish in the casts he purchased from the Florentine artist Massimiliano Soldani, who maintained a thriving business in both life-size and small bronze casts well into the 18th century.

For spreading knowledge and appreciation of the style of classical antiquity and its most famous sculptural embodiments beyond the wealthy elite, engravings, illustrated books, and plaster casts were far more important. The great scholar of ancient art J. J. Winckelmann, the son of a poor cobbler, wrote his first study of the imitation of Greek painting and sculpture in 1755, on the basis of knowledge of the ancient works that he had acquired solely from illustrated books. Meanwhile, extensive collections of life-size plaster casts, which were also costly, were displayed in impressive galleries in palaces of the nobility, and demand for them increased as art academies throughout Europe followed the French model in depending on casts for training artists in proper classical form. Plaster casts continued to serve for more than two centuries to educate not only artists but also, beginning in the late 19th century, archaeologists, for at that time classical archaeology consisted primarily of the study of sculpture. Eventually, no serious institution of learning could afford to be without at least a modest number of plaster casts. Some collections grew to contain hundreds of them as the corpus of Greek and Roman artworks expanded with each new archaeological discovery.

Political fortunes also propelled the production and collecting of plaster casts. In an ironic twist of fate, when the Italians lost the wars with Napoleon and the French laid claim to many of the most famous ancient sculptures as war booty, those taken from the Vatican galleries were replaced with plaster casts. But, following the French defeat at Waterloo, most of the ancient statues were returned, whereupon the cast atelier of the Louvre, established under Napoleon, went on to produce casts of the returned antiquities for many European and American collections.

As early as the time of Mantegna the training of painters as well as sculptors involved drawing from casts, and in some cases painters, like sculptors, made three-dimensional replicas of them. Poussin, for example, made a small wax model, now in the Louvre, of the Ariadne-Cleopatra. In the academies, such as the famous École des Beaux-Arts in Paris, the training of artists extended to their copying from the works of approved masters of the High Renaissance, such as Raphael and his followers, who were regarded as founders of the classical tradition.

As scholars employed them for their own scientific ends, the very casts that had enabled the widespread appreciation of classical forms were devalued aesthetically along with many of their ancient models, which in the wake of Winckelmann were increasingly classified as Roman rather than Greek. Impelled by changing attitudes, which placed a distinctly higher value on all that was seen as Greek, scholars adopted a method known as copy criticism in a quest to recover the appearance of lost originals by Greek masters mentioned in ancient texts, an experiment that had far-reaching consequences. The science of reconstructing the Ur-model, which became ever more refined in the course of the 19th century and much of the 20th, depended heavily on the notion that multiples of a given Roman marble sculpture had been mechanically produced and were therefore reliable evidence of the lost bronze original. Further, supporting struts on the marble statues were adduced as evidence that the marble image reproduced a bronze, a material that did not require support. These and other assumptions of those who employ copy criticism have recently been challenged, but in the meantime, this method of studying classical art—along with both Romanticism's and Modernism's worship of artistic genius—led to the devaluation of ancient Roman sculptures that had for so long been admired.

With the discovery of Herculaneum and Pompeii in the 18th century, the story of replicas of the antique, which had up to then been about classical sculptures, began to involve paintings as well. Drawings and engravings of individual Roman murals and views of entire rooms with their painted walls in situ were produced by many artists, and publishers such as Fausto and Felici Niccolini brought out books that circulated widely through Europe. Not until the early decades of the 20th century, however, did painters undertake large-scale replicas of Roman murals. These served as accurate records at a time when color photography was not yet widely available and as a hedge against deterioration. In the process, replicas after the antique were once again used for political purposes.

One particularly informative example is a nearly full-scale watercolor replica of the bacchic murals in the Villa of the Mysteries, discovered in Pompeii in 1909. In 1924 an American classicist, Francis W. Kelsey, commissioned an Italian artist, Maria Barosso, to provide an accurate, "scientific" record of the murals primarily for study purposes. Barosso, while committed to making a fully accurate copy, also tried to recapture the original beauty of her ancient model. But more than a scientific tool and aesthetic re-creation, the replica became a political statement as Mussolini laid claim to Italy's past glory as the model for his new Italian state. Before the replica was sent to the United States, the Italian Ministry of Public Education arranged to have it exhibited at the Galleria Borghese, and the government press duly proclaimed the show a great Fascist triumph. Replicas of Roman antiquities were also displayed in the service of the Italian Fascist agenda at other venues, but most comprehensively in the Mostra Augustea della Romanità of 1937–1938, an immense exhibition that opened on the 2,000th birthday of Augustus, with whom Mussolini identified. The exhibition relied extensively on replicas of archaeological artifacts as well as models of Roman buildings, works of engineering, machinery, and other inventions to celebrate the genius of the Italian race, tracing its roots to Roman antiquity. In effect, because the majority of copies and models were works of the Fascist era, they presented the lauded Roman achievements as products of the regime.

Despite the prominent role given to replicas in Fascist states, in the early decades of the 20th century replicas after the antique were not widely regarded as artworks in themselves. They were, in fact, thoroughly rejected by Modernist aesthetic values that reigned throughout most of the period. Though plaster casts were still collected by some universities for teaching purposes and were eagerly analyzed by archaeologists and art historians, few artists studied them. Eventually many collections were dismantled and put into storage or destroyed.

Following the Fascist era, replicas did not reemerge as significant sources of artistic inspiration until postmodern times. In the 1980s in particular, ironic appropriations of classical artworks were seen as a potent vehicle of aesthetic and social critique. The British artist Edward Allington, for example, reflects broadly on the authority of the original, the inherent role of reproduction in the making of sculpture, and the role of the creative artist in relation to what is essentially a collaborative process. His theoretically informed, multireferential works incorporate multiple replicas of classical sculptures—the Discobolus, the Medici Venus, the Nike of Samothrace—which he obtains from museum shops and commercial suppliers and further reproduces. Nor does he ignore the ironies implicit in the making of replicas, which may include the relation of a work of art to its replication as a tourist souvenir.

Nonironic replication continues as well in both popular and elite culture. In 1972–1974 J. Paul Getty commissioned a re-creation of the Villa of the Papyri in Herculaneum for his museum in Malibu, California, and furnished it with full-size bronze casts and marble replicas of the ancient villa's sculpture. The Chiurazzi foundry in Naples, active since the late 19th century, produced the Getty casts, but demand for replicas made from its large stock of molds is not what it once was. Dust gathers on the shelves of the foundry's storerooms, where the molds and models, most as old as the business itself, appear as relics of a venerable craft not likely to revive, overshadowed by reproductions of all sorts generated by media more suited to the digital age.

BIBL.: Leonard Barkan, *Unearthing the Past: Archaeology and Aesthetics in the Making of Renaissance Culture* (New Haven 1991). Victoria C. G. Coates and Jon L. Seydl, eds., *Antiquity Recovered: The Legacy of Pompeii and Herculaneum* (Los Angeles 2007). Elaine K. Gazda, ed., *The Ancient Art of Emulation: Studies in Artistic Originality and Tradition from the Present to Classical Antiquity* (Ann Arbor 2002). Francis Haskell and Nicholas Penny, *Taste and the Antique: The Lure of Classical Sculpture, 1500–1900* (New Haven 1981). Anthony Hughes and Erich Ranfft, eds., *Sculpture and Its Reproductions* (London 1997). Jennifer Trimble and Jas Elsner, eds., *Art and Replication: Greece, Rome and Beyond,* special issue, *Art History* 29, no. 2 (2006).

E.GA.

Republicanism

Since Greek and Roman antiquity, republicanism has signified a series of often converging and sometime contradictory traditions in political theory, constitutional theory, political rhetoric, and political practice. The history of both the idea and the legal-political practice of republicanism suggests moments of convergence and also of conflict between the principal features of the republican state, public participation and the pursuit of the public good. Following the Greek democratic city-state and the early Roman Republic, the rhetoric of government for the people has often tended to eclipse the practice of actual citizens' participation. The concept of civic virtue cultivated in democratic Athens stressed political participation in the assemblies, councils, and particularly the courts as institutions of self-governance, and the defining purpose of serving the public rather than a private good. In *Antigone,* Sophocles's Creon says that "silver currency . . . destroys the state" and "drives citizens to acts of shame" (*Antigone,* 300). In the course of the history of Rome, actual commitment to the democratic form of citizens' self-government, based on rotating popular participation in government, was weakened as emphasis shifted to the content of a government bound to serve the public good. The virtue of public regard became increasingly attached to worthy and legitimate leaders, while the principal virtue of the citizen emerged correspondingly as obedience to the law and self-sacrifice on the battlefield. Although a republican state could be democratic in the sense of a state actually ruled by the people, it became more characteristically a state where varying leadership at different periods, sometimes elected representatives or an aristocratic elite, and at times even a single man, a Caesar or a monarch, would claim to represent the people and to govern for the public good. If a tyrannical or despotic regime came to be regarded as the polar opposite of republicanism, this was not primarily because the government did not take the form of self-governing citizenry, but because of its arbitrary use of power by a leader or ruling elite in violation of the public good.

As emphasis on the service ethics of the ruling few came to eclipse the requirement of government by the people, popular sovereignty has become a more abstract political imaginary only partially, and particularly symbolically, supported by actual constitutional and political practices. Regardless of its many inconsistencies with political practice, however, as a vision of political order combining the idea of self-government by a sovereign people (or its elected representatives) with pursuit of the collective public good, republican democracy has acquired a hegemonic status as the most influential Western, and gradually global, imaginary of legitimate government. Because its commitment to the principle of popular sovereignty has been combined with inherent ambiguities and sometimes nondemocratic constitutional and political forms, republicanism could be and has been used as an ideological and a political resource in the justification of a wide spectrum of political movements and regimes ranging from republican Sparta and Rome through early Renaissance Italian city-states like Venice and Florence, continuing through English, North American, and French revolutionaries to Mussolini's Fascist Italy. Depending on which elements of republicanism are stressed, it has been enlisted as a political resource to criticize and delegitimate hierarchic governments, leaders who do not seem to serve the public good, constitutions that do not secure appropriate channels of influence for citizens, liberal political regimes that privilege the individual over the community, citizens and elected representatives corrupted by greed and self-interest, and the corrosive effect of commercial market values on republican civic solidarities. Doubts concerning the possibility and sustainability of a government by a virtuous, public-regarding, and tolerant citizenry have generated a variety of alternative republican political imaginaries and institutional arrangements. These have translated the principle of popular sovereignty into various forms of credible legally or institutionally vicarious and virtual public controls, intended to serve as effective checks on the powers of the ruling few. The history of republicanism and of its legal-political discourse is, therefore, a record of continual assessments of alternative constitutions and constitutional amendments. Put differently, driven by fear of the volatility of aroused masses and the ease with which a civically disciplined public can degenerate into a violent mob, republicanism to date has produced a series of attempts to constitutionally channel and limit actual public participation, as well as to curb the corruption and abuse of governmental powers. These attempts have characteristically been accompanied by efforts to cultivate the often declining civic virtues of a service-oriented elite and a law-abiding citizenry.

The most influential and historically durable democratic-republican principle, though frequently too abstract to be translatable into practice, has three components: free citizens possess the ultimate right to govern themselves; they are therefore the source of government authority, whatever its structure; and when they cannot run the government themselves, they have the authority to elect and demote their governors as they assess those public servants' will and ability to serve the people's interest.

In the Roman constitution and during the early Republic, such orientations encouraged the emergence of the senate as the surrogate sovereign endowed with the people's power to constrain the Caesar. In modern republics, parliaments, as legislative bodies that are often similarly given the authority to oversee the executive branch of government, have continued this constitutional-institutional tradition. The citizens of the ancient republic enjoyed freedoms not yet grounded, as they were in later centuries, in universally recognized innate rights exercised within legal strictures. Greek and Roman freedoms (not yet problematized by ideas such as individual free will, individual conscience, and individual personality) were regarded as primarily political and social, a matter of relations within a sociopolitical context. This does not mean that the individual did not enjoy the privacy of family life, the free choice of religious practice, and reasonable protection of private property. Despite traditions of contemplative life and care for the self cultivated by ancient philosophical schools like Epicureans, Cynics, and some Stoics, it was not until the emergence of Christianity and Renaissance Humanism that the idea of individual freedom markedly moved beyond the civic context into a delineated private sphere where individual creativity and self-expression could flourish in relative and always precarious autonomy. In the course of time, advanced modern cultures of selfhood and self-interest would pose new challenges to the normative status of public-oriented civic individualism, while reinforcing economic, romantic, and other alternative forms of apolitical individualism.

Though republicanism has always stressed the value of civic service, the civic virtues of its rulers have only partly converged with those of the ruled. Informally the aristocracy, as in Rome, was the matrix of the regime, and such political freedoms as free speech and deliberation on public affairs were exercised by and within aristocratic circles in forums more exclusive than those symbolized by Athens' *agora.* In Rome, as in the Greek polis, rhetoric, the ultimate democratic political skill, was preserved and cultivated as a vital political skill exercised mostly by and among members of the upper classes. The practical constraints on mass political self-government in large societies further reinforced this primarily Roman aristocratic model of republicanism in the modern state, which entrusts the power to govern to an elite and diverts popular political controls of governmental power to vicarious and virtual channels of participation. The Roman concept of honor or social standing (*dignitas*) not derived solely from privileges of family and birth showed great flexibility in accommodating changing social values and extending to include acquired qualities like military excellence, rhetorical competence, and wealth.

The republican emphasis on the collective, or the people's, good over that of the individual or of the small group, has raised a host of perennial questions about the boundaries of the collective whose good is primary, the nature of the collective adhesive, and the relations between the collective and its parts, conceived as individuals or smaller groups. More specifically, this has raised the issue of privileging varying conceptions of the whole. Is the whole the polity, the people, the body of a legally defined community of citizens, the nation defined in ethnic and local terms, or the state? And what are the parts that compose the whole: the individual person or citizen, or ethnic, religious, local, or exterritorial groups? In what sense can a politically defined majority and consequent minorities coexist as parts of the same whole? Are women, immigrants, and resident aliens excluded, and if not, which conceptions of a whole include them as parts? To a large extent the historical variability of republican regimes and doctrines reflects different ideological, political, and legal responses to these questions and a correspondingly different distribution of freedoms between the whole and the parts.

Reflecting this preoccupation with imagining and conceptualizing the social or political whole, one of the most lasting and politically significant legacies of Roman jurists was the development of the concept of a corporation as an entity composed of individuals, yet distinct from its parts. With the rise of Christianity the imaginary of the corporation also acquired a religious significance as *corpus mysticum,* for example, came to signify the entire Christian community of believers. In the course of the Middle Ages and modernity this concept was increasingly attached to secular collectives such as universities, economic organizations, cities, the people, the kingdom, and the state. Such attachments of concepts of corporation as *corpus civile, corpus rei publicae mysticum,* and the like to political entities have often signified an additional shift of the idea of the corporation toward illiberal and coercive holism, including mystical conceptions of the nation and the state, further removed from its classical roots in imaginaries of civic bodies composed of free citizens.

Whereas Roman jurists developed the concept of corporate body in the context of private law transactions, the imaginary of a collective body that keeps its identity despite changes and transformations of its members has become a principal foundation of the emergence of the modern state as an agency whose life expectancy is longer than that of its mortal citizens. The legal-political development of the state as a *persona ficta,* as an artificial and therefore immortal person, for instance in Thomas Hobbes's influential *Leviathan,* has, despite Hobbes's radical individualism, further reinforced the special value and weight accorded to the collective vis-à-vis the individual. This trend was already embedded in Roman republican patriotism, as expressed for instance in Cicero's endorsement of the ethics of individual self-sacrifice for the state. This Roman prototype of a state embodying a sovereign people represented by magistrates and a monarch facilitated the integration of republican values with undemocratic oligarchic and monarchic political structures. What is important from the perspective of political history is that the flexibility of this Roman model led to its wide dissemination among other peoples and nations. The legal-political fiction of the state as a corporation, a fictitious person legally (and often also politically and spiritually) embodying the people, has been appropriated and contextualized in numerous distinct and often rival political and legal traditions. Continental countries like France developed an organic imaginary of the people consisting of a head and members, while the English opted for a more mechanistic imaginary of the political whole that facilitates a more moderate integration of parts with whole; the English adaptation is thereby more accommodating to the protection of the equality, integrity, and responsibility of individuals as the parts that compose its polity.

Despite the legal and political adaptability of republicanism to nondemocratic hierarchical forms of government, the republican idea of the sovereignty of the people, of a government legitimated from below, and the primacy of the purpose of service to the public good have retained considerable power to nurture resistance and revolt against tyranny and corrupt governments. A major document of the rise of Renaissance Humanism, Nicolas Machiavelli's *Discorsi* (ca. 1513)—based on a conversation with classical political thought and experience—was a prominent and influential channel for the revival of republican political imaginaries in the early modern era. In Machiavelli's view the most important lesson to be learned from Roman republicanism is the crucial role of the citizen-soldier in securing freedom from both external and internal subordination. For Machiavelli, soldiers' discipline and solidarity are fungible, convertible into vital assets of civic republican life. Although favoring a mixed republican constitution that balances monarchic, aristocratic, and democratic elements, he held that the public goods of stability and freedom depend primarily on virtuous citizenry. Since his republican ideal links patriotism, civic militia, and civic political service, he objected to the mercenary army and was preoccupied with the causes and destructive consequences of the spread of corruption among both citizens and their magistrates. Stress on the character and conduct of citizens and governors together with concern about corruption led Machiavelli in the *Discorsi* to advance a moral discourse on the good republic. He did not ignore the potential contribution of religion to civic discipline, but he was also concerned that Christian virtues and the belief in otherworldly rewards and punishments might actually weaken mundane civic culture.

The English republican imaginary also reflects and refracts republicanism's salient tensions. In contrast to earlier orthodoxy, Shakespearean scholars have recently emphasized the extent to which many of Shakespeare's plays reflect the opposition between Caesarism and republicanism through themes such as the corruption of centralized or personalized power. James Harrington, the author of the influential *Oceana* (1656), which he dedicated to Oliver Cromwell, contributed to the revival and contextualization of Graeco-Roman imaginaries of participatory civic commonwealth in the crucial period of the English civil war. Combining Humanistic civic values with neo-Roman Machiavellian republicanism, Harrington presented an idealized history of Renaissance Venice as an exemplary model of the legacy of Sparta and Rome. Like Machiavelli, he regarded the armed citizen-soldier, combining military and political civic virtues (the very foundation of the republican order), as a necessary check on the oligarchic tendencies of aristocratic magistrates. In addition to his influence on 17th-century English republicans, Harrington's advocacy of the advantages of a constitution combining democratic, aristocratic, and limited monarchic elements, his constitutional suggestions for controlling destructive factionalism, and his commitment to the equal distribution of land assured his intellectual presence in the constitutional debates of both revolutionary America and France.

It is evident that the revival of the democratic-republican ideas of participatory citizenship, channeled, empowered, and modernized during the 18th century (also through the influential writings of Rousseau and Montesquieu), was directed not only against the monarchy but also in opposition to the Church. Machiavelli, Harrington, Rousseau, and Montesquieu all held that the faith cultivated by the clergy weakens civic virtues and trust in human legislation. Rousseau preferred the citizens of martial Sparta to the self-cultivated citizens of Athens. He idealized the moral sensibilities and civic virtues of simple, hardworking farmers over those of the urban bourgeoisie and Parisian intellectuals. Rousseau was profoundly concerned with the corrosive effects of city life on the soul, and his republicanism became a principal weapon in his own discourse and in subsequent critiques of modernism. Karl Marx's critique of capitalism used the classical republican vocabulary inspired by Rousseau in his criticism of the enslavement of the laborer by his capitalist master and the corruption of civic virtues by selfish materialism. Rousseau's importance to the modern republican debate has also been augmented by the fact that his attempts to integrate democratic-republican values into a viable system of government exposed the fundamental theoretical contradictions and practical impossibilities that produced ambiguous, albeit influential, ideas such as the "general will" and "civil religion." Yet one can say that it is precisely the many possible interpretations and constitutional expressions to which such an appealing idea as the "general will" lends itself that have made it so central to republican political and constitutional debates both during and since the French Revolution.

In the second half of the 18th century Montesquieu advanced the view that a stable political order depends on a good constitution, which in turn requires the application of the science of government and legislation. Although he valued civic egalitarian patriotism, Montesquieu was skeptical that Graeco-Roman civic virtues could sustain republican government in large populous states. But he certainly believed that good institutions, including an independent judiciary and the introduction of checks and balances among the various branches of government, are vital to producing good citizens and good governments. The American Federalists did not share Montesquieu's pessimism about the viability of a large republic, but they affirmed his faith in the good of a balancing constitution and deliberative legislation. Madison combined the two when he suggested constitutional constraints on the consequences of the pursuit of private interests and against the destructive effects of factionalism, in particular containment of the unrestrained passions of the majority faction. The republican vocabulary has continued to be invoked in American politics, particularly in connection with issues such as the corruption of representatives or clerks, the role of the jury system, and debates between communitarians and liberal individualists on American values and policies.

From a more general perspective, modern and postmodern republicanism has been faced with five formidable, partly mutually reinforcing challenges: the spread of the market economy and its influence on the privatization of the citizen, compounded by the massive concentration of international economic power; globalization as the convergence of trans-state economic, technological, legal, political, communications, and cultural networks and institutions undermining the ethos and practices of popular participatory government; the emergence of radically fragmented and fluid individual identities coexisting with socially encumbered identities, thereby creating a hardly bridgeable gap between rationales and modes of political engagement; the decline of ethnically and culturally homogeneous societies; and the upsurge of Christian, Muslim, and Jewish fundamentalisms as well as other "otherworldly" worlds of meaning. These developments have led quite a few scholars to wonder whether the end of classical politics is not imminent.

There are solid grounds for skepticism concerning the capacity of contemporary multicultural and ethnically heterogeneous societies to generate sufficient agreement on public values to ground key elements of classical civic culture. Contemporary commercial mass media, which repeatedly address the public as potential purchasers (in a unilateral rather than a dialogical mode), seem to gradually "train" their publics to think and act as consumers rather than as citizens. This trend has penetrated contemporary arenas of mass politics, where policies and candidates are marketed by advertisers, the modern heirs of the ancient rhetoricians, like other consumer products. Radical postmodern individualism seems to corrode commitments to civic political participation, just as communitarianism, often buttressed by ethnic and organic holism and fundamentalist reactions to liberal individualism, seems incompatible with the cultivation of individual freedoms and republican egalitarianism. A death certificate for republicanism may nevertheless be premature, underestimating its record of and potential for transformations and adaptations to new circumstances.

BIBL.: G. Bock, Q. Skinner, and M. Viroli, eds., *Machiavelli and Republicanism* (Cambridge 1990). C. Dougherty and L. Kurke, eds., *The Cultures within Ancient Greek Culture: Contact, Conflict, Collaboration* (Cambridge 2003). E. H. Kantorowicz, *The King's Two Bodies: A Study in Mediaeval Political Theology,* with a new preface by W. C. Jordan (Princeton 1997). C. Rowe and M. Schonfield, eds., *The Cambridge History of Greek and Roman Political Thought* (Cambridge 2005). J. Shklar, *Montesquieu* (Oxford 1987). C. Wirszubski, *Libertas as a Political Idea at Rome during the Late Republic and the Early Principate* (Cambridge 1950).

Y.E.

Revolution, French

The last great political event to take its inspiration, iconography, and institutions primarily from classical antiquity. French revolutionaries depended heavily on Roman and Greek history for ideas and for the courage to apply them. But even if their understanding of history had been accurate (it seldom was), French politicians could never settle on which ancient model to follow. Classical antiquity provides innumerable conflicting moral and political examples, and the French came close to trying them all, running through the whole of Roman history in 15 years. Eighteenth-century Frenchmen postured as Romans, Athenians, and Spartans, without ever achieving liberty against arbitrary power, or any consistent rule of law. The French Revolution's ostentatious classicism, comprehensive experimentation, and obvious failure discredited Roman and Greek antiquity as practical models for political reform. Later revolutions would need new models, including the experience of France itself, and the transatlantic successes of the United States of America.

Classicism had been sapping the foundations of French absolutism for more than 40 years before the people of Paris finally stormed the Bastille in 1789. Camille Desmoulins, whose fiery rhetoric (according to his own account) precipitated the uprising of July 14, attributed the strike against "despotism" to the writings of "enlightened" authors who had prepared France for freedom, "just as Rome's vices prepared the way for Caesar" at the end of the Roman Republic (*La France libre,* 1789). This example was typical of the era, in that it recalled Rome's collapse into despotism and sought to reverse it. Desmoulins hoped that the French deficit would shock the people into fighting for their freedom, "just as the death of Virginia shocked the Romans" into fighting for liberty in Rome.

Four years later, when the king was dead and France had become a republic, Desmoulins would recount in his *Secret History* of the Revolution how the French first learned to love liberty and hate despotism by reading Cicero at school. "They brought us up in the schools of Rome and Athens," he complained, "to live under Claudius and Vitellius." Admiring the Roman past, young men came to hate the present and to hope for change (*Histoire des Brissotins; ou, Fragment de l'histoire secrète de la révolution et des six premiers mois de la République,* 1793). Nor were young women unaffected. The celebrated Madame Roland recalled how as the young Marie Phlipon she smuggled her copy of Plutarch instead of a prayer book into church. Plutarch inspired her to love liberty and to mourn the ancient republics, although she never imagined such virtue would ever come to France (*Mémoires,* 1793).

Admiration for Greek and Roman antiquity was the natural product of the classical reading of any educated child in 18th-century France, and growing prosperity meant that there were many more such educated children by midcentury than there had ever been before. Plutarch (read in translation), Cicero, Sallust, Livy, and even Tacitus (for more advanced students) helped shape a neo-Roman sensibility throughout the Republic of Letters, not only in France but across all Europe and America. With the possible exception of Cicero, who still hoped to save the Republic (but was known to have failed), these authors all shared a nostalgic attitude toward Roman liberty as something precious and evanescent, now regrettably lost and never to be regained. At most, the best-known Roman authors had hoped to moderate the excesses of imperial rule. This made Roman thinking acceptable in Bourbon France, where enlightened opinion guided absolute kings toward the rule of law and government for the common good, as endorsed by Aristotle and Livy. French enthusiasts for classical antiquity at first proposed not to replace the monarchy but to reform it, by introducing elements from the famous "mixed" constitution of republican Rome.

The history of England and (more recently, but exotically) America gave French reformers practical models for modern "mixed" government. The English Commonwealth (which failed) and the Glorious Revolution of 1688 (which was viewed by many as an inspiring success) both embraced the vocabulary of Roman liberty to reform an ancient monarchy that had fallen into fiscal and moral corruption, as Rome had. Americans never fully suffered the excesses of the Ancien Régime, but they too followed the Roman model of mixed government to balance their new state and federal constitutions in the light of book 6 of Polybius' *Histories* and other ancient and modern assessments of the political history of Rome. French translations of James Harrington's *Commonwealth of Oceana* (1656), Algernon Sidney's *Discourses concerning Government* (1698), John Adams's *Defence of the Constitutions of Government of the United States of America* (1787–1788), and other English and American commentaries on the ancient republics helped situate the French debate in the broader context of the universal struggle against despotism, inspired by the liberty of Rome.

French authors played a large part in this conversation about Roman and Greek political institutions. Among the most influential were Montesquieu in his *Considérations sur les causes de la grandeur des Romains et de leur décadence* (1734) and *De l'esprit des lois* (1748); Gabriel Bonnot de Mably in his *Observations sur les Romains* (1751), *Entretiens de Phocion, sur le rapport de la morale avec la politique* (1763), and *Observations sur l'histoire de la Grèce* (1766); and Jean-Jacques Rousseau through numerous writings and particularly in *Du contrat social* (1762). These meditations on government, which continued to find an avid audience throughout the Revolution, concurred in several important respects: their admiration for the mixed constitutions of Sparta and Rome; their awe at Roman and Greek (particularly Spartan) virtue; and their sad realization (which they shared with their classical sources) that neither was possible beyond the confines of small, stable, and homogenous republics, such as had existed in Sparta and during the early years of Rome. When Rome became too large and too prosperous, most such authors explained, the Romans became corrupt, the balance in the constitution failed, and imperial despotism supplanted republican liberty forever.

Despite their consensus on these main points, French attitudes toward antiquity had already begun to diverge into two main tendencies, best described, for the sake of simplicity, as the Roman and the Spartan camps, partially anticipated by Montesquieu and Rousseau. Where the Romanists emphasized the checks and balances of republican government, their application in England's Glorious Revolution, and the possibility of liberty through law, admirers of Sparta stressed the necessity of virtue, the example of England's Commonwealth government, and the importance of popular sovereignty, expressed though votes of the people. Neither set of views directly contradicted the other. Most educated men and women found it easy to praise both Sparta and Rome and usually to put Rome first, as reflected in the names they assumed in their pseudonymous publications and the themes they chose for their public art. But Rousseau and Mably encouraged French readers to assimilate the early institutions of the two republics and to prefer the simple, uncompromising virtue of Sparta to the commercial exuberance and complicated checks and balances of later republican Rome.

The French Revolution began with the classical appeal against despotism. England had shown how recourse to the "ancient constitution" could advance the cause of liberty, and French reformers tried to revive the Estates-General as a check against arbitrary power. But when the Estates-General met resistance, they declared themselves a "National Constituent Assembly" in July 1789 and embraced the new mission of creating a stable constitution for France. This brought the delegates back to the Roman political agenda endorsing the rule of law (*imperium legum*), popular sovereignty (*imperium populi*), and natural justice (*ius naturale*), embodied in a Declaration of Rights, much as the newly independent United States of America had done. But the French delegates would not accept Roman bicameralism, as proposed by the Assembly's constitutional committee under Jean-Joseph Mounier and the Count de Mirabeau. This reminded French patriots too much of British monarchy. Instead, they endorsed Rousseau's neo-Spartan conception of the "general will" (*la volonté générale*), which implied unicameral government and undermined the checks and balances of the traditional Roman constitution, as promoted by Montesquieu, Polybius, and the Glorious Revolution in Britain. The French Constitution of 1791 established a single National Legislative Assembly and vested executive power in the king, who had a suspensive rather than (as in Britain) an absolute veto over proposed legislation.

The presence of the king was not in itself a barrier to French Neoclassicism. Sparta had kings and so did Rome for the first several centuries of its existence (and the *rex sacrorum* afterward). Louis XVI could present himself as a Numa or Lycurgus, but educated Frenchmen perceived him more readily as Tarquin or Nero. He had come to represent the despotism and corruption of feudal France, and his flight to Varennes in June 1791 destroyed his remaining authority. Finally, the Legislative Assembly suspended the monarchy and summoned a new Constitutional Convention, whose first act, on September 22, 1792, declared France a republic. This released a new frenzy of Neoclassicism. Having severed their last link with political tradition, the French needed practical models for their new republican government and found them in the ancient world. Montesquieu, Rousseau, and Mably had all taught that republics could never survive in a country as large and corrupt as France. Circumstances having made France a republic, the French needed republican remedies for the maladies of republican rule. They returned to Greek and Roman classics to understand the dangers that threatened their new liberty in France.

"Faction" in the face of foreign and internal enemies was the first great challenge of republican government, as identified by Cicero and Sallust in Rome. The Romans had recourse to the *senatus consultum ultimum,* which liberated magistrates to take extraordinary measures to protect the Republic. The French National Assembly created similar procedures and had already declared that the "country was in danger" when the Convention began to take charge of the emergency. Louis de Saint-Just and Maximilien Robespierre denounced the former king as a threat to the republic, and he was put on trial by the Convention and on January 21, 1793, executed, like the English Charles I before him. This opened the floodgates of political killings in France. If Cicero could kill Catiline to save the Republic, if Cincinnatus could kill Maelius and Brutus could kill Caesar, if the Roman Senate could condemn Gaius Gracchus and Marcus Fulvius for undermining the Republic, why should the Convention not act just as firmly against factious demagogues and unrepentant royalists? Jean-Paul Marat called openly for a dictator, on the Roman model, to suppress enemies of the republic, and the Convention compromised by creating a nine-member Committee of Public Safety, recalling the American committees, and (more chillingly) the *decemviri* of early republican Rome. So France found itself repeating the least salubrious episodes of Roman history, and the Committee of Public Safety ordered or approved the arrest and execution of thousands of recalcitrant citizens and legislators.

Robespierre and Saint-Just, the two primary instigators and ideologues of what came to be known as the Terror both embraced the Spartan view of republican government. They perceived from the beginning, as Saint-Just explained in *Esprit de la Révolution et de la constitution de France* (1791), the great difficulty of recovering lost liberty once virtue has decayed. The Greeks after Philip of Macedon, like the Romans at the time of Sulla, no longer had the moral fortitude to be free. They spoke of liberty but wanted license. The Jacobin party of Saint-Just and Robespierre perceived that the Spartan scheme of simplicity and equality, so effective in a small, poor country, was almost impossible in France. So neither man proposed a republic at first. Driven by circumstances to remove their king, they used extreme measures to face an extreme challenge. The absence of virtue called for constant purification of the people, as if by the neo-Roman censors, in the manner once proposed by Rousseau (*Considérations sur le gouvernement de Pologne,* 1765). Idealists proposed a strict Laconian system of education and limits on commerce and the consumption of luxury goods.

The French Terror never developed any systematic program of reform, on the classical or any other model, beyond the Jacobins' frenzied efforts to root out corruption. Centralization under the Committee of Public Safety simply confirmed the necessity of Polybian checks and balances, as practiced in republican Rome. This explains the continuing popularity of Roman models after the fall of Robespierre, despite his close association with classical virtue and the Jacobin cult of antiquity. The Convention had completed a new constitution in 1793 that provided for a unicameral legislature, maintained by annual elections. Robespierre prevented its implementation and when in July 1794 the Convention finally reasserted its authority against the Jacobins, Rousseau's Spartan model had lost its allure. François-Noël (the self-styled Gracchus) Babeuf tried to raise a popular revolt in support of the Constitution of 1793 through his journal, *Le tribun du peuple,* without success. Instead, the Convention imposed a new republican constitution on France, designed to moderate the republic's recent extremes of tyranny and terror.

When the French National Convention met in the Tuileries to reform the French Constitution, they faced, from their benches, a series of statues showing Brutus, Camillus, Cincinnatus, and Publicola (on one wall) and Lycurgus, Solon, Demosthenes, and Plato (on the other). There were *fasces,* laurel wreaths above the statues, and a rostrum from which to speak. Small wonder then that, as the passion for Greece and Sparta departed with Saint-Just and Robespierre, the delegates simply turned to the opposite side of their faux-marble hall and drafted a neo-Roman document, the Constitution of the Year III, with a second chamber of elders (*Anciens*), like the Roman Senate, to control the popular assembly, a plural executive (the Directors), as in Rome, and a complicated system of elections by census class (in the manner of Roman *comitia*) to curb the influence of the more improvident and excitable citizens of France.

François-Antoine de Boissy d'Anglas introduced the new constitution in the name of the commission that had drafted it, directing the public to consider the sober Polybian checks and balances set out by John Adams in his neo-Roman *Defence of the Constitutions.* (*Projet de constitution pour la République française,* 1795). The government subsidized a new edition of Polybius. Other members of the commission invoked the "great models" of Cicero and Cato (Baudin des Ardennes, *Anecdotes et réflexions générales sur la constitution,* 1795). Critics mocked the commissioners for speaking so incessantly about Rome (Louis-Philippe de Ségur, *Réflexions sur la plan de constitution presentée par la commission des onze,* 1795), but advocates of the constitution clearly expected their language to be persuasive. In the Convention's debates confirming the new text, Jean-Jacques Cambacérès exalted its bicameralism as constituting the *palladium* of liberty (*Moniteur* 25:275–277). The Constitution of the Year III excluded all regular troops from a wide radius around Paris, just as proconsular armies had been excluded from Italy, and consular *imperium* kept strictly outside the *pomoerium* of Rome.

This prudent concern about military despotism reflected bitter republican experience in Cromwell's England and in Caesar's Rome. But the politicians and generals had studied their history too, and in September 1797 the Directors Paul Barras, Jean-François Reubell, and Louis-Marie de La Révellière-Lépeaux, known to their contemporaries as *triumviri,* brought troops into the capital, ousted their two colleagues, subverted the constitution, and seized governmental power, just as Caesar, Pompey, and Crassus had made themselves *triumviri* in Rome. Thenceforth, though the facade of the constitution would be maintained (as it had been in Rome), real control rested in the hands of those who had the power to enforce their will. Extraconstitutional coups d'état and countercoups among the directors controlled the republic whenever constitutional checks and balances might have inhibited their will. Finally, in November 1799 Director Emmanuel Joseph (the Abbé) Sieyès called in General Napoleon Bonaparte to impose a more stable government by three "consuls": Pierre-Roger Ducos, Bonaparte, and himself, and the consuls extracted a new constitution (Constitution of the Year VIII) to perpetuate their power.

With the dominance of the successful general, Bonaparte, the French Republic had found its Caesar. Just as Octavian had manipulated existing forms and claimed to restore the Republic as he established his domination in Rome, so Bonaparte gradually consolidated his power in the revised Constitutions of the Year VIII (December 1799), the Year X (August 1802), and the Year XII (May 1804). The Constitution of the Year VIII retained three consuls but gave the First Consul (Bonaparte) all power to name ministers, officers of the army, ambassadors, and judges, and to make all other important decisions on behalf of the republic, with the purely consultative assistance of his two colleagues. There was a senate of eighty members, serving for life (as in Rome), there were tribunes to discuss the laws proposed by the government, and there was a legislative assembly to vote on them. Two years later, the Constitution of the Year X made Bonaparte Consul for Life, pursuant to a *senatus consultum* of the French Senate, which also strengthened the Senate's own ability to modify the laws and constitution through *sénatus-consultes* proposed by the First Consul. Finally, the Constitution of the Year XII made Napoleon Bonaparte a hereditary emperor, retained the Senate and Tribunate, but added some subordinate "princes Français" and a Grand Council of the Emperor to support him. The Revolution had run its full course, from Brutus to Domitian, in less than 15 years.

The consuls declared the French Revolution to be at an end when they presented the Constitution of the Year VIII to the people, because the institutions of state had finally fulfilled the principles with which the Revolution began (*Proclamation des consuls de la République du 24 Frimaire an VIII*). With the Constitution of the Year XII the Revolution was finally over in fact, having abandoned the commitment to liberty against despotism that had animated French Neoclassicism from the start. Napoleon had not turned away from Rome. He simply followed the thread of Roman history from Caesar's dictatorship into the imperial age. The Constitution of the Year XII considered it still useful to create pseudo-Roman quaestors for the new empire, pursuant to a *sénatus-consulte*, and the art, architecture, and ambitions of Bonaparte's France clung closely to the precedents and examples of imperial Rome.

The Revolution had been a political event, a struggle to establish the constitution of liberty in France. But the culture of classicism was all-pervasive, as artists and citizens supported their new institutions by wearing the *pileus,* or Phrygian cap, of the Roman goddess Libertas, by naming their children (or themselves) Brutus, Gracchus, or Scaevola, and by depicting ancient heroes in their theaters, paintings, and sculpture, and in numerous other public ceremonies and festivals. Jacques-Louis David gave a particularly vivid example in his paintings of the same desperate cycle of classicism in art that was also progressing through the political institutions of France throughout his long career. A few of David's best-known works can illustrate the change. *The Combat of Minerva and Mars* (1771) is a typical allegorical scene in which learning triumphs over the sword. *Belisarius Receiving Alms* (1781) makes a mild criticism of ungrateful monarchs, as the blind, old general is reduced to begging in the streets. *The Oath of the Horatii* (1784) exults the simple bravery of three young men, prepared to die for their country. *Lictors Bringing Brutus the Bodies of His Sons* (1789) shows the austere virtue of a man prepared to kill his children to save the republic. *The Sabine Women* (1799) makes a more sensual plea for reconciliation. *Bonaparte Crossing the Great St. Bernard* (1801) compares the general to Hannibal. *The Consecration of the Emperor Napoleon I* (1807) is frankly imperial. But *Leonidas at Thermopylae* (1814) is just an excuse to paint nudes, and *Cupid and Psyche* (1817) is almost pornographic, showing two sated teenagers smirking on a divan.

The lesson of the French Revolution, for students of antiquity, which is to say for all educated Europeans at the end of the 18th century, was eerily similar to the lessons of Greece and Rome. Virtue was admirable, they agreed, and much to be desired as the only sure basis of liberty and justice, but not attainable by the citizens of large, complicated commercial states such as France. The people gathered in public assemblies would be turbulent and unjust, and no amount of tinkering with constitutional checks and balances could control this defect. Government by a reasonable emperor seemed the best that could be hoped for, so long as he committed himself (as in the Constitution of the Year XII) to the "interests, welfare, and glory" of the French people. Benjamin Constant expressed the jaded view of many former republicans in 1819 when he distinguished "the liberty of the moderns" from "the liberty of the ancients." The liberty of the ancients, he suggested, following Rousseau, was the right of the people to participate directly in *making* the laws that would rule them, but the liberty of the moderns, as enjoyed in the United States, England, and France, was the personal freedom to be *governed* by stable laws, to be free from arbitrary arrest, and to control one's own property (*De la liberté des anciens comparée a celle des modernes,* 1819). The dream of the old republics had finally died, and new models emerged to replace them. The French Revolution discredited classical antiquity by following it too closely, too blindly, and too much.

BIBL.: Keith Michael Baker, "Transformations of Classical Republicanism in Eighteenth-century France," *Journal of Modern History* 73 (2001) 32–53. Jacques Bouineau, *Les toges du pouvoir (1789–1799) ou la révolution de droit antique* (Toulouse 1986). Fernando Díaz-Plaja, *Griegos y Romanos en la revolución francesa* (Madrid 1960). François Furet and Mona Ozouf, eds., *Le siècle de l'avènement républicain* (Paris 1993). Claude Mossé, *L'antiquité dans la Révolution française* (Paris 1989). Harold T. Parker, *The Cult of Antiquity and the French Revolutionaries: A Study in the Development of the Revolutionary Spirit* (Chicago 1937). M.N.S.S.

Rhetoric

Although no single figure looms larger than Cicero in the history of rhetoric, Cicero himself throughout his career acknowledged his debt to the older, mostly Greek rhetoricians and orators who shaped his theory and practice. In the *De inventione,* an early work that so dominated medieval rhetoric that it was called simply the "old rhetoric" (*rhetorica vetus*), Cicero identifies Aristotle, Isocrates, and their pupils as sources for his own handbook (2.2.4–9). In *De oratore,* a more mature work in the form of a Platonic dialogue, unknown in the Middle Ages but inspirational for the Renaissance, Cicero has one of his principal interlocutors, the renowned orator Crassus, recall the well-established *ars dicendi* that he learned as a young boy at school (1.137–145). By the 1st century BCE, therefore, rhetoric was already a fully institutionalized art that looked back to a classical tradition for its theoretical principles and practical models.

But the long list of rules that Cicero's Crassus recites does more than unearth rhetoric's past; it also anticipates its future. For the history of rhetoric up through the 18th century at least—and arguably even longer—continues to move forward by looking back. "More than any other subject," according to one appraisal that captures scholarly consensus (France 1972, 8), "rhetoric was a classical inheritance; whatever modifications it might undergo, it built on the foundation of an ancient and rich tradition."

Rehearsing the foundations of this tradition in *De oratore,* Cicero's Crassus begins with the Aristotelian claim that rhetoric is an art of accommodation that aims at persuasion. (Aristotle was expressing his opposition to his own teacher, Plato, who not only denied rhetoric the status of an art but also discredited persuasion as a worthwhile goal.) Crassus continues with the (equally Aristotelian) three kinds of oration: deliberative, forensic or judicial, and epideictic. Also Aristotelian is the priority of invention over the other four divisions, or *partes,* of rhetoric. Aristotle had devoted two of the three books of his manual to this first division, which Crassus calls "hit[ting] on what to say" (1.142). Book 3 of Aristotle's *Rhetoric* then covers the second and third divisions—arrangement and style—whereas the fourth, delivery, is mentioned in passing as dependent on natural talent and therefore untreatable in an art. The fifth, memory, Aristotle handles not in his rhetorical but in his biological writings. Though looking back to Aristotelian—and Isocratean—rhetorical theory, in other words, the five traditional *partes* were systematized later in the tradition, perhaps for the first time by Roman rhetoricians.

In addition to Aristotelian (and Isocratean) influences, Crassus's rules also show signs of Plato, Theophrastus, and Hermagoras. Outspokenly antagonistic to public speaking, Plato nevertheless imagined an ideal rhetorician as someone who combined natural talent, a true art, and practice (*Phaedrus* 269D). Crassus ends his recitation with this winning threesome. Much more positively disposed toward rhetoric than Aristotle's teacher, his most famous student, Theophrastus, quantified his own teacher's prescription for a successful style into a number of stylistic qualities. Crassus's list includes the four Theophrastan virtues of correctness, clarity, ornament, and appropriateness. On the other hand, Crassus's reference to the crucial distinction between general and particular questions and the so-called status system, designed to isolate the main issue under debate in forensic rhetoric, suggests that his teacher administered a heavy dose of Hermagoras. Both Hermagorean elements aim to enhance the young orator's ability to find his arguments—that is, in rhetorical terms, to invent.

Despite its dependence on Aristotle, Crassus's list somewhat surprisingly omits a principle central to his *Rhetoric:* the three sources of persuasion—argument, the character of the speaker, and the emotions of the audience. Omitted here, however, this Aristotelian principle is featured elsewhere, in *De oratore* as well as in some of Cicero's other rhetorical writings. Crassus's partner in conversation, Antonius, acknowledges these three sources only to put greatest stock in the third. In keeping with this priority, Antonius stresses both decorum and, like Demosthenes before him, delivery. Both decorum and delivery belong to the *ars rhetorica* but, like Antonius himself, have a less than straightforward relation to the rules. Last of the five rhetorical *partes,* delivery depends almost entirely on talent, to the exclusion of art, whereas decorum is that rule that trumps all others in giving the orator the flexibility to accommodate the particularities of his case, including the demands of a particular audience. Crassus's list also fails to mention the three levels of style (grand, middle, plain), the three intentions they perform (teaching, delighting, and moving), or the figures of thought and speech.

In the *De oratore* Cicero stages a debate between two of republican Rome's most accomplished orators regarding the rules of their profession—rules that look back to the Greek rhetorical tradition. But Roman rhetoric, Cicero admits, owes at least as much—if not more—to Greek philosophy as it does to Greek rhetoric. Speaking in his own voice in a treatise dedicated to his friend and fellow orator Brutus, Cicero announces that what he learned from "the spacious grounds of the Academy" contributed more to his oratorical success than his time spent in the "workshops of the rhetoricians" (*Orator* 12). In *De oratore,* meanwhile, he has Crassus lament the rift between these two disciplines. In the days before Socrates, Crassus claims, the same professors that taught us to think also taught us to speak (3.15.57). Like the rules of rhetoric, the rivalries as well as the synergies between rhetoric and the other humanistic arts, especially philosophy, were by the 1st century BCE part and parcel of the tradition.

If Cicero and his recent Roman predecessors looked back to the Greeks (whether they admitted it or not), Cicero's successors for centuries to come looked back to Cicero. By the early imperial period his name was synonymous with eloquence. Some rhetoricians, therefore, set as their own professional agenda the revival of Ciceronian rhetoric. Among these, Quintilian is most notable. His *Institutio oratoria* in 12 books covers the complete training of the orator from his earliest preparation by the grammarian to his most mature aspirations for oratorical preeminence. Nearly everything about Quintilian's plan, moreover, is traditional: the three sources of persuasion, the three kinds of oratory, the five *partes* or divisions of rhetoric, and so on. Quintilian also supplemented the familiar rules of the art with the pedagogical practice of imitation, recommending that the student take none other than Cicero as his principal model. But the imitation of Cicero, whose history in the rhetorical tradition reached its climax in the 16th century, did not for Quintilian entail the exclusive appropriation of Ciceronian style, for Cicero himself imitated the force of Demosthenes, the fluency of Plato, and the charm of Isocrates (10.1.108–109).

Quintilian's approbation of the Ciceronian method of selecting what is best from among a number of models sets in high relief the attention paid by the rhetorical theorists of the first centuries CE not only to Cicero but to questions of style. In his *Dialogue on the Orators* (*Dialogus de oratoribus*), modeled on *De oratore,* Tacitus replaces philosophy with poetry as rhetoric's chief rival; his interlocutors debate whether the oratorical style of their day is enhanced or corrupted by the poetical flourishes then in fashion. Those on either side of the debate claim Cicero, who is variously considered to be the last of the ancients or the first of the moderns. This disagreement over Cicero's place in the tradition further calls into question the applicability of his own cardinal rule, namely decorum. Decorum requires that the orator accommodate the circumstances of the case, among other things, subject matter, speaker, time, place, and especially audience. As audiences change and so make different demands on the orator, should his style change to accommodate them? Tacitus challenged the conception of a Ciceronian style, in other words, with the competing concept of Ciceronian decorum—a principle of changing tastes in place of a fixed stylistic standard.

Like the Roman rhetoricians, their Greek counterparts often focused on questions of style in ways that at once preserved and transformed the tradition. An anonymous treatise, *On Style* (*Peri hermeneias*), attributed to Demetrius and probably written sometime between the 1st century BCE and the 1st century CE, takes Aristotelian and Theophrastan principles concerning stylistic excellence as its starting point and then grafts onto these principles not the traditional three (grand, middle, plain) but rather four "characters" of style. The additional, fourth character, combining elements of the plain and the grand, is the "forceful," used to describe the distinguishing features of Demosthenes' oratory. Demetrius also added a brief section on epistolary writing to his discussion of the plain style—a section with a noteworthy afterlife beginning in the Renaissance. Dionysius of Halicarnassus (1st cent. BCE) resembled his contemporaries, Greek as well as Roman, in adhering to three stylistic characters, in advocating imitation, and in pointing to Demosthenes as the single most accomplished model to be imitated.

Like Dionysius, "Longinus" advocated not only imitating but imitating Demosthenes. And like Demetrius, he featured a style other than the Ciceronian grand. For Longinus (or whoever wrote *On Sublimity*), this most excellent style does more than merely persuade; it transports. And its power derives as much from the outstanding part—Horace's "purple patch" (*Ars poetica* 15–16) —as from the unified composition of the whole. Whereas Cicero excelled at the invention, disposition, and elocution that builds steadily to a climax, Demosthenes won over his listeners in an instant with an unexpected flourish. Both Demosthenes and Cicero, however, were masters at creating pathos, the heightened emotional state indispensable to sublimity. While retaining two of the three Aristotelian sources of persuasion, in other words, Longinus made the very un-Aristotelian move of subordinating one to the other.

Aiming beyond the grand style, moreover, Longinian sublimity at the same time retains for itself that privileged position of the Aristotelian mean between extremes, a stylistic virtue flanked by vice. In this case, the stylistic vices are turgidity, at one extreme, and puerility, at the other. This fascinating little treatise stakes out its positions in recognizably traditional terms; and its balancing act between tradition and innovation is epitomized by Longinus' position on innovation itself. Whereas he exhorts the orator in search of sublimity to startle his audience's expectations with the unusual and the wondrous (35.5), he cautions against the "passion for novel ideas which is the prevalent craze of the day" (5.1).

Though the rhetorical theory of the late Republic and early empire, both Greek and Latin, reflects a rich tradition of principles and practices that the orator would first encounter at school, the *progymnasmata* (Latin *praeex-*

ercitationes), dating back to this same period, represent pedagogical exercises in actual use in the classroom. Attested as early as the 4th century BCE and, according to Quintilian, very much a part of grammatical training during the 1st century CE, these *progymnasmata* usually offered both instructions for composing relatively simple literary forms and sample compositions illustrating the instruction. Among the forms offered were fables, maxims, speeches in character, descriptions, comparisons, and refutations. Most notable among the *progymnasmata* still extant are those of Hermogenes and Aphthonius. Hermogenes' school exercises entered the Western curriculum through the Latin adaptation of the 6th-century grammarian Priscian. More forthcoming than Hermogenes with examples, Aphthonius' 6th-century exercises were more popular both in the schools of the Byzantine Empire and in those of Renaissance Europe.

During the Middle Ages rhetoric was no less grounded in the classical tradition; and that tradition was no less at home in the classroom. Regularly considered among the liberal arts, rhetoric followed grammar and complemented—when it did not compete with—dialectic in teaching students to read, write, and speak well. These three discursive arts constituted the Trivium. Together with the Quadrivium—arithmetic, geometry, astronomy, and music—the Trivium formed the foundation of the full round of learning—what the Greeks called encyclopedic learning.

During this time, as before, Cicero dominated the rhetorical curriculum. The encyclopedists of the 5th through 7th centuries, including Cassiodorus, Martianus Capella, and Isidore of Seville, defined the discursive arts in Ciceronian terms. So did the rhetoricians, including Fortunatianus and Julius Victor. Beginning in the 4th century with Victorinus, the two most popular rhetorical treatises, Cicero's early *De inventione* and the pseudo-Ciceronian *Ad Herennium,* came under the careful scrutiny of the commentators. And at court as well as at school, teachers such as Alcuin (8th cent.) undertook the training of their royal charges like Charlemagne by using Ciceronian dialogue to inculcate Ciceronian rhetorical principles. Indeed, Cicero alone among the ancient rhetoricians found his way during this period into the vernacular.

Fully fitted for the medieval classroom, Ciceronian rhetoric also met the needs of the pulpit. From Hrabanus Maurus's 9th-century *On the Education of Clerics* to Alain of Lille's 13th-century *Summa,* the classical art of rhetoric thoroughly informed the medieval art of preaching. The preacher so trained, moreover, would get a double dose of Cicero: first in the form of the *magister eloquentiae* himself and his commentators, then as appropriated by Augustine in his singularly influential manual for the preacher, *On Christian Doctrine* (397–427).

This duly famous treatise occupies a unique position in the gradual process that began with Paul of Christianizing the classical rhetorical tradition. The first three of its four books set out a number of principles for interpreting Scripture. Passing on to his readers Cicero's legacy from Aristotle, Augustine refers to this major portion of the treatise as the *ars inveniendi*—the art of discovering or inventing. Like his ancient predecessors, Augustine considers the preacher's first and most important task that of "hitting on what to say." For without having found "the truth" in Scripture, the preacher has nothing to teach his listeners. Only in the fourth book does Augustine turn to the art of professing the truth found, which combines rules for arrangement, style, and delivery. Quoting long passages of Cicero here, he considers the three characters of style—plain, middle, and grand—and how they teach, delight, and move the preacher's audience. The Augustinian transformations of classical rhetoric are easily recognized.

In Augustine's hands, the first Ciceronian ground of controversy, the discrepancy between the writer's words and his intention, becomes the distinction between literal and spiritual interpretation. The second and third grounds of controversy, ambiguity and contradiction, remain the same. Augustine also broadens the Ciceronian distinction between things and words (or content and form)—to things and signs, reducing language to only one—even if the most important—instrument of signification; and though he aligns things and signs with the equally rhetorical pairing made famous by Horace, the useful and the pleasant, he reverses the classical priority by characterizing as useful everything but God, in whom we find our ultimate delight. Augustine skillfully filled the new bottles of an emerging Christianity with the old wine of the rhetorical tradition, thereby joining the ranks of other influential Christian intellectuals, including Basil, Tertullian, Lactantius, Ambrose, and Jerome, who gave their rhetorical talents, both practical and theoretical, to the early Church.

Like the teachers and preachers of the Middle Ages, the officials of medieval Church and State, along with the lawyers who served their interests, could not have fulfilled their professional responsibilities without rhetorical training, and especially without training in the art of letter writing. This art both established the rules of composition for official documents in epistolary form and provided model letters for imitation. Often traced to a Benedictine monk of the 11th century, Alberic of Monte Cassino, the widely practiced epistolary art, like the art of preaching, actually had its roots in Ciceronian rhetoric, with its attention to the different parts of an oration, readily adapted to the parts of the letter, and to the effects of prose rhythm.

Throughout the Middle Ages, other classical authorities from the rhetorical tradition, most notably Aristotle and Quintilian, enjoyed occasional preeminence. William of Moerbeke's 13th-century translation of Aristotle's *Rhetoric* into Latin, for instance, inspired a number of commentaries on this all-but-forgotten treatise. And Quintilian, known throughout the Middle Ages in a partial text of the *Institutio oratoria,* first figured prominently in the work of the encyclopedists and then experienced a brief revival during the 12th century. Only after the Italian Humanist Poggio Bracciolini discovered a complete text early in 1416 did Quintilian finally come to exert a deep and lasting influence on rhetorical theory and practice. Thereafter, other Humanists, like Poliziano, made him the subject of their public lectures (1480–1481). And still others, such as the self-taught rhetorician and scholar Lorenzo Valla and Roger Ascham, the tutor to Queen Elizabeth, openly preferred him to Cicero. Between 1470 and 1539 Quintilian's masterwork became readily accessible through more than 40 editions.

Thus, until the 15th century no other classical authority exerted anything like the influence of Cicero on rhetorical training in its various forms. Even after 1400 Cicero commanded the field. The Humanists' Cicero, in contrast to the medieval one, wielded his authority from his later works: *De oratore, Orator,* and *Brutus.* These works of the mature Cicero were rediscovered in 1421. Indeed, the recovery of key classical texts, coupled with their increased availability through the new technology of printing, went a long way to explain the sharp rupture between medieval and Renaissance rhetoric—a rupture that rhetorically minded Humanists were themselves the first to announce.

Disengaged from its routine subordination to dialectic as part of the medieval Trivium, Renaissance rhetoric made league instead with poetry, philosophy, and history to form a new liberal arts—the *studia humanitatis.* In the hands of the Humanists, this liberal or humanistic study supported both the recovery of ancient Greek and the restoration of classical—more or less Ciceronian—Latin. With the recovery of Greek came the recovery of Greek rhetoric, aided in large part by the work of one man, George of Trebizond.

In addition to providing a new, improved translation of Aristotle's *Rhetoric* (printed ca. 1475), this native of Crete, equally fluent in ancient Greek and Latin, also composed the first full-scale Renaissance handbook designed to marry Hermogenes to Cicero, the Eastern to the Western rhetorical tradition. Through George's efforts, in fact, Hermogenes took his place beside Cicero and Quintilian as the principal authorities of antiquity. As late as the mid-16th century, professors of rhetoric at Oxford and Cambridge structured their lecture courses around this rhetorical triumvirate. Immodestly offered as a replacement for the *Institutio oratoria,* moreover, George's *Five Books of Rhetoric* (1433 or 1434) threatened to supplant more than Quintilian. For, as one contemporary Spanish academic put the case, "Our Trebizond falls between the tiresome prolixity of Quintilian and the concise brevity of Cicero" (quoted in Monfasani 1976, 319).

Building on "our Trebizond," influential educators such as Johann Sturm in Germany and Thomas Elyot in England championed Hermogenes' rhetorical theory without jettisoning Quintilian. In *The boke named the Governour* (1531), Elyot paired these two recently recovered ancient theorists together (1.11). So did Richard Rainolde in *A Booke called the Foundacion of Rhetorike* (1563), which added to the rhetorical pantheon another Greek authority, Aphthonius. Translated into Latin by Rudolf Agricola in the 15th century, Aphthonius' *Progymnasmata* formed the very bedrock of Renaissance rhetorical education and consequently of Renaissance literary production. Beginning in the 15th and well into the 16th century, then, Roman, and especially Ciceronian, rhetoric shared the stage with an increasing number of Greek rhetorical luminaries. It was only a matter of time before the Greek rhetorical theorists caught up to and in some quarters even surpassed the Roman rhetoricians, including Cicero. In the mid-17th century Milton proposed a rhetorical curriculum in his tract *Of Education* (1644) that included five Greeks—Plato, Aristotle, Demetrius, Longinus, and Hermogenes—and Cicero.

If the scholarly work of George of Trebizond proved decisive in the advance of Greek rhetoric, so did the publishing efforts of Aldus Manutius. In 1508 his revered Aldine Press in Venice brought out the first edition of the *Rhetores Graeci,* which featured Hermogenes (whose works with supplementary material take up over half a volume), Aphthonius, Demetrius, Dionysius of Halicarnassus, and Aristotle. Although this same press had earlier brought out an eagerly awaited edition of Aristotle's philosophical works (1495–1498), his *Rhetoric* and *Poetics* were excluded from that publication and included here instead.

No longer *the* classical authority on all matters rhetorical, Cicero nevertheless maintained well into the 16th century the undisputed status of master of style. Throughout Europe, especially in Italy and France, men of letters labored to imitate him, some refusing to use locutions unprecedented in his extant works. This program of a pure Ciceronian imitation had its defenders, most notably Pietro Bembo. It also had detractors, among them Erasmus, who responded to these imitators of Cicero's style with his *Ciceronianus* (1528), a satiric dialogue that sets in high and humorous relief the folly of imposing an inflexibly classical language on the discourse of Christians. Like Tacitus before him, however, Erasmus defended this position as more authentically Ciceronian on the grounds that it, rather than a slavish reproduction of style, promotes that most fundamental rhetorical principle of decorum. By the end of the 16th century and into the 17th, Ciceronian style lost ground to a simpler, less ornamental, Attic style.

Ciceronian rhetoric also came under attack by the French academic Peter Ramus, who rejects not only Ciceronianism but the classical tradition more broadly, writing polemics against Aristotle and Quintilian as well as Cicero. Reverting instead to a hierarchy familiar from the medieval Trivium, Ramus subordinated rhetoric to dialectic in an educational program that influenced the Protestant countries of northern Europe. In England he found a following in, among others, Gabriel Harvey and Abraham Fraunce. Meanwhile, the Jesuits embarked on their own educational mission to bring rhetorical training grounded in Aristotle, Cicero, and Quintilian to Catholics all over the world. Chief among the handbooks written for this effort is Father Cipriano Soarez's *De arte rhetorica libri tres ex Aristotele, Cicerone et Quintiliano deprompti* (1560).

Like the Jesuits, moreover, many of the most influential theorists of the 17th and 18th centuries continued to promote the cause of ancient rhetoric against its opponents. Fervently anti-Ramist, Gerardus Joannes Vossius wrote four rhetorics in Latin during the first half of the 17th century; all of them depend on Cicero, Quintilian, and especially Aristotle. In France and in the vernacular, René Rapin championed a classical rhetorical tradition that featured these same three figures, whereas his countryman François Fénelon added to the threesome Plato, Longinus, and Augustine. Largely inconsequential in earlier centuries, Longinian rhetoric came into its own in the 17th with, in addition to attention by Fénelon, the translation of *On Sublimity* into French by Nicolas Boileau (1674), followed in England by Edmund Burke's *A Philosophical Enquiry into the Origin of Our Ideas of the Sublime and Beautiful* (1757). Other British rhetorical manuals, like John Ward's *A System of Oratory* (1759), preserved Longinus' status among the more traditional threesome, Aristotle, Cicero, and Quintilian. Even those rhetorical movements in Britain at this time that seemed to depart from the classical tradition—the belletristic, for instance, represented by Hugh Blair's wildly popular *Lectures on Rhetoric and Belles Lettres* (1783), or the elocutionary, represented by Thomas Sheridan's *Lectures on Elocution* (1762)—arguably took ancient rhetoric and its principal theorists as their point of departure.

In Italy, on the other hand, where the earliest Humanists first labored to recover the Greek and Roman rhetorical texts that came to form the backbone of this tradition, Giambattista Vico openly countered the more scientific approaches to communication heralded throughout Europe with a return to more "humanistic" methods of persuasion sanctioned by the ancients. And in the fledgling United States, classical rhetoric still reigned supreme. Lecturing at Harvard as the first Boylston Professor of Rhetoric and Oratory (1806), John Quincy Adams assured his listeners that "a subject which has exhausted the genius of Aristotle, Cicero, and Quintilian can neither require nor admit much additional illustration. To select, combine, and apply their precepts, is the only duty left for their followers of all succeeding times, and to obtain a perfect familiarity with their instructions is to arrive at the mastery of the art" (quoted in Kennedy 1980, 240). Before too long, however, Adams's academic chair in rhetoric was replaced by a chair in poetry.

Thus, by the 19th century rhetoric suffered for being not only an art (as opposed to a science) but an art of persuasion. Identified (not for the first time) with sensory deception and only probable conclusions and therefore dismissed by the likes of Descartes, Locke, and Kant, rhetoric gradually lost its foothold both in the curriculum and in public life. Unlike Aldus's two-volume *Rhetores Graeci,* which galvanized the theoretical and practical efforts of accomplished rhetoricians throughout Europe, Christian Walz's nine volumes with the same title, published in the 1830s, brought in its wake no such flurry of rhetorical activity. And more recent attempts at revival, including the Chicago School of Neo-Aristotelians beginning in the 1930s, as represented by the work of R. S. Crane and Richard McKeon, or the attention to argument along classical rhetorical lines in the 1950s by such philosophers as Chaïm Perelman and Stephen E. Toulmin, have reached only very limited audiences, and those largely within a university setting. During the last hundred years and more the classical rhetorical tradition has remained almost exclusively an advanced academic specialty with little or no direct effect on general education or political life. I use the word *direct,* however, because the rhetorical principles forged as part of the classical tradition belong ineradicably to—because woven imperceptibly into—the fabric of contemporary intellectual life.

BIBL.: Thomas M. Conley, *Rhetoric in the European Tradition* (Chicago 1990). Kathy Eden, *Hermeneutics and the Rhetorical Tradition: Chapters in the Ancient Legacy and Its Humanist Reception* (New Haven 1997). Peter France, *Rhetoric and Truth in France: Descartes to Diderot* (Oxford 1972). Wilbur Samuel Howell, *Eighteenth-century British Logic and Rhetoric* (Princeton 1971). George A. Kennedy, *Classical Rhetoric and Its Christian and Secular Tradition from Ancient to Modern Times* (Chapel Hill 1980). John Monfasani, *George of Trebizond: A Biography and a Study of His Rhetoric and Logic* (Leiden 1976). Michael Mooney, *Vico in the Tradition of Rhetoric* (Princeton 1985). James J. Murphy, *Rhetoric in the Middle Ages* (Berkeley 1974).

K.E.

Rhōmaioi

A generic term for Greek-speaking citizens of the Roman Empire. With the Antonine Constitution of 212 CE all freeborn citizens of the empire were awarded Roman citizenship. Soon after Constantine the Great founded at Byzantium the imperial city of Constantinople (330), it was given the name New Rome (Nova Roma). Thereafter the eastern portion of the Roman Empire, which came to be called the Byzantine Empire, developed and persistently guarded its identity as the Roman Empire par excellence, especially after the collapse of the western half of the empire in 476. The increasing dominance of the Greek language in administration and legislation, especially after the 6th century, did not diminish this attitude, as all things labeled Hellenic were identified as pagan and hence were to be rejected by Christian citizens. Preference for the term *Rhōmaios* and its derivatives went so far as to term the Greek language as Roman (*rhōmaikē glōssa*), in distinction to Latin. With the emperor Heraclius (610–641) the official title of all Byzantine emperors became *pistos basileus autokrator Rhōmaiōn,* "faithful king and emperor of the Romans." The "Roman name" without any ethnic qualification was the constant label applied to all subjects of the "Roman" emperor and all state institutions. Occasional use of the expression "Roman nation" (*to Rhōmaiōn ethnos*) for the Byzantines as the political body was therefore deprived of any ethnic connotation. What counted was the allegiance of the citizens to the Roman emperor in Constantinople. They constituted the "kingdom" or, rather, "empire of the Romans," *basileia Rhōmaiōn* (Anna Comnena, *Alexiad* 3.173.4–7 passim). In Comnena and also in many other sources we also see terms such as *Rhōmaiōn chōra* or *gē* (territory), *Rhōmaiōn archē* and *hēgemonia* (leadership). The same term is abundantly used in connection with the army, the navy, the borders, and other geopolitical entities. The emperor Leo VI (886–912) applied to his own subjects the classical definition of the 2nd-century jurist Ulpian: "Those who live on Roman [i.e., Byzantine] soil are citizens of Rome" (*Basilica* 46.1.1.14). In the 12th century the canonist Theodore Balsamon further asserted that those who live an orthodox (Christian) life are *Rhōmaioi* even if they dwell beyond the empire's borders (Rhalles-Potles, *Syntagma* 4:454).

The empire's eastern neighbors did not hesitate to apply the same terminology (Rome is *Rum* in Syriac and Arabic). In the West, however, the kings of the successor states to the fallen Western empire, especially the Franks and later the Saxons, as pretenders to sovereignty over Rome and its imperial prerogatives, avoided and occasionally deliberately questioned the Latin term *Romani* as applied to the Byzantines, whom they preferred to call *Graeci* or *Greci*. Thus it came about that with his coronation in Rome in 800 Charlemagne claimed the Roman name for his title (*nomen Romanum*). *Romanitas* was to become the apple of discord in the two medieval empires' rivalry over identity. From the 7th century onward the term *Romania* was increasingly applied in Western colloquial usage to the territory and the populace of the Eastern Roman Empire. In the East, Constantine Porphyrogenitus distinguished the *Rhōmaioi,* all the subjects of the Byzantine emperor, from a small portion of them whom he called *Rhōmanoi:* those were the Latin-speaking citizens of Dalmatia, "from their having been removed from Rome," and this name attaches to them until this day (*De administrando imperio* 29.6). As late as the 15th century Joseph Bryennius would distinguish so between the Byzantines (*Rhōmaioi*) and the Westerners (*Latinoi*).

Even today *Rhōmioi* (the modern spelling) is another name of the Greeks, and *Rum-Orthodox* is the official name of Orthodox Christians in the Middle East; even the Muslims of Eastern Anatolia who still speak the Pontic dialect of Greek call their tongue *Rumtsa*.

BIBL.: Evangelos Chrysos, "Romans and Foreigners," in *Fifty Years of Prosopography,* ed. Averil Cameron, Proceedings of the British Academy 118 (London 2003) 119–136. E.C.

Roads, Roman

The Romans were not the first to build roads, but they were the first to create a great system of roads. At its fullest range this network covered more than 50,000 miles throughout the empire. Bridges carried roads across rivers and allowed travelers, including armies, merchants, and individuals of all kinds, to cross easily rather than to ford, ferry, or come to a complete halt. The Romans thought of their roads as "monuments" or enduring testimonies, and they often named them after great families or emperors. The vast system of Roman roads has been called the longest monument in the world. Most of the European road system up to the 18th century followed the Roman one. Even today, the Roman system profoundly influences the trajectory of roads and highways. Various modern terms for streets and roads in all European languages derive from Latin terms used in antiquity.

Roman roads were marked with cylindrical columns called milestones, which measured the distance in *milia passuum* (thousands of steps) whether from the beginning of the road, from the last town, or to the next one. We still speak today of passing milestones in life or on the way to a particular goal, a tribute to the lasting influence of the Roman invention.

The Romans built paved roads with the materials at hand depending on location. They created a special foundation by digging a trench to create the roadbed and then filling it with layers of various materials compressed with heavy rollers. The immediate subsurface layer was of sand; upon this the surface pavement was constructed with slabs cut from basalt, granite, or other hard stones. The roads were slightly pitched to ensure proper drainage, and lined with stones on each side to enclose and hold the pavement together. In towns and cities, streets included curbstones or stepping stones and were flanked with sidewalks.

Medieval people traveled Roman roads but did not maintain them well. They built new roads on different principles, using stones or cobbles on a loose foundation of sand, a road that could expand or contract in heat and cold and could be repaired easily. In the eastern Mediterranean and North Africa, vehicular traffic declined and then disappeared, as camels, which do not need roads, became the primary mode of transport.

Yet interest in Roman roads is evident from medieval times. For example, in 1265 a monk from Colmar (Alsace) made a copy of a Roman road map on 12 sheets of parchment. Now in the Nationalbibliothek in Vienna, it was found in 1494 by Conrad Celtis, who named it the Peutinger Table, after his friend Konrad Peutinger of Augsburg. Numerous charters and other documents of the time clearly show that medieval people also often used Roman roads to demarcate boundaries and areas of jurisdiction. Roman roads are frequently mentioned in descriptions of pilgrimages, guidebooks, and travelers' accounts, including that by Michel de Montaigne in his *Travel Journal* of the 1580s. The great 16th-century architect Andrea Palladio was particularly fascinated by Roman roads and bridges and described some of them in detail. Roman roads inspired him to provide access roads to his villas. In 17th-century France, Jean-Baptiste Colbert (1619–1683), minister of finance to Louis XIV, rehabilitated in Lyon the network of Roman roads originally constructed in the reign of the emperor Agrippa. In the

18th century the Scottish engineer John Loudon McAdam (1756–1836) went back to Roman ideas in his construction of "macadam" roads, draining the subsoil, grading the materials, and packing them in layers. Subsequent road builders again took up the Roman practice of creating embanked highways.

The Romans built bridges to extend roads (and sometimes aqueducts) across rivers. They built pontoon bridges (constructed out of boats), timber bridges, stone arch bridges, and masonry bridges. Pontoon and timber bridges are known through literary and visual evidence, such as the relief sculptures on two great monuments in Rome, Trajan's Column (113 CE) and the Column of Marcus Aurelius (193). Perhaps the most famous timber bridge is the one constructed by Julius Caesar over the Rhine in 55 BCE, described by him in his *Gallic War* (4.17). More than 350 Roman stone and brick bridges are extant, many of them still in use. Arch bridges, made of stone or brick, a form brought to perfection by the Romans, remained the major form of bridge construction until the mid-18th century.

BIBL.: R. Chevallier, *Roman Roads,* trans. N. H. Field (Berkeley 1976). D. Hill, *A History of Engineering in Classical and Medieval Times* (1984; repr. London 1996) 76–89. I. D. Margary, *Roman Roads in Britain,* 3rd ed. (London 1973). C. O'Connor, *Roman Bridges* (Cambridge 1993). A. Palladio, *The Four Books on Architecture,* trans. R. Tavernor and R. Schofield (Cambridge, Mass., 1997) 3:1–14. R. A. Staccioli, *The Roads of the Romans,* trans. S. Sartarelli (Los Angeles 2003).

P.O.L.

Roman Monuments, Reuse of

Despoiling and recycling of architectural monuments in ancient Rome, if not routine practice, was subject to imperial sanction. Alexander Severus, reenacting a law introduced by Vespasian, prohibited speculators from scavenging of building debris. In the 3rd century, however, reuse of *spolia* came to depend not just on the intrinsic value of dressed marble but on symbolic associations —whether the fluted Pentelic shafts conspicuously embedded in the pediment of the Porticus Octaviae during its Severan restoration, or the Antonine reliefs inserted on the north face of the Arco di Portogallo when Aurelian rebuilt it a century later. There were arguably similar propagandistic aims in the decision by Constantine to revet his triumphal arch with reliefs from earlier honorific monuments of Trajan, Hadrian, and Marcus Aurelius. In the case of the Janus Quadrifrons, also from the Constantinian period, the incorporation of figurated keystones and entablature fragments—probably of Flavian date—does not appear programmatic.

The 6th century saw the first systematic attempts to convert the city's abandoned ruins for Christian worship: the basilica of Santi Cosma e Damiano, once the audience hall of the city prefect's office (Templum urbis Romae) and an adjoining library of the Temple of Peace, was consecrated in 527 by Felix IV; Santa Maria ad Martyres, formerly the Pantheon, was dedicated in 609 by Boniface IV; and Sant'Adriano was transformed by Honorius I (625–638) from the Curia Senatus in the Roman Forum. During the 11th and 12th centuries Rome's baronial families constructed fortified residences over abandoned ruins: the Conti inside the precinct walls of the Forum of Augustus (Palatium Nervae, later inhabited by the Knights of Rhodes), the Orsini and Savelli over the Markets of Trajan (Torre delle Milizie), and the Frangipani addorsed to the Arch of Titus (Turris Cartularia). The Pierleoni clan dominated the Forum Holitorium, giving its name to the original sanctuary of San Nicola in Carcere. Rebuilt in 1128, the exterior flanks of the church were immured around colonnades from two adjacent temples from the late republican period, one Tuscan the other Ionic. The mansion erected by Nicola Crescenzi in the Forum Boarium around 1100, its brick walls adorned with a pastiche of ancient marble putti, sphinxes, and coffers, bears an inscription over its entrance attesting to the owner's desire to recover the beauty of the ancient city (*Romae veterem renovare decorem*).

Despite a series of papal bulls to protect Roman antiquities, the first by Pius II in 1462, quarrying went on unabated, most heavily from the Colosseum. Raphael, as *praefectus* of antiquities under Leo X, prosecuted against the defiling of marbles bearing inscriptions. In his famous memorandum to the pope, composed around 1518 with the collaboration of Baldassare Castiglione, Raphael deplored the incursions of the Goths and later barbarians, while observing that in imperial times often monuments would be restored (*ristaurati*), but always in concordance with the original design (*con la medesima maniera e ragione*). He pointed to the Domus Aurea, on which Titus later constructed his baths, as well as the Flavian amphitheater, which rose on the site of Nero's artificial lake. In this way the ancients maintained a consistently high standard in the building arts, which came to an abrupt end with the Arch of Constantine. Its sculptural reliefs, Raphael judged, were a stylistic anomaly (*sciochissime, senza arte o disegno alcuno buono*).

In the same way that Raphael understood the act of *ristorare* as a process of ongoing adaptation by successive emperors, so too contemporaries saw a continuum between the physical fabric of ancient Rome, such as it survived, and the emerging Renaissance style *all'antica.* It would have seemed appropriate not to preserve these ruins in archaeological isolation but instead to blend old and new, refitting forms as dictated by the functions these structures had come to assume. An early example is the Theater of Marcellus, which had fallen into disuse by 525, when a Roman prefect hauled away portions of the masonry to restore the nearby Pons Cestius. In the 14th century the ruin passed from the Pierleoni to the Savelli—its exterior so obscured by defensive towers that Petrarch mistook it for an amphitheater ("quliseo de' Saveli"). In 1523 Cardinal Giulio Savelli commissioned Baldassare Peruzzi to design a palace on the attic story, which, according to his pupil Sebastiano Serlio, presented the architect an opportunity to break through medieval tenements wedged between the interior *caveae* and to discern for the first time its original plan. Yet Peruzzi, constrained by the preexisting partitions, made no effort to align the Ghibelline windows on the facade with the arcades below.

In these same years Count Orsini di Pitigliano charged Peruzzi with converting the Baths of Agrippa to a grandiose palace. The project, known only from a detailed survey in the Uffizi, would have preserved the largest thermal rooms, most notably the *caldarium,* called the Arco della Ciambella from the portion of its dome still standing. In 1525 excavations were undertaken, perhaps at Orsini's own behest, to widen and straighten a road from the Pantheon to the baths (*ex dicta platea rotunde per directum ad plateam vulgariter nuncupatam la Sciampella*). According to Peruzzi's plan, however, the Via di Tor Argentina and Via de' Cestari, which bounded the ruins on the west and east respectively, were to be closed off. As the thermae were not laid out symmetrically, Peruzzi corrected for this "deficiency" by creating a new axis centered on the rectangular courtyard (labeled *cortiletto ovvero giardino*) egressing into a barrel-vaulted vestibule. Rather than linking north to the Pantheon, the palace would have turned its face to the south directly onto the Via Papalis. A scholar of Vitruvius, Peruzzi interpreted the *caldarium* along the lines of the *cavum aedium* in the ancient *domus,* specifically the type called *testudinate,* that is, covered by vaults (*De architectura* 6.3). Leon Battista Alberti had identified just such a room in describing the layout of the imperial baths: "In the middle, as in the center of a house, there is an atrium, roofed, spacious, and majestic" (*De re aedificatoria* 8.10). As no foundations of Roman houses had yet been unearthed, it was impossible to construe accurately what Vitruvius meant by the progression from vestibule to atrium to peristyle. Conversely, the centrifugal flow of rooms from a central core, which is typical of the imperial thermae, gave some basis for Renaissance architects to visualize such a disposition.

The Baths of Nero (Thermae Alexandrinae), extensive portions of which survived into the 16th century, similarly provided a blueprint for the invention of Renaissance architects. Its foundations stretched along Via dei Lombardi on the eastern fringes of Piazza Navona all the way to the medieval church of San Salvatore delle Terme. In 1509 a palace and adjacent properties "con vestigia e pareti delle antiche Terme" were acquired by Alfonsina Orsini, widow of Pietro de' Medici. About six years later Leo X commissioned Antonio da Sangallo the Younger to expand the palace, which required transforming what remained of the ancient *palestrae* into flanking courtyards for the papal quarters and the residences of the other Medici branch (its axis rotated 90 degrees). The drawings for this project (Uffizi A. 1259r–v) overlap with Sangallo's reconstruction of the Vitruvian *domus.*

Private habitations had also sprouted amid the ruins of the Thermae of Diocletian. Cardinal Jean du Bellay established his villa in the vast area enclosed by the south exedra. In 1541 the Sicilian priest Antonio Lo Duca experienced a mystical vision of seven angels hovering in the stucco vaults of the frigidarium and entreated Pope Paul III to dedicate a church on the site. In 1547 the pope conceded one of the corner *torrioni* of the bath complex (originally a *sphaeristerion*). The rotunda of San Bernardino alle Terme, its coffered dome resembling that of the Pantheon, was dedicated in 1600. Meanwhile, Pius IV endowed the ruins of the frigidarium and adjoining *natatio* to a community of Carthusian monks and in 1561 charged Michelangelo with converting the groin-vaulted hall for the basilica of Santa Maria degli Angeli. Earlier, Giuliano da Sangallo, Baldassare Peruzzi, and Giovan Antonio Dosio had drawn elevations of the frigidarium with the intention of transforming it into a nave, paralleling their designs for the interior of the new St. Peter's. These proposals largely anticipated Lo Duca's intentions, whereas Michelangelo reoriented the plan at 90 degrees by screening the frigidarium on its long axis to form an enclosed transept. He pushed out the choir to the northeast and converted the tepidarium to a round vestibule. The resultant plan followed a Greek cross, rather than the longitudinal form favored by Counter-Reform prelates.

Early guides affixed various names to the complex of *tabernae* making up the Aula Magna and Markets of Trajan. It was probably the senator Pandolfo de Subura who erected the infamous Torre delle Milizie in 1232 "in Montem (Quirinalem) . . . Ballea Neapolis dicitur." The toponyms "Balnea Neapolis," "Bagnanapoli," and "Magnanapoli" in time became interchangeable; Renaissance architects interpreted the great hemicycle facing the Forum of Trajan as an open-air courtyard belonging to the Palatium Militiarum. Pomponio Leto traced its origin to the Roman *aedile,* L. Aemilius Paullus, noting that *Balneapolis* was a vulgarized form of *Balneum Paulli.* This false etymology steered Renaissance antiquarians, who saw a further affinity of the hemicycle to either the ancient theater (Bartolomeo Marliani) or the ancient baths (Bernardo Gamucci). Sallustio Peruzzi's extensive studies of the area date to 1563, when Porzia Massimi founded the convent of Santa Caterina da Siena on the former palace of Prince Giovan Battista dei Conti, to which were annexed both the Torre delle Milizie and ancient markets. The shops along the Via Biberatica were to be redisposed for a choir, cistern, refectory, and poultry farm (*pollaio*). In one sketch, Peruzzi contemplated transforming the hemicycle into a *frons scaenae,* inverting the plan of the Roman theater by placing the spectators on the site of Trajan's Forum. Shortly after 1574 the papal architect Ottavio Mascarino proposed a more conservative reutilization of the hemicycle to accommodate a *lavatorio, anditone,* and *parlatorio delle monache.*

The Castel Sant'Angelo, originally the mausoleum of Hadrian, lost much of its travertine base during the pontificate of Alexander VI, who added battlements and redoubts for use as a fortress beginning in 1496. As late as the pontificate of Gregory XIII (1566–1572), marble tituli were still being stripped for the revetment of his chapel in the new St. Peter's. In the case of the Mausoleum of Augustus, an enclave of the Colonna going back to the 12th century, the exterior of travertine blocks was carted off during the laying of the Via Ripetta (Leonina) in 1519, at which time the obelisk from the ancient meridian was unearthed. In 1546 Francesco Soderini bought the ruinous mound and undertook excavations that resulted in the discovery of numerous ancient statues. The interior was rearranged with circular hedges forming a labyrinth garden, as depicted in a famous engraving by Étienne du Pérac. In the 18th century its Portuguese proprietor, Vincenzo Correa, refitted the grounds as a bull ring. The master plan of 1909 called for refurbishing the mausoleum as a concert hall, renamed the Augusteo, and disencumbering it from annexed buildings. In 1933 Mussolini, in preparation for the bimillennial of Augustus's birth, targeted this area for urban renewal. Vittorio Ballo Mopurgo's project called for reintegrating the mausoleum with the two Renaissance churches along the Via di Ripetta, San Girolamo and San Rocco, to create a grander aspect on the west. Two new buildings for the Fascist administration sporting classical porticoes would define the piazza on the north.

The Flavian amphitheater lay abandoned by the 6th century. In the 12th century the Frangipani claimed two levels of arcades on the eastern side toward the Lateran for their *palatium.* On the occasion of Ludwig of Bavaria's visit in 1332, the arena was outfitted for bullfights and wooden scaffolding had to be erected, as most of the marble seating had perished in limekilns. In 1366 the Compagnia dei Nobili Romani Sancta Sanctorum began purchasing houses clustered around the arena. This prepared the way for the Compagnia del Gonfalone, which in 1490 gained permission to perform passion plays and other sacred representations. In 1519 they erected a modest chapel dedicated to Santa Maria della Pietà, but the spectacles were discontinued in 1539. Sixtus V earmarked the Colosseum as part of his grand scheme to reconfigure Rome on a stellar plan: the amphitheater would be converted to a monumental church with an esplanade all around; a road under construction would link it to San Giovanni in Laterano. Only two years later he had Domenico Fontana revamp the ruins as a wool factory, with covered shops on the ground floor and artisans' lodgings on the second story. The Meta Sudans and newly dug fountains extending as far as the Tor de' Conti would supply water for washing and dyeing fabrics. According to Fontana, the project was one year from realization when Sixtus's death put an end to it. Bernini, when approached by Clement X to erect a Tempio de' Martiri on the site for the Jubilee of 1675, advocated leaving the Colosseum unaltered as a testimony both to Christian martyrdom and to the grandeur of imperial Rome. His pupil Carlo Fontana, however, undertook a round peripteral church at one end of the long axis by commission of Innocent XI. Its design, published posthumously in his *L'anfiteatro Flavio* (1725), never saw realization.

BIBL.: Michela di Macco, *Il Colosseo: Funzione simbolica, storica, urbana* (Rome 1971). Hellmut Hager, "Carlo Fontana's Project for a Church in Honour of the 'Ecclesia Triumphans' in the Colosseum, Rome," *Journal of the Warburg and Courtauld Institutes* 36 (1973) 319–337. Christian Huelsen, *Die Thermen des Agrippa: Ein Beitrag zur Topographie des Marsfeldes in Rom* (Rome 1910). Spiro Kostof, "The Emperor and the Duce: The Planning of Piazzale Augusto Imperatore in Rome," in *Art and Architecture in the Service of Politics,* ed. H. A. Millon and L. Nochlin (Cambridge, Mass., 1978) 270–322. Rodolfo Lanciani, *Storia degli scavi di Roma e notizie intorno le collezioni Romane di antichità,* vol. 1, ed. L. Malvezzi Campeggi (Rome 1989). Roberto Meneghini, "Il foro ed i mercati di Traiano nel medioevo attraverso le fonti storiche e d'archivio," *Archeologia medievale* 20 (1993) 79–120. Patrizio Pensabene and Clementina Panella, "Reimpiego e progettazione architettonica nei monumenti tardo-antichi di Roma," *Rendiconti della Pontificia Accademia Romana di Archeologia* 66 (1993–1994) 111–283. Joachim Poeschke, ed., *Antike Spolien in der Architektur des Mittelalters und der Renaissance* (Munich 1996). Anna Maria Riccomini, "A Garden of Statues and Marbles: The Soderini Collection in the Mausoleum of Augustus," *Journal of the Warburg and Courtauld Institutes* 58 (1995) 265–283. Ronald T. Ridley, *The Eagle and the Spade: Archaeology in Rome during the Napoleonic Era* (Cambridge 1992). Herbert Siebenhünner, "S. Maria degli Angeli in Rom," *Münchner Jahrbuch der bildenden Kunst,* ser. 3, 6 (1955) 179–206. Heinrich Würm, *Baldassare Peruzzi: Architekturzeichnungen: Tafelband* (Tübingen 1984).

P.J.

Romance, Medieval

In the minds of the writers of medieval romance, there existed an unbroken continuity between the literature of the ancient world and their own endeavors. This was attributable to the process of *translatio studii,* whereby Greek texts and learning were appropriated by a Roman culture that in turn left its own legacy for the Middle Ages. Chrétien de Troyes, the earliest and most important author of verse romance, opens his tale of Cligés with a tribute to his ancient models: "Our books have taught us how Greece ranked first in chivalry and learning; then chivalry passed to Rome along with the fund of transcendent learning that has now come to France" (1997, 93). The characterization of the ancient world as a locus of chivalry and learning is as much a compliment to the courtly culture of the 12th century, which prized both, as it is an acknowledgment of the debt owed by medieval romance to classical epic and history.

Many romances allude to the medieval myth of origin that held that the dynasties of Western Europe were founded by Trojan descendants such as Brutus, mythical founder of London. The anonymous 14th-century English masterpiece *Sir Gawain and the Green Knight* opens with an account of how Ennias (Aeneas) and "his highe kynde" (noble kin) "depreced prouinces, and patrounes bicome/Welneȝe of al þe wele in þe west iles" ("subjugated provinces and became rulers of almost all the wealth in the lands of the west," 5–6). The transformation of the matter of Troy from epic to romance occurred in two stages, the first of which was the rendition of the Trojan legend into quasi-historical form, in the shape of the versions composed between 400 and 600 CE and attributed to Dares and Dictys (*De excidio Trojae historia* and *Ephemeris belli Troiani,* respectively). These texts were the sources for Benoît de Sainte Maure's lengthy *Roman de Troie* (ca. 1165), which treats the epic material in a manner consistent with medieval religion and the secular ideologies of chivalry and *fin amor* ("refined love"). Benoît's *Roman de Troie* was itself adapted into Latin prose by Guido delle Colonne as *Historia destructionis Troiae* (1287), which was widely read and translated. Other *romans d'antiquité,* as they are called, were the *Roman de Thèbes* (ca. 1150, based on Statius's *Thebaid*), and the *Roman d'Eneas* (ca. 1160, based on the *Aeneid*). English translations or adaptations were made of all these romances, notably Chaucer's *Knight's Tale* and *Troilus and Criseyde* in the 14th century (which employed Boccaccio's *Teseide* and *Il filostrato* as intermediary texts), and in the 15th century John Lydgate's *Troy Book* and *Siege of Thebes.* In *Troilus,* Criseyde and her ladies are depicted listening to a "romaunce . . . of Thebes" (2.106). Chaucer's version of antiquity reflects a medieval fascination with the noble pagan, of whom Troilus and Theseus are the exemplars. Both are granted a proto-Christian sensibility as Chaucer weaves into his romances a 6th-century Christian text, Boethius's *De consolatione philosophiae,* which contributes the material for Theseus's meditation on the workings of the "Firste Moevere" in the *Knight's Tale* (2987–3074) and Troilus's speech on destiny and free will (*Troilus* 953–1078). The antiquity of Chaucer's romances is, therefore, simultaneously pagan and Christian, just as his classical protagonists are also types of the ideal medieval lover.

The prodigal achievements of Alexander (356–323 BCE), and the ancient tradition of blending fact and fantasy in accounts of his life, meant that his story seemed ideal matter to 12th-century romancers, whose various efforts were combined into the *Roman d'Alexandre.* The treatment of Alexander in medieval romance emphasizes his roles as conqueror and ruler and presents him as the embodiment of the ideal medieval prince—courageous, liberal, and magnanimous. A further attraction of the Alexander narrative lay in its fabulous content, which featured oriental marvels like Candace's palace and Alexander's famous attempt at flight.

The ancient world, as a consequence of its temporal distance and its reputation for learning, often figures as a site of magic and marvel in romance. The city of Carthage in the *Roman d'Eneas,* for example, becomes an architectural marvel, its decorations and wonders reminiscent of the gems and creatures described in medieval lapidaries and bestiaries. Technological devices such as Alexander's flying contraption drawn by birds, or the lifelike brass statues erected by Virgil in *The Seven Sages of Rome* and designated as "meruail" (line 1986), inspired wonder at the mechanical and quasi-magical skill of antiquity. Classical literature was often granted an aura of the magical. Virgil was frequently cast as a magician in medieval legend, and ancient texts include famous examples of magical practice, such as Circe's isle in the *Odyssey* and Dido's deployment of magic in the *Aeneid.*

Not surprisingly, mythological references are found predominantly in learned romances written by the likes of Chaucer and Lydgate rather than in popular metrical romance. One romance, the early 14th-century *Sir Orfeo,* is a medievalized version of the legend of Orpheus found in Virgil's *Georgics* and Ovid's *Metamorphoses.* Various changes are made in the English version; for example, its debt to Celtic mythology is shown by the fact that Orfeo's wife, Heurodis, is abducted by the King of the Fairies. The poem also has a happy ending, because Orfeo's musical skill secures the rescue of his wife. The focus of the story on the love of Orfeo and Heurodis is, however, blurred by the addition of a concluding section in which Orfeo tests the loyalty of his steward. Two other romances concerned with love, *Apollonius of Tyre* and *Floris and Blauncheflur,* both of which were popular throughout medieval Europe, are also ancient stories of probably Greek or Byzantine origin. Though classical epic and history contributed much to the narrative matter of medieval romance, its presentation of love is heavily indebted to the works of Ovid because of the influence exerted by the *Ars amatoria* and the *Remedia amoris* on the ideology of *fin amor.* This influence and the medieval tradition of moralizing Ovid's works is clearly seen in the 12th-century allegory of love, *Le Roman de la rose.* The *roman antique* also participated in the romancing of Ovid by enhancing the quantity and importance of erotic material in the historical narratives and by introducing Ovidian analyses of love. A notable example of this tendency is the story of Dido and Aeneas, in which the Virgilian and Ovidian versions are typically combined.

BIBL.: Peter L. Allen, *The Art of Love: Amatory Fiction from Ovid to the "Romance of the Rose"* (Philadelphia 1992). C. David Benson, *The History of Troy in Middle English Literature* (Woodbridge, U.K., 1980). George Cary, *The Medieval Alexander* (Cambridge 1956). Chrétien de Troyes, *Cligés,* in *Arthurian Romances,* ed. and trans. D. D. R. Owen (Rutland, Vt., 1997). Barbara Nolan, *Chaucer and the Tradition of the "Roman Antique"* (Cambridge 1992). H.M.

Romanticism

At the end of the 18th century, both the inventory and the ground map of the ancient world had expanded. Artworks of Greek and Roman antiquity were available in increasingly large numbers. Excavations, prominently at Pompeii and Herculaneum from 1748, had brought to light new objects abroad and created new tastes at home (based, for example, on William Hamilton's multivolume *Greek Vases,* 1791–1794), and travelers, images, and artifacts were circulating. Johann Joachim Winckelmann's seminal writings in the 1760s and 1770s on the history of ancient art had made Greek sculpture synonymous with the self-contained, clearly delineated cultural perfection of classical civilization. Romanticism would blur this contour, building on that same notion of the classical while interrogating it. Thus, it is no coincidence that the worlds of Romantic literature are filled with statues that uncannily mix the classical and the pagan with Christian elements (as in Eichendorff's prose work *The Marble Effigy,* 1817), which are distantly veiled (Novalis' *The Novices of Sais,* 1802), or which are relocated to modern or exotic surroundings.

Romanticism, as a European cultural movement or attitude, is notoriously hard to pin down in its temporal, geographical, and disciplinary reach. The deceptive looseness of the term *romantic,* and the tendency toward paradox, however, are part and parcel of the ambitious Romantic project as a whole, perhaps best captured in the programmatic call of the young German Romantics (Novalis, the brothers Schlegel, Schleiermacher) in the 1790s, to "romanticize the world"—in a continuous, reflective, even analytical, process that relied on the energies set free in the tension between ancient and modern, particular and universal, fragment and whole, own and foreign, self and other, individual and society, elite and democracy, national and global—all pairings that reappear in Romanticism's varied treatments of themes, forms, and contexts from classical antiquity.

To a large extent the association of Romanticism with an anti-classical position is the result of Romantic (and anti-Romantic) polemic, subsequently entrenched in literary historiography. It did not, however, spell the end of an engagement with the cultures of classical antiquity. Most practitioners of Romanticism had received a solid classical education, and in turn many of their ideas also manifestly permeated the steep career of institutionalized classical scholarship across Europe.

Against the normative authority of classical artistic forms and works of art, the historicizing position had come to prevail that ancient and modern art belonged in the first instance to their respective proper spheres. The focus shifted to what it meant to be modern (*romantic* becoming almost a synonym of *modern* and *vernacular*) and in what novel ways to conceive of tradition. The dangerous calibration between tradition and violent innovation, and the challenge of becoming a tradition, the "short circuit of Revolution and Restoration" (Moretti 2000), are among the guiding issues besetting the movement as a whole. As a historical period, likewise, Romanticism can be roughly framed in inception by the French Revolution, considered not only by many Romantics to have been the defining and catalytic moment of the age, and in closure by the restorative events of the 1830s in France and the revolutions of 1848 across Europe on the other hand, which formed the backdrop to the last debates surrounding the movement as a viable program.

Again, those boundaries, like those between classicism and Romanticism, were fluid. The intellectual commotions of the late Enlightenment, early Idealist philosophy, and the movements, for instance, of Sturm und Drang and sentimentality before 1789 had a strong bearing on Romanticism across Europe, especially in the close mutual observation of England, Germany, and France. The transformations of the Romantic repertoire in northern, eastern, and southern Europe, in places such as Russia, Poland, and Greece, on the other end, reached far into the mid- and even late 19th century, by which time Romanticism itself had developed the weight of a tradition to be reckoned with or to resist. In addition, notions of Romanticism were here often mediated through the example of France, especially Madame de Staël's seminal account *De l'Allemagne* (1813). Take the example of Italy: here the debate about Romanticism was about national literature and its position toward France and Europe; but its authors, such as Ugo Foscolo in his poem *On Funerary Monuments* (1807) and in his political tragedies on Greek mythological themes, or Giacomo Leopardi in his scholarly *Essay on the Popular Errors of the Ancients* (1815) and in his poems and dialogues of the 1820s and 1830s, combine elements of formal Neoclassicism and Romanticism in a range of genres and registers, and in equal and often inseparable measures.

In its terminology Romanticism had arisen out of a literary debate that tied into the then current fascination with the boundaries of the ancient and premodern. Until the end of the 18th century, "romantic" had been used, in several languages, to denote matters pertaining to romance and the *roman,* that is, to the genre of chivalric literature, composed in the vernaculars of the medieval romance languages (which themselves become the focus of Romantic attention); or, by extension, to indicate the fantastic, enchanted, or mysterious, as it manifested itself in the plots and landscapes of that genre, and as it could also be applied to modern works of art. With Romanticism, the term came in to use in contradistinction to the "classical," to mean both anything post-classical and that which emphasizes a valuable departure from classical norms. Like Schiller's dichotomy between the Naïve and the Sentimental (1795), the classical and the Romantic are a pairing that describes a historical development as well as an ongoing conceptual difference, a set of "modes" that can be perceived only from the self-conscious point of modernity.

The changing view of history, as something itself subject to historical change and analysis, laid the foundation for perceiving antiquity as an elusive and compelling medium for self-reflection. Such cultural critique had already been a strong impetus in the pre-Romantic period. The writings of Jean-Jacques Rousseau paradigmatically offered a response to restrictive modernity, combining an interest in the history of past civilizations, and the institutions that shaped them, with enthusiasm for the vision of a premodern, more natural state. This impetus arrived just as Homer became revalorized across Europe as a natural or naive poet, in the sense of offering the immediate distillation of the people's voice, uninflected by models (famously so in Robert Wood's *Essay on the Original Genius and Writings of Homer,* 1769). Although the natural was a highly valued attribute of antiquity, its relationship with culture was of prime interest to the Romantic perspective, and in general the Romantic approach to antiquity mined the dynamic affinities of the political, the personal, and the aesthetic. An illustrative example from the threshold of the Romantic era is Wilhelm Heinse's novel *Ardinghello; or, The Islands of the Blest* (1787), whose main character, a visionary artist in the Renaissance, seeks to establish a utopian colony in the Greek Mediterranean, based on Platonic models and combining natural law with moral and artistic freedom.

On this premise of self-reflection, reactions to the ancient past could range from the enthusiastic to the paralyzed. Constantin François Volney in *The Ruins; or, Meditations on the Revolutions of Empires* (1791), a universal history based on his travels to ancient monuments in the Near East, drew conclusions for the present that were of a strongly republican kind as much as they were about the overwhelming mental experience of the sublime in the face of lost grandeur. For him the ancient past posed a potentially liberating challenge to the political and aesthetic imagination alike. Yet perception of the ancient past was not restricted to the Graeco-Roman world, but inclusive of other civilizations, such as Egypt, the ancient Near East, and India. The study of Sanskrit, in particular, as an original language in the history of culture, is itself a product of Romantic scholarship (perhaps most prominently thanks to the untiring Friedrich Schlegel).

The challenge to the imagination also revalorized classical mythology to suggest new ways of signifying and understanding, appealing to a novel sense of creativity. Among the motifs most passionately adopted, the Titans loom large, the most paradigmatic of them perhaps Prometheus. Whether in Goethe's early poem of that name (1773) or in Shelley's *Prometheus Unbound* (1820) we find a youthful, rebellious figure at the risk of individuality and of solitude alike, yet impelled by a visionary commitment to mankind.

The pull against a perceived tradition also governed engagement with literary genres, including those of the classical canon. Like the past, these might not (and perhaps should not) be accessible any longer, but neither did they disappear. A wide and deliberate range of hybrid forms emerged: the lyrical drama, such as Shelley's *Hellas* (1822) or Hölderlin's fragmentary *Death of Empedocles* (1797–1800); epic, both in the appeal to the primitive voice of the poet (as in Macpherson's Ossian) and as self-conscious and eventually mocking grand narrative filtered through the Latin and the Renaissance traditions (Pushkin's *Eugene Onegin,* 1833), to name only the extremes; the ode (in Hölderlin, or Wordsworth, where the quasi-religious form deflects from religious orthodoxies to divinity in other guises)—all these emerged alongside experimentation with vernacular styles, such as the ballad, or forms inspired by song or folk culture.

Just as modern culture was envisaged as something radically different from yet potentially equal to ancient culture, canonicity was replaced by simultaneity. Schleiermacher's translations of the dialogues of Plato (1804–1810) were undertaken almost literally side by side with A. W. Schlegel's translations of Shakespeare (from 1797) and Tieck's translation of Cervantes (1799–1801)—translation itself being a mediation entirely in line with the self-understanding of Romanticism. Shelley's 1818 translation of Plato's *Symposium,* arising from the same Neoplatonic fascination with how to approach the world of the ideal, coexists with his transformation of Aeschylus' *Persians* into the guise of modern history in the lyrical drama *Hellas* (1822) and the philosophical overhaul of universal history in his visionary narrative poem *Queen Mab* (1813), which in turn takes much from Volney's *Ruins.* Friedrich Hölderlin likewise revolutionized language in his translations of Sophocles, then integrated these translations into philosophical analysis and produced his experimental novel *Hyperion* (1798), set in a modern Greek landscape on the brink of revolution, an account of the modern, visionary individual and his failings.

Insofar as Romanticism needed history to position itself, historiography, as the critical charting of the development of human culture and spirit, became a byproduct of the Romantic program. Along with universal cultural histories, some of the most influential works on the Romanticism debate across Europe were histories of literature, such as A. W. Schlegel's *Lectures on Dramatic Poetry* (1809–1811) and J.-C.-L. S. Sismondi's *De la littérature du midi de l'Europe* (1813), which did much to give new canonical status to vernacular writers such as Dante, Cervantes, and Shakespeare.

History writing also included histories of the self, as seen in such projects as Wordsworth's *Prelude* (begun in 1799, with a full version in 1805–1806) and Goethe's *Poetry and Truth* (*Dichtung und Wahrheit,* 1811–1833). For all their differences, and even though Goethe famously refused to be counted among the Romantics, the two share a complex textual history that reveals patterns of constant rewriting and revising of their life stories. The same may be said of another of the programmatic works of English Romanticism, Coleridge's *Biographia literaria* (1817). Influenced by German Idealist and Romantic philosophy, and informed with a sound knowledge of classical scholarship (Coleridge had studied at Göttingen with the German philologist C. G. Heyne), it is a new critical account of the poetic imagination, infused with classical allusions (again the Socratic dialogues), integrated into a mythology and narrative of the nascent self.

The thrilling need to account for the development of the self, of what is peculiar to the self, is a central reference point and organizing metaphor chosen by Romanticism itself. This may in part explain both the radical momentum and the self-obsession that fit under the umbrella of the movement, the egalitarian impulses and the elitist and nationalist tendencies, as well as the openness and the violent inwardness that have made it difficult to account for the diversity of Romanticism. As Friedrich Schlegel put it: "Everyone has always been able to find in the ancients whatever he needed or desired, especially himself" (*Athenäum-Fragmente,* 1798). (Incidentally, no synoptic view of the European Romantic classical tradition has yet been published, although the trend is toward a critical examination of the interactions of the different Romanticisms, as they are themselves part of the Romantic worldview.)

The focus on the self may also provide a framework for linking Romantic literature and Romantic scholarship on classical antiquity. *Bildung,* the formation of the individual, was seen in analogy to the development of human history from antiquity, and its charting became formalized in the institutions of classical scholarship, first and foremost in Germany, where program and institutional authority combined in the figure of Wilhelm von Humboldt and the foundation of the University of Berlin in 1810. What had been the regulated contour of formation could be extended to the infinitely risky, formative power of the individual and of a modern subjectivity. Formulated through a discourse of naturalness, the discourse of *Bildung* relied on images of organic growth that had already been a focus of the late Enlightenment, and which grew, in Romanticism, to include the more threatening aspects of nature as uncontrolled or deficient, not unlike the "romantic," that is, disordered and unreal, landscapes of the medieval romances. Hölderlin perhaps best expressed the Romantic structural longing toward antiquity in a letter to his brother in January 1799: "I, too, with all good intentions can only stumble behind those singular [ancient Greek] people in everything I do and say, and often I do it all the more clumsily and out of tune, because I, like the geese, stand flat-footed in the waters of modernity, flapping my powerless wings up towards the Greek sky."

A corollary of the organic conception (and alienation) of antiquity was the attempt by the new classical scholarship to understand as fully as possible the character and life story of antiquity (its rise and decline) and to make antiquity come alive in new ways. The primary method for exploring the cultures of antiquity was through philology, that is, through critical analysis of ancient languages and textual evidence, assuming that language shapes cultures and their thought (after all, this same period saw an increasing differentiation between a Greek and a Roman antiquity). This approach may at first seem very different from the radical longing of Romantic literature and its deliberate departure from things strictly classical, but the anguished conception of a necessarily fragmented modernity is just as visible in the scholarship of the Romantic period: the Romantics in fact appreciated the fragment as a literary form. At the same time, the German philologist Friedrich August Wolf, who most likely thought himself unrelated to the stirrings of the literary world, revolutionized Homeric scholarship in his *Prolegomena ad Homerum* (1795) by claiming that there was no single authorship of the ancient Homeric epics but rather a gradual synthesis of older, fragmented, largely oral traditions.

In the course of the next century, August Böckh could define the position of *Altertumswissenschaft* (ancient studies) as a scholarly institution in his compendium on philological science, *Encyclopädie und Methodologie der Philologischen Wissenschaften* (1877):

> Pythagoras is said to have invented the name *philosophia,* because it is only a striving for *sophia* . . . It is in this same way that philology does not possess the *logos,* but is philology because it strives for it . . . To the extent that science is realized, it exists as a whole only as the sum of its carriers, partially fragmented in a thousand heads, broken, deformed, as if we were speaking a broken language; and yet, the great love with which many have embraced it guarantees the reality of the idea, which is none other than the reconstruction of the constructions of the human spirit in their totality.

Here we see the same seeking for a new dialogue with antiquity, an acknowledgment of the desire to approximate its lost totality. Nietzsche's accusations, later in the 19th century, against a dry, diminished, and overspecialized philology would arise from the same desire to infuse antiquity with new meaning and life.

Altertumswissenschaft was not only philology but claimed to study ancient culture in its totality. The disintegration of a normative understanding of the "classical" also meant relativism in terms of the periods and areas of antiquity studied, as well as the products of its culture. Like the syncretism of Romantic literary expression, the period of Romanticism therefore saw the institutional rise of comparative subjects (Indo-European linguistics, comparative mythology, anthropology), as well as the integration of archaeology, epigraphy, and history into the remit of the new discipline.

Archaeology in particular fit into the dynamic of the fragment and the whole, as well as the past and the present (just as the ruin did in Romantic literature). Especially during the Napoleonic Wars, travel and archaeological exploration shifted from their traditional center in Italy to Greece (then still part of the Ottoman Empire), a shift that tied in well with the increasing favor for Greek antiquity over its Roman successor. The Philhellenism that mobilized a large section of Europe to support modern Greek national aspirations coincided in many ways with the expressive range of Romanticism and also with its paradoxes, and was in many ways the most tangible challenge of bringing antiquity alive in a novel way. Byron, the epitome of the Romantic philhellene and poet because of his immediate involvement with Greece and his early death there, conceived of his early travels in Greece as an antidote to the normative, classical schooling he had received in England: a "modern" Greece must necessarily be "romantic," and Greece, like Romanticism itself, remained practically impossible to disentangle from the memory of its classical tradition.

Thirty-five years before Byron, the young Goethe had traveled to Italy to seek a landscape there that expressed the desired formation of his self. But amid the growing enthusiasm for Greek antiquity, what happened subsequently to Rome as the object of Romantic scholarship? Although they did not vanish from the discourse of Romanticism, or as reference points for political thought, Rome and the Latin language were gradually steered toward their long career as the "purloined letter" of the classical tradition, hidden in plain view, yet overshadowed by an ever more prominent Hellenism. Within the cultural history told by Romanticism, Rome, which after all is at the linguistic root of the movement's name, had a very peculiar position. Still bound into classical antiquity, it was nevertheless part of the modern age, yet not counted among the vernacular romance cultures. Rome may have featured more visibly in English, French, and Italian Romanticism than in Germany, but it certainly held a universally prominent place in European historical scholarship (e.g., Barthold Niebuhr's *Römische Geschichte,* 1811–1832, and Thomas Babington Macaulay's *Lays of Ancient Rome,* 1842). Yet Friedrich Schlegel, expanding on Quintilian (*Institutio Oratoria* 10.1), granted Rome only one original genre: just as Greece's dominant genre was tragedy, and Romantic modernity could claim the novel, Rome had produced satire as its proper medium of expression—and that was all he had to say. Here, where the neat distinction between classical and Romantic, between ancient and modern could break down, Romanticism retained its blind spot.

BIBL.: Chryssanthi Avlami, *L'antiquité greque à la française: Modes d'appropriation de la Grèce au XIXe siècle* (Paris 2001). J. M. Bernstein, ed., *Classic and Romantic German Aesthetics* (Cambridge 2002). Hans Eichner, ed., *"Romantic" and Its Cognates: The European History of a Word* (Toronto 1972). Angela Esterhammer, ed., *Romantic Poetry* (Amsterdam 2002). Suzanne Marchand, *Down from Olympus: Archaeology and Philhellenism in Germany, 1750–1970* (Princeton 1996). Franco Moretti, *The Way of the World: The Bildungsroman in European Culture,* trans. Albert Sbragia (New York 2000). Thomas Pfau and R. F. Gleckner, eds., *Lessons of Romanticism: A Critical Companion* (Durham 1998). Carolyn Springer, *The Marble Wilderness: Ruins and Representation in Italian Romanticism, 1775–1850* (Cambridge 1987). Jennifer Wallace, *Shelley and Greece: Rethinking Romantic Hellenism* (Basingstoke 1997).
C.M.G.

Rome

I. Antiquity to Renaissance

Without Rome there would be no classical tradition, at least in the visual arts. Rome was the conduit through which the artistic legacy of Greece passed into later Western culture, and Romans created the Graeco-Italic language of art and architecture that was received as classical in later times. But however obvious it seems to us, the history of the classical tradition in Rome was not necessarily perceived as such by those who made it. The Romans themselves did not speak of "classical" art, although they followed the Greeks in celebrating a body of canonical works as exemplary. In the Renaissance, "classical" denoted the painting of Raphael, whereas Graeco-Roman art was "ancient." In the 18th century scholars and connoisseurs began to distinguish Greek statues and buildings from Roman ones and to reserve the designation "classical" for the Greek, specifically for Greek works from the time before Alexander the Great (356–323 BCE). At that point Rome lost its preeminence as the site where classical art from antiquity was most perfectly represented, but it remained the best place to study it. Art collections and libraries amassed over several centuries and a culture of scientific archaeology nurtured since the 15th century ensured Rome's enduring role in the academic transmission of the classical tradition, and artists continue to be inspired by its abundant, accessible, and ever more carefully stewarded physical remains.

Rome's role as a vehicle of classical art and architecture falls broadly into three epochs: the constitution of the body of ancient work received as "classical" by other eras and cultures; the dissipation of that patrimony through destruction, alienation, and neglect; and the academic reconstitution of classical culture and its dissemination through reproductive media, including print, graphic representations, and casts.

Before the Romans began to invade the Greek cities of southern Italy in the 3rd century BCE, Rome was an unexceptional Italic center with temples of tufa, terracotta cult statues, and little public decoration. The historian Livy (25.40), writing in the time of Augustus (r. 27 BCE–14 CE), traced the Romans' enthusiasm for Greek art to the sack of Syracuse in 211 BCE, in which for the first time the loot included statues and paintings. More than 1,000 statues in bronze and marble were brought back from Greece in 187 BCE (Livy 39.5.13–16); the paintings and statues captured by Aemilius Paulus in 168 filled 250 chariots (Plutarch, *Aemilius Paulus* 32); Lucius Mummius "filled the city with statues" after his destruction of Corinth in 146 (Pliny the Elder, *Natural History* 34.17.36); and so on down to Sulla's plunder of Athens in 86 BCE and Octavian's victory over Egypt in 29 (he assumed the title Augustus in 27). In addition to painting and sculpture, trophy art included gemstones and objects of chased silver and ivory. Pliny accused Pompey of having inspired the Roman "fashion" for gems and pearls with his extravagant triumph in 61 (37.6.12), during which he had ritually dedicated on the Capitol the "ring cabinet" (*dactyliotheca*) of King Mithridates of Pontus as part of the spoils of his victories in Asia (37.5.1). Six such cabinets were later dedicated in the temple of Venus Genetrix by Julius Caesar and one in the temple of Palatine Apollo by Marcellus.

J. J. Pollitt (1978) calculated that by the 1st century CE Rome had collected, by conquest or other means, 14 sculptures by Praxiteles, 8 by Scopas, 4 by Lysippus, 3 by Myron, and 2 each by Phidias and Polyclitus, as well as paintings by Apelles (3), Zeuxis (2), Parrhasius (2), Aristides (4), Nicias (4), Polygnotus, Timanthes, and other notable artists in various media. Few of these masterworks survived the imperial era. As spoils they were subject to destructive acts of appropriation, as when Claudius (r. 41–54 CE) had the faces of Alexander cut out from two paintings by Apelles in order to insert portraits of Augustus (Pliny 35.36.94). Statues melted in fires; paintings faded into invisibility. One of the few works that remained intact and on view into the Middle Ages was Lysippus' colossal bronze statue *Seated Hercules,* which had been taken from Taranto in 209 BCE and set up as a spoil on the Capitol. The *Hercules* was reproduced for Roman collectors in table-sized bronze and marble statuettes for 400 years; then around 325 CE it was taken to Constantinople, where it was displayed in the Hippodrome until at least 1204. Byzantine artisans used it as a model for biblical figures.

Whatever its consequences for individual objects, the encounter with Greek art in the 2nd century BCE forever transformed Roman artistic culture. Despite a strong current of opinion (still reflected in Pliny, writing in the latter half of the 1st cent. CE) that disdained the aesthetic and material refinement of Greek art as decadent and un-Roman, powerful Romans began to emulate Hellenistic kings and magnates by collecting it. Art dealers (who were sometimes also artists) appeared, ready to supply them with old masterworks, and many Greek artists followed the market to Rome. Equally adept at copying old originals and executing their own designs in the gamut of Hellenistic styles, from archaizing to baroque, these artists produced cult statues, portraits, garden sculptures, and luxury objects like candelabra, urns, basins, and furniture for public and private consumption throughout the later 2nd and 1st centuries BCE.

The value of this art was determined by a tradition of art writing born in Greece in the 5th century, which identified the objects and personalities that marked a progressive history of technical and aesthetic development. From works such as the treatise by Pasiteles (1st cent. BCE) on the world's greatest artworks (*opera nobilia*), the Romans inherited the still familiar canon of artists that extends from Phidias and Polyclitus to Lysippus, from Zeuxis and Parrhasius to Apelles. Yet they did not necessarily privilege a marble carved by one of these masters over a copy or a variant signed by a much later sculptor. The influential collection of Asinius Pollio, victor over the Parthini in 39 BCE, seems to have contained a mix of works by famous artists of the past, modern copies, and new inventions in recognizable styles. One of its most prized items was a contemporary group of Zethus, Amphion, Dirce, and a bull (possibly the Farnese Bull, now in the Museo Archeologico Nazionale, Naples) by Apollonius and Tauriscus, which he had imported from Rhodes (Pliny 36.4.33–34).

The hellenization of Roman artistic culture also embraced architecture, as conquering generals brought back to Rome their experience of the grand and showy buildings of Greek and Asian capital cities. The first basilicas were constructed in the early 2nd century BCE. Despite the Greek name, the basilica was not necessarily an imported form, and its subsequent dissemination was due to its success in Rome. The most celebrated early example was the Basilica Paulli (Basilica Aemilia) in the Forum, magnificently rebuilt in the second half of the 1st century BCE and again after 14 CE. Pliny considered it one of the wonders of the city, "marvelous" for its columns of mottled Phrygian marble (36.24.102).

Hellenization also affected temples. The first marble temple in Rome, designed by the Greek architect Hermodorus of Salamis, was the Temple of Jupiter Stator (146–143 BCE) in the Portico of Cecilius Metellus. It was distinguished from the local Etruscan-Italic temple type by its peripteral Ionic colonnade, its low platform instead of the high Italic podium, and its Pentelic material. Another purely Greek design appeared toward the end of the 2nd century BCE in the Corinthian round temple of Hercules Victor in the Forum Boarium, also of Pentelic marble. But the prostyle Italic type, emphatically frontal and built of travertine or tufa, persisted, and eventually a compromise was reached in the pseudoperipteral temple exemplified by the Ionic Temple of Portunus (1st cent. BCE) near the Theater of Marcellus.

Like the basilica, the stone theater was a Roman form with Greek associations. The type sprang into being with the Theater of Pompey in the Campus Martius, dedicated in 55 BCE. Unlike its Greek precedents, the Roman theater was a freestanding masonry structure in which the stepped *cavea* and the stage wall (*scaenae frons*) formed a single integral block. The Theater of Marcellus, completed ca. 13 BCE, may have been the first in which the external face of the *cavea* featured stone arcades framed by Greek orders. The arcades express the internal radial vaults of the interior, while the framing columns and entablatures—Doric at ground level and Ionic above—express concepts of harmonic design inherited, like the canons of sculpture and painting, from a rich Hellenistic tradition. Some of that tradition is preserved in the encyclopedic treatise *On Architecture* (*De architectura*) by Vitruvius, composed around the time the Theater of Marcellus was begun (ca. 30 BCE). Conceived largely in terms of Greek architectural history and theory (book 7, preface), Vitruvius's work presents a view of architectural canons and types that was only fitfully reflected in 1st-century Rome. The treatise is dedicated to Octavian, whose programmatic rebuilding of the city during his years as Augustus famously transformed it, although not entirely along Vitruvian lines (Suetonius, *Divus Augustus* 28.3).

The Augustan cultural program was deliberately classicizing. In public works, the baroque forms and hedonistic (Dionsyiac) vocabulary of later Hellenistic art were rejected in favor of the sober and dignified (Apollonian) paradigms of the 5th and 4th centuries BCE, exemplified in sculpture by the statue of Augustus from Primaporta, which recalls the *Doryphorus* (*Spear Bearer*) of ca. 450 BCE, renowned even in antiquity, and by the Parthenon-like friezes of the Ara Pacis (13–9 BCE). Classical and Archaic originals took on a "holy aura," according to Paul Zanker (1988), and some, like the *Thundering Zeus* by

Leochares, were moved to temples (Pliny 34.19.79). In architecture, marble became de rigueur for temple fronts, and ornament reproduced Athenian models, as in the exquisite lotus-and-palmette friezes in the Forum of Augustus, where there were also copies of the Erechtheum caryatids. Contrary to Vitruvius's even-handed prescription of three genera of temple columns, however, Augustan temples were nearly always Corinthian; Ionic and Doric evidently were considered too plain. An even more elaborate capital, combining Ionic volutes with the Corinthian acanthus basket, was invented. In the 15th century Leon Battista Alberti would regard this capital as a Roman synthesis of all three Greek types, dubbing it "Italian" in his *On Architecture* (*De re aedificatoria* 7.6). Sebastiano Serlio named it "Composite" in his *Rules of Architecture* (*Regole generali di architettura*).

The sobriety of Augustan public art was relaxed in luxury objects made for private use. The silver cups with relief decoration in the Hildesheim Treasure (dated 1st cent. CE), sardonyx cameos like the Gemma Augustea now in the Kunsthistorisches Museum in Vienna (10–14 CE), and the extraordinary cameo glass Portland Vase (5–25 CE) now in the British Museum in London share a Hellenistic classicism focused on consummate craftsmanship, otherworldly atmosphere, and languorous physical grace. Because of their portability, it is usually impossible to be certain where such objects were made, but the Portland Vase seems to have been found inside a sarcophagus that was excavated in the 1580s just outside Rome, in the tumulus grave of the family of the emperor Alexander Severus (r. 222–235 CE), where it had been reused as an ash urn. The vase has been attributed to the famous gemcutter Dioscourides, who carved a number of exquisite stone cameos for Augustus and his circle in the latter half of the 1st century BCE.

The decoration of domestic interiors—walls and ceilings or vaults—was not constrained by the programmatic classicism of public art. That painters were as able as sculptors to reproduce 5th-century Attic style, as well as any other Greek style, is demonstrated by the paintings-within-paintings in the house discovered under the Farnese villa (Farnesina) in Trastevere, which may have belonged to the statesman and general Agrippa, who married Augustus's elder daughter, Julia (ca. 20 BCE). But the Augustan era saw a move away from Hellenistic principles of wall painting, founded on the imitation of nature and architecture, toward the rendition of painters' fantasies, like the hybrid monsters and structures supported by "reeds" and candelabra decried by Vitruvius (7.5.3–4). This trend continued into the reigns of Augustus's early successors, culminating under Nero (r. 54–68) in the wall paintings and stucco reliefs of the notorious Golden House (Domus Aurea), which according to Pliny (35.27.120) were the work of the "dignified" but also "florid" painter Famulus.

The Attic classicism of the Augustan era was not consistently carried forward. It left a lasting impression on public sculpture, but individuals continued to prize diversity, and some of the greatest creations of the Hellenistic "baroque" style were made for Romans in the 1st and 2nd centuries CE, a notable example being the marble Laocoön group (now in the Vatican Museum). The chapters on art history in Pliny's *Natural History* (books 33–37, ca. 79 CE) reflect the artistic pluralism of his day as well as its ideological justification: Rome, as the center of the world, rightly displayed the best examples of all the artistic achievements of its empire. While repeating the criteria of value inherited from Greek art criticism, which emphasized the progressive conquest of mimetic representation, Pliny also asserted a Roman enthusiasm for ostentatious qualities like colossal scale, fine materials, technical virtuosity, and high price. He judged the best work of art in Rome to be the recently carved Laocoön (which not incidentally belonged to the dedicatee of his treatise, the emperor Titus) because of the "marvelous" coils of serpents carved by three different sculptors from what he thought was a single block of marble (36.4.37).

Pliny and other 1st-century CE authors also reflect a newly articulated sense of artistic decorum that distinguished Greek from Roman art on the basis of function. Greek styles, including conventions like nudity, expressed aesthetic qualities such as harmony, balance, and perfection of nature, whereas Roman painting and sculpture were commemorative and veristic; in short, Greek art was the visual language of allegory and myth, and Roman art was the language of history. The apparent eclecticism of later Roman art reflects the use of this opposition to signal different registers of meaning, as, for example, in the theomorphic (from *theos,* god) portraits of the 1st through 4th centuries CE, in which a veristic Roman portrait head is combined with the idealized nude body of a Hellenistic statue.

After Augustus, Roman art and architecture moved in directions unforeseen by and in many respects incompatible with the Greek-based framework developed by Vitruvius and Pliny. In architecture the language of columns and entablatures was retained as ornament, a visual rhetoric that signaled cultural continuity but sometimes masked revolutionary structural and functional innovations. In the figural arts, Greek canons and types remained available for quotation but were gradually debased through repetition, as inventiveness was focused on new art forms and the representation of history and the imperial regime. The Column of Trajan (dedicated in 113 CE) exemplifies this new direction. The form of the monument—a Doric column 100 feet in height—is ultimately Greek, but the shaft is transformed by a spiral band of bas-relief into a circular billboard advertising the deeds of the Roman army in Dacia (Romania and Moldova). Echoes of Hellenistic battle imagery are combined with mundane details of routine military operations in a continuous narrative format, periodically interrupted by static figures of the emperor rendered in slightly larger scale for emphasis and visibility.

A new vehicle of the classical tradition emerged in the 2nd century CE with the importation of figured marble sarcophagi from Attica and Asia Minor, which were decorated with mythological scenes in Hellenistic compositions and styles. The battle scenes that became popular in the later 2nd and 3rd centuries also contain Pergamene allusions, packed into dense fields of increasingly formulaic groups and poses. Toward the end of the 3rd century these residually hellenizing sarcophagi disappeared, and a new market of Christians (and occasionally Jews) called for sarcophagi with biblical subjects in a simple style devoid of aesthetic pretensions.

In architecture Vitruvian temples declined in prominence as emperors increasingly preferred to build for spectacle and pleasure, and as architects increasingly exploited the possibilities of concrete. Concrete had come into common use following the great fire in 64, when Nero decreed that new buildings were to be "untimbered" to promote safety (Tacitus, *Annals* 15.43). Durable and relatively inexpensive, concrete favored curves (arches, vaults, domes) and towering unencumbered spaces, as in the Pantheon (ca. 118–128) and the groin-vaulted halls of the imperial baths (Trajan, ca. 109; Caracalla, ca. 216; Diocletian, ca. 305). The concrete shells of these buildings were disguised externally with plastered brick and internally by sheets of colored marble, and columns and pieces of entablature were set against the walls as ornament. The basilica form remained conservative, however, with load-bearing colonnades and flat ceilings; its apogee was the Basilica Ulpia in the Forum of Trajan (ca. 112). The groin-vaulted Basilica of Maxentius (ca. 307) was an exception.

Roman columns differed from Greek columns in material, mode of production, and aesthetic effect. The shafts were monoliths, usually of colored stone, and they were made in modular sizes (30, 40, 50 Roman feet) that could be shipped and warehoused for future use. Capitals and bases were of white marble, but coloristic variation was the norm for shafts. The most prized materials for shafts were purplish *pavonazzetto* from Docimium in Phrygia, green-veined *cipollino* from Karystos (Euboea), yellow *giallo antico* from Chemtou (Tunisia), red granite from Aswan, grey *granito del foro* (so called because of its extensive use in Trajan's Forum) from Mons Claudianus (Gebel Fatireh) in Egypt, red and black *marmor luculleum* from Teos (Sigacik) in modern Turkey, and porphyry from Mons Porphyrites (Gebel Dokhan) in Egypt. Vitruvius's strict prescriptions for combinations of bases, shafts, capitals, and entablatures were ignored; and rather than the gender associations he imagined (Doric/masculine, Ionic/feminine, Corinthian/virginal, 4.1.5–8), columnar ornament connoted the expanse, wealth, and privilege of empire. Rome monopolized the market for some of the imported stones in the 2nd and 3rd centuries, and long after the quarry system collapsed, stockpiles of shafts and marble blocks remained in warehouses along the Tiber and in the port of Ostia.

The Pantheon exemplifies the hybrid classicism of post-Augustan architecture. The domed rotunda, inscribing a perfect circle, is a triumph of Roman engineering in concrete; affixed to it is a traditional pedimented temple front supported by Corinthian columns with monolithic granite shafts 40 feet in height; inside, pairs of *pavonazzetto* and *giallo antico* pseudo-structural columns at ground level create axes through color accents and contrast; above them, a different rhythm is created by a zone of interior windows and small porphyry pilasters. The forms of Greek architecture survive, but they are materialized in spaces and for purposes that Vitruvius never imagined.

The economic, political, and social turmoil of the later 3rd century disrupted all art production in Rome. The great surviving project of this period is the fortified Wall of Aurelian (begun 271), an 11-mile-long enclosure surrounding the city's seven hills and the Trastevere, with imposing but brutally functional openings on the main roads. Renewal under the tetrarchy (293–313) was marked by lavish imperial constructions like the Baths of Diocletian and the Basilica Nova of Maxentius, but from this time forward much of the ornament, including statues and architectural elements, was recycled.

Constantine's conquest of Rome in 312 began a new era. If the cathedral he sponsored (the Basilica Lateranensis; now St. John Lateran) was not the first Christian basilica, it was arguably the most influential. Like the Basilica Ulpia, which it rivaled in size, the Lateran basilica had four long colonnades with colored shafts, but only along the longitudinal axes. The components of these colonnades were of reused material (*spolia*), and in a very unclassical manner they supported walls rather than a second order of columns. The design established at the Lateran was taken up for the basilica erected over the tomb of Saint Peter in the Vatican, with the addition of a transverse space (transept) between the nave and the apse. St. Peter's colonnades were more heterogeneous than the Lateran's, and art historians still debate whether the visible differences among the shafts and capitals reflect necessity or choice.

Whatever the motivation, the effects of these colorful and diverse assemblages can be compared to similar qualities and concepts in late antique poetry and rhetoric and seem to correspond to a period taste that privileged brilliance and diversity of materials, artful recombination, antithesis and rhythm over Vitruvian symmetry, rationality, and order. Because of their connotations of obsolescence and renewal, perdurance and transience, *spolia* were also compatible with the metaphorical and symbolic discourse of architecture that originated in biblical exegesis and was applied to Christian buildings in the time of Constantine and throughout the Middle Ages.

In a further departure from classical usage, columns were combined with arches rather than horizontal entablatures, as in the mausoleum of Constantine's daughter (now the Church of Santa Costanza) and the imperial basilica over the tomb of Saint Paul (San Paolo Fuori le Mura), begun in 384. With this innovation the parameters of the Roman church basilica were fixed for a millennium: a flat-ceilinged basilica with long walls carried on two colonnades, entablatures or arches, transept or not. After the 5th century the colonnades were always made of *spolia*. The columned basilica was emulated in France, Germany, and England by builders eager to demonstrate Roman connections, down to the 11th century, when it was reimagined in a new style (Romanesque). Rome resisted this innovation, and in the 16th century Giorgio Vasari acknowledged that the spoliate colonnades of basilicas like St. Peter's had kept medieval architecture in closer alignment with antique norms than other art forms, because the *spolia* provided constant models for the architects (proem, *Lives of the Most Excellent Architects, Painters, and Sculptors; Le Vite de' più eccellenti architetti, pittori, e scultori,* 1550).

The triumphal arch erected in honor of Constantine's conquest of Rome was also decorated with heirloom ornament, including parts of the battle frieze made for the Forum of Trajan, eight roundels with hunting scenes of Hadrian (r. 117–138), and eight rectangular panels showing ceremonies of Marcus Aurelius (r. 161–180). In homage to the conqueror, the portrait heads of Trajan and other emperors were replaced with images of Constantine, an ambiguous gesture that both confirms and depletes the importance of the original reliefs. Eight crudely carved friezes representing the history of Constantine's military campaign complete the ensemble and highlight the contrast in style and skill between the 2nd and the 4th centuries CE. Although archaeologists still debate the intended meaning of this assemblage, and whether the older pieces were true *spolia* (that is, ripped from standing monuments) or salvaged from warehouses, the Arch of Constantine unquestionably marks the end of Roman historical relief.

The sudden emergence of an overtly Christian culture after Constantine's conversion in 312 provoked a backlash later in the 4th century among aristocrats who sought to preserve Rome's traditional religion, politics, and way of life. Unable to change the course of state patronage, they commissioned and circulated luxury objects that emulated the look of classical art with sometimes remarkable precision. One of the finest examples is the ivory diptych of the Nicomachi and the Symmachi, one leaf of which represents a Roman matron at an altar in the style of the Ara Pacis, and the other depicts a goddess (Kore?) in a Hellenistic manner as old as the 2nd century BCE. Another example is the Vatican Virgil (Vat. lat. 3225; ca. 400), a manuscript originally embellished with as many as 275 miniature paintings, in which Hellenistic pictorial devices such as foreshortening, converging orthogonals, atmospheric horizons, modulation of light and shadow, and a painterly treatment of contours were reproduced with varying degrees of competence. The scene of Laocoön's sacrifice even quotes the famous sculpture group praised by Pliny, preserving its iconography if not its dynamic style.

Because artisans worked for patrons of all persuasions, retrospective styles and higher standards of craftsmanship carried over into works with Christian subject matter, inaugurating a series of classicizing episodes or, as Erwin Panofsky called them, "renascences," that continued throughout the Middle Ages. Rather than in Rome, however, these renascences occurred in the new imperial city of Constantinople, created in 330 at the established Greek trading city of Byzantion; in the Carolingian courts and monasteries of Francia, where late antique books and carved ivories were avidly collected as exempla for copying; and again in the monasteries and cathedral schools of 12th-century France and England. The history of the Vatican Virgil shows how such objects could figure in these revivals, even beyond the Middle Ages. In 846 the Virgil was in the monastery of St. Martin of Tours, where a painter traced some of its figures for use in the illuminated Bible of Count Vivian (Paris, Bibliothèque Nationale MS lat. 1). In 1514 it was back in Rome, an object of study by Raphael and his circle, one of whom copied all its surviving illustrations (Princeton University Library, MS 104). Pietro Bembo took it to Padua in 1521, and in 1579 it was acquired by another Humanist, Fulvio Orsini, who bequeathed it to the Vatican Library in 1600. The diptych of the Nicomachi and Symmachi wound up in the Frankish monastery of Montier-en-Der as doors on a late 12th-century reliquary, despite its obviously pagan character and the virtual nudity of the goddess's generous bosom. Paradoxically, it survived intact until the height of Neoclassicism in the 1790s, when the destruction of the reliquary by antireligious zealots ruined one plaque.

The pagan–Christian polemic of the 4th century occasioned a resorting of the classical heritage into what could be retained for Christian use and what could not. The iconography of pagan gods and spirits was evidently tolerable in relief or in two dimensions, as shown by the Dionysiac cherubs and grapevines in the vault mosaics at Santa Costanza, so unadulterated that they misled Renaissance antiquarians into identifying the site as a temple of Bacchus. Statues of gods, on the other hand, were demonized by some Christians as idols. In the 4th century these statues still stood by the hundreds or thousands in the porticoes, gardens, and temples where they had been originally set up, or in later relocations in the imperial baths, the fora, the imperial palace, and private mansions. Marble ornament of all sorts, including columns, wall revetments, and historiated reliefs as well as statues, became vulnerable to predation in the 3rd century. Because burning marble produces lime, a necessary ingredient of concrete, marble had pragmatic as well as ornamental value, and the obvious fate of offensive or demon-housing statues was incineration. In the short term, however, marble in the public domain was protected by laws against spoliation and the belief that the marble patrimony was the sign of a great past and of a civilized present. Laws from the end of the 4th century required that statues receiving worship be removed or destroyed (Theodosian Code 16.10.18, 16.10.19), but some argued that even temple statues could be exorcised and returned to a pure aesthetic state, as famously expressed by the Christian poet Prudentius just after 400, countering a petition by the pagan senator Symmachus (*Contra Symmachum* 1.501–504).

Despite these early protective measures, all but a handful of Rome's classical statues disappeared in the course of the Middle Ages, through a combination of natural and man-made disasters, venality, political impotence, and neglect. The last glimpse of their ancient installation is an aside by the Greek historian Procopius, who accompanied the Byzantine army to Rome in the 530s and mentioned seeing many bronze statues by Pheidias, Myron, and other Greek masters standing on inscribed bases in the area of the Temple of Peace (*De bello gothico* 4.21.12–14). The popular medieval story that the statues were all destroyed by Pope Gregory I (r. 590–604), which was repeated into the 16th century, contains a kernel of truth: following the death of the Ostrogothic King Theodoric (526), who assiduously conserved the public ornament of Rome through legislation and funding, the official treatment of antique remains became purely utilitarian. Statues in precious metals and bronze were plundered for their material (Procopius, *De bello vandalico* 1.5.3–5; [various authors], *Liber pontificalis, vita Vitaliani* 3–4). The fate of marble statues is indicated by Procopius's description of the siege of Castel Sant'Angelo (Mausoleum of Hadrian) in 537, when the defenders broke up "most" of its statues to throw down on the attackers (*De bello gothico* 1.22.22); by the limekilns found in the ruins of many ancient monuments; and by the medieval toponym de Calcarario, which designated an entire neighborhood of lime-burners near the Pantheon. Many statues were buried before they could be burned, when the buildings in which they stood collapsed; others were put into the ground deliberately by owners or guardians who never returned to exhume them.

The war chronicled by Procopius was a watershed. The senatorial families who had not followed the imperial court to Constantinople after the Visigoth and Vandal invasions of the 5th century did so now. Without their patronage, the imperial baths, theaters, amphitheater—any public building for which no Christian purpose could be found—were not maintained. They remained defining features of the cityscape, however, and the Frankish monk who composed the Einsiedeln Itinerary (MS 326, Einsiedeln Monastery, Switzerland) of Christian sites in Rome toward the end of the 8th century named baths, theaters, and statues (though not pagan ones) as landmarks, while also copying many of their ancient inscriptions.

The papal alliance with the Frankish kings inaugurated by Pope Stephen II (r. 752–757), culminating in the coronation of Charlemagne as "emperor and augustus" at St. Peter's in 800, revivified Rome's place in the European imaginary as a seat of empire, although in practice no emperor resided there except, for a brief and ill-fated moment, Otto III (983–1002). Pieces of Rome consequently acquired talismanic value, as famously illustrated by Charlemagne's desire to incorporate "columns and marble" from Rome and Ravenna into his court church at Aachen (Einhard, *Vita Karoli* 26). The political allure of such *spolia* was enhanced by the aura of marble, now an antique substance all but unobtainable except from the quarry sites of Roman ruins. Marble columns and capitals were the architectural equivalent of ancient cameos and intaglios, which princely patrons in Francia and Germany applied to reliquaries and book covers for their craftsmanship and material value, regardless of their profane or pagan imagery. The Lothar Cross in Aachen (ca. 1000), displaying a giant sardonyx cameo portrait of the Emperor Augustus, is an example. The Ottonian fascination with Rome also produced original Christian versions of Roman monuments, like the bronze column with scenes of the life of Christ, modeled on the Column of Trajan, commissioned by Abbot Bernward of Hildesheim just after 1000.

The pace of Rome's decay accelerated rapidly after the earthquake of 847, which brought down several ancient structures in the Forum. Debris from fallen buildings and the frequent inundations of the Tiber was no longer cleared away, and in many places the ancient topography became unrecognizable, buried under accumulations as much as 30 feet high. Place names and history were forgotten. The ancient buildings that survived this period were those that had been converted into churches (the Pantheon, dedicated to Mary and all the martyrs in 604; the Temple of Portunus, dedicated to Mary ca. 872) and those that could be occupied as strongholds (the Mausoleum of Hadrian; Theaters of Pompey, Marcellus, and Balbus; the Colosseum). The strongholds were occupied by warring families who claimed de facto ownership, and the decay of Rome's physical fabric was mirrored by a decline in polity.

The discrepancy between the ideal Rome of political discourse and poetry and the imperfect reality of a crumbling urban landscape sharply increased after the 9th century. As the symbolic Rome remained vital as an ideal of Christian order, and the real Rome became a hazardous terrain of tottering relics, a third Rome came into being: the emblem of loss and mourning of a glorious past. This Rome mediated between the discursive abstraction of the political symbol and the desolate reality of the city itself. Ruins became the symptom of past greatness as well as the sign of present decline. The first great expression of this elegiac role of Rome in the classical tradition is the poem "Par tibi, Roma, nihil," written by Hildebert of Lavardin (bishop of Le Mans, later archbishop of Tours) before 1125. It is paired with a second poem that celebrates Rome's ruin as the proof of Christian triumph.

Inhabitants of the city took a pragmatic approach to its ruin. Although the extent of medieval depredation has been exaggerated, for Romans of the 10th and 11th centuries the antique marble lying on or just under the surface was an economic resource. By the 11th century there was an organized market for *spolia,* illustrated by the story of Abbot Desiderius of Montecassino, who went to Rome to find columns for his new abbey church and got them for "handfuls of money" (Leo of Ostia, *Chronicon Monasterii Casinensis* 3.26). Roman marbles were also exported to Pisa and other centers where the symbolism of authentic *romanitas* was desired. Around 1100 there may have been a connection between the hunt for *spolia*

110 From the Nicetas Codex. An assistant helps the expert reduce a lower jaw luxation by holding the head of the patient, first half of the 10th century.

Nicetas Codex (110)

This illuminated medical manuscript, written in Constantinople in the first half of the 10th century, contains the commentary by Apollonius of Citium on **Hippocrates'** treatise *On Joints* as well as a section on bandaging from Soranus of Ephesus. Both Apollonius and Soranus flourished toward the end of the 2nd century BCE. Illustrations from the Nicetas Codex were continually reproduced for centuries and strongly influenced later depictions of surgery.

111 Maarten van Heemskerck, *View from the Capitoline Hill toward the Colosseum in Rome,* ca. 1532–1536.

112 Princeton University Library MS Garrett 158 (Marcanova), fol. 6v: Rome. Vatican obelisk, ca. 1470.

Obelisk (111, 112)

Rome's **Egyptian** obelisks were all imported between the reigns of **Augustus** and Theodosius. Ancient obelisks were an important part of Pope Sixtus V's plans for the urban development of the city. Between 1585 and 1590, he oversaw the excavation, restoration, and redeployment of four of Rome's most impressive obelisks. The Vatican obelisk, moved to its current site in 1586 by the architect Domenico Fontana, became the centerpiece of Bernini's magnificent Saint Peter's Square. Maarten van Heemskerck's *View of Rome from the Capitoline Hill toward the Colosseum* depicts an obelisk then standing near Santa Maria in Aracoeli but later removed and now in the park of the Villa Mattei. This obelisk is first recorded in the Capitoline Square in the early 15th century, when it stood on the back of four lions in Romanesque style. Scholars have dated the new setting of the monument, with its reference to the political values and power of ancient Rome, either to the years of the Commune (in the mid-12th century), to the Jubilee Year 1300, or to the republican government of Cola di Rienzo (in the mid-14th century).

113 William Blake, *Ulysses and Diomed Swathed in the Same Flame,* ca. 1824–1827.

114 Jean Auguste Dominique Ingres, *Oedipus and the Sphinx,* 1808.

Odysseus (113)

In the *Divine Comedy,* Dante chose **Virgil** as his guide through Hell, where they encountered Ulysses (Odysseus) and Diomedes who were enveloped in the same flame. Virgil, who had written of Ulysses from the perspective of the Trojan Aeneas, cited three offenses for which these two friends were united in their punishment: devising and supporting the wicked stratagem of the wooden horse; luring Achilles into the war and away from the island of Skyros where he had been hidden by his mother; and stealing the Palladium, the sacred statue of the armed goddess Athena on which the safety of Troy depended.

Oedipus (114)

One of the most famous episodes in the story of Oedipus is his encounter with the Sphinx, the premise for his winning the kingdom of Thebes and for his incestuous marriage to Jocasta. According to the myth, Oedipus successfully answered the riddle posed by the Sphinx, who threatened anyone wishing to enter Thebes, and thus won the gratitude of the inhabitants of the city. They appointed Oedipus as their king and gave him the recently widowed queen's hand. In Ingres's painting *Oedipus and the Sphinx,* the scene is dominated by the hero who stands naked and luminescent in a deliberate pose of reflection and reasoning.

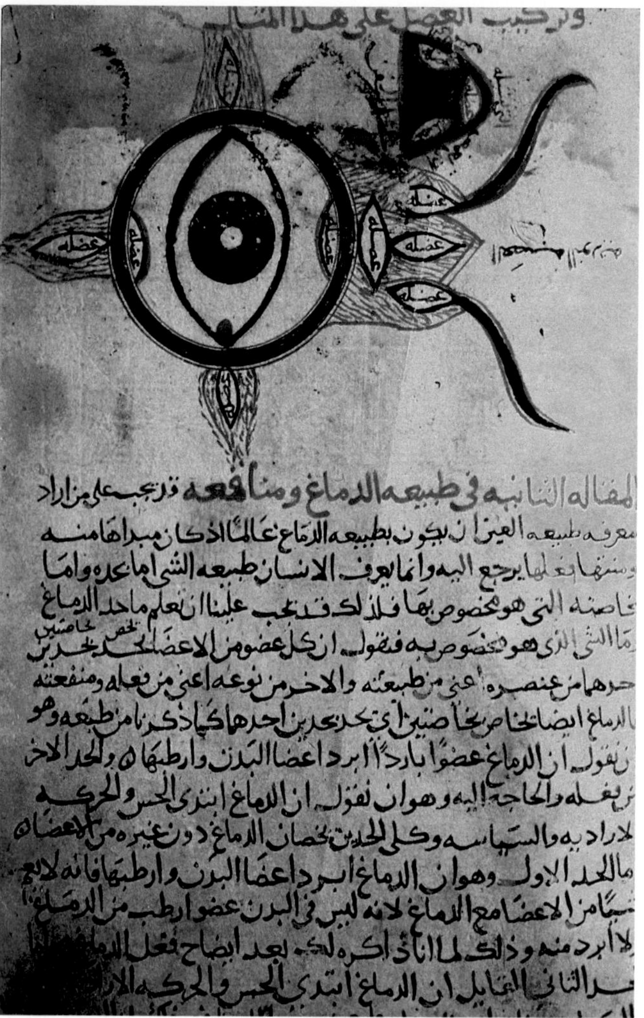

115 Anatomy of the eye, 12th century manuscript copied from Hunayn ibn-Ishāq, *The Book of the Ten Treatises on the Eye,* 9th century.

116 Medal with all-seeing eye, Italian, ca. 1450. Reverse of a medal bearing a portrait of Alberti on the obverse.

Optics (115, 116)

One of our main sources for the classical study of optics is a treatise by the 9th century scholar **Hunayn ibn-Ishāq,** who translated a large number of medical and scientific works from Greek into Arabic. His textbook on ophthalmology shows his impressive skills not only as a translator, but also as a physician and a surgeon. Debate continues over whether the theory of linear perspective developed by Florentine artists during the 15th century should be attributed to the rediscovery of ancient optical texts. **Leon Battista Alberti's** influential treatise *On Painting* drew extensively on **Euclid's** theory of vision to explain the mathematical basis of the new technique. According to Alberti, the eye itself (which he had portrayed as a hieroglyph on the reverse of a medal bearing his own portrait) was the source of inspiration for artists in their pursuit of an all-embracing knowledge.

Paestum (117)

The fame of Poseidonia (Paestum in Roman times) comes chiefly from its three **temples** in the Doric style, which were rediscovered in the mid-18th century. Paestum soon became a favorite destination for travelers on the **Grand Tour** and an important site for modern Hellenism. With their unexpected proportions and apparently essential design, the temples of Paestum played a significant role in architects' debates over the traditional **Vitruvian** canon.

117 Giovanni Battista Piranesi, *The Temples at Paestum*, ca. 1770–1778.

118 Reconstruction model of the Palace of Diocletian at Split, 1937.

119 Prothyron from the Palace of Diocletian, early 4th century.

Palace (118, 119)

Diocletian's palace at **Split,** in Dalmatia, had a regular plan which combined the qualities of a luxurious villa with those of a military camp, encompassing watchtowers, courtyards, arcades, and a **mausoleum.** Following a long period of abandonment in Late Antiquity, during the Middle Ages the walled complex provided a safe stronghold for nearby residents, who occupied the whole palace with new houses and buildings. The mausoleum was then restored as the Cathedral of St. Domnius. After the Middle Ages, the palace was virtually unknown in the West until the **Neoclassical** architect **Robert Adam** had the opportunity to survey and map its ruins, which became a major source of inspiration for his architectural style (see 1). Since then, Diocletian's palace has become a fundamental point of reference in the design vocabulary of European **architecture.**

Palladio (120)

Having studied both the extant Roman monuments and **Vitruvius'** treatise, Palladio developed a deep appreciation for classical **architecture,** which he displayed in his own buildings and writings. In the early 18th century, the renovation of Burlington House, a building on Piccadilly in London, proved a key moment in the reception of Palladian style. The aesthetic preferences and the strict Palladianism of Lord Burlington and his architect Colen Campbell would become the leading strand in English architecture and interior decoration for a long time to come.

Pandora (121)

The most famous version of the Pandora myth comes from **Hesiod's** *Works and Days*, in which the poet presents her as the first woman, created by the gods to inflict misery on mankind by means of her deceitful feminine nature. In his painting, Jean Cousin the Elder equates Eve, guilty of the original sin and responsible for human wretchedness, with Pandora, who unleashed all the evils that have afflicted mankind when she curiously opened the box entrusted to her by the gods. Cousin stresses the beauty and the seductive power of his Eve/Pandora, but a skull under her right forearm ominously portends her dark role in the future of mankind, while the jar rests partially hidden beneath her body.

120 Andrew Ingamells, *The Royal Academy of Arts, Burlington House, Piccadilly, London,* 1997.

121 Jean Cousin the Elder, *Eva Prima Pandora,* ca. 1540–1550.

122 The Pantheon, Paris (formerly Ste. Geneviève), ca. 1790.

Pantheon (122)

The building commissioned by Marcus Agrippa as a **temple** to all the gods of Rome, and later rebuilt by Hadrian, has exerted enormous influence over Western **architecture** at least since the Renaissance. During the **French Revolution** the church of St. Geneviève in the Latin Quarter of Paris, which overtly imitated the Roman Pantheon, was deconsecrated and turned into a secular **mausoleum** for prominent Frenchmen. Since then, the term "pantheon" has been applied to any building in which illustrious dead are honored or buried.

Parnassus (123)

According to classical myth, this massif was considered to be the dwelling place of **Apollo** and the **Muses. Raphael's** fresco at the Vatican portrays a mountain on which Apollo sits under laurels, playing the lyre, surrounded by the Muses and a group of poets from all eras. Raphael's depiction played a central role in shaping the imagery of Parnassus throughout modernity. (For details of this fresco, see **104, 105**.)

123 Raphael, *Parnassus*, 1510–1511.

Pasquino (124)

Pasquino is the name ordinary Romans gave to a mutilated ancient statue, which probably represents Menelaus holding the body of Patroclus. In 1501 Cardinal Carafa placed it on a pedestal outside his palace near Piazza Navona. Soon after, Pasquino became the repository for anonymous and usually satiric comments (*pasquinades*) on contemporary events, the first of several "talking statues" in Rome.

Pederasty (125)

After settling in Taormina in the early 1880s, the German photographer Wilhelm von Gloeden specialized in pastoral nude studies of Sicilian boys. Combined with the erotic implications of his images, the clothing and other items such as wreaths or amphoras featured in von Gloeden's photographs suggest a setting in ancient Greece or Italy.

124 Statue call the *Pasquino*, near Piazza Navona, Rome.

125 Wilhelm von Gloeden, Photograph of two boys in a Sicilian landscape, ca. 1900.

126 The Mobil Pegasus logo prominently displayed at a gas station in New York City, 1979.

Pegasus (126)

In contemporary visual culture, the winged horse of Greek mythology is widely used as a symbol for every form of flying, as well as for the ideas of speed and universal reach. In this photograph (taken during a fuel shortage in 1979), the Mobil Pegasus logo occupies a highly visible spot next to the window of a gas station at 42nd Street and 11th Avenue in New York City.

Pergamon (127, 128)

The ancient city of Pergamon, which lies in modern-day Turkey, became the capital of a kingdom under the Attalid dynasty during the **Hellenistic** period. It remained so until Attalus III bequeathed the kingdom to the Roman Republic in 133 BCE to avoid a likely succession crisis. The modern fame of Pergamon is linked primarily to an exceptional discovery in the late 19th century: a large, stately altar with its frieze, dated to around 160 BCE, which commemorated the triumph of Attalus I Soter over the Galatians in the 230s BCE. Moved to Berlin soon after its discovery, the altar is now the most spectacular exhibit in the Pergamon Museum.

127 Marble head of Attalus I Soter, ca. 200 BCE.

128 West side of the Pergamon Altar, ca. 160 BCE.

129 Michelangelo, *The Fall of Phaethon,* 1533.

130 André Legrand, *Three eagle heads and three human heads in relation to the eagle*, ca. 1806.

Phaethon (129)

According to **Ovid's** account, the young Phaethon insisted on driving the chariot of his father, Helios, the sun god. He lost control of the vehicle but was prevented from destroying the earth by Zeus, who struck him down with a thunderbolt. The dramatic image of tumbling horses, chariot, and driver has been a favorite subject of Western art. **Michelangelo's** drawing, now at the British Museum, includes the whole cast of characters involved in the story: Zeus sitting on his eagle and hurling a thunderbolt at the boy, the falling Phaethon, his weeping sisters, and the river god, Eridanus.

Physiognomy (130)

The classical theories of physiognomy achieved a philosophical and scientific synthesis during the Middle Ages, and later on, entered into artistic practice during the Italian **Renaissance.** Since the representation of corporeal forms was thought to imply an understanding of the natural laws behind them, the study of physiognomy became a key to the correct representation of character and emotions in the human figure.

131 Pablo Picasso, *Head of a Faun*, 1937.

Picasso (131)

The classical world was a great influence in shaping Picasso's imagery, providing him with a rich repertoire of legends and characters, such as **centaurs**, pipers, nymphs, shepherds, and **fauns.** Mythological figures from the Greek and Roman tradition became an integral part of this visual language, which Picasso exploited in a wide variety of contexts and attitudes.

132 Sculpture of Pliny the Elder on the facade of the cathedral, Como, Italy, ca. 1490–1495.

133 Sculpture of Pliny the Younger on the facade of the cathedral, Como, Italy, ca. 1490–1495.

Pliny the Elder (132)

Unlike other ancient encyclopedic works, the *Natural History* written by Pliny the Elder during the 1st century CE never ceased to be copied. Because of this exceptional uninterrupted tradition, it became one of the first Latin texts ever printed. The influence of Pliny and his vast treatise closely tracked the shifting cultural emphases of successive ages, during which the *Natural History* provided first a repository of information about nature, and then a model for systematic classification.

Pliny the Younger (133)

With his large corpus of letters on a wide variety of topics, the nephew of the Roman naturalist Pliny the Elder inspired many later authors and left his mark on several literary genres. The famous descriptions of his luxury villas have stirred imaginations for centuries, and they remain even now one of the most important sources for understanding the function and features of ancient country **palaces.**

134 Tomb of Frederick II Hohenstaufen, ca. 1220.

135 Porphyry statues of the Tetrarchs, ca. 300–310.

Porphyry (134, 135)

This white-flecked **purple** stone, quarried in **Egypt,** has always been associated with the ideas of empire, sacredness, and permanence. The group of the Tetrarchs, brought to Venice from Constantinople after its sack in 1204, counts among the most famous ancient porphyry sculptures. The unity and stability of the Roman Empire are effectively portrayed in the embrace of the four porphyry rulers, notable for their stiff rigidity and uniformity. The ideal link between this stone and imperial power persisted in later centuries. The body of the Holy Roman Emperor Frederick II Hohenstaufen, for example, lies in a red porphyry sarcophagus in the cathedral of Palermo, beside those of his parents.

136 Portico along the Main Quad, Stanford University.

Portico (136)

Soon after their introduction during the 2nd century BCE, porticoes became an essential feature of both Roman public architecture and domestic buildings. The portico has remained a key element in the vocabulary of classical **architecture** ever since and still provides a common solution for the layout of streets, squares, and courts.

Praeneste (137)

The town of Praeneste (now called Palestrina) in Latium was famous for its sanctuary dedicated to Primordial **Fortune.** Its structure, based on Hellenistic prototypes, consisted of a spectacular succession of terraces, exedras, and porticoes, arranged on multiple levels down the hillside and linked by monumental ramps. During the Middle Ages the town spread over the terraces of the sanctuary, while the upper part was rebuilt as a **palace** for the princely Colonna family. The site was greatly admired throughout the Renaissance and Baroque periods, and its unusual composition became a source of inspiration for countless villas and gardens.

137 Temple of Fortuna and Palazzo Barberini, Praeneste.

DIE

GEBURT DER TRAGÖDIE

AUS DEM

GEISTE DER MUSIK.

VON

FRIEDRICH NIETZSCHE,

ORDENTL. PROFESSOR DER CLASSISCHEN PHILOLOGIE AN DER UNIVERSITÄT BASEL.

LEIPZIG.

VERLAG VON E. W. FRITZSCH.

1872.

138 Title page. Nietzche's *Birth of Tragedy,* 1872.

139 Jean Leon Gérôme, *Pygmalion and Galatea,* ca. 1890.

Prometheus (138)

The Titan Prometheus was the hero of a tragedy, *Prometheus Bound,* attributed to **Aeschylus** and probably the first of a trilogy. In Greek legend, he was a benefactor of humanity who taught men the whole range of civilized skills and stole fire from Zeus to give it to mortals. Zeus then punished Prometheus by having him bound to a rock while an eagle ate his liver every day. During the 19th century, interest in the lost parts of the Greek trilogy grew increasingly keen, as evidenced by the choice of **Friedrich Nietzsche** to use a woodcut of the newly freed Prometheus on the title page of his *Birth of Tragedy.*

Pygmalion (139)

Jean Leon Gérôme was a noted exponent of a 19th century so-called **Greek Revival** style, which was popularized in the decorative arts during the reign of Napoleon III. Among the many classical subjects he put on canvas, Gérôme was particularly intrigued by the story of Pygmalion, which he portrayed in two paintings representing the same scene from diverse perspectives. Disgusted by the shameless behavior of real women, Pygmalion carved a miraculously lifelike ivory statue of an ideal woman. He fell in love so devotedly with the statue that Venus allowed the ivory to soften into flesh and art to turn into real life.

140 Exterior view of I. M. Pei's Pyramid at the Louvre, 1989.

141 John William Waterhouse, *Thisbe*, 1909.

Pyramids (140)

As enduring symbols of pharaonic power and the afterlife, pyramids were sometimes imitated by tomb builders in the Hellenistic and Roman periods. Among the Greeks, the best-known example was the stepped pyramid on the upper portion of the **Mausoleum** at Halicarnassus. The tomb of the Augustan official Gaius Cestius is the best-preserved of several pyramidal tombs built in Rome during the imperial era. The **Egyptian** pyramids have always been deemed one of the **Seven Wonders of the World,** and their suggestive power is still an influence in today's architecture.

Pyramus and Thisbe (141)

In his *Metamorphoses,* **Ovid** tells the story of the two young lovers from feuding families in Babylon, whose attempt to meet outside the walls of the city led to their mutual suicide. Among later literary variations on their story of tragic love was the play-within-a-play in **Shakespeare's** *A Midsummer Night's Dream.* John William Waterhouse portrays Thisbe during her years of secret love for Pyramus when the two could only speak through a hole in the wall between their neighboring houses.

142 Mosaic of the Palace of Theodoric the Great, Ravenna, ca. 500–525.

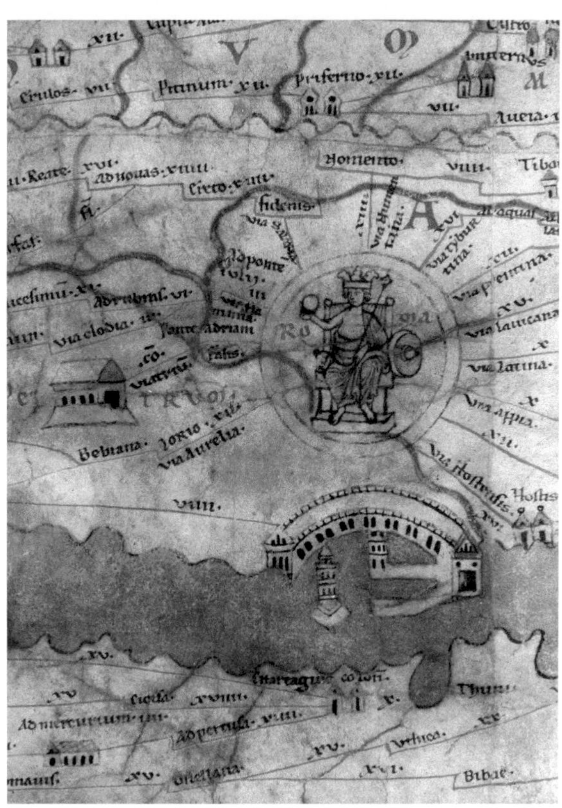

143 *The Peutinger Map,* Segment IV, Rome and the port of Ostia, 12th–13th century copy after a Late Antique original.

Ravenna (142)

The court of the Western Roman Empire settled in Ravenna during the first years of the 5th century because the city was deemed unconquerable because of its marshy surroundings. In addition, proximity to the suburban harbor of Classe facilitated connections with **Constantinople,** the Eastern imperial capital. Later, the Ostrogoth Theodoric ruled his kingdom of Italy from Ravenna. In his palace chapel, erected during the first quarter of the 6th century and known as Sant' Apollinare Nuovo, the late-antique tradition of **mosaics,** which reached its peak in Ravenna, blends with characteristic Eastern iconographies and compositions.

Roads, Roman (143)

The best known example of the interest in Roman roads during the Middle Ages is the Peutinger Table (or Peutinger Map), named for a German humanist and antiquarian. The map is a parchment scroll that shows the road network in the Roman Empire, covering Europe, parts of Asia, and North Africa. Even today, the ancient Roman system profoundly influences the trajectory of roads and highways throughout Europe.

144 Giambattista Tiepolo, *Sacrifice of Iphigenia,* ca. 1760.

145 Karl Friedrich Schinkel, Rotunda of the Altes Museum, ca. 1820.

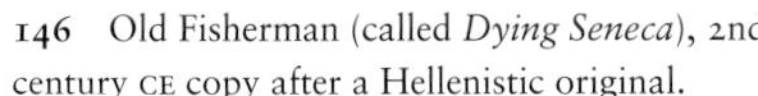

146 Old Fisherman (called *Dying Seneca*), 2nd century CE copy after a Hellenistic original.

147 Peter Paul Rubens, *The Dying Seneca*, 1615.

Sacrifice in the Arts (144)

The most famous modern depictions of **Homer's** tale of the sacrifice of **Iphigenia** are two paintings by Tiepolo: a fresco in the Villa Valmarana at Vicenza and this canvas, which was created for Palazzo Giustiniani Recanati. In each painting, the story takes place in a different environment and is seen from an opposite point of view. But in both works, the moment portrayed is the arrival of the deer sent by Diana to save Iphigenia, accompanied by two putti.

Schinkel, Karl Friedrich (145)

Karl Friedrich Schinkel was a prominent Prussian architect, city planner, and painter who designed both **Neoclassical** and Neogothic buildings. His large Rotunda for the Altes Museum in Berlin, built in the 1820s, was modeled on the Roman **Pantheon** and covered by a hemispheric dome which reproduced that of the Roman **temple.**

Seneca the Younger (146, 147)

The **suicide** of Seneca under **Nero's** order became one of the most significant elements in his influence over posterity. A Hellenistic image of an old fisherman, with his body bowed by age and a pathetic expression, was taken for the philosopher in his dying bath, an idea presumably inspired by the similarity of the head to a portrait bust which Fulvio Orsini identified as Seneca. **Rubens's** portrait of *Dying Seneca* drew inspiration from the ancient statue, now at the Louvre, which had been restored according to the contemporary interpretation and placed on a vase of marble that appeared to be full of water reddened with blood.

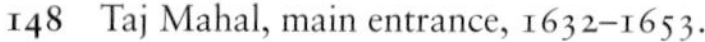

148 Taj Mahal, main entrance, 1632–1653.

149 The Great Wall of China, 5th century BCE–.

Seven Wonders of the World (148, 149)

The most common list of the Seven Wonders, drafted during the 2nd century BCE, included a series of monuments from ancient Mesopotamia, **Egypt,** and the Hellenistic world: the walls and hanging gardens of Babylon; the **pyramids** of Gizeh and the lighthouse of **Alexandria;** the statue of Zeus in his **temple** at Olympia; the Temple of Artemis at Ephesus and the **Mausoleum** at Halicarnassus (both in modern day Turkey); and the Colossus on the island of Rhodes. Today, many other spectacular examples of world architecture are commonly referred to as belonging to the Wonders of the World, such as the Indian Taj Mahal and the Great Wall in China.

Sewers (150)

Roman sewers not only served as models for those built in modern cities but also held great symbolic and aesthetic meaning for artists and writers. In Victor Hugo's *Les Misérables* (1862), as well as in director Carol Reed's film *The Third Man* (1949), dark visions of Paris and Vienna respectively find vivid visualization in the role of sewers as a **labyrinthian** underworld of hiding places and escape routes.

Soane, John (151)

An English architect who specialized in the **Neoclassical** style, Sir John Soane's most important work was the Bank of England, a building that significantly influenced later commercial architecture. Soane designed his remarkable London house not just to live in, but also as a setting for his collection of art, antiques, and casts, which he constantly added to and rearranged until his death. In his will, he directed that the house be established as a museum accessible to students and the general public.

150 Orson Welles hides from the police in the sewers of Vienna in a scene from *The Third Man,* 1949.

151 The cast of *Apollo Belvedere* in the Dome of Sir John Soane's Museum, 1820–1837.

152 The house of Laurentius Manlius, Rome, 1476.

Spolia (152, 153)

The house of Laurentius Manlius, built in Rome during the late 15th century, is an excellent example of the meaningful reuse of ancient remnants. Sculptural and architectural **fragments,** inscriptions, reliefs, and portraits were carefully selected for mounting in the building's facade, sometimes with a note explaining the place and circumstances under which they were found. The choice of spolia hinted at episodes in Roman history and was meant to suggest an ideal link between the family who lived there and antiquity. Spolia served as a concrete expression of continuity with the past and its legacy through the means of a fictional genealogy.

153 The house of Laurentius Manlius, Rome, 1476.

154 Opening ceremonies for the 1936 Olympic Games in Berlin.

Stadium (154)

Begining with the revival of the **Olympic Games** in the 1890s, the design of ancient stadia became a strong influence on modern architecture and imagery. For his 1936 Olympic stadium in Berlin, Adolf Hitler insisted that the German spirit demanded "something gigantic." The impressive stateliness of the building provided the perfect setting for the Olympic athletic contests and, above all, for a series of pompous ceremonies.

Statius (155)

The completed first book of Statius' fragmentary **epic** Achilleid relates the episode of **Achilles'** concealment in woman's clothing among the daughters of King Lycomedes and his impregnation of Deidamia. In his *Achilles at the Court of Lycomedes,* Pompeo Batoni portrays the hero, still disguised as a woman, testing the sword in Ulysses' pack a few moments before the shocking revelation of his real identity.

155 Pompeo Batoni, *Achilles at the Court of Lycomedes,* 1745.

156 Apollonius, son of Nestor, *The Belvedere Torso,* 1st century CE.

157 Honoré-Victorin Daumier, *The Plea of Tantalus,* 1842.

Suicide (156)

Classical history and myth are replete with stories of people who have ended their own lives, from **Homer's Ajax** and **Virgil's Dido** to intellectuals like **Socrates** and **Seneca,** and even emperors such as **Nero.** The famous **Belvedere Torso** has recently been identified as the figure of the Greek hero Ajax contemplating suicide. According to this reading, Ajax would have been seated on a rock, brooding and despondent, in the instant when he realized that only death can make amends for his folly and cleanse his honor.

Tantalus (157)

Once favored among all mortals by the gods, Tantalus was imprisoned for a grievous offense in Tartarus, the deepest portion of the underworld. His punishment was confinement up to his chin in a pool of water that receded whenever he bent down and tried to drink, beneath a fruit tree with low branches that withdrew from his reach whenever he came near them. Honoré Daumier's print caricatures Tantalus to ridicule the bourgeoisie and their insatiable greed.

158 The four complexions. *The Guild Book of the Barber-Surgeons of the City of York,* 15th century.

Temperament (158)

The distinction among four temperaments (sanguine, choleric, **melancholy,** and phlegmatic) traces its origin to the ancient idea that natural constitution or disposition was caused by the dominance of one in a foursome of bodily fluids, or humors. Countless images of the four temperaments can be found in manuscripts, such as this 15th century illustration of the four complexions from *The Guild Book of the Barber-Surgeons of the City of York*.

159 Jacques-Louis David, *Leonidas at the Thermopylae,* 1814.

160 Leonidas Monument, Thermopylae, 1955.

161 Arc de Triomphe du Carrousel, Paris, France, 1806–1808.

Thermopylae (159, 160)

In his canvas, **Jacques-Louis David** immortalized the hopeless struggle of the **Spartan** king Leonidas and his cohort against a far superior **Persian** force in 480 BCE. In both ancient and modern imageries, the Battle of Thermopylae has always been a symbol of unconditional obedience and courage against overwhelming odds. Today, a modern bronze monument honors Leonidas and his sacrifice at the site where the Spartans and their allies fought bravely to the death in one of history's most famous last stands.

Triumphal Arch (161)

The freestanding triumphal arch was revived by Napoleon, who exploited its associations with imperial power and its rich urbanistic possibilities. In commemoration of Napoleon's 1805 victory at Austerlitz, Charles Percier and Pierre-François Fontaine designed the Arch de Triomphe du Carrousel which was built in 1806–1808. Connecting the Louvre and the Tuileries, this edifice is modeled after the Arch of Septimius Severus in Rome.

162 Edward Burne-Jones, *Troilus and Criseyde* from *The Kelmscott Chaucer,* 1896.

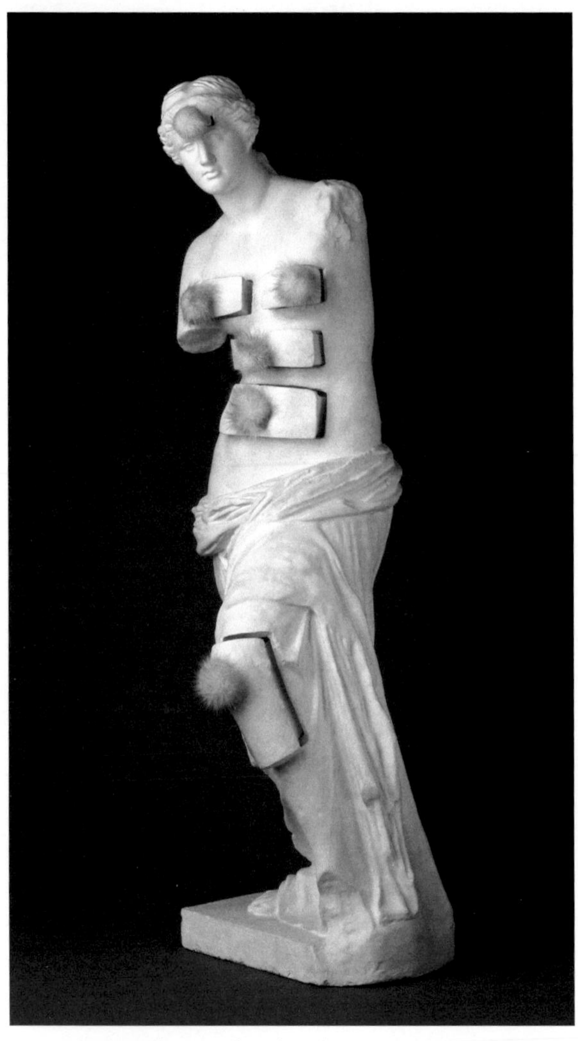

163 Salvador Dalí, *Venus de Milo with Drawers,* 1936.

Troilus (162)

Although Troilus is a character from ancient Greek literature, his identity as a lover was first suggested during the medieval period. The expanded story of his courtship, and ultimate loss, of the false Criseyde became the topic of numerous literary accounts. **Geoffrey Chaucer's** poem *Troilus and Criseyde,* probably completed in the mid-1380s, portrays the young man as an idealistic and constant lover and sets his unlucky affair against the backdrop of the siege of Troy.

Venus de Milo (163)

Venus de Milo with Drawers is certainly one of Salvador Dalí's most popular works. The original ancient statue became a veritable obsession for Dalí, who engaged in a continuous development of paradoxes on it throughout most of his career. An inconsistent and puzzling addition, such as drawers, distracts the viewer's attention away from the classical masterpiece, thus challenging the concepts of its value and immutability.

164 Andrea Palladio, Detail of the entablature, interior of S. Giorgio Maggiore, Venice, 1560–1563.

165 Luca Giordano, *Xanthippe Pours Water into Socrates' Collar,* ca. 1684.

Vitruvius and the Classical Orders (164)

The reading and translating of Vitruvius' *De architectura,* the only surviving treatise on **architecture** from classical times, deeply affected the development of architectural theory in the Renaissance. From the end of the 15th century on, comprehension of the text slowly increased, and Vitruvius was no longer seen merely as a literary model. Instead, readers began consulting the treatise as an actual guide for analyzing Roman buildings in order to work out a rational method of applying classical language to modern architecture. **Palladio** himself wrote a vernacular treatise on architecture, largely based on Vitruvius' *De architectura,* to advance the understanding and use of the classical orders.

Xanthippe (165)

The notoriety engendered by a hint about her character in **Xenophon's** *Symposium* has made Xanthippe a byword for a scolding wife. For centuries, writers and artists have relished anecdotes in which the lofty thinker **Socrates** is humbled by his bickering wife. In one, told by **Diogenes Laertius** and later incorporated in Jerome's treatise *Against Jovinianus,* Xanthippe empties a bucket of water onto her husband, to which he responds by saying that he had known her thundering would eventually be followed by rain.

110. Florence, Biblioteca Medicea Laurenziana, ms. Plut.74.7, c. 198v. By permission of the Ministero per i Beni e le Attività Culturali.

111. Staatliche Museen, Berlin, Germany. Bildarchiv Preussischer Kulturbesitz/Art Resource, NY.

112. Robert Garrett Collection of Medieval and Renaissance Manuscripts No. 158. Manuscripts Division. Department of Rare Books and Special Collections. Princeton University Library.

113. Illustration to Dante's *Divine Comedy,* 1824–1827. National Gallery of Victoria, Melbourne, Australia, Felton Bequest, 1920.

114. Louvre, Paris, France. Scala/Art Resource, NY.

115. Science Museum, London, England. SSPL/Science Museum/Art Resource, NY.

116. British Museum, London, England. Erich Lessing/Art Resource, NY.

117. Staatliche Museen, Berlin, Germany. Bildarchiv Preussischer Kulturbesitz/Art Resource, NY.

118. Mostra Augustea, Rome, Italy. Alinari/Art Resource, NY. The Mostra Augustea della Romanità closed in 1937. The model is now in the Museo della Civiltà Romana, Rome.

119. Palace of Diocletian, Split, Croatia. Vanni/Art Resource, NY.

120. Aquatint etching. Private Collection/ Capital Prints, London, England/ The Bridgeman Art Library.

121. Louvre, Paris, France. Erich Lessing/Art Resource, NY.

122. Vanni/Art Resource, NY.

123. Vatican Palace. Erich Lessing/Art Resource, NY.

124. Rome, Italy. Vanni/Art Resource, NY.

125. Erich Lessing/Art Resource, NY.

126. Getty Images.

127. Staatliche Museen, Berlin, Germany. Erich Lessing/Art Resource, NY.

128. Pergamon Museum, Berlin, Germany/ The Bridgeman Art Library.

129. © The Trustees of The British Museum/Art Resource, NY.

130. Engraving after Charles Le Brun, *Studies of the physiognomy of man in relationship with the animals,* ca. 1668. Louvre, Paris, France. Réunion des Musées Nationaux/Art Resource, NY.

131. Staatliche Museen, Berlin, Germany. Bildarchiv Preussischer Kulturbesitz/Art Resource, NY. © 2010 Estate of Pablo Picasso/Artists Rights Society (ARS), New York.

132. Alinari/Art Resource, NY.

133. © DeA Picture Library/Art Resource, NY.

134. Cathedral of Palermo, Italy. Vanni/Art Resource, NY.

135. S. Marco, Venice, Italy. Erich Lessing/Art Resource, NY.

136. © 2010 Ellen Isaacs and World of Stock.

137. Vanni/Art Resource, NY.

138. Friedrich Wilhelm Nietzsche, *Die Geburt der Tragödie* (Leipzig, 1872), GC8.N5588.872g, Houghton Library, Harvard University.

139. Image © The Metropolitan Museum of Art/Art Resource, NY.

140. Louvre, Paris, France. Réunion des Musées Nationaux/Art Resource, NY.

141. Private collection. Fine Art Photographic Library, London/Art Resource, NY.

142. S. Apollinare Nuovo, Ravenna, Italy. Cameraphoto Arte, Venice/Art Resource, NY.

143. Austrian National Library, Vienna. © ÖNB, Picture Archive, E 8213-C.

144. Coll. Contessa Giustiniani, Venice, Italy. Cameraphoto Arte, Venice/Art Resource, NY.

145. Staatliche Museen, Berlin, Germany. Bildarchiv Preussischer Kulturbesitz/Art Resource, NY.

146. Louvre, Paris, France. Réunion des Musées Nationaux/Art Resource, NY.

147. Bildarchiv Preussischer Kulturbesitz/Art Resource, NY.

148. Agra, Uttar Pradesh, India. Vanni/Art Resource, NY.

149. Erich Lessing/Art Resource, NY.

150. Getty Images.

151. Getty Images.

152. Photo courtesy of Pier Luigi Tucci.

153. Photo courtesy of Pier Luigi Tucci.

154. Getty Images.

155. Uffizi Gallery, Florence, Italy. Finsiel/Alinari/Art Resource, NY.

156. Museo Pio Clementino, Vatican Museums. Scala/Art Resource, NY.

157. Harvard Art Museum, Fogg Art Museum, The Program for Harvard College, M13724. Photo: Imaging Department © President and Fellows of Harvard College.

158. British Library, London, England. HIP/Art Resource, NY.

159. Louvre, Paris, France. Erich Lessing/Art Resource, NY.

160. Vanni/Art Resource, NY.

161. Art Resource, NY.

162. *The Works of Geoffrey Chaucer: now newly imprinted* [with pictures designed by Sir Edward Burne-Jones] (1896), Typ 805K.96.275 PF, Houghton Library, Harvard University.

163. Through prior gift of Mrs. Gilbert W. Chapman, 2005.424. Photograph by Robert Hashimoto. Reproduction, The Art Institute of Chicago. © 2010 Salvador Dalí, Gala-Salvador Dalí Foundation/Artists Rights Society (ARS), New York.

164. Cameraphoto Arte, Venice/Art Resource, NY.

165. Erich Lessing/Art Resource, NY.

and the revival of the craft of carving marble, by a succession of marble-working families who are today called Cosmati after the progenitor of the last of them (Cosmatus, son of Petri Mellini, fl. 1264–1280). These *marmorarii* recut *spolia* into bits and slices for their famous mosaic floors ("atomized antiquity," as Arnold Esch described it), and ultimately into ambitious cloisters and tombs. Their ability to imitate ancient architectural ornament, especially capitals, was so convincing that their work is sometimes difficult to distinguish from antique originals. Their popularity waned toward the end of the 13th century, however, as taste shifted to the Gothicizing style of Arnolfo di Cambio (1235–1310).

Fragmentary inscriptions in Cosmatesque pavements suggest that a primary source of marble was the abandoned cemeteries outside the city walls of Rome, which also yielded the figured sarcophagi that prominent citizens began to desire for their own tombs. These reused containers, decorated with pagan myths and rituals, began to appear in churches at the beginning of the 12th century and were also reused about the city for more mundane functions, such as fountains and mangers. In the 15th and 16th centuries they were a prime source of figural motifs and compositions for Renaissance artists who went to Rome in search of the visual vocabulary of antiquity.

Harbingers of interest in classical remains for their own sake occurred throughout the 12th through 14th centuries, but they did not cohere into the purposeful, collective effort that distinguished the Renaissance. Clerics educated in the cathedral schools of northern Europe were capable of a historical appreciation of antique monuments: John of Salisbury (ca. 1120–1180), for example, pondered the inscriptions on the Arch of Constantine (prologue, *Policraticus*). But he was not moved to study the monuments further, and in his *Memoirs of the Papal Court* (*Historia Pontificialis,* ca. 1163; ed. Chibnall, 79) he disparaged the desire of Bishop Henry of Winchester to export Roman marble statues to England.

The most influential medieval study of Rome's classical monuments was the lower-brow *Marvels of the City of Rome* (*Mirabilia urbis Romae,* ca. 1143), written by a Roman who may have been affiliated with St. Peter's, which relies on oral tradition and popular mythology in lieu of classical erudition. The tales reported in the *Mirabilia* lived on for centuries, influencing the reconstruction of ancient Roman topography into modern times. Although it bears some resemblance, the *Narracio de mirabilibus urbis Romae* by the 13th-century Englishman "Master Gregory" was more sophisticated. Like Pliny, Gregory categorized statues by material and judged them in terms of the emulation of nature. He also consistently (if not always correctly) attempted to match statues with ancient texts (Venus with Ovid, for example), although the *Spinario* (*Boy with Thorn*) is identified in medieval fashion as a figure of Priapus on the basis of a rumor that its genitals were oversized. Unlike the *Mirabilia,* Master Gregory's text had little circulation or influence.

Petrarch, the most famous exponent of the classical tradition in the 14th century, visited Rome only briefly between 1337 and 1350. He was an early supporter of Cola di Rienzo, whose revolution of 1347 aimed to restore republican government. Petrarch and Cola represent the literary and empirical approaches to classical remains that would be integrated in the 15th century. Petrarch's reminiscence of walking through Rome is a memory picture of sites known from Virgil and Livy, which he could not have actually seen (*Letters on Familiar Matters; Familiarium rerum liber* 6.2.5–14). Cola confronted ancient buildings directly to read their inscriptions; he was said to be the only person of the day who could decipher them ([anonymous, ca. 1358], *Life of Cola di Rienzo* 1.1). Petrarch lamented the ignorance of history among the local populace ("Nowhere is Rome less known than in Rome"), but his contemporary Giovanni Cavallini de Cerronibus was one of the first to attempt a description of the city that integrates the evidence of literary texts, coins, and inscriptions, in his *Comprehensive History of the Virtues and Qualities of the Romans* (*Polistoria de virtutibus et dotibus Romanorum,* 1343–1352). Around 1375 the polymath Giovanni de' Dondi of Padua added the element of measure, counting columns, pacing off lengths and widths, and estimating the heights of major buildings, classical and Christian, in his *Roman Journey* (*Iter romanum*). Dondi's list of the "remarkable things of the pagans which are partly still in Rome and show how great they were, the equal of which one doesn't see elsewhere," represents the core survivors that shaped the understanding of classical antiquity for later ages: Pantheon, Column of Trajan, Arch of Constantine, Arch of Septimius Severus, Colosseum, the *Horse Tamers* (or *Dioscuri*) and "Mensa Imperatoris" (Temple of Serapis?) on the Quirinal, Castel Sant'Angelo, equestrian statue of Marcus Aurelius, Septizonium, Baths of Diocletian, and Temple of Peace (Basilica of Maxentius).

Between 1308, when the pope decamped for Avignon, and 1417, when the Council of Constance restored the papacy to Rome, the city slid into squalor. An English chronicler described it in 1417 as filled with "huts, thieves, wolves, and vermin," and Bartolomeo Platina (ca. 1475) added "falling-down houses, collapsed temples, deserted streets, a filthy and defiled city" (Gregorovius 7:669). Popes Martin V (r. 1417–1431), Eugenius IV (r. 1431–1441), and Nicholas V (r. 1447–1455) ushered in an era of dramatic renovation, including the construction of massive cardinals' palaces (Palazzo di Venezia, 1455–1464; Cancelleria, 1485–1513), which consumed ancient remains for their stone and lime on a scale unimagined in the Middle Ages. The daily disappearance of antiquities became a woeful refrain of 15th- and 16th-century artists and Humanists who sought to study them.

The foundations of Roman Humanism were laid even before Martin V returned to Rome. Poggio Bracciolini (1380–1459) arrived ca. 1403; Manuel Chrysoloras (1355–1415) wrote his *Comparison of Old and New Rome* in 1411; Antonio di Tuccio Manetti claimed that

Filippo Brunelleschi (1377–1446) and Donatello (1386 or 1387–1466) were in Rome for "many years" beginning in 1401; and quotations of Roman monuments in the north door of the Florence Baptistery indicate that Lorenzo Ghiberti (1378–1455) studied there before 1416. Ultimately, however, the Roman Renaissance was due to a stable, increasingly wealthy, intermittently sympathetic, princely and culturally ambitious papacy, which attracted the critical mass of scholars and artists that made Rome the place where archaeology was born, in turn engendering a rebirth of the classical tradition. Other factors critical to the rebirth included a revolution in the technology of drawing, which made the graphic transcription of antiquities a desirable part of artists' training; the invention of printing, which made Roman antiquities familiar throughout Europe through graphic and verbal representations; the influence of Greek émigrés on Latin Humanism; a new appreciation of texts, artifacts, and ruins as interrelated traces of a single, historically bounded culture; the gathering of ancient artworks into public and private collections where they could be conveniently studied; and the resources to create new buildings on the scale of Roman imperial ones, which fostered the study of classical ruins as models even as it entailed their demise.

Chrysoloras' *Three Letters Comparing Old and New Rome* (*Epistolae tres de comparatione veteris et novae Romae,* 1411) is remarkable for his unprecedented recognition of ancient reliefs, like those of the Column of Trajan, as "eyewitness" historical documents; his testimony that "many" Greek monuments, statues, and inscriptions still survived in Rome; and his unified vision, in which ruins and churches were equally vital. The last of these perceptions was crucial to the development of a Christian classicism in which Rome continued to figure as the head of the Church rather than relapsing into paganism. Poggio's description of the ruins of Rome, *On the Inconstancy of Fortune* (*De varietate Fortunae,* 1432–1448) is more pessimistic: "a rotted giant corpse" of an age better known through historical writings, many of which (including Vitruvius) he had unearthed himself in medieval libraries.

By mid-century Poggio, Flavio Biondo (1392–1463), Leon Battista Alberti (1404–1472)—all employed as papal secretaries—and Pomponio Leto (1425–1498), who taught Latin eloquence, were residing in Rome and engaged in the recovery of the classical tradition. Biondo's *Restoration of Rome* (*De Roma instaurata,* ca. 1446) is considered the first systematic attempt to correlate every kind of evidence—classical texts of all genres, coins, inscriptions, physical remains—to reconstruct the topography of ancient Rome. Alberti studied Ptolemy's *Geography* (the translation of which was initiated by Chrysoloras) to devise a mathematical means of mapping Rome, outlined in his *Descriptio urbis Romae.* He wrote a treatise on ancient architecture, *Ten Books on Architecture* (*De re aedificatoria,* ca. 1452), based on Vitruvius, whose text he attempted to decipher by comparing it to extant buildings in Rome.

At the same time the invention and rapid spread of printing (a press was established in Rome in 1467; the *editio princeps* of Virgil, promoted by Pomponio Leto, was printed in Rome two years later) spurred the production of paper, and paper—abundant and relatively inexpensive—encouraged drawing. Manetti's account of Brunelleschi and Donatello sketching "almost all the buildings in Rome," as well as measuring them and making excavations, better corresponds to the practices of his own time (1480s) than of theirs, although drawings of sarcophagi and statues, often on parchment, by Pisanello (ca. 1390–ca. 1455, in Rome 1431–1432) and artists close to him survive. The second half of the 15th century also saw a revolution in technique, as artists mastered the skills of perspective, codified by Alberti in *On Painting* (*De pictura,* 1435), and orthogonal projection, recommended by Alberti for drawing architecture. Drawing proved to be a tool for understanding the structure, proportions, and vocabulary of classical art, and Rome was a drawing laboratory. Artists' sketchbooks became sought-after repertories of authentic antique forms and motifs, like the influential manuscript (now Vat. lat. 4464) of Giuliano da Sangallo (ca. 1445–1516, in Rome ca. 1465–1470, 1505–1506, 1513).

Drawing was done in the field, in churches, and in the collections of antiquities that were amassed by artists, Humanists, and popes. Pope Paul II (r. 1464–1471), though antagonistic to Humanists, collected ancient statues to be displayed in his palace (Palazzo di Venezia). His successor, Sixtus IV (r. 1471–1484), donated most of the bronze statues at the Lateran—including the *Spinario* and the bronze wolf, but not the statue of Marcus Aurelius—to the people of Rome for public display on the Capitol, where everyone could see them; from this core grew the Capitoline Museums. Chance finds and purposeful excavations accelerated the pace of new acquisitions. A few painted rooms of the Golden House, discovered underground and thought of as "grottoes," inspired the reinvention of "grotesque" candelabra, used as ornament by Perugino (ca. 1450–1523), Luca Signorelli (ca. 1450–1523), Pinturicchio (ca. 1452–1513), and other painters who were in Rome in the 1480s and 1490s. By 1500 statues representing the complete range of Roman styles and subjects, including the *Sleeping Hermaphrodite* (mentioned by Ghiberti), a copy of Lysippus' *Hercules Resting,* the Belvedere Torso (owned by the sculptor Andrea Bregno), and the Apollo Belvedere, had been unearthed, purchased, drawn, and assimilated into the formal repertoire of a new Christian classical art.

Most of the statues that came out of the ground were broken, including the Apollo, which was missing much of its extended left arm, and contemporary artists were called on to complete them. Pier Jacopo di Antonio Alari-Bonacolsi, called Antico (1460–1528), was one of the first sculptors to be known for his restorations. In addition to working directly on ancient marbles, Antico made imaginative restorations in the medium of bronze statuettes, which were avidly collected, especially by Isabella d'Este in Mantua. Like Hellenistic artists before them, Renaissance sculptors were asked to make new statues to complement the subjects and style of the classical works owned by collectors. Michelangelo's *Bacchus,* made in Rome ca. 1496 for Cardinal Raffaele Riario for display among his antiques, is an example. The encouragement to work *all'antica* facilitated the development of a style that was perceived as like the manner of the ancients without being simply reproductive. Vasari called this new style "modern"; for later eras it was "classical."

Most of the exponents of the modern style created their greatest works in Rome, including Donato Bramante (1443 or 1444–1514), Raphael (1483–1520), and Michelangelo (1475–1564); Leonardo da Vinci, who made a celebrity visit in 1513, is an exception. The egomaniacal Pope Julius II (r. 1503–1513) brought these and other artists to the Vatican to design a new Church of St. Peter (begun 1506), to make his grandiose tomb, and to paint the vault of the Sistine Chapel (1508–1512) and the rooms (*Stanze*) of the palace adjoining it. These works epitomized the new classical style for their own and later generations. The pope also had Bramante design an enormous terraced courtyard (Cortile del Belvedere) for the staging of spectacles, *otium* (leisure), and the display of antique sculpture. When the Laocoön was excavated in 1506—and immediately recognized as the group admired by Pliny—the pope acquired it for this courtyard, where it joined the Apollo and was later joined by other statues that were thought to represent the best of classical antiquity.

The Cortile del Belvedere exemplifies the new interest in secular forms of art and architecture that had been completely neglected in the Middle Ages. Architects were fascinated by theaters and villas. The Villa Farnesina in Trastevere was designed by Baldassare Peruzzi (1481–1536) as a re-creation of an ancient Roman villa with frescoes of carefully researched classical subjects by Raphael, his pupil Giulio Romano (ca. 1499–1546), and Sodoma (1477–1549) among others; the Villa Madama, originally designed by Raphael with Antonio da Sangallo the Younger (1484–1546) and completed by Giulio Romano, also evoked classical precedents.

The first two decades of the 16th century were a particularly intense and fruitful time for the study of Roman antiquity. Francesco Albertini published a critical revision of the medieval *Mirabilia,* entitled *A Short Survey of the Marvels of the New and Old City of Rome* (*Opusculum de mirabilibus novae et veteris urbis Romae*) in 1510; among other advances it gives evidence of the first art historical interest in the classical *spolia* incorporated in early Christian and medieval churches. Peruzzi (in Rome from 1503), Jacopo Sansovino (1486–1570, in Rome from 1506), and Antonio da Sangallo the Younger deepened the study of ancient Roman architecture, and Peruzzi mentored Sebastiano Serlio (1475–1553 or 1555) when he arrived in Rome in 1514. The first book on ancient numismatics, Andrea Fulvio's *Images of Famous Men* (*Illustrium imagines*), was published in Rome in 1517, followed by a milestone in the study of epigraphy, Jacopo Mazzocchi's *Inscriptions of the Ancient City* (*Epigrammata antiquae urbis*) in 1521. Raphael was commissioned by Pope Leo X (r. 1513–1521) to make a "drawing" of ancient Rome that would record and identify all the extant classical remains. The project was not completed, but the drawings for it influenced later publications, notably Fabio Calvo's *An Image of the Ancient City of Rome, with Its Regions* (*Antiquae urbis Romae cum regionibus simulachrum,* 1527).

Even as these artists and scholars were at work, however, the objects of their study were being consumed by the enormous building projects of the papacy. Raphael, named papal commissioner of antiquities (*commissario delle antichità*) in 1515, publicly complained in a letter to Leo X, probably ghostwritten by Baldassare Castiglione (1478–1529), that ancient foundations were being undermined for their pozzolana (a valuable type of cement), which caused the buildings they supported to collapse; marble ornamentation and statues were burned for lime; and whole monuments, including much of the Basilica Aemilia in the Forum, had just recently disappeared. The letter is notable for its periodization of buildings by style: "good antique," "wholly without style" (medieval), and "modern," which is very close to the antique but built with less precious materials; it is also the first recorded acknowledgment that the Arch of Constantine contains "*spoglie* [*spolia*] from the time of Trajan and Antoninus Pius," to be distinguished from its "tasteless" 4th-century decorations.

The invasion of Rome by the mutinous armies of the Holy Roman Emperor Charles V on 6 May 1527 and the savage looting that followed brought this fecund period to a shocking halt. Libraries and collections were damaged, dispersed, or destroyed. Some artists were killed and many fled, taking with them what drawings and sketchbooks they could salvage. Many never came back. Sansovino went to Venice and established a version of Roman classicism there. Serlio also went to Venice, where he began to publish the results of his study of Roman antiquities, using drawings by Peruzzi as well as his own: *General Rules of Architecture Regarding the Five Styles of Building* (*Regole generali di architettura sopra le cinque maniere de gli edifici . . . ,* 1537) and *Third Book, on the Characteristics of Roman Antiquities* (*Il terzo libro nel quale si figurano . . . le antichità di Roma,* 1540). The artists who did return to Rome found a different climate, especially after the Council of Trent (1545–1563), and a different attitude toward classical antiquity. Though Andrea Palladio (1508–1580; in Rome 1541, 1545, 1546–1547, 1549, 1554) brought a new precision to the study of ancient Roman architecture in the tradition of Serlio, contemporary art was dominated by Michelangelo (in Rome 1534–1564), who was held to have surpassed antiquity and who eclipsed the classical with his *terribilità.*

BIBL.: Leonard Barkan, *Unearthing the Past: Archaeology and Aesthetics in the Making of Renaissance Culture* (New Haven 1999). Francesco Paolo Fiore, ed., with Arnold Nesselrath,

La Roma di Leon Battista Alberti: Umanisti, architetti e artisti alla scoperta dell'antico nella città del Quattrocento (Milan 2005). Ferdinand Gregorovius, *History of the City of Rome in the Middle Ages,* trans. Annie Hamilton, 8 vols. (London 1894–1902). Richard Krautheimer, *Rome: Profile of a City, 312–1308* (Princeton 1980). *Master Gregorius: The Marvels of Rome,* trans. John Osborne (Toronto 1987). Jerome J. Pollitt, "The Impact of Greek Art in Rome," *Transactions of the American Philosophical Association* 108 (1978) 155–174. David H. Wright, *The Vatican Vergil: A Masterpiece of Late Antique Art* (Berkeley 1993). Paul Zanker, *The Power of Images in the Age of Augustus,* trans. Alan Shapiro (Ann Arbor 1988). D.KN.

II. Renaissance and After

The city that signifies for Western European cultures the very source of the classical tradition stood in the Middle Ages more as an absence than a presence. "Nothing, Rome, is equal to you; even when you are nearly all in ruins, you teach us how great you would be if your fragments were whole," wrote Hildebert of Lavardin in the 12th century. Both the ruins and the prospect of learning something from them remained for several hundred years the framework within which Rome was viewed. Many chroniclers, from the medieval observers themselves to great 19th-century historians such as Ferdinand Gregorovius and Leopold von Ranke, wrote about the city's degradation during this period: the lawlessness of the Roman mob, the diminution and poverty of the population, the struggles among pope, emperor, and other temporal powers. The antique city in the midst of all this lay forgotten, abandoned, and looted, the citizens themselves living not in the formerly monumental regions but rather in the flatlands near the Tiber, where they had access to water. What remained of the imperial order was a set of political terms—"Holy Roman Empire," "Senate," "Tribunes"—whose meanings would scarcely be recognizable to the ancients who had coined them. During the fleeting periods when more effective popes or less hostile external powers produced enough stability for the city to flourish, most of the constructive efforts were devoted to the building and rebuilding of churches.

There was, to be sure, a strand of what we would consider authentic classical consciousness, even in the early Middle Ages. The famous expression "As long as the Colosseum stands, Rome shall stand; when the Colosseum falls, Rome shall fall," attributed to the Venerable Bede in the 8th century, defines the city quite clearly in terms of what was an unmistakably ancient and pagan landmark. In a different key of classicism, and nearly contemporaneous, was the crowning of Charlemagne at St. Peter's in 800 and the export of legitimizing imperial relics to his capital at Aix-la-Chapelle. A collection of ancient bronze statues, including the *Spinario* and the *She-Wolf,* began to be displayed outside the papal Lateran Palace perhaps as early as this same period, and, though it was probably intended as an antipagan gesture, it became a mode of preserving and displaying antiquities. Itineraries written largely for the benefit of pious pilgrims nevertheless made mention of the classical monuments as early as the 9th century; and by the 12th century works like the *Mirabilia urbis Romae* and the travel notes of Magister Gregorius included enthusiastic (if historiographically half-baked) accounts of many visible antiquities, including the *Dioscuri* and the *Marcus Aurelius* as well as structures like Hadrian's Tomb and the Pantheon. Political movements militating for an independent or republican Rome, from the time of Arnold of Brescia in the 12th century to that of Cola di Rienzo in the 14th, tended to celebrate seats of ancient power like the Capitol, and in 1162 the Senate decreed capital punishment for anyone who mutilated Trajan's Column.

These classicizing gestures are not necessarily equivalent to the Humanist reception of antiquity that we associate with the Renaissance. Ironically, the real change toward a more genuine comprehension of and love for ancient culture may well have begun with the period of Rome's lowest fortunes as a center of power, when the popes had moved their residence to Avignon (1309–1377). This catastrophe for the city left its mark on two greatly influential literary and public figures by inspiring an intense desire for the renewal of a past time when Rome—particularly in the age of Augustus and Virgil—achieved every form of cultural dominance. For Dante (1265–1321) in *De monarchia,* arguing against Pope Boniface VIII's claims of the Church's temporal supremacy, it was a transhistorical idea of empire that legitimated a universal order both Christian and Rome-centered. That is also why, in the *Inferno,* Brutus and Cassius, as the assassins of Julius Caesar, share the deepest pit of hell with Judas Iscariot, betrayer of Christ. For Petrarch (1308–1374), a generation later, the worship of classical culture became far more all-consuming, and also more historicist. Among the landmarks of a life devoted to rediscovering and reenacting classical culture were his elaborate ceremony of coronation on the Capitoline Hill as Poet Laureate; the writing of an important letter (*Familiares* 6.2) in which he minutely describes his promenade through the ancient and modern topography of Rome while postulating (perhaps for the first time) the differentiation of *ancient* and *modern* as periods of history; the composition of a Latin epic (the *Africa*) celebrating the triumph of Scipio Africanus over the Carthaginian Hannibal in the Second Punic War; and earnest support for the revolution led by Cola di Rienzo, in the hopes that it would herald the rebirth of ancient culture as centered in Rome.

The Renaissance of the 15th century may have been born elsewhere, but its antiquarian and archaeological underpinnings defined the notion of classical rebirth by reference to what remained of ancient Rome. Poggio Bracciolini (1380–1459) retained some of the medieval *sic transit* when he contemplated the antique ruins, but he also began to connect monuments with texts so as to separate history from legend. Flavio Biondo (1392–1463) applied careful and wide-ranging philology in a project of reconstructing the ancient city in its archaeological completeness. Pomponio Leto (1425–1498) not only studied monuments and inscriptions but also founded an academy whose members gave themselves antique names and performed classical reenactments. In 1471 Bernardo Rucellai visited Rome in the company of Lorenzo de' Medici and the great Humanist and architect Leon Battista Alberti as part of a large-scale effort to correlate historical texts, monuments, coins, and inscriptions in an attempt (ultimately unrealized) to construct a complete historical and archaeological account of the ancient city.

If Humanists were finding new ways of studying the classical tradition, the occupants of the Holy See were reviving antiquity in their own way. Once the seat of the Church had been definitively wrested from Avignon and from schism, a series of powerful popes acted in different ways to aggrandize themselves and their office by identifying with Rome and the classical tradition. Nicholas V (r. 1447–1455) was an urban builder, a commissioner of translations, and the founder of the Vatican Library; Pius II (r. 1458–1464) was a significant Humanist author in his own right; and Paul II (r. 1464–1471) was a collector of classical gems, coins, and statuettes. But the classicizing glorification of Rome and the papacy gained real momentum with Sixtus IV (r. 1471–1484), who founded a museum of antiquities on the Capitol and reshaped the topography of Rome to better integrate the papal city with the classical city; with Julius II (r. 1503–1513), who was a patron of both classical and contemporary arts; and with Leo X (r. 1513–1521), who was a generous patron of art, music, and poetry as well as an unstinting bon vivant whose feasting followed the extravagance of ancient Roman tradition.

Alongside Humanists and popes, the third focal point of the classical tradition in Renaissance Rome was the artists. Painters, sculptors, and architects—few, if any, native to the city—were imported for the purpose of endowing both churchly and public spaces with a magnificence that would replicate as well as compete with ancient glory. Meanwhile, the decades at the end of the 15th and the beginning of the 16th century witnessed an extraordinary rediscovery under Roman soil of ancient art objects, including the decorative paintings in Nero's palatial Domus Aurea and statues like the Laocoön and the Apollo Belvedere. The combination of recently excavated classical masterpieces and generous opportunities for the making of new art was galvanic. Painters such as Botticelli and Perugino, whom Sixtus IV brought to decorate his eponymous chapel (finished 1482), found themselves operating in a style influenced by classical architecture, by the *grotteschi* in the Domus Aurea, and by ancient canons for representing the human body. In the next generation, and in the same space, Michelangelo conceived of a ceiling (finished 1512) that placed Judeo-Christian history in a frame that is classical both in its physical design and in its iconographic conception; at the same time, and virtually next door, Raphael was integrating the history of the Church with the celebration of such pagan utopias as Parnassus and the School of Athens (finished 1517). Nor did the work of these two geniuses stop at this early moment. Michelangelo, though, like the rest of his contemporaries, by the 1530s had turned away from the unproblematic embrace of the ancients and continued to furnish architectural designs for the city that were both highly classical and highly idiosyncratic. Raphael at the time became involved in protecting the fabric of the classical city and creating a new representation of it as it appeared in its glory days—an undertaking cut short by his early death.

This integration of sacred glory and secular power under the humanizing and aesthetically pleasing banner of classicism could not survive the dislocations occasioned by the Protestant Reformation (begun in 1517) and the Sack of Rome (1526). Pope Paul III (r. 1534–1549) was a Church reformer, but he possessed the same passion for *all'antica* construction projects—for example, the Farnese Palace for his family and the new design of the Capitol, both projects bearing the stamp of Michelangelo—as his immediate predecessors. The rest of the 16th century, however, saw papal administrations in various degrees of fundamentalist severity regarding anything that smacked of antique style, though Sixtus V (r. 1585–1590) was dedicated to rebuilding the city's infrastructure in ways that inevitably drew on its ancient topography. For all the urban construction in the 100 years between the two Sixtuses, it was really the subsequent age, defined by Paul V (r. 1605–1621), Urban VIII (r. 1623–1644), and Innocent X (r. 1644–1655), and, above all, by two great architects, Bernini and Borromini, that left the greatest mark on Rome as we see it today. The glories of the Baroque as they appeared in the city's churches, palaces, piazzas, and fountains did not take their cue from the classical tradition in the same way as, say, Bramante's Tempietto or Pinturicchio's frescoes of the evangelists, sibyls, and Church Fathers in Santa Maria del Popolo (both ca. 1508). But they employed the language of arch and column in the service of a high-altitude magnificence that, while stylistically unlike anything precisely classical, still served to glorify Rome as the once and future imperial city.

The story of the classical tradition in Rome after the 17th century boasts one great genius: Giovanni Battista Piranesi (1729–1778), who went as a young man to Rome from the Veneto and produced sets of etchings illustrating the ancient, the modern, and the ruined city in a manner that combined scrupulous archaeology with almost psychedelic fantasy. But this body of work, impossible to categorize among such terms as *classical, neoclassical, Romantic,* and so on, stands alone. In fact, throughout the last three centuries Rome's relation to the classical tradition has largely been one of reception rather than production; in other words, it is not the place where classicizing art is created but rather where visitors come to revel in the survival, whether in pristine or ruined form, of ancient works and to see the masterpieces of the early modern period that were themselves produced by classical inspiration. There had, of course, been tourists before (Rome was already a tourist town when Ammianus Marcellinus wrote about the visit of the Constantinople emperor in 357 CE), but in the 18th and 19th centuries the roster of visitors to the city included virtually every culturally aware European (and, eventually, American) who had the means to travel. Many of them—for instance, Boswell, Byron, Chekhov, Dickens, George Eliot, Flaubert, Goethe, Hawthorne, Henry James, Stendhal, Twain, Edith Wharton, Zola—left written records of their own reactions (sometimes rapturous, sometimes disappointed) to the remains of the classical tradition. And some of them, like Winckelmann, Gibbon, and Burckhardt, produced their own masterpieces in response to the experience of this tradition. If these individuals represent the literary side of Rome's allure, there developed in the same years a consciousness throughout the West that young graphic artists (as well as writers and scholars) required a sojourn among the city's treasures; hence, the formation of national academies—more than 20 at present—for Hungarians and Japanese, for Egyptians and Swiss, for Swedes and Slovaks, all of which institutions owe their origins to a sense that the classical tradition should be the foundation of an education and that it resided in Rome.

The darkest side of Rome's classicism also represents the most vivid topographical presence in the city since the 17th century. The term *fascism* itself derives from an ancient Roman symbol of office, and during the two decades of Mussolini's ascendancy (1923–1943), the imagery of the ancient empire was at the heart of the regime's propaganda. A special program, called the *Renovatio Romanorum,* was instituted to produce both a moral and an urbanological return to what were perceived as classical ideals. Some of these efforts turned in archaeological directions, such as the excavation and display of antiquities in the Largo Argentina; some involved the demolition of medieval neighborhoods so that ancient monuments like the Forum and the Colosseum could be suitably cleared of postimperial debris; some involved new construction on a colossal classicizing scale, like the Olympic Stadium, which went unused in its designated year of 1940, or the ludicrously ambitious Forum of Mussolini, which was never realized. Amid these opportunistic and propagandistic enterprises, the classical impetus behind Fascist construction in Rome also managed on occasion to express its stylistic eclecticism by producing quite breathtakingly original interpretations of the classical tradition, such as the Palazzo della Civiltà Italiana at the Esposizione Universale Roma, a showpiece village constructed outside the center of Rome for a planned exposition in 1942. This gorgeously original structure, which seems to have stepped out of a de Chirico painting, is fittingly known as *Il Colosseo quadrato,* the square Colosseum; it may be the most beautiful piece of classical architecture in Rome since the days when Bernini and Borromini were vying for the pope's attention.

As it turns out, one of the most significant urbanological efforts of the Fascist period proves that debates about Rome and the classical tradition are still alive in the 21st century. The Ara Pacis, or Altar of Peace, was a magnificently complex structure erected by the Emperor Augustus (completed ca. 9 BCE) in celebration of victories in the Western empire. Though a detailed written record of it survived, the vast array of decorative friezes had been lost or dispersed until a massive set of archaeological projects, dating back to the 16th century but culminating in the 1930s, managed to collect the fragments and reassemble them inside a glass-walled building constructed for the purpose next to the Tomb of Augustus. But the installation itself found little praise in the postwar years, partly because it was so nakedly propagandistic and partly because the economic exigencies of its time had resulted in somewhat shabby construction. The choice of the American architect Richard Meier, after decades of proposals and delays, and the postmodern concrete-and-glass style of his design have inspired one of Rome's great controversies, dividing the center-left politicians, who have supported it as part of an effort to bring the city into European contemporaneity, from the right and center-right politicians, who have seen it as an affront to the classical traditions that had spread through the world from this very spot. Whether one hates or loves Meier's building, whether one associates the 1930s installation with glorious antiquity or propagandistic Fascism, it may all depend on what we mean by "eternal" when we call Rome the Eternal City. In any event, the controversy is a reminder that Roman ruins still have something to teach us.

BIBL.: Leonard Barkan, *Unearthing the Past: Architecture and Aesthetics in the Making of Renaissance Culture* (New Haven 1999). Catharine Edwards, *Writing Rome: Textual Approaches to the City* (Cambridge 1996). Ferdinand Gregorovius, *History of the City of Rome in the Middle Ages* (Stuttgart 1889–1903). Francis Haskell and Nicholas Penny, *Taste and the Antique: The Lure of Classical Sculpture, 1500–1900* (New Haven 1981). Christopher Hibbert, *Rome: The Biography of a City* (New York 1985). Richard Krautheimer, *Rome: Profile of a City, 312–1308* (Princeton 1980). Borden Painter, *Mussolini's Rome: Rebuilding the Eternal City* (New York 2005). Charles L. Stinger, *The Renaissance in Rome* (Bloomington 1985).

L.B.

Ronsard, Pierre de

French poet, 1524–1585. Ronsard is the prime exponent in 16th-century France of a classically inspired form of poetry that was meant to rival the works of the Italian Renaissance as well as those of Greece and Rome.

The defining moment in his career came when he was entrusted to the care of Jean Dorat, an eminent Hellenist who had been employed by Lazare de Baïf to instruct his son. Ronsard lived with the Baïf family from 1544 until Lazare's death in 1547, receiving an education that paid greater attention to Greek than Latin writers and expounded a view of antiquity in which inspired poets such as Homer were considered to have acted as intermediaries between the divine and the human worlds. A firm believer in poetic inspiration, Ronsard set out in his own poetry to "create fictions and to conceal stories in an apt manner, and properly to disguise reality with a cloak of fables" (*Hymne de l'Automne* 80–81).

The first major work that he published, the *Odes* of 1549, put this theory into practice. Although models for the Horatian lyric ode existed among French Neo-Latin poets such as Salmon Macrin, Ronsard is the first French poet in either the vernacular or Latin to compose Pindaric odes, with their typically triadic verse pattern of strophe, antistrophe, and epode. Ronsard includes examples of both triadic and monostrophic poems, ranging in tone from lofty celebrations of the great and the good to playful and sensual love poems, but despite critical acclaim in the more erudite sections of society, many felt that his poetry was too obscure. Even his love poetry, *Les Amours,* a series of sonnet cycles published from 1552 onward, did not escape this criticism, which led to the eminent Humanist Marc-Antoine Muret writing a commentary on them in 1553, which was unheard of for a French vernacular poet.

In the mid-1550s Ronsard turned to another ancient genre with close links to the ode as a vehicle for his poetic talents. The first collection of *Hymnes* (1555), written in both decasyllabic verse and in alexandrines and variously inspired by the Homeric hymns, Callimachus, and the hymns attributed to Orpheus, took as its themes a mixture of real, allegorical, and mythological figures. The following year, two epyllia drawn from the legend of Jason and the Argonauts ("Hymne de Calaïs, et de Zetes" and "Hymne de Pollux et de Castor") show Ronsard at his best as a mythographical writer: the sensuality of the poetry, coupled with a rich vein of allegory, often conveyed through a complex tissue of intertextual allusions, exemplifies successfully the "cloak of fables" approach he had learned from Dorat. The four hymns devoted to the seasons (*Les IIII saisons de l'an,* 1563) continue equally successfully in this vein.

To rival both the ancients and the Italians, however, Ronsard felt the need to compose an epic, which he set out to do with his *Franciade.* Modeled (as he says in the preface "Au lecteur apprentif") "on the natural facility of Homer rather than the scrupulous industry of Virgil," this poem takes as its subject the French foundation myth of Francus, or Astyanax, son of Hector and Andromache. Ronsard completed only four books, published in 1572, and the work never achieved the status he desired for it.

Enormously prolific, he composed in many other forms—elegies, satires, court entertainments, and poems for royal entries—and his works offered a model of lofty poetry that was admired in England as well as France. With the reforms of Malherbe, however, he swiftly fell from favor in the following century.

BIBL.: Terence Cave, ed., *Ronsard the Poet* (London 1973). Philip Ford, *Ronsard's* Hymnes: *A Literary and Iconographical Study* (Tempe 1997). Gilbert Gadoffre, *Ronsard* (Paris 1960; rev. 1994). Michel Simonin, *Pierre de Ronsard* (Paris 1990).

P.J.F

Roswitha

German canoness, dramatist, and poet (ca. 935–after 975). Roswitha lived in the Benedictine abbey for aristocratic women in Gandersheim, Saxony, the cradle of the Ottonian dynasty, which brought to the region a cultural development similar to the Carolingian renaissance. She wrote during the period when Gerberga, the niece of Otto I, was abbess, in the second half of the 10th century. Roswitha is linked to ancient tradition by two original characteristics of her writing: she was committed to the systematic, reasoned, and critical imitation of ancient forms, and she kept up a constant yet discreet, even elusive, intertextual game with classical authors.

Most of her work was written in dactyl verse with internal rhyme, a form that brought together the ancient and the new medieval aesthetics. Two of her works extol the Ottonian dynasty and the beginnings of Gandersheim Abbey (*Gesta Oddonis* and *Primordia coenobii Gandeshemensis*); her third work, a metric rewriting of hagiographic legends in prose, represented the first installment in a program aimed at transposing Christian topics into ancient forms. These legends formed a diptych with her best-known work, a collection of dramas, written in rhymed prose, that sought, not without some humor, to replace the dangerous pagan plays of Terence—a very popular author among the scholars of the time—with works of Christian inspiration. She wrote six dramatic transpositions of hagiographic narratives of late antiquity. Written to celebrate the glory of God through his saints—female saints, in particular—these works include situations just as improper and lustful as those described by Terence: rapes (*Dulcitius*) and necrophilia, prostitutes and hermits dressed (for a good cause, of course) as brothel patrons (*Abraham* and *Dulcitius*). Roswitha tried to revive ancient theater by dressing up her Christian themes in the attire of Terence's *dulcedo sermonis:* her first drama, *Gallicanus,* follows closely, at times literally, Terence's *Adria,* whereas in other plays she freed herself a little from her model. Her literary project of *imitatio* and *emulatio,* unique in the Middle Ages, led the Humanists who discovered her at the end of the 15th century, and historians of the 19th and even the 20th century, to consider her the inventor of medieval theater. Actually, the books of hagiographic legends and dramas that she called simply *Liber primus* and *Liber secundus* are not essentially different from each other; as modern critics today recognize, both forms are works to be read aloud as "stage readings," similar to ancient recitations.

Ancient inspiration was for Roswitha a general aesthetic principle, expressed primarily in her choice of literary form rather than in the letter of the text. Besides Terence, Virgil was the only pagan poet—and Prudence the only Christian one—whom she quoted literally a few times; these were short passages fully integrated with Roswitha's own very personal style, and it is quite difficult to speak of real borrowings. Classical reminiscence and intertextual games were part of her search for literary authority and her project to create a referential world she could inscribe as her own.

BIBL.: Walter Bershin, ed., *Hrotsvit opera omnia* (Munich 2001). Marco Giovini, *Indagini sui poemetti agiografici di Rosvita di Gandersheim* (Genoa 2001) and *Rosvita e l'imitari dictando terenziano* (Genoa 2003). M.G.

Translated by Jeannine Routier Pucci and Elizabeth Trapnell Rawlings

Rubens

Flemish artist, collector, scholar, and diplomat (1577–1640). Hailed by Wolfgang Stechow as a "radiant favorite of the gods," Rubens enjoyed a life, both public and private, in which he was highly successful in his many diverse activities. His love of classical antiquity informed and intertwined with these activities in such a way that it is impossible to separate the various spheres of his existence as an artist (painter, designer, and architect), collector of antiquities and contemporary art, scholar of classical philology and archaeology, and diplomat who traveled widely and enjoyed the confidence of royal figures at the courts of England, France, and Spain. His personal life, too, reflects his lifetime association with the antique, in that his brother Philip and his son Albert both distinguished themselves as classical scholars. Many of his closest friendships, though formed in public life and in connection with artistic commissions or diplomatic missions, were sealed by mutual love of the classics.

The subject of Rubens and the antique is a vast topic that has been in the forefront of Rubens studies at least since the pioneering monograph of Friedrich Göler von Ravensburg, *Rubens und die Antike* (1882). Scholars of the 20th and early 21st centuries have labored to bring together the massive documentation that provides the details of where Rubens traveled and visited collections of antiquities, which objects he studied and drew, which items he had in his own collection in Antwerp, and how he fit into the intellectual currents of the 17th century.

Rubens's correspondence reveals that he was fluent in Latin. His letters, written mainly in Italian, are laced with spontaneous Latin phrases of his own devising as well as quotations from classical authors. The long list of authors cited includes on the Latin side Plautus, Catullus, Cicero, Virgil, Ovid, Petronius, Juvenal, Sallust, and Tacitus, and on the Greek (a language he knew less well), Homer, Euclid, Archimedes, Menander, Plutarch, Marcus Aurelius, and Procopius. He received an early education in the classics at the Latin School of Rumoldus Verdonck in Antwerp (1589–1590) and further absorbed the traditions of antiquity in his apprenticeship to the Antwerp painter and Humanist Otto van Veen, from whose shop he emerged as a master in 1598. His travels to Italy (1600–1608) completed his basic education in that they allowed him to visit the grand collections of antiquities of Rome, such as the Belvedere, Borghese, Farnese, Mattei, and de' Medici, as well as the less heralded but important assemblages of Lelio Pasqualini, Tiberio Ceoli, the Cesi, the Savelli, and Alessandro Peretti (Cardinal Montalto). Of course, he was exposed to the great monuments of sculpture and architecture still standing in the city; his designs survive from the Column of Trajan, the Temple of Vespasian in the Forum, and the Arch of the Argentarii.

He began to collect his own antiquities at this time, including his well-known marble then believed to represent Seneca, which he took back to Antwerp and displayed in his exquisitely designed Italianate home. One room there, compared by his biographers with the Pantheon, featured a rotunda with niches for the display of his statuary. In addition, he maintained a private study (his *cantoor,* or *studiolo secreto*) in which he must have kept his archives of drawings and smaller, precious items such as gems and coins.

Like most artists of the Renaissance and Baroque, Rubens made copies from the antique as a facet of study and training, and with the aims of an artist, not an antiquarian. His approach was not always objective, but rather more aesthetic, as we know from the famous statement in his fragmentary treatise, *De imitatione statuarum,* in which he advised artists to seek to give the appearance of flesh rather than stone in their copies of ancient statues. On the other hand, he was involved from time to time with publishing projects in which he endeavored to provide more literal and precise renderings of objects, as for example in the illustrations he contributed to the book by his brother Philip, *Electorum libri II* (1608). Most interesting of all was his ambitious project, never realized, to publish a book on all the most famous ancient cameos of Europe; from this undertaking there survive drawings and engravings of such splendid objects as the Gemma Augustea, the Gemma Tiberiana, and a number of fine cameos he once owned (now in the Cabinet des Médailles, Paris). Surely the book would have included the engraving after Rubens of the spectacular Rubens Vase, a honey-colored carved agate vessel once owned by the artist (now in Walters Art Museum, Baltimore). Some reflection of the high level of scholarship of Rubens and his chief collaborator, the French scholar Nicolas-Claude Fabri de Peiresc, may be found in their notes and correspondence and also in treatises on the Gemma Augustea and the Gemma Tiberiana published by Albert Rubens (*De re vestiaria veterum,* 1665).

Peiresc was one of Rubens's closest antiquarian friends (though they met only once). Their correspondence, from the 1620s and 1630s, touches on a wide variety of antique subjects—*The Aldobrandini Wedding* and the nature of ancient painting, tripods, ancient weights and measures, numismatics, and of course gems. Rubens also took considerable interest in ancient customs of dress, as can be seen not only from the publications of Philip and Albert, but from Rubens's numerous paintings and designs on ancient subjects (e.g., the tapestry designs for the series on the Roman consul Decius Mus and on the life of Constantine).

His relationship to the group around the famous Flemish scholar Justus Lipsius is ambiguous. Though he must have found their revival of the Stoicism of Seneca an inspiration for a way of life, there is little reference to this doctrine in his writings. Rubens's view of antiquity as revealed by his many paintings is extrovert and ardent and shows little tempering by the austerity of Neostoicism. He did refer to Stoicism in talking about his sorrow over the death of his first wife, Isabella Brant, but he noted that it was impossible and inappropriate to show Stoic restraint in his grief over her passing. Most revealing is the portrait named *The Four Philosophers* (Pitti Palace, Florence), painted ca. 1611, which shows Lipsius seated at a table with his star pupils, Philip Rubens and Jan Woverius. The artist stands to one side, an individual who is sympathetic but at the same time slightly apart from the group.

BIBL.: Marjon van der Meulen, *Copies after the Antique,* Corpus Rubenianum Ludwig Burchard, vol. 23, 3 vols. (London 1994) and *Petrus Paulus Rubens Antiquarius* (Alphen aan den Rijn 1975). Mark Morford, *Stoics and Neostoics: Rubens and the Circle of Lipsius* (Princeton 1991). Jeffrey M. Muller, "Rubens's Collection in History," in *A House of Art: Rubens as Collector,* ed. Kristin Belkin and Fiona Healey (Schoten 2004) 10–85. Wolfgang Stechow, *Rubens and the Classical Tradition* (Cambridge, Mass., 1968). N.T.G.

Ruins

From antiquity onward architectural ruins, both natural and artificial, furnished the landscape of the classical world with a strongly evocative symbolic evidence of the transience of human existence, as well as the precarious destiny of great civilizations. By the 18th century ruins had also developed as an art form in landscape design and, along with the emergence of the gothic revival, exercised a profound influence on the literary imagination.

Although there is little sign of a cult of ruins in the art of classical antiquity, literature shows the Romans contemplating the ruins of past civilizations, such as those of Carthage and Troy, as warnings of the fate of overproud and morally corrupt societies. With the emergence of Christian iconography, Roman ruins began to appear in the background of Nativity and Adoration scenes as signifying the overthrow of the past order by the New Dispensation; this fashion was to reach its most ambitious expression in Renaissance paintings by artists such as Botticelli and Perugino. The 15th century also saw the first significant transfer of ruins from religious to a secular and aesthetic expression in the woodcuts of the Venetian author Francesco Colonna's *Hypnerotomachia Poliphili* (1499), a literary fantasy describing the romantic journey of two lovers through a landscape of ruined temples, obelisks, and shattered columns. Here ruins became an expression of human love, its pains and pleasures. Within a few decades (ca. 1530) there appeared the first documented case of an artificial ruin (recorded in Vasari's *Lives of the Artists,* 1550): Girolamo Genga's Barchetto, a hermitage in the park at Pesaro belonging to Francesco Maria della Rovere, the Duke of Urbino. This combination—the hermitage, as a retreat from worldly cares, and a natural setting—introduced a long-standing symbolic role for ruins as a reminder of human frailty in the passage of time and the growth of nature. Ruins became a serious art form with the emergence of Mannerism in later Renaissance art, as expressed by Giulio Romano's celebrated dropped triglyphs in the courtyard of his Palazzo del Te in Mantua (ca. 1524–1534) and by the collapsing columns in the frescoed *Fall of the Giants* inside the same building. In the next century Bernini was to introduce a ruined bridge (1678) at the rear of his Palazzo Barberini in Rome, fashioned in such a way that the structure seemed composed of earlier classical fragments.

In England a highly significant development occurred in 1709 with the architect Sir John Vanbrugh's unsuccessful appeal to the Duchess of Marlborough for the medieval ruins of Woodstock Priory to be retained as a landscape feature viewed from the newly constructed Blenheim Palace in Oxfordshire. Vanbrugh pointed out that aside from its historical associations with Henry II and his mistress Rosamund Clifford, the site included the ancient manor house, framed by trees, "so that all the buildings left might appear in two risings amongst 'em, [and] it would make one of the most agreeable objects that the best of Landskip painters can invent" (*Works* 4:29–30). Within the next decades the use of ruins as evocative and visual features in informal landscape parks and gardens became well established. The architect Batty Langley made the important transition from medieval to classical ruins in a collection of designs in his *New Principles of Gardening* (1728) with eight designs for "Ruins after the old Roman manner for the termination of Walks, avenues &c." Among the most significant examples following this development were the triumphal arch at Shugborough in Staffordshire (ca. 1749), attributed to Thomas Wright of Durham, and William Chambers's surviving arch of 1759 in the royal gardens at Kew, outside London. In 1751 Chambers had also drawn a projected design for a mausoleum for Frederick, Prince of Wales, in the form of a ruin. Both this design and the arch clearly reflected the growing influence of Piranesi's arresting etchings of ruined antiquity in his *Vedute di Roma* (1745), which celebrated the triumph of Rome over destructive Time. Ruins also conveyed political and philosophical messages, as at Stowe, Buckinghamshire, where Lord Temple, a disaffected Whig, commissioned William Kent in 1736 to produce two contrasting buildings: the Temple of Ancient Virtue as an intact peripteral temple, and the Temple of Modern Virtue as ruins. Meanwhile, the pictorial effect of classical ruins was also popularized through a range of architectural fantasies, or *capricci,* notably in the paintings of Gian Paolo Panini and Hubert Robert (the latter was admitted to the French Academy in 1766 specifically as *peintre des ruines*), to serve Grand Tour patrons. A vogue for illusionistic interiors in this taste reached its ultimate expression in the Ruin Room (ca. 1766), painted by Charles-Louis Clérisseau in the convent of Santissima

Trinità dei Monti in Rome, which conveyed an impression of living in the interior of a decomposing temple, complete with furnishings created from fragments. By the close of the century the fashion for gardens with classical ruins was widespread throughout Continental Europe, particularly in Germany and France (as, for example, the Ruinenberg of 1748 at Frederick the Great's Sans Souci at Potsdam, and the sequence of monuments at Ermenonville, laid out 1765–1778 for Rousseau's patron, the Marquis de Girardin). At the Désert de Retz in Chambourcy, the ultimate act of empathy was achieved with a four-story dwelling (ca. 1780), in the form of a vast, truncated Roman column.

The rise of Neoclassicism in the 18th century was not confined to art and architecture. Edward Gibbon was inspired by the remains of the Roman Forum to write his *Decline and Fall of the Roman Empire* (1776–1788). A theoretical justification for the appeal of ruins was formulated by philosophers such as Lord Kames (*Elements of Criticism,* 1762) and Thomas Whately (*Observations on Modern Gardening,* 1770). New archaeological discoveries also had an influence on landscape features involving ruins. General Henry Seymour Conway constructed a set of ruins at Park Place, Berkshire, inspired by Robert Wood's *Ruins of Palmyra* (1753). This historicist tendency reached its climax with the arrangement of authentic architectural fragments imported from Leptis Magna in a "ruinscape" laid out for George IV by the architect Jeffrey Wyattville at Virginia Water, near Windsor, in 1826.

By that time the role of ruins had become deeply bound up with the introspective world of Romanticism. The architect Sir John Soane (1753–1837) used ruins as an element of intensely personal expression. He had the Bank of England, perhaps his best-known commission, morbidly portrayed as ruins in paintings by Joseph Gandy; he devised from a multitude of classical and gothic fragments a total ruin environment within his London house (now the Soane Museum), reflecting his deeply troubled temperament. Not much later, coming full circle, the association of ruins with apocalyptic visions was revived in the American painter Thomas Cole's picture cycle of classical civilization, *The Course of Empire* (1836, now in the collection of the New-York Historical Society). The same mood would be reflected in Gustav Doré's engraved views in *London: A Pilgrimage* (1872) in the image of a visitor from New Zealand contemplating the ruins of Sir Christopher Wren's classical masterpiece, St. Paul's Cathedral.

BIBL.: Rose Macaulay, *The Pleasures of Ruins* (London 1953). Sir John Vanbrugh, *Complete Works,* ed. Bonamy Dobrée and Geoffrey Webb, 5 vols. (London 1927–1928). David Watkin, "Built Ruins: The Hermitage as a Retreat," in *Visions of Ruins: Architectural Fantasies and Designs for Garden Follies* [Soane Gallery exhibition catalogue] (London 1999) 5–14. Christopher Woodward, *In Ruins* (London 2001). Paul Zucher, *Fascination of Decay, Ruins: Relic—Symbol—Ornament* (Ridgewood, N.J., 1968).

J.W.-E.

S

Sacrifice in the Arts

Sacrificial rituals and in particular animal sacrifices occupied a central position in both Greek and Roman religious practice and in related imagery. Most follow a somewhat typical scheme whereby the sacrificial animal is driven to the altar, has water and barleycorns thrown at it, and is then slaughtered. Yet despite the indisputable importance of sacrifice in Greek everyday life, the actual killing of the animal remained with some exceptions a visual taboo, analogous to the Greek unwillingness to present homicide or suicide on the theatrical stage. The procession accompanying the animal to the altar, perhaps the most luxurious and representative part of the sacrificial ritual, dominates Greek images related to ritual animal killing. Among the numerous human sacrifices narrated by myth, the killing of the Mycenean princess Iphigenia and of the Trojan princess Polyxena, both on altars, were favorite themes owing to their inherently dramatic situation.

In Roman iconography sacrifices are depicted most often on stone reliefs or appear among the various themes of wall painting. Most commonly the emperor is shown on stone reliefs during the preliminary sacrifice, accompanied by a few participants and the sacrificial assistants. Roman wall paintings dominated by mythological scenes also show detailed depictions of sacrifices.

The triumph of Christianity over the religions of the Graeco-Roman world marked the end of representations of sacrificial rituals in art. An exquisite ivory panel belonging to a diptych from the end of the 4th century CE (now in the Victoria and Albert Museum, London), which depicts in the classical tradition a priestess during a preliminary sacrifice before an altar, is among the last known evidence of attempts by the Roman nobility to challenge Christianity. The art of the following centuries in Europe was almost exclusively inspired by the Old and New Testaments. Despite its high achievements, Byzantine art never managed to escape that tradition.

In Italy, at the dawn of the 15th century, revived interest in classical traditions generated its first artistic products: a bronze panel made by Lorenzo Ghiberti in 1401 depicting the sacrifice of Isaac indirectly incorporates classical treatments through the nudity of the youth and the decoration of the altar with floral ornaments, reminiscent of Roman altars. Toward the end of the same century the works of painters such as Sandro Botticelli show the contribution of classical iconographic traditions and themes to the creation of a new artistic identity. Despite the resurrected affection for the Greek and Roman tradition, from the 16th through the 18th centuries sacrifice appears only in art within a Christian or a mythological context. Raphael's *Sacrifice at Lystra* (1515–1516) refers to the visit of Paul and Barnabas at Lystra and the attempted sacrifice by the citizens in honor of the apostles. The scene is full of pagan motifs, and the depiction of the priest lifting the ax and a sacrificial assistant holding down the bull's head can rival any Roman relief. This tradition of detailed depiction of pagan elements was followed in 1611 by Domenichino in his fresco of Saint Cecilia refusing to sacrifice to the pagan gods (Chapel of San Luigi dei Francesi, Rome). In the 17th and 18th centuries the sacrifice of Polyxena and especially that of Iphigenia became popular themes in Italy, as well as in France and the Netherlands. Pietro de Cortona rose to fame with his *Sacrifice of Polyxena* (1625). About a century later Giambattista Pittoni created in 1733 at least three different paintings on this subject: the one now in the J. Paul Getty Museum (Los Angeles) shows Polyxena approaching the priest peacefully and elegantly and has nothing to do with the brutality of the ancient Greek depictions of the same scene. The sacrifice of Iphigenia inspired, among others, Philippe Millereau (1590–1610), Jan Stehen (1671), and

Pompeo Batoni (1740). The most famous depiction is certainly the fresco in the Villa Vilmarana at Vicenza, a work by Giambattista Tiepolo (1757). The owner of the villa, Giustino Valmarana, had chosen themes inspired by Homer, Virgil, Ariosto, and Tasso for the frescoes as a means of demonstrating his literary erudition. In the same period Ignazio Collino created a statue representing a Vestal virgin sacrificing (1754), but not in the context of a mythical narrative. Paintings like *Penelope Sacrifices to Minerva* (after 1756) by Johann Heinrich Tischbein the Older (in Castle Wilhelmsthal, near Kassel), inspired by Fénelon's *Aventures de Télémaque* (1694–1699), demonstrate that modern literary reinterpretations of ancient myths usually served as the sources of such works.

Although the 19th century French impressionists were dedicated to portraying contemporary life, the most successful painter of the Victorian era, Sir Lawrence Alma-Tadema, concentrated on the extremely detailed depictions of the classical world. His paintings *A Dedication to Bacchus* (1889, now in the Kunsthalle, Hamburg) and *Spring* (1894, J. Paul Getty Museum, Los Angeles) illustrate the perception of classical sacrificial rituals in England at the end of the 19th century.

Themes from classical mythology played a dominant role also in the world of operatic artistic expression from the very beginnings of the genre in Florence, Mantua, and Rome, at the end of the 16th century, until the first half of the 20th century. The 17th and the 18th centuries appear to have been the Golden Age of mythological operas, whereas the two succeeding centuries have been inspired more by historical or semihistorical themes from the Middle Ages and the Renaissance or by contemporary issues. Some instances where sacrificial rituals were explicitly part of the plot display interesting but nonetheless erroneous reinterpretations or mixtures of Greek, Roman, and Egyptian elements. For example, in the third act of Jean-Baptiste Lully's *Phaëton* (1683) the main character, son of the Greek sun god Helios, is about to sacrifice not to a Greek deity but to Isis.

Animal sacrifices are rarely an important part of the plot of an opera, serving rather as background staging, as in the second act of Handel's *Hercules* (1745), which features a sacrifice celebrating the hero's victory over Oechalia; in the second act of *Antigona* by Tomaso Traetta (1772), which shows Oedipus sacrificing to Zeus; in the first act of Berlioz's *Troyens* (1863), a Trojan sacrifice; and in Strauss's *Elektra* (1909), Clytemnestra sacrificing. Not unlike the visual arts, opera also gives a central role to human sacrifice. In operas like Vivaldi's *Olimpiade* (1734) human sacrifice is just one of the plot elements, but the ritual is a pivotal element in Schuster's *Demofonte* (1776), Mozart's *Idomeneo* (1781), and Gluck's *Iphigénie en Aulide* (1774) and *Iphigénie en Tauride* (1779). A more Aristophanic view of sacrifice appears in Offenbach's comic opera *La belle Hélène* (1864): in the first act the seer Calchas expresses his profound disappointment at the unbloody sacrifice and bemoans the loss of the happy time of steaming ox-dung and sheep's entrails.

BIBL.: F. Fless, *Opferdiener als Kultmusiker auf stadtrömischen historischen Reliefs* (Mainz 1995). L. Impelluso, *Gods and Heroes in Art* (Los Angeles 2003). S. Leopold, *Die Oper im 17. Jahrhundert* (Laaber 2004). H. Schneider and R. Wiesend, eds., *Die Oper im 18. Jahrhundert* (Laaber 2001). F. T. van Straten, *Hierà kalá: Images of Animal Sacrifice in Archaic and Classical Greece* (Leiden 1995). J.MY.

Sallust

One of the most widely read and influential of Roman historians, along with Caesar, Livy, and Tacitus, Sallust (86–34 or 35 BCE) has been studied, quoted, and imitated not only as a historian but also as a moral philosopher, political thinker, and stylist. The continuing popularity of his work testifies especially to the adaptability of his thought and writing to changing political and intellectual climates, from classicizing to archaizing fashions in Latin prose, republican to monarchical ideologies, and civic to prudential ethics.

Born as C. Sallustius Crispus in the Sabine town of Amiternum and educated in Rome, Sallust entered politics in the turbulent era of the late 50s BCE and served under Julius Caesar in the civil war. After the death of his patron in 44 BCE, he retired (or was expelled) from the Senate and devoted the remaining years of his life to the writing of history. In addition to two monographs, *Bellum Catilinae* (or *De coniuratione Catilinae liber*) on the conspiracy of L. Sergius Catilina in 63 BCE and *Bellum Iugurthinum* on the Roman war with Jugurtha in North Africa 112–105 BCE, he wrote an account (*Historiae*) in five books, in annalistic format, on the events of 78–67 BCE, which survives only in a collection of speeches and letters (preserved in MS Vat. lat. 3864), and some 500 fragments (mostly through indirect transmission). Central to each work is the theme of moral, social, and political breakdown of the Roman Republic, from an early golden age of civic harmony at home and expanding power abroad to increasing factionalism, foreign and domestic crises, and civil strife. Two minor works, *Epistulae ad Caesarem* and *Oratio* (or *Invectiva*) *in Ciceronem,* have been attributed to Sallust, although the authorship is still debated.

By the 1st century CE Sallust had secured a prominent place in the canon of Latin authors, a place he retained through the Middle Ages and Renaissance and well into early modern times. In the school curriculum, the two monographs (*Catilina* and *Jugurtha*) and, later, the other works supplied lessons in Latin grammar and rhetoric, information on Roman history and government, maxims of moral and political wisdom, and memorable examples of virtues and vices. The monograph format itself offered a model for recounting recent or contemporary events of limited scope (but wide significance), and authors imitated his philosophizing prologues, digressions into the social-political background or geographical setting, dramatic speeches, battle scenes, and "paradoxical portraits." Distinctive features of his syntax and vocabulary, many of them influenced by Thucydides and the elder Cato (and by shared moral and political views), and an abrupt, rapid prose (the famed Sallustian *brevitas*) with variety of expression, including a preference for archaisms and antithesis, introduced a new style into Roman historical writing and in turn influenced Tacitus and numerous later authors.

Between the 9th century and the 15th, some 500 manuscripts of *Catilina* and *Jugurtha* (separately or in combination) were copied, many of them annotated by teachers and students and, in the case of *Jugurtha,* often illustrated with a small map of the world. From 1470, when the *editio princeps* of these monographs appeared, until 1600, more than 200 editions of Sallust's works were put into print, placing him at the top of the best-seller list of ancient historians. According to a 16th-century commentator, his work was in the hands of "nearly everybody," and Machiavelli remarked in *Discorsi* 3.6 that "everyone" had read Sallust's *Catilina.* The monographs were also familiar in the vernacular, from the early 13th-century French compilation *Li fait des Romains* and the early 14th-century *volgarizzamento* by Bartolomeo da San Concordio to the dozens of printed translations that followed in the modern languages. Maxims as well as prologues, speeches, and letters were extracted from his works and collected in compendia. The earliest surviving manuscript commentaries date to the 12th century; the first printed commentary, ascribed to Lorenzo Valla, was published in 1491.

Catilina, and its protagonist in particular, inspired works of history, literature, art, and theater: medieval legends of the rivalry between Fiesole and Florence; character studies of Renaissance popes (e.g., Guicciardini's Alexander VI and Benedetto Varchi's Clement VII); a painting by Salvator Rosa (1663); dramas by Ben Jonson (1611), Voltaire (1752), and Henrik Ibsen (1850), among many; an opera libretto by Giambattista Casti with music by Salieri (1792); and countless conspiracy histories. Most Renaissance (and later) accounts of conspiracies, like Angelo Poliziano's *Coniurationis commentarium* on the Pazzi plot against the Medici (1478), drew on Sallust chiefly as a moral and literary model, appropriating speeches and rhetorical techniques to dramatize the dangers of the plot and the threat to existing governments. Only from the later 1600s onward did authors also investigate more closely the social and economic conditions underlying a conspiracy. Moreover, though it has been argued that a romanticized cult of Catiline (Catilinarianism) inspired certain Renaissance idealists to overthrow "tyrannical" popes or princes in the name of republican liberty, it was not (with very few exceptions) until the era of the French Revolution and the Italian Risorgimento that the image of the Roman rebel was transformed from villain into hero. In general, the name Catiline has been applied to the enemies of established order, whether discontented nobles in Renaissance Italy, Catholic revolutionaries in Jacobean England, "plebeians" threatening the "honest freeholders" of Pennsylvania in the early 1700s, or Socialist agitators in Italy in the first decades of the 20th century.

Sallust's own ethico-political view of history, rooted in the notion that *libertas* fostered the display of *virtus,* the pursuit of *gloria,* and, hence, the rise of the early Roman Republic (*Catilina* 6–9), helped shape—together with Cicero's praises of the commonwealth and Livy's celebration of patriotic virtues—the ideals of civic Humanism that emerged in the Renaissance. Sallustian arguments, already introduced in late medieval treatises on rhetoric and civic government, provided an explanatory model for the impressive growth of Florence in Leonardo Bruni's *Historiarum Florentini populi libri XII* (begun 1415–1416) and *Oratio in funere Johannis Strozzae* (1428); the defense of personal merit in Marius' speech in *Jugurtha* 85 supplied material for 15th-century debates on "true nobility."

A century later Machiavelli too drew on Sallust for the republican themes of his *Discorsi,* but by developing the idea of *virtus* and the competitive forces it engendered into a dynamic concept of the historical process, he located Sallust's thought in a new context of pragmatic statecraft. In the atmosphere of political crisis in Italy at the turn of the 16th century, historians like Giovanni Pontano and Bernardo Rucellai responded to still other aspects of Sallust's writing, notably his bitter, skeptical mood and probing analysis of moral corruption and the hypocrisy of party leaders. As Sir Ronald Syme observed, Sallust "belongs to the company of searching and subversive writers, preoccupied with power and the play of chance . . . , finding their delectation in disillusionment" (1964, 256). During the religious wars of the late 16th century in France and well into the 17th century, he was cited increasingly in conjunction with Tacitus and Seneca to support absolutist theories of government and a Neostoic philosophy of prudence. In Stuart England he could be read, even more safely than either Tacitus or Seneca, as a "faithful patriot" and "deep statist." On the other hand, it was the republican Sallust, "enemy of tyrants," whom John Milton admired and who bolstered the cause of liberty in the Lowlands during the war with Spain and, later, in France and on the American continent. It is thus not surprising that Justus Lipsius, who considered Sallust second only to Tacitus, should elect him "leader of the Senate of historians" (*Notae,* 1574), or that the German philologist Cristoph Coler should claim in the preface to his 1599 edition of Sallust's collected works that his relevance to both republics *and* monarchies made him more useful even than Tacitus.

Thanks chiefly to the authority of Saint Augustine, who described him as "a historian of ennobled truthfulness" (*De civitate Dei* 1.5), and to Petrarch, who repeated this judgment, Sallust long enjoyed a reputation for accurate reporting and objectivity. For authors of late Renaissance treatises on *ars historica,* he was also a valuable source of law and political science, linked with such pragmatic historians as Thucydides and Polybius, Caesar and Tacitus, Commynes, Machiavelli, and Guicciardini. A dissonant note had already been struck, however, when the young Italian Humanist Costanzo Felici, author of a "revised version" of *Coniuratio Catilinae* (1518), accused Sallust of being unfair to Cicero, introducing criticisms that were echoed by later generations of Ciceronians and amplified with charges of pro-Caesarian bias by Paolo Beni in the early 1600s and again by Theodor Mommsen and Eduard Schwartz in the mid- to late 1800s. More recently scholars have pointed out the rhetorical and dramatic strategies that distorted his representation and chronology of events. As for the ancient attacks on Sallust's personal life and the alleged discrepancy between his lofty ideals and his own mores, reactions have varied over the centuries. With increasing knowledge of the sources, historians have tended, nevertheless, to dissociate such criticisms from an evaluation of his work, or to explain them as part of the polemics of his age.

Today Sallust no longer occupies a central place in the Latin curriculum, but further studies of the manuscript tradition have led to new critical editions, including a recent edition of the complete works by L. D. Reynolds and an edition with commentary and English translation of the fragments of the *Historiae* by Patrick McGushin. Moreover, since the 1960s a number of scholars, including Karl Büchner, Donald C. Earl, Antonio La Penna, and Ronald Syme, have reexamined his work in the context of Roman political thought, literature, and socioeconomic history. Catiline's *post mortem* adventures continue onstage and in the pages of historical novels and political pamphlets. But leading themes and debates in Sallust's account of the Roman revolution—concern for constitutional procedures versus the appeal, in times of national emergency, to extraordinary measures; the role of *metus hostilis* (the "counterweight of fear") in domestic politics; the interplay of *virtus* and *fortuna;* and the competing claims of an active and a contemplative life—offer important insights into issues of our own time.

BIBL.: Patricia J. Osmond and Robert W. Ulery, Jr., "Sallustius Crispus, Gaius," in *Catalogus translationum et commentariorum: Mediaeval and Renaissance Latin Translations and Commentaries,* 8 vols. (Washington, D.C., 1960–), vol. 8 (2003), ed. Virginia Brown, James Hankins, and Robert A. Kaster, 183–326 (including "Fortuna," 186–217, and Bibliography, 217–220); addenda to appear in vol. 9. P.O.

Sappho

Early Greek lyric poet. Antiquity's foremost woman writer, she was known above all for passionate love poetry, though her repertoire includes other themes. From early on, her reputation followed separate yet intertwining strands. Her poetic standing was of the highest: she was called The Poetess (as Homer was The Poet) and Tenth Muse. She was credited with poetic inventions, including the sapphic stanza (three hendecasyllabics and a fourth line comprising a dactyl and trochee), and was canonized as one of nine major Greek lyric poets by Alexandrian scholars, who collected her work into eight or nine books. Her poetry was imitated by later Greek and Roman writers, including Theocritus, Horace, and Catullus, and was quoted admiringly by Longinus.

Alongside her poetic reputation and sometimes overshadowing it is her fictional career as a lover. Although the word *lesbian* derives from the island on which she lived, Lesbos, that is far from the only sexual identity to have been attributed to her. In the classical period she was assigned an implausible collection of male lovers: most famous is the mythical ferryman Phaon, for unrequited love of whom she reputedly committed suicide by leaping off the Leucadian Cliff. This colorful fantasy was popularized by Ovid (or an imitator) in *Heroides* 15, a fictional verse letter from an abandoned Sappho to Phaon, which had a far-reaching influence on the interpretation of her poems. Ovid also evokes a third, more submerged account of Sappho as a tribad—a scandalously mannish pursuer of women—which circulated from Roman times onward.

Sappho's poetry is largely lost. Like most other early lyric, her texts did not survive in a direct manuscript tradition, probably because of factors such as the perceived obscurity of her dialect rather than, as some sources claim, because of censorship by Christian emperors. The latest surviving copies, on parchment, date to the 6th and 7th centuries CE; for most of the modern period her poetry was known only through quotations in other authors, first collected under her name by Henri Estienne in 1560.

Sappho's reputation and the fortunes of her poetry were often mediated through those of male writers who imitated, quoted, or represented her. Estienne's first edition tellingly prints her poems only as an appendix to Anacreon's. The two best-known, the prayer to Aphrodite (1) and fragment 31, in which a female speaker sees a beloved woman with a man, were repeatedly translated as poems of heterosexual love, a move facilitated for fragment 31 by Catullus' influential imitation, in which the voice is male. A complex relationship with his poetic forebear is also hinted at in Catullus' pseudonym for the addressee of his love poetry, Lesbia. A gendered rivalry, both poetic and sexual, likewise informs Ovid's fictional account, sometimes printed alongside the poems as contextualizing fact, in which the male author speaks for a fictional Sappho whose love for Phaon has superseded her love for her own sex.

This complex heritage made Sappho both an inevitable and a problematic role model and subject for women. As early as the Hellenistic period women writers such as Nossis claimed Sapphic lineage; from the 16th century onward it became commonplace for women writers and artists all over Europe to be hailed as "the modern Sappho." But like Sappho's own soubriquet as the Tenth Muse, with its implication that no mortal woman could produce such poetry, the title could be double-edged, not only because of the paucity of alternatives but also because of its continuing undertones of sexual scandal. As Cowley put it, "They talk of Sappho, but alas! the shame/Ill manners soil the lustre of her fame" ("On Orinda's Poems" 60–61), an accusation embracing both lesbian sexuality (still equated with tribadism) and general licentiousness.

Fragment 31, with its famous description of the physical effects of intense passion, attained greater prominence when Longinus' *On the Sublime* was translated by Boileau into French in 1674. Sappho's poem, the only lyric quoted by Longinus (who thus preserved it) as exemplifying sublimity, may have contributed to the increasing feminization of lyric in the 19th century.

At the same time the expressive theory of poetry developed by Longinus and continued in Romanticism gave new impetus to the fiction of Sappho as a passionate, and usually disappointed, lover. Madeleine de Scudéry, in *Artamène* (1649–1653), had already rendered the story of Phaon and Sappho (as *salonnière*) in prose, giving it an unusually happy ending; from the mid-18th century onward a host of narratives in different media reinvented it in predominantly tragic mode, from Verri's novel *Le avventure di Saffo* (1782) to plays by Madame de Staël (1811) and Grillparzer (1818), to pictorial representations such as David's *Sappho and Phaon* (1809). There were also operatic versions, most famously Pacini's *Saffo* (1840) and Gounod's *Sapho* (1851).

But the focus then shifted away from Phaon to Sappho herself, as exemplar of the suffering but supremely inspired Romantic artist. Visual images of Sappho poised on the cliff or in mid-fall proliferated, and many 19th-century poets scripted "last songs" for Sappho, including Lamartine (1823) and Leopardi (1824). A growing number of women writers, though, questioned Sappho's subjection to love, asking with Caroline Norton, "Was it History's truth, that tale of wasted youth . . . and Love forsaken pining?" ("The Picture of Sappho" 7–8).

The 18th and 19th centuries saw new editions of all the then known poems of Sappho by German scholars, one of whom (Bergk) made a key emendation in the text of poem 1 that renders it unambiguously a poem of lesbian love. Sappho was increasingly viewed as lesbian, though still for some time linked with scandal and despair, notably in "Les Lesbiennes," three poems originally intended for collection in Baudelaire's *Fleurs du Mal* (1857). At the same time her range as a poet started to be more widely known: Michael Field's *Long Ago* (1889), based on her fragments, conveys an unprecedentedly rich sense of the occasions and relationships that inspired her poems, from weddings, rituals, and poetic sisterhood to motherhood, friendship, and partings.

At the turn of the 20th century Sappho's corpus was increased by the excavation of ancient papyrus texts, mainly in Egypt and dating from the early centuries CE, which included several important new poems. These rediscovered scraps, often literally tattered at the edges but all the more hauntingly evocative for it, made an impression on early Modernist poets, especially Ezra Pound, whose 1916 poem "Papyrus" wittily renders a recently published fragment (95):

> Spring . . . . . .
> Too long . . . . . .
> Gongula . . . . . .

This poem's minimalism and its use of lacunae as an expressive device have continued to influence Sappho translations to the present day.

In 2005 the application of new technology to papyri revealed a poem by Sappho hitherto only partially preserved, and for the first time in nearly a century more new discoveries now seem likely.

BIBL.: F. Budelmann, ed., *The Cambridge Companion to Greek Lyric* (Cambridge 2009). J. de Jean, *Fictions of Sappho, 1546–1937* (Chicago 1989). E. Greene, ed., *Re-reading Sappho* (Berkeley 1995). H. Rüdiger, *Sappho: Ihr Ruf und Ruhm bei der Nachwelt* (Leipzig 1933). On Sappho papyri: www.papyrology.ox.ac.uk/Poxy/.

M.W.

Sarcophagi

No other genre of ancient art had a greater influence on European art and art history than the reliefs of Roman sarcophagi. Many of the most significant works in painting and sculpture, in particular during the Middle Ages and the early Renaissance, were created by artists who engaged directly with the rich repertoire of motifs and stylistic forms offered by ancient sarcophagus reliefs. This happened under constantly changing epistemological conditions and with greatly varying motivations. In addition to the phenomena of artistic emulation, selective adaptation, and competitive re-creation, a complex antiquarian and scholarly occupation with sarcophagi emerged in the Renaissance and has lasted into the present. An inevitable consideration, too, has been the frequent and manifold reuses of sarcophagi and their reliefs as parts of tombs, as spoils put on display on the facades of churches and palaces, as fountain basins and reliquaries—indeed, even as wine presses and drinking troughs for cattle.

The sarcophagi decorated with reliefs that held such a strong appeal for the artists and antiquarians of later times came into fashion with the gradual transition from cremation to inhumation that took place during the 2nd century CE. In keeping with inhumation's seemingly paradoxical attempt at preserving the integrity and unity of the body even beyond death (the word *sarcophagus* means "flesh-eater" and was already in use, alongside other terms, in the Roman imperial period), the elaborate figural reliefs of sarcophagi functioned as a "screen" that could hide the actual body from view and respond to decay and decomposition by displaying the splendid and permanent marble bodies of half-naked Greek heroes and heroines, as well as other allegorical and nonmythological personages. Although such decorated sarcophagi were produced and commonly used in various parts of the Roman Empire, the most important center of production was Rome, where the widest spectrum of motifs and themes could be found. About 12,000–15,000 sarcophagi (or fragments thereof) are preserved from the city of Rome (Koch 1993); if that accounts for about 10 percent of what once existed, there would have been more than 100,000 sarcophagi produced over a period of about 180 years in a city of close to 1 million inhabitants.

In accordance with the culturally charged atmosphere under Hadrian and the Antonines, mythological sarcophagi in particular employed an elaborate allegorical "language" that made it possible not only to praise the virtues of the deceased, their physical qualities, and the emotional bonds that they shared with their partners and to mourn their deaths, but also to celebrate the values of life itself. Through portraits, these mythological and nonmythological figures were often marked out as symbolic representations of the deceased and their relatives. The materiality of the sarcophagus itself—usually marble and, for members of the imperial family in the 4th century CE, also the especially precious purple porphyry—was intended to make this honoring of the dead permanent and, in that way, to preserve their memory.

Sarcophagi were—particularly in the 3rd century and beyond—frequently reused for secondary burials, however, despite inscriptions that were meant (by curses or threat of a fine) to prevent precisely such reuse. In these reuses, the specific relief decoration of the sarcophagus was of little or no significance; what mattered most was the material value of the marble, which, owing to the partial breakdown of infrastructure in late antiquity, had become increasingly difficult to obtain. (Consequently, these reuses do not differ greatly in principle from the many marble works that were recycled as building material or met their end in lime kilns.)

It is a symptom of the regained authority of Roman antiquity in the Middle Ages that Roman sarcophagi became charged with new symbolic meanings beyond their material value. The symbolic capital of the sarcophagi depended in large part on their Roman provenance: sarcophagi became, together with other *spolia* (despoiled antiques), mobile media for the idea of Rome, from which a claim to legitimacy and power could be derived. In many medieval cities, Roman sarcophagi were put on display in and on the public faces of churches and palaces, thus reinforcing claims of being a "new Rome" (as at the cathedral in Pisa, where an installation bears the inscription "Romanitas Pisana"). In this context, the burial of emperors and popes, clerics and aristocrats in Roman sarcophagi took on the character of a symbolic practice. Charlemagne (d. 814) was buried (perhaps not until the reign of Otto III, 983–1002) in a Roman Persephone sarcophagus; likewise, Otto III himself, who wanted his own reign to be understood as a revival of the Roman imperial system (*renovatio imperii Romanorum*), articulated these claims through burial in an ancient sarcophagus. From the 11th century onward such reuses of sarcophagi can be found in many medieval cities; on these occasions, the sarcophagi were often appropriated through the addition of inscriptions or coats of arms, through reworking or, later, through insertion into larger funerary monuments, such as the Roman marriage sarcophagus in the tomb of Cardinal Guglielmo Fieschi in Rome (San Lorenzo fuori le Mura, mid-13th cent.) or the Attic sarcophagus in the tomb of Giovanni Arberini in Rome (Santa Maria sopra Minerva, ca. 1476). A particularly striking example is again provided from Pisa, where in the 11th century several dozen sarcophagi were imported and quickly became popular for burials of the local elite. A beginning was made by the countess Beatrice di Lorena, who in 1076 was buried in a Roman sarcophagus of high quality depicting the myth of Hippolytus and Phaedra (the sarcophagus was later put on display in the Camposanto). Where no original Roman sarcophagi were readily available, medieval artists produced their own, which were understood by their contemporaries as perfectly legitimate substitutes for the actual Roman pieces.

Though the perceived "Romanity" of the sarcophagi was key in these adaptations, their materiality continued to play a certain role, as porphyry could increase imperial connotations. This in part explains why in the cathedral of Palermo the Norman kings were buried in porphyry sarcophagi (which were not ancient, but rather carved from ancient *spolia*). Similarly, for the burial of the emperor Otto II (d. 983) in St. Peter's Basilica in Rome, an ancient porphyry basin was used as a lid for the sarcophagus. (It was, in turn, later reworked into a baptismal font.) Consequently, during the 12th century popes such as Innocent II (d. 1143) and Anastasius IV (d. 1154) also employed porphyry to emphasize their own status and rank in contradistinction to the emperor's.

The reliefs of ancient marble sarcophagi, on the other hand, must have been understood primarily as a form of precious decor. When conscious attempts at their explanation were made, the figural reliefs could—in perfect analogy to the Roman ruins and antiquities in the *mirabilia* literature of the same time—be inserted into new narratives and fabrics of meaning, which in turn could themselves be illustrated and authorized by the sarcophagus. (An example is the description of a Roman Dionysiac sarcophagus in Cortona by Restoro d'Arezzo in his *Compositione del Mondo* of 1282.) But even after the complex mythological references of the sarcophagus reliefs had fallen into oblivion with the decline of the culture that had produced them, later viewers were of course always able to recognize single figures and the actions in which they were involved (e.g., a hunt).

Artistic adaptation and appreciation of Roman sarcophagi became especially prevalent in the 13th century. In its beginnings this adaptation aimed, in a highly selective manner, at the emulation of single figures, poses, and gestures, as well as the formal properties of the ancient reliefs. In this context, the drawings after antiquities that survive from the circle of Gentile da Fabriano and Pisanello in the early to mid-15th century are particularly instructive, combining as they do single figures from different reliefs. "The power of individual forms," writes Barkan, "when it is particularly intense, suppresses the referentiality of the image as a whole and produces misreadings or nonreadings of that image" (1999, 261). What the artists of the late Middle Ages and the early Renaissance were interested in was not so much a "revival of antiquity" but the *buona maniera* of the ancients: namely, the valid schemes found by ancient artists for organic, naturalistic, and mimetic representation, as well as the means that they had developed for expressing (often highly dramatic) emotions and various psychological states and energies. In the realm of sculpture, Nicola Pisano provides the most prominent examples: his figures of the Virgin in the Adoration of the Magi and the Nativity on the pulpit in the baptistery in Pisa (1260) adapt motifs from the Phaedra figure on the Roman Hippolytus sarcophagus mentioned above. Similarly the mourning women in the representation of the infanticide at Bethlehem on the pulpit in the cathedral at Siena (1268) owe much to the figures of the mourning mother (Altheia) and sisters of Meleager on Roman sarcophagi. The figure of the dead hero Meleager and his desperate and mourning relatives seems to have been a particular source of fascination for Renaissance artists; one of the most striking examples is provided by a relief of the Entombment of Christ executed in 1447–1450 by Donatello for the high altar in the Basilica of Sant'Antonio in Padua.

The collecting of Roman antiquities that began in the 15th century reached its climax in the 16th through 18th centuries. During that period the great collections (Medici, Ludovisi, Borghese, Mattei, Giustiniani, Albani, and Torlonia, among others) emerged, amassing numerous sarcophagi. Antiquities, including sarcophagi, began to be studied, inventoried, documented, published, and interpreted by artists and antiquarians, who also began to map onto the material remains the discourses available in newly edited ancient authors. A clear sense of "historical distance" emerged; chronologies and taxonomies were established. Some of those taxonomies underlie common classifications that are still employed today. For example, in the Paper Museum (Museum Chartaceum) compiled by Cassiano dal Pozzo in the mid-17th century, a compendium of drawings of antiquities from the hands of various artists, the underlying primary classification of themes was between *res divinae* and *res humanae*, which is by no means identical to but does in some ways anticipate the present-day distinction between "mythological" and "nonmythological" (*vita humana*) themes (although this latter rationale also owes much to the 18th-century differentiation between "genre" themes on the one hand and mythological and historical themes on the other). Similarly, in Bernard de Montfaucon's *L'antiquité expliquée* (1719–1724) sarcophagus reliefs serve as sources for ancient *realia* and are (together with other antiquities) grouped according to themes such as "myth and religion," "dress and furniture," "funeral rites," and "military and warfare."

Although artistic preoccupation with sarcophagi became perhaps less intense during this time, reliefs from Roman sarcophagi (often cut to size for the purpose) were used to decorate the facades of Roman palaces as parts of elaborate decorative programs (as at Casino dell'Aurora in the Palazzo Pallavicini-Rospigliosi, 1616, and at the Villa Doria Pamphilj, both in Rome). In their new contexts the sarcophagus reliefs served both as objects of aesthetic appreciation and as referents to Roman glory and virtue.

The positivism of the late 19th century prompted efforts at complete documentation of all known sarcophagi. In 1890 Carl Robert inaugurated a project to compile and publish a comprehensive corpus of ancient sarcophagi (*Die antiken Sarkophagreliefs*), which remains in progress today. Around 1900, Roman sarcophagi were further drawn into contemporary controversies about both the formal evolution and the "Romanness" of Roman art. Alois Riegl in his *Problems of Style* (*Stilfragen*, 1893), on the history of ornament, cited the reliefs to illustrate the transition from a "tactile" to an "optical" manner of perception that, in his system, would ultimately lead to the *Kunstwollen* (artistic impetus) for the Arch of Constantine. Gerhart Rodenwaldt (1939), on the other hand, described the formal change of sarcophagus reliefs during the late 2nd and 3rd centuries CE, in highly political terms, as the victorious struggle of an expressive and inorganic relief style in which "Roman nature" found its true expression, having both absorbed and overcome a more refined Greek "naturalistic" and "classicistic" style. A very different road was taken by Aby Warburg, who in the 1920s collected numerous photographs of Roman sarcophagi for his *Mnemosyne* project, an archive of ancient images. He was interested in the "pathos formulae" (*phobische Engramme,* as he called them) that the sarcophagus reliefs had provided, in the manner of "visual topoi," for later artists, most especially those of the Renaissance. Current scholarly approaches (often unknowingly closer to Warburg than to Rodenwaldt) have further broadened the agenda not only by examining Roman sarcophagi as sources for social and economic history and for the understanding of ancient visual narratives and the formal development of ancient art, but also by reconstructing the function of the images on sarcophagi in their original contexts and in their anthropological dimension (e.g., as objects created for consolation). Particularly cruel myths (e.g., the killing of the Niobids, the death of Kreusa), which were often deemed "inappropriate" or read symbolically by interpreters arguing from a modern (Christian or humanistic and rationalizing) perspective, can in fact best be explained with reference to the original consolatory and complex psychological functions of sarcophagus imagery. Beyond these concerns, current scholarship has analyzed long-term changes in the thematic range of Greek and Roman sarcophagus reliefs as symptoms and configurations of changes in the mentalities, worldviews, and self-images of their patrons. In doing so, it recognizes the important role of sarcophagus reliefs as a significant source in their own right for the understanding of the transformation of the Roman world in the 2nd to 4th centuries.

BIBL.: B. Andreae and S. Settis, eds., *Colloquio sul reimpiego dei sarcofagi Romani nel Medioevo, Pisa 5.–12. settembre 1982*, Marburger Winckelmann-Programm 1983 (Marburg 1984). L. Barkan, *Unearthing the Past* (New Haven 1999). M. Greenhalgh, *The Classical Tradition in Art* (New York 1978) and *The Survival of Roman Antiquities in the Middle Ages* (London 1989) 183–201. G. Koch, *Sarkophage der römischen Kaiserzeit* (Darmstadt 1993). G. Koch and H. Sichtermann, *Römische Sarkophage* (Munich 1982) 627–634. A. Nagel and C. S. Wood, "Toward a New Model of Renaissance Anachronism," *Art Bulletin* 87, no. 3 (2005) 403–415. *Der Neue Pauly* 15, no. 3 (2003) 195–208 s.v. Spolien (R. Müller). E. Panofsky, *Studies in Iconology* (Oxford 1939) and *Renaissance and Renascences in Western Art* (Stockholm 1960). A. Riegl, *Spätrömische Kunstindustrie* (1901; Vienna 1927) 139–154. G. Rodenwaldt, "The Transition to Late-Classical Art," *Cambridge Ancient History* (1939) 12:544–570. S. Settis, ed., *Memoria dell'antico nell'arte italiana*, 3 vols. (Turin 1984–1986). A. Warburg, "Einleitung zum *Mnemosyne* Atlas" (1929), repr. in I. Barta-Fliedl, C. Geissmar-Brandi, and N. Sato, *Rhetorik der Leidenschaft*, exhibition catalogue (Hamburg 1999) 225–228. P. Zanker and B. C. Ewald, *Mit Mythen leben: Die Bilderwelt der römischen Sarkophage* (Munich 2004) 9–27. B.E.

Satire

As John Dryden (1631–1700) observed in the influential preface to his English translations of the Roman satirists Juvenal (ca. 60–140 CE) and Persius (34–62 CE), "Discourse concerning the Original and Progress of Satire" (1692): "If we take satire in the general signification of the word, as it is used in all modern languages, for an invective, it is certain that it is almost as old as verse." True to his word, Dryden proceeded to trace satire back to a most venerable source—the original curse laid by God on Adam and Eve that evicted them from paradise. Even if we confine ourselves to the classical tradition we can still observe many varieties of satiric literature. Some are as old as Greek verse, such as Homer's *Margites,* a mock-epic poem about a legendary "Dunce the First," claimed by Alexander Pope (1688–1744), writing as Martin Scriblerus, to be the original *Dunciad,* "anterior even to the *Iliad* or *Odyssey*" (*The Dunciad Variorum,* 1723); or the famous mimes of Epicharmus and Sophron (both 5th cent. BCE), admired by Plato; or the outrageous caricatures of Aristophanes and Old Comedy (5th cent. BCE). All these varieties and others—such as the comic-satiric tradition about the legendary mute, blind slave-savant Aesop (6th cent. BCE)—would have been known to later satirists and parodists such as the Cynics Diogenes, Crates, and Menippus (4th–3rd cents. BCE) and the inimitable Lucian (2nd cent. BCE), a significant figure in his own right as well as a conduit of earlier traditions. And this is not to mention the pseudo-Homeric mock epic *Battle of Frogs and Mice,* so popular in the Renaissance—or Roman satire.

In fact, the plethora of satiric forms and the vagaries of the term *satire*—surely not mere "invective," pace Dryden—make the classical genealogy of the genre even more complex than those of tragedy or comedy. Fortunately, the bewildering variety of the ancient traditions has been ruthlessly reduced by the historical process of forgetting, also known as reception, to two main branches: a Greek branch consisting of the Cynic-Lucianic tradition (also known as "Menippean"), its roots in Socratic dialogue and Old Comedy; and a Roman branch comprising both an indigenous tradition of formal verse satire (from *satur:* "chockfull," "saturated") written in hexameters that runs from the fragments of Lucilius (ca. 180–101 BCE) to the extant satires of Horace (65–8 BCE)—which he called *sermones* or conversations—to Persius and Juvenal, and the Roman adaptation of the Greek Menippean form (which mixes prose and verse), known as Varronian, since it is exemplified solely by the fragments of Varro's *Saturae Menippeae* (1st cent. BCE) and Seneca's (ca. 4 BCE–65 CE) saturnalian parody of the deification of the emperor Claudius entitled *Apocolocyntosis.* (Since the Renaissance the *Satyrica* of Petronius (d. 66 CE) has often been lumped in with the Menippean family, but it is better seen as a novelized cousin.) When the Roman rhetorician Quintilian (late 1st cent. CE) boasts that "satire, at least, is all ours" (*Institutes* 10.1.93–95), he is referring to *satura,* the indigenous poetic kind originating with Lucilius and written only by Romans, not to satire in the broader, modern sense of Dryden.

The ancient traditions of satire were far from forgotten in the Middle Ages. Though the Roman satirists continued to be copied and annotated in the West, and Dante (1205–1321) saluted *Orazio satiro* in the *Commedia* (*Inferno* 4.89), Lucian inspired various forms of calque and imitation in Byzantium from the 10th century until its fall in the 15th century. At the same time, new forms of Christian or medieval satire emerged that show only mediated or fragmentary knowledge of the classical traditions, such as the "complaint" focusing on sin and death, estates satire, poetic flyting, and the bawdy French fabliaux, but the comic-satiric masterpieces of the 14th century—Giovanni Boccacio's *Decameron* (1351–1353) and Geoffrey Chaucer's *Canterbury Tales* (1387–1400)—were written by learned Humanists with a state-of-the-art knowledge of the classical past. Nevertheless, it was really only with proliferation of classical texts "after providence had permitted the invention of printing as a scourge for the sins of the learned" (Pope, *Dunciad Variorum*) that concerted attempts to emulate or reinvent the classical tradition of satire in contemporary form began.

Though the Greek tradition had obviously influenced the Roman (by way of Old Comedy, iambic poetry, the Socratics, and the Cynics), the two traditions differ fundamentally in both means and ends, and these differences are reflected in the divergent trajectories of their afterlives. From the 16th through the 18th centuries Horace and Juvenal were integral to the development of European poetry, not just to satire. From Ludovico Ariosto's

(1474–1533) Horatian-inspired satires to Nicolas Boileau (1636–1711)—"legislator of Parnassus" and founder of the French Neoclassical tradition—and the English Augustans, generations of poets writing in the vernacular started to find their own voices and acquire a critical distance from their contemporaries by experimenting with the voices of the wily, "temporizing" Horace or "the more vigorous and masculine" Juvenal, "the greater poet" (Dryden). Perhaps the most ambitious attempt to reinvent Roman satire in a contemporary vernacular idiom was that of the Elizabethans, whose false belief that satire comes from shaggy satyrs drew them more to Persius and Juvenal than to Horace as stylistic models. Yet for all their blustering brio—"Let custards quake; my rage must freely run" (Marston)—*The Scourge of Villainy* by John Marston (ca. 1575–1634) and *Vigedemarium* by Joseph Hall (1574–1656) are justly forgotten curiosities, whereas John Donne (1572–1631) is better remembered for his *Songs and Sonnets* than his *Satyres*. The most memorable satiric voices of the time were those of Ben Jonson's scheming con men (as in *Volpone,* 1606, which reworks elements of Lucian and Petronius), and Shakespeare's Thersites (in *Troilus and Cressida,* 1602, inspired by George Chapman's translation of Homer, 1598), or Hamlet in the graveyard, a scene clearly modeled on the Lucianic tradition of *Dialogues of the Dead,* which generated original satires in English by many hands from the Restoration through the 19th century.

We might expect Dryden and Pope—famous as translators of Horace, Persius, and Juvenal—to see their own most ambitious satiric poems as a reinvention in English of the venerable Roman tradition of formal verse satire. But neither their great theme—the spurious authority of what passed for high culture and the consequent triumph of Dulness as the Muse of the Day—nor their weapon of choice—the wittily rhymed heroic couplet used as a building block for grand mock-epic allegories modeled on famous biblical or epic narratives—owes much to Roman satire. Dryden even argued that his major satires—*Absalom and Achitophel* and *MacFlecknoe*—are actually Varronian (or Menippean), while acknowledging that they do not alternate verse with prose, often considered the defining formal feature of the tradition. Similarly, Pope (modestly) places his *Dunciad* in a mock-epic tradition as old as epic itself. The most important classical subtext of this masterpiece is provided not by satire but by the *Aeneid,* of which its plot is a satiric derogation, as its author dutifully notes. Indeed, the most memorable responses to Roman satire in 18th-century form—and the high point of its reception in English—are Pope's verse epistles, modeled on Horace (e.g., To Arbuthnot, To Augustus, To Burlington), and Samuel Johnson's adaptation of Juvenal's tenth satire, "The Vanity of Human Wishes" (1749).

It is in fact not Roman satire but the Cynic-Lucianic tradition that provided the principal sources of invention for the new forms of satiric literature that emerged in early modern and modern Europe. The Lucianic Renaissance began in the 15th century with translations into Latin and Italian and complex imitations such as Leon Battista Alberti's *Momus* (ca. 1450), a political satire in the form of a mythological burlesque. The Florentine press (of Laurentius de Alopa) produced the *editio princeps* of Lucian's oeuvre in 1496. But it was the remarkable intervention of Erasmus (1466–1536) and Thomas More (1478–1535) that created a vogue for Lucian that swept Renaissance Europe. First, their Latin translations of Lucian, often reprinted, elicited a new audience for his work in northern Europe; but, more important, they were the first to discover how the essential ingredients of Lucian—the fantastic journey, the satiric-philosophic dialogue, the paradoxical encomium, and the subtleties of his seriocomic (or ironic) manner—could be made into vehicles of the most original satiric literature written since antiquity: More's *Utopia* (1516) and Erasmus's *Praise of Folly* (or *Moriae encomium;* 1509–1522)—the only Neo-Latin works to become part of the European canon.

François Rabelais took the next Gargantuan step in *Pantagruel* (1532–1533). Working like an alchemist, as his pseudonym, "Master Alcofribas, abstractor of the quintessence," suggests, he transmuted the seriocomic essence of Lucian into the vernacular—"Pantagruelism"—and compounded it with the giants of French romance, medieval parodic traditions of mocking the sacred, and his own vast erudition to concoct a carnivalization of the classically learned Humanist culture of the Renaissance that More, Erasmus, and Rabelais himself personified. *The Histories of Gargantua and Pantagruel* provides a cornucopia of satiric and parodic forms. Rabelais's Lucianic play with scale and perspective looks back to More's *Utopia* as well as to Lucian's *A True Story, Icaromenippus,* and *Menippus,* as does Cyrano de Bergerac, whose *Histoire comique des états et empires de la lune et du soleil* (1656–1661) launched the fantastic voyage back into outer space (following Lucian's example) while accentuating its Cynical possibilities. But such journeys reach their satiric zenith in Jonathan Swift's *Gulliver's Travels* (1726), in which the voyage to other worlds is punctuated by satiric-philosophic dialogues (with the giant Brobdingnagians, the tiny Lilliputians, and rational horses) that elucidate the stages of Gulliver's progressive estrangement from his own kind—and himself.

At this point the Cynic-Lucianic tradition bifurcates: one can follow it into the history of the English novel or the history of the satiric-philosophical dialogue (and aphorism) written in French and German. The first is exemplified by Henry Fielding (1707–1754), who owned nine editions of the complete Lucian, and while imitating him overtly in such works as *Journey from This World to the Next* and *The History of the Late Jonathan Wilde the Great* called him "almost . . . the father of true humour," ranking him with Cervantes and Swift and claiming nothing less than to have formed his own "style upon that very author" (*Covent Garden Journal* no. 52, 1752). From Fielding the novelistic response to Lucian runs from Laurence Sterne's (1713–1768) play with the fictions of narrative form to Thomas Love Peacock's (1785–1866) peculiar amalgamation of romance and satire in essayistic novels of witty conversation that look ahead to the early novels of Aldous Huxley (1894–1963).

The high point of the second line of the Cynic-Lucianic reception—the satiric-philosophic dialogue—is represented by Denis Diderot (1713–1784) in France and Christoph Martin Wieland (1733–1813) in Germany. Wieland was addressed by Napoleon as "the German Voltaire"; his entire career was devoted to finding forms to express what Lucian and the Cynics had to say to an Age of Enlightenment and Revolution. He was the first German translator of the complete works of Lucian (1788–1789)—whose corpus is as large as Plato's and whose vocabulary is larger. Writing in response to a long French tradition of imitating the *Dialogues of the Dead,* which runs from Boileau's *Héros de roman* through dialogues by Fénelon (1651–1715), Fontenelle (1657–1757), and Voltaire (1694–1773), he succeeded in producing the most sophisticated adaptation of this perennial genre, *Conversations in Elysium* (1780). He wrote many other Lucianic works, including a novel in the form of a dialogue in which Lucian is one of two speakers, *Peregrinus Proteus* (1791), but his most philosophically—and politically—significant work was his novelistic elaboration of the figure of Diogenes in *Socrates Gone Mad; or, The Dialogues of Diogenes of Sinope* (1770), which was translated into French, admired by Diderot, and enormously influential in its day. But the satiric-philosophic tradition received its most profound expression in dialogue form at the hands of Diderot in *Rameau's Nephew,* which he called a satire. Goethe writing to Schiller (21 December 1804) called it "a bomb that exploded right in the middle of French literature": it is a literary and philosophical tour de force that would have astonished Plato and that begins and ends under the sign of his nemesis, Diogenes.

Like other writers in the Cynic-Lucianic tradition (such as Erasmus and Rabelais) Diderot was quite simply one of the most learned men alive. As an architect of the *Encyclopédie* (1751–1772) and author of the article on the Cynics, his grasp of their literary and philosophic significance would not be equaled until Friedrich Nietzsche (1844–1900). A Hellenist by training who did philological work on our primary source for the ancient Cynics, Diogenes Laertius (early 3rd cent. CE), Nietzsche reflected throughout his career on the value to the philosopher of Cynicism, satire, and laughter. He also transformed the aphorism—a hallmark of the original Cynics—into an integral part of his own dazzling stylistic repertoire. Nietzsche was a practicing *spoudogeloios* (or seriocomic) philosopher: near the conclusion of *Beyond Good and Evil* he proposes that philosophers be ranked by the quality of their laughter and speaks of a "new and super-human way of laughing—at the expense of everything serious!" (sect. 294), echoing the last words of advice that Lucian's Tiresias gives to Menippus in Hades: "Laugh a great deal and take nothing seriously" (*Menippus* 21).

When we turn to the 20th century we find many lively translations and learned studies of ancient satire—most notably the work of Mikhail Bakhtin (1895–1975) on the significance of ancient *Menippea* for Rabelais, Dostoyevsky, and the modern European novel—but does it live on as a source of invention in literature and the arts? The Roman tradition continued to recede from the horizon, with the telling exception of Petronius, who provided the epigraph for the most famous poem of the century, T. S. Eliot's "The Waste Land" (1922); a classical model for one of the most admired American novels, F. Scott Fitzgerald's *The Great Gatsby* (1925), originally entitled "Trimalchio at West Egg"; and the basis for a film adaptation by Federico Fellini, *Fellini Satyricon* (1969). There are also many recognizably Menippean literary experiments, even if they reflect a knowledge of the tradition mediated by Rabelais, Swift, or Sterne. To cite only a few examples: Aldous Huxley's first and best novel, *Crome Yellow,* which thematizes carnival and is set at an estate inherited from Lilliputian-like ancestors; Flann O'Brien's unclassifiable novel, *The Third Policeman,* which includes the most hilarious trip to eternity before the advent of psychedelics; Vladimir Nabokov's *Pale Fire,* with its over-the-top Scriblerian mock commentary on a perfectly dull poem; John Self, the debauched, scabrous, preternaturally eloquent narrator of Martin Amis's masterpiece, *Money: A Suicide Note,* who sounds like a cross between Petronius and Juvenal bred in a bad neighborhood in the late 20th century. No less remarkable is Tom Stoppard's transformation of the genre of *Dialogues of the Dead* into a postmodern dramatic form in the *Invention of Love,* which actually lives up to its title.

Since film as a medium inevitably treats preexisting forms of expression as content, it is inherently multiform and receptive to Menippean methods. Films exemplifying Menippean motifs would include Monty Python's use of a mythic frame for timely cultural and religious satire in *The Life of Brian* (1979); and Woody Allen's use of a mock-tragic chorus and Tiresias in *Mighty Aphrodite* (1995) and a journey to Hell by elevator in *Deconstructing Harry* (1997), whose subject—the relation of literary fictions to the life of their author—is originally Lucianic (as in *Lovers of Lies* or *A True Story*). The list could easily be extended.

When Juvenal wrote memorably in his first satire that "it is hard *not* to write satire," he expressed an alienation from his own time shared by many a modern author. When Aldous Huxley was once asked by a relative why he wrote such cynical novels, he is said to have replied simply, "Bow-wow"—mocking the pejorative sense of "cynical" and identifying himself with the ancient inventors of philosophical satire—the Cynics (from *kuōn,* the Greek word for dog). In the most searching reflection on the nature and place of satire in the 20th century, the painter and novelist Wyndham Lewis's book-length essay *Men without Art* (1933), the author argues that "there is nothing written or painted today of any power which could not be brought under the head of *satire.*" Though he mentions Juvenal (and Hogarth), his paradigmatic example of the art of satire is Swift's use of perspective to magnify to the point of estrangement—"of horror and disgust" (Gulliver)—the mottled flesh and noisome bodies of the giant Maids of Honour in Brobdingnag: "These are very painful images," comments Lewis; or as Swift put it in a maxim, "A nice man is a man of nasty ideas" (*Thoughts on Various Subjects,* 1727). Swift is the linchpin linking ancient satire to modern self-perception. In the only portrait he had made, Swift is sitting in his study surrounded by his books, but only three titles are legible: the Bible, Horace, and Lucian.

BIBL.: R. Bracht Branham, *Unruly Eloquence: Lucian and the Comedy of Traditions* (Berkeley 1989). R. Bracht Branham and M.-O. Goulet-Cazé, eds., *The Cynics: The Cynic Movement in Antiquity and Its Legacy* (Berkeley 1996). D. Duncan, *Ben Jonson and the Lucianic Tradition* (Cambridge 1999). K. Freudenburg, ed., *Cambridge Companion to Roman Satire* (Cambridge 2005). Charles A. Knight, *The Literature of Satire* (Cambridge 2004). F. M. Koenor, *English Dialogues of the Dead: A Critical History, an Anthology, and a Check List* (New York 1973). Wyndham Lewis, *Men without Art* (London 1933). J. Relihan, *Ancient Menippean Satire* (Baltimore 1993). C. Robinson, *Lucian and His Influence in Europe* (London 1979). B.BR.

Saturnalia. *See* Bacchanalia and Saturnalia.

Scaliger, Joseph Justus

Just before Joseph Justus Scaliger (1540–1609) published his *Thesaurus temporum* (1606), his massive and technical work on the chronology of the ancient world, he told the French students who boarded with him, "I am doing the history of 8,000 years, according to the pagans" (*Secunda Scaligerana,* 1740). This was a bold statement. The Old Testament, even in its ancient Greek version, which offered a longer chronology than the Hebrew, allowed for at most 6,800 years between Creation and Scaliger's time. In both tone and content, the project was typical of Scaliger. No scholar of his time or later did more to make the study of the ancient world a historical enterprise. Born in Agen in 1540, Joseph was the son of the natural philosopher, medical man, literary theorist, and con man Julius Caesar Scaliger, who pretended to be descended from the noble della Scala family of Verona. A prodigy, Joseph impressed his tutors at the Collège de Guienne in Bordeaux with his prodigious speed in learning.

After his father died in 1558, Joseph went to Paris. There he pursued the study of Latin literature, which had chiefly occupied Julius Caesar in his last years, and came into contact with the erudite Latinists and Hellenists of the Collège des Lecteurs Royaux, Jean Dorat, Denis Lambin, and Adrien Turnèbe. His Parisian fellow students included such highly gifted scholars and poets as Willem Canter and Janus Dousa. Inspired by their love of Greek, Scaliger mastered the language—by his own, much later account—not through attending lectures but through private study of Homer, whose works he read in three weeks, composing his own grammar and glossary as he went. Even if Scaliger exaggerated his youthful independence and speed on the uptake, his brilliance was quite impressive. Three years after he arrived in Paris, Lambin inserted a number of Scaliger's conjectural emendations, which he lavishly praised, into his famous commentaries on Horace.

During 1562 and 1563 Scaliger traveled through Europe with a young nobleman, Louis Chasteigner de la Roche-Posay. In Italy he met erudite antiquaries, particularly Onofrio Panvinio; at Avignon he encountered Jews, whom he impressed by speaking to them in their own language. From the first, Scaliger dedicated himself to the study and emendation of Latin texts, grammatical and poetic, and he published a series of innovative commentaries and editions: Varro (1565, 1573); the Virgilian Appendix (1572–1573); Ausonius (1573); Festus (1575); Catullus, Tibullus, and Propertius (1577); Manilius (1579). His work stood out in many ways: partly for the fertility with which he produced conjectural emendations, some of which remain in other texts, though many have been rejected; partly for the radical character of his theses about transmitted texts: for example, his removal of the Appendix from the Virgilian Corpus. Scaliger himself recalled that he had been "mad as a young hare" when he wrote his early commentary on Varro's *De lingua Latina.* Two years of study (1570–1572) with the lawyer and bibliophile Jacques Cujas gave Scaliger extensive knowledge of Latin manuscripts and Roman institutions. Gradually he began to apply innovative historical approaches to his work as an editor. In his edition of Catullus he attempted to reconstruct the lost archetype from which surviving manuscripts descended, down to the details of its script. In his edition of Manilius he used the text as the basis for an effort to retell the history of ancient astronomy and astrology, following lines laid down long before by Pico della Mirandola, as a critical story of progress over time, made possible by human effort rather than divine revelation.

Early in the 1580s Scaliger decided to enter a new field, one then fashionable in both Protestant and Catholic Europe: technical chronology, the study of ancient and modern, Western and Eastern calendars and dates. Chronology addressed both tightly defined practical problems, like the reform of the calendar, and broader intellectual questions. In his *Opus novum de emendatione temporum,* which appeared in 1583, he synthesized the work of two generations of astronomers and historians who had already demonstrated that historical studies could derive a new precision from the data preserved by Ptolemy. Scaliger drew heavily on numerous predecessors, but none of them matched his intellectual range or daring. He traced the history of calendars, arriving at new and radical results. Using fragmentary evidence, he argued that the Jewish rabbinical calendar had taken shape not in biblical times but during the Babylonian exile, and that it rested on Mesopotamian astronomy. Scaliger also argued at length that the history of the ancient world could be reconstructed only by close, comparative study of the Greek and Roman historians, the Old and New Testaments, and the evidence of astronomy—which began, for practical purposes, with the accession of Nabonassar to the throne of Babylon in 747 BCE.

Though controversial and sometimes arbitrary, Scaliger's book made his name. In 1593 he accepted a call to the new University of Leiden in Holland, administered by his old friend Dousa, where Justus Lipsius had created a center for classical studies. Scaliger did not lecture, but he served as a research professor and worked with talented individual students, such as Hugo Grotius and Philip Cluverius. His presence and example helped establish the principle that Leiden, unlike many contemporary universities, officially encouraged its staff and students to carry out original research on ancient texts and history. At Leiden Scaliger reworked his edition of Manilius (1599–1600) and drew up the 24 systematic indexes to Janus Gruter's massive corpus of Greek and Roman inscriptions (1602–1603), which remained the standard collection for more than two centuries. He also argued, in polemical and sometimes bizarre publications on the quadrature of the circle and the precession of the equinoxes, that he, as a scholar, could master the scientific issues treated by Aristarchus and Ptolemy more profoundly than could contemporary mathematicians and astronomers. Like his scientific arguments, his views on method stimulated withering refutations from Henry Savile, Tycho Brahe, and many other specialists in astronomy and mathematics, who rightly believed that they had emancipated their disciplines from philology. Scaliger's Leiden years were also embittered by his efforts to defend his father's claims to noble ancestry—he wore purple on public occasions—against Catholic opponents who printed Julius Caesar's genuine diploma from Padua, but also slandered Joseph unmercifully.

Neither Scaliger's side projects nor his misfortunes diminished his energy. Working even harder than the industrious Dutch, he brought together and published, in the *Thesaurus temporum,* a vast range of new historical sources. At first Scaliger set out to reconstruct the lost first book of the *Chronicle* of Eusebius, chiefly from materials preserved in the Byzantine world chronicle of George Syncellus. This enterprise led him into deep and difficult waters. Among the Eusebian rubble in Syncellus, he discovered the lost remains of the Egyptian history of Manetho (3rd century BCE). Manetho's name was not one to conjure with in historical circles, since Annius of Viterbo had published a forged version of his work, along with those of Berossus and "Metasthenes," in 1498, and Scaliger had spent much of his career showing that these texts were fakes. The real Manetho, moreover, listed Egyptian dynasties that began not only before the Flood but before the Creation itself. Nonetheless, Scaliger included these new materials—along with Ptolemy's Canon Basileion and much more—in the *Thesaurus,* which set the baseline for the vast and polemical 17th-century literature on chronology. Packed with dangerous information, Scaliger's book provoked criticism from Johannes Kepler and refutation from the erudite Jesuit Denys Petau. It also indirectly helped inspire another Jesuit, Martino Martini, to believe that Chinese history, like Egyptian, could have begun before the Flood. By the end of the century many scholars acknowledged that Scaliger's hoped-for synthesis of biblical and secular history could not be carried out without undermining the authority of the Bible—a paradoxical conclusion that Scaliger himself glimpsed, as he confessed to his pupils, though he also told them that he "did not dare" to publish on such issues (*Secunda Scaligerana* 399). Scaliger died in 1609, long before his work had its most powerful influence. He left his massive collection of Oriental manuscripts to the Leiden University Library. His example of fearless polyglot philology inspired great 19th-century scholars like Barthold Georg Niebuhr, who took Scaliger's interdisciplinary approach to ancient history as his model, and Jakob Bernays, who wrote a profound account of Scaliger's life and work.

BIBL.: *Autobiography of Joseph Scaliger,* ed. and trans. G. W. Robinson (Cambridge, Mass., 1927). Jacob Bernays, *Joseph Justus Scaliger* (Berlin 1855). Robert Goulding, "Studies on the Mathematical and Astronomical Papers of Sir Henry Savile" (Ph.D. diss., University of London 1999). Anthony Grafton, *Joseph Scaliger: A Study in the History of Classical Scholarship,* 2 vols. (Oxford 1983–1993). Henk Jan de Jonge and Anthony Grafton, *Joseph Scaliger: A Bibliography, 1850–1993,* 2nd ed. (Leiden 1993).

A.G.

Scaliger, Julius Caesar

The Humanist Scaliger (not to be confused with his more famous son, Joseph Justus Scaliger) was prolific in every sense of the word and had an extraordinarily inflated ego, an unusual talent for controversy, and almost superhuman capacities for sustained work.

The first 40 years of his life are shrouded in obscurity. Born in April 1484, probably in Padua, as a son of the miniaturist Benedetto Bordone, his real name was Giulio Bordone. Part of his childhood and youth were spent in Venice, where he gained access to the scholars working at the presses of Aldus Manutius. Scaliger would later pretend (though he would pretend to many other things, too) that between approximately 1509 and 1515 he had been pursuing a military career in the service of Emperor Maximilian I, fighting at the Battle of Ravenna (1512), but for this no independent evidence remains. Around 1515 he seems to have benefited from the protection of the Este family at Ferrara, to whom he dedicated his first major verse composition (*Elysium Atestinum,* not published until 1962). Registering at the University of Padua, he earned his M.A. in 1519 but refused the appointment to the chair of logic (accepted by Sperone Speroni) in order to study medicine. His last years in Italy were spent translating the second half of Plutarch's *Lives* into Italian (Venice 1526).

The year 1525 marked a fundamental break in Scaliger's

life. Accompanying Antonio della Rovere as personal physician across the Alps to the latter's distant bishopric of Agen in the Aquitaine, Giulio Bordone changed his name to Giulio Cesare Scaligero, thereby programmatically usurping the cognomen of the conqueror of the Gauls and vaingloriously pretending to be the last descendant of the famous noble family Della Scala of Verona. (Scaliger's fraudulent claims were exposed many times, and most violently by Kaspar Schoppe in his *Scaliger hypobolimaeus,* Mainz 1607.) Naturalized as a French citizen in 1529, Scaliger soon afterward acquired from a well-to-do family a young wife (age 16), Andiette de la Roque Loubejac, who bore him 15 children. He remained in Agen, where he practiced medicine with considerable success, becoming physician to the king and queen of Navarre in 1548. His last years were overshadowed by debilitating gout, and he died, almost certainly a Catholic, on 21 October 1558.

The works for which Scaliger is justly remembered were all written after he had settled in France. Living far away from the great Humanist centers of the day, he had an unquenchable, almost pathological, urge to position himself as a self-made man in the Republic of Letters. Eristic by temperament and unforgiving by choice, Scaliger wrote primarily *against.* His first major work, *Oratio pro M. T. Cicerone* (Paris 1531), is self-consciously directed against Erasmus and the latter's move away from Cicero as sole paragon of Latin style; his *De causis linguae Latinae* (Lyon 1540) gives a systematic exposition of Latin grammar against the universally accepted precedents set by Priscian and Linacre; his translations of and commentaries on (pseudo-)Aristotle (*De plantis,* Paris 1556; *Historia de animalibus,* Toulouse 1619) emphasize the inadequacies of the translations of these works made by Theodorus Gaza; his *Exotericae exercitationes* (Paris 1557) treats of natural philosophy in an Aristotelian vein against Cardano; and his *Poetices libri septem* (Geneva 1561), proclaiming the superiority of Latin poetry in general and of Virgil in particular over everything Greek, is written in an often polemical style against George of Trebizond, Erasmus, Dolet, and a host of other authors. Even as a poet, Scaliger wrote against current trends: he was one of the first to introduce the genres of the epigram (*Nova epigrammata,* Paris 1533) and of hendecasyllabic verse in France, against the then prevailing fashions.

The fame that Scaliger sought was denied him during his lifetime, but his posthumous reputation as one of the most learned men who had ever seen the light of day spread all over Europe and established itself firmly until well into the 18th century. Kant was not even half-joking when, in his *Anthropologie in pragmatischer Hinsicht* (Königsberg 1798), he reckoned Scaliger among the "prodigies of memory . . . , who carry around in their head a hundred camel-loads of books fit to serve the advancement of learning."

BIBL.: Myriam Billanovich, "Benedetto Bordon e Giulio Cesare Scaligero," *Italia medioevale e umanistica* 11 (1968) 187–256. Vernon Hall, Jr., "Life of Julius Caesar Scaliger," *Transactions of the American Philosophical Society,* n.s. 40, no. 2 (1950) 87–170.

L.D.

Schinkel, Karl Friedrich

The most prolific of German Neoclassical architects, Karl Schinkel (1781–1841) was the only one to be an inspirational figure for the Modernist movement. A designer of uncommon versatility, he was also a painter, decorator, and influential theorist. He served Prussia at the moment it became a major European power, and was pushed to think systematically about the full scope of building activity in a modern country. In his methodical attempt to reconcile classicism with the materials and building types of the modern world, he can be regarded as the first truly modern classicist.

Schinkel was born in Neuruppin, near Berlin, and attended the Bauakademie, the school of architecture established in 1797 by the Prussian state to provide officials for its highly rationalized building bureaucracy. His mentors were David Gilly and his son Friedrich, who practiced a richly imaginative Neoclassicism but who also, as state officials, stressed the importance of building frugally and practically. Schinkel's architectural tastes were expanded during the course of a prolonged study trip (1803–1805), during which he came to admire the Gothic monuments of Germany, the vernacular farmhouses of Italy, and even the Arab-Norman architecture of Sicily. Coming at a formative age, these encounters ensured that he would never be a doctrinaire classicist but would apply the lessons he extracted from these buildings to his classical designs.

Rising through the ranks of the Prussian building bureaucracy to become its director in 1830, Schinkel built the principal monuments of Neoclassical Berlin, including the Neue Wache (royal guardhouse, 1816–1818), the Schauspielhaus (theater, 1818–1821), and the Altes Museum (1824–1830). Each was unusually inventive in its free handling of classical form: in the Altes Museum Schinkel used a colossal Ionic colonnade for its facade and a deeply coffered, oculus-crowned dome for its central room—creatively fusing the Greek stoa to the Roman Pantheon. Schinkel's later projects were often astylar, classical only by virtue of their formal rhythms and the clear expression of their trabeated or arcuated construction. Most influential was the Bauakademie (1831–1836), which stood in central Berlin until its demolition after World War II. A nearly cubical mass of red brick and terra-cotta, it was remarkable for the even and uninflected rhythm of its bays, marked by crisp pilaster strips, and for the suppression of the roof (which sloped inward to a central court, in the manner of a Roman impluvium). Here was the culmination of Schinkel's efforts to synthesize classical and medieval principles, and to make of them a rational and economical system for modern construction.

If Schinkel was an artist of great idealism, with aesthetic views strongly colored by German Romanticism, he was also a civil servant who administered the state's immense building budget with conspicuous probity; his reputation rests in part on the inspired way he reconciled these two parts of his character. Though he never completed his proposed theoretical treatise, his characteristic blend of rationalism and idealism is nonetheless apparent in his *Sammlung architektonischer Entwürfe* (1819–1840), a portfolio of elegant engravings that emphasize the stereometric clarity of his designs. This work was widely influential and was admired by such diverse architects in the 20th century as Albert Speer, Philip Johnson, and James Stirling. Schinkel's encyclopedic versatility, however, ensured that he has been admired at different times for different reasons. His 19th-century followers admired his synthetic eclecticism, which seemed to offer a truce in architecture's Battle of the Styles. The 20th-century architect Mies van der Rohe, on the other hand, valued the abstraction and not the historicism; the lucid tectonic structure of Schinkel's work suggested a link between the form of the classical Greek temple and the gridded modularity of modern architecture. In this way, Schinkel has exerted a continuous, and continuously changing, authority as perhaps the most influential classicist since Palladio. M.J.L.

Schlegel, Friedrich

German writer and philosopher (1772–1829). "When I was about seventeen years old, the writings of Plato, the tragic poetry of the Greeks, and the enthusiastic works of Winckelmann constituted my spiritual world." Thus Schlegel described in 1822 his autodidactic affinity for the ancients, which was in a certain sense consummated in 1789 by his "viewing" of the casts of Dresden's Greek statues. When he was a law student in Göttingen in 1790, his brother August Wilhelm took him to Christian Gottlob Heyne's philology seminar. There he learned, among other things, the need for a periodization of ancient culture and the concept of mythology as a "language" of primitive humanity. Schlegel's aesthetic theories about antiquity took shape between 1794 and 1798 in a series of projects, sketches, outlines, and essays. One such was "On the Study of Greek Poetry" (1797), which draws the distinction between "objective" ancient poetry and "interesting" modern poetry. For Schlegel, modern poetry must be built on the study of the ancients. Ancient and modern were not antithetical categories for him but complementary ones. The one represents the finite, the closed circle, whereas the other is progressive development, that which is permanently *in fieri*. The completeness and totality of Greek culture are such that it cannot be revived through imitation, and thus every kind of classicism loses its raison d'être. *Classical* is the word used for a work of art that is aesthetically "a complete example." This completeness, which excites no ulterior expectations, constitutes the "relative maximum" achieved by Homer, Sophocles, and Greek poetry in general. The aim it did not achieve, however, and the one that is unachievable for all poetry, is the "absolute maximum." Thus Schlegel reached his solution to the quarrel of the ancients and moderns, for it was out of the "true" imitation of the ancients that the harmony between classical and Romantic had to develop. "The task of our poetry," he wrote to his brother, "is to unite the essence of the modern with the essence of the ancient" (24 February 1794).

Understanding the ancients thus means being aware of our distance from them, and this understanding must therefore be historical. Schlegel's project was to construct a system that would do for poetry what Winckelmann's work had done for art history. To that end he employed two concepts in combination: that of schools, corresponding to Winckelmann's concept of "style," with which he grouped artists into classes; and that of ages (*Zeitalter*), across which he charted the historical development of each school (*On the Schools of Greek Poetry,* 1794). As a principle or guide to the various ages of human history, and thus also to the history of Greek literature, Schlegel adopted one of the axioms of early idealism (Fichte, Schiller): the antagonism between freedom and nature (*History of Greek and Roman Poetry,* 1798). The world of the Homeric epic (the Ionic school) originated in barbaric roughness, and Nature still prevailed there over freedom. In the lyric age (Doric school), to which corresponded the political form of republic, the ego's freedom and self-determination grew. The culmination of this development is represented by Athenian tragedy (Athenian school), which depicts the struggle between freedom and necessity —that is, between man and destiny. Tragedy contains a synthesis of the objective nature of epic (action) and the subjective freedom of lyric (choral song). This tripartite division of epic, lyric, and tragedy recalls the scheme of thesis, antithesis, and synthesis used by Kant in his *Critique of Pure Reason* (1781). Schlegel's history of Greek literature is thus at the same time a theory of the idea of beauty and of its instantiation in the various ages. It is an aesthetic theory, and hence philology is both historical and philosophical knowledge. It is necessary to create a "philosophy of philology," wrote Schlegel in his *On Philology,* unconsciously following in the footsteps of Giambattista Vico.

Of the three tragedians, Sophocles achieved the "highest beauty," whereas decline began with the "philosophical" Euripides. If Schlegel was not the originator of the contrast between the Apollonian and the Dionysian, certainly he was the first to put it at the center of a reconstruction of Greek culture. The Apollonian world is that of epic poetry. There the Bacchic invasion had not yet occurred. All was order and harmony. The Bacchic dances expressed the sense of the infinite, and it is to the birth of the idea of infinity, according to Schlegel, that the birth of philosophy must be connected. In "On the Aesthetic Value of Greek Comedy" (1794) Schlegel theorizes that the idea of the comic is tied to the joyous Dionysian sense of life. On the other hand, his observations on Aristophanes' breaking of the illusion of the stage, with continual allusions to himself and his own work, anticipated Schlegel's later concept of Romantic irony. In general, it is wrong to think that Schlegel's studies of classical antiquity were only a preparatory phase, detached from his conversion to philosophy, which began with his move to Jena in 1796.

Schlegel's criticism has an anti-Aristotelian streak, for in his view art criticism first became a technique with Aristotle. Plato, on the other hand, possessed the true understanding of the value of imagination and poetic enthusiasm. Of post-Aristotelian critics, Schlegel's preference was for Dionysius of Halicarnassus. He used rhythm to assimilate prose to poetry and claimed that the works of Herodotus and Thucydides were also two poems, thus anticipating the synthesis and the transcendence of literary genres to which, according to Schlegel, modern poetry must aspire.

BIBL.: Ernst Behler, "Einleitung," in Friedrich Schlegel, *Studien des klassischen Altertums,* ed. E. Behler (Paderborn 1979). Glenn W. Most, "Schlegel, Schlegel und die Geburt eines Tragödienparadigmas," *Poetica* 25 (1993) 155–175. S.F.

Translated by Patrick Baker

Sculpture

The classical tradition in sculpture depended, for much of its history, on the absence of surviving antiquities. The ancient Greek and Roman worlds had been famous for their figurative works in metal and stone: portraits, cult images, funerary reliefs, triumphal scenes, animals, architectural ornaments. After Constantine transferred the capital of his empire from Rome to Constantinople in the early 4th century, however, the local quarrying of marble and mining of copper for the purpose of statuary largely ceased, and what was once a vast number of sculptures began to disappear. The conversion of the empire to Christianity led to the closing of temples and the removal of their decorations. Earthquakes and floods broke and buried stone figures, and what nature spared, humans did not. Fires, some of them set intentionally, cleared whole neighborhoods. Participants in political revolts targeted public statues associated with the rulers, and invaders trucked off trophies. The gravest threat to ancient sculptures of defunct gods and heroes, however, was the recognition that the materials with which they were made could be put to other ends. Bronzes could be recast to make tools, new works of art, and, by the later Middle Ages, artillery. Stone figures, once broken, could be used in foundation walls. Marbles could be reduced in kilns to lime, providing the basic ingredient in plaster.

Some statues from the ancient world survived because they had been buried, either by natural disasters or by owners hoping to secure them from approaching marauders. Others, like the bronze horses of San Marco in Venice, were preserved by the captors into whose hands they had come. Still others were felicitously misidentified: had the Capitoline equestrian monument to Marcus Aurelius not been mistaken for Constantine, who was admired as the first Christian emperor, it would never have made it to the Renaissance. Occasionally the recycling of sculptures worked to their advantage, as happened with the 2nd-century sarcophagus used for the burial of Charlemagne in Aachen Cathedral in 814, one of several put to such a purpose. Others were protected by their incorporation into particularly impressive large monuments, such as Trajan's Column and the Arch of Constantine. On the whole, though, the tiny fraction of antiquities that survived into modern centuries did so because they were hidden from view, whether because they were in a foreign land, beneath the ground, or simply not seen for what they were.

There are indications that by the late Middle Ages, the rare antiquities still on view were coming to be regarded as curiosities. The earliest guidebooks to the city of Rome, where more ancient sculptures survived than anywhere else, grouped them collectively under the rubric of *mirabilia,* marvels, and these provoked both awe and fear. Another signal that antiquities were starting to be greeted with admiration rather than indifference was the placement of ancient figures on fountains, as was done in the main squares of Siena and Verona in the 1350s and 1360s. The Sienese case, however, also illustrated the local resistance that such practices could occasion, and the *Venus* that had been put on display there was removed shortly thereafter (and reburied in Florentine territory) when the townsfolk began to worry that they had created an "idol," perhaps even a maleficent talisman. At the end of the century, a similar fate befell a statue of Virgil that had been erected in the poet's hometown of Mantua. The records that have reached us of these episodes are themselves significant, as they come largely from early Humanists who had qualms about the iconoclasm they saw. Pier Paolo Vergerio in Bologna and Coluccio Salutati in Florence both immediately wrote of the Virgil episode as a desecration. And we know of the events in Siena because they were reported by the goldsmith Lorenzo Ghiberti, the author of one of the first post-classical histories of ancient art.

Ghiberti was also a collector of ancient sculptures, and he was not the only one in the 15th century to show an interest in the preservation of ancient figural works. Humanists and their patrons, including Niccolò de' Niccoli in Florence, Poggio Bracciolini at Terranuova, Cristoforo Buondelmonti in Venice, and, most impressively, Lorenzo de' Medici, assembled ancient statues in the courtyards and especially in the gardens of their palaces and villas. Ghiberti nevertheless represents the decisive conjunction of two artistic sensibilities: the poetic idea, first articulated by Petrarch, that the writer stood at a distance from a lost ancient world, some traces of which were visible in its ruins, and an aesthetic self-consciousness, initially exemplified by the likes of the sculptors Nicola Pisano and his son Giovanni, that pushed him to imitate the antiquities he knew. Ghiberti essentially justified the treatment of ancient statues as objects of study and encouraged followers to think of their own productions as works that recovered a lost tradition.

Still, the nature of the surviving ancient sculptural record made it easier for artists to regard that tradition more as a set of ideas than as a repertory of subjects. Nicola and Giovanni Pisano had shown how many sculptural inventions could come out of a few fragments of sarcophagus, and many artists, to be sure, drew images based on the statues they knew, all the more so when the advent of the printing press made paper more readily available. At least as early as the Quattrocento, moreover, some were also making three-dimensional models of ancient works. But early on, texts about ancient sculpture played at least as important a role in artists' aspirations as did any actual surviving works. Tales from the Hermetica, of demons being summoned to enter statues and make them move and speak, complemented Ovid's Pygmalion, who persuaded Venus to bring his ivory statue of Galatea to life. Such legends encouraged artists to invest their works with signs of life: veins that all but pulsed, mouths that seemed to breathe, limbs looking capable of action. The Greek Anthology, a collection of poems known at least from 1301 and first published in 1494, augmented the mythical status of artists like Myron, and encouraged both the undertaking of ambitious bronze casts and the response to them in poetry. Galen familiarized readers with Polyclitus's *Canon,* an idealized statue governed by the principle of commensuration, according to which each part of the body stood in a determinate proportional relationship to every other. Callistratus (available somewhat later) praised sculptures that achieved an illusionistic softness belying the hard materials of which they were made. And Vitruvius established conventional architectural roles for sculpture, such as the prisoner or Atlas figure condemned to bear a building's weight.

Most important of all was Pliny the Elder's *Natural History,* which was known in manuscript to writers from Boccaccio to Ghiberti, but which became especially influential after its publication, going through some 15 editions between 1469 and 1500 and appearing in a vernacular Italian translation by Cristoforo Landino in 1476. Book 34 of the *Natural History* is on metals and book 36 is on stones; both include capsule histories of ancient sculptors, their innovations, and the achievements for which they were admired, establishing standards against which sculptors assigned to work on contemporary projects could be measured. Pliny reported, for example, on statues by Polyclitus that threw their weight onto a single leg, an arrangement that became basic to Renaissance and later conceptions of grace. He wrote of Praxiteles' *Venus* for the city of Cnidus, a statue that was "equally admirable from every angle" and was made for a shrine that was "entirely open so as to allow the image of the goddess to be viewed from every side." The idea encouraged Renaissance draftsmen to study surviving sculptures from multiple vantages, as Maarten van Heemskerk, for example, did with the Farnese Flora (*Flora Maggiore*) in the 1530s, and it spurred sculptors to conceive works that offered multiple interesting points of view—when Gian Lorenzo Bernini included in his *Pluto and Proserpina* a Cerberus that looks in three different directions, he was attempting to outdo earlier Renaissance versions of the trope. Pliny also introduced the category of the "colossus," the sculpture "as tall as a tower," the most famous of which was the 105-foot-high Colossus of Rhodes. No later reader of Pliny could have seen any of the works he described, but his awe over these giant monuments, which he framed as demonstrations of the sculptors' *audacia,* encouraged artists to think big: when Bartolomeo Ammanati made his 21-foot-high *Hercules* for the courtyard of Marco Mantova Benavides's house in Padua, or when Giambologna made his multistory *Apennine* for the Medici villa at Pratolino, they surely had Pliny's visions in mind.

One indication of the power of Pliny's text is the later history of the monolithic sculpture, the multifigure work carved from a single block of stone. Pliny cited a number of examples, including one showing the fable of Dirce; another with Apollo, Diana, a chariot, and a team of four horses; and a third, "superior to any painting and any bronze," of the priest Laocoön and his two sons being killed by snakes. The discovery in 1506 of a marble work corresponding to this last description, and later the unearthing of the sculpture known as the Farnese Bull, depicting the death of Dirce, revealed that these works had not been carved from one piece of stone after all, but by then, emulating what Pliny had described was enshrined as a fundamental challenge for the virtuoso. From Michelangelo, in his late *Pietà* sculptures, to the young Bernini, in the multifigure compositions commissioned by Scipione Borghese, sculptors repeatedly responded to it.

In addition to providing aesthetic criteria against which Renaissance sculptures could be judged, Pliny helped encourage the resurrection of particular formats. His observation that the ancients placed statues on columns "to elevate them above all other mortals" came to trump the medieval association of such arrangements with idolatry; Donatello's patrons regularly placed his figures, sacred as well as profane, on elevated platforms, and a column topped by the Virgin Mary or the patron saint of a city became a standard feature in late 16th- and 17th-century city squares, especially in Catholic countries. More generally, Pliny presented sculpture as an agonistic enterprise; sculptors met in competition and strove to defeat and surpass one another. When Florentine sculptors sought to win the commission for the baptistery doors or for the Neptune fountain that would go in the Piazza della Signoria, they were reenacting the battle between Phidias and Polyclitus to determine who could carve the best Amazon. Nor did it seem insignificant that Pliny had organized his history of sculpture by material and included an account of ancient bronze in a chapter that also treated the medicinal uses of metals, and a review of marble sculpture alongside discussions of the origins, natural and geographical, of various types of stone. Readers were shown that marbles and bronzes might be considered to belong to different categories and were encouraged to reflect on the meaning of the materials of which statues were made.

In the early Renaissance the works that ancient authors helped readers imagine probably made a greater impression than the actual sculptures they could see. A series of major discoveries, however—the Belvedere Antinous and the Farnese Hercules in the 1540s, the Uffizi Niobe group in the 1580s, the Prado Castor and Pollux in the early 1620s—required sculptors to come to a closer understanding of real objects, especially marbles. Those like Pier Jacopo Alari Bonacolsi (called Antico), Willem van Tetrode, and Pietro da Barga, who were capable of casting metal, were asked to make bronze reductions of the best-known figures, often for installation on elaborate desks or in studies. Those who specialized in stone, meanwhile, often earned much of their income, especially in their early years, as restorers. Benvenuto Cellini, Bartolomeo Ammanati, Giovanni Caccini, and, later, Gian Lorenzo Bernini and Alessandro Algardi, all made arms, legs, heads, and identifying attributes so that newly discovered fragments could be displayed, as collectors preferred, in a completed state. Only in the 19th century did artists, archaeologists, and collectors begin to admire the fragment as such. Antonio Canova's refusal to restore the Elgin Marbles is surprising, coming when it does, especially given that his most important contemporary, Bertel Thorvaldsen, continued to undertake this kind of work. When, in 1908, Rainer Maria Rilke wrote his "Archaischer Torso Apollos," the taste for the unrestored fragment was still relatively new.

The tasks of restoration that marble sculptors were assigned played a role in the way they understood their own inventive projects: Bernini's *Apollo and Daphne,* for example, is in a sense an elaborate amplification of the Apollo Belvedere, dramatizing its movement, reinterpreting its gesture, and adding a second character, while Michelangelo's *Prisoner* sculptures, with their highly finished stomachs and barely sketched heads and hands, remind us what was and was not to be seen in the Belvedere Torso. Such exercises, moreover, facilitated the development of a more empirical, materialist approach to antiquities, one that focused on the analysis of surviving statues as much as on the written record. Especially consequential was the distinction, first possible in the 17th century, between Greek and Roman sculptural styles. A hallmark, notably, of the Fleming François Duquesnoy (who had worked as a restorer for a variety of Roman collectors in the early 1620s) was that artist's propensity for thin, transparent, seemingly wet draperies and delicate, subtle contours. These features distinguished his inventions sharply from the muscular nudes that were central to the Roman legacy of Michelangelo, and it was on account of them that Duquesnoy's *Saint Susanna* became the most copied sculpture of the 17th century.

It was only after 1700, with Anton Mengs's recognition that many of the marbles in Roman collections were in fact Roman copies of Greek originals, and with the 1764 publication of Johann Joachim Winckelmann's monumental *History of Ancient Art,* that the study of Greek art became systematic. The *History of Ancient Art* offered the first real periodization of ancient sculpture, and its proposed chronology remained the basis of antiquarian studies until the birth of modern archaeology more than a century later. Winckelmann proposed a cyclical model of artistic perfection and decadence, arguing that an "archaic" Greek style had given way to a "high" and a "beautiful" manner, and then to a decline. Ostensibly, the decline at issue was that of ancient Roman art, which Winckelmann regarded as inferior to, even a corruption of, its Greek antecedent. Yet in the modern manner that, through Bernini and his followers, had come to dominate Europe, Winckelmann identified many of the same weaknesses, and this lent his history an art-critical edge. In addition, Winckelmann moved away from the biographical approach to art history that Giorgio Vasari had standardized, treating ancient sculptures as the products not just of artists but of cultures, as representations of the nobility and beauty of the ancient Greek people rather than as the products of individual geniuses. This made the choice to seek out and imitate the Greeks, in sculpture and otherwise, a moral decision as much as an aesthetic one.

The association of the Greeks with an ethic and even with a democratic state carried an appeal in late 18th- and early 19th-century France and the United States, though the idea that the Greeks represented heroic grandeur made it equally attractive to autocrats. Canova, who seems to have been as hostile to French revolutionaries as he was to Napoleon, made a portrait of George Washington (subsequently destroyed) that "breathed," according to one contemporary, "with Greek elegance," but he also became a favorite of the Bonaparte family, personally insisting on showing the emperor nude, on the grounds that "the Greek way is to cover nothing," and deifying Pauline Bonaparte as Venus. Much the same can be said of Bertel Thorvaldsen, Canova's most important contemporary. Thorvaldsen had trained in Copenhagen under Johannes Wiedewelt, who had lived with Winckelmann in Rome, but he spent much of his career completing commissions for royal patrons in northern Europe, and works like his 1815 sculpture of Countess Elizabeth Ostermann-Tolstaya recalls Roman imperial portraiture in a way that is difficult to reconcile with Winckelmann's ideals.

Even during the years that the Greek style, especially in its more archaic forms, was being promoted, Roman statues continued to be central to the education of sculptors, especially with the foundation throughout Europe of art academies, most of which assembled collections of plaster casts. From the 16th to the 19th century, drawing and modeling from these were a basic part of the sculptor's training; only when Romantic critics succeeded in making the claim that art was a matter of genius or personal expression rather than education did sculptors stop looking to the ancients for their fundamental lessons.

Other circumstances likewise separated 19th-century and later sculptors from their early modern predecessors. The advent of photography, significantly, made it seem obsolete to look to antique art for the study of movement, and the introduction of a public-exhibition culture turned ambitious art more pointedly toward studies of nature, modern society, and the new. When Rodin, in his *Burghers of Calais,* tried to redefine what sculpture of a figure walking looked like, or when Giacometti, taking inspiration from the art of Africa, Polynesia, and ancient Etruria, made jointless, muscleless totems, both were working as pointedly against the classical tradition as they were learning from it. The classical tradition could even seem oppressive, especially when, in the early 20th century, modern sculptures in that tradition figured so insistently in the art promoted by Hitler, Mussolini, and Stalin. Though many early 20th-century sculptors continued to work primarily in bronze and marble, the media most strongly associated with surviving antiquities and thus with the idea of what a museum sculpture should be, this vestige of the classical tradition, too, was doomed when Duchamp's "found objects" broke all limits on the kinds of things from which sculpture could be made. Today, as the boundaries even of the category of sculpture have vanished, sculptural practice is more distant than it has ever been from its ancient models.

BIBL.: Isabella Teotochi Albrizzi, *Opere di scultura e di plastica di Antonio Canova,* ed. Manlio Pastore Stocchi and Gianni Venturi (Bassano del Grappa 2003). Leonard Barkan, *Unearthing the Past: Archaeology and Aesthetics in the Making of Renaissance Culture* (New Haven 1999). Charles Dempsey, "The Greek Style and the Prehistory of Neoclassicism," in *Pietro Testa, 1612–1650,* exhibition catalogue, ed. Elizabeth Cropper (Philadelphia 1988) xxxvii–lxv. Chiara Frugoni, "L'antichità: Dai *Mirabilia* alla propaganda politica," in *Memoria dell'antico nell'arte italiana,* vol. 1, ed. Salvatore Settis (Turin 1984) 5–72. Jorgen Birkedal Hartmann, *Antike Motive bei Thorvaldsen: Studien zur Antikenrezeption des Klassizismus* (Tübingen 1979). Francis Haskell and Nicholas Penny, *Taste and the Antique: The Lure of Classical Sculpture, 1500–1900* (New Haven 1981). Rodolfo Lanciani, *The Destruction of Ancient Rome: A Sketch of the History of the Monuments* (London 1899) and *Storia degli scavi di Roma e notizie intorno le collezioni romane di antichità* (1902–1912; Rome 1998). Alina Payne et al., eds., *Antiquity and Its Interpreters* (Cambridge 2000). Pliny the Elder, *Natural History,* trans. H. Rackham, vol. 9 (London 1952). Alex Potts, *Flesh and the Ideal: Winckelmann and the Origins of Art History* (New Haven 1994) and "Greek Sculpture and Roman Copies I: Anton Raphael Mengs and the Eighteenth Century," *Journal of the Warburg and Courtauld Insitutes* 43 (1980) 150–173. Roberto Weiss, *The Renaissance Discovery of Classical Antiquity* (Oxford 1988).

M.CO.

Seneca the Elder

L. Annaeus Seneca (ca. 55 BCE–39 CE), historian, critic of declamation; father of Seneca the philosopher and grandfather of the poet Lucan. Seneca was a wealthy landowner at Cordoba, in Spain, whose life was spent there and at Rome. Of his *History of Rome* only two doubtful fragments remain. In old age he recorded (from memory, he said) extracts from declamations that he had heard as a young man, with lively recollections and criticism. This collection, *Oratorum et rhetorum sententiae, divisiones, colores* (*Quotations, divisions, and colors from the orators and rhetors*), often referred to as his *Declamations,* consisted of ten books of *Controversiae* (rhetorical exercises on debating hypothetical cases) and two of *Suasoriae* (rhetorical exercises on giving advice to a prominent figure faced with a difficult decision). Of these, five books of the former and one of the latter are extant; excerpts from all ten books of the *Controversiae* (compiled in the 4th cent.) have also survived. A unique source for the arts of declamation, the *Controversiae* and *Suasoriae* became the basis of Roman rhetorical education and an influence on the writings of the younger Seneca and Lucan. Although Quintilian does not mention him by name, the elder Seneca's collection reveals the practices of orators (including Livy and Ovid) of the late Roman republic and the early empire, whose oratory is otherwise lost to us.

The earliest manuscripts reporting two different versions of the *Controversiae* were written in France in the 9th century. Seneca's influence is apparent chiefly in medieval florilegia and the late medieval *Gesta Romanorum,* a collection of 150 tales of the ancient Romans garnished with Christian *envois;* 11 of these tales repeat themes from Seneca. Senecan influence on a number of authors, including John of Salisbury and Boccaccio, is probable but not certain.

The excerpts were first printed at Naples in 1475. The *editio princeps* of the full text was printed in Venice in 1490, included in an edition of the younger Seneca's complete works. In his *Miscellanea* (1489) Angelo Poliziano mentioned the rarity of available texts, but he was able still to quote several significant Senecan passages. The distinction between the two Senecas was suggested by Raphael Maffei of Volterra (d. 1529), but Justus Lipsius gave the definitive proof in 1580. Erasmus, who included the elder Seneca in his editions of the younger (1515, 1529), wrote in his preface of 1529: "Of all of Seneca's monuments I think it would be most important for scholarship if the complete books of *Declamations* were extant, for it would have made a great difference both for research and for criticism."

In 1534 the French translation of Pierre Grognet was published in Paris: *The Authoritative Writings, Maxims, and Unique Instruction of the Great Critic, Poet, Orator, and Moral Philosopher, Seneca* (*Les authoritez, sentences et singuliers enseignements du grant censeur poète orateur et philosophe moral Seneque*). Thus the fragmentary recollections of the father gained in importance from his identification with the son. The edition by Andreas Schott printed in Strasbourg in 1604 included the notes of Lipsius and was the first definitive edition: it had been reissued six times by 1665.

Seneca has always been more important in France than elsewhere, especially during the debates about rhetoric in the 17th century, during which there appeared two more French translations (by M. de Chavet in 1604 and by B. de Lesfargues in 1658). Nevertheless, he was insignificant among classical models compared with Aristotle, Demosthenes, Cicero, and the younger Seneca. Even Michel de Montaigne quotes him only five times in his *Essais* (1580). Jean-François Le Grand was typical in his *Discours sur la rhétorique françoise* (1658): "When I speak of eloquence I do not mean the kind of eloquence recorded by Seneca [the Elder]." In England Seneca was known but largely ignored. Only Ben Jonson in his *Timber, or Discoveries* (1640) quotes him at length, including a description of his powers of memory and a character sketch, both of which are largely translated from Seneca himself.

Since the 17th century the elder Seneca has been generally ignored, and the first reliable modern text did not appear until 1887. Despite the recent text and translation of Winterbottom (1974), Seneca is still little read, and modern appreciation of Silver Latin style has therefore suffered.

BIBL.: S. F. Bonner, *Roman Declamation* (Liverpool 1949). H. Bornecque, *Les Déclamations et les déclamateurs d'après Sénèque le Père* (Lille 1902) and *Sénèque le Rhéteur: Controverses et Suasoires,* 2nd ed. (Paris 1932). W. A. Edward, *The Suasoriae of Seneca the Elder* (Cambridge 1928). J. Fairweather, *Seneca the Elder* (Cambridge 1981). L. A. Sussman, *The Elder Seneca* (Leiden 1978). H. D. L. Vervliet, "De gedruckte overlevering van Seneca Pater," *De Gulden Passer* 35 (1957) 179–222. M. Winterbottom, *The Elder Seneca: Declamations* (Cambridge, Mass., 1974).

M.MO.

Seneca the Younger

Lucius Annaeus Seneca, ca. 4 BCE (before 1 CE)–65 CE; Roman philosopher, politician, and tragedian. The younger Seneca has always been controversial, attacked for his Latin style, his political compromises, and his wealth. Tacitus gives the most balanced estimate from antiquity of Seneca's significance as a writer, philosopher, and political figure, and he composes the speeches that Seneca and Nero might have made when Seneca attempted to retire from court in 62 (a legal impossibility for a senator and an *amicus principis,* counselor of the emperor). Seneca did in fact stay away from Rome and devoted himself to philosophy, finally being charged with complicity in the conspiracy of Piso in 65. His suicide (ordered by Nero) is described by Tacitus, omitting only Seneca's final speech. This death scene, *imago vitae suae* ("the image of his life"), has been a significant element in Seneca's influence on posterity.

During the 90s Quintilian was critical of Seneca, focusing chiefly on his style and its effect. Quintilian acknowledged his versatility but found his philosophy careless and his style corrupt and likely to corrupt young students. Because philosophy is a subject for study and a part of the education of the young, Quintilian's focus was right; but he did not explore the wider goals of Seneca's teaching. Seneca did not found a school or lecture, as the Greek philosophers had done before him, or Epictetus after him. Lacking a structured curriculum or a coterie of students, he was closer to the Cynics in needing to make his philosophy approachable to a general audience. He admired the Cynic Demetrius, quoting him extensively in *On Benefits* (*De beneficiis*). His goal as spiritual director ("directeur d'âmes," Guillemin 1952–1954) was to make his doctrines available and attractive. Popular doctrine is easily dismissed as superficial: the popular philosopher becomes a "spare-time amateur philosopher" (F. H. Sandbach, *The Stoics* 1994, 149), and his teaching not worth the effort of serious examination.

Seneca's new Latin style was urgent, colorful, and pointed, appropriate for the fragmented ethical and political ambiguities of his time, and it ultimately proved to be an effective vehicle for the Latin Church Fathers. It was revived in the Renaissance with the anti-Ciceronianism of Erasmus (d. 1536) and in the pointed style (influenced as much by Tacitus as by Seneca) of Justus Lipsius (d. 1606). Seneca was indeed the second founder of Latin prose, after Cicero, but his style was an easy target for his detractors. In the 2nd century Fronto, orator and tutor to Marcus Aurelius, wrote that Seneca's style should be "completely uprooted," and Fronto's contemporary Aulus Gellius dismissed Seneca as "a useless writer, whose books are not worth looking at. Their style is vulgar and commonplace, their matter is . . . superficial." This was the low point in antiquity for Seneca's reputation.

Similarly, the more coherent and consistent doctrines of Epictetus (in the 90s) superseded Seneca's philosophical authority, supported by the perceived superiority of Greek as a vehicle for philosophy. The Greek philosophical diary of the emperor Marcus Aurelius (r. 161–180) has been considered a more authentic expression of Stoicism; his sincerity appears less contrived than the pointed style of Seneca. Yet Seneca's range of inquiry is wider than either of these Stoic successors, and his involvement in the dilemmas, aspirations, and disappointments of the search for personal happiness was as genuine as theirs.

Seneca's philosophy has been further devalued by the contrast between Stoic doctrine in his *Letters* and *Dialogues* and his wealth and worldly success, summarized in Milton's jibe, "Seneca, *in his books* a philosopher." Seneca himself was candid in *On the Happy Life* (*De vita beata*), acknowledging the charge that he spoke one way and lived another. "The wise man," he said, "does not love wealth but prefers it. He admits it not into his mind but into his house . . . He wishes to make his greater means the servants of his virtue . . . If my wealth disappeared, it would take away nothing except itself." This defense, a comfortable compromise between Cynic austerity and luxury, has never impressed Seneca's critics. Nevertheless, when Seneca did give up his wealth in the last year of his life, his austere way of living came closer to his doctrine. Yet Stoic doctrine was too inflexible for the realities of life. Seneca admitted that the ideal wise man had never actually lived: the closest example was Cato the Younger (an ambiguous figure in Seneca).

He was more practical in the doctrine of the *proficiens* ("the student making progress"), elaborated in Letter 75, by which he defined grades of progress, differentiated by success in freeing oneself from moral faults, toward the goal of a life based on reason and virtue. He begins this same letter, "I want my letters to be like my conversation if we were sitting or walking together, easy and not artificial," words that explain why his teaching was attractive and why many philosophers have despised it.

Seneca's influence has been almost entirely in ethics. He did attempt an account of Stoic natural philosophy in his *Natural Questions* (*Naturales quaestiones*), and he says in Letter 65 that study of "the nature of things" (*rerum natura*), including cosmology, lifts the human mind to the contemplation of the universe and of god. Although *Natural Questions* is the most complete extant exposition of Stoic natural philosophy, its influence has been limited. Lipsius died before he could finish his commentary on this work; the first edition of his Seneca (1605) included a commentary by Muretus (Marc-Antoine Muret, d. 1585), replaced by that of Libertus Fromond in later editions. In his *Natural Philosophy of the Stoics* (*Physiologia Stoicorum,* 1604), Lipsius considered the Stoic doctrine of fate, which Seneca had discussed most effectively in *On Providence* (*De providentia*) and Letter 107. Seneca's logic and epistemology were at best summary. His discussion of causes in Letter 65 is superficial, and in Letter 58 he rejects Plato's Ideas by doubting that they can improve him morally. He approved of logic only if it was subordinated to moral improvement.

Seneca's views on suicide were ambiguous: he seems to have accepted Zeno's doctrine of suicide as a "reasonable exit" from life in response to incurable disease or inexorable pain, but he saw it also as a means to freedom, for example, under tyranny, and he died in accordance with this doctrine. In discussing the nature of the divine, he is unclear. In Letter 107 he recommends conforming the human will to fate, and he quotes Cleanthes' *Hymn to Zeus* to show that the wise man will follow where fate wills.

In Letter 41 he appeals to the innate divinity of human nature to show that ordinary people can approach the wise man's perfection: "God is close to you, he is with you, he is in you . . . The divine spirit has his home within us." This divine spirit is reason, which by itself leads a human being to live in accordance with nature. Although Lipsius admired this letter and found much in it to be consistent with Christianity, its doctrine was unacceptable to Catholic orthodoxy.

Seneca extended the dualism of animal and divine natures in the human being, "an animal endowed with reason" (*rationale animal*), to dualism in human social and political life, which he discussed in *On Tranquillity of Mind* (*De tranquillitate animi*) and the (fragmentary) *On Leisure* (*De otio*). The double citizenship of the Stoic had been poetically expressed in Cicero's *On the Republic* (*De re publica*), and it was revived by Marcus Aurelius.

The early Christians both appropriated features of Senecan Stoicism and helped make it obsolete. That Seneca and Saint Paul were in Rome at the same time led to the creation in the 4th century of a forged correspondence between them, known to Jerome and Augustine, neither of whom considered Seneca to have been a Christian (a possibility that Letter 14 implied). The early Christians considered Seneca to be a philosopher above all. For Tertullian (d. ca. 240) he was "often our Seneca" (*Seneca saepe noster*) and for Lactantius (d. ca. 320) "the sharpest mind among all the Stoics" (*omnium Stoicorum acutissimus*). Lactantius in fact advised reading Seneca if one "wished to know everything, for he was the truest recorder and most vigorous critic of public vices."

By the 4th century Seneca's reputation, as a human being and as a philosopher, had recovered. In his *Consolation of Philosophy* Boethius (d. 524) expresses Senecan doctrine on fate and the emotions in the fourth poem, and in the sixth poem he describes the tyranny of Nero. Cassiodorus (d. ca. 585) used Seneca's *Description of the World* (*De forma mundi,* no longer extant) and gave his copy to his monastery at Vivarium. In the same period Martin (d. ca. 579), bishop of Braga in northwest Spain, wrote two short essays for the Suevian king Miro, both of which are extant. The first, *On Anger* (*De ira*), is a series of extracts from Seneca's *On Anger.* The second, *Formula for an Honest Life* (*Formula vitae honestae*), was based on Seneca's lost *On Duties* (*De officiis*) and was significant in the revival of Senecan studies in the Italian Renaissance. Yet elsewhere in Spain by the 7th century Seneca's philosophy was no longer directly known. There is no sure evidence for it in the encyclopedic *Etymologies* of Isidore of Seville (d. 636), beyond a mention of Seneca's improvement of *notae Tironianae* (Roman shorthand). After the 7th century, knowledge of Seneca seems to have faded in Spain and Italy—although it did not entirely disappear, for *On Benefits* and *On Clemency* (*De clementia*) were copied in Italy in about 800—until its revival in the 12th and 13th centuries.

In northern Europe the *Letters* were copied at the court of Louis the Pious in the early 9th century, but the *Dialogues* and the *Tragedies* did not emerge until late in the 11th century, when the former (and possibly the latter) were copied at Monte Cassino. The *Dialogues,* however, were not well known in northern Europe until late in the 13th century, although Seneca's *sententiae* (pithy sayings) from the *Letters, On Benefits,* and *On Clemency* frequently appeared in medieval florilegia. From the 13th century onward Seneca was widely read, especially after the invention of printing. Four editions of the *Letters* were printed in Naples (along with the *Dialogues, On Benefits,* and *On Clemency*), Rome, Paris, and Strasbourg (in the *Complete Works*), by 1475; the *Tragedies* were first printed at Ferrara in 1484. The *Natural Questions* were first printed at Venice in 1490, and *The Pumpkinification of the Divine Claudius* (*Apocolocyntosis divi Claudii*) in 1513.

In the late Middle Ages the compatibility of Senecan doctrine with Christianity became a prominent problem. Peter Abelard (d. 1142) and Roger Bacon (d. 1294) drew on Seneca's *Dialogues* to extend the bounds of philosophical inquiry. Seneca was well known to the Dominicans Albertus Magnus (d. 1280) and Thomas Aquinas

(d. 1274), who argued against Seneca's doctrine of fate. Dante (d. 1321), in the fourth canto of *Inferno,* placed "Seneca morale" with other great pre-Christian figures in Limbo. By the 14th century it was possible to consider Seneca without reference to Christianity, a goal brilliantly achieved by the proto-Humanist Petrarch in his *On the Remedies for Good and Bad Fortune* (*De remediis utriusque fortunae,* ca. 1365) and *On His Own Ignorance and That of Many Others* (*De sui ipsius et multorum ignorantia,* 1368). Petrarch modeled his *Familiar Letters* (*Epistolae familiares,* ca. 1350–1366) on the letters of Cicero, Pliny the Younger, and Seneca, and he hoped that his correspondent, Socrates (Ludwig van Kempen), would be to him as Lucilius was to Seneca. Petrarch prepared the way for the work of the great Italian Humanists of the 15th century, notably Angelo Poliziano (d. 1494). By the 16th century the time was ripe for a complete revaluation of Seneca, and in that century and the next his reputation and influence reached their zenith.

The Senecan renaissance advanced with the editions of Erasmus, printed at Basel, the unsatisfactory first, *Lucubrations of Seneca* (*L. Annaei Senecae . . . Lucubrationes*) in 1515, without commentary, and the second, *Works of Seneca Emended* (*Opera L. Annaei Senecae . . . emendata*), vastly improved, in 1529. In the preface to the latter Erasmus gives a lively account of the problems in establishing a reliable text, and his critical review of Seneca's style is still valuable. Joseph Scaliger (d. 1609) admired this preface and thought it better than the equally weighty preface by Lipsius. Erasmus included the *Pumpkinification,* providing a reliable text for the first time. He also included the correspondence of Seneca and Saint Paul (which he proved, in a separate preface, to be spurious), several pseudo-Senecan fragments, and the *Declamations* of the elder Seneca. The text of the *Natural Questions* (established by Beatus Rhenanus) was edited for him by the Hungarian scholar Matthaeus Fortunatus (d. 1528).

John Calvin published his commentary on *On Clemency* in 1532, but later he opposed Seneca's doctrine on fate and free will. The text and commentary of Muretus, first published at Rome in 1585–1586, were included in Jan Gruter's edition of Seneca's works printed at Heidelberg in 1592, along with the *Castigationes* of Pincianus (Fernando Núñez de Toledo y Guzmán), first published at Basel in 1519. Muretus, who believed that Lipsius had plagiarized his notes, taught *On Providence* at Rome in 1575, when he defended Seneca as one who was "a good and profitable master of speaking" and a source of "true wisdom."

In his edition of Seneca's prose works (1605), Lipsius grudgingly acknowledged his debt to Erasmus and his successors, and he did little to improve the text beyond establishing correct punctuation and divisions of words and phrases. The strengths of his edition lay in its preface, its commentary, and its publisher. In the preface Lipsius gave a more historical and favorable account of the life and works of Seneca than had Erasmus, and he quoted Tacitus verbatim for Seneca's death. His commentary, while economical by modern standards, was fuller than that by Erasmus. The introductory paragraphs to each section were lucid, concise, and often enthusiastic. *Legite iuvenes senesque!* ("Read this, young men and old!") is a frequent exhortation, typical of Lipsius' primary goal, which was to teach. He wished "to reveal Seneca and put him in the hands of Everyman . . . to adapt these works for ordinary readers," and he instructed his readers to select *sententiae* that would be of practical use, and to read the text "with the eyes of a philosopher, not a grammarian." His final instruction was "to make practical use of these [works]."

Seneca's reputation (and that of Lipsius) was enhanced by the magnificent printing of Balthasar Moretus and the elaborate title pages for it engraved by T. Galle (1605) and C. Galle (1615, 1632, 1652). Moretus had been Lipsius' student, and he was a friend of Peter Paul Rubens, whom he commissioned to design, for the 1615 edition and its successors, a portrait of Lipsius and two full-page engravings of Seneca, one of an ancient bust believed to be of Seneca and owned by the artist, and the other of Seneca entering the bath in which he died. The latter engraving was related to Rubens's 1608 painting of Seneca's death, which further spread the fame of Seneca as a martyr to tyranny who died true to his philosophical principles.

The editions of Erasmus and Lipsius, with the latter's assessment of Seneca in his *Guide to Stoic Philosophy* (*Manuductio ad Stoicam philosophiam,* 1604), assured the reputation of Seneca through the 16th and 17th centuries, the former by establishing the text, the latter by making Seneca practically useful for people in troubled times. The paintings and engravings of Rubens—including *The Four Philosophers* (1611) and the title page to Lipsius' *Complete Works* (*Opera omnia,* 1637)—were also influential, as was the prominent role of Seneca in Monteverdi's opera *L'Incoronazione di Poppea,* first performed at Venice in 1642.

In France, Michel de Montaigne admired Seneca and borrowed heavily from him. The form of his *Essays* (1580–1592) follows that of Seneca's *Letters,* as vehicles for moral philosophy, each of limited length and focus, with the exception of the long "Apology for Raymond Sebond" (2.12). He quoted Seneca extensively and twice (2.10 and 2.32) defended him and compared him with his favorite ancient author, Plutarch. Some of the *Essays* are based closely on Senecan material, for example, "That to be a philosopher is to learn how to die" (1.20, "Que philosopher, c'est apprendre à mourir") and "On anger" (2.31, "De la colère"). His early letter on the death of Étienne de La Boétie (published in 1570, seven years after La Boétie's death) owes much to Stoic ideas of a good man's death (including that of Seneca), supplying the dying man's speeches to his family and friends. Yet Montaigne criticizes Senecan doctrine in the "Apology for Raymond Sebond," which he concludes by affirming the superiority of Christian faith. In this essay he is more favorable to Pyrrhonian skepticism, quoting his motto "Que sçay-je?" ("What do I know?"), which he had had engraved as his device, or seal, in 1576. Still, he never lost his affection for Seneca and continued to quote him frequently. Senecan influence in France and Spain continued into the 17th century with the Neostoic writings of Pierre Charron (d. 1603) and Guillaume du Vair (d. 1621), and the *Stoic Doctrine* (*Doctrina Estoica*) of Francisco de Quevedo (d. 1645). In the next century the last work of Denis Diderot was his *Essay on the Reigns of Claudius and Nero* (*Essai sur les règnes de Claude et de Néron,* 1782), whose second part was a commentary on and defense of Seneca's works.

In the 19th century Seneca was studied by philologists and despised as a philosopher. Thomas Macaulay found his philosophy "a philosophy of thorns" and opined that reading Seneca "is like living on anchovy sauce." By the mid-20th century Seneca was little read and less regarded in the English-speaking world, although he was still appreciated in France, Spain, and Germany. In *The Oxford Classical Dictionary* (1st ed., 1949) he became "a tortured egoist" displaying "the common stigmata of paranoiac abnormality." In 1975 F. H. Sandbach added chauvinism to criticism: "It is hard for the Englishman of to-day to approach Seneca with sympathy." But wiser judgments were already being heard. Seneca's *Letters* (1965) and *Dialogues* (1977) were included in the standard Oxford Classical Text series, and Miriam Griffin (1976, 1992) and Brad Inwood (2005) have led a revival of serious interest in him as a philosopher. Similar appreciation has been shown in France and Germany. Seneca may not be "the best in philosophy" (as Lipsius called him), but his doctrines are now admitted to be important.

There is now widespread agreement that Seneca's tragedies are important dramas and that the question whether they were composed for recitation or for performance is largely irrelevant. (Of the ten tragedies assigned to Seneca, *Octavia* is not by him, and his authorship of *Hercules Oetaeus* is doubtful.) Modern opinion is divided over the extent of Stoic doctrine in them; the majority incline toward judging them solely as dramas.

Knowledge of the tragedies was spotty in late antiquity: at Carthage Dracontius (late 5th cent.) drew on Seneca's *Agamemnon* for his *Orestis tragoedia,* a narrative poem in Latin hexameters, and several poems in Boethius' *Consolation of Philosophy* were influenced by Seneca's choruses. The earliest complete manuscript is the *Codex Etruscus,* from Italy in the 11th century. It was read by Poliziano and was the basis of the edition by J. F. Gronovius (Amsterdam 1661), the first reliable printed text. The *editio princeps* was printed at Ferrara in 1484: the first edition with a critical text and commentary of any value was that of Jodocus Badius (Paris 1514), which included the conjectures of Erasmus. Lipsius compiled a brief commentary, which the younger Raphelengius included in his edition (1589). The modern text was established by Friedrich Leo (Berlin 1878–1879) and improved by Otto Zwierlein (Oxford 1986). Several recent editions (notably those of Richard Tarrant) have firmly reestablished the independence and importance of the tragedies, and John Fitch has provided an accurate modern English translation (2002).

Seneca was by far the most important classical model for Renaissance tragedy, at a time when Greek tragedy was hardly known. His tragedies are declamatory but not exclusively so, and few would agree with T. S. Eliot's jibe (1927) that "[Seneca's] characters all seem to speak with the same voice, and at the top of it." There is philosophical reflection, especially in the choruses, but that is not their main purpose, and there is psychological subtlety, despite the rhetoric. Medieval appreciation of the tragedies' literary and dramatic value is evidenced by the commentary (1314–1316) of the English Dominican Nicolas Trevet. At the same time (1315) Albertino Mussato produced his Latin tragedy *Ecerinis* at Padua, the first Renaissance drama to imitate Seneca in theme, diction, and meter. Senecan influence blossomed in France and England in the 16th and 17th centuries. Julius Caesar Scaliger in his *Poetics* (*Poetices libri septem,* 1561) maintained that Seneca surpassed the Greek tragedians in dignity (*maiestas*) and had greater polish and brilliance (*cultus ac nitor*) than Euripides. *Cléopatre captive* (1552) by Étienne Jodelle was the earliest Senecan drama in French, followed by the dramas of Robert Garnier (d. 1590), who described their content as "swollen with lines full of blood and horror, of tears and sobs, of anger and madness." The tragedies of Pierre Corneille (d, 1684) and Jean Racine's *Phèdre* (1677) were the climax of Senecan influence in France.

In England the earliest Senecan drama was *Gorboduc* (1561), by Thomas Norton and Thomas Sackville: although its subject was taken from British legend, its rhetoric and spirit are Senecan. Thomas Newton published Seneca's tragedies in English translation (by several authors) in 1581. There are many references, direct and indirect, to Seneca in Shakespeare, especially in the tragedies. Most notable is by Hamlet's Stoic friend, Horatio:

> As one, in suff'ring all, that suffers nothing,
> A man that Fortune's buffets and rewards
> Has ta'en with equal thanks . . .
> . . . Give me that man
> That is not passion's slave. (3.2.68–7)

The melodramatic *Titus Andronicus* is in the tradition of Seneca's *Thyestes.* Other Elizabethan dramatists are even more indebted to Seneca: in Thomas Kyd's *Spanish Tragedy* (1592), Hieronimo, like Seneca's Hercules, threatens that his "restles passions" will "Beat at the windowes of the highest heavens,/Solliciting for justice and revenge." Seneca was the model for declamatory and psychological power, which at its best has never since been equaled. Later English tragedy was derived from different classical models: Joseph Addison's *Cato* (1713), for example, owes more to Lucan than to Seneca.

Seneca's tragedies were undervalued during the 19th

and most of the 20th centuries in England, France, and Germany, when many classical scholars dismissed them as worthless. Better judgments have prevailed, not least because of modern stage performances, starting with Peter Brook's production of *Oedipus* in London (1968).

BIBL.: K. A. Blüher, *Seneca in Spanien* (Munich 1969). G. Braden, *Renaissance Tragedy and the Senecan Tradition: Anger's Privilege* (New Haven 1985). C. D. N. Costa, ed., *Seneca* (London 1974). J. G. Fitch, ed. and trans., *Seneca: Tragedies* (Cambridge, Mass., 2002). M. T. Griffin, *Seneca: A Philosopher in Politics* (Oxford 1976; 2nd ed. 1992). A.-M. Guillemin, "Sénèque directeur d'âmes," *Revue des Études Latines* 30 (1952) 202–219; 31 (1953) 215–234; 32 (1954) 250–274. B. Inwood, *Reading Seneca: Stoic Philosophy at Rome* (Oxford 2005). R. Mayer, "*Personata Stoa:* Neostoicism and Senecan Tragedy," *Journal of the Warburg and Courtauld Institutes* 57 (1994) 151–174. R. J. Tarrant, *Seneca: Agamemnon* (Cambridge 1976). A. Tarrête, "Sénèque," in *Dictionnaire de Michel de Montaigne,* ed. P. Desan (Paris 2004) 904–908. M.MO.

Seven Sages of Rome

A medieval collection of *exempla* in frame-narrative form, the ultimate sources of which lie in preclassical India and Persia (*The Book of Sindbad the Philosopher,* 10th cent. BCE). The collection eventually spread in more than 40 distinct versions and cyclical continuations into all European languages.

The story that gives the collection its name runs (generically) as follows:

> A young prince is tempted by his stepmother, the [empress]. She, being rebuffed by him, accuses him of attempting to violate her, and he is condemned to death. His life is saved by seven wise men, who secure a stay of execution . . . by entertaining the [emperor] through seven days with tales showing the wickedness of woman, the [empress] meantime recounting stories [of filial disloyalty] to offset those of the sages. On the eighth day the prince, who has remained silent up to that time [as astrologically recommended], speaks in his own defense, and the [empress] is put to death. (Campbell 1907, xi–xii)

The stories that the sages tell, embedded within this frame, constitute the collection as a whole.

There is little that is truly Roman or classical in the frame and its stories, even though some of the stories and the frame as a whole are set in Rome (or, in a few versions, in Constantinople) under the emperor Diocletian (or, depending on the version, Vespasian or Pontianus); the emperor's first wife is only occasionally named (Auguste, for example), as is his son (Lucinius, Florentine, Stefano, Erasto, Phiseus); the son's stepmother is named (Aphrodisia) in only one version; and among the sages one finds Ancilles, Lentulus, and Cato. Embedded stories variously feature Hippocrates as his nephew's murderer, Virgil the magician as defender of Rome (*salvatio Romae*), Merlin curing the emperor Herod of blindness, and the unfaithful Matron of Ephesus from Petronius' *Satyricon.*

Fancifully fictitious as these appropriations of Rome may be, they nevertheless show how the prestigious classical tradition could be evoked in the Middle Ages to lend authority and persuasiveness to a body of texts that are pointedly misogynistic but that also fit in the traditions of *Fürstenspiegel* (manuals for princes), of fables and wisdom literature, and of oral source materials metamorphosing into literature. Demonstrable borrowings from classical authors (including Herodotus, Pausanias, Virgil, and Petronius, among others) are in fact rare, as if the medieval collectors of *exempla* did not know, or did not wish to acknowledge, Greece, Rome, and the Arab world as the bridge between East and West. At the same time, if stripped of the thematic straitjacket of the frame, the individual stories do recall the long history of what has been called "conduct literature" preserved in numerous collections of fables, *exempla* (Mosher 1966; Welter 1927), sermonic parables (Crane 1983; Schmitt 1985), folktales, etc., and reaching back to the *Panchatantra* of Bidpai, the *Hitopadesa,* and Aesop. Besides the last, Greek antiquity knew fables, and wisdom literature in general, through Hesiod (*Works and Days*), Archilochus, Crates of Thebes (*Games*), and Theophrastus (*Characters*). In Rome the genre is represented by Plautus, Ennius (*Satires*), Lucilius, Horace, Ovid, and Manilius. Aesop's tradition was continued by Phaedrus, Babrius, and Avianus in the early Christian era. Later on, the essentially anonymous *Catonis Disticha* (couplets attributed to Cato) and the *Thousand and One Nights* are early medieval sources from the West and the East, respectively, followed around the zenith of the Middle Ages by the very influential *Disciplina clericalis* of Petrus Alphonsus, by Alexander Neckam, by Vincent de Beauvais, and by Jacques de Vitry's oft-raided *exempla* in his *Sermones vulgares.* Two anonymous literary works also yielded source material for didactic writing: the *Gesta Romanorum* and the multibranched *Roman de Renart.* For the late medieval period should be mentioned Jacobus de Voragine's *Legenda aurea,* Étienne de Bourbon's *Anecdotes historiques,* John of Capua's pertinently titled *Directorium vitae humanae,* and the pedagogical *Book of the Knight of La Tour Landry* by Geoffroy IV de la Tour Landry.

After nearly two centuries of modern research into origins, transmission, manuscripts, versions, and filiations, and after the relatively recent completion of much of the fundamental editorial work, *Seven Sages* now is available to less philological and more properly literary and cultural investigations. Three major studies have opened up promising avenues for future interpretations. For Foehr-Janssens (1994), historically *Seven Sages* marks the transition from chivalric romance to a new genre celebrating wisdom and an incipient medieval humanism. For Steinmetz (2000), structurally the collection deserves detailed analyses of its narrative dialectic, which is based on medieval readings of classical rhetoricians (Aristotle, Cicero).

Lundt (2002) views *Seven Sages* culturally in light of gender studies and socialization theories: rather than advocating a class society, the didactic discourse proposes a rational community of men and women, each one of whom strives for an individuality tested by society.

BIBL.: Killis Campbell, *The Seven Sages of Rome* (Boston 1907). Thomas Frederick Crane, *Medieval Sermon-Books and Stories* (Ithaca 1883). Yasmina Foehr-Janssens, *Le temps des fables: Le Roman des sept sages, ou l'autre voie du roman* (Paris 1994). Bea Lundt, *Weiser und Weib* (Munich 2002). Joseph Albert Mosher, *The Exemplum in the Early Religious and Didactic Literature of England* (1911; repr. New York 1966). Hans R. Runte et al., *The Seven Sages of Rome [. . .]: An Annotated Bibliography* (New York 1984), continued at http://myweb.dal.ca/hrunte/seven_sages.html. Jean-Claude Schmitt, *Prêcher d'exemples: Récits de prédicateurs du Moyen Âge* (Paris 1985). Ralf-Henning Steinmetz, *Exempel und Auslegung: Studien zu den* Sieben weisen Meistern (Freiburg, Switzerland, 2000). Jean Thiébaut Welter, *L'exemplum dans la littérature religieuse et didactique du Moyen Âge* (Paris 1927).

H.R.R.

Seven Wonders of the World

The most common list of the Seven Wonders of the World includes the following outstanding buildings and monumental sculptures: (1) the Pyramids of Gizeh and (2) the Lighthouse (Pharos) of Alexandria, in Egypt; (3) the walls and the hanging gardens of Babylon, in Mesopotamia; (4) the Temple of Artemis at Ephesos and (5) the Mausoleum at Halicarnassus, in Asia Minor; (6) the Colossus, on the Aegean island of Rhodes; and (7) the Statue of Zeus in his temple at Olympia, in Greece. This canon, first formulated in the 2nd century BCE, could vary slightly and also include, for instance, the Tower of Babylon or the Colosseum in Rome. The criteria for excluding other famous buildings, such as the Palace of Darius and Xerxes at Persepolis or the Temple of Solomon in Jerusalem, which is mentioned only occasionally, are not obvious. All of these monuments, except for the Pyramids, were destroyed in antiquity or during the Middle Ages and are therefore known today only from written sources enlarged with legends.

Individual monuments or the group as a whole was frequently cited as a standard of comparison for spectacular buildings or projects proposed for addition to the canon as an eighth wonder. The Colossus of Rhodes, a giant statue of the sun god Helios placed at the entrance to the harbor at Rhodes, became the prototype for any colossal statue, from Nero's in Rome, which lent its name to the adjacent Colosseum, to the Statue of Liberty in New York harbor. The Mausoleum at Halicarnassus, a block-like tomb surmounted by a stepped pyramid, which was erected for King Mausolos by his widow Artemisia, gave the name to the species of sumptuous architectural tombs. Similarly, the Pharos at Alexandria forged notions of lighthouses throughout the Western world. The Babylonian monuments were also studied in the biblical context, particularly the stepped or spiral tower, which was regarded as an example of hubris, since God had punished the builders by confusing their languages.

Various graphic reconstructions of single wonders have been made from the Middle Ages onward. The first engraved cycle, by Jan Philipp Galle after Maarten van Heemskerk, was not published until 1572. It was soon followed by the series by Antonio Tempesta (1608) and Crispijn de Passe, after Marten de Vos (1614). The global perspective inherent in these cycles appears to be indicative of the period of discoveries and the colonization of the world by the Western empires in the 16th and 17th centuries. It is characteristic that images of the Seven Wonders were used as decorations of the margin of a map of the world published by Willem Janszoon Blaeuw in Amsterdam in 1606. The next series was published by Johann Bernhard Fischer von Erlach in Vienna in 1721 as an introductory section to his outline of world architecture, dedicated to the emperor Charles VI. In this context the Seven Wonders were linked to the worldwide claims of the Habsburg Empire.

During the 19th and 20th centuries architects and archaeologists focused their attention on excavations and reconstruction drawings, searching for archaeological evidence and shying as far as possible away from earlier, fanciful representations. Toward the end of the 20th century a rise in global tourism fostered increasing interest in visiting the sites of the Ancient Wonders, and some of these, such as the Pharos and Colossus, have been considered for reconstruction by local authorities.

BIBL.: Kai Brodersen, *Reisefuhrer zu den Sieben Weltwundern* (Frankfurt-am-Main 1992). Werner Ekschmitt, *Die Sieben Weltwunder: Ihre Erbauung, Zerstörung und Wiederentdeckung* (Mainz 1984). Max Kunze, ed., *Die Sieben Weltwunder der Antike. Wege der Wiedergewinnung aus sechs Jahrhunderten,* exhibition catalogue (Mainz 2003). M. L. Madonna, "*Septem mundi miracula come templi della virtu:* Pirro Ligorio e l'interpretazione cinquecentesca delle meraviglie del mondo," *Psicon* 3, no. 7 (1976) 24–63.

J.M.M.

Sewers

The ancient Romans constructed sewers for the disposal of human waste in urban areas. Such waste could also be dumped into cesspools or removed manually as night soil for use as fertilizer. Sewers are to be distinguished from drains, which were constructed for the disposal of surplus rainwater, for overflow water from constantly running fountains fed by aqueducts, and for the drainage of cultivated fields. Nevertheless, urban drains often doubled as sewers. In contrast to Greek cities, many Roman cities, including all newly founded ones, were built with a protected water supply and a carefully designed and constructed sewerage system.

The best-known ancient Roman drain is the Cloaca Maxima in Rome, which probably began as an open ditch that drained a swamp from the area that became the Roman Forum. An all-purpose drain and sewer, it collected water from the swamp, and water and sewage from smaller drains, and then discharged its contents into the Tiber River. Some ancient sewers consisted of open ditches running down the middle of the streets. Such open sewers existed even in Rome itself, a city supplied by numerous aqueducts. Roman drain openings visible today include the arched Cloaca Maxima, which still discharges runoff water into the Tiber River, and the Roman drain at Cologne that discharged into the Rhine.

Although open conduits for sewage were far more common in the ancient world than is generally believed, medieval cities were not as filthy as is often supposed. As medieval cities developed from the 11th through the 14th centuries, laws for cleaning the streets and disposing of waste proliferated. Neither ancient nor medieval cities came close to modem standards of waste disposal. Premodern peoples in general were more accustomed to close proximity to open accumulations of sewage than are many of their their modern counterparts.

Renaissance writers on architecture admired ancient Roman sewers and drains. For example, in his treatise *On the Art of Building* (ca. 1450) Leon Battista Alberti emphasized the importance of drains and sewers for cities, remarking that "the drains are considered the most astonishing of all the works of the city of Rome" (1988, 113). He distinguished various types of sewers (cesspools and conduits) and pointed to cities that egregiously stank because of their lack of adequate sewers and drains.

In 19th-century Paris the reform of the sewer system was undertaken for complex reasons involving the rationalization of urban space. During this process Roman sewers and drains were very much in the intellectual background. The emperor Napoleon III and his prefect of the Seine, Georges Haussmann, undertook the reconstruction of Paris that would make it worthy of Augustan Rome. Haussmann's chief water engineer, Eugène Belgrand, was not only an expert in his field but also a student of Roman hydraulic engineering, especially as it was evident in France. His engineers employed newer technologies to construct the massive Parisian sewers, but Roman sewers served as significant models. They also possessed great symbolic and aesthetic value for artists and writers. Victor Hugo's dark vision of Parisian sewers in *Les misérables* (1862) encompassed a long history that extended back to Roman times.

BIBL.: L. B. Alberti, *On the Art of Building in Ten Books,* trans. J. Rykwert, N. Leach, and R. Tavernor (Cambridge, Mass., 1988) 113–114. A. Trevor Hodge, *Roman Aqueducts and Water Supply,* 2nd ed. (London 2002) 332–345. D. Reid, *Paris Sewers and Sewermen: Realities and Representations* (Cambridge, Mass., 1991).

P.O.L.

Sexuality

There may be no afterlife of ancient Greek and Roman sexuality, if one subscribes to an important body of recent scholarship, influenced by Michel Foucault, that claims there really was no such thing in the first place. Antiquity was an age of "sex before sexuality," before the great discursive explosion of the late 18th century that produced "sexuality as an especially dense transfer point for relations of power," and before the categories through which we think about these matters today—homosexual, heterosexual, masturbator, hysteric, nymphomaniac—came into being. The Greek words that made their way into Latin—*pedico, pathicus, cinaedus, catamitus,* and *malacus*—that refer to anal intercourse, passivity, or male softness do not translate into our terms *fairy* or *homosexual.* (The 18th-century "mollie," something like what we would call a "queen," was probably not far off from what the Romans meant by *malacus,* from the same root.) There is no general term for masturbator in Greek or Latin, nor is there a word for our abstraction "sexuality." That said, one could trace the continuities and ruptures in the history of various fragments that would, by the middle of the 19th century, come uneasily together in its broad embrace.

First, the continuities. Much of the afterlife of sexuality in antiquity tracks the contours of classicism more generally. The social practices of Greek boy love ended in the 4th century BCE; its ideals of beauty and erotic attraction resurfaced in the Renaissance and again with the Enlightenment and Romantic neoclassicism. Some in its thrall—the art historian Johann Joachim Winckelmann or the Regency amateur classicist and friend of Byron's, Thomas Hope—moved to Italy or Greece in search of a lost, fantasmic, pederastic dream; Winckelmann was murdered in pursuit of his dream. Mann's *Death in Venice* is in this tradition. The antisodomy and friendship literature of the medieval cloister was written in the shadow of half-remembered ancient exemplars.

Ancient eroticism and interests in priapic cults too were reborn in the Renaissance and Enlightenment, and their fortunes followed the fortunes of the political and aesthetic causes to which they were linked. The capacity of classical art and literature to arouse readers and viewers easily crossed the millennia: copies of Praxiteles' infamous Aphrodite of Cnidus from the 4th century BCE, naked with her hand over her pudenda, were arousing when they were dug up during the Renaissance; William Gladstone, the greatest politician of 19th-century England, stealthily excited himself by sneaking a peak at Catullus in antiquarian bookshops. When Renaissance artists and the public imagined sexually explicit images, they were of gods and goddesses or of ancient mortals engaged in various erotic pursuits. The capacity of classical words and images to arouse did not diminish until the demise of general classical learning among the educated, and the advent of photography and film in the late 19th and early 20th centuries.

Ancient medical understanding of sexual difference, of sexual pleasure, and of the pangs of orgasm also had a remarkably long run. Galen's view of male and female bodies as inverted versions of each other—the penis an extruded vagina, the ovaries as internal testicles—was given new life by the investigations of Renaissance anatomists and new credence by their exquisite and detailed illustrations. Anatomical advances over the ancients—the discovery that the human uterus has no horns, for example—only made the old homologies look more plausible. The "discovery" of the clitoris by Renaldus Columbus in the mid-16th century, a seemingly damaging bit of evidence for this view, was easily assimilated to vague classical references and to the overarching framework of sexual difference.

Likewise, the ancient physiology of sexual bodies and pleasures—bits of the Hippocratic corpus, Galen, Soranus, and others—made their way directly and via Byzantine and Arabic medicine into the learned and popular culture of the Renaissance and succeeding centuries. Bodily fluids—milk, blood, semen—were understood and treated in clinical practice as fungible; monks were bled regularly, as were peasants after the long winter, to give men the benefit of purgation that women gained naturally through menses. Hot, spicy foods were prescribed for both sexes in need of heating. Orgasm still seemed to signal that the body of both male and female had sufficiently concocted the blood to generate new life; it was still a relief from a genital "itch," however else it might be interpreted.

More generally, an understanding of dietary regimes, of the economy of humors, and of the balance of bodily fluids that would have governed medical advice on matters of sexuality in antiquity would still hold sway. In fact, Galenism as a clinical practice outlived its underlying theory; Hippocrates enjoyed a revival in the early 19th century. Thus, a boy or girl asking questions about sex in 1800 would have found answers in the many vernacular translations and editions of books like *Aristotle's Masterpiece* (a 17th-century mishmash based on a medieval mishmash attributed to Albertus Magnus, based on an ancient mishmash attributed to the philosopher himself) or Nicholas de Venette's *Tableau de l'amour conjugal* (translated into English as *The Art of Conjugal Love Revealed,* 1698), which contained advice more or less similar to what a Roman boy might have heard.

Even in cases in which there was a genuine discontinuity—the 18th-century discovery of the unique moral and medical dangers of masturbation is the clearest case—the physiological and clinical basis for the jeremiads of Enlightenment doctors was thoroughly indebted to classical texts. S. A. D. Tissot, the distinguished and thoroughly modern physician whose 1759 *Onanisme* was translated into scores of languages and the single most important authority on the dire consequences of masturbation, cites prominently cases in Hippocrates that purportedly illustrate a connection between seminal loss and spinal degeneration. The pathophysiology that he so starkly recounts is based on his reading of Galen (the idea that 1 ounce of semen is worth 40 of blood echoes from Pergamon through the centuries). Galen's observation that rubbing the vulva relieved stress was still being cited in favor of hydrothermy and mechanical message devices in the late 19th and early 20th centuries. The "sin of Diogenes"—the fact that the Cynic philosopher masturbated in the agora—has an almost continuous history from classical times to the 18th century.

Thus, even when the valences of a sexual act had changed dramatically—masturbation was neither medically nor morally interesting before 1712—it was talked about in the language of ancient medicine. And even as references to Greek and Roman medical writers on questions of sexuality in the learned literature declined in the 19th century, they lived on in countless popular guides through vague and hoary resonances. The loss of semen was still said to harm the backbone long after its origin was known, because semen looked, as the Greeks had pointed out, like spinal fluid.

There were thus remarkable continuities in the history of sexuality from antiquity to the very recent past. In addition to tracking the fortunes of classicism generally, it followed other microtrajectories as well. Progressives in the 18th century, for example, construed pagan sexuality as the sexuality of freedom, specifically of republicanism. And ancient erotic art was treated accordingly. The Pompeian phalluses and the frescoes of copulating couples—clearly not married and not thinking about procreation—unearthed from the ashes of Mount Vesuvius were hidden after the European Restorations of 1815, resurfaced with the short-lived success of the 1848 revolution in Naples, went underground again when it failed, reemerged with Garibaldi, went back into hiding when the radical moment passed, and went back on display in the 1960s. Montaigne's views came straight from the Stoics and continued to have a certain purchase even as they were increasingly challenged by other views.

The rise of Christianity has long been taken to have caused the most radical rupture in the history of Western sexuality. Roman sexual openness and tolerance were said to have given way to Christian prudery and hostility to the body, especially to the sexually desiring body; the collapse of the pagan world signaled the end of sexual freedom and the advent of repression. After the work of Paul Veyne, Michel Foucault, and Peter Brown, this view is no longer tenable on the discursive level. In fact, late Roman writers on the family, and on ethics more generally—Plutarch and Musonius, in particular—began a conversation that Christian writers would sharpen and extend: marriage was an arena for moral self-government before marital sexuality became, as it did later, a second-best alternative through which the laity might manage concupiscence. More generally, ancient traditions of sexual restraint within marriage survived for millennia. Montaigne argued that the counsel to have sex purely hygienically—only to satisfy the body's needs—was perhaps too strict, but that Aristotle was basically right: a man should touch his wife "prudently and soberly."

But Christianity did shift the ground under classical sexuality in at least three ways—in addition, of course, to leading to the destruction of the social and economic system under which the male Roman elite had essentially untrammeled access to the bodies of slaves and other dependents. First, virginity came to have a moral resonance it had not had before. No longer regarded as a temporary condition, it came to be regarded as a spiritual and corporeal ideal superior to the married state. Second, sexuality came to be more sharply embodied; no longer a diffuse state of the body, it was localized in the male organ. Seminal loss, of little concern in antiquity, became a window into the state of the soul. And finally, Augustine made sexual desire—concupiscence—a sign of humanity's fallen nature. It was outside the bounds of reason and the will to control because it represented the estrangement of the soul from God occasioned by the Fall.

There are two further great discontinuities between, broadly speaking, the sexuality of modernity and that of antiquity. The first has to do with the sexuality of women. Sometime in the late 17th century it became possible to think of women not only as chaste or not chaste but also as being ethical subjects themselves. A sexual ethics—pagan and Christian—that had been almost entirely about men and the male body came to include women and the female body as well. So, for example, concern about masturbation represented a shift away from the focus on the married couple or the supposedly celibate priest, monk, or philosopher—or the older man and his young lover, for that matter—and toward the morally autonomous self, male or female, within and, increasingly, outside marriage. Speaking generally, the fate of classical sexuality—in antiquity and in the millennia following—has depended on the fortunes of classical ideals of what constituted the good life and of new answers to very old questions with the advent of Christianity and the Enlightenment.

BIBL.: Peter Robert Lamont Brown, *The Body and Society: Men, Women, and Sexual Renunciation in Early Christianity* (New York 1988). Vern Bullough and James A. Brundage, eds., *Handbook of Medieval Sexuality* (New York 1996). Thomas Laqueur, *Making Sex: Body and Gender from the Greeks to Freud* (Cambridge, Mass., 1990). Katharine Park, *Secrets of Women: Gender, Generation, and the Origins of Human Dissection* (New York 2006).

T.L.

Shakespeare

English playwright and poet (1564–1616). Even in rural Stratford in the second half of the 16th century, young Shakespeare, the bright son of a modestly comfortable family, was able to achieve at least the early stages of a standard Humanist education, including the "small Latin" with which Ben Jonson later credited him (enough that in due course he could read the story of Lucretia in Ovid's *Fasti*). There is no record of his attendance at any university, an absence sometimes cited as reason for denying his authorship of the works attributed to him, as if the wealth of classical references and quotations in those works could only be the product of higher education. Yet the London theater and literary world to which Shakespeare found his way in the late 1580s was already saturated with classical lore, accessible in any number of unrecondite ways. Several important classical texts had become available in vigorous and popular English translations, some of which we can verify to have been on Shakespeare's reading list; a well-furnished arsenal of classical names and stories was a stock-in-trade of the playhouse, among the means by which the audience expected to be dazzled. Serious study of this dimension to Shakespeare's classicism begins with Richard Farmer's *Essay on the Learning of Shakespeare* (1767), though Farmer's discoveries have often been treated as unhappy ones, evidence of haste and shallowness on Shakespeare's part. In a wider view, however, they characterize both Shakespeare's own resourcefulness and that of his milieu; the difficulty involved in discriminating erudition from popular and casual resources in his relation to the classics locates one of his strengths.

Classical drama is not itself in the top tier of classical influences on Shakespeare. Greek drama was still a subject of specialized knowledge even among the learned, and most of Shakespeare's direct access to it would have been through the numerous but brief quotations in Plutarch's *Lives*. Shakespeare's dramatic practice has almost nothing to do with the model of neoclassical dramaturgy that evolved on the Continent, primarily from the elaboration of Aristotelian theory as abstracted from the newly rediscovered *Poetics* and from re-creations of the dramatic form of Senecan tragedy by Neo-Latin and French playwrights. That tradition is represented in England by a modest line of translations and original plays, most of them related to a literary circle that formed around the Countess of Pembroke; this is the tradition to which the countess's brother, Philip Sidney, looks in his *Defense of Poetry* (written in the early 1580s) for the future of English drama. Yet it is a tradition that in England remains in its closet; by the standards of the playhouses, it is static and arid and gains no foothold there. Shakespeare occasionally seems to be reflecting certain features of this tradition; the last four acts of *Othello* (ca. 1604) appear to manifest something like Neo-Aristotelian unity of time as the tragic action comes to its crisis. But this happens within the context of the famous "double-time scheme," wherein evidence that perhaps 33 hours are passing is mingled with implications that longer periods of time have transpired: an artful messiness wholly consistent with the ethos of the playhouses and seldom if ever noticed in performance. In France the conscious attempt at reviving the formal structures and constraints of classical tragedy eventually finds a successful outcome in the theater of Corneille and Racine; Shakespeare and his English colleagues take a different road from the start.

They did have a serious professional affinity with the quick dialogue and clever plot management of Roman comedy. Terence was widely read in schools and not uncommonly performed in Latin, though Shakespeare's encounter with him and Plautus would also have been in the context of their strong influence on 16th-century Italian comedy, both the deliberately classicizing *commedia erudita*—which attracted authors as distinguished as Machiavelli and Ariosto—and the improvisational, free-form *commedia dell'arte*. The 16th century saw the creation of an international staple of stage comedy carrying many of the chromosomes of the New Comedy of antiquity: young love troubled with elderly opposition or interference, beset by extravagant narrative complications often having to do with mistaken identity. Italian playwrights are particularly inventive on that last score, which they extend beyond classical precedent to include young women passing as men. Shakespeare entered this tradition perhaps as early as 1589 with *The Comedy of Errors,* an homage to one of Plautus's most imitated plays, with a characteristically contemporary twist: not one pair of identical twins, but two. Perhaps a decade later Shakespeare reworked a well-known *commedia erudita* as *Twelfth Night* (1601) and gave the gendered version of Plautus's conceit—identical twin brother and sister—its richest and most durable dramatic incarnation.

The classical sibling to *Errors* among Shakespeare's earlier plays is *Titus Andronicus* (1594), testimony to his interest in Roman tragedy as well as comedy. The entire Senecan dramatic corpus, including the pseudo-Senecan *Octavia,* was available in English by 1581, when an inclusive volume of translations was published; trace evidence suggests that Shakespeare knew them, though we know that he looked at the Latin as well (two bits of Seneca's Latin appear in *Titus*). If Seneca's dramaturgy was largely irrelevant to English public theater, the themes and the rhetoric of his plays were not: the defiantly proud villain, the code of competitively escalating violence ("worse than Philomel you used my daughter,/And worse than Progne I will be revenged"; *Titus* 5.2.194–195), and the habit of cosmically aggressive declamation ("Threatening the world with high astounding terms," as Christopher Marlowe has it in the prologue to his *Tamburlaine*) all became famously at home on the Elizabethan stage. In *Titus* they served in the creation of a lurid vision of imperial Rome on the verge of a catastrophic implosion, a kind of phantasmagoric *praetexta* (a Roman history play, like *Octavia*) that was Shakespeare's first attempt at imagining classical Rome as a civilization. The narrative is wildly unhistorical and possibly Shakespeare's own creation, though the culminating outrage, when the Goth queen Tamora is fed the cooked remains of her two sons, conflates the climactic events of two of Seneca's strongest plays, *Thyestes* and *Medea.*

Seneca is, however, not the only source for such things, and here he shares the stage with an author whose influence is notably wider and stronger throughout Shakespeare's career. The banquet in *Titus* is in revenge for the rape and mutilation of Titus's daughter Lavinia, an act modeled on the fate of Philomela in Ovid's *Metamorphoses;* the tongueless victim eventually explains her condition by using a book identified as an edition of that poem ("My mother gave it me," says young Lucius; 4.1.43). Another copy turns up in *Cymbeline* (1610–1611), where another woman in peril has been reading the same story. A Latin tag from the poem appears in *Titus,* but we are confident that in this case Shakespeare's main form of access was an English translation, Arthur Golding's frequently reprinted version in fourteener couplets (first published in its complete form in 1567). Shakespeare's eye was caught not just by Ovid's stories but also by Golding's phrasing; scholars continue to find new evidence. The most expansive appropriation is one of the last; Prospero's summoning of his supernatural powers in the last scene of *The Tempest* (1611)—"Ye elves of hills, brooks, standing lakes and groves" (5.1.33)—begins with a near transcription of a chant of Medea's as Englished by Golding—"Ye airs and winds, ye elves of hills, of brooks, of woods alone,/Of standing lakes" (translating *Metamorphoses* 7.196ff)—and continues to echo its original over the next dozen or so lines. The play famously makes Prospero's magic difficult to distinguish from Shakespeare's craft as a playwright, and Ovid's presence inside this key invocation of that magic suggests an intimacy that can be detected in other, less solemn contexts as well:

> TOUCHSTONE: I am here with thee and thy goats, as the most capricious poet, honest Ovid, was among the Goths.
> JACQUES: O knowledge ill-inhabited, worse than Jove in a thatch'd house!
> (*As You Like It* 3.3.7–11)

About Ovid's name and the memory of his misfortune, a cleverly Latinate pun (the root sense of "capricious" is "goat-like") balances against a memory of Golding, who in translating the story of Jupiter's visit to Baucis and Philemon gave the pious couple an honest English thatched house not quite attested in the original.

It is tempting to read Shakespeare's own experience in the testimony of Montaigne, another writer whom Shakespeare knew exceedingly well: "The first taste I had for books came to me from my pleasure in the fables of the *Metamorphoses* of Ovid. For at about seven or eight years of age I would steal away from any other pleasure to read them" (Montaigne, *Essays* 1.26; trans. Donald Frame). The *Metamorphoses,* occasionally supplemented by some of Ovid's other works, is Shakespeare's single greatest source for references to classical mythology; the briefest often carry evidence of their Ovidian provenance. The connection was sufficiently visible to contemporaries to inspire the judgment that "the sweet witty soul of Ovid lives in mellifluous and honey-tongued Shakespeare" (Francis Meres, 1598). Shakespeare's two narrative poems, *Venus and Adonis* (1593) and *The Rape of Lucrece* (1594), are sustained expansions of Ovidian stories (in the latter case from the *Fasti,* with ancillary information from Livy) in a late-Elizabethan fashion first set by Thomas Lodge with *Scilla's Metamorphosis* (1589). Shakespeare published them as part of a bid for aristocratic patronage, possibly in hope of exchanging the theater for a different kind of poetic career. Ovid's relevance, however, works on other levels as well. Even Shakespeare's sonnets, which in defiance of sonneteering custom avoid all but the briefest mythological references, incorporate significant material from the *Metamorphoses,* notably a series of near quotations from that poem's last book, near the midpoint of the poems to the young man (Sonnets 55, 60, 64). The dominant theme of these passages is that of Pythagoras' speech, a vision of the cosmos in unending and irresistible metamorphosis, of immortal but infinitely malleable raw material constantly being recast. Golding directed his reader's attention to the speech as "a sum of all the former work"; some recent critics have sensed in it a template for Shakespeare's own deepest instincts for characterization and plot construction, and they have described his lifelong affinity for Ovid in terms that subtend the whole range of his achievement: "by reading Shakespeare's reading of Ovid we may come to a remarkably full . . . picture of the sort of artist that Shakespeare was" (Bate 1993, vii).

One other book on Shakespeare's classical shelf can inspire comparably broad claims: Sir Thomas North's translation of Plutarch's *Lives* (first ed. 1579). There is no likelihood of Shakespeare's recourse to the Greek or evidence that he consulted the French translation from which North himself worked. North's English seems to have been fully absorbing on its own; its wording is even more extensively visible in Shakespeare's own text than is that of Golding's Ovid (a line dropped from the First Folio text of *Coriolanus* can be restored from North). There are signs that Shakespeare was reading the *Lives* as early as *Titus* and *Midsummer Night's Dream* (1595–1596), but in the late 1590s that reading acquired a new dimension of seriousness. *Julius Caesar* (1599) is based in careful detail on the Plutarchan lives of Caesar, Brutus, and Antony; very possibly written to open the new Globe, it also marks an important return on Shakespeare's part to the genre of tragedy and inaugurates the run of plays (*Hamlet* was probably written the next year) that has long rested at the center of his reputation. Extravagant assertions have been made in this connection: "It was from Plutarch that Shakespeare learned how to make a tragedy of the kind exemplified in *Hamlet* and *Othello, Macbeth* and *Lear.* It was . . . in the course of writing *Julius Caesar* that he learned it" (Thomson 1952, 242).

Julius Caesar certainly marks an entirely new approach, after *Titus,* to the enterprise of dramatizing classical antiquity, and it also reveals a newly serious interest on Shakespeare's part in specifically Roman antiquity. Classical Greece, when he goes there, is primarily a site for recklessly venomous satire: *Troilus and Cressida* (ca. 1601; mostly medieval in its sources but including an almost comically abbreviated version of the plot of the *Iliad*) and *Timon of Athens* (perhaps 1607–1608; developed from a brief passage in Plutarch's *Life of Antony*). The Rome of *Julius Caesar,* however, is researched and imagined with obvious care and respect; the action is historically specific, with a modest amount of compressing and rearranging of events, and the whole presentation bespeaks a sober curiosity about the institutions and culture of a world that from the perspective of Christian Europe seemed both admirable and alien. The enterprise was sufficiently successful that a decade later Shakespeare returned to it twice; *Antony and Cleopatra* (1606–1607, a sequel of sorts to *Julius Caesar,* with some of the same characters) and *Coriolanus* (1608–1609) are focused even more tightly on Plutarchan sources, each play dramatizing an individual life.

Costuming was probably not much less eclectic than that displayed in a surviving drawing of a performance of *Titus* (our only contemporary drawing of any Shakespearean performance), where the attempt at a toga mingles with medieval and unabashedly modern attire; the plebeians and soldiers in *Coriolanus* wear "caps" and toss them into the air. There are some colorful anachronisms, such as the clock that strikes in *Julius Caesar.* Yet there are also some impressive feats of passionately informed re-creation. The rendering in *Coriolanus* of the political and class tensions connected with the creation of the tribunate in the early Republic is especially remarkable; unmistakable allusions to the Midland Revolt of 1607 show it to have been an achievement energized by a clear sense of contemporary relevance. More broadly, Shakespeare's three Plutarchan plays involve a sustained effort to dramatize a particular sense of what it might have meant and felt like to be a classical Roman. The playwright is scrupulous in remembering that the culture is one that had never heard of Christianity; references to an afterlife are avoided, in some cases even when they are present in North. The consolation toward which characters usually reach in times of crisis is, rather, a stern code of personal honor and self-sufficiency, whose ultimate expression is suicide. North prepares the way here by infusing his narratives with the idiom of Neostoicism, centered on the value of "constancy"; that idiom is something of a misrepresentation of Plutarch, who was anti-Stoic in his philosophical allegiances, but it fits the contours of his storytelling without serious disruption as one way of articulating a character's dignified self-possession. North's way of putting it can pass into Shakespeare with minimal alteration: "When you do find him, or alive or dead,/He will be found like Brutus, like himself" (*Julius Caesar* 5.4.24–25). In the Greek, the prediction is merely that Brutus's dead body will be found lying "worthily of himself"; North tightens this into the heroic tautology "like himself," which Shakespeare clinches with a repetition of the proper name.

Other depictions of classical Rome on the English Renaissance stage are generally more in the spirit of *Titus.* Shakespeare's Plutarchan plays present a different and in the long run more powerful image. The nearly automatic association in English of "noble" with "Roman" is part of their legacy; the version of Roman selfhood on view specifically in *Julius Caesar*—the most widely read Shakespearean play in American secondary education—remains the central image of classical Rome in anglophone popular culture. Yet Shakespeare does not simply make a Roman style of personal dignity dramatically vivid; his Plutarchan cycle also becomes, with its latter two plays, an exploration of the pathology and the limits of that style. *Coriolanus*—an almost unprecedented choice of subject for a Renaissance dramatist—is about the civic and personal carnage caused by a hero who by wide consent is one of the purest embodiments of Rome's signal virtues. In *Antony and Cleopatra,* a Roman ideal of manliness comes into spectacular conflict with the power of heterosexual desire, and it is notoriously hard to say which prevails; dying by his own hand, Antony prides himself on being "a Roman by a Roman/Valiantly vanquished"

(4.15.57–58), but he also looks to an afterlife in which he and Cleopatra rewrite the rules:

Where souls do couch on flowers, we'll hand in hand.
And with our sprightly port make the ghosts gaze.
Dido and her Aeneas shall want troops,
And all the haunt be ours.
(4.14.51–54)

The first sentiment comes from Plutarch, but the second does not. From the story as he found it Shakespeare coaxed some unguardedly romantic intimations of immortality, in which his Roman world dreams of a redemptive transcendence of which it elsewhere knows nothing.

BIBL.: T. W. Baldwin, *William Shakspere's Small Latine and Lesse Greeke*, 2 vols. (Urbana 1944). Jonathan Bate, *Shakespeare and Ovid* (Oxford 1993). Reuben A. Brower, *Hero and Saint: Shakespeare and the Graeco-Roman Heroic Tradition* (New York 1971). Charles Martindale and Michelle Martindale, *Shakespeare and the Uses of Antiquity* (Cambridge 1990). Geoffrey Miles, *Shakespeare and the Constant Romans* (Oxford 1996). A. B. Taylor and Charles Martindale, eds., *Shakespeare and the Classics* (Cambridge 2004). J. A. K. Thomson, *Shakespeare and the Classics* (New York 1952). G.B.

Sibyls

According to Ovid's *Metamorphoses,* in exchange for sexual favors Apollo granted the Sibyl as many years of life as grains in a heap of sand. When the seer refused the god's advances, he withheld the gift of lasting youth, so she shriveled to almost nothing, recognizable only by her voice: "Only by voice am I known; the Fates will leave me my voice" (*Metamorphoses* 14.152–153). This story predicted the Sibyl's fate in the four centuries after the spurious nature of the books that circulated under her name was revealed, but the history of the Sibyl's influence before 1600 was quite different. During these centuries her message was widely diffused and her fame led to depiction by noted artists, such as Van Eyck, Perugino, Pinturrichio, Michelangelo, and Raphael, and even to musical settings of her verses.

The female seer known as the Sibyl (etymology disputed), a manifestation of the ancient hunger for oracles, first appears in the 6th century BCE in connection with Erythrae in Asia Minor. The earlier Greek witnesses (Heraclitus, Aristophanes, Plato) speak of a single seer, but by the mid-4th century CE multiple Sibyls are found. The popular list of 10 that comes from Varro shows scattered Sibyls around the ancient world, including Cumae and Tibur in Italy (Varro in Lactantius, *Divine Institutes* 1.6). The Sibyl's fame as a guide to the underworld (*Aeneid* 6) and as a prophetess of political and natural crises gave her an official place in Roman religion through the collection and consultation of the Sibylline books. Only fragments of these obscure hexameters survive, owing to their destruction by Stilicho around 408 CE.

The Sibylline books that became important in the later Western tradition were the product of Jews and Christians who seized on this form of revelatory literature for their own purposes. Written under the pseudonyms of such seers of great antiquity (one Sibyl announces herself as Noah's daughter), these Greek hexameters proclaimed the superiority first of Judaism and then of Christianity by casting the prophetess's message as a critique of the false gods and immorality of pagans and a prediction of their impending doom. Eight books were produced between the mid-2nd century BCE and the 4th century CE and were put together as a collection in the 6th century. (Four other books had little influence and were not discovered until the 19th century.) The Sibylline oracles fell out of favor with Jews, but they were widely used by Christians of East and West as evidence that God had employed Gentile female seers along with the Jewish male prophets to announce Christ's first coming and his impending judgment on those who did not accept him. Augustine of Hippo, although generally opposed to apocalyptic prophecy, accepted the Sibyl as a member of the City of God because of the acrostic poem found in book 8 that hymned Christ's return (*City of God* 18.23, citing *Sibylline Oracles* 8.217–250).

The Greek Sibyllines were widely used by many patristic authors (Justin, Theophilus of Antioch, Clement of Alexandria, Tertullian, pseudo-Constantine, Eusebius, Lactantius) and survived into the Byzantine world. In the West only parts of the books were available in Latin translation, but because of the citations of the seer in Lactantius, Augustine, and the influential sermon *Against the Jews, Pagans, and Arians* ascribed to Augustine, the Sibyl remained a potent authority throughout the Middle Ages. This strand of the Sibylline story, which can be called the inherited tradition, was associated with the Christian messianic interpretation of Virgil's Fourth Eclogue and emphasized the Sibyl as a witness to the revelation made to the Gentiles. It was summarized in the opening verse of Thomas of Celano's famous sequence, the *Dies irae:*

Day of wrath, that day
That will dissolve the world in flames,
As David and the Sibyl attest.

There were two other strands in the Sibylline tradition in the Middle Ages and Renaissance. The first, the legendary or folkloric Sibyl, enshrined popular beliefs about the seer. According to a legend that began in the East in the 6th century, the Tiburtine Sibyl had revealed the birth of Christ to Emperor Augustus by showing him a heavenly vision of the Christ child on Mary's lap. This tale became popular in Rome and spread throughout the West in text and art. In Italian folklore, beginning ca. 1400, more sinister legends about the Sibyl as a Venus-like temptress hidden in a cave in the Apennines began to spread. The third strand of the medieval history of the Sibyl was the production of new Sibylline texts, mostly in prose. This literature used the Sibyl's authority to promote forms of apocalypticism with strong political overtones. Like the original Sibyls' texts, most of this literature was written in Greek, but in Latin and vernacular translation it became popular in the West. The two most famous texts are the *Tiburtine Sibyl,* which goes back to the 4th century and spread throughout Western Europe from the 11th century on; and the *Erythraean Sibyl,* which originated in the 12th century and was widely read through the 16th century, when it was printed three times.

Interest in the Sibyl was at its height in the 16th century, as is reflected in the editions and artistic renditions of the seers. The first printing of the Greek text, made by Sixtus Birck, appeared in Basel in 1545. Sebastian Castellio published another edition in 1555, with a full Latin translation. But the 1599 Paris edition of Joseph Koch expressed doubts about the antiquity and authority of the verses. A "battle of the books" ensued in the 17th century as classical scholars, such as Isaac Casaubon and Richard Simon, mounted arguments against the authenticity of the oracles, while increasingly beleaguered apologists, such as Cardinal Baronius and Isaac Vossius, sought to defend their witness to Christian faith. By the beginning of the 18th century, "the Moderne Criticks," as William Whiston, one of the last apologists, called them, had won. Those grandes dames who had proudly stood beside the prophets at the entrance to medieval cathedrals were fading into the small voice left them by the fates. In the 19th century critical editions were produced, and in the 20th century the oracles began to be studied for what they tell us about Judaism and Christianity in the Hellenistic and Roman worlds.

BIBL.: Monique Bouquet and Françoise Morzadec, eds., *La Sibylle: Parole et Représentation* (Paris 2004). J. J. Collins, "Sibylline Oracles (Second Century B.C.–Seventh Century A.D.)," in *The Old Testament Pseudepigrapha,* vol. 1, *Apocalyptic Literature and Movements,* ed. James L. Charlesworth (Garden City 1983) 317–472. I. C. Colombo and T. Seppilli, eds., *Sibille e linguaggi oracolari: Mito, storia, tradizione* (Pisa 1998). Bernard McGinn, "*Teste David cum Sibylla:* The Significance of the Sibylline Tradition in the Middle Ages," in *Women of the Medieval World,* ed. Julius Kirshner and Suzanne F. Wemple (Oxford 1985) 7–35. David Potter, *Prophets and Emperors: Human and Divine Authority from Augustus to Theodosius* (Cambridge, Mass., 1994). Karl Prümm, "Das Prophetenamt der Sibyllen in der kirchlichen Literatur mit besonderer Rücksicht auf der Deutung der 4. Ekloge Virgils," *Scholastik* 4 (1929) 498–533.

B.M.

Sicily

Largest island in the Mediterranean; in recent history, the southernmost region of Italy. Sicily's central position in the Mediterranean makes its history one of migration and cultural exchange. The Greeks, who established settlements in Sicily starting in the 8th century BCE, confronted both indigenous inhabitants and Punic settlers. Later the island, together with Magna Graecia, introduced Rome to Greek culture. It was in Sicily that the First Punic War developed, which ultimately led Rome to imperial power. Sicily's multilayered cultural history and its ties to mainland Greece resulted in a rich and unique classical tradition.

Thucydides wrote the first account we have of Sicily, memorably describing Athens' doomed Sicilian expedition but also the island's pre-Greek populations, the Sicels (Siculi) in eastern Sicily, the Sicans in central Sicily, and the Elymians in the northwest, as well as the Punic settlements Palermo and Motya, which halted Greek expansion westward. The island underwent powerful hellenization, as shown by the Greek-style temple at the Elymian site of Segesta. The Greek *poleis,* successful centers like Syracuse, Zancle (modern Messina), Catania, Selinus, and Agrigentum, fought bitterly with one another, and tyrannies were a fixture of Greek Sicilian history. Syracuse became the most prominent city, both politically and culturally. In 480 BCE the fleet of its tyrant Gelon was the largest in Greece; his brother Hiero was celebrated by the poets Pindar, Bacchylides, and Simonides; the brothers' successor, Dionysius, played host to Plato. With Archimedes' help, Syracuse long resisted the Romans. The final sack of the city in 212 BCE resulted in one of the largest importations of Greek art to Rome in ancient history.

Throughout classical antiquity, starting with the *Odyssey,* Sicily was a charged place. Scylla and Charybdis, the Cyclops, Polyphemus, and Galatea were legendarily located there, and Theocritus' bucolic poems were inspired by the Sicilian landscape. Mount Etna (Latin Aetna), mythologized by Virgil, became a tourist attraction, climbed by the emperor Hadrian.

Post-classical times brought still other cultures to Sicily, from the Vandals and Ostrogoths to the Byzantines, Arabs, Normans, and Swabians. By the end of the Middle Ages the island's varied architecture reflected this rich history. Alongside the best-preserved Greek temples could be found both Greek temples and Arab mosques that had been converted into Christian churches, such as the cathedral of Syracuse and the church of San Giovanni degli Eremiti in Palermo. The first deliberate turn to its classical past was taken by Frederick II of Swabia, king of Sicily from 1198 and Holy Roman Emperor from 1220 until his death in 1250. Palermo was his favorite city, and there he revived Roman and Greek traditions by appealing to Roman imperial models, by making Greek a chancellery language, and by investigating Greek science. This was Sicily's last period of cultural splendor and political independence. Subsequently it was ruled by the Anjou dynasty and then by Aragonese kings. In 1479 it became a province of Spain, and in 1734 it was annexed by the Bourbons into the Kingdom of the Two Sicilies, with Naples as its capital.

In 1558 the first modern study of Sicily's past appeared: *De rebus siculis decades duo* by the Dominican friar Tommaso Fazello. It offered a topographical survey of the island based on Humanist historical geography. Classical authors were Fazello's models and sources, and his goal was to revive Sicily's classical past. He proudly demonstrated that Selinus was to be located at the abandoned site of the three preserved temples, rather than at modern Mazara, as its citizens claimed. He was also responsible for many wrongly attributed names still in use today, including the Temple of Concordia in Agrigentum (modern Agrigento), but in general the information he painstakingly collected proved of long-lasting value. The second half of the book narrated Sicilian history as a succession of foreign invasions. In this work A. Momigliano (1984) identified the origins of Sicilian historical identity, which he defined mainly as a lack of identification with any of the island's invaders, including the Greeks.

A new interest in Sicily's past developed in the 18th century, among Sicilians and foreigners as well. The Dutch traveler J.-P. D'Orville visited the island as early as 1727 to record its classical remains, but his book was published posthumously, in 1764. By then the main inspiration to travel to Sicily was J. J. Winckelmann. Though he never visited Greece himself or indeed any Greek site south of Paestum, Winckelmann in 1759 had published an essay on the temples of Agrigentum, based on drawings and notes by the Scotsman Robert Mylne. Winckelmann directed the travels of his pupil Baron Riedesel to Sicily and southern Italy in 1767, which were reported in *Reise durch Sizilien und Grossgriechenland,* published in 1771 and soon translated into English, French, and Italian. Riedesel looked primarily for the classical past and found traces of the ancient Greeks even in the features of Sicilian women, and his account inspired the many travelers of the late 18th century. Within a few years, two *Voyages pittoresques,* by the Abbé de Saint-Non (1781–1786) and J.-P. L. Houël (1782–1787), made images of Sicilian ruins, landscapes, and people that became famous all over Europe.

Sicilian scholars of these times, unlike their counterparts in other classical lands, not only acted as hosts and figured in travelers' narratives but were published authors themselves with European reputations. Pride and a sense of ownership of the entire Sicilian past, beyond the Greek period privileged by foreigners, can be detected in their writings. The two most famous Sicilian antiquarians, G. L. Castelli, prince of Torremuzza (d. 1794) in Palermo and Prince Ignazio of Biscari (d. 1784) in Catania, were the first officially appointed curators of the island's cultural heritage. But the late 18th century was the golden age for the Sicilian classical tradition. Goethe, traveling with texts by both Riedesel and Biscari, wrote that it was in Sicily that one could experience Greece. The fragmented mass of the colossal temple of Zeus at Agrigentum, first revived by Winckelmann's imagination, inspired ideal reconstructions and shaped modern architecture for decades.

During the 19th century, however, Sicily, together with Greek southern Italy, was progressively marginalized in the study of the classical world. Mainland Greece became better known and more accessible, whereas the strict Sicilian antiquities legislation prohibited exports. When two English architects in the early 1820s discovered the archaic sculpted and painted metopes of Selinus and planned to convey them to London, like the Elgin Marbles, they were intercepted and allowed to export only casts. As Athens and its art came to define the classical canon, Sicilian temples and vases were judged to be of lesser quality. Gradually a colonial paradigm developed that viewed these artifacts in terms of the negative influences of non-Greek races. Something of this approach can be detected in T. J. Dunbabin's *The Western Greeks* (1948). Sicily's peculiarity remained of interest, but often to authors out of the mainstream of classical scholarship. In his *History of Sicily* (1891–1894) E. A. Freeman cherished the unity of Sicily's history, in which past and present were inextricable. Samuel Butler's *The Authoress of the Odyssey* (1897) argued that the Homeric epic was in fact written by a young Sicilian girl and set entirely in Sicily.

Garibaldi's famous expedition of 1866 annexed Sicily to the Kingdom of Italy. But the island's strong regional identity persisted, and in 1946 it was recognized as an autonomous region of the Italian Republic. For Italian scholars, unification offered both new resources and new challenges. Paolo Orsi, the first superintendent of antiquities at Syracuse (beginning in 1888), painstakingly excavated both native and Greek sites, thus anticipating modern concerns, but he never produced a synthesis. The historians Ettore Pais, with his *Storia della Sicilia e della Magna Grecia* (1894), and Emanuele Ciaceri, in his *Storia della Magna Grecia* (3 vols., 1927–1932), both strove to blend Sicilian ancient history with that of the new nation. Italian archaeologists reclaimed Sicilian classical art from the idea that it was a distorted and derivative version of the art of mainland Greece. Developments in terminology (*anti-classical,* coined by Pirro Marconi in the 1930s, soon followed by *hetero-classical* and *aclassical*) are indicative of their predicament. Nationalist bias at its strongest simply dismissed Greek influence and lauded only the autochthonous genius, as in Biagio Pace's *Arte e civiltà della Sicilia antica* (1935). Momigliano (1984) saw in this work a modern version of the Fazello model of Sicilian identity. On the other hand, residues of classical culture were often given especial notice in folkloric studies, beginning with the 19th-century work of Giuseppe Pitré.

Today, in accord with a renewed interest in Mediterranean history and because of the political turn within the European Union from nation-states to regional cultures, Sicily is appreciated as a site of dynamic cultural exchange throughout its history. The process of hellenization is now a major focus of archaeological research.

Among the most long-standing, attentive, and devoted interpreters of the multifaceted and layered history of the Sicilian classical tradition should be mentioned the island's literary authors, notably the novelist Giuseppe Tomasi di Lampedusa (*The Siren,* 1958); the poet Salvatore Quasimodo, winner of the Nobel Prize for Literature in 1959, in poems like "Wind at Tindari" and "Street in Agrigentum," and in his translation of ancient Greek lyric; and, most recently, Vincenzo Consolo.

BIBL.: M. Amari, *Storia dei Musulmani di Sicilia,* 3 vols. (Florence 1854–1872). G. Ceserani, "The Charm of the Siren: The Place of Classical Sicily in Historiography," in *Sicily from*

Aeneas to Augustus, ed. C. Smith and J. Serrati (Edinburgh 2000) 174–193. M. Cometa, *Duplicità del classico: Il mito del tempio di Giove Olimpico da Winckelmann a Leo von Klenze* (Palermo 1993). F. De Angelis, "Ancient Past, Imperial Present: The British Empire in T. J. Dunbabin's *The Western Greeks,*" *Antiquity* 72 (1998) 539–549. S. De Vido, *Gli Elimi: Storie di contatti e di rappresentazioni* (Pisa 1997) esp. 445–500. A. Momigliano, "The Rediscovery of Greek History: The Case of Sicily," in *Settimo contributo alla storia degli studi classici e del mondo antico* (Rome 1984) 133–153. S. Settis, "Idea dell'arte greca d'occidente fra otto e novecento: Germania e Italia," in *Un secolo di ricerche in Magna Grecia* (Taranto 1989) 135–176.

G.CE.

Sirens

Since the first written description of them in the 12th book of Homer's *Odyssey,* Sirens have appeared in numerous guises. Their significance has fluctuated according to time and place, emphasis shifting among three main aspects of their mythological character: their hybrid physical form (part woman, part bird, part fish), their compelling song, and the means used to withstand their charms.

Greek vases and figurines from the 7th century BCE depict the Sirens as bird-women, often showing them as a trio: one singing, one playing a flute, and one playing a lyre. Homer gives no physical description of his pair of Sirens and says only that their voices are "clear" and "honeyed." The most influential aspects of the Homeric source are Circe's detailed advice to Odysseus about how to resist the Sirens' charms—by filling his men's ears with wax and lashing himself (hearing unimpaired) to the mast of his ship—and the suggestion that the Sirens' power lies in the access to knowledge and history that they promise their targets. The philosopher Adriana Cavarero argued that the classical tradition gradually transformed the Siren from a bearer of voice and Logos in balance to a more purely feminine and eroticized fount of pure voice and wordless song. The Sirens have a kinship with Orpheus: their song—like his—is seen as impossible to represent or imitate, yet it inspires endless attempts to imagine it in words and music. An apparently independent tradition links the Sirens to the Muses, as in the myth of Er in the *Republic,* in which Sirens are positioned at the pinnacle of eight concentric circles representing the heavens, each emitting a single pure tone and combining to form a celestial concord. Commentaries on Homer, from the 3rd century BCE onward, locate the Sirens specifically in the Mediterranean, perhaps on Capri, name them, and introduce connections with Persephone and with Melpomene, the Muse of tragedy, said to be their mother. From this branch of commentary came the myth that Naples was founded on the site where the body of the distraught Siren Parthenope washed up after she was spurned by Odysseus.

In bestiaries, theological writings, and musical treatises through the 14th century, the Siren was often depicted as part bird and grouped with other birds to symbolize the attractions of the female body and the ungovernable power of music. In *Purgatorio* 19 Dante stresses the ugly reality thought to lie behind such charms. The poet dreams of a Siren who is deformed, frozen, and speechless until his gaze fixes on her and she begins to sing; immobilized by her song, he is freed only when she is stripped bare and the stench of her body is released. In the 16th century, in Ariosto's epic poem *Orlando furioso* (canto 6), Astolfo is captured by Alcina (herself a sort of Siren) when she invites him to step onto the back of a whale and sail across the water to see Sirens and other mythical creatures. The poet Torquato Tasso, in his *Gerusalemme liberata* (canto 16), equates birdsong and the voice of love. As Rinaldo's men approach Armida's island they hear a chorus of birds and other creatures singing in praise of momentary pleasure, then they come upon Armida, described as a Siren who has paralyzed Rinaldo's reason. A number of Italian madrigals assign music to Sirens, as do some operas based on Tasso or Ariosto (F. Caccini, *La liberazione di Ruggiero,* 1625; Lully, *Roland,* 1685; Handel, *Rinaldo,* 1711). These Sirens sing in ensembles or choruses, enchanting mainly through the timbral richness of combining two or more female voices in harmony.

Depictions of Sirens with fishlike characteristics are found as far back as Greek ceramics, but the first verbal description did not appear until the 8th century. Through the Middle Ages, wings and birds' feet became less common in images of Sirens, and the purely aqueous Siren has prevailed since about 1600, intersecting with the various mermaid figures in world folklore. Undines, rusalkas, and the water spirit Melusine all share the Siren's hybrid and watery form and her role as a fatal temptress, but song rarely figures in these legends. The Siren's closest folkloric relation is Lorelei, who uses song to lure sailors to disaster from her rock above the Rhine. Sirens surface infrequently in literature, music, and art after about 1650, possibly banished by Enlightenment skepticism toward mystical beings. Their folkloric kin enjoyed a boom in the 19th century; influential treatments were produced by Goethe and Mendelssohn (on Melusine), Friedrich de la Motte Fouqué and E. T. A. Hoffmann (Undine), Clemens Brentano and Heinrich Heine (Lorelei), and Pushkin and Dvořák (Rusalka). The Romantic reaction against classical sources meant that actual Sirens were rare until the fin de siècle, when the new fears and freedoms of the Freudian era sparked a renewed interest in mermaids and Sirens. Paintings by Gustave Moreau and Edward Burne-Jones, among many others, show them as embedded in nature, indistinguishable from the water, rock, and vegetation from which they emanate.

Musical representations in the 19th century focused on the legend of Lorelei (e.g., the settings of Heine's "Die Lorelei" by Robert Schumann, Clara Schumann, and Franz Liszt), the only Siren figure who operates alone and could thus be cast as a questing, self-questioning individual in the Romantic mold. By midcentury groups of Sirens again enjoyed a musical vogue, led by the nonsense-spouting Rhine Maidens in Wagner's *Das Rheingold* and the Siren chorus heard briefly in the opening scene of *Tannhäuser.* The Norns who introduce Wagner's *Götterdämmerung* might also be seen in this vein, reasserting the old tradition of Sirens as bearers of historical truth and fate. In France the final movement of Debussy's *Nocturnes* (1899) was only the most famous of several works to use Sirens as an excuse for the wordless *jouissance* of female voices dissolved in a lush shimmer of sound.

The early 20th century saw a return to the classical Siren, and specifically to Homer. In *Ulysses* (1922), James Joyce brings the Sirens down to earth by casting them as slangy barmaids, and the novel's "Sirens" episode shares the fin de siècle view of the Siren's song as an escape from the constraints of language and meaning, an excuse to experiment. Both Rilke ("Die Insel der Sirenen," 1907) and Kafka ("Das Schweigen der Sirenen," 1927) explore the idea of Sirens who do not sing. Rilke's sailors are terrified by silence as they approach the Island of the Sirens, perhaps because what they imagine is more disturbing than any actual music could be. Kafka's Odysseus, proud of his ruse of plugging his own ears with wax, is outwitted by Sirens who refuse to sing. Kafka mocks the bluntness of Odysseus's trick while suggesting that his swaggering and utterly secure subjectivity might have vanquished the Sirens. After World War II the Sirens migrated into the realm of philosophy, inspiring influential readings by Theodor Adorno and Max Horkheimer (*Dialectic of Enlightenment,* 1944) and Maurice Blanchot (*Le livre à venir,* 1959). In both these texts, the Siren myth is reinterpreted as a tale about human subjectivity in the face of artistic creation. Adorno and Horkheimer show Odysseus eager to dissolve his self in the song of the Sirens but prevented from doing so by the disenfranchised laborers who sail his ship. If the listener cannot abandon himself, they suggest, the fascination of the Sirens' music is neutralized, reduced to nothing more than ordinary entertainment. Perhaps the logical endpoint of this modern narrative of disenchantment is the gradual denaturing of the Siren's body that can be traced in iterations of the logo for the Starbucks coffee company since 1971—a design that concealed first the breasts and abdomen and then the fish tail, leaving the Siren as little more than a pretty face framed by a graphic pattern of repeating waves.

BIBL.: Linda Austern and Inna Naroditskaya, eds., *Music of the Sirens* (Bloomington 2006). Maurizio Bettini and Luigi Spina, *Il mito delle sirene: Imaggini e racconti dalla Grecia a oggi* (Turin 2007). Adriana Cavarero, *For More Than One Voice: Philosophy of Vocal Expression* (Stanford 2005). Siegfried de Rachowiltz, *De Sirenibus: An Inquiry into Sirens from Homer to Shakespeare* (New York 1987). M.A.S.

Sisyphus

Mythical founder and sometime ruler of Corinth; in Hades he is eternally condemned to push a huge boulder up a hill, which invariably rolls back down and must be retrieved. Classical literature preserves several stories about his life, all stressing his cleverness and talents as a trickster; in one of them he is the father of Odysseus by grace of a prenuptial seduction of Laertes' bride, Anticleia. Accounts vary as to which of his exploits earned him eternal punishment. Later mythography adds some variants—for instance, that he was one of the Isthmian robbers slain by the young Theseus. For the Ovidian translator George Sandys (1636), that particular version legitimates his fate as "the reward of treachery, injustice, and oppression." For the most part, however, Sisyphus' life is of little interest in post-classical venues; his story is almost exclusively that of his endless, pointless labor. His punishment is often linked with the similarly ingenious punishments of other famous sinners (Ixion, Tantalus, Tityus). In a series of paintings on the topic by Titian (1548–1549, now in the Prado, Madrid), Sisyphus carries his boulder instead of pushing it. In a lithograph by Daumier (1869) the burden is instead a huge sack labeled Budget. During the 19th century the terms *sisyphist* and *sisyphism* acquired some currency in connection with forcibly repetitive tasks in industrial manufacture or penal servitude.

As early as the 16th century Sisyphus in Hades was sometimes used as an emblem of the human condition at large; for Abraham Fraunce (*The Countesse of Pembrokes Yvychurch,* 1592) Sisyphus symbolized "the soul and mind of man, which, included in this prison of the body, striveth and contendeth by all means possible to attain to eternal rest and perfect felicity." In the 20th century this equation was turned by Albert Camus into one of the most memorable formulations of philosophical existentialism, *Le mythe de Sisyphe* (1942). Here Sisyphus' sole but nevertheless stirring consolation is his continuous self-consciousness as he walks back down the hill to resume his pointless task: "Sisyphus, proletarian of the gods, powerless and rebellious, knows the whole extent of his wretched condition: it is what he thinks of during his descent. The lucidity that was to constitute his torture at the same time crowns his victory. There is no fate that cannot be surmounted by scorn." In a later essay (1954) Camus proffered Prometheus as the mythic representation of existential heroism, an altogether more positive and hopeful figure, as Prometheus suffers for trying to benefit mankind and may eventually be released. *Le Mythe de Sisyphe,* written and published in more desperate times, is starker and more influential.

In Camus's wake various writers crafted further articulations of Sisyphean absurdity. "What you do is hopeless. Good," begins Hans Magnus Enzensberger's "anweisung an sisyphos" ("instructions to sisyphus," 1957). The Mexican poet José Emilio Pacheco turns the load so painfully carried up the hill into a grain of sand; when it falls back down, part of Sisyphus' hopeless task is to find it "in the plurality of this desert" ("Le nouveau mythe de Sisyphe," 1973). The Scots poet Robert Garioch offers his own version of what the walk downhill is all about; his Sisyphus, now literally proletarian, gets the stone securely to the top and then,

> houpan the Boss wadna spy him,
> had a wee look at the scenery, feenisht a pie and a
> cheese-piece.

Whit was he thinkin about, that he jist gied the
boulder a wee shove?
Bumpity doun in the corrie gaed whuddran the pitiless
whun stane,
Sisyphus dodderan eftir it, shair of his checque at the
month's end. ("Sisyphus," 1977)

BIBL.: B. Seidensticker and A. Wessels, eds., *Mythos Sisyphos: Texte von Homer bis Günter Kunert* (Leipzig 2001).

G.B.

Skepticism

A doctrine according to which it is impossible to decide the truth or falsity of any proposition. Of the two principal branches into which Hellenistic skepticism is divided, Academic skepticism persisted longer in European culture, whereas Pyrrhonian skepticism was almost totally eclipsed in the Middle Ages. Cicero's authority bears the responsibility for having perpetuated the first by obscuring the second. Deeply marked by the debates between Stoics and Academics over "comprehensive representation," the skepticism passed down by Cicero revolves around the notions of verisimilitude and probability and arrives at an explicit conclusion, the "knowledge of not knowing." Thus, the notion of phenomenon remains foreign to Cicero, and he does not grasp the importance of the suspension of judgment (*epoche*), which for Pyrrhonians constituted the principal remedy for slipping back into dogmatism. In fact, *epoche* indicates the halting of judgment, such that "we neither reject nor affirm a thing" about which there is no certainty. The doctrine of Pyrrho of Elis (ca. 350–ca. 270 BCE) is transmitted especially by texts that Sextus Empiricus (ca. 160–210 CE) redacted five centuries later. There Pyrrhonism is clearly separated from the Neo-academic position and is presented as a philosophy always open to searching and oriented toward an ethical goal, tranquility of the mind, which is freed from the passions produced by the obstinate attachment to the dogmas of the schools.

Among Christian philosophers, Lactantius and Augustine see in Academic skepticism an opportune ally in the polemic against pagan philosophies. In point of fact, Augustine did not know other skeptics besides the Academics, and it is they whom he criticized for falling into self-contradiction. More generally, the ethics of uncertainty and the idea that searching has no end seemed to him incompatible both with the Ciceronian description of wisdom as "the knowledge of things human and divine" and with Christian doctrine. For Trygetius (one of the characters in the *Contra academicos*), "he who lives in error and not in conformity with reason could not be happy. But searching and never finding is like being in error." Augustine therefore completely rejected the Pyrrhonian idea of the suspension of judgment as a condition of tranquility; it even became for him synonymous with anguish (*desperatio veri*) and thus with estrangement from God.

In early Humanism, Florence and Rome were the centers of the renascent interest in the Greek work of Sextus. Giovanni Pico della Mirandola(1463–1494) used it for his polemic against the astrologers, and his nephew Gianfrancesco made use of it to demolish the "pagan" dogmatism of the Aristotelians and of the other philosophical schools. The use of Pyrrhonian tropes (amply displayed and paraphrased in the *Examen vanitatis doctrinae gentium*) was for Pico closely connected to the idea that Christian revelation would be better set up on the ruins of philosophical reason, after the corrosive effect produced by the attacks of skepticism. From then on an understood alliance was consolidated in European culture between skepticism and fideism, which in the 17th century took the name of Christian Pyrrhonism, finding a fervent supporter in Blaise Pascal (1623–1662). Thus the long invective of Henricus Cornelius Agrippa's *De incertitudine et vanitate scientiarum* (1530) counterposed the ignorance of simple believers with the pride of knowledge, considered a "veritable plague."

The accusation of arriving at a de facto skepticism in theology was hurled at Erasmus by Martin Luther in his *De servo arbitrio* (*On the Bondage of the Will,* 1525). Against the humanistic defense of human freedom, the reformer maintained the arguments of a faith undergirded by dogmatic certainties about the truth of predestination: "The Holy Spirit is not a skeptic," he warned, maintaining that the believer ought to nourish solid certainties in this regard. "Indeed, how will he be able to believe in a thing he doubts?" In reality, the Flemish Humanist's *Diatriba de libero arbitrio* (*On Free Will,* 1524) was anything but skeptical. There Erasmus used rational and scriptural arguments to defend the existence of a middle path between Pelagianism and extreme determinism, maintaining a fundamentally Thomist conception of human freedom and responsibility. What could have seemed "skeptical" in Erasmus was, rather, a general attitude of hostility or indifference toward an excessive theological determination to investigate intrinsically controversial subjects. This attitude had found clear expression in his youthful *Praise of Folly,* written as a reaction to the Scholastic theology of the University of Paris: "The variety and obscurity of human affairs is so great that nothing can be known clearly, as was well said by our Academics, the least reckless of all the philosophers." Nevertheless, although he translated Galen's opusculum *De optimo genere docendi,* which is an important source for the knowledge of ancient skepticism, it would be difficult to find in Erasmus skeptical propositions in a technical sense, such as the suspension of judgment or the impossibility of determining the truth of knowing. What was polemically exchanged for skepticism (by Luther) was in reality a profound hostility to investigations that were too exclusively or unilaterally dogmatic, and the affirmation of moderation against theological *rabies*, or attacks, all to the good of the prevalently moral ends that according to Erasmus ought to characterize Christianity. This Humanist idea of a "moderate theology," tied to a firm defense of the value of tolerance in religious disputes, was put to use in Sebastian

Castellio's *De arte dubitandi et confitendi, ignorandi et sciendi* (1563). In this work the Humanist, who defended Michael Servetus against Calvin, considered it permissible not to know things that have not been commanded by God and that are not necessary for knowing Him or for performing one's duty. In Castellio's polemic with Theodore Beza, which culminated in his *De haereticis non puniendis* (1555), it is the arguments of Academic skepticism (not Pyrrhonian) that characterize the debate. Socrates is contrasted with Aristotle and the Peripatetic school, whereas the principles of Academic skepticism are identified in many New Testament passages that warn against judging controversial issues too quickly, issues like those debated by supposed "orthodox" and "heretics."

In the inflamed atmosphere of the religious disputes triggered by the Reformation, the accusation of promoting skepticism ricocheted between Catholics and Protestants. It is in this atmosphere that the first printed editions (in Latin) of Sextus's works appeared: *Pyrrhoniae hypotyposes,* at the hands of the Calvinist Henri Estienne (1562), and *Adversus mathematicos,* edited by the Catholic Gentian Hervet (1569); but it was necessary to wait until 1621 for the *editio princeps* of the Greek text. In their prefaces, the two Humanists highlighted the antidogmatic character of Sextus's arguments and also emphasized their utility from the theological point of view. Nevertheless, though Estienne, adhering to the positions of the Reformation, presented skeptical teaching in terms of moral reform and knowledge, Hervet, ensconced in the cultural atmosphere of the Counter-Reformation, made use of it to stigmatize Protestant positions as fresh examples of dogmatism.

Michel de Montaigne's *Essays* (1580–1588) and especially the *Apologie de Raimond Sebond* disseminated Pyrrhonian doctrines, clearly distinguished from Academic contaminations. The critical analysis of sensible representation, the irremediable contradictions between the philosophical schools on the grand topics of knowledge (God, the soul, immortality, the ontological foundations of reality, the laws of nature, morals, and politics), the more refined tropes such as reciprocity (circular reasoning) and infinite regression, the discussions of phenomena and of the criterion for truth, knowing as a "mixed" outcome of subjectivity and objectivity—these are the grand themes of ancient skepticism that come to life in the *Essays,* marking the beginning of a rather lively and convincing modern version of the "life without dogmas." Furthermore, Montaigne elaborated a new concept of belief, emphasizing its emotional character and giving prominence —in the field of religion—to that particular instinct from above that is divine grace. In spite of these overtures to fideism, the *Essays* presented a disenchanted view of the all-too-human form that religion takes when it is transformed into superstition and intolerant fanaticism.

After Montaigne, the epistemological aspect of skepticism decidedly prevailed over its original ethical connotation. It was above all René Descartes who forged its modern image. In works like *Discours de la méthode* (1637) and especially *Meditationes de prima philosophia* (1641), the arguments of skepticism are taken up as the dialectical test to which knowledge must be subjected to achieve a clearness that is certain precisely because it ends up "indubitable." With Descartes skepticism reached heights that had never been touched by the ancients. In particular, the problem of the existence of the external world (and even of one's own body) was for the first time clearly formulated, which resulted in the crisis of direct realism. At the same time Descartes stressed the unlivability of skepticism in practice, thus limiting it to purely speculative questions and separating it from the ethical ends with which *epoche* was originally connected. Descartes's radicalization of skepticism was actually in the service of a search for a kind of certainty that for him could not be less than absolute: metaphysical certainty. Conversely, 17th-century thinkers who did not share this search for metaphysical clarity also rejected this kind of exaggerated skepticism, instead achieving a compromise between probable certainty and moderate doubt, not the artificial doubt of Descartes. In Marin Mersenne and Pierre Gassendi this ideal took the form of a clear distinction between scientific knowledge (limited to appearances) and metaphysical knowledge of the essences of substances. Thus reemerged the probabilistic approach that Descartes had programmatically ruled out. It was made use of in the scientific milieu of the Royal Society (particularly Robert Boyle), and in latitudinarian ecclesiastical circles (Chillingworth and the Tew Circle), all interested in graduating the various forms of certainty depending on circumstances and context. Different again was the case of French "erudite libertines" in the first half of the 17th century. With them doubt (more Academic in Pierre Charron, more Pyrrhonian in La Mothe Le Vayer) had a direct effect on all kinds of beliefs: moral, cultural, historical, and even religious. Although Charron's Stoic critique differed from Le Vayer's philosophical indifference, it was nevertheless libertine circles that affirmed the corrosive and antireligious style of skepticism that, as a synonym for unbelief, had become a commonplace.

The "dogmatics" against whom the *Dictionnaire historique et critique* (1696–1701) was aimed were above all Descartes and the Cartesians, whose intellectual criterion of certainty Pierre Bayle challenged as a tool for accessing indubitable truths—although he also targeted Christian theologians of the Reformation and Counter-Reformation. Bayle pointed out that the new Newtonian science could easily coexist with a profession of antimetaphysical and antitheological skepticism, just as ethics and politics could do without dogmatic convictions. "Only religion has something to fear from Pyrrhonism," since its beliefs require certainty and firm conviction; ultimately, Arcesilaus would have been "a thousand times harder on our theologians than he was on the dogmatic philosophers of ancient Greece" ("Pyrrhon" rem. B).

Traditionally considered a golden age of *raison,* the Enlightenment was nevertheless marked by a profound awareness of the limits of human knowledge. It was Locke and Newton who steered Enlightenment thought in this sphere as well. In Voltaire, the Lockean theme of the "limits of the human mind" (which cannot penetrate to the first principles) was joined with Newton's finalistic vision of the grand divine architect who orders the world according to his will and intelligence. Diderot affirmed a clear distinction between two different kinds of doubt. "Make a Pyrrhonian become sincere and you'll have a skeptic": thus the philosophe reacted both to Cartesian exaggerations of doubt and to the fideistic temptations of "semi-skepticism," typical of the "weak minds" that claim to safeguard such "privileged notions" as those of religion. The necessity of overcoming the paradoxes of skepticism by incorporating them into an immaterialist view (already delineated by Bayle) was addressed by an author not unknown to Diderot: George Berkeley, who identified the cause of skepticism in dogmatic materialism. But it was above all David Hume who made extensive use of skeptical themes: in a radical or Pyrrhonian form in his *Treatise* (1739–1740), more moderate and Academic in his *First Enquiry* (1748). The "Pyrrhonian crisis" of the *Treatise* assails both rational knowledge and the sensible world, even if its doubt is accompanied by the awareness that nature is always too strong to submit to the dictates of reasoning, no matter how subtle. But even when he draws closer to the authentic spirit of the skeptical position, Hume gives it an original and innovative reading. Such is the case in the decisive realm of beliefs, among which causal inferences stand out. The drive to go "beyond the impressions of our senses" (to the point of inquiring about "existences and objects, which we do not see or feel") is manifested, according to Hume, not only in the dogmatic formulations of the metaphysicians, but even more so in the common beliefs of ordinary life, such as the belief in the effective power of causes or the uniform course of nature, or the opinion that external objects exist. Hume pushed his critique to the point of attacking two strongholds that had theretofore remained more or less intact: the idea of "necessary connection," on which the belief in the "power and efficacy of causes" is based, and "the supposition that the future resembles the past," which is the basis for induction. It was instead in *An Enquiry concerning Human Understanding* that he laid the foundation for overcoming the most destructive doubt: the "more *mitigated* skepticism or *academical* philosophy" is characterized by the "limitation of our enquiries to such subjects as are best adapted to the narrow capacity of human understanding," in addition to the preference accorded to the probabilistic approach. This form of "mitigated skepticism," then, is for Hume a remedy both to the "illusion" of which dogmatic philosophies are prisoners and to the "stupidity" that permeates the common way of thinking.

"Hume is perhaps the subtlest of all the skeptics, and without dispute the most important for the influence that the skeptical method can have on the revival of a well-grounded examination of reason": thus in his *Critique of Pure Reason* (1781–1787) did Immanuel Kant recognize the importance of skepticism as a "preliminary exercise" for the "critique of the intellect." Attentively describing the conflict of opposed dogmatisms (theism and atheism, determinism and freedom, and so on), he criticized the supporters of orthodoxy for claiming to halt conflict with arguments that actually constituted a "blinding" and spread "prejudices." In an ideal reconstruction of the history of pure reason, its first step, its childhood, is represented by dogmatism, but its second, decisive step is taken by the skeptic. In this view Kant praises Hume's concerted attempt to "undermine, with laboriously devised difficulties," even "consoling and useful" convictions, such as the one that "rational speculation" suffices "for conceiving and definitively affirming a supreme Being." It remained clear for Kant, however, that a "skeptical satisfaction of reason at variance with itself" was not possible and that a third step, beyond simple criticism, was instead necessary. Indeed, "critique" subjects not only "the facts of reason" to examination but "reason itself" in its entire capacity for a priori knowledge, thereby precisely describing its limits. Skepticism thus represented for Kant a temporary phase: in the course of its "dogmatic wanderings" doubt could offer a "place of rest," but it could not in any way constitute "a habitat fit for stable residence."

Unlike critiques such as those of Karl L. Reinhold and Salomon Maimon, who considered Kant a skeptic for having maintained the unknowability of *noumena,* the attitude of Georg W. F. Hegel aimed instead to recover the systematic aspect of doubt. In his short work *The Relationship of Skepticism to Philosophy* (1802), he portrayed skepsis as "the negative side of knowledge of the Absolute, which immediately presupposes reason as the positive side." It is therefore the first step toward philosophy. As the antithesis of Stoicism, skepsis embodies in the *Phenomenology of Spirit* (1807) one of the forms in which self-consciousness affirms "its own freedom": "skeptical self-consciousness is the ataraxia of thinking one's self." Since it is "conscious and universal negativity," wrote Hegel in his *Lectures on the History of Philosophy* (ca. 1820s; publ. posthumously), doubt must be considered not as "the most dangerous adversary of philosophy" but as the moment that does not deny either the changeability of things or the necessity of the thinking consciousness.

To these views Søren Kierkegaard counterposed a quite individual interpretation, centered on the existential categories of self-interest, risk, and paradox. This interpretation is contained above all in two works published under the pseudonym Joannes Climacus: *De omnibus dubitandum est* (1842–1843) and *Philosophical Fragments* (1844). In the first (whose title is taken from Descartes's *Principia philosophiae*), the Danish philosopher enunciates three propositions: "1) Philosophy begins with doubt; 2) It is necessary to have doubted to practice philosophy; 3) Modern philosophy begins with doubt." In the case of the moderns, this is "a speculative and comprehensive doubt, not at all easy in practice" and such that he who embraces it frees himself with difficulty ("falls victim to his own knowledge"). Rejecting Hegel's "universal constitutive doubt," Kierkegaard showed himself instead to be interested in the skepticism of Pyrrho and Sextus, in which he found the idea that *epoche* was a matter of will and, like faith, expressed an act of freedom. Unlike reflection, which is disinterested, doubt embodies for Kierkegaard "a form superior to all objective reasoning," since it contains something more, which is "self-interest or -consciousness." Thus, skepticism constituted for him "the introduction to the highest form of life," in the end unassailable by modern philosophy and its "disinterested systematic knowledge." Actually, for the author of *Fragments,* not even "suspension" constituted a definitive stage, since Climacus ended up recommending faith, as long as it was recognized (as by the skeptics) to be a rationally baseless leap.

Although positivism and then neopositivism established the model of science as a philosophical paradigm, nevertheless the problem of certainty and the criterion for truth, and thus the challenge of skepticism, continued to capture the attention of some of the greatest thinkers of the 20th century. Among these the first to be mentioned must be Bertrand Russell, the author of (inter alia) *Skeptical Essays* (1928) and *Our Knowledge of the External World* (1914), in which the problem of skepticism is explicitly taken up: how is the certainty of knowledge possible, since we are acquainted with our own ideas directly but only indirectly with their origin in the outside world? His theory distinguished between sense data ("primitive knowledge" or "knowledge by acquaintance"), on the one hand, and inferences or derived knowledge (or knowledge "by description"), on the other; Russell intended to provide a conclusive response to the challenge of skepticism, asserting that foundational knowledge cannot be erroneous. He was, however, forced to admit a certain amount, however weak, of ineradicable doubt: once inference comes into play, error immediately becomes possible. The very notion of "data" ends up being a rather borderline concept, which at best "we can approach asymptotically."

To the problems that skepticism poses in the form of phenomenalism (according to which it makes no sense to talk about an external object, since the only things with which we are acquainted are our interior sense perceptions), Ludwig Wittgenstein replied in his *Philosophical Investigations* (1953) with his famous "Private Language Argument." Therein he demonstrated that the skeptical idea, according to which each of us is encapsulated in the circle of his or her own ideas, actually makes no sense from the point of view of language. For language, even in the case of the most immediate sense perceptions, is always public and verifiable by other speakers. In *On Certainty* (1969) the Austrian philosopher developed an even more decisive refutation of skepticism that was based on the idea that total and omni-comprehensive doubt (like the exaggerated doubt of Descartes) is devoid of meaning: "A doubt that doubted everything would not be a doubt"; "A doubt without an end is not even a doubt."

That the account with skepticism remains open, however, was emphasized by Avrum Stroll and Richard H. Popkin, the greatest historian of modern skepticism (as Mario Dal Pra was for ancient skepticism): "The fact that skepticism has had such a long and lively career suggests that it must have real substance, and that the commonsense view, when scrutinized, is less compelling than it seems. The skeptic is urging this scrutiny, asking that we look deep into and beyond the obvious" (2002, 36).

BIBL.: Luciano Floridi, *Sextus Empiricus: The Transmission and Recovery of Pyrrhonism* (Oxford 2002). John Christian Laursen, *The Politics of Skepticism in the Ancients: Montaigne, Hume, and Kant* (New York 1992). José R. Maia Neto, *The Christianization of Pyrrhonism: Scepticism and Faith in Pascal, Kierkegaard, and Shestov* (Boston 1995). Pierre-François Moreau, ed., *Le scepticisme au XVIe et au XVIIe* siècle (Paris 2001). Gianni Paganini, ed., *The Return of Scepticism: From Hobbes and Descartes to Bayle* (Boston 2003) and Paganini, *Skepsis: Le débat des modernes sur le scepticisme* (Paris 2008). Gianni Paganini and José R. Maia Neto, eds., *Renaissance Scepticisms* (Dordrecht 2008). Richard H. Popkin, *The History of Scepticism: From Savonarola to Bayle* (Oxford 2003). Richard H. Popkin and Avrum Stroll, *Skeptical Philosophy for Everyone* (Amherst, N.Y., 2002).

G.PA.

Translated by Patrick Baker

Slavery

The study of slavery from classical antiquity to the present is the last bastion of Whig history. The general public takes for granted that every time slavery gives way to another form of labor, progress has been made. Even in academe, where progress now has the status of myth, the history of slavery, more than any other historical subject, allows its investigators a moral investment in their task. No one in or out of academe can promote the legalization of slavery without incurring social censure.

Nevertheless, a wide gulf separates popular perceptions from academic treatments of slavery in the classical world. For most of the 20th century, ancient Greece and Rome were exempted from modern dictates of propriety that deplore making light of human bondage. The moviegoing public who paid to watch the aquatic film star Esther Williams in the musical *Jupiter's Darling* (1955) were likely not offended by a blond Goth captive romancing a blond slave girl at a Roman slave auction to the tune "If This Be Slavery, I Don't Want to Be Free." Whether musical comedy or historical epic, made in Hollywood or in Europe, films reflect a widespread perception that ancient slavery was pervasive, could ensnare anyone regardless of skin color, often involved sexual as well as domestic service, and did not always entail a harsher life than a poor free person's in the same period. In this the public happens to be mostly right.

In movies set in the classical period, however, historical accuracy also happens to be beside the point. What matters more is resonance. This is not to say that classical antiquity has survived in the imagination of the West because subsequent generations understood the societies and cultures of Greece and Rome in all their complexity. On the contrary, for as long as people of Europe and the Americas have felt nostalgic for classical antiquity—a sentiment that emerged in the late 8th century, when Charlemagne dusted off the long-unused title of emperor in the West—they have been selective in their memories of it. Since then, philosophers, theologians, historians, political theorists, novelists, filmmakers, and artists of all kinds have picked through Greek and Roman history for models of individual and collective behavior that they felt their contemporaries should either aspire to or avoid. In either case, inconvenient truths have always been left out.

Slavery figures prominently among the inconvenient aspects of the ancient world that clash with the stature that Athens and Rome have enjoyed as the progenitors of republican virtue. Likewise, until relatively recently, slavery—from chattel slavery to indentured servitude to sex trafficking—has not been a vital feature whose absence or presence indicates a country's position on the scale of more or less admirable systems of government. In more parts of the world than many people would like to admit, the practice of slavery is still not a civic barometer. As slave societies of the past, classical Greece and Rome have traditionally enjoyed almost complete immunity from the censure of posterity. Drawing on ancient Greek democracy and Roman republicanism for inspiration, the founding fathers of the United States, most of whom learned Latin and Greek at school, ignored classical slavery or considered it to be incidental to the value they otherwise found in the works of Cicero and Livy. Believing themselves to be enlightened men, George Washington, Thomas Jefferson, and the other statesmen of the early American republic viewed slavery as an evil that would eventually wither away. Until then, it had to be endured. They took comfort in the belief that over time and as a matter of course, progress would improve the condition of the slave as well as that of all free men in the newly constituted United States.

Christian reformers, antiquarians, and radical economists in the 18th and 19th centuries shared the founding fathers' belief, but they turned slavery into an object of study. Christian reformers in Britain and the United States exhorted their coreligionists to support the abolition of the international slave trade by aligning the practice with pre-Christian morality. Antiquarian historians both for and against slavery studied Latin and Greek texts for ammunition in debates over slavery's future. Critics of capitalism regarded slavery as the precursor of serfdom and wage labor. Karl Marx assigned modern slavery an important role in the technological transformation of the European economy but distinguished it from the ancient system. The modern slave's role in the mode of production differed from that of the ancient slave: the former was a proletarian; the latter was not. For or against it, commentators all viewed slavery as a stage in human society, beyond which humanity would progress when the moral or economic conditions were right.

Once the American Civil War brought an end to slavery in North America, the subject of slavery was demobilized until after World War II, when belligerents in the Cold War drafted it once again into service. Scholars on both sides of the ideological divide argued over what ended ancient and modern slavery. On the side of Western liberalism, the eminent Anglo-American classicist Moses I. Finley rejected the primacy of the means of production in favor of social causes to explain the transition from slavery to serfdom and onward to capitalism. The British scholar G. E. M. de Ste. Croix downplayed the role of social and cultural factors. Using class analysis to study the ancient economy, he supported Marx's idea that each economic system contains the seeds of its own demise. In the West, Finley's approach to the study of slavery helped prepare the ground for the burgeoning disciplines of social history and cultural history; the Marxist school of history may be credited with inserting the concept of class into standard accounts of slavery's modern and premodern history.

As ideologically driven as it often has been, the polemical debate between the proponents of Western liberalism and Marxism has at least brought the distinctions between ancient and modern slavery into sharp focus. Beyond the primitive violence inherent in both systems, ancient slavery differed from the modern in three important respects. First, it was not unusual for Greek and Roman slaves to be literate. Elite owners put slaves to work as scribes, record keepers, and managers, unlike slave masters in the southern United States, who regarded literacy among slaves as a threat to owners' domination. Second, in contrast to slave societies in the Americas, Greek and Roman slaves had a reasonable hope of attaining free status before dying. Manumission, the legal act of releasing a slave from bondage, could come as a reward for a life of service or, in the Christian period, as a master's pious act of expiation. The Greek city-states forbade freed slaves from participating in political life, but the only bar that Romans placed against freed slaves was at the Senate door. Descendants of freed Roman slaves blended into the free population without impediment; conditions in the United States proved more ambivalent.

Third, in contrast to the modern period, no one actively opposed slavery in premodern times. Throughout history, the wretched condition of slaves has always aroused pity in people with the capacity for compassion. And at least as far back as the ancient Greeks there have been individuals who believed that all human beings were born free by nature. Before the modern period, however, very few people linked—at least in writing—the belief that humans are by nature free to the proposition that slavery was morally wrong. The early Christians believed that although God had created all human beings equally free, humanity's sinful nature made slavery a penalty necessary to endure. The jurists of the late Roman Empire enshrined this belief in the multivolume collection of imperial legislation and legal opinions known formally as the Body of Civil Law (*Corpus iuris civilis*) but informally as Roman law.

Legitimized through its associations with Rome and

Roman law in particular, slavery outlasted the Roman Empire in the West. At no point between the 5th and the 15th centuries did the sale and possession of slaves cease along the northern coastline of the Mediterranean Sea, although it had died out north of the Alps by 1100. The business of slave trading became as complicated as the many other kinds of economic exchanges taking place in the reinvigorated economy of medieval Europe. Twelfth-century jurists in the merchant cities of Italy and southern France turned to Roman law for formulae to safeguard the financial interests of slave buyers and sellers, protect the fiscal rights of governments to collect duty on imported slaves, and ensure that only the right people were being enslaved.

The danger of enslavement had become so prevalent in the Mediterranean world that by the 13th and 14th centuries the people of what is today Western Europe—distinguishing themselves from others in this context mostly by their obedience to the pope—stood inside a circle that protected them by law from enslavement. Greeks, Serbs (but not Bosnians), Albanians, Bulgarians (but not Hungarians), Russians, Tatars, Circassians, Corsicans, Sardinians, Turks, and all Muslims stood outside the circle and were lawfully held as slaves in Italy, southern France, and the Iberian Peninsula. In contrast, the Greeks and Romans had had no use for circles, being willing to enslave anyone, including each other. It was only in the 17th century that the Iberians and the English reversed tactics, by drawing a circle around people of African descent and considering everyone outside the circle to be legally free. Much of the motivation to draw ethno-religious circles lay at first in the need to protect people from enslavement. Later on, it became the preferred strategy to justify it.

The change over centuries in how slavery related to ancestry may have something to do with why most people living in Europe and the United States are under the mistaken impression that slavery in Europe died out not long after the Roman Empire, only to be revived in the late 15th century, when Iberian vessels sailed down the West African coast in search of new goods. The responsibility for this view belongs in large part to early 20th-century medieval historians, whose assertions that serfdom supplanted slavery derived from their apparent belief that what was true of a small area in northeastern France during the Middle Ages held true for the rest of the continent. But the 19th-century concept of race and the template of slavery in the United States are so deeply connected, not just in popular culture but also in scholarly debates about slavery, that it often seems as though the absence of black African slaves has, until very recently, been taken to mean the absence of slaves.

By the end of the Middle Ages, slavery had become so entrenched in Western culture that theologians, philosophers, and political theorists in the early modern and modern periods had no trouble finding texts, ranging from Aristotle to Roman law, to justify the practice of slavery. Those few who looked to the past for weapons against it had a harder time. Even both books of the Bible offered more support for slavery than against it. In a famous debate over the treatment of New World natives in Spanish colonies, held in Vallolidid, Spain, in 1550, the Dominican friar and missionary Bartolomé de las Casas challenged Bishop Juan Ginés de Sepúlveda's use of Aristotle to defend the enslavement of native peoples. Rather than refute the Greek philosopher's belief that some humans are born slaves, Las Casas insisted that the Indians were not the kind of people Aristotle had in mind. Although Las Casas never rejected slavery outright, his writings about the ill treatment endured by indigenous peoples of the Western Hemisphere furnished future generations searching for arguments against slavery with better material.

When opponents first developed rationales against slavery, their arguments focused on the contemporary trade and on Africans and their descendants. The prevalence of the danger of enslavement for Europeans gradually receded from historical memory. Classical slavery was a benign issue from then on. To this day, Roman slaves are taken as figures of fun; American kitsch has even embraced the dark side of Roman and Greek culture in Caesar's Palace in Las Vegas. The Greeks' and the Romans' enslavement of people who today are considered European and even of people who may yet be considered European occurred too far in the past to hold much emotional meaning for those raised in countries dominated by European culture. Would the public's sensitivity to issues of slavery extend chronologically back to Rome and Greece if the knowledge came into common currency that slavery and slave trading in Europe lasted through the Middle Ages and on to the Middle Passage? Probably not.

Erasing from time lines the long hiatus between classical and modern slavery would not make Zero Mostel's Pseudolus, the scheming slave in *A Funny Thing Happened on the Way to the Forum* (1966), less funny. Nor should it invite invidious comparisons between the treatment of enslaved people from Europe and that of African slaves in the southern United States. Instead, the recovery of collective memory in this instance might undermine the general sense of detachment in the West from the ongoing problem of slavery in many parts of the world. No abolition movement ended the enslavement of Europeans or, by Europeans, of everyone except those of African ancestry. But recognition that slavery in Europe did not end with the Roman Empire should render the sense of entitlement to liberty that undergirds Western liberalism vulnerable to historical contingency.

BIBL.: Robin Blackburn, *The Making of New World Slavery: From the Baroque to the Modern, 1492–1800* (London 1998). K. R. Bradley, *Slavery and Society at Rome* (Cambridge 1994). David Brion Davis, *Inhuman Bondage: The Rise and Fall of Slavery in the New World* (New York 2006). G. E. M. de Ste. Croix, *Class Struggle in the Ancient Greek World from the Archaic Age to the Arab Conquests* (London 1981). Moses I. Finley, *Ancient Slavery and Modern Ideology* (1980; repr. New York 1998). Orlando Patterson, *Slavery and Social Death: A*

Comparative Study (Cambridge, Mass., 1982). Alan Watson, *Roman Slave Law* (Baltimore 1987). S.MC.

Soane, John

Humbly born as the son of a bricklayer, Sir John Soane (1753–1837) rose to be head of the architectural profession in England, was appointed professor of architecture at the Royal Academy in 1806, and was knighted by William IV in 1831. His works include numerous country houses, government buildings, and the Bank of England. A passionate believer in the continuing vitality of the architectural language of ancient Greece and Rome, he claimed (referring to the column order) that "art cannot go beyond the Corinthian."

He learned from his study of French theory that each building should have an appropriate character and should express its purpose. This was part of the hierarchical system of ancien régime France, which rose, architecturally, from a simplified Doric construction in timber, suitable for a garden building, to the Corinthian order, fit for the palace of the monarch. Soane often hinted at the classical orders with incised lines that he called "sunk mouldings," so that some of his work has an understated appearance. This approach has made his style appealing to late 20th- and 21st-century architects who are normally seen as modernist.

Trained from 1768 by the younger George Dance, an inventive classical architect, Soane entered the recently founded Royal Academy in 1771 and was taken up by its leading architect, Sir William Chambers, thanks to whose help he won the Gold Medal in 1776 with a design for a triumphal bridge. This gave him funding to study ancient architecture in Italy, following the pattern that Chambers had adopted from the French Royal Academy of Architecture. Soane's Grand Tour of 1778–1780 was the making of his entire career, as he was always to acknowledge, for it was in Rome that he met his most important future patrons, including Thomas Pitt, Philip Yorke, and the bishop of Deny.

In 1784 he married Elizabeth Smith, through whom, on her uncle's death in 1790, he had access to a large fortune; this, added to the considerable fruits of his own extensive architectural practice, enabled him to form a valuable library and collection of antiquities. These were intended to play a role in improving the skills of modern architects, and for that purpose he built Pitzhanger Manor, Baling (1800–1803), to help educate his own two sons in architecture. When this experiment failed, he developed No. 13, Lincoln's Inn Fields, London, from 1808 until 1824, leaving it on his death as a museum for "the study of Architecture and the Allied Arts." He described "those fanciful effects that constitute the poetry of Architecture" in the Breakfast Parlour (1812) in Sir John Soane's Museum (still open today), with its floating pendentive dome.

Similar spaces recurred in his most important building, the Bank of England, on which he worked from 1788 to 1833 during its expansion to help pay for the Revolutionary and Napoleonic Wars. It was through the backing of the younger William Pitt, cousin of his friend Thomas Pitt, that he helped gain this commission. Soane's Dulwich Picture Gallery (1811–1814), the first public art gallery in England, featured top-lighting, which was widely influential.

Soane had a prickly personality and even a persecution complex, perhaps caused by his modest upbringing but also influenced by his reading of Rousseau's self-absorbed *Confessions*. He wrote numerous books on his own buildings, but his idiosyncratic style found few significant imitators.

BIBL.: Gillian Darley, *John Soane: An Accidental Romantic* (New Haven 1999). Pierre du Prey, *John Soane: The Making of an Architect* (Chicago 1982). Margaret Richardson and Mary-Anne Stevens, eds., *John Soane: Master of Space and Light* (London 1999). David Watkin, *Sir John Soane: Enlightenment Thought and the Royal Academy Lectures* (Cambridge 1996).
D.W.

Socrates

Already a local celebrity in his lifetime, the Athenian philosopher Socrates (ca. 470–399 BCE) was given permanent importance by his death—he was executed by his own city for religious nonconformity and fomenting moral corruption in the young—and by his pupils' posthumous use of him as a spokesman for philosophical truth. From the beginning he was a figure of controversy. Condemnation and satire continued throughout antiquity side by side with lavish praise from his admirers, though even they argued over the true nature of his legacy and who best represented it. It is in large part this ambivalence in the ancient record that has given Socrates his continuing life, as perhaps the best of the ancients to think with and argue over.

As a thinker, Socrates came to be remembered both for his place in the history of philosophy and for his distinctive method. In influential portrayals by his younger contemporaries Plato and Xenophon he became the man who first identified the true essence of *philosophia* as being the pursuit of moral excellence and the good life rather than the acquisition of knowledge about nature: not only "calling philosophy down from the heavens" (Cicero, *Tusculan Disputations* 5.4.10) but also making himself the shared ancestor of Platonists, Peripatetics, Stoics, Cynics, and even—on an alternative interpretation of his method and legacy—Skeptics. From Hellenistic times onward he has thus been emblematic of ancient (pagan) philosophy and of philosophy more generally, as well as being taken to have marked a great turning point in the development of thought. In the former, emblematic role he has been of particular interest, from the 2nd century CE onward, to Christian thinkers concerned about determining the relationship between pagan and Christian wisdom. Both their interest and their caution have been intensified by a constantly tempting, and regularly revisited, comparison of Socrates to Christ—also martyred by the State, also commemorated in his pupils' rather than his own words, also through their commemoration the founder of a durable spiritual movement. Erasmus' "Saint Socrates, pray for us!" in his *Godly Feast* (*Colloquies* 16)—a comment on Socrates' deference to the will of heaven—and his enrollment of Socrates along with Christ as one of "Alcibiades' Sileni" (individuals in whom a contemptible outer appearance gives no clue as to inner worth, *Adages* 3.3.1) are particularly celebrated instances of the general trend. The perception of Socrates as a turning point has produced both positive and negative variants: on the one hand, Hegel's account of Socrates ushering in the transition from tradition (*Sittlichkeit*) to real morality (*Moralität*); on the other, Nietzsche's depiction of the destruction of tragedy as the "Cyclops gaze" of Socrates' new optimistic rationality swept away older and better modes of awareness.

In point of distinctive method, again because of variations in the ancient depictions, Socrates has been commemorated both as an inspiring moral preacher, urging high-minded antimaterialism, and as a constant critical questioner, whose wisdom resided in his acknowledgment of his own ignorance. As instructive extremes, one can contrast the near-Cynic ascetic Socrates of medieval Arabic and Jewish wisdom literature with Kierkegaard's embodiment of "infinite absolute negativity"; or, in visual depiction, the heaven-pointing preacher of David's *Socrates at the Moment of Taking the Hemlock* (1787) with the pungent dialectician of Raphael's *School of Athens* (1510). The insistence on the necessity of unremitting self-examination in pursuit of true self-knowledge, attached to Socrates by Plato, can easily be made to fit with either understanding.

Among philosophical interpreters, since the early 19th century a central issue has often been seen in the "Socratic question" (or "problem"): the recurring challenge to extricate a real, historical Socrates with philosophical views identifiably distinct from those of his first commemorators (above all, Plato). Consensus is as far away as ever, as scholars remake the philosophical Socrates in the light of their own views of the history of thought and their own moral and philosophical identities: witness the tentative, fallibilist Socrates of Karl Popper's *Open Society* (1945), and the cheek-turning but undeceptive ironist of Gregory Vlastos' *Socrates* (1991), the most influential recent contribution.

In political reflection there has been recurrent argument over how to understand Socrates' execution. Was it a just measure of self-defense, taken against a confessed enemy of democracy? A condemnation of democracy, showing to what depths of injustice the mob can sink when not suitably restrained? A lesson in the dangers of suppressing free speech and nonconformist criticism? Or, as Hegel interpreted it, is it a case of the destructive clash of irreconcilable but equally justified outlooks? Such questions were hotly debated in the 18th century, when opinions were particularly sharply divided between the antirepublican perception of Socrates' death as proof of the danger of mob rule (e.g., Beval and Thorneycroft's *Socrates Triumphant,* 1716; or William Mitford's *History of Greece,* 1784–1816), and the democratic conviction that he fully deserved his fate, represented most notably in the essays of N. Fréret (*Observations,* 1736) and L. Dreisig (*Epistle on the Justice of Socrates' Condemnation,* 1738). They returned to prominence in the 20th century, when the democratic Socrates of Karl Popper's *Open Society* was to be contrasted with the oligarchic fellow traveler of I. F. Stone's *Trial of Socrates* (1988), and when Socrates' name and fate were regularly invoked in the 1950s and 1960s in debates over civil disobedience, freedom of opinion, and the right to dissent.

Thanks on the one hand to Plato's *Symposium* and *Phaedrus* (with lesser input from Xenophon's *Symposium* and *Memorabilia*) and on the other to anecdotes about his womenfolk, Socrates has also claimed a regular place in discussions of sex and sexuality. Here too there is disagreement over what he can be made to stand for. On one reading—popular especially in the 17th and 18th centuries and embodied in visual and operatic as well as in verbal form—he is the stereotypic henpecked intellectual, roughly treated by one or even two termagant wives. Examples include Niccolò Minato's *The Patience of Socrates* (1680), set to music successively by Antonio Draghi, Georg Philipp Telemann, Antonio Caldara, and Francisco de Almeida; and Otto van Veen's 1607 engraving of the drenching by Xanthippe, done to illustrate the Horatian maxim "Patience conquers misfortunes." On another reading Socrates appears as an expert tutor in affairs of the heart, steering impressionable youths—particularly the incipiently dissolute Alcibiades—to a sounder understanding of love: J.-B. Regnault's *Socrates Snatching Alcibiades from the Embrace of Sensuality* (1785, 1791) is just one example of a mass of 18th- and 19th-century paintings on this theme; in textual form, it can be seen in the *Alcibiades* of Marmontel's *Moral Tales* (1755). On yet another reading, particularly fashionable in the 19th and 20th centuries, Socrates can be made into an inspiring example or a polemical weapon in the exploration of homosexual self-understanding and the battle for homosexual rights. Symptomatic of this trend is Magnus Hirschfeld's decision to entitle his first campaigning work *Sappho and Socrates* (1896).

Socrates' personal moral example, too, has been felt to operate on a range of different levels. His trial and death (in Plato's portrayal in *Apology* and *Phaedo*) made him a model of principled dedication to a high cause, and of steadfastness in the face of persecution to the point of martyrdom. A more everyday form of patience was shown in his dealings with his wife or wives. Other aspects of his lifestyle—those made most of in the Cynic tradition—presented him as exemplary of the simple life and of material self-denial. His military career (sketched in Plato's *Symposium*) allowed him to be lauded as a war hero: straightforwardly in 18th- and 19th-century visual depictions, such as those of Antonio Canova (1797) and P. V. Basin (1828); with a cynical modern twist in Georg Kaiser's *Alcibiades Saved* (1919) and Bertolt Brecht's *Socrates Wounded* (1938). Finally, his fascinating but mysterious personal guardian spirit (*daimonion*), repeatedly reinterpreted over the centuries, made him into a special case revealing the possibilities of contact between human intelligence and that of higher powers.

Visual representation of Socrates has tended to concentrate on a limited number of themes, over and above portraits and the various symbolic groups in which he can be included. Scenes in the death cell (before, during, or after the fatal moment) are by far the most common, as well as the most liable to Christianizing elements. But Socrates and Alcibiades, the drenching by Xanthippe, and Socrates with his mirror (a concretization of the self-knowledge theme) are popular choices too. Socrates in battle, Socrates in court, and Socrates with his *daimonion* are also found, though more rarely. His distinctively and paradoxically ugly facial features, embodied in varying degrees in ancient portrait sculptures and made a topic of in antiquity by Plato and Xenophon (and more recently by physiognomonic writers and by Nietzsche), are sometimes emphasized and sometimes not.

When all forms of representation—musical and dramatic, as well as textual and visual—are taken together, Socrates emerges as by a long way the most diversely portrayed and multifariously contested of all ancient intellectuals. He may even be among the most diversely represented and appropriated of all figures from antiquity in any category. In the face of this purposeful variety, the philosophical search for the "real" Socrates, initiated in 18th-century scholarship and still going strong, seems less central than has sometimes been assumed.

BIBL.: M. B. Trapp, ed., *Socrates from Antiquity to the Enlightenment* (Aldershot 2007) and *Socrates in the Nineteenth and Twentieth Centuries* (Aldershot 2007). M.B.T.

Sophocles

Greek tragedian (ca. 496–406/405 BCE). Seven of his tragedies are extant in a complete state: *Oedipus the King (Oedipus Tyrannus* or *Oedipus Rex*), *Oedipus at Colonus, Antigone, Electra, The Trachinian Women* (*Trachiniae*), *Ajax,* and *Philoctetes.* Indomitable, inexorable, ruthless, excessive, their protagonists—Oedipus, his daughter Antigone, Electra, Heracles, Ajax, Philoctetes—compose an image of the "Sophoclean hero." The challenge they present to ideas of what is normal and reasonable has inspired artists, thinkers, and performers both ancient and modern to refashion them and their stories again and again.

Most notable are Oedipus and Antigone: it is through the three "Theban plays" that they dominate, *Antigone, Oedipus the King,* and *Oedipus at Colonus,* that Sophocles has had his greatest significance for Western culture and beyond. Aristotle prized *Oedipus the King* as the model for all tragic drama, and from the Renaissance onward the influence of his *Poetics* established this as conventional wisdom. An alternative preference arose ca. 1800 for *Antigone,* an elevation in status vigorously promoted by the philosopher G. W. F. Hegel and others. A century later Sigmund Freud gave new impetus to the story of Oedipus by claiming it as the master myth for psychoanalysis. Meanwhile, *Antigone* has provided a continuing focus for debates about politics, idealism, psychology, gender, sexuality, mourning, and death. In this the protagonist has shared the limelight with the other powerful daughter and sister figure created by Sophocles in the play named after her, *Electra.*

The surviving plays were first printed by Aldus Manutius in Venice in 1502. Later that century Sir Philip Sidney praised Sophocles as one of "the great Captaines of Sweete poesie," but for English readers without Greek (or Italian) access was limited until the late 18th century, when Thomas Francklin produced a complete version of "the Shakespeare of antiquity" (1759). Few translations enjoy more than half a century of shelf life, but exceptions must be made for the difficult but magnificent German versions of *Oedipus the King* and *Antigone* by Friedrich Hölderlin (1804), and Ezra Pound's crazed *Women of Trachis* (1956) and (with Rudd Fleming) *Electra* (1989).

The history of appropriating Sophocles for modern performance begins with the staging of *Oedipus the King* in an Italian translation at Palladio's Teatro Olimpico at Vicenza in 1585. Other significant moments include versions of *Oedipus* by Pierre Corneille (1659), John Dryden and Nathaniel Lee (1679), and Voltaire (1718). We can see their difficulties with those features of Sophocles' play that Aristotle's praise for its formal achievement serves to mask: disturbing questions of justice, blame, responsibility, and agency; the horror of parricide and incest; self-ignorance and self-punishment. More recent landmarks in the history of *Oedipus* onstage are the French version starring Jean Mounet-Sully, which opened in 1881, and the contrastingly turbulent production by the Austrian director Max Reinhardt that shook British audiences in 1912.

Whether designed for performance or not, the translation or adaptation of Greek tragedies has always had a political aspect. Robert Garnier's *Antigone* (1580, after Sophocles and Seneca, with additional help from Statius) addressed the civil and religious strife in contemporary France. Similarly, a royalist version of *Electra* by Christopher Wase appeared in 1649, immediately after the execution of Charles I. In recent years *Electra* has spoken vividly to communities with intimate knowledge of internecine bloodshed (a 1992 production in Derry, Northern Ireland, e.g., directed by Deborah Warner). From 1800 onward *Antigone* has also proved particularly evocative in politically troubled contexts. Notable versions have included Jean Anouilh's during the German occupation of France (1944), Bertolt Brecht's restaging of Hölderlin's translation in postwar Europe (1948), Athol Fugard's *The Island* in apartheid South Africa (1973), Tom Paulin's *The Riot Act* (1984), and Seamus Heaney's *The Burial at Thebes* (2004). *Philoctetes* too has been amenable to political readings and rewritings, by the (then East) German dramatist Heiner Müller (1968) and by Heaney in *The Cure at Troy* (1991), for the Irish Field Day theater company.

The plays have also inspired reenactment through music and dance. There have been operatic versions of *Antigone* by Arthur Honneger (1927) and Carl Orff (1949) and of *Oedipus Rex* by Igor Stravinsky (1927) and George Enescu (1936). Particularly significant for its effect on the larger cultural sense of what "Greek tragedy" stands for were the shocking first performances of Richard Strauss's *Elektra* (1909), in the version by Hugo von Hofmannsthal (1903). As for dance, Martha Graham's *Night Journey* (1947) is one of several adaptations to reimagine the role of Jocasta in *Oedipus the King,* including Rita Dove's *The Darker Face of the Earth* (1996), set in antebellum South Carolina.

Other rewritings have posed increasingly explicit questions about the grounds on which the modern world addresses its ancient materials, and vice versa. In his film *Edipo Re* (1967) Pier Paolo Pasolini places his retelling of the classical myth in a modern Italian setting. Steven Berkoff's play *Greek* (1980) resituates the Oedipus story in London's East End, and in *The Trackers of Oxyrhynchus* (1991) Tony Harrison embeds his translation of a fragment from Sophocles' satyr play *Ichneutae* (*The Tracking Satyrs*) within the context of its modern reception. References to Sophocles have erupted disconcertingly in films by Woody Allen, such as *Mighty Aphrodite* (1995) and *Match Point* (2005).

The 19th-century literary figure Matthew Arnold believed that Sophocles "saw life steadily, and saw it whole." Yet such an idea was always at odds with the turbulent material in the plays and its effect on audiences and readers. We might date the emergence of a darker perception of Sophocles from the moment in 1885 when the young Freud saw Mounet-Sully's *Oedipe* in Paris. If the Freudian Oedipus has been challenged by other stories about psychic formation, there is plenty of material still to be found and refigured in Antigone, Electra, and Sophocles' other great troublemakers.

BIBL.: Peter Burian, "Tragedy Adapted for Stages and Screens: The Renaissance to the Present," in *Greek Tragedy,* ed. P. E. Easterling (Cambridge 1997) 228–283. Edith Hall and Fiona Macintosh, *Greek Tragedy and the British Theatre, 1660–1914* (Oxford 2005). Edith Hall, Fiona Macintosh, and Amanda Wrigley, *Dionysus since 69: Greek Tragedy at the Dawn of the Third Millennium* (Oxford 2004). George Steiner, *Antigones* (Oxford 1984).

A.PL.

Sororities. *See* Fraternities and Sororities.

Sparta

Sparta, for better or worse, is a brand, not just a name. Whenever we casually drop into our everyday conversation the two little epithets *spartan* and *laconic,* we are, unwittingly for the most part, paying silent tribute to our Spartan cultural ancestors—or rather to the Spartan "tradition" (Rawson 1969), "myth" (Finley 1962), "legend" (Tigerstedt 1965–1978), or "mirage" (Ollier 1933–1943), which descends more or less unbroken from at least the 5th century BCE to our own 21st.

Of those four nouns, "mirage" probably best captures the essential nature of the stories about Sparta and the Spartans that have been invented and handed down from the historian Herodotus and the extremist politician Critias to the writer of the latest historical novel or Hollywood movie. A mirage is always an unfaithful reflection of reality, but sometimes it reflects nothing whatsoever and is a purely imaginary phenomenon, a mere trompe l'oeil.

Gardens, it might be supposed, are more naturally associated with Babylon or Eden, but in Scotland the late poet and sculptor Ian Hamilton Finlay created a remarkable space that he called Little Sparta. That is as good a reminder as any of the quite extraordinary contemporary reach of ideas (however imaginary) about ancient Sparta. Given the remarkable multiplicity of the mirage's scope, this essay will confine itself to just three key themes that recur with striking regularity: the myth of patriotic self-sacrifice, the status and role of women, and utopia. A problem that bedevils much scholarship on the classical tradition is the tendency to line up references and images of antiquity in a linear chronological series, all taken—or yanked, rather—out of the original context or contexts that provide a large and essential part of their meaning. That problem cannot, unfortunately, be entirely circumvented within the restricted scope of this brief essay.

The myth of patriotic self-sacrifice. In 480 BCE King Leonidas of Sparta, along with all but 2 of his 300 chosen champions, perished in an act of gloriously heroic self-sacrifice at Thermopylae. They were defending Greece and, it was claimed both at the time and yet more stridently later, a notion of political freedom against a massive Persian invasion. Scholars still debate furiously why exactly Leonidas and his Spartans came to die in this way, but there is no dispute over the mythical fallout of that famous deed. Simonides the praise-singer was an early contributor to the tradition, with his archetypally laconic epigram that begins, "Go, tell the Spartans . . ." From here there ran a direct line in antiquity to Horace's *dulce et decorum est pro patria morii* ("it is sweet and fitting to die for one's country"), though few other Greeks or Romans emulated Leonidas' men.

The supposed site of Leonidas' last stand was marked by a stone lion, and in Sparta itself the Spartans later established a shrine in his permanent honor, the remains of which can still be seen today not far from the ancient Spartan acropolis. At the foot of that acropolis stands a modern statue of Leonidas. Like its relative stationed at Thermopylae itself, the modern image is modeled on a genuine early 5th-century BCE marble statue, the upper half of which was excavated in a fill in the ancient theater in 1926. A local workman immediately baptized him Leonidas, which was a tribute to the continuing power of the Leonidas legend, if not, alas, to historical authenticity (since for various reasons this statue cannot have been a portrait of Leonidas).

In the Renaissance everyone's favorite ancient Spartan had been another king, Agesilaus II (r. ca. 400–360 BCE), who embodied temperance, affability, military virtue, and regal laconism of speech. All he lacked, indeed, was beauty—or at any rate, physical perfection, since he was lame in one leg from birth. Leonidas' post-antique heyday was yet to come, but when it came, in the late 18th and early 19th centuries, so great was his renown that we may fairly speak of an "age of Leonidas." He was then coopted to support the cause of nascent nationalism in France and England, as well as—naturally—in his native Greece. This apotheosis produced a more famous portrait of him by far than any putative 5th-century model, as the centerpiece of a history painting begun in 1800 (and completed in 1814) by Napoleon's court painter Jacques-Louis David. Here are David's own view and vision of his masterwork (as conveyed in a printed note accompanying the exhibition of the painting in his studio):

> Leonidas, king of Sparta, seated on a rock in the midst of his three hundred heroes, reflects, rather moved, on the near and inevitable death of his friends. At Leonidas' feet, in the shade, there is his wife's brother, Agis, who, after putting down the crown of flowers he had worn during the sacrifice, is about to place his helmet on his head; with his eyes on the general, he awaits his orders. Next to him, at the sound of the trumpet two young men run to take their weapons that are hanging from the branches of trees. Farther away, one of his officers, a devotee of the cult of Hercules, whose arms and outfit he wears, rallies his troops into battle formation. He is followed by the high priest, who calls on Hercules to grant them victory. He points his finger at the sky. Farther back the army parades.

Elsewhere David is plausibly reported to have told a former pupil of his that in the painting he had wanted "to characterize that profound, great, and religious sentiment that is inspired by the love of one's country." Hence the warrior at the upper left, who appears to be carving a rupestral inscription with the hilt of his sword; it transpires that this is a slightly altered French translation of part of the Simonidean epigram "Go, tell the Spartans . . ." To that uncontroversial motive we must surely add, if not as a conscious motive at least as a palpable effect, the strong homoerotic (not just homosocial) charge that the painting conveys. David himself had strong homoerotic proclivities, and he surely would not have been unaware of this key dimension of ancient Spartan social life or blind to the legitimacy that an appeal to the authorizing Spartan archetype might confer. As for David's principal patron, the Emperor Napoleon Bonaparte, he at first could not begin to fathom why David should have wasted so much time and effort on depicting a bunch of losers. Later, however, he happily changed his mind and tune.

Not to be outdone, Germany too laid claim to Leonidas and the Thermopylae legend. Under the Nazi Third Reich "Sparta-maniacs," as the historian Stefan Rebenich has feelingly called them, "were now fascinated by the idea that the people on the Rhine and on the Eurotas were racially connected and had a common Nordic background." It was this race myth, for example, that prompted a frenzy of excitement when in 1936 (the year of the propaganda-ridden Berlin Olympics) the German Archaeological Institute's excavations of the Athenian Cerameicus, the official state-cemetery of Athens, yielded the actual skeletons of Spartans, some of whom were even named in the accompanying honorific inscription (still visible on the site today).

These were among those who had been killed in 403 in the process of ending the bloodstained reign of the originally Sparta-backed junta of the Thirty Tyrants, led by the fanatical laconizer Critias. Germany's leading physical anthropologist was at once dispatched to Athens to verify and confirm that the skeletons conformed to the classic Nordic type. It was the same spirit of racist identification that animated Reichsmarshal Hermann Göring when he addressed his failing troops during the last days of the siege of Stalingrad in 1942; he reminded them of Leonidas and the 300 and predicted a new reading of the famous Simonides epitaph: "If you come to Germany, tell them you have seen us fighting in Stalingrad, obedient to the law of honor and warfare" (trans. Rebenich). It also inspired Hitler himself, who, according to Martin Bormann, enjoined the members of his last-ditch bunker on his fiftieth birthday on April 20, 1945, to "Just think of Leonidas and his 300 Spartans" (trans. Rebenich).

Women. The status and role of Spartan women was a matter of high controversy as early as the 6th century BCE. One problem they had to contend with was that they were avatars of Helen of Sparta (as she of course was both before and after she became Helen of Troy). That may have caused the Delphic Oracle to hail Spartan women collectively as the most beautiful in all Greece, but it also led to claims by hostile non-Spartan Greeks, especially in Athens, that congenitally they were utterly incapable of sexual propriety and continence. Spartan female dress was loose, in more senses than one, giving rise to the approbrious epithet "thigh-flashers." Their morals were believed to be even looser. No matter how much a Spartan supporter like the Athenian exile Xenophon might try to spin the circumstances, it remained a fact that Spartan wives had sex with Spartan men other than their husbands and yet were not punished or even morally stigmatized, as they would have been elsewhere in Greece, for their blatant adultery. Aristotle took such examples of sexual and social indiscipline to be a sign of a regime of gynecocracy, the rule of the women over the men, in Sparta, and he consistently blamed the women in significant part for Sparta's eventual military demise (when the Spartans were decisively defeated by the Thebans in pitched battle in 371 and then had their own home territory invaded for the first time in recorded history).

The Spartans themselves naturally fought back against such calumnies. In their standard representation, the women were properly and formally educated to be upholders to the end of the masculine, martial values on which the state's power and well-being were based. This unusual social prominence and public outspokenness of Spartan women gave rise to a number of apothegms, preserved in collections under the name of Plutarch. These are anecdotes or witty sayings, doubtless for the most part inauthentic, which were attributed either to the generic Spartan wife or to specific Spartan women. The classic example of the former is the saying—or rather injunction—"With it or on it!" allegedly barked by the good Spartan wife at her husband as he was leaving home for battle. "It" was the Spartan soldier's shield, and the message was shorthand for "Come back *with* your shield, victorious and alive, or come back carried *on* your shield, having died gloriously for the sake of your city and fatherland."

A more custom-made response, tailored specially to Gorgo (Gorgon), the wife of the great Leonidas, required a more elaborate buildup. Once upon a time a non-Spartan woman asked Gorgo, enviously, how it was that of all Greek women only the Spartans were able to rule their men, to which Gorgo gave the cryptic reply: "Because we alone give birth to (real) men." Aristotle would at least have agreed with the alleged fact of gynecocracy, even if he could not have pardoned or perhaps comprehended Gorgo's witty sidestepping of it. For he shared the standard Greek male view of the congenital, unalterable because of the "natural" inferiority of women as a species.

Laconizers of subsequent ages, admirers of all things Spartan, have found Spartan sexual mores and institutions worthy of both praise and imitation, though by no means always in precisely identical ways. For example, Claude-Adrien Helvétius argued in his *De l'esprit* (1758) that Lycurgus the Spartan lawgiver should have gone further even than he already had. Helvétius supposed that Lycurgus had introduced the practice of women dancing half-naked at religious festivals to spur on the Spartan men to virtue and valor. He would have done so even more effectively, Helvétius opined, if he had promised the fairest woman as a sexual prize to the most valorous and virtuous, since "the force of virtue is always proportionate to the degree of pleasure assigned to it as its reward." By contrast, his contemporary Jean-Jacques Rousseau, the "arch-priest of Laconism" (as Rawson has aptly dubbed him), approved the Spartan girls' vigorously physical upbringing, inasmuch as that conduced to potent motherhood of healthy sons, and he commended their power, but only to send their menfolk to a glorious patriotic death rather than to rule over them in any other sense.

Utopia. When Sir Thomas More coined the ancient Greek-derived and Greek-sounding word *Utopia* in 1516, he was well aware, as a good classical scholar, that the *U-* prefix was ambiguous. It could stand either for *eu,* meaning "well," or for *ou,* meaning "not," so that Utopia could be construed either as No-Place, in the manner of Samuel Butler's reversed-world Erewhon (almost *Nowhere* backward), or as Place of Well(Faring). More, in his supporting writings, made it clear that he himself had conceived of his Utopia as a No-Place, an imaginary construct pleasant to think about in contrast to the sad shortcomings of his own contemporary England in the early years of Henry VIII's reign but in no sense intended as a blueprint for a future ideal society. And most utopiographers since, of which there have been a huge number, have followed his lead. Indeed, in the 20th century a subbranch of dystopian or cacotopian literature was profitably established, George Orwell's *1984* probably being its best-known exemplar.

On the other hand, there have been idealist utopiographers of various sorts who have sketched out what they consider to be ideal societies that are practically realizable, and that is a tradition reaching back at least to the town planner Hippodamus of Miletus in the 5th century BCE. Such writers have often taken inspiration, as More himself did up to a point, from what they took to have been a really existent society, a society of virtue, namely classical Sparta—by which they understood the Sparta described most fully in Plutarch's alleged biography (ca. 100 CE) of the wondrously omniscient and omniprovident legislator Lycurgus. More knew his Plutarch well and, through him, was able to trace the Spartan tradition of (e)utopia back to Plato—whose two significantly different ideal republics, sketched in the *Republic* (in Greek *Politeia*) and more than just sketched in the *Laws,* have a distinctly Spartan tinge.

All such Sparta-derived political utopias—whether the inspiration was direct and conscious or not—were austere, self-denying, and need-satisfying rather than want-gratifying commonwealths. But had their authors read the essay on the Spartan *politeia* by Plato's fellow pupil of Socrates, Xenophon, they would or should have been given pause. After what seems for the most part right up until the end to be an unqualified eulogy of Spartan social arrangements regarding reproduction, education, communal dining in messes, contempt for private wealth and so forth, Xenophon in a stinging conclusion observes that the Spartans of his own day have utterly abandoned the wise legislation of their aboriginal lawgiver and are now as a direct result in a fine mess (of a different kind). Nevertheless, the distinction drawn by Xenophon and Aristotle between the ideals and wishes of the legislator and the less-than-ideal Spartan practice was one that many subsequent laconizers were keen to adopt. For example,

Rousseau, if somewhat paradoxically for a thinker who is associated more with liberation than repression, was unstinting in his eulogy of Lycurgus the lawgiver, who fastened an "iron yoke" of ceaseless constraint and restraint on his fellow citizens.

In a certain sense Sparta has been in a constant process of rebranding since antiquity. Above all, today the brand needs to be rescued from any shadow or taint of totalitarianism that may still linger from the 20th-century Nazi-Fascist appropriation. The idea that modern Germany had some special connection with ancient Greece was of course by no means a new one in 1933. Scholars had even spoken of the "tyranny" of Greece over Germany in the 19th century—meaning that ancient Greece served as an essential cultural reference point, a standard of value, a measure of aspiration. But in the Nazi era it was quite specifically Sparta that was appealed to as the (genetic) ancestor and model—the home of the "Nordic" Dorian Spartans, with their ruthless devotion to the common good, their sacrifice of private enjoyment, their fierce physical training, their public educational program aimed at producing mighty and patriotic warriors, and, not least, their eugenic practices involving the disposal of unfit or disabled infants. This has made it impossible any longer to appeal straightforwardly to ancient Sparta as a political-social ideal or model for today and tomorrow. But there is still a case for recalling the morally virtuous, relatively selfless ideal community imagined by Rousseau and to some extent Plato, and especially the real-life community of Leonidas: one that could not only conceive but also put into practice the ideal of fighting and dying for a concept of shared Greekness and a concept of freedom. Had it not been for the Spartans, I suggest, what we call "the Glory that was Greece" would largely either not have happened at all or have been forgotten by posterity.

BIBL.: P. Cartledge, *Spartan Reflections* (London 2001) esp. ch. 12. M. I. Finley, "The Myth of Sparta," *The Listener* (August 2, 1962) 171–173. F. Ollier, *Le mirage spartiate,* 2 vols. (1933–1943; repr. in 1 vol., New York 1973). A. Powell and S. Hodkinson, eds., *The Shadow of Sparta* (London 1994). E. Rawson, *The Spartan Tradition in European Thought* (Oxford 1969). S. Rebenich, "From Thermopylae to Stalingrad: The Myth of Leonidas in German Historiography," in *Spartan Society,* ed. T. Figueira (London 2004) 323–349. E. N. Tigerstedt, *The Legend of Sparta in Classical Antiquity,* 2 vols. + index (Göteborg 1965, 1974, 1978).

P.C.

Spartacus

Soldier, probably from Thrace (ca. 109–71 BCE); slave and gladiator, signal figure in the slave revolt termed the Third Servile War that paralyzed southern Italy 73–70 BCE. Opponents of slavery in the 19th century saw him as symbolic of a human being's innate right to resist domination. Whether Spartacus shared this view of the human condition will forever remain a matter of speculation, as everything that is known about him comes from those who most certainly would not have agreed. The ancient historians who wrote about his revolt respected him as a feared enemy, not as the leader of a cause. Then again, legends are most powerful when we know the least about them.

What little there is to know about him resembles a bad epic movie: long on action, short on motivation. Most classical writers agree that he came from Thrace, served in the Roman army, and then deserted. Captured and enslaved, he joined the ranks of gladiators at a famous gladiator school in Capua. He and his fellow gladiators escaped and established a base on the slopes of Mount Vesuvius, where other escaped slaves joined them. So many runaway slaves and disaffected people sought him out that Spartacus found himself in charge of an army, one whose pillaging of the region alarmed the authorities in republican Rome. His forces repeatedly defeated attempts by the Roman army to suppress them. When he and his followers approached the port of Brindisi, where they hoped to find ships that would carry them away from Italy, Roman legions under the command of Marcus Licinius Crassus defeated them in battle. Crassus ordered the crucifixion of more than 6,000 of Spartacus' followers. No one knows how Spartacus died.

Nearly two millennia later his story was resurrected first in the service of political reform and then in the struggle to end slavery. In late 18th-century Bavaria Adam Weishaupt, the radical deist and founder of the freethinking Illuminati, took the sobriquet Brother Spartacus. Toussaint Louverture, the leader of the Haitian slave revolt of 1791–1804, acquired among the French a reputation as a modern-day Spartacus. For the remainder of the 19th century the memory of Spartacus receded somewhat, as if the awful reality of a war to end slavery in the United States had superseded the need for a heroic model of a slave revolt.

During World War I Spartacus found new employment when a group of Marxists founded the Spartacist League in 1917. In 1919 the self-proclaimed leaders of oppressed wage slaves, Rosa Luxemburg, Karl Liebknecht, and Clara Zetkin, launched a revolution in the hopes of overthrowing bourgeois democracy and establishing in Germany a democratic socialist government like the one that in their view had emerged from the Russian Revolution the year before. Their attempt ended in defeat.

Film rather than politics has offered Spartacus the best chance of survival in historical memory. Several adaptations of the ancient slave revolt have appeared on film, but none as successful as Stanley Kubrick's *Spartacus* (1960), based on the popular 1951 novel of the same name by the novelist Howard Fast. Politics, however, lies just below the surface of the film's plot. Released a few years after the 1954 *Brown v. Board of Education* desegregation case and the 1956 bus boycott in Montgomery, Alabama, Kubrick's film sought to extend the white moviegoing public's sympathy for the Civil Rights Movement beyond the liberal and progressive circles that read Fast's novels. Kubrick, Dalton Trumbo, Fast (who was also the movie's scriptwriter, blacklisted and one of the Hollywood Ten), and Kirk Douglas, the executive producer and star of the movie, brought the meaning of Spartacus' search for an exit out of servitude up to date for audiences in the 20th and 21st centuries. Given how easily Spartacus has accommodated every generation searching for symbols of resistance, it is possible that the long-dead Thracian gladiator has still more life left in him.

S.MC.

Speculum Romanae Magnificentiae

Renaissance print album, first issued mid-1570s in Rome by the French publisher Antoine (Antonio) Lafréry with a title page by Etienne Dupérac. It contained the largest collection of prints of the monuments and statues of ancient Rome assembled to that date and remains one of the largest of all time.

The Parisian Etienne Dupérac (ca. 1525–1604) arrived in Rome around 1559. A talented draftsman with a passion for the ruins, he first appears as the artist who drew 13 maps of Europe for the Loggia della Cosmografia in the Vatican in 1560, working under Pirro Ligorio. Ligorio, an imaginative interpreter of antiquity and encyclopedic recorder of the entire material culture of the ancient world, would be a formative influence on his younger French colleague. Dupérac's tribute to Ligorio was a fine plan of Villa d'Este in Tivoli, done in 1573. He published two plans of ancient Rome in 1573 and 1574, where the debt to Ligorio's celebrated reconstruction of the ancient city, the *Antiquae urbis imago* of 1561, is patent. Dupérac also studied Michelangelo's drawings, especially for the unfinished architectural projects, which he incorporated into engravings of St. Peter's Basilica and the Capitoline Palaces published in 1569. In 1575 he engraved the *Vestigi dell'antichità di Roma,* 40 views of the most famous ruins, and in 1578 an ambitious plan of modern Rome, edited by Lafréry. In 1578 (or slightly later) he returned to France for his last two decades, working for Henri IV at Fontainebleau and the Louvre.

A sketchbook by Dupérac from ca. 1573–1575 shows a novel format: views of the ruins are mirrored by views showing what the same buildings might have looked like at the height of the empire. The Tiber Island with its crumbling medieval churches is juxtaposed with the ancient island-as-ship replete with temples and obelisk; the Campo Vaccino with its ruins is juxtaposed with a Forum resplendent with temples; the Aventine and Marmorata, looking ruined and sylvan, are juxtaposed with a built-up palatial hillside and dockside; the ruined theater of Marcellus and the Colosseum are juxtaposed with images of these monuments as new; and so forth. The popular genre of picture book, "Rome (or Pompeii) as it was and as it is today," originated with Dupérac.

It was near the end of his Roman period, ca. 1574–1578, that the *Speculum* was born in partnership between Dupérac and Lafréry. Lafréry (ca. 1512–1577) was born in the Franche-Comté but arrived in Rome in 1544 and ran a large publishing house and print shop there until his death. From 1553 to 1562 he joined in partnership with his older rival, Antonio Salamanca, who had been active in publishing immediately following the Sack of Rome in 1527. We have an inventory of Lafréry's extensive stock from 1573, which lists more than 500 prints, among them 107 of Roman statues and buildings.

Dupérac's title page for the *Speculum* announces a book (*liber*). The title hints at prints of Rome in the manner of his sketchbook: "Mirror of Roman Magnificence, nearly all the monuments that exist in the Urbs accurately drawn, partly in ancient form and partly as they appear today." But in practice Lafréry used the title page to assemble portfolios of prints from his stock that varied with the taste and purse of each customer. It was a bespoke book, and no two copies today are identical.

Christian Hülsen (1858–1935) reconstructed what he thought was an ideal *Speculum* of 167 plates, and although there probably never was such a copy, his list serves as a useful guide. Copies often include plates engraved much earlier for Lafréry but also for Salamanca. The draftsmen sought out celebrated statues, sometimes in public, like the colossal river gods in the Vatican Belvedere, the Dioscuri on the Quirinal, the Marcus Aurelius, or the Trophies of Marius, but sometimes inside palaces, such as the Farnese or the Della Valle. Triumphal arches and amphitheaters are represented, but so are the tomb of Cecilia Metella, the pyramid of Caius Cestius, and the theater of Marcellus. Seven of Ligorio's meticulous reconstructions of ancient circuses and similar monuments, done for the printer Tramezzino between 1552 and 1558, are often included. Among buildings of modern Rome one often finds Bramante's Palazzo Caprini, Palazzo Farnese, the tomb of Julius II with the Moses, and the St. Peter's projects of Sangallo and Michelangelo.

Hülsen first pointed to the existence of "monster" *Specula,* in which 19th-century collectors inserted many prints of Rome, indeed, sometimes entire dismembered books. There are three super-*Specula:* the Quaritch *Speculum* now in the Metropolitan Museum, with 374 plates; the *Speculum* formed by James Ludovic Lindsay, the 26th Earl of Crawford, bought by the Avery Library at Columbia University in New York in 1951, with 601 plates; and the *Speculum* sold to the University of Chicago by the Calvary firm in Berlin in 1891, with 994 plates (formerly 996).

Before Piranesi, it was through copies of the *Speculum* that many foreign dilettanti would first encounter the monuments of ancient and modern Rome.

BIBL.: Silvia Bianchi, "Note allo *Speculum Romanae Magnificentiae* di Antonio Lafrery," *Grafica d'arte: Rivista di storia dell'incisione antica e moderna e storia del disegno* 22 (1995). Michael Bury, *The Print in Italy 1550–1620* (London 2001) 48–50, 59–60, 121–135. Stefano Corsi, *Speculum Romanae Magnificentiae: Roma nell'incisione del Cinquecento,* exhibition catalogue (Florence 2004). [Etienne Dupérac] and Antonio Lafréry, *Speculum Romanae magnificentiae: Omnia fere quaecunq[ue] in Urbe monumenta extant partim iuxta anti-*

quam partim iuxta hodiernam formam accuratiss. delineata repraesentans. Christian Hülsen, "Das Speculum Romanae Magnificentiae des Antonio Lafreri," in *Collectanea variae doctrinae Leoni S. Olschki bibliopolae florentino sexagenario* (Munich 1921) 121–170. Bates Lowry, "Notes on the *Speculum Romanae magnificentiae* and Related Publications," *Art Bulletin* 34 (1952) 46–50. Lawrence McGinniss with Herbert Mitchell, *Catalogue of the Earl of Crawford's Speculum Romanae Magnificentiae Now in the Avery Architectural Library* (New York 1976). Rebecca Zorach, *The Virtual Tourist in Renaissance Rome: Printing and Collecting the Speculum romanae magnificentiae* (Chicago 2008). J.C.

Split

Croatian coastal city that developed inside the Palace of Diocletian, eventually absorbing the functions of nearby Salona, which once had been the capital of Roman Dalmatia but was destroyed during the Avar and Slav incursions of the 630s. Diocletian began the palace ca. 295 CE and spent the last years of his life there after his abdication on 1 May 305. The building was a combination of luxurious imperial villa and armed camp, and there were elements of a city as well. In the central *temenos* lay the octagonal Imperial Mausoleum and a small rectangular temple adorned with pantheist iconography. The smaller, southern section of the complex was residential; the larger, northern section housed workshops and storerooms of the great imperial weaving shop, the Gynaeceum Iovense Dalmatiae-Aspalatho, mentioned in the *Notitia dignitatum* (ca. 400 CE), a manual of "dignities," that is, of governmental offices and occupations in the empire.

Diocletian was a most ardent persecutor of Christians, and in the centuries after his death there occurred in Split a systematic settling of accounts with his memory. The mausoleum was transformed during the 5th century into a church. The Temple of Jupiter, one of the best-preserved smaller antique temples, was remodeled into a baptistery. Its stone coffer vault influenced the early Renaissance baptistery of the cathedral in nearby Trogir (1460–1467) as well as the chapel of the Blessed John (started in 1468) in the same church. On the other hand, because Diocletian had been the first to withdraw voluntarily from power, ostensibly at least, he was held to be a philosopher-emperor. Aurelius Victor (ca. 362 CE), by way of confirmation, records the answer that Diocletian made to his heirs when they called upon him to return to the throne in 308: "Oh, if you saw the vegetables around the Palace that I have planted with my own hand, you would not assail me with such offers." Voltaire made this bon mot from the imperial gardener famous in *Candide.* But the Croatian Humanists of the Renaissance and Baroque periods (Coriolano Cipiko, Petar Hektorovik, Jerolim Kavanjin, and others) attempted to imitate Diocletian in their eulogy of *otium,* the secluded life in contact with nature. In the emperor's retreat from the confusion of the world they saw an ideal example.

Antiquity was never completely interred in Split. The dialogue with it, even when it was consciously negated, would remain lastingly alive. The proto-Renaissance campanile was begun in the mid-13th century on the site of the prostasis of the mausoleum. This would be the most authentic Dalmatian medieval building. The ground floor was an idealized triumphal arch, and the elevation echoed the peristyle of the palace.

The Church of Split drew legitimacy from the alleged transfer of the metropolis from Salona and with it an apostolic link. The first bishop of Salona, Doimus, who was martyred by Diocletian in 304, was somehow said to be a disciple of the apostle Peter. But aside from this pious fiction there was no need to manufacture antique origins, which were there for all to see in the early Renaissance. There are learned disquisitions and encomia on the palace by local Humanists like Marko Marulic, the central figure in the Croatian literature of the Renaissance, by Franjo Bozicevic Natalis, and by others.

Because of its high degree of preservation and the harmonious impression given in the whole and in details, the palace attracted numerous investigators. In 1436 Cyriac of Ancona recorded a sarcophagus featuring a representation of Meleager and the Calydonian Boar, thought to be the tomb of Diocletian. A ground plan by Palladio (now in London at the Royal Institute of British Architects) is the first inventory of the visible parts. The first idealized reconstruction was drawn by J. B. Fisher von Erlach in *Entwurf einer historischer Architektur* (Vienna 1721). In London in 1764 Robert Adam published *The Ruins of the Palace of the Emperor Diocletian at Spalatro in Dalmatia,* with 61 folio views of the palace. His team of draftsmen was headed by Charles-Louis Clérisseau. The etchings, the most important part of the book, show a building of crestfallen majesty, which lent itself to Romantic capriccios. The monographs on Diocletian's palace published by Georg Niemann and Ernest Hébrard at the beginning of the 20th century are still basic works, although research done after World War II has filled in gaps in our knowledge of the original appearance of the imperial building and of its medieval and later *Nachleben.*

BIBL.: J. Belamaric, "Gynaeceum Iovense Aspalathos Dalmatie," in *Diokletian und die Tetrarchie: Aspekte einer Zeitenwende,* ed. A. Demandt (Berlin 2004) 141–162. E. Hébrard and J. Zeiller, *Spalato: Le palais de Dioclétien* (Paris 1912). J. Marasovic and T. Marasovic, *Diocletian's Palace* (Zagreb 1968). G. Niemann, *Der Palast Diokletians in Spalato* (Vienna 1910).

J.B.

Spolia

Remnants of ancient artifacts reused in the Middle Ages. The reuse of ancient remnants occurred in all genres, from architecture to sculpture to small decorative objects. Such remnants served either a function analogous to their original use (as when a column capital was reused as a column capital) or an altered function (e.g., a column capital hollowed out for use as a baptismal font). Reuse in a new context transformed the individual fragment or artifact from an antiquarian object into a historical one: *spolia* represent an adoption of antiquity and are the most concrete expression of its legacy.

In the field of architecture the use of spolia began with Constantine. The end of paganism, the disintegration of the Roman Empire in the West, and a drop in population beginning in the 5th century brought an enormous increase in the number of structures, both sacred and profane, that could be plundered. The huge collection of available architectural elements saved a trip to the quarry, and many were reused randomly in the early Middle Ages. Not until the Romanesque era did the reuse of ancient remnants begin to reflect sensitivity to the ancient architectural canon, proportions, harmony, and quality. From the late 11th century onward and particularly during the 12th century, spolia were employed systematically in architecture in Italy, southern France, and Spain: in rows of columns in church interiors and externally in particularly prominent places (such as portals, apses, and campaniles), where antique friezes, reliefs, inscriptions, and the like were inserted into the new works as decoration. By then remnants of ancient structures were being transported over considerable distances: entire shiploads of spolia were sent from Rome to Pisa. Spolia are also mentioned in written sources (e.g., by Abbot Suger of St.-Denis). They were adapted and reworked as church fixtures and even augmented by new pieces made in the ancient style, a tangible step toward the imitation of antiquity. For the Cosmati in Rome, antiquity served simultaneously as a source of raw materials and as a model.

Among the motives for using spolia, the most obvious was akin to modern recycling: new building projects could be carried out faster and more cheaply by reemploying already finished blocks of stone; these were often placed on the inner side of walls, where they would be invisible. At the other end of the spectrum of motives stood admiration for the beautiful forms and costly marble composition of ancient remnants. In between these poles further motives sometimes existed in combination, including turning spolia into instruments of politics and "ideology": because reused elements from antiquity added not only beauty and monumentality to a structure but also a semblance of age, and thus of status and *auctoritas,* spolia could be co-opted to legitimate claims to power—and were so used by emperors (Charlemagne used spolia from Rome and Ravenna in Aachen), popes (especially in Roman churches of the 12th century), and kings (the Norman dynasty in southern Italy even reused porphyry, which was supposed to be reserved for the emperor). Italian towns typically used spolia in cathedrals and town halls to identify the location of law courts and as official gauges for volume and length, thus affirming the legitimacy of their newly won political autonomy and reconstructing a long past in rivalry with other towns.

That the use of spolia did not result simply from the availability of many ancient remnants in various locales is demonstrated by the example of towns and cities (e.g., Venice, Genoa, Pisa) that lacked much ancient history but desired that attribute and therefore imported its evidence from elsewhere. Pisa even attached importance to the fact that its spolia came from Rome, as a way of demonstrating its *romanitas.* After the mid-13th century the use of spolia became rarer, as there was no place for them in Gothic church architecture. Their use simply as building material continued in Rome even into the Renaissance and Baroque periods, however; Roman builders seem to have had few qualms about stripping and dismantling ancient structures, even if they were still almost completely intact. During the Counter-Reformation the tendency was instead to remove or cover up "heathen" spolia.

Sculpture presented problems for reuse. Statues, particularly of nudes, were considered a symbol of paganism (as idols, to which martyrs had been forced to offer sacrifices). Statues were not understood, were to be feared, and were not easily exploited for other purposes: hence of all the genres in the legacy of antiquity they had by far the poorest chances for survival. Only a very few statues were preserved above ground in the Middle Ages. Some were spared by being given a Christian interpretation (Marcus Aurelius as Constantine, Pan as John the Baptist). But expressions of admiration and imitations began to appear from the 12th and 13th centuries onward. The reuse of reliefs posed fewer problems, particularly those on sarcophagi, which could serve as tombs of saints (that is, as reliquaries), emperors (Charlemagne), popes, princes, knights, merchants, and other prominent persons. (In the Camposanto in Pisa there are more than 60 reused ancient sarcophagi, many of them from Rome.) Sarcophagi were also often used as fountain basins or troughs.

Stones (gems, cameos) cut or carved in antiquity were frequently reused in small decorative artifacts such as reliquaries, crucifixes, and book covers in Italy and beyond (e.g., the cameo of Augustus on the Lothar crucifix in Aachen, made ca. 1000 CE), and also as seals and in jewelry. Even though their iconography was not understood, their obvious value and extraordinary beauty made them attractive, and for that reason they were reused or preserved in the treasure collections of churches and rulers (e.g., the church of San Marco in Venice, the collection of Emperor Frederick II). Ivory reliefs were popular as well, such as the "consular diptychs" that were created for Roman consuls in late antiquity. A special ritual existed to consecrate ancient vases and vessels for use in churches: *benedictio super vasa reperta in antiquis locis.*

The inclusion of ancient objects in medieval contexts was noticed as early as the 15th century and was later described by Giorgio Vasari. Up until the 18th century the practice was felt to denote disrespect toward antiquity, and later it was assessed as being at the very least an indication of the later era's low level of productivity and imagination (see Jacob Burckhardt in *Cicerone,* 1855). Not until the 1930s did the reuse of spolia become a topic of research, but the field has experienced massive growth since the 1970s, and there is a new appreciation of spolia as the reception and adoption of antiquity from various motives.

BIBL.: Richard Brilliant and Dale Kinney, eds., *The Ethics of Spolia* (forthcoming). Friedrich Wilhelm Deichmann, *Die Spolien in der spätantiken Architektur* (Munich 1975). Arnold Esch, *Wiederverwendung von Antike im Mittelalter: Die Sicht des Archäologen und die Sicht des Historikers* (Berlin 2005). Michael Greenhalgh, *The Survival of Roman Antiquities in the Middle Ages* (London 1989). Dale Kinney, "*Spolia. Damnatio* and *renovatio memoriae*," *Memoirs of the American Academy in Rome* 42 (1997) 117–148. Joachim Poeschke, ed., *Antike Spolien in der Architektur des Mittelalters und der Renaissance* (Munich 1996). Salvatore Settis, *Sopravvivenza dell'antichità* (Padua 2001) and Settis, ed., *Memoria dell'antico nell'arte italiana,* 3 vols. (Turin 1984–1986). A.E.

Translated by Deborah Lucas Schneider

Sports

From the name and the shape of our stadia to the range of disciplines we practice in track and field athletics, the modern legacy of ancient sports is undeniable. But it is also puzzling, since no classical language offered a close equivalent of *sport* (a word of French medieval origin). Greek had *agon,* usually translated as "competition"; athletics was its characteristic core, but it also applied to poetic contests. To give an example of the implications of such categorization, hunting was a well-known pastime but, since it was not practiced competitively, it would not count as *agon.* Latin had *ludus.* It referred to the games of the circus (particularly in the plural *ludi*) and generally to performances for spectators, but also to play and to dance.

The transition from the ancient civilizations of the Mediterranean to the world of medieval Europe shows contrasting signs of continuity and hiatus in sporting traditions. On the one hand, the interdiction of paganism brought the suppression of the Olympic games (393 CE). Christians loathed Roman blood sports, which they perceived as both brutal and pagan and associated with their own persecutions—the lion scenes of the movie *Quo Vadis?* brilliantly immortalized in the 20th-century mind the myth of the martyrdoms in the Colosseum (of doubtful historical foundation). On the other hand, the popularity of chariot racing in Byzantium arguably rivaled its Roman precedents. Continuity can also be noticed in the practice of betting on sporting results: the *Corpus iuris civilis* (6th cent. BCE) comprised laws for regulating it (Digest 11.5.1–4 and Code 3.43.1–2). From those norms and their medieval glosses we have inherited the common habit of distinguishing between games of chance and games of skill.

In late antiquity, Jews and Christians were often hostile toward Greek sport; nevertheless, they could be influenced by its legacy, as embodied in the will to excel and win. Athletic metaphors are frequent in the New Testament; Christian life is often presented as a race that requires training and endurance and promises a prize, and Jesus is portrayed as the supreme athlete. Drawing on this tradition, the Byzantine lexicon Suda (10th cent.) outlined the biblical figure of Job, undefeated by all trials, by portraying him as a wrestler, in the technical vocabulary of Greek athletics. Furthermore, at the heart of the medieval Christian experience, monastic life was frequently presented in muscular terms as a competition with the devil and its temptations. Despite such cultural legacy and continuity in some leisure activities, the sporting tradition at the heart of Western civilization in the Middle Ages—the military exercises featuring the knight and his horse—was chiefly an original development that had little connection with classical precedents.

A renewed direct interest in ancient athletics and gymnastics was the result of Renaissance antiquarianism and of the Humanist passion for every aspect of the classical world. A telling example was offered in the 1570s by the architect and antiquarian Pirro Ligorio, who devised the iconographic program for a stately apartment in the Este Castle in Ferrara. There Ligorio, who had been engaged in the excavations of Hadrian's villa and was impressed by its structures designed for physical exercise, filled the ceilings of two adjoining halls with scenes of Greek and Roman sports, from muscular athletic contests to educational games. In the same years, an example of the Renaissance fashion for dignifying contemporary sports by providing them with classical origins can be found in the Italian Humanist Antonio Scaino's 1555 treatise on a ball game (*jeu de paume,* or tennis): Nausicaa had probably invented it, and its mentors and keen practitioners included Alexander the Great and Julius Caesar.

Ball games had been a favorite also of medical literature from the times of Galen (2nd cent. BCE), who recommended one of them as the most efficacious form of physical exercise because all limbs participated in a balanced way. Consistently, the medical Renaissance of the 16th century also played a role in the renewed attention to ancient sports. If physical exercise was recommended, ancient and Renaissance physicians alike warned their readers against excessive training: rather than working as a model to imitate, the massive body of an athlete offered a negative example from which to steer away.

In the new context of the 19th-century genesis of modern sport, the German school was the first one to adopt ancient Greece as its predominant cultural model—a choice that also led to the systematic archaeological excavations of the site of Olympia. Nationalism, militarism, and racist notions of healthiness played a role in this phase in the cultural history of European sports; the historical example of Sparta occupied center stage. Eventually it was English public school sports that triumphed in the reestablished Olympic games. Most key features of the neo-Olympic movement bore little resemblance to their historical precedent, which was reinvented for the purpose as a powerful myth—from its programmatic amateurism to the slogan on the importance of participation. (For the Greeks, instead, only winning mattered: arriving second offered little consolation.)

In the work of early anthropologists such as the French Jesuit Joseph-François Lafitau (1681–1746), the comparison between games and other rituals of ancient Europeans and contemporary North American natives was used to support an evolutionary theory of human civilization. Later on, ancient sports played a central role in some influential accounts of the development of Western civilization. In his lectures on the history of Greek civilization (1872), the Swiss historian Jacob Burckhardt described the whole pre-classical period (until ca. 500 BCE) under the headline *Der koloniale und agonale Mensch* (the colonial and agonal man), defining *agon* as "the paramount feature of life." Half a century later the Dutch historian Johan Huizinga turned *agon* into a fundamental category of human experience throughout time, which found expression in a wide variety of fields, from poetry to war (*Homo ludens,* 1938).

BIBL.: Alessandro Arcangeli, *Recreation in the Renaissance* (Basingstoke 2003). N. C. Croy, *Endurance in Suffering: Hebrews 12:1–13 in Its Rhetorical, Religious, and Philosophical Context* (Cambridge 1998). R. D. Mandell, *Sport: A Cultural History* (New York 1984). Michael Poliakoff, "Jacob, Job, and Other Wrestlers: Reception of Greek Athletics by Jews and Christians in Antiquity," *Journal of Sport History* 11 (1984) 48–65. D. C. Young, *The Olympic Myth of Greek Amateur Athletics* (Chicago 1984).

A.AR.

Squaring the Circle

The geometrical problem known as squaring the circle (or quadrature of the circle) requires the construction of a square equal in area to any given circle. When the geometer is limited to using compasses and an unmarked straightedge (that is, the tools permitted by the postulates of Euclid's *Elements*), the problem is insoluble. This was finally demonstrated in 1882, by Ferdinand von Lindemann.

The problem was well known as early as the 5th century BCE. In *The Birds* Aristophanes satirizes geometers who turned circles into squares. Aristotle describes two early 4th-century BCE quadratures, those of Bryson and Antiphon, which he rejects as fallacies. Through Aristotle's remarks and later commentaries, Renaissance geometers also came to know of Hippocrates of Chios, whose valid quadratures of lunules formed from circular arcs assured them that *some* curvilinear shapes were quadrable.

In his *Categories* Aristotle observes that the fact that the quadrature of the circle was not yet known did not imply that it was not knowable, a dictum that was repeated in almost every Renaissance text on circle quadrature. Nicholas of Cusa prefaced his own attempted quadrature by recounting a discussion with fellow churchmen concerning this passage; as Johannes Regiomontanus showed in his published refutation, however, the possibility of solution provided no support for a false quadrature (printed with Cusa's quadrature in *De triangulis*, 1533).

Ironically, Aristotle was also the authority for the opposite opinion, that the quadrature of the circle was, in principle, impossible. In the *Physics* he seems to argue that rectilinear and circular motions are incommensurable, and hence so too are the paths that they describe; this implies that the circle cannot be squared. Such a position was to be adopted by Averroës and Jean Buridan; and Jakob Christmann, in his 1595 refutation of Joseph Scaliger's circle quadrature, based his argument almost entirely on incommensurability. Though it may seem prescient to have contended that quadrature is impossible, this argument carried no weight with most Renaissance mathematicians, who admired both Hippocrates' quadrature of lunules and Archimedes' quadrature of the parabola. Philosophical objections notwithstanding, it was clear that curvilinear figures *could* be equal to rectilinear ones.

Recent scholarship has emphasized that ancient mathematicians attacked—and solved—the problem of quadrature with a variety of tools, including marked straightedges and higher curves such as spirals. A "planar" solution (using only Euclidean tools) was considered the most elegant; but, lacking this, other solutions were entirely acceptable. It was not until late antiquity that mathematicians insisted on *only* planar solutions to the quadrature problem—a condition that rendered the problem insoluble, as we now know.

Archimedes' solutions demonstrate the flexibility of approaches in the earlier period. In his work *On Spirals,* he found a precise construction for the square equal to a given circle, but only by employing a curve—the spiral—that cannot be constructed with straightedge and compasses. In his *Measurement of the Circle* (the most influential ancient work), he inscribed and circumscribed a 96-sided polygon in a circle, in effect establishing narrow limits for the value of pi.

Because of the enormous influence of Euclid's *Elements* and late-antique commentaries and textbooks, Renaissance mathematicians generally supposed that the problem was limited to planar tools. Jean Borrel, in his important work *De quadratura circuli* (1559) had no doubts that quadrature using Euclidean methods was possible, and he interpreted Aristotle's opinion in the *Categories* to refer specifically to such a solution. He had, moreover, strong mathematical intuitions that a planar quadrature was possible. The *Elements* provides the means to square every rectilinear figure, but not the circle; on the other hand, the same book contains many theorems concerning circles, including comparisons between the area of two different circles. To Borrel it was prima facie obvious that the two kinds of results could be combined. The fact that Euclid had not done so should not be considered evidence for its impossibility, but only for Euclid's limitations as a mathematician.

The primary focus of Borrel's book was, however, the

rash of circle squarers who had appeared in the century before its publication, from Cusa to the French mathematics professor Oronce Fine. Borrel subtitled his work "A Defense of Archimedes against Every Attack," a reflection of the fact that attempts to square the circle were often accompanied by criticisms of Archimedes and other ancient mathematicians. Most false quadratures fell outside the numerical limits Archimedes set in his *Measurement of the Circle,* so that their authors were obliged to cast doubt on the value of his proof. They also extolled their use of exact, Euclidean methods over Archimedes' successive approximations and laborious calculations. Borrel's book explains and defends Archimedes' proof with unmatched lucidity, while it also reveals the errors in each of the supposed exact quadratures.

In his sumptuous *Cyclometrica* (1594), Joseph Scaliger claimed not only to have squared the circle, but also to have trisected the angle and duplicated the cube. In his preface to this work, he took the customary attack on Archimedes to intemperate lengths; and in his subsequent *Apology* (in which little contrition can be found) Scaliger accused contemporary mathematicians of slavish devotion to Archimedes. His charges were roundly defeated in several mathematical responses to his quadrature, most comprehensively by the Flemish mathematician Adriaan van Roomen, who defended the entire Archimedean tradition of mathematics against Scaliger in his *In Archimedis circuli dimensionem* (*On Archimedes' Measurement of the Circle,* 1597). Scaliger's public reputation never entirely recovered from this episode.

Neither the attempts to square the circle nor their refutations led to important mathematical discoveries in the Renaissance. They did, however, raise important issues of mathematical *possibility* and encouraged a deeper understanding of Archimedes' mathematical methods. Circle squaring took off as an activity primarily of Humanists and philosophers at precisely the time when the content of mathematics was expanding at such a rate that only those who dedicated themselves to it entirely could hope to master it. Scaliger's writings are filled with bitter attacks on those who pursued mathematics separately from the rest of the humanities, and thus (as he saw it) had little regard for his philological and historical contributions to the problem of quadrature. As the Scaliger affair showed and as the later debate between Thomas Hobbes and John Wallis confirmed, circle squaring helped define mathematics as a specialized activity requiring singular technical skills; it was no longer simply a part of the liberal arts, to which any philosophically or humanistically trained scholar could make a contribution.

BIBL.: R. Goulding, "Polemic in the Margin: Henry Savile against Joseph Scaliger's Quadrature of the Circle," in *Scientia in Margine,* ed. D. Jacquart and C. Burnett (Geneva 2005) 241–259. A. T. Grafton, *Joseph Scaliger: A Study in the History of Classical Scholarship* (Oxford 1983). D. M. Jesseph, *Squaring the Circle: The War between Hobbes and Wallis* (Chicago 1999). W. R. Knorr, *The Ancient Tradition of Geometric Problems* (Boston 1986). P. Mancosu, *Philosophy of Mathematics and Mathematical Practice in the Seventeenth Century* (Oxford 1996).

R.G.

Stadium

The early Greek stadium was often little more than a running track. The term signified a unit of linear measurement, a *stadion* or, stade, about 200 yards. By the 4th century BCE seats had been added to one or both sides. Subsequently the form was developed by the Greeks for other athletic contests that characterized their Olympic Games. Distinct from the Roman amphitheater and circus, the stadium proper was limited to the Hellenic world, although it would form the model for the Stadium of Domitian, inaugurated in Rome in 92–96 CE with athletic games called the Agones Capitolini and conforming to the hellenizing ceremonies Domitian held in the Campus Martius. This stadium came to enjoy widespread influence because in the Renaissance it provided the ground plan for the Piazza Navona, although this was in fact misidentified as a circus by eminent masters of the era such as Bernini and Borromini, an error that persisted until the correct identification in the 1840s; thus, the influence was in form and not in name.

It was therefore left to the modern era for the Hellenistic stadia to find true influence, through the revival of the Olympic Games in the 1890s. For his 1936 stadium Adolf Hitler insisted that the German spirit demanded "something gigantic," and with the secularization of Western society and the attendant rise in the importance of sport, the huge stadia built for the modern Olympics and World Cup soccer have come once again to symbolize the aspirations of entire nations. In modern arenas, such as the Stade de France (host to the World Cup in 2002), something of the ancient spirit lives on.

BIBL.: David Larmour, *Stage and Stadium: Drama and Athletics in Ancient Greece* (Hildesheim 1999). David Romano, *Athletics and Mathematics in Archaic Corinth: The Origins of the Greek Stadion,* Memoirs of the American Philosophical Society 206 (Philadelphia 1993).

V.H.

Statius

Roman poet (ca. 50–ca. 96 CE). He was roughly a decade younger than Lucan, whom he admired and imitated. Most of his own career played out under the psychopathic emperor Domitian, as Lucan's did under Nero, though not, for Statius, with the same fatal outcome. In the early 90s Statius published his *Thebaid,* an impassioned, highly wrought epic about the civil war between the sons of Oedipus, contesting power over the Grecian city of Thebes. It would prove extraordinarily popular during the Middle Ages. An especially inventive allegorization of the *Thebaid* was attributed to Fulgentius (ca. early 6th cent.); there are more than a hundred extant manuscripts, the earliest from the 9th century.

Dante goes so far as to make Statius a Christian, apparently on his own authority. Dante and Virgil find Statius on the penultimate cornice in Purgatory (*Purgatorio* 21–22); he has risen there after atoning for the slothful sin of keeping his conversion secret. He accompanies them in their encounters with the poets Guido Guinizelli and Arnaut Daniel and then ascends to heaven with Dante and Beatrice. Petrarch, on being crowned with laurel on the Capitoline Hill in 1341, saluted Statius (not quite accurately) as the last poet previously to receive that honor.

The *Thebaid* informed widespread medieval interest in the matter of Thebes. Boccaccio relies on it for his *Teseide* (1341), the proximate source for Chaucer's *Knight's Tale*—though Chaucer is sufficiently cognizant of Boccaccio's predecessor to enshrine "Stace" next to Homer in his *House of Fame* (ca. 1380). The *Thebaid* was translated into, among other things, Middle Irish prose (*Togail na Tebe,* surviving in a 15th-century manuscript), French octosyllabics (*Le roman de Thèbes,* 12th cent.), and Italian ottava rima (by Erasmo di Valvasone, 1570), though the appetite for an English version was sluggish: the teenaged Alexander Pope turned the first book into heroic couplets (ca. 1703), but the first complete English translation was W. L. Lewis's in 1766.

The particular distinction of the *Thebaid* during the Middle Ages and the Renaissance was as a repertory of moments of exemplary horror. Dante is explicit that when Ugolino gnaws on the head of Archbishop Ruggieri (*Inferno* 22–23), he is replicating the assault of the dying Tydeus on the body of Melanippus (*Thebaid* 8.751–762); the reaction of Milton's Adam to the chilling sight of the newly fallen Eve (*Paradise Lost* 9.888–893) mirrors the shock of Bacchus at the impending spoliation of Thebes, his beloved city (*Thebaid* 7.145–150).

There also survive from Statius a fragmentary second epic, the *Achilleid,* and five books of occasional poems, entitled *Silvae.* The *Achilleid* accompanies the *Thebaid* in many manuscripts and generally travels in its company, though its popularity did not really rise until interest in the longer poem had waned. The completed first book covers the episode of Achilles' concealment in women's clothing and his impregnation of Deidemia, a story that found a home in musical theater. Pietro Metastasio's libretto *Achille in Sciro* has attracted the talents of numerous composers, beginning with Antonio Caldara (1736); John Gay's ballad opera *Achilles* debuted in 1733 and in 1773 was restaged with new music by Thomas Arne (the composer of "Rule, Britannia!") as *Achilles in Petticoats.*

Survival of the *Silvae* has been more precarious, apparently dependent at one point on a single manuscript; the collection was rediscovered by Poggio Bracciolini on one of his book-hunting expeditions in 1417. Some poems in the collection have nevertheless enjoyed a vigorous afterlife—especially 1.2, an epithalamion that outdoes its Catullan precedent with a florid (and floral) extravagance that sets a new standard for the genre. Together with Claudian's later performances (late 4th cent.) in the same vein, it provided a template for a wide tradition of wedding poems in the 16th and 17th centuries. The name of the collection also captured the early modern imagination, as we see, for instance, with Milton's *Sylvarum liber* (1645), a selection of his Latin poems. When Ben Jonson included in his *Works* (1616) a collection of 15 poems named *The Forest,* he was bringing Statius' title into English. G.B.

Stephanus, Henricus. *See* Estienne, Henri II.

Stoicism

The Stoic tradition derives largely from the Roman philosophers Cicero (1st cent. BCE), Seneca the Younger (1st cent. CE), and Epictetus (1st–2nd cents. CE). The doctrines of the founders (Zeno, Cleanthes, and Chrysippus) in the 4th and 3rd centuries BCE were modified by Panaetius and Posidonius in the 2nd and the 1st, and the doctrines of the former on duty and of the latter on the physical world were especially important for Cicero and Seneca. The original divisions of Stoic philosophy between logic, physics, and ethics were blurred, and Cicero and Seneca focused more on ethics than on the other areas. Cicero's *On Duties* (*De officiis,* books 1 and 2, based on Panaetius) and *On the Ends of Goods and Evils* (*De finibus bonorum et malorum,* esp. book 3); Seneca's *Letters,* or *Epistulae, On Benefits* (*De beneficiis*), and *Dialogues* (notably on anger, *De ira;* and on providence, *De providentia*); and the *Handbook* or *Enchiridion* of Epictetus (more accessible, owing to its brevity, than his *Discourses*) were the principal founts of the Stoic ethical tradition. Cicero's *On the Nature of the Gods* (*De natura deorum,* esp. book 2), many of Seneca's letters (e.g. Letter 41) and *On Providence,* and Epictetus were the principal sources for Stoic theology (part of physics). Stoic doctrine on fate has been continually important in the tradition, not least because of its relevance to Christianity. Seneca's distaste for logic (to be valued only if it improved one's morality) has been an important element in the weakness of that field in the tradition. Although Seneca's *Natural Questions* (*Quaestiones naturales*) is the fullest extant text for Stoic physics, it has not had a great influence. Notable in the Roman philosophical tradition has been the emphasis on the *sapiens* (wise man), especially in Seneca and Epictetus; on the double citizenship of the Stoic in the material world and in the cosmos (expressed most brilliantly in Cicero's *Dream of Scipio* [*Somnium Scipionis*] and developed by Seneca and Marcus Aurelius); on the necessity of conforming to fate (expressed in Cleanthes' *Hymn to Zeus*); and on the control of the individual will (emphasized by Epictetus).

Stoicism was especially potent in hard times under Nero and the Flavians, for example, and in the religious wars of 16th- and 17th-century Europe. Many of its ethical doctrines were attractive to the early Christians, who appropriated them and so helped (along with the rise of Neoplatonism) weaken the formal system of Stoic thought. By the time Justinian closed the schools of philosophy in 529, Stoicism was a spent force, yet its doctrines lived on in the texts of the Roman philosophers, to be revived in Scholastic writings of the 12th and 13th centuries and in Renaissance Humanism and systematized in the Neostoicism of Justus Lipsius (1547–1606), whose influence lasted well into the 18th century. In modern times the publication of Stoic fragmentary texts by Hans von Arnim between 1905 and 1924, Ludwig Edelstein and Ian Kidd from 1972 to 1999, and A. A. Long and David Sedley in 1987 has recovered the original Stoic system and mandated serious interaction with its doctrines by philosophers. Thus, a just evaluation of Stoicism, which before had been partly obscured by hostility toward Seneca and Lipsius, has become possible.

Three doctrines in the Stoic system have significantly affected the tradition: that happiness is the goal of rational action; that virtue is attained by living in accordance with nature; and that virtue, achieved through reason, is the only good. Other things generally considered to be good and necessary for happiness (such as wealth, good health, social status) or bad and to be avoided (such as poverty, exile, pain) are "indifferent." The consequent focus on the "indifference" of bad things and on nature as a divine entity, both immanent and transcendent, was easily assimilated into Christian doctrine, as is evident in the writings of Clement of Alexandria and Tertullian (late 2nd and early 3rd cents.), Lactantius (late 3rd cent.), and Augustine (late 4th to early 5th cents.). Although Tertullian and Lactantius approved of Stoic moral doctrine, and Lactantius, following Seneca, identified nature with God, the early Christians argued from the superiority of Christian revelation and doctrine to pagan philosophy, even as they used it to support their arguments. Boethius (d. ca. 525), more subtly, used Senecan moral doctrine and the Stoic idea of fortune objectively and not merely as props for Christian theology.

Manuscripts of Seneca and Cicero were diffused from the 11th century onward, especially in France and Germany. In the first decades of the 12th century Peter Abelard gave new life to logic with his theory of universals, which, as the Stoics taught, were not real objects but utterances, and his reconciliation of human free will with divine providence was similar to Stoic doctrine. In the 13th century Albertus Magnus and his pupil Thomas Aquinas, seeking to reconcile Aristotelian with Christian tenets, were concerned with Stoic ethics and doctrine on fate and free will. Thomas Aquinas taught that virtue (*honestum*) was the essence of moral goodness, without reference to pleasure or self-interest. This Stoic doctrine was later expanded by Francisco Suárez, who in his *Metaphysical Disputations* (*Disputationes metaphysicae,* 1597), explained that virtue was appropriate (*conveniens*) to rational beings and was attained through reason. Aquinas further allowed a place for the emotions (*pathē*) in ethical decisions. The Stoic condemnation of the emotions as obstacles to right reason, he wrote, was in fact close to the Aristotelian view that the emotions should be moderated, for emotion (*pathos*), rightly felt, could move a rational being to right action. He disagreed with the Stoic view that human will should follow the dictates of fate (as Cleanthes taught in his *Hymn to Zeus,* quoted in Seneca's Letter 107), nor did he follow Chrysippus' definition of fate as "an inexorable series of things and a chain unrolling itself and involving eternal series of consequences," for human beings are free to make moral choices, even though divine providence knows of all things that were, are, and will be.

In Petrarch's *On the Remedies of Good and Bad Fortune* (*De remediis utriusque fortunae,* 1366), Reason, largely from a Stoic point of view, answers the misplaced optimism of Joy and Hope (book 1) and the complaints of Pain and Fear (book 2) about good and bad fortune, Stoic "indifferents" (health, wealth, etc.), and fear of death. Petrarch concludes that it is harder to bear good fortune than adversity, a doctrine that he found scarcely present in Seneca. In *On His Own Ignorance and That of Many Others* (*De sui ipsius et multorum ignorantia,* 1371) he followed Cicero and Seneca as "our philosophers," adding that "it is better to will what is good than to know the truth." Petrarch followed the Stoic emphasis on right action as the effect of right choice. He wrote that Cicero (with regard to book 2 of *On the Nature of the Gods*) "spoke not as a philosopher but as an apostle," and he found Cicero's Stoic doctrine that the world was created by divine providence compatible with Christianity. Nevertheless, he argued (unlike Seneca) that all human knowledge is minute compared with divine wisdom and that those who say they are wise are fools. Thus, Petrarch disagreed with the Stoics on the self-sufficiency of human beings to attain virtue through reason.

Petrarch's selective Stoicism influenced Coluccio Salutati (d. 1406), who rejected the Stoic denial of the emotions (*apatheia*), for even Christ had wept at the death of Lazarus. Nor did he or many others agree with the doctrine that virtue, not God, was the supreme good (*summum bonum*). Humanists' knowledge of Stoicism was advanced by Angelo Poliziano's Latin translation of Epictetus' *Handbook* in 1479 and by his defense of Stoic doctrine: "In the speech (*sermo*) of Epictetus," he wrote, "anyone can recognize his own emotions (*affectus*)."

The age-old tension between Stoicism and Christianity became acute in the 16th century, especially in northern Europe. Three issues were particularly irreconcilable: the Stoic doctrine of divinity immanent in human beings; the Stoic denial of the emotions; and Stoic views on suicide. Erasmus, in the preface to his 1529 edition of Seneca, said that human beings were not the source of their own virtue but owed it to the munificence of God. John Calvin, who was sympathetic to Stoicism at first, taught in his *Institutes of Christian Religion* (*Institutio Christianae religionis,* 1536) that human beings have a natural "sense of divinity" (*sensus divinitatis*), which opens their eyes to behold God. He too was totally opposed to the Stoic denial of the emotions, and he maintained that freedom of will was compatible with the doctrine of predestination.

Among other Reformation thinkers sympathetic to Stoicism was Philipp Melanchthon (d. 1560), whose fourth proof of the existence of God was drawn from Cicero's assertion that "in all human beings there is an innate belief that the gods exist" (*De natura deorum* 1.44).

The troubles of the Counter-Reformation, especially in the Spanish Netherlands, formed the background to the transformation of the Stoic tradition by its greatest interpreter, Justus Lipsius, who in the later 16th century developed the first systematic exposition of Stoicism since antiquity. His inconstancy in religion, his limited knowledge of Greek (compared to that of his contemporaries Joseph Scaliger and Isaac Casaubon), his focus on Seneca and Epictetus, and his attempts to reconcile Stoicism with Christianity earned the contempt of Scaliger and of many modern philosophers. A. A. Long, for example, has described his work as "a disaster for the interpretation of Stoicism as systematic philosophy" (2003, 379). Lipsius was above all a teacher, and the popularity of his work and its lasting influence are proofs of his success in communicating a systematic version of Stoicism, which is known as Neostoicism, a term first used by Calvin. Lipsius had a powerful memory, and his method of exposition was to support a thesis with quotations from ancient authors so as to produce what Michel de Montaigne called, with reference to Lipsius' *Six Books of Politics or Civil Doctrine* (*Politicorum sive civilis doctrinae libri sex,* 1589), "this learned and laboriously woven web" (*ce docte et laborieux tissu*). By quoting Stoic and Christian authors selectively, Lipsius created a "web" that was immensely influential in the confused religious context of the Counter-Reformation. He began his study of Seneca under Muretus (Marc-Antoine Muret) during a visit to Rome in 1568–1570, and his work built on the foundations laid by the editions of Seneca by Erasmus (2nd ed., 1529) and Muretus himself (1585). Nevertheless, in his appreciation of Seneca (and, to a lesser extent, of Epictetus) he far excelled his predecessors. His Neostoicism was a practical philosophy for troubled times, but, as Anthony Grafton has pointed out, he failed in his responsibility as a Humanist "to understand the past on its own terms" (2001, 241).

Lipsius' Neostoicism was explained in four works (his *Six Books of Politics* more properly belongs to political philosophy): *On Constancy* (*De constantia,* 1584); *Guide to Stoic Philosophy* (*Manuductio ad Stoicam philosophiam,* 1604); *Natural Philosophy of the Stoics* (*Physiologiae Stoicorum libri tres,* 1604); and his edition of Seneca's *Works* (*Opera,* 1605). *On Constancy,* the most influential, consists of two books, dialogues between the young Lipsius (the dramatic date is 1571) and a wise older teacher, Langius (Charles de Langhe). Lipsius represents himself as trying to escape from the disasters that were afflicting Belgium; but Langius shows him that he cannot escape from himself and that therefore he needs constancy, "the right and immovable strength of mind that is neither elated nor depressed by external events." To achieve constancy, he will need patience, and the principle for judging "things human and divine" must be reason. With these attributes he can free himself from the emotions (specifically, fear and grief), which Langius systematically discusses, showing that constancy is derived from providence (the directing intelligence of God), from necessity, and from fate. As Seneca had taught, one must follow one's commander like a good soldier, for obedience to God is liberty (*deo parere libertas est*). In the second book Langius proves the goodness of God's purposes; he explains the advantages of adversity and shows that the present troubles are comparable to the disasters of past history. Lipsius' presentation was enlivened by his Latin style, outdoing Seneca in its brevity (*brevitas*) and in his varied metaphors, particularly military and marine images. His defense of Stoic constancy made ancient philosophy relevant to the contemporary world. His goal was to bring "consolations against public evils" and to direct his voyage "to the haven of a tranquil mind."

Lipsius' effort to reconcile Stoicism with Christianity persuaded neither Catholic leaders nor philosophers. Some Stoic doctrines (for example, on suicide) were obviously incompatible with Christian tenets, and these Lipsius rejected or ignored, whereas Stoic nature and reason became the Christian God, and "living according to nature" became "living in obedience to God." Catholic leaders recognized the effectiveness of Lipsius' exposition of pagan Stoicism and pressured him to make changes. To the 1585 edition of *On Constancy* he added a preface (*praescriptio*) arguing that he was a philosopher and not a theologian, a Christian and not a heretic. But for countless readers in dangerous times the Neostoicism of *On Constancy* brought comfort and hope: it was a practical handbook for the realities of life. This was the source of its influence, whatever philosophers and theologians might say.

The climax of Lipsius' exposition of Senecan Stoicism was to be his edition of Seneca's prose works, published a few months before his death. Realizing that his time was short, he prepared for it with two systematic expositions of Stoicism, both published in 1604 and neither as elegant or convincing as *On Constancy.* In his *Guide to Stoic Philosophy* Lipsius reviewed the history of Stoicism and discussed the Stoic wise man and Stoic epistemology. He identified the supreme good and its attributes with the Christian God, and his discussion of the Stoic paradoxes in book 3 was selectively oriented toward Christian doctrines.

In *The Natural Philosophy of the Stoics* Lipsius set forth Stoic scientific doctrines essential for understanding Stoic ethics. Because theology was part of Stoic physics, much of the first book is devoted to discussion of fate and the nature of God. Here and in the remaining two books, in discussing the physical world and its creation, animals and human beings, the human soul and its functions, Lipsius endeavored to reconcile Stoicism with Christianity. By this time he was inescapably under Catholic scrutiny in Leuven. The censor's approval (*approbatio*) of the treatise noted that in it "many things were asserted in the

Stoic sense, not the author's," a grudging admission that Lipsius had succeeded in bringing ancient Stoicism into the modern world. Lipsius presented his edition of Seneca to the pope, who in reply urged him to devote his scholarship to the "excellence and greatness of the Catholic Church."

Fortunately, Lipsius did not live to satisfy the pope, and Neostoicism would be widely studied until late in the 18th century. The involvement of Lipsius' contemporary Michel de Montaigne with Senecan Stoicism was long, complex, and ambiguous. He admired Lipsius as a scholar but was wary of him as a philosopher, although, like Lipsius, he focused on the practical goals of philosophy, its applicability to life (*ad usum vitae*). Among his voluminous essays, written from 1571 until his death in 1592, those on philosophy as a preparation for death (*Essais* 1.20, "Que philosopher c'est apprendre à mourir") and on anger (2.31, "De la colère") largely draw on Senecan doctrine (respectively Seneca's Letter 24 and *On Anger*), and he never lost his affection for Seneca, whom he quoted frequently and followed in the form of his essays. But in his "Apology for Raymond Sebond" (2.12) he strongly criticized the Stoic doctrines of denial of the emotions, of the supremacy of reason, and, especially of the innate divinity of human beings. He concluded: "To make a fistful larger than the fist, an armful larger than the arm . . . is impossible and monstrous. Neither can man rise above himself and humanity . . . It is for our Christian faith, not Stoic virtue, to lay claim to this divine and miraculous metamorphosis."

Kaspar Schoppe (Scioppius), a Catholic controversialist, friend of the Rubens brothers, and would-be acolyte of Lipsius, published his *Elements of Stoic Moral Philosophy* (*Elementa philosophiae Stoicae moralis*) in 1606, but it added nothing to Lipsius' work and was didactically Christian. Much more significant were Guillaume du Vair and Pierre Charron. Du Vair translated Epictetus into French (1586), adding as a preface *The Moral Philosophy of the Stoics* (*La philosophie morale des Stoiques*). His *On Constancy* (*De la constance*) was published in 1594, along with reissues of his other Stoic essays. He relied on Epictetus more than Lipsius had, as he sought to reconcile Neostoicism with Christianity, but his practical experience in public life made his doctrines on mastering the emotions more convincing. Pierre Charron published *On Wisdom* (*De la sagesse*) in 1601, in which he discussed the Stoic wise man and provided a detailed guide for progress toward becoming one. He acknowledged his debts to Lipsius and Du Vair; his book was often reprinted. François de Sales (1567–1622) saw in Epictetus and the Stoics "the best of heathen men" but found their philosophy inferior to Christianity, which taught self-denial and the bearing of the Cross as the true way to inner peace, rather than Stoic freedom from the emotions.

Significant also was the Neostoicism of the painters Peter Paul Rubens and Nicolas Poussin. Philip Rubens, the painter's brother (and Lipsius' favorite student), appears with Lipsius in the *Self-Portrait with Friends* (1602) and in *Four Philosophers* (1611), in which a bust of Seneca is posed in the background. Rubens also painted and engraved *The Death of Seneca* (ca. 1615), an icon of Stoic constancy. His design for the title page of Lipsius' *Complete Works* (*Opera omnia*, 1637) is a symbolic summary of the author's work. Poussin's Neostoicism appears particularly in his *Death of Germanicus* (1627) and *Funeral of Phocion* (1648), reflections on the unjust death of a good man.

In Spain Neostoicism was advanced by Francisco Sanchez (El Brocense), editor of Epictetus (1600) and a believer in the primacy of reason, who was condemned by the Inquisition and died under house arrest, and by Francisco de Quevedo. In his *Stoic Doctrine* (*Doctrina Estoica,* 1635) Quevedo made a determined attempt to reconcile Stoicism with Christianity, and he traced the philosophy of Epictetus to the Book of Job (in this, developing a hint taken from Lipsius' *Guide*). But he found the Stoic doctrine that suicide is permissible in certain circumstances so abhorrent that he suppressed even the arguments against it that Seneca and Lipsius had made. He likewise found the Stoic denial of the emotions impossible to reconcile with Christianity unless it could be modified to apply only to certain ones, implying that the emotions were an inevitable feature of human experience but that we should not give in to them.

In England Neostoicism also flourished. Lipsius' *On Constancy* was translated in 1594, and Du Vair's *Moral Philosophy of the Stoics* in 1598. Thomas Lodge published the translation *Workes both Morall and Naturall of Lucius Annaeus Seneca* in 1614. In Shakespeare's *Hamlet* (1600) Horatio is a Stoic, a man whose "blood and judgment . . . are not a pipe for Fortune's finger . . . A man that is not passion's slave" (3.2.69–72). In *Heaven upon Earth* (1606) Bishop Joseph Hall, called (by Thomas Fuller) "our English Seneca," followed Seneca as a philosopher but found that Neostoicism was inadequate for "a Christian and a divine," for whom the Stoic denial of the emotions was unacceptable. Edward Herbert of Cherbury in *On Truth* (*De veritate,* 1623) and *The Layman's Religion* (*De religione laici,* 1645) developed from Neostoicism a kind of deism: he posited an innate *instinctus naturalis* (like Stoic *oikeiōsis,* "natural affinity") that leads human beings, through reason and piety, to belief in God, without the intervention of priest or church. Much later, Elizabeth Carter published a translation of Epictetus in 1758.

Of the great 17th-century founders of modern philosophy, René Descartes, Baruch Spinoza, and Gottfried Leibniz, all were indebted to Neostoicism, particularly its doctrine of the primacy of reason; Spinoza's *Ethics* (published in 1677, soon after his death) developed the Neostoic concept of God as immanent in nature, free of Christian dogma. His ethics (coincidentally, rather than as a direct appropriation of Neostoicism) were similar to those of Lipsius' *On Constancy.* After the 17th century all philosophers had to take Stoicism into account, and some were strongly influenced by it, including David Hume (*Treatise on Human Nature,* 1739–1740) and Bishop Joseph Butler (*Fifteen Sermons,* 1726). In France Denis Diderot focused particularly on the Stoic wise man in his article "Stoïcisme" in the *Encyclopédie* (1767), and he defended Seneca in his last work, *Essay on the Reigns of Claudius and Nero* (*Essai sur les règnes de Claude et de Néron,* 1782). Stoic influence continued well into the 19th century. Friedrich Nietzsche praised Epictetus in *Human, All Too Human* (*Menschliches, Allzumenschliches,* 1878), and Ralph Waldo Emerson was a Stoic in his doctrines of the "spirit present throughout nature" (*Nature,* 1849) and of individual potential (*Self-Reliance,* 1847).

The philosophical foundations of Stoicism, however, were largely overlooked by the end of the 19th century, and the term *stoic* became generalized to represent resistance to fear or pain and defiance of one's destiny. Typical was W. E. Henley, whose *Invictus* (1875) ends, "I am the master of my fate: I am the captain of my soul," a sentiment more in accord with the defiance of Lucan than of Cleanthes' *Hymn to Zeus.* In the later 20th century and into the 21st the serious study of Stoicism has been revived by philosophers. Martha Nussbaum (1994) has renewed Epictetus' doctrine that the philosopher is a healer of souls; Pierre Hadot (1994) has studied the spiritual discipline of Marcus Aurelius; and Lawrence Becker (1994) has reconstructed Stoic ethics on the basis of Stoic logic and physics.

BIBL.: L. Becker, *A New Stoicism* (Princeton 1994). H. Ettinghausen, *Francisco de Quevedo and the Neostoic Movement* (Oxford 1972). A. Grafton, "Portrait of Justus Lipsius," in *Bring Out Your Dead: The Past as Revelation* (Cambridge, Mass., 2001) 227–259. P. Hadot, *The Inner Citadel* (Cambridge, Mass., 1998), a translation of *La Citadelle intérieure* (Paris 1994). B. Inwood, ed., *The Cambridge Companion to the Stoics* (Cambridge 2003). J. Lagrée, *Juste Lipse et la restauration du Stoïcisme* (Paris 1994). A. A. Long, *Epictetus* (Oxford 2002) and "Stoicism in the Philosophical Tradition: Spinoza, Lipsius, Butler," in Inwood 2003, 365–392. P.-F. Moreau, ed., *Le Stoïcisme au XVIe et au XVIIe siècle* (Paris 1999). M. Morford, *Stoics and Neostoics: Rubens and the Circle of Lipsius* (Princeton 1991). Martha Nussbaum, *The Therapy of Desire* (Princeton 1994). A. Tarrête, "Stoïcisme," in *Dictionnaire de Michel de Montaigne,* ed. P. Desan (Paris 2004) 933–938.

M.MO.

Suda

Encyclopedia in lexicon form compiled in the second half of the 10th century, perhaps around 975–980, in Constantinople. The title could mean "fortification" or "moat" or it is, more probably, an acrostic, roughly, "a collection in alphabetical order of onomastic material" (or "of illustrious men"). The critical reference edition (A. Adler, 1928–1938) has a total of 31,438 items on 2,856 pages, and the aim of the work was to provide material for learned conversation in a literary and historical context. Previous works were lexicons in alphabetical order or encyclopedias arranged by subject; the novelty of the Suda lay in its combination of these two organizing principles, whereby it became the first encyclopedia of language (many of the entries deal with the correct use of vocabulary, particularly verbs), literature, and history that could be consulted alphabetically. The practicality of this structure explains its enormous success in the Byzantine world (Eustathius of Thessalonica was the first to mention it, in the late 12th cent.) and then in the West (the *editio princeps* was printed in Milan in 1499); every modern encyclopedia derives its organization from the Suda.

The compiler or compilers of the Suda seldom drew from classical authors but generally used intermediate sources: etymological and lexicographical lists, scholia (above all to Homer and Aristophanes), collections of proverbs, historiographical extracts (the *Excerpta Constantiniana,* compiled mid-10th cent.), and biographies. The most relevant historiographical exception seems to be John of Antioch, whom the Suda places alongside the *Excerpta Constantiniana* as the most reliable and authoritative historical guide in the entire span of Roman history.

Perhaps the most interesting aspect for the modern user of the Suda is the view it gives of the Greek and Roman past; we have in effect a compendium of the historical knowledge available in 10th-century Byzantium: how the middle Byzantine era preserved the historical memory of its Greek and Roman roots. Greek history here is the history of the affirmation and defense of Greek liberty against Persian and Macedonian tyrannies, following a "classicist" canon that was present as early as Pausanias (2nd cent. CE). Roman history is seen as having ended between the 4th and 5th centuries. Most of the entries concerning the Roman Empire (approx. 65 percent), whether biographical or not, date from after Diocletian, and the death of Theodosius I in 395 is seen as the founding act of the totally eastern Byzantine Empire, the fatherland of the author or authors of the Suda. The following subjects and events are recorded about the Rome that went before: archaic institutions and the exempla of early republican Rome; the Punic Wars; the events occurring in borderlands such as Dacia and Parthia (relevant perhaps because of contemporary tensions with the Bulgars, Arabs, and Persians; the line of succession of the emperors; and the relationship between the empire and Christianity.

The Web site http://www.stoa.org/sol/, active since 1998, aims to complete the first modern translation of the lexicon (into English and with a commentary); a great majority of entries have already been translated.

BIBL.: P. Lemerle, *Le premier humanisme byzantin* (Paris 1967) esp. 297–300. N. G. Wilson, *Scholars of Byzantium* (London 1983) esp. 145–147. G. Zecchini, ed., *Il lessico Suda: La memoria del passato a Bisanzio* (Bari 1999). G.Z.

Suetonius

The Roman Suetonius (late 1st–early 2nd century CE) was the most influential and best-known biographer in the Latin language. He composed lives of the Roman emperors down to Domitian (*De vita Caesarum*). He chose to begin the series not with Augustus but with Julius Caesar, whom Trajan, under whom he wrote, publicly commemorated as the founder of the imperial line. Suetonius held several high administrative posts under both Trajan and Hadrian, including the powerful office of *ab epistulis,* which put him in charge of the emperor's correspondence and presumably gave him access to archival material. He was a contemporary of Plutarch, whose *Parallel Lives,* written in Greek at about the same time as Suetonius' *Lives,* has always enjoyed tremendous popularity. Suetonius, like Plutarch, believed that a person's character could be revealed in small and insignificant details. But he chose, as Plutarch did not, to organize his *Lives* by topics (*per species*) rather than chronologically (*per tempora*). Suetonius also composed biographies of rhetoricians, grammarians, poets, orators, and other men of letters, although only the more famous figures are represented in texts that survive.

Suetonius' biographies built on an earlier biographical tradition in Latin that is represented by Varro and Nepos, but his twelve *Lives of the Caesars* swept the field after his death. His work induced Marius Maximus to write biographies of twelve later emperors. Although Maximus' work is now lost, it can be recovered in part through imperial biographies that have survived under the name *Historia Augusta.* This is a biographical confection of fact and fiction that was compiled toward the end of the 4th century and covers imperial personalities of the 2nd and 3rd centuries. The author drew heavily on Marius Maximus as far as he could, and that means that the lives into the early 3rd century are markedly superior to those that follow.

It is certain that Suetonius was known in the early middle ages; Einhard, the biographer of Charlemagne, was clearly inspired to construct his work along the lines of a Suetonian life. But from the Renaissance onward it was Plutarch, not Suetonius, whose name was synonymous with biography. Translations of the *Parallel Lives* by Amyot, North, and Dryden influenced writers throughout the 16th and 17th centuries. Although Casaubon worked on the Latin text of Suetonius at the end of the 16th century, the biographies were largely neglected until the great edition of Graevius at Utrecht in 1672. In the early 18th century Richard Bentley was preparing an edition that he never completed.

The positive assessment of Suetonius' *Lives* by Pierre Bayle in his *Dictionnaire* toward the end of the 17th century marked the start of a new and positive appreciation of the biographer as a reliable and honest writer. Those few clerics who had read him earlier had thought him gross and obscene, largely on the basis of a few explicit comments about sex (particularly in the *Life of Tiberius*). But Bayle's opinion gathered force in the 18th century both on the Continent and in England, and Gibbon famously praised Suetonius for his strict dedication to historical truth. Samuel Johnson undoubtedly had the Suetonian biographical form in mind when he wrote his *Life of Savage,* and he must have been aware of Suetonius' *De poetis* as a precedent for his *Lives of the Poets.* Even so, when Boswell came to compose his biography of Johnson, it was Plutarch to whom he appealed for inspiration, not Suetonius. The scabrous detail in Suetonius has tended recently to eclipse his value as a source for imperial history. Historians of Rome take him more seriously than do literary critics.

BIBL.: G. W. Bowersock, "Suetonius in the Eighteenth Century," in *Biography in the Eighteenth Century,* ed. J. D. Browning (New York 1980) 8–42, and "*Vita Caesarum:* Remembering and Forgetting the Past," in *La biographie antique,* ed. W. W. Ehlers, Entretiens sur l'antiquité classique, vol. 44 (Geneva 1998) 193–215. E. K. Rand, "On the History of the *De Vita Caesarum* of Suetonius in the Early Middle Ages," *Harvard Studies in Classical Philology* 37 (1926) 1–48. Andrew Wallace-Hadrill, *Suetonius: The Scholar and His Caesars* (London 1983).

G.W.B.

Suicide

Classical experiences of suicide were passed down to posterity along three channels: history, philosophy, and law. The dominant picture in all three was one of tolerance and even admiration for suicide, in a cultural background where considerations of honor and shame, enduring after death, were more likely guides to conduct than such ideas as existed of sanctions in an afterlife. Thus, history (with myth and epic) was star-studded with figures who had ended their own lives, from Homer's Ajax and Virgil's Dido down to hundreds of military and political Romans, headed by emperors like Nero and Otho and including privileged celebrities like Seneca, who were allowed a "voluntary death" in lieu of execution.

Philosophy was more equivocal. Several prominent schools—the Cynic, Cyreniac, Epicurean, and Stoic—nevertheless recommended suicide in some circumstances. Seneca even taught that the right to commit suicide was so central that to stop a man from committing it was worse than to kill him. Roman law, finally, bore the same mixed but predominantly tolerant message. The philosopher-jurists of its classical period (to ca. 250 CE) sought to remove suicide altogether from law's remit, as an act intrinsically innocent, allowing exceptions only where a suicide's breach of social obligation was beyond dispute, as for slaves and soldiers.

Despite this apparent acceptance of suicide, all three currents of tradition bore marks, confirmed by monumental inscriptions, of an apparently older, Mediterranean-wide taboo against suicide. The Pythagoreans referred to in Plato's *Phaedo* (62B) had given the taboo a religious rationale by comparing human beings with prisoners, who may not set themselves free, and sentries, bound to their watch until relieved. In late imperial times this anti-suicide current reemerged and was buttressed with new rationales simultaneously, if differently, by Neoplatonists and Christians. Most conspicuous of the latter was Saint Augustine (d. 430), whose *City of God* (1.16–27) gathered up the few relevant biblical texts, said suicides went to

Hell, and—at some length, perhaps reflecting an awareness that some pagan suicides could be confused with some Christian martyrdoms—blew apart the pagan case for treating two particular Roman suicides as "martyrs" of the republican era in Rome. These were Lucretia, whose self-stabbing in vindication of her honor after rape (allegedly in 509 BCE) had led to the overthrow of King Tarquin and the birth of the republic, and Cato of Utica, whose suicide by sword, in protest at Julius Caesar's victory in 46 BCE, had marked its end.

By the early Middle Ages, when Christianity was the sole official orthodoxy, suicide had become more taboo than ever, not only as an act but as a subject of discussion. A four-line decree of the Council of Braga in 561, denying public prayer for suicides, would remain the linchpin of all canon law on the subject for the next ten centuries. For half of that period theologians too would confine their rare utterances to snatches from *The City of God.* But some priests and monks are known to have prayed privately for suicides, and secular law, in a feudal world where most people "belonged" to someone else (whom they injured by suicide), had its own anti-suicide agenda, which included the confiscation of property and maltreatment of the corpse (the latter also suggestive of antipollution ritual). The 12th-century revival of Roman law, it might be thought, would erode this consensus, but it did not (except in some towns), for the relevant law was easily turned on its head by the extension of its strictures for slaves and soldiers to the population as a whole.

The 12th-century classical revival also saw the birth of moral theology, which welcomed the philosophers' moral doctrines and examples—as in Diogenes' contempt for the world, and Seneca's exaltation of virtue. Hence came all the greater shock at encountering their teachings on suicide. This dismay occasioned the first discussions of suicide since Augustine and also, incidentally, the creation of the Latin word *suicida,* a hostile neologism coined ca. 1179 in a refutation of Seneca. (The term was forgotten and would be reinvented in 1637 in a similar context by Sir Thomas Browne.) Scholastic theologians were finally rescued from their shyness of the subject when a second, pre-Stoic philosophical current appeared in the form of Aristotle's *Nicomachean Ethics,* available complete in Latin from ca. 1250. The *polis*-minded, convention-loving Aristotle had rationalized an Athenian anti-suicide ritual (much like several in medieval Europe) by explaining that all suicide was antisocial. Thomas Aquinas (d. 1274) and his colleagues leapt hungrily on this doctrine and installed it at the heart of subsequent theological utterances on the subject, which consequently became less rare.

If Roman law could be thus inverted, and Stoic philosophy diluted, it was left to the mythical and historical heroes and heroines to maintain the classical suicide culture. They did so effectively. From the 12th century, poets retold the stories of Dido, and of Pyramus and Thisbe, and their success inspired other story spinners to develop the same plots with new names and settings. An act hitherto unmentionable thus entered into the general repertoire of vernacular romance: coyly at first, but boisterously after Boccaccio (d. 1375), so that by 1500 it was entirely naturalized in the Italian *novelle* from which Shakespeare took his suicide-laden plots (those, that is, not set expressly in antiquity). *Romeo and Juliet* is just one example, its plot from a *novella* indirectly based on Pyramus and Thisbe, a medieval favorite. A similar account of derivation ultimately from classical roots could be given for many figures in the history of romance (as the word itself suggests), which means, inter alia, that even the most "romantic" representations of suicide—of the kind that burst on Europe with Goethe's *Werther* in 1774—can trace their ancestry back to the star-crossed lovers of antiquity.

Their star-crossed counterparts among ancient historical figures gained credence more gradually but with fewer disguises. From long before the invention of printing, oral and written popularizations of Roman history had begun to make classical heroes and heroines into household names. The Italian Renaissance multiplied that effect, so that Portia, Marius, and other historical suicides of antiquity began appearing in pictures, medals, and personal forenames. Three in particular soared above the rest: Lucretia, Cato, and Seneca. The first two, Rome's republican "martyrs," survived Augustine's deconstruction. The medieval Lucretia tradition crescendoed in the 16th century and, having dropped her revolutionary associations (compromising in a world of princes), made her a martyr not to virginity, by then well-represented by old Christian martyrs, but to wifely virtue. This role licensed narrators to speculate on female psychology, and illustrators to paint female flesh—even (especially after 1500, when a statue found in Rome was dubiously identified as Lucretia) to represent her sinuous nude form, its erotic charge grounded by a bloody dagger.

The fortunes of Cato rose in counterpoint with those of his fellow Stoic, Seneca, and peaked later. Seneca was Stoicism's Wise Man, who wrote; Cato, its Free Man, who stood firm. The Humanist preoccupation with texts, and the Counter-Reformation's preoccupation with moral rectitude to the point of martyrdom (taught in word and example by the Jesuits, schoolmasters to Catholic Europe), combined to raise Seneca to his highest-ever apotheosis, in a movement now called Neostoicism. Minds otherwise self-consciously critical strained their rules to make "mi santo" (as Seneca's Spanish apostle, Francisco de Quevedo, called his famous compatriot) almost into a Christian, while minds otherwise self-consciously Christian did the same with Seneca's disqualifications for baptism, especially the thorniest, his unapologetic suicide, which had to be either padded with excuses or discreetly ignored. It might, even more discreetly, be actually exalted, as it may have been by Rubens, an admiring friend of Justus Lipsius, fount of Neostoicism. In his uncommissioned painting *The Death of Seneca* (1611–1612, now in Munich) the Catholic artist endowed the philosopher's face (on a figure otherwise modeled on a Roman statue as *ben trovato,* and misidentified as capriciously as that slightly later "discovery" of Lucretia's) with the ecstatic expression of a martyr. Such discretion was thrown to the winds in the 18th century. The *philosophes,* denouncing the law's inhumane treatment of suicides' bodies, openly espoused Stoic suicide doctrine, against the Church. Because their words were aimed at a public schooled to memorize and enact classical literature, the more aristocratic of whom cultivated a "death before dishonor" ethic that fed on Stoicism, Seneca's suicide gradually became so fashionable as to be chosen as the set subject for Paris's prestigious art competition in 1773—the origin of Jacques-Louis David's huge picture on the theme now in the Petit Palais (though it did not win).

The less textual Cato had meanwhile to be content with supremacy in plain-speaking, liberty-loving England. Addison's play *Cato,* a runaway success in 1713, brought tears to the eyes of Alexander Pope and thousands of his contemporaries. Nor was any Whig palace complete without a bust of Cato. In France, Cato's day came only with the Revolution, when early Roman republicanism became the reigning classical ideal. Thus, in the end it was Cato, not Seneca, who hovered before the eyes of Condorcet and the Montagnards in 1794, when they cheated the guillotine by following his example.

Cato's zenith can be dated to 1828. By then a version of the western "death before dishonor" culture had reached Russia, complete with its classical heroes. A young artist of servile birth, Miasnikov, had won a reputation such that well-wishers offered to buy his freedom—a boon all the more desirable because he wanted to marry a freeborn woman. When his owner refused to sell him, Miasnikov went to the local gallery of antiquities, where Cato's bust presided over a phalanx of sages, locked the doors, and shot himself. His choice of method (firearms having long replaced blades as the mark of noble suicide, by contrast with the peasant's noose) amplified the message conveyed by the venue, a message spelled out, for good measure, in his suicide note: "I died for freedom."

BIBL.: H. Galinsky, *Der Lucretia-Stoff in der Welt-Literatur* (Breslau 1932). M. MacDonald and T. R. Murphy, *Sleepless Souls: Suicide in Early Modern England* (Oxford 1990) 86–95, 146–164, 179–190. J. McManners, *Death and the Enlightenment* (Oxford 1981) 409–433. S. Morrissey, "In the Name of Freedom: Suicide, Serfdom and Autonomy in Russia," *Slavonic and East European Review* 82 (2004) 268–291. A. Murray, *Suicide in the Middle Ages,* 2 vols. (Oxford 1998, 2000).

A.MU.

Symposium

Ancient drinking party or banquet. Today a symposium is an academic meeting of specialists for the purpose of presenting papers and discussing preestablished topics. This kind of event can also be called a colloquium, a conference, or a congress, words that share with symposium the prefix *cum-* (Greek *syn-*), indicating an activity that is done "together"—in the case of *col-loquium* "talking," of *con-ference* "bringing," and of *con-gress* "moving." The less sober sense of the term symposium refers to *potein,* the drinking of wine in company. The modern symposium has none of the characteristics that marked the Greek practice: a religious component; a clear separation from the meal; a small number of participants, exclusively men; the election of a symposiarch; the regulation of the consumption of wine through rituals (such as mixing with water by various degrees) in order to pursue equality through a shared state of inebriation; the symposiasts' taking turns in concocting and performing songs; the discussion of political topics; games, *eros,* and joy; the reinforcement of the group's ties; the dialectic between inclusion and exclusion, between friend and enemy, between equality and inequality, between private and public; experimentation with norms, sometimes creating and then breaking them; the value connected to active participation in the symposium as opposed to mechanical formalities; and so on. The Greek symposium was part of a complex and articulated system of conviviality whose characteristics varied according to time, place, and occasion.

Distinct developments can be perceived in the function and form of symposiastic practice—such as its flourishing in the 7th and 6th centuries BCE, its function and characteristics in democratic Athens, and the traces of it that are still visible in the convivial practices of Hellenistic cities and courts—by keeping track of the dilution of its characteristic aspects (e.g., the drinking of wine as a distinct occasion) in various forms of conviviality. A historical account of the symposium covering a long period of time must neglect its specificities and speak instead about Greek conviviality, or what in various periods is perceived as *graeco modo bibere* (drinking in the Greek fashion) (Cicero, *In Verrem* 2.1.66) or pagan conviviality. Thus emerge similarities and differences with Christian communal meals (*agapai*) and Roman dinners (*cenae*) and feasts, including the Jewish Passover Seder. These themes were present in the minds of ancient Roman writers, such as those who—like Saint Paul (e.g., 1 Corinthians) or Clement of Alexandria (*Paedagogus*)—undertook to provide Christian communal meals with a new etiquette and new functions different from those of the Roman banquet; and also of those who, participating in a banquet on a *triclinium* in a house in Rome or Pompeii, or in an imperial palace, or in a house in Antioch, or lying on a *stibadium* in a late antique house, adhered to an etiquette and to rules very different from those of the symposium, yet beheld pictures or mosaics or cups bearing images of stories, furnishings, behavior, and drinking parties of the past.

Generalizing to a greater degree, we can find similarities between the values and functions of the ancient banquet and convivial phenomena pertaining to certain medieval guilds and confraternities, to court banquets and feasts of the 15th and 16th centuries, to the conviviality practiced in Parisian cafés of the 18th century, to the *Kneipe* of certain German student associations of the 19th century, even to the formal meal at high table in an English college.

The more specific and enduring survival of Greek conviviality exists not on the level of convivial practice but on that of literature and scholarship, which we shall illustrate according to three intertwined and related lines, and which was powered by the Humanists' desire to establish a new kind of etiquette and to study and imitate ancient texts. Texts representative of the genre of the literary symposium are Plato's *Symposium,* Xenophon's *Symposium,* Plutarch's *Table Talk* and *The Symposium of the Seven Wise Men,* Lucian's *The Carousel; or, The Lapiths,* Athenaeus' *Deipnosophists,* Macrobius' *Saturnalia,* and, albeit only partially, Aulus Gellius' *Attic Nights.* (Petronius' *Satyricon,* although partially known in the 12th century, had an unsteady reception and did not achieve popularity until the 17th century, reaching its acme in the 19th.)

First, ancient conviviality was considered a microcosm for encyclopedically observing all aspects of human life, since its mixture of the word with the consumption of food was thought to conjoin physical and spiritual needs. As such its study attracted figures in the 15th and 16th centuries like Marsilio Ficino, in *De sufficientia, fine, forma, materia, modo, condimento, authoritate convivii* (*On the Sufficiency, Purpose, Form, Material, Manner, Seasoning, and Authority of the Symposium,* ca. 1476), and Montaigne, in book 3 of *Essays* (1575), scholars like J. W. Stuck, in *Antiquitatum convivialium libri III* (*Three Books of Convivial Antiquities,* 1597), and the many other Humanists who studied the phenomenon through texts handed down from antiquity, often in the context of commenting on them or of lexicographical studies. The subject of ancient banquets could also provide a stimulus and relevant examples for works on other topics. We might cite here, for example, the physician Andrea Bacci's *De naturali vinorum historia* (*Natural History of Wines,* 1596), a section of which is dedicated to ancient feasting, and the *De diversorum vini generum natura liber* (*The Nature of Different Types of Wine,* 1559) of Giacomo Profetti, another physician. In the 15th and especially the 16th centuries, antiquarian interest in customs and institutions, pursued either on the basis of texts alone or also in the light of images taken from ancient artifacts, put a great focus on the banquet. On the basis of written sources, Flavio Biondo affirmed in his *Roma triumphans* (*Rome Triumphant,* 1472) that the ancients reclined on *triclinia* and compared this custom to that of contemporary Turks and Greeks; Marsilio Ficino's work showed the importance of convivial customs in Hebrew texts and the Eucharist and, although not treating it specifically, noted the attested custom of reclining at banquets. A strong comparative character increasingly marked successive analyses of the banquet, many of which (produced during the Counter-Reformation) declared their intention to demonstrate that Jesus did not sit at table but reclined in the Roman manner, with important consequences—mediated through a complex tradition of visual sources—for the correct way to depict the Last Supper and other biblical feast scenes, as well as for interpreting certain passages of the Gospels. The custom of reclining at banquets was taken up in the context of a comparison with other peoples by the Neapolitan jurist Alessandro d'Alessandro in his *Genialum dierum libri sex* (*Six Books of Festive Days,* 1552). From the visual point of view, however, a turning point was reached in the physician Girolamo Mercuriale's *De arte gymnastica* (*Art of Gymnastics,* 1559), whose second edition (1573) provides a visual depiction of the textual evidence for the custom of reclining at banquets. Indeed, he includes among his illustrations two engravings, one from a drawing by Pirro Ligorio, the other of an ancient relief. Pedro Chacón's *De triclinio romano* (*On the Roman Eating Couch*) also contains illustrations. It was published in Rome in 1588 by Fulvio Orsini, who added his own appendix, and republished in 1664 by Frisius with additional illustrations and an appendix by Mercuriale (1601) entitled *De accubitus in coena antiquorum et semel dumtaxat in die cenandi consuetudinis origine* (*On the Origin of the Ancients' Habit of Reclining at Dinner and of Dining Just Once a Day*). In 1585 Justus Lipsius not only set his *Saturnalium sermonum libri duo* (*Two Books of Saturnalian Discourses*) in the narrative frame of a banquet, but he illustrated it with the banqueters lying on beds to show that gladiatorial games also took place on such occasions. The richness and variety of research on the banquet can be seen in Jules-César Boulenger's *De conviviis libri quattuor* (*Four Books on Banquets,* 1627), which, in a note to the reader, lists the most important scholars on the subject. Early interest, then, in the visual study of banquets focused on Roman feasting and made use of Roman artifacts or images evoked in written sources. On the other hand, the most important attempts at the iconographic interpretation of Greek vases, long considered Etruscan, did not flourish (after a few earlier spurts of interest) until the 18th century, and without any specific interest in the symposium. The 18th-century quarrel between Tuscans and Neapolitans over the Etruscan or Greek origin of these objects gave rise to a lively debate and provided the impulse for the production of important works, such as Thomas Dempster's *De Etruria regali* (*Royal Etruria,* published 1723), G. B. Passeri's *Picturae Etruscorum in vasculis* (*Etruscan Vase Painting,* 1767–1775), and P. F. H. D'Hancarville's *Collection of Etruscan, Greek and Roman Antiquities from the Cabinet of Sir Wm. Hamilton* (1766–1776). The exquisite plates that accompanied this work not only helped painted vases enter into the field of interest of scholars and historians, but it also inspired numerous ceramic productions, beginning with the Wedgwood factory founded in 1768 and named Etruria. With few exceptions, interest in Greek vases was long focused on their form and function (in line with the inquiries of anthropology and the history of civilization) rather than the images painted on them. And this despite a tradition of collecting dating back to the 15th century and the entrance of these objects, beginning at least in the 17th century, into the libraries of scholars like Giuseppe Valletta.

Second, treatises on good manners, on *civilitas,* beginning with Baldassarre Castiglione's *Il cortegiano* (*The Book of the Courtier,* 1528), Erasmus's *De civilitate puerum* (*On Civility in Boys,* 1530), Giovanni della Casa's

Galateo (1558), or Stefano Guazzo's *La civil conversazione* (1574), dedicate ample space to feasting. They sometimes use it as a narrative frame for dialogues, drawing on ancient sources and discussing the customs attested there, especially in their affirmation of the strict relationship between conversation and table manners, between the word and food. Some treatises portray this relationship more precisely as joining good manners and good eating. An ancient representative of this line of thought is Archestratus of Gela (4th cent. BCE), who wittily put the wisdom of the gourmet and the gourmand into hexameters in a work known under various titles (*Gastronomia, Hedypatheia, Deipnologia, Opsopoeia*). It was translated into Latin by Ennius (*Hedyphagetica*), and its fragments were preserved by Athenaeus. Equally influential was a collection of recipes in ten books, *De re coquinaria*. Attributed to Apicius but actually the product of long compilation, it was very well known in the Middle Ages. The most illustrious modern example is Jean-Anthelme Brillat-Savarin's *Physiologie du goût, ou Meditations de gastronomie transcendante: Ouvrage théorique, historique et à l'ordre du jour,* published in Paris in 1826.

And third, the tradition of the philosophical-literary symposium progressively developed in the direction of renouncing the written description of the feast and focusing exclusively on words, one of the two components of the symposium that in actual practice was indissolubly linked to food and wine. The unity of these aspects is nevertheless recovered on the literary level: poetry and the word, significantly the spoken word, are metaphorically food, wine, and banquet. A popular Pindaric topos envisions poetry as the cup of wine offered to a man who has just been married, "distilled nectar, gift of the Muses, sweet fruit of my mind" (*Olympians* 7.1–9); or again, "when a symposium of men comes to life, we pour a second crater of the Muses' songs" (*Pythians* 6.1–3). This is the basis of the popular metaphor, present in pagan authors but principally transmitted to medieval poetry by the Bible, of poetry as a banquet and as food, quite obvious in Dante's *Convivio*. Humanists, however, preferred to draw on the declarations of Plutarch and Athenaeus, such as the *excerptum* of the first book of the *Deipnosophists* (1.1b.7–10): "In short, the plan of the discourse (*he tou logou oikonomia*) reflects the rich bounty (*polyteleia*) of a banquet, and the arrangement of the book, the course of the banquet. Such is the delightful banquet of words (*logodeipnon*) which this wonderful steward (*oikonomos*), Athenaeus, introduces" (trans. Loeb, slightly modified). The banquet has become a stylistic vehicle for miscellany and variety, for a mimesis of extemporaneous spoken discourse, for an absence of plot. In contrast with the most ancient known literary symposia (Plato and Xenophon), this genre has come slowly to privilege, in narrative form, the spoken word over the concrete event of the feast, which becomes an imaginary setting—to which brief and desultory allusions are made—for the speeches to be recorded. It retains, however, its important characteristic of hosting the expression, in a nonhierarchical and miscellaneous way, of different points of view on the same topic (e.g., *Letter of Aristeas;* Methodius, *Symposium*). The banquet could thus become a narrative pretext for gathering together a large amount of information and erudite quotations, even quite heterogeneous, on the most disparate topics and in a nonhierarchical manner. This is the case with the symposiastic-encyclopedic texts known in the Renaissance, which provided, alongside the principal model, Plato's *Symposium,* an important prototype for the production of many literary banquets in the 16th century, such as Erasmus's six *Convivia* (*Banquets*) and Giordano Bruno's *Cena de le Ceneri* (*The Ash Wednesday Supper*). A special case is Marsilio Ficino's *Commentarium in convivium Platonis de amore* (*Commentary on Plato's Banquet, on Love,* 1469), and its vernacular translation, *El libro dell' Amore* (1475). In the prologue Ficino describes a banquet, portrayed as real, whose organization Lorenzo de' Medici supposedly entrusted to Francesco Bandini. According to Ficino, it was held in the Villa at Careggi in 1468, paired with a similar event held in Florence. The guests took turns commenting on the speeches about Eros given by the participants in the symposium narrated by Plato, and the *De amore* is supposedly a summary of this banquet. Although the banquet itself is functionally irrelevant in the *De amore,* it is portrayed, in line with the tradition of the literary symposium, as actually having taken place. And it was supposedly a cultivated revival: the date was 7 November 1468, which the learned Neoplatonic Humanists had calculated to be the anniversary of Plato's death and birth.

Rabelais offers an extraordinary example of the uses to which the banquet can be put as a stylistic vehicle, in terms both of the metaphor of the text as food and wine and of a literary work as a banquet, which presents the written word as if spoken. In his work the presence of food and the banquet, as in ancient models (Plato, Plutarch, and Lucian, but also in late medieval grotesque banquets), is highly important. The prologues to the five books emphasize the imaginary setting of the banquet. The story is a piece of entertainment during a drinking party and is directed to "you most illustrious guzzlers" (*Gargantua,* prologue 5; *Tiers livre,* prologue 345; *Quart livre,* prologue 535; *Quint livre,* prologue 723, 728). It is situated in the tradition of the literary symposium through a reference to the episode in Plato's *Symposium* in which Alcibiades compares Socrates to a Silenus, which becomes for Rabelais a guide to the interpretation of his own text (*Gargantua,* prologue 5–6). Narrator and readers (the fictive audience) are brought together by drinking and eating, for the author has composed his book in the space of a meal (*Gargantua,* prologue 7). Through illustrious predecessors like Ennius, Aeschylus, Cato, and Homer, the link between drinking and storytelling is reaffirmed. In the prologue to *Book Three,* the author, just like Athenaeus, portrays himself as the organizer of the feast (*Tiers livre,* prologue 349–352). It is no surprise that the model of the banquet could also be used for putting together a written collection of heterogeneous speeches, as in Luther's *Tischreden,* or to affirm the equality of opinions, as in the "Avis au lecteur" of the first issue of *Le banquet,* a journal founded by friends of Marcel Proust (in which the presence of the banquet and of food has extraordinary importance) in 1892. Ivan Illich, in a conscious innovation, makes metaphorical use of the concept of conviviality in his book *La convivialità* (*Tools of Conviviality,* 1973): "The convivial society is one which generally guarantees each individual's ability to use tools for his own purposes . . . The person who finds joy in the use of the convivial tool I call austere . . . Austerity . . . for Aristotle, as for Thomas Aquinas, is the foundation of friendship."

BIBL.: E. Auerbach, *Mimesis: The Representation of Reality in Western Literature,* trans. W. R. Trask (Princeton 1953). M. Aurel, O. Demoulin, and F. Thelamon, eds., *La sociabilité à table* (Rouen 1992). Mikhail Bakhtin, *Rabelais and His World,* trans. Hélène Iswolsky (Cambridge, Mass., 1968). L. Beschi, "La scoperta dell'arte greca," in S. Settis, ed., *Memoria dell'antico nell'arte italiana,* vol. 3, *Dalla tradizione all'archeologia* (Turin 1986) 293–372. F. Braudel, *Civilisation matérielle, économie et capitalisme, XVe–XVIIIe siècle,* vol. 1, *Les structures du quotidien: Le possible et l'impossible,* 2nd ed. (Paris 1979). D. Braund and I. Wilkins, *Athenaeus and His World: Reading Greek Culture in the Roman Empire* (Exeter, U.K., 2000). L. Bruit, F. Lissarrague, P. Schmitt-Pantel, A. Zografou, S. Estienne, V. Huet, N. Gilles, "Banquet," in *Thesaurus cultus et rituum antiquorum* (Los Angeles 2004) 2:4. E. R. Curtius, *European Literature and the Latin Middle Ages,* trans. W. R. Trask (Princeton 1990). N. Elias, *The Civilizing Process,* vol. 1, *The History of Manners* (New York 1978). I. Herklotz, *Cassiano dal Pozzo und die Archäologie des 17. Jahrhunderts* (Munich 1999). M. Jeanneret, *A Feast of Words: Banquet and Table Talk in the Renaissance,* trans. J. Whiteley and E. Hughes (Chicago 1991). C. Levi-Strauss, *The Origins of Table Manners* (New York 1978). J. C. Margolin and R. Sauzet, eds., *Pratiques et discours alimentaires à la Renaissance* (Paris 1982). J. Martin, *Symposion: Die Geschichte einer literarischen Form* (Paderborn 1931). M. E. Masci, *Picturae Etruscorum in vasculis: La raccolta Vaticana e il collezionismo di vasi antichi nel primo Settecento* (Rome 2008). Giuseppe Pucci, "Antichità e manifatture: Un itinerario," in S. Settis, ed., *Memoria dell'antico nell'arte italiana,* vol. 3, *Dalla tradizione all'archeologia* (Turin 1986) 251–292. S. Settis and M. C. Parra, eds., *Magna Graecia: Archeologia di un sapere* (Milan 2005). *La table et le partage,* Rencontres de l'École du Louvre (Paris 1986). F. Thelamon, ed., *Sociabilité, pouvoirs et société* (Rouen 1987). "La tradition des oeuvres morales de Plutarque de l'antiquité au début de la Renaissance," *Pallas* 67 (2005) 73–210. G. Vagenheim, "Des inscriptions Ligoriennes dans le Museo Cartaceo: Pour une étude de la tradition des dessins d'après l'antique," *Cassiano dal Pozzo's Paper Museum* 1 (1992) 79–104.

M.L.C.

Translated by Patrick Baker

Syriac Hellenism

The influence of Greek culture in Christian Aramaic tradition. Syriac is a dialect of classical Aramaic that originated around the city of Edessa (modern Urfa, in southeastern Turkey), in the Syrian province of Osrhoene; it became the common language of liturgy and written tradition from at least the 3rd century until the present for Christians of the Middle East and Iran and farther east. Syriac tradition was always hellenized to some degree, emerging in a region where local culture had over centuries come under the shadow of the proud, interregional prestige of Greek culture. From the 3rd century until the Middle Ages, scholars bilingual in Greek and Aramaic made a very large number of Syriac translations from Greek secular and ecclesiastical works. Thus, late antique Hellenism (together with Judaean, Mesopotamian, and Iranian traditions) was a major formative component of Syriac literary culture.

Brock (1982) has divided Syriac hellenization into three periods: a relatively unhellenized stage when traditional Aramaic forms of expression predominated (through the 4th century); a period of more enthusiastic assimilation of Greek works (5th and 6th centuries); and the acme of hellenization in the 7th century, when Byzantine and Persian rule of the Middle East was overthrown by the Arabs. In this period original Syriac writings most imitated the style of Greek works, and many more translations were made. The number of translations into Syriac diminished in the middle of the 8th century, from which time onward Arabic increasingly replaced Aramaic as the chief language of learned discourse among Christians in the Middle East.

Of the pre-Islamic translators, Sergius of Resaina (d. 536) is especially noteworthy. After studying at Alexandria, he translated works of Galen and Aristotle and the pseudo-Dionysian corpus into Syriac and composed his own works on medicine and philosophy. A full account of the translators and the works they rendered into Syriac must be found elsewhere, but mention should be made of the high prestige of the first three books of Aristotle's Organon (*Categories, On Interpretation,* and *Prior Analytics* up to 1.7) together with Porphyry's *Introduction* to Aristotle's logic, which became part of the curriculum of the School of Nisibis (founded 489). Thereafter the methods of linguistic and logical analysis found in these works became part of Syriac biblical exegesis.

During the 9th and 10th centuries a number of highly educated, polyglot translators fluent in Syriac, Greek, and Arabic were employed by the Arabic intelligentsia to translate Greek works into Arabic in an effort—unprecedented in scale—to revive and adopt classical Greek thought. During this time, which may be regarded as a fourth period of hellenization, translations of Greek science, medicine, and philosophy into Syriac increased in number again. A still-unknown proportion of the works translated into Arabic were rendered first from Greek into Syriac and then from Syriac into Arabic. The translators, such as the famous Hunayn ibn Ishaq and Thabit ibn Qurra, were quite often superb scholars in their own right and composed original contributions to Hellenistic science, medicine, philosophy, and mathematics in both Syriac and Arabic. These translators are often seen as cultural intermediaries whose "home culture" was Syriac. The Greek-Arabic translators were full participants in the culture of their day, however, most of them as at home in Arabic as they were in Syriac (and some not knowing Syriac at all). They were not the property of any single tradition but products of their own multicultural environment.

In time Arabic almost completely supplanted Syriac as a language of science, medicine, and philosophy, all of which were founded in Greek tradition. Middle Eastern Christians from the 10th century onward were more likely to compose such works in Arabic, and to use Syriac, the language of their Scriptures, for matters of religion. It is unknown how much material was translated from Greek into Syriac and then lost when Arabic versions became more current. There were, however, some instances of Syriac literary revival. The most outstanding example is the polymath Barhebraeus (Bar-ʿEbrāyā, d. 1286), who used Avicenna's Arabic synthesis of Aristotelian philosophy in his original Syriac philosophical works. Thereafter, Syriac tradition, like Persian, came to depend on the prestigious Arabic for its Greek learning.

As in Latin tradition, translations from Greek were classics of inestimable influence in Syriac tradition. Therefore the history of Syriac Hellenism is inseparable from an account of the entirety of Syriac tradition. Most modern scholarship on Syriac has been concerned primarily with Church history and doctrine. In addition to the large number of ecclesiastical texts still unstudied, many nonecclesiastical texts translated from Greek or inspired by Greek scientific traditions remain untouched in manuscripts today.

BIBL.: Anton Baumstark, *Geschichte der syrischen Literatur* (Bonn 1922). Adam H. Becker, *The Fear of God and the Beginning of Wisdom: The School of Nisibis and Christian Scholastic Culture in Late Antique Mesopotamia* (Philadelphia 2006). Sebastian Brock, "From Antagonism to Assimilation: Syriac Attitudes to Greek Learning," in *East of Byzantium: Syria and Armenia in the Formative Period*, ed. Nina Garsoïan, Thomas Mathews, and Robert Thomson (Washington, D.C., 1982) 17–34, and *From Ephrem to Romanos: Interactions between Syriac and Greek in Late Antiquity* (Aldershot 1999).

K.V.B.

T

Tacitus and Tacitism

Publius (or Gaius) Cornelius Tacitus (ca. 56–ca. 118 CE), celebrated in his own era and in later centuries both for his acuity of political insight and for his prose style, recorded the history of his time (roughly 18–96). His first, shorter works appeared in the 90s: a life of his father-in-law, the general, *Agricola,* with an implicit critique of Domitian, and an ethnographic study of peoples east of the Rhine, *Germania.* The *Dialogus,* an inquiry into the decline of oratory came next. The *Histories* (*Historiae,* ca. 100–110) describe the reigns of emperors after Nero (d. 68) until the time of Domitian (d. 96); the *Annals,* written near the end of his life, look back at the reigns of Tiberius, Caligula, Claudius, and Nero. The last two works, regarded as his greatest, survive only in incomplete form. His reputation waned in later antiquity, and thereafter his works remained little known until the 14th century, when part of the *Annals* and a copy of the *Histories* were brought to Florence from Montecassino. In the turbulent political and military world of the 15th and 16th centuries his genius as a political analyst commanded increasing attention—and so did his idiosyncratic style, noted for its brevity and unusual, deliberately difficult turns of thought and phrase. Gradually he won admirers and found critics in large numbers.

The Tacitism that emerged with the Renaissance was a complex, even protean phenomenon. Its creators included Humanists and administrators, Protestants and Catholics, Italians and Germans. It had a powerful influence on the history of literary style, in Latin and several modern languages, as well as on historical and political thought. And it followed a number of separate—and sometimes radically opposed—directions. Yet the whole phenomenon clearly began in the 15th century, when Tacitus' historical and literary work, barely read in the Middle Ages, began to circulate and to provoke discussion in intellectual circles. And Tacitus himself provided his interpreters not only with the historical material they discussed, but also with many of the intellectual tools they applied to it.

The first distinctive intellectual implement that Tacitus offered his Renaissance readers was the principle that cultural life changes, radically, in response to changes in its political and social environment. He explains, in the beginning of the *Histories,* that "outstanding minds" had vanished from historiography at the end of the Republic, and he argues at length in his *Dialogue on Orators* (ca. 102) that the art of rhetoric had declined at Rome as the emperors took sole power. These theories were not original with Tacitus, but he stated them in characteristically forceful, lapidary ways, making them accessible and easy to use. At the very beginning of the 15th century the Florentine Humanist Leonardo Bruni drew on the *Histories* to argue that Florence, as a colony settled by republican Rome, had inherited the special virtues that Rome itself eventually lost under the emperors. Later he would invoke Tacitus again when he tried to show in his *History of Florence* (1415–1444) that the fall of Rome had proved a blessing for the rest of Italy: the destruction of one overwhelmingly powerful center had enabled many smaller cities to rise and flourish.

Bruni's high estimate and strategic use of Tacitus were unusual: most 15th-century teachers and readers of history continued to think Livy, rather than Tacitus, the ideal historian, a reliable narrator whose moral tales of Brutus and Regulus provided perfect guidance for young patricians and courtiers. But in the late 15th and early 16th centuries discussion became livelier. Scholars debated the great divergence evident between Tacitus' style and that of Cicero and Livy. Fashionable purists (such as Paolo Cortesi and Pietro Bembo) who insisted on taking Cicero as the sole model for modern Latin prose argued that no one should teach or imitate later writers like Tacitus. They met opposition from eclectics (like Angelo Poliziano and Desiderius Erasmus) who believed in composing a modern style from multiple sources. In 1505 the first six books of the *Annals,* with their powerful and disturbing account of the early Roman empire, appeared in print. At least one of the most erudite scholars in northern Europe, Guillaume Budé, denounced Tacitus in 1508 for his malevolence toward Christianity.

For the most part, Tacitus came to his own rescue. Poliziano drew on the *Dialogue on Orators* to argue that in the realm of style "what is different is not necessarily worse." And the learned jurist Jean Bodin pointed out that Tacitus had lived in a pagan, rather than a Christian, world. To criticize him for his remarks about the Christians was to fail, once again, to understand that societies and cultures changed with time. Tacitus deserved praise for his loyalty to beliefs, however wrong to later ages, that were naturally his.

Historical change, moreover, was hardly limited to the world of books and scholarship. In the course of the 15th and early 16th centuries, Florence—one of Italy's two last great republics—came under the domination of the Medici family. The restored republics of 1494–1512 and 1527–1530 both failed. Meanwhile, the New Monarchies were taking shape in England, France, and Spain after a century and more of plague, civil war, and divided inheritances, and the vast Holy Roman Empire of Charles V had raised and deployed military power on a scale not seen in centuries. The Italian states found themselves overwhelmed and dominated when Charles VIII of France invaded the peninsula in 1494, making it a battleground for more than a generation and depriving great states like Naples and Milan of their long-held independence. Both within the Italian principalities and outside, courts became a dangerous, if profitable, theater of operations. Intellectuals and military men had to make their careers by deft performances before harsh critics.

As urban patricians who had specialized in bookkeeping turned into courtiers who fenced and danced, Tacitus' account of the early empire in ancient Rome, written from a senatorial point of view and impregnated with a deep and ironic sense of political corruption and its inevitability, seemed increasingly relevant. Francesco Guicciardini, a member of a great Florentine family who spent his career, to his own disgust, in the service of the Medici and the papacy, saw in Tacitus the one true guide for those involved in the awful revolution of modern times: he "teaches well the mode of life under tyrants, just as he teaches tyrants how to establish tyranny." Guicciardini's *History of Italy* (1540) emulates Tacitus' work in its scale, its reflective analysis of events, and its sense of universal corruption.

Guicciardini's close friend Machiavelli did not use Tacitus heavily in his own notorious reflection on the age of the Italian wars, *The Prince,* which he wrote in 1512—though he did draw a good many citations from Tacitus to adorn his great republican work, the *Discourses on Livy* (1513–1517). During the first half of the 16th century, however, many learned readers decided that Tacitus had been right to insist that "once the constitution has been overturned," only the sort of history he wrote could instill in the young the prudence they needed to survive without compromising their honor. As early as 1541, the Florentine scholar Thomas Sertinus told readers of a new critical edition of the *Annals* and the *Histories* by Emilio Feretti that "no historian is superior to Tacitus, either in terms of the resemblance to our times or in the gravity of his reflections and his skillful analysis of courtly ways."

Some influential men resisted the Tacitean vogue, usually motivated chiefly by religious scruples. Early in the 1570s two cardinals urged Marc-Antoine Muret not to lecture on Tacitus at Rome because Tacitus had slandered Christians and Jews. But in the course of the 1570s and 1580s, these barriers fell. Popes and kings became known for the pleasure they took in reading and discussing Tacitus in their private moments. What had once been suspect rapidly turned into a pervasive intellectual fashion. When Muret's pupil Justus Lipsius published his commentary on the *Annals* in 1581, he declared publicly that Tacitus' descriptions of lost liberty, failed revolutions, vicious civil wars, and mad emperors amounted to "a theater of our modern life."

Muret and Lipsius were prolific writers and effective, influential teachers. They prized Tacitus above all as a teacher of vital political lessons. Both scholars argued that the young aristocrat who came to a university to read the classics in preparation for an active life needed lessons of a new kind. It was not the nostalgic republican ideals openly propagated by Livy but the courtly and military prudence subtly taught by Tacitus that could ensure survival in the cold, shark-filled waters of a 16th-century court. By reading the *Annals* and the *Histories,* the student could learn what could and could not be said at court, how honor could be preserved even as dangers were avoided, and—most important—what constructive role the members of a social elite could play in the creation of a political and military system as successful as that of the Roman empire.

In his *Politics* (1589)—a brilliant textbook in mosaic form, composed of passages from the ancients, far more of them taken from Tacitus than from any other source—Lipsius showed how to make a version of Tacitus' analysis of empire fit the practical needs of the modern governing classes. So did a host of other writers, like Carlo Pasquale, the first of many Latin writers who composed what became known as "political commentaries" on Tacitus: bite-size nuggets of political advice, quarried from the *Annals* and *Histories,* rather than interpretations of those difficult, demanding texts as a whole. Meanwhile, Scipione Ammirato, Michel de Montaigne, and others wrote extended essays and treatises in Italian, French, and other vernacular languages interpreting the political lessons of Tacitus' work, sometimes at staggering length.

Muret and Lipsius acknowledged the difficulty of Tacitus' language and worked hard to eliminate textual corruptions in the extant works. But they also held that his obscure, provocative discourse could serve as the model for a new kind of writing: a prose more clipped, more rapid, more aphoristic than the Ciceronian Latin usually cultivated in Renaissance schools and universities. In the last two decades of the 16th and the first half of the 17th century, a Tacitean mode developed in England, Holland, the Holy Roman Empire, and elsewhere across Europe. Tacitean "brevity," with its central quality of "emphasis" or striking expression, was never considered appropriate for all genres in Latin and the vernacular. But historians, political publicists, and essayists as influential as Francis Bacon and P. C. Hooft developed their styles in a kind of protracted dialogue with Tacitus and Lipsius.

At some universities—like Leiden, the intellectual powerhouse of the new Dutch Republic, which the appeal of Lipsius' teaching transformed in less than two decades from a tiny Protestant college to the largest university in Europe—dozens of young intellectuals busied themselves in what they called the study of "politics." They studied and summarized in pointed, abrupt, witty Latin theses the Tacitean lessons about absolute monarchy. Throughout the Holy Roman Empire, publicists drew on Tacitus as they wrote their exposés of what Arnold Clapmarius, following Tacitus, called the *Arcana imperii*—the secret arts by which rulers maintained the mystery and authority that they needed.

The original Tacitists, like Muret and Lipsius, saw themselves as realistic analysts rather than bitter critics when they called attention to the similarities between the theater of power and cruelty that had ruled Julio-Claudian Rome and the courts of their own day. In Counter-Reformation Italy and Germany, many theorists saw Tacitus as a prime source for the doctrine of what Giovanni Botero called "reason of state"—the rational politics that would enable a pious ruler to survive in a dangerous world. Commenting on Tacitus could provide a way to teach the realistic politics of Machiavelli without citing him—or a pretext for insisting that Catholic doctrine required a prince to abstain from at least some of the ruses and forms of deceit that Tacitus and Machiavelli seemed to recommend. Some Jesuits criticized Tacitus for revealing the secret arts of government. But the most influential moralists of the 17th century, like Baltasar Gracián and Nicolas Amelot de la Houssaye, described Tacitus, and used him, as the preeminent guide to prudence, the best authority on the subtle, deadly arts of dissimulation that every courtier needed. Even those who reviled Tacitus for his impiety cited him, often with relish.

By the middle of the 17th century the distinguished librarian Gabriel Naudé could lay out in his bibliography for the study of politics a comprehensive and enthusiastic argument that history should play a central role in the understanding of the state. History was, as Cicero had stated in *De oratore,* a *magistra vitae,* a teacher of life—a form of philosophy, but one cast in attractive, factual examples rather than in wordy, ineffective precepts. History also meant what it had meant to Petrarch, Valla, and Erasmus: ancient history as recorded by the best of the Greek and Roman historians, such as Thucydides and Polybius, Sallust and Livy, who had perfectly obeyed "the laws of composing history." But those early Humanists had erred in their assessment of Tacitus, who in Naudé's view had offered a version of history superior to any other. Like a monarch taking the central seat in a theater at which a masque was to be performed, or a scene designer manipulating the stage machinery that produced spectacular effects of drifting clouds and flying gods, Tacitus had "resolved all the difficulties of politics." Students of politics could reasonably begin preparing to rule their states simply by memorizing the Roman historian's unique stock of "examples and oracles." Writers after Bacon and Descartes, in their various ways, had challenged the authority of the ancients; but Naudé insisted on Tacitus' preeminence in a central field of human thought and activity, political history. And he agreed with the many writers in the centuries from 1400 to 1800 who held that Tacitus offered an incomparably profound form of political instruction.

Tacitus, of course, was a more complex thinker and writer than most of his political analysts admitted. Early on, Guicciardini had suggested that Tacitus offered instruction not only to subjects but also to monarchs of an illegitimate kind, that is, tyrants. By doing so, Guicciardini had showed that Tacitism could function not only as pragmatic instruction in the arts of political survival but also as a form of critique, a way, if not to power, at least to tell the truth about it. In the extended political crisis that began in the mid-16th century and reached its denouement in the 1640s, these suggestions proved fertile. Another, republican form of Tacitism—sometimes called red—arose alongside the black Tacitism of monarchists like Lipsius.

Victims and opponents of monarchical excesses—the Spanish courtier Antonio Perez, the Italian journalist Trajano Boccalini, the English playwright Ben Jonson—found in Tacitus the raw materials for a critique of courtly life. Using Tacitus in this way could be dangerous, even when one stuck to the text. So Jonson found when his tragedy *Sejanus* was scrutinized for evidence of seditious teachings, despite the careful footnotes he had used to show that he had drawn his story entirely from Tacitus and other Roman sources. Even Tacitean historical scholarship could prove dangerous—as the Dutchman Isaac Dorislaus, the first professor of history at Cambridge, found in 1627. He filled his course on Tacitus with insistent references to the freedom that the Romans had enjoyed and the popular basis of sovereignty, which the Roman emperors had never formally repealed. His lectures were immediately denounced as republican and subversive. Dorislaus was silenced by the court—though he later found revenge in helping draw up the charges used to condemn King Charles I.

This red form of Tacitism was bolstered by a second, rather different current of interpretation—one that also began in Italy but flourished most extravagantly in the German states of the Holy Roman Empire. As early as 1458 Aeneas Silvius Piccolomini had drawn from Tacitus' *Germania* a detailed description of the ancient inhabitants of what was then the Holy Roman Empire, contrasting the rough customs, illiteracy, and simple life of the early Germans with the corruption of their modern descendants, in order to show how much Germany owed to the Roman Church, the only institution that could enable a return to ancient virtues. But German scholars like Jacob Wimpheling and Conrad Celtes, writing a few decades later, used the same evidence to insist that contemporary German peoples did possess the virtues of their forefathers. All Germans were pure-blooded, autochthonous, brave. All scorned luxury, even if they tended to eat and drink too much. All despised lawyers, since they had had no written laws. And all loved freedom, since the original Germans had elected their kings, who ruled only with the consent and advice of their subjects.

Tacitus offered ammunition for many intellectual battles—often to both sides. In the early 17th century, when Hugo Grotius and others wished to show that their new Dutch Republic rested on solid historical foundations, they turned to Tacitus, who made clear that their ancestors, the Batavi, had resisted the tyranny of Rome just as the modern citizens of Holland and Zeeland resisted that of Spain. Other Dutch writers agreed with Grotius about the virtues of the ancient Batavians, as Tacitus depicted them, but preferred monarchical to republican government. This was the form of Tacitism that shaped Dorislaus—one radically different from the Tacitism of Muret and Lipsius.

The new myth of German freedom proved intellectually fertile as well as politically provocative. Tacitus' picture in *Germania* of a society outside the bounds of conventional Graeco-Roman traditions—a work that found favor with the public and went through many editions—offered a potent model to Western Europeans who wanted to describe the alien societies they encountered in the New World and elsewhere. Tacitus' ethnography of a barbarian society suggested a set of topics that should be covered when describing any other culture—from that of the Maya of Yucatán to the almost equally foreign culture of the Jews who lived in Italian ghettos. More important, Tacitus' detailed and not unsympathetic account of a society at the periphery of the civilized world implicitly cast the exemplary virtue of the center into question. Thus, the historian of court and empire helped create the powerful imaginary figure of the noble savage, who could unmask the hollowness of imperial propaganda with one deadly phrase.

Even more challenging were the political implications of the fact that the ancient Germans, however peripheral, belonged to Europe and its tradition. François Hotman cited the *Germania* when he argued in his *Francogallia* (1573) that the original monarchy of the Franks was also Germanic and elective. Ancient German democracy made a potent additive to the other ingredients used by Hotman and his fellow Protestant propagandists when they tried to fix the limits of royal power. In the 17th century critics of the English monarchy went further, calling on Tacitus in support of their denunciation of the "Norman yoke" that William the Conqueror and his successors had imposed on the free Germanic tribesmen of England several centuries before. Throughout the 18th and early 19th centuries nostalgic evocations of primitive freedom mingled with sharp denunciations of court intrigue in the language of English journalists and French philosophes. Rebellious Americans and French critics of Napoleon agreed that Tacitus had definitively described the ways of emperors and revolutionaries. Tacitean history remained the prudent man's best teacher. But it now taught him to subvert the authorities that it had previously counseled him to conciliate and serve.

In the course of the 19th century Tacitus gradually fell from scholarly credit. New forms of analysis, often based on an assumption of the primacy of economic considerations, replaced politics as the most powerful tools at the historian's disposal. Tacitus himself, moreover, came to be seen as an interpreter of, rather than a primary source for, most of the events he recounted—and one whose dour, subtle style made him all the less reliable. Yet even the 19th-century scholarly revolution, which brought Tacitism in its classic form to a close, was in a distant sense the product of the Tacitist movement.

Tacitus himself remarked that the early Germans had no written histories; instead, they used songs to preserve their traditions. Sixteenth-century scholars compared this form of oral tradition to parallel cases—like those of the New World peoples. Evidently—so François Baudouin and Justus Lipsius remarked—all early peoples transmitted the outlines of their past by singing rather than by writing. Even the Romans had used the songs they sang at banquets to similar effect. Thus, Roman tradition too might be no more solid at its core than that of the antique Batavi or the newfound Aztecs—at least for the earliest period of the Republic, before the Gauls sacked the ancient city in 387 BCE. Romulus and Numa, those heroes of a thousand anecdotes repeated ad nauseam to schoolboys, might never have lived. These suspicions in turn stimulated later scholars, like Barthold Georg Niebuhr, to rethink the nature of historical tradition and source criticism itself. To that extent, Tacitus—who became, like few other ancient writers, the intellectual father of a coherent movement in modern thought—also helped bring about his own demise. But he has come back to life in more recent times. In Germany reverence for early Germanic virtues had scholarly consequences no Renaissance Tacitist could have imagined. In Britain, by contrast, he inspired Sir Ronald Syme, who took a Tacitean point of view and used a Tacitean style to reinterpret the history of the later Roman Republic and Empire—and wrote (Syme 1958) what remains the deepest study of Tacitus himself.

BIBL.: Morris Croll, *Style, Rhetoric and Rhythm,* ed. J. Max Patrick and Robert Evans, with John Wallace (Princeton 1966). Elsie-Luise Etter, *Tacitus in der Geistesgeschichte des 16. und*

17. Jahrhunderts (Basel 1966). Jeroen Jansen, *Brevitas: Beschouwingen over de beknoptheid van vorm en stijl in de Renaissance,* 2 vols. (Hilversum 1995). T. J. Luce and A. J. Woodman, eds., *Tacitus and the Tacitean Tradition* (Princeton 1993). Ronald Mellor, *Tacitus: The Classical Heritage* (New York 1995). Arnaldo Momigliano, *The Classical Foundations of Modern Historiography,* ed. Riccardo di Donato (Berkeley 1990), and *Essays in Ancient and Modern Historiography* (Oxford 1977). Mark Morford, *Stoics and Neostoics: Rubens and the Circle of Lipsius* (Princeton 1991). Gerhard Oestreich, *Antiker Geist und moderner Staat bei Justus Lipsius (1547–1606)* (Göttingen 1989). José Ruysschaert, *Juste Lipse et les Annales de Tacite: Une méthode de critique textuelle au XVIe siècle* (Turnhout 1949). Kenneth Schellhase, *Tacitus in Renaissance Political Thought* (Chicago 1976). Jacob Soll, *Publishing The Prince* (Ann Arbor 2005). Jürgen von Stackelberg, *Tacitus in der Romania: Studien zur literarischen Rezeption des Tacitus in Italien und Frankreich* (Tübingen 1960). Ronald Syme, *Tacitus,* 2 vols. (1958; repr. Oxford 1985), and *Ten Studies in Tacitus* (Oxford 1970). Richard Tuck, *Philosophy and Government, 1572–1651* (Cambridge 1993). H. Wansink, *Politieke wetenschappen aan de Leidse universiteit, 1575–±1650* (Utrecht 1981).

A.G.

Tantalus

Imprisoned in Tartarus by Zeus for grievous offense against the gods. His punishment was confinement up to his chin in water that receded whenever he tried to drink, in proximity to fruits that withdrew from reach every time he approached. Thus derives the verb—English *to tantalize,* Portuguese *tantalizar*—and the expression "to seek fruit from the garden of Tantalus," crystallizing the ironic experience of desiring the very thing that frustrates one. A *tantalus* is a case for spirits in which the liquor is enticingly displayed but locked up; Sherlock Holmes had a tantalus in his rooms at 221B Baker Street. The "apples of Tantalus" are false or inherently unsatisfying objects of desire, turning to ash at the touch: the serpentine devils of John Milton's epic *Paradise Lost* (1674) take the bait of a fruit-filled grove springing up before them in Hell, but "instead of Fruit/Chew'd bitter Ashes" (10.565–566). Love poetry is populated with unrequited lovers akin to Tantalus; the speaker of Luis de Góngora's 1584 sonnet "La dulce boca que a gustar convida" has learned that the roses of love are really poisoned apples:

> manzanas son de Tántalo, y no rosas,
> que después huyen dél que incitan ahora
> y sólo de el Amor queda el veneno.

Moralists from late antiquity through the mid-17th century used Tantalus variously to represent intemperance, miserliness, delusion, the vanity of desire, covetousness, avarice, self-deprivation in the midst of abundance, theft, the breaking of ritual fasts, even poverty itself. These economic crimes aroused punitive attitudes to the sinner among moralists. Honoré Daumier's 1843 print caricatures Tantalus to ridicule the bourgeoisie; in the modern age the writer Giora Shoham has used Tantalus and Sisyphus to make a punitive argument that Israeli Jews are hardworking, persistent, goal-oriented, organized, ambitious builders, whereas their enemies are the opposite.

In the visual arts Tantalus is often linked with his fellow criminals in Tartarus who suffer unique torments (chiefly Sisyphus, Ixion, and Tityus), most remarkably in a miniature by Hans Holbein the Younger (1532–1543), an engraving by Hendrik Goltzius (1588), Titian's life-size oils *The Damned in Hell* (1547–1549), and Bernard Picart's engravings on Hell's prisoners (1730s).

Challenges to the inevitability of violent punishment by a supreme power are evident in a drawing by Jan Harmensz Muller (Dutch, 1571–1628) in which we see Zeus observing his prisoner; in Countee Cullen's sonnet "Yet do I marvel," where the mystery of Tantalus' torture parallels the mystery of God's making "a poet black, and bid him sing" (1925); in Mati Unt's Estonian, anti-Soviet short story "Tantalus," narrated by Tantalus himself (1986). Sympathy for Tantalus also appears in accounts in which Tantalus briefly forgets his torment (Boethius) or is allowed to drink (Robert Henryson's 15th-century *Orpheus and Eurydice*):

> Than Orpheus had reuth of his grete need;
> Tuke out his harp and fast On it can clink;
> The water stude, and Tantalus got drink. (11.286–288)

Pity shades into admiration for Tantalus. Since at least the 2nd century CE, Tantalus could be taken as a culture hero, revealing divine secrets or divine gifts for the good of humankind. Maxim Gorky praised Tantalus as culture's fabling recognition of the heroic labors achieved by primitive, that is, materialist man: "All the myths and legends of ancient times find their consummation, as it were, in the Tantalus myth. Tantalus stands up to his neck in water, he is racked by thirst, but unable to allay it—there you have ancient man amid the phenomena of the outer world, which he has not yet learned to know" (speech delivered at Soviet Writers' Congress 1934).

T.KR.

Television

In its first decades television did not share cinema's appetite for the classical world. The expensiveness of movies set in antiquity may be a sufficient explanation; networks and stations sometimes paid to broadcast them as special events. Generally, the ancient world was the business of self-consciously educational programming. The CBS series *You Are There* (1953–1957) was on the edge of that category; it dramatized historical occurrences as if they were contemporary news stories (reported by Walter Cronkite), including such classical events as the assassination of Julius Caesar (twice), the fall of Troy, and the death of Socrates. The future of the ancient world is resolved in an episode of *Star Trek* (NBC, 1967) when the crew of a 23rd-century spaceship destroys the last surviving Olympian god on a distant planet.

Some serious dramatic efforts remain memorable from the middle decades: Jonathan Miller's modern-dress rendition of Plato's *Symposium* (*The Drinking Party,* BBC, 1965); Roberto Rossellini's two-part *Socrate* (RAI, 1971, one of several period pieces that he made for Italian television); Lars von Trier's *Medea* (Danish Broadcasting, 1987, from a treatment by Carl-Theodor Dreyer). The most impressive television drama with a classical setting is still the 13-part rendition of Robert Graves's novels about the fourth Roman emperor, *I, Claudius* (BBC, 1976; directed by Herbert Wise from a script by Jack Pulman). An attempt to make a feature film of the novels had failed expensively in 1937; the television version has been rebroadcast several times and marketed widely on tape and disk. As a representation of the ancient world it remains almost unique: an epic political story presented with drawing-room intimacy and knowingness, both avoiding excessive cost and focusing on the kind of drama that small-screen television can do extremely well (though with a psychopathic edge that initially required softening for American distribution).

In the 1990s the ancient world became a more viable possibility for television programming. An antic version of that world flourishes in two linked series filmed in New Zealand for international distribution: *Hercules: The Legendary Journeys* (1995–1999) and *Xena: Warrior Princess* (1995–2001), the latter recounting the adventures of a previously unattested Amphipolitan woman whom Hercules turns from evil to good. Ostensibly set in mythic times, both shows supplement the traditional stories with gamesome additions (Xena arranges the assassination of Julius Caesar); their mood is by turns tragic and inventively frivolous. Different ambitions are manifested in some handsomely mounted if dramatically conventional productions that recreate the movie epic in economical form (computer-generated imagery having reduced the need for expensive and vulnerable sets). Internationally financed, usually running three to four hours, these shows are marketable for two-part television broadcast, theatrical release, or by sale on DVD. They have included *The Odyssey* (1997), *Cleopatra* (1999), *Jason and the Argonauts* (2000), *Helen of Troy* (2003), *Spartacus* (2004), *Julius Caesar* (2004), and *Hercules* (2005). RAI is involved in a cycle of six such productions, covering the Roman Empire from beginning to end; the first two are *Augustus* (2003) and *Nero* (2004)—the latter presenting its title character as an idealistic reformer who eventually receives a loving funeral from his Christian girlfriend.

Two especially notable recent projects, the six-part *Empire* (broadcast by ABC in 2005) and the two-season *Rome* (HBO/BBC, 2005–2007), dramatize Rome's brutal transition from republic to empire (with Caesar's assassination as a focus). Both create roles for previously unreckoned figures: Caesar's gladiator bodyguard in one case, two soldiers from Caesar's army (their names lifted from his *Gallic Wars*) in the other. Both are dark in their vision, and *Rome* is especially seamy and graphic, in the spirit of *I, Claudius* but also reminiscent of HBO's long-running Mafia series, *The Sopranos.* The imperial theme looms menacingly on the television screens of the early 21st century. G.B.

Temperament

The four temperaments—sanguine, choleric, melancholy, and phlegmatic—still occupy a firm place in the popular study of character. This tetrad traces its origin to the ancient foursome of bodily fluids, or humors: blood (*sanguis*), yellow bile (*chole*), black bile (*melaina chole*), and phlegm (*phlegma*). The notion of a natural constitution or disposition caused by the dominance of one humor in the body originated in antiquity. In the Galenic (*In librum Hippocratis, de Natura Humana* 1.40K.15, 97; *Animi mores* 3.K4, 777) and post-Galenic texts by pseudo-Galen, pseudo-Soranus, the Venerable Bede, Isidore of Seville, and so on, which combine cosmological doctrines (on the four elements and qualities) with medical theories (the pathology of the humors) and observations of physiognomy, one finds an "increasingly clear acceptance of the idea of the humors' power to determine character types" (Klibansky et al., 1964). A reevaluation of the humors appears in post-Galenic times that remained dominant throughout the Middle Ages and into the modern period: blood creates "well-tempered" individuals who are cheerful, good-looking, and good-natured, whereas yellow bile makes people bad-tempered and prone to vehement outbreaks of anger. The character types produced by black bile and phlegm are less clearly defined but invariably seen in negative terms until the 12th century, when the reception of the idea of "ennobled melancholy" set in, as described in the (pseudo-)Aristotelian problem 30.1, and a better day dawns for melancholiacs, at least. The reassessment of the character-forming power of the humors that took place in late antiquity resulted from the transfer of the Galenic doctrine of eucrasia-dyscrasia as determined by the qualities of the humors. The doctrine of temperaments thus became an important component of a tetradic formula of the universe in which elements, qualities, humors, seasons, stages of life, cardinal organs, colors, modes of church music, planets, apostles, evangelists, archangels, and winds were linked together by way of analogy. In this context the doctrine offered a plausible and popular explanation for the variety of human physiognomies, characters, types of behavior, and changes in health.

The four temperaments were not systematized until the 12th century, however. William of Conches (ca. 1080–ca. 1154) mentions them in his *Philosophia* and Hugo de Folieto (ca. 1100–1172) in his work *De medicina animae.* A model for numerous later treatises on temperaments is the *Tractatus de complexionibus* from the late 13th century, ascribed to one Johannes de Nova Domo (printed 1495, 1511, 1514). From then onward the four temperaments became a fixture of Western culture. For the late

Middle Ages and early modern period the following ideas are dominant: the temperaments are hierarchically ordered, the sanguine temperament being considered ideal and occasionally even being compared with the human condition before the Fall. Furthermore, the temperaments are mutable, like the seasons, stages of life, planets, and *sex res naturales* (air; food and drink; rest and motion; waking and sleeping; excretions; and moods) that influence them. Thus, everyone is called on to optimize his or her temperament through diet and appropriate habits and with the aid of supporting therapeutic measures. To this extent the doctrine of temperaments became part of the general culture. The goal of such efforts was not only physical health and elevated mood, but also the attainment of firm moral and religious principles. This is because an unfavorable configuration, such as an excess of black bile, creates entries for the evil machinations of devils and demons, who luxuriate in its blackness, deceive the powers of reason with false images of God and Creation, and lead human beings into temptation. People could protect themselves from threats such as religious wars, the Inquisition, and the persecution of witches by optimizing their temperament; this was an important strategy for survival with regard to both this world and the next. The arts, which according to Horace are meant to delight as well as instruct, serve this same purpose. Joy and laughter promote the sanguine component in the temperament, offering protection against the corroding effect of black bile, the consuming effect of yellow bile, and the deadening effect of phlegm. Art thus functions not only as a mirror of the doctrine of temperaments and as a means of representing it, but also as a quasi-therapeutic agency for converting bad temperament to good.

Countless images of the four temperaments can be found in manuscripts, guild books, broadsheets, calendars, woodcuts, copper engravings, frontispieces, drawings, and oil paintings. Further stations in the development of the doctrine of temperaments are represented by Philipp Michel Novenianus' *De temperamentis* (1534); the *Disputatio* (August 14, 1588) of Johann Possel the younger, the later rector of the Humanistic gymnasium in Rostock; the *Disputatio arithmetica de complexionibus* with which Leibniz earned his faculty position at the University of Leipzig in 1666; Johann Daniel Longolius' *Wahrhafftiger Temperament* (*Veritable Temperament*, 1716); Jakob Böhme's theosophical work of consolation *De quatuor complexionibus* (1730); and Kant's *Anthropologie in pragmatischer Hinsicht* (*Anthropology from a Pragmatic Point of View*, 1798). Echoes of them persist in stereotypes of "national characters" and the doctrine of four races (red, black, yellow, white). The doctrine of temperaments influenced both the early modern Neostoic doctrine of four "passions" and modern biblical exegesis (e.g., Job; the apostle Paul; Luke 9:51–62). Like a groundwater channel, it runs below the unhappy consciousness of Hegel, Nietzsche's no longer gay science, Kierkegaard's melancholy, and Sartre's bad conscience. It found expression in countless doctoral dissertations in medicine, theology, and law between 1550 and 1850, in which the temperaments' physical, mental, and spiritual effects were investigated and their legal consequences discussed. It permeates theories of laughter and enthusiasm, notions of genius and anthropological theories. We encounter it in portrait collections, in the Neoclassical school of Jacques-Louis David, and in our everyday language. The idea of temperaments lives on today in sermons, theatrical comedies, choreography, musical compositions, cookbooks, personality tests, Waldorf pedagogy, and popular psychology, and it continues to be productively expanded in Jerome Kagan's developmental psychology and Hans-Jürgen Eysenck's theory of personality.

BIBL.: Noga Arikha, *Passions and Tempers: A History of the Humours* (New York 2007). J. Kagan, *Galen's Prophecy: Temperament in Human Nature* (New York 1994). R. Klibansky, E. Panofsky, and F. Saxl, *Saturn and Melancholy: Studies in the History of Natural Philosophy, Religion, and Art* (New York 1964). H. G. Schmitz, "Das Melancholieproblem in Wissenschaft un Kunst der frühen Neuzeit," *Sudhoffs Archiv* 60 (1976) 135–162. E. Schöner, *Das Viererschema in der antiken Humoralpathologie* (Wiesbaden 1964). W. Seyfert, "Ein Komplexionentext einer Leipziger Inkunabel (angeblich eines Johann von Neuhaus) und seine handschriftliche Herleitung aus der Zeit nach 1500," *Arhiv für Geschichte der Medizin* 20 (1928) 272–299, 372–380. L. Thorndike, "De complexionibus," *Isis* 49 (1958) 398–408.

T.R.

Translation by Deborah Lucas Schneider

Temple

With the triumph of Christianity in the late 4th century CE, the long age of classical temple building came to an end. Many temples were wrecked, but a few, such as the Athenian Parthenon and the Roman Pantheon, were converted to Christian use, resident pagan spirits having been banished with overpowering ceremonies. It was only in the context of Humanist and Renaissance revivals of classical values that ancient temple forms entered the broad stream of the history of Western architecture, where their expressive, orderly symmetries prospered.

Religious rituals in early classical times centered on an altar standing in consecrated open ground, with a primitive shelter alongside for the effigy and treasure of the deity. Both Greek and Roman temples evolved from these shelters, but at different times and with different results. The mature Greek temple, with its continuous lines of columns around a rectangular chamber, was well established by the 6th century BCE; circular temples came later. This was well before the Roman temple, based on Etruscan practice, took its characteristic shape: a boxlike structure usually raised on a high podium and originally unadorned except for a columned porch at one end, reached by a flight of stairs. The Greek temple persisted well into Roman times, but Roman temples, like Roman culture, became internationalized, much under the influence of the Hellenistic thought and art of the last three centuries BCE, so that in the Roman Empire (from 27 BCE) the sober simplicities of the past were augmented by more complex and theatrical designs and experiments with both rectilinear and circular forms and combinations thereof. In these later developments creative use was made of poured concrete.

The best-preserved traditional Greek temple is that of Hephaestus, god of the forge, standing beside the Agora in Athens. Incomplete but instructive examples survive in the Greek homelands (Greece, the islands, and western Turkey) and in the colonies of southern Italy, Sicily, and even Libya; temples preserved in part inside later buildings can be seen in Syracuse (the cathedral) and Rome (San Nicola in Carcere). Good examples of Roman traditional temples exist in Rome (the Temple of Portunus by the Tiber) and in France (Nîmes, Vienne). Grand imperial examples include the Pantheon in Rome and the temples at Baalbek (Lebanon); it should be pointed out that such creations were unknown to Vitruvius, whose invaluable textbook on Roman architecture (1st century BCE) is sometimes taken as an inclusive authority.

Church builders before the Renaissance might make internal use of fallen temple columns, as in Rome in San Giorgio in Velabro and Santa Sabina, and the classical circular plan of the Church of the Holy Sepulchre in Jerusalem (4th century CE, rebuilt twice) was reworked for Western baptisteries, rarely for churches. The facade of San Miniato al Monte in Florence and the colonnade in front of the cathedral of Civita Castellana, both from the early 13th century, are examples of the occasional late-medieval interpretations of classical temple forms. Neither then nor in the Renaissance were Greek temples much studied; travel between the city-states of Italy was difficult enough, and exploring the temples of Magna Graecia was unheard of. The travels of Cyriacus of Ancona, a learned antiquarian, were unique. For years in the 15th century he traveled in Greek lands, recording inscriptions, sculpture, and temples, and made drawings, one of them an approximation of the Parthenon's west facade, that were redrawn and published by Serlio in the next century. The work of Vitruvius, which includes explanations of Greek practice, first appeared in print in 1476.

With the exception of the Pantheon, the Roman temple as a building type played almost no role in Renaissance architecture. But the temple front itself—the elevated columned porch with its sheltering triangular pediment—became indispensable. The proportions of ancient plans and building elements, above all those of the orders (the various styles of columns) were closely studied; both Serlio (1475–1554) and Vignola (1507–1573) published their results. Vignola was the more successful, a gifted architect who, like many other northerners, went to Rome to participate in the renewal of the ruined city begun in the previous century. He made major contributions, there and elsewhere, and built two modest Pantheon-like churches, both with oval domes and temple fronts executed in high relief. His contemporary Andrea Palladio (1508–1580) is even more important, largely because of his *Four Books of Architecture* of 1570, the most influential treatise in the history of Western architecture; the adjective "Palladian" dates from the early 18th century. His fourth "book" is about ancient temples, of which the Pantheon gets the most attention, with ten plates. Elsewhere he treats villas and offers his own designs.

Palladio, like other architects then and later, measured the Pantheon. (This habit was long-lived: when John Russell Pope arrived in Rome in the 1890s, measuring the porch was his first project.) Well before Palladio's time two porch columns had fallen, the ancient sculpture had vanished, and a Christian altar had been placed before the large axial niche (the temple's conversion dates to the early 7th cent.). The great building was and is sound, available, unique, bathed in light, the best-preserved vaulted Roman temple. Brunelleschi, author of the mighty dome of the Florence cathedral, studied the Pantheon, as did Bramante, who proposed a Pantheon dome for the new St. Peter's Cathedral. In modern literature the Pantheon is often said to be a rebuilding of an earlier temple, but this is misleading, for Hadrian's Pantheon, built in the 120s CE, was entirely new. (It may be that the dome, a hemisphere made of some 5,000 tons of concrete, is still the largest such vault there is.) In any event, it is the most copied and reinterpreted building in the Western world.

Palladio's usual elegant sobriety gave way to flamboyance in his Loggia del Capitano in Vicenza, which wouldn't have been out of place at Baalbek. To some extent it implies the Baroque architecture of the next century, of the kind seen in the architectural displays inside St. Peter's by Gian Lorenzo Bernini (1598–1680), who also invoked the Pantheon in two churches, Sant'Andrea al Quirinale in Rome and another at Ariccia to the south. By 1700 domed churches entered through temple fronts were almost stock-in-trade for European architects, and at the time it may have seemed that the influence of classical temples had run its course. But that wasn't the case, in fair part because some intrepid architects managed, in the 18th century, to travel to distant locales to study and measure major structures all but unknown previously: for example, Robert Adam and Charles-Louis Clérisseau (the imperial palace at Split on the Adriatic coast), James Stuart and Nicholas Revett (Athenian temples), Robert Wood (Baalbek), and James Dawkins and Robert Wood (Palmyra); now there were images of Greek and Roman temples aplenty, all published. And in 1738 Palladio's *Four Books* appeared in English, dedicated to Richard Boyle, Earl of Burlington, the chief figure in a group of confirmed English Palladians responsible for numerous temples erected in new, artificially natural gardens—round temples and modest Pantheons, as at Chiswick and Stourhead. Thomas Jefferson owned a copy of the *Four Books,* but for public buildings he chose Roman sources as models: the Nîmes temple for the Virginia state capitol, the Pantheon for the library at the University of Virginia.

From the 18th century onward architects could consult illustrated books of antiquities. The discovery of Pompeii and Herculaneum caused a sensation when the settings of Roman life in the 1st century CE were revealed by early archaeologists. With the Enlightenment and its insistence on reason and the rejection of repetitive tradition, Greek and Roman thought and art came to be seen as life enhancing and productively instructive. The superiority of classical art was first argued in print, in 1764, by Johann Winckelmann, for whom sculpture was the mistress art. The faith of patrons and architects in the symbolic potency of ancient temples goes far to explain the proliferation of classical temples and temple forms that lasted until the mid-20th century, by which time they had been used for nearly every imaginable purpose.

Although the religious content of classical temple forms never disappeared, it was diluted by the Enlightenment, and from the mid-18th century onward inherent visual and sensory qualities of Greek and Roman sacred architecture were increasingly put to use in secular buildings. The formal scheme of the temple front, for example, came to imply stability and security and soon became the hallmark of portentous buildings of widely varying purposes. Stability is proclaimed by the powerful and precise symmetrical balance secured around an invisible center line rising to the tip of a broad-based triangle, the most stable geometric figure (in the more sophisticated designs, this effect is reinforced by placing the two central columns slightly farther apart than the flanking ones). The center line, the steps with their flanking podium arms, and the sheltering pediment invite entrance. Being tall, the columns are in sympathy with human verticality; being round, they are free of lateral connections. Their effect on the senses is unlike that of square pillars, which are essentially vertical slices of walls and retain something of a wall's denial (this is well illustrated by American temple fronts with pillars). Long rows of columns, with their staccato pattern of light and shade, solid and void, are the essence of precise order, more expressive in this sense than rows of identical windows or buttresses. The allusive power of classical temples lies in an eloquent geometry both satisfying and harmonious.

As wars and social crises intensified in the 1770s, the creation of grand architectural statements of classical design increased rather than lessened; authority usually led the way, and private patrons followed suit. The results are found from Britain to Russia and in the European colonies; they include whole temples and an incalculable number of impressive temple fronts and porticoes. This expansion was energized by books both practical and cerebral, by vastly increased travel (Italian and British architects worked in Russia, for example), and, in due time, by teaching architecture, first in the studios of masters and later in architecture schools. All of this, in addition to the increasing patronage of commercial firms, carried the image and standing of the classical temple design well into the 20th century. Meanwhile, the word *temple* was used ever more freely, for buildings described as temples of glory, liberty, science, or learning, for example, as well as for certain categories of buildings irrespective of their purpose, such as French Protestant churches, Jewish synagogues, and Mormon places of worship.

Neoclassicism is the term applied to art and architecture derived from or inspired by Greek and Roman originals, from about 1750 to roughly 1840. Grand temples of the period survive across Europe, from the Church of the Madeleine in Paris (by A. P. Vigion, begun in 1807 as Napoleon's Temple of Glory) to the Bourse in St. Petersburg (T. de Thomon, 1805–1810). The Madeleine, splendidly sited at the end of the rue Royale, sits girdled by stately Corinthian columns on a high podium the size of a football field, and in scale and design it recalls huge ancient temples like Hadrian's of Venus and Rome, and that of Zeus Olympios in Athens that had remained half built for several centuries before Hadrian completed it. Equally impressive is Ludwig of Bavaria's Walhalla, which rises high above the Danube east of Regensburg (L. von Klenze, 1830–1842). Huge staircases and transverse ramps lead up to a crowning Parthenon; architect von Klenze studied the rows of classical temples at Paestum, south of Naples, and Agrigento in Sicily, and he may have seen what remained of the long ramps of the outsize Roman sanctuary built on the steep hillside of Palestrina near Rome.

The Pantheon's popularity persisted. The sculptor Canova built in Possagno in northern Italy a Pantheon with a version of the Parthenon's porch (1819–1833); the clash of styles is rather disconcerting and most architects used Roman porches, as C. Amati did at San Carlo al Corso (1832–1846) in Milan, and G. Grognet de Vassé did with the Rotunda of Santa Marija Assunta at Mosta on Malta (1833–1860), where the Pantheon-shaped dome is made of horizontal rings of stone. The interiors of the rectangular buildings are rarely classical—that of the Madeleine, for example, has a file of shallow domes supported on arches and pendentives in the Byzantine manner. Classical temples, mostly on a small scale, were built in urban cemeteries in every Western country and colony, well into the 20th century; memorials consisting of domed circles of columns are fairly common and often quite elegant. Designers of domed buildings large or small rarely refrained from providing coffering, so powerful was the Pantheon's image.

In spite of the quickened pace and complexity of 19th-century life, ancient temples weren't forgotten. In Germany, for example, K. F. Schinkel, a Neoclassical master, built both major civic temples and elegant smaller works, such as a domed rotunda of columns in a park near Potsdam, crowned by a translation of the Lysicrates monument in Athens (1845); the entry to his Berlin Schauspielhaus (1819–1821) is a stately and archaeologically correct temple front in the late-Greek manner—slender Ionic columns support a low, spreading pediment. In Paris, A.-T. Brongniart created a grand Roman temple for the Bourse, P. von Nobile built a copy of the temple of Hephaestus in Vienna (1820s), and H. C. and T. F. Hansen began work in Athens on civic temples for the government of the new kingdom of Greece. Classical architecture was brought to America by English professionals, above all by Benjamin Latrobe (1764–1820), the benefactor of the native-born Robert Mills (1781–1855) and William Strickland (1788–1854), and it was these men, together with Thomas Jefferson, Clérisseau assisting, who established classical architecture as the primary public style of the new country.

Meanwhile, the number of architectural styles increased rapidly in both Europe and America. One historian identifies 21 in the United States, where illustrated books on architectural styles and building types proliferated together with hands-on manuals in which craftsmen could find, for instance, drawings of classical capitals and moldings from which working patterns and templates could be made. Latrobe's Catholic cathedral in Baltimore (1804–1818), with a somewhat inelegant exterior and a splendid interior centered on a wide dome, was the country's first major classical building. In Washington, Mills produced grand classical works such as the Treasury Building (1836–1842), with its mighty colonnades; the Washington Monument is also his. Strickland showed his considerable talent in the Philadelphia Merchants Exchange (1832–1834), a half-round temple whose columns support a low roof with a Lysicrates monument; his Tennessee State Capitol in Nashville is outstanding. T. U. Walter (1804–1887) produced what is perhaps the best American temple, Girard College in Philadelphia (1833–1848), in which he demonstrated his knowledge of fireproofing, as he did that of metal construction in his dome for the U.S. Capitol.

These early examples bred a number of domed state capitols and temple-style civic and commercial buildings across the land. The term *Greek Revival,* though, refers chiefly to the classical facades of dwellings, whether great mansions or simple single-family houses, all without any other Greek features whatsoever except for a bit of classical decor here and there: perhaps simply some columns and a pediment. For this very popular style, Carpenter Grecian isn't a bad name, for wooden temple fronts appeared on houses from eastern Maine to the frontier—signs of national pride, of keeping up with the times, and perhaps to some extent of an assumed superiority of ancient classical culture. The evidence runs from grand mansions, such as the 75-room Belle Grove in Louisiana, whose elegant porch, columns and all, was carved from cypress, to many hundreds of ordinary houses, most of them painted white, in ordinary towns throughout the country.

The French-led Beaux-Arts style, popular in the decades leading up to the First World War, produced no temples—the terms are antithetical: at the Chicago World's Fair of 1893, none of the scores of Beaux-Arts buildings was a temple. But classical examples weren't forgotten, as is shown by the Pantheon-like library built at Columbia University in New York (McKim, Mead and White, 1893–1902) and by B. Maybeck's domed octagonal centerpiece of the Palace of Fine Arts in San Francisco (1913), perhaps inspired by the Temple of Minerva Medica in Rome, just as Michelozzo was inspired when planning an addition to the Church of the Annunziata in Florence in 1444. For a fair in Nashville in 1897, a replica of the Parthenon was built of timber and plaster, then redone at full scale in concrete in the 1920s.

As modernist architects and critics denounced historical styles, such interest as there was in classical temples lapsed—except in Washington, D.C. Across the river, a simple, open and domed Temple of Fame once stood in Arlington, Virginia (M. C. Meigs, late 1860s); a similar building, a 1920s memorial to District men who died in the First World War, stands on the Mall. The powers who chose architects for major public buildings wanted classical forms in harmony with the past. They chose H. Bacon's proposal for the Lincoln Memorial (1912–1922); he had visited the site of the Greek city of Assos, where he studied, with his archaeologist brother, the remains of a major Greek Doric temple of the 6th century BCE. The Lincoln Memorial follows Greek precedence except that it is entered on the long side and has a flat Attic roof (C. F. McKim had drawn a classical temple with the same unclassical roof). C. Gilbert's Supreme Court Building (1929–1935) is a historically correct Roman temple with flanking wings; an ancient precedent for this is the Roman capitol that survives in Brescia, near Milan.

Our last classicist is J. R. Pope (1874–1937), who produced the National Gallery of Art's West Building, which encloses a circular domed temple; the National Archives Building, whose main hall is half a Pantheon; and the House of the Temple, a Scottish Rite temple of a square, ancient design that supports a stepped pyramid, based on what was thought at the time to be a proper Greek precedent. Pope's Jefferson Memorial, finished by his associates, has two encircling rings of supports for the dome, ingeniously placed to emphasize axial views of the interior. The building is well sited and, like that of the Lincoln Memorial, the workmanship is excellent.

A thought should be given to the pictorial life of ancient temples on metal and paper currency, and in the shape of the traditional Rolls Royce radiator and dozens of logos, including that of the British Museum. Finally, there is the case of the Guatemalan dictator Manuel Estrada Cabrera (r. 1898–1920), who built Temples of Minerva across the country, where schoolchildren were given prizes and writers gave readings, famous visitors were feted, and the dictator appeared as an apostle of learning. Only one of the temples survives, at Quetzaltenango—just columns and the roof.

BIBL.: Axel Boëthius and John B. Ward-Perkins, *Etruscan and Early Roman Architecture* (Harmondsworth 1970). William B. Dinsmoor, *The Architecture of Ancient Greece* (London 1950). William L. MacDonald, *The Pantheon: Design, Meaning, and Progeny* (Harmondsworth 1976, 2002). Andrea Palladio, *Four Books on Architecture,* trans. R. Tavernor and R. Schofield (Cambridge, Mass., 1997). Catherine Rendón, "Temples of Tribute and Illusion," *Américas* (August 2002) 16–23. John Summerson, *The Classical Language of Architecture* (London 1980).

W.L.M.

Terence

Publius Terentius Afer (ca. 195–159 BCE), Roman comic playwright. He wrote *fabulae palliatae,* "plays in Greek clothing," dramas adapted from Greek originals and set in Athens. This New Comedy, as it came to be called, popularized by Terence and his earlier contemporary Titus Maccius Plautus (ca. 254–184 BCE), featured stock characters such as the *senex* (old man), *virgo* (girl), *adulescens* (youth), and *miles gloriosus* (braggart soldier) clashing in domestic conflicts and intrigues. Only six of Terence's comedies have survived, though one legend (recalled by Suetonius) poignantly reports that he died while carrying back from Africa 108 new plays. Cicero praised Terence prophetically for *quiddam come loquens atque omnia dulcia dicens,* "speaking with a certain graciousness and with sweetness in every word," and Terence became for later generations a model for elegant Latin. More critically, Caesar called Terence *dimidiate Menander,* "half Menander," and lamented his lack of *vis,* "force" (both quoted by Suetonius, *Vita Terenti*). Unlike the more boisterous Plautus, Terence presented thoughtful discussions of ethical problems in well-constructed, often double plots and hardly ever used lyric meters (fewer than 30 lines total, compared with 14 percent of Plautus' canon).

Terence is the only Latin author besides Virgil whose complete work has survived in a manuscript written before the 6th century CE, the Codex Bembinus in the Vatican library. The survival of 650 manuscripts written after 800 CE attests to Terence's enduring popularity from late antiquity through the Middle Ages as a dramatist and model of Latinity. In the 4th century Donatus and Evanthius wrote grammatical and rhetorical commentaries on Terence, which were often reprinted. Terence is one of the few canonical classical authors who maintained a continuous presence in medieval literacy. He had a well-established place in European curricula and in the minds and hearts of schoolteachers long before the plays of Plautus emerged from obscurity.

Early modern Humanists delighted in Terence. Fragments of the earliest Neo-Latin comedy, Petrarch's *Philologia* (before 1336, now lost), reveal interest in the standard Terentian meter, iambic senarius. Another early comedy, Vergerio's *Paulus* (ca. 1390), adapted Terence's *Andria* and *Eunuchus.* After the *editio princeps* (1470) appeared in Strasbourg, productions of the plays increased. In 1476 *Andria* was performed at least three times in Florence—in the school of Giorgio Vespucci, in the Medici palace, and in the Palazzo della Signoria. Students from Verdun put on comedies of Terence in 1514. A 1538 statute in Salamanca stipulated that a comedy by Plautus or Terence or a tragicomedy be presented at the feast of Corpus Christi and on the Sundays following. Early modern annotators flocked to the text—Jodocus Badius (1493), Petrus Marsus (1502), and many others. In Wittenberg, Stephanus Riccius (Stephen Reich) gathered various commentaries together, including that of Philipp Melanchthon, to publish a Protestantized variorum edition (1568). Furnished with copious grammatical notes, this edition, like many that preceded (including the magnificent *Terentius, in quem triplex edita est P. Antesignani . . . commentatio,* Lyon 1560) and many that followed, drew numerous moral lessons from the action, reading characters as various virtues or vices. Pamphilus and Charinus in *Andria,* for example, love virtuously in contrast to the lustful Phaedria, Chaerea, and Thraso of *Eunuchus.* Micio in *Adelphi* illustrates a noble paternal clemency. In his *Defense of Poesy* (1595) Sir Philip Sidney defended the right use of comedy by citing the admonitory display "of a niggardly Demea, of a crafty Davus, of a flattering Gnatho, of a vainglorious Thraso"—all Terentian characters who illustrate some vice to be avoided. That such reading could not account for much of any play's action (especially the ending) reveals the essentially microscopic and analytical nature of the moralistic hermeneutic, also evident, though to a lesser extent, in Humanist appropriations of Plautus. Commentators routinely extracted lessons piecemeal from individual moments and scenes of the play, wholly removed from context.

Translations of Terence into vernacular languages proliferated. G. Rippe (1466), G. Cybille (1470), and J. Bourlier (1566) turned the plays into French; R. Bernard (1598), into English; Brant and Locher (attributed) (1499), V. Boltz von Ruffach (1539), and J. Bischoff (1566), into German; G. da Borgofranco (1533) and G. Fabrini (1556), into Italian; and P. Simón Abril (1577), into Spanish. There also appeared many translations of individual plays, including an Italian *Andria* by Niccolò Machiavelli (1517, 1520) and a French *Eunuchus* by Jean Antoine de Baïf (1565). Richard Bernard's 1598 English rendering shows that translators, no less than editors and commentators, aggressively managed and mined the Latin texts. Bernard's introductory epistle presents Terence as a "comical poet, pithy, pleasant, and very profitable, as merry as Eutrapeles, as grave as Cato, as ethical as Plato; he can play craftily the cozener and cunningly the clown. He will tell you the nature of the fraudulent flatterer, the grim and greedy old sire, the roisting ruffian, the mincing minion, and beastly bawd, that in telling the truth by these figments men might become wise to avoid such vices and learn to practice virtue." This edition, like many others, provides moral expositions of scenes, marginal notes, lists of sententiae, and Latin phrases (*formulae loquendi*).

Such didactic presentation sought to render Latin comedy safe for young, impressionable minds. Beginning at least with Cicero's commendations in *De oratore* and elsewhere, Terence lived a long and influential life in schools as a model for Latin language and rhetoric. In *On the Method of Teaching and Learning* (*De ordine docendi et discendi,* 1459) Battista Guarino recommended Terence's plays (along with Juvenal's satires) for elegance of speech. The 16th-century Venetian senate instructed publicly paid Humanists to teach Cicero in the morning and Terence or another suitable text in the afternoon. Notable teachers such as Gasparino da Barzizza (Gasparinus of Bergamo, d. 1431) lectured on him, compiled excerpts from his work, and encouraged students to do the same. Early in *De ratione studii* (1511), a central text for European curricula, Erasmus encouraged study of Terence for his language and moral utility: "Among Latin writers, who is more valuable as a standard of language than Terence? He is pure, concise, and closer to everyday speech and, by the very nature of his subject matter, is also congenial to youth." Handbooks and florilegia appeared to help students learn Terentian Latin. Nicholas Udall compiled for pupils at Eton *Flovres for Latine Spekynge* (1533, often reprinted and enlarged), which induced principles of Latin grammar and rhetoric from phrases culled line by line from *Andria, Eunuchus,* and *Heautontimorumenos.* Aldus Manutius' phrasebook *Locutioni di Terentio: Overo, modi famigliari di dire* (Venice 1585), furnished with lengthy Italian and Latin indices, taught Italian students to greet a friend, express dismay, or look for a street in Terentian Latin. Joseph Webbe's edition of *Andria* (1629) employed his influential method of instruction, consisting of an English translation printed next to the Latin text, both arranged on a grid of corresponding parallel lines and columns. Citing Erasmus, Scaliger, and Heinsius, Webbe in his preface commended Terence as "pleasing to be read . . . accommodated to the capacities of young beginners . . . profitable for matter of eloquence or behavior."

Not everyone agreed. Many objected to Terence's plays for their zestful depictions of lust, deceit, and greed. In 1553, for example, Ignatius Loyola banned Terence from the wide network of Jesuit schools. Earlier Roswitha, a 10th-century canoness of the Saxon Imperial Abbey of Gandersheim and perhaps Europe's first post-classical Latin playwright, had observed that many who delighted in Terence's sweet style and diction became corrupted by his depictions of wicked deeds. Consequently, as "the strong voice of Gandersheim," she stated in a preface to her dramas that she imitated the pagan dramatist with a difference, "so that in that selfsame form of composition in which the shameless acts of lascivious women were phrased, the laudable chastity of sacred virgins may be praised." In Terence's *Eunuchus,* for example, Chaerea disguises himself as a eunuch to gain entrance to a courtesan's house and access to his beloved; in two of Roswitha's Latin plays (*Abraham* and *Pafnutius*) a man disguises himself as a lover to enter a brothel, not to enjoy a woman but to reclaim her to virtue and penance. This sort of eristic adaptation flourished in a later movement that became known as Terence *moralisé.* One early, important example is Gulielmus Gnaphaeus' *Acolastus sive de filio prodigo* (1529). This play rephrases the New Comedic conflict between *adulescens* and *senex* as the biblical story of the prodigal son. Acolastus falls prey to a Terentian parasite and meretrix but finally repents and receives forgiveness from his father. *Acolastus* ran to about 60 editions during the 16th century and appeared in numerous translations and adaptations. Similarly neoclassical prodigal son plays became a minor genre in Europe, including Macropedius' *Asotus* (1510) and *Rebelles* (1535), Stymmelius' *Studentes* (1549); in England, *Nice Wanton* (1560), *Misogonus* (1571), and Gascoigne's *The Glass of Government* (1575); in Florence, Cecchi's *Figluol prodigo* (1569–1570), a brilliant mingling of New Comedy, Christian moralization, and bourgeois comedy. In Holland Cornelius Schonaeus (d. 1611) published 17 sacred comedies in the Latin style of Terence.

Of course most imitations of Terence were not so adversative. Along with Plautus, Terence served as a prototype for dramatic comedy, furnishing plots, characters, and ideas to all the West. Terence specifically bequeathed to later playwrights, including the cantankerous Ben Jonson, the argumentative prologue, wherein the author answers his detractors and defends the play. Commentators on Terence articulated an influential formal dynamics of play making, consisting of three major movements—*protasis* (introduction), *epitasis* (stretching out), and *catastrophe* (overturning)—organized into a five-act structure. Terence's canon also inspired a long list of direct adaptations and imitations throughout the theatrical repertories of early modern Europe. *Eunuchus,* for example, especially Chaerea's disguised entrance into the courtesan's house and the figure of the braggart soldier Thraso, had many and various descendants. Lodovico tried Chaerea's trick only to find the lady a disguised man and to receive a beating in George Chapman's *May Day* (1611). In William Wycherley's *The Country-Wife* (1675) Horner more successfully worked the ruse to facilitate several affairs. Lionel's disguise brought him both sexual satisfaction and reunion with his lost love in Sir Charles Sedley's *Bellamira* (1687). The strutting and bragging Thraso had many descendants. The Spanish dramatic novel *Celestina* (1502) featured an early offspring, Centurio. Nardi presented an Italian Trasone in *I due felice rivali* (1513). Adding romantic intrigue and local color, Aretino transformed Thraso in *Talanta* (1542), as did Oddi in *L'erofilomachia* (1572). In the 16th century Thraso entered the English language as a synonym for a boaster. Later, incorporating as well elements from Plautus' *Miles Gloriosus,* Thomas Cook undertook an extensive rewriting in *The Eunuch; or, The Darby Captain* (1737). This farce adds songs, invents a scene for the *virgo,* rechristened Dorinda and here given a voice, and transforms Thraso into a kidnapper named Captain Brag.

Many other transformations of Terence played on European stages. In Spain Bartolomé de Torres Naharro adapted *Heautontimorumenos* in *Comedia calamita* (1519). The comedies of Juan Ruiz de Alarcón (1581–1639), remarkable for their superb plot structure and ethical emphases, earned for the playwright (a native of Mexico) the title "the Spanish Terence." Thomas Shadwell's *The Squire of Alsatia* (1688) featured a blithe *adulescens* who ignored former lovers (and his illegitimate child) to marry the chaste Isabella. Molière lightly adapted *Adelphi* in *L'école des maris* (1661), and *Phormio* in *Les fourberies de Scapin* (1671), giving new life to the clever slave. Richard Steele turned *Andria* into sentimental comedy in *The Conscious Lovers* (1722), in which the chaste and modest Bevil Jr., neither callow youth nor braggart soldier, pointedly avoids a duel.

About the same time the classicist Richard Bentley brought out his great edition of Terence (1726, with Aesop and Publilius Syrus), which featured careful consideration of the text, an essay on meter, and copious philological notes. George Colman the elder published a verse translation of Terence (1765), and Richard Cumberland, "the Terence of England" in Oliver Goldsmith's phrase, reworked *Adelphi* into *The Choleric Man* (1774). The prologue to this play (from the London edition of 1775) shows the persistence of the moralizing tradition:

> Micio's mild virtue and mad Demea's rage,
> With bursts alternate shook the echoing stage;
> And from these models 'tis your poet draws
> His best, his only hope of your applause.
> A tale it is to chase that angry spleen,
> Which forms the mirth and moral of his scene.

Later playwrights such as George Bernard Shaw, Oscar Wilde, and Eugène Ionesco did not imitate any play of Terence per se but assimilated, adapted, and parodied New Comedy deftly and fluently. Notably in recent times Thornton Wilder transformed *Andria* into a novel, *The Woman of Andros* (1930), a lambent, melancholy fable that gives voice to Chrysis, the deceased courtesan of Terence's play.

BIBL.: George E. Duckworth, *The Nature of Roman Comedy* (Princeton 1952). Marvin T. Herrick, *Italian Comedy in the Renaissance* (Urbana 1960). Gilbert Norwood, *Plautus and Terence* (New York 1932). Bruce R. Smith, *Ancient Scripts and Modern Experience on the English Stage, 1500–1700* (Princeton 1988). R.MI.

Teubner

Publishing house for classical scholarship. The printing company was founded on 21 February 1811 in Leipzig by the book dealer Benedictus Gotthelf Teubner (1784–1856). Teubner first printed philological texts, then mathematical ones as well. Like other printers and publishers in Leipzig, he fostered contacts with scholars in Saxony, especially the classical philologists Gottfried Hermann and Friedrich Wilhelm Ritschl. In view of the expanding market for academic books, Teubner decided in 1823 to found his own publishing house in Leipzig, the capital of the book trade. On the initiative of Franz Passow, a scholar in Breslau, the journal *Jahrbücher für Philologie und Pädagogik* (*Philology and Pedagogy Yearbooks*) was launched in 1826; it was issued until 1944 under various names, most recently as *Neue Jahrbücher für Antike und deutsche Bildung* (*New Yearbooks for Antiquity and German Education*). This periodical profited from the middle-class "reading revolution" at the beginning of the 19th century and satisfied the desire of a humanistically educated elite for the scholarly discussion of philological and pedagogical subjects.

Teubner became famous in the mid-19th century in the areas of classical philology and higher education in Germany and Europe. The first editions of the *Bibliotheca scriptorum Graecorum et Romanorum* (*Library of Greek and Roman Writers*) appeared at the beginning of 1850. Within 60 years the works of about 250 ancient authors were available in 550 volumes. The series came to embody the editorial efficiency of German classical scholarship. It symbolized the methodological and theoretical direction taken by classical philology in the age of historicism. Thus, in his letters Friedrich Nietzsche spoke snidely of "the Teubners." The goal was to make the entire literary patrimony of Greek and Roman antiquity available in critical editions; it went without saying that new editions would be issued periodically to reflect improvements in the reconstruction of texts. Inexpensive school editions of the Greek and Latin classics were also produced, with little or no critical apparatus, for German high school students. The *Thesaurus linguae Latinae* (*Thesaurus of the Latin Language*) began appearing in 1900, edited by the five German-language academies of Berlin, Göttingen, Leipzig, Munich, and Vienna.

Teubner published not just works of classical scholarship, however. By the second half of the 19th century the company was starting to develop into an all-purpose publisher. Its catalogue reflected the rise of mathematics, especially geometry, of Neo-Kantianism, and of humanities pedagogy. In 1892 the direction of the department for philology and pedagogy was taken over by Alfred Giesecke, a doctor of classical philology influenced by the Protestant milieu of Leipzig and by Friedrich Naumann's Christian Socialist movement. He was the intellectual of the business. He consistently pressed ahead—partly out of economic considerations—with the disciplinary diversification of the catalogue, although he clung to the ideal of the "unity of scholarship." With high-circulation journals like the *Deutsche Literaturzeitung* (*German Literary News,* begun in 1892) and series like *Kultur der Gegenwar* (*Contemporary Culture,* begun in 1906), Teubner contributed to the popularization of scholarship and influenced the intellectual discourse of the late empire.

Teubner produced most of its titles in its own print shop, and before the First World War its size as well as the scholars represented in its series made it one of the German Empire's most distinguished publishers. Its catalogue contained tens of thousands of titles; in 1913 the company had well over 1,000 employees in Leipzig, Dresden, and Berlin.

The publishing house survived the inflation of the Weimar Republic and the indoctrination of the National Socialists. It was maintained as a private publisher in Leipzig until after World War II. But because of the political and economic changes resulting from the 1949 founding of the German Democratic Republic, the company split and part of it moved to Stuttgart, in West Germany, in 1952. B. G. Teubner continued to operate in Leipzig and to maintain the house's tradition of classical scholarship. After German reunification the two publishers were at first merged by the heirs, but then they were broken up again for economic reasons. Bertelsmann bought the scientific and technical portion of the Leipzig house in 1999; the branch devoted to classical scholarship was acquired by the publisher K. G. Saur, which since 2006 has belonged to Walter de Gruyter.

BIBL.: Helen Müller, *Wissenschaft und Markt um 1900* (Tübingen 2004). Friedrich Schulze, ed., *B. G. Teubner, 1811–1911: Geschichte der Firma* (Leipzig 1911). S.R.

Translated by Patrick Baker

Theater Architecture

The Roman writer Vitruvius describes in some detail the colonnades, scenes, and semi-circular cavea ("bowl" form) of the ancient theaters of Greece and Rome in his influential architectural treatise of the 1st century BCE. Surviving ruins of Greek theaters, such as that of Dionysus in Athens, remained relatively obscure until the 18th century, but Roman theaters that survived at various imperial outposts in the West became the object of much scrutiny at a far earlier date. In Renaissance Rome the vast size and relatively good state of preservation of the Theater of Marcellus gave it enormous prestige among architects and patrons. Together with the Septizonium in the Palatine, it demonstrated in particular how antique columns could be superimposed on facades of more than one story—thus becoming a focal point, in the Renaissance, for detailed studies by, among others, Baldassare Peruzzi (d. 1536 or 1537) and Andrea Palladio (d. 1580). Leon Battista Alberti had discussed the ancient theater in some depth in his unillustrated treatise of the 1450s. Sebastiano Serlio's representations of the grandeur of Roman civilization in his multivolume treatise on antiquities (begun in 1537) included woodcuts of the Theater of Marcellus as well as those in Pula and in the ruined Ferentium. Palladio's antiquarian interests are attested in particular by his drawings of the ancient theater for Daniele Barbaro's *Vitruvius* (1556) and by his design for a wooden theater similar to that of the ancient Romans erected in the Salone della Basilica in Vicenza in 1561–1562. He developed this design in his famous Teatro Olimpico in Vicenza (1585) with its permanent palace facade backdrop, as did his pupil Vincenzo Scamozzi in his theater in the ducal palace at Sabbioneta, near Mantua (1590).

Interest in the ancient theater among the Italian aristocracy marked their privileged status and represented an important means by which they affirmed their power. In his work on perspective, published in 1545, Serlio illustrated an adaptation of the ancient theater conceived as the perfect vehicle for the expression of social rank. The most eminent nobles sat at the base of the tiered seats, with the lesser nobles behind and standing room at the back for the "common people." His theater followed ancient precedent as regards its orchestra and proscenium, but the curved seating arrangement of the cavea was now truncated to fit within the ubiquitous modern rectangular courtyard. With a remnant cavea but with rigid social gradation, rectangular perimeter, and perspective scenery, Serlio's theater was a hybrid building, caught between the ancient and modern worlds. As if to emphasize its growing impracticality, the ground plan of the ancient theater reappeared during the 17th century in imaginary buildings. In England ca. 1620 Inigo Jones used the ancient theater plan to idealize Stonehenge as a Roman temple to the god Coelus, and Robert Fludd used it as a moral emblem and the basis of an imaginary memory theater in his *Ars memoriae* (1619). In the same era, the ancient theater form was changing to fit new functions in the real world. Jones had visited the Roman theater at Orange in Provence in 1609, and he and his pupil John Webb adapted the ancient theater in their scheme for the Barber-Surgeons' Anatomy Theatre of 1636–1637 in London. Giambattista Aleotti used the same ancient model for his Teatro Farnese at Parma of 1618, built with a greatly enlarged orchestra to facilitate elaborate intermezzi and opera seria.

Jones's Banqueting House of 1619–1622 in Whitehall, designed for the Stuart court masque, inaugurated the use of a rectangular hall, proscenium arch, and perspective sets in England, and its form came to dominate theater design for the next four centuries. In Paris the great hall of the Hôtel du Petit Bourbon, converted into a theater around 1614 and used by Molière's company in 1659, demonstrated the ease with which rectangular spaces could be used to satisfy the needs of modern drama. Ceremonial buildings based on the ancient theater continued to be built, however, one example being Christopher Wren's Sheldonian Theatre in Oxford of 1664–1669, with its painted sky; but these buildings performed modern functions, such as increasingly secular university ceremonial, which had little need of the perspective sets more suited to rectangular spaces.

The discovery of an ancient amphitheater at Herculaneum beneath the lava of Vesuvius in the early 18th century led to something of a revival of the ancient theater, especially among a rising generation of French architects who identified in the ancient stage an ability to meet the growing literary demand for new spaces of theatrical illusion. Jacques-Germain Soufflot's new theater for Lyon (1753–1756, demolished in 1826) led the way in introducing freestanding theaters into French towns and sought in the arrangement of its auditorium to compromise between existing social hierarchies and older ideals of communality and equality of sight lines, typical of the ancient theater.

The physical divorce between audience and action that the proscenium arch had introduced, together with the dominance in the Baroque theater of optical effect and perspective scenery, was nevertheless apparently confirmed by the advent of modern cinema. Yet the questioning of the role of perspective in optical perception by, among others, 20th-century Cubists helped stimulate a new revival of interest in the use of the ancient theater form, this time by architects of the Modern Movement. The Finnish architect Alvar Aalto had sketched the theater at Delphi in 1953, and its form became the basis of his main lecture theater in the Otaniemi Institute of Technology in Finland (1955–1964). The Greek theater, so much a part of the landscape, suggested to Aalto a new beginning for architecture based not on the machine but on nature. Similarly, Denys Lasdun's National Theatre in London (1967–1973) was also influenced by the Greek theater. In this case the ancient theater model helped confirm the mood of revival of a classical age under the second Queen Elizabeth. The desire to abandon the curtain and forge a new link between audience and actor led in the 1970s to a fashion for theater "in the round" (e.g., the Royal Exchange in Manchester, opened 1976), thereby reviving the ancient theater's most fundamental quality. This quest for simplicity and a reconnection with the landscape has also led in recent times to a worldwide vogue for open-air theaters. The modern era thus cast off the expression of social hierarchy that Serlio had regarded as fundamental and that the Baroque theater had reinforced with its private boxes and privileged views. Through a romantic understanding of the Greek theater, the ancient spirit of democracy was apparently reborn.

BIBL.: Vaughan Hart and Peter Hicks, *Sebastiano Serlio on Architecture,* vol. 1: *Books I–V* of *Tutte l'opere d'architettura et prospetiva* (London 1996). John Orrell, *The Human Stage: English Theatre Design, 1567–1640* (Cambridge 1988). Glynne Wickham, *A History of the Theatre* (London 1985). V.H.

Thermopylae

Persian War battle site in central Greece. Friedrich Schiller's well-known line, "Foreigner, go tell the Lacedaimonians that we lie here obedient to their commands," is a translation of a Greek epigram, attributed to the poet Simonides (ca. 556–468 BC), that exalts the hopeless struggle of the Spartan king Leonidas and his cohort against a far superior Persian force in 480 BCE.

Scholars have adduced numerous reasons that Leonidas, together with 300 Spartan citizens and 1,100 other Greek soldiers, held their position at Thermopylae despite the hopelessness of the situation. Some attribute it to military incompetence. The most likely explanation is that the king sacrificed himself and his men to save the Greek cause, which was supported only by a minority. If after a short struggle the Spartans had retreated for strategic reasons behind the Isthmus of Corinth and thus onto their own territory, the anti-Persian defensive alliance, composed of few Greek city-states, would have collapsed.

Leonidas' unconditional obedience has been glorified again and again as the highest example of the fulfillment of duty. In the 1st century BCE Cicero translated Simonides' epigram into Latin (*Tusculan Disputations* 1.42.101). In the 18th century the English poet Richard Glover portrayed the king dying for the fatherland, and in the next the French artist Jacques-Louis David immortalized *Léonidas aux Thermopyles* on canvas. Allusions to the battle of Thermopylae were used to justify pointless bloodshed during the American Civil War. And in "Död amazon," a poem written in April 1941, the Swedish lyric poet Hjalmar Gullberg commemorated the bravery of the small cohort that, scorning death, opposed a superior enemy.

Classical scholarship also idealized the death of Leonidas. In the 19th century, the age of historicism and nationalism, the Spartan king was discovered anew. The historical interpretation of the battle of Thermopylae was focused on meticulous source criticism, precise topographical reconstruction, military history analysis, and the search for historical causes. The moral relevance of the battle was also emphasized in specialist publications. Most scholars considered Leonidas a shining example of patriotism and heroism. Critics like Jacob Burckhardt and Karl Julius Beloch were in the minority.

In the 1920s and 1930s the battle of Thermopylae fascinated an entire generation of intellectuals marked by their horrifying experiences in the trenches of the First World War. Poets like Theodor Däubler and ancient historians like Helmut Berve commemorated Leonidas for his Doric virility, and they celebrated his cohort at Thermopylae for exhibiting the state-prescribed breeding of the perfect man and the unbreakable fighting spirit of the Spartan soldiers. After the First World War and especially after 1933, German historians held up the polis on the Eurotas as the lone historical model of an ideal *Volksgemeinschaft* (society composed of one pure people or race) and portrayed Leonidas as a role model for the *Führer*-state. The revival of the Romantic dichotomy between Ionians and Dorians, the glorification of the fulfillment of military duty, the longing for a strong leader, the mystical evocation of the German people, and the categories of an obscure racial doctrine all laid the foundation for a reassessment of the Leonidas legend. Under the influence of fascism and Nazism, according to Arnaldo Momigliano, classical scholarship integrated the battle of Thermopylae into "a religion that had its major sanctuaries at Dachau and Auschwitz." The soldiers of Thermopylae were a popular subject in courses on ancient history and languages in the schools of Nazi Germany. Hermann Göring demagogically invoked the ancient event to justify the senseless loss of the sixth army at Stalingrad in January 1943.

The battle of Thermopylae ceased to be a central issue of German scholarship after 1945. It was left especially to English and French scholars to develop new perspectives in academic discourse and to furnish insightful interpretations of the historical event.

BIBL.: Anuschka Albertz, *Exemplarisches Heldentum: Die Rezeptionsgeschichte der Schlacht an den Thermopylen von der Antike bis zur Gegenwart* (Munich 2006). Ian MacGregor Morris, "'To Make a New Thermopylae': Hellenism, Greek Liberation and the Battle of Thermopylae," *Greece & Rome* 47 (2000) 211–230. Stefan Rebenich, "From Thermopylae to Stalingrad: The Myth of Leonidas in German Historiography," in *Sparta: Beyond the Mirage,* ed. A. Powell and S. Hodkinson (London 2002) 323–349. S.R.

Translated by Patrick Baker

Thomas Magister

Byzantine politician and humanist (ca. 1280–ca. 1347); a central figure not only in the scholarly revival but also in the active, politically determined revival of Atticizing Greek rhetoric in the early 14th century. Almost nothing is known about his own upbringing. He was very likely born into the ranks of the senatorial elite of the thriving city of Thessalonica, where he spent his life. In the 1320s he became a monk, adopting the name of Theodoulos; most probably he was also ordained a priest.

After about 1310, at the latest, he taught grammar as well as rhetoric mostly to the sons of the civil elite of Thessalonica. Demetrius Triclinius may or may not have been his master pupil. Thomas himself, a typical "gentleman scholar," was not dependent on collecting fees. He admitted boys of little means to the classes he held in his private lodgings, presumably in a deliberate effort to spread the already dwindling knowledge of classicizing Greek. Most notable among those latter were Philotheus Coccinus, the future patriarch of Constantinople, and Gregory Acyndynus, who was to become the major opponent of Gregory Palamas and the hesychast doctrine. (The notion that Thomas late in life showed sympathies toward hesychasm—an ascetic withdrawal into prayer—must now be abandoned.)

He composed his own schoolbooks; he commented on the traditional dramatic poets (Euripides, Aeschylus, Sophocles, Aristophanes) as well as Pindar. Somewhat innovatively and unlike his contemporary Manuel Moschopoulos, he cross-referenced these commentaries. His *Selection of Attic Words,* a highly popular lexicon, is noteworthy because it marked an abrupt shift from more traditional late antique and Byzantine lexicography: he consciously disregarded the chain of Byzantine lexicographers from Saint Cyril of Alexandria to pseudo-Zonaras and looked back to the lexicographers of the Second Sophistic (mid-1st–mid-3rd cents. CE), when the "Attic dogma" was first coined, thus promoting for his own readers an "uncontaminated" Attic style.

Another, more vigorous aspect to Thomas's pervasive interest in the Second Sophistic, beyond his adoption of its lexicography, was that he also turned to the oratory of that period for practical, political advice. The crumbling late Byzantine Empire had come to resemble (entirely by accident) the "archipelago of cities" (Kaster 1988, 21) that had characterized the Eastern Roman Empire in late antiquity, albeit on a much smaller scale. With the weakening of imperial power, there was room once again for rhetors to strive for concord in their torn cities. Thomas became the first Byzantine scholar since the days of Aristides and Dio Chrysostom to compose an oration "On Concord"; he also showed interest in the public duties of citizens, in "On the Proper Conduct of a City."

In October 1312 he traveled, like the Christian Sophist Synesius many centuries earlier, to Constantinople, where he delivered an oration before the emperor (in Thomas's case, Andronicus II). His performance seems to have been a major success. He enjoyed the privilege of expressing himself to the emperor in candid terms (*parrhēsia*) and was offered, like many a contemporary, a career at court. He declined, however, styling himself as an Odysseus eager to return home—thus confirming his attachment to his native city of Thessalonica yet maintaining close links to the imperial court ever after. This ostentatious self-fashioning as a civic humanist, along with his self-identification with the authors of the Second Sophistic, made him a protagonist of what might be called a "third sophistic" movement, just before the decline of imperial power reduced Byzantine humanism to learned circles at the imperial courts at Constantinople and Mystras.

BIBL.: N. Gaul, *Die dritte Sophistik: Thomas Magistros (um 1280–um 1347/48) als Protagonist eines stadtischen Humanismus im spaten Byzanz* (Wiesbaden 2006). Robert A. Kaster, *Guardians of Language: The Grammarian and Society in Late Antiquity,* Transformation of the Classical Heritage 11 (Berkeley 1988).

N.G.

Thucydides

Notable Greek historian (ca. 460–ca. 395 BCE), admired since antiquity for his *History of the Peloponnesian War,* a minutely researched and ostensibly detached history of the first 20 years of the Peloponnesian conflict of 431–404 BCE. In post-classical antiquity Thucydides was never as popular as Herodotus (ca. 484–ca. 425 BCE). He was always found difficult: in Augustan times Dionysius of Halicarnassus wrote a treatise about him, remarking (chapter 33) that he was better when he stuck to normal language than when he resorted to strange words and forced figures. Cicero, like modern readers, had especial trouble with the speeches (*Orat.* 30). The Byzantine scholiasts or commentators, who probably transmitted material from ancient predecessors, spent much of their time explicating the Greek, though they did make the occasional helpful remark about style. (At 6.18.4, for example, the metaphor "lay low [lit. spread smooth] their pride," is said to be harsh but characteristic of Alcibiades.) But even in the 4th century BCE and in the Hellenistic period Thucydides was already read and influential. Conscious and explicit imitation, as by his near-contemporary the Sicilian historian Philistus, is rare. Polybius (203–120 BCE) surely knew the methodological sections at least. Nor should we confine ourselves to historians: parts of Plato and Aristotle are in nonexplicit argument with Thucydides.

That said, his lack of popularity in the Hellenistic period, relative to Herodotus, needs explaining. There were always barbarians to be fought, and Herodotus' Persians could be redefined, as new enemies appeared. Also, in the aftermath of Alexander's conquests Herodotus provided a way of looking at new worlds. By contrast, Thucydides' subject, a weary war between Greeks, was rebarbative, though we should not overstate this: a late Hellenistic inscription shows that the Peloponnesian War was honored in Athenian collective memory (*Supplementum Epigraphicum Graecum* 26.41).

After the mid-1st century BCE, as stylistic tastes changed, Thucydides gained greatly in popularity. Cicero evidently made a careful study of him from a rhetorical point of view. Imitators writing in Greek include Josephus, Cassius Dio, and Procopius. But the closest admirer, in style and substance, was the Roman historian Sallust (86–34 or 35 BCE). Quintilian in the 1st century CE even said that he would have "no hesitation matching Sallust with Thucydides" (10.1.101).

As for content, we must distinguish between direct and

indirect reception. If the ancient world knew Thucydides' narrative well, it was as filtered through the 4th-century BCE moralizing historian Ephorus, a popular writer in Hellenistic times, used in turn by Diodorus (1st cent. BCE). Similarly, Renaissance Europe knew Plutarch (ca. 46–120 CE) better than it knew Thucydides, partly because he too was a moralist and so was preferred; but Plutarch himself had used Thucydides. (The shift in taste from virtue to prudence, from Plutarch and Livy to Tacitus and Thucydides, came with the 17th century.)

Humanists of the early Renaissance were interested in Greek writers like Thucydides not so much for themselves as for the better understanding of their Latin successors. Before this, direct knowledge of Thucydides had been lost for centuries. The first serious figure influenced by Thucydides directly was Leonardo Bruni in his history of Florence, begun early in the 15th century. By contrast, there is surprisingly little specific trace of him in the writings of Machiavelli in the next century, only a general similarity of approach.

In between these two historians came the important Latin translation of Thucydides by Lorenzo Valla, commissioned by the Humanist Pope Nicholas V. This has attained almost the status of a separate line of textual tradition. The Greek of the second half of 6.89.6, for example, makes no sense as printed in the standard Oxford text, but Valla's Latin shows that he had read some words missing from the accepted text, which can thus be restored (see G. Alberti's new and better rendition). Though the first printed edition of Thucydides, that of Aldus Manutius (1502), was in Greek alone, the good 1564 edition of Henri Estienne (Stephanus) was accompanied by Valla's translation. Valla's translation did much to disseminate knowledge of Thucydides among the intellectual and political elite of Europe; the speeches were a special focus of attention.

In the turbulent 17th century Thucydides was much favored by conservatives, who saw him as one of themselves. This was partly due to a simple but still common error, that of confusing Thucydides' own views with those of his speakers. Hugo Grotius states, for example, in a letter to Jacques-Auguste de Thou, that "I embrace that dictum of Thucydides, that whatever form of government we have received, that we should keep" (Trevor-Roper 1987, 193 and 294 n.78). This is not Thucydides, but a simplified version of something said by that slippery figure Alcibiades, as "reported" by Thucydides—as it happens, in the first half of the difficult sentence mentioned above (6.89.6).

This reactionary "Thucydides" was shared by Thomas Hobbes the philosopher, whose extraordinarily accurate translation of Thucydides (1629) is still in print. In a Latin verse autobiography (1672) he says that Thucydides showed him "the ineptness of democracy." His friend Edward Hyde, Earl of Clarendon (1609–1674), has been called "the English Thucydides" (Hicks 1996). He knew Greek but read Thucydides in Hobbes's translation, on which he made notes, as can be seen from his manuscript commonplace books in the Bodleian Library. (As in the Renaissance, it was the speeches that most appealed.) Hyde's *History of the Rebellion and Civil Wars in England* (published posthumously in 1702) is the product of many literary and philosophical influences, not least the Bible, but Thucydides is importantly present in the work's detail, structure, and general philosophy of history. "Holding (as Thucydides said of the Athenians) for honourable that which pleased, and for just that which profited" (Hyde, 1:149) is unmistakably from Hobbes's version of the Melian Dialogue in Thucydides—but it was actually said by Athenians about Spartans: "They hold for honourable that which pleaseth, and for just that which profiteth" (5.105.4). Hyde, a royalist, reacted against the history of the parliamentarian Thomas May, but without citing him, just as Thucydides does not cite Herodotus. Hyde's treatise *An essay on the Active and Contemplative Life* (1668) shows he subscribed to the Polybian view of history, a view also popular among Roman historians: "There was," he says, "never yet a good history made but by men of business." He mentions Polybius and Tacitus; he could have added Thucydides. Herodotus and May, he believed, were not "pragmatic." If Thucydides had in his veins the blood of kings, as Hobbes said, Hyde was the grandfather of queens: Mary II and Anne of England.

Edward Gibbon's *Decline and Fall of the Roman Empire* (1776–1788) is Thucydidean in its concentration on war and politics. Specific awareness of Thucydides is rare in the work, but "all that is human must retrograde if it do not advance," from chapter 71 (the final chapter), may elegantly render part of Thucydides 6.18.6 (Alcibiades).

In the 19th century Thucydides was enthroned as *the* scientific historian. Whether Leopold Ranke's 1824 dictum "bloss sagen, wie es eigentlich gewesen" ("just to say what actually occurred") was a previously unnoticed quotation of Thucydides on the plague is disputed (for references see Hornblower, *Commentary* on 2.48.3). But Ranke certainly devoted great attention to Thucydides. German philology venerated Thucydides as the founder of the exact discipline of historical inquiry. Only in the last quarter of the 20th century did antipositivist reaction set in, and Thucydides' text is now being revalued as literature. But already for Macaulay in the 19th century, Thucydides' narrative of the Sicilian disaster was the "*ne plus ultra* of human art."

Thucydides lives on, even among thinkers who cannot read him in Greek. In 2004 the Greekless Marshall Sahlins entitled a book of comparative anthropology *Apologies to Thucydides*. In it a 19th-century Polynesian war is read alongside, and illuminated by, *The Peloponnesian War*. It will not be the last war to be so read. Just before another war, W. H. Auden wrote, in "September 1, 1939":

Exiled Thucydides knew
All that a speech can say
About Democracy,

And what dictators do,
The elderly rubbish they talk
To an apathetic grave.

BIBL.: P. Hicks, *Neoclassical Historians and English Culture: From Clarendon to Hume* (London 1996). S. Hornblower, *A Commentary on Thucydides,* 3 vols. (Oxford 1991–2008), and "The Fourth-century and Hellenic Reception of Thucydides," *Journal of Hellenistic Studies* 115 (1995) 47–68. O. Luschnat, "Die Thukydidesscholien," *Philologus* 98 (1954) 14–58. M. Pade, "Thucydides' Renaissance Readers," in A. Rengakos and A. Tsakmakis, eds., *Brill's Companion to Thucydides* (Leiden 2006) 779–810. H. G. Strebel, *Wertung und Wirkung des Thukydideischen Geschichtswerkes in der griechisch-römischen Literatur* (diss., Munich 1935). H. R. Trevor-Roper, "The Great Tew Circle," in *Catholics, Anglicans and Puritans: Seventeenth-century Essays* (London 1987) 166–230. S.H.

Thyestes

In Greek mythology, grandson of Tantalus and brother of Atreus. A struggle with Atreus for the throne of Mycenae culminated in a feast at which Thyestes unknowingly ate the flesh of his own sons, served to him by his brother under a pretense of reconciliation. Sophocles and Euripides composed tragedies on the subject, as did several Roman tragedians; the only dramatic treatment to survive from antiquity is Seneca's *Thyestes.* Seneca's Atreus speaks of his crime in perversely competitive terms: "You do not avenge crime unless you surpass it" (lines 95–96); a chorus before the final scene reports cosmic testimony that Atreus has indeed taken the prize, as the stars flee from the sky in horror. Horace cites the *cena Thyestae* as a touchstone subject for tragedy (*Ars poetica* lines 90–91); in later times the banquet served as a benchmark for deliberate evil at a pitch of extremity, and a stimulus to imagining even worse.

When the Venetian playwright Lodovico Dolce rewrote Seneca's play for the 16th-century Italian stage (1543), the story took its place in the international dramatic repertoire. Over the next three centuries subsequent versions appeared in Italian (by Ugo Foscolo, 1797; Tommaso Sgricci, 1827) and in other languages, including English (John Crowne, 1680), German (Christian Felix Weisse and Johann Jakob Bodmer, 1767), Spanish (the Cuban poet José María Heredia, 1825), and modern Greek (Petros Katsaitis, 1720). Some of these were inspired by the story's striking run in the French theater; Prosper Jolyot de Crébillion's *Atrée et Thyeste* (1707) preceded similar plays by Simon-Joseph Pellegrin (1710) and Voltaire (1771), and was itself performed at the Comédie-Française until 1866. Edgar Allan Poe's sleuth Auguste Dupin uses a villainous boast from Crébillon's play to effect a coded communication with his adversary at the end of "The Purloined Letter" (1845): "If a plan so deadly is worthy of Atreus, it is worthy of Thyestes." In the 20th century plays about Thyestes were composed by the Spanish playwright José María Pemán (1955) and the Flemish playwright Hugo Claus (1966). The English playwright Caryl Churchill, finding in the early 1990s that the Latin original "felt oddly topical," produced a spare verse translation that had its stage debut in London in 1994; a German version by the poet Durs Grünbein premiered in Mannheim in 2001, and Jan van Vlijmen's opera of Claus's play was first performed in Brussels in 2005.

Seneca's play includes a chorus on kingship that is a magnet for English translators, including Thomas Wyatt and Andrew Marvell. Thyestes is never mentioned by Shakespeare, but his story, blended with the story of Procne and Philomela from Ovid's *Metamorphoses* (to which Seneca's Atreus himself appeals), is part of the inspiration for *Titus Andronicus* (1593–1594); the Senecan competition in outrage is explicit in the title character's motivation: "Worse than Philomel you used my daughter,/And worse than Progne I will be avenged" (*Titus Andronicus* 5.2.194–195). When Edward Ravenscroft adapted Shakespeare's play in the Restoration (1687), he added another episode of child murder and worse in just this spirit: "She has outdone me in my own art,/Outdone me in murder: killed her own child./Give it me, I'll eat it!" In *Paradise Lost* (1667–1674) John Milton has Eve's feeding on the apple prompt a cosmic reaction overtly linked to that in Seneca: "At that tasted fruit/The sun, as from Thyestean banquet, turned/His course intended" (10.687–689). Eve's meal is Thyestean in both present and future effect: her dining ensures death for children yet to be born.

Palaeontology has taken Thyestes as the name for a genus of agnathan (lamprey-like) fish from the Silurian period. G.B.

Toga

A large, roughly semicircular woolen garment, worn draped over the left shoulder and then around the back, beneath the right arm, across the chest, and again over the left shoulder, the end falling loose down the back; the traditional costume of the Roman male citizen.

The toga was a marker of Roman civic identity, distinguishing citizens from noncitizens, Romans from foreigners. Ancient authors represent the Romans as toga-clad from the beginning and suggest that this drapery bound the Roman world together. Wearing the toga in one's portraiture signaled membership in a Rome-governed collective.

Modern scholarship on the toga arose in the 17th century as antiquarians supplemented their literary interests with research into the material culture of the classical world. Ottavio Ferrari's *On Matters of Dress* (*De re vestiaria,* vol. 7, 1642) and *On Matters of Dress among the Ancients, Especially the Toga* (*De re vestiaria veterum, praecipue de lato clavo,* 1665) by Albert Rubens (the painter's son) are the leading voices. (*Latus clavus,* "broad border," a reference to the wide purple band along the edge of togas worn by senators and other eminent officials, was a common metonym for the garment itself.)

Their arguments over how to wear the garment were referred to in the preface of G. Bosso's specialized toga commentary published in 1671. So influential was Rubens's study that its contents are cited alongside Locke and Pope in Laurence Sterne's *Tristram Shandy* (1759–1767).

Even earlier, in the 16th century, Cesare Vecellio's study of national costumes (*Degli habiti antichi et moderni di diverse parti del mondo,* Venice 1590) had opened with an image of a toga-clad Roman. As the author emphasizes, *toga* was also the name of a garment with wide sleeves, worn by Venetian senators, magistrates, and noblemen in his own era. The revision of this work in 1598 to include a Latin version of its Italian text strengthens the resonance of this "coincidence." Like Vecellio's return to classical language, the toga makes the comparison of past and present, Venice and Rome, explicit.

The toga became a culturally transferable symbol of the kind of qualities that had made Rome or, less specifically, classical culture great. In the 17th century English aristocrats were depicted wearing "the toga or civil vest, wide sleev'd and loosely flowing to the knees" (R. Flecknoe, *Erminia,* 1661); by the end of the 18th century, with its more traditional form in vogue, they went so far "as hardly to bear a statue in any other drapery" (J. Reynolds, *Discourses,* 1778). Neoclassicism needed it, from the history paintings of Jacques-Louis David and Benjamin West to sepulchral monuments such as Joseph Nollekens's memorial to Sir Thomas and Lady Salusbury (1777). Pompeo Batoni drew on its drapery for the folds of the tartan in his painted portrait of William Gordon (1765–1766).

For statesmen like Benjamin Franklin and George Washington, and for Charles James Fox and William Pitt the Younger, whose toga-clad images include statues by Richard Westmacott (1775–1856) and busts by Nollekens, the toga carried an obvious yet adaptable political message. For Britain's governors and governors-general of India, togate portraits tapped Rome's imperial might to emblematize civilizing conquest. Native Americans were represented in togas by settlers or missionaries as a borrowed signifier of their patriotism and eloquence (e.g., J. F. Lafitau, *Moeurs des sauvages amériquains,* 1724, with his engraving of the Iroquois in council).

Despite, if not because of, the toga's symbolic heritage, people are still intrigued by what it really looked like. Part I of Winckelmann's *Geschichte der Kunst des Alterthums* (1764) includes what he believes a modern sculptor should know about it, and Thomas Hope's frequently reprinted *Costumes of the Ancients* (1800) sells itself as a pattern book for artists. These sources in turn influenced the appearance of the "ancients" in reconstructions of Rome by Victorian artists such as Lawrence Alma Tadema (1836–1912) and pioneering filmmakers such as Cecil B. DeMille. "Toga movies" of the 1950s and 1960s continued this quest for authenticity, while also prompting fashion designers such as Yves Saint Laurent to find freer inspiration in its fabric. Toga parties became part of popular culture later in the 20th century; it is the hope of every participant that the toga will enable the wearer to feel like a Roman.

BIBL.: A. Miller, "Re-dressing Classical Statuary: The Eighteenth Century 'Hand-in-Waistcoat' Portrait," *Art Bulletin* 77, no. 2 (1995) 45–64. J. L. Sebesta and L. Bonfante, eds., *The World of Roman Costume* (Madison 1994). T. E. Timmons, "Habiti antichi et moderni di tutto il mondo and the 'Myth of Venice,'" *Athanor* 15 (1997) 28–33.

C.V.

Topos

Source of argumentative patterns that can be adapted to different lines of argument; also a commonplace expression or idea (pl. topoi). The first systematic account of topoi as logical patterns of argumentation was developed by Aristotle; the term was probably widely used in his time not only in its literal sense ("place"), but also as a technical term in rhetoric and philosophy. It then referred to collections of arguments metaphorically associated with distinct places. With his *Topica* Aristotle confronted those collections, which lacked systematic accuracy. He organized topoi by their logical structure rather than their content and tried to give a systematic account of argumentation in everyday communication. In his *Rhetoric* Aristotle focused on the inventive character of topoi. Though the *Topica* contained more than 300 topoi, here he distinguished 28 general topoi (e.g., the topos of the more and the less) from a range of specific topoi, which are connected to the three species of rhetoric (deliberative, judicial, epideictic) and provide argumentative patterns for different occasions (accusation, praise, etc.) (*Rhetoric* 1396b).

In the Roman tradition, Auctor ad Herennium and Cicero conflated the Aristotelian theory with Hermagoras' systematic stasis theory, which offers a set of questions for analyzing a judicial conflict. Cicero developed a list of *loci* (the Latin word for topos), which had basically a twofold structure, and distinguished between *loci a persona* and *loci a re.* Compared to Aristotle, Cicero characterized topoi by content rather than by their logical structure. Yet in *De oratore* he made a move toward the Aristotelian concept by adding logical patterns to his list of *loci.* Moreover, he complicated matters by introducing *loci communes,* general ideas and beliefs shared by a society or a majority of an audience, which can be employed in many different cases because they are not intimately related to a certain person or case. In the Roman tradition lists of *loci* were also frequently created in another form: as collections of fixed expressions, phrases, or ideas appropriate to standard situations such as the beginning and the end of a speech. Thus, the more structural approach intermingled with a more content-oriented definition of topos in Roman rhetoric. Both understandings can be found from late antiquity through the Middle Ages and into the 18th century. Whenever the knowledge of rhetoric was incorporated into dialectics, there was a tendency to put emphasis on the structural understanding (e.g., Boethius). When ancient rhetoric was drawn on as a productive art, lists of concrete expressions, phrases, and ideas were the focus—as in jurisprudence, letter writing, and literature, most radically in the Baroque tradition (e.g., Georg Philipp Harsdörffer, Magnus Omeis).

Historically the use of topos as a resource for acquiring knowledge was challenged because it discouraged innovation and fostered endless repetition of the same expression or idea. The decline of rhetoric in the 18th century can, to some extent, be explained by the Enlightenment critique of topos, from Bacon's disapproval of the *idola fori* ("idols of the marketplace") to Kant's rejection to grant rhetoric any intellectual value at all. It was Ernst Robert Curtius who reestablished topos as an analytic category and proved that it was a powerful tool for interpreting literature. He laid the foundations for a reviving interest in topoi in the 20th century. Another promising new approach is the study of topoi with an ideological perspective. Commonplace phrases and repetitive patterns of thought can be used to identify and understand ideological assumptions behind current or historic texts. From this viewpoint, Michael McGee's ideograph comes close to the content-driven understanding of topos and makes this concept fertile for critical thinking.

BIBL.: Aristotle, *On Rhetoric: A Theory of Civic Discourse,* ed. and trans. G. A. Kennedy (New York 1991). Ernst Robert Curtius, *European Literature and the Latin Middle Ages,* ed. and trans. W. R. Trask (Princeton 1973). Michael C. Leff, "The Topics of Argumentative Invention in Latin Rhetorical Theory from Cicero to Boethius," *Rhetorica* 1 (1983) 23–44. W. A. de Pater, *Les topiques d'Aristote et la dialectique platonicienne* (Fribourg 1965). Gert Ueding and Thomas Schirren, eds., *Topik und Rhetorik: Ein interdisziplinäres Symposium* (Tübingen 2000). O.K.

Tourism and Travel

The connotations of "tourism" as it is largely understood in the modern world are undeniably different from the phenomena that might be defined by the application of the term to antiquity. Above all, modern tourism—with its implications of leisure as opposed to work and of a secular escape into a distant space of rest, pleasure, or cultural edification—is for most people without a sacred dimension. Graeco-Roman antiquity, however, was a world enchanted by the presence of many gods; travel and sightseeing could never be wholly divorced from the effects of pilgrimage. Indeed, the Greek word for pilgrimage—*theōria*—means "spectacle" or "vision," as in the concept of "sightseeing."

Yet the importance of what remains a modern combination of nature (sun, sex, good food) and an interest in antiquities lay at the heart of ancient tourism, especially in the Roman imperial era and before that in the kingdoms of the Hellenistic world. As the Western world is now, so were the Hellenistic and Roman worlds multicultural and interconnected conglomerates controlled by an educated and wealthy elite, who in the Roman period communicated via excellent, imperially maintained roads from which bandits were cleared by the imperial armies, and who enjoyed a passion for travel. The Roman empire produced both a prolific literature of travel and a large network of attractions to be traveled to, which included sights of natural interest (such as volcanoes) as well as man-made attractions, from the Seven Wonders of the World (sites distributed around the Eastern Mediterranean area and into Mesopotamia) to many local monuments and shrines. There is copious evidence of imperial travels: the emperors Hadrian and Septimius Severus, for example, spent significant portions of their reigns on the road, overseeing the extent and variety of their domains (rather than the battlefield). Such mobility at the highest social level set patterns of emulation in a much wider constituency, much as the travels of media stars and celebrities do today. This mobility was aided by sophisticated patterns of mapping, by milestones and signposts along roads, and by "itineraries," texts that offered examples and models of given journeys (both by land and by sea), describing all the manageable stopping points along the way (for resting horses, for sleep, for food and water). Thus, tourism in the imperial era came to depend on a culture of movement—not only religious travel but also pragmatic and institutionalized travel in many social arenas.

Within this context the pull of a religiously flavored antiquarianism—an educated interest in antiquities, monuments redolent of ancient history or myth, relics of heroes, gods, or famous persons—was particularly strong during the Second Sophistic (ca. 50 CE into late antiquity), an era of revival for Greek culture, education, and letters within the Roman empire. The geographer Pausanias (2nd cent. CE) is our most extensive and intriguing source for this phenomenon, but we find elements of more or less sacred tourism also in the *Sacred Tales* of Aelius Aristides, *On the Syrian Goddess* by Lucian, the *Heroicus* of Philostratus, and many comments in the various works of Plutarch. Sightseeing and the search for wonders and origins (for instance, the sources of the Nile, a topic also much taken up in the 19th century) were essential to tourism in this period, as witnessed by ample evidence of the graffiti left by tourists at some of the prime sites (e.g., the statue of Memnon in Egypt). The Second Sophistic also produced a fictionalized image of travel, in an idealized past, as a basic component in the pattern of romantic love and separation that characterized ancient novels—a narrative trope that was appropriated for hagiography and for the writing of ideal lives (e.g., Philostratus' *Life of Apollonius of Tyana*). Pausanias' *Periēgēsis,* or *Description of Greece,* is the most complete version to survive of what might have passed as a tourist's guidebook, but we have fragments of others, such as the vivid descriptions that survive in *On the Greek Cities,* a Hellenistic text transmitted under the names of Heraclides Criticus or pseudo-Dichaearchus. The extent and institutionalization of tourism may be measured by the fact that we even find a polemic against tourism in the pseudo-Virgilian *Aetna* (1st cent. CE).

The rise of Christianity as the dominant religion within late antiquity had certain significant effects on tourism. One result of Christianity's insistence on a new kind of faith-based religion was its simultaneous creation of the conceptual category of the "secular" or "profane" (that which is not touched by religion) and its attempt, never wholly successful but in some contexts strikingly so, to drain the secular out of culture. In relation to travel, this development underlies the medieval concern with two antithetical motivational models—curiosity and pilgrimage—the former of which was dubiously tainted, though it could never be got rid of, as accounts of medieval pilgrimage such as Chaucer's *Canterbury Tales* well attest. Clearly this separation of curiosity from pilgrimage radically rewrote the Graeco-Roman reality of a form of travel where the two had coexisted unproblematically within *theōria*. But it also prepared the ground in the longer term for tourism as a cultural concept and practice in its own right, derived from curiosity, something like the phenomenon of tourism we recognize today and fundamentally different from how modernity regards pilgrimage.

In particular, the advent of Christian dominance focused patterns of pilgrimage around a single religion marked not by multiple and ancient civic shrines with intricate networks of local myths but by a scriptural model of privileged sites (where the heroes of the Old and New Testaments had lived and died) and, subsequently, a pattern of sacred centers focused on the bodies and relics of the saints. What had been a culture of travel to sights of natural and antiquarian curiosity remained so, but was inflected by a new Christian emphasis on the kinds of wonders and the kinds of heritage that mattered. What had been a vibrant search for multiple and varied mythologies, sacred epiphanies, and ancient histories in the landscape and monuments of the antique past—especially as evidenced in the great description of Greece by Pausanias—became a much more specific exploration of the scriptural past in the lands of Palestine and Egypt, where the Old and New Testaments were set, and in the landscapes where the saints had taken Christianity, struggled with paganism, and left their physical remains as a kind of sanctification, fortified by monastic foundations and the production of hagiographic and miracle texts.

The earliest Christian tourists—such as the Bordeaux Pilgrim of 333 CE, traveling in the later years of Constantine's reign—still visited some of the ancient non-Christian sites hallowed by antiquity, such as the birthplace of the wonder-worker Apollonius at Tyana and the tomb of Hannibal at Libissa near Nicomedia. But the imaginative focus of such travels—at least as represented by the narratives left by these tourists—is on the places of Scripture, where the prophets lived and the events of Christ's life took place. The vivid account of a Palestinian pilgrimage in the 380s by Egeria, an aristocratic woman from Gaul, mixes descriptions of monuments and landscape with retellings of scriptural narratives and much discussion of liturgical activity at the sites, commemorating and making vivid the sacred events which those sites had witnessed. Such sacred tourism must have been significant in Palestine—a rather unimportant province of the empire until suddenly it became a holy land where all the key events of the new religion had taken place. Even during the reign of Constantine, his biographer Eusebius, a bishop in Palestine, had complied a gazetteer of the holy places in his *Onomasticon* (ca. 330), which may in part have been designed to function as a sacred guidebook.

The fundamental shift of emphasis—comparable in the extent of its effects on travel to the shift in the 20th century from Old World–centered tourism to globalization—led, by the 5th century, to the removal of many of the most privileged and sacred monuments of antiquity (such as Phidias' cult statue of Olympian Zeus and Praxiteles' Aphrodite of Cnidos) from their former temples to museum collections in Constantinople. Objects that had a century before been imbued with resonance and wonder became the furniture of a theme park to the memory of a past whose religious life was discredited. Their eventual loss to the depredations of time, neglect, and fire was mourned by few in Byzantium. On the other hand, as the Western empire collapsed at the hands of invaders and as centralized armies became overstretched, harder to maintain, and fewer, the ease and safety on which Roman travel had been predicated was fundamentally undermined. Broadly speaking, tourism depends on safety; the increasingly precarious conditions of the Middle Ages massively reduced it except as a concomitant to military expeditions and war.

Despite the hugely increased difficulties of travel in the Middle Ages, it would be wrong to deny the existence of tourism even then. Exceptional figures of the period include Liudprand of Cremona, who wrote a colorful account of an embassy to Constantinople on behalf of the Ottonian court in the late 10th century; Gerald of Wales (Giraldus Cambrensis), who wrote an interesting travelogue about the wonders of Ireland in the 12th century; and Marco Polo, whose account of his sojourn in China (published ca. 1300) was widely disbelieved in his own time. Chance, patronage, and money brought these men unique opportunities to make uncommon journeys, which might be compared to the expeditions of professional travel writers or mountaineers today rather than to ordinary tourism. One reason such figures are exceptional is that among writings on travel, their works stood alongside and indeed were not easily distinguishable from entirely fictional accounts such as *The Travels of Sir John Mandeville,* which retold in the 1350s numerous tropes, stories, and narratives culled from a long litany of earlier texts. As in more recent eras, there was a strong antiquarian and archaeological impetus in medieval tourism, especially connected with travel to Rome, as is evidenced, for example, by such guidebooks as the Einsideln Itinerary (mid-9th cent.), the *Mirabilia* of Benedetto Canonico (mid-12th cent.), and *De mirabilibus urbis Romae* (later 12th cent.), by the English churchman Magister Gregorius.

With the rise of Humanism in the Renaissance and a concomitant dissatisfaction with ancient cliché (on the pattern of Mandeville) as an adequate account of the world, even if it was sanctioned by the Church, travel became positively aligned again with pursuits of curiosity. Empiricism in response to questions about what was really the case in foreign lands, the need to find discourses and vocabularies to frame the foreign in terms of the familiar, the imperial and missionary projects associated with the discovery of the New World and with Counter-Reformation ventures into the East—all this was to feed fundamentally into the cosmopolitanism that came increasingly to define European intellectual culture, especially in the Enlightenment. These were all long and diverse processes, whose effect was slow and varied. The first travelers and writers of the early modern era were all as exceptional in their own times as the major medieval travelers had been before them. But the proliferation of their texts, especially in the context of printed books and pictures, and readers' appetite for them, was to lead to a new rise in tourism among the wealthy elites and aristocrats of Europe. In this process antiquity became a fundamental inspiration, both as a series of literary and historical paradigms not constrained by the limitations of religious dogma, and as offering a key series of sites and monuments to be scientifically explored.

A fascination with antiquity—no less a geographical urge to search out the lands that once had cradled Greek and Roman civilization than an archaeological urge to dig up ancient remains beneath the soil—was essential to Humanism's reconstitution of tourism. Such remarkable figures as Cyriac of Ancona, an Italian antiquarian who in the early decades of the 15th century traveled in Greece, Egypt, Asia Minor, and the Greek islands, recording and sketching monuments and especially inscriptions, were pioneers of the revival of a tradition to which Pausanias was an ancient witness. Much of the recording of this kind of tourism to the Greek world in the early modern period comes in a combination of texts and sketches that have themselves become central to the study of antiquities no longer in situ. One thinks of Jacques Carrey's sketches of the Parthenon sculptures before they were blown off the building by the explosion of 1687, and the 16th-century description of Constantinople by Pierre Gilles and the related drawings in the Freshfield Album, which show the Column of Arcadius (early 5th cent. CE) before it was dismantled and its sculptures destroyed.

Travel to Greece before its liberation from Ottoman dominion in the early 19th century was always a difficult enterprise, but during the 17th and 18th centuries the dual impulses of naturalistic interest in foreign fauna and flora and antiquarian enthusiasm for Graeco-Roman remains bred a kind of super-tourism. Texts by the likes of Jacob Spon and George Wheler, James Stuart and Nicholas Revett, Robert Wood and James Adam, rapidly became classics of their type—spreading the enthusiasm for the exotica of antiquity and, simultaneously, spurring that revival of antiquity at home (in France, England, and Germany) through those emulations we have come to call neoclassical.

Strikingly, one key to the development of mass tourism remains the model of pilgrimage—and especially pilgrimage from all parts of Europe to Rome, the center of pan-European empire transformed into the prime See of the universal Church. The Grand Tour, perhaps the most significant paradigm for and origin of tourism as we now know it, was born in the wake of pilgrimage to Rome. But with the Reformation, many of those who continued to make the journey southward to Italy were no longer making it as a form of Catholic pilgrimage but out of curiosity. That curiosity was both about the unfamiliar world that the travelers were going to explore and about each other as fellow participants in a secular ritual of licensed self-discovery in Italy. Indeed, one way that children of the German or British nobility might become acquainted personally and informally in preparation for a lifetime's potential political association was as Grand Tourists. The removal of a religious dimension to tourism meant its opening to all manner of discoveries and activities hardly possible at home but easily procured abroad. Sex tourism, in the sense of illicit sexual encounters in a cultural space not one's own, is no less a child of the Grand Tour than the collecting of antiquities.

Alongside the shrines, saints, and sites of apostolic burial central to religious tourism (not only in Rome but along the route through Italy to get there), the Renaissance engaged in an extraordinary venture of disinterring the remains of classical antiquity, especially in the form of marble statues and sculptures, and of exhibiting them in some of the earliest modern museums in Rome. By the 17th century antiquity itself, as well as modern art, natural wonders such as Mount Vesuvius, and the tombs of revered figures such as Virgil (visited at the Grotta di Posillipo near Naples) had become the most substantive goal of the tourist. Not only were the numerous relics of antiquity to be seen on-site and in museums, but the immense wealth of the class that was so assiduously committed to the Grand Tour meant that such artifacts could be collected and carried back home. Private collections of grand antiquities or curiosities in museums attached to town or country houses were the province of the wealthy; smaller personal cabinets of natural wonders and collectibles—like the remarkable 17th-century cabinet of John Bargrave now in Canterbury Cathedral—or collections of prints and pictures (paper museums) were available to less wealthy tourists. The fragmentary nature of ancient remains was itself the spur of an aesthetic of ruin and sublimity that came to characterize the late 18th and 19th centuries, spanning the Enlightenment and Romanticism and giving rise to such visionary engagements with the antique as the works of G. B. Piranesi, J. M. W. Turner, and John Soane.

The extraordinary popularity of travel (which came to be a dominant theme in popular fiction from the 18th century) led to its development into a mass movement by the 19th century, as tourists went ever farther afield. This was especially the case after Thomas Cook turned international travel for the masses into a tremendously successful business in the 1860s. Europeans pushed beyond Italy and Greece into Asia Minor, the Near East, and Egypt. Americans began coming in numbers to Europe. In this process antiquity not only was an originator of such tourism but also became one of the prime goals to which it was directed. At the same time, though it may have been the core from which European travel evolved, soon tourism had transcended antiquity, venturing ever further into a global dimension and a global sense of pasts to be experienced. By a potent irony, tourism has come to be a prime frame for popular reception of the ancient world, the financial and ideological underpinning of archaeological excavation and museum display. What was once the need to justify nationalistic ambitions by grounding them in ancient paradigms (as in Mussolini's archaeological projects in Italy) has become the urge to make the past intelligible and available to the foreign visitor. In the modern era of global tourism, the classical tradition plays a small part—one of the privileged destinations alongside other ancient cultures, natural beauties, spectacular beaches. Tourists originating from the lands that were once the Roman empire and the bastion of Christendom no longer dominate world travel either in numbers or in financial clout.

BIBL.: L. Casson, *Travel in the Ancient World* (London 1974). E. Chaney, *The Evolution of the Grand Tour* (London 1998). C. Chard, *Pleasure and Guilt on the Grand Tour* (Manchester 1999). R. Eisner, *Travelers to an Antique Land: The History and Literature of Travel to Greece* (Ann Arbor 1993). J. Elsner and J.-P. Rubiés, eds., *Voyages and Visions: Towards a Cultural History of Travel* (London 1999). J.E.

Tragedy and the Tragic

Tragedy is a dramatic genre of formal constraint and serious intent, a construction of the experience of human suffering. Behind any modern play called a tragedy loom the towering shadows of Sophocles, Aeschylus, and Euripides, who achieved great fame as dramatists in Athens in the 5th century BCE. Even those who have sought to rebel against their influence have been inevitably shaped by it. When we invoke the notion of tragedy today, we may mean one of two concepts rooted in the classical past: tragedy as a dramatic genre, defined by specific formal conventions, or the tragic as a figuration of human suffering. We often loosely use the word "tragic" or "tragedy" to refer to any compelling spectacle of human suffering or catastrophe, but when we do so we are surely struggling, however inchoately, to find in those events the profound civic and religious meaning forged in Greek tragedy.

Greek tragedy was created for performance in a particular moment of history, but its long afterlife was shaped by its uses for teaching and rhetoric. After their original production, the plays were passed down in writing and performed for subsequent generations. Many plays were collected and edited in Alexandria, Egypt, in the 3rd century BCE, and by the dawn of the Roman Empire, some two centuries later, Greek tragedies had already become "classics," texts abstracted from the circumstances of their origin and valued as repositories of eloquence and wisdom. What survives today in more than just fragments—the 7 plays of Aeschylus, the 7 plays of Sophocles, and the 19 plays of Euripides (if we count *Rhesus,* of which the authorship is disputed)—is the much smaller number transmitted to succeeding generations as texts for teaching rhetoric and grammar in the schools of the 2nd century CE.

Later reception of tragedy was also mediated by its treatment in Plato's *Republic* and Aristotle's *Poetics* (both 4th cent. BCE). Plato was a student of Socrates, and in his youth both Sophocles and Euripides were still producing plays; Aristotle was a student of Plato. In *The Republic* Plato portrays Socrates as having been vehement against the power of tragedy to delude its spectators and to excite their emotions; tragedy is here seen as disruptive to the rule of reason in the individual and thus a danger to the state. In his *Poetics* Aristotle responds to Plato's focus on tragedy's dangerous emotional effects by asserting that tragedy can in fact subdue irrationality through the power of art. This combination of aesthetics and ethics was to exert an enormous influence on later generations of writers and theorists of tragedy.

In later centuries Aristotle's most influential idea was his notion of imitation (*mimēsis*) as defining the genre of tragedy. In his view tragedy is concerned with verisimilitude, that is, the representation of what the audience thinks is likely according to its standards of decorum or social expectations. Similarly, what is represented onstage needs to approximate formally what the mind can grasp as lifelike. Aristotle thus declared that the best tragedy represents a unified action, with no extraneous events, preferably encompassed within a short time span. The focus of the tragic event should be the turn in the hero's fortune, ideally triggered by a "mistake of great weight and consequence" (*hamartia*), a notion that later tragic theory translated as referring to a moral failing or character flaw. It was this reversal of fortune that Aristotle saw as arousing pity and fear in the audience and producing a "purification" (*catharsis*) of those effects. Critics still speculate just what it was that Aristotle actually meant in implying that in the tragic experience suffering, pain, pleasure, and healing are somehow intertwined.

Thus mediated by both education and philosophy, the Greek tragic legacy was further transformed in Roman culture through both theory and practice. In his *Art of Poetry* (*Ars poetica,* 18 BCE) the poet Horace developed a framework for understanding poetry's capacity to produce both edification and delight, such that it provided a social benefit. In his discussion of tragedy's social function, he was concerned with order and decorum, so that what is presented as true and lifelike will meet audience expectations of how old and young, female and male, master and slave, should act. By contrast, Seneca the Younger (1st cent. CE), who was both philosopher and playwright, drove tragedy to excess. He has now long been held in lower esteem than the Greek tragedians, but his plays deeply influenced tragedy as it emerged in European vernacular traditions many centuries later. Seneca's tragedies re-create their Greek models, featuring themes of incest, tyranny, and rage constrained by highly formal discourse.

Between the moment of Seneca's plays in imperial Rome and the recovery of ancient drama in Italy more than a millennium later, production of tragic drama ceased; but the West did not lose the idea of the tragic. The 4th-century grammarian Donatus transmitted to posterity the notion that tragedy concerns itself with the disasters that befall exalted characters who are drawn from historical truth rather than fiction. In one particularly influential text, Boethius in the early 6th century offered a simple definition of what was seen as tragic in the Middle Ages: "What else does the cry of tragedy do but lament how fortune overturns happy kingdoms with undiscriminating blows?" (*Consolation of Philosophy* 2, Prosa). Geoffrey Chaucer's translation of Boethius adds a gloss: "Tragedye is to seyn a dite of a prosperite for a tyme, that endeth in wrecchidness." In this context one can understand how Chaucer came to call his own poem *Troilus and Criseyde* a tragedy, as it relates the story of the downfall of the princes of Troy. In such a formulation the Aristotelian reversal of fortune is overlaid by the idea that tragedy represents "deeds of Fortune," who overthrows those of high estate. Medieval poetic theory thus insisted that the tragic was in some essential way political and not solely moral. Though Aristotle spoke of tragedy as happening to those who are better than we are, for medieval writers tragedy was what happened to those in power.

The recovery of tragedy as a distinct dramatic genre, as opposed to merely a term for the misfortunes of the great, began in Italy in the 14th century, at a time of intense political conflict. Seneca's plays were already in circulation in manuscript by the mid-13th century, but Greek tragedy had to wait until the 14th century to be read in Humanist circles. Seneca's plays were published in printed form in Italy between 1480 and 1490, and Greek tragedies came into print in the beginning of the 16th century (Sophocles in 1502, Euripides in 1503, and Aeschylus in 1518). The first significant (if somewhat premature) event in that classical revival was the appearance of Albertino Mussato's *Ecerinis* (ca. 1315). Composed in Latin, the play was a full-blown Senecan imitation, a tragedy in theatrical form (although it is unlikely that it was ever performed), with five acts of dialogue and a chorus. A landmark in its formal innovation, it was also prophetic in its subject matter, which represented the recent tyranny of Ezzelino III da Romano (d. 1259) in a way that was meant as a warning to the present rulers of Padua. This topicality pointed to the future of Renaissance tragedy as a genre obsessed with the excesses of power, merging the medieval idea of the misfortunes of the great with the Senecan type of the hero of overweening ambition.

As such, *Ecerinis* meant a breakthrough in the renovation of tragedy in Europe. Italy had to wait for a long time, however, for the first classical tragedy written in the vernacular: Gian Giorgio Trissino's *Sofonisba,* which was completed in 1515 but not performed until 1562. Modeled on both Sophocles' *Antigone* and Euripides' *Alcestis,* the play not only paved the way for vernacular tragedy but also introduced a tragic protagonist, an African queen, who was neither a classical heroine nor an Italian prince. The first Italian Senecan tragedy performed onstage was Giambattista Giraldi Cinthio's *Orbecche,* produced in Ferrara in 1541, a particularly gruesome tale of violence, cannibalism, and incest, which caused a scandal in its own time and set the standard for later Italian tragedy. Cinthio himself was adamant in defending his belief that Seneca was preferable to the Greeks for the audiences of his day. Although the formal imitation of Seneca did not produce memorable drama, it did shape the model for later tragedy rooted in the excesses of power and assertion of individual will.

The rebirth of tragedy also coincided with the rediscovery of Aristotle's *Poetics.* It had not completely disappeared during the Middle Ages, but it was lost to the West until Byzantine scholars undertook the translation of Aristotle's works into Latin. William of Moerbeke was the first to translate a text of the *Poetics* into Latin, in 1278. A commentary on the *Poetics* had been written in the 12th century by the Arabic scholar and philosopher Averroës; this was translated into Latin by Hermannus Alemannus a century later (1256) in Toledo. That translation was printed in Italy in 1481. Giorgio Valla's Latin translation of the *Poetics* appeared in Italy in 1498, although it had little effect at the time. It was not until the mid-16th century that Neoaristotelian poetic theory began to take hold, with the appearance of Bernardo Segni's Italian translation in 1549, with commentaries by Francesco Robortello (1548) and Lodovico Castelvetro (1570), and with the influential discussion by Julius Caesar Scaliger in his *Poetics* (1561). These and other commentators extracted from Aristotle a set of rules or a literary code and developed their own theories of poetics in conjunction with Horatian ethical principles. All these critics placed a high value on decorum and the exactitude of imitation, which they interpreted as conveying an impression of verisimilitude or likelihood. They sought to constrict the time frame of the tragic action represented, many limiting it to 12 hours in the belief that this was the most that could be imagined to transpire, in the minds of the audience, within the time that elapsed in actual viewing of the play; and they stipulated that plot and action should be confined to a single place and set of circumstances.

The powerful combination of Aristotelian theory and Senecan drama cast a long shadow on the national theaters of early modern England and France. It was in the English theaters that the rhetorical power and violent life of Seneca was transformed into plays that were politically engaged, fulfilling the Platonic nightmare, whereas in France the severity of neoclassical dramatic theory managed to produce brilliant theater indebted to Aristotle.

Classical plays were read and translated in Spain, whose great tragic writers were aware of neoclassical poetic theory, but it had little influence on the form and style of the genre. The Germanic states had to wait more than a century longer for the development of a neoclassical theater, although 17th-century Baroque writers like Andreas Gryphius and Daniel Caspar von Lohenstein experimented with the form of the *Trauerspiel,* in plays that were excessive in style and often both historical and allegorical in character. Walter Benjamin would use these plays to develop an alternative theory of tragedy in his *Origins of German Tragic Drama* (*Ursprung des deutschen Trauerspiels,* 1928).

In England the influence of classical drama was both more subtle and more contested than in either Italy or France. By the beginning of the 16th century English scholars and courtiers had begun to produce some Latin translations of Greek tragedy (Roger Ascham translated *Philoctetes* and Thomas Watson took on *Antigone*), but no English translations were printed before 1649. Greek plays in any language were performed only in schools and colleges and not on the public stage. More significant was the "englishing" of Seneca, culminating in the publication in 1581 of Thomas Newton's *Tenne Tragedies,* a collection of translations from Seneca made by several different authors during the years 1559–1566. The collection made the work of Seneca more widely available and spread an image of Seneca identified with strong rhetoric and themes of blood and revenge. Beginning with Thomas Kyd's *The Spanish Tragedy* (ca. 1587), this revival sparked an impressive string of revenge tragedies, haunted by ghosts and madmen and obsessed with the failures of human justice.

Senecanism also joined with a vernacular tradition of morality plays to fashion a new kind of political tragedy. *Gorboduc,* created jointly by Thomas Norton and Thomas Sackville and acted at the Inns of Court in 1561 and before Queen Elizabeth at Whitehall in 1562, usually counts as the first classical tragedy in English. The play depicts the disasters that ensue when the aged king Gorboduc decides to abdicate and divide his land between his two sons. Its image of ancient Britain's descent into bloody civil war served as a message to Elizabeth to look to her succession. Indirectly modeled on Euripides' *Phoenissae,* Thomas Hughes's *Misfortunes of Arthur* (printed in 1587) also used Senecan motifs of tyranny and revenge to stage the story of the defeat of King Arthur and his tyrannical son Mordred as a similar *exemplum* or warning to the monarch.

Sir Philip Sidney's *Defence of Poesy* (or *Apologie for Poetry*) reveals that by the 1580s tragedy could be understood as designed to have a political effect through its emotional force. Tragedy, as Sidney wrote, "openeth the greatest wounds and showeth forth the ulcers that are covered with tissue; that maketh kings fear to be tyrants, and tyrants manifest their tyrannical humors; that with stirring the effects of admiration and commiseration teacheth the uncertainty of this world, and upon how weak foundations gilden roofs are builded." This mixture of Aristotelian ideas of pity and fear ("admiration and commiseration") and medieval notions of tragic fortune and the role of art as a "mirror for magistrates" encapsulates how the Senecan and vernacular traditions could merge to produce some of the most remarkable tragedies of the European Renaissance. As the great playwrights took from the classical tradition tragedy's stern rhetoric and the discipline of a five-act structure, they also fashioned a new type of hero, a figure of titanic power and ambition who was most distinctly not the medieval Everyman.

At the same time, the English Renaissance was remarkable for the production of tragedy in defiance of the new classicism. For all the nominal status accorded to the classical tradition, the neoclassical ideas of tragic decorum and the unities that Sidney himself introduced into English poetic discourse did not flourish there. Having produced two unpopular tragedies in the classical mode, *Sejanus* (1603) and *Catiline* (1611), Ben Jonson often complained that his audiences were like pigs that preferred acorns (a common fodder for swine) to the pure wheat of classical drama (see his "Ode to Himself"). In the preface to *Sejanus,* he refers with pride to having observed "truth of argument, dignity of persons, gravity and height of elocution, fullness and frequency of sentence," yet he confesses to having neglected observation of the "strict laws of time" and a chorus, only because his audience would not stand for it. In his preface to *The White Devil* (ca. 1609–1612) John Webster acknowledges that his play was "no true dramatic poem," but he also blames his audience: "For, should a man present to such an auditory the most sententious tragedy that ever was written, observing all the critical laws, as height of style and gravity of person, enrich it with the sententious chorus, and as it were, life'n death, in the passionate and weighty Nuntius: yet, after all this divine rapture . . . the breath that comes from the uncapable multitude, is able to poison it."

The most eminent example of a writer who produced brilliant tragedy in tension with Senecan and neoclassical models is William Shakespeare. His early tragedies, such as *Titus Andronicus* (1593–1594) and *The Tragedy of Richard III* (ca. 1592) are rife with Senecan elements, both in terms of character types (the overweening villain, the tyrant) and ornate rhetorical structures. But in his later Roman tragedies, such as *Julius Caesar* (1599), *Coriolanus* (1607–1608), and *Antony and Cleopatra* (1607), he turned to Plutarch's histories, rather than to Seneca, to structure his complex vision of the inherently tragic world of ancient Rome, riven by the clash of its ambitions and destiny. Of all his tragedies *Antony and Cleopatra* seems to be the one most self-consciously defiant of classical formality or decorum. That play wildly violates the unities of time, place, and action, but apparently not because he did not know any better; the play itself shows signs that he knew the Countess of Pembroke's translation of Robert Garnier's *Tragedy of Antony,* as well as Samuel Daniel's closet drama *The Tragedy of Cleopatra,* both of which observe the neoclassical rules. In a sense, in this play we can see Shakespeare pitting the social and aesthetic values of constraint—all that is Rome—against a deeper tragic consciousness embedded in the powers of imagination that Cleopatra and Egypt embody.

Given that most efforts at a popular classical theater failed to please anyone, the only acknowledged masterpiece of early modern English literature written explicitly in imitation of classical form is John Milton's *Samson Agonistes* (published 1671). A dramatic poem not intended for popular performance, the play depicts the spiritual struggle of Samson as a form of Christian heroism. In the preface to his play Milton defended tragedy as "the gravest, moralest, and most profitable of all other poems" and lauded its power to "purge" the mind of the passions. He cited Aeschylus, Sophocles, and Euripides as "the best rule to all who endeavor to write tragedy," but he also made it clear he believed that his tragedy was structured according to Aristotelian standards. In *Samson Agonistes* he is widely credited with having successfully created a drama of spiritual tragedy working within the tensions of formal constraints.

In France the classical tradition took quite another turn. Whereas the English resisted the strictures of classical form while drawing on the essence of classical heroic types, French writers realized formal classicism in ways unmatched in any other national dramatic literature. Around the end of the 15th century French writers began to craft Latin imitations of Greek tragedies, and the Greek plays themselves, including Sophocles' *Electra* and Euripides' *Hecuba* and *Iphigenia at Aulis,* were translated into French. Like the Italians, the French emulated Seneca, first in Latin and then in the vernacular. In 1544 Marc-Antoine de Muret produced a *Julius Caesar,* a Senecan imitation that drew on the Roman tragedian's Hercules plays but contained many more speeches and a considerably reduced sense of *furor* (in this case denoting madness). The first Senecan tragedy in the vernacular was Étienne Jodelle's *Cléopâtre captive* (1552), based on Plutarch's account of the death of the Egyptian queen. Although this play was hardly a masterpiece, Jodelle did introduce to the French the model of a five-act tragedy focused on the dignified suffering of an individual hero. French theater would have to wait until the 17th century for the full flowering of neoclassicism in the plays of Corneille and Racine. Throughout the end of the 16th and the first decades of the 17th centuries the stage was dominated by Baroque tragedies and tragicomedies of playwrights like Robert Garnier and Alexandre Hardy. Garnier took classical materials as his subject, including *Hippolyte* (1573) and *Antigone* (1580), but eventually, like Hardy, he turned to tragicomedy in *Bradamante* (1582). Hardy's plays more resembled Elizabethan and Spanish tragedies, full of complications and gore.

The catalyzing force in the creation of French neoclassical taste was the evolution of literary theory that transformed Aristotle's *Poetics* into a strict code for tragic composition. After it faltered in Renaissance England and Spain, neoclassical dramatic theory flourished in France with Cardinal Richelieu's founding of the Académie Française in 1635. By the mid-17th century French writers had taken the lead in stipulating the standard for a classical tragic production based on verisimilitude and decorum. Jean Chapelain was the first to advocate moving observance of the unities from theory to actual practice on the stage, but the most developed expression of this theory was produced by the Abbé d'Aubignac in his *Pratique du théâtre* (begun in the 1640s and published 1657). Commissioned by Richelieu, the *Pratique* elaborated all aspects of the rules for "regular drama," including proper subjects, verisimilitude (*vraisemblance*), the unities of time, place, and action, the importance of high diction and tone in speeches, and the observance of decorum, whereby no character should ever be shown to deviate from his or her social type. He emphasized that "the principal rule of dramatic poetry is that the virtues should always be rewarded, or at least always praised, in spite of the outrages of fortune, and that the vices are always punished, or at least always held in horror, even when they triumph." Thus, at this moment in history tragic theory articulated the primacy of reason and order. As such, it radically remade a genre that from its beginnings had represented what in human experience most defied reason and order: lust, crime, madness, ambition. What was inexplicable was to be explained and rationalized.

The two greatest neoclassical French playwrights, Pierre Corneille and Jean Racine, managed to convert strict conventions that could be deadening into a powerful theater of desire caught in conflict and constraint. After producing his first Baroque tragedy, *Médée,* in 1635, Corneille burst fully upon the theatrical scene in 1636, causing a furor with the performance of *Le Cid*—precisely because, despite its popular success, the work was censured by members of the Académie for violating the neoclassical rules (although they admitted it was a wonderful play). *Le Cid* indeed just barely observed the unities and in the end strained the limits of both decorum and verisimilitude. The controversy served to clarify and publicize the formal conventions, and Corneille himself brilliantly adapted his themes to the rules, producing in succession three remarkable "regular" tragedies, *Horace* (1640), *Cinna* (1641), and *Polyeucte* (1643). With these four plays he established his reputation and gained admission to the Académie in 1647. All of his tragedies recall the legacy of Seneca and Baroque drama insofar as they engage political ideas, but they lack Seneca's obsession with political ambition. More profoundly, they explore the tension between personal desire or individual will and the demands of duty and the state.

Whereas Corneille emerged as a playwright chafing against the constraints of the rules, his rival Racine embraced them to create a world of exquisite oppression, focused on familial conflict. After his first tragedy, *La Thébaïde* (1664), a version of Aeschylus' *Seven against Thebes,* he made his mark with *Andromaque* (1667), a tale of frustrated love and hate set after the end of the

Trojan War. He wrote two tragedies on Roman themes, *Britannicus* (1669) and *Bérénice* (1670), then returned to Greek tragic roots with *Iphigénie* (1674) and *Phèdre* (1677), acknowledged as his masterpiece. After his retirement from writing for the Parisian stage, he wrote two biblical tragedies, *Esther* (1689) and *Athalie* (1691), for girls of the convent at Saint-Cyr. In all these plays the strictures of time and place embody and intensify the characters' entrapment in their desires, which hurtle them headlong into disaster.

Although Racine's and Corneille's tragedies scrupulously observed decorum yet brilliantly transcended it, not all tragedies in this mode were as successful. Racine was careful to point out that he understood his moral obligations as a playwright. In his preface to *Phèdre* he protested that he had never before written a play that so celebrated virtue: "the smallest faults are severely punished, the mere thought of crime is regarded with as much horror as the crime itself." In general, however, the critical demand for moral endings led to the ossification of neoclassical tragedy. At the end of the 17th century English critical taste dictated a tragic economy of reward for virtue and punishment of vice. One of the most influential treatises of the latter part of the century was Thomas Rymer's *Tragedies of the Last Age* (1678), which observed "the necessary relation and chain, whereby the causes and effects, the virtues and rewards, the vices and their punishments are proportion'd and link'd together, how deep and dark soever are laid the springs, and however intricate and involv'd are their operations." Rymer strictly judged that the "tragedies of the last age"—for example, Shakespeare's—did not generally live up to this standard. But even while he was declaring such high principles, popular and elite taste called for comedy, heroic drama, and then melodrama (as well as revivals of Shakespeare). Only John Dryden's *All for Love* (1677), a rewriting of *Antony and Cleopatra* in neoclassical form, and Joseph Addison's *Cato* (1713), dramatizing the republican hero's resistance to Julius Caesar in North Africa, are remembered today as tragedies from that era that achieved some distinction in the neoclassical tradition. In his own *Defense of Poetry* (1821), Percy Shelley declared an end to Sidney's hope for neoclassicism and its moral imperative, lamenting that in the hands of the neoclassicists "tragedy becomes a cold imitation of the form of the great masterpieces of antiquity, divested of all harmonious accompaniment of the kindred arts; and often the very form misunderstood, or a weak attempt to teach certain doctrines, which the writer considers as moral truths."

Romanticism thus linked neoclassical tragedy with morality and formal constraint and embraced Shakespeare in defiance of the Greeks as represented by their 18th-century avatars. With that revolt came a new sense of the relationship between the political and the emotional power of classical tragedy. In the 1827 preface to his never-performed play *Cromwell,* Victor Hugo railed against neoclassical rules and what he saw as the death grip of the unities, preventing the creation of a living new drama for a new age. To exemplify his conviction that the genre could represent outsize emotions and a broad narrative sweep, he produced a series of vigorous and immensely popular tragedies, including *Hernani* (which opened to riots in the winter of 1830), *Lucretia Borgia* (1833), and *Ruy Blas* (1838).

In Germany, as in England, formal neoclassicism never really took hold in the theater, but the *idea* of classical tragedy did flourish in the 18th century through a reinvention of the tragic sublime. J. C. Gottsched introduced neoclassical formal rules to German culture early in the century though his *Essay on a German Critical Poetic Theory* (*Versuch einer kritischen Dichtkunst vor die Deutschen,* 1730), but in the end he was less influential through what he said than through the revolt his work produced. Gotthold Ephraim Lessing reacted against Gottsched and the imitation of French drama by urging German writers to follow Shakespeare in producing a German national drama. But in doing so he claimed that he invoked a new classicism, a return to Aristotle through a focus on the evocation of tragic pity and fear, not poetic justice. By refocusing the theory of tragedy on catharsis as the release of emotion, he argued that tragedy would lead the spectator to virtue through the *mimēsis* of suffering, not through seeing virtue rewarded and vice punished. Lessing's best-known productions of that tragic vision were in his *Trauerspielen* or bourgeois tragedies *Miss Sara Sampson* (1755) and *Emilia Galotti* (1772), both depictions of the exquisite suffering of young middle-class women ruined by aristocratic vice.

In the late 18th century, taking Lessing's ideas a step further, Friedrich Schiller formulated more explicitly the idea of the tragic sublime, a distinctly non-Greek conception of the tragic experience rooted in pity and fear and the alienation of the heroic individual. Schiller himself composed tragedies that also sought to achieve a Shakespearean range, most notably *The Robbers* (*Die Räuber,* 1780), with its outsize and defiant hero, Karl Von Moor, and later sprawling historical tragedies that explored critical political issues in Schiller's own time, including *Don Carlos* (1787), *Maria Stuart* (1800), and *Wallenstein* (1799). In contrast, Johann Wolfgang von Goethe experimented with a more direct translation of Hellenism in German culture and drama. As an expression of that new classicism he wrote *Iphigenie auf Tauris* (1779), a recreation of Euripides' play that Schiller later called "astonishingly modern and un-Greek" for its transformation of divine forces into human thought and action.

Although in Germany classical tragedy was thus for the most part repudiated as a formal model, at the same time Greek tragedy became a touchstone for German philosophy, most notably in the works of G. W. F. Hegel and Friedrich Nietzsche, who both drew on Greek tragedy as a profound expression of the human condition. In his *Phenomenology of Mind* (*Phänomenologie des Geistes,* 1807) Hegel used Sophocles' *Antigone* as a vehicle for exploring the dialectical nature of truth. For Hegel, tragedy arose through the conflict of two equally justifiable positions, thus harkening back, before Aristotle's focus on the structure and reception of tragedy, to Plato's concern with the ethical condition of tragedy. In a very different way, in his bold first book, *The Birth of Tragedy* (*Die Geburt des Tragödie,* 1872), Nietzsche used his reading of Greek tragedy to articulate the tension between two truths, in this case between what he called the Apollonian power of art and the Dionysian life force. For Nietzsche, Greek tragedy was the product of art's mediation of Dionysus' power; it was destroyed, in turn, by Socratic rationalism.

Nietzsche may have dreamed that tragedy could be reborn in the modern age, and for a while he thought this was happening in Wagnerian opera. Today we still ask whether tragedy in the classical tradition could live again in our time. In *The Death of Tragedy* (1961) George Steiner has argued that tragedy must die, for "the decline of tragedy is inseparably related to the decline of the organic world view and of its attendant context of mythological, symbolic, and ritual reference" (292). Writers have nevertheless sought to transform classical tragic themes to reflect contemporary politics, philosophy, and aesthetics. Some have believed that tragedy might live again through Freud's and Jung's conversion of its themes into psychoanalytic or spiritual paradigms, such that classical plays and their attendant mythologies become templates for familial tragic drama. Eugene O'Neill's *Mourning Becomes Electra* (1931) set the essential plot and themes of the *Oresteia* as a tangled web of sexual betrayal, incest, and repression in 19th-century America. In a very different way, T. S. Eliot experimented with the formal conventions of Greek tragedy to shape Christian tragedies. In his *Murder in the Cathedral* (1935), which portrays the assassination of Thomas Becket, classical tragic conventions accord with the solemnity of the themes and setting; in *The Family Reunion* (1939), a retelling of the Orestes myth, the reintroduction of a chorus in the setting of a modern living room typically unsettles the audience.

In France 20th-century playwrights once again looked to Greek plays and myth as a cultural touchstone, but this time they sought in them not order and reason but rather the nerve of irrationality and power embedded in their symbolism. During the 1920s and 1930s Jean Cocteau and Jean Giraudoux re-created Greek tragedies in modern prose, both poetic and banal. They reveled in the anachronisms of their modern recreations of myths that are still mysterious: Cocteau in his *Antigone* (1922) and *La machine infernale* (1934) (based on the Oedipus story), and Giraudoux in his *Amphitryon 38* (1929), *La Guerre de Troie n'aura pas lieu* (*The Trojan War Will Not Take Place,* 1935), and *Électre* (1937). During World War II the emulation of Greek tragedy provided both thematic material and a screen for playwrights handling political material. Whereas O'Neill's treatment had extracted family angst from the *Oresteia,* Jean-Paul Sartre's *The Flies* (*Les mouches,* 1943) used the story to grapple with the power of blood guilt and cowardice during the German Occupation of France. Jean Anouilh's *Antigone* (1944), likewise produced during the Occupation, is a profoundly ambivalent study of political defiance and capitulation.

In the latter part of the 20th century tragedy that looks to the classical past continued to embrace themes of political striving. In that sense it sought to incite the disruptive effects that Plato feared so much. The movie theaters and television screens are now filled with stories that might be called tragic, but these have lost their connection to the past in their obsessive repetition of violence tempered with some form of justice or redemption. It is noteworthy, however, that we find classical tragedy re-created in the literary culture of Africa and the Caribbean, if never without a sense of irony and difference. The Nigerian Nobelist Wole Soyinka's *Bacchae* (1973) is his work that most explicitly evokes Greek tragedy, transfiguring Euripides' play within the current political context of the postcolonial moment and also within Yoruba myth; but other African playwrights, such as Ola Rotimi (also Nigerian), in his *The Gods Are Not to Blame* (1968), a reworking of *Oedipus the King,* also use the old plays both to shape dramatic stories and to defy aspects of Western tradition that are profoundly alien to African cultures. What these and other plays indicate is that the heritage of classical tragedy is still very much alive, even in resistance.

BIBL.: Gordon Braden, *Renaissance Tragedy and the Senecan Tradition: Anger's Privilege* (New Haven 1985). Rebecca Bushnell, ed., *A Companion to Tragedy* (Oxford 2004). Terry Eagleton, *Sweet Violence: The Idea of the Tragic* (Oxford 2003). Rita Felski, ed., *Special Issue: Rethinking Tragedy, New Literary History* 35, no. 1 (2004). Glenn W. Most, "Generating Genres: The Idea of the Tragic," in *Matrices of Genre: Authors, Canons, and Society,* ed. Mary Depew and Dirk Obbink (Cambridge, Mass., 2000) 15–35. Timothy Reiss, *Tragedy and Truth* (New Haven 1980). George Steiner, *The Death of Tragedy* (New York 1961). Bernard Weinberg, *A History of Literary Criticism in the Italian Renaissance,* 2 vols. (Toronto 1961). Raymond Williams, *Modern Tragedy* (London 1966).

R.BU.

Translatio Imperii

Literally, "transfer of imperial power." The concept grew from the desire to explain the succession of diverse empires through history in a way consistent with Jewish tradition (in which God punished sinful people by depriving them of power). *Translatio imperii* thus refers to a sweeping view of the removal and transfer of (imperial) power over successive regimes from the kingdom of Babylon in earliest-known history to the Holy Roman Empire that arose with Charlemagne and prevailed through the Middle Ages.

One of the earliest medieval accounts, if not the very first, of voluntary *translatio imperii* is found in the Donation of Constantine, a fraudulent decree forged either in Rome around the middle of the 8th century (at about the time that the papacy was turning to the Frankish Pippins for protection) or in northern France in the millieu of the opposition to Louis the Pious around 830/833. According to the Donation, the Roman emperor Constantine (d. 337), after moving to Byzantium and making Constantinople his capital, had supposedly granted dominion over the Western Roman Empire to Pope Sylvester I, who had baptized him. In the 9th century this idea was adopted by the Franks for their own benefit: refusing to recognize the legitimacy of the Roman (Byzantine) empress Irene (d. 802), Charlemagne acceded to the new Western (Holy Roman) Empire in 800, a restoration that transferred the seat of imperial power to the Franks. The first expression of this view that *imperium* was passed in succession is found in the life of Willehad (8th cent.), an Anglo-Saxon missionary to Germany during Charlemagne's reign as king of the Franks.

The notion of the succession of empires according to a divine plan is even older, however: it rests notably on a biblical story (mid-2d cent. BCE) that reverted to the idea of the succession of empires already described three centuries earlier by the Greek historian Herodotus (ca. 484–425) and on the exegesis of it by the Church Fathers. The concept of *translatio imperii* was thus based on the vision of Nebuchadnezzar (Daniel 2:31–45): the king had seen a statue with a golden head, a torso of silver and brass, iron legs, and feet partly of iron and partly of clay. This statue was struck by a rock, and the parts were scattered by the wind; the rock became a mountain. The prophet Daniel interpreted the different parts of the statue as four successive kingdoms, the last of which would be replaced by an eternal kingdom. Saint Jerome (d. ca. 420) was the first to use the term *regnum transferre* (transfer of sovereignty) in this sense. According to the Christian interpretation of the vision, the earlier Greek succession trilogy of Assyrians, Medes, and Persians was replaced by a quartet consisting of Assyrians, Persians, Greeks, and Romans. The latter arrangement was expected to endure until the Second Coming of Christ. Thus, it became important to find the link of continuity between the ancient Roman Empire and the medieval empire acquired by the Franks. (An analogous idea that would flourish during the 12th century was *translatio studii,* the transfer of studies, a succession of learning believed to have taken place between Athens and Rome and then between Rome and the realm of Charlemagne's "France.")

Until the end of the 12th century, discussion of the idea of *translatio imperii* was always historiographical, making it possible to justify, by hindsight, earlier political actions. Pope Innocent III was the first to use the concept as a political tool, employing it to pressure the candidate for succession to the imperial crown by claiming to have a say in his election (the papal decree of 1202, *Per Venerabilem*). Toward the middle of the 13th century the idea of *translatio imperii* disappeared from historiographical analysis once and for all, to become, for about a century, a matter of legal debate and the subject of treatises. Ludwig IV the Bavarian finally ended the controversy by establishing that the emperor derived his power solely by the choice of royal electors (constitution *licet iuris* of 4 August 1338).

BIBL.: J. H. Burns, ed., *The Cambridge History of Medieval Political Thought, c. 350–c. 1450* (Cambridge 1988). Werner Goez, *Translatio imperii: Ein Beitrag zur Geschichte des Geschichtsdenkens und der politischen Theorien im Mittelalter und in der frühen Neuzeit* (Tübingen 1948). Reinhard G. Kratz, *Translatio imperii: Untersuchungen zu den aramäischen Danielerzählungen und ihrem theologiegeschichtlichen Umfeld* (Neukirchen-Vluyn 1991).

PH.D.

Translated by Jeannine Routier Pucci and Elizabeth Trapnell Rawlings

Translation

Translation was central to Roman culture: it is taken for granted as much in modern as it was in ancient times that Latin literature grew expressly out of translation from the Greek epic and dramatic tradition. Livius Andronicus (ca. 284–204 BCE), sometimes claimed as the "father of Roman literature," introduced Greek writing to the Romans by translating the *Odyssey* into the Italian Saturnian meter and adapting Greek tragedy to the Roman stage. Others soon followed with closer or looser forms of translation and adaptation: Gnaeus Naevius with plays on the Trojan War; Ennius, Pacuvius, and Accius with tragedy; Caecilius Statius with comedy. Translation, that is, had the effect of directly inaugurating ancient Roman literature at a time when it was barely emergent in its own right.

This is an emphatic but not a unique instance of such a phenomenon: in the European Renaissance the medieval literary tradition was invigorated and the literary idiom much enriched by fresh contact with classical sources through translation and imitation, sometimes of a directly experimental kind. It might be said that in every phase of English literature, and many phases of other Western literatures too, something is owed to translation from ancient Greek and Roman texts, and that in some eras their influence is fundamental. Yet the debt is often one that is hidden or hard to discern, partly because of the frequent difficulty of determining whether originals or translations were being used in a given instance—did Shakespeare know Ovid's Latin text, Arthur Golding's English *Metamorphoses,* or both? (The answer here is both.) What is certain is that translations from the classics have been enormously well-read texts in the West, and that their readers and their creators too have over the centuries included the most influential of figures (not only artistic ones). Even today, the number of individuals who will read a major classic in one of the readily available paperback series in English and other modern languages is many times the number who will read it in Greek or Latin, whether as part of an educational program or not.

What continuity might be said to exist in terms of individual praxis between, say, Livius Andronicus' translation of the *Odyssey* and today's Penguin Classics version of it is a good question. In respect at least to how translation has been theorized in the West, marked continuity has been ensured over the centuries by the influential, though hardly extensive, remarks on the subject by Cicero in *De oratore* and *De optimo genere oratorium,* Horace in the *Ars poetica,* Pliny the Younger in his letter *To Fuscus,* Quintilian in the *Institutio oratoria,* and Aulus Gellius in the *Noctes Atticae* (almost all these are cited in English translations in Weissbort and Eysteinsson 2006, 20–33). Much Renaissance thinking on translation was done around Horace's and Cicero's brief statements in particular; their drift is against overscrupulous, word-for-word translation. But Christianity has successfully intervened in this tradition; Saint Jerome and Saint Augustine, in particular, battled over the translatability of the Word in a 4th-century controversy. Many of the subsequent striations of Western theory derive from Augustine's promotion of the notion of a single true translation (see Robinson 1992).

The growth and development over time of the corpus of classical texts translated into vernaculars still needs further analysis. By the 18th century publishing activity was so voluminous that comprehensive information has not been assembled (but see for English-language material the bibliographical information in France and Gillespie 2005–2008).

This account is primarily of anglophone translation, but for the Middle Ages the narrative begins elsewhere, with translation from Greek into Latin. The legacy of Boethius (480–ca. 525), who made literal Latin versions of the Greek philosophers that he intended would create an archive for civilization, together with Jerome (ca. 341–420), whose methods of biblical translation emphasized accuracy, gave the lead to the Roman senator Cassiodorus (ca. 480–ca. 550), who founded a monastery where monks were to translate works of philosophy and theology from Greek into Latin. The Greek East and Latinate West had to communicate, and there was a Greek presence along the northern coast of the Mediterranean for much of the early Middle Ages. By the 8th century it was the Muslim world that was taking the lead in translating Greek material: at Toledo or Baghdad, in Sicily or Seville, could be found Muslims active in turning classical Greek works of philosophy and physical science into Arabic. When Aristotle and other Greek philosophers were introduced into European universities in the 12th and 13th centuries, it was through Latin versions of these Arabic translations, one result being that Aristotle was condemned by some authorities as a pagan influence. Direct translation from the Greek was undertaken by the 12th century, through the agency of such figures as James of Venice (fl. 1125–1150).

In northern Europe some translations of classics were made into Old English, but here the limits on our knowledge are severe. A tantalizing indication of the nonsurvival of such texts is a mid-11th-century manuscript fragment of the Greek romance *Apollonius of Tyre,* translated from a Latin text that John Gower would later use in his *Confessio amantis,* and on which Shakespeare would base the play *Pericles.* After the Norman conquest Marie de France claimed to have translated a collection of Aesop's *Fables* from an English rendering by King Alfred, but if anything along these lines was available to her, neither it nor other mentions of it survive. Greek texts were more often translated into Latin than English; in the 1240s the Anglo-Norman Robert Grosseteste, bishop of Lincoln, made several works accessible to a learned European audience in this way, among them Aristotle's *Nicomachean Ethics* and *De caelo.*

The Humanist translation tradition began in 14th-century Italy, as Greek scholars fled Turkish incursions into the Byzantine Empire. Both Galen and Hippocrates were translated into Latin by Niccolo da Reggio (1280–1350). The first Humanist rendering of Aristotle (again into Latin) was Leonardo Bruni's of 1423. Bruni, more than any other, made the treasures of the Hellenic world accessible to the Latin scholar through his literal translations of Greek authors, among them Plato, Plutarch, Demosthenes, and Aeschines. These were considered excellent models of Latinity. Marsilio Ficino, Georgio Valla, Theodore Gaza, and Angelo Poliziano followed in Bruni's footsteps with further translations of Plato, Aristotle, and others. In Britain it was not until the arrival of Greek instruction at Oxford during the second half of the 15th century, along with the contemporaneous expansion of printing, that translations of Greek texts of any kind appeared in significant numbers.

Publishers such as Froben of Antwerp and the Estienne family of Paris worked as editors and did some translation on their own account. The "father of English printing," William Caxton (ca. 1422–1491), issued several of the first printed English versions of classics (such as Chaucer's translation of Boethius' *Consolation of Philosophy*), likewise offering some (such as Aesop's *Fables*) in his own renderings. Caxton's English *Aeneid* (*Eneydos,* 1490) is, however, drawn from a French romance, and his *Metamorphoses* remained in manuscript. On a European overview from this point to 1600, and quantitatively speaking, classical translation moved fastest in Italy and France, and German, Spanish, and English followed at some distance (Bolgar 1954, app. 2). Material translated is broad in range, including medical, military, and technical texts. In this era there were as many printed vernacular translations from Greek as from Latin overall, mainly because far fewer readers knew Greek. Hence, around Europe there were more Plutarch translators than Ovid translators, and many more of Lucian than of, say, Martial. Among the first Greek texts translated directly into English were Thomas Elyot's version of Lucian's *Necromantia* (bilingually in English with Thomas More's Latin, 1530), and Gentian Hervet's *Oeconomicus* of Xenophon (1532). Many of the translators, such as Étienne Dolet and Philipp Melanchthon, produced Latin versions of Greek works as well as translations into the vernacular. From Petrarch's time many writers had been *poetae utriusque linguae* ("poets of both languages"), and translation of vernacular works into Latin was also a regular phenomenon, especially in France. Secondary translation from intermediate versions in other languages was common, for example in the Plutarch *Lives* by Sir Thomas North via Jacques Amyot's French (1579), and Aristotle's *Politics,* rendered in English by I.D., sometimes identified as John Dee, from Louis Le Roi's French (1598).

By the Renaissance period vernacular writing consciously sought to remodel itself according to Latin standards, whether of linguistic purity or literary quality; in fact, translation was often felt to reveal the poverty of the vernacular. The problem is that this seems to impose a servile role on the translator; but at the highest level the instinct of Renaissance translators was competitive. Edmund Spenser's ambition was to "overgo" his sources; Ben Jonson invoked the classics as "guides, not commanders." Moreover, translation could be and was seen not just as a method of fertilization, but in another light, as a form of invasion, colonization, or conquest.

In England the early Tudor period in the 1540s and 1550s saw the pioneering work of Thomas Wyatt in translating Horatian satire, and of Henry Howard, Earl of Surrey, on Horace, Martial, and the *Aeneid* books 2 and 4 (drawing on the compelling 15th-century *Aeneid* of the Scottish poet Gavin Douglas). Moreover, the Earl of Surrey's best original poems, with their close attention to individual words and phrases, are those of a poet who has appreciated Martial, Virgil, and Horace—the 18th-century literary historian Thomas Warton called him "the first English classical poet." Certainly the effort to discover new possibilities in English literary writing was an impetus to translation of the classics; and a few years later Thomas Hoby suggested others, in the dedication to his English text of Castiglione (1561):

> The translation of Latin or Greeke authors, doeth not onely not hinder learning, but it furthereth it, yea it is learning it self, and a great stay to youth . . . and a vertuous exercise for the unlatined to come by learning, and to fill their minds with the morall vertues, and their body with civil condicions, that they may bothe talke freely in all company, live uprightly though there were no lawes, and be in a readinesse against all kinde of worldlye chaunces that happen, whiche is the profit that cometh of Philosophy.

Such sentiments would echo through translators' prefaces over many decades to come. Though their conventionality is apparent, their rehearsal reveals that justification had to be offered for English translations of the classics.

By 1600 there was still in English no full translation of Lucretius, Persius, or Quintilian. But developments toward the end of the 16th century had been rapid: new arrivals included Euripides and Sophocles, Moschus and Musaeus, Theocritus, Achilles Tatius, and Tacitus. The early Elizabethans experimented with the historians Sallust, Pliny, and Livy; with the playwrights Plautus and Terence; with Apuleius and Lucan; with the poets Horace, Martial, Ovid, and Virgil. Older favorites such as Cicero were being freshly translated, but there was also a taste for later, sometimes post-classical, texts. Renaissance English translators produced work that has remained squarely within the English literary canon, and indeed the translators were often major authors in their own right: for example, the playwrights Christopher Marlowe (who translated Ovid and Lucan) and George Chapman (Hesiod, Juvenal, Homer, and Musaeus). In England translators usually worked outside the academic world, unlike their contemporaries abroad. They were courtiers, writers, students at the Inns of Court, gentleman-soldiers. They regularly used French or Italian intermediate texts instead of Latin or Greek originals, and they were accused (often by the Church) of other kinds of amateurishness; but many of their versions have proved to have greater durability than more scholarly renderings.

"After the age of Jonson, ancient culture acquired in England that straddling status it already possessed on the Continent: it was foreign but at the same time it *belonged.* It had undergone its process of reception, and now it was progressively a native possession" (Greene 1982, 293). For "reception" we could read "translation," which for most readers—as contemporary discussion shows—was easily the most significant aspect of the process. Greene's generalization works better for Latin than Greek: Plato might have been translated into Latin by Jonson's time, but a full-scale English *Works* took until 1701, and even then it was from André Dacier's French. But on the whole, by the 17th century classical texts were no longer there to be "discovered" by the translator, and were used instead to broaden the range of what translators themselves wished to write about. "Even those works which to us read like a translation, like Francis Beaumont's wooden *Remedia amoris,* in fact often diverge in ways the author himself wished to expand" (Stoneman 1982, 10). The many classical translations of Abraham Cowley, John Dryden, and their contemporaries, though not lacking in respect for the originals, often conscript the classic for modern purposes of whatever kind—and hence the boundaries between translation and imitation start to blur. The first major translations of the Renaissance began to look dated, so that new versions were needed—of Plutarch (several hands, 1683–1685), Virgil (Dryden, 1697), Josephus (Roger L'Estrange, 1702), Ovid (Samuel Garth and others, 1717), and Homer (Alexander Pope, 1715–1726). But translators are often deeply aware of their predecessors, and they may seek deliberately to use and embody within their work the best parts of the tradition in which they stand—Dryden's *Works of Virgil* draws on previous English Virgils repeatedly for its phrasing, becoming a sort of summation of English Virgilianism. Finally, new markets emerged among readers: women and the non–classically educated middle classes were targeted by publishers of literary translation such as Jacob Tonson (ca. 1656–1736). At least some classical translation over this whole period had been aimed at a popular audience, however; the Elizabethan Seneca, for example, in the *Tenne Tragedies* of 1581, seems to have spoken to all those who enjoyed the Elizabethan stage.

Notable over the 18th century is the popularity and longevity of the leading classical translations. Dryden's Virgil went through ten editions by 1790, whereas Pope's *Iliad* and *Odyssey* can fairly be said to make Homer a classic for the Enlightenment English reader. But different kinds of translation had differing purposes. Utilitarian cribs met pedagogical needs. At another level, Dryden appealed in 1693 to "Gentlemen and Ladies, who tho they are not Scholars are not Ignorant: Persons of Understanding and good Sense . . . not . . . conversant in the Original." For readers who had good Latin or Greek, a translation could become a sort of commentary on its original, generating at the highest artistic pitch a complex intertextual play, an example being Pope's satirical *Imitations of Horace* (1733–1738), which appeared with the Latin *Sermones en face*. Such effects are likely only with the most familiar of classics. Much misunderstanding is caused by ignorance of a translation's ambitions: Pope's Horace simply should not be taken as a guide to the verbal meaning of the *Sermones*. Once again, a divide opens up between today's scholarly expectations and the very different assumptions of previous eras: the prime objective in the 18th century was understood not to be semantic accuracy but the reproduction of "classic" aesthetic qualities by any available means. Hence the centrality of the medium to the movement later known as English Augustanism, which took as its guiding lights Virgil, Ovid, and Horace: translations were meant as stylistic experiments or as models for modes of English verse writing.

The classical translations of this era include those (usually selections from the classic named) by Dryden (in 1700 Homer and Ovid, before that date Horace, Juvenal, Lucretius, Persius, Theocritus, and the complete Virgil), Pope (Boethius, Martial, Ovid, Statius, Tibullus, Homer, Horace), Samuel Johnson (Anacreon, Boethius, Euripides, Homer, Horace, Juvenal), and Christopher Smart (Horace, Phaedrus). As this roll call suggests, the period from Dryden's maturity in the 1680s to the end of Johnson's life in 1784 has a good claim to be regarded, with the Renaissance, as a golden age of English classical translation. It should be noted, too, that the work of these high-profile hands is underpinned by extensive activity from lesser names. Examples of specialist translators are Gilbert West (Euripides, Lucian, Pindar, Apollonius Rhodius) and Thomas Gordon (Tacitus, Sallust). Some 120 book-length translations and imitations (the distinction, as already noted, is vexed) of Horace, mostly selections but including about a dozen collected translations, appeared in the 18th century.

As that century went on the rise of Hellenism had significant effects on the mix of translated classics. Before the 19th century the works most commonly translated from the Greek into English were philosophical, broadly defined; after 1800 they were literary, and within this particularly the previously seldom-translated texts of Greek drama began to take precedence. In spite of Romantic theories of original genius, poets of this era engaged in classical translation across Europe. The central English Romantic in this respect was Shelley (1792–1822), who made direct versions of Euripides' *Cyclops*, the *Homeric Hymns*, Theocritus, and the *Symposium*, and modeled other works on texts by Aeschylus and Bion. The central German one is perhaps Hölderlin (1770–1843), who made his Pindar and Sophocles translations crucial to his work. And so it was into the mid-19th century, when Homer, then generally preferred over Virgil, was at the center of the debate about translation conducted publicly between Matthew Arnold and his opponent, F. W. Newman, in the 1860s. Should the archaic and alien be registered by a translator, disrupting the English-language norms of his day (as Newman argued), or should Homer be made to sound simple, natural, unquaint (as Arnold did)? Subsequent English versions of Homer—and there was no shortage—could go in either direction. Some adapted Johann Heinrich Voss's German Homer to arrive at an English dactylic hexameter as they went.

The 19th century also saw English treatments of some previously little-translated authors. Poems and fragments of Sappho were translated by Byron, George Eliot, Walter Savage Landor, and D. G. Rossetti, among others. Theocritus attracted Arnold, Elizabeth Barrett Browning, Charles Stuart Calverley, Leigh Hunt, Andrew Lang, John Addington Symonds, and others. Nonnus appealed to Thomas Love Peacock and Elizabeth Barrett Browning.

There is still plenty of distance between different types of translation, both in the product and in the intended audience. Shelley or Hölderlin did not carry out their work for the benefit of those who wanted cribs or plain translations, but others did. From the early 19th century many volumes of translation, which before then could normally be marketed only as discrete publications, were issued in series intended for readers who would not have possessed copies of the originals. Henry Bohn (1796–1884) became the best known of the series publishers, the hundred volumes of *Bohn's Classical Library* (issued mainly 1848–1863) being a core part of his list. This type of series publishing, it has been claimed, needed to aim at radically changing the potential audience for classical literature: "to find new markets for classics and to break the upper-class monopoly on classical learning" (France and Gillespie 2006, 4:165). But publishers had targeted classical translation at the middle classes as early as Dryden's time.

For all this activity, it is with some justice that the 19th century has been found wanting in the quality and durability of its achievements in this arena. That it is also a period in which the prestige of the classics reached a very high pitch is only superficially paradoxical, the explanation regularly advanced being that the "inhibiting force of excessive respect"—the "accepted inequity in the relation" between past and present—explains the lack of confidence with which translators approached the classics (Poole and Maule 1995, xlv). An archaizing technique was one tangible outcome of a felt distance between classics and moderns. The resulting vocabulary was apt to be stilted; instead of "hungry," for example, C. S. Calverley's Theocritus is made to say, "not on an o'erfull stomach." But it was remote from contemporary norms in its own day, too.

The next generation, of Pound and the modernists, it has been urged, would "not have anything to do with this cripplingly reverential position" (Poole and Maule 1995, xlv). Does this mean their work is of a different order? Appearances suggest this. Ezra Pound (1885–1972) made a point of irreverence. His *Homage to Sextus Propertius* (1919) is not quite offered as a translation of Propertius, but it outraged the establishment by an apparently cavalier attitude to interpretation and by implicitly claiming that intuition can be more productive than scholarship. Pound's belief, at least fairly well founded, in his having world literary history at his fingertips led to translations and imitations from many languages. One classical transaction had special significance: he went to Homer to begin his epic *Cantos,* which set out in 1915 with a version of part of Andreas Divus's Latin redaction of *Odyssey* 11. Sophocles (*Trachiniae*) and Euripides (*Elektra*) were much later targets, in quirkily idiomatic but not universally acclaimed versions of the 1950s. The nature of the poetic he promoted meant that Pound's contemporary and later followers were also often Hellenic in their tastes; Richard Aldington and his wife, Hilda Doolittle (H.D.), for example, produced versions of Euripides and Sappho.

There is no doubt that the work of this school sought to overturn Victorian and Georgian conventions in both poetry and translation. Its experimental free verse won praise for its freshness and clarity; it was sometimes claimed that it broke the Greek down to a preverbal level and reconstituted it so as to "make it new," as Pound's motto ran. Certainly Pound can resuscitate elements of diction and syntax "unfamiliar enough to sound startlingly new" and confront us with "ancient texts that we know could only have been written in [the 20th] century" (Carne-Ross 1990, 137). But at the distance of 100 years or so, it is possible to discern more continuity between the Victorians and the early modernists than might have made the latter comfortable, not least in respect of archaism. *Canto 1* ends "with golden/Girdles and breast bands, thou with dark eyelids," where it is not the pronoun but the Tennysonian "girdles" that strike us as redolent of the Victorian-Edwardian era.

The 20th century also had its fair share of classics in translation series. The establishment of the Penguin Classics in 1946 under the editorship of E. V. Rieu was a popularizing move for classical translation, enabling more works to be made widely available. Rieu promoted prose translations written in "plain English," without extensive annotations. Over time, with emphases shifting in schools and universities in the United Kingdom and United States, more use was made of translations in classrooms (in Great Books and in Classics in Translation courses, e.g.) and a more scholarly flavor was sought. This was developed by Rieu's assistant and eventual successor, Betty Radice, herself a translator of Roman comedy. Today there are two or three Penguin translations of some major classical texts (three *Aeneids* to date)—a sign of success, or of a fast track to obsolescence?

In the late 20th and early 21st centuries it has become fairly common, as it was in the Renaissance, for poets to undertake classical translation at some point in their writing careers. Rendering a few passages or poems from Ovid or Horace is routine, but in some cases a more regular commitment is apparent. Between translating a chunk of the *Odyssey* in 1960 and Euripides' *Alcestis* in 1993–1998, Ted Hughes undertook Seneca's *Oedipus* and selections from Ovid's *Metamorphoses* at volume length. Tony Harrison has translated the *Oresteia,* Euripides' *Hecuba,* and Aristophanes' *Lysistrata* (twice). Seamus Heaney's *The Cure at Troy* resets Sophocles' *Philoctetes* in present-day Ireland. But there are, as ever, many further layers of activity beyond this highest-profile level. The career-long classical translator is alive and well (C. H. Sisson, with Catullus, Horace, Lucretius, and Virgil to his credit, being a 20th-century example). A recent bibliography records more than 40 book-length translations and imitations of Ovid in English from 1950 to 2004. It should give pause that a much larger number of translations of the classics was published in the 20th century than in any previous one.

If classical literature has been formative of Western literary traditions, translations of it have probably been no less so. This is partly a practical matter: a writer cannot be influenced by a work that that writer cannot read. But it is also a more subtle question of how the most ambitious and creative kinds of translations make a text "available" to the native tradition. Through translation, and only through translation, it could be argued, can a classic fully take its place in the vernacular culture, an adoptive child, an immediate member of the family, rather than a distant (or dead) cousin—however deeply respected a cousin. Translations are crucial to the process described above as making the classic "belong."

Many practitioners of the art of translation have themselves been novelists, poets, and playwrights, and their own activity outside translation has often been affected by their translating work. Other writers can be shown to have read classics in translation and to have been influenced by those translations. In many eras, readers of all descriptions engage with given classics far more intensively once a translation accords it a vigorous vernacular existence. In 17th-century Italy Lucretius was a model for Neo-Latin poets but, in the absence of an Italian translation (largely because of Church suppression), far from widely read. In contrast, English interest in Lucretius was exponentially greater after the standard complete translation of Thomas Creech (1682) and the poetically impressive selection by Dryden (1685)—both reprinted for the following 100 years and more.

The effect of translations on modern literatures has taken many forms. Meters were discovered or developed through translation: blank verse derived in English from Surrey's *Aeneid* samples of the 1550s, and the heroic couplet evolved in part from the English Augustans' attempt to find an equivalent for Ovid's elegiacs. Swinburne and Tennyson adopted versions of the sapphics and alcaics of Greek verse. Poetic forms arrived: the Pindaric ode of the 18th century was popularized by Cowley's not terribly authentic versions of Pindar (1656). Poetic diction was strongly colored by translations: Pope's Homer was felt to have made available a highly influential new poetic idiom; Samuel Johnson wrote a couple of generations later in his *Life of Pope* that "Pope's version may be said to have tuned the English tongue, for since its appearance no writer, however deficient in other powers, has wanted melody."

Classical translation has been decisive in the formation of vernacular literary canons. In English the major works of translation were by 1800 established as integral parts of the English literary canon itself. Their proud inclusion in the several large-scale editions of *English Poets* from the late 18th century onward bespeaks a situation like that of Roman literature, in which translation helped create a national literature of universal aspirations. Johnson took occasion in his *Lives of the English Poets* (1779–1781) to comment on the rare examples of English poets who are *not* translators. Classical translations could even be said to act sometimes as a suppressant of native writing: it is often remarked how Dryden and Pope failed to write epics of their own while producing highly successful versions of Virgil and Homer. To use the word *failure* here, however, is to accept purely post-Romantic priorities. Pope became the equivalent of a multimillionaire through his Homer, whereas Milton sold the rights to *Paradise Lost* for a few pounds.

On a larger scale still, as we have seen, classical translation can also aim to alter the nature of classical learning, or at least which social groups possess it. It could be said to have an inherently democratic tendency, bringing material from the few to the many, turning the esoteric into the everyday. Some theorists (distantly related to Newman and Schlegel) have advocated "foreignization" in translations, that is, retaining texts' foreign features as a means of respecting their otherness, but it is doubtful that their otherness can really be preserved at all, and the price would be that they remain esoteric. In practice, too, different periods and different literatures are open to this type of effect to different degrees: Latinism in a 20th-century English translation would serve to distance and estrange, but not so in an era in which Latinism is more a part of the literary idiom (as in, say, *Paradise Lost*).

Nevertheless, various choices are open to any translator, perhaps reducible to two: either accommodating the translation's texture to the source's features, or accommodating the source to a smooth and "invisible" translation. Robert Browning's *Agamemnon of Aeschylus* (1877) was written, he noted, "in as Greek a fashion as English will bear," whereas Alexander Tytler had maintained in his *Essay on the Principles of Translation* (1795) that a translation "should have all the ease of original composition." Dryden tried to break away from the binary in proposing a tripartite scheme in the "Preface concerning Ovid's *Epistles*" (1680): "metaphrase" is literal, "paraphrase" involves "latitude," and "imitation" is looser still. Dryden's own translations usually mix these approaches so promiscuously as to suggest strict limitations on the usefulness of the generalizations. Moreover, a term like *imitation* has been used to mean different things in different eras. As with the ancients, so with the moderns, then; for in Rome translation was seen as a technically demanding version of the much wider practice of imitation of Greek models, and "what counted as translation . . . often allowed considerable leeway for adaptation and variation"; hence, "the precise point at which translation stops and imitation begins is often very hard indeed to discern" (Most 2003, 388).

Dryden defined imitation as writing what the ancient might have written had he been alive in contemporary England. This is by no means indefensible, but the principle can sanction a very broad range of approaches. Christopher Logue's is at one contemporary extreme: his "accounts" or "rewritings" (as he variously calls them) of the *Iliad,* appearing piecemeal since 1962, can take a page to deal with a couple of Homeric lines. Better creativity than slavishness: "What we do not want," Logue has written, "is bad writing hiding behind efficiency in ancient languages." But what is indispensable to authenticity? Form, meter, sense, sound, and many other elements have their claims. The experiments of the Americans Celia and Louis Zukofsky led to a complete "homophonic" Catullus in 1969, in which sound is primary, sense secondary. In Catullus 55 the line *Oramus, si forte non molestum est* is translated "A rum asks me—see, fortune won't molest you." This is not meant to be readable. It brings us back to "foreignization," and the esoteric outcome of excessive respect for the alienness of the classical and the foreign. What Catullus would have written had he lived in the world today would presumably have been, first of all, a poem.

BIBL.: R. R. Bolgar, *The Classical Heritage and Its Beneficiaries* (Cambridge 1954). D. S. Carne-Ross, "Jocasta's Divine Head: English with a Foreign Accent," *Arion,* 3rd ser., 1 (1990) 106–141. Peter France and Stuart Gillespie, eds., *The Oxford History of Literary Translation in English,* 5 vols. (Oxford 2005–2008). Thomas M. Greene, *The Light in Troy: Imitation and Discovery in Renaissance Poetry* (New Haven 1982). Glenn W. Most, "Violets in Crucibles: Translating, Traducing, Transmuting," *Transactions of the American Philological Association* 133 (2003) 381–390. Adrian Poole and Jeremy Maule, eds., *The Oxford Book of Classical Verse in English Translation* (Oxford 1995). Douglas Robinson, "The Ascetic Foundations of Western Translatology: Jerome and Augustine," *Translation and Literature* 1 (1992) 3–25. Richard Stoneman, ed., *Daphne into Laurel: Translations of Classical Poetry from Chaucer to the Present* (London 1982). Daniel Weissbort and Astradur Eysteinsson, eds., *Translation—Theory and Practice: A Historical Reader* (Oxford 2006).

S.GI.

Travel. *See* Tourism and Travel.

Triclinius, Demetrius

Byzantine philologist (ca. 1280–ca. 1330). He was arguably the most gifted in his field in the early 14th century. Although his work foreshadowed modern achievements by several centuries, his effect on intellectual life in his own time remained remarkably small. In the only extant work from his pen that shows an interest beyond philology, a treatise on lunar theory, he calls himself a son of the "wealthy city of Thessalonica." Next to nothing is known about his upbringing there. Some kind of a connection to Thomas Magister may be assumed, but it is no more than an educated guess that he was Thomas's disciple. At some point he cooperated with a certain Nicholas Triclines, perhaps his brother. It has been proposed on palaeographical grounds that he spent some time in Constantinople in the second decade of the 14th century, enjoying access to the manuscripts of Maximus Planudes' former circle; perhaps it is sufficient to assume that manuscripts traveled quite frequently between Thessalonica and Constantinople, the two intellectual centers of the late Byzantine world. Triclinius adopted that form of his name (from Triclines) ca. 1319. A curious parallel for this act is that a colleague or student, John Catrares, renamed himself Catrarius.

It is only by means of autograph manuscripts that the chronology of Triclinius' academic career can be established. The earliest and oldest known codex written by him dates to 1308 (Oxford, New College, MS gr. 258); the latest dates to ca. 1325–1330 (Naples, MS gr. II.F.31). The former is a deluxe version of Hermogenes' rhetorical treatises; the latter contains his own state-of-the-art edition of the tragedies of Aeschylus. In between those two fall several important renditions of classical Greek texts: Hesiod, from 1316–1319 (Venice, Marcianus graecus 464); Euripides, from ca. 1315–1325 (Rome, Bibliotheca Angelica, MS gr. 14); and Aristophanes, ca. 1320–1330 (Paris, Supplement grec 463). These contain, first and foremost, his own recension of the texts in question, informed, for the first time since late antiquity, by considerations of meter. Grasping the significance of the Alexandrian scholar Hephaestion's treatise on that subject (2nd cent. CE), he restored many verses and even strove to reintroduce strophic responsion into often quite corrupt texts. He usually composed a metrical commentary to go with his recensions, referring to these scholia as "ours" (that is, "mine"). The margins of the recensions feature a slightly revised version of Thomas Magister's commentaries (marked by a capital letter), silently correcting some of the latter's more obvious blunders; at a later stage, he also added Moschopoulos' commentaries (marked by a cross). It is only fair to refer to these precious autographs as masterpieces of late Byzantine scholarship.

Beyond these must also be mentioned his crucial role in the recovery of the nine "alphabetic plays" of Euripides: the surviving portion of an ancient alphabetized collection, comprising titles beginning epsilon through kappa (that is, *Electra* through *Kyklops*). In addition to drama he seems to have dealt with poetry—Pindar, Theocritus, the Planudean Anthology—and the rather uncommon fables of Babrius.

Marcus Musurus, in the early 15th-century printing workshop of Aldus Manutius in Venice, drew heavily on Triclinius' work. In most cases, modern editorial techniques have superseded Triclinius' emendations. But his name is still frequently spotted in the critical apparatuses of modern editions, and it has been rightly remarked that after the fall of Byzantium and the transfer of Greek philology to the West, it took classical scholarship centuries to reach the point where Triclinius had left off.

BIBL.: M. H. Shotwell, "On the Originality of Demetrius Triclinius in Editing and Commenting on the Byzantine Triad of Aeschylus" (Ph.D. diss., Brown University 1982). O. L. Smith, "Tricliniana," *Classica & Mediaevalia* 33 (1981–1982) 239–262, and "Tricliniana II," *Classica & Medievalia* 43 (1992) 187–229. N. G. Wilson, *Scholars of Byzantium,* rev. ed. (London 1996) 249–256. N.G.

Triumphal Arch

Not all Roman arches were erected to commemorate triumphs, but those most visible in subsequent centuries undoubtedly were, especially the Arches of Titus, Septimius Severus, and Constantine in Rome itself. These provided the principal models for later interpretations. They were conceived as freestanding rectangular solids pierced by passageways through which a triumph or similar ceremony could pass. The Arch of Titus had a single passageway, whereas the others have three, the center arch larger than the others. All had attics with inscriptions and were decorated with statues and reliefs alluding to the triumph they celebrated, though in some cases these were *spolia*, reused parts of earlier structures. The design of these monumental constructions was drawn on in later centuries not only for new triumphal arches but also for other building types and for temporary structures for civic festivities modeled on Roman triumphs.

In the early Christian period the term came to be applied to the arch between the nave and apse of a basilican church, alluding to Christian triumph over death. In the Renaissance the motif of the arch with a single passageway, such as the Arch of Titus or the Arch of Trajan at Ancona, provided Leon Battista Alberti with the elements of the nave and facade articulation at the Church of Sant'Andrea in Mantua (1470–1476). The three-bay type exemplified by the Arch of Constantine proved suitable for the fountains that terminated aqueducts, such as the Acqua Felice (1587) and Trevi Fountain (1732–1762) in Rome. It was a popular motif with Neoclassical architects, more for antique than triumphal associations, as with the south front of Kedleston Hall in Derbyshire by Robert Adam (1759–1765).

Temporary arches based on antique triumphal arches were a feature of royal entries from the early 16th century onward. Numerous antique-inspired triumphal arches were erected for the various entries into French cities by Henri II of France (r. 1547–1559), some designed by Jacques Androuet du Cerceau; for Henri III's visit to Venice (1574) an arch was designed by Andrea Palladio. These arches handled the traditional form with great freedom. So did the printed triumphal arch of the Emperor

Maximilian I, a huge compound woodcut supervised by Albrecht Dürer (1515), which recorded no event but took the image of a triumphal arch composed of allegorical scenes as a vehicle for imperial propaganda.

In Rome it was possible to use the original imperial triumphal route through the Forum to the Capitol (in reverse) for part of the *possesso,* the papal coronation procession. Temporary arches would be erected on the Campidoglio (by the Popolo Romano) and in the Forum across the Via Sacra near the Arch of Titus and the Farnese Gardens (by the Farnese dukes of Parma and, after 1748, the king of the Two Sicilies). These arches, designed by architects such as Carlo and Girolamo Rainaldi, Pompeo Aldrovandini, Alessandro Specchi, and Ferdinando Fuga, treated their models with great stylistic freedom, playing down the blockiness of the Roman models in favor of complex conjunctions of freestanding columns and expansive sculptural forms creating interesting silhouettes, often stepped inward on the upper levels. The use of triumphal arches in the *possesso* ended with the Napoleonic wars, but the return of Pius VII from exile in 1814 gave the idea of the triumphal entry new impetus. An arch informed by the new Neoclassical permanent arches of Paris was erected in Piazza Venezia on the design of Giuseppe Valadier. For the Feast of the Birth of the Virgin in 1849 Pius IX ordered construction in the Piazza del Popolo of an arch based on the Arch of Constantine, the emperor whom "God appointed to make the Church triumph." The erection of temporary arches for comparable occasions has since been revived sporadically, one notable example being the triumphal arch on Princes Bridge, Melbourne, made to commemorate Australian Federation in 1901.

Permanent structures modeled formally and functionally on Roman triumphal arches began in the Renaissance with the frontispiece (ca. 1452–1471) to the Castel Nuovo in Naples erected by Alfonso I to commemorate his triumphal entry into Naples; it "tells of the deeds of the first Alfonso, like that in Rome which witnesses Septimius' victories, or as the worthy Flavian arch shows forth." There were few subsequent attempts to create a permanent triumphal arch on the antique model until Nicolas-François Blondel created city gates for Paris, such as the Porte St.-Denis (1671), which returned to the antique conception of the arch as a rectilinear slab pierced by passageways. The freestanding triumphal arch was revived by Napoleon, who exploited its associations with imperial power and its richer urbanistic possibilities, as in the Arc de Triomphe du Carrousel (1806–1808) by Charles Percier and Pierre-François Fontaine based on the Arch of Septimius Severus, and the Arc de Triomphe (1806–1836) by Jean-François-Thérèse Chalgrin, which later became the centerpiece of Haussmann's boulevards.

The British equivalents, John Nash's Marble Arch (ca. 1825–1828) and Decimus Burton's Constitution Arch (1827–1828), likewise played important urbanistic roles in their original positions. In the later 19th century the significance of permanent "triumphal" arches was likely to be memorial rather than imperial, as is the case with the Soldiers and Sailors Memorial Arch, Brooklyn (by John H. Duncan, 1889–1892). After the First World War, when new memorial forms were being sought, the triumphal arch had its final flowering, most notably in Sir Edwin Lutyens's Memorial to the Missing of the Somme, in Thiepval (1928–1932), which ingeniously interlocks a triple arch with smaller triple arches at right angles to it to form a truly three-dimensional triumphal arch, well adapted to an isolated site and with ample space for the names of the dead.

BIBL.: Marcello Fagiolo, *Corpus delle Feste a Roma,* vol. 2, *Il Settecento e l'Ottocento* (Rome 1997). George L. Hersey, *The Aragonese Arch at Naples, 1443–1475* (New Haven 1973). Richard Jenkyns, *The Legacy of Rome: A New Appraisal* (Oxford 1992). J. R. Mulryne and Elizabeth Goldring, *Court Festivals of the European Renaissance: Art, Politics and Performance* (Aldershot 2002). Margaret A. Zaho, *Imago Triumphalis: The Function and Significance of Triumphal Imagery for Italian Renaissance Rulers* (New York 2004). D.R.M.

Triumphal Bridge

The Triumphal Bridge (Pons Triumphalis) was a Renaissance invention stemming from Flavio Biondo's identification in *Rome Restored* (*Roma instaurata,* written 1444–1446, printed 1471) of the *via "triumfalis"* of the Regional Catalogues with a road that crossed the Ager Vaticanus near the site of St. Peter's Basilica. This road linked up with the remains of a bridge at the Tiber bend near the Church of Santo Spirito in Sassia, which thus acquired the designation Pons Triumphalis. In fact, this bridge was the Pons Neronianus, built by Nero to connect his garden in the Ager Vaticanus with the Campus Martius. Subsequent Renaissance antiquarians assumed that ancient triumphators had approached Rome along this Via Triumphalis (a road in the area bearing that name has since been confirmed by inscriptions) and thus had entered Rome by crossing the Pons Triumphalis, from there making their way across the Campus Martius to the Capitol, where triumphs were known to have ended. A significant gate, the Porta Triumphalis recorded in antique sources and today thought to be at the foot of the Capitol, was often associated with the bridge; Biondo, Lucio Fauno (1542), Bernardo Gamucci (1569), and Onofrio Panvinio (1569) envisioned it as sited on the Vatican side of the bridge, but Pirro Ligorio's maps of ancient Rome (*Antiquae urbis imago,* 1553, 1561) placed it on the Campus Martius side. In an engraved view in Giacomo Lauro's popular compilation of antiquarian images, *Antiquae urbis splendor* (1612–1628), the Porta Triumphalis takes the form of a three-passageway triumphal arch, associated with, although not attached to, the Pons Triumphalis.

The idea of a bridge, increasingly thought of as magnificent, associated with a triumphal arch was given new impetus by Johann Bernhard Fischer von Erlach's envisioned Bridge of Augustus, from his *Entwurff einer histo-*

rischen architectur (Vienna 1721), in which (on the basis of antique coins) a triumphal arch, crowned by a statue of a chariot drawn by elephants, was placed in the center of the bridge. Combined with elements from reconstructions of Hadrian's Pons Aelius (the Ponte Sant'Angelo), the notion of a triumphal bridge inspired festival designs by Paolo Posi (for the Chinea of 1755) and *capricci* (follies) and theater sets by Filippo Juvarra.

Giovanni Battista Piranesi, whose influential illustrations of Roman antiquities appeared in the mid-18th century, had his own ideas about the location of the Pons Triumphalis. Rejecting its identification with the remains of the Pons Neronianus, he identified a structure that jutted into the Tiber at an angle near the Tor' di Nona, slightly upstream from the Pons Neronianus and Pons Aelius, as one of the abutments of this bridge, though it is now thought merely to have been a wharf. In his map of the ancient Campus Martius area in *Campo Marzio* (1762), he invented a Via Triumphalis that ran from a Temple of Mars located in the Vatican area across this Pons Triumphalis to the Campus Martius and the Capitol. Subsequent archaeologists had little patience with Piranesi's ideas, but the possibility of a triumphal Tiber crossing persisted and in fact was given physical form in 1814 in the festivities commemorating the return of Pius VII from exile in France. A rich bourgeois, Giovanni Rotti, paid for a bridge supported on boats to facilitate the movement of the crowd from the Piazza del Popolo to St. Peter's. The central boat, supporting a triumphal arch dedicated to religion, alluded to the *navicella* (fishing boat) of Saint Peter.

BIBL.: David R. Marshall, "Piranesi, Juvarra, and the Triumphal Bridge Tradition," *Art Bulletin* 85 (2003) 321–352.

D.R.M.

Troilus

Son of Priam and Hecuba; a minor character in classical accounts of the Trojan War. In the *Iliad* he is mentioned in only one line (24.257), in which Priam compares him (rather unfavorably) to his brother Hector; in Virgil's *Aeneid* his death at the hands of Achilles is depicted on the walls of Dido's temple. These brief appearances, along with several other equally minor allusions to him in classical literature, in no way predict the enormous literary afterlife of Troilus, in which he figured not only as a great military hero but also as the paragon of faithful love during his courtship, and ultimate loss, of the false Criseida.

It was in the medieval period that Troilus's identity as a lover was first suggested. In Benôit de Sainte-Maure's Anglo-Norman *Roman de Troie* (ca. 1155–1170) Troilus is an exemplum of the tragedy that awaits knights who fall too deeply in love, and in Guido delle Colonne's Latin *Historia destructionis Troiae* (1287), considered in the medieval period to be an authoritative account of the Trojan War, Troilus's tragic romance serves to underscore the work's theme that humanity will never fully understand the workings of destiny. Giovanni Boccaccio imaginatively expanded on Troilus's love affair in his *Filostrato* (ca. 1335), a work that was the source for Geoffrey Chaucer's *Troilus and Criseyde* (1382–1386). Both works portray Troilus as an idealistic and constant lover; Chaucer's poem attributes to him a probing interest in philosophy as well.

For the next several centuries Troilus's story was largely confined to literature produced in Britain. In the 15th century John Lydgate and William Caxton both cursorily retold the story of Troilus's love affair, the former in his *Troy Book* (1412–1420) and the latter in a prose work about the Trojan War (ca. 1474) that served as an important source for Renaissance writers. Robert Henryson's *Testament of Cresseid*, a continuation (in Middle Scots) of Chaucer's poem, dramatizes a poignant later meeting between the two former lovers: Troilus is knightly and generous, Cresseid so ill that they cannot quite recognize each other. Shakespeare's *Troilus and Cressida* (1601–1602) uses the character of Troilus to explore, in cynical fashion, the failure of youthful illusions in the face of political, economic, and social crisis. Troilus's tenderhearted idealism becomes replaced by corrosive sarcasm and militancy, as the hero slowly relinquishes thoughts of love in favor of action on the battlefield.

Refusing to accept Shakespeare's hard-edged account of Troilus's psychological fate, later writers returned to Chaucer to recover a more enduringly idealistic Troilus; Dryden, for example, rewrote Shakespeare's play in 1679 by adding Chaucerian touches. By the 19th century the character of Troilus stood as a model of idealistically faithful love. Wordsworth translated parts of Chaucer's *Troilus and Criseyde* in 1801, and Keats alludes to the love affair in his *Endymion* (1818). In the modern period Christopher Morley's novel *The Trojan Horse* (1937) idealizes Troilus as a young artist and lover; Louis MacNeice's poem "The Stygian Banks" (1948) envisages Troilus on the banks of the Styx, awaiting passage to the other shore. William Walton's 1954 opera *Troilus and Cressida* reinvents the ending of Troilus's story—he is killed by Cressida's father, not by Achilles.

The 20th century saw Troilus revivified on the European continent. In 1910 Paul Antonin Vidal's opera about Troilus and Criseyde was produced in Paris, and in 1951 two operas, written by Winfried Wolf and Winfried Zillig and both based on the Shakespeare play, were produced in Vienna and Wurzburg, respectively. Jean Giraudoux's *La Guerre de Troie n'aura pas lieu* (1935) characterizes Troilus largely as a poet, and Christa Wolf's *Cassandra* (1986) depicts, through Troilus, the ways in which war and its attendant political crises destroy youthful happiness.

BIBL.: C. David Benson, *The History of Troy in Middle English Literature* (Cambridge 1980). Piero Boitani, ed., *The European Tragedy of Troilus* (Oxford 1989). E. T. Donaldson, *The Swan at the Well: Shakespeare Reading Chaucer* (New Haven 1985), chs. 4 and 5. R. K. Gordon, ed. and trans., *The Story of Troilus* (New York 1964).

L.J.K.

Tzetzes, John

Together with that of his contemporary Eustathius of Thessalonica, one of the most important and prolific 12th-century Byzantine contributors to the survival and interpretation of Greek classical literature. Tzetzes' work is evidence for the state of knowledge and level of scholarship in Byzantium before the losses caused by the Fourth Crusade (1204) and illustrates the context and customs of cultural production in the Constantinople of his time. He often combines classical erudition with facts of his own life—a combination of scholarship and personal experiences that would be endearing if his character were less egotistical and quarrelsome.

He was born ca. 1110, perhaps in Constantinople. He worked for some time as a civil servant but then had to give up his post, probably after accusations in conjunction with a sentimental *affaire.* Neither an influential courtier nor an ecclesiastical dignitary or a monk, he became "one of the first men in European society to live by his pen" (Browning 1975, 26). He knew extreme poverty and was even compelled to sell his books. And yet he was among the protégés of the court; some of his works were the result of the patronage of either the consort of the emperor Manuel I Comnenus or of Manuel's sister-in-law and *sebastokratorissa* (both ladies were called Irene). He was even given accommodations in an imperial foundation and had access to the treasures of the Imperial Library. It seems that his finances improved toward the end of his life (ca. 1180).

His works are evidence of the central importance of Homer to Byzantine culture. His *Carmina Iliaca* (*Trojan Verses*), in hexameters, follows a chronological arrangement (*Antehomerica, Homerica, Posthomerica*) in order to report the "facts" connected with Homeric poems. His *Iliad Allegories* and *Odyssey Allegories*, devoted to the explication of Homeric texts, are all composed in the 15-syllabic "political" verse popular in his era. The *Iliad* is also the subject of a prose commentary (*Exēgēsis*) that has not survived in its entirety and was perhaps never completed. This work is rich in grammatical remarks that would have been suitable for classroom use, whereas the *Allegories,* initially conceived for Empress Irene and an audience at court, combine erudition with entertainment. Despite the errors and discrepancies in *Exēgēsis* and the *Allegories,* Tzetzes' effort is remarkable in that he tries to understand Homer in the poet's own historical, geographical, and religious setting. He was thus the first Byzantine to search for a proper context for Homer.

He also wrote works of different length and depth on many other classical authors. His scholia on Hesiod's *Works and Days* and on Aristophanes are among his best achievements. He also commented on Pindar, Euripides, Lycophron, Nicander, and others but showed rather less interest in ancient prose works, though his autograph notes on Thucydides' *History of the Peloponnesian Wars* show him striving to gain a proper understanding of a text he did not fully appreciate.

In his readings of texts and textual criticism he is particularly keen on prosody, orthography, and grammar. When discussing authors, he carefully considers their chronology. One of his lost works deals with, inter alia, tragedies of Euripides that were not part of the usual school curriculum (the "Alphabetic tradition"). In addition to lesser-known sources, he also seems to have had access to ancient works that are now lost, especially of Callimachus, Hipponax, and Stephen of Byzantium, among others.

Tzetzes' contribution to the classical tradition is passionate and personal, as witnessed also by his impressive iambic compendium *Chiliades* (lit. *Thousands,* more than 12,000 lines of verse on a great variety of topics and authors). He deserves to be appreciated more than he has been.

BIBL.: Robert Browning, "Homer in Byzantium," *Viator* 6 (1975) 15–34. Paolo Cesaretti, *Allegoristi di Omero a Bisanzio: Ricerche ermeneutiche (XI–XII secolo)* (Milan 1991) esp. 125–221. Maria J. Luzzatto, *Tzetzes lettore di Tucidide, Note autografe sul Codice Heidelberg Palatino Greco 252* (Bari 1999). C. Wendel, "Tzetzes," in *Paulys Realencyclopädie der classischen Altertumswissenschaft, Neue Bearbeitung,* Zweite Reihe, VII 2.2 (Stuttgart 1948) 1959–2010. Nigel G. Wilson, *Scholars of Byzantium* (London 1983) 190–196.

P.CE.

UV

Ulysses. *See* Odysseus.

Ut pictura poesis

"As is painting, so is poetry": an analogy between the figurative arts and the literary arts, it is one of the most fertile and enduring topoi in the history of Western culture. According to Plutarch (*Moralia* 346f), it was the poet Simonides of Cheos (who lived in the 6th and 5th cents. BCE) who first defined painting as a "mute poem" and poetry as "a talking painting."

In the exposition of Plato's and Aristotle's political, ethical, and literary theories, painting and, more generally, the figurative arts are occasionally invoked as a useful comparison (negative for Plato, neutral or basically positive for Aristotle) for better understanding poetry, theater, and rhetoric. When Horace (*Ars poetica* 361–365) coined the wildly successful phrase *ut pictura poesis,* he was actually concerned only with poetry, and he limited himself to emphasizing some of its commonalities with painting, whose conventions he presumed were well known to his readers.

In part because of the loss of ancient literature on art, the Middle Ages and the Renaissance handed down the same formula to modern times, but with an inverted sense: it was painting that was being measured by the yardstick of the arts of the word, and in multiple senses.

In the Middle Ages the figurative arts were often perceived as a kind of "visible speech" (Dante, *Purgatorio* 10.28–99), sometimes as a translation of the Scriptures and of doctrine for the illiterate. Renaissance writing on art (starting with Alberti), however, used *ut pictura poesis* to endow painting (and, more laboriously, sculpture) with the status of liberal, and also to transfer to it the formal laws of the literary arts. It is in this sense that the topos became one of the fundamental keystones to the Humanist theory of painting. Indeed, it was the process of drawing analogies between poetry and rhetoric that helped define certain central issues: the aim of the figurative arts (the imitation of the visible, but also of that which is not seen, such as the passions, loves, the motions of the soul, rendered through their expression); the hierarchy of genres (history at the top); the necessity or the possibility of adhering to certain norms (decorum, Aristotelian unities) or of achieving certain ends (education, moral edification).

The adoption of the literary tradition led, on the one hand, to minutely prescriptive theoretical systems that tended to efface the peculiarities of painting (especially in Italy in the late 16th century). On the other hand, it triggered a process of revision that tended to emphasize not the commonalities but the differences between the means and ends of poetry and painting. Leonardo made the most penetrating and unconventional observations in this regard, and he even ended up overturning the hierarchy implicit in the topos, claiming the primacy of the figurative.

The subtle speculation of the Carracci circle transmitted to the 16th century a renewed attention to the methods and limits of painting. And it is distinctive that the obvious transformation into a literary figure of the figurative was coupled with an increasingly vivid awareness that the language of forms cannot be reduced to that of the word. (The work of Giovan Pietro Bellori is a fine example of this fertile ambiguity.)

Leonardo's line of thought, which emphasized the differences over the commonalities between the two sister arts, reached its logical conclusions in Lessing's *Laokoon* (1766), and the *ut pictura poesis* topos was explicitly refuted. Yet it did not disappear. The age-old analogy may no longer be the hinge of a theoretical system, but exchanges between poets and artists multiplied in the 19th and 20th centuries, and their collaboration in avant-garde movements became increasingly common.

Today the *ut pictura poesis* topos continues to have a more or less clear influence. But its effects are perhaps to be felt less in the complex dynamics of the relationship between art and literature (which is still very much alive) than in art history, where it inspires hermeneutical currents such as iconology and semiology.

BIBL.: Antonio Franceschetti, ed., *Letteratura italiana e arti figurative* (Florence 1988). Jean H. Hagstrum, *The Sister Arts* (Chicago 1958). Rensselaer W. Lee, *Ut pictura poesis: The Humanistic Theory of Painting* (New York 1967). Mario Praz, *Mnemosyne: The Parallel between Literature and the Visual Arts* (Princeton 1970).

T.M.

Translated by Patrick Baker

Valla, Lorenzo

If Nietzsche was the philosopher with the hammer, Lorenzo Valla (1406–1457) must be regarded as the Humanist with the hammer. Like Nietzsche in his time, Valla loved to attack received theological and philosophical dogmas. It has earned him the reputation of being a skeptic and a relativist, and his name even features in a fictive discussion of the classical tradition in a novel by the Nobel Laureate J. M. Coetzee, *Elizabeth Costello* (2003, "Lesson" 5). But for Valla, unlike Nietzsche, God was far from dead, and it was particularly his religious convictions that brought him into conflict with many trends of his own time. Far from being a skeptic or a relativist in any strict sense, Valla was deeply concerned to rescue the Christian faith from the hands of theologians and philosophers, who in his view had contaminated religion and morality by dogmatically imposing their own abstractions and theories on human experience and understanding.

Valla's attitude toward what we now call the classical tradition was ambivalent: he was a tireless campaigner for the revival of Classical Latin and the rhetorical outlook of Cicero and Quintilian, but he rejected much of classical philosophy. Moreover, for him—as for most Humanists—the classical tradition had petered out by the time Boethius had begun to compose his philosophical and theological works in the late 5th century.

Valla led an itinerant life. Born in Rome to a family with close connections to the papal Curia, he moved to Pavia in 1431, where he lectured on rhetoric and wrote his famous dialogue on the highest good, entitled *De voluptate* (*On Pleasure*) in the earliest version, in which several major Humanists of his day figured as interlocutors. He had to flee Pavia after provoking the fury of the law professors and went to the court of King Alfonso in Naples, where he worked as a court Humanist and polemicist, supporting his patron by writing antipapal treatises. In 1447 he returned to the Vatican to become an apostolic scriptor and, two years later, a papal secretary. He died in 1457 and was buried in the Lateran.

Valla made numerous contributions to classical scholarship. He translated Thucydides, 33 fables of Aesop, the first book of Xenophon's *The Education of Cyrus,* 16 books of Homer's *Iliad,* Demosthenes' *In Defense of Ctesiphon,* and most of Herodotus. He studied and emended the text of Livy, working on a manuscript that had once belonged to Petrarch, whose emendations he sometimes corrected. One important project was his glossing of Quintilian's *Education of an Orator,* the full text of which had been discovered by his archenemy, Poggio, in 1416. He is most noted for an extremely influential handbook, *Elegantiae linguae latinae* (*The Fine Points of the Latin Language*), which elucidates, from a thorough reading of an impressively wide range of (late) classical sources, a great variety of morphological, syntactical, and semantic features of Latin. Behind the mass of detail, a clear program can be discerned: the replacement of a philosophical approach to the study of language by grammatical and philological methods grounded on the premise that only a close study of the usage of ancient authors can teach us to read and write Latin correctly. Unlike most medieval grammarians, who constructed abstract rules first and then assessed the correctness and validity of expressions on the basis of these artificial constraints, Valla stressed that linguistic practice, convention, and custom (*consuetudo*) should sanction the rules of grammar.

His sensitivity to the semantic nuances of words and expressions not only served the aesthetic ideal of restoring Latin to its classical form but also helped him use it as a weapon in criticizing philosophical theories and in exposing the Donation of Constantine, one of the pillars of the papal claim to worldly power, as a forgery. Extending his linguistic expertise to Greek, he also critically reviewed the Latin Vulgate of Jerome by comparing it to the Greek text of the New Testament, occasionally drawing theologically daring conclusions. These efforts had an enormous influence on Erasmus, who published Valla's annotations and further developed his text-critical approach to the Bible. No one before Valla had realized the power of philology.

With this sensitivity to the ordinary meaning of words naturally went an awareness that language is culturally and historically embedded. Valla regarded language primarily as a vehicle for debate, persuasion, and communication rather than as a scientific, formalized tool to be studied in abstraction from its living context of speech and discussion. In his *Dialecticae disputationes* (*Dialectical Disputations*) he attempted to transform Aristotelian and Scholastic logic by loosening the severe restrictions that medieval logicians had imposed on argumentation and validity. Inspired by the ideal of the orator as portrayed by Cicero and Quintilian—as a man full of wisdom, devoted to applying rhetorical teaching to public life—Valla sought to broaden considerably the range of acceptable arguments, rhetoricizing the syllogism and other forms of argumentation. What was important, in his view, was whether an argument worked, that is, whether it induced conviction in the hearer. Formal validity was only one way of looking at argumentation, and a rather narrow way at that. Rejecting the approach of the Scholastics, Valla wanted to ground dialectic in real language by studying arguments in context, and for him context embraced far more than the individual sentences of the traditional Scholastic example. Similar attempts to transform the study of language and argument were later undertaken by Rudolph Agricola, Philipp Melanchthon, and other Humanists.

The basic assumption behind his project is that language offers the key to our understanding of the world: without a sound grasp of the nuances of Latin, one cannot think correctly about human life and the world. This comes close to a conviction that Classical Latin, properly (to his mind) the alpha and omega of all our intellectual activities, adequately mirrors the world. It was a conviction that ignored the rise of the vernacular and the importance of specialized idioms in various disciplines. Moreover, in rejecting post-classical developments of Latin, Valla refused to generalize his own valuable insight into the cultural and historical embeddedness of language. But it would be unfair to criticize him for not having realized all the implications of his own views. These sustained a fruitful conviction that inspired future generations of Humanists to study and appropriate the riches of classical antiquity, laying the foundations of modern historical and textual scholarship.

BIBL.: Ottavio Besomi and Mariangela Regoiosi, eds., *Lorenzo Valla e l'umanesimo italiano* (Padua 1986). Salvatore Camporeale, *Lorenzo Valla: Umanesimo e teologia* (Florence 1972). Peter Mack, *Renaissance Argument: Valla and Agricola in the Tradition of Rhetoric and Dialectic* (Leiden 1993). Lodi Nauta, *In Defense of Common Sense: Lorenzo Valla's Humanist Critique of Scholastic Philosophy* (Cambridge, Mass., 2009) and "Lorenzo Valla and the Rise of Humanist Dialectic," in *The Cambridge Companion to Renaissance Philosophy*, ed. James Hankins (Cambridge 2007). L.N.

Vegetarianism

The idea that it is wrong to eat animals was a popular one, if not a majority view, in the ancient world. There were at least four reasons for vegetarianism.

Many of the ancient vegetarians believed in transmigration, which led them to spare animals in the belief that animals were, or would be, human beings. This belief has had little effect on subsequent history in the West.

Another reason for ancient abstention from meat was the belief that flesh eating was injurious to the health of either body or soul. The former belief was tied to ancient medical thought, whereas the latter was often associated with a more general commitment to moderation or asceticism. Here a greater influence on later eras can be detected, as in the popular claim made today by Keith Akers, among others, that a vegetarian lifestyle is especially healthy, and also in the rich history of vegetarianism in monastic and mendicant communities. Saint Francis of Assisi in the 13th century exemplifies this latter tendency.

There was also among the ancients a concern for animals themselves. The ancient and contemporary argument from sentiency involves the idea that because animals suffer when they are killed (or are deprived of a life that is theirs if killed painlessly), and because we can live healthy lives on vegetal food, eating meat involves violence that ought to be avoided. This argument has been the cornerstone of the subsequent history of vegetarianism, especially for vegetarians in the utilitarian philosophical tradition, such as Peter Singer, but also in the modern animal rights movement exemplified by Evelyn Pluhar and among recent feminist thinkers such as Martha Nussbaum.

Perhaps the most sophisticated grounds for ancient vegetarianism, however, are found in Porphyry (ca. 233–ca. 309). His argument from marginal cases (*On Abstinence from Killing Animals* 3.19), echoed in the present-day vegetarian thought of Tom Regan and many others, involves the claim that rationality is not a defensible criterion for receiving moral respect, because on this basis many members of our own species (the marginal cases of humanity, including the mentally defective) would not be protected. If we lowered the criterion for receiving moral respect to sentiency, so as to protect the marginal cases of humanity, we must, in order to be consistent, also protect sentient animals. In this regard, contemporary philosophical vegetarians are in agreement with Porphyry. Indeed, many contemporary vegetarian philosophers (e.g., Dale Jamieson) still see this as the most formidable argument for vegetarianism.

Vegetarianism flourished along an axis that traveled through the Platonic tradition, as is emphasized by the contemporary thinker Stephen R. L. Clark. In book 2 of Plato's *Republic* there is evidence that his perfect city was to have been a vegetarian paradise, as was the Garden of Eden in the biblical tradition. Elsewhere in Plato's writings vegetarianism is treated favorably.

Various predecessors who had influenced Plato's thought—the Pythagoreans, members of the Orphic cult, and Empedocles, among others—either were vegetarians or took vegetarianism seriously. There is also ample evidence in many Greek authors (e.g., Hesiod) that the original citizens of the lost golden age of perfection were vegetarian; utopian thinkers throughout the ages, including Tolstoy, have often returned to this Pythagorean view.

Further, after Plato several thinkers who were influenced by him show clear evidence of taking vegetarianism seriously: Plutarch, Plotinus, and especially Porphyry, whose *On Abstinence from Killing Animals,* a book-length treatment of the topic, is an encyclopedia of ancient vegetarian and antivegetarian thought. The influence of this Pythagorean–Platonic–Neoplatonic tradition can be seen in famous vegetarians like Leonardo da Vinci and George Bernard Shaw, who objected to eating meat both on moral grounds and because of a concern for bodily health.

Antivegetarian thought runs along an axis that goes from Aristotle to the Stoics, whose view of animals had a great effect on Immanuel Kant's influential Enlightenment view in the 18th century, a view that still runs strong today. Indeed, it is at present the dominant view. Because animals lack sophisticated language and rationality, it is argued, they can be used for human purposes.

The absolute nadir regarding animals, however, came in the 17th century, when René Descartes held that animals were machines who could not feel pain. No ancient thinker would have gone this far, although the mechanism of some of the atomists may have come close. Even Aristotle and the Stoics were firmly committed to the belief, now famously associated with Darwin, that human beings are sentient animals themselves, though rational ones. Hence it is not surprising that Aristotle's student Theophrastus was a defender of vegetarianism, according to Porphyry.

In any event, it should be noted that most people in the ancient world would have been largely vegetarian in practice, if not in theory, in that foods such as barley meal, wheaten loaves, and vegetables were the dietary staples. Further, not even antivegetarian thinkers in antiquity would have killed animals with equanimity, as has been done throughout the modern period as a result of the market commodification of animals. Ancient meat eaters had to petition for permission from the gods if they desired to kill besouled, sentient animals.

Clearly there are differences between contemporary vegetarianism and that practiced in the ancient world: ancient vegetarianism was often associated with a belief in transmigration; the ancients did not have our modern liberal notion of rights; and ancient vegetarians were probably more concerned than their modern counterparts with a life of *aretē*, or virtue. But the similarities between vegetarianism today and that practiced in the ancient world are more prominent: in both periods there is a noticeable concern for animals themselves; in both periods there is a tendency to see continuity between human and nonhuman animals without a major gap between the two, although there was no developed theory of evolution in the ancient period; and among both ancient and modern vegetarians there is a tendency to believe that abstinence from animal flesh tends to promote both bodily and psychic health, a healthiness that functions as a countercultural protest against the dominant society.

BIBL.: Keith Akers, *A Vegetarian Sourcebook* (Arlington, Va., 1989). Stephen R. L. Clark, *The Moral Status of Animals* (Oxford 1977). Daniel Dombrowski, *Babies and Beasts: The Argument from Marginal Cases* (Chicago 1997); "Nussbaum, the Ancients, and Animal Entitlements," *The Modern Schoolman* 81 (2004) 193–214; *The Philosophy of Vegetarianism* (Amherst, Mass., 1984); and "Two Vegetarian Puns at *Republic* 372," *Ancient Philosophy* 9 (1990) 167–171. Johannes Haussleiter, *Der Vegetarismus in der Antike* (Berlin 1935). Dale Jamieson, "Review of Stephen R. L. Clark," *Nous* 15 (1981) 230–234. Martha Nussbaum, ed., *Animal Rights* (Oxford 2004). Evelyn Pluhar, *Beyond Prejudice: The Moral Significance of Human and Nonhuman Animals* (Durham, N.C., 1995). Porphyry, *On Abstinence from Killing Animals,* trans. Gillian Clark (Ithaca 2000). Tom Regan, *The Case for Animal Rights* (Berkeley 1983). Steve Sapontzis, ed., *Food for Thought: The Debate over Eating Meat* (Amherst, N.Y., 2004). Peter Singer, *Animal Liberation* (New York 2001). Richard Sorabji, *Animal Minds and Human Morals* (Ithaca 1993). D.A.D.

Venice

The only major city in Italy without a history that reaches back into monumental classical antiquity, Venice was nonetheless built with ancient stones transported from the Italian mainland, the Dalmatian coast, and islands in the Aegean. But the city's classical architectural heritage was initially mediated through Byzantium—the model for political legitimacy. The Basilica of San Marco, built in the 9th century on the model of the 6th-century Church of the Holy Apostles in Constantinople, was embellished over the years with Byzantine spoils, both genuine and fake, that implied an early Christian past. Around the end of the 12th century, Piazza San Marco was framed with arcaded buildings on the model of a late antique forum.

During the 15th century *Romanitas* began to inform Venetian architecture, as the formal vocabulary of classical antiquity was incorporated piecemeal into the Byzantine and Gothic urban fabric. Classicizing tombs were built for doges and eminent citizens, and Venice became a major center for the production of medals, small bronzes, and portrait busts—new artistic genres based on classical prototypes. Under Doge Andrea Gritti (1455–1538) and the architect Jacopo Sansovino (1486–1570) the area around Piazza San Marco, the political and religious center of the city, was rebuilt as a "new Rome," with the construction of the Zecca (mint), Loggetta, and Biblioteca Marciana (Library of Saint Mark's).

The revival of classical literature, stimulated early on by Petrarch and Humanist circles in Padua, coupled with the fall of Constantinople to the Ottoman Turks in 1453 and the arrival of the printing press in 1469, made Venice a center for the dissemination of classical scholarship. Andrea Mantegna and other artists worked with antiquarians to revive classical epigraphy, and printers invented new typefaces based on classical principles. Aldus Manutius founded the Aldine Neakademia in 1502 to promote the teaching of Greek and to publish classical texts through his Aldine Press. By the time of his death in 1515, Aldus could confidently assert that Venice "can truly be called a second Athens."

Venetian pictorial artists likewise offered a new vision of classical antiquity. Evoking a lost world of Arcadian myth, Giorgione gave visual form to pastoral poetry, such as the idylls of the Greek poet Theocritus and the eclogues of Virgil, and invented the pastoral landscape that they evoked. Titian, Veronese, and Tintoretto turned their attention to Ovid and ekphrastic literature, as well as to Roman history. As antique sculpture became rare and costly to collect, sculptors such as Tullio Lombardo and Alessandro Vittoria revived the classical portrait bust. Nor did music escape the seductive imprint of the classical world; early operas, such as Monteverdi's *Orfeo* (1607), were inspired by a variety of classical themes.

Venetians more than made up for the lack of classical artifacts on the ground by collecting them elsewhere. Antiquarian interests were already evident in the 1330s when Oliviero Forzetta, a notary in Treviso, wrote of a market in antiquities in Venice. Over the course of the 15th century Venetians became avid collectors of, and dealers in, ancient texts, coins, inscriptions, and artifacts, primarily from the Aegean. By the end of the 16th century, aside from the princely collections of Florence and Mantua, Venice was exceeded only by Rome in its collections of antiquities in private hands. Among the most notable in Rome was the collection of ancient marbles amassed by Cardinal Domenico Grimani and later augmented by his nephew Giovanni; the collection eventually was left to the Republic of Venice and was installed in the specially built Statuario Pubblico. The bequest is one of the earliest examples of a private collection turned over to public use in Renaissance Italy.

BIBL.: Patricia Fortini Brown, *Venice and Antiquity: The Venetian Sense of the Past* (New Haven 1996). Margaret King, *Venetian Humanism in an Age of Patrician Dominance* (Princeton 1986). Alison Luchs, *Tullio Lombardo and Ideal Portrait Sculpture in Renaissance Venice, 1490–1530* (Cambridge 1995). Manfredo Tafuri, *Venice and the Renaissance,* trans. Jessica Levine (Cambridge, Mass., 1989). P.F.B.

Venus. *See* Aphrodite.

Venus de Milo

Statue of the goddess Aphrodite (130–100 BCE), of Parian marble; height 203.8 cm (80.2 inches). Found in 1820 on the Aegean island of Milos (Greek *Mēlos*), for which it is named. Now in the Louvre (inv. no. Ma 399).

Soon after the statue was discovered, the French ambassador to Turkey, the marquis de Rivière, arranged its purchase for King Louis XVIII. Once in Paris, the statue was exhibited at the Louvre and immediately inspired a lively debate among archaeologists and amateurs about the position of its missing arms and possible attributes. Toward the end of the century a fiery dispute erupted concerning the loss of a plinth that was said to have been found with the statue, inscribed with the name of its sculptor. Some German scholars suspected that the inscription had been intentionally concealed to permit attribution of the statue to a much more famous Greek master than was perhaps the case.

The statue's great fame throughout the 19th century did not depend entirely on its being an original work of ancient Greek art but was also due to a major propaganda effort by French authorities. Sculptures and paintings honoring this rendering of Venus as the embodiment of concepts such as Tradition and Taste appeared in some of the most prominent public settings in Paris (e.g., Jean-Jules Cambos, *La Tradition,* marble statue, 1867; Charles-Louis Müller, *Le Goût,* oil on canvas, 1864–1866). Its literary celebrity followed close on its first exhibition to the public (starting with a poem by Wilhelm Waiblinger in 1827) and increased exponentially over the decades. As early as 1822 a plaster cast was made for the Preussische Akademie der Künst, in Berlin.

By the 20th century the Venus de Milo had become a cultural icon in its own right, established as an epitome of beauty and antiquity by a century of praise and unceasing attention. During the 1930s artists belonging to the Surrealist movement began to use its image as a focus for free association of concepts and objects. René Magritte painted in bright colors a miniaturized plaster version of the Venus (*Les Menottes de cuivre*) in 1931; a few years later the statue became a veritable obsession for Salvador Dalí, who for more than 40 years engaged with its archetype in a continuous development of paradoxes, making several new painted or sculpted renditions in absurd settings, with inconsistent additions or inverted anatomical features.

From these innovative beginnings the statue has grown into a favorite archetype for exploring, challenging, or desecrating tradition in art. One perhaps unexpected effect of this process of deconstruction has been the standardization of metaphors and links with the ideal, thus strengthening the powerful significance of the statue and increasing its exceptional status among the entire repertoire of extant ancient statuary.

The virtually unlimited possibilities of creative exploitation of a model like the Venus de Milo continued to be widely explored in the late 20th century, for humorous effects (Clive Barker), by changing its character through new colors and materials (Jim Dine), and by destabilizing the viewer's expectations through the attachment of musical instruments to the well-known features of the classical body (Arman).

The statue's fortunes in cinema have been tied to its suggestive powers of combined sensuality and mutilation—that is, female vulnerability. Shots of the Venus de Milo appear throughout Jennifer Lynch's *Boxing Helena* (1993), a macabre tale of erotic fascination about a man who amputates the arms and legs of the woman he loves, turning her into his own living version of the statue. In Bernardo Bertolucci's *The Dreamers* (2003) the quotation is playful: the heroine engages in a mischievous game with her lover and poses as the Venus, standing in a dark doorway and wearing black gloves to mimic its missing arms.

The widespread presence of this statue in contemporary popular culture can also be seen in its appearance in comics and advertising. Comic strips often explore the humorous potential of the missing limbs and depict a Venus losing more anatomical parts or engaging in activities that require a firm grip. In advertising the image conveys a wide set of meanings, alluding to graceful female beauty, everlasting perfection, or carelessness leading to accidents, breaks, and fractures.

BIBL.: Gregory Curtis, *Disarmed: The Story of the Venus de Milo* (New York 2003). Jean-Pierre Cuzin, Jean-René Gaborit, and Alain Pasquier, eds., *D'après l'antique: Paris, Musée du Louvre, 16 octobre 2000–15 janvier 2001,* exhibition catalogue (Paris 2001) 430–499. Francis Haskell and Nicholas Penny, *Taste and the Antique: The Lure of Classical Sculpture 1500–1900* (New Haven 1981) 328–330, no. 89. Gisbert Kranz, *Meisterwerke in Bildgedichten: Rezeption von Kunst in der Poesie* (Frankfurt am Main 1986) 59–99. Dimitri Salmon, *La Vénus de Milo: Un mythe* (Paris 2000). A.AN.

Veterinary Medicine

Ancient veterinary medicine as an independent branch of learning and a subject of literary activity is understood here, as it probably was in antiquity, as *mulomedicina*—that is, the medical treatment of horses and mules and (in all likelihood) donkeys. (No Greek term is attested; practitioners were called *hippiatroi* in Greek and *mulomedici* or *ueterinarii* in Latin.) Farm animals would in general be covered in agricultural treatises (Cato the Elder, Varro, Columella, Palladius in Latin, the Byzantine collective work *Geoponika* in Greek), although some overlap did occur (Columella book 6 and Palladius book 14). We can only surmise that animals kept for hunting (like falcons and dogs) were dealt with in treatises on hunting, which probably were extant in late antiquity, although no convincing trace of them has yet been detected. (Both agriculture and hunting are excluded from this discussion.)

Surviving treatises on veterinary medicine can be dated to the 4th century CE, and curiously enough, they are in Latin. Both the work with the modern title of *Mulomedicina Chironis* (in ten books, authors and redactor unknown) and the treatise in epistolary form by the otherwise unknown Pelagonius draw on Latin and Greek sources going back at least to the 1st century CE; among these, Apsyrtos (fl. between 150 and 250 or in the early 4th cent. CE) features prominently. He was a horse doctor in the Roman army and drew on earlier writings (usually not specified). His keen interest in the subject extended to practices in human medicine and medical theory, a trait not discernible, at least not to the same degree, in other veterinary writers. What has been preserved of his veterinary writings has been incorporated into the Greek collection known as *Hippiatrika* (9th cent.), a digest of treatises in Greek or translated into Greek (i.e., Pelagonius and Vegetius, late 4th cent.). It is clear that veterinary medicine in antiquity enjoyed less prestige than did human medicine, that it was often based on experience and probably oral tradition rather than theory (only the Methodist school seems to have had some influence, for example on Apsyrtos), and that at best it strove to make advances in human medicine, first of all surgery, available to veterinarians. In drug treatment, no real difference exists. The knowledge that some diseases are infectious—that is, that a sick animal may pass certain diseases on to others (and should therefore be isolated or slaughtered, the pasture changed)—was thoroughly neglected by human physicians before the advent of bacteriology in the 19th century.

In antiquity and beyond, information on the treatment of animals would in many cases have been passed on orally by practitioners who were not necessarily literate. This applies especially to the period before roughly 1100, when a gulf emerged in both West and East between spoken forms of Latin and Greek and the written classicizing forms of these languages. Unfortunately, the written record is our only means of determining what and how much of ancient veterinary lore was passed on. Whereas in the Greek East an epitome of horse medicine in medieval (vernacular) Greek was transmitted in a number of manuscripts perhaps from as early as the 10th century onward and in several versions (although the earliest Greek and Latin manuscripts date from the 14th century), we know of only two fragments of Latin manuscripts of Vegetius and one of Pelagonius from the early Middle Ages. A decisive change regarding treatises on horse medicine in the West occurred in the second half of the 13th century, when Vegetius' work (itself based largely on the *Mulomedicina Chironis* and Pelagonius) was in its turn incorporated piecemeal into Theodoric of Cervia's (1205–1298) *Liber de equorum medela* or *Mulomedicina* and translated at least four times into Italian before the end of the 15th century. The 1260s were also the time when two Greek manuals on horse medicine (the epitome mentioned above and the work of Hierocles, reconstituted from the excerpts in the *Hippiatrika*) were translated, first into Latin and then into Italian. This occurred not long after the first Western medieval author known to us by name, Jordanus Ruffus, published his treatise on horse medicine (ca. 1250), a work that became immensely popular in its original Latin as well as in translations into Italian, French, Provençal, and Catalan. Surprisingly, neither the terminology used by Jordanus Ruffus nor the contents of his work show a clear link with ancient veterinary medicine. Vegetius became a major source for the Italian treatise by Dino Dini, completed in 1359, and was quoted, roughly a hundred years later, in the Renaissance Humanist L. B. Alberti's *De equo animante.*

The first printed editions of ancient veterinary treatises appeared rather late—a generation after two medieval Latin works had been printed—beginning with Vegetius in 1528 (followed by a translation into German in 1532 and another in 1565, as well as renderings into Italian and French), and the *Hippiatrika* in 1537 (Ruellius's Latin translation had been published a little earlier, in 1530; there were also translations into Italian, French, and German). It may be assumed that these translations were intended for practical use; however, the total absence of studies seriously addressing this question does not allow us to assert this, because apart from manuscripts and books as the only positive witnesses, we remain, for the time being, reduced to guesswork.

So far, surprisingly little work has been done on translations of Greek veterinary texts into Arabic. The most promising is the Arabic version of Theomnestus (4th century CE), of which only excerpts survive in Greek in the *Hippiatrika.* The 12th-century agricultural author Ibn al-ʾAwwam also quotes from (unspecified) Greek sources (Ar-Rum) that need to be studied in greater detail. Medieval Arabic treatises on horse medicine seem to outnumber those extant in the West and Byzantium, but very few have been studied, edited, or translated. The Arabic word for horse doctor, *baitar,* derives from Greek *hippiatros,* which might suggest that ancient Greek horse lore had played a considerable role, at least at the beginning. Moses of Palermo translated one or two short Arabic treatises into Latin in the 1270s, but these would hardly have been representative of the best that was available in Arabic. Nevertheless, no other translations from Arabic into Latin are on record.

BIBL.: Klaus-Dietrich Fischer, "'A horse! A horse! My kingdom for a horse!' Versions of Greek Horse Medicine in Medieval Italy," *Medizinhistorisches Journal* 34 (1999) 123–138. Martin Heide, *Buch der Hippiatrie: Kitāb al-Baytara von Muhammad ibn Ya'qūb ibn ahi Hizām al-Huttalī,* vol. 1, *Einleitung, Übersetzung, Indizes;* vol. 2, *Kritische Edition* (Wiesbaden 2008). Robert G. Hoyland, "Theomnestus of Nicopolis, Hunayn ibn Ishaq, and the Beginnings of Islamic Veterinary Science," in *Islamic Reflections, Arabic Musings: Studies in Honour of Professor Alan Jones,* ed. R. G. Hoyland and Philip F. Kennedy (Oxford 2004) 150–169. Vincenzo Ortoleva, *La tradizione manoscritta della "Mulomedicina" di Publio Vegezio Renato* (Acireale 1996). Susanne Saker, *Die Pferdeheilkunde des Theomnest von Nikopolis* (Wiesbaden 2008). Domizia Trolli, *Studi su antichi trattati di veterinaria* (Parma 1990).

K.-D.F.

Vico, Giambattista

Italian rhetorician, jurist, and philosopher (1668–1744). His major works contain some of the most inventive thinking about the culture of archaic Greece and Rome, the origins of epic poetry, and the methods of the human sciences written in the 18th century.

His life and learning were profoundly shaped by the city of Naples one of Europe's largest cities and a vibrant intellectual and artistic milieu. His *Autobiography* (1725, 1731) details his unsystematic and idiosyncratic education but does not mention his acquisition of a doctorate in civil and canon law in 1694. He was appointed to the chair of rhetoric at the University of Naples in 1699, a duty he fulfilled until 1741. His major professional disappointment was his failure to win the chair of civil law in 1723. He composed the poems, orations, and Latin inscriptions expected of an Italian intellectual; he wrote history and biography and three volumes on Roman law in Latin. This last work was reviewed and praised by the Dutch classicist and Protestant biblical scholar Jean Le Clerc. Among his Neapolitan friends were the classical scholars and antiquarians Domenico Aulisio, Matteo Egizio, and Gianvincenzo Gravina, as well as the poet Pietro Metastasio.

Vico's literary reputation and his significance as a theorist are based on his *New Science* (*Scienza nuova*), written in Italian. It was first published in 1725; five years later he issued a massive revision; the third, definitive and posthumous edition appeared in 1744. In these various editions he imaginatively reconstructs the mental framework of ancient mythologies and customs. Vico believed that the thoughts and emotions of the first people were radically different from the modern rational perspective; evidence of their way of thinking appeared in language, popular expressions, and metaphor. He approached religious experience in terms of ritual and symbolism rather than by articles of a creed and matters of doctrine. His theory aimed to reveal the historical pattern followed by all nations. The first edition of *New Science* is structured around his analysis of ideas or mental concepts of the first peoples, and the language and words they used to express their feelings. In the second and third editions he adopts a mathematical format to describe the "poetic wisdom" of the first peoples and the patterns of the historical development followed by all nations. The centerpiece is his solution to the Homeric problem (whether Homer existed and whether he was a single author) and the origins of epic poetry. The scholarly core of his work is his analysis of the political and legal practices of the early Roman Republic.

Vico relied on historical methods developed by Renaissance legal scholars such as Jacques Cujas, François Hotman, and François Baudouin; an edition of Cujas was published in Naples in 1723. He cites these authors but never suggests that he was seriously engaged by their work. This is similar to his relation to J. C. Scaliger's *Poetices libri VII,* which he cites but does not exploit. He claims instead to have studied little except the ancient sources; he was a master of Latin and concealed his weak Greek. His reading and involvement with the early modern scholarship of law, language, and chronology were far more nuanced than his text ever allows. His first readers did not recognize these connections with his intellectual predecessors and thus failed to find a meaningful context for this gallimaufry of a book. The title *New Science* indicated a work of political theory, but instead of speculations on the state of nature or historical examples, the reader encountered a collection of wild etymologies of words and bizarre interpretations of classical myths. From its first publication *New Science* has had enthusiastic readers, but until the 20th century it remained outside the mainstream. The disordered character of Vico's thought makes him a frustrating but fascinating figure whose work continues to stun and even offend but can also astound and inspire.

BIBL.: *The Autobiography of Giambattista Vico,* trans. M. H. Fisch and T. G. Bergin (Ithaca 1962), Introduction. Isaiah Berlin, *Vico and Herder* (London 1976). Peter Burke, *Vico* (Oxford 1985). Arnaldo Momigliano, "Roman 'bestioni' and Roman 'eroi' in Vico's *Scienza Nuova,*" in his *Essays in Ancient and Modern Historiography* (Oxford 1977) 253–276. Fausto Nicolini, *Commento storico alla seconda Scienza Nuova* (Rome 1949–1950). Harold Stone, *Vico's Cultural History* (Leiden 1997). F. A. Wolf, *Prolegomena to Homer (1795),* trans. Anthony Grafton, Glenn W. Most, and James E. G. Zetzel (Princeton 1988).

H.S.

Virgil

Publius Vergilius Maro (70–19 BCE), Roman poet, author of *Bucolics* (*Eclogues*), *Georgics,* and the *Aeneid.* To adapt a bon mot of Bernard Williams's on the relation between Greek philosophy and Western philosophy, we might say that Virgil's legacy to Western literature is Western literature. Perhaps it is only with regard to Virgil that T. S. Eliot could begin a lecture entitled "What Is a Classic?" (1944) by asserting as self-evidently true that "whatever the definition we arrive at, it cannot be one that excludes Virgil—we may say confidently that it must be one which will expressly reckon with him." For Virgil became a European classic, not only in the sense that he was a central author for many European readers for many centuries, but also in the further sense that his works crucially helped such readers to define themselves as Europeans. Virgil's contribution to Western culture is in that sense not merely literary: he became an indispensable element in its self-understanding. Like his hero Aeneas, he rescued his idols from historical oblivion by betraying them, by transporting them, with considerable reluctance and many a backward glance, to a new world, where he laid the foundation for a novel cultural and political empire that he would not live to experience himself and that in many regards would no doubt have profoundly troubled him.

For the Romans, Virgil was already a classic, with a speed and completeness that have few if any parallels in earlier or later world literature: his works are quoted so often in antiquity that even if they had been lost, they could still be reconstructed in large measure. During his own lifetime, fellow poets like Horace and Propertius admired him, from a distance; parodies of his works (e.g., *Antibucolica*) flourished; but no poet earlier than Ovid (in his *Metamorphoses*) seems to have dared to try to rival him. Very early he became a model author who provided pedagogical material for teachers of grammar and rhetoric; and throughout antiquity the *Aeneid* remained one of the fundamental school texts, replacing epic poets of the Republic (such as Ennius) and thereby condemning their works to full or partial extinction. One surviving papyrus (P. Tebt. 2.686) transmits *Georgics* 4.1–2 written six times, another (P. Hawara 24) *Aeneid* 2.601 written seven times and 4.174 written five times. But scholars also vilified his poetry: *obtrectatores Vergili,* "detractors of Virgil," wrote polemical tractates with titles like *Aeneidomastix* (*The Whip of the Aeneid,* modeled on the Greek *Homeromastix*) and *Homoiotetes* (*Similarities*), in which, misconstruing Virgil's profound traditionality, they attempted to demonstrate his lack of originality by collecting what they called his *furta,* "thefts," from earlier authors.

In the 1st century CE Virgil remained the supreme Latin author (even if, during the reign of Nero, Seneca the Younger and his circle sought originality by ostentatiously preferring Ovid). It is to this period that most of the minor imitations of his poetry, later gathered into the *Appendix Vergiliana,* are likely to belong. His verses are found scratched on the walls of Pompeii; and Petronius delighted in creating variations, sometimes obscene ones, on verses of the *Aeneid.* Toward the end of the century, Virgil's popularity seems to have reached a high point (coinciding, perhaps not accidentally, with Quintilian's conspicuous anti-Senecan polemics): Statius asked his *Thebaid* (at 12.816–817) to follow the *Aeneid* "at a distance" and to revere its footsteps; Silius Italicus not only imitated Virgil's poetry with almost religious scrupulosity but even collected mementos of the poet, bought the land on which his tomb was located, and celebrated his birthday every year as his own.

The foundations of the scholarly tradition of exegesis of Virgil's poems were laid in the 1st and 2nd centuries CE by Valerius Probus and thereafter especially by C. Julius Hyginus, L. Annaeus Cornutus, and Aemilius Asper. Though the running commentaries for students that have survived (especially that by Servius, but also the smaller collections of scholia and the rhetorical commentary of Tiberius Donatus) all date from the 4th century, they preserve a considerable amount of earlier material, much of it deriving from this period; and the essays on Virgil in Macrobius' *Saturnalia* (ca. 400) give us an idea of what earlier scholarly treatises might have looked like. The rhetoricians, too, took their examples from Virgil's poems and debated whether he was more an orator or a poet; one declamation by Ennodius (6th cent.) survives, purporting to be a speech by Dido upon the departure of Aeneas. The ancient allegorical tradition of Virgil exegesis, already established by the time of Donatus and Servius, culminated in the 6th century in the work of Fulgentius, who interpreted the 12 books of the *Aeneid* as the 12 stages of human life from infancy to old age. The widespread conviction that Virgil knew everything, including the future, led to the practice, attested in the *Historia Augusta,* of consulting his verses as oracles and prophecies (*sortes Vergilianae*). Through late antiquity Virgil continued to be a favorite object for scholastic poetry: exercises on Virgilian themes and in Virgilian style flourished (in the 4th century, for example, Avienus wrote a summary of Virgil's *Aeneid* in iambic verses), as did centos like Hosidius Geta's *Medea* (ca. 200) and Ausonius' *cento nuptialis* (ca. 374).

No other Latin author survives so massively, so anciently, and so excellently as Virgil. We have three ancient manuscripts, almost complete (Florence, Laur. 39.1 + Vatican lat. 3225, fol. 76, the Codex Mediceus; Vatican Pal. lat. 1631, the Codex Palatinus; and Vatican lat. 3867, the Codex Romanus), all written in the 5th to 6th centuries in rustic capital scripts (known in the early Middle Ages as *litterae Virgilianae,* Virgilian letters, precisely because so few codices in this script survived for any other author), and four others, in more fragmentary condition (Vatican lat. 3225, the Schedae Vaticanae; Verona XL [38]; Vatican lat. 3256 + Berlin lat. 416, the Codex Augusteus; and St. Gall 1394), dating from the 4th and 5th centuries. Two of these ancient manuscripts, the Codex

Romanus and the Schedae Vaticanae, have important illustrations, and one, the Augusteus, has decorated initials. Of all the surviving Latin papyri whose authors can be identified, Virgil appears on more than half (one or two may have been written only a century after his death).

For Christian late antiquity, Virgil was by far the most popular Latin poet. Jerome was intimately familiar with his works, which, like Servius, he studied at the feet of the great Virgil commentator Donatus, and though he notoriously felt keen anxiety about his fondness for Cicero (*Epistles* 22.30), Virgil never seems to have disquieted him. Augustine cannot retell the story of his own life without seeing crucial episodes through the lens of the *Aeneid;* he condemns himself for weeping at Dido's sufferings instead of at his own (*Confessions* 1.20–21), yet he cannot do so without quoting a line from that beloved poem, and he returns to it constantly throughout his works, as an indispensable textbook teaching finely tuned language, emotionally effective rhetoric, and the development of human, national, and cosmic destiny. The Christian poetess Proba even composed a Virgilian cento about the history of salvation, from the Creation through the life of Jesus.

Virgil's centrality continued unchanged throughout the Middle Ages, when (despite occasional protests by such figures as Alcuin and Ermenrich) he remained a fundamental school author, and the Fourth Eclogue and the *Aeneid* were the most widely read Latin poems. At the beginning of Chaucer's *House of Fame* (1386) the narrator dreams that he finds the *Aeneid* engraved in brass in a temple of Venus and goes on to provide an extended summary of the poem (140–467), emphasizing especially the story of Dido; and later he assigns Virgil a uniquely prominent position amid all the celebrities of human history, standing alone on a column of gleaming tinned iron (1481–1485). Throughout this period, Macrobius' widely read *Saturnalia,* in which four of the seven books are devoted to Virgil, propagated the view that he was the perfect rhetorician, learned in ancient religious lore and other scholarly matters, and indeed thoroughly omniscient, and at the same time taught readers how to understand his poetry in relation to that of some other Latin and even Greek authors.

Of course the pagan poet often had to be Christianized if he was to remain a supreme authority for the changed world of the Middle Ages. According to medieval legend, Saint Paul visited Virgil's tomb in Naples and wept because Virgil had died too soon to be converted by him. Yet in mystery plays Virgil appeared together with the Sibyl and the Prophets as a witness to the Incarnation. For those with eyes to see, the Fourth Eclogue was obviously an announcement of the birth of the Redeemer: so it had already seemed in late antiquity to Lactantius and Eusebius (who reports a speech of Constantine to this effect), and somewhat later to Augustine and Prudentius, among countless others; and Vincent of Beauvais in the 13th century (*Speculum historiale* 11.50) could still report that three pagans had been converted to Christianity by reading this eclogue (and who can be sure that he was not right?). But it was predominantly the *Aeneid* that not only, particularly in book 6, furnished ample material for the many medieval legends of Virgil as a sage, a magician, a prophet, and a saint (confusion with *virga,* the term for a magician's wand, may even have contributed to the transformation of the Latin Vergilius into the vernacular Virgil), but also provided the greatest challenges and the greatest rewards to allegorical interpretation. The epic was seen as an image of human life, in which wisdom and virtue (represented by Aeneas) triumphed with the help of the gods over folly and passion (represented by Dido and Turnus): Fulgentius' 12-book allegory was drawn on more than six centuries later by Bernardus Silvestris, who explained *Aeneid* books 1–6 as the six stages of life (shipwreck on the shores of Carthage in book 1 is birth, the fires of Troy in book 2 are the passions of youth, and the visit to the Underworld in book 6 is the passage to the next life); similar readings are expressed or implied by such authors as John of Salisbury.

By the Middle Ages Virgil's birthplace, Mantua, had come to pride itself on its famous son: there are at least three medieval monuments to the poet in the city, and even today Virgil's face is to be found on the city's coat of arms. But it is the Florentine poet Dante's reverence for Virgil that represents one of the very highest points of the Latin poet's literary fortunes and one of the deepest sources for the Italian poet's creativity: *tu se' solo colui,* he tells him in *Inferno* 1.86–87, *da cu'io tolsi/lo bello stile che m'ha fatto onore,* "You alone are the one from whom I acquired that beautiful style which has made me honored." He respects *l'altissimo poeta,* "the loftiest poet," not only for his irresistible eloquence (which was one of the main reasons Beatrice chose him to intervene with Dante, so as to rescue him from his troubles) but also as the embodiment of the highest limits attainable by human wisdom unaided by Christian Revelation, and he chooses him as his guide through *Inferno* and most of *Purgatorio* (where, in canto 30, Beatrice takes over from him in the Earthly Paradise). But the *Divine Comedy* was only one of many poetic forms assumed by Virgil's medieval reception: from the 9th through the 12th centuries Virgil spawned a variety of new medieval epic genres, especially the medieval romances, influencing such poems as Ekkehard's *Waltharius* and Walter of Châtillon's *Alexandreis;* in the second half of the 12th century the *Roman d'Énéas* (adapted in Heinrich von Veldeke's *Eneide*) provided an Ovidian continuation to the *Roman de Troie,* elaborating in detail on Aeneas' love affair with Lavinia.

Virgil's fortunes continued to prosper in the Renaissance. In the 14th century Petrarch, who admired Virgil and Cicero above all other Latin authors and whose carefully annotated manuscript of Virgil is preserved in Milan in the Biblioteca Ambrosiana (now Sala Prefetto, Arm. 10, scat. 27)—indeed, legend has it that he died while reading this very manuscript—wrote 12 Latin eclogues and an epic, the *Africa,* closely modeled on the *Aeneid.* His contemporary Boccaccio composed a *Theseid* that contained not only the same number of books as the *Aeneid* (which is not particularly remarkable) but even the same number of lines (which is). Most of the Italian Humanists worked intensely on elucidating Virgil's poetry; one, Maffeo Vegio, went so far in 1427 as to write a 13th book to complete Virgil's unfinished epic—his pious if not especially inspired contribution continued to be reprinted in editions of Virgil's works for centuries.

Virgil remained one of the most important school authors throughout the modern period (though, unsurprisingly, in the 16th century Jesuit schools banned certain of the *Eclogues* and the fourth book of the *Aeneid*). Imitations of his poems continued to dominate literature in the Renaissance and for another couple of centuries. The *Eclogues* found in Baptista Mantuan a writer of Latin bucolic poems whose very pen name (his real name was Spagnuoli, for he was of Spanish origin) betrayed his literary affiliation with the Latin poet who was born in Mantua, and in Jacopo Sannazaro an imitator so influential that his sentimental nostalgia for a lost Arcadia distorted readings of Virgil's tougher-minded and more politically involved bucolic poetry for centuries. In English poetry Edmund Spenser's *Shepheardes Calendar* (1579) created a tradition that was deconstructed in John Milton's *Lycidas* (1638) and resynthesized in Alexander Pope's four *Pastorals* (1709). So too, the *Georgics* generated a spate of 17th- and 18th-century didactic poems on agricultural subjects ranging from the long-forgotten *Cyder* of John Philips (1708), *The Fleece* of John Dyer (1757), and *The Sugar-Cane* of James Grainger (1764) to such masterpieces as Pope's *Windsor-Forest* (1713) and James Thomson's *Seasons* (1730).

But in the early modern period what captured readers even more than the *Eclogues* (except for the vague sentimentality of the pastoral mode that was retrojected into them) and the *Georgics* (except for the heartrending story of Orpheus and Eurydice, which Virgil may possibly have invented and which in any event received at his hands its definitive formulation for the Western tradition, inspiring for example Monteverdi's *Orfeo* and thereby founding modern lyric opera) was the *Aeneid:* the epic was studied closely by Humanist scholars, many of whom still accepted allegorical interpretations of it (so, for example, Leon Battista Alberti, Cristoforo Landino, and Coluccio Salutati, who cited Bernardus Silvestris); it was set above Homer as the most perfect ancient epic (so by Vida, *De arte poetica,* in 1527, and J. C. Scaliger, *Poetices libri septem,* in 1561, and in fact quite generally until such 18th-cent. critics as Lessing); and it founded the Renaissance genre of historical epic, which went on from Petrarch's *Africa* (1338–1343) to flourish in such grand poetic monuments as Luís Vaz de Camões's *Os Lusíadas* (1572), Torquato Tasso's *Gerusalemme liberata* (1580–1581, also of course much influenced by the tradition of chivalric epic, by Boairdo and Ariosto), and Milton's *Paradise Lost* (1667), and to subside in such more problematic works as Ronsard's *Franciade* (1572, unfinished, in four books), Pope's *Brutus* (1743, unfinished, only eight lines survive), and Voltaire's *Henriade* (1723, finished, but hardly read now). Parallel, parasitic, and complementary to these serious epics flourished another tradition of burlesques and travesties in which the historical distance between Virgil and modernity was transposed into a stylistic tension between lofty characters and vulgar or obscene language and incidents (Giambattista Lalli, *Aeneida travestita,* 1633; Paul Scarron, *Le Virgile travesty,* 1648–1653).

Virgil continued to be read as a Latin author for centuries: Shakespeare probably knew at least the earlier books of the *Aeneid* in Latin, and Milton's *Paradise Lost* often gives the impression of attempting to provide an equivalent in the English language not only of Virgil's epic themes, but even of his syntax, diction, and (as far as possible) meter. But in Britain he was also particularly well served by translations: in the 16th century, into Scottish verse by Gawin Douglas (the *Aeneid,* 1553) and into English by Henry Howard, Earl of Surrey (*Aeneid* 2 and 4, 1557); in the 17th century, by Dryden (the *Aeneid,* 1697); and in the 18th century, by Christopher Pitt (the *Aeneid,* 1740) and Joseph Warton (the *Eclogues* and *Georgics,* 1753)—and at the end of the same century Eugenios Voulgaris translated the *Georgics* and the *Aeneid* "back" into Homeric Greek hexameters, printed with the Latin and Greek texts on facing pages in four sumptuous volumes (1786, 1791–1792) by the St. Petersburg Academy of Sciences at the behest of Catherine the Great for the edification of Russian youth. (In antiquity a Greek poet named Arrian had translated the *Georgics* into Greek.) Even those who could read Virgil in no language at all had ample opportunity to become familiar with his themes: though never anywhere near as popular in music and the visual arts as Ovid was, he did provide material for operas like Purcell's *Dido and Aeneas* (1689, Nahum Tate composed the words), Gluck's *Orfeo ed Euridice* (1762), and Berlioz's *Les Troyens* (1858) and for paintings by Tiepolo, Claude Lorrain, Turner, and others. For that matter, all Americans are in constant contact with a particularly concrete form of the reception of Virgil: every U.S. one-dollar bill contains two Virgilian tags, *novus ordo seclorum* ("a new order of the ages," *Eclogues* 4.5) and *annuit coeptis* ("he has assented to our plans," *Georgics* 1.40).

Schiller admired Virgil and translated parts of books 1, 2, and 4 of the *Aeneid;* Goethe read him enthusiastically, in the original and in translation, throughout his life, though he once confessed to Eckermann that he preferred Longus's *Daphnis and Chloe.* But with the advent of Romanticism, Virgil's fortunes began to suffer a gradual decline: for certain tastes he could no doubt seem too literary, too reflective, too elitist, and the very eloquence that had so impressed earlier generations could now come to seem suspect. And though he has continued to remain one of the most popular school authors wherever Latin is taught, over the past two centuries he has gradually been displaced to the margins of modern culture—or to its epigraphs: *flectere si nequeo superos, Acheronta movebo,* "If I am unable to bend the gods above, I shall arouse

Acheron" (*Aeneid* 7.312), is to be found on the title pages of revolutionary works as different from one another as the Socialist Ferdinand Lasalle's *Der italienische Krieg und die Aufgabe Preussens* (*The Italian War and Prussia's Task,* 1859) and the psychoanalyst Sigmund Freud's *Traumdeutung* (*The Interpretation of Dreams,* 1900). Probably Ezra Pound was speaking for many 20th-century readers when he quoted what he described as a favorite anecdote of Yeats: "A plain sailor man took a notion to study Latin, and his teacher tried him with Virgil; after many lessons he asked him something about the hero. Said the sailor: 'What hero?' Said the teacher: 'What hero, why, Aeneas, the hero.' Said the sailor: 'Ach, a hero, him a hero? Bigob, I t'ought he waz a priest' " (*ABC of Reading,* 1934). Yet during the same period Virgil's verbal mastery has continued to fascinate lyric poets, in France (Victor Hugo, Charles Baudelaire, Paul Valéry), in Italy (Giovanni Pascoli), and in England (Alfred Lord Tennyson, T. S. Eliot); and at least one novelist, Hermann Broch, has used the story of the poet's dying wish to burn the *Aeneid* as the basis for a profound meditation on life, death, art, politics, and history, *Der Tod des Vergil* (*The Death of Virgil,* 1945). Virgil continues to fascinate even very recent poets, especially in America, such as Robert Frost, the Russian-born Joseph Brodsky, and Rosanna Warren.

Beyond the influence exercised by his individual works, Virgil has also provided the Western literary tradition with its most compelling and durable model of a poetic career, one beginning with small, unambitious, personal works (the *Eclogues*), moving on to more difficult tasks of greater intellectual complexity and social significance (the *Georgics*), and culminating in a single massive work that subsumes all the earlier ones and provides an epic mirror for the destiny of a nation (the *Aeneid*). The influence exercised by this model can be traced as early as the 1st century CE in some of the poems of the *Appendix Vergiliana* and in Lucan. For many centuries it continued to provide poets with a guideline for their own development and with suggestions for what kind of poem to write next, through the Middle Ages (when the three genres involved were known as the *rota Virgilii,* the "wheel of Virgil") and the early modern period (when it fascinated such poets as Spenser, Milton, and Pope), and even into Romanticism (it stands behind William Wordsworth's, and the other English Romantic poets', dream of a career culminating in a single great philosophical epic) and the 20th century (Marcel Proust, James Joyce, and Robert Musil all began with smaller and more personal works before moving on to their larger epics).

Although the 19th century sometimes read Virgil as an apologist for imperialism and the various fascist movements of the 20th century sought to canonize him as a propagandist of ruthless service to the state, since the Second World War he has tended more to be prized as a poet of peace, who loved bucolic tranquility and abhorred the horrors of war. Over the last several decades, with the rise of environmentalism, first the *Eclogues* and then the *Georgics* have enjoyed modest waves of renewed popularity. But it is the *Aeneid* that always has been, and still remains, the central vehicle for transmitting Virgil's complex and nuanced view of the world to posterity; it is not accidental that this is surely the most often translated classical poem in English.

I conclude with four snapshots, all taken from the middle of the 20th century, of American men of letters turning to Virgil's epic in an attempt to come to terms with variously difficult circumstances. Allen Tate's poem "Aeneas at Washington" (1933) begins with Aeneas recalling the horrors of the old world, the sack of Troy and his desperate escape, "Saving little—a mind imperishable/If time is, a love of past things tenuous/As the hesitation of receding love"—but concludes in the ambiguous new world he has founded, anxious and self-doubting:

> I stood in the rain, far from home at nightfall
> By the Potomac, the great Dome lit the water,
> The city my blood had built I knew no more . . .
> Stuck in the wet mire
> Four thousand leagues from the ninth buried city
> I thought of Troy, what we had built her for.

In the last year of the Second World War, Bernard Knox, pinned down together with Italian partisans by a German machine gun in a ruined house, discovers there Sabbadini's sumptuous Fascist edition of Virgil's collected works and opens it at random, to find the desperate protest at war and suffering from the end of the first Georgic ("Here right and wrong are reversed; so many wars in the world, so many faces of evil")—and thinks to himself as he escapes (without the book, too big to fit into his pocket), "If I ever get out of this, I'm going back to the classics and study them seriously." At the very same moment, on the other side of the world, Robert Fitzgerald, stationed on an island in the Pacific, lessens the tedium of military life at his remote encampment and distracts himself from the appallingly gleeful bloodthirstiness of some of his colleagues by spending his evenings studying Virgil's epic, of which he will go on one day to publish a distinguished translation—"More than literary interest, I think, kept me reading Virgil's descriptions of desperate battle, funeral pyres, failed hopes of truce or peace." And Robert Lowell's poem "Falling Asleep over the *Aeneid*" (1947) shows us a very old man doing just that: his dream starts off from the scene of Pallas's funeral at the beginning of *Aeneid* 11 but mixes distorted elements from Virgil's Italian wars with distant family memories from the American Civil War and with the catastrophic urban firestorms, industrial crematoria, and pompous Nazi celebrations familiar from the Second World War to create a harrowingly hallucinatory vision of fire and metal, of guilt and bloodlust, of barbarous rites and human sacrifice and never-ending suffering:

> Left foot, right foot—as they turn,
> More pyres are rising: armored horses, bronze,

And gagged Italians, who must file by ones
Across the bitter river, when my thumb
Tightens into their wind-pipes.

In the 60 years since Lowell's poem was written, our world has not become any easier; Virgil is as indispensable as ever. He will never cease to find admirers as long as Western literature, which he helped found, itself persists—as long, that is, as human beings continue to be fascinated, troubled, and consoled by reading about the ineluctable sufferings imposed by the necessities of mortal time, political action, and desperate passion on the ineradicable but unfulfillable desire for happiness and peace, all formulated in the most exquisitely controlled yet irreducibly suggestive language.

BIBL.: Richard A. Cardwell and Janet Hamilton, eds., *Virgil in a Cultural Tradition* (Nottingham 1986). John Chalker, *The English Georgic: A Study in the Development of a Form* (Baltimore 1969). Domenico Comparetti, *Virgil in the Middle Ages,* trans. E. F. M. Benecke, 2nd ed. (London 1966). T. S. Eliot, "What Is a Classic?" (1945) in *On Poetry and Poets* (London 1957) 52–71. Marcello Gigante, ed., *La Fortuna di Vergilio* (Naples 1986). Craig Kallendorf, *In Praise of Aeneas: Virgil and Epideictic Rhetoric in the Early Renaissance* (Hanover, N.H., 1989) and *Virgil and the Myth of Venice: Books and Readers in the Italian Renaissance* (Oxford 1999). Sabine MacCormack, *The Shadows of Poetry: Vergil in the Mind of Augustine* (Berkeley 1998). Charles Martindale, ed., *The Cambridge Companion to Virgil* (Cambridge 1997). Glenn W. Most and Sarah Spence, eds., *Re-Presenting Virgil: Special Issue in Honor of Michael C. J. Putnam, Materiali e discussioni per l'analisi dei testi classici* 52 (2004). David Quint, *Epic and Empire: Politics and Generic Form from Virgil to Milton* (Princeton 1992). Richard F. Thomas, *Virgil and the Augustan Reception* (Cambridge 2001). Jan Ziolkowski and Michael C. J. Putnam, eds., *The Vergilian Tradition: The First Fifteen Hundred Years* (New Haven 2007). Theodor Ziolkowski, *Virgil and the Moderns* (Princeton 1993).

G.W.M.

Vitruvius and the Classical Orders

The popularity of *De architectura* (*On Architecture*) by Marcus Vitruvius Pollio (1st cent. BCE), Roman architect and engineer, was limited in the ancient world. The few citations of Vitruvius's name that have been found—for example, in Pliny the Elder (index of *auctores* for books 16, 35, and 36), Frontinus (*De aquae ductu urbis Romae* 25.1–2), and Servius (*Ad Aeneid,* 6.43)—are bibliographical references that have no bearing on the theoretical or practical contents of the works in question. Vitruvius is also mentioned by Sidonius Apollinaris (*Epistulae* 4.3.5; 8.16.10) in the late imperial age, and that is when Faventinus assembled an epitome of his work. It reduced the size of the text and simplified its language, thus giving readers access to those parts of the treatise in particular that had a direct practical application, such as passages dedicated to materials or to various building techniques, which are prefaced by Vitruvian precepts transformed into simple formulas. Faventinus' digest was quite likely the vehicle by which some of the contents of *De architectura* reached the most important encyclopedia of the High Middle Ages, Isidore of Seville's *Etymologiae* (7th cent.). In turn, Isidore supplemented Vitruvius's theoretical precepts with observations drawn from other classical works (such as passages of Pliny the Elder on the four types of columns and their proportions, as well as on techniques and materials, *Natural History,* 36.56–64), thus facilitating their entrance into the later encyclopedic compendia of Hrabanus Maurus and, particularly, of Vincent of Beauvais.

In the course of the Middle Ages and its "renaissances" of ancient culture, the growing awareness that Vitruvius's *De architectura* was the only surviving text on architecture from classical times increased interest in the treatise substantially. Indeed, it is highly probable that it was Alcuin of York, one of the most important thinkers involved in the Carolingian program of *renovatio imperii,* who, called to direct the Schola Palatina, took back from the British Isles to continental Europe the copy of the work from which the entire manuscript tradition descends. In 840 Eginard, a student of Alcuin and Charlemagne's superintendent of buildings in Aachen, asked his pupil Vussinus for help in interpreting the "obscure verbs and nouns in Vitruvius's books" (*verba et nomina obscura ex libris Vitruvii*), perhaps those related to the parts of columns. From the 11th to the 13th century knowledge of the treatise was steadily diffused, and manuscripts have been preserved in numerous libraries, especially in Germany and France. The text was sometimes accompanied by *excerpta* dedicated to the anthropomorphic origin of Vitruvius's system of proportions (highly prized in the Christian sphere), technical prescriptions, or drawings (of bases, capitals, and trabeations, the proportions altered with respect to the classical ones, but their various parts named correctly enough). These *excerpta* provide evidence that the text was studied in search of rules applicable to practical issues of the day. Such study is reflected in certain isolated monumental works, both sacred and profane, in which the general proportions or the morphology of the columns appears in effect to reveal a Vitruvian influence. Some of the most oft-cited cases are the Torhalle of Lorsch, today dated to the late Carolingian period; St. Michael's Church in Hildesheim, consecrated in 1022; and the abbey of Montecassino, constructed by the abbot Desiderius between 1066 and 1071. *De architectura,* in addition to its circulation in learned circles and in *scriptoria,* was probably also diffused in the workshops of artisans, through oral transmission, and in partial vernacular translations of which no trace has remained.

It was in early Italian Humanism, however, that the treatise reentered the realm of culture. This is thanks in particular to Francesco Petrarch, who introduced it into the circle of his learned friends. Manuscripts of Vitruvius were possessed by Giovanni Boccaccio, Giovanni de' Dondi, and Nicolò Acciaiuoli. Starting in the mid-14th century, *De architectura* proceeded to be diffused without interruption in northern Italy and in Florence, thus anticipating by more than 50 years its supposed rediscovery, in 1414, by Poggio Bracciolini.

In the course of the 15th century, in the now widespread enterprise for the rebirth of ancient culture, Vitruvius became the undisputed protagonist of architectural thought. This was despite a highly critical judgment of him in Leon Battista Alberti's *De re aedificatoria,* composed for the most part around 1452. Alberti was nevertheless also the first to reconsider *De architectura* in its entirety, as opposed to merely extracting from it an ample variety of quotations and prescriptions. After Alberti's organic analysis, the Renaissance approach to Vitruvius moved essentially on two fronts: that of the translation and exegesis of a text rendered difficult by its technical nature and lexical heterogeneity (not to mention by the irreparably corrupt form of some of the copies consulted by the Humanists), and that of the composition of original theoretical works, for which the ancient treatise was the model—for structure, content, and language—to which architects generally ended up referring, although their dependence on it varied. There were three fundamental stages in the process of stabilizing the text of the *De architectura:* the publication of the *editio princeps* in Rome, edited by Giovanni Sulpicio da Veroli, around 1486; an illustrated edition of the Latin text, edited by Fra Giocondo, which appeared in Venice in 1511; and, finally, Daniele Barbaro's translation with commentary, published in Venice in 1556, with illustrations by Andrea Palladio. At the same time, the chief treatises in the vernacular—of Francesco di Giorgio Martini (ca. 1470) and then of Sebastiano Serlio (1537), of Jacopo Barozzi da Vignola (1562), and of Palladio himself (1570)—demonstrate the different ways in which the reading and interpretation of *De architectura* affected the development of architectural theory in the Renaissance. From them it can be deduced that, beginning at the end of the 15th century, as comprehension of the text slowly progressed, Vitruvius was no longer looked to merely as a literary model. He was also consulted as a guide in analyzing Roman buildings in order to work out a rational method of applying classical language to modern architecture. Yet the ancient treatise, in part because of the particular sociocultural conditions in which it had been written, was not up to that task. Indeed, 16th-century reflection on the concept of architectural order and its progressive establishment in a proper canon illustrates well the dialectical tension that arose between *De architectura,* the study of ancient remains, and the functional needs of contemporary architecture, a tension that the first volume of Serlio's treatises, of 1537, forcefully expresses right from its title: *General Rules of Architecture for the Five Manners of Buildings . . . with Examples from Antiquity, That Are* for the Most Part *in Accord with Vitruvius* (*Regole generali di Architettura sopra le cinque maniere de gli edifici . . . con gli essempi della antichità, che,* per la magior parte *concordano con la dottrina di Vitruvio*). As is known, Vitruvius used neither the word *order* nor a periphrasis for the concept as it has been understood ever since the Renaissance. In books 3 and 4 he speaks of different kinds of temples named, according to their historico-ethnographical origins, Doric, Ionic, and Corinthian. The precepts expounded always refer to the entire building. Columns, capitals, and trabeations, despite their individual morphological peculiarities, are described as elements of comprehensive structures and not as isolatable in independent formal configurations.

Once again it was Alberti (*De re aedificatoria* 7.6) who, acquainted with structures quite different from the Hellenistic models on which Vitruvius had based his codification, furnished the definition lacking in the ancient treatise and founded modern thought on the order. He understood it as a formal—and above all a conceptual—system, detached from the structural reality of the building. Thanks to this powerful foundation, and then to the isolation, in the endless repertory of solutions offered by ancient structures, of the linguistic and logical constants of building, the orders were transformed within the first two decades of the 16th century into a sequence of modular systems measured according to precise standards of proportion. This resulted in particular from Raphael's "protoarchaeological" investigations. He combined excavations and field measurements with the philological study of the Latin text, assisting the Ravennese Humanist Fabio Calvo in his 1516 translation of *De architectura* (two manuscript versions survive today in Munich, the codices Ital. 37 and 37a of the Bayerische Staatsbibliothek). Marginal notes in the artist's hand multiply directly in proportion to the passages relating to the three genera of Vitruvian columns, whose progression—as Raphael would later explain in his famous *Lettera a Leone X* (*Letter to Leo X,* drafted ca. 1518)—was ultimately rounded out with the inclusion of the Tuscan and the composite. Vignola closed the circle, definitively freeing the proportions of each order (understood as pedestal, column, and trabeation) from the real measurements of its various parts, and using an abstract magnitude as a dimensional unit (the module, i.e., half the diameter of a column at the *imo scapo,* bottom of the shaft). This was a level of systematic rigor unknown to Vitruvius and even to Vignola's own predecessors. At this point, the canon was ready for universal application and its appearance in the form of an autonomous manual. It had now been completely reinvented with respect to its ancient source, down to the physical form of the object that conveyed it: a book.

BIBL.: James S. Ackerman, "The Tuscan/Rustic Order: A Study in the Metaphorical Language of Architecture," *Journal of the Society of Architectural Historians* 42 (1983) 15–34. Pierre Gros, "Vitruve et les ordres," in *Les traités d'architecture de la Renaissance* (Paris 1988) 49–59. Vaughan Hart with Peter Hicks, eds., *Paper Palaces: The Rise of the Renaissance Architectural Treatise* (New Haven 1998). John Onians, *Bearers of Meaning: The Classical Orders in Antiquity, the Middle Ages, and the Renaissance* (Princeton 1988). Pier Nicola Pagliara, "Vitruvio da testo a canone," in *Memoria dell'antico nell'arte italiana,* vol. 3, *Dalla tradizione all'archeologia,* ed. Salvatore Settis (Turin 1986) 3–85. Ingrid Rowland, "Raphael,

Angelo Colocci, and the Genesis of the Architectural Orders," in *Sixteenth-century Italian Art,* ed. Michael Wayne Cole (Oxford 2006) 511–536. Stefan Schuler, *Vitruv im Mittelalter: Die Rezeption von "De Architectura" von der Antike bis in die frühe Neuzeit* (Cologne 1999). Christof Thoenes, *Gli ordini architettonici: Rinascita o invenzione?* (1985), in *Opus incertum: italienische Studien aus drei Jahrzehnten* (Munich 2002) 199–213. *Vitruvius: Ten Books on Architecture: The Corsini Incunabulum, with the Annotations and Autograph Drawings by Giovanni Battista da Sangallo,* ed. Ingrid D. Rowland (Rome 2003). *Vitruvius' On Architecture,* ed. Richard V. Schofield (London, forthcoming). M.BE.

Translated by Patrick Baker

Volcanoes

The Mediterranean is one of the world's main areas of volcanic activity: in classical times there were eruptions of Etna, the Lipari islands, Ischia, Methana, Vesuvius; submarine eruptions in the bay of Santorini; and low-level activity in the Phlegraean fields. Volcanoes feature in classical literature in a variety of contexts, including imaginative poetry in which a god or monster lives beneath the volcano, geographical descriptions, accounts of particular eruptions, and philosophical and scientific speculation about the causes of eruptions.

From Albertus Magnus in the 13th century onward, scholars and scientists writing about volcanoes knew and drew on classical writers. Still, in the 17th century Descartes's brief explanation of volcanism (*Principia philosophica* 4.78; 1644) closely resembles classical ideas, and the more extensive discussion by Athanasius Kircher (*Mundus subterraneus* 4.1; 1665) quotes extensively from classical sources while incorporating new information from more recent periods and from other parts of the world unknown in the classical period.

Classical writers influenced the development of modern volcanological thinking, although that influence has not yet been traced in detail. They bequeathed some of the terminology that is still used, such as *basalt, crater,* and *eruption,* though the word *volcano,* alluding to the myth of Vulcan having a workshop beneath the mountain, was apparently first coined by sailors in the 15th century. The universal ancient assumption that in volcanoes something is burning—a natural but erroneous assumption—was first challenged in the 17th century by Edward Jorden, but it retained adherents as late as the 19th century. There were various ancient theories of volcanic activity, which fell into two broad types, the one treating volcanoes as intermittent, localized phenomena, like huge furnaces, the other regarding them as linked to a network of underground channels perpetually filled with fire. In the modern period debate about volcanic activity was for a long time polarized between comparable views.

Classical writers also give descriptions of specific eruptions, and these have helped the reconstruction of the volcanic history of the Mediterranean area. In the 19th century field volcanology, and the excavations at Pompeii, Herculaneum, and other sites around Vesuvius, started to yield more detailed evidence of the great eruption of 79 CE. Nevertheless, the ancient literary sources remain important too, and indeed scientific discovery confirms the accuracy of the foremost of these sources, the letters (6.16, 6.20) in which the younger Pliny describes the death of his uncle, the elder Pliny, and his own experiences during the eruption. Today those two letters must be among the most widely disseminated of classical Latin prose texts, for most textbooks on volcanoes, and various television documentaries, include extracts from Pliny's vivid narrative. Since the late 19th century the term *Plinian,* in honor of Pliny the Elder, has been applied to the type of explosive eruption that occurred in 79 CE.

Classical volcanoes have also inspired writers of fiction. The fanciful *Baron Münchausen's Narrative of His Marvellous Travels and Campaigns in Russia* (1786) contains an episode in which the baron jumps into Etna's crater, falls to the bottom, and finds that Vulcan really does live there (the narrative was originally published anonymously by R. E. Raspe, who also published serious work on volcanoes). The fate of Pompeii and Herculaneum provides the backdrop to Edward Bulwer-Lytton's novel *The Last Days of Pompeii* (1834) and Robert Harris's *Pompeii* (2003); the former has inspired several films.

BIBL.: Haraldur Sigurdsson, *Melting the Earth: The History of Ideas of Volcanic Eruptions* (New York 1999). H. Sigurdsson, S. Carey, W. Cornell, and T. Pescatore, "The Eruption of Vesuvius in A.D. 79," *National Geographic Research* 1/3 (1985) 332–387. H.M.H.

War, Just

The concept of just war (*bellum iustum*) had its origins in pagan Rome. The Romans were the first to regard war as a form of legal self-help if another state had committed wrong by denial of justice. The ancient rules for declaring a formal war prescribed by Roman sacral law are reported in Livy (1.32.6 ff.). Cicero reflects this legal tradition under the influence of Stoic philosophy. His definition (*De re publica* 3.23/35): "Those wars are unjust which are undertaken without cause. For apart from the cause of revenge or defence no just war can be waged" was quoted by Saint Isidore of Seville in the 7th century (*Etymologiae* 18.1.2). Two centuries earlier Saint Augustine had combined the Roman and the Judeo-Christian traditions of just war, too. Avenging wrongs and defense are causes for a *bellum iustum.* The "natural order" (*ordo naturalis*) ordains that only the monarch (or state) has the power of undertaking war. Christian morals demand also that wars be waged only for securing peace, not out of cruelty or lust to dominate, or for glory.

This concept of *bellum iustum* expressed by the Latin Fathers of the Church, which stressed moral and religious aspects, surpassed the more formal Roman law. When in 12th-century Bologna the Camaldolese monk Gratian compiled his textbook of canon law (completed ca. 1140), he defined the just war by citing texts of Saint Augustine and Saint Isidore (*Decretum Gratiani* 2.23.2). Here Gratian also reports a leading example for *bellum iustum* that Saint Augustine had found in the Old Testament (Numbers 21.24 ff.): The Israelites had waged a just war against the Amorites, who had denied them the right of passage across their territory. In this legal and theological tradition Saint Thomas Aquinas formulated around 1270 his famous definition of just war, which specified the three requirements of state authority for warfare, *auctoritas principis,* a just cause for a war—*iusta causa,* and the just intention of the belligerents, *recta intentio* (Summa Theologiae 2.2.q40.1).

The Scholastic just-war doctrine of Aquinas was adapted and interpreted by the great Spanish authors of the 16th and early 17th centuries, who as theologians contributed considerably to the modern law of nations just developing. The Dominican Francisco de Vitoria (ca. 1483–1546), who was a professor of theology at the University of Salamanca, expounded the theory of Aquinas, concluding that a war could be just on either side: one party having the just cause in an objective sense, the other party fighting in excusable ignorance regarding the cause, and therefore without guilt. This was a great step forward in the direction of the modern principle that belligerents have equal duties and equal rights.

This further adaption of the just-war concept was begun by the secular jurists who combined the European tradition of Roman law with ample knowledge of ancient Greek and Roman authors who had been rediscovered in the Age of Humanism. A Spanish writer who had served as a military auditor in the army of Philip II in the Netherlands, Balthasar Ayala (1548–1584) had published in 1582 *On the Law and Duties of War and Military Discipline* (*De iure et officiis bellicis et disciplina militari libri III*). Ayala discussed the term *bellum iustum* in the scholastic sense and in comparison with Roman law sources. As a practical jurist, Ayala concluded that since "the right to wage war is a prerogative of sovereign princes, the discussion of the equity of the cause is inappropriate" (1.2.33). Therefore the "legal effects" of war and the "validity of the laws of war" require only that "war is waged by parties who have the right to wage war" (1.2.34). Hugo Grotius (1583–1645), the Dutch "father of international law," preserved the scholastic and humanistic traditions. In his famous work *On the Law of War and Peace* (*De iure belli ac pacis,* 1625), Grotius stresses that only one party can fight for the right cause, but that it is possible that both parties wage war in good faith (2.23.13.2). The legal effects of war, according to the law of nations, are therefore connected with every formal statal war (3.3).

The post-Grotian development led to the definite separation of morals and strict international law in the 18th and 19th centuries. An unjust war, declared by a sovereign monarch, was legal in the sense that the laws of war were valid for both parties. The theoretical distinction between just and unjust wars was without notable practical consequences. Sovereign states claimed the exclusive right to resort to war.

Since World War I a renaissance of just-war ideas could be observed. The Covenant of the League of Nations (1919) and the Briand-Kellogg Pact for the renunciation of war (1928) set positive rules for distinguishing between legal and illegal wars. This was confirmed and expanded by the United Nations Charter (1945).

An odd doctrine was formulated in the former Soviet Union: "Socialist states" could "by their nature" wage only just wars. Reality (including military conflicts between communist states) was faded out.

The old just-war doctrine is still in our minds. In 2004 the Roman Cardinal Ratzinger remembered the invasion of France by the anti-Nazi Allies (1944) as a *bellum iustum.* And in a military hymn (of 1814) Americans still sing: "Then conquer we must, when our cause is just."

BIBL.: A. Calore, ed., *Seminari di storia e di diritto III: "Guerra giusta"? Le metamorfosi di un concetto antico* (Milan 2003). P. Haggenmacher, *Grotius et la doctrine de la guerre juste* (Paris 1983). F. H. Russell, *The Just War in the Middle Ages* (Cambridge 1975). K.-H. Ziegler, "Zum 'gerechten Krieg' im späteren Mittelalter und in der Frühen Neuzeit—vom Decretum Gratiani bis zu Hugo Grotius," *Zeitschrift der Savigny-Stiftung für Rechtsgeschichte, Romanistische Abteilung* 122 (2005) 177–194. K.-H.Z.

Warburg, Aby

German art and cultural historian (1866–1929), founder of the Warburg Institute, now at the University of London, one of the leading sites in the world for the study of the classical tradition.

The original idea for the Warburg Institute, and the core of its library, go back to Warburg. Born into a family of bankers in Hamburg, he studied art history, classical philology, and other subjects in Bonn, Munich, and Florence. He wrote a dissertation on Botticelli and received a doctorate from the University of Strasbourg in 1892. Subsequently he entered medical school in Berlin, but he left before finishing his degree. In 1895 and 1896 he traveled to America, where he sought out ethnologists and occupied himself with the religion and art of Native Americans. From then on Warburg lived the life of a private scholar, serving from 1912 until his death as an honorary professor in Hamburg.

Warburg identified the central theme of his research as an attempt to answer one question: What does the influence of antiquity mean for European thought? His topic was thus not simply collecting examples of the classical tradition; rather, his goal was to understand the complex significance for Western civilization of the survival of paganism. Warburg regarded antiquity as ambivalent: "Athens has constantly to be won back again from Alexandria; rationality must always be defended against the danger of irrationalism and magic fears" ("Heidnisch-antike Weissagung in Wort und Bild zu Luthers Zeiten," 1919). He saw that the use of ancient images could both encourage careful reflection and endanger it. In brilliant and detailed studies, Warburg analyzed the influence of the classical world through such topics as Botticelli's use of formulaic images from antiquity for pathos, the preservation of ancient astrological ideas in the frescoes of the Palazzo Schifanoia in Ferrara, and why contemporary postage stamps depicted ancient goddesses or the Italian Fascists drew on ancient models to convey status and authority.

Warburg assembled a unique library and collection of photographs on all aspects of the legacy of antiquity. In 1921 the Warburg Library in Hamburg was expanded into a site for research and lectures and producing its own publications, largely through the efforts of Warburg's assistant, Fritz Saxl (1890–1948). The art historians Saxl and Erwin Panofsky contributed studies on classical antiquity and the Renaissance; Ernst Cassirer worked out his ideas on myth and symbol there, and noted historians of religion studied the effect of paganism on early Christianity. The Warburg Library of Cultural Studies became a highly respected cultural institution in Weimar Germany. When Aby Warburg died in 1929, Saxl succeeded him as director.

After the Nazis came to power in 1933, Saxl, who like Warburg was Jewish, moved the institute and its library to London; it became part of the University of London in 1944. Saxl served as director until his death in 1948; he was followed by Henri Frankfort, Gertrud Bing, Ernst H. Gombrich, J. B. Trapp, Nicholas Mann and, Charles Hope. In 1994 the Warburg Institute was one of the founding member institutions of the School of Advanced Studies at the University of London. Today the institute, located in Woburn Square, near the British Museum, devotes itself to the study of the classical tradition—that is, all the elements of European civilization, philosophy, literature, art, and science (including magic, astrology, and alchemy) that originated in the ancient world, as well as their reception history in Arabic and Hebrew. Its research, academic courses, conferences, and publications address continuities and discontinuities in the reception history of antiquity, the history and paths of transmission, and the interpretation and transformation of ancient texts, images, and ideas.

The Warburg Institute's library now contains some 350,000 volumes, arranged, as in Aby Warburg's day, so that publications on specific topics in the legacy of antiquity are shelved together. As the institute's *Guide to the Library* explains, this system preserves four of Warburg's fundamental categories: *action,* the survival and transformation of ancient patterns in social customs and political institutions; *orientation,* the gradual transition, in Western thought, from magical beliefs to religion, science, and philosophy; *word,* the persistence of motifs and forms in Western languages and literatures; and *image,* the tenacity of symbols and images in European art and architecture. Warburg's intentions can also still be discerned in the collection of approximately 300,000 photographs of works of art from antiquity to the modern era, all filed in iconographical order.

BIBL.: Ernst H. Gombrich, *Aby Warburg: An Intellectual Biography* (London 1970). Roland Kany, *Die religionsgeschichtliche Forschung an der Kulturwissenschaftlichen Bibliothek Warburg* (Bamberg 1989). Nicholas Mann, "Two-way Traffic: The Warburg Institute as a Microcosm of Cultural Exchange between Britain and Europe," in *The British Contribution to the Europe of the Twenty-first Century,* ed. B. Markenisis (Oxford 2002) 93–104. Aby Warburg, *The Renewal of Pagan Antiquity: Contributions to the Cultural History of the European Renaissance* (Los Angeles 1999). Dieter M. Wuttke, *Aby M. Warburg—Bibliographie, 1866–1996* (Baden-Baden 1998).

R.K.

Translated by Deborah Lucas Schneider

Warfare

"Because the Romans devoted themselves to warfare and considered this to be the only art, they applied all their genius and thoughts to its perfection": Montesquieu, in an anonymously published critique of Louis XIV's imperialistic plans, couched in terms of Rome's greatness and decline (*Considérations sur les causes de la grandeur des Romains et de leur décadence,* 1734), was neither the only writer nor the first to see and admire Roman discipline and tactics as the very basis of military and political success. As early as the 4th century, the Christian author Vegetius had dedicated his influential military handbook *De re militari* (or *Epitoma rei militaris*) to the emperor Theodosius I with the clear message that "the idea of forming a legion was inspired in the Romans by a god." From antiquity onward war itself was considered an art. The ancients themselves commonly regarded Homer as a first-class instructor in this field, and special ancient textbooks on military practice such as Xenophon's *Hipparchus* (on the duties and the functions of a cavalry officer) and *On Horsemanship,* from the 4th century BCE, were read for practical use until the 19th century. Although Greek and Roman historians such as Thucydides, Xenophon, and Polybius all showed appreciation for the art of war as an important factor in history, the generals and captains, dukes and kings of later centuries also turned diligently to technical writers on military strategy, ballistics, siege operations, fortifications. and the arts of war, most of them dating from the Hellenistic and Roman period, such as Aeneas the Tactician (4th cent. BCE), Asclepiodotus (1st cent. BCE), Onasander (1st cent. CE), Frontinus (1st cent. CE), and Aelian (1st–2nd cents. CE).

Formerly it was believed that medieval armies had little planning or organization, but it is now acknowledged that strategy and tactics were a constant part of medieval warfare. The benefits of tactical positioning and surprise, of using hidden forces and reserves, were recognized; the importance of training was understood, as shown in tournaments and by practice maneuvers of militias. To this end classical Roman writers on warfare were studied for information. They not only influenced medieval chroniclers, who were among the few then able to obtain copies of their work and read them; they also influenced leaders who were educated or had educated advisers. The most telling example is provided by John of Marmoutier in his *Historia Gaufredi Ducis,* about his hero, Geoffrey V le Bel, Count of Anjou and Duke of Normandy (1113–1151). When the duke's siege of Montreuil-Bellay in 1149 reached a stalemate, he consulted Vegetius' *De re militari,* the only ancient manual of Roman military institutions to have survived intact into his era. The manual's account of incendiary devices inspired him to try the most advanced technology of his time: this marked the first known use of Greek fire in the West.

Although incendiary weapons had been used in antiquity, Greek fire was a post-classical invention; it had come into use in the 7th century as Constantinople waged war on early Muslim invaders. The new formulation had been invented by the Greek engineer Callinicus of Heliopolis in Syria, during the time of Constantine Pogonatus (r. 668–685). Like their Graeco-Roman antecedents, Byzantine forces had relied on science and technique to create a secret weapon with which to surprise the enemy and prevail against overwhelming odds. Geoffrey's knowledge of it, centuries later in Anjou, came via the Holy Land; his father, Fulk V le Jeune (1092–1143), had been king of Jerusalem (r. 1131–1143) and probably brought this knowledge home with him. Montreuil-Bellay, fortified with double walls and a keep that "rose to the stars," was isolated from approach by a natural escarpment. When efforts to breach the wall ultimately failed because the damage was repaired overnight, Geoffrey hurled pots of Greek fire from a catapult. Success was immediate; the castle surrendered.

As with tactics, so with strategy. Modern historians once denigrated medieval methods, even denying that strategy existed. More recent studies, however, have demonstrated that most military leaders followed a cautious strategy, avoiding pitched battle and favoring control through sieges and garrisons. Medieval military handbooks that contained views on strategy were in fact popular. Generals and leaders read and used the works of contemporary authors such as Pierre Dubois, James I of Aragon (the king who had played an important part in the Reconquista and recovered the Balearic Islands), and Christine de Pizan. Yet Vegetius' *De re militari,* offering practical material, remained immensely popular as well. In the 9th century the encyclopedist Hrabanus Maurus had written an updated extract of Vegetius for the Carolingian emperor Lothar II. Julius Caesar's *Commentaries* on his campaigns in Gaul were not translated until the time of Charles the Bold of Burgundy (by Jean Duchesne in 1473), but Vegetius' manual had been translated into French by 1271. In fact, Vegetius' technical work now rivals Pliny's *Natural History* in the number of extant copies dating from the 14th century. From the 5th until the 15th century Vegetius was the most famous author who dealt with war and military matters. Admittedly, in the 15th century Ferdinand of Aragon discovered in the Greek historian Procopius' *History of the Wars of Justinian* (6th cent.) a tactic that enabled him to conquer Milan by using an aqueduct; but more often medieval commanders seem to have seen in Vegetius an enduring prescription for invincibility, especially in the "general rules of war" (*regulae bellorum generales*) expounded in chapter 26 of the third book of his manual.

From the 9th century onward manuscripts containing Vegetius' *De re militari* in the Latin original or in translation could be found in the collections of the most prominent and educated princes and military commanders of Western Europe, such as Lothar II and Edward I, and from the 15th century onward an increasing number of European kings, princes, and statesmen personally owned a copy. Latin manuscripts of Vegetius were, for instance, owned by Charles the Bold, Charles IX, Louis XII, Francis I, Henri IV, Cardinal Mazarin, and Colbert, by Alfonso of Aragon, Casimir IV of Poland, and Queen Christina of Sweden. Translations into French—the important ones were by Jean de Meun (1284) and Philippe de Vitry (1332)—were read by Philip the Good, Duke of Burgundy; John II, Duke of Bourbon; John, Duke of Berry; and Louis de Bourbon. Edward VI, members of the Strozzi family, Queen Isabella I of Castile, and Count Duke Olivares read their Vegetius in English, Tuscan, and Castilian respectively. Christine de Pizan (1364–1430), who had used Vegetius' *De re militari* in several of her political works, incorporated major parts of Jean de Vignay's French translation of Vegetius in her own treatise *The Book of Deeds of Arms and of Chivalry* (*Livre des fais d'armes et de chevalerie,* 1410). This work became so widely read that it was translated into English by 1489; its content was sufficiently similar to Vegetius' that Christine was often thought to be Vegetius himself. Indeed, French translations of Vegetius and her *Fais d'armes et chevalerie* were often placed together in a single manuscript. Not surprisingly, manuscript copies of Vegetius were in great demand. After having defeated the Lombard Ardoin, the Holy Roman Emperor Henry II (r. 1014–1024) took back to France an important manuscript that contained Vegetius' *De re militari* (now in the Vatican, Palatinus lat. 909); when pillaging Pavia in 1499, the French king Louis XII (r. 1498–1515) took five Latin manuscripts of Vegetius' manual from the Visconti, and he later deprived the Medici of another.

Vegetius was not only read but used in practical ways. On a basic level *De re militari* offered medieval generals a theoretical model, such as that created centuries later by the great Prussian military theorist Carl von Clausewitz, whose *On War* (*Vom Kriege,* 1832–1834) emphasized the close relationship between war and national policy and the importance of the principles of mass, economy of force, and the destruction of enemy forces. Vegetius' tactical ideas and military insights on the organization, preparation, and exercise of a legion were similarly applied. The question was rather, as the Franciscan Gilbert of Tournai (d. 1284) put it in 1259, "Who does *not* keep a copy of Vegetius when he is preparing to defend or to besiege a camp or a city?" The maneuvering and positioning of armies, the fortification of encampments, the use of catapults and machines in storming walls, the procuring of bitumen, sulphur, liquid pitch, and oil while conducting a defense—all this was put into practice in the battles of Hastings (1066), Steppes (1213), Bouvines (1214), and Agincourt (1415) and at the sieges of Arques (1053), Jerusalem (1099), and Neuss (1475), as it had been in an earlier century at the siege of Paris by the Normans (885–886).

Vegetius remained useful for naval engagements as well. The first to use his naval precepts were the Byzantines: the 6th-century writer Anonymous of Byzantium transmitted the naval combat chapters almost verbatim. Italian galleys, a type of war vessel recommended by Vegetius, dominated the Mediterranean from the 12th century into the 17th (the last major engagement involving these was the Battle of Lepanto in 1571).

Between the end of the 15th century and the middle of the 17th the arts of war were revolutionized. Infantry became the chief arm, and the heavily armed horsemen who had dominated the battlefields of the Middle Ages virtually disappeared, their efficiency challenged first by the longbows of the English, then by the dense pike squares of the Swiss, and finally by the advent of cannon and small arms with the arrival (in the mid-13th century) of gunpowder and its weaponry. The radical changes that gunpowder introduced had many ramifications. By the mid-16th century the scientist and thinker Francis Bacon would be moved to call it one of the three critical discoveries in the history of mankind, along with printing and the directional compass.

Amid such changes the question was frequently raised whether the long-used military models from antiquity were still relevant. The invention of firearms certainly brought novel problems; but modern armies of the time, which relied more on infantry than on the heavily armed cavalry of medieval forces and had begun to adopt less dense, more extended battle formations, had in some ways moved closer to classical principles rather than further away. Along with preparation, discipline, and morale, strategy was common to all wars, and on these topics the ancients had spoken definitively and could still be heeded.

Other innovations demonstrated how new science, technology, and engineering had entered the battlefield, bringing changes in military strategy. This was not to say that science had played no part in military strategy before. The Greek mathematician, astronomer, philosopher, physicist, and engineer Archimedes (287–212 BCE) had been the classical example par excellence for Renaissance scientists and polymaths who addressed the arts of war. They knew quite well the crucial role that Archimedes was said to have played in the defense of Syracuse against the siege laid by the Romans in 213, when he devised technology so effective that it forestalled the capture of the city and devastated a substantial Roman invading force. Plutarch's widely read biographies of famous Greeks and Romans included (in the life of the Roman general Marcellus) an account of how Archimedes had single-handedly defended the city by arranging reflecting lenses to focus the sun's rays on Roman ships, setting fire to them in the harbor—as well as deploying huge cranes that could seize ships and turn them upside down. Recognition of ancient inventions of this kind had created an enduring and robust interest in scientific developments that might have military applications. The eminent Renaissance scientist Galileo Galilei (1564–1642), upon receiving a description of a telescope that had been developed the year before in the Netherlands by Hans Lippershey, an optician, applied his own knowledge of optical science to the idea and built a telescope or *occhiale* for himself—and offered it in turn, in August 1609, to Leonardo Donato, doge of Venice, for secret use in warfare. With it, ships could be discovered at sea two hours before they could be seen with the naked eye; their number, quality, and strength could be distinguished and judged; on land, similarly, in open country all details, movements, and preparations of the enemy could be seen from a great distance. And although the gunpowder that so changed Western warfare had come originally from the East, the tide of ideas did not flow entirely in one direction. It was the introduction of Christophorus Clavius's Latin edition of the Greek mathematician Euclid's *Elements* (ca. 300 BCE), brought by the Italian Jesuit missionary Matteo Ricci (1552–1610), that changed the art of warfare in China during the Ming era: telescopes could now be fabricated, fortifications built, and cannons calibrated.

When discussing war machinery in his *Remedies of Good and Ill Fortune* (*De remediis utriusque fortunae* 1.99), the Italian Humanist and poet laureate Petrarch (1304–1374) did not omit to mention that gunpowder had been known by the ancients and was said to have been invented by Archimedes himself. Believing that the ancients had anticipated everything, some Renaissance Humanists visualized in terms of guns the ancient accounts of sieges that had employed prototypes of Greek fire. The Sienese Humanist and statesman Aeneas Silvius Piccolomini (1405–1464), later to become Pope Pius II, opined in referring to the passage in Virgil's *Aeneid* (6.585) on Salmoneus' new flaming machine, that "in Homer and Virgil could be found descriptions of every kind of weapon which our age used."

The science of ballistics (the use of projectiles), as applied to firearms, was not welcomed immediately or without critique. Medieval moralists erroneously believed that mechanical siege technology had not been used by the great heroes of antiquity. Guns were considered a coward's weapon. Scorn for missile weapons went back to a saying in Euripides' *Hercules* (159–162) that denigrated even archery in comparison to the courage and valor demonstrated in direct combat. In a later age the emperor Napoleon III of France (r. 1852–1870), author of a history of firearms, would still cite the exclamation of Archidamus, king of Sparta, on first viewing a catapult: "This is the tomb of bravery!" (Plutarch gives the anecdote twice in his *Moralia,* 191e, 219a, trans. Babbitt.) Despite this undercurrent of negative attitude, Christine de Pizan's translation of Vegetius, written for knights and courtiers, clearly explained the obvious advantage of using guns in siegecraft. Moreover, the appeal of guns was so strong that 15th-century manuscript illuminations showed the armies of Alexander the Great and of the Crusaders conducting sieges with cannon. In the earliest printed editions of the Roman historian Livy, battles were depicted with gunpowder effects. Still, on the battlefield itself the design of artillery remained essentially unchanged. Military opinion was content with a surviving tradition of chivalry that valued close combat as more honorable than long-range bombardment between invisible foes.

Another innovation with far-reaching results occurred in 1575 with a publication by the great architectural theorist Andrea Palladio (1518–1580) that initiated a revolutionary departure in the visual depiction of military history: an illustrated commentary on Julius Caesar's *Commentaries* (1st cent. BCE), which describe his military campaigns. Earlier works describing military campaigns had usually been illustrated only with schematic diagrams symbolizing troop formations and tactics. Palladio's were the first military illustrations to present a mise-en-scène in which individual figures were depicted in realistically rendered geographic locations. The edition proved immensely popular and became a standard textbook for students of military history well into the British Augustan age, in the early 18th century.

Visual considerations such as these, in fact, demonstrate how the study of ancient warfare had become a branch of what might be called applied antiquarianism, an instance in which detailed scholarship on the institutions and material culture of antiquity served present needs. A long tradition, through the Middle Ages, of illustrations of Roman military devices had been based on ancient or late antique prototypes. The accuracy of detail in the reliefs on Trajan's Column (early 2nd cent. CE), down to the eye-protectors for the horses of the Dacian armored cavalry, for instance, did not escape the notice of Renaissance artists and antiquaries. Mantegna, Raphael, and Giulio Romano all consulted the reliefs for details in representing Roman armor and weapons, and antiquarian scholars such as Guillaume Du Choul, Alfonso Chacón, and Justus Lipsius all drew on this evidence to show their contemporaries what a Roman "shield roof" (*testudo*) actually looked like and how it was used during sieges.

The strongest link, however, among war, art, mathematics, and engineering in the study of ancient sources lay in the subject of fortification. This strong connection was overwhelmingly demonstrated in the lectures on fortification given by Galileo at Padua and by the *New Method of Fortification* (*Nieuwe Maniere van Sterctebou*, 1617) written by the Flemish mathematician Simon Stevin (1548–1620), at one time quartermaster general in the Dutch army under Prince Maurice of Nassau, and director of public works. The Italianate ideal of the cultivated warrior, the courtier famously depicted by Baldassare Castiglione (1478–1529), was already in general currency. In his *Book of the Courtier* (1528) Castiglione commended to the courtier the art of drawing, not only as a skill excellent in itself but also as a tool of great use in planning military operations and designing fortifications. Giorgio Vasari (1511–1574) mentions in his biographical survey of famous artists of his time several notable Florentine artists who became involved in the design of fortifications, among them Arnolfo, Giotto, Brunelleschi, Leonardo da Vinci, and Michelangelo. Michelangelo saw the artist's role in war as especially apt for designing the form and proportions of citadels and defensive works, and of bastions, ditches, mines, gunports, and other utilitarian structures.

The arts of fortification had, of course, a very ancient tradition, which had periodically absorbed significant innovations. In antiquity fortifications had become increasingly sophisticated from the 4th century BCE onward, and surviving technical treatises from the era, such as those of Aeneas the Tactician (4th cent.) and Philo of Byzantium (3th cent.) demonstrated how innovations had affected patterns of warfare. The new style of bastioned fortification that had emerged in the 15th century, developed especially in Italy, was in its best examples geometrically designed by architect-engineers who for once could outdistance the ancients. This style of fortification revolutionized the defensive–offensive pattern of conducting war by providing a stout form of resistance to the new artillery while also furnishing platforms for heavy guns used in counterattack or defense.

Technical discussion of fortification did not end with the Italian Renaissance. In 1631 Adam Freitag (1602–1664) dedicated his *Architectura militaris nova* to Wladislaus Sigismund, prince of Poland and Sweden. Intending to offer a comprehensive work on the latest fortification design and practice in the Netherlands, Freitag not only established the canon for 17th-century design but also dealt both with the historical developments of fortress design and with the attack and defense of geometrical and irregular fortresses.

The building of fortifications also aroused both technical and political debates in which ancient views were echoed and evaluated. In the preface to his *De re aedificatoria* (1449, printed in Florence in 1485) Leon Battista Alberti (1404–1472) pointed out that "if you were to examine the expeditions that have been undertaken, you would come close to finding that most of the victories were gained more by the art and the skill of the architects than by the conduct or fortune of the generals; and that the enemy was oftener overcome and conquered by the architect's wit without the captain's arms, than by the captain's arms without the architect's wit." Alberti, following Egidio Romano and other medieval philosophers, also looked to Aristotle's *Politics*, where doubts were expressed about the military and psychological effectiveness of fortifications. (Aristotle had in fact taken up the discussion of the topic from Plato's *Laws*.) A similar dual questioning can be found in the Florentine political thinker Niccolò Machiavelli (1469–1527). Contributing to the Renaissance debates concerning whether internal or external defenses had greater effect and whether national armies were more trustworthy than mercenary forces, Machiavelli first offered a technical discussion on fortification in the seventh book of his *Arts of War* (*Arte della guerra*, 1521), analyzing the function of fortifications during the sieges of Pisa and Padua (1509), and in his *Account of a Journey Made to Fortify Florence* (*Relazione di una visita fatta per fortificare Firenze*, 1526). Later, moving the issue of the significance of fortifications closer to the center of current political and military debate, he connected the usefulness of fortification to the qualities and attitudes of military leadership, both in *The Prince* (*Il Principe*, written in 1513, published 1532) and in the later *Discorsi*. He not only recounted Roman examples and contemporary cases in which walls and citadels had or had not protected tyrants or princes but also pointed to conflicting political and military views that had emerged in antiquity—views that Renaissance political thinkers such as Justus Lipsius, Giovanni Botero, Scipione Ammirato, and Jean Bodin would repeat: while the Athenians had considered their walls admirable, the Romans built no fortresses, and the Spartans did not even permit their city to be protected by walls, as they wanted to rely solely on the valor and fortitude of their soldiers and citizens for their defense, not on the strength of citadels. Thus it came about that although fortifications yielded relatively good value in the wasteful economy of warfare, military theorists in the late Renaissance often mentioned admiringly what they called Spartan walls, that is, the effective citizen armies of that ancient military state, which had allowed Sparta to avoid altogether the expense of permanent walls.

Alongside this Renaissance debate concerning internal or external defenses and national or mercenary armies, one other suggestion was made at intervals throughout the 16th century: that a return should be made to some form of the Roman battle order. For infantry, a new role opened for the classical *triplex acies* of *hastati*, a triple line in which a front of spearmen (who had made the initial engagement after the enemy had been harassed by cavalry attacks from the flanks) would yield ground to the *principes*, who held a second line of defense through which the *hastati* could retire if sorely pressed, both these supported by the third and anchoring line of the *triarii*. By 1531 the French had experimented with something like the Roman legion. In his *Instructions sur le faict de la guerre,* published in 1548 and translated into German in 1594, Raymond de Fourquevaux recommended the formation of bodies based on units of 10 under a decurion, grouped in units of 100 under a centurion, and drawn up in what was basically Roman battle formation, supplemented by flanks of combined shot and pike. As with the Roman legion, Fourquevaux's *princes* (second front) were to be trained to absorb the first-front *hastaires,* and the *triairies* to admit them both, while the flanks telescoped back correspondingly. Under the conditions of discipline and pay that prevailed at the time, it was, however, virtually impossible to submit an army to the painstaking drill that alone could have made this Roman system work. The success of any battle formation, so it was repeated time and again, depended on the steadiness of an army and its ability to perform evolutions in formation without falling into disorder. Two of the main disadvantages of the Spanish square, for instance, were its unwieldiness and the fact that large numbers of men inside it were unable to bring their weapons to bear; they acted as ballast rather than as part of the unit's striking power. Various schemes, therefore, were worked out for breaking an army up into smaller units.

The first important experiments were those of the princes of Orange, Maurice of Nassau (1567–1625) and his cousin William Louis of Nassau (1560–1620), when confronting a Spanish imperial force of enormous size in a desperate struggle for political, religious, and economic freedom. The basis of this freedom was war and military life; constant war, since 1572, seemed the essential condition for natural unity and survival. Dutch Humanism of the period and its study of classical philology aided the technical and tactical evolution of the Dutch army and thus in the military protection of the Dutch Provinces' independence and liberty. In fact, three great military treatises of the eminent Humanist Justus Lipsius (1547–1606), ranging from a general consideration of war and military matters in his *Politica* (1589) to the more specialized study of ancient military organization in *De militia Romana* (1595) and early armaments, fortifications, and sieges in *Poliorcetica* (1596; the Greek title refers to siegework), inspired and guided Dutch military reform and organization after the pattern of the ancients and on the principles of Roman Stoicism, the ancient philosophy of discipline and self-control propagated by Lipsius at that time. In 1583–1584 Maurice of Nassau had been a student of Lipsius when he was a philologist and classical scholar at the newly founded university of Leiden, and in 1590 William Louis had recommended that his younger brothers likewise study there with Lipsius. Lipsius' interest in military topics was obvious: although his writings were of a purely philological nature, he also commented on contemporary issues as well. Having noted that the Dutch army had no discipline at all, he observed that whoever understood how to rule the troops of his day with the Roman art of war would be able to dominate the Earth. When *De militia Romana* appeared in 1595, the Dutch States General at once sent a copy to Maurice. Maurice, who always referred to Lipsius as his teacher, also approached him for clarification on the undecided question whether soldiers (rather than other laborers) should be assigned to dig fortifications, a matter of considerable moment in the siege warfare the Dutch were predominantly engaged in. Lipsius, basing his answer on Vegetius, Caesar, and Plutarch, pointed to the example of the Roman legionaries, who were indeed employed in the construction of siegeworks. His treatise was in fact a commentary on the chapters on the Roman army in the *Histories* (6.19–40) of Polybius (2nd cent. BCE), the Greek historian of Rome's rise to Mediterranean dominion in the years 220–146. The *Histories,* in 40 books of which only books 1–5 and part of book 6 have survived intact (the rest is known to some extent through excerpts in other sources), had been fairly unknown in the Middle Ages but was not entirely new to readers of Lipsius' time. Polybius' value as a historian had been discovered by 15th-century Florentine Humanists; Machiavelli's *Arte della guerra,* a comprehensive attempt to augment, modernize, illustrate, and supplement Vegetius in the light of all evidence of classical warfare available to him, had made notable use of Polybius, along with Frontinus and Livy, in order to bring modern warfare into line with ancient practice. In a similar line Francesco Patrizi (1529–1597), the first professor of Platonic philosophy at Ferrara, whom Lipsius in the preface to *De militia Romana* explicitly names as his predecessor, had based his first book on the Roman army, *La militia Romana* (1583), on ancient historians, especially Polybius' sixth book and the work of Dionysius of Halicarnassus. Patrizi's *Military Parallels* (*Paralleli militari: Della milita riformata,* 1594–1595), published during a renewal of the Ottoman Wars (1593–1606), suggested strategies drawn from ancient writers such as Polybius which might defeat the "great multitude of Turks" with only a few troops. Following both of these publications, Lipsius too explained how Polybius' information on the Roman army could offer solutions to contemporary problems. His successor at Leiden University, Joseph Justus Scaliger (1540–1609), dismissed these views as "rubbish" (*asinina*) and predicted that "if the Prince of Orange were to rely only on counselors who cannot get beyond Livy," his Spanish adversaries "would soon tear out his beard."

Maurice, however, having read in Lipsius' *De militia Romana* that the Romans themselves knew and stated that it was not only virtue, discipline, and arms but also their *opus* (work) that gave them victory over their enemies, reformed the Dutch military system entirely. Lipsius' emphasis on the idea of daily drill was effectively backed up by literal translations of ancient instructions and commands into modern languages. The value to a military unit of the cohesiveness to be attained through continuous practice, and based on these new drill techniques, was recognized. Each of the newly formed small tactical bodies, shallow units now, was trained to enhance mobility and maneuverability. Lipsius' explanations of the ancient orders of battle, marching, and encampment were likewise adopted as a direct model. With their new discipline, inspired by Lipsius' Stoic philosophy of constancy and self-control, and with the ample pay they offered, the princes of Orange saw to it that their soldiers were now ready to engage in digging fortifications for their encampments. Having secured his position by circumvallation and countervallation (systems of walls) and having besieged Gertruidenborg successfully, William Louis wrote: "This siege can definitely be called the second Alesia [the site of Caesar's definitive victory in Gaul], and it means the restoration of a great part of the ancient art and science of war, which until now has been prized very little and laughed at by ignorant men, and which has not been understood by even the greatest modern generals or at least has not been practiced by them."

Much more, so it appears, was needed to bring this new art of warfare into being than simple knowledge of a real situation and a simple decision or command. The princes of Orange studied everything available concerning the military skills practiced by the ancient Greeks and Romans, and they spared no trouble, work, or expense in transferring the tenets found there into practice. They commissioned learned philologists to carry out projects of military science. Joseph Scaliger, despite his skepticism of Lipsius' ideas, produced a new edition of Caesar's *Commentaries* in 1606; Joannes Meursius (1579–1639), a pupil of Lipsius' at Leiden, brought out in 1612 the first Greek edition of the *Tactics* of the Byzantine emperor Leo VI (the Wise) (r. 866–912), to which he added a Latin translation at the request of Maurice. At the suggestion of William Louis an edition of Aelian (Aelianus Tacticus, 2nd cent. CE), an author virtually unknown outside Byzantium and the Muslim world in the Middle Ages, was edited by Sixtus Arcerius in 1613. Their choice of Leo and Aelian was deliberate. The work of the first consisted, for the most part, of somewhat systematized extracts from older authors, particularly Aelian, whereas Aelian himself was one of the most renowned and reliable of the ancient Greek military writers who had dealt with the organization, drilling, arming, and battle formations of armies. He was held in such high esteem by Maurice that the prince had a Dutch translation prepared for his officers. Captain John Bingham, who was serving in Holland under Maurice, not only translated Aelian's *Tactics* or "Embattailing of an Army after ye Graecian Manner" (London 1616) but also included in his work the special exercises issued by order of Maurice for the English troops in the service of the United Provinces. In 1623 he would translate into English Lipsius' *De militia Romana* (or at least parts of it), giving it a highly topical relevance. Like Clement Edmondes's *Observations upon the Five First Books of Caesar's Commentaries, Setting Forth the Practice of the Art Military in the Time of the Roman Empire . . . Together with Such Instructions as May Be Drawn from Their Proceedings, for the Better Direction of Our Modern Wars* (1600), all these translations had practical purposes. In the company of their closest associates and generals, the princes of Orange spent nights at their desks, poring over these classical military authors and practicing elementary movements and orders of battle with miniature lead soldiers before training their men on the field.

Maurice of Orange's successes had brought him such great prestige that the devotees of Mars from all of Protestant Europe gathered in his camp to be initiated into the new military system. The art of war of the Netherlands was no longer based on simple experience, but on study and knowledge. In 1617 Count Johann of Nassau (1561–1623) established in Siegen a military and knightly school that instructed young nobles and the sons of patricians in the arts of engineering, fortification, artillery, tactics, mathematics, Latin, French, and Italian.

Although all aspects of the new training had been exercised and applied in battles and sieges, Maurice's order of battle was never tested on a full scale, and its effectiveness remained a matter for debate. The man who perfected Maurice's art of war was Gustavus Adolphus (1594–1632), who regarded Maurice as his teacher. The grandson of Gustavus Vasa, he ascended the Swedish throne in 1611 at the age of 17. Not only did he expand on the new tactics, he also established a new system, with a large number of musketeers, well-trained and disciplined after the Netherlandish pattern and armed with improved weapons, as the base of a large-scale strategy. He achieved some notable victories in the Thirty Years' War. Many of his commanders and military leaders had previously served or been trained in the Dutch army camps, and it was in Sweden that Lipsius' first proposal for reform, the selection of subjects for military service, was put into practice. Because the small Swedish army, consisting of simple citizens who were committed to unconditional obedience in military service, had to be supplemented by troops recruited from other countries, the original intention as well as the ethical element contained in Lipsius' Neostoic concept of discipline was lost—this despite the fact that literary and scholarly exchanges continued between Sweden and the Netherlands and that Gustavus's daughter, Queen Christina (1626–1689), in whose scholarly circle Stoicism was deeply cultivated, gathered a circle of the most important Dutch philologists around her. If not all of them devoted their scholarly life to ancient warfare, Johann Scheffer (1621–1679), professor of eloquence and political science at Uppsala, dedicated his treatise on ancient naval warfare, *De militia navali veterum libri IV,* to Christina in 1654. Years later Scheffer was the first to edit and translate into Latin the *Strategikon,* a military handbook supposedly written by the Byzantine emperor Maurice (r. 582–602), known for his army reform and incorporation of Avar tactics into Byzantine warfare. Yet Scheffer's dedication did not match that of Heinrich von Rantzau (Henricus Ranzovius, 1526–1599), the German historian, genealogist, astrologer, Humanist, and Danish governor of Schleswig-Holstein, whose learned, encyclopedic summary of military science, the *Commentarius bellicus* (1595), laden with precepts, advice, and stratagems for terrestrial and naval combat, demonstrated a glowing admiration for Lipsius' Neostoic *constantia.* Similarly, the French writer J. de Billon, who had trained in the Netherlands, when describing the Dutch reforms in his *Principles* (*Principes de l'art militaire,* 1612), echoed Lipsius in praising prudence, force, justice, and temperance as guiding principles important for the soldier and necessary for the commander.

By the first half of the 18th century awareness that Roman Stoicism had provided, via Lipsius, the ethical basis for the modern army remained only vaguely present. Yet Lipsius, still present in military handbooks together with Polybius and Vegetius, could be discerned, especially in the spiritual background of Prussian military reforms. The Prussian general Gerhard von Scharnhorst (1755–1813) drew on the Orange-Nassau tradition and resurrected Neostoic ideals for the modern conscript army at a time when military life had become ossified and lacking in moral content and army organization was dominated by mathematical calculation and soulless discipline. Carl von Clausewitz (1780–1831), the other great Prussian military theorist, also described the moral forces of army life in his *Vom Kriege* (1832–1834) in Lipsian terms of constancy and firmness.

In the middle of the 18th century a new type of military literature appeared. The earliest representative of the new wave was a volume by a French officer, Armand-François de La Croix, entitled *Traité de la petite guerre* (1752)—the French phrase (lit. "little war") is parallel with the now universally recognized Spanish term *guerrilla.* Precisely during the years when the theory of tactics and of grand operations was pushed to an extreme of almost geometric precision ("maneuver strategy"), irregular warfare for the first time became a common concern of military thinkers. By the end of the 18th century vital changes had taken place in the organization and equipment of French forces and had been adopted to a varying extent by other Continental services. The cumbersome structure of the army was recast into divisions; artillery was made more mobile and more powerful, the number of its guns was increased, and new tactics were evolved to exploit artillery's new potential. In addition, a decisive innovation in infantry fighting consisted in the acceptance of open-order tactics by the line infantry. In contrast to the prevailing doctrine of scientific warfare, in which soldiers had to fight like the living marionettes and clockwork musketeers of the line, the writers on irregular war taught the soldier and his commander that one must learn to live with the unexpected. Here convention had no place; success depended on the individual initiative of many. Strikingly, immediately after the collapse of Prussia, there appeared in Königsberg a manual on firearms tactics for infantry and cavalry officers, *Der Schützen-Dienst für Jäger- und Schützen-Offiziere bey der Infanterie und Kavallerie* (1807), which discussed certain weaknesses of linear tactics and argued in favor of the more flexible methods of the French.

This did not mean that the classical tradition evaporated. However radical the changes in tactics had been from the Renaissance to the time of Frederick the Great (1712–1786), the principles of tactics had remained the same. Frederick, in refuting the theoreticians of his day who (in his view) wanted to force Caesar's ancient mode of warfare into the schema of the strategy of attrition, observed that only a few classical works were extant in which one could truly study the art of war: "Caesar teaches us in his *Commentaries* little more than what we see in Pandour [irregular, brutal] warfare; his move to Great Britain is hardly anything different, and a general of our time could use from Caesar only the employment of his cavalry on the day of [the Battle of] Pharsalus." (The Pandours were rapacious East European forces enlisted by Frederick's opponents in the War of Austrian Succession.)

The military genius Charles-Joseph de Ligne (1735–1814), who had served as field marshal to Catherine II of Russia and to Francis II (the last Holy Roman Emperor) and who at the age of 15 had composed a *Discours sur la profession des armes* based on Livy, Caesar, and Quintus Curtius, declared in 1805, late in his life, regarding Vegetius' *De re militari:* "It is a golden book. Vegetius says that a god inspired [the Romans] to organize a legion, and I say that a god inspired Vegetius." In his monumental 34-volume miscellany of his military, literary, and personal writings (*Mélanges militaires, littéraires et sentimentaires,* 1795–1811) he called the *Tactics* of the Byzantine emperor Leo VI "immortal" and claimed that Leo was the equal of Frederick the Great and superior to Caesar. In a time when firearms dominated battlefields Napoleon I Bonaparte (1769–1821), who in a way was more a statesman than a soldier, kept a copy of the 1806 edition of Vegetius' *De re militari* at Fontainebleau. Neither as a young person nor later did he pursue military history or theoretical studies. Contrary to his contemporaries among military men, such as Johann Gottfried Hoyer in his excellent *History of the Art of War* (*Geschichte der Kriegskunst,* 1797), he did not concern himself with the question whether one should revert from the thin-lines battle formation to the deep column. Whereas Frederick the Great had read everything there was in the way of old and more modern literature on the nature of war and military history, Napoleon, though convinced that a soldier had to study the deeds of the great commanders such as Alexander, Hannibal, Caesar, Gustavus Adolphus, Marshal Henri de la Tour Turenne, and Frederick the Great, was himself essentially familiar with Caesar and with Plutarch's quite unmilitary biographies. Just as Charles VIII, Charles V, Süleyman II, Henry IV, Louis XIII, Louis XIV, Condé, and Christina of Sweden had been inspired by the image and deeds of Caesar, Napoleon, who read and annotated Caesar's *Commentaries* in long nights of study, discerned usable elements in the memoirs of the Roman general who had defeated Vercingetorix and Pompey the Great. The annotations in his copy of a French translation of the *Commentaries*—they would later result in the *Précis des guerres de César* dictated to Louis-Joseph Marchand during his exile on St. Helena, ultimately published in 1836—reveal that Napoleon deplored the lack of precise information on places, dates, distances, and the exact number of legions deployed, which prevented Caesar's tactical genius from being imitated, used, or adapted in truly practical ways.

Napoleon's approach in reading ancient military authors is still practiced today. Modern military academies such as the École Polytechnique in Paris, the U.S. Military Academy at West Point, the Frunze Academy in Moscow, and the Royal Military Academy at Sandhurst continue to study and analyze famous ancient battles (Marathon, Thermopylae, Plataea, Leuctra, Chaeronea, Gaugamela, Cannae, Zama, Pharsalus, and Adrianopolis) and sieges (Syracuse and Alesia). Classification of actual types of military maneuvers and their variations has remained part of military science, for new technology and weapons have not drastically altered some of the classical types of offensive tactics. The famous single envelopments (flank attacks) by Alexander the Great at Gaugamela (331 BCE) and by Erwin Rommel at Gazala (1942) have both acquired the status of classics, and the double envelopment (pincer movement) of Hannibal's forces at the Battle of Cannae (216 BCE) is as much a classic as the destruction of the 7th German Army at the Falaise Gap (1944).

BIBL.: Jeremy Black, ed., *Warfare in Europe, 1650–1792* (Aldershot 2005). Peter Burke, "Images as Evidence in Seventeenth-century Europe," *Journal of the History of Ideas* 64, no. 2 (2003) 273–296. Hans Delbrück, *History of the Art of War within the Framework of Political History*, vol. 4, *The Modern Era*, trans. Walter J. Renfroe Jr. (Westport, Conn., 1985). Anthony Grafton, "Rhetoric, Philology and Egyptomania in the 1570s: J. J. Scaliger's Invective against M. Guilandinus's Papyrus," *Journal of the Warburg and Courtauld Institutes* 42 (1979) 167–194. Werner Hahlweg, *Die Heeresreform der Oranier und die Antike* (Berlin 1941). John R. Hale, *Renaissance War Studies* (London 1983). Peter N. Miller, "Nazis and Neo-Stoics: Otto Brunner and Gerhard Oestreich before and after the Second World War," *Past & Present* 176, no. 1 (2002) 144–186. Arnaldo Momigliano, "Polybius' Reappearance in Western Europe" and "Polybius between the English and the Turks," in *Sesto contributo alla storia degli studi classici e del mondo antico* (Rome 1980) 1:103–123, 1:125–141. Gerhard Oestreich, *Antiker Geist und moderner Staat bei Justus Lipsius (1547–1606): Der Neustoizismus als politische Bewegung* (Göttingen 1989); *Neostoicism and the Early Modern State*, ed. Brigitta Oestreich and H. G. Koenigsberger, trans. David McLintock (Cambridge 1982); and "Der römische Stoïzismus und die oranische Heeresreform," in *Geist und Gestalt der frühmodernen Staates* (Berlin 1969) 11–34. Charles C. W. Oman, *A History of the Art of War in the Middle Ages*, 2 vols. (London 1924–1991). Geoffrey Parker, "The Limits to Revolutions in Military Affairs: Maurice of Nassau, the Battle of Nieuwpoort (1600), and the Legacy," *Journal of Military History* 71, no. 2 (2007) 331–372, and *The Military Revolution: Military Innovation and the Rise of the West, 1500–1800* (Cambridge 1988; 2nd ed. 1996). Wolfgang Reinhard, "Humanismus und Militarismus: Antike-Rezeption und Kriegshandwerk in der oranischen Heeresreform," in *Krieg und Frieden im Horizont des Renaissancehumanismus*, ed. Franz Joseph Worstbrock (Weinheim 1986) 185–204. Philippe Richardot, *Végèce et la culture militaire au Moyen Âge (Ve–XVe siècles)* (Paris 1998).

J.P.

Water Supply

In classical antiquity people gathered water from springs and rivers, collected rainwater in cisterns, and dug wells. In addition, the Romans adopted hydraulic technologies from the Etruscans and other sources to build numerous aqueducts in which water flowed from outlying springs to urban centers by force of gravity. These massive aqueducts supplied the vast water requirements of the Roman baths, which the Romans considered essential for any civilized town or city.

Ancient structures such as baths and aqueducts were highly visible to subsequent generations even when they no longer functioned as originally intended. Ancient writings concerning the water supply and the appropriate uses of water also exerted an ongoing influence. Such writings included book 7 of *On Architecture* by the Roman architect Vitruvius (1st cent. BCE), *On Aqueducts* by Frontinus (1st cent. CE), and book 31 of the *Natural History* of Pliny the Elder. Pliny's chapter on water treated many medicinal uses of water, as did the Hippocratic Corpus and the writings of Celsus and Galen.

The Etruscans and ancient Romans devoted much attention to thermal medicine and the therapeutic value of mineral springs. The health-giving powers of water were elaborated in detail and formed the rationale for the Roman baths and aqueducts. Yet attitudes toward water, and therefore toward the water supply, varied greatly with time and place. After 1350, especially in central and northern Italy, a flourishing tradition of writings emerged on thermal baths and hot springs. Important examples include Giovanni de' Dondi's *De fontibus calidis agri patavini consideratio* (*On the Hot Springs of the Paduan Countryside*, ca. 1372) and Michele Savonarola's *De balneis et thermis naturalibus omnibus Italiae* (*Concerning all the Baths and Natural Spas of Italy*, 1448–1449).

A new spa culture developed around thermal springs in the countryside. Some of these were newly rediscovered Roman springs surrounded by classical ruins that were often rebuilt. In northern Europe spas were developed for specific therapeutic purposes. Ancient writings on baths and the medicinal properties of water became widely available with the encyclopedic publication of *De balneis omnia quae extant* (*All Extant Writings on Baths*), published by the Giunta Press of Venice in 1553. Numerous writings on the characteristics and medicinal virtues of various springs and other waters appeared subsequently, such as the 16th-century writings of the physician Andrea Bacci.

In succeeding centuries baths continued to be utilized, although the rationales for using them changed. For example, the use of alternating hot and cold baths to achieve a balance of the four humors, characteristic of classical medicine, had become transformed by the 18th century into the use of the bath for hygienic purposes and for the treatment of specific diseases utilizing particular waters. Such treatments were accompanied by controversy involving rival claims and techniques. In the 19th century balneology became a form of "alternative medicine," pure, natural, and unadulterated by drugs. In the 20th century spas and hot springs became an adjunct of the tourist industry; but though people sought them out for many of the traditional health-related reasons, most were no longer endorsed by the medical establishment.

To maintain proper water flow from natural sources to urban areas, aqueducts were designed with a gradual downward slope. Because of the need to maintain a constant gradient, the builders constructed massive arches to span low-lying valleys. Some of these arches survived as awesome monuments that have attracted numerous sightseers from medieval times to the present day. The aqueducts of the city of Rome were particularly well known because of their spectacular arches and because of the treatise by Frontinus describing them in detail. One Roman aqueduct, the Aqua Virgo, remained in partial use during the medieval period, but many others fell into disrepair. Of the eleven original Roman aqueducts, only the Aqua Virgo (subsequently called the Acqua Virgine) was partially functioning by the 15th century.

In the mid-16th century the Humanist and Vatican librarian Agostino Steuco set out to trace the original source of the Acqua Virgine and discovered it at the Salone Springs, about 8 km from Rome. He advocated the restoration of the ancient aqueduct as a way vastly to improve the city and create dramatic fountains along widened streets, thereby glorifying the city of the popes and the papacy itself. Aqueduct repair was part of a *renovatio imperii,* a renewal of imperial power in which the pope was seen as heir to the political power of the ancient empire. Steuco's ambition to restore an ancient aqueduct was achieved only later in the century, when the Acqua Virgine was restored in 1570. By 1612 two additional aqueducts had been repaired, the Acqua Felice and the Acqua Paola. As a result the city was transformed by the construction of numerous fountains, and an adequate water supply was finally available for a growing population.

These aqueduct restorations were accompanied by numerous tracts providing the history of aqueducts, locating ancient aqueducts, and offering plans for (or accounts of) aqueduct repair. Practitioners and learned men alike penned such writings, including the Roman magistrate Luca Peto, the architect and antiquarian Pirro Ligorio, and the architect Antonio Trevisio. Writings on aqueducts continued to be published in the following centuries. They include the earliest topographical work focused on the aqueducts of the ancient city, Raffaello Fabretti's *De aquis et aquaeductibus veteris Romae* (*Concerning the Waters and Aqueducts of Ancient Rome,* 1680).

In the late Renaissance and in the 17th century hydraulic projects and the study of hydraulics took new directions. Elaborate gardens with fountains requiring massive supplies of water were constructed, such as the gardens at the Villa d'Este at Tivoli, created by Pirro Ligorio, and the gardens of Versailles, created under the auspices of the Sun King, Louis XIV. Among other hydraulic projects came the construction of dams and canals. For example, numerous canals and waterworks were constructed on or near the Po River and its tributaries in northern Italy. The mathematical analysis of hydraulic problems and other "scientific" methods became features of hydraulic engineering in the late 16th century and beyond—approaches not entirely alien to Frontinus' measurements of aqueduct water flow more than a millennium earlier.

BIBL.: T. Ashby, *The Aqueducts of Ancient Rome* (Oxford 1935). D. R. Coffin, *Pirro Ligorio: The Renaissance Artist, Architect, and Antiquarian* (University Park, Pa., 2004). R. K. Delph, "From Venetian Visitor to Curial Humanist: The Development of Agostino Steuco's 'Counter-Reformation' Thought," *Renaissance Quarterly* 47 (Spring 1994) 102–139. H. B. Evans, *Aqueduct Hunting in the Seventeenth Century: Raffaello Fabretti's De aquis et aquaeductibus veteris Romae* (Ann Arbor 2002). A. Fiocca, D. Lamberini, and C. Maffioli, *Arte e scienza delle acque nel Rinascimento* (Venice 2003). A. Trevor Hodge, *Roman Aqueducts and Water Supply,* 2nd ed. (London 2002). C. Mukerji, *Territorial Ambitions and the Gardens of Versailles* (Cambridge 1997). K. Park, "Natural Particulars: Medical Epistemology, Practice, and the Literature of Healing Springs," in *Natural Particulars: Nature and the Disciplines in Renaissance Europe,* ed. A. Grafton and N. Siraisi (Cambridge, Mass., 1999) 347–367. R. Porter, ed., *The Medical History of Waters and Spas* (London 1990).

P.O.L.

West. *See* East and West.

Widow of Ephesus

The protagonist of a famous lewd story of antiquity: after having theatrically mourned her dead husband by remaining enclosed in his tomb for days, a widow overcomes all resistance and yields to the seducing embrace of a young *miles,* a soldier standing guard nearby.

If it is true that interpreting always means judging to some degree, it sometimes happens that the reception of a classical literary character takes on, through history, the features of a never-ending trial. In other words, though attempts to reduce the character and narrative context to a structure of unambiguous meaning may result, over the course of time, in a verdict of "guilty" or "not guilty," such a verdict is destined to be soon overturned. This has been the case with the widow of Ephesus, a character handed down to modernity principally in her Petronian version—the protagonist of the story in *Satyricon* that has enjoyed the greatest independent success. None of the later "charges" against the widow of Ephesus appears in Petronius' text. The original tale—the narrative version of a folkloric motif that merges the taboos of death and sex in order to exorcise them—has the typical features of the *fabula Milesia,* a short fable of erotic love and adventure. With ironic cynicism, it makes the widow the epitome of deceiving appearances, and a parody of the chaste heroines of Greek romance.

The widow's life in the Middle Ages, in contrast, began with an unappealable verdict of guilty. Medieval reprises of the Milesian tale were strictly dependent on the *Satyricon,* which in the 12th and 13th centuries was widely read among scholars, especially in France. Nevertheless, the more striking examples, like the section "De mulieris Ephesiae, et similium, fide" of John of Salisbury's *Policraticus,* and the retelling in Marie de France's *Fables* (fable 25, "De vidua"), paradoxically resemble the misogynist version by Phaedrus, which until the discovery in 1809 of the *Appendix Perottina* circulated only in Romulus's highly revised adaptation. If in Petronius the *fabula* celebrates the liberating power of sexual pleasure in opposition to the repressive chains of a particularly ostentatious prudery, medieval interpretations used the widow as a tool for the promotion of chastity.

For her next chance of an appeal the widow of Ephesus had to wait until the 17th century, when her rehabilitation began. The first to push for her acquittal was Jean de La Fontaine. Omitting certain details of the original plot (the widow's singular beauty, the spectacular portrayal of her mourning) and modifying others (eros alone is responsible for the passion between the woman and the guard), La Fontaine managed to transform the widow of Ephesus into the prototype of the wise woman, capable of making life rise from death, and he seems to have anticipated Bakhtin in interpreting Petronius' *fabula* as "an uninterrupted series of life's victories over death." In the same century, a similar attitude of acquittal underlay Walter Charleton's *Ephesian Matron,* which, influenced by Hobbesian materialism, sees in Petronius' tale the just triumph of eros as a natural physical impulse and the defeat of the whole mirage of Platonic *amor.* It was not, however, until the 18th century, and primarily in France (although Gotthold Lessing's unfinished play *Die Matrone von Ephesos* should be mentioned), that the widow's full acquittal was achieved. Rousseau advised a contemporary widow to take the widow of Ephesus as her model rather than Andromache or Dido. And Voltaire, who saw in the widow's yielding to the soldier's advances vindication for an old abuse by her husband, seems even to anticipate decidedly feminist 20th-century interpretations. After some revivals of the widow's guilt in the 19th century—as in Chamisso's poem "Ein Lied von der Weibertreue," which rehabilitates the moralistic censure of the Middle Ages in a Romantic form—she was destined in the 20th century to be graced with increasingly unconditional redemption. Christopher Fry arrived at a particularly Christian sense of redemption in his play *A Phoenix Too Frequent,* in which the infidelity of Petronius' character is transformed into a hymn to life, but in a sense opposed to Bakhtin: bread and wine, in fact, far from representing the first step toward a festive, carnivalesque rebirth, are revealed to be thoroughly Christian symbols. The idea of resurrection, although interpreted hedonistically, is also central to the role played by the widow of Ephesus in Federico Fellini's film *Satyricon.* Obviously deviating from Petronius' tale, the director set the story, which he put into the mouth of a young homosexual, during the course of a visit to the tomb of Trimalchio. In Jean Cocteau's play *L'école des veuves* (1936), doubts raised about the moral integrity of the deceased husband endow the widow's tale with the character of a long-deferred but ultimately achieved emancipation. Cocteau's comedy also features a trial, but with a new defendant: it is in fact the husband who is accused and then found guilty. An equally resonant conviction is reserved for him in J. M. Synge's *In the Shadow of the Glen,* with an unexpected twist: not only does the widow free herself from a tyrannical husband—who in this play only pretends to be dead, to test his wife's fidelity—but she also chooses to flee in the face of the *Miles* character, a young shepherd. The roles have been completely reversed: Petronius' widow ultimately dons the judge's robes herself and irrevocably condemns the entire male sex.

BIBL.: S. B. Carleton, "The Widow of Ephesus in Restoration England," *Classical and Modern Literature* 9 (1988) 51–63. R. E. Colton, "The Story of the Widow of Ephesus in Petronius and La Fontaine," *Classical Journal* 71 (1975–1976) 35–52. Roseann Runte, "The Matron of Ephesus in Eighteenth-century France: The Lady and the Legend," *Studies in Eighteenth-century Culture* 6 (1977) 361–375. M.T.

Translated by Patrick Baker

Wilamowitz-Moellendorff, Ulrich von

German Hellenist and classical philologist (1848–1931). He was considered by his admirers the *princeps philologorum,* and his life and works are an exemplary reflection of the tension at the turn of the 20th century in German classical scholarship between relativizing historicism and normative classicism.

He was born the third child of an East Elbian Junker at the Markowitz manor in Posen (today Poznán) and grew up in East Prussia. He attended the renowned Schulpforta boarding school (near Naumburg) and received his *Abitur* there in 1867. His *Valediktionsarbeit,* "In wieweit befriedigen die Schlüsse der erhaltenen griechischen Trauerspiele?" ("How Satisfying Are the Endings of Preserved Greek Tragedies?"), indicated the direction his life would take. He decided against becoming a military officer or large landowner, as would have befit his station, and instead pursued an academic career. He commenced his studies in Bonn, but after the death of Otto Jahn in September 1869 he moved to Berlin, where he received his doctorate in 1870. During his time in Bonn he developed an aversion to Friedrich Nietzsche, and in 1872 he bombarded Nietzsche's *Birth of Tragedy* with a damning polemic in the pamphlet "Zukunftsphilologie" ("Philology of the Future").

After volunteering to serve in the Franco-Prussian War in 1870–1871, Wilamowitz went to Italy and Greece on an archaeological fellowship, for which he was recommended by Theodor Mommsen. In 1875 he dedicated his *Habilitationsschrift* in philology, on Euripides, to Mommsen. Three years later he married Mommsen's eldest daughter, Marie.

He was appointed to a full professorship in classical philology at the University of Greifswald in 1876. In 1883 he moved to Göttingen, and then in 1897, after difficult and exhausting negotiations, to the University of Berlin, where he also became a member of the Prussian Academy of Sciences. Wilamowitz's detailed research on Greek poetry, conducted on the basis of historical source criticism, together with his seminal syntheses of Greek culture, religion, philosophy, and literature, put his stamp not only on Greek studies but on all of classical philology. His numerous students, including Felix Jacoby, Wolfgang Schadewaldt, Eduard Fraenkel, Werner Jaeger, Johannes Geffcken, Paul Maas, Eduard Schwartz, and Gilbert Murray, promoted his teaching and fame both at home and abroad. He played a part in transforming the German academic system into a major enterprise of international renown. Nor did he conduct his work cooped up in the ivory tower: the educated citizenry of Berlin sat at the feet of the "born lecturer." He also energetically defended the preservation of the elite humanistic *Gymnasium.*

He failed, however, in his ambitious attempt to preserve antiquity as an interdisciplinary ideal and, through the conception of an overarching, all-encompassing *classical* studies, to overcome its fracturing into discrete disciplines. For his own research remained beholden to historicism and was of limited value to the future, as even his best pupils noted after World War I. As for his belief, inherited from Winckelmann, in the ideal nature of classical antiquity and his exaltation of the art-producing individual, neither was the product of theoretical reflection.

In his final, fragmentary work, *Der Glaube der Hellenen* (*The Faith of the Greeks,* 2 vols., 1931–1932), he elaborated a cultural-historical developmental model of Greek religion. The romantically transfigured "faith of the Greeks" culminated in Plato, the embodiment not only of Greek religiosity but of human religiosity generally; Wilamowitz claimed to have opted for it even as a student.

Politically, Wilamowitz was conservative. He glorified the Prussian monarchy his whole life. During the First World War he supported the annexation of territory as a military objective and called for unlimited submarine warfare. He rejected the Weimar Republic as "parliamentary ochlocracy." He was no anti-Semite. He laid no groundwork for Nazism and its racial doctrine. But his open rejection of the democratic system of the Weimar Republic made the Nazi state acceptable to many among the educated classes.

BIBL.: M. Armstrong, W. Buchwald, and W. M. Calder III, eds., *Ulrich von Wilamowitz-Moellendorff: Bibliography, 1867–1990* (Hildesheim 1991). W. M. Calder III, H. Flashar, and T. Lindken, eds., *Wilamowitz nach 50 Jahren* (Darmstadt 1985). W. M. Calder III et al., eds., *Wilamowitz in Greifswald* (Hildesheim 2000). William M. Calder III and Robert Kirstein, eds., *"Aus dem Freund ein Sohn": Theodor Mommsen und Ulrich von Wilamowitz-Moellendorff: Briefwechsel, 1872–1903,* 2 vols. (Hildesheim 2003). Stefan Rebenich, "Der alte Meergreis, die Rose von Jericho und ein höchst vortrefflicher Schwiegersohn: Mommsen, Harnack und Wilamowitz," in *Adolf von Harnack: Theologe, Historiker, Wissenschaftspolitiker,* ed. K. Nowak and O. G. Oexle (Göttingen 2001) 39–69, and "'Dass ein strahl von Hellas auf uns fiel': Platon im Georgekreis," *George-Jahrbuch* 7 (2008–2009) 115–141. Claudia Ungefehr-Kortus, "Nietzsche-Wilamowitz-Kontroverse," *Der Neue Pauly* 15, no. 1 (2001) 1062–1070. S.R.

Translated by Patrick Baker

Winckelmann, Johann Joachim

Internationally famed German historian of classical culture, especially of the arts (1717–1768). His major influence, both on specialist studies of ancient Greek and Roman art, and more generally on late Enlightenment and early 19th-century thought concerning the aesthetic and ethical ideals embodied in classical Greek culture, derived largely from his formidable achievements as an antiquarian scholar. His *History of the Art of Antiquity,* first published in 1764, quickly became established as the standard text on the subject, functioning as by far the fullest compendium of the existing evidence, verbal and visual, relating to the art of the ancient Greeks and Romans and, more marginally, that of the ancient Etruscan and Egyptians. At the same time, it offered a bold new synthesis of this material, set out as a history unfolding in time.

Winckelmann's attempt to reconstitute such a history was by no means entirely new. His work developed out of a tradition of antiquarian and classical scholarship, already well-established in the Renaissance, that by his time had made almost all the evidence on which he drew available in published form. He, however, was the one to take the step of elaborating a speculative history that attempted to integrate the commentaries on the history of ancient Greek and Roman sculpture in the ancient literature with the existing material remains of this art excavated in Italy. This he did at a point where there was precious little visual evidence, aside from a few early Greek coins, that could be ascribed to the crucial earlier phases of that history as documented in the ancient literature. He in effect projected a new history of Greek art, concrete evidence of which became available only after his death, once explorations in sites in Greece and the Near East made early Greek remains, such as the sculpture from the Parthenon, available to classical scholars. In a funeral oration delivered in 1820 on Ennio Quirino Visconti (Winckelmann's successor as the leading international authority on classical Greek and Roman art), the French art theorist and antiquarian scholar Quatremère de Quincy devoted a moment to the contribution of Winckelmann himself:

> It was precisely the pretension of the work to appear to be what it could not be, and precisely again this title [*History of Art*] that constituted its success and

> merit. Yes, the name *history* was a grand idea and produced a grand effect. It devalued the narrow methods of the antiquarians, who saw only one fact and object after another, and had no sense of the connection between them.

Winckelmann is often characterized as the father of modern classical archaeological studies. But he is in fact the father of a very particular tradition, one that sought to effect a historical reconstruction of the work of the classical Greek masters cited in the ancient literature by correlating the Graeco-Roman artifacts that could be identified as copies or adaptations of this earlier work with the fragmentary evidence provided by surviving examples of early Greek sculpture. He was no archaeologist in the modern sense of the word. He carried out no fieldwork and only occasionally availed himself of evidence about the excavated source of the material he analyzed, very little of which existed for the ideal Graeco-Roman works that interested him. The more abundant archaeological evidence relating to sculpture specifically identifiable as Roman was a secondary concern, given that he envisioned the fully developed Roman tradition as merely a pale afterglow of the Greek one, with no distinctive character of its own.

Although his speculative history of the rise and decline of ancient Greek art was new, his way of working was firmly anchored in a long-standing tradition of antiquarian scholarship in which the study of ancient artifacts was envisioned primarily as an exercise in the iconographical decoding of motifs. The purpose of such study was to identify visual images of the mythological and historical figures and stories, rituals, and material culture of the ancients described or mentioned in ancient literary texts. Winckelmann's last major publication (*Monumenti inediti,* 1767), a catalogue of ancient monuments he had inspected firsthand in collections in Rome that either had not been published before or had been incorrectly interpreted by earlier scholars, took the form, aside from its brief historical introduction, of a conventional iconographical compendium, not that different in conception from Bernard de Montfaucon's *Antiquity Explained in Figures* (1719). There was little attempt to date or to analyze the style of the artifacts being catalogued. The same held true for his treatise on ancient allegory (*Attempt at an Allegory, Particularly for Art*) published in the same year. Indeed, the present-day reader of *The History of the Art of Antiquity* will be struck by the frequent displays of virtuoso decoding of obscure motifs—including the 23 pages of densely detailed text on items of clothing rendered on ancient statuary.

The key role Winckelmann played in shaping the understanding of ancient Greek and Roman art in the years immediately after his death in 1768 derives to a considerable degree from a feature of his writing that was somewhat at odds with the antiquarian tradition in which his scholarship was based, namely his passionate invocations to the aesthetic quality of many of the sculptures he cited. His lyrical ecphrases or descriptions of works considered at the time to be the key masterpieces of ancient art, such as the Laocoön, the Apollo Belvedere, the so-called Antinoüs and the Belvedere Torso in the Vatican, were widely reproduced and quoted and became a staple for many who embarked on an artistic pilgrimage to Italy. Also important were his disquisitions on the distinctive beauty of ancient Greek art, as well as his discussions of the environmental circumstances and conditions of political freedom he saw as accounting for its peculiar excellence. Aesthetic considerations intermingled with antiquarian interests in the attitudes of many who collected or studied ancient art, but Winckelmann stood out as unique for effecting such a compelling synthesis of the aesthetic and the scholarly in the very conception and rhetoric of his *History of the Art of Antiquity.*

This dimension to his work was an important inspiration for later, more far-reaching historical inquiries seeking to differentiate the formation of ancient and modern culture by German writers and intellectuals such as Goethe and Hegel. For them Winckelmann stood as the inventor of a new, more richly invested understanding of the informing spirit of ancient Greek art and culture and of its unique realization of what Nietzsche later called an Apollonian ideal of pure yet sensuous beauty. Hegel's introduction to a collection of lectures on aesthetics that he delivered in the 1820s invokes Winckelmann with praise:

> Winckelmann was inspired by his contemplation of the ideals of the ancients to fashion a new sense for contemplating art, which saved art from perspectives dictated by common aims and mere imitation of nature, and set up a powerful stimulus to discover the [true] idea of art in art works and in the history of art. For Winckelmann is to be seen as one of those men who managed to open up a new organ and a whole new way of looking at things for the human spirit.

Goethe was getting at something similar when, in conversation with Johann Peter Eckermann in 1827, he reminisced about how Winckelmann's writings offered a model for coming to terms with the deeper values embodied in ancient art and sculpture: "One learns nothing when one reads him, but one becomes something."

For some time afterward, Winckelmann continued to function as a cultural icon for writers and scholars preoccupied with things Greek and with the lost values they embodied. Indeed, there was a major Winckelmann revival in the late 19th century: Carl Justi published his magisterial intellectual biography *Winckelmann: His Life, His Works, His Contemporaries* (1866–1872), Walter Pater devoted a whole chapter to him in his influential *Studies in the History of the Renaissance* (1873), and Nietzsche critiqued what he identified as a still pervasive Winckelmannian understanding of ancient Greek art and culture for its exclusively Apollonian bias in his *Birth of Tragedy from the Spirit of Music* (1872). Winckelmann at this point had become a figure who was seen as embodying a Platonic vision of the ancient Greek ideal, not only through the vivid picture he offered of its sculptural creations but also through his own persona and way of life. Pater, like Goethe before him, envisaged Winckelmann as a true ancient somehow reborn in the modem world. In Pater's case, this image of Winckelmann acquired a particular charge because Winckelmann had written so eloquently and openly about the Greek cult of homoerotic beauty. Winckelmann for Pater was a true Platonist.

Winckelmann's reputation as a major intellectual of the late Enlightenment derives not only from his achievements as a scholar whose studies on the art and material remains of the classical Greek and Roman world marked a transition from post-Renaissance antiquarian studies to modern art-historical and archaeological scholarship. It also partly rests on the unusual circumstances of his life. These became a source of fascination for later German intellectuals who saw themselves as escaping the narrow confines of the world in which they had been brought up. Winckelmann hardly conformed to the type of the enlightened gentleman scholar, having started life in a world very different from the one where he eventually made his mark. He was born in the small Prussian town of Stendal in 1717, the son of a cobbler and a weaver's daughter. By the time of his death in 1768 he had become an internationally renowned intellectual as well as a key figure in the artistic life of Rome and recipient of several prestigious honorary titles, including that of *commissario delle antichità della camera apostolica,* or antiquary to the pope. The pattern of his educational career, though, was relatively conventional. Like almost all antiquarian scholars of his time, he came to the study of ancient art by way of classical texts. He was trained at the universities of Halle and Jena in classical Greek and Latin, as well as theology, and his first job was as a classics teacher and private tutor in the town of Seehausen in rural Prussia. His entry into a larger intellectual world came when he was hired in 1747 as a librarian by Graf von Bünau, a prominent figure at the court of Friedrich August II, Elector of Saxony. The contacts Winckelmann made with the German art world in Dresden as part of his experience there of major works of art, made possible by the Saxon court's famous collections of Italian Renaissance and ancient art, set him on a new career as a passionate apologist for the classical Greek ideal.

His first publication, a polemical treatise arguing for the overriding excellence of ancient Greek art and detailing the "causes" of this excellence in the uniquely favorable material and political conditions enjoyed by the ancient Greeks, *Thoughts on the Imitation of the Works of the Greeks in Painting and Sculpture* (1755), was such a success (2nd ed. 1756) that it was almost immediately translated from German into French and English. At the time he was still living in Dresden and had not yet seen firsthand the antique sculptures, such as the Laocoön in the Vatican, that he celebrated as the highest models, which modern artists should imitate more closely. For Winckelmann the ideal that he was championing, of "a noble simplicity and a calm grandeur" embodied in ancient Greek sculpture, was as much imagined as real. He had to reconstitute this ideal from textual sources and from indications provided by engravings and plaster casts. Later on, once he settled in Rome in late 1755, he was still faced with a similar problem: trying to envisage from the Graeco-Roman works he came to know there, such as the Apollo Belvedere, what the pure, early Greek sculpture of the age of Pericles and Alexander the Great, celebrated by writers such as Pliny, actually looked like.

In Rome, supported by the patronage of figures at the papal court such as Cardinal Alberico Archinto, whom he had met in Dresden, and Cardinal Albani, Winckelmann embarked on a comprehensive study of the ancient sculpture in major Roman collections, such as in the Vatican, and soon formulated the plan of his most famous and influential work, *History of the Art of Antiquity.* The first version was delivered to his publisher in Dresden late in 1761, and the book finally came out in 1764. This was a work of a breathtaking ambition that was spelled out in his declaration in the preface: "The history of art should tell us about its origin, growth, change and fall, as well as the various styles of different peoples, periods and artists, and demonstrate this as far as possible with reference to the remaining works of antiquity." Earlier antiquarians had obviously examined the look of the material remains they were studying, trying to decode motifs, establish a work's authenticity, and even make rough distinctions between work that appeared Greek, or Roman, or Etruscan, or Egyptian. Winckelmann went a stage further. Following in the footsteps of a prominent figure in the French art world, Anne-Claude-Philippe de Tubières, comte de Caylus, author of the multivolume *Collection of Egyptian, Etruscan, Greek and Roman Antiquities* (1752–1767), he was the first to bring stylistic discriminations of the kind practiced by connoisseurs and collectors of modem art to bear in a concerted way on the scholarly study of antiquities. Like Caylus, whose output was much more fragmentary and less systematic, Winckelmann was unusual in having close connections with the contemporary art world. His first project when he arrived in Rome, a treatise on the taste of the ancient Greek artists based on descriptions of the famous classicizing sculptures in Rome then assumed to be the purest embodiments of the principles of the best Greek art, was undertaken in collaboration with the German painter Anton Raphael Mengs—a figure who later became the first to propagate the view that all the masterpieces of classical sculpture in Rome, even the very best, were most probably copies of earlier Greek originals.

Despite Winckelmann's insistence on being the first properly to base his account of ancient art on close firsthand examination of actual works, his reconstruction of the history of the ancient Greek artistic ideal was still very much based on textual evidence. Anything he knew about the work of the major artists of the Greek tradition, such as the sculptors Phidias, Polyclitus, Praxiteles, and Lysippus, came from mentions in the ancient literature, and his attempts to identify existing sculptures on stylistic grounds that might have originated from the classical phase of ancient Greek sculpture were extremely hypothetical. In a way this problematic has persisted in subsequent studies of classical Greek sculpture. Even after quantities of early Greek sculpture were excavated in Greece and Asia Minor, almost all the most famous works singled out by ancient Greek and Roman writers, particularly the bronze sculptures and the large chryselephantine cult statues, remain lost, and their appearance has had to be inferred on the basis of analysis of textual evidence and putative copies. This situation makes it less puzzling than it might seem at first that the periodization of the history of ancient Greek art that Winckelmann established has persisted so long: a pattern of rise and decline beginning with an archaic phase, followed by a high early classical phase associated with artists such as Phidias and Polyclitus, then a later, more sensual classical phase identified with Praxiteles and Lysippus, and finally a Hellenistic phase that many still see as in some sense a falling off from the classical moment, ending in the Roman appropriation of the Greek tradition.

The afterlife of Winckelmann's account of ancient Greek art also owes something to the complex publishing history of his *History of the Art of Antiquity.* He envisioned this work both as a bold new speculative venture and as a handbook collating all the significant existing evidence, verbal and visual, relating to the arts of antiquity. To keep it up to date, he published a supplement in 1767 and was working on a new edition in 1768 when he met his death on his way back from Vienna to Rome, murdered by a Venetian pimp while he was waiting for a ferry in Trieste. This sudden death, the circumstances of which have played a significant role in the modern mythologizing of Winckelmann, set the stage for the unusual posthumous history of his text. The manuscript on which he had been working was published in Vienna in 1776 and formed the basis for countless new scholarly editions that continued to come out in French, Italian, and German well into the 19th century. Through their ever-expanding apparatus of notes and commentaries, these editions updated Winckelmann's text and enabled it to maintain its status as the standard handbook for several decades.

As late as 1849 Henry Lodge began publication of an English translation, still envisaged as a handbook on classical Greek and Roman art. The last volume came out in 1872, the year that Nietzsche launched his famous diatribe against a Winckelmannian view of the art and culture of Greek antiquity. These circumstances illustrate the continuing importance of Winckelmann's vision of a Greek ideal, both for those who saw in it the embodiment of a simple beauty and sensuous self-fulfillment lost to the modern world, and for those reacting against it who began to be fascinated, as Freud later was, by the irrational forces in ancient Greek culture, which were more evident in its literature than its art. If one returns to Winckelmann's writing, however, it is clear that this duality tends to obscure the complex undercurrents animating his own vision of ancient Greek art. It was not for nothing that he made the Laocoön one of his key exemplars, and his vivid evocation of the central figure's spasms of bodily pain, resisting and succumbing to the bite of the writhing snake, hardly makes for a vision of simple, calm plenitude. There is some logic to Sacher-Masoch's evocation of Winckelmann's hymn to the seductive and violent beauty of the Apollo Belvedere in a description of the man about to humiliate the masochistic "hero" of his novel *Venus in Furs* (1870).

BIBL.: A. H. Borbein, "Winckelmann und die Klassische Archäologie," in *Johann Joachim Winckelmann, 1717–1768,* ed. T. W. Gaehtgens (Hamburg 1986) 289–299. Whitney Davis, "Winckelmann's 'Homosexual' Teleologies," in *Sexuality in Ancient Art,* ed. N. B. Kampen (Cambridge 1996) 262–276. A. A. Donohue, "Winckelmann's History of Art and Polyclitus," in *Polykleitos, the Doryphorus, and Tradition,* ed. W. G. Moon (Madison 1995) 327–353. Pascal Griener, *Winckelmann, les langues et l'histoire de l'art (1755–1784)* (Geneva 1998). A. D. Potts, *Flesh and the Ideal: Winckelmann and the Origins of Art History* (New Haven 1994). J. J. Winckelmann, *History of the Art of Antiquity,* trans. H. F. Mallgrave from the 1764 German ed. (Los Angeles 2006). A.PT.

Wolf, Friedrich August

German philologist (1759–1824); the most eloquent prophet of the new method that transformed classical studies ca. 1800. "Our whole question," he wrote in the preface to his edition of Homer, "is historical and critical: it has to do not with what we would prefer but with what actually happened" (1804, xxvi). With these crisp words he confirmed the thesis he had advanced in his most provocative and successful work, *Prolegomena ad Homerum* (1795): that the *Iliad* and the *Odyssey* were not the work of a single, peerless poet but rather were assemblies of ancient songs that had been put into their definitive shape, centuries after their creation, by the critics of Hellenistic Alexandria. More generally, he offered an iconoclastic vision of the nature of classical studies, which he defined as a purely historical science. And yet he had the title page of his edition adorned with a Neoclassical bust of Homer—just as he had insisted, in his *Prolegomena,* that the *Iliad* and *Odyssey* still glowed with all the peerless beauty that Neoclassical criticism had ascribed to them. Much of the power and fascination of his work lay in his ability to hold historical and Neoclassical views of antiquity in productive tension.

Wolf studied at Göttingen, where he registered, as a number of others had before him, as a student of philology, not theology, even though the great Christian Gottlob Heyne told him he would never find employment. Though Wolf found Heyne's famous lectures unenlightening, he profited from the matchless Göttingen library, and within a few years he began to publish modest editions of texts. After teaching at Ilfeld, in 1783 he became a professor at the Pietist University of Halle, where he soon established his own reputation as a great teacher. In his lectures on methodology he reconfigured Heyne's broad-gauged approach to antiquity in his own more explicit and dramatic terms. He urged his students to master every discipline from philology and hermeneutics to geography and metrology, and then to fuse them in a single interdisciplinary "science of antiquity." By doing so, he promised, they would see the ancient Greeks in three dimensions and in color. Wolf applied these precepts in his own celebrated courses on classical texts, which attracted the great and the good as well as his enrolled students (even Goethe hid behind a curtain to hear him teach). His seminar, which he designed for those who wanted to become classical scholars, emphasized original research rather than teacher preparation. It became a nursery of great philologists, notably Immanuel Bekker and August Böckh.

Wolf published a wide range of minor works, most notably an edition of Demosthenes' oration *Against Leptines* (*Adversus Leptinem,* 1789) in which he followed the French antiquarian tradition and took a historical approach to the Athenian institutions mentioned in the text. But his real loves, in the Neoclassical spirit of his time, were Plato and Homer. Heyne too was fascinated by Homer and had drawn on earlier 18th-century writers—especially Thomas Blackwell and Robert Wood—to argue that the *Iliad* and *Odyssey* showed clear signs of having been written in a primitive age. Wolf also did much to illuminate the erudite, scholarly culture of the Hellenistic world, in which Alexandrian and Pergamene scholars had concerned themselves with the correction and explication of the Homeric epics. Though he loathed theology, at Göttingen he was exposed to the most advanced Old Testament scholarship of his day, as perfected by Michaelis and Eichhorn, who traced the history of the biblical text and argued that later Jewish grammarians had edited and altered its original, primitive contents. As a professor at Halle he spent much time with his theological colleague Johann Salomo Semler, who also specialized in hermeneutics and the history of texts and insisted on a historical approach to understanding Scripture.

Accordingly, Wolf was ready to spring in 1788, when d'Ansse de Villoison's edition of the Venice scholia on Homer provided him with a rich Greek counterpart to the critical apparatus that Jewish grammarians, or Masoretes, had assembled around the Old Testament text in the second half of the first millennium. He analyzed in minute detail the critical remarks and comments by ancient Homeric scholars that had been preserved in the margins of Codex Venetus A and printed by Villoison. He set out to build a new edition of Homer from this material, and in 1795 the first volume of his *Prolegomena* stated his views in a clipped, elegant Latin prose that excited readers across Europe. Homer, he argued, must have been an oral poet, illiterate. Despite his powers of memory, moreover, he could not have produced works on the scale of the *Iliad* and the *Odyssey.* Later Greeks added to and compiled the early texts after they were written down. Still later, Wolf showed, Aristarchus and Zenodotus redacted these and, in the process, gave them the appearance of large-scale coherence and order that they still undeniably possessed—just as the Masoretes had edited, and imposed a new coherence on, the varied texts that went into the Five Books of Moses and the rest of the Hebrew Bible. In his radical account, the *Iliad* and *Odyssey* had come into being over an almost geological timescale, thanks to the industry of generations rather than the inspiration of an individual poet. Like biblical scholarship, Homeric scholarship now had as its central task the creation of a history of a text—one whose original form proved endlessly elusive.

Over the next few decades Wolf's dangerous idea provoked many refutations and as many panegyrics. Heyne infuriated Wolf by claiming that he had advanced similar arguments in his courses. In truth, Wolf did not treat the Homeric text itself more radically than Vico and d'Aubignac had, decades before. But he went about his work with a philological precision they had not attained. He thus both challenged the entire notion of the classical and offered powerful new models for research on Homer and on the formation and transmission of classical texts. The Homeric Question, which occupied so many 19th-century scholars, stemmed largely from his work. So, more generally, did the new, more historical approach to editing texts that he had called for (though he did not practice it himself) and that established itself over the next half century in the practice of Lachmann and others.

Wolf's later career did not unfold as smoothly as his early years at Halle, which he left when the university closed in 1806–1807. He never completed the second volume of the *Prolegomena,* and though he joined the new University of Berlin at its founding in 1810, his most successful pupil there was not a classicist but instead the future Judaist Leopold Zunz. In 1807, however, Wolf published a manifesto of the new historical approach, his *Darstellung der Altertumswissenschaft* (*Representation of the Study of Antiquity*). By approaching the Greeks from all points of the scholarly compass, Wolf argued, in terms partly borrowed from his younger friend Wilhelm von Humboldt, scholars and students would encounter "human nature in antiquity, knowledge of which comes from the observation of an organically developed, significant national culture, founded on study of the ancient remains" (1869, 2:883). Here he combined, in an unstable but influential way, a call for a new, interdisciplinary and historical approach to the classics and a statement of Neoclassical ideals that transcended history—and that seemingly left little space for comparison of Greeks with Jews, or of Homer's fate with that of the Bible. Wolf's radical historicism and passionate Neo-Hellenism would both inspire students of the classics—including many of the Americans who came to study the field in German universities—long after Wolf himself died in 1824, isolated and embittered, in Marseilles, on his way to see Greece at last.

BIBL.: Salvatore Cerasuolo, ed., *Friedrich August Wolf e la scienza dell'antichita: Atti del Convegno internazionale (Napoli, 24–26 maggio 1995)* (Naples 1997). William Clark, *Aca-*

demic Charisma and the Origins of the Research University (Chicago 2006). Manfred Fuhrmann, "Friedrich August Wolf," *Deutsche Vierteljahrsschrift für Literaturwissenschaft und Geistesgeschichte* 33 (1959) 187–236. Anthony Grafton, *Defenders of the Text* (Cambridge, Mass., 1991) 214–243. Reinhard Markner and Giuseppe Veltri, eds., *Friedrich August Wolf: Studien, Dokumente, Bibliographie* (Stuttgart 1999). Friedrich August Wolf, *Darstellung der Altertumswissenschaft*, in *Kleine Schriften*, ed. G. Bernhardy, 2 vols. (Halle 1869); *Esposizione della scienza dell'antichita*, ed. Salvatore Cerasuolo (Naples 1999); and *Prolegomena to Homer*, trans. A. T. Grafton, G. W. Most, and J. E. G. Zetzel (Princeton 1985). A.G.

Wonders

Unusual phenomena that evoke wonder, an emotion related to surprise, pleasure, and awe. Although wonders appear in the works of earlier Greek writers, including Homer, Hesiod, and Herodotus, the first known treatises devoted explicitly to this topic date from the 3rd century BCE. Modern scholars refer to this genre as *paradoxography*, because the authors of such works usually referred to their subject matter as *thaumasia, thaumata* ("wonders"), or *paradoxa* ("contrary to expectation or opinion"). Almost all the wonders retailed by Greek paradoxographers belonged to the natural world: animals (including humans), plants, and minerals with unexpected properties, as well as unusual topographical and meteorological phenomena. For example, we know from Apollonius (ca. 2nd cent. BCE) that there is a spring in the Arabian Gulf whose water, when rubbed on the feet, gives any man an erection, and that the lodestone attracts iron during the day but not at night; Antigonus of Carystus (3rd cent. CE) informs us that no bird can fly over the temple of Achilles on the island of Leuke, and that the bat is the only bird endowed with teeth and breasts. Although authors sometimes gave textual sources for their information, they almost never attempted to explain it or to say whether it was true. Judging by their numbers, these works enjoyed great popularity; embracing a host of counterintuitive phenomena, they showed their readers that the world was not fully known or catalogued, mixing instruction with the pleasure of surprise.

The enduring appeal of Greek paradoxography is confirmed by the stability and longevity of the tradition. It flourished in the Byzantine and Islamic worlds, inspiring works such as the *ʿAjāʾib al-makhlūqāt* (*Wonders of Created Things*) of the 13th-century Persian physician Zakariyaʾ ibn Muhammad al-Qazwini. It also had great influence in the medieval West, mediated through the Latin encyclopedias of Pliny the Elder (1st cent. CE), Solinus (4th cent.), and Isidore of Seville (d. 636). Like Greek writers before them, medieval authors integrated wonders into their histories, travel narratives, and fictions, where they were usually placed in distant lands. Although Giraldus Cambrensis (Gerald of Wales) described Ireland as an island of wonders in his *Topography of Ireland* (*Topographia Hiberniae*, ca. 1187), wonders were associated predominantly with the East—northern Africa, Ethiopia, and especially Asia—as in vernacular romances set in Troy or Carthage and travel narratives such as Marco Polo's *Division of the World* (*Devisament du monde*, 1299).

Eastern wonders also graced the portals of the late 13th-century world map that hung in Hereford Cathedral, where the sections devoted to Asia and Africa show springs with marvelous properties, unicorns, mandrakes, and a variety of monstrous human races, including Androgynes and the headless Blemmyes. The presence of wonders in medieval churches testifies to their importance within the Christian tradition, where they were used (as by Qazwini) to demonstrate the fertility and variety of God's creative power. In this context they often shaded into the miracles performed by saints—the Latin words *mirabile* and *miraculum* could be used interchangeably—or were read as signs of moral lessons that God had built into the structure of the world. Thus, according to one anonymous 14th-century writer, the poisonous herb sardonia, which causes its victims to die laughing, "shows that the pleasures of this world bring death."

The Western fascination with the wonders of paradoxography reached its peak in the early modern period. Over the course of the 15th and 16th centuries the voyages of exploration flooded Europe with new marvels—pineapples, armadillos, "Indians" with unfamiliar customs, if disappointingly familiar physiques—while increasing attention to Greek and Roman writers confirmed the pedigree of old ones. During the same period the religious struggles of the Reformation led to a new focus on reading prodigies, such as monsters and celestial apparitions, as signs of God's will. This interest in marvels went beyond the textual: princes, merchants, and scholars created extensive collections, sometimes referred to as *Wunderkammern* ("cabinets of wonders"), that mixed natural marvels—including human specimens—with antiquities and works of human art.

In part because of the increasing tangibility of wonders, there arose a new commitment on the part of 16th- and 17th-century writers and scholars to sort out true wonders from false ones and to find natural causes to account for them. This impulse was not entirely new; in the 13th century the Holy Roman Emperor Frederick II had sent messengers to look for geese hatched from barnacles and to test the powers of petrifying springs, and the Dominican philosopher Albertus Magnus explained some marvels, including fossils and monstrous births, as due to celestial influences. But early modern Europeans collected, dissected, and tested wonders as never before. The Danish medical professor Olaus Worm, for example, determined that lemmings had standard mammalian reproductive organs, which meant that they were not generated by falling from the sky. Many of the most progressive thinkers of the Scientific Revolution, most notably Francis Bacon, came to see the study of wonders as a key element in the reform of natural philosophy, precisely because their peculiarity challenged old certainties and demanded new explanatory principles. For these reasons, wonders began to colonize a new genre of literature: the reports of scientific societies such as the Royal Academy of London and the Académie Royale des Sciences of Paris.

In the end these hopes were largely unfulfilled. By the middle of the 18th century the wonders of ancient paradoxography were no longer a major focus of scientific inquiry (except perhaps to debunk them), and the rhetoric of wonder that had surrounded them for two millennia had disappeared in favor of a sensibility that privileged natural uniformity and regularity. Deprived of its unifying principles, the traditional canon of wonders split apart over the course of the 19th and 20th centuries: physicists studied magnetism, astronomers monitored comets, palaeontologists scrutinized fossils, and teratologists investigated monsters. The wonder that had originally accrued to the old *paradoxa* now enhanced new and completely different types of phenomena that became, at least temporarily, objects of serious scientific inquiry: spiritualism, extrasensory perception, UFOs, the Kirlian effect. But the old paradoxographical wonders have by no means faded from view. Many still grace institutional and commercial collections, such as the Mutter Museum of the College of Physicians of Philadelphia and Ripley's *Believe It or Not!* as well as the pages (paper or electronic) of the *Guinness Book of Records* and the *Weekly World News*. In many respects these 21st-century manifestations of the paradoxographical tradition are more faithful to its classical roots than were the attempts of medieval theologians and early modern natural philosophers to find higher meanings in phenomena that were originally prized almost entirely for their power to delight and amaze.

BIBL.: L. Daston and K. Park, *Wonders and the Order of Nature* (New York 1998). Phlegon of Tralles, *Phlegon of Tralles' Book of Marvels,* trans. W. Hansen (Exeter 1996). R. Wittkower, "Marvels of the East: A Study in the History of Monsters," *Journal of the Warburg and Courtauld Institutes* 5 (1942) 159–197. K. Ziegler, "Paradoxographoi," in Pauly-Wissowa, *Realencyclopädie der classischen Altertumswissenschaft (RE)* 49 vols. in 58 (Stuttgart 1894–1980) 18:1137–1166.

K.P.

Writing

Although the invention and history of writing intrigued ancient thinkers and continued to fascinate the inheritors of the classical tradition, modern conceptions of this history, based on archaeology, scientific epigraphy, and historical linguistics, did not exist until about 1800. Instead of a fact-based history of writing, earlier scholars possessed a mythology, a body of traditional narratives about individual "inventors" and transmitters of writing, and about books attributed to them. These myths concerning writing were transmitted largely through writing itself. This closed circuit persisted into the 17th century in part because of the lack of a felt need—almost an inability to imagine a need—for nonwritten evidence about humanity, history, and the world.

Like other branches of mythology, myths relating to writing gradually became the subject of mythography, a metadiscourse or second-order discipline that brought them under increasingly critical scrutiny. Yet until about 1600, the mythography of writing lagged behind the critical study of other myths. This was partly because myths of writing seemed to require no ideological apologies or excuses: they entailed no obvious conflict with the monotheistic religious traditions of the observant Jews, Christians, and Muslims who dominated the study of the classics between the age of Constantine and the time of Nietzsche. Other forms of myth regularly told of bodily metamorphoses and of humans' encounters with gods and demigods: such tales required allegorical or euhemeristic (historicizing) interpretation to make them theologically acceptable. But there was no a priori connection between writing and polytheism: Cadmus the Phoenician, legendary founder of the Greek city of Thebes, for instance, might well have invented the Greek alphabet even if some of the personages he interacted with were not truly gods. Indeed, even when the invention or transmission of writing was attributed to pagan deities or founders of non-Abrahamic religions, mythographers tended to domesticate such figures, envisioning them as forerunners or alternative identities of patriarchal figures. Thus, Hermes Trismegistus had perhaps inherited or duplicated revelations made to Moses and the biblical patriarchs; Zoroaster was perhaps another name for Noah's son Ham.

Even in the Middle Ages, however, dissonant stories were known. Thanks to an early Latin translation of Plato's *Timaeus* (Calcidius, 4th cent. CE), many medieval authors in Western Europe knew of the Egyptians' sarcastic dismissal of Greek and Roman pretensions to cultural antiquity: "Ah, Solon, Solon, you Greeks are ever children. There isn't an old man among you" (*Timaeus* 22B). This was in reference to Solon of Athens' journey to the holy city of Sais, on the Nile Delta, sometime in the 6th century BCE, during which he was shown written archives said to date from 9,000 years before his own time. It was explained that the priestly archivists of Sais maintained such records because other cultural centers in the world were prone to floods and fires that destroyed their written history; as a result, those cultures remained constantly in a state of childhood or adolescence. Thus, says the Latin translation, human societies are constantly beginning over, and "new" peoples continually require a new written memory (*memoria litterarum*). Like Aeschylus in Greek antiquity (*Prometheus,* 460–461), the Latin translator speaks of writing as *containing* memory.

In the early modern period several factors encouraged scholars to begin thinking relativistically about traditional myths of writing. Increasing literacy in Greek after 1400 led Western European scholars indirectly to the study of ancient Near Eastern cultures and religions, whose mythologies regarding writing were strikingly different from those of ancient Greece, Rome, and Judea. Ancient Greek writers like Herodotus, Plato, and Diodorus Siculus, and

Byzantine scholars such as "Suidas" (the Suda) and Georgius Syncellus, who were unknown or largely unread in the Latin Middle Ages and were not translated into Latin or edited until sometime between 1450 and the mid-17th century, gave an unexpectedly more complex account of ancient Egyptian and Babylonian religions and their attendant myths of writing. The newly accessible accounts included the Chaldean Creation story told by Berossus (3rd cent. BCE), in which writing was described as a gift of the gods to humanity, taught by a creature (half man and half fish) named Oannes, who emerged from the ocean; at a later point in the story, writing preserved the arts and sciences during a great flood.

Increasing travel and exploration from the 14th century onward, including ventures by Christian missionaries, exposed Europeans to living cultures in Asia and the Americas that were alien and shocking not only in their theologies and their visual arts but also, in some cases, in their practices of and tales about writing and books. Some traditions, both ancient and modern, described the world as much older than the 5,000 or 6,000 years posited by Jews, Christians, and Muslims; these fantastic-sounding chronologies often set the invention of writing at dates unimaginably early to Christians who went by the chronology of the Old Testament. The discovery and exploration of archaeological sites, the development of methods for dating artifacts independently of writing, and techniques for classifying and deciphering monumental inscriptions, all of which accelerated after 1600, gradually weakened or invalidated the authority of writing mythologies based on Graeco-Roman and Judaic literature.

Berossus' story about the origin of writing was unknown to the Latin Middle Ages, but his name, and a few scraps of his texts, was familiar from a medieval Latin translation (late 6th cent.) of Flavius Josephus' *Jewish Antiquities* (Greek, ca. 100 CE). Josephus' paraphrase of the Hebrew Bible added numerous details to the biblical account of early human history, including a tale about the origins of writing much like the accounts of Plato and Berossus. In this story the sons of Adam's third son, Seth, hearing from Adam that the world would be destroyed once by flood and again by fire, inscribed their astronomical discoveries on two columns or stelae, one of stone and the other of brick, to memorialize both their astronomy and their creation of the columns. Practically every European author who discussed the history of writing, from Isidore of Seville in the 7th century to Giambattista Vico in the 18th, cited this story to credit or refute its implications (Stephens 2005).

Equally stimulating, though in different ways, were other tales about writing that derived from Graeco-Roman antiquity itself, such as Homer's reference (*Iliad* 6.156–190) to a "folding tablet" inscribed with "murderous symbols . . . enough to destroy life" that Bellerophon was instructed to carry to King Iobates: its "wicked symbols" contained an order that the bearer of the tablets be killed—a sentence that the hero managed to evade; the passage suggests that writing might have magical powers. In Plato's *Phaedrus* Socrates explains that an Egyptian god, Theuth, had invented writing as an improvement on memory, "a recipe for memory and wisdom." Thamus, king of Thebes (in Egypt, not Cadmus's Thebes in Greece), to whom Theuth praised his innovation, rebuked him, deprecating writing as a recipe "not for memory, but for reminder," which would destroy memory—and which, unlike speech, could not adapt itself to new audiences or new needs: indeed, writing depends on speech "to defend or help itself" if it is "ill-treated and unfairly abused" (274C–276A). This view of writing, which seems to oppose the view Plato offered in the *Timaeus,* nonetheless makes room for writing as a "refreshment" of memory against "oblivious old age," both for the writer and for those who come after him (276D). Of course, Socrates' hostility to writing, and Plato's possible ambivalence to it, can be known only through the latter's written representations of living dialogue, an irony that was probably not unintended.

A wider range of historical traditions concerning the origin and invention of writing was available to Western Europeans in Pliny the Elder's *Natural History* (Latin, 1st cent. CE). Pliny asserted (on the assumption that the world and humanity were eternal) that the Assyrians had "always" had writing. But he also noted (as would Aulus Gellius and other later Roman authors) that writing was invented in Egypt by Mercury (or Hermes), whereas still others believed it was discovered in Syria. Both schools of thought agreed, however, that Cadmus had adapted the Phoenician alphabet to create a Greek system of 16 letters, to which others were added by later inventors. Pliny also quoted Greek authors who asserted that the Egyptians had letters 15,000 years before the Greeks; the Babylonians—among them Berossus—claimed to have either 730,000 or 490,000 years of astronomical observations recorded on baked bricks. The Pelasgians (pre-Hellenistic Greeks) were said to have brought the alphabet to Latium on the west coast of the Italian Peninsula, where Rome was eventually founded. Thus, Pliny concluded, the use of writing was *aeternum*—very ancient or even eternal (7.56.192–193).

Elsewhere in his *Natural History* Pliny surveyed writing materials in conjunction with a catalogue of plants. Discussing the papyrus reed, he observed that "our civilization or at all events our records" depended on this abundant resource. He then quoted Marcus Varro's chronology of writing materials: palm leaves were used in earliest times, then the inner bark of trees (*libri arborum,* from which books, *libri,* had taken their name), then sheets of lead and linen; during an embargo on papyrus imports from Egypt (3rd cent. BCE), parchment (Greek *pergamēnē,* Latin *pergamina*) had been invented at Pergamon (in what is now Turkey), whose library came to rival that of Egyptian Alexandria. *Chartae* (sheets of papyrus or parchment), Pliny concluded, are "the thing on which the immortality of men depends" (13.21.68–70). (As if in an echo of this sentiment, Melchior Guilandinus, who ca. 1562 became director of the botanical garden in Padua, drew on Pliny's material when he compiled the first systematic modern treatise on papyrus in antiquity, published in 1572.) However impressive these ancient writing materials were, though, they remained vulnerable, as Aulus Gellius had pointed out in the 2nd century. The public library in ancient Athens, established by Pisistratus and enlarged by later efforts, had been stolen by Xerxes (ca. 480 BCE) and was returned much later by Seleucus I (d. 281 BCE). And the vast library assembled by the Ptolemies (r. 305–30) was destroyed by fire "in our first war with Alexandria [48 BCE, under Julius Caesar], not intentionally or by anyone's order, but accidentally by the auxiliary soldiers" (7.17)—one of many hyperbolic testimonies to the size and fragility of the greatest ancient collection of books.

Since the time of Petrarch (1304–1374), the Middle Ages have been stereotyped as an epoch of massive textual losses, when the classical heritage was neglected in favor of saints' lives and compendia. Yet few medieval writers accepted the ancient legends' presupposition that writing was a fragile medium for preserving personal and cultural immortality, especially when not engraved on monuments of stone, brick, or metal. Between Isidore of Seville (d. 636) and Vincent of Beauvais (d. 1264), Josephus' tale about the columns erected by Adam's grandsons was the dominant literary legend, endlessly repeated and embellished to emphasize the durability, rather than the fragility, of written memory. But the paradox is more apparent than real; as Jean Seznec and modern scholars have observed, until Petrarch, most medieval Latin writers saw their own efforts as a continuation of ancient cultures, rather than as a revival after degeneration or hiatus.

This perspective changed rapidly over the 14th and 15th centuries. As Europeans' interest in recovering and preserving ancient texts became more urgent, scholars expressed increasing pessimism about preserving the classical textual heritage. The English writer Richard de Bury composed a treatise on the love of books (*Philobiblon,* 1345) that included a lament for the destruction of these antidotes to oblivion. Rather than focusing on the divinely sent or natural floods and fires that had menaced writing in the ancient and earlier medieval mythologies, he concentrated on human neglect and destruction. Though he tried to describe the wartime biblioclasms of ancient Troy and Carthage, he dwelt most extensively on the destruction of the Library of Alexandria, accepting Gellius's figure, stated some 200 years after the conflagration, of 700,000 incinerated volumes or book rolls. Among the books irrevocably lost, de Bury imagined not only the archives of Plato's Egyptian priests, but also works by Adam, Enoch, Noah, Moses, Solomon, Asclepius, Cadmus, Jason, "and infinite other secrets of science."

This new awareness of cultural loss, still mythic and based in large degree on Christian veneration of the Bible as Scripture or Holy Writ (both terms notably refer to writing), was progressively historicized over the next several generations. Petrarch, who had met de Bury at the papal court of Avignon in 1333, was keenly interested in works of Cicero, Quintilian, and other ancient Romans and regretted his inability to read Homer in Greek. His recovery in 1345 of several ancient texts, particularly Cicero's letters to Atticus, though personally satisfying, could not dispel his depression over the apparent total loss of other writings. Like de Bury, Petrarch blamed humanity for the loss of written memory; more systematic than the Englishman, he sifted surviving documents for references to specific textual losses. Like its architecture, which Petrarch also mourned, Rome's literary monuments lay in ruins. His pessimism had limits, however: he himself wrote an *Epistle to Posterity* describing his life and works for future ages.

Both writers excluded ancient texts of the Judeo-Christian Bible from their catalogues of loss. Presumably this derived from their acceptance of the doctrine that the original recording of the Scriptures had been overseen by divine Providence, dictated by the Holy Spirit, and canonized, translated into Latin, and scribally transmitted under the same divine auspices. All other writings, lacking such protection, were subject to catastrophic loss; although some books of the Bible were attributed to Solomon, de Bury decried the loss of the great Hebrew king's nonbiblical writings, some of them nevertheless divinely inspired, and of lost books attributed to other biblical personages.

Petrarch's widely disseminated notion that Europe was living through an age of cultural decline and decadence galvanized scholars' awareness that great losses had occurred and were doubtless still happening through neglect. Petrarch's contemporary Boccaccio (d. 1375) lamented that "books dealing with our subject have fallen into disuse, and straightway quickly perished," victims of "the silent and adamantine tooth of fleeting time, which slowly eats away not books alone, but hardest rocks, and even steel." Classical literature was like a human body "torn limb from limb and scattered among the rough and desert places of antiquity"; only a godlike scholar, a literary Prometheus or Asclepius, could "bring to light and life again minds long since removed in death." Although Petrarch and Boccaccio made some monumental discoveries, Humanists of the next few generations recovered ever larger numbers of texts. The history of these recoveries, and of scientific progress in philology, textual criticism, and historical and comparative linguistics, is given elsewhere in this volume but all these developments influenced European scholars' thinking about the nature, origin, and progress of writing.

After 1500, discussions of writing found their place in three venues: general histories of human achievement; introductory or ancillary discussions in histories of language, literature, and philosophy; and, increasingly, in specialized treatises on the history of writing, including exposés of forgery and falsification. In the first group the most conspicuous presence is Polydore Vergil's *On Discovery* (*De inventoribus rerum*), first published in 1499 and thereafter reissued more than 100 times in eight languages. Book 1, chapter 6, was concerned with the inventors of writing: "Since only the use of letters makes memory endure and protects things worthy of memory from all damage of forgetfulness . . . we should treat letters before anything else" (77). Only divinity, the elements or "first principles," and the human institutions of language, marriage, and religion were more fundamental to human existence. Believing that alphabetic writing, which "confined the seemingly infinite sounds of the voice in a few written signs" was the work of a single genius, Polydore rehearsed much of the lore discussed above, including the stories of antediluvian literature. Similar treatises were produced by later writers such as Celio Calcagnini, Ravisius Textor, and Caelius Rhodiginus, who searched classical and biblical literature for notable human achievements.

In his book *On the Honorable Profession (De honesta disciplina,* 1504), a compendium of philological information, Pietro Riccio (Petrus Crinitus) recorded some old verses that he claimed to have found in an ancient book—and which commentators on the history of writing were still quoting without irony in the 18th century:

> Moses first wrote Hebrew letters.
> The wise-minded Phoenicians founded the Greek ones.
> The Latin ones we write were invented by Nicostrata [Carmentis].
> Abraham discovered both the Syrian and Chaldaean ones.
> Isis with no less art brought forth the Egyptian ones.
> Ulfila produced the ones of the Goths, which we see are the latest.

"The inventors of writing" was an endlessly stimulating topos for early modern scholars. When Pope Sixtus V (r. 1585–1590) enlarged the premises of the Vatican Library, he commissioned a number of frescoes on the history of books and writing, including a series of perhaps 24 full-length portraits of the inventors of writing. The program for the Salone Sistino, designed by Angelo Rocca, included Adam, the sons of Seth, Abraham, Moses, Isis, Hermes Trismegistus, Cadmus, and Carmentis, the mother of Evander. Each was accompanied by a caption (e.g., "Adam, divinely taught, the inventor of sciences and letters") and the complete alphabet or individual letters that he or she supposedly invented. Rocca published a large book to celebrate the library, the frescoes, and the history of writing (*Bibliotheca Apostolica Vaticana,* Rome 1591).

The fascination of erasure (the irretrievable loss of texts known to have once existed) was still a major theme among writers of the 16th century, despite their success in recalling many manuscripts from the grave. Publishing a Greek grammar for the use of Lutheran youth in 1565, Michael Neander (Neumann) prefaced it with a 340-page canon of the best books from antiquity to his own time in every field. He began his preface with a remarkable threnody for erasures throughout history: "My dear young people, innumerable thousands of excellent books, in every kind of science, studies, and discipline, have died a sad and miserable death through the injury and iniquity of time, the long passage of years, age which consumes all, the turmoil and malignity of wars, the devastation of lands by floods, the unexpected accidents of fire, and sometimes through shameful, detestable hatred and envy (which has moved the dull and stupid burners of books even in our own time), or being eaten by roaches, worms, and other plagues of literature." The roll call of the disappeared commences with the declaration that "nowhere today can be found the innumerable treasures of histories and other books written before Noah's Flood."

Histories and surveys of alphabets and writing began in the early 16th century, but the most influential treatise was published by an early 17th-century Jesuit, Hermann Hugo. His *First Origin of Writing and Antiquity of Literary Endeavor* (*De prima scribendi origine et universa rei literariae antiquitate,* Antwerp 1617) was inspired, he wrote, when he noticed that the history of writing was frequently mentioned but hitherto had been examined unsystematically and in parentheses, as it were. Careful to defend his "few little pages" as "not only about letters" and as "a treatise not of Grammar, but of Philology," Hugo stipulated that the work examined "everything relative to the antiquity of the whole literary endeavor." Noting that not only the ancient Hebrews but also modern Brazilian "savages" were in awe of writing, Hugo exclaimed:

> And if we ourselves consider the wondrous power of writing, I doubt we can easily find anything worthy of greater wonderment in all of creation. What then is more wondrous, than the fact that so few letters, which all together number twenty-three [the classical Latin alphabet, conflating *i* and *j,* also *u* and *v,* omitting *w*], can compose so many various words in so many languages? Indeed, there are practically infinite numbers of words as yet unthought-of and unheard, which anyone can make up for himself. That fact makes this whole matter practically unbelievable, unless we perceive it with our own eyes, that so many words have been made—and made up!—only from the interspersing of vowels and consonants. And if words composed only of consonants could be pronounced as easily as they can be written, good God! what a great and incredible power of new words could be observed!

Throughout the 17th and 18th centuries, as philology expanded its historical and geographic reach, histories of literature and philosophy incorporated histories of writing and books. Study of the classics and study of the Bible were far more closely linked than is the case today, and both disciplines relied heavily on refining literary history, which depended to a considerable degree on continual reexamination of the authors and lore of ancient traditions and their later elaborators. The scientific archaeological study of Egyptian, Assyrian, and Chinese antiquity was still in the future, but the attempt to write the history of writing did more than simply mark time. Joseph Justus Scaliger's attempt to reconstitute the lost Greek text of Eusebius's chronicle of universal history from scattered quotations of it in Byzantine authors led to a much fuller knowledge of Berossus' and Manetho's Chaldaean and Egyptian histories, and of the Book of Enoch, an apocryphal book of the Hebrew Bible that had been all but erased in Western Christendom owing to its heretical notions of human and angelic history and sin (Grafton 1990, 99–103, 118–123). Antiquaries copied, published, and tried to decipher the hieroglyphs that appeared on Egyptian monuments, such as some of the obelisks that Sixtus V and his successors excavated, repaired, and erected in Rome's most public places. Daniel Morhof's massive *Polyhistor litterarius* (4th ed., 1747) attempted a complete survey of everything relating to the nature and history of *litera-tura*—in our terms, both writing and literature in its broadest sense. Johann Albert Fabricius compiled enormous multivolume histories of classical, biblical, and early Christian literature. His immense *Bibliotheca graeca* (1705–1728) devoted more than 300 pages to lost works from before the time of Homer, whether written in Greek or discussed by Greek writers.

These scholars, and others more specialized, such as Vincent Placcius (d. 1699) and Christoph August Heumann (*De libris anonymis ac pseudonymis,* 1711) confronted the problem of attribution of authorship and provenance, including the need to detect forged, pseudonymous, plagiarized, apocryphal, and pseudepigraphic works. Their labors, though aimed at establishing or contesting authorship, were often vitally important for advancing the historiography of writing systems and materials. Outright forgeries of ancient texts by *docti impostores* ("learned impostors") were especially important. The most infamous and influential of all were the 11 texts published at Rome in 1498 and attributed to Berossus, Manetho, Xenophon, Archilochus, Cato the Elder, Fabius Pictor, "Metasthenes the Persian," and other ancient authors. For 200 years these forgeries stimulated research into biblical history, Greek and Roman archaeology, ancient Near Eastern languages, Egyptology, and the history of the Etruscan civilization, language, and alphabet. Above all, they stimulated speculation about the antiquity of writing, even before Noah's Flood, and inspired a thorough search of ancient literature for clues to the history of writing and books (Stephens 2004, 2005). In the early 17th century a pseudo-Etruscan forgery, largely inspired by those mentioned above, posed as the diary of a priestly potentate recounting the devastation of his city-state by Roman armies (Rowland 2004). The teenaged forger's ill-considered choice of writing materials—modern Italian linen-rag paper with its watermarks incompletely removed—inspired decades of investigation into the chronology and durability of writing materials, especially papyrus, parchment, and cotton- and linen-rag papers. By the 18th century numerous dissertations were being written on the chronology of writing and the morphology of ancient books, by students of law and medicine as well as of classics.

Research into the history of writing was also stimulated by the creation of new kinds of libraries, outside the religious context of cathedrals and monastic orders and the political confines of civic and princely archives. The collections of classical and secular books by Humanists like Petrarch and Boccaccio enriched older civic and conventual libraries soon after their deaths; the Vatican Library grew into one of the premier collections under 15th- and 16th-century popes from Nicholas V to Sixtus V; magnificent libraries were created or consolidated in major capitals and university towns by bibliophilic nobles and scholars throughout the 17th and 18th centuries. To celebrate and publicize these collections, and to instruct scholars in their contents and organization, a number of books, some now recognized as foundational to library science, were published, including Angelo Rocca's *Bibliotheca Apostolica Vaticana* (1591), Justus Lipsius' *On Libraries* (*De bibliothecis syntagma,* 1602), Thomas Bartholin's *On Reading Books* (*De libris legendis,* 1676; 1711), Joachim Johann Mader's *On Libraries* (*De bibliothecis atque archivis,* 1666; 1702), Johannes Lomeier's *Book of Libraries* (*De bibliothecis liber singularis,* 1669; 1680), Jacob Friedrich Reimmann's *Survey of Literary Antiquity* (*Idea systematis antiquitatis literariae,* 1718), and Burcard Gotthelf Struve's *Introduction to Literary Knowledge and the Use of Libraries* (*Introductio in notitiam rei litterariae et usum bibliothecarum,* 1706; 1754). These and many other books combined traditional lore and contemporary scholarship to examine the history of writing and books, libraries, classical and biblical literature, and numerous other topics relating to the written transmission of cultural knowledge. Debates over the genuineness of documents—especially, but not only, monastic privileges—motivated Jean Mabillon and others to assemble collections of documents they saw as genuine and to draw up histories of script in Latin, Greek, and other languages, in order to help with authentication. Mabillon's fellow Benedictine Bernard de Montfaucon gave this new field of study a name: palaeography. More ambitious genres of publication repeated this information, from highly specialized works, such as Johann Jakob Brucker's *Critical History of Philosophy* (*Historia critica philosophiae,* 1742), to that most ambitious invention, the modern general encyclopedia (e.g., Ephraim Chambers's *Cyclopaedia, or Universal Dictionary of Arts and Sciences,* 1738; and Diderot and d'Alembert's *Encyclopédie, ou dictionnaire raisonné,* 1751–1772, with later supplements).

Along with improvements in mechanical typography, the spread of vernacular literacy made the history of writing available to a vast audience by the mid-18th century. Specialized works on writing, such as those in English by William Massey (1763) and Thomas Astle (1784; 2nd ed. 1803), made the complexities of lore and history available to 18th-century readers who had little or no classical training. Such works illustrated the wonders of writing with quotations from recent vernacular authors as well as the ancient classics: Massey and Astle both allude to Alexander Pope's lyric "Heloisa to Abelard," and Massey includes "a poem, in praise of the invention of writing, said to be wrote by a lady"; both poems extol writing as a means whereby lovers conquer distance as surely as scholars and historians conquer time.

Vernacular literature had long maintained a recreational or ludic relation to the history of writing. Ancient sequels and forgeries such as the apocryphal Trojan histories of "Dares of Phrygia" and "Diktys of Crete" inspired medieval romances such as the *Roman de Troie,* both by their ambition to continue or modify well-known stories and by the literary ruses they adopted to lend verisimilitude to their revisionist "histories." Ancient, often decomposing books, rediscovered in tombs, temples, or libraries, were regularly cited as the sources of new stories about familiar characters and legends. The 16th century, following on two centuries of intensive research into the history of books and writing, produced a plethora of fictions posing as forgeries, among which Rabelais' genealogy of Pantagruel, discovered in an ancient giant's bronze tomb (*Gargantua,* chap. 1) and Cervantes' Arabic manuscript source for the "history" of *Don Quixote* (chap. 9), rescued from a fishmonger's stock of wrapping paper, are the best-known. Such philological fictions of historicity continued strongly in the 17th and 18th centuries and adorned 19th-century classics such as Jan Potocki's *Manuscript Found in Saragossa* (1815) and Alessandro Manzoni's *The Betrothed (I promessi sposi,* 1842). The novels of Umberto Eco, especially *The Name of the Rose* (1980) and *Foucault's Pendulum* (1988), use postmodern literary theory to enrich philological fictions even further by complicating their supposed relation to historical truth, often by reference to the vertiginous fictions and essays of Jorge Luís Borges (d. 1985).

BIBL.: Berossus, *Berossos and Manetho,* trans. with introduction, in *Native Traditions in Ancient Mesopotamia and Egypt,* ed. Gerald P. Verbrugge and John M. Wickersham (Ann Arbor 1996). Phyllis Walter Goodhart Gordan, trans., *Two Renaissance Bookhunters: The Letters of Poggius Bracciolini to Nicolaus de Niccolis* (New York 1974). Anthony Grafton, *Forgers and Critics: Creativity and Duplicity in Western Scholarship* (Princeton 1990). Ingrid D. Rowland, *The Scarith of Scornello: A Tale of Renaissance Forgery* (Chicago 2004). John Edwin Sandys, *A History of Classical Scholarship,* 3 vols., 3rd ed. (1920; repr. New York 1958). Walter Stephens, "*Livres de haulte gresse:* Bibliographic Myth from Rabelais to Du Bartas," in *La littérature engagée aux XVIe et XVIIe siècles: Études en l'honneur de Gérard Defaux (1937–2004),* Supplement to *Modern Language Notes* 120, no. 1, Italian issue (2005) S60–S83, and "When Pope Noah Ruled the Etruscans: Annius of Viterbo and His Forged *Antiquities,* 1498," in *Studia Humanitatis: Essays in Honor of Salvatore Camporeale,* Supplement to *Modern Language Notes* 119, no. 1, Italian issue (2004) S201–S223. Polydore Vergil, *On Discovery,* trans. Brian P. Copenhaver (Cambridge, Mass., 2006). W.ST.

Xanthippe

Nothing is certain about Xanthippe except her name and marriage to Socrates (469–399 BCE). The union produced a son named Lamprocles and lasted until the philosopher's death. When the two were married and how old she was when he died have been disputed.

Xanthippe has long been a byword for a scolding wife. In this capacity she is mentioned in Shakespeare's comedy *The Taming of the Shrew* (1593): "Be she . . . as curst and shrewd/As Socrates' Xanthippe, or a worse,/She moves me not" (1.2). Henry Fielding interjected the name in *The History of Tom Jones* (1749) apparently seeing no need to explain to his audience who she was: "An arrant vixen of a wife . . . By this *Xanthippe* he had two sons" (8.11).

But Xanthippe's character had been besmirched for two millennia before Shakespeare. In *Phaedo* (60A) Plato (ca. 429–347 BCE) records how Socrates had had this wife and their son (he had another wife and two other sons as well) dismissed from his prison cell, so that he could be left alone to speak with his male friends who had come to visit him. Xenophon, supporter of Socrates and contemporary of Plato, records in his *Symposium* (2.10) how Antisthenes characterized Xanthippe as being the most difficult woman of all time. Socrates explains that he used her poor temper to develop patience in dealing with people. This defamation of Xanthippe had a long afterlife, being repeated by Plutarch in his *Moralia* ("How to Profit from One's Enemies," 90e) in the late 1st century CE and by Aulus Gellius (*Attic Nights* 1.17.1) in the mid- to late 2nd.

For centuries writers relished anecdotes in which the lofty thinker was humbled by his bickering wife. In one, Xanthippe angrily emptied a bucket (some say a chamberpot) onto her husband; he responds by saying that he had known her thundering would eventually be followed by rain. This story, told ca. 275 CE by Diogenes Laertius (2.37), was incorporated into the catalogue of bad wives in Jerome's treatise *Against Jovinianus* (1.48), written in 393. It reappeared in the late 1300s in Chaucer's *Canterbury Tales* (*Wife of Bath's Prologue* 3.727–732) and John Gower's *Confessio amantis* (3.639–713). It was later depicted in art and dramatized in comic operas and comedies about Socrates (e.g., in 1721 by Johann Ulrich von König, in 1809 by Louis-Sébastien Mercier, and in 1885 by Théodore Faullain de Banville). Xanthippe also appears interestingly in dialogue in Erasmus's *Colloquia familiaria,* no. 21, "Uxor mempsigamos" ("The Scolding Wife"), published in 1518. She continues to be employed to humorous ends, most recently in the *Xanthippic Dialogues* (1993) of Roger Scruton, but here the humor derives from parody of Socratic dialogue rather than mockery of her.

Although a strong tide of prejudices and proverbs has run against her, Xanthippe has had defenders. At the turn of the 15th century Christine de Pizan presented her laudatorily in *The Book of the City of Ladies* (2.21.1). In 1865 Eduard Zeller published an essay, "To Save the Honor of Xanthippe" (in *Vorträge und Abhandlungen geschichtlichen Inhalts*); in 1884 Fritz Mauthner made a case in her favor in a novel, *Xanthippe;* in 1944 the Austrian Hanns Sassmann also wrote a novel in her cause; and in 1960 Stefan Paul Andres published 12 stories in her defense. She has been the title character in many novels and plays, most of them easily located through her name (with attention to differences in spelling, such as Santippe in Italian) or through that of Socrates, as in the novel *Madame Socrate* (2000) by Gérald Messadié. A successful mid-20th-century treatment was *Xanthippe* (1959), by the Flemish author Paul Lebeau.

The name has been invoked often, both pro and con, in discussions of women's rights and in other feminist causes, as in a dialogue entitled "Xanthippe on Woman Suffrage" by Duffield Osborne in the *Yale Review* for 1915 (4:590–607); in a pamphlet, *Xanthippe: San Jose Women's Liberation,* issued in 1971 by the Xanthippe Collective of San Jose, California; in the names of bookshops and printing presses; and in a section of a novel by Cynthia Ozick, *The Puttermesser Papers* (1997).

BIBL.: Michael W. Weithmann, *Xanthippe und Sokrates: Eros, Ehe, Sex und Gender im antiken Athen: Ein Beitrag zu höherem historischem Klatsch* (Munich 2003). J.M.Z.

Xenophon

Greek historian and philosopher (ca. 430–354 BCE), noted author on various subjects. Born into an aristocratic family in Athens, he trained as a cavalry officer and studied with Socrates. In 401 he joined a large expedition of mercenaries in the *anabasis* or inland march mounted by Cyrus the Younger to conquer the Persian kingdom. When Cyrus was killed, Xenophon helped lead the difficult retreat of the surviving forces from Anatolia to Greece. After his return to Athens he fell afoul of the governing oligarchs and was exiled. He moved to Sparta and then settled on an estate near Olympia. Later he moved to Scillus in the western Peloponnese. His exile was eventually revoked, and he may have spent his last years in Athens.

His extant works reveal an astonishing variety and versatility. Xenophon the historian provides a continuation of Thucydides' *History of the Peloponnesian War* in his *Hellenica,* and his *Anabasis* (*Expedition of Cyrus*) offers an eyewitness account of the Greek expedition into Persia. (In his *New Science* [1725] Giambattista Vico calls him "the first to learn about Persian institutions with any certainty.") As a philosopher, Xenophon records the teachings of Socrates in his *Memorabilia* and *Oeconomicus.* An admirer of other cultures, he composed a biography of King Agesilaus of Sparta and an outline of the Spartan constitution, as well as a historical romance about Cyrus the Great of Persia, known as the *Education of Cyrus.* His experience as a soldier and sportsman inspired his treatises on horsemanship and hunting, and his tract *Ways and Means* proposes fiscal reforms for the city of Athens.

Xenophon's fluent and perspicuous prose was so admired in antiquity that he was dubbed the Attic Bee. During the Hellenistic era he was especially admired by the Cynics and Stoics, who valued his Spartan writings for their illustration of rigorous physical and ethical self-discipline. He is included as a Socratic thinker in Diogenes Laertius' *Lives of the Philosophers* (2.48–59). Among Greek writers his popularity culminated during the Second Sophistic (late 1st cent. CE–mid-3rd cent.), when grammarians cited him as a model of Atticism, and various authors imitated his simple style. The orator Dio Chrysostom commended him as "the best among the Socratics" (*Orations* 18), and the historian Arrian emulated him by composing a treatise on hunting and by giving the title *Anabasis* to his history of Alexander the Great.

Xenophon's combination of piety and common sense in moral reflections held a particular appeal for Roman readers. Cicero translated the *Oeconomicus* (only fragments survive) and quoted the *Education of Cyrus* in his dialogue *On Old Age.* Roman noblemen were clearly inspired by Xenophon's tributes to great men such as Cyrus, Lycurgus, and Socrates. His *Agesilaus* served as a model for the encomia in Tacitus' *Agricola* and for Pliny the Younger's *Panegyric of Trajan.*

During the Middle Ages, Xenophon was unknown in the Latin West, and his fortune declined in the Greek East. The learned patriarch of Constantinople Photius (ca. 810–895) seems to have read some of his works, and Greek grammarians continued to cite Xenophon for examples of Attic usage, often from anthologies. Yet if Byzantine grammarians and rhetoricians seldom read Xenophon firsthand, his variety of information on Greek life made him a useful source for historians and polymaths such as John Zonaras (d. after 1159), John Tzetzes (ca. 1110–1185), and Theodorus Metochites (1270–1332).

After the Western revival of Greek studies ca. 1400, Xenophon rapidly became a favorite author among European Humanists. Leonardo Bruni's 1402 translation of his short dialogue *Hiero,* which contrasts the ethics of public command and private conduct, became one of the most widely read texts of the early Renaissance. It survives in some 200 manuscripts, was printed in eight incunabula, and was included in the first Latin collection of Xenophon's major works, printed at Milan ca. 1501.

For Renaissance readers Xenophon remained a philosopher and historian, an idealist who recorded the exemplary lives and sayings of Socrates and Cyrus. Even the pragmatic Machiavelli in *The Prince* commends the idealized ruler as described in the *Education of Cyrus.* The publication of Xenophon's complete works in parallel (Greek with Latin) editions, redacted by Henricus Stephanus (1561) and Johannes Levvenklaius (1569), assured his canonical authority. He also attracted anthologizers, who mined the speeches from his historical works for their edifying content.

Two texts enjoyed especial popularity in the 16th century and beyond. *Oeconomicus* was printed at least 18 times between 1506 and 1603 in the version of Raphael Maffeius Volaterranus (Raffaele Maffei); it was also translated by Lampus Biragus, Bernardinus Donatus, Joachim Camerarius, Jacobus Lodoicus Strebaeus, and Johannes Levvenklaius. Even more popular was Prodicus' tale of Hercules at the Crossroads (*Memorabilia* 2.1), an allegorical anecdote in which the young hero is wooed by two maidens representing Vice and Virtue and chooses to follow the latter. It was translated by Saxolus Pratensis, Philipp Melanchthon, Guillaume Budé, and Vincentius Obsopoeus, also (as verse) by Johannes Spangenbergus and Johannes Stigelius. The popularity of this moral apologue in Germany extended well into the Enlightenment. It provided the subject of Bach's cantata of the same name, *Hercules auf dem Scheideweg* (1733), Handel's oratorio *The Choice of Hercules* (1751), and Christoph

Martin Wieland's singspiel *Die Wahl des Herkules* (*The Choice of Hercules,* 1773).

Xenophon was a basic school text in colonial America. His *Memorabilia* was valued for its moral instruction; Thomas Jefferson advocated reading the *Anabasis* and *Hellenica.* In 1776 John Adams proposed the Choice of Hercules (in an engraving by Simon Gribelin) for the national seal of the fledgling American republic. In the 19th century Xenophon's self-reliance inspired New England essayists: Thoreau recalled the river crossings of the *Anabasis* as he navigated the Merrimack in 1839, and Emerson lauded Xenophon and his "gang of great boys" in his essay titled "History." The disciplined perseverance of ancient Greek soldiers, so vividly described in the *Anabasis,* served as an obvious model for officers and officials in the heyday of the British Empire. As Tim Rood (2004) has brilliantly demonstrated, the celebrated cry *thalatta thalatta* ("The sea! The sea!"), raised by the Ten Thousand on beholding the Black Sea after their perilous march from the interior, became both a popular cliché of classical history and a resonant catchphrase for writers as disparate as Heinrich Heine (in his poem "The North Sea") and James Joyce (most notably, Buck Milligan's ruminations on Dublin Bay in *Ulysses*).

As classical scholarship became more specialized in the 19th century, the variety of Xenophon's writings inevitably caused his reputation to suffer among philologists: he was judged inferior to Thucydides as a historian, and to Plato as a thinker and stylist. Nevertheless, his *Anabasis, Hellenica,* and *Memorabilia* remained school texts that inspired generations of youth with an ideal of personal achievement. As in antiquity, Xenophon was read as a source of information about the Spartans and Persians. His reflections on economy, both public and private, are cited by thinkers as diverse as John Ruskin and Karl Marx.

The 20th century witnessed a new appreciation both of Xenophon's originality and of his limitations. His political and religious views, and even his prose style, provide a key to the emergence of Hellenistic culture, and his expertise as soldier and cavalry officer makes him invaluable to students of Greek warfare.

BIBL.: J. K. Anderson, *Xenophon* (London 1974). David Marsh, "Xenophon," in *Catalogus Translationum et Commentariorum* 7 (Washington, D.C., 1992), 75–196. Erwin Panofsky, *Hercules am Scheideweg und andere antike Bildstoffe in der neueren Kunst* (Leipzig 1930; repr. 1997). Elizabeth Rawson, *The Spartan Tradition in European Thought* (Oxford 1969). Tim Rood, *The Sea! The Sea! The Shout of the Ten Thousand in the Modern Imagination* (London 2004).

D.M.

Z

Zeno's Paradoxes

The fame of Zeno of Elea (ca. 490–ca. 430 BCE) rests on his invention of a number of paradoxes intended to prove that plurality and change, though evident to the senses, are in fact unintelligible. Evidently these were given as arguments in a book designed to support the philosophy of his mentor, Parmenides, by paying back his detractors in kind. Although only a few brief fragments of his work have survived, and his reasoning has often been dismissed as sophistical or naive, Zeno's paradoxes have had an enormous influence on subsequent developments in philosophy and science, chiefly on theories of the continuum in mathematics and natural philosophy.

Perhaps the most famous of Zeno's paradoxes is the Achilles (Aristotle, *Physics* 239b): in a race with a tortoise that runs, say, a tenth as fast, a demigod gives the tortoise a head start of, say, one league. By the time Achilles has run that distance, the tortoise has crawled 1/10 league farther; by the time Achilles has covered that, the tortoise is still 1/100 league ahead, and so forth. Each time Achilles runs the distance that remains, the tortoise is still 1/10 as far ahead; so Achilles never catches the tortoise. Worse, according to Zeno's Dichotomy Paradox, Achilles could never begin to move; for in order to run one league he would first have to run a half; before that a quarter; and so on to infinity, there being no first subinterval. And according to the Arrow Paradox, motion is in any case impossible, since an arrow in flight (for example) is stationary at every instant of its flight and therefore never moves.

A common reaction to the paradoxes is to see them as soluble by mathematics. Thus, René Descartes was able to show by a nice geometrical argument that Achilles will reach the tortoise after running precisely 1 1/9 leagues: assuming that the subintervals "exhaust" the distance, he proved that the sum 1/10 + 1/100 + 1/1000 . . . converges to 1/9, and he dismissed the paradox as mere "captiousness." The American philosopher Charles Sanders Peirce gave a 19th-century version of this argument using the theory of limits, adding that "this silly little catch presents no difficulty at all to a mind trained in mathematics and logic." In the 20th century, philosophers such as Bertrand Russell insisted that even this was not sufficiently rigorous, until the German mathematician Richard Dedekind had laid down axioms for the real number system that guaranteed the existence of such limits.

Many philosophers, though, have seen such arguments as missing an essential point. Leibniz inverted Zeno's Dichotomy, arguing that because motion is real, it must have a beginning; but this beginning cannot lie in the right half of any subinterval and therefore cannot lie in any extended subinterval; so it must be infinitely small, yet unextended. This was part of a theory of infinitesimal elements of the continuum, which within four years Leibniz had developed into his differential calculus. And with the calculus in hand, he could distinguish the moving arrow from one at rest in terms of its instantaneous velocity, defined as a ratio of infinitesimal intervals of space and time.

But Russell joined the founder of set theory, Georg Cantor, in rejecting the adequacy of such solutions, arguing that the very axioms of mathematics which establish the one-to-one correspondence between the points on a line and the real numbers also preclude the existence of infinitesimal intervals in the continuum. Motion, argued Russell, Adolf Grünbaum, and Wesley Salmon, consists in being at a different point of space at each different instant, and this is sufficient to dispose of Zeno's Arrow. Yet ever since Abraham Robinson's rehabilitation of infinitesimals in 1967 through nonstandard analysis, this Russellian consensus has been contested, and there now exist several rival accounts of infinitesimals in modern mathematics.

Other philosophers have refused the mathematical solutions by inventing variations on Zeno's paradoxes. Max Black has identified the root of the problem identified by Zeno to be the impossibility of performing an infinite series of tasks; he compares Achilles' task with Hercules' cutting off heads of a hydra faster and faster in geometrical progression, though the hydra regenerates only one head each time a head is cut off. If Hercules' task is impossible, why isn't Achilles'? And in an ingenious variation of the Dichotomy, José Benardete asks us to imagine a book whose first page is ½ inch thick, and each of whose subsequent pages is ½ as thick as the one before. It follows mathematically both that the book is one inch thick and that there is no last page. So what does one see when one turns it over and lifts the back cover? There is no last page to greet one's gaze.

The latter objection is related to the controversy over infinitesimals. There is no assignable difference between the series of half-intervals and its limit 1, or between 1.111 . . . and 10/9. Do we therefore conclude with the Cantorians that they are identical, and define them to be so? Or do we side with the infinitesimalists, who deny that the unassignable difference between such a series and its limit—the missing last page of Benardete's diminishing book—is nothing? Zeno continues to stir controversy.

BIBL.: Jonathan Barnes, *Early Greek Philosophy* (New York 1987). J. L. Bell, "Infinitesimals," *Synthese* 75 (1988) 285–315. José Benardete, *Infinity: An Essay in Metaphysics* (Oxford 1964). Wesley Salmon, ed., *Zeno's Paradoxes* (Indianapolis 1970, 2001). R.T.W.A.

Zoology

The word *zoology* was coined in the 17th century to denote the medical and scientific study of animals—just as intense classical influence on that study was waning. From the mid-15th to the early 17th centuries, classical texts and careful observation went hand in hand in the study of the animal world.

Many classical sources contributed to the medieval and Renaissance understanding of animals. By far the most important were Aristotle's biological works: *History of Animals, Generation of Animals, Parts of Animals, Motion of Animals,* and *Progression of Animals,* and also his *On the Soul* and parts of the *Parva naturalia.* The first five, known collectively as *De animalibus* (*On Animals*), were translated into Latin in the 13th century by William of Moerbeke and in the 15th by George of Trebizond and Theodore Gaza. Other classical sources on animals include Pliny the Elder's *Natural History;* Aelian's *On the Nature of Animals;* the agricultural treatises of Cato the Elder, Columella, and Palladius; the hunting and fishing poems attributed to Oppian; Pausanias's chorography; and scattered works by Plutarch and other writers. The heterogeneity of these sources underscores the fact that ancient writers took a variety of interests in animals; there was no single sustained tradition of writing about them. With the significant exception of Aristotle, who concentrated on comparative anatomy, classification, and philosophical explanation, ancient texts emphasized animal husbandry or fabulous stories about animals as well as, or even more than, their anatomy and behavior.

Medieval writers were equally heterogeneous. In the 13th century Albertus Magnus produced a paraphrase-commentary on Aristotle's *History, Parts,* and *Generation of Animals* in *De animalibus,* including his own personal observations, but he appended an encyclopedia of individual animals drawn from the *De naturis rerum* of Thomas of Cantimpré. Another medieval tradition, that of the bestiary (a moral and allegorical work about the strange properties of animals), had roots in the late antique *Physiologus* but otherwise owed little to classical sources. Aristotle's *On the Soul* formed part of the scholastic curriculum in natural philosophy, introducing students to the notion that animals' souls possessed the faculties of sensation and (with some exceptions) motion, distinguishing them from plants, but that they lacked reason, a belief that would persist long after the demise of Aristotelian psychology. (Some ancient and medieval tales of animals' astonishing sagacity seem to undermine this conclusion.) Otherwise, zoology was not part of the standard medieval university curriculum.

In the 15th century, the Humanists' interest in Latin and Greek writings led them to seek out, acquire, and edit ancient texts on animals and to translate (or retranslate) the Greek texts into Latin. Gaza's translation of Aristotle's books on animals, intended to replace Moerbeke's literal, word-for-word version, was completed in 1454. The printing press soon made this and other ancient sources widely available, some for the first time in Latin.

Renaissance scholars pursued two main approaches to the study of animals. In the universities, particularly in Italy, some professors lectured on Aristotle's zoological books, producing commentaries in the vein of Albertus, but with up-to-date philology and exegesis. This tradition began in 1521 with Pietro Pomponazzi and continued through the end of the 16th century. Few commentators, apart from Agostino Nifo, managed to cover the whole Aristotelian zoological corpus, and, as was the case in the Middle Ages, the books on animals never became standard university subjects.

Other writers took an encyclopedic approach, mining classical (and medieval) works, making their own observations, and corresponding with colleagues to gather as much information as they could about animals. Shaped in part by their sources, these scholars included medical, agricultural, and cultural lore in their works. The most important of these writers was the Zurich physician Konrad Gesner, whose four-volume *Historia animalium* (1551–1558) has been described as a *summa* of Renaissance zoology. Gessner specified that his work was not intended to supplant that of Aristotle, whose philosophical framework he retained. The English physician Edward Wotton restated Aristotle's principles and used them to organize the animal kingdom in his *De differentiis animalium* (1552). In Bologna, Ulisse Aldrovandi gathered an extensive collection of preserved animal parts, along with animal drawings, observation notes, and excerpts from classical sources that were published (mostly posthumously) in massive folios. Renaissance collectors urged patrons to support their study of animals, citing Pliny's story of the specimens sent to Aristotle by Alexander the Great during his Asian campaigns.

By the early 17th century classical texts were themselves no longer necessary sources for descriptive zoology; Renaissance compilations had rendered them superfluous. In his otherwise derivative work, John Johnston omitted "philology" from ancient sources. Nonetheless, anatomists and zoologists continued to engage with specific aspects of the classical tradition. Physiology, generation, and classification, all problems raised by Aristotle, were taken up in the 17th century by Harvey, Borelli, Swammerdam, Malpighi, Tournefort, Ray, and others, though most rejected Aristotle's approach. In his *Histoire naturelle, générale et particulière* (1749–1788), Buffon mentions Aristotle more than 200 times, often critically but sometimes with appreciation for his careful observations.

From the 18th century onward, Aristotle was the only ancient writer on zoology whose works continued to be regularly consulted by working zoologists. In particular, with the rise of invertebrate zoology in the 19th century, his remarks on fishes and marine invertebrates received new attention. Ridiculing Aristotle for his implausible errors has long been a zoologist's sport, and it is true that his works and other ancient zoological books contain much that is wrong or secondhand. But in the 20th century some of Aristotle's odder claims and subtle observations were confirmed. Aristotle's views on classification and biological method still interest philosophers of science and ethnobiologists.

BIBL.: Scott Atran, *Cognitive Foundations of Natural History: Towards an Anthropology of Science* (Cambridge 1990). Änne Bäumer, "Edward Wotton: Aristotelische Zoologie aristotelischer als bei Aristoteles," in *Vorträge des ersten Symposions des Bamberger Arbeitskreises "Antike Naturwissenschaft und ihre Rezeption,"* ed. Klaus Döring and Georg Wöhrle (Wiesbaden 1990). Paula Findlen, *Possessing Nature: Museums, Collecting, and Scientific Culture in Early Modern Italy* (Berkeley 1994). Michel Foucault, *The Order of Things: An Archaeology of the Human Sciences* (London 1970). Roger French, *Ancient Natural History: Histories of Nature* (London 1994). Allan Gotthelf and James G. Lennox, eds., *Philosophical Issues in Aristotle's Biology* (Cambridge 1987). Stefano Perfetti, *Aristotle's Zoology and Its Renaissance Commentators* (Louvain 2000). Laurent Pinon, "Conrad Gessner and the Historical Depth of Renaissance Natural History," in *Historia: Empiricism and Erudition in Early Modern Europe,* ed. Gianna Pomata and Nancy G. Siraisi (Cambridge, Mass., 2005), and *Livres de zoologie à la Renaissance* (Paris 1995). Jason A. Tipton, "Aristotle's Study of the Animal World," *Perspectives in Biology and Medicine* 49 (2006) 369–383.

B.O.

CONTRIBUTORS

A.A.	Alexander Alexakis, Department of Philology, University of Ioannina
A.Ak.	Anna Akasoy, Oriental Institute, University of Oxford
A.An.	Anna Anguissola, Institut für Klassische Archäologie, Ludwig-Maximilians-Universität München
A.Ar.	Alessandro Arcangeli, Dipartimento di Arte, Archeologia, Storia e Società, Università di Verona
A.-B.R.	Almut-Barbara Renger, Institut für Religionwissenschaft, Freie Universität Berlin
A.B.T.	A. B. Taylor, Centre for Medieval and Early Modern Research, Swansea University
A.E.	Arnold Esch, Deutsches Historisches Institut, Rome
A.E.H.	Ann Ellis Hanson, Department of Classics, Yale University
A.G.	Anthony Grafton, Department of History, Princeton University
A.K.	Andreas A. M. Kinneging, Faculty of Law, University of Leiden
A.L.	André Laks, UFR de Philosophie et Sociologie, Université Paris-Sorbonne/Paris IV
A.M.	Alexander Marr, Department of Art History, University of Southern California
A.Mu.	Alexander Murray, University College, Oxford
A.P.	Anthony Pagden, Department of Political Science, University of California Los Angeles
A.Pl.	Adrian Poole, Faculty of English, University of Cambridge
A.Pt.	Alex Potts, Department of History of Art, University of Michigan
A.Py.	Andrew Pyle, Department of Philosophy, University of Bristol
A.S.	Alessandro Scafi, Warburg Institute, University of London
A.V.	Amy Vail, Indianapolis, Indiana
B.Br.	Bracht Branham, Department of Classics, Emory University
B.C.	Brian Copenhaver, Departments of Philosophy and History, University of California Los Angeles
B.Cu.	Brian Curran, Department of Art History, Pennsylvania State University
B.E.	Björn Ewald, Department of Art, University of Toronto
B.M.	Bernard McGinn, Divinity School, University of Chicago
B.O.	Brian W. Ogilvie, Department of History, University of Massachusetts Amherst
B.R.	Bruce Redford, Department of Art History, Boston University
B.S.	Bernd Seidensticker, Seminar für Klassische Philologie, Freie Universität Berlin
B.T.	Bette Talvacchia, Department of Art and Art History, University of Connecticut
B.V.	Bernard Vitrac, Centre National de la Recherche Scientifique (ANHIMA), Paris
B.v.R.	Barbara von Reibnitz, Deutsches Seminar der Universität Basel
B.Y.	Bernard Yack, Department of Politics, Brandeis University
C.A.S.	Christopher Stray, Department of History and Classics, Swansea University
C.B.	Carolina Brown, Department of Art History, Uppsala University
C.Br.	Charles Burnett, Warburg Institute, University of London
C.C.	Christopher Celenza, Department of German and Romance Languages, Johns Hopkins University, and Director, American Academy in Rome

C.Ch. Catherine Chin, Program in Religious Studies, University of California Davis
C.D.A. Christopher Drew Armstrong, Department of History of Art and Architecture, University of Pittsburgh
C.F. Claudio Franzoni, Reggio Emilia, Italy
C.G. Cathy Gere, Department of History, University of California San Diego
C.Gn. Christian Gnilka, Institut für Klassische Philologie, Westfälische Wilhems-Universität Münster
C.H. Craig Hanson, Department of Art and Art History, Calvin College
C.J.M. Constant Mews, School of Philosophical, Historical and International Studies, Monash University
C.K. Craig Kallendorf, Departments of English and of European and Classical Languages and Cultures, Texas A & M University
C.Ke. Christopher Kelly, Corpus Christi College, Cambridge
C.M. Christopher Martin, Department of English, Boston University
C.M.G. Constanze Güthenke, Department of Classics, Princeton University
C.M.S.J. Christopher M. S. Johns, Department of History of Art, Vanderbilt University
C.R. Claudia Rapp, Department of History, University of California Los Angeles
C.S. Carlos Steel, Institute of Philosophy, University of Leuven
C.V. Caroline Vout, Faculty of Classics, University of Cambridge
C.V.-A. Catherine Volpilhac-Auger, Institut d'Histoire de la Pensée Classique, Ecole Normale Supérieure de Lyon
C.W. Caroline Winterer, Department of History, Stanford University
D.A.D. Daniel A. Dombrowski, Department of Philosophy, Seattle University
D.F. David Friedman, History, Theory and Criticism Section, Department of Architecture, Massachusetts Institute of Technology
D.G. Dimitri Gutas, Department of Near Eastern Languages and Civilizations, Yale University
D.H. Deborah Howard, Faculty of Architecture and History of Art, University of Cambridge
D.K. Dilwyn Knox, Department of Italian, University College London
D.Ka. David Karmon, Department of Visual Arts, College of the Holy Cross
D.Kn. Dale Kinney, Department of History of Art, Bryn Mawr College
D.L. Domenico Laurenza, Istituto e Museo di Storia della Scienza, Firenze
D.M. David Marsh, Department of Italian, Rutgers University
D.R. David Richter, Department of English, Queens College and Graduate Center, City University of New York
D.R.M. David R. Marshall, Art History Discipline, School of Culture and Communication, University of Melbourne
D.R.W. Daniel R. Woolf, Department of History, Queen's University, Kingston, Ontario
D.Ri. David Ricks, Centre for Hellenic Studies, King's College London
D.Rm. Daniela Romagnoli, Dipartimento di Storia, Università degli Studi di Parma
D.Ro. David Roessel, Department of Languages and Culture Studies, Richard Stockton College of New Jersey
D.Ru. H. Darrel Rutkin, Institute for the Study of the Ancient World, New York University
D.S. David Summers, McIntire Department of Art, University of Virginia
D.T.R. David T. Runia, Queen's College, Centre for Classics and Archaeology, University of Melbourne
D.v.M. Dirk van Miert, Huygens Instituut, Koninklijke Nederlandse Akademie van Wetenschappen
D.W. David Watkin, Department of History of Art, University of Cambridge
E.B. Eve Borsook, Villa I Tatti, Florence, Italy
E.C. Evangelos Chrysos, Hellenic Parliament Foundation, Athens
E.F. Elizabeth Fisher, Department of Classical and Near Eastern Languages and Civilizations, George Washington University
E.G. Ernst Gamillscheg, Sammlung von Handschriften und alten Drucken, Österreichische Nationalbibliothek
E.Ga. Elaine Gazda, Department of History of Art, University of Michigan
E.H. Ellen T. Harris, Department of Music and Theater Arts, Massachusetts Institute of Technology
E.J.A. E. Jennifer Ashworth, Department of Philosophy, University of Waterloo
E.L. Elisabeth Ladenson, Department of French and Romance Philology, Columbia University

E.Le.	Eleanor Winsor Leach, Department of Classical Studies, Indiana University
E.M.H.	Elizabeth M. Hull, Department of English, Bethany College
E.R.	Eileen Reeves, Department of Comparative Literature, Princeton University
E.Se.	Elizabeth Sears, Department of History of Art, University of Michigan
E.T.	Edmund Thomas, Department of Classics and Ancient History, Durham University
E.Tr.	Erich Trapp, Institut für Griechische und Lateinische Philologie, Universität Bonn
E.W.	Emily Wilson, Department of Classical Studies, University of Pennsylvania
F.C.	Francis Cairns, Department of Classics, Florida State University
F.Ch.	François Charette, Independent Scholar
F.D.	Francesca Dell'Acqua, Facoltà di Lettere, Università degli Studi di Salerno
F.M.P.	Filippomaria Pontani, Dipartimento di Scienze dell'Antichità, Università Ca' Foscari, Venezia
F.Pu.	Frederick Purnell, Jr., Department of Philosophy, Queens College-City University of New York
F.R.	Federica Rossi, Storia dell'Architettura, Scuola Normale Superiore di Pisa
F.S.	Fred Schreiber, New York, New York
F.W.	Françoise Waquet, Centre National de la Recherche Scientifique, Paris
G.A.B.	Gauvin Bailey, Department of History of Art, University of Aberdeen
G.B.	Gordon Braden, Department of English, University of Virginia
G.C.	Gordon Campbell, School of English, University of Leicester
G.Ca.	Guglielmo Cavallo, Dipartimento di Studi sulle Società e le Culture del Medioevo, Università di Roma "La Sapienza"
G.Ce.	Giovanna Ceserani, Department of Classics, Stanford University
G.G.	Giuseppe Gerbino, Department of Music, Columbia University
G.Gi.	Guido Giglioni, Warburg Institute, University of London
G.M.	George McClure, Department of History, University of Alabama
G.M.C.	Gian Mario Cao, Department of History, Princeton University
G.P.	Guido Paduano, Dipartimento di Filologia Classica, Università di Pisa
G.Pa.	Gianni Paganini, Facoltà di Lettere e Filosofia, Università degli Studi del Piemonte Orientale
G.Pr.	Grant Parker, Department of Classics, Stanford University
G.S.	Gregory Shaw, Department of Religious Studies, Stonehill College
G.W.B.	G. W. Bowersock, Institute for Advanced Study, Princeton
G.W.M.	Glenn W. Most, Scuola Normale Superiore di Pisa and Committee on Social Thought, University of Chicago
G.Z.	Giuseppe Zecchini, Dipartimento di Scienze Storiche, Università Cattolica del Sacro Cuore
H.B.	Hervé Brunon, Centre André Chastel, Centre National de la Recherche Scientifique, Paris
H.C.	Hubert Cancik, Klassische Philologie, Eberhard-Karls-Universität Tübingen
H.J.	Howard Jones, Department of Classics, McMaster University
H.K.	Helen King, Department of Classics, University of Reading
H.M.	Helen Moore, Faculty of English, University of Oxford
H.M.H.	Harry Hine, School of Classics, University of St Andrews
H.P.	Hélène Parenty, Lyon, France
H.Pa.	Holt Parker, Department of Classics, University of Cincinnati
H.R.R.	Hans R. Runte, Department of French, Dalhousie University
H.S.	Harold Stone, Department of Humanities, Shimer College
I.C.	Ian Campbell, Edinburgh School of Architecture and Landscape Architecture, University of Edinburgh
I.D.K.	Ignace De Keyser, Dienst Etnomusicologie, Koninklijk Museum voor Midden-Afrika, Tervuren
I.D.R.	Ingrid D. Rowland, Rome Studies Center, University of Notre Dame
I.D.S.	Ingrid De Smet, Centre for the Study of the Renaissance, University of Warwick
I.S.	Ivo Schneider, Universität der Bundeswehr München and Münchner Zentrum für Wissenschafts- und Technikgeschichte
I.W.	Ian White, St John's College, University of Cambridge

J.A. Jan Assmann, Department of Egyptology, University of Heidelberg
J.-A.D. Jens-Arne Dickmann, Zentrum für Altertumswissenschaften, Institut für Klassische Archaeologie, Ruprecht-Karls-Universität Heidelberg
J.B. Joško Belamarić, Institute of Art History, Republic of Croatia
J.B.G. Julia Beatrice Griffin, Department of Literature and Philosophy, Georgia Southern University
J.B.S. J. B. Schneewind, Department of Philosophy, Johns Hopkins University
J.C. Joseph Connors, Villa I Tatti, Florence, Italy
J.D. Janet DeLaine, Faculty of Classics, Ioannou Centre for Classical and Byzantine Studies
J.D.L. John D. Lyons, Department of French, University of Virginia
J.E. Jaś Elsner, Corpus Christi College, University of Oxford
J.E.C. Julie E. Cumming, Schulich School of Music, McGill University
J.Ev. James Evans, Program in Science, Technology, and Society, The University of Puget Sound
J.G. John Gage, Department of History of Art, University of Cambridge
J.Go. Jaime Goodrich, Department of English, Wayne State University
J.H.G. Julia Haig Gaisser, Department of Greek, Latin and Classical Studies, Bryn Mawr College
J.K. Jill Kraye, Warburg Institute, University of London
J.La. Joachim Latacz, Seminar für Klassische Philologie, Universität Basel
J.Le. Jonathan Lear, Committee on Social Thought, University of Chicago
J.Ln. John Leonard, Department of English, University of Western Ontario
J.M. Jürgen Malitz, Lehrstuhl für Alte Geschichte, Katholische Universität Eichstätt-Ingolstadt
J.M.M. Jörg Martin Merz, Institut für Kunstgeschichte, Westfälische Wilhelms-Universität Münster
J.M.Z. Jan M. Ziolkowski, Department of the Classics, Harvard University, and Dumbarton Oaks Research Library and Collection, Washington, D.C.
J.Mo. John Monfasani, Department of History, University at Albany-SUNY
J.My. Ioannis Mylonopoulos, Department of Art History and Archaeology, Columbia University
J.O. James O'Donnell, Provost, Georgetown University
J.P. Jan Papy, Faculteit Letteren, Katholieke Universiteit Leuven
J.Pe. Jed Perl, Art Critic, *The New Republic*
J.Pi. John Pinto, Department of Art and Archaeology, Princeton University
J.R. Jessica Rawson, School of Archaeology, University of Oxford
J.S. Joshua Scodel, Departments of English Language and Literature and Comparative Literature, University of Chicago
J.Se. John Sellars, Department of Philosophy, University of the West of England Bristol
J.Sh. Jonathan Sheehan, Department of History, University of California Berkeley
J.Ss. Jacques Sesiano, Section de Mathématiques, École Polytechnique Fédérale de Lausanne
J.T.H. John T. Hamilton, Department of Comparative Literature, Harvard University
J.T.K. Joshua T. Katz, Department of Classics, Princeton University
J.W.-E. John Wilton-Ely, Department of Art History, University of Hull
K.B. Kai Brodersen, Präsident, Universität Erfurt
K.-D.F. Klaus-Dietrich Fischer, Institut für Geschichte, Theorie und Ethik der Medizin, Johannes-Gutenberg-Universität Mainz
K.E. Kathy Eden, Department of English and Comparative Literature, Columbia University
K.G. Karl Galinsky, Department of Classics, University of Texas at Austin
K.H. Kristine Haugen, Division of the Humanities and Social Sciences, California Institute of Technology
K.-H.Z. Karl-Heinz Ziegler, Fakultät für Rechtswissenschaft, Universität Hamburg
K.P. Katharine Park, Department of the History of Science, Harvard University
K.S. Klaus Sallmann, Seminar für Klassische Philologie, Johannes-Gutenberg-Universität Mainz
K.T. Karl Toepfer, College of Humanities and Arts, San José State University
K.v.B. Kevin van Bladel, Department of Classics, University of Southern California
K.W.C. Kathleen Wren Christian, Department of History of Art and Architecture, University of Pittsburgh

L.B. Leonard Barkan, Department of Comparative Literature, Princeton University
L.Bo. Lina Bolzoni, Classe di Lettere, Scuola Normale Superiore di Pisa
L.Br. Leslie Brubaker, Institute of Archaeology and Antiquity, University of Birmingham
L.C. Luciano Canfora, Dipartimento di Scienze dell'Antichità, Università degli Studi di Bari
L.D. Luc Deitz, Bibliothèque nationale de Luxembourg and Institut für Klassische Philologie, Universität Trier
L.F. Lucia Faedo, Dipartimento di Scienze Archeologiche, Università di Pisa
L.F.B. Larry F. Ball, Department of Art and Design, University of Wisconsin Stevens Point
L.Fr. Luba Freedman, Department of the History of Art, The Hebrew University of Jerusalem
L.G. Lionel Gossman, Department of French and Italian, Princeton University
L.H.-S. Leofranc Holford-Strevens, Classics Department, Oxford University Press, Oxford
L.J.K. Lisa J. Kiser, Department of English, Ohio State University
L.L. Luther Link, Aoyama Gakuin University, Tokyo
L.Li. Lawrence Lipking, Department of English, Northwestern University
L.N. Lodi Nauta, Department of Philosophy, University of Groningen
L.Ne. Lolita Nehru, Independent Scholar, New Delhi
L.No. Larry Norman, Department of Romance Languages and Literatures, University of Chicago
L.P. Laurent Pinon, Département d'Histoire, École Normale Supérieure Paris
L.R. Lois Rosow, School of Music, Ohio State University
L.S. Lambert Schneider, Archäologische Institut, Universität Hamburg
L.T. Liba Taub, Department of History and Philosophy of Science, University of Cambridge
M.A. Michael J. B. Allen, Department of English, University of California Los Angeles
M.A.B. Mary Beagon, Department of Classics and Ancient History, University of Manchester
M.A.G. Miguel Angel Granada, Departament d'Història de la Filosofia, Universitat de Barcelona
M.A.S. Mary Ann Smart, Department of Music, University of California Berkeley
M.B. Mary Beard, Faculty of Classics, University of Cambridge
M.B.H. Marcia B. Hall, Department of Art History, Temple University
M.B.T. Michael Trapp, Department of Classics, King's College London
M.Ba. Manuel Baumbach, Seminar für Klassische Philologie, Ruhr-Universität Bochum
M.Be. Maria Beltramini, Facoltà di Lettere e Filosofia, Università degli Studi di Roma-Tor Vergata
M.Bl. Malcolm Bell, Department of Art, University of Virginia
M.C. Monica Centanni, Centro studi Classici, Università IUAV di Venezia
M.C.F. Michele C. Ferrari, Mittellatein und Neulatein, Universität Erlangen
M.Co. Michael Cole, Department of Art History and Archaeology, Columbia University
M.Cr. Michael Crawford, Department of History, University College London
M.D. Martin Davies, London, England
M.De. Marilynn Desmond, Department of English and Comparative Literature, Binghamton University
M.Dt. Marcel Detienne, Department of Classics, Johns Hopkins University
M.G. Monique Goullet, Laboratoire de Médiévistique Occidentale de Paris, Université de Paris Sorbonne
M.Gf. Mark Griffith, Department of Classics, University of California Berkeley
M.Gr. Miriam Griffin, Faculty of Classics, University of Oxford
M.H.L. Maria H. Loh, Department of the History of Art, University College London
M.J. Max Jones, School of Arts, Histories and Cultures, University of Manchester
M.J.L. Michael J. Lewis, Department of Art, Williams College
M.L.C. Maria Luisa Catoni, Classe di Lettere, Scuola Normale Superiore di Pisa
M.M. Maria Mavroudi, Departments of History and Classics, University of California Berkeley
M.M.W. Martin M. Winkler, Department of Modern and Classical Languages, George Mason University
M.Mc. Michael McCarthy, Department of the History of Art, University College Dublin
M.Mo. Mark Morford, Department of Classics, University of Virginia
M.Mu. Martin Mulsow, Forschungszentrum Gotha, Universität Erfurt

M.N.S.S.	Mortimer N. S. Sellers, Center for International and Comparative Law, University of Baltimore School of Law
M.Pe.	Mario Pereira, Department of History of Art and Architecture, Brown University
M.R.	Melvin Richter, Department of Political Science, Hunter College
M.R.S.	Michele Renee Salzman, Department of History, University of California Riverside
M.S.	Michael Squire, Faculty of Classics, University of Cambridge
M.Su.	Mihoko Suzuki, Department of English, University of Miami
M.T.	Mario Telò, Department of Classics, University of California Los Angeles
M.T.C.	Mary T. Crane, English Department, Boston College
M.V.	Martin Vöhler, Institut für Griechische und Lateinische Philologie, Freie Universität Berlin
M.W.	Margaret Williamson, Department of Classics, Dartmouth College
M.Z.	Mauro Zonta, Dipartimento di Studi Filosofici ed Epistemologici, Università di Roma "La Sapienza"
N.C.	Nigel Crowther, Department of Classical Studies, University of Western Ontario
N.G.	Niels Gaul, Department of Medieval Studies, Central European University
N.L.	Noel Lenski, Department of Classics, University of Colorado
N.T.	Nathan Tarcov, Committee on Social Thought, University of Chicago
N.T.G.	Nancy Thomson de Grummond, Department of Classics, Florida State University
O.K.	Olaf Kramer, Seminar für Allgemeine Rhetorik, Eberhard-Karls-Universität Tübingen
O.R.C.	Olivia Remie Constable, Department of History, University of Notre Dame
O.V.C.	Olga Vassilieva-Codognet, Ecole des Hautes Etudes en Sciences Sociales, Paris
P.B.	Paul Barolsky, Department of Art, University of Virginia
P.Bu.	Peter Burian, Department of Classical Studies, Duke University
P.C.	Paul Cartledge, Faculty of Classics, University of Cambridge
P.Ce.	Paolo Cesaretti, Facoltà di Scienze Umanistiche, Università degli Studi di Bergamo
P.D.P.	Pierre du Prey, Department of Art, Queen's University, Kingston, Ontario
P.E.F.	Paula E. Findlen, Department of History, Stanford University
P.F.B.	Patricia Fortini Brown, Department of Art and Archaeology, Princeton University
P.H.	Phillip Harding, Department of Classical, Near Eastern and Religious Studies, University of British Columbia
Ph.D.	Philippe Depreux, Faculté des Lettres et des Sciences Humaines, Université de Limoges / Institut Universitaire de France
P.J.	Philip Jacks, Department of Fine Arts and Art History, George Washington University
P.J.D.	Penelope J. E. Davies, Department of Art and Art History, University of Texas at Austin
P.J.F.	Philip J. Ford, Department of French, University of Cambridge
P.M.	Peter Mack, Department of English and Comparative Literary Studies, University of Warwick
P.M.K.	Paschalis M. Kitromilides, Department of Political Science, University of Athens
P.Ma.	Peter Mackridge, Faculty of Medieval and Modern Languages, University of Oxford
P.Mg.	Paul Magdalino, Koç University, Istanbul
P.Mu.	Penelope Murray, Department of Classics, University of Warwick
P.N.	Paul Nelles, Department of History, Carleton University
P.O.	Patricia Osmond, College of Design, Iowa State University
P.O.L.	Pamela O. Long, Washington, D.C.
P.R.H.	Philip Hardie, Trinity College, University of Cambridge
P.V.	Phiroze Vasunia, Department of Classics, University of Reading
P.v.d.E.	Philip van der Eijk, Institut für Klassische Philologie, Humboldt-Universität zu Berlin
R.A.K.	Robert Kaster, Department of Classics, Princeton University
R.B.	Reinhold Bichler, Institut für Alte Geschichte und Altorientalistik, Universität Innsbruck
R.Bu.	Rebecca Bushnell, Department of English, University of Pennsylvania
R.C.K.	Robert C. Ketterer, Department of Classics, University of Iowa
R.E.G.	Richard E. Goodkin, Department of French and Italian, University of Wisconsin-Madison

R.G.	Robert Goulding, Program of Liberal Studies, University of Notre Dame
R.H.	Ralph Hexter, President, Hampshire College
R.J.	Richard Jenkyns, Faculty of Classics, University of Oxford
R.K.	Roland Kany, Katholisch-Theologische Fakultät, Universität München
R.L.	Robert Lamberton, Department of Classics, Washington University in St. Louis
R.Mi.	Robert Miola, Department of English and Classics, Loyola University Maryland
R.Ne.	Robert S. Nelson, Department of the History of Art, Yale University
R.No.	Robert E. Norton, Department of German and Russian, University of Notre Dame
R.R.R.S.	R. R. R. Smith, Faculty of Classics, University of Oxford
R.T.	Richard Tarrant, Department of the Classics, Harvard University
R.T.R.	Ronald T. Ridley, Department of History, University of Melbourne
R.T.W.A.	Richard T. W. Arthur, Department of Philosophy, McMaster University
R.W.	Ruth Webb, UMR 8163 "Savoirs, Textes, Langage," Université Lille 3
R.W.G.	Robert Gaston, Department of Art History, La Trobe University
R.W.T.	Robert W. Thomson, Oriental Institute, University of Oxford
S.A.B.	Sarah Annes Brown, Department of English, Anglia Ruskin University
S.B.	Shane Butler, Department of Classics, University of California Los Angeles
S.B.B.	Suzanne Butters, Department of Art History, University of Manchester
S.Br.	Stefano Bruni, Dipartimento di Scienze Storiche, Università degli Studi di Ferrara
S.E.	Sabrina Ebbersmeyer, Fakultät für Philosophie, Ludwig-Maximilians-Universität München
S.F.	Sotera Fornaro, Facoltà di Lettere e Filosofia, Università degli Studi di Sassari
S.G.	Stephen Gersh, Medieval Institute, University of Notre Dame
S.Gi.	Stuart Gillespie, Department of English Literature, University of Glasgow
S.Go.	Simon Goldhill, King's College, University of Cambridge
S.H.	Simon Hornblower, All Souls College, University of Oxford
S.Hu.	S. C. Humphreys, University of Michigan
S.K.	Sachiko Kusukawa, Trinity College, University of Cambridge
S.M.	Suzann Marchand, Department of History, Louisiana State University
S.Mc.	Sally McKee, Department of History, University of California Davis
S.R.	Stefan Rebenich, Historisches Institut, Universität Bern
S.S.	Salvatore Settis, Storia dell'Arte e dell'Archeologia Classica, Scuola Normale Superiore di Pisa
S.Sh.	Steven Shankman, Departments of English and Classics, University of Oregon
T.B.	Tommaso Braccini, Centro Antropologia del Mondo Antico, Università di Siena
T.Ch.	Thomas Christensen, Department of Music, University of Chicago
T.G.	Timo Günther, Baumgart-Stiftung, Germany
T.H.	Tomas Hägg, Department of Linguistic, Literary and Aesthetic Studies, University of Bergen
T.H.-T.	Teresa Huguet-Termes, Departmento de Historia de la Ciencia, Institución Milá y Fontanals
T.Hu.	Thomas Hubbard, Department of Classics, University of Texas at Austin
T.J.M.	Thomas J. Mathiesen, Jacobs School of Music, Indiana University
T.K.	Ted Kaizer, Department of Classics and Ancient History, University of Durham
T.Kr.	Theresa Krier, Department of English, Macalester College
T.Ku.	Taneli Kukkonen, Department of History, University of Jyväskylä, Finland
T.L.	Thomas Laqueur, Department of History, University of California Berkeley
T.M.	Tomaso Montanari, Dipartimento di Discipline Storiche, Università degli Studi di Napoli Federico II
T.R.	Thomas Rütten, School of Historical Studies, Newcastle University
T.S.	Tilo Schabert, Fach Politische Wissenschaft, Friedrich-Alexander Universität Erlangen-Nürnberg
U.L.	Uta Lindgren, Wissenschaftsgeschichte, Universität Bayreuth
U.P.B.	Peter Burke, Faculty of History, University of Cambridge
U.V.	Umberto Vincenti, Dipartimento di Storia e Filosofia del Diritto, Università degli Studi di Padova
V.H.	Vaughan Hart, Department of Architecture and Civil Engineering, University of Bath

V.K.	Victoria Kirkham, Department of Romance Languages, University of Pennsylvania
V.L.	Volker Losemann, Seminar für Alte Geschichte, Philipps-Universität Marburg
V.N.	Vivian Nutton, Wellcome Trust Centre for the History of Medicine, University College London
V.P.	Verity Platt, Departments of Classics and History of Art, Cornell University
W.C.	Walter Cupperi, Classe di Lettere e Filosofia, Scuola Normale Superiore di Pisa
W.H.	Wendy Heller, Department of Music, Princeton University
W.J.K.-K.	W. Julian Korab-Karpowicz, Anglo-American University of Prague
W.L.M.	William L. MacDonald, Department of Art History, Smith College
W.N.	Wilfried Nippel, Humboldt University, Berlin, Germany
W.Ne.	William Newman, Department of History and Philosophy of Science, Indiana University
W.R.J.	W. Ralph Johnson, Department of Classics, University of Chicago
W.S.	William Stenhouse, Department of History, Yeshiva University
W.S.M.	William Morison, Department of History, Grand Valley State University
W.St.	Walter Stephens, Department of German and Romance Languages, Johns Hopkins University
W.W.	Wes Williams, Faculty of Medieval and Modern Languages, University of Oxford
Y.E.	Yaron Ezrahi, Department of Political Science, Hebrew University
Y.H.	Yasmin Haskell, Classics and Ancient History, University of Western Australia
Z.B.	Zygmunt Baranski, Department of Italian, University of Cambridge
Z.S.	Zeph Stewart, Department of the Classics, Harvard University
Z.Sh.	Zur Shalev, Departments of General History and Land of Israel Studies, University of Haifa

INDEX

Bold numbers denote the page on which articles begin. In cross-references, extended discussions are indicated with Roman type.

Aalto, Alvar. *See* Modernism; Theater Architecture
Abano, Pietro d'. *See* Magic; Medicine
Abaris. *See Philosophy*
Abbasids. *See* Avicenna; Islam; Ptolemy; *Philosophy*
Abbo of Fleury. *See Philosophy*
Abd al-Latif al-Baghdadi. *See* Medicine
Abelard, Peter. *See* Chartres; Philosophy; Seneca the Younger; Stoicism; *Astronomy; Book, Manuscript: Development; Macrobius*
Abildgaard, Nicolai. *See Demon*
Abraham. *See* Fathers, Church; Paganism; *Aristotle; Historiography*
Abraham, Karl. *See* Arachne
Abraham bar Hiyya. *See* Judaism
Abravanel, Isaac. *See Judaism*
Abravanel, Judah (Leone Ebreo). *See Judaism*
Abril, P. Simón. *See Terence*
Abulafia, Abraham. *See Pico della Mirandola*
Abulcasis. *See* Pharmacology
Abulfaragius. *See* Medicine
Abū Maʿshar (Albumasar). *See* Astrology; Cosmology
Abū-Sulaymān al-Sijistānī. *See Baghdad Aristotelians*
Abu Taher Tarsusi. *See* Persia
Abu Ya'qub Yusuf. *See Averroës*
Abu Yusuf al-Mansur. *See Averroës*
Academy, **1**. *See also* Plato; *Athens; Brutus; Dialogue; Fathers, Church; Neoplatonism; Philosophy; Renaissance*
Acciaiuoli, Nicolò. *See Vitruvius*
Accius. *See* Achilles; Translation
Accursius. *See* Law, Roman
Achaemenides. *See Cyclops*
Achaemenids. *See* East and West; *Colony; Gandhara*
Achelous. *See Hercules*
Achilles, **3**. *See also* Ajax; Alexander the Great; Amazons; Epic; Helen; Hero; Pope, Alexander; Statius; Zeno's Paradoxes; *Centaur; Cinema; Iphigenia; Knossos; Labyrinth; Novel; Nudity; Papyrology; Parmenides; Troilus*
Achilles Tatius. *See* Photius; Translation
Achillini. *See Philosophy*
Achmat. *See* Caesar, as Political Title
Acis. *See Galatea*
Acosta, José de. *See* Cartography; *Atlantis; Ethnography*
Acrisius. *See Danaë*
Acropolis. *See* Architecture; Athens; Replicas
Actaeon, **5**. *See also* Paganism; *Centaur; Locus Amoenus; Ovid*
Actuarius, Johannes. *See* Medicine
Acyndynus, Gregory. *See* Thomas Magister
Adam. *See* Devil; Epic; Giants; Progress and Decline; *Alexander the Great; Nudity; Numismatics; Ornament; Petrarch; Pico della Mirandola; Statius; Writing*
Adam, James. *See* Adam, Robert; *Piranesi; Tourism*
Adam, Jean-Pierre. *See* Pliny the Younger
Adam, Robert, **6**. *See also* Architecture; Grand Tour; Hadrian's Villa; Neoclassicism; Pompeii; Split; Triumphal Arch; *Piranesi; Temple*
Adam, William. *See* Adam, Robert
Adamantius. *See Physiognomy*
Adams, Francis. *See* Medicine
Adams, John. *See* Cicero; Constitution, Mixed; Democracy; Founding Fathers; Revolution, French; Xenophon
Adams, John Quincy. *See* Rhetoric; *Juvenal*
Addams, Jane. *See* Museum
Addison, Joseph. *See* Cato the Younger; Comedy; Dulce et decorum est; Founding Fathers; Imitation; Milton; Pastoral; Seneca the Younger; Suicide; Tragedy; *Dialogue; Genius*
Adela (daughter of William the Conqueror). *See Ovid*
Adelard of Bath. *See Boethius*
Admetus. *See* Alcestis; *Euripides*
Adonis, **7**. *See also* Aphrodite; *Elegy; Names*
Adorno, Theodor. *See* Divination; Sirens
Adrian VI. *See* Nudity; *Pasquino*
Aedesius. *See Julian*
Aeëtes. *See Medea*
Aegeus. *See Opera*
Aegisthus. *See Cassandra*
Aelian. *See* Egypt; Natural History; Physiologus; Warfare; Zoology; *Basilisk; Korais; Moschopoulos*
Aelius Aristides. *See* Cities, Praise of; Tourism; *Atticism; Byzantium; Dream Interpretation; Poetics; Renaissance; Thomas Magister*
Aelius Herodianus. *See Palimpsest*
Aelius Stilo. *See* Etymology
Aemilius Asper. *See* Virgil
Aemilius Paulus. *See* Rome
Aeneas, **8**. *See also* Aphrodite; Cupid; Dido; Epic; Europe; Greek, Ancient; Romance, Medieval; *Hercules; Hero; Imitation; Names; Popular Culture; Virgil*
Aeneas the Tactician. *See Warfare*
Aeolus. *See Neptune*
Aeschines. *See* Dialogue; Translation; *Athens; Demosthenes*
Aeschylus, **10**. *See also* Achilles; Athens;

Aeschylus *(continued)*
Book, Printed; Cassandra; Classical; East and West; Electra; Epic; Euripides; Liberty; Matriarchy; Milton; Opera; Orpheus; Parody; Political Theory; Prometheus; Racine; Renaissance; Romanticism; Tragedy; Translation; Writing; *Anthology; Aristophanes; Art History; Barbarians; Book, Manuscript: Development; Byzantium; Estienne, Henri II; Moschopoulos; Mycenae; Nietzsche; Symposium; Thomas Magister; Triclinius*
Aeson. *See Medea*
Aesop. *See* Ancients and Moderns; Comedy; Education; Rabelais; Seven Sages of Rome; Translation; *Donatus; Judaism; Melanchthon; Poliziano; Valla*
Aesthetics, **11**. *See also* Apollo
Aethicus Ister. *See Geography*
Aëtius of Amida. *See* Doxography; Gynecology; Medicine; *Diels, Hermann*
Affecti, **18**
Africanus. *See Opera*
Agamemnon. *See* Ajax; Electra; Europe; Helen; Iphigenia; Mycenae; *Achilles; Allegory; Cassandra; Names*
Agatharchus of Samos. *See* Aesthetics; *Art History*
Agathias. *See* Greek Anthology; Plutarch; Renaissance; *Anthology; Iranian Hellenism*
Agathodaimon. *See Cartography*
Agave. *See Euripides*
Agenor. *See Europe*
Agesilaus II. *See* Biography; Sparta; Xenophon; *Persia*
Agis IV. *See* Constitution, Mixed
Agostini, Leonardo. *See Cameos*
Agricola. *See Names*
Agricola, Rudolph. *See* Petrarch; Rhetoric; Valla
Agrippa, Marcus Vipsanius. *See* Guidebooks to Ancient Rome; Pantheon; Roads, Roman; Rome; *Cartography; Geography; Maison Carrée*
Agrippa von Nettesheim, Heinrich Cornelius. *See* Demon; Harmony of the Spheres; Magic; Mnemonics; Skepticism; *Hermes Trismegistus*
Agrippina. *See Nero*
Agucchi, Giovan Battista. *See Bellori*
Aguilonius. *See* Color
Agustín, Antonio. *See* Coins; Epigraphy; Fragments; Guidebooks to Ancient Rome; Numismatics; *Historiography; Inscriptions; Ligorio; Nudity*
Ahala, C. Servilius. *See Brutus*
Ahrun. *See* Medicine
Aidoneus. *See Empedocles*
Ajax, **19**. *See also* Sophocles; Suicide; *Achilles; Cassandra; Melancholy; Mythology; Poetics*
Akers, Keith. *See* Vegetarianism
Akhenaten. *See* Egypt
Akropolites, Constantine. *See* Metaphrasis
Aksyonov, Vasily. *See* Aristophanes; Epic
Alain de Lille. *See* Immortality of the Soul; Paganism; Plato; Rhetoric; *Boethius; Martianus Capella*
Alamanni, Luigi. *See* Elegy
Alarcón, Juan Ruiz de. *See* Terence
Alardus, Wilhelm. *See Anacreon*
Alaric. *See Ovid*
Albani, Cardinal Alessandro. *See* Winckelmann; *Collecting; Paper Museum*
Albani, Francesco. *See Hermaphroditus*
Albani collection. *See Sarcophagi*
Albee, Edward. *See* Comedy
Alberic of Monte Cassino. *See* Education; Letters; Rhetoric
Alberti, Leandro. *See* Etruscans
Alberti, Leon Battista, **21**. *See also* Aesthetics; Architecture; Art History; Atrium; Book, Manuscript: Development; Cartography; City Planning; Color; Consolation; Dialogue; Domus Aurea; Epigraphy; Guidebooks to Ancient Rome; Hieroglyphs; Historiography; History Painting; Households; Hypnerotomachia Poliphili; Imitation; Inscriptions; Lucian; Neoclassicism; Nudity; Optics; Ornament; Palace; Palladio; Plato; Plautus; Pliny the Younger; Portico; Pythagoras; Roman Monuments, Reuse of; Rome; Satire; Sewers; Theater Architecture; Triumphal Arch; Ut pictura poesis; Veterinary Medicine; Virgil; Vitruvius; Warfare; *Diogenes Laertius; Etruscans; Herodotus; Obelisk; Petrarch*
Albertini, Francesco. *See* Guidebooks to Ancient Rome; Rome; *Art History*
Alberto Pio da Carpi. *See Greek, Ancient*
Albertus Magnus. *See* Alchemy; Astrology; Botany; Bronze; Demon; Liberal Arts; Logic; Melancholy; Mnemonics; Monsters; Natural History; Philosophy; Physiognomy; Seneca the Younger; Sexuality; Stoicism; Volcanoes; Wonders; Zoology; *Automata; Macrobius; Magic*
Albinoni, Tomaso. *See Opera*
Albinus. *See Concord, Philosophical; Isagoge*
Albizzi, Albiera degli. *See Elegy*
Albucasis (al-Zahrawi). *See* Medicine
Alcaeus. *See* Allegory; Horace
Alcestis, **22**. *See also Euripides; Hercules*
Alchemy, **23**
Alciato, Andrea. *See* Ajax; Cupid; Emblem; Guidebooks to Ancient Rome; Hercules; Natural History; Nudity; Paganism; *Centaur; Hercules*
Alcibiades. *See* Erasmus; Thucydides; *Aristophanes; Socrates; Symposium*
Alcinous. *See Isagoge*
Alcmaeon of Croton. *See* Immortality of the Soul
Alcman. *See* Pastoral; Purple
Alcmene. *See Amphitryon*
Alcubierre, Rocco de. *See* Herculaneum
Alcuin, **25**. *See also* Grammar; Horace; Liberal Arts; Notitia Dignitatum; Pastoral; Renaissance; Virgil; Vitruvius; *Book, Manuscript: Development; Letters*
Aldelmus. *See Book, Manuscript: Development*
Alderotti, Taddeo. *See* Medicine
Aldington, Richard. *See* Translation
Aldobrandini, Tommaso. *See Diogenes Laertius*
Aldrich, Henry. *See* Logic
Aldrovandi, Ulisse. *See* Collecting; Etruscans; Guidebooks to Ancient Rome; Natural History; Pliny the Elder; Zoology
Aldrovandini, Pompeo. *See* Triumphal Arch
Aleander, Hieronymus. *See Greek, Ancient*
Aleandro, Girolamo. *See Raphael*
Alegreto, Antonio. *See* Guidebooks to Ancient Rome
Alemanno, Yohanan. *See Judaism; Pico della Mirandola*
Alemannus, Hermannus. *See* Tragedy
Aleotti, Giambattista. *See* Theater Architecture
Alessandro, Duke of Florence. *See Numismatics*
Alessi, Galeazzo. *See* Grotto
Alessi, Marco Attilio. *See Etruscans*
Alexander VI. *See* Annius of Viterbo; Colony; Giants; Names; Paganism; Roman Monuments, Reuse of; *Etruscans; Historiography; Janus; Pasquino; Sallust*
Alexander VII. *See* Pantheon; *City Planning*
Alexander, Jason. *See* Plautus
Alexander of Aphrodisias. *See* Al-Fārābī; Aristotle; Immortality of the Soul; Logic; *Averroës; Baghdad Aristotelians; Commentary; Judaism; Philosophy*
Alexander of Hales. *See* Immortality of the Soul
Alexander of Villedieu. *See* Grammar; *Liberal Arts*
Alexander Severus. *See* Guidebooks to Ancient Rome; Horace; Roman Monuments, Reuse of; Rome
Alexander the Great, **25**. *See also* Alexandria; Alexandrianism; Aristotle; Cartography; East and West; Epic; Gandhara; Gellius; Hellenistic Age; Hero; Historiography; India; Iranian Hellenism; Islam; Judaism; Novel; Ornament; Persia; Popular Culture; Rabelais; Romance, Medieval; Rome; Sports; Thucydides; Warfare; Winckelmann; Xenophon; *Achilles; Armenian Hellenism; Barbarians; Basilisk; Coins; Colony; Cynicism; Divination; Genre; Geography; Liberal Arts; Mystery Religions; Ode; Oracles; Plutarch; Zoology*
Alexander the Sophist. *See Poetics*

Alexandria, **31**. *See also* Alexandrianism; Book, Manuscript: Production; Greek Anthology; Libraries; Museum
Alexandrianism, **32**
Alexios I Komnenos. *See* Caesar, as Political Title; Renaissance
Alexios III. *See* Caesar, as Political Title
Alfanus, bishop of Salerno. *See* Medicine
Al-Fārābī, **20**. *See also* Doxography; Immortality of the Soul; Judaism; Music; Neoplatonism; Philosophy; Plato; *Astrology; Averroës; Baghdad Aristotelians; Concord, Philosophical*
Alfieri, Vittorio. *See* Alcestis; *Brutus; Latin Language; Livy*
Alfonso I of Naples. *See* Caesars, Twelve; Triumphal Arch
Alfonso de Portugal. *See Numismatics*
Alfonso of Aragon. *See* Donation of Constantine; Valla; *Historiography; Warfare*
Alfred the Great. *See* Translation; *Boethius; City Planning*
Algardi, Alessandro. *See* Hydra; Sculpture
Algarotti, Francesco. *See* Iphigenia; Opera; *Maecenas*
Alkaios. *See* Achilles
Allacci, Leone. *See* Forgery
Allatius, Leo. *See* Greek Anthology
Allegory, **34**. *See also* Paganism
Allen, Woody. *See* Aphrodite; Satire; Sophocles; *Comedy*
Allington, Edward. *See* Replicas
Allori, Alessandro. *See* Etruscans
Alma-Tadema, Sir Lawrence. *See* Fin de Siècle Art; Pompeii; Sacrifice in the Arts; Toga; *Baths; Maenads*
Almeida, Francisco de. *See Socrates*
Almogáver, Juan Boscán. *See* Hero and Leander
Alopa, Laurentius de. *See* Satire
Alpers, Svetlana. *See Ecphrasis*
Alsop, Anthony. *See* Horace
Alsted, Johann Heinrich. *See* Mnemonics
Altheim, Franz. *See Nietzsche*
Altilio, Gabriele. *See* Genre
Amalasuntha. *See* Ravenna
Amalthea. *See Grotto*
Amarcius. *See* Horace
Amaseo, Romulo. *See Names*
Amati, Carlo. *See* Temple
Amazons, **41**. *See also* Matriarchy; Sculpture; *Achilles; Pegasus*
Ambrose. *See* Cicero; Fathers, Church; Horace; *Anthology; Aristotle; Consolation; Erasmus; Isidore; Philo; Physiologus; Rhetoric*
Amcott, Vincent. *See* Parody
Amerbach, Johannes. *See* Book, Printed
Amigoni, Jacopo. *See* Aeneas; *Adonis*
ʾĀmirī, al-. *See* Aristotle; *Baghdad Aristotelians*
Amīr Khusrow Dehlawī. *See* Persia
Amis, Martin. *See* Satire
Ammanati, Bartolomeo. *See* Sculpture; *Herm; Nudity*
Ammianus Marcellinus. *See* Fathers, Church; Hieroglyphs; Mirabilia Urbis; Obelisk; *Barbarians; Julian; Renaissance*
Ammirato, Scipione. *See* Tacitus; Warfare; *Etruscans*
Ammonius. *See* Al-Fārābī; Logic; *Aristotle; Philosophy*
Ammonius Hermiae. *See* Aristotle
Ammonius Saccas. *See* Fathers, Church
Amon. *See Hermes Trismegistus*
Ampère, Jean-Jacques. *See* Renaissance
Amphion. *See* Rome
Amphitrite the Nereid. *See Neptune*
Amphitryon, **42**
Amyot, Jacques. *See* Cleopatra; Plutarch; Suetonius; Translation; *Biography; Daphnis*
Anabaptists. *See* Progress and Decline
Anacharsis, **42**. *See also* Barbarians
Anacreon and Anacreontics, **43**. *See also* Allegory; Cupid; Homosexuality; Ode; Prosody; Rabelais; Sappho; Translation; *Dacier*
Anastasius I. *See* Ravenna
Anastasius IV. *See* Sarcophagi
Anastasius Bibliothecarius. *See* Greek, Ancient
Anaxagoras. *See* Allegory; Censorship; Cosmology; Plato; Presocratics; Rabelais; *Art History; Atoms*
Anaximander. *See* Cartography; Fragments; Heidegger; Meteorology; Presocratics; *Liberal Arts*
Anaximenes. *See* Meteorology; Presocratics
Anchises. *See* Aeneas
Ancients and Moderns, **44**
Ancilles. *See* Seven Sages of Rome
Andernach, Johann Guinther von. *See* Medicine
Anderson, Judith. *See Medea*
André, Elie. *See* Ode
Andres, Stefan Paul. *See* Xanthippe
Andrew of Caesarea. *See Renaissance*
Andromache. *See* Helen; Names; Ronsard; *Widow of Ephesus*
Andromeda. *See Pegasus*
Andronicus II Paeaeologus. *See Byzantium; Moschopoulos; Planudes; Renaissance; Thomas Magister*
Andronicus of Rhodes. *See* Aristotle; Logic; Lyceum; *Philosophy*
Angelo, Jacopo d'. *See* Cartography; Geography
Angeloni, Francesco. *See Bellori*
Angelopoulos, Theo. *See* Odysseus; *Cinema*
Anghiera, Pietro Martire d'. *See* Ethnography
Angiolini, Gasparo. *See Mime*
Anguillara, Aloysius. *See Dioscorides*
Anguillara, Giovanni Andrea dell'. *See* Ariadne
Anguisciola, Sofonisba. *See Names*
Anhacht, David. *See* Medicine
Anicia Juliana. *See* Renaissance; *Book, Manuscript: Development*
Anne of England. *See Thucydides*
Annianus. *See* Ptolemy; *Calendars*
Annius of Viterbo, **46**. *See also* Book, Manuscript: Development; Commentary; Etruscans; Forgery; Fragments; Giants; Guidebooks to Ancient Rome; Hieroglyphs; Historiography; Inscriptions; Janus; *Scaliger, Joseph Justus*
Anonymus Bruxellensis. *See* Doxography
Anonymus Latinus. *See Physiognomy*
Anonymus Londinensis. *See* Doxography
Anonymus Parisinus. *See* Doxography
Anouilh, Jean. *See* Sophocles; Tragedy; *Antigone; Orpheus*
Anscombe, G. E. M. *See* Ethics
Anselm. *See* Philosophy; Plato; Renaissance
Antaeus. *See Hercules*
Anthemius of Tralles. *See* Archimedes; Hagia Sophia
Anthologia Planudea. *See Bessarion*
Anthology and Florilegium, **47**
Anthony, Saint. *See* Popular Culture; *Paganism*
Anthony, Susan B. *See Lyceum*
Anthony Abbott, Saint. *See* Biography; *Centaur*
Anthony of Novgorod. *See Constantinople*
Anthropology, **48**
Anticleia. *See Sisyphus*
Antigone, **50**. *See also* Sophocles
Antigonus of Carystus. *See* Wonders; *Art History*
Antinous. *See* Portraits, Reception of Ancient; Raphael; Sculpture; Winckelmann
Antiochus. *See Opera*
Antiochus I. *See Mithras*
Antiochus IV. *See Judaism*
Antiochus of Ascalon. *See* Concord, Philosophical; *Brutus*
Antiope. *See Amazons; Paganism*
Antipater. *See Mausoleum*
Antiphon. *See* Squaring the Circle
Antiquarianism, **51**
Antisthenes. *See* Dialogue; Xanthippe; *Cynicism*
Antonines. *See* Gibbon; *Sarcophagi*
Antoninus Pius. *See* Architecture; *Annius of Viterbo; Baalbek; Portraits, Reception of Ancient; Rome*
Antonius Diogenes. *See Photius*
Antony, Mark. *See* Brutus; Caesar, Julius; Cleopatra; Plutarch; Shakespeare; *Barbarians*
Anubis. *See Paganism*
Apelles. *See* Aesthetics; Alexander the Great; Art History; Color; Pompeii; Rome
Aphrodite, **53**. *See also* Adonis; Aeneas; Aesthetics; Cupid; Europe; Hercules;

Aphrodite *(continued)*
Homosexuality; Mithras; Neoclassicism; Nudity; Paganism; Popular Culture; Pygmalion; Raphael; Sappho; Sculpture; Sibyls; Venus de Milo; *Allegory; Cinema; Galatea; Grotto; Helen; Hermaphroditus; Hero and Leander; Hesiod; Hypnerotomachia Poliphili; Locus Amoenus; Mars; Opera; Phaedra; Rome*
Aphthonius. *See* Poetics; Rhetoric; *Armenian Hellenism*
Apianus, Petrus (Peter Bierewitz). *See* Names; Ptolemy; *Calendars*
Apicius. *See Symposium*
Apion. *See* Forgery
Apis. *See Paganism*
Apollinaire, Guillaume. *See* Orpheus
Apollo, **54**. *See also* Marsyas; Orpheus; Paganism; Parnassus; Philosophy; Pythagoras; Raphael; Rome; Sculpture; Sibyls; *Cassandra; Gandhara; Grotto; Hippocrates; Laocoön; Leda; Matriarchy; Midas; Muses; Names; Opera; Oracles; Pasquino; Pegasus; Plutarch; Popular Culture*
Apollo Belvedere, **55**. *See also* Apollo; Replicas; Rome; Sculpture; Winckelmann; *Plaster Casts*
Apollodorus of Athens. *See* Aesthetics; Education; *Anthology; Calendars; Heyne; Pegasus*
Apollodorus of Pergamum. *See* Genre
Apollonius. *See Wonders*
Apollonius Dyscolus. *See* Aristotle; Grammar; *Liberal Arts*
Apollonius of Athens. *See* Belvedere Torso
Apollonius of Citium. *See* Nicetas Codex
Apollonius of Perga. *See* Archimedes; *Astronomy; Euclid*
Apollonius of Rhodes. *See* Alexandrianism; Castor and Pollux; Ecphrasis; Epic; Medea; Orpheus; Translation; *Cinema; Homer; Novel; Opera*
Apollonius of Tralles. *See* Rome
Apollonius of Tyana. *See* Aesthetics; Tourism
Apollonius of Tyre. *See* Romance, Medieval; *Popular Culture*
Apostolis, Michael. *See* Greek, Ancient
Appian of Alexandria. *See Caesar, Julius; Corneille, Pierre; Racine*
Apsines. *See Poetics*
Apsyrtos. *See* Veterinary Medicine
Apted, Michael. *See* Novel
Apuleius, **56**. *See also* Book, Manuscript: Development; Book, Printed; Cupid; Demon; Divination; Egypt; Hypnerotomachia Poliphili; Magic; Marsyas; Natural History; Novel; Plutarch; Translation; *Archimedes; Cicero; Commentary; Libraries*
Aquarius. *See Pegasus*
Arachne, **57**. *See also Ovid*
Aratus of Soli. *See* Astronomy; Divination; Education; Meteorology; Ptolemy; *Book, Manuscript: Development; Commentary; Melanchthon; Planudes*
Arberini, Giovanni. *See* Sarcophagi
Arcadia, **58**
Arcadius. *See* East and West; Renaissance
Arcerius, Sixtus. *See* Warfare
Arcesilaus. *See* Skepticism
Archelaus. *See* Presocratics
Archestratus of Gela. *See* Symposium
Archidamus. *See* Warfare
Archigenes of Apamea. *See Melancholy*
Archilochus. *See* Fragments; Papyrology; *Annius of Viterbo; Poetics; Prosody; Seven Sages of Rome; Writing*
Archimedes, **59**. *See also* Alexandria; Commentary; Liberal Arts; Sicily; Squaring the Circle; Warfare; *Automata; Book, Manuscript: Development; Byzantium; Judaism; Renaissance; Rubens*
Archinto, Cardinal Alberico. *See* Winckelmann
Architecture, **60**
Archytas. *See* Gellius; *Automata*
Arcimboldo, Giuseppe. *See* Color; *Physiognomy*
Arendt, Hannah. *See* Political Theory
Aretaeus of Cappadocia. *See* Medicine; Melancholy
Arethas of Caesarea. *See* Epictetus; Greek Anthology; Inscriptions; Renaissance; *Book, Manuscript: Development; Byzantium; Constantinople; Lucian*
Aretino, Pietro. *See* Comedy; Genius; History Painting; Pornography; Terence; *Color; Livy; Nudity; Pasquino*
Argenterius, Ioannes. *See Galen*
Argoli, Andrea. *See Astrology*
Argonauts, **67**. *See also* Ronsard
Argus. *See* Elegy; *Names*
Argyropoulos, John. *See* Greek, Ancient; Medicine
Ariadne, **67**. *See also* Knossos; *Catullus; Ovid; Phaedra; Popular Culture; Portraits, Reception of Ancient*
Arianna. *See* Nudity
Ariosto, Lodovico. *See* Ariadne; Epic; Hero; Horace; Imitation; Locus Amoenus; Lucan; Parasite; Pegasus; Plautus; Satire; Shakespeare; Sirens; Virgil; *Amazons; Comedy; Cyclops; Parody; Sacrifice in the Arts*
Aristaeus. *See Orpheus*
Aristarchus of Samos. *See* Archimedes; Aristotle; Cosmology; *Scaliger, Joseph Justus*
Aristarchus of Samothrace. *See* Commentary; Homer; Wolf, Friedrich August; *Asterisk*
Aristides of Thebes. *See* Rome; *Aesthetics*
Aristides Quintilianus. *See* Music
Aristippus, Henricus. *See* Diogenes Laertius; Greek, Ancient; Philosophy
Aristocracy, **68**
Aristophanes, **69**. *See also* Aeschylus; Allegory; Book, Manuscript: Production; Comedy; Empedocles; Homosexuality; Menander; Olympus; Parody; Pindar; Poetics; Political Theory; Presocratics; Prosody; Rabelais; Racine; Renaissance; Sacrifice in the Arts; Satire; Schlegel; Squaring the Circle; Suda; Translation; *Bentley; Book, Manuscript: Development; Byzantium; Calendars; Censorship; Dacier; Herm; Hunayn ibn-Ishāq; Melanchthon; Philosophy; Sibyls; Thomas Magister; Triclinius; Tzetzes*
Aristophanes of Byzantium. *See* Menander; *Asterisk*
Aristotle and Aristotelianism, **70**. *See also* Academy; Aeschylus; Aesthetics; Alchemy; Alexander the Great; Al-Fārābī; Allegory; Ancients and Moderns; Anthropology; Archimedes; Art History; Astronomy; Atoms; Averroës; Avicenna; Baghdad Aristotelians; Boethius; Book, Manuscript: Production; Book, Printed; Botany; Byzantium; Cartography; Censorship; City Planning; Color; Comedy; Commentary; Concord, Philosophical; Constitution, Mixed; Corneille, Pierre; Cosmology; Dante; Democracy; Despotism, Oriental; Deus ex Machina; Dialectic; Dialogue; Diels, Hermann; Diogenes Laertius; Divination; Doxography; Dramatic Unities; Dream Interpretation; Education; Empedocles; Epic; Epicurus; Ethics; Ethnography; Etruscans; Euclid; Euripides; Fathers, Church; Fortune; Founding Fathers; Fragments; Galen; Galileo; Genius; Geography; Grammar; Greek, Ancient; Gynecology; Harmony of the Spheres; Heidegger; Heraclitus; Historiography; History Painting; Homer; Households; Humors; Imitation; Immortality of the Soul; Iranian Hellenism; Irony; Islam; Judaism; Lessing; Liberal Arts; Liberty; Libraries; Logic; Lyceum; Lyric Poetry; Magic; Melancholy; Metaphysics; Meteorology; Milton; Mnemonics; Monsters; Muses; Museum; Music; Mystery Religions; Natural History; Neoplatonism; Novel; Opera; Optics; Parmenides; Petrarch; Philosophy; Physiognomy; Physiologus; Pico della Mirandola; Plato; Plutarch; Poetics; Political Theory; Popular Culture; Presocratics; Progress and Decline; Prosody; Psellus; Ptolemy; Purple; Pythagoras; Rabelais; Racine; Renaissance; Revolution, French; Rhetoric; Scaliger, Julius Caesar; Schlegel; Seneca the Elder; Seven Sages of Rome; Sexuality; Shakespeare; Skepticism; Slavery; Sophocles; Sparta; Squaring the Circle; Suicide; Thucydides; Topos; Tragedy; Translation; Ut pictura poesis; Valla; Vegetarianism; Warfare; Zoology; *Affecti;*

Armenian Hellenism; Astrology; Athens; Atlantis; Automata; Barbarians; Bellori; Bessarion; Book, Manuscript: Development; Catharsis; Chrēsis; Christine de Pizan; Cicero; Donation of Constantine; Erasmus; Hippocrates; Horace; Humanism; Isagoge; Jesuits; Korais; Latin and the Professions; Melanchthon; Names; Papyrology; Pegasus; Photius; Poliziano; Pope, Alexander; Raphael; Symposium; Syriac Hellenism
Aristoxenus. *See* Music
Arius Didymus. *See* Doxography
Armenian Hellenism, 77
Armenini, Giovanni Battista. *See Color*
Armenopoulos, Konstantinos. *See* Law, Roman
Arminius (Hermann). *See Barbarians*
Arne, Thomas. *See* Statius
Arnim, Hans von. *See* Doxography; Stoicism
Arnobius. *See* Epicurus; Immortality of the Soul; Paganism
Arnold, Gottfried. *See* Progress and Decline
Arnold, Matthew. *See* Elegy; Empedocles; Lucretius; Macaulay; Pastoral; Sophocles; Translation; *Antigone; Cavafy; Laocoön*
Arnold, Thomas. *See* Education; Macaulay
Arnold of Brescia. *See* Rome
Arnold of Villanova. *See* Medicine
Arnolfo di Cambio. *See* Rome; Warfare
Arp, Hans. *See* Modernism
Arp, Jean. *See Laocoön*
Arrian of Nicomedia. *See* Alexander the Great; Epictetus; Xenophon
Artavazdes. *See* Armenian Hellenism
Artaxerxes II. *See Persia*
Artemidorus of Ephesus (diviner). *See* Dream Interpretation; Oracles
Artemidorus of Ephesus (geographer). *See* Cartography; Papyrology; *Fragments*
Artemis. *See* Actaeon; *Allegory; Iphigenia*
Artemisia. *See* Mausoleum; Seven Wonders of the World
Artemon. *See Danaë*
Art History and Criticism, 78
Arthur, King. *See* Alexander the Great; Amphitryon; Novel; Tragedy
Arundel, Richard Fitzalan, 1st Earl of. *See* Grand Tour
Arundel, Thomas Howard, 3rd Earl of. *See* Collecting
Ascanius. *See Aeneas*
Ascham, Roger. *See* Rhetoric; Tragedy
Asclepiades of Prusa. *See Judaism*
Asclepiads. *See Hippocrates*
Asclepiodotus. *See Warfare*
Asclepius. *See* Writing; *Centaur; Hermes Trismegistus; Pergamon; Philosophy*
Asconius Pedianus. *See Commentary*
Ashmole, Elias. *See Astrology*
Asplund, Erik Gunnar. *See* Architecture
Asser. *See Biography*
Asterisk, 83
Asterius, king of Crete. *See Europe*
Asterius, Turcius Rufius Apronianus. *See Book, Manuscript: Development*
Astérix, 83
Astle, Thomas. *See* Writing
Astraea. *See* Progress and Decline; *Popular Culture*
Astrampsychus. *See* Oracles
Astrology, 84. *See also* Divination; Magic
Astronomy, 89
Astyanax. *See* Ronsard
Athanasius of Alexandria. *See* Alexandria; Immortality of the Soul; *Biography; Cities, Praise of; Philosophy*
Atheism, 96
Athena. *See* Arachne; Raphael; *Allegory; Comic Books; Iphigenia; Matriarchy; Names; Pegasus; Prometheus*
Athenaeus. *See* Natural History; Parody; Poetics; Prosody; Symposium; *Anthology; Bessarion; Hippocrates; Marxism; Music; Renaissance*
Athenagoras. *See* Epicurus
Athens, 97. *See also* Alexandrianism; *Armenian Hellenism; Böckh; City Planning*
Atkinson, Kate. *See* Ovid
Atlantis, 100
Atlas, 102. *See also* Paganism; *Hercules*
Atoms and Atomism, 103. *See also* Plato
Atreus. *See* Thyestes
Atrium, 105
Attalid dynasty. *See Athens; Pergamon*
Atticism, 106
Atticus (Platonist). *See* Fathers, Church
Atticus, Titus Pomponius. *See* Writing; *Grotto; Letters*
Attila. *See* Epic; *Barbarians; Corneille, Pierre; Names*
Attis. *See Mystery Religions*
Atwood, Margaret. *See* Demeter and Persephone; Penelope; *Medea*
Aubrey, John. *See Biography*
Auden, W. H. *See* Dionysus; Elegy; Horace; Ode; Thucydides; *Euripides; Ganymede; Maenads*
Auer, Christoph. *See* Nicetas Codex
Auerbach, Erich. *See* Novel
Augier, Emile. *See Livy*
Augustine, 107. *See also* Aesthetics; Alcuin; Allegory; Antiquarianism; Apuleius; Architecture; Biography; Cato the Younger; Cicero; Collecting; Commentary; Consolation; Cynicism; Danaë; Demiurge; Dialogue; Dido; Dionysus; Divination; Education; Epicurus; Erasmus; Ethics; Fathers, Church; Ficino; Fortune; Geography; Giants; Grammar; Greek, Ancient; Historiography; Horace; Immortality of the Soul; Interpretatio Christiana; Letters; Liberal Arts; Liberty; Magic; Metaphrasis; Monsters; Music; Neoplatonism; Nudity; Orpheus; Pan; Papyrology; Philosophy; Plato; Pliny the Younger; Plutarch; Poetics; Political Theory; Progress and Decline; Pythagoras; Renaissance; Rhetoric; Sallust; Seneca the Younger; Sexuality; Sibyls; Skepticism; Stoicism; Suicide; Translation; Virgil; War, Just; *Art History; Astrology; Atoms; Barbarians; Boethius; Censorship; Chaos; Chrēsis; Dante; Hercules; Hermes Trismegistus; Isidore; Livy; Martianus Capella; Persia; Petrarch; Philo; Planudes*
Augustine of Denmark. *See* Poetics
Augustus, 108. *See also* Aeneas; Alexander the Great; Architecture; Aristotle; Brutus; Caesar, as Political Title; Caesar, Julius; Censorship; Cleopatra; Empire; Epic; Fascism; Forum; Genre; Gibbon; Guidebooks to Ancient Rome; Historiography; Liberty; Maecenas; Mausoleum; Numismatics; Obelisk; Ode; Palace; Pergamon; Pornography; Portraits, Reception of Ancient; Revolution, French; Rome; *Astrology; Calendars; Cartography; Corneille, Pierre; Etruscans; Geography; Horace; Livy; Maison Carrée; Nero; Ovid; Poetics; Popular Culture; Replicas; Roman Monuments, Reuse of; Sibyls; Suetonius*
Augustus III of Poland. *See Maecenas*
Auletta, Robert. *See* Ajax
Aulisio, Domenico. *See Vico*
Aurelian. *See* Roman Monuments, Reuse of; *Museum*
Aurelian of Réôme. *See* Music; Plato; *Isidore*
Aurelius, Marcus. *See* Aristotle; Gibbon; Philosophy; Portraits, Reception of Ancient; Rome; Sculpture; Seneca the Younger; Stoicism; *Brutus; Korais; Lucian; Michelangelo; Mirabilia Urbis; Moschopoulos; Renaissance; Roman Monuments, Reuse of; Rubens; Spolia*
Aurelius Victor. *See* Split; *Dacier*
Aurispa, Giovanni. *See* Byzantium; Panegyric; *Bessarion*
Ausonius (Delphin editor). *See Delphin Classics*
Ausonius, Decimus Maximus. *See* Augustine; Cento; Horace; Virgil; *Commentary; Genre; Mirabilia Urbis; Scaliger, Joseph Justus*
Austen, Jane. *See Commentary*
Autels, Guillaume des. *See* Pléiade
Autolycus of Pitane. *See Judaism*
Automata, 109
Avempace. *See Averroës*
Averlino, Antonio di Pietro (Filarete). *See* Architecture; Museum; Replicas; *Art History; Etruscans; Labyrinth*
Averroës, 111. *See also* Al-Fārābī; Aristotle; Avicenna; Ficino; Imitation; Immortality of the Soul; Judaism; Logic; Squaring the Circle; Tragedy; *Astrology; Baghdad Aristotelians; Philosophy; Plato*

Avianus. *See* Seven Sages of Rome; *Donatus*
Avicebron. *See* Immortality of the Soul
Avicenna, 112. *See also* Aristotle; Galen; Humors; Immortality of the Soul; Judaism; Medicine; Melancholy; Metaphysics; Mnemonics; Neoplatonism; Philosophy; Plato; Syriac Hellenism; *Astrology; Averroës; Baghdad Aristotelians; Commentary; Magic; Natural History; Physiognomy*
Avienus. *See* Virgil
Avitus. *See Genre*
Ayala, Balthasar. *See* War, Just
Aylesford, Earl of. *See* Grand Tour
Ayyubids. *See Islam*
ʿAyyūqī. *See* Persia
Azariah de' Rossi. *See* Philo; *Commentary*

Baal. *See Olympus*
Baalbek, 115
Babbitt, Irving. *See Laocoön*
Babeuf, François-Noël (Gracchus). *See* Niebuhr; Revolution, French; *Names*
Babrius. *See* Seven Sages of Rome; Triclinius; *Byzantium*
Bacchanalia and Saturnalia, 116
Bacchylides. *See* Achilles; *Fragments; Papyrology; Sicily*
Bacci, Andrea. *See* Water Supply; *Symposium*
Bach, Johann Sebastian. *See* Endymion; Xenophon; *Midas*
Bachofen, Johann Jakob. *See* Ethnography; Professionalization of Classics; *Anthropology; Burckhardt; Matriarchy*
Bacon, Francis. *See* Ancients and Moderns; Astrology; Commentary; Dialectic; Divination; Endymion; Europe; Galen; Gibbon; Historiography; Maxims; Paganism; Philosophy; Progress and Decline; Prometheus; Ptolemy; Tacitus; Topos; Warfare; Wonders; *Atlantis; Atoms; Biography; Cartography; Colony; Doxography; Letters; Livy; Neo-Latin*
Bacon, Henry. *See* Temple
Bacon, Roger. *See* Alchemy; Aristotle; Astrology; Calendars; Grammar; Greek, Ancient; Magic; Optics; Paganism; Ptolemy; Seneca the Younger; *Book, Manuscript: Development; Philosophy*
Badius Ascensius (Jodocus Badius). *See* Book, Printed; Seneca the Younger; Terence
Baer, Karl von. *See* Presocratics
Baghdad Aristotelians, 116. *See also* Al-Fārābī; Avicenna
Baglione, Giovanni. *See Art History*
Baïf, Jean-Antoine de. *See Pléiade; Terence*
Baïf, Lazare de. *See Ronsard*
Baillou, Guillaume de. *See* Plague
Bailly, Jean-Sylvain. *See Astronomy*
Bakhtin, Mikhail. *See* Cynicism; Epic; Novel; Satire; Widow of Ephesus
Bakhtishū' family. *See* Hunayn ibn-Ishāq
Balaam. *See Magic*
Balami, Ferdinando. *See* Nicetas Codex
Balanchine, George. *See* Apollo; Gesture; Modernism; Orpheus
Balanos, Nicholas. *See Parthenon*
Balbi, Giovanni. *See* Grammar
Balbi, Pietro. *See Philosophy*
Balbillus, Tiberius Claudius. *See* Astrology
Balbus. *See* Liberal Arts
Balde, Jacob. *See* Jesuits; *Horace*
Baldi, Bernardino. *See* Automata
Baldinucci, Filippo. *See Art History*
Balīnās. *See* Alchemy
Balsamon, Theodore. *See* Rhōmaioi
Balthasar, Hans Urs von. *See Fathers, Church*
Bandello, Matteo. *See* Phaedra
Bandinelli, Baccio. *See* Apollo Belvedere; Nudity; Replicas; *Laocoön*
Bandini, Francesco. *See Symposium*
Banville, Théodore Faullain de. *See* Alexandrianism; Xanthippe
Baptista Fulgosus. *See* Cupid
Bara, Theda. *See Cleopatra*
Barbarians, 117
Barbaro, Daniele. *See* Atrium; Theater Architecture; Vitruvius; *City Planning; Palladio*
Barbaro, Ermolao (Hermolaus Barbarus). *See* Botany; Commentary; Dioscorides; Geography; Natural History; Philosophy; *Aristotle*
Barbaro, Francesco. *See* Households; *Petrarch*
Barbedienne, Ferdinand. *See* Bronze
Barber, Samuel. *See Medea*
Barberini, Francesco. *See* Barberini Faun
Barberini family. *See* Praeneste
Barberini Faun, 120
Barbo dynasty. *See Cameos*
Barclay, John. *See* Petronius
Barclay, William. *See* Poetics
Bardi, Giovanni de'. *See* Music; Opera; *Affecti*
Barga, Pietro da. *See* Sculpture
Bargagli, Girolamo. *See* Plautus
Bargrave, John. *See* Tourism
Barhebraeus (Bar-ʿEbrāyā). *See* Syriac Hellenism
Barker, Clive. *See* Venus de Milo
Barlow, Joel. *See* Comedy; Epic
Barlowe, Arthur. *See* Arcadia
Barnabas. *See* Sacrifice in the Arts
Barnes, Jonathan. *See* Aristotle
Barnes, Joshua. *See* Homer
Barney, Matthew. *See Faun*
Baron, Hans. *See* Renaissance
Baronio, Cesare. *See* Donation of Constantine; Sibyls; *Casaubon; Corneille, Pierre*
Barosso, Maria. *See* Replicas
Barozzi, Pietro. *See* Immortality of the Soul
Barras, Paul. *See* Revolution, French
Barrett, Francis. *See Astrology*
Barrio, G. *See Magna Graecia*
Barrit, Desmond. *See* Plautus
Barros, Homero do Rêgo. *See Names*
Barry, Edward Middleton. *See Herm*
Barth, Caspar. *See Anacreon*
Barth, Heinrich. *See Olympus*
Barthélemy, Jean-Jacques. *See* Anacharsis; Palmyra; *Antigone; Barbarians*
Bartholin, Thomas. *See* Writing
Bartholomaeus Anglicus. *See* Ethnography; Natural History; Purple; *Isidore*
Bartholomew, Saint. *See Names*
Bartholomew of Messina. *See* Divination
Bartoli, Pietro Santi. *See Bellori; Mausoleum*
Bartolomé de las Casas. *See Ethnography*
Bartolomeo da San Corcordio. *See* Gellius; Sallust
Bartolus de Saxoferrato. *See* Law, Roman
Barye, Antoine-Louis. *See* Bronze
Barzizza, Gasparino. *See* Petrarch; *Alberti; Terence*
Basil I. *See* Renaissance
Basil II, the Bulgar-Slayer. *See* Caesar, as Political Title; *Renaissance*
Basilaces, Nicephoros. *See Atticism*
Basilides. *See* Fathers, Church
Basilisk, 121
Basil of Caesarea. *See* Allegory; Anthology; Fathers, Church; Interpretatio Christiana; *Armenian Hellenism; Byzantium; Erasmus; Philosophy; Physiologus; Renaissance; Rhetoric*
Basin, P. V. *See Socrates*
Bate, Henry, of Malines. *See* Concord, Philosophical
Baths, 121
Batoni, Pompeo. *See* Sacrifice in the Arts; Toga
Battānī, al-. *See* Astronomy; *Cartography*
Batteux, Charles. *See* Imitation; *Lessing*
Battus. *See Pastoral*
Baucis and Philemon. *See* Shakespeare
Baudelaire, Charles. *See* Dionysus; Endymion; Midas; Progress and Decline; Sappho; *Cities, Praise of; Lyric Poetry; Virgil*
Baudin des Ardennes, Pierre-Charles-Louis. *See* Revolution, French
Baudouin, François. *See* Calendars; Forgery; Historiography; Tacitus; *Vico*
Baudri, Abbot of Bourgeuil. *See* Ovid
Bauer, Georg. *See* Bronze; *Names*
Bauhin, Gaspard. *See* Botany; Natural History
Baumgarten, Alexander. *See* Aesthetics
Bausch, Johann Lorenz. *See* Academy
Bava, Mario. *See* Cinema
Baxter, Richard. *See Epicurus*
Bayer, Johann. *See* Astronomy
Bayle, Pierre. *See* Atheism; Cynicism; Re-

naissance; Skepticism; Suetonius; *Biography; Censorship; Dacier; Fragments*
Beardsley, Aubrey. *See Catullus*
Beatrice. *See Statius*
Beatus Rhenanus (Beat Bild). *See* Book, Printed; Classical; Commentary; Historiography; Livy; Seneca the Younger; *Liberal Arts*
Beauchamp, Alphonse de. *See* Caesar, Julius
Beaufort, Louis de. *See* Historiography
Beaumarchais, Pierre de. *See* Comedy; Imitation
Beaumont, Francis. *See* Translation; *Hermaphroditus*
Beauvais, Vincent de. *See* Seven Sages of Rome
Beazzano, Agostino. *See Raphael*
Beccadelli, Antonio (Il Panormita). *See* Neo-Latin; *Hermaphroditus; Letters; Petrarch*
Beccari, Agostino. *See* Pastoral
Beccaria, Cesare. *See* Law, Roman; *Korais*
Becket, Thomas. *See Tragedy*
Beckett, Samuel. *See* Comedy; Dramatic Unities; *Lyric Poetry*
Bede. *See* Architecture; Art History; Calendars; Education; Fathers, Church; Glass; Grammar; Horace; Liberal Arts; Ovid; Pliny the Elder; Poetics; Purple; Rome; Temperament; *Biography; Book, Manuscript: Development*
Beeby, Thomas. *See* Architecture
Beethoven, Ludwig van. *See Deus ex Machina; Nudity; Opera*
Beguin, Jean. *See* Alchemy
Behn, Aphra. *See* Ovid; *Juvenal*
Bekker, August Immanuel. *See* Aristotle; *Wolf, Friedrich August*
Bel. *See* Paganism
Bélanger, François-Joseph. *See Piranesi*
Beldeanu, Ovidiu. *See Names*
Belgrand, Eugène. *See* Sewers
Bell, Charles. *See Physiognomy*
Bellarmine, Cardinal Robert. *See* Paganism
Bellay, Guillaume de. *See Rabelais*
Bellay, Jean du. *See* Roman Monuments, Reuse of; *Rabelais*
Bellay, Joachim du. *See Rabelais*
Belleau, Remy. *See* Ode; Pastoral; Pléiade; *Anacreon*
Bellerophon. *See* Popular Culture; Writing; *Melancholy; Pegasus*
Belli, Valerio. *See Cameos*
Bellini, Giovanni. *See* Paganism; *Centaur*
Bellini, Vincenzo. *See* Opera
Belloc, Hillaire. *See* Epigram
Bellori, Giovan Pietro, **122**. *See also* Aesthetics; Coins; Forma Urbis Romae; Raphael; Ut pictura poesis; *Atlas*
Bellow, Saul. *See Carpe diem*
Beloch, Karl Julius. *See* Thermopylae; *Democracy*
Belon, Pierre. *See* Natural History
Belvedere collection. *See Rubens*
Belvedere Torso, **123**. *See also* Raphael; Rome; Sculpture; Winckelmann
Bembo, Bernardo. *See* Horace
Bembo, Pietro. *See* Cicero; Collecting; Greek, Ancient; Historiography; Humanism; Hypnerotomachia Poliphili; Imitation; Immortality of the Soul; Letters; Neoplatonism; Raphael; Rhetoric; Rome; Tacitus
Benardete, José. *See* Zeno's Paradoxes
Benavides, Marco Mantova. *See* Sculpture
Benedetti, Alessandro. *See* Medicine
Benedict, Saint. *See* Liberal Arts; Libraries; Philosophy
Benedict XIV. *See Colosseum*
Benedict XVI (Joseph Alois Ratzinger). *See* War, Just
Benedict Biscop. *See* Glass
Beni, Paolo. *See* Sallust
Benjamin, Walter. *See* Fragments; Portico; Tragedy; *Cities, Praise of; Nietzsche*
Benjamin of Tudela. *See Baalbek; Constantinople*
Benn, Gottfried. *See* Fascism
Benoît de Sainte-Maure. *See* Romance, Medieval
Bentham, Jeremy. *See Law, Roman*
Bentley, Richard, **123**. *See also* Ancients and Moderns; Commentary; Education; Forgery; Greek, Ancient; Progress and Decline; Prosody; Suetonius; Terence; *Astrology; Fragments; Horace*
Beowulf. *See* Epic
Béranger, Jean-Pierre. *See* Horace
Berceo, Gonzalo de. *See Isidore*
Bergerac, Cyrano de. *See* Lucian; Satire; *Lucretius*
Bergk, Theodor. *See* Sappho
Bergman, Ingmar. *See Maenads*
Bergson, Henri. *See Parmenides*
Berkeley, George. *See* Philosophy; Progress and Decline; Skepticism; *Dialogue*
Berkoff, Steven. *See* Oedipus; Sophocles
Berlin, Isaiah. *See* Political Theory; *Philosophy*
Berlioz, Hector. *See* Aeneas; Dido; Opera; Sacrifice in the Arts; Virgil
Bernard, Sir Francis. *See* Empire
Bernard, Richard. *See* Terence
Bernard de Ventadour. *See Narcissus*
Bernardi, Giovanni. *See Cameos*
Bernard of Chartres. *See* Chartres; Concord, Philosophical; Neoplatonism
Bernard of Clairvaux. *See Book, Manuscript: Development*
Bernard of Tours. *See* Neoplatonism
Bernard Silvestris. *See* Cosmology; Cyclops; Divination; Paganism; Poetics; Virgil; *Boethius; Martianus Capella*
Bernays, Jakob. *See* Catharsis; Diels, Hermann; Historiography; Poetics; *Scaliger, Joseph Justus*
Bernhard, Christoph. *See Affecti*
Berni, Francesco. *See Comedy*
Bernier, François. *See Atoms*
Bernini, Gian Lorenzo. *See* Aeneas; Apollo; Architecture; Demeter and Persephone; Forum; Hypnerotomachia Poliphili; Neoclassicism; Nudity; Pantheon; Roman Monuments, Reuse of; Rome; Ruins; Sculpture; Stadium; Temple; *Belvedere Torso; Herm*
Bernini, Pietro. *See Herm*
Bernoulli, Daniel. *See Latin Language*
Bernoulli, J. J. *See* Portraits, Reception of Ancient
Bernward, Abbot. *See* Rome
Beroaldo, Filippo, the Elder. *See* Apuleius; Classical; Commentary; *Cicero; Education*
Berossus. *See* Book, Manuscript: Development; Forgery; Giants; Writing; *Calendars; Fragments; Historiography; Scaliger, Joseph Justus*
Berry, Jean de France, duc de. *See* Book, Manuscript: Development; *Coins*
Bersuire, Pierre (Petrus Berchorius). *See* Atlas; Demeter and Persephone; Poetics
Bertelsmann. *See* Teubner
Berthold of Moosburg. *See* Plato
Bertoldo di Giovanni. *See* Nudity
Bertolucci, Bernardo. *See* Venus de Milo
Berve, Helmut. *See* Thermopylae
Bes. *See* Devil
Bessarion of Nicaea (Cardinal Basileos Bessarion), **125**. *See also* Academy; Apuleius; Book, Manuscript: Development; Byzantium; Concord, Philosophical; Demosthenes; Diogenes Laertius; Fathers, Church; Ficino; Greek Anthology; Immortality of the Soul; Libraries; Medicine; Planudes; Plato; Renaissance; *Cartography; Letters; Music; Philosophy*
Betencourt, Rómulo. *See Names*
Béthune, Évrard de. *See* Grammar
Beza, Theodore (Théodore de Bèze). *See* Renaissance; Skepticism; *Estienne, Henri II*
Bialas, Günter. *See Hero and Leander*
Bianchini, Francesco. *See* Forma Urbis Romae; Historiography; *Calendars*
Bianco, P. Zanotti. *See* Paestum
Bibbiena, Cardinal (Bernardo Dovizi). *See* Plautus; Raphael; *Color*
Bickel, Ernst. *See Nietzsche*
Bickerman, E. J. *See Calendars*
Bidpai. *See* Seven Sages of Rome
Biel, Gabriel. *See Numismatics*
Bigot, Paul. *See Forma Urbis Romae*
Billi, Antonio. *See Art History*
Billon, Jean de. *See* Warfare
Bing, Gertrud. *See Warburg*
Bingham, John. *See* Warfare
Biography, **126**
Bion. *See* Adonis; Elegy; Translation
Biondo, Flavio. *See* Antiquarianism; Atrium; Cartography; Guidebooks to Ancient

Biondo, Flavio *(continued)*
Rome; Hadrian's Villa; Historiography; Livy; Petrarch; Renaissance; Rome; Symposium; Triumphal Bridge; *Alberti*

Biragus, Lampus. *See* Households; *Xenophon*

Biringuccio, Vanoccio. *See* Bronze

Bīrūnī, al-. *See* Ethnography; Geography; *Cartography*

Bischoff, Johannes. *See Terence*

Bismarck, Otto von. *See* Caesar, Julius

Bisticci, Vespasiano da. *See* Book, Manuscript: Development; Cartography; *Biography; Historiography*

Black, Max. *See* Zeno's Paradoxes

Blackwell, Thomas. *See* Goethe; Wolf, Friedrich August

Blaeuw, Willem Janszoon. *See* Seven Wonders of the World

Blair, Hugh. *See* Panegyric; Rhetoric

Blake, William. *See* Demiurge; Hesiod; *Centaur; Laocoön*

Blanchot, Maurice. *See* Sirens

Blavatsky, Madame. *See* Mithras; *Epic*

Blemmydes, Nicephorus. *See Atticism; Metaphrasis*

Bletterie, Abbé de la. *See Julian*

Blondel, Maurice. *See Neo-Latin*

Blondel, Nicolas-François. *See* Triumphal Arch

Bloom, Harold. *See* Homer; Imitation

Blüher, Hans. *See Nietzsche*

Blundell, John. *See* Mercuriale

Bobadilla, Nicolas. *See* Greek, Ancient

Boccaccio, Giovanni, **130**. *See also* Actaeon; Aeneas; Ancients and Moderns; Antigone; Apuleius; Book, Manuscript: Development; Chaucer; Cupid; Cynicism; Dido; Europe; Greek, Ancient; Helen; Historiography; Horace; Inscriptions; Livy; Locus Amoenus; Medea; Muses; Nudity; Orpheus; Paganism; Palmyra; Pandora; Pastoral; Pegasus; Penelope; Petrarch; Philosophy; Plague; Popular Culture; Pyramus and Thisbe; Renaissance; Romance, Medieval; Satire; Sculpture; Seneca the Elder; Statius; Suicide; Tacitus; Troilus; Virgil; Vitruvius; Writing; *Academy; Aphrodite; Art History; Atlas; Biography; Boethius; Centaur; Cicero; Cleopatra; Hypnerotomachia Poliphili; Isidore*

Boccalini, Trajano. *See* Historiography; Tacitus

Bock, Hieronymus. *See* Botany

Böckh, August, **131**. *See also* Inscriptions; Romanticism; *Burckhardt; Calendars; Greek, Ancient; Marxism; Pindar; Wolf, Friedrich August*

Bode, Johann. *See Astronomy; Music*

Bodin, Jean. *See* Anthropology; Demon; Despotism, Oriental; Forgery; Tacitus; Warfare; *Historiography*

Bodmer, Johann Jakob. *See Thyestes*

Bodoni, Giambattista. *See* Book, Printed

Boemus, Joannes. *See* Ethnography

Boerhaave, Herman. *See* Maxims; Medicine

Boethius, **131**. *See also* Aristotle; Commentary; Concord, Philosophical; Consolation; Cosmology; Dialectic; Dialogue; Donatus; Fathers, Church; Fortune; Greek, Ancient; Harmony of the Spheres; Horace; Logic; Muses; Music; Musical Instruments; Neoplatonism; Numbers; Orpheus; Paganism; Philosophy; Plato; Ptolemy; Pythagoras; Ravenna; Renaissance; Romance, Medieval; Seneca the Younger; Stoicism; Tantalus; Topos; Tragedy; Translation; Valla; *Automata; Boccaccio; Chartres; Chaucer; Dante; Delphin Classics; Isagoge; Judaism; Liberal Arts; Macrobius; Martianus Capella; Planudes*

Boetus of Sidon. *See Judaism*

Böhme, Jakob. *See* Chaos; Temperament

Bohn, Henry. *See* Translation

Boiardo, Matteo Maria. *See* Apuleius; Virgil; *Parody*

Boileau-Despréaux, Nicolas. *See* Ancients and Moderns; Comedy; Epigram; Genius; Horace; Parody; Poetics; Rhetoric; Sappho; Satire; *Juvenal; Latin Language*

Boillot, Joseph. *See Herm*

Boissard, Jacques. *See Guidebooks to Ancient Rome*

Boissy d'Anglas, François-Antoine de. *See* Revolution, French

Boito, Arrigo. *See Hero and Leander*

Boivin, Jean. *See* Historiography

Bol, Ferdinand. *See Adonis*

Boldù, Zuan. *See* Nudity

Bolingbroke, Henry St. John, Viscount. *See* Horace

Boll, Franz. *See Magic*

Bologna, Guidotto da. *See* Poetics

Boltz von Ruffach, Valentin. *See Terence*

Bolzanio, Urbano. *See* Grammar

Bonacolsi, Pier Jacopo Alari (L'Antico). *See* Faun; Hydra; Replicas; Rome; Sculpture

Bonaparte, Luciano. *See Etruscans*

Bonaparte, Pauline. *See* Sculpture

Bonaventure, Saint. *See* Demon; *Petrarch; Philosophy*

Boncompagno da Signa. *See* Consolation; Liberal Arts

Boner, Hieronymus. *See Ethnography*

Boniface IV. *See* Roman Monuments, Reuse of

Boniface VIII. *See* Rome

Bonincontri, Lorenzo. *See Astrology*

Bonitz, Hermann. *See Aristotle*

Bonnard, Pierre. *See* Modernism

Bonnaud, Jacques-Julien. *See Atlantis*

Bonomi, Joseph. *See* Grand Tour

Bonomo, Pietro. *See Genre*

Bonvesin de la Riva. *See* Mirabilia Urbis

Book, Manuscript: Development and Transmission, **133**

Book, Manuscript: Production, **139**

Book, Printed, **142**

Boole, George. *See* Logic

Bopp, Frana. *See Greek, Ancient*

Bordone, Benedetto. *See Maenads; Scaliger, Julius Caesar*

Borelli, Giovanni Alfonso. *See Zoology*

Borges, Jorge Luis. *See* Poetics; *Labyrinth*

Borghese, Paolina. *See Nudity*

Borghese, Scipione. *See* Sculpture

Borghese collection. *See Rubens; Sarcophagi*

Borghesi, Bartolomeo. *See* Inscriptions; Numismatics

Borghini, Vincenzo. *See* Paganism; Plautus; *Etruscans*

Borgia, Cesare. *See* Giants; *Names*

Borgia, Lucrezia. *See Names; Plautus*

Borgia, Stefano. *See* Papyrology

Borgofranco, Giambattista de. *See Terence*

Borheck, August C. *See* Ajax

Borja, Cesare. *See Names*

Borja, Lucrezia. *See Names*

Bormann, Martin. *See Sparta*

Born, Ignaz von. *See* Egypt

Borrel, Jean. *See* Squaring the Circle

Borromeo, Carlo. *See* Atrium; Portico; *Bacchanalia*

Borromeo, Federico. *See* Pliny the Elder; *Museum; Nudity*

Borromini, Francesco. *See* Architecture; Hadrian's Villa; Ornament; Pantheon; Rome; Stadium; *Herm*

Börtz, Daniel. *See Maenads*

Boscoli, Pietro Paolo. *See* Caesar, Julius

Boscovich, Roger. *See Atoms*

Bosio, Antonio. *See* Catacombs

Bosio, François. *See Hermaphroditus*

Bosso, Girolamo. *See* Toga

Bossuet, Jacques. *See Delphin Classics*

Boswell, James. *See* Suetonius; *Biography; Juvenal; Rome*

Botany, **146**

Botero, Giovanni. *See* Tacitus; Warfare

Bottai, Giuseppe. *See* Fascism

Bottesini, Giovanni. *See Hero and Leander*

Botticelli, Sandro. *See* Aphrodite; Centaur; Cupid; Faun; Historiography; Nudity; Popular Culture; Rome; Ruins; Sacrifice in the Arts; Warburg; *Martianus Capella*

Bouchardon, Edmé. *See* Barberini Faun

Bouché-Leclercq, Auguste. *See Magic*

Boucher, François. *See* Apollo; Cupid

Bouchet, Jules. *See* Pliny the Younger

Bouguereau, Adolphe. *See Maenads*

Boulanger, Nicolas. *See Atheism*

Boulenger, Jules-César. *See* Symposium

Boullée, Étienne-Louis. *See* Architecture; Neoclassicism; Pyramid; *Mausoleum*

Boulton, Matthew. *See* Adam, Robert

Bourbon, Étienne de. *See* Seven Sages of Rome

Bourdelle, Antoine. *See Hercules*
Bourguet, Louis. *See Etruscans*
Bourlier, Jean. *See Terence*
Bowen, John. *See Maenads*
Boyle, Charles. *See* Ancients and Moderns
Boyle, Richard, Earl of Burlington. *See Temple*
Boyle, Robert. *See* Academy; Atoms; Epicurus; Skepticism
Bozicevic-Natalis, Franjo. *See Split*
Bracciolini, Poggio. *See* Academy; Architecture; Book, Manuscript: Development; Collecting; Epicurus; Epigraphy; Fragments; Guidebooks to Ancient Rome; Historiography; Humanism; Libraries; Lucretius; Petrarch; Philosophy; Rhetoric; Rome; Sculpture; Statius; Vitruvius; *Atoms; Cartography; Hieroglyphs; Petronius; Valla*
Bracton, Henry. *See* Law, Roman
Bradford, Edwin Emmanuel. *See Pederasty*
Bradley, Francis Herbert. *See* Maxims
Bradley, Marion Zimmer. *See Cassandra*
Bradwardine, Thomas. *See* Philosophy; *Aristotle*
Brahe, Tycho. *See* Astronomy; Cosmology; Ptolemy; *Astrology; Scaliger, Joseph Justus*
Bramante, Donato. *See* Architecture; Hadrian's Villa; Mausoleum; Michelangelo; Ornament; Palace; Pantheon; Praeneste; Raphael; Replicas; Rome; Temple; *City Planning; Janus; Speculum Romanae Magnificentiae*
Bramer, Leonaert. *See Ajax*
Bramwell, Edward. *See Hero and Leander*
Brancusi, Constantin. *See* Caryatid; Modernism
Brandis, Christian August. *See Aristotle*
Brant, Isabella. *See* Rubens
Brant, Sebastian. *See Aeneas; Juvenal; Terence*
Brantôme, Pierre de Boureille, seigneur de. *See* Pornography
Braque, Georges. *See* Modernism; *Hesiod*
Brass, Tinto. *See Cinema*
Braun, Richard Emil. *See Cassandra*
Brecht, Bertolt. *See* Deus ex Machina; Empedocles; Horace; Lucretius; Plautus; Sophocles; *Antigone; Lyric Poetry; Socrates*
Bregno, Andrea. *See* Rome
Brentano, Clemens. *See* Sirens
Brentano, Franz. *See Aristotle*
Breuer, Josef. *See Catharsis*
Breug, Jörg. *See* Emblem
Bridges, Robert. *See* Demeter and Persephone
Bridges, Thomas. *See* Dido; *Comedy*
Briffault, Robert. *See Matriarchy*
Brillat-Savarin, Jean-Anthelme. *See Symposium*
Briseis. *See* Helen; *Achilles; Cinema; Ovid*
Britannicus. *See* Nero
Britten, Benjamin. *See* Phaedra; *Euripides*
Broch, Hermann. *See* Aeneas; Virgil
Brock, Arthur. *See Galen*
Brodsky, Joseph. *See* Horace; *Virgil*
Brome, Alexander. *See* Ode
Brongniart, Alexandre-Théodore. *See* Temple
Bronze, 147
Bronzino (Agnolo di Cosimo). *See* Aphrodite
Brook, Peter. *See Seneca the Younger*
Brooke, Rupert. *See* Epic; *Hero*
Brookes, William Penny. *See Olympic Games*
Brophy, Aaron Quinn. *See Belvedere Torso*
Brougham, Henry, Lord. *See Demosthenes*
Brown, Joe E. *See Comedy*
Brown, Peter. *See* Sexuality
Browne, Moses. *See Pastoral*
Browne, Sir Thomas. *See* Egypt; Museum; Pliny the Elder; Suicide
Browning, Elizabeth Barrett. *See* Translation
Browning, Robert. *See* Alcestis; Aristophanes; Education; Horace; Lyric Poetry; Orpheus; Translation; *Cavafy; Euripides*
Brucker, Johann Jakob. *See* Neoplatonism; Pico della Mirandola; Philosophy; Plato; Presocratics; Writing; *Diogenes Laertius; Doxography; Fragments*
Brueghel, Pieter, the Elder. *See* Orpheus; *Bacchanalia*
Brugghen, Hendrick ter. *See Maenads*
Brugmann, Karl. *See Greek, Ancient*
Brühl, Heinrich, Count von. *See Heyne; Maecenas*
Brumidi, Constantino. *See* Pompeii
Brumoy, Pierre. *See* Jesuits
Brunck, R. F. P. *See* Greek Anthology
Brunelleschi, Filippo. *See* Aesthetics; Alberti; Architecture; Bronze; Domus Aurea; Michelangelo; Optics; Ornament; Rome; Temple; Warfare; *Art History*
Brunfels, Otto. *See* Botany; Natural History; *Dioscorides; Hippocrates*
Bruni, Leonardo. *See* Ancients and Moderns; Anthology; Cato the Younger; Cities, Praise of; Commentary; Dialogue; Diogenes Laertius; Etruscans; Fathers, Church; Greek, Ancient; Historiography; Homer; Households; Humanism; Immortality of the Soul; Letters; Livy; Neo-Latin; Neoplatonism; Petrarch; Philosophy; Plautus; Progress and Decline; Renaissance; Sallust; Tacitus; Thucydides; Translation; Xenophon; *Aristotle; Augustus; Cicero; Demosthenes; Epicurus*
Bruno, Giordano. *See* Actaeon; Cosmology; Dialogue; Egypt; Irony; Lucretius; Mnemonics; Neoplatonism; Pegasus; Philosophy; Plato; Presocratics; Symposium; *Hermes Trismegistus; Magic*
Brunot, Ferdinand. *See Latin Language*
Bruscambille. *See Comedy*
Brutus, 149. *See also* Caesar, as Political Title; Caesar, Julius; Greek, Ancient; Names; Portraits, Reception of Ancient; Revolution, French; Rhetoric; Romance, Medieval; Rome; Shakespeare; Tacitus; *Censorship; Historiography; Numismatics*
Brutus, Lucius Junius. *See* Brutus
Brutus, Stephanus Junius. *See Brutus*
Bryars, Gavin. *See Medea*
Bryaxis. *See Mausoleum*
Bryennius, Joseph. *See* Rhōmaioi
Bryennius, Manuel. *See* Music
Bryson. *See* Squaring the Circle
Bucephalus. *See* Alexander the Great
Buchanan, George. *See Euripides*
Bücheler, Franz. *See Petronius*
Büchenschütz, Bernhard. *See* Dream Interpretation
Buchler, Johann. *See* Genre; Poetics
Buckle, Henry Thomas. *See* Anthropology
Buddha. *See* Alexander the Great; Gandhara
Budé, Guillaume, 150. *See also* Book, Printed; Classical; Coins; Commentary; Grammar; Greek, Ancient; Hercules; Rabelais; Tacitus; *Doxography; Eustathius; Numismatics; Xenophon*
Bufalini, Andrea. *See* Forma Urbis Romae
Bufalini, Leonardo. *See City Planning*
Buffon, Georges-Louis Leclerc, Comte de. *See* Pliny the Elder; Zoology; *Physiognomy*
Bulgaro. *See Law, Roman*
Buller, John. *See Maenads*
Bullinger, Heinrich. *See* Immortality of the Soul
Bulwer-Lytton, Edward. *See* Comic Books; Novel; Pompeii; Popular Culture; Volcanoes
Bünau, Graf von. *See Winckelmann*
Bunting, Basil. *See Catullus; Ode*
Buonarroti, Filippo. *See* Etruscans
Buondelmonti, Cristoforo. *See* Constantinople; Sculpture
Buoninsegni, Giovan Battista. *See* Epicurus
Buontalenti, Bernardo. *See* Grotto; Harmony of the Spheres
Burckhardt, Jacob, 151. *See also* Antiquarianism; Biography; Constantine; Democracy; Historicism; Names; Nudity; Pergamon; Petrarch; Professionalization of Classics; Raphael; Renaissance; Rome; Spolia; Sports; Thermopylae; *Art History; Magic*
Burgess, Anthony. *See Censorship*
Burgundio of Pisa. *See* Medicine; *Greek, Ancient*
Buridan, Jean. *See* Logic; Philosophy; Squaring the Circle; *Aristotle*

Burke, Edmund. *See* Empire; Europe; Liberty; Professionalization of Classics; Rhetoric; *Neoclassicism*
Burkert, Walter. *See* East and West; *Magic*
Burley, Walter. *See Diogenes Laertius; Hippocrates; Philosophy*
Burlington, Earl of. *See* Grand Tour; Portico
Burn, William. *See* Architecture
Burnaby, William. *See Petronius*
Burne-Jones, Edward. *See* Sirens; *Apuleius; Circe; Elgin Marbles*
Burnet, Thomas. *See* Ancients and Moderns
Burnham, Daniel. *See* Architecture
Burns, Christopher. *See Hero and Leander*
Burns, Robert. *See* Martial
Burton, Decimus. *See* Triumphal Arch
Burton, Richard. *See Cleopatra*
Burton, Richard F. *See Catullus*
Burton, Robert. *See* Consolation; Melancholy
Bury, Richard de. *See* Writing
Busbecq, Augier Ghislain de. *See* Letters; *Inscriptions*
Busenello, Giovanni Francesco. *See* Opera; *Dido*
Bush, George W. *See Cicero*
Busiris. *See Mythology*
Bussi, Giannandrea. *See* Book, Printed
Butler, H. M. *See* Education
Butler, Joseph. *See* Epicurus; Ethics; Stoicism
Butler, Samuel. *See* Parody; Sicily; Sparta; *Comedy*
Butzer, Martin. *See Constitution, Mixed*
Byres, James. *See* Etruscans
Byron, George Gordon, Lord. *See* Anthology; Apollo Belvedere; Comedy; Elgin Marbles; Epic; Hero and Leander; Homosexuality; Horace; Parody; Philhellenism; Professionalization of Classics; Pronunciation of Greek and Latin; Romanticism; Translation; *Parthenon; Rome; Sexuality*
Byron, Henry James. *See Comedy*
Byzantium, **152**

Cabrera, Manuel Estrada. *See* Temple
Caccini, Giovanni. *See* Sculpture
Caccini, Giulio. *See* Music; Opera
Cacoyannis, Michael. *See* Cinema
Cadmus the Phoenician. *See* Writing
Caecilius Statius. *See* Translation
Caecina Alienus, Aulus. *See Etruscans*
Caelius Aurelianus. *See* Doxography; Gynecology; Medicine
Caesar, as Political Title, **159**. *See also* Fortune; Republicanism
Caesar, Caius. *See Maison Carrée*
Caesar, Julius, **161**. *See also* Aeneas; Alexander the Great; Alexandria; Alexandrianism; Brutus; Caesar, as Political Title; Cato the Younger; Censorship; Cleopatra; Comic Books; Daphnis; Dictatorship; Education; Elegy; Epic; Forum; Founding Fathers; Historiography; Lucan; Novel; Plutarch; Popular Culture; Revolution, French; Roads, Roman; Rome; Sallust; Shakespeare; Sports; Suetonius; Suicide; Terence; Warfare; Writing; *Astérix; Augustus; Calendars; Cicero; Guidebooks to Ancient Rome; Names; Opera; Palladio; Scaliger, Joseph Justus; Television; Tragedy*
Caesar, Sir Julius. *See Names*
Caesar, Lucius. *See Maison Carrée*
Caesarius of Arles. *See* Progress and Decline; *Names*
Caesarius of Nazianzus. *See* Hippocratic Oath
Caesars, Twelve, **163**
Cain. *See* Giants
Caius, John. *See* Medicine
Cajetan, Cardinal Thomas. *See* Immortality of the Soul
Calasso, Roberto. *See* Demeter and Persephone; *Martianus Capella*
Calcagnini, Celio. *See* Raphael; Writing
Calchas. *See* Sacrifice in the Arts
Calcidius. *See* Astronomy; Commentary; Cosmology; Demiurge; Dream Interpretation; Music; Neoplatonism; Plato; *Writing*
Caldara, Antonio. *See* Statius; *Socrates*
Calder, Alexander. *See Laocoön*
Calderini, Domizio. *See* Commentary
Calderón de la Barca, Pedro. *See* Adonis; Comedy; Cupid; Plautus
Calendars, Chronicles, Chronology, **165**
Caligula. *See* Tacitus; *Caesars, Twelve; Censorship*
Callas, Maria. *See Cinema; Medea*
Callimachus. *See* Actaeon; Alexandrianism; Apollo; Epic; Forgery; Fragments; Genre; Lyric Poetry; Museum; Pindar; Prosody; Ronsard; *Bentley; Book, Manuscript: Development; Commentary; Dacier; Muses; Pastoral; Tzetzes*
Callinicus of Heliopolis. *See* Warfare
Calliope. *See* Orpheus; *Comic Books; Muses*
Callisto. *See Opera*
Callistratus. *See* Ecphrasis; Sculpture; *Aesthetics*
Calpurnius Siculus. *See* Pastoral
Calverley, Charles Stuart. *See* Horace; Translation
Calvin, John. *See* Immortality of the Soul; Maxims; Paganism; Progress and Decline; Renaissance; Seneca the Younger; Skepticism; Stoicism; *Astrology; Constitution, Mixed; Estienne, Henri II; Latin and the Professions*
Calvino, Italo. *See* Hero; Lucian
Calvo, Fabio. *See* Atrium; Guidebooks to Ancient Rome; Medicine Rome; Vitruvius; *City Planning; Raphael*
Calvus, Licinius. *See* Alexandrianism; *Genre*
Calypso. *See Locus Amoenus*
Calzabigi, Ranieri de'. *See* Alcestis; Opera; Orpheus; *Deus ex Machina; Mime*
Calzolari, Francesco. *See Museum*
Cambacérès, Jean-Jacques. *See* Revolution, French
Cambiaso, Luca. *See Pegasus*
Cambos, Jean-Jules. *See* Venus de Milo
Cambyses. *See* Persia
Camden, William. *See* Antiquarianism; Cartography
Cameos and Gems, **168**
Camerarius, Joachim. *See Herodotus; Households; Xenophon*
Cameron, Charles. *See* Hadrian's Villa
Cameron, Julia Margaret. *See* Endymion
Camillo, Giulio. *See* Mnemonics
Camillus. *See* Revolution, French
Camões, Luís Vaz de. *See* Ancients and Moderns; Epic; Locus Amoenus; Pastoral; Virgil
Campanella, Tommaso. *See* Maxims; Mnemonics; *Atlantis; Galen; Grammar; Janus; Magic*
Campano, Giannantonio. *See Letters; Petrarch*
Campanus of Novara. *See* Astronomy; Ptolemy
Campbell, John. *See Colony*
Campe, Heinrich. *See* Dionysus
Camper, Pieter. *See* Physiognomy
Campion, Thomas. *See Catullus; Midas*
Camus, Albert. *See* Pindar; Plague; Sisyphus
Camus, Marcel. *See Cinema; Orpheus*
Canclini, Néstor. *See Names*
Candace. *See Hero*
Candaules. *See Historiography*
Candelori brothers. *See Etruscans*
Canfora, Luciano. *See* Forgery
Canina, Luigi. *See* Forma Urbis Romae; Praeneste
Canonico, Benedetto. *See* Tourism
Canova, Antonio. *See* Centaur; Cupid; Endymion; Neoclassicism; Nudity; Orpheus; Sculpture; *Adonis; Elgin Marbles; Socrates; Temple*
Cantacuzenos, John. *See* Plague
Canter, Willem. *See* Book, Manuscript: Development; *Aristophanes; Scaliger, Joseph Justus*
Cantone, Pier Francesco. *See* Atrium
Cantor, Georg. *See* Zeno's Paradoxes
Canutt, Yakima. *See Cinema*
Capella, Martianus. *See* Astronomy; Cosmology; Education; Epicurus; Paganism
Capitein, Jacobus. *See* Neo-Latin
Capodiferro, Evangelista Maddaleni. *See Raphael*
Capponi, Gino. *See Etruscans*

Caracalla. *See* Architecture; Guidebooks to Ancient Rome; Rome; *Baths*
Carafa, Cardinal Oliviero. *See Pasquino*
Caravaggio, Michelangelo Merisi da. *See* Narcissus; Nudity; Pornography
Caravaggio, Polidoro da. *See* Color
Cardano, Girolamo. *See* Astrology; Commentary; Consolation; Divination; Galen; Monsters; Nero; Ptolemy; Scaliger, Julius Caesar; *Diogenes Laertius; Magic; Philosophy*
Carducci, Giosue. *See* Horace
Carion, Johannes. *See Melanchthon*
Carli, Gian Rinaldo. *See Atlantis*
Carlisle, Charles Howard, Earl of. *See Mausoleum*
Carlyle, Thomas. *See* Biography
Carmenta. *See Guidebooks to Ancient Rome*
Carmines, Al. *See* Aristophanes
Carnap, Rudolf. *See* Metaphysics
Carné, Marcel. *See Mime*
Caro, Annibale. *See* Guidebooks to Ancient Rome
Caro, Miguel Antonio. *See* Education
Carpe diem, 169
Carpi, Iacopo Berengario da. *See Isagoge*
Carpini, John de Plano. *See* Ethnography
Carpioni, Giulio. *See Maenads*
Carpus of Antioch. *See* Archimedes
Carrà, Carlo. *See* Metaphysics; Modernism
Carracci, Annibale. *See* Ariadne; Circe; Galatea; Hercules; *Adonis; Atlas; Bellori; Cyclops; Hermaphroditus; Maenads; Names; Physiognomy*
Carracci circle. *See* Ut pictura poesis
Carrara family. *See Humanism*
Carretto, Galeotto del. *See* Cupid
Carrey, Jacques. *See* Elgin Marbles; Tourism; *Athens*
Carrier-Belleuse, Albert-Ernest. *See Maenads*
Carson, Anne. *See Catullus*
Cartari, Vicenzo. *See* Paganism; *Hercules*
Carter, Elizabeth. *See* Stoicism
Carter, Lynda. *See* Amazons
Cartography, 170
Carvilius Maximus, Spurius. *See* Bronze
Cary, Elizabeth. *See Cleopatra*
Caryatid, 175
Casa, Giovanni della. *See Symposium*
Casaubon, Isaac, 175. *See also* Education; Egypt; Forgery; Fragments; Geography; Greek, Ancient; Hermes Trismegistus; Historiography; Humanism; Magic; Neoplatonism; Pliny the Younger; Sibyls; Stoicism; Suetonius; *Diogenes Laertius; Herodotus*
Casaubon, Méric. *See Diogenes Laertius; Epicurus*
Casimir IV of Poland. *See Warfare*
Cassandra, 176. *See also Comedy; Dido*
Cassatt, Mary. *See Maenads*
Cassian, John. *See* Poetics
Cassianus Bassus Scholasticus. *See Iranian Hellenism*
Cassiodorus. *See* Chrēsis; Education; Fathers, Church; Grammar; Greek, Ancient; Horace; Letters; Liberal Arts; Libraries; Philosophy; Ravenna; Rhetoric; Seneca the Younger; Translation; *Boethius; Book, Manuscript: Development; Cartography; Music*
Cassirer, Ernst. *See* Parmenides; Warburg; *Magic; Mythology; Pico della Mirandola*
Cassius Longinus, Gaius. *See* Brutus; Rome; *Censorship; Historiography*
Cassius Severus. *See Censorship*
Castagno, Andrea del. *See* Ornament
Castell, Robert. *See* Grand Tour; Pliny the Younger
Castellamonte, Carlo di. *See* Portico
Castellejo, Cristóbal de. *See Cyclops*
Castelli, Gabriele Lancilotto. *See* Sicily
Castellio, Sebastian. *See* Skepticism; *Sibyls*
Castello, Giovanni Battista. *See Ajax*
Castelvetro, Lodovico. *See* Dramatic Unities; *Catharsis; Tragedy*
Casti, Giambattista. *See Sallust*
Castiglionchio, Lapo da, the Younger. *See* Academy
Castiglione, Baldassare. *See* Aesthetics; Dialogue; Elegy; Gellus; Neoplatonism; Plato; Raphael; Roman Monuments, Reuse of; Rome; Translation; Warfare; *Montaigne; Symposium*
Castiglione, counts of. *See* Raphael
Castor and Pollux, 177. *See also Helen; Leda*
Catacombs, 177
Catel, Charles Simon. *See Musical Instruments*
Catharsis, 178
Catherine, Saint. *See* Alexandria; *Paganism*
Catherine II. *See* Warfare; *Hadrian's Villa; Virgil*
Catherine de Médicis. *See* Gesture; Helen
Catherine of Aragon. *See Households*
Catiline. *See* Caesar, Julius; Revolution, French; Sallust; *Poliziano*
Cato (as name). *See* Founding Fathers; *Names*
Cato the Elder. *See* Book, Manuscript: Production; Botany; East and West; Epigram; Historiography; Sallust; Veterinary Medicine; Writing; Zoology; *Annius of Viterbo; Barbarians; Cato the Younger; Liberal Arts; Opera; Petrarch; Poetics; Symposium; Terence*
Cato the Younger, 179. *See also* Brutus; Education; Epic; Plutarch; Revolution, French; Seneca the Younger; Suicide; *Lucan*
Catrares (Catrarius), John. *See* Triclinius
Cattaneo, Carlo. *See* Europe
Cattaneo, Pietro. *See* City Planning
Cattius Catullus, Lucius. *See* Papyrology
Catullus, 181. *See also* Achilles; Aesthetics; Alexandrianism; Anacreon; Ariadne; Carpe diem; Cupid; Elegy; Genre; Homosexuality; Lyric Poetry; Opera; Pornography; Propertius; Sappho; Statius; Translation; *Book, Manuscript: Development; Censorship; Commentary; Lachmann; Magic; Renaissance; Rubens; Scaliger, Joseph Justus; Sexuality*
Cavafy, C. P., 182. *See also* Alexandria; Alexandrianism; Endymion; Metaphrasis; *Barbarians; Julian*
Cavalier, P.-J. *See* Nudity
Cavalieri, Tommaso. *See Ganymede*
Cavalli, Francesco. *See* Dido; Endymion; Opera; *Medea*
Cavendish, Margaret. *See* Penelope; *Cleopatra*
Caxton, William. *See* Achilles; Translation; Troilus; *Hercules*
Caylus, Anne-Claude-Philippe de Tubières, comte de. *See* Winckelmann
Cazzati, Maurizio. *See Cupid*
Ceauşescu, Nicolae. *See Palace*
Cecchi, Giovanni Maria. *See* Terence; *Plautus*
Cecilia, Saint. *See* Sacrifice in the Arts
Celan, Paul. *See* Empedocles
Celer. *See* Domus Aurea
Cellini, Benvenuto. *See* Bronze; Narcissus; Sculpture; *Ganymede; Laocoön*
Celsus. *See* Allegory
Celsus, Aulus Cornelius. *See* Botany; Doxography; Medicine; Water Supply; *Hippocrates*
Celsus, Publius Juventius. *See* Law, Roman
Celtis, Conrad. *See* Education; Greek, Ancient; Horace; Roads, Roman; Tacitus; *Cartography*
Cennini, Cennino. *See* Color
Censorinus. *See Antiquarianism; Calendars; Music*
Censorship, 183
Centaur, 187
Cento, 189
Ceoli, Tiberio. *See Rubens*
Cephalas, Constantine. *See* Greek Anthology; *Anthology*
Cerberus. *See* Sculpture; *Orpheus*
Cerceau, Jacques Androuet du. *See* Triumphal Arch
Ceres. *See Demeter and Persephone*
Cerronibus, Giovanni Cavallini de. *See* Rome
Cervantes, Miguel de. *See* Ajax; Apollo; Comedy; Galatea; Novel; Romanticism; Writing; *Melancholy; Plutarch; Renaissance*
Cesalpino, Andrea. *See* Botany

Cesare, Giulio. *See* Demeter and Persephone
Cesariano, Cesare. *See Caryatid; Hypnerotomachia Poliphili*
Cesi, Federico. *See* Academy
Cesi collection. *See Rubens*
Cesti, Pietro. *See Cupid*
Cestius, Gaius. *See* Guidebooks to Ancient Rome; Pyramid
Ceva, Tommaso. *See* Lucretius
Cézanne, Paul. *See* Modernism
Cha, Theresa Hak Kyung. *See Hesiod*
Chacón, Alfonso. *See* Warfare
Chacón, Pedro. *See* Numismatics; Symposium
Chagall, Marc. *See Daphnis*
Chalcondyles, Demetrius. *See* Grammar; Greek, Ancient; Homer; *Eustathius*
Chalcondyles, Laonicus. *See* Herodotus; Historiography
Chaldaean Oracles. *See Hermes Trismegistus*
Chalgrin, Jean-François-Thérèse. *See* Triumphal Arch
Chambers, Ephraim. *See* Writing
Chambers, William. *See* Neoclassicism; Ruins; Soane; *Adam, Robert*
Chamisso, Adelbert von. *See* Widow of Ephesus
Champier, Symphorien. *See* Galen
Champollion, Jean-François. *See* Forgery; Obelisk; *Hieroglyphs*
Chandler, Richard. *See* Dilettanti, Society of; *Olympia*
Chandragupta Maurya. *See* India
Chanwook, Park. *See* Odysseus
Chaos, **190**
Chapelain, Jean. *See* Tragedy
Chaplin, Charlie. *See Comedy; Mime*
Chapman, George. *See* Achilles; Hero and Leander; Homer; Pope, Alexander; Satire; Terence; Translation; *Estienne, Henri II; Juvenal*
Chariton. *See* Novel
Charlemagne. *See* Alcuin; Collecting; David; Education; Empire; Historiography; Law, Roman; Libraries; Livy; Martial; Mosaic; Notitia Dignitatum; Palace; Pastoral; Renaissance; Rhetoric; Rhōmaioi; Rome; Sarcophagi; Sculpture; Slavery; Spolia; Translatio Imperii; Vitruvius; *Augustus; Book, Manuscript: Development; Greek, Ancient; Liberal Arts; Novel; Suetonius*
Charles I of England. *See* Caesars, Twelve; Constitution, Mixed; Founding Fathers; Revolution, French; Sophocles; Tacitus; *Apuleius; Biography; Brutus; Epicurus; Milton; Ode; Portico*
Charles II of England. *See Academy; Astrology; Augustus; Brutus*
Charles III Bourbon. *See Forum*
Charles III of Naples. *See* Epicurus
Charles III of Spain. *See* Herculaneum
Charles IV. *See* Numismatics
Charles V. *See* Caesar, Julius; *Atlas; Christine de Pizan*
Charles V, Holy Roman Emperor. *See* Palace; Rome; Tacitus; *Augustus; Colony; Historiography; Neptune; Warfare*
Charles VI, Emperor. *See* Seven Wonders of the World
Charles VII. *See Rabelais*
Charles VIII. *See* Tacitus; *Budé; Demosthenes; Warfare*
Charles IX. *See Warfare*
Charles the Bald. *See* Empire; *Philosophy*
Charles the Bold. *See* Alexander the Great; Warfare
Charleton, Walter. *See* Epicurus; Widow of Ephesus; *Atoms*
Charpentier, Marc-Antoine. *See Medea*
Charron, Pierre. *See* Seneca the Younger; Skepticism; Stoicism; *Philosophy*
Chartier, Alain. *See* Classical
Chartier, René. *See Doxography*
Chartres, **191**
Chasteigner de la Roche-Posay, Louis. *See Scaliger, Joseph Justus*
Chateaubriand, Vicomte François-Auguste-René de. *See* Hannibal; *Elgin Marbles*
Chaucer, Geoffrey, **192**. *See also* Achilles; Aeneas; Ajax; Ariadne; Boethius; Comedy; Donatus; Elegy; Epicurus; Locus Amoenus; Lodging; Lucan; Martianus Capella; Medea; Midas; Ovid; Palmyra; Parody; Ptolemy; Pyramus and Thisbe; Romance, Medieval; Satire; Statius; Tourism; Tragedy; Translation; Troilus; Virgil; Xanthippe; *Astronomy; Boccaccio; Cleopatra; Euripides; Isidore; Livy; Macrobius*
Chaucer, Lewis. *See Astronomy*
Chaussard, P. J. B. *See Anacharsis*
Chavet, M. de. *See* Seneca the Elder
Cheke, John. *See* Pronunciation of Greek and Latin; *Demosthenes*
Chekhov, Anton. *See Rome*
Chénier, André. *See* Greek, Ancient; *Maenads*
Chénier, Marie-Joseph. *See* Electra
Chersiphron. *See Art History*
Cherubini, Luigi. *See Cupid; Euripides; Medea; Opera*
Chesterfield, Philip Dromer Stanhope, 4th Earl of. *See* Horace
Chesterton, Gilbert Keith. *See* Pliny the Younger
Chevalier, Étienne. *See* Book, Manuscript: Development
Chigi, Agostino. *See Astrology; Color*
Chillingworth, William. *See* Skepticism
Chilperic. *See Numismatics*
Chimera. *See Pegasus*
Chirico, Giorgio de. *See* Ariadne; Castor and Pollux; Metaphysics; Modernism; *Hercules; Pegasus*
Chiron. *See Centaur*
Chloe. *See* Daphnis; *Pastoral*
Choerospactes, Leo. *See Moschopoulos*
Chomsky, Noam. *See Grammar*
Choniates, Michael. *See Athens; Eustathius*
Choniates, Nicetas. *See* Constantinople; *Atticism; Byzantium; Eustathius; Metaphrasis*
Choricius of Gaza. *See Genre*
Chorier, Nicolas. *See* Censorship
Chortasmenos, John. *See Bessarion*
Chosroes I. *See* Aristotle; Caesar, as Political Title; Iranian Hellenism; *Islam*
Chrēsis, **193**
Chrétien de Troyes. *See* Fortune; Romance, Medieval
Chrétien le Gouays. *See Hercules*
Christina of Sweden. *See* Warfare; *Faun; Warfare*
Christine de Pizan, **194**. *See also* Aeneas; Demeter and Persephone; Fortune; Helen; Medea; Ovid; Penelope; Pyramus and Thisbe; Warfare; Xanthippe; *Hermaphroditus*
Christine of Lorraine. *See Deus ex Machina*
Christmann, Jakob. *See* Squaring the Circle
Christodorus of Coptus. *See* Greek Anthology
Chromatius. *See Palace*
Chrysaor. *See Pegasus*
Chrysippus. *See* Classical; Isagoge; Logic; Stoicism
Chrysokokkes, George. *See Bessarion*
Chrysologus, Peter. *See* Nudity
Chrysoloras, Manuel. *See* Byzantium; Cartography; Constantinople; Grammar; Greek, Ancient; Hagia Sophia; Philosophy; Renaissance; Rome; *Cities, Praise of; Lucian*
Chrysostom, John. *See* Alexander the Great; *Consolation*
Churchill, Caryl. *See* Thyestes; *Maenads*
Churchill, Winston. *See* Education
Churchyard, Thomas. *See Ovid*
Chytraeus, David. *See Herodotus*
Ciaceri, Emanuele. *See* Sicily
Ciatti, Felice. *See* Etruscans
Cicero, Quintus Tullius. *See Letters*
Cicero and Ciceronianism, **194**. *See also* Aeschylus; Aesthetics; Ancients and Moderns; Antiquarianism; Archimedes; Aristocracy; Aristotle; Astronomy; Augustine; Book, Manuscript: Development; Book, Manuscript: Production; Book, Printed; Botany; Calendars; Cato the Younger; Chaucer; Classical; Collecting; Color; Commentary; Concord, Philosophical; Consolation; Constitution, Mixed; Cosmology; Cynicism; Dante; Demosthenes; Dialectic; Dialogue; Divination; Dream Interpretation; Education; Empire; Epicurus; Erasmus; Ethics; Fashion; Fathers,

Church; Forgery; Founding Fathers; Fragments; Galileo; Gesture; Grammar; Grotto; Herodotus; Historiography; Homer; Humanism; Imitation; Immortality of the Soul; Letters; Liberal Arts; Liberty; Macrobius; Magic; Melancholy; Mnemonics; Monsters; Muses; Neo-Latin; Paganism; Petrarch; Plato; Pliny the Younger; Plutarch; Poetics; Political Theory; Poliziano; Portico; Presocratics; Progress and Decline; Prosody; Purple; Rabelais; Renaissance; Revolution, French; Rhetoric; Sallust; Scaliger, Julius Caesar; Seneca the Elder; Seneca the Younger; Seven Sages of Rome; Skepticism; Slavery; Socrates; Stoicism; Symposium; Tacitus; Terence; Thermopylae; Thucydides; Topos; Translation; Valla; Virgil; War, Just; Writing; Xenophon; *Academy; Affecti; Allegory; Art History; Astrology; Atheism; Athens; Atticism; Barbarians; Boccaccio; Boethius; Brutus; Ficino; Hippocrates; Horace; Households; Irony; Jesuits; Judaism; Latin and the Professions; Latin Language; Libraries; Machiavelli; Melanchthon; Montaigne; Palimpsest; Philosophy; Pronunciation of Greek and Latin; Racine; Rubens*
Cicognini, Giacinto Andrea. *See* Opera
Cid, the. *See* Epic
Cieza de Léon, Pedro de. *See Ethnography*
Cimabue, Giovanni. *See* Renaissance; *Art History; Biography*
Cimarosa, Domenico. *See* Opera
Cincinnatus. *See* Founding Fathers; Revolution, French
Cinczio, G. B. Giraldi. *See* Aeneas
Cinema, **197**
Cinna, Helvius. *See* Alexandrianism; *Genre*
Cinthio, Giambattista Giraldi. *See* Imitation; Tragedy
Cipiko, Coriolano. *See Split*
Circe, **200**. *See also* Paganism; Romance, Medieval; Sirens; *Lucian; Medea; Odysseus*
Cities, Praise of, **201**
City Planning, **202**
Cixous, Hélène. *See* Ovid
Clapmarius, Arnold. *See* Tacitus
Clarendon, Edward Hyde, Earl of. *See* Livy; Thucydides
Claretus de Solentia. *See* Donatus
Clark, Stephen R. L. *See* Vegetarianism
Classical, **205**
Claudel, Paul. *See* Aeschylus
Claudian. *See* Aphrodite; Comedy; Demeter and Persephone; Genre; Horace; Locus Amoenus; Statius
Claudius. *See* Nero; Revolution, French; Rome; Satire; Tacitus; *Etruscans; Plutarch*
Claudius Gothicus. *See* Palace
Claus, Hugo. *See Thyestes*
Clausewitz, Carl von. *See* Warfare
Clavius, Christophorus. *See* Warfare; *Astrology; Euclid*
Clay, Cassius. *See Names*
Cleanthes. *See* Classical; Seneca the Younger; Stoicism
Clearchus. *See Persia*
Clearchus of Soli. *See Iranian Hellenism*
Cleitus. *See* Alexander the Great
Clémanges, Nicholas de. *See* Progress and Decline
Clemenceau, Georges. *See Demosthenes*
Clement, Saint. *See Etruscans*
Clement III. *See* Replicas
Clement VII (Giulio de' Medici). *See* Nicetas Codex; Replicas; *Cicero; Laocoön; Ornament; Sallust*
Clement X. *See* Roman Monuments, Reuse of
Clement XI. *See Paper Museum*
Clement XII. *See* Etruscans; *Porphyry*
Clement XIII. *See Piranesi*
Clement XIV. *See* Collecting; Jesuits
Clement, Claude. *See* Museum
Clement of Alexandria. *See* Anthology; Egypt; Epicurus; Fathers, Church; Hieroglyphs; Orpheus; Philo; Plutarch; Stoicism; Symposium; *Atticism; Chrēsis; Philosophy; Sibyls*
Cleomedes. *See Planudes*
Cleon. *See* Founding Fathers
Cleonides. *See Isagoge; Music*
Cleopatra, **206**. *See also* Alexandria; Alexandrianism; East and West; Ode; Plutarch; Shakespeare; *Helen; Names; Numismatics; Portraits, Reception of Ancient; Tragedy*
Clérisseau, Charles-Louis. *See* Hadrian's Villa; Neoclassicism; Pompeii; Ruins; *Maison Carrée; Split; Temple*
Clifford, Rosamund. *See* Ruins; *Ovid*
Clinton, Henry Fynes. *See Calendars*
Clio. *See Muses*
Clitomachus. *See Atheism*
Clodius, Publius. *See* Founding Fathers
Cloots, Jean-Baptiste (Anacharsis). *See Anacharsis; Names*
Clusius, Carolus. *See* Botany
Cluverius, Philip. *See* Cartography; Historiography; *Scaliger, Joseph Justus*
Clytemnestra. *See* Sacrifice in the Arts; *Cassandra; Castor and Pollux; Helen; Iphigenia; Leda; Names; Penelope*
Coccinus, Philotheus. *See* Thomas Magister
Coccio, Marc Antonio (Sabellicus). *See* Livy
Cocteau, Jean. *See* Modernism; Oedipus; Orpheus; Tragedy; Widow of Ephesus; *Cinema*
Codex Iustinianus. *See* Renaissance
Codussi, Mauro. *See* Alexandria
Coelius Sedulis. *See Poetics*
Coelus. *See Theater Architecture*
Coen, Ethan. *See* Cyclops; Odysseus; *Cinema*
Coen, Joel. *See* Cyclops; Odysseus; *Cinema*
Coetzee, J. M. *See* Barbarians; Valla
Coins and Medals, **207**
Coiter, Volcher. *See* Medicine
Coke, Roger. *See Matriarchy*
Coke, Thomas, 1st Earl of Leicester. *See* Grand Tour
Cola di Rienzo. *See* Antiquarianism; Inscriptions; Livy; Rome; *Augustus*
Colbert, Claudette. *See Cleopatra*
Colbert, Jean-Baptiste. *See* Roads, Roman; *Atlas; Warfare*
Cole, Thomas. *See* Ruins
Coler, Cristoph. *See* Sallust
Coleridge, Samuel Taylor. *See* Endymion; Horace; Lyric Poetry; Neoplatonism; Psellus; Romanticism
Collas, Achille. *See* Bronze
Collecting, **208**
Collenuccio, Pandolfo. *See* Natural History; Pliny the Elder
Colleoni, Bartolommeo. *See* Caesars, Twelve
Collingwood, William Gershom. *See* Households
Collino, Ignazio. *See* Sacrifice in the Arts
Collins, William. *See* Horace; Ode; *Pindar*
Colman, George, the elder. *See* Terence
Colmanus, Irish monk. *See* Genre
Colocci, Angelo. *See Cartography*
Colomiès, Paul. *See Bentley*
Colonna, Fabrizio. *See Machiavelli*
Colonna, Francesco. *See* Emblem; Hieroglyphs; Hypnerotomachia Poliphili; Nudity; Pyramid; Ruins; *Maenads*
Colonna, Giovanni. *See* Historiography
Colonna, Cardinal Prospero. *See* Guidebooks to Ancient Rome
Colonna di San Vito, Giovanni. *See* Guidebooks to Ancient Rome
Colonne, Guido delle. *See* Achilles; Aeneas; Paganism; Romance, Medieval; Troilus
Colony, **211**
Color, **213**
Colosseum, **216**. *See also* Roman Monuments, Reuse of; Sports
Columbus, Christopher. *See* Cartography; India; Ptolemy; *Colony; Renaissance*
Columbus, Renaldus. *See* Sexuality
Columella. *See* Botany; Veterinary Medicine; Zoology; *Renaissance*
Comanini, Gregorio. *See* Color
Comatas. *See Pastoral*
Comedy and the Comic, **217**
Comenius, John Amos. *See* Greek, Ancient
Comestor, Peter. *See* Paganism
Cometas. *See Book, Manuscript: Development*
Comic Books, **225**

Commandino, Federico. *See Automata*
Commentary, **225**
Commodus. *See* Gibbon
Commynes, Philippe de. *See* Sallust
Comnena, Anna. *See* Grammar; Renaissance; Rhōmaioi; *Atticism; Constantinople; Metaphrasis*
Comnenus, Alexius. *See* Nicetas Codex
Comparetti, Domenico. *See* Allegory
Comte, Auguste. *See* Progress and Decline; *Magic*
Concord, Philosophical, **233**
Condé, Louis II, prince of. *See Warfare*
Condillac, Étienne Bonnot de. *See Neoclassicism*
Condivi, Ascanio. *See Michelangelo*
Condorcet, marquis de. *See* Liberty; Progress and Decline; Suicide; *Korais*
Congreve, William. *See* Comedy; Horace
Conington, John. *See Homosexuality*
Conrad-Martius, Hedwig. *See* Chaos
Conrad of Hirsau. *See* Donatus
Consolation, **234**
Constans II. *See* Pantheon; *Book, Manuscript: Development*
Constant, Benjamin. *See* Democracy; Despotism, Oriental; Empire; Political Theory; Revolution, French
Constantine I, **236**. *See also* Architecture; Byzantium; Collecting; Constantinople; Donation of Constantine; Empire; Fathers, Church; Forgery; Glass; Guidebooks to Ancient Rome; Portico; Progress and Decline; Renaissance; Rhōmaioi; Roman Monuments, Reuse of; Rome; Sculpture; Spolia; Translatio Imperii; Virgil; *Barbarians; Catacombs; Forma Urbis Romae; Julian; Mirabilia Urbis; Novel; Tourism*
Constantine II. *See* Caesar, as Political Title
Constantine IV Pogonatus. *See Warfare*
Constantine V, emperor. *See* Iconoclasm
Constantine VI, emperor. *See* Iconoclasm
Constantine VII Porphyrogenitus. *See* Antiquarianism; Cartography; Renaissance; Rhōmaioi; *Byzantium*
Constantine IX Monomachus. *See* Psellus; *Byzantium*
Constantine the African. *See* Medicine; Melancholy; Pharmacology
Constantine the Rhodian. *See Cities, Praise of*
Constantinople, **237**. *See also* Byzantium; Cities, Praise of; *Athens*
Constantius I. *See* Constantine
Constantius II. *See Julian; Mirabilia Urbis*
Constitution, Mixed, **239**
Contarini, Gasparo. *See* Constitution, Mixed
Conti, Antonio. *See Brutus*
Conti, Giovan Battista dei. *See* Roman Monuments, Reuse of
Conti, Natale. *See* Genre; Paganism; *Hercules*
Conti family. *See* Roman Monuments, Reuse of
Contini, Francesco. *See* Hadrian's Villa
Conway, Henry Seymour. *See* Ruins
Cook, James. *See Geography*
Cook, Thomas. *See* Terence; Tourism
Cooper, Anthony Ashley, Third Earl of Shaftesbury. *See* Epictetus
Copeau, Jacques. *See* Comedy
Copernicus, Nicolai. *See* Archimedes; Astronomy; Commentary; Cosmology; Galileo; Geography; Melanchthon; Progress and Decline; Ptolemy; Pythagoras; *Academy; Astrology; Martianus Capella; Philosophy; Renaissance*
Copp, Guillaume. *See* Medicine
Corax of Sicily. *See* Isagoge
Corcoran, John. *See* Logic
Cordus, Valerius. *See* Botany; *Melanchthon*
Coriolanus. *See Opera*
Cornarius, Janus. *See* Dream Interpretation; Medicine; *Dioscorides*
Corneille, Pierre, **240**. *See also* Dramatic Unities; Oedipus; Opera; Racine; Seneca the Younger; Shakespeare; Tragedy; *Catharsis; Cleopatra; Lessing; Livy; Medea; Sophocles*
Corneille, Thomas. *See* Hannibal
Cornelia. *See Cleopatra*
Cornelius Labeo. *See* Etruscans
Cornutus, Annaeus L. *See* Allegory; Fragments; Virgil
Cornwallis, Charles. *See Cato the Younger*
Cornwallis, William. *See Comedy*
Corot, Jean-Baptiste-Camille. *See* Modernism; Orpheus; *Daphnis; Maenads; Picasso*
Corpus Iuris Civilis. *See* Law, Roman; Renaissance; Slavery; Sports; *Judaism*
Corradini, Enrico. *See Brutus*
Correa, Vincenzo. *See* Roman Monuments, Reuse of
Correggio, Antonio Allegri da. *See* Cupid; Danaë; Leda; *Actaeon; Art History; Ganymede; Hercules*
Correggio, Niccolò da. *See* Apuleius
Corso, Rinaldo. *See Nudity*
Cortés, Donoso. *See* Dictatorship
Cortés, Hernán. *See* Ethnography
Cortesi, Paolo. *See* Cicero; Neo-Latin; Poliziano; Tacitus
Corti, Matteo. *See Medicine*
Cortona, Pietro da. *See* Demeter and Persephone; Praeneste; Sacrifice in the Arts
Corvinus, Matthias. *See* Book, Manuscript: Development
Corvo, Baron. *See Homosexuality*
Corydon. *See* Elegy; *Pastoral*
Cosmas. *See Book, Manuscript: Development*
Cosmas Indicopleustes. *See* Geography; India
Cosmati family. *See* Rome; *Spolia*
Cosmology, **241**
Cossa, Francesco del. *See* Cupid
Costabili, Beltrando. *See* Raphael
Costellion. *See* Skepticism
Cottam, Samuel Elsworth. *See Pederasty*
Cotton, Charles. *See* Comedy; Dido
Cotton, Sir Robert. *See* Caesars, Twelve
Coubertin, Pierre de. *See* Olympia; *Olympic Games*
Courtois, Jehan. *See* Purple
Cowley, Abraham. *See* Epic; Horace; Lucan; Ode; Pindar; Sappho; Translation; *Comedy*
Cox, Stephen. *See* Porphyry
Coyzevox, Antoine. *See* Bronze
Cranach, Lucas, the Elder. *See* Aphrodite; Cupid; *Hercules*
Crane, Ronald Salmon. *See* Rhetoric
Crantor. *See Atlantis; Consolation*
Crassi, G. P. *See* Medicine
Crassus, Lucius Licinius. *See* Rhetoric
Crassus, Marcus Licinius. *See* Caesar, Julius; Revolution, French; Spartacus; *Cato the Younger*
Crastone, Giovanni. *See* Greek, Ancient
Cratander, Andreas. *See* Book, Printed
Crates of Thebes. *See* Satire; Seven Sages of Rome; *Cynicism*
Cratevas. *See* Botany
Cratinus. *See* Pronunciation of Greek and Latin
Crébillion, Prosper Jolyot de. *See Thyestes*
Creech, Thomas. *See* Epicurus; Translation; *Lucretius*
Cremonini, Cesare. *See Philosophy*
Cremutius Cordus. *See Censorship*
Creon. *See* Republicanism; *Antigone*
Crescenzi, Nicola. *See* Roman Monuments, Reuse of
Cresilas. *See Amazons*
Crespin, Jean. *See Biography*
Creuzer, Georg Friedrich. *See* Apollo; Fragments; Mithras; Paganism; *Neoplatonism*
Crichton, Michael. *See Chaos*
Criseida. *See Troilus*
Crispus, Flavius Julius. *See Constantine*
Critias. *See* Atheism; Sparta
Croce, Benedetto. *See* Hercules
Croce, Giulio Cesare. *See Names*
Croesus. *See* East and West
Cromwell, Oliver. *See* Constitution, Mixed; Revolution, French; *Ode; Republicanism*
Cronkite, Walter. *See* Television
Cronos. *See* Demiurge; *Mythology*
Crowley, Aleister. *See Astrology*
Crowne, John. *See Thyestes*
Cruquius, Jacobus. *See Horace*
Crusius, Martin. *See Censorship*
Crusius, Otto. *See Nietzsche*
Crusius, Paulus. *See Calendars; Herodotus*
Cruz, Sor Juana Inés de la. *See* Adonis; Narcissus

Ctesias of Cnidos. *See* Herodotus; India; *Barbarians; Ethnography; Persia; Photius*
Ctesibius. *See Automata*
Ctesiphon. *See Byzantium*
Cudworth, Ralph. *See* Egypt; Neoplatonism; Plato; *Fragments*
Cueva, Juan de la. *See* Ajax
Cuffe, Henry. *See* Historiography
Cujas, Jacques. *See* Law, Roman; *Petronius; Scaliger, Joseph Justus; Vico*
Cullen, Countee. *See* Endymion; Tantalus
Cumberland, Richard. *See* Terence
Cumont, Franz. *See* Mithras
Cunha, Euclides da. *See Names*
Cunningham, James Vincent. *See* Epigram; Horace; *Ode*
Cunningham, William. *See Atlas*
Cupid, **244**. *See also* Aphrodite; Endymion; Paganism
Curtius, Ernst. *See* Olympia; Professionalization of Classics; Topos; *Olympic Games*
Cuspinian, Johannes. *See* Calendars; *Hippocrates*
Cuvier, Georges. *See* Pliny the Elder
Cybele. *See* Herculaneum; *Mystery Religions*
Cybille, Gilles. *See Terence*
Cyclops, **246**. *See also* Sicily; *Locus Amoenus*
Cydones (Cydonius), Demetrius. *See* Renaissance
Cynicism, **247**. *See also* Judaism; Seneca the Younger; Socrates; Suicide; Xenophon; *Philosophy; Republicanism; Satire*
Cyprian, Saint. *See* Anthology; Fathers, Church; Forgery; *Erasmus; Horace*
Cyrenaics. *See Consolation*
Cyriac of Ancona. *See* Antiquarianism; Calendars; Cartography; Collecting; Constantinople; Elgin Marbles; Epigraphy; Hagia Sophia; Hypnerotomachia Poliphili; Inscriptions; Oracles; Pyramid; Replicas; Split; Temple; Tourism; *Athens; Hieroglyphs*
Cyriacus. *See* Constantine
Cyril, Saint. *See* Renaissance
Cyril of Alexandria. *See* Egypt; *Anthology; Thomas Magister*
Cyrus the Great. *See* East and West; Xenophon; *Households; Machiavelli*
Cyrus the Sophist. *See* Poetics
Cyrus the Younger. *See* Xenophon

Dacier, André. *See* Translation; *Dacier; Delphin Classics; Lessing*
Dacier, Anne, **249**. *See also* Ancients and Moderns; Book, Printed; *Delphin Classics*
Dacre, Lady. *See* Petrarch
Daedalus. *See* Knossos; *Automata; Labyrinth*
D'Ailly, Pierre. *See* Astrology; Cartography; Forgery; *Aristotle*
Dalberg, Johann von. *See Numismatics*
D'Alembert, Jean le Rond. *See* Livy; Writing; *Latin Language; Lucian*
D'Alessandro, Alessandro. *See Symposium*
Dalí, Salvador. *See* Venus de Milo; *Hercules; Laocoön*
Dalou, Aimé Jules. *See Maenads*
Dal Pozzo, Carlo Antonio. *See* Paper Museum
Dal Pozzo, Cassiano. *See* Paper Museum
Dalton, John. *See Atoms; Philosophy*
Dalton, Richard. *See Elgin Marbles*
Damascius. *See* Epictetus
Damasus, Pope. *See* Catacombs; Fathers, Church
Damoetas. *See Alcuin*
Danaë, **250**. *See also Ganymede*
Danaides. *See Montaigne*
Dance, George, the Younger. *See* Neoclassicism; Soane; *Mausoleum*
D'Andeli, Henri. *See* Alexander the Great
Dandolo, Enrico. *See* Alexander the Great
Danet, Pierre. *See Delphin Classics*
Daniel (prophet). *See* Alexander the Great; Translatio Imperii; *Ornament*
Daniel, Arnaut. *See* Statius
Daniel, Samuel. *See* Tragedy; *Cleopatra*
Daniélou, Jean. *See Fathers, Church*
D'Annunzio, Gabriele. *See* Inscriptions; Phaedra; *Cinema; Etruscans; Hermaphroditus; Mycenae*
D'Ansse de Villoison, Jean-Baptiste Gaspard. *See* Book, Manuscript: Development; Commentary; Wolf, Friedrich August
Dante Alighieri, **250**. *See also* Aeneas; Alexander the Great; Ancients and Moderns; Arachne; Astronomy; Boethius; Book, Printed; Cato the Younger; Centaur; Cosmology; Cynicism; Demeter and Persephone; Donatus; East and West; Empire; Epic; Epicurus; Fortune; Ganymede; Helen; Hercules; Horace; Liberty; Livy; Locus Amoenus; Lucan; Marsyas; Mnemonics; Nudity; Odysseus; Ovid; Paganism; Parnassus; Pastoral; Poetics; Ptolemy; Pyramus and Thisbe; Renaissance; Romanticism; Rome; Satire; Seneca the Younger; Sirens; Statius; Ut pictura poesis; Virgil; *Academy; Aesthetics; Aristotle; Art History; Boccaccio; Brutus; Censorship; Chaucer; Cleopatra; Dialogue; Hesiod; Homer; Isidore; Macrobius; Martianus Capella; Mirabilia Urbis; Petrarch; Philosophy; Symposium*
Danti, Vincenzo. *See* Aesthetics; Bronze
Danton, Georges. *See Dionysus*
Daphne. *See Names; Ovid*
Daphnis, **252**. *See also* Elegy; Pastoral
Da Ponte, Lorenzo. *See* Endymion
Darab. *See Persia*
D'Aragona, Tullia. *See Names*
D'Arco, Nicolò. *See* Genre
Dares the Phrygian. *See* Achilles; Aeneas; Cassandra; Historiography; Romance, Medieval; Writing; *Dacier; Delphin Classics*
D'Arezzo, Restoro. *See* Sarcophagi
Darius I. *See Persia*
Darius II. *See Persia*
Darius III. *See* Persia; *Alexander the Great*
Darré, Richard Walther. *See* Fascism
Darwin, Charles. *See* Anthropology; Empedocles; Ethnography; Presocratics; Progress and Decline; Vegetarianism; *Aristotle; Cicero; Lucretius*
Darwin, Erasmus. *See* Lucretius
Dassin, Jules. *See* Phaedra; *Cinema*
Dasypodius, Conrad. *See* Ptolemy
Dati, Agostino. *See* Neo-Latin
Dati, Leonardo. *See Alberti*
D'Aubignac, François Hédelin, Abbé d'. *See* Dramatic Unities; Tragedy; Wolf, Friedrich August
D'Aubigné, Agrippa. *See* Epic; Lucan; Plague
Däubler, Theodor. *See* Thermopylae
Daumier, Honoré. *See* Sisyphus; Tantalus; *Cynicism; Physiognomy*
Davanzati, Bernardo. *See* Galileo
Davenant, Charles. *See* Empire
Davenant, William. *See Comedy*
D'Averara, Pietro. *See* Ajax
David (king). *See* Orpheus; Pléiade
David, Jacques-Louis, **252**. *See also* Aesthetics; Helen; History Painting; Modernism; Neoclassicism; Nudity; Revolution, French; Sappho; Socrates; Sparta; Suicide; Temperament; Thermopylae; Toga; *Apuleius; Picasso*
David of Dinant. *See* Philosophy
Davie, Donald. *See* Demeter and Persephone; Horace; *Ode*
Davies, Robertson. *See* Apuleius
Davis, Lindsey. *See* Palmyra
Davison, Francis. *See* Epigram
Dawkins, James. *See Temple*
Dawkins, Richard. *See Bacchanalia*
Day, Angel. *See Daphnis*
D'Eaubonne, Françoise. *See Matriarchy*
Deburau, Jean Gaspard. *See* Comedy; *Mime*
Debussy, Claude. *See* Faun; Pastoral; Sirens; *Inscriptions*
Decembrio, Angelo. *See* Alexander the Great; Historiography
Decembrio, Pier Candido. *See* Alexander the Great; *Cities, Praise of; Petrarch*
Decius Mus. *See* Rubens
De Conty, Évrart. *See Hermaphroditus*
Decroux, Etienne. *See* Comedy
Dedekind, Richard. *See* Zeno's Paradoxes
Dee, John. *See* Aristophanes; Translation
Defoe, Daniel. *See* Novel; *Juvenal*
Degas, Edgar. *See* Modernism; Nudity; *Picasso*
Dehio, Georg. *See* Atrium
Deianeira. *See Centaur; Hercules*

Deidameia. *See* Statius; *Achilles*
Deiphobus. *See Helen*
Dekker, Thomas. *See* Plague
Delacroix, Eugène. *See* David; Nudity; Orpheus; *Cleopatra; Medea*
De la Mare, Walter. *See* Epigram
Delambre, Jean-Baptiste-Joseph. *See* Astronomy
Delaunay, Robert. *See* Orpheus
Delaunay, Sonia. *See* Orpheus
DeLillo, Don. *See* Novel
Della Robbia, Luca. *See* Alberti
Della Rovere, Galeotto. *See* Guidebooks to Ancient Rome
Della Scala family. *See* Scaliger, Julius Caesar
Delphin Classics, **253**
Del Rio, Martín. *See Automata*
Delsarte, François. *See* Gesture
Demeter and Persephone, **254**. *See also* Orpheus; Sirens; *Chaucer; Demeter and Persephone; Locus Amoenus; Paganism; Popular Culture*
Demetrius. *See* Allegory; Rhetoric
Demetrius Chalcondylas. *See* Book, Printed
Demetrius of Phaleron. *See* Demosthenes; Museum; Poetics
Demetrius the Cynic. *See Seneca the Younger*
DeMille, Cecil B. *See Cleopatra; Toga*
Demiurge, **255**
Democracy, **256**
Democritus. *See* Atoms; Classical; Galileo; Philosophy; Portraits, Reception of Ancient; Presocratics; Purple; Rabelais; *Anthology; Art History; Hippocrates; Magic; Melancholy; Nietzsche; Philosophy*
Demodocus. *See Mythology*
Demon, **259**
Demonax. *See Cynicism*
Demosthenes, **260**. *See also* Ancients and Moderns; Book, Manuscript: Production; Grammar; Imitation; Maxims; Metaphrasis; Portraits, Reception of Ancient; Revolution, French; Rhetoric; Seneca the Elder; Translation; Wolf, Friedrich August; *Athens; Bessarion; Book, Manuscript: Development; Byzantium; Commentary; Erasmus; Melanchthon; Photius; Valla*
Dempster, Thomas. *See* Etruscans; Grand Tour; *Symposium*
Denis, Saint. *See* Neoplatonism
Dennis, George. *See Etruscans*
Denon, Vivant. *See* Bronze
Depardieu, Gérard. *See Astérix*
D'Épinay, Prosper. *See Maenads*
De Quincey, Thomas. *See Antigone*
Derain, André. *See* Modernism
Dermée, Paul. *See* Modernism
De' Rossi, Giovanni Giacomo. *See Bellori*
Derrida, Jacques. *See Chaos; Hieroglyphs*
Derveni Papyrus. *See Orpheus*
Derzhavin, Gavrila. *See* Horace; Ode
De Sales, François. *See* Stoicism
Desbillons, François. *See* Jesuits
Descartes, René. *See* Ancients and Moderns; Archimedes; Automata; Commentary; Cosmology; Dialectic; Hermes Trismegistus; Historiography; Immortality of the Soul; Logic; Metaphysics; Montaigne; Optics; Philosophy; Physiognomy; Rhetoric; Skepticism; Stoicism; Tacitus; Vegetarianism; Volcanoes; Zeno's Paradoxes; *Aesthetics; Affecti; Aristotle; Atheism; Atoms; Dialogue; Latin Language; Lucretius; Magic; Medicine*
Desgodetz, Antoine. *See* Dilettanti, Society of
Desiderio da Settignano. *See* Caesars, Twelve
Desiderius, Abbot. *See* Rome; Vitruvius; *Book, Manuscript: Development*
Desiderius, King. *See Historiography*
Desmoulins, Camille. *See* Revolution, French; *Cicero*
Despautère, Jean. *See Grammar*
Despotism, Oriental, **261**
Desprez, Louis. *See Horace*
D'Este, Alfonso I. *See* Raphael; *Maenads*
D'Este, Alfonso II. *See Etruscans*
D'Este, Borso. *See* Book, Manuscript: Development; *Magic*
D'Este, Cesare. *See Martianus Capella*
D'Este, Ercole I. *See* Caesars, Twelve; *Names; Plautus*
D'Este, Isabella. *See* Book, Printed; Collecting; Rome; *Mime; Museum*
D'Este, Leonello. *See* Historiography; *Alberti; Museum*
D'Este, Niccolò. *See Phaedra*
De Ste. Croix, G. E. M. *See* Slavery
D'Este family. *See* Numismatics; Scaliger, Julius Caesar; *Hercules*
Deucalion. *See Mythology*
Deus ex Machina, **263**
Devil, **264**
De Vitry, Philippe. *See Warfare*
Dewey, John. *See* Liberty
D'Hancarville, P. F. H. *See Symposium*
Dhu'-l Qarnayn. *See Persia*
Diacceto, Francesco da. *See* Immortality of the Soul
Diaghilev, Serge. *See* Modernism; *Daphnis; Picasso*
Diagoras of Melos. *See Atheism*
Dialectic, **265**
Dialogue, **266**
Diana. *See* Endymion; Paganism; Sculpture; *Locus Amoenus; Names; Ovid; Popular Culture*
Diane de Poitiers. *See* Names
Dias, Bartholomew. *See* India
Dias, Cícero. *See Names*
Díaz del Castillo, Bernal. *See* Ethnography
Dicaearchus. *See* Aristotle; *Art History; Judaism*
Dickens, Charles. *See* Parasite; *Cities, Praise of; Rome*
Dickinson, Emily. *See Asterisk; Lyric Poetry*
Dickinson, John. *See* Founding Fathers
Dictatorship, **267**
Dictys of Crete. *See* Achilles; Aeneas; Cassandra; Historiography; Romance, Medieval; Writing; *Dacier*
Diderot, Denis. *See* Aeschylus; Cynicism; Horace; Imitation; Iphigenia; Livy; Lucretius; Plato; Satire; Seneca the Younger; Skepticism; Stoicism; Writing; *Atheism; Dialogue; Ecphrasis*
Dido, **268**. *See also* Aeneas; Ariadne; Cleopatra; Cupid; Elegy; Ovid; Rabelais; Romance, Medieval; Suicide; Virgil; *Catullus; East and West; Helen; Machiavelli; Opera; Popular Culture; Troilus; Widow of Ephesus*
Didymus Chalcenterus. *See* Commentary
Didymus the Blind. *See Philo*
Diels, Hermann, **269**. *See also* Doxography; Fragments; Historiography; Presocratics
Dieterich, Albrecht. *See Magic*
Dietrich of Freiberg. *See* Plato
Dietz, Friedrich Reinhard. *See* Medicine
Digges, Thomas. *See* Cosmology
Dihle, Albrecht. *See Fathers, Church*
Dilettanti, Society of, **270**. *See also* Athens; Collecting; Grand Tour; Greek Revival
Dilmen, Güngör. *See Midas*
Dindorf, Wilhelm. *See* Forgery
Dine, Jim. *See* Venus de Milo
Dini, Dino. *See* Veterinary Medicine
Dio Cassius. *See* Cato the Younger; Palace; Pantheon; *Augustus; Bessarion; Byzantium; Corneille, Pierre; Livy; Racine; Thucydides*
Dio Chrysostom. *See* Homer; Xenophon; *Cities, Praise of; Philosophy; Renaissance; Thomas Magister*
Diocles. *See Archimedes*
Diocles of Carystus. *See Hippocrates*
Diocletian. *See* Caesar, as Political Title; Palace; Porphyry; Purple; Seven Sages of Rome; Split; Suda; *Adam, Robert; Michelangelo; Mosaic*
Diodati, Charles. *See Milton*
Diodorus Siculus. *See* Aesthetics; Egypt; Hieroglyphs; Historiography; India; Muses; Writing; *Annius of Viterbo; Atlas; Book, Manuscript: Development; Estienne, Henri II; Machiavelli; Magic; Thucydides*
Diogenes Laertius, **271**. *See also* Book, Manuscript: Production; Cosmology; Cynicism; Doxography; Empedocles; Logic; Philosophy; Presocratics; Pythagoras; Rabelais; Satire; Xanthippe; Xenophon; *Anthology; Aristotle; Asterisk; At-*

las; Atoms; Biography; Epicurus; Nietzsche; Racine; Raphael
Diogenes of Apollonia. *See* Fragments; Presocratics
Diogenes of Sinope. *See* Cynicism; Diogenes Laertius; Sexuality; Suicide
Diogenianus. *See Anthology*
Diomedes. *See* Poetics
Dionigi of Sansepolcro. *See* Petrarch
Dionysius, Saint. *See Diophantus*
Dionysius Exiguus (the Small). *See* Calendars; Greek, Ancient
Dionysius of Furna. *See* Art History
Dionysius of Halicarnassus. *See* Caesar, Julius; Herculaneum; Historiography; Maxims; Poetics; Rhetoric; Schlegel; Thucydides; Warfare; *Atticism; Book, Manuscript: Development; Calendars; Estienne, Henri II; Historiography; Poetics; Pope, Alexander*
Dionysius Periegetes. *See Eustathius*
Dionysius the Areopagite. *See* Fathers, Church; Ficino
Dionysius Thrax. *See* Grammar; *Armenian Hellenism*
Dionysus, **272**. *See also* Apollo; Ariadne; Bacchanalia; Barberini Faun; Fathers, Church; Faun; Maenads; Orpheus; Parnassus; Philosophy; Picasso; Pornography; Rabelais; Rome; Schlegel; Statius; *Dilettanti, Society of; Grotto; Midas; Names; Popular Culture*
Diophantus, **273**. *See also Planudes*
Dioscorides (gem cutter). *See* Rome
Dioscorides (physician), **274**. *See also* Botany; Medicine; Natural History; Pharmacology; Renaissance; *Averroës; Byzantium; Melanchthon*
Dioscorus of Aphrodito, Flavius. *See* Papyrology
Diotima, **275**
Dirce. *See* Rome; Sculpture
Disney, Walt. *See* Amphitryon; *Centaur*
Disraeli, Benjamin. *See* Colony; Empire
Dittersdorf, Carl Ditters von. *See* Phaethon
Divination, **275**
Divus, Andreas. *See* Translation
Dobson, Austin. *See* Horace
Doimus, bishop of Salona. *See* Split
Dolce, Lodovico. *See* Aesthetics; Thyestes; *Color; Comedy; Hermaphroditus; Plautus*
Dolet, Étienne. *See* Scaliger, Julius Caesar; Translation; *Epicurus*
Domat, Jean. *See* Law, Roman
Dominic, Saint. *See* Nudity
Domitian. *See* Domus Aurea; Forum; Palace; Philosophy; Plutarch; Stadium; Statius; Suetonius; Tacitus; *Censorship; Juvenal; Martial; Revolution, French*
Domitius Ahenobarbus, Gnaeus. *See Nero*
Domitius Apollinaris. *See* Pliny the Younger
Domus Aurea, **279**. *See also* Adam, Robert; Raphael; Roman Monuments, Reuse of; Rome; *Ornament*
Donatello. *See* Bronze; Cupid; Etruscans; Faun; Nudity; Portraits, Reception of Ancient; Rome; Sarcophagi; Sculpture
Donation of Constantine, **280**. *See also* Forgery; Translatio Imperii; Valla; *Historiography*
Donato, Leonardo. *See* Warfare
Donato, Pietro. *See Notitia Dignitatum*
Donatus, **281**. *See also* Book, Printed; Commentary; Grammar; Imitation; Irony; Terence; Tragedy; *Boccaccio; Liberal Arts*
Donatus, Alexander. *See Catharsis*
Donatus, Bernardinus. *See Households; Xenophon*
Donatus, Tiberius. *See* Commentary; Virgil
Dondi, Giovanni de'. *See* Ptolemy; Water Supply; *Vitruvius*
Donen, Stanley. *See Cinema*
Dongo, Fabrizio del. *See* Epic
Doni, Anton. *See Comedy*
Doni, Giovanni Battista. *See Ligorio; Mime*
Donne, John. *See* Comedy; Consolation; Metaphysics; Ovid; Propertius; Satire; *Biography*
Donnelly, Ignatius. *See Atlantis*
Doolittle, Hilda (H.D.). *See* Apuleius; Helen; Phaedra; Translation; *Centaur*
Dorat, Jean. *See* Greek, Ancient; Pléiade; Ronsard; *Allegory; Education; Scaliger, Joseph Justus*
Doré, Gustave. *See* Arachne; Ruins
Dorion. *See* Metaphrasis
Dorislaus, Isaac. *See* Commentary; Historiography; Tacitus
Dornavius, Caspar. *See* Comedy
Dorotheus of Sidon. *See* Astrology; Divination; *Iranian Hellenism*
Dörpfeld, Wilhelm. *See* Olympia
Dörrie, Heinrich. *See Plato*
D'Orville, Jacques-Philippe. *See* Sicily
Dosio, Giovanni Antonio. *See* Forma Urbis Romae; Guidebooks to Ancient Rome; Roman Monuments, Reuse of
Dossi, Battista. *See* Maenads
Dossi, Dosso. *See* Aeneas; Circe; Maenads
Doué, Bertin de la. *See* Ajax
Douglas, Gavin. *See* Translation; Virgil
Douglas, Kirk. *See Cinema; Spartacus*
Douglass, Frederick. *See Lyceum*
Doukas, Demetrios. *See* Poetics
Douris of Amos. *See* Penelope
Dousa, Janus. *See Scaliger, Joseph Justus*
Dove, Rita. *See* Sophocles
Dover, Sir Kenneth James. *See Calendars*
Dover, Robert. *See Olympic Games*
Doxography, **282**
Dracontius. *See* Seneca the Younger
Draghi, Antonio. *See Socrates*
Dramatic Unities, **284**
Drayton, Michael. *See* Endymion; Locus Amoenus; Ovid; Pastoral
Dream Interpretation, **285**
Dreisig, L. *See* Socrates
Dreyer, Carl-Theodor. *See* Television; *Cinema*
Droysen, Johann Gustav. *See* Alexander the Great; Hellenistic Age; *Böckh; Burckhardt*
Druids. *See Magic*
Druillet, Philippe. *See* Popular Culture
Drumann, Wilhelm. *See Brutus*
Dryden, John. *See* Amphitryon; Comedy; Elegy; Epic; Epicurus; Horace; Imitation; Juvenal; Lucretius; Metaphysics; Ode; Oedipus; Ovid; Parody; Plautus; Satire; Suetonius; Tragedy; Translation; Troilus; Virgil; *Cleopatra; Milton; Pindar; Sophocles*
Du Bellay, Guillaume. *See* Rabelais
Du Bellay, Jean. *See* Guidebooks to Ancient Rome; Rabelais
Du Bellay, Joachim. *See* Aristophanes; Hercules; Ovid; Pléiade; Poetics; Rabelais; *Comedy; Martial*
Dubois, Pierre. *See* Warfare
Du Cange, Charles. *See* Greek, Ancient
Du Cange, Dominique. *See* Museum
Duchamp, Marcel. *See* Sculpture
Duchesne, Jean. *See* Warfare
Du Choul, Guillaume. *See* Warfare
Ducos, Pierre-Roger. *See* Revolution, French
Duff, William. *See Genius*
Duffy, Carol Ann. *See* Midas; *Circe*
Duffy, Maureen. *See Maenads*
Dugonics, András. *See* Neo-Latin
Dulce et decorum est pro patria mori, **286**
Dumas, Alexandre, père. *See* Electra
Dunbabin, T. J. *See Magna Graecia*
Duncan, Isadora. *See* Gesture
Duncan, John H. *See* Triumphal Arch
Duns Scotus, John. *See* Demon; Grammar; Immortality of the Soul; Metaphysics; Philosophy; *Erasmus*
Dunton, John. *See Comedy*
Dupérac, Étienne. *See* Forma Urbis Romae; Speculum Romanae Magnificentiae
Duquesnoy, François. *See* Sculpture
Dürer, Albrecht. *See* Apollo; Apollo Belvedere; Centaur; City Planning; Cupid; Demeter and Persephone; Faun; Genius; Melancholy; Orpheus; Triumphal Arch; *Divination; Hercules; Magic; Modernism; Nudity*
Duret, Claude. *See* Progress and Decline
Duris of Samos. *See Art History*
Durkheim, Emile. *See* Mythology; *Anthropology*
Durrell, Lawrence. *See* Alexandria; Alexandrianism
Dürrenmatt, Friedrich. *See* Hercules
Dutton, Paul. *See Chartres*

Du Vair, Guillaume. *See* Seneca the Younger; Stoicism
Dvořák, Antonín. *See* Sirens
Dyer, John. *See* Virgil
Dying Gaul. *See Plaster Casts*

East and West, **288**
Ebb, Fred. *See Cities, Praise of*
Eber, Paul. *See* Natural History
Eberhard, Johann August. *See* Presocratics
Eberhard of Béthune. *See* Greek, Ancient; *Liberal* Arts
Echo. *See Narcissus*
Eckermann, Johann Peter. *See* Virgil; *Winckelmann*
Eckhart, Meister. *See* Plato
Eckhel, Joseph-Hilaire. *See* Coins
Eco, Umberto. *See* Poetics; Writing; *Book, Manuscript: Development; Comedy*
Ecphrasis, **291**
Edelstein, Ludwig. *See* Stoicism
Edmondes, Clement. *See* Warfare
Education, **292**
Edward I. *See Warfare*
Edward III. *See Chaucer*
Edward VI. *See Warfare*
Egeria. *See* Tourism
Egidio da Viterbo. *See* Historiography
Eginard. *See* Vitruvius
Egio, Benedetto. *See* Guidebooks to Ancient Rome
Egizio, Matteo. *See Vico*
Egnazio, Giovanni Battista. *See Numismatics*
Egypt, **299**. *See also Athens; Barbarians*
Eichendorff, Joseph, Freiherr von. *See* Romanticism
Eichhorn, Johann Gottfried. *See* Wolf, Friedrich August
Einhard. *See* Gellius; Historiography; Livy; Rome; Suetonius; *Biography; Cicero; Renaissance*
Einstein, Albert. *See* Genius; *Archimedes; Ovid*
Eirene. *See* Iconoclasm
Ekkehard the Elder. *See* Virgil
Eleanora of Toledo. *See* Palace; Penelope
Eleatics. *See* Philosophy
Eleazar, son of Jair. *See Masada*
Electra, **302**. *See also* Sophocles
Elegy, **303**
Elephantis. *See* Pornography
Elgin, Thomas Bruce, 7th Earl of. *See* Athens; Collecting; Elgin Marbles; Parthenon; *Caryatid; Dilettanti, Society of*
Elgin Marbles, **306**. *See also* Pergamon; Sicily; *Plaster Casts*
El Greco. *See Laocoön*
Eliot, George. *See* Academy; Education; Greek, Ancient; Neoclassicism; Translation; *Antigone; Rome*
Eliot, T. S. *See* Aeschylus; Alexandrianism; Comedy; Electra; Greek, Modern Uses of Ancient; Lyric Poetry; Modernism; Satire; Seneca the Younger; Tragedy; Virgil; *Centaur; Euripides; Juvenal; Ovid*
Elizabeth, Countess of Ulster. *See Chaucer*
Elizabeth I. *See* Dido; Endymion; Gesture; Historiography; Tragedy; *Boethius; Cleopatra; Demosthenes; Latin and the Professions; Rhetoric*
Elizabeth II. *See Theater Architecture*
Elizabeth of Shrewsbury. *See* Penelope
Ellet, Elizabeth Fries. *See Biography*
Elliott, Spencer H. *See* Education
Ellis, Bret Easton. *See Ovid*
Elssler, Fanny. *See* Gesture
Elyot, Thomas. *See* Rhetoric; Translation
Elysian Islands. *See Achilles*
Elzeviers. *See* Book, Printed
Emblem, **307**
Emerson, Ralph Waldo. *See* Biography; Plutarch; Stoicism; Xenophon; *Lyceum*
Emmanuel, Maurice. *See* Music
Empedocles, **308**. *See also* Allegory; Freud; Mythology; Papyrology; Plato; Poetics; Presocratics; Pythagoras; Vegetarianism; *Allegory; Aphrodite; Fragments; Judaism*
Empereur, Jean-Yves. *See* Alexandrianism
Empire, **310**
Empson, William. *See Pastoral*
Endelechius. *See* Pastoral
Endymion, **312**. *See also* Barberini Faun
Enescu, George. *See Sophocles*
Engels, Friedrich. *See* Aeschylus; Dialectic; Dictatorship; Ethnography; Marxism; Matriarchy; *Caesar, Julius; Cities, Praise of; Historiography; Philosophy*
Ennius, Quintus. *See* Epic; Fragments; Seven Sages of Rome; Translation; Virgil; *Horace; Muses; Symposium*
Ennodius. *See* Classical; Virgil
Enoch. *See* Writing
Enright, Dennis Joseph. *See* Alexandrianism
Enzensberger, Hans Magnus. *See* Sisyphus
Epaphroditus. *See Liberal Arts*
Ephorus. *See* Thucydides; *India*
Ephraem. *See Byzantium*
Ephrem, Saint. *See Julian*
Epic, **313**
Epicharmus. *See* Parasite; Satire
Epictetus, **319**. *See also* Ethics; Philosophy; Seneca the Younger; Stoicism; *Anthology; Book, Manuscript: Development; Heyne; Poliziano*
Epicurus and Epicureanism, **320**. *See also* Atheism; Atoms; Cosmology; Diogenes Laertius; Ethics; Etymology; Fathers, Church; Galileo; Homer; Horace; Judaism; Lucretius; Meteorology; Montaigne; Parasite; Philosophy; Political Theory; Presocratics; Suicide; *Allegory; Anthology; Consolation; Martial; Nietzsche; Novel; Pastoral; Plutarch; Republicanism*
Epigram, **324**
Epigraphy, **325**
Epimetheus. *See* Prometheus; *Pandora*
Epiphanius. *See* Doxography; *Asterisk; Physiologus*
Epirus. *See Achilles*
Episcopius, Nicolaus. *See Diogenes Laertius*
Er, myth of. *See* Harmony of the Spheres
Erasistratus. *See* Gynecology
Erasmus, Desiderius, **327**. *See also* Anacharsis; Book, Printed; Centaur; Cicero; Comedy; Commentary; Cynicism; Dialectic; Diogenes Laertius; Education; Emblem; Epicurus; Etymology; Euripides; Fathers, Church; Forgery; Grammar; Greek, Ancient; Hero; Historiography; Households; Humanism; Imitation; Iphigenia; Letters; Lucian; Maxims; Melanchthon; Mnemonics; Neo-Latin; Paganism; Pandora; Panegyric; Parody; Petrarch; Philosophy; Pindar; Plato; Pronunciation of Greek and Latin; Prosody; Rabelais; Renaissance; Rhetoric; Satire; Scaliger, Julius Caesar; Seneca the Elder; Seneca the Younger; Skepticism; Socrates; Stoicism; Tacitus; Terence; Valla; Xanthippe; *Aristotle; Atlas; Biography; Boethius; Budé; Chrēsis; Demosthenes; Isagoge; Janus; Pliny the Younger; Symposium*
Erato. *See Muses*
Eratosthenes. *See* Calendars; Cartography; Geography; *Astronomy*
Ercilla, Alonso de. *See* Lucan
Eriugena, Johannes Scotus. *See* Cosmology; Demon; Gellius; Greek, Ancient; Neoplatonism; Philosophy; Plato
Erizzo, Sebastiano. *See* Coins; Numismatics; *Mars*
Erlach, Johann Bernhard Fischer von. *See* Praeneste; Pyramid; Seven Wonders of the World; Split; Triumphal Bridge
Ermenrich. *See* Virgil
Ernesti, Johann August. *See Lachmann; Lessing*
Ernst, Max. *See Laocoön*
Eros. *See* Freud; *Dilettanti, Society of*
Eschenbach, Ulrich von. *See* Hero
Essex, Duke of. *See* Historiography
Estaço, Achille. *See Herm*
Estensi of Ferrara. *See Historiography*
Esther, Queen. *See Penelope*
Estienne, Charles. *See* Natural History; *Comedy*
Estienne, François. *See* Book, Printed
Estienne, Henri I. *See Estienne, Henri II*
Estienne, Henri II (Henricus Stephanus), **330**. *See also* Anacreon; Book, Printed; Fragments; Greek, Ancient; Greek Anthology; Montaigne; Philosophy; Sappho; Skepticism; Thucydides; *Comedy; Diogenes Laertius; Herodotus; Hesiod; Xenophon*
Estienne, Robert. *See* Book, Printed; Estienne, Henri II; Ode
Estienne family. *See* Translation

Ethics, 331
Ethnography, 335
Etienne du Castel. *See Christine de Pizan*
Etruscans, 338. *See also* Annius of Viterbo; Giants; Hypnerotomachia Poliphili; Neoclassicism; Piranesi, Giovanni Battista; Water Supply
Etty, William. *See Hero and Leander; Maenads*
Etymology, 342
Euclid, 345. *See also* Alexandria; Archimedes; Commentary; Cosmology; Liberal Arts; Optics; Squaring the Circle; Warfare; *Astronomy; Book, Manuscript: Development; Judaism; Music; Philosophy; Planudes; Renaissance; Rubens*
Eudemus. *See* Doxography; *Aristotle*
Eudocia, empress. *See* Cento; *Book, Manuscript: Development*
Eudoxia, empress. *See* Renaissance
Eudoxus. *See* Cosmology; *Astronomy*
Eugénie, Empress. *See* Purple
Eugenius IV. *See* Guidebooks to Ancient Rome; Rome; *Alberti*
Eugenius of Palermo. *See Lucian*
Euler, Leonhard. *See Latin Language*
Eumenes II. *See Pergamon*
Eumenes of Cardia. *See* Alexander the Great
Eunapius. *See* Constantine; Plutarch; *Biography; Philosophy*
Euphemus. *See Atheism*
Euphorbus. *See Pythagoras*
Euphorion. *See* Alexandrianism
Euphratas. *See Constantine*
Eupolis. *See* Fragments; Pindar
Euripides, 346. *See also* Achilles; Actaeon; Aeschylus; Alcestis; Ancients and Moderns; Antigone; Aristophanes; Athens; Book, Manuscript: Production; Book, Printed; Cassandra; Centaur; Classical; Comedy; Cyclops; Deus ex Machina; Dionysus; Electra; Helen; Iphigenia; Liberty; Medea; Milton; Olympus; Parody; Phaedra; Philosophy; Political Theory; Portraits, Reception of Ancient; Prosody; Racine; Renaissance; Schlegel; Seneca the Younger; Thyestes; Tragedy; Translation; Warfare; *Anthology; Barbarians; Byzantium; Cinema; Erasmus; Eustathius; Moschopoulos; Mycenae; Nietzsche; Opera; Thomas Magister; Triclinius; Tzetzes*
Europa. *See* Europe; *Ganymede; Ovid; Phaedra*
Europe, 347
Euryalus. *See Homosexuality*
Eurydice. *See* Elegy; Orpheus; *Names*
Eurylochus. *See Circe*
Eusden, Laurence. *See* Pyramus and Thisbe
Eusebius of Caesarea. *See* Alexandria; Allegory; Biography; Censorship; Constantine; Constantinople; Egypt; Fathers, Church; Fragments; Historiography; Orpheus; Paganism; Tourism; Virgil; Writing; *Aristotle; Armenian Hellenism; Calendars; Cartography; Commentary; Isagoge; Philo; Philosophy; Scaliger, Joseph Justus; Sibyls*
Eusebius of Nicomedia. *See Constantine*
Eustace. *See* Actaeon
Eustathius, 350. *See also* Allegory; Homer; Renaissance; Suda; *Atticism; Bessarion; Book, Manuscript: Development; Byzantium; Constantinople; Tzetzes*
Euterpe. *See Muses*
Eutocius of Ascalon. *See Archimedes*
Eutropius. *See Dacier; Delphin Classics; Historiography; Livy; Renaissance*
Euzoius. *See Philo*
Evander. *See Guidebooks to Ancient Rome; Writing*
Evans, Arthur. *See* Knossos
Evans-Pritchard, Edward Evan. *See Magic*
Evanthius. *See* Imitation; Poetics; Terence
Eve. *See* Devil; Giants; Pandora; Progress and Decline; Statius; *Alexander the Great; Numismatics; Ornament; Ovid*
Evelyn, John. *See* Epicurus
Everett, Edward. *See* Professionalization of Classics
Evliya Çelebi. *See* Parthenon
Ewers, Hanns H. *See* Arachne
Eyck, Jan van. *See Sibyls*
Eysenck, Hans Jürgen. *See* Temperament
Ezechiel. *See Judaism*
Ezzelino III da Romano. *See* Tragedy

Fabius Maximus, Quintus. *See Education; Popular Culture*
Fabius Pictor, Quintus. *See* Writing; *Annius of Viterbo*
Fabretti, Raffaello. *See* Water Supply
Fabriano, Gentile da. *See* Sarcophagi; *Hercules*
Fabricius, Johann Albert. *See* Writing; *Doxography; Fragments; Philo*
Fabricius of Aquapendente, Hieronymus. *See* Medicine
Facio, Bartolomeo. *See Art History; Petrarch*
Faerno, Gabriele. *See* Commentary; Guidebooks to Ancient Rome; *Bentley*
Fakhr al-Din al-Razi. *See Astrology*
Falcone, Mattea. *See Elegy*
Falconet, Maurice. *See* Pygmalion
Famulus. *See* Rome
Faraday, Michael. *See Philosophy*
Farghānī, al-. *See* Ptolemy
Farmer, Richard. *See* Shakespeare
Farnell, L. R. *See Pausanias*
Farnese, Alessandro. *See Centaur*
Farnese, Francesco. *See* Forma Urbis Romae
Farnese, Odoardo. *See Hercules*
Farnese collection. *See Rubens*
Farnese family. *See* Triumphal Arch; *Hercules*
Fascism, 352
Fashion, 354
Fast, Howard. *See* Spartacus
Fates. *See Harmony of the Spheres*
Fathers, Church, 355. *See also* Greek, Ancient; Immortality of the Soul; *Fragments; Hellenes; Philosophy*
Faun, 359
Fauno, Lucio. *See* Triumphal Bridge
Faunus. *See* Pan; Pastoral
Faure, Élie. *See Colony*
Fauré, Gabriel. *See* Aeschylus
Fausta Flavia Maxima. *See Constantine*
Faventinus. *See* Vitruvius
Favorinus. *See* Plutarch
Fawcett, Henry. *See* Households
Fazello, Tommaso. *See* Sicily
Fedele, Cassandra. *See Names*
Fedeli, Vencenzo. *See* Etruscans
Félibien, André. *See Art History; History Painting*
Félibien des Avaux, Jean-François. *See* Pliny the Younger
Felici, Costanzo. *See* Sallust
Feliciano, Felice. *See* Book, Manuscript: Development; Epigraphy; Inscriptions
Felix IV. *See* Roman Monuments, Reuse of
Fellini, Federico. *See* Cinema; Satire; Widow of Ephesus; *Petronius*
Fénelon, François. *See* Rhetoric; Sacrifice in the Arts; Satire; *Dialogue; Lucian*
Ferdinand I. *See Etruscans*
Ferdinand of Aragon. *See* Warfare
Ferdowsi. *See* Persia
Feretti, Emilio. *See* Tacitus
Ferguson, Mary Nisbet. *See Elgin Marbles*
Fermat, Pierre de. *See* Diophantus
Fernandez, Armand Pierre (Arman). *See* Venus de Milo
Fernández de Oviedo, Gonzalo. *See* Natural History
Fernel, Jean-François. *See Philosophy*
Ferrante (Ferdinand I), king of Naples. *See* Portico
Ferrari, Benedetto. *See* Cupid
Ferrari, Ottavio. *See* Toga
Festus, Sextus Pompeius. *See* Etymology; Guidebooks to Ancient Rome; Numismatics; Poetics; *Commentary; Fragments; Renaissance; Scaliger, Joseph Justus*
Fetti, Domenico. *See Herm*
Feuerbach, Ludwig. *See* Atheism; Dialectic
Fichte, Johann Gottlieb. *See* Greek, Ancient; Humanism; Schlegel; *Historicism*
Ficino, Marsilio, 360. *See also* Academy; Aesthetics; Calendars; Censorship; Centaur; Commentary; Concord, Philosophical; Cosmology; Cupid; Demiurge; Demon; Diotima; Egypt; Harmony of the Spheres; Hermes Trismegistus; Hieroglyphs; Immortality of the Soul; Magic; Mars; Melancholy; Michelangelo; Music; Neoplatonism; Orpheus; Paganism;

Ficino, Marsilio *(continued)* Petrarch; Philosophy; Pico della Mirandola; Plato; Poliziano; Psellus; Pythagoras; Symposium; Translation; *Affecti; Aphrodite; Apuleius; Astrology; Cartography; Letters*
Ficoroni, Francesco. *See Collecting*
Field, Michael. *See* Sappho
Fielding, Henry. *See* Comedy; Epic; Imitation; Novel; Parody; Plautus; Satire; Xanthippe; *Juvenal*
Fieschi, Cardinal Guglielmo. *See* Sarcophagi
Filelfo, Francesco. *See* Consolation; Greek, Ancient; *Bessarion; Epicurus; Horace; Letters; Petrarch; Philosophy; Pindar*
Filip, Traian. *See Names*
Fin de Siècle Art, **361**
Fine, Oronce. *See* Squaring the Circle
Finlay, George. *See* Philhellenism
Finlay, Ian Hamilton. *See* Sparta
Finley, Moses I. *See* Slavery
Fioravanti, Aristotele. *See Names*
Fiorentino, Rosso. *See* Centaur; Pornography
Fiorillo, Johann Domincus. *See* Art History
Firdausi. *See* Alexander the Great
Firenzuola, Agnolo. *See Comedy*
Firmicus Maternus. *See* Astrology; Demeter and Persephone
Fischer von Erlach, Johann Bernhard. *See Herm*
Fisher, John. *See Medea*
Fitch, John. *See Seneca the Younger*
Fittschen, Klaus. *See* Portraits, Reception of Ancient
Fitzgerald, F. Scott. *See* Satire
Fitzgerald, Robert. *See* Horace
Fitzstephen, William. *See* Palace
Flaccus, Valerius. *See* Pan
Flaccus, Verrius. *See Calendars; Etruscans*
Flaubert, Gustave. *See* Hannibal; Lucian; Popular Culture; *Censorship; Rome*
Flaxman, John. *See* Grand Tour; Hydra; Neoclassicism; *Elgin Marbles*; *Hesiod*
Flecknoe, Richard. *See* Comedy and the Comic; Toga
Fleming, Rudd. *See* Sophocles
Fletcher, Andrew. *See Colony*
Fletcher, John. *See* Daphnis
Fletcher, Phineas. *See* Pastoral
Fliotson, Anne. *See* Comedy
Florio, John. *See* Montaigne
Florus. *See Dacier; Guidebooks to Ancient Rome; Livy; Racine; Renaissance*
Fludd, Robert. *See* Harmony of the Spheres; Pythagoras; Theater Architecture; *Hermes Trismegistus; Magic*
Foggini, Giovanni Battista. *See Faun*
Fogliano, Lodovico. *See* Music
Folard, Melchior. *See* Oedipus
Folengo, Teofilo. *See* Rabelais
Folieto, Hugo de. *See* Temperament
Fomenko, Anatoly. *See* Forgery
Fonseca, Alonso III. *See* Classical
Fontaine, Jean de la. *See* Ancients and Moderns; Comedy
Fontaine, Pierre-François. *See* Triumphal Arch
Fontana, Carlo. *See* Roman Monuments, Reuse of
Fontana, Domenico. *See* Castor and Pollux; Roman Monuments, Reuse of; *Obelisk*
Fontana, Giovanni. *See Labyrinth*
Fontana, Lavinia. *See* Cleopatra; *Names*
Fontanini, Giusto. *See* Etruscans
Fontenelle, Bernard le Bovier de. *See* Ancients and Moderns; Elegy; Ethnography; Imitation; Lucian; Mythology; Pastoral; Satire; *Catharsis; Dialogue; Homer*
Foot, Philippa. *See* Ethics
Foppa, Caradosso. *See* Coins
Forbonnais, Verron de. *See Colony*
Forcellini, Egidio. *See* Mosaic
Foreest, Pieter van (Petrus Forestus). *See* Medicine; Plague; *Hippocrates*
Foresti, Jacopo. *See* Historiography
Forgery, **361**
Forman, Simon. *See* Astrology
Forma Urbis Romae, **364**
Forster, E. M. *See* Alexandrianism; Censorship; Homosexuality
Forster, Georg. *See Geography*
Forsyth, Malcolm. *See* Electra
Fortuna. *See* Fortune; Praeneste
Fortunatianus. *See* Rhetoric
Fortunatus, Matthaeus. *See* Seneca the Younger
Fortunatus, Venantius. *See* Glass; Horace; Ravenna; *Genre*
Fortune, **365**
Fortuny, Mariano. *See Fashion*
Forum, **366**
Forzetta, Oliviero. *See* Venice
Foscarini, Marco. *See Piranesi*
Foscarini, Paolo Antonio. *See* Divination
Foscolo, Ugo. *See* Ajax; Petrarch; Romanticism; *Thyestes*
Fossa, Girolamo. *See Herm*
Fossombrone, Tolomeo Egnazio da. *See Guidebooks to Ancient Rome*
Foucault, Michel. *See* East and West; Households; Philosophy; Sexuality; *Cynicism*
Fouché, Joseph. *See* Caesar, Julius
Founding Fathers, American, **367**
Fouqué, Friedrich de la Motte. *See* Sirens
Fourier, Charles. *See* Professionalization of Classics
Fourmont, Étienne. *See* Historiography
Fourmont, Michel. *See* Inscriptions
Fourquevaux, Raymond de. *See* Warfare
Fox, Charles James. *See Toga*
Foxe, John. *See Biography*
Fracastoro, Girolamo. *See* Lucretius; Plague; Poetics; *Atlantis*
Fraenkel, Eduard. *See* Commentary; *Wilamowitz*
Fragments, **371**
Fragonard, Jean-Honoré. *See* Endymion; Faun; Hadrian's Villa
Francesca, Piero della. *See* Cupid
Francesco II da Carrara. *See* Coins
Francis I. *See* Book, Manuscript: Development; Book, Printed; Bronze; Greek, Ancient; Libraries; Nicetas Codex; Renaissance; Replicas; *Automata; Budé; Centaur; Guidebooks to Ancient Rome; Laocoön; Palace; Warfare*
Francis II. *See* Warfare
Francisci, Pietro. *See* Cinema
Francis of Assisi, Saint. *See* Nudity; Vegetarianism
Francis of Meyronnes. *See Aristotle*
Franck, J. W. *See* Aeneas
Francklin, Thomas. *See* Sophocles
Franco, Battista. *See Cameos*
Franco of Liège. *See Liberal Arts*
Francus (Astyanax). *See* Ronsard
Frangipani family. *See* Roman Monuments, Reuse of; *Colosseum*
Frankfort, Henri. *See Warburg*
Frankl, Viktor. *See* Consolation
Franklin, Benjamin. *See* Plutarch; *Philosophy; Toga*
Fraternities and Sororities, **377**
Fraunce, Abraham. *See* Rhetoric; Sisyphus; *Hermaphroditus*
Frazer, James G. *See* Ethnography; Magic; Mithras; Pausanias; *Bacchanalia; Catharsis; Ovid*
Frederick, Prince of Wales. *See* Ruins; *Neoclassicism*
Frederick I (Holy Roman Emperor). *See* Empire; *Mirabilia Urbis*
Frederick II (Holy Roman Emperor). *See* Liberal Arts; Spolia; Wonders; *Averroës; Book, Manuscript: Development; City Planning; Numismatics*
Frederick II of Prussia (the Great). *See* Greek, Ancient; Ruins; Warfare; *Demosthenes*
Frederick II of Sicily. *See* Sicily
Frederick III (Holy Roman Emperor). *See* Caesar, as Political Title
Frederik Hendrik, Prince of Orange. *See* Caesars, Twelve
Freeman, E. A. *See* Sicily
Freemasons. *See* Egypt
Frege, Gottlob. *See* Logic; Parmenides; *Philosophy*
Freinsheim, Johannes. *See Livy*
Freitag, Adam. *See* Warfare
Fréret, Nicolas. *See* Historiography; Socrates; *Atheism*
Freud, Sigmund, **377**. *See also* Anthropol-

ogy; Athens; Centaur; Consolation; Dream Interpretation; Empedocles; Euripides; Hannibal; Matriarchy; Mithras; Modernism; Narcissus; Oedipus; Ovid; Parthenon; Physiognomy; Poetics; Sophocles; Tragedy; Virgil; Winckelmann; *Brutus; Catharsis*
Friedlaender, Carl. *See* Purple
Friedrich August II, Elector of Saxony. *See* Winckelmann
Friel, Brian. *See* Phaedra; *Euripides*
Frischlin, Nicodemus. *See* Poetics
Frisius, Andreas. *See Symposium*
Fritzlar, Herbort von. *See* Cassandra
Froben, Hieronymus. *See Diogenes Laertius*
Froben, Johann. *See* Book, Printed; Erasmus; Translation
Fromm, Erich. *See Matriarchy*
Fromond, Libertus. *See* Seneca the Younger
Frontinus. *See* Guidebooks to Ancient Rome; Vitruvius; Warfare; Water Supply
Fronto, Marcus Cornelius. *See* Classical; Comedy; Seneca the Younger
Frost, Robert. *See* Horace; *Virgil*
Froumund of Tegernsee. *See* Genre
Fry, Christopher. *See* Widow of Ephesus
Fuchs, Leonhart. *See* Botany; *Dioscorides; Medicine*
Fuentes, Carlos. *See* Hydra
Fuga, Ferdinando. *See* Triumphal Arch
Fugard, Athol. *See Antigone; Sophocles*
Fugger, Ulrich. *See Estienne, Henri II*
Fulbert of Chartres. *See Chartres*
Fulgentius. *See* Aeneas; Alexander the Great; Allegory; Apuleius; Classical; Cyclops; Demeter and Persephone; Hercules; Martianus Capella; Muses; Orpheus; Paganism; Pegasus; Prometheus; Statius; Virgil; *Aphrodite; Genre*
Fulk V le Jeune. *See* Warfare
Fuller, Thomas. *See* Paganism; *Stoicism*
Fulvio, Andrea. *See* Coins; Guidebooks to Ancient Rome; Rome; *City Planning; Numismatics*
Fulvius, Marcus. *See* Revolution, French
Furies. *See Orpheus*
Furtwängler, Adolf. *See* Olympia
Fuseli, Henry. *See* Barberini Faun; *Cyclops; Elgin Marbles*
Füssli, Johann Heinrich. *See Ajax*
Fust, Johann. *See* Book, Printed
Fustel de Coulanges, Numa Denis. *See* Democracy; Ethnography; Professionalization of Classics
Fux, Johann Joseph. *See* Parnassus

Gabriel, archangel. *See Pegasus*
Gadamer, Hans-Georg. *See* Philosophy; *Aristotle*
Gaffurio, Franchino. *See* Harmony of the Spheres; Music; *Affecti*
Gager, William. *See* Aeneas
Gaguin, Robert. *See Letters*
Gaia. *See Hesiod*
Gaiman, Neil. *See* Comic Books
Gaius. *See* Empire; Law, Roman; *Isagoge; Niebuhr*
Galatea, 380. *See also* Sculpture; Sicily; *Cyclops*
Galateo, Antonio. *See Magna Graecia*
Galba, Servius Sulpicius. *See* Numismatics; Portraits, Reception of Ancient
Gale, Phillips. *See Adonis*
Gale, Theophilus. *See* Paganism
Gale, Thomas. *See Bentley*
Galen, 381. *See also* Aesthetics; Aristotle; Book, Printed; Botany; Commentary; Dioscorides; Doxography; Dream Interpretation; Education; Forgery; Greek, Ancient; Gynecology; Humors; Hunayn ibn-Ishāq; Islam; Judaism; Medicine; Natural History; Nicetas Codex; Optics; Pharmacology; Plague; Rabelais; Sculpture; Sexuality; Skepticism; Sports; Temperament; Translation; Water Supply; *Allegory; Art History; Averroës; Avicenna; Erasmus; Gymnasium; Judaism; Latin and the Professions; Melancholy; Melanchthon; Mercuriale; Palimpsest; Philosophy; Physiognomy; Syriac Hellenism*
Galfridus de Vino Salvo. *See* Poetics
Galilei, Vincenzo. *See* Music; Opera
Galileo Galilei, 383. *See also* Academy; Aesthetics; Ancients and Moderns; Archimedes; Astrology; Commentary; Cosmology; Dialogue; Optics; Philosophy; Plato; Ptolemy; Warfare; *Aristotle; Euclid; Magic; Neo-Latin; Paper Museum; Pliny the Elder; Renaissance*
Gall, Franz. *See* Physiognomy
Galla Placidia. *See* Mosaic; *Byzantium*
Galle, Cornelius. *See* Seneca the Younger
Galle, Jan Philipp. *See* Seven Wonders of the World
Galle, Theodore. *See* Seneca the Younger
Gallego, Rómulo. *See Names*
Gallienus. *See* Portico
Gallio, Marco. *See Museum*
Gallitzin, Amalie. *See* Diotima
Gallus, Constantius. *See Julian*
Gallus, Cornelius. *See* Elegy; Papyrology; *Fragments*
Gallus, Thomas. *See* Plato
Galton, Francis. *See* Genius
Galvani, Luigi. *See Latin Language*
Gama, Vasco da. *See* Epic; India; *Ancients and Moderns*
Gamon, Christophe de. *See* Pastoral
Gamucci, Bernardo. *See* Guidebooks to Ancient Rome; Roman Monuments, Reuse of; Triumphal Bridge
Gandhara, 384
Gandy, Joseph. *See* Ruins; *Pausanias*
Ganymede, 385. *See also* Parody
Garamond, Claude. *See* Book, Printed
Garcilaso de la Vega. *See* Horace; *Herodotus*
Gardiner, Stephen. *See* Pronunciation of Greek and Latin
Gardner, Ava. *See* Aphrodite
Gardner, John. *See* Argonauts
Garibaldi, Giuseppe. *See* Caesar, Julius; Names; Sexuality; Sicily
Garimberto, Hieronimo. *See Atlantis*
Garioch, Robert. *See* Sisyphus
Garnier, Jean-Louis-Charles. *See* Architecture; Greek Revival
Garnier, Robert. *See* Seneca the Younger; Sophocles; Tragedy; *Cleopatra*
Garth, Samuel. *See* Pyramus and Thisbe; Translation; *Ovid*
Gascoigne, George. *See* Parasite; Plautus; *Terence*
Gassendi, Pierre. *See* Atoms; Cosmology; Epicurus; Ethics; Lucretius; Philosophy; Skepticism; *Atheism; Biography; Diogenes Laertius; Fragments; Hermes Trismegistus*
Gasteiger, Mathias. *See* Hydra
Gates, Ellen. *See Museum*
Gatterer, Johann Christoph. *See Heyne*
Gatti, Guglielmo. *See* Forma Urbis Romae
Gaurico, Pomponio. *See Physiognomy*
Gautier, Théophile. *See Parnassus*
Gautier de Châtillon. *See* Alexander the Great
Gay, John. *See* Daphnis; Galatea; Pastoral; Statius; *Comedy; Deus ex Machina; Ovid*
Gaza, Theodore. *See* Calendars; Grammar; Greek, Ancient; Natural History; Poetics; Scaliger, Julius Caesar; Translation; Zoology; *Atticism; Erasmus; Genre*
Gedike, Friedrich. *See Heyne*
Geffcken, Johannes. *See Wilamowitz*
Gehe, E. H. *See* Aeneas
Gehry, Frank. *See* Museum
Geiser, Konrad. *See Plato*
Gelbart, Larry. *See* Plautus; *Cinema*
Gelenius, Sigismund. *See* Guidebooks to Ancient Rome
Gell, Sir William. *See* Pompeii
Gelli, Giambattista. *See* Etruscans; *Art History*
Gellius, Aulus, 386. *See also* Antiquarianism; Book, Printed; Classical; Fragments; Horace; Humanism; Isagoge; Macrobius; Plutarch; Poetics; Poliziano; Seneca the Younger; Translation; Writing; Xanthippe; *Commentary; Hippocrates; Pronunciation of Greek and Latin; Symposium*
Gelon. *See Sicily*
Geminus of Rhodes. *See Judaism*
Gemistus Pletho, George. *See* Aristotle; Calendars; Cartography; Concord,

Gemistus Pletho, George *(continued)* Philosophical; Ficino; Fragments; Immortality of the Soul; Plato; Psellus; Renaissance; *Bessarion; Byzantium*
Genaru, Ovidiu. *See Names*
Genga, Girolamo. *See* Ruins
Genghis Khan. *See* Caesar, as Political Title; *Hercules*
Genius, **387**
Gennadios Scholarios (George Scholarius). *See Aristotle; Bessarion*
Gennadius I. *See Isidore*
Genre, **388**
Gentile, Giovanni. *See* Fascism
Gentileschi, Artemisia. *See* Cleopatra
Gentili, Alberico. *See* Poetics
Geoffrey V le Bel. *See* Warfare
Geoffrey of Monmouth. *See* Amphitryon; Greek, Ancient
Geoffrey of Vinsauf. *See* Imitation
Geoffroy IV de la Tour Landry. *See* Seven Sages of Rome
Geography, **391**
George I. *See Augustus*
George II of Georgia. *See* Caesar, as Political Title
George III. *See* Founding Fathers; *Adam, Robert; Paper Museum*
George IV. *See Ruins*
George, Stefan. *See* Historicism
George of Pisidia. *See Byzantium*
George of Trebizond. *See* Caesar, as Political Title; Concord, Philosophical; Plato; Poetics; Ptolemy; Rhetoric; Scaliger, Julius Caesar; Zoology; *Aristotle; Commentary; Education; Isagoge; Philosophy*
Georgides, John. *See Anthology*
Gerald of Wales. *See* Tourism
Gerard, Alexander. *See Genius*
Gerard of Cremona. *See* Astronomy; Medicine; Ptolemy
Gerberga. *See* Roswitha
Gerbert of Aurillac. *See Liberal Arts; Philosophy*
Gerhard, Eduard. *See* Etruscans
Géricault, Théodore. *See* David; *Laocoön*
Gerischer, Carl Friedrich. *See Museum*
Germain, Michel. *See Museum*
Germanicus Caesar. *See* Ptolemy
Gernet, Louis. *See* Parmenides
Gérôme, Jean-Léon. *See* Fin de Siècle Art; Nudity; Pygmalion; *Cleopatra; Daphnis; Maenads*
Gerson, Jean. *See* Donatus
Gersonides (Levi ben Gershom). *See* Immortality of the Soul
Gervase of Tilbury. *See Mirabilia Urbis*
Gesner, Konrad. *See* Libraries; Natural History; Zoology; *Doxography; Hippocrates*
Gessner, Salomon. *See* Elegy
Gesture and Dance, **394**
Geta, Hosidius. *See* Virgil; *Cento*
Getty, J. Paul. *See* Replicas
Ghazālī, al-. *See* Aristotle; Immortality of the Soul; Philosophy; *Averroës; Martianus Capella*
Ghedini, Giorgio Federico. *See Maenads*
Gherardi da Prato, Giovanni. *See* Etruscans
Ghiberti, Lorenzo. *See* Alberti; Art History; Renaissance; Rome; Sacrifice in the Arts; Sculpture; *Hermaphroditus*
Ghiglia, Oscar. *See Etruscans*
Ghini, Luca. *See Dioscorides*
Giacometti, Alberto. *See* Sculpture; *Etruscans*
Giambologna (Jean Boulogne). *See* Bronze; Centaur; Sculpture
Giamboni, Bono. *See* Poetics
Giambullari, Pier Francesco. *See* Etruscans
Giannone, Pietro. *See* Livy
Giants, **397**
Gibbon, Edward, **398**. *See also* Antiquarianism; Constantine; Empire; Epic; Europe; Grand Tour; Historiography; Livy; Panegyric; Professionalization of Classics; Progress and Decline; Rome; Ruins; Suetonius; Thucydides; *Art History; Augustus; Barbarians; Cavafy; Censorship; Julian; Macaulay; Petrarch*
Gibson, Mel. *See Cinema*
Gide, André. *See* Demeter and Persephone; Modernism; Narcissus; Novel; Oedipus; Prometheus
Giedion, Sigfried. *See* Neoclassicism
Giesecke, Alfred. *See* Teubner
Gigli, Giovanni. *See* Genre
Gilbert, Cass. *See* Architecture; Temple
Gilbert, W. S. *See Comedy*
Gilbert of Poitiers. *See* Chartres
Gilbert of Tournai. *See* Warfare
Giles of Rome. *See* Households; Philosophy
Giles of Viterbo. *See* Actaeon; Raphael
Gilio da Fabriano, Andrea. *See Color; Nudity*
Gilleragues, Vicomte de. *See* Ovid
Gilles, Pierre. *See* Constantinople; Tourism; *Natural History*
Gilly, David. *See* Schinkel
Gilly, Friedrich. *See* Neoclassicism; Schinkel
Ginzel, Friedrich Karl. *See Calendars*
Giocondo, Giovanni. *See* Epigraphy; Raphael; Vitruvius; *Architecture; Caryatid*
Giorgi, Francesco. *See Hermes Trismegistus*
Giorgio, Francesco di. *See City Planning*
Giorgione. *See* Aphrodite; Hypnerotomachia Poliphili; Pornography; Venice
Giotto. *See* Modernism; Renaissance; Warfare; *Art History; Mosaic; Picasso*
Giovanni, Bartolomeo di. *See Centaur*
Giovanni da Udine. *See* Color; Neoclassicism; Raphael
Giovio, Giulio. *See* Museum
Giovio, Paolo. *See* Emblem; Museum; Pliny the Younger; Raphael; Renaissance; *Art History; Astrology; Biography*
Giraldi, Lilio Gregorio. *See Martianus Capella; Raphael*
Giraldus Cambrensis. *See* Wonders; *Palace*
Girardin, René-Louis, marquis de. *See* Ruins
Girardon, François. *See* Bronze; Demeter and Persephone
Giraudoux, Jean. *See* Amphitryon; Helen; Plautus; Tragedy; Troilus
Giraud-Teulon, Alexis. *See Matriarchy*
Girodet-Trioson, Anne-Louis. *See* Endymion; Nudity
Gismondi, Italo. *See Forma Urbis Romae*
Giunta Press. *See* Water Supply
Giustiniani collection. *See Sarcophagi*
Gladstone, William. *See* Horace; Sexuality; *Mycenae*
Glanvill, Joseph. *See Epicurus*
Glarean, Heinrich. *See* Calendars; *Affecti*
Glass, **399**
Glauber, Johannes. *See Hermaphroditus*
Gloeden, Baron Wilhelm. *See Pederasty*
Glover, Richard. *See* Thermopylae; *Medea*
Gluck, Christoph Willibald. *See* Alcestis; Iphigenia; Opera; Orpheus; Sacrifice in the Arts; Virgil; *Demeter and Persephone; Deus ex Machina; Euripides; Mime*
Glück, Louise. *See* Demeter and Persephone
Glykys, John. *See* Grammar
Gnaphaeus, Gulielmus. *See* Terence
Gnostic Christian community. *See* Papyrology
Gnosticism. *See* Alchemy; Alexandrianism; Fathers, Church; *Aristotle; Hermes Trismegistus*
Goad, John. *See Astrology*
Goclenius, Rudolph, the Elder. *See* Divination
Godard, Jean-Luc. *See Cinema*
Goddio, Franck. *See* Alexandrianism
Godley, A. D. *See Horace*
Goehr, Alexander. *See* Ariadne
Goethe, Johann Wolfgang von, **400**. *See also* Achilles; Alcestis; Anacreon; Apollo Belvedere; Athens; Catharsis; Classical; Commentary; Demeter and Persephone; Epic; Galatea; Ganymede; Grand Tour; Greek Anthology; Helen; Hercules; Humanism; Inscriptions; Iphigenia; Martial; Novel; Nudity; Ode; Olympus; Orpheus; Ovid; Paestum; Pandora; Parnassus; Pindar; Prometheus; Propertius; Purple; Romanticism; Satire; Sicily; Sirens; Suicide; Tragedy; Virgil; Winckelmann; Wolf, Friedrich August; *Academy; Antigone; Biography; Burckhardt; Euripides; Laocoön; Melancholy; Nietzsche; Rome*
Gog and Magog. *See* Alexander the Great
Goldberg, Whoopi. *See* Plautus
Golding, Arthur. *See* Comedy; Pyramus and Thisbe; Shakespeare; Translation; *Hermaphroditus; Ovid*
Goldoni, Carlo. *See* Menander; Plautus

Goldschmidt, Viktor. *See Music*
Goldsmith, Oliver. *See Terence*
Goliath. *See* Giants
Goltzius, Hendrik. *See* Apollo Belvedere; Phaethon; Tantalus; *Belvedere Torso*
Goltzius (Goltz), Hubert. *See* Coins; Numismatics; *Magna Graecia*
Gombauld, Jean. *See* Endymion
Gombrich, Ernst. *See* Aesthetics; Pausanias; Renaissance; *Warburg*
Gómes de Mora, Juan. *See* Forum
Góngora, Luis de. *See* Cyclops; Epigram; Hero and Leander; Tantalus
Gontard, Susette. *See* Diotima
Gonzaga, Federico. *See* Caesars, Twelve
Gonzaga family. *See* Replicas; *Hercules*
Goodman, Godfrey. *See* Progress and Decline
Goodwin, Thomas. *See* Paganism
Goodyear, Howard. *See Ornament*
Goold, G. P. *See* Loeb Classical Library
Gordianus. *See* Guidebooks to Ancient Rome
Gordon, Thomas. *See* Translation; *Founding Fathers*
Gordon, William. *See Toga*
Gorgani, Fakhraddin. *See* Persia
Gorges, Arthur. *See Lucan*
Gorgias of Leontini. *See* Aesthetics; Helen
Gorgo. *See* Sparta
Gorgon. *See Basilisk*
Gori, Anton Francesco. *See* Etruscans; *Cameos*
Göring, Hermann. *See* Sparta; Thermopylae
Gorky, Maxim. *See* Tantalus
Gorlaeus, Abraham. *See* Collecting
Goscinny, René. *See* Popular Culture
Gossaert, Jan (Mabuse). *See Hermaphroditus*
Gossec, François-Joseph. *See Musical Instruments*
Goths. *See Barbarians*
Gottsched, Johann Christoph. *See* Tragedy; *Lessing*
Goulet-Cazé, Marie-Odile. *See Cynicism*
Gounod, Charles-François. *See* Sappho; *Opera*
Goupylus, Jacobus. *See Dioscorides*
Gournay, Marie de. *See Montaigne*
Goutsos, Dionysis. *See Names*
Gouvy, Théodore. *See* Electra
Gower, John. *See* Epicurus; Ovid; Pyramus and Thisbe; Translation; Xanthippe; *Isidore*
Goya, Francisco José de. *See* Aphrodite; *Hesiod*
G. P. Putnam's Sons. *See Loeb Classical Library*
Grabbe, Christian Dietrich. *See* Olympus
Gracchus. *See* Names
Gracchus, Gaius. *See* Revolution, French; *Niebuhr*
Gracchus, Tiberius. *See Niebuhr*
Gracián, Baltasar. *See* Epigram; Maxims; Tacitus
Graevius, Johannes Georgius. *See Letters*
Graham, Martha. *See* Gesture; Sophocles; *Euripides; Medea*
Grainger, James. *See* Virgil
Grammar, **401**
Gramsci, Antonio. *See* Caesar, Julius
Grand Tour, **404**
Grant, Ulysses S. *See Names*
Grassi, Orazio. *See Galileo*
Gratian. *See* Donation of Constantine; Purple; War, Just; *Book, Manuscript: Development; Cento*
Graupner, Christoph. *See Pegasus*
Graves, Charles. *See* Horace
Graves, Michael. *See Ornament*
Graves, Robert. *See* Argonauts; Novel; Television; *Matriarchy*
Gravina, Gianvincenzo. *See Vico*
Gray, Elizabeth Caroline Hamilton. *See Etruscans*
Gray, Thomas. *See* Elegy; Horace; Macaulay; Ode; Pindar; *Comedy*
Greek. *See* Pronunciation of Greek and Latin
Greek, Ancient, **405**
Greek, Modern, **409**
Greek, Modern Uses of Ancient, **410**
Greek Anthology, **410**. *See also* Sculpture
Greek Revival, **411**
Green, T. H. *See* Ethics
Greenberg, Clement. *See* Alexandrianism; *Laocoön*
Greene, Robert. *See Penelope*
Gregoras, Nicephorus. *See* Plague; *Metaphrasis*
Gregorius, Magister. *See* Tourism; *Mirabilia Urbis*
Gregorovius, Ferdinand. *See* Rome
Gregory I (the Great). *See* Progress and Decline; Renaissance; Rome; *Book, Manuscript: Development; Nudity*
Gregory XIII. *See* Roman Monuments, Reuse of
Gregory, Caspar René. *See* Book, Manuscript: Production
Gregory of Corinth. *See* Grammar; Psellus
Gregory of Cyprus. *See* Planudes
Gregory of Nazianzus. *See* Anthology; Fathers, Church; Hippocratic Oath; *Anthology; Armenian Hellenism; Atticism; Byzantium; Palimpsest; Philosophy; Photius*
Gregory of Nyssa. *See* Fathers, Church; *Anthology; Byzantium; Chrēsis; Philosophy*
Gregory of Tours. *See* Martianus Capella
Grenfell, Bernard P. *See* Papyrology
Grès, Madame (Germaine Krebs). *See Fashion*
Greuze, Jean-Baptiste. *See Maenads*
Grévin, Jacques. *See* Plautus
Grey, Lady Jane. *See Ovid*
Gribelin, Simon. *See* Xenophon
Grien, Hans Baldung. *See* Alexander the Great
Griffith, D. W. *See Cinema*
Grillparzer, Franz. *See* Greek, Ancient; Hero and Leander; Sappho; *Medea*
Grimani, Domenico. *See* Replicas; Venice; *Collecting; Numismatics*
Grimani, Giovanni. *See* Collecting; Venice
Grimani dynasty. *See Cameos*
Grimm, Friedrich Melchior von. *See* Nudity
Grimm, Jacob. *See* Neo-Latin; *Greek, Ancient*
Gris, Juan. *See* Modernism
Gritti, Andrea. *See* Venice
Grognet, Pierre. *See* Seneca the Elder
Grognet de Vassé, Giorgio. *See* Temple
Grolier, Jean. *See* Book, Printed
Gronovius, Jacobus. *See Museum*
Gronovius, Johannes Fredericus. *See* Coins; Seneca the Younger; *Museum*
Groot, Hugo de. *See Livy*
Gropius, Walter. *See* Architecture
Gross, Otto. *See Matriarchy*
Grosseteste, Robert. *See* Astrology; Plato; Translation; *Philosophy*
Grossman, Allen. *See* Lyric Poetry
Grote, George. *See* Democracy; Demosthenes; Professionalization of Classics; *Historiography*
Grotius, Hugo. *See* Commentary; Despotism, Oriental; Ethics; Greek Anthology; Tacitus; Thucydides; War, Just; *Law, Roman; Martianus Capella; Scaliger, Joseph Justus*
Grotto, **412**
Grünbaum, Adolf. *See* Zeno's Paradoxes
Grünbein, Durs. *See* Horace; Ovid; *Juvenal; Thyestes*
Gruter, Jan. *See* Antiquarianism; Epigraphy; Inscriptions; Seneca the Younger; *Ligorio; Scaliger, Joseph Justus*
Gruyer, François-Anatole. *See* Raphael
Grynaeus, Simon. *See Livy*
Gryphius, Andreas. *See* Plautus; Tragedy
Guarini, Camillo-Guarino. *See Ornament*
Guarini, Giovanni Battista. *See* Pastoral; *Martianus Capella; Mime; Opera*
Guarino, Battista. *See* Anthology; Commentary; Education; Terence
Guarino da Verona. *See* Education; Grammar; Greek, Ancient; Historiography; Lucian; Pliny the Younger; Renaissance; *Commentary; Herodotus; Letters*
Guazzalotti, Andrea. *See* Nudity
Guazzo, Stefano. *See Symposium*
Guccione, Bob. *See Cinema*
Guercino (Giovanni Francesco Barbieri). *See* Endymion; *Cleopatra*
Guérin, Pierre-Narcisse. *See* Aeneas
Guicciardini, Francesco. *See* Commentary; Maxims; Sallust; Tacitus; *Livy*
Guidebooks to Ancient Rome, **413**

Guidi, Guido (Vidus Vidius). *See* Nicetas Codex
Guido of Arezzo. *See* Music
Guignes, Joseph de. *See* Progress and Decline
Guilandinus, Melchior. *See* Papyrology; Writing; *Dioscorides*
Guillaume de Machaut. *See* Orpheus
Guillaume du Choul. *See* Coins; *Neptune*
Guimarães, Ulysses. *See Names*
Guimond de la Touche, Claude. *See* Iphigenia
Guinizelli, Guido. *See* Statius
Guizot, François. *See* Democracy
Gullberg, Hjalmar. *See* Thermopylae
Gunn, Thom. *See* Demeter and Persephone
Gurlitt, Ludwig. *See Nietzsche*
Gustavus Adolphus. *See* Warfare
Gutenberg, Johannes. *See Donatus*
Guthrie, Tyrone. *See* Cinema
Guy de Chauliac. *See* Medicine
Gyges. *See Historiography*
Gymnasium, **415**
Gynecology, **416**

Habsburgs. *See* Aeneas; *Hercules*
Hades. *See Demeter and Persephone; Demiurge*
Hadfield, George. *See* Praeneste
Hadith. *See* Immortality of the Soul
Hadot, Pierre. *See* Philosophy
Hadrian. *See* Architecture; Caesar, as Political Title; Collecting; Color; Greek Anthology; Historiography; Neoclassicism; Palace; Pantheon; Rome; Sicily; Suetonius; Tourism; Triumphal Bridge; *Athens; Caesars, Twelve; Caryatid; Elgin Marbles; Names; Nero; Plutarch; Portraits, Reception of Ancient; Roman Monuments, Reuse of; Sarcophagi*
Hadrian's Villa, **418**. *See also Color, Herm*
Haemon. *See Antigone*
Haemstede, Adrian Cornelis van. *See Biography*
Hagedorn, Friedrich von. *See* Horace
Hagia Sophia, **419**. *See also* Architecture; Domus Aurea
Hagiopetrites, Theodore. *See* Book, Manuscript: Development
Hakewill, George. *See* Progress and Decline
Hakluyt, Richard. *See* Colony; Paganism
Hale, Nathan. *See* Dulce et decorum est
Hall, Donald. *See Ode*
Hall, Joseph. *See* Juvenal; Satire; Stoicism
Hall, Peter. *See* Aeschylus; *Cassandra*
Halley, Edmond. *See* Astronomy
Halma, Nicholas. *See* Ptolemy
Haly Abbas al-Majusi. *See* Medicine
Ham. *See* Writing
Hamilton, Alexander. *See* Democracy; Empire; Founding Fathers; Plutarch
Hamilton, Emma. *See* Grand Tour; *Maenads*
Hamilton, Gavin. *See* Neoclassicism
Hamilton, Thomas. *See* Architecture
Hamilton, Sir William. *See* Collecting; Dilettanti, Society of; Glass; Grand Tour; Romanticism; *Adam, Robert*
Hampden, John. *See* Founding Fathers
Hancock, John. *See* Founding Fathers
Handel, George Frideric. *See* Galatea; Opera; Sacrifice in the Arts; *Achilles; Cleopatra; Cyclops; Deus ex Machina; Hercules*
Hanegraaff, Wouter. *See Hermes Trismegistus*
Hannibal, **419**. *See also* David; Epic; Names; Portraits, Reception of Ancient; Revolution, French; Rome; Tourism; *Historiography; Machiavelli; Warfare*
Hansen, Hans Christian. *See* Temple
Hansen, Theophilus Eduard. *See* Temple
Hardouin, Jean. *See* Forgery; Historiography; Jesuits; *Delphin Classics*
Hardouin-Mansart, Jules. *See* Forum
Hardy, Alexandre. *See* Tragedy
Hardy, Thomas. *See* Education; Epic; Epigram; Horace
Hare, Francis. *See Bentley*
Hare, Kenneth. *See Hermaphroditus*
Harington, John. *See* Ajax; Epigram
Harlays family. *See Names*
Harman, Barry. *See* Amphitryon
Harmonia. *See Mars*
Harmony of the Spheres, **420**
Harrington, James. *See* Constitution, Mixed; Dictatorship; Empire; Liberty; Maxims; Republicanism; Revolution, French; *Founding Fathers*
Harriot, Thomas. *See* Optics
Harris, Robert. *See* Pompeii; Volcanoes
Harrison, Jane Ellen. *See* Magic; Professionalization of Classics; *Catharsis; Matriarchy; Pausanias*
Harrison, Tony. *See* Aeschylus; Phaedra; Sophocles; Translation; *Euripides; Medea*
Harryhausen, Ray. *See Cinema*
Harsdörffer, Georg Philipp. *See Topos*
Hart, Lorenz. *See* Plautus
Harvard University Press. *See Loeb Classical Library*
Harvey, Gabriel. *See* Erasmus; Rhetoric
Harvey, William. *See* Commentary; Galen; Humors; Medicine; *Neo-Latin; Pliny the Elder; Zoology*
Hase, Karl-Benedikt. *See Censorship*
Haskins, Charles Homer. *See* Renaissance
Haudebourt, Louis-Pierre. *See* Pliny the Younger
Hauptmann, Gerhart. *See* Apollo
Haussmann, Georges-Eugène. *See* Sewers; Triumphal Arch
Hawking, Stephen. *See Music*
Hawkins, Erick. *See Cupid*
Hawkins, Sir John. *See* Music
Hawksmoor, Nicholas. *See* Forum; Palace; Pyramid; *Mausoleum*
Hawthorne, Nathaniel. *See* Faun; Midas; *Circe; Rome*
Haydon, Benjamin. *See Elgin Marbles*
Hayez, Francesco. *See* Nudity
Hazlitt, William. *See* Imitation; *Elgin Marbles*
Heaney, Seamus. *See* Translation; *Hesiod; Sophocles*
Hebe. *See Ganymede*
Hébrard, Ernest. *See* Split
Hecataeus of Abdera. *See* Egypt
Hecataeus of Miletus. *See* Egypt; India; Mythology
Hector. *See* Helen; Hero; Racine; Ronsard; *Achilles; Ajax; Poetics; Troilus*
Hecuba. *See Euripides; Helen; Troilus*
Hedges, Chris. *See* Dulce et decorum est
Heemskerk, Maarten van. *See* Helen; Sculpture; Seven Wonders of the World
Heffernan, George. *See Isagoge*
Hege, Walter. *See* Apollo
Hegel, G. W. F. *See* Aesthetics; Antigone; Aristotle; Catharsis; Cynicism; Despotism, Oriental; Dialectic; Diogenes Laertius; Empedocles; Ethics; Europe; Hannibal; Heraclitus; Irony; Metaphysics; Neoplatonism; Nudity; Philosophy; Plato; Political Theory; Presocratics; Skepticism; Socrates; Sophocles; Temperament; Tragedy; Winckelmann; *Burckhardt; Demon; Elgin Marbles; Greek, Modern Uses of Ancient; Heidegger; Historicism; Magic; Renaissance*
Heiberg, Johan Ludvig. *See* Archimedes; Ptolemy
Heidegger, Martin, **421**. *See also* Antigone; Empedocles; Heraclitus; Metaphysics; Neoplatonism; Parmenides; Philosophy; Plato; Presocratics; *Aristotle; Nietzsche*
Heine, Heinrich. *See* Dionysus; Greek, Ancient; Sirens; Xenophon
Heinemann, William. *See* Loeb Classical Library
Heinichen, Johann. *See Affecti*
Heinse, Wilhelm. *See* Novel; Romanticism
Heinsius, Daniel. *See* Book, Printed; Philosophy; Terence; *Catharsis; Comedy*
Heinsius, Nicolaus. *See* Book, Printed
Heinze, Richard. *See Nietzsche*
Heiric of Auxerre. *See* Renaissance; *Book, Manuscript: Development*
Hektorovik, Petar. *See Split*
Helena. *See Constantine*
Helen of Troy, **422**. *See also* Europe; Paganism; Popular Culture; Sparta; *Castor and Pollux; Cinema; Leda; Names; Novel; Ovid; Penelope*
Helicon. *See Pegasus*
Heliodorus. *See* Novel; *Basilisk; Book,*

Manuscript: Development; Korais; Petronius; Racine
Heliogabalus. *See Opera*
Helios (Helius). *See Circe; Medea; Phaethon; Seven Wonders of the World*
Hellenes, **423**
Hellenistic Age, **423**
Helmholtz, Hermann von. *See* Presocratics
Helmont, Jan Baptista van. *See* Alchemy
Héloïse. *See Astronomy*
Helvétius, Claude-Adrien. *See* Sparta
Hemsterhuis, Frans. *See* Diotima
Hen, Zerahyah. *See Judaism*
Henderson, Jeffrey. *See* Loeb Classical Library
Henderson, John. *See* Etymology
Henley, W. E. *See* Stoicism
Hennin, H. C. *See* Prosody
Henri II. *See* Triumphal Arch; *Centaur; Names; Pindar*
Henri III. *See* Triumphal Arch
Henri IV. *See* Speculum Romanae Magnificentiae; *Casaubon; Warfare*
Henry I. *See Ovid*
Henry II. *See* Ruins; *Ovid*
Henry II, Holy Roman Emperor. *See Genre; Warfare*
Henry III. *See* Law, Roman
Henry VII. *See Genre; Mausoleum*
Henry VIII. *See* Palace; Sparta
Henry, Patrick. *See* Founding Fathers; *Brutus*
Henry of Blois, bishop of Winchester. *See* Palace; Rome
Henry of Ghent. *See Aristotle*
Henry of Hesse (Henry of Langenstein). *See* Ptolemy; *Astrology*
Henryson, Robert. *See* Orpheus; Tantalus; Troilus
Henze, Hans Werner. *See* Dionysus; *Adonis; Euripides; Maenads*
Hephaestion (grammarian). *See* Poetics; *Triclinius*
Hephaestion (son of Amyntor). *See* Alexander the Great
Hephaestus. *See Demiurge; Pandora*
Hepworth, Barbara. *See Orpheus*
Hera. *See* Amphitryon; *Allegory; Empedocles; Helen; Olympus*
Heraclides Criticus. *See* Tourism
Heraclitus, **424**. *See also* Allegory; Egypt; Empedocles; Fragments; Heidegger; Portraits, Reception of Ancient; Presocratics; *Judaism; Sibyls*
Heraclitus (1st cent. CE). *See* Allegory
Heraclius. *See* Caesar, as Political Title; Rhōmaioi; *Byzantium; Corneille, Pierre; Islam*
Herbert, Edward. *See* Stoicism
Herbert, George. *See Biography*
Herbert, Victor. *See Hero and Leander*
Herculaneum, **425**. *See also* Pompeii; Pornography; Portraits, Reception of Ancient; Replicas; Romanticism; Theater Architecture; Volcanoes; *Architecture; Temple*
Hercules, **426**. *See also* Aesthetics; Alcestis; Amphitryon; Atlas; Devil; Herculaneum; Hydra; Olympia; Paganism; Pompeii; Sophocles; Sparta; Television; Xenophon; Zeno's Paradoxes; *Boethius; Byzantium; Centaur; Cinema; Gandhara; Hero; Mythology; Names; Ode; Olympic Games; Opera; Oracles; Pasquino; Petrarch; Seneca the Younger; Tragedy*
Herder, Johann Gottfried von. *See* Aeschylus; Alcestis; Athens; Ethnography; Goethe; Greek Anthology; Horace; Prometheus
Heredia, José María. *See Thyestes*
Herm, **429**
Hermagoras. *See* Rhetoric; Topos
Hermann, Albert. *See Atlantis*
Hermann, Gottfried. *See* Inscriptions; Professionalization of Classics; Prosody; *Böckh; Teubner*
Hermaphroditus, **429**. *See also Locus Amoenus; Ovid*
Hermapion. *See Obelisk*
Hermes. *See* Apollo; Divination; Herm; Paganism; Raphael; Writing; *Allegory; Circe; Grammar; Hermaphroditus; Magic; Names; Pegasus; Popular Culture; Portraits, Reception of Ancient*
Hermesianax. *See Pastoral*
Hermes Trismegistus and Hermeticism, **430**. *See also* Alchemy; Egypt; Fathers, Church; Ficino; Forgery; Hieroglyphs; Immortality of the Soul; Magic; Neoplatonism; Pyramid; Pythagoras; Sculpture; Writing; *Casaubon; Concord, Philosophical; Iranian Hellenism; Martianus Capella; Philosophy*
Hermodorus of Salamis. *See* Rome
Hermogenes of Tarsus. *See* Poetics; Rhetoric; *Censorship; Planudes; Triclinius*
Hernández, Francisco. *See* Natural History
Hero, **432**
Hero and Leander, **433**. *See also Popular Culture*
Herod. *See* Seven Sages of Rome; *Masada*
Herodas. *See Papyrology*
Herodian. *See* Grammar; Maxims; *Machiavelli*
Herodianus. *See* Aristotle; *Palimpsest*
Herodotus, **434**. *See also* Allegory; Antiquarianism; Barbarians; Biography; Book, Printed; Cartography; Dionysus; Dulce et decorum est; East and West; Egypt; Ethnography; Europe; Fathers, Church; Forgery; Helen; Historiography; Homer; India; Magic; Matriarchy; Mithras; Monsters; Mythology; Parody; Political Theory; Pyramid; Renaissance; Schlegel; Seven Sages of Rome; Sparta; Thucydides; Translatio Imperii; Wonders; Writing; *Anacharsis; Anthology; Anthropology; Byzantium; Cavafy; Diogenes Laertius; Herm; Jesuits; Natural History; Papyrology; Photius; Valla*
Heron of Byzantium. *See Metaphrasis*
Hero of Alexandria. *See* Automata; *Liberal Arts*
Herophilus. *See* Gynecology
Herrick, Robert. *See* Carpe diem; Epigram; Genre; Horace; Ode; *Anacreon*
Herschel, William. *See* Astronomy
Herulians. *See Lyceum*
Hervé (Florimond Ronger). *See Opera*
Hervet, Gentian. *See* Skepticism; Translation
Hesiod, **435**. *See also* Allegory; Anthology; Anthropology; Astronomy; Chaos; Cupid; Cyclops; Epic; Giants; Homer; Locus Amoenus; Muses; Pandora; Pergamon; Pléiade; Poetics; Presocratics; Progress and Decline; Prometheus; Prosody; Renaissance; Seven Sages of Rome; Translation; Vegetarianism; Wonders; *Bessarion; Book, Manuscript: Development; Circe; Commentary; Households; Liberal Arts; Melanchthon; Modernism; Moschopoulos; Mythology; Natural History; Neo-Latin; Pegasus; Poliziano; Triclinius; Tzetzes*
Hesychius of Miletus. *See* Constantinople; *Philosophy*
Heumann, Christoph August. *See* Writing
Hevelius, Johannes. *See Astronomy*
Heyne, Christian Gottlob, **436**. *See also* Commentary; Fragments; Historiography; Professionalization of Classics; Romanticism; Schlegel; Wolf, Friedrich August; *Education; Niebuhr*
Heywood, Thomas. *See* Apuleius; Ovid; Plautus; *Hercules*
Hiero I. *See* Pindar; *Sicily*
Hiero II. *See Archimedes*
Hieroglyphs, **437**
Highet, Gilbert. *See* Propertius
Hilaeira. *See* Castor and Pollux
Hilary of Poitiers. *See Erasmus*
Hildebert of Lavardin. *See* Rome
Hilduinus. *See Neoplatonism*
Hill, Geoffrey. *See* Ode
Hill, Walter. *See Cinema*
Himerius. *See Genre*
Himmler, Heinrich. *See* Fascism
Hipparchus. *See* Astronomy; Cartography; Commentary; Ptolemy; *Astronomy; Liberal Arts*
Hippocrates, **438**. *See also* Aristotle; Bronze; Dream Interpretation; Education; Galen; Geography; Gynecology; Humors; Islam; Judaism; Maxims; Medicine;

Hippocrates *(continued)* Melancholy; Nicetas Codex; Pharmacology; Rabelais; Seven Sages of Rome; Sexuality; Translation; *Guidebooks to Ancient Rome; Korais; Latin and the Professions; Mercuriale*
Hippocrates of Chios. *See* Squaring the Circle
Hippocratic Corpus. *See* Ethnography; Gynecology; Water Supply
Hippocratic Oath, **439**
Hippodamus of Miletus. *See* Sparta
Hippolyta. *See* Amazons
Hippolytus. *See* Sarcophagi; *Phaedra*
Hippolytus of Rome. *See* Doxography; Fathers, Church; *Armenian Hellenism*
Hipponax. *See* Parody; *Book, Manuscript: Development; Tzetzes*
Hirsch, William. *See Melancholy*
Hirschfeld, Magnus. *See* Socrates
Historicism, **440**
Historiography, **441**
History Painting, **448**
Hitchcock, Alfred. *See* Comedy
Hitler, Adolf. *See* Architecture; Fascism; Olympia; Sculpture; Sparta; Stadium; *Forum*
Hittorff, Jacques Ignace. *See* Greek Revival
Hoadly, Benjamin. *See Founding Fathers*
Hobbes, Thomas. *See* Aristotle; Commentary; Despotism, Oriental; Dictatorship; Ethics; Historiography; Immortality of the Soul; Law, Roman; Metaphysics; Philosophy; Political Theory; Republicanism; Squaring the Circle; Thucydides; Widow of Ephesus; *Brutus; Lucretius; Ode*
Hoby, Thomas. *See* Translation
Hoffmann, E. T. A. *See* Sirens
Hoffmann, Friedrich W. *See* Medicine
Hofhaimer, Paul. *See Horace*
Hofmannsthal, Hugo von. *See* Ariadne; Electra; Greek Anthology; Oedipus; *Sophocles*
Hogarth, William. *See Cities, Praise of; Physiognomy; Satire*
Holbach, Paul-Henri Thiry, Baron d'. *See Atheism*
Holbein, Hans, the Younger. *See* Nudity; Tantalus
Hölderlin, Friedrich. *See* Achilles; Antigone; Dionysus; Diotima; Empedocles; Hercules; Horace; Nietzsche; Novel; Ode; Paganism; Philhellenism; Pindar; Political Theory; Romanticism; Sophocles; Translation; *Heidegger; Olympus; Philosophy*
Holinshed, Raphael. *See* Matriarchy
Holkham, Duke of. *See Etruscans*
Holkot, Robert. *See* Philosophy
Holland, Philemon. *See* Pliny the Elder; *Livy*
Hollanda, Francisco da. *See* Color
Holmes, Oliver Wendell. *See* Horace
Holmes, Sherlock. *See* Tantalus
Holtz, Louis. *See Commentary*
Holy Spirit. *See Leda; Muses; Paganism*
Holzer, Ernst. *See Nietzsche*
Holzer, Johann Evangelist. *See* Castor and Pollux
Homer, **449**. *See also* Achilles; Aesthetics; Alexander the Great; Allegory; Ancients and Moderns; Atlas; Barbarians; Book, Manuscript: Production; Book, Printed; Cassandra; Censorship; Centaur; Cento; Circe; Comedy; Comic Books; Cyclops; Demiurge; Divination; Dulce et decorum est; Ecphrasis; Education; Empedocles; Epic; Eustathius; Fathers, Church; Ganymede; Genius; Genre; Goethe; Grammar; Greek, Ancient; Grotto; Heidegger; Helen; Hero; Historiography; Imitation; Judaism; Knossos; Labyrinth; Leda; Locus Amoenus; Maxims; Menander; Metaphrasis; Milton; Mycenae; Mythology; Neoplatonism; Novel; Odysseus; Olympus; Oracles; Paganism; Papyrology; Parnassus; Parody; Pastoral; Penelope; Plague; Pléiade; Plutarch; Poetics; Poliziano; Pope, Alexander; Prosody; Pythagoras; Rabelais; Racine; Renaissance; Romance, Medieval; Romanticism; Ronsard; Sappho; Satire; Schlegel; Sicily; Sirens; Statius; Suda; Suicide; Translation; Troilus; Tzetzes; Vico; Virgil; Warfare; Wolf, Friedrich August; Wonders; Writing; *Alcuin; Asterisk; Augustine; Automata; Biography; Boccaccio; Book, Manuscript: Development; Byzantium; Cavafy; Chaucer; Cinema; Commentary; Dacier; Dante; David; Estienne, Henri II; Forgery; Heyne; Jesuits; Korais; Lessing; Liberal Arts; Lucan; Lyric Poetry; Machiavelli; Melanchthon; Muses; Natural History; Neoclassicism; Neo-Latin; Ovid; Palimpsest; Petrarch; Philosophy; Rubens; Sacrifice in the Arts; Scaliger, Joseph Justus; Symposium; Valla*
Homeric Hymns. *See* Apollo; Castor and Pollux; Demeter and Persephone; Pan; Ronsard; Translation
Homosexuality, **453**
Honneger, Arthur. *See Antigone; Sophocles*
Honorius I. *See* Roman Monuments, Reuse of
Honorius III (Cencio Savelli). *See Mirabilia Urbis*
Honorius, Flavius. *See* East and West; *Barbarians*
Honour, Hugh. *See* Neoclassicism
Hood, Thomas. *See* Endymion
Hooft, Pieter Corneliszoon. *See* Ajax; Tacitus
Hooker, Richard. *See* Paganism
Hope, Charles. *See Warburg*
Hope, Thomas. *See* Neoclassicism; Philhellenism; Sexuality; Toga; *Herm*
Hopkins, Charles. *See Hermaphroditus*
Hopkins, John. *See Hermaphroditus*
Horace, **454**. *See also* Achilles; Aesthetics; Alcuin; Alexandrianism; Anacreon; Book, Printed; Carpe diem; Catullus; Circe; Commentary; Dante; Deus ex Machina; Dulce et decorum est; East and West; Education; Fathers, Church; Fragments; Genre; Grammar; Hero; Homosexuality; Hydra; Imitation; Leda; Letters; Lyric Poetry; Maecenas; Novel; Nudity; Numismatics; Ode; Orpheus; Philosophy; Pindar; Poetics; Pope, Alexander; Rhetoric; Ronsard; Sappho; Satire; Seven Sages of Rome; Sparta; Temperament; Thyestes; Tragedy; Translation; Ut pictura poesis; Virgil; *Art History; Astronomy; Augustus; Bentley; Boccaccio; Censorship; Color; Comedy; Epicurus; Erasmus; Fascism; Galileo; Jesuits; Juvenal; Lessing; Libraries; Lucan; Michelangelo; Muses; Poliziano; Racine; Renaissance; Scaliger, Joseph Justus; Socrates*
Horapollo. *See* Egypt; Emblem; Hieroglyphs; Physiologus
Horatius. *See* Opera; *Corneille, Pierre*
Horkheimer, Max. *See* Sirens
Horsley, John. *See* Censorship
Horus. *See Paganism*
Hotman, François. *See* Tacitus; *Budé; Vico*
Houël, J.-P. L. *See* Sicily
Households and Householding, **460**
Housman, A. E. *See* Comedy; Commentary; Dulce et decorum est; Epigram; Parody; *Astrology; Bentley; Lachmann; Magic*
Houssaye, Nicolas Amelot de la. *See* Tacitus
Hoyer, Johann Gottfried. *See* Warfare
Hrabanus Maurus. *See* Demeter and Persephone; Epicurus; Gellius; Renaissance; Rhetoric; Vitruvius; Warfare; *Book, Manuscript: Development; Chrēsis; Genre*
Hubaish. *See* Medicine
Hubbard, Margaret. *See* Commentary
Hubert. *See* Actaeon
Hucbald. *See* Music
Huerta, Gerónimo de. *See* Natural History
Huerta, Vincente Antonio de la. *See* Electra
Huet, Pierre-Daniel. *See* Book, Printed; Commentary; *Dacier; Delphin Classics*
Hufeland, Christoph Wilhelm. *See Hippocratic Oath*
Hughes, Ted. *See* Ovid; Phaethon; Pyramus and Thisbe; Translation; *Hermaphroditus; Phaedra*
Hughes, Thomas. *See* Tragedy
Hugh of St. Victor. *See* Liberal Arts; Mnemonics; Plato
Hugo, Hermann. *See* Writing
Hugo, Victor. *See* Aeschylus; Diogenes Laertius; Epic; Philhellenism; Sewers; Tragedy; *Virgil*
Hugo of Santalla. *See* Divination
Hugucio (Hugutio). *See* Greek, Ancient; *Isidore*

Huizinga, Johan. *See* Sports
Hülsen, Christian. *See* Speculum Romanae Magnificentiae
Humanism, **462**. *See also* Academy; Alberti; Ancients and Moderns; Antiquarianism; Architecture; Book, Manuscript: Development; Bronze; Philosophy; Political Theory; Renaissance; *Affecti; Aristotle; Biography; Boethius; Plato*
Humann, Karl. *See Pergamon*
Humboldt, Alexander von. *See* Geography; *Heyne*
Humboldt, Wilhelm von. *See* Greek, Modern Uses of Ancient; Greek Anthology; Gymnasium; Humanism; Professionalization of Classics; Romanticism; Wolf, Friedrich August; *Bentley; Burckhardt; Greek, Ancient; Heyne*
Hume, David. *See* Democracy; Dictatorship; Ethics; Immortality of the Soul; Metaphysics; Philosophy; Progress and Decline; Skepticism; Stoicism; *Atheism; Marxism*
Humors, **467**
Humphrey, Duke of Gloucester. *See* Book, Manuscript: Development
Hunayn ibn-Ishāq, **467**. *See also* Judaism; Medicine; Pharmacology; *Commentary; Islam; Syriac Hellenism*
Hunibald. *See* Book, Manuscript: Development
Huns. *See Barbarians*
Hunt, Arthur S. *See* Papyrology
Hunt, Leigh. *See* Translation
Hursthouse, Rosalind. *See* Ethics
Hurtrelle, Simon. *See Herm*
Hus, Jan. *See* Progress and Decline
Hussein, Saddam. *See Palace*
Husserl, Edmund. *See* Heidegger; *Isagoge*
Huston, John. *See* Alexander the Great
Hutchinson, Lucy. *See* Epicurus; Lucretius
Hutten, Ulrich von. *See* Donation of Constantine; *Letters*
Huttich, J. *See Numismatics*
Huxley, Aldous. *See* Satire; *Etruscans*
Huyot, Jean-Nicolas. *See* Praeneste
Huysmans, Joris-Karl. *See* Progress and Decline
Hyde, Robin. *See* Arachne
Hyde, Thomas. *See* Persia
Hydra, **468**. *See also Hercules*
Hyginus, C. Julius. *See* Virgil; *Astronomy; Liberal Arts*
Hypatia. *See* Alexandrianism; Diophantus; Ptolemy; *Philosophy*
Hyperides. *See Papyrology*
Hypnerotomachia Poliphili, **469**
Hypsicles of Alexandria. *See* Astrology
Hypsipyle. *See Opera; Ovid*

Iamblichus (novelist). *See Photius*
Iamblichus (philosopher). *See* Demiurge; Egypt; Fathers, Church; Magic; Mystery Religions; Neoplatonism; Pythagoras; *Byzantium; Ficino; Julian; Philosophy*
Iapetus. *See Prometheus*
Iarbas. *See Dido*
Ibn Abi Usaibi'a. *See* Doxography
Ibn-ʿAdī, Yahyā. *See Baghdad Aristotelians*
Ibn Aknin. *See* Medicine
Ibn al-ʾAwwam. *See* Veterinary Medicine
Ibn al-Hakām, Hisham. *See* Aristotle
Ibn al-Haytham (Alhazen). *See* Aesthetics; Astronomy; Music; Optics; Ptolemy
Ibn al-Nadīm. *See* Music
Ibn al-Nafis. *See* Medicine
Ibn-al-Samh, ʿAlī. *See Baghdad Aristotelians*
Ibn al-Samh of Granada. *See Astronomy*
Ibn al-Shatir of Damascus. *See* Astronomy
Ibn al-Zarqallu. *See Astronomy*
Ibn at-Tayyib, Abū-l-Faraj. *See Baghdad Aristotelians*
Ibn Bajja. *See Philosophy*
Ibn Bakhtishūʿ, Djibril. *See* Medicine
Ibn Battuta. *See* Geography
Ibn Butlan. *See* Medicine
Ibn Daud, Abraham. *See* Judaism
Ibn Ezra, Moses. *See* Judaism
Ibn Falaquera, Shem Tob. *See* Medicine
Ibn Gabirol, Solomon. *See* Judaism; Philosophy
Ibn-Haylān, Yūhannā. *See* Al-Fārābī
Ibn Hayyān, Jābir (Geber). *See* Alchemy
Ibn ʿImrān, Ishāq. *See* Medicine
Ibn Isa, Ali. *See Astrology*
Ibn Khaldūn. *See Averroës*
Ibn Khurradadhbeh. *See* Persia
Ibn Luca, Qusta. *See* Doxography
Ibn-Māsawayh, Yhūannā. *See* Hunayn ibn-Ishāq
Ibn Muhammad al-Qazwini, Zakariyaʾ. *See* Wonders
Ibn Qurra, Thabit. *See Astronomy; Cartography; Syriac Hellenism*
Ibn Ridwan. *See* Medicine; Plague
Ibn-Suwār, al-Hasan. *See Baghdad Aristotelians*
Ibn Taymiyya. *See Astrology; Averroës*
Ibn Tibbon, Moses. *See Judaism*
Ibn Tibbon, Samuel. *See* Judaism; Medicine
Ibn Tufayl. *See Averroës; Philosophy*
Ibn Tumlus. *See Averroës*
Ibn Yahya, Harun. *See Constantinople*
Ibn Yaish of Seville, David. *See Judaism*
Ibn-Yūnus, Abū-Bishr Mattā. *See* Al-Fārābī; *Baghdad Aristotelians; Islam*
Ibn Zakariyyā al-Rāzī, Muhammad. *See* Alchemy
Ibn-Zura, Īsā. *See Baghdad Aristotelians*
Ibsen, Henrik. *See Julian; Sallust*
Ibycus. *See* Orpheus
Icarus. *See Names*
Iconoclasm, **471**
Idas. *See* Castor and Pollux
Ideler, Christian Ludwig. *See Calendars*
Idrisi, al-. *See* Geography; *Cartography*
Ignatius of Loyola. *See* Jesuits
Ignatius the Deacon. *See* Greek Anthology
Ignazio, Prince of Biscari. *See* Sicily
Igraine. *See* Amphitryon
Iktinos. *See Art History*
Ildefonsus, bishop of Toledo. *See Isidore*
Illich, Ivan. *See Symposium*
Illyricus, Flacius. *See Melanchthon*
Imhotep. *See Hermes Trismegistus*
Imitation and Mimesis, **472**
Immortality of the Soul, **475**
Inachus. *See Europe*
Indagine, Johannes de. *See Physiognomy*
India, **481**
Indicopleuste, Cosmas. *See* Inscriptions
Inghirami, Curzio. *See* Etruscans; Forgery
Ingrassia, Giovanni Filippo. *See Hippocrates*
Ingres, Jean-Auguste-Dominique. *See* Alexander the Great; Modernism; *Picasso*
Innocent II. *See* Sarcophagi
Innocent III. *See* Translatio Imperii
Innocent VII. *See* Immortality of the Soul
Innocent X. *See* Rome
Innocent XI. *See* Roman Monuments, Reuse of
Inscriptions, Greek and Latin, **483**
Interpretatio Christiana, **484**
Inwood, Henry. *See* Architecture; Caryatid
Inwood, Thomas. *See* Architecture
Inwood, William. *See* Caryatid
Io. *See* Europe; *Ganymede*
Iobates. *See* Writing
Iohannikios. *See* Medicine
Iolaus. *See Hydra*
Ionesco, Eugène. *See* Comedy; *Terence*
Ion of Chios. *See Biography*
Iphigenia, **485**. *See also* Sacrifice in the Arts; *Euripides*
Iranian empire. *See Armenian Hellenism*
Iranian Hellenism, **486**
Irenaeus. *See* Immortality of the Soul; *Cento; Chrēsis; Philosophy*
Irene (daughter of Theodore Hagiopetrites). *See* Book, Manuscript: Development
Irene, empress. *See* Translatio Imperii; Tzetzes, John
Irigaray, Luce. *See Antigone*
Irnerius. *See* Law, Roman
Irony, **487**
Irwin, David. *See* Neoclassicism
Isaac. *See* Fathers, Church; Sacrifice in the Arts
Isaac I Comnenus. *See* Psellus
Isaac Israeli. *See* Judaism; *Philosophy*
Isabella I. *See Warfare*
Isagoge, **488**
Isham family. *See Names*
Isidore of Miletus. *See* Hagia Sophia; *Archimedes*
Isidore of Seville, **489**. *See also* Academy; Cartography; Demeter and Persephone; Divination; Education; Empire; Epicurus; Ethnography; Etymology; Fathers,

Isidore of Seville *(continued)* Church; Geography; Glass; Grammar; Greek, Ancient; Historiography; Horace; India; Judaism; Liberal Arts; Macrobius; Meteorology; Monsters; Natural History; Paganism; Pan; Pliny the Elder; Poetics; Purple; Rhetoric; Seneca the Younger; Temperament; Vitruvius; War, Just; Wonders; Writing; *Allegory; Asterisk; Basilisk; Hercules; Hippocrates; Martianus Capella; Music; Palimpsest*
Isis. *See* Apuleius; Paganism; Sacrifice in the Arts; Writing; *Egypt; Mystery Religions; Pasquino*
Islam, **491**
Ismene. See Antigone
Isocrates. *See* Biography; Egypt; Genre; Historiography; Lyceum; Milton; Mythology; Pindar; Rhetoric; *Anthology; Athens; Byzantium; Comedy; Erasmus; Korais*
Italus, John. *See* Alexander the Great; Renaissance
Ivanov, Lev. *See Cupid*
Ivan the Terrible. *See* Caesar, as Political Title
Ixion. *See Orpheus; Sisyphus; Tantalus*

Jābirī, Muhammad Abid. *See Avicenna*
Jablonski, P. E. *See Hermes Trismegistus*
Jacob. *See* Fathers, Church
Jacobs, Friedrich. *See* Greek Anthology
Jacobus de Cessolis. *See* Gellius
Jacobus de Porta Ravennate. *See Law, Roman*
Jacobus de Voragine. *See* Centaur; Seven Sages of Rome; *Biography*
Jacobus Venetus. *See Greek, Ancient*
Jacoby, Felix. *See* Historiography; *Calendars; Herodotus; Wilamowitz*
Jacopo. *See Law, Roman*
Jacopo, Giovanni Battista di (Rosso Fiorentino). *See Pandora*
Jaeger, Werner. *See* Aristotle; Fascism; Gymnasium; Historicism; *Fathers, Church; Nietzsche; Wilamowitz*
Jahn, Friedrich Ludwig. *See* Gesture; Gymnasium
Jahn, Otto. *See Mommsen; Wilamowitz*
James I of Aragon. *See* Warfare
James I of England. *See* Demon; *Augustus; Casaubon; Cleopatra*
James II of England. *See Panegyric*
James, Henry. *See Rome*
James of Liège. *See* Plato
James of Venice. *See* Translation
Jameson, Mrs. Anna. *See* Pompeii
Jami, ʿAbd ar-Rahman. *See* Persia
Jamieson, Dale. *See* Vegetarianism
Jamnitzer family. *See* Bronze
Janssens, Abraham. *See Adonis*
Janus, **495**. *See also Etruscans; Pasquino*
Jaques-Dalcroze, Émile. *See* Gesture
Jarman, Derek. *See Censorship; Cinema*
Jaro, Benita Kane. *See Catullus*
Jarrell, Randall. *See* Alexandrianism
Jarvis, Harold John. *See* Dulce et decorum est
Jason. *See* Epic; Orpheus; Ronsard; Writing; *Centaur; Cinema; Hero; Medea; Opera; Petrarch*
Jaurès, Jean. *See Neo-Latin*
Jauss, Hans Robert. *See Catharsis*
Jay, John. *See* Founding Fathers
Jean d'Antioche de Harens. *See* Poetics
Jean de Meun. *See* Classical; Pygmalion; *Boethius; Warfare*
Jeffers, Robinson. *See* Phaedra; *Medea*
Jefferson, Thomas. *See* Architecture; Dictatorship; Empire; Epicurus; Founding Fathers; Neoclassicism; Pantheon; Professionalization of Classics; Slavery; Temple; Xenophon; *Aesthetics; Maison Carrée; Mythology*
Jenkins, Thomas. *See* Etruscans
Jens, Walter. *See Cassandra*
Jensen, Wilhelm. *See* Aeneas
Jenson, Nicolas. *See* Book, Printed
Jeppesen, Kristian. *See Mausoleum*
Jerome. *See* Alexander the Great; Augustine; Calendars; Cento; Cicero; Devil; Donatus; Education; Epicurus; Erasmus; Fathers, Church; Greek, Ancient; Historiography; Horace; Labyrinth; Letters; Lodging; Martial; Nudity; Pliny the Younger; Poetics; Renaissance; Seneca the Younger; Translatio Imperii; Translation; Valla; Virgil; Xanthippe; *Asterisk; Barbarians; Biography; Book, Manuscript: Development; Commentary; Consolation; Constantine; Isidore; Lucretius; Palimpsest; Petrarch; Philo; Rhetoric*
Jerome, abbot of Pomposa. *See* Libraries
Jerusalem. *See Athens*; *Constantinople*
Jesuits, **496**
Jesus Christ. *See* Actaeon; Alexander the Great; Devil; Elegy; Epic; Ethics; Fragments; Milton; Orpheus; Papyrology; Physiologus; Porphyry; Progress and Decline; Purple; Rome; Sarcophagi; Sibyls; Socrates; Sports; Stoicism; Translatio Imperii; *Europe; Hercules; Horace; Irony; Mithras; Muses; Nudity; Numismatics; Ode; Ornament; Ovid; Pan; Pastoral; Pico della Mirandola; Symposium; Tourism*
Jhering, Rudolf von. *See Law, Roman*
Joanna of Austria. *See Paganism*
Joan of Arc. *See Rabelais*
Job. *See* Sports; Temperament; *Nudity; Ornament*
Job of Edessa (Ayyub al-Ruhawi). *See* Medicine
Jocasta. *See* Oedipus; Sophocles
Jodelle, Étienne. *See* Pléiade; Seneca the Younger; Tragedy; *Cleopatra*
Johann Adam of Liechtenstein, Prince. *See* Replicas
Johannes de Nova Domo. *See* Temperament
Johann of Nassau. *See* Warfare
John (scribe). *See Byzantium*
John, Duke of Berry. *See Warfare*
John, the "philosopher." *See Moschopoulos*
John II, Duke of Bourbon. *See Warfare*
John III, king of Portugal. *See Atlas*
John VIII, emperor. *See* Coins
John XII. *See* Caesar, as Political Title
John Chrysostom. *See Armenian Hellenism; Byzantium; Erasmus; Palimpsest*
John Italus. *See Byzantium*
John of Antioch. *See* Suda
John of Capua. *See* Seven Sages of Rome
John of Damascus. *See* Anthology; East and West; Fathers, Church; Iconoclasm; *Doxography*
John of Garland. *See* Donatus; Grammar; Poetics
John of Gaunt. *See Chaucer*; *Ovid*
John of Jandun. *See Aristotle*
John of Marmoutier. *See* Warfare
John of Rupescissa. *See* Alchemy
John of Sacrobosco. *See* Numbers
John of Salisbury. *See* Anacharsis; Chartres; Divination; Epicurus; Humanism; Imitation; Macrobius; Plutarch; Renaissance; Rome; Seneca the Elder; Virgil; Widow of Ephesus; *Aristotle; Book, Manuscript: Development; Concord, Philosophical*
John of Stobi (Stobaeus). *See Hermes Trismegistus*
Johnson, Bob. *See* Comedy
Johnson, Charles Frederick. *See* Epicurus
Johnson, Philip. *See Schinkel*
Johnson, Samuel. *See* Comedy; Dramatic Unities; Imitation; Juvenal; Pope, Alexander; Satire; Suetonius; Translation; *Barbarians; Biography*
Johnston, John. *See* Zoology
John the Archiatros. *See* Medicine
John the Baptist. *See Cynicism; Etruscans; Spolia*
John the Grammarian. *See* Iconoclasm
Joinville, Jean, sire de. *See Biography*
Jonah. *See* Devil
Jones, Inigo. *See* Architecture; Forum; Gesture; Grand Tour; Palace; Palladio; Theater Architecture
Jones, Owen. *See* Ornament
Jones, Sir William. *See* East and West; Greek, Ancient
Jonson, Ben. *See* Ancients and Moderns; Aristophanes; Comedy; Consolation; Cupid; Dramatic Unities; Epigram; Hero and Leander; Historiography; Horace; Imitation; Martial; Ode; Plautus; Popular Culture; Satire; Seneca the Elder; Shakespeare; Statius; Tacitus; Terence; Tragedy; Translation; *Catullus; Gesture; Sallust*

Jonston, Jan. *See* Natural History
Jordaens, Jacob. *See* Centaur; Midas; *Amazons; Heraclitus*
Jordan, Heinrich. *See* Forma Urbis Romae
Jorden, Edward. *See* Volcanoes
Jorio, Andrea de. *See* Gesture
Joseph. *See* Portraits, Reception of Ancient; Pyramid
Joseph (husband of Mary). *See* Alexander the Great; *Lodging*
Josephine, Empress. *See* Neoclassicism
Josephus, Flavius. *See* Fathers, Church; Forgery; Historiography; Homer; Judaism; Masada; Translation; Writing; *Armenian Hellenism; Philo; Thucydides*
Josquin des Prez. *See* Dido
Jouffroy, François. *See Herm*
Jovian. *See Julian*
Jowett, Benjamin. *See* Ethics; Professionalization of Classics
Joyce, James. *See* Cyclops; Epic; Homer; Lyric Poetry; Modernism; Odysseus; Parody; Pornography; Sirens; Xenophon; *Cavafy; Circe; Hypnerotomachia Poliphili; Philosophy; Virgil*
Judah Halevi. *See* Philosophy
Judaism, **497**
Judas Iscariot. *See* Papyrology; Rome; *Divination*
Jugurtha. *See* Sallust
Julia (daughter of Augustus). *See Rome*
Julia (granddaughter of Augustus). *See Censorship*
Julian, **500**. *See also* Allegory; Caesar, Julius; Constantine; Fathers, Church; Gibbon; Hellenistic Age; Interpretatio Christiana; Palace; *Cavafy; Philosophy*
Julius II. *See* Apollo Belvedere; Collecting; Names; Paganism; Palace; Raphael; Rome; *Cicero; Concord, Philosophical; Herm; Janus; Michelangelo; Nudity; Pasquino*
Julius III. *See Herm*
Julius Valerius. *See* Alexander the Great
Julius Victor. *See* Letters; Rhetoric
Jung, Carl. *See* Apuleius; Demeter and Persephone; Dream Interpretation; Hercules; Mithras; Mnemonics; Pan; Pandora; Tragedy; *Matriarchy*
Junius, Franciscus. *See* Color; *Art History*
Juno. *See Europe; Ganymede; Names; Phaedra*
Jupiter. *See* Paganism; Parody; Prometheus; Raphael; Shakespeare; *Danaë; Ganymede; Neptune; Ovid; Paganism; Phaedra*
Justi, Carl. *See* Winckelmann
Justin. *See* Book, Printed; Education; Greek Anthology; *Machiavelli; Sibyls*
Justinian. *See* Academy; Alexander the Great; Commentary; Constantinople; Fathers, Church; Hagia Sophia; Law, Roman; Lodging; Lyceum; Names; Neoplatonism; Portico; Purple; Ravenna; Renaissance; Stoicism; *Byzantium; Cities, Praise of; Etruscans; Islam; Philosophy; Plutarch*
Justinian II. *See* Caesar, as Political Title
Justin Martyr. *See* Chrēsis; Epicurus; Fathers, Church; Immortality of the Soul; Interpretatio Christiana; *Philosophy*
Juvarra, Filippo. *See* Triumphal Bridge
Juvenal, **500**. *See also* Classical; Education; Fashion; Genre; Homosexuality; Horace; Martial; Pornography; Satire; Translation; *Barbarians; Book, Manuscript: Development; Cities, Praise of; Poliziano; Renaissance; Rubens; Terence*
Juventius. *See Catullus; Homosexuality*

Kabbalah. *See* Magic; Philosophy; *Pico della Mirandola*
Kafka, Franz. *See* Comedy; Sirens; *Ovid*
Kagan, Donald. *See Historiography*
Kagan, Jerome. *See* Temperament
Kaibel, Georg. *See Diels, Hermann*
Kaiser, Georg. *See* Amphitryon; *Socrates*
Kakalos, Christos. *See Olympus*
Kallierges, Zacharias. *See Medicine*
Kallman, Chester. *See* Dionysus; *Euripides*
Kalojan of Bulgaria. *See* Caesar, as Political Title
Kalokairinos, Minos. *See* Knossos
Kames, Henry Home, Lord. *See* Ruins
Kander, John. *See Cities, Praise of*
Kane, Sarah. *See* Phaedra; *Euripides*
Kant, Immanuel. *See* Aesthetics; Aristotle; Cosmology; Ethics; Europe; Genius; Horace; Humanism; Immortality of the Soul; Liberty; Logic; Metaphysics; Philosophy; Pico della Mirandola; Plato; Political Theory; Presocratics; Prosody; Rhetoric; Schlegel; Skepticism; Temperament; Topos; Vegetarianism; *Heidegger; Law, Roman; Magic; Physiognomy*
Kanter, Albert Lewis. *See* Comic Books
Kapuściński, Ryszard. *See* Historiography; *Herodotus*
Kassia. *See Renaissance*
Kaster, Robert. *See Commentary*
Katsaitis, Petros. *See Thyestes*
Kauffmann, Angelica. *See* Grand Tour; Pompeii; *Apuleius; Ariadne; Maenads*
Kaufmann, Emil. *See* Neoclassicism
Kaulbach, Wilhelm von. *See Barbarians*
Kavanjin, Jerolim. *See Split*
Kazantzakis, Nikos. *See* Epic; Odysseus
Keaton, Buster. *See* Plautus; *Comedy*
Keats, John. *See* Elegy; Endymion; Epic; Horace; Ode; Ovid; Troilus; *Ecphrasis; Elgin Marbles; Estienne, Henri II; Hesiod*
Keckermann, Bartholomew. *See* Historiography
Keiser, Reinhard. *See Pegasus*
Keller, Michael. *See* Amazons
Kelly, Emmett. *See Comedy*
Kelsey, Francis W. *See* Replicas
Kempen, Ludwig van. *See Seneca the Younger*
Kennett, White. *See* Panegyric
Kent, William. *See* Grand Tour; Ruins; *Herm*
Kepler, Johannes. *See* Aesthetics; Archimedes; Astrology; Astronomy; Commentary; Cosmology; Geography; Harmony of the Spheres; Liberal Arts; Optics; Plato; Ptolemy; Pythagoras; *Calendars; Divination; Music; Scaliger, Joseph Justus*
Kerenyi, Carl. *See* Demeter and Persephone
Kerry, John. *See Cicero*
Keun, Bernard. *See Korais*
Keyser, Hendrick de. *See* Orpheus
Khorenatsi, Moses. *See* Armenian Hellenism
Khufu. *See* Pyramid
Khwārizmī, al-. *See* Astrology; Astronomy; Liberal Arts
Kidd, Ian. *See* Stoicism
Kien, Peter. *See Atlantis*
Kierkegaard, Søren. *See* Irony; Skepticism; Socrates; Temperament; *Antigone*
Kindī, Abū Yūsuf Yaʿqūb ibn Ishāq, al-. *See* Al-Fārābī; Astrology; Epictetus; Music; Pharmacology; *Baghdad Aristotelians; Cartography; Judaism; Philosophy*
King, B. B. *See Aristotle*
King, Edward. *See Elegy; Milton*
Kingsley, Charles. *See* Alexandrianism; Novel
Kipling, Rudyard. *See* Alexander the Great; Dulce et decorum est; Education; Horace; Macaulay
Kircher, Athanasius. *See* Harmony of the Spheres; Hieroglyphs; Music; Obelisk; Volcanoes; *Affecti; Atlantis; Collecting; Hermes Trismegistus; Heyne; Magic*
Kirchmeier, Thomas. *See Bacchanalia*
Kirchner, Néstor. *See Names*
Klee, Paul. *See* Fragments; Modernism; *Orpheus*
Klein, Melanie. *See* Euripides
Kleist, Heinrich von. *See* Achilles; Amphitryon; Comedy; Greek Anthology; Plautus
Kleisthenes. *See* Democracy
Klenze, Leo von. *See* Architecture; Neoclassicism; Palace; Temple; *Caryatid; Parthenon*
Klimt, Gustav. *See* Nudity
Klinger, Max. *See* Nudity; *Apuleius*
Klopstock, Friedrich Gottlieb. *See* Greek, Ancient; Ode; Pindar
Klotz, Christian Adolf. *See Lessing*
Knaust, Heinrich. *See* Aeneas
Knight, Richard Payne. *See* Censorship; Dilettanti, Society of; Elgin Marbles; Lucretius
Knobelsdorff, Georg Wenzeslaus von. *See Herm*
Knoop, Vera Ouckama. *See Orpheus*

Knossos, 503
Knox, Bernard. *See* Virgil
Koch, Gaetano. *See* Portico
Koch, Joseph. *See Sibyls*
Kochanowski, Jan. *See* Horace
Kochowski, Wespajzan. *See Names*
Koenig, Fritz. *See* Caryatid
Kokoshka, Oskar. *See Orpheus*
Komensky, Amos. *See* Mnemonics
Konchalovsky, Andrei. *See Cinema*
König, Johann Ulrich von. *See* Xanthippe
Korais, Adamantios, 504. *See also* Philhellenism
Köselitz, Heinrich (Peter Gast). *See Horace*
Koster, Henry. *See Cinema*
Kotlyarevsky, Ivan. *See* Comedy
Koun, Karolos. *See* Aeschylus; *Cassandra*
Krafft-Ebing, Richard von. *See* Censorship
Krämer, Hans-Joachim. *See Plato*
Kranz, Walther. *See Diels, Hermann; Nietzsche*
Krauss, F. S. *See* Dream Interpretation
Krenek, Ernst. *See* Aeschylus
Kretschmer, Ernst. *See Physiognomy*
Kretzschmar, Hermann. *See Affecti*
Kreusa. *See* Sarcophagi
Krieck, Ernst. *See Fascism*
Krieglstein, J. F. Binder von. *See Pegasus*
Krier, Léon. *See* Pliny the Younger
Kristeller, Paul Oskar. *See* Renaissance; *Pico della Mirandola*
Kristeva, Julia. *See* Imitation; *Antigone; Chaos*
Kroeber, Alfred L. *See* Geography
Kronos. *See Hesiod*
Krubsacius, Friedrich August. *See* Pliny the Younger
Kruse, Friedrich. *See Dilettanti, Society of*
Krylov, Ivan Andreyevich. *See Comedy*
Kubrick, Stanley. *See* Cinema; Ovid; Spartacus; *Cinema*
Kühn, Karl-Gottlob. *See* Medicine; *Galen*
Kupka, František. *See* Orpheus
Küster, Ludolf. *See Bentley; Museum*
Kwārizmī, al-. *See* Geography
Kyd, Thomas. *See* Seneca the Younger; Tragedy
Kydones, Demetrios. *See* Planudes

Labeo, Notker. *See Martianus Capella*
La Boétie, Étienne de. *See* Households; Montaigne; Seneca the Younger
Labrouste, Henri. *See* Greek Revival
La Bruyère, Jean de. *See Names*
Labyrinth, 505
Lacan, Jacques. *See* Narcissus; *Anthropology*
Lachmann, Karl, 506. *See also* Book, Manuscript: Development; Wolf, Friedrich August
Lacon. *See Pastoral*
La Croix, Armand-François de. *See* Warfare
Lactantius. *See* Epicurus; Ethics; Europe; Fathers, Church; Fortune; Founding Fathers; Horace; Lucian; Paganism; Seneca the Younger; Sibyls; Skepticism; Stoicism; Virgil; *Biography; Cicero; Donation of Constantine; Erasmus; Hermes Trismegistus; Isagoge; Philosophy; Rhetoric*
Laertes. *See Penelope; Sisyphus*
Laestrygonians. *See Locus Amoenus*
Lafitau, Joseph-François. *See* Ethnography; Mythology; Sports; *Matriarchy; Toga*
La Fontaine, Jean de. *See* Apuleius; Widow of Ephesus
Lafréry, Antoine. *See* Speculum Romanae Magnificentiae
Lagrenée, Louis-Jean-Francois. *See* Aphrodite
Laguna, Andrés. *See* Botany; *Dioscorides*
Laius. *See* Oedipus
Lajard, Félix. *See* Mithras
Lake, Simon. *See Argonauts*
Lalande, Joseph de. *See* Astronomy
Lalli, Giambattista. *See* Virgil
Lamartine, Alphonse de. *See* Cato the Younger; Sappho
Lamb, Charles. *See* Comedy
Lamb, George. *See Catullus*
Lambin, Denis (Dionysius Lambinus). *See* Horace; Lucretius; Scaliger, Joseph Justus; *Commentary; Education*
Lambranzi, Giorgio. *See Mime*
Lami, Giovanni (Clemente Bini). *See* Etruscans
La Mothe Le Vayer, François de. *See* Skepticism
La Motte, Antoine Houdar de. *See* Ancients and Moderns
Lamprecht. *See* Alexander the Great
Lamprocles. *See* Xanthippe
Lamy, Peronet. *See Notitia Dignitatum*
Lancel, Serge. *See* Hannibal
Lancellotti, Secondo. *See Progress and Decline*
Lanci, Cornelio. *See Comedy*
Lanciani, Rodolfo. *See* Forma Urbis Romae
Landini, Francesco. *See Cupid*
Landino, Cristoforo (Landinus). *See* Aeneas; Art History; Horace; Poetics; Sculpture; Virgil; *Aphrodite; Education; Epicurus*
Landivar, Rafael. *See* Jesuits
Landor, Walter Savage. *See* Epigram; Translation
Lane, Nathan. *See* Plautus
Lanfranc of Milan. *See* Medicine
Lang, Andrew. *See* Translation; *Horace*
Lang, Fritz. *See Cinema*
Lange-Eichbaum, Wilhelm. *See Melancholy*
Langhans, Carl Gotthard. *See* Greek Revival
Langius (Charles de Langhe). *See* Stoicism
Langley, Batty. *See* Ruins
Lanier, Nicholas. *See* Hero and Leander
Lanteri, Giacomo. *See* Households
Lanyer, Aemilia. *See Cleopatra*
Lanzi, Luigi. *See* Etruscans; *Art History*
Laocoön, 507. *See also* Replicas; Rome; Sculpture; Winckelmann; *Belvedere Torso; Cassandra; Pergamon*
Laplace, Pierre-Simon. *See* Cosmology; Presocratics
La Révellière-Lépeaux, Louis-Marie de. *See* Revolution, French
Larivey, Pierre. *See* Comedy
La Rochefoucauld, François, duc de. *See* Maxims
La Rue, Charles de. *See* Jesuits
Lasalle, Ferdinand. *See* Virgil
Lascaris, Constantine. *See* Grammar; Greek, Ancient; *Moschopoulos*
Lascaris, Janus (John). *See* Greek Anthology; Inscriptions; *Eustathius; Nicetas Codex*
Las Casas, Bartolomé de. *See* Ethnography; Slavery
Lasdun, Denys. *See* Theater Architecture
Lassen, Christian. *See* India
Latin and the Professions, 508
Latini, Brunetto. *See* Poetics
Latin Language, 509
Latinus. *See* Epic
Latomus. *See Dialectic*
La Tour d'Auvergne, Henri de, vicomte de Turenne. *See Warfare*
Latrobe, Benjamin. *See* Neoclassicism; Temple
Laugier, Marc-Antoine. *See* Architecture; Greek Revival; Neoclassicism; *Maison Carrée; Piranesi*
Laurenzi, Filiberto. *See* Cupid
Lauro, Giacomo. *See* Triumphal Bridge
Lausus. *See* Constantinople; Renaissance
Lavater, Johann. *See* Physiognomy
Lavinia. *See* Epic; Virgil
Lavisse, Ernest. *See Latin Language*
Lavoisier, Antoine-Laurent. *See* Alchemy; *Atoms*
Law, Roman, 512
Lawrence, D. H. *See Centaur; Etruscans*
Lawrence, T. E. *See* Alexandrianism
Lawrence, Thomas. *See Elgin Marbles*
Lazius, Wolfgang. *See Cartography*
Lazzarelli, Lodovico. *See* Hermes Trismegistus
Leander. *See Isidore*
Lebeau, Paul. *See* Xanthippe
Le Blanc du Roullet, Jacques. *See* Alcestis
Le Brun, Antoine-Louis. *See* Epigram
Le Brun, Charles. *See* Physiognomy; *History Painting*
Lebrun, Ponce Denis Écouchard. *See* Pindar
Le Camus de Mézières, Nicolas. *See* Neoclassicism
Le Clerc, Jean. *See* Forgery; Vico; *Bentley*
Leconte de Lisle, Charles-Marie-René. *See Parnassus*
Lecoq, Jacques. *See Comedy*

Le Corbusier. *See* Architecture; Hadrian's Villa; Modernism
Leda, **519**. *See also* Castor and Pollux; Pornography; *Ganymede; Helen; Novel; Paganism*
Ledoux, Claude-Nicolas. *See* Architecture; Greek Revival; Neoclassicism; Pyramid; *Piranesi*
Lee, Nathaniel. *See* Oedipus; *Sophocles*
Lee, Richard Henry. *See* Founding Fathers
Lee, Sidney. *See Biography*
Lefebvre, Claude. *See Atlas*
Lefèvre, Jacques. *See Aristotle*
Le Fèvre, Raoul. *See* Hercules
Le Fèvre, Tanneguy. *See Dacier*
Lefèvre d'Étaples, Jacques. *See Hermes Trismegistus; Philosophy*
Lefroy, E. C. *See Pederasty*
LeGeay, Jean-Laurent. *See Neoclassicism*
Léger, Fernand. *See* Modernism
Legouvé, Ernest. *See Medea*
Le Grand, Jean-François. *See* Seneca the Elder
Lehrer, Tom. *See Comedy*
Leibniz, Gottfried Wilhelm. *See* Archimedes; Concord, Philosophical; Immortality of the Soul; Law, Roman; Liberty; Metaphysics; Philosophy; Plato; Stoicism; Temperament; Zeno's Paradoxes; *Aristotle; Calendars; Martianus Capella; Numbers*
Leigh, Vivien. *See Cleopatra*
Leighton, Frederic. *See Elgin Marbles*
Leighton, Frederick, Lord. *See* Orpheus
Le Lorrain, Louis-Jospeh. *See Neoclassicism*
Lemaire de Belges, Jean. *See* Giants; *Greek, Ancient*
Lemerre, Alphonse. *See* Parnassus
Lenel, Otto. *See* Law, Roman
L'Enfant, Pierre. *See* Founding Fathers
Lenin, V. I. *See* Dictatorship; *Brutus; Pergamon*
Lenormant, François. *See* Coins; *Magna Graecia*
Lentulus. *See* Seven Sages of Rome
Leo, archpriest. *See* Alexander the Great
Leo I. *See Anthology; Europe*
Leo III, emperor. *See* Iconoclasm
Leo III, Pope. *See* Empire
Leo IV. *See* Aeneas
Leo V, emperor. *See* Iconoclasm
Leo VI. *See* Rhōmaioi
Leo VI, emperor. *See* Warfare
Leo X. *See* Aeneas; Architecture; Cicero; City Planning; Greek, Ancient; Guidebooks to Ancient Rome; Immortality of the Soul; Pliny the Younger; Poliziano; Replicas; Roman Monuments, Reuse of; Rome; *Academy; Color; Janus; Neoclassicism; Pasquino; Raphael*
Leo XIII. *See Aristotle*
Leo, Friedrich. *See* Seneca the Younger
Leochares. *See* Rome; *Mausoleum*
Leon, Judah Messer. *See* Judaism
Leonardo da Vinci. *See* Aesthetics; Color; Etruscans; Genius; Leda; Physiognomy; Renaissance; Rome; Ut pictura poesis; Vegetarianism; Warfare; *Automata; Cartography; Mercuriale; Nudity; Picasso; Piranesi*
Leoni, Leone. *See* Bronze
Leoni, Pompeo. *See* Bronze
Leoniceno, Niccolò. *See* Libraries; Medicine; Natural History; Plague; Pliny the Elder
Leonidas. *See* Sparta; Thermopylae; *Herodotus*
Leo of Ostia. *See* Rome
Leopardi, Giacomo. *See* Dialogue; Horace; Lucian; Romanticism; Sappho; *Diogenes Laertius*
Leopold I. *See Academy*
Leo the Philosopher. *See* Renaissance
Leo Tuscus. *See Greek, Ancient*
Lepidus. *See* Book, Manuscript: Development
Le Plat, Victor A. C. *See* Aeneas
Lepsius, Karl Richard. *See* Forgery
Le Roi, Louis. *See* Translation
Le Roy, Julien-David. *See* Architecture; Greek Revival; *Elgin Marbles; Piranesi*
Le Roy, Louis. *See* Progress and Decline
Le Roy, Loys. *See Montaigne*
Léry, Jean de. *See* Ethnography
Lesbia. *See* Sappho
Lescot, Pierre. *See Palace*
Lesfargues, Bernard de. *See* Seneca the Elder
Lessing, Gotthold Ephraim, **519**. *See also* Catharsis; Gesture; Greek Anthology; Horace; Humanism; Imitation; Laocoön; Tragedy; Ut pictura poesis; Widow of Ephesus; *Virgil*
Lester, Richard. *See Cinema*
L'Estrange, Roger. *See* Translation
Leto, Pomponio. *See* Academy; Colosseum; Guidebooks to Ancient Rome; Historiography; Plautus; Roman Monuments, Reuse of; Rome; *Calendars; Education*
Letters and Epistolography, **520**
Leucippus. *See* Atoms; Castor and Pollux
Leucothea. *See Lucian*
Lévesque de Pouilly, Louis Jean. *See* Historiography
Levi, Eliphas. *See Astrology*
Levi, Primo. *See* Epic
Levin, Harry. *See Comedy*
Lévi-Strauss, Claude. *See* Anthropology; Ethnography; Montaigne; Mythology
Levvenklaius, Johannes. *See* Xenophon; *Households*
Lewis, C. S. *See* Apuleius; *Ganymede*
Lewis, William Lillington. *See* Statius
Lewis, Wyndham. *See* Satire
Lewyn, Sir Justinian. *See Names*
Lhomond, Abbé. *See Latin Language*
L'Hôpital, Michel de. *See Letters; Ronsard*
Lhote, André. *See* Modernism
Libanius. *See* Fathers, Church; Gesture; *Armenian Hellenism*
Libavius, Andreas. *See* Alchemy
Liberal Arts, **523**
Libertas. *See Revolution, French*
Liberty, **529**
Libraries, **532**
Lichtenberg, Georg Christoph. *See* Maxims; *Physiognomy*
Lichtenberger, Johann. *See Divination*
Lichtenstein, Prince Joahnn Adam Andreas I von. *See Faun*
Licinio family. *See Belvedere Torso*
Licinius, Valerius Licinianus. *See* Constantine
Liddell, Robert. *See* Alexandrianism
Liebknecht, Karl. *See* Spartacus
Ligne, Charles-Joseph de. *See* Warfare
Ligneus, Petrus. *See* Aeneas
Ligorio, Pirro, **536**. *See also* Antiquarianism; Atrium; Cartography; Coins; Guidebooks to Ancient Rome; Hadrian's Villa; Inscriptions; Museum; Praeneste; Speculum Romanae Magnificentiae; Sports; Triumphal Bridge; Water Supply; *Calendars; City Planning; Etruscans; Mercuriale; Nudity; Paper Museum*
Lilly, William. *See* Astrology
Lily, John. *See* Gesture
Linacre, Thomas. *See* Medicine; Scaliger, Julius Caesar; *Grammar*
Lindemann, Ferdinand von. *See* Squaring the Circle
Linden, J. A. van der. *See* Medicine
Lindsay, James Ludovic. *See* Speculum Romanae Magnificentiae
Ling, Pehr Henrik. *See* Gymnasium
Linnaeus, Carolus. *See* Botany; Hydra; Natural History; Pliny the Elder; *Latin Language*
Lipchitz, Jacques. *See Orpheus*
Lippershey, Hans. *See* Warfare
Lippi, Filippino. *See* Color; *Herm*
Lippi, Filippo. *See* Centaur
Lipsius, Justus. *See* Book, Printed; Epictetus; Ethics; Historiography; Letters; Museum; Neo-Latin; Philosophy; Rubens; Sallust; Scaliger, Joseph Justus; Seneca the Elder; Seneca the Younger; Stoicism; Suicide; Symposium; Tacitus; Warfare; Writing; *Asterisk; Atlantis; Augustus; Inscriptions; Petronius; Pliny the Younger*
Liszt, Franz. *See* Aeschylus; Sirens; *Barbarians; Prometheus*
Littré, Émile. *See* Medicine
Liudprand of Cremona. *See* Constantinople; Greek, Ancient; Tourism
Liuzzi, Mondino dei. *See* Medicine
Livingstone, Sir Richard. *See* Education
Livius Andronicus. *See* Electra; Epic; Translation

Livy, 536. *See also* Alexander the Great; Book, Manuscript: Development; Book, Manuscript: Production; Book, Printed; Classical; Dictatorship; East and West; Epic; Etruscans; Fathers, Church; Founding Fathers; Historiography; Macaulay; Machiavelli; Political Theory; Popular Culture; Revolution, French; Rome; Sallust; Seneca the Elder; Slavery; Tacitus; Thucydides; Translation; War, Just; Warfare; *Annius of Viterbo; Augustus; Boccaccio; Calendars; Chaucer; Commentary; Corneille, Pierre; David; Epigraphy; Humanism; Libraries; Numismatics; Philosophy; Racine; Renaissance; Valla*

Llull, Ramon. *See* Alchemy; Isagoge; Mnemonics

Locher, Jakob. *See Terence*

Locke, John. *See* Commentary; Demiurge; Despotism, Oriental; Epicurus; Humanism; Immortality of the Soul; Liberty; Logic; Mythology; Philosophy; Rhetoric; Skepticism; *Aristotle; Founding Fathers; Law, Roman; Toga*

Locus Amoenus, 538

Lodge, David. *See Commentary*

Lodge, Henry. *See* Winckelmann

Lodge, Thomas. *See* Shakespeare; Stoicism

Lodging, 538

Lodoli, Carlo. *See* Piranesi

Lo Duca, Antonio. *See* Roman Monuments, Reuse of

Loeb, James. *See* Loeb Classical Library

Loeb Classical Library, 539

Loewy, Emanuel. *See* Raphael

Loggetta. *See* Architecture

Logic, 540

Logue, Christopher. *See* Epic; Translation

Lohenstein, Daniel Caspar von. *See* Nero; Tragedy

Lomazzo, Giovanni Paolo. *See* Automata; Color

Lombardi, Alfonso. *See* Hydra

Lombardo, Tullio. *See* Venice

Lombroso, Cesare. *See* Genius; *Melancholy; Physiognomy*

Lomeier, Johannes. *See* Writing

Lomonosov, Mikhail. *See* Ode

Long, Anthony A. *See* Stoicism

Long, Herbert Strainge. *See Diogenes Laertius*

Longfellow, Henry Wadsworth. *See* Endymion; Juvenal

Longinus. *See* Aesthetics; Genius; Homosexuality; Imitation; Poetics; Rhetoric; Sappho; *Pope, Alexander*

Longolius, Johann Daniel. *See* Temperament

Longus. *See* Daphnis; Novel; Pan; Pastoral; Virgil

Lonicerus, Johannes. *See* Pindar

Loos, Adolf. *See* Ornament

López, Gerónimo. *See* Education

López de Gómara, Francisco. *See* Ethnography; *Atlantis*

López de Villalobos, Francisco. *See* Plautus

Lorelei. *See* Sirens

Lorena, Beatrice di. *See* Sarcophagi

Lorichius, Reinhardus. *See* Poetics

L'Orme, Philibert de. *See* Hadrian's Villa

Lorrain, Claude. *See* Aphrodite; Ariadne; Cyclops; Dido; *Virgil*

Lorscher Arzneibuch. *See Hippocrates*

Loschi, Antonio. *See* Guidebooks to Ancient Rome

Lothar II. *See* Warfare

Loubejac, Andiette de la Roque. *See* Scaliger, Julius Caesar

Louis IX. *See Book, Manuscript: Development*

Louis XII. *See* Giants; *Academy; Budé; Machiavelli; Warfare*

Louis XIII. *See Warfare*

Louis XIV. *See* Apollo; Architecture; Book, Printed; Caesar, Julius; Despotism, Oriental; Gesture; Grotto; Palace; Renaissance; Replicas; Roads, Roman; Water Supply; *Augustus; Dacier; Delphin Classics; Deus ex Machina; Europe; Jesuits; Latin and the Professions; Metaphrasis; Warfare*

Louis XV. *See* Forum; *Nudity*

Louis XVI. *See* Revolution, French; *Atlas; City Planning*

Louis XVIII. *See* Venus de Milo

Louis Napoleon, Prince. *See* Pompeii

Louis de Bourbon. *See Warfare*

Louise of Savoy. *See Elegy*

Louis-Philippe. *See City Planning*

Louis the Pious. *See* Renaissance; Seneca the Younger; *Book, Manuscript: Development*

Louÿs, Pierre. *See Maenads*

Lovato dei Lovati. *See* Humanism

Lovelace, Richard. *See* Ode; *Catullus; Comedy*

Lowe, Robert. *See Greek, Modern Uses of Ancient*

Lowell, Robert. *See* Demeter and Persephone; Horace; Propertius; Virgil; *Euripides; Phaedra*

Loyer, Pierre le. *See* Aristophanes

Loyola, Ignatius. *See* Education; Terence

Lubac, Henri de. *See Fathers, Church*

Lucan, 543. *See also* Alcuin; Book, Printed; Caesar, Julius; Cato the Younger; Cleopatra; Education; Epic; Genre; Milton; Pastoral; Seneca the Elder; Seneca the Younger; Statius; Stoicism; Translation; Virgil; *Basilisk; Boccaccio; Brutus; Chaucer; Cinema; Corneille, Pierre; Dante; Genre; Historiography; Irony; Isidore; Livy; Opera; Renaissance*

Lucas, George. *See Cinema*

Lucchesi, Matteo. *See Piranesi*

Lucena, Ludovico. *See* Guidebooks to Ancient Rome

Lucian, 544. *See also* Alexander the Great; Cynicism; Dialogue; Galatea; Gesture; Greek, Ancient; Heraclitus; Hercules; Historiography; Locus Amoenus; Novel; Parasite; Parody; Rabelais; Satire; Tourism; Translation; *Art History; Book, Manuscript: Development; Byzantium; Centaur; Comedy; Erasmus; Renaissance; Symposium*

Lucian of Samosata. *See* Galileo; *Biography*

Lucilius. *See* Imitation; Satire; Seven Sages of Rome; *Horace; Juvenal; Seneca the Younger*

Lucius Septimius. *See* Historiography

Lucretia. *See* Popular Culture; Suicide; *Ovid*

Lucretius, 546. *See also* Academy; Aesthetics; Atoms; Book, Manuscript: Development; Cosmology; Empedocles; Epicurus; Etymology; Meteorology; Montaigne; Philosophy; Plague; Poetics; Political Theory; Portico; Progress and Decline; Purple; Translation; *Atheism; Homer; Lachmann; Nietzsche; Renaissance*

Ludovisi collection. *See Sarcophagi*

Ludwig I of Bavaria. *See* Collecting; Pompeii; Temple; *Barberini Faun; Horace*

Ludwig II of Bavaria. *See* Grotto; Palace; *Mosaic*

Ludwig IV of Bavaria. *See* Roman Monuments, Reuse of; Translatio Imperii

Luis de León. *See* Horace

Lukács, Georg. *See* Novel

Łukasiewicz, Jan. *See* Logic

Lully, Jean-Baptiste. *See* Alcestis; Apollo; Demeter and Persephone; Opera; Phaethon; Sacrifice in the Arts; *Deus ex Machina; Hercules; Pegasus*

Lumley, Lady Jane. *See* Iphigenia

Lupus of Ferrières. *See* Commentary; Renaissance; *Book, Manuscript: Development*

Luther, Martin. *See* Allegory; Aristotle; Donation of Constantine; Epicurus; Fortune; Greek, Ancient; Historiography; Immortality of the Soul; Law, Roman; Popular Culture; Progress and Decline; Renaissance; Skepticism; *Astrology; Biography; Cicero; Constitution, Mixed; Divination; Latin and the Professions; Magic; Melanchthon; Symposium*

Lutyens, Sir Edwin. *See* Architecture; Triumphal Arch

Luxemburg, Rosa. *See* Spartacus

Lyceum, 547

Lycidas. *See Pastoral*

Lycophron of Chalcis. *See* Alexandrianism; Book, Manuscript: Development; Cassandra; Penelope; Poetics; *Tzetzes*

Lycoris. *See Papyrology*

Lycosthenes, Conrad. *See* Monsters

Lycurgus. *See* Revolution, French; Sparta; Xenophon; *Athens; Democracy*

Lydgate, John. *See* Achilles; Aeneas; Romance, Medieval; Troilus
Lydus, John. *See* Antiquarianism; Calendars; Etruscans; *Byzantium*
Lyly, John. *See* Comedy; Endymion; *Midas*
Lynceus. *See* Castor and Pollux
Lynch, Jennifer. *See* Venus de Milo
Lyric Poetry, **547**
Lysias. *See Forgery*
Lysippus. *See* Aesthetics; Alexander the Great; Rome; Winckelmann; *Art History; Byzantium*
Lyttleton, Lord. *See* Lucian

Maas, Paul. *See Wilamowitz*
Mabillon, Jean. *See* Book, Manuscript: Development; Fathers, Church; Forgery; Writing; *Museum*
Mably, Gabriel Bonnot de. *See* Revolution, French
Macaulay, Thomas Babington, **551**. *See also* Progress and Decline; Romanticism; Seneca the Younger; *Livy*
Maccabees. *See Judaism; Masada*
MacDonald, William. *See* Neoclassicism
Machado, Aníbal. *See Names*
Machiavelli, Niccolò, **552**. *See also* Academy; Aristophanes; Book, Printed; Centaur; Commentary; Despotism, Oriental; Dictatorship; Diogenes Laertius; Ethnography; Europe; Fortune; Hannibal; Historiography; Liberty; Livy; Maxims; Parasite; Philosophy; Political Theory; Progress and Decline; Republicanism; Sallust; Shakespeare; Tacitus; Thucydides; Warfare; Xenophon; *Augustus; Biography; Comedy; Law, Roman; Terence*
MacIntyre, Alasdair. *See* Ethics; *Aristotle*
Mackail, John William. *See Cavafy*
Mackennal, Sir Bertram. *See Circe*
Mackenzie, Compton. *See Pederasty*
MacKinnon, Catharine. *See Censorship*
MacLeish, Archibald. *See* Endymion; Hercules
MacMonnies, Frederick William. *See Maenads*
MacNeice, Louis. *See* Horace; Troilus
Macpherson, James. *See* Macaulay; Romanticism
Macrin, Salmon (Salmonius Macrinus). *See* Horace; Ronsard
Macrobius, **553**. *See also* Aesthetics; Allegory; Astronomy; Cartography; Chaucer; Cicero; Commentary; Cosmology; Cynicism; Dido; Etruscans; Fragments; Harmony of the Spheres; Horace; Imitation; Immortality of the Soul; Interpretatio Christiana; Music; Paganism; Virgil; *Bacchanalia; Boccaccio; Book, Manuscript: Development; Chartres; Greek, Ancient; Hippocrates; Martianus Capella; Music; Symposium*
Macropedius. *See Terence*
Mader, Joachim Johann. *See* Writing
Madgearu, Virgil. *See Names*
Madison, James. *See* Colony; Democracy; Founding Fathers; Liberty; Republicanism
Madvig, Johan Nicolai. *See Lachmann*
Maecenas, **554**. *See also* Hagia Sophia; *Elegy; Horace*
Maelius, Spurius. *See* Revolution, French
Maenads, **554**
Maffei, Paolo Alessandro. *See* Barberini Faun; Faun; *Cameos*
Maffei, Raffaello. *See* Greek, Ancient; Households; Seneca the Elder; Xenophon; *Art History; Etruscans*
Maffei, Scipione. *See* Antiquarianism; Epigraphy; Inscriptions; Raphael; *Etruscans; Ligorio*
Magenta, Giovanni Ambrogio. *See* Pliny the Younger
Magi. *See* Magic; Sarcophagi
Magic, **555**
Magna Graecia, **562**
Magri, Gennaro. *See Mime*
Magritte, René. *See* Venus de Milo
Māhdī, al-. *See Astrology*
Mahon, Derek. *See Phaedra*
Mai, Angelo. *See* Book, Manuscript: Development; *Palimpsest*
Maillol, Aristide. *See* Modernism
Maimon, Salomon. *See* Skepticism
Maimonides, Moses (Moses ben Maimon). *See* Immortality of the Soul; Judaism; Medicine; Pharmacology; *Astrology; Averroës; Martianus Capella; Philo; Philosophy*
Maine, Sir Henry. *See* Empire; *Matriarchy*
Maiorano, Nicolao. *See Eustathius*
Mairet, Jean. *See* Dramatic Unities; *Livy*
Maison Carrée, **563**
Maistre, Joseph de. *See Latin Language*
Maiuri, Amedeo. *See Herculaneum*
Majo, Gian Francesco de. *See* Iphigenia
Makoto, Satoh. *See* Antigone
Malalas, John. *See* Book, Manuscript: Production; *Baalbek; Bentley; Byzantium*
Malaparte, Curzio. *See Etruscans*
Malatesta, Sigismondo, of Rimini. *See Renaissance*
Malherbe, François de. *See* Pléiade; Ronsard
Malinowski, Bronisław. *See* Magic
Mallarmé, Stéphane. *See* Alexandrianism; Faun; Orpheus; Pastoral; *Parnassus*
Malpighi. *See Zoology*
Mā'mūn, Caliph al-. *See* Aristotle; Medicine; Renaissance; *Cartography*
Manardi, Giovanni. *See* Medicine
Manasses, Constantine. *See Byzantium; Metaphrasis*
Mancinus, Gaius Hostilius. *See* Nudity
Mandela, Nelson. *See Brutus*
Mandelstam, Osip. *See* Demeter and Persephone; Ode
Mander, Karel van. *See Art History*
Mandeville, Sir John. *See* India; Tourism; *Herodotus*
Manet, Edouard. *See* Aphrodite; Faun; Nudity; Pornography; Raphael
Manetho. *See* Book, Manuscript: Development; Forgery; Scaliger, Joseph Justus; Writing; *Annius of Viterbo; Calendars; Fragments; Historiography*
Manetti, Antonio di Tuccio. *See* Rome; *Art History*
Manetti, Giannozzo. *See* Consolation; Philosophy; *Demon*
Mani. *See* Papyrology
Manicelli, Luigi. *See Hero and Leander*
Manilius, Gaius. *See* Dulce et decorum est; Lucretius; Seven Sages of Rome; *Astrology; Calendars; Commentary; Scaliger, Joseph Justus*
Manilius, Marcus. *See Bentley*
Manin, Bernard. *See* Political Theory
Mankiewicz, Joseph L. *See Cinema; Cleopatra*
Mann, Anthony. *See Cinema*
Mann, Heinrich. *See* Greek, Ancient
Mann, Nicholas. *See Warburg*
Mann, Thomas. *See* Caesar, Julius; Dionysus; Irony; Sexuality; *Hippocrates*
Manship, Paul. *See* Actaeon; Prometheus; *Hercules*
Mansionario, Giovanni. *See* Numismatics
Mantegna, Andrea. *See* Antiquarianism; Caesars, Twelve; Centaur; Dido; Epigraphy; Faun; Inscriptions; Notitia Dignitatum; Pegasus; Portraits, Reception of Ancient; Replicas; Venice; Warfare; *Art History; Hercules; Maenads; Plaster Casts*
Mantuan, Baptista. *See* Virgil; *Milton; Pastoral*
Manuel I Comnenus. *See Allegory; Tzetzes*
Manutius, Aldus. *See* Book, Manuscript: Development; Book, Printed; Emblem; Erasmus; Grammar; Greek, Ancient; Greek Anthology; Hypnerotomachia Poliphili; Libraries; Medicine; Paganism; Philosophy; Pindar; Poetics; Pronunciation of Greek and Latin; Renaissance; Rhetoric; Scaliger, Julius Caesar; Sophocles; Terence; Thucydides; Venice; *Bessarion; Demosthenes; Herodotus; Triclinius*
Manutius, Paulus. *See* Book, Printed
Manzoni, Alessandro. *See* Plague; Writing; *Opera*
Mapplethorpe, Robert. *See* Pornography
Marat, Jean-Paul. *See* Dictatorship; Revolution, French
Marc, Franz. *See Orpheus*
Marcanova, Giovanni. *See* Inscriptions
Marceau, Marcel. *See Comedy; Mime*
Marcellinus, Ammianus. *See* Pantheon; Rome
Marcellus. *See* Warfare; *Archimedes*
Marchand, Louis-Joseph. *See Warfare*

Marchetti, Alessandro. *See Lucretius*
Marchi, Francesco de'. *See Labyrinth*
Marco, Giovanni di. *See* Medicine
Marconi, Guglielmo. *See Obelisk*
Marconi, Pirro. *See* Sicily
Marcovich, Miroslav. *See Diogenes Laertius*
Maréchal, Pierre-Sylvain. *See* Pornography; *Censorship*
Margaret of Austria. *See Martianus Capella*
Marguerite de Navarre. *See* Rabelais
Mari, Febo. *See Faun*
Marie-Antoinette. *See* Grotto
Marie de France. *See* Translation; Widow of Ephesus
Mariette, Auguste. *See* Egypt
Mariette, Pierre Jean. *See Cameos*
Marini, Marino. *See Etruscans*
Marino, Giambattista. *See* Adonis; Endymion; Epigram; *Ecphrasis*
Marinus of Samaria. *See Orpheus*
Marinus of Tyre. *See* Cartography; Ptolemy
Marius, Gaius. *See* Sallust
Marius, Gaius, the Younger. *See* Suicide
Marius Maximus. *See* Suetonius
Marivaux, Pierre de. *See* Hannibal
Mark, Saint. *See* Alexandria
Marlborough, John Churchill, Duke of. *See* Hannibal; *Faun*
Marlborough, Sarah Churchill, Duchess of. *See* Ruins
Marliani, Bartolomeo. *See* Guidebooks to Ancient Rome; Roman Monuments, Reuse of
Marlowe, Christopher. *See* Aeneas; Dido; Helen; Hero and Leander; Hydra; Lucan; Ovid; Parody; Propertius; Shakespeare; Translation; *Ganymede*
Marmocchini, Santi. *See* Etruscans
Marmontel, Jean-François. *See* Socrates
Marolles, Michel de. *See* Epicurus
Marosi, Erik. *See* Pliny the Younger
Marot, Clément. *See* Elegy; Hero and Leander; Pastoral; *Comedy; Donatus; Martial*
Marpurg, Friedrich Wilhelm. *See* Music
Márquez, Pedro José. *See* Pliny the Younger
Marrou, Henri-Irenée. *See Commentary*
Mars, **564**. *See also Allegory; Comic Books; Nudity*
Marshfield, Alan. *See* Electra
Marsilius of Padua. *See* Democracy
Marston, John. *See* Juvenal; Satire
Marston, William Moulton. *See* Amazons
Marsus, Petrus. *See* Terence
Marsyas, **564**. *See also* Pan; *Belvedere Torso; Midas; Ovid; Paganism*
Martello, Pier Jacopo. *See* Alcestis
Martial, **565**. *See also* Book, Manuscript: Development; Book, Manuscript: Production; Catullus; Education; Epigram; Genre; Pornography; Translation; *Barbarians; Censorship; Commentary; Isidore; Pope, Alexander; Renaissance*
Martianus Capella, **566**. *See also* Apollo; Book, Manuscript: Development; Grammar; Macrobius; Muses; Music; Rhetoric; *Boethius; Delphin Classics; Liberal Arts*
Martin, bishop of Braga. *See* Seneca the Younger
Martin V. *See* Rome
Martin, Theodore. *See Catullus*
Martini, Arturo. *See Etruscans*
Martini, Francesco di Giorgio. *See* Atlas; Hadrian's Villa; Pantheon; Vitruvius
Martini, Giovanni Battista. *See* Music
Martini, Martino. *See Scaliger, Joseph Justus*
Martini, Simone. *See* Donatus; Pygmalion
Martino. *See Law, Roman*
Martino, Francesco De. *See* Caesar, Julius
Martin of Laon. *See Martianus Capella*
Martinus Gosia. *See Law, Roman*
Martín y Soler, Vicente. *See* Endymion
Martius Valerius. *See* Pastoral
Marulic, Marko. *See Split*
Marullus, Michael (Michele Marullo). *See* Lucretius; Ode; *Catullus*
Marvell, Andrew. *See* Carpe diem; Daphnis; Horace; Locus Amoenus; Ode; Pastoral; *Thyestes*
Marx, Adolph Bernhard. *See* Opera
Marx, Harpo. *See Comedy; Mime*
Marx, Karl. *See* Aeschylus; Caesar, Julius; Despotism, Oriental; Dialectic; Dictatorship; Ethnography; Lucretius; Marxism; Matriarchy; Republicanism; Slavery; *Anthropology; Aristocracy; Cicero; Historiography; Philosophy; Xenophon*
Marxism, **567**. *See also* Dialectic
Mary. *See* Progress and Decline; Purple; Rome; Sarcophagi; Sculpture; Sibyls; *Hercules; Leda; Ovid; Parthenon*
Mary II. *See Thucydides*
Mary Stuart. *See* Architecture; Penelope
Mary Tudor. *See Penelope; Pronunciation of Greek and Latin*
Masaccio. *See Alberti; Optics; Picasso*
Masada, **568**
Mascarino, Ottavio. *See* Roman Monuments, Reuse of
Mashtots, Mesrop. *See Armenian Hellenism*
Massaio, Pietro del. *See Cartography*
Massari, Francesco. *See* Natural History
Massenet, Jules. *See Opera*
Massey, William. *See* Gellius; Writing
Massimi, Porzia. *See* Roman Monuments, Reuse of
Masson, André. *See* Modernism
Master of the Die. *See Apuleius*
Masters, Edgar Lee. *See Cavafy*
Mästlin, Michael. *See* Ptolemy
Masʿūdī, al-. *See Geography*
Matal, Jean. *See Historiography*
Mates, Benson. *See* Logic
Matham, Jacob. *See Adonis*
Mather, Cotton. *See Fraternities*
Matilda (daughter of Henry I). *See Ovid*
Matisse, Henri. *See* Modernism
Matius, Gaius. *See Brutus*
Matociis, Giovanni de. *See* Historiography
Matriarchy, **569**
Matro of Pitane. *See* Comedy
Mattei collection. *See Rubens; Sarcophagi*
Mattheson, Johann. *See* Music; *Affecti*
Matthew of Vendôme. *See* Poetics
Mattioli, Andrea. *See* Cupid
Mattioli, Pier Andrea. *See* Botany; Dioscorides; *Medicine*
Maurice (emperor). *See* Warfare
Maurice of Nassau. *See* Historiography; Warfare
Mauro, Fra. *See* Cartography
Mauro, Lucio. *See* Guidebooks to Ancient Rome
Maurois, André. *See Biography*
Maurolyco, Francesco. *See* Archimedes
Mausoleum, **571**
Mausolos. *See* Mausoleum; Seven Wonders of the World
Mauss, Marcel. *See* Mythology
Mauthner, Fritz. *See* Xanthippe
Mavortius, Vettius Agorius Basilius. *See* Horace
Maxentius. *See* Constantine; Rome
Maximilian I. *See* Caesars, Twelve; Scaliger, Julius Caesar; Triumphal Arch; *Genre*
Maxims, **571**
Maximus of Ephesus. *See Julian; Philosophy*
May, Thomas. *See* Lucan; *Cleopatra; Thucydides*
Mayakovsky, Vladimir. *See* Comedy; Parasite
Maybeck, Bernard. *See* Temple
Mayrhofer, Johann Baptist. *See* Castor and Pollux
Mazarin, Jules. *See Warfare*
Mazo, Juan Bautista Martínez del. *See Midas*
Mazzocchi, Alessio Simmaco. *See Magna Graecia*
Mazzocchi, Jacopo. *See* Guidebooks to Ancient Rome; Rome; *Historiography*
McAdam, John Loudon. *See* Roads, Roman
McCrindle, John Watson. *See* India
McGee, Michael. *See* Topos
McKeon, Richard. *See* Rhetoric
McKim, Charles Follen. *See* Architecture
McKim, Mead and White. *See* Architecture; *Temple*
McLennan, John Ferguson. *See Matriarchy*
McWhirter, George. *See* Ovid
Mead, G. R. S. *See Hermes Trismegistus*
Méchain, Pierre. *See Astronomy*
Medea, **573**. *See also* Epic; Shakespeare; *Cinema; Euripides; Names; Opera; Ovid*
Medici, Cosimo de'. *See* Collecting; Consolation; Ficino; Hermes Trismegistus; *Cartography; Guidebooks to Ancient Rome; Humanism; Immortality of the Soul; Magic; Museum*

Medici, Cosimo I de. *See* Astrology; Etruscans; Libraries; Palace; Penelope
Medici, Cosimo II de'. *See* Etruscans; *Astronomy; Galileo*
Medici, Ferdinand de'. *See Deus ex Machina*
Medici, Francesco de'. *See Etruscans; Paganism*
Medici, Giuliano de'. *See* Poliziano
Medici, Lorenzo de'. *See* Ficino; Michelangelo; Poliziano; Renaissance; Rome; Sculpture; Symposium; *Epictetus; Etruscans; Immortality of the Soul*
Medici, Lorenzo di Pierfrancesco de'. *See* Michelangelo
Medici, Maria de'. *See Endymion*
Medici, Piero de'. *See* Replicas
Medici, Pietro de'. *See* Roman Monuments, Reuse of
Medici, Virginia de'. *See Martianus Capella*
Medici collection. *See Sarcophagi*
Medici court. *See* Opera
Medici family. *See* Architecture; Raphael; Tacitus; *Apuleius; Cameos; Faun; Machiavelli; Rubens*
Medicine, **573**
Medigo, Elia del. *See Pico della Mirandola*
Medusa. *See Names; Pegasus*
Megasthenes. *See* Herodotus; India; *Ethnography*
Megobacchus (Meckback), Johannes. *See* Dream Interpretation
Mehmed II. *See* Caesar, as Political Title; Constantinople; *Averroës*
Méhul, Étienne-Nicolas. *See Musical Instruments*
Mei, Girolamo. *See* Music; Opera; *Affecti*
Meibom, Marcus. *See* Music; *Diogenes Laertius*
Meidias Painter. *See* Castor and Pollux
Meier, Michael. *See Hermes Trismegistus*
Meier, Richard. *See* Rome
Meigs, Montgomery C. *See* Temple
Meinecke, Friedrich. *See Historicism*
Meineke, August. *See* Fragments; *Doxography*
Mela, Pomponius. *See* Book, Manuscript: Development; Geography; *Delphin Classics; Renaissance*
Melancholy, **579**
Melanchthon, Philipp, **581**. *See also* Alexander the Great; Classical; Grammar; Greek, Ancient; Historiography; Melancholy; Mnemonics; Renaissance; Stoicism; Translation; Valla; *Aristotle; Astrology; Biography; Constitution, Mixed; Dialectic; Education; Hippocrates; Irony; Isagoge; Magic; Medicine; Names; Terence; Xenophon*
Melanippus. *See* Statius
Meleager. *See* Anthology; Greek Anthology; Papyrology; Sarcophagi; Split; *Centaur*
Meletius of Sardes. *See Doxography*
Meliboeus. *See Poetics*
Méliès, Georges. *See Cinema*
Meliseus. *See* Elegy
Melissus of Samos. *See* Parmenides
Melpomene. *See* Sirens; *Muses*
Melusine. *See Sirens*
Ménage, Gilles. *See Diogenes Laertius*
Menander, **582**. *See also* Alexander the Great; Aristophanes; Book, Manuscript: Development; Comedy; Portraits, Reception of Ancient; Prosody; *Barbarians; Bentley; Fragments; Herm; Rubens; Terence*
Menander Rhetor. *See* Cities, Praise of; Genre; Panegyric; Poetics
Menasseh ben Israel. *See* Immortality of the Soul
Mendelssohn, Felix. *See* Sirens; *Antigone; Opera*
Mendelssohn, Moses. *See* Aristophanes; Immortality of the Soul; *Lessing*
Menelaus. *See* Europe; *Helen; Pasquino*
Menelaus of Alexandria. *See Judaism*
Menes. *See* Egypt
Ménestrier, Claude. *See* Jesuits
Mengs, Anton. *See* Parnassus; Sculpture; Winckelmann
Menippean satire. *See* Novel
Menippus. *See* Satire; *Cynicism; Lucian*
Meno. *See* Doxography
Menocchio. *See Chaos*
Menoeceus. *See Diogenes Laertius*
Mensendieck, Bess. *See* Gesture
Mercadante, Saverio. *See Opera*
Mercati, Michele. *See Hieroglyphs*
Mercator, Gerard. *See* Cartography; *Atlas; Calendars*
Mercier, Louis-Sébastien. *See* Nudity; Xanthippe
Mercier, Michel-Louis Victor. *See Herm*
Mercouri, Melina. *See Phaedra*
Mercuriale, Girolamo, **582**. *See also* Gymnasium; Plague; *Doxography; Medicine; Symposium*
Meredith, George. *See* Arachne; Demeter and Persephone; *Cassandra*
Meres, Francis. *See* Shakespeare
Merezhkovsky, Dmitry. *See Julian*
Mérimée, Prosper. *See Etruscans*
Merivale, Charles. *See Brutus*
Merkel, Inge. *See* Penelope
Merlin. *See* Amphitryon; Seven Sages of Rome
Merobaudes, Flavius. *See Niebuhr*
Merrill, James. *See* Homer
Mersenne, Marin. *See* Hermes Trismegistus; Skepticism
Mersmann, Hans. *See Affecti*
Mesarites, Nikolaus. *See Cities, Praise of*
Mesomedes. *See Music*
Messadié, Gérald. *See* Xanthippe
Messiaen, Olivier. *See* Music
Metagenes. *See Art History*
Metaphrasis, **583**
Metaphrastes, Symeon. *See* Renaissance
Metaphysics, **584**
Metastasio, Pietro. *See* Opera; Statius; *Vico*
Metasthenes the Persian. *See* Writing; *Annius of Viterbo; Historiography; Scaliger, Joseph Justus*
Metellus of Tegernsee. *See* Horace
Metellus Scipio. *See Cato the Younger*
Meteorology, **587**
Methodius, patriarch. *See* Iconoclasm
Methodius, Saint. *See* Renaissance
Metochites, George. *See* Planudes
Metochites, Theodore. *See* Byzantium; Constantinople; Music; Renaissance; Xenophon; *Constantinople; Philo*
Metrodorus of Lampsacus. *See* Allegory
Metternich, Klemens Wenzel, Prince von. *See* Professionalization of Classics
Meun, Jean de. *See* Adonis
Meursius, Joannes. *See* Warfare
Meyer, Eduard. *See* Caesar, Julius; *Democracy; Herodotus*
Meyer, Leonard. *See Affecti*
Miasnikov, Grigorii. *See* Suicide
Micali, Giuseppe. *See* Etruscans; Paestum
Michael, archangel. *See Pegasus*
Michael II. *See Book, Manuscript: Development*
Michael III. *See* Iconoclasm
Michael VIII. *See Byzantium*
Michael VIII Palaeologus. *See* Planudes; Renaissance
Michael IX. *See* Planudes
Michaelis, Johann David. *See* Wolf, Friedrich August
Michel, Claude (Clodion). *See Maenads*
Michelangelo, **588**. *See also* Aesthetics; Apollo Belvedere; Architecture; Atlas; Belvedere Torso; Calendars; Centaur; Cleopatra; Color; Cupid; Etruscans; Fragments; Ganymede; Genius; Leda; Nudity; Ornament; Paganism; Pantheon; Pornography; Raphael; Renaissance; Roman Monuments, Reuse of; Rome; Sculpture; Speculum Romanae Magnificentiae; Warfare; *Academy; Art History; Biography; Herm; Janus; Laocoön; Modernism; Neoclassicism; Picasso; Sibyls*
Michelet, Jules. *See* Renaissance; *Art History*
Michelozzo di Bartolomeo. *See* Temple
Michels, Robert. *See Democracy*
Michiel, Marcantonio. *See Art History; Raphael*
Midas, **589**. *See also* East and West; *Marsyas*
Middleton, Conyers. *See Bacchanalia*
Midler, Bette. *See Plautus*
Mies van der Rohe, Ludwig. *See* Architecture; Modernism; Schinkel
Milhaud, Darius. *See* Aeschylus; Electra; *Medea; Opera*

Mill, James. *See* Despotism, Oriental; East and West
Mill, John Stuart. *See* Democracy; Despotism, Oriental; Ethics; Households; Immortality of the Soul; Liberty
Millar, John. *See* Democracy; Matriarchy
Millay, Edna St. Vincent. *See* Endymion
Miller, Anna. *See* Grand Tour
Miller, Jonathan. *See* Television
Millereau, Philippe. *See* Sacrifice in the Arts
Mills, Robert. *See* Temple
Milosz, Czeslaw. *See Cavafy*
Milton, John, **589**. *See also* Aeneas; Ancients and Moderns; Apollo; Consolation; Demeter and Persephone; Elegy; Epic; Founding Fathers; Gesture; Hercules; Hero, Horace; Imitation; Immortality of the Soul; Livy; Locus Amoenus; Muses; Narcissus; Ode; Ovid; Parody; Pastoral; Rhetoric; Sallust; Seneca the Younger; Statius; Tantalus; Thyestes; Tragedy; Translation; Virgil; *Bentley; Brutus; Censorship; Chaos; Cyclops; Euripides; Hesiod; Labyrinth*
Mime and Pantomime, **591**
Minato, Niccolò. *See Socrates*
Minerva. *See* Paganism; *Grammar; Marsyas; Names; Ovid*
Minos. *See* Ariadne; Knossos; *Phaedra*
Minotaur. *See* Ariadne; Knossos; Labyrinth; Picasso
Minturno, Antonio Sebastiano. *See Catharsis*
Minucianus the Younger. *See Poetics*
Minucius Felix, Marcus. *See* Dialogue; Immortality of the Soul; *Horace*
Mirabeau, Honoré-Gabriel Riqueti, Comte de. *See* Revolution, French
Mirabeau, Victor Riqueti, Marquis de. *See* Empire
Mirabilia Urbis, **592**. *See also* Rome; *Art History*
Mirabilia Urbis Romae. *See* Art History; *Augustus; Inscriptions*
Miro. *See Seneca the Younger*
Misch, Robert. *See* Aristophanes
Mitchell, David. *See* Ovid
Mitford, William. *See* Demosthenes; Socrates
Mithras, **593**. *See also Mystery Religions*
Mithridates, Flavius. *See Pico della Mirandola*
Mithridates I. *See* Iranian Hellenism
Mithridates VI Eupator. *See* Rome; *Cavafy*
Mitterrand, François. *See* Astrology
Miyazaki, Hayao. *See* Ovid; Popular Culture
Mizler, Lorenz Christoph. *See* Music
Mnemonics, **594**
Mnemosyne. *See* Parnassus; *Muses; Museum; Paganism*
Mnouchkine, Ariane. *See* Aeschylus; *Cassandra*
Möbius, Paul Julius. *See Melancholy*
Modernism in Art, **595**
Modigliani, Amedeo. *See* Caryatid
Modoin of Autun. *See* Pastoral
Mohammed Ali Pasha. *See* Alexandria; Alexandrianism
Mola, Pier Francesco. *See Endymion*
Molière. *See* Amphitryon; Comedy; Dramatic Unities; Grammar; Menander; Parasite; Plautus; Terence; Theater Architecture; *Dacier; Latin Language*
Moloch. *See Paganism*
Molza, Francesco Maria. *See Raphael*
Molza, Tarquinia. *See* Diotima
Momigliano, Arnaldo. *See* Antiquarianism; Hannibal; Thermopylae; *Dilettanti, Society of; Ligorio*
Mommsen, Marie. *See Wilamowitz*
Mommsen, Theodor, **598**. *See also* Alexandrianism; Antiquarianism; Caesar, Julius; Cicero; Coins; Epigraphy; Historiography; Inscriptions; Sallust; Wilamowitz; *Böckh*
Moncino, Michele. *See* Atrium
Mondrian, Piet. *See* Modernism
Moneo, Rafael. *See* Architecture
Moninckx, Pieter. *See* Cupid
Monomakh, Vladimir. *See* Caesar, as Political Title
Monotropus, Philip. *See Atticism*
Monsters, **599**
Montagnone, Geremia da. *See Diogenes Laertius*
Montaigne, Michel de, **600**. *See also* Cato the Younger; Commentary; Dialectic; Diogenes Laertius; Epicurus; Estienne, Henri II; Ethics; Gellius; Heraclitus; Horace; Households; Humanism; Lucretius; Nudity; Petronius; Philosophy; Pliny the Elder; Plutarch; Roads, Roman; Seneca the Elder; Seneca the Younger; Sexuality; Shakespeare; Skepticism; Stoicism; Tacitus; *Atlantis; Byzantium; Livy; Renaissance; Symposium*
Montano, Benito Arias. *See Atlantis*
Montausier, Charles de Saint-Maure, Duke of. *See Delphin Classics*
Monte, Giambattista da. *See* Gynecology; Medicine
Montecuccoli, Raimondo. *See* Maxims
Montefeltro, Federico da. *See* Book, Manuscript: Development; Palace; *Alberti; Byzantium; Museum*
Montemayor, Jorge de. *See* Pastoral
Montes, Fernando. *See* Pliny the Younger
Montesquieu, Baron de. *See* Anacharsis; Anthropology; Cato the Younger; Democracy; Despotism, Oriental; Founding Fathers; Geography; Hannibal; Liberty; Matriarchy; Political Theory; Progress and Decline; Republicanism; Revolution, French; Warfare; *Barbarians; Dialogue; Korais; Law, Roman*
Monteverdi, Claudio. *See* Aeneas; Ariadne; Demeter and Persephone; Deus ex Machina; Endymion; Nero; Opera; Orpheus; Seneca the Younger; Venice; Virgil; *Affecti*
Montfaucon, Bernard de. *See* Antiquarianism; Barberini Faun; Book, Manuscript: Development; Etruscans; Forgery; Greek, Ancient; Mithras; Olympia; Sarcophagi; Winckelmann; Writing
Montorsoli, Giovanni Angelo. *See* Barberini Faun
Montuoro, P. Zancani. *See* Paestum
Monty Python. *See* Satire
Moor, Karl von. *See* Tragedy
Moore, Charles. *See Forum*
Moore, Thomas. *See Anacreon*
Mopsus. *See* Elegy
Mopurgo, Vittorio Ballo. *See* Roman Monuments, Reuse of
Moraes, Vinicius de. *See Orpheus*
Morandi, Orazio. *See Astrology*
Morata, Olimpia. *See Names*
Moravia, Alberto. *See* Oedipus
Morcillo, Sebastiano Fox. *See Colony*
Mordred. *See* Tragedy
More, Henry. *See* Immortality of the Soul; Metaphysics; Neoplatonism; Plato; *Magic*
More, Thomas. *See* Consolation; Cynicism; Gellius; Immortality of the Soul; Lucian; Plato; Rabelais; Satire; Sparta; Translation; *Boethius; Brutus; Erasmus; Pliny the Younger*
Moreau, Gustave. *See* Orpheus; Sirens; *Cyclops; Hesiod; Pegasus*
Moreelse, Paulus. *See Hermaphroditus*
Moretus, Balthasar. *See* Seneca the Younger
Moretus, Jan. *See* Book, Printed
Morgan, J. P. *See Atlas*
Morgan, Julia. *See Herm*
Morgan, Lewis Henry. *See* Ethnography; Matriarchy; *Marxism*
Morgan, Sidney Owenson, Lady. *See* Philhellenism
Morghen, Raffaello. *See* Barberini Faun
Morgues, Michel. *See Atheism*
Morhof, Daniel. *See* Writing
Mörike, Eduard. *See* Greek Anthology; Horace
Morisini, Francesco. *See Athens*
Morley, Christopher. *See* Troilus
Morley, John. *See* Maxims
Moro, Lodovico. *See* Pastoral
Morris, William. *See* Apuleius; Museum
Morrison, Grant. *See* Midas
Morrison, Toni. *See Medea*
Morton, John Maddison. *See* Comedy
Mosaic, **601**
Mosca, Gaetano. *See Democracy*
Moschopoulos, Manuel, **602**. *See also* Book, Manuscript: Development; Planudes; Triclinius; *Byzantium; Thomas Magister*

Moschopoulos, Nicephorus. *See Moschopoulos*
Moschus, John. *See* Elegy; Translation; *Book, Manuscript: Development*
Mosellanus, Petrus. *See* Greek, Ancient
Moses. *See* Egypt; Orpheus; Writing; *Machiavelli; Magic; Neoplatonism; Pico della Mirandola*
Moses of Bergamo. *See Greek, Ancient*
Moses of Palermo. *See* Veterinary Medicine
Mosheim, Johann Lorenz von. *See Gibbon, Edward*
Mostel, Zero. *See* Plautus; Slavery
Mounet-Sully, Jean. *See Sophocles*
Mounier, Jean-Joseph. *See* Revolution, French
Mozart, Wolfgang Amadeus. *See* Ajax; Anacreon; Apollo; Egypt; Electra; Opera; Sacrifice in the Arts; *Comedy*
Muhammad. *See* Aristotle; East and West; Islam; *Isidore; Philosophy*
Mulcaster, William. *See* Gymnasium
Mulla Sadrā. *See* Aristotle; Immortality of the Soul
Müller, Charles-Louis. *See* Venus de Milo
Müller, Heiner. *See* Achilles; Ajax; *Medea; Sophocles*
Muller, Jan Harmensz. *See* Tantalus
Müller, Karl Otfried. *See* Professionalization of Classics; *Etruscans*
Müller, Max. *See* Mythology
Mummius, Lucius. *See* Rome
Muncaster, Richard. *See Mercuriale*
Münchhausen, Gerlach Adolph von. *See Heyne*
Münster, Sebastian. *See* Ethnography; *Calendars*
Muqaddasi, Muhammad ibn Amed al-. *See* Geography
Muratori, Ludovico Antonio. *See Ligorio*
Murdoch, Iris. *See* Dialogue; Ethics
Muret, Marc-Antoine. *See* Ronsard; Seneca the Younger; Stoicism; Tacitus; Tragedy; *Education*
Murmellius, Johannes. *See* Poetics
Murphy, Eddie. *See* Comedy
Murray, Gilbert. *See* Iphigenia; *Nietzsche; Wilamowitz*
Murray, Les. *See Hesiod*
Musaeus (disciple of Orpheus). *See* Orpheus
Musaeus (Grammaticus). *See* Hero and Leander; Translation
Muscio. *See* Gynecology; Medicine
Muses, **603**. *See also* Apollo; Museum; Nudity; Parnassus; Pegasus; Raphael; *Hesiod; Olympus; Symposium*
Museum, **604**
Music, **607**
Musical Instruments, **611**
Musil, Robert. *See* Diotima; *Virgil*
Muslims. *See* Anthropology
Musonius Rufus, Gaius. *See* Sexuality
Mussato, Albertino. *See* Humanism; Seneca the Younger; Tragedy; *Boethius*
Mussolini, Benito. *See* Architecture; Caesar, Julius; Cinema; Dulce et decorum est; Fascism; Obelisk; Replicas; Republicanism; Roman Monuments, Reuse of; Rome; Sculpture; *Augustus; Forum; Inscriptions; Tourism*
Musurus, Marcus. *See* Triclinius; *Asterisk*
Mycenae, **612**
Myers, John Myers. *See* Circe
Mylius, Christlob. *See Lessing*
Mylne, Robert. *See* Neoclassicism; *Sicily*
Myron. *See* Aesthetics; Rome; Sculpture
Myrrha. *See Adonis; Ovid*
Myrsilus Lesbius. *See Annius of Viterbo*
Mystery Religions, **613**
Mythology, **614**

Nabokov, Vladimir. *See* Commentary; Etymology; Horace; Satire
Nabonassar. *See Scaliger, Joseph Justus*
Nadal, Jerónimo. *See* Education; *Jesuits*
Naevius, Gnaeus. *See* Epic; Translation
Naharro, Bartolomé de Torres. *See* Terence
Naldi, Naldo. *See* Etruscans; Orpheus; *Genre*
Namatianus, Rutilius. *See* Ovid
Names, **618**
Napoleon I. *See* Ajax; Alexander the Great; Alexandria; Alexandrianism; Caesar, as Political Title; Caesar, Julius; Collecting; David; Empire; Greek Anthology; Hannibal; Law, Roman; Museum; Nudity; Replicas; Revolution, French; Satire; Sculpture; Sparta; Tacitus; Triumphal Arch; Warfare; *Apollo Belvedere; Barbarians; Brutus; City Planning; Comedy; Europe; Gymnasium; History Painting; Horace; India; Islam; Laocoön; Names; Niebuhr; Philosophy; Portraits, Reception of Ancient*
Napoleon III. *See* Caesar, Julius; Democracy; Dictatorship; Sewers; Warfare; *Forum*
Narcissus, **620**. *See also* Pygmalion; *Locus Amoenus; Ovid*
Nardi, Jacopo. *See* Terence
Narmour, Eugene. *See Affecti*
Nash, John. *See* Portico; Triumphal Arch
Nashe, Thomas. *See* Hero and Leander
Nasser, Gamal Abdel. *See* Comedy; *Alexandria*
Natoire, Joseph. *See Maenads*
Natural History, **621**
Nauck, Johann August. *See* Fragments
Naudé, Gabriel. *See* Tacitus; *Atheism; Hermes Trismegistus*
Naumann, Friedrich. *See* Teubner
Nausicaa. *See* Sports; *Mythology; Odysseus*
Navagero, Andrea. *See Raphael*
Neander, Michael. *See* Pindar; Writing
Nebrija, Antonio de. *See* Grammar
Nebuchadnezzar. *See* Translatio Imperii; *Judaism*
Neckam, Alexander. *See* Aristotle; Seven Sages of Rome; *Basilisk; Martianus Capella*
Nectanebus II. *See* Alexander the Great
Nedham, Marchamont. *See Founding Fathers*
Nelson, Horatio Nelson, Viscount. *See* Inscriptions
Nemesianus, Marcus Aurelius Olympius. *See* Elegy
Nemesion. *See Papyrology*
Nemesius of Emesa. *See* Medicine; *Doxography*
Neoclassicism, **629**
Neo-Latin, **627**
Neopythagoreanism. *See Martianus Capella, Pythagoras*
Neoplatonism, **632**. *See also* Academy; Aesthetics; Al-Fārābī; Aristotle; Empedocles; Epictetus; Fathers, Church; Ficino; Irony; Lucretius; Mystery Religions; Plato; *Aristotle; Dante; Julian; Leda; Martianus Capella; Stoicism*
Neoptolemus. *See* Alexander the Great
Nepos, Cornelius. *See* Historiography; *Commentary; Suetonius*
Neptune, **636**. *See also Hero and Leander; Names; Popular Culture*
Nero, **636**. *See also* Alexander the Great; Aristotle; Astrology; Caesar, Julius; Domus Aurea; Guidebooks to Ancient Rome; Palace; Revolution, French; Roman Monuments, Reuse of; Rome; Seneca the Younger; Statius; Stoicism; Suicide; Tacitus; *Color; Colosseum; Education; Lucan; Names; Petronius; Plutarch; Popular Culture; Virgil*
Neruda, Pablo. *See* Ode
Nerva, Marcus Cocceius. *See* Forum
Nessus. *See Centaur; Hydra*
Nestis. *See Empedocles*
Nestle, Wilhelm. *See Nietzsche*
Nestor. *See Achilles; Names*
Nestorians. *See* Al-Fārābī
Nethuns. *See Neptune*
Neuber, Caroline. *See Lessing*
Neugebauer, Otto. *See* Ptolemy
Neumann, Erich. *See* Apuleius; Pandora
Neumann, Johann Balthasar. *See* Architecture
Newman, Barnett. *See* Modernism; *Obelisk; Orpheus*
Newman, Francis William. *See* Translation
Newman, John Henry. *See* Progress and Decline
Newman, John Kevin. *See* Alexandrianism
Newton, Charles. *See Mausoleum*
Newton, Huey. *See Carpe diem*
Newton, Isaac. *See* Academy; Ancients and Moderns; Archimedes; Astrology; Atoms; Cosmology; Demiurge; Genius;

Newton, Isaac *(continued)* Historiography; Philosophy; Progress and Decline; Skepticism; *Atheism; Calendars; Hermes Trismegistus; Latin Language; Magic; Neo-Latin*
Newton, Thomas. *See* Seneca the Younger; Tragedy
Nezāmi. *See* Persia
Nicander of Colophon. *See* Botany; *Melanchthon; Tzetzes*
Niccoli, Niccolò. *See* Book, Manuscript: Development; Cartography; Collecting; Guidebooks to Ancient Rome; Sculpture; *Cato the Younger; Hieroglyphs*
Niccolini, Fausto. *See* Pompeii; Replicas
Niccolini, Felici. *See* Pompeii; Replicas
Nicephorus I. *See* Iconoclasm; Metaphrasis
Nicetas Codex, **638**. *See also* Medicine
Nicholas V. *See* Guidebooks to Ancient Rome; Households; Loeb Classical Library; Pantheon; Rome; Thucydides; Writing; *Alberti; Bessarion; Colosseum*
Nicholas (Nectarius). *See Book, Manuscript: Development*
Nicholas of Autrecourt. *See Atoms*
Nicholas of Cusa. *See* Chaos; Constantine; Donation of Constantine; Plato; Squaring the Circle; *Philosophy; Plautus*
Nicholas of Damascus. *See* Natural History; *Averroës; Fragments; Judaism*
Nicholas of Lyra. *See* Giants
Nicholas of Poland. *See Hippocrates*
Nicholas of Reggio. *See* Inscriptions
Nicias. *See* Rome
Nicolai, Christoph Friedrich. *See Catharsis; Lessing*
Nicolini, Fausto. *See* Replicas
Nicomachus of Gerasa. *See* Liberal Arts; Music; *Isagoge; Judaism*
Nicomedia. *See Constantinople*
Nicostrata. *See* Writing
Niebuhr, Barthold Georg, **638**. *See also* Calendars; Livy; Macaulay; Professionalization of Classics; Romanticism; Tacitus; *Historiography; Scaliger, Joseph Justus*
Niebuhr, Carsten. *See Niebuhr*
Nieheim, Dietrich von. *See* Progress and Decline
Niehues-Pröbsting, Heinrich. *See Cynicism*
Niemann, Georg. *See* Split
Niemann, Johanna. *See* Ajax
Niethammer, Friedrich Immanuel. *See* Humanism
Nietzsche, Friedrich, **639**. *See also* Aesthetics; Alexandrianism; Apollo; Aristotle; Catharsis; Cynicism; Demiurge; Dionysus; Empedocles; Epictetus; Ethics; Euripides; Heraclitus; Historicism; Horace; Humanism; Liberty; Maxims; Metaphysics; Music; Paganism; Philosophy; Picasso; Poetics; Portico; Presocratics; Professionalization of Classics; Progress and Decline; Prometheus; Romanticism; Satire; Socrates; Stoicism; Temperament; Teubner; Tragedy; Valla; Wilamowitz; Winckelmann; *Atheism; Burckhardt; Chaos; Demon; Epic; Greek, Modern Uses of Ancient; Heidegger; Magic; Melancholy; Neo-Latin; Petronius; Phaedra*
Nifo, Agostino. *See* Zoology; *Aristotle; Philosophy*
Nigidius Figulus, Publius. *See Astrology*
Nigri, Francesco. *See* Letters
Niketas Byzantios. *See* East and West
Nimrod. *See Baalbek; Historiography*
Ninagawa, Yukio. *See Medea*
Niobe. *See* Elegy
Nisbet, Charles. *See* Education
Nisbet, Robin. *See* Commentary
Nissen, Heinrich. *See* Historiography
Nisus. *See Homosexuality*
Noah. *See* Barberini Faun; Forgery; Giants; Rabelais; Writing; *Janus; Nudity; Sibyls*
Nobile, Peter von. *See* Temple
Nodot, François. *See Petronius*
Nogarola, Isotta. *See Latin and the Professions*
Noguchi, Isamu. *See* Orpheus
Nointel, Charles Olier, Marquis de. *See Athens*
Nollekens, Joseph. *See* Toga
Nolli, Giambattista. *See* Forma Urbis Romae
Nonius Balbus, Marcus. *See* Herculaneum
Nonius Marcellus. *See* Epicurus; Poetics
Nonnus. *See* Galatea; Metaphrasis; Translation; *Byzantium; Cinema*
Nono, Luigi. *See* Diotima
Nordau, Max. *See* Progress and Decline; *Melancholy*
North, Frederick, Lord. *See* Gibbon
North, Thomas. *See* Plutarch; Shakespeare; Suetonius; Translation; *Biography; Cleopatra*
Norton, Caroline. *See* Sappho
Norton, Charles Eliot. *See* Loeb Classical Library
Norton, Thomas. *See* Seneca the Younger; Tragedy
Nossis. *See* Sappho
Nostradamus. *See* Atlas
Notitia Dignitatum, **640**
Notker III of St. Gall. *See Boethius*
Nott, John. *See Catullus*
Novalis (Georg Philipp Friedrich von Hardenberg). *See* Fragments; Neoplatonism; Romanticism
Novel, **641**
Novenianus, Philipp Michel. *See* Temperament
Noverre, Jean-Georges. *See* Ajax; *Mime*
Nucleo, Orazio. *See* Guidebooks to Ancient Rome
Nudity, **643**
Numa Pompilius. *See* Historiography; Revolution, French; Tacitus; *Guidebooks to Ancient Rome*
Numbers, Numerals, Notation, **647**
Numenius. *See* Demiurge; *Allegory*
Numismatics, **648**
Nussbaum, Martha. *See* Vegetarianism; *Aristotle*
Nymphs. *See Grotto*

Oannes. *See* Writing
Oates, Lawrence. *See Hero*
Obelisk, **650**
O'Brien, Flann. *See* Satire
O'Brien, Tim. *See* Dulce et decorum est
O'Brien, Willis. *See Cinema*
Obsopoeus, Vincentius. *See Xenophon*
Occo, Pompeius. *See Names*
Oceanus. *See Circe*
Ocland, Christopher. *See Latin Language*
Octavia. *See* Nero
Odaenathus, Lucius Septimius. *See* Palmyra
Oddi, Sforza degl'. *See* Plautus; Terence
Ode, **651**
Odoacer. *See* East and West; Empire
Odofred. *See Law, Roman*
Odo of Deuil. *See* Constantinople
Odysseus, **652**. *See also* Ajax; Cyclops; Dante; Epic; Hercules; Imitation; Mythology; Neoplatonism; Paganism; Penelope; Rabelais; Sirens; Sisyphus; *Achilles; Boethius; Circe; Parody; Popular Culture; Thomas Magister*
Oeagrus. *See Orpheus*
Oecolampadius, Johannes (Johannes Hausschein). *See Names*
Oedipus, **653**. *See also* Freud; Sacrifice in the Arts; Sophocles; Statius; *Antigone; Lucian; Mythology*
Oenomaus of Gadara. *See* Judaism
Offenbach, Jacques. *See* Ajax; Opera; Orpheus; Sacrifice in the Arts
Ogle, William. *See Aristotle*
Og of Bashan. *See* Giants
O'Hara, Kane. *See Midas*
Older, Julia. *See Hermaphroditus*
Oldham, John. *See Juvenal*
Olearius, Gottfried. *See Diogenes Laertius*
Olivares, Count Duke. *See Warfare*
Oliveira, Sócrates de. *See Names*
Olivi, Giovan Battista. *See* Museum
Olson, Charles. *See* Hesiod
Olympia, **654**
Olympias. *See Alexander the Great*
Olympic Games, **654**
Olympiodorus of Alexandria. *See* Epictetus
Olympiodorus of Thebes. *See Photius*
Olympus, **655**
Omeis, Magnus Daniel. *See Topos*
Omphale. *See* Pompeii
Onasander. *See Warfare*

Onassis, Aristotle. *See Names*
Ondaatje, Michael. *See* Historiography
O'Neill, Eugene. *See* Aeschylus; Electra; Phaedra; Tragedy; *Euripides*
Ongaro, Antonio. *See* Pastoral
Opera, **656**
Opitz, Martin. *See* Apollo; Dionysus; Epigram; Horace
Oppermann, Hans. *See* Fascism
Oppian. *See* Natural History; Zoology
Optics, **659**
Oracles, **660**
Orcagna, Andrea. *See Centaur*
Orellana, Francisco de. *See Amazons*
Orelli, Johann Caspar von. *See Lachmann*
Oresme, Nicole. *See* Monsters; *Astrology; Christine de Pizan*
Orestes. *See* Electra; Tragedy; *Iphigenia; Opera*
Orff, Carl. *See* Aeschylus; *Antigone; Sophocles*
Oribasius. *See* Gynecology; Medicine
Origen. *See* Alexandrianism; Allegory; Anthology; Asterisk; Chaos; Commentary; Fathers, Church; Immortality of the Soul; Poetics; *Augustus; Biography; Chrēsis; Erasmus; Philo; Philosophy*
Orion. *See Opera*
Ornament, **660**
Orosius, Paulus. *See* Alexander the Great; Augustine; Geography; Hero; India; Judaism; Persia; Progress and Decline; *Augustus; Barbarians; Boccaccio; Cartography; Dante; Livy*
Orpheus, **664**. *See also* Dante; Egypt; Elegy; Fathers, Church; Ficino; Fragments; Poliziano; Prosody; Rabelais; Romance, Medieval; Ronsard; Sirens; Virgil; *Affecti; Boethius; Deus ex Machina; Maenads; Musical Instruments; Paganism; Papyrology; Philosophy; Popular Culture; Tantalus*
Orphic cult. *See* Vegetarianism
Orphic poems. *See* Demiurge; *Hermes Trismegistus*
Orphics. *See* Presocratics; Pythagoras
Orphism. *See Martianus Capella*
Orsi, Paolo. *See* Sicily
Orsini, Alfonsina. *See* Roman Monuments, Reuse of
Orsini, Fulvio. *See* Coins; Forma Urbis Romae; Fragments; Guidebooks to Ancient Rome; Historiography; Numismatics; Portraits, Reception of Ancient; Rome; Symposium; *Herm; Hieroglyphs*
Orsini family. *See* Roman Monuments, Reuse of
Orwell, George. *See* Comedy; Sparta
Osborne, Duffield. *See Xanthippe*
Osiris. *See* Dionysus; Fathers, Church; Pyramid; *Egypt; Hieroglyphs; Historiography; Mystery Religions; Paganism*
Osman, Jane. *See Asterisk*
Ossian. *See* Genius; Macaulay; *Opera*
Ostermann-Tolstaya, Elizabeth. *See* Sculpture
Osthoff, Hermann. *See Greek, Ancient*
Ostrogoths. *See Ravenna*
Oswald, Sydney. *See* Dulce et decorum est
Otho, Marcus Salvius. *See* Palace; Suicide; *Caesars, Twelve; Corneille, Pierre*
Otis, James. *See* Founding Fathers
Ottheinrich, Count Palatine. *See* Notitia Dignitatum
Otto I (the Great). *See* Caesar, as Political Title; *Renaissance; Roswitha*
Otto II. *See* Sarcophagi; *Renaissance*
Otto III. *See* Rome; Sarcophagi; *Renaissance*
Otto IV. *See Mirabilia Urbis*
Otto, Walter F. *See* Nietzsche
Ottomans. *See Islam*
Otto of Freising. *See Chartres*
Ouranos. *See Hesiod*
Ovid, **667**. *See also* Achilles; Actaeon; Adonis; Aeneas; Ajax; Alcuin; Alexandrianism; Allegory; Antiquarianism; Arachne; Arcadia; Ariadne; Atlas; Book, Manuscript: Production; Book, Printed; Caesar, Julius; Carpe diem; Cassandra; Censorship; Centaur; Chaos; Chaucer; Consolation; Cupid; Cyclops; Demeter and Persephone; Dido; Education; Elegy; Epic; Ethnography; Fashion; Forgery; Galatea; Ganymede; Genre; Giants; Grotto; Helen; Hermaphroditus; Hero and Leander; Historiography; Homosexuality; Letters; Locus Amoenus; Lucretius; Lyric Poetry; Marsyas; Medea; Midas; Montaigne; Names; Narcissus; Opera; Orpheus; Paganism; Palace; Pan; Parody; Penelope; Phaedra; Phaethon; Poliziano; Pope, Alexander; Pornography; Prometheus; Propertius; Pygmalion; Pyramus and Thisbe; Rabelais; Renaissance; Romance, Medieval; Sappho; Sculpture; Seneca the Elder; Seven Sages of Rome; Shakespeare; Sibyls; Thyestes; Translation; Venice; Virgil; *Boccaccio; Byzantium; Catullus; Christine de Pizan; Cinema; Cities, Praise of; Commentary; Dante; David; Delphin Classics; Epicurus; Horace; Labyrinth; Latin Language; Lucan; Melanchthon; Michelangelo; Neoclassicism; Neptune; Parnassus; Picasso; Planudes; Racine; Rome; Rubens; Sisyphus*
Oviedo y Valdés, Gonzalo Fernández de. *See Ethnography*
Owen, John. *See* Epigram; Martial
Owen, Wilfred. *See* Dulce et decorum est; Hero; Horace
Oxyrhynchus. *See* Astrology; Calendars; Forgery; Papyrology
Ozenfant, Amédée. *See* Modernism
Ozick, Cynthia. *See Xanthippe*

Pabst, Georg Wilhelm. *See* Pandora
Pace, Biagio. *See* Sicily
Pacheco, José Emilio. *See* Sisyphus
Pachymeres, George. *See* Music; *Atticism; Metaphrasis*
Pacini, Giovanni. *See* Sappho; *Opera*
Pacioli, Luca. *See* Aesthetics
Pacuvius. *See* Translation
Paestum, **674**. *See also Architecture*
Paganism, **675**
Page, Thomas Ethelbert. *See* Loeb Classical Library
Paine, Thomas. *See* Founding Fathers
Painter, William. *See Livy*
Pais, Ettore. *See* Sicily; *Livy*
Palace, **679**
Palaemon, Quintus Remmius. *See* Grammar
Palamas, Gregory. *See Thomas Magister*
Paleotti, Gabriele. *See Nudity*
Palerne, Jean. *See* Ethnography
Palestrina, Giovanni Pierluigi da. *See* Endymion
Palimpsest, **680**
Palingenius, Marcellus. *See* Lucretius
Palladas of Alexandria. *See Anthology*
Palladio, Andrea, **681**. *See also* Architecture; Atrium; City Planning; Domus Aurea; Hadrian's Villa; Pantheon; Plato; Praeneste; Roads, Roman; Rome; Schinkel; Split; Temple; Theater Architecture; Triumphal Arch; Vitruvius; Warfare; *Aesthetics; Baths; Maison Carrée; Mausoleum; Neoclassicism; Ornament; Sophocles*
Palladius, Peder. *See Isagoge*
Palladius, Rutilius Taurus Aemilianus. *See* Botany; Households; Veterinary Medicine; Zoology
Palmerio, Mattia. *See Ethnography*
Palmieri, Niccolò. *See* Nudity
Palmyra, **681**
Palomino, Antonio. *See Art History*
Pamphilus of Amphipolis. *See* Art History
Pan, **682**. *See also* Devil; Faun; Penelope; Rabelais; *Grotto; Plutarch; Popular Culture; Spolia*
Panaetius of Rhodes. *See* Stoicism
Pandectarius. *See Natural History*
Pandoni, Giannantonio. *See Numismatics*
Pandora, **683**. *See also* Prometheus; *Hesiod*
Panegyric, **684**
Panini, Gian Paolo. *See* Ruins
Pannartz, Arnold. *See* Book, Printed; Donatus
Panodorus. *See* Ptolemy; *Calendars*
Panofsky, Erwin. *See* Renaissance; Rome; Warburg
Pan Painter. *See* Actaeon
Pantaenus. *See Philo*

Pantheon, **684**. *See also* Architecture; Roman Monuments, Reuse of; *Temple*
Panvinio, Onofrio. *See* Calendars; Guidebooks to Ancient Rome; Triumphal Bridge; *Biography; Historiography; Scaliger, Joseph Justus*
Paper Museum, **685**
Papias. *See* Grammar; Greek, Ancient; *Isidore*
Pappas, Irene. *See Cinema*
Pappus of Alexandria. *See* Ptolemy; *Armenian Hellenism; Euclid*
Papyrology, **686**
Paracelsus. *See* Alchemy; Demon; Galen; Humors; Medicine; *Philosophy*
Parasite, **688**
Pardus, Gregory. *See* Renaissance
Parini, Giuseppe. *See* Horace
Paris. *See Cassandra; Cinema; Helen; Ovid*
Paris, Pierre-Adrien. *See* Praeneste
Parker, Dorothy. *See Catullus*
Parmenides, **689**. *See also* Atoms; Egypt; Empedocles; Heidegger; Presocratics; Zeno's Paradoxes; *Magna Graecia*
Parmigianino (Francesco Mazzola). *See* Pornography; *Herm*
Parnassus, **690**
Parody and Burlesque, **691**
Parrasio, Giano. *See* Guidebooks to Ancient Rome
Parrhasius. *See* Aesthetics; Rome; *Aesthetics; Art History*
Parry, Milman. *See Homer*
Pars, William. *See* Dilettanti, Society of
Partch, Harry. *See* Music; *Maenads; Music*
Parthenius of Nicaea. *See* Genre
Parthenon, **692**. *See also* Architecture; Collecting; Elgin Marbles; Ornament; Rome; *Athens; Temple*
Parthenope. *See* Sirens
Parthey, Gustavus. *See Hermes Trismegistus*
Parthians. *See Armenian Hellenism*
Parton, James. *See Biography*
Pas, Gerald. *See Phaethon*
Pascal, Blaise. *See* Cosmology; Epictetus; Maxims; Skepticism
Pascal, Gabriel. *See Cleopatra*
Pascalis Romanus. *See* Dream Interpretation
Paschasius Radbertus. *See* Elegy
Pascoli, Giovanni. *See* Horace; *Virgil*
Pasiphaë. *See* Ariadne; Knossos; *Phaedra*
Pasiteles. *See* Rome
Pasolini, Pier Paolo. *See* Oedipus; Sophocles; *Cinema; Medea*
Pasquale, Carlo. *See* Tacitus
Pasqualini, Lelio. *See Rubens*
Pasquino, **693**
Passe, Crispijn de. *See* Seven Wonders of the World
Passeri, Giovan Battista. *See* Etruscans; *Art History; Symposium*
Passow, Franz. *See* Teubner
Pasti, Matteo de'. *See* Alberti
Pastoral, **694**
Pastrone, Giovanni. *See* Cinema
Pater, Walter. *See* Apuleius; Dionysus; Epicurus; Fin de Siècle Art; Homosexuality; Novel; Winckelmann; *Cavafy*
Pătrăşcanu, Lucreţiu. *See Names*
Patrizi, Francesco. *See* Diotima; Warfare; *Affecti; Hermes Trismegistus; Historiography*
Patroclus. *See* Alexander the Great; *Achilles; Pasquino*
Patton, George S. *See* Dulce et decorum est
Paul, Saint. *See* Alcuin; Anthology; Chrēsis; Consolation; Constantine; Fathers, Church; Ficino; Forgery; Immortality of the Soul; Letters; Neoplatonism; Nudity; Paganism; Plato; Pliny the Younger; Rhetoric; Sacrifice in the Arts; Seneca the Younger; Symposium; Temperament; Virgil; *Aristotle; Catacombs; Epictetus; Mirabilia Urbis; Philosophy; Rome*
Paul II. *See* Academy; Numismatics; Rome
Paul III. *See* Jesuits; Roman Monuments, Reuse of; Rome; *Michelangelo; Natural History; Popular Culture*
Paul V. *See* Rome
Paul, Jean (Johann Paul Friedrich Richter). *See Olympus; Opera*
Paulin, Tom. *See* Aeschylus; *Sophocles*
Paulinus of Nola. *See* Augustine; Horace; *Genre*
Paullus, L. Aemilius. *See* Roman Monuments, Reuse of
Paul of Aegina. *See* Gynecology; Medicine
Paul of Middelburg. *See Calendars*
Paul of Taranto. *See* Alchemy
Paul the Deacon. *See* Horace; *Corneille, Pierre*
Paul the Hermit, Saint. *See Centaur*
Paul the Persian. *See Iranian Hellenism*
Paul the Silentiary. *See* Constantinople; Ecphrasis; Hagia Sophia
Paulus Aemilius. *See* Popular Culture
Pausanias, **697**. *See also* Collecting; Hydra; Museum; Oracles; Pan; Seven Sages of Rome; Suda; Tourism; Zoology; *Art History; Athens; Byzantium; Inscriptions; Music; Mycenae*
Pausanias of Athens. *See* Pederasty
Pavese, Cesare. *See* Demeter and Persephone; Dialogue; Lucian
Pavić, Milorad. *See* Hero and Leander
Pazzi de' Medici, Alessandro. *See* Aeneas
Peacock, Thomas Love. *See* Satire; Translation; *Philhellenism*
Peale, Charles Willson. *See* Founding Fathers
Pecham, John. *See* Optics
Pecock, Reginald. *See* Constantine; Donation of Constantine
Pederasty, **698**
Peele, George. *See* Comedy
Peend, Thomas. *See Hermaphroditus*
Pegasus, **698**. *See also Hercules*
Pei, I. M. *See* Pyramid
Peirce, Charles Sanders. *See* Zeno's Paradoxes
Peiresc, Nicolas-Claude Fabri de. *See* Collecting; Rubens; *Inscriptions; Nudity*
Pelagonius. *See* Veterinary Medicine
Peletier, Jacques. *See* Pléiade
Peleus. *See* Ariadne; *Centaur*
Pellegrin, Simon-Joseph. *See Thyestes*
Peloponnesian War. *See Achilles*
Pelops. *See Olympic Games*
Pemán, José María. *See Thyestes*
Pember, Clifford. *See* Pliny the Younger
Pembroke, Mary Sidney Herbert, Countess of. *See* Shakespeare; Tragedy
Pembroke, Philip Herbert, 4th Earl of. *See* Portico
Pena, Jean. *See* Cosmology
Penelope, **699**. *See also Helen; Names*
Penrose, Roger. *See Music*
Penthesilea. *See* Amazons; Rabelais; *Achilles*
Pentheus. *See Dionysus*
Pepys, Samuel. *See Censorship*
Pérac, Étienne du. *See* Roman Monuments, Reuse of
Percier, Charles. *See* Triumphal Arch
Perctarit. *See Corneille, Pierre*
Percy, Thomas. *See* Macaulay
Perdiccas. *See Hippocrates*
Pereira, Gómez. *See Galen*
Perelman, Chaïm. *See* Rhetoric
Peretti, Alessandro. *See Rubens*
Peretti, Camilla. *See Guidebooks to Ancient Rome*
Perez, Antonio. *See* Tacitus
Pérez d'Oliva, Fernan. *See* Plautus
Pérez-Galdós, Benito. *See* Alcestis
Pergamon, **700**
Pergolesi, Giovanni. *See* Opera
Peri, Giovanni Domenico. *See* Etruscans
Peri, Jacopo. *See* Music; Opera; Orpheus; *Affecti*
Pericles. *See* Architecture; Athens; Historiography; Political Theory; Presocratics; Winckelmann; *Cities, Praise of; Fascism; Herm; Olympus; Plutarch*
Périon, Joachim. *See Philosophy*
Peripatetics. *See* Aristotle; *Consolation*
Perizonius, Jacob. *See* Historiography; Livy; *Macaulay; Niebuhr*
Perkin, William. *See* Purple
Perkins, Anthony. *See Phaedra*
Pernambucano, Ulisses. *See Names*
Perotti, Niccolò. *See* Commentary; Epictetus; Grammar; Letters; Petrarch
Perrault, Charles. *See* Ancients and Moderns; Homer
Perrault, Claude. *See* Architecture; Ornament
Perrault, William. *See* Households
Perrier, François. *See* Faun

Perrière, Guillaume de la. *See* Emblem
Perrucci, Andrea. *See Mime*
Perse. *See Circe*
Perseus. *See* Atlas; *Art History; Basilisk; Cinema; Danaë; Pegasus*
Persia, **701**. *See also Aristotle; Astrology; Astronomy; Athens*
Persius. *See* Allegory; Education; Horace; Satire; Translation; *Poliziano; Renaissance*
Perugino, Pietro. *See* Color; Rome; Ruins; *Sibyls*
Peruzzi, Baldassare. *See* Demeter and Persephone; Raphael; Roman Monuments, Reuse of; Rome; Theater Architecture; *Adam, Robert; City Planning; Ganymede; Maenads; Neoclassicism*
Peruzzi, Sallustio. *See* Roman Monuments, Reuse of
Petau, Denis. *See* Calendars; *Scaliger, Joseph Justus*
Peter. *See* Constantine; Guidebooks to Ancient Rome; Split; *Catacombs; Mausoleum; Mirabilia Urbis*
Peter, Hermann. *See* Gymnasium
Peter Damian. *See Philosophy*
Peter Lombard. *See Book, Manuscript: Development; Commentary*
Peter of Alexandria. *See Physiologus*
Peter of Spain. *See* Philosophy
Peter Pan. *See Devil*
Peters, Randolph. *See* Apuleius
Petersen, Wolfgang. *See* Achilles; Novel; *Cinema*
Peter the Great. *See* Caesar, as Political Title; *Latin Language*
Peto, Luca. *See* Water Supply
Petracco, Ser. *See* Petrarch
Petrarch, **703**. *See also* Academy; Alexander the Great; Ancients and Moderns; Apollo; Art History; Book, Manuscript: Development; Book, Printed; Caesar, Julius; Caesars, Twelve; Calendars; Cicero; Collecting; Commentary; Consolation; Cosmology; Cupid; Dialogue; Dido; Donatus; Elegy; Epic; Fathers, Church; Forgery; Fortune; Fragments; Gellius; Grammar; Greek, Ancient; Guidebooks to Ancient Rome; Herodotus; Historiography; Horace; Humanism; Letters; Liberty; Libraries; Livy; Lyric Poetry; Muses; Narcissus; Neo-Latin; Numismatics; Orpheus; Ovid; Parnassus; Pastoral; Philosophy; Plato; Pliny the Elder; Poetics; Pygmalion; Renaissance; Roman Monuments, Reuse of; Rome; Sallust; Sculpture; Seneca the Younger; Statius; Stoicism; Tacitus; Terence; Translation; Valla; Venice; Virgil; Vitruvius; Warfare; Writing; *Aesthetics; Apuleius; Aristotle; Biography; Boccaccio; Boethius; Chrēsis; Cyclops; Isidore; Milton; Pliny the Younger*
Petrarch, Gherardo. *See Pastoral*
Pétrequin, J. P. E. *See* Medicine
Petri, Sebastian Henric. *See* Petrarch
Petronius, **706**. *See also* Book, Manuscript: Development; Cinema; Horace; Lucan; Novel; Satire; Seven Sages of Rome; Virgil; Widow of Ephesus; *Censorship; Martianus Capella; Pope, Alexander; Renaissance; Rubens; Symposium*
Petrus Alphonsus. *See* Seven Sages of Rome
Petrus Helias. *See* Grammar
Petrus Padubanensis. *See* Dioscorides
Peucer, Kaspar. *See* Divination; Natural History; *Melanchthon*
Peurbach, Georg. *See* Astronomy; Commentary; Ptolemy
Peutinger, Konrad. *See* Roads, Roman; *Inscriptions*
Peutinger map. *See* Cartography; Geography; Roads, Roman
Pevsner, Nikolaus. *See* Neoclassicism
Peyre, Marie-Joseph. *See Neoclassicism*
Phaedo. *See Homosexuality*
Phaedra, **707**. *See also* Sarcophagi; *Euripides*
Phaedria. *See Donatus*
Phaedrus. *See* Seven Sages of Rome; Translation; Widow of Ephesus
Phaethon, **708**. *See also Ovid*
Phalaris. *See* Ancients and Moderns; Forgery; *Bentley*
Phanocles. *See* Orpheus
Phaon. *See* Sappho
Pharmacology, **709**
Pharnabazus. *See* Persia
Pherecydes of Syros. *See Allegory*
Pheres. *See* Alcestis
Phialites, Theodore. *See Atticism*
Phidias. *See* Aesthetics; Michelangelo; Olympia; Renaissance; Replicas; Rome; Sculpture; Tourism; Winckelmann; *Amazons; Belvedere Torso*
Philanthropenos, Alexios. *See Moschopoulos; Planudes*
Philaretus. *See* Medicine
Philastre, Guillaume. *See* Cartography
Philemon. *See* Divination; *Raphael*
Philetas. *See* Pastoral
Philhellenism, **710**
Philip II of Spain. *See* Caesars, Twelve; Palace; *Atlas; Education; Europe; History Painting; War, Just*
Philip III of Spain. *See Martianus Capella*
Philip of Macedon. *See* Alexander the Great; Demosthenes; Revolution, French; *Persia*
Philip of Opus. *See* Book, Manuscript: Production
Philipps, Jenkin Thomas. *See Atheism*
Philippus of Thessalonica. *See* Greek Anthology
Philips, Ambrose. *See* Pastoral
Philips, John. *See* Virgil
Philips, Katherine. *See Cleopatra*
Philip the Good. *See Warfare*
Philip the Handsome. *See Panegyric*
Philistus. *See* Thucydides
Philo, **712**. *See also* Allegory; Commentary; Fathers, Church; Historiography; Immortality of the Soul; Judaism; Pandora; Poetics; *Annius of Viterbo; Armenian Hellenism*
Philoctetes. *See* Sophocles; *Belvedere Torso*
Philodemus of Gadara. *See* Allegory; Epicurus; *Papyrology*
Philolaus. *See* Cosmology; Geography; Harmony of the Spheres; Presocratics
Philomela. *See* Shakespeare; *Ovid*
Philon of Eleusis. *See Art History*
Philo of Byblos. *See Commentary*
Philo of Byzantium. *See* Warfare
Philoponus, John. *See* Logic; Music; *Astronomy; Commentary; Philosophy*
Philosophy, **713**
Philostorgius. *See Constantine*
Philostrati. *See* Ecphrasis
Philostratus, Flavius. *See* Aesthetics; Lodging; Nudity; Tourism; *Art History; Biography; Cities, Praise of*
Philostratus Lemnius. *See* Collecting; Ecphrasis; Galatea; Grammar; *Centaur; Moschopoulos; Museum; Philosophy*
Philoxenos. *See* Galatea
Phocylides. *See Judaism*
Phoebe. *See* Castor and Pollux; *Names*
Phoebus. *See Chaucer*
Phoenicians. *See* Glass
Pholus. *See Centaur*
Phoroneus. *See Mythology*
Photius, **724**. *See also* Book, Manuscript: Development; Byzantium; Epictetus; Fragments; Lucian; Music; Prosody; Renaissance; Xenophon; *Anthology; Bessarion; Constantinople; Doxography*
Phradmon. *See Amazons*
Phyllis. *See* Alexander the Great; *Popular Culture*
Physiognomy, **725**
Physiologus, **726**. *See also* Egypt; Zoology
Piacentini, Marcello. *See* Fascism
Piaggio, Antonio. *See* Papyrology
Picard, Jean. *See Greek, Ancient*
Picart, Bernard. *See* Paganism; Tantalus
Picasso, Pablo, **727**. *See also* Centaur; Faun; Modernism; Phaethon; *Maenads*
Piccinni, Niccolò. *See* Iphigenia
Piccolomini, Alessandro. *See Households*
Picinelli, Filippo. *See* Emblem
Pico della Mirandola, Gianfrancesco. *See* Aristotle; Astrology; Cicero; Divination; Philosophy; Pico della Mirandola; Skepticism
Pico della Mirandola, Giovanni, **728**. *See also* Aesthetics; Anacharsis; Astrology; Dionysus; Hieroglyphs; Libraries; Magic; Mystery Religions; Neoplatonism;

Pico della Mirandola, Giovanni *(continued)* Paganism; Philosophy; Plato; Scaliger, Joseph Justus; Skepticism; *Concord, Philosophical; Judaism; Letters*
Pictor, Georg. *See* Paganism
Pierleoni family. *See* Roman Monuments, Reuse of
Piero di Cosimo. *See* Centaur; Faun
Pigalle, Jean-Baptiste. *See* Nudity
Pighius, Stephanus. *See Herm*
Pignoni, Zenobi. *See* Etruscans
Pignoria, Lorenzo. *See* Nudity; *Hieroglyphs*
Pigres of Halicarnassus. *See Comedy*
Pilato, Leonzio. *See* Greek, Ancient; *Boccaccio*
Pilatus. *See Palace*
Pincianus (Fernando Núñez de Toledo y Guzmán). *See* Seneca the Younger
Pindar, **729**. *See also* Achilles; Ajax; Anacreon; Castor and Pollux; Genius; Genre; Geography; Horace; Locus Amoenus; Lyric Poetry; Medea; Mythology; Ode; Olympus; Poetics; Purple; Ronsard; Translation; *Book, Manuscript: Development; Byzantium; Centaur; Eustathius; Heyne; Melanchthon; Moschopoulos; Muses; Nietzsche; Pegasus; Renaissance; Sicily; Symposium; Thomas Magister; Triclinius; Tzetzes*
Pinet, Antoine du. *See* Natural History
Pino, Paolo. *See Color*
Pinsky, Robert. *See* Horace
Pinter, Harold. *See* Plautus; *Lyric Poetry*
Pinto, John. *See* Neoclassicism
Pinturicchio. *See* Color; Paganism; Pyramid; Rome; *Janus; Sibyls*
Pio, Giovanni Battista. *See Cicero*
Piombo, Sebastiano del. *See Color*
Piranesi, Francesco. *See* Hadrian's Villa; Piranesi
Piranesi, Giovanni Battista, **730**. *See also* City Planning; Forma Urbis Romae; Greek Revival; Hadrian's Villa; Neoclassicism; Ornament; Paestum; Rome; Triumphal Bridge; *Adam, Robert; Herm; Speculum Romanae Magnificentiae; Tourism*
Pirgoteles. *See* Alexander the Great
Pisançon, Albéric de. *See* Alexander the Great
Pisanello, Antonio. *See* Alexander the Great; Coins; Rome; Sarcophagi
Pisano, Giovanni. *See* Nudity; Sculpture; *Etruscans*
Pisano, Nicola. *See* Nudity; Sarcophagi; Sculpture; *Art History; Etruscans*
Pisistratus. *See* Homer; Writing
Pithou, Pierre. *See Petronius*
Pitigliano, Niccolò, Count Orsini di. *See* Roman Monuments, Reuse of
Pitré, Giuseppe. *See* Sicily
Pitt, Brad. *See Hero*
Pitt, Christopher. *See* Virgil
Pitt, Thomas. *See* Soane
Pitt, William, earl of Chatham. *See* Founding Fathers
Pitt, William, the Younger. *See* Soane; *Toga*
Pitti, Luca. *See* Palace
Pittoni, Giambattista. *See* Sacrifice in the Arts
Pius II (Aeneas Silvius Piccolomini). *See* Caesar, as Political Title; Education; Hadrian's Villa; Plautus; Roman Monuments, Reuse of; Rome; Tacitus; Warfare; *Biography; Letters; Names; Petrarch; Pliny the Younger*
Pius IV. *See* Roman Monuments, Reuse of; *Ligorio*
Pius VI. *See* Greek Anthology; *Collecting*
Pius VII. *See* Triumphal Arch; *Triumphal Bridge*
Pius IX. *See* Triumphal Arch
Pizolpasso, Francesco. *See* Pliny the Younger; *Notitia Dignitatum*
Pizzano, Tommaso da. *See Christine de Pizan*
Placcius, Vincent. *See* Writing
Plague, **732**
Planché, James Robinson. *See Comedy*
Plantin, Christophe. *See* Book, Printed
Planudean Anthology. *See Inscriptions*
Planudes, Maximus, **732**. *See also* Anthology; Byzantium; Cartography; Grammar; Greek Anthology; Music; Plutarch; Poetics; Ptolemy; Renaissance; Triclinius; *Book, Manuscript: Development; Moschopoulos*
Plaster Casts, **733**
Platearius, Mattheus. *See* Dioscorides; Pharmacology; *Natural History*
Platen, August von. *See* Horace; *Cassandra*
Plath, Sylvia. *See Maenads*
Platina, Bartolomeo. *See* Rome; *Biography*
Plato and Platonism, **734**. *See also* Academy; Aeschylus; Aesthetics; Alcestis; Allegory; Ancients and Moderns; Anthropology; Aphrodite; Apuleius; Aristotle; Astronomy; Atlantis; Augustine; Boethius; Book, Manuscript: Production; Book, Printed; Bronze; Byzantium; Censorship; Chaos; Commentary; Concord, Philosophical; Constitution, Mixed; Cosmology; Cupid; Cynicism; Demiurge; Democracy; Demon; Dialectic; Dialogue; Dionysus; Diotima; Dream Interpretation; East and West; Education; Egypt; Empedocles; Epicurus; Erasmus; Ethics; Ethnography; Etymology; Fathers, Church; Ficino; Fragments; Freud; Galen; Galileo; Ganymede; Genius; Geography; Greek, Ancient; Grotto; Harmony of the Spheres; Heidegger; Helen; Heraclitus; Homer; Homosexuality; Households; Humanism; Hydra; Imitation; Immortality of the Soul; Interpretatio Christiana; Irony; Judaism; Liberal Arts; Liberty; Locus Amoenus; Logic; Lyceum; Macrobius; Marsyas; Maxims; Metaphysics; Muses; Music; Mystery Religions; Mythology; Neoplatonism; Orpheus; Paganism; Parmenides; Pederasty; Petrarch; Philosophy; Picasso; Pico della Mirandola; Pliny the Younger; Plutarch; Poetics; Political Theory; Presocratics; Progress and Decline; Ptolemy; Pythagoras; Rabelais; Renaissance; Revolution, French; Rhetoric; Romanticism; Satire; Schlegel; Sirens; Socrates; Sparta; Suicide; Symposium; Thucydides; Tragedy; Translation; Ut pictura poesis; Vegetarianism; Warfare; Wilamowitz; Wolf, Friedrich August; Writing; Xanthippe; Xenophon; *Affecti; Anthology; Asterisk; Athens; Atlas; Atoms; Averroës; Bellori; Bessarion; Böckh; Book, Manuscript: Development; Brutus; Cato the Younger; Chartres; Chrēsis; Dante; Divination; Epictetus; Estienne, Henri II; Hermes Trismegistus; Hippocrates; Horace; Isidore; Korais; Labyrinth; Latin and the Professions; Lucian; Magic; Modernism; Opera; Photius; Planudes; Racine; Raphael; Sibyls; Sicily; Television; Terence*
Plautius Lateranus. *See Etruscans*
Plautus, **740**. *See also* Amphitryon; Aristophanes; Book, Manuscript: Production; Comedy; Education; Fathers, Church; Galileo; Hypnerotomachia Poliphili; Menander; Opera; Parasite; Popular Culture; Prosody; Seven Sages of Rome; Shakespeare; Terence; Translation; *Book, Manuscript: Development; Cinema; Dacier; Forgery; Lessing; Renaissance; Rubens*
Playfair, William Henry. *See* Greek Revival
Pléiade, **743**. *See also* Horace
Pleiades. *See Atlas*
Pliny the Elder, **744**. *See also* Aesthetics; Alexander the Great; Alexandria; Antiquarianism; Architecture; Aristotle; Art History; Astronomy; Atrium; Book, Printed; Botany; Bronze; Collecting; Color; Cosmology; Divination; Egypt; Ethnography; Forgery; Galileo; Geography; Glass; Grotto; Imitation; India; Liberal Arts; Macrobius; Magic; Marsyas; Mausoleum; Medicine; Meteorology; Monsters; Mosaic; Museum; Natural History; Nudity; Obelisk; Pharmacology; Physiologus; Pliny the Younger; Pompeii; Pornography; Portico; Progress and Decline; Purple; Pyramid; Raphael; Rome; Sculpture; Translation; Vitruvius; Volcanoes; Warfare; Water Supply; Winckelmann; Wonders; Writing; Zoology; *Annius of Viterbo; Atlas; Basilisk; Baths; Belvedere Torso; Cameos; Commentary; Delphin*

Classics; Guidebooks to Ancient Rome; Hippocrates; Jesuits; Laocoön; Masada; Montaigne; Papyrology; Pausanias; Physiognomy; Renaissance
Pliny the Younger, **745**. *See also* Horace; Letters; Panegyric; Raphael; Seneca the Younger; Translation; Volcanoes; Xenophon; *Geography; Magic; Museum; Renaissance*
Plotinus. *See* Academy; Aesthetics; Alexandrianism; Al-Fārābī; Aristotle; Demiurge; Fathers, Church; Ficino; Imitation; Irony; Macrobius; Magic; Neoplatonism; Philosophy; Plato; Vegetarianism; *Allegory; Averroës; Avicenna; Boethius; Byzantium; Concord, Philosophical; Hermes Trismegistus; Hieroglyphs*
Plouton. *See Demeter and Persephone*
Pluhar, Evelyn. *See* Vegetarianism
Plutarch, **747**. *See also* Aesthetics; Alexander the Great; Alexandrianism; Allegory; Archimedes; Aristophanes; Biography; Book, Printed; Botany; Caesar, as Political Title; Caesar, Julius; Cato the Younger; Cleopatra; Constitution, Mixed; Cynicism; Democracy; Demosthenes; Dialogue; Egypt; Epic; Erasmus; Ethics; Ethnography; Herodotus; Historiography; Homer; Horace; Households; Humanism; Imitation; Machiavelli; Macrobius; Maxims; Menander; Metaphrasis; Michelangelo; Milton; Montaigne; Mystery Religions; Pan; Philosophy; Political Theory; Psellus; Revolution, French; Scaliger, Julius Caesar; Seneca the Younger; Sexuality; Shakespeare; Sparta; Suetonius; Thucydides; Tourism; Tragedy; Translation; Ut pictura poesis; Vegetarianism; Warfare; Xanthippe; Zoology; *Anthology; Armenian Hellenism; Art History; Atticism; Barbarians; Book, Manuscript: Development; Brutus; Byzantium; Cinema; City Planning; Corneille, Pierre; Estienne, Henri II; Hippocrates; Korais; Labyrinth; Libraries; Livy; Lucian; Magic; Melanchthon; Music; Opera; Papyrology; Petrarch; Planudes; Racine; Renaissance; Rubens; Symposium*
Pluto. *See* Orpheus; *Chaucer; Demiurge; Locus Amoenus; Popular Culture*
Pocock, J. G. A. *See Barbarians*
Poe, Edgar Allan. *See* Lucian; Lyric Poetry; Thyestes
Poetics, **750**
Poghirc, Cicerone. *See Names*
Polanco, Juan de. *See Jesuits*
Polemo. *See Physiognomy*
Polignac, Melchior de. *See* Lucretius
Politi, Ambrogio. *See Nudity*
Political Theory, **755**
Poliziano, Angelo, **761**. *See also* Book, Printed; Catullus; Commentary; Dionysus; Elegy; Epictetus; Fragments; Genre; Grammar; Greek, Ancient; Humanism; Hypnerotomachia Poliphili; Letters; Michelangelo; Music; Neo-Latin; Orpheus; Philosophy; Poetics; Rhetoric; Sallust; Seneca the Elder; Seneca the Younger; Stoicism; Tacitus; Translation; *Art History; Carpe diem; Cicero; Education; Eustathius; Hermaphroditus; Horace*
Pollaiuolo, Antonio del. *See* Centaur; Hercules; Hydra
Pollio, Asinius. *See* Rome
Pollux. *See* Poetics; *Music*
Polo, Marco. *See* Ethnography; India; Tourism; Wonders
Polybius. *See* Arcadia; Aristocracy; Book, Printed; City Planning; Commentary; Constitution, Mixed; Founding Fathers; Historiography; Judaism; Political Theory; Progress and Decline; Revolution, French; Sallust; Tacitus; Thucydides; Warfare; *Book, Manuscript: Development; Byzantium; Fragments; Libraries; Machiavelli; Magna Graecia; Palladio*
Polyclitus. *See* Aesthetics; Architecture; Art History; Rome; Sculpture; Winckelmann; *Amazons; Plaster Casts*
Polyeuktos. *See Demosthenes*
Polygnotus. *See* Rome; *Aesthetics*
Polyhymnia. *See Muses*
Polynices. *See Antigone*
Polyphemus. *See* Sicily; *Cyclops; Galatea; Odysseus*
Polyxena. *See* Sacrifice in the Arts; *Achilles; Euripides*
Pomeroy, Sarah. *See* Households
Pompeii, **763**. *See also* Pornography; Replicas; Romanticism; Sexuality; Volcanoes; *Architecture; Temple*
Pompey. *See* Brutus; Caesar, Julius; Cato the Younger; Epic; Revolution, French; Rome; *Lucan; Names; Warfare*
Pomponazzi, Pietro. *See* Immortality of the Soul; Zoology; *Aristotle; Magic; Philosophy*
Ponet, John. *See Founding Fathers*
Ponsard, François. *See* Horace
Pontano, Giovanni. *See* Catullus; Elegy; Herodotus; Historiography; Ode; Pastoral; Sallust; *Astrology; Lucian; Petrarch; Pindar*
Pontano, Jacopo. *See* Genre
Pontianus, emperor. *See Seven Sages of Rome*
Pope, Alexander, **764**. *See also* Ancients and Moderns; Comedy; Commentary; Elegy; Epic; Epigram; Grotto; Horace; Juvenal; Midas; Ovid; Parody; Pastoral; Pyramus and Thisbe; Satire; Statius; Suicide; Translation; Virgil; Writing; *Toga*
Pope, John Russell. *See* Pantheon; Temple
Popelinière, Henri de la. *See Colony*
Popkin, Richard H. *See* Skepticism
Poppaea. *See Popular Culture*
Popper, Karl. *See* Poetics; Socrates
Popular Culture, **765**
Pornography, **767**
Porphyrio, Demetri. *See* Architecture
Porphyrio, Pomponius. *See* Horace
Porphyrogenitus, Constantine. *See* Hellenes
Porphyry (Neoplatonist). *See* Allegory; Aristotle; Commentary; Egypt; Fathers, Church; Forgery; Grotto; Homer; Liberal Arts; Logic; Macrobius; Magic; Music; Neoplatonism; Philosophy; Plato; Pythagoras; Vegetarianism; *Baghdad Aristotelians; Boethius; Byzantium; Cavafy; Concord, Philosophical; Ficino; Isagoge; Mithras; Paganism; Poliziano; Syriac Hellenism*
Porphyry (Egyptian stone), **771**
Porsenna. *See Etruscans*
Porson, Richard. *See* Professionalization of Classics; Prosody
Porta, Giacomo della. *See City Planning*
Porta, Giambattista della. *See* Optics; Physiognomy; Plautus; *Magic*
Porta, Guglielmo della. *See* Bronze; Caesars, Twelve
Porter, Cole. *See* Amphitryon
Porter, Peter. *See Hesiod*
Portia. *See* Suicide
Portico, **772**
Portland, William Henry Cavendish-Bentinck, Duke of. *See* Glass
Portland Vase. *See* Glass
Portman, John. *See* Atrium
Portoghesi, Paolo. *See* Architecture
Portraits, Reception of Ancient, **773**
Porus. *See Alexander the Great*
Porzio, Leonardo. *See* Numismatics
Poseidon. *See* Devil; *Demiurge; Neptune; Paganism; Pegasus*
Posi, Paolo. *See* Pantheon; Triumphal Bridge
Posidippus. *See* Papyrology
Posidonius. *See* Stoicism; *Etruscans*
Possel, Johann, the younger. *See* Temperament
Possevino, Antonio. *See* Caesar, as Political Title; *Herodotus*
Postel, Guillaume. *See* Etruscans; *Greek, Ancient*
Potârcă, Virgil. *See Names*
Pothier, Robert Joseph. *See* Law, Roman
Potocki, Jan. *See* Writing
Potocki, Stanislaw Kostka. *See* Etruscans
Potter, Robert. *See* Aeschylus
Poulenc, Francis. *See* Opera
Pound, Ezra. *See* Aeneas; Alexandrianism; Demeter and Persephone; Epic; Fragments; Hercules; Homer; Horace; Modernism; Pindar; Propertius; Sappho; Sophocles; Translation; Virgil; *Catullus; Cavafy; Lyric Poetry; Ovid*

Poussin, Nicholas. *See* Aeneas; Aphrodite; Barberini Faun; Color; Cyclops; Endymion; Faun; Galatea; History Painting; Midas; Modernism; Muses; Orpheus; Parnassus; Replicas; Stoicism; *Achilles; Art History; Cynicism; Herm; Maenads; Paper Museum; Picasso*
Poynter, Edward. *See Baths*
Pozzo, Cassiano dal. *See* Antiquarianism; Barberini Faun; Museum; Sarcophagi
Pra, Mario Dal. *See* Skepticism
Prado Júnior, Caio. *See Names*
Praeneste, **775**
Pratensis, Saxolus. *See Xenophon*
Praxiteles. *See* Aesthetics; Humanism; Neoclassicism; Pornography; Renaissance; Rome; Sculpture; Sexuality; Tourism; Winckelmann; *Belvedere Torso; Faun*
Preisendanz, Karl. *See Magic*
Presocratics, **776**. *See also* Cosmology; East and West; Heidegger; *Aristotle; Fragments; Nietzsche; Philosophy*
Preti, Girolamo. *See Hermaphroditus*
Prévost, Antoine François, abbé. *See* Novel
Prey, Pierre du. *See* Neoclassicism
Priam. *See* Epic; *Achilles; Cassandra; Troilus*
Priapus. *See* Paganism; Pornography; *Rome*
Price, John. *See* Greek, Ancient
Prigogine, Ilya. *See Chaos*
Primaticcio, Francesco. *See* Nicetas Codex; Replicas; *Laocoön*
Prince. *See* Purple
Prior, Matthew. *See* Horace; Lucian; *Juvenal*
Priscian. *See* Donatus; Epicurus; Grammar; Rhetoric; Scaliger, Julius Caesar; *Chartres; Liberal Arts; Philosophy*
Priscianus of Lydia. *See Iranian Hellenism*
Proba, Faltonia Betitia. *See* Cento; Virgil
Probus, Marcus Valerius. *See* Epicurus; Epigraphy; Horace; Virgil
Proclus. *See* Allegory; Aristotle; Demiurge; Diotima; Egypt; Etruscans; Fathers, Church; Ficino; Magic; Mystery Religions; Orpheus; Philosophy; Plato; Ptolemy; Renaissance; *Astronomy; Boethius; Byzantium; Commentary; Concord, Philosophical; Isagoge; Paganism*
Procne and Philomela. *See Thyestes*
Procopius. *See* Constantinople; Hagia Sophia; Plague; Renaissance; Rome; Warfare; *Armenian Hellenism; Biography; Cities, Praise of; Historiography; Rubens; Thucydides*
Prodicus of Ceus. *See* Atheism; Xenophon; *Hercules*
Prodromus, Theodore. *See Byzantium; Lucian*
Professionalization of Classics, **779**
Profetti, Giacomo. *See Symposium*
Progress and Decline, **782**
Prohaeresius. *See Armenian Hellenism*
Prometheus, **785**. *See also* Paganism; Romanticism; Sisyphus; Writing; *Centaur; Hercules; Hesiod; Pandora*
Pronunciation of Greek and Latin, **785**
Propertius, **786**. *See also* Achilles; Book, Manuscript: Development; Elegy; Galatea; Historiography; Horace; Maecenas; Parnassus; Virgil; *Catullus; Censorship; Commentary; Galileo; Lachmann; Muses; Renaissance; Scaliger, Joseph Justus*
Propylaea. *See* Architecture; Athens
Prosody, **787**
Protagoras. *See* Lyceum; Political Theory
Proteus. *See Helen*
Protogenes. *See* Aesthetics; Galileo; *Art History*
Proust, Marcel. *See* Fragments; Novel; *Symposium; Virgil*
Prudence. *See* Roswitha
Prudentius, Aurelius Clemens. *See* Allegory; Glass; Homer; Horace; Rome; Virgil
Psellus, Michael, **789**. *See also* Byzantium; Ficino; Hellenes; Historiography; Metaphrasis; Music; Neoplatonism; Renaissance; *Atticism; Book, Manuscript: Development; Constantinople; Doxography; Philo*
Pseudo-Acro. *See* Horace; *Commentary*
Pseudo-Aetius. *See Atheism*
Pseudo-Apollinaris of Laodicea. *See* Metaphrasis
Pseudo-Apuleius. *See* Medicine; Pharmacology
Pseudo-Aristotle. *See* Botany; Divination; Genius; Households; Poetics; Scaliger, Julius Caesar; *Judaism; Melancholy*
Pseudo-Berosus of Chaldea. *See Annius of Viterbo*
Pseudo-Callisthenes. *See* Alexandria; *Judaism; Persia*
Pseudo-Cato. *See Education*
Pseudo-Cicero. *See* Education; Irony; Rhetoric; *Judaism*
Pseudo-Constantine. *See Sibyls*
Pseudo-Demetrius. *See* Letters
Pseudo-Demetrius (author of *On Style*). *See* Letters
Pseudo-Democritus. *See Alchemy*
Pseudo-Dichaearchus. *See* Tourism
Pseudo-Dionysius of Halicarnassus. *See* Genre
Pseudo-Dionysius the Areopagite. *See* Demon; Greek, Ancient; Neoplatonism; Philosophy; Plato; *Book, Manuscript: Development; Syriac Hellenism*
Pseudo-Galen. *See* Doxography; Temperament; *Doxography; Hippocrates; Isagoge*
Pseudo-Geber. *See* Alachemy
Pseudo-Homer. *See* Satire
Pseudo-Justin. *See* Orpheus
Pseudo-Libanius. *See* Letters
Pseudo-Lucian. *See* Apuleius
Pseudo-Lull. *See* Alchemy
Pseudo-Matthew. *See* Nudity
Pseudo-Maximus. *See Anthology*
Pseudo-Plutarch. *See* Doxography; *Judaism*
Pseudo-Quintilian. *See* Renaissance
Pseudo-Seneca. *See* Consolation; Shakespeare
Pseudo-Soranus. *See* Temperament; *Doxography; Isagoge*
Pseudo-Virgil. *See* Tourism; *Carpe diem*
Pseudo-Xenophon. *See* Gynecology
Pseudo-Zonaras. *See Thomas Magister*
Psyche. *See* Apuleius
Ptolemies. *See* Book, Manuscript: Production; Libraries; Ptolemy; Writing; *Egypt; Judaism*
Ptolemy, **789**. *See also* Ancients and Moderns; Astrology; Astronomy; Cartography; Commentary; Cosmology; Divination; Ethnography; Galileo; Geography; Harmony of the Spheres; India; Liberal Arts; Magic; Melanchthon; Music; Optics; Rome; Scaliger, Joseph Justus; *Armenian Hellenism; Byzantium; Erasmus; Iranian Hellenism; Judaism; Planudes; Raphael; Renaissance*
Ptolemy I Sotor. *See* Euclid; Museum
Ptolemy II Philadelphus. *See* Museum
Ptolemy III Euergetes. *See* Museum
Ptolemy V. *See Hieroglyphs*
Ptolemy XII. *See* Cleopatra
Ptolemy XIII. *See* Alexandrianism; Cleopatra
Ptolemy of Lucca. *See Names*
Publicola. *See* Revolution, French
Publius Victor. *See Guidebooks to Ancient Rome*
Puccini, Giacomo. *See* Opera
Pucheymer, Philipp. *See* Dream Interpretation
Puchstein, Otto. *See Baalbek*
Puchta, Georg Friedrich. *See Law, Roman*
Pückler-Muskau, Hermann von. *See* Olympia
Pufendorf, Samuel von. *See* Democracy; Despotism, Oriental
Puget, Pierre. *See Atlas; Herm*
Pulcheria. *See Corneille, Pierre*
Pulci, Luigi. *See* Comedy
Pulman, Jack. *See Television*
Pulp (musical group). *See* Ovid
Purcell, Henry. *See* Aeneas; Dido; Virgil; *Amphitryon*
Purchas, Samuel. *See* Europe; Paganism
Purple, **792**
Pushkin, Alexander. *See* Horace; Ovid; Romanticism; Sirens; *Aristophanes*
Puttenham, George. *See* Lyric Poetry
Puvis de Chavannes, Pierre. *See* Modernism
Pygmalion, **793**. *See also* Galatea; Sculpture

Pynchon, Thomas. *See* Novel
Pyramid, **794**
Pyramus and Thisbe, **795**. *See also* Suicide; *Ovid; Popular Culture*
Pyrgoteles. *See* Cameos
Pyrrhonism. *See* Skepticism
Pyrrho of Elis. *See* Skepticism
Pyrrhus. *See* Racine
Pythagoras and Pythagoreanism, **796**. *See also* Aesthetics; Anthropology; Censorship; Color; Cosmology; Divination; East and West; Egypt; Empedocles; Galileo; Harmony of the Spheres; Immortality of the Soul; Liberal Arts; Music; Musical Instruments; Mythology; Neoplatonism; Presocratics; Ptolemy; Rabelais; Romanticism; Shakespeare; Suicide; Vegetarianism; *Anthology; Aristotle; Bentley; Biography; Geography; Judaism; Magic; Magna Graecia; Plato; Raphael*
Pytheos of Priene. *See* Mausoleum
Pythocles. *See Diogenes Laertius*

Qaddafi, Muammar. *See* Amazons
Qalonymos ben Qalonymos of Arles. *See Judaism*
Qazwini. *See* Wonders
Qotb al-Din al-Shirazi. *See Astrology*
Quasimodo, Salvatore. *See* Sicily
Quatremère de Quincy, Antoine-Chrysostome. *See* Nudity; Winckelmann; *Elgin Marbles*
Questenberg, G. A. *See Numismatics*
Quevedo, Francisco de. *See* Epigram; Seneca the Younger; Stoicism; Suicide
Quiccheberg, Samuel. *See* Museum
Quinault, Philippe. *See* Alcestis; Phaethon
Quincy, Josiah. *See Founding Fathers*
Quine, Willard. *See* Metaphysics
Quintilian. *See* Aesthetics; Alberti; Ancients and Moderns; Classical; Collecting; Dialectic; Education; Etymology; Fathers, Church; Gesture; Grammar; Horace; Imitation; Letters; Menander; Metaphrasis; Mnemonics; Philosophy; Poetics; Poliziano; Propertius; Replicas; Rhetoric; Romanticism; Satire; Seneca the Elder; Seneca the Younger; Thucydides; Translation; Valla; Virgil; Writing; *Affecti; Art History; Cicero; Cities, Praise of; Color; Commentary; Donation of Constantine; Erasmus; Hippocrates; Irony; Isagoge; Isidore; Judaism; Melanchthon; Philosophy; Pope, Alexander; Renaissance*
Quintus Smyrnaeus. *See* Ajax
Quirinus, Saint. *See Horace*

Rabelais, François, **800**. *See also* Allegory; Aristophanes; Comedy; Cynicism; Gellius; Giants; Greek, Ancient; Guidebooks to Ancient Rome; Lucian; Mnemonics; Novel; Plutarch; Satire; Symposium; Writing; *Epicurus; Estienne, Henri II; Interpretatio Christiana*
Rachilde (Marguerite Valette-Eymery). *See* Adonis
Racine, Jean Baptiste, **801**. *See also* Ancients and Moderns; Aristophanes; Commentary; Corneille, Pierre; Dramatic Unities; Iphigenia; Menander; Opera; Phaedra; Progress and Decline; Seneca the Younger; Shakespeare; Tragedy; *Antigone; Catharsis; Euripides*
Radice, Betty. *See* Translation
Radzivil, Prince Mikołaj. *See Baalbek*
Raimondi, Cosma. *See Atheism*
Raimondi, Marcantonio. *See* Apollo; Caesars, Twelve; Pornography; Raphael
Rainaldi, Carlo. *See* Triumphal Arch
Rainaldi, Girolamo. *See* Triumphal Arch
Rainolde, Richard. *See* Rhetoric
Rains, Claude. *See Cleopatra*
Raleigh, Sir Walter. *See* Catullus; Maxims
Rameau, Jean-Philippe. *See* Castor and Pollux; *Maenads*
Ramsay, Andrew Michael, Chevalier. *See Hermes Trismegistus*
Ramses II. *See* Obelisk
Ramus, Petrus (Pierre de la Ramée). *See* Commentary; Erasmus; Grammar; Logic; Mnemonics; Philosophy; Rhetoric; *Dialectic; Greek, Ancient; Isagoge*
Ramusio, Giambattista. *See Atlantis*
Ramusio, Paulo. *See Mercuriale*
Randolph, Thomas. *See* Aristophanes
Ranke, Leopold von. *See* Rome; Thucydides; *Burckhardt*
Ransmayr, Christoph. *See* Arachne; Ovid
Ransome, Arthur. *See* Amazons
Rantzau, Heinrich von (Henricus Ranzovius). *See* Warfare
Raphael, **802**. *See also* Aeneas; Aesthetics; Alexander the Great; Architecture; Aristotle; Art History; Athens; Atrium; City Planning; Color; Concord, Philosophical; Faun; Galatea; Guidebooks to Ancient Rome; Hadrian's Villa; History Painting; Horace; Lyceum; Muses; Neoclassicism; Nero; Nudity; Ornament; Paganism; Pantheon; Parnassus; Pliny the Younger; Pornography; Ptolemy; Pyramid; Replicas; Roman Monuments, Reuse of; Rome; Sacrifice in the Arts; Socrates; Vitruvius; Warfare; *Adam, Robert; Apuleius; Cynicism; Forma Urbis Romae; Janus; Laocoön; Magic; Sibyls*
Raphelengius, Franciscus. *See* Book, Printed; Seneca the Younger
Rapin, René. *See* Elegy; Livy; Pastoral; Rhetoric; *Jesuits; Lessing*
Rasario, Giovanni Battista. *See* Medicine
Raschdorff, Julius. *See* Architecture
Rashīd al-Dīn. *See* Persia
Raspe, Rudolf Erich. *See* Volcanoes
Ratherius of Verona. *See Book, Manuscript: Development; Catullus; Martianus Capella*
Ravel, Maurice. *See* Daphnis; Pastoral
Ravenna, **806**
Ravensburg, Friedrich Göler von. *See* Rubens
Ravenscroft, Edward. *See* Thyestes
Ravisius Textor, Johannes. *See* Writing
Rawlinson, Henry. *See Persia*
Rawls, John. *See Law, Roman*
Ray, John. *See Zoology*
Rāzi, al- (Rhazes). *See* Medicine; Plague; *Physiognomy*
Reade, Simon. *See Hermaphroditus*
Reagan, Ronald. *See* Astrology
Rebenich, Stefan. *See* Sparta
Recanati, Menahem. *See Pico della Mirandola*
Rechberg, Adam. *See Museum*
Redditi, Filippo. *See Numismatics*
Redon, Odilon. *See* Apollo; Modernism
Reed, Evelyn. *See Matriarchy*
Reeves, Steve. *See Hercules*
Regan, Tom. *See* Vegetarianism
Reggio, Niccolò Deoprepio da. *See* Medicine; Translation
Regino of Prüm. *See* Music
Regiomontanus, Johannes. *See* Astronomy; Cartography; Commentary; Oracles; Ptolemy; Squaring the Circle; *Bessarion*
Regnault, Jean-Baptiste. *See* Socrates
Regnier, Nicolas. *See Hero and Leander*
Regulus, Publius Memmius. *See* Tacitus
Rehberg, Frederick. *See Grand Tour*
Rehfisch, Hans José. *See* Ajax
Reich, Wilhelm. *See Matriarchy*
Reimmann, Jacob Friedrich. *See* Writing; *Atheism*
Reinesius, Thomas. *See Ligorio*
Reinhard, Karl. *See* Parmenides; *Nietzsche*
Reinhardt, Max. *See Cassandra; Sophocles*
Reinhold, Karl Leonhard. *See* Egypt; Skepticism
Reisch, Gregor. *See* Numbers
Rekkared. *See Isidore*
Remarque, Erich Maria. *See* Dulce et decorum est
Rembrandt Harmenszoon van Rijn. *See* Cupid; Demeter and Persephone; *Ganymede*
Remigius of Auxerre. *See* Grammar; *Martianus Capella*
Remus. *See Guidebooks to Ancient Rome*
Renaissance, **807**
Renan, Ernest. *See* Empedocles; Mithras; *Greek, Ancient*
Renault, Mary. *See* Novel
Reni, Guido. *See* Centaur; Helen; *Cleopatra; Hercules*
Renoir, Auguste. *See* Modernism
Replicas, **815**
Republicanism, **819**

Rettenbacher, Simon. *See Horace*
Retz, Franciscus de. *See* Danaë
Reubell, Jean-François. *See* Revolution, French
Reuchlin, Johannes. *See* Greek, Ancient; *Demosthenes; Melanchthon*
Revett, Nicholas. *See* Architecture; Athens; Caryatid; Dilettanti, Society of; Grand Tour; Greek Revival; *Elgin Marbles; Temple; Tourism*
Revolution, French, 822
Reynolds, Sir Joshua. *See* Apollo Belvedere; Belvedere Torso; Dido; Fashion; Grand Tour; Toga; *Maenads*
Reynolds, Tim. *See* Aristophanes
Rezzonico family. *See Piranesi*
Rhazes (al Rāzi). *See* Medicine; Plague; *Physiognomy*
Rhea Silvia. *See Mars*
Rheticus, Georg Joachim. *See Astronomy*
Rhetoric, 826
Rhoades, James. *See* Dulce et decorum est
Rhodiginus, Caelius. *See* Writing
Rhōmaioi, 830
Rhuphus. *See Anthology*
Riario, Cardinal Raffaele. *See* Rome
Ricci, A. *See* Medicine
Ricci, Matteo. *See* Epictetus; Warfare
Ricci, Sebastiano. *See* Faun
Riccio, Andrea. *See* Faun; *Atlas*
Riccio, Pietro (Petrus Crinitus). *See* Writing
Riccioli, Giambattista. *See* Commentary; Harmony of the Spheres; Ptolemy; *Calendars*
Riccius, Stephanus (Stephen Reich). *See* Terence
Riccobono, Antonio. *See* Historiography
Rich, Adrienne. *See Medea*
Rich, Barnabe. *See Ethnography*
Rich, John. *See Mime*
Richard III. *See Comedy*
Richard of Wallingford. *See* Ptolemy
Richardson, Samuel. *See* Novel; Ovid
Richard the Bishop. *See Chartres*
Richelieu, Armand-Jean du Plessis, Cardinal. *See* Tragedy; *Academy*
Ridolfi, Niccolò. *See* Nicetas Codex
Riedesel, Friedrich Adolf, Baron. *See* Sicily; *Magna Graecia*
Riefenstahl, Leni. *See* Olympia
Riegl, Alois. *See* Ornament; Sarcophagi; *Ornament*
Riesener, Léon. *See Maenads*
Rieu, Emile Victor. *See* Translation
Rigg, Diana. *See Medea*
Righetti, Francesco. *See Faun*
Rilke, Rainer Maria. *See* Apollo; Endymion; Fragments; Orpheus; Sculpture; Sirens; *Ecphrasis; Euripides; Maenads; Mystery Religions; Ovid*
Rinaldi, Giovanni. *See* Mercuriale
Rinuccini, Ottavio. *See* Ariadne; Music; Opera; Orpheus
Ripa, Cesare. *See* Emblem; Nudity; *Hercules; Martianus Capella*
Ripheus. *See* Education
Rippe, Guillaume. *See Terence*
Risner, Friedrich. *See* Optics
Ristori, Adelaide. *See Medea*
Ritschl, Friedrich Wilhelm. *See Lachmann; Teubner*
Rittershusius, Conrad. *See* Pliny the Younger
Roads, Roman, 831
Robert, Carl. *See* Sarcophagi; *Diels, Hermann*
Robert, Hubert. *See* Grotto; Hadrian's Villa; Ruins; *Neoclassicism*
Robert, King of Naples. *See* Elegy; *Petrarch*
Robert of Anjou. *See Boccaccio*
Robert of Clari. *See Constantinople*
Robert of Crichlade. *See* Pliny the Elder
Roberts, David. *See Baalbek*
Robertson, Edward. *See Masada*
Robertson, William. *See* Ethnography; Gibbon
Robespierre, Maximilien. *See* Caesar, Julius; Cicero; Democracy; Dictatorship; Law, Roman; Revolution, French; *David; Dionysus; Education*
Robinson, Abraham. *See* Zeno's Paradoxes
Robinson, Edward Arlington. *See* Epigram
Robinson, Hugh. *See* Education
Robortello, Francesco. *See* Commentary; *Catharsis; Horace; Tragedy*
Rocca, Angelo. *See* Writing
Rochester, John Wilmot, 2nd Earl of. *See* Comedy; Horace; Parody
Rodenwaldt, Gerhart. *See* Sarcophagi
Rodgers, Richard. *See* Plautus
Rodin, Auguste. *See* Apollo; Caryatid; Faun; Fragments; Orpheus; Sculpture; *Daphnis; Maenads*
Roederer, Pierre-Louis. *See* Nudity
Roger II of Sicily. *See Cartography*
Rogers, Ernesto. *See* Architecture
Rogers, Will. *See* Comedy
Rohault, Jacques. *See Astrology*
Rohde, Erwin. *See Nietzsche*
Roland (epic hero). *See* Alexander the Great; Epic
Roland, Madame (Marie-Jeanne). *See* Revolution, French
Rolland, Romain. *See* Empedocles
Rolli, Domenico. *See* Etruscans
Rollin, Charles. *See Historiography*
Roman, Jean-Baptiste. *See Cato the Younger*
Romance, Medieval, 834
Roman Monuments, Reuse of, 832
Romano, Egidio. *See* Warfare
Romano, Giulio. *See* Apuleius; Architecture; Donation of Constantine; Palace; Pornography; Rome; Ruins; Warfare; *Adam, Robert; Ajax; Amazons; Cupid; Hercules*
Romanticism, 835
Rome, 839. *See also* Aeneas; Alexandrianism; Athens; Byzantium; Cities, Praise of; City Planning; Constantinople; Guidebooks to Ancient Rome; Mirabilia Urbis; Speculum Romanae Magnificentiae
Rommel, Erwin. *See Warfare*
Romney, George. *See Maenads*
Romulus. *See* Caesar, Julius; Tacitus; *Guidebooks to Ancient Rome; Historiography; Machiavelli; Mars; Names; Petrarch*
Romulus Augustulus. *See* Empire; Ravenna
Ronsard, Pierre de, 850. *See also* Adonis; Cupid; Epic; Estienne, Henri II; Greek, Ancient; Helen; Hercules; Horace; Lucretius; Ode; Pindar; Pléiade; Virgil; *Anacreon; Atlas; Carpe diem; Catullus; Cyclops*
Roomen, Adriaan van. *See* Squaring the Circle
Roosevelt, Franklin Delano. *See* Alcestis
Roper, William. *See Biography*
Rops, Daniel. *See Etruscans*
Rosa, Salvator. *See Nudity; Sallust*
Rosenberg, Alfred. *See* Dionysus; Fascism
Rosetta Stone. *See Hieroglyphs*
Rosinus, Johannes. *See* Antiquarianism
Rossellini, Roberto. *See* Television
Rossetti, Dante Gabriel. *See* Translation
Rossi, Aldo. *See* Architecture
Rossi, Domenico de. *See Faun*
Rossi, Franco. *See Cinema*
Rossi, Gabriele de'. *See* Raphael
Rossi, Giovanni Battista de. *See Catacombs*
Rossi, Properzia de'. *See Names*
Rossini, Gioachino Antonio. *See Opera*
Rostand, Edmond. *See Asterisk*
Roswitha, 851. *See also* Gesture; Horace; Renaissance; Terence
Rota, Bernardino. *See* Pastoral
Rota, Giulio. *See Doxography*
Rotimi, Ola. *See* Tragedy
Rotrou, Jean. *See* Antigone; Plautus; *Hercules*
Rotti, Giovanni. *See* Triumphal Bridge
Rouillé, Guillaume. *See* Numismatics
Rouse, Christopher. *See* Phaethon
Rousseau, Jean-Jacques. *See* Cato the Younger; Daphnis; Democracy; Dictatorship; Europe; Founding Fathers; Galatea; Households; Humanism; Liberty; Montaigne; Novel; Political Theory; Professionalization of Classics; Progress and Decline; Pygmalion; Republicanism; Revolution, French; Romanticism; Soane; Sparta; Widow of Ephesus; *Biography; Cynicism; Law, Roman; Livy; Neoclassicism; Ruins*
Rovere, Antonio della. *See* Scaliger, Julius Caesar
Rovere, Francesco Maria della. *See* Ruins
Rowe, Colin. *See* Architecture
Rowling, J. K. *See Basilisk*
Roxana. *See* Alexander the Great

Royal High School (Edinburgh). *See* Architecture
Royal Society of London. *See* Ancients and Moderns
Rubens, **852**. *See also* Antiquarianism; Aphrodite; Apollo; Arachne; Ariadne; Caesars, Twelve; Castor and Pollux; Centaur; Color; Demeter and Persephone; Dido; Dionysus; Faun; Midas; Phaethon; Portraits, Reception of Ancient; Seneca the Younger; Stoicism; Suicide; *Achilles; Amazons; Art History; Belvedere Torso; Cynicism; Hercules; Hero and Leander; Hesiod; Laocoön; Modernism; Pegasus*
Rubens, Albert. *See* Rubens; Toga
Rubens, Philip. *See* Rubens; Stoicism
Rubruck, William. *See* Ethnography
Rucellai, Bernardo. *See* Rome; Sallust
Rucellai family. *See* Academy; *Historiography*
Rückert, Friedrich. *See* Greek Anthology
Rudbeck, Olof, the Elder. *See Atlantis*
Rude, François. *See Cato the Younger*
Rudolf II. *See Centaur; Liberal Arts*
Rudolph Agricola. *See* Dialectic
Rueda, Lope de. *See* Plautus
Ruel, Jean (Ruellius, Johannes). *See* Botany; Veterinary Medicine; *Dioscorides*
Ruffus, Jordanus. *See* Veterinary Medicine
Rufinus of Aquileia. *See* Constantine; Egypt
Rufus, Quintus Curtius. *See* Alexander the Great; Historiography; Maxims; Warfare; *Racine*
Rufus of Ephesus. *See* Medicine; *Melancholy*
Ruhnkenius, David. *See Doxography*
Ruins, **853**
Rush, Benjamin. *See* Education
Ruskin, John. *See* Apollo; Households; *Xenophon*
Russell, Bertrand. *See* Skepticism; Zeno's Paradoxes; *Philosophy*
Ruzé, Antoine Coëffier, Marquis d'Effiat. *See Atlas*
Ryder, Albert Pinkham. *See Pegasus*
Ryff, Walter Hermann. *See* Dream Interpretation
Rymer, Thomas. *See* Tragedy

Saadia Gaon. *See* Judaism; *Philosophy*
Sabine women. *See Cinema; Penelope*
Sacchini, Antonio Maria Gasparo. *See* Aeneas
Sacher-Masoch, Leopold von. *See* Winckelmann
Sachs, Hans. *See* Aristophanes; Plautus
Sackville, Thomas. *See* Seneca the Younger; Tragedy
Sacrifice in the Arts, **855**
Sacro Bosco, Johannes de. *See* Astronomy; Liberal Arts
Sadoleto, Jacopo. *See* Letters; *Cicero*
Sahlins, Marshall. *See* Thucydides
Said, Edward. *See* East and West; *Barbarians*
Sailly, Abbé de. *See* Historiography
Saint-Amant, Marc-Antoine Girard, sieur de. *See* Locus Amoenus
Sainte-Beuve, Charles Augustin. *See* Classical; Menander
Sainte-Maure, Benoît de. *See* Achilles; *Troilus*
Saint-Évremond, Charles de Marguetel de Saint-Denis de. *See Catharsis*
Saint-Just, Louis de. *See* Revolution, French; *Livy*
Saint Laurent, Yves. *See* Toga
Saint-Non, Abbé de. *See* Sicily
Saint-Saëns, Charles-Camille. *See* Demeter and Persephone; *Opera*
Salaman, Clement. *See Hermes Trismegistus*
Salamanca, Antonio. *See* Speculum Romanae Magnificentiae
Salel, Hugues. *See* Rabelais
Salem, Ali. *See* Comedy
Salgado, Plínio. *See Names*
Salieri, Antonio. *See Sallust*
Sallust, **856**. *See also* Cato the Younger; Education; Empire; Europe; Fathers, Church; Founding Fathers; Geography; Historiography; Political Theory; Poliziano; Progress and Decline; Revolution, French; Tacitus; Thucydides; Translation; *Book, Manuscript: Development; Cartography; Commentary; Horace; Melanchthon; Renaissance; Rubens*
Sallustius. *See Palace*
Salmacis. *See Hermaphroditus; Locus Amoenus*
Salmon, André. *See* Modernism
Salmon, Wesley. *See* Zeno's Paradoxes
Salomon, Bernard. *See* Phaethon
Saltonstall, Wye. *See Ovid*
Salusbury, Sir Thomas and Lady. *See Toga*
Salutati, Coluccio. *See* Academy; Book, Manuscript: Development; Consolation; Etruscans; Greek, Ancient; Hercules; Historiography; Humanism; Letters; Libraries; Nicetas Codex; Petrarch; Renaissance; Sculpture; Stoicism; Virgil; *Atlas; Boethius; Cicero; Petrarch*
Salvage, Jean-Galbert. *See* Nudity
Salvi, Nicola. *See* Neoclassicism; *Adam, Robert*
Salviani, Ippolito. *See* Natural History
Salvian of Marseilles. *See Barbarians*
Samain, Albert. *See Maenads*
Sambin, Hugues. *See Herm*
Sambucus, Johannes. *See* Emblem
Samuel. *See* Paganism
Samuel, Richard. *See* Muses
Samuel of Marseilles. *See Judaism*
Sanchez de las Brozas, Francisco. *See* Grammar; Stoicism; *Philosophy*
Sanchuniathon. *See* Commentary
Sandrart, Joachim von. *See Art History*
Sandys, George. *See* Cyclops; Prometheus; Pyramus and Thisbe; *Midas; Ovid; Sisyphus*
Sangallo, Antonio da, the Elder. *See* Atrium
Sangallo, Antonio da, the Younger. *See* Etruscans; Palace; Roman Monuments, Reuse of; Rome; *Speculum Romanae Magnificentiae*
Sangallo, Francesco da. *See Laocoön*
Sangallo, Giuliano da. *See* Atrium; Hagia Sophia; Praeneste; Rome; *Herm*
Sannazaro, Jacopo. *See* Actaeon; Arcadia; Elegy; Galatea; Pastoral; Petrarch; Virgil; *Catullus*
Sanravius (Jean de Saint-Ravy). *See* Aeschylus
Sanseverino, Roberto da. *See* Ethnography
Sansovino, Andrea. *See* Etruscans
Sansovino, Jacopo. *See* Architecture; Raphael; Replicas; Rome; Venice; *Herm; Laocoön*
Santacroce, A. *See* Numismatics
Santayana, George. *See* Dialogue
Santi, Giovanni. *See Art History*
Santorinos of Rhodes. *See* Nicetas Codex
Sappho, **858**. *See also* Achilles; Cupid; Homosexuality; Locus Amoenus; Lyric Poetry; Translation; *Book, Manuscript: Development; Dacier; Papyrology; Parnassus*
Saraceni, Carlo. *See Hermaphroditus*
Saracenus, Janus Antonius. *See Dioscorides*
Sarapis. *See Egypt*
Sarbiewski, Maciej Kazimierz. *See* Jesuits; Ode; *Horace*
Sarcophagi, **859**
Sargent, John Singer. *See* Hydra; Phaethon
Sarmiento de Gamboa, Pedro. *See Atlantis*
Sarpi, Paolo. *See* Progress and Decline
Sarrazin, Jean François. *See* Comedy
Sarti, Giuseppe. *See* Opera
Sartre, Jean-Paul. *See* Dramatic Unities; Orpheus; Temperament; Tragedy; *Cassandra*
Sassmann, Hanns. *See* Xanthippe
Satan. *See* Epic; Magic; Milton; *Demiurge; Mithras; Nudity*
Satie, Eric. *See* Modernism
Satire, **862**
Saturn. *See* Paganism; Progress and Decline
Saumaise, Claude. *See* Geography
Sauppe, Hermann. *See Lachmann*
Saussure, Ferdinand de. *See Grammar*
Savelli, Cardinal Giulio. *See* Roman Monuments, Reuse of
Savelli collection. *See Rubens*
Savigny, Friedrich Carl von. *See* Law, Roman
Savile, Henry. *See Scaliger, Joseph Justus*
Savinio, Alberto. *See* Alcestis; Castor and Pollux; *Etruscans*
Savonarola, Girolamo. *See* Historiography; Nudity; Pico della Mirandola; Poliziano; Porphyry; Renaissance

Savonarola, Michele. *See* Water Supply
Săvulescu, Traian. *See Names*
Saxl, Fritz. *See* Warburg
Sayf al-Dawla. *See* Al-Fārābī
Scaino, Antonio. *See* Sports
Scala, Bartolomeo. *See* Poliziano; *Epictetus*
Scalfurotto, Giovanni. *See Piranesi*
Scaliger, Joseph Justus, **865**. *See also* Allegory; Book, Manuscript: Development; Book, Printed; Commentary; Etymology; Forgery; Fragments; Greek, Ancient; Historiography; Humanism; Inscriptions; Progress and Decline; Propertius; Seneca the Younger; Squaring the Circle; Stoicism; Warfare; Writing; *Aristophanes; Art History; Astrology; Bentley; Calendars; Education; Herodotus; Petronius; Scaliger, Julius Caesar*
Scaliger, Julius Caesar, **866**. *See also* Dramatic Unities; Genre; Imitation; Pastoral; Petrarch; Plague; Pléiade; Poetics; Prosody; Scaliger, Joseph Justus; Seneca the Younger; Terence; Tragedy; Vico; Virgil; *Grammar*
Scamozzi, Vincenzo. *See* Pliny the Younger; Theater Architecture; *Ornament; Palladio*
Scarlatti, Alessandro. *See* Endymion; *Opera*
Scarron, Paul. *See* Epic; Parody; Virgil; *Comedy*
Scève, Maurice. *See* Narcissus; *Chaos*
Schadewaldt, Wolfgang. *See Wilamowitz*
Schaefer, Arnold. *See* Demosthenes
Scharnhorst, Gerhard von. *See* Warfare
Schechner, Richard. *See* Aeschylus; Dionysus; *Euripides; Maenads*
Schedel, Hartmann. *See* Cartography; Historiography; *Athens*
Scheffer, Johann. *See* Ethnography; Warfare
Scheiner, Christoph. *See* Galileo
Schelling, Friedrich Wilhelm Josef von. *See* Chaos; Dionysus; Mythology; Neoplatonism; Paganism
Schiavone, Andrea. *See Pegasus*
Schickele, Peter. *See* Comedy
Schiller, Friedrich. *See* Aeschylus; Apollo Belvedere; Goethe; Greek Anthology; Hero and Leander; Humanism; Martial; Pegasus; Poetics; Political Theory; Professionalization of Classics; Romanticism; Satire; Schlegel; Thermopylae; Tragedy; Virgil; *Cassandra; Mystery Religions; Olympus*
Schiller, Julius. *See Astronomy*
Schinkel, Karl Friedrich, **867**. *See also* Architecture; Neoclassicism; Pliny the Younger; Temple; *Caryatid*
Schlegel, August Wilhelm. *See* Greek Anthology; Romanticism; Schlegel; Translation; *Heyne*
Schlegel, Friedrich, **868**. *See also* Diotima; Fragments; Greek, Ancient; Irony; Romanticism; *Heyne*
Schlegel, Johann Elias. *See* Aeneas
Schleicher, August. *See Greek, Ancient*
Schleiermacher, Friedrich Daniel. *See* Fragments; Plato; Presocratics; Romanticism; *Böckh; Historicism*
Schlesinger, Kathleen. *See* Music
Schlieffen, Alfred, Count von. *See* Hannibal
Schliemann, Heinrich. *See* Knossos; Mycenae
Schlözer, Ludwig August von. *See* Antiquarianism
Schmidt, Wilhelm. *See Matriarchy*
Schnitzler, Arthur. *See* Comedy
Schnur, Harry. *See Juvenal; Petronius*
Schoeffer, Peter. *See* Book, Printed
Scholderer, Victor. *See* Book, Printed
Schonaeus, Cornelius. *See* Terence
Schöner, Johann. *See Astronomy*
Schopenhauer, Arthur. *See* Aesthetics; Metaphysics; Nudity; Presocratics; *Melancholy; Nietzsche; Philosophy*
Schoppe, Kaspar. *See* Scaliger, Julius Caesar; Stoicism
Schott, Andreas. *See* Seneca the Elder
Schow, Niels Iversen. *See* Papyrology
Schreckenfuchs, Erasmus Oswald. *See Calendars*
Schröder, Alexander. *See* Horace
Schubert, Franz. *See* Castor and Pollux; *Ganymede*
Schumann, Clara. *See* Sirens
Schumann, Robert. *See* Sirens
Schünzel, Reinhold. *See* Amphitryon
Schürer, Matthias. *See* Classical
Schuster, Joseph. *See* Sacrifice in the Arts
Schütz, Hans. *See* Apollo
Schwartz, Eduard. *See* Sallust; *Calendars; Wilamowitz*
Schwarzenegger, Arnold. *See Cinema; Hercules*
Schwendi, Lazarus. *See* Historiography
Scipio Africanus the Elder. *See* Dulce et decorum est; Epic; Hannibal; Rome; *Historiography; Petrarch*
Scipio Africanus the Younger. *See Cicero; Etruscans*
Scopas. *See* Aesthetics; Rome; *Mausoleum*
Scot, Michael. *See* Physiognomy; *Averroës*
Scott, Ridley. *See* Cinema
Scott, Sir Walter. *See* Epic; Macaulay
Scribonius Largus. *See* Medicine; *Hippocrates*
Scruton, Roger. *See* Xanthippe
Scudéry, Georges. *See* Plague
Scudéry, Madeleine de. *See* Sappho
Scully, Vincent. *See* Neoclassicism
Sculpture, **869**
Scutellius, Nicolaus. *See Philosophy*
Scylax of Caryanda. *See* India
Scylla and Carybdis. *See* Sicily; *Popular Culture*
Seale, Bobby. *See Carpe diem*
Seba, Albert. *See Latin Language*
Sebastian, Saint. *See Cinema*
Sebillet, Thomas. *See* Classical
Sebokht, Severus. *See* Astrology; *Astronomy*
Secundus, Janus. *See* Catullus
Sedley, Sir Charles. *See* Terence
Sedley, David. *See* Stoicism
Sedulius Scotus. *See Book, Manuscript: Development*
Segni, Bernardo. *See* Tragedy
Ségur, Louis-Philippe de. *See* Revolution, French
Seiter, Daniel. *See Endymion*
Selden, John. *See Calendars*
Seleucus I Nicator. *See* Gandhara; Writing
Sellars, Peter. *See* Aeschylus; Ajax
Semiramis. *See Mirabilia Urbis*
Semler, Johann Salomo. *See* Wolf, Friedrich August
Semper, Gottfried. *See* Forum; Ornament
Seneca the Elder, **872**. *See also* Metaphrasis; *Isidore*
Seneca the Younger, **873**. *See also* Aeschylus; Alexander the Great; Antigone; Atheism; Book, Manuscript: Development; Book, Printed; Cassandra; Consolation; Cosmology; Cynicism; Education; Electra; Elegy; Epictetus; Erasmus; Ethics; Forgery; Galileo; Genius; Heraclitus; Horace; Imitation; Letters; Macrobius; Maxims; Medea; Meteorology; Nero; Oedipus; Phaedra; Plague; Pliny the Younger; Portraits, Reception of Ancient; Progress and Decline; Racine; Rubens; Sallust; Satire; Seneca the Elder; Shakespeare; Stoicism; Suicide; Thyestes; Tragedy; Translation; Virgil; *Boccaccio; Cicero; Corneille, Pierre; Dante; Delphin Classics; Hippocrates; Isidore; Latin Language; Lessing; Lucan; Martianus Capella; Montaigne; Philosophy; Renaissance; Sophocles*
Senfl, Ludwig. *See Horace*
Sennert, Daniel. *See Atoms*
Sennett, Richard. *See* Apollo
Sepúlveda, Juan Ginés de. *See* Despotism, Oriental; Ethnography; Slavery
Serapio. *See Natural History*
Şerban, Andrei. *See Medea*
Seregni, Vincenzo. *See* Names
Seregni, Vitruvius. *See Names*
Serenus, Quintus. *See* Medicine
Sergel, Johan Tobias. *See Herm*
Sergius of Resaina. *See* Aristotle; Medicine; Syriac Hellenism
Sergius the Confessor. *See Photius*
Serlio, Sebastiano. *See* Architecture; City Planning; Guidebooks to Ancient Rome; Ornament; Portico; Praeneste; Rome; Temple; Theater Architecture; Vitruvius; *Roman Monuments, Reuse of*
Séroux d'Agincourt, Jean Baptiste. *See Art History*
Serres, Michel. *See* Lucretius

Sertinus, Thomas. *See* Tacitus
Servatus Lupus. *See* Gellius
Servetus, Michael. *See* Skepticism
Servilia. *See Brutus*
Servius Honoratus, Marius. *See* Allegory; Atrium; Commentary; Elegy; Etymology; Hercules; Horace; Imitation; Macrobius; Mars; Parnassus; Poetics; Virgil; Vitruvius; *Atlas; Guidebooks to Ancient Rome; Martianus Capella; Neptune*
Seth. *See* Writing
Sethos I. *See* Obelisk
Settembrini, Luigi. *See* Dialogue; Lucian
Seurat, Georges. *See* Modernism
Seven Sages of Rome, **877**
Seven Wonders of the World, **878**
Severus (architect). *See* Domus Aurea
Severus, Septimius. *See* Architecture; Tourism; *Cartography; Forma Urbis Romae; Portraits, Reception of Ancient*
Sewers, **878**
Sextus Afranius Burrus. *See* Nero
Sextus Empiricus. *See* Estienne, Henri II; Logic; Montaigne; Parmenides; Philosophy; Skepticism; *Astrology; Music*
Sextus Rufus. *See Guidebooks to Ancient Rome*
Sexuality, **879**
Sforza, Bianca Maria. *See Genre*
Sforza, Galeazzo Maria. *See Astrology*
Sforza, Ludovico. *See City Planning*
Sgricci, Tommaso. *See Thyestes*
Shabbetai ben Donnolo. *See* Medicine
Shadwell, Thomas. *See* Parody; Terence
Shaftesbury, Anthony Ashley Cooper, 3rd Earl of. *See* Ethics; Progress and Decline; *Dialogue*
Shakespeare, **881**. *See also* Achilles; Adonis; Aeneas; Ajax; Alexandria; Alexandrianism; Amazons; Brutus; Caesar, as Political Title; Cleopatra; Comedy; Commentary; Cupid; Dramatic Unities; Education; Endymion; Ethnography; Genius; Helen; Hero; Hero and Leander; Historiography; Horace; Imitation; Juvenal; Lodging; Lucretius; Lyric Poetry; Medea; Menander; Montaigne; Odysseus; Opera; Ovid; Parasite; Parody; Pastoral; Phaethon; Philosophy; Plautus; Pliny the Elder; Plutarch; Popular Culture; Pygmalion; Pyramus and Thisbe; Republicanism; Romanticism; Satire; Seneca the Younger; Stoicism; Suicide; Thyestes; Tragedy; Translation; Troilus; Virgil; Xanthippe; *Aristophanes; Biography; Boccaccio; Carpe diem; Cassandra; Cinema; Euripides; Livy; Melancholy; Midas; Racine; Renaissance*
Shaw, George Bernard. *See* Comedy; Plautus; Pygmalion; Vegetarianism; *Cleopatra; Terence*
Sheffield, John, Duke of Buckingham. *See Brutus*
Shelley, Mary Wollstonecraft. *See* Demeter and Persephone; Prometheus; *Midas*
Shelley, Percy Bysshe. *See* Aeschylus; Consolation; Demeter and Persephone; Devil; Elegy; Epic; Lucan; Midas; Ode; Petrarch; Philhellenism; Prometheus; Romanticism; Tragedy; Translation; *Antigone; Juvenal; Maenads*
Shepherd, Reginald. *See* Endymion
Sherburne, Edward. *See Bentley; Hermaphroditus*
Sheridan, Thomas. *See* Rhetoric; *Comedy*
Sheringham, Robert. *See* Greek, Ancient
Shevelove, Burt. *See* Plautus; *Cinema*
Shimshon ben Shlomo. *See* Medicine
Shirley, James. *See* Ajax; Cupid
Shirley, William. *See* Electra
Shoham, Giora. *See* Tantalus
Sibyls, **884**
Sicarii. *See Masada*
Siciliano, Angelo. *See Atlas*
Siciliano, Teodoro. *See* Etruscans
Sicily, **885**
Sidgwick, Henry. *See* Ethics; Greek, Modern Uses of Ancient
Sidney, Algernon. *See* Despotism, Oriental; Dictatorship; Founding Fathers; Revolution, French; *Brutus*
Sidney, Mary. *See Cleopatra*
Sidney, Sir Philip. *See* Arcadia; Dramatic Unities; Harmony of the Spheres; Lyric Poetry; Ovid; Pastoral; Shakespeare; Sophocles; Terence; Tragedy; *Carpe diem*
Sidonius Apollinaris. *See* Horace; Pliny the Younger; Vitruvius; *Genre*
Sienkiewicz, Henryk. *See* Novel; Popular Culture; *Nero; Petronius*
Sieyès, Emmanuel Joseph. *See* Revolution, French
Siger of Brabant. *See Philosophy*
Signorelli, Luca. *See* Color; Nudity; Rome
Signorili, Niccolò. *See* Guidebooks to Ancient Rome
Sigonio, Carlo. *See* Collecting; Forgery; *Historiography*
Sikelianos, Angelos. *See Cavafy*
Silenus. *See* Devil; Rabelais; *Midas; Symposium*
Silius Italicus. *See* Book, Printed; Epic; Virgil; *Livy*
Silvanus. *See* Pan
Silvers, Phil. *See* Plautus
Simeon I. *See* Caesar, as Political Title
Simeon Seth. *See* Medicine; *Galen*
Simichidas. *See Pastoral*
Simocattes, Theophylactus. *See* Alexander the Great
Simon, Richard. *See* Sibyls
Simonides, Constantine. *See* Cartography; Forgery
Simonides of Amorgos. *See* Anthropology
Simonides of Ceos. *See* Aesthetics; Danaë; Dulce et decorum est; Epigram; Papyrology; Sparta; Thermopylae; Ut pictura poesis; *Barbarians; Sicily*
Simplicius of Cilicia. *See* Aristotle; Epictetus; Logic; Parmenides; *Commentary; Concord, Philosophical; Diels, Hermann; Philosophy*
Simpson, John. *See* Neoclassicism
Singer, Peter. *See* Vegetarianism
Sirens, **887**
Sironi, Mario. *See* Modernism
Sismondi, Jean-Charles-Léonard Sismonde de. *See* Romanticism
Sisson, Charles Hubert. *See* Horace; Translation; *Ovid; Phaedra*
Sisyphus, **888**. *See also Cassandra; Orpheus; Tantalus*
Sitte, Camillo. *See* City Planning
Sixtus IV. *See* Collecting; Portico; Replicas; Rome; *Augustus; Etruscans*
Sixtus V. *See* Castor and Pollux; Forum; Guidebooks to Ancient Rome; Obelisk; Roman Monuments, Reuse of; Rome; Writing; *City Planning; Color; Colosseum; Inscriptions*
Skeaping, Mary. *See Cupid*
Skepticism, **889**. *See also* Ethics; Heraclitus; Socrates; *Judaism; Philosophy*
Skylax of Caryanda. *See Biography*
Slavery, **892**
Slavitt, David. *See* Ovid
Sleidan, Johann. *See* Progress and Decline
Sloane, Sir Hans. *See Museum*
Sloterdijk, Peter. *See* Cynicism
Słowacki, Juliusz. *See* Plague
Smart, Christopher. *See* Horace; Translation; *Comedy*
Smet, Bonaventura de (Vulcanius). *See Names*
Smet, Martin. *See Guidebooks to Ancient Rome; Inscriptions*
Smirke, Robert. *See* Architecture; Greek Revival
Smith, Adam. *See* Colony; Households; Progress and Decline; *Matriarchy*
Smith, Eli. *See Masada*
Smith, Elizabeth. *See* Soane
Smith, Horace. *See* Horace
Smith, James. *See* Horace
Smith, Stevie. *See Catullus*
Smith, Sir Thomas. *See* Pronunciation of Greek and Latin
Smith, Thomas Gordon. *See* Pliny the Younger
Smith, William Robertson. *See Catharsis*
Snell, Willebrord. *See* Optics
Snow, C. P. *See* Maxims
Snyder, Zack. *See Cinema*
Soane, John, **895**. *See also* Architecture; Neoclassicism; Ruins; *Caryatid; Pausanias; Piranesi; Tourism*
Soarez, Cipriano. *See* Rhetoric
Socrates, **895**. *See also* Aesthetics; Allegory; Aristophanes; Censorship; Democracy;

Socrates *(continued)*
Demon; Dialogue; East and West; Erasmus; Ethics; Ethnography; Etymology; Fathers, Church; Homosexuality; Households; Irony; Lyceum; Marsyas; Mythology; Plato; Political Theory; Presocratics; Rhetoric; Romanticism; Satire; Skepticism; Sparta; Tragedy; Writing; Xanthippe; Xenophon; *Biography; Cato the Younger; Cynicism; Divination; Epictetus; Immortality of the Soul; Philosophy; Popular Culture; Raphael; Symposium; Television*
Socrates Scholasticus. *See* Byzantium; *Armenian Hellenism*
Soderini, Francesco. *See* Roman Monuments, Reuse of
Soderini, Piero. *See* Historiography
Sodoma, Apelles. *See Names*
Sodoma, Giovanni. *See* Names; Rome
Soldani, Massimiliano. *See* Replicas
Solinus, Gaius Julius. *See* Ethnography; Geography; India; Natural History; Pliny the Elder; Wonders; *Delphin Classics; Masada*
Solomon. *See* Paganism; Palace; Writing; *Aristotle; Baalbek; Pindar; Rabelais*
Solomon, Simeon. *See Demon*
Solon. *See* Egypt; Liberty; Mythology; Revolution, French; Writing; *Anacharsis; Barbarians; Democracy*
Sombart, Werner. *See* Households
Sömmering, Samuel Thomas. *See Hippocrates*
Sondheim, Stephen. *See* Plautus
Soner, Ernst. *See* Immortality of the Soul
Sopater of Apamea. *See Anthology*
Sophianos, Nikolaos. *See* Grammar
Sophists. *See* Allegory; Genre; Mythology; Presocratics; *Hydra; Liberal Arts*
Sophocles, **897**. *See also* Achilles; Aeschylus; Ajax; Antigone; Athens; Book, Manuscript: Production; Book, Printed; Comedy; Electra; Euripides; Genre; Grotto; Heidegger; Irony; Liberty; Milton; Oedipus; Olympus; Plague; Political Theory; Racine; Renaissance; Republicanism; Romanticism; Schlegel; Thyestes; Tragedy; Translation; *Book, Manuscript: Development; Byzantium; Centaur; Cinema; Hercules; Lessing; Moschopoulos; Mycenae; Nietzsche; Ovid; Phaedra; Thomas Magister*
Sophoulis, Themistocles. *See Names*
Sophron of Syracuse. *See* Satire
Sorabji, Richard. *See Diels, Hermann*
Soranus of Ephesus. *See* Gynecology; Medicine; Nicetas Codex; Sexuality; *Hippocrates; Melancholy*
Sostratus of Nisa. *See* Etruscans
Soufflot, Jacques-Germain. *See* Architecture; Neoclassicism; Theater Architecture
Sousa, Otávio Tarquínio de. *See Names*
Southern, Richard. *See Chartres*
Southey, Robert. *See* Epic
Soutsos, Panagiotis. *See Olympic Games*
Soyinka, Wole. *See* Tragedy; *Euripides; Maenads*
Sozomen, Salminius Hermias. *See Constantine*
Spangenbergus, Johannes. *See Xenophon*
Spanheim, Ezechiel. *See Ligorio*
Spani, Prospero. *See Herm*
Spark, Muriel. *See* Nudity
Sparta, **898**
Spartacus, **901**. *See also Caesar, Julius*
Specchi, Alessandro. *See* Triumphal Arch
Speculum Romanae Magnificentiae, **902**
Speer, Albert. *See* Architecture; Neoclassicism; *Pergamon; Schinkel*
Speiss, Eric. *See Hero and Leander*
Spence, Joseph. *See Maison Carrée*
Spencer, Herbert. *See* Progress and Decline; *Anthropology*
Spencer, John. *See* Egypt
Spengler, Oswald. *See* Alexandrianism; Progress and Decline
Spenser, Edmund. *See* Adonis; Chaos; Cyclops; Daphnis; Demeter and Persephone; Elegy; Epic; Genre; Harmony of the Spheres; Helen; Hercules; Hydra; Locus Amoenus; Lyric Poetry; Ovid; Pastoral; Plato; Translation; Virgil; *Circe; Comedy; Macrobius; Martianus Capella; Ode*
Sperelli, Andrea. *See Hermaphroditus*
Speroni, Sperone. *See* Households; Scaliger, Julius Caesar
Speusippus. *See* Aristotle
Spielberg, Steven. *See* Purple
Spina, Bartolomeo della. *See* Immortality of the Soul
Spinoza, Baruch. *See* Democracy; Dictatorship; Immortality of the Soul; Metaphysics; Stoicism; *Aristotle; Atheism; Philosophy*
Spinoza, Benedict. *See* Harmony of the Spheres
Spitteler, Carl. *See Hercules*
Spitzer, Leo. *See* Ecphrasis
Spizel, Gottlieb. *See Atheism*
Split, **903**
Spolia, **903**
Spon, Jacob. *See* Elgin Marbles; *Athens; Tourism*
Sports, **905**
Sprat, Thomas. *See* Horace; *Epicurus*
Squarcione, Francesco. *See* Plaster Casts; Replicas
Squaring the Circle, **906**
Stadium, **907**
Staël, Madame de. *See* Romanticism; Sappho
Stalin, Joseph. *See* Sculpture
Stampa, Gaspara. *See Carpe diem*
Stampiglia, Silvio. *See* Opera
Stanhope, Lady Hester. *See* Palmyra
Stanislavsky, Konstantin. *See* Gesture
Stanley, Thomas. *See* Philosophy; *Anacreon; Diogenes Laertius; Fragments*
Stanyan, Temple. *See Historiography*
Starke, Marianna. *See* Grand Tour
Statius, **907**. *See also* Achilles; Alcuin; Antigone; Book, Manuscript: Development; Education; Elegy; Epic; Genre; Horace; Lucan; Poetics; Poliziano; Translation; Virgil; *Boccaccio; Chaucer; Cicero; Cinema; Commentary; Dante; Letters; Ovid; Pope, Alexander; Renaissance; Sophocles*
Stearne, John. *See* Maxims
Stebbins, Genevieve. *See* Gesture
Steele, Richard. *See* Terence
Stefan IV Dušan. *See* Caesar, as Political Title
Stefan V Dušan. *See* Caesar, as Political Title
Stehen, Jan. *See* Sacrifice in the Arts
Stein, Peter. *See* Aeschylus; *Cassandra*
Steinem, Gloria. *See Comic Books*
Steiner, George. *See* Tragedy
Steiner, Heinrich. *See* Emblem
Stemplinger, Eduard. *See* Horace
Stendhal (Marie-Henri Beyle). *See* Epic; Raphael; *Etruscans; Rome*
Stephanus. *See* Islam
Stephanus the Philosopher. *See* Astrology
Stephen I. *See* Law, Roman
Stephen II. *See* Rome
Stephen, Leslie. *See Biography*
Stephen of Byzantium. *See Hippocrates; Tzetzes*
Sterne, Laurence. *See* Comedy; Novel; Raphael; Satire; Toga; *Asterisk*
Stesichorus. *See* Daphnis; Helen; Pastoral
Steuco, Agostino. *See* Concord, Philosophical; Donation of Constantine; Water Supply; *Hermes Trismegistus*
Stevens, George. *See Cinema*
Stevens, Wallace. *See* Epic
Stevin, Simon. *See* Warfare
Stigelius, Johannes. *See Xenophon*
Stilicho, Flavius. *See Barbarians; Sibyls*
Stillingfleet, Edward. *See* Paganism; *Bentley*
Stirling, James. *See* Architecture; *Schinkel*
Stobaeus, John. *See* Anthology; *Doxography; Papyrology*
Stoddart, Alexander. *See* Neoclassicism
Stoicism, **908**. *See also* Allegory; Cato the Younger; Chrēsis; Cosmology; Egypt; Empire; Epictetus; Epicurus; Ethics; Fathers, Church; Heraclitus; Homer; Horace; Isagoge; Judaism; Liberal Arts; Logic; Philosophy; Plato; Political Theory; Presocratics; Progress and Decline; Ptolemy; Seneca the Younger; Sexuality; Skepticism; Socrates; Suicide; Vegetarianism; War, Just; Warfare; Xenophon; *Consolation; Cynicism; Martianus Capella; Nietzsche; Novel; Plutarch; Republicanism*

Stone, I. F. *See* Socrates
Stone, Oliver. *See* Alexander the Great; Novel; *Cinema*
Stoppard, Tom. *See* Satire
Strabo. *See* Aesthetics; Book, Printed; Egypt; Ethnography; Europe; Geography; Herculaneum; Herodotus; India; Lodging; Museum; Olympic Games; Parnassus; *Barbarians; Byzantium; Cartography; Eustathius; Korais; Magna Graecia; Masada; Natural History; Pegasus; Planudes*
Strachey, Lytton. *See Biography*
Stradanus. *See* Caesars, Twelve
Strategopoulos, Alexios. *See Planudes*
Strato. *See* Aristotle; Greek Anthology; *Anthology*
Strauss, Botho. *See* Dionysus
Strauss, Leo. *See* Political Theory
Strauss, Richard. *See* Ariadne; Electra; Opera; Sacrifice in the Arts; *Iphigenia; Sophocles*
Stravinksy, Igor. *See* Apollo; Gesture; Modernism; Opera; Orpheus; *Sophocles*
Strawson, Peter. *See* Metaphysics
Strebaeus, Jacobus Lodoicus. *See Households; Xenophon*
Strickland, Agnes. *See Biography*
Strickland, William. *See* Temple
Striggio, Alessandro. *See* Deus ex Machina; Orpheus
Strindberg, August. *See* Comedy
Stroll, Avrum. *See* Skepticism
Strozzi family. *See Warfare*
Struve, Burcard Gotthelf. *See* Writing
Stuart, James. *See* Architecture; Athens; Caryatid; Dilettanti, Society of; Grand Tour; Greek Revival; Neoclassicism; *Elgin Marbles; Temple; Tourism*
Stuck, Johann Wilhelm. *See Symposium*
Stückelberger, Alfred. *See Geography*
Stufa, Sigismondo della. *See Elegy*
Sturiale, Grant. *See* Amphitryon
Sturm, Johann. *See* Rhetoric; *Demosthenes*
Stymmelius, Christopher. *See Terence*
Suárez, Francisco. *See* Ethics; Metaphysics; Stoicism; *Philosophy*
Subura, Pandolfo de. *See* Roman Monuments, Reuse of
Suckling, Sir John. *See Comedy*
Suda, **912**. *See also* Writing; *Renaissance; Sports*
Suetonius, **912**. *See also* Biography; Book, Printed; Caesars, Twelve; Domus Aurea; Historiography; Horace; Nero; Numismatics; Pliny the Younger; Pornography; *Caesar, Julius; Censorship; Colosseum; Commentary; David; Machiavelli; Maecenas; Novel; Petrarch; Racine; Renaissance; Rome; Terence*
Sufi ʿAbd al-Rahman Ibn ʿUmar al-Razi, al-. *See* Astronomy
Suger, abbé, of St. Denis. *See* Architecture; Plato; Porphyry; *Spolia*
Suhrawardī, Shahāb al-Dīn, al-. *See* Aristotle; *Astrology*
Suicide, **913**
Süleyman the Magnificent. *See Byzantium; Constantinople*
Süleyman II. *See Warfare*
Sulla. *See* Dictatorship; Portraits, Reception of Ancient; Revolution, French; Rome; *Etruscans; Lyceum*
Sullivan, Louis. *See Ornament*
Sulpicius Severus. *See Historiography*
Sulpitius, Johannus. *See* Lucan
Summonte, Pietro. *See Art History*
Supple, Tim. *See Hermaphroditus*
Surgères, Hélène de. *See* Helen
Suriano, Francesco. *See* Ethnography
Surrey, Henry Howard, Earl of. *See* Translation; Virgil
Susannah. *See Nudity*
Susini, Giovanni Francesco. *See Hermaphroditus*
Svendsen, Torben Anton. *See Cinema*
Swammerdam, Jan. *See Zoology*
Sweynheym, Conrad. *See* Book, Printed; Donatus
Swift, Jonathan. *See* Ancients and Moderns; Comedy; Horace; Lucian; Parody; Satire; *Asterisk; Atlas; Brutus*
Swinburne, Algernon Charles. *See* Aeschylus; Aphrodite; Demeter and Persephone; Phaedra; Translation; *Hermaphroditus*
Swinton, John. *See* Palmyra
Sydenham, Thomas. *See* Medicine; *Hippocrates*
Sylvaticus, Matthaeus. *See* Dioscorides
Sylvester I. *See* Constantine; Donation of Constantine; Forgery; Translatio Imperii
Sylvester II. *See* Liberal Arts; Renaissance
Sylvius, Franciscus. *See Medicine*
Sylvius, Jacobus. *See* Medicine
Syme, Ronald. *See* Tacitus; *Augustus*
Symeon Metaphrastes. *See* Metaphrasis; *Atticism; Psellus*
Symmachus, Quintus Aurelius. *See* Pliny the Younger; Rome
Symmachus, Quintus Aurelius Memmius. *See* Macrobius; *Book, Manuscript: Development; Greek, Ancient*
Symonds, John Addington. *See* Homosexuality; Translation
Symposium, **915**
Syncellus, George. *See* Calendars; Writing; *Scaliger, Joseph Justus*
Syncellus, Michael. *See* Grammar
Synesius of Cyrene. *See* Comedy; *Ficino; Renaissance; Thomas Magister*
Synge, J. M. *See* Widow of Ephesus
Syriac Hellenism, **918**
Syrianus. *See* Demiurge
Syrinx. *See* Pan
Szymanowski, Karol. *See Maenads*
Tacitus and Tacitism, **920**. *See also* Augustus; Book, Manuscript: Development; Book, Printed; Commentary; Dialogue; Domus Aurea; Empire; Ethnography; Forgery; Founding Fathers; Guidebooks to Ancient Rome; Historiography; Maxims; Nero; Nietzsche; Plutarch; Political Theory; Portraits, Reception of Ancient; Progress and Decline; Revolution, French; Rhetoric; Sallust; Seneca the Younger; Thucydides; Translation; Xenophon; *Barbarians; Censorship; Cicero; Corneille, Pierre; Galileo; Letters; Libraries; Novel; Opera; Petronius; Racine; Renaissance; Rome; Rubens*
Tadda, Francesco Ferrucci del. *See* Porphyry
Tages. *See Etruscans*
Taglioni, Marie. *See* Gesture
Taillasson, Jean-Joseph. *See Hero and Leander*
Takashi. *See* Ovid
Talleyrand, Charles-Maurice de. *See* Colony
Taneyev, Sergei. *See* Aeschylus
Tantalus, **924**. *See also Orpheus; Sisyphus; Thyestes*
Tarasius. *See* Iconoclasm; *Photius; Renaissance*
Tardieu, Ambroise. *See* Censorship
Tarquin. *See* Revolution, French; Suicide; *Ovid; Popular Culture*
Tarquitius Priscus. *See Etruscans*
Tarrant, Richard. *See Seneca the Younger*
Tarrutius of Firmum, Lucius. *See* Calendars
Tasso, Bernardo. *See* Hero and Leander
Tasso, Torquato. *See* Arcadia; Ariadne; Demeter and Persephone; Dialogue; Epic; Faun; Grotto; Households; Imitation; Locus Amoenus; Lucretius; Opera; Pastoral; Sirens; Virgil; *Circe; Cyclops; Labyrinth; Milton; Sacrifice in the Arts*
Tassoni, Alessandro. *See* Comedy
Tat. *See Hermes Trismegistus*
Tatarkiewicz, Wladislaw. *See* Classical
Tate, Allen. *See* Ode; Virgil
Tate, Nahum. *See* Dido; Virgil; *Opera*
Tatian. *See* Allegory; Fathers, Church; Immortality of the Soul
Tauriscus. *See* Rome
Taurus, L. Calvenus. *See* Plutarch
Taviani, Paolo. *See Cinema*
Taviani, Vittorio. *See Cinema*
Taylor, Elizabeth. *See Cleopatra*
Taylor, John. *See Comedy*
Taylor, Thomas. *See* Ethics; Neoplatonism; *Pausanias*
Taymor, Julie. *See Cinema*
Tazze, Aldrobrandini. *See* Caesars, Twelve
Tebaldeo, Antonio. *See* Raphael
Telamon. *See Ajax*
Telchines. *See Mythology*
Telegonus. *See Circe*
Telemachus. *See Allegory; Penelope*

Telemann, Georg Philipp. *See Opera; Socrates*
Telephus. *See Papyrology*
Telesio, Bernardino. *See Galen*
Television, **924**
Tellenbach, Hubertus. *See Melancholy*
Temperament, **925**
Tempesta, Antonio. *See* Caesars, Twelve; Seven Wonders of the World
Tempier, Étienne. *See* Cosmology; Immortality of the Soul
Temple, **926**
Temple, Richard Grenville, 2nd Earl of. *See* Ruins
Temple, Sir William. *See* Ancients and Moderns; Empire; Epicurus
Temps, Jean du. *See* Calendars; Historiography
Tennemann, Wilhelm Gottlieb. *See* Pico della Mirandola; *Doxography*
Tennyson, Alfred, 1st BaronTennyson. *See* Consolation; Demeter and Persephone; Epicurus; Horace; Lucretius; Odysseus; Translation; *Cavafy; Virgil*
Tepper, Sherri. *See* Iphigenia
Terence, **929**. *See also* Aristophanes; Book, Printed; Comedy; Danaë; Donatus; Education; Fathers, Church; Gesture; Horace; Menander; Parasite; Plautus; Poetics; Popular Culture; Prosody; Renaissance; Roswitha; Shakespeare; Translation; *Augustine; Bentley; Book, Manuscript: Development; Commentary; Dacier; Dante; Jesuits; Latin Language; Lessing; Melanchthon; Poliziano*
Terentianus Maurus. *See Pastoral*
Terentius Scaurus, Quintus. *See* Horace
Tereus. *See Ovid*
Terminus. *See* Herm
Terpsichore. *See Cinema; Muses*
Terry, Philip. *See* Ovid
Terry, Quinlan. *See* Architecture
Tertullian. *See* Anacharsis; Doxography; Epicurus; Fathers, Church; Paganism; Philosophy; Seneca the Younger; Stoicism; *Chrēsis; Horace; Rhetoric; Sibyls*
Tervel of Bulgaria. *See* Caesar, as Political Title
Tesauro, Emanuele. *See* Oedipus
Testi, Fulvio. *See* Horace
Testori, Giovanni. *See* Oedipus
Tetrode, Willem Daniëlsz van. *See* Bronze; Sculpture
Teubner, **932**. *See also* Book, Printed; Loeb Classical Library
Teucer of Babylon. *See Iranian Hellenism*
Texier, Charles. *See Pergamon*
Tezi, Girolamo. *See* Barberini Faun
Thackeray, William Makepeace. *See* Horace
Thales of Miletus. *See* Diogenes Laertius; Presocratics
Thalia. *See Muses*
Thamus. *See* Writing
Thamyris. *See Muses*
Thanatos. *See* Alcestis
Theagenes of Rhegium. *See Allegory; Homer*
Theater Architecture, **933**
Theias. *See Adonis*
Theiler, Willy. *See Plato*
Themistius. *See* Immortality of the Soul; Logic; *Averroës; Baghdad Aristotelians; Book, Manuscript: Development; Concord, Philosophical; Genre; Jesuits; Judaism; Philosophy; Renaissance*
Themistocles. *See Herm; Persia*
Theobald, Lewis. *See Comedy*
Theocritus. *See* Adonis; Alexandrianism; Arcadia; Castor and Pollux; Cyclops; Daphnis; Elegy; Galatea; Genre; Judaism; Locus Amoenus; Pan; Pastoral; Pederasty; Penelope; Pindar; Poetics; Sappho; Sicily; Translation; Venice; *Cavafy; Ecphrasis; Melanchthon; Moschopoulos; Opera; Poliziano; Triclinius*
Theoderic. *See* Boethius; *Barbarians*
Theodora (wife of Emperor Theophilus). *See* Iconoclasm
Theodora, empress. *See* Lodging; Ravenna; *Censorship*
Theodora Palaeologina. *See* Book, Manuscript: Development
Theodore. *See Book, Manuscript: Development*
Theodore I Lascaris. *See Atticism*
Theodoret of Cyrrhus. *See Doxography*
Theodoretus. *See* Nudity
Theodoric of Cervia. *See* Veterinary Medicine
Theodoric the Great. *See* Greek, Ancient; Palace; Ravenna; Rome; *Guidebooks to Ancient Rome*
Theodorus of Cyrene. *See Atheism*
Theodorus of Samos. *See Art History*
Theodosian Code. *See* Renaissance
Theodosius I. *See* East and West; Olympia; Oracles; Purple; Renaissance; Suda; Warfare; *Athens; Barbarians; Mithras; Obelisk*
Theodosius II. *See* East and West; *Book, Manuscript: Development*
Theodosius of Alexandria. *See* Grammar
Theodosius of Tripoli. *See Judaism*
Theodotion. *See Asterisk*
Theodotus. *See Judaism*
Theodulus. *See* Pastoral
Theognis of Megara. *See* Mythology; *Nietzsche*
Theomnestus. *See* Veterinary Medicine
Theon, Aelius. *See Armenian Hellenism*
Theon of Alexandria. *See* Ptolemy; *Astronomy; Diophantus*
Theon of Smyrna. *See* Astronomy
Theophilus, emperor. *See* Iconoclasm
Theophilus of Antioch. *See* Fathers, Church; *Sibyls*
Theophilus of Edessa. *See* Astrology; Medicine
Theophilus Presbyter. *See* Art History; Glass
Theophilus Protospathario. *See* Medicine
Theophrastus. *See* Aristotle; Atheism; Botany; Divination; Doxography; Etruscans; Logic; Melancholy; Meteorology; Museum; Natural History; Philosophy; Poetics; Rhetoric; Seven Sages of Rome; Vegetarianism; *Art History; Averroës; Byzantium; Casaubon; Diels, Hermann; Korais*
Theophylactus of Ohrid. *See Atticism*
Theopompus of Chios. *See Etruscans; Historiography*
Thermopylae, **934**
Theron. *See* Pindar
Thersites. *See Ajax*
Theseus. *See* Amazons; Ariadne; Novel; Romance, Medieval; *Labyrinth; Machiavelli; Parody; Phaedra; Popular Culture; Sisyphus*
Thetis. *See* Ariadne; *Popular Culture*
Theuth. *See* Writing; *Philosophy*
Thevet, André. *See* Ethnography
Thierry of Chartres. *See* Chartres; Cosmology; Neoplatonism; Plato; *Boethius*
Thomas (apostle) (Didymus Judas Thomas). *See* India; Papyrology
Thomas, Kristin Scott. *See Historiography*
Thomas Aquinas. *See* Alchemy; Automata; Chaos; Cicero; Demon; Divination; Ethics; Ficino; Fortune; Immortality of the Soul; Liberal Arts; Logic; Magic; Metaphysics; Mnemonics; Paganism; Philosophy; Political Theory; Renaissance; Seneca the Younger; Skepticism; Stoicism; Suicide; War, Just; *Aristotle; Averroës; Boccaccio; Boethius; Censorship; Juvenal; Latin and the Professions; Names; Symposium*
Thomas Magister, **934**. *See also* Atticism; Byzantium; Triclinius
Thomas of Cantimpré. *See* Zoology
Thomas of Celano. *See* Sibyls
Thomon, Thomas de. *See* Temple
Thompson, Francis. *See Maenads*
Thompson, Homer. *See Names*
Thomson, Alexander. *See* Architecture
Thomson, George. *See Matriarchy*
Thomson, James. *See* Virgil
Thon, Konstantin. *See* Praeneste
Thoreau, Henry David. *See* Xenophon; *Lyceum*
Thorvaldsen, Bertel. *See* Neoclassicism; Sculpture; *Ganymede; Maenads*
Thoth. *See Hermes Trismegistus*
Thou, Jacques-Auguste de. *See Budé; Thucydides*
Thrasyllus of Mendes. *See* Astrology
Thucydides, **935**. *See also* Antiquarianism; Book, Manuscript: Production; Book,

Printed; Commentary; Ethnography; Forgery; Herm; Herodotus; Historiography; Judaism; Mythology; Plague; Political Theory; Renaissance; Sallust; Schlegel; Sicily; Tacitus; Tzetzes; Warfare; Xenophon; *Athens; Atticism; Cities, Praise of; Herm; Machiavelli; Melanchthon; Photius; Valla*
Thyestes, **937**
Tiberius. *See* Astrology; Censorship; Grotto; Portraits, Reception of Ancient; Tacitus; *Names*
Tiberius II Constantinus. *See* Constantine
Tibullus, Albius. *See* Book, Printed; Homosexuality; Translation; *Catullus; Commentary; Lachmann; Pope, Alexander; Renaissance; Scaliger, Joseph Justus*
Tieck, Ludwig. *See* Romanticism; *Melancholy*
Tiedemann, Dietrich. *See Hermes Trismegistus*
Tiepolo, Giambattista. *See* Aeneas; Aphrodite; Ariadne; Maecenas; Phaethon; Sacrifice in the Arts; *Achilles; Cleopatra; Hercules; Pegasus; Virgil*
Tiepolo, Giandomenico. *See* Centaur
Tigranes the Great. *See* Armenian Hellenism
Timaeus of Taormina. *See* Calendars; Dido
Timanthes of Cythnus. *See* Rome
Timoneda, Juan de. *See* Plautus
Timotheos. *See Mausoleum*
Tintoretto (Jacopo Robusti). *See* Arachne; Ariadne; Demeter and Persephone; Dionysus; History Painting; Ornament; Venice; *Herm*
Tiresias. *See Lucian*
Tiro, Marcus Tullius. *See Letters*
Tischbein, Johann Heinrich, the Older. *See* Galatea; Sacrifice in the Arts; *Achilles*
Tischendorf, Konstantin von. *See* Forgery
Tissot, Samuel-Auguste. *See* Censorship; Sexuality
Titans. *See* Romanticism; *Dionysus; Hesiod; Mythology*
Titi, Placido. *See Astrology*
Titian (Tiziano Vecelli). *See* Aphrodite; Arachne; Ariadne; Caesars, Twelve; Color; Cupid; Danaë; Faun; History Painting; Pornography; Sisyphus; Tantalus; Venice; *Actaeon; Adonis; Art History; Janus; Laocoön; Maenads; Modernism; Picasso*
Titius, Johann. *See Music*
Titus Flavius Vespasianus. *See* Roman Monuments, Reuse of; Rome; *Colosseum; Corneille, Pierre; Papyrology*
Tityrus. *See* Pastoral; *Poetics*
Tityus. *See Sisyphus; Tantalus*
Tizio, Sigismondo. *See Etruscans*
Tocqueville, Alexis de. *See* Democracy; Despotism, Oriental; Law, Roman; *Aristocracy; Colony*
Toga, **937**
Toland, John. *See* Livy
Tolkien, J. R. R. *See Ganymede*
Tolomei, Claudio. *See* Grotto
Tolstoy, Leo. *See* Education; Epic; *Latin Language*
Tomasi, Henri. *See Atlantis*
Tomasi di Lampedusa, Giuseppe. *See* Sicily
Tomlin, Lily. *See Plautus*
Tommasi, Francesco. *See* Households
Tonson, Jacob. *See* Translation
Topos, **938**
Torlonia collection. *See Sarcophagi*
Torre, Alfonso de la. *See* Martianus Capella
Torrejón, Tomás de. *See Adonis*
Toscanella, Orazio. *See* Education
Tostado, Alfonso. *See* Poetics
Toulmin, Stephen E. *See* Rhetoric
Tourism and Travel, **939**
Tournefort, Joseph Pitton de. *See Zoology*
Toussaint Louverture. *See* Spartacus
Tower of the Winds. *See* Architecture
Townley, Charles. *See* Grand Tour; *Collecting*
Toynbee, Arnold. *See* Hannibal; Progress and Decline
Traetta, Tomaso. *See* Iphigenia; Sacrifice in the Arts
Tragedy and Tragic, **942**
Trajan. *See* Forum; Names; Numismatics; Panegyric; Pliny the Younger; Rome; Suetonius; *Caesars, Twelve; Color; Mirabilia Urbis; Roman Monuments, Reuse of; Rome*
Trajan Decius. *See Palace*
Tramezzino, Michele. *See* Guidebooks to Ancient Rome; *Speculum Romanae Magnificentiae*
Translatio Imperii, **947**
Translation, **948**
Trapp, Joseph Burney. *See Warburg*
Traube, Ludwig. *See* Book, Manuscript: Development
Traversari, Ambrogio. *See* Cynicism; Philosophy; Pythagoras; *Diogenes Laertius*
Travis, Roy. *See Maenads*
Trenchard, John. *See Founding Fathers*
Trendelenburg, Friedrich Adolf. *See Aristotle*
Trevelyan, George Otto. *See* Horace
Trevet, Nicolas. *See* Historiography; Seneca the Younger
Trevisani, Francesco. *See* Galatea
Trevisio, Antonio. *See* Water Supply
Triclines, Nicholas. *See* Triclinius
Triclinius, Demetrius, **953**. *See also* Byzantium; Renaissance; Thomas Magister; *Aristophanes; Book, Manuscript: Development*
Tridentone, Antonio. *See* Book, Printed
Trier, Lars von. *See* Television; *Cinema*
Trincavella, Vittorio. *See* Medicine
Trippault, Léon. *See* Greek, Ancient
Triptolemus. *See Poetics*
Trissino, Gian Giorgio. *See* Palladio; Tragedy; *Circe*
Trithemius, John. *See* Book, Manuscript: Development; Renaissance
Triton. *See Neptune*
Tritonius, Petrus. *See Horace*
Triumphal Arch, **954**
Triumphal Bridge, **955**
Trivet, Nicholas. *See* Orpheus; Philosophy
Troeltsch, Ernst. *See* Historicism
Troilus, **956**. *See also* Romance, Medieval
Trojan War. *See Helen; Hero*
Troost, Paul. *See* Neoclassicism
Troy. *See* Romance, Medieval; *Popular Culture; Television*
Trumbo, Dalton. *See Spartacus*
Tryon, Thomas. *See* Maxims
Tsountas, Christos. *See* Mycenae
Tsvetaeva, Marina. *See* Phaedra
Tuditanus, Caius Sempronius. *See Annius of Viterbo*
Tullus Hostilius. *See Corneille, Pierre*
Turberville, George. *See* Dido
Turgenev, Ivan. *See* Aeneas
Turgot, Anne-Robert-Jacques. *See* Colony; Progress and Decline
Turnèbe, Odet de. *See Comedy*
Turnebus, Adrian (Adrien Turnèbe). *See Education; Hermes Trismegistus; Philo; Scaliger, Joseph Justus*
Turner, J. M. W. *See* Cyclops; Dido; *Tourism; Virgil*
Turner, William. *See* Natural History
Turnus. *See* Aeneas; Ajax; Epic; Virgil
Tūsī, Naṣīr al-Dīn al-. *See* Astronomy; Ptolemy
Tüzün, Ferit. *See Midas*
Twain, Mark. *See* Aphrodite; Comedy; Nudity; Pornography; *Rome*
Twombly, Cy. *See Hero and Leander*
Tyard, Pontus de. *See* Pléiade
Tyche. *See* Fortune
Tydeus. *See* Statius
Tylor, Edward Burnett. *See* Mythology; *Magic*
Tyndale, William. *See* Immortality of the Soul
Tyndareus. *See* Castor and Pollux; *Leda*
Typhon. *See* Paganism
Tyrtaeus. *See* Dulce et decorum est
Tytler, Alexander. *See* Translation
Tzavellas, George. *See* Cinema
Tzetzes, John, **957**. *See also* Allegory; Archimedes; Aristophanes; Homer; Renaissance; Xenophon; *Book, Manuscript: Development; Byzantium; Hippocrates; Lucian*

Uc Faidit. *See* Donatus
Udall, Nicholas. *See* Comedy; Parasite; Terence
Uderzo, Albert. *See* Popular Culture
Udine, Hercole. *See* Cupid

Uggeri, Angelo. *See Forum*
Ugo de Porta Ravennate. *See Law, Roman*
Ugonio, Pompeo. *See* Guidebooks to Ancient Rome
Uguccione of Pisa. *See* Grammar
Ulfila. *See* Writing
Ullmann, Viktor. *See Atlantis*
Ulpian. *See* Empire; Purple; Rhōmaioi
Ulrichs, Karl Heinrich. *See Homosexuality*
Underwood, John. *See Horace*
'Unsuri, Abul Qasim Hasam. *See* Persia
Unt, Mati. *See* Tantalus
Updike, John. *See Centaur*
Upton, John. *See* Epictetus
Urania. *See* Paganism; *Muses*
Uranios. *See* Forgery
Urban VIII. *See* Astrology; Barberini Faun; Pantheon; Paper Museum; Rome
Urceo, Antonio Cortesi. *See Education*
Urfé, Honoré d'. *See* Pastoral
Usener, Hermann. *See* Diogenes Laertius; *Diels, Hermann; Fathers, Church*
Ustinov, Peter. *See Nero*
Uther Pendragon. *See* Amphitryon
Ut pictura poesis, **958**

Vaballathus. *See* Palmyra
Vacarius, Roger. *See Law, Roman*
Vair, Guillaume du. *See* Epictetus
Valadés, Diego de. *See* Atrium
Valadier, Giuseppe. *See* Obelisk; Triumphal Arch; *Neoclassicism*
Valens, Flavius Julius. *See Barbarians*
Valentinus. *See* Fathers, Church
Valeriano, Pierio. *See* Commentary; Raphael; *Hieroglyphs*
Valerius Flaccus, Gaius. *See* Epic; *Olympus*
Valerius Maximus. *See* Cynicism; Education; Historiography; *Petrarch; Renaissance*
Valéry, Paul. *See* Alexandrianism; Hydra; Modernism; Narcissus; Parmenides; *Virgil*
Valla, Giorgio. *See* Botany; Music; Poetics; Tragedy; Translation; *Automata; Medicine*
Valla, Lorenzo, **959**. *See also* Ancients and Moderns; Constantine; Dialectic; Donation of Constantine; Epicurus; Erasmus; Etruscans; Forgery; Grammar; Greek, Ancient; Herodotus; Historiography; Homer; Humanism; Letters; Livy; Philosophy; Professionalization of Classics; Progress and Decline; Renaissance; Rhetoric; Sallust; Thucydides; *Boethius; Budé; Calendars; Cities, Praise of; Commentary; Education; Ethnography; Petrarch; Philosophy; Tacitus*
Valle, Andrea della. *See Numismatics*
Valletta, Giuseppe. *See Symposium*
Valmarana, Giustino. *See Sacrifice in the Arts*
Valpy, Abraham John. *See* Book, Printed; *Metaphrasis*
Vanbrugh, John. *See* Architecture; Atrium; Comedy; Ruins
Van Dyck, Anthony. *See* Adonis; *Achilles; Apuleius*
Vannucci, Atto. *See Etruscans*
Vanvitelli, Luigi. *See* Forum; *Adam, Robert; Herm*
Varchi, Benedetto. *See* Aesthetics; *Art History; Sallust*
Varen, Bernhard. *See* Geography
Varro, Marcus Terentius. *See* Antiquarianism; Atrium; Botany; Calendars; Divination; Etymology; Forgery; Grammar; Guidebooks to Ancient Rome; Historiography; Humanism; Liberal Arts; Prosody; Satire; Veterinary Medicine; *Book, Manuscript: Development; Cicero; City Planning; Commentary; Fragments; Horace; Isagoge; Martianus Capella; Museum; Scaliger, Joseph Justus; Sibyls; Suetonius*
Varuna. *See Mithras*
Vasa, Gustavus. *See* Warfare
Vasari, Giorgio. *See* Aesthetics; Art History; Ecphrasis; Etruscans; Imitation; Paganism; Penelope; Porphyry; Progress and Decline; Raphael; Renaissance; Rome; Ruins; Sculpture; Spolia; Warfare; *Bellori; Belvedere Torso; Biography; Cleopatra; Michelangelo; Nudity*
Vasilevič, Ivan. *See* Caesar, as Political Title
Vaughn, Henry. *See Juvenal*
Vavasseur, François. *See Petronius*
Vecellio, Cesare. *See* Toga
Veen, Otto van. *See* Rubens; *Socrates*
Vega, Lope de. *See* Arcadia; Comedy; Phaedra; Plautus
Vegetarianism, **960**
Vegetius Renatus, Flavius. *See* Veterinary Medicine; Warfare
Vegio, Maffeo. *See* Aeneas; Epic; Neo-Latin; Petrarch; Virgil
Velázquez, Diego. *See* Aphrodite; Arachne; Cynicism; Midas
Veldeke, Heinrich von. *See* Aeneas; Cupid; Virgil
Velleius Paterculus, Marcus. *See* Book, Printed; Progress and Decline; *Commentary; Nudity*
Venette, Nicholas de. *See* Sexuality
Veneziano, Agostino. *See* Raphael
Venice, **961**. *See also* Alexandria; Constitution, Mixed
Ventris, Michael. *See* Mycenae
Venturi, Robert. *See* Architecture; *Ornament*
Venus de' Medici. *See Fashion*
Venus de Milo, **962**. *See* Aphrodite; *Fashion*
Venus Genetrix. *See* Rome
Venus of Cnidus. *See* Neoclassicism; Nudity; Pornography; Renaissance; Sculpture; Sexuality; Tourism
Vercingetorix. *See Astérix; Warfare*
Verdi, Giuseppe. *See* Egypt; Opera
Verdonck, Rumoldus. *See* Rubens
Vergerio, Pier Paolo. *See* Petrarch; Renaissance; Sculpture; Terence
Vergil, Polydore. *See* Raphael; Writing
Verhaeren, Émile. *See* Hercules
Verino, Ugolino. *See* Etruscans
Verlaine, Paul. *See Orpheus; Parnassus*
Vernant, Jean-Pierre. *See* Parmenides
Verne, Jules. *See Atlantis*
Verney, Pierre. *See Hippocrates*
Vernia, Nicoletto. *See* Immortality of the Soul; *Aristotle; Philosophy*
Veroli, Giovanni Sulpicio da. *See* Vitruvius
Veronese, Paolo. *See* Aphrodite; Demeter and Persephone; Venice; *Hercules; Nudity*
Verres, Gaius. *See Barbarians; Cicero*
Verri, Alessandro. *See* Sappho
Verrocchio, Andrea del. *See* Bronze
Vertumnus. *See Etruscans*
Verus, Lucius. *See Portraits, Reception of Ancient*
Vesalius, Andreas. *See* Galen; Medicine; Melanchthon; Progress and Decline; *Neo-Latin; Pliny the Elder*
Vespasian. *See* Caesar, Julius; Numismatics; Roman Monuments, Reuse of; Seven Sages of Rome; *Antiquarianism; Colosseum*
Vespucci, Amerigo. *See* India
Vespucci, Giorgio. *See Terence*
Vestris, Auguste. *See Cupid*
Veterinary Medicine, **963**
Vettius Valens. *See* Astrology; *Iranian Hellenism*
Vettori, Francesco. *See* Academy; Book, Printed; *Machiavelli*
Vettori, Piero (Petrus Victorius). *See* Aeschylus; Commentary; Greek, Ancient; *Aristophanes*
Veyne, Paul. *See* Sexuality
Viau, Théophile de. *See Lucretius*
Vicentino, Nicola. *See* Music
Vico, Enea. *See* Numismatics; *Cameos*
Vico, Giambattista, **964**. *See also* Calendars; Cato the Younger; Ethnography; Historiography; Liberty; Progress and Decline; Rhetoric; Schlegel; Wolf, Friedrich August; Writing; Xenophon; *Atheism*
Victoria, Queen. *See* Empire; Pompeii; Purple
Victorinus, Gaius Marius. *See* Neoplatonism; Prosody; Rhetoric; *Judaism; Labyrinth*
Victorius of Aquitaine. *See* Liberal Arts
Vida, Girolamo. *See* Epic; Imitation
Vidal, Gore. *See* Novel; *Cinema; Julian*
Vidal, Paul Antonin. *See* Troilus
Vidius, Vidus. *See* Medicine
Vien, Joseph-Marie. *See Cupid; David*
Vienne, Philibert de. *See Comedy*
Viète, François. *See* Archimedes; Ptolemy

Vigée-Lebrun, Marie Louise Élisabeth. *See Maenads*
Vigion, A. P. *See* Temple
Vignay, Jean de. *See Warfare*
Vignola, Giacomo Barozzi da. *See* Architecture; Portico; Temple; Vitruvius; *Herm; Neoclassicism; Ornament*
Vikelas, Demetrios. *See Olympic Games*
Villani, Filippo. *See* Renaissance; *Art History*
Villani, Giovanni. *See* City Planning; Etruscans
Villani, Matteo. *See Astrology*
Villard de Honnecourt. *See* Liberal Arts
Villena, Enrique de. *See* Hercules; Poetics
Villey, Pierre. *See Montaigne*
Villiers, George. *See Comedy*
Vincent of Beauvais. *See* Botany; Cicero; Historiography; Households; Paganism; Virgil; Vitruvius; Writing; *Hippocrates; Isidore; Macrobius*
Vionnet, Madeleine. *See Fashion*
Viperano, Giovanni Antonio. *See Catharsis*
Virgil, **965**. *See also* Achilles; Aeneas; Ajax; Alcuin; Alexandrianism; Allegory; Ancients and Moderns; Arcadia; Ariadne; Atlas; Book, Manuscript: Development; Book, Manuscript: Production; Book, Printed; Caesar, as Political Title; Caesar, Julius; Cassandra; Catullus; Cento; Chaucer; Circe; Cleopatra; Collecting; Comedy; Comic Books; Commentary; Cupid; Cyclops; Dante; Daphnis; Dido; Divination; Donatus; East and West; Ecphrasis; Education; Elegy; Empire; Epic; Europe; Fathers, Church; Galatea; Galileo; Ganymede; Genre; Grotto; Guidebooks to Ancient Rome; Helen; Hercules; Hero and Leander; Historiography; Homer; Homosexuality; Horace; Imitation; Labyrinth; Laocoön; Locus Amoenus; Lucretius; Machiavelli; Macrobius; Maecenas; Milton; Mirabilia Urbis; Neo-Latin; Odysseus; Orpheus; Paganism; Parnassus; Parody; Pastoral; Petrarch; Plague; Plato; Poetics; Poliziano; Pope, Alexander; Popular Culture; Portraits, Reception of Ancient; Progress and Decline; Rabelais; Romance, Medieval; Rome; Ronsard; Roswitha; Scaliger, Julius Caesar; Seven Sages of Rome; Sibyls; Sicily; Statius; Suicide; Translation; Troilus; Venice; Warfare; *Astronomy; Augustine; Augustus; Boccaccio; Calendars; Cato the Younger; Censorship; Christine de Pizan; Cinema; David; Epicurus; Erasmus; Etymology; Fascism; Heyne; Jesuits; Juvenal; Libraries; Lyric Poetry; Mars; Melanchthon; Metaphrasis; Mirabilia Urbis; Montaigne; Muses; Neptune; Opera; Ovid; Paper Museum; Philosophy; Pléiade; Racine; Renaissance; Rubens; Sacrifice in the Arts; Scaliger, Joseph Justus; Terence; Tourism*
Virgilio, Giovanni del. *See* Pastoral
Virgilius, Marcellus. *See Dioscorides*
Virunio, Pontico. *See* Letters
Vischer family. *See* Bronze
Visconti, Ennio Quirino. *See* Etruscans; Portraits, Reception of Ancient; Winckelmann
Visconti, Filippo Maria. *See* Caesars, Twelve
Visconti family. *See Humanism*
Visscher, Roemer. *See* Emblem
Vitali, Girolamo. *See Astrology*
Vitelli, Lorenzo. *See Etruscans*
Vitellius, Aullus. *See* Portraits, Reception of Ancient; Revolution, French
Vitoria, Francisco de. *See* War, Just; *Philosophy*
Vitruvius and the Classical Orders, **969**. *See also* Aesthetics; Alberti; Architecture; Art History; Atrium; Caryatid; Etruscans; Forum; Greek Revival; Hypnerotomachia Poliphili; Liberal Arts; Mars; Ornament; Palace; Palladio; Piranesi; Plato; Pompeii; Purple; Raphael; Replicas; Roman Monuments, Reuse of; Rome; Sculpture; Temple; Theater Architecture; Water Supply; *Atlas; Augustus; Baths; City Planning; Fascism; Guidebooks to Ancient Rome; Museum; Nudity; Paestum; Renaissance*
Vitry, Jacques de. *See* Seven Sages of Rome
Vittone, Bernardo Antonio. *See Ornament*
Vittoria, Alessandro. *See* Venice
Vittorino da Feltre (Vittorino Ramboldini). *See* Education; Greek, Ancient; Music; *Mercuriale; Petrarch*
Vittorio Emanuele II. *See* Praeneste
Vivaldi, Antonio. *See* Sacrifice in the Arts; *Opera*
Vives, Juan Luis. *See* Greek, Ancient; Herodotus; Historiography; Households; Letters; Penelope; Petrarch; Philosophy; *Atlas; Macrobius*
Viviani, Vincenzo. *See* Galileo
Vivien, Renée. *See Maenads*
Vladimir, Saint. *See* Caesar, as Political Title
Vlasto, Gregory. *See* Socrates
Vlastos, Nicolaos. *See Medicine*
Vlijmen, Jan van. *See Thyestes*
Voigt, Georg. *See* Petrarch; Renaissance
Volcanoes, **971**
Volfius, Jacobus Jacobaeus. *See* Poetics
Volkmann, Richard. *See Doxography*
Volney, Constantin François. *See* Romanticism
Volpato, Giovanni. *See* Barberini Faun
Volpi, Giuseppe. *See Ligorio*
Volsungs. *See Novel*
Voltaire. *See* Constantine; Cosmology; Dialogue; Empire; Etymology; Europe; Horace; Humanism; Law, Roman; Lucian; Oedipus; Philhellenism; Pindar; Progress and Decline; Prometheus; Renaissance; Satire; Skepticism; Split; Virgil; Widow of Ephesus; *Art History; Brutus; Nudity; Sallust; Sophocles; Thyestes*
Volterra, Daniele da. *See Nudity*
Vos, Marten de. *See* Seven Wonders of the World
Voss, Johann Heinrich. *See* Translation; *Achilles*
Vossius, Gerardus Joannes. *See* Fragments; Paganism; Rhetoric; *Demon; Diogenes Laertius; Heyne*
Vossius, Isaac. *See* Prosody; Sibyls; *Bentley*
Voulgaris, Eugenios. *See* Virgil
Vries, Adriaen de. *See* Bronze
Vulcan. *See* Volcanoes; *Mars*
Vussinus. *See* Vitruvius

Wackernagel, Jacob. *See* Greek, Ancient; Nietzsche
Wagner, Richard. *See* Aeschylus; Alcestis; Aphrodite; Dionysus; Grotto; Music; Nietzsche; Opera; Sirens; Tragedy; *Comedy; Greek, Modern Uses of Ancient; Iphigenia*
Waiblinger, Wilhelm. *See* Venus de Milo
Wailly, Charles De. *See Neoclassicism*
Walafrid Strabo. *See Renaissance*
Walcott, Derek. *See* Achilles; Cyclops; Epic; Helen; Ovid; Penelope; *Lyric Poetry*
Waldseemüller, Martin. *See* Cartography
Walker, Alice. *See* Purple
Wallace, Lew. *See* Novel; Popular Culture
Wallenstein, Albrecht von. *See Liberal Arts*
Waller, Edmund. *See Carpe diem*
Wallis, John. *See* Academy; Music; Squaring the Circle
Walpole, Horace. *See Dilettanti, Society of*
Walpole, Sir Robert. *See* Progress and Decline
Walter, Thomas Ustick. *See* Architecture; Temple
Walter of Châtillon. *See* Genre; Virgil
Walton, Izaak. *See Biography*
Walton, William. *See* Troilus
Walz, Christian. *See* Rhetoric
Wandschneider, Wilhelm. *See* Nudity
War, Just, **972**
Warburg, Aby, **973**. *See also* Magic; Paganism; Sarcophagi
Warburton, William. *See* Egypt
Ward, Artemus (Charles Farrar Browne). *See* Comedy
Ward, John. *See* Rhetoric
Ward, John Quincy Adams. *See Belvedere Torso*
Ware, William. *See* Palmyra
Warfare, **974**
Warmington, Eric Herbert. *See* Martial
Warner, Deborah. *See* Sophocles
Warren, Joseph. *See* Founding Fathers; *Cicero*
Warren, Rosanna. *See Virgil*
Warton, Joseph. *See* Virgil

Warton, Thomas. *See* Translation
Wase, Christopher. *See* Sophocles
Washington, George. *See* Founding Fathers; Sculpture; Slavery; *Cato the Younger; Toga*
Waterhouse, John William. *See* Circe; Penelope
Water Supply, 981
Watson, Thomas. *See* Tragedy
Watteau, Jean-Antoine. *See Modernism*
Watts, George Frederick. *See Elgin Marbles; Endymion*
Wauquelin, Jean. *See* Alexander the Great
Weaver, John. *See Mime*
Webb, John. *See* Theater Architecture
Webbe, Joseph. *See* Terence
Webber, Andrew Lloyd. *See Comedy*
Weber, Bruce. *See Fashion*
Weber, Karl. *See* Herculaneum; Pompeii
Weber, Max. *See* Antiquarianism; Historicism; Households; *Historiography*
Webster, John. *See* Tragedy
Weddell, William. *See* Grand Tour
Wedderburn, Alexander D. *See* Households
Wedekind, Frank. *See* Pandora; *Hercules*
Wedgwood, Josiah. *See* Glass; Grand Tour; Neoclassicism; *Faun*
Weill, Kurt. *See Cinema*
Weir, Peter. *See Horace*
Weishaupt, Adam. *See* Spartacus
Weiss, Peter. *See* Pergamon
Weisse, Christian Felix. *See Thyestes*
Welcker, Friedrich. *See* Matriarchy
Weller, Hermann. *See* Neo-Latin
Welles, Orson. *See Caesar, as Political Title*
Wellesz, Egon. *See Maenads*
Wellington, Arthur Wellesley, Duke of. *See* Castor and Pollux
Welser, Markus. *See Cartography*
Welty, Eudora. *See* Apuleius
Werfel, Franz. *See Cassandra*
West, Benjamin. *See* History Painting; Neoclassicism; Pompeii; Toga; *Elgin Marbles*
West, Gilbert. *See* Translation
West, Martin Litchfield. *See* East and West; Prosody
Westmacott, Richard. *See* Castor and Pollux; Toga
Wharton, Edith. *See Rome*
Whately, Thomas. *See* Ruins
Whately, William. *See* Epicurus
Wheler, George. *See* Elgin Marbles; Parthenon; *Athens; Tourism*
Whewell, William. *See* Ethics
Whistler, James Abbott McNeill. *See* Elgin Marbles
Whiston, William. *See* Sibyls
Whitehead, William. *See Euripides*
Whitelock, John. *See* Education
Whitman, Walt. *See* Epic; Lyric Poetry
Whitney, Geoffrey. *See Hercules*
Wibald of Corvey. *See Book, Manuscript: Development; Martianus Capella*
Widow of Ephesus, 982
Wiedewelt, Johannes. *See* Sculpture
Wiegand, Theodor. *See Baalbek*
Wieland, Christoph Martin. *See* Alcestis; Dialogue; Dionysus; Diotima; Lucian; Novel; Satire; Xenophon
Wiesel, Elie. *See* Consolation
Wijnants, Etienne (Pighius). *See Etruscans*
Wikström, Emil. *See Herm*
Wilamowitz-Moellendorff, Ulrich von, 983. *See also* Epigraphy; Herodotus; Historiography; Prosody; *Democracy; Diels, Hermann; Galen; Lachmann; Nietzsche; Pausanias*
Wilbur, Richard. *See* Horace; *Phaedra*
Wilde, Oscar. *See* Alexandrianism; Anthology; Comedy; Homosexuality; Maxims; *Cavafy; Terence*
Wilder, Thornton. *See* Novel; Terence; *Centaur*
Wilhelm II. *See* Caesar, as Political Title; *Baalbek; Greek, Modern Uses of Ancient*
Wiligelmo. *See* Nudity
Wilkes, John. *See* Founding Fathers
Willehad of Bremen. *See* Translatio Imperii
William I (the Conqueror). *See* Tacitus; *Ovid*
William III. *See* Founding Fathers
William IV. *See* Soane
William Louis, Count of Nassau-Dillenburg. *See* Warfare
William of Auvergne. *See* Immortality of the Soul; *Philosophy*
William of Conches. *See* Chartres; Cosmology; Grammar; Macrobius; Neoplatonism; Orpheus; Pythagoras; Temperament; *Boethius*
William of Malmesbury. *See Biography; Livy*
William of Moerbeke. *See* Archimedes; Greek, Ancient; Philosophy; Rhetoric; Tragedy; Zoology
William of Ockham. *See* Immortality of the Soul; Liberal Arts; Logic; Philosophy
William of Orange. *See* Architecture
Williams, Bernard. *See* Ethics; Philosophy
Williams, Esther. *See* Slavery
Williams, Jonathan. *See Carpe diem*
Williams, Tennessee. *See Orpheus*
Williams, William Carlos. *See* Demeter and Persephone
Wills, Richard. *See* Genre
Wilson, James. *See* Colony; Democracy
Wilson, Nigel. *See Commentary*
Wilson, Robert. *See Medea*
Wimpheling, Jacob. *See* Tacitus
Winckelmann, Johann Joachim, 984. *See also* Aesthetics; Antiquarianism; Apollo; Apollo Belvedere; Art History; Athens; Barberini Faun; Belvedere Torso; Classical; Collecting; Color; Etruscans; Goethe; Greek, Ancient; Greek Revival; Gymnasium; Homosexuality; Humanism; Inscriptions; Neoclassicism; Nietzsche; Nudity; Olympia; Paestum; Paganism; Parnassus; Pausanias; Pergamon; Philhellenism; Philosophy; Pindar; Piranesi; Pompeii; Portraits, Reception of Ancient; Professionalization of Classics; Progress and Decline; Raphael; Replicas; Romanticism; Rome; Schlegel; Sculpture; Sexuality; Sicily; Temple; Toga; Wilamowitz; *Burckhardt; Cameos; Heyne; Laocoön; Lessing; Magna Graecia; Maison Carrée; Mercuriale*
Windscheid, Bernhard. *See Law, Roman*
Wise, Herbert. *See Television*
Wise, Robert. *See Cinema*
Witelo, Erazmus Ciolek. *See* Optics; Ptolemy
Wittgenstein, Ludwig. *See* Metaphysics; Skepticism
Wladislaus Sigismund. *See Warfare*
Wodehouse, P. G. *See* Comedy
Wolf, Christa. *See* Achilles; Epic; Hero; Troilus; *Cassandra; Medea*
Wolf, Friedrich August, 987. *See also* Aristophanes; Classical; Commentary; Fragments; Historiography; Homer; Papyrology; Professionalization of Classics; Romanticism; *Achilles; Böckh; Education; Greek, Ancient; Heyne*
Wolf, Hieronymus. *See Byzantium*
Wolf, Winfried. *See* Troilus
Wolff, Christian. *See Metaphysics; Philosophy*
Wonders, 989
Woo, John. *See* Castor and Pollux
Wood, John. *See Endymion*
Wood, Robert. *See* Romanticism; Ruins; Wolf, Friedrich August; *Baalbek; Heyne; Palmyra; Temple; Tourism*
Woodville, Elisabeth. *See Genre*
Woolf, Virginia. *See* Greek, Ancient; Greek, Modern Uses of Ancient; Novel; *Ovid*
Wordsworth, William. *See* Elegy; Epic; Horace; Lucretius; Lyric Poetry; Ode; Pastoral; Romanticism; Troilus; Virgil; *Euripides; Juvenal*
Worm, Ole (Olaus). *See* Antiquarianism; Wonders
Wotton, Edward. *See* Zoology
Wotton, William. *See* Philosophy; *Ancients and Moderns*
Woverius, Jan. *See Rubens*
Wren, Christopher. *See* Architecture; Palace; Ruins; Theater Architecture; *Herm; Mausoleum*
Wright, Frank Lloyd. *See* Architecture; City Planning
Wright, Georg Henrik von. *See* Ethics
Wright, Joseph. *See* Penelope
Wright, Thomas. *See* Ruins
Writing, 990
Wyatt, James. *See* Neoclassicism; *Adam, Robert*

Wyatt, Thomas. *See* Translation; *Thyestes*
Wyattville, Jeffrey. *See* Ruins
Wycherley, William. *See* Comedy; Hero and Leander; Terence
Wyclif, John. *See Asterisk*
Wyler, William. *See Cinema*
Wylson, Thomas. *See Demosthenes*

Xanthippe, **996**. *See also Socrates*
Xanthus of Lydia. *See Biography*
Xenakis, Iannis. *See* Aeschylus; Music
Xenarchus. *See* Aristotle
Xenocrates. *See* Aristotle; Demon; *Art History*
Xenophanes. *See* Homer; Magic; Mythology; *Allegory*
Xenophon, **997**. *See also* Aesthetics; Biography; Dialogue; Hero; Households; Machiavelli; Magic; Presocratics; Socrates; Sparta; Symposium; Translation; Warfare; Writing; Xanthippe; *Annius of Viterbo; Byzantium; Cinema; Erasmus; Korais; Philosophy; Valla*
Xerxes. *See* Writing; *Armenian Hellenism; Opera*
Xylander, Wilhelm. *See* Psellus

Yaddus. *See* Judaism
Yadin, Yigael. *See Masada*
Yanase, Takashi. *See Cinema*
Yates, Dame Frances. *See* Egypt; Hermes Trismegistus; Magic
Yeats, William Butler. *See* Aeneas; Demeter and Persephone; Elegy; Epigram; Fin de Siècle Art; Helen; Pornography; Virgil; *Catullus; Centaur; Cinema*
Yorke, Philip. *See* Soane
Young, Edward. *See* Genius
Young, Thomas. *See Hieroglyphs*
Young, William. *See* Architecture
Yourcenar, Marguerite. *See* Alcestis; Electra; Epic; Phaedra; *Euripides*
Youssef, Saadi. *See* Aristotle

Zabarella, Francesco. *See Epicurus*
Zabarella, Jacopo. *See* Logic; *Aristotle; Philosophy*
Zahn, Wilhelm. *See* Pompeii
Zahran, Yasmine. *See Palmyra*
Zalmoxis. *See Philosophy*
Zamkauskas, Walter. *See* Amazons
Zampieri, Domenico (Domenichino). *See* Sacrifice in the Arts; *Actaeon; Bellori*
Zanker, Paul. *See* Portraits, Reception of Ancient
Zappas, Evangelis. *See Olympic Games*
Zarate, Agustin de. *See Atlantis*
Zarides, Andronikos. *See* Planudes
Zarides, John. *See* Planudes
Zarlino, Gioseffo. *See* Music; *Affecti*
Zarqallu, al-. *See Astronomy*
Zeller, Eduard. *See* Presocratics; Xanthippe; *Aristotle; Diels, Hermann*
Zeno. *See* Paganism; Parmenides; Seneca the Younger; Stoicism; Zeno's Paradoxes; *Allegory; Erasmus; Homer; Magna Graecia*
Zeno, Apostolo. *See* Iphigenia; Opera
Zenobia. *See* Palmyra; *Museum*
Zenodotus. *See* Commentary; Wolf, Friedrich August
Zeno's Paradoxes, **999**
Zerclaere, Thomasin von. *See* Cupid
Zethus. *See* Rome
Zetkin, Clara. *See* Spartacus
Zeus. *See* Castor and Pollux; Demiurge; Olympia; Ovid; Pornography; Prometheus; Renaissance; Tantalus; *Allegory; Amphitryon; Comic Books; Danaë; Demeter and Persephone; Empedocles; Europe; Ganymede; Grotto; Helen; Hercules; Hermes Trismegistus; Homosexuality; Leda; Muses; Museum; Novel; Olympic Games; Olympus; Oracles; Pandora; Pegasus; Pergamon; Phaethon*
Zeus-Ammon. *See* Alexander the Great
Zeuxippus. *See* Greek Anthology
Zeuxis. *See* Aesthetics; Imitation; Marsyas; Rome; *Art History*
Ziegler, Jakob. *See Raphael*
Zillig, Winfried. *See* Troilus
Zimmerman, Mary. *See* Midas; Ovid; Penelope
Zimmermann, Dominikus. *See* Architecture
Zimmermann, Johann Jacob. *See Atheism*
Zoffoli, Giacomo. *See Faun*
Zola, Émile. *See Rome*
Zolotas, Xenophon. *See Names*
Zonaras, John. *See* Xenophon
Zoology, **1000**
Zoroaster. *See* Egypt; Ficino; Magic; Paganism; Persia; Writing; *Hermes Trismegistus; Mithras*
Zosima brothers. *See Korais*
Zosimos of Panopolis. *See* Alchemy
Zosimus. *See* Constantine; *Julian*
Zukofsky, Celia. *See* Translation
Zukofsky, Louis. *See* Translation; *Catullus*
Zumpt, Karl Gottlob. *See Lachmann*
Zunz, Leopold. *See Wolf, Friedrich August*
Zwierlein, Otto. *See* Seneca the Younger
Zwingli, Ulrich. *See* Immortality of the Soul